Robert W. Corrigan

PROFESSOR OF DRAMATIC LITERATURE
NEW YORK UNIVERSITY

THE
MODERN
THEATRE

THE MACMILLAN COMPANY, NEW YORK

LIBRARY OF CONGRESS CATALOG CARD NUMBER: 64–12541

THE MACMILLAN COMPANY, NEW YORK
COLLIER–MACMILLAN CANADA, LTD., TORONTO, ONTARIO

Printed in the United States of America

For My Parents
ELIZABETH AND DANIEL

Preface

No anthology ever completely satisfies anyone, including its editor. For various reasons —space, cost, permission difficulties, balance, utility—I have had to omit plays which should unquestionably be included in any large and general anthology of modern drama. My initial table of contents included seventy-five plays. Such a volume would have been preposterous. Who could have carried it? But amputation is a painful process, and a dangerous one too, for there is always the possibility of destroying the patient. I trust this has not occurred, but I do wish to express my regret that some thirty playwrights could not be represented in the book.

As I have indicated in the general introduction that follows, the modern theatre's general pattern of development has been involved with a gradual but steady shift away from universal philosophical and social concerns toward the crises and conflicts of man's inner and private life. Another dominant characteristic of all the arts, and especially the theatre, in the past century has been its extremism. It has been an era of movements and radical counter-movements; a time of bold experimentation, rebellion, and change. In making my selections for the book, I hoped I could demonstrate the pattern and at the same time capture this sense of flux as it has occurred in the theatre.

Since this is a textbook to be used in college courses in modern drama, it was obviously necessary to include a good representation of the established masterpieces. At the same time, I wanted to open up a few new areas of the modern theatre that are not usually made available in anthologies of this kind. Frisch's *The Chinese Wall,* Betti's *The Queen and the Rebels,* Sastre's *Anna Kleiber,* and Fry's *A Sleep of Prisoners* fall into this category.

A few words also should be said about the general arrangement of the book and some of its special features. For the most part, I have organized the volume chronologically by country because to do it in any other way seemed to me misleading or confusing. To do it by styles or forms would involve the use of labels which would tend to destroy the vitality and meaning of many of the plays. Is *The Wild Duck,* for instance, a naturalistic drama or a symbolist play? A tragedy or a comedy? Good cases have been made for each of these positions, but finally how much difference does it make? The play itself is more important than what we call it. I am fully aware that the modern theatre, more than any other in history, is predominantly an international theatre; and yet, a writer tends to write out of his own national milieu, and as a result he will usually have more in common with the other dramatists of his own country than with anyone else. Frisch, for instance, has been greatly influenced by Wilder, and there are many similarities between *The Chinese Wall* and *The Skin of Our Teeth.* But Frisch is as distinctly a Germanic writer as Wilder is an American; their stylistic similarities, while important, are secondary and not generic. For these reasons I believe that the organization of the text by nationality will minimize confusion for students and make for the greatest possible flexibility for the teacher.

It might be argued that the arrangement of the plays is finally an arbitrary matter, and this may be so, but the question of translations can never be. Today, largely because of Eric Bentley's efforts, we are finally aware of the great importance of good translations in the theatre. True translation is, of course, not possible, for one can never bring completely the richness, subtlety, and texture of one language into another. It is nonetheless essential that translations of plays express, as far as possible, the dynamics of performance—the sense of actors speaking lines in a theatre—as well as the literary qualities of the text. Unfortunately, too many of the standard translations of modern European plays lack both of these qualities. I saw the editing of this book as an opportunity to improve that situation, with the result that sixteen of the plays in the volume appear in new or heretofore unpublished translations.

Finally, a word must be said about the essays that precede each play. The dramatists represented have written about the theatre in general, and their own work in particular, and what they have written is very revealing and, for the most part, not widely known nor readily available. Thus, by introducing each playwright with one of his own essays, it has been possible to make available both an anthology of plays and a collection of essays and letters on the modern theatre by the makers of that theatre. This, it seems to me, will be far more valuable to both the teacher and the student of the theatre than anything I might have written in a limited space about the plays.

At last, I come to the pleasant task of acknowledging the assistance of the many people whose advice, encouragement, and hard work have helped to make this book possible. First, I must thank the translators, Carl Mueller, Fred Wahr, James Rosenberg, Otto Reinert, Evert Sprinchorn, Henry Burke, Paul Mayer, Eric Bentley, and Leonard Pronko, whose talents can never be overestimated. In particular, I want to thank Mr. Mueller, who undertook the huge task of making new translations of most of the German plays in the volume.

I must also acknowledge the many people who not only assisted me in getting new translations, but also did much to make several of the plays available to me. In this regard, I should like to express my appreciation to Mrs. Andrienna Betti, Mrs. Ninon Tallon Karlweis, Miss Isabel Wilder, Miss Toby Cole, Miss Margaret Ramsey, Dr. Suzanne Czech, Alfonso Sastre, Jean-Pierre Giraudoux, and Professor Robert Weiss.

A book such as this could never be published without the cooperation of many other publishers, and so I should also like to thank the many permissions departments with which I had to correspond for their helpfulness. And I am particularly grateful to Barney Rosset, Jason Epstein, Cyril Nelson, and my good friend Arthur Wang, who helped me solve many difficulties.

It should be apparent by now that this book is the result of large-scale collaboration; but there was a small group of people whose help was indispensable, and to whom this acknowledgment can at best be but a token of my gratitude. First, thanks to my friends and colleagues, Earle Gister, Ted Hoffman, and Eric Bentley, who were a constant source of advice and strength; next, to my secretaries, Mrs. Karen Haller, Mrs. Catherine Radcliffe, and Mrs. Mary Kline, who typed hundreds of letters and prepared the manuscript for publication; and thanks also to one of my students, Gerald Bradley, who prepared the bibliographies. Finally, I must express my gratitude to my editor, J. G. Case, whose participation in the work on the book has been invaluable.

ROBERT W. CORRIGAN

Pittsburgh, Pa.

Introduction

After visiting the United States, Alexander de Tocqueville prophetically described the kind of literature which he believed an industrialized democratic society would produce. "I am persuaded," he wrote in *Democracy in America,* "that in the end democracy diverts the imagination from all that is external to man and fixes it on man alone. . . . It may be foreseen in like manner that poets living in democratic times will prefer the delineation of passions and ideas to that of persons and achievements. The language, the dress, and the daily actions of men in democracies are repugnant to conceptions of the ideal. . . . This forces the poet constantly to search below the external surface which is palpable to the senses, in order to read the inner soul. . . . The destinies of mankind, man himself taken aloof from his country, and his age, and standing in the presence of Nature and of God, with his passions, his doubts, his rare prosperities and inconceivable wretchedness, will become the chief, if not the sole theme of poetry." Any examination of the arts of the past century would seem to indicate that Tocqueville's prophecy has been fulfilled, and it is certainly clear that the theatre's general pattern of development during this time can be best described as a gradual but steady shift away from universal philosophical and social concerns toward the crises and conflicts of man's inner and private life. It is possible to discover foreshadowings of this change in direction and emphasis in the works of early nineteenth-century romantics—Buechner, Hebbel, Kleist, Gogol, Musset—but it is not until Ibsen that the theatre's revolutionary break with the past becomes clearly discernible. In fact, Ibsen's development as a playwright, beginning with his large philosophical dramas (*Brand* and *Peer Gynt*), though the plays of social protest and reform (*Pillars of Society, A Doll's House, Ghosts, An Enemy of the People*), to the autobiographical and almost pathologically introspective plays of his later years (*Rosmersholm, The Master Builder, When We Dead Awaken*), to a large extent embodies in a microcosmic way both in form and theme the modern theatre's increasing tendency to be more concerned with the conflicts of the individual's interior world than with the significance of his public deeds.

The causes of any revolution are always as difficult to untangle as its consequences are to assess, and any attempt on the part of the critic to describe them will inevitably result in oversimplification. But it is possible to discover certain basic changes in attitude which had been evolving in Europe since the time of Luther and had begun to crystallize in continental thought by the second half of the nineteenth century. And the works of the revolutionary playwrights—Ibsen, Strindberg, Chekhov, Shaw, and Hauptmann—were the first to express in the theatre certain of these radical shifts in the way man had come to think of nature, society, and himself. What follows is an attempt to set forth briefly some of the more important aspects of this revolution in the drama which Ibsen referred to as "a war to the knife with the past."

Probably no force in the nineteenth century did more to destroy man's belief in an established norm of human nature, and hence begin the process of internalization in the theatre, than the advent of psychology as a systematized field of study. In his book *"Modernism" in the Modern Drama,* Joseph Wood Krutch argued that the basic issue confronting all the dramatists of the past one hundred years was the problem of "modernism." Briefly, modernism involves both the conviction and practice that to be modern is to be, in many important ways, different from anyone who ever lived before. This does not mean that man has changed; human nature is the same, but man's way of looking at himself has changed in a way that is significantly new. It is this new view of man that creates the problem for the dramatist.

Good examples of this changed perception can be found in Ibsen's *Hedda Gabler* (1890) and Strindberg's *Miss Julie* (1888). Hedda and Julie have the distinction of being the first fully and consciously developed neurotic heroines in dramatic literature. By neurotic we mean that they are neither logical nor insane (in the sense of being random and unaccountable), but that the aims and motives of each of them have a secret personal logic of their own. Both are motivated as dramatic characters on the premise that there is a secret, and sometimes unconscious, world of aims and methods—a secret system of values—which is more important in human experience than rationality. The significant difference is that neither of these characters can be explained or judged by a common standard; the actions of each dramatic character (and, by extension, each human being) are explicable only in terms of that peculiar combination of forces, frustrations, and desires which is unique to himself.

For us, living in the middle of the twentieth century, there is nothing very new in these psychological ideas; but, coming when they did, they were quite revolutionary, and they have created problems for the playwright that have not yet been solved. By convincingly demonstrating that normal people are not as rational as they seem, and that abnormal people do not act in a random and unintelligible way, psychology has made it difficult, if not impossible, for the dramatist to present his characters directly. In earlier times, when it was believed that there was a sharp distinction between the sane and the insane, the irrational "aberrations" of human behavior were dramatically significant because they could be defined in terms of a commonly accepted standard of sane human conduct. It seems clear, for instance, that in Shakespeare's presentation of them, Lear on the heath is insane while Macbeth at the witches' cauldron is not. But, for the modern dramatist, deeds do not necessarily mean what they appear to mean, and in themselves they are not directly revelatory of the characters who commit them. Like Othello, Miss Julie, Hedda Gabler, and Kostya Treplev of Chekhov's *The Sea Gull* are suicides; but, in the case of these three, the meaning of each death cannot be clearly ascertained from the actions that preceded it. The plight of the modern dramatist in this regard becomes apparent when we realize that without Strindberg's Preface to *Miss Julie* or Ibsen's Notes for *Hedda Gabler,* we could never know for certain what, in each instance, the significance of the heroine's death really was. And the ambiguity of almost every interpretation of *The Sea Gull* is largely due to the fact that Chekhov never made the meaning of Treplev's suicide explicit.

All drama of the past is based upon the axiom "By their deeds shall ye know them." The significance of the dramatic hero was revealed by his deeds, and there was a direct relationship between the hero's overt acts and his inner spiritual condition. The significance of Oedipus, for instance, is revealed by what he does, not by some explanation that he is suffering from an Oedipus complex; and there is a direct relationship between the act of tearing out his own eyes and his solving the riddle of the Sphinx. Even when a character commits a dissembling deed, it is to deceive the other characters in the play, not the spectators. Certainly one of the chief functions of the soliloquy in Elizabethan drama was to keep the audience continually informed as to what was going on. Hamlet may put an antic disposition on, but not before he tells the audience he is going to do so. However, beginning in the nineteenth century, the drama began to reflect man's growing distrust in the ability of his senses to comprehend the true nature of reality. Appearances are no longer believed to be direct reflections of ideal reality, like the shadows on the wall of Plato's cave; rather, they are thought of as a mask which hides or distorts reality. And by the time of Pirandello, particularly in such plays as *Right You Are, If You Think You Are* (1916), *Six Characters in Search of an Author* (1921), and *The Emperor [Enrico IV]* (1922), appearances not only do not express reality, they contradict it, and the meaning of these plays is not to be found in appearance or reality but in the contradiction itself.

One of the great achievements of the Elizabethan dramatic form was its ability to express several levels of experience simultaneously. The world of *Hamlet* is both public and private, a world in which personal and familial relationships, fantasy and mystery, and political and psychological conflict coexist in a state of constant dramatic tension. One of the main reasons why the Elizabethan dramatic form works so successfully is that appearances can be taken at their face value. But when the dramatist begins to distrust the validity of the information yielded by his sensory perceptions, it becomes difficult, if not impossible, for him to dramatize the complex totality of experience in a single form. Reality must be broken down into its component parts, and each part can only be expressed in a form peculiar to itself. Admitting the existence of individual differences in the work of each dramatist writing in any given period, it is nonetheless possible to describe with some accuracy the dramatic form employed by the playwrights of the fifth-century Greek theatre, the Elizabethan and Restoration theatres of England, and the French neo-classic theatre of the seventeenth century. But in discussing the modern theatre we must always speak of forms, for there is no single, dominant form in the serious theatre of the past hundred years. It is for this reason that the evolution of the drama since the time of Shakespeare has been so aptly described as a process of fragmentation.

Nothing, by the way, illustrates the eclectic and schizoid character of the modern drama more succinctly than a brief examination of the sixteen plays written by Strindberg between the years 1899 and 1902. During this period he wrote the most brutal of his naturalistic dramas (*The Dance of Death*, Parts I and II), six of his greatest history plays (including *Gustavus Vasa* and *Eric XIV*), his most important religious play (*Easter*), several folk fantasies (including *The Bridal Crown*), a fascinating, almost Chekhovian melodrama of indirection (*There Are Crimes and Crimes*), and his monumental dream plays (*To Damascus, I and II,* and *The Dream Play*). Strindberg wrote about almost every aspect of reality in this most productive time of his career, but we are not conscious of any apparent order or progression in his writing, and there seems to be little or no formal or thematic relationship between the plays.

It is very likely that every serious dramatist believes that it is his artistic duty to be true to his presuppositions about the real nature of the world in which he lives. However, once a playwright believes that the meaning of every human action is relative and intelligible only in terms of a unique and subsurface combination of forces, the dramatic events of the plot cease to have meaning in themselves, and they take on significance only as the secret motivations of the characters who participate in them are revealed. (The technique of earlier drama is just the reverse: the motivations of the characters are revealed by the events of the plot.) But how does the dramatist objectify the hidden and unconscious, and what happens to the theatre when he feels obligated to explain and probe into his characters' hidden lives? Explanation is always a dangerous business in the theatre (since the time of the ancient

Greeks, exposition has always been the dramatist's most difficult problem), but the moment a playwright assumes that if he explains his characters he has written a play, that danger becomes mortal. All too often the writers of the modern theatre have forgotten that a dramatic situation requires not that we should *understand* a character but simply that we should *believe* in him. Dramatic action always leads to a judgment; it requires that something shall happen to and through the characters— something that is embodied in the events of which the characters are a part. Whenever the personality of the character, rather than the action of which the character should be a part, becomes the playwright's chief concern, dramatic process dissolves into explanation; and when that occurs, the range of the theatre is drastically reduced, if not unalterably damaged.

One has only to compare the plays of the mid-twentieth century with those of Ibsen, Shaw, or Strindberg to realize just how much the scope of the theatre has been narrowed. However, evidence of the gradual loss of belief in dramatic heroes, who needed no explaining, can initially be found in the sentimental bourgeois drama of the eighteenth century. For the first time a character was no longer noble, responsible, or morally significant—and, therefore, dramatically interesting—just because of his birth, position, power, or wealth. As a result, the dramatist was obliged to justify both his choice of characters and the situations in which they are engaged. The Romantic drama of the eighteenth and nineteenth centuries resisted a break with the past and attempted unsuccessfully to perpetuate the forms and figures of earlier times. Certainly, the revolt of Ibsen and his contemporaries in the last quarter of the nineteenth century was at least in some measure due to their conviction that the dramatic conflicts of the Romantic drama were inflated and without significance, and that the nobility of its characters was artificial and contrived. In rejecting these artificialities the modernists changed the theatre in many ways; but nothing that they could do would forestall the attrition of belief in the possibility of heroic characters who needed no explaining.

This was largely due to the fact that, as a literary movement, nineteenth-century naturalism was so closely related to nineteenth-century biology. Darwin's theories of evolution (*The Origin of Species,* 1859) and the discovery of new genetic laws had convinced many writers that man's existence, including his personality, was a phenomenon that could be explained in terms of scientific laws. As a result, increasingly, man's complex biological needs rather than his capacity to make moral choices were thought to be his most significant characteristic. Once such a view was accepted, however, the exceptional man, who because of his position and power had the greatest freedom of choice, ceased to be the fullest embodiment, and therefore the best representative, of those conflicts and choices that most clearly define the human condition. Instead, the lives of the poor—where the role of natural necessity is most readily observable—became the playwright's most suitable subjects. The drama of the common man, then, did not happen by accident, nor did it evolve because some dramatist or group of dramatists wanted it to. Given the problem of creating in a world in which all human actions tend to be explained in terms of some kind of psychological or sociological cause and effect, a world in which the possibility of deliberate and moral choice is doubted if not rejected outright, it is difficult, if not impossible, for the playwright to fashion a character of traditional heroic stature.

There is an old saw about no man being a hero to his valet. Neither is he one to his psychoanalyst. Nor can he be one to a playwright who views his actions as behavioral phenomena explicable in terms of some kind of laws—scientific or otherwise. Oedipus, for example, remains a hero of great stature so long as he is not suffering from an Oedipus complex. But once we learn to explain him in terms of repressed hopes and fears, traumatic childhood experiences, or a vitamin deficiency in infancy, he may remain interesting—in fact, he will gain a new kind of interest, as Cocteau's *The Infernal Machine* attests—but he loses stature. Or while, temporarily, we accept the Elizabethan attitude toward them, which of us can understand a Hamlet or a Lear? And which of us can forgive an Othello or a Macbeth? But it is precisely that they seem mysteriously beyond our powers of understanding that they remain heroes for us. And it is a belief in a mysterious quality in men which passeth all understanding that affirms the importance of man in his universe. However, if a playwright comes to believe that all human actions are in reality predictable behavioral responses, and that his moral judgments of these actions can be dissolved by psychological understanding, how can he pattern a tragedy or create characters with stature? If there can be no possibility for an appraisal of personality as such, why should Hamlet's death be any more significant than that of Rosencrantz and Guildenstern?

That there has been a shift in our attitude toward the heroic is easily seen when we examine any one of the many modern adaptations of the Greek tragedies. For example, today most people find Anouilh's *Antigone* much more compatible with their attitudes and, thus, more interesting than Sophocles' tragic working of the theme. The characters and the dilemma of their situation seem more human. Antigone is not a hard and almost inhuman girl, with such a monomaniacal fixity of purpose that she rejects all other feelings and desires. In the modern version she is, humanly, both weak and strong. She has a lover in Haemon, whom she rejects, but she is also a helpless little girl who runs to "Nanny" for comfort and strength; as she approaches death, she is afraid and seeks the consolations of even the most calloused of guards. Creon is not a blind and power-mad tyrant; he is a businessman–king who is caught in the complex web of compromise and expediency which will not allow abstract moral principles to upset the business of government.

However, what the play gains in humanity it loses in tragic force. The sense of Antigone's aloneness and Creon's moral blindness has been softened. Anouilh's Antigone is not alone and unloved, and his Creon is not blind. We pity their situation in that they are two quite attractive people caught up in a situation which neither of them likes but which they cannot control. They are victims in a disordered world which they have not created and which they have no moral obligation to correct. As the play ends, we are left with an ambiguity that allows for no reconciliation.

While the advent of psychology as a systematized field of study may have been the most powerful single force to shape the modern theatre, actually the process of internalization had begun much earlier. For instance, it is clear from Hebbel's essays on the drama that the despair of old Anton's "I don't understand the world any more" in the final scene of *Maria Magdalena* is much more than an expression of the age-old frustration of the parent who does not understand the behavior of his children. It also reflects his dimly understood but tremendously painful realization that it is no longer possible for him to comprehend what the world has become or to imagine what the future will be like. Until the Industrial Revolution, patterns of life were passed on from father to son with the confidence that these patterns would satisfy the needs and desires of each new generation. Such confidence was justified, for life changed so gradually and imperceptibly that when changes did occur they were easily assimilated into the shared life of the community. But by the middle of the nineteenth century the effects of the Industrial Revolution had begun to be felt on all levels of society. Technology, with its ever-increasing capacity to transform man's way of living, not only made the future so unpredictable that it soon became impossible for him to imagine what his life would be like twenty years hence, but in its singular concern with the individual's functional qualities technology tended to isolate him from his fellows and invalidate his spiritual values and metaphysical concerns. At the same time, the discoveries of the nineteenth-century archeologists and the ensuing interest in anthropology tended to break down provincial and absolutist attitudes concerning human nature. Early anthropologists like Mannhardt, Robertson-Smith, Tylor, and the great James Frazer made it clear that human nature was not something fixed and unchanging but only that kind of behavior exhibited in each culture. In fact, as early as 1860 scholars were demonstrating that human nature is so plastic that it can, as Frazer was later to point out in the Preface to the first edition of *The Golden Bough* (1890), "exhibit varieties of behavior which, in the animal Kingdom could only be exhibited by different species." Furthermore, by the middle of the century, democracy was finally beginning to be established both as a way of life and as a form of government. Today we tend to forget what a revolutionary idea democracy is and the shattering effects that it had upon the values of eighteenth- and nineteenth-century Europe. We also forget what Tocqueville told us long ago: "not only does democracy make every man forget his ancestors, but it hides his descendants and separates his contemporaries from him, it throws him back forever upon himself alone and threatens in the end to confine him entirely within the solitude of his own heart." In short, by the middle of the nineteenth century, every established view of God, human nature, social organization, and the physical universe was beginning to be seriously challenged if not invalidated. And this revolutionary climate had a profound effect on the theatre.

Of all the Arts, theatre is the only one which has always concerned itself with human destinies. Dramatic action is historical in the sense that the perpetual present of each moment on the stage is created out of past events and is directed toward a definite, if yet unknown, future. In previous ages the destiny of any dramatic action was significant because the everchanging events in the lives of dramatic heroes could be meaningfully related to eternity —that is, to some permanent value or idea such as Fate, the Gods, or Heaven and Hell—which transcends the human condition and which is believed in by the dramatist, or his audience, or both.

In the plays of Buechner and Hebbel we discover the first indications in the theatre of that sense of alienation both from God and from Society which underscores the fact that man's belief in eternity had been shaken. And one of the most significant aspects of Ibsen's work (at least after *Peer Gynt,* 1867) is that the realm of ultimate value has either disappeared or has become so mysterious that it has ceased to have dramatic relevance. In its place we find instead a belief in some form of social ideal or societal structure—first, as the agent of some unknown Destiny and, then, as Destiny itself. But when Society begins to assume the role of Destiny—that is, is thought of as the determining force for good or evil in the lives of men—man cannot help but feel eventually that the meaning of his Destiny has been drastically reduced. For Society, as Robert Bolt writes in the Preface to his *A Man for All Seasons,* "can only have as much idea as we have what we are about, for it has only our brains to think with. And the individual who tries to plot his position by reference to our society finds no fixed points, but only the vaunted absence of them, 'freedom' and 'opportunity'; freedom for what, opportunity to do what, is nowhere indicated. The only positive he is given is 'get and spend' . . . and he did not need society to tell him that. In other words we are thrown back by our society upon ourselves, which of course sends us flying back to society with all the force of rebound."

Any mind capable of spiritual aspiration seeks in the actions of the dramatic hero that which affirms the vitality of the free will in any given situation. Man's free will may be defeated by the forces of Destiny—in fact, the great plays have always testified that the destroying forces of Destiny are as much a part of the hero's character as his free will; it may be paralyzed and thus incapable of action; it may be submerged by the battle in such a way as to become part of that Destiny; it may even turn out to be an illusion; but it must always be an active force if we are to believe that we are partaking in human greatness. Such a Destiny must be greater than an aggregate of human beings or an expression of social patterns.

Ironically, the revolt of Ibsen and Shaw against the conventional nineteenth-century drama was motivated by a desire to enlarge the range of Destiny in the theatre. In their attempts to present man in his total historical and social setting, they were rebelling against the narrow and private worlds that had been dominating the stage since the Restoration. But in spite of their efforts, nothing could change the fact that in the two hundred years since Shakespeare the world of the spirit had greatly diminished. The Ekdals' attic and Mrs. Warren's drawing room were not—and never could be—the same as Elsinore or Cleopatra's barge.

Nonetheless, the pioneers of the modern drama had revitalized the theatre precisely because they believed that significant social issues should be dealt with there. Thus for nearly three decades the theatre had a vitality of spirit and a forcefulness of manner which it had lacked for better than a century, for the very reason that its context had been reduced. To the playwright writing at that time, the human and social problems, which were the source materials of the naturalistic play, appeared capable of solution if only man and society would learn to use their common sense. This usually meant one of two things: the acceptance of a less rigid standard of social morality or the espousal of some form of socialism. But with the collapse of the established social order in the First World War, the validity of these too-easy solutions was impugned, and, beginning with the plays of the early German Expressionists (written between 1912 and 1916), the positive optimism of the Edwardian era gave way to a sense of bewilderment, exasperation, and defeatism, only occasionally tempered by the slim hope that the war had brought man to the threshold of a "New Age." The theatre reflects these changes from confidence to doubting and despair; from complacent faith in cherished values to an anxious questioning; from a rigorous, but rigid, morality to the mystic evangelism, the fanatical polemics, and the frivolous apathy of a disintegrating world. These changes are most apparent in the Jekyll-and-Hyde theatre of the German Expressionists, whose nerve-shattered playwrights alternated between militant idealism and grotesque nightmares. But one need only compare Shaw's *Heartbreak House* to *Major Barbara,* Pirandello's *Right You Are, If You Think You Are* to *Liola,* or Hauptmann's *Winter Ballad* to *The Weavers* to realize that the effects of the collapse of the old order were widespread and were reflected in the works of established writers as well as those of the new generation. Immediately after the war the theatre on the continent was dominated by

attitudes of emotionalism and cynicism, but these gradually gave way to feelings of frustration, futility, and despair, and by the middle of the 1920's the serious drama of Europe had become almost totally introspective and psychological in its orientation.

Because they were essentially isolated from the main currents of European history in the first two decades of the century, the Irish and American Theatres were not immediately affected by the spreading paralysis that was transforming the rest of modern drama. But it is clear from O'Casey's *The Plow and the Stars* (1926) and *The Silver Tassie* (1927) that the Abbey Theatre could not withstand for long the theatre's introspective tendencies, and there was no serious American drama until O'Neill's plays were first produced right after the war. In the twenty years between *Beyond The Horizon* (1920) and *The Iceman Cometh* (1941) the American Theatre repeated the continental cycle in its own terms, and by the beginning of the Second World War all of the Western Theatre had reached that No Man's Land between comedy and tragedy, between pathetic aspirations and ridiculous bewilderment, between never-beginning action and never-ending talk.

Obviously, this tendency towards paralyzing introspection has by no means been accepted by everyone writing for the theatre. In fact, a large segment of the modern theatre might be best described as a reaction against the despair and dehumanizing implications of the modernist position. These "resistance movements" have sought to discover the means, both formal and substantive, whereby the possibility and validity of selfhood and human integrity, personal responsibility, and morally significant judgments could be reasserted in the theatre. The first of these groups are those playwrights like Eliot, Fry, Betti, and Claudel who have used some form of orthodox Christian belief to provide the metaphysical basis for their drama. Each of these playwrights understands the despair of modernism, and they are fully conscious of man's sense of isolation and estrangement. But, unlike most writers in the modern theatre, they believe that man's alienation is spiritual and not social or psychological; for them the modern condition is one of estrangement from God. As a result, almost all of their plays are intended to lead us to a state of spiritual awareness; they are attempts to envisage some form of the Christian community by dramatizing the need to recognize and accept the supernatural in experience. This is a mysterious realm, and it is this area of mystery that Eliot is describing in his essay "Poetry and Drama" when he writes:

> It seems to me that beyond the nameable, classifiable emotions and motives of our conscious life when directed toward action there is a fringe of indefinite extent, of feeling which we can only detect so to speak out of the corner of the eye and can never completely focus; of feeling of which we are only aware in a kind of temporary detachment from action.

The reason this kind of theatre has not been very successful in counteracting the debilitating effects of modernism—apart from the crucial fact that it does not seem relevant to a large segment of the modern audience and, therefore, has had only a very limited impact on them—is that the theatre is an art form which deals with the nameable and classifiable. An action that is a "detachment from action" does not find the theatre to be a very hospitable home, and only the "true believers" are satisfied by such plays—and this, probably, for theological and not theatrical reasons.

A second group might be called the "folk dramatists." They are writers such as Lorca, Synge, and, to a certain extent, Betti and the early Pirandello, who write out of the traditions and value systems of pre-modern hieratic societies. There is no doubt that they succeed artistically. Lorca's tragedies of Spain and Synge's plays of the Aran Islands are among the most moving and effective pieces in the modern repertoire. They are filled with human significance, and they celebrate affirmatively man's greatness, his inevitable defeat, and the possibility of spiritual victory. But as much as we are moved by these plays, we must ultimately reject them as irrelevant to our times. For most people living in highly industrialized urban situations, these rural dramas can at best evoke only nostalgia. And all attempts by more recent writers to imitate them have been self-conscious, precious, and sentimental. This is quite understandable, for the world of Synge's and Lorca's plays is, by contemporary standards, a comparatively simple one. It is a world in which the individual insists upon making every relationship a personal one—an heroic society based upon the feudal aristocratic values of honor, generosity, and revenge. These are values which we, in our economic society, have chosen to deny. We may admire or sympathize with a Yerma, a Christy Mahon, or a Maurya, but it is impossible for us to identify ourselves with them. After our brief experience of uplift and exaltation (and for some it is boredom), we return to our city and

suburban homes having enjoyed these folk dramas but not having been nourished by them. (In this regard, I believe it is significant that, in spite of the praise of the critics and scholars, neither Lorca nor Betti has ever been successfully produced on Broadway, and there certainly hasn't been a successful New York production of Synge since the Abbey Theatre's visit in the 1930's.)

The third, and last, group is by far the largest and probably the most important one: those who have sought to escape the deadly strictures of modernism by turning to classical mythology. This group is represented in the text by such playwrights as Hofmannsthal, Yeats, Giraudoux, Anouilh, and O'Neill. The use of myth in modern art has become commonplace. It has been successfully employed in poetry and the novel by Yeats, Pound, and Joyce. T. S. Eliot, in his famous review of Joyce's *Ulysses*, pointed out its great value when he wrote: "In using the myth, in manipulating a continuous parallel between contemporaneity and antiquity, Mr. Joyce is pursuing a method which others must pursue after him. . . . It is simply a way of controlling, of ordering, of giving shape and a significance to the immense panorama of futility and anarchy which is contemporary history. . . . It is a step toward making the modern world possible for art. . . ." Myth used in this way provides the playwright with a form for the expression of his experience, rather than the subject matter itself. In a world seen as constantly changing, myth orders the chameleon-like present with a calculable objectification of reality. It permits the modern dramatist to present the here and now in terms of the universal and historical. As a method, the use of myth has often been very successful, and some great plays have been written in that form. But the universality of such achievements is finally artificial, and the use of myth as a means of dramatic expression, while attractive to the playwright, is usually employed with fear and trembling. It is too obviously a compensatory technique, a substitute for that community of belief which most dramatists find lacking in the modern world.

It is this public truth which in earlier periods of history provided the artist with his means of communication. It enabled him to communicate emotion and attitude by simply describing incidents; it gave him a storehouse of symbols with guaranteed responses; it enabled him to construct a plot by selecting and patterning events which, by means of this public criterion, were significant. But once public truth is shattered into innumerable separate and mutually incommunicable private truths, the drama is seriously threatened. The use of myth makes it possible for the dramatist to create a theatrical world that has a meaning which he is unable to find in the world outside of the theatre, and thus he is able, temporarily at least, to communicate with the disparate world that his audience represents. In a sense, by playing with the themes and forms of a now nonexistent ordered world, the playwright has solved the problem of the artist in modern society. However, the fact that he *plays* with these themes and forms reminds the audience all over again that it does not live in such an ordered world.

All these writers shared one common and fundamental attitude: each of them was in some way rebelling against the conditions of the modern world. They were not only conscious of that lack of a sense of community which inevitably occurs in an increasingly democratic society; more important, they were aware of man's growing sense of his own isolation. The modern world, with its growing collectivism, paradoxically tends to throw man back upon himself, while at the same time it increasingly tends to destroy the individual's sense of his own selfhood. This creates an impasse which the modern dramatist, for the most part, has been unable to overcome.

Joseph Warren Beach, in analyzing the problems of modern fiction, describes the reaction of many writers to this condition in this way: "One of the hardest things for man to bear is spiritual isolation. The sense that he stands alone in the universe goes terribly against his gregarious instincts. He has an overpowering impulse to construct a system which will enable him to feel that he does not stand alone but is intimately associated with some force or group infinitely more powerful and significant than himself." It is clearly evident in the work of all those playwrights who have rebelled against modernism that they too are seeking to construct a system that will restore meaning to life and validity to art. In the end, however, they have not been completely successful, because they have all too often had to deny the realities of the modern world in the process. Furthermore, they have not accepted the wisdom of Brecht's statement that "when one sees that our world of today no longer fits into the drama, then it is merely that the drama no longer fits into the world." By insisting upon values that we may once have cherished but which no longer in actuality exist, the playwrights of the resistance have not been able to revitalize the theatre or its audiences.

And most important, they have not succeeded in stretching the imaginations of men in order that they might conquer that sense of isolation and despair which pervades the modern world. And this brings us to the playwrights of the mid-twentieth century.

In an age dominated by space orbits and artificial satellites, the fear of nuclear war, the tension of cold-war diplomacy, and the insecurity of a defense economy, our greatest uncertainty is whether or not, in the midst of epochal disorder, man has any good chance (to borrow Faulkner's phrase) of prevailing; and if he does, what kind of man will prevail.

This atmosphere has had a profound effect on our theatre, and if there is one thing that characterizes the work of almost all of our serious playwrights of the last decade, it is that their plays express the contemporary theatre's tremendous concern to find a metaphor for universal modern man as he lives on the brink of disaster. We sense that our condition is much like that of those helpless travelers described by Kafka in his *Notebooks*:

> We are in the situation of travelers in a train that has met with an accident in a tunnel, and this at a place where the light of the end is so very small a glimmer that the gaze must continually search for it and is always losing it again, and, furthermore, both the beginning and the end are not even certainties. Round about us, however, in the confusion of our senses, or in the supersensitiveness of our senses, we have nothing but monstrosities and a kaleidoscopic play of things that is either delightful or exhausting according to the mood and injury of each individual. What shall I do? or: Why should I do it? are not questions to be asked in such places.

The train of our national and international—indeed interglobal—life seems to be wrecked, too; and as a result, in despair and desperation, our writers have become increasingly preoccupied with finding a metaphor of the theatre that is symbolic of the inalienable part of every man—that irreducible part of each of us which exists after all the differences have been stripped away, and which is beyond and beneath all that is social, political, economic, religious, and ideological. In short, they are searching for a metaphor of man left face to face with himself.

But what happens to the theatre when our dramatists believe that their chief obligation is to reveal man in a condition of isolation? One of the reasons that the works of our new playwrights seem so difficult to audiences and critics alike is the fact they are so different. Until recently—Chekhov, of course, is the notable exception—we went to the theatre expecting to see a story about someone doing something; "character in action" is the way our critics put it. This story also usually involved some kind of "message" or "statement" about an aspect of human experience. In short, one of the things we expected of a dramatic action was that it express some kind of completion to the statement: "Life is. . . . . !" But increasingly the modern dramatist—this is certainly so of Pinter, and of Beckett, Ionesco, and Ghelderode on the continent—has come to doubt that "Life is something"; and all of their plays are expressions of the proposition that "Life is."

Such an idea of the theatre has tremendous implications for the drama, and we are just now becoming aware of them. First of all, it abolishes the traditional linear plot, because our contemporary playwrights are not interested in presenting an action in any Aristotelian sense. They are, rather, dramatizing a condition. Whenever one asks what the central action of a Beckett, Ionesco, or Pinter play is, he comes a cropper; "action" for the contemporary playwright is an artificial concept. He is concerned with showing life as it is, and in life there is no central action, there are only people, and the only thing that is basic to each individual is the ontological solitude of his being. These playwrights, then, are not interested in telling stories. What do stories have to do with life? To be about life, a story must either be myth, invention, or chronicle; it must have a protagonist or center. But then it becomes a personal narrative or history, either real or imaginary. It is a commonplace that there are no great figures (one can't even think of using the word *hero*) in the plays of our new writers. But it has not been pointed out strongly enough that perhaps the chief reason for this is the fact that they are not interested in describing personal histories. The reason there is no Oedipus, Lear, or Macbeth is that, in his concern to show us life as it is, the contemporary playwright has no use for seeing particular men in particular world systems. His only concern is to create in his plays a situation that will reveal the private drama which every man has inside himself and which is enacted every day in the random, apparently meaningless, and undramatic events of our common routine. "History," said Stephen Daedalus, "is a nightmare from which I must awake." The rapidity of historical change and the apparent powerlessness of the individual to affect Collective History has led in the theatre to a retreat from history. Instead of tracing the his-

tory of an individual who is born, grows old, and dies, many modern playwrights have devoted their attention to the timeless passionate moments of life, to states of being.

But such radical shift in intention has brought with it equally revolutionary experiments with dramatic form. Earlier, we said that these plays were not imitations of an action in any Aristotelian sense. Most serious contemporary playwrights are dramatizing a condition, and therefore they need a dramatic form which, as Ionesco put it, "progressed not through a predetermined subject and plot, but through an increasingly intense and revealing series of emotional states." Such a drama must from the beginning, then, dispense with the traditional linear plot. The traditional plot is sequential; it starts at a certain moment in time and then moves through a series of events to a conclusion. Everything that occurs in this kind of play—each speech, every action, any symbol—is a part of the play's forward movement and is causally related to the sequence of events. It is this sequential nature of dramatic action, of which plot is the first form, that Aristotle was referring to when he said that tragedy is an imitation of an action "which has a beginning, a middle, and an end."

But the new playwrights—first in Europe, and now in the United States—are not interested in "imitations of actions"; they want to show "life as it is," and life as it is lacks direction, the external causality, the cathartic effect of completed events. Like so many painters, composers, poets, and novelists before them, our dramatists are aware that the crises which are so neatly resolved by the linear form of drama are not so neatly resolved in life. To be alive is to be in a continual state of crisis; in life, as one crisis is resolved another is always beginning. Today the playwright wants his plays to express the paradox, the contradiction, and the incompleteness of experience; he wants to suggest the raggedness, the confusion, the complexity of motivation, the "discontinuous continuity," and the basic ambiguity of all human behavior. The contemporary playwrights have rejected the traditional forms of theatre because they are convinced that these forms, ruled by the destructive tyranny of a sequential and chronological structure, are incapable of expressing the "is-ness" of experience. So they have developed a form (Chekhov was the first to use it fully) which might be called—to use the terminology of the new criticism of poetry—*contextual* or *concentric*. The structure of these plays, then, is epiphanic; its purpose is to reveal—literally "to show forth"—the inner lives of the characters. In such drama the plot has been twisted into a situation that is to reveal the psychic lives of the characters. There are many dramatic situations in a plot; in these new plays a single situation has been stretched to take the place of the plot. This inflation of the situation into the source of the dramatic action so that it replaces the plot is the vital secret of the dramaturgy of the new theatre. The new playwrights, in an attempt to capture "the aimless unclimactic multiplicity" of their characters' lives, have created a form of drama based on what Marvin Rosenberg has called "the tensions of context, rather than direction, of vertical depth, rather than horizontal movement."

But once you assert that the meaning of life is absurdity, that the laws of logic are spurious, that action is meaningless, that individuality is illusory, that social interaction is unimportant, and that communication is impossible, you have denied every assumption upon which the art of the theatre as we have known it in the Western world is based. The playwrights of the Absurd did not really set out to destroy the modern theatre; they maintain, to the contrary, that they are seeking the means to revivify it. Rather, they are pursuing to their fullest and most logical conclusions the premises of modernism. These dramatists are facing the "facts of life." If the dramatic meaning of their plays is that drama is no longer possible, they would contend that any other meaning would be artificial, illusory, false; if the dialogue in their plays consists of meaningless clichés and stereotyped phrases, they would insist that this is the way we talk; if their characters are constantly changing their personalities, these playwrights would point out that no one today is really consistent or truly integrated. If the people in their plays seem to be helpless puppets without any will of their own, the Absurdists would argue that we are all passively at the mercy of blind fate and meaningless circumstance. They call their theatre "Anti-Theatre," and this they insist is the true theatre of our times. If they are correct, so be it! Then history has again followed its own inexorable laws. The very forces which gave life and strength to the modern theatre have caused its decline and death.

But the theatre is always dying, and with equal regularity, like the phoenix, it is resurrected. No one can say with certainty what its new form will be, although it would seem that the increasing influence of Brecht on the work of new dramatists all over the world indicates that the conflicts of men living in industrialized collective societies will provide the themes for the theatre of the future, and that the narrative structure of epic drama is the most appropriate form within which to embody these conflicts. But no matter what the future of the theatre will be like, that there will be a future is certain. First, largely because of the development of college and university theatre programs in this country, and the large increase in the number of professional repertory theatres here and abroad, there are more people who have experienced good theatre than ever before. And this enlarged audience wants and needs theatre, and it will not be satisfied for long with the maimed rites of psychological and moral cliché, or impassioned Jeremiads from prophets of doom, or the meandering contemplations of writers who are morbidly consumed in introspection and self-analysis. Fortunately, audiences still go to the theatre in the spirit of expectancy, in the hopeful anticipation that the stage will be capable of accommodating all of the terrible-wonderful emotions and insoluble dilemmas of our shared life together. This demand bid made by our new and increasingly informed and aware audiences for a drama that deals with the significant issues and concerns of our public life will, I believe, force our playwrights to open up new frontiers in the drama and thus extend the boundaries of the theatre. The second great hope of the theatre is that, in spite of the overriding temper of despair and the current dominance of anti-theatricality, our playwrights still find human action significant, still find it necessary to write plays, and in the very act of writing attest to the miracle of life that contemporary despair would deny. We live in one of the most dramatic ages in the history of mankind, and if the past is any kind of reliable guide to what the future of the theatre will be, we have good reason to believe that the theatre of tomorrow can be as dramatic as the world in which we live today.

R.W.C.

Contents

CONTENTS

ITALY AND SPAIN—Continued

GERMANY
AUSTRIA
SWITZERLAND

GEORG BUECHNER (1813–1837) is usually referred to as the first truly modern dramatist. His career as a playwright was a case of "instantaneous ripeness"; he wrote his first play at the age of twenty and his meteoric career ended with his tragic death at the age of twenty-three. Buechner's modernity lies in the fact that he was the first to fuse the realistic social concerns—which we generally associate with Ibsen, Hauptmann, and Zola—with the anguish of isolation and social alienation that did not become a dominant theme in the theatre until the twentieth century. His profoundly moving plays, with their episodic structure, their staccato-like language, and their serious concern for the conflicts of the little man, strangely prefigure the work not only of Brecht but also the writers of the Theatre of the Absurd.

FRIEDRICH HEBBEL (1813–1863) was the first successful writer of serious middle-class drama in the modern theatre. Although Hebbel's name is usually linked with those writers of the "Storm and Stress" period of nineteenth-century German romanticism, it is probably more correct to consider him as a forerunner of that revolution in the theatre usually attributed to Ibsen and Strindberg. In fact, Hebbel openly rejected both the sentimentality and the romantic neo-Shakespeareanism which dominated early nineteenth-century drama, and sought to dramatize the essential social and moral conflicts of his own time. He lived in a period of great social, economic, political, and philosophical ferment, and the sense of upheaval and change is mirrored in all his work. Furthermore, he was greatly influenced by the philosophy of Hegel, whose theories of the dialectic in history led Hebbel to believe that the most significant dramas of life were the result of the conflicts of historical process. "Great drama," he wrote, "occurs at the transition from one epoch to the

[FRIEDRICH HEBBEL, *Cont.*]
next and expresses the clash of world views." In Hebbel's view, then, a time of crisis was the essential condition of drama, and in all his work he sought to represent in powerful images the issues and conflicts of an emerging middle-class morality.

GERHART HAUPTMANN (1862–1946) once described himself as "an Aeolian Harp whose strings are stirred by every slightest breeze," and the wide variety in tone, style, and theme of his more than forty plays tends to substantiate the aptness of this self-evaluation. However, as our perspective on Hauptmann and his works broadens with time, his greatest contributions to the modern theatre appear to have been his leadership in creating a strong free theatre in Germany and his naturalistic dramatization of the struggles of the working classes. Hauptmann was the first modern playwright to employ the mob as a collective hero and *The Weavers* is probably his most important achievement in this regard. In dramatizing the revolt of a group of Silesian weavers in the 1840's, Hauptmann used a loose, almost symphonic, form to express the swirling character of a great upheaval in which ideals and ambitions, humanity and inhumanity, justice and injustice, courage and cowardice are entangled. His choice of form and his concern for the individual as submerged in and identified by the group began what has become a dominant type of drama in the modern theatre, and Hauptmann has been followed by such diverse writers as Galsworthy, Odets, and Wesker.

ARTHUR SCHNITZLER (1862–1931) had a crazy-quilt career in the theatre, but in his most memorable plays (*The Affairs of Anatol, Light-o-Love,* and *La Ronde*) he captured the spirit of gaiety and sensuality that pervaded the city of Vienna at the turn of the century. Schnitzler, like Chekhov, was a physician, and he viewed the amoral hi-jinks of his fellow Viennese with a compassion tinged with skepticism and melancholic sadness. As his heroes and heroines danced from one amorous adventure to another, we sense the fun and charm of the life of sensuality, but we are equally conscious of its transiency and ultimate emptiness. Schnitzler was a moralist who never moralized. His judgments were always disguised by a mask of slightly grotesque bantering, but underneath the glossy surface of this gay society we soon discover a biting discontent and a gnawing sense of disillusionment. Looking back, Schnitzler's greatest achievement was

his almost infallible ability to dramatize with psychological accuracy the promptings of extreme sexuality without having to resort to the case-book details of a Havelock Ellis or Krafft-Ebbing. Sex was an escape, the life-giving illusion, for a people who were trying to maintain a former grandeur at the same time that their world was crumbling about them. With the fall of Austria in World War I, Vienna ceased to be one of the theatrical capitals of the world. Schnitzler had no heirs, but his dramas expressed the autumnal flowering of one of the Western world's greatest cultures.

FRANK WEDEKIND (1864–1918) was the first modern dramatist to use expressionist techniques openly in the theatre. All of the German writers at the turn of the century were beginning to turn the searchlight on bourgeois values, and it is in the drama of Wedekind that we discover the clearest indication of the cynical despair and skepticism with which contemporary values were being regarded. The world of his theatre expresses the grotesque disequilibrium of middle class society, and it is peopled by fascinating and demonically dislocated bourgeois characters. From the beginning, German expressionism was schizophrenic in nature. On the one hand, it was idealistic and celebrated in a mystical way the need for love and universal brotherhood in a bewildering and confusing world. On the other, it stridently encouraged the grotesque dramatization of every form of brutality, cruelty, bestiality, and sensuality. Wedekind most fully embodies the Jekyll-Hyde character of this frenzied movement. All of his work is stamped with a kind of level-headed lunacy that defies analysis, and each of his plays tends to be a strange combination of grand guignol and farce. In Wedekind's view, the civilized world is a menagerie of wild animals, and his plays are brutal satires in which he strips the individual down to the horrifying moral nakedness of the jungle. Morality is seen as the most lucrative of all rackets, and sexual emancipation is hailed as the only means of curing a diseased society. Variations on these two anti-bourgeois ideas appear again and again in his plays, and finally serve as the foundation for everything Wedekind ever wrote.

HUGO VON HOFMANNSTHAL (1874–1929) was always violent in his reaction against materialism in philosophy and naturalism in art. Even as a young man, living in the morally debilitated pre-World War I city of Vienna, Hofmannsthal saw the limitations of an art that

[HUGO VON HOFMANNSTHAL, *Cont.*]
was committed to an external view of reality. Naturalism in the drama, with its convention of environmental credibility, had tended to show life as it existed on the surface; it was all too often sociological in its orientation and failed to capture the multiple complexities of man's inner life. It was because of this tendency to ordinariness in most of the drama written at the turn of the century that Hofmannsthal turned to symbolism, the shrine of all the disenchanted young poets and dramatists of his time.

Hofmannsthal's early plays reflect this allegiance, but despite his lyrical tendencies and the fact that he was strongly influenced by the symbolist ideals of verse, he soon broke with many writers of his generation who included a social art like the theatre in the world they rejected. From that point on, Hofmannsthal's work is a continuing effort to achieve a theatrical form that would combine the symbolists' rich and colorful language with an action that was dramatically rather than lyrically conceived.

Hofmannsthal believed that the function of the theatre was to show that sublime and true moment in a man's life when the motivating "passion-power" of his existence is expressed. He was convinced that in life, although the process may be slower and less apparent, man is ultimately destroyed by that very passion which gives him the power to live. It is that moment when man's motivating passion-power drives him to the conflict of life and death that must be captured in the drama.

BERTOLT BRECHT (1898–1956) was a Marxist and the prophet for the drama of the collective. But he never wore his prophet's mantle with ease, nor was he ever comfortable with his Marxist position. He was, however, the first playwright of the modern theatre to comprehend fully the effects of industrialization and collectivism upon our social structures, and he realized that these forces were creating new kinds of conflicts which were not being dealt with in the theatre. As early as 1925, he wrote: "When one sees that our world of today no longer fits into the drama, then it is merely that the drama no longer fits into the world." Brecht's epic theatre is an attempt to express the drama of a world that was gradually being transformed from a traditional community into a highly organized collective state. In using the term "epic theatre," Brecht was thinking of the drama as episodic and narrative and, therefore, more like the structure of an epic poem

than the well-made play. He rejected the traditional Aristotelian idea that a play should have a beginning, middle, and end, because he believed that the dramatic processes of history do not end, but only move on to the next episode. He wanted to translate this episodic nature of history into the theatre. Brecht's epic form, then, is his way of expressing the complexity, multiplicity, variety, and even the contradiction of a collective world while still maintaining that unity of form which is essential for art. Furthermore, it is a form that seeks to achieve the capacity of the novel in dealing with the central issues of the modern world, without sacrificing the immediacy and force of the actor on a stage.

The second important point that must be made about Brecht is that he was a poet. A large number of the serious dramatists of the twentieth century have been involved in the revolt against the tyranny of words in the modern theatre. They believe that the language of drama has become stereotyped and wooden because it has lost that gestural quality which is essential to all language in theatre. They realize, as George Steiner has pointed out, "that drama is language under such high pressure of feeling that the words carry a necessary and immediate connotation of gesture." In their attempts to revitalize the language of the theatre, they hope to force audiences into a new awareness of the world in which they live. But most of these dramatists, in order to achieve these ends, have tended to dislocate the very mechanism of language itself; they have practically destroyed the syntax of rational discourse. This Brecht did not do. As a poet he believed in the power of verse to deal with the contradictions of reality. He believed poetry could advance discordant persuasions simultaneously and still retain that gestural quality which is essential to the theatre.

Now, nearly a decade after his death, Brecht's work is just being evaluated with thoroughness and objectivity, and it seems clear that he has made more important contributions to the modern theatre than any other playwright writing in the first half of the twentieth century.

MAX FRISCH (1911–   ) is one of two important dramatists in the post-Second World War renaissance of the Swiss theatre. He had an abortive career as a writer when he was a young man, and it was not until the first appearance of his plays and novels after 1946 that he emerged as an artist of great stature and a dramatist to be reckoned with in any account

[MAX FRISCH, *Cont.*]
of the European drama of the twentieth century.

Frisch shares many things in common with his fellow countryman, Duerrenmatt. Both are openly theatrical and anti-illusionistic in their approach to dramatic form; they have been greatly influenced by Brecht both in form and idea; and their plays express much of the irony, cynicism, and pacificism which we associate with Brecht's work. They both are conscious of man's helplessness before the forces of anonymous world powers, and both have been wildly experimental with theatrical forms. But Frisch is much more eclectic than his younger colleague. Like Strindberg's, his development as a dramatist cannot be charted. He jumps from form to form and idea to idea without apparent rhyme or reason, and this gives his total accomplishment as a dramatist an uneven quality. When he is good, he is absolutely brilliant; but he has also had some terrible misses. Frisch's work also has a compassion that is lacking in the steely and bitter vision of life which Duerrenmatt's plays present. Frisch is absorbed by the realization that man is incapable of learning any lessons from the catastrophes of history; but he is not cynical about this incapacity so much as he is deeply saddened by it.

The most striking characteristic of Frisch's plays is their universality. He has come as close as anyone writing for the modern theatre in successfully creating the "Everyman" of the mid-twentieth century. He has achieved this by fusing the dramatic forms of all periods in history with a theatricality that is not in any way limited by the logic of space and time. His chief device, in this regard, is the use of historical anachronisms. By juxtaposing fabled figures from past history and literatures with men of the present, he creates the effect of all time, no time, every time.

Frisch, like Lorca, Brecht, and Betti, failed in his first attempt to be widely accepted by American audiences. But just as the work of those who failed before him gradually came to impose their dramatic power on the American popular imagination, it seems safe to assume that Frisch will soon come to be regarded as one of the mid-twentieth century's most important dramatists.

FRIEDRICH DUERRENMATT (1921–   )
is probably the most important representative of the new theatre movement that has emerged in Switzerland since the Second World War. It was almost as if the dramatic impulse in Europe had been kept in incubation during the war, and then reappeared in that one country which had been able to avoid involvement in the continental holocaust, a country which heretofore had made no significant contributions to dramatic literature. But these new Swiss plays were remarkably different from the mainstream of prewar continental drama, and they pointed in some directions—directions that many playwrights have followed in the past decade or so.

Duerrenmatt is chiefly concerned with two ideas: man's collective sense of guilt for the disasters of global upheaval, and the sense of helplessness people feel living under the shadow of imminent atomic destruction. There can be no heroes in such a world—only victims; and the possibility of freely chosen noble actions is doubted, if not flatly denied. Like Kafka, Duerrenmatt describes the human condition as living in a tunnel with no beginning and no end, in which there can be no meaningful action, and from which there can be no escape. The result of such a belief is a grotesque drama that combines fantastic comedy with bitterness, and a mordant satire with an awareness of profound human suffering. It is, in short, a drama that is impossible to classify in terms of traditional genres. All of Duerrenmatt's plays have a strange and haunting power that overwhelms our minds, arouses our feelings, and heightens in us that sense of guilt and helplessness which Duerrenmatt believes is our true condition. It would be a mistake, however, to think that for this reason Duerrenmatt is only a didactic pamphleteer. In an interview in 1958, he said: "When you write a play you don't do it to teach a lesson or prove a point or build a philosophy, because you can never force art to prove anything. I describe human beings, not marionettes; an action, not an allegory; I set forth a world, not a moral." The world that Duerrenmatt presents to us is the world made by a poet, and he has had a tremendous impact on the modern theatre because he has found powerful theatrical means to express the central concerns of modern man's shared life.

Georg Buechner

1813-1837

FROM GEORG BUECHNER'S LETTERS

LETTER TO HIS FIANCÉE, NOVEMBER 1833

I have been studying the history of the French Revolution. I have felt as if crushed beneath the gruesome fatalism of History. I find in human nature a terrifying sameness, in the human condition an inexorable force, granted to all and to none. The individual mere froth on the wave, greatness sheer chance, the mastery of genius a marionette play, a ridiculous struggle against brazen law; to recognize it, the supreme achievement, to control it impossible. . . .

I intend to bow no more before the parade horses and bystanders of History. I have accustomed my eyes to the sight of blood. But I am no guillotine blade. *Must* is one of the curses which baptized man. The dictum: "for it must needs be that offenses come; but woe to that man by whom the offense cometh!"—is terrifying. What is it in us that lies, murders, steals? I do not want to pursue this thought any further. Oh, if I could but lay this cold and tormented heart on your breast!

LETTER TO GUTZKOW[1] FROM DARMSTADT, FEBRUARY 21, 1835

Dear Sir!

Perhaps you may have observed; or even, in less fortunate instance, your own experience may already have told you that there is a degree of misery which makes one forget every consideration and benumbs every feeling. True, there are people who maintain that in such a case one ought rather starve himself out of this world; but I came upon the living refuta-

tion of this position in an only recently blinded captain I met on the street who declared he would shoot himself were he not forced to live in order to support his family. That is terrible. You will easily perceive that there could be similar circumstances hindering one from making an anchor of one's body to be thrown from the wreck of this world into the water; and you will therefore not wonder at my breaking open your door, bursting into your room, thrusting a manuscript[2] onto your breast, and demanding charity. I ask you to read this manuscript as quickly as possible and, in the event your conscience as a critic will allow, to recommend it to Mr. Sauerländer, and to answer forthwith.

As to the work itself, I can tell you no more than that the most unfortunate circumstances forced me to write it in at most five weeks. I say this to motivate your judgment of the author, not of the drama as such. What I should make of it, I myself do not know; I know only that I have every reason to blush as far as History is concerned; still, I console myself with the thought that, with the exception of Shakespeare, all poets stand like schoolboys before History and Nature. . . .

Should the tone of this letter perhaps cause you to wonder, consider that it is easier for me to beg in rags than to extend a supplication in dresscoat; and almost easier, with pistol in hand, to say: "la bourse ou la vie!" than to whisper with trembling lips: "God bless you!"

LETTER TO HIS FAMILY FROM STRASSBURG, JULY 28, 1835

I must say a few words about my play. First let me observe that permission to make a few

---

Excerpts from Georg Buechner's *Letters*, translated by Maurice Edwards, reprinted by permission of *The Tulane Drama Review*.

[1] Karl Ferdinand Gutzkow (1811–1878), German dramatist, theorist, and Director of the Court Theatre at Dresden.

[2] *Danton's Death.*

changes has been liberally abused: on well-nigh every page, something omitted, something added, and nearly always in a way most detrimental to the whole. Often the sense is entirely distorted or else totally gone, and almost downright nonsense takes over. Besides, the book literally abounds in the most dreadful misprints. They sent me no proofs. The title page is insipid, and it bears my name—which I had expressly forbidden; moreover, it is not on the title page of my manuscript. In addition, the editor stuck several vulgarities into my mouth which never in my life would I have uttered. I have read Gutzkow's brilliant critique and noted there to my joy that I have no inclination to conceit. Moreover, as to the so-called immorality of my book, my answer is as follows:

The dramatic poet is, in my eyes, nothing but a writer of history, but is superior to the latter in that he creates history for the second time. He transplants us directly into the midst of the life of an era, giving us, instead of a dry account of it, characters rather than characteristics, and figures rather than descriptions. His foremost task is to get as close as possible to history as it really happened. His book must be neither more nor less moral than history itself; but history was not created by the good Lord to provide suitable reading matter for young females, and so I must not be blamed either if my drama is so little suited to that. I can hardly make paragons of virtue out of a Danton and the bandits of the Revolution! If I wished to describe their dissoluteness, I had to make them dissolute; if I wished to show their godlessness, I had to let them speak like unbelievers. If a few indecent expressions result, one need only reflect on the well-known obscenity of the speech of that time—of which what I let my people utter is only a weak distillation. There remains but to reproach me for having chosen such a subject. But this objection was refuted long ago. Were one to let it stand, the greatest masterpieces of literature would have to be repudiated. The poet is not a teacher of morals; he invents and creates characters, he brings past epochs back to life, and people may then learn from these as they learn from the study of history and their observation of what happens around them in human life. . . . In that case (if one *so* wished), one ought not to study history at all because so very many immoral things are reported therein; one would have to go blindfold through the streets not to see the indecencies, and must needs cry out against a God who created a world in which so much debauchery takes place. If, moreover, someone were then to tell me that the poet should not represent the world as it is, but rather as it should be, I would answer that I don't wish to make it better than the good Lord who surely created the world as it ought to be.

Further, as to the so-called idealist poets, I find that they have given us almost nothing but marionettes with sky-blue noses and affected pathos, certainly not people of flesh and blood who make me feel their joy and suffering, and whose comings and goings fill me with horror or admiration. In short, I think highly of Goethe or Shakespeare, but very little of Schiller. That, moreover, the most unfavorable critiques are yet to appear is understood; for governments must demonstrate through their paid penmen that their opponents are stupid asses or immoral yokels. Besides in no way do I consider my work perfect and will gratefully accept any genuine aesthetic criticism. . . .

Three more refugees have drifted in here; Nievergelder is among them; in Giessen two students were arrested again. I am extremely careful. Here we know of no one arrested on the border. History must be a fairy tale.

LETTER TO HIS FAMILY FROM STRASSBURG, JANUARY 1, 1836

. . . By the way, I definitely do not belong to the so-called Young Germany, the literary party of Gutzkow and Heine. Only a total misunderstanding of our social conditions could make people believe it possible to effect a complete reform of our religious and social ideas. Then too, though I by no means share their concept of marriage and Christianity, I am nevertheless annoyed when people a thousandfold more sinful in practice than these are in theory pull moral faces and throw stones at young, diligent talent. I go my own way and remain in the field of drama which has nothing to do with all these controversial issues. I draw my characters in accordance with Nature and History and laugh at those who would like to make me responsible for their morality or immorality. I have my own thoughts about that. . . .

LETTER TO HIS FAMILY, SEPTEMBER 1836

I have not let my two plays out of my hands yet; I am still dissatisfied with much in them and do not wish it to go as it did the first time. This is work one cannot be ready with at a set time as a tailor with his clothes.

Translated by Maurice Edwards

WOYZECK

Translated by Carl Richard Mueller

CAST OF CHARACTERS

WOYZECK
MARIE
CAPTAIN
DOCTOR
DRUM-MAJOR
SERGEANT
ANDRES
MARGRET
PROPRIETOR OF THE BOOTH
CHARLATAN
OLD MAN WITH BARREL ORGAN
JEW
INNKEEPER

FIRST APPRENTICE
SECOND APPRENTICE
KATHY
KARL THE FOOL
GRANDMOTHER
FIRST CHILD
SECOND CHILD
THIRD CHILD
FIRST PERSON
SECOND PERSON
SOLDIERS, STUDENTS, YOUNG
    MEN AND GIRLS, CHILDREN,
    AND PEOPLE

Scene One

AT THE CAPTAIN'S

(*The* CAPTAIN *in a chair.* WOYZECK *shaving him*)

CAPTAIN   Not so fast, Woyzeck, not so fast! One thing at a time! You're making me dizzy. What am I supposed to do with the ten extra minutes that you'll finish early today? Just think, Woyzeck: You still have thirty beautiful years to live! Thirty years! That makes three-hundred-sixty months! And days! Hours! Minutes! What do you think you'll do with all that horrible stretch of time? Have you ever thought about it, Woyzeck?

WOYZECK   Yes, sir, Captain.

CAPTAIN   It frightens me when I think about the world . . . when I think about eternity. Busyness, Woyzeck, busyness! There's the

Woyzeck by Georg Buechner, translated by Carl Richard Mueller, printed by permission of the translator.

eternal: that's eternal, that is eternal. That you can understand. But then again it's not eternal. It's only a moment. A mere moment. Woyzeck, it makes me shudder when I think that the earth turns itself about in a single day! What a waste of time! Where will it all end? Woyzeck, I can't even look at a mill-wheel without becoming melancholy.

WOYZECK   Yes, sir, Captain.

CAPTAIN   Woyzeck, you always seem so exasperated! A good man isn't like that. A good man with a good conscience, that is. Well, say something, Woyzeck! What's the weather like today?

WOYZECK   Bad, Captain, sir, bad: Wind!

CAPTAIN   I feel it already. Sounds like a real storm out there. A wind like that has the same effect on me as a mouse. (*cunningly*) I think it must be something out of the North-South.

WOYZECK   Yes, sir, Captain.

CAPTAIN   Ha! Ha! Ha! North-South! Ha! Ha! Oh, he's a stupid one! Horribly stupid! (*moved*) Woyzeck, you're a good man, but, (*with dignity*) Woyzeck, you have no morality! Morality, that's when you have morals, you understand. It's a good word. You have a

[7]

child without the blessings of the Church, just like our right reverend garrison chaplain says: "Without the blessings of the Church." It's not *my* phrase.

WOYZECK   Captain, sir, the good Lord's not going to look at a poor worm just because they said Amen over him before they went to it. The Lord said: "Suffer little children to come unto me."

CAPTAIN   What's that you said? What kind of a strange answer's that? You're confusing me with your answers!

WOYZECK   It's us poor people that . . . You see, Captain, sir . . . Money, money! Whoever hasn't got money . . . Well, who's got morals when he's bringing something like *me* into the world! We're flesh and blood, too. Our kind is miserable only once: in this world and in the next. I think if we ever got to heaven we'd have to help with the thunder.

CAPTAIN   Woyzeck, you have no virtue! You're not a virtuous human being! Whenever I rest at the window, when it's finished raining, and my eyes follow the white stockings along as they hurry across the street . . . Damnation, Woyzeck, you've got me talking about love again! I'm made of flesh and blood, too. But, Woyzeck: Virtue! Virtue! How was I supposed to get rid of the time? I always say to myself: "You're a virtuous man, (*moved*) a good man, a good man."

WOYZECK   Yes, sir, Captain: Virtue. I haven't got much of that. You see, us common people, we haven't got virtue. That's the way it's got to be. But if I could be a gentleman, and if I could have a hat and a watch and a walking-stick, and if I could talk refined, I'd want to be virtuous, all right. There must be something beautiful in virtue, Captain, sir. But I'm just a poor good-for-nothing!

CAPTAIN   Good, Woyzeck. You're a good man, a good man. But you think too much. It eats at you. You always seem so exasperated. Our discussion has affected me deeply. You can go now. And don't run so! Slowly! Nice and slowly down the street!

Scene Two

AN OPEN FIELD, THE CITY IN THE DISTANCE

(WOYZECK *and* ANDRES *cut twigs from the bushes*)

ANDRES   (*whistles*)

WOYZECK   Andres? You know this place is cursed? Look at that light streak on the grass. Over there where the toadstools grow. That's where the head rolls every night. One time somebody picked it up. He thought it was a hedgehog. Three days and three nights, and he was in a box. (*low*) Andres, it was the Freemasons, don't you see, it was the Freemasons!

ANDRES   (*sings*)
> Two little rabbits sat on a lawn
> Eating, o eating the green, green
> grass . . .

WOYZECK   Quiet! Can you hear it, Andres? Can you hear it? Something's moving!

ANDRES   (*sings*)
> Eating, o eating the green, green
> grass
> Till all the grass was gone.

WOYZECK   It's moving behind me! Under me! (*stamps on the ground*) Listen! Hollow! It's all hollow down there! It's the Freemasons!

ANDRES   I'm afraid.

WOYZECK   Strange how still it is. You almost want to hold your breath. Andres!

ANDRES   What?

WOYZECK   Say something! (*looks about fixedly*) Andres! How bright it is! It's all glowing over the city! A fire's sailing around the sky and a noise coming down like trumpets. It's coming closer! Let's get out of here! Don't look back! (*drags him into the bushes*)

ANDRES   (*after a pause*) Woyzeck? Do you still hear it?

WOYZECK   It's quiet now. So quiet. Like the world's dead.

ANDRES   Listen! I can hear the drums inside. We've got to go!

Scene Three

THE CITY

(MARIE *with her child at the window.* MARGRET. *The Retreat passes, the* DRUM-MAJOR *at its head*)

MARIE   (*rocking the child in her arm*) Ho, boy! Da-da-da-da! Can you hear? They're coming! There!

MARGRET   What a man! Built like a tree!

MARIE   He walks like a lion.

DRUM-MAJOR   (*salutes* MARIE)

MARGRET   Oh, what an eye he gave you, neighbor! We're not used to such things from you.

MARIE   (*sings*)
>   Soldiers, o you pretty lads . . .

MARGRET   Your eyes are still shining.

MARIE   And if they are? Take *your* eyes to the Jew's and let him clean them for you. Maybe he can shine them up enough so you can sell them for a pair of buttons.

MARGRET   Look who's talking! Just look who's talking! If it isn't the Virgin herself! I'm a respectable person. But *you*! Everyone knows *you* could stare your way through seven layers of leather pants!

MARIE   Slut! (*slams the window closed*) Come, boy! What's it to them, anyway! Even if you are just a poor whore's baby, your dishonorable little face still makes your mother happy! (*sings*)
>   I have my trouble and bother
>   But, baby dear, where is your father?
>   Why should I worry and fight
>   I'll hold you and sing through the
>   night:
>   Heio popeio, my baby, my dove
>   What do I want now with love.

(*a knock at the window*) Who's there? Is it you, Franz? Come in!

WOYZECK   Can't. There's roll-call.

MARIE   Did you cut wood for the Captain?

WOYZECK   Yes, Marie.

MARIE   What is it, Franz? You look so troubled.

WOYZECK   Marie, it happened again, only there was more. Isn't it written: "And behold, there was a smoke coming up from the land like the smoke of an oven"?

MARIE   Oh, Franz!

WOYZECK   It followed me, all the way to the city. Something that I can't put my hands on, or understand. Something that drives us mad. What's going to happen?

MARIE   Franz!

WOYZECK   I've got to go. Tonight at the fair! I saved something again. (*He leaves*)

MARIE   That man! Seeing things like that! He didn't even look at his own child! He'll go crazy if he keeps thinking like that! Why are you so quiet, boy? Are you afraid? It's growing so dark. It's like we were going blind. Only that lantern shining in from outside. I can't stand it! It makes me shiver. (*She goes out*)

Scene Four

FAIR BOOTHS, LIGHTS, PEOPLE

OLD MAN   (*sings while a child dances to the barrel-organ*)
>   There's nothing on this earth will last
>   Our lives are as the fields of grass
>   Soon all is past, is past.

WOYZECK   Ho! Ho! Poor man, old man! Poor child, young child! Trouble and happiness!

MARIE   My God, when fools still have their senses, then we're all fools. Oh, what a crazy world! What a beautiful world!

(*They both go over to the* CHARLATAN *who stands in front of a booth, his wife in pants, and a costumed monkey*)

CHARLATAN   Gentlemen, gentlemen! You see here before you a creature as God created it! But it's nothing this way! Absolutely nothing! But now look at what Art can do. It walks upright! Wears coat and pants. And even carries a sabre! This monkey here is a regular soldier. So what if he *isn't* much different! So what if he *is* still on the bottom rung of the human ladder! Ho, there, take a bow! That's the way! Now you're a Baron, at least. Give us a kiss! (*The monkey trumpets*) This little customer's musical, too. And, gentlemen, in here you will see the astronomical horse and the little lovebirds. Favorites of all the crowned heads of Europe. They'll tell you anything: how old you are, how many children you have, what your ailments are. The performance is about to begin. And at the beginning. The beginning of the beginning!

WOYZECK   You want to?

MARIE   Sure. That must be nice in there. Look at the tassels on him! And his wife's got pants on! (*They both go inside*)

DRUM-MAJOR   Wait a minute! Did you see her? What a piece!

SERGEANT   Hell, she could whelp a couple regiments of cavalry!

DRUM-MAJOR   And breed Drum-Majors!

SERGEANT   Look at the way she carries that head! You'd think that black head of hair would pull her down like a weight. And those eyes!

DRUM-MAJOR   Like looking down a well . . . or up a chimney. Come on, let's go after her!

Scene Five

INTERIOR OF THE BRIGHTLY LIGHTED
BOOTH

MARIE All these lights!

WOYZECK Sure, Marie. Black cats with fiery eyes. Ho, what a night!

PROPRIETOR OF THE BOOTH (*bringing forward a horse*) Show your talent! Show your brute reason! Put human society to shame! Gentlemen, this animal you see here, with a tail on its torso, and standing on its four hoofs, is a member of all the learnéd societies. As well as a professor at our university where he teaches students how to ride and fight. But that requires simple intelligence. Now think with your double reason! What do you do when you think with your double reason? Is there a jackass in this learned assembly? (*The nag shakes its head*) How's that for double reasoning? That's physiognomy for you. This is no dumb animal. This is a person! A human being! A human brute! But still an animal. A beast. (*The horse conducts itself indecently*) That's right, put society to shame. As you can see, this animal is still in a state of nature. Not ideal nature, of course! Take a lesson from him! But ask your doctor first, otherwise it might prove highly dangerous! What we have been told by this is: Man must be natural! You are created of dust, sand and dung. Why must you be more than dust, sand and dung? Look there, at his reason. He can figure even if he can't count it off on his fingers. And why? Because he cannot express himself, can't explain. A metamorphosed human being. Tell the gentlemen what time it is! Which of you ladies and gentlemen has a watch? A watch?

SERGEANT A watch? (*He pulls a watch imposingly and measuredly from his pocket*) There you are, my good man!

MARIE I've got to see this. (*She clambers down to the first row of seats; the* SERGEANT *helps her*)

DRUM-MAJOR What a piece!

Scene Six

MARIE'S ROOM

MARIE (*sitting, her child on her lap, a piece of mirror in her hand*) The other one gave him orders, so he had to go! (*looks at herself in the mirror*) Look how the stones shine! What kind are they, I wonder? What kind did he say they were? Sleep, boy! Close your eyes! Tight! Stay that way now. Don't move, or he'll get you! (*sings*)
Hurry, lady, close up tight
A gypsy boy is out tonight
And he will take you by the hand
And lead you into gypsyland.

(*continues to look at herself in the mirror*) They must be gold! I wonder how they'll look on me at the dance? Our kind's got only a little corner in the world and a piece of broken mirror. But my mouth is just as red as any of the fine ladies with their mirrors from top to bottom, and their handsome gentlemen that kiss their hands for them! I'm just a poor common piece! (*The child sits up*) Quiet, boy. Close your eyes! There's the sandman! Look at him run across the wall! (*She flashes with the mirror*) Eyes tight! Or he'll look into them and make you blind!

(WOYZECK *enters behind her. She jumps up, her hands at her ears*)

WOYZECK What's that?

MARIE Nothing.

WOYZECK There's something shining in your hands.

MARIE An earring. I found it.

WOYZECK I never found anything like that! Two at a time!

MARIE Am I human or not?

WOYZECK I'm sorry, Marie.—Look at the boy asleep! Lift his arm, the chair's hurting him. Look at the shiny drops on his forehead. Everything under the sun works! We even sweat in our sleep. Us poor people! Here's some money again, Marie. My pay and something from the Captain.

MARIE God bless you, Franz.

WOYZECK I've got to get back. Tonight, Marie! I'll see you!

MARIE (*alone, after a pause*) Why am I so bad! I could run myself through with a knife! Oh, what a life, what a life! We'll all end up in hell, anyway, in the end: man, woman and child!

Scene Seven

AT THE DOCTOR'S

DOCTOR I don't believe it, Woyzeck! And a man of your word!

WOYZECK What's that, doctor, sir?

DOCTOR I saw it all, Woyzeck. You pissed

on the street! You were pissing on the wall like a dog! And here I'm giving you three groschen a day plus board! That's terrible, Woyzeck! The world's becoming a terrible place, a terrible place!

WOYZECK   But, doctor, sir, when Nature . . .

DOCTOR   When Nature? When Nature? What has Nature to do with it? Did I or did I not prove to you that the *musculus constrictor vesicae* is controlled by your will? Nature! Woyzeck, man is free! In Mankind alone we see glorified the individual's will to freedom! And you couldn't hold your water! (*shakes his head, places his hands behind the small of his back, and walks back and forth*) Have you eaten your peas today, Woyzeck? Nothing but peas! *Cruciferae!* Remember that! There's going to be a revolution in science! I'm going to blow it as high as the heavens! Urea, Oxygen, Ammonium hydrochloratem hyperoxidic. Woyzeck, couldn't you just *try* to piss again? Go in the other room there and make another try.

WOYZECK   Doctor, sir, I can't.

DOCTOR   (*disturbed*)   But you could piss on the wall! I have it here in black and white. Our contract is right here! I saw it. I saw it with these very eyes. I had just stuck my head out the window, opening it to let in the rays of the sun, so as to execute the process of sneezing. (*going towards him*) No, Woyzeck, I'm not going to vex myself. Vexation is unhealthy. Unscientific. I'm calm now, completely calm. My pulse is beating at its accustomed 60, and I'm speaking to you in utmost coldbloodedness. Why should I vex myself over a man, God forbid! A man! Now if he were a Proteus, it would be worth the vexation! But, Woyzeck, you really shouldn't have pissed on the wall.

WOYZECK   You see, doctor, sir, sometimes a person's got a certain kind of character, like he's built a certain way. But with Nature it's not the same, you see. With Nature, (*He snaps his fingers*) it's like that. How should I explain it, it's like . . .

DOCTOR   Woyzeck, you're philosophizing again.

WOYZECK   (*confidentially*)   Doctor, sir, did you ever see anything with double nature? Like when the sun stops at noon, and it's like the world's going up in fire. That's when I hear a terrible voice saying things to me!

DOCTOR   Woyzeck, you have an *aberratio!*

WOYZECK   (*places his finger at his nose*)   It's in the toadstools, doctor, sir, that's where it is. Did you ever see the shapes the toadstools make when they grow up out of the earth? If only somebody could read what they say!

DOCTOR   Woyzeck, you have a most beautiful *aberratio mentalis partialis* of a secondary order! And so wonderfully developed! Woyzeck, your salary is increased! *Idée fixe* of a secondary order, and with a generally rational state. You go about your business normally? Still shaving the Captain?

WOYZECK   Yes, sir.

DOCTOR   You eat your peas?

WOYZECK   Just like always, doctor, sir. My wife gets the money for the household.

DOCTOR   Still in the army?

WOYZECK   Yes, sir, doctor.

DOCTOR   You're an interesting case. Subject Woyzeck, you're getting an increase in salary. So behave yourself! Let's feel your pulse. Ah, yes.

Scene Eight

MARIE'S ROOM

(DRUM-MAJOR. MARIE)

DRUM-MAJOR   Marie!

MARIE   (*looking at him, with expression*) Go on, show me how you march! A chest broad as a bull's and a beard like a lion! There's not another man in the world like that! And there's not a prouder woman in the world than me!

DRUM-MAJOR   Wait till Sunday when I wear my helmet with the plume and my white gloves! Damn, that'll be a sight for you! The Prince always says: "My God, there goes a real man!"

MARIE   (*scoffing*)   Ha! (*goes towards him*) A man?

DRUM-MAJOR   You're not such a bad piece either! Hell, we'll plot a whole brood of Drum-Majors! Right? (*He puts his arm around her*)

MARIE   (*annoyed*)   Let go!

DRUM-MAJOR   Bitch!

MARIE   (*fiercely*)   Just touch me!

DRUM-MAJOR   There's devils in your eyes.

MARIE   Let there be, for all I care! What's the difference!

Scene Nine

STREET

(CAPTAIN. DOCTOR. *The* CAPTAIN *comes panting along the street, stops; pants, looks about*)

CAPTAIN   Ho, Doctor, don't run so fast!

Don't paddle the air so with your walking-stick! You're only courting death that way. A good man, with a good conscience, never walks as fast as that. A good man . . . (*He catches him by the coat*) Doctor, permit me to save a human life!

DOCTOR   I'm in a hurry, Captain, in a hurry!

CAPTAIN   Doctor, I'm so melancholy. I have such fantasies. I start to cry every time I see my coat hanging on the wall.

DOCTOR   Hm! Bloated, fat, thick neck: apoplectic constitution. Yes, Captain, you'll be having *Apoplexia Cerebria* anytime now. Of course you may have it on only one side, in which case you'll be paralyzed down that one side. Or if things go really well you'll be mentally disabled so that you can vegetate away for the rest of your days. You can look forward to something approximately like this during the next four weeks! And furthermore, I can assure you that you give promise of being a most interesting case. And if it is God's will that only half of your tongue become paralyzed, then we will conduct the most immortal of experiments.

CAPTAIN   Doctor, you mustn't scare me that way! People are said to have died of fright. Of pure, sheer fright. I can see them now with lemons in their hands. But they'll say: "He was a good man, a good man." You devil's casket-nailmaker!

DOCTOR   (*extending his hat towards him*) Do you know who this is, Captain? This is Sir Hollowhead, my most honorable Captain Drill-theirassesoff!

CAPTAIN   (*makes a series of folds in his sleeve*)   And do you know who this is, Doctor? This is Sir Manifold, my dear devil's Casketnail-maker! Hahaha! But no harm meant! I'm a good man, but I can play, too, when I want to, Doctor, when I want to . . .

WOYZECK   (*comes towards them and tries to hurry past*)

CAPTAIN   Ho, Woyzeck, where are you off to in such a hurry? Stay a while, Woyzeck! Running through the world like an open razor, you're liable to cut someone. He runs as if he had to shave a castrated regiment, and would be hung before he discovered and cut the longest hair that wasn't there. But on the subject of long beards . . . What was it I wanted to say? Woyzeck, why was I thinking about beards . . .

DOCTOR   The wearing of long beards on the chin, remarks Pliny, is a habit of which soldiers must be broken . . .

CAPTAIN   (*continues*) Ah, yes, this thing about beards! Tell me, Woyzeck, have you found any long hairs from beards in your soupbowl lately? Ho, I don't think he understands!

A hair from a human face, from the beard of an engineer, a Sergeant, a . . . a Drum-Major? Well, Woyzeck? But then he's got a good wife. It's not the same as with the others.

WOYZECK   Yes, sir, Captain! What was it you wanted to say, Captain, sir?

CAPTAIN   What a face he's making! Well, maybe not in his soup, but if he hurries home around the corner, I'll lay a wager he might still find one on a certain pair of lips. A pair of lips, Woyzeck. I know what love is, too, Woyzeck. Look at him, he's white as chalk!

WOYZECK   Captain, sir, I'm just a poor devil. And I've got nothing else in the world. Captain, sir, if you're just playing with me . . .

CAPTAIN   Playing with you? Me? Playing with you, Woyzeck?

DOCTOR   Your pulse, Woyzeck, your pulse! Short, hard, skipping, irregular.

WOYZECK   Captain, sir, the earth's as hot as the coals in hell. But I'm as cold as ice, cold as ice. Hell is cold. I'll bet you. I don't believe it! God! God! I don't believe it!

CAPTAIN   Look here, you, how would you . . . how'd you like a pair of bullets in your skull? You keep stabbing at me with those eyes, and I'm only trying to help you. Because you're a good man, Woyzeck, a good man.

DOCTOR   Facial muscles rigid, taut, occasionally twitches. Condition excitable, strained.

WOYZECK   I'm going. Anything's possible. The bitch! . . . Anything's possible. The weather's nice, Captain, sir. Look, a beautiful, hard, grey sky. You'd almost like to pound a nail in up there and hang yourself on it. And just because of that little dash between Yes and Yes again . . . and No. Captain, sir: Yes and No: did No make Yes, or did Yes make No? I've got to think about that. (*He goes off with long strides, slowly at first, then faster and faster*)

DOCTOR   (*shouting after him*)   Phenomenon! Woyzeck, you get a raise!

CAPTAIN   I get so dizzy around people like that. Look at him go! Long-legged rascals like him step out like a shadow running away from its spider. But short ones only dawdle along. Long-legged ones are the lightning, the short ones are the thunder. Haha . . . Grotesque! Grotesque!

Scene Ten

MARIE'S ROOM

(WOYZECK. MARIE)

WOYZECK   (*looks fixedly at her and shakes his*

head) Hm! I don't see it! I don't see it! My God, I should be able to see it. I should be able to take it in my fists!

MARIE (*frightened*) What is it, Franz? You're raving.

WOYZECK A sin, so fat and big . . . It stinks enough to smoke the angels out of heaven! You have a red mouth, Marie! No blisters on it? Marie, you're as beautiful as sin. How can mortal sin be so beautiful?

MARIE Franz, it's your fever making you talk this way!

WOYZECK Damn you! Did he stand here? Like this? Like this?

MARIE While the day's long and the world's old, a lot of people can stand in one spot, one right after the other.

WOYZECK I saw him here!

MARIE You can see a lot with two eyes while the sun shines.

WOYZECK Whore! (*He goes after her*)

MARIE Don't you touch me, Franz! I'd rather have a knife in my body than your hands touch me. When I looked at him, my father didn't dare lay a hand on me from the time I was ten.

WOYZECK Whore! No, it should show on you! Something! Every man's a chasm. It makes you dizzy when you look down in. It's got to show! And she looks like innocence itself. So, innocence, there's a spot on you. But I can't prove it. Can't prove it. Who can prove it? (*He goes*)

Scene Eleven

THE GUARD HOUSE

(WOYZECK. ANDRES)

ANDRES (*sings*)
Our hostess she has a pretty maid
She sits in her garden night and day
She sits within her garden . . .

WOYZECK Andres!

ANDRES Hm?

WOYZECK Nice weather.

ANDRES Sunday weather. They're playing music outside the city tonight. All the whores are already there. And the men stinking and sweating. Nice, uh?

WOYZECK (*restlessly*) They're dancing, Andres, they're dancing!

ANDRES At the *Horse and Star Inn*.

WOYZECK They're dancing, dancing!

ANDRES Sure, for all I care. (*sings*)

She sits within her garden
But when the bells have tollèd late
Then she waits at the garden-gate
That's what the soldiers say.

WOYZECK Andres, I'm so restless.

ANDRES You're a fool!

WOYZECK I've got to see them. It keeps turning and turning in my head. They're dancing, dancing! Will her hands be hot, Andres? God damn her, Andres! God damn her!

ANDRES What do you want?

WOYZECK I've got to go. I've got to see them.

ANDRES What if they are? What's all this for a whore?

WOYZECK I've got to get out of here! I can't stand the heat!

Scene Twelve

THE INN

(*The windows are open. Dancing. Benches in front of the Inn.* APPRENTICES)

FIRST APPRENTICE (*sings*)
This shirt I've on, it is not mine
And my soul it stinketh of brandywine . . .

SECOND APPRENTICE Brother, let me be a real friend and knock a hole in your nature! Come on! I'll knock a hole in his nature! Hell, I'm as good a man as he is! I'll kill every flea on his body.

FIRST APPRENTICE My soul, my soul stinketh of brandywine! And even money passeth into decay! Forget me not, but the world's a beautiful place! Brother, my sadness could fill a barrel with tears! I wish our noses were two bottles, so we could pour them down each other's throats.

OTHERS (*in chorus*)
A hunter from the Rhine
Once rode through a forest so fine
Hallei-hallo, he called to me
From high on a meadow, open and free
A hunters' life for me.

(WOYZECK *stands at the window.* MARIE *and the* DRUM-MAJOR *dance past, without noticing him*)

WOYZECK Both of them! God damn her!

MARIE (*dancing past*) Don't stop! Don't stop!

WOYZECK (*choking*) Don't stop! Don't stop! (*He starts up passionately then sinks down onto the bench*) Don't stop! Don't stop! (*beating his hands together*) Turn and roll and roll and turn! God! Blow out the sun so they can roll on each other in their lechery! Man and woman and man and beast! They'll do it in the light of the sun, they'll do it in the palm of your hand like flies! Whore! That whore's red as coals, red as coals! Don't stop! Don't stop! (*jumps up*) Watch how the bastard takes hold of her! Touching her body! He's holding her, holding her now . . . like I held her once. (*He slumps down dizzily*)

FIRST APPRENTICE (*preaching from a table*) I say unto you, forget not the wanderer who standeth leaning against the stream of time, and who giveth himself answer with the wisdom of God, and saith: What is Man? What is Man? Yea, verily, I say unto you: How should the farmer, the cooper, the shoemaker, the doctor live, had not God created Man for their use? How should the tailor live, had not God implanted in Man his sense of shame? And the soldier, had not God endowed Man with the need to slaughter himself? And therefore, doubt ye not, for all things are sweet and lovely! Yet the world with all its things is an evil place, and even money passeth into decay. In conclusion, my belovèd brethren, let us piss once more upon the Cross, so that somewhere a Jew may die!

(*Amid the general yelling* WOYZECK *wakens and rushes off*)

Scene Thirteen

AN OPEN FIELD

WOYZECK   Don't stop! Don't stop! Hishh! Hashh! That's the way the fiddles and pipes go. Don't stop! Don't stop! Stop your playing! There's someone talking down there! (*He stretches himself on the ground*) What? What are you saying? Louder! Louder! Stab? Stab the goat-bitch dead! Should I? Must I? Do I hear it there, too? Does the wind say so, too? Will it never stop! Don't stop! Don't stop! Stab her! Stab her! Dead! Dead!

Scene Fourteen

A ROOM IN THE BARRACKS

(*Night.* ANDRES *and* WOYZECK *in a bed*)
WOYZECK (*softly*)   Andres!

ANDRES (*murmurs in his sleep*)
WOYZECK (*shaking Andres*)   Hey, Andres! Andres!
ANDRES   Mmm! What do you want?
WOYZECK   I can't sleep! When I close my eyes everything turns and turns. I hear voices in the fiddles: Don't stop! Don't stop! And then the walls start to talk. Can't you hear it?
ANDRES   Sure. Let them dance! I'm tired. God bless us all, Amen.
WOYZECK   All I hear is: Stab! Stab! And it cuts at my eyes like a knife.
ANDRES   Go to sleep, you fool! (*goes back to sleep*)
WOYZECK   Don't stop! Don't stop!

Scene Fifteen

THE DOCTOR'S COURTYARD

(STUDENTS *and* WOYZECK *below, the* DOCTOR *in the attic window*)

DOCTOR   Gentlemen, I find myself on the roof like David when he beheld Bathsheba. But all I see are the Parisian panties of the girls' boarding-school drying in the garden. Gentlemen, we are concerned with the weighty question of the relationship of the subject to the object. If, for example, we were to take one of those innumerable things in which we see the highest manifestation of the self-affirmation of the Godhead, and examine its relationship to space, to the earth, and to the planetary constellations . . . Gentlemen, if we were to take this cat and toss it out the window: how would this object conduct itself in conformity with its own instincts towards its *centrum gravitationis*? Well, Woyzeck? (*roars*) Woyzeck!

WOYZECK (*picks up the cat*)   Doctor, sir, she's biting me!

DOCTOR   Damn, why do you handle the beast so tenderly! It's not your grandmother! (*He comes down*)

WOYZECK   Doctor, I'm shaking.

DOCTOR (*utterly delighted*)   Excellent, Woyzeck, excellent! (*He rubs his hands. He takes the cat*) What's this, gentlemen? The new species of rabbit louse! A beautiful species . . . (*He pulls out a magnifying-glass, the cat runs off*) Animals, gentlemen, simply have no scientific instincts. But in its place you may see something else. Now, observe: for three months this man has eaten nothing but peas. Notice the effect. Feel how irregularly his pulse beats! And look at his eyes!

WOYZECK Doctor, sir, everything's going dark! (*He sits down*)

DOCTOR Courage, Woyzeck! Just a few more days, and then it will be all over with. Feel, gentlemen, feel! (*They fumble over his temples, pulse and chest*) Apropos, Woyzeck, wiggle your ears for the gentlemen! I've meant to show you this before. He uses only two muscles. Let's go, let's go! You stupid animal, shall I wiggle them for you? Trying to run out on us like the cat? There you are, gentlemen! Here you see an example of the transition into a donkey: frequently the result of being raised by women and of a persistent usage of the Germanic language. How much hair has your mother pulled out recently for sentimental remembrances of you? It's become so thin these last few days. It's the peas, gentlemen, the peas!

Scene Sixteen

THE INN

(WOYZECK. THE SERGEANT)

WOYZECK (*sings*)
 Oh, daughter, my daughter
 And didn't you know
 That sleeping with coachmen
 Would bring you low?

What is it that our Good Lord God cannot do? What? He cannot make what is done undone. Ha! Ha! Ha!—But that's the way it is, and that's the way it should be. But to make things better is to make things better. And a respectable man loves his life, and a man who loves his life has no courage, and a virtuous man has no courage. A man with courage is a dirty dog.

SERGEANT (*with dignity*) You're forgetting yourself in the presence of a brave man.

WOYZECK I wasn't talking about anybody, I wasn't talking about anything, not like the Frenchmen do when they talk, but it was good of you.—But a man with courage is a dirty dog.

SERGEANT Damn you! You broken mustache cup! You watch or I'll see you drink a pot of your own piss and swallow your own razor!

WOYZECK Sir, you do yourself an injustice! Was it *you* I talked about? Did I say *you* had courage? Don't torment me, sir! My name is science. Every week for my scientific career I get half a guilder. You mustn't cut me in two

or I'll go hungry. I'm a *Spinosa pericyclia;* I have a Latin behind. I am a living skeleton. All Mankind studies me.—What is Man? Bones! Dust, sand, dung. What is Nature? Dust, sand, dung. But poor, stupid Man, stupid Man! We must be friends. If only you had no courage, there would be no science. Only Nature, no amputation, no articulation. What is this? Woyzeck's arm, flesh, bones, veins. What is this? Dung. Why is it rooted in dung? Must I cut off my arm? No, Man is selfish, he beats, shoots, stabs his own kind. (*He sobs*) We must be friends. I wish our noses were two bottles that we could pour down each other's throats. What a beautiful place the world is! Friend! My friend! The world! (*moved*) Look! The sun coming through the clouds—like God emptying His bedpan on the world. (*He cries*)

Scene Seventeen

THE BARRACKS YARD

WOYZECK What have you heard?

ANDRES He's still inside with a friend.

WOYZECK He said something.

ANDRES How do you know? Why should I be the one to tell you? Well, he laughed, and then he said that she was some piece. And then about her thighs. And that she was as hot as a red poker.

WOYZECK (*quite coldly*) So, he said that? What was it I dreamed about last night? About a knife? What stupid dreams we get!

ANDRES Friend! Where are you off to?

WOYZECK Get some wine for the Captain. Andres, you know something? There aren't many girls like she was.

ANDRES Like who was?

WOYZECK Never mind. I'll see you. (*He goes off*)

Scene Eighteen

THE INN

(DRUM-MAJOR. WOYZECK. PEOPLE)

DRUM-MAJOR I'm a man! (*He pounds his chest*) A real man, you hear me? Anybody say different? Anybody who isn't as crocked as the

Lord God himself better keep off. I'll screw his nose up his own ass if he doesn't! I'll . . . (*to* WOYZECK) You, there! Get drunk! I wish the world was schnapps, schnapps! You better start drinking! (WOYZECK *whistles*) Son-of-a-bitch, you want me to pull your tongue out and wrap it around your middle? (*They wrestle,* WOYZECK *loses*) Should I leave enough wind in you for a good old lady's fart? Uh? (*Exhausted and trembling,* WOYZECK *seats himself on the bench*) The son-of-a-bitch can whistle himself blue, for all I care. (*sings*)

> Brandy's all my life, my life
> Brandy gives me courage!

A MAN   He sure got more than he came for.
ANOTHER   He's bleeding.
WOYZECK   One thing after another.

Scene Nineteen

PAWNBROKER'S SHOP

(WOYZECK. THE JEW)

WOYZECK   The pistol costs too much.
JEW   So, you want it or not? Make up your mind.
WOYZECK   How much was the knife?
JEW   It's straight and sharp. What do you want it for, to cut your throat? So, what's the matter? You get it as cheap here as anyplace else. You'll die cheap enough, but not for nothing. What's the matter? It'll be a cheap enough death.
WOYZECK   This'll cut more than bread.
JEW   Two groschen.
WOYZECK   There! (*He goes out*)
JEW   There, he says! Like it was nothing! And it's real money. Dog!

Scene Twenty

MARIE'S ROOM

FOOL   (*lying down telling fairy tales on his fingers*)   This one has the golden crown. He's the Lord King. Tomorrow I'll bring the Lady Queen her child. Bloodsausage says: Come on, Liversausage . . .
MARIE   (*paging through her bible*)   "And no guile is found in his mouth." Lord God,

Lord God! Don't look at me! (*paging further*) "And the scribes and Pharisees brought unto him a woman taken in adultery, and set her in the midst . . . And Jesus said unto her: Neither do I condemn thee; go, and sin no more." (*striking her hands together*) Lord God! Lord God! I can't! Lord God, give me only so much strength that I can pray. (*The child presses himself close to her*) The child is a sword in my heart. (*to the* FOOL) Karl! The only happy dog under the sun! (*The* FOOL *takes the child and grows quiet*) Franz hasn't come. Not yesterday. Not today. It's getting hot in here! (*She opens the window and reads further*) "And stood at his feet weeping, and began to wash his feet with tears, and did wipe them with the hairs of her head, and kissed his feet, and anointed them with ointment." (*striking her breast*) Everything dead! Savior! Savior! If only I could anoint your feet!

Scene Twenty-One

AN OPEN FIELD

WOYZECK   (*buries the knife in a hole*)   Thou shalt not kill. Lay here! I can't stay here! (*He rushes off*)

Scene Twenty-Two

THE BARRACKS

(ANDRES. WOYZECK *rummages through his belongings*)

WOYZECK   Andres, this jacket's not part of the uniform, but you can use it, Andres.
ANDRES   (*replies almost numbly to everything with*)   Sure.
WOYZECK   The cross is my sister's. And the ring.
ANDRES   Sure.
WOYZECK   I've got a Holy Picture, too: two hearts, real gold. I found it in my mother's Bible, and it said:

> O Lord, with wounded head so sore
> So may my heart be evermore.

My mother only feels now when the sun shines on her hands . . . that doesn't matter.
ANDRES   Sure.

WOYZECK (*pulls out a paper*) Friedrich Johann Franz Woyzeck, Soldier. Rifleman, Second Regiment, Second Battalion, Fourth Company. Born on the Feast of the Annunciation, the twentieth of July. Today I'm thirty years old, seven months and twelve days.

ANDRES Go to the hospital, Franz. Poor guy, you've got to drink some schnapps with a powder in it. That'll kill the fever.

WOYZECK You know, Andres, when the carpenter puts those boards together, nobody knows who it's made for.

Scene Twenty-Three

THE STREET

(MARIE, *with little* GIRLS, *in front of the house door.* A GRANDMOTHER. *Later,* WOYZECK)

GIRLS (*sing*)
The sun shone bright on Candlemas-day
And the corn was all in bloom
And they marched along the meadow-way
They marched by two and two.
The pipers marched ahead
The fiddlers followed through
And their socks were scarlet red . . .
FIRST CHILD I don't like that one.
SECOND CHILD Why do you always want to be different?
FIRST CHILD *You* sing for us, Marie!
MARIE I can't.
FIRST CHILD Why?
MARIE Because.
SECOND CHILD But *why* because?
THIRD CHILD Grandmother, *you* tell us a story!
GRANDMOTHER All right, you little crabapples! Once upon a time there was a poor little girl who had no father and no mother. Everyone was dead, and there was no one left in the whole wide world. Everyone was dead. And the little girl went out and looked for someone night and day. And because there was no one left on the earth, she wanted to go to heaven. And the moon looked down so friendly at her. And when she finally got to the moon, it was a piece of rotten wood. And so she went to the sun. And when she got to the sun, it was a faded sunflower. And when she got to the stars, they were little golden flies, stuck up there like they were caught in a spider's web. And when she wanted to go back to earth, the earth was an upside down pot. And she was

all alone. And she sat down there and she cried. And she sits there to this day, all, all alone.
WOYZECK (*appears*) Marie!
MARIE (*startled*) What!
WOYZECK We have to go, Marie. It's getting time.
MARIE Where to?
WOYZECK How should I know!

Scene Twenty-Four

A POND BY THE EDGE OF THE WOODS

(MARIE *and* WOYZECK)

MARIE The city's out that way. It's dark.
WOYZECK You can't go yet, Marie. Come, sit down!
MARIE But I've got to get back.
WOYZECK You don't want to run your feet sore.
MARIE What's happened to you?
WOYZECK You know how long it's been, Marie?
MARIE Two years from Pentecost.
WOYZECK You know how much longer it'll last?
MARIE I've got to get back. Supper's not made yet!
WOYZECK Are you freezing, Marie? And still you're so warm. Your lips are hot as coals! Hot as coals, the hot breath of a whore! And still I'd give up heaven just to kiss them again. Are you freezing? When you're cold through, you won't freeze any more. The morning dew won't freeze you.
MARIE What are you talking about?
WOYZECK Nothing. (*silence*)
MARIE Look how red the moon is! It's rising.
WOYZECK Like a sword washed in blood.
MARIE What are you going to do? Franz, you're so pale. (*He raises the knife*) Franz, stop! For heaven's sake! Help me! Help me!
WOYZECK (*stabs madly*) Take that and that! Why can't you die? There! There! Ha, she's still shivering! Still not dead? Still not dead? Still shivering? (*stabbing at her again*) Are you dead? Dead! Dead! (*He drops the knife and runs away*)
(*Some people approach*)
FIRST PERSON Wait!
SECOND PERSON You hear something? Shh! It's over there!
FIRST PERSON Whh! There! What a sound!

SECOND PERSON   It's the water, it's calling. It's a long time since anyone drowned here. Let's go! I don't like hearing things like that!

FIRST PERSON   Whh! There it is again! Like a man, dying!

SECOND PERSON   This is a gloomy place! So foggy, nothing but grey mist as far as you can see . . . and the hum of beetles like broken bells. Let's go!

FIRST PERSON   No, it's too clear, too loud! Up there! Come on!

Scene Twenty-Five

THE INN

WOYZECK   Dance! Everybody! Don't stop! Sweat and stink! He'll get you all in the end! (sings)

> O daughter, my daughter
> And didn't you know
> That sleeping with coachmen
> Would bring you low?

(He dances) Ho, Kathy! Sit down! I'm so hot, so hot! (He takes off his coat) That's the way it is: The devil grabs hold of one and lets the other get away. Kathy, you're hot as coals! Why are you so hot? You'll be cold, too, one day, Kathy. Have some sense. Can't you sing?

KATHY (sings)

> That Swabian land I cannot bear
> And long, long dresses I will not wear
> For long, long dresses and pointed shoes
> Are clothes a chamber-maid never should
>   choose.

WOYZECK   No shoes, no shoes! We can get to hell without shoes.

KATHY (sings)

> To such and like I'll not be prone
> Take back your gold and sleep alone.

WOYZECK   Sure, what do I want to get all bloody for?

KATHY   What's that on your hand then?

WOYZECK   Me? Me?

KATHY   Red! It's blood! (People gather round them)

WOYZECK   Blood? Blood?

INNKEEPER   Blood!

WOYZECK   I think I cut myself. Here, on my right hand.

INNKEEPER   Then why's there some on your elbow?

WOYZECK   I wiped it off.

INNKEEPER   Your right hand and you wiped it off on your right elbow? You're a smart one!

FOOL   And then the Giant said: "I smell, I smell the flesh of man." Pew, it stinks already!

WOYZECK   What do you want from me? Is it your business? Out of my way, or the first one who . . . Damn you! Do I look like I murdered somebody? Do I look like a murderer? What are you looking at? Look at yourselves, why don't you! Out of my way! (He runs out)

Scene Twenty-Six

AT THE POND

(WOYZECK alone)

WOYZECK   The knife? Where's the knife? I left it here. It'll give me away! Closer! And closer! What is this place? What am I hearing? Something's moving. Now it's quiet. It's got to be here. Marie? Ha, Marie! It's quiet now. It's all so quiet! Why are you so pale, Marie? Why are you wearing those red beads around your neck? Where did you earn that necklace with your sins? Your sins made you black, Marie, they made you black! Did I make you so pale? Why is your hair so wild? Did you forget to twist your braids today? The knife, the knife! I've got it. There! (He runs towards the water) There, into the water! (He throws the knife into the water) It dives like a stone into the black water. No, it's not out far enough for when they swim! (He goes into the pond and throws it out farther) There! Now! But in the summer when they dive for mussels? Ha, it'll get rusty, who'll ever notice it! Why didn't I break it first! Am I still bloody? I've got to wash myself. There, there's a spot, and there's another . . . (He goes out farther into the water)

Scene Twenty-Seven

THE STREET

(CHILDREN)

FIRST CHILD   Let's go find Marie!

SECOND CHILD   What happened?

FIRST CHILD   Don't you know? Everybody's out there. They found a body!

SECOND CHILD   Where?

FIRST CHILD   By the pond, out in the woods.

SECOND CHILD   Hurry, so we can still see something. Before they bring it back. (*They rush off*)

Scene Twenty-Eight

IN FRONT OF MARIE'S HOUSE

(IDIOT. CHILD. WOYZECK)

IDIOT (*holding the* CHILD *on his knee, points to* WOYZECK *as he enters*)   Looky there, he fell in the water, he fell in the water, he fell in the water!

WOYZECK   Boy! Christian!

IDIOT (*looks at him fixedly*)   He fell in the water.

WOYZECK (*wanting to embrace the* CHILD *tenderly, but it turns from him and screams*) My God! My God!

IDIOT   He fell in the water.

WOYZECK   I'll buy you a horsey, Christian.

There, there. (*The* CHILD *pulls away. To the* IDIOT) Here, buy the boy a horsey! (*The* IDIOT *stares at him*) Hop! Hop! Hip-hop, horsey!

IDIOT (*shouting joyously*)   Hop! Hop! Hip-hop, horsey! Hip-hop, horsey!

(*He runs off with the* CHILD. WOYZECK *is alone*)

Scene Twenty-Nine

THE MORGUE

(JUDGE, COURT CLERK, POLICEMAN, CAPTAIN, DOCTOR, DRUM MAJOR, SERGEANT, IDIOT, *and others.* WOYZECK)

POLICEMAN   What a murder! A good, genuine, beautiful murder! Beautiful a murder as you could hope for! It's been a long time since we had one like this!

(WOYZECK *stands in their midst, dumbly looking at the body of* MARIE; *he is bound, the dogmatic atheist, tall, haggard, timid, good-natured, scientific*)

Friedrich Hebbel

1813-1863

PREFACE TO
MARIA MAGDALENA

The function of drama, as the summit of all art, is to clarify the existing state of the world and man in its relationship to the Idea, that is, to that moral center which conditions all things, and which we must accept as existing, if only for the sake of the preservation of those things. The drama is possible only when in this state of affairs a decisive change takes place. By drama I mean the highest, epoch-making drama, because there exist a second and third kind, a partial-nationalistic and a subjective-individual kind, which are to the first as single scenes and characters are to the complete play, but which must represent the drama until a universal genius appears, and which, if he does not, must take his place as *disjecti membra poetae*. It is therefore in every way a product of the age, but only in the sense in which such an age is the product of all preceding ages, the connecting link between a series of centuries about to close, and a new series about to begin.

Until the present, history has produced only two ages of crisis in which the highest drama could have been possible; accordingly it has appeared only twice: once among the Ancient Greeks when classical antiquity's concept of the world proceeded from its original simplicity to the stage of reflection, a progress at first disintegrative and finally destructive; and once among the moderns when a similar self-division proceeded from the Christian concept of the world. When paganism was on the wane, Greek drama evolved itself and devoured it. It laid bare the nerve of the idea which wound its way through all the variegated divine forms of Olympus, or, if you prefer, it gave form to Fate. Thus we have the unmitigated suppression of the individual by those moral forces with which he finds himself not in accidental but in necessary conflict, the very conflict which in *Oedipus* reaches such dizzying heights. Shakespearean drama developed along the lines of Protestantism and emancipated the individual. Thus we have the terrible dialectic of his characters, who, inasmuch as they are men of action, in their unrestrained expansion crowd out and impinge upon all those living about them; and, inasmuch as they are men of thought, like Hamlet, are equally unrestrained in their introspection, and attempt, through the boldest and most terrifying questions, to drive God from the world as though He were a bungled piece of work.

After Shakespeare, Goethe was the first to lay again the foundation for a great drama; this he accomplished with his *Faust* and his *Elective Affinities*,[1] a work rightly called dramatic. He did, or rather he began to do, the only thing remaining: he placed the dialectical problem directly in the Idea; he placed the contradiction, which for Shakespeare existed only in the individual, directly in the center around which the individual turns, that is, in such comprehensible aspects of the Idea as the individual can grasp; and in so doing, he tried to divide that point, that Idea, into two parts: the point towards which the straight line of Greek drama and the crooked line of Shakespearean drama seemed both to lead. It need surprise no one that I pass over Calderón, to whom many assign an equal position. Calderón's dramas are indeed admirable in their logical development,

"Preface to *Maria Magdalena*" by Friedrich Hebbel, translated by Carl Richard Mueller, printed by permission of the translator.

[1] *Wahlverwandtschaften*—a novel written by Goethe in 1804.

and he has incorporated into the literature of the world an imperishable symbol with his play, *Life is a Dream*. This play, however, contains only past, no future; in its rigid dependence on dogma it assumes what it should prove. It is because of content, then, and not of form that it must be assigned a subordinate position.

Goethe, however, only showed the way. One can scarcely say he took the first step, for when, in *Faust,* he rises too high up into the cold regions where the blood begins to freeze, he turns around; and in his *Elective Affinities* he assumes, like Calderón, what he is to prove or demonstrate. I cannot explain how Goethe, in every respect an artist, and a great artist, was able in his *Elective Affinities* to offend so against the inner form or logic of this work, in that, not unlike an absent-minded analyst who brings an automaton into the dissecting room instead of a real body, he made the central point of his work a marriage, like that between Eduard and Charlotte, which from the start was not only invalid but immoral as well, and that he treated and used it as though it were its exact opposite, a marriage completely justified. The fact that he did not go more deeply into the main problem of the novel, and that just as in *Faust,* when he had to choose between an enormous perspective and a signboard painted over with figures from the catechism, he chose the signboard—and in so doing degraded the birth pangs of a humanity struggling for a new form, which we justly see in Part One, but which in Part Two is reduced to mere phases of a sickness which is cured later through an arbitrary and makeshift-psychological act—all this emanated from his quite particularly complicated individuality which I have no need to analyze here, since I have only to indicate how far he went. I hope it is not necessary to note that the foregoing, quite well motivated objections to *Faust* and *Elective Affinities* are by no means meant to cast aspersions on the immeasurable worth of these two world-famous and historical works, but to show the relationship which existed between the poet and the ideas incorporated in the works, and to prove where these ideas remained formless.

Goethe therefore, to use his own expression, indeed entered upon the great heritage of his time, but he did not consume it. He realized well enough that human consciousness was trying to expand, that it wanted to burst another ring, but he could not resign himself to a child-like trust in history; and since he was not able to resolve the dissonances which arose from the transitory conditions, into which he as a youth was violently drawn, he turned from them with decision, indeed with repugnance and disgust. But these conditions were not therefore eliminated. They have passed down to the present day. They have, in fact, increased, and all fluctuations and ruptures in our public as well as in our private lives are to be traced back to them. Nor are they by any means as unnatural or even as dangerous as one would like to make them seem. For the man of this century does not, as he is accused of, want new and unheard of institutions: he wants merely a better foundation for those which already exist. He wants them to rest on nothing less than morality and necessity, which are identical, and thus exchange for that external hook onto which till now they have in part been attached the internal center of gravity from which they are completely to be derived. This, I am convinced, is the world-wide historical process which is taking place in our day. Philosophy since Kant, indeed since Spinoza, has in its demoralizing and disintegrating way prepared for this, and dramatic art, assuming it still has anything left to do, must help to end it; for the circle which we have known till now has been described, and duplicates are superfluous and have no place in the household of literature. Dramatic art must show—just as in a similar age of crisis Aeschylus, Sophocles, Euripides, and Aristophanes did—it must show through great and powerful pictures how those elements set free as a result of the last great historical movement but which have not completely and absolutely been absorbed into a living organism but only partially formed themselves into a seeming body—dramatic art must show how these elements, surging about confusedly and in reciprocal conflict, are begetting a new form of humanity in which all things will return to place, in which woman will once again stand face to face with man, as man stands face to face with society, and society with the Idea. Bound up with this of course is the disadvantage that dramatic art must have to do with the most delicate and dubious of problems, because a breaking up of general world-wide conditions can appear only insofar as individual conditions are broken up, just as the earthquake cannot appear except through the collapse of churches and houses and the unrestrained inrushing of the sea. Of course I call this a disadvantage only in regard to those harmless souls for whom a tragedy and a game of cards are unconsciously reduced to serving the same purpose, because they grow uncomfortable when a spade is no longer to be a spade. They want new combinations within the game, but no new rules.

I say to you who call yourselves dramatic poets, that if you satisfy yourselves with putting on stage anecdotes, historical or otherwise, they are all one; or, at the most, if you satisfy yourself with analyzing the psychological clockwork of a character, then, no matter how often you put pressure on our tearducts or convulse us with laughter, you are not one whit better than your famous Thespian cousin who lets his puppets dance in his booth. The only basis for your art is where a problem exists. But when such a problem occurs to you, when life confronts you in its brokenness, together with that aspect of the Idea, for both must coincide, in which the lost unity is found again, then seize upon it and do not worry yourself with the thought that the aesthetic-minded rabble demands that the state of health be shown in the very disease itself, because all you are doing is showing the transition to that state of health and are quite unable to heal the fever unless you concern yourself with it. Let me add expressly to this that it is not the allegorical dressing up of the Idea which need concern us here, nor any philosophical dialectic, but that dialectic which is directly a part of life itself.

I said that dramatic art must help to end that world-wide historical process of our day, that process which does not desire the overthrow of existing human institutions—political, religious, and moral—but to give them a firmer foundation and thereby secure them from overthrow. In this sense dramatic art must be timely, like all poetry which does not restrict itself to empty representations and arabesquings; in this sense and in no other is all real poetry timely. It was also in this sense that in my preface to *Genoveva* I designated my dramas as artistic offerings of the time, for I am aware that the individual life processes which I have represented, and which I have still to represent, stand in closest relationship with the general problems which presently concern us.

Poetry, we seem to say now, is not to remain either what it was or what it is: the mirror of the century and the movement of mankind in general. It seems it is to become the mirror of the day, indeed of the very hour itself. But it is the drama that comes off worst of all, not because too much or the wrong thing is demanded of it, but because nothing at all is demanded. It is meant merely to amuse, it is meant merely to bring forward a thrilling anecdote, carried, at best, in order to be piquant, by characters of unusual psychology. But on no account must it do more.

There is one question which I cannot circumvent: is our philosophy, thus far advanced, able, alone, to solve the great problem of our age, and is the point of view of art to be regarded as outdated or capable of being outdated? If art were nothing more than what most people see in it, a dreamlike spinning on of the physical world, interrupted now and then by a so-called ironic remark about itself, almost a comedy of forms [*Gestalten-komoedie*], transferred from the external theatre to the internal one, in which the veiled Idea plays hide-and-seek with itself the same as ever—if this were true, then one must of necessity answer Yes, and lay upon it the task of atoning for the four thousand-year-old sin of usurped existence with a voluntary death. But art is not only infinitely more, it is something completely different. It is realized philosophy, just as the world is realized Idea; and that philosophy which desires no traffic with art, and which does not want to manifest itself in appearance and thereby give highest proof of its reality—that philosophy had best forget the world entirely. It is a matter of indifference whether it deny the first or the last phase of the life-process, from which it must presume itself to be excluded, if it believes itself able to manage without representation; for philosophy cannot relate to the world, as is possible through representation, without at the same time relating to art, for it is in art alone that the world becomes a totality. No productive and natural philosophy has ever done this; it always realized that it had not the right to suppress a proof which its nakedly reproduced Idea could not save itself from; and therefore it saw in art not merely a point of view, but its own goal and culminating point.

Now, if the drama is to solve no less a problem than the world-wide historical one itself, if it is to mediate between the Idea and the condition of the world and mankind, does it not follow that it must give itself completely to history, that it must be historical? I have said elsewhere in regard to this important point, that the drama in and of itself and without any special tendency is historical, and that art is the highest form of historical recording. This statement will be contested by no one who is versed in the skill of looking to the past as well as to the future, for he will remember that all that remains to us of the peoples of the ancient world are pictures, a skill which they developed into an art, and through which they recorded their being and their works in an unbreakable form; herein, above all, lies factual proof which ought never to be despised. He will see, too, that the presently strengthening historical process of elimination, which separates for us the significant from the insignificant—that which for us is wholly dead though still important in itself, from that which is still relevant in the historical organism—is in continuous advance. He will see that at some future time it will thin out the ranks of illustrious names, even to the Alexanders and the Napoleons; and that even later it will retain only the physiognomies of races, and finally perhaps even only the most general developmental epochs of mankind, brought about through the phases of religion and philosophy.

Since the great achievements of art are far less numerous than other great achievements, for the simple reason that they result from these other achievements, and since, for that reason, they increase in number far less rapidly, it becomes evident that art will long be with us, and that it will pass on to posterity the general essence of history, not the extensive and indifferent list of gardeners who planted and fertilized the tree, but the fruit with its body and core, which alone is of importance, and which furthermore can offer posterity the fragrance of the atmosphere in which it ripened.

But so much for generalities. Now a word more about the drama that I am offering to the public. It is a bourgeois tragedy. The bourgeois tragedy in Germany has fallen into discredit, and chiefly because of two abuses. Principally because it has not been constructed of those inner elements which are inherent in it: the harsh determination with which the individuals, incapable of dialectic, stand face-to-face with one another in the most confined of spheres; and the terrible constraint of life in all its one-sidedness which results from this condition. Rather they have patched it together out of all kinds of externalities: lack of money, for example, surplus of hunger; but above all out of the conflict between the third estate and the first and second estates in love-affairs. This undoubtedly gives rise to much that is pathetic, but not tragic, for the tragic must appear from the start as something necessary, as something postulated in life itself, such as death, as something which is utterly unavoidable. As soon as one can help himself with a: If only he had (thirty dollars, which a touching sentimentality bolsters with a: If only he had come to me, I live in No. 32), or a: If only she had been (a lady, etc.)—when one can help himself with the like of these, then the impression, which was meant to stir us deeply, becomes trivial, and

the effect, if it is not utterly scattered to the winds, exists in the fact that the next day the spectator will pay his poorhouse taxes more readily than before or that he will treat his daughter with more consideration: facts for which the supervisor of the poorhouse and the daughter, respectively, may be grateful, but which are not dramatic art.

The second reason why bourgeois tragedy has fallen into discredit is that once our poets let themselves down to the people, because it occurred to them that perhaps one need only be human to have a fate, and in certain circumstances a terrible fate, they assumed it necessary to ennoble the common people with whom they occupy themselves during such lost hours through beautiful speeches which they bestow upon them from their treasure chest; or else these poets thought it necessary to force them down below their actual station in life by imposing on them a wooden stupidity, so that their characters appear to us partly as bewitched princes and princesses—whom the magician out of sheer malice refused to turn into dragons and lions and other respectable worthies of the animal kingdom, but turned instead into base bakery maids and tailor's apprentices—but also partly as living blocks of wood, whose very ability to say Yes and No is cause for no little surprise. This, if possible, was even worse, because to the absurd and the ridiculous it added the trivial, and furthermore in a most obvious manner, for it is well known that the citizen and the farmer do not pluck their figures of speech, which they use just as well as the heroes of the salon and the promenade, from the starry firmament nor fish them from the sea; rather the artisan gathers them in his workshop, and the farmer from behind his plow, and many of us have learned that these simple people, though they may not be adept in the art of conversation are nevertheless capable of lively speech, and know how to combine and illustrate their ideas.

These two abuses explain the prejudice against bourgeois tragedy, but they cannot justify it, because they are the fault not of the *genre* but of inferior tradesmen who have bungled so badly in it. It is in and of itself a matter of indifference whether the hands of a clock are made of gold or of brass; nor does it matter whether an action which is in itself significant, that is, symbolic, takes place in a lower or in a socially higher sphere. Whereas in the heroic tragedy the seriousness of the subject matter and the reflections directly bound up in it may compensate up to a point for the deficiency in the tragic form, in the bourgeois tragedy everything depends on whether the circle of the tragic form is completed, that is, whether the point has been reached where we no longer care about the fate of a single individual, arbitrarily chosen by the playwright, but are able to see in that individual fate a fate which is universally human. The tragic outcome, too, whatever the particular form it may assume, must be recognized as wholly inevitable and incontestable.

These are the only points to be concerned about in a play: the relationship of the story to the positive and negative aspects of the moral powers moving in its background—family, honor, the choice between good and evil. Never ask for the so-called "flowery diction" of the false poets, that lamentably colorful calico in which marionettes strut themselves about; nor for the number of pretty figures, splendid aphorisms and descriptions and other spurious adornments, to be poor in which is the first result of richness. Those hereditary sins of the bourgeois tragedy, which I have mentioned above, are the very ones which I have avoided, of that I am certain. But I have undoubtedly committed others in their place. What are they?   [*Paris, March 4, 1844*]

Translated by Carl Richard Mueller

A WORD ABOUT THE DRAMA

Art has to do with life, inner and outer life, and one may well say that it represents both simultaneously: purest form and highest content. The main categories of art and their laws result directly from the difference of the elements which in every instance are taken from life and worked over. Life, however, appears in two-fold form, as Being and as Becoming, and art fulfills its task most completely when it maintains an even balance between the two. Only in this way can it assure itself of both present and future, which must be of equal importance; only in this way can it become what it ought to become: life in life. For that which is wholly complete stifles the creative spirit,

"A Word About the Drama" by Friedrich Hebbel, translated by Carl Richard Mueller, printed by permission of the translator.

without which it remains ineffectual, and the quivering embryo excludes form.

Drama represents the life-process as such. And indeed not merely in the sense that it presents life to us in its entire breadth, an aspect also characteristic of epic poetry, but in the sense that it visualizes for us the critical relationship which the individual, released from the original nexus, bears to the whole, a part of which, despite his incomprehensible freedom, he still remains. Drama, therefore, as is fitting for the highest form of art, refers itself equally to Being as to Becoming: to Being, in that it may never tire in repeating the eternal truth, that life as individualization, which knows no moderation or bounds, does not engender guilt merely by accident, but necessarily and essentially contains and conditions it; and to Becoming, in that with the ever new material furnished it by changing time and its deposit, history, it must prove that man, however the things about him may change, remains according to his nature and his destiny eternally the same. In this regard we may not overlook the fact that dramatic guilt does not, like the original sin of Christianity, originate in the direction of the human will, but emanates directly from the will itself, from the inflexible, arbitrary expansion of the ego, and that therefore it is a matter of complete indifference dramatically whether the hero founders while engaged in an excellent or in reprehensible endeavor.

The stuff of drama consists of plot and characters. The former we will not discuss here, for among the moderns at least it has been assigned a subordinate position, and anyone who doubts this may prove it to himself by examining a play of Shakespeare and asking himself what it was that fired the author to write the play, the plot or the people he lets appear in it. The treatment of characters, on the other hand, is of the utmost importance. These must never appear as finished persons, as people who can play their way through all kinds of relationship and, like actors, enjoy or suffer good fortune or misfortune respectively, but only externally, not inwardly, not in heart and spirit. This is the death of drama, death before birth. Drama only comes alive when it visualizes for us how the individual attains form and firmness of character and resolution in the struggle between his personal will and the general will of the world, which always modifies and changes his deed, the expression of freedom, through the event, the expression of necessity; and in so doing it explains to us the nature of all human action, which as soon as it tries to manifest a personal (*inneres*) motive, always simultaneously releases a resisting motive which is intended to restore equilibrium. And although the fundamental Idea, upon which the, here presumed, dignity and worth of the drama depend, provides the circle within which all must move in planetary fashion, nevertheless the poet must still provide for a diversification of interest, both properly and without violating the true unity; or more properly, for the realization of the totality of life and the world; and also guard against placing all of his characters at an equal distance from the center, as so often happens in the so-called lyrical dramas. The most complete picture of life arises when the principal character is to the subordinate and opposing characters what fate, with which he wrestles, is to him; and when, in the same manner, everything, down to the lowest level, is mutually developed, conditioned, and mirrored.

The question now is: what is the relationship between drama and history and to what extent must it be historical? To the same extent, I think, that it is now in and of itself, and insofar as art may be considered the highest form of historical recording; because art cannot possibly represent the most imposing and significant life-processes without those decisive historical crises which history evokes and calls forth, the integration or the gradual disintegration of the religious and political forms of the world, as the principal conductor and fundament of all civilization—in a word: art and history must conjointly provide us with the atmosphere of the times. Recorded history, which even Napoleon called a fable agreed upon, this motley chequered, monstrous chaos of dubious facts and one-sided or badly drawn character sketches, will sooner or later exceed the capacity of human comprehension, and in this way the newer drama, especially the plays of Shakespeare, which is to say all of them and not merely those specifically called historical, might quite naturally assume the same relationship to distant posterity as the Greek drama has assumed to us. Then, and very likely not before, will we cease narrowmindedly trying to discover a common identity between art and history, and cease anxiously comparing the historical situation and character with their artistic counterparts: for then we will have learned to understand that through such means the almost non-existent agreement between the first and the second portrayal can be brought out, not, however, that between image and truth; we will have learned to understand that the drama is sym-bolic, not merely in its totality, which is self-evident, but that it is symbolic in each of its elements, and that it must be regarded as symbolic; in the same way the painter, when he endows his figures with red cheeks and blue eyes, does not distill his colors from human blood, but quite naturally and as a matter of course uses cinnabar and indigo.

But the content of life is inexhaustible and the medium of art is limited. Life knows no conclusion; the thread on which it spins its phenomena merges into the infinite. Art on the other hand must come to a conclusion, it must, as best it can, tie the thread into a circle. This is the point Goethe must have had in mind when he said, that in all the forms of art there is something untrue. This something untrue can, of course, be detected in life itself, for not even life can offer a single form into which all of its elements are equally merged; it cannot, for example, fashion the most perfect man without withholding from him the merits which constitute the most perfect woman; and the two buckets in the well, only one of which can always be full, are the most characteristic symbol of all creation. This fundamental lack shows itself to be far worse and more critical in art than in life, where the totality always intercedes and compensates for the individual, and this for the reason that in art a lack in one place must absolutely be compensated for in another.

I will illustrate this thought by applying it to the drama. The most superior dramas of all literatures demonstrate that only by giving one or more of the main characters a measure of consciousness of the world and of himself which far exceeds reality can the poet complete the invisible ring in which the picture of life which he has set up moves. Omitting the Greeks whose treatment of character was something else, I will only remind the reader of Shakespeare, and, omitting the perhaps too compelling evidence of Hamlet, draw attention to the monologues in *Macbeth* and *Richard*, as well as those of the Bastard in *King John*. Some, be it remarked in passing, have at times wanted to see in this obvious defect in Shakespeare a virtue, a particular excellence (even Hegel did so in his *Aesthetics*), instead of being content with the proof that the reason lay not in the poet but in art. But what is accordingly found in the greatest dramatists as a consistent trait in whole characters is also often met with in single culminating moments when the word accompanies the deed or perhaps even precedes it. It is this, to draw a most important conclusion, which differentiates the conscious presentation in art from the unconscious presentation in life; that art, if it does not want to fail in its effect, must bring to itself sharp and complete outlines, while life, which does not first have to fight to establish itself in our belief, and which in the end may be indifferent to whether or not and how it has been understood, may content itself with a half-hearted Ah! or Oh!, with a facial expression or a gesture. Goethe's statement, with which he dared to touch on the most dangerous secret of art, is often repeated, but mostly in regard to what is superficially called form. The boy sees in the most profound Bible verse only his good friends, the twenty-four letters of the alphabet, which were used to express it.

The German drama seems to be in the ascendant again. What task has it now to solve? The question might be cause for surprise, for the most obvious answer in any case must be: The same which drama has had to solve in all ages. But one can ask further: Shall it come to grips with the present? Shall it turn back to the past? Or shall it be social, historical, or philosophical? Respectable talents have already entered upon these three different directions. Gutzkow has taken up the social theme. Four of his plays are available to us, and they make a better impression in their totality than taken separately, because they are obviously correlates which illuminate the heights and the depths of the social condition with sharp, cutting lights.

Others have taken up historical drama. I believe, and I have explained it above, that the true historical character of the drama does not lie in its subject matter, and that a pure creation of fancy, even a love story, can be very historical if only the spirit of life moves in it and keeps it fresh for posterity, which does not want to know what our grandfathers looked like to us in our imaginations, but what we ourselves really were. I do not wish to imply in any way that our poets should fabricate their works out of this air; on the contrary, when history or legend offers them a point of reference they ought not to scorn it in a ridiculous self-conceit of invention, but make grateful use of it. I want only to contest the widespread delusion that the poet can give anything but himself, anything but his own life-process. This he cannot do, nor need he do it: for if he lives truthfully, if he does not creep pettily and obstinately into his own paltry ego, but permits himself to become permeated with those unseen elements which are in flux at all times, preparing new forms and figures, then he can confidently follow the inclination of his spirit, he can be certain that in expressing his needs he is expressing the needs of the world, that in the efforts of his imagination are the pictures of the future; it follows from this that it lies not in his province to become personally involved in any street fight which might come about. For the poet, history is the vehicle for the embodiment of his views and ideas; whereas, to turn the statement around, he is not the resurrecting angel for history. Those who understand me will find that Shakespeare and Aeschylus confirm my view rather than contradict it. Philosophical dramas are also available. In these everything rests upon whether metaphysics issues from life, or whether life is to issue from metaphysics. In the first case something healthy will result, though by no means a new *genre*; in the other a monstrosity.

Now there is a possibility for a fourth kind of drama, one which unites the various tendencies characterized here, and which for that very reason permits no single tendency to predominate. This drama is the goal of my own endeavors, and if I have failed to make myself clear in the efforts themselves, in my *Judith* and my soon to appear *Genoveva*, then it would be foolish to try to help them with abstract explanations.

Translated by Carl Richard Mueller

MARIA MAGDALENA

Translated by Carl Richard Mueller

CAST OF CHARACTERS

MASTER ANTON *a cabinet-maker*
HIS WIFE
KLARA *his daughter*
KARL *his son*
LEONARD
A SECRETARY
WOLFRAM *a merchant*
ADAM *a court bailiff*
A SECOND COURT BAILIFF
A BOY
A YOUNG GIRL

SCENE   *A town of moderate size*

ACT ONE

A ROOM IN THE HOUSE OF THE
CABINET-MAKER

Scene One

(KLARA. THE MOTHER)

KLARA   Your wedding-dress? Oh, how nice it looks on you. It's like it was just made.

MOTHER   Well, child, a fashion can go only so far and then it turns around again and has to come back. This dress has been out of fashion ten times, and every time it came back in.

KLARA   This time, mother, I don't think it

Maria Magdalena by Friedrich Hebbel, translated by Carl Richard Mueller, printed by permission of the translator.

quite made it. Look here, the sleeves are too wide. But you mustn't let that worry you.

MOTHER   (*smiling*)   I'd have to be *you* to let *that* happen.

KLARA   So this is what you looked like. But you must have worn a wreath too, didn't you?

MOTHER   I should hope! Why else would I have tended that myrtle-bush in the big flower-pot for all those years.

KLARA   I remember how often I'd beg you to put it on, but you never would; you'd always say: "It's not my bridal-dress anymore, it's my burial-dress, and not a plaything." Finally it got to where I didn't want to see it, because when I'd look at it hanging there, so white, it would always remind me of your death, and of the day when the old women would pull it over your head. But why today?

MOTHER   When a person is as sick as I was, and doesn't know if she'll ever get well again, all kinds of things come into her mind. Death is more terrible than we think. Oh, it's a bitter thing. It wraps the world in gloom; it blows out all the lights, one after another, that glitter around us so gay and happy. The friendly eyes of husband and children don't shine anymore like they used to, and there's darkness everywhere; except that in our hearts a light is kindled that makes everything bright, and we see so much, so very much that we don't want to see. I know of no evil in my life. I have always followed the ways of God. I did as much in my own home as I was able; I raised you and your brother in the fear of the Lord and have held together the fruits of your father's hard labor. But I always knew how to save an extra penny for the poor, and sometimes when I sent one of them away because I was out of humor or because there were too many of them, well, it wasn't such a disaster after all, because I'd always call him back and end up by giving him twice as much as the others. And what does it all mean? It doesn't keep us from trembling when the hour of our death comes round. When death threatens us, we writhe like worms, we plead to God for life, like a servant pleading to his master to let him do again the work that he's done so badly, so that when he's paid he won't be given less than his due.

KLARA   Mother, you mustn't! You mustn't strain yourself this way!

MOTHER   No, my child, it does me good. Don't you see me standing here well and healthy again? Didn't the Lord God call me only to tell me that my festive dress isn't quite spotless and clean yet; and didn't He let me come back from the very gates of death and give me time to deck myself out for my wedding in Heaven? He wasn't as merciful as all that to those seven virgins in the Gospel that you read me about yesterday! That's why I made up my mind that today when I go to the Lord's Supper I would wear this dress. I wore it on the day when I made the best and most devout promises of my life. I want it to remind me today of the promises that I have still to keep.

KLARA   You're talking like you did when you were sick!

Scene Two

KARL   (*entering*)   Good morning, mother! Tell me something, Klara, would you put up with me if I weren't your brother?

KLARA   A golden necklace? Where did you get it?

KARL   What do I work for? Why do I stay at work two hours later every evening than the others? You're being impertinent!

MOTHER   Quarrelling on Sunday morning! Shame on you, Karl!

KARL   Have you a guilder for me, mother?

MOTHER   The only money I have is for the household.

KARL   Then give me some of that. I promise I won't complain if the pancakes aren't as rich as usual for the next two weeks. You've done it often enough before, I know *that* much! When you were saving up for Klara's white dress we had nothing special on the table for months. I didn't say anything, but I knew what to expect: a new hat or something else to show off. Let *me* have something of it, too, for a change!

MOTHER   Aren't you ashamed!

KARL   If I had time now, I'd . . . (*He starts to leave*)

MOTHER   Where are you going?

KARL   Why do you always want me to tell you that? When I do you only get embarrassed when the old bear asks where I've gone and you have to say you don't know. Well, now you won't have to be embarrassed because you *won't* know, and you won't be lying. And besides that I don't need your guilder. It's a good thing there's water in more wells than one! (*He goes off*)

Scene Three

KLARA   What did he mean by that?

MOTHER   He's such a worry to me! Yes, yes, his father was right, this is what comes of it. He was just as defiant now when he demanded that guilder as he was lovable when he was a curly-headed little boy and asked me for a piece of sugar. I wonder, would he have demanded that guilder just now if I hadn't given him those pieces of sugar? It plagues me so often. I don't think he even loves me. Did you see him cry, just once, while I was so sick?

KLARA   I saw him seldom enough; most of the time only at the table. His appetite was somewhat better than mine!

MOTHER   (*quickly*)   That was only natural, his work isn't easy!

KLARA   I suppose so! Men are such strange things! They're more ashamed of their tears than of their sins! A clenched fist is something else again. But tears? Father's the same way. The time they tried to let blood from your veins but nothing would come, he sat there on his joiner's bench the whole afternoon, sobbing, till I thought I couldn't bear it any longer. And then when I went over to him and put my hand to his cheek, what do you think he said? "Get this confounded splinter out of my eye! I have so much work to do and I can't get at it!"

MOTHER   I know, I know!—I never see Leonard anymore. Why's that?

KLARA   If he wants to stay away, let him!

MOTHER   I hope you're seeing him nowhere but in this house!

KLARA   Have I ever given you reason to suspect me? Do I stay too long in the evening when I go to the well?

MOTHER   No, of course you don't. But that's why I said he could come *here* to see you, so that he wouldn't have to watch for you like a thief in the night. My mother would never put up with that either.

KLARA   I don't see him.

MOTHER   Are you angry with one another? I like him well enough, he's a serious young man. I only wish he had some position in the world. In *my* day he couldn't have waited *too* long! The men would scramble around an able scribe like cripples for a crutch, because they were hard to come by. Even unimportant people like us could make use of him. One day he would write out a New Year's Greeting from a son to his father and get paid enough for the gilt letters alone to buy a doll for a child! Then the next day the father would call in the scribe and have him read him the greeting secretly where they couldn't be seen; that way they wouldn't be taken unawares and the father have to admit his ignorance. That's the way scribes got paid double. That's why they were always better off than others and made the beer more expensive. Things are different now, now old people like your father and me, who know nothing about reading and writing, have to let nine-year-old school-boys make fun of us. The world gets smarter all the time, and maybe the time will even come when we'll have to be ashamed for not knowing how to walk a tight-rope!

KLARA   The church bells are ringing.

MOTHER   Well, child, I'll pray for you. And as for Leonard, you may love him just as much as he loves God, no more, no less. That's what my old mother said to me when she gave me her blessing before she died. I think I've kept it long enough now, so now I'll give it to *you!*

KLARA   (*giving her a bouquet of flowers*) Here!

MOTHER   Is it from Karl?

KLARA   (*nods, then aside*)   How I wish it were! The only real happiness she can ever know has to come from him!

MOTHER   Oh, he *is* good! He *does* love me! (*She goes off*)

KLARA   (*watching her from the window*) There she goes. Three times I dreamt I saw her lying in a coffin, and then . . . why must these terrible dreams clothe themselves in our fears and frighten us so! I must never again pay attention to dreams, never be happy because of a good one, and so never be afraid because of the bad one that always follows. How firm and steady she walks. I wonder who'll be the first to meet her? I know it doesn't mean anything, but . . . (*startled*) the grave-digger! He's climbing out of a grave that he's just finished digging. She's bowing to him and smiling as she looks down into that hole. And now she throws her bouquet of flowers into it and goes into the church. (*The sounds of a choral heard*) They're singing: "Now thank we all our God." (*She folds her hands*) God, my God, if my mother had died, I would never have found peace again. (*She looks toward heaven*) But Thou art merciful, Thou art compassionate! I wish that I believed like the Catholics do, so that I could offer something to You. I would take all the money I have and buy You a lovely golden heart and wreathe it with roses. Our pastor says that offerings mean nothing to You because all things are Yours already, and we ought not to want to give You what You already possess. But everything in this house belongs to my father, and still it makes him happy when for his birthday I buy him a handkerchief with his own money and put it on his plate to surprise him. Yes, and then he always honors my gift by wearing it only on the highest holy-days, at Christmas or Pentecost. One time I saw a tiny Catholic girl carrying cherries to the altar as an offering. It made me so happy to watch her! They were the first cherries of the year that they'd given the child, and I saw how much she wanted to eat them. But still she fought against her innocent desire, and to put an end to her temptation she put down the cherries so quickly that the priest who had just raised the chalice looked at her so threateningly that he frightened the child away. And then I saw the Blessed Virgin smiling so tenderly above the altar, as if she wanted to step down out of her frame to hurry after the child and kiss her. I did it for her—Leonard's coming!

Scene Four

LEONARD   (*outside the door*) Are you proper?

KLARA   Why so tender all of a sudden, so thoughtful? I'm no princess!

LEONARD   (*entering*) I didn't think you were alone. When I walked past I thought I saw your neighbor's daughter Barbara at the window.

KLARA   Oh, so that's the reason!

LEONARD   Why are you always so cross! A person can stay away for two whole weeks but he'll always find the same rain-clouds around you!

KLARA   It wasn't always like this.

LEONARD   I should hope not! If you'd always looked like this we'd never have become friendly.

KLARA   Would that have been so terrible?

LEONARD   You're very open, aren't you! That suits me, too. Then that (*with reference to something*) toothache recently didn't mean anything!

KLARA   Oh, Leonard, that wasn't right of you!

LEONARD   Not right of me to want to possess completely my most priceless possession? Isn't that what you are? And at a time when I was in danger of losing you? Do you think I was blind to the looks you and the Secretary gave to one another that evening? That was quite a happy day for me! I took you to a dance and . . .

KLARA   When will you stop tormenting me this way! Yes, I looked at the Secretary, why should I say I didn't? But it was only because of the moustache he had grown at the university, it made him look . . . (*She stops*)

LEONARD   So handsome, isn't that what you wanted to say? Women, women! They'd sit up at the grossest caricature of a soldier's brush! I've had enough of him! Why should I hide the way I feel? He's stood in my way long enough! That round laughable little face of his, and that forest of hair on his head that he combs down the middle, looks like a white rabbit hiding behind a bush!

KLARA   I haven't praised him yet, so you needn't insult him!

LEONARD   Yet your interests in him aren't exactly cool!

KLARA   We played together as children, and afterwards . . . you know well enough.

LEONARD   Yes, I know! And that's just what I'm talking about!

KLARA   It was only natural for me to want to look at him. I was seeing him for the first time after so long. I was surprised to see how tall he had grown and . . . (*She interrupts herself*)

LEONARD   Then why were you embarrassed when he looked back at you?

KLARA   I thought he was looking at the mole on my left cheek, to see if it had grown larger. You know that's what I always think when anybody stares at me very hard, and that I always get embarrassed. It seems like the mole grows bigger as long as they're looking at me.

LEONARD   I don't care what your reasons were! It frightened me to see the two of you looking at one another. I said to myself that I'd make sure of you that same night. "If she wants to be my wife then she'll know it and won't try anything else," I said. "If she says no, then . . ."

KLARA   I'll never forget what you said when I pushed you from me. I wanted to run away but I felt myself held back. At first I thought it was you, but it was a rosebush that held to my dress with its thorns as though they were teeth. After that night I couldn't even trust *myself* anymore. You stood in front of me like someone demanding payment for a debt, And I . . . my God!

LEONARD   I'm not sorry for that yet. I knew that it was the only way I could keep you. I swore to myself that I would make you forget him.

KLARA   When I got back home I found my mother sick, deathly sick; suddenly struck down as if by some unseen hand. My father wanted to send for me earlier, but she wouldn't let him; she didn't want to destroy my happiness. I can't tell you how I felt when I heard. I didn't go near her, I didn't dare touch her, I trembled. She took it all for childish fear and nodded for me to come to her. As I slowly went towards her she pulled me down beside her and kissed me here on the mouth. I was ashamed, I wanted to confess to her, I wanted to cry out to her what I thought and felt: that it was *my* fault she was lying there! I *did* tell her, but my tears and sobbing choked my words. She reached for my father's hand and looked up at me so peacefully and said: "She's too good to me!"

LEONARD   And now she's well. I came to congratulate her and . . . what do you think?

KLARA   What?

LEONARD   To ask your father for your hand.

KLARA   Oh!

LEONARD   Aren't you well?

KLARA   Well? I'd be dead soon if I weren't your wife. But you don't know my father. He has no idea why it has to be soon. He mustn't know and we can't tell him. I've heard him say a hundred times that he would only give his daughter to someone who had more than love in his heart for her, but bread on the table, too. He's going to say: "Wait another year, my son, or maybe two!" And what will you say to that?

LEONARD   That problem doesn't exist anymore. I have the position. I'm Treasurer now.

KLARA   Treasurer? And the other candidate? The pastor's nephew?

LEONARD   He was drunk when he arrived at the examination. He bowed to the stove instead of to the Mayor, and when he sat down he knocked three cups from the table. You know how hot-tempered the old man is. "Sir!" he roared, still trying to control himself and biting his lip. His eyes blazed through his glasses like a pair of snakes ready for the spring, and his patience was at the breaking-point. Finally we got down to computing figures and (*he chuckles*) my competitor used a multiplication-table of his own finding that produced some quite novel results. "His calculations are wrong!" said the Mayor, giving me a look that told me the appointment was mine. I took his tobacco-stinking hand in mine and kissed it in all humility. And here it is, signed and sealed!

KLARA   It's all so . . .

LEONARD Unexpected? Well, it didn't quite happen by chance, you see. Why do you think I stayed away for two whole weeks?

KLARA I have no idea. I thought because of our quarrel that Sunday.

LEONARD I slyly set up that little disagreement myself, so that I could stay away without it seeming too unusual.

KLARA I don't understand.

LEONARD I mean it. I used the time well. I used it to court that hunchbacked little niece of the Mayor's, the one he's so fond of. She's as much his *right* hand as the bailiff is his *left*. Don't misunderstand me! I didn't say anything too pleasant to her, except to compliment her on her hair which, as you know, is red. In fact I said only one thing that really pleased her . . . about *you*.

KLARA Me?

LEONARD Why should I keep it a secret? It was done with the best of intentions. I let her think that there had never been anything between us, that there was—but that's enough of that! It lasted only long enough for me to get my hands on *this*. That gullible man-crazy little fool will find out just how much I meant of what I said when she hears our wedding banns read in church.

KLARA Leonard!

LEONARD Child! Child! You be harmless as a dove, my sweet, and I'll be sly as a snake, and that way, since they say man and wife are one, we'll satisfy the Gospel all the way round. (*He laughs*) Of course it wasn't quite an accident that our young Hermann happened to be drunk at the most important moment of his life. I suppose you've never heard that he goes in for drinking?

KLARA No.

LEONARD That made our plan all the easier. Three glasses and that was it! A couple of friends of mine helped. "Are congratulations in order?"—"Not yet!"—"Well, it's a pretty sure thing! After all, your uncle . . ." And then: "Have a drink with us, friends!"—On my way over here this morning I found him standing looking dejectedly over the railing of the bridge into the water. I greeted him mockingly and asked if he had lost something in the river. "Yes," he said, without looking up, "and maybe it'd be better if I jumped in after it."

KLARA How could you! I never want to see you again!

LEONARD Really? (*He starts as if to leave*)

KLARA My God, why must I be chained to him like this!

LEONARD Stop being a child! I want you to tell me something now in confidence. Does your father still have the thousand thalers invested in the pharmacy?

KLARA How should I know?

LEONARD Even about something as important as that?

KLARA My father's coming.

LEONARD Don't misunderstand me! The only reason I asked is that the pharmacist is about to go bankrupt.

KLARA I have to get to the kitchen! (*She goes off*)

LEONARD (*alone*) Well, I guess there's not much to get *here*! Master Anton's the kind of man who if he found one letter too many on his tombstone would haunt his grave till he'd scratched it out, and only because he'd think it dishonorable to take more of the alphabet than is his due!

Scene Five

THE FATHER, MASTER ANTON (*enters*) Good morning, Mr. Treasurer! (*He takes off his hat and puts on his woolen cap*) Will you permit an old man to cover his head?

LEONARD Then you know . . .

MASTER ANTON I knew yesterday evening. Yesterday at dusk I went to take the measurements for the casket of my good friend Müller who just died. I heard some of your friends complaining about you. I thought right away that you must have made it. And then in the dead man's house I heard the details from the sexton. He got there just ahead of me to console the widow, and to get drunk.

LEONARD And Klara had to learn of it from me?

MASTER ANTON If *you're* not interested in making her happy with the news, why should *I* be? I light no candles in my house till they belong to me. That way I can be sure that no one will come along and blow them out just when we're enjoying them most.

LEONARD Surely you couldn't think that I . . .

MASTER ANTON Think? About you? Or anyone else? I plane my boards smooth like they ought to be with iron tools, but I never let my thoughts do the same with people. I cured myself of that foolishness a long time ago. When I see a tree that's green I have good cause to think that it will blossom soon. And when it's blossomed that it will soon have fruit. And I have never been deceived. That's why I have kept up the custom. But about people I have no thoughts, none whatever, neither good ones nor bad ones. That way I have no need one time to grow red with embarrassment and the next pale with disappointment, when one time they deceive my fears and the next time my hopes. I only learn from them and take examples with my two eyes, but they don't think either, they only see. I thought I had learned all there was to learn about you, and now I find you here and have to admit that I only learned the half of it.

LEONARD   I think you have it all wrong, Master Anton. A tree depends on wind and weather, but human beings have laws and standards inside them.

MASTER ANTON   Really? Yes, I suppose we old people owe death a great debt for allowing us to chase around here for so long with all these young people, and for the chance to educate ourselves by them. It used to be the stupid world believed the father was put in it to educate the son. They had it all backwards. The son is here to put the last lick of polish on the father so that the poor simple old man needn't be ashamed when he goes to meet the worms in his grave. God be praised, I have a good teacher in my son Karl. He wages a terrible war against my prejudices, and he doesn't pamper the old child with too much indulgence. This morning he taught me two new lessons and in the most skillful way, without opening his mouth, in fact without even showing himself. First of all he proved to me that we needn't keep our word, and second that it is unnecessary to go to church in order to renew in ourselves the Commandments of the Lord. Yesterday evening he promised me that he would, and I relied on him to come, because I thought: He will want to render thanks to the Gracious Creator for the recovery of his mother. But he didn't come. I found my pew, which of course is a bit narrow for two persons, quite comfortable. I wonder how it would please him if I took up his lesson at once and made it my own and failed to keep my *own* word? I promised him a new suit of clothes for his birthday, and so I have the chance to test his delight with my teachable nature. But . . . prejudice, prejudice! I won't do it.

LEONARD   Maybe he wasn't well . . .

MASTER ANTON   Possible! All I need to do is ask my wife and I'll know for sure he was sick. She tells me the truth about everything under the sun, except about the boy. And if he wasn't sick . . . this younger generation's got the better of us there, too, they can be moved to devotion anywhere, they can say their prayers whether they're catching birds, taking a walk, or even at the tavern. "Our Father, Which art in Heaven!"—"Hello, Peter, will you be at the dance?"—"Hallowed be Thy Name!"

—"Don't worry, Catherine, we'll find it!"—"Thy will be done!"—"Damnation, I'm not shaved yet!"—And so on to the end. And then they give themselves their own blessing, because they're as human as the preacher, and the power that proceeds from his black coat can just as well come from a blue one. I'm not against it, I'd just as soon they'd drink down seven glasses of beer between the seven petitions of *The Lord's Prayer*. What's the difference? I can't prove that beer and religion don't mix. And besides that it might come into the liturgy as a new way of taking the Lord's Supper. Of course an old sinner like me, I'm not strong enough to go along with the new custom. I can't catch up my devotions like I can a beetle in the street; the chirping of sparrows can never take the place of the organ for me; when I'm to feel my heart lifted up then I must first hear the heavy iron doors of the church close behind me and imagine them the gates to the world; the dark high walls of the church, with their narrow windows that let in the light only dimly as though they filter it through, must press upon me; and in the distance I must see the charnel-house with the death's-head imbedded in its wall. Well . . . it's best to be on the safe side!

LEONARD   You take the matter too seriously.

MASTER ANTON   Of course! Of course I do! And today, being an honorable man, I have to confess that I was all wrong. I lost my devotion in church because of the empty place next to me. But outside under the pear-tree in my garden I found it again. Does it surprise you? You see, I went home depressed and downcast, like a man who has had his harvest ruined by hail-storms, because children are like fields, you sow good seed and weeds grow up. I stood there quietly under the pear-tree that the caterpillars had eaten away. "Yes," I thought, "the boy is like this tree, empty and bare!" And then suddenly it seemed to me I was terribly thirsty and had to get to the tavern at once. I deceived myself, it wasn't a glass of beer I wanted; all I was after was to find the boy and chide him; I knew well enough I could find him at the tavern. Just as I was about to leave, the wise old tree let a juicy pear fall at my feet as if to say: "This is for your thirst, and for insulting me by comparing me with your son!" I thought for a moment, bit into the pear, and went into the house.

LEONARD   Do you know the pharmacist is about to go bankrupt?

MASTER ANTON   It's not my worry.

LEONARD   Not at all?

MASTER ANTON   Of course! I'm a Christian. The man has many children.

LEONARD   And even more creditors. Even children could be called creditors.

MASTER ANTON   How is that *my* business?

LEONARD   It was my belief that you . . .

MASTER ANTON   That was settled long ago.

LEONARD   You're a cautious man. I suppose you called in your money when you saw things weren't going too well with the pharmacy.

MASTER ANTON   No, I have no worry about losing it now; I lost it a long time ago.

LEONARD   You're joking!

MASTER ANTON   Dead serious!

KLARA (*looking through the doorway*)   Did you call, father?

MASTER ANTON   Are your ears burning already? We haven't even talked about you yet!

KLARA   Here's the weekly paper. (*She goes out*)

LEONARD   You're a philosopher, too, I see.

MASTER ANTON   What is that supposed to mean?

LEONARD   You know how to compose yourself.

MASTER ANTON   I carry a mill-stone around my neck at times as a ruff, instead of drowning myself with it . . . it gives one a stiff bearing.

LEONARD   Let whoever can follow your example!

MASTER ANTON   Anyone who finds as brave a man to share his burden with as I seem to have found in *you*, ought to be able to *dance* under the weight. You became downright pale. That's what I call sharing.

LEONARD   I'll prove to you that you haven't misjudged me!

MASTER ANTON   Of course! (*He pounds on a chest-of-drawers*) Isn't it strange how we can't see through wood?

LEONARD   I don't understand.

MASTER ANTON   What a fool our grandfather Adam was to take Eve so naked and unprotected, without even a fig-leaf. You and I would have whipped her from Paradise for a tramp. What have you to say to that?

LEONARD   You're angry because of your son. I came to talk to you about your daughter's . . .

MASTER ANTON   That's enough! Perhaps I won't say no!

LEONARD   I hope you won't. I'd also like to tell you what I think. Not even the Holy Patriarchs, you know, scorned their women's dowries. Jacob loved Rachel and strove for her hand for seven years, but at the same time he was pleased with the fat ewes and rams he earned in her father's service. I don't think it

was disgraceful of him, and to out-do him would only be to embarrass him. I would have been pleased, too, if your daughter had brought along a couple hundred thalers with her, and that would have been natural enough. Things would have been easier for her: when a girl brings her own bed along into the new house then she has no need to start right in by combing wool and spinning yarn. But that's not the case here. But no matter. We'll eat on Sundays as if it were Lent, and our Sunday roasts we'll save for our Christmas feast! It'll work out!

MASTER ANTON (*extending his hand*)   Well said, and I can see the Lord God nodding His approval. And so . . . I suppose I can forget that every evening for two weeks my daughter set an extra cup of tea on the table to no purpose. And now that you're to become my son-in-law I'll tell you what has become of the thousand thalers.

LEONARD (*aside*)   So it *is* gone! Son-in-law or not, I needn't smile at everything he says!

MASTER ANTON   Things were bad for me in my young days. I wasn't born into this world a prickly hedgehog, but as time went on I got to be one. At first all my quills were turned inwards on me, and people amused themselves by pressing and pinching my bare soft skin, and they were happy when I winced because they knew the stingers were pressing my heart and entrails. I wasn't satisfied with that so I turned my skin inside out, that way the quills pricked *their* fingers and I was left in peace.

LEONARD   With the devil himself, no doubt!

MASTER ANTON   My father worked himself to death by the time he was thirty because he allowed himself no rest either day or night. My poor mother helped to raise me as well as she could by her spinning. I grew up without learning anything, and the older I became, still unable to earn, the happier I would have been if at least I could have given up eating. But even if sometimes at noon I had said I was sick and pushed the plate from me, what good would it have done? That evening my stomach would have forced me to say I was well again. The thing that tormented me most was that I had no skill. I could have argued with myself as if it had been my own fault, as if I was tied to the apron-strings of my mother's love and purposely left behind in her everything that could have made me useful and skilled. I could have shamed myself every time the sun shone on me. Just after I was confirmed a man came to visit us in our tiny room, Master Gebhard, the one they buried yesterday. He wrinkled his brow and twisted up his face like he always did when he had something good in mind; then he said to my mother: "Did you bring this boy into the world to eat you out of house and home?" I was just about to cut a piece from a loaf of bread, but he shamed me so, that I quickly put it back into the cupboard. My mother took offence at what he meant well, and taking a firm hold on her spinning-wheel she fired back at him that her son was honest and good. "Well, we'll have to see about that," the Master said. "If he wants he can come along with me to my workshop just as he is. It won't cost him a penny, he'll be fed, and I'll take care of his clothes, too; and if he wants to get up early and go to bed late then there'll be plenty of times for him to earn a little something extra for his old mother." My mother started to cry, and I started to dance, and when we finally got around to talking about it the Master stopped his ears, started out and waved for me to come along. There was no need for me to put on my hat, because I didn't have one. Without even saying goodbye to my mother I followed him out, and on the next Sunday when I had my first time off to go back, he gave me half of a ham to take to her. God bless that good man in his grave! I can still hear his half-angry: "Damnation, put it under your jacket so my wife can't see it!"

LEONARD   Does it make you cry even now?

MASTER ANTON (*drying his eyes*)   Yes, as sure as the well of my tears is choked up inside me, I can't think about it without it tearing at my heart. God! If I ever come down with dropsy, at least they won't have to draw *this* water off me! (*suddenly wheeling about*) Tell me: what would you do if one Sunday afternoon you went to visit a man that you owed everything to, and you found him confused and troubled, with a knife in his hand, the same knife that he used a thousand times before to cut the bread with for your tea, but you found him with the bloody knife at his throat, and his other hand pulled a scarf up high around his neck . . .

LEONARD   He wore the scarf like that until he died.

MASTER ANTON   Because of the scar. And suppose you got there in time to save him and help him, but not only by taking the knife from his hand and binding his wound, but by having to give him a miserable thousand thalers that you'd saved, yes, you *had* to give it to him so that the sick man would take it . . . and this happened just between the two of you, what would you do?

LEONARD   Since I'm single and without wife or child, I'd have sacrificed the money.

MASTER ANTON   And if you'd had ten wives like the Turks and as many children as were promised our father Abraham, and you had one second to think it over in, you'd have . . . well, you're to be my son-in-law! Now you know what happened to the money. I can tell you this now because my old Master is in his grave. But a month ago, if I had been on my own deathbed, I would have taken the secret with me to my grave. I placed his promise to pay back the money under his head before they nailed his coffin closed. If I'd known how to write I'd have written across it first: *Honorably paid!* But being an ignorant man, all there was left me was to tear the paper through. He'll sleep in peace now, and I hope to do the same when the time comes for me to lay myself down by his side.

Scene Six

THE MOTHER (*enters quickly*)   Do you still know me?

MASTER ANTON (*indicating the wedding dress*)   The frame's all right but the picture's not the same. It seems the cobwebs have covered it over, but it's been so many years.

MOTHER   As you can see I have an honest husband. But there's no need for me to praise him specially, because honesty, they say, is the virtue of husbands.

MASTER ANTON   Are you sorry your hair was more golden at twenty than it is now at fifty?

MOTHER   Of course not. If it were the other way around I'd have to be ashamed for both of us.

MASTER ANTON   Then give me a kiss. I shaved today and better than usual.

MOTHER   The only reason I'll agree is to see if you still know anything about the art. It's been a long time since you thought of it.

MASTER ANTON   You're a good wife. When I die I don't want you to be the one to close my eyes for me. It's a hard thing to do. I want to be the one to do it for *you*. I want to be able to do that last kindness for you. But you must give me time for it, you hear? I'll have to steel myself first and find the courage, and not do it all wrong. But it's too soon to think of that now.

MOTHER   I thank God that we'll be together for a while longer.

MASTER ANTON   I hope so, too. Your cheeks are even rosy again.

MOTHER   What a strange man our new grave-digger is. He was digging a grave as I cut across the church-yard this morning, and I asked him who it was for. "For whoever God wants it to be for," he said, "maybe even for me. It can happen to me just like to my grandfather who dug an extra grave once, and that night on the way home from the tavern he fell into it and broke his neck."

LEONARD (*who till now has been reading the newspaper*) Since he's not from these parts, he can lie to us all he wants.

MOTHER I asked him: "Why don't you wait till somebody orders a grave from you?"—"I'm invited to a wedding tonight," he said, "and I'm enough of a prophet to know what I'll feel like tomorrow. And somebody's bound to play a trick on me and die so that I'll have to get up early tomorrow and dig instead of sleep it off."

MASTER ANTON I would have told him he was a fool, because what if the grave didn't fit?

MOTHER That's what I said, too, but he spit out his sharp answers at me like lies out of a devil's mouth. "I went by the measurements of our weaver Mr. Veit," he said, "he's like King Saul himself and towers a whole head above us all. Let come who will, he won't find his house too small for him, and if it's too big then I'm the one to lose, because being an honorable man I never charge for more than the length of the coffin." Then I threw my bouquet of flowers into it and said: "There now, it's been ordered."

MASTER ANTON I think the fellow was only joking, and that's sinful enough. Digging graves beforehand is like setting up a trap for death. The good-for-nothing who does such things ought to be chased from his job. (*to* LEONARD *who is reading*) Anything new? Is some kind soul looking for an old widow who can use a few hundred thalers? Or the other way around, the old widow looking for a kind soul who can give her some?

LEONARD The police give notice of a jewelry theft. That's amazing enough in itself. At least we can see that no matter how bad the times are there are still people around us with jewelry stuck away.

MASTER ANTON A jewelry theft? Where was this?

LEONARD At Wolfram's, the merchant.

MASTER ANTON At Wol . . . That's impossible! That's where my son Karl polished a writing-desk a few days ago!

LEONARD Yes, it disappeared from the writing-desk.

MOTHER (*to* MASTER ANTON) May God forgive you for that!

MASTER ANTON Yes, it was a terrible thought!

MOTHER You have never been more than half a father to your son.

MASTER ANTON We are not going to talk about that today!

MOTHER Just because he's not like you do you have to think he's evil?

MASTER ANTON Where is he now? The noon bells rang long ago. I'll wager our food is overcooked and that Klara has secret orders not to set the table before he comes.

MOTHER Where do you *expect* him to be? At most he's out playing at bowling, and of course he has to play in an alley as far away as possible so that you won't be able to find him. The way back for him is bound to be long. And besides that I don't know what you have against the harmless game.

MASTER ANTON Against the game? Nothing! Fashionable gentlemen *need* something to pass their time with. Without a king of cards a real king would be bored often enough, and if bowling hadn't been invented who knows whether princes and barons wouldn't play at it with our heads. But there is nothing more deceitful or outrageous than when a craftsman stakes his hard earned pay on gaming. A man must respect what he has gained through hard labor in the sweat of his brow, he must hold it high and value it, unless he wants to lose faith in himself, unless he wants to find all he does contemptible. When I think of what a thaler means to me and then . . .

(*The bell on the outside door rings*)

MOTHER There he is.

Scene Seven

(ADAM *the bailiff, and a* SECOND BAILIFF *enter*)

ADAM (*to* MASTER ANTON) You may go and pay off your wagers now. People in red coats with blue lapels (*He emphasizes this strongly*) would never enter your house, eh? Well, here the two of us are. (*to the* SECOND BAILIFF) Why did you take your hat off? Why bother when you're with your own kind?

MASTER ANTON What do you mean "with your own kind"?

ADAM You're right, we're not with our own kind, scoundrels and thieves are not our kind. (*He points to the chest*) I want that unlocked. And then you will back up three paces. So that you don't sneak anything out of it.

MASTER ANTON What's this! What this!

KLARA (*enters with a table-cloth*) Shall I . . . (*She is suddenly silent*)

ADAM (*showing a paper*) Can you read?

MASTER ANTON How should I be able to do what my own teacher couldn't?

ADAM Then you'll listen. Your son stands

accused of stealing jewels. We already have the thief. Now we want to search your house.

MOTHER Sweet Jesus! (*She collapses and dies*)

KLARA Mother! Mother! Look at her eyes!

LEONARD I'll get a doctor!

MASTER ANTON That won't be necessary. I know that look. I have seen it a hundred times before. Good night, Therese. You died as you heard the truth. That will be written on your grave.

LEONARD But maybe if . . . (*leaving*) It's horrible! But it saved my neck. (*off*)

MASTER ANTON (*pulling out a ring of keys and tossing it from him*) There! Unlock them! One cabinet after another! Bring an axe here! The key to that trunk is lost. Scoundrels and thieves, uh? (*He turns his pockets inside out*) Nothing here.

SECOND BAILIFF Master Anton, get hold of yourself. We all know you for the most honest man in the town.

MASTER ANTON Really? Really? (*laughs*) In that case I must have used up all the honesty in my family! My poor son. There was nothing left for him. And she . . . (*indicating the dead* MOTHER) she was too virtuous, too. Who knows, maybe my daughter has . . . (*suddenly to* KLARA) What has my innocent daughter to say?

KLARA Father!

SECOND BAILIFF (*to* ADAM) Don't you have *any* pity?

ADAM Pity? Do you see me digging in his pockets? Am I forcing him to take his stockings off or shake out his boots? That's what I *should* have done because of how I hate that man! Ever since the time at the tavern when he took his glass and . . . he knows the story and he couldn't help but feel insulted if he had any honor in his body. (*to* KLARA) Where is your brother's room?

KLARA (*showing him*) Back there.

(BOTH BAILIFFS *go off*)

KLARA Father, he *isn't* guilty. He *can't* be guilty.

MASTER ANTON Not guilty, and yet he murdered his mother? (*He laughs*)

A GIRL (*enters with a letter, to* KLARA) It's from Leonard, the Treasurer. (*off*)

MASTER ANTON There's no need to read it. He's got himself rid of you. (*striking his hands together*) Bravo, the scoundrel!

KLARA (*having read the letter*) Yes! Yes! My God!

MASTER ANTON Let him be.

KLARA Father, father, I can't!

MASTER ANTON Can't? You can't? What do you mean, you can't? Are you . . .

(BOTH BAILIFFS *return*)

ADAM (*spitefully*) Seek and ye shall find!

SECOND BAILIFF (*to* ADAM) What are you talking about? Were you right or not?

ADAM Keep quiet!

(*Both go off*)

MASTER ANTON He's innocent, but you . . . you . . .

KLARA Father, how can you be this way!

MASTER ANTON (*takes her tenderly by the hand*) Dear Klara . . . my Karl is no more than a scoundrel. He murdered his own mother, what else can you call it? But the father stayed behind. Will you help him? You can't ask him to do everything alone. Give me some rest. The old trunk looks as gnarled as ever, but it too, is beginning to tremble. It won't take much strength to fell it, too. You won't have to put your hands to an axe. You have a lovely face. I've never praised you before in any way, but I want to tell you this today to give you courage and confidence. Your eyes, your nose, your mouth will always . . . find approval, will always . . . you know what I'm saying. You must tell me, I can't help feeling that . . . that something has already happened.

KLARA (*almost frantic, she falls with raised arms at the feet of her* MOTHER's *body and calls to her like a child*) Mother! Mother!

MASTER ANTON Take her hand in yours and swear to me that you are the same as on the day that she gave you birth!

KLARA I . . . swear . . . that . . . I . . . will . . . never . . . bring . . . shame . . . upon . . . you!

MASTER ANTON Good! (*He puts on his hat*) It's fine weather out. I must take a long walk in it, up one street and down another. (*off*)

ACT TWO

A ROOM IN THE HOUSE OF THE CABINET-MAKER

Scene One

(MASTER ANTON *rises from the table.* KLARA *starts to clear the table*)

MASTER ANTON You haven't eaten anything again.

KLARA Father, I've had enough.

MASTER ANTON Of nothing?

KLARA I ate in the kitchen.

MASTER ANTON A bad appetite means a bad conscience. Well, all things come to light in the end. Or was there poison in the soup, like I dreamt yesterday? Maybe a sprig of hemlock got picked into your basket of herbs by mistake? That would have been the wise thing to do.

KLARA My God in Heaven!

MASTER ANTON Forgive me, I . . . Oh, the devil take you and that woeful face that you stole from the Mother of God herself! Your face should be full of life when you're young. There's only one person to show off a face like that, but do you see him doing it? A man who cries over nothing but a cut finger ought to have his face slapped. No one has that right any more . . . but then self-praise is no recommendation. What was it I did when our neighbor was about to nail shut your mother's coffin?

KLARA You tore the hammer from his hand and nailed it shut yourself. You said: "This is my masterpiece!" The choir-master thought you had gone mad.

MASTER ANTON Gone mad! (*laughs*) Gone mad! Yes, it's a wise head that lops itself off when the time's right. Mine is put on a little too tight for that, otherwise . . . A man squats himself down in the world and thinks he's sitting in good quarters behind a warm stove, and then someone puts a light on the table and he finds himself in a den of thieves; but there's no harm done, because his heart is made of stone.

KLARA Yes, father. that's the way it is.

MASTER ANTON What do you know about it? Do you think just because your Treasurer's run off you have the right to curse the world along with me? There'll be another one to take you out on Sunday afternoons walking. There'll be another one to tell you your cheeks are red and your eyes blue. And another to take you for his wife, if you deserve it. When you've borne up under the burden of life for thirty long years, when without complaining you have patiently accepted sorrow and death and every other misfortune, and then your son comes along, who was to console you in your old age, and instead heaps shame upon you till you want to cry out to the earth: "Swallow me, unless I disgust you, for I am filthier than you!" —When you've lived through this, then you can cry out all the curses that I hold back inside me; then you can tear your hair and beat your breast; you're not a man, you have that advantage over me.

KLARA Oh, Karl!

MASTER ANTON I wonder what I'll do when I see him here in front of me again, when he comes into this room in the evening before we've lighted the lamps, and his head is shaved, because hair isn't allowed in prison, and he stutters good-evening with the latch of the door still in his hand. I'll do something, that's for sure, but what? (*gnashing his teeth*) And if they keep him there ten years, he'll find me. I'll live long enough for that, I know that much. And as for death, I give him notice now that from this moment on I am a stone in front of his sickle, and that his sickle will break to pieces before I'll move out of his path.

KLARA (*takes his hand*) Father, you *must* lie down for half an hour.

MASTER ANTON So that I can dream that you've gone into child-bed? So that I can fly up and lay hands on you and only come to my senses afterwards and say: "Dear Klara, I didn't know what I was doing." I thank you. My sleep has dismissed its charlatan and taken on a prophet in its place. He points out hideous things to me with his bloody finger, and I don't know why but everything seems possible to me now. I shudder as much when I think of the time to come as when I think of the glass of water that they looked through a microscope at!—Is that right, choir-master? You've spelled it out to me often enough!—I did it once in Nürnberg at the Fair, and I wouldn't drink a glass of water the rest of the day. Last night I saw my son Karl with a pistol in his hand, and as I kept my eyes on him he pulled the trigger, I heard a scream, but the powder-smoke kept me from seeing. And then after it cleared away there was no shattered skull to see. In between my son had become a rich man, he stood there counting gold-pieces from one hand into the other, and his face . . . the devil take me, he couldn't have looked more satisfied if he had worked all day and then locked his shop up behind him! But we ought to beware of that. We ought to beware of passing judgment and then standing in front of the Highest Judge ourselves.

KLARA Calm yourself.

MASTER ANTON "Get well," is what you meant to say! And why am I sick? Yes, doctor, hand me the drink that will make me well! Since your brother is the worst of sons you must become the best of daughters. I stand in view of the world like a worthless bankrupt. I owed the world a good man to take my place when I could no longer fill it, but I deceived it with a scoundrel. If you become a woman like your mother was, then they'll say: "It wasn't the parents' fault the boy went wrong, because look at the daughter, she's as honorable as any, she's the best of us all." (*with terrible coldness*) But I'll do my part too, I'll make it easier for you. And at the moment when I see people pointing accusing fingers at you in the street,

I'll go inside and . . . (*with a movement of his hand at his throat*) shave myself. And then, and I give you my solemn assurance of this, I'll shave this old fool away. You can tell them I was scared by the sound of a horse dashing through the street outside, or because the cat jumped onto the floor and overturned a chair or a mouse ran up my leg. The people who know me will shake their heads because I'm not one to scare easy, but what's the difference. Why should I want to live in a world where people have to feel sympathy for you when they wouldn't even bother spitting at your feet!

KLARA   Merciful Heaven, what can I do!

MASTER ANTON   Nothing, nothing, my poor child . . . I'm too hard on you, I know that . . . nothing . . . just stay what you are and I'll be satisfied. I've suffered such wrong that I have to do wrong too when it takes hold of me so that it doesn't crush me. The other day as I was crossing the street I met that scoundrel of a thief with the pock-marks on his face, the one I had thrown in jail a couple of years ago for stealing three times from me. Before this the scoundrel didn't have the nerve to look at me, but now he comes up to me without any shame and reaches out his hand. I wanted to give him a slap on the ear but I thought better of it and didn't even bother to spit at his feet. After all, we've been cousins now for eight days and it's only right for relatives to greet one another. That compassionate man our pastor paid me a visit yesterday and said that a man has no one but himself to account for and that it was unchristian pride in me that I wanted to accept responsibility for my son; that way, he said, our father Adam would have to feel the same as I do. Lord, I can well believe that the peace of our forefather Adam in Paradise can no longer be disturbed just because one of his great-grandsons begins to murder or to steal! But canst Thou tell me that he did not tear his hair in torment over his son Cain? No, no, it's too much! Sometimes I want to turn around and see if my shadow hasn't grown blacker. I can bear up under anything, anything, and I have proved it . . . except shame. Hang around my neck what you like, but don't you touch the nerve that gives me life!

KLARA   Father, Karl has confessed nothing yet, and they haven't found anything either.

MASTER ANTON   What's that supposed to prove? I went around the town from one tavern and inn to the other, asking about his debts, and they came to more than he could have earned working for me for the next three months, even if he worked three times as hard.

I know now why he always worked two hours later and why in spite of that he always got out of bed two hours earlier than me. But then he saw that even all this didn't help or else that it was too much trouble and took too long, so he took the advantage when an opportunity came.

KLARA   You always think the worst of Karl. You always did. Do you still remember . . .

MASTER ANTON   You're talking like your mother would have, and I'll answer you the same way that I answered her, by keeping silent.

KLARA   And what if they let Karl free? What if they find the jewels again?

MASTER ANTON   If that happens I'll hire a lawyer, and if it costs me my last penny I'll learn whether or not the Mayor has the right to send the son of an honorable man to prison. And if he has the right, then I'll bow to his will, because what others have to bear up under I must be satisfied with too, even if it costs me a thousand times as much as the others. If it happens, then it was destined to happen, and when God strikes me down I shall fold my hands and answer Him: "Lord, Thou knowest the why and the wherefore of all things!" And if he hasn't the right, if that man with the golden chain around his neck was overhasty for no other reason but that the merchant whose jewels were stolen is his brother-in-law, then we will see whether there are holes in the law! They say the King knows he must pay his subjects for their loyalty and obedience with justice, and that he would want least of all to be in debt to the humblest of his subjects; well then, we'll see whether the King will leave this hole unstopped. But why should I bother even talking about such things. The boy won't come any cleaner out of this trial than his mother will rise from her grave. I'll never find any comfort in him, and therefore you must never forget the debt you owe to me, you must keep your oath, so that I will never have to keep mine. (*He starts to leave but turns around again*) I won't be back till late tonight. I'm going to visit the timber-dealer in the hills. He's the only man who can still look me in the eyes, and only because he knows nothing about my shame. He's deaf. No one can tell him anything because they'd have to shout too loud, and even then he gets it all backwards. That's why no one ever tells him anything. (*off*)

Scene Two

KLARA   (*alone*)   God! God! Have mercy! Have mercy on that old man! Please take my life instead of his. There's no other way to help him.—Look there, how golden the sunlight is on the street, the children grab for it with their hands. Everything's alive, everything wants to live. Listen to me, death, because I cry out to you now! Spare just one being whose soul still trembles at the thought of you, give him time till the world grows grey and desolate for him, and take *me* in his place. I won't shudder when you reach out your cold hand to me. I'll take it bravely in mine and follow you more happily than any child of man has ever followed you.

Scene Three

THE MERCHANT WOLFRAM (*enters*) Good-day, Miss Klara, is your father at home?

KLARA He just went off.

WOLFRAM I came to . . . my jewels have been found again.

KLARA Oh, I wish he were here! He went off without his glasses, look! If only he'll notice it and come back. How did you find them? Where? Who had them?

WOLFRAM It was my wife who . . . tell me something very honestly, Miss. Have you ever heard anything strange concerning my wife?

KLARA Yes.

WOLFRAM That she . . . (*He indicates his forehead*)

KLARA Yes, that she's not right in her mind.

WOLFRAM (*bursting out*) My God! My God! It was all for nothing! Every servant I ever hired I kept with me, I paid each one twice his salary and ignored their carelessness, just to buy their silence, and for all that . . . the deceitful, ungrateful creatures! And my poor children. I wanted to hide it for their sake.

KLARA There's no need to blame your servants. They're not the ones at fault. We've known it since the time your neighbor's house burned down. Your wife leaned out the open window and laughed and clapped her hands, she even blew into the smoke like she wanted to blow it into a flame. We had only the choice of thinking that either she was a devil or mad. Hundreds of us saw her that day.

WOLFRAM That's true enough. In that case, I suppose it would be foolish of me to ask you to keep it silent. All right I'll tell you. The theft that put your brother in prison was the fault of her madness.

KLARA Your own wife . . .

WOLFRAM There was a time when she was the noblest, most sympathetic soul in the world. But I've known for a long time now that she's become malicious and that she gloats over other people's misfortunes. She shouts with delight when she sees an accident, when the maid breaks a glass or cuts her finger. Unfortunately I didn't learn till too late, till this afternoon, that she was in the habit of secreting things, of hiding money, of destroying documents. I had just laid down across the bed and wanted to fall asleep when I noticed her coming towards me very quietly, she watched me intently to see whether I had fallen asleep yet. I closed my eyes tighter, and then she took a key from the pocket of my waistcoat lying across a chair. She opened the writing-desk, grabbed for a roll of money, locked it up again and returned the key to where she had found it. I was horrified, even though I controlled myself so as not to disturb her. She left the room then and I followed her. She climbed up to the top floor and threw the roll of money into a chest that had been empty since my grandfather's time, then she looked around as if she were afraid, and hurried away without noticing me. I lighted a taper and looked through the chest. There I found some toys belonging to my youngest daughter, a pair of the maid's slippers, an account-book, letters, and then, fortunately or unfortunately, I don't quite know how to say it, down at the bottom, I found the jewels.

KLARA My poor mother! It's too shameful even to talk about.

WOLFRAM God only knows I'd gladly give up the jewels if only I could undo what has already been done. But I'm not the one who's at fault. With due respect for your father, it was only natural that I should suspect your brother. He had just finished polishing the writing-desk, and the jewels seemed to disappear with him. I noticed it almost at once because I had to take some papers from the compartment where the jewels were placed. But I had no intention of using such strong measures against him. I mentioned it only provisionally to Adam the court bailiff and asked him to investigate the matter quietly. But he'd hear of no consideration being shown, he said he had to and would report the case at once, because your brother is a drunkard and a trouble-maker. Unfortunately he carries enough weight with the Mayor to be able to do what he wants. I don't know why, but the man seemed enraged against your father almost to the extreme. There was little chance of calming him because he held his ears shut and hurried off. He called back to me that if I had given him the jewels as a gift he couldn't be happier.

KLARA One time at the tavern the bailiff put his glass next to my father's on the table and nodded to him like he wanted to drink a toast. My father took his glass away and said that people in red coats with blue lapels used to have to drink out of wooden steins, and that they had to wait outside by the window, or when it rained by the door, and be modest enough to take their hats off when the inn-keeper handed them a drink; and if they wanted to drink a toast with anyone they'd wait till one of their own kind came by.—My God, isn't there anything impossible in this world! And my mother had to pay for this with her death!

WOLFRAM   We ought never to provoke any-one, and bad people especially. Where is your father?

KLARA   In the hills visiting the old timber-dealer.

WOLFRAM   I'll ride out there and try to find him. I've already been to see the Mayor. Un-fortunately I didn't find him at home otherwise your brother would be here by now. But the Secretary sent off a message at once. You'll have your brother back before evening. (*off*)

Scene Four

KLARA (*alone*)   I should be so happy now. God! God! And all I can think of is that now I am the only one who can still hurt him. And yet I have the feeling that something must come soon to make everything turn out well.

Scene Five

THE SECRETARY (*entering*)   Good-day.

KLARA (*holding onto a chair as though about to collapse*)   He's come! Why did he have to come back . . .

SECRETARY   Isn't your father at home?

KLARA   No.

SECRETARY   I have some good news to de-liver to you. Your brother . . . No, Klara, I can't talk to you in this tone of voice. It seems as if the table and chairs and cabinets, all our old friends that we used to skip around in circles when we were children—Good-day! (*He nods to a cabinet*) How are you? You haven't changed!—it seems like they're about to put their heads together and make fun of this fool unless he comes up with something else pretty quickly! I *must* call you Klara like this, like I used to; and if it displeases you then you must think: "This grown calf of a boy is just a dreamer, I must waken him, I must go to him and (*with gestures*) pull myself up tall so that he can see that the girl in front of him isn't a child anymore"—this is how tall you were when you were eleven (*He points to a mark on the doorpost*)—"not a child anymore but a grown girl, who can reach the sugar even when it's set on top of the cabinet." Do you still remember? That was the place, the mighty fortress, where it was safe from our hands even without being locked up. When the sugar was up there we used to kill time by slapping at the flies because we couldn't bear seeing them so happy flying about up there, able to get at what we couldn't have ourselves.

KLARA   I thought people forget things like that, especially when they have to study through hundreds and thousands of books.

SECRETARY   Oh, they forget alright. And what don't we forget about Justinian and Gaius too. These young school boys who fight so hard against learning their ABCs, they know well enough why they do it; they have premo-nitions even at that age. And then without any shame whatever we lead those innocent souls astray; we show them just enough behind the scenes to whet their appetites; and from then on there's no stopping them, they go like a streak of lightning from A to Z and so on and on until suddenly they find themselves in the middle of a *Corpus Juris*. And it's only then that they learn with dismay into what a wilder-ness that blasted alphabet has lured them, those same twenty-six letters that at the start promised such wonderful things.

KLARA   And what happens then?

SECRETARY (*disinterestedly*)   That's where temperaments differ. Some of them go through with it. Generally they see the light of day again after three or four years, somewhat more lean and pale however, but we shouldn't hold that against them. I belong to this group. Others lie down in the middle of a forest with the intention of merely taking a nap, but they seldom ever get up again. I have a friend who for the last three years has been drinking his beer under the shade of the *Lex Julia*. He picked the place because it calls up such pleasant memories. And there are others who grow desperate and turn back. They're the dumbest of the lot because they're let out of one thicket only on the condition that they im-mediately lose themselves in another one. And then there are some who are even more terrible, who never make an end. (*to himself*) Why can't I say what I want instead of this babble!

KLARA   Everything's so bright and lively today, that's why it's so lovely.

SECRETARY   Yes, it's the kind of weather that makes owls fall out of their nests, and bats commit suicide because they think they're made by the devil. And then there's the mole who digs himself so deep into the earth that he can't find his way back and has to suffocate, poor mole, unless he can find his way through to the other side and come to light again in America. It's the kind of day when an ear of corn grows twice as much, and poppies grow twice as red, ashamed for not being red enough in the first place. Why should people be left behind? Why should they want to cheat God of the sole tribute that His world yields Him, a happy face and clear sparkling eyes that mirror all the glory of His creation and give it back to Him transfigured? In the morning when I see some hermit or other creeping out from under his doorway, his forehead wrinkled, gaping up at the sky like a sheet of blotting paper, I can't help but think: "There's bound to be rain soon; how can God help but bring on a layer of black clouds if only in anger over that man's face." We ought to summon these scoundrels to court for spoiling country picnics and destroying our harvest weather. How else would you want to give thanks for life except by living! The only way a bird can earn its voice is by singing.

KLARA   Yes, I know how right you are, how right. It almost makes me want to cry.

SECRETARY   Please, I didn't say that against you. I realize how badly things have gone for you these past eight days. I know your father, too. But, thank God, I can make things easier for you, that's why I've come. You'll see your brother again this evening; and instead of pointing at *him*, it'll be the ones who threw him into prison that people will point at. Doesn't that deserve a kiss, maybe only a sister-like one, if nothing else? Or shall we play blind-man's buff? If I don't tag you in ten minutes I'll leave empty-handed and with a slap on the face to top it off.

KLARA   (*to herself*)   Suddenly I feel like a thousand years old, and time standing still above me, I can't back up and I can't go forward. Why must the sun be so bright and the world so happy.

SECRETARY   Why don't you answer me? Of course, I forgot, you're engaged. Oh, Klara, why did you have to do this to me? But then . . . what right have I to complain? You're like everything that's precious and wonderful, and everything precious and wonderful should have reminded me of you, but then for years you seemed to be out of my world entirely. And it was for that reason that you . . . If only it had been a person you could have some respect for. But this Leonard . . .

KLARA   (*suddenly as she hears the name*) I've got to go to him . . . Don't you see, my brother's not a thief any longer. God, what more do I want? Leonard *will* listen to me, he

has to. If only he'll listen to reason, it can all be like it was before. (*to the* SECRETARY) I'm sorry, Frederick.—Why am I so weak all of a sudden?

SECRETARY   Then you're going to . . .

KLARA   Yes, I'm going to find Leonard. What else is there for me to do? There's no other way open for me now.

SECRETARY   Then you love him?

KLARA   (*impetuously*)   Love him? Either I'll have Leonard or I'll kill myself! Does it surprise you now that I'd choose *him*? I'd never do it if it were only for myself.

SECRETARY   Leonard or your death? Klara, either you tell me what this is about or . . .

KLARA   Please don't make it worse than it is! Don't say that word again! It's you, it's you I love! There, I've said it, I've said it! I can call it out to you now as if I were a ghost on the other side of my grave, where there is no more shame, where we pass each other by, naked and cold, because the terrible nearness of God's Presence has consumed to the very roots every thought of anyone else!

SECRETARY   *Me?* You still love *me?* Klara, I felt that, too, that night I saw you in the garden.

KLARA   Did you? Yes, he felt it, too. (*hollow as though alone*) And then he came to me. "It has to be one or the other of us," he said. Oh, my God, my God! And then to prove to him, but to prove it to .nyself, too, that it wasn't true, or if it was true, to smother it inside me, I let him do what now I . . . (*bursting into tears*) Dear God in Heaven, have mercy on me as I would have on You if You were me!

SECRETARY   Be my wife, Klara. I came here to look at you just once more like I used to. If you hadn't understood my reason for coming, I would have left without saying a word. But I offer you everything now, everything I am and everything I have. It isn't much, but there'll be more. I would have come long before this, but your mother was sick, and then she died. (KLARA *laughs distractedly*) You mustn't be frightened, Klara. You're afraid because you've given him your promise. That's a terrible enough thing in itself. How could you . . .

KLARA   Why don't you ask to hear the rest of the story! I had mockery and scorn thrown in my face everytime I turned around when you went off to the university and were never heard from again. "She's still dreaming about him!"—"She must think children's play is serious business!"—"Does she get letters?"—And then my mother: "Stay with your own kind!" she said. "Pride never helped anything. This Leonard's a good enough boy, and nobody can understand why you always look down on him."—And then my own heart would say: "If he's forgotten you, then why can't you show him that you . . ." Oh, God!

SECRETARY   I *am* at fault. I *know* it. But just because something's difficult doesn't mean it's impossible. I'll get your promise back. Perhaps . . .

KLARA   My promise! Here! (*She tosses him* LEONARD's *letter*)

SECRETARY   (*reads*)   "Since I am Treasurer now . . . your brother . . . thief . . . I'm sorry . . . I have no choice with regard to my position . . ." (*to* KLARA) He wrote this on the same day that your mother died? He expresses his condolences over her sudden death, too, I see!

KLARA   I think he does!

SECRETARY   Are you blind? Klara, there's nothing to worry about now. (*wanting to embrace her*) Come here. I'll never let you go. Let me kiss you . . .

KLARA   (*leaning against him*)   No . . . I mustn't . . . just don't let me fall . . .

SECRETARY   But, Klara, you don't love him, he's released you from your promise . . .

KLARA   (*hollowly, straightening up again*) There's nothing else for me to do but go to him, to fall at his feet and beg him to take me if he has any pity for my father.

SECRETARY   My poor Klara . . . do I understand you . . .

KLARA   Yes.

SECRETARY   And now you want to humble yourself in front of this man instead of spitting in his face. (*taking* KLARA *impetuously into his arms*) My poor Klara! My poor Klara!

KLARA   Go now, please go.

SECRETARY   (*moodily to himself*)   A dog like that ought to be packed from the world! If only he'd agree. If only I could force him.

KLARA   Please, Frederick.

SECRETARY   (*going*)   When it's dark. (*He turns around again and takes* KLARA's *hand*) You can count on me. I know now just how much I owe you. (*off*)

Scene Six

KLARA   (*alone*)   Please, God, don't let me feel hope when I know that there can be none. —I'm going, father, I'm going. Your life is safe.—God, I'm not begging You for happiness . . . I beg You for *unhappiness*, for eternal unhappiness . . . and I know that You will give me that unhappiness.—Where's the letter? (*She takes it*) There are three wells that you

must pass on your way to him. And *you must go past them!* That right is still not yours. (*off*)

ACT THREE

Scene One

A ROOM AT LEONARD'S

LEONARD   (*at a table covered with documents; writing*)   This will make the sixth sheet since supper. It makes a man feel good to have steady work to do. There's not a man in the world who could step through that door now, not even the King himself, but I could stand up and look him straight in the eye without embarrassment. There is one person though, the old cabinet-maker Master Anton. But then there's not much that he can do to me either. Poor Klara. I do feel sorry for her, I can't think about her without feeling uneasy. If only it hadn't been for that one evening. The fact is I did it more out of jealousy than out of love, and the only reason she gave herself was to disprove my blaming her, because she was as cold in my arms as death. She's in for some bad times. But then it won't be so easy for me either. Every man to his own troubles. The important thing now is to see that the affair with the little hunchback is set, to make sure she doesn't get away from me when the storm breaks. With that in hand I'm sure to have the Mayor on my side and there'll be nothing to worry about.

Scene Two

KLARA   (*enters*)   Good evening, Leonard.

LEONARD   Klara! What are you doing here? Didn't you get my letter? But then . . . perhaps you've come on your father's business, to pay his taxes. Let's see, how much would that come to? (*paging through a day-book*) I should know it without bothering to look it up.

KLARA   I came to give you back your letter. Here it is. Would you read it again?

LEONARD   (*reading it in great seriousness*) It's quite a reasonable letter. How can a man to whom public monies are entrusted marry into a family to which . . . (*He slurs over his words*) to which your brother belongs?

KLARA   Leonard!

LEONARD   But then perhaps the whole town is wrong! And your brother isn't locked up in jail! That he's never been in jail! And that you are not the sister of a . . . of your brother!

KLARA   Leonard, I am my father's daughter, and I'm standing here in front of you not as the sister of a wrongly accused brother who has been set free, and he *has* been set free, not as a girl who trembles out of undeserved shame, because (*half-voice*) I tremble more on your account, but only as the daughter of an old man who gave me life.

LEONARD   And you want what?

KLARA   I didn't think you would have to ask. Oh, if only I could leave this place. My father will cut his own throat if I . . . marry me.

LEONARD   Your father . . .

KLARA   He's sworn it . . . marry me, you can kill me afterwards, I'll be more grateful to you for the one than for the other!

LEONARD   Do you love me? Did you come here because your heart forced you to it? Am I the one human being without whom you can neither live nor die?

KLARA   Answer that yourself.

LEONARD   Can you swear to me that you love me? That you love me in the way that a girl must love the man who is to bind himself to her for all eternity?

KLARA   No, I can't swear it. But I can swear *this* to you: that whether I love you or whether I do not love you is something that you will never learn. I will serve you, I will work for you, but you must never put food on my plate because I will support myself, at night I will sew and spin for others, I will go hungry when there's no work for me to do, and I would rather bite into my own flesh than be forced to go back to my father so that he can see for himself. And if you strike me because your dog isn't at hand or because you've got rid of him, I will rather swallow my tongue than utter a cry so that the neighbors can gossip about what happens between us. I can't promise that my skin won't show the welts of your lash, because I have no power over that, but I will lie, I will say that I struck my head on a cabinet or that I fell on the pavement because it was too slippery, I'll answer them even before they ask me what the bruises are from. Marry me . . . my life can't go on for too long. And if it does and you don't want to put out the costs for separation to rid yourself of me, then buy poison from the pharmacist and place it somewhere as though it were for the rats, and without your even looking in its direction I will take it, and in dying I will say to the neighborwoman that I thought it was crushed sugar.

LEONARD   But if the person from whom you expect all this happens to say no, you won't be too taken unawares?

KLARA   Then God must not look at me too terribly if I come before I'm called. If I were the only one concerned, I wouldn't complain, I'd take it upon myself patiently as deserved punishment for . . . for I don't know what. And if the world were to ridicule me instead of standing by me in my torment I would love my child all the more, even if he bore the features of this man, and I would weep so often in the presence of that poor innocent that when it grew older and more intelligent it could neither scorn nor curse its mother. But I'm *not* the only one concerned, and on the Day of Judgment I will find it far easier to answer the question: "Why didst thou lay hand upon thyself?" than: "Why didst thou drive thy father to such extreme?"

LEONARD   The way you're talking you'd think you were the only person in the world. How many thousands of people do you think have gone through this same thing before you and given in to it; how many thousands do you think will do it after you and find their fate the same as yours? Are they all such pigheaded fools that you think you're the only one who has to stand herself in the corner for what you've done? They had fathers, too, that invented a whole stock of new curses when they first heard and talked about murder and homicide; afterwards they were ashamed of themselves and did penance for their curses and blasphemies and they sat down and rocked the cradle or fanned flies from it.

KLARA   I can see now how you could never believe that anyone could ever keep his word.

Scene Three

A BOY (*enters*)   Some flowers for you. But I'm not supposed to tell you who they're from.

LEONARD   How lovely! (*striking his forehead*) Damnation! How stupid! I was supposed to send some too! Now how do I get out of a thing like this? I'm afraid I'm not experienced in these matters even if the little hunchback *does* take them seriously, but then she has nothing else to think about. (*He takes the flowers*) However, I won't take them all. (*to* KLARA) If I remember correctly these are for shame and remorse. Wasn't it you who told me that once?

(KLARA *nods*)

LEONARD (*to the* BOY)   I want you to pay attention to this now, boy. *These* flowers are for me. As you see I'm placing them here inside my shirt, next to my heart. But these dark ones that burn like smouldering fire, these I want you to take back to her. Understand? And when my apples are ripe you can remind me of it.

BOY   That'll be a long time yet! (*off*)

Scene Four

LEONARD   Yes, Klara, now, you were talking about keeping one's word. It is simply because I *am* a man of my word that I have answered you as I have. I wrote you off my ledger eight days ago, and you can't deny it because there's the letter. (*He hands her the letter; she takes it mechanically*) I had my reason: your brother. You tell me now that he's been set free, and I'm happy for you. Within the last eight days I have entered into a new "liaison"; I had the right because you failed to protest my letter within the proper amount of time. I felt as justified in my own regard as I felt justified in regard to the law. And now you make an appearance, but I have already given my word as well as accepted that of another—(*to himself*) if it were only true—the fact is that my new "interest" already finds herself in the same condition as you. I *do* feel sorry for you (*He smoothes back her hair, which she allows as though she were unaware of it*), but I know you'll understand. There's no playing around where the Mayor's concerned.

KLARA   (*absentmindedly*)   No, not where the Mayor's concerned.

LEONARD   You see, you *are* being reasonable about it. And as far as your father's concerned, you can tell him to his face that he's the one at fault. You needn't look at me like that and shake your head, it's the truth, Klara, it's the truth! You tell him that and he'll understand what I mean, he'll turn over a new leaf, I can guarantee you that. Or would you rather I talk with him myself? He can be as uncivil to me as he likes, he can throw the boot-jack at my head, but colic or no colic he's going to have to swallow the truth, hard as it may be, and leave you in peace. Is he at home?

KLARA   (*raising herself proudly*)   I thank you. (*wanting to leave*)

LEONARD   Shall I walk over with you? I'm not afraid of him.

KLARA   I thank you as I would a serpent that had wound itself about me and then suddenly let me go to prey on something else. I know that I've been bitten, I know the only reason you're leaving me is that it doesn't seem worth your pains to suck the little marrow from my bones, and still I thank you, because now my

death will be peaceful. Please, you must believe me, I'm not mocking you, I *do* thank you. It seems as if through you I was able to see down to the very depths of hell itself, and whatever awful share eternity may have in store for me at least I have nothing further to do with you, and that's a consolation. A man stung by a snake is never blamed when he horribly opens the veins in his body to let the poisoned life inside him out. Perhaps God's eternal kindness will have mercy upon me in the same way when he looks at you and at me and sees what you have made of me, because why should I be *able* to do such a thing when I haven't the *right* to do it? There's one more thing: my father knows nor suspects nothing of this; to keep him from ever learning I will take my life, tonight. If I ever thought that you . . . (*She takes a step toward him distractedly*) But that would be foolish! You can only be grateful for the fact that they'll all stand around my grave shaking their heads to no purpose, asking why such a thing happened.

LEONARD   Accidents happen! What can *we* do? Klara!

KLARA   Let me out of here! People can talk. (*wanting to leave*)

LEONARD   Do you really think I believe you?

KLARA   No.

LEONARD   Don't forget that you can't kill yourself without killing your own child as well.

KLARA   I'd rather do both than kill my own father! I know that we can't wash one sin away with another. But what I have to do concerns no one but myself. Placing the knife in my father's hand would hurt him as much as me. There's no way out for me. This is the only thing that gives me the courage and strength to ignore my fears. You will have nothing to worry about. (*off*)

Scene Five

LEONARD   (*alone*)   I have to. I have to marry her. And why do I have to? Because she wants to commit an insane action to keep her father from committing an insane action. Then why should I commit a *more* insane action simply to keep her from hers? I'll agree to nothing. At least not until I'm faced with the man who'll threaten me with the insanest action of all. And if we both happen to think alike there'll never be an end to it. That sounds sensible enough, but then . . . I've got to go after her. Someone's coming. Thank God for that. What's worse than having it out with your own thoughts.

Scene Six

SECRETARY (*enters*) Good evening.

LEONARD Oh, it's you. And to what do I owe the honor of . . .

SECRETARY You'll find out soon enough.

LEONARD I see, you're very frank. But then we were school-comrades together, weren't we.

SECRETARY And may be comrades in death. (*He lays out a pair of pistols*) Are you versed in the art?

LEONARD I'm afraid I don't quite understand.

SECRETARY (*cocks one of the pistols*) See that? That's the way it's done. Then you take aim at me, like I'm aiming at you now and you pull the trigger. Like this.

LEONARD What are you talking about?

SECRETARY That one of the two of us must die.

LEONARD Die?

SECRETARY There's no need to explain.

LEONARD I don't understand.

SECRETARY That's not important. It'll come to you at the last minute.

LEONARD I have no idea . . .

SECRETARY Then think hard. I could shoot you down now for a mad dog that's bitten someone dear to me, without thinking anything of it. But my conscience tells me that I must take you for a human being, at least for the next half-hour.

LEONARD You needn't talk so loud. Suppose someone hears you?

SECRETARY If there were anyone around you would have called him by this time. Well?

LEONARD If you're doing this for Klara's sake, yes, I can marry her. In fact, I half-way decided it while she was still here.

SECRETARY She was here and left without seeing you at her feet? Come with me. Come on.

LEONARD All right, listen to me . . . I'll do everything you say. I'll ask her to marry me, tonight.

SECRETARY Either I'll be the one to do that or no one. I'll see that you never so much as touch the hem of her dress again even if the world depends on it. Come on. We're going into the woods. I'm going to take you by the arm, like this, and if you make a sound on the way there, I'll . . . (*He holds up the pistol*) just as long as we understand each other. But just so that you won't be tempted, we'll take the back way through the garden.

LEONARD If one of those is for me . . . then let me have it.

SECRETARY So that you can throw it away and force me either to murder you or let you run off? You can wait. When we get to where we're going I'll give you as good a one as I'll have.

LEONARD (*goes to the table and inadvertently pushes a glass from it*) I suppose I've had my last drink.

SECRETARY You musn't give up so easily, my friend. It seems God and the Devil are always fighting for the upper hand in the world. Who knows which one's on top at the moment. (*takes him by the arm and they go off*)

Scene Seven

A ROOM IN THE HOUSE OF THE CABINET-MAKER. EVENING

KARL (*enters*) Nobody here. If it hadn't been for the rathole under the door where they hide the key when they go out I'd never have got in. Not that that would have mattered. I could run around the city twenty times now and imagine there's no greater pleasure in the world than using your legs. Let's have some light in here. (*He lights a lamp*) I'll bet the matches are in the same place as ever. In this house we have *two times* Ten Commandments. My hat belongs on the third nail and not on the fourth. At half-past nine every night you have to be tired. There's no freezing before St. Martinsmas and no sweating afterwards. All this goes side-by-side with: "Thou shalt fear and love the Lord thy God!" I'm thirsty. (*calls*) Mother! Damn! I'd forgotten she's gone to where not even the inn-keeper's servant-boy has to come when he's called. I didn't cry when I heard the funeral-bells in my dark hole in the tower, but . . . you, bailiff Adam, you wouldn't let me have my last shot in the alley even though I already had the ball in my hand. If I find you, you won't have time to draw your last breath, and that may be tonight because I know where to find you at ten o'clock. After that I'll go to sea. What's keeping Klara out so late? I'm as hungry as I am thirsty. Today's Thursday, they had veal-broth. If it was winter now there would have been cabbage, too, white cabbage before Shrove Tuesday, green cabbage after. That's as sure as that Thursday *has* to come once Wednesday's been so that Thursday can't ask Friday to take his place because his feet are tired.

Scene Eight

(KLARA *enters*)

KARL   It's about time! You shouldn't kiss so much! Where four lips get together, they say, there's the devil's bridge for sure! What's that?

KLARA   Where? What?

KARL   "Where?" "What?" That in your hand?

KLARA   Nothing!

KARL   Nothing? Something I'm not supposed to see? (*He tears* LEONARD's *letter from her*) Give it here! When father's not home I'm the one you listen to.

KLARA   I held so tight to it that not even the wind could tear it from my hand. It's so strong it's pulling tiles off roofs. On my way past the church one of them fell so close in front of me that I kicked it with my foot. "O God," I thought, "send another!" And I waited there. That would have been the best way, and they would have buried me and said: "It was an accident." But the second tile never came.

KARL   (*who has read the letter*)   Damn him, I'll . . . I'll tear the arm off that wrote this! Bring me a bottle of wine! Or is the money-box empty?

KLARA   There's still another bottle. I bought it secretly for mother's birthday and set it aside. It would have been tomorrow . . . (*She turns away*)

KARL   Then bring it here.

(KLARA *brings the wine*)

KARL   (*drinking hurriedly*)   We could begin all over again now. Planing, sawing, hammering, and in between eating and drinking and sleeping so that we can keep on planing and sawing and hammering, and with a bend of the knee thrown in on Sundays: "I thank Thee, Lord, for permitting me to plane and saw and hammer!" (*drinks*) Long live the good dog that doesn't bite his chain! (*He drinks again*) Here's to him again!

KLARA   Karl, you mustn't drink so much. Father says there's the devil in wine.

KARL   And the priest says there's God in wine! (*He drinks*) We'll see who's right. The bailiff was here, wasn't he? How did he behave?

KLARA   Like in a den of thieves. Mother collapsed and died as soon as she heard.

KARL   Good! Then tomorrow when you hear that he's been found murdered you won't condemn the murderer.

KLARA   Karl, you couldn't . . .

KARL   Am I his only enemy? Hasn't he been attacked before this? It'd be a hard thing to try to find the right man out of all those who could have done it, unless he leaves behind his hat or his cane. (*He drinks*) But whoever it is, I wish him luck!

KLARA   You're talking like a . . .

KARL   Don't you like the idea? Then don't think about it. You won't have to put up with me much longer.

KLARA   (*shuddering*)   Karl, no!

KARL   No? Do you know already that I'm going to sea? Are my thoughts as obvious as all that that you can read my mind? Or has the old bear been raging and threatening again to lock me out of the house? Hell, that's about like the warden threatening that he can't keep me in jail any longer!

KLARA   You don't understand.

KARL   (*sings*)

The ship's stout sail blows hearty, oh,
And briskly blows the wind!

Yes, and now there's nothing to keep me here at this joiner's-bench. Mother's dead, there's nobody now to keep me from eating fish after every storm like I liked to do from the time I was little. I've got to get out into the world! I'll never make a go of it here, or at least not until I'm sure that there's no hope for a man who's willing to risk his life.

KLARA   And you'd leave your father alone? He's sixty years old.

KARL   Alone? Won't you be here?

KLARA   Me?

KARL   Yes, you! His pet! Why ask such silly questions? He'll be happy to see me go, he'll have nothing more to grumble about . . . so why shouldn't I do it? We don't belong together. There's nothing too cramped for him. He'd like to ball up his fist and crawl into it if he could, and I'd like to burst out of my skin like a baby out of its clothes! (*sings*)

The heaving anchor wails,
The rudder trims the sails,
And leaves the shore behind!

Tell me, did he doubt for even one minute that I was guilty? Didn't he console himself like he always does with his: "Just what I expected!" If it had been you he would have committed suicide. I'd like to see him if you'd gone the way a lot of women do. He'd go around like he was in labor himself! And what's more, with the devil!

KLARA   I wish you wouldn't talk like that! I've got to get out of here! I've got to!

KARL   What is it?

KLARA   I've got to get to the kitchen (*putting her hand to her forehead*) Yes, of course, that's the only reason I came back. (*off*)

KARL   Why is she acting like that? (*sings*)

A daring seabird greets me,
And circles round the mast!

KLARA   (*re-enters*) The last thing's done,

father's evening drink is on the fire. When I pulled closed the kitchen door behind me and thought: "You will never again come through that door," I shuddered to my very soul. I'll leave this room in the same way, this house, and then my life.

KARL (*he walks back and forth, singing;* KLARA *remains in the background*)
And fishes bright and merry
Boldly encircle their guest!

KLARA Why don't you do it? Aren't you ever going to do it? Are you going to put it off from day to day like now you're putting it off from minute to minute? I've got to do it. And all I do is stand here. I feel as if two tiny hands were raising themselves inside me here, as if two eyes . . . (*sits on a chair*) What's the matter with you? Are you too weak? Then ask yourself if you're strong enough to see your father with his throat . . . (*She rises*) No! No! "Our Father, Which art in Heaven . . . hallowed be Thy Kingdom . . ." God, my head, my head . . . I can't even pray anymore. Karl! Karl! Help me . . .

KARL What is it?

KLARA *The Lord's Prayer!* (*She recollects*) I felt like I was in the water already and sinking and had forgotten to pray! I . . . (*suddenly*) "Forgive us our trespasses, as we forgive those who trespass against us!" That's it. Yes, yes, I forgive him, I don't even think about him anymore. Good night, Karl!

KARL Why are you going to bed so early? Good night.

KLARA (*like a child repeating the Lord's Prayer*) Forgive us . . .

KARL Would you bring me a glass of water? But I want it fresh.

KLARA (*quickly*) I'll get it from the well!

KARL If it isn't too much trouble. It isn't far.

KLARA Thank you. Thank you. That was the only thing that held me back. They would never have believed it otherwise. Now they'll say: "It was an accident. She tumbled in."

KARL And be careful, they still haven't renailed that board on yet.

KLARA The moon is out . . . O God, if it were not myself it would be my father! Forgive me, as I . . . Have mercy on me . . . have mercy . . . (*off*)

Scene Nine

KARL (*sings*)
How gladly I'd have joined them
For my kingdom's there below!
Let's see, what comes before that . . . (*He looks at the clock*) What time its it? Nine. (*sings*)

My heart and head are youthful,
I came for the ride, to be truthful,
I care not where the winds blow!

Scene Ten

MASTER ANTON (*enters*) I had an apology to make to you, but if I forgive you for making debts secretly and besides that pay them off, then I'll consider my apology made.

KARL The one's good and the other's not necessary. If I sell my Sunday clothes I can pay the people myself the few thalers I owe them. I'll take care of that tomorrow. As a sailor I won't be needing them.

MASTER ANTON What's all this talk about?

KARL It's not the first time you've heard it, but say what you like today, I've made up my mind.

MASTER ANTON You're old enough, that's for sure.

KARL It's *because* I'm old enough that I'm not going to argue about it. Fishes and birds have no right arguing which is better: air or water. There's just one more thing: either you'll never see me again or you'll put your hand on my shoulder and tell me that what I'm doing is right!

MASTER ANTON We'll see first what happens. At least I won't have to discharge the man I called in to do your work. What else is there?

KARL I thank you!

MASTER ANTON I want you to tell me, when the bailiff caught you did he take you to the Mayor by the shortest route or is it true he led you through the whole town . . .

KARL Up one street, down another, onto the market-place like the Shrove-Tuesday ox, but don't worry, I'll pay him off, too, before I leave.

MASTER ANTON I can't blame you for that, but I forbid you to do it!

KARL Ho!

MASTER ANTON I won't let you out of my sight, and if you lay hands on the scoundrel I'll come to his defence!

KARL I thought *you* loved mother, *too*!

MASTER ANTON And I will prove it!

Scene Eleven

THE SECRETARY (*enters pale and unsteadily, pressing a cloth to his chest*) Where's Klara? (*He falls back into a chair*) My God! I didn't think I would make it here. Where is she?

KARL She went to the . . . What's keeping her? She said something about . . . my God! (*off*)

SECRETARY He's paid for his . . . he's lying out there . . . but he struck me, too . . . why, God, why . . . now I'll never . . .

MASTER ANTON What is it? What's happened to you?

SECRETARY It'll all be over soon. Give me your hand and promise me that you will never disown your daughter . . . Do you understand? You must never disown your daughter if she . . .

MASTER ANTON You're talking very strangely. Why should I . . . yes, I begin to see now. Maybe I wasn't unjust to her!

SECRETARY Give me your hand!

MASTER ANTON No! (*sticks both hands in his pockets*) But I won't stand in her way, and she knows that, I have already promised.

SECRETARY (*horrified*) You've promised her . . . My God, I'm beginning to understand you!

KARL (*rushing in*) Father, father, someone's fallen into the well! It can't be . . .

MASTER ANTON Bring the tall ladder! The hooks and the ropes, too! What are you standing there for? Hurry! I don't care if it's the bailiff!

KARL They already have all they need. The neighbors got there before me. It can't be Klara!

MASTER ANTON Klara? (*holding onto a table*)

KARL She went to get some water, and they found her handkerchief.

SECRETARY Now I know why I was struck. It *is* Klara.

MASTER ANTON Go and see! (*seats himself*) I can't. (KARL *goes off*) But . . . (*rises again*) if I (*to the* SECRETARY) understood you right . . . then it has all turned out for the best.

KARL (*returns*) Klara's dead. She cracked her head horribly on the rim of the well when she . . . Father, she didn't fall in, she jumped, a girl saw her!

MASTER ANTON She should consider more carefully before she talks! It's too dark out there for her to be so certain!

SECRETARY Do you *doubt* what happened? Yes, you'd like to, but you can't. Think of what you said to her. You were the one who pointed out to her the way to her death, and I, I'm the one to blame for her not turning back. When you suspected her all you thought about was the tongues that would hiss, but not about the worthless snakes they belonged to. What you said to her drove her to desperation; and I, instead of taking her in my arms when she opened her heart to me, I could only think of the scoundrel who could mock at me and . . . well, I'm paying now with my life for making myself dependent on a man who was worse than me. And you, standing there like a rod of iron, someday you, too, will have cause to cry out: "Klara, I wish now that you had not spared me the scorn and disapproval of these Pharisees; it humiliates me even more not to have you here beside my deathbed to wipe the sweat of anguish from my brow!"

MASTER ANTON She spared me *nothing*! They *saw* her!

SECRETARY She did all she could. But you weren't worthy enough for her to succeed!

(*Noises outside*)

KARL They're coming with her . . . (*wanting to leave*)

MASTER ANTON (*stands there immovably till the end; calls after him*) In the backroom, where they put her mother!

SECRETARY I've got to see her! (*He tries to rise but falls back*) Oh, Karl!

(KARL *helps him up, leads him out*)

MASTER ANTON I don't understand the world any more! (*He continues standing there reflectively*)

Gerhart Hauptmann

1862-1946

ON THE DRAMA

The origin of everything dramatic is in any case the split or twofold ego. The first two actors were *homo* and *ratio*,[1] or also You and I. The earliest drama which expressed itself outwardly was the first loud soliloquy. The first stage was erected nowhere else than in the head of man. It remains the smallest and yet the largest which can be erected. It represents the world, and encompasses the world more than the greatest theatres of the world.

*   *   *

Human speech contains the Yes and the No. And there where human speech is alive, namely in the human spirit, there the Yes and the No are the two leading antagonists. The conflict or dialogue between these two forces begins in the child, when thinking begins, and ends only in death. In this Yes and No we have the first actors in the primal drama [*Urdrama*], two words, which can disguise themselves indeed in the I and the Non-I or the You. Much can be said about this primal drama, the *dramatis personae* of which will become more and more numerous as life goes on and will play their roles without interruption upon the stage of consciousness longer than even the Chinese drama, namely for an entire lifetime. Unfortunately we have not time for that. *Faust,* however, is such a primal drama in objective form, Faust himself the willful Yes, Mephisto the willful No.

*   *   *

Perhaps there takes place in the poet's soul agglomerations in tempestuous rotation, which in dynamic concentration create heat, light, and finally life. There is in this something like the struggle between Ormuzd[2] and Ahriman.[3] Above all, Ormuzd and Ahriman, god and devil, are in combat with one another, and the stage where this drama takes place is in the human breast.

Every man might then be a dramatist? I believe that to be the case. Goethe sought the *Urpflanze*.[4] One might more justly seek the *Urdrama*, and indeed in the human psyche itself. It is perhaps the earliest thought-process.

*   *   *

If I do not possess the advantages of this high calling, in the view of mankind perhaps the most objective, in any case I possess its weaknesses, and one of them is the inability to let one voice speak for itself out of the polyphony of my inner spirit, even though it be my own voice. As it is today, so it always was; there were always many voices seeking to speak out within me, and I found no other possibility of bringing about some sort of order than by giving utterance to these many voices —by writing dramas. I shall have to continue to do this; for it has been up to now the highest means of expression of my spiritual life.

*   *   *

The drama represents one of the many efforts of the human spirit to form a cosmos out of chaos. This effort begins already in the child and continues throughout life. The stage in the human mind grows from year to year,

"On the Drama" by Gerhart Hauptmann, translated by F. B. Wahr, reprinted with the friendly permission of Ullstein Verlag, GmbH., Frankfurt/Main, Berlin.

[1] *Man* and *reason*.
[2] The creator of the world in Zoroastrian religion.
[3] The spirit of evil in Zoroastrian religion.
[4] The source of life.

[49]

and the company of players becomes larger and larger. Its director, the intellect, is soon no longer able to keep it all in hand, for the actors grow into a countless throng.

The earliest members of the large-small world-theatre in the child's mind are mother, father, brothers and sisters, relatives and whatever other human beings enter into the circle of experience. In the child's games this drama begins theatre-like to project itself outward. It imitates the mother, the father and their relation to the children. And this imitative impulse expands farther and farther, enabling the child to establish and build up its dramatic world. This world possesses throughout universal character. In it little analogies to the greatest moments of art taken as a whole are to be found, which are at the same time always seeking to represent themselves objectively. Not only the drama performed on the stages of the world go back to them, but likewise the Olympian Zeus of Pheidias, the Moses, the Pietà, and the Last Judgment of Michelangelo.

If we intend to limit ourselves to the art of the theatre our task becomes complicated at the first hasty glance. In point of time and so historically, there is the Indian, Greek, Roman, Italian, French, Spanish, English, and German theatre. One might designate their summits by the following names: Kalidasa,[5] Aeschylus, Plautus, Goldoni, Molière, Calderon, Shakespeare, Goethe, and Richard Wagner. But it would be a matter here of only a few happenstances, as we say, unique instances, in which great poets ennoble the theatre and lift it up into the divine, whereby human tragedy as well as human comedy find their highest expression. On the other hand, however, the theatre born out of the populace's need for sensation is of extreme variety. As regards ancient times I would point only to the Roman Coliseum. What a great span of time to it from the cart of Thespis! Within the modern theatre a similar lapse of time can be fixed; from Verdi and Richard Wagner, let us say, to the puppet play, from the little stage of strolling players to the joy in decorative fittings and stage equipment in the drama and pantomime of the Reinhardt [6] theatre, and from there on to Barnum and Bailey and the universal circus world.

Recent times afford the utmost in satisfying the human need for entertainment, especially in the cinema. Its rule extends in countless theatres over all five parts of the world. Millions of human beings of all races crowd through its doors daily. Who would not get dizzy in the presence of this great and general phenomenon, when he seeks to understand its significance in the mind of the folk and in that of the individual? And there still remains the satisfaction derived from the great love of potpourri on the part of the people, which the radio meets universally, in that it directs through millions and millions of channels all that is spoken, sung, fiddled and trumpeted into palaces and citizens' homes, even into the snow-covered huts of poor mountain dwellers.

At the Festival plays at Heidelberg on July 21, 1928, I gave a short address much like this. Later they called it "The Tree of Gallowayshire." Upon the ruins of the wall of New Abbey in Gallowayshire there grows a kind of maple tree. Forced by lack of space and nutriment it sent forth a strong root, which found firm footing in the earth beneath and grew into a sturdy trunk. And after it had freed the roots from the height of the wall, the whole tree, released from the wall, became independent. The tree in this way left its original place. It sought the strength of mother earth and penetrated it with all its roots.

The German drama for over a century and a half has passed through a similar process. Only in recent times has it reached root-soil completely. Thus I have treated in the drama peasant conditions in my homeland in *Before Dawn*, in *Drayman Henschel*, in *Rose Bernd*, the misery of poor mountain weavers, the struggles of a washerwoman to "get ahead," the sufferings of a beggar child in *The Ascension of Hannele*, of two workhouse inmates in *Schluck und Jau*,[7] and in *The Rats* an underworld of suffering, depravity, and crime.

Then in *Florian Geyer* I have extended my drama by presenting the sufferings of our people in the historical past. But I shall not speak further of myself; I had to do so in order to honor the truth; for I am to be regarded as one of the roots of the tree of Gallowayshire.

The individual is born into the elementally dramatic nature of his people, whose natural mirror he is, more or less clearly, more or less inclusively. The genius, however, is a divinely magic mirror, and thus, as Shakespeare says, in the living drama is the mirror of the age. . . .

Struggle is the father of all things and the

---

[5] India's greatest dramatist (c. 450 A.D.), best known for *Shakuntala*.

[6] Named for Max Reinhardt (1873–1943), the most famous director in the modern German theatre.

[7] A play written by Hauptmann in 1899.

drama one of the many forms of representing this struggle in its tragical, its comical, or in its tragi-comical manifestations. A drama ranks higher in so far as it keeps itself aloof from party or prejudice . . . A challenge to combat is to be presupposed, and an evil quarrel is now and then inescapably forced upon the good as well as the bad. Some kind of victory over life should be attained at the close of the drama, tragic or comic. Advocacy of dogmas as an essential aim makes a drama second-rate. The drama is not meant to prove anything, and when it is thus abused it is destroyed as an art-form.

❋　　❋　　❋

In so far as Germany is concerned, the theatre has been freed and ennobled by the thoughts and deeds of a Lessing, Goethe, Schiller, Wagner and Nietzsche. Its task, which it fulfilled a long time ago in the music of Mozart, was formulated by these men. If nothing human is to be foreign to the theatre, then it must also preserve the dignity of man, things often difficult to unite. The theatre oftentimes makes itself effective like a natural event in such a manifold manner that its high meaning is not infrequently obscured. But religious ideas too become obscured. And there exists no bright, guiding star which is never hidden by clouds. What the stage, the actor requires is an emotional existence. In addition he must bear as a *conditio sine qua non* [8] the burden of talent or even of genius; both stand under special laws. If a chemist deals with dangerous materials, so much more perhaps, transferred into the spiritual realm, does the actor. No wonder, if at times the god-like light is extinguished for him. And yet ever and again the heavenly fixed stars shine upon the stage, which represents the world; names like Aeschylus, Sophocles, Euripides, Calderon, Shakespeare, Molière, Goethe, Schiller, Kleist, and Grillparzer beam forth, the supernatural music of Mozart, Beethoven, Richard Wagner resounds, and even the poorest comedian feels himself exalted by their rays.

❋　　❋　　❋

Among other things I have written dramas. . . . In these dramas all kinds of figures step forth, characters imbued with the fullest vitality by my spirit. One will not find the so-called villain in these works which are meant for the theatre. I would much rather claim to have been the seemingly incorruptible and, if

possible, loving counsel for almost all of my figures. Of course I could not overlook the human-all-too-human, because if one wishes to present the lot of human beings, whether tragically or comically, it is an inevitable life-giving and also fateful factor. Whoever desires the theatre, the drama, whoever desires the genuine, clear, purifying and clarifying mirror of life, must also most decisively say Yes to the human-all-too-human. . . . The poetic art, as I understand it, reckons with fully developed human beings, spiritually strong men and women, who have become capable of making judgments and are not oversensitive and pampered by sickly vanity. It reckons with such hearers and auditors who have the courage, seeking their own instruction and purification, to look down into the abyss of life, even where it is deepest.

❋　　❋　　❋

Recently I was speaking in Berlin of what Henrik Ibsen once said to me after he had read my early drama *Before Dawn*,—namely that it was brave and courageous. That seemed to him to contain the greatest praise. . . . He was right! Courage belongs to truth to oneself, to the love of truth! Without the high courage of youth we can accomplish nothing successfully. . . . It has been said, I have turned in my art too much to the affairs of the little man, the common man, and too little to that which lies just at the heart of the human beings of our own day. Well, not only in nature is the greatest and the smallest equally astonishing. The human is the truly great and is not changed so very much by the spirit of the time, that elemental things and destinies retreat behind the variations. Thus the eternal fate of man will always be a greater theme than the cerebrally conscious fate of an epoch.

Every man, and also every gifted man, is timed. He not only goes his own way through the darkness, but carries his own lantern. Many others go forth, indeed, on better paths and light the world differently. For me it is chiefly a matter of leaving behind me a work as phraseless and as rich in human experience as possible.

❋　　❋　　❋

Perception lies at the basis of all thinking. To think is to contend—thus dramatic. Every philosopher who presents to us his system of logical constructions has erected it by decisions which he has formulated out of the conflicting voices of his inner self. Accordingly I consider the drama to be the expression of primary

---

[8] An indispensable condition.

thought processes upon a higher level of development and of course without having to make those decisions which concern the philosopher.

From this kind of perception there arise series of consequences which extend the field of the drama in all directions infinitely beyond the ruling dramaturgies, so that nothing which presents itself to the outer or inner senses can be excluded from this form of thinking, which has become an art form.

So much and no more shall I say to accompany this first collection of my dramatic works; they are to be understood as a natural expression of a personality. After all it must be left to them to achieve any vital success, such as they have at present, in the struggle between love and hatred.

* * *

Translated by F. B. Wahr

THE WEAVERS

Translated by Carl Richard Mueller

CAST OF CHARACTERS

DREISSIGER, *fustian manufacturer*
FRAU DREISSIGER, *his wife*
PFEIFER, *manager*
NEUMANN, *cashier*
AN APPRENTICE
JOHANN, *coachman*
A SERVANT GIRL
} *in Dreissiger's service*
WEINHOLD, *tutor to Dreissiger's sons*
PASTOR KITTELHAUS
FRAU PASTOR KITTELHAUS, *his wife*
HEIDE, *Police Superintendent*
KUTSCHE, *a policeman*
WELZEL, *an innkeeper*
FRAU WELZEL, *his wife*
ANNA WELZEL, *their daughter*
WIEGAND, *a joiner*
A TRAVELING SALESMAN
A PEASANT
A FORESTER
SCHMIDT, *a surgeon*
HORNIG, *a ragpicker*
OLD WITTIG, *blacksmith*

Weavers

BAECKER
MORITZ JAEGER
OLD BAUMERT
MOTHER BAUMERT, *his wife*
BERTHA BAUMERT, *their daughter*
EMMA BAUMERT, *another daughter*
FRITZ, *Emma's son, four years old*
AUGUST BAUMERT, *Baumert's son*
OLD ANSORGE
FRAU HEINRICH
OLD HILSE
FRAU HILSE, *his wife*
GOTTLIEB HILSE, *their son*
LUISE HILSE, *his wife*
MIELCHEN, *their daughter, six years old*
REIMANN
HEIBER
A BOY, *eight years old*
DYEWORKERS
A large crowd of young and old weavers and weaver women.

The events described in this play take place in the 1840s in Kasbach in the Eulengebirge, as well as in Peterswaldau and Langenbielau at the foot of the Eulengebirge.

ACT ONE

(*A large whitewashed room in* DREISSIGER'S *house in Peterswaldau. It is the room where*

The Weavers by Gerhart Hauptmann, translated by Carl Richard Mueller, printed by permission of the translator.

the weavers must deliver their finished products. To the left there are windows without curtains; in the back wall a glass door; and to the right a similar glass door through which we see a continuous flow, in and out, of weavers, men, women, and children. The right wall, like the others, is for the most part hidden by wooden shelves for storing cotton. Along this wall stands a bench on which the in-coming weavers spread their goods. They step forward in order of their arrival and present their goods for inspection. PFEIFER, *the manager, stands behind a large table on which the goods to be inspected are placed. This he does with the use of dividers and a magnifying glass. The inspection finished, the weavers place the cloth on the scale where an* APPRENTICE *tests it for weight. The same* APPRENTICE *then places the accepted goods on a shelf. Each time,* PFEIFER *calls out loudly to* NEUMANN, *the cashier, sitting at a small table, the amount to be paid.*

It is a sultry day towards the end of May. The clock is at the stroke of twelve. Most of the weavers resemble persons standing in front of a bar of justice where with tortuous expectation they must wait for a life-and-death decision. There is something of the oppressed about them, something characteristic of the receiver of charity, who, having passed from one humiliation to another, is conscious of the fact that he is merely tolerated and is accustomed to making himself as inconspicuous as possible. Add to this an inflexible feature in their bearing of irresolute, harassed brooding. The men all resemble one another, half dwarf-like, half schoolmaster-like. They are, for the most part, flat-chested, coughing, miserable creatures with pallid faces: creatures of the loom, whose knees are bent as a result of excessive sitting. Their women, at first glance, are less of a type; they are broken individuals, harassed, worn out—whereas the men still have about them a look of pathetic gravity. The clothes of the women are ragged, while those of the men are patched. The young girls among them are not without a certain charm: a wax-like paleness, delicate figures and large, protruding, melancholy eyes)

CASHIER NEUMANN (*counting out money*) That leaves sixteen silver groschen and two pfennig.

FIRST WEAVER WOMAN (*about thirty, very emaciated. She puts away the money with trembling fingers*) Thank you.

NEUMANN (*When the* WOMAN *fails to move on*) Well? Something wrong again?

FIRST WEAVER WOMAN (*excitedly, begging*) I was wondering, could I have a few pfennig in advance, I need it awful bad.

NEUMANN And I need a couple hundred thalers. Nice if all we had to do is need it—! (*already busy counting out money to another weaver, curtly*) Herr Dreissiger's the one who takes care of advance payments.

FIRST WEAVER WOMAN Then maybe I could talk with Herr Dreissiger for a minute?

MANAGER PFEIFER (*Formerly a weaver himself, his type is unmistakable, except that he is well fed, well groomed, cleanly shaven, and a heavy user of snuff. He calls across brusquely*) God knows, Herr Dreissiger'd have enough to do if he had to worry about every petty request. That's what *we're* here for. (*He measures and then inspects with the magnifying glass*) Damn! There's a draft! (*He wraps a heavy scarf around his neck*) Close the door when you come in.

APPRENTICE (*loudly to* PFEIFER) Might as well talk to a stone wall.

PFEIFER All right, that's done! Weigh it! (*The* WEAVER *places his web on the scale*) Why don't you learn to do your work better? It's full of lumps again. I don't even have to look at it. A good weaver doesn't put off the winding for God knows how long.

BAECKER (*enters. He is a young and exceptionally strong weaver whose unconstrained deportment is almost impudent.* PFEIFER, NEUMANN *and the* APPRENTICE *exchange knowing glances at his entrance*) Damn! Sweating like a dog again!

FIRST WEAVER (*in a low voice*) This heat means rain.

OLD BAUMERT (*pushes through the glass door at the right. On the other side of the door one can see the weavers waiting, crowded together, shoulder to shoulder.* OLD BAUMERT *has hobbled his way forward and laid down his pack on the bench near* BAECKER'S. *He sits down beside it and wipes the perspiration from his face*) I can use a rest after that.

BAECKER Rest's better than money anytime.

OLD BAUMERT I could use a little money too. Good day to you, Baecker!

BAECKER Good day to you, Father Baumert! Looks like another long wait here, uh?

FIRST WEAVER What's the difference? A weaver can wait an hour or a day. He don't count.

PFEIFER Quiet back there! How can I hear myself think?

BAECKER (*softly*) One of his bad days again.

PFEIFER (*to the* WEAVER *in front of him*) How many times do we have to tell you to clean up your webs better! What do you call a mess like this? Clots of dirt in here long as my finger, and straw and all kinds of muck.

WEAVER REIMANN But there's always a pound waste figured in.

PFEIFER I haven't got time. That's done with.—What have *you* got?

WEAVER HEIBER (*puts down his web. While* PFEIFER *examines it he steps up to him and talks to him in a low and eager voice*) Beg pardon, Herr Pfeifer, sir, I wanted to ask you a favor, sir, if maybe you'd be so kind and wanted to do me a good turn, sir, and not have my advance pay come off my salary this time.

PFEIFER (*measuring and inspecting, scornfully*) Well, now! Very well done. Looks like half of the woof was left on the spool again.

WEAVER HEIBER (*continues in his own way*) I'll be sure to make it up this week, sir. Last week I had to work two days on the estate. And then my wife's home sick too . . .

PFEIFER (*placing the web on the scales*) Here's another fine piece of sloppy work. (*already beginning to inspect a new web*) You call this a selvage? Broad here, narrow there! In one place the woof's all drawn together, God knows how much, and then here the reed's been pulled apart. And you've hardly got seventy threads to the inch. Where's the rest of it? You call this honest work? Whoever heard of such a thing?

(WEAVER HEIBER, *suppressing his tears, stands there humiliated and helpless*)

BAECKER (*in a low voice, to* BAUMERT) Looks like those bastards would like to make us pay for our own yarn too.

FIRST WEAVER WOMAN (*who has stepped back only a few paces from the cashier's table and has looked staringly about her from time to time, seeking help, without moving from the place. She now takes heart and turns again beseechingly toward the cashier*) I can hardly . . . I just don't know if you don't give me any advance . . . O Jesus, Lord Jesus . . .

PFEIFER (*calls across*) What's all this calling the Lord Jesus! Let Him in peace for a while! You never bothered much about your Lord Jesus up to now. Give a little more mind to your husband, you'd be better off, so we don't see him sitting at a tavern window all day long. We can't give any advances. We have to account here for every pfennig. Besides that, it's not our money. They'd be after *us* for it later. People who work hard and understand their business and do their work in the fear of the Lord don't need advances. So that's the end of that.

NEUMANN And if a weaver from Bielau got paid four times as much, he'd waste just four times as much and still be in debt.

FIRST WEAVER WOMAN (*loudly as if appealing to everyone's sense of justice*) There's nobody can say I'm lazy, but I can't go on like this anymore. Two times I had a miscarriage. And for my husband, he can do only half his part too. He even went to the shepherd at Zerlau but he couldn't help him with his trouble either . . . there's nobody can do more than he's able. We do our work here, all right, we do all we can. I've not had much sleep these past weeks, but everything'll be all right soon if only I can get some strength back into my bones. But you must have a little bit of consideration then. (*beseeching him fawningly*) You'll be good enough, won't you, sir, and allow me a few groschen this time.

PFEIFER (*without interrupting himself*) Fiedler: eleven silver groschen.

FIRST WEAVER WOMAN Just a few groschen to buy our bread. The farmer, he won't give no more credit. And then there's all our children . . .

NEUMANN (*in a low voice, with comic earnestness, to the* APPRENTICE) Every year the linen-weaver has another kid, lálalala, lálalala, lá, lá, lá!

APPRENTICE (*takes it up*) And the little brat is as blind as a lid, lálalala, lálalala, lá, lá, lá!

WEAVER REIMANN (*not touching the money which the cashier has counted out for him*) We always used to get thirteen and a half groschen for a web.

PFEIFER (*calling over*) If it don't suit you, Reimann, all you got to do is say so. There's enough weavers around. Especially your kind. You get full pay when your web's full weight.

WEAVER REIMANN How could anything be wrong with the weight . . .

PFEIFER Bring us a flawless piece of cotton sometime and your pay'll be all right, too.

WEAVER REIMANN I don't understand how there are any mistakes in it.

PFEIFER (*as he inspects*) Weave well, live well.

WEAVER HEIBER (*has stayed near* PFEIFER, *looking for another favorable opportunity. He smiled together with the others over* PFEIFER'S *witticism, and now he starts towards him again and addresses him as before*) What I wanted to ask you, Herr Pfeifer, sir, is if perhaps you'd be so kind as not to take the five groschen advance off this week's pay. My wife she's been a-bed since Shrove Tuesday. There's nothing she can do to help me. So I have to pay the girl to tend the spools. So you see . . .

PFEIFER (*taking snuff*) Heiber, you're not the only one I've got to take care of here. The others want their turn too.

WEAVER REIMANN This is how I got the warp—so this is how I wound it up and took it off again. I can't bring back better yarn than I got.

PFEIFER If you don't like it then don't bother picking up anymore. We got enough around here who'd run their soles off for it.

NEUMANN (*to* REIMANN) Do you want the money or not?

WEAVER REIMANN How could I feel right if I took that money?

NEUMANN (*no longer troubling himself with* REIMANN) Heiber: ten silver groschen. Take off five for advance, that leaves five silver groschen.

WEAVER HEIBER (*steps forward, looks at the money, shakes his head as though there were something he can't believe, then puts the money slowly and carefully into his pocket*) My God, my God—(*sighs*) Well——

OLD BAUMERT (*looking* HEIBER *in the face*) Yes, yes, Franz! There's cause enough for sighing.

WEAVER HEIBER (*speaking with difficulty*) Then, you see, I got a sick girl at home too. She needs a bottle of medicine.

OLD BAUMERT What's she got?

WEAVER HEIBER Well, you see, she's been a sick one from when she was born. I don't know . . . well, I can tell you this much: she's brought it with her into the world. All kinds of troubles break out over and over on her. It's in the blood.

OLD BAUMERT There's trouble all over. Wherever there's poor people there's bad luck after bad luck. There's no end to it and no saving us.

WEAVER HEIBER What's that there in the bundle?

OLD BAUMERT We had nothing at all to eat at home. And so I had our little dog killed. There's not much on him, he was half starved away. He was a nice little dog. I didn't want to kill him myself. I couldn't find the heart for that.

PFEIFER (*has inspected* BAECKER's *web, calls*) Baecker: thirteen and a half silver groschen.

BAECKER That's a shabby piece of charity, not pay.

PFEIFER Whoever's been taken care of has to leave. We can't even move around for all the crowd.

BAECKER (*to the people standing about, not lowering his voice*) This is a shabby tip, that's all it is. And for this we're supposed to work our treddle from early morning to late at night. And when you've worked eighteen days over the loom, night after night, worn out, half dizzy with the dust and the burning heat, then you're lucky if you made thirteen and a half silver groschen.

PFEIFER We don't allow back-talk here.

BAECKER You don't tell *me* what not to say!

PFEIFER (*jumps up shouting*) We'll see about that! (*goes to the glass door and calls into the office*) Herr Dreissiger, Herr Dreissiger, if you'd be so kind, sir!

DREISSIGER (*enters. He is in his early forties, fat, asthmatic, with a severe look*) What is it, Pfeifer?

PFEIFER (*angrily*) Baecker here says he won't keep his mouth shut.

DREISSIGER (*draws himself up, throws back his head, stares at* BAECKER *with quivering nostrils*) Yes, of course—Baecker! (*to* PFEIFER) Is this the one?

(*The* CLERK *nods*)

BAECKER (*impudently*) Right enough, Herr Dreissiger! (*pointing to himself*) This is *this* one—(*pointing to* DREISSIGER) and that's *that* one.

DREISSIGER (*with indignation*) Who does he think he's talking to?

PFEIFER He's too well off, that's what! He'll skate on thin ice just once too often.

BAECKER (*roughly*) You shut your mouth, you stinking toad. Your mother must have rode a broomstick with Satan himself to get a devil like you!

DREISSIGER (*bellowing in sudden anger*) Hold your tongue! Hold your tongue this minute or I'll . . . (*He trembles, comes forward a few steps*)

BAECKER (*awaiting him with determination*) I'm not deaf. My hearing's all right.

DREISSIGER (*controls himself and asks with apparent business-like calm*) Isn't this one of those who . . .

PFEIFER He's a weaver from Bielau. You find them wherever there's trouble.

DREISSIGER (*trembling*) Just let me warn you of one thing: if ever it happens again like it did yesterday evening that a horde of half-drunken wet-nosed young louts passes my house again—and singing that vile song . . .

BAECKER I guess it's *The Song of Bloody Justice* you mean, uh?

DREISSIGER You know which one I mean. You just let me warn you: if I ever hear it again, I'll get hold of one of you and—I promise you this on my word of honor, I'm not joking—he will be turned over to the state's attorney. And if I ever find out who's responsible for that vile thing you call a song . . .

BAECKER It's a beautiful song!

DREISSIGER One more word out of you and I'll send for the police—and at once. I don't fool around. We know how to take care of young louts like you. I've taken care of people a lot different from you.

BAECKER I take your word for it. Sure, a factory owner like you can take care of two or three hundred weavers before a man can turn around, and not even a bone left over. A man like that's got four bellies like a cow and the jaws of a wolf. For him it's nothing, nothing!

DREISSIGER (*to the* CLERK) This one gets no more work from us.

BAECKER What do I care whether I go hungry over a loom or at the side of a road!

DREISSIGER Get out of here! Get out!

BAECKER (*firmly*) First I'll take my pay.

DREISSIGER What's he got coming, Neumann?

NEUMANN Thirteen silver groschen, five pfennig.

DREISSIGER (*takes the money overhastily from the cashier and tosses it onto the counter so that some of the coins roll onto the floor*) There you are! Now—get out of my sight!

BAECKER First I'll get my pay.

DREISSIGER There's your pay; and unless you get out of here, and quick . . . It's exactly twelve . . . My dyers are just now taking off for lunch . . .

BAECKER I get my pay in my hand. My pay belongs here. (*He touches the palm of his left hand with the fingers of his right hand.*)

DREISSIGER (*to the* APPRENTICE) Pick it up, Tilgner.

(*The* APPRENTICE *does so and places the money in* BAECKER's *hand*)

BAECKER Everything done proper. (*Without hurrying he places the money in an old purse*)

DREISSIGER Well? (*impatiently, since* BAECKER *does not leave*) Shall I *help* you out? (*Agitation has risen among the crowd of weavers. A long, deep sigh is heard. Then someone falls. All interest is turned towards the new event*)

DREISSIGER What's the matter here?

VARIOUS WEAVERS AND WEAVER WOMEN Someone fainted.—It's a sick little boy.—Is it the falling sickness, or what?

DREISSIGER What . . . what's that? Fainted, you say? (*He goes nearer*)

AN OLD WEAVER He just lays there.

(*Room is made. An eight-year-old* BOY *is seen lying on the ground as if dead*)

DREISSIGER Does anybody know the boy?

THE OLD WEAVER Not from our village.

OLD BAUMERT He looks like one of the Heinrichs. (*looks at him more closely*) Yes, yes! It's Heinrich's boy Gustav.

DREISSIGER Where do these people live?

OLD BAUMERT Up around us, in Kasbach, Herr Dreissiger. He goes around playing music, and in the daytime he works at his loom. They have nine children, the tenth on the way.

VARIOUS WEAVERS AND WEAVER WOMEN They've got a lot of trouble, those people.—It rains through their roof.—The wife can't get two shirts for all the nine children.

OLD BAUMERT (*grabbing hold of the* BOY) Hey there, boy, what's the matter with you? Wake up now!

DREISSIGER Get hold of him there, we'll pick him up. Whoever heard of such foolishness, letting a child weak as him make such a long trip! Pfeifer, bring some water!

WEAVER WOMAN (*helps him sit up*) You're not going to go and die on us now, boy, are you?

DREISSIGER Or some cognac, Pfeifer, cognac's better.

BAECKER (*Forgotten by everyone, he has stood there watching. Now, with one hand on the doorknob, he calls across loud and mockingly*) Give him something to eat, too, and he'll come round all right. (*off*)

DREISSIGER That one'll come to no good end. —Grab him under the arms, Neumann. Slowly, slowly . . . there . . . there . . . we'll take him into my office. What is it?

NEUMANN He said something, Herr Dreissiger! He moved his lips.

DREISSIGER What do you want, boy?

THE BOY (*whispering*) I'm hungry!

DREISSIGER (*turning pale*) I can't understand him.

WEAVER WOMAN I think he wants . . .

DREISSIGER We'll see what it is. Just don't hold us up.—He can lie down on my sofa. We'll hear what the doctor has to say.

(DREISSIGER, NEUMANN *and the* WEAVER WOMAN *take the* BOY *into the office. Excited agitation arises among the weavers as though they were school children whose teacher had just left the room. They stretch their limbs, they whisper, they shift from one foot to another, and within a few seconds their conversation is loud and general*)

OLD BAUMERT I do believe Baecker was right.

SEVERAL WEAVERS AND WEAVER WOMEN The boy said something that sounded like that. —It's nothing new around here, people fainting with hunger.—And what'll happen with us this winter if this cutting our wages keeps up?—And with the potatoes like they are, it'll be a bad year.—They won't do anything here until they find us all laying flat on our backs.

OLD BAUMERT The best thing to do is what the weaver in Nentwich did, put a rope around your neck and hang yourself to your loom. Here, take yourself a pinch of snuff. He gave me a few grains to take along. What have you got in your handkerchief there that's nice?

AN OLD WEAVER   A little bit of pearl barley, that's all. The wagon from the miller in Ullbrich drove along ahead of me. One of the sacks had a little hole in it. That was a very handy thing, you can believe me.

OLD BAUMERT   Twenty-two mills there are in Peterswaldau and for us there's nothing left over.

OLD WEAVER   We mustn't ever lose our courage. There's always something to come along and help us on a little farther.

WEAVER HEIBER   When we're hungry the thing to do is pray to the Fourteen Helping Saints, and if that don't fill you up then you must put a pebble in your mouth and suck away. Right Baumert?

(DREISSIGER, PFEIFER *and the cashier return*)

DREISSIGER   Nothing serious. The boy's wide awake again. (*He walks about excited and puffing*) Still and all it remains a disgrace. The child's as strong as a piece of straw in a windstorm. It's quite impossible to understand how people . . . how parents could be so unreasonable. Loading him down with two bundles of cotton and making him come all that way. I'll simply have to make it clear that goods brought by children will not be accepted. (*He walks back and forth in silence again for a while*) In any case, I urgently hope that such a thing will never happen again.—Who's to be blamed for it in the end? The factory owners, of course. We get blamed for everything. If a little fellow like this one gets stuck in the snow in wintertime and falls asleep there'd be a reporter there before we know it and the gruesome story would be in all the papers in two days. The father, the parents who send a child like that out . . . why, of course, why should *they* be blamed? The factory owner's the one, the factory owner's the scapegoat. The weaver is always the one they let off easy, and the factory owner is the one who gets the lash: he's the one with no feelings, the one with a heart of stone, he's the dangerous one that every presshound can bite in the leg. He lives as splendid and happy as a prince and pays his weavers starvation wages.—They forget in all their high-sounding phrases that a man like that has troubles, too, and sleepless nights, and he runs tremendous risks that the worker doesn't even dream about; that there are times when he's so confused that his head swims with all the addition and multiplication and division that he has to do, with calculations and recalculations; that he has a hundred different things to think about

and consider and has to fight competition tooth and nail, so to speak; that not a single day goes by without aggravation and losses; but these they never mention. Think of all the dependents the factory owner has around his neck, all the people who try to suck him dry to live off him! No, no! You ought to be in *my* shoes for a while, you'd have your fill of it soon enough. (*after a moment of reflection*) And what about *that* fellow, *that* one, *Baecker*, how did he act! Now he'll go out and shout all over town what a hard-hearted creature I am, how I discharge my weavers over insignificant matters. Is that true? Am I as hardhearted as all that?

MANY VOICES   No, Herr Dreissiger!

DREISSIGER   Well, that's the way I see it, too. And still these young louts come around singing their vile songs about us factory owners. They talk about being hungry, yet they have so much left over to be able to drink their liquor by the quart. They ought to snoop around a little more and see what conditions are like with the linen weavers. Those are the people who can talk about being in need. But those of you here, you cotton weavers, you can still thank God quietly that you're as well off as you are. And I ask you now, you old, industrious and efficient weavers that are here: can a worker who knows what a good job is make a living working for me?

A GREAT MANY VOICES   Yes, Herr Dreissiger!

DREISSIGER   There, you see!—One like that Baecker, of course, couldn't. Let me advise you to keep fellows like him in check. If things go too far, then I'll just quit. I'll give up the whole business, and then you'll see how things really are. Then you can see about finding work for yourselves. And I can assure you, it won't be from your honorable Herr Baecker that you'll get work.

FIRST WEAVER WOMAN (*has made her way up to* DREISSIGER *and with servility and humility brushes some dust from his coat*) You've gone and brushed yourself up against something, Herr Dreissiger, sir.

DREISSIGER   Business is miserable right now, you know that yourselves. I'm losing money instead of making it. And if, in spite of this, I always see to it that my weavers have work, then I expect a little gratitude in return. I have piles of cloths by the thousands, and right now I don't know if I'll ever be able to get rid of them.—But then I heard how many weavers around here are out of work entirely, and so . . . well, Pfeifer can give you the rest of the details.—But the fact is simply that in order to show you my good intentions . . . I can't, of course, hand out charity, I'm not rich enough for that, but up to a certain point I *can* give the unemployed the opportunity to earn at least *something*. The fact that I am running a tremendous risk is, of course, *my* worry.—It has always been my opinion that it is better for a man to earn a piece of cheese each day than to have to starve. Am I right?

MANY VOICES   Yes, yes, Herr Dreissiger.

DREISSIGER   And therefore I am more than happy to give work to another two hundred weavers. Pfeifer will explain to you under what conditions. (*He is about to go*)

FIRST WEAVER WOMAN (*steps into his path, speaks hastily, imploringly and urgently*) Herr Dreissiger, if you'd be so good, sir, what I wanted to ask you in a friendly way, if maybe you'd . . . well you see I been laid up two times already.

DREISSIGER (*hastily*)   You'll have to speak with Pfeifer, my good woman, I'm late as it is. (*He leaves her standing there*)

WEAVER REIMANN (*also steps into his path; in an injured and accusing tone*)   Herr Dreissiger, I'm sorry, I have a complaint to make. Herr Pfeifer there has . . . Well, I always used to get twelve and a half groschen a web . . .

DREISSIGER (*interrupting him*)   My manager is over there. You may go to him: he's the great offence over a piece of kindling wood.

WEAVER HEIBER (*stopping* DREISSIGER) Herr Dreissiger, sir— (*stuttering and with confused haste*) What I wanted to ask you, sir, was if maybe you could be so kind as to . . . that is maybe you could be so kind as to . . . that is maybe if Herr Pfeifer could . . . if I could . . .

DREISSIGER   What is it you want?

WEAVER HEIBER   That advance pay I had last time, well, what I mean is that . . .

DREISSIGER   I don't understand a word you're saying.

WEAVER HEIBER   Things were awful hard up for me, sir, because . . .

DREISSIGER   That's Pfeifer's business, that is all Pfeifer's business. There is really nothing I can . . . settle your business with Pfeifer. (*He escapes into the office*)

(*The suppliants look helplessly at one another. One after another they step back, sighing*)

PFEIFER (*starts his inspecting again*)   Well there, Annie, what have you got for us today?

OLD BAUMERT   How much do we get for a web, Herr Pfeifer?

PFEIFER   Ten silver groschen a web.

OLD BAUMERT   Now what do you think of that!

(*Excitement rises among the weavers, a whispering and murmuring*)

ACT TWO

(*A room in the house of* WILHELM ANSORGE *in Kaschbach in the Eulengebirge. It is a narrow room, not six feet high, the floor is decayed and the rafters black with soot. In the room are two young girls:* EMMA *and* BERTHA BAUMERT, *sitting at their looms;* MOTHER BAUMERT, *a stiff-limbed old woman, sitting on a stool by her bed, in front of a spooling-wheel; her son* AUGUST, *twenty-years-old, an idiot, with a small body and head, and long spidery limbs, sitting on a footstool, also spooling yarn.*

The weak, rose colored light of evening forces its way through two small windows, holes in the left wall which are partially stuffed with paper and straw. It falls onto the whitish-blond loose hair of the girls, on their bare, lean shoulders and thin waxen necks, on the folds of their coarse blouses which except for a short skirt of the roughest linen, constitutes their entire clothing. The warm glow falls fully upon the face, neck and chest of the old woman: a face emaciated to a skeleton, with folds and wrinkles in its bloodless skin, with sunken eyes which are inflamed and watery as a result of the lint, the smoke, and from working by lamplight; a long goiter neck with folds and sinews; a sunken chest which is packed in cloths and scarfs.

A part of the right wall, along with the stove and the stove bench, the bedstead and several loudly tinted holy pictures, also stands in light. On the bar of the stove rags are hung up to dry, while behind the stove all the old, worthless rubbish is piled. On the stove bench are several old pots and cooking utensils; potato-peelings are laid out on a paper to dry. From the rafters there hang skeins and reels of yarn. Baskets with spools stand beside the looms. In the back wall there is a door without a lock. Leaning against the wall beside the door is a bundle of willow-switches. Several damaged quarter-bushelbaskets lie about near them. The room is filled with the sounds of the looms, the rhythmic movement of the lathe which shakes both floor and walls, the shuffle and clicking of the rapid shuttle moving back and forth. Mixed into this is the deep constant whirring of the spooling-wheels which resembles the humming of bumble-bees)

MOTHER BAUMERT (*in a pitiful, exhausted voice as the girls leave off their weaving and lean over their looms*) Do you have to make knots again?

EMMA (*the elder of the two girls, twenty-two-years-old; while knotting threads*) This is sure some yarn!

BERTHA (*fifteen-years-old*) This warp is giving us trouble, too.

EMMA Where is he? He left at nine o'clock.

MOTHER BAUMERT Yes, I know, I know! Don't you know where he could be?

BERTHA Don't you worry, mother.

MOTHER BAUMERT It's always a worry to me.

(EMMA *goes on with her weaving*)

BERTHA Wait a minute, Emma!

EMMA What's the matter?

BERTHA I thought I heard a noise like somebody coming.

EMMA More likely Ansorge coming home.

FRITZ (*A small barefoot, ragged little boy of four comes in crying*) Mother, I'm hungry.

EMMA Wait a while, Fritzy, wait a while! Grandpa'll be here soon. He'll bring some bread with him and some grain.

FRITZ I'm still hungry, mother!

EMMA I just told you. Don't be so stupid. He'll be here right away. He'll bring some nice bread with him and some coffee beans.—When work's over, mother'll take the potato peelings and she'll go to the farmer with them, and then he'll give her a nice swallow of milk for her little boy.

FRITZ Where'd grandpa go?

EMMA To the factory owner's, to deliver a web, Fritzy.

FRITZ The factory owner?

EMMA Yes, Fritzy, yes! Down to Dreissiger's, in Peterswaldau.

FRITZ That where he gets the bread?

EMMA Yes, yes, he gets money there, and then he can buy the bread.

FRITZ Will he get much money?

EMMA (*intensely*) Oh, stop it, boy, with your talking.

(*She goes on weaving like* BERTHA. *Then they both stop again*)

BERTHA August, go and ask Ansorge if we could have a little light.

(AUGUST *leaves.* FRITZ *goes with him*)

MOTHER BAUMERT (*with increasing, childlike fear, almost whining*) Children, children, where could he be so long?

BERTHA He probably only dropped in to see Hauffen.

MOTHER BAUMERT (*cries*) I only hope he's not in a tavern!

EMMA You mustn't cry, mother! Our father's not that kind.

MOTHER BAUMERT (*beside herself with a multitude of fears*) Well, well . . . well, tell me what will happen if he . . . if he comes home and . . . and if he's drunk everything up and don't bring nothing home? There's not a handful of salt in the house, not a piece of bread. We need a shovel of fuel . . .

BERTHA Don't worry, mother! The moon's out tonight. We'll take August with us and gather some wood for the fire.

MOTHER BAUMERT So you can be caught by the forester?

ANSORGE (*an old weaver with a gigantic body frame, who must bend low in order to enter the room, sticks his head and upper body through the doorway. His hair and beard are quite unkempt*) What's the matter here?

BERTHA You *could* give us some *light!*

ANSORGE (*in a subdued voice, as though speaking in the presence of a sick person*) It's light enough here.

MOTHER BAUMERT Now you even make us sit in the dark.

ANSORGE I do the best I can. (*He pulls himself out through the doorway*)

BERTHA You see there how stingy he is?

EMMA So now we sit here and wait till he's ready.

FRAU HEINRICH (*enters. She is a woman of thirty and pregnant. Her tired face expresses tortuous anxieties and fearful tensions*) Good evening, everyone.

MOTHER BAUMERT Well, Mother Heinrich, any news?

FRAU HEINRICH (*limping*) I stepped on a piece of glass.

BERTHA Come here, then, sit down. I'll see if I can get it out for you.

(FRAU HEINRICH *sits down, while* BERTHA *kneels in front of her and works with the sole of the woman's foot*)

MOTHER BAUMERT How are you at home, Mother Heinrich?

FRAU HEINRICH (*breaks out in despair*) It can't go on like this.

(*She fights in vain against a torrent of tears. Then she cries silently*)

MOTHER BAUMERT It would be better for our kind, Mother Heinrich, if the Good Lord had a little understanding and took us from the world altogether.

FRAU HEINRICH (*Her self-control gone, she cries out, weeping*) My poor children are starving! (*She sobs and moans*) I don't know what to do. You can do what you want, but all you ever do is chase around till you drop.

I'm more dead than alive, and still there's no use. Nine hungry mouths I've got to feed, and how will I do it? Last evening I had a little piece of bread, it wasn't even enough for the two littlest. Which one was I to give it to? They all cried out to me: Me, mama, me, mama . . . No, no! This is what happens when I can still get about. What'll happen the day I can't get up out of bed no more? The flood's washed away the couple potatoes we had. We haven't got bread nor food to eat.

BERTHA (*has removed the piece of glass and washed the wound*) We'll tie a rag around it now. (*to* EMMA) See if you can find one.

MOTHER BAUMERT It's no better here with us, Mother Heinrich.

FRAU HEINRICH You still got your girls at least. You got a husband who can work, too. Last week my husband just broke down. He had such a fit and I was so scared to Heaven I didn't know what to do with him. Whenever he has an attack like that he just has to lay in bed for a good eight days.

MOTHER BAUMERT Mine's not so much better either anymore. He's about to give out, too. It's in his chest and his back. And there's not a pfennig in the house now. If he don't bring a couple of groschen home tonight, I don't know what'll happen.

EMMA You can believe her, Mother Heinrich. We're so hard up, father had to take Ami along with him. He had to let them butcher him so we could have something solid in our bellies again.

FRAU HEINRICH Don't you have a handful of flour left over, maybe?

MOTHER BAUMERT Not even that much, Mother Heinrich; not even a grain of salt left in the house.

FRAU HEINRICH Well, then, I don't know! (*She rises, remains standing and broods*) Then I just don't know!—I just can't help it. (*crying out in rage and fear*) I'd be happy if we only had pig-swill! But I can't go home with empty hands. I just can't. God forgive me. I just don't know what else there is to do. (*She limps out quickly, stepping on the heel of her left foot*)

MOTHER BAUMERT (*calls after her, warningly*) Mother Heinrich, Mother Heinrich, you musn't go and do nothing foolish.

BERTHA She won't do no harm to herself. Don't you worry.

EMMA She's always like that. (*She sits down and weaves again for a few seconds*)

(AUGUST *lights the way for his father,* OLD BAUMERT, *with a tallow candle, as the old man drags in a bundle of yarn*)

MOTHER BAUMERT Jesus, Lord Jesus, where were you all this time, father.

OLD BAUMERT There, don't snap at me all at once. Let a man catch his breath a minute first. Why don't you go and see who's come in with me?

MORITZ JAEGER (*enters through the doorway, stooping. He is a robust, average-sized, red-cheeked reservist. His Hussar's cap is worn jauntily on his head, and his clothes and shoes are in good repair; he also wears a clean shirt without a collar. Having entered, he takes a military stance and salutes; energetically*) Good evening, Aunt Baumert!

MOTHER BAUMERT Well, well, now, you're home again, are you? And you didn't forget us. Sit down over here, then. Come over here, sit down.

EMMA (*wipes off a wooden chair with her skirt and pushes it over towards* JAEGER) Good evening, Moritz! Did you come home again to see how us poor people live?

JAEGER Tell me, now, Emma, I almost didn't want to believe it. And you've got a youngster here almost old enough to be a soldier. Where'd you get him?

BERTHA (*takes the little food her father has brought, puts the meat in a pan and places it in the oven, while* AUGUST *builds a fire*) You know the weaver named Finger?

MOTHER BAUMERT He used to live with us here once. He wanted to marry her all right, but even then he had it awful bad in the lungs. I warned the girl enough. You think she listened? Now he's long dead and forgotten and she has to see about raising the boy. But you tell me now, Moritz, how things went with you.

OLD BAUMERT You be quiet there, mother, can't you see how good he's fed? He'll laugh us all out, he will. He brought clothes with him like a prince. And a silver watch. And on top of all that ten thalers cash.

JAEGER (*takes a boastful stance, with a swaggering, self-important smile on his face*) I can't complain. I never knew a bad time in the army.

OLD BAUMERT He was orderly to a cavalry captain. Listen to him, he talks like a regular gentleman.

JAEGER I got so used to all their fine talk I can't get rid of it.

MOTHER BAUMERT No, no, now I want you to tell me! And such a good-for-nothing as you was, too, and coming into all that money. No, you weren't fit for nothing; you couldn't spool one bobbin after another without having to stop. You were always gone; setting up traps for titmice and robin snares was what you really liked. Now, ain't that the truth?

JAEGER   True enough, Aunt Baumert. It wasn't robins I caught, it was swallows.

EMMA   And all we used to tell him was: swallows are poison.

JAEGER   It was all the same to me. But how have you all got on, Aunt Baumert?

MOTHER BAUMERT   Oh, Lord Jesus, so bad, so bad these last four years. I had these pains, you see. Just you look at my fingers here. I don't know if I got rheumatism or what. I'm in such misery. I can hardly move a limb. No-body'd believe the pains I had to suffer.

OLD BAUMERT   She's in a real bad way now. She can't hold out much longer.

BERTHA   Mornings we have to put her clothes on, nights we have to take them off for her. We've got to feed her like a child.

MOTHER BAUMERT   (continues in a doleful, tearful voice)   They have to help me every which way. I'm more than sick, I'm a burden. How have I prayed to the good Lord God that He should just take me. O Jesus, my Jesus, it's too much for me. I just don't know . . . may-be people think that . . . but I been used to working since I was just a little one. I could always do my job, then all of a sudden (She tries in vain to raise herself) it just won't go anymore. I have a good husband and good children, but if all I can do is watch . . . Just you look there at those girls! They got almost no blood in them anymore. White as a sheet. It never stops here with this treadle, even if they get nothing for it. What kind of life is that for them? They never get away from that bench the whole year. There's not a dress they own that they can show for their work so that they can cover themselves sometimes and go out among the other people or go to church sometimes and find some comfort. They look like they was cut down from the gallows, girls of fifteen and twenty.

BERTHA   (at the stove)   It's smoking again now.

OLD BAUMERT   Just you look at that smoke. Can anything be done about it, you think? It'll fall to pieces soon, that stove. Well, we'll just have to let it fall to pieces, and as for the soot, we'll just have to swallow it. We all cough, one more than the other. If you cough, you cough, and if it gets you and you choke to death, what's it matter, nobody'll ask no ques-tions.

JAEGER   But that's Ansorge's business, he's got to fix it.

BERTHA   He'd only look at us like we was crazy. He already grumbles too much.

MOTHER BAUMERT   We take up too much room for him as is.

OLD BAUMERT   And if we start to grumble, we'll be out on our ears. He's had no rent from us this half-year.

MOTHER BAUMERT   A man like him that ain't married could be a little more friendly.

OLD BAUMERT   He's got nothing either, mother, things are as bad for him, too, just be glad he didn't raise the roof on us.

MOTHER BAUMERT   Still, he's got his own house.

OLD BAUMERT   There, mother, what are you talking about! There's hardly a board in this house he can call his.

JAEGER   (sits down and removes a short pipe with a nice tassle hanging from one pocket, and from the other pocket a bottle of brandy)   This can't go on much longer like this. I'm amazed how things look. Why, the dogs in the city live better than you people here do.

OLD BAUMERT   (eagerly)   That's right, isn't it, isn't it? You know that! And if any one of us makes a complaint about it they just say it's the bad times.

ANSORGE   (enters with an earthenware bowl of soup in one hand and a half-finished quarter-bushelbasket in the other)   Welcome home, Moritz! You've come back, I see.

JAEGER   Thank you, Father Ansorge.

ANSORGE   (pushing his bowl into the oven)   Just look at him now, if he don't look almost like a count.

OLD BAUMERT   Show him the nice watch you got. He brought along a new suit and ten thalers cash.

ANSORGE   (shaking his head)   Well, well, well!

EMMA   (puts the potato peelings into a little sack)   I'm going over now with the peelings. Maybe it'll be enough for a little milk. (She goes out)

JAEGER   (while they all watch him with attention and admiration)   You think back and remember how many times you made things hot as hell for me. That'll teach you a thing or two, Moritz, you always used to say, when you get in the army. Well, you can see, things went pretty good for me. I had my stripe in half a year. You got to be willing to work, that's the main thing. I polished the sergeant's boots; I brushed his horse, got his beer. I was fast as a weasel. I was sharp as a tack; my stuff really shined. I was the first to the stables, the first to roll-call, the first in the saddle; and then when we attacked— forward march! Holy Moses and damnation! I watched like a bloodhound! I always said to myself: you'll get no help here, it's up to you now; and then I pulled myself together, and I was all right. I did so much that one time the captain said in front of the whole squadron: This is what a Hussar ought to be. (*Silence. He lights his pipe*)

ANSORGE (*shaking his head*) Then you were lucky, uh? Well, well, well!—Well, well, well! (*He sits down on the floor with the willow switches beside him, and with the basket between his legs he continues mending it*)

OLD BAUMERT Let's hope now you brought some luck with you.—Well, maybe we'll have a drink with you now, uh?

JAEGER Sure, Father Baumert, sure, and when that's gone, there'll be more. (*He puts a coin onto the table*)

ANSORGE (*with stupid, grinning amazement*) Lord in Heaven, what goings-on . . . a roast there in the oven, and here a quart of brandy— (*He drinks from the bottle*) Your health, Moritz! Well, well, well! Well, well, well! (*From here on the brandy bottle is handed around*)

OLD BAUMERT If only on Holy Days we could have a little roast like this instead of never seeing meat for months and months.—So now we'll have to wait till another little dog comes by like this one four weeks ago: and a thing like that don't happen so often in a life.

ANSORGE Did you have to have Ami killed?

OLD BAUMERT He would have starved to death anyway . . .

ANSORGE Well, well, well—well, well, well.

MOTHER BAUMERT And he was such a nice, friendly little dog.

JAEGER Are you still so eager around here for roast dog?

OLD BAUMERT O Jesus, Jesus, if we only had enough of it.

MOTHER BAUMERT Well, a little piece of meat is a good thing.

OLD BAUMERT Don't you have taste for things like that anymore? Well, you just stay with us, Moritz, you'll get it back soon enough.

ANSORGE (*sniffing*) Well, well, well—that's something good there, good smell, too.

OLD BAUMERT (*sniffing*) The real thing, you might say.

ANSORGE Tell us what you think now, Moritz. You know the way it is out there in the world. Do you think things'll ever be different here with us weavers?

JAEGER I really hope so.

ANSORGE We can't live here and we can't die. It's bad for us here, you can believe that.

You fight to the last, but in the end you got to give in. Poverty tears the roof off from over your head and the floor from under your feet. In the old days when you could still work at the loom you could just about half get by with all kinds of trouble and misery. Nowadays month after month can go by and I can't find a piece of work. Weaving baskets is all over with too now, all you can do is stay alive at it. I weave till late into the night, and when I fall into bed I've made a groschen and six pfennigs. You got education, you tell me: can anybody get by nowadays with these rising prices? I have to toss out three thalers for house tax, one thaler for property tax and three thalers for interest. I can count on fourteen thalers pay. That leaves seven thalers the year for myself. Out of it I have food to pay for, and heat and clothes and shoes and patches and thread for mending and then I got to have a place to live in and God knows what else.—Is there any wonder when you can't pay the interest?

OLD BAUMERT Somebody ought to go to Berlin and explain to the King how things are with us.

JAEGER There wouldn't be much good in that, Father Baumert. There's been enough said about it in the newspapers. But these rich people, they turn and they twist the news so that . . . they can bedevil the best Christians.

OLD BAUMERT (*shaking his head*) Not to know better than that in Berlin!

ANSORGE Tell me, Moritz, you think that's possible? Aren't there laws for such things? If a person works the skin right off his hands and still can't pay the interest, can the farmer take my house away from me? He's a farmer who wants his money. I just don't know what'll come of it all.—If I have to get out of the house . . . (*speaking through his tears*) I was born here, my father sat here at his loom for more than forty years. How many times did he tell my mother: If ever I'm not here anymore, don't let the house go, he said. I worked for this house, he said. Every nail in it I paid for with a night of work, and every beam is worth a year's bread. Wouldn't you think that . . .

JAEGER They're able to take the last thing you've got.

ANSORGE Well, well, well! If it ever comes to that, I'd rather they carry me out than have to walk out in my old age. What's there to dying! My father was glad enough to die.—It was only at the last he got a little scared. But then when I crawled into bed with him he quieted down a bit.—When I think about it, I was just a boy of thirteen then. I was so tired out I went to sleep right beside that sick man

—I didn't know no better—and when I woke up he was already cold.

MOTHER BAUMERT (*after a pause*) Reach into the stove, Bertha, and give Ansorge his soup.

BERTHA Here you are, Father Ansorge!

ANSORGE (*weeping as he eats*) Well, well, well—well, well, well!

(OLD BAUMERT *has begun to eat the meat out of the pan*)

MOTHER BAUMERT Now, father, father, you can wait a while. Let Bertha set the table right first.

OLD BAUMERT (*chewing*) It was two years ago I went to the Lord's Supper last. Just after that I sold my Sunday clothes. We bought a little piece of pork with the money. Since then I've had no meat till tonight.

JAEGER What do we need meat for? The factory owners eat it for us. They wade in fat up to here. Whoever don't believe that can go down to Bielau and Peterswaldau and see for himself. He'd have an eyeful there: one factory owner's mansion after another. With glass windows and little towers and iron fences. Believe me, they don't know what bad times are. There's enough money down there for roasts and cakes, for carriages and coaches, for governesses and who knows what else! They're so stuffed with their greed they don't know what to do with all their riches out of cockiness.

ANSORGE It was all a different thing in the old days. Then they gave the weavers enough to live on. Today they waste it all on themselves. But I say that's because those people in high places don't believe in God no more or in the devil either. What do they know about commandments and punishments? They all but steal our last piece of bread from our mouths and make us weak and eat up the little food we got whenever they can. Those are the people our troubles come from. If the factory owners was good men, there wouldn't be no bad times for us.

JAEGER Listen to me now. I want to read you something real nice. (*He pulls some pieces of paper from his pocket*) Come on, August, you run down to the tavern and get another quart. What's the matter, August, why are you laughing?

MOTHER BAUMERT I don't know what it is with the boy. He's always happy. He'll laugh himself sick no matter what happens. Well, run now, run! (AUGUST *goes off with the empty brandy bottle*) Ha, you know what it is tastes good, don't you, father!

OLD BAUMERT (*chewing, stimulated by the food and drink*) Moritz, you're our man. You can read, you can write. You know how things are with us weavers. And you have a heart for the weavers, too. You ought to step in and take up our cause for us around here.

JAEGER If that's all. Sure, I'd like to teach those mangy factory owners a thing or two. Wouldn't bother me at all. I'm an easygoing enough person, but once I get my temper up and get mad, I could take Dreissiger in one hand and Dietrich in the other and knock their heads together till sparks fly from their eyes. If we could manage to stick together we could really make a racket for those factory owners. We wouldn't need a king for that, *or* a government, all we'd have to do is say: we want this and this and we want it done this way and not that, and they'd whistle another tune soon enough. Once they see we got some guts, they'll calm down. I know their kind. They're a bunch of cowardly bastards.

MOTHER BAUMERT That's the truth. I'm sure not bad. I was always one to say: there have to be rich people, too. But when it comes to this . . .

JAEGER For all of me the devil can take them, they deserve it.

BERTHA Where did father go?

(OLD BAUMERT *has left quietly*)

MOTHER BAUMERT I don't know where he is.

BERTHA Do you think maybe his stomach's not used to meat anymore?

MOTHER BAUMERT (*beside herself, crying*) You see now, there you see! He can't even keep it down. He'll vomit up that nice little piece of food.

OLD BAUMERT (*returning, crying in rage*) No, no! It can't go on much longer with me. It has to end soon! When you finally get something good to eat you can't even keep it down.

(*He sits down crying on the stove bench*)

JAEGER (*in a sudden frantic outburst*) And to think there are people, judges, not far from here, with their pot-bellies, who've got nothing to do all year long but steal a day from the Lord God. And they're the ones who say the weavers could get along well and good if they wasn't so lazy.

ANSORGE They're not people. Those are monsters.

JAEGER Don't you worry, he's got what he asked for. Red Baecker and me gave him a piece of our mind, and before we left, we even sang *Bloody Justice* for him.

ANSORGE Good Lord, is that the song?

JAEGER Yes, yes, I've got it here.

OLD BAUMERT They call it *Dreissiger's Song*, don't they?

JAEGER I'll read it to you.

MOTHER BAUMERT Who wrote the song?

JAEGER Nobody knows. Now listen. (*He reads, spelling like a schoolboy, stressing poorly, but with unmistakably strong feeling. Despair, pain, rage, hatred, and a thirst for vengeance are felt in his reading*)

A bloody justice rages here,
A law that's worse than lynching,
Where courtroom trials are not the
  rule,
They kill us without flinching.

A man is slowly tortured here,
A man is tortured long,
His sighs are counted as the proof
Of his affliction's song.

OLD BAUMERT (*gripped by the song and deeply moved, he has several times had to control himself from interrupting* JAEGER. *Now he can contain himself no longer; stammering, amid tears and laughter, to his wife*) "A man is tortured long." Whoever wrote that, he knew what he knew. "His sighs are proof . . ." How does it go? "His sighs . . . affliction's song . . ." Is that it? "Counted as the proof . . ."

JAEGER (*reads*)

His sighs are counted as the proof
Of his affliction's song.

OLD BAUMERT You know how we sigh, mother, day after day, in bed or on our feet.

JAEGER (*while* ANSORGE, *who has stopped his work, sits brokenly on the floor, deeply moved, and while* MOTHER BAUMERT *and* BERTHA *constantly wipe their eyes, he continues to read*)

Our hangmen are the Dreissigers,
Their servants are their henchmen,
And each one takes his pound of flesh
As though it were no sin.

You scoundrels all, you brood of
  hell . . .

OLD BAUMERT (*trembling with rage and stamping on the floor*) Yes! "Brood of hell! Brood of hell!"

JAEGER (*reads*)

You demons of the fire,
You eat the poor from house and
  home—
May curses pay your hire.

ANSORGE Yes, yes, that's worth a curse.

OLD BAUMERT (*clenching his fists, threateningly*) "You eat the poor from house and home!"—

JAEGER (*reads*)

Pleading gets you nowhere here,
Begging's all in vain;
"If you don't like it, then go starve
Elsewhere," they complain.

OLD BAUMERT How does it go? "Begging's all in vain"? Every word . . . every word . . . it's all as true as the Bible itself. "Pleading gets you nowhere here!"

ANSORGE Well, well, well! Nothing does any good.

JAEGER (*reads*)

Let every man regard our need,
Whom misery doth bow,
With not a bite of bread at home—
Where is your pity now!

Pity! that you've never known,
And never did ask why;
But every man must know your aim,
To bleed us till we die.

OLD BAUMERT (*jumps up, almost in a frenzy*) "Till we die." That's what it is, "bleed us till we die." Here I stand, Robert Baumert, master weaver of Kaschbach. Who can step forward and say . . . ? I have been a good man all my days, but look at me now! What do I have to show? What do I look like? What have they done to me? "A man is slowly tortured here." (*He holds out his arms*) Here, feel me, feel me . . . skin and bones. "You scoundrels all, you brood of hell!!" (*He collapses into a chair with anger and despair*)

ANSORGE (*tosses his basket into the corner, lifts himself, his whole body trembling with rage; stammers out*) And it's got to change, I say it's got to change now! We won't stand it no more! We won't stand it no more, no matter what happens!

ACT THREE

(*The taproom of the Peterswaldau village tavern. It is a large room with a beamed ceiling supported by a wooden center column, around which runs a table. In the rear wall, to the right of the column, is an entrance door, one jamb of which is hidden by the column. Through the door there is a large storeroom with barrels and brewing utensils. In the corner of the taproom, to the right of the door, is a bar: a wooden partition, the height of a man, with compartments for bar utensils; behind it is a cupboard containing rows of whisky bottles; between the partition and the liquor cabi-*

net is a small area for the bartender. In front of the bar stands a table decorated with a multicolored cloth. A pretty lamp hangs above it, and round about it are a number of cane chairs. Not far off, in the right wall, there is a door with "Weinstube" written above it leading into a room for more prominent guests. Farther downstage right stands an old grandfather's clock. To the left of the entrance door in the back wall there is a table with bottles and glasses, and farther on, in the corner, is the great tiled stove. There are three small windows in the left wall, below them runs a bench, and in front of each window is a large wooden table with one of its ends towards the wall. Along the sides of these tables are benches with backs, while at the window end of each table is a single wooden chair. The entire room is whitewashed almost blue, covered over with advertisements, pictures, and colored prints, including the portrait of Friedrich Wilhelm IV.

SCHOLZ WELZEL *a good-natured colossus of more than fifty is drawing beer from a barrel into a glass.*

FRAU WELZEL *is ironing at the stove. She is a dignified, cleanly dressed woman not yet thirty-five.*

ANNA WELZEL *a seventeen-year-old, pretty girl with beautiful reddish-blond hair, and nicely dressed, sits behind the table with the colored cloth and embroiders. She looks up for a moment from her work and listens as the sounds of a funeral hymn sung by school children are heard in the distance.*

MASTER WIEGAND *the joiner, sits in his working clothes at the same table with a glass of beer in front of him. One can see that he is a man who knows what it takes to be a success in the world, namely cunning, quickness, and ruthless determination.*

A TRAVELING SALESMAN *sitting at the column table is vigorously chewing at a chopped steak. He is of medium height, well fed, stout, inclined to be cheerful, lively and impudent. His clothes are in fashion. His traveling effects— handbag, sample case, umbrella, overcoat and blanket—are on the chair beside him)*

WELZEL (*carrying a glass of beer to the* SALESMAN, *aside to* WIEGAND) Seems like the devil's loose in Peterswaldau today.

WIEGAND (*with a sharp trumpetlike voice*) Sure, because it's delivery day at Dreissiger's.

FRAU WELZEL But they don't usually make such a stir.

WIEGAND Well, it's maybe because of the two hundred new weavers that he wants to take on now.

FRAU WELZEL (*continues ironing*) Yes, I

suppose that would be it. If it's two hundred he wants, at least six hundred must have showed up. There's enough of that kind around.

WIEGAND O Jesus, yes, there's enough of them. Their kind don't ever die out even when times are bad. They put more children into the world than we know what to do with. (*For a moment the hymn is heard more clearly*) Then there's a funeral today too. The weaver Fabish died.

WELZEL He's been at it long enough. Running around like a ghost all this long time.

WIEGAND Believe me, Welzel, never in my life did I ever glue together such a tiny little casket. That was a corpse for you, couldn't have weighed ninety pounds.

SALESMAN (*chewing*) I don't understand it . . . wherever you look, in whatever paper, all you ever read is gruesome stories about the need of the weavers. You get the impression that people in this neighborhood are three-quarters dead from starvation. And take this funeral. I just got to the village. Brass band, school master, school children, the pastor, and that procession of people behind them—my God, it's like the Emperor of China was being buried. Well, if these people have money to pay for something like that . . . (*He drinks the beer. After putting down his glass, with frivolous levity*) Isn't that right, miss? Am I right or not?

(ANNA *smiles with embarrassment and eagerly continues her embroidering*)

SALESMAN I'll bet those are a pair of slippers for your papa.

WELZEL You won't catch *my* feet in any such thing.

SALESMAN Let me tell you that I'd give half of what I'm worth if those slippers were for me.

FRAU WELZEL He just don't understand things like that.

WIEGAND (*after having coughed several times, moved his chair about, and made an attempt to speak*) The gentleman seemed surprised about the funeral. Wouldn't you say, miss, that it's a rather small funeral?

SALESMAN Yes, but the question is . . . Why, that must cost a monstrous lot of money. Where do these people come by it?

WIEGAND If you will excuse me, sir, but there's a kind of lack of reasonableness among these poor classes of people. With your permission, I will say that they have an exaggerated idea of the respect and duty they owe to those taken from them. And if it happens to be the parent who died, you never saw such superstitiousness. The children and nearest relatives scrape together whatever they can get their hands on. And what they can't get, they borrow from the nearest man of wealth. His Eminence the pastor finds himself borrowed from, not to mention the sexton and everyone else standing about. And then there's the food and drinks and all the other things they need. I have nothing against a child's respect for his parents, but when the mourners are put in debt for the rest of their lives, then it's too much.

SALESMAN If I may say so, the pastor should talk them out of such foolishness.

WIEGAND If you'll excuse me, sir, I must say something in support of this, that every little community has its own house of God and has to support the shepherd of its flock. The clergy has its advantages from large funerals. The more people at a burial, the richer flows the offertory. Whoever knows the working conditions around here, sir, can tell you with unauthoritative certainty that the pastors regard quiet funerals with little favor.

(HORNIG *enters. He is a small bow-legged old man with a draw-rope around his shoulders and chest. He is a rag-picker*)

HORNIG Good day to you all. Could I have a small glass of schnapps? Well now, miss, have you any rags for me? Miss Anna! I have beautiful hair ribbons, and shirt bands, and garters in my cart, nice pins, hairpins, and hooks and eyes. It's all yours for a couple of rags. (*in a changed tone of voice*) A nice white piece of paper will be made from those rags, and then your sweetheart will write you a lovely letter on it.

ANNA Thank you, no. I don't want a boy friend.

FRAU WELZEL (*putting a heating iron into her flatiron*) That's the way the girl is. She won't hear a word about marrying.

SALESMAN (*jumps up, apparently pleasantly surprised, goes to the covered table and holds his hand across it towards* ANNA) That's the way to be, miss, do like me. Agreed? Give me your hand on it! We'll both of us stay single.

ANNA (*red as a beet, gives him her hand*) But you're already married, aren't you?

SALESMAN God forbid! You think that because I wear this ring? I only do that to protect my irresistible personality from the sordid attacks of people. But I'm not afraid of you. (*He puts the ring in his pocket*) But seriously, miss, wouldn't you like to get even just a little bit married?

ANNA (*shaking her head*) You leave me alone!

FRAU WELZEL She'll stay single unless something awful special comes along.

SALESMAN Well, why not? I know of a rich Silesian grandee who married his mother's chambermaid, and the rich factory owner Dreissiger, he married an inkeeper's daughter, who isn't half as pretty as you are, miss, and she rides around now in a carriage and with servants in livery. So why not? (*He wanders about, stretching himself and his legs while walking*) How about a cup of coffee here?

(ANSORGE *and* OLD BAUMERT *enter, each with a pack, and sit quietly and humbly at the table to the front and left with* HORNIG)

WELZEL Welcome, Father Ansorge! Good to see you again!

HORNIG Did you really crawl out again from that smoked-up nest of yours?

ANSORGE (*awkward and obviously embarrassed*) Yes, I went and took another web again.

OLD BAUMERT He'll do the work for ten groschen.

ANSORGE I would never have done it, but now there's an end to my basket-weaving, too.

WIEGAND It's better than nothing, I always say. And he's doing it so that you'll have something to work at. I know Dreissiger good enough. A week ago I took out his storm windows. We talked about it then. He's doing it out of pity.

ANSORGE Sure, sure, sure—I believe every word you say.

WELZEL (*placing a shot of schnapps in front of the weavers*) There you are. Tell me now, Ansorge, how long's it been since you had a shave?—The gentleman over there wants to know.

SALESMAN (*calls over to them*) Now, Herr Welzel, I said no such thing. I was merely struck by our good weaver's venerable appearance. It's not often you get to see a giant like him.

ANSORGE (*scratches his head in embarrassment*) Sure, sure, sure—well . . .

SALESMAN Primeval men of nature like him are rather rare nowadays. We've been licked so smooth by civilization . . . but I can still take pleasure in nature in the rough. Bushy eyebrows! Wild beard . . .

HORNIG Now you let me tell you something, sir; people like them can't afford a barber, and a razor is even more out of the question. What grows grows. They can't afford to worry about what they look like.

SALESMAN I beg your pardon, sir, but I had no intention . . . (*quietly to the inn-*

keeper) Would it be all right to offer the hairy one a glass of beer?

WELZEL   I wouldn't try it. He wouldn't take it anyway. He's got strange ideas.

SALESMAN   Well, then I won't. Will you allow me, miss? (*He takes a place at* ANNA's *table*) I can assure you, miss, I noticed your hair the moment I came in. It's gentle brilliance, it's softness, and the fullness of it! (*At the same time he kisses his finger tips as though enchanted*) And it's color . . . like ripe wheat. Come to Berlin with hair like that and you'll be the toast of the town. On my word of honor, you could even go to the court with such hair . . . (*Leaning back he looks at her hair*) Magnificent! Absolutely magnificent!

WIEGAND   That's why they've given her the name she's got.

SALESMAN   What is it then?

ANNA (*laughing constantly to herself*)   Oh, don't listen to him!

HORNIG   They call you the chestnut filly, don't they?

WELZEL   Now, now, that's enough! Don't you be confusing the girl more than she is! She already has enough silly ideas in that head of hers. Today she wants a count and tomorrow it'll be a prince.

FRAU WELZEL   You let the girl alone now, father! It's no crime if a person wants to get ahead in the world. It's a good thing everybody doesn't think like you; if they did nobody'd ever get anywhere. They'd all still be sitting here. If Dreissiger's grandfather had thought like you, they'd all of them still be poor weavers. Now they're rich as kings. And old Tromtra was nothing but a poor weaver, too, and now he's got twelve estates and besides that they made him a nobleman.

WIEGAND   Be fair now, Welzel; this time your wife knows what she's talking about. I'll vouch for it. If I thought like you, would I be boss over seven journeymen now?

HORNIG   You know your way around all right, no denying that. While a weaver's still running about on two legs, you're already busy with his coffin.

WIEGAND   If a man's to get ahead in the world, he has to stick by his business.

HORNIG   Yes, and you do stick by your business, don't you! You know better than a doctor when death's coming for a weaver's child.

WIEGAND (*no longer smiling, suddenly furious*)   And you know better than the police where the thieves are among the weavers, and which of them end each week with a nice spool of yarn left over. You come for rags, but you don't object if there's a little yarn among them.

HORNIG   And luck comes your way in the churchyard. The more of us that go to sleep on wooden planks, the better for you. When you look at all the children's graves, you pat yourself on the belly and say: another good year; the little brats have fallen like June-bugs from the trees again. That means another extra quart for me each week.

WIEGAND   At least that don't make me a receiver of stolen goods.

HORNIG   The most you ever do is bill the rich manufacturer twice, or take a couple extra planks from Dreissiger's new building when the moon happens not to be shining.

WIEGAND (*turns his back on him*)   Babble on all you want but don't bother me with it. (*then suddenly*) Hornig the liar!

HORNIG   Deadmen's butler!

WIEGAND (*to the others*)   He can put a hex on cattle.

HORNIG   You watch yourself, or I'll put one on you.

(WEIGAND *grows pale*)

FRAU WELZEL (*who had gone out, returns now and places a cup of coffee in front of the* SALESMAN)   Should I serve your coffee in the little room, sir?

SALESMAN   I should say not! (*with a languishing glance at* ANNA) I shall sit here until I die.

A YOUNG FORESTER *and* A PEASANT (*enter. The* PEASANT *carries a whip. Together*)   Good day to you! (*They remain standing at the bar*)

PEASANT   Two gingers.

WELZEL   Welcome to both of you! (*He pours them their drink; they both take up their glasses, clinking them together, drink down, and place the glasses back on the bar*)

SALESMAN   Well, young forester, have a good march?

FORESTER   Not bad. I come from Steinseifersdorf.

(TWO OLD WEAVERS *enter and seat themselves beside* ANSORGE, OLD BAUMERT *and* HORNIG)

SALESMAN   Excuse me, but aren't you one of Count Hochheim's foresters?

FORESTER   I work for Count Keil.

SALESMAN   Of course, of course, that's what I meant to say. It's a little confusing with all these counts and barons and other worthy gentlemen. One needs a giant's memory to remember so much. Why do you carry an axe?

FORESTER   I took it from some wood thieves.

OLD BAUMERT   These lords of ours take

great offense over a piece of kindling wood.

SALESMAN Well, if you don't mind my saying so, suppose everyone took what he wanted . . .

OLD BAUMERT With your permission, sir, there's the same difference here between big and little thieves. There are some here with wholesale lumber businesses who get rich off their stolen wood. But when a poor weaver does it . . .

FIRST OLD WEAVER (*interrupts* BAUMERT) We don't dare take a twig, but these lords they skin us alive. We got protection fees to pay, spinning fees, fees in kind, we got to run here and there.

ANSORGE That's how it is: what the factory owners leave behind for us, their lordships steal from our pockets.

SECOND OLD WEAVER (*has taken a place at the next table*) I said so myself to his lordship. I said, you'll pardon me, my lord, I just can't manage to work so many field days this year, I just can't! And why? You'll pardon me, my lord, but the rain ruined everything for me. The flood's carried off the little field I had. I have to work day and night if I'm to live. What a terrible storm! My God, my God, all I could do was stand there and wring my hands! All that good soil came rushing down the hill and into the hut. And all my good, fine seeds! O Jesus, Jesus, I screamed out at the clouds, and for eight days I cried until I almost couldn't see the road anymore. And afterwards I had to lug eighty heavy loads of soil back up the mountain.

PEASANT (*roughly*) You sure do know how to send up a terrible complaint here. What heaven sends us, we got to take. And then if things don't go well, whose fault is it but your own? What did you do when business was good? Gambled it all away and drank it up. If you'd saved something then, you'd have something to fall back on now, instead of stealing yarn and wood.

FIRST YOUNG WEAVER (*with some of his comrades in the hallway, talks loudly through the doorway*) A peasant's a peasant even if he sleeps till nine!

FIRST OLD WEAVER That's just the way it is: a peasant and a nobleman, they pull at the same rope. When the weaver needs a place to live, the peasant says to him: I'll give you a little hole to live in, and you'll pay me a nice rent and help me get in my hay and my grain; and if you don't want to, you'll see where you'll land. And then you go to another one and he says the same thing.

OLD BAUMERT (*enraged*) A weaver's like an apple that everybody takes his bite out of.

PEASANT (*flaring up*) Oh, you poor hungry bastards, what are you good for anyway? Can you force a plow down into the soil? Can you plow a straight furrow? Or toss a bundle of oats onto the wagon? You're good for nothing but being lazy and laying with your women! You dirty bastards, what help are you? (*He has paid and now goes off. The* FORESTER, *laughing, follows him*)

(WELZEL, *the joiner, and* FRAU WELZEL *laugh loudly;* SALESMAN *laughs to himself. When the laughter dies down there is a moment of silence*)

HORNIG A peasant like that is as dumb as his own ox. Talking like he didn't know there was any misery here. What don't a person see in these villages around here? I seen four, five people lay naked on one sack of straw.

SALESMAN (*in a mildly reproving tone of voice*) If you'll permit me, my good man, there is some divided opinion about the misery in these mountains, if you can read . . .

HORNIG Oh, I can read straight on down the page, just as good as you. No, no, I know what I've seen. I've been around enough with these people. When a man's had a draw-rope around his shoulders for forty years, he knows what's going on. What happened to Fuller? His children played around with the neighbor's geese in dung heaps. They died, those people, naked, on the flagstones in their house. They was so hungry they ate that stinking weaver's glue in fear of death. Death took them off by the hundreds.

SALESMAN If you can read, as you say, then you must know that the government has investigated the matter and that . . .

HORNIG Yes, we know, we know: A man comes from the government who knows all about it better than if he'd seen it. He wanders about a bit in the village, down there by the brook, where the nicest houses are. Why should he dirty his nice polished boots? And then he thinks: well, the rest of the place must look as good as this, and climbs back in his carriage and rides on home. And then he writes to Berlin that there was no poverty here. But if he'd had a little more patience and climbed up higher in the village where the brook comes in, or across the brook on the narrow side, or even off the road, where the little single shacks are, the old thatch huts on the side of the hill that are so black, so dirty and broken down sometimes that it's not even worth a match to set them on fire—maybe then he'd have something to write about to Berlin. It's to me they should have come, these government gentle-men who wouldn't believe there was any need here. I'd have showed them something. I'd have opened their eyes for them in these starvation pits.

(*The weaver's song is heard from outside*)

WELZEL   They're singing the devil's song again.

WIEGAND   They're turning the whole village upside down.

FRAU WELZEL   It's like there was something in the air.

(JAEGER *and* BAECKER, *arm in arm, at the head of a group of* YOUNG WEAVERS, *enter the hall-way noisily and go into the taproom*)

JAEGER   Squadron, halt! Dismount!

(*The new arrivals take places at the various ta-bles at which weavers are already seated, and engage them in conversation*)

HORNIG   (*calls out to* BAEKER)   What does this mean, your running around in a mob like this?

BAECKER   (*significantly*)   Who knows, maybe something might happen. Right, Moritz?

HORNIG   Wouldn't that be something! Don't get yourself into trouble.

BAECKER   There's already been some blood spilt. Want to see it? (*He pulls up his sleeve and shows bloody tattoo marks on his bare upper arm. As he does so, the young weavers at the other tables do the same*)

BAECKER   We've been to Barber Schmidt's to get tattooed.

HORNIG   I see now. No wonder there's such an uproar in the streets, with louts like you bab-bling all over the village.

JAEGER   (*swaggeringly, in a loud voice*)   Two quarts here, Welzel! I'll pay. You think maybe I ain't got enough to pay? Wait and see! If we wanted to we could sit here drinking schnapps and sipping coffee till tomorrow morning, just like any traveling salesman.

(*Some of the young weavers laugh*)

SALESMAN   (*with comic surprise*)   Are you re-ferring to me?

(*The innkeeper, his wife, and her daughter, the joiner* WIEGAND, *and the* TRAVELING SALESMAN *laugh*)

JAEGER   If the cap fits, wear it.

SALESMAN   If I may say so, young man, your business seems to be going quite well.

JAEGER   No complaints. I travel around sell-ing ready-to-wear goods. I go in halves with the manufacturers. The hungrier the weaver is, the better I eat. The more they need, the better I feed.

BAECKER   Well said, Moritz! Well said!

WELZEL   (*has brought the corn-schnapps; on his way back to the bar he stops and slowly turns himself, with all the power of his nature and bulk, to face the weavers again; calmly, but emphatically*)   You will let the gentleman alone, he's done nothing to you.

VOICES OF THE YOUNG WEAVERS   Who's hurt-ing him?

(FRAU WELZEL *has exchanged some words with the* SALESMAN; *she lifts his coffee cup with the remainder of the coffee and takes it into the next room. The* SALESMAN *follows her as the weavers laugh*)

VOICES OF THE YOUNG WEAVERS   (*singing*)
    Our hangmen are the Dreissigers,
    Their servants are their henchmen . . .

WELZEL   Psst! Quiet! You can sing that song wherever you want, but not in *my* house!

FIRST OLD WEAVER   He's right, you stop singing.

BAEKER   (*shouts*)   But we're going to pass by Dreissiger's once more, we want to make sure *he* hears the song again.

WIEGAND   You better not go too far so that he takes it all wrong!

(*Laughter and cries of "Ho-ho!"*)

OLD WITTIG   (*a grey-haired old smith, enters. He has on a leather apron and wooden shoes, and is sooty as though he had just come from his workshop. He waits, standing at the bar, for a glass of brandy*)   Let them do what they want. Dogs that bark, don't bite.

VOICES OF THE OLD WEAVERS   Wittig! Wittig!

WITTIG   Here's Wittig. What do you want with him?

VOICES OF THE OLD WEAVERS   Wittig's here —Wittig, Wittig—Come over here, Wittig, sit down with us!—Come over here, Wittig!

WITTIG   I better be careful sitting with rascals like you.

JAEGER   Come on, have a drink with us.

WITTIG   You can keep your brandy. When I drink I pay by myself. (*He takes his schnapps glass and sits with* BAUMERT *and* ANSORGE. *Tap-ping* ANSORGE *on the belly*)   What do you weavers use for food, sauerkraut and louse meat?

OLD BAUMERT   (*ecstatically*)   And what would you say if we're not happy with that no more?

WITTIG   (*stares dumbly at the weavers, with affected surprise*)   No, no, no, don't tell me it's you, Heinerle! (*bursts out into laughter*) Lord in Heaven, I could die laughing! Old Baumert wants rebellion. That really does it: next it'll be the tailor's turn, and then the baa-

baa sheep will want a rebellion and then the mice and the rats. My God if that ain't going to be a fine dance! (*almost helpless with laughter*)

OLD BAUMERT   I'm no different now than I ever was, Wittig, and I still say it'd be better if it worked out peaceable.

WITTIG   It'll work out, the dirty way, but not peaceable. What was ever worked out peaceable? Did they work it out peaceable in France? Maybe Robespierre patted the hands of the rich? What he said was: Away with them all! To the guillotine with them! That's the way it has to work, *allong sangfang*. Did you ever see a roast duck fly into your open mouth?

OLD BAUMERT   If only I could make just half a living . . .

FIRST OLD WEAVER   We're in water up to our chins already, Wittig.

SECOND OLD WEAVER   We almost don't want to go home again. Work or lay abed, you starve both ways.

FIRST OLD WEAVER   At home a man's like to go mad.

ANSORGE   It's all the same to me. It'll come one way or the other.

VOICES OF THE OLD WEAVERS (*with mounting excitement*)   No peace anywhere anymore.—No spirit left to work.—Up there by us in Steinkunzendorf there's a man who sits beside the brook the whole day and washes himself, naked as the Lord God made him. It's made him lose his senses.

THIRD OLD WEAVER (*raises himself up, moved by the Spirit, and begins to talk with "tongues", raising his finger threateningly*)   A judgment is nigh. Forsake your dealings with the rich and the great. A judgment is nigh. The Lord God of Sabaoth . . .

(*A number of the weavers laugh; he is pushed back into his seat*)

WELZEL   He can't even drink a little glass without going out of his head.

THIRD OLD WEAVER (*jumps up again*)   Alas, they believe not in God, nor in Heaven nor Hell. Religion is a mockery . . .

FIRST OLD WEAVER   Let that be enough!

BAECKER   You let the man pray his sermon. There might be somebody who could take it to heart.

MANY VOICES (*tumultuously*)   Let him speak!—Let him!

THIRD OLD WEAVER (*with his voice raised*)   And therefore hell opened wide its soul, and its jaws gaped without measure, so that all who bend the right of the poor, and use force upon them in misery, might descend into it—thus speaks the Lord.

(*A great commotion*)

THIRD OLD WEAVER (*suddenly declaims in schoolboy fashion*)

If one regard it well
How strange it is to tell
Why anyone should scorn the linen-weaver's ware.

BAECKER   But we're only fustian-weavers.

(*Laughter*)

HORNIG   Linen-weavers are even more miserable. They wander about in the hills like ghosts. You people here still have enough nerve to talk back.

WITTIG   You think maybe the worst is over for us here? The little bit of strength they still got left in their bodies the factory owners will beat out of them soon enough.

BAECKER   He even said it: Before I'm through with these weavers they'll work for a crust of bread.

(*A great commotion*)

VARIOUS OLD AND YOUNG WEAVERS   Who said that?

BAECKER   That's what Dreissiger said about the weavers.

A YOUNG WEAVER   We ought to sling the filthy bastard up by his ass!

JAEGER   Listen here, Wittig, you're always the one telling us about the French Revolution. You always had a lot to say. Well, maybe a time's coming soon when a man can show himself for what he is: a big-mouth or an honest man.

WITTIG (*infuriated*)   You say just one more thing! Have you heard the whistle of bullets? Have you ever stood guard in an enemy country?

JAEGER   I never said you were a bad one. We're friends, aren't we? I didn't mean anything bad by that.

WITTIG   I don't give a damn for your friendship, you bloated oaf!

(POLICEMAN KUTSCHE *enters*)

A NUMBER OF VOICES   Shhh! Shhh! The police!

(*There is a sound of hissing which continues for an extremely long time, until finally there is complete silence*)

KUTSCHE (*who takes a place at the center column, while the others maintain a deep silence*)   A small brandy, please. (*Silence again*)

WITTIG   Well, Kutsche, you've come to see that everything's all right with us here?

KUTSCHE (*without listening to* WITTIG)
Good morning Master Wiegand!

WIEGAND (*still in the corner in front of the bar*)   Thank you, Kutsche.

KUTSCHE   How's business?

WIEGAND   Thanks for asking.

BAECKER   The Superintendent's afraid we're ruining our stomachs with all the pay we're getting.

(*Laughter*)

JAEGER   Isn't it right, Welzel, we've been sitting here eating roast pork, and sauce, and dumplings, and sauerkraut, and now we've settled back for some champagne.

(*Laughter*)

WELZEL   Your world's upside down today, eh?

KUTSCHE   And even if you had champagne and roast pork I still wouldn't be satisfied. I don't have champagne either and still I have to get on.

BAECKER (*with reference to* KUTSCHE's *nose*)
He waters that beet-red pickle of his with brandy and beer, that's why it's so ripe.

(*Laughter*)

WITTIG   It's a hard life for a policeman like him: one time he has to lock up a starving beggar boy, another time he has to lead a pretty young weaver girl astray; then he's got to get stone drunk so he can beat his wife up, so that she can go running to the neighbor's in mortal terror; and then he has to ride around on horseback, lay in bed until nine. I tell you, it's not easy!

KUTSCHE   Talk all you want! Sooner or later you'll talk a rope around your neck. We already know what kind *you* are. Even the Magistrate knows that seditious tongue of yours. I know someone who'd bring his wife and child to the poorhouse with his drinking and squatting in the village tavern, and get himself into jail. He'll keep on agitating and agitating until he ends up with what he deserves.

WITTIG (*laughs bitterly*)   Who knows what's to come? You may be right about that last bit. (*bursting out even more furiously*) But if it ever comes to that, I know who I've got to thank for it, who blabbed to the factory owners and to the lords, who shamed me and blackened my character, so that I can't get work anywhere—who turned the peasants against me and the millers, so that all week long I don't have a single horse to shoe, or a wheel to fix. I know who it is. Once I pulled this miserable beast off his horse because he was beating a poor dumb boy with a horsewhip, for stealing a few unripe pears. But let me tell you

this, and you know me, if you ever get me in jail, you'd better write up your will. And if ever I hear even a whisper of it, I'll take up anything I can get, whether it's a horseshoe or a hammer, the spoke of a wheel or a waterbucket, and I'll search you out, even if I have to pull you out of bed from next to your wife, and I'll beat your skull in, just as sure as my name is Wittig. (*He has jumped up and wants to attack* KUTSCHE)

OLD AND YOUNG WEAVERS (*holding him back*)   Be reasonable, Wittig, be reasonable!

(KUTSCHE *has risen involuntarily; his face is pale*)

KUTSCHE (*retreating during the following. The nearer he gets to the door the braver he becomes. His last words are spoken on the threshold, so as to be able to disappear immediately thereafter*)   What do you want from me? I never had anything to do with you. I never hurt you. I've got no business with you. What I came to say was to you weavers: the Superintendent of Police forbids you to sing that song, the *Dreissiger Song*, or whatever you call it. And if it doesn't stop in the streets at once, he'll take pains to give you ample time and leisure for it in jail. You can sing there on water and bread as long as you like. (*He goes off*)

WITTIG (*shouts after him*)   He can't forbid us a damned thing! And if we shout it till the windows shake, and they hear us in Reichenbach, and if we sing until all the factory owners' houses tumble down on their heads, and the helmets of the Superintendents dance around on their skulls, that's nobody's business but ours.

BAECKER (*has risen in the meanwhile, given the sign to sing, and begins himself as they all join in*)

A bloody justice rages here,
A law that's worse than lynching,
Where courtroom trials are not the rule,
To kill us without flinching.

(*The innkeeper attempts to keep them quiet, but they pay no attention to him.* WIEGAND *covers his ears and runs away. The weavers rise and while the following verses of the song are sung follow* WITTIG *and* BAECKER *who by means of nods, etc., have given signs to break up*)

A man is slowly tortured here,
A man is tortured long,
His sighs are counted as the proof
Of his affliction's song.

(*The greater number of the weavers sing the following verses on the street; only a few of the younger men are still inside the tavern paying.*

At the end of the next line the room is empty except for WELZEL, *his wife, his daughter,* HORNIG *and* OLD BAUMERT)

You scoundrels all, you brood of hell,
You demons of the fire,
You eat the poor from house and home—
May curses be your hire.

WELZEL (*calmly gathers the glasses together*) They've sure gone wild today.

(OLD BAUMERT *is about to leave*)

HORNIG   What in God's name are they up to now, Baumert?

OLD BAUMERT   They're on their way to Dreissiger's to see that he adds something to their wages.

WELZEL   Do you go along with all this crazy goings on?

OLD BAUMERT   It's like this, Welzel, I can't help it. Sometimes a young man *can* go, but an old man *must.* (*He goes off somewhat embarrassed*)

HORNIG (*rises*)   It'll surprise me if this don't turn out bad.

WELZEL   Even these old ones are losing their heads!

HORNIG   Well, everybody's got a dream.

ACT FOUR

(*Peterswaldau.—A private room in the house of* DREISSIGER, *the textile manufacturer. It is a room luxuriously decorated in the frosty taste of the first half of the century. The ceiling, stove, and doors are white; the wallpaper is of a cold lead-grey tone, with straight rows of small flowers on it. The furniture is of mahogany and upholstered in red, carved and richly decorated; the cupboard and chairs are of the same material. To the right, between two windows, with cherry-red damask curtains, stands the secretary with a drop front; on the wall directly opposite it is the sofa, not far from the iron safe; in front of the sofa are table, easy-chairs, and other chairs. A gun cabinet stands at the back wall. All the walls are partially hidden by bad pictures in gold frames. Above the sofa hangs a mirror with a sturdy, gilt, rococo frame around it. A single door, left, leads into the hallway, an open double door in the rear wall leads into a salon, decorated in the same uncomfortable splendor. There are two women in the salon,* FRAU DREISSIGER *and* FRAU PASTOR KITTELHAUS, *busy looking at pictures. In addi-*tion, PASTOR KITTELHAUS *is in conversation with* WEINHOLD, *the tutor, and theology student*)

KITTLEHAUS (*a small, friendly little man, enters into the front room with the tutor, both of them smoking and talking pleasantly; he looks around and finding no one there shakes his head in surprise*)   There's nothing at all surprising about it, Herr Weinhold; the fact is you are still young. When we old folks were your age—I don't mean to say we had the same ideas, but similar ones. Yes, by all means similar. And then there's always something nice about youth—all those wonderful ideals. But, alas, they are fleeting, fleeting as the April sunshine. Wait till you get to be my age! When for thirty years a man has had his say from the pulpit fifty-two times a year, not counting saints' days, then he must of necessity become more calm. Think of me sometimes, Herr Weinhold, when you have come as far as I.

WEINHOLD (*nineteen years of age, pale, thin, tall, with simple long blond hair. His movements are very restless and nervous*)   With all due respect, Herr Pastor . . . I simply don't know . . . After all, there is a great diversity in our natures.

KITTELHAUS   My dear Herr Weinhold, however restless an individual you may be—(*in a tone of reproof*)—and you are exactly that—however violently and unrestrainedly you may attack existing conditions, you will calm down in the end. Oh, yes, I quite admit that among our brethren in office there are individuals of advanced age who still play youthful pranks. One preaches against the evils of drinking, and founds temperance societies; the other composes proclamations which make undeniably gripping reading, but what good are they? They do not lessen the distress among the weavers, wherever it may exist, whereas social freedom is undermined. No, no, in cases of this sort one would really rather say: cobbler, stick to your last! And you who are keeper of souls, do not become keeper of bellies! Preach the pure Word of God, and leave the rest to Him Who provides shelter and food for the birds and will not suffer the lily of the field to perish. —But now I should like to know what has happened to our good host, that he has disappeared so suddenly.

(FRAU DREISSIGER *enters the front room now with* FRAU KITTELHAUS. *She is in her thirties, a pretty woman of a healthy, robust sort. A certain discrepancy between her manner of speaking, or the way in which she moves, and her elegant, rich way of dressing is obvious*)

FRAU DREISSIGER   You're quite right, Herr

Kittelhaus, Wilhelm does this all the time. Whenever he gets an idea he runs away and lets me sit here. I've said enough about it already, but what good does it do?

KITTELHAUS   My dear, good woman, that's why he is a business man.

WEINHOLD   Unless I'm mistaken something's happened downstairs.

DREISSIGER (*enters; hot, excited*)   Well, Rosa, have you served the coffee?

FRAU DREISSIGER (*sulking*)   Why must you always run off?

DREISSIGER (*lightly*)   Oh, you wouldn't understand!

KITTELHAUS   I beg your pardon, Herr Dreissiger, but have you had any trouble?

DREISSIGER   I have trouble every day that the Good Lord lets be, my good Herr Kittelhaus. I'm used to it. Well, Rosa! Are you taking care of it?

(FRAU DREISSIGER *walks ill-humoredly to the wide, embroidered bell-pull, and tugs violently at it several times*)

DREISSIGER   I wish—(*after a few strides*)—Herr Weinhold, that you had been along just now. You would really have seen something. And besides . . . But come, what do you say to a game of whist?

KITTELHAUS   Why, of course, Herr Dreissiger, of course! Shake the dust and burden of the day from your shoulders, and join the company!

DREISSIGER (*has walked to a window, pulls aside one of the curtains; involuntarily*)   Hoodlums!—Come here, Rosa! (*She goes to him*) Do you see that tall red-haired man over there?

KITTELHAUS   They call him Red Baecker.

DREISSIGER   Tell me, is that the same man who insulted you the day before yesterday? You remember what you told me about when Johann was helping you into the carriage?

FRAU DREISSIGER (*pouts*)   I don't remember.

DREISSIGER   Will you stop sulking! I must know. I've had enough of his impudence. If he's the one, then I will make him answer for it. (*The weavers' song is heard*) Will you listen to that, will you listen!

KITTELHAUS (*extremely angry*)   When will this nonsense stop! I must confess I think it is time the police step in. If you please. (*He goes to the window*) Do you see, Herr Weinhold! Those aren't merely young people out there, there are old, steady, weavers out there, too, who for many years I have thought to be respectable, God-fearing men. And there they are. There they are, taking part in this unheard of nonsense. They are trampling God's law

under foot. Do you still insist on defending these people?

WEINHOLD   Certainly not, Herr Kittelhaus. That is, Herr Kittelhaus, *cum grano salis*. They are nothing but hungry, ignorant people. They are expressing their dissatisfaction in the only way they know. I couldn't possibly expect that such people . . .

FRAU KITTELHAUS (*small, thin, faded, looks more like an old maid than an aging wife*)   Herr Weinhold, Herr Weinhold, how *can* you!

DREISSIGER   Herr Weinhold, I'm terribly sorry . . . I did not take you into my house so that you could lecture me on humanitarianism. I must ask that you confine yourself to educating my sons, and to leave my own affairs entirely to me! Do you understand?

WEINHOLD (*stands rigid and white as death for a moment, then bows with a forced smile; softly*)   Of course, of course, I quite understand. I saw this coming; it is my wish as well. (*He goes off*)

DREISSIGER (*brutally*)   Then see to it as soon as possible, we need the room.

FRAU DREISSIGER   But, Wilhelm, Wilhelm!

DREISSIGER   Have you lost your senses? Would you protect a man who would stand up in defence of such vulgar, villainous libel as this song?

FRAU DREISSIGER   But, Wilhelm, he didn't, he didn't at all, he didn't . . .

DREISSIGER   Herr Kittelhaus, did he defend it or did he not defend it?

KITTELHAUS   Herr Dreissiger, you must consider his youth.

FRAU KITTELHAUS   I just don't understand, that young man comes from such a good, respectable family. His father held public office for forty years and was never guilty of the slightest misdemeanor. His mother was overjoyed when he found such a wonderful position here. But now, now he hasn't the least idea how to make the most of it.

PFEIFER (*tears open the halldoor and shouts into the room*)   Herr Dreissiger, Herr Dreissiger! They've caught him.

DREISSIGER (*hastily*)   Did someone go for the police?

PFEIFER   The Superintendent is coming up the stairs now.

DREISSIGER (*in the doorway*)   Your servant, sir! I am happy that you have come.

(KITTELHAUS *indicates to the women through gestures that it were better if they retire. He, his wife, and* FRAU DREISSIGER *go into the salon*)

DREISSIGER (*in extreme excitement to the* POLICE SUPERINTENDENT *who in the meanwhile has entered*)   Sir, I have finally had one of the chief singers of this mob taken captive by my dye-workers. I could stand it no longer. Their impudence simply knows no bounds. It's disgraceful. I have guests in my house and these scoundrels have the nerve to . . . They insult my wife whenever she goes out; my sons' lives are not safe. I risk having my guests pummeled about. I assure you that if it is possible in a well-ordered community for unoffending people like myself and my family to be publicly put to ridicule time and again . . . well then . . . then I must regret to having different ideas about law and morality.

SUPERINTENDENT (*a man of about fifty, of medium height, fat, with high blood pressure. He wears a cavalry uniform with a long sabre and spurs*) Certainly not . . . No, certainly not, Herr Dreissiger! I am completely at your disposal. You may rest at ease, I am completely at your disposal. Everything is quite in order . . . In fact I'm delighted that you've caught one of the chief trouble-makers. I'm pleased that this matter is finally coming to a head. There are a few disturbers of the peace around here on whom I've had my eye for a long time.

DREISSIGER A few young brats, that's right, a lazy rabble of louts afraid to work, that lead disgusting lives, and hang around day after day in the taverns until they've drunk down their last pfennig. But I am determined once and for all to put an end to the trade of these professional foul-mouths. It is in the public interest, not merely in my interest.

SUPERINTENDENT No doubt about it! No doubt about it, Herr Dreissiger. No one could possibly blame you. And whatever lies in my power . . .

DREISSIGER This pack of louts should be gone after with a bullwhip.

SUPERINTENDENT Quite right, quite right. We must make an example of them.

KUTSCHE (*enters and stands at attention. With the door to the hallway open, the sound of heavy footsteps coming up the stairs is heard*) I wish to report, sir, that we've taken one of the men.

DREISSIGER Would you care to see this man, sir?

SUPERINTENDENT Why, certainly, certainly. First of all we must see him at close range. Would you oblige me, Herr Dreissiger, and not speak to him just at first. I assure you every satisfaction, or my name is not Heide.

DREISSIGER I cannot be satisfied with that, the man must be turned over to the Magistrate without fail.

JAEGER (*is led in by five of the dye-workers whose faces, hands, and clothes are covered with dye, having come directly from work. The prisoner, his cap set cockily on his head, behaves with impudent gaiety and finds himself, as a result of his earlier consumption of liquor, in high spirits*) Oh, you poor sons-of-bitches! You call yourselves workers, you call yourselves comrades? Before I ever did a thing like that— before I ever took one of my fellow workers prisoner, I'd think my hand would wilt on my arm first!

(*At a sign from the* SUPERINTENDENT, KUTSCHE *signifies to the dye-workers that they take their hands from the captive.* JAEGER *stands there free and impudent, while around him all doors are being guarded*)

SUPERINTENDENT (*shouts at* JAEGER) Off with your hat, you lout!

(JAEGER *removes his cap, but very slowly, without relinquishing his ironic smile*)

SUPERINTENDENT What's your name?

JAEGER What do you think I am, your swineherd?

(*His words create a great commotion among those present*)

DREISSIGER Who does he think he is!

SUPERINTENDENT (*changes color, is about to blow up, but controls his rage*) We'll see about that! I asked you what your name is! (*since he receives no answer, wildly*) Answer me or you will get twenty-five lashes!

JAEGER (*with absolute cheerfulness, and without so much as batting an eyelid at the fury of words, calls over the heads of those present to a pretty servant girl who, about to serve coffee, stands wide-eyed looking at the unexpected scene*) Well, ironing-board Emily, what are you doing with this crowd? You better see to it that you get out of here, there might come a wind that will blow everything away over night.

(*The girl stares at* JAEGER, *and as soon as she is aware that it is she who is being spoken to, she grows red with embarrassment, covers her face with her hands and runs out, leaving the dishes behind her just as they are*)

SUPERINTENDENT (*almost beside himself, to* DREISSIGER) I have never in my life come across such unheard of impudence in . . .

JAEGER (*spits on the floor*)

DREISSIGER May I remind you that this is not a stable!

SUPERINTENDENT I have reached the end of my patience. Now for the last time: what is your name?

KITTELHAUS (*has during the last scene looked through the slightly open door to the salon and listened; he comes forward now, shaking with excitement, to intervene, unable to restrain himself any longer*) His name is Jaeger, Herr Superintendent. Moritz. Right? Moritz Jaeger. (*to* JAEGER) Well, say something, Jaeger, don't you remember me?

JAEGER (*seriously*) You are Pastor Kittelhaus.

KITTELHAUS Yes, Jaeger, the keeper of your soul! The same one who accepted you into the Community of Saints when you were but a babe in swaddling clothes. The same one out of whose hands you first received the Lord's Supper. Do you still remember? I took every pain to bring home the Word of God to your soul. Is this the thanks I have?

JAEGER (*darkly, like a humiliated schoolboy*) I put a thaler in the plate.

KITTELHAUS Money, money . . . Do you perhaps believe that that filthy, miserable piece of money . . . Keep your money, I prefer it that way. What nonsense! Be good. Be a Christian! Think of what you once promised. Keep the Lord's Commandments, be good and be pious. Money, money . . .

JAEGER I'm a Quaker, Herr Kittelhaus, I don't believe in anything anymore.

KITTELHAUS Quaker! What are you talking about! See to it that you better yourself, and forget these words that you know nothing about! The Quakers are pious people, not heathens like you. Quaker! Quaker!

SUPERINTENDENT With your permission, Herr Kittelhaus. (*He steps between him and* JAEGER) Kutsche, bind his hands!

VOICES FROM OUTSIDE (*yelling wildly*) Jaeger! Jaeger! Come out!

DREISSIGER (*slightly frightened like the others present, steps automatically to the window*) What's the meaning of this?

SUPERINTENDENT Oh, I understand all right. It means they want this scoundrel outside again. But I'm afraid we can't do them the favor. Do you understand, Kutsche? He goes to jail.

KUTSCHE (*the rope in his hand, hesitant*) With all due respect, sir, we may have some trouble. That's a damned big crowd down there. A regular band of devils. There's Baecker, and there's the smith . . .

KITTELHAUS With your permission—so as not to incense them any more, would it not be better, Herr Superintendent, if we tried to do this peaceably. Perhaps Jaeger will promise to come along quietly, or . . .

SUPERINTENDENT Do you know what you are saying! He's my responsibility! I couldn't possibly allow such a thing. Come on, Kutsche, don't waste time!

JAEGER (*puts his hands together and holds them out, laughing*) Tighter, tighter, tight as you can. It won't be for long.

(KUTSCHE *binds him with the help of his men*)

SUPERINTENDENT All right now, off with you, march! (*to* DREISSIGER) If you're worried about him escaping, let six of your dye-workers go along. They can form a guard around him. I'll ride in front and Kutsche will follow. And if anyone gets in the way he'll be beaten down.

VOICES FROM BELOW (*shouting*) Cockadoodledo! Bowwowwow!

SUPERINTENDENT (*threateningly toward the window*) Rabble! I'll cockadoodle and bowwow you! Now march! (*He strides out ahead of them with sabre drawn. The others follow with* JAEGER)

JAEGER (*shouts as he goes off*) Let her highness Frau Dreissiger act as proud as she wants, but she's no better than us. There's hundreds of times she served my father three pfennigs of schnapps. Squadron, left. March!

(*He goes off laughing*)

DREISSIGER (*after a pause, seemingly calm*) Well, what do you think, Herr Kittelhaus! Shall we have a game of whist? I think there's nothing to prevent us now. (*He lights a cigar, emitting short laughs as he does so; as soon as it is lighted he laughs loudly*) I'm beginning to see the thing as quite amusing. That scoundrel! (*in a nervous burst of laughter*) It's incredibly ludicrous. First the row at table with Weinhold —then five minutes later he takes his leave, wherever that may be! Then *this* business. And now we'll have a game of whist.

KITTELHAUS Yes, but . . . (*Roaring is heard from downstairs*) Yes, but . . . That crowd is making a terrible noise down there.

DREISSIGER Then let's retire to another room. We won't be disturbed there.

KITTELHAUS (*shaking his head*) If only I knew what has got into these people. I must agree with Herr Weinhold, at least until quite recently I was of the opinion that these weavers were a humble, patient, and easily handled class. Wouldn't you say so, Herr Dreissiger?

DREISSIGER Of course they were once patient and easily handled; of course they were once well mannered and orderly. At least as long as these humanitarians left them alone. These people have had it made clear enough to them for a long time in what terrible misery they find themselves. Just think of it: all those societies and committees for the relief of distress among the weavers. Finally the weaver believes it himself, and now they've all gone out of their minds. Now let one of them come back and set their heads straight again. Now that they're started they grumble at everything. They don't like this and they don't like that. Now they want nothing but the best.

(*Suddenly a loud, swelling cry of "Hurray!" is heard from the crowd*)

KITTELHAUS   And so with all their humanitarianism all they've succeeded in doing is making wolves out of lambs.

DREISSIGER   I wouldn't say that, Herr Kittelhaus. If you look at the matter with calm understanding, something good might come of it even yet. Perhaps such occurrences as this will not go unnoticed in leading circles. It is possible they will be convinced that this can go on no longer, that something must happen, unless our local industry is to be completely ruined.

KITTELHAUS   Tell me then, what is the cause of this enormous depression?

DREISSIGER   Foreign markets have barricaded themselves from us through high import duty. We lose our best markets there, and here at home we have to fight all kinds of competition. We're being abandoned, completely abandoned.

PFEIFER   (*totters in, pale and breathless*) Herr Dreissiger, Herr Dreissiger!

DREISSIGER   (*already in the doorway to the salon and about to leave, turns, irritated*) Well, what is it now, Pfeifer?

PFEIFER   No, no . . . leave me alone!

DREISSIGER   What's the matter?

KITTELHAUS   You're frightening us. Say something.

PFEIFER   (*not yet recovered*)   No, leave me alone! I never saw anything like it! The Superintendent . . . they really got themselves into it this time.

DREISSIGER   For God's sake, man, what is it? Has someone broken his neck?

PFEIFER   (*almost crying with fear, cries out*) They've set Moritz Jaeger free. They thrashed the Superintendent and chased him off, and then they thrashed the policeman and chased him off. Without his helmet . . . his sabre broken . . . No, no!

DREISSIGER   Pfeifer, you've gone mad!

KITTELHAUS   This could mean revolution.

PFEIFER   (*sitting in a chair, his whole body trembling, whimpering*) It's serious Herr Dreissiger, it's serious!

DREISSIGER   That whole damned police force can go and . . .

PFEIFER   It's serious, Herr Dreissiger!

DREISSIGER   Oh, shut your mouth, Pfeifer! For God's sake!

FRAU DREISSIGER   (*enters from the salon with* FRAU KITTELHAUS)   This is disgraceful, Wilhelm. Our whole evening has been ruined. Frau Kittelhaus just said she thought that she'd rather go home.

KITTELHAUS   My dear Frau Dreissiger, perhaps it is the best solution for right now . . .

FRAU DREISSIGER   But, Wilhelm, why don't you do something really drastic about it?

DREISSIGER   Go on and try! Go on! Go on! (*standing helplessly in front of the* PASTOR) Am I a tyrant? Am I a slave driver?

JOHANN, THE COACHMAN   (*enters*)   Ma'am, I've got the carriage ready. Herr Weinhold's already put Jorgel and Karlchen in the wagon. If it gets much worse, we can leave.

FRAU DREISSIGER   What's there to get worse?

JOHANN   Well, I don't know, ma'am. I just thought I'd tell you. There are more people coming all the time. They already ran off the Superintendent and the policeman.

PFEIFER   It's serious, Herr Dreissiger, it's serious!

FRAU DREISSIGER   (*with mounting fear*) What's going to happen? What do these people want? Surely they can't attack us, Johann.

JOHANN   There are some awful rough ones down there, ma'am.

PFEIFER   It's serious, it's serious.

DREISSIGER   Shut up, you fool! Are the doors barred?

KITTELHAUS   Do me one favor . . . do me this favor . . . I've come to a decision . . . just one favor . . . (*to* JOHANN) What do the people want?

JOHANN   (*embarrassed*)   They want more pay, the crazy bastards.

KITTELHAUS   Very well!—I shall go out and do my duty. I shall speak seriously with these people.

JOHANN   But, Herr Kittelhaus, Herr Kittelhaus, you mustn't! They won't listen to words.

KITTELHAUS   My dear Herr Dreissiger, one word more. I should like to ask you to station some people behind the door, and as soon as I have gone out, to close it behind me.

FRAU KITTELHAUS   Joseph, you're not really going to do it.

KITTELHAUS   I am. I am. I know what I am doing. Have no fear, the Lord will protect me.

(FRAU KITTELHAUS *presses his hand in hers, steps back and wipes tears from her eyes*)

KITTELHAUS   (*while the incessant dull rumbling of a great mob of people forces its way up from below*) I shall pretend . . . I shall pretend that I am on my way home. I want to see whether my spiritual office . . . whether or not there is still that much respect left in these people . . . I want to see . . . (*He takes his hat and walking stick*) I go forward in the Name of God.

(*He goes off accompanied by* DREISSIGER, PFEIFER, *and* JOHANN)

FRAU KITTELHAUS My dear Frau Dreissiger —(*She breaks into tears and throws her arms around* FRAU DREISSIGER)—They mustn't hurt him!

FRAU DREISSIGER (*lost in thought*) I really don't know, Frau Kittelhaus . . . what I feel. Things like this aren't possible. If that's how it is . . . then it's just like saying it's a sin to be rich. If someone had told me all this, Frau Kittelhaus, I don't know but I would rather have remained with the little I had at first.

FRAU KITTELHAUS My dear Frau Dreissiger, there are troubles and disappointments in every way of life.

FRAU DREISSIGER Of course, of course, that's what I tell myself, too. And just because we have more than other people . . . Lord only knows we didn't steal it. We came by every pfennig honestly. Such things are simply not possible, that people come and attack you. Is it my husband's fault if business is bad?

(*A tumultuous roaring is heard from below. While the two women still look at one another, pale and frightened,* DREISSIGER *rushes into the room*)

DREISSIGER Quick, Rosa, throw something over your shoulders and get into the carriage; I'll be right there! (*He rushes toward the safe, opens it and removes various valuable articles*)

JOHANN (*entering*) Everything's ready! But hurry before they take the back door, too!

FRAU DREISSIGER (*in panicked fright, throws her arms around the coachman*) Dear, dear Johann! Save us, dear, dear Johann! Save my boys, oh, oh . . .

DREISSIGER Be reasonable! Let go of Johann!

JOHANN Ma'am, ma'am! You mustn't worry. Our horses are in good shape. Nobody can overtake us. If anyone gets in my way I'll run over him. (*He goes off*)

FRAU KITTELHAUS (*in helpless fear*) But my husband? But, but my husband? But, Herr Dreissiger, my husband?

DREISSIGER Frau Kittelhaus, Frau Kittelhaus, he's all right. You must calm yourself, he's all right.

FRAU KITTELHAUS Something terrible has happened to him. You just won't tell me, you just won't tell me.

DREISSIGER Oh, never mind, they'll regret it. I know exactly who's to blame. Such a nameless, shameless piece of impudence will not stay unavenged. The devil take the community that would manhandle its own pastor. Mad dogs, that's what they are, beasts gone mad, and they will be handled accordingly. (*to* FRAU DREISSIGER *who stands there as though in a trance*) Go on now, move. (*Pounding is heard against the front door*) Don't you hear? The rabble has lost its senses. (*The clatter of broken glass panes on the ground floor is heard*) The rabble's gone mad. There's nothing we can do but get ourselves out of here.

INDIVIDUAL VOICES FROM OFFSTAGE Bring Pfeifer out!—Bring Pfeifer out!

FRAU DREISSIGER Pfeifer, Pfeifer, they want Pfeifer out there.

PFEIFER (*rushes in*) Herr Dreissiger, there are people at the back door already. We can't hold the front door more than three minutes longer. Wittig's banging at it with a pail, like a madman.

VOICES FROM BELOW (*louder and clearer*) Bring out Pfeifer!—Bring out Pfeifer!

(FRAU DREISSIGER *runs off as though chased;* FRAU KITTELHAUS *follows her*)

PFEIFER (*listens, grows pale, understands the calling and is gripped with maddening fear. The following is spoken at a frantic pace, while he cries, whimpers, begs, and whines. He overwhelms* DREISSIGER *with childish affections, he caresses his cheeks and arms, kisses his hands, and finally clings to him like a drunken man, thereby restraining and fettering* DREISSIGER *without letting him go*) Dear, good, kind, Herr Dreissiger, don't leave me behind, I always served you faithfully; and I always handled the people good, too. I couldn't give them more wages than you'd set. Don't leave me here, they'll kill me. If they find me they'll beat me to death. My God, my God! My wife, my children . . .

DREISSIGER (*tries in vain to free himself from* PFEIFER) At least let go of me, man! We'll see, we'll see about it.

(*He goes off with* PFEIFER. *The room is empty for several seconds. Window glass is shattered in the salon. A loud crack reverberates through the house, from below there is heard a roar of "Hurray!" And then silence. Several seconds pass, then the sounds of quiet, cautious footsteps are heard on the stairs leading to the second floor, as well as quiet, timid exclamations*)

VOICES To the left!—Upstairs!—Psst!—Slowly! Slowly! Don't slip!—Take it easy!—Damn, what's this!—Get on there!—We're going to a wedding!—Go on in!—Go on!

(*Young weavers, both boys and girls, appear at the door to the hallway; they dare not enter, and one tries to push the other on into the room from behind. After a few seconds their shyness is overcome and the poor, thin, often sickly figures dressed in rags or mended clothes, spread themselves out across* DREISSIGER's *room and across the salon. They are curious at first and look shyly at things, then they touch them. The girls try out the sofas; groups form and admire their reflections in the mirror. Some climb up on the chairs to look at the pictures and to take them down; in the meanwhile other miserable forms stream in from the hallway*)

AN OLD WEAVER (*enters*) No, no, I don't want no part of it! They're already tearing things apart downstairs. It's all madness! There ain't no sense or reason in it. It will all turn out a bad thing in the end. No man who's got a clear head would do such a thing. I'll be careful and take no part in such crime!

(JAEGER, BAECKER, WITTIG *with a wooden pail,* OLD BAUMERT, *and a number of young and old weavers rush in as though chasing after something, shouting to one another with hoarse voices*)

JAEGER Where's he gone?

BAECKER Where is the slave driver?

OLD BAUMERT If we can eat grass he can eat sawdust.

WITTIG When we catch him we'll string him up.

FIRST YOUNG WEAVER We'll take him by the legs and throw him out the window onto the stones, so that he'll never get up again.

SECOND YOUNG WEAVER (*enters*) He's gone.

ALL Who's gone?

SECOND YOUNG WEAVER Dreissiger.

BAECKER Pfeifer too?

VOICES Let's get Pfeifer! Let's get Pfeifer!

OLD BAUMERT Come, Pfeifer, come, here's a weaver you can starve.

(*Laughter*)

JAEGER Even if we don't get that Dreissiger brute . . . we'll make a poor man of him.

OLD BAUMERT We'll make him poor as a churchmouse. We'll make a poor man of him.

(*They all rush towards the salon door with the intention of demolishing it*)

BAECKER (*runs ahead, turns around and halts the others*) Halt, listen to me! When we've finished here we haven't even begun. From here we go to Bielau, to Dietrich's, where they've got mechanical looms. All our misery comes from these factories.

ANSORGE (*enters from the hallway. After he has entered a few steps he remains standing, looks around, bewildered, shakes his head, strikes his forehead and says*) Who am I? A weaver, Anton Ansorge. Has he gone mad, this Ansorge? It's true, my head is going round like a wheel. What's he doing here? What he wants to do he'll do. Where is he, Ansorge? (*He strikes his forehead again*) I've gone crazy! I'm not responsible. I'm not right in the head. Get out, get out! Get out, you rebels. Heads out, legs out, hands out! You take my shack and I'll take your shack, come on, let's go! (*With a howl, he goes into the salon. Those present follow him with shouting and laughter*)

ACT FIVE

(*Langenbielau.—The small weaving-room of* OLD HILSE. *To the left is a small window, in front of it a loom; to the right there is a bed with a table pushed close to it. In the right corner, a stove with a bench. Sitting around the table on a footstool, on the bed and on a wooden stool are:* OLD HILSE, *his equally old, blind, and almost deaf wife* FRAU HILSE, *his son* GOTTLIEB, *and his wife* LUISE. *They are at morning prayers. A spooling-wheel with bobbins stands between the table and the loom. All kinds of spinning, spooling, and weaving implements are stored on top of the smoke-browned ceiling beams. Long strands of yarn hang down. All sorts of trash lie about in the room. In the backwall of this very narrow, low, and shallow room is a door leading into the hallway. Opposite this door, at the other end of the hallway, is another door which is open, and through which we can see into a second, similar weaving room. The hallway is paved with stone and the plaster is cracked; a flight of unsteady wooden stairs leads up into the attic living quarters. A washtub on a stool is partially visible; ragged pieces of clothes and the household implements of poverty stricken people lie about in disorderly fashion. The light falls from the left into all three rooms*)

OLD HILSE (*a bearded, heavy-boned man, who now as a result of age, work, sickness and hardships is a bent and wasted man. A war veteran, he has only one arm. He has a pointed nose, his face is pale, he trembles, and he is obviously only skin, bones and sinews, and has the deep-set sore eyes so characteristic of the weavers. He, his son, and daughter-in-law rise; he prays)* Dear God, we cannot thank you enough that you in your goodness and graciousness have had pity on us on this night, too. That on this night, too, we have suffered no grief. Lord, so far does your graciousness reach, and we are poor, evil, sinful children of men, not worthy that your foot should stamp us out, so sinful and all bad are we. But you, dear Father, you want to see and accept us for the sake of your dear son, Our Lord and Savior Jesus Christ. Jesus' blood and righteousness are my adornment and my clothes of honor. And if at times we are too much cast down by your chastisement—when the oven which is to purify us burns with too terrible heat—then do not take us too sorely to task, forgive us our sins. Give us patience, Heavenly Father, so that after this suffering we may be made partakers in your eternal bliss. Amen.

MOTHER HILSE *(who is bent forward, straining to hear, weeping)* Oh, father, what a beautiful prayer you always say.

(LUISE goes to the washtub, GOTTLIEB goes into the opposite room)

OLD HILSE   Where's the girl?

LUISE   She went over to Peterswaldau—to Dreissiger's. She spooled a few more bobbins last night.

OLD HILSE *(speaking very loudly)* You want me to bring you your wheel now, mother?

MOTHER HILSE   Yes, father, bring it, bring it.

OLD HILSE *(setting it down in front of her)* Oh, how I wish I could do it for you.

MOTHER HILSE   No . . . no . . . what could I ever do with all the time I'd have?

OLD HILSE   I'll wipe your fingers for you, so you won't get grease on the yarn, you hear?

(He wipes her hands with the rag)

LUISE *(from the washtub)* From where would she get grease on her fingers?

OLD HILSE   When we got no grease, we eat our bread dry—when we got no bread, then we eat potatoes—and when we got no potatoes either, then we eat dry bran.

LUISE *(sneering)* And when we've got no black flour, we'll do like that Wengler woman down below, we'll find where a skinner has buried a rotten horse. Then we'll dig it up and live off the carrion for a few weeks. That's what we'll do, ain't it?

GOTTLIEB *(from the backroom)* You sure do like to jabber!

OLD HILSE   You should watch yourself with that Godless talk! *(He goes to the loom, calls)*

Will you help me, Gottlieb—there's still a few threads to pull through.

LUISE *(from the washtub)* Gottlieb, you're to help your father.

(GOTTLIEB enters. The old man and his son now begin the troublesome task of putting up the threads. The threads of the warp are pulled through the eyes of the comb, or shaft of the loom. They have scarcely begun when HORNIG appears in the hallway)

HORNIG *(in the doorway to the room)* Good luck with your work!

OLD HILSE *and* GOTTLIEB   Thank you Hornig!

OLD HILSE   Tell me now, when do you ever sleep? In the daytime you make your rounds and at night you stand guard.

HORNIG   I can't sleep no more!

LUISE   Welcome, Hornig!

OLD HILSE   Well, what's the good news?

HORNIG   It's fine news, too, master. The weavers at Peterswaldau have risked the devil and chased Dreissiger and his whole family out of the place.

LUISE *(with signs of emotion)* Hornig's lying again as sure as he's talking.

HORNIG   Not this time, ma'am, not this time —I've got some nice children's aprons in the wagon. No, no, I'm telling you the God's truth. They chased them right out. They got to Reichenbach last night. And believe it or not, they didn't want to let them stay—for fear of the weavers. So off he went again to Schweidnitz this time.

OLD HILSE *(carefully takes up the threads of the warp and brings them near the shaft, while from the other side his son uses a wire hook to pull them through one of the eyes)* It's about time you stopped, Hornig!

HORNIG   May I never leave this room in one piece if it's not true. Why, every child knows as much.

OLD HILSE   Tell me, am I crazy, or are you?

HORNIG   What I told you is as true as the Word of God. I wouldn't say nothing about it if I hadn't seen it, but I seen it with my own eyes. With my own eyes, just the same as I see you here, Gottlieb. They tore up the factory owner's house from the cellar to the roof. They threw his china from the attic windows— right out over the roof—I wonder how many bolts of fustian are laying in the brook now? Water can't get through, you can believe it. It's running over its sides. It looked real sulfur blue from all the indigo they threw out the window. Those sky-blue clouds of dust just came floating down. Yes, they sure tore that house apart. And not just the house, the dye-works, too, and the warehouse! The banister's knocked in pieces, the floor's torn up and mirrors shattered, sofa and chairs, everything torn and slashed, cut and thrown, kicked and hacked to pieces—damnation, believe me, it's worse than in wartime.

OLD HILSE   They were weavers from around here? (*He shakes his head slowly and unbelievingly*)

(*Curious tenants of the house have gathered at the door*)

HORNIG   Who else would it be? I could name every one of them. I led the Commissioner through the house. So I talked to a lot of them. They was as friendly as ever. They went about their business real slow, but they did it good. The Commissioner talked to a lot of them. And they was as humble as ever. But they wouldn't be stopped. They hacked up beautiful pieces of furniture like they was getting paid for it.

OLD HILSE   You took the Commissioner through the house?

HORNIG   Well, what would I be afraid of? Those people all know me like I was a bad coin. I never have trouble with them. We're all friends. As sure as my name's Hornig, I went through the house. And you can believe it or not, but it got all soft here around my heart—and I saw it happen to the Commissioner, too—it touched him real close. And why? You couldn't hear a single word, they did their work so quietlike. It made a man feel downright solemn to see those poor hungry bastards finally take their revenge.

LUISE   (*with tears in her eyes, drying them with her apron*)   Yes, yes, that's what has to happen!

VOICES OF THE NEIGHBORS   There's enough slave drivers around here, too.—There's one just across the street.—He's got four horses and six carriages in his stables and lets his weavers go hungry so that he can pay for it.

OLD HILSE   (*still incredulous*)   Why did it start, over there?

HORNIG   Who knows, who knows? Once there's one thing and another time another.

OLD HILSE   What do they say?

HORNIG   Well, they say Dreissiger said that if the weavers are hungry they can eat grass. That's all I know.

(*There is a commotion among the neighbors who angrily pass the word from one to the other*)

OLD HILSE   You listen to me, Hornig. For all I care, you could say to me: Father Hilse, tomorrow you're to have a visit from the King of Prussia. But when you tell me that weavers,

men like me and my son, should have done things like that—no! No, I will never believe it.

MIELCHEN   (*A pretty girl of seven years with long, open flaxen hair, carrying a basket, comes running in. She holds out a silver spoon toward her mother*)   Mummy, look here what I got. You can buy me a dress with this.

LUISE   Why do you come running in like that, girl? (*with increased excitement and tension*)   What's that you've got there, tell me? You're all out of breath. And the bobbins are still in your basket. What do you mean by this, girl?

OLD HILSE   Child, where did that spoon come from?

LUISE   Maybe she found it.

HORNIG   It's worth at least two or three thalers.

OLD HILSE   (*beside himself*)   Get out, girl, get out! I said get out of here now! Will you behave or do I have to beat you! And you take that spoon back from where you got it. Get out! Do you want to make all of us thieves, eh? You little brat, I'll teach you to steal.—(*He looks for something to strike her with*)

MIELCHEN   (*clinging to her mother's skirt, weeping*)   No, grandfather, no, don't hit me, we—we found it. All the . . . all the bobbin children have them.

LUISE   (*between fear and anxiety, bursts out*)   There now, you see, she found it. Where did you find it?

MIELCHEN   (*sobbing*)   We found it in Peterswaldau, in front of Dreissiger's house.

OLD HILSE   Don't make it worse. You get out of here now or I'll teach you what it means to move.

MOTHER HILSE   What's all this?

HORNIG   I'll tell you what, Father Hilse. You let Gottlieb put on a coat and take that spoon over to the police station.

OLD HILSE   Gottlieb, put on a coat!

GOTTLIEB   (*already putting it on, eagerly*)   I'll go to the station and say: You mustn't blame her too much, a child like her don't understand such things. And here I'm bringing the spoon. Stop crying, girl!

(*The crying child is taken by her mother into the backroom, closing the door. She comes back*)

HORNIG   That's worth at least three thalers.

GOTTLIEB   Give me a cloth, Luise, to wrap this up in. My, my, what an expensive thing.

(*There are tears in his eyes, while he wraps the spoon*)

LUISE   If we kept it we could eat for a couple weeks.

OLD HILSE   Go on, go on, hurry up! As fast

as you can! Wouldn't that be something! That's all I need. See that you get that devil's spoon out of my house!

(GOTTLIEB *goes off with the spoon*)

HORNIG   Well, I'd better get on my way, too. (*He goes out, talks for a few seconds in the hallway, then goes off*)

SURGEON SCHMIDT (*a round, quick-silvery little man with a wine-red, cunning face, enters the hallway*) Good morning, people! What lovely stories I've heard here this morning. You take care! (*threateningly with his finger*) Pretty sly lot, that's what you are. (*in the doorway to the front room, without entering*) Good morning, Father Hilse! (*to a woman in the hallway*) Well now, mother, how's the pain? Better, eh? There, you see! Well, Father Hilse, I thought I'd come to see how you're getting on. What's the matter with mother?

LUISE   Doctor, the veins are dried up in her eyes, she can't see no more.

SCHMIDT   That's from the dust and from weaving by candlelight. Tell me, do you know what this is all about? All Peterswaldau is on its way here. I got into my carriage this morning like usual, thinking nothing at all was wrong, and then I started to hear such strange things. What the devil has taken hold of these people, Father Hilse? They're raging like a pack of wolves. It's a regular revolution, a rebellion; they're plundering and marauding . . . Mielchen! Where's Mielchen? (MIELCHEN, *her eyes still red from crying, is pushed in by her mother*) Say, Mielchen, look into my coat pocket. (MIELCHEN *does so*) The ginger snaps are for you. Now, now, not all at once. A song first though! "Fox, you have . . ." Well? "Fox, you have stolen our goose . . ." You just wait, I know what you did; you called the sparrows on the pastor's fence a dirty name because of what they do to it. And they went and told the choir-master. What do you have to say to that? —Almost fifteen hundred people are on the march. (*The pealing of bells in the distance*) Listen to that: they're sounding the alarm bell in Reichenbach. Fifteen hundred people. It's like the world was coming to an end. It makes a person uneasy!

OLD HILSE   Are they really on their way to Bielau?

SCHMIDT   Of course, of course, I just now drove through them, right through the middle of that whole mob. What I should have done was gotten down and given them all a powder. There they were, jogging along one behind the other, grey as death and singing so that it al-

most turned a man's stomach. It makes you want to be sick. My Frederick up in the driver's seat was wailing like an old woman. As soon as we were past them we had to go and buy us a good stiff drink. I wouldn't be a factory owner now even if I could have rubber rims on my wheels. (*Singing in the distance*) Listen to that! Like somebody knocking with his knuckles on an old, cracked boiler. It won't be five minutes before they're here. Good-bye, my friends. Don't do anything foolish. Soldiers are right behind them. Don't lose your heads. These people from Peterswaldau have sure lost theirs. (*Bells are rung close by*) By God, now they're ringing our bells. That'll drive them crazy for sure. (*He goes upstairs*)

GOTTLIEB (*returns; from the hallway, out of breath*) I saw them, I saw them. (*to a woman in the hallway*) They're here, Auntie, they're here! (*in the doorway*) They're here, father, they're here! They've got beanpoles and stickers and axes. They're already up there at Dietrich's house, making a terrible racket. I think they're getting paid money. O Jesus, what's going to happen here! I won't look at it. I never seen so many people in all my life! Once they get started—my God, my God, our factory owners will be really hard put.

OLD HILSE   Why did you run so! You'll chase around till you get your sickness again, then you'll be flat on your back waving your arms around like before.

GOTTLIEB (*almost joyously excited*) I had to run, or they would have caught me. They were already screaming at me to join them. Godfather Baumert was there, too. He said to me: Go get your five groschen, too; you're one of those poor, starving weavers, too. He even said: Go tell your father . . . Father, I'm supposed to tell you to come and help pay the factory owners back for cutting our wages. (*passionately*) Times are changing, he said. Now things are going to be different for us weavers. He wants us to all come and help bring it about. We're all going to have our half-pound of meat on Sundays, and Holy Days we'll have a nice blood sausage with sauerkraut. It's all going to change, he told me.

OLD HILSE (*with suppressed indignation*) And he calls himself your godfather! And he tells you to take part in such terrible deeds! You stay out of such things, Gottlieb. There's the devil's hand in such business. They're doing the devil's work.

LUISE (*overcome with passionate excitement, vehemently*) Yes, Gottlieb, yes, go crawl there behind the stove, in the corner, take a spoon in your hand and a bowl of buttermilk on your knee, put on a dress and say your prayers, then you'll be what your father wants. —And he calls himself a man!

(*Laughter from the people in the hallway*)

OLD HILSE (*trembling, with suppressed rage*) And you call yourself a good wife, eh? Just you let me tell you something. You call yourself a mother with that evil tongue of yours, you want to teach your little girl what's right, and you stir your husband up to crime and wickedness!

LUISE (*without control*) You and all your big talk . . . did it ever give us enough food to feed even one child? Just because of that they've laid in dirt and rags . . . all four of them. They never even had a dry diaper. Yes, I call myself a mother all right, if you want to know! And if you want to know something else, that's the reason I wish these factory owners to hell and damnation—just because I am a mother.—How was I to keep such little things alive? I have cried more than I have breathed, from the minute one of the poor things came into the world, till death had pity on it and took it. And you never gave a damn. You prayed and you sang, while I ran my feet bloody trying to find a bowl of buttermilk. How many hundreds of nights have I wracked my brain how just once I could cheat the churchyard and keep my child! What did the child ever do to deserve such a miserable end!—And over there in Dietrich's house, they get bathed in wine and washed in milk. No, no . . . if it ever starts here—there aren't ten horses could hold me back. And I tell you this: if ever they storm Dietrich's house, I'll be in front of them all, and pity the man who tries to hold me back. I've had enough, and that's a fact.

OLD HILSE You're a lost soul; there's no help for you.

LUISE (*in a frenzy*) You're the one there's no help for. Ragpickers, that's what you are. You're disgraces, you're not men. You're no better than the gutter scrapers they spit at in the street. You're weaklivered cowards, that get scared at the sound of a child's rattle. Fools who thank their beaters for a sound thrashing. They've bled you so white you can't even turn red in the face anymore. Somebody ought to take a whip to you and beat some life into your dead bones. (*Breathless, she goes off quickly*)

(*An embarrassed pause*)

MOTHER HILSE What is it with Luise, father?

OLD HILSE Nothing, mother dear, what should be the matter with her?

MOTHER HILSE Tell me, father, are the bells really ringing, or am I hearing things?

OLD HILSE They must be burying someone, mother.

MOTHER HILSE And still there's no end to my life. Why can't I die?

(*Pause*)

OLD HILSE (*leaves his work, holds himself straight, solemnly*) Gottlieb—you heard what your wife told us. Gottlieb, look at this! (*He opens his shirt*) There was a bullet here once, big as a thimble. And the king knows where I lost my arm. It wasn't the mice ate it off. (*He walks back and forth*) Your wife—before she was ever thought of, I was spilling my blood for my country. And that's why she can jabber on all she wants. It's all right with me. I don't care.—Afraid? Me, afraid? What's there to be afraid of, tell me? Of a few soldiers, maybe, who'll be coming after the rioters? O Jesus, if that was all! That'd be nothing. No, no, maybe I'm a little stiff in the back, but if it ever comes to that, I got bones as strong as ivory. I'd stand up all right against a couple of miserable bayonets.—And if it really got bad? How glad I'd be, oh, how glad I'd be to leave this world behind. No need for them to ask me twice to die. Better today than tomorrow. No, no. How glad I'd be! For what would I leave behind? Who would cry over this old torture box of aches and pains, that little heap of fear and torment that we call our life, how glad I'd be to leave that behind.—But then, Gottlieb! Then there comes something else—and when we've thrown that away, then there's nothing left.

GOTTLIEB Who knows what's to come after you're dead? Nobody's ever seen it.

OLD HILSE You listen, Gottlieb, don't you be throwing doubt on the one thing that we poor people got left. Why else would I have sat here—why would I have worked this treadle here for forty years until I was almost dead? And why would I have sat here and watched him over there living in pride and gluttony, making himself rich on my hunger and misery? Why? Because I had hope. In all this misery I still have something. (*pointing out the window*) You've got your share here in this world, I've got mine in the other. That's what I've been thinking all this time. And you can tear my body to pieces—but I know what I know. We've been promised. The day of judgment is coming; but we are not the judges: Vengeance is Mine, saith the Lord Our God.

A VOICE (*through the window*) Weavers, come out!

OLD HILSE Go, do what you want! (*He sits down at his loom*) But you'll never make me leave.

GOTTLIEB (*after a brief struggle with himself*) I'm going to work, too. Come what will. (*He goes off*)

(*The sound of the weaver's song, sung by hundreds of voices, is heard in the immediate vicinity; it sounds like a dull monotonous wailing*)

VOICES OF THE NEIGHBORS (*in the hallway*) O Jesus, Lord Jesus, they're coming like ants.— Where did all them weavers come from.—Stop pushing, I want to see, too.—Look at that beanpole walking in front of them all.—My God, my God, now they're coming in swarms!

HORNIG (*steps among the people in the hallway*) How's that for a show? You don't see something like that every day. Come on up to Dietrich's house. There's a *real* show up there. He ain't got a house, or a factory, or a wine-cellar, or a nothing anymore. They're drinking down the bottles like they was water. They don't even bother to take out the corks anymore. One, two, three, and the necks are off even if they cut their mouths open on the glass. Some of them run around bleeding like pigs— they'll do the same now for Dietrich across the street.

(*The singing of the crowd has stopped*)

VOICES OF THE NEIGHBORS They don't look like such bad people.

HORNIG Never mind! You just wait! They're taking time now to look the place over first. See there, how they're looking that palace over? Look at that little fat man—he's got a horse pail along, he's the smithy from Peterswaldau, he's a dangerous man. Believe me, he can break down the thickest doors like they was pretzels. If he ever gets one of those factory owners in his hands, there'll be no helping him!

VOICES OF THE NEIGHBORS Bang, something happened there!—That was a stone flying in the window!—I bet old Dietrich's afraid now— Look, he's hanging a sign out.—He's hanging a sign out?—What does it say?—Can't you read? —What do you think would happen to me if I couldn't read?—Well then, read it!—"You will all get satisfaction. You will all get satisfaction."—

HORNIG He might have spared himself that one. That won't do him much good. They got

their own ideas. It's the factory they want. It's the mechanical looms they want to get rid of. The looms are what's ruining the weavers; any blind man can see that. No, no! These people won't be stopped today. No Magistrate or Councillor could change their minds—and least of all a sign. If you ever saw them work, you'd know what they was up to.

VOICES OF THE NEIGHBORS My God, my God, who ever saw such a crowd!—What can they want?—(*rapidly*) They're coming across the bridge now! (*fearfully*) They're coming over here? (*in utmost surprise and fear*) They're coming, they're coming.—They're coming to get the weavers out of their houses. (*They all run off. The hallway is left empty*)

(*A swarm of rioters surges into the hallway, dirty, dusty, their clothes torn, rumpled as though they had been up all night, their faces flushed with strain and whisky; they cry out: "Weavers, come out!" Then they disperse themselves through the house.* BAECKER *and several young weavers enter* OLD HILSE's *room, they are armed with clubs and sticks. When they recognize* OLD HILSE, *they stop, slightly cooled off*)

BAECKER Father Hilse, stop your slaving away. Let whoever wants to run the treadle. You won't have to do yourself anymore harm by working. That'll all be taken care of.

FIRST YOUNG WEAVER You won't have to go to bed hungry anymore.

SECOND YOUNG WEAVER The weavers'll have a roof over their heads and a shirt for their backs.

OLD HILSE What the devil are you doing here with sticks and axes?

BAECKER We'll break them on Dietrich's back.

SECOND YOUNG WEAVER We'll get them red hot and stuff them down these factory owners' throats so that they'll know how hunger can burn.

THIRD YOUNG WEAVER Come with us, Father Hilse! We give no quarter.

SECOND YOUNG WEAVER Nobody took pity on us. Neither God nor man. And now we're seeing to our own rights.

OLD BAUMERT (*enters, already somewhat unsteady on his feet, a newly killed rooster under his arm. He stretches out his arms*) My brothers—we are all brothers! Come to my arms, my brothers!

(*Laughter*)

OLD HILSE So this is what you look like now, Wilhelm!

OLD BAUMERT Gustav, is it really you,

Gustav! Poor starving weaver, come to my arms. (*He is deeply moved*)

OLD HILSE (*muttering*) Leave me in peace.

OLD BAUMERT Gustav, that's the way it is. A man must have luck. Gustav, look here at me once. How do I look? A man must have luck! Don't I look like a count? (*striking his belly*) What do you think I've got here in my belly? There's a king's dinner in this belly. A man must have luck, that's when he gets champagne and roast rabbit.—Let me tell you something: we've made a great mistake: we've got to help ourselves.

ALL (*together*) We've got to help ourselves! Hurray!

OLD BAUMERT No sooner you get the first bite of good food in your belly, that's when you start feeling you're alive again. Jesus, Jesus, you feel the power come back into you like you was a bull. And the strength flies out of your arms so that you don't see where you're hitting any more. It's a damned good feeling!

JAEGER (*at the door, armed with an old cavalry sabre*) We made a couple of pretty good attacks.

BAECKER We know what we're doing now. One, two, three and we're inside the house, and then it's like a fire run wild, so that everything crackles and shakes, and sparks fly like at the smithy's.

FIRST YOUNG WEAVER What do you say we have a nice little fire? We'll march to Reichenbach and burn the roofs right off of people's houses.

JAEGER There's nothing they'd like better. Think of all the insurance money they'd get.

(*Laughter*)

BAECKER From here we march to Trumtra's in Freiburg.

JAEGER We ought to see about them government officials for once. I read that all our bad luck comes from these bureaucrats.

SECOND YOUNG WEAVER And then we'll go to Breslau. More people are joining us all the time.

OLD BAUMERT (*to* HILSE) Here, have a drink, Gustav!

OLD HILSE I never drink whisky.

OLD BAUMERT That was in the old world, Gustav, we're in a new one now!

FIRST YOUNG WEAVER Christmas don't come every day.

(*Laughter*)

OLD HILSE (*impatiently*) You hounds of hell, what do you want from me!

OLD BAUMERT (*somewhat startled, in an over-friendly manner*) Why, look here, Gustav, I meant to bring you a chicken. You have to cook mother a nice soup out of it.

OLD HILSE (*touched, in a half friendly manner*) Well, you tell mother herself about it.

MOTHER HILSE (*with her hand cupped at her ear has, with some strain, been listening to them; now she waves him off with her hands*) Leave me in peace. I don't want no chicken soup.

OLD HILSE That's right, mother, I don't want none either. Least of all, not that kind. And you, Baumert, I want to tell you something! The devil stands on his head for joy when he sees us old people jabbering away like we was little children. And just so you know! Just so all of you know: me and you, we got nothing in common. I gave you no leave to come in here!

A VOICE Who's not with us is against us.

JAEGER (*threatening, brutally*) You got it all wrong, old man, we're not thieves.

A VOICE We're hungry, that's all.

FIRST YOUNG WEAVER All we want to do is live. And so we cut the rope we was hung to.

JAEGER And we were right! (*his fist in front of the old man's face*) Another word out of you and you'll get this right in the face.

BAECKER Stop it now, stop it! Let the old man alone. Father Hilse, we felt this way, too, once; better dead, we used to say, than start another life like this again.

OLD HILSE Haven't I lived it sixty years and more?

BAECKER It makes no difference; it's got to change.

OLD HILSE When, on Saint Nevercomes' Day?

BAECKER What we don't get from them peaceably we'll take by force.

OLD HILSE By force? (*laughs*) Then you can start digging your graves right here. They'll teach you where force is. You just wait a while, sonny!

JAEGER Because of the soldiers? We were soldiers, too. We can take care of a few companies.

OLD HILSE With your tongues. I believe it. And even if you do, for every two you chase away, ten will come back at you.

VOICES (*through the window*) The soldiers are coming. Watch out!

(*Suddenly there is a general silence. For a moment the weak sound of fife and drum is heard. Into the silence there comes a short involuntary cry: "The hell with it! I'm taking off!" General laughter*)

BAECKER   Who's talking about taking off? Who said that?

JAEGER   Who's afraid here of a few miserable helmets? I'll take the command. I was in the army. I know their tricks.

OLD HILSE   What will you use for guns? You going to use clubs?

FIRST YOUNG WEAVER   Let the old fool alone, he ain't right upstairs.

SECOND YOUNG WEAVER   He's out of his head, that's what.

GOTTLIEB   (*without being noticed has entered among the rioters; he takes hold of the speaker*) Is that how you talk to an old man?

FIRST YOUNG WEAVER   Get your hands off me, I didn't say it.

OLD HILSE   (*interrupting*)   Let them jabber, Gottlieb. Have nothing to do with them. He'll know soon enough which of us is crazy: him or me.

BAECKER   Are you coming with us, Gottlieb?

OLD HILSE   No, he ain't going with you!

LUISE   (*enters the hallway, calls in*)   Don't stop for them. Don't waste your time with these prayerbook jackasses. Come out on the square! You've got to come out on the square! Godfather Baumert, come out as quick as you can! The major's talking to the people from up on his horse. They're to go home. If you don't hurry it'll be all over.

JAEGER   (*going off*)   That's a brave husband you've got!

LUISE   Where's my husband! I see no husband here!

VOICES   (*singing in the hallway*)
    Once there was a man so small,
    Heigh, diddle diddle!
    He wanted a woman big and tall,
    Heigh, diddle, heigh diddle,
    Heigh, diddle diddle!

WITTIG   (*come down from the upper story, the horse pail still in his hand, is about to go out but remains standing for a moment in the hallway*)   Come on! Anyone who ain't a coward follow me! Hurray! (*He storms out*)

(*A group of people, with* LUISE *and* JAEGER *among them, follow him, crying:* "Hurray!")

BAECKER   Stay well, Father Hilse, we'll see each other again. (*about to go*)

OLD HILSE   I don't think so. I won't last five more years. And you won't be out before then.

BAECKER   (*stops suddenly, surprised*)   Out of where, Father Hilse?

OLD HILSE   Out of prison; where else?

BAECKER   (*laughing wildly*)   I'd never argue with that. At least you get enough to eat there, Father Hilse! (*He goes off*)

OLD BAUMERT   (*had been sitting on a stool, in a dull, brooding mood; he now rises*)   You're right, Gustav, I am a little bit drunk. But I'm still clear enough in my head. You've got your opinion of this business and I've got mine: I say that Baecker is right, even if he ends up in chains; it's always better in prison than at home. You're taken care of there; and you don't starve either. I would have been happy not to have joined them. But you must understand, Gustav, a man has got to breathe just once in his lifetime. (*He goes slowly towards the door*) Good-bye, Gustav. If anything happens, say a little prayer for me, you hear? (*He goes off*)

(*The rioters have all gone now. The hallway gradually becomes full again with curious neighbors.* OLD HILSE *knots at his web.* GOTTLIEB *has taken an axe from behind the stove and tests the blade unconsciously. Both of them are silently shaken. Outside one hears the hum and roar of a great crowd of people*)

MOTHER HILSE   Look, father, look, the floors are trembling—what's happening? What will become of us?

(*Pause*)

OLD HILSE   Gottlieb!

GOTTLIEB   What do you want?

OLD HILSE   Put down that axe.

GOTTLIEB   Then who'll cut the kindling?

(*He leans the axe against the stove.—Pause—*)

MOTHER HILSE   Gottlieb, you listen to what your father tells you.

A VOICE   (*singing in front of the window*)
    Stay home, stay home, my little man,
    Heigh, diddle diddle!
    Clean the dish and clean the pan,
    Heigh, diddle, heigh, diddle,
    Heigh, diddle diddle!

(*He goes past*)

GOTTLIEB   (*jumps up, rushes to the window with his fist clenched*)   Bastard! You try me once more!

(*The crack of a volley is heard*)

MOTHER HILSE   (*drawn together with fright*) O Jesus, Jesus, it's thundering again!

OLD HILSE   (*his hand on his chest, praying*) O Lord in Heaven, protect the poor weavers, protect my poor brothers!

(*There is a short silence*)

OLD HILSE   (*who is shaken, to himself*) There's blood flowing now.

GOTTLIEB   (*at the sound of the volley, has jumped up and taken the axe into his hands with firm grip; he is pale, almost beside himself with his deep inner excitement*) Am I still supposed to stay here like a scared dog!

A WEAVER GIRL (*calls into the room from the hallway*) Father Hilse, Father Hilse, get away from the window. A bullet went right through our upstairs. (*She disappears*)

MIELCHEN (*sticks her laughing face in through the window*) Grandfather, grandfather, they shot with their guns. Some of them fell down. One of them's turning himself all around like a wheel. And the other one's kicking like a sparrow when you tear its head off. And you should see all the blood that's coming out! (*She disappears*)

A WEAVER WOMAN Some of those will never get up again.

AN OLD WEAVER (*in the hallway*) You just wait, they're going to make a run at the soldiers.

A SECOND WEAVER (*beside himself*) Look there at the women, look at the women, look at them! Lifting their skirts up! Spitting at the soldiers!

A WEAVER WOMAN (*calls in*) Gottlieb, take a look at your wife out there, she's more man than you ever were, running around out there in front of the bayonets, like it was a dance.

(*Four men carry a wounded man through the hallway. Silence. Then a voice is heard saying clearly: "It's Weaver Ulbrich." After another few moments of silence, the voice is heard again: "It won't last long with him; he got a bullet right through the ear." Men are heard ascending the wooden stairs. Suddenly from outside: "Hurray, hurray!"*)

VOICES (*from inside the house*) Where did you get the stones?—You better clear out! From the road they're building.—Bye-bye, soldiers.—It's raining paving stones now.

(*Screams of terror and roaring spread from the street into the house itself. The door is banged shut with a cry of terror*)

VOICES (*in the hallway*) They're loading up again.—They'll fire another volley soon.— Father Hilse, get away from the window.

GOTTLIEB My God, my God, my God! Are we mad dogs! Are we to eat gun powder and bullets instead of bread! (*He hesitates for a moment with the axe in his hand. To* OLD HILSE) Do you want my wife to be shot? I won't let them! (*He rushes out*) Let me through! I'm coming! (*He goes off*)

OLD HILSE Gottlieb, Gottlieb!

MOTHER HILSE Where has Gottlieb gone?

OLD HILSE To the devil.

VOICES (*from the hallway*) Get away from the window, Father Hilse!

OLD HILSE Not me! Not even if you all go mad! (*to* MOTHER HILSE, *with mounting ecstasy*) Here is where the Heavenly Father has placed me. Isn't that right, mother? Here we will sit and do what is our duty, though the snow itself catch fire. (*He begins to weave*)

(*There is a loud volley. Struck,* OLD HILSE *raises himself up and falls forward across his loom. At the same moment there is a strengthened, resounding cry of "Hurray!" Joining the cry, the people who till now have stood in the hallway surge outside*)

OLD MOTHER HILSE (*repeats several times*) Father, father, what's the matter with you?

(*The uninterrupted cry of "Hurray!" gradually fades into the distance. Suddenly in a great hurry* MIELCHEN *runs into the room*)

MIELCHEN Grandfather, grandfather, they're chasing the soldiers out of town, they tore down Dietrich's house, it's just like over at Dreissiger's. Grandfather!? (*The child is suddenly frightened, she grows alert, sticks her finger in her mouth and cautiously approaches the dead man*)

MIELCHEN Grandfather!?

MOTHER HILSE Why don't you say something, father! You're scaring me.

Arthur Schnitzler

1862-1931

FROM *BOOK OF APHORISMS AND CONSIDERATIONS*

We sense from the works of many a writer that somehow there is genius in him; unfortunately, however, it is not precisely in his works that this genius resides.

❖   ❖   ❖

Every writer is at once a realist and an idealist, an impressionist and an expressionist, a naturalist and a symbolist, otherwise he is no writer at all. It is natural that one of these will dominate his views of art and the world according to his temperament, his natural tendencies, the age in which he writes, and his disposition toward the age and its attributes. But as soon as one of these dominates the others to the extent of serious hurt, or to the extent that one or the other of them is utterly atrophied, then there can be no doubt of his lack of talent as well as his lack of organization.

❖   ❖   ❖

The writer with a comic sense, alone among all other writers, is permitted the use of verbosity; indeed, under certain circumstances it is more a tool of his art than a hindrance, a tool which he neither dare nor can do without.

❖   ❖   ❖

Enjoyment is the intrinsic primary condition of the comic in the subjective as well as in the objective sense, and the idea of enjoyment is irreconcilable with limitations of any sort. In a certain sense the writer with a comic sense can make no end; in fact he can scarcely make a beginning. Only technical necessities force him to do so.

❖   ❖   ❖

The writer with a comic sense walks inside infinity.

❖   ❖   ❖

The tragic *Weltanschauung*,[1] regarded from the heights for the comic, in every instance gives the impression of somehow being limited, if not ridiculous or absurd.

❖   ❖   ❖

The human imagination is capable of descending as deeply into the tragic as it desires, in fact to its very depths—with the comic this is impossible.

❖   ❖   ❖

The comic, that veritable child of God, is denied nothing: not even when it comes to playing with pain, misery, and death. But permit irony, wit, or satire to attempt the same and it will appear to us as tasteless, crude, if not quite frankly blasphemous.

❖   ❖   ❖

The only valid claim which irony, wit, and satire can make in regard to the artistic is insofar as they are incidental phases or aspects of the comic. When utterly dependent upon themselves, they are capable of producing all sorts of effects—political, moral, literary; but these effects have nothing whatever to do with art in its highest sense.

❖   ❖   ❖

Excerpts from *Book of Aphorisms and Considerations* by Arthur Schnitzler, translated by Carl Richard Mueller, printed by permission of the translator.

---

[1] World view.

The comic is always demonic in its nature; the realm of wit, irony, and satire—those fallen angels of the imagination—is held prisoner within the satanic.

*   *   *

Not every literary artist of genius possesses the comic sense, but every comic literary artist (not the jokester) is a genius. The comic is a higher and more inclusive concept. It is the proper genius of the heart, for whereas kindness might well exist without the comic sense, the comic sense cannot possibly exist without kindness.

*   *   *

He who possesses the comic sense is very near to possessing genius. He who possesses wit alone, scarcely possesses even that.

*   *   *

In light plays authors generally tend to betray the deficiency of their characters; in serious dramas they betray the deficiency of their understanding.

*   *   *

A genuine tragedy ascends to the heavens like a tower on whose open storm-battered heights the body of the hero lies in state—but also at the basis of every proper comedy, buried deep down in walled up areas, there rests a tragic secret—even though the master who erected the structure knows nothing of it.

*   *   *

The reposeful effect of a work of art is primarily due to the fact that that which we call chance is totally excluded from it.

In the same way it seems that chance is also excluded from history (insofar as it is the past), and all things historical operate as necessity.

Only the present, and in particular our personal existence, is exposed and subjected to what we call chance.

There exists, therefore, no universal difference between necessity and chance, rather it is entirely a question of the spectator's point of view.

We always command a view of only a certain number of causal chains, and even so only to a certain point, while every moment we live presents to us the intersecting point of an infinite number of causal chains which emanate from infinity and return to infinity.

History, however, tells only of those causal chains which have proven themselves to have had important consequences in the highest sense of the word, and ignores the others.

An example: A great man chokes on a cherry pit. The life of this great man from birth to death is an open fact. The cherry pit, however, was important only at the moment when it took its wrong course down the great man's larynx, not during the course of his gradual rise; furthermore, we are indifferent towards any other part of the man's history.

But the cherry pit has no part in tragedy, even though it gave rise to the death of this great man. For in works of art we require that the causal chains whose intersection brings on the moment of tragedy develop with an approximately equal intensity.

The hero may be brought low through his antagonist who has causally, so to speak, attached himself to him, or through such threatening causalities as exhaustion, suicide as a result of revulsion, and so forth. He may only be brought low as a result of the cherry pit, if perhaps the basic idea of the drama is that the history of the world is capable of being directed from its course by a cherry pit. We will never permit ourselves to be convinced by the work of art (even though it conform to our philosophical or religious convictions), that the cherry pit was willed by God—even if we believe that for God all lines of causality are equal, because they all come from and return to Him. God, as it were, has always had his reasons, because He is reason itself. But in art God can only be that against which the hero revolts. A pious hero, in the dogmatic sense of the word, is an impossibility. No causal chain can be significant enough that in its intersection with the causal chain of the hero it may destroy it. Furthermore, death cannot in any way terminate the causal effects of any human being; the death of a great man in particular has consequences in the same way as the deeds of his life, often they are even more significant.

*   *   *

In the soul of the born dramatist, the individual case, tragic as well as comic, comes into being as symbol; or at least it raises itself to that level in the course of the work. Yet every attempt to invest the individual case intentionally with symbolic significance by means of such appendages as lights (as an afterthought), must of necessity fail; and it will be precisely these boasting and supercilious airs, here as in other areas, which will reveal the parvenu or the snob.

*   *   *

Playwrights who are capable of writing their fourth act before their second have always been somewhat suspect in my regard. They have obviously never experienced anything of the surprises and adventures which tend to befall a poet on his course, and which signify for him those precious, though at times not wholly accidental enticements of his travels.

* * *

Even the dilettante at times has sudden ideas which are capable of amazing even the most exacting of critics. But in contrast to the artist he generally forgets that the idea is merely a necessary prerequisite and is often nothing more than a temptation which can lead to the abyss. In any case it is necessary to know what developmental possibilities are present in the idea; to feel when the proper moment has come to conduct one of these possibilities into the light of day, and—in the event that for certain external or internal reasons it fails to materialize—to have the heart to reject it like an unwanted child.

* * *

Translated by Carl Richard Mueller

LA RONDE

Translated by Carl Richard Mueller

CAST OF CHARACTERS

THE PROSTITUTE
THE SOLDIER
THE PARLOR MAID
THE YOUNG GENTLEMAN
THE YOUNG WIFE
THE HUSBAND
THE SWEET YOUNG THING
THE POET
THE ACTRESS
THE COUNT

TIME   *The eighteen-nineties*

PLACE   *Vienna*

Scene One

THE PROSTITUTE AND THE SOLDIER

(*Late evening. On the Augarten Bridge. The* SOLDIER *comes along whistling, on his way home*)

PROSTITUTE   Hey there, honey. Come here. (*The* SOLDIER *turns around to look, then continues on*)

PROSTITUTE   Don't you want to come with me?

SOLDIER   You talking to me?

PROSTITUTE   Sure, who else? Hey, come on. I live right around here.

SOLDIER   I haven't got time. I've got to get back to the barracks!

La Ronde by Arthur Schnitzler, translated by Carl Richard Mueller, printed by permission of the translator.

PROSTITUTE   You'll get back to the barracks okay. It's nicer here with me.

SOLDIER   (*near her*)   You think so?

PROSTITUTE   Psst! A policeman could come by anytime.

SOLDIER   You're crazy! A policeman! Anyway, I'm armed!

PROSTITUTE   Come on, what do you say?

SOLDIER   Cut it out. I haven't got any money.

PROSTITUTE   I don't need money.

SOLDIER   (*stops; they are at a street light*) You don't need money? Who the hell are you?

PROSTITUTE   It's these civilians that got to pay. A guy like you can get it free anytime he wants.

SOLDIER   I think you must be the one Huber was talking about.

PROSTITUTE   I don't know any Huber.

SOLDIER   Sure, you're the one. You know— the coffee-house in Schiff Gasse? He went home with you from there.

PROSTITUTE   I've gone home with more guys than him from *that* coffee-house. Eh! Eh!

SOLDIER   Okay, let's go, let's go.

PROSTITUTE   What's the matter, you can't wait now?

SOLDIER   Well, what's there to wait for? And I got to be back at the barracks by ten.

PROSTITUTE   How long you been in?

SOLDIER   None of your business! You live far?

PROSTITUTE   About ten minutes walk.

SOLDIER   Hell, that's too far. Give me a kiss.

PROSTITUTE   (*kisses him*)   I figure that's the best part of it when you really like a guy.

SOLDIER   Oh, yeah? Hell, I can't go with you, it's too far.

PROSTITUTE   Well then, why not come tomorrow afternoon?

SOLDIER   Great. What's the address?

PROSTITUTE   Ah, but you won't come.

SOLDIER   If I promise?

PROSTITUTE   Hey, you know what? If you

[91]

don't want to go all the way home with me tonight—what about—over there?—

(*She points toward the Danube*)

SOLDIER   What's over there?

PROSTITUTE   It's nice and quiet there, too. Nobody around at this time of night.

SOLDIER   Ah, that's no good.

PROSTITUTE   Everything I got's good. Come on, stay awhile with me. Who knows, we might be dead tomorrow.

SOLDIER   All right, come on—but make it quick!

PROSTITUTE   Careful, it's awful dark over here. One slip and you'll end up in the Danube.

SOLDIER   That might be the best bet after all.

PROSTITUTE   Psst, not so fast. We'll come to a bench soon.

SOLDIER   You're right at home, uh?

PROSTITUTE   I'd like one like you for a sweetheart.

SOLDIER   I'd only make you jealous.

PROSTITUTE   I could take care of that.

SOLDIER   Ha—

PROSTITUTE   Not so loud. Sometimes these policemen get lost down here. Who'd ever think us in the middle of Vienna?

SOLDIER   Come over here, come on.

PROSTITUTE   What's the matter with you, if we slip we end up in the river.

SOLDIER   (*takes hold of her*)   There, that's better—

PROSTITUTE   You just hold tight.

SOLDIER   Don't worry . . .

*   *   *

PROSTITUTE   It would have been better on the bench.

SOLDIER   Hell, what's the difference!—Well, come on, get up.

PROSTITUTE   What are you running for?

SOLDIER   I've got to get back to the barracks, I'll be late as it is.

PROSTITUTE   Hey, uh, what's your name?

SOLDIER   What's it to you what my name is!

PROSTITUTE   My name's Leocadia.

SOLDIER   Ha!—Who ever heard of a name like that!

PROSTITUTE   You!

SOLDIER   Well, what do you want?

PROSTITUTE   Well, uh, how about a little something for the janitor?

SOLDIER   Ha! What do you think I am! So long! Leocadia . . .

PROSTITUTE   Tightwad! Son-of-a-bitch!

(*He has disappeared*)

Scene Two

THE SOLDIER AND THE PARLOR MAID

(*The Prater. Sunday evening. A path leading from the Wurstelprater, an amusement park, out into the dark avenues. The confused sounds of the park are still audible, along with the music of the Fünfkreuzertanz, a banal polka, played by a brass band. The* SOLDIER. *The* PARLOR MAID)

PARLOR MAID   Why did we have to leave just now?

(*The* SOLDIER *laughs stupidly; he is embarrassed*)

PARLOR MAID   It was so nice in there. And I just love to dance.

(*The* SOLDIER *takes her by the waist*)

PARLOR MAID (*letting him*)   But we're not dancing now. Why are you holding me so tight?

SOLDIER   What's your name? Kathi?

PARLOR MAID   You must have Kathi on the brain!

SOLDIER   I know, I know, don't tell me . . . Marie.

PARLOR MAID   Oh, it's so dark here. I'm going to be afraid.

SOLDIER   As long as I'm here you don't have to be afraid. You just leave it to me!

PARLOR MAID   But where are we going now? There are no people around. Come on, let's go back!—And it's so dark!

SOLDIER (*draws on his Virginia cigar, making the tip glow red*)   How's that for light? Haha! Oh, you beautiful . . .

PARLOR MAID   Hey, what are you doing. If I had only known!

SOLDIER   I'll be damned if you aren't the softest one of the bunch, Fräulein Marie.

PARLOR MAID   I suppose you tried them all.

SOLDIER   You notice things like that, dancing. You notice a lot of things! Ha!

PARLOR MAID   You sure danced more with that pie-faced blonde than with me.

SOLDIER   She's a friend of a friend of mine.

PARLOR MAID   The Corporal with the turned-up moustache?

SOLDIER   No, the civilian at the table with me earlier, the one with the big mouth.

PARLOR MAID   Oh, I remember. He sure is fresh.

SOLDIER   Did he do anything to you? I'll teach him a . . . What did he do to you?

PARLOR MAID   Oh, nothing—I only watched him with the others.

SOLDIER   Tell me something, Fräulein Marie . . .

PARLOR MAID   You'll burn me with that cigar.

SOLDIER   Sorry!—Fräulein Marie, why are we being so formal?

PARLOR MAID   Because we aren't well acquainted yet.

SOLDIER   A lot of people who can't stand each other aren't as formal as we are.

PARLOR MAID   The next time maybe, when we . . . oh, Herr Franz—

SOLDIER   So you *do* know my name.

PARLOR MAID   But, Herr Franz . . .

SOLDIER   Just call me Franz, Fräulein Marie.

PARLOR MAID   Then don't be so fresh— Come on, what if somebody sees us!

SOLDIER   So let them look. They couldn't see two feet in front of their own faces out here.

PARLOR MAID   But, Herr Franz, where are you taking me?

SOLDIER   Look there—two more just like us.

PARLOR MAID   Where? I can't see a thing.

SOLDIER   There—right in front of us.

PARLOR MAID   Why did you say 'two just like us'?

SOLDIER   Well, what I meant was, they like each other, too.

PARLOR MAID   Oh, be careful there! What is it? I almost fell.

SOLDIER   Just the railing around the grass.

PARLOR MAID   Stop pushing me like that, I'll fall.

SOLDIER   Psst, not so loud.

PARLOR MAID   I'm really going to scream in a minute.—Why, what are you doing . . . why . . .

SOLDIER   There's not a soul in sight out here.

PARLOR MAID   Then let's go back where there are.

SOLDIER   What do we need people for, Marie . . . what we need is . . . come on . . . come on.

PARLOR MAID   Oh, but, Herr Franz, please, for Heaven's sake, listen to me, if I'd only . . . known . . . oh . . . oh . . . yes! . . .

* * *

SOLDIER   (*blissfully*)   My God, don't . . . don't stop . . . ah . . .

PARLOR MAID   . . . I can't even see your face.

SOLDIER   My God—my face . . .

* * *

SOLDIER   Well, are you going to lay there all night, Fräulein Marie?

PARLOR MAID   Please, Franz, help me.

SOLDIER   Oh, come on.

PARLOR MAID   Oh, God, Franz.

SOLDIER   Well, what's all this with Franz all of a sudden?

PARLOR MAID   You're a terrible man, Franz.

SOLDIER   Sure, sure. Hey, wait for me.

PARLOR MAID   Why did you let go of me?

SOLDIER   Do you mind if I light my cigar again?

PARLOR MAID   It's so dark.

SOLDIER   It'll be light again tomorrow.

PARLOR MAID   At least tell me if you like me.

SOLDIER   What's the matter, Fräulein Marie, didn't you feel anything? Ha!

PARLOR MAID   Where are we going?

SOLDIER   Back.

PARLOR MAID   Please, not so fast!

SOLDIER   What's the matter now? Do you think I like walking in the dark?

PARLOR MAID   Tell me, Franz, do you like me?

SOLDIER   But I just told you I liked you!

PARLOR MAID   Don't you want to give me a kiss?

SOLDIER   (*kindly*)   There . . . Listen—you can hear the music again now.

PARLOR MAID   You mean you want to go back dancing again?

SOLDIER   Sure, why not?

PARLOR MAID   Well, Franz, I've got to go home. They'll be angry with me as is, my mistress is such a . . . she'd rather we never go out.

SOLDIER   All right, then, go home.

PARLOR MAID   Well, I was thinking, Herr Franz, that you would walk home *with* me.

SOLDIER   Walk home *with* you? Ah!

PARLOR MAID   Well, you see, it's always so lonely walking home alone.

SOLDIER   Where do you live?

PARLOR MAID   Not at all far—in Porzellan Gasse.

SOLDIER   I see! We've got quite a walk ahead of us . . . but it's too early now . . . I want to have some fun. I've got a late pass tonight . . . I don't have to be back before twelve. I'm going to dance some more.

PARLOR MAID   Sure, I know. Now it's the blonde's turn, with the pie-face!

SOLDIER   Ha!—She's no pie-face.

PARLOR MAID   Oh, God, why are men so terrible. I'll bet you treat them all that way.

SOLDIER   Oh, I wouldn't say that!

PARLOR MAID Franz, please, not tonight again—stay with me tonight, won't you?

SOLDIER All right, all right. But I'm still going back in dancing.

PARLOR MAID I wouldn't dance with another soul tonight!

SOLDIER We're almost there.

PARLOR MAID Where?

SOLDIER The Swoboda! We made good time. Listen, they're still playing it . . . tata-tatum tatatatum . . . (*He sings along*) . . . Okay, if you want to wait for me, I'll take you home . . . if not . . . so long!

PARLOR MAID I'll wait.

(*They enter the dance hall*)

SOLDIER I'll tell you what, Fräulein Marie, why not buy yourself a glass of beer? (*turning to a blonde as she dances past in the arms of a young man*) May I have this dance?—

Scene Three

THE PARLOR MAID AND THE YOUNG GENTLEMAN

(*A hot summer afternoon. His parents are already off to the country. The cook is having her day off. The* PARLOR MAID *is in the kitchen writing a letter to the* SOLDIER *who is her lover. A bell rings from the room of the* YOUNG GENTLEMAN. *She rises and goes to the room of the* YOUNG GENTLEMAN. *The* YOUNG GENTLEMAN *is lying on the divan, smoking and reading a French novel*)

PARLOR MAID Did the young gentleman ring?

YOUNG GENTLEMAN Oh, yes, Marie, yes, I, uh, rang. Yes, now what was it I . . . ? Oh, yes, of course, the blinds, would you let them down, Marie? It's cooler with the blinds down . . . yes . . .

(*The* PARLOR MAID *goes to the window and lowers the blinds*)

YOUNG GENTLEMAN (*continues reading*) What are you doing, Marie? Oh, yes. Well, now it's too dark to read, isn't it?

PARLOR MAID The young gentleman is always so studious.

YOUNG GENTLEMAN (*ignores this genteelly*) There, that's fine.

(MARIE *goes out. The* YOUNG GENTLEMAN *tries to continue reading; soon, however, he drops his book and rings again. The* PARLOR MAID *appears*)

YOUNG GENTLEMAN Oh, Marie . . . what I wanted to say was . . . uh . . . would you have any cognac in the house?

PARLOR MAID Yes, but it would be locked up.

YOUNG GENTLEMAN Well, who has the key?

PARLOR MAID Lini has the key.

YOUNG GENTLEMAN Who is Lini?

PARLOR MAID The cook, Herr Alfred.

YOUNG GENTLEMAN Well then, tell Lini to do it.

PARLOR MAID Yes, but she's on her day off.

YOUNG GENTLEMAN I see . . .

PARLOR MAID Shall I run down to the café for the young gentleman?

YOUNG GENTLEMAN No, no . . . it's warm enough as is. I don't think I'll need the cognac. But, Marie, you might bring me a glass of water. And, Marie—let it run so it will be nice and cold.—

(*The* PARLOR MAID *goes off. The* YOUNG GENTLEMAN *watches her leave. At the door she turns around to him—the* YOUNG GENTLEMAN *looks into space. The* PARLOR MAID *turns the handle on the tap and lets the water run. Meanwhile she goes into her little room, washes her hands, and arranges her curls in front of the mirror. Then she brings the* YOUNG GENTLEMAN *his glass of water. She goes to the divan. The* YOUNG GENTLEMAN *raises up half-way, the* PARLOR MAID *hands him the glass of water, their fingers touch*)

YOUNG GENTLEMAN Thank you.—Well, what is it?—Be careful; put the glass back on the saucer . . . (*He lies down again and stretches himself out*) What time is it?

PARLOR MAID Five o'clock, sir.

YOUNG GENTLEMAN Oh, five o'clock. Good.

(*The* PARLOR MAID *goes out; she turns around at the door; the* YOUNG GENTLEMAN *has followed her with his eyes; she notices this and smiles.*

The YOUNG GENTLEMAN *remains on the divan for a while, then rises suddenly. He walks as far as the door, then comes back, lies down again on the divan. He tries to continue reading. After a few moments he rings again. The* PARLOR MAID *appears with a smile which she does not try to hide*)

YOUNG GENTLEMAN Oh, Marie, what I

meant to ask you—did Doctor Schueller come by this morning?

PARLOR MAID   No, there was no one here this morning.

YOUNG GENTLEMAN   How strange. You're sure he didn't come? Would you know him if you saw him?

PARLOR MAID   Yes. He's the tall man with the black beard.

YOUNG GENTLEMAN   That's right. Was he here?

PARLOR MAID   No, sir, there was no one here.

YOUNG GENTLEMAN   (*having decided*) Come here, Marie.

PARLOR MAID   (*steps a bit closer*) Yes, sir?

YOUNG GENTLEMAN   Closer . . . there . . . why . . . I always thought . . .

PARLOR MAID   What is it, sir?

YOUNG GENTLEMAN   I thought . . . I always thought . . . About that blouse . . . What's it made of . . . Well, come on, come closer. I won't bite.

PARLOR MAID   (*goes to him*)   What about my blouse? Doesn't the young gentleman like it?

YOUNG GENTLEMAN   (*takes hold of her blouse and pulls her down to him*)   Blue? It's quite a lovely blue, isn't it? (*simply*) You're very nicely dressed, Marie.

PARLOR MAID   Oh, but the young gentleman . . .

YOUNG GENTLEMAN   Why, what is it? (*He has opened her blouse. Pertinently*) You have such lovely white skin, Marie.

PARLOR MAID   The young gentleman flatters me.

YOUNG GENTLEMAN   (*kisses her breast*) That can't hurt you, can it?

PARLOR MAID   No.

YOUNG GENTLEMAN   It's your sighing! Why are you sighing so, Marie?

PARLOR MAID   Oh, Herr Alfred . . .

YOUNG GENTLEMAN   And what nice slippers you have on . . .

PARLOR MAID   . . . But . . . Herr Alfred . . . what if someone rings!

YOUNG GENTLEMAN   Who'd ring at a time like this?

PARLOR MAID   But doesn't the young gentleman . . . look . . . how light it is . . .

YOUNG GENTLEMAN   You needn't be ashamed in front of me. You needn't be ashamed in front of anyone . . . not as lovely as you are. My God, Marie, you're so . . . Even your hair smells wonderful.

PARLOR MAID   Herr Alfred . . .

YOUNG GENTLEMAN   Don't be so silly, Marie . . . I've seen you—look quite different. One night just after I came home I went to the kitchen for a glass of water; the door to your room was open . . . well . . .

PARLOR MAID   (*hides her face*) Oh, God, I never thought you would do such a terrible thing, Herr Alfred!

YOUNG GENTLEMAN   I saw everything, Marie . . . here . . . and here . . . and here . . . and—

PARLOR MAID   Oh, Herr Alfred!

YOUNG GENTLEMAN   Come here, come here . . . come . . . there, that's right . . .

PARLOR MAID   But someone might ring!

YOUNG GENTLEMAN   Now you stop that . . . we simply won't answer . . .

❀   ❀   ❀

(*The bell rings*)

YOUNG GENTLEMAN   Goddamn! . . . Couldn't he make a little *more* noise!—He probably rang earlier and we didn't hear it.

PARLOR MAID   Oh, I was listening the whole time.

YOUNG GENTLEMAN   Well, go and see who it is—through the peep-hole.

PARLOR MAID   Herr Alfred . . . you're . . . no . . . you're a terrible man.

YOUNG GENTLEMAN   Please, go see who it is . . .

(*The* PARLOR MAID *goes out. The* YOUNG GENTLEMAN *opens the blinds*)

PARLOR MAID   (*appears again*) He must have left again. There's no one there now. It might have been Doctor Schueller.

YOUNG GENTLEMAN   (*unfavorably moved*) That will be all.

(*The* PARLOR MAID *draws nearer to him*)

YOUNG GENTLEMAN   (*avoids her*)   Oh, Marie —I'm going to the coffee-house now.

PARLOR MAID   (*tenderly*) So soon . . . Herr Alfred?

YOUNG GENTLEMAN   (*sternly*) I'm going to the coffee-house now. If Doctor Schueller should call—

PARLOR MAID   He won't come anymore today.

YOUNG GENTLEMAN   (*more sternly*) If Doctor Schueller should call, I'll . . . I'll be in the coffee-house. (*He goes into the other room*)

(*The* PARLOR MAID *takes a cigar from the smoking table, puts it in her pocket and goes off*)

Scene Four

THE YOUNG GENTLEMAN AND THE YOUNG WIFE

(*Evening. A salon in the house on Schwind Gasse, furnished with cheap elegance. The* YOUNG GENTLEMAN *has just entered, and, while still wearing his topcoat and with hat still in his hand, lights the candles. He then opens the door to the adjoining room and looks in. The light from the candles in the salon falls across the inlaid floor to the four-poster against the back wall. The reddish glow from a fireplace in the corner of the room diffuses itself on the curtains of the bed. The* YOUNG GENTLEMAN *also inspects the bedroom. He takes an atomizer from the dressing-table and sprays the pillows on the bed with a fine mist of violet perfume. He then goes through both rooms with the atomizer, pressing continuously on the little bulb, until both rooms smell of violet. He then removes his topcoat and hat, sits in a blue velvet armchair, and smokes. After a short while he rises again and assures himself that the green shutters are down. Suddenly he goes back into the bedroom, opens the drawer of the night-table. He feels around in it for a tortoise-shell hairpin. He looks for a place to hide it, then finally puts it in the pocket of his topcoat. Then he opens a cabinet in the salon, removes a tray with a bottle of cognac on it and two small liqueur glasses which he places on the table. He goes to his overcoat and removes a small white package from the pocket. He opens it and places it beside the cognac, returns to the cabinet, and takes out two small plates and eating utensils. From the small package he takes a maroon glacé and eats it. He then pours himself a cognac and drinks it. He looks at his watch. He paces the room, back and forth.— He stops in front of the large wall mirror and combs his hair and his small moustache with a pocket comb. He now goes to the door of the hallway and listens. Not a sound. The bell rings. The* YOUNG GENTLEMAN *starts suddenly. He then seats himself in the armchair and rises only when the door is opened and the* YOUNG WIFE *enters. She is heavily veiled, closes the door behind her, remains standing there for a moment while she brings her left hand to her heart as though to master an overwhelming emotion. The* YOUNG GENTLEMAN *goes to her, takes her left hand in his and imprints a kiss on the white black-trimmed glove*)

YOUNG GENTLEMAN (*softly*) Thank you.

YOUNG WIFE Alfred—Alfred!

YOUNG GENTLEMAN Come in, gracious lady . . . come in, Frau Emma.

YOUNG WIFE Please, leave me alone here for a while—please . . . please, Alfred! (*still standing at the door*)

(*The* YOUNG GENTLEMAN *stands in front of her, holding her hand*)

YOUNG WIFE Where am I?

YOUNG GENTLEMAN With me.

YOUNG WIFE This house is a fright, Alfred.

YOUNG GENTLEMAN But why? It's a very distinguished house.

YOUNG WIFE I passed two gentlemen on the stairs.

YOUNG GENTLEMAN Did you know them?

YOUNG WIFE I'm not sure. But it's possible.

YOUNG GENTLEMAN My dear lady, you must know your own friends.

YOUNG WIFE I couldn't see a thing.

YOUNG GENTLEMAN Even if they had been your *best* friends—they could never have recognized you. With that veil on I would never have recognized you myself, unless I knew.

YOUNG WIFE There are two of them.

YOUNG GENTLEMAN Won't you come in? And you must at least take your hat off.

YOUNG WIFE Oh, but, Alfred, I couldn't possibly! I told you before I came: five minutes . . . no, not a moment longer . . . I assure you—

YOUNG GENTLEMAN Well, at least your veil.

YOUNG WIFE There are two of them.

YOUNG GENTLEMAN Well, yes, then both veils . . . but at least let me see you.

YOUNG WIFE Do you really love me, Alfred?

YOUNG GENTLEMAN (*deeply hurt*) Emma—how *can* you . . .

YOUNG WIFE It's so warm in here.

YOUNG GENTLEMAN Well, you still have on your fur cape—you're sure to catch a cold.

YOUNG WIFE (*finally enters the room and throws herself into the armchair*) I'm dead tired.

YOUNG GENTLEMAN May I? (*He takes off her veils; takes the pin out of her hat, and places the hat, the pin, and the veils to the side. The* YOUNG WIFE *does not stop him. The* YOUNG GENTLEMAN *stands in front of her, shakes his head*)

YOUNG WIFE What's the matter?

YOUNG GENTLEMAN You have never been so lovely.

YOUNG WIFE Why, what do you mean?

YOUNG GENTLEMAN Alone . . . alone with you—Emma—(*He kneels beside her arm-*

chair, takes her hands in his and covers them with kisses)

YOUNG WIFE And now . . . now I must go. I've done all you asked of me.

(*The* YOUNG GENTLEMAN *lets his head sink onto her lap)*

YOUNG WIFE You promised me to be good.

YOUNG GENTLEMAN Yes.

YOUNG WIFE I'm about to suffocate in this room.

YOUNG GENTLEMAN (*rises)* You still have your fur cape on.

YOUNG WIFE Here, put it beside my hat.

YOUNG GENTLEMAN (*takes off her cape and places it beside the other things on the divan)* There.

YOUNG WIFE And now—adieu—

YOUNG GENTLEMAN Emma—Emma!

YOUNG WIFE Those five minutes are long past.

YOUNG GENTLEMAN Not a single minute has gone by!

YOUNG WIFE Now, Alfred, for once I want you to tell me exactly what time it is.

YOUNG GENTLEMAN It's a quarter to seven, exactly.

YOUNG WIFE I should have been at my sister's long ago.

YOUNG GENTLEMAN Your sister can see you anytime.

YOUNG WIFE Oh, God, Alfred, why did you ever mislead me into this?

YOUNG GENTLEMAN Because I . . . worship you, Emma.

YOUNG WIFE How many others have you told that to?

YOUNG GENTLEMAN Since I first saw you, no one.

YOUNG WIFE What a frivolous woman I've become! If anyone had told me of this . . . even just a week ago . . . even yesterday . . .

YOUNG GENTLEMAN And it was the day before yesterday that you promised me . . .

YOUNG WIFE You tormented me so. But I didn't want to do it. God as my witness, I didn't want to do it . . . Yesterday I was firmly resolved . . . Do you know that yesterday evening I wrote you a long letter?

YOUNG GENTLEMAN I didn't receive it.

YOUNG WIFE I tore it up. Oh, how I wish now I'd sent you the letter!

YOUNG GENTLEMAN It's better this way.

YOUNG WIFE Oh, no, it's disgraceful . . . of me. I don't even understand myself. Adieu, Alfred, you must let me go.

(*The* YOUNG GENTLEMAN *embraces her and covers her face with passionate kisses)*

YOUNG WIFE Is this how you . . . keep your promise?

YOUNG GENTLEMAN Just one more kiss . . . just one.

YOUNG WIFE And the last. (*He kisses her; she returns the kiss; their lips remain locked together for a long while)*

YOUNG GENTLEMAN Shall I tell you something, Emma? I know now, for the first time, what happiness is.

(*The* YOUNG WIFE *sinks back into the armchair)*

YOUNG GENTLEMAN (*sits on the arm of the chair, places his arm lightly about her neck)* . . . or better still, I know now what happiness *could* be.

(*The* YOUNG WIFE *sighs deeply. The* YOUNG GENTLEMAN *kisses her again)*

YOUNG WIFE Alfred, Alfred, what are you making of me!

YOUNG GENTLEMAN Tell me now . . . it's not really so uncomfortable here, is it? And we're so safe here, too. It's a thousand times more wonderful than our meetings in the open.

YOUNG WIFE Oh, please, don't remind me of it.

YOUNG GENTLEMAN I will think of those meetings with a great deal of joy. Every moment that I've been able to spend with you will be with me forever!

YOUNG WIFE Do you still remember the Industrial Ball?

YOUNG GENTLEMAN Do I remember it? I sat beside you during supper, quite close beside you. Your husband ordered champagne . . .

(*The* YOUNG WIFE *looks protestingly at him)* I was only going to mention the champagne. Emma, would you like a glass of cognac?

YOUNG WIFE Just a drop, but I'd like a glass of water first.

YOUNG GENTLEMAN Yes . . . Well now, where is the—ah, yes . . . (*He pushes back the doors and enters the bedroom. The* YOUNG WIFE *watches him. The* YOUNG GENTLEMAN *enters with a decanter of water and two drinking glasses)*

YOUNG WIFE Where were you?

YOUNG GENTLEMAN In the . . . the next room. (*pours a glass of water)*

YOUNG WIFE I want to ask you something now, Alfred—and promise me you will tell me the truth.

YOUNG GENTLEMAN I promise.

YOUNG WIFE Has there ever been another woman in these rooms?

YOUNG GENTLEMAN Well, Emma—this house is twenty years old!

YOUNG WIFE You know what I mean, Alfred . . . with you!

YOUNG GENTLEMAN With me—here—Emma!—It's not at all nice that you should think of such a thing.

YOUNG WIFE Then you . . . how shall I say it . . . But no, I'd rather not ask you. It's better if I don't. I'm the one to blame. Nothing goes unavenged.

YOUNG GENTLEMAN What is it? I don't understand! What doesn't go unavenged?

YOUNG WIFE No, no, no, I mustn't come to myself, or I'll sink into the earth in shame.

YOUNG GENTLEMAN (*with the decanter of water in hand, shakes his head sadly*) Emma, if you only knew how you're hurting me.

(*The* YOUNG WIFE *pours herself a glass of cognac*)

YOUNG GENTLEMAN I want to tell you something, Emma. If you are ashamed to be here—if I mean absolutely nothing to you—if you are unable to feel that for me you are all the joy in the world—then I think you had best leave.

YOUNG WIFE Yes, I'll do exactly that.

YOUNG GENTLEMAN (*taking her by the hand*) But if you are able to realize that I cannot live without you, that to kiss your hand means for me more than the endearments of all the women of the world . . . Emma, I'm not like these other young people who know how to court women—perhaps I'm too naive . . . I . . .

YOUNG WIFE And what if you *were* like these other young people?

YOUNG GENTLEMAN Then you wouldn't be here—because you aren't like other women.

YOUNG WIFE How do you know?

YOUNG GENTLEMAN (*has pulled her to the divan, seated himself close beside her*) I have thought a great deal about you. I know that you are unhappy.

(*The* YOUNG WIFE *is pleased*)

YOUNG GENTLEMAN Life is so empty, so futile—and then—so short—so terribly short! There's only one happiness . . . to find another person who will love you.

(*The* YOUNG WIFE *has taken a candied pear from the table and puts it into her mouth*)

YOUNG GENTLEMAN Give me half! (*She proffers it to him with her lips*)

YOUNG WIFE (*takes hold of his hands which threaten to go astray*) What are you doing, Alfred . . . is this the way you keep your promise?

YOUNG GENTLEMAN (*swallowing the pear, then more boldly*) Life is so short.

YOUNG WIFE (*weakly*) But that's no reason to—

YOUNG GENTLEMAN (*mechanically*) Oh, but it is.

YOUNG WIFE (*more weakly*) Now you see, Alfred, and you promised to be good . . . And it's so light . . .

YOUNG GENTLEMAN Come, come, my only, only . . . (*He lifts her from the sofa*)

YOUNG WIFE What are you doing?

YOUNG GENTLEMAN It's not at all light in *there*.

YOUNG WIFE You mean there's another room?

YOUNG GENTLEMAN (*takes her with him*) A beautiful room . . . and very dark.

YOUNG WIFE But I'd rather stay here.

(*The* YOUNG GENTLEMAN *is already through the doorway with her, into the bedroom, and begins to unbutton her blouse*)

YOUNG WIFE You're so . . . oh, God, what are you making of me!—Alfred!

YOUNG GENTLEMAN I worship you, Emma!

YOUNG WIFE Please, wait, can't you at least wait . . . (*weakly*) Go on, I'll call you.

YOUNG GENTLEMAN Please let me—let me —let me help you.

YOUNG WIFE You're tearing my clothes.

YOUNG GENTLEMAN Don't you wear a corset?

YOUNG WIFE I never wear a corset. And neither does Dusé. But you can unbutton my shoes.

(*The* YOUNG GENTLEMAN *unbuttons her shoes, kisses her feet*)

YOUNG WIFE (*has slipped into bed*) Oh, I'm so cold.

YOUNG GENTLEMAN You'll be warm enough soon.

YOUNG WIFE (*laughing softly*) Do you think so?

YOUNG GENTLEMAN (*unfavorably moved, to himself*) She shouldn't have said that. (*He undresses in the dark*)

YOUNG WIFE (*tenderly*) Come, come, come!

YOUNG GENTLEMAN (*suddenly in a better mood*) Right away—

YOUNG WIFE I smell violets.

YOUNG GENTLEMAN It's you who smell that way . . . Yes—(*to her*)—it's you.

YOUNG WIFE Alfred . . . Alfred!!!!

YOUNG GENTLEMAN Emma . . .

❋   ❋   ❋

YOUNG GENTLEMAN   It's obvious I love you too much . . . I feel like I've lost my senses.

YOUNG WIFE   . . .

YOUNG GENTLEMAN   These past days I've felt like I were going mad. I knew it would happen.

YOUNG WIFE   Don't worry about it.

YOUNG GENTLEMAN   Of course not. It's natural for a man to . . .

YOUNG WIFE   No . . . no . . . You're all excited. Calm yourself now . . .

YOUNG GENTLEMAN   Are you familiar with Stendhal?

YOUNG WIFE   Stendhal?

YOUNG GENTLEMAN   His *Psychology of Love?*

YOUNG WIFE   No, why do you ask?

YOUNG GENTLEMAN   There's a story in it that's very significant.

YOUNG WIFE   What kind of story is it?

YOUNG GENTLEMAN   There's a large crowd of cavalry officers that's gotten together—

YOUNG WIFE   And?

YOUNG GENTLEMAN   And they tell about their love affairs. And each one reports that with the woman he loves most, that is, most passionately . . . that he, that they—well, to come to the point, that the same thing happened to each of them that happened to us just now.

YOUNG WIFE   I see.

YOUNG GENTLEMAN   I find that very characteristic.

YOUNG WIFE   Yes.

YOUNG GENTLEMAN   Oh, I'm not through yet. One of them claims that it never happened to him in his entire life. But, Stendhal adds—he was a notorious braggart.

YOUNG WIFE   I see.

YOUNG GENTLEMAN   Still, it does give one a jolt, that's the stupid thing about it, even if it doesn't mean anything.

YOUNG WIFE   Of course. And besides, don't forget you promised me to be good.

YOUNG GENTLEMAN   Don't laugh, it doesn't help matters any.

YOUNG WIFE   Oh, but I'm *not* laughing. What you said about Stendhal is really very interesting. I always thought it only happened to older men . . . or with very . . . well, you understand, with men who have lived a great deal . . .

YOUNG GENTLEMAN   What are you talking about! That has nothing to do with it. Besides I forgot to tell you the nicest of all of Stendhal's stories. One of the cavalry officers even tells how he spent three nights—or was it six, I don't remember—with a woman he had wanted for weeks on end—*désirée,* you understand—and all they did during those nights was cry with happiness . . . both of them . . .

YOUNG WIFE   Both of them?

YOUNG GENTLEMAN   Yes. Isn't that remarkable? I find it so understandable—especially when you're in love.

YOUNG WIFE   But surely there must be many who *don't* cry.

YOUNG GENTLEMAN   (*nervously*)   Surely . . . that was an exceptional case, too.

YOUNG WIFE   Oh—I thought Stendhal said that *all* cavalry officers cry under the circumstances.

YOUNG GENTLEMAN   There now, you see, you're making fun of me.

YOUNG WIFE   What are you talking about! Don't be so childish, Alfred!

YOUNG GENTLEMAN   It makes me nervous, that's all . . . and I have the feeling that you can think of *nothing else.* That's what embarrasses me most.

YOUNG WIFE   I'm not thinking about it at *all.*

YOUNG GENTLEMAN   Oh, yes, you are. If only I were convinced that you love me.

YOUNG WIFE   What more proof can you want?

YOUNG GENTLEMAN   You see . . . ? You're always making fun of me.

YOUNG WIFE   What do you mean? Come here, give me your sweet little head.

YOUNG GENTLEMAN   I like that.

YOUNG WIFE   Do you love me?

YOUNG GENTLEMAN   Oh, I'm *so* happy!

YOUNG WIFE   But you needn't cry, too.

YOUNG GENTLEMAN   (*pulling himself from her, highly irritated*)   Again, again! And I begged you so.

YOUNG WIFE   All I said was you shouldn't cry.

YOUNG GENTLEMAN   You said: "You needn't cry, *too!*"

YOUNG WIFE   You're nervous, my sweet.

YOUNG GENTLEMAN   I know that.

YOUNG WIFE   But you shouldn't be. I find it rather nice that . . . that we . . . well, that we, so to speak, are good . . . comrades . . .

YOUNG GENTLEMAN   You're at it again!

YOUNG WIFE   Don't you remember! That was one of our first talks together. We wanted to be good comrades, nothing more. Oh, that was a lovely time . . . it was at my sister's, the big ball in January, during the quadrille . . . Oh, for God's sake, I should have been gone long ago . . . my sister's waiting for me —what will she say . . . Adieu, Alfred . . .

YOUNG GENTLEMAN   Emma! Are you going to leave me this way?

YOUNG WIFE   Yes—just like that!

YOUNG GENTLEMAN   Just five more minutes . . .

YOUNG WIFE   All right. Just five more minutes. But you must promise me . . . not to move. All right? . . . I'll give you another kiss when I leave. Psst . . . quiet . . . don't move, I said, or I shall get up at once, my sweet . . . sweet . . .

YOUNG GENTLEMAN   Emma . . . my dearest . . .

* * *

YOUNG WIFE   My dear Alfred—

YOUNG GENTLEMAN   It's Heaven to be with you.

YOUNG WIFE   But now I really must go.

YOUNG GENTLEMAN   Oh, let your sister wait.

YOUNG WIFE   I must get home. It's far too late for my sister. What time is it?

YOUNG GENTLEMAN   Well, how am I to find *that* out?

YOUNG WIFE   You'll have to look at your watch.

YOUNG GENTLEMAN   But my watch is in my waistcoat.

YOUNG WIFE   Then get it.

YOUNG GENTLEMAN   (*gets up with a mighty push*)   Eight.

YOUNG WIFE   (*rises quickly*)   Oh, my God! . . . Quick, Alfred, give me my stockings. What am I to tell him? They're sure to be waiting for me at home . . . Eight o'clock . . . !

YOUNG GENTLEMAN   When will I see you again?

YOUNG WIFE   Never.

YOUNG GENTLEMAN   Emma! Don't you love me anymore?

YOUNG WIFE   That's *why*. Give me my shoes.

YOUNG GENTLEMAN   Never again? Here are your shoes.

YOUNG WIFE   There's a buttonhook in my bag. Please hurry, I beg of you . . .

YOUNG GENTLEMAN   Here's the buttonhook.

YOUNG WIFE   Alfred, this can cost both of us our necks.

YOUNG GENTLEMAN   (*quite unfavorably moved*)   Why's that?

YOUNG WIFE   Well, what shall I answer him when he asks me: Where have you been?

YOUNG GENTLEMAN   At your sister's.

YOUNG WIFE   If only I could lie.

YOUNG GENTLEMAN   You'll simply have to.

YOUNG WIFE   All this for someone like you!

Oh, come here . . . let me kiss you again. (*She embraces him*)—And now—leave me alone, go in the other room. I can't dress myself with you here.

(*The* YOUNG GENTLEMAN *goes into the salon and dresses himself. He eats some of the pastry and drinks a glass of cognac*)

YOUNG WIFE   (*calls after a while*)   Alfred!

YOUNG GENTLEMAN   My sweet.

YOUNG WIFE   I think it better that we didn't cry.

YOUNG GENTLEMAN   (*smiling not without pride*)   How can one be so flippant—

YOUNG WIFE   What do you think will happen—if just by chance we should meet again one day at a party?

YOUNG GENTLEMAN   By chance?—One day? Surely you'll be at Lobheimer's tomorrow, won't you?

YOUNG WIFE   Why, yes. And you?

YOUNG GENTLEMAN   Of course. May I ask you for the cotillion?

YOUNG WIFE   Oh, but I *can't* go! What can you be thinking of!—Why I would . . . (*She enters the salon fully dressed, takes a chocolate pastry*) . . . sink into the earth.

YOUNG GENTLEMAN   Well, then, tomorrow at Lobheimer's, that will be lovely.

YOUNG WIFE   No, no . . . I'll excuse myself; absolutely—

YOUNG GENTLEMAN   Then the day after tomorrow . . . here.

YOUNG WIFE   What are you talking about?

YOUNG GENTLEMAN   At six . . .

YOUNG WIFE   Are there carriages here on the corner?

YOUNG GENTLEMAN   As many as you like. The day after tomorrow, then, here, at six. Say yes, my dearest, sweetest . . .

YOUNG WIFE   . . . We'll talk about that tomorrow during the cotillion.

YOUNG GENTLEMAN   (*embraces her*)   My angel.

YOUNG WIFE   Don't muss my hair again.

YOUNG GENTLEMAN   Tomorrow at Lobheimer's, then, and the day after tomorrow, here in my arms.

YOUNG WIFE   Goodby . . .

YOUNG GENTLEMAN   (*suddenly troubled again*)   But what will you tell him—today?

YOUNG WIFE   You mustn't ask . . . you mustn't ask . . . it's too terrible to think about. —Why do I love you so!—Adieu.—If I meet anyone on the stairs again, I'll have a stroke.— Ha!

(*The* YOUNG GENTLEMAN *kisses her hand once again. The* YOUNG WIFE *goes off. The* YOUNG

GENTLEMAN *stays behind alone. Then he sits on the divan*)

YOUNG GENTLEMAN (*smiles and says to himself*) At last an affair with a respectable woman.

Scene Five

THE YOUNG WIFE AND THE HUSBAND

(*A comfortable bedroom. It is 10:30 P.M. The* YOUNG WIFE *is reading in bed. The* HUSBAND *enters the bedroom in his bathrobe*)

YOUNG WIFE (*without looking up*) Have you stopped working?

HUSBAND Yes. I'm too tired. And besides . . .

YOUNG WIFE Well?

HUSBAND Suddenly at my writing table I felt very lonely. I felt a longing for you.

YOUNG WIFE (*looks up*) Really?

HUSBAND (*sits beside her on the bed*) Don't read anymore tonight. You'll ruin your eyes.

YOUNG WIFE (*closes the book*) What is it?

HUSBAND Nothing, my child. I'm in love with you! But of course you know that!

YOUNG WIFE One might almost forget it at times.

HUSBAND At times one *has* to forget it.

YOUNG WIFE Why?

HUSBAND Because marriage would be imperfect otherwise. It would . . . how shall I say it . . . it would lose its sanctity.

YOUNG WIFE Oh . . .

HUSBAND Believe me—it's true . . . If during these last five years we hadn't forgotten at times that we are in love with one another— well, perhaps we wouldn't be.

YOUNG WIFE That's beyond me.

HUSBAND The matter is simply this: we have had perhaps twelve love affairs with one another . . . Wouldn't you say so?

YOUNG WIFE I haven't kept count!—

HUSBAND If we had fully experienced our first love affair to its logical end, if from the beginning I had surrendered myself involuntarily to my passion for you, then we would have ended the same as every other pair of lovers. We would have been through with one another.

YOUNG WIFE Oh . . . is that what you meant.

HUSBAND Believe me—Emma—in the early days of our marriage I was afraid it would turn out that way.

YOUNG WIFE Me, too.

HUSBAND You see? Wasn't I right? That's why I think it well, for short periods of time, to live together merely as good friends.

YOUNG WIFE I see.

HUSBAND That way we can always experience *new* honeymoons with one another, simply because I never let our honeymoons . . .

YOUNG WIFE Last for months.

HUSBAND Right.

YOUNG WIFE And now . . . would you say another of these periods of friendship has come to an end?

HUSBAND (*tenderly pressing her to him*) It just might be.

YOUNG WIFE But just suppose that . . . that it were different with *me*.

HUSBAND But it's *not* different. You are the cleverest, most enchanting creature there is. I'm very fortunate to have found you.

YOUNG WIFE It's really very nice this way you . . . court me . . . from time to time.

HUSBAND (*has also gone to bed*) For a man who's been around a bit in the world—come, lay your head on my shoulder—well, marriage is something far more mysterious than it is for a young girl out of a good family. You come to us pure and . . . at least to a certain degree, ignorant, and therefore you have a far clearer conception of the nature of love than we.

YOUNG WIFE (*laughing*) Oh!

HUSBAND Of course. Because we're completely confused, made insecure by the various experiences we are forced into before marriage. You women hear a great deal and know far too much, in fact you even read too much, but you have no proper conception of what we men have to experience. What is commonly called love is made absolutely repellent to us; for, after all, what *are* those creatures on whom we are so dependent!

YOUNG WIFE Yes, what are they?

HUSBAND (*kisses her on the forehead*) Be glad, my sweet, that you have never had to become aware of such relationships. Besides that, they're mostly pitiable creatures—so let us not cast stones!

YOUNG WIFE I'm sorry—but this pity—it doesn't seem to me quite properly placed.

HUSBAND (*with gentle mildness*) They deserve it. You young girls from good families, who enjoyed the protection of your parents until a bridegroom came along to ask for your hand—you know nothing of the misery that drives most of these poor creatures into the arms of sin.

YOUNG WIFE   So they all sell themselves?

HUSBAND   I wouldn't want to say *that*. And I'm not talking only about material misery. There is also such a thing—I might say—as moral misery; a faulty comprehension of what is proper, and especially of what is noble.

YOUNG WIFE   But why are they pitiable?—They seem to be doing rather well.

HUSBAND   You have rather strange notions, my child. You oughn't to forget that such creatures as they are destined by nature to sink deeper and deeper. There's no end to it.

YOUNG WIFE   (*snuggling close to him*)   It sounds rather nice.

HUSBAND   (*rather pained*)   How can you talk like that, Emma! I should think that for a respectable woman there could be nothing more repulsive than a woman who is not . . . respectable.

YOUNG WIFE   Of course, Karl, of course. I only said it. But tell me more. I like it when you talk this way. Tell me more.

HUSBAND   About what?

YOUNG WIFE   Well—about these creatures.

HUSBAND   What are you talking about!

YOUNG WIFE   Don't you remember when we were first married, I always begged you to tell me something of your youth?

HUSBAND   Why should that interest you?

YOUNG WIFE   Well, aren't you my husband? And isn't it rather unfair that I should know absolutely nothing about your past?

HUSBAND   Surely you can't think me so tactless as to—That will do, Emma . . . it would be an absolute profanation.

YOUNG WIFE   Nevertheless . . . who knows how many other women you've held in your arms, just like you're holding me now.

HUSBAND   Women, perhaps—but not like you.

YOUNG WIFE   But you must answer me one question . . . otherwise . . . otherwise . . . there will be no honeymoon.

HUSBAND   You have a way of talking that . . . don't forget you're a mother . . . that our little girl is sleeping right in there . . .

YOUNG WIFE   (*snuggling close to him*)   But I'd like a boy, too.

HUSBAND   Emma!

YOUNG WIFE   Oh, don't be that way . . . Of course I'm your wife . . . but I'd like sometimes to be your mistress, too.

HUSBAND   Would you really?

YOUNG WIFE   Well—but first my question.

HUSBAND   (*accommodating*)   Well?

YOUNG WIFE   Was there . . . was there ever a . . . a married woman among them?

HUSBAND   What's that?—How do you mean?

YOUNG WIFE   You know what I mean.

HUSBAND   (*mildly disturbed*)   What makes you ask?

YOUNG WIFE   I wondered whether . . . that is—I know there *are* such women . . . yes. But did *you* ever . . .

HUSBAND   (*seriously*)   Do you know such a woman?

YOUNG WIFE   Well, I'm not really sure.

HUSBAND   Is there such a woman among your female friends?

YOUNG WIFE   How can I possibly say yes or no to such a thing and—and be certain?

HUSBAND   Perhaps one of your friends . . . well, people talk a great deal . . . women, when they get together—did one of them confess?

YOUNG WIFE   (*uncertainly*)   No.

HUSBAND   Have you ever *suspected* that any of your friends . . .

YOUNG WIFE   Suspect . . . oh . . . suspect . . .

HUSBAND   Then you have.

YOUNG WIFE   Of course not, Karl, absolutely not. Now that I think about it—I wouldn't suppose them capable of it.

HUSBAND   Not even one of them?

YOUNG WIFE   No—not my friends.

HUSBAND   Promise me something, Emma.

YOUNG WIFE   Well?

HUSBAND   That you will have nothing to do with a woman of whom you have the slightest suspicion that she . . . whose life is not completely above reproach.

YOUNG WIFE   I have to promise you a thing like that?

HUSBAND   Of course I *know* you would *never* seek out such acquaintances. But it could just by chance happen that . . . Well, it's not uncommon that such women whose reputations aren't exactly the best seek out the companionship of respectable women, partly as a relief for them, and partly—how shall I say it—partly as a longing for virtue.

YOUNG WIFE   I see.

HUSBAND   Yes. I believe it's quite true, what I've just said. A longing for virtue. One thing you can believe for certain, that all of these women are very unhappy.

YOUNG WIFE   Why?

HUSBAND   How can you even ask? Emma! —How *can* you?—Just imagine the kind of existence these women lead! Full of lies, viciousness, vulgarity, and full of danger.

YOUNG WIFE   Why, of course. You're quite right.

HUSBAND   Absolutely.—They pay for their bit of happiness . . . their bit of . . .

YOUNG WIFE   Pleasure.

HUSBAND   Why pleasure? How do you come to call it pleasure?

YOUNG WIFE   Well—there must be something to recommend it—or they wouldn't do it.

HUSBAND   It has *nothing* to recommend it . . . mere intoxication.

YOUNG WIFE   (*reflectively*)   Mere intoxication.

HUSBAND   No, it's not even intoxication. But it is bought at a high price, that is for certain!

YOUNG WIFE   Then you . . . then you must have known it at first hand?

HUSBAND   Yes, Emma.—It is my saddest recollection.

YOUNG WIFE   Who is it? Tell me! Do I know her?

HUSBAND   How can you think such a thing?

YOUNG WIFE   Is it long past? Was it very long before you married me?

HUSBAND   Don't ask me. Please, don't ask me.

YOUNG WIFE   But, Karl!

HUSBAND   She's dead.

YOUNG WIFE   Seriously?

HUSBAND   Yes . . . I know it sounds ridiculous, but I have the feeling that *all* these women die young.

YOUNG WIFE   Did you love her very much?

HUSBAND   One doesn't love a liar.

YOUNG WIFE   Then why . . .

HUSBAND   Intoxication . . .

YOUNG WIFE   Then it does have something to . . .

HUSBAND   Don't talk about it, please. It's all long past. I have loved only one woman— and you are that woman. One can love only purity and truth.

YOUNG WIFE   Karl!

HUSBAND   How secure, how happy I feel in these arms. Why didn't I know you as a child? I am sure I wouldn't have looked at other women.

YOUNG WIFE   Karl!

HUSBAND   How beautiful you are! . . . beautiful! . . . come here . . . (*He puts out the light*)

*   *   *

YOUNG WIFE   Do you know what I can't help thinking about tonight?

HUSBAND   About what, my sweet?

YOUNG WIFE   About . . . about . . . about Venice.

HUSBAND   That first night . . .

YOUNG WIFE   Yes . . . it was so . . .

HUSBAND   What—? Tell me!

YOUNG WIFE   Do you love me like that now?

HUSBAND   Just like that.

YOUNG WIFE   Oh . . . if you would always . . .

HUSBAND   (*in her arms*)   What?

YOUNG WIFE   Dear Karl!

HUSBAND   What did you mean to say? If I would always . . .?

YOUNG WIFE   Yes.

HUSBAND   Well, what would happen if I would always . . .?

YOUNG WIFE   Then I would always know that you love me.

HUSBAND   Yes. But you must know that already. One can't always be the loving husband, at times one must venture out into the hostile world, he must fight and struggle for an existence! You must never forget that, my child! In marriage everything has its place—that's the beauty of it all. There aren't many couples five years later who can remember their . . . their Venice.

YOUNG WIFE   Of course.

HUSBAND   And now . . . good night, my child.

YOUNG WIFE   Good night!

Scene Six

THE HUSBAND AND THE SWEET YOUNG THING

(*A private room in the Riedhof Restaurant. Comfortable, modest elegance. The gas stove is burning.—On the table are the remains of a meal, meringues with whipped cream, fruit, cheese*

The HUSBAND *smokes a Havana cigar; he leans in the corner of the divan. The SWEET YOUNG THING sits beside him on a chair and spoons the whipped cream out of a bowl, which she sucks up with great pleasure*)

HUSBAND   Taste good?

SWEET YOUNG THING   (*not letting herself be disturbed*)   Oh!

HUSBAND   Would you like another?

SWEET YOUNG THING   No, I've had too much already.

HUSBAND   You're out of wine. (*He pours her some*)

SWEET YOUNG THING   No . . . I'll just let it sit there, sir.

HUSBAND   You said "sir" again.

SWEET YOUNG THING Did I?—Well, I guess I just always forget—don't I, sir?

HUSBAND Karl!

SWEET YOUNG THING What?

HUSBAND "Don't I, Karl?" not "Don't I, sir?"!—Come, sit over here, by me.

SWEET YOUNG THING Just a minute . . . I'm not through yet.

(*The* HUSBAND *rises, places himself behind the chair and embraces her, while turning her head toward him*)

SWEET YOUNG THING What is it?

HUSBAND I'd like a kiss.

SWEET YOUNG THING (*gives him a kiss*) You're a very forward man, sir—I mean, *Karl*.

HUSBAND Are you just discovering that?

SWEET YOUNG THING Oh, no, I knew that before . . . on the street.—You certainly must have a nice impression of me, sir.

HUSBAND Karl!

SWEET YOUNG THING Karl.

HUSBAND Why?

SWEET YOUNG THING That I came here with you so easily—to a private room and . . .

HUSBAND Well, I wouldn't say it was *that* easy.

SWEET YOUNG THING But you have such a nice way of asking.

HUSBAND Do you think so?

SWEET YOUNG THING And after all, what's the difference?

HUSBAND Of course.

SWEET YOUNG THING What's the difference if we go for a walk or . . .

HUSBAND Oh, it's much too cold for a walk.

SWEET YOUNG THING Of course it's too cold.

HUSBAND And it *is* nice and warm here, isn't it?

(*He has seated himself again, puts his arms around the* SWEET YOUNG THING *and pulls her to his side*)

SWEET YOUNG THING (*weakly*) Oh!—

HUSBAND Tell me now . . . you've noticed me before, haven't you?

SWEET YOUNG THING Naturally. In Singer Strasse.

HUSBAND I don't mean today. But yesterday and the day before yesterday, when I followed you.

SWEET YOUNG THING A lot of people follow me.

HUSBAND I can well imagine. But did you notice me?

SWEET YOUNG THING Do you know what happened to me the other day? My cousin's husband followed me in the dark without recognizing me.

HUSBAND Did he speak to you?

SWEET YOUNG THING Don't be silly! Do you think everyone is as forward as you?

HUSBAND It happens.

SWEET YOUNG THING Naturally it happens.

HUSBAND What did you do?

SWEET YOUNG THING Why, nothing.—I simply didn't answer.

HUSBAND Hm . . . but you answered *me*.

SWEET YOUNG THING Well, are you sorry I did?

HUSBAND (*kisses her violently*) Your lips taste like whipped cream.

SWEET YOUNG THING Yes, they're always sweet.

HUSBAND How many other men have told you that?

SWEET YOUNG THING How many others! The way you talk!

HUSBAND Be honest for once. How many other men have kissed that mouth of yours?

SWEET YOUNG THING Are you asking me? You'd never believe it if I told you!

HUSBAND And why shouldn't I?

SWEET YOUNG THING Guess!

HUSBAND Well, let's say—but you mustn't be angry . . .

SWEET YOUNG THING Why should I be angry?

HUSBAND Well then, let's say—twenty.

SWEET YOUNG THING (*pulling away from him*) Well—why didn't you say a hundred right off?

HUSBAND I was only guessing.

SWEET YOUNG THING It wasn't a very good one.

HUSBAND Well then, ten.

SWEET YOUNG THING (*insulted*) Sure! a girl who lets herself be approached on the street and goes right to a private room!

HUSBAND Don't be so childish. What's the difference between running around the streets or sitting in a room . . . ? Here we are in a restaurant. The waiter could come in any time—there's nothing to it.

SWEET YOUNG THING That's what I thought, too.

HUSBAND Have you ever been in a private room in a restaurant before?

SWEET YOUNG THING Well, if you want me to be honest about it: yes.

HUSBAND There, you see, I like the way you answered that: at least you're honest about it.

SWEET YOUNG THING But not the way you think. It was with a friend of mine and her husband, during the Fasching Carnival last year.

HUSBAND   It wouldn't exactly be a tragedy if sometime you had been . . . well, with your lover—

SWEET YOUNG THING   Naturally it wouldn't have been a tragedy. But I don't have a lover.

HUSBAND   Now really!

SWEET YOUNG THING   Believe me, I haven't.

HUSBAND   Are you trying to tell me that I'm the . . .

SWEET YOUNG THING   The what?—It's just that I don't have one . . . well, for the last six months, I mean.

HUSBAND   I see.— But before that? Who was it?

SWEET YOUNG THING   You're awfully inquisitive.

HUSBAND   I'm inquisitive because I love you.

SWEET YOUNG THING   Do you mean it?

HUSBAND   Of course. Surely you must have noticed. But tell me about it. (*presses her close to him*)

SWEET YOUNG THING   What do you want me to tell you?

HUSBAND   Why must I always beg you? I'd like to know who it was.

SWEET YOUNG THING   (*laughing*) Oh, just a man.

HUSBAND   Well—well—who was he?

SWEET YOUNG THING   He looked a little bit like you.

HUSBAND   Oh?

SWEET YOUNG THING   If you hadn't looked so much like him—

HUSBAND   What then?

SWEET YOUNG THING   Why ask, if you already know . . .

HUSBAND   (*understands*) Then that's why you let me talk to you?

SWEET YOUNG THING   Well, I suppose.

HUSBAND   I really don't know now whether to be happy or angry.

SWEET YOUNG THING   If I were in your place, I'd be happy.

HUSBAND   Well, yes.

SWEET YOUNG THING   And even the way you talk reminds me of him . . . the way you look at a person . . .

HUSBAND   What was he?

SWEET YOUNG THING   And your eyes—

HUSBAND   What was his name?

SWEET YOUNG THING   No, you mustn't look at me that way, please.

(*The* HUSBAND *embraces her. A long passionate kiss*)

HUSBAND   Where are you going?

SWEET YOUNG THING   It's time to go home.

HUSBAND   Not yet.

SWEET YOUNG THING   No, I really must get home. What do you think my mother will say!

HUSBAND   You live with your mother?

SWEET YOUNG THING   Naturally I live with my mother. Where did you think?

HUSBAND   I see—with your mother. Do you live alone with her?

SWEET YOUNG THING   Yes, of course, alone! Five of us! Two brothers and two more sisters.

HUSBAND   Why do you sit so far away from me? Are you the eldest?

SWEET YOUNG THING   No, I'm the second. Kathi comes first, she works, in a flower shop. And then I come next.

HUSBAND   Where do you work?

SWEET YOUNG THING   I stay home.

HUSBAND   All the time.

SWEET YOUNG THING   *Somebody* has to stay home.

HUSBAND   Of course. Yes—and what do you tell your mother when you—come home so late?

SWEET YOUNG THING   It doesn't happen often.

HUSBAND   Then today for example. Won't your mother ask?

SWEET YOUNG THING   Naturally she'll ask. I can be quiet as a mouse when I come home, but she'll hear me every time.

HUSBAND   Then, what will you tell her?

SWEET YOUNG THING   Well, I'll say I went to the theatre.

HUSBAND   And she'll believe you?

SWEET YOUNG THING   Well, why *shouldn't* she believe me? I go to the theatre quite often. Just last Sunday I went to the Opera with my girl-friend and her husband and my elder brother.

HUSBAND   Where did you get the tickets?

SWEET YOUNG THING   My brother's a barber!

HUSBAND   Oh, a barber—you mean a theatrical barber.

SWEET YOUNG THING   Why are you questioning me?

HUSBAND   It interests me, that's all. And what is your other brother?

SWEET YOUNG THING   He's still in school. He wants to be a teacher. Imagine . . . a teacher!

HUSBAND   And then you have still a younger sister?

SWEET YOUNG THING   Yes, she's a little brat, you have to keep an eye on her. You have no idea how a girl can be ruined at school! Why, just the other day I found her out with a boy.

HUSBAND   What?

SWEET YOUNG THING   Yes! With a boy from the school across from us; she went out walking with him at half-past seven in Strozzi Gasse. The little brat!

SWEET YOUNG THING   And what did you do about it?

SWEET YOUNG THING   Well, she got a spanking!

HUSBAND   Are you that strict?

SWEET YOUNG THING   If *I'm* not, who *will* be? My elder sister works, my mother does nothing but nag;—everything lands on *me*.

HUSBAND   My God, but you're sweet! (*kisses her and grows more tender*) You remind me of someone, too.

SWEET YOUNG THING   Oh?—Who?

HUSBAND   Of no one in particular . . . perhaps—perhaps of my youth. Come, my child, have some wine!

SWEET YOUNG THING   How old are you? My goodness . . . I don't even know your name.

HUSBAND   Karl.

SWEET YOUNG THING   Not really! Your name is Karl?

HUSBAND   Was his name Karl, too?

SWEET YOUNG THING   No, I don't believe it, it's a miracle . . . it's an absolute—why, those eyes . . . that look . . . (*shakes her head*)

HUSBAND   And still you haven't told me who he was!

SWEET YOUNG THING   He was a terrible man—that's for sure, or else he wouldn't have walked out on me.

HUSBAND   Did you love him very much?

SWEET YOUNG THING   Of course I loved him very much.

HUSBAND   I know his kind—he was a lieutenant.

SWEET YOUNG THING   No, he wasn't a soldier. They wouldn't take him. His father had a house in . . . but why do you want to know all this?

HUSBAND   (*kisses her*)   Do you know your eyes are grey? At first I thought they were black.

SWEET YOUNG THING   Well, aren't they pretty enough for you?

(*The* HUSBAND *kisses her eyes*)

SWEET YOUNG THING   No, no—I can't stand that . . . oh, please—oh, God . . . no, let me up . . . just for a moment—please.

HUSBAND   (*ever more tenderly*)   Oh, no, no.

SWEET YOUNG THING   Please, Karl, please . . .

HUSBAND   How old are you?—Eighteen? Hm?

SWEET YOUNG THING   Nineteen.

HUSBAND   Nineteen . . . and how old am *I*?

SWEET YOUNG THING   You're . . . thirty . . .

HUSBAND   And a little more.—But let's not talk about that.

SWEET YOUNG THING   He was thirty-two when I first got to know him.

HUSBAND   How long ago was that?

SWEET YOUNG THING   I don't remember . . . You know, I think there was something in that wine.

HUSBAND   What makes you think so?

SWEET YOUNG THING   I'm all . . . well, you know—my head's turning.

HUSBAND   Just hold tight to me. There . . . (*He presses her to him and grows increasingly more tender, she scarcely repulses him*) You know something, my sweet, I think we could go now.

SWEET YOUNG THING   Yes . . . home.

HUSBAND   Not home exactly . . .

SWEET YOUNG THING   What do you mean? . . . Oh, no, oh, no . . . I won't go anywhere, what are you thinking of—

HUSBAND   Now, just listen to me, child, the next time we meet, we'll arrange it so that . . . (*He has sunk to the floor, his head in her lap*) Oh, that's nice, oh, that's so nice.

SWEET YOUNG THING   What are you doing? (*She kisses his hair*) You know, I think there *was* something in that wine—I'm so . . . sleepy . . . whatever will happen to me if I can't get up? But, but, look here, but, Karl . . . what if someone comes in . . . oh, please . . . the waiter.

HUSBAND   No waiter . . . 'll come in here . . . if he knows . . . what's . . .

* * *

(*The* SWEET YOUNG THING *leans, with her eyes closed, in the corner of the divan. The* HUSBAND *walks back and forth in the small room after lighting a cigarette. A long silence*)

HUSBAND   (*looks at the* SWEET YOUNG THING *for a long while; to himself*)   Who knows what kind of person she really is—Damn! . . . It happened so quickly . . . It wasn't very careful of me . . . Hm . . .

SWEET YOUNG THING   (*without opening her eyes*)   There must have been something in the wine.

HUSBAND   Really? Why?

SWEET YOUNG THING   Otherwise . . .

HUSBAND   Why blame it all on the wine?

SWEET YOUNG THING   Where are you? Why are you way over there? Come over here by me.

(*The* HUSBAND *goes to her, sits down*)

SWEET YOUNG THING   Tell me, do you really like me?

HUSBAND   You should know that . . . (*He quickly interrupts himself*) Of course.

SWEET YOUNG THING   You know . . . I still . . . Come on now, tell me the truth, what was in the wine?

HUSBAND   What do you think I am . . . a poison-mixer?

SWEET YOUNG THING   I just don't understand it. I'm not that way . . . We've only known each other for . . . I tell you, I'm just not like that . . . I swear to God—and if you believe that of me—

HUSBAND   There now, what are you worrying about! I don't think anything bad of you. I only think that you like me.

SWEET YOUNG THING   Yes . . .

HUSBAND   And besides, when two young people are alone together in a room, having dinner and drinking wine . . . there needn't be anything at all in the wine . . .

SWEET YOUNG THING   I was just talking.

HUSBAND   Yes, but why?

SWEET YOUNG THING   (*somewhat obstinately*)   Because I was ashamed of myself.

HUSBAND   That's ridiculous. There's no reason for it. And besides, I reminded you of your first lover.

SWEET YOUNG THING   Yes.

HUSBAND   Your first.

SWEET YOUNG THING   Why, yes . . .

HUSBAND   Now I'd be interested in knowing who the others were.

SWEET YOUNG THING   There were no others.

HUSBAND   That's not true, it can't be true.

SWEET YOUNG THING   Come on, please, don't pester me.—

HUSBAND   Cigarette?

SWEET YOUNG THING   No, thank you.

HUSBAND   Do you know what time it is?

SWEET YOUNG THING   What?

HUSBAND   Half-past eleven.

SWEET YOUNG THING   Really?

HUSBAND   Well, uh . . . what about your mother? She's used to it, uh?

SWEET YOUNG THING   You really want to send me home already?

HUSBAND   But, just a while ago you . . .

SWEET YOUNG THING   How you've changed. What have *I* done to you?

HUSBAND   Child, what's the matter, what are you talking about?

SWEET YOUNG THING   It was the look in your eyes, I swear, otherwise you'd have had to . . . a lot of men have begged me to go to private rooms like this with them.

HUSBAND   Well, would you like to . . . come here again soon . . . or somewhere else, too—

SWEET YOUNG THING   I don't know.

HUSBAND   What does *that* mean: I don't know?

SWEET YOUNG THING   Well then, why did you ask?

HUSBAND   All right, when? I just want to explain that I don't live in Vienna. I come here now and then for a few days.

SWEET YOUNG THING   Go on, you aren't Viennese?

HUSBAND   Oh, I'm from Vienna. But I don't live right in town . . .

SWEET YOUNG THING   Where?

HUSBAND   Why, what difference can *that* make?

SWEET YOUNG THING   Don't worry, I won't come looking for you.

HUSBAND   My God, if it will make you happy, come anytime you like. I live in Graz.

SWEET YOUNG THING   Seriously?

HUSBAND   Well, yes, why should that surprise you?

SWEET YOUNG THING   You're married, aren't you?

HUSBAND   (*greatly surprised*)   Why do you say *that*?

SWEET YOUNG THING   It just seemed that way to me.

HUSBAND   And that wouldn't bother you?

SWEET YOUNG THING   Well, of course I'd rather you were single.—But you *are married!*

HUSBAND   You must tell me what makes you think so!

SWEET YOUNG THING   When a man says he doesn't live in Vienna and hasn't always got time—

HUSBAND   That's not so improbable.

SWEET YOUNG THING   I don't believe him.

HUSBAND   And it wouldn't give you a bad conscience to make a married man be unfaithful to his . . .

SWEET YOUNG THING   My God, your wife probably does the same thing!

HUSBAND   (*highly indignant*)   I forbid you to say such a thing! Such remarks are . . .

SWEET YOUNG THING   I thought you said you had no wife.

HUSBAND   Whether I have or not—one doesn't make such remarks. (*He has risen*)

SWEET YOUNG THING   Karl, now, Karl, what's the matter? Are you angry? Look, I really *didn't* know that you were married. I only said it. Come on, be nice again.

HUSBAND   (*comes to her after a few seconds*) You're really such strange creatures, you . . . women. (*He becomes tender again at her side*)

SWEET YOUNG THING   No . . . please . . . besides, it's too late—

HUSBAND All right, now listen to me. Let's talk together seriously for once. I want to see you again, see you often.

SWEET YOUNG THING Really?

HUSBAND But if so, then it will be necessary . . . well, I must be able to depend on you. I can't be careful *all* the time.

SWEET YOUNG THING Oh, I can take care of myself.

HUSBAND You're . . . well, I can't say inexperienced—but you're young—and—men in general are an unscrupulous lot.

SWEET YOUNG THING Oh, Lord!

HUSBAND I don't necessarily mean that in a moral sense.—But, you understand what I mean.

SWEET YOUNG THING Tell me, what do you really think of me?

HUSBAND Well—if you *do* want to love me —only me—then I think we can arrange something—even if I *do* usually live in Graz. A place like this, where someone could come in at any moment, just isn't right.

(*The* SWEET YOUNG THING *snuggles close to him*)

HUSBAND The next time . . . we'll get together somewhere else, all right?

SWEET YOUNG THING Yes.

HUSBAND Where we can't be disturbed.

SWEET YOUNG THING Yes.

HUSBAND (*embraces her passionately*) We'll talk the rest over walking home. (*rises, opens the door*) Waiter . . . the check!

Scene Seven

THE SWEET YOUNG THING AND THE POET

(*A small room furnished in comfortable good taste. The drapes keep it in semi-darkness. Red curtains. A large writing table upon which paper and books lie about. An upright piano against the wall. The* SWEET YOUNG THING *and the* POET *enter together. The* POET *locks the door*)

POET There, my sweet. (*kisses her*)

SWEET YOUNG THING (*in hat and cape*) Oh! Isn't this nice! But you can't see anything!

POET Your eyes have to get used to this semi-darkness.—These sweet eyes!—(*kisses her eyes*)

SWEET YOUNG THING I'm afraid my sweet little eyes won't have time for that.

POET Why not?

SWEET YOUNG THING Because I'm going to stay here just one minute.

POET Won't you take your hat off?

SWEET YOUNG THING For one minute?

POET (*removes the pin from her hat and places the hat at a distance*) And your cape—

SWEET YOUNG THING What are you doing? —I have to leave right away.

POET But you must rest first! We've been walking for three hours.

SWEET YOUNG THING We were in a carriage.

POET Yes, on the way home—but in Weidling-am-Bach we walked for a full three hours. So why don't you sit down, my child . . . wherever you like;—here at the writing table; —but no, it's not comfortable enough. Sit here on the divan.—There (*He urges her down onto the divan*) If you're very tired you can even lie down. (*He makes her lie down on the divan*) There, your little head on the pillow.

SWEET YOUNG THING (*laughing*) But I'm not tired at all!

POET You just think so. There—and if you're sleepy you can sleep a bit. I shall be quite still. Besides, I can play a lullaby for you . . . one of my own (*goes to the piano*)

SWEET YOUNG THING One of your own?

POET Yes.

SWEET YOUNG THING Why, Robert, I thought you were a doctor.

POET How so? I told you I was a writer.

SWEET YOUNG THING Writers are always doctors.

POET No, not all. Myself for example. But why did you think of that?

SWEET YOUNG THING Well, because you said the piece you were going to play was your own.

POET Well . . . perhaps it isn't my own. But that's unimportant. Isn't it? It never really matters who does a thing—as long as it's beautiful—isn't that right?

SWEET YOUNG THING Of course . . . as long as it's beautiful—that's the main thing!

POET Do you know what I meant when I said that?

SWEET YOUNG THING What you meant?

POET Yes, what I just said.

SWEET YOUNG THING (*sleepily*) Oh . . . of course.

POET (*rises, goes to her and strokes her hair*) You didn't understand a word of it.

SWEET YOUNG THING Go on, I'm not that stupid.

POET Of course you're that stupid. And that's why I love you. It's a wonderful thing for a woman to be stupid. I mean, in *your* way.

SWEET YOUNG THING Why are you making fun of me?

POET You angel, you sweet little angel! Do you like lying on a soft Persian rug?

SWEET YOUNG THING Oh, yes. Go on, why don't you play the piano?

POET No, I'd rather be here with you (*He strokes her*)

SWEET YOUNG THING Say, why don't you turn on the light?

POET Oh, no . . . This twilight is very comforting. We spent the whole day bathed in sunlight. And now, you might say, we've just climbed from the bath and are about to wrap the . . . the twilight around us like a bathrobe—(*He laughs*)—or, no—that should be put differently . . . Wouldn't you say so?

SWEET YOUNG THING I don't know.

POET (*gently moving from her*) How divine this stupidity can be! (*takes out a notebook and writes down a few words*)

SWEET YOUNG THING What are you doing? (*turning towards him*) What are you writing?

POET (*softly*) Sun, bath, twilight, robe . . . there . . . (*pockets the notebook. Out loud*) Nothing . . . Tell me now, my sweet, would you like something to eat or drink?

SWEET YOUNG THING I'm not really thirsty. But I'm hungry.

POET Hm . . . I'd rather you were thirsty. I have some cognac at home, but I'll have to go out for the food.

SWEET YOUNG THING Can't you send out for it?

POET That will be difficult—the maid's not around anymore—well, all right—I'll go myself . . . what would you like?

SWEET YOUNG THING Oh, I don't think it'll be worth it—I have to be getting home anyway.

POET Child, you musn't think such a thing. But I'll tell you what: when we leave, let's go somewhere and have supper.

SWEET YOUNG THING Oh, no. I don't have time. And besides, where would we go? We might meet friends.

POET Have you that many friends?

SWEET YOUNG THING It's bad enough if even *one* of them sees us.

POET What do you mean "bad enough"?

SWEET YOUNG THING Well, what would happen do you think if my mother heard about it?

POET We could go somewhere where no one could see us; there are restaurants with private rooms, you know.

SWEET YOUNG THING (*singing*) "Oh, take me to supper in a private room!"

POET Have you ever been to one of those private rooms?

SWEET YOUNG THING Well, to tell you the truth—yes.

POET And who was the fortunate gentleman?

SWEET YOUNG THING Oh, it's not what you're thinking . . . I was there once with my girl-friend and her husband. They took me along.

POET I see. And you expect me to believe that?

SWEET YOUNG THING I didn't ask you to believe it!

POET (*close to her*) Are you blushing? It's too dark in here! I can't even make out your features. (*He touches her cheek with his hand*) But I recognize you this way, too.

SWEET YOUNG THING Just be careful you don't confuse me with someone else.

POET How strange! I can't remember anymore what you look like.

SWEET YOUNG THING Thanks!

POET (*seriously*) Isn't that uncanny! I can't even picture you.—In a certain sense I've forgotten you.—And if I couldn't recognize you by the tone of your voice either . . . what would you be?—Near and far at the same time . . . uncanny.

SWEET YOUNG THING Go on, what are you talking about—?

POET Nothing, my angel, nothing. Where are your lips . . . (*He kisses her*)

SWEET YOUNG THING Don't you want to turn on the light?

POET No . . . (*He grows very tender*) Tell me, do you love me?

SWEET YOUNG THING Very . . . oh, very much!

POET Have you ever loved anyone else as much as me?

SWEET YOUNG THING I already told you—no.

POET (*sighs*) But . . . (*He sighs*)

SWEET YOUNG THING Well—he was my fiancé.

POET I'd rather you didn't think about him.

SWEET YOUNG THING Go on . . . what are you doing . . . look . . .

POET We can imagine ourselves now in a castle in India.

SWEET YOUNG THING I'm sure they couldn't be as bad there as you are.

POET What nonsense! What a divine thing you are! If only you could guess what you mean to me.

SWEET YOUNG THING Well?

POET Stop pushing me away like that all

the time; I'm not doing anything to you—yet.

SWEET YOUNG THING You know what?—my corset hurts.

POET (*simply*) Take it off.

SWEET YOUNG THING Well—but you mustn't be bad if I do.

POET No.

(*The* SWEET YOUNG THING *has risen and removes her corset in the dark*)

POET (*in the meanwhile sits on the divan*) Say, aren't you at all interested in knowing my last name?

SWEET YOUNG THING Sure, what is it?

POET I'd rather not tell you my name, but what I call myself.

SWEET YOUNG THING What's the difference?

POET Well, the name I write under.

SWEET YOUNG THING Oh, you don't write under your real name?

(*The* POET *is close to her*)

SWEET YOUNG THING Oh . . . go on! . . . no.

POET What a wonderful fragrance rises from you. How sweet it is. (*He kisses her breasts*)

SWEET YOUNG THING You're tearing my blouse.

POET Here . . . let me . . . it's so unnecessary.

SWEET YOUNG THING But, Robert!

POET And now—enter our Indian castle.

SWEET YOUNG THING Tell me first if you really love me.

POET But I worship you. (*kisses her passionately*) I worship you, my sweet, my springtime . . . my . . .

SWEET YOUNG THING Robert . . . Robert . . .

* * *

POET That was unearthly bliss . . . I call myself . . .

SWEET YOUNG THING Robert . . . my Robert!

POET I call myself Biebitz.

SWEET YOUNG THING Why do you call yourself Biebitz?

POET My name isn't Biebitz—I just call myself that . . . well, don't you recognize the name?

SWEET YOUNG THING No.

POET You don't know the name Biebitz? Oh, how divine you are! Really? You're just saying that now, aren't you?

SWEET YOUNG THING I swear, I never heard of it!

POET Don't you go to the theatre?

SWEET YOUNG THING Oh, yes—just recently I went with . . . with the uncle of a girl-friend of mine, and the girl-friend—we went to the Opera—*Cavalleria Rusticana*.

POET Hm, then you don't go to the Burg Theatre.

SWEET YOUNG THING Nobody gives me tickets for there.

POET One day soon I'll send you a ticket.

SWEET YOUNG THING Oh, please! But don't forget! And to something funny.

POET I see . . . to something funny . . . you wouldn't want to see anything sad?

SWEET YOUNG THING Not really.

POET Not even if it's a play by me?

SWEET YOUNG THING Oh! . . . a play by you? You write for the theatre?

POET Excuse me, may I light a candle? I haven't seen you since you became my love. —Angel! (*He lights a candle*)

SWEET YOUNG THING No, don't, I'm ashamed. At least give me a cover.

POET Later! (*He approaches her with the candle and looks at her for a long while*)

SWEET YOUNG THING (*covers her face with her hands*) Robert, you mustn't!

POET You're beautiful. You are Beauty. Perhaps you are even Nature herself. You are sacred simplicity.

SWEET YOUNG THING Oh! You're dripping on me! Look at that, why can't you be careful!

POET (*places the candle aside*) You are what I have sought for for a long time. You love only me, you would love me even if I worked in a shop as an assistant. That's very comforting. I must confess to you that up to this moment I have harbored a certain suspicion. Tell me, honestly, didn't you have even the slightest idea that I was Biebitz?

SWEET YOUNG THING Look, I don't know what you want with me, but I don't know any Biebitz.

POET Oh, fame, fame! No, forget what I said, even forget the name I told you. I'm Robert to you, that's all. I was only joking. (*lightly*) I'm not even a writer, I'm a shop assistant, and in the evening I play the piano for folk singers.

SWEET YOUNG THING Now you've *really* got me mixed up . . . oh, and the way you look at a person. What is it, what's the matter?

POET It's very strange—it's almost never happened to me before, my sweet, but I could almost cry. You move me very deeply. We'll stay together for now. We'll love each other very much.

SWEET YOUNG THING Did you mean that about the folk singers?

POET Yes, but no more questions. If you really love me, then you will have no question.

Tell me, could you be free for a couple of weeks?

SWEET YOUNG THING How do you mean "free"?

POET Well, away from home.

SWEET YOUNG THING Oh!! How could I do *that!* What would my mother say? And then, well, without me around the house everything would go wrong.

POET I thought it might be nice to be alone with you somewhere where there's solitude, in the woods, surrounded by Nature, for a few weeks . . . to live there with you. Nature . . . surrounded by Nature . . . And then one day just to say goodby—to part from one another without knowing where.

SWEET YOUNG THING You're already talking about saying goodbye! And I thought you loved me so.

POET That's *why*—(*bends down to her and kisses her on the forehead*) You precious creature!

SWEET YOUNG THING Yes, hold me tight, I'm so cold.

POET It's about time you were getting dressed. Wait, I'll light a few more candles for you.

SWEET YOUNG THING (*rises*) But don't look.

POET No. (*at the window*) Tell me, child, are you happy?

SWEET YOUNG THING How do you mean?

POET I mean, in general, are you happy?

SWEET YOUNG THING It could be better.

POET You don't understand. You've told me enough about the conditions at home. I know that you're no princess. I mean, when you set all that aside, do you feel alive? Do you really feel you're living?

SWEET YOUNG THING Got a comb?

POET (*goes to the dressing-table, gives her a comb, then looks at her*) My God, but you're charming!

SWEET YOUNG THING Now . . . don't!

POET Come on, stay a while longer, stay, I'll get something for supper, and—

SWEET YOUNG THING But it's much too late.

POET It's not even nine.

SWEET YOUNG THING Oh, well then, I've got to hurry.

POET When will we see each other again?

SWEET YOUNG THING Well, when do you *want* to see me again?

POET Tomorrow.

SWEET YOUNG THING What day is tomorrow?

POET Saturday.

SWEET YOUNG THING Oh, I can't tomorrow, I have to take my little sister to see our guardian.

POET Sunday, then . . . hm . . . Sunday . . . on Sunday . . . I must explain something to you.—I am not Biebitz, but Biebitz is a friend of mine. I'll introduce you sometime. There's a play of his next Sunday; I'll send you some tickets and come to get you at the theatre. And you must tell me what you think of the play. All right?

SWEET YOUNG THING And now all this about Biebitz!—I really must be stupid!

POET I'll know you fully only when I know what you thought about the play.

SWEET YOUNG THING There . . . I'm ready.

POET Come, my sweet. (*They go out*)

Scene Eight

THE POET AND THE ACTRESS

(*A room in a country inn. It is an evening in spring; the moon shines across the hills and the meadows. The windows are open. Complete silence. The* POET *and the* ACTRESS *enter; as they enter the candle in the* POET's *hand goes out*)

POET Oh!

ACTRESS What is it?

POET The candle.—But we don't need it. Look, it's light enough. Wonderful!

(*The* ACTRESS *suddenly sinks to her knees beside the window, her hands folded*)

POET What's the matter?

(*The* ACTRESS *is silent*)

POET (*goes to her*) What are you doing?

ACTRESS (*indignant*) Can't you see I'm praying?

POET Do you believe in God?

ACTRESS Of course—do you think I'm as mean as all that!

POET I see!

ACTRESS Come here to me, kneel down beside me. For once in your life you can pray, too. You won't lose any jewels out of your precious crown.

(*The* POET *kneels beside her and puts his arms around her*)

ACTRESS Libertine!—(*He rises*) And do you know to whom I was praying?

POET God, I suppose.

ACTRESS (*with great scorn*) Of course! Of course! I was praying to you.

POET Why did you look out the window then?

ACTRESS Suppose *you* tell *me* where you've *brought* me, you abductor!

POET But, child, it was all your idea. You wanted to go to the country. You wanted to come here.

ACTRESS Well, wasn't I right?

POET Of course, it's charming here. When you think it's only two hours from Vienna—and all this absolute solitude. What wonderful country!

ACTRESS Yes, isn't it. If you had any talent you could write some poetry here.

POET Have you been here before?

ACTRESS Been here before? Ha! I lived here for years!

POET With whom?

ACTRESS Why, with Fritz, of course.

POET I see!

ACTRESS Oh, how I worshipped that man!

POET Yes, you've told me.

ACTRESS Well—I'm sorry—I can leave if I bore you!

POET Bore me? You have no idea what you mean to me. You're a world in yourself. You're Divinity, you're Spirit. You are . . . you are sacred simplicity itself. Yes, you . . . But you mustn't talk about Fritz now.

ACTRESS Yes, that *was* a mistake! Well!

POET I'm glad you see that.

ACTRESS Come here, give me a kiss!

(*The* POET *kisses her*)

ACTRESS But now it's time we said goodnight! Goodbye, my sweet!

POET How do you mean that?

ACTRESS I'm going to bed!

POET Yes—that's fine, but what do you mean goodnight . . . where am *I* supposed to sleep?

ACTRESS Surely there must be other rooms in the house.

POET But the others have no attraction for me. What do you say I light a candle?

ACTRESS Yes.

POET (*he lights the candle on the night-table*) What a pretty room . . . and how pious these people are. Nothing but holy pictures. It might be interesting to spend some time among these people. It's quite another world. We really know so little about our fellow men.

ACTRESS Don't talk so silly, and hand me my pocketbook from the table, will you?

POET Here, my only love!

(*The* ACTRESS *takes a small, framed picture from her pocketbook and places it on the night-table*)

POET What's that?

ACTRESS A picture of the Madonna.

POET Do you always have it with you?

ACTRESS It's my talisman. Go on now, Robert!

POET You must be joking! Don't you want me to help you?

ACTRESS No, I want you to go.

POET And when shall I come back?

ACTRESS In ten minutes.

POET (*kisses her*) Goodbye!

ACTRESS Where will you go?

POET I'll walk back and forth in front of your window. I'm very fond of walking outdoors at night. I get my best ideas that way. And especially when I'm near you, surrounded with my longing for you . . . wafted along by your art.

ACTRESS You're talking like an idiot . . .

POET (*painfully*) There are women who might have said . . . like a poet.

ACTRESS Go on now. But don't you start anything with the waitress.—

(*The* POET *goes out. The* ACTRESS *undresses. She hears the* POET *as he goes down the wooden stairs and as he walks back and forth in front of her window. As soon as she is undressed she goes to the window, looks down and sees him standing there; she calls down to him in a whisper*)

ACTRESS Come!

(*The* POET *hurries upstairs, rushes to her. She has in the meanwhile gone to bed and put out the candle; he locks the door*)

ACTRESS There now, you sit down here next to me and tell me a story.

POET (*sits down beside her on the bed*) Shall I close the window? Aren't you cold?

ACTRESS Oh, no!

POET What shall I tell you?

ACTRESS Well, to whom are you being unfaithful at this very moment?

POET Unfortunately I'm *not* being unfaithful—yet.

ACTRESS You mustn't worry about it, because I'm deceiving someone, too.

POET I can imagine.

ACTRESS Who do you think?

POET Well, child, I haven't any idea.

ACTRESS Just guess.

POET Let me see . . . Well, your producer.

ACTRESS My dear, I'm *not* a *chorus girl*.

POET It was only a guess.

ACTRESS Guess again.

POET One of the actors then . . . Benno—

ACTRESS Ha! That man never *looked* at a woman . . . didn't you know? That man's having an affair with his postman!

POET You must be joking!

ACTRESS Why don't you kiss me!

(*The* POET *embraces her*)

ACTRESS Why, what are you doing?

POET Why must you torture me this way.

ACTRESS May I suggest something, Robert? Why don't you come to bed with me?

POET Accepted!

ACTRESS Quickly, quickly!

POET If it had been up to me, I'd long ago have . . . You hear that?

ACTRESS What?

POET The crickets chirping outside.

ACTRESS You're mad, child, there are no crickets here.

POET Don't you hear them?

ACTRESS Come here, why are you taking so long?

POET Here I am. (*goes to her*)

ACTRESS There now, you lie there quietly now . . . now . . . I said quietly.

POET What do you mean quietly!

ACTRESS You mean you'd like to have an affair with me?

POET I thought you'd already have guessed.

ACTRESS A great many men have wanted to . . .

POET But at the moment the chances seem to be more in *my* favor.

ACTRESS Come, my cricket! I shall call you my cricket from now on.

POET I like that . . .

ACTRESS Well—who am I deceiving?

POET Who? Me, perhaps . . . ?

ACTRESS My dear child, are you sure you're all right?

POET Or someone . . . you've never even seen . . . someone you don't know, someone— destined for you, but you've never found him . . .

ACTRESS Why must you talk so silly!

POET . . . Isn't it strange . . . even you— and one would have thought.—But no, it would be depriving you of all that's best about you if one . . . Come, come—come . . .

*   *   *

ACTRESS This is so much nicer than acting in those idiotic plays . . . don't you think so?

POET Well, I think it's nice that you have the chance to play in reasonable plays now and then.

ACTRESS You arrogant dog, do you mean *your* play?

POET Of course!

ACTRESS (*seriously*) It's a magnificent play!

POET There, you see!

ACTRESS Yes, Robert, you're a great genius!

POET Now that you have the chance why not tell me why you cancelled your performance the day before yesterday. And don't tell me you were ill.

ACTRESS No, I wanted to antagonize you.

POET But why? What did I do to you?

ACTRESS You were arrogant.

POET In what way?

ACTRESS Everyone at the theatre thinks so.

POET I see.

ACTRESS But I told them: That man has every right to be arrogant.

POET And what did they say to that?

ACTRESS What *should* they have said? I never speak to them.

POET Is that right?

ACTRESS They would all like to poison me. But they'll never succeed.

POET Don't think about other people now. Be happy that we're here together, and tell me you love me.

ACTRESS Do you need even *more* proof?

POET You don't prove such things.

ACTRESS How nice! What more do you want?

POET How many others have you tried to prove it to this way? Did you love them all?

ACTRESS No. I've loved only one.

POET (*embracing her*) My . . .

ACTRESS Fritz.

POET My name is Robert. What can I *possibly* mean to you if you can think of Fritz at a time like *this*!

ACTRESS You are a whim.

POET Thanks for telling me.

ACTRESS Tell me, aren't you proud?

POET What's there to make me proud?

ACTRESS I think you have good reason to be.

POET Oh, because of *that*!

ACTRESS Of course, because of that, my little cricket!—And what about the chirping? Are they still chirping outside?

POET Certainly. Can't you hear them?

ACTRESS Of course, I hear them. But those are frogs you hear.

POET You're mistaken: frogs croak.

ACTRESS That's right, they're croaking.

POET But not here, my child, they're chirping.

ACTRESS You are the stubbornnest man I have ever come across. Give me a kiss, my little frog!

POET   Please, don't call me that. It makes me nervous.

ACTRESS   Well, what *shall* I call you?

POET   I have a name, don't I? Robert.

ACTRESS   But that's too silly.

POET   But I would *rather* you call me by my proper name.

ACTRESS   Kiss me, then—Robert.—Oh! (*She kisses him*) Are you happy now, my little frog? Hahahaha.

POET   Do you mind if I light a cigarette?

ACTRESS   I'll have one, too.

(*He takes the cigarette case from the night-table, takes out two cigarettes, lights both, and hands her one*)

ACTRESS   Incidentally, you said nothing about my performance last night.

POET   Performance?

ACTRESS.   Really . . .!

POET   Oh! That one! I wasn't at the theatre.

ACTRESS   You must like to joke.

POET   Why, no. After your cancellation the day before yesterday I assumed you wouldn't be in full possession of your powers, so I thought I'd rather forgo it.

ACTRESS   You missed something.

POET   Oh?

ACTRESS   I was sensational. The audience turned pale.

POET   Could you really see them?

ACTRESS   Benno said: My child, you were a goddess!

POET   Hm! And so ill the day before.

ACTRESS   That's *right,* and I *was,* too. And do you know why? Out of longing for you.

POET   A little while ago you said you cancelled out because you wanted to antagonize me.

ACTRESS   What do you know of my love for you! All this leaves you cold. I had a fever for nights on end. Over a hundred and five!

POET   That's quite a temperature for just a whim.

ACTRESS   You call that a whim? Here I am dying of love for you, and you call it a whim—!

POET   And what about Fritz?

ACTRESS   Fritz? . . . Don't talk to me about that terrible creature!—

Scene Nine

THE ACTRESS AND THE COUNT

(*The bedroom of the* ACTRESS. *Very sumptuously decorated. It is twelve noon, the blinds are still down, a candle burns on the small night-table, the* ACTRESS *lies in her canopied bed. Numerous newspapers are strewn across the bed cover.*

The COUNT *enters in the uniform of a Captain of the Dragoons. He remains standing at the door*)

ACTRESS   Oh, Herr Count.

COUNT   Your dear mother gave me permission, or I should never have—

ACTRESS   Please, do come in.

COUNT   I kiss your hand. Excuse me—when one enters directly from the street . . . the fact is I still can't see a thing. Ah, yes . . . here we are—(*at the bed*)—I kiss your hand.

ACTRESS   Won't you have a seat, Herr Count.

COUNT   Your mother said that you weren't feeling well, Fräulein. I do hope it's nothing serious.

ACTRESS   Nothing serious? I was on the verge of death!

COUNT   Good heavens, is that possible?

ACTRESS   In any case I think it very nice of you to have troubled yourself on my account.

COUNT   On the verge of death! And last night you played like a goddess.

ACTRESS   Yes, it was rather a triumph, wasn't it?

COUNT   Colossal! The audience was absolutely carried away. And I won't even tell you what I thought.

ACTRESS   Thank you for the lovely flowers.

COUNT   Don't mention it.

ACTRESS   (*indicates with her eyes a large basket of flowers sitting on a small table at the window*)   There they are.

COUNT   Yesterday you were absolutely overwhelmed with flowers and garlands.

ACTRESS   They are all still in my dressing room. I brought only your basket with me.

COUNT   (*kisses her hand*)   That was very sweet of you. (*The* ACTRESS *suddenly takes his hand and kisses it*) But, my dear!

ACTRESS   Don't be afraid, Herr Count, that doesn't oblige you in any way.

COUNT   What an extraordinary creature you are . . . one might almost say an enigma.— (*pause*)

ACTRESS   Fräulein Birken might be easier to . . . solve.

COUNT   Oh, little Birken is no problem, although . . . but of course I know her only superficially.

ACTRESS   Ha!

COUNT   Believe me. But you are a problem. A kind that I have always lorged for. I never realized until last night, when I saw you act for the first time, what an extraordinary pleasure I had let slip from me.

ACTRESS   Is that possible?

COUNT   Yes. You see, I find it rather difficult to get to the theatre. I'm accustomed to dining late . . . so that when I *do* arrive the best part of the play has already gone by.

ACTRESS   From now on you must eat earlier.

COUNT   Yes, I've considered that. Or perhaps not dining at all. Actually dining is no pleasure for me anymore.

ACTRESS   What *does* a young old man like you take pleasure in?

COUNT   I often ask myself the same question! But I am not an old man. There must be another reason.

ACTRESS   Do you think so?

COUNT   Yes. For example, Louie says I'm a philosopher. What he means, Fräulein, is that I think too much.

ACTRESS   Think . . . yes, well that *is* a misfortune.

COUNT   I have too much time on my hands, and so I think. But then, you see, I thought that if they were to transfer me to Vienna things might be different. There's amusement and stimulation here. But the fact is, it's not much different here than it was there.

ACTRESS   Where is "there"?

COUNT   Why, in Hungary . . . the small towns where I was generally stationed.

ACTRESS   Whatever did you do in Hungary?

COUNT   Well, I just told you, Fräulein, the Army.

ACTRESS   Well then why did you stay *so long* in Hungary?

COUNT   That's the way it happens.

ACTRESS   That must be enough to drive one mad.

COUNT   Why do you say that? Of course there's more to do there than here. Such things as training recruits, breaking in the horses . . . and then, too, the region isn't all as bad as they say. It's really quite lovely, the low-lying plains —and those sunsets . . . It's a pity I'm not a painter; I've often thought that if I were, I should paint it. There *was one* young man in the regiment, his name was Splany, he could have done it.—But why am I telling you all these dull stories, Fräulein?

ACTRESS   Oh, please, I'm terribly amused.

COUNT   You know, Fräulein, it's quite easy talking to you. Louie told me it would be. And that's something you don't often find.

ACTRESS   Well, in Hungary, I suppose not.

COUNT   And definitely not in Vienna! People are the same everywhere. The only difference is that where there are more people, the crowds are larger. Tell me, Fräulein, are you fond of people?

ACTRESS   Fond? I hate them! I can't *look* at a human being! I *never* see them! I am always alone, no one *ever* enters this house.

COUNT   You see, I was right when I thought you a misanthrope! It happens often where artists are concerned. When one exists in those higher regions . . . well, it's alright for you, at least you know why you're living!

ACTRESS   Whoever told you that? I have no idea why I'm living!

COUNT   But I beg to differ—you're famous —celebrated . . .

ACTRESS   Is that what you call happiness?

COUNT   Happiness? I'm sorry, but there is no such thing as happiness. Most of the things that people talk about so freely don't really exist . . . love, for example. It's the same there, too.

ACTRESS   You're quite right.

COUNT   Pleasure . . . intoxication . . . fine, there's nothing to say against them . . . they are something positive. If I take pleasure in something, fine, at least I *know* I take pleasure in it. Or else I feel myself intoxicated, excellent. That's positive, too. And when it's past, well then, it's past.

ACTRESS   (*grandly*)   It's past!

COUNT   But as soon as one fails to, how shall I say it, as soon as one fails to live for the moment, and starts thinking about the future or the past . . . well, then it's all over with. The future . . . is sad . . . the past is uncertain. In short, it only confuses one. Am I right?

ACTRESS   (*nods, her eyes large*)   You have gone to the heart of the matter.

COUNT   So you see, my dear madam, once you have perceived the truth of this, it really makes little difference whether you live in Vienna or in Pussta or even in Steinamanger. For example . . . excuse me, where can I put my cap? . . . Oh, thank you . . . now what were we talking about?

ACTRESS   Steinamanger.

COUNT   Ah, yes. It's just as I said, the difference is very slight. It's all the same to me whether I spend my evenings at the Casino or at the Club.

ACTRESS   And how does all this relate to love?

COUNT   If one believes in it, he'll always find someone around to love him.

ACTRESS   Fräulein Birken, for example.

COUNT   Really, my dear, I don't know why you always seem to return to poor little Birken.

ACTRESS   She's your mistress, isn't she?

COUNT Whoever said that?

ACTRESS Everyone knows.

COUNT Except me. Isn't that remarkable!

ACTRESS You even fought a duel for her sake!

COUNT Perhaps I was even killed and didn't notice.

ACTRESS Yes, Count, you *are* a man of honor. Won't you sit closer?

COUNT May I?

ACTRESS Here. (*She draws him to her and runs her fingers through his hair*) I knew you would come today!

COUNT How?

ACTRESS I knew yesterday at the theatre.

COUNT Could you see me from the stage?

ACTRESS My dear man, couldn't you tell that I was playing for no one but you?

COUNT How can that be?

ACTRESS I felt like I was walking on air when I saw you in the first row!

COUNT Walking on air? On my account? I had no idea you even saw me!

ACTRESS You know, you can drive a woman to desperation with your "dignity."

COUNT Fräulein!

ACTRESS "Fräulein"!—At least take off your sabre!

COUNT If I may. (*He unbuckles the belt and leans it against the bed*)

ACTRESS And now kiss me.

(*The* COUNT *kisses her, she does not let loose of him*)

ACTRESS Oh, how I wish I had never seen you!

COUNT It's much better like this!—

ACTRESS Count, you are a *poseur*!

COUNT I? How so?

ACTRESS How happy do you think many a man would be to find himself in your place right now!

COUNT But I *am* happy. Very.

ACTRESS I thought there was no happiness. Why are you looking at me that way? I do believe you are afraid of me, Herr Count!

COUNT As I said, madam, you are a problem.

ACTRESS Oh, don't bother me with your philosophizing . . . come here. And now, ask me for something. You can have anything you like. You're far too handsome.

COUNT If I have your permission then— (*kissing her hand*)—I will return tonight.

ACTRESS Tonight? . . . But I'll be playing.

COUNT After the theatre.

ACTRESS Is that all you're asking for?

COUNT I shall ask for everything else *after* the theatre.

ACTRESS (*offended*) And you'll have to ask for a long time, you miserable *poseur*.

COUNT Well, you see, you see, we've been so open with one another up till now. I would really find all that so much nicer *after* the theatre . . . more comfortable than now. Well, I have the feeling that a door could open on us at any moment . . .

ACTRESS The door doesn't open from the outside.

COUNT Don't you feel it would be careless to spoil something at the start, something that might quite possibly turn out to be beautiful?

ACTRESS "Quite possibly"!

COUNT To be quite honest, I find love in the morning really rather ghastly.

ACTRESS Well—you are easily the most insane man I have ever met!

COUNT I'm not talking about just *any* woman . . . after all, in general it scarcely matters. But women like you . . . no, call me a fool a hundred times over if you like . . . women like you . . . aren't to be had before breakfast. And so . . . you see . . .

ACTRESS My God, but you're sweet!

COUNT You do see what I mean, don't you. The way I see it . . .

ACTRESS *Tell* me how you see it!

COUNT I thought that . . . I would wait for you after the theatre in a carriage, and then we could drive somewhere together and have supper—

ACTRESS I am not Fräulein Birken.

COUNT I didn't say you were. It's that one must be in the mood. And I always find myself in the mood after supper. It's always nicer that way, when after supper you drive home together, and then . . .

ACTRESS And then what?

COUNT Well, then . . . then it simply depends on how things develop.

ACTRESS Sit closer to me. Closer.

COUNT (*sitting on the bed*) I must say there's a lovely aroma coming from your pillows—mignonette, isn't it?

ACTRESS Don't you find it terribly hot in here?

(*The* COUNT *bends down and kisses her throat*)

ACTRESS Oh, but, my dear Count, that's not on your program.

COUNT Who says so? I have no program.

(*The* ACTRESS *draws him to her*)

COUNT Yes, it *is* warm.

ACTRESS Isn't it? And so dark, as though it

were evening . . . (*pulls him to her*) It *is* evening . . . it's night.—Close your eyes if it's too light for you. Come! Come!

(*The* COUNT *no longer resists*)

*   *   *

ACTRESS   What was that about being in the mood, you *poseur*?

COUNT   You're a little devil.

ACTRESS   What a thing to say!

COUNT   Well then, an angel.

ACTRESS   You should have been an actor! Really! You understand women! Do you know what I shall do now?

COUNT   Well?

ACTRESS   I shall tell you that I will never see you again.

COUNT   But why?

ACTRESS   No, no. You're too dangerous for me! You'd drive a woman mad. There you are, standing in front of me now, as though nothing had happened.

COUNT   But . . .

ACTRESS   I beg you to remember, Herr Count, that I have just been your mistress.

COUNT   I shall never forget it!

ACTRESS   And what about tonight?

COUNT   How do you mean that?

ACTRESS   Well—you were going to wait for me after the theatre?

COUNT   Yes, fine, what about tomorrow?

ACTRESS   What do you mean 'tomorrow'? We were talking about tonight.

COUNT   But that wouldn't make sense.

ACTRESS   You old fool!

COUNT   Don't misunderstand. I mean it more, how shall I say, from the spiritual standpoint.

ACTRESS   What's your soul got to do with it?

COUNT   Believe me, that's part of it, too. I find it completely false that the two can be kept apart.

ACTRESS   Don't bother me with your philosophizing. When I want that, I'll read books.

COUNT   One doesn't learn from books.

ACTRESS   I agree! That's why you should wait for me this evening. We'll come to some agreement about the soul, you scoundrel!

COUNT   Well then, with your permission, I shall have my carriage waiting—

ACTRESS   . . . After the theatre.

COUNT   Of course. (*He buckles on his sabre*)

ACTRESS   What are you doing?

COUNT   I think it's time I were going. For a formal call I think I've overstayed my time a bit.

ACTRESS   But tonight it won't be a formal call.

COUNT   Really?

ACTRESS   You let me take care of that. And now give me another kiss, my little philosopher. Here, you seducer, you . . . sweet child, you slave-dealer, you polecat . . . you . . . (*After having kissed him vigorously several times, she pushes him vigorously from her*) Count, it was a great honor!

COUNT   I kiss your hand, Fräulein! (*at the door*) Au revoir!

ACTRESS   Adieu, Steinamanger!

Scene Ten

THE COUNT AND THE PROSTITUTE

(*Morning, around six o'clock. A miserable little room with one window; the dirty yellow blinds are down; worn green curtains on the window. A chest-of-drawers with a few photographs on it and a conspicuously tasteless, cheap woman's hat. A number of cheap Japanese fans behind the mirror. On the table, covered over with a reddish cloth, stands a kerosene lamp, still feebly alight and emitting its odor, with a yellow paper lampshade. Beside it is a jug with left-over beer and a half empty glass. On the floor beside the bed there is a disarray of woman's clothing, as though they had rapidly been thrown down. The* PROSTITUTE *is asleep in the bed; she breathes quietly. Fully dressed on the divan lies the* COUNT *in his overcoat, his hat on the floor at the head of the divan*)

COUNT (*moves, rubs his eyes, rises quickly, remains sitting, looks around*)   How did I get . . . Oh yes . . . then I did go home with that female . . . (*He rises quickly, sees her bed*) And here she is . . . The things that happen to a man my age! I can't remember . . . did they carry me up here? No . . . I saw—I came into the room . . . yes, I was still awake . . . or . . . or is it that this room reminds me of somewhere else?—My God, yes, yes . . . I saw it yesterday all right . . . (*looks at his watch*) Hm! Yesterday! A couple hours ago, that's when I saw it—But I knew that something had to happen . . . I felt it . . . yesterday when I started drinking, I felt that something . . . And what *did* happen?—Nothing . . . Or did I . . . ? My God . . . not for . . . not for ten years has anything happened to me that I haven't remembered. Well, in any case I was drunk. If only I could remember when I got that way.—At least I remember when I went into that whores' café with Louie and . . . no, no . . . it was after we left Sacher's . . . and then on the way . . . Yes, that's right, I was driving along with Louie . . . But what am I wracking my brains for! It doesn't matter. Just see that you get out of here. (*gets up; the lamp shakes*) Oh! (*He looks at the sleeping girl*) At least *she's* sleeping soundly. I don't remember a thing, but I'll put the money on the night-table . . . and goodbye . . . (*He stands looking at her a long while*) If only one didn't know what she is! (*He looks at her thoughtfully for a long while*) I've known a lot of her kind that didn't look so virtuous even in their sleep. My God . . . Louie would say I'm philosophizing . . . but it's true, it seems to me Sleep washes away all differences—like his brother, Death.—Hm, I wish I knew whether . . . no, I'd remember that. No, no, I came straight in and fell onto the divan . . . and nothing happened . . . Isn't it remarkable how sometimes all women look alike.—Well, time to go. (*He is about to leave*) Oh, I forgot. (*He takes out his wallet and is about to remove a bill*)

PROSTITUTE (*wakes up*)   What! . . . who's here so early? (*recognizing him*) Hello!

COUNT   Good morning. Sleep well?

PROSTITUTE (*stretches herself*)   Oh! Come here. Give me a little kiss.

COUNT (*bends down to her, considers, pulls up*)   I was just going . . .

PROSTITUTE   Going?

COUNT   It's about time.

PROSTITUTE   You want to go like this?

COUNT (*almost embarrassed*)   Well . . .

PROSTITUTE   All right, so long; come back some other time.

COUNT   Yes. Goodbye. Won't you give me your hand? (*The* PROSTITUTE *extends her hand from under the cover*)

COUNT (*takes the hand and kisses it mechanically, becomes aware of himself, laughs*)   Like a princess. After all, if one saw only. . . .

PROSTITUTE   What are you looking at me like that for?

COUNT   If one saw only that little head, like now . . . when they wake one looks as innocent as the next . . . my God, one could imagine all sorts of things, if only it didn't smell so of kerosene . . .

PROSTITUTE   Yes, that lamp's always a bother.

COUNT   How old are you?

PROSTITUTE   Guess.

COUNT   Twenty-four.

PROSTITUTE   Sure, sure.

COUNT   You mean you're older?

PROSTITUTE   I'm going on twenty.

COUNT   And how long have you . . .

PROSTITUTE   How long have I been in the business? A year.

COUNT   You started early.

PROSTITUTE   Better early than too late.

COUNT (*sits down on the bed*)   Tell me something, are you really happy?

PROSTITUTE   What?

COUNT   Well, what I mean is, how are you getting on?

PROSTITUTE   Oh, right now I'm doing all right.

COUNT   I see.—Tell me, didn't it ever occur to you that you could become something else?

PROSTITUTE   Like what?

COUNT   Well . . . you're really quite a lovely girl. You could have a lover, for example.

PROSTITUTE   What makes you think I don't have one?

COUNT   Yes, of course—what I meant was one who, you know, one who would support you, so that you wouldn't have to go around with just anyone who came along.

PROSTITUTE   I *don't* go around with just anyone. Thank God I'm not that hard up. I pick and choose.

(*The* COUNT *looks around the room*)

PROSTITUTE (*noticing this*)   Next month we're moving into town. Spiegel Gasse.

COUNT   We? Who do you mean?

PROSTITUTE   Why, the madam and the couple other girls who still live here.

COUNT   There are others living here?

PROSTITUTE   Next door . . . can't you hear? . . . that's Milli, she was in the café, too.

COUNT   Someone's snoring.

PROSTITUTE   That's Milli all right! She'll snore like that all day long till ten at night. Then she gets up and goes to the café.

COUNT   That must be a terrible life.

PROSTITUTE   Sure. The madam gets fed up enough, too. I'm out on the street everyday by noon.

COUNT   What do you do on the street at noon?

PROSTITUTE   What do you think I do? I walk my beat.

COUNT   Oh, I see . . . of course . . . (*He rises, takes out his wallet, and places a bill on the night-table*)   Goodbye.

PROSTITUTE   Going so soon?—So long.— Come back again soon. (*turns on her side*)

COUNT (*stops again*)   Say, tell me something; does it really mean anything to you anymore?

PROSTITUTE   What?

COUNT   I mean, there's no enjoyment in it for you anymore?

PROSTITUTE   (*yawns*)   I'm sleepy.

COUNT   It makes no difference whether a man is young or old . . .

PROSTITUTE   Why are you asking all this?

COUNT   . . . Well—(*suddenly struck by an idea*) My God, now I remember who you remind me of, it's . . .

PROSTITUTE   I remind you of someone?

COUNT   It's unbelieveable, unbelieveable! Please, now, don't say a word, just for a moment . . . (*looks at her*) The same face exactly, the same face exactly. (*He kisses her suddenly on the eyes*)

PROSTITUTE   Say . . .

COUNT   My God, what a pity that you . . . that you aren't something else . . . you could really be a success.

PROSTITUTE   You're just like Franz.

COUNT   Who is Franz?

PROSTITUTE   A waiter at the café.

COUNT   How am I like Franz?

PROSTITUTE   He's always saying I could be a success, and that I should get married.

COUNT   Why don't you?

PROSTITUTE   No, thanks . . . no, I don't want to get married, not for all the money in the world. Later, maybe.

COUNT   Your eyes . . . it's your eyes that . . . Louie would say I'm a fool—but I do want to kiss your eyes, just once more . . . there . . . and now, goodbye, now I really must go.

PROSTITUTE   So long . . .

COUNT   (*at the door*)   Say . . . tell me . . . doesn't it surprise you that . . .

PROSTITUTE   That what?

COUNT   That I want nothing of you?

PROSTITUTE   A lot of men aren't in the mood for it in the morning.

COUNT   Yes, I suppose . . . (*to himself*) How silly of me to want her to be surprised . . . Well, goodbye . . . (*He is at the door*) Still, it does annoy me. I know that girls like this do it only for the money . . . but why did I say: 'girls like this'? . . . it's nice at least that . . . that she doesn't pretend, that should be some satisfaction . . . (*to her*) Say—I'll tell you what . . . I'll come back again soon.

PROSTITUTE   (*with her eyes closed*)   Good.

COUNT   When are you at home?

PROSTITUTE   I'm always in. Just ask for Leocadia.

COUNT   Leocadia . . . Good.—Well then, goodbye. (*at the door*) I can still feel that wine. Isn't it remarkable . . . here I am with one of her kind, and I did nothing more than kiss her eyes, just because she reminded me of someone . . . (*turns to her again*) Say, Leocadia, does it happen often that a man leaves you . . . like this?

PROSTITUTE   Like what?

COUNT   Like me.

PROSTITUTE   In the morning?

COUNT   No . . . I wondered whether it happened often that a man comes to you . . . and doesn't ask for anything.

PROSTITUTE   No, that never happened to me.

COUNT   What do you mean? Do you think I don't like you?

PROSTITUTE   Why shouldn't you like me? You liked me well enough last night.

COUNT   And I like you now, too.

PROSTITUTE   But you liked me better last night.

COUNT   Why do you say *that?*

PROSTITUTE   Why all the silly questions?

COUNT   Last night . . . yes, well, didn't I fall onto the divan right away?

PROSTITUTE   Sure you did . . . with me.

COUNT   With you?

PROSTITUTE   Sure, don't you remember?

COUNT   You mean I . . . that we . . . yes . . .

PROSTITUTE   But you went right to sleep.

COUNT   Right to sleep . . . I see . . . So that's the way it was . . .

PROSTITUTE   Sure, lovey. You must have had a real load on, not to remember.

COUNT   I see . . .—Still . . . there *is* a faint resemblance . . . So long . . . (*he listens*) What's that noise?

PROSTITUTE   The parlor maid's up already. Why not give her a little something on the way out. The door's open, so you'll save on the janitor.

COUNT   Of course. (*in the entrance hall*) Well . . . it would have been beautiful even if I had only kissed you on the eyes. That would almost have been an adventure in itself . . . Well, I suppose it wasn't meant to be.

(*The* PARLOR MAID *stands at the door, holding it open for him*) Oh—here you are . . . Good night.—

PARLOR MAID   Good morning.

COUNT   Yes, of course . . . good morning . . . good morning.

Frank Wedekind

1864-1918

THE ART OF ACTING: A GLOSSARY

MAX REINHARDT

Our hope and our unhappy love. The unfathomable sorcerer Klingsor.[1] What utter and tremendous delight would Nietzsche have found in Max Reinhardt. A man for whom the impossible became possible. A cultural phenomenon of first rank. The after-effects of Bismarck in the intellectual life of the German people are gradually becoming less political and far more poetic. On the other hand, the foundation of Reinhardt's theatre, in addition to its artistic importance, is gradually also becoming politically important. The reawakening of intellectual independence in southern Germany lures him from the theatre-satiated and literature-jaded city of Berlin to Frankfurt and Munich.

In Munich Georg Stollberg had of course favorably prepared the way for him for half a generation. If Georg Stollberg hasn't the expansion-drive of Reinhardt, then he has at least proven from the first day of his activity to the present to have an equal amount of energy, consistency, and independence as Reinhardt when it comes to the question of fighting for new dramatic works for the theatre, even when it is in contradiction to the momentarily authorative literary current. The theatre battles which raged in the Munich *Schauspielhaus*[2] were the direct result of the uncompromising artistic convictions of Georg Stollberg, and with every day that passes it becomes clearer that it was the Munich *Schauspielhaus* which

was victorious. For that reason Munich for Max Reinhardt is not a city to be conquered, but a brother-in-cause, ready to receive him with open arms. However, in Stuttgart, Darmstadt, Mannheim, Karlsruhe, Heidelberg and Konstanz the appearance of Max Reinhardt would with a single stroke call together and unite all those in southern Germany who delight in theatre and who have only to wait for that great event which will set them in motion toward achieving their own independence. Bismarck once spoke of the "putrid fermenting of southern German lack of discipline." This appears equally as rash to me as if a southern German were to speak of the "boastful and unwarranted pride of northern German narrow-mindedness." But surely the successful development of German culture rests not upon the conflict between the southern German lack of discipline and the northern German narrow-mindedness; it rests rather upon the cooperation between northern German proficiency and southern German richness of soul, between northern German freshness of intellect and southern German depth of feeling. If ever there was a common leader for this cooperative effort, one who stands high enough to make both elements serve his purpose, then it is Max Reinhardt.

Why then do we say "our unhappy love"?

Because in the metropolis of Berlin he is the only one who can be considered as being interested in a new art. Because he, like all others who are alone in their endeavor, very often have not enough time. Because he is laid claim to by the illustrious dead—all of these are facts which add only to his fame and glory. That he can make possible the impossible is something

---

"The Art of Acting" by Frank Wedekind, translated by Carl Richard Mueller, printed by permission of the translator.

[1] A magician in Wagner's *Parzival*, and who is the main enemy of the Knights of the Holy Grail.
[2] Theatre.

which he has proven with my tragedy of childhood, *The Awakening of Spring.* But his sorcery does not always work advantageously with the plainly possible. Since it is his profession to change water into wine, it happens at times, when there is no water at hand, that he changes wine into a beverage which bears little relationship to its original vine. But these are small failings which are inseparable from the great phenomena of all ages.

❋   ❋   ❋

TRANSITION

The works of the naturalist playwrights owe their uncommonly rapid dissemination not least of all to the advantage that they were childishly simple to act. This is no objection to their literary and social qualities. The actor stuck his hands in his pockets, placed himself with his back to the audience next to the prompt-box, and waited with the greatest of ease until he heard the word called out to him by the prompter. If he happened to misunderstand the word, then there was no particular harm done, because his audience for the most part consisted of stagehands playing cards behind the scenes. For years the spectator demanded nothing more of the actor than that he should not break the mood with the spoken word.

The actors who celebrated their triumphs in this form of art are no longer of any use to us. The drama of today concerns itself with far more serious problems and cultivates a far higher art form than the naturalists could ever manage. The fact that the literary production of today cannot point to a series of successes is surely no proof whatever that its stage technique exists on a lower level than those dramas of twenty years ago. More than one of today's practicing dramatists has found himself dissatisfied not because his stagecraft was too bad, but on the contrary because it was too good for the abilities of today's literary theatre.

❋   ❋   ❋

COMPENSATION

The collected thrashings which the press has seen fit to bestow upon me for my dramas I would now like to pass on undiminished and unmitigated to today's German acting profession. It has for years now proven itself unfit to present effectively the works of today's aspiring German dramatists.

❋   ❋   ❋

IBSEN

Ibsen gave us a new conception of life [*Weltanschauung*], a new picture of man, new knowledge of the soul, but no new drama. Hebbel was a stronger dramatist than Ibsen, and Goethe and Schiller were stronger dramatists than Hebbel. How could it have been otherwise? For just as surely as the life of the German people is dramatically weaker than that of the Neo-Latin people, it is certain that it is ten times more dramatic than the life of the Norwegians. German mirth is more lively than Scandinavian; a pair of German lovers is far more ardent and bold; German wit is sharper and more spicy; a fight between Germans ends more bloodily than in Sweden or in Norway. The blood of Ibsen's women of fate, Rebecca West and Hedda Gabler, flows in the veins of our old maids. This conviction led me to believe twenty years ago that the highest ideal of art would be to unite the unsurpassed mastery of Ibsen's picture of man with the equally unsurpassed dramatic technique of Schiller's *Love and Intrigue.*

For twenty years now the modern German actor has known no higher ideal than to be able to play Ibsen. This means lamentably little to the art of acting. To be sure, Ulrik Brendal and Eilert Lövborg require a passion of spirit and liveliness. Both are episodic figures. Herbert Eulenberg is not the only dramatist writing today whose plays demand to be carried by the passion of spirit and liveliness of an Eilert Lövborg. Should an Ibsen-actor tackle such a problem, then the play will be lost, because the actor lacks the endurance. He grows short of breath, he hasn't learned enough. In the most exciting situations he tiredly drags himself from one couch to the next in order to rally new strength.

And the reviews—the divinely inspired X. X. has truly outdone himself in this role. His ingenious ability deserved a more challenging task. It is a pity that today's theatre cannot produce more such works for these thespian demi-gods.

❋   ❋   ❋

STRANGE HAPPENSTANCE

In face of the most grateful roles to be found in my plays, the German actor has for twenty years now been playing the *timid lover.* Unfortunately I have never written a role for precisely this department of acting.

❋   ❋   ❋

BERLIN

The ten-year old, almost absolute control of a single direction of taste which made it possible to exhaust the situation artistically in the widest measure is understandable only when one realizes that Berlin considers as its own cause the battle for this direction of taste. Since the interest in Naturalism is on the decline, Germany has only one great artistic event to record, an event which, save for the lively interest manifested by Berlin, would never have reached such heights of development. This event is *Max Reinhardt.*

Considering that both these artistic events of Germany were in every respect the children of Berlin and are only to be understood in regard to the favorable conditions predominating in Berlin at the time, it would be utterly against reason to suppose that suddenly this fertile mother should fail to bring forth and nourish other children. It may be true that at the moment Berlin is somewhat tired and in need of rest. But for this reason suddenly to let fly with the damning: "Down with Berlin!" would be screaming ingratitude.

I say: No, on the contrary! Let us continually hold up Berlin as a shining example for all German towns. Let us demand that every German town try, within the limits of its powers, to rival Berlin. There must be no slavish imitations, but there must also be no envy or injustice. When our art possesses an invigorating power, then it will harm neither Berlin nor any other towns. And we could not possibly render German culture a greater service.

❈   ❈   ❈

ON THE MISERY AND DEATH OF THE GERMAN ART OF ACTING [REPLY TO THE ATTACK: "ON THE MISERY AND DEATH OF THE GERMAN DRAMA"]

Those actors whose art exceeds that of any critic, whose ability decides absolutely and without argument the fate of today's dramatic productions, storm out of a performance of *The Bride from Messina,* in which they have acted the lead roles, and cry: "Schiller! The inept idiot! Just ask the public what an abominable impression this miserable play made on it! The scribbler! Just think, if it weren't for us!"

Not one of them has the least idea about the world-historical charade which Schiller builds up through powerful verses, compared with which Ibsen's *Master Builder* is a broken-winded eccentricity, which they idolize as

revelation only because for twenty years they learned nothing more demanding.

And so Schiller becomes our companion in misery, parodying himself in so doing: it is not that the hero is destroyed while the idea conquers; no one is at all concerned about the idea; rather the play fails while the direction succeeds.

How is that possible?

The actor who today is praised as exemplary lacks the ability to carry a play, as well as lacking endurance. He is unsurpassed in charges and episodes and for that reason the darling of directors. The fact that he can sing-song out conversation-pieces is certainly not to his discredit; it misleads him, however, into passing over the author's passion of spirit and liveliness in the tone of voice of the conversation-piece. Then the critics scream out that the author is utilizing a wooden German. Unfortunately he hasn't the ability to portray greatness as something self-evident, to remain exultantly naive, to show human warmth and depth of feeling convincingly bound up with strength and liveliness. If he speaks naively, obviously, then what he says is not understood, because he has neglected his speech techniques for twenty years. Should he want to appear powerful, heroic, vivacious, then every word will appear deliberately stressed, overworked, conscious, intellectualized, so that there will be no trace of naturalness or of the obvious. The actor of today makes of every God-created human being, who is not naturalistically lazy intellectually, a bloodless, overdrawn, desk-created whim.

An art of acting which grows into an unbridgeable yawning gap between author and audience.

❈   ❈   ❈

ALBERT STEINRÜCK

In the character of my Lulu in *Earth Spirit* I tried to draw a fine example of a woman, and how it happens that a creature highly gifted by nature, even though she may have sprung from the dregs of society, achieves an unrestrained development in the company of men to whom she is far superior in the matter of common sense.

Under the command of the bourgeois narrow-mindedness of German Naturalism the splendid creature I intended became a paragon of malevolent unnaturalness, and through the years I was decried as a fanatical, pitiless inquisitor of woman, an exorcising misogynist.

This fact can in no way do damage to the acting genius of a Gertrud Eysoldt. On the contrary, I was convinced from the beginning that had my *Earth Spirit* been played ten years ago as I had envisioned it, and without the interpretation of Gertrud Eysoldt, it would have aroused only displeasure and moral indignation. Frau Eysoldt played precisely that type of woman and beauty which was in current literary and artistic vogue in Berlin. Moreover, Albert Steinrück's Dr. Schön was from the beginning the most fascinating embodiment of a brutal beast of prey that I could have imagined. Albert Steinrück, a deeply moving Gabriel Borkmann, a demonic Master Builder Solness, is spoken of far more in regard to his presentations of active, determined characters than passive, brooding ones, and this by virtue of the acting energy inherent in him. Today's drama does not feel so much inclined to give extravagant praise to the paralytic condition as did the drama of the 1890s. But it is all the more inclined to extol the unflinching intellect, passion, and high-spiritedness. And for that it no longer needs a theatrical interpreter of dreams, but theatrical energy. When Albert Steinrück has his hands free he is one of our greatest hopes.

✿   ✿   ✿

DILLETANTISM

In view of the literary minds of all nations—and I believe that today my voice may also be heard abroad—I herewith appeal to the professional honor of the German actor:

For five years now actors everywhere in Germany where I have appeared in one of my own plays have acknowledged and eulogized me for the work I have done, but these same actors seem unable to concern themselves in the least about the fact. Of every role I have played during the last five years, the critics have written that any actor could have played it immeasurably better, and that in these roles I show myself to be a miserable, incapable, obtrusive dilletante. To the present it has never occurred to any actor to oppose this observation whether by word or deed. I have no desire to contradict the critics; I could wish nothing better for myself than for them to be right; but then, my most honored actors, when will you finally set about to prove in those places where I have appeared that you are qualified to praise my taste? Just for once play an unmutilated *The Tenor*, especially since the mutilated ones are more than a hundred years

in the past. Play a Karl Hetmann, a King Nicolo, a Marquis of Keith, a Marquis Casti Piani. Do you consider it an honor for the German art of acting that a playwright is compelled to act the leading roles in his own plays, unless he wants the critics to make nothing more of him than a bungling author of unstagable literary dramas? Answer that for me. If I hadn't acted, then, of course, you would have had as easy a time with me as with my companions in misfortune: Arthur Vollmöller, Herbert Eulenberg, Josef Ruederer, Wilhelm von Scholz, and others, whose stage techniques even today are a Book of Seven Seals to you, and who must let themselves be dismissed by the critics with a sympathetic shrug of the shoulders. And so, of course, you found just recently in regard to me as well, that I too am a justification for your convenience. You maintain that my plays are so lacking in content and are so superficial that no spectator could possibly find any interest in them, unless for the same money there were thrown into the bargain the added sensation of seeing the author on stage as an utterly incompetent dilletante. Besides that you spread the rumor that unless I am personally able to star in my own plays I will withhold them from production. But all this will no longer be of any avail to you. According to the way that for five years now you have with cheerful openness relished the work I have done, I challenge you today, on the honor of your profession, to show at last how the roles of Gerardo, Karl Hetmann, King Nicolo, and the Marquis of Keith can be acted more artfully and with greater effect than they have been by me. It is only after you have proven this to me that you will be justified in disparaging me to your own high honor.

Should you ignore this summons, then I believe we will know what to expect of you.

✿   ✿   ✿

EXECUTIONS

Today's theatre seems to have more to do with executions than with productions. My own experience is meager by comparison with those of my professional comrades. My play *Such Is Life* was executed in Munich, Berlin, and Frankfurt on the Main. My *Marquis of Keith* was twice broken on the wheel in Berlin during a ten year period. My *Earth Spirit* was executed in Hamburg and Breslau prior to its Berlin production. My harmless farce *Game of Love* was pilloried in Leipzig, Nürnberg, and Breslau. I should think that for premieres actors would prefer to change the word 'production' to 'supreme penal court,' something more in keeping with the effect they produce. The office of executioner has its professional honor too, as soon as it stops bothering itself with worthless subjects.

❊   ❊   ❊

FIORENZA

In a country in which not a day goes by but one reads in the papers of a new and immortal feat performed by some immeasurably gifted genius of a director, it must seem somewhat odd that a work such as the *Fiorenza* of Thomas Mann, a work so richly poetic in the plasticity of its characters, in the dramatic soundness of its dialogue, in the stage worthiness of its technique, should become four years old and in these years have known only two stage productions.

It deserves by virtue of its poetic greatness and beauty long ago to have been made a repertory piece of every German theatre, those same theatres which claim to be the guardians of art. And every director and stage designer worth his salt will already have in his mind a particular conception of how *Fiorenza* must be staged. Such a thing is as self-evident as that the same directors and designers must have preconceived, personal ideas about staging Goethe's *Faust* and Schiller's *The Robbers*.

But what happens instead?

German theatres and the art of German acting have successfully hushed up this distinguished play for four whole years, despite the fact that in its final scene, between Savanarola and the dying Lorenzo di Medici, there exists the most exalted, ingenious, and dramatically effecting writing which has ever been done for the German stage. Or is there something missing in dramatic effectiveness in the remaining four acts of *Fiorenza*? The first act offers as its high point the relation of what happened in the cathedral. The second act shows the splendid band of artists, the dialogue between the two brothers, and then the love dialogue between Fiore and Piero.

Despite this, the play has lain fallow for four years while our directors permit their art to be praised to the skies and at the same time publicly proclaim the misery and death of the German drama.

❊   ❊   ❊

FOR THE PUBLIC

When I recently appeared at Düsseldorf, I elicited a general headshaking and shrugging of shoulders, because I rolled my R's, because I failed to turn my back to the audience, and because I did not veil my plays in muslin. In short, because I proceeded on the barbaric assumption that the spectator wanted to hear and see something for his money. I am firmly of the conviction that for the past twenty years our literary theatre has, first, had far too little theatre in it, and, second, that it has been far too literary. I am convinced that for the past twenty years our literary theatre has offered far too little pleasure and amusement. I am for that reason an abomination to the snobs and philistines of art.

Moreover I know of two actors who share my opinion in this regard, Josef Kainz and Josef Jarno.

By chance I heard both of them express the conviction that even the gloomy Ibsen is made excessively gloomy by his contemporary high priests. Engstrand and Pastor Manders, whose comic elements go back to the Hofmarschall von Kalb, must willy-nilly hold fast to a gloomy human destiny for their characterizations. I retorted dryly: It's good box office. It will be done even in despite of Ibsen, even if it makes Ibsen turn over in his grave.

In the entire range of my plays there is not a single leading male role which I did not write for either one or the other of those two incomparably great actors: Kainz and Jarno. Jarno has thanked me by his unexcelled characterization of my Marquis of Keith, and Kainz by his warmhearted, honest interest in my Karl Hetmann. Both actors have one thing in common: the exceedingly rare gift of being able to play a role almost immediately as though they were riding a hurdle-race. The acting routine of the routine actor enchants the public by the way it lightly pushes aside with a red pencil every hurdle it encounters and plays only the remaining platitudes. That is how they have managed to ruin my *The Tenor* through the years. The great, celebrated actor, on the other hand, persists in each single hindrance as though it were a labor of Hercules, while during the intermissions he celebrates wild orgies which seem never to end. When and how he arrives at his mark does not bother him in the least. Nevertheless, naturalism has drummed into the public a hardy endurance, one which is scarcely to be outdone.

❊   ❊   ❊

DICTATORIAL DIRECTION

The expression dictatorial direction stems from Wilhelm von Scholz, to whom I herewith express my thanks for it.

The dictatorial director is a man who will not be shoved into the shadows by any theatre piece, regardless of its strength and virtues.

In one of my plays the dictatorial director was afraid of being shoved into the shadows by one of my most effective scenes. What was he to do? He came to his own rescue in that without any cause whatever he brought onto stage a real, live donkey. The experiment was a spendid success. My play failed, but the donkey found himself extolled to the high heavens by all the critics.

❁   ❁   ❁

CONCLUSION

. . . I am not fighting against a profession, but against a state of things. I am not fighting to repress, but to awaken new life. I am firmly convinced that this quarrel will be dispatched remarkably soon. Afterwards the former friendship will continue on an even firmer basis, and perhaps we will be able to be more mutually thankful to one another than has been the situation till now.

Translated by Carl Richard Mueller

THE MARQUIS OF KEITH

Translated by Carl Richard Mueller

CAST OF CHARACTERS

CONSUL CASIMIR, *a merchant*
HERMANN CASIMIR, *his son, fifteen years old*
THE MARQUIS OF KEITH
ERNST SCHOLZ
MOLLY GRIESINGER
ANNA, COUNTESS WERDENFELS, *a widow*
SARANIEFF, *a painter*
ZAMRIAKI, *a composer*
SOMMERSBERG, *a writer*
RASPE, *a police inspector*
OSTERMEIER, *proprietor of a brewery*
KRENTZL, *a master-builder*

GRANDAUER, *a restaurateur*
FRAU OSTERMEIER
FRAU KRENTZL
BARONESS VON ROSENKRON, *divorcée*
BARONESS VON TOTLEBEN, *divorcée*
SASCHA
SIMBA
A BUTCHER'S HELPER
A BAKERY WOMAN
A PORTER
PATRONS OF THE HOFBRÄUHAUS

The place of the action is Munich, late summer, 1899.

ACT ONE

(*A workroom, the walls of which are covered with pictures. In the rear wall to the right there is a door leading into the hallway, and to the left, a door leading into a waitingroom. A door in the right wall leads into the living-room. Downstage left is a writing-table on which unrolled plans are lying; on the wall beside the writing-table is a telephone. There is a divan downstage right, with a smaller table in front of it; somewhat upstage center is a larger table. Bookcases with books; musical instruments, bundles of notes and documents.*

The MARQUIS OF KEITH *is seated at the writing-table, engrossed in one of the plans. He is*

The Marquis of Keith by Frank Wedekind, translated by Carl Richard Mueller, printed by permission of the translator.

a man of about twenty-seven: medium height, slender and bony; he would have an exemplary figure were it not for the limp in his left leg. His features are vigorous, though at the same time nervous and somewhat hard. He has piercing grey eyes, a small blond mustache. His unmanageable short, straw-blond hair is carefully parted in the middle. He is dressed in a suit well chosen for its social elegance, but by no means foppishly. He has the rough red hands of a clown.

MOLLY GRIESINGER *enters from the living-room and places a covered tray on the small table in front of the divan. She is a plain sort of creature, brunette, somewhat shy and harassed, wearing a plain house dress, but at the same time she possesses large, black, soulful eyes*)

MOLLY   There you are, my dear, tea, caviar and cold cuts. Do you realize you were up by nine this morning?

KEITH   (*without moving*)   Thank you, my dear child.

MOLLY   You must be terribly hungry. Have you had word yet whether the Fairyland Palace will be built?

KEITH   Can't you see I'm busy with some work?

MOLLY   Yes, you're always busy when I come in. That means that all I ever learn about you and your enterprises has to come from your lady friends.

KEITH   (*without turning in his chair*)   I once knew a woman who stopped up both her ears whenever I talked about plans. She would say: "Come and tell me when you've *done* something!"

MOLLY   Well, I suppose it's my misfortune that you've already known every kind of woman. (*A bell rings*) Merciful heaven, now who could *that* be! (*She goes into the hall to open the door*)

KEITH   (*to himself*)   That poor miserable creature!

MOLLY   (*returns with a card*)   A young gentleman would like to see you. I told him you were very busy with some work.

KEITH   (*after reading the card*)   Just who I wanted to see!

(MOLLY *brings in* HERMANN CASIMIR *and goes off into the living-room*)

HERMANN CASIMIR   (*a fifteen-year-old student in a very elegant cycling costume*)   Good morning, Herr Baron.

KEITH   To what do I owe the honor?

HERMANN   I suppose it were best if I come right out with it. I was at the Café Luitpold last night with Saranieff and Zamriaki. I told them that I absolutely had to have a hundred marks. And so Saranieff thought I might come to you for it.

KEITH   All Munich must think I'm an American railroad baron!

HERMANN   Zamriaki said you always have money on hand.

KEITH   I've patronized Zamriaki because he's the greatest musical genius since Richard Wagner. But these highway robbers certainly aren't proper kind of company for you!

HERMANN   I find these highway robbers interesting. I met the gentlemen at an anarchist meeting.

KEITH   Your father must be delightfully surprised to find you spend your time at revolutionary meetings.

HERMANN   Why doesn't my father let me leave Munich!

KEITH   Because you're still too young for the great world.

HERMANN   But I find that a person my age can learn infinitely more by direct experience than by scooting about on a school-bench till he's come of age.

KEITH   Actual experience merely causes you to lose the abilities you brought with you into the world along with your flesh and blood. And this is especially true of you, the son and sole heir of our greatest German financial genius. What has your father to say about me?

HERMANN   My father never speaks to me.

KEITH   But he does speak to others.

HERMANN   That's possible. I spend as little time at home as I can.

KEITH   I'm afraid you're at fault there. I have followed your father's financial operations ever since I was in America. Your father completely rejects the possibility that there is another soul alive who can be as clever as he. That's why, up till now, he's so obstinately refused to join my enterprise.

HERMANN   However I may try, I can't imagine ever finding pleasure in leading the kind of life my father does.

KEITH   It's simply that your father lacks the ability to interest you in his profession.

HERMANN   The important thing in this world is not merely to live; the important thing is to learn to know both life *and* the world.

KEITH   Your desire to learn to know the world will only end you in a ditch at the side of the road. Just remember that the most important thing is to learn to put the greatest value on the circumstances into which you were born. That will guard you against degrading yourself quite so cheerfully.

HERMANN   Do you mean by pumping you for money? And yet I'm certain there must be things of a higher value than wealth!

KEITH   Theoretically perhaps. These things are called "higher" because they are the *products* of material possessions and are only made possible *through* material possessions. You, of course, are free to devote yourself to either an artistic or a scientific profession because your father has already made a fortune. If in doing so, however, you disregard the primary guiding principle of the world, then you are merely dropping your inheritance into the hands of swindlers.

HERMANN   If Jesus Christ had chosen to act according to this guiding principle of the world . . .

KEITH   You will kindly remember that Christianity liberated two-thirds of mankind from slavery. There's not a single idea—social, scientific or artistic—that deals with anything other than goods and property. That's why anarchists are the sworn enemies of ideas. And don't think that the world will ever change itself in this regard. Man either adjusts or he is eliminated. (*He has seated himself at the writing-table*) I'll give you the hundred marks. But do come around sometime when you aren't in need of money. How long is it since your mother died?

HERMANN   It will be three years this spring.

KEITH (*giving him a sealed note*) You will take this note to the Countess Werdenfels, Brienner Strasse number twenty-three. Give her my best regards. I seem not to have any cash today.

HERMANN   Thank you, Herr Baron.

KEITH (*leading him out; as he closes the door behind him*) Thank you, it was my pleasure. (*With this he returns to the writing-table; rummages in the plans*) You would think his old man were a dog-catcher the way he treats me. Let's see, I must arrange a concert as soon as possible. That way public opinion will force him into joining my enterprise. If worst comes to worst I will simply have to do without him. (*A knock at the door*) Come in!

(ANNA, THE WIDOWED COUNTESS WERDENFELS, *enters. She is a voluptuous beauty of thirty. White skin, turned-up nose, sparkling eyes, luxuriant chestnut-brown hair*)

KEITH (*going to meet her*) Well, here you are, my queen! I've just sent young Casimir to you with a small request.

ANNA   Oh, so that was the young Herr Casimir, was it?

KEITH (*after kissing her hastily on the mouth which she has offered him*) He'll be back if he finds you not at home.

ANNA   He doesn't look in the least like his father.

KEITH   Let's forget about his father. I've just approached a number of people whose social ambitions assure me their burning enthusiasm for my enterprise.

ANNA   But everyone knows that old Casimir loves to patronize young actresses and singers.

KEITH (*devouring* ANNA *with his eyes*) Anna, as soon as you appear in front of me I become another person; it's as though you were the living pledge of my good fortune. But won't you have some breakfast? There's tea here, and caviar and cold cuts.

ANNA (*seats herself on the divan and eats*) I have a lesson at eleven. I dropped in for only a moment. Madame Bianchi tells me that in a year's time I could be the leading Wagnerian soprano of Germany.

KEITH (*lighting a cigarette*) Perhaps in a year you'll have improved so much that the best Wagnerian sopranos will be seeking *your* patronage.

ANNA   That's alright with me. With my limited woman's intelligence I really can't see

how I could possibly reach the top so soon.

KEITH   I'm afraid *I* can't tell you that beforehand either. I simply let myself be driven along without resistance until I arrive at a place where I feel comfortable enough and say to myself: "This is the place to build!"

ANNA   And in that, my dear, I shall be your most faithful accomplice. For some time now my delirious love of life has brought me round to thoughts of suicide.

KEITH   One man steals what he wants, the other receives it as a gift. When I came out into the world my boldest aspiration was to die a village school-master somewhere in Upper Silesia.

ANNA   You would have had a hard time dreaming then that someday Munich would be lying at your feet.

KEITH   My only knowledge of Munich was from a class in geography. If my career till now hasn't been exactly spotless, then one oughtn't to forget the depths out of which I rose.

ANNA   I pray fervently to God every night that He may transfer some of your remarkable energy to *me*.

KEITH   Nonsense, I haven't the slightest bit of energy.

ANNA   Yet it's a necessity of your existence to keep running your head through stone walls.

KEITH   My talent is restricted by the unfortunate fact that I'm unable to breathe in a bourgeois atmosphere. If for that very reason I also achieve what I want, then I certainly will never assume the least bit of credit for it. There are other people, of course, who find themselves planted on a certain level of society on which they can vegetate their whole lives away without ever coming into conflict with the world.

ANNA   You on the other hand fell from the heavens an utterly individualized personality.

KEITH   I'm a bastard. Intellectually my father was a very prominent man, especially in matters concerning mathematics and other such exact sciences, and my mother was a gypsy.

ANNA   If only I had your skill in reading the secrets in men's faces! Then I could grind their noses into the dirt with the tip of my toe.

KEITH   These are accomplishments which cause more distrust in people than they are likely to give benefit to you. That's why bourgeois society has harbored a secret aversion of me ever since I came into this world. This bourgeois society by means of its cautiousness, and against its own will, has made my fortune for me. The higher I climb the more I'm trusted. In fact I'm waiting for the time when the crossing of the philosopher with the horse-thief will be appreciated at its full value.

ANNA   There's no other topic of conversation in the city besides your Fairyland Palace.

KEITH   This Fairyland Palace is nothing more than a rallying-point for my powers. I know myself too well to suppose that I could ever start auditing account books at this time in my life.

ANNA   Then what's to become of *me*? Do you suppose I thrill to the prospect of taking singing lessons for the rest of my life? You said only yesterday that the Fairyland Palace was being built especially for me.

KEITH   But not for you to dance around on your hind legs the rest of your life and be crucified by those nitwits of the press. What you need are more highpoints in your past.

ANNA   Well it's certain I can't produce a family-tree like Mesdames von Rosenkron and von Totleben.

KEITH   And you needn't envy either of them because of it.

ANNA   I should hope not! What feminine attributes *should* I be jealous of them for?

KEITH   I inherited these two ladies as legacies from my predecessor when I took over the concert agency. As soon as I've established my position they can peddle radishes or write novels for a living if they like.

ANNA   I'm more concerned about my boots than about your love for me. And do you know why? Because you are the most inconsiderate being in the world, and because you care about nothing else in this world than your sensual gratifications! That's why if you were to leave me all I could feel for you would be pity. But just you take care that you aren't the one who gets left!

KEITH   (*caressing* ANNA)   I have a life of sudden reversals behind me, but now I am seriously considering building a house; a house with the highest ceilings possible, a park and a broad flight of stairs leading to the entrance. And there must be beggars, too, to decorate the driveway. I'm through with the past and I have no desire to turn back. There were too many times when I had to fight for my existence. I would never advise a friend to take my life as an example.

ANNA   Of course. You're indestructible.

KEITH   I can attribute everything I've achieved up to now to that fact. You know, Anna, I believe that even had we been born in two separate worlds we would have had to find one another after all.

ANNA   I'm indestructible too.

KEITH   Even if Providence hadn't destined us for one another because of our fabulous similarity of taste, there's still one other thing that we have in common . . .

ANNA   Robust healthiness.

KEITH   (*seats himself beside her and caresses her*)   As far as women are concerned, cleverness, good health, sensitivity and beauty are inseparable; any one of them leads inevitably to the other three. If this inheritance is increased in our children . . .

(SASCHA, *a thirteen-year-old errand boy in livery jacket and knee breeches, enters from the hallway and places an armful of newspapers on the center table*)

KEITH   What does Councillor Ostermeier have to say?

SASCHA   The Herr Councillor gave me a letter. It's there with the newspapers. (*He goes off into the waiting-room*)

KEITH   (*having opened the letter*)   I can thank your being with me for this! (*reads*) ". . . I have been told several times now about your plans and find myself extremely interested. I shall be at the Café Maximilian at noon today . . ." The world just now has been placed in the palm of my hand! Now I can turn my backside on old Casimir if he decides to come along. With these "worthy" gentlemen on my side my absolute power remains undisputed.

ANNA   (*has risen*)   Could you give me a thousand marks?

KEITH   Do you mean to tell me you're broke again?

ANNA   The rent is due.

KEITH   That can wait till tomorrow. Just don't worry about it.

ANNA   Whatever you think best. Count Werdenfels prophesied on his deathbed that one day I would learn about the less agreeable side of life.

KEITH   If he had known you for your true worth he might even still be alive today.

ANNA   Up till now his prophecy has remained unfulfilled.

KEITH   I'll send you the money tomorrow noon.

ANNA   (*while* KEITH *accompanies her out*) No, please don't; I'll come for it myself.

(*The stage remains empty for a moment. Then* MOLLY GREISINGER *enters from the living-room and clears away the tea things.* KEITH *returns from the hallway*)

KEITH   (*calling*)   Sascha! (*removes one of the pictures from the wall*) This will have to help me through the next two weeks.

MOLLY Do you mean to say you hope we can continue living this way?

SASCHA (*enters from the waiting-room*) Herr Baron?

KEITH (*gives him the picture*) Go over to Tannhäuser's. He's to place this Saranieff in his window. I'll let it go for three thousand marks.

SASCHA Very well, Herr Baron.

KEITH I'll be along in five minutes. Wait! (*He takes a card from his writing-table on which "3000 M" is written and fastens it to the frame of the picture*) Three thousand marks! (*goes to the writing-table*) First I'll have to dash off a newspaper article about it. (SASCHA *goes off with the picture*)

MOLLY I'd like just once to see a single trace of success from all this talking so big!

KEITH (*writing*) "The Aesthetical Ideal in Modern Landscape Painting."

MOLLY If this Saranieff knew how to paint you wouldn't have to write newspaper articles about him.

KEITH (*turning around*) I beg your pardon?

MOLLY I know, you're busy.

KEITH What was it you wanted to say?

MOLLY I received a letter from Bückeberg.

KEITH From your mama?

MOLLY (*finds the letter in her pocket and reads*) "You are both welcome at any time. You could move into the two front rooms on the third floor. That way you could wait quietly till your transactions in Munich are completed."

KEITH Can't you understand, my dear child, that you're undermining my credit with these little letters of yours?

MOLLY We haven't even any bread for tomorrow.

KEITH Then we'll eat at the Hotel Continental.

MOLLY I wouldn't be able to swallow a mouthful in fear that meanwhile the bailiff would lay hold of our beds.

KEITH He's still deliberating that prospect. Why is it the only things you can think about in that little head of yours are food and drink? You could make your existence so endlessly more enjoyable if only you appreciated its lighter side more. You cherish the most unyielding affection for misfortune.

MOLLY I think it's *you* who cherish this affection for misfortune! Other people seem to have an awfully easy time of it; they never have to give a second thought to their professions. That's why they exist for one another in comfortable homes where nothing ever threatens their happiness. And you, with all your talents, run about endangering your health like a madman, and for all that there's never so much as a penny in the house for days on end.

KEITH Still, you've always had enough to eat! If you never spend anything for clothes, that's scarcely *my* fault. As soon as I've finished writing this newspaper article I'll have three thousand marks in the palm of my hand. Then you can take a cab and buy up everything you can think of at the moment.

MOLLY He'll pay three thousand marks for that picture like I'll put on silk stockings for your sake.

KEITH (*rises unwillingly*) You're a real jewel!

MOLLY (*throws her arms around his neck*) Have I hurt you, darling? Please, forgive me! But what I just told you, I'm solemnly convinced of it.

KEITH Even if the money only lasts till tomorrow evening I still won't regret the sacrifice.

MOLLY (*wailing*) I know it was hateful of me. Why don't you beat me!

KEITH The Fairyland Palace is as good as built.

MOLLY Then at least let me kiss your hand! Please let me kiss your hand!

KEITH If only I can maintain my composure for the next couple of days.

MOLLY Why won't you let me? How can you be so inhuman?

KEITH (*pulls his hand out of his pocket*) It's high time, I think, you took council with yourself; otherwise the enlightenment may suddenly come of its own accord.

MOLLY (*covering his hand with kisses*) Why won't you beat me? I know I deserve it!

KEITH You're cheating yourself of happiness with all the means a woman has at her disposal.

MOLLY (*jumps up indignantly*) Don't ever suppose that I'll let myself be frightened by these flirtations of yours! We're bound too closely together. Once that band breaks I won't hold you anymore; but as long as you're in misery you belong to me.

KEITH It will be your undoing, Molly, this fearing my good fortune more than death. If tomorrow my hands are free you won't stay here another moment.

MOLLY As long as you know that, then everything's fine.

KEITH But I am not in misery!

MOLLY Just let me keep on working here for you until your hands *are* free.

KEITH (*seats himself again at the writing-table*) All right, do what you have to do. But you know there's nothing I like less about a woman than seeing her have to work.

MOLLY I won't make a monkey or a parrot out of myself for your sake. I can't very well ruin you by standing over a washtub, instead of running around half-naked with you to fancy-dress balls.

KEITH This doggedness of yours is something superhuman.

MOLLY I can well believe that it's above your capacity for understanding.

KEITH Even if I *did* understand you, it still wouldn't help you.

MOLLY (*triumphantly*) I don't have to put one over on you, but I can give it to you in black and white if you like! I wouldn't be one bit happier if I constrained myself and made me think myself better than God had made me—*because you love me!*

KEITH That goes without saying.

MOLLY (*triumphantly*) Because you can't live without my love! Keep your hands as free as you want! My staying here only depends on whether I let you have some love left over for other women! Let your women dress themselves up as vulgarly as they can and idolize you as much as they please; it saves me going to comedies. You and your ideals! I know all about that! If it ever came to your doing anything about your ideals—and a lot of chance there is of that—I'd happily let myself be buried alive.

KEITH If only you'd be happy with what fortune offers you!

MOLLY (*tenderly*) But what *does* it offer me, my sweet? We knew these same endless fears in America too. And in the end everything always went to pieces. In Santiago you weren't elected president and you were nearly shot because you didn't have brandy on the table on the decisive evening. Do you still remember how you cried out: "A dollar, a dollar, a republic for a dollar!"

KEITH (*jumps up enraged and goes to the divan*) I was born into this world a cripple. I do not feel myself condemned to be a slave because of it, any more than I feel I should hinder myself from regarding the most luxurious pleasures of life as my rightful inheritance, just because I was born a beggar.

MOLLY You'll never do anything *but* regard those pleasures as long as you live.

KEITH Only death can change what I've just said. And death would never have the nerve to come near to me for fear of making a fool of himself. If I die without having lived, then I'll come back as a ghost.

MOLLY Your only trouble is a swelled head.

KEITH But I *am justified!* When you were just an irresponsible fifteen-year-old child you left school and ran off with me to America. If we were to part now and you were left to your own resources, you'd come to the worst end possible.

MOLLY (*throws her arms around his neck*) Then come to Bückeberg with me. My parents haven't seen their Molly for three whole years. They'll be so happy they'll give you half their wealth. And the two of us could live there together.

KEITH In Bückeberg?

MOLLY There would be no more troubles for you!

KEITH (*freeing himself*) I'd rather have to pick up cigar butts in cafés.

SASCHA (*returns with the picture*) Herr Tannhäuser says he can't put the picture in his window. Herr Tannhäuser says he already has a dozen pictures by Herr Saranieff.

MOLLY I knew that from the start!

KEITH That's why I keep you here! (*goes to the writing-table and tears up the writing paper*) At least I needn't write a newspaper article about it anymore!

(SASCHA *goes into the waiting-room after putting the picture on the table*)

MOLLY These Saranieffs and Zamriakis are people of an entirely different sort from us. They know how to turn people's pockets inside out. The two of us are just too simple for the great world!

KEITH Your kingdom hasn't come yet. Leave me alone. Bückeberg will just have to wait.

MOLLY (*as the bell rings in the corridor, claps her hands maliciously*) The bailiff! (*She hurries to open the door*)

KEITH (*looks at his watch*) What else can we sacrifice to fortune?

MOLLY (*accompanies* ERNST SCHOLZ *into the room*) The gentleman refuses to give me his name.

(ERNST SCHOLZ *is a slender, extremely aristocratic figure of about twenty-seven years of age; black wavy hair, a vandyke beard, and under his strong elongated eyebrows large water-blue eyes with an expression of helplessness*)

KEITH Gaston! Where have you come from?

SCHOLZ Your welcome is a good sign. I've changed so, that I presumed you would never recognize me.

(MOLLY, *after looking at* SCHOLZ, *decides against removing the breakfast dishes for fear of disturbing the two men. She goes into the living room without the dishes*)

KEITH   You seem worn out; but then life never was a game!

SCHOLZ   At least not for me. That's precisely why I've come. It's only because of you that I've come to Munich.

KEITH   I thank you; whatever I have left over from my business is yours.

SCHOLZ   I know how bitter a struggle life is for you. But now I want to get to know you personally. I would like to place myself under your moral guidance for a time, but only on the condition that you allow me to help you as much as you need with my financial resources.

KEITH   But why? I'm just now at the point of becoming director of a gigantic company. And I rather assume you're doing well too? If I'm not mistaken, we saw each other last four years ago.

SCHOLZ   At the legal convention in Brussels.

KEITH   You had passed your State examination just a while before.

SCHOLZ   And you were already writing for every conceivable newspaper. You may recall how I reproached you for your cynicism that time at the ball in the Palace of Justice.

KEITH   You had fallen in love with the daughter of the Danish ambassador, and you broke out in a rage when I maintained that women are by nature far more materialistic than men, even after we've experienced the finest of luxuries.

SCHOLZ   I find you no different now than I did during the whole of our youth, a monster of unscrupulousness; however, you were perfectly right.

KEITH   I've never had a more flattering compliment in all my life.

SCHOLZ   I'm a broken man. Although I detest your entire conception of life from the depths of my soul, I entrust to you as of now the unsoluble riddle of my existence.

KEITH   God be praised you're finally escaping your gloom and turning round to the sun!

SCHOLZ   Don't think this a cowardly capitulation on my part. I've tried every means at my disposal to solve this riddle, and failed every time.

KEITH   All the better for you to have that behind you. During the Cuban revolution I was to have been shot along with twelve conspirators. I naturally fell down with the first shot and stayed "dead" until they came to bury me. It was from that day that I actually felt myself the master of my fate. (*jumping up*) We assume no obligations at birth, and we have nothing to throw away except our life. Anyone who lives on after death is outside the rules. That time in Brussels you intended to go into the civil service, didn't you?

SCHOLZ   I decided on our ministry of railroads.

KEITH   I never understood why, with your great wealth, you never chose to live like a great lord, according to your tastes.

SCHOLZ   I intended first to become a useful member of human society. Had I been born the son of a day-laborer than it would have happened as a matter of course.

KEITH   One can help his fellow man best in this world by working to his own advantage in as far-reaching a manner as possible. The farther my interests extend, the greater the number of people I can provide with a means of livelihood. Whoever imagines that by standing by his post and feeding his children he's accomplishing something useful is only pulling the wool over his own eyes. The children would thank their creator if they had never been brought into the world, and a hundred poor devils are struggling for the same post!

SCHOLZ   The fact is I could see no compelling reason why I should saunter around the world like a worthless idler just because I was a rich man. I have no artistic talent, and I didn't think myself insignificant enough to believe my only vocation in life was to marry and nurture children.

KEITH   Then you've given up the civil service?

SCHOLZ   (*hangs his head*)   Because I was the cause of a terrible disaster while I still held office.

KEITH   When I came back from America someone who had met you the year before in Constantinople told me that you had travelled for two years but that now you were at home and on the verge of being married.

SCHOLZ   I broke my engagement just three days ago. Up till now I'd been only half a man. Since that day on which I became my own master I allowed myself to be guided by the single conviction that I could not enjoy my existence until I had justified it through honest work. This one-sided point of view has led me today to where I seek nothing but material satisfaction, and this out of a sheer sense of duty, nothing else, as though I were doing penance. But no sooner do I want to open my arms to life than I'm paralyzed by remembering those unfortunate people who lost their lives in the most horrible way as a result of my exaggerated conscientiousness.

KEITH   What's all this about?

SCHOLZ   I had changed one of the regulations of the railroad. There was a constant danger that this regulation could not be carried out to the letter. Naturally my fears were exaggerated, but with every day that passed I saw this disaster draw nearer. I lack that intellectual equilibrium which those people have who come from a home worthy of human beings. The first day after my new regulation was introduced there was a collision of two express trains; it cost the lives of nine men, three women and two children. I even had to inspect the scene of the disaster. It isn't my fault that I'm still alive after seeing the sight.

KEITH   And then you began to travel?

SCHOLZ   I went to England, to Italy, but I still felt myself completely cut off from all human activity. In gay, happy surroundings, amid deafening music, I suddenly hear a shrieking cry, because I am unexpectedly reminded of the disaster. Even in the Orient I lived like a frightened owl. To be quite honest, ever since the day of the disaster I have been convinced that I can only buy back my joy in living through self-sacrifice. But in order to do that I must have access to life. I had hoped to find that access to life a year ago when I became engaged to a lovely girl of humble origins.

KEITH   And you wanted to turn the creature into the Countess Trautenau?

SCHOLZ   I am no longer the Count Trautenau. That's something you can't understand. The press placed my name and rank in effective contrast with the disaster I had caused. I felt myself bound by duty to my family to assume another name. For two years now my name has been Ernst Scholz. That way, too, my engagement could surprise no one; but some disaster would have emerged from that too. In her heart, not a spark of love; in mine, only the need to sacrifice myself; our association, an endless chain of trivial misunderstandings. I've given the girl an ample enough dowry to make her a desirable choice for anyone of her station in life. She was so happy with her newly won freedom that she could scarcely express herself. And now, finally, I must learn the difficult art of forgetting myself. We can look death in the eye with clear consciousness; but no one can really live until he can forget himself.

KEITH   (*throws himself into a chair*)   My father would turn over in his grave if he knew that you . . . were asking me for my advice.

SCHOLZ   In that way life contradicts theoretical wisdom. Your father contributed his share towards my one-sided development too.

KEITH   My father was as selfless and conscientious as the mentor and tutor of a Count Trautenau had to be. You were his model student, and I his whipping-boy.

SCHOLZ   Don't you remember how, when you were at our castle, the chambermaids used to kiss you with such tenderness, and then with even greater preference when *I* happened to be around! (*rising*) I shall spend the next two to three years singly and solely (*with tears in his voice*) teaching myself to be an epicurean.

KEITH   (*jumping up*)   What do you say we go to the dance this evening at the Nymphenburg! That's as unworthy of our sort of people as you can possibly imagine. But with all the rain and sleet pouring itself down over my head I feel enticed to bathe myself in the mire again.

SCHOLZ   I don't particularly want to hear market cries.

KEITH   You won't hear a single loud word spoken, just a hollow roar as though the ocean had been uprooted from its depths. Munich is Arcadia and Babylon at the same time. The silent Saturnalian frenzy here that seizes upon the soul at every opportunity has a fascination for even the most jaded beings.

SCHOLZ   How could I possibly be jaded! To this day I have quite literally never enjoyed a moment of my life.

KEITH   We'll have to guard ourselves against the people on the dance floor! In such places my appearance attracts them like flies to carrion. But I'll lay you a wager that you'll forget yourself for all that. In three months from now you'll even be able to forget yourself when you think back to this evening.

SCHOLZ   I have also asked myself in all seriousness whether it is not my tremendous wealth, perhaps, which is the single source of my misfortune.

KEITH   (*indignant*)   That's blasphemy!

SCHOLZ   In fact I have already debated whether I should not also renounce my wealth as I have my title. As long as I am alive this renunciation could only be for the benefit of my family. In any case, I can decide upon an advantageous disposition of my property on my death bed, that is to say, after it has ruined my life. If from my youth on I had had to struggle for my livelihood, then, with my moral earnestness and industry, I'd be in the midst of a brilliant career instead of being an outcast.

KEITH   Or else you'd be revelling with your lower-class girl in the most common sort of trashy lovemaking and then clean the dirty boots of your "fellow men."

SCHOLZ   I'd gladly exchange that for my lot anytime.

KEITH   Just don't ever make yourself believe that this railroad disaster is what's standing between you and your life. The only reason you find satisfaction in these hideous memories is that you're too dull to provide yourself with a more delicate nourishment.

SCHOLZ   You may be right. That's precisely why I should like to submit myself to your spiritual guidance.

KEITH   We'll find something to sink our teeth into tonight. I'm afraid I can't invite you to have breakfast with me. I have a business meeting at twelve with a local big-wig. But I'll give you a few lines to take to my friend Raspe. Spend the afternoon with him; we'll meet at six tonight at the Hofgarten Café. (*He has gone to the writing-table and writes a note*)

SCHOLZ   What sort of business are you in?

KEITH   I'm an art dealer, I write for the newspapers, I have a concert agency—none of it worth talking about. You've come just at the right time to see the founding of a large-scale concert hall which is being built exclusively for my artists.

SCHOLZ   (*takes the pictures from the table and looks at it*)   You have a nice picture gallery.

KEITH   (*jumping up*)   I wouldn't give ten thousand marks for that. A Saranieff. (*turns the picture around in his hands*)   This is the way you have to hold it.

SCHOLZ   I know nothing about art. While travelling I didn't set foot inside a single museum.

KEITH   (*gives him the note*)   The gentleman is an international authority on crime; so you mustn't be too open with him at first. Really a charming man. People never know whether they ought to keep an eye on me, or whether I'm here to keep an eye on them.

SCHOLZ   Thank you for your kind reception. Well then, at six tonight, at the Hofgarten Café.

KEITH   Then we'll drive out to the Nymphenburg. And I thank you that you have finally come around to having faith in me.

(KEITH *accompanies* SCHOLZ *out. The stage is empty for a moment. Then* MOLLY GRIESINGER *enters from the living-room and clears the tea-service from the table.* KEITH *returns immediately*)

KEITH   (*calling*)   Sascha! (*goes to the telephone and rings*)   Seventeen thirty-five. Inspector Raspe!

SASCHA   (*enters from the living-room*)   Herr Baron!

KEITH   My hat! My overcoat! (SASCHA *hurries into the hall*)

MOLLY   I beg of you, don't have anything to do with this patron! He wouldn't have come unless he wanted to exploit us.

KEITH   (*speaking into the telephone*)   Thank God you're there! Just wait ten minutes. You'll see for yourself. (*to* MOLLY *while* SASCHA *helps him into his overcoat*)   I must hurry to the newspaper offices.

MOLLY   What should I answer mama?

KEITH   (*to* SASCHA)   A carriage!

SASCHA   Yes, Herr Baron! (*goes off*)

KEITH   Give her my deepest regards. (*goes to the writing-table*)   The plans—the letter from Ostermeier—tomorrow morning all Munich must know that the Fairyland Palace will be built!

MOLLY   Then you're not coming to Bückeburg?

KEITH   (*the plans rolled up together under his arm, takes his hat from the table, center, and crams it onto his head*)   I can't help but wonder how he's going to turn himself into an epicurean! (*goes off hurriedly*)

ACT TWO

(*In the study of the* MARQUIS OF KEITH *the center table is laid for breakfast: champagne and a large dish of oysters. The* MARQUIS OF KEITH *is seated on the writing-table with his left foot on a stool, while* SASCHA, *kneeling in front of him, buttons his shoes with a buttonhook.* ERNST SCHOLZ *stands behind the divan as he tries out a guitar which he has taken from the wall*)

KEITH   What time did you get back to your hotel this morning?

SCHOLZ   (*with a radiant smile*)   At ten.

KEITH   Wasn't I right to leave you alone with that charming creature?

SCHOLZ   (*smiling blissfully*)   After last night's discussions about art and modern literature I'm beginning to ask myself whether I shouldn't start taking lessons from this girl. I was even more surprised that she asked you whether she could wait on your guests at the garden party that you plan to astonish all Munich with.

KEITH   She quite simply considers it an honor. Besides, there's time enough to talk about the garden party later. I'm leaving for Paris tomorrow for a couple of days.

SCHOLZ   This comes at a most inopportune time for me.

KEITH   Come along then. I want one of my artists to sing for Madame Marquesi before she makes her debut here.

SCHOLZ   Must I bring back those mental torments that I once lived through in Paris?

KEITH   Won't last night's experience help you to jump that hurdle? Well then, spend your time during my absence with Saranieff the painter. He's bound to run into us sometime today.

SCHOLZ   The girl told me that this Saranieff's studio is a regular chamber of horrors full of the most terrifying abominations ever perpetrated on man. And then she ran on in the most delightfully charming way about her childhood, how when she was a girl in the Tyrol she spent all summer long sitting in the cherry trees and how on winter evenings till dark came on she would go sleighing with the village children. How can a girl like this possibly consider it an honor to serve at your party!

KEITH   The girl considers it an honor because it accords her an opportunity to fight against the unbounded contempt with which our bourgeois society treats her.

SCHOLZ   But how do they justify this contempt? How many hundreds of women in the best social circles have their lives ruined because the stream of life has dried up inside them, in the same way that in this girl it overflows its banks. This girl in all her exuberant joy can never be guilty of a sin like the soul-killing discord which my parents endured together for twenty years!

KEITH   What is sin!

SCHOLZ   Yesterday I was certain that I knew. But today I can confess without despair what thousands upon thousands of other well established persons like myself have experienced: that the man who has failed in life looks with bitter envy at the creature who has wandered from the path of virtuous living!

KEITH   The happiness of these creatures would never be so despised were it not the most unprofitable of all businesses imaginable. Sin is a mythological name for bad business. Good business always works its way into the existing social order! No one knows that better than I. I, the Marquis of Keith, despite that I am the talk of all Munich, and despite my reputation in Europe, I am just as much outside the boundaries of society as that girl. That's the only reason that I'm giving the garden party. I'm unspeakably sorry that I can't receive the poor thing as one of my guests. It will be in far better taste if she appears among my hired help.

SASCHA   (*has risen*)   Would the Herr Baron like me to call a carriage?

KEITH   Yes.

(SASCHA *goes off*)

KEITH   (*stamping his feet into his boots*)   You've read, I suppose, that the Fairyland Palace Company was established yesterday?

SCHOLZ   How could I have seen a newspaper since yesterday?

(*They both take their places at the breakfast table*)

KEITH   The entire enterprise rests on a beer-brewer, a master-builder, and a restaurant owner. They are the Caryatids that support the pediment of the temple.

SCHOLZ   Incidentally, your friend Raspe, the police inspector, is a charming person.

KEITH   He's a scoundrel; yet I like him for another reason.

SCHOLZ   He told me he was originally a theology student, but lost his faith through too much studying and then tried to regain it the same way as the prodigal son.

KEITH   He sank deeper and deeper till finally the arm of the law caught him up and made good his lost faith again by detaining him for two years under lock and key.

SCHOLZ   The girl absolutely couldn't understand why I had never learned to ride a bicycle. She thought it very reasonable of me not to have ridden a bicycle in Asia and Africa because of the wild animals. But she thought I ought certainly to have begun in Italy!

KEITH   I'll warn you again, my friend, don't be too open with people! The truth is our most priceless possession and we can never be too sparing with it.

SCHOLZ   Is that why you laid on to the title "Marquis of Keith?"

KEITH   I have as much right to be called the Marquis of Keith as you have to be called Ernst Scholz. I am the adopted son of Lord Keith, who in the year 1863 . . .

SASCHA   (*enters from the hall, announcing*)   Herr Professor Saranieff!

(SARANIEFF *enters. He wears a black walking coat with sleeves which are somewhat too long, light trousers which are somewhat too short, thick shoes and glaring red gloves; his rather long, straight, black hair is cut straight all the way around; on a black ribbon in front of his promising eyes he wears a pincenez à la Murillo; his profile is expressive; he wears a small Spanish mustache. After greeting them he hands his top hat to* SASCHA)

SARANIEFF   I wish you good fortune from the bottom of my heart, my good friend. At last the cables are cut and the balloon may rise!

KEITH   The Command of my enterprise is

awaiting me; I'm afraid there isn't time to invite you to breakfast.

SARANIEFF (*sitting down at the table*) Then I shall release you from the obligation to invite me.

KEITH   Sascha, set another place!

(SASCHA *has hung up the hat in the hall and goes off into the living-room*)

SARANIEFF   I am amazed that the name of the great Casimir isn't listed among the members of the Fairyland Palace Company.

KEITH   That's simply because I don't wish to waive credit for being the creator of my own work. (*introducing them*) Saranieff, the painter —Count Trautenau.

SARANIEFF (*taking a glass and plate and helping himself; to* SCHOLZ) Count, I already know you inside and out. (*to* KEITH) Simba was just with me; she is presently sitting for a Böcklin.

KEITH (*to* SCHOLZ) Böcklin was a great artist himself. (*to* SARANIEFF) You really needn't boast about such tricks!

SARANIEFF   Make me famous, and I'll no longer have need for such tricks! I'll pay you thirty percent for life. Zamriaki's mind is already tottering like a rotting fencepost because he utterly insists on becoming immortal through honorable means.

KEITH   My only concern is his music. For a genuine composer the mind is always a hinderance.

SCHOLZ   To want to be immortal one must first have an extraordinary love for life.

SARANIEFF (*to* SCHOLZ) Incidentally, our Simba described you to me as a highly interesting person.

SCHOLZ   Yes, I can well imagine she doesn't meet old grumpusses like me every day.

SARANIEFF   She categorized you with the Symbolists. (*to* KEITH) And then she raved about an imminent party for the Fairyland Palace, with an extraordinary fireworks display.

KEITH   You can't very well dazzle a dog with fireworks. But the rational man always feels insulted if you fail to give him any. In any case, I'll be going to Paris for a few days beforehand.

SARANIEFF   Undoubtedly they want your opinion on a joint German-French mutual-aid treaty?

KEITH   But don't say anything about it!

SCHOLZ   I had no idea you were active in politics too!

SARANIEFF   Can you think of a single thing in which the Marquis of Keith isn't active?

KEITH   I don't want people to say that I don't take an interest in my own times!

SCHOLZ   Doesn't one find enough to occupy his time if he takes life seriously?

SARANIEFF   In any case, you take it too damned seriously! Did a washer-woman in Gizeh, at the foot of the pyramids, exchange one of your collars by mistake?

SCHOLZ   You seem to have been quite thoroughly informed about me. Would you permit me to visit you someday in your studio?

SARANIEFF   If you have no objection we can have our coffee there right now. You'll even find your Simba still there.

SCHOLZ   Simba?—Simba? You always seem to be talking about Simba. The girl told me her name was Kathi!

SARANIEFF   Her real name is Kathi; but the Marquis of Keith dubbed her Simba.

SCHOLZ   Undoubtedly because of her wonderfully red hair.

KEITH   Goodwill or no goodwill, I have no information on the subject.

SARANIEFF   She has made herself comfortable on my Persian divan and at the moment is sleeping off her hangover from yesterday.

(MOLLY GRIESINGER *enters from the living-room and lays a place for* SARANIEFF)

SARANIEFF   My heartiest thanks, dear madam; but as you can see, I have already finished. You will pardon me, I hope, if I haven't yet taken the opportunity of kissing your hand.

MOLLY   Save your compliments for more worthy opportunities!

(*The bell rings in the corridor;* MOLLY *goes to answer it*)

KEITH (*looks at his watch and rises*) You will have to excuse me, gentlemen. (*calls*) Sascha!

SARANIEFF (*wiping his mouth*) We shall go with you, of course. (*He and* SCHOLZ *rise*)

(SASCHA *enters from the waiting-room with the coats and helps* KEITH *and* SCHOLZ *put theirs on*)

SCHOLZ (*to* KEITH) Why didn't you tell me you were married?

KEITH   Here, let me straighten your tie. (*He does so*) You must give more attention to your outward appearance.

(MOLLY *returns from the hall with* HERMANN CASIMIR)

MOLLY   The young Herr Casimir wishes to see you.

KEITH (*to* HERMANN) Did you deliver my kind regards yesterday?

HERMANN   The Countess herself was waiting for money from you!

KEITH   Would you wait here just a moment? I shall be right back. (*to* SCHOLZ *and* SARANIEFF) Ready, gentlemen?

SARANIEFF (*takes his hat from* SASCHA) With you through thick and thin!

SASCHA   The carriage is waiting, Herr Baron.

KEITH   Sit with the driver!

(SCHOLZ, SARANIEFF, KEITH *and* SASCHA *go off*)

MOLLY (*gathering the breakfast dishes together*)   I wish I knew what you wanted in this madhouse! You would be much more sensible to stay at home with your mama!

HERMANN (*wanting to leave the room at once*)   My mother is no longer alive, my dear madam; but I wouldn't want to bother you.

MOLLY   Oh, for Heaven's sake, don't go! You're not bothering anyone. I just can't understand these inhuman parents who don't keep their children from associating with such highway thieves! I had a happy home like you and was neither older nor wiser than you are when without thinking I jumped into the bottomless abyss.

HERMANN (*very agitated*)   My God, I *must* find a way! I'll be ruined if I stay in Munich any longer! But the Marquis is bound to refuse me his help if he even suspects what I have in mind. I beg you, madam, don't betray me!

MOLLY   If only you knew how I feel you wouldn't have any fear of my being concerned with your stories! I hope things don't turn out worse for you than for me! If my mother had let me work like I'm working now, instead of sending me ice-skating every free afternoon, I'd still have a life of happiness ahead of me!

HERMANN   But—if you're so terribly unhappy and you know—that you could still be happy, why—why don't you get a divorce?

MOLLY   Oh, for Heaven's sake, don't talk about things you don't understand! You have to be married first if you want to get a divorce.

HERMANN   I'm sorry, I—I thought you *were* married.

MOLLY   God only knows, I don't want to complain about anyone! But in order to get married anywhere in the world you first need papers. And to have papers is something beneath his dignity! (*as a bell rings in the corridor*) This place is like a post office from morning till night! (*goes off into the hall*)

HERMANN (*pulling himself together*)   Why do I go shooting my mouth off like that!

(MOLLY *leads in the* COUNTESS WERDENFELS)

MOLLY   You may wait here for my husband if you like. He should be back very soon. May I introduce you?

ANNA   Thank you. We've met.

MOLLY   Of course! Then I won't be needed. (*goes into the living-room*)

ANNA (*sits down on the bench of the writing-table beside* HERMANN *and places her hand on his*)   Now, I want you to tell me honestly and openly, my dear young friend, what you do at school with so much money?

HERMANN   I won't tell you.

ANNA   But I'd like very much to know!

HERMANN   I can believe it!

ANNA   Aren't you stubborn!

HERMANN (*pulls his hands from hers*)   I will not be bargained with!

ANNA   And who's bargaining you? Don't flatter yourself! You see, I divide human beings into two large classes. The young and interesting and the old maids.

HERMANN   In your opinion, of course, I'm an old maid.

ANNA   Yes, unless you can tell me why you need all that money.

HERMANN   But I couldn't possibly because I'm an old maid!

ANNA   Oh, but I could tell from the first time I laid eyes on you that you were young and interesting!

HERMANN   And I am, too; otherwise I'd be content to stay here in Munich.

ANNA   But you want to go out into the world!

HERMANN   And you would like very much to know where. To Paris—to London.

ANNA   Nowadays Paris isn't at all fashionable.

HERMANN   I don't really care about going to Paris.

ANNA   Now why wouldn't you rather stay here in Munich? You have a father with more money than . . .

HERMANN   Because there's nothing here to experience! I'll die if I stay here in Munich, and especially if I have to spend anymore time at school. An old school-friend writes me from Africa that when you're unhappy in Africa you're ten times happier than when you're happy in Munich.

ANNA   Let me tell you something: your friend is an old maid. Don't go to Africa. Stay here in Munich with us and really experience something.

HERMANN   But there's no chance of that here!

(MOLLY *shows in* POLICE INSPECTOR RASPE. RASPE, *in his early twenties, is dressed in a light-colored summer suit and straw hat and has the innocent childlike features of an angel by Guido Reni. Short blond hair, the start of a mustache. When he feels himself being watched he clamps his blue pincenez onto his nose*)

MOLLY My husband will be back very soon, if you would care to wait. May I introduce you . . .

RASPE I really don't know, my good madam, whether it would be of any real service to the Baron if you introduce me.

MOLLY Well, all right then!—For Heaven's sake!

(*She goes into the living-room*)

ANNA May I say your precautions are quite superfluous. We have met.

RASPE (*seating himself on the divan*) Hmm —I'm afraid I shall have to recollect . . .

ANNA When you have sufficiently recollected yourself, then I should like to ask you not to introduce me either.

RASPE How is it that I've never heard you spoken of here?

ANNA Only a change of name. I was told that you had spent two years in absolute solitude.

RASPE Whereupon you naturally concealed the fact that you had known me during my days of glory.

ANNA Whom haven't we known in his day of glory!

RASPE You're quite right. Pity is blasphemy. What could I do? I was the sacrifice of the insane confidence which everyone offered me.

ANNA But now you're young and interesting again?

RASPE Now I make use of that same insane confidence which everyone offered me for the well being of my fellow human beings. By the way, can you tell me something more specific about this epicurean?

ANNA I'm very sorry; no one has put him through his paces for me yet.

RASPE I'm extremely surprised. A Herr Scholz wants to train himself here in Munich to be an epicurean.

ANNA And for that reason the Marquis of Keith introduces him to a Police Inspector?

RASPE He's quite harmless. I scarcely knew what to do with him. For his education's sake I took him to the Hofbräuhaus. It's right next door here.

(MOLLY *opens the entrance door and shows in* CONSUL CASIMIR. *He is a man in his middle-forties, rather heavy-set, dressed in opulent elegance; a full face with a luxuriant black beard, powerful mustache, bushy eyebrows, and hair parted carefully down the center*)

MOLLY My husband is not at home. (*off*)

CASIMIR (*without greeting anyone, goes straight toward* HERMANN) There is the door! To think that I had to hunt you down in a robbers' den like this!

HERMANN You'd never have looked for me here if you weren't afraid for your business!

CASIMIR (*threatening him*) Will you be quiet! I'll show you what it means to move!

HERMANN (*pulls out a pocket revolver*) Don't touch me, papa! Don't touch me! I'll shoot myself if you touch me!

CASIMIR I'll make you pay for this when I get you home!

RASPE Why should he let himself be treated like an animal?

CASIMIR Must I be insulted as well here?

ANNA (*approaches him*) If you please, sir, this is bound to cause an accident. You must calm yourself first. (*to* HERMANN) Be reasonable; go with your father.

HERMANN I have nothing to go home for. He doesn't even notice when I drink myself senseless because I don't know why I'm alive!

ANNA Then tell him quietly what you have in mind; but don't threaten your father with that revolver. Give me that thing.

HERMANN Is that what you thought I wanted?

ANNA You won't regret it. I'll give it back to you when you've quieted down. Do you take me for a liar?

(HERMANN *hesitantly gives her the revolver*)

ANNA Now you ask your father to forgive you. If you have a spark of honor in your body you couldn't possibly expect your father to make the first move.

HERMANN· But I will not be ruined!

ANNA You will first ask for forgiveness. You can be quite certain then that your father can be reasoned with.

HERMANN I—I beg you to . . . (*He sinks to his knees and sobs*)

ANNA (*tries to stand him up*) Aren't you ashamed of yourself! Look your father in the eye!

CASIMIR He has his mother's nerves!

ANNA Prove to your father that he can have confidence in you. Now you will go home and when you've quieted down you will tell your father all about your plans and your wishes.

(*She leads him out*)

CASIMIR (*to* RASPE) Who is this woman?

RASPE Today is the first time I've seen her in two years. At the time she was a saleswoman in a shop on Perus Strasse and her name was Huber if I'm not mistaken. However if you want to know anything further . . .

CASIMIR I thank you. Your faithful servant! (*goes off*)

(MOLLY *enters from the living-room to remove the breakfast dishes*)

RASPE Pardon me, my good woman; did the Baron really intend to be back before dinner?

MOLLY Oh, for God's sake, don't ask me such ridiculous things!

ANNA (*re-enters from the hall; to* MOLLY) May I help you carry something off?

MOLLY You're asking me if you can help me . . . (*She puts the serving tray back down on the table*) Whoever wants to can clear the table; I didn't eat off it! (*goes off into the living room*)

RASPE That bit with the boy was extremely well done.

ANNA (*sits down at the writing-table*) I envy him the carriage his father is taking him home in.

RASPE Tell me, whatever happened to the Count Werdenfels who used to give one champagne party after another two years ago?

ANNA That happens to be my own name now.

RASPE I should have guessed! Would you be so good as to convey to the Count my sincerest congratulations on his choice.

ANNA I'm afraid that is no longer possible.

RASPE Obviously then you've separated.

ANNA Yes, obviously. (*as voices are heard in the hallway*) I'll explain it to you some other time.

(KEITH *enters with* HERR OSTERMEIER, HERR KRENZL, *and* HERR GRANDAUER, *all of them more or less large-bellied, bleary-eyed Munich Philistines.* SASCHA *follows them*)

KEITH What a remarkable stroke of luck! I can introduce you at once to one of our leading artists. Sascha, remove this stuff!

(SASCHA *goes into the living-room with the breakfast dishes*)

KEITH (*introducing them*) Herr Ostermeier, the brewery proprietor; Herr Krenzl, the master builder; Herr Grandauer, the restauranteur: the Caryatids of the Fairyland Palace—the Countess Werdenfels. But your time is limited, gentlemen, and you did come to see the plans. (*Takes the plans from the writing-table and unrolls them on the center table*)

OSTERMEIER Take your time, my honored friend. Five minutes one way or the other won't matter.

KEITH (*to* GRANDAUER) Would you hold this, please.—What you see here is the large concert hall with its sliding ceiling and skylight, so that in the summer it can serve as an exhibition palace. Next to it here there is a smaller theatre which I intended to make popular by means of the most modern of artistic

decorations, something, you know, which is a cross between a dancehall and a death chamber. The most modern of styles is always the cheapest and the most effective advertising.

OSTERMEIER Hm—didn't you forget the toilets?

KEITH Here you can see a completely detailed sketch of the cloak room and the toilet facilities.—And here, Herr Master Builder, is the façade: the driveway, pediment and caryatids!

KRENZL I sure wouldn't want being one of them caryatids!

KEITH Just a little joke of mine, my good sir!

KRENZL What'd my old lady have to say if I let myself be chiselled into one of them caryatids way up there, and even more on a Fairyland Palace!

GRANDAUER Let me tell you, the main thing I want to have as the owner of the restaurant is room.

KEITH My dear Herr Grandauer, we have proposed to devote the entire ground floor to the restaurant.

GRANDAUER You can't go crowding folks into a place for eats and drinks like you can for listening to that there music.

KEITH And for afternoon coffee, my dear Herr Grandauer, here you have a terrace on the mezzanine with a magnificent view overlooking the grounds of the Isar.

OSTERMEIER And now, my good friend, I'd like to ask you to let us have a look at your preliminary expense sheet.

KEITH (*producing a sheet of writing*) Four thousand shares at five thousand makes approximately twenty million marks.—I'm operating on the assumption, gentlemen, that each of us subscribes to forty preferred shares, and that we pay for them at once. You see, the estimated profit is extraordinarily low.

KRENZL The only question now is if the local authorities say all right to what we want.

KEITH That's why, in addition to the shares, we are going to issue a number of interest-drawing bonds and place a portion of them at the city's disposal for worthy purposes. —It is proposed that members of the governing board receive ten percent of the net profit before deductions for depreciation reserves.

OSTERMEIER All as it should be. Can't ask for more than that.

KEITH As far as the stock-exchange is concerned, we'll need to work some on that. I'm going to Paris tomorrow for that very purpose. In two weeks from today we shall have our founders' party at my villa on Brienner Strasse.

(ANNA *starts*)

OSTERMEIER   Sure would be nice to get Consul Casimir to come along with us by the time of the party!

KRENZL   That'd be the smartest thing, all right. Get Consul Casimir with us and the authorities would say yes to anything.

KEITH   I hope, gentlemen, that we shall be able to call a general meeting of the board before the party. You will see then how I shall take into consideration your suggestions regarding Consul Casimir.

OSTERMEIER   (*shakes his hand*) Have a nice trip to Paris, then, my good friend. Let's have a word out of you from Paris. (*bowing to* ANNA) May I take the liberty of bidding you farewell; my compliments.

GRANDAUER   Farewell; may I take the liberty of wishing you a good afternoon.

KRENZL   My best regards. Good day!

(KEITH *leads the gentlemen out*)

ANNA   (*after he has returned*) What can you possibly be thinking of, announcing your founders' party at my house?!

KEITH   I shall have a dress made for you in Paris that will make it wholly unnecessary for you to be able to sing.—(*to* RASPE) And you, Herr Police Inspector, I shall expect you at our founders' party to utilize all the charm of your personality in bewitching the wives of our three caryatids.

RASPE   The ladies will find nothing to complain of.

KEITH   (*giving him some money*) Here are three hundred marks. I'm bringing fireworks back from Paris, the likes of which the city of Munich has never seen.

RASPE   (*pocketing the money*) He got this from the epicurean.

KEITH   (*to* ANNA) I use every mortal according to his talents, and I must recommend a certain degree of caution in regard to my close friend, Police Inspector Raspe.

RASPE   When a man looks as though he had been cut down from the gallows, like yourself, getting through life honestly is no art. I'd like to see where you'd be today if you had my angelic face!

KEITH   With your face I'd have married a princess.

ANNA   (*to* RASPE) If I'm not mistaken, you were first introduced to me under a French name.

RASPE   I no longer use French names since I've become a useful member of human society. —Permit me to pay you my respects. (*goes off*)

ANNA   With my serving staff I am not equipped to give big suppers!

KEITH   (*calls*) Sascha!

SASCHA   (*enters from the waiting room*) Herr Baron?

KEITH   Would you like to help serve at a garden party for my friends?

SASCHA   That would be a real pleasure, Herr Baron. (*goes off*)

KEITH   May I introduce you today to my oldest boyhood friend, the Count Trautenau?

ANNA   I've never had much luck with counts.

KEITH   That's all right. All I ask is that you don't discuss my domestic relations with him. The fact is he is a moralist, both by nature and by conviction. He's already questioned me closely today about my family life.

ANNA   Good Heavens, this man doesn't really want to become an epicurean, does he?

KEITH   That makes it all the more contradictory! Ever since I've known him he's lived a life of sacrifice, without realizing that there are really two souls in his breast.

ANNA   That too! I find that just one is too many. But isn't his name Scholz?

KEITH   One of his souls is named Ernst Scholz, the other Count Trautenau.

ANNA   Thank you anyway, but I want nothing to do with people who can't make up their minds!

KEITH   Why, he's a paragon of decision. The world has no more pleasures to offer him unless he starts from the bottom up.

ANNA   But man is always supposed to climb higher!

KEITH   Why are you so upset?

ANNA   Because you are trying to pair me off with this frightful monster!

KEITH   He's gentle as a lamb.

ANNA   I thank you very much, but no personification of disaster will even enter my boudoir!

KEITH   But you don't understand me. At the moment I cannot do without his confidence, and for that reason I don't want to expose myself to his disapproval. If he fails to get to know you, all the better for me, because I won't have his reproaches to look forward to.

ANNA   Who can ever tell where your calculations are going to lead!

KEITH   What did you have in mind?

ANNA   I thought you wanted to use me as a whore for your friend.

KEITH   Do you really think me capable of such a thing?

ANNA   You said just a moment ago that you use every mortal according to his talents. And who could ever doubt that I possess the talent of a whore?

KEITH   (*taking* ANNA *in his arms*) Anna—I

am going to Paris tomorrow, not to work out the stock-exchange or to buy fireworks, but because I must breathe some fresh air, because I must stretch out my arms unless I want to see the façade topple that I have so carefully erected here in Munich. Anna, would I be taking you with me to Paris if you weren't everything to me?—Do you know something, Anna? Not a night goes by but I see you in my dreams with a diadem in your hair. If you were ever to ask me to get a star for you from the firmament, I wouldn't be afraid, I'd find the ways and means to do it.

ANNA Use me as a whore!—You'll see whether or not I yield a profit!

KEITH All I can think of at this moment is the concert dress that I will have made for for you at St. Hilaire's . . .

SASCHA (*enters from the hall*) A Herr Sommersberg would like to see you.

KEITH Show him in. (*to* ANNA, *describing the dress*) A silvery torrent of mauve silk and paillettes from shoulder to knee, so tightly laced and cut so deep in front and back that the dress will appear a glittering jewel on your slender body!

(SOMMERSBERG *has entered. In his late thirties, deeply-lined face, hair and beard streaked with grey and unkempt. A heavy winter overcoat covers his shabby clothes, torn kid gloves*)

SOMMERSBERG I am the author of *Songs of a Happy Man*. I don't look it.

KEITH I looked like that once myself.

SOMMERSBERG I would never have found the courage to come to you if it weren't for the fact that I have had almost nothing to eat for almost two days.

KEITH That's happened to me a hundred times. How can I help you?

SOMMERSBERG Just a little something—for my lunch . . .

KEITH Is that all the use you think I can be to you?

SOMMERSBERG I'm an invalid.

KEITH But you still have half a lifetime ahead of you!

SOMMERSBERG I have wasted my life living up to the expectations people had set for me.

KEITH Perhaps you may still find a current which will take you out to the open sea. Or are you afraid for your life?

SOMMERSBERG I can't swim; and here in Munich resignation isn't so hard to bear.

KEITH Why don't you come to our founders' party in two weeks from today? Brienner Strasse. You'll be able to make some necessary contacts there. (*gives him some money*) Here are a hundred marks. Keep enough of this

money in reserve so that you can rent a dress suit for the evening.

SOMMERSBERG (*hesitantly taking the money*) I feel as if I were deceiving you . . .

KEITH Just don't deceive yourself! And in doing so you will be doing a good turn for the next poor devil who comes to me.

SOMMERSBERG Thank you, Herr Baron. (*goes off*)

KEITH Don't mention it! (*after he has closed the door behind him, putting his arms around* ANNA) And now, my queen, we're off to Paris!

ACT THREE

(*A room overlooking a garden is lighted with electric lamps; a wide glass door in the right side wall leads into the garden. The middle door in the back wall leads into the diningroom in which dinner is being served. When the door is opened one sees the upper end of the table. In the left wall is a curtained door into the gameroom. Near the door is an upright piano. Downstage right, a lady's writing-table; downstage left, a settee, chairs and table, etc. In the upstage right corner there is a door which leads into the hallway. A toast is being drunk in the diningroom. As the classes clink,* SOMMERSBERG, *in shabbily elegant evening dress, and* KEITH, *in a full-dress suit, enter the salon through the center door*)

KEITH (*closing the door behind him*) You've composed the telegram?

SOMMERSBERG (*a paper in hand, reading*) "The Founders of the Munich Fairyland Palace Company brought together yesterday evening the notable citizens of the gay city on the Isar for a highly spirited garden party at the villa of the Marquis of Keith on Brienner Strasse. Until after midnight a magnificent fireworks display delighted the residents of the neighboring streets. We wish to extend to this enterprise begun under such favorable auspices . . .

KEITH Excellent!—Whom can I send to the telegraph office . . .?

SOMMERSBERG Let me take care of that. After all the champagne I've had, a little fresh air will do me good.

(SOMMERSBERG *goes off into the hallway; at the same time* ERNST SCHOLZ *enters; he is in a full-dress suit and an overcoat*)

KEITH You've certainly kept us waiting long enough.

SCHOLZ And I've merely come to tell you I can't stay.

KEITH They're making a laughing stock of me! Old Casimir has already left me in the lurch; but at least he sent a congratulatory telegram.

SCHOLZ I don't belong with people! You complain about being outside society; I'm outside humanity!

KEITH Haven't you every pleasure now that a man can dream of?

SCHOLZ Pleasure? What pleasure? This frenzied whirl of pleasurable sensations I'm reveling in now leaves no line of distinction between myself and a barbarian. To be sure, I have learned to go into raptures over Rubens and Richard Wagner. The disaster which earlier aroused pity in me has become almost insupportable in its ugliness. And so I've become an all the more devout enthusiast of the artistic achievements of dancers and acrobats.—If only, after all this, I had made just one step of progress! It's for my money's sake that I'm treated like a human being. But as soon as I actually want to be one I find myself ramming against invisible walls!

KEITH If you can envy those lucky dogs who take root wherever they find room and then are blown away as soon as the wind changes, then don't look to me for pity! This world is a damned sly beast, and it's no easy thing to conquer. But once succeed and you're proof against any misfortune.

SCHOLZ If such phrases give you any sort of satisfaction then I'm afraid there's nothing I can hope for from you. (*He is about to leave*)

KEITH (*holds him back*) They are not phrases! There's no misfortune today that can touch me. We're too well acquainted with one another, misfortune and I. Misfortune for me is as favorable an opportunity as anything else. Any stupid ass can suffer misfortune; the trick of the matter is to know how to exploit it to one's own advantage!

SCHOLZ You hang around the world's neck like a whore to a pimp. You can't understand that a man can become as loathesome to himself as carrion if he exists only for himself.

KEITH Then in the name of all the devils in hell will you be satisfied with your godly way of life! Once you have this purgatory of earthly vice and joy behind you you'll look down on this poor miserable sinner as if I were a Father of the Church!

SCHOLZ If only I were in possession of my human birthright! Better to crawl into the wilderness like a wild animal than to have to beg to be excused for my existence every step of the way!—I can't stay here!—I met the Countess Werdenfels yesterday.—How I could have offended her is something I cannot understand. I suppose I unintentionally assumed the tone I've grown accustomed to using with our Simba.

KEITH I've received more slaps on the ear from women than I have hairs on my head! But no one has ever laughed at me behind my back because of it!

SCHOLZ I'm a man without breeding!—And with a woman for whom I have the highest regard!

KEITH A man like you, whose every step from his youth on has given rise to a spiritual conflict, can be the master of his times and rule the world long after the rest of us have become food for worms!

SCHOLZ And then there's our little Simba who's playing the waitress here tonight!—The most experienced diplomat never had to deal with as ticklish a situation as this!

KEITH Simba doesn't know you!

SCHOLZ I'm not afraid that Simba will be too friendly with me; I'm afraid Simba will be insulted if I ignore her here without the slightest provocation.

KEITH How could you insult her by doing that! She understands class distinctions a hundred times better than you!

SCHOLZ Believe me, I've learned all there is to know about class distinctions! God knows, they're the fetters that show man his utter weakness in its most extreme form!

KEITH I suppose you think *I* have no weakness to combat! It makes no difference whatever whether my conduct is as correct as the course of the planets, or whether my dress is as elegant and well-chosen as possible, these things are no more capable of changing these plebeian hands of mine than you can make an intellect out of an imbecile! With my intellectual endowments I should long ago have enjoyed a better position in society were it not for these hands.—Come, you'd do best to put your overcoat in the next room!

SCHOLZ Leave me alone! I couldn't talk calmly with the Countess today if I wanted to.

KEITH Then talk with the two divorcées; they're both experiencing conflicts similar to yours.

SCHOLZ Both at the same time?!

KEITH Neither one of them is over twenty-five, absolute beauties, ancient Nordic aristocracy, and so ultra-modern in their principles that they make me feel like an old flintlock beside them.

SCHOLZ   I rather feel that I'm not far from being a modern myself. (SCHOLZ *goes off into the gameroom;* KEITH *is about to follow him but at that moment* SARANIEFF *enters from the hallway*)

SARANIEFF   Tell me, is there anything left to eat?

KEITH   Please leave your coat outside! I haven't eaten all day long.

SARANIEFF   One needn't worry so about it in here. But first I must ask you something very important. (SARANIEFF *hangs his hat and coat in the hallway; meanwhile* SASCHA *in frock coat and satin breeches enters from the gameroom with a filled champagne cooler on his way into the diningroom*)

KEITH   When you set off the fireworks later, Sascha, be sure you're careful with the big mortar! There's all hellfire in that one!

SASCHA   Oh, I'm not scared, Herr Baron! (*goes off into the diningroom, closing the door behind him*)

SARANIEFF   (*re-enters from the hallway*) Have you any money?

KEITH   But you've just sold a picture! Why do you think I sent my friend to see you?

SARANIEFF   What do you expect me to get from a squeezed lemon like him?! Why, you've already stripped him to his shirt. He has to wait three days before he can pay me a pfennig.

KEITH   (*gives him a note*) Here are a thousand marks.

(SIMBA, *a typical Munich girl, ruddy complexion, with nimble movements, luxuriant red hair, in a tasteful black dress with white pinafore, enters from the diningroom with a serving tray of half-empty wine glasses*)

SIMBA   The Herr Councillor wants to drink another toast to the Herr Baron.

(KEITH *takes one of the glasses from the tray and goes to the table through the open door.* SIMBA *goes off into the gameroom*)

KEITH   Ladies and gentlemen! This evening's celebration signifies the beginning of an era for Munich which will eclipse everything that has gone before. We are creating here in this city a center for the arts in which all the arts of the world will find a welcome home. If our project has been the cause of general astonishment, then you must be mindful of the fact it is always only the truly astounding which wins the crown of greatest success. I empty my glass in honor of the principle which has ordained Munich a city of the arts, in honor of Munich's citizens and its lovely women. (*While the glasses are still clinking,* SASCHA *enters from the diningroom, closes the door behind him and goes into the gameroom.* SIMBA *enters from the gameroom with a platter of cheese under a glass cover on her way into the diningroom*)

SARANIEFF   Simba! Have you been struck blind?! Can't you see, Simba, that this epicurean of yours is about to escape from your snare and be gathered up again by this Countess from Perusa Strasse?!

SIMBA   What are you doing out here? Go on, sit at the table!

SARANIEFF   Me sit with the Caryatids!— Simba! Do you want all that lovely money that your epicurean has in his pockets to be devoured by the insane Marquis of Keith?!

SIMBA   Go on, now, let me alone! I have to serve!

SARANIEFF   The Caryatids don't need anymore cheese! It's time they wiped their mouths and put an end to it! (*He places the cheese platter on the table and takes* SIMBA *on his knee*) Simba! Don't you feel anything for me anymore! Am I to have to beg for twenty mark pieces from the Marquis of Keith amid wailing and the gnashing of teeth, while you can fetch thousand mark notes fresh from their source!

SIMBA   Thanks! Nobody in the world ever plagued me like this epicurean with his compassion, that stupid compassion of his! He's trying to tell me I'm a martyr of civilization! Ever hear anything like that? Me a martyr of civilization! I said to him, I said: "Tell your society ladies that! They'll like it when you call them martyrs of civilization, because otherwise they're nothing!" A martyr of civilization he calls me, when I can drink champagne and have all the fun I want!

SARANIEFF   Simba! If I were a woman of your qualities this epicurean would have to pay for every muggy glance with an ancestral castle!

SIMBA   That's the way he talks all right! He asks me why he's a man. Like there aren't enough ghosts in the world! Ever hear me ask why I'm a girl?

SARANIEFF   Nor do you ask us to throw away fifty million marks on some confounded idea of yours!

SIMBA   Oh, those sad millions! You know, there's only once I've seen this epicurean laugh since I met him. I told him, this epicurean, that he had to learn to ride a bicycle. And so he learned. We took a ride to Schleissheim and while we were in the woods looking around a thunderstorm broke out like I thought the world would come to an end. It was then, for the first time since I met him, that he started to laugh. Oh, and how he laughed! "There," I said, "now you're a real epicurean!" He laughed at every stroke of lightning! The more it lightninged and thundered the crazier he laughed!—"Don't stand there under the trees," I said, "that's where the lightning'll hit!"—"No lightning's going to hit me," he said, and laughed and laughed!

SARANIEFF   Simba! Simba! At that very moment you could have become an imperial countess!

SIMBA   Thanks! What I could have become is a Social Democrat. World betterment, humanitarianism, those are his specialties. No thanks, I wasn't made for the Social Democrats. They're too moralistic for me! Let them get into power once and goodbye champagne suppers.—Have you seen my lovey?

SARANIEFF   Have I seen your lovey? I thought I was your lovey!

SIMBA   That could be almost anybody!— You see, I have to keep close watch on him, otherwise the Marquis of Keith won't engage him for his new Fairyland Palace.

(SOMMERSBERG *enters from the hallway*)

SIMBA   Here he is! Where in Heaven's name have you been all this time?

SOMMERSBERG   I was sending off a telegram to the newspapers.

SARANIEFF   My God, the graves have begun to open! Sommersberg! Aren't you ashamed to come back from the dead to be secretary of this Fairyland Palace?!

SOMMERSBERG   (*indicating* SIMBA) This angel has restored me to the world.

SIMBA   Oh, go on, lovey!—He comes and asks me where he can get some money.—"Go to the Marquis of Keith," I said. "If he's all out, you won't find another pfennig in the city of Munich."

RASPE   (*dressed in the most elegant evening clothes, a small chain with an Order on his chest, enters from the gameroom*) Simba, this is simply scandalous, making the Fairyland Palace Company wait for its cheese!

SIMBA   (*catches up the cheese platter*) Holy Mother of God!—I'll be there!

SARANIEFF   Why don't you just stay with the old crones you are hired to take care of!

SIMBA   (*taking* RASPE'S *arm*) You let this

boy alone, you hear?—You'd both be happy enough if you were as handsome as he is!

SARANIEFF   Simba—you are a born whore!

SIMBA   I'm what?

SARANIEFF   You are a born whore!

SIMBA   Say that again?

SARANIEFF   You are a born whore!

SIMBA   I'm not a born whore. I'm a born cheese spit. (*goes off into the diningroom with* RASPE)

SOMMERSBERG   I even dictate her love letters for her.

SARANIEFF   Then it's you I have to thank for destroying my castles in the air!

(SASCHA *enters from the gameroom with a lighted lantern*)

SARANIEFF   My God, what are you all got up for! You want to marry a countess too?

SASCHA   I'm going to set off the fireworks in the garden now. Wait'll I set off the big mortar, that'll open their eyes! The Herr Marquis said there's all hellfire in that one! (*goes off into the garden*)

SARANIEFF   His master's afraid if he sets off the fireworks himself he might go up with them!—There's no wonder fortune never lets him up in the saddle! He's no sooner mounted than he rides the poor beast to its shame till there's not a shred of flesh on its ribs! (*as the center door opens and the guests leave the diningroom*) Come, Sommersberg! Now our Simba can dish us up a real Lucullan feast!

(*The guests stream into the salon; at their head,* RASPE *between* FRAU COUNCILLOR OSTERMEIER *and* FRAU KRENZL; *then* KEITH *with* OSTERMEIER, KRENZL, *and* GRANDAUER; *then* ZAMRIAKI *with* BARONESS VON ROSENKRON *and* BARONESS VON TOTLEBEN, *and finally* SCHOLZ *and* ANNA. —SARANIEFF *and* SOMMERSBERG *sit down at the table in the diningroom*)

RASPE   Will your royal highnesses join me in a cup of exquisite coffee?

FRAU OSTERMEIER   My, I don't think there could possibly be another cavalier as gracious as you in all southern Germany!

FRAU KRENZL   The noblemen of our Royal House could certainly take you as an example!

RASPE   I give you my absolute word of honor that this is the most blessed moment of my life. (*goes off with both ladies into the gameroom*)

OSTERMEIER   (*to* KEITH) All the same it was nice of old Casimir, you know, to send us a congratulatory telegram. But then, you see, my dear friend, old Casimir is a very cautious man!

KEITH   Never mind! Never mind! We'll have old Casimir with us by the time of our first general meeting.—Won't you gentlemen have some coffee?

(OSTERMEIER, KRENZL *and* GRANDAUER *go off into the gameroom*)

BARONESS VON ROSENKRON (*to* KEITH, *who is about to follow the gentlemen*)   Promise me now, Marquis, that you will let me study to be a dancer at the Fairyland Palace.

BARONESS VON TOTLEBEN   And that you'll let me learn to be a trick-rider!

KEITH   I swear to you, my lovely goddesses, that we will not open the Fairyland Palace without you!—What's the matter with you, Zamriaki? You're as pale as a corpse . . .

ZAMRIAKI (*a slender, short conservatory musician, with long, black, wavy hair parted down the middle; speaks with a Polish accent*)   On my symphony I am working day and night. (*takes* KEITH *to one side*) If you permit me, Herr Marquis, I like to ask for advance of twenty marks on salary of conductor for Fairyland Palace Orchestra.

KEITH   With the greatest pleasure. (*gives him the money*) Could you perhaps give us a sampling soon of your new symphony in one of my Fairyland Palace concerts?

ZAMRIAKI   I play the Scherzo. Scherzo will be great success.

BARONESS VON ROSENKRON (*at the glass door into the garden*)   My, just look at this sea of light! Look, Martha, look!—Come, Zamriaki, take us into the garden!

ZAMRIAKI   I come, ladies! I come! (*He goes into the garden with* BARONESS VON ROSENKRON *and* BARONESS VON TOTLEBEN)

KEITH (*following them*)   Damnation, people, stay away from the big mortar! It's loaded with my most splendid rockets! (*goes off into the garden*)

(SIMBA *closes the center door from inside the diningroom.*—ANNA *and* SCHOLZ *stay behind alone in the salon*)

ANNA   I can't imagine what in the world I could have taken amiss. Have you ever experienced this tactlessness you speak of in your relations with any other women?

SCHOLZ   Quite impossible. But you see, I'm as happy now as a person who has been locked inside a prison since his earliest childhood, and now for the first time in his life breathes the free air. That's why I'm still so distrustful of myself with every step I take; I'm that afraid of losing my newfound happiness.

ANNA   I can imagine it must be fascinating to live one's life in the dark without ever opening one's eyes!

SCHOLZ   You see, Countess, if I could exchange my existence for one which strives for the common good, I could never render my Creator sufficient thanks.

ANNA   I thought you came to Munich to learn to be an epicurean?

SCHOLZ   This learning to be an epicurean is only a means to an end for me. I give you my most sacred assurance of that! But you mustn't think me a hypocrite because of it!—Oh, there's still so much good still to fight for in this world! I'll find my rightful place. The more blows Fortune rains down upon my head, the more precious this bag of bones will be to me, that seemed so unspeakably burdensome till now. And I am absolutely certain of this one fact: if I am ever successful at putting myself at the service of my fellow men I shall never, never once assume any credit for it! Whether my path lead me upwards or whether it lead me downwards I belong solely to that terrible and pitiless race whose interest resides in self-preservation!

ANNA   Maybe the only reason famous people become famous is that they couldn't endure traffic with us common run-of-the-mill people!

SCHOLZ   You still do not understand me, Countess.—As soon as I have found my proper sphere of activity I shall be the most modest and grateful member of society. I've even begun riding a bicycle here in Munich. It made me feel as though I hadn't seen the world since the days of my childhood. Every tree, every body of water, the mountains, the heavens, they were all one great revelation which I seemed to have had a presentiment of in a former life.—May I invite you to a cycling party sometime?

ANNA   What would you say to tomorrow morning at seven? Or aren't you one for getting up early?

SCHOLZ   Tomorrow morning at seven! I see my life spread out before me like an endless spring landscape!

ANNA   Just don't keep me waiting!

(ZAMRIAKI, BARONESS VON ROSENKRON *and* BARONESS VON TOTLEBEN *return from the garden.*—SIMBA *enters from the gameroom*)

BARONESS VON ROSENKRON   Oh, but it's cold! —Martha, we'll have to take our shawls the next time we go out. Play us a cancan, Zamriaki! (*to* SCHOLZ) Do you dance the cancan?

SCHOLZ   I regret that I do not, madam.

BARONESS VON ROSENKRON (to BARONESS VON TOTLEBEN)   Then let us dance together!

(ZAMRIAKI has seated himself at the piano and begun a waltz)

BARONESS VON ROSENKRON   Do you call that a waltz, Maestro?

ANNA (to SIMBA)   But you can do the waltz, can't you?

SIMBA   If madam wishes . . .

ANNA   Come on!

(BARONESS VON ROSENKRON, BARONESS VON TOTLEBEN, ANNA and SIMBA dance the waltz)

BARONESS VON ROSENKRON   More tempo, please!

(KEITH returns from the garden and turns off all the electric lights but one, so that the salon is only dimly lighted)

ZAMRIAKI (breaks off playing with annoyance)   I come with each beat closer to my symphony.

BARONESS VON TOTLEBEN   But why is it so dark all of a sudden?

KEITH   So that my rockets make more of an impression! (He opens the door to the dining-room) If you please, ladies and gentlemen . . .

(RASPE, HERR and FRAU OSTERMEIER and HERR and FRAU KRENZL enter the salon. SIMBA goes off)

KEITH   It pleases me to be able to announce to you that in the course of the next few weeks the first of our great Fairyland Palace concerts will take place. These concerts shall serve as publicity for our enterprise. Countess Werdenfels will introduce us to some songs of very recent composition, while our conductor Herr Zamriaki will personally direct excerpts from his symphonic poem The Wisdom of the Brahmans.

(General applause. In the garden a rocket rises hissingly into the air, casting a reddish shimmer into the salon. KEITH turns off all the electric lights and opens the glass door)

KEITH   Into the garden, ladies and gentlemen! Into the garden if you care to see something!

(A second rocket rises into the air as the guests leave the salon. KEITH, who is about to follow them, is held back by ANNA. The stage remains dark)

ANNA   Just what do you mean announcing I'm to take part in your Fairyland Palace concert?

KEITH   If you want to wait until your teacher declares you ready for the public, you might grow old and grey without ever having

sung a note. (throws himself into a chair) At last, at last this perilous rope-dancing bit is coming to an end! For ten years I had to dissipate my powers so as not to lose my equilibrium. From this day on my way is upwards!

ANNA   And just where am I supposed to get the cheek to step in front of the Munich public with my so-called singing?!

KEITH   I thought you were going to be the best Wagnerian singer in Germany inside of two years.

ANNA   I said that only in jest.

KEITH   How was I to know that!

ANNA   Other concerts are prepared for months in advance!

KEITH   I haven't denied myself thousands of times in my lifetime only to pattern myself after other people. If your so-called singing doesn't please them, then they'll be intoxicated by the brilliance of your Parisian concert dress.

ANNA   If only the others saw me with your eyes!

KEITH   I'll see they use the right glasses!

ANNA   I no sooner come within your sight than you hear and see the most fantastic sort of day-dreams. You overrate my appearance as much as you overrate my art.

KEITH (jumping up)   I have never been suspected of overrating women, but I knew all there was to know about you from the first moment I laid eyes on you! Is it any wonder I looked for you for ten years on two separate continents! You might have made my acquaintance several times, but at the time you were either in the clutches of a bandit like myself or else I was reduced to such a level that there would have been little point in my entering your luminous circle of society.

ANNA   Just because you're losing your mind out of love for me, is that any reason why I should heap the scorn of all Munich on my own back?

KEITH   Other women have heaped quite different things on themselves for my sake!

ANNA   I haven't become infatuated with you yet!

KEITH   That's what they all say! You might as well surrender to your inevitable good fortune. I shall inspire you with the necessary degree of ingenuousness for your first appearance—even if I have to drive you out there with a loaded revolver!

ANNA   You just keep pushing me around like an animal and you'll see how soon it will be over between us!

KEITH   You can be confident in the fact that I'm a man who takes life damned seriously!

Perhaps I may like to bathe in champagne, but for all that I can deny myself every one of life's pleasures, like few other people can. Not a single moment of my existence is bearable to me unless I've made at least one step of progress towards my goal!

ANNA   And it's about time you reached that goal!

KEITH   Do you really think, Anna, that I would arrange this Fairyland Palace concert if I were not absolutely certain of the fact that it will yield a brilliant triumph for you?!—Let me tell you something: I am a man of *faith* . . . (*In the garden a rocket rises hissingly into the air*) . . . I believe in nothing so firmly as in the fact that our efforts and sacrifices are rewarded in this world!

ANNA   You'd *have* to believe like that to overwork yourself like you do!

KEITH   And if we are not rewarded then our children will be.

ANNA   But you haven't any children!

KEITH   Then you will give them to me, Anna—children with my intelligence, with robust, healthy bodies and aristocratic hands. And for that I shall build you a home fit for a queen, such as a woman of your stamp deserves! And I shall place a spouse at your side with the power of fulfilling every desire mirrored in your great, black eyes (*He kisses her passionately. In the garden some fireworks are set off which for a moment bathe the couple in a dark red glow*)—Go into the garden. The Caryatids are dying for the privilege of kneeling before our Divinity!

ANNA   Aren't you coming too?

KEITH   (*turns on two of the electric lights so that the salon is dimly lighted*)   I want to dash off a newspaper article about our concert. The notice must appear in tomorrow morning's paper. In it I shall congratulate you in advance for your eminent triumph. (ANNA *goes into the garden.* KEITH *sits at the table and notes down a few words.* MOLLY GRIESINGER, *a colored shawl over her head, enters excitedly and provoked from the hallway*)

MOLLY   I have to speak to you for a moment.

KEITH   As long as you want, my child; you aren't disturbing me at all. I told you though that you wouldn't be able to hold out at home alone.

MOLLY   I pray to Heaven for some dreadful disaster to overtake us! That's the only thing left that can still save us!

KEITH   But why won't you come with me if I ask you to?

MOLLY   (*shuddering*)   To your friends?

KEITH   The people in these rooms are the business on which we both live! But you find it unbearable that I should be here with my thoughts and not with you!

MOLLY   Can that surprise you?—You know, when you're with these people you're an entirely different person; you're someone I've never known, whom I've never loved, whom I would never in my life have followed so much as a single step, to say nothing of sacrificing home, family, happiness, everything.—You're so good, so wonderful, so dear!—But with these people —to me you're worse than—than dead!

KEITH   Go home and dress yourself up a little; Sascha will go with you. You *mustn't* be alone tonight.

MOLLY   Yes, I'm just in the mood to get dressed up. The way you're carrying on frightens me so that I feel as if the world's going under tomorrow. I have the feeling that I must do something, whatever it may be, to keep these horrors from us.

KEITH   As of yesterday I am drawing a yearly salary of one-hundred-thousand marks. You needn't fear any longer that we'll die of hunger.

MOLLY   Don't joke like that! You're sinning against *me*! I can scarcely express any more what it is that frightens me!

KEITH   Then tell me what I can do to calm you. I'll do it at once.

MOLLY   Come with me! Come with me out of this murderers' den where all they want to do is destroy you. It's true that I've complained to people about you; but I did it because I couldn't look at your childish delusions any longer. You're so stupid! Really you are! You let yourself be taken in by the lowest, commonest swindlers, and you patiently let them cut your throat!

KEITH   It's better, my child, to suffer evil than to do evil.

MOLLY   Yes, if you only knew!—But they make certain your eyes stay closed. These people flatter you by saying you're a marvel of cleverness and diplomacy! And only because your vanity strives towards nothing higher than to be just that! At the same time they are quietly and cold-bloodedly placing the rope around your neck!

KEITH   What is this terrible thing you're so afraid of?

MOLLY   (*whimpering*)   I can't tell you! I can't make myself say it!

KEITH   Please, you *must* say it; you'll be able to laugh about it then.

MOLLY   I'm afraid that . . . I'm afraid that . . . (*A muffled report sounds from the garden;* MOLLY *screams and falls to her knees*)

KEITH (*helping her up*) That was the large mortar.—You must calm yourself!—Come, have a couple glasses of champagne; then we'll go out and look at the fireworks together . . .

MOLLY Those fireworks have been burning inside me for fourteen days now!—You were in Paris!—Who was with you in Paris!—I swear to you by everything that's holy that I never trembled for you, that I never suffered anything, if only you will come with me now!

KEITH (*kisses her*) Poor creature!

MOLLY (*throws her arms passionately around his neck and covers him with kisses*) You're dear!—You're wonderful!—You're good!—(*She lets loose of him, smiling*) All I wanted was to see you today, just once, with your friends. You know there are times when I'm a little . . .

(*She turns her fist in front of her forehead*)

KEITH (*wants to keep her back*) You're staying here, girl . . .!

(MOLLY *rushes out through the hall door.* SCHOLZ *enters from the garden through the glass door, limping and holding his knee*)

SCHOLZ (*very pleased*) Please don't be alarmed!—Put out the light so the people outside can't see me. No one noticed anything.

(*He drags himself to the chair into which he lets himself down*)

KEITH What's the matter with you?

SCHOLZ Turn the lights out first.—It's nothing. The big mortar exploded! A piece of it struck me in the knee!

(KEITH *has put the light out; the stage is dark*)

KEITH That could only happen to you!

SCHOLZ (*in a blissful voice*) The pains are already beginning to subside.—Believe me, I'm the most fortunate creature under the sun! In any case I won't be able to go cycling tomorrow with the Countess Werdenfels. But what does that matter? (*jubilantly*) I have overcome the evil spirits; happiness lies before me; I belong to life! From this day forward I am another man . . .

(*A rocket rises from the garden and bathes* SCHOLZ's *features in a dark red glow*)

KEITH Damnation!—I almost didn't recognize you then!

SCHOLZ (*jumps up from the chair and hops about the room triumphantly on one foot, while holding onto his injured knee with his hands*) For ten long years I took myself to be an outcast! Outlawed by society! Now I realize that it was all just my imagination! All just my imagination! Nothing but imagination!

ACT FOUR

(*In the gardenroom of the* COUNTESS WERDENFELS *a number of rather large laurel wreaths are lying about on the arm chairs; a splendid bouquet of flowers is placed in a vase on the table.* ANNA, COUNTESS WERDENFELS, *dressed in an attractive morning costume, is found in conversation with* POLICE INSPECTOR RASPE *and* HERMANN CASIMIR. *It is forenoon*)

ANNA (*a piece of colored paper in her hand, to* HERMANN) Let me thank you, my young friend, for the lovely verses you composed for me after our first Fairyland Palace concert yesterday evening.—(*to* RASPE) But I find it highly unusual that you, sir, should come to me, especially on this particular morning, with such serious rumors concerning your friend and benefactor.

RASPE The Marquis of Keith is neither my friend nor my benefactor. Two years ago I asked him to give evidence at my trial as a psychiatric expert. He might have saved me a year and a half in prison. But instead, he absconded to America with a fifteen-year-old girl!

(SIMBA, *in a tasteful maid's uniform, enters from the hallway and hands* ANNA *a card*)

SIMBA The gentleman would like to see you.

ANNA (*to* HERMANN) Good Lord, your father!

HERMANN (*frightened, looking at* RASPE) How could my father suspect I came here!

RASPE He didn't hear it from me.

ANNA (*lifts the curtain to the gameroom*) Go in there. I'll send him on his way.

(HERMANN *goes into the gameroom*)

RASPE It's best, then, if I pay my respects and be on my way too.

ANNA Yes, I should like that.

RASPE (*bowing*) Madam! (*off*)

ANNA (*to* SIMBA) You may show the gentleman in.

(SIMBA *shows* CONSUL CASIMIR *in; he is followed by a lackey from whom he has taken a bouquet of flowers;* SIMBA *goes off*)

CONSUL CASIMIR (*handing her the flowers*) You will permit me, madam, to extend to you my sincere congratulations on your triumph of yesterday evening. Your debut has taken all Munich by storm; you could not, however, have made a more lasting impression on any of your listeners than you did on me.

ANNA   Even if that were the case, I must still be overwhelmed with your coming personally to tell me so.

CASIMIR   Do you have a moment?—It has to do with a purely practical matter.

ANNA   (*invites him to be seated*)   I'm certain you'll find yourself on the wrong track.

CASIMIR   (*after both have been seated*)   We shall see presently.—I wanted to ask you if you would be my wife.

ANNA   How am I to understand you?

CASIMIR   That is why I am here, so that we can come to an understanding over it. Permit me to make it clear to you from the start that you will naturally be required to give up the enticing artistic career which you embarked on yesterday evening.

ANNA   Surely you can't have considered this step thoroughly enough yet.

CASIMIR   A man of my age, madam, takes no step that is ill-considered. Later, yes—or earlier. Would you care to tell me what other scruples may come to mind?

ANNA   Surely you must know that I cannot give an answer to such a proposal.

CASIMIR   I'm quite aware of that. I am speaking, however, for that time in the not too distant future, when you shall be utterly free to make your own decisions concerning yourself and your future.

ANNA   At this moment I really can't imagine any such possibility.

CASIMIR   Today, as you see, I am the most respected man in Munich, but tomorrow I might be under lock and key. I should not find fault with my best friend if by chance he should ask himself whether to stand by me in such a reversal of fortune.

ANNA   Would you also not find fault with your wife if *she* should consider the same question?

CASIMIR   My wife, certainly; my mistress, never. I want no answer from you just yet. I am speaking only for the time when you may find yourself with nowhere to turn or when the situation alters and frees you from all obligations; in short then, for the time when you need someone to turn to.

ANNA   And then you will make me your wife?

CASIMIR   At all events that must appear almost insane to you; yet that is all to the honor of your modesty. But in such a case one is only accountable to oneself. As you may perhaps know, I have two small children at home, girls of three and six. Then, as you might well imagine, there are other considerations . . . As for you, I shall take all responsibility upon myself that you do not disappoint my expectations—even in spite of yourself.

ANNA   I must admire your self-confidence.

CASIMIR   You may have absolute confidence in me.

ANNA   But after a success like yesterday evening!—It seemed as though an entirely different spirit came over the Munich public.

CASIMIR   Believe me, I sincerely envy the founder of the Fairyland Palace for this subtle shrewdness of his. Incidentally, I must express to you my particular compliments on your choice of a concert dress for yesterday. You displayed so aristocratic an assurance in it, and it showed your figure to such extraordinary effect, that I must confess I found it quite impossible to devote proper attention to your recital.

ANNA   Please don't think that I in any way overrate the applause in regard to my artistic accomplishments.

CASIMIR   I certainly would not blame you for it in any case; but your teacher has told me that a success like yours last night has brought misfortune to many people. And then there is one thing that you must not forget; where would the most celebrated singer today be if rich men did not consider it their moral duty to listen to her without hope of return. No matter how splendid the salary may be in individual cases, the fact remains that these people almost always live on charity.

ANNA   I was amazed at the reception the public gave every one of the numbers.

CASIMIR   (*rising*)   Until the unfortunate symphony of this Herr Zamriaki. Furthermore, I have no doubt whatever that with time we shall come around to praising the noise occasioned by this Herr Zamriaki as a divine artistic revelation. Let us allow the world its ways, hope for the best, and be prepared for the worst. You will permit me, madam, to bid you good day. (*off*)

(ANNA *seizes both her temples, goes to the gameroom, lifts the curtain and steps back*)

ANNA   You didn't even close the door!

(HERMANN CASIMIR *enters from the gameroom*)

HERMANN   How could I ever have dreamed I could live through an experience like this!

ANNA   Go on now, so that your father will find you at home.

HERMANN   (*notices the second bouquet*)   The flowers are from him?—I seem to have inherited *that* from him too.—Except that to him the expense means nothing.

ANNA Where do you get the money for such insane expenses?

HERMANN (*significantly*) From the Marquis of Keith.

ANNA Please, you must go now! You look tired. I hope your round of drinking didn't last too long last night!

HERMANN I helped save the composer Zamriaki's life.

ANNA Do you consider that one of your worthy accomplishments?

HERMANN What better have I to do?

ANNA It is nice of you, of course, to have a heart for unfortunate people; but you mustn't sit at the same table with them. Misfortune is contagious.

HERMANN (*significantly*) The Marquis of Keith told me the same thing.

ANNA Go now! Please!

(SIMBA *enters from the hallway and hands* ANNA *a card*)

SIMBA The gentleman would like to see you.

ANNA (*reading the card*) "Representative of the South German Concert Agency."—Tell him to come back in two weeks. (SIMBA *goes off*)

HERMANN What answer will you give my father?

ANNA I think it's time you left! You're becoming impertinent!

HERMANN I'm going to London—even if I have to steal the money. Then my father won't have any reason to complain about me.

ANNA That will be more to your benefit than to his.

HERMAN (*uneasily*) I owe that much to my two little sisters. (*off*)

ANNA (*reflects a moment, then calls*) Kathi!

(SIMBA *enters from the diningroom*)

SIMBA Yes, madam?

ANNA I want to get dressed.

(*A bell rings in the corridor*)

SIMBA At once, madam. (*goes to open the door*)

(ANNA *goes off into the diningroom. Immediately following,* SIMBA *shows in* ERNST SCHOLZ; *he walks supported by an elegant crutch, limping on his stiff knee, and carrying a large bouquet of flowers*)

ERNST SCHOLZ I've had no opportunity, my dear child, to thank you for your tactful, sensitive conduct recently at the garden party.

SIMBA (*formerly*) Does the Herr Baron wish to be announced to my mistress?

(KEITH *enters from the hallway in a light-colored overcoat, with a bundle of newspapers in his hand*)

KEITH (*removing his overcoat*) It's an act of Providence that I should find you here! (*to* SIMBA) What are you still doing here?

SIMBA Madam has taken me on as a housemaid.

KEITH You see, I brought you luck.—You may announce us!

SIMBA Very well, Herr Baron. (*goes off into the gameroom*)

KEITH The morning papers are already coming out with the most enthusiastic reviews of our concert yesterday! (*He sits down at the table downstage left and pages through the newspapers*)

SCHOLZ Have you had any word yet where your wife is staying?

KEITH She's with her parents in Bückeberg. Where did you suddenly disappear to yesterday during the banquet?

SCHOLZ I had the most vital need to be alone. How *is* your wife?

KEITH Thank you: her father is about to go bankrupt.

SCHOLZ Surely you'll have enough left over to protect her family from such an extremity!

KEITH Have you any idea what the concert yesterday cost me?

SCHOLZ I find you take things too lightly!

KEITH Do you really want me to help you hatch the eggs of eternity?

SCHOLZ I would consider myself fortunate if I could cede some of my excess sense of duty to you.

KEITH God protect me from that! I need all the elasticity possible to make the most of this success.

SCHOLZ (*self-confidently*) I have to thank you that today I can stand up to life calmly and confidently. Therefore I consider it my duty to speak as frankly to you as you spoke to me two weeks ago.

KEITH The only difference is that I didn't ask you for your advice.

SCHOLZ To my mind that's merely another reason for complete and open frankness. Through my exaggerated zeal for duty I was guilty for the death of twenty people; but *you* behave as though one had absolutely *no* duty to his fellow men. You take great pleasure in playing with the lives of others!

KEITH No one ever got away from me with more than a black eye.

SCHOLZ (*with growing self-confidence*) That is your personal good fortune! But you are not conscious of the fact that others have precisely the same claims to the pleasures of life as you. And as far as morality is concerned, that sphere in which we see Man's highest achievement, why, you haven't the slightest understanding of it.

KEITH   You do remain true to yourself, don't you!—You come to Munich with the express purpose of training yourself to be an epicurean and through some oversight train yourself to be a moralist.

SCHOLZ   By means of the variegated life here in Munich I have arrived at a modest yet all the more reliable self-evaluation of myself. During these last two weeks I have passed through such tremendous inner transformations that if you wanted to listen to me I actually *could* speak as a moralist.

KEITH   (*irritated*)   The fact is you can't endure my good fortune!

SCHOLZ   I don't believe in your good fortune! I'm so unspeakably happy that I could embrace the entire world, and quite honestly and frankly I wish you the same. But you will never have it as long as you jeer in your puerile way at the highest values of life. Before I came to Munich I was able only to appreciate the *spiritual* significance of the relationship between men and women, because at the time sensual gratification seemed vulgar to me. I've learned that it's the other way around. But you, in your entire life, have never valued a woman for anything higher than her sensual gratification. As long as you refuse to make those concessions to the moral order, as I have had to do, you will find that just that long will your good fortune stand on feet of clay!

KEITH   (*to the point*)   Things are really quite different. I can thank these last two weeks for my *material* freedom, and as a result I am finally able to enjoy my life. And you can thank these last two weeks for your *spiritual* freedom, and as a result *you* are finally able to enjoy *your* life.

SCHOLZ   With the difference that all *my* pleasures are concerned with becoming a useful member of human society.

KEITH   (*jumping up*)   Why should anyone even *want* to become a useful member of human society?!

SCHOLZ   Because otherwise one has no justification for his existence!

KEITH   I need no justification for my existence! I asked no one for my existence and I deduce from that my justification for existing according to my own dictates.

SCHOLZ   And so with extraordinary calm of spirit you give over your wife to misery, she who shared every danger and hardship with you these last three years!

KEITH   What am I to do! My expenses are so horrendous that I never have so much as a pfennig left over for my own use. I paid up my share of the founding capital with the first installment of my salary. For a moment I considered laying hold of the money that had been placed at my disposal to defray the costs of the preliminary work. But I can't do that.—Or would you advise me to?

SCHOLZ   I can let you have ten or twenty thousand marks if you find it necessary, if you can't help yourself in any other way. Just by chance I received a draft today from my steward for more than ten thousand marks. (*takes the draft from his portfolio and hands it to* KEITH)

KEITH   (*tears the paper from his hand*)   Just don't come to me tomorrow and say you want the money back!

SCHOLZ   I don't need it just now. The other ten thousand marks I'll have to have sent through my banker in Breslau. (ANNA *enters from the gameroom, dressed in elegant street clothes*)

ANNA   Pardon me for keeping you waiting, gentlemen.

SCHOLZ   (*hands her his flowers*)   I could not deny myself the pleasure, madam, of wishing you luck with all my heart on the first morning of your very promising career.

ANNA   (*places the flowers in a vase*)   Thank you. In last night's excitement I completely forgot to ask how your injuries are coming along.

SCHOLZ   Heaven knows, they're not worth talking about. My doctor says that if I wanted to I could be climbing mountains inside of a week. What pained me yesterday was the resounding and scornful laughter that Herr Zamriaki's symphony occasioned.

KEITH   (*has seated himself at the writing-table*)   I can do nothing more than give people the opportunity of showing what they can do. Whoever can't play his part will be left behind. I can find any number of conductors in Munich.

SCHOLZ   Wasn't it you who said of him that he's the greatest musical genius since Richard Wagner?

KEITH   Just because I *own* a nag, do you think I'd *call* it that? I must be prepared at every moment to answer for the accuracy of my accounts. (*rising*) I've just been to the municipal council with the Caryatids. They're questioning whether the Fairyland Palace is something which Munich really needs. The answer was unanimously in the affirmative. A city like Munich could not even begin to dream of all it needs!

SCHOLZ (*to* ANNA) I presume madam has world-embracing plans to discuss with her fortunate impressario.

ANNA Thank you, no; we have nothing to discuss with one another. Are you planning on leaving us already?

SCHOLZ May I have the honor of calling on you again in the next few days?

ANNA I should be pleased; you are always welcome.

(SCHOLZ *has shaken* KEITH's *hand; goes off*)

KEITH The morning papers have come out with enthusiastic critiques of your performance yesterday.

ANNA Have you had any news about Molly?

KEITH She's with her parents in Bückeberg. She's reveling in an ocean of petit bourgeois sentimentality.

ANNA The next time we won't let ourselves be so frightened for her! And besides that, she really needed to prove to you how completely unnecessary she is to you!

KEITH God be praised that passion for you is a book with seven seals. If a woman isn't capable of making a man happy then the least she wants to do is set the roof afire over his head!

ANNA Nevertheless you ought to inspire somewhat more confidence in your business enterprises! It isn't particularly pleasant sitting on top a volcano day and night!

KEITH Why must everything I hear today be a moral lecture!

ANNA Because you act as though you were in constant need of a sedative! You don't know what rest is. I've found that as soon as one is in doubt about doing one thing in preference to another, the best thing to do is *nothing at all.* It's only by doing things that one makes himself susceptible to all kinds of unpleasantries. I do as little as I possibly can and I've always been happy because of it. You can't blame anyone for not trusting you when all you do is chase after your own good fortune day and night like a starving wolf.

KEITH I can't help it if I'm insatiable.

ANNA But sometimes there are people sitting in sleighs with loaded rifles, and then they go bang-bang.

KEITH I'm bullet-proof. I still have two Spanish bullets from Cuba here in my limbs. And besides that I possess the most inviolable guarantee of my good fortune.

ANNA This is the absolute limit!

KEITH The limit, at least, of the human herd-mentality!—It must be twenty years now since that young Trautenau and I stood in short pants at the altar of the village church. My father was playing the organ. The village priest handed each of us a picture with a Bible verse on it. Since that time I have scarcely seen the inside of a church, but my confirmation verse has fulfilled itself in such ways that I've often been amazed beyond belief. And even today when some calamity or other arises I always smile scornfully in recollection of that saying: "We know that all things work together for good to them that love God."

ANNA "Them that love God"?—And you want to be capable of this love?

KEITH Concerning the question *whether I love God,* I have tested all existing religions and in no religion have I found that there is any difference between love of God and love of one's own well-being. Love of God is everywhere only a summary and symbolic way of expressing love of oneself.

(SIMBA *enters from the hallway*)

SIMBA Would the Marquis care to come out for a moment. Sascha is here.

KEITH Why doesn't the boy come in?

(SASCHA *enters with a telegram*)

SASCHA I didn't know if I should or if I shouldn't, because the Herr Baron said not to deliver telegrams in company.

KEITH (*breaks the seal on the telegram, wads it into a ball in his hand and throws it away*) Damnation!—My overcoat!

ANNA From Molly?

KEITH No!—I only hope to God nobody finds out about it!

ANNA Then she isn't with her parents in Bückeberg?

KEITH (*while* SASCHA *helps him into his coat*) No!

ANNA But you just said . . .

KEITH Is it *my* fault she's not in Bückeberg? You no sooner have a bit of luck in the world than you find a noose around your neck!

(KEITH *and* SASCHA *go off*)

SIMBA (*picks up the telegram and hands it to* ANNA) The Marquis forgot his telegram.

ANNA Do you know where Sascha came from?

SIMBA Sascha's from the country. His mother's a housekeeper.

ANNA Surely then his name can't be Sascha?

SIMBA At first his name was Seppi, but the Herr Marquis christened him Sascha.

ANNA Bring me my hat.

(*The bell rings in the corridor*)

SIMBA Right away, madam. (*goes to open the door*)

ANNA (*reads the telegram*) ". . . Molly is not here. Please answer by return wire if you have any sign of Molly. In anxious fear . . ."

(SIMBA *returns*)

SIMBA The Herr Baron forgot his gloves.

ANNA Which Baron?

SIMBA The epicurean.

ANNA (*searches hastily*) Merciful Heaven, where could his gloves be . . . !

(ERNST SCHOLZ *enters*)

SCHOLZ Will you permit me two more words, madam?

ANNA I was just about to go out. (*to* SIMBA) My hat, quickly!

(SIMBA *goes off*)

SCHOLZ My friend's presence prevented me from expressing myself as openly as I . . .

ANNA Perhaps you might care to wait for a more suitable opportunity.

SCHOLZ I hoped to be able to wait a few days for your decision. But my feelings, Countess, have overcome me! And so that there can be no doubt in your mind that my offer seeks only to gain you happiness, permit me to say, to confess to you that I—that I am quite unspeakably—in love with you.

ANNA Well? And what were your offers?

SCHOLZ Before you, as an artist, are able to reap the fruits of uncontested recognition you will find many obstacles in your path . . .

ANNA I know that, however, I don't expect to sing anymore!

SCHOLZ You don't want to sing anymore? How many unfortunate artists would give up half their lives to be able to buy your talent!

ANNA Is that all you have to say to me?

SCHOLZ I'm afraid I have offended you again without even realizing it. Naturally you expected me to offer you my hand . . .

ANNA You mean to say that isn't what you intended?

SCHOLZ I wanted to ask you if you would be my *mistress*.—I could not honor you as my wife any more highly than I could honor the mistress in you. (*From here on he speaks with the ruthless, aggressive deportment of a madman*) Whether as wife or mistress, I offer you my life, I offer you everything that I possess. You know that it was only after the most absolute self-conquest that I was able to accept the moral attitudes that are the standard here in Munich. If my happiness should be dashed to pieces on that conquest which I won over myself in order to be able to share in the happiness of my fellow man, that would be the most *revolting of farces!*

ANNA I thought you were doing it only to become a useful member of human society!

SCHOLZ I dreamed of bettering the world like a prisoner behind iron bars dreams of snow-covered mountains! Now I can hope for only one thing more, to make this woman happy whom I love so unspeakably, so that she will never regret her choice.

ANNA I'm sorry to have to tell you that I find myself indifferent towards you.

SCHOLZ Indifferent towards me? I have never had more proof of dedication from *any* woman than I have from you!

ANNA That's not my fault. Your friend described you to me as a philosopher who couldn't be bothered with reality.

SCHOLZ It was reality that wrested me from my philosophy! I'm not one of those who rail against earthly vanity all their lives, and who, when they are deaf and lame, have to be kicked along by death before they will accept him!

ANNA The Marquis of Keith is helped out of his misfortunes by his confirmation verse! He considers it an infallible magic formula before which police and bailiff take to their heels!

SCHOLZ I do not lower myself to the level of believing in omens! If this fortune-hunter is right, then I received just as infallible a magic formula against misfortune at my confirmation as he did. The priest gave me the verse: "Many are called, but few are chosen."—But that doesn't bother me! Even if I had the most certain proofs that I do *not* belong to the chosen, it could only strengthen me in my fearless battle against my destiny!

ANNA Please spare me this fearless battle of yours!

SCHOLZ I swear to you that I would rather renounce my reason than let myself be convinced through this reason that there are certain people who through no fault of their own are from the very beginning shut off from all happiness!

ANNA Complain about that to the Marquis of Keith.

SCHOLZ But I'm not complaining! The longer the hard school of misfortune endures the more hardened my intellectual resistance will become. It is an enviable transformation which people like myself enter into. *My soul is indestructible!*

ANNA I congratulate you!

SCHOLZ Therein lies my irresistible power! The less you feel for me the greater and more powerful becomes my love for you, and the sooner do I see the moment when you will say:

"I fought against you with all at my command, and still I love you!"

ANNA   Heaven protect me from it!

SCHOLZ   Heaven will *not* protect you from it! When a man of my strength of will, which has remained unbroken through all adversity, concentrates all his thought and endeavor on *one* design, then there are only two possibilities: either he achieves his goal or he loses his mind.

ANNA   Yes, I'm inclined to agree.

SCHOLZ   I will take the chance! It all depends on which is more resistant, your lack of feeling or my mind. I'm counting on the worst outcome and I will not look back till I have reached my goal; because if I cannot fashion a happy life out of the bliss which fills me at this moment, then there's no hope for me. The opportunity will never offer itself again!

ANNA   I thank you from the bottom of my heart for reminding me of that! (*She sits down at the writing-table*)

SCHOLZ   This is the last time that the world will be spread out before me in all its glory!

ANNA   (*writing a note*)   That applies to me too!—(*calls*) Kathi—(*to herself*) The opportunity will never offer itself to me again either.

SCHOLZ   (*suddenly coming to himself*)   Why are you so suspicious, madam?—Why are you so suspicious? You are mistaken, Countess!—You are harboring a terrible suspicion . . .

ANNA   Are you still unaware of the fact that you are detaining me?—(*calls*) Kathi!

SCHOLZ   I couldn't possibly leave you like this! Give me your assurance that you do not doubt my sanity!

(SIMBA *enters with* ANNA'*s hat*)

ANNA   Where were you so long?

SIMBA   I was afraid to come in.

SCHOLZ   Simba, you know better than anyone else that I'm in possession of my five senses . . .

SIMBA   (*pushing him back*)   Go on, don't talk so dumb!

ANNA   You will leave my maid alone. (*to* SIMBA) Do you know the address of Consul Casimir?

SCHOLZ   (*suddenly petrified*)   I bear the mark of Cain on my brow . . .

ACT FIVE

(*All the doors in the* MARQUIS OF KEITH'*s workroom are wide open. While* HERMANN CASIMIR *seats himself at the center table* KEITH *calls into the livingroom*)

KEITH   Sascha! (*Receiving no answer he goes to the waitingroom; to* HERMANN) Excuse me. (*calls into the waitingroom*) Sascha! (*comes downstage; to* HERMANN) So, you're going to London with your father's consent. I can give you the best of recommendations to take with you to London. (*throws himself onto the divan*) In the first place I recommend you leave your German sentimentality at home. Social Democracy and Anarchism won't even bring on a raised eyebrow in London anymore. But let me tell you one thing more: the only proper way to make use of one's fellow man is to play up to the good in him. Therein lies the art of being liked, the art of getting what one wants. The more abundantly you take advantage of your fellow man, the more careful you have to be that you have the right on your side. Never seek your own gain to the detriment of a virtuous man, but only to the detriment of scoundrels and blockheads. And now let me endow you with the philosophers' stone: the most splendid business in the world is morality. I'm not at the point yet of having made it my business, but I wouldn't be the Marquis of Keith if I let the opportunity slip from me.

(*The bell rings in the corridor*)

KEITH   (*calls*)   Sascha! (*rising*) I'll slap that rascal's ears! (*He goes into the hallway and returns with* COUNCILLOR OSTERMEIER)

KEITH   You couldn't have come at a more opportune moment, my dear Herr Ostermeier . . .

OSTERMEIER   My colleagues on the Board of Directors, my dear friend, have commissioned me to . . .

KEITH   I have a plan to discuss with you which will increase our intake a hundredfold.

OSTERMEIER   Do you want me to say at the general meeting that I failed again today to inspect your account books?

KEITH   You're raving, my dear Herr Ostermeier! Why don't you explain to me calmly and impartially what this is all about?

OSTERMEIER   It is about your account books, dear friend.

KEITH   (*irritably*)   I slave away for these bleary-eyed numbskulls . . .

OSTERMEIER   So he's right then! (*turning to leave*) Your servant!

KEITH   (*tears open the drawer of the writing-table*)   Here, you may revel in the account books if you like! (*turning to face* OSTERMEIER) And who is it who's right?

OSTERMEIER   A certain Herr Raspe, a police inspector, who bet five bottles of Pommery last night in the American Bar that you don't keep account books.

KEITH (*giving himself airs*) Well, yes, I don't keep account books.

OSTERMEIER Then show me your notebook.

KEITH Where would I have found time since establishing the Company to set up an office!

OSTERMEIER Then show me your notebook.

KEITH (*giving himself airs*) I have no notebook.

OSTERMEIER Then show me the deposit receipts the bank gave you.

KEITH Do you think I took your money to let it out on interest?!

OSTERMEIER Don't excite yourself, my dear friend. If you don't have any books then surely you must make notations of your expenditures somewhere. An errand boy does that much.

KEITH (*tosses his memorandum book onto the table*) There you have my memorandum book.

OSTERMEIER (*opens it and reads*) "A silvery torrent of mauve silk and paillettes from shoulder to knee—" That's all!

KEITH If, after I've scored up one success after another, you care to place obstacles in my path, then you may rest assured of one thing, that you will never again see so much as one pfennig of your money whether in this world or in the next!

OSTERMEIER Our shares in the Fairyland Palace, my dear friend, aren't so bad off. We'll see our money again. Your servant! (*about to leave*)

KEITH (*holding him back*) Your snooping about is undermining our enterprise! You must pardon me, sir; but I am excited because I feel towards the Fairyland Palace like a father towards his child.

OSTERMEIER Then you needn't worry for your child's sake anymore. The Fairyland Palace is secured and will be built.

KEITH Without *me?*

OSTERMEIER If necessary, then without you, my dear friend!

KEITH But you can't do that!

OSTERMEIER At all events you are the last one who would hinder us!

KEITH That would be a low and infamous trick!

OSTERMEIER That would be better yet! Because we won't let ourselves be cheated by you any longer. And you call *us* the cheats!

KEITH If you believe yourself cheated then you ought to bring an action against me for payment of your money!

OSTERMEIER Excellent idea, my friend, if

only we didn't belong to the Board of Directors!

KEITH What are you talking about! You sit on the Board of Directors in order to support me in my work.

OSTERMEIER That's why I've come; but you don't seem to have anything to work at.

KEITH My dear Herr Ostermeier, you cannot expect me as a man of honor to submit myself patiently to so base an act as this. You take over the business side of the enterprise, why don't you, and let me manage the artistic side. I admit to certain faults in my managing of the business, but I was able to forgive myself for them because I knew they would never happen again, and that as soon as my position had been consolidated I would never be found at fault in even the slightest matter.

OSTERMEIER We could have talked of this yesterday when I and the other gentlemen were here; but you were more determined to talk our ears off. I might even say to you today: let's try again—if you had only shown yourself to be an honorable person. But when all we hear are lies, well . . .

KEITH (*giving himself airs*) Then you may tell the gentlemen that I shall build the Fairyland Palace just as surely as the idea was mine in the first place. If, however, *you* build it— and you may tell the gentlemen this too!—then I shall blow the Fairyland Palace, together with its Board of Directors and its stockholders—sky high!

OSTERMEIER I shall give them an exact account, good neighbor! You know, I really don't like to insult people to their faces, not to mention throwing them out on their . . . Your servant! (*goes off*)

KEITH (*starting after him*) . . . on their butts! I thought as much. (*to* HERMANN) Don't leave me alone now or I'm afraid I'll go to pieces till there's nothing left of me.—How can this be possible? (*with tears in his eyes*) After all those fireworks!—Am I to be driven like an outcast again from country to country? —No! No!—I mustn't let myself be pushed against a wall!—This is the last time in this life that the world will be spread out before me with all its glory! (*pulling himself up straight*) No!—I'm not only not tottering yet, but I'll take a leap that will set all Munich gaping. And while it's still shaking with astonishment, I'll fall on its prostrate body to the accompaniment of trumpets and drums, and tear it to pieces. We'll see then who'll be the first to get on his feet!

(*The* COUNTESS WERDENFELS *enters*)

KEITH (*rushing towards her*) My queen . . .

ANNA (*to* HERMANN) Would you excuse us for a moment?

(KEITH *shows* HERMANN *into the livingroom*)

KEITH (*closing the door behind him*) You look terribly self-confident today.

ANNA That's quite possible. Every day now since our Fairyland Palace concert I've received a good half-dozen proposals of marriage.

KEITH That means damned little to me!

ANNA But not to me.

KEITH (*scornfully*) Have you fallen in love with him?

ANNA Whom do you mean?

KEITH The epicurean!

ANNA Are you making fun of me?

KEITH Then whom *do* you mean?

ANNA (*indicating the livingroom*) His father.

KEITH And you want to talk with me about this?

ANNA No, I wanted only to ask whether you had had any sign of Molly.

KEITH No, but what's this about Casimir?

ANNA What's this about Molly—Are you keeping her disappearance a secret?

KEITH (*uneasily*) To be quite honest, I'm less afraid *she* has met with some misfortune than that her disappearance might pull the ground out from under *my* feet. If that seems somewhat inhuman, then I've paid for it by sitting out the last three nights in the telegraph office.—My only crime against her is that since we have known one another she has never once heard an angry word from me. She lets herself be eaten up with longing for her petit bourgeois world where, brow to brow, they drudge and humiliate themselves, and love one another! No free view, no free breath! Nothing but love! As much as possible and of the commonest sort!

ANNA Suppose they don't find Molly, what then?

KEITH I can be comforted with the prospect that once my house has collapsed about me she will come back penitent and smiling and say: "I'll never do it again!"—She's reached her goal; I can start packing.

ANNA And what's to become of *me*?

KEITH Up till now you've gained the most from our enterprise, and I hope you'll continue to gain by it. You can't lose anything because you haven't invested anything.

ANNA Are you so sure?

KEITH —I see . . . !

ANNA I'm glad!

KEITH —What did you answer him?

ANNA I wrote him that I couldn't give him an answer just yet.

KEITH That's what you wrote him?

ANNA I wanted to talk with you about it first.

KEITH (*takes her by the wrist and thrusts her from him*) If all you had in mind was to talk with me about it—then marry him!

ANNA A person as contemptuous of feelings as you surely ought to be able to discuss a purely practical matter calmly!

KEITH My feelings have nothing to do with this! What infuriates me is that you have so little family pride as to sell your birthright for a mess of pottage!

ANNA Whatever you have no part in is a mess of pottage!

KEITH I know my weaknesses; but these men are domestic animals! The one of them is weak in the head and the other weak in the spine! Do you want to bring creatures into the world who can't see before the eighth day?—If it's all over with me, I will gladly give you whatever glow of spirit I've imbued you with for use in your career. But if you take refuge from your artist's fate behind a sack of money, then you are worth no more today than the grass that one day will grow on your grave!

ANNA —If only you had the faintest idea where Molly could be!

KEITH You needn't revile me on top of it all! (*calls*) Sascha!

ANNA If you absolutely insist that we should part . . .

KEITH Of course I insist on it.

ANNA Then give me back my letters!

KEITH (*scornfully*) Do you plan to write your memoirs?

ANNA No, but they *could* find their way into the wrong hands.

KEITH (*jumping up*) Sascha!

ANNA What is it you want Sascha for?—I sent him on an errand.

KEITH How did you come to do that?!

ANNA Because he came to me. I've done so a number of times. When worst comes to worst the boy always knows where he can earn something.

KEITH (*sinks into the chair by the writing-table*) My Sascha! (*wipes a tear from his eye*) You didn't forget him either!—If you leave the room now, Anna, I shall break down like an ox in a slaughterhouse.—Give me a reprieve!

ANNA I have no time to lose.

KEITH Only until I've accustomed myself to doing without you, Anna!—I need mental clarity now more than ever . . .

ANNA   Are you going to give me back my letters?

KEITH   You're dreadful!—But of course you're doing it out of pity! I should at least be able to curse you now that you are no longer my mistress.

ANNA   As long as you live you'll never learn to judge a woman properly!

KEITH   (*straightening himself up proudly*) I will not renounce my belief even on the rack! You're on the road to good fortune; that's human enough. You will always remain to me what you once were.

ANNA   Then give me back my letters.

KEITH   No, my child! Your letters I shall keep for myself. Otherwise I shall doubt one day on my deathbed whether perhaps you were not a phantom after all. (*kissing her hand*) Good luck!

ANNA   Even without you! (*goes off*)

KEITH   (*alone, wrenched by spasms of the heart*)   —Ah!—Ah! This is my death!—(*He plunges for the writing-table, removes a handful of letters from the drawer and hurries after her*) Anna! Anna!

(*In the open doorway he is met by* ERNST SCHOLZ. SCHOLZ *walks without even a trace of his injury*)

KEITH   (*starting back*)   . . . I was just going to drive to your hotel.

SCHOLZ   There's no sense in that. I'm leaving.

KEITH   Then at least give me the twenty thousand marks you promised me yesterday!

SCHOLZ   You'll get no more money from me.

KEITH   The Caryatids will crush me! They want to take my directorship away from me!

SCHOLZ   That only confirms me in my resolution.

KEITH   It's a matter of overcoming a momentary crisis!

SCHOLZ   My wealth is far more important than you! My wealth will secure for the members of my family a free and lofty position of power for all time! Whereas you will never arrive at any point where you will be able to be of use to anyone!

KEITH   You parasite, where do you have the gall to accuse me of being useless?

SCHOLZ   Let's not argue!—I am finally fulfilling the greatest renunciation which many a man must agree to in this life.

KEITH   What's that?

SCHOLZ   I've torn myself from my illusions.

KEITH   (*scornfully*)   I suppose you're revelling again in the love of a girl from the lower classes?

SCHOLZ   I've torn myself from everything.— I am entering a private sanatorium.

KEITH   (*crying out*)   There is nothing more shameful than the betrayal of your own person!

SCHOLZ   I can well understand your anger. —During these last three days I have fought through the most terrible battle that can be allotted a mortal man.

KEITH   So that you could crawl away a coward?—So that as the victor you could renounce your worth as a human being?

SCHOLZ   (*flaring up*)   I am not renouncing my worth as a human being! You have no cause to insult or to jeer at me!—If a man is forced against his will into accepting the restraints in which I find myself now, then he may very well lose his worth as a human being. And because of that he remains relatively happy; he protects his illusions.—A man who settles his account with reality dispassionately, like myself, has to forfeit neither the respect nor the sympathy of his fellow men.

KEITH   (*shrugs his shoulders*)   If I were you I'd take a little more time to think it over.

SCHOLZ   I've thought it through thoroughly. It is the last duty which my fate has left to fulfill.

KEITH   Once you're in it's not so easy to get out.

SCHOLZ   If I had even the slightest hope of getting out again, I'd never go in. The renunciation which I have burdened myself with, the self-conquest and joyful hope which I have been able to wrest from my soul, I undertook in order to change my fate. God be damned that there is no longer any doubt that I am different from other men.

KEITH   (*very proudly*)   God be praised that I have never *doubted* that I was different from other men!

SCHOLZ   (*very calmly*)   God be damned or God be praised—up till now I have always thought of you as the most cunning of scoundrels!—I have given up even this illusion. A scoundrel can count on good fortune just as surely as an honorable man can count on his good conscience staying with him through an irrevocable misfortune. Your good fortune exists no more than mine, except that you don't realize it. Therein lies the horrible danger that hangs over you!

KEITH   The only danger hanging over me is that tomorrow I will have no money!

SCHOLZ   However long you live you'll never have money tomorrow!—I wish I knew that you were safe from your hopeless delusion. That's why I've come to see you this last time.

I am profoundly convinced that the best thing for you is to come with me.

KEITH (*with impatient suspicion*) Where?

SCHOLZ To the sanatorium.

KEITH Give me the thirty-thousand marks and I'll come with you!

SCHOLZ If you come with me you won't need money anymore. You'll find a more comfortable home than perhaps you may ever have known. We'll have a carriage and horses, we'll play billiards . . .

KEITH (*embracing him*) Give me the thirty-thousand marks! Do you want me to fall prostrate at your feet? I could be arrested on the spot!

SCHOLZ Has it really gone that far? (*pushing him back*) I don't give sums like that to madmen!

KEITH (*shouts*) You're the madman!

SCHOLZ (*calmly*) I'm the one who has come to his senses.

KEITH (*scornfully*)—If you want to go to a lunatic asylum just because you've come to your senses, then—go ahead!

SCHOLZ You're one of those they bring there by force!

KEITH I suppose you'll resume your title again once you've got into the lunatic asylum?

SCHOLZ Haven't you gone bankrupt on two continents in every conceivable way that bourgeois life permits?!

KEITH (*venomously*) If you consider it your moral duty to free the world of your superfluous existence then I'm certain you can find more radical means than going for drives or playing billiards!

SCHOLZ I tried that long ago.

KEITH (*shouts at him*) Then what are you still doing here?!

SCHOLZ (*gloomily*) I failed at that like I have at everything else.

KEITH I suppose you shot someone else by mistake!

SCHOLZ They cut the bullets from between my shoulders, quite near the spinal colunm.—This is the last time in your life that someone will extend you a helping hand. You already know the kind of experiences that are in store for you.

KEITH (*throws himself on his knees in front of* SCHOLZ *and clasps* SCHOLZ's *hands*) Give me the forty-thousand marks and I'm saved!

SCHOLZ That won't save you from the penitentiary!

KEITH (*starts up in terror*) Shut up!

SCHOLZ (*pleading*) Come with me, then you'll be out of danger. We grew up together; I see no reason why we shouldn't wait for the end together too. Bourgeois society judges you a criminal and subjugates you to all kinds of inhuman medieval tortures . . .

KEITH (*moaning*) If you won't help me, then go, I beg you!

SCHOLZ (*tears in his eyes*) Don't turn your back on your only refuge! I know you didn't choose your pitiable fate anymore than I chose mine.

KEITH Go away! Go away!

SCHOLZ Come with me. Come.—You have a companion in me as gentle as a lamb. It would be a dim ray of light in the night of my life if I knew how to rescue my boyhood friend from his terrible fate.

KEITH Go away! I beg you!

SCHOLZ —From this moment on you must entrust yourself to my guidance, like I once wanted to entrust myself to you . . .

KEITH (*cries out in despair*) Sascha! Sascha!

SCHOLZ —You must never forget that you have a friend who will welcome you at any time. (*goes off*)

KEITH (*crawls about, searching*)—Molly!—Molly!—This is the first time in my life that I have whimpered on my knees in front of a woman! (*He suddenly hears a sound from the direction of the livingroom*) There. . . ! There. . . ! (*after opening the door to the livingroom*) Oh, it's you?

(HERMANN CASIMIR *enters from the livingroom*)

KEITH I can't ask you to stay here any longer. I'm—I'm not quite well. I must first—sleep on it—for a night, to be master of the situation again.—Have a good . . . a good . . .

(*Heavy footsteps and many voices are heard from the stairs*)

KEITH Listen . . . The noise! The uproar! —That's bad . . .

HERMANN Lock the door then, why don't you?

KEITH I can't!—I can't!—It's her!

(*A number of patrons from the neighboring Hofbräuhaus drag in* MOLLY's *lifeless body. Water drips from her body, her clothes hang from her in shreds. Her undone hair covers her face*)

A BUTCHER'S HELPER Here's the bastard we want!—(*to the others behind him*) Right? —All right! (*to* KEITH) Look here what we fished up! Look here what we're bringin' you! Look here—if you got the guts!

A PORTER We pulled her out of the sewer! From under the iron bars! She must have been in the water a whole week!

A BAKERY WOMAN   And all the while the filthy little scoundrel runs around with his shameless crew! He hasn't paid for his bread in six weeks! He let his poor wife go begging at all the shops to see what she could get to eat! It would have made a stone cry to see the way she looked at the end!

KEITH   (*retreats to his writing-table, while the crowd presses around him with the body*) I beg of you, just calm yourselves!

THE BUTCHER'S HELPER   Shut your mouth, you swindler! Or I'll clout you one in the face that'll knock you off your feet!—Look here!— Is it her or not?—Look at her, I said!

KEITH   (*has taken hold of* HERMANN's *revolver which the* COUNTESS WERDENFELS *had left there earlier*)   Keep your hands off me unless you want to make me use this weapon!

THE BUTCHER'S HELPER   What's the coward say?—What's he say?—You goin' to give me the revolver?—Haven't you done enough to *her*, you dog? Give it here, I said . . . !

(THE BUTCHER'S HELPER *grapples with* KEITH *who has succeeded in getting close to the doorway through which at that moment* CONSUL CASIMIR *enters.* HERMANN CASIMIR *in the meanwhile has gone to the body; he and the* BAKERY WOMAN *carry the body to the divan*)

KEITH   (*defending himself like a desperate man, calls*)   Police!—Police! (*notices* CASIMIR *and clings to him*) Save me, for God's sake! They're going to hang me!

CONSUL CASIMIR   (*to the people*)   You listen to me now, because if this goes any further you'll learn to know another side of me!— Leave the woman there on the divan!—Now get out!—Or must I show you what a door's made for?—(*He pulls forward his son who wants to leave with the crowd*) Just a minute there, little friend! You're going to take a nice lesson with you on your trip to London!

(*The Hofbräuhaus people have left now*)

CASIMIR   (*to* KEITH)   I was going to invite you to leave Munich within twenty-four hours; now, however, I think it best for you if you leave on the next train.

KEITH   (*still holding the revolver in his left hand*)   I—I am not responsible for this—this disaster . . .

CASIMIR   You can settle that with yourself! But you *are* responsible for the forgery of my signature on a congratulatory telegram delivered to your founders' party on Brienner Strasse.

KEITH   I can't leave . . .

CASIMIR   (*hands him a paper*)   You will sign this receipt. In it you are certifying that a sum of ten-thousand marks owed to you by the Countess Werdenfels has been received from me.

(KEITH *goes to the writing-table and signs*)

CASIMIR   (*counting the money from his wallet*) As your successor in the directorship of the Fairyland Palace Company I will request of you that in the interests of our enterprise's successful development you do not show yourself again in Munich for some time!

(KEITH, *standing at the writing-table, hands the paper to* CASIMIR *and mechanically receives the money*)

CASIMIR   (*pocketing the paper*)   Pleasant journey! (*to* HERMANN) And you come with me!

(HERMANN *slips out shyly.* CASIMIR *follows him*)

KEITH   (*the revolver in his left hand, the money in his right, takes a few steps toward the divan, but recoils in horror. Then he looks irresolutely from the revolver to the money in turn. As he lays down the revolver behind him on the center table, with a grin on his face*) Life is one switchback after another . . .

Hugo von Hofmannsthal

1874-1929

ON CHARACTERS IN NOVELS AND PLAYS

An imaginary conversation between Balzac and Hammer-Purgstall, the Orientalist, in a garden near Vienna, 1842.

HAMMER You will permit me, dear sir, a question which for a long time has been burning on my tongue. Please excuse my liberty; you are aware that before you stands one of the most ardent admirers of your stupendous art of narration: but will you not now, in the prime of your creative imagination, present us with an equal, a similar series of works for the theatre?

You remain silent? You do not wish to answer me? Am I to presume that you do not love the dramatic form—that the theatre means nothing to you?

* * *

BALZAC Of course I love the theatre. The theatre as I understand it. The theatre where everything happens, everything. All vices, all absurdities, every manner of speech! How puny, how symmetrical in comparison is the theatre of Victor Hugo! Mine, the one I dream of, is the world, the chaos. And it did once exist, my theatre, it did exist. Lear on the heath, and the fool beside him, and Edgar and Kent and the voice of thunder mingled with their voices! Volpone, who worships his gold, and his servants—the dwarf, the eunuch, the hermaphrodite and the villain! And the legacy

hunters, offering him their wives and daughters, dragging those wives and daughters by the hair into his bed! And the daemonic voices of beautiful things, of alluring possessions, of golden vessels, of cut stones, of glittering candelabra, mingling with the human voices just as did the thunder. Yes, there was a theatre once.

HAMMER You mean in England around 1590?

BALZAC Yes, they had it. And later still. There have been belated flashes of lightning. Do you know Otway's *Venice Preserved*?

HAMMER I believe I saw it in Weimar.

BALZAC My Vautrin considers it the best of all plays. I set great store by such a person's judgment.

HAMMER Your lively interest in this subject is most gratifying to me. We will, I now see, have a Comédie humaine on the stage! We will see the wig fly from Vautrin's head and the convict's ghastly skull reveal itself. We will spy on Goriot while he, lonely in his ice-cold attic, conjures up the vision of his beautiful daughters. Why are you shaking your head, sir? From now on nothing can stand in your way.

BALZAC Nothing, apparently nothing whatever. Not even in my intentions, apparently. Nor do I lack dramaturgic collaborators. You cannot walk from the Opéra to the Palais Royal without meeting one or two of them. For I have wanted to create collaborators for myself. I wanted to creep into someone else. But I was wrong. One cannot hide in the ass's skin. I wanted to find something which I did not carry in myself. I wanted to commit a dishonesty, one of the great secret dishonesties. It lies in the nature of most authors to commit quantities of such dishonesties, and to remain unpunished. They resemble the rider in the German ballad who, without knowing it, rides across the frozen Lake Constance. But such people don't realize it even afterwards and so do not drop dead, as

---

"On Characters in Novels and Plays" by Hugo von Hofmannsthal, translated by Mary Hottinger and James and Tania Stern, is from *Hofmannsthal's Selected Prose*, Bollingen Series 33, and is reprinted by permission of the Bollingen Foundation.

did this rider. To make use of an art form and to do it justice: what an abyss lies between the two! The greater man is, the clearer he sees such things. Let others violate the forms; I, for my part, know that I am no dramatist, as little as—

Here M. de Balzac mentioned the names of all his compatriots who, in the preceding decade, had achieved a great, on occasion a European, reputation for their dramatic works, and continued:

The reason for this? The deepest reason? Perhaps I don't believe that characters exist. Shakespeare believed it. He was a dramatist.

HAMMER   You don't believe that human beings exist! That's good! You yourself have created between six and seven hundred of them, and given them life! And they've existed ever since.

BALZAC   I don't know whether these people could live on the stage. Are you familiar with what, in mineralogical science, is known as allotropy? The same matter appears twice in the realm of things, in completely different forms of crystallization, in quite unexpected shapes. The stage character is an allotropy of the corresponding real one. In the figure of Goriot I have the phenomenon of Lear; I have the chemical process of Lear, but I could not be further removed from the crystallization of Lear.—You, Baron, like all Austrians, are a born musician. You are, moreover, a learned musician. Let me tell you that characters in the theatre are nothing but contrapuntal necessities. The stage character is a contraction of the real one. What enchants me in the real one is precisely its breadth. Its breadth, which is the basis of its destiny. As I've said, I don't see people, I see destinies. And one must not confound destiny with catastrophe. Catastrophe as a symphonic composition, that's the business of the dramatist who is so closely related to the musician. The destiny of man—that is something whose reflection probably didn't exist before I wrote my novels. My people are nothing but litmus-paper which reacts by turning red or blue. The living, the great, the real, are the acids—the powers, the destinies.

HAMMER   You mean the passions?

BALZAC   You can use that word if you like, but you must give it a breadth such as it has never had, and then again narrow it down into the particular as has never been done before. I said "the powers." The power of the erotic for him who is the slave of love. The power of weakness for the weak. The power of glory for the ambitious. No, not just love, just weakness, just glory: but the love by which man is enslaved, his individual weakness, his specific glory. What I mean, Napoleon called his star: this is what compelled him to go to Russia, what compelled him to attach such importance to the notion of "Europe" that he could not rest until he had "Europe" lying at his feet. What I mean, unhappy people—glimpsing their lives in a flash of lightning—call their doom. For Goriot it is embodied in his daughters. For Vautrin, in human society, whose foundation he wants to blow up. For the artist, in his work.

HAMMER   And not in his experiences?

BALZAC   There are no experiences but the experience of one's own nature. This is the key which unlocks everyone's lonely prison cell, whose impenetrably thick walls, to be sure, are hung with the phantasmagoria of the universe as with colorful carpets. No one can escape from his world. Have you ever taken a long journey by steamer? Do you remember seeing there an odd, almost pitiful figure emerging towards evening from a corner of the engine-room, to spend a quarter of an hour on deck for a breath of fresh air? The man was half-naked; he had a blackened face and red, inflamed eyes. You'd been told that he was a stoker. Each time he came up, he swayed; he greedily drank a large jug of water to its last drop, lay down on a heap of oakum and played with the ship's dog; he cast a few shy, almost idiotic glances at the gay and elegant first-class passengers assembled on deck to delight in the stars of the Southern sky; he breathed, this man, as greedily as he had drunk, the air which was moistened by a night-cloud dissolving in dew and the perfume of virgin palm-islands floating over the ocean; and he disappeared again into the belly of the ship without having so much as noticed the stars or the aroma of the mysterious islands. Such are the sojourns of the artist among men, when he emerges staggering and with dim-sighted eyes from the fiery belly of his work. But this creature is no poorer than those up on deck. Even if, among those fortunate ones up there, among those chosen by life, there were two lovers who, leaning against one another with intertwined fingers, oppressed by the flood of their emotions, were to experience the crashing down of immeasurably distant stars as the Southern sky lets fall in sheafs, in swarms and cataracts from the unfathomable to the unfathomable—if they were to experience this as the strongest pulse-beat of bliss resounding to the periphery of their existence—even measured by this, he would not be the poorer. The artist is no poorer than any other among living beings, no poorer than Timur the Conqueror, no poorer than Lucullus, the Glutton, no poorer than Casanova the Seducer, no poorer than Mirabeau the Man of Destiny. But his destiny is nowhere but in his work. He should look nowhere else for his depths and his peaks: otherwise he will take a puny sand-hill for a Mont Blanc, will climb it breathlessly, will stand up there with arms akimbo and be the laughing-stock of all who live twenty years later. In his work he has everything; he has the nameless voluptuousness of conception, the rapturous ether-trance of inspiration, and he has the inexhaustible torment of execution. There he has experiences for which the language has no word and the most sinister dreams no comparison. Like the ghost from the bottle of Sinbad the Sailor, he will dilate like smoke, like a cloud, and cast a shadow over lands and seas. And the following hour will press him back into his bottle, where, suffering a thousand deaths, an imprisoned vapour suffocating itself, he will sense his limits, the merciless limits which fetter him, a despairing demon on a narrow glass prison, through whose invincible walls he sees with grinning torment the world spread out, the whole world over which but an hour ago he was hovering in meditation, a cloud, an immense eagle, a God.

But to such a point, so utterly is his work the whole destiny of the artist that in the entire world about him he can recognize only the counterparts of those conditions which he is accustomed to experience in the torments and delights of work. The poets have made a poet out of the highest being. And they are so clever at projecting into the ups and downs of all human souls the reflection of their own ecstasies and exhaustions that gradually—with the increase of the reading public and the sinister levelling of the classes from which we are suffering—the strangest phenomena will appear, and this, incidentally, not in isolated instances but in masses. Around 1890 the intellectual sicknesses of the poets, their excessively aggravated sensibility, the indescribable anxiety of their depressed hours, their disposition to succumb to the symbolic power even of insignificant things, their incapacity to remain content with existing words for the expression of their feelings—all this will be a common disease among the young men and women of the upper classes. For the artist resembles that Midas under whose hands everything turned to gold. The same curse fulfils itself, but always in an infinitely more subtle way. Benvenuto Cellini lies in the deepest dungeon of the Castel Sant' Angelo; he has a broken leg, his teeth are falling from his jaws; for days he has been left without nourishment; he's convinced he's dying: and then his agonizing deliriums condense into a lovely, comforting dream in which he sees the sun, but without blinding rays, as a bath of the purest gold. Its centre blows itself out and ascends into the heights: out of it there forms a Christ on the Cross of the same substance. All this he actually saw while continually thanking God in a loud voice. He lay in agony, but he was the greatest goldsmith of his century, and the vision in which Heaven sweetened his agony was the vision of a goldsmith's work. Twisting on the threshold of death, his dreams were of no other substance but that in which his hands were able to create a work of art. And do you know the painter, Frenhofer?

HAMMER   The hero of *Le Chef-d'oevre inconnu?* Yes, indeed.

BALZAC   He is Mabuse's only pupil. He received from his master the prodigious secret of form, or true form, that of the human body modelled by light and shade. He knows that contour does not exist. His sketches have the luminous power of Giorgione and the flesh tints of Titian; and he despises these sketches. Pourbus adores him, and Nicolas Poussin, who makes his acquaintance, trembles before him as before a demon. This man has worked for ten years on a nude female figure, and no one has set eyes on the picture. You remember how the story continues. Poussin is so roused, so overwhelmed by this demon of painting, that he offers him his mistress, an enchanting twenty-year-old creature, as his model. It is said that this Gilette had the most beautiful body on which the eyes of a painter had ever rested. To offer her to the old man was the most delirious sacrifice of love to art, to genius, to glory. It was a devilish attempt to surrender the most precious possession in order to buy one's way into the inhuman magnificence of creation. And the old man? He barely notices her. For ten years he has been living in his picture. In a delirium now almost continuous, he feels this painted body live, feels the air play round it, feels this nudity breathe, sleep, grow animated, come close to life. What could a living woman, a real body, give him? By now he sees this palpable body of a woman, he sees all forms and colors, all shadows and half-shadows, all harmonies of the world, only as a negative picture, in a secret relationship to his work, comprehensible only to himself. To him the world is the shell of an eaten egg. What exists of the world for his soul he has carried over into his picture. How vain to offer him a fruit, even were it the most enchanting on earth, against which the doors of his soul have closed themselves forever! What a grotesque and vain sacrifice! Here you have the artist: when he's young, when he gives himself to art —Poussin. And when he is mature, when he is almost Pygmalion, when his statue, his goddess, the creation of his hands begins to walk towards him—Frenhofer. And Gilette—she is Experience, she is the sweet fullness of life's possibilities: and one of them, the youth, is ready to hand her over, while the other no longer has eyes to see her.

Life! The world! The world is in his work, and his work is his life. Talk to a gambler, a real one, about the world at the moment he is going to lay his stake. Tell a collector that his wife has just been seized with convulsions, that his son has been arrested, that his house is on fire—tell him this at the moment when in an antique shop, his eye has lighted on some Nardon Pénicaud enamel from Limoges, or on a screen of the genre that has begun to be known as Pompadour and whose bronze-work is modelled by Clodion. He will gaze at you with the expression with which Lear on the heath gazed at anyone who tried to convince him that it was not his ungrateful daughters who had caused Edgar's misery and the misery of every unfortunate creature. There are times when every eye finds the sublime expression of the soul which refuses to recognize that anything in the world exists beyond its own concern.

HAMMER (*humbly*) That is Lear in the Third Act. At this point he may be considered mad.

BALZAC That, dear Baron, can be said of any man, and particularly in the beautiful, in the sublime, in the true moments of his life. I mean, of course, just as mad as Lear.

HAMMER What, M. de Balzac! You want to set such narrow, such sad limits to your genius? The atmosphere of existences consuming themselves pathologically, the hideous, blind, devouring mania—are these the sinister and constricted subjects you want to choose as the topic of your narrative, instead of plunging into the colorful variety of human life? Have you not always known how to seize what is new, what is interesting?

BALZAC My creating, Baron, has never known other laws than those which I am explaining here. But I have never felt the urge to explain them to myself. It would appear that the philosophic Germany has begun to infect me. But I fear, Baron, that you thoroughly misunderstand me when you assume that I consider anything between heaven and earth as lying outside my subject matter. I don't know what you call "pathological": but I know that every human existence worthy of presentation consumes itself, and that to maintain this flame it absorbs out of the whole world nothing but the elements expedient to its burning, as the candle devours the oxygen from the air. I know who brought into fashion the word "pathological" in relation to poetic creation: it was Herr von Goethe, a very great genius, perhaps the greatest your nation has ever produced, a man whose power of throwing armies of ideas and perceptions from one field of thought into another is not less surprising than that with which Napoleon threw armies of soldiers across the Po or the Vistula—save that his ideas could be as little handled by weaker hands as the bow of Odysseus. But I accept your word: "pathological," "maniacal"—I will tolerate them all. Yes, the world which I've fetched forth from my brain is peopled with madmen. They are all as mad, my creatures, as obsessed by their fixed ideas, as incapable of seeing anything in the world which they themselves do not project into it with their feverish eyes, as out of their senses as Lear when he takes a wisp of straw for Goneril. But they are so, because they are human. For them experiences do not exist, because there is no such thing as experience; because the inner core of man is a fire consuming itself, a fire of agony, a glass furnace in which the viscous liquid matter of life receives its forms, as graceful as flowers, like the stemmed vases from the isles of Murano, or hero-like, sparkling with metallic reflexes, like the potteries from Deruta and Rhodes; because each generation is more conscious than the preceding one; because a peculiar chemistry fulfilling itself with every breath will disintegrate life more and more until even disappointments, the loss of illusions, this inevitable experience, will not tumble down into the deep well of the soul like a single rock, but will be powdered to dust, into atoms, with each breath—so much so that around the year 1890 or 1900 it will no longer be possible to understand what we meant by the word "experience."

Pathological! Let us please conceive the notions in the broadest terms, and Heaven and Hell will find in them their place. I, at any rate, do not intend to renounce either of them. There is in everything the germ of a fetish, of a God, of an all-embracing God. Let us leave faith to him who has made faithfulness his god. I also have a vision of him who has made his god out of faithlessness. One must understand how to envisage Beethoven side by side with Casanova or Lauzun. The one who needed no woman next to him who needed all women. Everything is an empire, and each person is a Napoleon in his. They do not disturb one another, these empires, they are spiritual spheres: happy is he who can hear their music.

Yes, they are demons, all my creatures, and I have put the smoldering fire of madness into their heads. Admitted! But you must also admit, dear Baron, that your German Apollo, your Olympian, that your wizard of Weimar was a demon, and not one of the least awe-inspiring. I will not judge him by his *Werther*: he has repudiated this fever of his youth. But the whole man, the whole poet, the whole Being! I could imagine having known him, his eye must have been more uncanny than that of Medusa. He could kill, this prodigious man, with one glance, with one breath from his mouth, with one lift of his Olympian shoulders: he could turn a human heart to stone; he could kill a soul and then turn his back on it as if nothing had happened, and then walk off to his plants, to his stones, to his colors—which he called the sufferings and labors of light and with which he carried on conversations profound enough to cause the stars of the firmament to waver. There were times when men would have burned him, and there were other times when he would have been worshipped. He allowed his destiny—all the sacrifices demons require. What Napoleon called his star, he called the harmony of his soul. And this glittering enchanted castle which he fashioned out of immortal substance—do you imagine it had no dungeons where prisoners moaned their way towards a lingering death? But he designed not to hear them, for he was great. Yes, who killed the soul of Heinrich von Kleist,[1] who was it? Oh, I see him, the wizard of Weimar. I will paint his picture, I will recreate him completely. He is bigger and more sinister than the Trojan horse, but I will break down the doorposts of my work and lead him in. Next to

Seraphitus-Seraphita [2] he will stand—as in the cemetery at Pisa the leaning tower beside the baptistry, gazing at one another, silent, immense, defying the centuries.

Oh, I see him, and what a shudder of delight to see him! There, I see him, where he lives, where his real life is—in the thirty or forty volumes of his work which he left behind him, not in the nonsense of his biographers. For all that matters is to be able to recognize destinies where they are stamped in divine substance. I know a woman, an obscure woman who will never be famous: she is the daughter of an enslaved country—a demon in imagination, a child in simplicity, a sage in experience, with the brain of a man, the heart of a woman; her love, her faith, her sufferings, her hopes, her dreams, are like chains strong enough to hold a world over the bottomless abyss: and her life, her destiny, her soul, are sometimes written in her face for him who can see it: thus Goethe's destiny can be seen in his works.

To read destinies where they are written— that is everything. To have the power to see them all as they consume themselves, these living torches. To see them all at once bound to the trees of the enormous garden which is illuminated by their blaze alone: and to stand on the uppermost terrace, to be the only spectator, and to search among the strings of the lyre for those sounds which bind together heaven, hell, and this vision.

At this moment, at the outer garden gate, a carriage pulled up in which sat Madame Hanska, née Rzewuska. Balzac, with a movement reminiscent of Mirabeau, swung round to watch the newcomer make her appearance between the chestnut trees; and no one would have dared attempt to resume a conversation which had been broken off by so great a gesture.

Translated by Mary Hottinger
and James and Tania Stern

---

[1] German dramatist and poet (1777–1811).

[2] A reference to Balzac's novel *Seraphita*.

ELECTRA

Translated by Carl Richard Mueller

DRAMATIS PERSONAE

CLYTEMNESTRA
ELECTRA } *her daughters*
CHRYSOTHEMIS
AEGISTHUS
ORESTES
THE GUARDIAN OF ORESTES
CLYTEMNESTRA'S WOMAN

THE TRAIN BEARER
A YOUNG SERVING MAN
AN OLD SERVING MAN
THE COOK
THE WOMAN OVERSEER
THE WOMEN SERVANTS

(*The inner court, bounded by the back of the Palace and the low buildings in which the servants live.* WOMEN SERVANTS *at the draw-well, downstage left.* WOMEN OVER-SEERS *among them*)

FIRST WOMAN SERVANT (*lifting her water jug*)
    Where is Electra?
SECOND WOMAN SERVANT   Time has come again,
    the hour when she howls out for her father,
    till all the walls resound.

(ELECTRA *enters running from the already darkened hallway. They all turn toward her.* ELECTRA *recoils like an animal into its lair, one arm covering her face*)

FIRST WOMAN SERVANT   Did you see the look she gave us?
SECOND WOMAN SERVANT   Furious
    as any wildcat
THIRD WOMAN SERVANT   A moment past I saw her
    lie and moan—
FIRST WOMAN SERVANT   She always lies and moans
    when the sun is low.
THIRD WOMAN SERVANT   The two of us went towards her,
    but came too close—
FIRST WOMAN SERVANT   One thing she'll not endure
    is to be looked at.
THIRD WOMAN SERVANT   Yes, we came too close.
    And then she screeched out at us like a cat:
    "Away with you, you flies!" she cried, "away!"
FOURTH WOMAN SERVANT   "Blow-flies, away!"
THIRD WOMAN SERVANT   "Must you eat at my wounds!"
    And struck out at us with a straw.
FOURTH WOMAN SERVANT   "Away,
    blow-flies, away!"

ELECTRA by Hugo von Hofmannsthal, translated by Carl Richard Mueller, printed by permission of the translator.

[165]

THIRD WOMAN SERVANT   "You shall not feed upon
    the sweetness of my agony nor smack
    your lips to lick the foam from off my madness."
FOURTH WOMAN SERVANT   "Go on, crawl to your beds," she screamed at us.
    "Eat sweets and fats and sneak to bed with your men,"
    she screamed, and you—
THIRD WOMAN SERVANT   I was not idle—
FOURTH WOMAN SERVANT   —answered her!
THIRD WOMAN SERVANT   Yes: "If you are hungry," I answered her,
    "then you eat, too." She sprang up then and shot
    horrible glances at me, stretched her fingers
    claw-like towards me and cried out: "I am feeding
    a vulture here within my body," she cried.
SECOND WOMAN SERVANT   And you?
THIRD WOMAN SERVANT   I said to her: "And that is why
    you're always crouching where there's smell of carrion,
    and scratching the ground for a body long since dead!"
SECOND WOMAN SERVANT   What did she say to that?
THIRD WOMAN SERVANT   She howled and cast herself
    back to her corner.
(*They have finished drawing the water*)
FIRST WOMAN SERVANT   I can't but be amazed
    that the queen should let this demon run about
    freely in house and court to do her mischief.
THIRD WOMAN SERVANT   Her own child, too!
SECOND WOMAN SERVANT   If she were mine, by God,
    I'd keep her under lock and key.
FOURTH WOMAN SERVANT   Don't you feel
    they're hard enough on her now? Don't they place
    her bowl so she eats with the dogs?
                     (*softly*) Haven't you seen
    the master strike her?
FIFTH WOMAN SERVANT (*young, with a tremulous, excited voice*)
                 I will throw myself
    down before her feet and kiss those feet.
    Is she not the daughter of a king, and
    made to endure such outrage! I will anoint
    her feet with oil and wipe them with my hair.
WOMAN OVERSEER   Get on with you! (*pushes her*)
FIFTH WOMAN SERVANT   There's nothing to be found
    in all the world more royal than she. She lies
    in rags upon the threshold, but not one, (*crying out*)
    not one in all this house can look in her eyes!
WOMAN OVERSEER   Get on! (*pushes her through the low open doorway downstage
left*)
FIFTH WOMAN SERVANT (*jammed in the doorway*)
                     Not any one of you is worthy
    to breathe the air that she breathes! O if only
    I could see all of you, all, hanged by the neck,
    see you strung up in some dark granary,
    for all that you have done against Electra!
WOMAN OVERSEER (*shuts the door, stands with her back against it*)
    Did you hear that? What we've done against Electra!
    When told to eat with us, she knocked her bowl
    clear off the table and spat at us and called us
    dirty female dogs.

FIRST WOMAN SERVANT   What? What she said was,
    there's no dog can be humiliated,
    and that's why they broke us in like animals
    to wash away with water, with fresh water,
    the everlasting blood of murder from the floor—

THIRD WOMAN SERVANT   —and to sweep, said she, the outrage into the corner,
    the outrage that renews itself day and night—

FIRST WOMAN SERVANT   —and our bodies, she cried out, are stiffening
    with the dirt that we are bound in bondage to!

(*They carry their jugs into the house left*)

WOMAN OVERSEER (*who has opened the door for them*)
    And screams out when she sees us with our children,
    that there is nothing, nothing, so accursed
    as children that we've littered in this house,
    slipping upon the stairs in blood like dogs.
    Did she say that or not?

THE WOMEN SERVANTS (*already inside*)
                  Yes! Yes!

FIFTH WOMAN SERVANT   They're beating me!

(*The* WOMAN OVERSEER *goes in. The door falls shut.* ELECTRA *steps from the house. She is alone with the splashes of red light which fall obliquely from the branches of the figtrees upon the ground and upon the walls like splashes of blood*)

ELECTRA   Alone! All, all alone. My father gone,
    held prisoner in the coldness of the grave.

(*toward the ground*)

    Father, where are you? Have you not the strength
    to make your way to earth again and me?
    The hour is come, the hour that is our own!
    The same cold hour in which they slaughtered you,
    your wife and the thing that shares her bed with her,
    who sleeps with her in your once royal bed.
    They slew you in your bath, your blood ran red
    down across your eyes, and all the bath
    steamed with your blood; this coward took you then
    and lugged you by the shoulders from the chamber,
    head first, your legs trailing on behind you;
    your eyes, staring, open, saw into the house.
    And so you'll come again, and set one foot
    in front of the other, and suddenly appear,
    your eyes wide open, and a royal round
    of purple placed upon your brows that eats
    upon the open wound it finds there.
                     Father!
    I must see you, don't leave me here alone!
    Show me yourself, if only as a shadow,
    there, in the wall's niche, like yesterday!
    Father! Your time will come! The stars decree
    our times, and so a time will come when blood
    from a hundred throats will gush upon your grave,
    will flow as from a hundred upset jugs,
    stream from the throats of shackled murderers,
    and round the naked bodies of their helpers,
    like marble jugs, from men and women both,
    and in a single flood, one swollen stream,
    shall all of their life's life gush out of them;

and we shall slaughter the horses of your house,
and drive them to your grave, and they shall snuff
death, and neigh in the air laden with death,
and die; and we shall slaughter for you the hounds,
because they are the litter of the litter
of that same pack you hunted with, and who
would lick your feet, to whom you threw the morsels,
their blood must flow to serve you, and we, we,
your blood, your son Orestes and your daughters,
we three, when all is done and purple canopies
are raised high by the steam of your royal blood,
which the sun sucks to itself, then shall we dance,
then shall your blood dance round about your grave:
and over every corpse my knee shall rise
higher with every step, and they who see me,
dancing thus, yea, they who see from afar
only my shadow dancing, they shall say:
How great must be this king whose flesh and blood
would celebrate so grand a feast for him;
happy that king with children who would dance
so royal a dance of victory round his tomb!

(CHRYSOTHEMIS, *the younger sister, stands in the doorway of the house. She looks anxiously at* ELECTRA, *then calls softly*)

CHRYSOTHEMIS   Electra!

(ELECTRA *starts like a sleep-walker who hears his name called out. She staggers. She looks about as though not quite able to find her way. Her face becomes distorted as she sees the anxious features of her sister.* CHRYSOTHEMIS *stands depressed in the doorway*)

ELECTRA   Ah, that face!
CHRYSOTHEMIS   Is it so hateful?
ELECTRA   What is it? Tell me, speak, what do you want?
         Then go away and leave me!

(CHRYSOTHEMIS *raises her hands as though warding off a blow*)

ELECTRA   You raise your hands?
         Our father once raised both his hands that way
         and then the axe struck down cleaving his flesh.
         What is it you want, daughter of my mother?
CHRYSOTHEMIS   They're planning something terrible, I know it.
ELECTRA   *Both* the women?
CHRYSOTHEMIS   Who?
ELECTRA   Why, my mother, of course,
         and then that other woman, the cowardly one,
         Aegisthus, yes, Aegisthus, the brave assassin,
         whose only hero's deeds are done in bed.
         What have they in mind?
CHRYSOTHEMIS   They mean to throw you
         in a dark tower where neither sun nor moon
         will visit you again.

(ELECTRA *laughs*)

CHRYSOTHEMIS   They will, I know,
         I've heard them.
ELECTRA   Yes, I think I've heard it, too.
         At table, wasn't it? Just before finishing?
         He loves to raise his voice then and brag about,
         I think it helps his digestion.

CHRYSOTHEMIS   No, not at table,
    nor was he boasting. He and she together
    discussed it secretly.
ELECTRA   Oh, secretly?
    How did you hear them then?
CHRYSOTHEMIS   I heard at the door.
ELECTRA   Let no doors ever be opened in this house!
    There's nothing in these rooms but gasping for air
    and the death-rattle of strangulation. Never
    open a door that stifles a groan behind it:
    for surely they cannot always be in there killing,
    at times they are alone in there together!
    Open no doors! Do not prowl about.
    Sit on the ground like me and wish for death
    and for judgment upon her and him.
CHRYSOTHEMIS   I cannot sit and stare into the dark
    like you. O there's a burning in my heart
    that makes me rove the house incessantly.
    There's not a room to comfort me, and so
    I wander up the stairs and down the stairs,
    from one place to another; O it seems a
    room will call to me, and once I'm there,
    there's nothing but an empty, staring room.
    I'm so afraid, my knees tremble beneath me
    day and night; it seems as if two hands
    are here at my throat; I can't even cry;
    I've turned to stone! Sister, pity, pity!
ELECTRA   Pity whom?
CHRYSOTHEMIS   It's you who have bound me here
    with hoops of iron. Were it not for you,
    they would not keep us here. Were it not for your hate,
    for your unsleeping and excessive temper,
    which makes me tremble, they would not keep us
    locked and chained here in this prison, sister!
    I *will* get out! I *will not* sleep each night
    here until my death! Before I die
    I want to know what life is! I want children
    before my body withers, and even though
    they marry me with a peasant, I will bear him
    children and will warm them with my body
    through cold nights when storms beat at our hut!
    But there is one thing I'll endure no longer,
    this living here like animals with servants
    who are not our kind, locked in here day and night
    with mortal fear! Are you listening to me?
    Speak to me, sister!
ELECTRA   Pitiable creature!
CHRYSOTHEMIS   Have pity on yourself, have pity on me.
    Who profits from this anguish? Father perhaps?
    Our father is dead. Our brother does not come home.
    Day after day time graves his token
    in your face and in mine, and there, outside,
    the sun rises and sets, and women I knew
    when they were slender are heavy now with blessing;
    they make their way to the well, scarcely able
    to lift the pail; then suddenly they're loosed
    of their burden and they come again to the well,

and out of them there flows a draught of sweetness,
and a new life clings sucking to their bodies,
and their children grow—and we sit here on our perch
like captive birds, turning our heads to left
and right, and no one comes, no brother comes
no news of our brother, no news of any news,
nothing! I were better dead than live without life.
No! I'm a woman, I will bear a woman's lot.

ELECTRA   Shame on the thought! Shame on the thinker of it!
To be the hollow where the murderer
is safe after the murder; play the beast
for the pleasure of a beast—that's even worse!
Ah, she slept with one and pressed her breasts
on both his eyes, and nodded to another
who crept from behind the bed with net and axe.

CHRYSOTHEMIS   How terrible you are!

ELECTRA   Why terrible?
Are you such a woman? You will become one.

CHRYSOTHEMIS   Why is it you cannot forget, Electra?
My mind is a wasteland. I cannot remember
from one day to the next. Sometimes I lie here
like this, and then I am what once I was,
and do not know why I am young no longer.
Where has it gone, Electra, where has it gone?
This is not water flowing on its way,
this is not yarn flying back and forth
on a spool, it is no one but myself!
I want to pray some god will kindle a flame
here in my breast that I may find myself
again. Were I not here, how soon I would
forget these evil dreams—

ELECTRA   Forget? Forget?
Am I a beast then that I should forget?
The beast will sleep with its half-eaten prey
hanging from its jaws; the beast forgets itself
and starts to chew, the while death sits on him,
strangling out life; the beast forgets what crept
from its own body, and with its own young
allays its hunger—I am no beast, *I cannot
forget!*

CHRYSOTHEMIS   O must my soul forever feed
upon this food it loathes, that it so loathes!
the smell of which makes me shudder, which I ought never
have touched, never have known that there existed
anything so horrible as that,
never to have known that, never to have seen,
never heard! So terrible a thing is
not for the hearts of men! And when it comes,
and when it shows itself, then we must flee
our houses, flee to the vineyards, to the mountains!
And then when it stands astride the mountain tops,
we creep down to hide again in our houses;
we must never be with it, never live
together in one house! I must get out!
I must conceive children, I must bear them,
who will know nothing of this. I'll wash my body
in every stream, dive deep, deep in the water,

wash every part of me, wash clean the sockets
of my eyes—they must never be afraid
when they look up into their mother's eyes!

ELECTRA   When they look up into their mother's eyes!
And how will you look into our father's eyes?

CHRYSOTHEMIS   O stop!

ELECTRA   May your children, when you have them,
do unto you as you do to our father!

(CHRYSOTHEMIS *cries out*)

ELECTRA   Why must you howl so? Get in! That's your place.
There's a noise broken out. Are they preparing
your wedding? I hear running. Everyone's up.
Either they are in birthpangs or at murder.
Should there be corpses lacking, they must make some,
or else they'll not sleep soundly in their beds!

CHRYSOTHEMIS   Stop, O stop! That's past and done, it's done!

ELECTRA   Past and done? They're up to some new crime now!
Do you think I don't know the sound of bodies
as they drag them down the stairs, whispering
and wringing out cloths sopped in blood!

CHRYSOTHEMIS   Sister!
You must not stay.

ELECTRA   This time I *will* be here!
Not as before. This time I will be strong.
I'll throw myself upon her, I'll tear the axe
out of her hands and swing it over her head—

CHRYSOTHEMIS   You must not stay here, hide before she sees you.
Don't cross her path today, she scatters death
Wherever she looks. She's had terrible dreams.

(*The noise of people approaching draws nearer*)

You must not stay. They're coming through the passage.
They'll come by here. She's had terrible dreams;
I don't know what, I heard it from her women,
I don't know if it's true, sister, but they say
she has had terrible dreams of Orestes,
and that she cried out in the middle of night
like one about to be strangled.

ELECTRA   I! I!
I sent it to her. I sent her this dream
from my own breast! I lie in bed and hear
the footsteps of the spectre haunting her.
I hear him make his way from room to room
and lift the curtain from her bed: screaming
she leaps from the bed, but he is always there,
close behind her on the stairs, the chase continues
from one vault to another and another.
It is far darker now than any night,
far quieter and darker than the grave,
she gasps and staggers in darkness, but he is there:
he swings the torch to right and left of the axe.
And I like a hunting-hound am at her heels:
should she hide in a hollow, I spring after,
sideways, upon her trail, and drive her on
till a wall end her flight, and there in darkness,
there in deepest darkness—I see him still,
his shadow, and his limbs, the light of his eyes—

there sits our father, who neither sees nor hears,
and yet, it must happen: we drive her to his feet,
and the axe falls!

(*Torches and figures fill the passage, left of the door*)

CHRYSOTHEMIS   They're coming now. She's driving her women on
with torches. Look, they're dragging animals
and sacrificial knives. O sister, Electra,
she is most dreadful when she is afraid;
you must not cross her path today, not now!

ELECTRA   I have a mind to speak with my mother now
as I have never spoken!

(*A noisy and shuffling procession hurries past the glaringly lighted windows. There is a tugging and hauling of animals, a subdued chiding, a quickly stifled cry, the swish of a whip, a pulling back and a staggering forward again*)

CHRYSOTHEMIS   I will not hear it.

(*She rushes off through the door of the court*)

(*The figure of* CLYTEMNESTRA *appears in the wide window. Her sallow, bloated face, in the light thrown from the glaring torches, appears even more pale above her scarlet dress. She supports herself upon one of her women, dressed in dark violet, and upon an ivory staff embellished with precious jewels. Her train is carried by a yellow figure, whose black hair is combed back like an Egyptian, and whose sleek face resembles a poised snake. The* QUEEN *is almost completely covered with precious stones and talismans. Her arms are full of bracelets, her fingers almost rigid with rings. The lids of her eyes seem excessively large, and it appears to be a great effort for her to hold them open.* ELECTRA *stands rigid, her face toward the window.* CLYTEMNESTRA *suddenly opens her eyes and trembling with anger goes towards the window and points at* ELECTRA *with her staff*)

CLYTEMNESTRA   (*at the window*)
What do you want? Look there! Look at it there!
See how it rears its swollen neck at me
and hisses! And this thing I let run free
in my own house!
O how she'd like to kill me with those eyes!
Gods, why must you weigh so heavy on me?
Why must you send destruction on me? Why
do you cripple all the strength within me, why am
I, a living being, like a wasteland,
covered with weeds and nettles that grow on me,
and I have not the strength to root them out!
Why must I suffer this, immortal gods?

ELECTRA   Gods? The gods? But you are a goddess yourself!
The same as they.

CLYTEMNESTRA   What? What was that she said?
Did you understand what she said?

THE WOMAN   That you, too
stem from the gods.

TRAIN BEARER   (*hissingly*)   But she means it only in spite.

CLYTEMNESTRA   (*as her heavy eyelids fall shut*)
How familiar it sounds, like a thing forgotten
long, long ago. How well she knows me.
Yet no one ever knows what she will do.

(*The* WOMAN *and the* TRAIN BEARER *whisper together*)

ELECTRA   You are yourself no longer. Reptiles hang
from your body. What they hiss into your ear
severs your thoughts forever; you go about
in a frenzy, as though living in a dream.

CLYTEMNESTRA   I will go down to her. I will speak to her.
   She is no beast today—talks like a doctor.
   The hours hold our fate firm in their hands.
   Nothing is so unbearable but once
   must show a pleasant aspect in its nature.

(*She walks from the window and appears at the doorway, her* WOMAN *at her side, the* TRAIN BEARER *behind her, and torches bringing up the rear*)

CLYTEMNESTRA   (*from the threshold*)
   You call me a goddess. Why? Did you say it
   in malice? Then take care. For this may be
   the last time you will see the light of day
   and breathe the free air.

ELECTRA   If you are not
   a goddess, tell me, then, where are the gods!
   There's nothing in this world makes me tremble so
   than to think your body was the dark door
   through which I crept into the light of the world.
   Have I lain here naked upon this lap?
   Have you lifted me up to reach these breasts?
   Well, then, I must have crept from my father's grave
   and played about in swaddling-clothes upon
   the place where my father was murdered. Then you must be
   a colossus whose brazen hand I never escaped.
   You have me by the bridle and can tie me
   to what you will. You have cast up like the sea
   a living being, a father, and a sister.
   I do not know how I should ever die—
   unless you died before me.

CLYTEMNESTRA   Is this how you honor me? Is there so little
   respect in you?

ELECTRA   I lack not of respect!
   What troubles me troubles you as well.
   I grow ill to see Aegisthus, your husband,
   wear the robes of my father, who's dead, as you know,
   he was the former king. It makes me ill,
   believe me, for they do not fit him well.
   I think they are too broad across the chest.

THE WOMAN   What she says is not what she means.

TRAIN BEARER   Every word a lie.

CLYTEMNESTRA   (*angrily*)   I will not listen. Whatever comes from you
   is only Aegisthus' breath. I do not want
   to find fault everywhere. But say to me
   what I would gladly hear, then I will listen
   to what you say. Truth is not so easily
   discovered by mortal man. No man on earth
   can know the truth of any hidden thing.
   Are there not certain men in prison here
   who dare to call me murderess, and Aegisthus
   assassin? When I wake you in the night,
   does not each of you give different answer?
   Do you not cry out that my eyes are swollen
   and that I am sick within, and that all this
   is but that I am sick; and do you not
   whimper in my other ear that you've seen demons
   with long pointed beaks sucking my blood,
   and show me the marks on my body? Do I not
   believe you then and slay, and slay, and slay one

sacrifice after another? Am I not torn
to death between your words and your replies?
I will no longer listen when you tell me:
this is truth and this is not the truth.
Should anyone speak pleasantly to me,
were it even my daughter, were it that one,
    I would remove the veils around my soul
and let soft breezes, come from where they may,
envelop me, as they do those sick people
who in the evening sit beside a pool
and bare to the cool air their boiled and reeking
bodies, and think only of relief.
And so I must begin to serve myself.
Leave me alone with her.

(*With her stick, she impatiently motions the* WOMAN *and the* TRAIN BEARER *into the
house. They hesitantly disappear through the doorway. The torches disappear, too,
and now only a faint light emerges from the inside of the house across the paved
corridor and into the courtyard, so that the figures of the two women are lightly
touched by the light*)

CLYTEMNESTRA (*after a puse*)   I do not sleep at night. Do you know
    some remedy for dreams?
ELECTRA (*moving closer*)   For dreams, mother?
CLYTEMNESTRA   Have you no other words to comfort me?
    Tell me what you know. Yes, yes, I dream.
    When one grows old, he dreams. But that can be
    dispelled. Why are you standing there in darkness?
    We must learn to make use of our own powers
    that lie scattered. There are customs. Yes,
    there must be customs, usages for all things.
    How one articulates a word or sentence
    can make much difference. Even the hour it's spoken.
    And whether one's fed or fasting. Many a man
    has perished for entering too soon into his bath.
ELECTRA   Are you thinking of my father?
CLYTEMNESTRA   That is why
    I am so behung with jewels. In every one
    exists a certain power. One must but know
    how to use them. If it were your pleasure,
    I know that you could tell me how to use them.
ELECTRA   I, mother, I?
CLYTEMNESTRA   Yes, you! For you are wise.
    Your mind is sound. You talk of old things
    as if they happened yesterday. But I
    decay. I think, but all things are confused.
    And when I start to speak, Aegisthus cries,
    and what he cries out is hateful to me,
    and then I would rise up and would be stronger
    than all his words, but I find nothing, nothing!
    I do not even know if what he said,
    which makes me tremble with rage, was said today,
    or long ago; I grow dizzy then
    and no longer know who I am: it's a terrible thing
    to sink, alive and breathing, into chaos!
    And then Aegisthus! then Aegisthus scorns me!
    But I can find nothing, find no terrible thing
    to silence him and turn him pale as myself,
    staring into the fire. But you have words.

You could tell me much to help me now.
And even if a word is but a word?
What is a breath? And yet between night and day,
as I lie with eyes open, a something creeps
across my body, it is not a word,
it is not a grief, it does not press upon me,
it does not choke me, but leaves me lying there
just as I am, and there, there at my side
Aegisthus lies, and beyond him, there, is the curtain:
and all things look at me as though it were
from eternity unto eternity:
and it is nothing, no, not even a nightmare,
and yet it is so dreadful that my soul
longs to be hanged, and every part of me
thirsts after death; and yet I am alive,
and am not even sick. You see me here:
do I look sick? Is it then possible
to perish like a foul carcass while still alive?
to decompose and still not even be sick?
to have a waking mind decay, like a garment
eaten by moths? And then I sleep and dream,
dream till the marrow runs liquid in my bones!
I stagger from my bed again and not
the tenth part of an hour has passed by,
and what I see grinning beneath the curtain
is still not the ashgrey dawn, no, but only
the torch outside the door that starts and quivers
horribly like some living thing, spying
upon my sleep.
I do not know them who play this game with me,
whether they are at home above or below,
but when I see you standing there before me
as now you are, I cannot but believe
but you are in league with them. Who are you really?
Why can't you speak, now, when I would hear you?
Who is it could be so much helped or hurt
by whether you live or die? Why do you look
so hard at me? I will not have you look
that way. I say these dreams must have an end.
Whoever sent me them, whatever the demon,
we will be left in peace to sleep our nights
when the right blood is spilt.

ELECTRA   Are you so certain!
CLYTEMNESTRA   And must I let blood each beast that creeps and flies,
      and rise each day and sleep each night in the steam
      of their blood, like the race that lives in farthest Thule
      in bloodred mist: I will not dream again.
ELECTRA   Your dreams will end when the right blood-sacrifice
      falls beneath the axe.
CLYTEMNESTRA (*steps closer*)   Then you must know
      what sacred beast must fall—
ELECTRA   A most profane beast!
CLYTEMNESTRA   That lies within there?
ELECTRA   No! It still runs free.
CLYTEMNESTRA (*eagerly*)   What rites must we use?
ELECTRA   Wonderful rites, that must
      be strictly observed.
CLYTEMNESTRA   Why do you keep silent?

ELECTRA   Can't you divine my meaning?

CLYTEMNESTRA   Why would I ask?
Tell me the name of the victim.

ELECTRA   It is a woman.

CLYTEMNESTRA (*eagerly*)   One of my women-servants? Is it? Tell me!
A child? A young virgin? Has this woman
known a man yet?

ELECTRA   Known a man? Yes! Yes,
that's it!

CLYTEMNESTRA   And for the sacrifice? What hour?
And where?

ELECTRA   Anywhere, at any hour,
day or night.

CLYTEMNESTRA   And tell me what rites to use!
How must I do it? I myself will—

ELECTRA   No.
This time you will not hunt the victim down.

CLYTEMNESTRA   Then who? Who'll bring it here?

ELECTRA   A man.

CLYTEMNESTRA   Aegisthus?

ELECTRA   I said a man!

CLYTEMNESTRA   Who? Tell me! Tell me who!
Someone of the house? Or must a stranger come
and—

ELECTRA   Yes, yes, a stranger. But of course
he is of our house.

CLYTEMNESTRA   Why must you speak in riddles?
Electra, you listen to me. How pleased I am
to find you not so headstrong for a change.
When parents must act harshly towards their child,
the child forces them to it. There's no word
so stern it can't be revoked; and when a mother
sleeps ill, how rather would she know her child
sleeps in a marriage-bed and not in chains.

ELECTRA (*to herself*)   It's different with the child: the child would rather
the mother were dead than in her marriage-bed.

CLYTEMNESTRA   What are you murmuring there? I say that nothing
is irrevocable. Do not all things pass
before our eyes, changing like the mist?
And we ourselves, we, we and our deeds!
Our deeds! We and our deeds! Those are mere words.
Am I still she who did it? And if so!
Did is done, is done! What's done is done!
Don't throw these words at me! There, there he stood,
that one you can't forget, he stood there,
and there I stood and over there Aegisthus,
then all our glances met: and nothing done:
all still to do! How your father's look
changed in death, so slowly, horribly,
but always looking at me—then it was done:
nothing between the doing and the deed!
First it was undone, and then it was done—
and in that moment between, I did nothing.

ELECTRA   Of course, the axe that slew him lifted itself.

CLYTEMNESTRA   You cut me with your words.

ELECTRA   But not so nimbly
and well as your axe cut him.

CLYTEMNESTRA   I'll hear no more
of this. Be silent. If your father came
to meet me here today—I would speak with him
the same as I speak with you. It may well be
I'd shudder here before him, yet it may be
I could be tender with him and could weep,
like two old friends meeting together again.
ELECTRA (*to herself*)   Horrible! She talks about the murder
like a quarrel before supper.
CLYTEMNESTRA   Tell your sister
she need not run from me like a frightened dog
into darkness. Bid her speak more friendly with me,
as becomes her station, and give me civil greeting.
And then I do not know what should hinder me
from giving you both in marriage before winter.
ELECTRA   And our brother? May our brother not come home?
CLYTEMNESTRA   I have forbidden you to speak of him.
ELECTRA   Then you're afraid of him?
CLYTEMNESTRA   Who says that?
ELECTRA   Mother,
you're trembling!
CLYTEMNESTRA   Do you think I'd be afraid
of an imbecile?
ELECTRA   An imbecile?
CLYTEMNESTRA   They say
he stammers, lies in the courtyard with the dogs
and knows no difference between man and beast.
ELECTRA   He was sound as a child.
CLYTEMNESTRA   They say they gave him
a wretched hole to live in and the animals
of the courtyard for companions.
ELECTRA   Ah!
CLYTEMNESTRA (*with lowered eyelids*)   I sent
gold on top of gold for them to keep him
as befits a king's child.
ELECTRA   You're lying, mother!
You sent gold for them to strangle him.
CLYTEMNESTRA   Who told you that?
ELECTRA   I see it in your eyes.
And by your trembling I know that he lives.
I know that day and night you think of nothing
but him. And that your heart dries up with dread
because you know he's coming.
CLYTEMNESTRA   Don't lie to me.
Who lives without this house is not my concern.
I live here and I am mistress here.
I have enough servants to guard the gates,
and when I will, I shall have three armed servants
stand guard, day and night, before my chamber.
I quite ignore these things that you have told me.
Nor do I know this one you're speaking of.
I'll never see him; so what concern is it
of mine, whether he be live or dead.
But I have dreamt of him enough. These dreams
are signs of illness, they fatten on our strength,
and I would live and be the mistress here.
I will not have another such attack,

to bring me here like any hawker-woman,
and pour out to you the secrets of my nights.
I am as good as sick, and the sick, they say,
prattle of their ills, and nothing more.
But I will no longer be sick. I will have from you

(*She raises her stick threateningly against* ELECTRA)

one way or another the word I must have.
You have already betrayed yourself once
that you know the proper sacrifice and rites
that I have need of. If you will not tell me
in freedom, then you'll tell me so in chains;
if not well fed, then you shall tell me fasting.
One can be rid of dreams. Who suffers from them
and does not find the means to cure himself,
he is a fool. I will learn some way
who must be let blood, that I may sleep.

ELECTRA (*leaps out at her from the darkness, approaching her closer and closer,
growing increasingly more frightening*)

Who must be let blood? You! Your own neck,
when the hunter has hunted you down! And he will hunt you:
but only in the chase! Who slaughters a beast
of sacrifice in its sleep! He'll hunt you down,
he'll chase you through the house! And if you turn right,
there is the bed; and left, your bath, foaming
like blood! The darkness and the torches cast
black-red nets of death across your body—

(CLYTEMNESTRA, *shuddering with speechless fear, wants to enter the house.* ELECTRA
pulls her back by her robe. CLYTEMNESTRA *shrinks back to the wall. Her eyes are
wide open; the stick falls from her trembling hands*)

ELECTRA   You want to cry out, but the air strangles
the unborn cry in you and lets it fall
silent upon the ground; your neck stretches out,
as brooding on the deed, and you feel the sharp blade
to the very marrow of you, though he holds back:
the rites are not yet fulfilled. He takes you by
the tresses of your hair, and all is silence,
you hear your heart beat against your ribs;
this time—yes, this time spreads out before you
like a dark gulf of years—this time is given you
to know the fear that shipwrecked men must know
when their vain cry gnaws at the dark clouds
and the blackness of death; this time is given you
to envy those chained to prison walls,
those who cry out from the bottom of a well
for death as though for deliverance; for you,
you lie so prisoned up within yourself
as though in the glowing belly of a beast
of bronze and, just as now, you cannot cry out!
And I stand there beside you, and your eyes
can never leave me, for you hope in vain
to read that word upon my silent face;
you roll your eyes, you'd grasp at any thought,
you'd have the gods smile down at you from the clouds:
but the gods, the gods are at supper, just as when
you slew our father, they're sitting there at supper
and are just as deaf now to any death-rattle!
Only a half-mad god, the god of laughter,
staggers in: he thinks it's all a game,

a love-game that you're playing with Aegisthus,
but when he sees his error, he laughs at once,
loud and shrill, and vanishes like that.
And you have had enough. The bile drops bitter
upon your heart, and dying you would recall
one word, would speak one single word more,
no matter which, instead of weeping tears
of blood, which are denied no dying beast.
I stand before you there, and now you read
with staring eyes the monstrous word that's written
upon my face, for my face is composed
of the features of my father and of you;
and I with my silent presence here
have brought to nothing your last word, your soul
is caught up in your self-turned noose, the axe
falls with a rush, and here I stand and see you
die at last! You will dream no longer then,
and I will dream no more, and who lives after,
let him rejoice and be happy in his life!

(*They stand eye to eye,* ELECTRA *in wildest intoxication,* CLYTEMNESTRA *breathing horribly with fear. At this moment the passageway grows light and the* WOMAN *comes running from the house. She whispers something in* CLYTEMNESTRA's *ear. She appears not to understand at first. She gradually comes to herself. Beckons for lights!* SERVING WOMEN *enter with torches and stand behind* CLYTEMNESTRA. *She beckons for more lights! More are brought in, station themselves behind her, so that the entire court is full of light and a reddish-yellow blaze floods the walls.* CLYTEMNESTRA's *features slowly change now, and the tension of her fear gives way to an evil triumph. She lets the message be whispered to her again, at the same time never permitting* ELECTRA *out of her sight. Satisfied to the full, with a wild joy she extends both her hands threateningly toward* ELECTRA. *Then her* WOMAN *lifts her stick from the ground and, leaning on them both, hurriedly, eagerly, snatching up her robe from the stairs, runs into the house. The* SERVING WOMEN, *as though chased, follow her in*)

ELECTRA (*meanwhile*) What are they saying to her? Why is she happy?

Why, why can't I think? Why is this woman
so happy?

(CHRYSOTHEMIS *enters, running, through the door of the court, howling loudly like a wounded animal*)

ELECTRA Chrysothemis! Quickly! Quickly!
I must have help. Tell me what in this world
could make a person happy!

CHRYSOTHEMIS (*crying out*) Orestes! Orestes
is dead!

ELECTRA (*motions her to keep away, as though demented*)
Be silent!

CHRYSOTHEMIS (*close to her*) Orestes is dead!

(ELECTRA *moves her lips*)

CHRYSOTHEMIS I came
from the house, and they knew of it already.
They all stood about and knew already,
only not we.

ELECTRA No one knows it.

CHRYSOTHEMIS Every one knows!

ELECTRA No one knows: because it isn't true.

(CHRYSOTHEMIS *throws herself to the ground*)

ELECTRA (*pulls her up*) It isn't true, I tell you! No! I tell you,
it isn't true!

CHRYSOTHEMIS   The strangers stood against the wall, the strangers
    sent here to tell us of it: there were two,
    an old man and a young man. They had told
    everyone already, they made a circle
    around them and they all knew already.

ELECTRA   It isn't true.

CHRYSOTHEMIS   Only they didn't tell *us*!
    No one thinks of us. Dead! Dead, Electra!

YOUNG SERVING MAN (*hurries from the house, stumbling over the figure lying at the threshold*)
    Make way here! What's this loitering at the door?
    Ah, I should have known! Bring out a groom here!

COOK (*enters through the door, right*)
    What is it?

YOUNG SERVING MAN   I call out for a stableboy,
    and what creeps from the hold but the old cook.

OLD SERVING MAN (*with a gloomy face, appears at the door to the courtyard*)
    What's needed from the stable?

YOUNG SERVING MAN   Saddle something up,
    as quick as you can, you hear? A carthorse, an ass,
    a cow, for all I care, but do it quickly!

OLD SERVING MAN   Who for?

YOUNG SERVING MAN   For him who orders you to do it!
    Don't gape at me! Be about it! Quickly!
    For me! Hurry! Don't stand there! I must ride out
    to find and bring our master from the field,
    for I have news for him, news great enough
    to ride one of your mares to death for it.

(*The* OLD SERVING MAN *disappears*)

COOK   What news is it? Just one word!

YOUNG SERVING MAN   Just one word,
    my good cook, really wouldn't serve you well.
    And then to sum up everything I know
    and must tell my master, and all this in a word,
    and so offhandedly, is no small task:
    be satisfied with knowing that a message
    of highest import has arrived just now,
    a message that—how long it takes an old man
    to saddle up a horse!—that ought to please you
    as a faithful servant; whether you know or not
    what it's about, it ought to please you still.

(*shouting into the court*)

    A whip, too, you fool! How can I ride
    without a whip? It's you and not the nag
    who's keeping me here!

(*to the* COOK, *ready to rush out*)

                Well then, in a word:
    the young lad Orestes, the son of the house
    who never was at home and for that reason
    as good as dead: in short then let me say
    this son who, so to speak, has always been dead,
    this son, so to speak, is really dead now! (*rushes off*)

COOK (*turns toward* ELECTRA *and* CHRYSOTHEMIS, *who lie pressed so closely to one another that they seem one body, shaken by* CHRYSOTHEMIS' *sobbing, and from which the death-pale, silent face of* ELECTRA *raises itself*)

Yes, yes, I have it now. They say dogs howl
when the moon is at its full, but you howl now
because your moon will always be a new one.
Dogs are run out when they disturb the house.
Take care, they may treat you the same.

(*He goes in again*)

CHRYSOTHEMIS (*half raised up*)

To die among strangers! Dead, buried, there,
in a strange land. Killed and cut to pieces
by his own horses! His face, they say, was torn,
unrecognizable. We never saw his face!
We think of him, but always as a child.
But he was a man. I wonder if his mind
thought of us when he died. I could not ask them:
they were crowded out with people. O Electra,
we must find the men and speak with them.

ELECTRA (*to herself*)   Then we must do the deed.

CHRYSOTHEMIS   Electra, listen,
we must go in. There are two of them,
an old man and a young one. When they learn
that we are his sisters, his poor sisters,
they will tell us everything.

ELECTRA   What more should we know?
We know that he's dead.

CHRYSOTHEMIS   That they should bring us nothing,
no lock, no single lock from his dear head!
As though we no longer exist, his two sisters.

ELECTRA   Therefore we must prove we are his sisters.

CHRYSOTHEMIS   Electra?

ELECTRA   We! We must do the deed.

CHRYSOTHEMIS   Electra, what?

ELECTRA   It must be done today,
tonight.

CHRYSOTHEMIS   But, sister, what?

ELECTRA   What? The work
that's fallen to us now that he will not
return, the work that cannot be left undone.

CHRYSOTHEMIS   Work? What work?

ELECTRA   You and I together
must go inside to that woman and her husband,
and kill them.

CHRYSOTHEMIS   Sister—not our mother. No.

ELECTRA   Our mother. And her husband. We must do it
unafraid.

(CHRYSOTHEMIS *is speechless*)

ELECTRA   Be still. Our words are nothing.
There's nothing to consider, only: how,
how we will do it.

CHRYSOTHEMIS   I?

ELECTRA   Yes. You and I.
Who else? Has our father other children
hidden in this house to help us now?
No. I know that much.

CHRYSOTHEMIS   Must we both go?
We? The two of us? With both our hands?

ELECTRA   That will be mine to do.

CHRYSOTHEMIS   If you had a knife—

ELECTRA *(contemptuously)*   A knife!

CHRYSOTHEMIS   Or else an axe—

ELECTRA   *An* axe! *The* axe!

The same axe they used when they killed our—

CHRYSOTHEMIS   You?

You have the axe? You horror!

ELECTRA   For our brother,

that's why I kept it. Now it's ours to use.

CHRYSOTHEMIS   You mean you'd kill Aegisthus with these arms?

ELECTRA   First him, then her; first her, then him; no matter.

CHRYSOTHEMIS   You frighten me. You're not in your right senses.

ELECTRA   They have no one guarding at their door now.

CHRYSOTHEMIS   You'd murder them in their sleep, and then live on?

ELECTRA   The question is of him, and not of us.

CHRYSOTHEMIS   If only you could see how mad you are!

ELECTRA   A man asleep is an offering already bound.

If they do not sleep together, I can do it
alone. But you must come with me.

CHRYSOTHEMIS   Electra!

ELECTRA   You!

You must! For you are strong!

(close to her)   How strong you are!

How strong your virginal nights have made you grow.
Your loins, your loins are slender here and lithe!
You can slip through any crevice, raise yourself
to the window! Let me, let me feel your arms:
how cool they are and strong! I feel their strength
by the way you push me from you. You could crush
what you embrace in them. You could press
me or any man to these cool, firm breasts
till we suffocate in them! O every part
of you is powerful! It streams like cool
damned water from a rock. It floods with your hair
down your strong shoulders!

CHRYSOTHEMIS   Let me go!

ELECTRA   No! No!

I'll hold you! With my wretched withered arms
I'll wind about your body, and if you resist
the knot is pulled tighter; I'll twist myself
like tendrils round your body, sink my roots
deep inside you and engraft my will
into your blood!

CHRYSOTHEMIS   Let me go! *(She escapes a few steps)*

ELECTRA *(goes after her wildly, grasps her by her garment)*

                        No! No!

CHRYSOTHEMIS   Electra!

Let me go!

ELECTRA   I will not let you go.

We two must grow like one, so that the knife
that severs both our bodies will bring death
at once, for we are alone now in this world.

CHRYSOTHEMIS   Electra, listen. I know how shrewd you are,
help us escape from here, help us get free.

ELECTRA *(without hearing her)*

You are full of strength, your sinews here
are like a colt's, and how slender your feet are,
how easily I can catch them in my arms

as though they were a rope. And here beneath
the coolness of your skin I feel your warm blood
flowing, with my cheek I feel the down
on your young arms: you are like a fruit
on the day that it grows ripe. From this time on
I will be your sister as I have never
been your sister yet! I'll sit in your chamber
with you and wait for the bridegroom, and for him
I will anoint your body; you shall plunge
like a young swan into the fragrant bath
and hide your precious head upon my breast
until he draws you—you, glowing like a torch
beneath your veils—draws you with his arms,
his strong arms, into the marriage-bed.

CHRYSOTHEMIS (*closes her eyes*)
No, sister, no, you must never utter
such words inside this house.

ELECTRA   O I shall be more
than ever a sister was from this day on.
I'll serve you, be a slave. When you are in labor
I'll stand there day and night beside your bed,
protect you from the flies, draw cool water,
and then when suddenly some living thing
lies there between your legs, almost afraid,
I'll lift it up, this high, so that its smile
shall fall into the deepest and most secret
fissures of your soul, and like the sun,
melt in you that last icy horror
and let you weep bright tears.

CHRYSOTHEMIS   O take me from this!
I shall die if I stay here!

ELECTRA (*on her knees*)   Your mouth is beautiful:
but when will it open wide and cry in rage!
Out of your chaste strong mouth a terrible cry
must come, a cry as terrible as that
of the Death goddess, when someone should awaken
suddenly and see you standing there
above his head like the Death goddess; when someone
should lie bound at your feet and look up at you,
as I do now, look up at your slender body
with fixed eyes like shipwrecked men look up
at the rocky crag above them as they die.

CHRYSOTHEMIS   What are you saying?

ELECTRA (*rising*)   Before you can escape
this house and me, you must help me.

(CHRYSOTHEMIS *tries to speak.* ELECTRA *puts her hand across her mouth*)

ELECTRA   There is
no way for you but this. I'll hold you here
till you have sworn to me, mouth upon mouth,
that you will help me.

CHRYSOTHEMIS (*wrenches herself loose*)   Let me go!

ELECTRA (*grabbing her again*)   Swear to me
that you will come to the foot of the stairs tonight
when all is silent.

CHRYSOTHEMIS   Let me go!

ELECTRA (*holding her by her garment*)   Stay still!
No drop of blood will light upon your body;

you will slip quickly from your bloody garment
and clothe your clean body in your bridal dress.

CHRYSOTHEMIS   Let me go!

ELECTRA   You must not be a coward!
The fear you conquer now will be repaid
night after night with raptures of joy—

CHRYSOTHEMIS   I cannot!

ELECTRA   Say that you will come!

CHRYSOTHEMIS   I cannot!

ELECTRA   Look at me,
lying here at your feet—I'll kiss your feet!

CHRYSOTHEMIS (*escapes through the house gate*)
I cannot!

ELECTRA (*after her*)   Then be damned! (*to herself with wild determination*)
Well then—alone!

(*She begins to dig passionately at the wall of the house, beside the threshold, noise-lessly, like an animal. She leaves off for a moment, looks around, then digs again*)

(ORESTES *stands in the door to the court, black against the last rays of light. He enters.* ELECTRA *looks up at him. He turns around slowly until he looks at her.* ELECTRA *starts violently, trembling*)

ELECTRA   Who are you? What do you want? Why do you prowl
about here in the dark spying upon what
others do? It may be that you, too,
intend what you would not have others know.
So leave me here in peace. I have some business
to do. It's none of your concern! Get out,
and let me grub about upon the ground.
Didn't you hear? Or has your curiosity
too strong a will? I am not burying,
I'm digging up. And not the dead bones
of a little child I buried some days ago.
No, my friend, I have given no one life,
and so I have no need to take a life,
nor to bury it. If the body of earth
should ever receive anything from my hands,
then it must be what I came forth from, not
any being that ever came forth from me.
What I dig up—O you will have scarcely gone
and I will have it and hold it to my heart
and kiss it as it were both brother and son.

ORESTES   Have you nothing on earth that you can love,
that you must dig this something from the ground
to kiss? Are you really so much alone?

ELECTRA   I am no mother, nor have I any mother.
I am no sister, nor have I brother or sister.
I lie at the door, and yet I am no watchdog.
I speak and yet I do not speak. I live
and do not live. I have long hair and feel
nothing they say a woman must feel:
in short, then, please go! Leave me! Leave me!

ORESTES   I must wait here.

ELECTRA   Wait?

(*Pause*)

ORESTES   Are you of this house?
Are you a maid of this house?

ELECTRA   Yes, I serve them.
    But you have no deed to do here. Let that please you
    and go.
ORESTES   I told you once that I must wait
    until they call me.
ELECTRA   They inside? You're lying.
    I know myself the master isn't home.
    And she, what would she want with you?
ORESTES   I
    and another who came with me have a message
    for the lady of the house.

(ELECTRA *is silent*)

ORESTES   We were sent to her
    to testify the death of her son Orestes
    which we ourselves saw. For his own horses
    dragged him to his death. I was the same age
    as he and his companion day and night;
    the other who came with me is an old man,
    he was guardian and servant to us both.
ELECTRA   Why must I see you here? Why did you have to
    make your way here to my sad corner,
    O herald of misfortune! Why can't you trumpet
    your news there where it will make them rejoice!
    You live—and he who was better than you
    and nobler a thousand times, a thousand times
    more needed now to be alive—is dead!
    Your eyes stare at me now, and his are clouded.
    Your mouth speaks to me now, but his is stopped
    with earth. O could I stop your mouth with curses!
    Get out of my sight.
ORESTES   What do you want of me?
    The others here received the news with joy.
    Let the dead be. Forget Orestes.
    Orestes is dead now, what's come is come,
    and had to be. He took too much pleasure
    in living, and the gods cannot endure
    the far too bright and ringing sound of joy;
    the far too heavy rush or wings at evening
    repulses them; they grasp the nearest arrow
    and nail the creature to the dismal tree
    of his dark fate that somewhere has grown in silence
    a long while. And so he had to die.
ELECTRA   How knowingly he speaks of death, this—creature!
    As if he'd tasted it and spat it out.
    But I! But I! I must lie here and know
    that the child will never again come home,
    that those inside the house rejoice and live,
    that this vile brood lives on inside its hole
    and eats and drinks and sleeps and multiplies,
    while down below the child lingers in the chasm
    of horror, and dare not approach its father.
    And here am I, alone upon the earth,
    living as no beast ever lived, alone
    and monstrously!
ORESTES   Who are you?
ELECTRA   Why should you care
    who I am. Did I ask you who you were?

ORESTES   I can think nothing else but that you are
          closely related in blood to them who died,
          Agamemnon and Orestes.

ELECTRA   Related? I?
          I *am* that blood! That blood spilt so brutishly!
          King Agamemnon's blood! I'm called Electra.

ORESTES   No!

ELECTRA   He doesn't believe me. He scorns me first
          and then takes from me my name. Even the children
          ridicule me because my father and brother
          are dead! And everyone who comes this way
          kicks at me, and now they want even my name!

ORESTES   Electra must be ten years younger than you.
          Electra is tall; her eyes are sad, but gentle,
          while yours are filled with blood and hate. Electra—
          Electra lives apart from the common people,
          she spends her days guarding at a tomb.
          She has always two or three women about her,
          who serve her silently, and animals
          steal timidly about the house she lives in,
          and nestle to her when she walks.

ELECTRA *(clapping her hands)*   True! True!
          What other pretty stories can you tell me!
          I'll tell it to her when I—(*with choked voice*)
                                     —see her again.

ORESTES   Is it true then? Is it really true?
          You? (*quickly*)
                      And have they left you here to starve or—
          have they beaten you?

ELECTRA   You with your questions—
          who are you?

ORESTES   Have they? Have they? Tell me! Please!

ELECTRA   Both! Both! Both! Queens do not flourish
          fed with the refuse from the garbage-heap,
          and a priestess is not made to spring about
          when she's been whipped, nor go about in rags
          in place of flowing robes. Leave go my dress,
          why must you muss it so to wipe your eyes!

ORESTES   Electra!
          Where have they made you sleep your terrible nights!
          Your eyes are dreadful.

ELECTRA *(sullenly)*   Go into the house there,
          inside you'll find my sister always ready
          for festivities!

ORESTES   Electra, listen to me.

ELECTRA   Don't come near me, I don't want to know
          who you are. I will not see anyone!
(She cowers, her face against the wall)

ORESTES   Listen, I haven't time. Listen. I dare not
          speak too loud. Listen: Orestes lives.

*(*ELECTRA *turns sharply)*

ORESTES   Don't make a sound. One movement from you now
          and you betray him.

ELECTRA   Then he's free? Where is he?
          You know where he is? Is he hidden? He is
          a prisoner, cowering in some corner,
          waiting for his death! And I must see him die!

They sent you here to torture me, to tie
my soul with a rope, and draw it high, and then
dash it to earth again.

ORESTES   He's as unharmed
as I.

ELECTRA   Then rescue him! Before they kill him.
Why can't you warn him? O I kiss your feet
that you may warn him. By your father's body
I beg you, run as quickly as you can,
run and bring him away! The child must die
if he should spend one night inside that house.

ORESTES   And by my father's body that is why
the child entered the house, so that this night
those who *must* die *will* die—

ELECTRA (*struck by his tone*)   Who are you?

(*The gloomy* OLD SERVANT *rushes in silently from the court, throws himself down at* ORESTES' *feet, kisses them, collects himself, looking about fearfully, and rushes out again silently*)

ELECTRA (*almost without control*)
Who are you then? Tell me! You frighten me.

ORESTES (*softly*)   The dogs that lie in the yard remember me,
but not my own sister.

ELECTRA (*cries out*)   No! Orestes!

ORESTES (*feverishly*)   If anyone inside the house there heard you,
he holds my life in his hands.

ELECTRA (*very softly, trembling*)   O Orestes!
No one's moving. Look at me, Orestes!
Look at me! No, no, you mustn't touch me!
Step back, I'm so ashamed that you should see me.
I do not know how you can look at me.
I am but the dead body of your sister,
my poor child. I know it makes you shudder
to see me. Still, I was a King's daughter!
I believe I was beautiful once: when I'd blow
the lamp out at my mirror, I would feel
a virgin thrill run through me as my naked
body's chastity glowed through the sultry night
like a thing divine. I would feel the moon's thin rays
bathe me in her snowwhite nakedness
as in a pond; my hair, O my hair then
was such as made men tremble, this same hair,
straggled, dirtied now, humiliated!
These, my brother, are the sweet delights
I had to sacrifice to my father.
Do you think if I enjoyed my body
that his sighs and groans would not throng so
about my bed? For the dead are jealous:
and he has sent me hatred, hollow-eyed hatred,
as a bridegroom. And so to my sleepless bed
I took this horror that breathed like a viper,
and let him crawl on top of me and force me
to know all that happens between man and woman.
The nights, O, O the nights that taught me this!
My body was cold as ice, though hot as coals,
charred in its depths. And then when I knew all,
then I knew what wisdom was, and the murderers—
my mother, I mean, and that one with her—

they could no longer look into my eyes!
Why do you look about so anxiously?
Speak to me, speak! Why are you trembling so?

ORESTES   Let my body tremble. Do you think
it would not tremble otherwise if it knew
the way that it must go, the way I'll lead it?

ELECTRA   You'll do it? You? Alone? O my poor child!
And you have brought no friends along with you?

ORESTES   You must not speak of it. My old servant
is with me here. But I will do the deed.

ELECTRA   I've never seen the gods, and yet I'm certain
that they will be here with you, they will help you.

ORESTES   I do not know the gods, but I know this:
they have laid this deed upon my conscience,
and they will scorn me if I tremble at it.

ELECTRA   You *will* do it!

ORESTES   Yes, yes. I only wish
I need not look my mother in the eyes.

ELECTRA   Then look and see what she has made of me.

(ORESTES *looks sadly at her*)

ELECTRA   O child, O child! How stealthily you've come here,
speaking of yourself as though dead,
and yet you are alive!

ORESTES (*softly*)   Be careful!

ELECTRA   Who
am I, that you should cast such loving looks
at me? See, I am nothing. All I was
I had to sacrifice: even that modesty,
that sweetest thing of all, which, like the silvery,
milky haze of the moon, hovers about
a woman and protects her and her soul
from all things horrible! My modesty
was sacrificed as though I'd fallen among thieves
who stripped my last garment from me! I have
known the wedding-night, as no other virgins,
have known the pangs of women who bear children,
but have brought nothing into the world, nothing;
I have become a perpetual prophetess,
and have brought nothing forth from my body
except eternal curses and despair.
At night I never slept, but made my bed
high on the tower and cried down to the court
and whimpered with the dogs. I have been hated,
I have seen everything, have had to see everything
just like the watchman on the tower,
and day is night and night becomes day again,
and I have found no joy in sun or stars,
for all things, for his sake, were nothing to me,
all things were but signs, and every day
a marker on the road.

ORESTES   O my sister.

ELECTRA   What is it?

ORESTES   Does our mother look like you
in any way?

ELECTRA (*wildly*)   Like me? No. I will not
have you look her in the face. When she is dead,
then we together will look her in the face.

O my brother, she threw a white shirt
upon our father, and then she struck away
at that which stood before her, helpless, sightless,
which could not turn its face to hers, whose arms
could not work free—are you listening to me?—
she struck down at this with her axe raised high
above him.

ORESTES   Electra! No!

ELECTRA   O now her face
is mirror to the deeds that she has done.

ORESTES   I *will* do it! I must do it quickly!

ELECTRA   Happy the man who *does*! Who dares to do!
A deed is like a bed on which the soul
can rest, a bed of balsam where the soul
that is a wound, a blight, a running sore,
a sore that flames like fire!

(ORESTES' GUARDIAN *stands in the door to the court, a strong old man with flashing
eyes*)

ELECTRA   Who is this man?

GUARDIAN (*quickly to them*)
Are you both mad? Can't you hold your tongues
when a breath, a sound, when nothing might undo
both us and our work together—

ELECTRA   Who is this man?

ORESTES   Don't you know him? If you love me, thank him.
You must thank him I am here. This is Electra.

ELECTRA   You! You! O everything is true now!
Everything comes to me now! Here, let me kiss
your hands! I know nothing of the gods,
I do not know them, therefore I would rather
kiss your hands.

GUARDIAN   Be still, Electra, be still!

ELECTRA   No, I will rejoice over you, for you
have brought him here. When I was steeped in hatred
I kept nothing but silence. Hatred is nothing,
it consumes itself, and love is still less
than hatred, it grasps out at everything,
but fastens onto nothing, its hands are like flames
that cannot grasp; and thought, too, is nothing,
and all that comes from our mouths is feeble air:
that man alone is happy who comes to *do*!
And happy who dares to touch him and who digs
his axe from the earth, who holds the torch for him,
who opens the door, who listens there.

GUARDIAN (*takes hold of her roughly and presses his hand to her mouth*)
Be silent!

(*to* ORESTES *in great haste*)
She's waiting inside. Her maids are looking for you.
There's not a man in all the house. Orestes!

(ORESTES *collects himself, controls his terror. The doorway of the house grows bright,
and a* WOMAN SERVANT *appears with a torch, behind her* CLYTEMNESTRA'S WOMAN.
ELECTRA *has sprung back; she stands in darkness. The* WOMAN *does obeisance to the
two men and nods for them to follow her inside. The* WOMAN SERVANT *secures the
torch in an iron ring at the doorpost.* ORESTES *and the* GUARDIAN *go inside.* ORESTES
closes his eyes momentarily as though dizzy; the GUARDIAN *is close behind him; they
exchange a quick glance. The door closes behind them.*)

ELECTRA *is left alone in dreadful suspense. She runs back and forth in front of the door, her head bent forward, like a captive animal in its cage. Suddenly she stands still and says:*)

ELECTRA   I didn't give him the axe! They've gone inside,
    and I didn't give him the axe. There are no gods
    in heaven!

(*Another fearful waiting. From inside there comes the shrill cry of* CLYTEMNESTRA)

ELECTRA (*cries out as though possessed*)   Again! Again!

(*A second cry from inside. From the servants' quarters, left, enter* CHRYSOTHEMIS *and a crowd of* WOMEN SERVANTS. ELECTRA *stands at the door, her back pressed against it*)

CHRYSOTHEMIS   Something has happened.

FIRST WOMAN SERVANT   She cries like that in her sleep.

SECOND WOMAN SERVANT   There must be men inside. I heard men's footsteps.

THIRD WOMAN SERVANT   All the doors are locked.

FOURTH WOMAN SERVANT   They're murderers!
    There are murderers in the house!

FIRST WOMAN SERVANT (*cries out*)
                               O!

ALL   What is it?

FIRST WOMAN SERVANT   Don't you see? There's someone at the door!

CHRYSOTHEMIS   That's Electra! That must be Electra!

SECOND WOMAN SERVANT   Why is she standing there so quiet?

CHRYSOTHEMIS   Electra,
    why do you stand there so quiet?

FIRST WOMAN SERVANT   I must get out.
    I must get the men. (*runs off left*)

CHRYSOTHEMIS   Open the door, Electra!

SEVERAL WOMEN SERVANTS   Electra, let us in the house!

FIRST WOMAN SERVANT (*comes running back through the courtyard gate crying out*)
                            Get back!

(*They all grow startled*)

FIRST WOMAN SERVANT   Aegisthus! Aegisthus! Quick! Get back to our rooms!
    Aegisthus is crossing the court! If he finds us,
    and something's happened inside, he'll have us killed!

ALL   Quick! Get back! Get back!

(*They disappear into the house, left*)

AEGISTHUS (*at the entrance on the right*)   Is there no one here
    to light my way? Will none of these scoundrels help me?
    Impossible to teach these people manners!

(ELECTRA *takes the torch from the ring, runs down toward him, and bows*)

AEGISTHUS (*startled at the wild-looking figure in the flickering light, steps backward*)
    What ghastly thing is this? I have forbidden
    that an unknown face approach me!

(*recognizes her, angrily*)   What? Is it you?
    Who bade you to come near me?

ELECTRA   May I not
    light your way?

AEGISTHUS   Well, I suppose the news
    concerns you most. Where will I find these strangers
    who tell us of Orestes?

ELECTRA   Why—inside.
    They found a gracious hostess there to greet them.
    They're amusing themselves with her.

AEGISTHUS   And their news?
    That he is dead? Is it true beyond a doubt?

ELECTRA My lord, their proof is not in words alone,
 O no, they have bodily signs with them,
 which cannot be denied.
AEGISTHUS   What's that in your voice?
 What's happened to you that you even speak to me?
 Why do you stagger back and forth this way
 with this light you hold!
ELECTRA   I am become wise at last
 and hold myself with them that are the stronger.
 May I light your way?
AEGISTHUS   As far as the door.
 Why are you dancing? Be careful!
ELECTRA (*while circling about him, as though doing a sinister dance, suddenly bows
deeply*)   Have care! The steps!
 You mustn't fall.
AEGISTHUS (*at the door to the house*)   Why is there no light here?
 Who are those people?
ELECTRA   They are the very ones
 who'd pay you their respects in person, my lord.
 And I who've often disturbed you with the arrogant
 impudence of my presence have learned at last
 to withdraw myself at the proper moment.

(AEGISTHUS *enters the house. A short silence. Then noise inside.* AEGISTHUS *appears
at once at a small window at the right, tears back the curtain and cries out*)

AEGISTHUS Help! Murder! Help your master! Murder, murder!
 They're murdering me! (*He is dragged away*)
       Will no one listen to me?
 No one listen? (*Once again his face appears at the window*)
ELECTRA   Agamemnon listens!
AEGISTHUS (*torn from the window*)   Ah!

(ELECTRA *stands breathing fearfully, turned toward the house. The* WOMEN *run
out wildly,* CHRYSOTHEMIS *among them. As though unconscious they run toward the
door of the court. They suddenly stop there and turn around*)

CHRYSOTHEMIS Electra! Sister! Come, O come with us!
 It's our brother there inside! It's Orestes
 who did it!

(*A confusion of voices, tumult outside*)

CHRYSOTHEMIS   Come! He's in the entrance hall,
 they're round about him in circles, kissing his feet;
 all who hated Aegisthus in their hearts
 have thrown themselves on the others, everywhere,
 in all the courts, the dead are lying about;
 those who are still alive are spattered with blood
 and bear wounds themselves, but their faces are radiant,
 all embrace one another—

(*The noise outside increases, the* WOMEN *have run out,* CHRYSOTHEMIS *is alone. Light
spills in from outside*)

CHRYSOTHEMIS   —and rejoice;
 a thousand torches are lighted. Don't you hear it?
 Don't you?
ELECTRA (*crouching on the threshold*)   Don't I hear it? Hear the music?
 That music comes from me. Those thousands and thousands
 with torches, they whose boundless myriad footsteps
 make hollow rumbling round the earth, all these,
 these, wait upon me: I know that they all,
 all, wait upon me to lead the dance,

and yet I cannot; the ocean, the monstrous ocean,
the manifold ocean weighs me down with its burden
in every limb; I cannot lift myself!

CHRYSOTHEMIS (*almost screaming with excitement*)
Don't you hear them? Listen! They're carrying him,
they're carrying him upon their hands, their faces
are all changed, their eyes and the cheeks of the old
glisten with tears! They're crying. Don't you hear?
Ah! (*She runs out*)

(ELECTRA *has raised herself. She strides down from the stairs, her head thrown back like a Maenad. She thrusts forward her knees, she stretches out her arms: it is an indescribable dance in which she strides forward.* CHRYSOTHEMIS *appears again at the door, behind her are torches, a throng, faces of men and women*)

CHRYSOTHEMIS Electra!

ELECTRA (*stops short, stands staring at them*)
                    Be silent and dance. All must come!
All must join with me! I bear the burden
of joy, and I dance here before you all.
One thing alone remains for him who is happy:
to be silent and dance!

(*She does a few more steps of her most tense dance of triumph, and collapses.* CHRYSOTHEMIS *rushes to her.* ELECTRA *lies motionless.* CHRYSTHEMIS *runs to the door of the house and knocks*)

CHRYSOTHEMIS Orestes! Orestes!

(*Silence*)

Bertolt Brecht

1898-1956

ON EXPERIMENTAL THEATRE

For at least two generations the serious European drama has been passing through a period of experiment. So far the various experiments conducted have not led to any definite and clearly established result, nor is the period itself over. In my view these experiments were pursued along two lines which occasionally intersected but can none the less be followed separately. They are defined by the two functions of *entertainment* and *instruction*; that is to say that the theatre organized experiments to increase its ability to amuse, and others which were intended to raise its value as education.

[Brecht then lists various experiments from Antoine on, designed to increase the theatre's capacity to entertain, and singles out Vakhtanghov and the constructivist Meyerhold—who 'took over from the asiatic theatre certain dance-like forms and created a whole choreography for the drama'—Reinhardt, with his open-air productions of *Faust, Jedermann* and *Midsummer Night's Dream,* and his seating of actors among the audience in Büchner's *Danton's Death;* Okhlopkov, and the elaboration of crowd scenes by Stanislavsky, Reinhardt and Jessner.[1] But 'on the whole the theatre has not been brought up to modern technological standards'.

[1] All famous directors of the theatre of the twentieth century.

"On Experimental Theatre" and "A New Technique of Acting" by Bertolt Brecht are from *Brecht on Theatre,* translated by John Willett. Copyright © 1957, 1963, 1964 by Suhrkamp Verlag, Frankfurt am Main. Translation and notes © 1964 by John Willett. Reprinted by permission of Hill & Wang, Inc.

The second line he sees as pursued primarily by the playwrights, instancing Ibsen, Tolstoy, Strindberg, Gorki, Tchekov, Hauptmann, Shaw, Georg Kaiser and Eugene O'Neill, and mentioning his own *Threepenny Opera* as 'a parable type plus ideology-busting'. Piscator's theatre was 'the most radical' of all such attempts. 'I took part in all his experiments, and every single one was aimed to increase the theatre's value as education.']

These discoveries [he goes on] have not yet been taken up by the international theatre; this electrification of the stage has been virtually forgotten; the whole ingenious machinery is rusting up, and grass is growing over it. Why is that?

The breakdown of this eminently political theatre must be attributed to political causes. The increase in the theatre's value as political education clashed with the growth of political reaction. But for the moment we shall restrict ourselves to seeing how its crisis developed in aesthetic terms.

Piscator's experiments began by causing complete theatrical chaos. While they turned the stage into a machine-room, the auditorium became a public meeting. Piscator saw theatre as a parliament, the audience as a legislative body. To this parliament were submitted in plastic form all the great public questions that needed an answer. Instead of a Deputy speaking about certain intolerable social conditions there was an artistic copy of these conditions. It was the stage's ambition to supply images, statistics, slogans which would enable its parliament, the audience, to reach political decisions. Piscator's stage was not indifferent to applause, but it preferred a discussion. It didn't want only to provide its spectator with an experience but also to squeeze from him a practical decision to intervene actively in life. Every means was justified which helped to secure this. The

[193]

technical side of the stage became extremely complicated. Piscator's stage manager had before him a book that was as different from that of Reinhardt's stage manager as the score of a Stravinsky opera is from a lute-player's part. The mechanism on the stage weighed so much that the stage of the Nollendorftheater had to be reinforced with steel and concrete supports; so much machinery was hung from the dome that it began to give way. Aesthetic considerations were entirely subject to political. Away with painted scenery if a film could be shown that had been taken on the spot and had the stamp of documentary realism. Up with painted cartoons, if the artist (e.g. George Grosz) had something to say to the parliamentary audience. Piscator was even ready to do wholly without actors. When the former German Emperor had his lawyers protest at Piscator's plan to let an actor portray him on his stage, Piscator just asked if the Emperor wouldn't be willing to appear in person; he even offered him a contract. In short, the end was such a vast and important one that all means seemed justified. And the plays themselves were prepared in much the same way as the performance. A whole staff of playwrights worked together on a single play, and their work was supported and checked by a staff of experts, historians, economists, statisticians.

Piscator's experiments broke nearly all the conventions. They intervened to transform the playwright's creative methods, the actor's style of representation, and the work of the stage designer. *They were striving towards an entirely new social function for the theatre.*

Bourgeois revolutionary aesthetics, founded by such great figures of the Enlightenment as *Diderot* [2] and *Lessing*,[3] defines the theatre as a place of entertainment and instruction. During the Enlightenment, a period which saw the start of a tremendous upsurge of the European theatre, there was no conflict between these two things. Pure amusement, provoked even by objects of tragedy, struck men like Diderot as utterly hollow and unworthy unless it added something to the spectators' knowledge, while elements of instruction, in artistic form of course, seemed in no wise to detract from the amusement; in these men's view they gave depth to it.

If we now look at the theatre of our day

we shall find an increasingly marked conflict between the two elements which go to make it up, together with its plays—entertainment and instruction. Today there is an opposition here. That 'assimilation of art to science' which gave naturalism its social influence undoubtedly hamstrung some major artistic capacities, notably the imagination, the sense of play and the element of pure poetry. Its artistic aspects were clearly harmed by its instructive side.

The expressionism of the postwar period showed the World as Will and Idea and led to a special kind of solipsism. It was the theatre's answer to the great crisis of society, just as the doctrines of Mach [4] were philosophy's. It represented art's revolt against life: here the world existed purely as a vision, strangely distorted, a monster conjured up by perturbed souls. Expressionism vastly enriched the theatre's means of expression and brought aesthetic gains that still have to be fully exploited, but it proved quite incapable of shedding light on the world as an object of human activity. The theatre's educative value collapsed.

In Piscator's productions or in *The Threepenny Opera* the educative elements were so to speak *built in:* they were not an organic consequence of the whole, but stood in contradiction to it; they broke up the flow of the play and its incidents, they prevented empathy, they acted as a cold douche for those whose sympathies were becoming involved. I hope that the moralizing parts of *The Threepenny Opera* and the educative songs are reasonably entertaining, but it is certain that the entertainment in question is different from what one gets from the more orthodox scenes. The play has a double nature. Instruction and entertainment conflict openly. With Piscator it was the actor and the machinery that openly conflicted.

This is quite apart from the fact that such productions split the audience into at least two mutually hostile social groups, and thus put a stop to any common experience of art. The fact is a political one. Enjoyment of learning depends on the class situation. Artistic appreciation depends on one's political attitude, which can accordingly be stimulated and adopted. But even if we restrict ourselves to the section of the audience which agreed politically we see the sharpening of the conflict between ability to entertain and educative

---

2 Denis Diderot (1713–1784), French philosopher and aesthetician of The Enlightenment.

3 Gotthold Ephraim Lessing (1729–1781), German playwright and critic.

---

4 A philosophy of "critical positivism" developed by Austrian physicist and philosopher Ernst Mach (1838–1916).

value. Here is a new and quite specific kind of learning, and it can no longer be reconciled with a specific old kind of entertainment. At one (later) stage of the experiments the result of any fresh increase in educative value was an immediate decrease in ability to entertain. ('This isn't theatre, it's secondary-school stuff.') Conversely, emotional acting's effects on the nerves was a continual menace to the production's educative value. (It often helped the educational effect to have bad actors instead of good ones.) In other words, the greater the grip on the audience's nerves, the less chance there was of its learning. The more we induced the audience to identify its own experiences and feelings with the production, the less it learned; and the more there was to learn, the less the artistic enjoyment.

Here was a crisis: half a century's experiments, conducted in nearly every civilized country, had won the theatre brand-new fields of subject-matter and types of problem, and made it a factor of marked social importance. At the same time they had brought the theatre to a point where any further development of the intellectual, social (political) experience must wreck the artistic experience. And yet, without further development of the former, the latter occurred less and less often. A technical apparatus and a style of acting had been evolved which could do more to stimulate illusions than to give experiences, more to intoxicate than to elevate, more to deceive than to illumine.

What was the good of a constructivist stage if it was socially unconstructive; of the finest lighting equipment if it lit nothing but childish and twisted representations of the world; of a suggestive style of acting if it only served to tell us that A was B? What use was the whole box of tricks if all it could do was to offer artificial surrogates for real experience? Why this eternal ventilating of problems that were always left unsolved? This titillation not only of the nerves but of the brain? We couldn't leave it at that.

The development tended towards a fusion of the two functions, instruction and entertainment. If such preoccupations were to have any social meaning, then they must eventually enable the theatre to project a picture of the world by artistic means: models of men's life together such as could help the spectator to understand his social environment and both rationally and emotionally to master it. [Brecht goes on, in terms that anticipate the Short Organum and perhaps reflect his work on the first version of *Galileo*, to lament

man's failure to understand the laws governing his life in society. His knowledge of these has not kept pace with his scientific knowledge, so that 'nowadays nearly every new discovery is greeted with a shout of triumph which transforms itself into a shout of fear'. (Cf. the long speech in Scene 14 of *Galileo*.) But art ought to be able to give 'a workable picture of the world'.

As it is, he argues, art gets its effects more by empathy than by accuracy. He attacks empathy on the same grounds as before, and describes the attempt to stave it off by methods of 'alienation'. This technique was developed at the Theater am Schiffbauerdamm [5] in Berlin with 'the most talented of the younger generation of actors . . . Weigel, Peter Lorre, Oskar Homolka, (Carola) Neher and Busch', and also with amateur groups, workers' choruses, etc.]

This all represented a continuation of previous experiments, in particular of Piscator's theatre. Already in his last experiments the logical development of the technical apparatus had at last allowed the machinery to be mastered and led to a beautiful simplicity of performance. The so-called *epic* style of production which we developed at the Schiffbauerdamm Theater proved its artistic merits relatively soon, and the *non-aristotelian school of playwriting* tackled the large-scale treatment of large-scale social objects. There was some prospect of changing the choreographic and grouping aspects of Meyerhold's school from artifice into art, of transforming the Stanislavsky school's naturalistic elements into realism. Speech was related to gestics; both everyday language and verse speaking were shaped according to the so-called *gestic principle*. A complete revolution took place in stage design. By a free manipulation of Piscator's principles it became possible to design a setting that was both instructive and beautiful. Symbolism and illusion could be more or less dispensed with, and the *Neher principle* of building the set according to the requirements established at the actors' rehearsals allowed the designer to profit by the actors' performance and influence it in turn. The playwright could work out his experiments in uninterrupted collaboration with actor and stage designer; he could influence and be influenced. At the same time the painter and the composer regained their independence, and were able to express their view of the theme by their own artistic means. The integrated work of art (or 'Gesamtkunst-

---

[5] Brecht's theatre in Berlin.

werk') appeared before the spectator as a bundle of separate elements.

From the start the *classical repertoire* supplied the basis of many of these experiments. The artistic means of alienation made possible a broad approach to the living works of dramatists of other periods. Thanks to them such valuable old plays could be performed without either jarring modernization or museum-like methods, and in an entertaining and instructive way.

It plainly has a particularly good effect on the contemporary amateur theatre (worker, student and child actors) when it is no longer forced to work by hypnosis. It seems conceivable that a line may be drawn between the playing of amateur actors and professionals without one of the theatre's basic functions having to be sacrificed.

Such very different ways of acting as those of, say, the Vakhtangov or Okhlopkov companies and the workers' groups can be reconciled on this new foundation. The variegated experiments of half a century seem to have acquired a basis that allows them to be exploited.

None the less these experiments are not so easy to describe, and I am forced here simply to state our belief that we can indeed encourage artistic understanding on the basis of alienation. This is not very surprising, as the theatre of past periods also, technically speaking, achieved results with alienation effects—for instance the Chinese theatre, the Spanish classical theatre, the popular theatre of Brueghel's [6] day and the Elizabethan theatre.

So is this new style of production *the* new style; is it a complete and comprehensible technique, the final result of every experiment? Answer: no. It is *a* way, the one that *we* have followed. The effort must be continued. The problem holds for all art, and it is a vast one. The solution here aimed at is only *one* of the conceivable solutions to the problem, which can be expressed so: How can the theatre be both instructive and entertaining? How can it be divorced from spiritual dope traffic and turned from a home of illusions to a home of experiences? How can the unfree, ignorant man of our century, with his thirst for freedom and his hunger for knowledge; how can the tortured and heroic, abused and ingenious, changeable and world-changing man of this great and ghastly century obtain his own theatre which will help him to master the world and himself?

['Über experimentelles Theater', from *Theater der Zeit,* East Berlin, 1959, No. 4. Also *Schriften zum Theater* 3, pp. 79–106. Two long passages have been summarized to save repetition of Brecht's arguments]

NOTE: This lecture is published in full in another translation in *The Tulane Drama Review* for Autumn 1961. Brecht delivered it to a student theatre in Stockholm in May 1939, revising it and repeating it in Helsinki in October 1940 (by which time he had temporarily settled in Finland). A draft version (Brecht-Archive 60/06–10) shows that he was conscious of addressing 'a scientifically-trained body, not just ordinary theatre lovers'.

Here is the first indication that Brecht wanted to strike a balance between didacticism and entertainment. Ever since the *Lehrstücke* his theoretical writing had been consistently on the side of the former; thus compare this essay with 'Theatre for Pleasure or Theatre for Instruction', where learning is supposed to contain its own amusement. Soon, however, he was writing in his diary (12 January 1941, quoted in Mittenzwei, *Bertolt Brecht,* East Berlin, 1962, p. 332):

> It must never be forgotten that *non-aristotelian theatre* is only *one* form of theatre; it furthers specific social aims and has no claims to monopoly as far as the theatre in general is concerned. I myself can use both aristotelian and non-aristotelian theatre in certain productions.

It was the period of his greatest plays—the first version of *Galileo* was finished in November 1938, *Mother Courage* by the end of 1939, *The Good Person of Szechwan* 'more or less finished' in June 1940—and he was heading for the theoretical compromise of the 'Short Organum'.

Translated by John Willett

SHORT DESCRIPTION OF A NEW TECHNIQUE OF ACTING WHICH PRODUCES AN ALIENATION EFFECT

What follows represents an attempt to describe a technique of acting which was applied in certain theatres (1) with a view to taking the incidents portrayed and alienating them from the spectator. The aim of this technique, known as the alienation effect, was to make the spectator adopt an attitude of inquiry and

---

[6] Pieter Bruéghel (1520–1569), Flemish painter, best known for his grotesque style.

criticism in his approach to the incident. The means were artistic.

The first condition for the A-effect's application to this end is that stage and auditorium must be purged of everything 'magical' and that no 'hypnotic tensions' should be set up. This ruled out any attempt to make the stage convey the flavour of a particular place (a room at evening, a road in the autumn), or to create atmosphere by relaxing the tempo of the conversation. The audience was not 'worked up' by a display of temperament or 'swept away' by acting with tautened muscles; in short, no attempt was made to put it in a trance and give it the illusion of watching an ordinary unrehearsed event. As will be seen presently, the audience's tendency to plunge into such illusions has to be checked by specific artistic means (2).

The first condition for the achievement of the A-effect is that the actor must invest what he has to show with a definite gest of showing. It is of course necessary to drop the assumption that there is a fourth wall cutting the audience off from the stage and the consequent illusion that the stage action is taking place in reality and without an audience. That being so, it is possible for the actor in principle to address the audience direct.

It is well known that contact between audience and stage is normally made on the basis of empathy. Conventional actors devote their efforts so exclusively to bringing about this psychological operation that they may be said to see it as the principal aim of their art (3). Our introductory remarks will already have made it clear that the technique which produces an A-effect is the exact opposite of that which aims at empathy. The actor applying it is bound not to try to bring about the empathy operation.

Yet in his efforts to reproduce particular characters and show their behaviour he need not renounce the means of empathy entirely. He uses these means just as any normal person with no particular acting talent would use them if he wanted to portray someone else, i.e. show how he behaves. This showing of other people's behaviour happens time and again in ordinary life (witnesses of an accident demonstrating to newcomers how the victim behaved, a facetious person imitating a friend's walk, etc.), without those involved making the least effort to subject their spectators to an illusion. At the same time they do feel their way into their characters' skins with a view to acquiring their characteristics.

      ✿   ✿   ✿

When reading his part the actor's attitude should be one of a man who is astounded and contradicts. Not only the occurrence of the incidents, as he reads about them, but the conduct of the man he is playing, as he experiences it, must be weighed up by him and their peculiarities understood; none can be taken as given, as something that 'was bound to turn out that way', that was 'only to be expected from a character like that'. Before memorizing the words he must memorize what he felt astounded at and where he felt impelled to contradict. For these are dynamic forces that he must preserve in creating his performance.

When he appears on the stage, besides what he actually is doing he will at all essential points discover, specify, imply what he is not doing; that is to say he will act in such a way that the alternative emerges as clearly as possible, that his acting allows the other possibilities to be inferred and only represents one out of the possible variants. . . . Whatever he doesn't do must be contained and conserved in what he does. In this way every sentence and every gesture signifies a decision; the character remains under observation and is tested. The technical term for this procedure is 'fixing the "not . . . but" '.

The actor does not allow himself to become completely transformed on the stage into the character he is portraying. He is not Lear, Harpagon, Schweik; he shows them. . . . Once the idea of total transformation is abandoned the actor speaks his part not as if he were improvising it himself but like a quotation (4). At the same time he obviously has to render all the quotation's overtones, the remark's full human and concrete shape; similarly the gesture he makes must have the full substance of a human gesture even though it now represents a copy.

Given this absence of total transformation in the acting there are three aids which may help to alienate the actions and remarks of the characters being portrayed:

1. Transposition into the third person.
2. Transposition into the past.
3. Speaking the stage directions out loud.

Using the third person and the past tense allows the actor to adopt the right attitude of detachment. In addition he will look for stage directions and remarks that comment on his lines, and speak them aloud at rehearsal ('He stood up and exclaimed angrily, not having eaten: . . .', or 'He had never been told so before, and didn't know if it was true or not', or 'He smiled, and said with forced nonchalance: . . .') (5). Speaking the stage directions out loud in the third person results in a clash between two tones of voice, alienating the second of them, the text proper. This style of acting is further alienated by taking place on the stage after having already been outlined and announced in words. Transposing it into the past gives the speaker a standpoint from which he can look back at his sentence. The sentence too is thereby alienated without the speaker adopting an unreal point of view; unlike the spectator, he has read the play right through and is better placed to judge the sentence in accordance with the ending, with its consequences, than the former, who knows less and is more of a stranger to the sentence.

This composite process leads to an alienation of the text in the rehearsals which generally persists in the performance too (6). The directness of the relationship with the audience allows and indeed forces the actual speech delivery to be varied in accordance with the greater or smaller significance attaching to the sentences. Take the case of witnesses addressing a court. The underlinings, the characters' insistence on their remarks, must be developed as a piece of effective virtuosity. If the actor turns to the audience it must be a whole-hearted turn rather than the asides and soliloquizing technique of the old-fashioned theatre. To get the full A-effect from the poetic medium the actor should start at rehearsal by paraphrasing the verse's content in vulgar prose, possibly accompanying this by the gestures designed for the verse. A daring and beautiful handling of verbal media will alienate the text. (Prose can be alienated by translation into the actor's native dialect.)

Gesture will be dealt with below, but it can at once be said that everything to do with the emotions has to be externalized; that is to say, it must be developed into a gesture. The actor has to find a sensibly perceptible outward expression for his character's emotions, preferably some action that gives away what is going on inside him. The emotion in question must be brought out, must lose all its restrictions so that it can be treated on a big scale. Special elegance, power and grace of gesture bring about the A-effect.

❖   ❖   ❖

Whatever the actor offers in the way of gesture, verse structure, etc., must be finished and bear the hallmarks of something rehearsed and rounded-off. The impression to be given is one of ease, which is at the same time one of difficulties overcome. The actor must make it possible for the audience to take his own art, his mastery of technique, lightly too. He puts an incident before the spectator with perfection and as he thinks it really happened or might have happened. He does not conceal the fact that he has rehearsed it, any more than an acrobat conceals his training, and he emphasizes that it is his own (actor's) account, view, version of the incident.

❖   ❖   ❖

The attitude which he adopts is a socially critical one. In his exposition of the incidents and in his characterization of the person he tries to bring out those features which come within society's sphere. In this way his performance becomes a discussion (about social conditions) with the audience he is addressing. He prompts the spectator to justify or abolish these conditions according to what class he belongs to (7).

The object of the A-effect is to alienate the social gest underlying every incident. By social gest is meant the mimetic and gestural expression of the social relationships prevailing between people of a given period (8).

It helps to formulate the incident for society, and to put it across in such a way that society is given the key, if titles are thought up for the scenes. These titles must have a historical quality.

This brings us to a crucial technical device: historicization.

The actor must play the incidents as historical ones. Historical incidents are unique, transitory incidents associated with particular periods. The conduct of the persons involved in them is not fixed and 'universally human'; it includes elements that have been or may be overtaken by the course of history, and is subject to criticism from the immediately following period's point of view. The conduct of those born before us is alienated[1] from us by an incessant evolution.

It is up to the actor to treat present-day events and modes of behaviour with the same detachment as the historian adopts with regard to those of the past. He must alienate these characters and incidents from us.

Characters and incidents from ordinary life, from our immediate surroundings, being familiar, strike us as more or less natural. Alienating them helps to make them seem remarkable to us. Science has carefully developed a technique of getting irritated with the everyday, 'self-evident', universally ac-

---

[1] *Entfremdet.*

cepted occurrence, and there is no reason why this infinitely useful attitude should not be taken over by art (9). It is an attitude which arose in science as a result of the growth in human productive powers. In art the same motive applies.

As for the emotions, the experimental use of the A-effect in the epic theatre's German productions indicated that this way of acting too can stimulate them, though possibly a different class of emotion is involved from those of the orthodox theatre (10). A critical attitude on the audience's part is a thoroughly artistic one (11). Nor does the actual practice of the A-effect seem anything like so unnatural as its description. Of course it is a way of acting that has nothing to do with stylization as commonly practised. The main advantage of the epic theatre with its A-effect, intended purely to show the world in such a way that it becomes manageable, is precisely its quality of being natural and earthly, its humour and its renunciation of all the mystical elements that have stuck to the orthodox theatre from the old days.

APPENDIX
[*selected notes*]

1. *Edward II* after Marlowe (Munich Kammerspiele).

Trommeln in der Nacht (Deutsches Theater, Berlin).

The Threepenny Opera (Theater am Schiffbauerdamm, Berlin).

Die Pioniere von Ingolstadt (Theater am Schiffbauerdamm).

Aufstieg und Fall der Stadt Mahagonny, opera (Aufricht's Kurfürstendammtheater, Berlin).

Mann ist Mann (Staatstheater, Berlin).

Die Massnahme (Grosses Schauspielhaus, Berlin).

The Adventures of the Good Soldier Schweik (Piscator's Theater am Nollendorfplatz, Berlin).

Die Plattköpfe und die Spitzköpfe (Riddersalen, Copenhagen).

Señora Carrar's Rifles (Copenhagen, Paris).

Furcht und Elend des Dritten Reiches (Paris).

2. E.g. such mechanical means as very brilliant illumination of the stage (since a half-lit stage plus a completely darkened auditorium makes the spectator less level-headed by preventing him from observing his neighbour and in turn hiding him from his neighbour's eyes) and also *making visible the sources of light*.

MAKING VISIBLE THE SOURCES OF LIGHT

There is a point in showing the lighting apparatus openly, as it is one of the means of preventing an unwanted element of illusion; it scarcely disturbs the necessary concentration. If we light the actors and their performance in such a way that the lights themselves are within the spectator's field of vision we destroy part of his illusion of being present at a spontaneous, transitory, authentic, unrehearsed event. He sees that arrangements have been made to show something; something is being repeated here under special conditions, for instance in a very brilliant light. Displaying the actual lights is meant to be a counter to the old-fashioned theatre's efforts to hide them. No one would expect the lighting to be hidden at a sporting event, a boxing match for instance. Whatever the points of difference between the modern theatre's presentations and those of a sporting promoter, they do not include the same concealment of the sources of light as the old theatre found necessary.

(Brecht:
'Der Bühnenbau des epischen Theaters')
* * *

3. Cf., Rapaport, 'The Work of the Actor', *Theater Workshop*, October 1936:

'. . . On the stage the actor is surrounded entirely by fictions. . . . The actor must be able to regard all this as though it were true, as though he were convinced that all that surrounds him on the stage is a living reality and, along with himself, he must convince the audience as well. This is the central feature of our method of work on the part. . . . Take any object, a cap for example; lay it on the table or on the floor and try to regard it as though it were a rat; make believe that it is a rat, and not a cap. . . . Picture what sort of a rat it is; what size, colour? . . . We thus commit ourselves to believe quite naïvely that the object before us is something other than it is and, at the same time, learn to compel the audience to believe. . . .'

This might be thought to be a course of instruction for conjurers, but in fact it is a course of acting, supposedly according to Stanislavsky's method. One wonders if a technique that equips an actor to make the audience see rats where there aren't any can really be all that suitable for disseminating the truth. Given enough alcohol it doesn't take acting to persuade almost anybody that he is seeing rats: pink ones.

4. *Quotation*

Standing in a free and direct relationship to it, the actor allows his character to speak and move; he presents a report. He does not have to make us forget that the text isn't spontaneous, but has been memorized, is a fixed quantity; the fact doesn't matter, as we anyway assume that the report is not about himself but about others. His attitude would be the same if he were simply speaking from his own memory. [. . .]

5. The epic actor has to accumulate far more material than has been the case till now. What he has to represent is no longer himself as king, himself as scholar, himself as grave-digger, etc., but just kings, scholars, grave-diggers, which means that he has to look around him in the world of reality. Again, he has to learn how to imitate: something that is discouraged in modern acting on the ground that it destroys his individuality.

6. The theatre can create the corresponding A-effect in the performance in a number of ways. The Munich production of *Edward II* for the first time had titles preceding the scenes, announcing the contents. The Berlin production of *The Threepenny Opera* had the titles of the songs projected while they were sung. The Berlin production of *Mann ist Mann* had the actors' figures projected on big screens during the action.

7. Another thing that makes for freedom in the actor's relationship with his audience is that he does not treat it as an undifferentiated mass. He doesn't boil it down to a shapeless dumpling in the stockpot of the emotions. He does not address himself to everybody alike; he allows the existing divisions within the audience to continue, in fact he widens them. He has friends and enemies in the audience; he is friendly to the one group and hostile to the other. He takes sides, not necessarily with his character but if not with it then against it. (At least, that is his basic attitude, though it too must be variable and change according to what the character may say at different stages. There may, however, also be points at which everything is in the balance and the actor must withhold judgment, though this again must be expressly shown in his acting.)

8. If *King Lear* (in Act I, scene 1) tears up a map when he divides his kingdom between his daughters, then the act of division is alienated. Not only does it draw our attention to his kingdom, but by treating the kingdom so plainly as his own private property he throws

some light on the basis of the feudal idea of the family. In *Julius Caesar* the tyrant's murder by Brutus is alienated if during one of his monologues accusing Caesar of tyrannical motives he himself maltreats a slave waiting on him. Weigel as *Maria Stuart* suddenly took the crucifix hanging round her neck and used it coquettishly as a fan, to give herself air. (See too Brecht: 'Übungsstücke für Schauspieler' in *Versuche 11*, p. 107.)

9. *The A-Effect as a Procedure in Everyday Life*

The achievement of the A-effect constitutes something utterly ordinary, recurrent; it is just a widely-practised way of drawing one's own or someone else's attention to a thing, and it can be seen in education as also in business conferences of one sort or another. The A-effect consists in turning the object of which one is to be made aware, to which one's attention is to be drawn, from something ordinary, familiar, immediately accessible, into something peculiar, striking and unexpected. What is obvious is in a certain sense made incomprehensible, but this is only in order that it may then be made all the easier to comprehend. Before familiarity can turn into awareness the familiar must be stripped of its inconspicuousness; we must give up assuming that the object in question needs no explanation. However frequently recurrent, modest, vulgar it may be it will now be labelled as something unusual.

A common use of the A-effect is when someone says: 'Have you ever really looked carefully at your watch?' The questioner knows that I've looked at it often enough, and now his question deprives me of the sight which I've grown used to and which accordingly has nothing more to say to me. I used to look at it to see the time, and now when he asks me in this importunate way I realize that I have given up seeing the watch itself with an astonished eye; and it is in many ways an astonishing piece of machinery. . . . The asking of the question has alienated it, and intentionally so. The very simplest sentences that apply in the A-effect are those with 'Not . . . But': (He didn't say 'come in' but 'keep moving'. He was not pleased but amazed). They include an expectation which is justified by experience but, in the event, disappointed. One might have thought that . . . but one oughtn't to have thought it. There was not just one possibility but two; both are introduced, then the second one is alienated, then the first as well. To see one's mother as a man's wife one needs an A-effect; this is provided, for instance, when one acquires a stepfather. If one sees one's teacher hounded by the bailiffs an A-effect occurs: one is jerked out of a relationship in which the teacher seems big into one where he seems small. An alienation of the motor-car takes place if after driving a modern car for a long while we drive an old model T Ford. Suddenly we hear explosions once more; the motor works on the principle of explosion. We start feeling amazed that such a vehicle, indeed any vehicle not drawn by animal-power, can move; in short, we understand cars, by looking at them as something strange, new, as a triumph of engineering and to that extent something unnatural. Nature, which certainly embraces the motor-car, is suddenly imbued with an element of unnaturalness, and from now on this is an indelible part of the concept of nature.

The expression 'in fact' can likewise certify or alienate. (He wasn't in fact at home; he said he would be, but we didn't believe him and had a look; or again, we didn't think it possible for him not to be at home, but it was a fact.) . . .

*　　*　　*

10. *About Rational and Emotional Points of View*

The rejection of empathy is not the result of a rejection of the emotions, nor does it lead to such. The crude aesthetic thesis that emotions can only be stimulated by means of empathy is wrong. None the less a non-aristotelian dramaturgy has to apply a cautious criticism to the emotions which it aims at and incorporates. Certain artistic tendencies like the provocative behaviour of Futurists and Dadaists and the icing-up of music point to a crisis of the emotions. Already in the closing years of the Weimar Republic the post-war German drama took a decisively rationalistic turn. Fascism's grotesque emphasizing of the emotions, together perhaps with the no less important threat to the rational element in Marxist

aesthetics, led us to lay particular stress on the rational. Nevertheless there are many contemporary works of art where one can speak of a decline in emotional effectiveness due to their isolation from reason, or its revival thanks to a stronger rationalist message. This will surprise no one who has not got a completely conventional idea of the emotions.

*　　*　　*

11. *Is the Critical Attitude an Inartistic One?*

An old tradition leads people to treat a critical attitude as a predominantly negative one. Many see the difference between the scientific and artistic attitudes as lying precisely in their attitude to criticism. People cannot conceive of contradiction and detachment as being part of artistic appreciation. Of course such appreciation normally includes a higher level, which appreciates critically, but the criticism here only applies to matters of technique; it is quite a different matter from being required to observe not a representation of the world but the world itself in a critical, contradictory, detached manner.

To introduce this critical attitude into art, the negative element which it doubtless includes must be shown from its positive side: this criticism of the world is active, practical, positive. Criticizing the course of a river means improving it, correcting it. Criticism of society is ultimately revolution; there you have criticism taken to its logical conclusion and playing an active part. A critical attitude of this type is an operative factor of productivity; it is deeply enjoyable as such, and if we commonly use the term 'arts' for enterprises that improve people's lives why should art proper remain aloof from arts of this sort?

['Kurze Beschreibung einer neuen Technik der Schauspielkunst, die einen Verfremdungseffekt hervorbringt', from *Versuche 11*, 1951.]

Translated by John Willett

THE CAUCASIAN CHALK CIRCLE

English Adaptation by Eric Bentley

CAST OF CHARACTERS

OLD MAN *on the right*
PEASANT WOMAN *on the right*
YOUNG PEASANT
A VERY YOUNG WORKER
OLD MAN *on the left*
PEASANT WOMAN *on the left*
AGRICULTURIST KATO
GIRL TRACTORIST
WOUNDED SOLDIER
THE DELEGATE *from the capital*
THE STORY TELLER
GEORGI ABASHWILI, *the*
  GOVERNOR
NATELLA, *the* GOVERNOR'S WIFE
MICHAEL, *their son*
SHALVA, *an Adjutant*
ARSEN KAZBEKI, *a fat prince*
MESSENGER *from the capital*
NIKO MIKADZE *and* MIKA
  LOLADZE, *doctors*
SIMON SHASHAVA, *a soldier*
GRUSHA VASHNADZE, *a kitchen*
  maid
OLD PEASANT *with the milk*
CORPORAL *and* PRIVATE
LAVRENTI VASHNADZE,
  Grusha's brother

PEASANT *and his wife*
ANIKO, *his wife*
PEASANT WOMAN, *for a while*
  Grusha's mother-in-law
JUSSUP, *her son*
MONK
AZDAK, *village scrivener*
SHAUWA, *a policeman*
GRAND DUKE
DOCTOR
INVALID
LIMPING MAN
BLACKMAILER
LUDOVICA
INNKEEPER, *her father-in-law*
STABLEBOY
POOR OLD PEASANT WOMAN
IRAKLI, *her brother-in-law, a bandit*
THREE WEALTHY FARMERS
ILLO SHUBOLADZE *and* SANDRO
  OBOLADZE, *lawyers*
OLD MARRIED COUPLE

SOLDIERS, SERVANTS,
  PEASANTS, BEGGARS,
  MUSICIANS, MERCHANTS,
  NOBLES, ARCHITECTS

Prologue

(*Among the ruins of a war-ravaged Caucasian village the members of two Kolkhoz villages, mostly women and older men, are sitting in a circle, smoking and drinking wine. With them is a delegate of the state reconstruction commission from Nuka, the capital*)

PEASANT WOMAN (*left, pointing*) In those hills over there we stopped three Nazi tanks, but the apple orchard was already destroyed.

OLD MAN (*right*) Our beautiful dairy farm; a ruin.

GIRL TRACTORIST I laid the fire, Comrade. (*Pause*)

THE DELEGATE Now listen to the report. Delegates from the goat-breeding Kolkhoz "Rosa Luxemburg" have been to Nuka. When Hitler's armies approached, the Kolkhoz had moved its goat-herds further east on orders from the authorities. They are now thinking of returning. Their delegates have investigated the village and the land and found a lot of it destroyed. (DELEGATES *on right nod*) The neighboring fruit-culture Kolkhoz (*to the left*) "Galinsk" is proposing to use the former grazing land of Kolkhoz "Rosa Luxemburg," a valley with scanty growth of grass, for orchards and vineyards. As a delegate of the Reconstruction Commission, I request that the two Kolkhoz villages decide between themselves whether Kolkhoz "Rosa Luxemburg" shall return here or not.

OLD MAN (*right*) First of all, I want to protest against the restriction of time for discussion. We of Kolkhoz "Rosa Luxemburg" have spent three days and three nights getting here. And now discussion is limited to half a day.

WOUNDED SOLDIER (*left*) Comrade, we haven't as many villages as we used to have. We haven't as many hands. We haven't as much time.

GIRL TRACTORIST All pleasures have to be rationed. Tobacco is rationed, and wine. Discussion should be rationed.

OLD MAN (*right, sighing*) Death to the fascists! But I will come to the point and explain why we want our valley back. There are a great many reasons, but I'll begin with one of the simplest. Makina Abakidze, unpack the goat cheese. (*A* PEASANT WOMAN *from right takes from a basket an enormous cheese wrapped in a cloth. Applause and laughter*) Help yourselves, Comrades, start in!

OLD MAN (*left, suspiciously*) Is this a way of influencing us?

OLD MAN (*right, amid laughter*) How could it be a way of influencing you, Surab, you valley-thief? Everyone knows you will take the cheese and the valley, too. (*laughter*) All I expect from you is an honest answer. Do you like the cheese?

OLD MAN (*left*) The answer is: yes.

OLD MAN (*right*) Really. (*bitterly*) I ought to have known you know nothing about cheese.

OLD MAN (*left*) Why not? When I tell you I like it?

OLD MAN (*right*) Because you can't like it. Because it's not what it was in the old days. And why not? Because our goats don't like the new grass as they did the old. Cheese is not cheese because grass is not grass, that's the thing. Please put that in your report.

OLD MAN (*left*) But your cheese is excellent.

OLD MAN (*right*) It isn't excellent. It's just

passable. The new grazing land is no good, whatever the young people may say. One can't live there. It doesn't even smell of morning in the morning.

(SEVERAL PEOPLE *laugh*)

THE DELEGATE Don't mind their laughing: they understand you. Comrades, why does one love one's country? Because the bread tastes better there, the air smells better, voices sound stronger, the sky is higher, the ground is easier to walk on. Isn't that so?

OLD MAN (*right*) The valley has belonged to us from all eternity.

SOLDIER (*left*) What does *that* mean— from all eternity? Nothing belongs to anyone from all eternity. When you were young you didn't even belong to yourself. You belonged to the Kazbeki princes.

OLD MAN (*right*) Doesn't it make a difference, though, what kind of trees stand next to the house you are born in? Or what kind of neighbors you have? Doesn't that make a difference? We want to go back just to have you as our neighbors, valley-thieves! Now you can all laugh again.

OLD MAN (*left, laughing*) Then why don't you listen to what your neighbor, Kato Wachtang, our agriculturist, has to say about the valley?

PEASANT WOMAN (*right*) We've not said all there is to be said about our valley. By no means. Not all the houses are destroyed. As for the dairy farm, at least the foundation wall is still standing.

DELEGATE You can claim State support— here and there—you know that. I have suggestions here in my pocket.

PEASANT WOMAN (*right*) Comrade Specialist, we haven't come here to bargain. I can't take your cap and hand you another, and say "This one's better." The other one might *be* better; but you *like* yours better.

GIRL TRACTORIST A piece of land is not a cap—not in our country, Comrade.

DELEGATE Don't get angry. It's true we have to consider a piece of land as a tool to produce something useful, but it's also true that we must recognize love for a particular piece of land. As far as I'm concerned, I'd like to find out more exactly what you (*to those on the left*) want to do with the valley.

OTHERS Yes, let Kato speak.

DELEGATE Comrade Agriculturist!

KATO (*rising, she's in military uniform*) Comrades, last winter, while we were fighting in these hills here as Partisans, we discussed how, after the expulsion of the Germans, we could build up our fruit culture to ten times its original size. I've prepared a plan for an irrigation project. By means of a cofferdam on our mountain lake, 300 hectares of unfertile land can be irrigated. Our Kolkhoz could not only cultivate more fruit, but also have vineyards. The project, however, would pay only if the disputed valley of Kolkhoz "Galinsk" were also included. Here are the calculations. (*She hands the delegate a briefcase*)

OLD MAN (*right*)   Write into the report that our Kolkhoz plans to start a new stud farm.

GIRL TRACTORIST   Comrades, the project was conceived during days and nights when we had to take cover in the mountains. We were often without ammunition for our half-dozen rifles. Even getting a pencil was difficult.

(*Applause from both sides*)

OLD MAN (*right*)   Our thanks to the Comrades of Kolkhoz "Galinsk" and all who have defended our country! (THEY *shake hands and embrace*)

PEASANT WOMAN (*left*)   In doing this our thought was that our soldiers—both your men and our men—should return to a still more productive homeland.

GIRL TRACTORIST   As the poet Mayakovski said: "The home of the Soviet people shall also be the home of Reason"!

(*The* DELEGATES *including the* OLD MAN *have got up, and with the* DELEGATE *specified proceed to study the Agriculturist's drawings . . . exclamations such as: "Why is the altitude of all 22 meters?"—"This rock must be blown up" —"Actually, all they need is cement and dynamite"—"They force the water to come down here, that's clever!"*)

A VERY YOUNG WORKER (*right, to* OLD MAN, *right*)   They're going to irrigate all the fields between the hills, look at that, Aleko!

OLD MAN (*right*)   I'm not going to look. I knew the project would be good. I won't have a revolver aimed at my chest.

DELEGATE   But they only want to aim a pencil at your chest.

(*Laughter*)

OLD MAN (*right, gets up gloomily, and walks over to look at the drawings*)   These valley-thieves know only too well that we can't resist machines and projects in this country.

PEASANT WOMAN (*right*)   Aleko Bereshwili, you have a weakness for new projects. That's well known.

DELEGATE   What about my report? May I write that you will all support the cession of your old valley in the interests of this project when you get back to your Kolkhoz?

PEASANT WOMAN (*right*)   I will. What about you, Aleko?

OLD MAN (*right, bent over drawings*)   I suggest that you give us copies of the drawings to take along.

PEASANT WOMAN (*right*)   Then we can sit down and eat. Once he has the drawings and he's ready to discuss them, the matter is settled. I know him. And it will be the same with the rest of us.

(*Delegates laughingly embrace again*)

OLD MAN (*left*)   Long live the Kolkhoz "Rosa Luxemburg" and much luck to your horse-breeding project!

PEASANT WOMAN (*left*)   In honor of the visit of the delegates from Kolkhoz "Rosa Luxemburg" and of the Specialist, the plan is that we all hear a presentation of the Story Teller Arkadi Tscheidse.

(*Applause.* GIRL TRACTORIST *has gone off to bring the* STORY TELLER)

PEASANT WOMAN (*right*)   Comrades, your entertainment had better be good. We're going to pay for it with a valley.

PEASANT WOMAN (*left*)   Arkadi Tscheidse knows about our discussion. He's promised to perform something that has a bearing on the problem.

KATO   We wired to Tiflis three times. The whole thing nearly fell through at the last minute because his driver had a cold.

PEASANT WOMAN (*left*)   Arkadi Tscheidse knows 21,000 lines of verse.

OLD MAN (*left*)   It's very difficult to get him. You and the Planning Commission should see to it that you get him to come North more often, Comrade.

DELEGATE   We are more interested in economics, I'm afraid.

OLD MAN (*left, smiling*)   You arrange the redistribution of vines and tractors, why not of songs?

(*Enter* THE STORY TELLER *Arkadi Tscheidse, led by* GIRL TRACTORIST. *He is a well-built man of simple manners, accompanied by* FOUR MUSICIANS *with their instruments. The* ARTISTS *are greeted with applause*)

GIRL TRACTORIST   This is the Comrade Specialist, Arkadi.

(THE STORY TELLER *greets them all*)

DELEGATE   I'm honored to make your acquaintance. I heard about your songs when I was a boy at school. Will it be one of the old legends?

THE STORY TELLER   A very old one. It's called "The Chalk Circle" and comes from the

Chinese. But we'll do it, of course, in a changed version. Comrades, it's an honor for me to entertain you after a difficult debate. We hope you will find that the voice of the old poet also sounds well in the shadow of Soviet tractors. It may be a mistake to mix different wines, but old and new wisdom mix admirably. Now I hope we'll get something to eat before the performance begins—it would certainly help.

VOICES Surely. Everyone into the Club House!

(*While everyone begins to move, the* DELEGATE *turns to the* GIRL TRACTORIST)

DELEGATE I hope it won't take long. I've got to get back tonight.

GIRL TRACTORIST How long will it last, Arkadi? The Comrade Specialist must get back to Tiflis tonight.

THE STORY TELLER (*casually*) It's actually two stories. An hour or two.

GIRL TRACTORIST (*confidentially*) Couldn't you make it shorter?

THE STORY TELLER No.

VOICE Arkadi Tscheidse's performance will take place here in the square after the meal.

(*And* THEY ALL *go happily to eat*)

1: THE NOBLE CHILD

(*As the lights go up,* THE STORY TELLER *is seen sitting on the floor, a black sheepskin cloak round his shoulders, and a little, well-thumbed notebook in his hand. A small group of listeners* —THE CHORUS—*sits with him. The manner of his recitation makes it clear that he has told his story over and over again. He mechanically fingers the pages, seldom looking at them. With appropriate gestures, he gives the signal for each scene to begin*)

THE STORY TELLER
In olden times, in a bloody time,
There ruled in a Caucasian city—
Men called it City of the Damned—
A governor.
His name was Georgi Abashwili.
He was rich as Croesus.
He had a beautiful wife
He had a healthy baby.
No other governor in Grusinia
Had so many horses in his stable
So many beggars in his doorstep
So many soldiers in his service
So many petitioners in his courtyard.
Georgi Abashwili—how shall I describe him to you?
He enjoyed his life.

On the morning of Easter Sunday
The governor and his family went to church.

(*At the left a large doorway, at the right an even larger gateway.* BEGGARS *and* PETITIONERS *pour from the gateway, holding up thin* CHILDREN, *crutches, and petitions. They are followed by* IRONSHIRTS, *and then, expensively dressed, the* GOVERNOR'S FAMILY)

BEGGARS AND PETITIONERS Mercy! Mercy, Your Grace! The taxes are too high.
—I lost my leg in the Persian War, where can I get . . .
—My brother is innocent, Your Grace, a misunderstanding . . .
—The child is starving in my arms!
—Our petition is for our son's discharge from the army, our last remaining son!
—Please, Your Grace, the water inspector takes bribes.

(ONE SERVANT *collects the petitions,* ANOTHER *distributes coins from a purse.* SOLDIERS *push the* CROWD *back, lashing at them with thick leather whips*)

THE SOLDIER Get back! Clear the church door!

(*Behind the* GOVERNOR, *his* WIFE, *and the* ADJUTANT, *the* GOVERNOR'S CHILD *is brought through the gateway in an ornate carriage*)

THE CROWD The baby!
—I can't see it, don't shove so hard!
—God bless the child, Your Grace!

THE STORY TELLER (*while the crowd is driven back with whips*)
For the first time on that Easter Sunday, the people saw the Governor's heir.
Two doctors never moved from the noble child, apple of the Governor's eye.
Even the mighty Prince Kazbeki bows before him at the church door.

(*A* FAT PRINCE *steps forward and greets the family*)

THE FAT PRINCE Happy Easter, Natella Abashwili! What a day! When it was raining in the night, I thought to myself, gloomy holidays! But this morning the sky was gay. I love a gay sky, a simple heart, Natella Abashwili. And little Michael is a governor from head to foot! Tititi! (*He tickles the* CHILD)

THE GOVERNOR'S WIFE What do you think, Arsen, at last Georgi has decided to start building the wing on the east side. All those wretched slums are to be torn down to make room for the garden.

THE FAT PRINCE   Good news after so much bad! What's the latest on the war, Brother Georgi? (*The* GOVERNOR *indicates a lack of interest*) Strategical retreat, I hear. Well, minor reverses are to be expected. Sometimes things go well, sometimes not. Such is war. It doesn't mean a thing, does it?

THE GOVERNOR'S WIFE   He's coughing. Georgi, did you hear? (*She speaks sharply to the* DOCTORS, *two dignified men standing close to the little carriage*) He's coughing!

THE FIRST DOCTOR (*to the second*)   May I remind you, Niko Mikadze, that I was against the lukewarm bath? (*to the* GOVERNOR'S WIFE) There's been a little error over warming the bath water, Your Grace.

THE SECOND DOCTOR (*equally polite*)   Mika Loladze, I'm afraid I can't agree with you. The temperature of the bath water was exactly what our great, beloved Misiko Oboladze prescribed. More likely a slight draft during the night, Your Grace.

THE GOVERNOR'S WIFE   But do pay more attention to him. He looks feverish, Georgi.

THE FIRST DOCTOR (*bending over the child*) No cause for alarm, Your Grace. The bath water will be warmer. It won't occur again.

THE SECOND DOCTOR (*with a venomous glance at the first*)   I won't forget that, my dear Mika Loladze. No cause for concern, Your Grace.

THE FAT PRINCE   Well, well, well! I always say: "A pain in my liver? Then the doctor gets fifty strokes on the soles of his feet." We live in a decadent age. In the old days one said: "Off with his head!"

THE GOVERNOR'S WIFE   Let's go into the church. Very likely it's the draft here.

(*The procession of* FAMILY *and* SERVANTS *turns into the doorway. The* FAT PRINCE *follows, but the* GOVERNOR *is kept back by the* ADJUTANT, *a handsome young man. When the crowd of* PETITIONERS *has been driven off, a young dust-stained* RIDER, *his arm in a sling, remains behind*)

THE ADJUTANT (*pointing at the* RIDER, *who steps forward*)   Won't you hear the messenger from the capital, Your Excellency? He arrived this morning. With confidential papers.

THE GOVERNOR   Not before Service, Shalva. But did you hear Brother Kazbeki wish me a happy Easter? Which is all very well, but I don't believe it did rain last night.

THE ADJUTANT (*nodding*)   We must investigate.

THE GOVERNOR   Yes, at once. Tomorrow.

(*They pass through the doorway. The* RIDER, *who has waited in vain for an audience, turns sharply round and, muttering a curse, goes off. Only one of the Palace Guards—*SIMON SHASHAVA—*remains at the door*)

THE STORY TELLER
The city is still.
Pigeons strut in the church square.
A soldier of the Palace Guard
Is joking with a kitchen maid
As she comes up from the river with
     a bundle.

(*A girl—*GRUSHA VASHNADZE—*comes through the gateway with a bundle made of large green leaves under her arm*)

SIMON   What, the young lady is not in church? Shirking?

GRUSHA   I was dressed to go. But they needed another goose for the banquet. And they asked me to go and get it. I know about geese.

SIMON   A goose? (*He feigns suspicion*) I'd like to see that goose. (GRUSHA *does not understand*) One has to be on one's guard with women. "I only went for a fish," they tell you, but it turns out to be something else.

GRUSHA (*walking resolutely toward him and showing him the goose*)   There! If it isn't a fifteen-pound goose stuffed full of corn, I'll eat the feathers.

SIMON   A queen of a goose. The Governor himself will eat it. So the young lady has been down to the river again?

GRUSHA   Yes, at the poultry farm.

SIMON   Really? At the poultry farm, down by the river . . . not higher up maybe? Near those willows?

GRUSHA   I only go to the willows to wash the linen.

SIMON (*insinuatingly*)   Exactly.

GRUSHA   Exactly what?

SIMON (*winking*)   Exactly that.

GRUSHA   Why shouldn't I wash the linen by the willows?

SIMON (*with exaggerated laughter*)   Why shouldn't I wash the linen by the willows! That's good, really good!

GRUSHA   I don't understand the soldier. What's so good about it?

SIMON (*slyly*)   "If something I know someone learns, she'll grow hot and cold by turns!"

GRUSHA   I don't know what I could learn about those willows.

SIMON   Not even if there was a bush opposite? That one could see everything from?

Everything that goes on there when a certain person is—"washing linen"?

GRUSHA What does go on? Won't the soldier say what he means and have done?

SIMON Something goes on. And something can be seen.

GRUSHA Could the soldier mean I dip my toes in the water when it is hot? There is nothing else.

SIMON More. Your toes. And more.

GRUSHA More what? At most the foot?

SIMON Your foot. And a little more. (*He laughs heartily*)

GRUSHA (*angrily*) Simon Shashava, you ought to be ashamed of yourself! To sit in a bush on a hot day and wait till someone comes and dips her leg in the river! And I bet you bring a friend along too! (*She runs off*)

SIMON (*shouting after her*) I didn't bring any friend along!

(*As* THE STORY TELLER *resumes his tale, the* SOLDIER *steps into the doorway as though to listen to the service*)

THE STORY TELLER
    The city lies still,
    But why are there armed men?
    The Governor's palace is at peace
    But why is it a fortress?
    And the Governor returned to his
        palace
    And the fortress was a trap
    And the goose was plucked and
        roasted
    But the goose was not eaten this time
    And noon was no longer the hour to
        eat:
    Noon was the hour to die.

(*From the doorway at the left the* FAT PRINCE *quickly appears, stands still, looks around. Before the gateway at the right* TWO IRONSHIRTS *are squatting and playing dice. The* FAT PRINCE *sees them, walks slowly past, making a sign to them. They rise:* ONE *goes through the gateway, the* OTHER *goes off at the right. Muffled voices are heard from various directions in the rear: "To your posts!" The palace is surrounded. The* FAT PRINCE *quickly goes off. Church bells in the distance. Enter, through the doorway, the* GOVERNOR'S FAMILY *and* PROCESSION, *returning from church*)

THE GOVERNOR'S WIFE (*passing the* ADJUTANT) It's impossible to live in such a slum. But Georgi, of course, will only build for his little Michael. Never for me! Michael is all! All for Michael!

(*The procession turns into the gateway. Again the* ADJUTANT *lingers behind. He waits. Enter the* WOUNDED RIDER *from the doorway.* TWO IRONSHIRTS *of the palace guard have taken up positions by the gateway*)

THE ADJUTANT (*to the* RIDER) The Governor does not wish to receive military reports before dinner—especially if they're depressing, as I assume. In the afternoon His Excellency will confer with prominent architects. They're coming to dinner too. And here they are! (*enter* THREE GENTLEMEN *through the doorway*) Go in the kitchen and get yourself something to eat, my friend. (*As the* RIDER *goes, the* ADJUTANT *greets the* ARCHITECTS) Gentlemen, His Excellency expects you at dinner. He will devote all his time to you and your great new plans. Come!

ONE OF THE ARCHITECTS We marvel that His Excellency intends to build. There are disquieting rumors that the war in Persia has taken a turn for the worse.

THE ADJUTANT All the more reason to build! There's nothing to those rumors anyway. Persia is a long way off, and the garrison here would let itself be hacked to bits for its Governor. (*noise from the palace. The shrill scream of a woman. Someone is shouting orders. Dumbfounded, the* ADJUTANT *moves toward the gateway. An* IRONSHIRT *steps out, points his lance at him*) What's this? Put down that lance, you dog.

ONE OF THE ARCHITECTS It's the Princes! Don't you know the Princes met last night in the capital? And they're against the Grand Duke and his Governors? Gentlemen, we'd better make ourselves scarce.

(*They rush off. The* ADJUTANT *remains helplessly behind*)

THE ADJUTANT (*furiously to the* PALACE GUARD) Down with those lances! Don't you see the Governor's life is threatened?

(*The* IRONSHIRTS *of the Palace Guard refuse to obey. They stare coldly and indifferently at* THE ADJUTANT *and follow the next events without interest*)

THE STORY TELLER
    O blindness of the great!
    They go their way like gods,
    Great over bent backs,
    Sure of hired fists,
    Trusting in the power
    Which has lasted so long.
    But long is not forever.
    O change from age to age!
    Thou hope of the people!

(*Enter the* GOVERNOR, *through the gateway, between* TWO SOLDIERS, *fully armed. He is in chains. His face is gray*)

Up, great sir, deign to walk upright!
From your palace the eyes of many
    foes follow you!
And now you don't need an architect,
    a carpenter will do.
You won't be moving into a new
    palace
But into a little hole in the ground.
Look about you once more, blind
    man!

(*The* GOVERNOR *looks round*)

Does all you had please you?
Between the Easter mass and the
    Easter meal
You are walking to a place whence
    no one returns.

(*The* GOVERNOR *is led off. A horn sounds an alarm. Noise behind the gateway*)

When the house of a great one
    collapses
Many little ones are slain.
Those who had no share in the *good*
    fortunes of the mighty
Often have a share in their *misfor-*
    tunes.
The plunging wagon
Drags the sweating oxen down with it
Into the abyss.

(*The* SERVANTS *come rushing through the gateway in panic*)

THE SERVANTS (*among themselves*) —The baskets!
—Take them all into the third courtyard! Food for five days!
—The mistress has fainted! Someone must carry her down.
—She must get away.
—What about us? We'll be slaughtered like chickens, as always.
—Goodness, what'll happen? There's bloodshed already in the city, they say.
—Nonsense, the Governor has just been asked to appear at a Princes' meeting. All very correct. Everything'll be ironed out. I heard this on the best authority . . .

(*The* TWO DOCTORS *rush into the courtyard*)

THE FIRST DOCTOR (*trying to restrain the other*) Niko Mikadze, it is your duty as a doctor to attend Natella Abashwili.

THE SECOND DOCTOR My duty! It's yours!

THE FIRST DOCTOR Whose turn is it to look after the child today, Niko Mikadze, yours or mine?

THE SECOND DOCTOR Do you really think, Mika Loladze, I'm going to stay a minute longer in this accursed house on that little brat's

account? (*They start fighting. All one hears is:* "You neglect your duty!" *and* "Duty my foot!" *Then the* SECOND DOCTOR *knocks the* FIRST *down*) Oh, go to hell! (*exit*)

(*Enter the soldier,* SIMON SHASHAVA. *He searches in the crowd for* GRUSHA)

SIMON Grusha! There you are at last! What are you going to do?

GRUSHA Nothing. If worst comes to worst, I've a brother in the mountains. How about you?

SIMON Forget about me. (*formally again:*) Grusha Vashnadze, your wish to know my plans fills me with satisfaction. I've been ordered to accompany Madam Natella Abashwili as her guard.

GRUSHA But hasn't the Palace Guard mutinied?

SIMON (*seriously*) That's a fact.

GRUSHA Isn't it dangerous to go with her?

SIMON In Tiflis, they say: Isn't the stabbing dangerous for the knife?

GRUSHA You're not a knife, you're a man, Simon Shashava. What has that woman to do with you?

SIMON That woman has nothing to do with me. I have my orders, and I go.

GRUSHA The soldier is pigheaded: he is getting himself into danger for nothing—nothing at all. I must get into the third courtyard, I'm in a hurry.

SIMON Since we're both in a hurry we shouldn't quarrel. You need time for a good quarrel. May I ask if the young lady still has parents?

GRUSHA No, just a brother.

SIMON As time is short—my second question is this: Is the young lady as healthy as a fish in water?

GRUSHA I may have a pain in the right shoulder once in a while. Otherwise I'm strong enough for my job. No one has complained. So far.

SIMON That's well-known. When it's Easter Sunday, and the question arises who'll run for the goose all the same, she'll be the one. My third question is this: Is the young lady impatient? Does she want apples in winter?

GRUSHA Impatient? No. But if a man goes to war without any reason and then no message comes—that's bad.

SIMON A message will come. And now my final question . . .

GRUSHA Simon Shashava, I must get to the third courtyard at once. My answer is yes.

SIMON (*very embarrassed*) Haste, they say, is the wind that blows down the scaffolding. But they also say: The rich don't know what haste is. I'm from . . .

GRUSHA Kutsk . . .

SIMON So the young lady has been inquiring about me? I'm healthy, I have no dependents, I make ten piasters a month, as paymaster twenty piasters and I'm asking—very sincerely—for your hand.

GRUSHA Simon Shashava, it suits me well.

SIMON (*taking from his neck a thin chain with a little cross on it*) My mother gave me this cross, Grusha Vashnadze. The chain is silver. Please wear it.

GRUSHA Many thanks, Simon.

SIMON (*hangs it round her neck*) It would be better for the young lady to go to the third courtyard now. Or there'll be difficulties. Anyway, I must harness the horses. The young lady will understand?

GRUSHA Yes, Simon.

(*They stand undecided*)

SIMON I'll just take the mistress to the troops that have stayed loyal. When the war's over, I'll be back. In two weeks. Or three. I hope my intended won't get tired, awaiting my return.

GRUSHA

Simon Shashava, I shall wait for you.
Go calmly into battle, soldier
The bloody battle, the bitter battle
From which not everyone returns:
When you return I shall be there.
I shall be waiting for you under the
    green elm
I shall be waiting for you under the
    bare elm
I shall wait until the last soldier has
    returned
And longer.
When you come back from the battle
No boots will stand at my door
The pillow beside mine will be empty
And my mouth will be unkissed.
When you return, when you return
You will be able to say: It is just as
    it was.

SIMON I thank you, Grusha Vashnadze. And goodbye!

(*He bows low before her. She does the same before him. Then she runs quickly off without looking round. Enter the* ADJUTANT *from the gateway*)

THE ADJUTANT (*harshly*) Harness the horses to the carriage! Don't stand there doing nothing, louse!

(SIMON SHASHAVA *stands to attention and goes off.* TWO SERVANTS *crowd from the gateway, bent low under huge trunks. Behind them, supported by her* WOMEN, *stumbles* NATELLA ABASHWILI. *She is followed by a* WOMAN *carrying the* CHILD)

THE GOVERNOR'S WIFE I hardly know if my head's still on. Where's Michael? Don't hold him so clumsily. Pile the trunks onto the carriage. Shalva, is there no news from the city?

THE ADJUTANT None. All's quiet so far, but there's not a minute to lose. No room for all these trunks in the carriage. Pick out what you need. (*exits quickly*)

THE GOVERNOR'S WIFE Only essentials! Quick, open the trunks! I'll tell you what I need. (*The trunks are lowered and opened. She points at some brocade dresses*) The green one! And, of course, the one with the fur trimming. Where are Niko Mikadze and Mika Loladze? I've suddenly got the most terrible migraine again. It always starts in the temples. (*enter* GRUSHA) Taking your time, eh? Go at once and get the hot water bottles! (GRUSHA *runs off, returns later with hot water bottles; the* GOVERNOR'S WIFE *orders her about by signs*) Don't tear the sleeves.

A YOUNG WOMAN Pardon, madam, no harm has come to the dress.

THE GOVERNOR'S WIFE Because I stopped you. I've been watching you for a long time. Nothing in your head but making eyes at Shalva Tzereteli. I'll kill you, you bitch! (*She beats the* WOMAN)

THE ADJUTANT (*appearing in the gateway*) Please make haste, Natella Abashwili. Firing has broken out in the city. (*exits*)

THE GOVERNOR'S WIFE (*letting go of the* YOUNG WOMAN) Oh dear, do you think they'll lay hands on us? Why should they? Why? (*She herself begins to rummage in the trunks*) How's Michael? Asleep?

THE WOMAN WITH THE CHILD Yes, madam.

THE GOVERNOR'S WIFE Then put him down a moment and get my little saffron-colored boots from the bedroom. I need them for the green dress. (*The* WOMAN *puts down the* CHILD *and goes off*) Just look how these things have been packed! No love! No understanding! If you don't give them every order yourself . . . At such moments you realize what kind of servants you have! They gorge themselves at your expense, and never a word of gratitude! I'll remember this.

THE ADJUTANT (*entering, very excited*) Natella, you must leave at once!

THE GOVERNOR'S WIFE Why? I've got to take this silver dress—it cost a thousand piasters. And that one there, and where's the wine-colored one?

THE ADJUTANT (*trying to pull her away*) Riots have broken out! We must leave at once. Where's the baby?

THE GOVERNOR'S WIFE (*calling to the* YOUNG WOMAN *who was holding the baby*) Maro, get the baby ready! Where on earth are you?

THE ADJUTANT (*leaving*) We'll probably have to leave the carriage behind and go on horseback.

(*The* GOVERNOR'S WIFE *rummages again among her dresses, throws some onto the heap of chosen clothes, then takes them off again. Noises, drums are heard. The* YOUNG WOMAN *who was beaten creeps away. The sky begins to grow red*)

THE GOVERNOR'S WIFE (*rummaging desperately*) I simply cannot find the wine-colored dress. Take the whole pile to the carriage. Where's Asja? And why hasn't Maro come back? Have you all gone crazy?

THE ADJUTANT (*returning*) Quick! Quick!

THE GOVERNOR'S WIFE (*to the* FIRST WOMAN) Run! Just throw them into the carriage!

THE ADJUTANT We're not taking the carriage. And if you don't come now, I'll ride off on my own.

THE GOVERNOR'S WIFE (*as the* FIRST WOMAN *can't carry everything*) Where's that bitch Asja? (THE ADJUTANT *pulls her away*) Maro, bring the baby! (*to the* FIRST WOMAN) Go and look for Masha. No, first take the dresses to the carriage. Such nonsense! I wouldn't dream of going on horseback! (*Turning round, she sees the red sky, and starts back rigid. The fire burns. She is pulled out by the* ADJUTANT. *Shaking, the* FIRST WOMAN *follows with the dresses*)

MARO (*from the doorway with the boots*) Madam! (*She sees the trunks and dresses and runs toward the baby, picks it up, and holds it a moment*) They left it behind, the beasts. (*She hands it to* GRUSHA) Hold it a moment. (*She runs off, following the* GOVERNOR'S WIFE)

(*Enter* SERVANTS *from the gateway*)

THE COOK Well, so they've actually gone. Without the food wagons, and not a minute too early. It's time for us to get out!

A GROOM This'll be an unhealthy neighborhood for quite a while. (*to one of the* WOMEN) Suliko, take a few blankets and wait for me in the foal stables.

GRUSHA What have they done with the governor?

THE GROOM (*gesturing throat cutting*) Fffft.

A FAT WOMAN (*seeing the gesture and becoming hysterical*) Oh dear, oh dear, oh dear, oh dear! Our master Georgi Abashwili! A picture of health he was, at the Morning Mass—and now! Oh, take me away, we're all lost, we must die in sin like our master, Georgi Abashwili!

THE OTHER WOMAN (*soothing her*) Calm down, Nina! You'll be taken to safety. You've never hurt a fly.

THE FAT WOMAN (*being led out*) Oh dear, oh dear, oh dear! Quick! Let's all get out before they come, before they come!

A YOUNG WOMAN Nina takes it more to heart than the mistress, that's a fact. They even have to have their weeping done for them.

THE COOK We'd better get out, all of us.

ANOTHER WOMAN (*glancing back*) That must be the East Gate burning.

THE YOUNG WOMAN (*seeing the* CHILD *in* GRUSHA'S *arms*) The baby! What are you doing with it?

GRUSHA It got left behind.

THE YOUNG WOMAN She simply left it there. Michael, who was kept out of all the drafts!

(*The* SERVANTS *gather round the* CHILD)

GRUSHA He's waking up.

THE GROOM Better put him down, I tell you. I'd rather not think what'd happen to anybody who was found with that baby.

THE COOK That's right. Once they get started, they'll kill each other off, whole families at a time. Let's go.

(*Exeunt all but* GRUSHA, *with the* CHILD *on her arm, and* TWO WOMEN)

THE TWO WOMEN Didn't you hear? Better put him down.

GRUSHA The nurse asked me to hold him a moment.

THE OLDER WOMAN She's not coming back, you simpleton.

THE YOUNGER WOMAN Keep your hands off it.

THE OLDER WOMAN (*amiably*) Grusha, you're a good soul, but you're not very bright, and you know it. I tell you, if he had the plague he couldn't be more dangerous.

GRUSHA (*stubbornly*) He hasn't got the plague. He looks at me! He's human.

THE OLDER WOMAN Don't look at *him*. You are a fool—the kind that always gets put upon. A person need only say, "Run for the salad, you have the longest legs," and you run. My husband has an ox cart—you can come with us if you hurry! Lord, by now the whole neighborhood must be in flames.

(BOTH WOMEN *leave, sighing. After some hesitation,* GRUSHA *puts the sleeping* CHILD *down, looks at it for a moment, then takes a brocade* blanket from the heap of clothes and covers it. Then BOTH WOMEN return, dragging bundles. GRUSHA starts guiltily away from the CHILD and walks a few steps to one side)

THE YOUNGER WOMAN Haven't you packed anything yet? There isn't much time, you know. The Ironshirts will be here from the barracks.

GRUSHA Coming. (*She runs through the doorway.* BOTH WOMEN *go to the gateway and wait. The sound of horses is heard. They flee, screaming*)

(*Enter the* FAT PRINCE *with drunken* IRON-SHIRTS. *One of them carries the governor's head on a lance*)

THE FAT PRINCE Here! In the middle! (ONE SOLDIER *climbs onto the other's back, takes the head, holds it tentatively over the door*) That's not the middle. Farther to the right. That's it. What I do, my friends, I do well. (*While, with hammer and nail, the soldier fastens the head to the wall by its hair:*) This morning at the church door I said to Georgi Abashwili: "I love a clear sky." Actually, I prefer the lightning that comes out of a clear sky. Yes, indeed. It's a pity they took the brat along, though, I need him. Urgently.

(*Exit with* IRONSHIRTS *through the gateway. Trampling of horses again. Enter* GRUSHA *through the doorway looking cautiously about her. Clearly she has waited for the* IRONSHIRTS *to go. Carrying a bundle, she walks toward the gateway. At the last moment, she turns to see if the* CHILD *is still there. Catching sight of the head over the doorway, she screams. Horrified, she picks up her bundle again, and is about to leave when* THE STORY TELLER *starts to speak. She stands rooted to the spot*)

THE STORY TELLER
    As she was standing between court-
        yard and gate,
    She heard or she thought she heard a
        low voice calling.
    The child called to her,
    Not whining, but calling quite sen-
        sibly,
    Or so it seemed to her.
    "Woman," it said, "help me."
    And it went on, not whining, but
        saying quite sensibly:
    "Know, woman, he who hears not a
        cry for help
    But passes by with troubled ears will
        never hear
    The gentle call of a lover nor the
        blackbird at dawn
    Nor the happy sigh of the tired
        grape-picker as the Angelus rings."

(GRUSHA *walks a few steps toward the* CHILD *and bends over it*)
    Hearing this she went back for one
        more look at the child:
    Only to sit with him for a moment or
        two,
    Only till someone should come,
    His mother, or anyone.

(*Leaning on a trunk, she sits facing the* CHILD)
    Only till she would have to leave, for
        the danger was too great,
    The city was full of flame and crying.

(*The light grows dimmer, as though evening and night were coming on*)
    Fearful is the seductive power of
        goodness!

(GRUSHA *now settles down to watch over the* CHILD *through the night. Once, she lights a small lamp to look at it. Once, she tucks it in with a coat. From time to time she listens and looks to see whether someone is coming*)
    And she sat with the child a long
        time,
    Till evening came, till night came, till
        dawn came.
    She sat too long, too long she saw
    The soft breathing, the small clenched
        fists,
    Till toward morning the seduction
        was complete
    And she rose, and bent down and,
        sighing, took the child
    And carried it away.

(*She does what* THE STORY TELLER *says as he describes it*)
    As if it was stolen goods she picked
        it up.
    As if she was a thief she crept away.

2: THE FLIGHT INTO THE NORTHERN MOUNTAINS

THE STORY TELLER
    When Grusha Vashnadze left the city
    On the Grusinian highway
    On the way to the Northern Moun-
        tains
    She sang a song, she bought some
        milk.
THE CHORUS
    How will this human child escape
    The bloodhounds, the trap-setters?
    Into the deserted mountains she
        journeyed
    Along the Grusinian highway she
        journeyed

She sang a song, she bought some milk.

(GRUSHA VASHNADZE *walks on. On her back she carries the* CHILD *in a sack, in one hand is a large stick, in the other a bundle. She sings*)

The Song of the Four Generals
Four generals
Set out for Iran.
With the first one, war did not agree.
The second never won a victory.
For the third the weather never was right.
For the fourth the men would never fight.
Four generals
And not a single man!

Sosso Robakidse
Went marching to Iran
With him the war did so agree
He soon had won a victory.
For him the weather was always right.
For him the men would always fight.
Sosso Robakidse,
He is our man!

(*A peasant's cottage appears*)

GRUSHA (*to the* CHILD) Noontime is meal time. Now we'll sit hopefully in the grass, while the good Grusha goes and buys a little pitcher of milk. (*She lays the* CHILD *down and knocks at the cottage door. An* OLD MAN *opens it*) Grandfather, could I have a little pitcher of milk? And a corn cake, maybe?

THE OLD MAN We have no milk. The soldiers from the city have our goats. Go to the soldiers if you want milk.

GRUSHA But grandfather, you must have a little pitcher of milk for a baby?

THE OLD MAN And for a God-bless-you, eh?

GRUSHA Who said anything about a God-bless-you? (*She shows her purse*) We'll pay like princes. "Head in the clouds, backside in the water." (*The* PEASANT *goes off, grumbling, for milk*) How much for the milk?

THE OLD MAN Three piasters. Milk has gone up.

GRUSHA Three piasters for this little drop? (*Without a word* THE OLD MAN *shuts the door in her face*) Michael, did you hear that? Three piasters! We can't afford it! (*She goes back, sits down again, and gives the* CHILD *her breast*) Suck. Think of the three piasters. There's nothing there, but you *think* you're drinking, and that's something. (*Shaking her head, she sees that the* CHILD *isn't sucking any more. She gets up, walks back to the door, and knocks again*)

Open, grandfather, we'll pay. (*softly*) May lightning strike you! (*when the* OLD MAN *appears*) I thought it would be half a piaster. But the baby must be fed. How about one piaster for that little drop?

THE OLD MAN Two.

GRUSHA Don't shut the door again. (*She fishes a long time in her bag*) Here are two piasters. The milk better be good. I still have two days' journey ahead of me. It's a murderous business you have here—and sinful, too!

THE OLD MAN Kill the soldiers if you want milk.

GRUSHA (*giving the* CHILD *some milk*) This is an expensive joke. Take a sip, Michael, it's a week's pay. Around here they think we earned our money just sitting around. Oh, Michael, Michael, you're a nice little load for a girl to take on! (*Uneasy, she gets up, puts the* CHILD *on her back, and walks on.* THE OLD MAN, *grumbling, picks up the pitcher and looks after her unmoved*)

THE STORY TELLER
As Grusha Vashnadze went north-ward
The Princes' Ironshirts went after her.

THE CHORUS
How will the barefoot girl escape the Ironshirts,
The bloodhounds, the trap-setters?
They hunt even by night.
Pursuers never get tired.
Butchers sleep little.

(TWO IRONSHIRTS *are trudging along the highway*)

THE CORPORAL You'll never amount to anything, blockhead, your heart's not in it. Your senior officer sees this in little things. Yesterday, when I made the fat gal, yes, you grabbed her husband as I commanded, and you did kick him in the stomach, at my request, but did you *enjoy* it, like a loyal Private, or were you just doing your duty? I've kept an eye on you blockhead, you're a hollow reed and a tinkling cymbal, you won't get promoted. (*They walk a while in silence*) Don't think I've forgotten how insubordinate you are, either. Stop limping! I forbid you to limp! You limp because I sold the horses, and I sold the horses because I'd never have got that price again. You limp to show me you don't like marching. I know you. It won't help. You wait. Sing!

THE TWO IRONSHIRTS (*singing*)
Sadly to war I went my way
Leaving my loved one at her door.

My friends will keep her honor safe
Till from the war I'm back once more.

THE CORPORAL   Louder!

THE TWO IRONSHIRTS (*singing*)

When 'neath a headstone I shall be
My love a little earth will bring:
"Here rest the feet that oft would
    run to me
And here the arms that oft to me
    would cling."

(*They begin to walk again in silence*)

THE CORPORAL   A good soldier has his heart
and soul in it. When he receives an order, he
gets a hard on, and when he drives his lance
into the enemy's guts, he comes. (*He shouts
for joy*) He lets himself be torn to pieces for
his superior officer, and as he lies dying he
takes note that his corporal is nodding approval, and that is reward enough, it's his
dearest wish. *You* won't get any nod of approval, but you'll croak all right. Christ, how'm
I to get my hands on the Governor's bastard
with the help of a fool like you!

(*They stay on stage behind*)

THE STORY TELLER

When Grusha Vashnadze came to the
    River Sirra
Flight grew too much for her, the
    helpless child too heavy.
In the cornfields the rosy dawn
Is cold to the sleepless one, only cold.
The gay clatter of the milk cans in
    the farmyard where the smoke rises
Is only a threat to the fugitive.
She who carries the child feels its
    weight and little more.

(GRUSHA *stops in front of a farm. A fat* PEASANT
WOMAN *is carrying a milk can through the door.*
GRUSHA *waits until she has gone in, then ap-
proaches the house cautiously*)

GRUSHA (*to the child*)   Now you've wet
yourself again, and you know I've no linen.
Michael, this is where we part company. It's
far enough from the city. They wouldn't want
you *so* much that they'd follow you all *this*
way, little good-for-nothing. The peasant
woman is kind, and can't you just smell the
milk? (*She bends down to lay the child on the
threshold*) So farewell, Michael, I'll forget
how you kicked me in the back all night to
make me walk faster. And you can forget the
meager fare—it was meant well. I'd like to
have kept you—your nose is so tiny—but it
can't be. I'd have shown you your first rabbit,
I'd have trained you to keep dry, but now I
must turn around. My sweetheart the soldier

might be back soon, and suppose he didn't
find me? You can't ask that, can you?

(*She creeps up to the door and lays the* CHILD
*on the threshold. Then, hiding behind a tree,
she waits until the* PEASANT WOMAN *opens
the door and sees the bundle*)

THE PEASANT WOMAN   Good heavens, what's
this? Husband!

THE PEASANT   What is it? Let me finish my
soup.

THE PEASANT WOMAN (*to the child*)
Where's your mother then? Haven't you got
one? It's a boy. Fine linen. He's from a good
family, you can see that. And they just leave
him on our doorstep. Oh, these are times!

THE PEASANT   If they think we're going to
feed it, they're wrong. You can take it to the
priest in the village. That's the best we can do.

THE PEASANT WOMAN   What'll the priest
do with him? He needs a mother. There, he's
waking up. Don't you think we could keep
him, though?

THE PEASANT (*shouting*)   No!

THE PEASANT WOMAN   I could lay him in
the corner by the armchair. All I need is a crib.
I can take him into the fields with me. See him
laughing? Husband, we have a roof over our
heads. We can do it. Not another word out of
you!

(*She carries the* CHILD *into the house. The*
PEASANT *follows protesting.* GRUSHA *steps out
from behind the tree, laughs, and hurries off
in the opposite direction*)

THE STORY TELLER

Why so cheerful, making for home?

THE CHORUS

Because the child has won new par-
    ents with a laugh,
Because I'm rid of the little one, I'm
    cheerful.

THE STORY TELLER

And why so sad?

THE CHORUS

Because I'm single and free, I'm sad.
Like someone who's been robbed
Someone who's newly poor.

(*She walks for a short while, then meets the*
TWO IRONSHIRTS, *who point their lances at her*)

THE CORPORAL   Lady, you are running
straight into the arms of the Armed Forces.
Where are you coming from? And when? Are
you having illicit relations with the enemy?
Where is he hiding? What movements is he
making in your rear? How about the hills? How
about the valleys? How are your stockings
fastened? (GRUSHA *stands there frightened*)

Don't be scared, we always stage a retreat, if necessary . . . what, blockhead? I always stage retreats. In that respect at least, I can be relied on. Why are you staring like that at my lance? In the field no soldier drops his lance, that's a rule. Learn it by heart, blockhead. Now, lady, where are you headed?

GRUSHA   To meet my intended, one Simon Shashava, of the Palace Guard in Nuka.

THE CORPORAL   Simon Shashava? Sure, I know him. He gave me the key so I could look you up once in a while. Blockhead, we are getting to be unpopular. We must make her realize we have honorable intentions. Lady, behind apparent frivolity I conceal a serious nature, so let me tell you officially: I want a child from you. (GRUSHA *utters a little scream*) Blockhead, she understood me. Uh-huh, isn't it a sweet shock? "Then first I must take the noodles out of the oven, Officer. Then first I must change my torn shirt, Colonel." But away with jokes, away with my lance! We are looking for a baby. A baby from a good family. Have you heard of such a baby, from the city, dressed in fine linen, and suddenly turning up here?

GRUSHA   No, I haven't heard a thing.

(*Suddenly she turns round and runs back, panic-stricken. The* IRONSHIRTS *glance at each other, then follow her, cursing*)

THE STORY TELLER
   Run, kind girl! The killers are coming!
   Help the helpless babe, helpless girl!
   And so she runs!

THE CHORUS
   In the bloodiest times
   There are kind people.

(*As* GRUSHA *rushes into the cottage, the* PEASANT WOMAN *is bending over the* CHILD'S *crib*)

GRUSHA   Hide him. Quick! The Ironshirts are coming! I laid him on your doorstep. But he isn't mine. He's from a good family.

THE PEASANT WOMAN   Who's coming? What Ironshirts?

GRUSHA   Don't ask questions. The Ironshirts that are looking for it.

THE PEASANT WOMAN   They've no business in my house. But I must have a little talk with you, it seems.

GRUSHA   Take off the fine linen. It'll give us away.

THE PEASANT WOMAN   Linen, my foot! In this house I make the decisions! "You can't vomit in *my* room!" Why did you abandon it? It's a sin.

GRUSHA (*looking out of the window*)   Look, they're coming out from behind those trees! I

shouldn't have run away, it made them angry. Oh, what shall I do?

THE PEASANT WOMAN (*looking out of the window and suddenly starting with fear*) Gracious! Ironshirts!

GRUSHA   They're after the baby.

THE PEASANT WOMAN   Suppose they come in!

GRUSHA   You mustn't give him to them. Say he's yours.

THE PEASANT WOMAN   Yes.

GRUSHA   They'll run him through if you hand him over.

THE PEASANT WOMAN   But suppose they ask for it? The silver for the harvest is in the house.

GRUSHA   If you let them have him, they'll run him through, right here in this room! You've got to say he's yours!

THE PEASANT WOMAN   Yes. But what if they don't believe me?

GRUSHA   You must be firm.

THE PEASANT WOMAN   They'll burn the roof over our heads.

GRUSHA   That's why you must say he's yours. His name's Michael. But I shouldn't have told you. (*The* PEASANT WOMAN *nods*) Don't nod like that. And don't tremble—they'll notice.

THE PEASANT WOMAN   Yes.

GRUSHA   And stop saying yes, I can't stand it. (*She shakes the* WOMAN) Don't you have any children?

THE PEASANT WOMAN (*muttering*)   He's in the war.

GRUSHA   Then maybe *he's* an Ironshirt? Do you want *him* to run children through with a lance? You'd bawl him out. "No fooling with lances in *my* house!" you'd shout. "Is that what I've reared you for? Wash your neck before you speak to your mother!"

THE PEASANT WOMAN   That's true, he couldn't get away with anything around here!

GRUSHA   So you'll say he's yours?

THE PEASANT WOMAN   Yes.

GRUSHA   Look! They're coming!

(*There is a knocking at the door. The* WOMEN *don't answer. Enter* IRONSHIRTS. *The* PEASANT WOMAN *bows low*)

THE CORPORAL   Well, here she is. What did I tell you? What a nose I have! I *smelt* her. Lady, I have a question for you. Why did you run away? What did you think I would do to you? I'll bet it was something dirty. Confess!

GRUSHA (*while the* PEASANT WOMAN *bows again and again*)   I'd left some milk on the stove, and I suddenly remembered it.

THE CORPORAL Or maybe you imagined I'd looked at you in a dirty way? Like there could be something between us? A lewd sort of look, know what I mean?

GRUSHA I didn't see it.

THE CORPORAL But it's possible, huh? You admit that much. After all, I might be a pig. I'll be frank with you: I could think of all sorts of things if we were alone. (*to the* PEASANT WOMAN) Shouldn't you be busy in the yard? Feeding the hens?

THE PEASANT WOMAN (*falling suddenly to her knees*) Soldier, I didn't know a thing about it. Please don't burn the roof over our heads.

THE CORPORAL What are you talking about?

THE PEASANT WOMAN I had nothing to do with it. She left it on my doorstep, I swear it!

THE CORPORAL (*suddenly seeing the* CHILD *and whistling*) Ah, so there's a little something in the crib! Blockhead, I smell a thousand piasters. Take the old girl outside and hold on to her. It looks like I have a little cross-examining to do. (*The* PEASANT WOMAN *lets herself be led out by the* PRIVATE, *without a word*) So, you've got the child I wanted from you! (*He walks toward the crib*)

GRUSHA Officer, he's mine. He's not the one you're after.

THE CORPORAL I'll just take a look. (*He bends over the crib.* GRUSHA *looks round in despair*)

GRUSHA He's mine! He's mine!

THE CORPORAL Fine linen!

(GRUSHA *dashes at him to pull him away. He throws her off and again bends over the crib. Again looking round in despair, she sees a log of wood, seizes it, and hits the* CORPORAL *over the head from behind. The* CORPORAL *collapses. She quickly picks up the* CHILD *and rushes off*)

THE STORY TELLER
  And in her flight from the Ironshirts
  After twenty-two days of journeying
  At the foot of the Janga-Tu glacier
  Grusha Vashnadze decided to adopt
    the child.

THE CHORUS
  The helpless girl adopted the helpless
    child.

(GRUSHA *squats over a half-frozen stream to get the* CHILD *water in the hollow of her hand*)

GRUSHA
  Since no one else will take you, son,
  I must take you.
  Since no one else will take you, son,
  You must take me.
  O black day in a lean, lean year,

  The trip was long, the milk was dear,
  My legs are tired, my feet are sore:
  But I wouldn't be without you any
    more.
  I'll throw your silken shirt away
  And dress you in rags and tatters.
  I'll wash you, son, and christen you
    in glacier water.
  We'll see it through together.

(*She has taken off the* CHILD'S *fine linen and wrapped it in a rag*)

THE STORY TELLER
  When Grusha Vashnadze
  Pursued by the Ironshirts
  Came to the bridge on the glacier
  Leading to the villages of the Eastern
    Slope
  She sang the Song of the Rotten
    Bridge
  And risked two lives.

(*A wind has risen. The bridge on the glacier is visible in the dark. One rope is broken and half the bridge is hanging down the abyss.* MERCHANTS, TWO MEN *and a* WOMAN, *stand undecided before the bridge as* GRUSHA *and the* CHILD *arrive.* ONE MAN *is trying to catch the hanging rope with a stick*)

THE FIRST MAN Take your time, young woman. You won't get across here anyway.

GRUSHA But I *have* to get the baby to the east side. To my brother's place.

THE MERCHANT WOMAN Have to? How d'you mean "have to"? I have to get there, too—because I have to buy carpets in Atum —carpets a woman had to sell because her husband had to die. But can *I* do what I have to? Can she? Andrei's been fishing for that rope for hours. And I ask you, how are we going to fasten it, even if he gets it up?

THE FIRST MAN (*listening*) Hush, I think I hear something.

GRUSHA The bridge isn't quite rotted through. I think I'll try it.

THE MERCHANT WOMAN *I* wouldn't—if the devil himself were after me. It's suicide.

THE FIRST MAN (*shouting*) Hi!

GRUSHA Don't shout! (*to the* MERCHANT WOMAN) Tell him not to shout.

THE FIRST MAN But there's someone down there calling. Maybe they've lost their way.

THE MERCHANT WOMAN Why shouldn't he shout? Is there something funny about you? Are they after you?

GRUSHA All right, I'll tell. The Ironshirts are after me. I knocked one down.

THE SECOND MAN Hide our merchandise!

(*The* WOMAN *hides a sack behind a rock*)

THE FIRST MAN Why didn't you say so right away? (*to the* OTHERS) If they catch her they'll make mincemeat out of her!

GRUSHA Get out of my way. I've got to cross that bridge.

THE SECOND MAN You can't. The precipice is two thousand feet deep.

THE FIRST MAN Even with the rope it'd be no use. We could hold it up with our hands. But then we'd have to do the same for the Ironshirts.

GRUSHA Go away.

(*There are calls from the distance: "Hi, up there!"*)

THE MERCHANT WOMAN They're getting near. But you can't take the child on that bridge. It's sure to break. And look!

(GRUSHA *looks down into the abyss. The* IRONSHIRTS *are heard calling again from below*)

THE SECOND MAN Two thousand feet!

GRUSHA But those men are worse.

THE FIRST MAN You can't do it. Think of the baby. Risk your life but not a child's.

THE SECOND MAN With the child she's that much heavier!

THE MERCHANT WOMAN Maybe she's *really* got to get across. Give *me* the baby. I'll hide it. Cross the bridge alone!

GRUSHA I won't. We belong together. (*to the* CHILD) "Live together, die together." (*She sings:*)

The Song of the Rotten Bridge

Deep is the abyss, son,
I see the weak bridge sway
But it's not for us, son,
To choose the way.

The way I know
Is the one you must tread,
And all you will eat
Is my bit of bread.

Of every four pieces
You shall have three.
Would that I knew
How big they will be!

Get out of my way, I'll try it without the rope.

THE MERCHANT WOMAN You are tempting God!

(*There are shouts from below*)

GRUSHA Please, throw that stick away, or they'll get the rope and follow me.

(*Pressing the* CHILD *to her, she steps onto the swaying bridge. The* MERCHANT WOMAN *screams when it looks as though the bridge is about to collapse. But* GRUSHA *walks on and reaches the far side*)

THE FIRST MAN She made it!

THE MERCHANT WOMAN (*who has fallen on her knees and begun to pray, angrily*) I still think it was a sin.

(*The* IRONSHIRTS *appear; the* CORPORAL's *head is bandaged*)

THE CORPORAL Seen a woman with a child?

THE FIRST MAN (*while the* SECOND MAN *throws the stick into the abyss*) Yes, there! But the bridge won't carry you!

THE CORPORAL You'll pay for this, blockhead!

(GRUSHA, *from the far bank, laughs and shows the* CHILD *to the* IRONSHIRTS. *She walks on. The wind blows*)

GRUSHA (*turning to the* CHILD) You mustn't be afraid of the wind. He's a poor thing too. He has to push the clouds along and he gets quite cold doing it. (*Snow starts falling*) And the snow isn't so bad, either, Michael. It covers the little fir trees so they won't die in winter. Let me sing you a little song. (*She sings:*)

The Song of the Child

Your father is a bandit
A harlot the mother who bore you.
Yet honorable men
Shall kneel down before you.

Food to the baby horses
The tiger's son will take.
The mothers will get milk
From the son of the snake.

3: IN THE NORTHERN MOUNTAINS

THE STORY TELLER
Seven days the sister, Grusha Vashnadze,
Journeyed across the glacier
And down the slopes she journeyed.
"When I enter my brother's house," she thought
"He will rise and embrace me."
"Is that you, sister?" he will say,
"I have long expected you.
This is my dear wife,
And this is my farm, come to me by marriage,
With eleven horses and thirty-one cows. Sit down.
Sit down with your child at our table and eat."
The brother's house was in a lovely valley.

When the sister came to the brother,
She was ill from walking.
The brother rose from the table.

(*A fat* PEASANT COUPLE *rise from the table.* LAVRENTI VASHNADZE *still has a napkin round his neck, as* GRUSHA, *pale and supported by a* SERVANT, *enters with the* CHILD)

LAVRENTI Where've *you* come from, Grusha?

GRUSHA (*feebly*) Across the Janga-Tu Pass, Lavrenti.

THE SERVANT I found her in front of the hay barn. She has a baby with her.

THE SISTER-IN-LAW Go and groom the mare.

(*Exit the* SERVANT)

LAVRENTI This is my wife Aniko.

THE SISTER-IN-LAW I thought you were in service in Nuka.

GRUSHA (*barely able to stand*) Yes, I was.

THE SISTER-IN-LAW Wasn't it a good job? We were told it was.

GRUSHA The Governor got killed.

LAVRENTI Yes, we heard there were riots. Your aunt told us. Remember, Aniko?

THE SISTER-IN-LAW Here with us, it's very quiet. City people always want something going on. (*She walks toward the door, calling*) Sosso, Sosso, don't take the cake out of the oven yet, d'you hear? Where on earth are you? (*Exit, calling*)

LAVRENTI (*quietly, quickly*) Is there a father? (*as she shakes her head*) I thought not. We must think up something. She's religious.

THE SISTER-IN-LAW (*returning*) Those servants! (*to* GRUSHA) You have a child.

GRUSHA It's mine. (*She collapses.* LAVRENTI *rushes to her assistance*)

THE SISTER-IN-LAW Heavens, she's ill—what are we going to do?

LAVRENTI (*escorting her to a bench near the stove*) Sit down, sit. I think it's just weakness, Aniko.

THE SISTER-IN-LAW As long as it's not scarlet fever!

LAVRENTI She'd have spots if it was. It's only weakness. Don't worry, Aniko. (*to* GRUSHA) Better, sitting down?

THE SISTER-IN-LAW Is the child hers?

GRUSHA Yes, mine.

LAVRENTI She's on her way to her husband.

THE SISTER-IN-LAW I see. Your meat's getting cold. (LAVRENTI *sits down and begins to eat*) Cold food's not good for you, the fat mustn't get cold, you know your stomach's your weak spot. (*to* GRUSHA) If your husband's not in the city, where is he?

LAVRENTI She got married on the other side of the mountain, she says.

THE SISTER-IN-LAW Oh, on the other side the mountain. (*She also sits down to eat*)

GRUSHA I think I should lie down somewhere, Lavrenti.

THE SISTER-IN-LAW If it's consumption we'll all get it. (*She goes on cross-examining her*) Has your husband got a farm?

GRUSHA He's a soldier.

LAVRENTI But he's coming into a farm—a small one—from his father.

THE SISTER-IN-LAW Isn't he in the war? Why not?

GRUSHA (*with effort*) Yes, he's in the war.

THE SISTER-IN-LAW Then why d'you want to go to the farm?

LAVRENTI When he comes back from the war, he'll return to his farm.

THE SISTER-IN-LAW But you're going there now?

LAVRENTI Yes, to wait for him.

THE SISTER-IN-LAW (*calling shrilly*) Sosso, the cake!

GRUSHA (*murmuring feverishly*) A farm—a soldier—waiting—sit down, eat.

THE SISTER-IN-LAW It's scarlet fever.

GRUSHA (*starting up*) Yes, he's got a farm!

LAVRENTI I think it's just weakness, Aniko. Would you look after the cake yourself, dear?

THE SISTER-IN-LAW But when will he come back if war's broken out again as people say? (*She waddles off, shouting*) Sosso! Where on earth are you? Sosso!

LAVRENTI (*getting up quickly and going to* GRUSHA) You'll get a bed in a minute. She has a good heart. But wait till after supper.

GRUSHA (*holding out the* CHILD *to him*) Take him.

LAVRENTI (*taking it and looking around*) But you can't stay here long with the child. She's religious, you see.

(GRUSHA *collapses.* LAVRENTI *catches her*)

THE STORY TELLER
　　The sister was so ill,
　　The cowardly brother had to give her shelter.
　　Summer departed, winter came.
　　The winter was long, the winter was short
　　People mustn't know anything,
　　Rats mustn't bite,
　　Spring mustn't come.

(GRUSHA *sits over the weaving loom in a workroom. She and the* CHILD, *who is squatting on the floor, are wrapped in blankets. She sings*)

GRUSHA (*sings*)

The Song of the Center
And the lover started to leave
And his betrothed ran pleading after
him
Pleading and weeping, weeping and
teaching:
"Dearest mine, dearest mine
When you go to war as now you do
When you fight the foe as soon you
will
Don't lead with the front line
And don't push with the rear line
At the front is red fire
In the rear is red smoke
Stay in the war's center
Stay near the standard bearer
The first always die
The last are also hit
Those in the center come home."

Michael, we must be clever. If we make ourselves as small as cockroaches, the sister-in-law
will forget we're in the house, and then we can
stay till the snow melts.

(*Enter* LAVRENTI. *He sits down beside his
sister*)

LAVRENTI   Why are you sitting there muffled up like coachmen, you two? Is it too cold
in the room?

GRUSHA (*hastily removing one shawl*)   It's
not too cold, Lavrenti.

LAVRENTI   If it's too cold, you shouldn't be
sitting here with the child. Aniko would never
forgive herself! (*pause*) I hope our priest didn't
question you about the child?

GRUSHA   He did, but I didn't tell him anything.

LAVRENTI   That's good. I wanted to speak to
you about Aniko. She has a good heart but she's
very, very sensitive. People have only to mention our farm and she's worried. She takes
everything hard, you see. One time our milkmaid went to church with a hole in her stocking. Ever since, Aniko has worn two pairs of
stockings in church. It's the old family in her.
(*He listens*) Are you sure there are no rats
around? If there are rats, you couldn't live here.
(*There are sounds as of dripping from the
roof*) What's that, dripping?

GRUSHA   It must be a barrel leaking.

LAVRENTI   Yes, it must be a barrel. You've
been here six months, haven't you? Was I
talking about Aniko? (*They listen again to the
snow melting*) You can't imagine how worried
she gets about your soldier-husband. "Suppose
he comes back and can't find her!" she says

and lies awake. "He can't come before the
spring," I tell her. The dear woman! (*The drops
begin to fall faster*) When d'you think he'll
come? What do *you* think? (GRUSHA *is silent*)
Not before the spring, you agree? (GRUSHA *is
silent*) You don't believe he'll come at all?
(GRUSHA *is silent*) But when the spring comes
and the snow melts here and on the passes,
you can't stay on. They may come and look
for you. There's already talk of an illegitimate child. (*The "glockenspiel" of the falling drops has grown faster and steadier*)
Grusha, the snow is melting on the roof. Spring
is here.

GRUSHA   Yes.

LAVRENTI (*eagerly*)   I'll tell you what
we'll do. You need a place to go, and, because
of the child (*He sighs*), you have to have a
husband, so people won't talk. Now I've made
cautious inquiries to see if we can find you a
husband. Grusha, I *have* one. I talked to a
peasant woman who has a son. Just the other
side of the mountain. A small farm. And she's
willing.

GRUSHA   But I *can't* marry! I must wait for
Simon Shashava.

LAVRENTI   Of course. That's all been taken
care of. You don't need a man in bed—you
need a man on paper. And I've found you one.
The son of this peasant woman is going to
die. Isn't that wonderful? He's at his last gasp.
And all in line with our story—a husband
from the other side the mountain! And when
you met him he was at the last gasp. So you're
a widow. What do you say?

GRUSHA   It's true I could use a document
with stamps on it for Michael.

LAVRENTI   Stamps make all the difference.
Without something in writing the Shah couldn't
prove he's a Shah. And you'll have a place
to live.

GRUSHA   How   much   does   the   peasant
woman want?

LAVRENTI   Four hundred piasters.

GRUSHA   Where will you find it?

LAVRENTI (*guiltily*)   Aniko's milk money.

GRUSHA   No one would know us there. I'll
do it.

LAVRENTI (*getting up*)   I'll let the peasant
woman know. (*quick exit*)

GRUSHA   Michael, you cause a lot of fuss. I
came to you as the pear tree comes to the
sparrows. And because a Christian bends down
and picks up a crust of bread so nothing will go
to waste. Michael, it would have been better
had I walked quickly away on that Easter
Sunday in Nuka in the second courtyard. Now
I *am* a fool.

THE STORY TELLER

The bridegroom was lying on his deathbed when the bride arrived.

The bridegroom's mother was waiting at the door, telling her to hurry

The bride brought a child along.

The witness hid it during the wedding.

(*On one side the bed. Under the mosquito net lies a very sick* MAN. GRUSHA *is pulled in at a run by her future* MOTHER-IN-LAW. *They are followed by* LAVRENTI *and the* CHILD)

THE MOTHER-IN-LAW Quick! Quick! Or he'll die on us before the wedding. (*to* LAVRENTI) I was never told she had a child already.

LAVRENTI What difference does it make? (*pointing toward the dying man*) It can't matter to him—in his condition.

THE MOTHER-IN-LAW To him? But *I'll* never survive the shame! We are honest people. (*She begins to weep*) My Jussup doesn't have to marry a girl with a child!

LAVRENTI All right, make it another two hundred piasters. You'll have it in writing that the farm will go to you: but she'll have the right to live here for two years.

THE MOTHER-IN-LAW (*drying her tears*) It'll hardly cover the funeral expenses. I hope she'll really lend me a hand with the work. And what's happened to the monk? He must have slipped out through the kitchen window. We'll have the whole village round our necks when they hear Jussup's end is come! Oh dear! I'll run and get the monk. But he mustn't see the child!

LAVRENTI I'll take care he doesn't. But why only a monk? Why not a priest?

THE MOTHER-IN-LAW Oh, he's just as good. I only made one mistake: I paid half his fee in advance. Enough to send him to the tavern. I only hope . . . (*She runs off*)

LAVRENTI She saved on the priest, the wretch! Hired a cheap monk.

GRUSHA You *will* send Simon Shashava over to see me if he turns up after all?

LAVRENTI Yes. (*pointing at the* SICK MAN) Won't you take a look at him? (GRUSHA, *taking* MICHAEL *to her, shakes her head*) He's not moving an eyelid. I hope we aren't too late.

(*They listen. On the opposite side enter* NEIGHBORS *who look around and take up positions against the walls, thus forming another wall near the bed, yet leaving an opening so that the bed can be seen. They start murmuring prayers. Enter the* MOTHER-IN-LAW *with a* MONK. *Showing some annoyance and surprise, she bows to the* GUESTS)

THE MOTHER-IN-LAW I hope you don't mind waiting a few moments? My son's bride has just arrived from the city. An emergency wedding is about to take place. (*to the* MONK *in the bedroom*) I might have known you couldn't keep your trap shut. (*to* GRUSHA) The wedding can take place at once. Here's the license. I myself and the bride's brother (LAVRENTI *tries to hide in the background, after having quietly taken* MICHAEL *back from* GRUSHA. *The* MOTHER-IN-LAW *waves him away*) who will be here in a moment, are the witnesses.

(GRUSHA *has bowed to* THE MONK. *They go to the bed. The* MOTHER-IN-LAW *lifts the mosquito net. The* MONK *starts reeling off the marriage ceremony in Latin. Meanwhile, the* MOTHER-IN-LAW *beckons to* LAVRENTI *to get rid of the* CHILD, *but fearing that it will cry he draws its attention to the ceremony.* GRUSHA *glances once at the* CHILD, *and* LAVRENTI *waves the* CHILD'S *hand in a greeting*)

THE MONK Are you prepared to be a faithful, obedient, and good wife to this man, and to cleave to him until death you do part?

GRUSHA (*looking at the* CHILD) I am.

THE MONK (*to the* SICK PEASANT) And are you prepared to be a good and loving husband to your wife until death do you part?

(*As the* SICK PEASANT *does not answer, the* MONK *looks inquiringly around*)

THE MOTHER-IN-LAW Of course he is! Didn't you hear him say yes?

THE MONK All right. We declare the marriage contracted! How about extreme unction?

THE MOTHER-IN-LAW Nothing doing! The wedding cost quite enough. Now I must take care of the mourners. (*to* LAVRENTI) Did we say seven hundred?

LAVRENTI Six hundred. (*He pays*) Now I don't want to sit with the guests and get to know people. So farewell, Grusha, and if my widowed sister comes to visit me, she'll get a welcome from my wife, or I'll show my teeth. (*Nods, gives the* CHILD *to* GRUSHA, *and leaves*)

(*The* MOURNERS *glance after him without interest*)

THE MONK May one ask where this child comes from?

THE MOTHER-IN-LAW Is there a child? I don't see a child. And you don't see a child either—you understand? Or it may turn out I saw all sorts of things in the tavern! Now come on. (*After* GRUSHA *has put the* CHILD *down and told him to be quiet, they move over left,* GRUSHA *is introduced to the* NEIGHBORS) This is my daughter-in-law. She arrived just in time to find dear Jussup still alive.

ONE WOMAN He's been ill now a whole year, hasn't he? When our Vassili was drafted he was there to say goodbye.

ANOTHER WOMAN Such things are terrible for a farm. The corn all ripe and the farmer in bed! It'll really be a blessing if he doesn't suffer too long, I say.

THE FIRST WOMAN (*confidentially*) You know why we thought he'd taken to his bed? Because of the draft! And now his end is come!

THE MOTHER-IN-LAW Sit yourselves down, please! And have some cakes!

(*She beckons to* GRUSHA *and* BOTH WOMEN *go into the bedroom, where they pick up the cake pans off the floor. The* GUESTS, *among them the* MONK, *sit on the floor and begin conversing in subdued voices*)

ONE PEASANT (*to whom the* MONK *has handed the bottle which he has taken from his soutane*) There's a child, you say! How can that have happened to Jussup?

A WOMAN She was certainly lucky to get herself hitched, with him so sick.

THE MOTHER-IN-LAW They're gossiping already. And gorging themselves on the funeral cakes at the same time! If he doesn't die today, I'll have to bake some more tomorrow!

GRUSHA I'll bake them for you.

THE MOTHER-IN-LAW Yesterday some horsemen rode by, and I went out to see who it was. When I came in again he was lying there like a corpse! So I sent for you. It can't take much longer. (*She listens*)

THE MONK Dear wedding and funeral guests! Deeply touched, we stand before a bed of death and marriage. The bride gets the veil; the groom, a shroud: how varied, my children, are the fates of men! Alas! One man dies and has a roof over his head, and the other is married and the flesh turns to dust from which it was made. Amen.

THE MOTHER-IN-LAW He's getting his own back. I shouldn't have hired such a cheap one. It's what you'd expect. A more expensive monk would behave himself. In Sura there's one with a real air of sanctity about him, but of course he charges a fortune. A fifty-piaster monk like that has no dignity, and as for piety, just fifty piasters' worth and no more! When I came to get him in the tavern he'd just made a speech, and he was shouting: "The war is over, beware of the peace!" We must go in.

GRUSHA (*giving* MICHAEL *a cake*) Eat this cake, and keep nice and still, Michael.

(*The* TWO WOMEN *offer cakes to the* GUESTS. *The* DYING MAN *sits up in bed. He puts his head out from under the mosquito net, stares at the*

TWO WOMEN, *then sinks back again. The* MONK *takes two bottles from his soutane and offers them to the* PEASANT *beside him. Enter* THREE MUSICIANS *who are greeted with a sly wink by the* MONK)

THE MOTHER-IN-LAW (*to the* MUSICIANS) What are you doing here? With instruments?

ONE MUSICIAN Brother Anastasius here (*points at the* MONK) told us there was a wedding on.

THE MOTHER-IN-LAW What? You brought them? Three more on my neck! Don't you know there's a dying man in the next room?

THE MONK A very tempting assignment for a musician: something that could be either a subdued Wedding March or a spirited Funeral Dance.

THE MOTHER-IN-LAW Well, you might as well play. Nobody can stop you eating in any case.

(*The* MUSICIANS *play a potpourri. The* WOMEN *serve cakes*)

THE MONK The trumpet sounds like a whining baby. And you, little drum, what have you got to tell the world?

THE DRUNKEN PEASANT (*beside the* MONK, *sings:*)

Miss Roundass took the old old man
And said that marriage was the thing
To everyone who met 'er.
She later withdrew from the contract
  because
Candles are better.

(*The* MOTHER-IN-LAW *throws the* DRUNKEN PEASANT *out. The music stops. The* GUESTS *are embarrassed*)

THE GUESTS (*loudly*) Have you heard? The Grand Duke is back! But the Princes are against him.

—They say the Shah of Persia has lent him a great army to restore order in Grusinia.

—But how is that possible? The Shah of Persia is the enemy . . .

—The enemy of Grusinia, you donkey, not the enemy of the Grand Duke!

—In any case, the war's over, so our soldiers are coming back.

(GRUSHA *drops a cake pan.* GUESTS *help her pick up the cake*)

AN OLD WOMAN (*to* GRUSHA) Are you feeling bad? It's just excitement about dear Jussup. Sit down and rest a while, my dear. (GRUSHA *staggers*)

THE GUESTS Now everything'll be the way it was. Only the taxes'll go up because now we'll have to pay for the war.

GRUSHA (*weakly*) Did someone say the soldiers are back?

A MAN I did.

GRUSHA It can't be true.

THE FIRST MAN (*to a* WOMAN) Show her the shawl. We bought it from a soldier. It's from Persia.

GRUSHA (*looking at the shawl*) They are here. (*She gets up, takes a step, kneels down in prayer, takes the silver cross and chain out of her blouse, and kisses it*)

THE MOTHER-IN-LAW (*while the* GUESTS *silently watch* GRUSHA) What's the matter with you? Aren't you going to look after our guests? What's all this city nonsense got to do with us?

THE GUESTS (*resuming conversation while* GRUSHA *remains in prayer*) You can buy Persian saddles from the soldiers too. Though many want crutches in exchange for them.
—The big shots on one side can win a war, the soldiers on both sides lose it.
—Anyway, the war's over. It's something they can't draft you any more.

(*The* DYING MAN *sits bolt upright in bed. He listens*)

THE GUESTS (*continuing*) What we need is two weeks of good weather.
—Our pear trees are hardly bearing a thing this year.

THE MOTHER-IN-LAW (*offering cakes*) Have some more cakes and welcome! There are more!

(*The* MOTHER-IN-LAW *goes to the bedroom with the empty cake pans. Unaware of the* DYING MAN, *she is bending down to pick up another tray when he begins to talk in a hoarse voice*)

THE PEASANT How many more cakes are you going to stuff down their throats? Think I'm a fucking goldmine?

(*The* MOTHER-IN-LAW *starts, stares at him aghast, while he climbs out from behind the mosquito net*)

THE FIRST WOMAN (*talking kindly to* GRUSHA *in the next room*) Has the young wife got someone at the front?

A MAN It's good news that they're on their way home, huh?

THE PEASANT Don't stare at me like that! Where's this wife you've hung round my neck?

(*Receiving no answer, he climbs out of bed and in his nightshirt staggers into the other room. Trembling, she follows him with the cake pan*)

THE GUESTS (*seeing him and shrieking*) Good God! Jussup!

(EVERYONE *leaps up in alarm. The* WOMEN *rush to the door.* GRUSHA, *still on her knees, turns round and stares at the* MAN)

THE PEASANT A funeral supper! You'd enjoy that, wouldn't you? Get out before I throw you out! (*as the* GUESTS *stampede from the house, gloomily to* GRUSHA) I've upset the apple cart, huh? (*Receiving no answer, he turns round and takes a cake from the pan which his mother is holding*)

THE STORY TELLER
O confusion! The wife discovers she
   has a husband.
By day there's the child, by night
   there's the husband.
The lover is on his way both day
   and night.
Husband and wife look at each other.
The bedroom is small.

(*Near the bed* THE PEASANT *is sitting in a high wooden bathtub, naked.* THE MOTHER-IN-LAW *is pouring water from a pitcher. Opposite,* GRUSHA *cowers with* MICHAEL, *who is playing at mending straw mats*)

THE PEASANT (*to his* MOTHER) That's *her* work, not yours. Where's she hiding out now?

THE MOTHER-IN-LAW (*calling*) Grusha! The peasant wants you!

GRUSHA (*to* MICHAEL) There are still two holes to mend.

THE PEASANT (*when* GRUSHA *approaches*) Scrub my back!

GRUSHA Can't the peasant do it himself?

THE PEASANT "Can't the peasant do it himself?" Get the brush! To hell with you! Are you the wife here? Or are you a visitor? (*to* THE MOTHER-IN-LAW) It's too cold!

THE MOTHER-IN-LAW I'll run for hot water.

GRUSHA Let me go.

THE PEASANT You stay here. (THE MOTHER-IN-LAW *exits*) Rub harder. And no shirking. You've seen a naked fellow before. That child didn't come out of thin air.

GRUSHA The child was not conceived in joy, if that's what the peasant means.

THE PEASANT (*turning and grinning*) You don't look the type. (GRUSHA *stops scrubbing him, starts back. Enter* THE MOTHER-IN-LAW)

THE PEASANT A nice thing you've hung around my neck! A simpleton for a wife!

THE MOTHER-IN-LAW She just isn't cooperative.

THE PEASANT Pour—but go easy! Ow! Go easy, I said. (*to* GRUSHA) Maybe you did something wrong in the city . . . I wouldn't be surprised. Why else should you be here? But I won't talk about that. I've not said a word about the illegitimate object you brought into my house either. But my patience has limits! It's against nature. (*to the* MOTHER-IN-LAW) More! (*to* GRUSHA) And even if your soldier does come back, you're married.

GRUSHA   Yes.

THE PEASANT   But your soldier won't come back. Don't you believe it.

GRUSHA   No.

THE PEASANT   You're cheating me. You're my wife and you're not my wife. Where you lie, nothing lies, and yet no other woman can lie there. When I go to work in the mornings I'm tired—when I lie down at night I'm awake as the devil. God has given you sex—and what d'you do? I don't have ten piasters to buy myself a woman in the city. Besides, it's a long way. Woman weeds the fields and opens up her legs, that's what our calendar says. D'you hear?

GRUSHA (*quietly*)   Yes. I didn't mean to cheat you out of it.

THE PEASANT   She didn't mean to cheat me out of it! Pour some more water! (*The* MOTHER-IN-LAW *pours*) Ow!

THE STORY TELLER

As she sat by the stream to wash the
    linen
She saw his image in the water
And his face grew dimmer with the
    passing moons.
As she raised herself to wring the
    linen
She heard his voice from the mur-
    muring maple
And his voice grew fainter with the
    passing moons.
Evasions and sighs grew more nu-
    merous,
Tears and sweat flowed.
With the passing moons the child
    grew up.

(GRUSHA *sits by a stream, dipping linen into the water. In the rear, a few* CHILDREN *are standing*)

GRUSHA (*to* MICHAEL)   You can play with them, Michael, but don't let them boss you around just because you're the littlest.

(MICHAEL *nods and joins the* CHILDREN. *They start playing*)

THE BIGGEST BOY   Today it's the Heads-Off Game. (to a FAT BOY) You're the Prince and you laugh. (to MICHAEL) You're the Governor. (to a GIRL) You're the governor's wife and you cry when his head's cut off. And I do the cutting. (*He shows his wooden sword*) With this. First, they lead the Governor into the

yard. The Prince walks in front. The Governor's wife comes last.

(*They form a procession. The* FAT BOY *is first and laughs. Then comes* MICHAEL, *then the* BIGGEST BOY, *and then the* GIRL, *who weeps*)

MICHAEL (*standing still*)   Me cut off head!

THE BIGGEST BOY   That's my job. You're the littlest. The Governor's the easy part. All you do is kneel down and get your head cut off—simple.

MICHAEL   Me want sword!

THE BIGGEST BOY   It's mine! (*He gives him a kick*)

THE GIRL (*shouting to* GRUSHA)   He won't play his part!

GRUSHA (*laughing*)   Even the little duck is a swimmer, they say.

THE BIGGEST BOY   You can be the Prince if you can laugh. (MICHAEL *shakes his head*)

THE FAT BOY   I laugh best. Let him cut off the head just once. Then you do it, then me.

(*Reluctantly, the* BIGGEST BOY *hands* MICHAEL *the wooden sword and kneels down. The* FAT BOY *sits down, slaps his thigh, and laughs with all his might. The* GIRL *weeps loudly.* MICHAEL *swings the big sword and "cuts off" the head. In doing so, he topples over*)

THE BIGGEST BOY   Hey! I'll show you how to cut heads off!

(MICHAEL *runs away. The* CHILDREN *run after him.* GRUSHA *laughs, following them with her eyes. On looking back, she sees* SIMON SHA-SHAVA *standing on the opposite bank. He wears a shabby uniform*)

GRUSHA   Simon!

SIMON   Is that Grusha Vashnadze?

GRUSHA   Simon!

SIMON (*formally*)   A good morning to the young lady. I hope she is well.

GRUSHA (*getting up gaily and bowing low*) A good morning to the soldier. God be thanked he has returned in good health.

SIMON   They found better fish, so they didn't eat me, said the haddock.

GRUSHA   Courage, said the kitchen boy. Good luck, said the hero.

SIMON   How are things here? Was the winter bearable? The neighbor considerate?

GRUSHA   The winter was a trifle rough, the neighbor as usual, Simon.

SIMON   May one ask if a certain person still dips her foot in the water when rinsing the linen?

GRUSHA   The answer is no. Because of the eyes in the bushes.

SIMON   The young lady is speaking of soldiers. Here stands a paymaster.

GRUSHA A job worth twenty piasters?

SIMON And lodgings.

GRUSHA (*with tears in her eyes*) Behind the barracks under the date trees.

SIMON Yes, there. A certain person has kept her eyes open.

GRUSHA She has, Simon.

SIMON And has not forgotten? (GRUSHA *shakes her head*) So the door is still on its hinges as they say? (GRUSHA *looks at him in silence and shakes her head again*) What's this? Is something not as it should be?

GRUSHA Simon Shashava, I can never return to Nuka. Something has happened.

SIMON What can have happened?

GRUSHA For one thing, I knocked an Ironshirt down.

SIMON Grusha Vashnadze must have had her reasons for that.

GRUSHA Simon Shashava, I am no longer called what I used to be called.

SIMON (*after a pause*) I do not understand.

GRUSHA When do women change their names, Simon? Let me explain. Nothing stands between us. Everything is just as it was. You must believe that.

SIMON Nothing stands between us and yet there's something?

GRUSHA How can I explain it so fast and with the stream between us? Couldn't you cross the bridge there?

SIMON Maybe it's no longer necessary.

GRUSHA It is very necessary. Come over on this side, Simon. Quick!

SIMON Does the young lady wish to say someone has come too late?

(GRUSHA *looks up at him in despair, her face streaming with tears.* SIMON *stares before him. He picks up a piece of wood and starts cutting it*)

THE STORY TELLER
So many words are said, so many left
    unsaid.
The soldier has come.
Where he comes from, he does not
    say.
Hear what he thought and did not
    say:
"The battle began, gray at dawn,
    grew bloody at noon.
The first man fell in front of me,
    the second behind me, the third at
    my side.
I trod on the first, left the second be-
    hind, the third was run through by
    the captain.

One of my brothers died by steel, the
    other by smoke.
My neck caught fire, my hands froze
    in my gloves, my toes in my socks.
I fed on aspen buds, I drank maple
    juice, I slept on stone, in water."

SIMON I see a cap in the grass. Is there a little one already?

GRUSHA There is, Simon. How could I conceal the fact? But please don't worry, it is not mine.

SIMON When the wind once starts to blow, they say, it blows through every cranny. The wife need say no more.

(GRUSHA *looks into her lap and is silent*)

THE STORY TELLER
There was yearning but there was
    no waiting.
The oath is broken. Neither could say
    why.
Hear what she thought but did not
    say:
"While you fought in the battle,
    soldier,
The bloody battle, the bitter battle
I found a helpless infant
I had not the heart to destroy him
I had to care for a creature that was
    lost
I had to stoop for breadcrumbs on
    the floor
I had to break myself for that which
    was not mine
That which was other people's.
Someone must help!
For the little tree needs water
The lamb loses its way when the
    shepherd is asleep
And its cry is unheard!"

SIMON Give me back the cross I gave you. Better still, throw it in the stream. (*He turns to go*)

GRUSHA (*getting up*) Simon Shashava, don't go away! He isn't mine! He isn't mine! (*She hears the* CHILDREN *calling*) What's the matter, children?

VOICES Soldiers! And they're taking Michael away!

(GRUSHA *stands aghast as* TWO IRONSHIRTS, *with* MICHAEL *between them, come toward her*)

ONE OF THE IRONSHIRTS Are you Grusha? (*She nods*) Is this your child?

GRUSHA Yes. (SIMON *goes*) Simon!

THE IRONSHIRT We have orders, in the name of the law, to take this child, found in your custody, back to the city. It is suspected that the child is Michael Abashwili, son and heir of the late Governor Georgi Abashwili, and his wife, Natella Abashwili. Here is the document and the seal. (*They lead the* CHILD *away*)

GRUSHA (*running after them, shouting*) Leave him here. Please! He's mine!

THE STORY TELLER

The Ironshirts took the child, the beloved child.
The unhappy girl followed them to the city, the dreaded city.
She who had borne him demanded the child.
She who had raised him faced trial.
Who will decide the case?
To whom will the child be assigned?
Who will the judge be? A good judge? A bad?
The city was in flames.
In the judge's seat sat Azdak.*

4: THE STORY OF THE JUDGE

THE STORY TELLER

Hear the story of the judge
How he turned judge, how he passed judgment, what kind of judge he was.
On that Easter Sunday of the great revolt, when the Grand Duke was overthrown
And his Governor Abashwili, father of our child, lost his head
The Village Scrivener Azdak found a fugitive in the woods and hid him in his hut.

(AZDAK, *in rags and slightly drunk, is helping an* OLD BEGGAR *into his cottage*)

AZDAK Stop snorting, you're not a horse. And it won't do you any good with the police, to run like a snotty nose in April. Stand still, I say. (*He catches the* OLD MAN, *who has marched into the cottage as if he'd like to go through the walls*) Sit down. Feed. Here's a hunk of cheese. (*From under some rags, in a chest, he fishes out some cheese, and the* OLD MAN *greedily begins to eat*) Haven't eaten in a long time, huh? (*The* OLD MAN *growls*) Why were you running like that, asshole? The cop wouldn't even have seen you.

THE OLD MAN Had to! Had to!

AZDAK Blue Funk? (*The* OLD MAN *stares, uncomprehending*) Cold feet? Panic? Don't

lick your chops like a Grand Duke. Or an old sow. I can't stand it. We have to accept respectable stinkers as God made them, but not you! I once heard of a senior judge who farted at a public dinner to show an independent spirit! Watching you eat like that gives me the most awful ideas. Why don't you say something? (*sharply*) Show me your hand. Can't you hear? (*The* OLD MAN *slowly puts out his hand*) White! So you're not a beggar at all! A fraud, a walking swindle! And I'm hiding you from the cops as though you were an honest man! Why were you running like that if you're a landowner? For that's what you are. Don't deny it! I see it in your guilty face! (*He gets up*) Get out! (*The* OLD MAN *looks at him uncertainly*) What are you waiting for, peasant-flogger?

THE OLD MAN Pursued. Need undivided attention. Make proposition . . .

AZDAK Make what? A proposition? Well, if that isn't the height of insolence. He's making me a proposition! The bitten man scratches his fingers bloody, and the leech that's biting him makes him a proposition! Get out, I tell you!

THE OLD MAN Understand point of view! Persuasion! Pay hundred thousand piasters one night! Yes?

AZDAK What, you think you can buy me? For a hundred thousand piasters? Let's say a hundred and fifty thousand. Where are they?

THE OLD MAN Have not them here. Of course. Will be sent. Hope do not doubt.

AZDAK Doubt very much. Get out!

(*The* OLD MAN *gets up, waddles to the door. A* VOICE *is heard off stage*)

A VOICE Azdak!

(*The* OLD MAN *turns, waddles to the opposite corner, stands still*)

AZDAK (*calling out*) I'm not in! (*He walks to door*) So you're sniffing around here again, Shauwa?

POLICEMAN SHAUWA (*reproachfully*) You've caught another rabbit, Azdak. And you promised me it wouldn't happen again!

AZDAK (*severely*) Shauwa, don't talk about things you don't understand. The rabbit is a dangerous and destructive beast. It feeds on plants, especially on the species of plants known as weeds. It must therefore be exterminated.

SHAUWA Azdak, don't be so hard on me. I'll lose my job if I don't arrest you. I know you have a good heart.

AZDAK I do not have a good heart! How often must I tell you I'm a man of intellect?

SHAUWA (*slyly*) I know, Azdak. You're a

---

* The name *Azdak* should be accented on the second syllable.

superior person. You say so yourself. I'm just a Christian and an ignoramus. And so I ask you: When one of the Prince's rabbits is stolen, and I'm a policeman, what should I do with the offending party?

AZDAK Shauwa, Shauwa, shame on you. You stand and ask me a question, than which nothing could be more seductive. It's like you were a woman—let's say that bad girl Nunowna, and you showed me your thigh—Nunowna's thigh, that would be—and asked me: "What shall I do with my thigh, it itches?" Is she as innocent as she pretends? Of course not. I catch a rabbit, but you catch a man. Man is made in God's image. Not so a rabbit, you know that. I'm a rabbit-eater, but you're a man-eater, Shauwa. And God will pass judgment on you. Shauwa, go home and repent. No, stop, there's something . . . (*He looks at the* OLD MAN *who stands trembling in the corner*) No, it's nothing. Go home and repent. (*He slams the door behind* SHAUWA) Now you're surprised, huh? Surprised I didn't hand you over? I couldn't hand over a bedbug to that animal. It goes against the grain. Now don't tremble because of a cop! So old and still so scared? Finish your cheese, but eat it like a poor man, or else they'll still catch you. Must I even explain how a poor man behaves? (*He pushes him down, and then gives him back the cheese*) That box is the table. Lay your elbows on the table. Now, encircle the cheese on the plate like it might be snatched from you at any moment—what right have you to be safe, huh?—now, hole your knife like an undersized sickle, and give your cheese a troubled look because, like all beautiful things, it's already fading away. (AZDAK *watches him*) They're after you, which speaks in your favor, but how can we be sure they're not mistaken about you? In Tiflis one time they hanged a landowner, a Turk, who could prove he quartered his peasants instead of merely cutting them in half, as is the custom, and he squeezed twice the usual amount of taxes out of them, his zeal was above suspicion. And yet they hanged him like a common criminal—because he was a Turk—a thing he couldn't do much about. What injustice! He got onto the gallows by a sheer fluke. In short, I don't trust you.

THE STORY TELLER
Thus Azdak gave the old beggar a bed,
And learned that old beggar was the old butcher, the Grand Duke himself,
And was ashamed.
He denounced himself and ordered

the policeman to take him to Nuka, to court, to be judged.

(*In the court of justice* THREE IRONSHIRTS *sit drinking. From a beam hangs a man in judge's robes. Enter* AZDAK, *in chains, dragging* SHAUWA *behind him*)

AZDAK (*shouting*) I've helped the Grand Duke, the Grand Thief, the Grand Butcher, to escape! In the name of justice I ask to be severely judged in public trial!

THE FIRST IRONSHIRT Who's this queer bird?

SHAUWA That's our Village Scrivener, Azdak.

AZDAK I am contemptible! I am a traitor! A branded criminal! Tell them, flat-foot, how I insisted on being chained up and brought to the capital. Because I sheltered the Grand Duke, the Grand Swindler, by mistake. And how I found out afterwards. See the marked man denounce himself! Tell them how I forced you to walk with me half the night to clear the whole thing up.

SHAUWA And all by threats. That wasn't nice of you, Azdak.

AZDAK Shut your mouth, Shauwa. You don't understand. A new age is upon us! It'll go thundering over you. You're finished. The police will be wiped out—poof! Everything will be gone into, everything will be brought into the open. The guilty will give themselves up. Why? They couldn't escape the people in any case. (*to* SHAUWA) Tell them how I shouted all along Shoemaker Street: (*with big gestures, looking at the* IRONSHIRTS) "In my ignorance I let the Grand Swindler escape! So tear me to pieces, brothers!" I wanted to get it in first.

THE FIRST IRONSHIRT And what did your brothers answer?

SHAUWA They comforted him in Butcher Street, and they laughed themselves sick in Shoemaker Street. That's all.

AZDAK But with you it's different. I can see you're men of iron. Brothers, where's the judge? I must be tried.

THE FIRST IRONSHIRT (*pointing at the hanged man*) There's the judge. And please stop "brothering" us. It's rather a sore spot this evening.

AZDAK "There's the judge." An answer never heard in Grusinia before. Townsman, where's His Excellency the Governor? (*pointing to the floor*) There's His Excellency, stranger. Where's the Chief Tax Collector? Where's the official Recruiting Officer? The Patriarch? The Chief of Police? There, there,

there—all there. Brothers, I expected no less of you.

THE SECOND IRONSHIRT What? *What* was it you expected, funny man?

AZDAK What happened in Persia, brother, what happened in Persia?

THE SECOND IRONSHIRT What did happen in Persia?

AZDAK Everybody was hanged. Viziers, tax collectors. Everybody. Forty years ago now. My grandfather, a remarkable man by the way, saw it all. For three whole days. Everywhere.

THE SECOND IRONSHIRT And who ruled when the Vizier was hanged?

AZDAK A peasant ruled when the Vizier was hanged.

THE SECOND IRONSHIRT And who commanded the army?

AZDAK A soldier, a soldier.

THE SECOND IRONSHIRT And who paid the wages?

AZDAK A dyer. A dyer paid the wages.

THE SECOND IRONSHIRT Wasn't it a weaver, maybe?

THE FIRST IRONSHIRT And why did all this happen, Persian?

AZDAK Why did all this happen? Must there be a special reason? Why do you scratch yourself, brother? War! Too long a war! And no justice! My grandfather brought back a song that tells how it was. I will sing it for you. With my friend the policeman. (*to* SHAUWA) And hold the rope tight. It's very suitable. (*He sings, with* SHAUWA *holding the rope tight around him*)

The Song of Injustice in Persia
Why don't our sons bleed any more?
Why don't our daughters weep?
Why do only the slaughter-house cat-
   tle have blood in their veins?
Why do only the willows shed tears
   on Lake Urmi?

The king must have a new province,
   the peasant must give up his savings.
That the roof of the world might be
   conquered, the roof of the cottage
   is torn down.
Our men are carried to the ends of
   the earth, so that great ones can
   eat at home.
The soldiers kill each other, the mar-
   shals salute each other.
They bite the widow's tax money to
   see if it's good, their swords break.

The battle was lost, the helmets were
   paid for.
      [*Refrain*]
Is it so? Is it so?
SHAUWA
      [*Refrain*]
Yes, yes, yes, yes, yes it's so.

AZDAK Do you want to hear the rest of it? (*The* FIRST IRONSHIRT *nods*)

THE SECOND IRONSHIRT (*to* SHAUWA) Did he teach you that song?

SHAUWA Yes, only my voice isn't very good.

THE SECOND IRONSHIRT No. (*to* AZDAK) Go on singing.

AZDAK The second verse is about the peace. (*He sings:*)

The offices are packed, the streets
   overflow with officials.
The rivers jump their banks and
   ravage the fields.
Those who cannot let down their
   own trousers rule countries.
They can't count up to four, but
   they devour eight courses.
The corn farmers, looking round for
   buyers, see only the starving.
The weavers go home from their
   looms in rags.
      [*Refrain*]
Is it so? Is it so?
SHAUWA
      [*Refrain*]
Yes, yes, yes, yes, yes it's so.

AZDAK
That's why our sons don't bleed any
   more, that's why our daughters
   don't weep.
That's why only the slaughter-house
   cattle have blood in their veins,
And only the willows shed tears by
   Lake Urmi toward morning.

THE FIRST IRONSHIRT Are you going to sing that song here in town?

AZDAK Sure. What's wrong with it?

THE FIRST IRONSHIRT Have you noticed that the sky's getting red? (*Turning round,* AZDAK *sees the sky red with fire*) It's the people's quarters. On the outskirts of town. The carpet weavers have caught the "Persian Sickness," too. And they've been asking if Prince Kazbeki isn't eating too many courses. This morning they strung up the city judge. As for us we beat them to pulp. We were paid one hundred piasters per man, you understand?

AZDAK (*after a pause*) I understand. (*He glances shyly round and, creeping away, sits down in a corner, his head in his hands*)

THE IRONSHIRTS (*to each other*) If there ever was a troublemaker it's him.

—He must've come to the capital to fish in the troubled waters.

SHAUWA Oh, I don't think he's a really bad character, gentlemen. Steals a few chickens here and there. And maybe a rabbit.

THE SECOND IRONSHIRT (*approaching* AZDAK) Came to fish in the troubled waters, huh?

AZDAK (*looking up*) I don't know why I came.

THE SECOND IRONSHIRT Are you in with the carpet weavers maybe? (AZDAK *shakes his head*) How about that song?

AZDAK From my grandfather. A silly and ignorant man.

THE SECOND IRONSHIRT Right. And how about the dyer who paid the wages?

AZDAK (*muttering*) That was in Persia.

THE FIRST IRONSHIRT And this denouncing of yourself? Because you didn't hang the Grand Duke with your own hands?

AZDAK Didn't I tell you I let him run? (*He creeps farther away and sits on the floor*)

SHAUWA I can swear to that: he let him run.

(*The* IRONSHIRTS *burst out laughing and slap* SHAUWA *on the back.* AZDAK *laughs loudest. They slap* AZDAK *too, and unchain him. They all start drinking as the* FAT PRINCE *enters with a* YOUNG MAN)

THE FIRST IRONSHIRT (*to* AZDAK, *pointing at the* FAT PRINCE) There's your "new age" for you! (*more laughter*)

THE FAT PRINCE Well, my friends, what is there to laugh about? Permit me a serious word. Yesterday morning the Princes of Grusinia overthrew the war-mongering government of the Grand Duke and did away with his Governors. Unfortunately the Grand Duke himself escaped. In this fateful hour our carpet weavers, those eternal troublemakers, had the effrontery to stir up a rebellion and hang the universally loved city judge, our dear Illo Orbeliani. Ts-ts-ts. My friends, we need peace, peace, peace in Grusinia! And justice! So I've brought along my dear nephew Bizergan Kazbeki. He'll be the new judge, hm? A very gifted fellow. What do you say? I want your opinion. Let the people decide!

THE SECOND IRONSHIRT Does this mean *we* elect the judge?

THE FAT PRINCE Precisely. Let the people propose some very gifted fellow! Confer among yourselves, my friends. (*The* IRONSHIRTS *confer*) Don't worry, my little fox. The job's yours. And when we catch the Grand Duke we won't have to kiss this rabble's ass any longer.

THE IRONSHIRTS (*between themselves*) Very funny: they're wetting their pants because they haven't caught the Grand Duke.

—When the outlook isn't so bright, they say: "My friends!" and "Let the people decide!"

—Now he even wants justice for Grusinia! But fun is fun as long as it lasts!

(*Pointing at* AZDAK)

—He knows all about justice. Hey, rascal, would you like this nephew fellow to be the judge?

AZDAK Are you asking me? You're not asking *me?!*

THE FIRST IRONSHIRT Why not? Anything for a laugh!

AZDAK You'd like to test him to the marrow, correct? Have you a criminal on hand? An experienced one? So the candidate can show what he knows?

THE SECOND IRONSHIRT Let's see. We do have a couple of doctors downstairs. Let's use them.

AZDAK Oh, no, that's no good, we can't take real criminals till we're sure the judge will be appointed. He may be dumb, but he must be appointed, or the Law is violated. And the Law is a sensitive organ. It's like the spleen, you mustn't hit it—that would be fatal. Of course you can hang those two without violating the Law, because there was no judge in the vicinity. But Judgment, when pronounced, must be pronounced with absolute gravity— it's all such nonsense. Suppose, for instance, a judge jails a woman—let's say she's stolen a corncake to feed her child—and this judge isn't wearing his robes—or maybe he's scratching himself while passing sentence and half his body is uncovered—a man's thigh *will* itch once in a while—the sentence this judge passes is a disgrace and the Law is violated. In short it would be easier for a judge's robe and a judge's hat to pass judgment than for a man with no robe and no hat. If you don't treat it with respect, the Law just disappears on you. Now you don't try out a bottle of wine by offering it to a dog; you'd only lose your wine.

THE FIRST IRONSHIRT　Then what do you suggest, hair-splitter?

AZDAK　I'll be the defendant.

THE FIRST IRONSHIRT　You? (*He bursts out laughing*)

THE FAT PRINCE　What have you decided?

THE FIRST IRONSHIRT　We've decided to stage a rehearsal. Our friend here will be the defendant. Let the candidate be the judge and sit there.

THE FAT PRINCE　It isn't customary, but why not? (*to the* NEPHEW) A mere formality, my little fox. What have I taught you? Who got there first—the slow runner or the fast?

THE NEPHEW　The silent runner, Uncle Arsen.

(*The* NEPHEW *takes the chair. The* IRONSHIRTS *and the* FAT PRINCE *sit on the steps. Enter* AZDAK, *mimicking the gait of the* GRAND DUKE)

AZDAK (*in the* GRAND DUKE's *accent*)　Is any here knows me? Am Grand Duke.

THE IRONSHIRTS　*What* is he?

—The Grand Duke. He knows him, too.

—Fine. So get on with the trial.

AZDAK　Listen! Am accused instigating war. Ridiculous! Am saying ridiculous! That enough? If not, have brought lawyers. Believe five hundred. (*He points behind him, pretending to be surrounded by lawyers*) Requisition all available seats for lawyers!

(*The* IRONSHIRTS *laugh, the* FAT PRINCE *joins in*)

THE NEPHEW (*to the* IRONSHIRTS)　You really wish me to try this case? I find it rather unusual. From the taste angle, I mean.

THE FIRST IRONSHIRT　Let's go!

THE FAT PRINCE (*smiling*)　Let him have it, my little fox!

THE NEPHEW　All right. People of Grusinia versus Grand Duke. Defendant, what have you got to say for yourself?

AZDAK　Plenty. Naturally, have read war lost. Only started on the advice of patriots. Like Uncle Arsen Kazbeki. Call Uncle Arsen as witness.

THE FAT PRINCE (*to the* IRONSHIRTS, *delightedly*)　What a screw-ball!

THE NEPHEW　Motion rejected. One cannot be arraigned for declaring a war, which every ruler has to do once in a while, but only for running a war badly.

AZDAK　Rubbish! Did not run it at all! Had it run! Had it run by Princes! Naturally, they messed it up.

THE NEPHEW　Do you by any chance deny having been commander-in-chief?

AZDAK　Not at all! Always *was* commander-in-chief. At birth shouted at wet nurse. Was trained drop turds in toilet, grew accustomed to command. Always commanded officials rob my cash box. Officers flog soldiers only on command. Landowners sleep with peasants' wives only on strictest command. Uncle Arsen here grew his belly at *my* command!

THE IRONSHIRTS (*clapping*)　He's good! Long live the Grand Duke!

THE FAT PRINCE　Answer him, my little fox. I'm with you.

THE NEPHEW　I shall answer him according to the dignity of the law. Defendant, preserve the dignity of the law!

AZDAK　Agreed. Command you to proceed with the trial!

THE NEPHEW　It is not your place to command me. You claim that the Princes forced you to declare war. How can you claim, then, that they—er—"messed it up"?

AZDAK　Did not send enough people. Embezzled funds. Sent sick horses. During attack, drinking in whore house. Call Uncle Arsen as witness.

THE NEPHEW　Are you making the outrageous suggestion that the Princes of this country did not fight?

AZDAK　No. Princes fought. Fought for war contracts.

THE FAT PRINCE (*jumping up*)　That's too much! This man talks like a carpet weaver!

AZDAK　Really? I told nothing but the truth.

THE FAT PRINCE　Hang him! Hang him!

THE FIRST IRONSHIRT (*pulling the* PRINCE *down*)　Keep quiet! Go on, Excellency!

THE NEPHEW　Quiet! I now render a verdict: You must be hanged! By the neck! Having lost war!

AZDAK　Young man, seriously advise not fall publicly into jerky clipped manner of speech. Cannot be employed as watchdog if howl like wolf. Got it? If people realize Princes speak same language as Grand Duke, may hang Grand Duke *and Princes*, huh? By the way, must overrule verdict. Reason? War lost, but not for Princes. Princes won their war. Got 3,863,000 piasters for horses not delivered, 8,240,000 piasters for food supplies not produced. Are therefore victors. War lost only for Grusinia, which as such is not present in this court.

THE FAT PRINCE　I think that will do, my friends. (*to* AZDAK) You can withdraw, funny man. (*to the* IRONSHIRTS) You may now ratify the new judge's appointment, my friends.

THE FIRST IRONSHIRT　Yes, we can. Take down the judge's gown.

(ONE IRONSHIRT *climbs on the back of the* OTHER, *pulls the gown off the hanged man*)

THE FIRST IRONSHIRT (*to the* NEPHEW) Now you run away so the right ass can get on the right chair. (*to* AZDAK) Step forward! Go to the judge's seat! Now sit in it! (AZDAK *steps up, bows, and sits down*) The judge was always a rascal! Now the rascal shall be a judge! (*The judge's gown is placed round his shoulders, the hat on his head*) And what a judge!

THE STORY TELLER
And there was civil war in the land.
The mighty were not safe.
And Azdak was made a judge by the Ironshirts.
And Azdak remained a judge for two years.

THE STORY TELLER AND CHORUS
When the towns were set afire
And rivers of blood rose higher and higher,
Cockroaches crawled out of every crack.
And the court was full of schemers.
And the church of foul blasphemers.
In the judge's cassock sat Azdak.

(AZDAK *sits in the judge's chair, peeling an apple.* SHAUWA *is sweeping out the hall. On one side an* INVALID *in a wheelchair. Opposite, a* YOUNG MAN *accused of blackmail. An* IRON-SHIRT *stands guard, holding the Ironshirt's banner*)

AZDAK In consideration of the large number of cases, the Court today will hear two cases at a time. Before I open the proceedings, a short announcement—I accept. (*He stretches out his hand. The* BLACKMAILER *is the only one to produce any money. He hands it to* AZDAK) I reserve the right to punish one of the parties for contempt of court. (*He glances at the* INVALID) You (*to the* DOCTOR) are a doctor, and you (*to the* INVALID) are bringing a complaint against him. Is the doctor responsible for your condition?

THE INVALID Yes. I had a stroke on his account.

AZDAK That would be professional negligence.

THE INVALID Worse than negligence. I gave this man money for his studies. So far, he hasn't paid me back a cent. It was when I heard he was treating a patient free that I had my stroke.

AZDAK Rightly. (*to a* LIMPING MAN) And what are *you* doing here?

THE LIMPING MAN I'm the patient, your honor.

AZDAK He treated your leg for nothing?

THE LIMPING MAN The wrong leg! My rheumatism was in the left leg, and he operated on the right. That's why I limp now.

AZDAK And you were treated free?

THE INVALID A five-hundred-piaster operation free! For nothing! For a God-bless-you! And I paid for this man's studies! (*to the* DOCTOR) Did they teach you to operate free?

THE DOCTOR Your Honor, it is actually the custom to demand the fee before the operation, as the patient is more willing to pay before an operation than after. Which is only human. In the case in question I was convinced, when I started the operation, that my servant had already received the fee. In this I was mistaken.

THE INVALID He was mistaken! A good doctor doesn't make mistakes! He examines before he operates!

AZDAK That's right. (*to* SHAUWA) Public Prosecutor, what's the other case about?

SHAUWA (*busily sweeping*) Blackmail.

THE BLACKMAILER High Court of Justice, I'm innocent. I only wanted to find out from the landowner concerned if he really *had* raped his niece. He informed me very politely that this was not the case, and gave me the money only so I could pay for my uncle's studies.

AZDAK Hm. (*to the* DOCTOR) You, on the other hand, can cite no extenuating circumstances for your offense, huh?

THE DOCTOR Except that to err is human.

AZDAK And you are aware that in money matters a good doctor is a highly responsible person? I once heard of a doctor who got a thousand piasters for a sprained finger by remarking that sprains have something to do with blood circulation, which after all a less good doctor might have overlooked, and who, on another occasion made a real gold mine out of a somewhat disordered gall bladder, he treated it with such loving care. You have no excuse, Doctor. The corn merchant, Uxu, had his son study medicine to get some knowledge of trade, our medical schools are so good. (*to the* BLACKMAILER) What's the landowner's name?

SHAUWA He doesn't want it mentioned.

AZDAK In that case I will pass judgment. The Court considers the blackmail proved. And you (*to the* INVALID) are sentenced to a fine of one thousand piasters. If you have a second stroke, the doctor will have to treat you free. Even if he has to amputate. (*to the* LIMPING MAN) As compensation, you will receive a bottle of rubbing alcohol. (*to the* BLACKMAILER) You are sentenced to hand over half the proceeds of your deal to the Public Prosecutor to keep the landowner's name secret. You are advised, moreover, to study medicine—you seem well suited to that calling. (*to the* DOCTOR) You have perpetrated an unpardonable error in the practice of your profession: you are acquitted. Next cases!

THE STORY TELLER AND CHORUS
Men won't do much for a shilling.
For a pound they may be willing.
For 20 pounds the verdict's in the
    sack.
As for the many, all too many,
Those who've only got a penny—
They've one single, sole recourse:
    Azdak.

(*Enter* AZDAK *from the caravansary on the highroad, followed by an old bearded* INNKEEPER. *The judge's chair is carried by a* STABLEMAN *and* SHAUWA. *An* IRONSHIRT, *with a banner, takes up his position*)

AZDAK   Put me down. Then we'll get some air, maybe even a good stiff breeze from the lemon grove there. It does justice good to be done in the open: the wind blows her skirts up and you can see what she's got. Shauwa, we've been eating too much. These official journeys are exhausting. (*to the* INNKEEPER) It's a question of your daughter-in-law?

THE INNKEEPER   Your Worship, it's a question of the family honor. I wish to bring an action on behalf of my son, who's on business on the other side of the mountain. This is the offending stable-man, and here's my daughter-in-law.

(*Enter the* DAUGHTER-IN-LAW, *a voluptuous wench. She is veiled*)

AZDAK (*sitting down*)   I accept. (*Sighing, the* INNKEEPER *hands him some money*) Good. Now the formalities are disposed of. This is a case of rape?

THE INNKEEPER   Your Honor, I caught the fellow in the act. Ludovica was in the straw on the stable floor.

AZDAK   Quite right, the stable. Lovely horses! I specially liked the little roan.

THE INNKEEPER   The first thing I did, of course, was question Ludovica. On my son's behalf.

AZDAK (*seriously*)   I said I specially liked the little roan.

THE INNKEEPER (*coldly*)   Really? Ludovica confessed the stableman took her against her will.

AZDAK   Take your veil off, Ludovica. (*She*

does so) Ludovica, you please the Court. Tell us how it happened.

LUDOVICA (*well-schooled*)   When I entered the stable to see the new foal the stableman said to me on his own accord: "It's hot today!" and laid his hand on my left breast. I said to him: "Don't do that!" But he continued to handle me indecently, which provoked my anger. Before I realized his sinful intentions, he got much closer. It was all over when my father-in-law entered and accidentally trod on me.

THE INNKEEPER (*explaining*)   On my son's behalf.

AZDAK (*to the* STABLEMAN)   You admit you started it?

THE STABLEMAN   Yes.

AZDAK   Ludovica, do you like to eat sweet things?

LUDOVICA   Yes, sunflower seeds!

AZDAK   Do you like to lie a long time in the bathtub?

LUDOVICA   Half an hour or so.

AZDAK   Public Prosecutor, drop your knife —there—on the ground. (SHAUWA *does so*) Ludovica, pick up that knife. (LUDOVICA, *swaying her hips, does so*) See that? (*He points at her*) The way it moves? The rape is now proven. By eating too much—sweet things, especially—by lying too long in warm water, by laziness and too soft a skin, you have raped that unfortunate man. Think you can run around with a behind like that and get away with it in court? This is a case of intentional assault with a dangerous weapon! You are sentenced to hand over to the Court the little roan which your father liked to ride "on his son's behalf." And now, come with me to the stables, so the Court may inspect the scene of the crime, Ludovica.

THE STORY TELLER AND CHORUS
When the sharks the sharks devour
Little fishes have their hour.
For a while the load is off their back.
On Grusinia's highways faring
Fixed-up scales of justice bearing
Strode the poor man's magistrate:
    Azdak.

And he gave to the forsaken
All that from the rich he'd taken.
And a bodyguard of roughnecks was
    Azdak's.
And our good and evil man, he
Smiled upon Grusinia's Granny.
His emblem was a tear in sealing
    wax.

All mankind should love each other.
But when visiting your brother
Take an ax along and hold it fast
Not in theory but in practice miracles
    are wrought with axes
And the age of miracles is not past.

(AZDAK's *judge's chair is in a tavern.* THREE RICH FARMERS *stand before* AZDAK. SHAUWA *brings him wine. In a corner stands an* OLD PEASANT WOMAN. *In the open doorway, and outside, stand* VILLAGERS *looking on. An* IRONSHIRT *stands guard with a banner*)

AZDAK   The Public Prosecutor has the floor.

SHAUWA   It concerns a cow. For five weeks the defendant has had a cow in her stable, the property of the farmer Suru. She was also found to be in possession of a stolen ham, and a number of cows belonging to Shutoff were killed after he asked the defendant to pay the rent on a piece of land.

THE FARMERS   —It's a matter of my ham, Your Honor.
—It's a matter of my cow, Your Honor.
—It's a matter of my land, Your Honor.

AZDAK   Well, Granny, what have *you* got to say to all this?

THE OLD WOMAN   Your Honor, one night toward morning, five weeks ago, there was a knock at my door, and outside stood a bearded man with a cow. "My dear woman," he said, "I am the miracle-working Saint Banditus and because your son has been killed in the war, I bring you this cow as a souvenir. Take good care of it."

THE FARMERS   —The robber, Irakli, Your Honor!
—Her brother-in-law, Your Honor!
—The cow-thief!
—The incendiary!
—He must be beheaded!

(*Outside, a* WOMAN *screams. The* CROWD *grows restless, retreats. Enter the* BANDIT IRAKLI *with a huge ax*)

THE BANDIT   A very good evening, dear friends! A glass of vodka!

THE FARMERS (*crossing themselves*)   Irakli!

AZDAK   Public Prosecutor, a glass of vodka for our guest. And who are you?

THE BANDIT   I'm a wandering hermit, Your Honor. Thanks for the gracious gift. (*He empties the glass which* SHAUWA *has brought*) Another!

AZDAK   I am Azdak. (*He gets up and bows. The* BANDIT *also bows*) The Court welcomes the foreign hermit. Go on with your story, Granny.

THE OLD WOMAN   Your Honor, that first night I didn't yet know that Saint Banditus could work miracles, it was only the cow. But one night, a few days later, the farmer's servants came to take the cow away again. Then they turned round in front of my door and went off without the cow. And bumps as big as a fist sprouted on their heads. So I knew that Saint Banditus had changed their hearts and turned them into friendly people.

(*The* BANDIT *roars with laughter*)

THE FIRST FARMER   I know what changed them.

AZDAK   That's fine. You can tell us later. Continue.

THE OLD WOMAN   Your Honor, the next one to become a good man was the farmer Shutoff —a devil, as everyone knows. But Saint Banditus arranged it so he let me off the rent on the little piece of land.

THE SECOND FARMER   Because my cows were killed in the field.

(*The* BANDIT *laughs*)

THE OLD WOMAN (*answering* AZDAK's *sign to continue*)   Then one morning the ham came flying in at my window. It hit me in the small of the back. I'm still lame, Your Honor, look. (*She limps a few steps. The* BANDIT *laughs*) Your Honor, was there ever a time when a poor old woman could get a ham *without* a miracle?

(*The* BANDIT *starts sobbing*)

AZDAK (*rising from his chair*)   Granny, that's a question that strikes straight at the Court's heart. Be so kind as to sit here.

(*The* OLD WOMAN, *hesitating, sits in the judge's chair*)

AZDAK (*sits on the floor, glass in hand, reciting*)
   Granny
   We could almost call you Granny
     Grusinia
   The Woebegone
   The Bereaved Mother
   Whose sons have gone to war
   Receiving the present of a cow
   She bursts out crying.
   When she is beaten
   She remains hopeful.
   When she's not beaten
   She's surprised.
   On us
   Who are already damned
   May you render a merciful verdict
   Granny Grusinia!

(*Bellowing at the* FARMERS)
Admit you don't believe in miracles, you atheists! Each of you is sentenced to pay five hundred piasters! For godlessness! Get out! (*The* FARMERS *slink out*) And you Granny, and you (*to the* BANDIT) pious man, empty a pitcher of wine with the Public Prosecutor and Azdak!

THE STORY TELLER AND CHORUS
> And he broke the rules to save them.
> Broken law like bread he gave them,
> Brought them to shore upon his crooked back.
> At long last the poor and lowly
> Had someone who was not too holy
> To be bribed by empty hands: Azdak.
>
> For two years it was his pleasure
> To give the beasts of prey short measure:
> He became a wolf to fight the pack.
> From All Hallows to All Hallows
> On his chair beside the gallows
> Dispensing justice in his fashion sat Azdak.

THE STORY TELLER
> But the era of disorder came to an end.
> The Grand Duke returned.
> The Governor's wife returned.
> A trial was held.
> Many died.
> The people's quarters burned anew.
> And fear seized Azdak.

(AZDAK's *judge's chair stands again in the court of justice.* AZDAK *sits on the floor, shaving and talking to* SHAUWA. *Noises outside. In the rear the* FAT PRINCE's *head is carried by on a lance*)

AZDAK Shauwa, the days of your slavery are numbered, maybe even the minutes. For a long time now I have held you in the iron curb of reason, and it has torn your mouth till it bleeds. I have lashed you with reasonable arguments, I have manhandled you with logic. You are by nature a weak man, and if one slyly throws an argument in your path, you *have* to snap it up, you can't resist. It is your nature to lick the hand of some superior being. But superior beings can be of very different kinds. And now, with your liberation, you will soon be able to follow your natural inclinations, which are low. You will be able to follow your infallible instinct, which teaches you to plant your fat heel on the faces of men. Gone is the era of confusion and disorder, which I find described in the Song of Chaos. Let us now sing that song together in memory of those terrible days. Sit down and don't do violence to the music. Don't

be afraid. It sounds all right. And it has a fine refrain. (*He sings:*)
> Sister, hide your face! Brother, take your knife!
> The times are out of joint!
> Big men are full of complaint
> And small men full of joy.
> The city says:
> "Let us drive the strong ones from our midst!"
> Offices are raided. Lists of serfs are destroyed.
> They have set Master's nose to the grindstone.
> They who lived in the dark have seen the light.
> The ebony poor box is broken.
> Sesnem wood is sawed up for beds.
> Who had no bread have barns full.
> Who begged for alms of corn now mete it out.

SHAUWA
> [*Refrain*]
> Oh, oh, oh, oh.

AZDAK
> [*Refrain*]
> Where are you, General, where are you?
> Please, please, please, restore order!
>
> The nobleman's son can no longer be recognized;
> The lady's child becomes the son of her slave.
> The councilors meet in a shed.
> Once, this man was barely allowed to sleep on the wall;
> Now, he stretches his limbs in a bed.
> Once, this man rowed a boat; now, he owns ships.
> Their owner looks for them, but they're his no longer.
> Five men are sent on a journey by their master.
> "Go yourself," they say, "we have arrived."

SHAUWA
> [*Refrain*]
> Oh, oh, oh, oh.

AZDAK
> [*Refrain*]
> Where are you, General, where are you?
> Please, please, please, restore order!

Yes. So it might have been, had order been neglected much longer. But now the Grand Duke has returned to the capital, and the

Persians have lent him an army to restore order with. The suburbs are already aflame. Go and get me the big book I always sit on. (SHAUWA *brings the big book from the judge's chair.* ADZAK *opens it*) This is the Statute Book and I've always used it, as you can testify. Now I'd better look in this book and see what they can do to me. I've let the down-and-outs get away with murder, and I'll have to pay for it. I helped poverty onto its skinny legs, so they'll hang me for drunkenness. I peeped into the rich man's pocket, which is bad taste. And I can't hide anywhere—everybody knows me because I've helped everybody.

SHAUWA   Someone's coming!

AZDAK (*in panic, he walks trembling to the chair*)   It's the end. And now they'd enjoy seeing what a Great Man I am. I'll deprive them of that pleasure. I'll beg on my knees for mercy. Spittle will slobber down my chin. The fear of death is in me.

(*Enter* NATELLA ABASHWILI, *the* GOVERNOR'S WIFE, *followed by the* ADJUTANT *and an* IRONSHIRT)

THE GOVERNOR'S WIFE   What sort of a creature is that, Shalva?

AZDAK   A willing one, Your Highness, a man ready to oblige.

THE ADJUTANT   Natella Abashwili, wife of the late Governor, has just returned. She is looking for her two-year-old son, Michael. She has been informed that the child was carried off to the mountains by a former servant.

AZDAK   The child will be brought back, Your Highness, at your service.

THE ADJUTANT   They say that the person in question is passing it off as her own.

AZDAK   She will be beheaded, Your Highness, at your service.

THE ADJUTANT   That is all.

THE GOVERNOR'S WIFE (*leaving*)   I don't like that man.

AZDAK (*following her to door, bowing*)   At your service, Your Highness, it will all be arranged.

5: THE CHALK CIRCLE

THE STORY TELLER
Hear now the story of the trial
Concerning Governor Abashwili's
    child
And the establishing of the true
    mother
By the famous test of the Chalk
    Circle.

(*The court of justice in Nuka.* IRONSHIRTS *lead* MICHAEL *across stage and out at the back.* IRONSHIRTS *hold* GRUSHA *back with their lances under the gateway until the child has been led through. Then she is admitted. She is accompanied by the former Governor's* COOK. *Distant noises and a fire-red sky*)

GRUSHA (*trying to hide*)   He's brave, he can wash himself now.

THE COOK   You're lucky. It's not a real judge. It's Azdak, a drunk who doesn't know what he's doing. The biggest thieves have got by through him. Because he gets everything all mixed up and the rich never offer him big enough bribes, the likes of us sometimes do pretty well.

GRUSHA   I *need* luck right now.

THE COOK   Touch wood. (*She crosses herself*) I'd better offer up another prayer that the judge may be drunk. (*She prays with motionless lips, while* GRUSHA *looks around, in vain, for the child*) Why must you hold on to it at any price if it isn't yours? In days like these?

GRUSHA   He's mine. I brought him up.

THE COOK   Have you never thought what'd happen when she came back?

GRUSHA   At first I thought I'd give him to her. Then I thought she wouldn't come back.

THE COOK   And even a borrowed coat keeps a man warm, hm? (GRUSHA *nods*) I'll swear to anything for you. You're a decent girl. (*She sees the soldier* SIMON SHASHAVA *approaching*) You've done wrong by Simon, though. I've been talking with him. He just can't understand.

GRUSHA (*unaware of* SIMON's *presence*)   Right now I can't be bothered whether he understands or not!

THE COOK   He knows the child isn't yours, but you married and not free "til death do you part"—he can't understand *that*.

(GRUSHA *sees* SIMON *and greets him*)

SIMON (*gloomily*)   I wish the lady to know I will swear I am the father of the child.

GRUSHA (*low*)   Thank you, Simon.

SIMON   At the same time I wish the lady to know my hands are not tied—nor are hers.

THE COOK   You needn't have said that. You know she's married.

SIMON   It needs no rubbing in.

(*Enter an* IRONSHIRT)

THE IRONSHIRT   Where's the judge? Has anyone seen the judge?

ANOTHER IRONSHIRT (*stepping forward*)   The judge isn't here yet. Nothing but a bed and a pitcher in the whole house!

(*Exeunt* IRONSHIRTS)

THE COOK   I hope nothing has happened to him. With any other judge you'd have about as much chance as a chicken has teeth.

GRUSHA (*who has turned away and covered her face*) Stand in front of me. I shouldn't have come to Nuka. If I run into the Ironshirt, the one I hit over the head . . .

(*She screams. An* IRONSHIRT *had stopped and, turning his back, had been listening to her. He now wheels around. It is the* CORPORAL, *and he has a huge scar across his face*)

THE IRONSHIRT (*in the gateway*) What's the matter, Shotta? Do you know her?

THE CORPORAL (*after staring for some time*) No.

THE IRONSHIRT She's the one who's stolen the Abashwili child, or so they say. If you know anything about it you can make some money, Shotta.

(*Exit the* CORPORAL, *cursing*)

THE COOK Was it him? (GRUSHA *nods*) I think he'll keep his mouth shut, or he'd be admitting he was after the child.

GRUSHA I'd almost forgotten him.

(*Enter the* GOVERNOR'S WIFE, *followed by the* ADJUTANT *and* TWO LAWYERS)

THE GOVERNOR'S WIFE At least there are no common people here, thank God. I can't stand their smell. It always gives me migraine.

THE FIRST LAWYER Madam, I must ask you to be careful what you say until we have another judge.

THE GOVERNOR'S WIFE But I didn't say anything, Illo Shuboladze. I love the people with their simple straightforward minds. It's only that their smell brings on my migraine.

THE SECOND LAWYER There won't be many spectators. The whole population is sitting at home behind locked doors because of the riots on the outskirts of town.

THE GOVERNOR'S WIFE (*looking at* GRUSHA) Is that the creature?

THE FIRST LAWYER Please, most gracious Natella Abashwili, abstain from invective until it is certain the Grand Duke appointed a new judge, and we're rid of the present one, who's about the lowest fellow ever seen in a judge's gown. Things are all set to move, you see.

(*Enter* IRONSHIRTS *from the courtyard*)

THE COOK Her Grace would pull your hair out on the spot if she didn't know Azdak is for the poor. He goes by the face.

(IRONSHIRTS *begin fastening a rope to a beam.* AZDAK, *in chains, is led in, followed by* SHAUWA, *also in chains. The three farmers bring up the rear*)

AN IRONSHIRT Trying to run away, were you? (*He strikes* AZDAK)

ONE FARMER Off with his judge's gown before we string him up!

(IRONSHIRTS *and* FARMERS *tear off* AZDAK'S *gown. His torn underwear is visible. Then someone kicks him*)

AN IRONSHIRT (*pushing him into someone else*) If you want a heap of justice, here it is!

(*Accompanied by shouts of* "You take it!" *and* "Let me have him, brother!" *they throw* AZDAK *back and forth until he collapses. Then he is lifted up and dragged under the noose*)

THE GOVERNOR'S WIFE (*who, during this* "Ball game," *has clapped her hands hysterically*) I disliked that man from the moment I first saw him.

AZDAK (*covered with blood, panting*) I can't see. Give me a rag.

AN IRONSHIRT What is it you want to see?

AZDAK You, you dogs! (*He wipes the blood out of his eyes with his shirt*) Good morning, dogs! How goes it, dogs! How's the dog world? Does it smell good? Got another boot for me to lick? Are you back at each other's throats, dogs?

(*Accompanied by a* CORPORAL, *a dust-covered* RIDER *enters. He takes some documents from a leather case, looks at them, then interrupts*)

THE RIDER Stop! I bring a dispatch from the Grand Duke, containing the latest appointments.

THE CORPORAL (*bellowing*) Atten—shun!

THE RIDER Of the new judge it says: "We appoint a man whom we have to thank for saving a life indispensable to the country's welfare—a certain Azdak of Nuka." Which is he?

SHAUWA (*pointing*) That's him, Your Excellency.

THE CORPORAL (*bellowing*) What's going on here?

AN IRONSHIRT I beg to report that His Honor Azdak was already His Honor Azdak, but on these farmers' denunciation was pronounced the Grand Duke's enemy.

THE CORPORAL (*pointing at the farmers*) March them off! (*They are marched off. They bow all the time*) See to it that His Honor Azdak is exposed to no more violence.

(*Exeunt* RIDER *and* CORPORAL)

THE COOK (*to* SHAUWA) She clapped her hands! I hope he saw it!

THE FIRST LAWYER It's a catastrophe.

(AZDAK *has fainted. Coming to, he is dressed again in judge's robes. He walks, swaying, toward the* IRONSHIRTS)

AN IRONSHIRT What does Your Honor desire?

AZDAK Nothing, fellow dogs, or just an occasional boot to lick. (*to* SHAUWA) I pardon you. (*He is unchained*) Get me some red wine, the sweet kind. (SHAUWA *stumbles off*) Get out of here, I've got to judge a case. (*Exeunt* IRONSHIRTS. SHAUWA *returns with a pitcher of wine*. AZDAK *gulps it down*) Something for my backside. (SHAUWA *brings the Statute Book, puts it on the judge's chair*. AZDAK *sits on it*) I accept. (*The prosecutors, among whom a worried council has been held, smile with relief. They whisper*)

THE COOK Oh dear!

SIMON A well can't be filled with dew, they say.

THE LAWYERS (*approaching* AZDAK, *who stands up, expectantly*) A quite ridiculous case, Your Honor. The accused has abducted a child and refuses to hand it over.

AZDAK (*stretching out his hand, glancing at* GRUSHA) A most attractive person. (*He fingers the money, then sits down, satisfied*) I declare the proceedings open and demand the whole truth. (*to* GRUSHA) Especially from you.

THE FIRST LAWYER High Court of Justice! Blood, as the popular saying goes, is thicker than water. This old adage . . .

AZDAK (*interrupting*) The Court wants to know the lawyers' fee.

THE FIRST LAWYER (*surprised*) I beg your pardon? (AZDAK, *smiling, rubs his thumb and index finger*) Oh, I see. Five hundred piasters, Your Honor, to answer the Court's somewhat unusual question.

AZDAK Did you hear? The question is unusual. I ask it because I listen in quite a different way when I know you're good.

THE FIRST LAWYER (*bowing*) Thank you, Your Honor. High Court of Justice, of all ties the ties of blood are strongest. Mother and child—is there a more intimate relationship? Can one tear a child from its mother? High Court of Justice, she has conceived it in the holy ecstasies of love. She has carried it in her womb. She has fed it with her blood. She has borne it with pain. High Court of Justice, it has been observed that even the wild tigress, robbed of her young, roams restless through the mountains, shrunk to a shadow. Nature herself . . .

AZDAK (*interrupting, to* GRUSHA) What's your answer to all this and anything else the lawyer might have to say?

GRUSHA He's mine.

AZDAK Is that all? I hope you can prove it. Why should I assign the child to you in any case?

GRUSHA I brought him up like the priest says "according to my best knowledge and conscience." I always found him something to eat. Most of the time he had a roof over his head. And I went to such trouble for him. I had expenses too. I didn't look out for my own comfort. I brought the child up to be friendly with everyone, and from the beginning taught him to work. As well as he could, that is. He's still very little.

THE FIRST LAWYER Your Honor, it is significant that the girl herself doesn't claim any tie of blood between her and the child.

AZDAK The Court takes note of that.

THE FIRST LAWYER Thank you, Your Honor. And now permit a woman bowed in sorrow—who has already lost her husband and now has also to fear the loss of her child—to address a few words to you. The gracious Natella Abashwili is . . .

THE GOVERNOR'S WIFE (*quietly*) A most cruel fate, Sir, forces me to describe to you the tortures of a bereaved mother's soul, the anxiety, the sleepless nights, the . . .

THE SECOND LAWYER (*bursting out*) It's outrageous the way this woman is being treated. Her own husband's palace is closed to her! The revenue of her estates is blocked! And she is cold-bloodedly told that it's tied to the heir. She can't do anything without that child. She can't even pay her lawyers!! (*to the* FIRST LAWYER, *who, desperate about this outburst, makes frantic gestures to keep him from speaking*) Dear Illo Shuboladze, surely it can be divulged now that the Abashwili estates are at stake?

THE FIRST LAWYER Please, Honored Sandro Oboladze! We agreed . . . (*to* AZDAK) Of course it is correct that the trial will also decide if our noble client can dispose of the Abashwili estates, which are rather extensive. I say "also" advisedly, for in the foreground stands the human tragedy of a mother, as Natella Abashwili very properly explained in the first words of her moving statement. Even if Michael Abashwili were not heir to the estates, he would still be the dearly beloved child of my client.

AZDAK Stop! The Court is touched by the mention of estates. It's a proof of human feeling.

THE SECOND LAWYER Thanks, Your Honor. Dear Illo Shuboladze, we can prove in any case that the woman who took the child is not the child's mother. Permit me to lay before the Court the bare facts. High Court of Justice, by an unfortunate chain of circumstances, Michael Abashwili was left behind on that

Easter Sunday while his mother was making her escape. Grusha, a palace kitchen maid, was seen with the baby . . .

THE COOK   All her mistress was thinking of was what dresses she'd take along!

THE SECOND LAWYER (*unmoved*)   Nearly a year later Grusha turned up in a mountain village with a baby and there entered into the state of matrimony with . . .

AZDAK   How did you get to that mountain village?

GRUSHA   On foot, Your Honor. And it was mine.

SIMON   I am the father, Your Honor.

THE COOK   I used to look after it for them, Your Honor. For five piasters.

THE SECOND LAWYER   This man is engaged to Grusha, High Court of Justice: his testimony is not trustworthy.

AZDAK   Are you the man she married in the mountain village.

SIMON   No, Your Honor, she married a peasant.

AZDAK (*to* GRUSHA)   Why? (*pointing at* SIMON)   Is he no good in bed? Tell the truth.

GRUSHA   We didn't get that far. I married because of the baby. So he'd have a roof over his head. (*pointing at* SIMON)   He was in the war, Your Honor.

AZDAK   And now he wants you back again, huh?

SIMON   I wish to state in evidence . . .

GRUSHA (*angrily*)   I am no longer free, Your Honor.

AZDAK   And the child, you claim, comes from whoring? (GRUSHA *doesn't answer*)   I'm going to ask you a question: What kind of child is it? Is it a ragged little bastard or from a well-to-do family?

GRUSHA (*angrily*)   He's just an ordinary child.

AZDAK   I mean—did he have refined features from the beginning?

GRUSHA   He had a nose on his face.

AZDAK   A very significant comment! It has been said of me that I went out one time and sniffed at a rosebush before rendering a verdict—tricks like that are needed nowadays. Well, I'll make it short, and not listen to any more lies. (*to* GRUSHA)   Especially not yours. (*to all the accused*)   I can imagine what you've cooked up to cheat me! I know you people. You're swindlers.

GRUSHA (*suddenly*)   I can understand your wanting to cut it short, now I've seen what you accepted!

AZDAK   Shut up! Did I accept anything from you?

GRUSHA (*while the* COOK *tries to restrain her*)   I haven't got anything.

AZDAK   True. Quite true. From starvelings I never get a thing. I might just as well starve, myself. You want justice, but do you want to pay for it, hm? When you go to a butcher you know you have to pay, but you people go to a judge as if you were going to a funeral supper.

SIMON (*loudly*)   When the horse was shod, the horse-fly held out its leg, as the saying is.

AZDAK (*eagerly accepting the challenge*)   Better a treasure in manure than a stone in a mountain stream.

SIMON   A fine day. Let's go fishing, said the angler to the worm.

AZDAK   I'm my own master, said the servant, and cut off his foot.

SIMON   I love you as a father, said the Czar to the peasants, and had the Czarevitch's head chopped off.

AZDAK   A fool's worst enemy is himself.

SIMON   However, a fart has no nose.

AZDAK   Fined ten piasters for indecent language in court! That'll teach you what justice is.

GRUSHA (*furiously*)   A fine kind of justice! You play fast and loose with us because we don't talk as refined as that crowd with their lawyers!

AZDAK   That's true. You people are too dumb. It's only right you should get it in the neck.

GRUSHA   You want to hand the child over to her, and she wouldn't even know how to keep it dry, she's so "refined"! You know about as much about justice as I do!

AZDAK   There's something in that. I'm an ignorant man. Haven't even a decent pair of pants under this gown. Look! With me, everything goes for food and drink—I was educated at a convent. Incidentally, I'll fine you ten piasters for contempt of court. And you're a very silly girl, to turn me against you, instead of making eyes at me and wiggling your backside a little to keep me in a good temper. Twenty piasters!

GRUSHA   Even if it was thirty, I'd tell you what I think of your justice, you drunken onion! (*incoherently*)   How dare you talk to me like the cracked Isaiah on the church window? As if you were somebody? For you weren't born to this. You weren't born to rap your own mother on the knuckles if she swipes a little bowl of salt someplace. Aren't you ashamed of yourself when you see how I tremble before you? You've made yourself their servant so no one will take their houses from them—houses they had stolen! Since when have houses belonged to the bedbugs? But you're on the watch, or they couldn't drag our men into their wars! You bribe-taker! (AZDAK *half gets up, starts beaming. With his little hammer he half-heartedly knocks on the table as if to get silence. As* GRUSHA's *scolding continues, he only beats time with his hammer*) I've no respect for you. No more than for a thief or a bandit with a knife! You can do what you want. You can take the child away from me, a hundred against one, but I tell you one thing: only extortioners should be chosen for a profession like yours, and men who rape children! As punishment! Yes, let *them* sit in judgment on their fellow creatures. It is worse than to hang from the gallows.

AZDAK (*sitting down*) Now it'll be thirty! And I won't go on squabbling with you —we're not in a tavern. What'd happen to my dignity as a judge? Anyway, I've lost interest in your case. Where's the couple who wanted a divorce? (*To* SHAUWA) Bring 'em in. This case is adjourned for fifteen minutes.

THE FIRST LAWYER (*to the* GOVERNOR'S WIFE) Even without using the rest of the evidence, Madam, we have the verdict in the bag.

THE COOK (*to* GRUSHA) You've gone and spoiled your chances with him. You won't get the child now.

THE GOVERNOR'S WIFE Shalva, my smelling salts!

(*Enter a very* OLD COUPLE)

AZDAK I accept. (*The* OLD COUPLE *don't understand*) I hear you want to be divorced. How long have you been together.

THE OLD WOMAN Forty years, Your Honor.

AZDAK And why do you want a divorce?

THE OLD MAN We don't like each other, Your Honor.

AZDAK Since when?

THE OLD WOMAN Oh, from the very beginning, Your Honor.

AZDAK I'll think about your request and render my verdict when I'm through with the other case. (SHAUWA *leads them back*) I need the child. (*He beckons* GRUSHA *to and bends not unkindly toward her*) I've noticed you have a soft spot for justice. I don't believe he's your child, but if he *were* yours, woman, wouldn't you want him to be rich? You'd only have to say he wasn't yours, and he'd have a palace and many horses in his stable and many beggars on his doorstep and many soldiers in his service and many petitioners in his courtyard, wouldn't he? What do you say—don't you want him to be rich?

(GRUSHA *is silent*)

THE STORY TELLER
Hear now what the angry girl thought
    but did not say:

Had he golden shoes to wear
He'd be cruel as a bear.
Evil would his life disgrace.
He'd laugh in my face.

Carrying a heart of flint
Is too troublesome a stint.
Being powerful and bad
Is hard on a lad.

Then let hunger be his foe!
Hungry men and women, no.
Let him fear the darksome night
But not daylight!

AZDAK I think I understand you, woman.

GRUSHA (*suddenly and loudly*) I won't give him up. I've raised him, and he knows me.

(*Enter* SHAUWA *with the* CHILD)

THE GOVERNOR'S WIFE It's in rags!

GRUSHA That's not true. But I wasn't given time to put his good shirt on.

THE GOVERNOR'S WIFE It must have been in a pigsty.

GRUSHA (*furiously*) I'm not a pig, but there are some who are! Where did you leave your baby?

THE GOVERNOR'S WIFE I'll show you, you vulgar creature! (*She is about to throw herself on* GRUSHA, *but is restrained by her* LAWYERS) She's a criminal, she must be whipped. Immediately!

THE SECOND LAWYER (*holding his hand over her mouth*) Natella Abashwili, you promised . . . Your Honor, the plaintiff's nerves . . .

AZDAK Plaintiff and defendant! The Court has listened to your case, and has come to no decision as to who the real mother is, therefore, I, the judge, am obliged to *choose* a mother for the child. I'll make a test. Shauwa, get a piece of chalk and draw a circle on the floor. (SHAUWA *does so*) Now place the child in the center. (SHAUWA *puts* MICHAEL, *who smiles at* GRUSHA, *in the center of the circle*) Stand near the circle, both of you. (*The* GOVERNOR'S WIFE *and* GRUSHA *step up to the circle*) Now each of you take the child by one hand. (*They do so*) The true mother is she who can pull the child out of the circle.

THE SECOND LAWYER (*quickly*) High Court of Justice, I object! The fate of the great Abashwili estates, which are tied to the child, as the heir, should not be made dependent on such a doubtful duel. In addition, my client does not command the strength of this person, who is accustomed to physical work.

AZDAK She looks pretty well fed to me. Pull! (*The* GOVERNOR'S WIFE *pulls the* CHILD *out of the circle on her side;* GRUSHA *has let go and stands aghast*) What's the matter with you? You didn't pull!

GRUSHA I didn't hold on to him.

THE FIRST LAWYER (*congratulating the* GOVERNOR'S WIFE) What did I say! The ties of blood!

GRUSHA (*running to* AZDAK) Your Honor, I take back everything I said against you. I ask your forgiveness. But could I keep him till he can speak all the words. He knows a few.

AZDAK Don't influence the Court. I bet you only know about twenty words yourself. All right, I'll make the test once more, just to be certain. (*The* TWO WOMEN *take up their positions again*) Pull!

(*Again* GRUSHA *lets go of the* CHILD)

GRUSHA (*in despair*) I brought him up! Shall I also tear him to pieces? I can't!

AZDAK (*rising*) And in this manner the Court has established the true mother. (*to* GRUSHA) Take your child and be off. I advise you not to stay in the city with him. (*to the* GOVERNOR'S WIFE) And you disappear before I fine you for fraud. Your estates fall to the city. They'll be converted into a playground for the children. They need one, and I've decided it shall be called after me: Azdak's Garden. (*The* GOVERNOR'S WIFE *has fainted and is carried out by the* LAWYERS *and the* ADJUTANT. GRUSHA *stands motionless.* SHAUWA *leads the child toward her*) Now I'll take off this judge's gown—it has grown too hot for me. I'm not cut out for a hero. In token of farewell I invite you all to a little dance outside on the meadow. Oh, I'd almost forgotten something in my excitement . . . to sign the divorce decree.

(*Using the judge's chair as a table, he writes something on a piece of paper, and prepares to leave. Dance music has started*)

SHAUWA (*having read what is on the paper*) But that's not right. You've not divorced the old people. You've divorced Grusha!

AZDAK Have I divorced the wrong couple? What a pity! And I never retract! If I did, how could we keep order in the land? (*to

the OLD COUPLE) I'll invite you to my party instead. You don't mind dancing with each other, do you? (*to* GRUSHA *and* SIMON) I've got forty piasters coming from *you*.

SIMON (*pulling out his purse*) Cheap at the price, Your Honor. And many thanks.

AZDAK (*pocketing the cash*) I'll need this.

GRUSHA (*to* MICHAEL) So we'd better leave the city tonight, Michael? (*to* SIMON) You like him?

SIMON With my respects, I like him.

GRUSHA Now I can tell you: I took him because on that Easter Sunday, I got engaged to you. So he's a child of love. Michael, let's dance.

(*She dances with* MICHAEL, SIMON *dances with the* COOK, *the* OLD COUPLE *with each other.* AZDAK *stands lost in thought. The dancers soon hide him from view. Occasionally he is seen, but less and less as* MORE COUPLES *join the dance*)

THE STORY TELLER

And after that evening Azdak vanished and was never seen again.
The people of Grusinia did not forget him but long remembered
The period of his judging as a brief golden age
Almost an age of justice.

(*All the couples dance off.* AZDAK *has disappeared*)

But you, you who have listened to the Story of the Chalk Circle,
Take note what men of old concluded:
That what there is shall go to those who are good for it,
Children to the motherly, that they prosper,
Carts to good drivers, that they be driven well,
The valley to the waterers, that it yield fruit.

TRANSLATOR'S NOTE

This adaptation is based on the German MS of 1946. A German version very close to this MS was published in a supplement to *Sinn und Form*, 1949. My English text has now appeared in three versions. Maja Apelman collaborated on the first one (copyrighted 1947, 1948). The second and third were respectively copyrighted in 1961 and 1963.

Max Frisch

1911-

ON THE NATURE OF THE THEATRE

Excerpts from the Diary of Max Frisch

Among those concepts which I use with partiality, without knowing precisely what they mean, which need mean nothing at all, but which might have a meaning, there belongs the concept of the theatrical.

Wherein does it exist?

On the stage there stands a human being, I see his physical form, his costume, his countenance, his gestures, as well as his wider surroundings, all of them things which, by chance, I do not have in a reading, at least not as sensible perceptions. And then something else is added: speech. I do not merely hear noises, in keeping with sensible perceptions, but speech. I hear what this human being says, which is to say that a second thing is added, another image, an image of another sort. He says: The night is like a cathedral! Besides that manifest image I also receive a verbal image, one which I gain not through perception, but through a mental image, through fancy, through imagination, evoked through the word. And I possess them both simultaneously: sensible perception and imagination. Their playing together, their relation to one another, the sphere of tension which is produced between them, this, it seems to me, is what one might designate as being the theatrical.

°   °   °

Hamlet with the skull of Yorick:—
When this scene is narrated one must con-

"On the Nature of the Theatre" by Max Frisch, translated by Carl Richard Mueller, reprinted by permission of the translator, *The Tulane Drama Review,* and Suhrkamp Verlag, Berlin and Frankfurt am Main.

ceive of both things, must imagine them both, the skull in the living hand of Hamlet and the jokes of the dead Yorick, of which Hamlet reminds himself. The narration, in opposition to the theatre, rests wholly and completely in language, and everything which the narrator has to impart reaches me on a single plane: namely that of imagination. The theatre performs in an essentially different way: the skull, which is only an object, the grave, the spade, all these things I already possess through sensible perception, involuntarily, in front of me, inevitably at every moment, while my imagination, wholly reserved for the words of Hamlet, has only to call up the vanished life, which it is capable of doing all the more intelligibly, since I use it for no other purpose. The past and the present, the once and the now: divided between imagination and sensible perception. . . . The poet of the theatre therefore uses two antennas in playing with me, and it is evident that the one, a skull, and the other, the jokes of a jokester, are of little significance in and of themselves; the complete statement of this scene, everything about it which moves us, rests in the relationship between these two images, and only herein.

°   °   °

It can be said of many a playwright who fails on the stage, that he possesses a more individual, a stronger, a more intrinsic language than Gerhart Hauptmann; nevertheless he drowns on stage, while a Hauptmann, whose magic is scarcely to be sought in individualistic language, is buoyed-up by this very same stage, much to our amazement. It seems as though language for the playwright were, after all, only a part. The other part, the sensibly perceptible part, which belongs essentially to the theatre, has the ability to be present even when the playwright forgets it, to be powerful even when the playwright fails to use it—to be against him, and indeed so much so, that no language, none whatever, may save him.

The most eminent example that language alone cannot bring this off is of course the second part of *Faust*, that felicitous marriage of the German language, which is playable only here and there: not because the statements of this poem are too exalted—Shakespeare is also exalted—but because they are not theatrical.

*   *   *

Theatrical diagnosis: what I see and what I hear—have they any relationship to one another? If not, if perhaps the statement lies exclusively in the word, so that in reality I could close my eyes, then the stage is fallow, and what, in this case, I see on the stage, when of course I do not close my eyes, is not a theatrical situation, but a superfluous sight, an apparently meaningless meeting of speakers, epic, lyric or dramatic.

(The dramatic, that dialectical wrestling match, wherein one may here and there perceive the sole possible theatre or at least the quintessence of the theatre, is desired by the stage only insofar as the stage actually always possesses something of the wrestling ring, of the arena, of the circus ring, of the public courtroom.)

*   *   *

The multiplication table of the clown: that at the moment when he appears heroic and respectable he stumbles over his own feet—I read once that the essence of the comic resides in the disproportionate, the inconsistent, the incongruous. In the case of the clown: the incongruous resides not within his utterance, but between his utterance and our perception. Self-confidence is not comical, stumbling is not comical; they are comical only when seen together. The incongruous, the disproportionate, which constitute the essence of all things comic, is divided between word and image, and particularly the theatrically comic—from the clumsy to the refined, from the clown to Shakespeare: we hear how blissful and tender are the phantasies of Titania in love, we hear her magnificent words, which are anything but witty, and we smile with delight because at the same time we see how with these selfsame sweet words, which enrapture us as well, she wins nothing more than the head of an ass—we see it.

*   *   *

The overwhelming aspect in Shakespeare is the way in which the situation (who stands opposite whom) is generally already composed as such, it is already significant as situation, so that nothing remains for the word to do but what is the most delightful of all: to reap, to pluck, to reveal the significance which is already present.

Who stands opposite whom.

The style itself of the classical plays indicates how essential this question is, even in the printed texts every entrance is noted, whereas very little else. Scene Ten: The King, the two Murderers. This is what is perceptible when the curtain rises, and when the two Murderers have their instructions, so that they leave the King alone, that which is perceptible changes; every entrance is a caesura. The King alone! If he says something now which reveals the burden of his increasing solitude, then it has the whole stage to itself, the emptiness of the stage—congruity between the outer and the inner situation. Another theatrical realization is the contrapuntal: Macbeth experiences the burden of his guilty solitude during a festive social gathering, he alone sees the ghost of Banquo, his solitude becomes manifest to such an extent that all his words which he wants to be sociable are powerless, the gathering disappears, only Macbeth and his Lady remain, each guilty in his own degree; again the entire working of a scene is visibly outlined, the ghost of the murdered Banquo says nothing—which is to say: I do not look in vain at the stage.

*   *   *

In the second play of Friedrich Duerrenmatt [*Der Blinde*] . . . there exists the following scene: a blind man, who does not perceive the destruction of his duchy, believes that he is still living in his secure fortress. In his belief, in his imagination, he rules over an unscathed and spared land. Thus he sits in the midst of ruins, which he of course, being blind, cannot see, surrounded by all kinds of the dissolute rabble of war, mercenaries, prostitutes, robbers, pimps, who in wanting to make a fool of the blind duke now deride his belief while allowing themselves to be received as dukes and generals, the prostitute, however, as a persecuted abbess. The blind duke addresses them in such a way as he imagines they deserve. We, however, see the repulsive individual whose blessing as abbess he believingly begs for—on his knees. . . . Model example of a theatrical situation: the statement resides wholly in the opposition between perception and imagination. Here the theatre can play alone.

*   *   *

In the Basel Museum there hangs a painting by Arnold Böcklin: *Odysseus and Calypso*, the relations between man and woman. He is in blue, she in red. She is in a hidden grotto, he on a projecting rock, his back towards her, as he looks out across the breadth of the open sea. . . . On my journey here I saw this painting again, without looking for it, and was amazed that the sea, the subject of his longing, is almost non-existent. There is only a tiny blue wedge of it. In my recollection it was a picture of the full sea—precisely because the sea is not shown. No theatre, anymore than a painting, is capable of showing the breadth of the sea. It must be left to the imagination. In Sartre there is a scene in which Zeus puts on airs concerning his starry firmament, in order to attract Orestes, the mortal, to a belief in the gods. Sartre does the only thing possible, he describes his starry firmament with words. Now if a director, as I have seen done, wants suddenly with these words to turn on a heaven of electric bulbs, thus wanting to make the stars sensible perceptions, then naturally the magic of the theatre is made a joke of; the starry firmament which Zeus has to describe is made so childish thereby that the scorn of the unbelieving Orestes is in itself made to seem foolish. The backbone of the scene is broken—despite good actors—broken by a brainstorm which fails to appreciate the limitations of the theatre.

The field of action is always the human soul! All things are subject to its decrees. One of these decrees: Compensation. If I perceive a dungeon, then the word which describes an open and cheerful landscape finds me particularly responsive; the sight of Calypso housed in a grotto, which wants to hold me there, makes me particularly responsive to each tiny word which speaks of the open sea and foreign coasts; my imagination, which desires this, answers my longing. Or if I perceive a happy and high-spirited festival, a voice which mentions death will have particular power; the imagination which desires it answers my fear. The theatrical relationship—the opposition between perception and imagination—will be particularly compelling, particularly productive, particularly positive, if it follows the wants of the human soul, if, by way of example, it is composed of compensation.

*   *   *

The enticement of the theatre for even the non-dramatic poet, perhaps the lyric poet: the stage will supply him, if he masters it, with a heightened background for the word.

*   *   *

No play will be constantly theatrical. It is scarcely important as regards its theatrical potency, whether it is often theatrical in its development. The realization of the theatrical, I believe, always concerns the infrequent, the rare, the eye on the surface of a face. What may be decisive is whether the essential or only the accessory statements become theatrical. In the latter case, where the theatrical remains incidental, accessory, eccentric, every production, even the consummate one, will, without fail, signify a distortion, a falsifying displacement of accent. The theatre, the playwright will then say, is in my opinion a terrible means whereby a word is made crude! Of course it is that, but it is not the fault of the theatre if such an occurrence, which never seems to destroy a Shakespeare, becomes more than what it is, that is, if it grows into distortion, disfigurement, misrepresentation, into a destruction of the poetic. It is not the fault of the theatre if the poet cannot make use of it. Whoever works for the stage and fails to use it will find the stage against him. By making use of the stage I mean: not writing *for* the stage, but *with* the stage.

*   *   *

I went to another rehersal today, and since I arrived an hour too early I withdrew into a private box, which is dark as a confessional. Fortunately the stage was cleared and without wings, and I knew nothing of the play which was to be rehearsed. There is nothing so stimulating as nothing, at least now and then. Just by chance a worker crossed the stage, a young man in brown overalls; he shakes his head, remains standing and scolds another, whom I cannot see, and the speech which sounds from the stage is utterly conventional, anything but literary—shortly thereafter an actress appears eating an apple, while with her coat and hat on she crosses the empty stage; she says good morning to the worker, nothing further, and then again the silence, the empty stage, the occasional rumble of a streetcar passing outside. This tiny scene, repeated a thousandfold on the street outside, why is it so different here, so much more powerful? These two people, just as they crossed the stage, had a being, a presence, a destiny, which naturally I know nothing of, nevertheless it was here, even if only secretly, it had a presence which filled all this large space. I must note, too, that there was the customary work-light, a light pale as ashes, devoid of magic, devoid of that so-called atmosphere, and so the entire impression produced was that nothing else existed save this little scene; all that surrounded it was night; for a moment's time there existed only a stage-hand, scolding, and a young actress, yawning and going into the checkroom; two human beings, who meet in space, who can walk and stand upright, who have resounding voices; and then everything is past, inexplicably, as if a human being had died, inexplicable that he ever existed, that he ever stood in front of us for us to see, that he spoke, conventionally and without consequence, but nevertheless stimulatingly.

There is something in this small event which seems significant to me, it also reminds me of the experience of taking an empty frame and hanging it tentatively on a bare wall, in a room perhaps in which we may have lived for a number of years: now, however, for the first time, we notice how the wall is really plastered. It is an empty frame which compels us to look. Our reason, of course, tells us that the plaster which I have framed can be no different from that on the rest of the wall; as a matter of fact, it is not the least bit different; but it becomes evident, it is there, it speaks. Why then are pictures framed? Why do they have a different effect when we release them from their frames? It is simply that they no longer set themselves off from the contingencies of their surroundings; for once removed from their frames, they are suddenly no longer secure; they no longer depend wholly on themselves; one has the feeling that they are falling apart, and one feels somewhat disillusioned in the fact; they suddenly appear worse; worse, that is, than they are. The frame, when it is there, severs the painting from nature; it is a window into an utterly different sphere, a window into the spirit, where the painted flower is no longer a flower which can fade, but the essence of all flowers. The frame places it beyond time. To that extent there is an exciting difference between the surface lying within a frame, and the surface which, as it were, is endless. It is a bad artist indeed who depends on a frame to rescue his work; it is not meant that everything, merely because it takes place within a frame, will assume the significance of a symbol; yet it assumes, whether it wills it or not, the claim to such a significance. It says: Look at me; here

you will see something worth looking at, which exists beyond chance and impermanence; here you will find a lasting significance, not the flower that fades, but the likeness of all flowers, or as has already been said: the symbol.

All this holds good for the frame of the stage as well, and naturally there would be other examples which would explain, at least here and there, the stimulating impression which even the empty stage makes; one need only think of those display-windows which exhibit whole supplies of wares, display-windows which could never attract our attention, and then of those other windows which circumscribe themselves to a modest peephole: we see there a single watch, a single bracelet, a single necktie. And this unusual thing appears to us from the very first to have value. There are small windows such as these, which at times are like tiny stages, one enjoys standing in front of them, looking into another world, which at least gives the appearance of having value. And its relation to the real stage lies in this: that on the stage I do not see thousands of fools, but only one, whom I can still love, not thousands of lovers, whose loves with their interminable protestations become obnoxious, but two or three, whose vows we can take as seriously as our own. There is profit in looking at them. I see people; I do not see millions of workers. In doing so, I would, unfortunately, no longer see the individual person. Rather, I see this individual who represents the millions and who alone is real: I see a stagehand, who scolds, and a young actress, who eats an apple and says good morning. I see what I would not otherwise see: two human beings.

*   *   *

One must naturally, having spoken of the frame of the stage, also speak of the stage's apron, which is a part of every such frame, and, indeed, the critical part. A stage without an apron would be a gate. And it is precisely that which it does not want to be. It keeps us from entering. It is a window through which we are allowed only to look. As part of a window it is called a sill, and there is a whole series of arrangements which serves that single purpose. All kinds of pedestals are possible. The concern is always with the separation of image and nature. There is a group by Rodin, the famous *Citizens of Calais*, which was conceived of without a base; the intention obviously lay in this, that the image presented by those bravely sacrificing Citizens of Calais was meant to be taken up into everyday life, as an example, and therefore it was placed on the same level as the living, who were to follow them, on the pavement of a public plaza. This is a special case, but for all that, it testifies in its own way, in the desire to avoid the pedestal, to the effectiveness and importance of this arrangement. It is well known that the temples of antiquity, too, stood on a pedestal of three or five or seven steps; steps are made for the precise purpose of being tread upon, as an aid for one who might hesitate at the thought of reaching the top elevation; it is only when the attempt is made that one realizes the steps are far too high; one may clamber up them, but a dignified gait is not possible, a gait with which one approaches a temple, and such an approach is indeed the very opposite of that which the pedestal desires. It severs the temple from us; but not only from us, rather from the countryside as well, from the contingencies of the region; it does not trouble itself over the incline of a hill, as, for example, we do when we build a country house. There it is our aim to nestle our house into that particular countryside in such a way that would not be possible anywhere else, but only in this solitary spot. That is: we recognize our limitations, and we make the most of them. There is a single Greek temple from the Golden Age which is adapted to the countryside, which plays with the summit on which it is placed, the Erechtheum on the Acropolis. All others, however, have the pedestal, which disregards the countryside, which dissociates the temple from the contingencies of the solitary countryside, which raises it above all earthly restrictions, which places it in another sphere: in the sphere of the Absolute.

Is this not universally the situation?

Time and again there are playwrights who reject the limits of the stage's apron; there is no lack of examples of actors approaching the stage from the orchestra floor, or of an actor stepping onto the apron and speaking into the orchestra, as though there were no gulf there, of which the apron is only a weak symbol; I am thinking of Thornton Wilder, of the time when Sabina turns towards the spectator with the passionate plea that he give up his seat to the fire so that Mankind may be saved. Here, too, just as with Rodin's sculpture, an example is to be carried out into real life, since the artwork is placed on the same level on which the spectator himself stands and walks. The question is whether the example becomes more effective when it rejects its removal. At all events, it has, when we consider Sabin's appeal, the momentary gain of surprise; that it can only

be momentary is a fact which Wilder, too, realized: he has the curtain fall immediately thereafter. It serves as an exception rather than as a rule. Every gesture which rejects the limits of the apron loses in magic. It opens the locks, which is stimulating; but it is scarcely done so that thereby the artistic form can stream out into the chaos which it wants to change, rather chaos rushes into the sphere which we call by another name, into the sphere of poetry, and the poet who demolishes the apron surrenders himself.

Does he do so because it is a vogue?

Does he do so out of desperation?

Perhaps it is no accident that it was precisely Sabina who occurred to us as an example, Sabina, who, with her appeal across the apron, wants to save Mankind: the self-surrender of poetry, which recognizes its own weakness, which shows its own weakness, has about it something which suggests a final alarm, which is all it has left.

* * *

Yesterday again we went to a puppet-play, and after it was over we were permitted to go behind the small stage. It is a narrow room filled with stale air. We regarded with astonishment the hanging puppets, somehow incredulous whether they were really the same ones which had just enchanted us. Even the devil hangs on the batten now, shabbier than we had expected. During the play they have a completely different effect, always in keeping with the scene, always in keeping with the word, which they themselves neither speak nor hear. This is established through the changing incidence of light, through the various positions of the head, and so on. Somehow one remains undeceived while the father-puppet soaps his hands, washes them, dries them and tells of further plans. Or at least one is silently disconcerted with the way in which the puppets suddenly stare into a void, lifeless, senseless, as though they no longer recognize us. . . .

* * *

What astonishes us everytime:

How easy it is for marionettes to succeed in representing other-than-human beings, an earth-spirit, a goblin, monsters and fairies, dragons, spirits of air and that which the heart desires. It can even happen that such forms must appear on the large stage as well, long-tailed monkeys or an Ariel; in this, however, there is always the danger that it will become embarrassing, and at best the actors can only succeed in not becoming ludicrous; nevertheless, the hoped for effect, namely ultimate horror or supernatural delight, which is supposed to emanate from such other-than-human beings, can scarcely be attained by the stage as long as it is bound to the use of human actors. Marionettes could carry it off. There is much to be said for the fact that this puppet which represents a human being, and that other puppet which represents an earth-spirit, are made of the same stuff. This means that the marionette which represents the earth-spirit for us is equally as believable or as unbelievable as the other which we are to believe a human being. On the large stage, I think, we cannot believe in the earth-spirit, because he is no match for the human being: because the human being who plays opposite him is really a human being, who is by nature of flesh and blood. The other, the earth-spirit, in comparison with him, remains an image, a symbol. And therewith the scene, however admirably it may be acted, plays from the very start on two different planes, which are not believable in the same manner. In the puppet-play there is a single level of belief. It is the same as in the drama of antiquity with its use of masks: when Athena and Odysseus both wear masks, when they both remain equally improbable and symbolic, then we can believe in the goddess.

❀   ❀   ❀

Another thing which enthuses one about marionettes is their relation to the word. Whether one wills it or not, the word in a puppet-play is always heightened, so that it can never be confused with our everyday speech. It is supernatural, just because it is separated from the puppet, because it is filled with activity over and above it; to that end, it is a larger language than ever the wooden chest of the puppet could make it. It it more than the accompanying noises which daily emanate from our mouths. It is the word, which was in the beginning, the autocratic, the all-creating word. It is speech. The puppet-play cannot for one moment confuse itself with nature. There is one possibility only, namely the world of poetry; that remains its only sphere of action.

❀   ❀   ❀

The comparison with the theatre of antiquity, which also possessed these rigid masks, forces

itself upon us in many respects. Both theatres, the large and the small, operate through the means of an altered dimension. In the theatre of antiquity it was the mask wherewith one magnified figures, and later also with the cothurnus; in the puppet-play one reduces the figures. And the impression produced is essentially the same: we can no longer stand, shoulder to shoulder, beside the acting figures, nor should we be able to; on the contrary, the altered scale prohibits every such familiarity: we are here, and they are there, and whatever happens on the stage, we see across an irreconcilable distance, no matter whether this is achieved through magnification or through diminution. We then observe with amazement that the marionettes, the longer their play succeeds, become alive for us in a compelling sort of way; after a while we completely forget that they are smaller than we, dwarfs, and, indeed, dwarfs made of wood, whom we might catch up in our hand and cast from the play; we discover, we observe the proportions of all outward dimensions, including our own, and as long as their play is not interrupted through some prank or other, through some accident of gesture, which falls beyond the frame of the stage, and which thereby betrays that frame, just that long will the spirit of the thing remain unbound to any scale of measure. These wooden dwarfs, while playing, take possession, as it were, of our being. They become more real than we ourselves, and there are moments of true magic; we are, quite literally, beside ourselves.

And when it is all over:

How shabbily they hang there on the batten, now that they no longer are in possession of our being, now that we are again in possession of ourselves.

❀   ❀   ❀

Christ as a puppet?

I recall as a student seeing a puppet-play in which the Last Supper was represented. It was deeply affecting. It was holy to such a degree that it would be thoroughly impossible for any human actor, trying to simulate a Christ for us, even to approach it. A Christ of linden-wood, such as Marion [1] makes: if we consider a crucifix, then we will sense nothing blasphemous in the puppet; the puppet, in opposition to the human actor, meets us from the very first as form, as image, as a creation

---

[1] A contemporary Swiss sculptor.

of spirit, which alone is able to represent that which is Holy. The human being, even when he plays as image, always remains a man of flesh and blood. The puppet is wood, an honorable and a fine piece of wood, which never lays claim to the deceitful pretension of presenting an actual Christ, nor should we take it to be such; it is merely a symbol, a formula, a text, which signifies, without wanting to be that which it signifies. It is play, not deception; it is spiritual in such a way as only play can be.

Translated by Carl Richard Mueller

THE CHINESE WALL

Translated by James L. Rosenberg

CAST OF CHARACTERS

THE CONTEMPORARY
HWANG TI, *Emperor of China*
MEE LAN, *his daughter*
WU TSIANG, *a Chinese prince*
OLAN, *a Chinese mother*
THE MUTE, *her son*
SIU, *a servant*
DA HING YEN I, II, III, *Masters of the Revels*
FU CHU, *a Chinese executioner*
A HERALD, SOLDIERS, MANDARINS, WAITERS, EUNUCHS, JOURNALISTS

The Maskers:
ROMEO AND JULIET
NAPOLEON BONAPARTE
COLUMBUS
L'INCONNUE DE LA SEINE
PONTIUS PILATE
DON JUAN
BRUTUS
PHILIP OF SPAIN
CLEOPATRA
MARY STUART
A GENTLEMAN IN A TAIL COAT
A GENTLEMAN IN A CUTAWAY

Prologue

(THE CONTEMPORARY *steps forward in front of a drop curtain on which is painted in realistic style the Chinese Wall*)

THE CONTEMPORARY Ladies and gentlemen. You are looking at the Chinese Wall, the greatest edifice in the history of mankind. It measures (according to the encyclopedia) over ten thousand li, or—to express it more concretely—the distance between Berlin and New York. According to newspaper reports, the structure is in poor condition; recently, indeed, there has been talk of the government's tearing it down, on the ground that here, as it stands, it no longer serves any real purpose. The Chinese Wall (or, as the Chinese say, the Great

Wall), planned as a defensive rampart against the barbaric peoples from the steppes of Central Asia, is another one of these constantly repeated attempts to hold back time, to dam up history, and, as we know today, it has not succeeded. Time will not be held back. This great work was completed under the reign of the glorious Emperor Tsin She Hwang Ti, who tonight will personally appear on our stage. As for the remainder of that with which this evening's action is concerned, and so that no false expectations may be aroused, let me read to you the additional characters in our play (*He reads from a list*) Romeo and Juliet; Philip of Spain; Mee Lan, a Chinese princess; Pontius Pilate; L'Inconnue de la Seine; Alexander the Great—oh, yes, after a consultation with the author, we have changed that: we will present Napoleon instead (in this play, it really makes no difference, and we've got to remember our wardrobe)—so, Napoleon Bonaparte; Brutus; Don Juan Tenorio; Cleopatra; Christopher Columbus. (*Two Chinese figures,* OLAN *and* WANG, *mother and son, appear*) In addition, you will see: Miscellaneous People, Courtiers, Mandarins and Boards of Directors, A Waiter, An Executioner, Eunuchs, Newspaper Reporters—(*The two Chinese bow to him*) Yes—what is it?

OLAN   I am a Chinese farmer's wife. My name is Olan. I am the eternal mother who plays no part in the great history of the world.

THE CONTEMPORARY (*aside*)   Naturally, she says that now, because later, as we shall see, she will play a most decisive role.

OLAN   We live in the time of the Great Exalted Emperor, Tsin She Hwang Ti, called the Son of Heaven, he who is always in the right. We come from the land of Chau. We have been on this pilgrimage for a year now. Seven times we came through floods, thirty times we were seized by soldiers, ninety times we lost our way—because there *was* no way. Just look at my poor feet! However, you are an honest man, sir, we can see that, and if you tell us that we are in Nanking——

THE CONTEMPORARY   We are in Nanking.

OLAN   Wang! You hear? (WANG *nods*) Wang! We're in Nanking! Wang! (OLAN *embraces her son*)

THE CONTEMPORARY   Why are you crying?

OLAN   A whole year, sir, a long year——

THE CONTEMPORARY   You have been on this pilgrimage; I understand.

OLAN   Do you know the Yangtse-Kiang?

THE CONTEMPORARY   In my atlas, yes.

OLAN   A whole year's walking straight ahead, then a sharp left; and there you are—our land: a lovely place, sir, a fruitful place, you can believe me, plenty of work for us, plenty of crops for the Emperor. Oats and millet, rice and tobacco, bamboo, cotton, poppies, oh, and we have typhoons there, too, and apes and pheasants——

THE CONTEMPORARY   I understand. And you've just come here from there?

OLAN   We have come here from there.

THE CONTEMPORARY   What do you want in Nanking?

OLAN   Wang! You hear? He asks what we want in Nanking. Wang! He asks that. You hear? (WANG *laughs silently*) We want to see our Emperor!

THE CONTEMPORARY   Ah.

OLAN   Tsin She Hwang Ti, called the Son of Heaven, he who is always in the right. They say it isn't true.

THE CONTEMPORARY   What isn't true?

OLAN   They say it through the whole land.

THE CONTEMPORARY   What?

OLAN   They say he is no Son of Heaven.

THE CONTEMPORARY   But rather—?

OLAN   A blood-sucking leech.

THE CONTEMPORARY   Hm.

OLAN   A hangman, a murderer.

THE CONTEMPORARY   Hm.

OLAN
   "What do we count on the day of
      victory,
   We, the farmers and folk in the land?
   We count our dead, we count our
      dead,
   While you jingle your gold in your
      hand."

THE CONTEMPORARY   Hm. Hm.

OLAN   They go around singing it, you know.

THE CONTEMPORARY   Who does?

OLAN   Whoever has a voice. That is my son over there. My son is mute. He doesn't get it from me.

THE CONTEMPORARY   Mute?

OLAN   Perhaps it's just as well that he is mute. Really, my son, really! There's enough stupid talk in this world simply because people know how to talk. And what's the result? For forty years people have been saying things have got to change. They've got to get better. Justice will come. Peace will come. Have you heard the latest, sir?

THE CONTEMPORARY   I haven't yet spoken to anyone here in Nanking. (OLAN *whispers in his ear*) Min Ko?

OLAN   That's what they call him. The Voice of the People! But no one has ever seen him. Only his sayings are known. Now the Emperor wants to have him killed. Does that mean that men have been singing the truth for forty years? (*Drum rolls are heard*) Here they come!

(*A Chinese* HERALD *enters, along with a* SOLDIER *with a drum, a* SOLDIER *with a lance, a* SOLDIER *with a footstool for the* HERALD)

HERALD   "We, Tsin She Hwang Ti, called the Great Exalted Emperor, the Son of Heaven, he who is always in the right, announce to the dutiful people of our realm the following proclamation: (*roll of drums*) Victory is ours. The barbarian hounds of the steppes, our last enemies, have been smashed! The barbarian hounds of the steppes lie, as promised, in the lake of their own blood. The world is ours." (*drum roll*)

OLAN   Heil. Heil. Heil.

(*The* HERALD *looks at* THE CONTEMPORARY *and waits*)

THE CONTEMPORARY   Heil. (*drum roll*)

HERALD   "People of our realm! There remains one last adversary today in our land, a single man, who calls himself the Voice of the People: Min Ko. We will seek him out and find him, even to the remotest corner of our land. His head on the block! And to anyone who is caught repeating his sayings, the same thing will happen: *His* head on the block!"

(*drum roll*) Long live our Great Exalted Emperor, Tsin She Hwang Ti, called the Son of Heaven, he who is always in the right.

OLAN   Heil. Heil. Heil.

(*The* HERALD *looks at* THE CONTEMPORARY *and waits*)

THE CONTEMPORARY   Heil.

(*The* HERALD *and the three* SOLDIERS *withdraw as they came, perfectly in step, like mechanical figures*)

OLAN   You hear, sir?

THE CONTEMPORARY   Min Ko, the Voice of the People—his head on the block—. It sounds like a crisis for that party in power, which has conquered everything—except the truth. I understand.

OLAN   Come, my son, come!

THE CONTEMPORARY   One more question—

OLAN   I don't know anything, sir, I don't know anything! Come, my son. And thank God you are mute! (OLAN *and* WANG *exit*)

THE CONTEMPORARY   So much for the situation in Nanking. You are going to ask, ladies and gentlemen, what is meant by all this? Where is this Nanking today? And who, today, is Hwang Ti, the Son of Heaven, he who is always in the right? And this poor mute boy who can't even say a single "Heil" and Wu Tsiang, the general with the bloody boots, and all the rest—what do they all mean? Who are they? I hope you won't be too upset, ladies and gentlemen, if you don't find any ready answer to this. All that is meant (word of honor!) is the truth, but, once you embrace it, you find it two-edged. (*the first gong*) On with the play! Place of the action: this stage. Or one might also say: our consciousness. Hence, for example, Shakespeare's characters, who exist only in our consciousness; and Biblical quotations, and so forth. Time of the action: this evening. And thus in an era when the building of Chinese Walls has become, you understand, a farce. (*second gong*) Tonight, I play the role of an intellectual. (*third gong*)

Scene One

(*The stage remains a stage: right, an outside staircase in the Chinese manner; left, in the foreground, a group of modern armchairs. Ceremonial music is heard and the voices of an unseen company. After a while (when the spectators have had a chance to get used to the stage) there appears a youthful pair in costumes which every theatergoer would recognize*)

SHE

Wilt thou be gone? it is not yet near day.
It was the nightingale and not the lark,
That pierced the fearful hollow of thine ear;
Nightly she sings on yond pomegranate tree.
Believe me, love, it was the nightingale.

HE

It was the lark, the herald of the morn—
I must be gone and live, or stay and die.

SHE

Yond light is not day-light, I know it, I;
Therefore stay yet; thou needst not to be gone.

HE

Let me be ta'en, let me be put to death;
I am content, so thou wilt have it so.

SHE

They come! I hear a sound! Farewell!

HE

Farewell!   ·

SHE

O, thinkst thou we shall ever meet again?

(*A* WAITER *in tails appears, right*)

WAITER   Ladies and gentlemen: the Polonaise is beginning on the terrace. The company awaits your pleasure. (*he disappears*)

HE

If I but knew, dear, where we are—
and when!
I shudder at these people here. It seems,
They've all ransacked their closets. Their costumes
Smell of mothballs, and in truth it is
As though they all were dead, and yet they talk
And dance about in circles endlessly
Like tiny figures on a musical clock.

SHE

What has happened?

HE

Time—Time is standing still.

SHE

Away, my love, away! and let us flee!

(*A* WAITER *in tails appears, left*)

WAITER Ladies and gentlemen: the Polonaise is beginning on the terrace. The company awaits your pleasure. (*the* WAITER *disappears*)

SHE

O God, I have an ill-divining soul!

HE

I know not what, but something strange has happened.
"Entropy" and "atom": what are these?
Somebody speaks, but no one understands.
"Death by radiation"—what is this?
The Time, my love, the Time is standing still.

SHE

Send news, my love, each hour, every day!
Too many seconds does the year contain;
Counting them all, I will grow old and die
Before we meet again, love, lip to lip.

HE

O Juliet! This night I'll lie with thee.

SHE

O Romeo! beloved Romeo!

HE

How oft when men are at the point of death
Have they been merry! O my love! My wife!
The world's become a single grave. O eyes,
Look, look your last! Arms, take your last
Embrace—thus, with a kiss, I die!

(*The* MEMBERS *of the Polonaise enter, in costumes of every type:* NAPOLEON, CLEOPATRA, DON JUAN, THE MAID OF ORLEANS, FREDERICK THE GREAT, HELEN OF TROY, WALLENSTEIN, MARY STUART, LOHENGRIN, *etc.*)

SOMEONE Here they are: Romeo and Juliet, the classic pair!

(ROMEO *and* JULIET *are swept up and carried away by the merrymakers.* NAPOLEON BONAPARTE *remains behind, in half profile, his hand in his white vest.* THE CONTEMPORARY, *also left behind, approaches him respectfully*)

THE CONTEMPORARY Excellency! Could I speak to you for a moment?

NAPOLEON We are not acquainted with thee, Monsieur.

THE CONTEMPORARY That's not surprising, Excellency. We live in different Times. Perhaps it would please you to hear, Excellency, that your fame—and I do not wish to startle you in any way—has survived its first century.

NAPOLEON What dost thou say?

THE CONTEMPORARY That which concerns my insignificance, Excellency, since I belong to the people who are living on the earth today and who would like to live.

NAPOLEON A century? sayst thou. And what—inform me!—has happened since then?

THE CONTEMPORARY I *will* inform you, Excellency; that's why I have come. You died, if I mistake not, in the spring of 1821. Yet even today you remain a sort of symbol. Your personality, your profile (the inner and the outer man), your glorious campaigns, and your hand's predilection for concealing itself in your vest, these are known to every educated person —indeed, to every half-educated person, and nowadays that's most of mankind. You are admired, Excellency, and not only in France. Your letters may be read in every library— even the most intimate ones (in facsimile, of course). If I may be explicit, Excellency; we are very well acquainted with you. You belong to those figures who people our brains, and to that degree, as a figure in our thoughts, you are still living—otherwise how could I be speaking to you, Emperor of France?— living and dangerous!

NAPOLEON I ask, what is happening? What are the French doing? And the British and the Russians? Tell me that they are at last defeated!

THE CONTEMPORARY Excellency——

NAPOLEON Russia can be defeated; it was an unusually hard winter when we marched against Russia.

THE CONTEMPORARY We all know that very well.

NAPOLEON Russia *must* be defeated!

THE CONTEMPORARY Excellency——

NAPOLEON Europe is the world—!

THE CONTEMPORARY No more, Excellency, no more——

NAPOLEON Who is the Master of Europe?

THE CONTEMPORARY Excellency!

NAPOLEON Why dost thou not speak, citizen?

THE CONTEMPORARY Excellency—the atom is fissionable!

NAPOLEON What does that mean?

THE CONTEMPORARY That means—with the the troops ready, Excellency, and the generals ready: the next war, which we believe to be inevitable, will be the last.

NAPOLEON And who will win it?

THE CONTEMPORARY No one. You can't grasp that, Excellency, I know. But it is so:

the deluge can now be re-enacted. It remains only for the order to be given, Excellency, which means we are faced with the simple choice, will there be a mankind or not? But who, Excellency, should make this choice: humanity itself—or you?

NAPOLEON   Thou art a democrat?

THE CONTEMPORARY   I am worried, yes. We can no longer stand the adventure of absolute monarchy, Excellency, nowhere ever again on this earth; the risk is too great. Whoever sits on a throne today holds the human race in his hand, their whole history, starting with Moses or Buddha, including the Acropolis, the Temple of Maia, Gothic cathedrals, including all of Western philosophy, Spanish and French painting, German music, Shakespeare and this youthful pair: Romeo and Juliet. And included in it all, our children and our children's children. A slight whim on the part of the man on the throne, a nervous breakdown, a touch of neurosis, a flame struck by his madness, a moment of impatience on account of indigestion—and the jig is up! Everything! A cloud of yellow or brown ashes boiling up toward the heavens in the shape of a mushroom, a dirty cauliflower—and the rest is silence— radioactive silence.

NAPOLEON   Why tellst thou this to us, Napoleon Bonaparte, banished to Saint Helena?

THE CONTEMPORARY   I don't know, Excellency, if you can grasp what a contemporary has to say to you?

NAPOLEON   Answer me!

THE CONTEMPORARY   Why do I come and report to you in your banishment? Quite frankly: You must not return, Excellency, not for a hundred days or even a hundred seconds. The era of great generals (even of a great one like yourself) is past.

NAPOLEON   And if the people call me?

THE CONTEMPORARY   They won't. The people want to live.

NAPOLEON   And what if I tell thee, Monsieur, that thou art wrong? I hear the call of the people day after day.

(*Laughter in the background.* THE CONTEMPORARY *turns to the audience*)

THE CONTEMPORARY   You see, ladies and gentlemen, how ticklish it is speaking with these great personages who people our brains, these evil spirits out of the bad dream of a history which must not be repeated, and who cannot grasp that which a contemporary has to tell them. However, I will not give up. . . .

(*A new pair of maskers now enters, an elderly man, seemingly a* SPANISH SEAFARER, *and a*

YOUNG GIRL, *who, barefooted and in laughing rapture, is dancing along before him*)

L'INCONNUE
Entrez dans la danse,
Voyez comme on danse,
Sautez, dansez,
Embrassez cell'que vous voudrez!

COLUMBUS   I don't understand it. . . .

L'INCONNUE
Entrez dans la danse,
Voyez comme on danse. . . .

(COLUMBUS *shakes his head*)

L'INCONNUE   It's a party, my friend, a great ball, such as I have envisioned a thousand times behind my closed lids when I couldn't sleep beneath the bridges of the Seine.

COLUMBUS   I don't understand it. . . .

L'INCONNUE   I love exciting parties, my friend—the formal gardens, which I have never entered; I love the silk, the music which seems to make all things possible. I love the lives of fine people. All this, you understand, I know only from reading the newspapers.

COLUMBUS   America, they call it. . . .

L'INCONNUE   We must hurry, my friend, or we'll miss out on the Polonaise. Give me your arm!

COLUMBUS   America, they call it. America! And so it's not India that I've discovered? Do understand that? Not India, not the truth! (*the two maskers disappear*)

NAPOLEON   Who was that?

THE CONTEMPORARY   Columbus, I think, the old Columbus.

NAPOLEON   I mean the girl.

THE CONTEMPORARY   She has no name.

NAPOLEON   She mentioned the Seine.

THE CONTEMPORARY   Her life was unknown, Excellency, no one inquired into it. We know only her death mask; it hangs in the shop windows and can be bought at any second-hand store. We call her "L'Inconnue de la Seine."

NAPOLEON   Does that mean that even this barefooted waif is on the guest list?

THE CONTEMPORARY   So it seems.

NAPOLEON   And why haven't we been informed whose guests we are?

THE CONTEMPORARY   I have already told you, Excellency. Nowadays whoever sits on a throne holds humanity in his hand, the whole kaleidoscopic history of deeds and dreams, Romeo and Juliet, Napoleon Bonaparte, Christopher Columbus, and the rest—and even those who are nameless: "L'Inconnue de la Seine"!

(*The crack of a whip is heard. A Chinese* MASTER-OF-CEREMONIES *appears, with a pack of coolies who drag in the throne and place it on the stage. All this is carried out like a swift and flawless military drill—left, right, left, right—while periodically the sharp crack of an invisible whip is heard. Then they all disappear)*

NAPOLEON   What is the meaning of all this chinoiserie?

THE CONTEMPORARY   That's the throne.

NAPOLEON   And who are these here . . .?

(From the opposite side there appear two new maskers, who promenade back and forth like men awaiting a ceremonious occasion—at which they are expected; back and forth in casual companionship. They are a ROMAN and a young SPANIARD who impatiently, while he listens, toys with a glove and peers mysteriously about)

PILATE   What is truth? Now in that time it happened that I was the governor of a province which was called in Hebrew Eriz Jisrael——

DON JUAN   I know, I know——

PILATE   One fine morning (it was the eve of Passover) they brought him to the place of judgment and I said to them: What kind of complaint bringest thou against this man? The Jews, however, answered and said so on and so forth. Then I went back to him and said to him: Art thou King of the Jews? But he replied: My kingdom is not of this world——

DON JUAN   I know!

PILATE   After this, when he had thus spoken, I went to the high priests and said: I find no fault in him. Then they cried and said: He has claimed to be the Son of God! Then, as I heard these words, I was greatly afraid and returned and spoke to him, saying: Whither comest thou? He, however, made no answer. I sat then, in the seat of judgment (that which in Hebrew is called Gabbatha) and waited his answer, but in vain. Everyone that is of the truth heareth my voice, he said; then I said: What is truth?

DON JUAN   I know, we all know.

PILATE   However, I am not fond of decisions. How can I decide what is the truth? There was an uproar, though, and before the place of judgment they cried: Crucify him! Crucify him! And I spoke and said: I have a custom of releasing one at Passover. Which do you want me to release? Then they all cried together and said: Not this one, but Barabbas!

DON JUAN   I know—I know.

PILATE   Yet, Barabbas was a robber.

DON JUAN   A murderer.

PILATE   Then I delivered unto them the other, that they might crucify him, and saw how he went out to the so-called Place of the Skull (in Hebrew called Golgotha)——

(DON JUAN approaches L'INCONNUE *and kisses her hand)*

DON JUAN   Mademoiselle de la Seine?

L'INCONNUE   Who does me this honor?

DON JUAN   A man who envies you! Not for the greatness of your fame, which, I fear, is inferior to mine. I envy you, Mademoiselle de la Seine, for the *manner* of your fame!

L'INCONNUE   How do you mean that, Monsieur?

DON JUAN   All the world imagines that it knows me. All wrong, Mademoiselle, all wrong! The world, on the other hand, admits that it knows nothing of you, nothing but the name: L'Inconnue de la Seine! How I envy you!

L'INCONNUE   But I am tubercular—and pregnant. . . .

DON JUAN   My name is Don Juan.

THE CONTEMPORARY   Of Seville? Don Juan Tenorio?

DON JUAN   You are mistaken! You know me from the theater. (*to the audience*) I come from the hell of literature. What things have been imputed to me! Once, after a night of revelry, it's true, I took a short-cut through the cemetery and stumbled over a skull. And I had to laugh, God knows why. I am young, I hate death, that's all. When have I blasphemed against God? The confessor of adulteries in Seville, a priest, Gabriel Tellez, put it into verse. I know. May God punish him for his poetical fantasies! Once there was a beggar, that's true, and I swore at him, for I am a Tenorio, son of a banker, and the alms-giving of the Tenorios disgusts me. But what else do Brecht and his crowd know about me? In the bordello, of which I have no need, I go and play chess. I am considered an intellectual! The love of geometry! Whatever I do or don't do, though, it's all misunderstood and poeticized. Who can put up with that? I am young and I simply want to be what I am. Where is there a land without literature? That's what I'm seeking, ladies and gentlemen: Paradise. I'm seeking the virgin land! (*he turns to* COLUMBUS) You are, I understand, the discoverer of America?

COLUMBUS   So they call it.

DON JUAN   We are compatriots!

COLUMBUS   I am in the service of the Spanish Crown, although born a Genovese——

DON JUAN   Honored friend and compatriot, I want to discuss with you the following——

COLUMBUS   It's a question of truth, that's all. We didn't voyage in the name of the

Spanish Crown to discover a piece of land which nowadays is called (I don't see why) *America!* To root out and destroy a whole race of people in the name of the Spanish Crown (as later happened)—this we did not voyage for! And that the fields should be torn up in the search for gold: That was not our purpose!

DON JUAN I know, I know.

COLUMBUS Five years I had to wait, talking and waiting, five years until they built the ships. I said, we will reach India. And then the storm! It was not a question of India, the treasures of India—it was a question of truth! Death and danger and hunger and thirst, God knows, these we endured, and then those nights that I stood chained and fettered to the mast; all those howling nights—I knew that we'd reach India! And we *did* reach India! Why does he shake his head?

DON JUAN I?

COLUMBUS Him, over there.

PILATE Yes, yes, what is truth?

DON JUAN I forgot to introduce you: Pontius Pilate. This is the situation, Captain—I want to leave Europe——

L'INCONNUE Ah!

DON JUAN I know. Mademoiselle, what you're thinking now. All honor to Mozart! but it has nothing to do with women. (*He turns to the men*) Gentlemen, Europe is Death. . . .

Scene Two

(DON JUAN *cannot go on speaking, since their attention is now distracted by a Chinese steward who bows to them ceremoniously*)

DA HING YEN My name is Da Hing Yen, Master of the Autumn Revels. I have the undeserved honor of announcing to our guests the bill of fare in honor of our victorious generalissimo, Tsin She Hwang Ti, our Great Exalted Emperor, called the Son of Heaven, he who is always in the right and therefore has taken possession of the world.

PILATE Who?

DA HING YEN Tsin She Hwang Ti.

PILATE Never heard of him.

THE CONTEMPORARY Two thousand years before Christ: unknown in Rome; builder of the Chinese Wall.

DA HING YEN First course: Soup of young tender bamboo sprouts, horse-radish sprinkled with dew from morning roses, fattened duck liver with rice wine, pheasant à la Peking, pomegranates in Siamese vinegar, stewed swallows' nests——

DON JUAN Stewed?

DA HING YEN Stewed. . . . Second course: Tibetan chicken stuffed with young apes' brains, butterfly salad with Indian cherries, broiled pigeons' eggs——

L'INCONNUE Broiled?

DA HING YEN Broiled.

L'INCONNUE Go on!

DA HING YEN Third course: Assorted fish, caught in the hours of dawn by the imperial cormorants, brought to Nanking by the imperial dispatch riders, garnished with sugared lotus pips, peppered oranges, mussels with sour ant eggs—

Scene Three

(*Church music; a black-clad monarch appears*)

THE CONTEMPORARY Sire!

PHILIP Knowest thou with whom thou speakest?

THE CONTEMPORARY Philip of Spain presumably.

PHILIP Why dost thou not kneel?

THE CONTEMPORARY Sire—it is urgent——

PHILIP Why dost thous not kneel? (THE CONTEMPORARY *kneels down*) Thou wouldst speak with me?

THE CONTEMPORARY Sire—I am—I must confess, Sire—I am really not prepared to clothe in words a subject which I as a citizen of this world have thought much about, especially since—I am not sure, Sire, if you have been informed about developments? We have, to put it briefly, Sire, the Second World War behind us, and now, concerning proud Spain—I wonder, Sire, if I might rise?

PHILIP Speak!

THE CONTEMPORARY We pay homage to Picasso, García Lorca, Casals——

PHILIP Thou hast yet more to say to me.

THE CONTEMPORARY I hope you know that the Netherlands are free. Gibraltar is British. Spain has not become a democracy, but rather a foothold for America. And so forth! I will not disturb you, Sire, if you really prefer not.

PHILIP The Netherlands—thou darest to say—!

THE CONTEMPORARY What the facts are.

PHILIP   Is there, then, no longer an Inquisition?

THE CONTEMPORARY   Not *exactly.*

PHILIP   I have done my duty.

THE CONTEMPORARY   For that, may God forgive you.

PHILIP   I know heretics. I burned them by the thousands and the ten thousands. There is no other way.

THE CONTEMPORARY   You are wrong, Sire. There is another way. Today we have the hydrogen bomb.

PHILIP   What does that mean?

THE CONTEMPORARY   That means that the others have it also. And what is the good of it, by your leave, for he who wants to burn up others because they believe differently than he must now burn up himself. It is no longer so simple, Sire, not so simple—to save Christianity! There only remains to us, in fact, the obligation to behave like Christians.

PHILIP   Mad dreamer!

THE CONTEMPORARY   Sire—(PHILIP *stands motionless with folded hands*) In a word: You shall not return, Sire. Remain in the Escorial! There stands your bed, with a peephole before the high altar.

PHILIP   Thou wast in my sleeping quarters?

THE CONTEMPORARY   As a tourist. . . . (*He turns to those standing about*) All of you, my lords, all of you, you must not return. It is too dangerous. Your victories, your kingdoms, your thrones by divine right, your crusades hither and thither, they just don't make sense any more. We want to live. Your way of making history—we can't put up with it any longer. It would be the end, a chain reaction of madness——

(*A* WAITER *appears offering apertifs*)

WAITER   With or without gin? With or without gin?

THE CONTEMPORARY   I beg you, gentlemen, to listen to me——

WAITER   With or without gin?

DON JUAN   With

THE CONTEMPORARY   Sire!—(*He falls to his knees*) Give us the four freedoms!

PHILIP   Four—?

THE CONTEMPORARY   First, the freedom of thought——

WAITER   With or without gin?

(THE CONTEMPORARY, *interrupted by the* WAITER, *cannot continue; he kneels, speechless, for a moment before the gently urgent politeness of the* WAITER, *who bows before him, lowering his tray a little*)

WAITER   With or without gin?

Scene Four

(*A fanfare. Sound of jubilant voices in the distance*)

DA HING YEN   Entry of our Great Exalted Emperor, called the Son of Heaven, into Nanking. . . . Do not miss the opportunity, my lords, of being eyewitnesses to this indescribable spectacle. An unparalleled kaleidoscope of color, gentlemen, a never-before-equaled crowd of people, all throwing themselves on their knees while forty thousand streaming pennants fill the streets of Nanking. An ear-splitting wave of joy, gentlemen, rolls on before our Emperor, who is not yet to be seen. (*Fanfare again*) Do not miss the opportunity, my lords, of being eyewitnesses to this historic spectacle: The entry of Tsin She Hwang Ti, called the Son of Heaven, into Nanking—which is to say, into the Center of the World. (DA HING YEN *motions toward the right, and* THE MASQUERADERS, *aperitifs in their hands, move toward the right in order to observe the goings-on to best advantage. Only* THE CONTEMPORARY, *who has arisen and dusted off his trousers, hangs back*) Who are you? Where do you come from? Who invited you? Are you a historical figure?

THE CONTEMPORARY   Don't trouble yourself.

DA HING YEN   At any moment the Great Exalted Emperor will appear——

THE CONTEMPORARY   Tsin She Hwang Ti— or however you pronounce it—the builder of the Chinese Wall. I know. I want to speak to him. (*He lights a cigarette*) Just think, my friend, today the remains of your wall still stand; every school child has seen pictures of it. And if humanity is destroyed—as seems more likely day by day—along with all these evil spirits who promenade about there and lie in wait for their historical return, deaf and blind to the evolutions of our consciousness— of all the works of man, your wall will be the only thing visible, say, from Mars—this serpent of stone, this monstrosity, this monument of madness, capable of being blown away like the ashes from a cigarette—so—dust of the centuries!

DA HING YEN   I am Da Hing Yen, Master of the Autumn Revels. If I do not know who someone is, that means: To the Mongolian dogs with him! If I do not understand what someone says, that means: To the Mongolian dogs with him! If I understand that which is not pleasing to our ears, that means——

THE CONTEMPORARY   Who is that?

DA HING YEN   Ssh!

(DA HING YEN *kowtows and* THE CONTEMPORARY *steps back so as not to be seen*)

Scene Five

(MEE LAN, *the young princess, enters, followed by her maid*)

DA HING YEN   Princess, called Mee Lan, which means Beautiful Orchid! God is gracious to thy simple servant who has the unmerited honor of announcing to you that which will bring sweet joy into the heart of our Princess: The barbarian hounds from the steppes are smashed, the victory is ours, the world is ours!

MEE LAN   What else is new?

DA HING YEN   Heil. Heil. Heil. (*He backs out kowtowing*)

MEE LAN   What else is new?

SIU   Yesterday, they say, our court jester died.

MEE LAN   Who do you think will take over his job? (*She sits*) Bring the tea. (*She fans herself*) What a world! I don't understand them, Siu, they're always talking about victory. I find men so boring. And so stupid. Papa, for example! Now he's sending his drummers all through the empire and he wants to arrest the voice of the people. How can he do *that*?

SIU   Not the voice of the people, Princess. You misunderstood me. They are looking for a man, Min Ko, who *calls* himself "The Voice of the People."

MEE LAN   One man?

SIU   So they say, Princess.

MEE LAN   What kind of man is he?

SIU   Oh, a bad man, they say, a liar, an unbeliever, a destroyer—a very bad man.

MEE LAN   What does he look like?

SIU   That, Princess, no one knows. Only his words are known. They are bad words, they say, lying, unfaithful, destructive, wicked words.

MEE LAN   And as a result Papa wants to kill him?

SIU   Nothing is sacred to him, they say, not even war.

MEE LAN   Ah.

SIU   Therefore they say: His head on the block!

MEE LAN   I am curious. So often I like what Papa considers bad! I'd like to see him!

SIU   Min Ko?

MEE LAN   Papa is comical. He always wants to forbid me whatever is displeasing to him. And the books he forbids me entice me most of all! He is called Min Ko?

SIU   Yes.

MEE LAN   Perhaps it is he?

SIU   Who?

MEE LAN   I want to see him!

SIU   Min Ko?

MEE LAN   Perhaps he is the man I love——

SIU   Princess!

MEE LAN   I love someone, somewhere—— (MEE LAN *has risen, fanning herself*) What else is new? (*She sits again*)

SIU   Perhaps, Mee Lan, the Prince will also return, the young hero who has been courting you, who won the battle of Liautung for love of you. Nothing has yet been heard of his death.

MEE LAN   Nothing yet?

SIU   Mee Lan——

MEE LAN   I don't love him.

SIU   This is the eighth prince, Mee Lan, the eighth!

MEE LAN   I haven't kept count.

SIU   One after another you have sent them into battle because you cannot love them——

MEE LAN   Love!

SIU   The gods will punish you.

MEE LAN   With a handsome head leaning on my breast, do you mean? And suddenly they get all fishy-eyed. And their hands get like slippery fins. Ugh! I have to laugh every time they try, these princes, and then they become angry and leap onto their horses and plunder some province somewhere so that I will take them seriously: If *that's* love—!

SIU   You are pledged to the Prince, Mee Lan, if he survives the war.

MEE LAN   And above all, this stupid blood pounding in my ears? I don't like that—no! Everything is so—so inexpressibly——(MEE LAN *breaks her fan*) I won't put up with it! (*She rises*) Bring us the tea! And inquire if it is true that nothing has yet been heard of the Prince's death (SIU *kowtows and exits*)

Scene Six

MEE LAN   You look at me and are silent. The eighth prince! I don't deny I hope he never returns. But what have I done that you are so silent? He will die for me—all of them say that. Then let them do it! I know, you find me common and base. You feel that a true Chinese girl should not speak like this, a daughter of the Great Exalted Emperor, called the Son of Heaven, a princess in silk and jade, whose duty it is to wait for a prince—(*She protests*) I am not a Chinese girl! (*She looks at the spectators*) You think you can prescribe my duty to me? You think I don't know that I am disguised, in costume? And you, who are grown up and know everything, do you really believe, for example, that Papa is always in the right? I am not stupid. You think I don't know that everything here (for example, this throne—even a schoolgirl can see it) everything here is nothing but theater? But you sit and look at one another. You, who are grown up and wise, you sit, your arms folded over your breast, and you are silent—and no one comes forward and says what it really is, and no one dares and is a man!

Scene Seven

(THE CONTEMPORARY *steps forward from his hiding place*)

THE CONTEMPORARY   Miss—(MEE LAN *sees him and screams*) Don't be afraid.

MEE LAN   Help! Siu! Help! Siu, Siu——

THE CONTEMPORARY   I haven't been spying on you. Please.

MEE LAN   Who are you?

THE CONTEMPORARY   Calm yourself. I'm sorry if I frightened you. Don't be afraid of me. I'm no prince.

MEE LAN   Who are you?

THE CONTEMPORARY   I want to speak with the Emperor of China. Why do you stare at me like that? This is the costume of our time; business suit, ready-made.

MEE LAN   Who are you?

THE CONTEMPORARY   Shall we sit down?

(*He leads her toward the chairs in the foreground*)

MEE LAN   Are you—Min Ko?

THE CONTEMPORARY   Me? But why?

MEE LAN   And you have dared to enter the imperial park——(*She falls silent with astonishment, then gestures toward the other chair*)

THE CONTEMPORARY   Thank you very much!

(*He sits down and crosses his legs*) An elegant park! Your papa, the Great Exalted Emperor, will be coming in at any moment, I believe. How old are you?

MEE LAN   Seventeen.

THE CONTEMPORARY   I really didn't mean to spy on you.

MEE LAN   But where have you come from so suddenly?

THE CONTEMPORARY   I—er—how shall I put it—? (*He takes a cigarette*) I come from another time. I am older than you, Princess, by some two thousand years.

MEE LAN   Then do you know our future?

THE CONTEMPORARY   In a certain sense, oh, yes. That which concerns the future of this empire, for example——

MEE LAN   And mine? Mine? Speak! Whom will I marry? I can't stand this prince. But who else is coming toward me in my future? I sit and wait—you can see—in hope and fear, with open eyes, yet blind, for not an hour can I see forward, not even a minute! And you know the future two thousand years from now? (*He snaps on his cigarette lighter*) Oh, tell me what you know!

(SIU, *the maid, brings tea. Silence. Soft music is heard in the distance.* SIU *kowtows and disappears*)

THE CONTEMPORARY   What we know?

MEE LAN   Speak!

THE CONTEMPORARY   Item: Energy equals mass times the speed of light squared. Whereby the speed of light (one hundred eighty-six thousand miles a second) is the single absolute power with which we are able to reckon nowadays. Everything else, we know, is relative.

MEE LAN   I don't understand that.

THE CONTEMPORARY   Item: Even time is relative. Seat yourself on a ray of light, Princess, and you will become convinced: There is (for you) no space, therefore likewise no time. And your every thought will be endlessly slow. "No!" you think, "I don't want to be eternal!" and you dismount from your ray of light. And you will return here (I swear it to you) not a second older. On our earth, however, there have been—look—two thousand years in the meantime——

MEE LAN   Two thousand years?

THE CONTEMPORARY   Irredeemably.

MEE LAN   And I?

THE CONTEMPORARY   You, Princess, live on —today.

MEE LAN   How do you sit on a ray of light?

THE CONTEMPORARY   Time is a function of

space. That, for example, is what we know. And there is actually neither time nor space! Nor truth, for we are so created that we can exist only in time and space. . . . You are seventeen?

MEE LAN   Yes.

THE CONTEMPORARY   I am thirty-four, twice as old as you, Princess. An impossible pair!

MEE LAN   Why?

THE CONTEMPORARY   Do you see that reddish star?

MEE LAN   Which one?

THE CONTEMPORARY   There, above my thumb! (*They gaze up, heads close together*) See it?

MEE LAN   Yes.

THE CONTEMPORARY   Suppose I emigrate to that reddish star, whizzing along at an ungodly speed (let's say, one hundred fifty thousand miles per second) and you, Princess, remain here——

MEE LAN   I remain here?

THE CONTEMPORARY   And now let's compare our ages. I will leave you my wrist watch. And look, you will be convinced: We are both seventeen!

MEE LAN   Really?

THE CONTEMPORARY   Suppose I am whizzing toward that reddish star and then, to be sure, we are the same age, according to your earth time. But also, Princess, I am adjusting our ages and measuring according to my then-and-there time, and behold: you are seventeen while I am almost sixty, a graybeard, no longer worthy your falling in love with.

MEE LAN   Ah!

THE CONTEMPORARY   So what happens now?

MEE LAN   Tell me!

THE CONTEMPORARY   Nothing to either of us, Princess, or something to both of us, but later, not now, where we are. On this earth, as I said, we are seventeen and thirty-four. But *tempus absolutum,* a universal time such as man hitherto believed in, a time that embraces all and everything—no, there is no such thing.

MEE LAN   That is what you know!?

THE CONTEMPORARY   Among other things.

MEE LAN   And what do you know about men?

THE CONTEMPORARY   That they measure wrong, always, in space that is not endless, yet is unlimited—space that curves back in upon itself at its borders.

MEE LAN   Ah.

THE CONTEMPORARY   Read Einstein.

MEE LAN   I can't picture it.

THE CONTEMPORARY   No one, Princess, not even a contemporary, can picture it, any more than he can picture God.

MEE LAN   You believe in a God?

THE CONTEMPORARY   What shall I say to that? Energy equals mass times the speed of light squared, which means: mass is energy, an ungodly ball of energy. And woe to the world if it goes wrong! And it *does* go wrong. It's been doing it presumably for two million years. What is our sun? An explosion. All the cosmos: one giant explosion. It's flying apart. And what will remain? The greater probability—so our modern physics teaches us—is that it will be chaos, the collapse of the mass. Creation—so our modern physics teaches us—was a vast improbability. Energy will remain, with no loss, with no possibility. Destruction by heat of the world! That is the end: unalterable endlessness, nothingness.

MEE LAN   I asked if you believe in a God.

THE CONTEMPORARY   Man discovered the microscope. But the deeper he was able to penetrate into creation, the less was there any creator to be seen. In order to compensate for the loss of God, man established the law of cause and effect. We considered everything else to be wrong. But suddenly behold: an atom with suicidal free will: the radium atom. And then the behavior of the electrons! And matter, the only thing we can count on, what is it? A dance of numbers, a ghostly diagram. So today we have come this far: God, who could not be found in the microscope, still calls us menacingly to the inevitable reckoning. Anyone who does not think of Him has ceased to think. Why are you looking at me like that?

MEE LAN   I don't know. . . .

THE CONTEMPORARY   What don't you know?

MEE LAN   If you are the one whom I have awaited. . . .

THE CONTEMPORARY   Awaited? Me?

MEE LAN   Oh, say that you are!

(DA HING YEN, *the Master of the Revels, comes in with three soldiers*)

DA HING YEN   There he is. To the Mongolian dogs with him!

(*The soldiers obey, throw a noose over* THE CONTEMPORARY, *but* MEE LAN *jumps up, removes the noose, and places it around the neck of the Master of the Revels*)

MEE LAN   To the Mongolian dogs with him!

(*The soldiers obey and haul out* DA HING YEN *howling fearfully*)

THE CONTEMPORARY   Thanks.

MEE LAN   Do you drink tea?

THE CONTEMPORARY   As I said, I have come to talk to the Emperor of China. For in view of all that we now know it's clear that things cannot go on like this. The calculations of our learned men have been proved correct: unfortunately, quite fatally correct. I don't know, Princess, if you have heard of the hydrogen bomb——

MEE LAN   Is that what you want to talk to Papa about?

THE CONTEMPORARY   It's a question of whether or not the rulers of the world understand that things can't go on like this. Others are of the opinion that the rulers of the world should not be persuaded reasonably, but simply hanged. Only I'm afraid that even the revolution which stands this moment before your gates is too late——(MEE LAN *offers him a cup*) Oh—thank you, Princess, thank you very much! (*He takes the cup and holds it*) By the way—what gave you the idea that I was Min Ko?

MEE LAN   Papa wants to kill him. His head on the block! Papa is looking for him throughout the whole empire. If you are are he——

THE CONTEMPORARY   Min Ko. That means "The Voice of the People"?

MEE LAN   Yes.

THE CONTEMPORARY   I am an intellectual. (*He drinks tea*) Delicious tea! Oh, yes, we have often thought, over and over, that one of us, an intellectual, might be "The Voice of the People," beginning with Kung Fu Tse, your teacher.

MEE LAN   You know Kung Fu Tse?

THE CONTEMPORARY   "Every man among the people earns his title according to what he can do. He enjoys the fruits of his labor in his time. He takes his position according to his labors. In this fashion, true brotherhood will be achieved. When the people live in brotherhood, then dissatisfaction will be rare and discord will not arise. This is the basis upon which state and home will build and long endure."

MEE LAN   Kung Fu Tse said that?

THE CONTEMPORARY   Kung Fu Tse said that. I wonder: Was Kung Fu Tse "The Voice of the People!"?

(DA HING YEN II, *the successor to his unfortunate predecessor of the same name, enters with the same three soldiers*)

DA HING YEN II   My name is Da Hing Yen, Master of the Autumn Revels. If I don't know who someone is, that means: To the Mongolian dogs with him! If I do not understand what someone says, that means: To the Mongolian dogs with him! If I understand that which is not pleasing to our ears, that means: To the Mongolians dogs with him!

(*The soldiers obey, and everything is repeated: they put the noose over* THE CONTEMPORARY, *but* MEE LAN *jumps up, takes it off and throws it over the neck of the Master of the Revels*)

MEE LAN   To the Mongolian dogs with him!

(*The soldiers obey and* DA HING YEN II *is dragged out howling even more fearfully than the first one*)

THE CONTEMPORARY   Do you have any more of these?

MEE LAN   It's a much sought-after job. (*They take up their cups again*) You were speaking of Kung Fu Tse. . . .

(*They look at one another*)

THE CONTEMPORARY   You are a lovely girl. (MEE LAN *drops her cup*) What is it, Mee Lan? You're crying?

(MEE LAN *jumps up and turns away*)

MEE LAN   No! I won't have it. No! And this stupid blood pounding in my ears. No! That everything is so—so inexpressibly——

THE CONTEMPORARY   Mee Lan! Your name is still Mee Lan?

MEE LAN   Don't touch me!

THE CONTEMPORARY   You're all mixed up. What's happened? You're confused, Princess; think of the two thousand years between us. . . .

MEE LAN   I love you in spite of them.

THE CONTEMPORARY   But seriously . . .

MEE LAN   I love you in spite of them.

THE CONTEMPORARY   Mee Lan . . . ?

MEE LAN   I love you.

(*She kisses him. And then he kisses her.* DA HING YEN III *enters, kowtows.* MEE LAN *and* THE CONTEMPORARY *remain in an embrace*)

DA HING YEN   My name is Da Hing Yen, Master of the Autumn Revels. God is gracious to thy simple servant who has the unmerited honor of announcing that which will bring joy into the heart of the Princess: Your father, Tsin She Hwang Ti, is here! (*drum roll*) Heil. Heil. Heil. (DA HING YEN *disappears*)

MEE LAN   What will I do when you are not beside me? Kiss the stones, embrace the pillars, kiss the leaves of the trees; oh, I will walk in the river embracing wave upon wave, I will talk with dogs and with clouds, and when I walk in the sun I will close my eyes in order to feel your warmth. I will go mad without you. And when I cannot sleep, the night winds will caress me, and if you do not come, I will be sick until I find you. . . . You are silent?

THE CONTEMPORARY   You are speaking.

MEE LAN Is it true? I don't know. Where did you get this scar? I feel you like a blind person. From a serpent's bite? No, it was in a child's game with bow and arrow.

THE CONTEMPORARY An accident.

MEE LAN I want to know everything about you!

THE CONTEMPORARY Your father was just announced.

MEE LAN Here in your arms like this I could hear them say over me: Tomorrow you will die, struck down by lightning, and your grave will be prepared! and I would not tremble, it would not touch me, if I could only feel myself in your arms!

THE CONTEMPORARY Mee Lan——

MEE LAN How I have planned and dreamed: You would be thus and so and such and such! And now you are simply what you are, and I am glad.

THE CONTEMPORARY Don't you hear me?

MEE LAN Don't tell me there's another woman!

THE CONTEMPORARY Your father was just announced.

MEE LAN There *is* another woman?

THE CONTEMPORARY I want to tell you how it is——

(*Fanfare*)

MEE LAN Hide yourself! They're coming! And wait for me!

THE CONTEMPORARY And you?

MEE LAN I will come—to your time!

Scene Eight

(*Deployment of* EUNUCHS *in preparation for the reception of the Emperor*)

DA HING YEN Line up on both sides, as I ordered! And here, where is the interval? Thirteen paces for eunuchs!

JOURNALIST Excuse me, but we're not the eunuchs, we're the gentlemen of the press!

DA HING YEN Thirteen paces, I said! (*A flash bulb explodes*) What—was—that?!

JOURNALIST Thank you!

(*Fanfare for the second time, and the* EUNUCHS *prostrate themselves. However, instead of the Emperor, two promenading masqueraders appear:* L'INCONNUE DE LA SEINE *and a man in a toga. They pause on the steps*)

THE TOGA I said to myself:
"It must be by his death; and for my part,
I known no personal cause to spurn at him
But for the general; he would be crowned."

(DA HING YEN *gestures that they should disappear*)

THE TOGA I said to myself:
"It is the bright day that brings forth the adder,
And that craves wary walking. Crown him? That—
And then, I grant, we put a sting in him
That at his will he may do danger with."

(DA HING YEN *gestures that they should disappear*)

THE TOGA
"And therefore think him as a serpent's egg
Which, hatched, would, as his kind, grow mischievous,
And kill him in the shell."

(L'INCONNUE *takes his arm*)

L'INCONNUE We mustn't pass through here.

THE TOGA What do you mean?

L'INCONNUE Something is going on here, it seems.

THE TOGA I don't like these ceremonies.

L'INCONNUE It doesn't concern us, my noble friend. They are honoring their emperor, that's all.

THE TOGA But I thought Caesar was dead!

(*Fanfare for the third time, and* TSIN SHE HWANG TI, *Emperor of China, appears on the steps. He has a round, soft face, a gentle voice. He is smiling. He is absolutely the opposite of the bloodthirsty tyrant we have expected. He seems almost timid*)

HWANG TI My loyal subjects!

THE EUNUCHS Heil! Heil! Heil!

(THE TOGA *steps forward toward the* EUNUCHS)

BRUTUS
My name is Brutus, whoever you may be.
(It's like an evil dream; the icy sweat
Runs on my forehead as I look at you,
There where you kneel and huzzah and exult
As though what we have done was done in vain.)
Listen to Brutus! I with my own hand

Struck down the mighty Caesar, he
who was
My friend, until, ambitious, deaf to
friends,
Who offered their advice, their pleas,
their warning,
He lay before us, dead, a fallen tyrant.
And what has happened since? Do
you permit
That bold and shameless tyranny
should thrive
Till all free will and action disappear?
Now is the time; do not delude yourselves;
You have, unquestioned by your
judgments,
Robbed yourselves of all your dearest rights;
And for the common good to fight
you have
(How long?) a single weapon, friends
—a dagger!

L'INCONNUE   Come on! We're only interrupting!

BRUTUS   Shall Rome (the world) quake before one man?

L'INCONNUE   It's no use, my noble friend.
They don't hear you. All that happened in a
completely different time.

BRUTUS
Is Caesar then not dead? And has not
Brutus
Atoned for his friend's blood upon
this dagger
With his dear wife's and his own poor
life?
Is this what history means, that men's
mistakes
Keep returning endlessly forever?

L'INCONNUE   Come!

BRUTUS
It's like an evil dream, whene'er I
see . . .

L'INCONNUE   Let's go to the pond, my noble
friend, I will show you the goldfish.

(*She takes* BRUTUS *away*)

HWANG TI   My loyal subjects! Since I have
been upon this throne, as you well know, I
have fought for only one thing: Peace—but not
for a barbarous peace, rather for a true peace,
a conclusive peace, which is to say—for the
Great Order, which we call the True Order
and the Happy Order and the Final Order.

THE EUNUCHS   Heil! Heil! Heil!

HWANG TI   My loyal subjects! It is achieved:
The world is free. That is all that I can say

to you at this moment: The world is free. I
stand before you with a full heart. The barbarian hordes of the steppes are silenced, they
who opposed the Great Peace—as you know,
they wanted a twenty-year peace treaty!—
and the world is ours, which is to say: there is
now in the world only one Order, our Order,
which we call the Great Order and the True
Order and the Final Order.

THE EUNUCHS   Heil! Heil! Heil!

HWANG TI   Here is my plan—(*He takes out
a parchment scroll*) Do not fear the future, my
loyal subjects. For, as things are now, so they
will remain. We will forestall any future. (*He
gives the scroll to* DA HING YEN) Read!

(DA HING YEN *kowtows, then reads*)

DA HING YEN   "The Chinese Wall, or the
Great Wall. In Chinese: Wan-li-chang-cheng;
literally, the Ten Thousand Li Wall. The
greatest structure in the world. Up to sixteen
meters high and (defensively) over five meters
wide. It begins west of Suchou and ends at
the Gulf of Liautung. Built as defense against
the northwestern barbarian hordes under Tsin
She Hwang Ti (221–210 B.C.)."

HWANG TI   It will be started tomorrow.

THE EUNUCHS   Heil. Heil. Heil.

HWANG TI   What remains for preparation
for the ceremonies is, I hope, in readiness; our
guests are all assembled?

DA HING YEN   A slight oversight, Your Majesty. A gentleman named Hitler, apparently a
German, is not to be admitted. My predecessors didn't trust him, since this gentleman made
such a terrible impression at first glance, and
my unfortunate predecessors felt that, generally
speaking, Germans don't look like that.

HWANG TI   Hm.

DA HING YEN   The gentlemen from Moscow
adhere to their "nyet."

HWANG TI   And the ladies?

DA HING YEN   A youthful Queen of Egypt,
Your Majesty, who is complaining that she has
nothing to wear—literally nothing. She protests that this is historically accurate.

HWANG TI   Lest we forget: Before we proceed to the great banquet in order to enjoy
ourselves, and so that your joy, my loyal subjects, shall be complete, one more word—there
now remains but one last enemy, a single
adversary in our empire, one man who calls
himself "The Voice of the People." You know
him as Min Ko. You know his sayings. With
abhorrence, I know, with abhorrence. Well,
you can take comfort now. Min Ko has been
captured.

MEE LAN   Min Ko?

HWANG TI   I am going to bring him to trial.

DA HING YEN   Before we dine?

HWANG TI   It won't take us long. You, however, my loyal subjects, prepare for the feast. It will the feast of our lives. Let there be music, classical music. Let there be nothing lacking for the delight of ourselves and our foreign guests. Let there be incense and theatre, cost what it may, fireworks and culture!

(*Gong.* DA HING YEN *and the others withdraw*)

Scene Nine

(HWANG TI *and* MEE LAN *are alone*)

HWANG TI   Greetings, my child, you above all!

MEE LAN   Papa . . .

HWANG TI   Mee Lan: my lovely orchid! (*He seats himself on the throne and relaxes*)   It is achieved. At last I can say it! A final adversary, a single one—I laugh at him, at all who hope to change the future. They will not survive their future. For power is ours. And we who have that power, we need no future. For we are happy. I will forestall the future. I will build a wall—that is, the people will build it——My child, why are you looking at me like that?

MEE LAN   I don't know, Papa, how much you know.

HWANG TI   About what?

MEE LAN   About the future. . . . I can't explain it. But, if I understand it rightly, our future, Papa lies behind us. We are (if I understand it rightly) two thousand years behind reality. And it's all untrue. I don't know, Papa, whether you know it or not.

HWANG TI   What is untrue?

MEE LAN   The show that's being played here. All. Your whole empire. Nothing but theater. . . .

(HWANG TI *gives a fatherly chuckle*)

HWANG TI   You have read too much, my child. You talk all this intellectual nonsense, my child, and you know I don't like that sort of thing. The Atomic Age! You read that in all the newspapers. Sit by me and be a child, as you ought to be: a happy child, a nice child, a positive child. Sit down! For I have my child, good tidings for you. (MEE LAN *sits on the steps*) He is alive!

MEE LAN   Who?

HWANG TI   Your prince, Wu Tsiang—Prince Charming! The Brave Prince, who has earned that title in action. It hung in the balance—unforeseen, they swooped down from the north and the south, the barbarian dogs of the steppes! We were surrounded!—that is to say, not us, of course, but our troops. Do you understand, my child, what that meant? Then up spoke Wu Tsiang the Brave: "We will fight to the last man!" And so it happened. He sacrificed his entire army, thirty thousand men——

MEE LAN   And he himself survived?

HWANG TI   He is a born general, no doubt about it! His fatherland owes him its praise. And now within the hour he will appear, my child, as your suitor before the assembled court. (MEE LAN *jumps up violently*) What is it? (MEE LAN *fans herself furiously, back to her father, silent*) What does this mean?

MEE LAN   What you already know, Papa: I will marry no prince.

HWANG TI   My dear child——

MEE LAN   It's out of the question.

HWANG TI   Why?

MEE LAN   I no longer believe in princes.

HWANG TI   Then whom do you wish to marry?

MEE LAN   Min Ko.

HWANG TI   What's that you say?

MEE LAN   I will marry Min Ko.

HWANG TI   A water-carrier?

MEE LAN   Laugh, Papa—I'm laughing too —Min Ko arrested, when no one even knows what he looks like!

HWANG TI   Now that he *is* arrested, we know very well how he looks—this water-carrier, this gaping fool, this mule-driver. Why do you smile? We paraded through the city and when people saw their emperor, they roared with joy. Only one man, once, did not roar. I saw him immediately. He gaped at me without making a sound. I said to my people: "I wonder what that voiceless one is thinking. Seize him after I have passed!"

MEE LAN   And?

HWANG TI   All the others, scarcely had I passed but they were roaring with joy——

MEE LAN   Then turned away, I can well imagine, and murmured their mocking words as always.

HWANG TI   True.

MEE LAN   With the exception of this one.

HWANG TI   True.

MEE LAN   And so he has been arrested, this lone brave man?

HWANG TI   Anyone who flaunts his bravery as openly as that, my child, is sure to be a pretty rascal, indeed. I don't like bravery. I don't trust it. Why didn't he roar with joy, eh? Tell me that.

MEE LAN   I don't know. Maybe he is mute.

HWANG TI   Mute?

MEE LAN   That happens, you know.

HWANG TI   Mute. Most amusing. We search for Min Ko, The Voice of the People, and now he wants us to believe that we have arrested a mute. What does that mean—that he is making fools of us again?

MEE LAN   Papa . . .

HWANG TI   Why should he be mute? Why him, of all people? (HWANG TI *gets up*) We'll see about this. We have a way of making him speak.

MEE LAN   You're going to have him tortured—?

HWANG TI   Until he confesses.

MEE LAN   Torture a mute—?

HWANG TI   Until he confesses! (*For the first time* HWANG TI *loses his gentle voice and bellows suddenly*) It must be *someone!* What's the good of all our victories, the greatness of all our victories, when the mocker goes on with his blasphemies? Am I never, never, to enjoy my peace? We can't win any more great victories; there are no enemies left. Do you grasp what that means? There are no more enemies left—(HWANG TI *who has been pacing about in his rage, stops suddenly*) Who is that?

Scene Ten

(THE CONTEMPORARY *steps forward from his place of concealment*)

THE CONTEMPORARY   Allow me to introduce myself——

HWANG TI   Are you Min Ko? (HWANG TI *draws his dagger*)

MEE LAN   Papa! (MEE LAN *springs between them*)

HWANG TI   Who are you?

THE CONTEMPORARY   An intellectual.

HWANG TI   A—what?

THE CONTEMPORARY   Doctor of Jurisprudence.

HWANG TI   You come most appropriately, Doctor of Jurisprudence! (*He replaces his dagger*) Go and call the mandarins of my court to assemble. Bring in the water-carrier whom we have arrested. I will hold trial—here and now.

THE CONTEMPORARY   Your majesty——

HWANG TI   Why don't you go?

THE CONTEMPORARY   I wanted to speak with you, Your Majesty.

HWANG TI   What?

THE CONTEMPORARY   My knowledge of history is not particularly extensive, and yet perhaps of some use to you.

HWANG TI   Do you know the future?

THE CONTEMPORARY   If you leave out of account certain modern scientific accomplishments—then yes, Your Majesty, generally.

HWANG TI   We are going to build a wall ——

THE CONTEMPORARY   Against the barbarians: I know. For the barbarians are always the others. That's still true today, Your Majesty. And culture, that's always us. And therefore we must liberate other people, for we (and not the others) are the Free World.

HWANG TI   Do you doubt it?

THE CONTEMPORARY   I have just seen your naked dagger, Your Majesty. How can I doubt it?

HWANG TI   What do you mean by that?

THE CONTEMPORARY   That I want to live.

HWANG TI   And why don't you do what I order?

THE CONTEMPORARY   Did you order me to speak the truth (insofar as we understand it) or did you order me to call the people to a Donkey Court?

HWANG TI   Donkey Court?

THE CONTEMPORARY   I'm only asking. (HWANG TI *draws his dagger again*) Your Majesty—I understand! (THE CONTEMPORARY *kowtows and goes*)

HWANG TI   But he didn't dare, you notice, he didn't dare! (MEE LAN *follows* THE CONTEMPORARY) Mee Lan? Mee Lan!

Scene Eleven

(HWANG TI, *left suddenly alone, turns toward the audience*)

HWANG TI   I know well enough what you're thinking, you out there. But I laugh at your hopes. You're thinking, this very evening you will see me hurled from this throne, for the play must have an ending and a moral, and when I am dethroned then you can complacently return home and drink your beer and nibble on a cracker. That's what you would like. You with your dramaturgy! I laugh. Go out and buy your evening newspaper, you out there, and on the first page you will find my name. For I do not intend to be dethroned. I don't believe in dramaturgy.

Scene Twelve

(*A young Egyptian princess, attractively un-clad, now appears*)

CLEOPATRA   I find you alone, my lord, and not in the serene good humor appropriate for such a masquerade party.

HWANG TI   Who are you?

CLEOPATRA   How can you ask? I am Cleopatra. Or have I disguised myself too thoroughly? (*She sits on his knee*) Why so grave?

HWANG TI   The situation is grave.

CLEOPATRA   Oh, well, hasn't it been for centuries?

HWANG TI   Never as grave as it is today.

CLEOPATRA   I remember, that's what Caesar said, too—and also Antony. I understand you great men who make history. Sometimes you are Roman, sometimes Spanish, sometimes Chinese. Only I, you notice, never change costumes. I love all men who make history. Indeed, I love all *men*—(*She caresses* HWANG TI) How lonely you must be!

HWANG TI   Since I have been on this throne, I have fought for one cause and one cause only: Peace! By which I mean, of course: for the Great Order, which we call the True Order and the Only Order and the Final Order! For thirteen years I have said, again and again and again, that I am their Savior. Why won't they believe me? For thirteen years they have gone around slandering me, and then, if I have one of these slanderers killed, I am considered a murderer.

CLEOPATRA   Really?

HWANG TI   Am I a bloodsucker?

CLEOPATRA   Who says that?

HWANG TI   Min Ko.

CLEOPATRA   Kill him! (*She caresses him*)

HWANG TI   They drive me to it, you know. For thirteen years they've been driving me to it. For thirteen years they've been saying: There's no such thing as a government that's always right. And so for thirteen years they've driven me from victory to victory. Do they think I make war because I *like* to? They don't want me to have any peace.

CLEOPATRA   I understand.

HWANG TI   But now what? The world is ours, yet no one understands what that means. The situation is now more serious than ever: There are no more victories possible! The world is ours! (CLEOPATRA *strokes him soothingly*) You say your name is Cleopatra?

CLEOPATRA   I am the girl who offers consolation to the victors. However I can! I was scarcely a child when Caesar came. He considered himself the Master of the World, and so naturally he moved me to pity. And then Antony! he needed me so desperately in order to enjoy his victories.

HWANG TI   Cleopatra!

CLEOPATRA   Yes?

HWANG TI   Tell me, just once——

CLEOPATRA   I believe in you!

(HWANG TI, *overjoyed by her correct answer, kisses her naked thigh, as* DA HING YEN *appears*)

HWANG TI   Yes. What is it *now*?

DA HING YEN   Wu Tsiang, better known as the Brave Prince, wishes to make known his arrival. He has just this moment leaped off the galloping horse which has dropped dead beneath him!

HWANG TI   Let him approach. (DA HING YEN *withdraws*) This prince comes as though in answer to my prayers. I will retire from the business of government. What do you think? The prince is going to marry my daughter and take over the burdens of history. What do I want here on this throne? I am not like this. People misunderstand me.

CLEOPATRA   I don't.

HWANG TI   Fundamentally, you see, I am a simple man.

CLEOPATRA   Make it short and sweet with this prince!

HWANG TI   I will retire—yes, that's it! That's all I've ever really wanted from the beginning. Somewhere in the country. I adore nature. Fundamentally, I'm an introvert. A little bungalow is all I ask. And I will read a good book, some books I've always wanted to read, perhaps by this Kung Fu Tse, and I will raise bees. Or I will go fishing. That's all I want to be on this earth: a poor, simple fisherman——

CLEOPATRA   And a landscape painter!

HWANG TI   How do you know that, my sweet?

CLEOPATRA Because, my sweet, I do *not* misunderstand you.

HWANG TI Cleopatra!

(HWANG TI, *again overjoyed by her answer, again kisses her naked thigh, as* WU TSIANG, *the Prince, appears*)

Scene Thirteen

THE PRINCE Long live Hwang Ti, our Great Exalted Emperor, called the Son of Heaven, he who is always in the right, the Savior of the Fatherland—all hail! (*drum roll*) All hail! (*drum roll*) All hail! (*drum roll.* HWANG TI *returns the elaborate gestures of greeting*)

HWANG TI You come in good time, Hero of Liautung. He who comes through such a battle as the only survivor of his entire army is an officer of stature, we know, and therefore I repeat: You come in good time, Prince, a time of celebration and gratitude.

THE PRINCE He who fulfills his duty because it *is* his duty has no need, Your Majesty, either of reward or thanks.

HWANG TI We know only too well, my Prince, of your noble disposition, which nevertheless will not hinder us from awarding you the highest order in our realm: for the medals are there, and the more dead there are, the more medals to go around for the survivors.

THE PRINCE Your Majesty, I have not fought for medals——

HWANG TI Not another word!

THE PRINCE I have fought for Peace, and for that Order which we call the True Order and the Happy Order and the Final Order.

HWANG TI We know that, Prince. The gratitude of the Fatherland awaits you. I will keep my word: My child shall be your wife, Hero of Liautung, this very night!

(*They repeat the complicated ceremony of soldierly greetings, then suddenly change their whole tone and manner;* THE PRINCE *takes off his Chinese helmet, puffs loudly, and mops the sweat from his brow*)

THE PRINCE Phew!

CLEOPATRA I take it you're thirsty?

THE PRINCE Talk about *hot!*

CLEOPATRA Vodka or whiskey—what do they drink hereabouts?

THE PRINCE These historical costumes are suffocating! I'm all chafed around my neck.

CLEOPATRA And you, my lord, what do you drink?

HWANG TI We drink no alcoholic beverages.

CLEOPATRA Ha! Do-gooder! (CLEOPATRA *mixes drinks*)

HWANG TI Now, to get down to business, my dear Prince: this affair of the Great Wall——

THE PRINCE Right!

HWANG TI You've received my letters?

THE PRINCE Right!

HWANG TI You take over the management. I will, of course, be Chairman of the Board of Directors. And, as noted, we'll stick to sandstone.

THE PRINCE I hear that granite would be better.

HWANG TI My sandstone is cheaper.

THE PRINCE Ah.

HWANG TI Your father advises us to use granite, I know. Your father is a loyal mandarin, and his province, I hear, is full of granite. Also full of timber. And my provinces, as far as I know, are poor in timber. What I *am* able to sell the Fatherland, however, is sandstone. Thus it has occurred to me: The construction will require lots of scaffolding. Lots of timber, which your worthy father can supply——

THE PRINCE At what price?

HWANG TI Oh, I don't understand prices——

(CLEOPATRA *hands* THE PRINCE *a glass*)

THE PRINCE Thank you very much! (*He starts to drink*)

HWANG TI I have still another concern, Prince——

THE PRINCE The labor supply?

HWANG TI We need a good million men, and many are going to die; nevertheless the figure of a million must remain stable, that's clear. And our people, I hear, are not enthusiastic over the plan.

THE PRINCE So much the better!

HWANG TI How is that?

THE PRINCE So much the cheaper! Whoever is not enthusiastic over the plan is obviously an enemy, and therefore becomes a slave-laborer. (*He lifts his glass*) Your health! (*He drinks.* THE CONTEMPORARY *enters*) Who is this?

HWANG TI My new court jester.

THE PRINCE Ah.

HWANG TI My Doctor of Jurisprudence.

Scene Fourteen

HWANG TI   What do you want?

THE CONTEMPORARY   The lords of your court, Your Majesty, are assembled, as ordered, for the Donkey Court. The defendant has been advised that it is useless for him to plead innocent and that things will go more smoothly if he accuses himself of high treason. The death sentence has already been drawn up.

HWANG TI   Good.

THE CONTEMPORARY   And that's no joke.

HWANG TI   You see, my dear Prince, how all things fulfill themselves this day: Min Ko, my last adversary, is in custody——

THE PRINCE   I have heard about that, Your Majesty—in no uncertain terms.

HWANG TI   Where?

THE PRINCE   I am delighted, Your Majesty, to find you in such good spirits in spite of the uproar before your gates. I couldn't have gotten through that mob without the aid of my trusty followers. They chased us, and when I cried: "Open in the name of the Emperor!" they hooted and threw stones at us. "Hand him over!" they bellowed. "Give us the Emperor!"

HWANG TI   Before my gates?

THE PRINCE   Nine of my men are dead, not to speak of my horse. We had to carve an alley through the mob with our naked sabers. Look, Your Majesty, see the blood on my boots!

HWANG TI   Rioting?

THE PRINCE   You didn't know about it?

(CLEOPATRA *hands a glass to* HWANG TI)

CLEOPATRA   That one's for you, my lord.

HWANG TI   No alcohol?

CLEOPATRA   Word of honor!

(HWANG TI *takes the glass*)

THE PRINCE   Your health!

HWANG TI   Why should there be rioting?

THE PRINCE   They want to set him free.

HWANG TI   Min Ko?

THE PRINCE   To keep him from being brought to trial.

HWANG TI   He will be brought to trial.

THE PRINCE   Anything else would be considered a sign of weakness.

HWANG TI   His head on the block! (HWANG TI *drinks, leaving himself with a milk mustache*)

THE CONTEMPORARY   And if the trial is not just?

HWANG TI   Be still.

THE CONTEMPORARY   Right.

HWANG TI   Was there something you wanted to say?

THE CONTEMPORARY   Nothing.

HWANG TI   We need a head, my dear Doctor of Jurisprudence. It *could* be yours. Was there something you wanted to say?

THE CONTEMPORARY   I just wanted to say— well, for example—er, if you will allow me, Your Majesty—you have milk on your upper lip.

HWANG TI   You had something else you wanted to say!

THE CONTEMPORARY   What?

HWANG TI   Would you like to be The Voice of the People?

THE CONTEMPORARY   I wanted to say: Nowadays—it's not very common for the people to go marching through the streets. Nowadays, after all, weapons—which the people don't have—keep getting better. Nevertheless, it happens. But nowadays—we don't get excited about these things, Your Majesty, we know as a matter of course: These are not the real people, out there in the streets, those are not *our* people!

THE PRINCE   But rather—?

THE CONTEMPORARY   Agitators. Spies. Terrorists. Undesirable Elements.

THE PRINCE   And what does that mean?

THE CONTEMPORARY   That means: The rulers determine who the people are. And those persons who are out there demonstrating in the streets today cannot be expected to be treated like people. For the real people—the *real* people—are always satisfied with their rulers.

HWANG TI   Good.

THE PRINCE   Very good.

THE CONTEMPORARY   Isn't it true? The blood on your splendid boots, Prince—how could that be the blood of the people? It would be a painful thought, wouldn't it? Very painful.

HWANG TI   What were those words again?

THE CONTEMPORARY   Terrorists, Undesirable Elements, Agitators. Very helpful words, Your Majesty; they nip truth in the bud.

HWANG TI   Doctor of Jurisprudence, you will remain in our service.

THE CONTEMPORARY   And this, too, Your Majesty, is no joke.

(HWANG TI *rises and repeats the ceremony of salutes*)

HWANG TI   Hero of Liautung! (THE PRINCE *rises and puts his helmet back on*) I greet you, Hero of Liautung, as my son-in-law and heir to my kingdom; *if* you are able to pass the final test!

THE PRINCE   Your Majesty.

HWANG TI   Undesirable Elements are at our gates. . . .

THE PRINCE   I understand.

HWANG TI   You know what hangs in the balance.

THE PRINCE   I will deal with them as they deserve, as Agitators, Spies, and Terrorists.

HWANG TI   I have complete confidence in you, Prince. You are loyalty personified. You battle for a kingdom that is sacred to you, my dear Prince, you battle for your own heritage! (THE PRINCE *repeats the ceremonial saluting*) We will meet again later, I hope, in fireworks and festivities!

(HWANG TI *goes off to the celebration, arm in arm with* CLEOPATRA. THE CONTEMPORARY *follows them. The music swells.* THE PRINCE, *left alone, turns to the audience*)

Scene Fifteen

THE PRINCE   You heard it yourselves: *If* I am able to pass the final test! And I swear to you, that's the way it's gone for years now. Patience! Over and over—patience, be patient, be patient! And always this talk about the Great Order and the True Order, which is going to make us all happy, of the Final Order, which is coming soon—*if* I am able to pass the final test! It's the old song, you know, the song of the Leaders—they can do everything except die. They drink milk and don't smoke, they take good care of themselves, until finally one finds oneself—you will come to understand my generation!—thinking of overthrowing the government. (*laughter from the company within*) And meanwhile where is the Princess —my betrothed?

Scene Sixteen

(*The company of masqueraders passes across the stage again.* L'INCONNUE DE LA SEINE *is going about with a little basket distributing masks*)

L'INCONNUE   A cotillion, gentlemen, a cotillion!

NAPOLEON   I must not return, they say! I *must* not! The Era of Great Leaders is past. What sort of nonsense is that? I *will* return. I will lead them against Russia——

L'INCONNUE   A cotillion, sir?

PHILIP   Not return! He said the same to me. Freedom of thought? Insane dreamer! At least, this is a novel idea, but, good heavens!——

L'INCONNUE   If I may, sir?

PHILIP   Yes? What are we to do now?

L'INCONNUE   Don't you know, sir, what a cotillion is? You are to dance with that mask which is a partner to your own.

PHILIP   What? Dance? With a death's-head?

L'INCONNUE   Try it again.

PHILIP   Ah.

L'INCONNUE   Again a death's-head!

PHILIP   Is the entire court to enjoy this performance?

(DON JUAN *stops with* COLUMBUS)

DON JUAN   You see: it's a dance of death. Didn't I say so? We are lost, Captain, if we don't get there.

COLUMBUS   Where?

DON JUAN   When I think of your world: Marco Polo, who discovered China, and it was as though he had arrived on the other side of time and space; Vasco da Gama; and you—ah, that was a world open in all directions, surrounded by mystery. There were islands which no human had ever set foot on, continents undiscovered by man, coasts of hope. A twig floating upon the sea was a twig of promise. Anything was possible, and everything; the earth was like a bride. There was poverty, too, I know, injustice, hunger, the tyranny of kings, but also (and as a result): Hope! There were fruits which belonged to no man, Paradise which was not yet lost—an answer to my longing. The Unknown was still possible; adventure was in the air. A virginal world. And the earth was not what it is today: a globe cut up into sections once and for all, a big ball that sits at one's elbow upon the writing desk, complete, contained, devoid of hope! For man is everywhere, and everything that we have now discovered has served to make the world, not greater, but smaller. . . . Let's fly, Captain! In seven days (or four, or less—I don't know any more) we can circle the entire world, and all those spaces that represented Hope to you will become transmuted into time, which we no longer need, for we —we have no more hope, we have no Beyond! —if you don't give it back to us, Captain.

COLUMBUS   And where, my dear young man, am I to find it?

DON JUAN   Discover it!!

COLUMBUS   So that they can call it *America* again?

(L'INCONNUE *comes forward*)

L'INCONNUE   A cotillion, my lords, a cotillion?

DON JUAN   Death's-heads, nothing but death's-heads.

L'INCONNUE   The young gentleman sounds as though he were in despair.

DON JUAN   Yes, indeed, I am—so we all are, those of us who are young——

COLUMBUS   There is no need to be.

L'INCONNUE   Really?

COLUMBUS   The India that I meant to find is still undiscovered.

DON JUAN   India?

COLUMBUS   There still remains for you, young man, the continent of your own soul, the adventure of truth. I never saw any other regions of hope.

Scene Seventeen

(MEE LAN *now appears. She is wearing a contemporary evening dress, which draws every eye toward her and produces a sudden silence*)

MEE LAN   Where is The Contemporary?

(THE PRINCE *falls on one knee before her.* THE MASKERS *disappear*)

THE PRINCE   Daughter of our Great Exalted Emperor, Mee Lan, which means: Beautiful Orchid——

MEE LAN   Yes, yes—I know.

THE PRINCE   —at your chaste feet, the Brave Prince, Wu Tsiang, kneels—he who woos you truly, who has fought and won for love of you in the thick of battle, who has done all things for love of you——

MEE LAN   So I hear.

THE PRINCE   —without thought of peril—

MEE LAN   Stand up.

THE PRINCE   —returning home as victor, unconquered by the enemy, but conquered only by your love, returning home to kiss your chaste feet!

(*While* THE PRINCE *kisses her feet,* MEE LAN *is looking all around for* THE CONTEMPORARY; THE MASKERS *have gone, the stage is empty*)

MEE LAN   Please. What's the good of all that Chinese nonsense? I'm looking for someone else——

THE PRINCE   Mee Lan?

MEE LAN   It's urgent. (THE PRINCE *jumps up and stands blocking her way*) Let me go. Seriously. This is urgent.

THE PRINCE   Mee Lan!

MEE LAN   You make me sorry for you. What do you want? I see that you have survived the war. All right. Congratulations.

THE PRINCE   Mee Lan?

MEE LAN   Speaking very frankly, you give me a pain.

THE PRINCE   Don't you remember the night before I went away? The moon was shining, the full moon, and we sat here in the park——

MEE LAN   And there was some kissing. I know. I was there.

THE PRINCE   Mee Lan——

MEE LAN   I remember too that whenever you couldn't think of anything else you always used to say: Mee Lan! Mee Lan! Mee Lan! (THE PRINCE *tries to kiss her*) Stop that! (THE PRINCE *lets go of her and steps back, proud and sulky*) Now you are insulted again. I remember you always get insulted when you can't think of anything else to say or do. (*She strokes his helmet*) Come. Not another word now!

THE PRINCE   Mee Lan—?

MEE LAN   I was a child. I'm sorry. I didn't know what love means. But then who doesn't misuse and misunderstand that word? Simply because the moon is shining. Isn't it true? One lets oneself go, simply because nobody else is at hand at the moment. And since one sometimes believes that no other man will ever appear—well, all these things are not altogether lies.

THE PRINCE   And now another man has appeared?

MEE LAN   I was a child, an inexperienced girl. Word of honor! And then one morning—it's quite natural: I fell in love with your new helmet (the way girls nowadays fall in love with a Porsche or a Mercedes), then one morning I awoke to discover I didn't believe in princes any more.

THE PRINCE   Now he has appeared?

MEE LAN   I hope so—yes. I hope so, very, very much—yes, oh, yes! (THE PRINCE *draws his Chinese saber*) What does this mean . . . ? Let me go . . . I mean it. Let me go. . . . Are you disappointed, is that it . . . ? What can I do for you . . . ? I don't want to insult you; I just don't love you. . . . Why so grim? You have all my best wishes for your future career. . . . Are you trembling with self-pity, Hero of Liautung?

THE PRINCE   He will learn to know me better!

MEE LAN   Who?

THE PRINCE   So this is my reward! This!

MEE LAN   I don't understand you.

THE PRINCE   I trusted in him. Who promised me fortune and success? I fought for him.

MEE LAN   Without thought of peril, I know.

THE PRINCE   Laugh now! We are not yet at the end.

MEE LAN   You are speaking of Papa?

THE PRINCE   Go ahead! Laugh!

MEE LAN   What did you think?

THE PRINCE   I thought an Emperor's word could be trusted.

MEE LAN   Now you are really talking like a Chinese prince.

THE PRINCE   It was I who won the victory!

MEE LAN   Who denies it?

THE PRINCE   I! I! No one else!

MEE LAN   You're sure to get a medal.

THE PRINCE   A *medal!!?*

MEE LAN   Is that what you really thought: that I would be the reward to hang on your breast?

THE PRINCE   I will not be cheated!

MEE LAN   Who is cheating you? You fought for the Emperor of China; what does that have to do with my love? I don't love you; what does that have to do with the Emperor of China? You are really comical.

THE PRINCE   Laugh!

MEE LAN   What do you expect to do with that sword?

THE PRINCE   Go on! Laugh.

MEE LAN   You imagine you've been cheated, whereas you've simply been told the bare truth. That's what it is. Fighting the bloodiest battles is easier for you, Hero of Liautung, than listening to the common, everyday truth spoken in confidence.

THE PRINCE   Laugh!

MEE LAN   I'm not laughing at all.

THE PRINCE   The laugh will be on you, now——(*He resheathes his sword and starts out*)

MEE LAN   Where are you going?

THE PRINCE   At this moment, the people are at the gates.

MEE LAN   So I've heard.

THE PRINCE   I am to disperse them.

MEE LAN   And?

THE PRINCE   And? If I don't disperse them? If I do not protect that empire which does not

reward my faith? If I open the very gates before which the people clamor?

MEE LAN   I understand.

THE PRINCE   I will not be cheated!

MEE LAN   You've said that already. . . .

(*They fall silent together*)

THE PRINCE   I am going to do it.

MEE LAN   I will never be your happiness.

THE PRINCE   And if I force you to it?

MEE LAN   That is all I can say: I will never be your happiness (THE PRINCE *kneels again*) Why don't you go?

THE PRINCE   Mee Lan——

MEE LAN   I don't love you.

THE PRINCE   For the last time——

MEE LAN   I don't love you.

THE PRINCE   Mee Lan!

MEE LAN   You are laughable. Go away. You believe in power, all experience to the contrary. You believe in happiness through power. You make me sick. You are stupid. (*a fanfare*) Go away! (*another fanfare*) The members of the court are coming. The farce is going on. . . .

Scene Eighteen

(*Entry of* MANDARINS *and* EUNUCHS; *grand procession to the Royal Court (choreography, drums, music), during which* THE PRINCE, *after some irresolution, stands up and goes away.* THE MASKERS *appear, in the meanwhile, and finally* THE EMPEROR, *in full regalia*)

HWANG TI   Mandarins of my realm! I have called you together, as so many times in the past, to give me the benefit of your collective wisdom. I am handing over to your court my last adversary, a man who calls himself The Voice of the People. Let wisdom rule! As for me, my faithful subjects, I will remain silent, otherwise it might be thought that I was trying to influence this court. Let that never be thought! I will remain silent. (HWANG TI *seats himself on his throne*)

DA HING YEN   Bring in the prisoner! (*drum roll*)

MEE LAN   Papa!—

HWANG TI   Don't interrupt now! What's the meaning of this costume?

MEE LAN   The Prince——

HWANG TI   Later! Later!

MEE LAN   Listen to me, Papa——

HWANG TI   Later!

(*A ceremony has begun:* DA HING YEN *and four* MANDARINS *stand up, each holding a large book open before him*)

DA HING YEN   Let us read, as the ceremony prescribes, the sentences from the handbook of ritual: "Li Gi, the Master, Spake."

FIRST MANDARIN   "The Master spake: When the path of righteousness is followed upon the earth, then it will happen that there will come forth a Son of Heaven, one who well deserves that name."

DA HING YEN   "It was not so, however, during the Tsin Dynasty."

SECOND MANDARIN   "The Master spake: It is of no importance how great the kingdom may be, but rather that the ruler is able to win the hearts of his subjects."

DA HING YEN   "It was not so, however, during the Tsin Dynasty."

THIRD MANDARIN   "The Master spake: If there is justice in the hearts of the rulers, then state and house will flourish and prosper; if the rulers are pure in heart, there will be no strife among the people, and no unrest need arise."

DA HING YEN   "It was not so, however, during the Tsin Dynasty."

FOURTH MANDARIN   "The Master spake: Justice is the root of true prosperity. But if men set prosperity at any cost as a goal, evil results."

DA HING YEN   "This, however, is how it was during the Tsin Dynasty: The rulers did not act according to justice and propriety, and the life of the people was not harmonious. People sought only for news of victories; the rulers were covetous of possessions; the strong were only concerned with cunningly hoarding their strength. They had a book of ritual, but the rulers did not live in accord with its precepts. The Prince had been placed on the throne by a eunuch who taught him how to prosecute all his enemies in mock trials. The most learned men of the court were assailed as dissidents and traitors, and no one dared to speak out against this injustice. Heaven however will always punish an unjust ruler, through the actions of his own people."

(*They close their books and resume their seats*)

MEE LAN   Papa——

HWANG TI   Ssssh!

MEE LAN   You will be sorry if you don't listen to me—

HWANG TI   Be quiet!

MEE LAN   The Prince, Papa, the Prince is going to open the gates—(*drum roll*)

DA HING YEN   The accused!

(*The prisoner is brought in*—WANG, *the mute son of the Prologue. Helpless and uncomprehending, he turns the wrong way and gapes out at the audience.* HWANG TI *involuntarily starts up, but then sinks down again*)

DA HING YEN   Here! Here! You must face us!

HWANG TI   Go on!

DA HING YEN   Accused, you are suspected of being the man who calls himself Min Ko, The Voice of the People, whose words are known to all. I ask in the name of Justice, do you know the words I refer to?

THE CONTEMPORARY   For example:
"What do we count on the day of
    victory,
We, the farmers and folk in the
    land?
We count our dead, we count our
    dead,
While you jingle your gold in your
    hand."

Or——

HWANG TI   Enough!

THE CONTEMPORARY
"He who sits on the throne:
He hopes the future never comes;
He who loves the Lord:
He hears the future in the drums."

HWANG TI   We're not interested in hearing all these rhymes!

THE CONTEMPORARY   I can well understand that, Your Majesty. Their literary value is slight. So slight that one wonders at the extraordinary price Your Majesty has placed upon their heads.

DA HING YEN   I ask in the name of Justice: Are you the man who invented these words and spread them from mouth to mouth through the entire realm?

THE CONTEMPORARY   He's not.

HWANG TI   Silence!

THE CONTEMPORARY   But I happen to know that——

DA HING YEN   If you remain silent, my boy, that means that you do not want to be recognized. If you do not want to be recognized, that means that you must be the man we are seeking. And *that* means: Your head on the block! Therefore I ask: Do you confess to the charge or do you deny it? (WANG *shakes his head*) You don't deny it? (WANG *nods vigorously*) You confess? (WANG *shakes his head*) Your Majesty, the accused denies——

HWANG TI   We will prove him guilty! Go on!

DA HING YEN   As you will, Your Majesty.

THE CONTEMPORARY   You are innocent, I

know. Why don't you speak out? They are afraid of your silence. Don't you see that? They suspect that you are thinking the truth, my son, simply because you *don't* speak.

HWANG TI   Go on!

THE CONTEMPORARY   Don't be silent, my boy, glorify them at the top of your lungs!

HWANG TI   Go on! Are we assembled to listen to the prattlings of a court fool? Go on!

DA HING YEN   It's an ancient custom, Your Majesty, that the man who defends the innocent before the lords of our land should be the Court Fool.

HWANG TI   The innocent?

DA HING YEN   In the eyes of a fool, of course, Your Majesty. We will demonstrate the opposite.

HWANG TI   So I hope.

DA HING YEN   As you will, Your Majesty. (*He makes a sign*) Fu Chu, the Executioner! (*In the brief pause which now occurs as they await the appearance of the executioner, two more* MASKERS *appear and promenade across the stage: Schiller's* MARY STUART *and* PONTIUS PILATE)

PILATE   But then as I sat in the seat of judgment (which is called in Hebrew: Gabbatha), I answered and spake unto him: What is truth?

DA HING YEN   Quiet!

PILATE   There was, though, an outcry before the place of judgment, and the high priests cried out and said: "Away with him! Crucify him!" Then I flogged him, but when I saw that this was accomplishing nothing, I took some water and washed my hands before the people, saying: "I am innocent of the blood of this just man."

DA HING YEN   Quiet!

PILATE   The other man was named Barabbas and was a robber——

DA HING YEN   Quiet!

PILATE   —or a murderer——

(*The Chinese executioner enters*)

DA HING YEN   Fu Chu, the Executioner! (MEE LAN *covers her face with her hands*) Let us continue in the name of Justice. Since the accused refuses to be accused and is not willing to incriminate himself——

THE CONTEMPORARY   He is mute!

HWANG TI   Silence.

THE CONTEMPORARY   I know it.

DA HING YEN   Mute?

THE CONTEMPORARY   I can't help it, Your Majesty. It's a joke, really—you have sought out The Voice of the People in order to silence

him, and now you have arrested—look—a mute!

HWANG TI   How do you know this?

THE CONTEMPORARY   Any man who sees your Justice and remains silent instead of praising your Justice in order to escape from your Justice *must* be a mute, it seems to me, or else a saint who is looking for martyrdom. Are you a saint? (WANG *shakes his head*) The accused denies being a saint.

HWANG TI   *Anyone* can deny that!

THE CONTEMPORARY   Except, of course, a saint. For if he is a saint, he can't lie, simply because he *is* one. Er—does Your Majesty follow the logic? Any man who sees your Justice in silence and is not posing can only be a saint or a mute, since, however, it's quite clear the accused is not a saint——

(HWANG TI *stands up*)

HWANG TI   The rack will teach him how to speak!

THE CONTEMPORARY   And what shall he speak, Your Majesty?

HWANG TI   The truth!

THE CONTEMPORARY   What for?

HWANG TI   Do you think I don't recognize the truth?

THE CONTEMPORARY   So much the better, Your Majesty; then we won't need any rack.

(HWANG TI *stares about him like a caged beast*)

HWANG TI   Mute? Now all at once? How can this be? After he has mocked me in every street and village square for ten years? Am I never, never to—(*He turns to the* MANDARINS) Haven't I taught my judges how to conduct trials properly?

DA HING YEN   To be sure, Your Majesty.

HWANG TI   Go on! I say. Or am I now to be mocked at by a mute? Go on! (*He sits down again*)

THE CONTEMPORARY   You see, my boy, how much simpler it would have been if you could have at least feigned respect, as everyone else does. Your silence is ruining everything. You'll wind up forcing them to speak the truth themselves.

DA HING YEN   Let us continue in the name of Justice. Accused! Your death sentence is prepared, and the Emperor, whose graciousness is dear to us, awaits your confession. For it is an old Chinese custom that no death sentence should be executed without proof or confession of guilt. Therefore why are you silent? If you refuse to confess that you are guilty of high treason, then in effect you are saying that the Son of Heaven, who is always in the right, is *not* in the right—and you are then for *that* reason guilty of high treason! Do you understand, my boy, what I am saying to you? In the name of Justice, although it makes no difference as far as your execution is concerned, I ask you for the last time: Do you confess to the crime of high treason or do you deny it? (WANG *shakes his head*) That means: you deny it? (WANG *nods*) That means: you confess? (WANG *shakes his head*) It is not becoming for you to shake your head at this court, my boy. Answer! I ask you for the last time: Do you confess or deny your guilt? (WANG *nods and shakes his head and nods, faster and faster*) To the dragons with you! I give up! Or—are you *really* mute? (WANG *nods*) Your Majesty . . .

(HWANG TI *springs off his throne*)

HWANG TI   Torture him! That's not true! Torture him! That's a lie, like everything else he has already said! Torture him!

THE CONTEMPORARY   What has he already said, Your Majesty?

HWANG TI   You traitor, you wretch, you hard-hearted beast! Do you think we don't know what you are thinking behind your dirty forehead, you gaping fool, you ragamuffin, you man of the streets! The Great Wall, you say, is nothing but a business deal! Millions dead, because of a business deal! Deny it, if you can! (WANG *is silent*) Bloodsucker, you say—my whole court, a company of bloodsuckers! Do you think I haven't heard? I, Tsin She Hwang Ti, the liberator of the people, the bringer of peace, I, a bloodsucker, you say—I suck the blood of the poor, I enjoy the fruits of your labor! *Your* labor! (HWANG TI *attempts a scornful laugh*) Ha! Ha! (WANG *is silent*) Gape at me, yes, and tremble! I'll force you to be silent, you chatterbox, you seditionist, and if you refuse to bring one word out of your stinking throat—I know what your kind thinks! I am not the Savior of the Fatherland. I am a robber of the people, a murderer of the people, a criminal—deny it if you can! (WANG *is silent*) You don't deny it!? (WANG *is silent*) You dare —to my face—a criminal!—you dare—before all the mandarins of my court—to my very face! I, the mightiest man in the world, I, you say, I: a coward, a laughable simpleton, an idiot, a scarecrow of my own fear, you say, I tremble and shake, I don't dare hear what my loyal subjects really think, for I know that they hate me, you say, and there's not an honest man in my empire, you say, who wouldn't like to spit in my face if he could—— (HWANG TI *turns toward his court, suddenly composed and smiling*) My loyal subjects, is

that true? I ask you in all honesty, is there a man in this assemblage who would like to spit in my face? (BRUTUS *steps forward*) I mean, among my *contemporaries* . . . ! (BRUTUS *steps back*) I ask you before all the world: Is there a man who would like to spit in my face? (*They all shake their heads*) That is to say— you love me? (*They all nod*)

MEE LAN   Papa! Stop it! This is nonsense! Everyone knows you have the power. Papa! You're not changing the truth! Who believes you? I don't. What good is all this? Stop this farce, Papa. . . .

(*A silence. A* MANDARIN *steps forward*)

THE MANDARIN   At last!

HWANG TI   What does my loyal subject mean?

THE MANDARIN   Out of the mouth of your own child. At last. You have heard it.

(HWANG TI *looks at him. The silence continues. Everyone stares.* HWANG TI *gives a tiny sign to* DA HING YEN. DA HING YEN *gives the same sign to* FU CHU, *who relays it to someone else, and* THE MANDARIN, *almost before he grasps it, is silently and almost magically removed as if on runners. No one moves; it is as if nothing had happened*)

HWANG TI   I ask you one more time before all the world: Is it true, my loyal subjects, that you are all feigning loyalty simply because you fear my torture chamber? (*Everyone shakes his head*) And you, man of the streets, you dare to tell me—to my very face—my power lies in my torture instruments. Well, you shall become acquainted with them, you liar, you damnable—ha! to my face! A criminal, you say, a man has to be a criminal to stay *out* of my prisons. And whoever is wise had better stay under cover. What do you know about wisdom, you nastynose? And I, you say, I kill all wisdom, I am the lie in person, I am the plague enthroned, and whoever stretches his hand toward me, it stinks of carrion; I am no Son of Heaven and no man, I am the spiritual sickness of my time—deny it, if you can! (WANG *is silent*) You can't deny it!! (WANG *is silent*) Shall I strangle you with my own hands, you—you *talker*? So that you are finally silenced, you with your wisdom, you Voice of the People, do you think I am going to be mocked at on the day of my victory—do you think— (HWANG TI *suddenly has a thought*) Do you have a father? (WANG *nods, then shakes his head*) What does that mean?

THE CONTEMPORARY   His father was killed in your last war.

HWANG TI   Do you have a mother? (WANG

nods, beaming) Then I will have your mother tortured—! (WANG *falls on his knees, unable to cry out*) Fu Chu! (*The executioner steps forward*) Is it true, Executioner, what this slanderous dog tells in every street and village square in the empire? I am the murderer of my friends, he says. I ask you, Hangman, before all the world: Of all the people you have tortured, was a single one of them a friend of mine? (FU CHU *shakes his head*) You hear that? (HWANG TI *kicks the mute*) Voice of the People—*you*—you hear? (MEE LAN *sobs loudly*) Enough. The truth, I think, has been demonstrated. I, Tsin She Hwang Ti, a bloodsucker, I fatten myself on your labor! I: the murderer of my friends, the destroyer of my people—I force them into the wars, you say this to my face! I create the wars myself, you say, in order to divert the people's rage toward others and to save myself through their patriotism—in my very face! Do you think I am going to let you drag our most sacred beliefs through the mud? Our wars, our battles for peace? The barbarian dogs of the steppes, you say—they wouldn't have done anything to us if I hadn't attacked them. How do you know that? How do you know what no one can know, you gaping lout who can't even read a newspaper, you water-carrier, you mule-driver, you ragamuffin, how do you know what would have happened if I hadn't attacked just in time —attacked! Yes, indeed! Naturally, I attacked them! (HWANG TI *grows angrier*) Shut up! I say. Shut up! (HWANG TI *seizes him and shakes him*) One word more and I'll strangle you! One word more! (HWANG TI *hurls him to the floor*) Thousands, hundreds of thousands, you say, slaughtered for a lie, bled white, crippled for the kingdom of spiritual sickness in our time—mine!—bled white, you say, for me! For a criminal! And this today—on the day of our victory! Do you think I am going to let you mock at all of them, the heroes of my army, thousands and hundreds of thousands, who have died for me—for *me*, yes! for *me!* (HWANG TI *is now almost voiceless*) Shut up! I say. (*He totters back to his throne, hoarse and shaking*) Torture him! He is the one. Torture him till he confesses. I will never listen to him. Torture him till he hears the cracking of his own bones!

(FU CHU, *the executioner, drags out the mute*) I've gotten overexcited, gentlemen of the court. You heard the slandering liar, though— enough! No more of him! He was our final adversary. My loyal subjects, assembled in honor

of this glorious day, let us now proceed to the joyous banquet!

(HWANG TI *rises with an effort. Music begins. Arm in arm with* CLEOPATRA, *he goes out, followed by his entire court, again with appropriate choreography.* MEE LAN—*in evening dress*—*and* THE CONTEMPORARY *are left behind*)

Scene Nineteen

THE CONTEMPORARY   You despise me, don't you? You are disillusioned. Well, what did you expect?

(DON JUAN *appears and bows to* MEE LAN)

MEE LAN   Thank you, but I don't dance the cha-cha-cha.

DON JUAN (*sadly*)   Ah. (*He bows again and withdraws*)

MEE LAN   You knew that he was mute.

THE CONTEMPORARY   Yes.

MEE LAN   And you are going to permit this mute boy to be tortured—you, who know everything?

THE CONTEMPORARY   Permit?

MEE LAN   You shrug your shoulders. And that's all! Shrug the shoulders, light another cigarette—while they torture a mute to force him to scream; and you, who can speak, stand there and keep silent—and that's all!

THE CONTEMPORARY   What can I do?

MEE LAN   You with your learning! Time and space are one; how comforting! Destruction of the world by heat; how exciting! And the speed of light is unsurpassable; how interesting! Energy equals mass times the speed of light.

THE CONTEMPORARY   —Squared.

MEE LAN   And what's the result of all this? You with your great formulas! You shrug your shoulders while a man is flayed alive, and light another cigarette!

(*He is silent for a moment or two, then suddenly shouts*)

THE CONTEMPORARY   What can I do? (*He automatically takes out a cigarette, then speaks very quietly*) He will be tortured. I know. As thousands before him have been. First the thumbscrew, then the nailed whip, then the business with the block and pulleys (which tears the tendons so that he will never again be able to lift his arms), then the white-hot wire, then the bone-breakers, repeated as often as necessary—all that, I know, has been going on right up to today. And whether we cry or laugh, whether we dance, sleep, read—there is probably not a single hour that goes by today in which some man somewhere is not being tortured, flayed, martyred, disgraced, murdered. (*He takes the cigarette out of his mouth again*) But has any intellectual ever been able to forestall destiny simply because he foresaw it? We can write books and make speeches, even angry speeches: "Why this can no longer go on!" And yet it goes on. Precisely so. Great and learned persons arise and call to mankind: "The cobalt bomb, which you are now producing, will be the end of you!"—and people go on making the cobalt bomb. (*He sticks the cigarette back in his mouth and snaps on his cigarette lighter*) You're right, Mee Lan—to shrug the shoulders and light another cigarette, that's all someone like me can do in times like these. (*He lights his cigarette*)

MEE LAN Talk! Nothing but talk! (*he smokes*) Don't you hear?

THE CONTEMPORARY What?

MEE LAN Through all of this—don't you hear? A mute, who is being tortured till he screams! Till he screams—a helpless, defenseless creature without a voice! And you hear only your own voice? I don't want to know the things you know. Why don't you cry? You with your sterile science! Why don't you cry for him? No! I hate you!

THE CONTEMPORARY Mee Lan——

MEE LAN I hate you! (*She throws herself into a chair*)

THE CONTEMPORARY And you—what have you done? I see you have gotten yourself dressed up. You want to be a modern woman, I see, and yet you still expect men to perform miracles. You were there, the same as I. Why didn't you save him? You put up with it, you wept, you hoped. For what? That the others would do something, that a man would, that I would? What were you able to do? Whether man or woman, we stand here, one human being facing another, and I ask you: What did *you* do? You changed clothes. That's all. (MEE LAN *sobs*) You hate me——

MEE LAN Yes!

THE CONTEMPORARY I don't know what you think love is. Did you hope that I would be something for you to admire and wonder at? And what do you find? A man who is not capable of changing the world——

MEE LAN You're no man!

THE CONTEMPORARY Otherwise I would

have committed suicide on the spot, is that what you mean? Is that what you expected? It wouldn't have changed the world—for there's never any shortage of deaths!—but you would have discovered that I was a man. Dead —but a man! (*He smiles teasingly*) And you're supposed to be a Chinese princess! (*She turns away*) You are young. And now you are sobbing. You are very young. You know what hope is, Mee Lan, but hope is not the measure of our actions—or inactions. You don't know what the world is. . . .

(*Two men with cigars came in: a* TAIL COAT *and a* CUTAWAY)

THE TAIL COAT A cigar of distinction!

THE CUTAWAY Isn't it?

THE TAIL COAT Have you had a chance to chat with Lohengrin?

THE CUTAWAY Lohengrin is here, too?

THE TAIL COAT The whole cultural world!

THE CUTAWAY Tell me, what's he like?

THE TAIL COAT Lohengrin? Not a bad fellow, if you can get him to stop singing.

THE CUTAWAY I've been chatting with Mary Stuart.

THE TAIL COAT Ah.

THE CUTAWAY People always think persons like that have no culture. But they know all sorts of things. A very fine person, this Stuart! And then, as I always say: What a fine gift of conversation these classical characters have! It's a shame·my wife isn't here. As she always says, she simply can't live without the classics —and she means it. (*They both nod with pompous courtesy to someone offstage*) Do you have any inkling who this Roman is who keeps watching us all the time?

THE TAIL COAT I do indeed.

THE CUTAWAY Really?

THE TAIL COAT Also a classic character.

(BRUTUS *enters, holding a newspaper rolled up like a parchment scroll*)

BRUTUS

A word, you citizens! If I seem sad,
Think only that the sorrow of my
    gaze
Goes not toward men of mediocre
    mind.
Consider that it is a bitter task,
The full reconstitution of the State
(The which I love, you know, more
    than myself),
And knowledge of these things, to
    freely speak,

Has cast the shades of gloom across
    my face.

THE TAIL COAT   Hm.

BRUTUS

The times are grave. Your evening
    paper here—
Which you had dropped—has roused
    my blood
(I understand your paper all too
    well!);
No longer will I stand aside, the
    while my heart
Buries its impulses at their birth.
What is the plan? You are, my friends,
If I have understood your paper right,
My brothers under the skin, O, busi-
    nessmen,
O, friends of Rome, who love the
    public weal,
Love Justice as I do, and will defend
Freedom with your lives, if necessary.
Have I, friends, read your thoughts
    aright?

THE CUTAWAY   Yes, yes—quite.

BRUTUS My name is Brutus.

THE CUTAWAY   Ah.

THE TAIL COAT   What did he say?

THE CUTAWAY   Brutus.

THE TAIL COAT   Hm.

BRUTUS

I hear the raging mob is threatening
Justice, that most noble work of man;
Is threatening with violence the State,
And in an hour of rage endangers
    Freedom
(But oh, how well I understand that
    rage
When I see the abuse of all these
    things!)
A suicidal passion of destruction!
Is it then something for the common
    good
(Do not conceal your thoughts from
    me!)
That you are planning? Hark! the
    shouts
Of uproar that now reach our ears—a
    flame
Whipped by a storm that whirls
    about us.
What is to come? Evil is on the march
And takes whatever path it will
    when men
Do not remove determinedly those
    things
Which harm the folk (be it a man's
    own friend!).

You know? Declare yourselves! What
    do the people want?

THE TAIL COAT   Higher wages. What else?

BRUTUS

Think not, my friends, I am an ad-
    vocate
Of nonsense when I question you—
I, enemy of mob rule as I am—
Concerning the true grounds of this
    uprising.

THE CUTAWAY   Higher wages are out of the
question, that's quite clear. Where will that
lead us? To higher prices! But try to explain
this to the mob! Apart from that, though, there
is nothing to worry about; the police have the
situation well in hand.

BRUTUS

I do not understand, my friends, the
    form
Your government doth take, but if I
    read
This paper here aright, 'tis a repub-
    lic——

THE CUTAWAY   Yes, yes—quite.

THE TAIL COAT   Absolutely!

THE CUTAWAY   Yes, sir!

THE TAIL COAT   And we won't have any
tampering with it!

BRUTUS Brutus is glad to hear it.

THE TAIL COAT   Particularly not by labor
unions and the like!

BRUTUS

I know not the condition of your
    state,
And yet I hope that these police you
    speak of
Are not the bodyguards of tyranny.
If this were so, oh, then, eternal God!
Then let us, brothers, let us bathe
    our hands
In Caesar's blood up to the very
    elbows.
Let us make our swords smoke red
    with blood!
And let us step forth in the market
    place
And, swinging round our heads our
    bloody weapons,
Cry to all the world: Rescue! Free-
    dom! Peace!

(*The* TAIL COAT *and the* CUTAWAY *exchange
uneasy glances*)

THE TAIL COAT   Er—if you have no objections—we can be heard here—(*They lead
their classic character aside*)

BRUTUS Give me your hands—one, then the other——

(*They disappear.* MEE LAN *and* THE CONTEMPORARY *remain. During the* BRUTUS *intermezzo, which has crossed the forestage, they have taken no notice of the interruption*)

THE CONTEMPORARY What did you expect from me? I ask you. What did you expect? I could have saved him? Is that what you think? I only had to speak up. Voluntarily. I only had to say: "I am the man you're looking for. Release this water-carrier, for he is not The Voice of the People. He is mute. Here is my head. Yes—I, an intellectual, a somewhat ordinary intellectual, a Doctor of Jurisprudence, unmarried, temporarily unemployed (since I quit my job with the life-insurance company), occupant of a two-room apartment without bath, contributor to leading literary quarterlies (which don't pay), cigarette smoker, unaffiliated, idler in the fields of Physics, History, Theology—arrest me as The Voice of the People! Please—don't laugh! Or arrest me (in selling out your titles and honors) as The Voice of the Spirit—it's all the same; my head won't change the course of history. But take it, you hangman. Otherwise I am no man in the eyes of this girl! Have pity, hangman, and take my head off my shoulders—show this girl who I am!" (MEE LAN *arises*) Is that what you expected from me?

MEE LAN (*taking a cigarette*) Will you give me a light?

THE CONTEMPORARY Can a man choose martyrdom the way he chooses a job? And yet you are right. I know! The only thing the mind can do is to offer itself as a sacrifice——

MEE LAN Will you give me a light?

THE CONTEMPORARY You have nothing more to say?

MEE LAN I see you talk, but I hear nothing. I only hear the mute. He is the only man in this whole stupid farce.

(*He takes out his cigarette lighter, but doesn't snap it on yet*)

THE CONTEMPORARY Maybe I'm a coward. Otherwise I would have seen what I have to do. But I don't see it——

(DON JUAN *appears and bows*)

DON JUAN This time, Princess, it's not a cha-cha-cha.

(MEE LAN *accepts him, smiling*)

THE CONTEMPORARY Mee Lan . . . ? Mee Lan . . . !

(MEE LAN *waltzes away with* DON JUAN)

Scene Twenty

(HWANG TI *comes in,* CLEOPATRA *on his arm, a glass in his hand, followed by his retinue, everyone in high spirits*)

HWANG TI No matter, my dear child, no matter—a wall is a wall, and therefore I say— hic!—I say: Let's build one! Today, tomorrow, yesterday, eh? Why do you laugh? A wall that will protect us from the future—hic!—I believe I'm beginning to feel this drink, but the situation is grave, my dear subjects, frankly grave, and therefore I say—Cleopatra, where are you? A toast! Wan-li-chang-cheng, I say, and all that dwells within it, which is the Republic and Freedom and Culture—hic!—and that means us, and as for everything outside the wall—. My dear, faithful, loyal subjects! Let us drink to the Great Wall, as it is called in the books, my faithful subjects, one more time—brr! but for a moment it seemed to me as though we were concluding an affair that already for centuries, so to speak—as though we were building a wall that—hic!—has already crumbled away—as though our future, so to speak, lay— hic!—behind us! (*He seats himself on the throne*) A toast! (*general clinking of glasses, laughter, then a sudden silence*) What was that? (*Machine guns are heard in the distance*) My loyal subjects, I feel unwell. All my life I have drunk milk and fruit juice so that I might see things clearly, as a Son of Heaven should; I have never smoked, never—the better to bring about that which we call the Great Order and the Final Order——(*He starts to laugh*) Suddenly I feel quite well again! (*another burst of machine-gun fire*) What *is* that?!

(THE CONTEMPORARY *steps forward*)

THE CONTEMPORARY That is the revolution.

HWANG TI Revolution?—why—?

THE CONTEMPORARY The people, my lords, are unpredictable. And who are the people? We all are; we stand behind the curtain when the neighbor is arrested and dragged away. And we become cautious in our dealings with neighbors. But in vain. One morning (around four o'clock) they come and drag your own father away; the next wave will swallow up your own brother. And every time that the sun rises again over this land, it seems that nothing has happened. On the contrary: the newspapers tell us of a disappointing wheat crop somewhere. And friends wonder whether their friend is still living, but they don't ask too many questions, lest they themselves be dragged away. And whoever is left alive lives harmlessly, and so, in truth, there is peace in the land. And yet now comes the revolution. Why? Suddenly a bagatelle is enough to start the avalanche—a harmless creature, someone whom we don't even know, a mute boy is tortured——

HWANG TI Harmless?

THE CONTEMPORARY —and the people, afraid for years, rush into the streets, unafraid in memory of their dead. But the people, my lords, have no voice, unless we lend them one —one of us!

HWANG TI What is he talking about?

THE CONTEMPORARY Arrest me, my lords, as The Voice of the People.

HWANG TI Hic!

THE CONTEMPORARY Precisely.

HWANG TI You are Min Ko? You?

THE CONTEMPORARY As much as anyone.

HWANG TI He thinks I am drunk. . . .

THE CONTEMPORARY If you want to find out what the people think, don't go on torturing a mute! I will tell you. Listen to me!

(HWANG TI *looks about*)

HWANG TI Where is Fu Chu?

FU CHU Here. (*The* EXECUTIONER *takes two strides toward* THE CONTEMPORARY)

HWANG TI We are listening. Speak!

THE CONTEMPORARY *stands before a huge half-circle which* THE MASKERS *and courtiers have formed about him. He has the typical manner of speaking of an intellectual: not loud, quite informal, somewhat ill at ease, but not disconcerted or confused, from time to time smiling or toying with a cigarette to mask his nervousness, the while his seriousness shows itself throughout in his objectivity*)

THE CONTEMPORARY What I have to say to you is banal; you can read it in the papers every morning. . . . We find ourselves, my lords, in the era of the hydrogen bomb, or, as the case may be, the cobalt bomb, which means—without going any further into contemporary physics—whoever is a tyrant today, wherever he may be on this planet, is a tyrant over the whole of humanity. He holds in his hand, for the first time in the history of mankind, the means to make an end of the human race—a possibility which up to now has seemed absurd; however, when you're dealing with neurotics, nothing is really strange. (*An unbeliever laughs*) My lords, I am not drawing up the plans for the Apocalypse. I am simply reminding you of certain medical findings

which are quite well known. The investigations of the survivors of Hiroshima, for example—and bear in mind that in Hiroshima we had, so to speak, a harmless bomb, one in which only the explosive effect was considered —these investigations showed among the women a definite gene damage as a result of radioactivity, a significant aftereffect which remains at least very much open to question. I can't go any further into this matter here; it involves various horrible throwbacks in certain carriers of the genes which produce various kinds of physical deformities and mental deficiencies. The slaying of the children of Bethlehem is perhaps comparable to Hiroshima, except that Hiroshima involved not only living children but those of the future as well—while Bethlehem, which was, to be sure, no idyl for those concerned, was of no real significance to mankind at large——(*a murmur of dissatisfaction*) But let me be brief. For the first time in the history of man (for up till now the tyrant who sent his Rome up in flames was always simply a temporary and quite local catastrophe)—for the first time (and therefore, my lords, the example of history will help us no longer!) we are face to face with the choice, will there be a human race or will there not? The end of the world can be manufactured. Technology—no problem. The more we become able to do (thanks to technology), the more nakedly we stand, like Adam and Eve, before the primal question: "What do we want?"—before what is ultimately a moral decision. However, if we decide "The human race must live!," that means your way of making history is no longer of any importance. We can no longer tolerate a civilization which considers war unavoidable, that much is clear——

HWANG TI What is he saying? I am no longer of any importance—!

THE CONTEMPORARY For war means the end of everything.

HWANG TI Hic!

THE CONTEMPORARY And I assure you, my lords: There is no ark we can board to save us from a radioactive flood!

HWANG TI Does he think I am drunk? I *am* of importance! What is this radioactivity? And really—am I a monster? Why can't I have some of this radioactivity, too? Does that mean that people don't trust me? (THE CONTEMPORARY *sees that he is interrupted and falls silent*) Am I a tyrant? (FU CHU *ostentatiously arranges his hangman's noose in order to be ready*) Why don't you answer?

THE CONTEMPORARY So far as I know, no

one who *was* a tyrant ever called himself one. The position is more desirable than the title.

HWANG TI   Answer: Yes or no!

THE CONTEMPORARY   What's this hangman doing here? Is he going to prove that I am wrong if I answer "Yes"?

HWANG TI   Am I a tyrant?

(THE CONTEMPORARY, *pausing a second, involuntarily sticks a cigarette in his mouth*)

THE CONTEMPORARY   Yes.

(FU CHU *throws the noose over his neck*)

HWANG TI   Release him! (FU CHU *takes the noose away again*) Speak further! I am going to prove you wrong. Speak further! I am a great admirer of your mental agility.

THE CONTEMPORARY   I have said what I have to say.

HWANG TI   We listen to you with pleasure.

(THE CONTEMPORARY, *uncertain about this behavior of* HWANG TI, *who is smiling benignly, looks about like someone who feels he is being mocked, then suddenly speaks quietly and directly*)

THE CONTEMPORARY   Smile, gentlemen, mock at me! I see what I see, what everyone who wants to see can see: I see our earth, which is no more, a planet without life, cruising through the darkness of eternity, illuminated by the sun, but no creature lives to feel the warmth of its rays, and dead is the brightness of day; I see the streaked shadows of its mountains and its violet-colored oceans—dead —clouds like silver fungi, and dead are the continents, pale as the moon, fruitless, bare—a barren, sterile star, revolving aimlessly like a million other stars. I see the cities and states of mankind, as they once were, the lost oases of time: Greece, Italy, Europe! Morning dawns, but no one is alive to see *this* morning, no bird, no child, no voice of greeting—not even a voice of lamentation. Nothing. Water, fire, and wind rage and roar, but silently, for no ear hears them. And the light—the same light as this here today: bluish in the sky, brown or green on the earth, white or purple on your walls, or yellow or red—the light is colorless! For no eye sees it. And empty and blind as His world is God, blind and empty and without creatures of His making: without the mirror of a dying human eye, without our human consciousness of time—timeless—continents, which once rose up shining out of the mists of timelessness and into the consciousness of man: Asia, Europe, America—meaningless! senseless! lifeless! spiritless! empty of man! empty of God! (*prolonged general silence*)

HWANG TI   Bravo! Bravo! Now I call that poetry! (HWANG TI *claps, and then they all clap. It mounts to an ovation, as at a concert or in the theatre*) Where is Da Hing Yen, the Master of the Revels?

DA HING YEN   Here.

(DA HING YEN *steps forward in place of the executioner*)

HWANG TI   Read the document!

DA HING YEN   (*unrolls a scroll*) "What would the mightiest empire in the world, victor over all barbarians, be without the lustrous splendor and adornment of its intelligentsia? Therefore is it an ancient custom to reward and honor the wise men of our realm, to whom we always listen with pleasure. And therefore do we hereby proclaim" (*drum roll*) "The Kung Fu Tse Award, established by our Great Exalted Emperor, Tsin She Hwang Ti, called the Son of Heaven, he who is always in the right, annually awarded to the wise man who dares to portray the world as it was before our reign and thereby dares to be our enemy— all honor in this sacred hour to the man who was able so strikingly and movingly to speak into the ears of the tyrant of the Chinese Wall the complete and utter truth." (*drum roll*)

HWANG TI   Place the golden chain about his neck! (DA HING YEN *lays a golden chain about* THE CONTEMPORARY's *neck*) All hail!

(*Hoisted onto the shoulders of the* EUNUCHS, THE CONTEMPORARY *covers his face*)

ALL   Heil! Heil! Heil!

CLEOPATRA   And a kiss from me——

(*The jubilation changes into equally loud laughter, everyone lifts his glass, a fanfare is sounded, then a sudden scream. Silence*)

Scene Twenty-One

(*The revolution is here: men with arm-bands and sub-machine guns: one sees them now as the people on the stage disperse and draw back.* HWANG TI *left standing alone, continues laughing for a moment in the general silence, then stops suddenly*)

HWANG TI   Hic!—Who are you?

(THE PRINCE *steps forward, now in plain trousers and white shirt*)

THE PRINCE   There he is—your Son of Heaven! Look, he can scarcely stand——

HWANG TI   My prince?

THE PRINCE   I am no prince!

HWANG TI   And in this costume—?

THE PRINCE   Liquidate him!

THE CONTEMPORARY   Stop!

THE PRINCE   Fire!

THE CONTEMPORARY   Stop! I said . . . Stop! (*He drags the Chinese mother out of the crowd of people*) Here is the Mother! (*It is suddenly still*) She is here to plead for the freedom of her son. (*He turns to the crowd*) Don't you all see the game that is being played here? Our prince, who has just been playing the part of a man of the people (as is customary in military *putsches*), this born general who has sacrificed his thirty thousand men in order to spare himself for the problems of the postwar world —naturally he would welcome the idea that The Voice of the People was a mute!

THE PRINCE   Him too! Liquidate him! All of them!

THE CONTEMPORARY   How well we have come to know this figure, so easy to see through; only the people, the unhappy people, always see through him too late. . . . The only hope left in this entire game, the last hope that I see, is you. (*He turns to the mother*) You are the Chinese Mother, the good and poor mother who thinks that she plays no role in the history of this world. Right?

OLAN   Yes, sir, yes. . . .

THE CONTEMPORARY   Tell me, haven't you informed me that your son is mute?

OLAN   Yes, sir, yes. . . .

THE CONTEMPORARY   (*gestures toward the right*) Bring him in. (FU CHU *brings in the tortured mute*)

OLAN   Wang!!!

THE CONTEMPORARY   Is this your son?

OLAN   My Wang! my poor Wang—!

THE CONTEMPORARY   Tell the whole world what you know, mother. Testify that he is mute.

OLAN   What have they done to you, Wang? Who has broken your fingers? Who has wrenched your shoulders? My poor Wang, my dear Wang, my stupid Wang! Don't you recognize me? Who has burned your tongue? Who has torn the skin from your arms? My blood, my blood, I kiss you! You shouldn't have stood out in front of the crowd that day; you should have listened to your mother! Oh, Wang, my son! Look at me! Why don't you at least listen, if you can't speak? Oh, Wang! Oh, Wang!

THE CONTEMPORARY   Control yourself.

OLAN   Why have they done this to you?

THE CONTEMPORARY   It will never happen again. If you speak the truth now before all of us—your son is a mute, isn't he?

OLAN   Yes, sir, he is my son.

THE CONTEMPORARY   He is not Min Ko, he is not the man who made up the verses. Say it!

OLAN   Verses?

THE CONTEMPORARY   Because he is mute!

OLAN   Wang—what have you done?

THE CONTEMPORARY   He has done nothing.

OLAN   Wang?

THE CONTEMPORARY   Testify to the truth, nothing more. Testify with a single word that he is a mute.

OLAN   Have I done you an injustice, Wang? I have always thought that you were stupid. My Wang, my poor Wang! Is that true, that you have made verses?

THE CONTEMPORARY   But, my good woman——

OLAN   My son is not stupid!

THE CONTEMPORARY   No one has claimed that.

OLAN   Why shouldn't he do it? My son! Why shouldn't he make verses?

THE CONTEMPORARY   It's not true——

OLAN   Oh, Wang, my sweet Wang, my unhappy Wang, my son, why have you never told your mother, my proud Wang, that you are the man?

THE CONTEMPORARY   It's not true!

OLAN   Why shouldn't my son be a man of importance?

THE CONTEMPORARY   Woman——

OLAN   Yes, he is the man! Yes! Yes!

(*The revolutionaries break out in jubilation, the crowd lifts* WANG *onto its shoulders and starts to carry him into the streets. Then—*MEE LAN *appears; it grows still once more. She stands there with disordered hair and torn clothing*)

MEE LAN   Here I am, Prince.

THE CONTEMPORARY   Mee Lan!

MEE LAN   Shamed and disgraced by the power you have unleased. I told you once: I will never be your happiness. Well, here I am.

THE PRINCE   Forward! (*No one stirs*) Forward! A savior of the world cannot trouble himself over a single individual! Forward!

THE CONTEMPORARY   Stop!

THE PRINCE   Liquidate them!

THE CONTEMPORARY   Stop, I say!

THE PRINCE   All of them! All of them!

(*Shots; the lights go out for a moment; shouts, cries of confusion; and when the lights come back on, the scene is empty of persons. The scenery has collapsed, and the stage is seen as a stage; the machinery is visible. Distant cries of confusion and rioting in the distance.* BRUTUS *and his two companions come in as if to view the ruins)*

Scene Twenty-Two

THE TAIL COAT   What do you say about this?

THE CUTAWAY   What do you say now?

BRUTUS
  The fury of the mob I understand,
  Though it be evil: impulse, passion,
  Sprung from the selfsame root as
    tyranny,
  Despite the work of human reason.
  Injustice reigns to kill injustice,
  And bloodily there ends what was a
    hope
  For freedom, right, a world of com-
    mon good.

THE CUTAWAY   That's the way it is here, all right.

BRUTUS
  Now upon the shoulders of the angry
    mob,
  So long neglected and suspected, now
  They hoist—they, throwers-down of
    tyranny—
  Their newest leader and their next
    oppressor.

THE TAIL COAT   At least he's a former general.

THE CUTAWAY   That's right.

THE TAIL COAT   You can do business with generals, I always say.

THE CUTAWAY   You're right.

THE TAILCOAT   Generals have behind them a certain tradition.

BRUTUS *(aside)*
  Oh you, Octavius and Mark Antony,
  How often shall we meet at Philippi?

THE CUTAWAY   What did you say?

BRUTUS   Nothing, nothing, I was lost in memory. . . .

THE CUTAWAY   Well, how do you judge our present situation?

BRUTUS *(aside)*
  And yet I will not deal unjustly with
    Mark Antony;
  He was an enemy of larger size than
    this,
  One who stood in person on the field!

(BRUTUS lays his hands on their shoulders)

  I tell you: be of cheer! The form and
    manner

Of your business dealings, honest
    men,
  You noble business-leaders, friends of
    Rome,
  I know too well; haven't you proved
    yourselves?
  I see you prosperous, well fed; what
    do you fear?
  As for the mob, consider only this:
  How can a mob like this, now here,
    now there,
  Free itself from your bland tyranny?
  If it really wants its freedom, yes! But
    does it?

THE TAIL COAT   Then you think . . . ?

BRUTUS
  As necessary as is daily bread
  Are despotism, arrogance, misrule
  To you—these things that make men
    great.
  He who freely tolerates injustice
  (Look into your hearts!) then sees
    himself
  As somehow thereby just—oh, irony!
  Oft have I thought of this. . . . Is it
    not true?

THE CUTAWAY   Very interesting—hmm. . . .

THE TAIL COAT   Yes, indeed. . . .

THE CUTAWAY   A rather psychological interpretation. . . .

BRUTUS
  How could it otherwise have hap-
    pened
  That such as you could for two thou-
    sand years
  Still hold the center of the stage
  Long after Caesar fell for your false
    sakes?

THE CUTAWAY   You mean—?

BRUTUS
  I mean: Be of good cheer! You'll not
    die out,
  O noble citizens with hollow hearts!
  And if one stabs you with a sudden
    dagger—

(Suddenly he has a dagger in each hand)

  (So bitter has the world converted
    me!)—

(He plunges the daggers into their bellies)

  Good cheer! As species, you will
    still survive!

(The two men, who have listened to their classic character with growing suspicion, clutch their sides where the daggers are sticking; meanwhile, BRUTUS, stepping forward two

steps, turns to THE CONTEMPORARY, *who now comes in from the side*)

BRUTUS   What is it?

THE CONTEMPORARY   The play is at an end.

BRUTUS   The reason?

THE CONTEMPORARY   Because the farce is going to start all over again; again we must repeat it——

Scene Twenty-Three

(ROMEO *and* JULIET *enter as at the beginning. Music again*)

JULIET

It was the nightingale and not the lark
That pierced the fearful hollow of
  thine ear;
Nightly she sings on yond pomegranate tree.
Believe me, love, it was the nightingale.

ROMEO

Our only hope is haste; delay is death.

JULIET

Oh, thinkst thou we shall ever meet
  again?

(*A* WAITER *in tails appears, right*)

WAITER   Ladies and gentlemen: the Polonaise is beginning on the terrace. The company awaits your pleasure. (*He disappears*)

JULIET

O God! I have an ill-divining soul;
The song of birds, the whisp'ring of
  the trees,
All make me fear we'll never meet
  again,
We pawns of love in a divided world,
By civil discord cruelly transposed.
Each look, each glance, but makes
  me newly fear,
As though each kiss, so sweet, were
  full of poison,
The fear that death is counting every
  kiss.
O pain of love! O pain of innocence!
So happy as we are, we also fear,
And fearfully the frailty of this world
We see. Is there no place for lovers
In this world? I want to live until the
  Day
Of Judgment if I can. And in that
  time,

No breath, no tears, no sorrow of the
  heart,
No bitter pangs of longing could
  there be
So keen to make me cry out: "No!
This world is not a lovely world! It
  shall not be!"
The song of birds, the whisp'ring of
  the trees
Still makes me glad. See, love, the
  shining moon!
The stars' white light is dazzling
  pure,
Blazing in the east. The river gleams,
A shining mirror underneath the stars,
And then the birds, chill in the frosty
  branches,
Loudly greet the morning's early
  beam.
The clouds, outlined in fire, shift and
  dissolve,
And soon, kissed by the dawn's first
  rays,
The dewdrops flash, the jewelry of
  the earth,
And shadows flee 'neath every bush
  and stone.
O day! O inconceivable rich gift!
O light! O lovely light! O morning
  breeze,
Waking light and hue in every
  flower—
Too lovely and too sweet to be en-
  dured!—
Remembrance in the sweet scent of
  the leaves,
The spice of berries, ah, like tender
  lips,
Remembrance of the rainbow-spar-
  kling sea,
Of all this wondrous world, the great,
  the small,
A day of dallying with a butterfly
While lounging on my sun-warmed
  window-ledge;
A mute smooth stone caressed by
  mute smooth hands;
And one's own image shimmering in
  a pond;
And oh, my dear beloved's voice and
  face—
Remembering, of all, one single day
When fearful longing stood before
  my eyes
And made me cry: "O God, to live is
  all!"
O holy world! O world! O bitter
  world!

We love you so; you shall not be de-
    stroyed!

(*A* WAITER *in tails appears, left*)

WAITER   Ladies and gentlemen: the company awaits your pleasure. (*the* WAITER *disappears*)

ROMEO
    If I but knew, love, where we are—
        and when!
    A swarm of costumes, and they smell
        of moth balls:
    It is as though they're dead, and
        yet they speak
    And dance about and form in circles
    Like little figures on a musical clock.

JULIET
    Away, my love, away! and let us flee!

ROMEO
    But where?

(THE MASKER'S *Polonaise enters. They circle
about like figures on a musical clock: every
figure, as he comes to the front of the stage,
speaks in his turn*)

NAPOLEON   I must not return! they say. I
must not! What is the sense in such remarks?
Russia must be beaten. It was a most unusually
severe winter. I will lead you against Russia. . . .

L'INCONNUE   I am the girl from the banks
of the Seine, the nameless one. I'm only known
by my death mask; you can buy it in any
second-hand shop. Nobody asks about my
life. . . .

PILATE   I do not like decisions. How am I
to decide what is the truth? I am innocent of
the blood of this just man. . . .

PHILIP   I understand heretics; I have burned
them by the thousands and the hundreds of
thousands; I have done my duty. . . .

DON JUAN   I search for Paradise. I am
young. I want to be, only to be. I search for
a virginal world. . . .

BRUTUS
    Is this what History means, that
        ignorance
    Returns forever, endlessly
        triumphing?
    When I see this, it's like an evil
        dream. . . .

CLEOPATRA   I am Cleopatra; I am the
woman who believes in victors, I love victors,
I love men who make history, but, above all,
I love *men!* . . .

COLUMBUS   I don't understand it. They call
it America, and they say it is not India I have
discovered—not India, not the truth . . . !

ROMEO
    O Juliet! this night I'll lie with thee.

JULIET
    O Romeo! beloved Romeo!

ROMEO
    How oft when men are at the point
        of death
    Have they been merry! O my love!
        my wife!
    The world's become a single grave!
        O eyes,
    Look, look your last! Arms, take your
        last
    Embrace—thus, with a kiss, I die!

(*Darkness, and the music ceases*)

Scene Twenty-Four

(*In the foreground, left and right of the stage,
stand* MEE LAN—*with disordered hair and torn
clothing—and* THE CONTEMPORARY—*with a
golden chain about his neck; they look at one
another*)

THE CONTEMPORARY   Look at me, the weak
and the helpless!

MEE LAN   You have said what you had to
say.

THE CONTEMPORARY   And achieved nothing!

MEE LAN   And still you had to say it.

THE CONTEMPORARY   Why? What for?

MEE LAN   This is the truth we have learned:
You, the helpless, and I, the shamed and insulted, we stand here in our time, and the
world rolls forward over us. This is our history.
Why do you hide your face? (*she kneels before him*) I love you. I have come to understand you, and I love you. I, the arrogant,
kneel before you, the scorned and despised,
and I love you. (*he is silent*) And now it is you
who are mute.

Friedrich Duerrenmatt

1921-

PROBLEMS OF THE THEATRE

Behold the drive for purity in art as art is practised these days. Behold this writer striving for the purely poetic, another for the purely lyrical, the purely epic, the purely dramatic. The painter ardently seeks to create the pure painting, the musician pure music, and someone even told me, pure radio represents the synthesis between Dionysos and Logos. Even more remarkable for our time, not otherwise renowned for its purity, is that each and everyone believes he has found his unique and the only true purity. Each vestal of the arts has, if you think of it, her own kind of chastity. Likewise, too numerous to count, are all the theories of the theatre, of what is pure theatre, pure tragedy, pure comedy. There are so many modern theories of the drama, what with each playwright keeping three or four at hand, that for this reason, if no other, I am a bit embarrassed to come along now with my theories of the problems of the theatre.

Furthermore, I would ask you not to look upon me as the spokesman of some specific movement in the theatre or of a certain dramatic technique, nor to believe that I knock at your door as the traveling salesman of one of the philosophies current on our stages today, whether as existentialist, nihilist, expressionist or satirist, or any other label put on the compote dished up by literary criticism. For me, the stage is not a battlefield for theories,

philosophies and manifestos, but rather an instrument whose possibilities I seek to know by playing with it. Of course, in my plays there are people and they hold to some belief or philosophy—a lot of blockheads would make for a dull piece—but my plays are not for what people have to say: what is said is there because my plays deal with people, and thinking and believing and philosophizing are all, to some extent at least, a part of human nature. The problems I face as playwright are practical, working problems, problems I face not before, but during the writing. To be quite accurate about it, these problems usually come up after the writing is done, arising out of a certain curiosity to know how I did it. So what I would like to talk about now are these problems, even though I risk disappointing the general longing for something profound and creating the impression that an amateur is talking. I haven't the faintest notion of how else I should go about it, of how not to talk about art like an amateur. Consequently I speak only to those who fall asleep listening to Heidegger.[1]

What I am concerned with are empirical rules, the possibilities of the theatre. But since we live in an age when literary scholarship and criticism flourish, I can not quite resist the temptation of casting a few side glances at some of the theories of the art and practice of the theatre. The artist indeed has no need of scholarship. Scholarship derives laws from what exists already; otherwise it would not be scholarship. But the laws thus established have no value for the artist, even when they are true. The artist can not accept a law he has not discovered for himself. If he can not find such a law, scholarship can not help him with one it has established; and when the artist does find

---

[1] Martin Heidegger (1889–   ), Swiss existentialist theologian.

one, then it does not matter that the same law was also discovered by scholarship. But scholarship, thus denied, stands behind the artist like a threatening ogre, ready to leap forth whenever the artist wants to talk about art. And so it is here. To talk about problems of the theatre is to enter into competition with literary scholarship. I undertake this with some misgivings. Literary scholarship looks on the theatre as an object; for the dramatist it is never something purely objective, something separate from him. He participates in it. It is true that the playwright's activity makes drama into something objective (that is exactly his job), but he destroys the object he has created again and again, forgets it, rejects it, scorns it, overestimates it, all in order to make room for something new. Scholarship sees only the result; the process, which led to this result, is what the playwright can not forget. What he says has to be taken with a grain of salt. What he thinks about his art changes as he creates his art; his thoughts are always subject to his mood and the moment. What alone really counts for him is what he is doing at a given moment; for its sake he can betray what he did just a little while ago. Perhaps a writer should not talk about his art, but once he starts, then it is not altogether a waste of time to listen to him. Literary scholars who have not the faintest notion of the difficulties of writing and of the hidden rocks that force the stream of art into oft unsuspected channels run the danger of merely asserting and stupidly proclaiming laws that do not exist.

Doubtless the unities of time, place and action which Aristotle—so it was supposed for a long time—derived from Greek tragedy constitute the ideal of drama. From a logical and hence also esthetic point of view, this thesis is incontestable, so incontestable indeed, that the question arises if it does not set up the framework once and for all within which each dramatist must work. Aristotle's three unities demand the greatest precision, the greatest economy and the greatest simplicity in the handling of the dramatic material. The unities of time, place and action ought to be a basic dictate put to the dramatist by literary scholarship, and the only reason scholarship does not hold the artist to them is that Aristotle's unities have not been obeyed by anyone for ages. Nor can they be obeyed, for reasons which best illustrate the relationship of the art of writing plays to the theories about that art.

The unities of time, place and action in essence presuppose Greek tragedy. Aristotle's unities do not make Greek tragedy possible; rather, Greek tragedy allows his unities. No matter how abstract an esthetic law may appear to be, the work of art from which it was derived is contained in that law. If I want to set about writing a dramatic action which is to unfold and run its course in the same place inside of two hours, for instance, then this action must have a history behind it, and that history will be the more extensive the fewer the number of stage characters there are at my disposal. This is simply an experience of how the theatre works, an empirical rule. For me a history is the story which took place before the stage action commenced, a story which alone makes the action on the stage possible. Thus the history behind Hamlet is, of course, the murder of his father; the drama lies in the discovery of that murder. As a rule, too, the stage action is much shorter in time than the event depicted; it often starts out right in the middle of the event, or indeed towards the end of it. Before Sophocles' tragedy could begin, Oedipus had to have killed his father and married his mother, activities that take a little time. The stage action must compress an event to the same degree in which it fulfills the demands of Aristotle's unities. And the closer a playwright adheres to the three unities, the more important is the background history of the action.

It is, of course, possible to invent a history and hence a dramatic action that would seem particularly favorable for keeping to Aristotle's unities. But this brings into force the rule that the more invented a story is and the more unknown it is to the audience, the more careful must its exposition, the unfolding of the background be. Greek tragedy was possible only because it did not have to invent its historical background, because it already possessed one. The spectators knew the myths with which each drama dealt; and because these myths were public, ready coin, part of religion, they made the feats of the Greek tragedians possible, feats never to be attained again; they made possible their abbreviations, their straightforwardness, their *stichomythia* and choruses, and hence also Aristotle's unities. The audience knew what the play was all about; its curiosity was not focused on the story so much as on its treatment. Aristotle's unities presupposed the general appreciation of the subject matter—a genial exception in more recent times is Kleist's *The Broken Jug*—presupposed a religious theatre based on myths. Therefore as soon as the theatre lost its religious, its mythical significance, the unities had to be reinterpreted or discarded. An audience facing an unknown story will pay more attention to the story than to its treatment, and by necessity then such a play has to be richer in detail and circumstances than one with a known action. The feats of one playwright can not be the feats of another. Each art exploits the chances offered by its time, and it is hard to imagine a time without chances. Like every other form of art, drama creates its world; but not every world can be created in the same fashion. This is the natural limitation of every esthetic rule, no matter how self-evident such a rule may be. This does not mean that Aristotle's unities are obsolete; what was once a rule has become an exception, a case that may occur again at any time. The one-act play obeys the unities still, even though under a different condition. Instead of the history, the situation now dominates the plot, and thus unity is once again achieved.

But what is true for Aristotle's theory of drama, namely its dependency upon a certain world and hence its validity relative to that world, is also true of every other theory of drama. Brecht is consistent only when he incorporates into his dramaturgy that *Weltanschauung*, the communist philosophy, to which he—so he seems to think—is committed; but in doing so he often cuts off his own nose. Sometimes his plays say the very opposite of what they claim they say, but this lack of agreement can not always be blamed on the capitalistic audience. Often it is simply a case where Brecht, the poet, gets the better of Brecht, the dramatic theorist, a situation that is wholly legitimate and ominous only were it not to happen again.

Let us speak plainly. My introducing the audience as a factor in the making of a play may have seemed strange to many. But just as it is impossible to have theatre without spectators, so it is senseless to consider and treat a play as if it were a kind of ode, divided into parts and delivered in a vacuum. A piece written for the theatre becomes living theatre when it is played, when it can be seen, heard, felt, and thus experienced immediately. This immediacy is one of the most essential aspects of the theatre, a fact so often overlooked in those sacred halls where a play by Hofmannsthal counts for more than one by Nestroy,[2] and a Richard Strauss opera more than one by Offenbach. A play is an event, is something that happens. In the theatre everything must be transformed into something immediate, something visible and sensible; the corollary to this thought, however, is that not everything can be translated into something immediate and corporeal. Kafka, for example, really does not belong on the stage. The bread offered there gives no nourishment; it lies undigested in the iron stomachs of the theatre-going public and the regular subscribers. As luck would have it, many think of the heaviness they feel not as a stomach ache, but as the heaviness of soul which Kafka's true works emanate, so that by error all is set aright.

The immediacy sought by every play, the spectacle into which it would be transformed, presupposes an audience, a theatre, a stage. Hence we would also do well to examine the theatres for which we have to write today. We all know these money-losing enterprises. They can, like so many other institutions today, be justified only on an idealistic basis: in reality, not at all. The architecture of our theatres, their seating arrangements and their stages, came down from the court theatre or, to be more precise, never got beyond it. For this reason alone, our so-called contemporary theatre is not really contemporary. In contrast to the primitive Shakespearean stage, in contrast to this "scaffold" where, as Goethe put it, "little was shown, everything signified," the court theatre made every effort to satisfy a craving for naturalness, even though this resulted in much greater unnaturalness. No longer was the audience satisfied to imagine the royal chamber behind the "green curtain"; every attempt was made to show the chamber. Characteristic of such theatre is its tendency to separate audience and stage, by means both of the curtain as well as having the spectators sit in the dark facing a well-lit stage. This latter innovation was perhaps the most treacherous of all, for it alone made possible the solemn atmosphere in which our theatres suffocate. The stage became a peep show. Better lighting was constantly invented, then a revolving stage, and it is said they have even invented a revolving house! The courts went, but the court theatre stayed on. Now to be sure, our time has discovered its own form of theatre, the movies. But no matter how much we may emphasize the differences, and how important it may be to emphasize them, still it must be pointed out that the movies grew out of theatre, and that they can at last achieve what the court theatre with all its machinery, revolving stages and other effects only dreamed of doing: to simulate reality.

The movies, then, are nothing more nor less than the democratic form of the court theatre.

[2] Johann Nestroy (1801–1862), Viennese actor and playwright—a writer of witty satires for the popular theatre.

They intensify our sense of intimacy immeasurably, so much so that the movies easily risk becoming the genuinely pornographic art. For the spectator is forced into being a "voyeur," and movie stars enjoy their immense popularity because those who see them come also to feel that they have slept with them; that is how well movie stars are photographed. A larger-than-life picture is an indecency.

Just what then is our present-day theatre? If the movies are the modern form of the old court theatre, what is the theatre? There is no use in pretending that the theatre today is anything much more than a museum in which the art treasures of former golden ages of the drama are put on exhibition. There is no way of changing that. It is only too natural, at a time like ours, a time which, always looking toward the past, seems to possess everything but a living present. In Goethe's time the ancients were rarely performed, Schiller occasionally, but mostly Kotzebue [3] and whoever else they were. It is worthwhile to point out that the movies preempt the theatre of its Kotzebues and Birch-Pfeiffers,[4] and it is hard to imagine what sort of plays would have to be put on today, if there were no movies and if all the scriptwriters wrote for the legitimate stage.

If the contemporary theatre is to a large extent a museum, then this has definite effects on the actors which it employs. They have become civil servants, usually even entitled to their pensions, permitted to act in the theatre when not kept busy making movies. The members of this once despised estate have settled down now as solid citizens—a human gain, an artistic loss. And today actors fit into the order of professional rank somewhere between the physicians and small industrialists, surpassed within the realm of art only by the winners of the Nobel prize, by pianists and conductors. Some actors are visiting professors of sorts, or independent scholars, who take their turn appearing in the museums or arranging exhibitions. The management, of course, takes this into account when it arranges its playbill more or less with an eye to its gueststars; says the management: what play should we put on when this or that authority in this or that field is available to us at such and such a date? Moreover actors are forced to move about in many different acting styles, now in a baroque style,

now in a classical one, today acting naturalism, tomorrow Claudel.[5] An actor in Molière's day did not have to do that. The director, too, is more important, more dominant than ever, like the conductor of an orchestra. Historical works demand, and ought to demand, proper interpretation; but directors as yet dare not be as true to the works they put on as some conductors are quite naturally to theirs. The classics often are not interpreted but executed, and the curtain falls upon a mutilated corpse. But then, where is the danger in it all? There is always the saving convention by which all classical things are accepted as perfection, as a kind of gold standard in our cultural life, with all things looked upon as gold that shine in Modern Library or Temple classics. The theatre-going public goes to see the classics, whether they be performed well or not; applause is assured, indeed is the duty of the educated man. And thus the public has legitimately been relieved of the task of thinking and of passing judgments other than those learned by rote in school.

Yet there is a good side to the many styles the present-day theatre must master, although it may at first glance appear bad. Every great age of the theatre was possible because of the discovery of a unique form of theatre, of a particular style, which determined the way plays were written. This is easily demonstrable in the English or Spanish theatre, or the Vienna National Theatre, the most remarkable phenomenon in the German-speaking theatre. This alone can explain the astounding number of plays written by Lope de Vega. Stylistically a play was no problem for him. But to the degree that a uniform style of theatre does not exist today, indeed can no longer exist, to that extent is writing for the theatre now a problem and thus more difficult. Therefore our contemporary theatre is two things: on one hand it is a museum, on the other an experimental field, each play confronting the author with new challenges, new questions of style. Yes, style today is no longer a common property, but highly private, even particularized from case to case. We have no style, only styles, which puts the situation in art today in a nutshell. For contemporary art is a series of experiments, nothing more nor less, just like all of our modern world.

If there are only styles, then, too, we have only theories of the art and practice of the the-

---

[3] August von Kotzebue (1761–1819), popular German dramatist and leader of the anti-romantic movement in the German theatre.

[4] Friedrich Birch-Pfeiffer, early 19th century popular German dramatist.

[5] Paul Claudel (1868–1955), French dramatist and poet—a Catholic writer, most famous for *The Tidings Brought to Mary* and *The Satin Slipper*.

atre, and no longer one dramaturgy. We now have Brecht's and Eliot's, Claudel's and that of Frisch or of Hochwaelder: [6] always a new theory of drama for each dramatic offering. Nevertheless one can conceive of a single theory of drama, a theory that would cover all particular instances, much in the same way that we have worked out a geometry which embraces all dimensions. Aristotle's theory of drama would be only one of many possible theories in this dramaturgy. It would have to be a new *poetics*, which would examine the possibilities not of a certain stage, but of the stage, a dramaturgy of the experiment itself.

What, finally, might we say about the audience without which, as we have said before, no theatre is possible? The audience has become anonymous, just "the paying public," a matter far worse than first strikes the eye. The modern author no longer knows his public, unless he writes for some village stage or Caux, neither of which is much fun. A playwright has to imagine his audience; but in truth the audience is he himself—and this is a danger which can neither be altered now nor circumvented. All the dubious, well-worn, politically misused notions which attach themselves to the concepts of "a people" and "society," to say nothing of "a community," have perforce also crept into the theatre. What points is an author to make? How is he to find his subjects, what solutions should he reach? All these are questions for which we may perhaps find an answer once we have gained a clearer notion as to what possibilities still exist in the theatre today.

In undertaking to write a play I must first make clear to myself just where it is to take place. At first glance that does not seem like much of a problem. A play takes place in London or Berlin, in the mountains, a hospital or on a battlefield, wherever the action demands. But it does not work out quite that way. A play, after all, takes place upon a stage which in turn must represent London, the mountains or a battlefield. This distinction need not, but can be made. It depends entirely on how much the author takes the stage into account, how strongly he wants to create the illusion without which no theatre can exist, and whether he wants it smeared on thickly with gobs of paint heaped upon the canvas, or transparent, diaphanous and fragile. A playwright can be

deadly serious about the place: Madrid, the Ruetli, the Russian steppe, or he can think of it as just a stage, the world, his world.

How the stage is to represent a given place is, of course, the task of the scene designer. Since designing scenes is a form of painting, the developments which have taken place in painting in our time have not failed to touch the theatre. But the theatre can really neither abstract man nor language, which is in itself both abstract and concrete, and scenery, no matter how abstract it would pretend to be, must still represent something concrete to make sense, and for both of these reasons, abstraction in scenic design has essentially failed. Nevertheless the "green curtain" behind which the spectators have to imagine the place, the royal chamber, was reinstituted. The fact was recalled that the dramatic place and the stage were not one and the same, no matter how elaborate, how verisimilar the stage setting might be. The fact is the place has to be created by the play. One word: we are in Venice; another in the Tower of London. The imagination of the audience needs but little support. Scenery is to suggest, point out, intensify, but not describe the place. Once more it has become transparent, immaterialized. And similarly the place of the drama to be shown on the stage can be made immaterial.

Two fairly recent plays which most clearly illustrate the possibility referred to as immaterializing the scenery and the dramatic place are Wilder's *Our Town* and *The Skin of Our Teeth*. The immaterializing of the stage in *Our Town* consists of this: the stage is nearly empty; only a few objects needed for rehearsals stand about—some chairs, tables, ladders and so on; and out of these everyday objects the place is created, the dramatic place, the town, all out of the world, the play, the wakened imagination of the spectators. In his other play Wilder, this great fanatic of the theatre, immaterializes the dramatic place: where the Antrobus family really lives, in what age and what stage of civilization, is never wholly clear; now it is the ice age, now a world war. This sort of experiment may be met quite often in modern drama; thus it is indefinite where in Frisch's play, *Graf Oederland*, the strange Count Wasteland abides; no man knows where to wait for Godot, and in *The Marriage of Mr. Mississippi (Die Ehe des Herrn Mississippi)* I expressed the indefiniteness of the locale (in order to give the play its spirit of wit, of comedy) by having the right window of a room look out upon a northern landscape with its Gothic cathedral and apple tree, while the left window of the

---

[6] Fritz Hochwaelder (1911–   ), Swiss playwright who writes on religious themes in historical settings.

same room opens on a southern scene with an ancient ruin, a touch of the Mediterranean and a cypress. The really decisive point in all this is that, to quote Max Frisch, the playwright is making poetry with the stage, a possibility which has always entertained and occupied me and which is one of the reasons, if not the main one, why I write plays. But then—and I am thinking of the comedies of Aristophanes and the comic plays of Nestroy—in every age poetry has been written not only *for*, but *with* the stage.

Let us turn from these incidental problems to more basic ones. What do the particular problems look like, which I—to cite an author whom I knew at least to some, though not the whole extent—have faced? In *The Blind Man (Der Blinde)* I wanted to juxtapose the word against the dramatic place, to turn the word against the scene. The blind duke believes he is living in his well-preserved castle whereas he is living in a ruin; he thinks he is humbling himself before Wallenstein,[7] but sinks to his knees before a Negro. The dramatic place is one and the same, but by means of the pretense carried on before the blind man, it plays a dual role: the place seen by the audience and the place in which the blind man fancies himself to be. So also, when in my comedy, *An Angel comes to Babylon (Ein Engel kommt nach Babylon)* I picked for my dramatic locale the city in which the Tower was built, I had essentially to solve two problems. In the first place the stage had to express the fact that there were two places of action in my comedy, heaven and the city of Babylon; heaven, which was the secret point of origin of the action, and Babylon the locale, where that action ran its course.

Well, I suppose heaven could have been simply represented by a dark background to suggest its infinity, but since I wanted to convey in my comedy the idea that heaven was not something infinite, but something incomprehensible and altogether different, I asked for the stage background, the heaven above the city of Babylon, to be occupied entirely by the Great Nebula in Andromeda, just as we might see it through the telescope on Mt. Palomar. What I hoped to achieve thereby was that heaven, the incomprehensible and inscrutable, would take on form, gain, as it were, its own stage presence. In this wise also heaven's rapprochement with the earth was to be brought out, reiterating the coming together of the two

that is expressed in the action through the angel's visiting Babylon. Thus, too, a world was constructed in which the result of the action, namely the building of the tower of Babylon, became possible.

In the second place I had to think of how to make the stage represent Babylon, the place in which the action unfolds. I found the idea of Babylon challenging because of its timeliness, its Cyclopean big-city character, its New-York-look with its skyscrapers and slums, and by having the first two acts take place along the banks of the Euphrates I wished to hint at Paris. Babylon, in brief, stands for the metropolis. It is a Babylon of the imagination, having a few typically Babylonian features, but as a modernized parodied version, with its modernities—for instance the convenience of electric streetlights. Of course the execution of the scenery, the building of the stage itself, is a job for the scene designer, but the playwright must always decide himself just what kind of stage he wants.

I love a colorful stage setting, a colorful theatre, like the stage of Theo Otto,[8] to mention an admirable example. I have little use for a theatre that uses black curtains as was the fashion once upon a time, or for the tendency to glory in threadbare poverty which some stage designers seem to aim for. To be sure the word is important above all else in the theatre; but note: above all else. For after the word there are many other things, which also rightfully belong to the theatre, even a certain wantonness. Thus when someone asked me quite thoughtfully with respect to my play *Mississippi*, where one of the characters enters through a grandfather-clock, whether or not I thought a four-dimensional theatre possible, I could only remark that I had not thought of Einstein when I did it. It is just that in my daily life it should give me great pleasure if I could enter into a company and astonish those present by coming into the room through a grandfather-clock or by floating in through a window. No one should deny us playwrights the opportunity to satisfy such desires now and then at least on the stage, where such whims can be fulfilled. The old argument of which came first, the chicken or the egg, can be transformed in art into the question of whether the egg or the chicken, the world as potential or as rich harvest, is to be presented. Artists might very well be divided then into those fa-

---

[7] The hero of Schiller's famous trilogy, written in 1799, based on the Thirty Years' War.

[8] Swiss scene designer and most famous for his designs for Brecht's plays.

voring the egg and those favoring the chicken. The argument is a lively one. Alfred Polgar [9] once said to me, it was odd that while in the contemporary Anglo-Saxon drama everything came out in the dialogue, there was always much too much happening on the stage in my plays and that he, Polgar, would sometimes like to see a simple Duerrenmatt play. Behind this truth, however, lies my refusal to say that the egg came before the chicken, and my personal prejudice of preferring the chicken to the egg. It happens to be my passion, not always a happy one perhaps, to want to put on the stage the richness, the manifold diversity of the world. As a result my theatre is open to many interpretations and appears to confuse some. Misunderstandings creep in, as when someone looks around desperately in the chicken coop of my plays, hoping to find the egg of Columbus which I stubbornly refuse to lay.

But a play is bound not only to a place, but also to a time. Just as the stage represents a place, so it also represents a time, the time *during* which the action takes place as well as the time *in* which it occurs. If Aristotle had really demanded the unity of time, place and action, he would have limited the duration of a tragedy to the time it took for the action to be carried out (a feat which the Greek tragedians nearly achieved), for which reasons, of course, everything would have to be concentrated upon that action. Time would pass "naturally," everything coming one after the other without breaks. But this does not always have to be the case. In general the actions on the stage follow one another but, to cite an example, in Nestroy's magical farce, *Death on the Wedding Day (Der Tod am Hochzeitstag)*, there are two acts taking place simultaneously and the illusion of simultaneity is skillfully achieved by having the action of the second act form the background noise for the first, and the action of the first act the background noise for the second. Other examples of how time is used as a theatrical device could be easily recalled. Time can be shortened, stretched, intensified, arrested, repeated; the dramatist can, like Joshua, call to his heaven's orbits, "Theatre-Sun, stand thou still upon Gideon! And thou, Theatre-Moon, in the valley of Ajalon!"

It may be noted further that the unities ascribed to Aristotle were not wholly kept in Greek tragedy either. The action is interrupted by the choruses, and by this means time is spaced. When the chorus interrupts the action,

it achieves as regards time—to elucidate the obvious like an amateur—the very same thing the curtain does today. The curtain cuts up and spreads out the time of an action. I have nothing against such an honorable device. The good thing about a curtain is that it so clearly defines an act, that it clears the table, so to speak. Moreover it is psychologically often extremely necessary to give the exhausted and frightened audience a rest. But a new way of binding language and time has evolved in our day.

If I cite Wilder's *Our Town* once again, I do so because I assume that this fine play is widely known. You may recall that in it different characters turn toward the audience and talk of the worries and needs of their small town. In this way Wilder is able to dispense with the curtain. The curtain has been replaced by the direct address to the audience. The epic element of description has been added to the drama. For this reason, of course, this form of theatre has been called the epic theatre.

Yet when looked at quite closely, Shakespeare's plays or Goethe's *Goetz von Berlichingen* are in a certain sense also epic theatre. Only in a different, less obvious manner. Since Shakespeare's histories often extend over a considerable period of time, this time span is divided into different actions, different episodes, each of which is treated dramatically. *Henry IV, Part I,* consists of nineteen such episodes, while by the end of the fourth act of *Goetz* there already are no less than forty-one tableaux. I stopped counting after that. If one looks at the way the over-all action has been built up, then, with respect to time, it is quite close to the epic, like a movie that is run too slowly, so that the individual frames can be seen. The condensation of everything into a certain time has been given up in favor of an episodic form of drama.

Thus when an author in some of our modern plays turns toward the audience, he attempts to give the play a greater continuity than is otherwise possible in an episodic form. The void between the acts is to be filled; the time gap is to be bridged, not by a pause, but by words, by a description of what has gone on in the meanwhile, or by having some new character introduce himself. In other words, the expositions are handled in an epic manner, not the actions to which these expositions lead. This represents an advance of the word in the theatre, the attempt of the word to reconquer territory lost a long time ago. Let us emphasize that it is but an attempt; for all too often the direct address to the audience is used to ex-

---

[9] Contemporary Swiss literary and drama critic.

plain the play, an undertaking that makes no
sense whatever. If the audience is moved by
the play, it will not need prodding by explanations; if the audience is not moved, all the
prodding in the world will not be of help.

In contrast to the epic, which can describe
human beings as they are, the drama unavoid-
ably limits and therefore stylizes them. This
limitation is inherent in the art form itself. The
human being of the drama is, after all, a talking
individual, and speech is his limitation. The
action only serves to force this human being
on the stage to talk in a certain way. The action
is the crucible in which the human being is
molten into words, must become words. This,
of course, means that I, as the playwright, have
to get the people in my drama into situations
which force them to speak. If I merely show
two people sitting together and drinking coffee
while they talk about the weather, politics or
the latest fashions, then I provide neither a
dramatic situation nor dramatic dialogue, no
matter how clever their talk. Some other ingredient must be added to their conversation,
something to add pique, drama, double meaning. If the audience knows that there is some
poison in one of the coffee cups, or perhaps
even in both, so that the conversation is really
one between two poisoners, then this little cof-
fee-for-two idyl becomes through this artistic
device a dramatic situation, out of which and
on the basis of which dramatic dialogue can
develop. Without the addition of some special
tension or special condition, dramatic dialogue
can not develop.

Just as dialogue must develop out of a situation, so it must also lead into some situation,
that is to say, of course, a new situation. Dramatic dialogue effects some action, some suffering, some new situation, out of which in turn
new dialogue can again develop, and so on
and so forth.

However, a human being does more than just
talk. The fact that a man also thinks, or at least
should think, that he feels, yes, more than anything feels, and that he does not always wish
to show others what he is thinking or feeling,
has led to the use of another artistic device, the
monologue. It is true, of course, that a person
standing on a stage and carrying on a conversation with himself out loud is not exactly natural; and the same thing can be said, only
more so, of an operatic aria. But the monologue
(like the aria) proves that an artistic trick,
which really ought not be played, can achieve
an unexpected effect, to which, and rightly so,
the public succumbs time and again; so much

so that Hamlet's monologue, "To be or not to
be," or Faust's, are among the most beloved
and most famous passages in the theatre.

But not everything that sounds like a monologue is monologue. The purpose of dialogue is
not only to lead a human being to a point where
he must act or suffer, but at times it also leads
into a major speech, to the explanation of some
point of view. Many people have lost the appreciation of rhethoric since, as Hilpert maintains, some actor who was not sure of his lines
discovered naturalism. That loss is rather sad.
A speech can win its way across the footlights
more effectively than any other artistic device.
But many of our critics no longer know what
to make of a speech. An author, who today
dares a speech, will suffer the same fate as
the peasant Dicaeopolis; he will have to lay
his head upon the executioner's block. Except
that instead of the Acharnians of Aristophanes,
it will be the majority of critics who descend
on the author—the most normal thing in the
world. Nobody is more anxious to bash out
someone's brains than those who haven't any.

Moreover, the drama has always embodied
some narrative elements; epic drama did not
introduce this. So, for instance, the background
of an action has always had to be related, or an
event announced in the form of a messenger's
report. But narration on the stage is not without its dangers, for it does not live in the same
manner, is not tangible the way an action taking place on the stage is. Attempts have been
made to overcome this, as by dramatizing the
messenger, by letting him appear at a crucial
moment, or by making him a blockhead from
whom a report can only be extracted with great
difficulties. Yet certain elements of rhetoric
must still be present if narration is to succeed
on the stage. Stage narratives can not exist without some exaggeration. Observe, for instance,
how Shakespeare elaborates on Plutarch's description of Cleopatra's barge. This exaggeration is not just a characteristic of the baroque
style, but a means of launching Cleopatra's
barge upon the stage, of making it visible there.
But while the speech of the theatre can not
exist without exaggeration, it is important to
know when to exaggerate and above all, how.

Furthermore, just as the stage characters can
suffer a certain fate, so also their language. The
angel that came to Babylon, for example, grows
more and more enthusiastic about the earth's
beauty from act to act, and hence his language
must parallel this rising enthusiasm until it
grows into a veritable hymn. In the same
comedy the beggar Akki relates his life in a
series of *makamat,* passages of a rich and stately

prose interspersed with rhymes, refined in grammar, rhetoric, poetic idiom and tradition, that come from the Arabic and flourished a thousand years ago. In this way I try to convey the Arabic character of this personage, his joy in inventing stories and in duelling and playing with words, without at the same time wandering off into another form, the chanson. The *makamat* or anecdotes of Akki are nothing less than the most extreme possibilities offered by his language, and therefore they intensify his being. Through the *makamat* Akki has become all language and this is just what an author must always strive for, so that there are moments in his plays in which the characters he has created with the written word become living language and nothing less.

A danger lurks here, too, of course. Language can lead a writer astray. The joy of being able all of a sudden to write, of possessing language, as it came over me, for instance, while I was writing *The Blind Man*, can make an author talk too much, can make him escape from his subject into language. To keep close to the subject is itself a great art, achieved only by masterful control of the impetus to talk. Dialogue, like playing on words, can also lead an author into byways, take him unawares away from his subject. Yet ideas flash into his mind again and again, ideas which he ought not resist, even if they disrupt his carefully laid plans. For in addition to being on guard against some of these tempting flashes of ideas, a writer must also have the courage to follow some of them.

These elements and problems of place, time, and action, which are all, of course, interwoven and are but hinted at here, belong to the basic material, to the artistic devices and tools of the craft of the drama. But let me make it clear here and now, that I make war upon the notion of "the craft of the drama." The very idea that anyone who makes a sufficiently diligent and steadfast endeavor to achieve something in that art will succeed in the end or even that this craft can be learned is a notion we thought discarded long ago. Yet it is still frequently met with in critical writings about the art of play-writing. This art is supposed to be a sound-and-solid, respectable and well-mannered affair. Thus, too, the relationship between a playwright and his art is considered by some to be like a marriage in which everything is quite legal when blessed with the sacraments of esthetics. For these reasons, perhaps, critics often refer to the theatre, much more than to any other form of art, as a craft which, depend-ing on the particular case, has been more or less mastered. If we investigate closely what the critics really mean by "the craft of the drama," then it becomes obvious that it is little else but the sum of their prejudices. There is no craft of the theatre; there is only the mastery of the material through language and the stage or, to be more exact, it is an overpowering of the material, for any creative writing is a kind of warfare with its victories, defeats and indecisive battles. Perfect plays do not exist except as a fiction of esthetics in which, as in the movies, perfect heroes may alone be found. Never yet has a playwright left this battle without his wounds; each one has his Achilles' heel, and the playwright's antagonist, his material, never fights fairly. It is cunning stuff, often not to be drawn out of its lair, and it employs highly secret and low-down tricks. This forces the playwright to fight back with every permissible and even non-permissible means, no matter what the wise exhortations, rules and adages of the masters of this craft and their most honored trade may say. Best foot forward won't get an author anywhere in the drama, not even his foot in the doorway. The difficulties in writing for the drama lie where no one suspects them; sometimes it is no more than the problem of how to have two people say hello, or the difficulty in writing an opening sentence. What is sometimes considered to be the craft of the drama can be easily learned inside half an hour. But how difficult it is to divide a given material into five acts and how few subjects there are which can be divided that way, how nearly impossible it is to write today in iambic pentameter, those things are hardly ever suspected by the hack writers who can slap a play together anytime and without trouble, who can always divide any subject into five acts, and who have always written and still write with facility in iambic pentameter. They really pick their material and their language in the way some critics think this is done. They are not so much amateurs when they talk about art as when they tailor art to their talk. No matter what the material is like, they always fashion the same bathrobe to be sure the audience will not catch cold and that it will sleep comfortably. There is nothing more idiotic than the opinion that only a genius does not have to obey those rules prescribed for writers of talent. In that case I should like to be counted among the geniuses. What I want to emphasize strongly is that the art of writing a play does not necessarily start out with the planning of a certain child, or however else a eunuch thinks love is made; but it starts out with love making of which a eunuch is incapable. Though really the difficulties, pains and also fortunes of writing do not lie within the realm of things we mean to talk about or even can talk about. We can only talk about the craft of the drama, a craft that exists only when one *talks* of drama, but not when one writes plays. The craft of the drama is an optical illusion. To talk about plays, about art, is a much more utopian undertaking than is ever appreciated by those who talk the most.

Employing this—really non-existent—craft, let us try and give shape to a certain material. Usually there is a central point of reference, the hero. In theories of the drama a difference is made between a tragic hero, the hero of tragedy, and a comic hero, the hero of comedy. The qualities a tragic hero must possess are well known. He must be capable of rousing our sympathy. His guilt and his innocence, his virtues and his vices must be mixed in the most pleasant and yet exact manner, and administered in doses according to well-defined rules. If, for example, I make my tragic hero an evil man, then I must endow him with a portion of intellect equal to his malevolence. As a result of this rule, the most sympathetic stage character in German literature has turned out to be the devil. The role of the hero in the play has not changed. The only thing that has changed is the social position of the character who awakens our sympathy.

In ancient tragedy and in Shakespeare the hero belongs to the highest class in society, to the nobility. The spectators watch a suffering, acting, raving hero who occupies a social position far higher than their own. This continues still to impress audiences today.

Then when Lessing and Schiller introduced the bourgeois drama, the audience saw itself as the suffering hero on the stage. But the evolution of the hero continued. Buechner's Woyzeck is a primitive proletarian who represents far less socially than the average spectator. But it is precisely in this extreme form of human existence, in this last, most miserable form, that the audience is to see the human being also, indeed itself.

And finally we might mention Pirandello who was the first, as far as I know, to render the hero, the character on the stage, immaterial and transparent just as Wilder did the dramatic place. The audience watching this sort of presentation attends, as it were, its own dissection, its own psychoanalysis, and the stage becomes man's internal milieu, the inner space of the world.

Of course, the theatre has never dealt only with kings and generals; in comedy the hero has always been the peasant, the beggar, the ordinary citizen—but this was always in comedy. Nowhere in Shakespeare do we find a comic king; in his day a ruler could appear as a bloody monster but never as a fool. In Shakespeare the courtiers, the artisans, the working people are comic. Hence, in the evolution of the tragic hero we see a trend towards comedy. Analogously the fool becomes more and more of a tragic figure. This fact is by no means without significance. The hero of a play not only propels an action on, he not only suffers a certain fate, but he also represents a world. Therefore we have to ask ourselves how we should present our own questionable world and with what sort of heroes. We have to ask ourselves how the mirrors which catch and reflect this world should be ground and set.

Can our present-day world, to ask a concrete question, be represented by Schiller's dramatic art? Some writers claim it can be, since Schiller still holds audiences in his grip. To be sure, in art everything is possible when the art is right. But the question is if an art valid for its time could possibly be so even for our day. Art can never be repeated. If it were repeatable, it would be foolish not just to write according to the rules of Schiller.

Schiller wrote as he did because the world in which he lived could still be mirrored in the world his writing created, a world he could build as a historian. But just barely. For was not Napoleon perhaps the last hero in the old sense? The world today as it appears to us could hardly be encompassed in the form of the historical drama as Schiller wrote it, for the reason alone that we no longer have any tragic heroes, but only vast tragedies staged by world butchers and produced by slaughtering machines. Hitler and Stalin can not be made into Wallensteins. Their power is so enormous that they themselves are no more than incidental, corporeal and easily replaceable expressions of this power; and the misfortune associated with the former and to a considerable extent also with the latter is too vast, too complex, too horrible, too mechanical and usually simply too devoid of all sense. Wallenstein's power can still be envisioned; power as we know it today can only be seen in its smallest part for, like an iceberg, the largest part is submerged in anonymity and abstraction. Schiller's drama presupposes a world that the eye can take in, that takes for granted genuine actions of state, just as Greek tragedy did. For only what the eye can take in can be made visible in art. The state today, however, can not be envisioned for it is anonymous and bureaucratic; and not only in Moscow and Washington, but also in Berne. Actions of state today have become *post-hoc* satyric dramas which follow the tragedies executed in secret earlier. True representatives of our world are missing; the tragic heroes are nameless. Any small-time crook, petty government official or policeman better represents our world than a senator or president. Today art can only embrace the victims, if it can reach men at all; it can no longer come close to the mighty. Creon's secretaries close Antigone's case. The state has lost its physical reality, and just as physics can now only cope with the world in mathematical formulas, so the state can only be expressed in statistics. Power today becomes visible, material only when it explodes as in the atom bomb, in this marvelous mushroom which rises and spreads immaculate as the sun and in which mass murder and beauty have become one. The atom bomb can not be reproduced artistically since it is mass-produced. In its face all of man's art that would recreate it must fail, since it is itself a creation of man. Two mirrors which reflect one another remain empty.

But the task of art, insofar as art can have a task at all, and hence also the task of drama today, is to create something concrete, something that has form. This can be accomplished best by comedy. Tragedy, the strictest genre in art, presupposes a formed world. Comedy—in so far as it is not just satire of a particular society as in Molière—supposes an unformed world, a world being made and turned upside down, a world about to fold like ours. Tragedy overcomes distance; it can make myths originating in times immemorial seem like the present to the Athenians. But comedy creates distance; the attempt of the Athenians to gain a foothold in Sicily is translated by comedy into the birds undertaking to create their own empire before which the gods and men will have to capitulate. How comedy works can be seen in the most primitive kind of joke, in the dirty story, which, though it is of very dubious value, I bring up only because it is the best illustration of what I mean by creating distance. The subject of the dirty story is the purely sexual, which because it is purely sexual, is formless and without objective distance. To be given a form the purely sexual is transmuted, as I have already mentioned, into the dirty joke. Therefore this type of joke is a kind of original comedy, a transposition of the sexual onto the plane of the comical. In this way it is possible today in a society domi-

nated by John Doe, to talk in an accepted way about the purely sexual. In the dirty story it becomes clear that the comical exists in forming what is formless, in creating order out of chaos.

The means by which comedy creates distance is the conceit. Tragedy is without conceit. Hence there are few tragedies whose subjects were invented. By this I do not mean to imply that the ancient tragedians lacked inventive ideas of the sort that are written today, but the marvel of their art was that they had no need of these inventions, of conceits. That makes all the difference. Aristophanes, on the other hand, lives by conceits. The stuff of his plays are not myths but inventions, which take place not in the past but the present. They drop into their world like bomb shells which, by throwing up huge craters of dirt, change the present into the comic and thus scatter the dirt for everyone to see. This, of course, does not mean that drama today can only be comical. Tragedy and comedy are but formal concepts, dramatic attitudes, figments of the esthetic imagination which can embrace one and the same thing. Only the conditions under which each is created are different, and these conditions have their basis only in small part in art.

Tragedy presupposes guilt, despair, moderation, lucidity, vision, a sense of responsibility. In the Punch-and-Judy show of our century, in this back-sliding of the white race, there are no more guilty and also, no responsible men. It is always, "We couldn't help it" and "We didn't really want that to happen." And indeed, things happen without anyone in particular being responsible for them. Everything is dragged along and everyone gets caught somewhere in the sweep of events. We are all collectively guilty, collectively bogged down in the sins of our fathers and of our forefathers. We are the offspring of children. That is our misfortune, but not our guilt: guilt can exist only as a personal achievement, as a religious deed. Comedy alone is suitable for us. Our world has led to the grotesque as well as to the atom bomb, and so it is a world like that of Hieronymus Bosch whose apocalyptic paintings are also grotesque. But the grotesque is only a way of expressing in a tangible manner, of making us perceive physically the paradoxical, the form of the unformed, the face of a world without face; and just as in our thinking today we seem to be unable to do without the concept of the paradox, so also in art, and in our world which at times seems still to exist only because the atom bomb exists: out of fear of the bomb.

But the tragic is still possible even if pure

tragedy is not. We can achieve the tragic out of comedy. We can bring it forth as a frightening moment, as an abyss that opens suddenly; indeed many of Shakespeare's tragedies are already really comedies out of which the tragic arises.

After all this the conclusion might easily be drawn that comedy is the expression of despair, but this conclusion is not inevitable. To be sure, whoever realizes the senselessness, the hopelessness of this world might well despair, but this despair is not a result of this world. Rather it is an answer given by an individual to this world; another answer would be not to despair, would be an individual's decision to endure this world in which we live like Gulliver among the giants. He also achieves distance, he also steps back a pace or two who takes measure of his opponent, who prepares himself to fight his opponent or to escape him. It is still possible to show man as a courageous being.

In truth this is a principal concern of mine. The blind man, Romulus, Uebelohe, Akki, are all men of courage. The lost world order is restored within them; the universal escapes my grasp. I refuse to find the universal in a doctrine. The universal for me is chaos. The world (hence the stage which represents this world) is for me something monstrous, a riddle of misfortunes which must be accepted but before which one must not capitulate. The world is far bigger than any man, and perforce threatens him constantly. If one could but stand outside the world, it would no longer be threatening. But I have neither the right nor the ability to be an outsider to this world. To find solace in poetry can also be all too cheap; it is more honest to retain one's human point of view. Brecht's thesis, that the world is an accident, which he developed in his street scene where he shows how this accident happened, may yield—as it in fact did—some magnificent theatre; but he did it by concealing most of the evidence! Brecht's thinking is inexorable, because inexorably there are many things he will not think about.

And lastly it is through the conceit, through comedy that the anonymous audience becomes possible as an audience, becomes a reality to be counted on, and also, one to be taken into account. The conceit easily transforms the crowd of theatre-goers into a mass which can be attacked, deceived, outsmarted into listening to things it would otherwise not so readily listen to. Comedy is a mousetrap in which the public is easily caught and in which it will get caught over and over again. Tragedy, on the other hand, predicated a true community, a kind of community whose existence in our day is but an embarrassing fiction. Nothing is more ludicrous, for instance, than to sit and watch the mystery plays of the Anthroposophists when one is not a participant.

Granting all this there is still one more question to be asked: is it permissible to go from a generality to a particular form of art, to do what I just did when I went from my assertion that the world was formless to the particular possibility for writing comedies today. I doubt that this is permissible. Art is something personal, and something personal should never be explained with generalities. The value of a work of art does not depend on whether more or less good reasons for its existence can be found. Hence I have also tried to avoid certain problems, as for example the argument which is quite lively today, whether or not plays ought to be written in verse or in prose. My own answer lies simply in writing prose, without any intentions of thereby deciding the issue. A man has to choose to go one way, after all, and why should one way always be worse than another? As far as my concepts of comedy are concerned, I believe that here, too, personal reasons are more important than more general ones that are always open to argument. What logic in matters of art could not be refuted! One talks best about art when one talks of one's own art. The art one chooses is an expression of freedom without which no art can exist, and at the same time also of necessity without which art can not exist either. The artist always represents his world and himself. If at one time philosophy taught men to arrive at the particular from the general, then unlike Schiller who started out believing in general conclusions, I can not construct a play as he did when I doubt that the particular can ever be reached from the general. But my doubt is mine and only mine, and not the doubt and problems of a Catholic for whom drama holds possibilities non-Catholics do not share. This is so even if, on the other hand, a Catholic who takes his religion seriously, is denied those possibilities which other men possess. The danger inherent in this thesis lies in the fact that there are always those artists who for the sake of finding some generalities to believe in accept conversion, taking a step which is the more to be wondered at for the sad fact that it really will not help them. The difficulties experienced by a Protestant in writing a drama are just the same difficulties he has with his faith. Thus it is my way to mistrust what is ordinarily called the building of the drama, and to arrive at my plays from the unique, the sudden idea or conceit, rather than from some general concept or plan. Speaking for myself, I need to write off into the blue, as I like to put it so that I might give critics a catchword to hang onto. They use it often enough, too, without really understanding what I mean by it.

But these matters are my own concerns and hence it is not necessary to invoke the whole world and to make out as if what are my concerns are the concerns of art in general (lest I be like the drunk who goes back to Noah, the Flood, original sin and the beginning of the world to explain what is, after all, only his own weakness). As in everything and everywhere, and not just in the field of art, the rule is: No excuses, please!

Nevertheless the fact remains (always keeping in mind, of course, the reservations just made) that we now stand in a different relationship to what we have called our material. Our unformed, amorphous present is characterized by being surrounded by figures and forms that reduce our time into a mere result, even less, into a mere transitional state, and which give excessive weight to the past as something finished and to the future as something possible. This applies equally well to politics. Related to art it means that the artist is surrounded by all sorts of opinions about art and by demands on him which are based not upon his capacities, but upon the historical past and present forms. He is surrounded therefore by materials which are no longer materials, that is possibilities, but by materials which have already taken on shape, that is some definitive form. Caesar is no longer pure subject matter for us; he has become the Caesar whom scholarship made the object of its researches. And so it happened that scholars, having thrown themselves with increasing energy not only upon nature but also upon the intellectual life and upon art, establishing in the process intellectual history, literary scholarship, philosophy and goodness knows what else, have created a body of factual information which can not be ignored (for one can not be conscious of these facts and at the same time pretend to be so naive that one need pay no attention to the results of scholarship). In this way, however, scholars have deprived the artist of materials by doing what was really the artist's task. The mastery of Richard Feller's *History of Berne* precludes the possibility of an historical drama about the city of Berne; the history of Berne was thus given shape before some literary artist could do it. True, it is a scholastic form (and

not a mythical one which would leave the way open for a tragedian), a form that severely limits the field for the artist, leaving to art only psychology which, of course, has also become a science. To rewrite such a history in a creative literary manner would now be a tautology, a repetition by means which are not suitable or fitting, a mere illustration of scholarly insights; in short, it would be the very thing science often claims literature to be. It was still possible for Shakespeare to base his Caesar upon Plutarch, for the Roman was not a historian in our sense of the word but a storyteller, the author of biographical sketches. Had Shakespeare read Mommsen he could not have written his Caesar because he would of necessity have lost the supremacy over his materials. And this holds true now in all things, even the myths of the Greeks which, since we no longer live them but only study, evaluate, investigate them, recognizing them to be mere myths and as such destroying them, have become mummies; and these, bound tightly round with philosophy and theology, are all too often substituted for the living thing.

Therefore the artist must reduce the subjects he finds and runs into everywhere if he wants to turn them once more into real materials, hoping always that he will succeed. He parodies his materials, contrasts them consciously with what they have actually been turned into. By this means, by this act of parody, the artist regains his freedom and hence his material; and thus material is no longer found but invented. For every parody presupposes a conceit and an invention. In laughter man's freedom becomes manifest, in crying his necessity. Our task today is to demonstrate freedom. The tyrants of this planet are not moved by the works of the poets. They yawn at a poet's threnodies. For them heroic epics are silly fairy tales and religious poetry puts them to sleep. Tyrants fear only one thing: a poet's mockery. For this reason then parody has crept into all literary genres, into the novel, the drama, into lyrical poetry. Much of painting, even of music, has been conquered by parody, and the grotesque has followed, often well camouflaged, on the heels of parody: all of a sudden the grotesque is there.

But our times, up to every imaginable trick there is, can handle all that and nothing can intimidate it: the public has been educated to see in art something solemn, hallowed and even pathetic. The comic is considered inferior, dubious, unseemly; it is accepted only when it makes people feel as bestially happy as a bunch of pigs. But the very moment people recognize the comic to be dangerous, an art that exposes, demands, moralizes, it is dropped like a hot potato, for art may be everything it wants to be so long as it remains *gemütlich*.

We writers are often accused of art that is nihilistic. Today, of course, there exists a nihilistic art, but not every art that seems nihilistic is so. True nihilistic art does not appear to be nihilistic at all; usually it is considered to be especially humane and supremely worthy of being read by our more mature young people. A man must be a pretty bungling sort of nihilist to be recognized as such by the world at large. People call nihilistic what is merely uncomfortable. Then also people say, the artist is supposed to create, not to talk; to give shape to things, not to preach. To be sure. But it becomes more and more difficult to create "purely" or however people imagine the creative mind should work. Mankind today is like a reckless driver racing ever faster, ever more heedlessly along the highway. And he does not like it when the frightened passengers cry out, "Watch out" and "There's a warning sign! Slow down" or "Don't kill that child!" What is more, the driver hates it even worse when he is asked, "Who is paying for the car?" or "Who's providing the gas and oil for this mad journey?", to say nothing of what happens when he is asked for his driver's license. What unpleasant facts might then come to light! Maybe the car was stolen from some relatives, the gas and oil squeezed from the passengers, and really not gas and oil but the blood and sweat of us all; and most likely he wouldn't even have a driver's license and it would turn out that this was his first time driving. Of course, it would be embarrassing if such personal questions were to be asked. The driver would much prefer the passengers to praise the beauty of the countryside through which they are traveling, the silver of the river and the brilliant reflection of the ice-capped mountains in the far distance, would even prefer to have amusing stories whispered into his ear. Today's author, however, can no longer confine himself with good conscience to whispering pleasant stories and praising the beautiful landscape. Unfortunately, too, he can not get out of this mad race in order to sit by the wayside, writing the pure poetry demanded of him by all the nonpoets. Fear, worry, and above all anger open his mouth wide.

How very nice it would be if we could end now on this emphatic note. It would be a conclusion that could be considered at least par-tially safe and not wholly impossible. But in all honesty we must ask ourselves at this point if any of this makes sense today, if it were not better if we practiced silence. I have tried to show that the theatre today is, in the best sense of the word to be sure, in part a museum, and in part a field of experimentation. I have also tried to show here and there what these experiments are. Is the theatre capable of fulfilling this, its latter destiny? Not only has the writing of plays become more difficult today but also the rehearsing and performing of these plays is harder. The very lack of time results at best in only a decent attempt, a first probing, a slight advance in what might be the right direction. A play that is to be more than a merely conventional piece, that is really to be an experiment, can no longer be solved at the writing desk. Giraudoux's fortune was that he had Jouvet.[10] Unhappily this happens only once or twice. The repertory theatre of Germany can afford less and less to experiment. A new play must be gotten rid of as quickly as possible. The museum's treasures weigh too heavily in the scales. The theatre, our whole culture, lives on the interest of the well invested intellect, to which nothing can happen any more and for which not even royalties have to be paid. Assured of having a Goethe, Schiller or Sophocles at hand, the theatres are willing now and then to put on a modern piece—but preferably only for a premiere performance. Heroically this duty is discharged, and sighs of relief are breathed all around when Shakespeare is performed next time. What can we say or do? Clear the stages completely! Make room for the classics! The world of the museum is growing and bursts with its treasures. The cultures of the cave dwellers have not yet been investigated to the nth degree. Let the custodians of the future concern themselves with our art when it is our turn. It does not make much difference then if something new is added, something new is written. The demands made of the artist by esthetics increase from day to day. What is wanted is the perfection which is read into the classics. And let the artist even be suspected of having taken one step backwards, of having made a mistake, just watch how quickly he is dropped. Thus a climate is created in which literature can be studied but not made. How can the

---

[10] Louis Jouvet (1887–1951), famous French actor—one of the founders of the *Théâtre du Vieux Colombier* and well known for his acting in the plays of Giraudoux.

artist exist in a world of educated and literate people? This question oppresses me, and I know no answer. Perhaps the writer can best exist by writing detective stories, by creating art where it is least suspected. Literature must become so light that it will weigh nothing upon the scale of today's literary criticism: only in this way will it regain its true worth.

Translated by Gerhard Nellhaus

THE VISIT

Translated by Patrick Bowles

CAST OF CHARACTERS

Visitors:
CLAIRE ZACHANASSIAN, *née*
Wascher, Multi-millionairess,
Armenian Oil
HER HUSBANDS, VII–IX
BUTLER

TOBY } *gum-chewers*
ROBY }

KOBY { *blind*
LOBY {

Visited:
ILL
HIS WIFE
HIS SON
HIS DAUGHTER
MAYOR
PRIEST
SCHOOLMASTER
DOCTOR
POLICEMAN
MAN ONE

MAN TWO
MAN THREE
MAN FOUR
PAINTER
FIRST WOMAN
SECOND WOMAN
MISS LOUISA

Extras:
STATION-MASTER
TICKET INSPECTOR
GUARD
BAILIFF

Distractors:
FIRST REPORTER
SECOND REPORTER
RADIO COMMENTATOR
CAMERAMAN

PLACE *Guellen, a Smalltown*

TIME *The Present*

ACT ONE

(Clangor of railway-station bell before curtain rises to discover legend: "Guellen." Obviously name of small, skimpily depicted township in background: a tumbledown wreck. Equally ramshackle station-buildings may or may not be cordoned off, according to country, and include a rusty signal-cabin, its door marked "No Entry." Also depicted in bare outline, center, the piteous Station Road. Left, a barren little building with tiled roof and mutilated posters on its windowless walls. A sign, at left corner: "Ladies." Another, at right corner: "Gents." This entire prospect steeped in hot autumn sun. In front of little building, a bench. On it, four men. An unspeakably ragged fifth—so are the other four—is inscribing letters in red paint on a banner clearly intended for some procession: "Welcome Clarie." Thunderous pounding din of express train rushing through. Men on bench show interest in express train by following its headlong rush with head movements from left to right)

MAN ONE The Goodrun. Hamburg-Naples.
MAN TWO The Racing Roland gets here at eleven twenty-seven. Venice-Stockholm.

The Visit, a tragicomedy by Friedrich Duerrenmatt, translated from the German by Patrick Bowles. Copyright © 1956 by Peter Schifferli, Verlag AG 'Die Arche,' Zürich. English version copyright © 1962 by Jonathan Cape Limited, London. Published by Grove Press, Inc., N. Y.

MAN THREE   Our last remaining pleasure: watching trains go by.

MAN FOUR   Five years ago the Goodrun and the Racing Roland stopped in Guellen. And the Diplomat. And the Lorelei. All famous express trains.

MAN ONE   World famous.

MAN TWO   Now not even the commuting trains stop. Just two from Kaffigen and the one-thirteen from Kalberstadt.

MAN THREE   Ruined.

MAN FOUR   The Wagner Factory gone crash.

MAN ONE   Bockmann bankrupt.

MAN TWO   The Foundry on Sunshine Square shut down.

MAN THREE   Living on the dole.

MAN FOUR   On Poor Relief soup.

MAN ONE   Living?

MAN TWO   Vegetating.

MAN THREE   And rotting to death.

MAN FOUR   The entire township.

(*Bell rings*)

MAN TWO   It's more than time that millionairess got here. They say she founded a hospital in Kalberstadt.

MAN THREE   And a kindergarten in Kaffigen. And a memorial church in the Capital.

PAINTER   She had Zimt do her portrait. That Naturalistic dauber.

MAN ONE   She and her money. She owns Armenian Oil, Western Railways, North Broadcasting Company and the Hong Kong—uh—Amusement District.

(*Train clatter.* STATION-MASTER *salutes.* MEN *move heads from right to left after train*)

MAN FOUR   The Diplomat.

MAN THREE   We were a city of the Arts, then.

MAN TWO   One of the foremost in the land.

MAN ONE   In Europe.

MAN FOUR   Goethe spent a night here. In the Golden Apostle.

MAN THREE   Brahms composed a quartet here.

(*Bell rings*)

MAN TWO   Bertold Schwarz invented gunpowder here.

PAINTER   And I was a brilliant student at the *École des Beaux Arts*. And what am I doing here now? Sign-painting!

(*Train clatter. Guard appears, left, as after jumping off train*)

GUARD   (*long-drawn wail*) Guellen!

MAN ONE   The Kaffigen commuter.

(*One passenger has got off, left. He walks past men on bench, disappears through doorway marked "Gents"*)

MAN TWO   The Bailiff.

MAN THREE   Going to distrain on the Town Hall.

MAN FOUR   We're even ruined politically.

STATION-MASTER   (*waves green flag, blows whistle*) Stand clear!

(*Enter from town,* MAYOR, SCHOOLMASTER, PRIEST *and* ILL—*a man of near sixty-five; all shabbily dressed*)

MAYOR   The guest of honor will be arriving on the one-thirteen commuting from Kalberstadt.

SCHOOLMASTER   We'll have the mixed choir singing; the Youth Club.

PRIEST   And the fire bell ringing. It hasn't been pawned.

MAYOR   We'll have the town band playing on Market Square. The Athletics Club will honor the millionairess with a pyramid. Then a meal in the Golden Apostle. Finances unfortunately can't be stretched to illuminating the Cathedral for the evening. Or the Town Hall.

(*Bailiff comes out of little building*)

BAILIFF   Good morning, Mister Mayor, a very good morning to you.

MAYOR   Why, Mister Glutz, what are you doing here?

BAILIFF   You know my mission, Mister Mayor. It's a colossal undertaking I'm faced with. Just try distraining on an entire town.

MAYOR   You won't find a thing in the Town Hall. Apart from one old typewriter.

BAILIFF   I think you're forgetting something, Mister Mayor. The Guellen History Museum.

MAYOR   Gone three years ago. Sold to America. Our coffers are empty. Not a single soul pays taxes.

BAILIFF   It'll have to be investigated. The country's booming and Guellen has the Sunshine Foundry. But Guellen goes bankrupt.

MAYOR   We're up against a real economic enigma.

MAN ONE   The whole thing's a Free Masons' plot.

MAN TWO   Conspired by the Jews.

MAN THREE   Backed by High Finance.

MAN FOUR   International Communism's showing its colors.

(*Bell rings*)

BAILIFF   I always find something. I've got eyes like a hawk. I think I'll take a look at the Treasury. (*exit*)

MAYOR   Better let him plunder us first. Not after the millionairess's visit.

(PAINTER *has finished painting his banner*)

ILL   You know, Mister Mayor, that won't do. This banner's too familiar. It ought to read, "Welcome Claire Zachanassian".

MAN ONE   But she's Clarie!

MAN TWO   Clarie Wascher!

MAN THREE   She was educated here!

MAN FOUR   Her dad was the builder.

PAINTER   O.K., so I'll write "Welcome Claire Zachanassian" on the back. Then if the millionairess seems touched we can turn it round and show her the front.

MAN TWO   It's the Speculator. Zürich-Hamburg.

(*Another express train passes, right to left*)

MAN THREE   Always on time, you can set your watch by it.

MAN FOUR   Tell me who still owns a watch in this place.

MAYOR   Gentlemen, the millionairess is our only hope.

PRIEST   Apart from God.

MAYOR   Apart from God.

SCHOOLMASTER   But God won't pay.

MAYOR   You used to be a friend of hers, Ill, so now it all depends on you.

PRIEST   But their ways parted. I heard some story about it—have you no confession to make to your Priest?

ILL   We were the best of friends. Young and hotheaded. I used to be a bit of a lad, gentlemen, forty-five years ago. And she, Clara, I can see her still: coming towards me through the shadows in Petersens' Barn, all aglow. Or walking barefoot in the Konrad's Village Wood, over the moss and the leaves, with her red hair streaming out, slim and supple as a willow, and tender, ah, what a devilish beautiful little witch. Life tore us apart. Life. That's the way it is.

MAYOR   I ought to have a few details about Madam Zachanassian for my little after-dinner speech in the Golden Apostle. (*takes a small notebook from pocket*)

SCHOOLMASTER   I've been going through the old school-reports. Clara Wascher's marks, I'm sorry to say, were appalling. So was her conduct. She only passed in botany and zoology.

MAYOR (*takes note*)   Good. Botany and zoology. A pass. That's good.

ILL   I can help you here, Mister Mayor. Clara loved justice. Most decidedly. Once when they took a beggar away she flung stones at the police.

MAYOR   Love of justice. Not bad. It always works. But I think we'd better leave out that bit about the police.

ILL   She was generous too. Everything she had she shared. She stole potatoes once for an old widow woman.

MAYOR   Sense of generosity. Gentlemen, I absolutely must bring that in. It's the crucial point. Does anyone here remember a building her father built? That'd sound good in my speech.

ALL   No. No one.

(MAYOR *shuts his little notebook*)

MAYOR   I'm fully prepared for my part. The rest is up to Ill.

ILL   I know. Zachanassian has to cough up her millions.

MAYOR   Millions—that's the idea. Precisely.

SCHOOLMASTER   It won't help us if she only founds a nursery.

MAYOR   My dear Ill, you've been the most popular personality in Guellen for a long while now. In the spring, I shall be retiring. I've sounded out the Opposition: we've agreed to nominate you as my successor.

ILL   But Mister Mayor.

SCHOOLMASTER   I can confirm that.

ILL   Gentlemen, back to business. First of all, I'll tell Clara all about our wretched plight.

PRIEST   But do be careful—do be tactful.

ILL   We've got to be clever. Psychologically acute. If we make a fiasco of the welcome at the station, we could easily wreck everything else. You won't bring it off by relying on the municipal band and the mixed choir.

MAYOR   Ill's right, there. It'll be one of the decisive moments. Madam Zachanassian sets foot on her native soil, she's home again, and how moved she is, there are tears in her eyes, ah, the old familiar places. The old faces. Not that I'll be standing here like this in my shirtsleeves. I'll be wearing my formal black and a top hat. My wife beside me, my two grandchildren in front of me, all in white. Holding roses. My God, if only it all works out according to plan!

(*Bell rings*)

MAN ONE   It's the Racing Roland.

MAN TWO   Venice-Stockholm eleven twenty-seven.

PRIEST   Eleven twenty-seven! We still have nearly two hours to get suitably dressed.

MAYOR   Kuhn and Hauser hoist the "Welcome Claire Zachanassian" banner. (*points at four men*) You others better wave your hats. But please: no bawling like last year at the Government Mission, it hardly impressed them at all and so far we've had no subsidy. This is no time for wild enthusiasm, the mood you want is an inward, an almost tearful sympathy for one of our children, who was lost, and has been found again. Be relaxed. Sincere. But above all, time it well. The instant the choir stops singing, sound the fire-alarm. And look out . . .

(*His speech is drowned by the thunder of the oncoming train. Squealing brakes. Dumbfounded astonishment on all faces. The five men spring up from bench*)

PAINTER   The Express!

MAN ONE   It's stopping!

MAN TWO   In Guellen!

MAN THREE   The lousiest—

MAN FOUR   Most poverty-stricken—

MAN ONE   Desolate dump on the Venice-Stockholm line!

STATION-MASTER   It's against the Laws of Nature. The Racing Roland ought to materialize from around the Leuthenau bend, roar through Guellen, dwindle into a dark dot over at Pückenried valley and vanish.

(*Enter, right,* CLAIRE ZACHANASSIAN. *Sixty-three, red hair, pearl necklace, enormous gold bangles, unbelievably got up to kill and yet by the same token a Society Lady with a rare grace, in spite of all the grotesquerie. Followed by her entourage, comprising* BUTLER BOBY, *aged about eighty, wearing dark glasses, and* HUSBAND VII, *tall and thin with a black moustache, sporting a complete angler's outfit. Accompanying this group, an excited* TICKET INSPECTOR, *peaked cap, little red satchel*)

CLAIRE ZACHANASSIAN   Is it Guellen?

TICKET INSPECTOR   Madam. You pulled the Emergency Brake.

CLAIRE ZACHANASSIAN   I always pull the Emergency Brake.

TICKET INSPECTOR   I protest. Vigorously. No one ever pulls the Emergency Brake in this country. Not even in case of emergency. Our first duty is to our time-table. Will you kindly give me an explanation.

CLAIRE ZACHANASSIAN   It is Guellen, Moby. I recognize the wretched dump. That's Konrad's Village Wood, yonder, with a stream you can fish—pike and trout; that roof on the right is Petersens' Barn.

ILL   (*as if awakening*)   Clara.

SCHOOLMASTER   Madam Zachanassian.

ALL   Madam Zachanassian.

SCHOOLMASTER   And the choir and the Youth Club aren't ready!

MAYOR   The Athletic Club! The Fire Brigade!

PRIEST   The Sexton!

MAYOR   My frock-coat, for God's sake, my top hat, my grandchildren!

MAN ONE   Claire Wascher's here! Claire Wascher's here! (*jumps up, rushes off towards town*)

MAYOR   (*calling after him*)   Don't forget my wife!

TICKET INSPECTOR   I'm waiting for an explanation. In my official capacity. I represent the Railway Management.

CLAIRE ZACHANASSIAN   You're a simpleton. I want to pay this little town a visit. What d'you expect me to do, hop off your express train?

TICKET INSPECTOR   You stopped the Racing Roland just because you wanted to visit Guellen?

CLAIRE ZACHANASSIAN   Of course.

TICKET INSPECTOR   Madam. Should you desire to visit Guellen, the twelve-forty commuter from Kalberstadt is at your service. Please use it. Like other people. Arrival in Guellen one thirteen p.m.

CLAIRE ZACHANASSIAN   The ordinary passenger train? The one that stops in Loken, Brunnhübel, Beisenbach and Leuthenau? Are you really and truly asking me to go puffing round this countryside for half an hour?

TICKET INSPECTOR   You'll pay for this, Madam. Dearly.

CLAIRE ZACHANASSIAN   Boby, give him a thousand.

ALL   (*murmuring*)   A thousand.

(BUTLER *gives* TICKET INSPECTOR *a thousand*)

TICKET INSPECTOR   (*perplexed*)   Madam.

CLAIRE ZACHANASSIAN   And three thousand for the Railway Widows' Fund.

ALL   (*murmuring*)   Three thousand.

(TICKET INSPECTOR *receives three thousand from* BUTLER)

TICKET INSPECTOR   (*staggered*)   Madam. No such fund exists.

CLAIRE ZACHANASSIAN.   Then found one.

(*The supreme* CIVIC AUTHORITY *whispers a word or two in* TICKET INSPECTOR'*s ear*)

TICKET INSPECTOR   (*all confusion*)   Madam is Madam Claire Zachanassian? O do excuse me. Of course it's different in that case. We'd have been only too happy to stop in Guellen if we'd had the faintest notion, O, here's your money back, Madam, four thousand, my God.

ALL   (*murmuring*)   Four thousand.

CLAIRE ZACHANASSIAN   Keep it, it's nothing.

ALL   (*murmuring*)   Keep it.

TICKET INSPECTOR   Does Madam require the Racing Roland to wait while she visits Guellen? I know the Railway Management would be only too glad. They say the Cathedral portals are well worth a look. Gothic. With the Last Judgment.

CLAIRE ZACHANASSIAN Will you and your express train get the hell out of here?

HUSBAND VII (*whines*) But the Press, poppet, the Press haven't got off yet. The Reporters have no idea. They're dining up front in the saloon.

CLAIRE ZACHANASSIAN Let them dine, Moby, let them dine. I can't use the Press in Guellen yet, and they'll come back later on, don't worry.

(*Meanwhile* MAN TWO *has brought* MAYOR *his frock-coat.* MAYOR *crosses ceremoniously to* CLAIRE ZACHANASSIAN. PAINTER *and* MAN FOUR *stand on bench, hoist banner: "Welcome Claire Zachanassi" . . . Painter did not quite finish it*)

STATION-MASTER (*whistles, waves green flag*) Stand clear!

TICKET INSPECTOR I do trust you won't complain to the Railway Management, Madam. It was a pure misunderstanding.

(*Train begins moving out.* TICKET INSPECTOR *jumps on*)

MAYOR Madam Zachanassian, my dear lady. As Mayor of Guellen, it is my honor to welcome you, a child of our native town . . .

(*Remainder of* MAYOR'S *speech drowned in clatter of express train as it begins to move and then to race away. He speaks doggedly on*)

CLAIRE ZACHANASSIAN I must thank you, Mister Mayor, for your fine speech.

(*She crosses to* ILL *who, somewhat embarrassed, has moved towards her*)

ILL Clara.

CLAIRE ZACHANASSIAN Alfred.

ILL It's nice you've come.

CLAIRE ZACHANASSIAN I'd always planned to. All my life. Ever since I left Guellen.

ILL (*unsure of himself*) It's sweet of you.

CLAIRE ZACHANASSIAN Did you think about me too?

ILL Of course. All the time. You know I did, Clara.

CLAIRE ZACHANASSIAN They were wonderful, all those days we used to spend together.

ILL (*proudly*) They sure were. (*to* SCHOOLMASTER) See, Professor, I've got her in the bag.

CLAIRE ZACHANASSIAN Call me what you always used to call me.

ILL My little wildcat.

CLAIRE ZACHANASSIAN (*purrs like an old cat*) And what else?

ILL My little sorceress.

CLAIRE ZACHANASSIAN I used to call you my black panther.

ILL I still am.

CLAIRE ZACHANASSIAN Rubbish. You've grown fat. And grey. And drink-sodden.

ILL But *you're* still the same, my little sorceress.

CLAIRE ZACHANASSIAN Don't be crazy. I've grown old and fat as well. And lost my left leg. An automobile accident. Now I only travel in express trains. But they made a splendid job of the artificial one, don't you think? (*She pulls up her skirt, displays left leg*) It bends very well.

ILL (*wipes away sweat*) But my little wildcat, I'd never have noticed it.

CLAIRE ZACHANASSIAN Would you like to meet my seventh husband, Alfred? Tobacco Plantations. We're very happily married.

ILL But by all means.

CLAIRE ZACHANASSIAN Come on, Moby, come and make your bow. As a matter of fact his name's Pedro, but Moby's much nicer. In any case it goes better with Boby; that's the butler's name. And you get your butlers for life, so husbands have to be christened accordingly.

(HUSBAND VII *bows*)

Isn't he nice, with his little black moustache? Think it over, Moby.

(HUSBAND VII *thinks it over*)

Harder.

(HUSBAND VII *thinks it over harder*)

Harder still.

HUSBAND VII But I can't think any harder, poppet, really I can't.

CLAIRE ZACHANASSIAN Of course you can. Just try.

(HUSBAND VII *thinks harder still. Bell rings*)

You see. It works. Don't you agree, Alfred, he looks almost demoniacal like that. Like a Brazilian. But no! He's Greek-Orthodox. His father was Russian. We were married by a Pope. Most interesting. Now I'm going to have a look round Guellen.

(*She inspects little house, left, through jewel-encrusted lorgnette*)

My father built this Public Convenience, Moby. Good work, painstakingly executed. When I was a child I spent hours on that roof, spitting. But only on the Gents.

(MIXED CHOIR *and* YOUTH CLUB *have now assembled in background.* SCHOOLMASTER *steps forward wearing top hat*)

SCHOOLMASTER Madam. As Headmaster of Guellen College, and lover of the noblest Muse, may I take the liberty of offering you a homely folk-song, rendered by the mixed choir and the Youth Club.

CLAIRE ZACHANASSIAN Fire away, Schoolmaster, let's hear your homely folk-song.

(SCHOOLMASTER *takes up tuning-fork, strikes key.* MIXED CHOIR *and* YOUTH CLUB *begin ceremoniously singing, at which juncture another train arrives, left.* STATION-MASTER *salutes.* CHOIR *struggles against cacophonous clatter of train,* SCHOOLMASTER *despairs, train, at long last, passes*)

MAYOR (*despondent*) The fire alarm, sound the fire alarm!

CLAIRE ZACHANASSIAN Well sung, Guelleners! That blond bass out there on the left, with the big Adam's apple, he was really most singular.

(*A* POLICEMAN *elbows a passage through mixed choir, draws up to attention in front of* CLAIRE ZACHANASSIAN)

POLICEMAN Police Inspector Hahncke, Madam. At your service.

CLAIRE ZACHANASSIAN (*inspects him*) Thank you, I shan't want to arrest anybody. But Guellen may need you soon. Can you wink a blind eye to things from time to time?

POLICEMAN Sure I can, Madam. Where would I be in Guellen if I couldn't!

CLAIRE ZACHANASSIAN Start learning to wink them both.

(POLICEMAN *goggles at her, perplexed*)

ILL (*laughing*) Just like Clara! Just like my little wildcat!

(*Slaps thigh with enjoyment.* MAYOR *perches* SCHOOLMASTER'S *top hat on his own head, ushers pair of* GRANDCHILDREN *forward. Twin seven-year-old girls, blond plaits*)

MAYOR My grandchildren, Madam. Hermione and Adofina. My wife is the only one not present.

(*Mops perspiration. The two little girls curtsy for* MADAM ZACHANASSIAN *and offer her red roses*)

CLAIRE ZACHANASSIAN Congratulations on your kids, Mister Mayor. Here!

(*She bundles roses into* STATION-MASTER'S *arms.* MAYOR *stealthily hands top hat to* PRIEST, *who puts it on*)

(PRIEST *raises top hat, bows*)

CLAIRE ZACHANASSIAN Ah, the Priest. Do you comfort the dying?

PRIEST (*startled*) I do what I can.

CLAIRE ZACHANASSIAN People who've been condemned to death as well?

PRIEST (*perplexed*) The death sentence has been abolished in this country, Madam.

CLAIRE ZACHANASSIAN It may be reintroduced.

(PRIEST, *with some consternation, returns top hat to* MAYOR, *who dons it again*)

ILL (*laughing*) Really, little wildcat! You crack the wildest jokes.

CLAIRE ZACHANASSIAN Now I want to go into town.

(MAYOR *attempts to offer her his arm*)

What's all this, Mister Mayor. I don't go hiking miles on my artificial leg.

MAYOR (*shocked*) Immediately, immediately, Madam. The doctor owns a car. It's a Mercedes. The nineteen thirty-two model.

POLICEMAN (*clicking heels*) I'll see to it, Mister Mayor. I'll have the car commandeered and driven round.

CLAIRE ZACHANASSIAN That won't be necessary. Since my accident I only go about in sedan-chairs. Roby, Toby, bring it here.

(*Enter, left, two herculean gum-chewing* BRUTES *with sedan-chair. One of them has a guitar slung at his back*)

Two gangsters. From Manhattan. They were on their way to Sing Sing. To the electric chair. I petitioned for them to be freed as sedan-bearers. Cost me a million dollars per petition. The sedan-chair came from the Louvre. A gift from the French President. Such a nice man; he looks exactly like his pictures in the newspapers. Roby, Toby, take me into town.

ROBY *and* TOBY (*in unison*) Yes Mam.

CLAIRE ZACHANASSIAN But first of all to the Petersens' Barn, and then to Konrad's Village Wood. I want to take Alfred to visit our old trysting-places. In the meanwhile have the luggage and the coffin put in the Golden Apostle.

MAYOR (*startled*) The coffin?

CLAIRE ZACHANASSIAN Yes, I brought a coffin with me. I may need it. Roby, Toby, off we go!

(*The pair of gum-chewing* BRUTES *carry* CLAIRE ZACHANASSIAN *away to town.* MAYOR *gives signal, whereon all burst into cheers which spontaneously fade as two more servants enter, bearing an elaborate black coffin, cross stage and exeunt, towards Guellen. Now, undaunted and unpawned, the fire-alarm bell starts ringing*)

MAYOR At last! The fire bell.

(*Populace gather round coffin. It is followed in by* CLAIRE ZACHANASSIAN'S *maidservants and an endless stream of cases and trunks, carried by Guelleners. This traffic is controlled by* POLICEMAN, *who is about to follow it out when* enter *at that point a pair of little old fat soft-spoken* MEN, *both impeccably dressed*)

THE PAIR   We're in Guellen. We can smell it, we can smell it, we can smell it in the air, in the Guellen air.

POLICEMAN   And who might you be?

THE PAIR   We belong to the old lady, we belong to the old lady. She calls us Koby and Loby.

POLICEMAN   Madam Zachanassian is staying at the Golden Apostle.

THE PAIR (*gay*)   We're blind, we're blind.

POLICEMAN   Blind? O.K., I'll take you there, in duplicate.

THE PAIR   O thank you Mister Policeman, thank you very much.

POLICEMAN (*with surprise*)   If you're blind, how did you know I was a policeman?

THE PAIR   By your tone of voice, your tone of voice, all policemen have the same tone of voice.

POLICEMAN (*with suspicion*)   You fat little men seem to have had a bit of contact with the police.

THE PAIR (*incredulous*)   Men, he thinks we're men!

POLICEMAN   Then what the hell are you?

THE PAIR   You'll soon see, you'll soon see!

POLICEMAN (*baffled*)   Well, you seem cheerful about it.

THE PAIR   We get steak and ham, every day, every day.

POLICEMAN   Yeah. I'd get up and dance for that too. Come on, give me your hands. Funny kind of humor foreigners have. (*goes off to town with pair*)

THE PAIR   Off to Boby and Moby, off to Roby and Toby!

(*Open scene-change: façade of station and adjacent little building soar into flies. Interior of the Golden Apostle: an hotel-sign might well be let down from above, an imposing gilded Apostle, as emblem, and left to hang in mid-air. Faded, outmoded luxury. Everything threadbare, tattered, dusty and musty and gone to seed. Interminable processions of porters taking interminable pieces of luggage upstairs: first a cage, then the cases and trunks.* MAYOR *and* SCHOOLMASTER *seated in foreground drinking schnapps*)

MAYOR   Cases, cases, and still more cases. Mountains of them. And a little while ago they came in with a cage. There was a panther in it. A black, wild animal.

SCHOOLMASTER   She had the coffin put in a special spare room. Curious.

MAYOR   Famous women have their whims and fancies.

SCHOOLMASTER   She seems to want to stay here quite a while.

MAYOR   So much the better. Ill has her in the bag. He was calling her his little wildcat, his little sorceress. He'll get thousands out of her. Her health, Professor. And may Claire Zachanassian restore the Bockmann business.

SCHOOLMASTER   And the Wagner Factory.

MAYOR   And the Foundry on Sunshine Square. If they boom we'll all boom—my Community and your College and the Standard of Living.

(*He has called a toast; they clink glasses*)

SCHOOLMASTER   I've been correcting the Guellen schoolchildren's Latin and Greek exercises for more than two decades, Mister Mayor, but let me tell you, Sir, I only learned what horror is one hour ago. That old lady in black robes getting off the train was a gruesome vision. Like one of the Fates; she made me think of an avenging Greek goddess. Her name shouldn't be Claire; it should be Clotho. I could suspect her of spinning destiny's webs herself.

(*Enter* POLICEMAN. *Hangs cap on peg*)

MAYOR   Pull up a chair, Inspector.

(POLICEMAN *pulls up a chair*)

POLICEMAN   Not much fun patrolling in this dump. But maybe now it'll rise from the ashes. I've just been to Petersens' Barn with the millionairess and that shopkeeper Ill. I witnessed a moving scene. Both parties maintained a meditative pause, as in church. I was embarrassed. I therefore did not follow them when they went to Konrad's Village Wood. Say, that was a real procession. The sedan-chair first, then Ill walking beside it, then the Butler, then her seventh husband last with his fishing-rod.

SCHOOLMASTER   That conspicuous consumption of husbands; she's a second Laïs.

POLICEMAN   And those two little fat men. The devil knows what it all means.

SCHOOLMASTER   Sinister. An ascent from the infernal regions.

MAYOR   I wonder what they're after, in Konrad's Village Wood.

POLICEMAN   The same as in Petersens' Barn, Mister Mayor. They're calling in on the places where their passion used to burn, as they say.

SCHOOLMASTER   Flame, flame. Remember Shakespeare: Romeo and Juliet. Gentlemen: I'm stirred. I sense the grandeur of antiquity in Guellen. I've never sensed it here before.

MAYOR   Gentlemen: we must drink a special toast to Ill—a man who's doing all a man can do to better our lot. To our most popular citizen: to my successor!

(*The Hotel Apostle floats away, back into the flies. Enter the four* CITIZENS, *left, with a simple, backless wooden bench, which they set down, left.* MAN ONE, *with a huge, pasteboard heart hanging from his neck, on it the letters* **A ↑ C**, *climbs on to the bench. The others stand round him in a half-circle, holding twigs at arm's length to designate trees*)

MAN ONE
We are trees, we're pine and spruce
MAN TWO
We are beech, and dark-green fir
MAN THREE
Lichen, moss and climbing ivy
MAN FOUR
Undergrowth and lair of fox
MAN ONE
Drifting cloud and call of bird
MAN TWO
We are the woodland wilderness
MAN THREE
Toadstool, and the timid deer
MAN FOUR
And rustling leaves; and bygone dreams.

(*The two gum-chewing* BRUTES *emerge from background bearing sedan-chair with* CLAIRE ZACHANASSIAN, ILL *at her side. Behind her,* HUSBAND VII. BUTLER *brings up rear, leading blind pair by the hand*)

CLAIRE ZACHANASSIAN   It's the Konrad's Village Wood. Roby, Toby, stop a moment.

BLIND PAIR   Stop, Roby and Toby, stop, Boby and Moby.

(CLAIRE ZACHANASSIAN *descends from sedan-chair, surveys wood*)

CLAIRE ZACHANASSIAN   There's the heart with our two names on it, Alfred. Almost faded away, and grown apart. And the tree's grown. The trunk and branches have thickened. The way we have ourselves.

(CLAIRE ZACHANASSIAN *crosses to other trees*) A woodland bower. It's a long time since I last walked through these woods, in my young days, frolicking in the foliage and the purple ivy. You brutes just go and chew your gum behind the bushes, and take your sedan-chair with you; I don't want to look at your mugs all the time. And Moby, stroll away over to that stream on the right, there, and look at the fish. (*Exit* BRUTES, *left, with sedan-chair.*

Exit HUSBAND VII, *right.* CLAIRE ZACHANASSIAN *sits on bench*) Look, a doe. (MAN THREE *springs off*)

ILL   It's the closed season. (*sits next to her*)

CLAIRE ZACHANASSIAN   We kissed each other on this spot. More than fifty years ago. We loved each other under these boughs, under these bushes, among these toadstools on the moss. I was seventeen, and you weren't quite twenty. Then you married Matilda Blumhard with her little general store, and I married old Zachanassian with his millions from Armenia. He found me in a brothel. In Hamburg. It was my red hair took his fancy; the old, gold lecher!

ILL   Clara!

CLAIRE ZACHANASSIAN   Boby, a Henry Clay.

BLIND PAIR   A Henry Clay, a Henry Clay.

(BUTLER *comes out of background, passes her a cigar, lights it*)

CLAIRE ZACHANASSIAN   I'm fond of cigars. I suppose I ought to smoke my husband's produce; but I don't trust them.

ILL   It was for your sake I married Matilda Blumhard.

CLAIRE ZACHANASSIAN   She had money.

ILL   You were young and beautiful. The future belonged to you. I wanted you to be happy. So I had to renounce being happy myself.

CLAIRE ZACHANASSIAN   And now the future's here.

ILL   If you'd stayed here, you'd have been ruined like me.

CLAIRE ZACHANASSIAN   Are you ruined?

ILL   A broken-down shopkeeper in a broken-down town.

CLAIRE ZACHANASSIAN   Now it's me who has money.

ILL   I've been living in hell since you went away from me.

CLAIRE ZACHANASSIAN   And I've grown into hell itself.

ILL   Always arguing with my family. They blame me for being poor.

CLAIRE ZACHANASSIAN   Didn't little Matilda make you happy?

ILL   Your happiness is what matters.

CLAIRE ZACHANASSIAN   Your children?

ILL   No sense of ideals.

CLAIRE ZACHANASSIAN   They'll develop one soon.

(*He says nothing. Both gaze at the wood of childhood memory*)

ILL   I lead a laughable life. I never once really managed to leave this township. One trip to Berlin and one to Tessin. That's all.

CLAIRE ZACHANASSIAN Why bother, any-way. I know what the world's like.

ILL Because you've always been able to travel.

CLAIRE ZACHANASSIAN Because I own it.

(*He says nothing; she smokes*)

ILL Everything's going to be different now.

CLAIRE ZACHANASSIAN Sure.

ILL (*watches her*) Are you going to help us?

CLAIRE ZACHANASSIAN I shan't leave my home-town in the lurch.

ILL We need thousands.

CLAIRE ZACHANASSIAN That's nothing.

ILL (*enthusiastically*) My little wildcat!

(*Moved, he slaps her on left shoulder, then painfully withdraws hand*)

CLAIRE ZACHANASSIAN That hurt. You hit one of the straps for my artificial leg.

(MAN ONE *pulls pipe and rusty door-key from trousers-pocket, taps on pipe with key*)

A woodpecker.

ILL Now it's the way it used to be when we were young and bold, when we went out walking in Konrad's Village Wood, in the days of our young love. And the sun was a dazzling orb, above the pine-trees. And far away a few wisps of cloud, and somewhere in the wood-land you could hear a cuckoo calling.

MAN FOUR Cuckoo, cuckoo!

(ILL *lays a hand on* MAN ONE)

ILL Cool wood, and the wind in the boughs, soughing like the sea-surge.

(*The three* MEN *who are trees begin soughing and blowing and waving their arms up and down*)

Ah, my little sorceress, if only time had really dissolved. If only life hadn't put us asunder.

CLAIRE ZACHANASSIAN Would you wish that?

ILL That above all, above all. I do love you!

(*kisses her right hand*)

The same, cool white hand.

CLAIRE ZACHANASSIAN No, you're wrong. It's artificial too. Ivory.

(ILL, *horrified, releases her hand*)

ILL Clara, are you all artificial?

CLAIRE ZACHANASSIAN Practically. My plane crashed in Afghanistan. I was the only one who crawled out of the wreckage. Even the crew died. I'm unkillable.

BLIND PAIR She's unkillable, she's unkill-able.

(*Ceremonial oom-pah music. The Hotel Apos-tle descends again.* GUELLENERS *bring in tables,* wretched, tattered tablecloths, cutlery, crock-ery, food. One table, center, one left, and one right, parallel to audience. PRIEST *comes out .of background. More* GUELLENERS *flock in, among them a* GYMNAST. MAYOR, SCHOOLMAS-TER *and* POLICEMAN *reappear. The* GUEL-LENERS *applaud.* MAYOR *crosses to bench where* CLAIRE ZACHANASSIAN *and* ILL *are sitting; the trees have metamorphosed back into citizens and moved away upstage*)

MAYOR The storm of applause is for you, my dear lady.

CLAIRE ZACHANASSIAN It's for the town band, Mister Mayor. It was a capital perform-ance; and the Athletic Club did a wonderful pyramid. I love men in shorts and vests. They look so natural.

MAYOR May I escort you to your place?

(*He escorts* CLAIRE ZACHANASSIAN *to her place at table, center, introduces her to his wife*) My wife.

(CLAIRE ZACHANASSIAN *examines wife through lorgnette*)

CLAIRE ZACHANASSIAN Annie Dummermut, top of our class.

(MAYOR *introduces her to a second woman, as worn out and embittered as his wife*)

MAYOR Mrs. Ill.

CLAIRE ZACHANASSIAN Matilda Blumhard. I can remember you lying in wait for Alfred behind the shop door. You've grown very thin and 'pale, my dear.

(*Doctor hurries in, right; a squat, thick-set fifty-year-old; · moustachioed, bristly black hair, scarred face, threadbare frock-coat*)

DOCTOR Just managed to do it, in my old Mercedes.

MAYOR Doctor Nuesslin, our physician.

(CLAIRE ZACHANASSIAN *examines* DOCTOR *through lorgnette as he kisses her hand*)

CLAIRE ZACHANASSIAN Interesting. Do you make out Death Certificates?

DOCTOR (*taken off guard*) Death Certifi-cates?

CLAIRE ZACHANASSIAN If someone should die?

DOCTOR Of course, Madam. It's my duty. As decreed by the authorities.

CLAIRE ZACHANASSIAN Next time, diagnose heart attack.

ILL (*laughs*) Delicious, simply delicious.

(CLAIRE ZACHANASSIAN *turns from* DOCTOR *to inspect* GYMNAST, *clad in shorts and vest*)

CLAIRE ZACHANASSIAN Do another exercise.

(*Gymnast bends knees, flexes arms*) Marvellous

muscles. Ever used your strength for strangling?

GYMNAST (*stiffens in consternation at knees-bend position*) For strangling?

CLAIRE ZACHANASSIAN Now just bend your arms back again, Mister Gymnast, then forward into a press-up.

ILL (*laughs*) Clara has such a golden sense of humor! I could die laughing at one of her jokes!

DOCTOR (*still disconcerted*) I wonder. They chill me to the marrow.

ILL (*stage whisper*) She's promised us hundreds of thousands.

MAYOR (*gasps*) Hundreds of thousands?

ILL Hundreds of thousands.

DOCTOR God Almighty.

(*The millionairess turns away from* GYMNAST)

CLAIRE ZACHANASSIAN And now, Mister Mayor, I'm hungry.

MAYOR We were just waiting for your husband, my dear lady.

CLAIRE ZACHANASSIAN You needn't. He's fishing. And I'm getting a divorce.

MAYOR A divorce?

CLAIRE ZACHANASSIAN Moby'll be surprised too. I'm marrying a German film star.

MAYOR But you told us it was a very happy marriage.

CLAIRE ZACHANASSIAN All my marriages are happy. But when I was a child I used to dream of a wedding in Guellen Cathedral. You should always fulfill your childhood dreams. It'll be a grand ceremony.

(*All sit.* CLAIRE ZACHANASSIAN *takes her place between* MAYOR *and* ILL. ILL'S WIFE *beside* ILL, MAYOR'S WIFE *beside* MAYOR. SCHOOLMASTER, PRIEST *and* POLICEMAN *at separate table, right. The four citizens, left. In background, more guests of honor, with wives. Above, the banner: "Welcome Claire."* MAYOR *stands, beaming with joy, serviette already in position, and taps on his glass*)

MAYOR My dear lady, fellow-citizens. Forty-five years have flowed by since you left our little town, our town founded by Crown Prince Hasso the Noble, our town so pleasantly nestling between Konrad's Village Wood and Pückenried Valley. Forty-five years, more than four decades, it's a long time. Many things have happened since then, many bitter things. It has gone sadly with the world, gone sadly with us. And yet we have never, my dear lady—our Claire (*applause*)—never forgotten you. Neither you, nor your family. Your mother, that magnificent and robustly healthy creature (ILL *whispers something to him*) tragically and prematurely torn from our midst by tuber-culosis, and your father, that popular figure, who built the building by the station which experts and laymen still visit so often (ILL *whispers something to him*)—still admire so much, they both live on in our thoughts, for they were of our best, our worthiest. And you too, my dear lady: who, as you gambolled through our streets—our streets, alas, so sadly decrepit nowadays—you, a curly-headed blonde (ILL *whispers something to him*)—red-headed madcap, who did not know you? Even then, everyone could sense the magic in your personality, foresee your approaching rise to humanity's dizzy heights. (*takes out his note-book*) You were never forgotten. Literally never. Even now, the staff at school hold up your achievements as an example to others, and in nature studies—the most essential ones—they were astonishing, a revelation of your sympathy for every living creature, indeed for all things in need of protection. And even then, people far and wide were moved to wonder at your love for justice, at your sense of generosity. (*huge applause*) For did not our Claire obtain food for an old widow, buying potatoes with that pocket money so hardly earned from neighbors, and thereby save the old lady from dying of hunger, to mention but one of her deeds of charity. (*huge applause*) My dear lady, my dear Guelleners, that happy temperament has now developed from those tender seeds to an impressive flowering, and our redheaded madcap has become a lady whose generosity stirs the world; we need only think of her social work, of her maternity homes and her soup kitchens, of her art foundations and her children's nurseries, and now, therefore, I ask you to give three cheers for the prodigal returned: Hip, Hip, Hip, Hurrah!

(*applause*)

(CLAIRE ZACHANASSIAN *gets to her feet*)

CLAIRE ZACHANASSIAN Mister Mayor, Guelleners. I am moved by your unselfish joy in my visit. As a matter of fact I was somewhat different from the child I seem to be in the Mayor's speech. When I went to school, I was thrashed. And I stole the potatoes for Widow Boll, aided by Ill; not to save the old bawd from dying of hunger, but just for once to sleep with Ill in a more comfortable bed than Konrad's Village Wood or Petersens' Barn. None the less, as my contribution to this joy of yours, I want to tell you I'm ready to give Guellen one million. Five hundred thousand for the town and five hundred thousand to be shared among each family.

(*Deathly silence*)

MAYOR (*stammers*) One million.

(*Everyone still dumbstruck*)

CLAIRE ZACHANASSIAN On one condition.

(*Everyone bursts into indescribable jubilation, dancing round, standing on chairs,* GYMNAST *performing acrobatics, etc.* ILL *pounds his chest enthusiastically*)

ILL There's Clara for you! What a jewel! She takes your breath away! Just like her, O my little sorceress! (*kisses her*)

MAYOR Madam: you said, on one condition. May I ask, on what condition?

CLAIRE ZACHANASSIAN I'll tell you on what condition. I'm giving you a million, and I'm buying myself justice.

(*Deathly silence*)

MAYOR My dear lady, what do you mean by that?

CLAIRE ZACHANASSIAN What I said.

MAYOR Justice can't be bought.

CLAIRE ZACHANASSIAN Everything can be bought.

MAYOR I still don't understand.

CLAIRE ZACHANASSIAN Boby. Step forward.

(BUTLER *steps forward, from right to center, between the three tables. Takes off his dark glasses*)

BUTLER I don't know if any of you here still recognize me.

SCHOOLMASTER Chief Justice Courtly.

BUTLER Right. Chief Justice Courtly. Forty-five years ago, I was Lord Chief Justice in Guellen. I was later called to the Kaffigen Court of Appeal until, twenty-five years ago it is now, Madam Zachanassian offered me the post of Butler in her service. A somewhat unusual career, indeed, I grant you, for an academic man, however, the salary involved was really quite fantastic . . .

CLAIRE ZACHANASSIAN Get to the point, Boby.

BUTLER As you may have gathered, Madam Claire Zachanassian is offering you the sum of one million dollars, in return for which she insists that justice be done. In other words, Madam Zachanassian will give you all a million if you right the wrong she was done in Guellen. Mr. Ill, if you please.

(ILL *stands. He is pale, startled, wondering*)

ILL What do you want of me?

BUTLER Step forward, Mr. Ill.

ILL Sure. (*steps forward, to front of table, right. Laughs uneasily. Shrugs*)

BUTLER The year was nineteen ten. I was Lord Chief Justice in Guellen. I had a paternity claim to arbitrate. Claire Zachanassian, at the time Clara Wascher, claimed that you, Mr. Ill, were her child's father. (ILL *keeps quiet*) At that time, Mr Ill, you denied paternity. You called two witnesses.

ILL Oh, it's an old story. I was young, thoughtless.

CLAIRE ZACHANASSIAN Toby and Roby, bring in Koby and Loby.

(*The two gum-chewing* GIANTS *lead pair of blind eunuchs on to center of stage, blind pair gaily holding hands*)

BLIND PAIR We're on the spot, we're on the spot!

BUTLER Do you recognize these two, Mr. Ill?

(ILL *keeps quiet*)

BLIND PAIR We're Koby and Loby, we're Koby and Loby.

ILL I don't know them.

BLIND PAIR We've changed a lot, we've changed a lot!

BUTLER Say your names.

FIRST BLIND MAN Jacob Chicken, Jacob Chicken.

SECOND BLIND MAN Louis Perch, Louis Perch.

BUTLER Now, Mr. Ill.

ILL I know nothing about them.

BUTLER Jacob Chicken and Louis Perch, do you know Mr. Ill?

BLIND PAIR We're blind, we're blind.

BUTLER Do you know him by his voice?

BLIND PAIR By his voice, by his voice.

BUTLER In nineteen ten, I was Judge and you the witnesses. Louis Perch and Jacob Chicken, what did you swear on oath to the Court of Guellen?

BLIND PAIR We'd slept with Clara, we'd slept with Clara.

BUTLER You swore it on oath, before me. Before the Court. Before God. Was it the truth?

BLIND PAIR We swore a false oath, we swore a false oath.

BUTLER Why, Jacob Chicken and Louis Perch?

BLIND PAIR Ill bribed us, Ill bribed us.

BUTLER With what did he bribe you?

BLIND PAIR With a pint of brandy, with a pint of brandy.

CLAIRE ZACHANASSIAN And now tell them what I did with you, Koby and Loby.

BUTLER Tell them.

BLIND PAIR The lady tracked us down, the lady tracked us down.

BUTLER Correct. Claire Zachanassian tracked you down. To the ends of the earth. Jacob Chicken had emigrated to Canada and

Louis Perch to Australia. But she tracked you down. And then what did she do with you?

BLIND PAIR   She gave us to Toby and Roby, she gave us to Toby and Roby.

BUTLER   And what did Toby and Roby do to you?

BLIND PAIR   Castrated and blinded us, castrated and blinded us.

BUTLER   And there you have the full story. One Judge, one accused, two false witnesses: a miscarriage of justice in the year nineteen ten. Isn't that so, plaintiff?

CLAIRE ZACHANASSIAN (*stands*)   That is so.

ILL (*stamping on floor*)   It's over and done with, dead and buried! It's an old, crazy story.

BUTLER   What happened to the child, plaintiff?

CLAIRE ZACHANASSIAN (*gently*)   It lived one year.

BUTLER   What happened to you?

CLAIRE ZACHANASSIAN   ·I became a prostitute.

BUTLER   What made you one?

CLAIRE ZACHANASSIAN·   The judgment of that court made me one.

BUTLER   And now you desire justice, Claire Zachanassian?

CLAIRE ZACHANASSIAN   I can afford it. A million for Guellen if someone kills Alfred Ill.

(*Deathly silence.* MRS. ILL *rushes to* ILL, *flings her arms round him*)

MRS. ILL   Freddy!

ILL   My little sorceress! You can't ask that! It was long ago. Life went on.

CLAIRE ZACHANASSIAN   Life went on, and I've forgotten nothing, Ill. Neither Konrad's Village Wood, nor Petersens' Barn; neither Widow Boll's bedroom, nor your treachery. And now we're old, the pair of us. You decrepit, and me cut to bits by the surgeons' knives. And now I want accounts between us settled. You chose your life, but you forced me into mine. A moment ago you wanted time turned back, in that wood so full of the past, where we spent our young years. Well I'm turning it back now, and I want justice. Justice for a million.

(MAYOR *stands, pale, dignified*)

MAYOR   Madam Zachanassian: you forget, this is Europe. You forget, we are not savages. In the name of all citizens of Guellen, I reject your offer; and I reject it in the name of humanity. We would rather have poverty than blood on our hands.

(*Huge applause*)

CLAIRE ZACHANASSIAN   I'll wait.

ACT TWO

(*The little town—only in outline. In background, the Golden Apostle Hotel, exterior view. Faded "art nouveau" architecture. Balcony. Right, a sign, "Alfred Ill: General Store," above a grimy shop-counter backed by shelves displaying old stock. Whenever anyone enters the imaginary door, a bell rings, tinnily. Left, a sign, "Police," above a wooden table, on it a telephone. Two chairs. It is morning.* ROBY *and* TOBY, *chewing gum, enter, left, bearing wreaths and flowers as at a funeral, cross stage and enter, back, the hotel.* ILL *at a window, watching them. His* DAUGHTER *on her knees scrubbing floor. His* SON *puts a cigarette in his mouth*)

ILL   Wreaths.

SON   They bring them in from the station every morning.

ILL   For the empty coffin in the Golden Apostle.

SON   It doesn't scare anyone.

ILL   The town's on my side. (SON *lights cigarette*) Mother coming dòwn for breakfast?

DAUGHTER   She's staying upstairs. Says she's tired.

ILL   You've a good mother, children. That's a fact. I just want you to know. A good mother. Let her stay upstairs, rest, save her energy. In that case, *we'll* have breakfast together. It's a long time since we've done that. I suggest eggs and a tin of American Ham. We'll do ourselves proud. Like in the good old days, when the Sunshine Foundry was still booming.

SON   You'll have to excuse me. (*stubs out cigarette*)

ILL   Aren't you going to eat with us, Karl?

SON   I'm going to the station. There's a railwayman off sick. Maybe they want a temporary.

ILL   Railroad work in the blazing sun is no job for my boy.

SON   It's better than no job.

(*Exit* SON. DAUGHTER *stands*)

DAUGHTER   I'm going too, father.

ILL   You too? I see. May one ask my lady where?

DAUGHTER   To the Employment Agency. They may have a vacancy.

(*Exit* DAUGHTER. ILL, *upset, takes out handkerchief, blows nose*)

ILL   Good kids, fine kids.

(*A few bars of guitar-music twang down from balcony*)

VOICE OF CLAIRE ZACHANASSIAN   Boby, pass me my left leg.

VOICE OF BUTLER   I can't find it, Madam.

VOICE OF CLAIRE ZACHANASSIAN   On the chest of drawers behind the wedding flowers.

(*Enter* MAN ONE, *as first customer; he goes through imaginary door into* ILL'S *shop*)

ILL   'Morning, Hofbauer.

MAN ONE   Cigarettes.

ILL   Same as usual?

MAN ONE   Not those, I want the green ones.

ILL   They cost more.

MAN ONE   On account.

ILL   Since it's you, Hofbauer, and we should all stick together.

MAN ONE   That's a guitar playing.

ILL   One of those Sing Sing gangsters.

(BLIND PAIR *walk out of hotel carrying rods and other appurtenances proper to fishing*)

BLIND PAIR   Lovely morning, Alfred, lovely morning.

ILL   Go to hell.

BLIND PAIR   We're going fishing, we're going fishing. (*Exit* BLIND PAIR, *left*)

MAN ONE   Gone to Guellen Pond.

ILL   With her seventh husband's fishing tackle.

MAN ONE   They say he's lost his tobacco plantations.

ILL   They belong to the millionairess.

MAN ONE   The eighth wedding will be gigantic. She announced their engagement yesterday.

(CLAIRE ZACHANASSIAN *appears on balcony in background, dressed for the morning. Moves her right hand, her left leg. Sporadic notes plucked on the guitar accompany the balcony scene which follows, after the fashion of opera-recitative, pointing the text now with a waltz, now with snatches of national or traditional songs, anthems, etc.*)

CLAIRE ZACHANASSIAN   I'm assembled again. Roby, the Armenian folk-song! (*Guitar music*) Zachanassian's favorite tune. He used to love listening to it. Every morning. An exemplary man, that old tycoon. With a veritable navy of oil tankers. And racing-stables. And millions more in cash. It was worth a marriage. A great teacher, and a great dancer; a real devil. I've copied him completely.

(*Two* WOMEN *come in, hand* ILL *milk-cans*)

FIRST WOMAN   Milk, Mr Ill.

SECOND WOMAN   My can, Mr Ill.

ILL   A very good morning to you. A quart of milk for the ladies. (*opens a milk-drum, prepares to ladle milk*)

FIRST WOMAN   Jersey milk, Mr Ill.

SECOND WOMAN   Two quarts of Jersey, Mr Ill.

ILL   Jersey. (*opens another drum, ladles milk*)

(CLAIRE ZACHANASSIAN *assesses morning critically through lorgnette*)

CLAIRE ZACHANASSIAN   A fine autumn morning. Light mist in the streets, a silvery haze, and the sky above precisely the shade of violet-blue Count Holk used to paint. My third husband. The Foreign Minister. He used to spend his holidays painting. They were hideous paintings. (*She sits, with elaborate ceremony*) The Count was a hideous person.

FIRST WOMAN   And butter. Half a pound.

SECOND WOMAN   And super-bread. Four large loaves.

ILL   I see we've had a legacy, ladies.

THE TWO WOMEN   On account.

ILL   Share the rough and share the smooth.

FIRST WOMAN   And a bar of chocolate.

SECOND WOMAN   Two bars.

ILL   On account?

FIRST WOMAN   On account.

SECOND WOMAN   We'll eat those here, Mr Ill.

FIRST WOMAN   It's much nicer here, Mr Ill.

(*They sit at back of shop eating chocolate*)

CLAIRE ZACHANASSIAN   A Winston. I will try that brand my seventh husband made, just once, now I've divorced him; poor Moby, with his fishing passion. He must be so sad sitting in the Portugal Express.

(BUTLER *hands her a cigar, gives her a light*)

MAN ONE   Look, sitting on the balcony, puffing at her cigar.

ILL   Always some wickedly expensive brand.

MAN ONE   Sheer extravagance. She ought to be ashamed, in front of the poor.

CLAIR ZACHANASSIAN   (*smoking*)   Curious. Quite smokeable.

ILL   Her plan's misfired. I'm an old sinner, Hofbauer—who isn't. It was a mean trick I played on her when I was a kid, but the way they all rejected the offer, all the Guelleners in the Golden Apostle unanimously, that was the finest moment of my life.

CLAIRE   ZACHANASSIAN   Boby.   Whisky. Neat.

(*Enter* MAN TWO, *as second customer, poor and tattered and torn, like everyone else*)

MAN TWO   'Morning. It'll be a hot day.

MAN ONE   Very fine and warm for the time of the year.

ILL   Extraordinary custom this morning. Not a soul for as long as you like and suddenly these past few days they're flocking in.

MAN ONE   We'll stick by you. We'll stick by *our* Ill. Come what may.

THE TWO WOMEN (*munching chocolate*) Come what may, Mr Ill, come what may.

MAN TWO   Remember, you're the town's most popular personality.

MAN ONE   Our most important personality.

MAN TWO   You'll be elected Mayor in spring.

MAN ONE   It's dead certain.

THE TWO WOMEN (*munching chocolate*) Dead certain, Mr Ill, dead certain.

MAN TWO   Brandy.

(ILL *reaches to shelf*)

(BUTLER *serves whisky*)

CLAIRE ZACHANASSIAN   Wake the new guy. Can't bear my husbands sleeping all the time.

ILL   Five and three.

MAN TWO   Not that.

ILL   It's what you always drink.

MAN TWO   Cognac.

ILL   It costs thirty-seven and nine. No one can afford that.

MAN TWO   Got to give yourself a treat sometimes.

(*A half-naked girl rushes headlong over stage, pursued by Toby*)

FIRST WOMAN (*munching chocolate*)   It's a scandal, the way Louisa behaves.

SECOND WOMAN (*munching chocolate*) And to make matters worse she's engaged to that blond musician in Gunpowder Street.

(ILL *takes down Cognac*)

ILL   Cognac.

MAN TWO   And tobacco. For my pipe.

ILL   Tobacco.

MAN TWO   The Export.

(ILL *totals account*)

(HUSBAND VIII *appears on balcony—the film star, tall, slender, red moustache, bath-robe. May be played by same actor as* HUSBAND VII)

HUSBAND VIII   Isn't it divine, Hopsi. Our first engagement breakfast. Really a dream. A little balcony, the lime-tree rustling, the Town Hall fountain softly plashing, a few hens scampering right across the sidewalk, housewives' voices chattering away over their little

daily cares and there, beyond the roof-tops, the Cathedral spires!

CLAIRE ZACHANASSIAN   Sit down, Hoby. Stop babbling. I can see the landscape. And thoughts aren't your strong point.

MAN TWO   She's sitting up there with her husband now.

FIRST WOMAN (*munching chocolate*)   Her eighth.

SECOND WOMAN (*munching chocolate*) Handsome gentleman. Acts in films. My daughter saw him as the poacher in a country-life feature.

FIRST WOMAN   I saw him when he was a priest in a Graham Greene.

(CLAIRE ZACHANASSIAN *is kissed by* HUSBAND VIII. *Guitar twangs chords*)

MAN TWO   You can get anything you want with money. (*spits*)

MAN ONE   Not from us (*bangs fist on table*)

ILL   One pound three shillings and three-pence.

MAN TWO   On account.

ILL   I'll make an exception this week; only you make sure you pay on the first, when the dole's due.

(MAN TWO *crosses to door*)

ILL   Helmesberger!

(MAN TWO *halts.* ILL *goes after him*)
You're wearing new shoes. New yellow shoes.

MAN TWO   So what?

(ILL *stares at* MAN ONE's *feet*)

ILL   You too, Hofbauer. You're wearing new shoes too. (*His gaze alights on the women; he walks slowly towards them, terror-stricken*) You too. New shoes. New yellow shoes.

MAN ONE   What's so extraordinary about new shoes?

MAN TWO   You can't go around in the same old shoes for ever.

ILL   New shoes. How did you all get new shoes?

THE TWO WOMEN   We got them on account, Mr Ill, we got them on account.

ILL   You got them on account. You got things on account from me too. Better tobacco, better milk, Cognac. Why are all the shops suddenly giving you credit?

MAN TWO   You're giving us credit too.

ILL   How are you going to pay? (*Silence. He begins throwing his wares at the customers. They all run away*) How are you going to pay? How are you going to pay? How? How? (*He rushes off, back*)

HUSBAND VIII   Township's getting rowdy.

CLAIRE ZACHANASSIAN   Village life.

HUSBAND VIII   Seems to be trouble in the shop down there.

CLAIRE ZACHANASSIAN   Haggling over the price of meat.

(*Chords on guitar, fortissimo.* HUSBAND VIII *leaps up, horrified*)

HUSBAND VIII   Hopsi, for heaven's sake! Did you hear that?

CLAIRE ZACHANASSIAN   The Black Panther. Spitting a little.

HUSBAND VIII   (*awestruck*)   A Black Panther?

CLAIRE ZACHANASSIAN   From the Pasha of Marakeesh. A present. He's loping around in the hall. A great wicked cat with flashing eyes. I'm very fond of him.

(POLICEMAN *sits down at table, left. Drinks beer. Slow, portentous manner of speech.* ILL *arrives from back of stage*)

CLAIRE ZACHANASSIAN   You may serve, Boby.

POLICEMAN   Ill. What can I do for you? Take a seat. (ILL *remains standing*) You're trembling.

ILL   I demand the arrest of Claire Zachanassian.

(POLICEMAN *thumbs tobacco into his pipe, lights it, comfortably*)

POLICEMAN   Peculiar. Highly peculiar.

(BUTLER *serves breakfast, brings mail*)

ILL   I demand it as future Mayor.

POLICEMAN   (*puffing clouds of smoke*)   We have not yet held the elections.

ILL   Arrest that woman on the spot.

POLICEMAN   What you mean is, you wish to charge this lady. It is then for the police to decide whether or not to arrest her. Has she infringed the law?

ILL   She's inciting the people of our town to kill me.

POLICEMAN   So now you want me to walk up to the lady and arrest her. (*pours himself beer*)

CLAIRE ZACHANASSIAN   The mail. One from Ike. Nehru. They send congratulations.

ILL   It's your duty.

POLICEMAN   Peculiar. Highly peculiar. (*drinks beer*)

ILL   It's only natural. Perfectly natural.

POLICEMAN   My dear Ill, it's not as natural as all that. Now let's examine the matter soberly. The lady makes an offer of one million

to the town of Guellen in exchange for your— you know what I'm talking about, of course. True, true, I was there. All this notwithstanding, no sufficient grounds are thereby constituted for the police taking action against Mrs Claire Zachanassian. We must abide by the law.

ILL   Incitement to murder.

POLICEMAN   Now listen here, Ill. We would only have a case of incitement to murder if the proposal to murder you were meant seriously. So much is obvious.

ILL   That's what I'm saying.

POLICEMAN   Exactly. Now, this proposal cannot be meant seriously, because one million is an exorbitant price, you have to admit that yourself. People offer a hundred, or maybe two hundred, for a job like that, not a penny more, you can bet your life on it. Which again proves the proposal wasn't meant seriously, and even if it had been the police couldn't take the lady seriously, because in that case she'd be mad. Get it?

ILL   Inspector. This proposal threatens *me*, whether the woman happens to be mad or not. That's only logical.

POLICEMAN   Illogical. You can't be threatened by a proposal, only by the execution of a proposal. Show me one genuine attempt to execute that proposal, for example one man who's been pointing a gun at you, and I'll be on the spot in a flash. But no one, in point of fact, has any wish to execute the proposal; quite the contrary. That demonstration in the Golden Apostle was extremely impressive. It was a while ago now, but allow me to congratulate you. (*drinks beer*)

ILL   I'm not quite so sure, Inspector.

POLICEMAN   Not quite so sure?

ILL   My customers are buying better milk, better bread, better cigarettes.

POLICEMAN   But you ought to be overjoyed! Business is better! (*drinks beer*)

CLAIRE ZACHANASSIAN   Boby, buy up Dupont Shares.

ILL   Helmesberger's been in buying Cognac. A man who hasn't earned a cent for years and lives on Poor Relief soup.

POLICEMAN   I'll have a tot of that Cognac this evening. Helmesberger's invited me over. (*drinks beer*)

ILL   Everyone's wearing new shoes. New yellow shoes.

POLICEMAN   Whatever can you have against new shoes? I've got a new pair on myself. (*displays feet*)

ILL   You too.

POLICEMAN   Look.

ILL   Yellow as well. And you're drinking Pilsener Beer.

POLICEMAN   Tastes good.

ILL   You always used to drink local beer.

POLICEMAN   Filthy stuff.

(*Radio music*)

ILL   Listen.

POLICEMAN   What?

ILL   Music.

POLICEMAN   *The Merry Widow.*

ILL   A radio.

POLICEMAN   It's Hagholzer next door. He ought to keep his window shut. (*makes note in little notebook*)

ILL   How did Hagholzer get a radio?

POLICEMAN   That's his business.

ILL   And you, Inspector, how are you going to pay for your Pilsener Beer and your new shoes?

POLICEMAN   That's my business. (*Telephone on table rings.* POLICEMAN *picks up receiver*) Policeman. Guellen Police Station.

CLAIRE ZACHANASSIAN   Boby, telephone the Russians and tell them I accept their offer.

POLICEMAN   O.K., we'll see to it.

ILL   And how are my customers going to pay?

POLICEMAN   That doesn't concern the police. (*stands, takes rifle from back of chair*)

ILL   But it does concern me. Because it's me they're going to pay with.

POLICEMAN   Nobody's threatening you.

(*begins loading rifle*)

ILL   The town's getting into debt. The greater the debt, the higher the standard of living. The higher the standard of living, the greater the need to kill me. And all that woman has to do is sit on her balcony, drink coffee, smoke cigars and wait. That's all. Just wait.

POLICEMAN   You're imagining things.

ILL   You're all just waiting. (*bangs on table*)

POLICEMAN   You've been drinking too much brandy. (*checks rifle*) There. Now it's loaded. Set your mind at rest. The police are here to enforce respect for the law, to maintain order and protect the individual. They know their duty. If the faintest suspicion of a threat to you arises, wheresoever it arises, from whatsoever source, the police will step in, Mr Ill, you can rely upon it.

ILL   (*softly*)   Then how do you explain that gold tooth in your mouth, Inspector?

POLICEMAN   What?

ILL   A gleaming new gold tooth.

POLICEMAN   Are you crazy? (*At this point,* ILL *perceives the gun-barrel is now directed at himself, and his hands go slowly up*) I've no time to argue over your ravings, man. I've got to go. That screwy millionairess has lost her little lapdog. The black panther. Now I have to hunt it down. (*goes towards back of stage and off*)

ILL   It's me you're hunting down, me.

(CLAIRE ZACHANASSIAN *is reading a letter*)

CLAIRE ZACHANASSIAN   He's coming, my dress-designer's coming. My fifth husband, my best-looking man. He still creates all my wedding-gowns. Roby, a minuet.

(*Guitar plays a minuet*)

HUSBAND VIII   But your fifth was a surgeon.

CLAIRE ZACHANASSIAN   My sixth. (*opens another letter*) From the Boss of Western Railways.

HUSBAND VIII   (*astonished*)   I've not heard of that one at all.

CLAIRE ZACHANASSIAN   My fourth. Impoverished. His shares belong to me. I seduced him in Buckingham Palace.

HUSBAND VIII   But that was Lord Ishmael.

CLAIRE ZACHANASSIAN   So it was. You're right, Hoby. I forgot all about him and his castle in Yorkshire. Then this letter must be from my second. Met him in Cairo. We kissed beneath the Sphinx. A most impressive evening.

(*Scene-change, right. The legend "Town Hall" descends.* MAN THREE *enters, carries off shop-till and shifts counter into position as desk.* MAYOR *enters. Puts revolver on table, sits.* ILL *enters, left. A construction-plan is affixed to wall*)

ILL   I want to talk to you, Mister Mayor.

MAYOR   Take a seat.

ILL   As man to man. As your successor.

MAYOR   By all means. (ILL *stays standing, watches revolver*) Mrs. Zachanassian's panther has escaped. It's climbing around in the Cathedral. So it's best to be armed.

ILL   Sure.

MAYOR   I've called up all men owning weapons. We're not letting the children go to school.

ILL   (*suspiciously*)   Somewhat drastic measures.

MAYOR   It's big game hunting.

(*Enter* BUTLER)

BUTLER   The World Bank President, Madam. Just flown in from New York.

CLAIRE ZACHANASSIAN I'm not at home. Tell him to fly away again.

MAYOR What's on your mind? Go on, feel free, unburden yourself.

ILL (*suspiciously*) That's a fine brand you're smoking there.

MAYOR A Pegasus. Virginia.

ILL Pretty expensive.

MAYOR Well worth the money.

ILL Your Worship used to smoke another brand.

MAYOR Sailor's Mates.

ILL Cheaper.

MAYOR Far too strong.

ILL New tie?

MAYOR Silk.

ILL And I suppose you bought a pair of shoes?

MAYOR I had some made in Kalberstadt. That's funny, how did you know?

ILL That's why I've come to see you.

MAYOR Whatever's the matter with you? You look pale. Are you sick?

ILL I'm scared.

MAYOR Scared?

ILL Living standards are going up.

MAYOR That's real news to me. I'd be glad if they were.

ILL I demand official protection.

MAYOR Eh! Whatever for?

ILL Your Worship knows very well what for.

MAYOR Don't you trust us?

ILL There's a million on my head.

MAYOR Apply to the police.

ILL I've been to the police.

MAYOR And that reassured you.

ILL When the Police Inspector opened his mouth, I saw a gleaming new gold tooth.

MAYOR You're forgetting you're in Guellen. A city of Humanist traditions. Goethe spent a night here. Brahms composed a quartet here. We owe allegiance to our lofty heritage.

(MAN THREE *enters, left, carrying typewriter*)

MAN The new typewriter, Mister Mayor. A Remington.

MAYOR It's to go in the office. (MAN *exits, right*) We've not deserved your ingratitude. If you're unable to place any trust in our community, I regret it for your sake. I didn't expect such a nihilistic attitude from you. After all, we live under the rule of law.

ILL Then arrest that woman.

MAYOR Peculiar. Highly peculiar.

ILL The Police Inspector said that too.

MAYOR God knows, the lady isn't acting so unreasonably. You did bribe two kids to commit perjury and fling a young girl into the lower depths.

ILL None the less there were quite a few millions down in those lower depths, Mister Mayor.

(*Silence*)

MAYOR Let me say a few frank words to you.

ILL I wish you would.

MAYOR As man to man, the way you wanted. You haven't any moral right to demand the arrest of that lady, and futhermore there's no question of your becoming Mayor. I'm extremely sorry to have to tell you.

ILL Officially?

MAYOR It's an all-party directive.

ILL I understand. (*crosses slowly to window, left, turns back on* MAYOR *and stares out*)

MAYOR The fact that we condemn the lady's proposal does not mean we condone the crime which led to that proposal. The post of Mayor requires certain guarantees of good moral character which you can no longer furnish. You must realize that. We shall continue of course to show you the same friendship and regard as ever. That goes without saying. (ROBY *and* TOBY *enter, left, with more wreaths and flowers. Cross the stage and disappear into the Golden Apostle*) The best thing is to pass over the whole affair in silence. I've also requested the local paper not to let any of it get into print.

(ILL *turns*)

ILL They've already begun adorning my coffin, Mister Mayor. For me, silence is too dangerous.

MAYOR But my dear Ill, what makes you think that? You ought to be thankful we're spreading a cloak of forgetfulness over the whole nasty business.

ILL You've already condemned me to death.

MAYOR Mr Ill!

ILL That plan proves it! It proves you have!

CLAIRE ZACHANASSIAN Onassis will be coming. The Prince and the Princess. Aga.

HUSBAND VIII Ali?

CLAIRE ZACHANASSIAN All the Riviera crowd.

HUSBAND VIII Reporters?

CLAIRE ZACHANASSIAN From all over the world. The Press always attend when I get married. They need me, and I need them. (*opens another letter*) From Count Holk.

HUSBAND VIII Hopsi, this is our first breakfast together. Must you really spend it reading letters from your former husbands?

CLAIRE ZACHANASSIAN I have to keep them under observation.

HUSBAND VIII I have problems too. (*rises to his feet, stares down into town*)

CLAIRE ZACHANASSIAN Something wrong with your Porsche?

HUSBAND VIII Small towns like this get me down. I know the lime-tree's rustling, the birds are singing, the fountain's plashing, but they were all doing all that half an hour ago. And nothing else is happening at all, either to the landscape or to the people, it's all a picture of deep, carefree peace and contentment and cosy comfort. No grandeur, no tragedy. Not a trace of the spiritual dedication of a great age.

(*Enter* PRIEST, *left, with a rifle slung round his shoulder. Over the table formerly occupied by* POLICEMAN *he spreads a white cloth marked with a black cross. Leans rifle against wall of hotel.* SEXTON *helps him on with soutane. Darkness*)

PRIEST Come in, Ill, come into the sacristy. (*Ill comes in, left*) It's dark in here, dark but cool.

ILL I don't want to bother you, Father.

PRIEST The doors of the Church are open to all. (*perceives that* ILL's *gaze has settled on the rifle*) Don't be surprised at this weapon. Mrs. Zachanassian's black panther is on the prowl. It's just been up in the choir-loft. Now it's in Petersens' Barn.

ILL I need help.

PRIEST What kind of help?

ILL I'm scared.

PRIEST Scared? Of whom?

ILL People.

PRIEST That the people will kill you, Ill?

ILL They're hunting me as if I were a wild animal.

PRIEST You should fear not people, but God; not death in the body, but in the soul. Sexton, button the back of my soutane.

(*The* CITIZENS *of Gullen materialize round the entire periphery of the stage;* POLICEMAN *first, then* MAYOR, *the* FOUR MEN, PAINTER, SCHOOLMASTER, *on patrol, rifles at the ready, stalking round*)

ILL My life's at stake.

PRIEST Your eternal life.

ILL There's a rise in the standard of living.

PRIEST It's the specter of your conscience rising.

ILL The people are happy. The young girls are decking themselves out. The boys have put on bright shirts. The town's getting ready to celebrate my murder, and I'm dying of terror.

PRIEST All they're doing is affirming life, that's all they're doing, affirming life.

ILL It's Hell.

PRIEST You are your own Hell. You are older than I am, and you think you know people, but in the end one only knows oneself. Because you once betrayed a young girl for money, many years ago, do you believe the people will betray you now for money? You impute your own nature to others. All too naturally. The cause of our fear and our sin lies in our own hearts. Once you have acknowledged that, you will have conquered your torment and acquired a weapon whereby to master it.

ILL The Siemethofers have acquired a washing-machine.

PRIEST Don't let that trouble you.

ILL On credit.

PRIEST You should rather be troubled by your soul's immortality.

ILL And the Stockers, a television set.

PRIEST Pray to God. Sexton, my bands. (SEXTON *positions bands round* PRIEST) Examine your conscience. Go the way of repentance, or the world will relight the fires of your terror again and again. It is the only way. No other way is open to us. (*Silence. Men and rifles disappear. Shadows round rim of stage. Fire bell begins clanging*) Now I must discharge my office, Ill, I have a baptism. The Bible, Sexton, the Liturgy, the Book of Psalms. When little children begin to cry they must be led to safety, into the only ray of light which illumines the world.

(*A second bell begins to sound*)

ILL A second bell?

PRIEST Hear it? Splendid tone. Rich and powerful. Just affirming life.

ILL (*cries out*) You too, Father! You too!

(PRIEST *flings himself on* ILL, *clings to him*)

PRIEST Flee! We are all weak, believers and unbelievers. Flee! The Guellen bells are tolling, tolling for treachery. Flee! Lead us not into temptation with your presence. (*Two shots are fired.* ILL *sinks to ground,* PRIEST *kneels beside him*) Flee! Flee!

CLAIRE ZACHANASSIAN Boby. They're shooting.

BUTLER Yes, Madam, they are.

CLAIRE ZACHANASSIAN What at?

BUTLER The black panther escaped, Madam.

CLAIRE ZACHANASSIAN Did they hit him?

BUTLER   He's dead, Madam, stretched out in front of Ill's shop.

CLAIRE ZACHANASSIAN   Poor little animal. Roby, play a funeral march.

(*Funeral march on guitar. Balcony disappears. Bell rings. Stage set as for opening of Act One. The station. On wall, however, is a new, untorn time-table and, stuck almost anywhere, a great poster depicting brilliant yellow sun, with the legend "Travel South." Further along same wall, another, with the legend "Visit the Passion Plays in Oberammergau." Amidst buildings in background, a few cranes and a few new roof-tops. Thunderous pounding din of express train rushing through.* STATION-MASTER *standing on station salutes.* ILL *emerges from background, one hand clutching little, old suitcase, and looks around. As if by chance,* CITIZENS *of Guellen come gradually closing in on him from all sides.* ILL *moves hesitantly, stops*)

MAYOR   Hallo, Ill.

ALL   Hallo! Hallo!

ILL (*hesitant*)   Hallo.

SCHOOLMASTER   Where are you off to with that suitcase?

ALL   Where are you off to?

ILL   To the station.

MAYOR   We'll take you there.

ALL   We'll take you there! We'll take you there!

(*More* GUELLENERS *keep arriving*)

ILL   You don't need to, you really don't. It's not worth the trouble.

MAYOR   Going away, Ill?

ILL   I'm going away.

POLICEMAN   Where are you going?

ILL   I don't know. First to Kalberstadt, then a bit further to—

SCHOOLMASTER   Ah! Then a bit further?

ILL   To Australia, preferably. I'll get the money somehow or other. (*walks on towards station*)

ALL   To Australia! To Australia!

MAYOR   But why?

ILL (*uneasily*)   You can't live in the same place for ever—year in, year out. (*begins running, reaches station. The others amble over in his wake, surround him*)

MAYOR   Emigrating to Australia. But that's ridiculous.

DOCTOR   The most dangerous thing you could do.

SCHOOLMASTER   One of those two little eunuchs emigrated to Australia.

POLICEMAN   This is the safest place for you.

ALL   The safest place, the safest place.

(ILL *peers fearfully round like a cornered animal*)

ILL   I wrote to the Chief Constable in Kaffigen.

POLICEMAN   And?

ILL   No answer.

SCHOOLMASTER   Why are you so suspicious? It's incomprehensible.

MAYOR   No one wants to kill you.

ALL   No one, no one.

ILL   The Post Office didn't send the letter.

PAINTER   Impossible.

MAYOR   The Postmaster is a member of the Town Council.

SCHOOLMASTER   An honorable man.

ALL   An honorable man! An honorable man!

ILL   Look at this poster: "Travel South."

DOCTOR   What about it?

ILL   "Visit the Passion Plays in Oberammergau."

SCHOOLMASTER   What about it?

ILL   They're building!

MAYOR   What about it?

ILL   And you're all wearing new trousers.

MAN ONE   What about it?

ILL   You're all getting richer, you all own more!

ALL   What about it?

(*Bell rings*)

SCHOOLMASTER   But you must see how fond we are of you.

MAYOR   The whole town's brought you to the station.

ALL   The whole town! The whole town!

ILL   I didn't ask you to come.

MAN TWO   We're surely allowed to come and say goodbye to you.

MAYOR   As old friends.

ALL   As old friends! As old friends!

(*Noise of train.* STATION-MASTER *takes up flag.* GUARD *appears, left, as after jumping down from train*)

GUARD (*with long-drawn wail*)   Guellen!

MAYOR   Here's your train.

ALL   Your train! Your train!

MAYOR   Well, have an enjoyable trip, Ill.

ALL   An enjoyable trip, an enjoyable trip!

DOCTOR   And long life and prosperity to you!

ALL   Long life and prosperity!

(*The* CITIZENS *of Guellen flock round* ILL)

MAYOR   It's time. Get on the Kalberstadt train, and God be with you.

POLICEMAN   And good luck in Australia!

ALL   Good luck, good luck!

(ILL *stands motionless staring at his compatriots*)

ILL (*softly*)   Why are you all here?

POLICEMAN   Now what do you want?

STATION-MASTER   Take your seats please!

ILL   Why are you all crowding me?

MAYOR   We're not crowding you at all.

ILL   Let me pass.

SCHOOLMASTER   But we're letting you pass.

ALL   We're letting you pass, we're letting you pass.

ILL   Someone'll stop me.

POLICEMAN   Nonsense. All you need do is get on the train, and you'll see it's nonsense.

ILL   Get out of the way.

(*No one moves. Several stand where they are, hands in pockets, and stare at him*)

MAYOR   I don't know what you're trying to do. It's up to you to go. Just get on the train.

ILL   Get out of the way!

SCHOOLMASTER   It's simply ridiculous of you to be afraid.

(ILL *falls on knees*)

ILL   Why have you all come so close to me!

POLICEMAN   The man's gone mad.

ILL   You want to stop me going.

MAYOR   Go on! Get on the train!

ALL   Get on the train! Get on the train!

(*Silence*)

ILL (*softly*)   If I get on the train one of you will hold me back.

ALL (*emphatically*)   No we won't! No we won't!

ILL   I know you will.

POLICEMAN   It's nearly time.

SCHOOLMASTER   My dear man, will you please get on the train.

ILL   I know, I know. Someone will hold me back, someone will hold me back.

STATION-MASTER   Stand clear!

(*Waves green flag, blows whistle.* GUARD *assumes position to jump on train as* ILL, *surrounded by the* CITIZENS *of Guellen, his head in his hands, collapses*)

POLICEMAN   Look! He's collapsed!

(*Leaving* ILL *crumpled in collapse, all walk slowly towards back of stage and disappear*)

ILL   I'm lost!

ACT THREE

(*Petersens' Barn.* CLAIRE ZACHANASSIAN *seated, left, immobile in sedan-chair, clad in white wedding-gown, veil, etc. Further left, a ladder. Further back, a hay-cart, an old hansom-cab, straw. Center, small cask. Rags and moulder-ing sacks hang from beams. Enormous outspun spiders' webs. Enter* BUTLER *from back*)

BUTLER   The Doctor and the Schoolmaster.

CLAIRE ZACHANASSIAN   Show them in.

(*Enter* DOCTOR *and* SCHOOLMASTER, *groping through the gloom. When at last they locate the millionairess, they bow. Both are clad in good, solid, very nearly fashionable bourgeois clothes*)

DOCTOR/SCHOOLMASTER   Madam.

(CLAIRE ZACHANASSIAN *raises lorgnette, inspects them*)

CLAIRE ZACHANASSIAN   You appear to be covered in dust, gentlemen.

(*Both rub away dust with hands*)

SCHOOLMASTER   Excuse us. We had to climb in over an old hansom-cab.

CLAIRE ZACHANASSIAN   I've retired to Petersens' Barn. I need peace and quiet. I found the wedding in Guellen Cathedral a strain. I'm not a dewy young maiden any more. You can sit on that cask.

SCHOOLMASTER   Thank you. (*He sits on it.* DOCTOR *remains standing*)

CLAIRE ZACHANASSIAN   Pretty hot here. Suffocating, I'd say. Still, I love this barn, and the smell of hay and straw and axle-grease. Memories. The dung-fork. The hansom-cab. That busted hay-cart, and all the other implements. They were here when I was a child.

SCHOOLMASTER   A suggestive spot. (*mops away sweat*)

CLAIRE ZACHANASSIAN   An uplifting sermon by the Priest.

SCHOOLMASTER   First Corinthians, thirteen.

CLAIRE ZACHANASSIAN   And a very stout performance on your part, Professor, with the mixed choir. It sounded grand.

SCHOOLMASTER   Bach. From the Saint Matthew Passion. My head is still spinning with it all. The place was packed with High Society, Financiers, Film Stars . . .

CLAIRE ZACHANASSIAN   Society went whizzing back to the Capital in its Cadillacs. For the wedding breakfast.

SCHOOLMASTER   My dear lady: we don't wish to take up more of your precious time than necessary. Your husband will be growing impatient.

CLAIRE ZACHANASSIAN   Hoby? I've sent him back to Geiselgasteig in his Porsche.

DOCTOR (*staggered*)   To Geiselgasteig?

CLAIRE ZACHANASSIAN   My lawyers have already filed the divorce.

SCHOOLMASTER   But Madam, the wedding guests!

CLAIRE ZACHANASSIAN   They're used to it.

It's my second-shortest marriage. Only the one with Lord Ishmael was a trifle quicker. What brings you here?

SCHOOLMASTER   We've come to discuss the Ill affair.

CLAIRE ZACHANASSIAN   O, has he died?

SCHOOLMASTER   Madam! We're still loyal to our Western principles.

CLAIRE ZACHANASSIAN   Then what do you want?

SCHOOLMASTER   The Guelleners have most, most regretably acquired a number of new possessions.

DOCTOR   A considerable number.

(*Both mop off sweat*)

CLAIRE ZACHANASSIAN   In debt?

SCHOOLMASTER   Hopelessly.

CLAIRE ZACHANASSIAN   In spite of your principles?

SCHOOLMASTER   We're only human.

DOCTOR   And now we must pay our debts.

CLAIRE ZACHANASSIAN   You know what you have to do.

SCHOOLMASTER   (*bravely*)   Madam Zachanassian. Let's be frank with each other. Put yourself in our melancholy position. For two decades, I have been sowing the Humanities' tender seeds in this poverty-stricken population, and our doctor too for two decades has been trundling around curing its rickets and consumption in his antediluvian Mercedes. Why such agony of sacrifice? For the money? Hardly. Our fee is minimal. Furthermore I received and flatly rejected an offer from Kalberstadt College, just as the doctor here turned down a chair in Erlangen University. Out of pure love for our fellow-beings? No, no, that would also be saying too much. No. We, and this entire little township with us, have hung on all these endless years because of a single hope: the hope that Guellen would rise again, in all its ancient grandeur, and the untold wealth in our native soil be once again exploited. Oil is waiting under Pückenried Valley, and under Konrad's Village Wood there are minerals for the mining. Madam, we are not poor; we are merely forgotten. We need credit, confidence, contracts, then our economy and culture will boom. Gullen has much to offer: the Foundry on Sunshine Square.

DOCTOR   Bockmann's.

SCHOOLMASTER   The Wagner Factory. Buy them. Revive them. And Guellen will boom. Invest a few hundred thousand, carefully, systematically. They'll produce a good return. Don't simply squander a million!

CLAIRE ZACHANASSIAN   I've two others.

SCHOOLMASTER   Don't condemn us to a lifelong struggle in vain. We haven't come begging for alms. We've come to make a business proposition.

CLAIRE ZACHANASSIAN   Really. As business goes, it wouldn't be bad.

SCHOOLMASTER   My dear lady! I knew you wouldn't leave us in the lurch.

CLAIRE ZACHANASSIAN   Only it can't be done. I can't buy Sunshine Square, because I own it already.

SCHOOLMASTER   *You* own it?

DOCTOR   And Bockmann's?

SCHOOLMASTER   The Wagner Factory?

CLAIRE ZACHANASSIAN   I own those too. And all the factories, Pückenried Valley, Petersens' Barn, the entire township; street by street and house by house. I had my agents buy the whole ramshackle lot and shut every business down. Your hopes were lunacy, your perseverance pointless, and your self-sacrifice foolish; your lives have been a useless waste.

(*Silence*)

DOCTOR   What a monstrous thing.

CLAIRE ZACHANASSIAN   It was winter, long ago, when I left this little town, in a schoolgirl sailor suit and long red plaits, pregnant with only a short while to go, and the townsfolk sniggering at me. I sat in the Hamburg Express and shivered; but as I watched the silhouette of Petersens' Barn sinking away on the other side of the frost-flowers, I swore a vow to myself, I would come back again, one day. I've come back now. Now it's me imposing the conditions. Me driving the bargain. (*calls—*) Roby and Toby, to the Golden Apostle. Husband number nine's on the way with his books and manuscripts.

(*The two* GIANTS *emerge from background, lift sedan-chair*)

SCHOOLMASTER   Madam Zachanassian! You are a woman whose love has been wounded. You make me think of a heroine from antiquity: of Medea. We feel for you, deeply; we understand; but because we do, we are inspired to prove you further: cast away those evil thoughts of revenge, don't try us till we break. Help these poor, weak yet worthy people lead a slightly more dignified life. Let your feeling for humanity prevail!

CLAIRE ZACHANASSIAN   Feeling for humanity, gentlemen, is cut for the purse of an ordinary millionaire; with financial resources like mine you can afford a new world order. The world turned me into a whore. I shall turn the world into a brothel. If you can't fork out when you want to dance, you have to put off dancing. You want to dance. They alone are eligible who pay. And I'm paying. Guellen for a murder, a boom for a body. Come on, the pair of you, off we go!

(*She is borne away into background*)

DOCTOR My God. What shall we do?

SCHOOLMASTER The dictates of our conscience, Doctor Nuesslin.

(ILL's *shop appears in foreground, right. New sign. Glittering new shop-counter, new till, costlier stock. Whenever anyone enters the imaginary door, a bell rings, magnificently. Behind shop-counter,* MRS ILL. *Enter, left,* MAN ONE—a thriving butcher. Scattered bloodstains on his new apron*)

MAN ONE That was a ceremony. The whole of Guellen was on Cathedral Square watching it.

MRS ILL Claire deserves a little happiness, after all she's been through.

MAN ONE Every bridesmaid was a film starlet. With breasts like this.

MRS ILL They're in fashion today.

MAN ONE And newspapermen. They'll be coming here too.

MRS ILL We're simple people, Mr. Hofbauer. They won't want anything from us.

MAN ONE They pump everybody. Cigarettes.

MRS ILL Green?

MAN ONE Camels. And a bottle of aspirins. Went to a party at Stocker's last night.

MRS ILL On account?

MAN ONE On account.

MRS ILL How's business?

MAN ONE Keeps me going.

MRS ILL Me too. Can't grumble.

MAN ONE I've got more staff.

MRS ILL I'm getting someone on the first.

(MISS LOUISA *walks across stage in stylish clothes*)

MAN ONE She's got her head full of dreams dressing up like that. She must imagine we'd murder Ill.

MRS ILL Shameless.

MAN ONE Where is he, by the way? Haven't seen him for quite a while.

MRS ILL Upstairs.

(MAN ONE *lights cigarette, cocks ear towards ceiling*)

MAN ONE Footsteps.

MRS ILL Always walking around in his room. Has been for days.

MAN ONE It's his bad conscience. Nasty trick he played on poor Madam Zachanassian.

MRS ILL It's upset me terribly too.

MAN ONE Getting a young girl in trouble. Rotten bastard. (*speaks with decision*) Mrs Ill, I hope your husband won't blabber when the journalists come.

MRS ILL Not really.

MAN ONE What with his character.

MRS ILL I have a hard time of it, Mr Hofbauer.

MAN ONE If he tries showing up Clara, and telling lies, claiming she offered something for his death, or some such story, when it was only a figure of speech for unspeakable suffering, then we'll *have* to step in. Not because of the million. (*He spits*) But because of public indignation. God knows he's already put that sweet Madam Zachanassian through enough. (*He looks round*) Is that a way up to the apartment?

MRS ILL It's the only way up. Most inconvenient. But we're having another one built in the spring.

MAN ONE I'd better just plant myself here. You can't be too sure.

(MAN ONE *plants himself there, very upright stance, arms folded, quietly, like a warder. Enter* SCHOOLMASTER)

SCHOOLMASTER Ill?

MAN ONE Upstairs.

SCHOOLMASTER It really isn't like me, but I need some kind of strong, alcoholic beverage.

MRS ILL How nice of you to come and see us, Professor. We've a new Steinhäger in. Would you like to try it?

SCHOOLMASTER A small glass.

MRS ILL You too, Mr Hofbauer?

MAN ONE No thanks. Still have to drive my Volkswagen into Kaffigen. There's pork to buy.

(MRS ILL *pours a glassful.* SCHOOLMASTER *drinks*)

MRS ILL But you're trembling, Professor.

SCHOOLMASTER I've been over-drinking lately.

MRS ILL One more won't harm.

SCHOOLMASTER Is that him walking about? (*cocks ear towards ceiling*)

MRS ILL Up and down, all the time.

MAN ONE God will punish him.

(*Enter, left,* PAINTER *with picture under arm. New corduroys, colourful neckerchief, black beret*)

PAINTER Watch out. Two reporters asked me about this shop.

MAN ONE Suspicious.

PAINTER I acted ignorant.

MAN ONE Clever.

PAINTER   For you, Mrs Ill. Fresh off the easel. It's still damp.

(*Exhibits picture.* SCHOOLMASTER *pours himself another drink*)

MRS ILL   It's my husband.

PAINTER   Art's beginning to boom in Guellen. How's that for painting, eh?

MRS ILL   A real likeness.

PAINTER   Oils. Last for ever.

MRS ILL   We could hang it in the bedroom. Over the bed. Alfred'll be old one day. And you never know what might happen, it's a comfort to have a souvenir.

(*The two* WOMEN *from Act Two, passing by outside, stop and examine wares in imaginary show-window. Both elegantly dressed*)

MAN ONE   Look at those women. Going to the films in broad daylight. The way they behave, you'd think we were sheer murderers!

MRS ILL   Expensive?

PAINTER   Thirty pounds.

MRS ILL   I can't pay now.

PAINTER   Doesn't matter. I'll wait, Mrs Ill, I'll be happy to wait.

SCHOOLMASTER   Those footsteps, those footsteps all the time.

(*Enter* MAN TWO, *left*)

MAN TWO   The Press.

MAN ONE   All stick together. It's life or death.

PAINTER   Watch out he doesn't come down.

MAN ONE   That's taken care of.

(*The* GUELLENERS *gather to right.* SCHOOLMASTER *having now drunk half the bottle remains standing at counter. Enter two* REPORTERS *carrying cameras*)

FIRST REPORTER   'Evening, folks.

GUELLENERS   How do you do.

FIRST REPORTER   Question one: How do you all feel, on the whole?

MAN ONE   (*uneasily*)   We're very happy of course about Madam Zachanassian's visit.

PAINTER   Moved.

MAN TWO   Proud.

FIRST REPORTER   Proud.

SECOND REPORTER   Question two for the lady behind the counter: the story goes, you were the lucky woman instead of Madam Zachanassian.

(*Silence.* GUELLENERS *manifestly shocked*)

MRS ILL   Where did you get that story?

(*Silence. Both* REPORTERS *write impassively in notebooks*)

FIRST REPORTER   Madam Zachanassian's two fat blind little mannikins.

(*Silence*)

MRS ILL   (*hesitant*)   What did the mannikins tell you?

SECOND REPORTER   Everything.

PAINTER   Goddam.

(*Silence*)

SECOND REPORTER   Forty years ago Claire Zachanassian and the proprietor of this shop nearly married. Right?

MRS ILL   That's right.

SECOND REPORTER   Is Mr Ill here?

MRS ILL   He's in Kalberstadt.

ALL   He's in Kalberstadt.

FIRST REPORTER   We can imagine the Romance. Mr Ill and Claire Zachanassian grow up together, maybe they're next-door kids, they go to school together, go for walks in the wood, share the first kisses, they're like brother and sister, and so it goes on till Mr Ill meets you, lady, and you're the new woman, his mystery, his passion.

MRS ILL   Passion. Yes, that's how it happened, just the way you said.

FIRST REPORTER   Foxy, foxy, Mrs Ill. Claire Zachanassian grasps the situation, in her quiet, noble fashion she renounces her claims, and you marry . . .

MRS ILL   For love.

GUELLENERS   (*on whom light dawns*)   For love.

FIRST REPORTER   For love.

(*Enter, right,* ROBY *leading the pair of eunuchs by their ears*)

THE PAIR   (*wailing*)   We won't tell any more stories, we won't tell any more stories.

(*They are dragged towards back of stage, where* TOBY *awaits them with whip*)

SECOND REPORTER   About your husband, Mrs Ill, doesn't he now and then, I mean, it'd be only human for him, now and then, to feel a few regrets.

MRS ILL   Money alone makes no one happy.

SECOND REPORTER   (*writing*)   No one happy.

FIRST REPORTER   That's a truth we in this modern world ought to write up in the sky of our hearts.

(*Enter* SON, *left, wearing suede jacket*)

MRS ILL   Our son Karl.

FIRST REPORTER   Splendid youngster.

SECOND REPORTER   Is he in the know about the relationship?

MRS ILL   There are no secrets in our family. What we always say is, anything God knows our children ought to know.

SECOND REPORTER   (*writing*)   Children ought to know.

(*Daughter walks into shop, wearing tennis-outfit, carrying tennis-racket*)

MRS ILL   Our daughter Ottilie.

SECOND REPORTER   Charming.

(SCHOOLMASTER *now calls up courage*)

SCHOOLMASTER   Guelleners. I am your old schoolmaster. I've been quietly drinking my Steinhäger and keeping my thoughts to myself. But now I want to make a speech. I want to talk about the old lady's visit to Guellen.

(*Scrambles on to the little cask left over from the scene in Petersens' Barn*)

MAN ONE   Have you gone mad?

MAN TWO   Stop him!

SCHOOLMASTER   Guelleners! I want to reveal the truth, even if our poverty endures for ever!

MRS ILL   You're drunk, Professor, you ought to be ashamed of yourself?

SCHOOLMASTER   Ashamed? You're the one to be ashamed, woman! You're paving your way to betray your own husband!

SON   Shut your trap!

MAN ONE   Drag him down!

MAN TWO   Kick him out!

SCHOOLMASTER   You've nearly contrived your doom!

DAUGHTER (*supplicating*)   Please, Professor!

SCHOOLMASTER   Child, you disappoint me. It was up to you to speak out, and now your old schoolmaster must unleash the voice of thunder!

(PAINTER *breaks painting over his head*)

PAINTER   There! You'll sabotage all my commissions!

SCHOOLMASTER   I protest! I wish to make a public appeal to world opinion! Guellen is planning a monstrous deed!

(*The* GUELLENERS *launch themselves at him as, simultaneously, in an old tatterdemalion suit,* ILL *enters, right*)

ILL   Just what is going on here, in my shop! (*The* GUELLENERS *fall back from* SCHOOLMASTER *to stare at* ILL, *shocked. Deathly silence*) Professor! What are you up to on that cask!

(SCHOOLMASTER *beams at* ILL *in happy relief*)

SCHOOLMASTER   The truth, Ill. I'm telling the gentlemen of the Press the truth. Like an archangel I'm telling them, in forceful ringing tones. (*wavers*) Because I'm a humanist, a lover of the ancient Greeks, an admirer of Plato.

ILL   Hold your peace.

SCHOOLMASTER   Eh?

ILL   Get down.

SCHOOLMASTER   But humanitarianism—

ILL   Sit down.

(*Silence*)

SCHOOLMASTER (*sobered*)   Humanitarianism has to sit down. By all means—if you're going to betray truth as well (*steps down from cask, sits on it, picture still round his neck*)

ILL   Excuse this. The man's drunk.

FIRST REPORTER   Mr Ill?

ILL   What is it?

FIRST REPORTER   We're very glad we finally got to meet you. We need a few pictures. May we? (*glances round*) Groceries, household wares, ironmongery—I've got it: we'll take you selling an axe.

ILL (*hesitant*)   An axe?

FIRST REPORTER   To the butcher. You gotta have Realism for a punch. Give me that homicidal weapon here. Your client takes the axe, weighs it in his hand, he puts an appraising expression on his face, while you lean across the counter, you're discussing it with him. O.K., let's go. (*He arranges the shot*) More natural, folks, more relaxed. (*Reporters click their cameras*) That's fine, just fine.

SECOND REPORTER   Now if you don't mind please, one arm round your good wife's shoulders. Son on the left, daughter on the right. That's fine. O.K., now, you're radiant with happiness, please, just brimming over with it, radiant, radiant and contented deep down inside, quietly, happily radiant.

FIRST REPORTER   Great, great, that sure was radiant.

(*Several* PHOTOGRAPHERS *come running in, downstage left, cross the boards and go running out, upstage left. One photographer bawls into shop—*)

PHOTOGRAPHER   Zachanassian's got a new one. They're taking a walk in Konrad's Village Wood, right now.

SECOND REPORTER   A new one!

FIRST REPORTER   That's good for a cover on *Life* magazine.

(*The two* REPORTERS *race out of shop. Silence.* MAN ONE *is left still gripping axe*)

MAN ONE (*relieved*)   That was a bit of luck.

PAINTER   Forgive us, Professor. If we still hope to settle this affair amicably, we've got to exclude the Press. Agreed?

(*Exit, followed by* MAN TWO. *But passing* ILL, MAN TWO *pauses*)

MAN TWO   Smart. Very smart you didn't shoot your mouth. No one would believe a word a bastard like you said anyway.

(*Exit* MAN TWO)

MAN ONE   We'll be in the illustrateds, Ill.

ILL   Yes.

MAN ONE   We'll be famous.

ILL   In a manner of speaking.

MAN ONE   A Corona.

ILL   Certainly.

MAN ONE   On account.

ILL   Of course.

MAN ONE   Let's face it: what you did to little Clara was a real worm's trick. (*begins to go*)

ILL   Hofbauer. The axe.

(MAN ONE *hesitates, then returns axe to* ILL. *Silence in shop.* SCHOOLMASTER *is still sitting on his cask*)

SCHOOLMASTER   I apologize. I've been trying the Steinhäger. Must have had two or three.

ILL   It's all right.

(*The family cross to right, and exit*)

SCHOOLMASTER   I wanted to help you. But they shouted me down, and you didn't want my help either. (*disengages himself from picture*) Ah, Ill. What kind of people are we. That infamous million is burning up our hearts. Pull yourself together, fight for your life. Enlist the sympathy of the Press. You haven't any more time to lose.

ILL   I'm not fighting any more.

SCHOOLMASTER (*amazed*)   Tell me, has fear driven you completely out of your senses?

ILL   I've realized I haven't the least right on my side.

SCHOOLMASTER   No right? No right compared to that damned old woman, that brazen arch-whore changing husbands while we watch, and making a collection of our souls?

ILL   That's all my fault, really.

SCHOOLMASTER   Your fault?

ILL   I made Clara what she is, and I made myself what I am, a failing shopkeeper with a bad name. What shall I do, Schoolmaster? Play innocent? It's all my own work, the Eunuchs, the Butler, the coffin, the million. I can't help myself and I can't help any of you, any more. (*takes up torn painting and examines it*) My portrait.

SCHOOLMASTER   Your wife wanted to hang it in your bedroom. Over the bed.

ILL   Kuhn will paint another.

(*Lays picture down on counter.* SCHOOLMASTER *stands with an effort, sways*)

SCHOOLMASTER   I'm sober. All at once. (*He reels across to* ILL) You are right. Absolutely. It's all your fault. And now I want to tell you something, Alfred Ill, something fundamental. (*Stands facing* ILL, *stiff as a ramrod and hardly swaying at all*) They will kill you. I've known it from the beginning, and you've known it too for a long time, even if no one else in

Guellen wants to admit it. The temptation is too great and our poverty is too wretched. But I know something else. I shall take part in it. I can feel myself slowly becoming a murderer. My faith in humanity is powerless to stop it. And because I know all this, I have also become a sot. I too am scared, Ill, just as you have been scared. And finally I know that one day an old lady will come for us too, and then what happened to you will also happen to us, but soon, perhaps in a few hours, I shall have lost that knowledge. (*Silence*) Another bottle of Steinhäger. (ILL *gets him a bottle,* SCHOOLMASTER *hesitates, then firmly takes and clutches bottle*) Put it on my account. (*walks slowly out*)

(*The family return.* ILL *looks round at his shop as if dreaming*)

ILL   It's all new. Our place looks so modern nowadays. Clean. Inviting. I've always dreamed of having a shop like this. (*takes* DAUGHTER'S *tennis-racket from her hand*) D'you play tennis?

DAUGHTER   I've had a couple of lessons.

ILL   Early mornings, eh? Instead of going to the Employment Agency?

DAUGHTER   All my friends play tennis.

(*Silence*)

ILL   I was looking out of my bedroom window, Karl, and I saw you in an automobile.

SON   It's only an Opel, they aren't so expensive.

ILL   When did you learn to drive?

(*Silence*)

Instead of looking for work on the railroad in the blazing sun, eh?

SON   Sometimes.

(SON, *embarrassed, crosses to cask on which the drunk has been sitting, shoves it to right and out*)

ILL   I was looking for my Sunday suit. I found a fur coat hanging beside it.

MRS ILL   It's on approval. (*Silence*) Everyone's making debts, Freddy. You're the only one throwing fits of hysterics. It's simply ridiculous of you to be scared. It's so obvious the thing's going to be settled peacefully, without anyone harming a hair of your head. Claire won't go the whole way, I know her, she's too good-hearted.

DAUGHTER   Of course, father.

SON   Surely you realize that.

(*Silence*)

ILL (*slowly*)   It's Saturday. Karl, I'd like to go for a drive in your automobile, just once. In *our* automobile.

SON (*uncertainly*) You'd like that?

ILL Put on your best clothes. We'll all go for a drive together.

MRS ILL (*uncertainly*) Am I to go with you? But surely that wouldn't do.

ILL And why wouldn't it do? Go and put on your fur coat, this'll be an opportunity to christen it. I'll be seeing to the till in the meantime.

(*Exit* MOTHER *and* DAUGHTER, *right. Exit* SON, *left.* ILL *busies himself at till. Enter, left,* MAYOR *carrying rifle*)

MAYOR Good evening, Ill. Don't let me trouble you. I'll just have a quick look round.

ILL By all means.

(*Silence*)

MAYOR Brought you a gun.

ILL Thanks.

MAYOR It's loaded.

ILL I don't need it.

(MAYOR *leans gun against counter*)

MAYOR There's a public meeting this evening. In the Golden Apostle. In the auditorium.

ILL I'll be there.

MAYOR Everyone'll be there. We're dealing with your case. We're under a certain amount of pressure.

ILL That's what I feel.

MAYOR The motion will be rejected.

ILL Possibly.

MAYOR People make mistakes, of course.

ILL Of course.

(*Silence*)

MAYOR (*cautiously*) In such a case, Ill, would you then submit to the judgment? Since the Press will be present.

ILL The Press?

MAYOR And the Radio. And the Television and Newsreel cameras. Very ticklish situation. Not only for you. For us too, believe you me. We're famous as the old lady's native town, and also because of her marriage in the Cathedral here. So now they're going to run a commentary on our ancient democratic institutions.

(ILL *busies himself at till*)

ILL Are you making public knowledge of the lady's offer?

MAYOR Not directly. Only the initiated will grasp the full meaning of the procedure.

ILL The fact that my life is at stake.

(*Silence*)

MAYOR I've let a few hints leak out to the Press that Madam Zachanassian may—there's just a possibility she may make an endowment and that you, Ill, as her childhood friend, will have negotiated that endowment. Of course, it's well known by now that you in fact were her childhood friend. This means that so far as appearances go, you'll have an absolutely clean record.

ILL That's kind of you.

MAYOR To be quite frank, I didn't do it for your sake. I was really thinking of your fine, upright, honest family.

ILL I see.

MAYOR You've got to admit we're playing fair with you. Up to now, you've kept quiet. Good. But will you go on keeping quiet? If you intend to talk, we'll have to settle the whole business without a public meeting.

ILL I understand.

MAYOR Well?

ILL I'm glad to hear an open threat.

MAYOR I'm not threatening you, Ill, you're threatening us. If you talk, we'll have to act accordingly. First.

ILL I'll keep quiet.

MAYOR However the decision turns out at the meeting?

ILL I'll accept it.

MAYOR Good. (*Silence*) I'm glad you'll abide by the ruling of our community court, Ill. You still have a certain glimmer of honor in you. But wouldn't it be better if we didn't even have to call on that community court to assemble?

ILL What are you trying to say?

MAYOR When I came in, you said you didn't need the gun. But now, perhaps, you do need it. (*Silence*) We might then tell the lady we had brought you to justice and that way, just the same, receive the money. You can imagine the sleepless nights I've spent on that suggestion. But isn't it your duty, as a man of honor, to draw your own conclusions and make an end of your life? If only out of public spirit, and your love for your native town. You're well aware of our wretched privations, the misery here, and the hungry children . . .

ILL You're all doing very well.

MAYOR Ill!

ILL Mister Mayor! I have been through a Hell. I've watched you all getting into debt, and I've felt death creeping towards me, nearer and nearer with every sign of prosperity. If you had spared me that anguish, that gruesome terror, it might all have been different, this discussion might have been different, and I might have taken the gun. For all your sakes. Instead, I shut myself in. I conquered my fear. Alone. It was hard, and now it's done. There is no turning back. You *must* judge me, now. I shall accept your judgment, whatever it may be. For me, it will be justice; what it will be for you, I do not know. God grant you find your judgment justified. You may kill me, I will not complain and I will not protest, nor will I defend myself. But I cannot spare you the task of the trial.

(MAYOR *takes back gun*)

MAYOR Pity. You're missing a chance to redeem yourself and be a more or less decent human being. I might have known it was too much to ask you.

ILL Match, Mister Mayor. (*lights cigarette for* MAYOR. *Exit* MAYOR.)

Enter MRS ILL *in fur coat,* DAUGHTER *in red dress*)

You look very distinguished, Matilda.

MRS ILL Persian lamb.

ILL Like a real lady.

MRS ILL Quite expensive.

ILL Pretty dress, Ottilie. But isn't it a little bold?

DAUGHTER O silly Daddy. You should just take a peek at my evening dress.

(*Shop disappears.* SON *drives up in motor-car*)

ILL Fine automobile. You know, I toiled a lifetime to get a little property, a mite of comfort, say for example an automobile like this, and now, my time's up, but still, I'd like to know how it feels to be inside one of these. Matilda, get in the back with me, you in the front, Ottilie, next to Karl.

(*They get into motor-car*)

SON It'll do eighty.

ILL Not so fast. I want to see a bit of the scenery, a bit of the town, I've lived here nearly seventy years. They've cleaned up the old streets. Lot of reconstruction, already. Grey smoke, coming out of those chimneys. Geraniums there in the window-boxes. Sunflowers. The Goethe Arch, they've planted roses in the gardens. Don't the children look happy; and sweethearts, all over the place. Brahms Square, that's a new apartment block.

MRS ILL They're re-doing the Café Hodel.

DAUGHTER There goes the Doctor, in his Mercedes 300.

ILL Look at the plain, and the light on the hills beyond, all golden, today. Impressive, when you go into the shadows and then out again into the light. Those cranes on the horizon by the Wagner Factory look like giants; and the Bockmann chimneys too.

SON They're starting up again.

ILL What's that?

SON (*louder*) They're starting up again. (*hoots horn*)

MRS ILL Funny little car.

SON Bubble-car: Messerschmidt. Every kid in the Technical College has one.

DAUGHTER *C'est terrible.*

MRS ILL Ottilie's taking advanced French and German.

ILL Useful. Sunshine Square. The Foundry. Long time since I've been out here.

SON They're going to build a bigger one.

ILL You'll have to talk louder at this speed.

SON (*louder*) They're going to build a bigger one. Stocker again, who else. Passing everybody in his Buick.

DAUGHTER *Un nouveau riche.*

ILL Now drive through Pückenried Valley. Go past the Moor and down Poplar Boulevard, round Prince Hasso's Hunting Lodge. Colossal clouds in the sky, banks of them, real summertime castles. It's a beautiful country in a soft twilight. I feel I'm seeing it today the first time.

DAUGHTER Atmosphere like Tennyson.

ILL Like what?

MRS ILL Ottilie's studying literature too.

ILL It'll give her advantages.

SON Hofbauer in his Volkswagen. Coming back from Kaffigen.

DAUGHTER With the pork.

MRS ILL Karl drives well. Very smart, the way he cut that corner. You don't feel frightened with him.

SON First gear. The road's getting steep.

ILL I always used to get out of breath walking up here.

MRS ILL I'm so glad I brought my fur coat. It's getting quite chilly.

ILL You've come the wrong way. This road goes to Beisenbach. You'll have to go back and then left, into Konrad's Village Wood.

(*Motor-car reverses into background. Enter, carrying wooden bench, and wearing dress-suits now, the four* CITIZENS *who designate trees*)

MAN ONE

We're standing in for trees again,
A spruce, a fir, a beech, a pine,

MAN TWO

We're bird and beast, we're timid deer,
We're woodpeckers;

MAN THREE

The cuckoos here
Sing songs of bygone nights and dawns,

MAN FOUR

Outraged today by motor horns.

SON (*hoots horn*) Another deer. The animal just won't get off the road.

(MAN THREE *jumps off the road*)

DAUGHTER They're so trusting. The poaching's stopped.

ILL Stop under these trees.

SON Sure.

MRS ILL What do you want to do?

ILL Walk through the woods. (*He gets out*) The Guellen bells are ringing. They sound so good from here. Time to stop work.

SON Four of them. First time they sound like real bells.

ILL Everything's yellow. The autumn's really here. The leaves on the ground are like layers of gold.

(*He tramples amongst leaves on the ground*)

SON We'll wait for you down by Guellen Bridge.

ILL You needn't wait. I shall walk through the wood into town. To the public meeting.

MRS ILL In that case we'll drive into Kalberstadt, Freddy, and see a film.

SON 'Bye, father.

DAUGHTER *Au revoir, papa.*

MRS ILL See you soon! See you soon!

(*Motor-car with family in it disappears, returns in reverse, the family waving;* ILL *watches them out of sight. Sits on wooden bench, left*

Rush of wind. Enter ROBY *and* TOBY, *right, bearing sedan-chair in which* CLAIRE ZACHANASSIAN, *seated, wearing her customary clothes.* ROBY *carries guitar slung at his back.* HUSBAND IX *comes striding in beside her—the Nobel Prize-winner, tall, slender, hair peppered grey, moustache.* [*May also be played by same actor as earlier husbands.*] BUTLER *brings up rear*)

CLAIRE ZACHANASSIAN It's the Konrad's Village Wood. Roby and Toby, stop a moment.

(CLAIRE ZACHANASSIAN *descends from sedan-chair, inspects wood through lorgnette, and strokes back of* MAN ONE)

Bark-beetle. This tree's withering away. (*notices* ILL) Alfred! How nice to see you! I'm visiting my Wood.

ILL Does Konrad's Village Wood belong to you as well?

CLAIRE ZACHANASSIAN Yes, it does. May I sit down beside you?

ILL By all means. I've just said goodbye to my family. They've gone to the cinema. Karl's got himself an automobile.

CLAIRE ZACHANASSIAN Progress. (*sits down beside* ILL, *right*)

ILL Ottilie's taking a course in literature. French and German as well.

CLAIRE ZACHANASSIAN You see, they have developed a sense of ideals after all. Zoby, come and make your bow. My ninth husband. Nobel Prize-winner.

ILL Very glad to meet you.

CLAIRE ZACHANASSIAN He's particularly interesting when he stops thinking. Stop thinking a moment, Zoby.

HUSBAND IX But Precious . . .

CLAIRE ZACHANASSIAN No showing off.

HUSBAND IX Oh all right. (*stops thinking*)

CLAIRE ZACHANASSIAN See? Now he looks like a diplomat. Reminds me of Count Holk, except that he couldn't write books. He wants to go into retirement, publish his memoirs and manage my property.

ILL Congratulations.

CLAIRE ZACHANASSIAN I feel uneasy about it. You only have husbands for display purposes, they shouldn't be useful. Zoby, go away and do some research. You'll find the historical ruins on the left.

(HUSBAND IX *goes away to do some research.* ILL *glances round*)

ILL What's happened to the two Eunuchs?

CLAIRE ZACHANASSIAN They were getting garrulous. I had them shipped off to Hong Kong. Put in one of my opium dens. They can smoke and they can dream. The Butler will follow them soon. I shan't be needing him either, any more. Boby, a Romeo and Juliet. (BUTLER *emerges from background, passes her a cigarette case*) Would you like one, Alfred?

ILL Thank you.

CLAIRE ZACHANASSIAN Here, then. Give us a light, Boby.

(*They smoke*)

ILL Smells good.

CLAIRE ZACHANASSIAN We often smoked together in this wood; do you remember? You used to buy the cigarettes from little Matilda. Or steal them. (MAN ONE *taps key on pipe*) That woodpecker again.

MAN FOUR Cuckoo! Cuckoo!

CLAIRE ZACHANASSIAN Would you like Roby to play for you on his guitar?

ILL Please.

CLAIRE ZACHANASSIAN My amnestied killer plays well. I need him for meditative moments. I hate gramophones. And radios.

ILL There's an army marching in an African valley.

CLAIRE ZACHANASSIAN Your favorite song. I taught it to him.

(*Silence. They smoke. Cuckoo call, forest sounds, etc.* ROBY *plays ballad*)

ILL You had—I mean, we had a child.

CLAIRE ZACHANASSIAN   True.

ILL   Was it a boy or girl?

CLAIRE ZACHANASSIAN   A girl.

ILL   And what name did you give it?

CLAIRE ZACHANASSIAN   Genevieve.

ILL   Pretty name.

CLAIRE ZACHANASSIAN   I only saw the thing once. At birth. Then they took it away. The Salvation Army.

ILL   Eyes?

CLAIRE ZACHANASSIAN   Not yet open.

ILL   Hair?

CLAIRE ZACHANASSIAN   I think it had black hair. But then new-born babies often have black hair.

ILL   Yes, they often do. (*Silence. They smoke. Guitar plays*) Where did it die?

CLAIRE ZACHANASSIAN   With some people. I've forgotten their name.

ILL   What of?

CLAIRE ZACHANASSIAN   Meningitis. Perhaps it was something else. I did receive a card from the authorities.

ILL   In cases of death you can rely on them.

(*Silence*)

CLAIRE ZACHANASSIAN   I've talked about our little girl. Now you talk about me.

ILL   About you?

CLAIRE ZACHANASSIAN   The way I was, when I was seventeen, when you loved me.

ILL   I had to look for you a long while once in Petersens' Barn; I found you in the old carriage with nothing on but a blouse and a long straw between your lips.

CLAIRE ZACHANASSIAN   You were strong and brave. You fought that railwayman when he tried to paw me. I wiped the blood off your face with my red petticoat. (*Guitar stops playing*) The ballad has ended.

ILL   One more: "Home Sweet Home."

CLAIRE ZACHANASSIAN   Yes, Roby can play that.

(*Guitar resumes play*)

ILL   Thank you for the wreaths, and for the chrysanthemums and roses. They'll look fine on the coffin in the Golden Apostle. Distinguished. They fill two rooms already. Now the time has come. It is the last time we shall sit in our old wood and hear the cuckoo calling and the sound of the wind. They are meeting this evening. They will sentence me to death, and one of them will kill me. I don't know who it will be, and I don't know where it will happen, I only know that my meaningless life will end.

CLAIRE ZACHANASSIAN   I shall take you in your coffin to Capri. I have had a mausoleum built, in my Palace Park. It is surrounded by cypress-trees. Overlooking the Mediterranean.

ILL   I only know it from pictures.

CLAIRE ZACHANASSIAN   Deep blue. A grandiose panorama. You will remain there. A dead man beside a stone idol. Your love died many years ago. But my love could not die. Neither could it live. It grew into an evil thing, like me, like the pallid mushrooms in this wood, and the blind, twisted features of the roots, all overgrown by my golden millions. Their tentacles sought you out, to take your life, because your life belonged to me, for ever. You are in their toils now, and you are lost. You will soon be no more than a dead love in my memory, a gentle ghost haunting the wreckage of a house.

ILL   "Home Sweet Home" has ended now as well.

HUSBAND IX   (*returns*)

CLAIRE ZACHANASSIAN   Here's the Nobel Prize-winner. Back from his ruins. Well, Zoby?

HUSBAND IX   Early Christian. Sacked by the Huns.

CLAIRE ZACHANASSIAN   What a pity. Give me your arm. Roby, Toby, the sedan. (*gets into sedan-chair*) Goodbye, Alfred.

ILL   Goodbye, Clara.

(*The sedan-chair is borne away to background. ILL remains seated on bench. The trees put away their twigs. Portal descends, with usual curtains and draperies, also inscription: "Life Is Serious, Art Serene." POLICEMAN emerges from background, in swashbuckling new uniform, sits beside ILL. A RADIO COMMENTATOR enters, begins talking into microphone while the GUELLENERS assemble. Everyone in new evening gowns and dress-suits. Hordes of PRESS PHOTOGRAPHERS, REPORTERS, CAMERAMEN*)

RADIO COMMENTATOR   Ladies and gentlemen: Radio Newsreel has been bringing you a Scene from the Birthplace and a Conversation with the Priest, and now it's time to go over to the Public Meeting. We're nearing the climax of this visit which Madam Claire Zachanassian has kindly accorded to her charming, friendly little home-town. Of course it's unfortunate the famous lady won't be putting in a personal appearance, on the other hand we will be hearing the Mayor, because he's slated to make an important announcement in her name. Right now we're coming to you from the auditorium of the Golden Apostle, an hotel which can boast of a bed where Goethe once spent the night. And now the townsmen are assembling on the stage, in less exciting days the scene of local club gatherings and guest shows by the Kalberstadt Repertory Players. The Mayor's just informed me this is an old custom.

The women are all down in the auditorium—it seems this is an old custom too. I can't tell you what a solemn atmosphere it is, the tension's really extraordinary. All the newsreel cameras are here, I can see my colleagues from T.V., there are reporters from all over the world, and now here comes the Mayor and he's going to begin his speech, we're crossing over to him now!

(RADIO COMMENTATOR *crosses over to* MAYOR, *who is standing in centre of stage, round him in a semi-circle the* MEN *of* GUELLEN)

MAYOR   Ladies and gentlemen, Citizens of Guellen. I'm very happy to welcome you all here this evening. I declare this meeting open. We have one, single item on our agenda. It is my privilege to announce that Madam Claire Zachanassian, daughter of our worthy fellow-citizen Godfrey Wascher—the architect—intends to make us a donation of one million pounds. (*Whispers among the* PRESS) Five hundred thousand for the town and five hundred thousand to be shared among all citizens.

(*Silence*)

RADIO COMMENTATOR (*subdued*)   What a sensation, listeners, what a colossal sensation. One endowment, and every inhabitant of this little town has suddenly become a well-to-do citizen. It must constitute one of the greatest social experiments of the age. The public here are gasping for breath, there's a deathly silence, O, they're awestruck, you can see it on every face.

MAYOR   I yield the floor to the Headmaster of our College.

(RADIO COMMENTATOR *crosses with microphone to* SCHOOLMASTER)

SCHOOLMASTER   Guelleners: I want to raise one point we must all clearly understand—namely, in making her donation, Madam Claire Zachanassian has a definite aim. What is her aim? Is it her aim to make us happy with money? Is it merely her aim to heap gold on our heads? To revive the Wagner Factory and Bockmann's and the Foundry on Sunshine Square? You know very well it is not. Madam Claire Zachanassian has a more important aim. Her aim is to have the spirit of this community transformed—transformed to the spirit of justice. We, staggered by this demand, ask: have we not always been a just community?

VOICE ONE   Never!
VOICE TWO   We fostered a crime!
VOICE THREE   A false judgment!
VOICE FOUR   A perjury!
WOMAN'S VOICE   A villain!

OTHER VOICE   Hear! Hear!

SCHOOLMASTER   O people of Guellen! Such is the bitter truth! We have connived at injustice! I am of course fully aware of the material possibilities inherent for all of us in a million. Nor am I blind to the fact that poverty is the root of much evil, nay, of great hardship. And yet, and yet: we are not moved by the money (*huge applause*) we are not moved by ambitious thoughts of prosperity and good living, and luxury: we are moved by this matter of justice, and the problem of how to apply it. Nor yet by justice alone, but also by all those ideals, for which our forebears lived and fought, and for which they died; and which constitute the values of our Western World. (*huge applause*) When individual persons slight the ideal of brotherly love, disobey the commandment to succor the weak, spurn the marriage vow, deceive the courts and plunge young mothers into misery, then Freedom is at stake. (*catcalls*) Now, in God's name, we must take our ideals seriously, even unto death. (*huge applause*) For what would be the sense of wealth, which created not a wealth of grace? Yet grace can only be accorded those who hunger after grace. People of Guellen, do you have that hunger? Or is all your hunger common hunger, physical and profane? That is the question. As Head of your College, I put it to you all. Only if you refuse to abide any evil, refuse to live any longer under any circumstances in a world which connives at injustice, can you accept a million from Madam Zachanassian, and thereby fulfill the conditions attaching to her endowment. (*thunderous applause*)

RADIO COMMENTATOR   Just listen to it, ladies and gentlemen, just listen to that applause. We're all overwhelmed. That speech by the Head evinced a moral grandeur we don't find everywhere these days. And a very brave denunciation it was too, aimed at all the little misdemeanors and injustices we find in every community, alas, all over the world.

MAYOR   Alfred Ill . . .

RADIO COMMENTATOR   It's the Mayor, I think he's going to take the floor again.

MAYOR   Alfred Ill, I would like to ask you one question.

(POLICEMAN *gives* ILL *a shove.* ILL *stands.* RADIO COMMENTATOR *crosses with microphone to* ILL)

RADIO COMMENTATOR   Ah. Now we're going to hear the voice of the man responsible for the Zachanassian endowment: it's the voice of Alfred Ill, our prodigal lady's childhood friend.

Alfred Ill—a vigorous man around seventy, an upright Guellener of the old school, and of course he's deeply moved, full of gratitude, full of quiet satisfaction.

MAYOR   Alfred Ill: it is owing to you we have been offered this endowment. Are you aware of that?

(ILL *says something in an undertone*)

RADIO COMMENTATOR   My dear sir, would you kindly speak a shade louder, our listeners are so eager to hear you.

ILL   All right.

MAYOR   Will you respect our decision as to acceptance or refusal of the Claire Zachanassian Endowment?

ILL   I shall respect it.

MAYOR   Are there any questions to Alfred Ill? (*Silence*) The Church? (PRIEST *says nothing*) The Medical Profession? (DOCTOR *says nothing*) The Police? (POLICEMAN *says nothing*) The Opposition Party? (*No one says anything*) I shall now put the issue to vote. (*Silence. Hum of movie-cameras, flash of flashlights*) All those pure in heart who want justice done, raise their hands (*All except* ILL *raise their hands*)

RADIO COMMENTATOR   There's a devout silence in the auditorium. Nothing but a single sea of hands, all raised, as if making one, mighty pledge for a better, juster world. Only the old man has remained seated, absolutely motionless, he's overcome with joy. His ambition has been fulfilled, and thanks to the generosity of his childhood friend the endowment's finally assured.

MAYOR   The Claire Zachanassian Endowment is accepted. Unanimously. Not for the sake of the money,

CITIZENS   Not for the sake of the money,

MAYOR   But for justice

CITIZENS   But for justice

MAYOR   And for conscience' sake.

CITIZENS   And for conscience' sake.

MAYOR   For we cannot connive at a crime:

CITIZENS   For we cannot connive at a crime:

MAYOR   Let us then root out the wrongdoer,

CITIZENS   Let us then root out the wrongdoer,

MAYOR   And deliver our souls from evil

CITIZENS   And deliver our souls from evil

MAYOR   And all our most sacred possessions.

CITIZENS   And all our most sacred possessions.

ILL (*screams*)   My God!

(*Everyone remains standing solemnly with raised hands, but at this point, however, the news-reel camera jams*)

CAMERAMAN   What a shame, Mister Mayor. There's a short in the light-cable. Would you just do that last vote again, please?

MAYOR   Do it again?

CAMERAMAN   For the newsreel.

MAYOR   O yes, certainly.

CAMERAMAN   O.K., spots?

A VOICE   O.K.

CAMERAMAN   O.K., shoot!

(MAYOR *assumes pose*)

MAYOR   The Claire Zachanassian Endowment is accepted. Unanimously. Not for the sake of the money,

CITIZENS   Not for the sake of the money,

MAYOR   But for justice

CITIZENS   But for justice

MAYOR   And for conscience' sake.

CITIZENS   And for conscience' sake.

MAYOR   For we cannot connive at a crime:

CITIZENS   For we cannot connive at a crime:

MAYOR   Let us then root out the wrongdoer,

CITIZENS   Let us then root out the wrongdoer,

MAYOR   And deliver our souls from evil

CITIZENS   And deliver our souls from evil

MAYOR   And all our most sacred possessions.

CITIZENS   And all our most sacred possessions.

(*Silence*)

CAMERAMAN   (*stage whisper*)   Hey! Ill! Come on!

(*Silence*)

CAMERAMAN   (*disappointed*)   O.K., so he won't. Pity we didn't get his cry of joy the first time. That "My God" was most impressive.

MAYOR   And now we invite the gentlemen of the Press, Cinema and Radio to a little Refreshment. In the Restaurant. The easiest way out of the auditorium is through the stage-door. Tea is being served for the ladies on the Golden Apostle lawn.

(*Those of the Press, Cinema and Radio cross to background, right, and go off.* MEN *of Guellen remain on stage, immobile.* ILL *stands, moves to go*)

POLICEMAN   You stay here!

(*He pushes* ILL *down on to bench*)

ILL   Were you going to do it today?

POLICEMAN   Of course.

ILL   I'd have thought it would be better at my place.

POLICEMAN   It'll be done here.

MAYOR   No one left in the stalls?

(MAN THREE *and* MAN FOUR *peer down into stalls*)

MAN THREE   No one.

MAYOR   What about the gallery?

MAN FOUR   Empty.

MAYOR   Lock the doors. Don't let anyone else into the auditorium.

(MAN THREE *and* MAN FOUR *step down into stalls*)

MAN THREE   Locked.

MAN FOUR   Locked.

MAYOR   Put out the lights. The moon is shining through the gallery window. It's enough. (*The stage dims. In the pale moonlight, people are only dimly visible*) Form a lane. (MEN *of Guellen form a lane: it ends at* GYMNAST, *clad now in elegant white slacks and vest, round which a red scarf*) Father. If you please.

(PRIEST *crosses slowly to* ILL, *sits beside him*)

PRIEST   Now, Ill, your hardest hour is at hand.

ILL   Give me a cigarette.

PRIEST   Mister Mayor, a cigarette.

MAYOR   (*warmly*)   But of course. A good one.

(*Passes packet to* PRIEST, *who offers it to* ILL, *who takes a cigarette;* POLICEMAN *proffers light,* PRIEST *returns packet to* MAYOR)

PRIEST   As the prophet Amos said—

ILL   Please don't.

(ILL *smokes*)

PRIEST   Are you not afraid?

ILL   Not much, any more.

(ILL *smokes*)

PRIEST   (*helpless*)   I'll pray for you.

ILL   Pray for Guellen.

(ILL *smokes.* PRIEST *gets slowly to his feet*)

PRIEST   God have mercy upon us.

(PRIEST *slowly rejoins the Guelleners' ranks*)

MAYOR   Alfred Ill. Stand up.

(ILL *hesitates*)

POLICEMAN   Get up, you bastard. (*Drags* ILL *to his feet*)

MAYOR   Inspector, control yourself.

POLICEMAN   Sorry. It just slipped out.

MAYOR   Alfred Ill. Come here. (ILL *drops cigarette, treads it out. Then walks slowly to center of stage, turns his back to audience*) Walk down that lane.

(ILL *hesitates*)

POLICEMAN   Get moving.

(ILL *walks slowly into lane of silent men. When he gets to the end, he comes up against* GYMNAST *planted facing him.* ILL *stops, turns round, and seeing lane close mercilessly in on him,*

sinks to his knees. The lane becomes a silent knot of men, swelling up, then slowly crouching down. Silence. Enter REPORTERS, *downstage, left. Lights up*)

FIRST REPORTER   What's going on here?

(*The knot of men opens, loosed. The men assemble quietly in background. Only* DOCTOR *remains, kneeling beside a corpse over which is spread, as if in an hotel, a chequered tablecloth.* DOCTOR *stands, puts away stethoscope*)

DOCTOR   Heart attack.

(*Silence*)

MAYOR   Died of joy.

FIRST REPORTER   Died of joy.

SECOND REPORTER   Life writes the most beautiful stories.

FIRST REPORTER   Better get to work.

(REPORTERS *hurry off to background, right. Enter, left.* CLAIRE ZACHANASSIAN, *followed by* BUTLER. *She sees corpse, stops, then walks slowly to center of stage, turns to face audience*)

CLAIRE ZACHANASSIAN   Bring him here.

(*Enter* ROBY *and* TOBY *with stretcher, on which they lay* ILL, *then bring him to* CLAIRE ZACHANASSIAN'S *feet*)

CLAIRE ZACHANASSIAN (*unmoving*)   Uncover him, Boby. (BUTLER *uncovers* ILL'S *face. She examines it at length, does not move*) Now he looks the way he was, a long while ago: the black panther. Cover him. (BUTLER *covers face*) Carry him to the coffin. (ROBY *and* TOBY *carry out body, left*) Take me to my room, Boby. Get the bags packed. We are going to Capri. (BUTLER *offers her his arm, she walks slowly out to left, then stops*) Mayor. (MAYOR *emerges from ranks of silent men in background, comes slowly forward*) The check. (*She passes him a piece of paper; and exit, with* BUTLER)

(*As the clothing, that outward visible form of a mounting standard of living, improves by degrees discreet and unobtrusive yet less and less to be ignored, and as the stage grows more inviting, while rung by rung it scales the social ladder and metamorphoses into wealth, like a gradual change of house from a slum to a well-to-do neighborhood, so the epitome of that ascent occurs in the concluding tableau. The erstwhile grey and dreary world has been transformed; it has grown rich and dazzling new, a flashy incarnation of up-to-the-minute technics, as if the world and all were ending happily. Flags and streamers, posters, neon-lights now surround the renovated railway station, and the men and women of Guellen clad in evening*

gowns and dress-suits form two choruses, re-
sembling those of Greek tragedy, nor is this
an accident but rather to orientate the close, as
if some stricken ship, borne far, far away, were
sending out its last signals)

CHORUS ONE

Many, many the monstrous things on earth,
The volcano spewing and spitting its fire,
The shattering earthquake and the tidal wave,
And wars:
    Across the corn the clatter of tanks
    While the radiant mushroom grows
    From the spoor of the atom bomb.

CHORUS TWO

These monstrous things
    do not exceed
The monstrous plight
    of poverty
Which excites
    no tragic deed
Is not heroic
    but condemns
Our human race
    to barren days
After hopeless
    yesterdays.

THE WOMEN

The mothers are helpless, they watch
    Their loved ones pining away;

THE MEN

But the men rumor rebellion.
    The men think treachery.

MAN ONE

In worn-out shoes they pace the town.

MAN THREE

A filthy fag-end in their mouths.

CHORUS ONE

For the jobs, the jobs that earned them bread,
    The jobs are gone.

CHORUS TWO

And the station scorned by the screaming trains.

ALL

Now God be praised

MRS ILL

For kindly fate

ALL

Has changed all that.

THE WOMEN

Our tender forms are clad in fitting frocks,

SON

Young guys with any future drive a Sports,

THE MEN

The business-men relax in limousines,

DAUGHTER

All tennis-girls play tennis on hard courts.

DOCTOR

Our operating-theatres are the best:

The instruments are new, the tiles green;
Medical morale will stand the test.

ALL

Our suppers now are simmering at home
And Everyman, contented and well-shod,
Buys cigarettes of quality at last.

SCHOOLMASTER

Assiduous students study their studies,

MAN TWO

Dynamic tycoons amass fortunes,

ALL

Rembrandts after Rubens,

PAINTER

        And the painters of today
Get an excellent living in Art.

PRIEST

At Christmas and at Easter and at Whitsun
The Cathedral is packed to the portals
With Flocks of the Christian religion.

ALL

And the trains, the trains come haughtily roaring
    In on the iron
        Railway to Guellen
Hurrying people from town to town,
    Commuting,
        Stopping.

(*Enter* GUARD, *left*)

GUARD

Guellen!

STATION-MASTER

Guellen-Rome Express! All seats please!
    Diner up front!

(*Enter from background* CLAIRE ZACHANASSIAN
*seated immobile in sedan-chair, like an old
stone idol, and moves down-stage with retinue,
between the two* CHORUSES)

MAYOR

Our lady and her noble retinue,

ALL

Her wealth endowed on Guellen town,

DAUGHTER

The benefactrice of us all

MAYOR

Is leaving now!

(*Exit* CLAIRE ZACHANASSIAN, *right, followed last
and very slowly by* SERVANTS *bearing coffin*)

MAYOR

Long may she live.

ALL

    She bears a precious charge.

(STATION-MASTER *whistles, waves green flag*)

STATION-MASTER

Stand clear!

PRIEST

Now let us pray to God

ALL

To protect us all

MAYOR

In these hustling, booming, prosperous times:

ALL

Protect all our sacred possessions,
Protect our peace and our freedom,
Ward off the night, nevermore
Let it darken our glorious town
Grown out of the ashes anew.
Let us go and enjoy our good fortune.

POSTSCRIPT

The Visit is the story of an action which takes place in a small town somewhere in Central Europe. It is told by someone who feels himself at no great remove from the people involved, and who is not so sure he would have acted differently. Any further meaning imputed to the story needs no mention here, and should not be imposed on the stage production. This applies even to the final scene, where the people, admittedly, speak in a more formal fashion than might be found in reality, more in the so-called poetical manner and use what could be described as fine words, but this is merely because the Guelleners have just acquired riches and speak as befits the newly rich, in a more select language. I have described people, not marionettes, an action and not an allegory. I have presented a world, not pointed a moral (as I have been accused of doing), and what is more I have not even tried to force my play on the public, for all that happens quite naturally in any case, so long as the audience too belong in the theatre. In my view, a play is acted in the theatre according to the limits and possibilities of the stage; it is not confined within the garb of some special style. When the Guelleners act trees, therefore, this is no Surrealism. Rather it is a somewhat distressing love story, enacted in that wood: an old man's attempt to approach an old woman; and this is placed in a "poetical" setting in order to make it more bearable. I write with an inherent confidence in the theatre and its actors—this is my fundamental inspiration; the material draws me into its charmed circle. To play his character, the actor needs little: only the very outer skin, the text, which of course accords with it. That is to say, just as any creature is sealed off inside its skin, so the play is sealed off inside speech. For speech is all the dramatist provides. It is his end-product. And it is consequently impossible to work on the element of speech alone, but only on that which gives rise to speech, namely thought and action; only dilettantes work on speech alone. I think the actor should aim to present that end-product afresh, whereby all that is art should seem to be nature. If the foreground I have provided be correctly played, the background will emerge of its own accord. I don't account myself a member of the contemporary avant-garde. I admit I have my Theory of Art as well, it's a thing one doesn't always enjoy having, and inasmuch as it's my own private opinion I withhold it (otherwise I'd be obliged to practise it) and prefer being regarded as a somewhat lunatic child of nature lacking a proper sense of form and structure. Producers and directors will probably come nearest the mark if they stage my plays after the style of folk-plays, and treat me as a kind of conscious Nestroy. They should follow the flights of my fancy and let the deeper meanings take care of themselves; they should change the sets without pause or curtain, play even the car scene simply and for preference with a stage-vehicle, equipped only with what the action requires: seats, steering-wheel, bumpers, the car seen from the front, rear seats raised and, of course, everything brand-new, like the shoes, etc. (This scene hasn't anything to do with Wilder—why not? Dialectical exercise for critics.) Claire Zachanassian doesn't represent Justice or the Marshall Plan or even the Apocalypse, she's purely and simply what she is, namely, the richest woman in the world and, thanks to her finances, in a position to act as the Greek tragic heroines acted, absolutely, terribly, something like Medea. She can afford to. This lady has a sense of humor and it mustn't be overlooked, for she is quite as detached from people as from saleable objects and detached from herself as well, and she has a rare grace, more, she has a wicked charm. None the less, moving as she does outside the human pale, she has grown into someone unalterable and rigid, contains within herself no further possibility of development and she, in consequence, is cast in a mould of stone, she is the one to be represented as a stone idol. She's a poetical apparition, so is her retinue, and her eunuchs too. The latter are not to be given a realistically unappetizing interpretation, complete with high-pitched gelded voices, but made on the contrary to seem quite improbable, legendary, fantastic, soft and ghostly in their vegetable contentment, a sacrifice to total revenge, logical as the law-books of antiquity. (To facilitate the playing of these roles the blind pair may speak alternately, instead of together, in which case they needn't repeat every phrase.) While Claire Zachanassian, fixed and unmoving, is a heroine from the very beginning, her onetime sweetheart still has to develop into a hero. At first, a disreputable shop-keeper, he is her unsuspecting victim and, guilty, believes life has been its own expiation of that guilt; he is a thoughtless figure of a man, a simple man in whose mind something slowly dawns, by the agency of fear and terror, something highly personal; a man who in recognizing his guilt lives out justice and who, in death, achieves greatness. (His death should not be without a certain monumental quality.) That death is both meaningful and meaningless. It would only have been entirely meaningful in the mythological kingdom of some ancient *polis*. But the action of this story unfolds in Guellen. In the present. The Guelleners who swarm round the hero are people like the rest of us. They must not, emphatically not, be portrayed as wicked. At first, they are firmly resolved to reject the offer, and although they incur debts that is not because they intend to kill Ill, but out of thoughtless irresponsibility and the feeling that somehow things will come to a happy settlement. Act Two should be directed accordingly. And then in the station scene, Ill is the only one to see his own plight and be afraid; not a harsh word has yet been uttered; events only take their decisive turn during the scene in Petersens' Barn. Disaster can no longer be averted. From that moment onward, the Guelleners steadily pave their way to the murder, waxing indignant over Ill's guilt, etc. The family alone keep on to the end trying to convince themselves things will somehow turn out all right; for they aren't wicked either, only weak, like everyone. It's a community slowly yielding to temptation, as in the Schoolmaster's case; but it must be a perceptible yielding. The temptation is too strong, the poverty too wretched. The old lady is a wicked creature, and for precisely that reason musn't be played wicked, she has to be rendered as human as possible, not with anger but with sorrow and humor, for nothing could harm this comedy with a tragic end more than heavy seriousness.

Friedrich Duerrenmatt

NORWAY
SWEDEN

HENRIK IBSEN (1828–1906) was a playwright whose life and work is a study in conflict and contradiction. The gadfly of bourgeoisie morality was helplessly bourgeois; the enemy of pietism was a guilt-ridden possessor of the worst kind of protestant conscience; the champion of the "love-life of the soul" was incapable of loving; the militant spokesman against hypocrisy and respectability tended to be pompous and was outraged at any breach of decorum. Ibsen's life, in short, was the contradiction of those values affirmed in his plays, and this contradiction is the source of his dramatic methods and techniques and also helps to explain the three major stages in his development as a playwright.

The "father" of the modern drama, who "fought a war to the knife" with the theatre of the past, began his career by writing sprawling romantic history plays. This was the customary practice of young Scandinavian playwrights, and it was not until the publication of *Brand* (1866) and *Peer Gynt* (1867) that it was evident that Ibsen was a revolutionary talent. These early plays were radically different, both in form and subject matter, from the conventional drama of Europe. But it was not until he turned to contemporary social, psychological, and moral concerns in such plays as *Pillars of Society* (1879), *A Doll's House* (1881), *Ghosts* (1883), and *An Enemy of the People* (1884) that Ibsen became the widely acknowledged leader of the new theatre of Europe. Beginning with *The Wild Duck* (1886), however, his attention drifted away from the conflicts of man living within restrictive social situations to those more personal conflicts of the individual's psychological life; and by the end of his career he was almost exclusively concerned with showing the destiny of each man's innermost soul. In the steady progression from his dramas of universal ideals to the plays of vigorous social protest, and finally to his portrayal of the drama of

[HENRIK IBSEN, *Cont.*]
man's inner life, Ibsen incorporated all the cross-currents of late nineteenth-century life and thought and, in so doing, opened up the theatre so that modernity could spread in the theatre throughout the rest of Europe.

AUGUST STRINDBERG (1849–1912) is the most frequently misunderstood of all modern dramatists. It has been said of him that no writer "had a shorter distance from the blood to the ink," and it is true that in reading Strindberg we are always conscious of the terrible subjectivity of his work. His plays seem to be eruptions out of his very entrails, as if the word and the experience were one. But for all the immediacy of his style, Strindberg is an enormously complex figure, and no fixed critical formula will work when one attempts to analyze and evaluate his plays. Unlike Ibsen, who is always predictable, Strindberg is full of surprises, and one can never tell in which direction this Swedish genius is going next. He wrote over fifty plays, but there is no pattern to his development as an artist. His career is usually broken down into three major divisions: the period between 1870–1880, when, like all Scandinavian apprentice playwrights, he wrote mostly romantic historical plays; the period of 1885–1890, in which he wrote his brutal contemporary naturalistic plays, plays in which a tough naturalistic dialogue is combined with the poetic language of madness; and his expressionist period, which began in 1898 after his longest bout with insanity. But such divisions are artificial, for there is no consistency within any of these periods, nor is there any inner relationship among them. The only constant in the works of this man so full of paradoxes and contradictions was his terrifying, intense vision. He always looked at life without blinders, but he was never able to find a completely satisfactory dramatic form in which to express this vision. All of his life, Strindberg sought the final answer to the meaning of life, but this quest was pervaded with a skepticism that doubted the validity of such a search.

Henrik Ibsen

1828-1906

THE TASK OF THE POET

. . . And what does it mean, then, to be a poet? It was a long time before I realized that to be a poet means essentially to see, but mark well, to see in such a way that whatever is seen is perceived by the audience just as the poet saw it. But only what has been lived through can be seen in that way and accepted in that way. And the secret of modern literature lies precisely in this matter of experiences that are lived through. All that I have written these last ten years, I have lived through spiritually. But no poet lives through anything in isolation. What he lives through all of his countrymen live through with him. If that were not so, what would bridge the gap between the producing and the receiving minds?

And what is it, then, that I have lived through and that has inspired me? The range has been large. In part I have been inspired by something which only rarely and only in my best moments has stirred vividly within me as something great and beautiful. I have been inspired by that which, so to speak, has stood higher than my everyday self, and I have been inspired by this because I wanted to confront it and make it part of myself.

But I have also been inspired by the opposite, by what appears on introspection as the dregs and sediment of one's own nature. Writing has in this case been to me like a bath from which

"The Task of the Poet" by Henrik Ibsen, from "Speech to the Norwegian Students, September 10, 1874," and originally published in *Speeches and New Letters* as translated by Arne Kildal (Boston: Richard G. Badger, 1910, pp. 49–52). Revised translation printed by permission of the translator, Evert Sprinchorn.

I have risen feeling cleaner, healthier, and freer. Yes, gentlemen, nobody can picture poetically anything for which he himself has not to a certain degree and at least at times served as a model. And who is the man among us who has not now and then felt and recognized within himself a contradiction between word and deed, between will and duty, between life and theory in general? Or who is there among us who has not, at least at times, been egoistically sufficient unto himself, and half unconsciously, half in good faith, sought to extenuate his conduct both to others and to himself?

I believe that in saying all this to you, to the students, my remarks have found exactly the right audience. You will understand them as they are meant to be understood. For a student has essentially the same task as the poet: to make clear to himself, and thereby to others, the temporal and eternal questions which are astir in the age and in the community to which he belongs.

In this respect I dare to say of myself that I have endeavored to be a good student during my stay abroad. A poet is by nature farsighted. Never have I seen my homeland and the true life of my homeland so fully, so clearly, and at such close range, as I did in my absence when I was far away from it.

And now, my dear countrymen, in conclusion a few words which are also related to something I have lived through. When Emperor Julian stands at the end of his career, and everything collapses around him, there is nothing which makes him so despondent as the thought that all he has gained was this: to be remembered by cool and clear heads with respectful appreciation, while his opponents live on, rich in the love of warm, living hearts. This thought was the result of much that I had lived through; it had its origin in a question that I had sometimes asked myself, down there in my solitude. Now the young people of Norway have come to me tonight and given me my answer in word and song, have given me my answer more warmly and clearly than I had ever expected to hear it. I shall take this answer with me as the richest reward of my visit with my countrymen at home, and it is my hope and my belief that what I experience tonight will be an experience to "live through" which will sometime be reflected in a work of mine. And if this happens, if sometime I shall send such a book home, then I ask that the students receive it as a handshake and a thanks for this meeting. I ask you to receive it as the ones who had a share in the making of it.

TRANSLATOR'S NOTE

After an absence of ten years, Ibsen spent some time in Norway during the summer of 1874. On September 10, Norwegian students marched in procession to Ibsen's home. The preceding excerpt is from Ibsen's reply to their greeting.

Revised Translation by Evert Sprinchorn

NOTES FOR *HEDDA GABLER*

I

¶ This married woman more and more imagines that she is an important personality, and as a consequence feels compelled to create for herself a sensational past—

¶ If an interesting female character appears in a new story or in a play, she believes that it is she who is being portrayed.

¶ The masculine environment helps to confirm her in this belief.

¶ The two lady friends agree to die together. One of them carries out her end of the bargain. But the other one who realizes what lies in store for her loses her courage. This is the reversal—

¶ "He has such a disgusting way of walking when one sees him from behind."

¶ She hates him because he has a goal, a

"Notes for *Hedda Gabler*" by Henrik Ibsen, translated by Evert Sprinchorn with Part VI translated by A. G. Chater. Printed by prmission of the translators.

mission in life. The lady friend has one too, but does not dare to devote herself to it. Her personal life treated in fictional form.

¶ In the second act the manuscript that is left behind—

¶ "The lost soul" apologizes for the man of culture. The wild horse and the race horse. Drinks—eats paprika. House and clothes. Revolution against the laws of nature—but nothing stupid, not until the position is secure.

II

¶ The pale, apparently cold beauty. Expects great things of life and the joy of life.

The man who has now finally won her, plain and simple in appearance, but an honest and talented, broad-minded scholar.

III

¶ The manuscript that H. L. leaves behind contends that man's mission is: Upward, toward the bearer of light. Life on the present foundations of society is not worth living. Therefore he escapes from it through his imagination. By drinking, etc.—Tesman stands for correct behavior. Hedda for blasé oversophistication. Mrs. R. is the nervous-hysterical modern individual. Brack represents the personal bourgeois point of view.

¶ Then H. departs this world. And the two of them are left sitting there with the manuscript they cannot interpret. And the aunt is with them. What an ironic comment on humanity's striving for progress and development.

¶ But Holger's double nature intervenes. Only by realizing the basely bourgeois can he win a hearing for his great central idea.

¶ Mrs. Rising is afraid that H., although "a model of propriety," is not normal. She can only guess at his way of thinking but cannot understand it. Quotes some of his remarks—

¶ One talks about building railways and highways for the cause of progress. But no, no, that is not what is needed. Space must be cleared so that the spirit of man can make its great turnabout. For it has gone astray. The spirit of man has gone astray.

¶ HOLGER: I have been out. I have behaved obscenely. That doesn't matter. But the police know about it. That's what counts.

¶ H. L.'s despair lies in that he wants to master the world but cannot master himself.

¶ Tesman believes that it is he who has in a way seduced H. L. into indulging in excesses again. But that is not so. It is as Hedda has said: that it was *he* she dreamed of when she talked about "the famous man." But she does not dare tell Tesman this.

¶ To aid in understanding his own character, L. has made notes in "the manuscript." These are the notes the two of them should interpret, want to interpret, but *cannot* possibly.

¶ Brack is inclined to live as a bachelor, and then gain admittance to a good home, become a friend of the family, indispensable—

¶ They say it is a law of nature. Very well then, raise an opposition to it. Demand its repeal. Why give way. Why surrender unconditionally—

¶ In conversations between T. and L. the latter says that he lives for his studies. The former replies that in that case he can compete with him.—(T. lives *on* his studies) that's the point.

¶ L. (Tesman) says: I couldn't step on a worm! "But now I can tell you that I too am seeking the professorship. We are rivals."

IV

¶ She has respect for his knowledge, an eye for his noble character, but is embarrassed by his insignificant, ridiculous appearance, makes fun of his conduct and remarks.

V

¶ The aunt asks all sorts of ambiguous questions to find out about those things that arouse her imagination the most.

¶ NOTES: One evening as Hedda and Tesman, together with some others, were on their way home from a party, Hedda remarked as they walked by a charming house that was where she would like to live. She meant it, but she said it only to keep the conversation with Tesman going. "He simply cannot carry on a conversation."

The house was actually for rent or sale. Tesman had been pointed out as the coming young man. And later when he proposed, and let slip that he too had dreamed of living there, she accepted.

He too had liked the house very much.

They get married. And they rent the house.[1]

---

[1] Both of them, each in his and her own way, have seen in their common love for this house a sign of their mutual understanding. As if they sought and were drawn to a common home. Then he rents the house. They get married and go abroad. He orders the house bought and his aunt furnishes it at his expense. Now it is their home. It is theirs and yet it is not, because it is not paid for. Everything depends on his getting the professorship. (*Ibsen's note.*)

But when Hedda returns as a young wife, with a vague sense of responsibility, the whole thing seems distasteful to her. She conceives a kind of hatred for the house just because it has become her home. She confides this to Brack. She evades the question with Tesman.

¶ The play shall deal with "the impossible," that is, to aspire to and strive for something which is against all the conventions, against that which is acceptable to conscious minds— Hedda's included.

¶ The episode of the hat makes Aunt Rising lose her composure. She leaves—That it could be taken for the maid's hat—no, that's going too far!

That my hat, which I've had for over nine years, could be taken for the maid's—no, that's really too much!

¶ *Hedda:* Yes, once I thought it must be wonderful to live here and own this house.

Brack: But now you are contradicting yourself.

Hedda: That may be so. But that's how it is anyway.

¶ *Hedda:* I don't understand these self-sacrificing people. Look at old Miss Rising. She has a paralyzed sister in her house, who has been lying in bed for years. Do you suppose she thinks it is a sacrifice to live for that poor creature, who is a burden even to herself? Far from it! Just the opposite. I don't understand it.

¶ *Hedda:* And how greedy they are for married men. Do you know what, Judge Brack? You don't do yourself any good by not getting married.

Brack: Then I can practically consider myself married.

Hedda: Yes, you certainly can—in one way—in many ways even—

Brack: In many ways? What do you mean by that?

Hedda: No thanks. I won't tell you.

¶ When Mrs. Elvsted says that the first part of Lövborg's book deals with the historical development of "Sociology," and that another volume will appear later, Tesman looks at her a little startled.

¶ Very few true parents are to be found in the world. Most people grow up under the influence of aunts or uncles—either neglected and misunderstood or else spoiled.

¶ Hedda rejects him because he does not dare expose himself to temptation. He replies that the same is true of her. The wager! . . . He loses . . . ! Mrs. Elvsted is present. Hedda says: No danger—He loses.

¶ Hedda feels herself demoniacally attracted

by the tendencies of the times. But she lacks courage. Her thoughts remain theories, ineffective dreams.

¶ The feminine imagination is not active and independently creative like the masculine. It needs a bit of reality as a help.

¶ Lövborg has had inclinations toward "the bohemian life." Hedda is attracted in the same direction, but she does not dare to take the leap.

¶ Buried deep within Hedda there is a level of poetry. But the environment frightens her. Suppose she were to make herself ridiculous!

¶ Hedda realizes that she, much more than Thea, has abandoned her husband.

¶ The newly wedded couple return home in September—as the summer is dying. In the second act they sit in the garden—but with their coats on.

¶ Being frightened by one's own voice. Something strange, foreign.

¶ NEWEST PLAN: The festivities in Tesman's garden—and Lövborg's defeat—already prepared for in the 1st act. Second act: the party—

¶ Hedda energetically refuses to serve as hostess. She will not celebrate their marriage because (in her opinion, it isn't a marriage)

¶ Holger: Don't you see? I am the cause of your marriage—

¶ Hedda is the type of woman in her position and with her character. She marries Tesman but she devotes her imagination to Eilert Lövborg. She leans back in her chair, closes her eyes, and dreams of his adventures. . . . This is the enormous difference: Mrs. Elvsted "works for his moral improvement." But for Hedda he is the object of cowardly, tempting daydreams. In reality she does not have the courage to be a part of anything like that. Then she realizes her condition. Caught! Can't comprehend it. Ridiculous! Ridiculous!

¶ The traditional delusion that one man and one woman are made for each other. Hedda has her roots in the conventional. She marries Tesman but she dreams of Eilert Lövborg. . . . She is disgusted by the latter's flight from life. He believes that this has raised him in her estimation. . . . Thea Elvsted is the conventional, sentimental, hysterical Philistine.

¶ Those Philistines, Mrs. E. and Tesman, explain my behavior by saying first I drink myself drunk and that the rest is done in insanity. It's a flight from reality which is an absolute necessity to me.

¶ E. L.: Give me something—a flower—at our parting. Hedda hands him the revolver. Then Tesman arrives: Has he gone? "Yes."

Do you think he will still compete against me? No, I don't think so. You can set your mind at rest.

¶ Tesman relates that when they were in Gratz she did not want to visit her relatives—He misunderstands her real motives.

¶ In the last act as Tesman, Mrs. Elvsted, and Miss Rising are consulting, Hedda plays in the small room at the back. She stops. The conversation continues. She appears in the doorway—Good night—I'm going now. Do you need me for anything? Tesman: No, nothing at all. Good night, my dear! . . . The shot is fired—

¶ CONCLUSION: All rush into the back room. Brack sinks as if paralyzed into a chair near the stove: But God have mercy—people don't *do* such things!

¶ When Hedda hints at her ideas to Brack, he says: Yes, yes, that's extraordinarily amusing—Ha ha ha! He does not understand that she is quite serious.

¶ Hedda is right in this: There is no love on Tesmans' part. Nor on the aunt's part. However full of love she may be.

Eilert Lövborg has a double nature. It is a fiction that one loves only *one* person. He loves two—or many—alternately (to put it frivolously). But how can he explain his position? Mrs. Elvsted, who forces him to behave correctly, runs away from her husband. Hedda, who drives him beyond all limits, draws back at the thought of a scandal.

¶ Neither he nor Mrs. Elvsted understands the point. Tesman reads in the manuscript that was left behind about "the two ideals." Mrs. Elvsted can't explain to him what E. L. meant. Then comes the burlesque note: both T. and Mrs. E. are going to devote their future lives to interpreting the mystery.

¶ Tesman thinks that Hedda hates E. L. Mrs. Elvsted thinks so too.

Hedda sees their delusion but dares not disabuse them of it. There is something beautiful about having an aim in life. Even if it is a delusion—

She cannot do it. Take part in someone else's.

That is when she shoots herself.

The destroyed manuscript is entitled "The ~~Philosophy~~ Ethics of Future Society."

¶ Tesman is on the verge of losing his head. All this work meaningless. New thoughts! New visions! A whole new world! Then the two of them sit there, trying to find the meaning in it. Can't make any sense of it. . . .

¶ The greatest misery in this world is that

so many have nothing to do but pursue happiness without being able to find it.

¶ "From Jochum Tesman there developed a Jørgen Tesman—but it will be a long, long time before this Jørgen gives rise to a George."

¶ The simile: The journey of life = the journey on a train.

H.: One doesn't usually jump out of the compartment.

No, not when the train is moving.

Nor stand still when it is stationary. There's always someone on the platform, staring in.

¶ *Hedda:* Dream of a scandal—yes, I understand that well enough. But commit one— no, no, no.

¶ *Lövborg:* Now I understand. My ideal was an illusion. You aren't a bit better than I. Now I have nothing left to live for. Except pleasure—dissipation—as you call it. . . . Wait, here's a present (The pistol)

¶ Tesman is nearsighted. Wears glasses. My, what a beautiful rose! Then he stuck his nose in the cactus. Ever since then—!

¶ NB: The mutual hatred of women. Women have no influence on external matters of government. Therefore they want to have an influence on souls. And then so many of them have no aim in life (the lack thereof is inherited)—

¶ Lövborg and Hedda bent over the photographs at the table.

He: How is it possible? *She:* Why not? *L.:* Tesman! You couldn't find words enough to make fun of him. . . . Then comes the story about the general's "disgrace," dismissal, etc. The worst thing for a lady at a ball is not to be admired for her own sake. . . . *L.:* And Tesman? He took you for the sake of your person. That's just as unbearable to think about.

¶ Just by marrying Tesman it seems to me I have gotten so unspeakably far away from him.

¶ *He:* Look at her. Just look at her! . . . *Hedda* (stroking her hair): Yes, isn't she beautiful!

¶ Men and women don't belong to the same century. . . . What a great prejudice that one should love only *one!*

¶ Hedda and Brack talk about traveling to the small university towns. *Hedda:* Now I'm not counting that little trip through the Tyrol—

¶ *Brack* (*to Tesman*): Are you blind and deaf? Can't you see? Can't you hear—

Tesman: Ah. Take the manuscript. Read to me!

¶ The demoniacal element in Hedda is this:

She wants to exert her influence on someone— But once she has done so, she despises him. . . . The manuscript?

¶ In the third act Hedda questions Mrs. Elvsted. But if he's like that, why is he worth holding on to. . . . Yes, yes, I know—

¶ Hedda's discovery that her relations with the maid cannot possibly be proper.

¶ In his conversation with Hedda, Lövborg says: Miss H—Miss—You know, I don't believe that you are married.

¶ *Hedda:* And now I sit here and talk with these Philistines—And the way we once could talk to each other—No, I won't say any more. . . . Talk? How do you mean? Obscenely? Ish. Let us say indecently.

¶ NB!! The reversal in the play occurs during the big scene between Hedda and E. L. *He:* What a wretched business it is to conform to the existing morals. It would be ideal if a man of the present could live the life of the future. What a miserable business it is to fight over a professorship!

Hedda—that lovely girl! *H.:* No! *E. L.:* Yes, I'm going to say it. That lovely, cold girl —cold as marble.

I'm not dissipated fundamentally. But the life of reality isn't livable—

¶ In the fifth act: *Hedda:* How hugely comic it is that those two harmless people, Tesman and Mrs. E., should try to put the pieces together for a monument to E. L. The man who so deeply despised the whole business—

¶ Life becomes for Hedda a ridiculous affair that isn't "worth seeing through to the end."

¶ The happiest mission in life is to place the people of today in the conditions of the future.

L.: Never put a child in this world, H.!

¶ When Brack speaks of a "triangular affair," Hedda thinks about what is going to happen and refers ambiguously to it. Brack doesn't understand.

¶ Brack cannot bear to be in a house where there are small children. "Children shouldn't be allowed to exist until they are fourteen or fifteen. That is, girls. What about boys? Shouldn't be allowed to exist at all—or else they should be raised outside the house."

¶ H. admits that children have always been a horror to her too.

¶ Hedda is strongly but imprecisely opposed to the idea that one should love "the family." The aunts mean nothing to her.

¶ It liberated Hedda's spirit to serve as a confessor to E. L. Her sympathy has secretly been on his side—But it became ugly when the public found out everything. Then she backed out.

¶ MAIN POINTS:

1. They are not all made to be mothers.

2. They are passionate but they are afraid of scandal.

3. They perceive that the times are full of missions worth devoting one's life to, but they cannot discover them.

¶ And besides Tesman is not exactly a professional, but he is a specialist. The Middle Ages are dead—

¶ *T.:* Now there you see also the great advantages to my studies. I can lose manuscripts and rewrite them—no inspiration needed—

¶ Hedda is completely taken up by the child that is to come, but when it is born she dreads what is to follow—

¶ Hedda must say somewhere in the play that she did not like to get out of her compartment while on the trip. Why not? I don't like to show my legs. . . . Ah, Mrs. H., but they do indeed show themselves. Nevertheless, I don't.

¶ Shot herself! Shot herself!

Brack (collapsing in the easy chair): But great God—people don't *do* such things!

¶ NB!! Eilert Lövborg believes that a comradeship must be formed between a man and woman out of which the truly spiritual human being can arise. Whatever else the two of them do is of no concern. This is what the people around him do not understand. To them he is dissolute. Inwardly he is not.

¶ If a man can have several male friends, why can't he have several lady friends?

¶ It is precisely the sensual feelings that are aroused while in the company of his female "friends" or "comrades" that seek release in his excesses.

¶ Now I'm going. Don't you have some little remembrance to give me—? You have flowers —and so many other things—(The story of the pistol from before)—But you won't use it anyhow—

¶ In the fourth act when Hedda finds out that he has shot himself, she is jubilant. . . . He had courage.

Here is the rest of the manuscript.

¶ CONCLUSION: Life isn't tragic. . . . Life is ridiculous. . . . And that's what I can't bear.

¶ Do you know what happens in novels? All those who kill themselves—through the head—not in the stomach. . . . How ridiculous —how baroque—

¶ In her conversation with Thea in the first act, Hedda remarks that she cannot understand how one can fall in love with an unmarried man—or an unengaged man—or an unloved man—on the other hand—[2]

¶ Brack understands well enough that it is Hedda's repression, her hysteria that motivates everything she does.

¶ On her part, Hedda suspects that Brack sees through her without believing that she understands.

¶ *H.:* It must be wonderful to take something from someone.

¶ When H. talks to B. in the fifth act about those two sitting there trying to piece together the manuscript without the spirit being present, she breaks out in laughter. . . . Then she plays the piano—then—d—

¶ Men—in the most indescribable situations how ridiculous they are.

¶ NB! She really wants to live a *man's* life wholly. But then she has misgivings. Her inheritance, what is implanted in her.

¶ Loving and being loved by aunts . . . Most people who are born of old maids, male and female.

¶ This deals with the "underground forces and powers." Woman as a minor. Nihilism. Father and mother belonging to different eras. The female underground revolution in thought. The slave's fear of the outside world.

¶ NB!! Why should I conform to social morals that I know won't last more than half a generation. When I run wild, as they call it, it's my escape from the present. Not that I find any joy in my excesses. I'm up to my neck in the established order. . . .

¶ What is Tesman working on?

¶ *Hedda:* It's a book on the domestic industries of Brabant during the Middle Ages.

¶ I have to play the part of an idiot in order to be understood. Pretend that I want to rehabilitate myself in the eyes of the mob— today's mob.

¶ When I had finished with my latest book, I conceived the idea for a brilliant new work. You must help me with it. I need women, Hedda—! In the Middle Ages the female conscience was so constituted that if she discovered she had married her nephew, she was filled with rancor——

¶ Shouldn't the future strive for the great,

---

[2] 1. But, my heavens, Tesm. was unmarried. *H.:* Yes, he was. *Th.:* But you married him. *H.:* Yes, I did. *Th.:* Then how can you say that . . . Well now—

2. But now he's married. *H.:* Yes, but not to someone else.

the good, and the beautiful as Tesman says it should? Yes! But the great, the good, the beautiful of the future won't be the same as it is for us—

¶ *H.:* I remember especially a red-headed girl whom I have seen on the street. *Br.:* I know whom you mean—*H.:* You called her— it was such a pretty name—*Br.:* I know her name too. But how do you know it was pretty? *H.:* Oh, Judge Brack, you are an idiot.

¶ The passenger and his trunk at the railway station. P. decides where he is going, buys his ticket. The trunk is attended to—

¶ *Hedda:* Slender figure of average height. Nobly shaped, aristocratic face with fine, wax-colored skin. The eyes have a veiled expression. Hair medium brown. Not especially abundant hair. Dressed in a loose-fitting dressing gown, white with blue trimmings. Composed and relaxed in her manners. The eyes steel-gray, almost lusterless.

¶ Mrs. Elvsted: weak build. The eyes round, rather prominent, almost as blue as water. Weak face with soft features. Nervous gestures, frightened expression—

¶ See above. E. L.'s idea of comradeship between man and woman. . . . The idea is a life-saver!

¶ If society won't let us live morally with them (women), then we'll have to live with them immorally—

¶ *Tesman:* The new idea in E. L.'s book is that of progress resulting from the comradeship between man and woman.

¶ Hedda's basic demand is: I want to know everything, but keep myself clean.

¶ I want to know everything—everything— everything—

H.:— —

H: If only I could have lived like him!

¶ Is there something about Brabant? *B.:* What on earth is that? . . .

¶ The wager about the use of both pistols.

¶ *Miss T.:* Yes, this is the house of life and health. Now I shall go home to a house of sickness and death. God bless both of you. From now on I'll come out here every day to ask Bertha how things are—

¶ In the third act H. tells E. L. that she is not interested in the great questions—nor the great ideas—but in the great freedom of man. . . . But she hasn't the courage.

¶ The two ideals! *Tesman:* What in the name of God does he mean by that? What? What do we have to do with ideals?

¶ The new book treats of "the two ideals." Thea can give no information.

VI

¶ NB! Brack had always thought that Hedda's short engagement to Tesman would come to nothing.

Hedda speaks of how she felt herself set aside, step by step, when her father was no longer in favor, when he retired and died without leaving anything. Then she realized, bitterly, that it was for his sake she had been made much of. And then she was already between twenty-five and twenty-six. In danger of becoming an old maid.

She thinks that in reality Tesman only feels a vain pride in having won her. His solicitude for her is the same as is shown for a thoroughbred horse or a valuable sporting dog. This, however, does not offend her. She merely regards it as a fact.

Hedda says to Brack that she does not think Tesman can be called ridiculous. But in reality she finds him so. Later on she finds him pitiable as well.

Tesman: Could you not call me by my Christian name?

Hedda: No, indeed I couldn't—unless they have given you some other name than the one you have.

Tesman puts Lövborg's manuscript in his pocket so that it may not be lost. Afterward it is Hedda who, by a casual remark, with tentative intention, gives him the idea of keeping it.

Then he reads it. A new line of thought is revealed to him. But the strain of the situation increases. Hedda awakens his jealousy.

¶ In the third act one thing after another comes to light about Lövborg's adventures in the course of the night. At last Lövborg himself comes, in quiet despair. "Where is the manuscript?" "Did I not leave it behind me here?" He does not know that he has done so. But after all, of what use is the manuscript to him now! He is writing of the "moral doctrine of the future"! When he has just been released by the police!

¶ Hedda's despair is that there are doubtless so many chances of happiness in the world, but that she cannot discover them. It is the want of an object in life that torments her.

When Hedda beguiles T. into leading E. L. into ruin, it is done to test T.'s character.

¶ It is in Hedda's presence that the irresistible craving for excess always comes over E. L.

Tesman cannot understand that E. L. could wish to base his future on injury to another.

¶ *Hedda:* Do I hate T.? No, not at all. I only find him boring.

¶ *Brack:* But nobody else thinks so.

Hedda: Neither is there any one but myself who is married to him.

Brack: . . . not at all boring.

Hedda: Heavens, you always want me to express myself so correctly. Very well then, T. is not boring, but I am bored by living with him.

Hedda . . . had no prospects. Well, perhaps you would have liked to see me in a convent (home for unmarried ladies).

Hedda: . . . then isn't it an honorable thing to profit by one's person? Don't actresses and others turn their advantages into profit. I had no other capital. Marriage—I thought it was like buying an annuity.

Hedda: Remember that I am the child of an old man—and a worn-out man too—or past his prime at any rate—perhaps that has left its mark.

Brack: Upon my word, I believe you have begun to brood over problems.

Hedda: Well, what cannot one take to doing when one has gone and got married.

VII

¶ *E. L.:* It's impossible for me to call you Mrs. T. You will always be H. G. to me.

¶ Both Miss T. and B. have seen what lies in store for Hedda. . . . T. on the other hand cries out: My God, I had no idea.

¶ When E. L. tells H. that he cannot possibly confess to Thea that their book has been lost, H. says: I don't believe a word of that. *E. L.:* No, but I know how terribly dismayed she will be.

TRANSLATOR'S NOTE

More preliminary notes have been preserved for *Hedda Gabler* than for almost any other play by Ibsen. These notes afford the student of playwriting a rare opportunity to trace the growth of a masterpiece from the first embryonic thoughts through its birth as a full-length draft. Nearly all of these preliminary notes are given here, grouped in seven sets to indicate their different sources: scattered loose sheets, notebooks, even a calling card. Of greatest interest are the notes in sets 1 and 5 taken from a little black book, now in the possession of Tancred Ibsen, which Ibsen carried about with him. According to Else Høst, *Hedda Gabler: En monografi* (Oslo: 1958), pp. 78 ff., the notes in set 1 were probably jotted down in the fall of 1889 and comprise the abortive ideas for a play about a prominent woman novelist, Camilla Collett, who imagined that Ibsen had used her as a model for the heroine of *The Lady from the Sea.* Ibsen made no progress with this play, but among the notes for it he had planted the seeds of another play: a play about a cowardly woman, the woman's jealousy of a man with a mission in life, and a misplaced manuscript which represents that mission. The lengthy sequence of notes in set 5, almost certainly in chronological order, was probably made during the winter and spring of 1890 and reveals the convolutions of Ibsen's thought as the characters, plot, and motives of *Hedda Gabler* take shape. In late July or early August, Ibsen began to write a full-length draft, most of which is translated in *From Ibsen's Workshop*, Vol. XII of the Archer edition of Ibsen's Collected Works. This draft was thoroughly revised in October, fair copied in October and November, and *Hedda Gabler* was published on December 4, 1890, in time for the Christmas season. The notes are arranged in the order given in the Centennial Edition of Ibsen's works (21 vols.; Oslo: 1928–1957), ed. Francis Bull, Halvdan Koht, and Didrik Arup Seip, XI, pp. 496–516.

Translated by Evert Sprinchorn and A. G. Chater

THE PRIMACY OF CHARACTER

Before I write down one word, I have to have the character in mind through and through. I must penetrate into the last wrinkle of his soul. I always proceed from the individual; the stage setting, the dramatic ensemble, all of that comes naturally and does not cause me any worry, as soon as I am certain of the individual in every aspect of his humanity. But I have to have his exterior in mind also, down to the last button, how he stands and walks, how he conducts himself, what his voice sounds like. Then I do not let him go until his fate is fulfilled.

* * *

As a rule, I make three drafts of my dramas which differ very much from each other in characterization, not in action. When I proceed to the first sketch of the material I feel as though I had the degree of acquaintance with my characters that one acquires on a railway journey; one has met and chatted about this or that. With the next draft I see everything

"The Primacy of Character" by Henrik Ibsen appeared in *Ibsen: The Master Builder* by A. E. Zucker, pp. 194, 208. Copyright 1929, Henry Holt and Company. Reprinted by permission of Holt, Rinehart and Winston, Inc.

more clearly, I know characters just about as one would know them after a few weeks' stay in a spa; I have learned the fundamental traits in their characters as well as their little peculiarities; yet it is not impossible that I might make an error in some essential matter. In the last draft, finally, I stand at the limit of knowledge; I know my people from close and long association—they are my intimate friends, who will not disappoint me in any way; in the manner in which I see them now, I shall always see them.

Translated by A. E. Zucker

THE WILD DUCK

Translated by Otto Reinert

CAST OF CHARACTERS

WERLE, *a manufacturer and merchant*
GREGERS WERLE, *his son*
OLD EKDAL
HJALMAR EKDAL, *his son, a photographer*
GINA EKDAL, *Hjalmar's wife*
HEDVIG, *their daughter, fourteen years old*
MRS. SØRBY, *Werle's housekeeper*
RELLING, *a physician*

MOLVIK, *a former student of theology*
GRÅBERG, *a bookkeeper in Werle's office*
PETTERSEN, *Werle's servant*
JENSEN, *a hired waiter*
A FLABBY GENTLEMAN
A THIN-HAIRED GENTLEMAN
A NEARSIGHTED GENTLEMAN
SIX OTHER GENTLEMEN, *Werle's dinner guests*
OTHER HIRED WAITERS

SCENE *The first act takes place at* WERLE'S; *the other four, in* HJALMAR EKDAL'S *studio.*

ACT ONE

(*An expensive-looking and comfortable study in* WERLE'S *house; bookcases and upholstered furniture; in the middle of the room a desk with papers and ledgers; lamps with green shades give the room a soft, subdued light. In the rear, open double doors with portieres pulled apart reveal a large, elegant drawing room, brightly illuminated by lamps and candles. Front right, a small door to the office wing. Front left, a fireplace with glowing coals in it. Farther back on the left wall, double doors to the dining room.*

PETTERSEN, WERLE'S *servant, in livery, and the hired waiter* JENSEN, *in black, are setting the study in order for the guests. In the drawing room, two or three other hired waiters are lighting candles, moving chairs, etc. Sounds of conversation and laughter of many people come from the dining room. Someone signals he wishes to make a speech by touching his glass with his knife. Silence follows, a short speech is made, there are noises of approval, then again conversation*)

PETTERSEN (*lights a lamp by the fireplace and puts a shade on it*) Just listen to that, Jensen. There's the old man now, proposing a long toast to Mrs. Sørby.

JENSEN (*moving an armchair*) Do you think it's true what people say, that the two of 'em—y'know—?

PETTERSEN Couldn't say.

JENSEN I bet he used to be quite a goat in the old days.

PETTERSEN Maybe so.

JENSEN They say this dinner is for his son.

PETTERSEN That's right. He came home yesterday.

JENSEN It's the first I've heard Werle has a son.

PETTERSEN He has a son, all right. But he's up at the works at Høydal all the time. He hasn't been home as long as I've been here.

A HIRED WAITER (*in the drawing room doorway*) Pst, Pettersen, there's an old fellow here, says he—

The Wild Duck by Henrik Ibsen, translated by Otto Reinert. Copyright © 1961, 1962, by Little, Brown and Company, Inc. Reprinted by permission of the publishers.

PETTERSEN (*under his breath*) Dammit! Can't have anybody in here now!

(OLD EKDAL *appears from the right in the drawing room. He is dressed in a shabby old coat with a high collar. Wool mittens. He carries a walking stick and a fur cap in his hand. Under his arm a parcel in thick paper. Dirty, reddish brown wig. Small, gray mustache*)

PETTERSEN (*going towards him*) Good Lord! What are *you* doing here?

EKDAL (*in the doorway*) Got to get into the office, Pettersen.

PETTERSEN The office closed an hour ago, and—

EKDAL They told me that downstairs. But Gråberg is still in there. Be a good boy, Pettersen; let me in this way. (*points to the small office door*) Been through here before.

PETTERSEN Oh well, all right. (*opens the door*) But see you go out the other way. We're having guests tonight.

EKDAL I know, I know—h'm! Thanks a lot, Pettersen, old boy. Good old friend. Thanks. (*mutters*) Ass!

(*He enters the office.* PETTERSEN *closes the door behind him*)

JENSEN Is he one of them office people, too?

PETTERSEN Oh no. He just does some extra copying for them, when they need it. But he's been a fine enough fellow in his day, old Ekdal has.

JENSEN You know, he sort of looked like that.

PETTERSEN Oh yes. He used to be a lieutenant!

JENSEN I'll be damned! a lieutenant!

PETTERSEN Yessir: Then he got mixed up in some forest deal or something. They say he pretty near ruined Werle once. The two of 'em were partners—owned the Høydal works together. Oh yes, Ekdal and I are good friends. We've had many a drink together at Madam Eriksen's place, we have.

JENSEN Didn't look to me like he'd have much to buy people drinks with.

PETTERSEN Good Lord, Jensen. It's my treat, of course. I always say one should be nice to people who've seen better days.

JENSEN So he went bankrupt?

PETTERSEN Worse than that. He went to prison.

JENSEN Prison!

PETTERSEN Or something.—(*listens*) Shhh. They are getting up from the table.

(*Servants open the doors to the dining room.*

MRS. SØRBY *appears, in conversation with a couple of the dinner guests. The rest of the company follows in small groups.* WERLE *is among them. The last to appear are* HJALMAR EKDAL *and* GREGERS WERLE)

MRS. SØRBY (*to the servant, in passing*) Pettersen, tell them to serve the coffee in the music room, will you?

PETTERSEN Very well, Mrs. Sørby.

(*She and the two guests go into the drawing room and disappear, right.* PETTERSEN *and* JENSEN *follow them out*)

A FLABBY GENTLEMAN (*to* A THIN-HAIRED *one*) Phew! That dinner—it was almost too much for me.

THE THIN-HAIRED GENTLEMAN Oh, I don't know. With a little bit of good will, it's amazing what one can accomplish in three hours.

THE FLABBY GENTLEMAN Yes, but afterwards, afterwards, my dear Chamberlain!

A THIRD GENTLEMAN I am told the coffee and liqueurs will be served in the music room.

THE FLABBY GENTLEMAN Wonderful! Then maybe Mrs. Sørby will play something for us.

THE THIN-HAIRED GENTLEMAN (*in a low voice*) If only she doesn't play us a different tune one of these days.

THE FLABBY GENTLEMAN Don't worry. Bertha isn't one to let old friends down.

(*They laugh and enter the drawing room*)

WERLE (*in a low and troubled voice*) I don't think anybody noticed, Gregers.

GREGERS (*looks at him*) Noticed what?

WERLE You didn't either?

GREGERS What?

WERLE We were thirteen at the table.

GREGERS Really? Were we thirteen?

WERLE (*with a glance at* HJALMAR EKDAL) Usually we are only twelve. (*to the other guests*) Gentlemen!

(*He and the remaining guests, except* HJALMAR *and* GREGERS, *leave through the drawing room, rear right*)

HJALMAR (*who has overheard the conversation*) You shouldn't have invited me, Gregers.

GREGERS Nonsense! This is supposed to be a party for *me*. Shouldn't I invite my one and only friend?

HJALMAR But I don't think your father approves. I never come to this house.

GREGERS So I hear. But I wanted to see you and talk to you.—Well, well, we two old school mates have certainly drifted apart. It must be sixteen—seventeen years since we saw each other.

HJALMAR Is it really that long?

GREGERS   It is indeed. And how are you? You look fine. You're almost stout.

HJALMAR   Stout is hardly the word, but I suppose I look a little more manly than I used to.

GREGERS   Yes, you do. Your appearance hasn't suffered any all these years.

HJALMAR   (*gloomily*)   But the inner man—! Believe me, that's a different story. You know, of course, how utterly everything has collapsed for me and mine since we last met.

GREGERS   (*in a lower voice*)   How is your father these days?

HJALMAR   I'd just as soon not talk about him. My poor, unfortunate father lives with me, of course. He has no one else in the whole world to turn to. But it is so terribly difficult for me to talk about these things. Tell me rather how you have been—up there at the works.

GREGERS   Lonely—blissfully lonely. I've had all the time in the world to think over all sorts of things.—Here. Let's make ourselves comfortable.

(*He sits down in an armchair near the fireplace and gets* HJALMAR *to take another chair beside him*)

HJALMAR   (*softly*)   All the same, I do want to thank you, Gregers, for inviting me to your father's table. It proves to me you no longer bear me a grudge.

GREGERS   (*surprised*)   Grudge? What makes you think I ever did?

HJALMAR   You did at first, you know.

GREGERS   When?

HJALMAR   Right after the tragedy. Of course, that was only natural. After all, your own father only escaped by the skin of his teeth. Oh, that terrible old business!

GREGERS   And so I bore you a grudge? Who told you that?

HJALMAR   I know you did, Gregers. Your father said so himself.

GREGERS   (*startled*)   Father! Really? H'm. So that's why you've never written—not a single word.

HJALMAR   Yes.

GREGERS   Not even when you decided to become a photographer?

HJALMAR   Your father thought it would be better if I didn't write about anything at all.

GREGERS   (*looking straight ahead*)   Oh well, maybe he was right, at that.—But tell me, Hjalmar—do you feel you have adjusted pretty well to your situation?

HJALMAR   (*with a small sigh*)   Oh yes, I think I have. Can't say I haven't, anyway. At first, of course, things seemed very strange. My circumstances were so completely different. But then, everything had changed. Father's great, ruinous tragedy—The shame—The disgrace— ·

GREGERS   (*feelingly*)   Yes, yes. I see.

HJALMAR   Of course there was no way in which I could pursue my studies. There wasn't a penny left. Rather the opposite; there was debt. Mainly to your father, I think.

GREGERS   H'm—

HJALMAR   Well—then I thought it best to take the bull by the horns and make a clean break with the past—you know, all at once. Your father thought so, too, and since he had been so helpful, and—

GREGERS   Father helped you?

HJALMAR   Yes, surely you know that? Where do you think I got the money to learn photography and to set up my own studio? Things like that are expensive, I can tell you.

GREGERS   And father paid for all that?

HJALMAR   Yes, didn't you know? I understood him to say he had written to you about it.

GREGERS   Not a word that it was *he*. He must have forgotten. We only write business letters. So it was father—!

HJALMAR   It certainly was. But he has never wanted people to know that. It was he who made it possible for me to get married, too. Or maybe—maybe you didn't know that, either?

GREGERS   No! How could I? (*shakes* HJALMAR's *arm*)   My dear Hjalmar, I can't tell you how happy all this makes me—and pains me, too. Perhaps I have been unfair to father. In some respects, anyway. For this shows he has a heart, you know. A kind of conscience—

HJALMAR   Conscience?

GREGERS   Or whatever you want to call it. No, really, I can't tell you how glad I am to hear this about father.—So you are married, Hjalmar. That's more than I ever will be. I trust you find yourself happy as a married man?

HJALMAR   Yes, I certainly do. She is as good and competent a wife as any man could ask for. And she is by no means without culture.

GREGERS   (*a little taken aback*)   No, of course not.

HJALMAR   Life itself is an education, you see. Being with me every day—And then there are a couple of remarkable men we see quite a lot of. I assure you, you'd hardly recognize Gina.

GREGERS   Gina?

HJALMAR   Yes. Surely you remember her name was Gina?

GREGERS   Whose name? I haven't the slightest idea—

HJALMAR   But don't you remember she was here in the house for a while?

GREGERS (*looks at him*) Is it Gina Hansen—?

HJALMAR Of course it is Gina Hansen.

GREGERS —who kept house for us the last year of mother's illness?

HJALMAR That's it. But my dear friend, I know for a fact that your father wrote you about my marriage.

GREGERS (*who has risen*) Yes, so he did, that's true, but not that—(*paces the floor*) Wait a minute—Yes, he did—now when I think back. But father always writes such short letters. (*sits down on the arm of the chair*) Listen, Hjalmar—this interests me—how did you make Gina's acquaintance—your wife, I mean?

HJALMAR Quite simply. You remember she didn't stay here very long. Everything was so unsettled during your mother's illness. Gina couldn't take that, so she gave notice and moved out. That was the year before your mother died. Or maybe it was the same year.

GREGERS It was the same year. I was up at Høydal at the time. Then what happened?

HJALMAR Well, Gina moved in with her mother, Madam Hansen, an excellent, hard-working woman, who ran a small eating place. And she had a room for rent, too. A nice, comfortable room.

GREGERS Which you were lucky enough to get?

HJALMAR Yes. Through your father, in fact. And it was there I really learned to know Gina.

GREGERS And then you got engaged?

HJALMAR Yes. It's easy for young people to fall in love, you know. H'm—

GREGERS (*gets up, walks up and down*) Tell me—after you'd become engaged, was that when father—I mean, was that when you took up photography?

HJALMAR That's right. Naturally, I wanted to get married and have a place of my own, the sooner the better. And both your father and I agreed that photography was the best thing I could get into. Gina thought so, too. Oh yes, that was another reason. It so happened that Gina had learned how to retouch.

GREGERS What a wonderful coincidence.

HJALMAR (*smiling contentedly*) Yes, wasn't it? Don't you think it worked out very well?

GREGERS Remarkably well, I should say. So father has really been a kind of Providence for you, Hjalmar; hasn't he?

HJALMAR (*moved*) He did not abandon his old friend's son in his days of need. That's one thing about your father: he does have a heart.

MRS. SØRBY (*enters on* WERLE'S *arm*) I don't want to hear another word, my dear sir.

You are not to stay in there staring at all those bright lights. It isn't good for you.

WERLE (*letting go of her arm and moving his hand across his eyes*) I almost think you are right.

(PETTERSEN *and* JENSEN *enter carrying trays with glasses of punch*)

MRS. SØRBY (*to the guests in the drawing room*) Gentlemen, if you want a glass of punch, you'll have to take the trouble to come in here.

THE FLABBY GENTLEMAN (*to* MRS. SØRBY) Dear Mrs. Sørby, please tell me it isn't so. You have not withdrawn your cherished permission to smoke?

MRS. SØRBY Yes, Chamberlain. No smoking here in Mr. Werle's own sanctum.

THE THIN-HAIRED GENTLEMAN And when did you append these harsh paragraphs to the tobacco regulations, Mrs. Sørby?

MRS. SØRBY After the last dinner, Chamberlain, when certain persons abused their liberties.

THE THIN-HAIRED GENTLEMAN And will not even the smallest infraction be tolerated, Mrs. Sørby? Really none at all?

MRS. SØRBY None whatsoever, Chamberlain.

(*Most of the guests are gathered in the study. The servants are serving punch*)

WERLE (*to* HJALMAR, *over by a table*) Well, Ekdal, what is that you are looking at?

HJALMAR Oh, just an album, sir.

THE THIN-HAIRED GENTLEMAN (*moving about*) Ah yes! Photographs! That's your line, of course.

THE FLABBY GENTLEMAN (*seated*) Haven't you brought some of your own along?

HJALMAR No, I haven't.

THE FLABBY GENTLEMAN Too bad. Looking at pictures is good for the digestion, you know.

THE THIN-HAIRED GENTLEMAN And then it would have contributed a mite to the general entertainment.

A NEARSIGHTED GENTLEMAN And all contributions are gratefully received.

MRS. SØRBY The chamberlains think that when one has been invited to dinner, one ought to work for one's food, Mr. Ekdal.

THE FLABBY GENTLEMAN With a cuisine like this that's only a pleasure.

THE THIN-HAIRED GENTLEMAN Oh well, if it's a question of the struggle for existence—

MRS. SØRBY You are so right!

(*They continue their conversation, laughing and joking*)

GREGERS (*in a low voice*) You must join in, Hjalmar.

HJALMAR (*with a twist of his body*) What am I to say?

THE FLABBY GENTLEMAN Don't you believe, sir, that Tokay may be considered relatively beneficial to the stomach?

WERLE (*by the fireplace*) I'll guarantee the Tokay you were served tonight, at any rate. It is one of the very best years. I am sure you noticed that yourself.

THE FLABBY GENTLEMAN Yes, it really was unusually delicate-tasting.

HJALMAR (*hesitantly*) Do the years differ?

THE FLABBY GENTLEMAN (*laughs*) Ah, Mr. Ekdal! Splendid!

WERLE (*with a smile*) I see it is hardly worth while to serve you fine wine.

THE THIN-HAIRED GENTLEMAN Tokay is like photographs, Mr. Ekdal. Both need sunshine. Or isn't that so?

HJALMAR Yes, sunshine has something to do with it.

MRS. SØRBY Just the same with chamberlains. They need sunshine, too—royal sunshine, as the saying goes.

THE THIN-HAIRED GENTLEMAN Ouch! That's a tired old joke, Mrs. Sørby.

THE NEARSIGHTED GENTLEMAN The lady will have her fun—

THE FLABBY GENTLEMAN —and at our expense. (*wagging his finger*) Madam Bertha! Madam Bertha!

MRS. SØRBY But it is true that vintages differ widely sometimes. The older the better.

THE NEARSIGHTED GENTLEMAN Do you count me among the older vintages?

MRS. SØRBY Far from it.

THE THIN-HAIRED GENTLEMAN Well, well! But what about me, Mrs. Sørby?

THE FLABBY GENTLEMAN And me? What vintages do we belong to?

MRS. SØRBY I reckon you among the sweet vintages, gentlemen.

(*She sips a glass of punch. The chamberlains laugh and flirt with her*)

WERLE Mrs. Sørby always finds a way out —when she wants to. But gentlemen, you aren't drinking! Pettersen, please see to that—! Gregers, lets have a glass together. (GREGERS *does not move*) Won't you join us, Ekdal? I had no opportunity at the table—

(GRÅBERG *comes in through the office door*)

GRÅBERG Beg your pardon, Mr. Werle, but I can't get out.

WERLE They've locked you in again, eh?

GRÅBERG Yes, they have, sir. And Flakstad has left with the keys.

WERLE That's all right. You just come through here.

GRÅBERG But there is somebody else—

WERLE Doesn't matter. Come on, both of you.

(GRÅBERG *and* OLD EKDAL *enter from the office*)

WERLE (*involuntarily*) Damn!

(*Laughter and talk among the guests cease.* HJALMAR *gives a start when he sees his father, puts down his glass, and turns away toward the fireplace*)

EKDAL (*does not look up but makes quick little bows to both sides, as he mutters*) Beg pardon. Came the wrong way. Gate's locked. Gate's locked. Beg pardon. (*He and* GRÅBERG *go out, rear right*)

WERLE (*between his teeth*) That idiot Gråberg!

GREGERS (*staring, his mouth hanging open, to* HJALMAR) Don't tell me that was—!

THE FLABBY GENTLEMAN What is it? Who was that?

GREGERS Nothing. Just the bookkeeper and somebody else.

THE NEARSIGHTED GENTLEMAN (*to* HJALMAR) Did *you* know that man?

HJALMAR I don't know—I didn't notice—

THE FLABBY GENTLEMAN (*getting up*) What the devil has gotten into everybody? (*He walks over to some other guests, who are talking in low voices*)

MRS. SØRBY (*whispers to the servant*) Give him something from the kitchen to take home. Something good.

PETTERSEN (*nods his head*) I'll do that, ma'am. (*goes out*)

GREGERS (*shocked, in a low voice to* HJALMAR) Then it really was he?

HJALMAR Yes.

GREGERS And you stood there and denied him!

HJALMAR (*in a fierce whisper*) But how could I—?

GREGERS —acknowledge your own father?

HJALMAR (*pained*) Oh, if you had been in my place, maybe—

(*The low conversation among the guests changes to forced gaiety*)

THE THIN-HAIRED GENTLEMAN (*approaching* HJALMAR *and* GREGERS, *in a friendly mood*) Aha! Reminiscing about university days, gentlemen?—Don't you smoke, Mr. Ekdal? Can I give you a light? Oh that's right. We are not allowed—

HJALMAR Thanks, I don't smoke.

THE FLABBY GENTLEMAN Don't you have a nice little poem you could recite for us, Mr. Ekdal? You used to do that so beautifully.

HJALMAR I am sorry. I don't remember any.

THE FLABBY GENTLEMAN That's a shame. Well, in that case, Balle, what do we do?

(*They both walk into the drawing room*)

HJALMAR (*gloomily*) Gregers—I am leaving! You see, when a man has felt Fate's crushing blow—Say goodbye to your father for me.

GREGERS Yes, of course. Are you going straight home?

HJALMAR Yes. Why?

GREGERS I thought I might come up and see you a little later.

HJALMAR No, don't do that. Not to my home. My home is a gloomy one, Gregers, particularly after a brilliant banquet such as this. We can meet somewhere in town.

MRS. SØRBY (*has come up to them; in a low voice*) Are you leaving, Ekdal?

HJALMAR Yes.

MRS. SØRBY Say hello to Gina.

HJALMAR Thank you. I'll do that.

MRS. SØRBY Tell her I'll be up to see her one of these days.

HJALMAR Fine. (*to* GREGERS) You stay here. I'll slip out without anybody noticing.

(*drifts off. A little later he goes into the drawing room and out right*)

MRS. SØRBY (*in a low voice to the servant who has returned*) Well, did you give the old man something?

PETTERSEN Oh yes. A bottle of brandy.

MRS. SØRBY Oh dear. Couldn't you have found something better?

PETTERSEN But Mrs. Sørby, there's nothing he likes better than brandy.

THE FLABBY GENTLEMAN (*in the doorway to the drawing room, with a sheet of music in his hand*) Will you play a duet, Mrs. Sørby?

MRS. SØRBY Yes, gladly.

THE GUESTS Good! Good!

(*She and all the guests go out rear right.* GREGERS *remains standing by the fireplace.* WERLE *is looking for something on the desk and appears to wish to be left alone. Since* GREGERS *does not leave,* WERLE *walks towards the drawing room door*)

GREGERS Father, do you have a moment?

WERLE (*stops*) What is it?

GREGERS I'd like a word with you.

WERLE Couldn't it wait till we're alone?

GREGERS No, it can't, for maybe we'll never be alone again.

WERLE (*coming closer*) What does that mean?

(*During the following scene, the sound of a piano is faintly heard from the music room*)

GREGERS How is it that that family has been allowed to go to ruin so miserably?

WERLE I suppose you refer to the Ekdals?

GREGERS Yes, I do mean the Ekdals. Lieutenant Ekdal was once your close friend.

WERLE Yes, unfortunately. Too close. I have felt that keenly enough for many years. It was his fault that my good name and reputation, too, were—somewhat tarnished.

GREGERS (*in a low voice*) Was he the only one who was guilty?

WERLE Who else, do you mean?

GREGERS The two of you were together on that big purchase of forest land, weren't you?

WERLE But it was Ekdal who surveyed the area—surveyed it fraudulently. It was he who felled all that timber on state property. He was responsible for everything that went on up there. I didn't know what he was doing.

GREGERS I doubt that Lieutenant Ekdal himself knew what he was doing.

WERLE That may well be. The fact remains that he was convicted and I was not.

GREGERS Yes, I know there were no proofs.

WERLE Acquittal is acquittal. Why do you want to bring back that miserable old business that gave me gray hairs before my time? Is that what has been on your mind all these years up there? I can assure you, Gregers, here in town that whole story has been forgotten long ago, as far as I am concerned.

GREGERS But what about that unfortunate family?

WERLE Well, now, exactly what do you want me to do for those people? When Ekdal got out, he was a broken man, beyond help altogether. Some people go to the bottom as soon as they've got some buckshot in them and never come up again. Believe me, Gregers, I've done all I possibly could do, if I didn't want to put myself in a false light and give people occasion for all sorts of talk and suspicion—

GREGERS Suspicion? I see.

WERLE I have given Ekdal copying work to do for the office, and I pay him far, far more than he is worth.

GREGERS (*without looking at him*) H'm. I don't doubt that.

WERLE You are laughing? Don't you think I am telling you the truth? Oh, to be sure, you won't find it in my books. I never enter expenses like that.

GREGERS (*with a cold smile*) No, I suppose there are certain expenses that are better not entered.

WERLE (*puzzled*) What do you mean?

GREGERS (*being brave*) Have you entered what it cost you to let Hjalmar Ekdal learn photography?

WERLE I? What do you mean—entered?

GREGERS I know now it was you who paid for it. And I also know it was you who set him up in business—quite comfortably, too.

WERLE All right! And you still say I have done nothing for the Ekdals! I assure you, Gregers, those people have cost me a pretty penny!

GREGERS Have you entered those expenses?

WERLE Why do you ask?

GREGERS I have my reasons. Listen—at the time you were providing so kindly for your old friend's son, wasn't that just when he was getting married?

WERLE Damn it, Gregers! How can I remember—! After so many years—!

GREGERS You wrote me a letter at the time. A business letter, of course. And in a postscript you mentioned very briefly that Hjalmar Ekdal had married one Miss Hansen.

WERLE That's right. That was her name.

GREGERS But you did not say anything about Miss Hansen being Gina Hansen, our ex-housekeeper.

WERLE (*with scornful but forced laughter*) No, to tell the truth, it didn't occur to me that you were particularly interested in our ex-housekeeper.

GREGERS I wasn't. But—(*lowers his voice*) somebody else in this house was.

WERLE What do you mean? (*flaring up*) Don't tell me you're referring to me!

GREGERS (*in a low but firm voice*) Yes, I am referring to you.

WERLE And you dare—! You have the audacity—! How can that ingrate, that—that photographer fellow—how dare he make accusations like that!

GREGERS Hjalmar hasn't said a word. I don't think he has the faintest suspicion of anything like this.

WERLE Then where do you get it from? Who could have said a thing like that?

GREGERS My poor, unfortunate mother. The last time I saw her.

WERLE Your mother! I might have thought so! You and she—you always stood together. It was she who first turned you against me.

GREGERS No, it was all she had to go through, till things became too much for her and she died in sheer misery.

WERLE Oh, nonsense! She didn't have to go through anything! No more than what others have had to, anyway. There's just no way of getting on with morbid, hysterical people—that's something *I* have had to learn! And here you are, with a suspicion like that—dabbling in old rumors and gossip against your own father. Listen here, Gregers. It really seems to me that at your age you might find something more useful to do.

GREGERS Yes, it is about time.

WERLE Then maybe your mind would be more at ease than it seems to be now. What is the point of working away, year in and year out, as just an ordinary clerk up there at Høydal, with not so much as a penny beyond regular wages? It's plain silly!

GREGERS I wish I could believe that.

WERLE Not that I don't understand, mind you. You want to be independent, don't want to be obliged to me for anything. But right now there is a chance for you to become independent, to be on your own in everything.

GREGERS Oh? How so?

WERLE When I wrote you that I needed you here in town right away—h'm—

GREGERS Yes, what is it you want of me? I've been waiting to hear all day.

WERLE I am offering you a partnership in the firm.

GREGERS I! In your firm? As a partner?

WERLE Yes. That doesn't mean we have to be together all the time. You could take over the business here in town and I could go up to Høydal.

GREGERS You would want to do that?

WERLE Well, you see, Gregers. I can't work as well as I used to. I'll have to save my eyes. They are getting weaker.

GREGERS You have always had weak eyes.

WERLE Not as bad as now. Besides—there are other things, too, that may make it advisable for me to live up there—for a while, anyway.

GREGERS Nothing like this has ever even occurred to me.

WERLE Look here, Gregers. I know there are many things that stand between us. But after all, we are father and son. It seems to me we ought to be able to come to some sort of understanding.

GREGERS For appearance's sake, I suppose you mean.

WERLE Well, that would be something, anyway. Think it over, Gregers. Wouldn't that be possible? What do you say?

GREGERS (*looks at him coldly*) There is something behind this.

WERLE   I don't understand.

GREGERS   You want to use me for something.

WERLE   In a relationship as close as ours I suppose one person can always be of use to the other.

GREGERS   Yes. So they say.

WERLE   I want to have you at home with me for a while. I am a lonely man, Gregers. I have always been lonely, but mostly now, when I am getting older. I need somebody around me.

GREGERS   You have Mrs. Sørby.

WERLE   So I do, and she has become almost indispensable to me. She is bright, she has an even temper, she brings life into the house—and I badly need that.

GREGERS   Well, then, everything is just as you want it.

WERLE   Yes, but I am afraid it won't last. A woman in her circumstances can easily have her position misconstrued in the eyes of the world. I'll almost go so far as to say it does a man no good either.

GREGERS   Oh, I don't know. When a man gives the kind of dinner parties you do he can take quite a few liberties.

WERLE   Yes, but what about *her*, Gregers? I am afraid she will not put up with it much longer. And even if she did, even if she ignored what people are saying and all that sort of thing, out of devotion to me—Do you really think, Gregers, you with your strong sense of justice, do you feel it would be—

GREGERS   (*interrupting*)   Just tell me this: are you going to marry her?

WERLE   What if I did? What then?

GREGERS   That's what I am asking. What then?

WERLE   Would it displease you very much?

GREGERS   No, not at all.

WERLE   Well, you see, I didn't know—I thought perhaps out of regard for your mother—

GREGERS   I am not given to melodramatics.

WERLE   Well, whether you are or not, you have lifted a stone from my heart. I can't tell you how pleased I am that I can count on your support in this matter.

GREGERS   (*looks intently at him*)   Now I see what you want to use me for.

WERLE   Use you for? What an expression!

GREGERS   Let's not be particular in our choice of words—not as long as we're by ourselves, at any rate. (*laughs*) So that's it. That's why I had to come to town at all costs. Because of Mrs. Sørby, there are arrangements being made for family life in this house. Touch-

ing scene between father and son! That would indeed be something new!

WERLE   I won't have you use that tone!

GREGERS   When were we ever a family here? Never in my memory. But now, of course, there is need for a display of domestic affection. It will look very well to have the son hastening home on wings of filial feeling to attend the aging father's marriage feast. What happens then to all the talk of what the poor, deceased mother had to suffer? It evaporates. Her son takes care of that.

WERLE   Gregers, I don't believe there is anyone you detest as much as me.

GREGERS   (*in a low voice*)   I have seen too much of you.

WERLE   You've seen me with your mother's eyes. (*lowers his voice a little*) But don't forget that those eyes were—clouded at times.

GREGERS   (*his voice trembles*)   I know what you have in mind. But who's to blame for mother's tragic weakness? You and all those—! The last one was that female you palmed off on Hjalmar Ekdal, when you yourself no longer—!

WERLE   (*shrugs his shoulders*)   Word for word as if I were hearing your mother.

GREGERS   (*paying no attention*)   —and there he is now, with his great, trusting child's soul in the middle of all this deceit—sharing his roof with a woman like that, unaware that what he calls his home is based on a lie! (*steps closer to* WERLE) When I look back upon all you have done, I seem to see a battlefield strewn with mangled human destinies.

WERLE   I almost think the gap between us is too wide.

GREGERS   (*with a formal bow*)   So I have observed. That is why I take my hat and leave.

WERLE   You're leaving? The house?

GREGERS   Yes. For now at last I see a mission to live for.

WERLE   What mission is that?

GREGERS   You'd only laugh if I told you.

WERLE   A lonely man doesn't laugh so easily, Gregers.

GREGERS   (*pointing to the rear*)   Look, father. The chamberlains are playing blind-man's buff with Mrs. Sørby.—Goodnight and good-bye.

(*He goes out rear right. The sound of people talking, laughing, and playing games can be heard from the drawing room, where the guests are now coming into view*)

WERLE   (*mutters scornfully*)   Hah—! The fool! And he says he is not melodramatic!

ACT TWO

(HJALMAR EKDAL's *studio, a large attic room. To the right, a slanting roof with skylights, half covered by blue cloth. The entrance door from the hallway is in the far right corner; the door to the living room farther forward on the same wall. There are two doors to the left, as well, with an iron stove between them. In the rear, wide, sliding, double doors. The studio is unpretentious but cozy. Between the two doors on the right and a little out from the wall is a sofa with a table and some chairs in front of it. On the table is a lighted lamp with a shade. Near the wall by the stove is an old armchair. Various pieces of photographic equipment here and there in the room. In the rear, to the left of the sliding doors, a shelf with a few books, bottles with chemical solutions, tools, and some other objects. Photographs, brushes, paper, etc., are lying on the table.*

GINA EKDAL *sits by the table, sewing.* HEDVIG *sits on the sofa, reading, her hands shading her eyes, her thumbs in her ears*)

GINA (*glances at* HEDVIG *a few times, as if secretly anxious*) Hedvig!

HEDVIG (*does not hear*)

GINA (*louder*) Hedvig!

HEDVIG (*takes away her hands and looks up*) Yes, mother?

GINA Hedvig, be a good girl. Don't read any more tonight.

HEDVIG Please, mother, just a little bit longer? Can't I?

GINA No. I want you to put that book away. Your father doesn't like you to read so much. He never reads at night.

HEDVIG (*closing her book*) Well, father doesn't care much for reading, anyway.

GINA (*puts her sewing aside and picks up a pencil and a small notebook from the table*) Do you remember how much we spent for the butter today?

HEDVIG One crown and sixty-five øre.

GINA That's right. (*writes it down*) We're using an awful lot of butter in this family. Then there was the sausage and the cheese—let me see—(*writing*)—and the ham—(*mumbles figures while adding up*) Goodness! It does add up—

HEDVIG And the beer.

GINA Right. (*writes*) It gets terrible expensive, but it can't be helped.

HEDVIG And you and I didn't need anything hot for supper since father was out.

GINA No, that's right. That helps some. And I did get eight crowns and fifty øre for the pictures.

HEDVIG Was it that much?

GINA Eight-fifty, exactly.

(*Silence.* GINA *picks up her sewing.* HEDVIG *takes paper and pencil and starts drawing, her left hand shading her eyes*)

HEDVIG Isn't it nice to think that father is at that big dinner party at Mr. Werle's?

GINA Can't rightly say he's *his* guest. It was the son who invited him. (*after a pause*) We have nothing to do with the old man.

HEDVIG I can't wait till father comes home. He promised to ask Mrs. Sørby if he could take home something good for me.

GINA Why yes, you can be sure there are plenty of good things in *that* house.

HEDVIG (*still drawing*) Besides, I think I am a little bit hungry, too.

(OLD EKDAL *enters right rear, the brown paper parcel under his arm, another parcel in his coat pocket*)

GINA So late you are today, Grandpa.

EKDAL They'd locked the office. Had to wait for Gråberg. And then I had to go through—h'm—

HEDVIG Did they give you any more copying to do, Grandpa?

EKDAL This whole parcel. Look.

GINA That's nice.

HEDVIG And you've got another one in your pocket.

EKDAL What? Oh never mind. That's nothing. (*puts his walking stick away in the corner*) This will keep me busy a long time, Gina. (*slides one of the double doors half open*) Shhh! (*peeks into the attic for a while, then he cautiously slides the door shut. Chuckling*) They're sound asleep the whole lot of 'em. And she herself's in the basket.

HEDVIG Are you sure she won't be cold in that basket, Grandpa?

EKDAL Cold? With all that straw? Don't you worry about *that*. (*goes towards the door left rear*) There are matches, aren't there?

GINA On the dresser.

(EKDAL *goes into his room*)

HEDVIG It's nice that he got all that new work to do.

GINA Yes, poor old thing. It will give him a little spending money.

HEDVIG And he won't be able to stay down at that awful Madam Eriksen's all morning.

GINA No; there's that, too.

HEDVIG Do you think they're still at the table?

GINA   Lord knows. Could be.

HEDVIG   Just think of all that delicious food. I'm sure he'll be in a good mood when he comes home. Don't you think so, mother?

GINA   Yes, but what if we could tell him we'd rented the room. Wouldn't that be nice?

HEDVIG   But we don't need that tonight.

GINA   Oh yes we do. We could always use the money. The room is no good to us as it is.

HEDVIG   No, I mean that father will be in a good mood tonight, anyway. It's better to have the room for some other time.

GINA   (*looking at her*)   You like it when you have something nice to tell father when he comes home nights, don't you?

HEDVIG   It makes things more pleasant.

GINA   (*reflectively*)   Yes, I guess you're right about that.

(OLD EKDAL *enters from his room, heads for the kitchen door, left front*)

GINA   (*turning half around in her chair*)   Do you need anything in the kitchen, Grandpa?

EKDAL   Yes. But don't you get up. (*goes out*)

GINA   I hope he isn't fooling around with the fire out there. (*after a while*) Hedvig, go out and see what he's doing.

(OLD EKDAL *enters with a pitcher of hot water*)

HEDVIG   Getting hot water, Grandpa?

EKDAL   That's right. Got some writing to do, but the ink's as thick as gruel. H'm—

GINA   But hadn't you better have supper first? It's all ready for you in your room.

EKDAL   Never mind supper, Gina. I tell you I'm busy. I don't want anybody coming in to me. Not anybody. H'm.

(*He goes into his room.* GINA *and* HEDVIG *look at each other*)

GINA   (*in a low voice*)   I can't think where he got the money from. Can you?

HEDVIG   From Gråberg, maybe.

GINA   No, it wouldn't be that. Gråberg always gives me the money.

HEDVIG   Maybe he got a bottle on credit.

GINA   Him! Who'd give him credit?

(HJALMAR EKDAL, *in overcoat and gray hat, enters right*)

GINA   (*throws down her sewing, gets up*) Heavens, Ekdal! Home already?

HEDVIG   (*getting up at the same time*) Father? So soon!

HJALMAR   (*lays down his hat*)   Most of them seemed to be leaving now.

HEDVIG   Already?

HJALMAR   Well, it was a dinner party, you know. (*takes his coat off*)

GINA   Let me help you.

HEDVIG   Me too. (*They help him off with his coat.* GINA *hangs it up in the rear*) Were there many there, father?

HJALMAR   Not too many. About twelve or fourteen at the table.

GINA   Did you get to talk to all of them?

HJALMAR   Oh yes, a little. Though Gregers kept me engaged most of the evening.

GINA   Is he as ugly as he used to be?

HJALMAR   Well—I suppose nobody would call him handsome. Is father back?

HEDVIG   Yes, he is in there writing.

HJALMAR   Did he say anything?

GINA   No. About what?

HJALMAR   He didn't mention—? I thought I heard he'd been with Gråberg. I think I'll go in to him for a moment.

GINA   No, you'd better not.

HJALMAR   Why not? Did he say he didn't want to see me?

GINA   He doesn't want to see anybody.

HEDVIG   (*making signs to her*)   Ahem!

GINA   (*doesn't notice*)   He's gotten himself some hot water.

HJALMAR   Ah! So he is—

GINA   Looks that way.

HJALMAR   Ah yes—my poor old white-haired father. Let him enjoy his little pleasures as best he can.

(OLD EKDAL, *a lighted pipe in his mouth, enters in an old smoking jacket*)

EKDAL   Home again? Thought it was you I heard talking.

HJALMAR   Yes. I just came back.

EKDAL   Guess you didn't see me, did you?

HJALMAR   No, but they told me you'd gone through, so I thought I'd catch up with you.

EKDAL   H'm. That's good of you, Hjalmar. Who were they—all those people?

HJALMAR   Oh—all sorts. Chamberlain Flor and Chamberlain Balle and Chamberlain Kaspersen and chamberlain this and that. I don't know—

EKDAL   (*nodding his head*)   Hear that, Gina? He's been with nothing but chamberlains all evening.

GINA   Yes, I hear as they've become quite fancy in that house now.

HEDVIG   Did the chamberlains sing, father? Or recite poetry?

HJALMAR   No. They just talked nonsense. They wanted *me* to recite, though, but I didn't want to.

EKDAL   They couldn't get you to, eh?

GINA   Seems to me you might have done that.

HJALMAR   No. I don't see any reason why one has to oblige every Tom, Dick, and Harry all the time. (*walks up and down*) At any rate, I won't.

EKDAL   No point in being too obliging, you know. That's Hjalmar for you.

HJALMAR   I don't see why *I* always have to be the one who provides entertainment on the rare occasions when I am out for dinner. Let the others exert themselves for a change. Those fellows go from one big meal to the next, stuffing themselves day in and day out. Let *them* do something for all the food they are getting!

GINA   You didn't tell them that though, did you?

HJALMAR   (*humming a little*)   Well, I don't know about that. They were told a thing or two.

EKDAL   The chamberlains?

HJALMAR   Mmm—(*casually*) Then we had a little controversy over Tokay wine.

EKDAL   Tokay, no less! Say, that's a fine wine!

HJALMAR   (*stops his walking*)   It *may* be a fine wine. But let me tell you: not all the vintages are equally fine. It depends on how much sunshine the grapes get.

GINA   If you don't know everything—!

EKDAL   And they quarreled with that?

HJALMAR   They tried to, but then it was pointed out to them that it was the same way with chamberlains. Not all vintages are equally fine among chamberlains, either—so they were told.

GINA   Goodness! What you don't think of!

EKDAL   Heh-heh! So they got that to put in their pipe.

HJALMAR   Right to their face. That's how they got it.

EKDAL   Gina, d'ye hear that? He gave it to them right to their face!

GINA   Right to their face! Imagine!

HJALMAR   Yes, but I don't want you to talk about it. One doesn't talk about such things. Of course, the whole thing was done in the friendliest possible way. They are all of them pleasant, easy-going people. Why should I hurt them? No!

EKDAL   Right to their face, though—

HEDVIG   (*ingratiatingly*)   It's so nice to see you all dressed up, father. You look very well in tails.

HJALMAR   Yes, don't you think so? And it really fits me perfectly. As if it were tailor-made. Possibly a trifle tight in the armpits, that's all. Help me, Hedvig. (*takes his dinner jacket off*) I'd rather wear my own coat. Where is it, Gina?

GINA   Here it is. (*helps him on with it*)

HJALMAR   There now! Be sure to have Molvik get his suit back first thing in the morning.

GINA   (*putting the clothes away*)   I'll take care of it.

HJALMAR   (*stretching*)   Aaahh. This feels cozier after all. And this kind of loose-fitting, casual wear is really more in keeping with my whole appearance; don't you think so, Hedvig?

HEDVIG   Oh yes, father!

HJALMAR   Especially when I tie my neck-cloth with loose, flying ends—like this? What do you think?

HEDVIG   Yes, it goes extremely well with your mustache. And with your curls, too.

HJALMAR   I'd hardly call my hair curly. Wavy, rather.

HEDVIG   Yes, for the curls are so large.

HJALMAR   Waves, really.

HEDVIG   (*after a moment, pulling his sleeve*) Father?

HJALMAR   What is it?

HEDVIG   Oh, you know very well what it is!

HJALMAR   I certainly don't.

HEDVIG   (*laughing and pleading*)   Oh come on, father! Don't tease me!

HJALMAR   But what is it?

HEDVIG   (*shaking him*)   Father! Give it to me! You know, you promised me. Something good to eat.

HJALMAR   Oh, dear! I completely forgot!

HEDVIG   You are teasing, father. Shame on you! Where is it?

HJALMAR   No, honest, I really did forget. But wait a moment. I have something else for you, Hedvig. (*goes and searches his coat pockets*)

HEDVIG   (*jumps up and down, clapping her hands*)   Oh mother, mother!

GINA   See what I mean? If you just give him time—

HJALMAR   (*with a piece of paper*)   Here it is.

HEDVIG   That? But that's just a piece of paper.

HJALMAR   It's the menu, Hedvig, the entire menu. Look here. It says "Menu." That means what you get to eat.

HEDVIG   Haven't you anything else for me?

HJALMAR   I tell you, I forgot all about it. But take my word for it: it's not such a great treat, all that rich food. You just sit down and read the menu, now, and I'll tell you later what the things taste like. Here you are Hedvig.

HEDVIG   (*swallowing her tears*)   Thank you.

(*She sits down but doesn't read.* GINA *signals to her.* HJALMAR *notices*)

HJALMAR (*pacing the floor*) It is really unbelievable all the things a father is supposed to keep in mind. And if he forgets the smallest item—! Long faces right away. Oh well. One gets used to that, too. (*stops by the stove where* OLD EKDAL *is sitting*) Have you looked at them tonight, father?

EKDAL I certainly have! She's in the basket!

HJALMAR No! Really? In the basket? She is getting used to it then, I guess.

EKDAL Didn't I tell you she would? But look, Hjalmar, there are still a few things—

HJALMAR —improvements, yes, I know.

EKDAL They've got to be done.

HJALMAR Right. Let's talk about it now, father. Come over here to the sofa.

EKDAL All right. H'm. Guess I want to fill my pipe first, though. Need to clean it, too— h'm—(*goes into his room*)

GINA (*with a smile, to* HJALMAR) Cleaning his pipe—

HJALMAR Oh well, Gina—let him. The poor shipwrecked old man.—About those improvements—We'd better get to them tomorrow.

GINA You won't have time tomorrow, Ekdal.

HEDVIG (*interrupting*) Oh, yes, mother.

GINA For remember those prints you were going to retouch? They came for 'em again today.

HJALMAR I see. It's those prints again, is it? Well, they'll get done. You can be sure of that. Perhaps there are some new orders come in, too?

GINA Not a thing, worse luck. Tomorrow I've got only those two portraits I told you about.

HJALMAR Is that all? Well, If one doesn't exert oneself, what can you expect?

GINA But what can I do? I advertise in the papers all I can, seems to me.

HJALMAR The papers, the papers—you see yourself how far that gets us. I suppose there hasn't been anyone to look at the room, either?

GINA No, not yet.

HJALMAR Just as I thought. Well, no—if one doesn't *do* anything—One has to make a real effort, Gina!

HEDVIG (*going to him*) Shall I get your flute, father?

HJALMAR No, not the flute. *I* need no pleasures. (*paces up and down*) You'll see if I don't work tomorrow! You don't need to worry about *that!* You can be sure I shall work as long as my strength holds out—

GINA But Ekdal, dear—I didn't mean it that way.

HEDVIG How about a bottle of beer, father?

HJALMAR Not at all. I don't need anything—(*stops*) Beer? Did you say beer?

HEDVIG (*brightly*) Yes, father; lovely, cool beer.

HJALMAR Oh well—all right—since you insist, I suppose you may bring me a bottle.

GINA Yes, do that. That'll be nice and cozy.

(HEDVIG *runs towards the kitchen door*)

HJALMAR (*by the stove, stops her, looks at her, takes her by the head and presses her to him*) Hedvig! Hedvig!

HEDVIG (*happy, in tears*) Oh father! You are so sweet and good!

HJALMAR No, no, don't say that. There I was—seated at the rich man's table—gorging myself on his ample fare—and I couldn't even remember—

GINA (*seated by the table*) Nonsense, Ekdal.

HJALMAR It is not nonsense. But you must not reckon too strictly. You know I love you, regardless.

HEDVIG (*throwing her arms around him*) And we love you, father, so much, so much!

HJALMAR And if I am unreasonable at times, remember—God forgive me—remember I am a man beset by a host of sorrows. Well, well! (*drying his eyes*) No beer at such a moment. Give me my flute.

(HEDVIG *runs to the shelf and fetches it*)

HJALMAR Thank you. There now. With my flute in my hand and you two around me—ah!

(HEDVIG *sits down by the table next to* GINA. HJALMAR *walks back and forth, playing a Bohemian folk dance. He plays loudly but in slow tempo and with pronounced sentiment*)

HJALMAR (*interrupts his playing, gives his left hand to* GINA, *and says with strong emotion*) Our home may be mean and humble, Gina. But it is our home. And I say to you both: here dwells contentment!

(*He resumes his playing. Presently there is a knock on the door*)

GINA (*getting up*) Shh, Ekdal. I think somebody's coming.

HJALMAR (*putting the flute back on the shelf*) Yes, yes of course. Somebody would—

(GINA *goes to open the door*)

GREGERS WERLE (*out in the hall*) I beg your pardon—

GINA (*taking a step back*) Oh!

GREGERS —isn't this where Mr. Ekdal lives, the photographer?

GINA Yes, it is.

HJALMAR (*going to the door*)   Gregers! So you did come, after all. Come in.

GREGERS (*entering*)   I told you I wanted to see you.

HJALMAR   But tonight—? Have you left the party?

GREGERS   Both party and home. Good evening, Mrs. Ekdal. I don't know if you recognize me.

GINA   Oh yes. Young Mr. Werle isn't hard to recognize.

GREGERS   No, for I look like my mother, and you remember her, I am sure.

HJALMAR   You have left your home?

GREGERS   Yes. I have taken a room at a hotel.

HJALMAR   Really?—Well, since you're here, take off your coat and sit down.

GREGERS   Thanks. (*removes his overcoat. He has changed clothes and is now dressed in a plain, gray suit, of somewhat unfashionable cut*)

HJALMAR   Here on the sofa. Make yourself comfortable.

(GREGERS *sits down on the sofa,* HJALMAR *on a chair by the table*)

GREGERS (*looking around*)   So this is your residence, Hjalmar. This is where you live.

HJALMAR   This is the studio, as you can see.

GINA   It's roomier in here, so this is where we mostly keep ourselves.

HJALMAR   The apartment we had before was really nicer than this, but there is one big advantage here: we have plenty of space.

GINA   And we have a room across the hallway that we're renting out.

GREGERS (*to* HJALMAR)   You have lodgers, too?

HJALMAR   No, not yet. These things take time, you see. One has to be on the lookout. (*to* HEDVIG) What about that beer?

(HEDVIG *nods her head and goes out into the kitchen*)

GREGERS   So that's your daughter.

HJALMAR   Yes, that's Hedvig.

GREGERS   Your only child, isn't she?

HJALMAR   Our only one. Our greatest joy in the world, and (*lowers his voice*) our greatest sorrow, as well.

GREGERS   What are you saying!

HJALMAR   Yes, Gregers, for there is every probability that she'll lose her sight.

GREGERS   Becoming blind!

HJALMAR   Yes. So far, there are only early symptoms, and things may be well with her for some time yet. But the doctor has warned us. It is coming, irresistibly.

GREGERS   But this is nothing less than a tragedy! How do you account for it?

HJALMAR (*with a sigh*)   Heredity, most likely.

GREGERS (*struck*)   Heredity?

GINA   Ekdal's mother had weak eyes.

HJALMAR   That's what father says. I of course don't remember her.

GREGERS   Poor child. How does she take it?

HJALMAR   Oh, we can't bring ourselves to tell her—I'm sure you can understand that. She suspects nothing. Joyous and carefree, chirping like a little bird, she'll flutter into life's endless night. (*overcome by emotion*) Oh Gregers, this is such a terrible burden for me.

(HEDVIG *enters with a tray with beer and glasses. She puts it down on the table*)

HJALMAR (*stroking her hair*)   Thanks. Thank you, Hedvig.

HEDVIG (*puts her arms around his neck and whispers something in his ear*)

HJALMAR   No. No sandwiches now. (*looks off*) That is—unless Gregers wants some?

GREGERS (*with a gesture of refusal*)   No. No thanks.

HJALMAR (*still in a melancholic mood*)   Oh well, you might as well bring in some, all the same. A crust, if you have one. And plenty of butter, please.

GREGERS (*who has followed her with his eyes*)   Otherwise she seems healthy enough.

HJALMAR   Yes, thank God, there is nothing else wrong with her.

GREGERS   I think she is going to look like you, Mrs. Ekdal. How old is she?

GINA   Hedvig is just about fourteen. Her birthday is day after tomorrow.

GREGERS   Quite big for her age, isn't she?

GINA   Yes, she has grown a lot lately.

GREGERS   It's by the children we tell we're growing older ourselves. How long have you two been married now?

GINA   We've been married for—let's see— fifteen years, pretty near.

GREGERS   Just imagine! Has it really been that long?

GINA (*taking notice, looks at him*)   It certainly has.

HJALMAR   That's right. Fifteen years, less a few months. (*changing topic*) Those must have been long years for you up there at the works, Gregers.

GREGERS   They were long while they lasted. Now afterwards I hardly know where they went.

(OLD EKDAL *enters from his room, without his pipe, but with his old-fashioned lieutenant's cap on his head. His walk is a trifle unsteady*)

EKDAL   I'm ready for you now, Hjalmar. Let's talk about this—h'm—What was it again?

HJALMAR   (*going towards him*) Father, there's someone here. Gregers Werle. I don't know if you remember him?

EKDAL   (*looks at* GREGERS, *who has stood up*) Werle? That's the son, isn't it? What does he want from me?

HJALMAR   Nothing. He has come to see me.

EKDAL   Then there's nothing wrong?

HJALMAR   Of course not.

EKDAL   (*swinging one arm back and forth*) Not that I am scared, mind you, but—

GREGERS   (*goes up to him*)   I just wanted to bring you greetings from your old hunting grounds, Lieutenant Ekdal.

EKDAL   Hunting grounds?

GREGERS   Yes, the woods up around the Høydal works.

EKDAL   Oh yes, up there. Yes, I used to know that country quite well in the old days.

GREGERS   You were quite a hunter then, weren't you?

EKDAL   Could be. Maybe I was. You're looking at my get-up. I don't ask anybody's permission to wear it in the house. Just as long as I don't go outside—

(HEDVIG *brings a plate with open-faced sandwiches, which she puts down on the table*)

HJALMAR   You sit down, father, and have a glass of beer. Help yourself, Gregers.

(EKDAL *mutters something and shuffles over to the sofa.* GREGERS *sits down on a chair next to him;* HJALMAR *is on the other side of* GREGERS. GINA *sits some distance from the table, sewing.* HEDVIG *is standing by her father*)

GREGERS   Do you remember, Lieutenant Ekdal, when Hjalmar and I used to come up and visit you summers and Christmas?

EKDAL   You did? No; can't say as I do. But it's true I used to be a good hunter, if I do say so myself. I've killed bears, too. Nine of 'em.

GREGERS   (*looks at him with compassion*) And now your hunting days are over.

EKDAL   Oh—I wouldn't say that. I still go hunting once in a while. Well, yes, not in the old way, of course. For you see, the woods—the woods—the woods—! (*drinks*) Nice-looking woods up there now?

GREGERS   Not as in your time. They have cut a great deal.

EKDAL   Cut? (*in a lower voice and as if afraid*) That's risky business, that is. It has consequences. The woods are vengeful.

HJALMAR   (*filling his glass*) Here, father. Have some more.

GREGERS   How can a man like you—such an outdoors man as you used to be—how can you stand living here in the middle of a musty city, within four walls?

EKDAL   (*chuckles, glancing at* HJALMAR) Oh, it's not so bad here. Not bad at all.

GREGERS   But surely—all the things your soul grew used to up there—? The cool, invigorating breezes? The free life in woods and mountains, among beasts and birds—?

EKDAL   (*smiling*) Hjalmar, shall we show it to him?

HJALMAR   (*quickly, a little embarrassed*) Oh no, father. Not tonight.

GREGERS   What is it he wants to show me?

HJALMAR   Oh, it's just—something. You can see it some other time.

GREGERS   (*continues addressing* OLD EKDAL) You see, this is what I had in mind, Lieutenant. Why don't you come up to Høydal with me? I'll probably be going back shortly. I'm sure you could get some copying work to do up there as well. For down here you can't have a thing to cheer you up and keep you occupied.

EKDAL   (*looks at him in astonishment*) Don't I have—!

GREGERS   Yes, of course, you have Hjalmar. But then he has his own family. And a man like you, who have always loved the outdoors—

EKDAL   (*striking the table*) Hjalmar, he *shall* see it!

HJALMAR   But father, do you really think so? It's dark and—

EKDAL   Nonsense. There's a moon. (*getting up*) I say he's got to see it. Let me out. Come and help me, Hjalmar!

HEDVIG   Oh yes, father! Do!

HJALMAR   (*getting up*) Oh well, all right.

GREGERS   (*to* GINA) What is it?

GINA   Oh, don't expect anything much.

(EKDAL *and* HJALMAR *have gone to the rear of the room. Each of them slides one of the double doors back.* HEDVIG *is helping the old man.* GREGERS *remains standing by the sofa.* GINA *keeps on sewing, paying no attention. Through the opened doors can be seen a big, elongated, irregular-shaped attic, with nooks and corners and a couple of chimneys standing free from the wall. Moonlight falls through several skylights, illuminating some parts of the room, while others are in deep shadow*)

EKDAL   (*to* GREGERS) You are welcome to come closer, sir.

GREGERS   (*goes up to them*) What is this really?

EKDAL   See for yourself. H'm.

HJALMAR   (*somewhat embarrassed*) This is all father's, you understand.

GREGERS   (*at the door, peering into the attic*) Do you keep chickens, Lieutenant?

EKDAL   Should say we do. They're roosting now. But you ought to see those chickens in daylight!

HEDVIG   And there is—

EKDAL   Hush, don't say anything yet.

GREGERS   And I see you've got pigeons, too.

EKDAL   Could be we have. We've got pigeons, all right! The roosts are up on the rafters, for pigeons like to be up high, you know.

HJALMAR   They aren't all of them just ordinary pigeons.

EKDAL   Ordinary! I should say not! We've got tumblers and even a couple of pouters. But come over here. Do you see that pen over by the wall?

GREGERS   Yes. What do you use that for?

EKDAL   That's where the rabbits are at night.

GREGERS   Oh? You have rabbits, too, do you?

EKDAL   Damn right we have rabbits! He asks if we have rabbits, Hjalmar! H'm. But now we're coming to the *real* thing. Here we are. Move, Hedvig. You stand here and look down —there; that's right. Now, do you see a basket with straw in it?

GREGERS   Yes, I do. And I see a bird.

EKDAL   H'm—A "bird."

GREGERS   Isn't it a duck?

EKDAL   (*offended*)   I'd say it's a duck!

HJALMAR   But what kind of duck, do you think?

HEDVIG   It's not just an ordinary duck.

EKDAL   Hush!

GREGERS   And it's not a muscovy duck, either.

EKDAL   No, Mr.—Werle; it's not a muscovy, for it's a wild duck!

GREGERS   Is it really? A wild duck?

EKDAL   That's what it is. The—"bird," as you called it. A wild duck. It's our wild duck.

HEDVIG   *My* wild duck. For it belongs to me.

GREGERS   And it lives here in the attic? It's thriving?

EKDAL   What's so odd about that? She's got a big pail of water to splash around in.

HJALMAR   Fresh water every other day.

GINA   (*turning to* HJALMAR)   Ekdal, please. I'm freezing.

EKDAL   H'm. All right; let's close up. Just as well not to disturb their night's rest, anyway. Help me Hedvig.

(HJALMAR *and* HEDVIG *slide the double doors shut*)

EKDAL   You can have a good look at her some other time. (*sits down in the armchair by the stove*) I'm telling you, they are strange birds, those wild ducks.

GREGERS   But how did you ever catch it, Lieutenant?

EKDAL   I didn't. There's a certain man in this town we can thank for her.

GREGERS   (*struck by a thought*)   Would that man be my father?

EKDAL   Indeed it is. It's your father, sure enough. H'm.

HJALMAR   Funny you'd guess that, Gregers.

GREGERS   You told me before that you owed a great deal to my father, so I thought that perhaps—

GINA   But we didn't get the duck from Werle himself.

EKDAL   It's Håkon Werle we have to thank for her all the same, Gina. (*to* GREGERS) He was out in a boat, see, and took a shot at her. But he doesn't see so well, your father doesn't. H'm. Anyway, she was only wounded.

GREGERS   I see. She got some buckshot in her.

HJALMAR   Yes. A little.

HEDVIG   Right under the wing, so she couldn't fly.

GREGERS   Then she went to the bottom, I suppose.

EKDAL   (*sleepily, his voice muffled*)   So it did. Always do that, wild ducks. Dive straight to the bottom—far as they can, sir. Bite themselves fast in the grasses and roots and weeds and all the other damn stuff down there. And never come up again.

GREGERS   But, Lieutenant, *your* wild duck did.

EKDAL   He had such a wonderful clever dog, your father. And that dog—it went down and got the duck up.

GREGERS   (*to* HJALMAR)   And so it came to you?

HJALMAR   Not right away. First your father took it home with him, but it didn't seem to get on too well there, and then he told Pettersen to get rid of it.

EKDAL   (*half asleep*)   H'm—Pettersen— Ass—

HJALMAR   That's how we got it, for father knows Pettersen a little, and when he heard about the wild duck, he asked Pettersen to give it to him.

GREGERS   And now it seems perfectly contented in there in the attic.

HJALMAR   Yes, you would hardly believe how well it gets on. It's becoming fat. I think perhaps it's been in there so long that it has forgotten what wild life is like. And that makes all the difference.

GREGERS   I am sure you are right, Hjalmar. The thing to do is never to let it look at sea and sky again.—But I don't think I should stay any longer. I believe your father is asleep.

HJALMAR   Oh, as far as that is concerned—

GREGERS   Oh yes, one thing more. You said you had a room for rent? A vacant room?

HJALMAR   We do. What of it? Do you know anyone who—?

GREGERS   Could I get it?

HJALMAR   You?

GINA   Oh, Mr. Werle, I'm sure *you* don't want to—

GREGERS   Couldn't I have it? If I can, I'll move in first thing in the morning.

HJALMAR   Yes, indeed, with the greatest pleasure.

GINA   No, but Mr. Werle, that's not a room for you.

HJALMAR   Gina! How can you say that?

GINA   It's not large enough or light enough, and—

GREGERS   That doesn't matter, Mrs. Ekdal.

HJALMAR   I think it's quite a nice room myself, and decently furnished, too.

GINA   But remember those two downstairs.

GREGERS   Who are they?

GINA   There's one who used to be a private tutor.

HJALMAR   Molvik is his name. He studied to be a minister once.

GINA   And then there's a doctor, name of Relling.

GREGERS   Relling? I know him slightly. He used to practice up at Høydal.

GINA   They are a couple of real wild characters those two. Out all hours of the night, and when they come home they aren't always— y'know—

GREGERS   One gets used to that sort of thing. I hope I'll be like the wild duck.

GINA   H'm. Well, *I* think you ought to sleep on it first.

GREGERS   I take it you don't really want me in the house, Mrs. Ekdal.

GINA   Good Lord! How can you say a thing like that?

HJALMAR   Yes, Gina. It really does seem very odd of you. (*to* GREGERS) Does this mean you'll be staying in town for a while?

GREGERS   (*putting on his overcoat*)   Yes, I think I'll stay.

HJALMAR   But not with your father? What do you intend to do?

GREGERS   If I knew that, Hjalmar, I'd be much better off. But when you're cursed with a name like "Gregers"—and then "Werle" after that—Did you ever hear of an uglier name?

HJALMAR   I don't think it's ugly at all.

GREGERS   Ugh! I feel like spitting in the face of anybody with a name like that. But since it's my cross in life to be Gregers Werle, such as I am—

HJALMAR   Ha-ha! If you weren't Gregers Werle, what would you like to be?

GREGERS   If I could choose, I'd like to be a really clever dog.

GINA   A dog!

HEDVIG   (*involuntarily*)   Oh no!

GREGERS   Yes, an exceptionally skillful dog —the kind that goes down to the bottom after wild ducks when they've dived down among the weeds and the grass down there in the mud.

HJALMAR   Honestly, Gregers. This makes no sense whatever.

GREGERS   I suppose it doesn't. But tomorrow morning, then, I'll be moving in. (*to* GINA) You won't have any trouble with me; I'll do everything myself. (*to* HJALMAR) The other things we can talk about tomorrow.—Goodnight, Mrs. Ekdal. (*nods to* HEDVIG) Goodnight!

GINA   Goodnight, Mr. Werle.

HEDVIG   Goodnight.

HJALMAR   (*who has lighted a candle*)   Wait a moment. I'll see you down. I'm sure it's all dark on the stairs.

(GREGERS *and* HJALMAR *go out through the entrance door, right rear*)

GINA   (*staring ahead, her sewing lowered in her lap*)   Wasn't it funny all that talk about wanting to be a dog?

HEDVIG   Do you know, mother—I think he really meant something else.

GINA   What would that be?

HEDVIG   No, I couldn't say, but it was just like he had something else in mind all the time.

GINA   You think so? It sure was funny, though.

HJALMAR   (*returning*)   The lamp was still burning. (*blows out the candle and sits down*) Ah, at last it's possible to get a bite to eat. (*starts on the sandwiches*) Now do you see what I mean, Gina—about seizing the opportunity?

GINA   What opportunity?

HJALMAR   Well—it was lucky, wasn't it, that we got the room rented? And then to somebody like Gregers, a dear old friend.

GINA   Well, I don't know what to say to that.

HEDVIG   Oh mother, you'll see it will be fun.

HJALMAR   I must say you are strange. First you wanted nothing more than to get a lodger; then when we do, you don't like it.

GINA   I know, Ekdal. If only it had been somebody else. What do you think old Werle will say?

HJALMAR   He? It's none of his business.

GINA   But don't you see that something's bound to be wrong between the two of 'em, since the young one is moving out. Sure you know how those two are.

HJALMAR   That may be so, but—

GINA   And maybe Werle will think you are behind it!

HJALMAR   All right! Let him think that. Oh, by all means, Werle has done a great deal for me—I'm the first to admit it. But that doesn't mean I everlastingly have to let him run my life.

GINA   But Ekdal, dear, it could hurt Grandpa. Perhaps he'll lose what little he's making from working for Gråberg.

HJALMAR   I almost wish he would! Is it not humiliating for a man like me to see his gray-haired father treated like dirt? Ah, but soon now the time will be ripe. I feel it. (*takes another sandwich*) As sure as I have a mission in life, it shall be accomplished!

HEDVIG   Oh yes, father!

GINA   Shhh! Don't wake him up.

HJALMAR   (*in a lower voice*)   I say it again: I *will* accomplish it! The day will come, when—That's why it's such a good thing we got the room rented out, for that makes me more independent. And that's necessary for a man with a mission in life. (*over by the armchair, with feeling*) Poor old white-haired father. Trust your Hjalmar. He has broad enough shoulders—powerful shoulders, at any rate. Some day you'll wake up, and—(*to* GINA) Or don't you believe that?

GINA   (*getting up*)   Sure I do, but let's first get him to bed.

HJALMAR   Yes, let us.

(*They tenderly lift the old man*)

ACT THREE

(*The studio. It is morning. Daylight comes in through the skylight, the blue cloth having been pulled aside.*

HJALMAR *sits at the table, retouching a photograph. Several other photographs are lying in front of him. After a while,* GINA, *in coat and hat, enters from outside. She is carrying a covered basket*)

HJALMAR   Back already, Gina?

GINA   Yes. I'm in a hurry. (*puts the basket down on a chair and takes off her coat and hat*)

HJALMAR   Did you look in at Gregers's?

GINA   I did. It looks real nice in there. He fixed up the place real pretty, soon as he moved in.

HJALMAR   Oh?

GINA   Remember, he was to take care of everything himself? Well, he built a fire in the stove, but he hadn't opened the flue, so the whole room got filled with smoke. Phew! It smelled like—

HJALMAR   Oh dear—

GINA   Then do you know what he does? This really beats everything. He wanted to put out the fire, so he pours the water from the wash basin into the stove. The whole floor is sloppy with filth!

HJALMAR   I am sorry.

GINA   I've got the janitor's wife to clean up after him, pig as he is, but the room can't be lived in till this afternoon.

HJALMAR   Where is he now?

GINA   He said he was going out for a while.

HJALMAR   I went in there for a moment, too—right after you had left.

GINA   He told me. You've asked him for breakfast.

HJALMAR   Just a bit of a late morning meal. It's the first day and all. We can hardly do less. I am sure you have something.

GINA   I'll have to find something, at any rate.

HJALMAR   Be sure it's plenty, though. I think Relling and Molvik are coming, too. I ran into Relling on the stairs just now, and so of course I had to—

GINA   So we are to have those two as well.

HJALMAR   Good heavens, one or two more or less—can that make any difference?

EKDAL   (*opens his door and looks in*)   Listen, Hjalmar—(*sees* GINA) Well, never mind.

GINA   Do you want something, Grandpa?

EKDAL   No. It doesn't matter. H'm! (*goes back inside his room*)

GINA   (*picking up her basket*)   Make sure he doesn't go out.

HJALMAR   Yes, I will.—Say, Gina—how about some herring salad? I believe Relling and Molvik made a night of it again last night.

GINA   If only they don't get here too soon.

HJALMAR   I'm sure they won't. Just take your time.

GINA   Well, all right. Then you can work some in the meantime.

HJALMAR   I *am* working! I'm working as hard as I can!

GINA   All I mean is you'd have it out of the way for later. (*goes into the kitchen*)

(HJALMAR *picks up the photograph and the brush and works for a while—slowly and with evident distaste*)

EKDAL   (*peeks in, looks around, says in a low voice*)   Pst! Are you busy?

HJALMAR Yes. I am struggling with these everlasting pictures—

EKDAL All right, all right. If you're busy, then you're busy. H'm! (*Goes back inside his room. The door remains open*)

HJALMAR (*works in silence for a while, puts his brush down, walks over to* EKDAL'*s door*) Are you busy, father?

EKDAL (*grumbling inside his room*) When *you* are busy, *I* am busy! H'm!

HJALMAR Oh all right. (*returns to his work*)

EKDAL (*appears in his door again after a while*) H'm Hjalmar, listen—I'm not so *terribly* busy, you know.

HJALMAR I thought you were writing.

EKDAL Dammit all! Can't that Gråberg wait a day or two? Didn't think it was a matter of life and death.

HJALMAR Of course not. And you aren't a slave, after all.

EKDAL And there is this other job in there—

HJALMAR Just what I was thinking. Do you want to go in there now? Shall I open the door for you?

EKDAL Good idea.

HJALMAR (*getting up*) Then we'd have that job out of the way.

EKDAL Exactly. It has to be ready for tomorrow, anyway. It *is* tomorrow, isn't it?

HJALMAR Sure it's tomorrow.

(*They slide the double doors open. The morning sun is shining through the skylight. Some pigeons are flying around; others are cooing on their perches. From farther inside the room the chickens are heard clucking once in a while*)

HJALMAR All right, father. Guess you can go ahead.

EKDAL (*entering the attic*) Aren't you coming?

HJALMAR Yes, do you know—I almost think I will. (*notices* GINA *in the kitchen door*) I? No, I don't have the time. I have to work. But then there is this thing—

(*He pulls a cord. A curtain comes down from within the attic. Its lower part is made out of a strip of old sailcloth; its upper part is a piece of stretched-out fish net. The attic floor is now no longer visible*)

HJALMAR (*returns to the table*) Now! Maybe I can have peace for a few minutes.

GINA Is he fooling around in there again?

HJALMAR Would you rather he went down to Madam Eriksen? (*sitting down*) Do you want anything? I thought you said—

GINA I just wanted to ask you if you think we can set the table in here?

HJALMAR Yes. There aren't any appointments this early, are there?

GINA No—only those two sweethearts who want their picture taken.

HJALMAR Damn! Couldn't they come some other time!

GINA Goodness, Ekdal, they'll be here after dinner, when you're asleep.

HJALMAR Oh, in that case it's all right. Yes, let's eat in here.

GINA Fine. But there's no hurry with the table. You're welcome to use it some more.

HJALMAR Can't you see I *am* using it?

GINA Then you'll be all done for afterwards, you know. (*goes into the kitchen*)

(*Brief silence*)

EKDAL (*in the door to the attic, inside the fish net*) Hjalmar!

HJALMAR What?

EKDAL Afraid we'll have to move the pail, after all.

HJALMAR What else have I been saying all along?

EKDAL H'm—h'm—h'm! (*disappears inside again*)

HJALMAR (*keeps on working for a moment, glances over towards the attic, half rises, as* HEDVIG *enters from the kitchen. He quickly sits down again*) What do you want?

HEDVIG Just to be with you, father.

HJALMAR (*after a short while*) Seems to me like you're snooping around. Have you been told to watch me, perhaps?

HEDVIG No, of course not.

HJALMAR What is mother doing?

HEDVIG Mother is in the middle of the herring salad. (*comes over to the table*) Isn't there any little thing I can help you with, father?

HJALMAR Oh no. It is better I do it all alone—as long as my strength lasts. There is no need for you to worry about anything, Hedvig, as long as your father is allowed to keep his health.

HEDVIG Oh father. I won't have you talk that horrid way. (*She walks around a bit, stops by the opening to the inner room and looks in*)

HJALMAR What is he doing in there?

HEDVIG Looks like a new ladder up to the water pail.

HJALMAR He'll never manage that by himself! And here I am condemned to sit—!

HEDVIG (*goes to him*) Give me the brush, father. I can do it.

HJALMAR I won't hear of it. You'll just be ruining your eyes.

HEDVIG No, I won't. Give me the brush.

HJALMAR (*getting up*) It would only be for a minute or two—

HEDVIG   What possible harm could that do? (*takes the brush*) There now. (*sits down*) And here is one I can use as model.

HJALMAR   But don't ruin your eyes! Do you hear me? I will not take the responsibility. It's all yours. I'm just telling you.

HEDVIG   (*working*)   Yes, of course.

HJALMAR   You are really very good at it, Hedvig. It will only be for a few minutes, you understand.

(*He slips into the attic by the edge of the curtain.* HEDVIG *keeps on working.* HJALMAR *and* EKDAL *can be heard talking behind the curtain*)

HJALMAR   (*appearing inside the net*)   Hedvig, please give me the pliers on the shelf. And the chisel. (*turns around*) See here, father. Just let me show you what I have in mind first.

(HEDVIG *fetches the tools from the shelf and gives them to him*)

HJALMAR   Thank you. It was a good thing I went in.

(*He leaves the doorway. Sounds of carpentering and conversation are heard from inside.* HEDVIG *remains watching them. After a while there is a knock on the entrance door. She does not notice*)

GREGERS   (*bareheaded and coatless, enters, stops near the door*)   H'm!

HEDVIG   (*turns around and walks towards him*)   Good morning! Won't you please come in?

GREGERS   Thank you. (*looks towards the attic*) You seem to have workmen in the house.

HEDVIG   Oh no. It's just father and Grandpa. I'll tell them you're here.

GREGERS   Please don't. I'd rather wait a while. (*sits down on the sofa*)

HEDVIG   It's such a mess in here—(*begins removing the photographs*)

GREGERS   Never mind. Are they pictures you are retouching?

HEDVIG   Yes. It is something I help father with.

GREGERS   I hope you won't let me disturb you.

HEDVIG   I won't.

(*She moves the things more within her reach and resumes work.* GREGERS *watches her in silence*)

GREGERS   Did the wild duck sleep well last night?

HEDVIG   Yes, thank you. I think so.

GREGERS   (*turning towards the attic*)   In daylight it looks quite different from last night when there was a moon.

HEDVIG   Yes, it varies so. In the morning it looks different than in the afternoon, and when it rains it looks different than when the sun is shining.

GREGERS   You have noticed that?

HEDVIG   Yes, of course.

GREGERS   Do you too spend much time with the wild duck?

HEDVIG   Yes, when I can.

GREGERS   I suppose you don't have much spare time, though. You are going to school, of course?

HEDVIG   Not any more. Father is afraid I'll ruin my eyes.

GREGERS   Then he reads with you himself?

HEDVIG   He has promised to, but he hasn't had the time yet.

GREGERS   But isn't there anyone else who can help you?

HEDVIG   Well, yes, there is Mr. Molvik, but he isn't always—you know—quite—

GREGERS   You mean he is drunk sometimes.

HEDVIG   I think so.

GREGERS   Well, in that case you have time for many things. And in there, I suppose, it's like a world all its own?

HEDVIG   Yes, quite. And there are so many strange things in there.

GREGERS   There are?

HEDVIG   Yes, there are big closets with books in them, and in many of the books there are pictures.

GREGERS   I see.

HEDVIG   And there is an old desk with drawers and drop-down leaves and a big clock with figures that come out. But the clock doesn't run any more.

GREGERS   So time has stopped in there where the wild duck lives?

HEDVIG   Yes. And there are old coloring sets and that sort of thing, and then all the books.

GREGERS   I expect you read the books.

HEDVIG   Yes, whenever I have a chance. But most of them are in English and I can't read that. But I look at the pictures. There is a great, big book that's called "Harrison's History of London." I think it is a hundred years old. There are ever so many pictures in it. In front it shows a picture of Death with an hourglass and a girl. I think that is horrible. But then there are all the pictures of churches and castles and streets and big ships that sail the seas.

GREGERS   Tell me—where do all those strange things come from?

HEDVIG   There was an old sea captain who used to live here. He brought them home. They called him The Flying Dutchman. And that's odd, I think, for he wasn't a Dutchman at all.

GREGERS   No?

HEDVIG   No. But finally he disappeared at sea, and all the things were left here.

GREGERS   Listen—when you sit in there looking at the pictures, don't you ever want to travel and see the real, big world for yourself?

HEDVIG   Oh no. I want to stay here at home always and help father and mother.

GREGERS   With the photographs?

HEDVIG   Not just with that. Best of all I'd like to learn how to engrave pictures like those in the English books.

GREGERS   H'm. And what does your father say to that?

HEDVIG   I don't think father likes the idea very much. He is funny about things like that. You know, he says I ought to learn basket-weaving and straw-plaiting. But I don't think that sounds like much of anything at all.

GREGERS   No, I don't think it does either.

HEDVIG   Though of course father is quite right in saying that if I had learned basket-weaving I could have made the new basket for the wild duck.

GREGERS   That's true. And that really ought to have been your job, you know.

HEDVIG   Yes. Because it is my wild duck.

GREGERS   So I hear.

HEDVIG   Oh yes. I own it. But father and Grandpa get to borrow it as often as they like.

GREGERS   So? And what do they do with it?

HEDVIG   Oh—they take care of it and build things for it and that sort of thing.

GREGERS   I see. For of course the wild duck is the noblest of all the animals in there.

HEDVIG   Yes, she is, for she is a real, wild bird. And then I feel sorrier for her than for any of the others, because she's all alone, poor thing.

GREGERS   No family, like the rabbits.

HEDVIG   No. And the chickens, so many were little chicks together. But she is all alone, with none of her own near by. And there is the strange thing about the wild duck. Nobody knows her and nobody knows where she is from.

GREGERS   And she has been down to the depths of the sea.

HEDVIG   (*glances quickly at him, suppresses a smile, asks*)   Why do you say "the depths of the sea"?

GREGERS   What should I say?

HEDVIG   You could say "the sea bottom" or "the bottom of the sea."

GREGERS   Can't I just as well say "the depths of the sea"?

HEDVIG   Yes, but I think it sounds so strange when other people say "the depths of the sea."

GREGERS   Why is that? Tell me.

HEDVIG   No, I won't, for it is so silly.

GREGERS   I don't think so. Please tell me why you smiled.

HEDVIG   It's because every time I think of what's in there—when it comes into my head all of a sudden, I mean—I always feel that the whole room and everything that's in it are the depths of the sea. But that's silly.

GREGERS   Don't say that.

HEDVIG   Yes, for it's just an old attic, you know.

GREGERS   (*looking intently at her*)   Are you sure?

HEDVIG   (*surprised*)   That it's an attic?

GREGERS   Yes. Are you sure it is?

(HEDVIG *stares at him in silence, her mouth open in astonishment.* GINA *enters from the kitchen with linen, silverware, etc., to set the table*)

GREGERS   (*getting up*)   I am afraid I am too early for you.

GINA   Oh well. You have to be somewhere. Things are almost ready now, anyway. Clear the table, Hedvig.

(*During the next scene* HEDVIG *clears the table and* GINA *sets it.* GREGERS *seats himself in the armchair and starts leafing through an album of photographs*)

GREGERS   I understand you know how to re-touch, Mrs. Ekdal.

GINA   (*looks at him out of the corner of her eye*)   That's right.

GREGERS   That was fortunate.

GINA   How—fortunate?

GREGERS   I mean since Ekdal is a photographer.

HEDVIG   Mother knows how to take pictures, too.

GINA   Oh yes, I've had to learn *that* business, all right.

GREGERS   Perhaps it is you who are responsible for the daily routine?

GINA   Yes, when Ekdal himself doesn't have the time—

GREGERS   I suppose he busies himself a great deal with his old father?

GINA   Yes, and then it's not for a man like Ekdal to waste his time taking pictures of everybody and his grandmother.

GREGERS   I quite agree, but since he did choose this as his profession, shouldn't he—?

GINA   You know just as well as I do, Mr. Werle, that Ekdal isn't just one of your common, ordinary photographers.

GREGERS   Of course not, but—nevertheless—

(*A shot is heard from the attic*)

GREGERS (*jumps up*) What was that?

GINA Ugh! There they go, firing away again!

GREGERS They shoot, too?

HEDVIG They go hunting.

GREGERS What? (*over by the door to the attic*) Do you go hunting, Hjalmar?

HJALMAR (*inside the curtain*) Have you arrived? I didn't know—I've been so busy— (*to* HEDVIG) And you—not letting us know—! (*comes into the studio*)

GREGERS Do you go shooting in the attic?

HJALMAR (*showing him a double-barreled pistol*) Oh, it's only this old thing.

GINA You and Grandpa are going to have an accident with that pestol of yours one of these days.

HJALMAR (*irritated*) I believe I have told you that this kind of firearm is called a pistol.

GINA I don't see that that makes it any better.

GREGERS So you have taken up hunting, too, Hjalmar?

HJALMAR Only a little rabbit hunting now and then. It's mostly for father's sake, you understand.

GINA Menfolks are strange. They always need something to diverge themselves with.

HJALMAR (*grimly*) That's right. We always need something to divert ourselves with.

GINA That's exactly what I'm saying.

HJALMAR Oh well—! H'm! (*to* GREGERS) Well, you see, we're fortunate in that the attic is situated so that nobody can hear the shots. (*puts the pistol on the top shelf*) Don't touch the pistol, Hedvig! Remember, one barrel is loaded!

GREGERS (*peering through the net*) You have a hunting rifle, too, I see.

HJALMAR That's father's old gun. It doesn't work any more. There's something wrong with the lock. But it's rather fun to have it around all the same, for we take it apart and clean it once in a while and grease it and put it back together again. It's mostly father, of course, who amuses himself with things like that.

HEDVIG (*standing next to* GREGERS) Now you can get a good look at the wild duck.

GREGERS I was just looking at it. One wing is drooping a bit, isn't it?

HJALMAR Well that's not so strange. She was hit, you know.

GREGERS And she drags her foot a little. Or doesn't she?

HJALMAR Perhaps a little bit.

HEDVIG Yes, for that is the foot the dog seized her by.

HJALMAR But aside from that she has no other hurt or defect, and that's really quite remarkable when you consider that she has a charge of buckshot in her and has been between the teeth of a dog.

GREGERS (*with a glance at* HEDVIG) Yes, and been to the depths of the sea—for so long.

HEDVIG (*smiles*) Yes.

GINA (*busy at the table*) Oh yes, that precious wild duck. They sure make enough of a fuss over it.

HJALMAR H'm. Will you be done setting the table soon?

GINA In a minute. Hedvig, I need your help. (GINA *and* HEDVIG *go into the kitchen*)

HJALMAR (*in a low voice*) You had better not watch father. He doesn't like it.

(GREGERS *leaves the attic door*)

HJALMAR And I ought to close this before the others arrive. (*shoos the birds away with his hands*) Shoo! Shoo—you! (*raising the curtain and sliding the doors back*) This arrangement is my own invention. It is really quite amusing to fool around with these things and to fix them when they get broken. And it's absolutely necessary to have something like it, for Gina won't stand for rabbits and chickens in the studio.

GREGERS No, I suppose not. And perhaps the studio is your wife's department?

HJALMAR I generally leave the daily run of the business to her. That gives me a chance to retire into the living room and give my thoughts to more important things.

GREGERS What things, Hjalmar?

HJALMAR I have been wondering why you haven't asked me that before. Or maybe you haven't heard about the invention?

GREGERS Invention? No.

HJALMAR Really? You haven't? Oh well— up there in the woods and wilderness—

GREGERS So you have invented something!

HJALMAR Not quite yet, but I am working on it. As you can well imagine, when I decided to devote myself to photography it was not my intent to do nothing but take portraits of all sorts of ordinary people.

GREGERS I suppose not. Your wife just said the same thing.

HJALMAR I made a pledge to myself that if I were to give my powers to this profession, I would raise it so high that it would become both an art and a science. That is how I decided to make some remarkable invention.

GREGERS What is it? What does it do?

HJALMAR Well, Gregers, you must not ask for details just yet. You see, it takes time. And don't think I am driven by vanity. I can truthfully say I am not working for my own sake. Far from it. It is my life's mission that is in my thoughts night and day.

GREGERS What mission?

HJALMAR The old man with the silver hair —can you forget him?

GREGERS Yes, your poor father. But what exactly do you think you can do for him?

HJALMAR I can resurrect his respect for himself by once again raising the name of Ekdal to fame and honor.

GREGERS So that is your life's mission.

HJALMAR Yes. I will rescue the shipwrecked man. For he was shipwrecked the moment the storm broke. During those terrible inquiries he was not himself. The pistol over yonder—the one we use to shoot rabbits with— it has played its part in the tragedy of the Ekdal family.

GREGERS The pistol? Really?

HJALMAR When sentence had been pronounced and he was to be confined—he had that pistol in his hand—

GREGERS He tried to—!

HJALMAR Yes, but didn't dare. He was a coward. So much of a wreck, so spiritually ruined was he already then. Can you understand it? He, an officer, the killer of nine bears, descended from two lieutenant colonels—I mean one after the other, of course—Can you understand it, Gregers?

GREGERS I can indeed.

HJALMAR Not I.—But the pistol came to figure in our family chronicle a second time. When he had begun to wear the garb of gray and sat there behind bolt and bar—oh, those were terrible days for me, believe me. I kept the shades down on both windows. When I looked out, I saw the sun shining as usual. I saw people in the street laughing and talking about nothing. I could not understand it. It seemed to me that all of existence ought to come to a standstill, as during an eclipse of the sun.

GREGERS I felt that way when mother died.

HJALMAR In such an hour Hjalmar Ekdal turned the pistol against himself—

GREGERS You too were thinking of—?

HJALMAR Yes.

GREGERS But you did not pull the trigger?

HJALMAR No. In the decisive moment I won a victory over myself. I remained alive. Take my word for it: it requires courage to go on living in a situation like that.

GREGERS That depends on how you look at it.

HJALMAR No, it doesn't. At any rate, it all turned out to be for the best. For soon now I will finish my invention, and when I do, Doctor Relling thinks, as I do myself, that father will be allowed to wear his uniform again. I shall claim that as my only reward.

GREGERS So it is this business with the uniform that mostly—

HJALMAR Yes, to be able to wear it again is what he dreams of and longs for. You have no idea how it cuts me to the quick to see him. Whenever we have a little family celebration here, like Gina's and my wedding anniversary or whatever it may be, then the old man appears in his lieutenant's uniform from happier days. But no sooner is there a knock on the door than he scuttles back to his own little room as fast as his old legs will carry him. He doesn't dare to show himself to strangers, you know. A sight like that lacerates a son's heart, Gregers!

GREGERS About when do you think the invention will be ready?

HJALMAR Heavens, you must not ask for details like that. An invention, you see, is something you don't altogether control yourself. It is very largely a matter of inspiration—a sudden idea—and it is next to impossible to tell beforehand when that may come.

GREGERS But it is progressing?

HJALMAR Certainly, it is progressing. It occupies my thoughts every day. It fills me. Every afternoon, after dinner, I shut myself up in the living room to ponder in peace. I just can't be hurried; it won't do any good. That is what Relling says, too.

GREGERS And you don't think that all this business in the attic interferes too much, distracts you from your work?

HJALMAR No, no, no. Quite the contrary. You must not say a thing like that. After all, I cannot everlastingly be pursuing the same exhausting train of thought. I need something else, something to occupy me during the waiting period. The inspiration, the sudden flash of insight, don't you see?—when it comes, it comes.

GREGERS My dear Hjalmar, I almost think there is something of the wild duck in you.

HJALMAR The wild duck? How do you mean?

GREGERS You have plunged down through the sea and got yourself entangled in the grasses on the bottom.

HJALMAR Are you perhaps referring to the well-nigh fatal shot that lodged in father's wing and hit me, too?

GREGERS Not to that so much. I won't say you are crippled. But you are in a poisonous marsh, Hjalmar. You have contracted an insidious disease and gone to the bottom to die in the dark.

HJALMAR I? Die in the dark? Honestly, Gregers. You really shouldn't say such things.

GREGERS Don't you worry. I'll get you up again. For I, too, have got a mission in life. I found it yesterday.

HJALMAR That may well be, but I shall ask you kindly to leave me out of it. I assure you that—aside from my easily explainable melancholia, of course—I am as contented a man as anybody could wish to be.

GREGERS The fact that you are—that is one of the symptoms of the poisoning.

HJALMAR No, really, Gregers. Please don't talk to me any more about disease and poison. I am not used to that sort of talk. In my house we never discuss unpleasant topics.

GREGERS That I can well believe.

HJALMAR No, for it isn't good for me. And there is no marshy air here, as you call it. The roof may be low in the poor photographer's home—I know very well it is—and my lot is lowly. But I am an inventor, and a provider as well. That is what raises me above my humble circumstances.—Ah! Here's lunch!

(GINA *and* HEDVIG *enter with bottles of beer, a decanter of brandy, glasses, and other appurtenances. At the same moment,* RELLING *and* MOLVIK *come through the entrance door. Neither one wears hat or coat.* MOLVIK *is dressed in black*)

GINA (*putting the things down on the table*) Well, you two arrive just in time.

RELLING Molvik thought he could smell herring salad, and then there was no holding him.—Good morning again, Ekdal.

HJALMAR Gregers, may I introduce you to Mr. Molvik—And Doctor—that's right, you two already know each other, don't you.

GREGERS Slightly.

RELLING Oh yes, young Mr. Werle. We used to do some skirmishing up at the Høydal works. I take it you have just moved in?

GREGERS This morning.

RELLING Well, Molvik and I live downstairs, so you don't have far to go for doctor and minister if you need them.

GREGERS Thank you; maybe I shall. We were thirteen at the table yesterday.

HJALMAR Come now! Please don't start any of that unpleasantness again!

RELLING Calm down, Ekdal. You are immune.

HJALMAR I hope so, for my family's sake.—Sit down. Let's eat, drink, and be merry.

GREGERS Aren't we going to wait for your father?

HJALMAR No, he'll eat later in his own room. Do sit down!

(*The men seat themselves and begin eating and drinking.* GINA *and* HEDVIG *wait on them*)

RELLING Molvik got pretty high last night, Mrs. Ekdal.

GINA Again?

RELLING Didn't you hear me bring him home?

GINA Can't say I did.

RELLING That's good, for Molvik was awful last night.

GINA Is that true, Molvik?

MOLVIK Let us consign last night's events to oblivion. They do not represent my better self.

RELLING (*to* GREGERS) It comes over him like an irresistible impulse. Then he has to go out and get drunk. You see, Molvik is demonic.

GREGERS Demonic?

RELLING That's right. Molvik is demonic.

GREGERS H'm.

RELLING And demonic natures aren't made to follow the straight and narrow path. They have to take off for the fields once in a while.—So you still stick it out up at that filthy old place?

GREGERS So far.

RELLING Did you ever collect on that claim you went around presenting?

GREGERS Claim? (*looks at him and understands*) Oh I see.

HJALMAR Have you been a bill collector, Gregers?

GREGERS Oh nonsense.

RELLING Oh yes, he has. He went around to all the cottages up there, trying to collect on something he called "the claim of the ideal."

GREGERS I was young.

RELLING You're right. You were very young. And the claim of the ideal—you never collected as long as I was up there.

GREGERS Not since then, either.

RELLING In that case, I suppose you have been wise enough to reduce the amount somewhat.

GREGERS Never when I have to do with a real and genuine human being.

HJALMAR I think that is reasonable enough. —Some butter, Gina.

RELLING And a piece of bacon for Molvik.

MOLVIK Ugh! Not bacon!

(*There is a knock from inside the door to the attic*)

HJALMAR   Go and open, Hedvig. Father wants to get out.

(HEDVIG *opens the door a little.* OLD EKDAL *enters with the skin of a freshly flayed rabbit.* HEDVIG *closes the door after him*)

EKDAL   Good morning, gentlemen! Good hunting today. Got me a big one.

HJALMAR   And you skinned it yourself, I see.

EKDAL   Salted it, too. It's nice, tender meat, rabbit is. It's sweet, y'know. Tastes like sugar. Good appetite, gentlemen! (*goes into his room*)

MOLVIK   (*getting up*)   Excuse me—I can't —Got to get downstairs—

RELLING   Drink soda water, you idiot!

MOLVIK   Uh—Uh—(*hurries out, right rear*)

RELLING   (*to* HJALMAR)   Let us drink to the old hunter.

HJALMAR   (*touching* RELLING'S *glass with his own*)   For the sportsman on the brink of the grave—yes.

RELLING   For the gray-haired—(*drinks*) Tell me, is his hair gray or is it white?

HJALMAR   In between, I think. Though I don't think there are many hairs left on his head at all.

RELLING   Oh well. One can live happily with a wig, too. Ah, yes, Ekdal. You are really a very happy man. You have this beautiful ambition of yours to strive for—

HJALMAR   Believe me, I am striving.

RELLING   Then you have your excellent wife, shuffling about in slippered feet with that comfortable waddle of hers, making things nice and pleasant for you.

HJALMAR   Yes, Gina—(*nods to her*)—you are a good companion on life's journey.

GINA   Aw, you don't need to sit there and dissectate me!

RELLING   And your Hedvig, Ekdal.

HJALMAR   (*moved*)   Ah yes, the child! The child above all. Hedvig, come to me. (*stroking her hair*) What day is tomorrow?

HEDVIG   (*playfully shaking him*)   Oh, stop it, father!

HJALMAR   It's like a knife through my heart, when I consider how little we can do. Just a small celebration here in the attic.

HEDVIG   But that's just the way I like it!

RELLING   You wait till the invention is all done, Hedvig.

HJALMAR   Yes! Then you'll see, Hedvig. I have decided to secure your future. You shall be made comfortable for as long as you live. I will ask for something for you, something or

other. That will be the impecunious inventor's sole reward.

HEDVIG   (*whispers, her arms around his neck*) Oh you good, sweet father!

RELLING   (*to* GREGERS)   Well, now, don't you think it's nice for a change to sit down to a good table in a happy family circle?

HJALMAR   Yes, I really relish these hours at the table.

GREGERS   I, for one, don't like to breathe marsh air.

RELLING   Marsh air?

HJALMAR   Oh, don't start all that again!

GINA   I'll have you know there is no marsh air here, Mr. Werle. The place is aired every single day.

GREGERS   (*leaving the table*)   The stench I have in mind you don't get rid of by opening windows.

HJALMAR   Stench!

GINA   Yes, how do you like that, Ekdal!

RELLING   Begging your pardon—it wouldn't by any chance be you yourself who bring the stench with you from the Høydal mines?

GREGERS   It's just like you to call stench what I bring to this house.

RELLING   (*walks over to* GREGERS)   Listen here, Mr. Werle junior, I strongly suspect that you still carry the claim of the ideal around in your rear pocket.

GREGERS   I carry it in my heart.

RELLING   I don't care where the hell you carry it as long as you don't go bill collecting here while *I* am around.

GREGERS   And if I do so, nevertheless?

RELLING   Then you'll go head first down the stairs. Now you know!

HJALMAR   No, really, Relling—!

GREGERS   Go ahead! Throw me out!

GINA   (*interposing*)   No, we won't have any of that, Relling. But I will say this to you, Mr. Werle, that it seems like you are not the right person to come here and talk about stench after what you did to the stove in your room this morning.

(*There is a knock on the door*)

HEDVIG   Mother, someone's knocking.

HJALMAR   Oh yes, let's have customers on top of everything else—!

GINA   I'll handle it. (*opens the door, gives a start, steps back*) Oh dear!

(WERLE, *in a fur coat, steps inside*)

WERLE   I beg your pardon, but I am told my son is here.

GINA   (*swallowing hard*)   Yes sir.

HJALMAR (*closer*) Sir, wouldn't you like to—?

WERLE Thanks. I just want a word with my son.

GREGERS Well. Here I am.

WERLE I want to talk with you in your room.

GREGERS In my room—? Oh, all right. (*is about to leave*)

GINA Good Lord, no! That's not a fit place!

WERLE All right; out here in the hall, then. I want to see you alone.

HJALMAR You may do that right here, Mr. Werle. Relling, come into the living room with me.

(HJALMAR *and* RELLING *go out, right front.* GINA *takes* HEDVIG *with her into the kitchen, left front*)

GREGERS (*after a brief silence*) Well. We are alone.

WERLE You dropped some hints last night. And since you have moved in with the Ekdals, I can only assume that you are planning something or other against me.

GREGERS I plan to open Hjalmar Ekdal's eyes. He is to see his position as it really is. That's all.

WERLE Is that the life mission you mentioned yesterday?

GREGERS Yes. You have left me no other.

WERLE So you feel it is I who have twisted your mind, Gregers?

GREGERS You have twisted my whole life. I am not thinking of all that with mother. But it is you I can thank for the fact that I am being haunted and driven by a guilty conscience.

WERLE Ah, I see. So your conscience is ailing.

GREGERS I should have opposed you the time you were laying traps for Lieutenant Ekdal. I should have warned him, for I suspected how things were going.

WERLE Yes, in that case you certainly ought to have said something.

GREGERS I didn't have the courage. I was a coward—frightened. I felt an unspeakable fear of you—both then and for a long, long time afterwards.

WERLE That fear appears to have left you now.

GREGERS Yes, fortunately. What has been done to Old Ekdal, both by me and by—others, for that there is no remedy. But Hjalmar I can rescue from the web of lies and deceit in which he is suffocating.

WERLE Do you think that is a good thing to do?

GREGERS I am sure it is.

WERLE I take it you think Mr. Photographer Ekdal is the kind of man who will be grateful for your friendly services?

GREGERS Yes! He is that kind of man.

WERLE H'm. We'll see.

GREGERS Besides, if I am to continue living, I have to find a way to heal my sick conscience.

WERLE It will never get well. Your conscience has been sickly from the time you were a child. It's hereditary, Gregers. You have it from your mother. The only inheritance she left you.

GREGERS (*with a contemptuous half smile*) I see you still haven't forgotten your disappointment when you found out mother wasn't rich.

WERLE Let's not change the subject. Am I to think, then, that you are firmly resolved to guide Hjalmar Ekdal into the path you consider the right one?

GREGERS Yes. That is my firm intent.

WERLE In that case I could have saved myself coming all the way up here. For then I suppose there is no point in my asking you to move back home again?

GREGERS No.

WERLE And you don't want to join the firm?

GREGERS No.

WERLE Very well. But since I am to marry again, your part of the estate will have to be paid you.

GREGERS (*quickly*) No, I don't want that.

WERLE You don't want it?

GREGERS I dare not, for my conscience's sake.

WERLE (*after a brief pause*) Are you going back up to Høydal?

GREGERS No. I consider myself released from your service.

WERLE But what do you want to do with yourself?

GREGERS Accomplish my mission. Nothing else.

WERLE But afterwards? What are you going to live on?

GREGERS I have saved some of my salary.

WERLE How long do you think that will last?

GREGERS I think it will do for the time I have left.

WERLE What is that supposed to mean?

GREGERS I won't answer any more questions.

WERLE Well, goodbye, Gregers.

GREGERS Goodbye.

(WERLE *leaves*)

HJALMAR (*looks in*) Did he leave?

GREGERS   Yes.

(HJALMAR *and* RELLING *enter from the living room,* GINA *and* HEDVIG *from the kitchen*)

RELLING   Now that was a very successful breakfast.

GREGERS   Put on your coat, Hjalmar. I want you to take a long walk with me.

HJALMAR   Gladly. What did your father want? Did it have to do with me?

GREGERS   Just come. We'll talk. I'll go and get my coat. (*goes out*)

GINA   You shouldn't go with him, Ekdal.

RELLING   No, don't. Stay here.

HJALMAR   (*taking his hat and coat*)   What! When an old friend feels the need to open his heart for me in private—!

RELLING   But goddamit! Can't you see that the fellow is mad, cracked, insane!

GINA   Yes, listen to Relling. His mother used to have physicological fits, too.

HJALMAR   All the more reason why he needs a friend's alert eyes. (*to* GINA) Be sure to have dinner ready at the usual time. Goodbye. (*goes out*)

RELLING   It's nothing less than a disaster that that man didn't go straight to hell down one of the shafts up at Høydal.

GINA   Heavens—! Why do you say that?

RELLING   (*mutters*)   I have my reasons.

GINA   Do you really think young Werle is crazy?

RELLING   No, unfortunately. He is no madder than most people. He is sick, though.

GINA   What do you think is wrong with him?

RELLING   That I can tell you, Mrs. Ekdal. He suffers from an acute attack of moral integrity.

GINA   Moral integrity?

HEDVIG   Is that a disease?

RELLING   Yes, it is a national disease, but it occurs only sporadically. (*nods to* GINA) That was a good meal, thank you. (*goes out*)

GINA   (*troubled, walks up and down*)   Ugh! That Gregers Werle—he's always been a weird fish.

HEDVIG   (*by the table, looks at her searchingly*)   I think this is very strange.

ACT FOUR

(*The studio. Photographs have just been taken. A cloth-covered camera on a tripod, a couple* of chairs, and a small table are standing about in the middle of the floor. Afternoon light. The sun is about to disappear. After a while darkness begins to fall.

GINA *stands in the open entrance door with a small box and a wet glass plate in her hand. She is talking to someone not in sight*)

GINA   Absolutely. When I promise something I keep it. I'll have the first dozen ready for you on Monday.—Goodbye.

(*Sounds of someone descending the stairs.* GINA *closes the door, puts the plate inside the box and the box into the camera*)

HEDVIG   (*enters from the kitchen*)   Did they leave?

GINA   (*putting things in order*)   Yes, thank goodness. I finally got rid of them.

HEDVIG   Can you understand why father isn't back yet?

GINA   You're sure he is not down at Relling's?

HEDVIG   No, he is not there. I just went down the kitchen stairs to ask.

GINA   His food is getting cold and everything.

HEDVIG   Yes. And father who is always so particular about having dinner on time.

GINA   Oh well. You'll see he'll be back soon.

HEDVIG   I wish he'd come. Everything seems so strange.

(HJALMAR *enters from outside*)

HEDVIG   (*towards him*)   Father! If you knew how we've been waiting for you!

GINA   (*glancing at him*)   You've been gone quite some time.

HJALMAR   (*without looking at her*)   Yes, I suppose I have.

(*He starts taking his coat off.* GINA *and* HEDVIG *both go to help him. He turns them away*)

GINA   Maybe you and Werle had something to eat some place?

HJALMAR   (*hanging up his coat*)   No.

GINA   (*towards the kitchen door*)   I'll get your dinner.

HJALMAR   Never mind. I don't feel like eating now.

HEDVIG   (*coming closer*)   Are you sick, father?

HJALMAR   Sick? No, I'm not sick—exactly. We had a strenuous walk, Gregers and I.

GINA   You shouldn't do that, Ekdal. You aren't used to it.

HJALMAR   H'm. There are many things in life a man has to get used to. (*paces up and down*) Anybody here while I've been gone?

GINA   Only that engaged couple.

HJALMAR   No new appointments?

GINA   No, not today.

HEDVIG   There will be some tomorrow, father, I am sure.

HJALMAR   I hope you are right, for tomorrow I plan to go to work in earnest.

HEDVIG   Tomorrow! But don't you remember what day is tomorrow?

HJALMAR   That's right. Well, then, the day after tomorrow. From now on I'll do everything myself. I want to assume the entire work load.

GINA   Whatever for, Ekdal? That's only making yourself miserable. I'll manage the pictures. You just go on with the invention.

HEDVIG   And the wild duck, father. And the chickens and the rabbits and—

HJALMAR   Don't ever mention all that junk to me again! Starting tomorrow, I'll never more set foot in the attic.

HEDVIG   But father, you promised that tomorrow we're having a celebration—

HJALMAR   H'm. That's right. Day after tomorrow then. That damn wild duck. I'd like to wring its neck!

HEDVIG   (*with a cry*)   The wild duck!

GINA   Now I've heard everything!

HEDVIG   (*shaking him*)   But father—it's *my* wild duck!

HJALMAR   That's why I won't do it. I don't have the heart—for your sake, Hedvig. But deep down I feel I ought to do it. I shouldn't harbor under my roof a creature that has been in those hands.

GINA   For heaven's sake! Even if Grandpa *did* get it from that awful Pettersen.

HJALMAR   (*walking up and down*)   There are certain demands—what shall I call them? Let me say ideal demands—certain claims, that a man disregards only at the peril of his soul.

HEDVIG   (*following after him*)   But think— the wild duck! That poor wild duck!

HJALMAR   (*halts*)   Didn't I tell you I'll spare it—for your sake? Not a hair on its head will be—h'm. Well, as I said, I'll spare it. After all, there are bigger tasks awaiting me. But you ought to go out for a little walk, Hedvig. The twilight is just right for you.

HEDVIG   I don't care to go out now.

HJALMAR   Yes, do. Seems to me you are squinting. The fumes in here aren't good for you. The air is close under this roof.

HEDVIG   All right. I'll run down the kitchen stairs and walk around a bit. My hat and coat? Oh yes, in my room. Father, please—don't do anything bad to the wild duck while I'm gone!

HJALMAR   Not a feather shall be plucked

from its head. (*clutches her to him*) You and I, Hedvig—we two! Be on your way now.

(HEDVIG *nods goodbye to her parents and goes out through the kitchen door*)

HJALMAR   (*pacing back and forth*)   Gina.

GINA   Yes?

HJALMAR   Starting tomorrow—or let's say the day after tomorrow—I'd like to keep account of the housekeeping expenses myself.

GINA   So you want to keep the accounts too, now?

HJALMAR   Keep track of what we take in, at any rate.

GINA   Lord knows, that's easily done!

HJALMAR   One wouldn't think so. It seems to me you make the money go incredibly far. (*stops and looks at her*) How do you do it?

GINA   It's because Hedvig and I need so little.

HJALMAR   Is it true that father is overpaid for the copying work he does for Werle?

GINA   I couldn't say about that. I don't know the rates.

HJALMAR   Well, what *does* he get? In round figures.—I want to know.

GINA   It differs. I guess it comes to about what he costs us, plus a little extra in spending money.

HJALMAR   What he costs us! And you haven't told me that!

GINA   No, I couldn't, for you were so happy because he got everything from you.

HJALMAR   And it has really been Werle all the time!

GINA   Oh well. He can afford it.

HJALMAR   Light the lamp!

GINA   (*lighting the lamp*)   And as far as that is concerned, how do we know it is Werle himself? It may be Gråberg—

HJALMAR   Really, Gina. You know that isn't so. Why do you say a thing like that?

GINA   I don't know. I just thought—

HJALMAR   H'm!

GINA   It wasn't me who got Grandpa all that copying to do. It was Bertha, when she took service there.

HJALMAR   It sounds to me like your voice is trembling.

GINA   (*putting the shade on the lamp*) Does it?

HJALMAR   And your hands are shaking. Aren't they?

GINA   (*firmly*)   You might as well tell me straight, Ekdal. What has he been saying about me?

HJALMAR   Is it true—*can* it be true—that

there was some kind of affair between you and Werle while you were in his house?

GINA   That's not so. Not then. He was after me, though. And Mrs. Werle thought there was something going on, and she made a fuss and a big hullaballoo about it, and she beat me and pulled me around—and so I quit.

HJALMAR   But afterwards—!

GINA   Well, then I went to live with mother. And you see—mother—she wasn't all the woman you thought she was, Ekdal. She talked to me about this, that, and the other. For Werle was a widower by that time—

HJALMAR   And then—?

GINA   You might as well know it, I guess. He didn't give up till he had his way.

HJALMAR   (*striking his hands together*) And this is the mother of my child! How could you keep a thing like this from me?

GINA   Yes, I know it was wrong. I should have told you long ago, I suppose.

HJALMAR   You should have told me right away; that's what you should have. Then I would have known what sort of woman you were.

GINA   But you would have married me, irregardless?

HJALMAR   Of course, I wouldn't!

GINA   I didn't think so, and that's why I didn't dare to tell you. I had come to care for you, you know—a whole lot I cared for you. And I just couldn't see making myself as unhappy as all that—

HJALMAR   (*walking about*)   And this is my Hedvig's mother! And to know that everything I lay my eyes on here (*kicks a chair*)—my whole home—I owe to a favored predecessor! Oh, that seducer, that damn Werle!

GINA   Do you regret the fourteen-fifteen years we've had together?

HJALMAR   (*fronting her*)   Tell me if you haven't felt every day and every hour to be one long agony of repentance for that web of deceitful silence you have woven around me, like a spider? Answer me! Haven't you lived here in perpetual torture of guilt and remorse?

GINA   Bless you, Ekdal! I've been plenty busy with the house and the pictures—

HJALMAR   So you never cast a probing glance at your past?

GINA   No, to tell the truth, I had almost forgotten all those old stories.

HJALMAR   Oh, this dull, apathetic calm! There is something shocking about it. Not even repentant—!

GINA   Just tell me this, Ekdal. What do you think would have become of you if you hadn't got yourself a wife like me?

HJALMAR   Like you—!

GINA   Yes, for you know I have always been more practical and able to cope with things than you. Of course, I am a couple of years older—

HJALMAR   What would have become of me!

GINA   For you've got to admit you weren't living exactly right when you first met me.

HJALMAR   So you call that living wrong! Oh, what do you know about a man's feelings when he sorrows and despairs—especially a man of my fiery temperament.

GINA   No, I guess I don't know. And I don't mean to execrete you for it, either, for you turned into as decent a man as they come as soon as you got a house and a family of your own to take care of. And now we were getting on so nicely here, and Hedvig and I were just thinking that pretty soon we might spend some money on clothes for ourselves.

HJALMAR   Yes, in the swamp of deceit!

GINA   That that fellow ever poked his nose inside here!

HJALMAR   I, too, thought our home a pleasant one. That was a mistake. Where now do I gather the necessary inner resilience to bring my invention into the world of reality? Perhaps it will die with me. If it does, it will be your past, Gina, that has killed it.

GINA   (*on the verge of tears*)   Please, Ekdal —don't be saying such things! I that have all my days only tried to make things nice and pleasant for you!

HJALMAR   I ask—what happens now to the breadwinner's dream? As I reclined in there on the sofa, pondering the invention, it came to me that it was going to drain me of my last drop of vitality. I knew that the day the patent was issued and in my hands—that day would be my—my day of farewell. And then it was my dream that you were to live on as the late inventor's well-to-do widow.

GINA   (*wiping her tears*)   I won't have you talk that way, Ekdal. May the good Lord never let me live the day when I'm your widow!

HJALMAR   Oh what difference does it all make! It is all over now, anyway. Everything!

(GREGERS *cautiously opens the entrance door and peers in*)

GREGERS   May I come in?

HJALMAR   Yes, do.

GREGERS   (*goes up to them with a beaming, happy face, reaches out his hands to them*) Now, then—you dear people—! (*looks from one to the other, whispers to* HJALMAR) It hasn't happened yet?

HJALMAR (*loud*)   It has happened.

GREGERS   It has?

HJALMAR   I have lived through the bitterest moment of my life.

GREGERS   But also, I trust, its most exalted one.

HJALMAR   Anyway, it's done and over with.

GINA   May God forgive you, Mr. Werle.

GREGERS (*greatly bewildered*)   But I don't understand—!

HJALMAR   What don't you understand?

GREGERS   As crucial a conversation as this— a conversation that is to be the foundation for a whole new way of life—a life, a partnership, in truth and frankness—

HJALMAR   I know. I know it very well.

GREGERS   I was so sure that when I came in here now I would be met with a splendor of revelation shining from both husband and wife. But all I see is this dull, heavy gloom—

GINA   So that's it. (*removes the lamp shade*)

GREGERS   You refuse to understand me, Mrs. Ekdal. Well, I suppose you need time. But you, Hjalmar? Surely, you must have felt a higher consecration in this great crisis.

HJALMAR   Of course I did. That is, in a way.

GREGERS   For surely nothing in the world can be compared to finding forgiveness in one's heart for her who has erred and lovingly lifting her up to one's own heights.

HJALMAR   Do you think a man so easily forgets the draught of wormwood I just drained?

GREGERS   An ordinary man, maybe not. But a man like you—!

HJALMAR   Oh, I know. But you must not rush me, Gregers. It takes time.

GREGERS   There is much of the wild duck in you, Hjalmar.

(RELLING *has entered*)

RELLING   Ah! Here we go with the wild duck again!

HJALMAR   Mr. Werle's crippled prey—yes.

RELLING   Werle? Is it him you're talking about?

HJALMAR   About him—and about ourselves.

RELLING (*in a low voice, to* GREGERS)   Damn you to hell!

HJALMAR   What are you saying?

RELLING   I am just expressing an ardent wish that this quack here would betake himself home. If he stays around he is likely to ruin both of you.

GREGERS   Those two cannot be ruined, Mr. Relling. Of Hjalmar I need say nothing. Him we know. But she, too, has surely in the depths of her being something reliable, something of integrity—

GINA (*almost crying*)   Why didn't you leave me alone then?

RELLING (*to* GREGERS)   Is it impertinent to ask exactly what you want in this house?

GREGERS   I want to lay the foundation for a true marriage.

RELLING   So you don't think the Ekdals' marriage is good enough as it is?

GREGERS   I daresay it is as good a marriage as most, unfortunately. But a true marriage it has yet to become.

HJALMAR   You have never had an eye for the claim of the ideal, Relling!

RELLING   Nonsense, boy!—Begging your pardon, Mr. Werle—how many—roughly— how many true marriages have you observed in your life?

GREGERS   Hardly a single one.

RELLING   Nor have I.

GREGERS   But I have seen a number of the other kind. And I have had occasion to witness what havoc a marriage like that can work in a pair of human beings.

HJALMAR   A man's whole moral foundation may crumble under his feet; that's the terrible thing.

RELLING   Well, I can't say I've ever been exactly married, so I can't judge about that. But I do know this, that the child belongs to marriage too. And you had better leave the child alone.

HJALMAR   Oh, Hedvig! My poor Hedvig!

RELLING   Yes—keep Hedvig out of it, you two! You are grown-ups. In God's name, do whatever fool things you like to your marriage. But I am warning you: be careful what you do to Hedvig. If you're not, there is no telling what may happen to her.

HJALMAR   Happen to her!

RELLING   Yes, she may bring a disaster upon herself—and perhaps on others, too.

GINA   But how can you tell about that, Relling?

HJALMAR   Are you saying there is some immediate danger to her eyes?

RELLING   This has nothing whatever to do with her eyes. Hedvig is in a difficult age. She may do all sorts of crazy things.

GINA   I know—she does already. She's taken to fooling around with the woodstove in the kitchen. Playing fire, she calls it. Sometimes I'm scared she'll burn the whole house down.

RELLING   There you are. I knew it.

GREGERS (*to* RELLING)   But how do you explain a thing like that?

RELLING (*sullenly*)   Her voice is changing, sir.

HJALMAR   As long as the child has *me*—! As long as *my* head is above the ground!

(*There is a knock on the door*)

GINA   Shhh, Ekdal. There are people outside.

(MRS. SØRBY *enters, wearing hat and coat*)

MRS. SØRBY   Good evening!

GINA (*going to her*)   Goodness! It is you, Bertha!

MRS. SØRBY   So it is. Maybe it's inconvenient—?

HJALMAR   Oh by no means! A messenger from *that* house—!

MRS. SØRBY (*to* GINA)   Frankly, I had hoped you'd be without your menfolks this time of day. I've just dropped in to have a word with you about something and say goodbye.

GINA   You're going away?

MRS. SØRBY   Tomorrow morning—to Høydal. Mr. Werle left this afternoon. (*casually, to* GREGERS)   He asked me to say hello.

GINA   Imagine—!

HJALMAR   So Mr. Werle has left? And you are going after him?

MRS. SØRBY   Yes. What do you say to that, Ekdal?

HJALMAR   Look out, is all I say.

GREGERS   I can explain. Father and Mrs. Sørby are getting married.

GINA   Oh Bertha! At long last!

RELLING (*his voice trembling a little*)   Surely, this cannot be true?

MRS. SØRBY   Yes, my dear Relling, true it is.

RELLING   You want to get married again?

MRS. SØRBY   That's what it amounts to. Werle has got the license. We'll have a quiet little party up at the works.

GREGERS   I suppose I should tender my felicitations like a good stepson.

MRS. SØRBY   Thank you, if you really mean it. I hope this will be for the best for both Werle and myself.

RELLING   I am sure you have every reason to think it will. Mr. Werle never gets drunk—at least not to my knowledge. Nor do I believe he is in the habit of beating up his wife, like the late lamented horse doctor.

MRS. SØRBY   Let Sørby rest quietly in his grave. He had his good sides, too.

RELLING   Mr. Industrialist Werle has better ones, I am sure.

MRS. SØRBY   At least he has not thrown away what is best in himself. The man who does that must take the consequences.

RELLING   Tonight I'll go out with Molvik.

MRS. SØRBY   Don't do that, Relling. Don't—for my sake.

RELLING   There's nothing else to do. (*to* HJALMAR)   Want to come along?

GINA   No, thank you. Ekdal doesn't go in for escapades like that.

HJALMAR (*angrily, in a half whisper*)   For heaven's sake! Keep your mouth shut!

RELLING   Goodbye—Mrs. Werle! (*goes out*)

GREGERS (*to* MRS. SØRBY)   It appears that you and Doctor Relling know each other quite well?

MRS. SØRBY   Yes, we've known each other for a good many years. At one time it looked as if we might have made a match of it.

GREGERS   I'm sure it was lucky for you that you didn't.

MRS. SØRBY   You may well say that. But I've always been wary of acting on impulse. A woman can't just throw herself away, you know.

GREGERS   Aren't you afraid I'll let my father know about this old acquaintanceship?

MRS. SØRBY   Do you really believe I haven't told him myself?

GREGERS   Oh?

MRS. SØRBY   Your father knows every little thing people might say about me with any show of truth at all. I have told him everything. That was the first thing I did when I realized what his intentions were.

GREGERS   It seems to me you are more than usually frank.

MRS. SØRBY   I have always been frank. For us women that's the best policy.

HJALMAR   What do you say to that, Gina?

GINA   Oh, women differ. Some do it one way, others do it different.

MRS. SØRBY.   Well, Gina, in my opinion I have followed the wiser course. And Werle hasn't kept back anything either. You see, that's what mainly brought us together. Now he can sit and talk to me as openly as a child. He has never been able to do that before. A healthy, vigorous man like him—all through his youth and all the best years of his life he had his ears drummed full with angry sermons. And very often sermons about sins he hadn't even committed—according to what I have been told.

GINA   That's the truth.

GREGERS   If you ladies want to pursue that topic any further, I had better absent myself.

MRS. SØRBY   You may just as well stay as far as that's concerned. I won't say another word.

I just wanted you to know I haven't kept anything back or played him false in any way. Maybe people will say I am a very fortunate woman, and in a way of course that's true. But I don't think I am getting any more than I am giving. I'll certainly never desert him. And I can be of more service and use to him than anybody else, now that he'll soon be helpless.

HJALMAR　Will he be helpless?

GREGERS　(to MRS. SØRBY)　Don't say anything about that here.

MRS. SØRBY　It can't be kept secret any longer, much as he'd like to. He is going blind.

HJALMAR　(struck)　Blind? That's strange. He, too?

GINA　Lots of people go blind.

MRS. SØRBY　And I'm sure you can tell yourself what that must mean to a businessman. Well, I'll try to be his eyes, the best I know how.—But I can't stay any longer. I have so much to do right now.—Oh yes, what I wanted to tell you, Ekdal, is that if Werle can be of any service to you, all you need to do is to get in touch with Gråberg.

GREGERS　That is an offer I am sure Hjalmar Ekdal will decline.

MRS. SØRBY　Really? It seems to me he hasn't always been so—

GINA　Yes, Bertha. Ekdal doesn't need to accept anything more from Mr. Werle.

HJALMAR　(slowly, with weight)　Tell your husband-to-be from me, that in the very near future I intend to go to Mr. Gråberg—

GREGERS　What! You want to do that!

HJALMAR　—I say, go to Mr. Gråberg, and demand an account of the sum I owe his employer. I desire to pay this debt of honor—ha-ha-ha!—let us call it a debt of honor! Enough! I shall pay it all, with five per cent interest.

GINA　But Ekdal—goodness! We don't have that kind of money!

HJALMAR　Be so good as to inform your fiancé that I am working incessantly on my invention. Please tell him that what sustains my mind during this exhausting enterprise is my ambition to free myself from a painful burden of debt. This is why I am an inventor. The entire proceeds from my invention are to be devoted to liberating myself from the obligation to remunerate your husband-to-be for his expenses on behalf of my family.

MRS. SØRBY　Something has happened here.

HJALMAR　Indeed, something has.

MRS. SØRBY　Well, goodbye. I had something else I wanted to talk to you about, Gina, but that will have to wait till some other time. Goodbye.

(HJALMAR and GREGERS return her greeting silently. GINA sees her to the door)

HJALMAR　Not beyond the threshold, Gina!

(MRS. SØRBY leaves. GINA closes the door)

HJALMAR　There, now, Gregers. I have that burdensome debt off my chest.

GREGERS　You soon will, at any rate.

HJALMAR　I believe my attitude must be deemed the proper one.

GREGERS　You are the man I have always taken you to be.

HJALMAR　In certain cases it is impossible to disregard the claims of the ideal. As provider for my family, I am bound, of course, to find my course of action difficult and painful. Believe me, it is no joke for a man situated as I am, without means, to assume a debt of many years' standing—a debt, you might say, covered by the sands of oblivion. But never mind. The man in me demands his rights.

GREGERS　(placing his hand on his shoulder)　Dear Hjalmar—wasn't it a good thing that I came?

HJALMAR　Yes.

GREGERS　That your whole situation was made clear to you—wasn't that a good thing?

HJALMAR　(a bit impatiently)　Of course it was. But there is one thing that shocks my sense of justice.

GREGERS　What is that?

HJALMAR　It is this that—But I don't know that I ought to speak so freely about your father—

GREGERS　Don't let that worry you. Say what you want.

HJALMAR　All right. Well, you see, there is something shocking in the notion that now it's he and not I who realizes the true marriage.

GREGERS　How can you say a thing like that!

HJALMAR　Well, it is. For your father and Mrs. Sørby are about to solemnify a union built on full mutual confidence, on complete, unconditional frankness on both sides. They conceal nothing from each other, there are no deceitful silences, there has been declared, if I may put it so, mutual absolution between them.

GREGERS　Well, what of it?

HJALMAR　Well, then—it's all there! All the difficult conditions you yourself said are prerequisites for the building of a true marriage.

GREGERS　But that's in quite a different way, Hjalmar. Surely, you won't compare either yourself or Gina with those two—? Oh I am sure you know what I mean.

HJALMAR　Yet I can't get away from the thought that in all this there is something that offends my sense of justice. It looks exactly as if there were no just order in the universe.

GINA Ekdal, for God's sake, don't talk like that!

GREGERS H'm. Let's not get involved in those issues.

HJALMAR Though, on the other hand, I do in a way discern fate's ruling finger, too. He is going blind.

GINA We don't know that yet.

HJALMAR There is no doubt about it. At least, we ought not to doubt it, for in that very fact lies the proof of just retribution. He did once hoodwink a trusting fellow being.

GREGERS I am afraid he has hoodwinked many.

HJALMAR And here comes the inexorable, the inscrutable, claiming Werle's own eyes.

GINA How you talk! I think it's scary.

HJALMAR It is salutary at times to contemplate the night side of existence.

(HEDVIG, *dressed for the outside, enters. She is happy, breathless*)

GINA Back so soon?

HEDVIG Yes. I didn't feel like walking any farther. It was a good thing, too, for I met somebody as I was coming in.

HJALMAR Mrs. Sørby, I suppose.

HEDVIG Yes.

HJALMAR (*pacing the floor*) I hope you have seen her for the last time.

(*Silence.* HEDVIG, *troubled, looks from one to the other in order to gauge their mood*)

HEDVIG (*approaching* HJALMAR, *ingratiatingly*) Father?

HJALMAR All right—what is it, Hedvig?

HEDVIG Mrs. Sørby had something for me.

HJALMAR (*halts*) For you?

HEDVIG Yes. Something for tomorrow.

GINA Bertha always brings you a little something for your birthday.

HJALMAR What is it?

HEDVIG No, you're not to find out now. Mother is to give it to me in the morning, when she brings me breakfast in bed.

HJALMAR What is all this mystification that I am to be kept in the dark about!

HEDVIG (*quickly*) I'll be glad to let you see it, father. It's a big letter. (*takes the letter out of her coat pocket*)

HJALMAR A letter too?

HEDVIG The letter is all there is. I suppose the other thing will come later. Just think—a letter! I never got a letter before. And it says "Miss" on the outside of it. (*reads*) "Miss Hedvig Ekdal." Just think—that's me!

HJALMAR Let me see that letter.

HEDVIG Here you are. (*hands it to him*)

HJALMAR It's Werle's handwriting.

GINA Are you sure, Ekdal?

HJALMAR See for yourself.

GINA How would I know?

HJALMAR Hedvig? May I open the letter? Read it?

HEDVIG If you like.

GINA Not tonight, Ekdal. It's supposed to be for tomorrow.

HEDVIG (*in a low voice*) Please let him read it! It's bound to be something nice, and then father will be in a good mood, and everything will be pleasant again.

HJALMAR You say I may open it?

HEDVIG Yes, please, father. I'd like to know what it is about, too.

HJALMAR Good. (*Opens the envelope, reads the letter inside. Appears confused*) What is this—?

GINA What does it say?

HEDVIG Please, father—tell us!

HJALMAR Be quiet. (*Reads the letter again. He is pale, but his voice is controlled*) It is a gift letter, Hedvig.

HEDVIG Imagine! What is it I get?

HJALMAR Read for yourself.

(HEDVIG *goes over to the lamp and reads*)

HJALMAR (*in a low voice, clenches his fists*) The eyes, the eyes! And now that letter!

HEDVIG (*interrupting her reading*) Seems to me like it's Grandpa who gets it.

HJALMAR (*taking the letter away from her*) You, Gina—can you make any sense out of this?

GINA I don't know a blessed thing about it. Why don't you just tell me?

HJALMAR Werle writes to Hedvig that her old grandfather no longer needs to trouble himself with the copying work he has been doing, but that he may go to the office every month and draw one hundred crowns—

GREGERS Aha!

HEDVIG One hundred crowns, mother! I read that.

GINA That will be nice for Grandpa.

HJALMAR —one hundred crowns for as long as he needs it. That means, of course, till he closes his eyes.

GINA So *he* is all taken care of, poor soul.

HJALMAR Then it comes. You can't have read that far, Hedvig. After his death, that money will be yours.

HEDVIG Mine? All of it?

HJALMAR He writes that the same amount has been set aside for you for the rest of your life. Are you listening, Gina?

GINA   Yes, I hear.

HEDVIG   Just think—all the money I'll be getting! (*shaking* HJALMAR's *arm*) Father! Father! But aren't you glad?

HJALMAR   (*going away from her*) Glad! (*walking about*) Oh what vistas, what perspectives, open up before me! It is Hedvig he is so generous to!

GINA   Well, she's the one with the birthday.

HEDVIG   And of course you will get it anyway, father! Don't you know I'll give it all to you and mother?

HJALMAR   To mother, yes! That's just it!

GREGERS   Hjalmar, this is a trap being prepared for you.

HJALMAR   You think this may be another trap?

GREGERS   When he was here this morning, he said, "Hjalmar Ekdal is not the man you think he is."

HJALMAR   Not the man—!

GREGERS   "You just wait and see," he said.

HJALMAR   You were to see me selling myself for money—!

HEDVIG   Mother, what *is* all this?

GINA   Go out and take your wraps off.

(HEDVIG, *about to cry, goes out into the kitchen*)

GREGERS   Well, Hjalmar—now we shall see who is right—he or I.

HJALMAR   (*slowly tearing the letter in two, putting the pieces down on the table*) Here is my answer.

GREGERS   Just as I thought.

HJALMAR   (*to* GINA, *who is standing near the stove; in a low voice*) No more concealment now. If everything was over between you and him when you—came to care for me, as you call it, then why did he make it possible for us to get married?

GINA   I guess he thought he'd make free of the house.

HJALMAR   Just that? He wasn't worried about a certain possibility?

GINA   I don't know what you're talking about.

HJALMAR   I want to know—if your child has the right to live under my roof.

GINA   (*drawing herself up, her eyes flashing*) You ask me that!

HJALMAR   Just tell me one thing. Is Hedvig mine or—?—Well?

GINA   (*looks at him with cold defiance*) I don't know.

HJALMAR   (*with a slight tremble*) You don't know!

GINA   How can I? A woman like me!

HJALMAR   (*quietly, turning away from her*) In that case I have nothing more to do in this house.

GREGERS   Think it over, Hjalmar!

HJALMAR   (*putting his overcoat on*) For a man like me there is nothing to think over.

GREGERS   Yes, there is ever so much to think over. You three must stay together if you are to attain to the sacrificial spirit of sublime forgivingness.

HJALMAR   I don't want to attain it! Never! Never! My hat! (*takes his hat*) My house is in ruins about me. (*bursts out crying*) Gregers! I have no child!

HEDVIG   (*who has opened the kitchen door*) Father! What are you saying!

GINA   Oh dear!

HJALMAR   Don't come near me, Hedvig! Go far away from me. I can't stand looking at you. Oh those eyes—! Goodbye. (*is about to go out*)

HEDVIG   (*clings to him, cries*) No! No! Don't leave me!

GINA   Look at the child, Ekdal! Look at the child!

HJALMAR   I will not! I cannot! I must get out—away from all this! (*He tears himself loose from* HEDVIG *and exits*)

HEDVIG   (*her eyes desperate*) He's leaving us, mother! He's leaving us! He'll never come back!

GINA   Just don't cry, Hedvig. Father will be back. You wait.

HEDVIG   (*throws herself sobbing down on the sofa*) No! No! He'll never come back to us any more!

GREGERS   Do you believe I meant all for the best, Mrs. Ekdal?

GINA   Yes, I suppose you did, but God forgive you all the same.

HEDVIG   (*on the sofa*) I want to die! What have I done to him, mother? You just have to get him back again!

GINA   Yes, yes, yes; only be quiet. I'll go out and look for him. (*putting on her coat*) Perhaps he's gone down to Relling's. But you're not to lie there, bawling like that. Promise?

HEDVIG   (*sobbing convulsively*) All right, I'll stop, if only father comes home again.

GREGERS   (*to* GINA, *who is leaving*) But would it not be better to let him fight his agony through by himself?

GINA   He can do that afterwards. First we've got to get the child quieted down. (*goes out*)

HEDVIG   (*sitting up, drying her eyes*) Now you have to tell me what this is all about. Why doesn't father want me any more?

GREGERS   You must not ask that till you're big and grown-up.

HEDVIG (*sobbing*)   But I just can't stay as miserable as this all the time till I'm grown up. —But I know what it is. Maybe I'm not really father's child.

GREGERS (*uneasily*)   How could that be?

HEDVIG   Mother might have found me. And now perhaps father has found out about it. I have read about things like that.

GREGERS   Well, if it really were so—

HEDVIG   I think he could love me just as much, regardless. More, almost. The wild duck is a gift, too, and I love her very, very much.

GREGERS (*glad to turn the conversation*) Oh yes, the wild duck. Let's talk about the wild duck, Hedvig.

HEDVIG   That poor wild duck. He can't stand the sight of her, either. Just think, he wants to wring her neck!

GREGERS   Oh, I don't think he'll do that.

HEDVIG   No, but he said it. And I think that was horrid of father, for I pray for the wild duck every night, that she may be kept safe from death and all that's evil.

GREGERS (*looks at her*)   Do you usually say prayers at night?

HEDVIG   Yes, I do.

GREGERS   Who taught you that?

HEDVIG   Myself, for father was terribly sick once and had leeches on his neck, and then he said that death was his dread companion.

GREGERS   And—?

HEDVIG   So I prayed for him when I went to bed. And I have done so ever since.

GREGERS   And now you pray for the wild duck, too?

HEDVIG   I thought it was best to mention her as well, for she was so sickly when we first got her.

GREGERS   Do you say morning prayers, too?

HEDVIG   Of course not.

GREGERS   Why is that so of course?

HEDVIG   Because it's light in the morning. There's not so much to be afraid of then.

GREGERS   And the wild duck you love so much—your father said he'd like to wring her neck?

HEDVIG   No, he said it would be better for him if he did, but he was going to spare her for my sake. And that was good of him.

GREGERS (*closer to her*)   How would it be if you decided to sacrifice the wild duck for *his* sake?

HEDVIG (*getting up*) The wild duck!

GREGERS   What if you willingly gave up the dearest thing in the whole world for him?

HEDVIG   Do you think that would help?

GREGERS   Try it, Hedvig.

HEDVIG (*softly, with shining eyes*)   Yes. I want to.

GREGERS   Do you think you have the right kind of strength for doing it?

HEDVIG   I shall ask Grandpa to shoot the wild duck for me.

GREGERS   Yes, do that. But not a word to your mother about this!

HEDVIG   Why not?

GREGERS   She doesn't understand us.

HEDVIG   The wild duck? I'll try it in the morning!

(GINA *enters from the hall*)

HEDVIG (*towards her*)   Did you find him, mother?

GINA   No, but I found out he's got Relling with him.

GREGERS   Are you sure?

GINA   Yes, the janitor's wife said so. Molvik's with them also.

GREGERS   Just now, when his soul so sorely needs to struggle in solitude—!

GINA (*taking off her coat*)   Yes, men are funny. God knows where Relling is taking him! I ran over to Madam Eriksen's, but they aren't there.

HEDVIG (*struggling with her tears*)   What if he never comes back!

GREGERS   He'll come back. I'll get word to him tomorrow, and then you'll see *how* he *comes* back. You count on that, Hedvig, and get a good night's sleep. Goodnight. (*goes out*)

HEDVIG (*throws herself sobbing on* GINA's *neck*)   Mother! Mother!

GINA (*patting her back, sighing*)   Yes, Relling was right. This is what happens when crazy people come around pestering us with the claim of the ordeal.

ACT FIVE

(*The studio. Cold, gray morning light. There is wet snow on the big panes of the skylight.*

GINA, *aproned, with broom and dust cloth in her hand, enters from the kitchen and goes towards the living room door.* HEDVIG *hurries in from the outside at the same moment*)

GINA (*stops*)   Well?

HEDVIG   Yes, mother, I almost think he's down at Relling's—

GINA   What did I tell you!

HEDVIG   —for the janitor's wife said she

heard Relling bring two others home with him last night.

GINA   I knew it.

HEDVIG   But what good does it do, if he doesn't come up here to us?

GINA   I want to go down and have a talk with him, anyway.

(OLD EKDAL, *in dressing gown and slippers and with his lighted pipe, appears in the door to his room*)

EKDAL   Eh—Hjalmar—? Isn't Hjalmar here?

GINA   No, he is out, Grandpa.

EKDAL   So early? In this blizzard? Well, I can walk by myself in the morning, I can, if it comes to that.

(*He slides the attic door open.* HEDVIG *helps him. He enters. She closes the door behind him*)

HEDVIG   (*in a low voice*)   Mother, what do you think will happen when poor Grandpa hears that father has left us?

GINA   Silly! Grandpa musn't hear anything about it, of course. It was a good thing he wasn't home last night, during all that hullaballoo.

HEDVIG   Yes, but—

(GREGERS *enters*)

GREGERS   Well? Have you traced him yet?

GINA   They say he's down at Relling's.

GREGERS   At Relling's! Has he really been out with those two?

GINA   It looks like it.

GREGERS   But he is so badly in need of solitude—to find himself in earnest—

GINA   Yes. I should think so, too.

(RELLING *enters*)

HEDVIG   (*goes towards him*)   Is father with you?

GINA   (*at the same time*)   Is he down there?

RELLING   He certainly is.

HEDVIG   And you haven't told us!

RELLING   I know. I am a big, bad beast. But I had this other big, bad beast to take care of, too—I mean the demonic one. And after that, I just fell asleep—sound asleep—

GINA   What does Ekdal say today?

RELLING   Not a thing.

HEDVIG   Doesn't he say anything at all?

RELLING   Not a blessed word.

GREGERS   I think I understand that.

GINA   But what is he doing?

RELLING   He is on the sofa, snoring.

GINA   Oh. Yes, Ekdal does snore a lot.

HEDVIG   He's asleep? Can he sleep now?

RELLING   It certainly looks that way.

GREGERS   That's reasonable enough, after

the spiritual turmoil he's just been through—

GINA   And he isn't used to being out revelling nights, either.

HEDVIG   It may be a good thing that he is sleeping, mother.

GINA   That's what I am thinking. Anyway, we'd better not wake him up too soon. Thank you, Relling. First of all I've got to clean things up a bit and make the place look nice. Come and help me, Hedvig. (*They go into the living room*)

GREGERS   (*turning to* RELLING)   Can you account for the present spiritual unrest in Hjalmar Ekdal?

RELLING   To tell you the truth, I haven't noticed any spiritual unrest in him.

GREGERS   What? At such a turning point—When his whole life is acquiring a new basis? How can you think that a personality like Hjalmar Ekdal—?

RELLING   Personality? He? If he ever had any tendency to sprout the kind of abnormal growth you call personality, I can assure you that all roots and tendrils were thoroughly extirpated in his boyhood.

GREGERS   That would indeed be strange, considering the loving upbringing he enjoyed.

RELLING   By those two crackpot, hysterical spinster aunts of his, you mean?

GREGERS   Let me tell you that they were women who never forgot the claim of the ideal—though I suppose you'll just be making fun of me again.

RELLING   No, I'm not in the mood. I do know about them, though. He has often enough held forth about "his soul's two mothers." Personally, I don't think he has much to be grateful to them for. Ekdal's misfortune is that he has always been looked upon as a shining light in his own circle.

GREGERS   And you don't think he is that? I mean, when it comes to depth of soul?

RELLING   I have never noticed it. That his father thought so is one thing. The old lieutenant has been an idiot all his days.

GREGERS   He has all his days been a man with a childlike mind. That is what you don't understand.

RELLING   All right. But after dear, sweet Hjalmar had taken up studying—after a fashion—right away he was the light of the future among his friends, too. He was handsome enough, the rascal—red and white, just the way little shop-girls like the fellows. And he had this sentimental temperament and this warm-hearted voice, and he could give such pretty declamations of other people's poetry and other people's thoughts—

GREGERS (*indignantly*) Is this Hjalmar Ekdal you are describing?

RELLING Yes, if you please. For this is what he looks like on the inside, the idol you are prostrating yourself for.

GREGERS I didn't know I was as blind as all that.

RELLING Well—not far from it. For you are sick, too, you see.

GREGERS That is true.

RELLING Yes it is. And yours is a complicated case. First, there is this pesky integrity fever you're suffering from, and then something worse—you are forever walking around in a delirium of adoration, always looking for something to admire outside of yourself.

GREGERS Yes, there certainly wouldn't be much point in looking for it within myself.

RELLING But you are always so hideously wrong about all those big, wonderful flies you see and hear buzzing around you. Once again you have entered a cottage with your claim of the ideal. People here just can't pay.

GREGERS If this is the way you think of Hjalmar Ekdal, what sort of pleasure can you derive from your constant association with him?

RELLING Oh well. I am supposed to be a kind of doctor, believe it or not, so the least I can do is to look after the poor patients I share quarters with.

GREGERS Ah, I see. Hjalmar Ekdal is sick, too?

RELLING Most people are, worse luck.

GREGERS And what treatment do you apply in Hjalmar's case?

RELLING My usual one. I see to it that his vital lie is kept up.

GREGERS Vital—lie? I am not sure I heard what you said.

RELLING That's right. I said the vital lie. You see, that's the stimulating principle.

GREGERS May I ask with what vital lie you have infected Hjalmar?

RELLING You may not. I never reveal professional secrets to quacks. You are capable of messing him up for me even more than you have. But the method is proven. I have used it with Molvik, too. I have made him demonic. That's the suppurative I have applied to *his* neck.

GREGERS But *isn't* he demonic?

RELLING What the hell does it mean—being demonic? It's just some nonsense I thought of to save his life. If I hadn't, the poor, pitiful swine would have succumbed to self-hatred and despair many a year ago. Not to mention the old lieutenant! Though he has found his own cure.

GREGERS Lieutenant Ekdal? What about him?

RELLING What do you think? There he is, the old slayer of bears, chasing rabbits in a dark attic. And yet, there isn't a happier hunter alive than that old man when he is playing with all that junk. The four or five dried-out Christmas trees he has saved are the whole big, wild Høydal forest to him. The rooster and the chickens are wild fowl in the tree tops, and the rabbits bouncing about on the floor are bears he's grappling with—the frisky old sportsman.

GREGERS Ah, yes—that unfortunate old Lieutenant Ekdal. He has certainly had to compromise the ideals of his youth.

RELLING While I think of it, Mr. Werle—don't use the foreign word "ideals." We have available a good native one: "lies."

GREGERS You think the two things are related?

RELLING About as closely as typhus and putrid fever.

GREGERS Doctor Relling! I won't give up till I have rescued Hjalmar from your clutches!

RELLING That might be his bad luck. Take his vital lie away from the average person, and you take his happiness, too. (*to* HEDVIG, *who enters from the living room*) Well, now, little duck mother. I am going down to see if papa is still in bed pondering that wonderful invention of his. (*goes out*)

GREGERS (*approaching* HEDVIG) I can tell from looking at you that it has not yet been accomplished.

HEDVIG What? Oh, that about the wild duck? No.

GREGERS Your strength of purpose deserted you, I suppose, when the time for action had come.

HEDVIG No, it wasn't that. But when I woke up this morning and remembered what we had talked about, it all seemed so strange.

GREGERS Strange?

HEDVIG Yes, I don't know—Last night, just at the time—I thought there was something very wonderful about it, but when I had slept and I thought about it again, it didn't seem like anything much.

GREGERS I see. I could hardly expect you to grow up in this environment without injury to your soul.

HEDVIG I don't care about that, if only father would come home again.

GREGERS If only your eyes were opened to what gives life its worth—if only you possessed the true, joyful, brave, sacrificial spirit, then you'd see he'll return. But I still have faith in you, Hedvig. (*goes out*)

(HEDVIG *walks around aimlessly. She is about to enter the kitchen, when there is a knock on the inside of the door to the attic.* HEDVIG *opens the doors wide enough for* OLD EKDAL *to come out. She shuts them again*)

EKDAL   H'm. Not much fun taking a walk by yourself, y'know.

HEDVIG   Wouldn't you like to go hunting, Grandpa?

EKDAL   It isn't hunting weather today. Too dark. Can hardly see a thing.

HEDVIG   Don't you ever want to shoot something beside rabbits?

EKDAL   Aren't the rabbits good enough, perhaps?

HEDVIG   Yes, but what about the wild duck?

EKDAL   Haw! So you're scared I'll shoot your wild duck? I'll never do that, Hedvig. Never.

HEDVIG   No, for I bet you don't know how. I've heard it's difficult to shoot wild ducks.

EKDAL   Don't know how! Should say I do!

HEDVIG   How would you do it, Grandpa?— I don't mean *my* wild duck, but another one.

EKDAL   Would try to get a shot in just below the breast; that's the best place. And try to shoot *against* the feathers, not *with*.

HEDVIG   Then they die?

EKDAL   Damn right they do—if you shoot right.—Well, better go in and dress up. H'm. Y'know. H'm—(*goes into his own room*)

(HEDVIG *waits a moment, glances towards the living room door, stands on tiptoe, takes the double-barreled pistol down from the shelf, looks at it.* GINA, *with broom and dust cloth, enters from the living room.* HEDVIG *quickly puts the pistol back, without* GINA's *noticing*)

GINA   Don't fool with father's things, Hedvig.

HEDVIG   (*leaving the shelf*)   I just wanted to straighten up some.

GINA   Why don't you go into the kitchen and see if the coffee is keeping hot? I am taking a tray with me when I go down.

(HEDVIG *goes into the kitchen.* GINA *starts putting the studio in order. After a short while, the door to the outside is hesitantly opened and* HJALMAR *looks in. He is wearing a coat but no hat. He looks unkempt and unwashed. His eyes are dull and lusterless*)

GINA   (*stands staring at him, still with the broom in her hand*)   Bless you, Ekdal—so you did come back, after all!

HJALMAR   (*enters, answers in a dull voice*)   I return—only to leave.

GINA   Yes, yes, I suppose. But good Lord! how you look!

HJALMAR   Look?

GINA   And your nice winter coat? I'd say that's done for.

HEDVIG   (*in the kitchen door*)   Mother, don't you want me to—(*sees* HJALMAR, *gives a shout of joy and runs towards him*) Father! Father!

HJALMAR   (*turning away, with a gesture*)   Go away! Go away! (*to* GINA) Get her away from me, I say!

GINA   (*in a low voice*)   Go into the living room, Hedvig.

(HEDVIG *leaves silently*)

HJALMAR   (*busy, pulling out the table drawer*)   I need my books with me. Where are my books?

GINA   Which books?

HJALMAR   My scientific works, of course— the technical journals I need for my invention.

GINA   (*looking on the shelf*)   Do you mean these over here, with no covers on them?

HJALMAR   Yes, yes, of course.

GINA   (*puts a pile of journals down on the table*)   Don't you want me to get Hedvig to cut them open for you?

HJALMAR   No. Nobody needs to cut any pages for me.

(*Brief silence*)

GINA   So you *are* going to leave us, Ekdal?

HJALMAR   (*rummaging among the books*) That goes without saying, I should think.

GINA   All right.

HJALMAR   (*violently*)   For you can hardly expect me to want to stay where my heart is pierced every single hour of the day!

GINA   God forgive you for thinking so bad of me!

HJALMAR   Proof—!

GINA   Seems to me, you're the one who should bring proof.

HJALMAR   After a past like yours? There are certain claims—I might call them the claims of the ideal—

GINA   What about Grandpa? What is *he* going to do, poor man?

HJALMAR   I know my duty. The helpless one goes with me. I'll go out and make arrangements—H'm (*hesitantly*) Has anybody found my hat on the stairs?

GINA   No. Have you lost your hat?

HJALMAR   I most certainly had it on when I came home last night; there isn't the slightest doubt about that. But now I can't find it.

GINA   Good Lord! Where did you go with those two drunks?

HJALMAR   Oh, don't ask about inessentials. Do you think I'm in a mood for remembering details?

GINA   I only hope you haven't got a cold, Ekdal. (*goes into the kitchen*)

HJALMAR (*speaking to himself, in a low voice, angrily, as he empties the drawer*) You're a scoundrel, Relling!—A villain is what you are!—Miserable traitor!—I'd gladly see you assassinated—!

(*He puts aside some old letters, discovers the torn gift letter from the day before, picks it up and looks at the two peices, puts them down quickly as GINA enters*)

GINA (*putting a tray with food down on the table*) Here's a drop of coffee, if you want it. And some salt meat sandwiches.

HJALMAR (*glancing at the tray*) Salt meat? Never under this roof! True it is, I haven't taken solid nourishment for almost twenty-four hours, but that can't be helped.—My notes! My incipient memoirs! Where is my diary—all my important papers! (*opens the door to the living room, but steps back*) If she isn't there, too!

GINA   Heavens, Ekdal. She's got to be somewhere.

HJALMAR   Leave! (*He makes room. HEDVIG, scared, enters the studio. With his hand on the door knob; to GINA*) During the last moments I spend in my former home I wish to be spared the sight of intruders—(*enters the living room*)

HEDVIG (*starts, asks her mother in a low and trembling voice*) Does that mean me?

GINA   Stay in the kitchen, Hedvig, or no— go to your own room. (*to HJALMAR, as she enters the living room*) Wait a minute, Ekdal. Don't make such a mess in the dresser. I know where everything is.

HEDVIG (*remains motionless for a moment, in helpless fright, presses her lips together not to cry, clenches her hands, whispers*) The wild duck!

(*She tiptoes over to the shelf and takes the pistol down, opens the doors to the inner attic, goes inside, closes behind her. HJALMAR and GINA are heard talking in the living room*)

HJALMAR (*appears with some notebooks and a pile of old papers, which he puts down on the table*) The bag obviously won't be enough. There are thousands of things I need to take with me!

GINA (*entering with the bag*) Can't you leave most of it behind for the time being and just pick up a clean shirt and some underwear?

HJALMAR   Phew—! These exhausting preparations—! (*takes off his overcoat and throws it on the sofa*)

GINA   And there's the coffee getting cold too.

HJALMAR   H'm. (*without thinking, he takes a sip, and then another one*)

GINA (*dusting off the back of chairs*) How are you ever going to find a large enough attic for the rabbits?

HJALMAR   You mean I have to drag all those rabbits along, too?

GINA   Grandpa can't do without his rabbits —you know that as well as I do.

HJALMAR   He'll have to get used to that. I shall have to give up higher values in life than a bunch of rabbits.

GINA (*dusting off the shelf*) Shall I put the flute in for you?

HJALMAR   No. No flute for me. But give me my pistol.

GINA   You want that old pistol?

HJALMAR   Yes. My loaded pistol.

GINA (*looking for it*) It's gone. He must have taken it inside with him.

HJALMAR   Is he in the attic?

GINA   Sure, he's in the attic.

HJALMAR   H'm. The lonely grayhead—(*He eats a sandwich, empties his cup of coffee*)

GINA   If only we hadn't rented that room, you could have moved in there.

HJALMAR   And stay under the same roof as—! Never! Never again!

GINA   But couldn't you stay in the living room for a day or two? There you'd have everything to yourself.

HJALMAR   Not within these walls!

GINA   How about down at Relling's and Molvik's, then?

HJALMAR   Don't mention their names to me! I get sick just thinking about them. Oh no—it's out into the wind and the snowdrifts for me—to walk from house to house seeking shelter for father and myself.

GINA   But you have no hat, Ekdal! You've lost your hat, remember?

HJALMAR   Oh, those two abominations! Rich in nothing but every vice! A hat must be procured. (*takes another sandwich*) Arrangements must be made. After all, I don't intend to catch my death. (*looks for something on the tray*)

GINA   What are you looking for?

HJALMAR   Butter.

GINA   Just a moment. (*goes out into the kitchen*)

HJALMAR (*shouting after her*) Oh never mind. Dry bread is good enough for me.

GINA (*bringing a plate with butter*) Here. This is supposed to be freshly churned.

(*She pours him another cup of coffee. He sits down on the sofa, puts more butter on his bread, eats and drinks in silence*)

HJALMAR (*after a pause*)   Could I, without being disturbed by anyone—and I mean *anyone*—stay in the living room for a day or two?

GINA   You certainly can, if you want to.

HJALMAR   You see, I don't know how to get all of father's things moved out on such short notice.

GINA   And there is this, too, that first you'd have to tell him that you don't want to live together with the rest of us any more.

HJALMAR (*pushing his cup away*)   Yes, yes —that, too. I shall have to go into all those intricate relationships once again, to explain—I must think, I must have air to breathe, I can't bear all the burdens in one single day.

GINA   Of course not. And in such awful weather too—

HJALMAR (*moving* WERLE's *letter*)   I notice this piece of paper still lying around.

GINA   Well, *I* haven't touched it.

HJALMAR   Not that it concerns *me*—

GINA   I'm sure *I* don't expect to make use of it—

HJALMAR   Nevertheless, I suppose we shouldn't let it get completely lost. In all the fuss of moving, something might easily—

GINA   I'll take care of it, Ekdal.

HJALMAR   For the gift letter belongs to father, first of all. It's his affair whether he wants to make use of it or not.

GINA (*with a sigh*)   Yes, poor old Grandpa—

HJALMAR   Just to make sure—Is there any glue?

GINA (*walks over to the shelf*)   Here's a bottle.

HJALMAR   And a brush?

GINA   Here. (*brings him both*)

HJALMAR (*picks up a pair of scissors*)   Just a strip of paper on the back—(*cuts and glues*) Far be it from me to lay hands on somebody else's property—least of all the property of a poverty-stricken old man.—Well—not on—that other one's, either.—There, now! Leave it to dry for a while. And when it's dry, remove it. I don't want to see that document again—ever!

(GREGERS *enters*)

GREGERS (*a little surprised*)   What? So this is where you are, Hjalmar!

HJALMAR (*quickly gets up*)   Sheer exhaustion drove me to sit down.

GREGERS   And I see you've had breakfast.

HJALMAR   The body, too, makes demands at times.

GREGERS   Well, what have you decided to do?

HJALMAR   For a man like me, there is only one way open. I am in the process of gathering up my most important possessions. Obviously, that takes time.

GINA (*a trifle impatient*)   Do you want me to make the living room ready for you, or do you want me to pack the bag?

HJALMAR (*after an irritated glance at* GREGERS)   Pack—and make the room ready.

GINA (*picking up the bag*)   All right. I'll just put into it the shirts and those other things.

(*She goes into the living room, closing the door behind her*)

GREGERS (*after a short silence*)   I had no idea this would be the end of it. Is it really necessary for you to leave house and home?

HJALMAR (*paces restlessly up and down*) What do you want me to do? I am not made to be unhappy, Gregers. I require peace and security and comfort around me.

GREGERS   But you can have all that, Hjalmar. Just try. It seems to me there is a firm foundation to build upon now. Start all over again. And remember, you still have your invention to live for.

HJALMAR   Oh don't talk about that invention. It may take a long time yet.

GREGERS   So?

HJALMAR   Well, yes, for heaven's sake, what do you expect me to invent, anyway? The others have invented most of it already. It's getting more difficult every day.

GREGERS   But all the labor you have put into it—?

HJALMAR   It was that dissipated Relling who got me started on it.

GREGERS   Relling?

HJALMAR   Yes, it was he who first called attention to my talent for making some fabulous invention or other in photography.

GREGERS   I see. It was Relling—!

HJALMAR   Ah—I have been so wonderfully happy about it. Not so much about the invention itself, but because Hedvig believed in it—believed with all the strength and power of a child's soul.—That is, I *thought* she did— fool as I was.

GREGERS   Can you really think that Hedvig would be false to you?

HJALMAR   I can believe anything now. It is Hedvig who is in the way. She it is who is shutting the sun out of my entire life.

GREGERS   Hedvig? You mean Hedvig? How in the world is she going to be an obstacle?

HJALMAR (*without answering*) I have loved that child more than I can ever say. You have no idea how happy I was whenever I came back to my humble dwelling and she rushed towards me with her sweet, squinting eyes. Ha, credulous fool that I was! She was so unspeakably dear to me—and so I lulled myself into the dream that I was equally dear to her.

GREGERS You call that a dream?

HJALMAR How can I tell? I can't get anything out of Gina. Besides, she completely lacks any sense of the ideal aspects of the issue. But to you I can open up, Gregers. It is this terrible doubt—perhaps Hedvig has never really loved me.

GREGERS Maybe you'll receive proof— (*listens*) Shh! What's that? The wild duck?

HJALMAR It's just quacking. Father's in the attic.

GREGERS He is! (*joy lights his face*) I tell you again, Hjalmar—maybe you will find proof that your poor, misunderstood Hedvig has always loved you!

HJALMAR Pah! What proof could she give? I dare not trust to mere asseverations.

GREGERS Surely, Hedvig doesn't know what deceit is.

HJALMAR Ah, Gregers—that is just what I cannot be certain of. Who knows what Gina and this Mrs. Sørby may have been whispering and scheming? And Hedvig's ears are big enough, believe you me. Maybe that gift letter didn't come as such a surprise to her. It seemed to me I noticed something like that.

GREGERS Good heavens, Hjalmar! What kind of spirit is this that's taken possession of you!

HJALMAR I have had my eyes opened. You just wait. It may turn out that the gift letter was just the beginning. Mrs. Sørby has always been very fond of Hedvig, and now, of course, it's in her power to do anything she likes for the child. They can take her away from me what day and hour they choose.

GREGERS Hedvig will never leave you, Hjalmar. Never.

HJALMAR Don't be too sure. If they beckon her with their arms full—? And I who have loved her so infinitely much! I, whose greatest joy it was to take her tenderly by the hand and lead her, as one leads a frightened child through a dark and deserted room! Now I feel this painful certainty that the poor photographer in his attic has never really meant very much to her. She has only cleverly managed to keep on good terms with him while she bided her time.

GREGERS You don't believe this, Hjalmar.

HJALMAR That is just what is so terrible— I don't know what to believe—I'll never be able to find out! But do you really doubt that I am right? Ah, Gregers, you put too much trust in the claim of the ideal! If those others were to come now, with their ample offerings, and called to the child: Leave him; life awaits you here with us—

GREGERS (*quickly*) Yes, what then—?

HJALMAR If then I were to ask her: Hedvig, are you willing to give your life for me? (*laughs scornfully*) Oh yes—you'd find out soon enough what answer I'd get!

(*A pistol shot is heard from within the attic*)

GREGERS (*with a shout of joy*) Hjalmar!

HJALMAR Must he go shooting today—!

GINA (*enters*) Can't say I like this, Ekdal —Grandpa is there all by himself, banging away.

HJALMAR I'll take a look—

GREGERS (*agitated, feelingly*) Wait! Do you know what that was?

HJALMAR Yes, of course, I do.

GREGERS No, you don't. But *I* know. It was the proof!

HJALMAR What proof?

GREGERS It was a child's sacrifice. She has got your father to shoot the wild duck.

HJALMAR Shoot the wild duck!

GINA Heavens—!

HJALMAR Whatever for?

GREGERS She wanted to sacrifice to you what she held dearest in the whole world. For then she thought you'd love her again.

HJALMAR (*softly, moved*) Oh that child!

GINA What she thinks of!

GREGERS All she wanted was your love, Hjalmar. Without it, life didn't seem possible to her.

GINA (*struggling with tears*) Now, do you see, Ekdal?

HJALMAR Gina, where is she?

GINA (*sniffling*) Poor thing. She is sitting out in the kitchen, I guess.

HJALMAR (*walks to the kitchen door, flings it open, says*) Hedvig—come! Come to me! (*looks around*) No. She isn't here.

GINA Then she must be in her own room.

HJALMAR (*off-stage*) No, she isn't there, either. (*re-entering the studio*) She must have gone out.

GINA Yes, for you know you didn't want to see hide nor hair of her in the house.

HJALMAR If only she'd come back soon— so I can tell her—Now I feel that everything will be all right, Gregers. Now I think we can start life over again.

GREGERS (*quietly*) I knew it. Restitution would come through the child.

(*Old* EKDAL *appears in the door to his room. He is in full uniform and is buckling on his sabre*)

HJALMAR (*surprised*) Father! You're in there!

GINA Do you go shooting in your room, now, Grandpa?

EKDAL (*approaches indignantly*) So you're off hunting by yourself, are you Hjalmar?

HJALMAR (*tense, confused*) You mean it wasn't you who fired that shot in the attic just now?

EKDAL I? Fired? H'm.

GREGERS (*shouts to* HJALMAR) She has shot the wild duck herself!

HJALMAR What *is* this? (*He hurriedly slides the attic doors open, looks in, gives a loud cry*) Hedvig!

GINA (*runs to the door*) Oh God! What is it?

HJALMAR (*going inside*) She is lying on the floor!

GREGERS Lying—! (*follows* HJALMAR *inside*)

GINA (*at the same time*) Hedvig! (*enters the attic*) No! No! No!

EKDAL Ho-ho! So *she* has taken to hunting too, now!

(HJALMAR, GINA, *and* GREGERS *drag* HEDVIG *into the studio. Her trailing right hand clasps the pistol tightly*)

HJALMAR (*beside himself*) The pistol went off! She's hit! Call for help! Help!

GINA (*running out into the hallway, shouts down*) Relling! Relling! Doctor Relling! Hurry up here, fast as you can!

(HJALMAR *and* GREGERS *put* HEDVIG *down on the sofa*)

EKDAL (*quietly*) The woods avenge themselves.

HJALMAR (*on his knees beside* HEDVIG) She's coming to now. She is coming to. Oh yes, yes, yes—

GINA (*having returned*) Where's she hit? I can't see a thing.

(RELLING *enters hurriedly, followed by* MOLVIK. *The latter is without vest and tie, his tailcoat thrown open*)

RELLING What's the matter?

GINA They say Hedvig has shot herself.

HJALMAR Come and help us!

RELLING Shot herself! (*He pulls the table back and begins to examine her*)

HJALMAR (*still on his knees, looking anxiously at* RELLING) It can't be dangerous, can it, Relling? What, Relling? She hardly bleeds at all. It can't possibly be dangerous?

RELLING How did this happen?

HJALMAR Oh, I don't know—

GINA She was going to shoot the wild duck.

RELLING The wild duck?

HJALMAR The pistol must have gone off.

RELLING H'm. I see.

EKDAL The woods avenge themselves. But I'm not afraid. (*enters the attic and closes the doors behind him*)

HJALMAR Relling—why don't you say anything?

RELLING The bullet has entered her chest.

HJALMAR Yes, but she's coming to!

RELLING Can't you see that Hedvig is dead?

GINA (*bursts into tears*) Oh, the child, the child—!

GREGERS (*hoarsely*) In the depths of the sea—

HJALMAR (*jumps to his feet*) She must live! I want her to live! For God's sake, Relling—just for a moment—just so I can tell her how unspeakably much I have loved her all the time!

RELLING Her heart has been pierced. Internal hemorrhage. She died instantly.

HJALMAR And I who chased her away from me like an animal! Frightened and lonely she crawled into the attic and died for love of me. (*sobbing*) Never to be able to make up for it! Never to tell her—! (*shakes his fists upwards*) You! You above! If thou are at all—! Why hast thou done this unto me?

GINA Shhh, shhh. You mustn't make such a fuss. We had no right to keep her, I suppose.

MOLVIK The child is not dead. It sleepeth.

RELLING Rubbish!

HJALMAR (*quieting down, walks over to the sofa, looks at* HEDVIG, *his arms crossed*) There she lies, so stiff and still.

RELLING (*trying to release the pistol*) She holds on so tightly, I can't—

GINA No, no, Relling. Don't break her fingers. Let the pistol be.

HJALMAR Let her have it with her.

GINA Yes, let her. But the child isn't going to lie out here for a show. She is going into her own little room, right now. Give me a hand, Ekdal.

(HJALMAR *and* GINA *carry* HEDVIG *between them*)

HJALMAR (*carrying*) Gina, Gina—do you think you can bear this?

GINA The one has to help the other. Seems to me like now we both have a share in her.

MOLVIK (*raising his arms, muttering*) Praise be the Lord, to dust thou returnest, to dust thou returnest—

RELLING (*whispers*) Shut up, man! You're drunk.

(HJALMAR *and* GINA *carry* HEDVIG *through the kitchen door.* RELLING *closes the door behind them.* MOLVIK *slinks quietly out into the hall*)

RELLING (*goes up to* GREGERS) Nobody is going to tell me this was an accident.

GREGERS (*who has remained stunned, moving convulsively*) Who is to say how this terrible thing happened?

RELLING There were powder burns on her dress. She must have placed the muzzle against her chest and pulled the trigger.

GREGERS Hedvig has not died in vain. Did you notice how grief released what is great in him?

RELLING There is a touch of greatness in most of us when we stand in sorrow by a corpse. How long do you think that will last with him?

GREGERS As if it won't last and grow throughout the rest of his days!

RELLING Within a year little Hedvig won't be anything to him but an occasion for spouting pretty sentiments.

GREGERS And you dare say that about Hjalmar Ekdal!

RELLING Let's talk about this again when the first grass has withered on her grave. You'll hear all about "the child so early taken from the father's heart." You'll see him wallow in sentimentality and self-admiration and self-pity. You just wait!

GREGERS If you are right and I am wrong, life isn't worth living.

RELLING Oh, life would be fairly tolerable if only we'd be spared these blasted bill collectors who come around pestering us paupers with the claim of the ideal.

GREGERS (*staring ahead*) In that case I am glad my destiny is what it is.

RELLING Beg your pardon—what *is* your destiny?

GREGERS (*about to leave*) To be the thirteenth man at the table.

RELLING The hell it is.

HEDDA GABLER

Translated by Otto Reinert

CAST OF CHARACTERS

JØRGEN TESMAN, *University Research Fellow in the History of Civilization*
HEDDA, *his wife*
MISS JULIANE TESMAN, *his aunt*
MRS. ELVSTED
JUDGE BRACK
EILERT LØVBORG
BERTE, *the Tesman's maid*

SCENE *The Tesman's villa in a fashionable residential section of the town*

ACT ONE

(*A spacious, handsome, tastefully furnished room. Dark décor. In the rear, a wide doorway with open portieres. Beyond is a smaller room, furnished in the same style as the front room. A door, right, leads to the front hall. Left, French doors, with portieres drawn aside, through which can be seen a part of a roofed verandah and trees with autumn foliage. Front center, an oval table covered with a cloth. Chairs around it. Front right, a wide, dark, porcelain stove, a high-backed easy chair, a footstool with a pillow, and two ottomans. In the corner far right, a sofa and a small, round table. Front left, a sofa, set out from the wall. Far left, beyond the*

Hedda Gabler by Henrik Ibsen, translated by Otto Reinert. Copyright 1962 by Chandler Publishing Company. All performance rights are the property of Literary Discoveries, Inc., and permissions for performances of any kind must be obtained from Literary Discoveries, Inc., 604 Mission Street, San Francisco.

French doors, an upright piano. On both sides of the doorway, rear center, whatnots with knickknacks. Against the rear wall of the inner room, a sofa, and in front of it a table and two chairs. Above the sofa, a portrait of a handsome, elderly man in general's uniform. Over the table hangs a lamp with milky, white glass. There are several bouquets of flowers, in vases and glasses, in various places in the front room. Others are lying on the tables. Thick carpets on the floors of both rooms. The morning sun is shining through the French doors.

MISS JULIANA TESMAN, *with hat and parasol, enters right, followed by* BERTE, *who carries a bouquet of flowers wrapped in paper.* MISS TESMAN *is a nice-looking woman of 65, of pleasant mien, neatly but not expensively dressed in a gray suit.* BERTE *is a middle-aged servant girl, of rather plain and countrified appearance*)

MISS TESMAN (*stops inside the door, listens, says in a low voice*) On my word—I don't think they are even up yet!

BERTE (*also softly*) That's what I told you, miss. When you think how late the steamer got in last night. And afterwards—! Goodness!— all the stuff she wanted unpacked before she turned in.

MISS TESMAN Well—just let them sleep. But fresh morning air—*that* we can give them when they come in here. (*goes and opens the French doors wide*)

BERTE (*by the table, lost, still holding the flowers*) Please, miss—I just don't see a bit of space anywhere! I think I'd better put these over here. (*puts the flowers down on the piano*)

MISS TESMAN Well, well, my dear Berte. So you've got yourself a new mistress now. The good Lord knows it was hard for me to let you go.

BERTE (*near tears*) What about me, then, miss! What shall *I* say? I who have served you and Miss Rina all these blessed years.

[384]

MISS TESMAN   We shall just have to make the best of it, Berte. There's nothing else to do. Jørgen can't do without you, you know. He just can't. You've looked after him ever since he was a little boy.

BERTE   Yes, but miss—I'm ever so worried about leaving Miss Rina. The poor dear lying there all helpless. With that new girl and all! She'll never learn how to make things nice and comfortable for an invalid.

MISS TESMAN   Oh yes, you'll see, I'll teach her. And of course, you know, I'll do most of it myself. So don't you worry yourself about my poor sister, Berte.

BERTE   Yes, but there's another thing, too, miss. I'm scared I won't be able to suit young Mrs. Tesman.

MISS TESMAN   Oh, well. Good heavens. So there is a thing or two—Right at first—

BERTE   For I believe she's ever so particular.

MISS TESMAN   Can you wonder? General Gabler's daughter? Just think of the kind of life she was used to when the General was alive. Do you remember when she rode by with her father? That long black riding habit she wore? And the feather in her hat?

BERTE   Oh, I remember, all right. But I'll be blessed if I ever thought she and the young master would make a pair of it.

MISS TESMAN   Nor did I. By the way, while I think of it, Berte. Jørgen has a new title now. From now on you must refer to him as "the Doctor."

BERTE   Yes, the young mistress said something about that, too, last night. Soon as they were inside the door. Then it's really so, miss?

MISS TESMAN   It certainly is. Just think, Berte—they have made him a doctor abroad. During the trip, you know. I hadn't heard a thing about it till last night on the pier.

BERTE   Well, I daresay he could be anything he put his mind to, *he* could—smart as *he* is. But I must say I'd never thought he'd turn to doctoring people, too.

MISS TESMAN   Oh, that's not the kind of doctor he is. (*nods significantly*) And as far as that is concerned, there is no telling but pretty soon you may have to call him something grander yet.

BERTE   You don't say! What might that be, miss?

MISS TESMAN (*smiles*)   Wouldn't you like to know! (*moved*) Ah yes, indeed—! If only dear Jochum could see from his grave what has become of his little boy! (*looking around*) But look, Berte—what's this for? Why have you taken off all the slip covers?

BERTE   She told me to. Said she can't stand slip covers on chairs.

MISS TESMAN   Do you think they mean to make this their everyday living room, then?

BERTE   It sure sounded that way. Mrs. Tesman did, I mean. For he—the doctor—he didn't say anything.

(JØRGEN TESMAN *enters from the right side of the inner room. He is humming to himself. He carries an open, empty suitcase. He is of medium height, youthful-looking thirty-three years old, somewhat stoutish. Round, open, cheerful face. Blond hair and beard. He wears glasses and is dressed in a comfortable, rather casual suit*)

MISS TESMAN   Good morning, good morning, Jørgen!

TESMAN (*in the doorway*)   Auntie! Dearest Aunt Julle! (*comes forward and shakes her hand*) All the way out here—as early as this! Hm?

MISS TESMAN   Well—I just had to drop in for a moment. To see how you are getting along, you know.

TESMAN   Even though you haven't had a good night's sleep.

MISS TESMAN   Oh, that doesn't matter at all.

TESMAN   But you did get home from the pier all right, I hope. Hm?

MISS TESMAN   Oh yes, certainly I did, thank you. The Judge was kind enough to see me all the way to my door.

TESMAN   We were so sorry we couldn't give you a ride in our carriage. But you saw for yourself—all the boxes Hedda had.

MISS TESMAN   Yes, she certainly brought quite a collection.

BERTE (*to* TESMAN)   Should I go and ask Mrs. Tesman if there's anything I can help her with?

TESMAN   No, thank you, Berte—you'd better not. She said she'll ring if she wants you.

BERTE (*going right*)   Well, all right.

TESMAN   But, look—you might take this suitcase with you.

BERTE (*takes it*)   I'll put it in the attic. (*exits right*)

TESMAN   Just think, Auntie—that whole suitcase was brimful of copies of old documents. You wouldn't believe me if I told you all the things I have collected from libraries and archives all over. Quaint old items nobody has known anything about.

MISS TESMAN   Well, no, Jørgen. I'm sure you haven't wasted your time on your honeymoon.

TESMAN   No, I think I may say I have not. But take your hat off, Auntie—for goodness' sake. Here! Let me untie the ribbon for you. Hm?

MISS TESMAN (*while he does so*) Ah, God forgive me, if this isn't just as if you were still at home with us!

TESMAN (*inspecting the hat*) My, what a fine-looking hat you've got yourself!

MISS TESMAN   I bought it for Hedda's sake.

TESMAN   For Hedda's sake? Hm?

MISS TESMAN   So she won't need to feel ashamed of me if we ever go out together.

TESMAN (*patting her cheek*) If you don't think of everything, Auntie! (*puts the hat down on a chair by the table*) And now—over here to the sofa—we'll just sit and chat for a while till Hedda comes.

(*They seat themselves. She places her parasol in the corner by the sofa*)

MISS TESMAN (*takes both his hands in hers and gazes at him*) What a blessing it is to have you back again, Jørgen, big as life! You—Jochum's little boy!

TESMAN   For me, too, Aunt Julle. To see you again. For you have been both father and mother to me.

MISS TESMAN   Ah, yes—don't you think I know you'll always keep a spot in your heart for these two old aunts of yours!

TESMAN   So Aunt Rina isn't any better, hm?

MISS TESMAN   Oh no. We mustn't look for improvement in her case, poor dear. She is lying there just as she has been all these years. Just the same, may the good Lord keep her for me a long time yet! For else I just wouldn't know what to do with myself, Jørgen. Especially now, when I don't have you to look after any more.

TESMAN (*pats her back*) There, there, now!

MISS TESMAN (*changing tone*) And to think that you are a married man, Jørgen! And that you were the one to walk off with Hedda Gabler. The lovely Hedda Gabler. Just think! As many admirers as she had!

TESMAN (*hums a little, smiles contentedly*) Yes, I daresay I have quite a few good friends here in town who'd gladly be in my shoes, hm?

MISS TESMAN   And such a lovely, long honeymoon you had! More than five—almost six months!

TESMAN   Well, you know—for me it has been a kind of study tour as well. All the collections I had to go through. And the books I had to read!

MISS TESMAN   Yes, I suppose. (*more confi-dentially, her voice lowered a little*) But listen, Jørgen—haven't you got something—something special to tell me?

TESMAN   About the trip?

MISS TESMAN   Yes.

TESMAN   No—I don't know of anything besides what I wrote in my letters. They gave me a doctor's degree down there—but I told you that last night; I'm sure I did.

MISS TESMAN   Well, yes, that sort of thing—What I mean is—don't you have certain—certain—expectations?

TESMAN   Expectations?

MISS TESMAN   Ah for goodness' sake, Jørgen! I am your old Auntie, after all!

TESMAN   Certainly I have expectations.

MISS TESMAN   Well!!

TESMAN   I fully expect to be made a professor one of these days.

MISS TESMAN   Professor—oh yes—

TESMAN   I may even say I am quite certain of it. But dear Aunt Julle—you know this just as well as I do!

MISS TESMAN (*laughing a little*) Of course I do. You're quite right. (*changing topic*) But we were talking about the trip. It must have cost a great deal of money—hm, Jørgen?

TESMAN   Well, now; you know that large stipend went quite a long way.

MISS TESMAN   I just don't see how you made it do for both of you, though.

TESMAN   No, I suppose that's not so easy to understand, hm?

MISS TESMAN   Particularly with a lady along. For I have always heard that is ever so much more expensive.

TESMAN   Well, yes, naturally. That *is* rather more expensive. But Hedda had to have this trip, Auntie! She really had to. Nothing less would do.

MISS TESMAN   No, I daresay. For a wedding journey is quite the thing these days. But now tell me—have you had a chance to look around here yet?

TESMAN   I certainly have. I have been up and about ever since dawn.

MISS TESMAN   And what do you think of it all?

TESMAN   Delightful! Perfectly delightful! The only thing is I don't see what we are going to do with the two empty rooms between the second sitting room in there and Hedda's bedroom.

MISS TESMAN (*with a chuckle*) Oh my dear Jørgen—you may find them useful enough—when the time comes!

TESMAN   Of course, you're right, Auntie! As my library expands, hm?

MISS TESMAN Quite so, my dear boy. It was your library I was thinking of.

TESMAN But I'm really most happy on Hedda's behalf. For you know, before we were engaged she used to say she wouldn't care to live anywhere but in Secretary Falk's house.

MISS TESMAN Yes, just think—wasn't that a lucky coincidence, that it was up for sale right after you had left?

TESMAN Yes, Aunt Julle. We've certainly been lucky. Hm?

MISS TESMAN But it will be expensive, my dear Jørgen. Terribly expensive—all this.

TESMAN (*looks at her, a bit crestfallen*) Yes, I daresay it will, Auntie.

MISS TESMAN Heavens, yes!

TESMAN How much, do you think? Roughly. Hm?

MISS TESMAN No, I couldn't possibly say till all the bills arrive.

TESMAN Well, anyway, Judge Brack managed to get very reasonable terms for us. He said so himself in a letter to Hedda.

MISS TESMAN Yes, and I won't have you uneasy on that account, Jørgen. Besides, I have given security for the furniture and the carpets.

TESMAN Security? You? But dear Aunt Julle —what kind of security could you give?

MISS TESMAN The annuity.

TESMAN (*jumps up*) What! Your and Aunt Rina's annuity?

MISS TESMAN Yes. I didn't know what else to do, you see.

TESMAN (*standing before her*) But are you clear out of your mind, Auntie! That annuity— that's all the two of you have to live on!

MISS TESMAN Oh well, there's nothing to get so excited about, I'm sure. It's all just a matter of form, you know. That's what the Judge said, too. For he was kind enough to arrange the whole thing for me. Just a matter of form—those were his words.

TESMAN That's all very well. Still—

MISS TESMAN For now you'll have your own salary, you know. And, goodness—what if we do have a few expenses—Help out a bit right at first—? That would only be a joy for us—

TESMAN Oh, Auntie! When will you ever stop making sacrifices for my sake!

MISS TESMAN (*gets up, puts her hands on his shoulders*) But what other happiness do I have in this world than being able to smooth your way a little, my own dear boy? You, who haven't had either father or mother to lean on? And now the goal is in sight, Jørgen. Things may have looked black at times. But heaven be praised; you're on top now!

TESMAN Yes, it's really quite remarkable the way things have worked out.

MISS TESMAN Yes—and those who were against you—who tried to block your way— now they are tasting defeat. They are down, Jørgen! He, the most dangerous of them all, his fall was the greatest! He made his bed, and now he is lying in it—poor, lost wretch that he is!

TESMAN Have you had any news about Eilert? Since I went away, I mean?

MISS TESMAN Just that he is supposed to have published a new book.

TESMAN What? Eilert Løvborg? Recently? Hm?

MISS TESMAN That's what they say. But I wonder if there can be much to it. What do you think? Ah—but when *your* new book comes, that will be something quite different, Jørgen! What is it going to be about?

TESMAN It will deal with the domestic industries of Brabant during the Middle Ages.

MISS TESMAN Just think—being able to write about something like that!

TESMAN But as far as that is concerned, it may be quite some time before it is ready. I have all these collections to put in order first, you see.

MISS TESMAN Yes, collecting and putting things in order—you certainly know how to do that. In that you are your father's son.

TESMAN Well, I must say I am looking forward to getting started. Particularly now, that I've got my own delightful home to work in.

MISS TESMAN And most of all now that you have the one your heart desired, dear Jørgen.

TESMAN (*embracing her*) Oh yes, yes, Aunt Julle! Hedda—she is the most wonderful part of it all! (*looks toward the doorway*) There—I think she is coming now, hm?

(HEDDA *enters from the left side of the inner room. She is twenty-nine years old. Both features and figure are noble and elegant. Pale, ivory complexion. Steel-gray eyes, expressive of cold, clear calm. Beautiful brown hair, though not particularly ample. She is dressed in a tasteful, rather loose-fitting morning costume*)

MISS TESMAN (*going toward her*) Good morning, my dear Hedda! A very happy morning to you!

HEDDA (*giving her hand*) Good morning, dear Miss Tesman! So early a call? That is most kind.

MISS TESMAN (*seems slightly embarrassed*) And—has the little lady of the house slept well the first night in her new home?

HEDDA Passably, thank you.

TESMAN (*laughs*)   Passably! You are a good one, Hedda! You were sleeping like a log when I got up.

HEDDA   Fortunately. And then, of course, Miss Tesman, it always takes time to get used to new surroundings. That has to come gradually. (*looks left*) Oh dear. The maid has left the verandah doors wide open. There's a veritable flood of sunlight in here.

MISS TESMAN (*toward the doors*)   Well, then, we'll just close them.

HEDDA   No, no, not that. Tesman, dear, please pull the curtains. That will give a softer light.

TESMAN (*over by the French doors*)   Yes, dear. There, now! Now you have both shade and fresh air, Hedda.

HEDDA   We certainly can use some air in here. Such loads of flowers— But, Miss Tesman, please—won't you be seated?

MISS TESMAN   No thanks. I just wanted to see if everything was all right—and so it is, thank goodness. I had better get back to Rina. I know she is waiting for me, poor thing.

TESMAN   Be sure to give her my love, Auntie. And tell her I'll be around to see her later today.

MISS TESMAN   I'll certainly do that!—Oh my! I almost forgot! (*searches the pocket of her dress*) I have something for you, Jørgen. Here.

TESMAN   What's that, Auntie? Hm?

MISS TESMAN (*pulls out a flat parcel wrapped in newspaper and gives it to him*)   Here you are, dear.

TESMAN (*opens the parcel*)   Well, well, well! So you took care of them for me, Aunt Julle! Hedda! Now, isn't that sweet, hm?

HEDDA (*by the whatnot, right*)   If you'd tell me what it is—

TESMAN   My old slippers! *You* know!

HEDDA   Oh really? I remember you often talked about them on the trip.

TESMAN   Yes, for I missed them so. (*walks over to her*) Here—now you can see what they're like, Hedda.

HEDDA (*crosses toward stove*)   Thanks. I don't know that I really care.

TESMAN (*following*)   Just think— Aunt Rina embroidered these slippers for me. Ill as she was. You can't imagine how many memories they hold for me!

HEDDA (*by the table*)   Hardly for me.

MISS TESMAN   That's true, you know, Jørgen.

TESMAN   Yes, but—I just thought that now that she's one of the family—

HEDDA (*interrupting*)   I don't think we'll get on with that maid, Tesman.

MISS TESMAN   Not get on with Berte?

TESMAN   Whatever makes you say that, dear? Hm?

HEDDA (*points*)   Look—she has left her old hat on the chair over there.

TESMAN (*appalled, drops the slippers*)   But Hedda—!

HEDDA   What if somebody were to come and see it!

TESMAN   No, no, Hedda—that's Aunt Julle's hat!

HEDDA   Oh?

MISS TESMAN (*picking up the hat*)   Yes, indeed it is. And it isn't old either, my dear young lady.

HEDDA   I really didn't look that closely—

MISS TESMAN (*tying the ribbons*)   I want you to know that this is the first time I have it on my head. On my word it is!

TESMAN   And very handsome it is, too. Really a splendid-looking hat!

MISS TESMAN   Oh, I don't know that it is anything so special, Jørgen. (*looks around*) My parasol—? Ah, here it is. (*picks it up*) For that is mine, too. (*mutters*) Not Berte's.

TESMAN   New hat and new parasol! What do you think of that, Hedda!

HEDDA   Very nice indeed.

TESMAN   Yes, don't you think so? Hm? But, Auntie, take a good look at Hedda before you leave. See how pretty and blooming she looks.

MISS TESMAN   Dear me, Jørgen; that's nothing new. Hedda has been lovely all her days. (*She nods and walks right*)

TESMAN (*following*)   Yes, but have you noticed how full-figured and healthy she looks after the trip? How she has filled out?

HEDDA (*crossing*)   Oh—stop it!

MISS TESMAN (*halts, turns around*)   Filled out?

TESMAN   Yes, Aunt Julle. You can't see it so well now when she wears that dress. But I, who have the opportunity—

HEDDA (*by the French doors, impatiently*)   Oh, you have no opportunity at all!

TESMAN   It must be the mountain air in Tyrol.

HEDDA (*curtly interrupting*)   I am just as I was when I left.

TESMAN   Yes, so you say. I just don't think you're right. What do you think, Auntie?

MISS TESMAN (*has folded her hands, gazes at HEDDA*)   Lovely—lovely—lovely; that is what Hedda is. (*goes over to her, inclines her head forward with both her hands, and kisses her hair*) God bless and keep Hedda Tesman. For Jørgen's sake.

HEDDA (*gently freeing herself*) There, there. Now let me go.

MISS TESMAN (*in quiet emotion*) Every single day I'll be over and see you two.

TESMAN Yes, please do, Auntie. Hm?

MISS TESMAN Goodbye, goodbye!

(*She leaves through door, right.* TESMAN *sees her out. The door remains ajar.* TESMAN *is heard repeating his greetings for* AUNT RINA *and his thanks for the slippers. In the meantime,* HEDDA *paces up and down, raises her arms, clenching her fists, as in quiet rage. Opens the curtains by the French doors and stands looking out. In a few moments,* TESMAN *re-enters and closes the door behind him*)

TESMAN (*picking up the slippers*) What are you looking at, Hedda?

HEDDA (*once again calm and controlled*) Just the leaves. They are so yellow. And so withered.

TESMAN (*wrapping the slippers in their paper, putting the parcel down on the table*) Well, you know—we're in September now.

HEDDA (*again restless*) Yes—just think. We are already in—September.

TESMAN Don't you think Aunt Julle acted strange, Hedda? Almost solemn. I wonder why. Hm?

HEDDA I hardly know her, you see. Isn't she often like that?

TESMAN Not the way she was today.

HEDDA (*turning away from the French doors*) Do you think she minded that business with the hat?

TESMAN Oh, I don't think so. Not much. Perhaps a little bit right at the moment—

HEDDA Well, I'm sorry, but I must say it strikes me as very odd—putting her hat down here in the living room. One just doesn't do that.

TESMAN Well, you may be sure Aunt Julle won't ever do it again.

HEDDA Anyway, I'll make it up to her, somehow.

TESMAN Oh yes, Hedda; if only you would!

HEDDA When you go over there today, why don't you ask her over for tonight?

TESMAN I'll certainly do that. And then there is one other thing you could do that she'd appreciate ever so much.

HEDDA What?

TESMAN If you could just bring yourself to call her Auntie. For my sake, Hedda, hm?

HEDDA No, Tesman, no. You really mustn't ask me to do that. I have already told you I won't. I'll try to call her Aunt Juliane. That will have to do.

TESMAN All right, if you say so. I just thought that now that you're in the family—

HEDDA Hmmm—I don't know about that—

(*She walks toward the doorway*)

TESMAN (*after a brief pause*) Anything the matter, Hedda? Hm?

HEDDA I'm just looking at my old piano. It doesn't quite go with the other furniture in here.

TESMAN As soon as I get my first pay check we'll have it traded in.

HEDDA No—I don't want to do that. I want to keep it. But let's put it in this inner room and get another one for out here. Whenever it's convenient, I mean.

TESMAN (*a little taken back*) Well—yes—we could do that—

HEDDA (*picks up the bouquet from the piano*) These flowers weren't here last night.

TESMAN I suppose Aunt Julle brought them for you.

HEDDA (*looking at the flowers*) There's a card here. (*takes it out and reads*) "Will be back later." Can you guess who it's from?

TESMAN No. Who? Hm?

HEDDA Thea Elvsted.

TESMAN No, really? Mrs. Elvsted! Miss Rysing that was.

HEDDA That's right. The one with that irritating head of hair she used to show off with. An old flame of yours, I understand.

TESMAN (*laughs*) Well, now—that didn't last long! Anyway, that was before I knew you, Hedda. Just think—her being in town.

HEDDA Strange, that she'd call on us. I have hardly seen her since we went to school together.

TESMAN As far as that goes, I haven't seen her either for—God knows how long. I don't see how she can stand living in that out-of-the-way place. Hm?

HEDDA (*suddenly struck by a thought*) Listen, Tesman—isn't it some place near there that he lives—what's his name—Eilert Løvborg?

TESMAN Yes, that's right. He is up there, too.

(BERTE *enters right*)

BERTE Ma'am, she's here again, that lady who brought those flowers a while back. (*pointing*) The flowers you're holding in your hand, ma'am.

HEDDA Ah, she is? Well, show her in, please.

(BERTE *opens the door for* MRS. ELVSTED *and exits.* MRS. ELVSTED *is of slight build, with a pretty, soft face. Her eyes are light blue, large, round, rather prominent, of a timid and query-*

ing expression. Her hair is strikingly light in color, almost whitish, and unusually rich and wavy. She is a couple of years younger than HEDDA. *She is dressed in a dark visiting dress, tasteful, but not quite in the most recent fashion)*

HEDDA (*walks toward her. Friendly*) Good morning, my dear Mrs. Elvsted. How very nice to see you again.

MRS. ELVSTED (*nervous, trying not to show it*) Well, yes, it is quite some time since we met.

TESMAN (*shaking hands*) And we, too. Hm?

HEDDA Thank you for your lovely flowers—

MRS. ELVSTED Please, don't—I would have come here yesterday afternoon. But I was told you were still traveling—

TESMAN You've just arrived in town, hm?

MRS. ELVSTED I got here yesterday, at noon. Oh, I was quite desperate when I learned you weren't home.

HEDDA Desperate? But why?

TESMAN But my dear Mrs. Rysing—I mean Mrs. Elvsted—

HEDDA There is nothing wrong, I hope?

MRS. ELVSTED Yes there is. And I don't know a single soul other than you that I can turn to here.

HEDDA (*putting the flowers down on the table*) Come—let's sit down here on the sofa.

MRS. ELVSTED Oh, I'm in no mood to sit!

HEDDA Of course you are. Come on. (*She pulls* MRS. ELVSTED *over to the sofa and sits down next to her*)

TESMAN Well, now, Mrs.—? Exactly what—?

HEDDA Has something—special happened at home?

MRS. ELVSTED Well, yes—and no. Oh, but I am so afraid you are going to misunderstand!

HEDDA In that case, it seems to me you ought to tell us exactly what has happened, Mrs. Elvsted.

TESMAN After all, that's why you are here. Hm?

MRS. ELVSTED Yes, yes, of course. Well, then, maybe you already know—Eilert Løvborg is in town.

HEDDA Is Løvborg—!

TESMAN No! You don't say! Just think, Hedda—Løvborg's back!

HEDDA All right. I can hear.

MRS. ELVSTED He has been here a week already. Imagine—a whole week! In this dangerous place. Alone! With all that bad company around.

HEDDA But my dear Mrs. Elvsted—why is he a concern of yours?

MRS. ELVSTED (*with an apprehensive look at her, says quickly*) He tutored the children.

HEDDA Your children?

MRS. ELVSTED My husband's. I don't have any.

HEDDA In other words, your stepchildren.

MRS. ELVSTED Yes.

TESMAN (*with some hesitation*) But was he—I don't quite know how to put this—was he sufficiently—regular—in his way of life to be thus employed? Hm?

MRS. ELVSTED For the last two years, there hasn't been a thing to object to in his conduct.

TESMAN No, really? Just think, Hedda!

HEDDA I hear.

MRS. ELVSTED Not the least little bit, I assure you! Not in any respect. And yet—knowing he's here—in the big city—And with all that money, too! I'm scared to death!

TESMAN But in that case, why didn't he remain with you and your husband? Hm?

MRS. ELVSTED After his book came out, he was too restless to stay.

TESMAN Ah yes, that's right. Aunt Julle said he has published a new book.

MRS. ELVSTED Yes, a big new book, about the course of civilization in general. It came out about two weeks ago. And since it has had such big sales and been discussed so much and made such a big splash—

TESMAN It has, has it? I suppose this is something he has had lying around from better days?

MRS. ELVSTED You mean from earlier?

TESMAN Yes.

MRS. ELVSTED No; it's all been written since he came to stay with us. During this last year.

TESMAN Well, now! That's very good news, Hedda! Just think!

MRS. ELVSTED Yes, if it only would last!

HEDDA Have you seen him since you came to town?

MRS. ELVSTED No, not yet. I had a great deal of trouble finding his address. But this morning I finally tracked him down.

HEDDA (*looks searchingly at her*) Isn't it rather odd that your husband—hm—

MRS. ELVSTED (*with a nervous start*) My husband! What about him?

HEDDA That he sends you to town on such an errand? That he doesn't go and look after his friend himself?

MRS. ELVSTED Oh, no, no—my husband doesn't have time for things like that. Besides, I have some—some shopping to do, anyway.

HEDDA (*with a slight smile*) Well, in that case, of course—

MRS. ELVSTED (*getting up, restlessly*) And now I beg of you, Mr. Tesman—won't you please receive Eilert Løvborg nicely if he calls on you? And I am sure he will. After all— Such good friends as you two used to be. And then you both do the same kind of work—the same studies, as far as I know.

TESMAN We used to, at any rate.

MRS. ELVSTED Yes. And that's why I implore you to please, please, try to keep an eye on him—you too. You'll do that, Mr. Tesman, won't you? Promise?

TESMAN With the greatest pleasure, Mrs. Rysing.

HEDDA Elvsted.

TESMAN I'll gladly do as much for Eilert as I possibly can. You may certainly count on that.

MRS. ELVSTED Oh, how good and kind you are! (*clasps his hands*) Thank you, thank you, thank you! (*nervously*) You see, my husband is so very fond of him.

HEDDA (*getting up*) You ought to write him a note, Tesman. Maybe he won't come without an invitation.

TESMAN Yes, I suppose that would be the right thing to do, Hedda. Hm?

HEDDA The sooner the better. Right away, *I* think.

MRS. ELVSTED (*pleadingly*) If only you would!

TESMAN I'll write this minute. Do you have his address, Mrs.—Mrs. Elvsted?

MRS. ELVSTED Yes. (*pulls a slip of paper from her bag and gives it to him*) Here it is.

TESMAN Very good. Well, then, if you'll excuse me—(*looks around*) By the way—the slippers? Ah, here we are. (*leaving with the parcel*)

HEDDA Be sure you write a nice, warm, friendly letter, Tesman. And a long one, too.

TESMAN Certainly, certainly.

MRS. ELVSTED But not a word that it is I who—!

TESMAN No, that goes without saying, I should think. Hm? (*goes out right through inner room*)

HEDDA (*goes over to* MRS. ELVSTED, *smiles, says in a low voice*) There! We've just killed two birds with one stone.

MRS. ELVSTED What do you mean?

HEDDA Didn't you see I wanted him out of the room?

MRS. ELVSTED Yes, to write that letter—

HEDDA And to speak to you alone.

MRS. ELVSTED (*flustered*) About the same thing?

HEDDA Exactly.

MRS. ELVSTED (*anxious*) But there *is* nothing more, Mrs. Tesman! Really, there isn't!

HEDDA Oh yes, there is. There is considerably more. I can see that much. Over here— We are going to have a real, nice, confidential talk, you and I. (*She forces* MRS. ELVSTED *down in the easy chair and seats herself on one of the ottomans*)

MRS. ELVSTED (*worried, looks at her watch*) But my dear Mrs. Tesman— I had really thought I would be on my way now.

HEDDA Oh, I am sure there is no rush. Now, then. Tell me about yourself. How are things at home?

MRS. ELVSTED That is just what I don't want to talk about.

HEDDA But to me—! After all, we are old schoolmates.

MRS. ELVSTED But you were a year ahead of me. And I used to be so scared of you!

HEDDA Scared of me?

MRS. ELVSTED Terribly. For when we met on the stairs, you always ruffled my hair.

HEDDA Did I really?

MRS. ELVSTED Yes. And once you said you were going to burn it off.

HEDDA Oh, but you know—I wasn't serious!

MRS. ELVSTED No, but I was such a silly, then. Anyway. Afterwards we drifted far apart. Our circles are so very different, you know.

HEDDA All the more reason for getting close again. Listen. In school we called each other by our first names.

MRS. ELVSTED Oh I'm sure you're wrong—

HEDDA I'm sure I'm not! I remember it quite clearly. And now we want to be open with one another, just the way we used to. (*moves the ottoman closer*) There now! (*kisses her cheek*) You call me Hedda.

MRS. ELVSTED (*seizes her hands*) Oh, you are so good and kind! I'm not used to that.

HEDDA There, there! And I'll call you my dear Thora, just as in the old days.

MRS. ELVSTED My name is Thea.

HEDDA So it is. Of course. I meant Thea. (*looks at her with compassion*) So you're not much used to goodness and kindness, Thea? Not in your own home?

MRS. ELVSTED If I even had a home! But I don't. I never have had one.

HEDDA (*looks at her for a moment*) I thought there might be something like this.

MRS. ELVSTED (*helplessly, looking straight ahead*) Yes—yes—yes—

HEDDA   I am not sure if I quite remember—
Didn't you first come to your husband as his
housekeeper?

MRS. ELVSTED   I was really hired as governess. But his wife—his first wife—was ailing
already then and was practically bedridden.
So I had to take charge of the household as
well.

HEDDA   But in the end you became his wife.

MRS. ELVSTED   (*dully*)   So I did.

HEDDA   Let's see. How long ago is that?

MRS. ELVSTED   Since my marriage?

HEDDA   Yes.

MRS. ELVSTED   About five years.

HEDDA   Right. It must be that long.

MRS. ELVSTED   Oh, those five years! Or
mostly the last two or three! Oh, Mrs. Tesman
—if you could just imagine!

HEDDA   (*slaps her hand lightly*)   Mrs. Tesman? Shame on you!

MRS. ELVSTED   Oh yes, all right; I'll try. Yes
—if you could just—conceive—understand—

HEDDA   (*casually*)   And Eilert Løvborg has
been living near you for some three years or so,
hasn't he?

MRS. ELVSTED   (*looks at her uncertainly*)
Eilert Løvborg? Yes—he has.

HEDDA   Did you know him before? Here in
town?

MRS. ELVSTED   Hardly at all. That is, of
course I did in a way. I mean, I knew *of* him.

HEDDA   But up there— You saw a great
deal of him; did you?

MRS. ELVSTED   Yes, he came over to us
every day. He was supposed to tutor the children, you see. For I just couldn't do it all by
myself.

HEDDA   Of course not. And your husband—? I suppose he travels quite a bit.

MRS. ELVSTED   Well, yes, Mrs. Tes—Hedda
—as a public magistrate, you know, he very
often has to travel all over his district.

HEDDA   (*leaning against the armrest on the
easy chair*)   Thea—poor, sweet Thea—now
you have to tell me everything—just as it is.

MRS. ELVSTED   You'd better ask me, then.

HEDDA   How *is* your husband, Thea? I mean
—you know—*really*? To be with. What kind
of person is he? Is he good to you?

MRS. ELVSTED   (*evasively*)   I believe he
thinks he does everything for the best.

HEDDA   But isn't he altogether too old for
you? He is more than twenty years older, isn't
he?

MRS. ELVSTED   (*with irritation*)   Yes, there
is that, too. But there isn't just one thing. Every
single little thing about him repels me! We

don't have a thought in common, he and I.
Not a thing in the world!

HEDDA   But isn't he fond of you all the
same? I mean in his own way?

MRS. ELVSTED   I don't know. I think I am
just useful to him. And I don't use much
money. I am inexpensive.

HEDDA   That is foolish of you.

MRS. ELVSTED   (*shakes her head*)   Can't be
changed. Not with him. I don't think he cares
for anybody much except himself. Perhaps the
children a little.

HEDDA   And Eilert Løvborg, Thea.

MRS. ELVSTED   (*looks at her*)   Eilert Løvborg? What makes you think that?

HEDDA   Well, it seems to me that when he
sends you all the way to town to look after
him—(*with an almost imperceptible smile*)
Besides, you said so yourself. To Tesman.

MRS. ELVSTED   (*with a nervous twitch*)   Did
I? I suppose I did. (*with a muted outburst*)
No! I might as well tell you now as later. For
it's bound to come out, anyway.

HEDDA   But my dear Thea—?

MRS. ELVSTED   All right. My husband
doesn't know I've gone!

HEDDA   What! He doesn't know?

MRS. ELVSTED   He wasn't even home. He's
away again. Oh, I just couldn't take it any
longer, Hedda! It had become utterly impossible. All alone as I was.

HEDDA   So what did you do?

MRS. ELVSTED   I packed some of my things.
Just the most necessary. Without telling anybody. And left.

HEDDA   Just like that?

MRS. ELVSTED   Yes. And took the next train
to town.

HEDDA   But dearest Thea—how did you
dare to do a thing like that!

MRS. ELVSTED   (*rises, walks*)   What else
could I do?

HEDDA   But what do you think your husband will say when you go back?

MRS. ELVSTED   (*by the table; looks at her*)
Go back to him?

HEDDA   Yes!

MRS. ELVSTED   I'll never go back.

HEDDA   (*rises, approaches her slowly*)   So
you have really, seriously—left everything?

MRS. ELVSTED   Yes. It seemed to me there
was nothing else I could do.

HEDDA   And quite openly, too.

MRS. ELVSTED   You can't keep a thing like
that secret, anyway.

HEDDA   But what do you think people will
say, Thea?

MRS. ELVSTED In God's name, let them say whatever they like. (*sits down on the sofa, dully, tired*) For I have only done what I had to do.

HEDDA (*after a brief silence*) And what do you plan to do with yourself? What sort of work will you do?

MRS. ELVSTED I don't know yet. I only know I have to live where Eilert Løvborg is. If I am to live at all.

HEDDA (*moves a chair from the table closer to* MRS. ELVSTED, *sits down, strokes her hands*) Thea—tell me. How did this—this friendship between you and Eilert Løvborg—how did it begin?

MRS. ELVSTED Oh, it grew little by little. I got some sort of power over him.

HEDDA Oh?

MRS. ELVSTED He dropped his old ways. Not because I asked him to. I never dared to do that. But I think he must have noticed how I felt about that kind of life. So he changed.

HEDDA (*Quickly suppresses a cynical smile*) So you have—rehabilitated him, as they say. Haven't you, Thea?

MRS. ELVSTED At least, that's what *he* says. On the other hand, he has turned me into a real human being. Taught me to think—and understand—all sorts of things.

HEDDA Maybe he tutored you, too?

MRS. ELVSTED No, not tutored exactly. But he talked to me. About so many, many things. And then came that lovely, lovely time when I could share his work with him. He let me help him!

HEDDA He did?

MRS. ELVSTED Yes! Whatever he wrote, he wanted us to be together about it.

HEDDA Just like two good comrades.

MRS. ELVSTED (*with animation*) Comrades! —that's it! Imagine, Hedda—that's just what he called it, too. Oh, I really ought to feel so happy. But I can't. For you see, I don't know if it will last.

HEDDA You don't trust him any more than that?

MRS. ELVSTED (*heavily*) The shadow of a woman stands between Eilert Løvborg and me.

HEDDA (*tensely, looks at her*) Who?

MRS. ELVSTED I don't know. Somebody or other from—his past. I don't think he has ever really forgotten her.

HEDDA What has he told you about it?

MRS. ELVSTED He has mentioned it only once—just casually.

HEDDA And what did he say?

MRS. ELVSTED He said that when they parted she was going to kill him with a gun.

HEDDA (*cold, controlled*) Oh, nonsense. People don't do that sort of thing here.

MRS. ELVSTED No, I know. And that is why I think it must be that red-headed singer he used to——

HEDDA Yes, I suppose so.

MRS. ELVSTED For I remember people said she carried a loaded gun.

HEDDA Well, then I'm sure it's she.

MRS. ELVSTED (*wringing her hands*) Yes, but just think, Hedda—now I hear that she— that singer—that she's here in town again, too! Oh, I'm just desperate—!

HEDDA (*with a glance toward the inner room*) Shhh! Here's Tesman. (*rises and whispers*) Not a word about all this to anybody, Thea!

MRS. ELVSTED (*jumps up*) No, no. For God's sake—!

(TESMAN, *carrying a letter, enters from the right side of the inner room*)

TESMAN There, now—here's the missive, all ready to go!

HEDDA Good. But I believe Mrs. Elvsted wants to be on her way. Wait a moment. I'll see you to the garden gate.

TESMAN Say, Hedda—do you think Berte could take care of this?

HEDDA (*takes the letter*) I'll tell her.

(BERTE *enters right*)

BERTE Judge Brack is here and wants to know if you're receiving.

HEDDA Yes, ask the Judge please to come in. And—here—drop this in a mailbox, will you?

BERTE (*takes the letter*) Yes, ma'am.

(*She opens the door for* JUDGE BRACK *and exits. The* JUDGE *is forty-five years of age. Rather thickset, but well-built and with brisk, athletic movements. Roundish face, aristocratic profile. His hair is short, still almost completely black, very neatly dressed. Lively, sparkling eyes. Thick eyebrows and mustache with cut-off points. He is dressed in an elegant suit, a trifle youthful for his age. He wears pince-nez glasses, attached to a string, and lets them drop from time to time*)

JUDGE BRACK (*hat in hand, salutes*) May one pay one's respects as early as this?

HEDDA One certainly may.

TESMAN (*shaking his hand*) You are always welcome. (*introducing*) Judge Brack—Miss Rysing—

HEDDA (*groans*)

BRACK (*bowing*) Delighted!

HEDDA (*looks at him, laughs*) How nice it is to see you in daylight, Judge!

BRACK You find me changed, perhaps?

HEDDA A bit younger, I think.

BRACK Much obliged.

TESMAN But what do you think of Hedda? Hm? Did you ever see her in such bloom? She positively—

HEDDA Will you please leave me out of this? You had better thank the Judge for all the trouble he has taken.

BRACK Oh, nonsense. It's been a pleasure.

HEDDA Yes, you are indeed a faithful soul. But my friend here is dying to be off. Don't leave, Judge. I'll be back in a minute.

(*Mutual goodbyes.* MRS. ELVSTED *and* HEDDA *exit, right*)

BRACK Well, now—your wife—is she tolerably satisfied?

TESMAN Yes, indeed, and we really can't thank you enough. That is, I understand there will have to be some slight changes made here and there. And there are still a few things— just a few trifles—we'll have to get.

BRACK Oh? Really?

TESMAN But we certainly don't want to bother you with that. Hedda said she's going to take care of it herself. But do sit down, hm?

BRACK Thanks. Maybe just for a moment— (*sits down by the table*) There's one thing I'd like to talk to you about, my dear Tesman.

TESMAN Oh? Ah, I see! (*sits down*) I suppose it's the serious part of the festivities that's beginning now. Hm?

BRACK Oh—there's no great rush as far as the money is concerned. Though I must say I wish we could have established ourselves a trifle more economically.

TESMAN Out of the question, my dear fellow! Remember, it's all for Hedda! You, who know her so well—! After all, I couldn't put her up like any little middle-class housewife—

BRACK No, I suppose— That's just it.

TESMAN Besides—fortunately—it can't be long now before I receive my appointment.

BRACK Well, you know—things like that have a way of hanging fire.

TESMAN Perhaps you have heard something? Something definite? Hm?

BRACK No, nothing certain—(*interrupting himself*) But that reminds me. I have some news for you.

TESMAN Oh?

BRACK Your old friend Eilert Løvborg is back in town.

TESMAN I know that already.

BRACK So? Who told you?

TESMAN The lady who just left.

BRACK I see. What did you say her name was again? I didn't quite catch—

TESMAN Mrs. Elvsted.

BRACK Ah yes—the Commissioner's wife. Yes, it's up in her part of the country that Løvborg has been staying, too.

TESMAN And just think. I am so glad to hear it. He is quite respectable again.

BRACK Yes, so they say.

TESMAN And he has published a new book, hm?

BRACK Oh yes.

TESMAN Which is making quite a stir.

BRACK Quite an unusual stir.

TESMAN Just think! Isn't that just wonderful! He—with his remarkable gifts. And I was so sure he'd gone under for good.

BRACK That seems to have been the general opinion.

TESMAN What I don't understand, though, is what he is going to do with himself. What sort of living can he make? Hm?

(*During the last remark* HEDDA *re-enters, right*)

HEDDA (*to* BRACK, *with a scornful little laugh*) Tesman is forever worrying about how people are going to make a living.

TESMAN Well, you see, we are talking about poor Eilert Løvborg, Hedda.

HEDDA (*with a quick look at him*) You are? (*sits down in the easy chair by the stove and asks casually*) What is the matter with him?

TESMAN Well, you see, I believe he's run through his inheritance a long time ago. And I don't suppose he can write a new book every year. Hm? So I really must ask how he is going to make out.

BRACK Maybe I could help you answer that.

TESMAN Yes?

BRACK Remember, he has relatives with considerable influence.

TESMAN Ah—unfortunately, those relatives have washed their hands of him long ago.

BRACK Just the same, they used to call him the hope of the family.

TESMAN Yes, before! But he has ruined all that.

HEDDA Who knows? (*with a little smile*) I hear the Elvsteds have rehabilitated him.

BRACK And then this book—

TESMAN Well, I certainly hope they will help him to find something or other. I just wrote him a letter. Hedda, dear, I asked him to come out here tonight.

BRACK Oh dear, I am sorry. Don't you remember—you're supposed to come to my little stag dinner tonight? You accepted last night on the pier, you know.

HEDDA   Had you forgotten, Tesman?

TESMAN   So I had.

BRACK   Oh well. I'm sure he won't come, so it doesn't really make any difference.

TESMAN   Why is that? Hm?

BRACK   (*gets up somewhat hesitantly, rests his hands on the back of the chair*)   Dear Tesman—and you, too, Mrs. Tesman—I cannot in good conscience let you remain in ignorance of something, which—which—

TESMAN   Something to do with Eilert?

BRACK   With both you and him.

TESMAN   But my dear Judge, do speak!

BRACK   You must be prepared to find that your appointment will not come through as soon as you hope and expect.

TESMAN   (*jumps up, nervously*)   Something's happened? Hm?

BRACK   It may conceivably be made contingent upon the result of a competition.

TESMAN   Competition! Just think, Hedda!

HEDDA   (*leaning farther back in her chair*)   Ah—I see, I see—!

TESMAN   But with whom? Don't tell me with—?

BRACK   Precisely. With Eilert Løvborg.

TESMAN   (*claps his hands together*)   No, no! This can't be! It is unthinkable! Quite impossible! Hm?

BRACK   All the same, that's the way it may turn out.

TESMAN   No, but Judge, this would amount to the most incredible callousness toward me! (*waving his arms*) For just think—I'm a married man! We married on the strength of these prospects, Hedda and I. Got ourselves deep in debt. Borrowed money from Aunt Julle, too. After all, I had practically been promised the post, you know. Hm?

BRACK   Well, well. I daresay you'll get it in the end. If only after a competition.

HEDDA   (*motionless in her chair*)   Just think, Tesman. It will be like a kind of contest.

TESMAN   But dearest Hedda, how can you be so unconcerned!

HEDDA   (*still without moving*)   I'm not at all unconcerned. I'm dying to see who wins.

BRACK   In any case, Mrs. Tesman, I'm glad you know the situation for what it is. I mean—before you proceed to make the little additional purchases I understand you threaten us with.

HEDDA   This makes no difference as far as that is concerned.

BRACK   Really? Well, in that case, of course— Goodbye! (*to* TESMAN) I'll pick you up on my afternoon walk.

TESMAN   What? Oh yes, yes, of course. I'm sorry; I'm just all confused.

HEDDA   (*without getting up, gives her hand*)   Goodbye, Judge. Come back soon.

BRACK   Thanks. Goodbye, goodbye.

TESMAN   (*sees him to the door*)   Goodbye, my dear Judge. You really must excuse me— (JUDGE BRACK *exits, right*)

TESMAN   (*pacing the floor*)   Oh, Hedda, Hedda! One should never venture into fairyland. Hm?

HEDDA   (*looks at him, smiles*)   Do *you* do that?

TESMAN   Well, yes—it can't be denied—it was most venturesome of me to rush into marriage and set up a home on the strength of mere prospects.

HEDDA   Well, maybe you're right.

TESMAN   Anyway—we do have our own nice, comfortable home, now. Just think, Hedda—the very home both of us dreamed about. Set our hearts on, I may almost say. Hm?

HEDDA   (*rises, slowly, tired*)   The agreement was that we were to maintain a certain position—entertain—

TESMAN   Don't I know it! Dearest Hedda— I have been so looking forward to seeing you as hostess in a select circle! Hm? Well, well, well! In the meantime, we'll just have to be content with one another. See Aunt Julle once in a while. Nothing more. And you were meant for such a different kind of life, altogether!

HEDDA   I suppose a footman is completely out of the question.

TESMAN   I'm afraid so. Under the circumstances, you see—we couldn't possibly—

HEDDA   And as for getting my own riding horse—

TESMAN   (*aghast*)   Riding horse!

HEDDA   I suppose I mustn't even think of that.

TESMAN   Good heavens, no! That goes without saying, I hope!

HEDDA   (*walking*)   Well—at least I have one thing to amuse myself with in the meantime.

TESMAN   (*overjoyed*)   Oh thank goodness for that! And what *is* that, Hedda, hm?

HEDDA   (*in the doorway, looks at him with suppressed scorn*)   My guns—Jørgen!

TESMAN   (*in fear*)   Your guns!

HEDDA   (*with cold eyes*)   General Gabler's guns. (*She exits left, through the inner room*)

TESMAN   (*runs to the doorway, calls after her*)   But Hedda! Good gracious! Hedda, dear! Please don't touch those dangerous things! For my sake, Hedda! Hm?

ACT TWO

(*The same room at the* TESMANS'. *The piano has been moved out and replaced by an elegant little writing desk. A small table has been placed near the sofa, left. Most of the flowers have been removed.* MRS. ELVSTED'S *bouquet is on the big table front center. Afternoon.*

HEDDA, *dressed to receive callers, is alone. She is standing near the open French doors loading a revolver. Its mate is lying in an open case on the desk*)

HEDDA (*looking down into the garden, calls*) Hello there, Judge! Welcome back!

JUDGE BRACK (*off-stage*) Thanks, Mrs. Tesman!

HEDDA (*raises the gun, sights*) Now I am going to shoot you, Judge Brack!

BRACK (*calls off-stage*) No—no—no! Don't point the gun at me like that!

HEDDA That's what you get for sneaking in the back door! (*fires*)

BRACK (*closer*) Are you out of your mind—!

HEDDA Oh dear—did I hit you?

BRACK (*still off-stage*) Stop that nonsense!

HEDDA Come on in, then.

(JUDGE BRACK, *dressed for dinner, enters, left. He carries a light overcoat over his arm*)

BRACK Dammit! Do you still fool around with that thing? What are you shooting at, anyway?

HEDDA Oh—just firing off into blue air.

BRACK (*gently but firmly taking the gun away from her*) With your permission, Mrs. Tesman. (*looks at it*) Ah yes, I remember this gun very well. (*looks around*) Where is the case? Ah, here we are. (*puts the gun in the case and closes it*) That's enough of that silliness for today.

HEDDA But in the name of heaven, what do you expect me to do with myself?

BRACK No callers?

HEDDA (*closing the French doors*) Not a soul. All my close friends are still out of town, it seems.

BRACK And Tesman is out, too, perhaps?

HEDDA (*by the desk, puts the gun case in a drawer*) Yes. He took off for the aunts' right after lunch. He didn't expect you so early.

BRACK I should have thought of that. That was stupid of me.

HEDDA (*turns her head, looks at him*) Why stupid?

BRACK I would have come a little—sooner.

HEDDA (*crossing*) If you had, you wouldn't have found anybody home. For I have been in my room ever since lunch, changing my clothes.

BRACK And isn't there the tiniest little opening in the door for negotiations?

HEDDA You forgot to provide one.

BRACK Another stupidity.

HEDDA So we'll have to stay in here. And wait. For I don't think Tesman will be back for some time.

BRACK By all means. I'll be very patient.

(HEDDA *sits on the sofa in the corner.* BRACK *puts his overcoat over the back of the nearest chair and sits down, keeping his hat in his hand. Brief silence. They look at one another*)

HEDDA Well?

BRACK (*in the same tone*) Well?

HEDDA I said it first.

BRACK (*leans forward a little*) All right. Let's have a nice little chat, Mrs. Tesman.

HEDDA (*leans back*) Don't you think it's an eternity since last time we talked? I don't count last night and this morning. That was nothing.

BRACK You mean—just the two of us?

HEDDA Something like that.

BRACK There hasn't been a day I haven't wished you were back again.

HEDDA My feelings, exactly.

BRACK Yours? Really, Mrs. Tesman? And I have been assuming you were having such a wonderful time.

HEDDA I'd say!

BRACK All Tesman's letters said so.

HEDDA Oh yes, he! He's happy just poking through old collections of books. And copying old parchments—or whatever they are.

BRACK (*with a touch of malice*) Well, that's his calling, you know. Partly, anyway.

HEDDA Yes, so it is. And in that case I suppose— But I! Oh, Judge! You've no idea how bored I've been.

BRACK (*with sympathy*) Really? You're serious?

HEDDA Surely you can understand that? For a whole half year never to see anyone who knows even a little bit about our circle? And talks our language?

BRACK Yes, I think I would find that trying, too.

HEDDA And then the most unbearable thing of all—

BRACK Well?

HEDDA —everlastingly to be in the company of the same person—

BRACK (*nods in agreement*) Both early and late—yes. I can imagine—at all possible times—

HEDDA I said everlastingly.

BRACK All right. Still, it seems to me that with as excellent a person as our Tesman, it ought to be possible—

HEDDA My dear Judge—Tesman is a specialist.

BRACK Granted.

HEDDA And specialists are not at all entertaining travel companions. Not in the long run, at any rate.

BRACK Not even—the specialist—one happens to love?

HEDDA Bah! That nauseating word!

BRACK (*puzzled*) Really, now, Mrs. Tesman—?

HEDDA (*half laughing, half annoyed*) You ought to try it some time! Listening to talk about the history of civilization, early and late—

BRACK Everlastingly—

HEDDA All right. And then this business about the domestic industry in the Middle Ages—! That's the ghastliest part of it all!

BRACK (*looking searchingly at her*) But in that case—tell me—how I am to explain—?

HEDDA That Jørgen Tesman and I made a pair of it, you mean?

BRACK If you want to put it that way—yes.

HEDDA Come now. Do you really find that so strange?

BRACK Both yes and no—Mrs. Tesman.

HEDDA I had danced myself tired, my dear Judge. My season was over—(*gives a slight start*) No, no—I don't really mean that. Won't think it, either!

BRACK Nor do you have the slightest reason to, I am sure.

HEDDA Oh—as far as reason is concerned—(*looks at him as if trying to read his mind*) And, after all, Jørgen Tesman must be said to be a most proper young man in all respects.

BRACK Both proper and substantial. Most certainly.

HEDDA And one can't say there is anything exactly comical about him. Do you think there is?

BRACK Comical? No—o. I wouldn't say that—

HEDDA All right, then. And he is a most assiduous collector. Nobody can deny that. I think it is perfectly possible he may go quite far, after all.

BRACK (*looks at her rather uncertainly*) I assumed that you, like everybody else, were convinced that he will in time become an exceptionally eminent man?

HEDDA (*with a weary expression*) Yes, I was. And then, you see—there he was, wanting so desperately to be allowed to provide for me —I don't know why I shouldn't have accepted?

BRACK No, certainly. From that point of view—

HEDDA For you know, Judge, that was considerably more than my other admirers were willing to do.

BRACK (*laughs*) Well! Of course I can't answer for all the others. But as far as I am concerned, I have always had a certain degree of—respect for the bonds of matrimony. You know—as a general proposition, Mrs. Tesman.

HEDDA (*lightly*) Well, I never really counted very heavily on *you*—

BRACK All I want is a nice, confidential circle, in which I can be of service, both in deed and in counsel. Be allowed to come and go like a true and trusted friend—

HEDDA You mean, of the master of the house—?

BRACK (*with a slight bow*) To be perfectly frank—rather of the mistress. But by all means —the master, too, of course. Do you know, that kind of—shall I say, triangular?—relationship can really be a great comfort to all parties involved.

HEDDA Yes, many were the times I missed a second travel companion. To be twosome in the compartment—brrr!

BRACK Fortunately, the wedding trip is over.

HEDDA (*shakes her head*) There's a long journey ahead. I've just arrived at a station on the way.

BRACK Well, at the station one gets out and moves around a bit, Mrs. Tesman.

HEDDA I never get out.

BRACK Really?

HEDDA No. For there's always someone around, who—

BRACK (*laughs*) —looks at one's legs; is that it?

HEDDA Exactly.

BRACK Oh well, really, now—

HEDDA (*with a silencing gesture*) I won't have it! Rather stay in my seat—once I'm seated. Twosome and all.

BRACK But what if a third party were to join the couple?

HEDDA Well, now—*that* would be something altogether different!

BRACK A proven, understanding friend—

HEDDA   —entertaining in all sorts of lively ways—

BRACK   —and not at all a specialist!

HEDDA (*with audible breath*) Yes, that would indeed be a comfort.

BRACK (*hearing the front door open, looking at her*) The triangle is complete.

HEDDA (*half aloud*) And the train goes on. (TESMAN, *in gray walking suit and soft hat, enters, right. He carries a pile of paperbound books under his arm. Others are stuffed in his pockets*)

TESMAN (*walks up to the table in front of the corner sofa*) Puuhh—! Quite some load to carry, all this—and in this heat, too. (*puts the books down*) I am positively perspiring, Hedda. Well, well. So you're here already, my dear Judge. Hm? And Berte didn't tell me.

BRACK (*rises*) I came through the garden.

HEDDA What are all those books?

TESMAN (*leafing through some of them*) Just some new publications in my special field.

HEDDA Special field, hm?

BRACK Ah yes—professional publications, Mrs. Tesman. (*He and* HEDDA *exchange knowing smiles*)

HEDDA Do you still need more books?

TESMAN Yes, my dear. There is no such thing as having too many books in one's special field. One has to keep up with what is being written and published, you know.

HEDDA I suppose.

TESMAN (*searching among the books*) And look. Here is Eilert Løvborg's new book, too. (*offers it to her*) Want to take a look at it, Hedda? Hm?

HEDDA No—thanks just the same. Or perhaps later.

TESMAN I glanced at it on my way home.

BRACK And what do you think of it? As a specialist yourself?

TESMAN It is remarkable for its sobriety. He never wrote like that before. (*gathers up all the books*) I just want to take these into my study. I am so much looking forward to cutting them open! And then I'll change. (*to* BRACK) I assume there's no rush to be off, is there?

BRACK Not at all. We have plenty of time.

TESMAN In that case, I think I'll indulge myself a little. (*On his way out with the books he halts in the doorway and turns*) That's right, Hedda—Aunt Julle won't be out to see you tonight, after all.

HEDDA No? Is it that business with the hat, do you think?

TESMAN Oh, no—not at all. How can you believe a thing like that about Aunt Julle! Just

think! No, it's Aunt Rina. She's feeling very poorly.

HEDDA Isn't she always?

TESMAN Yes, but it's especially bad today, poor thing.

HEDDA Well, in that case I suppose she ought to stay home. I shall have to put up with it; that's all.

TESMAN And you have no idea how perfectly delighted Aunt Julle was, even so. Because of how splendid you look after the trip, Hedda!

HEDDA (*half aloud, rising*) Oh, these everlasting aunts!

TESMAN Hm?

HEDDA (*walks over to the French doors*) Nothing.

TESMAN No? All right. Well, excuse me. (*exits right, through inner room*)

BRACK What is this about a hat?

HEDDA Oh, something with Miss Tesman this morning. She had put her hat down on the chair over there. (*looks at him, smiles*) So I pretended to think it was the maid's.

BRACK (*shakes his head*) But my dear Mrs. Tesman—how could you do a thing like that! And to that excellent old lady, too!

HEDDA (*nervously pacing the floor*) Well, you see—something just takes hold of me at times. And then I can't help myself—(*throws herself down in the easy chair near the stove*) Oh I can't explain it even to myself.

BRACK (*behind her chair*) You aren't really happy—that's the trouble.

HEDDA (*staring into space*) I don't know any reason why I should be. Do you?

BRACK Well, yes—partly because you've got the home you've always wanted.

HEDDA (*looks up at him and laughs*) So you too believe that story about my great desire?

BRACK You mean, there is nothing to it?

HEDDA Well, yes; there is *something* to it.

BRACK Well?

HEDDA There is this much to it, that last summer I used Tesman to see me home from evening parties.

BRACK Unfortunately—my route was in quite a different direction.

HEDDA True. You walked other roads last summer.

BRACK (*laughs*) Shame on you, Mrs. Tesman! So, all right—you and Tesman—?

HEDDA One evening we passed by here. And Tesman, poor thing, was practically turning himself into knots trying to find something to talk about. So I felt sorry for all that erudition—

BRACK (*with a doubting smile*) You did? Hm—

HEDDA I really did. So, just to help him out of his misery, I happened to say that I'd like to live in this house.

BRACK Just that?

HEDDA That was all—*that* evening.

BRACK But afterwards—?

HEDDA Yes, my frivolity had consequences, Judge.

BRACK Unfortunately—that's often the way with frivolities. It happens to all of us, Mrs. Tesman.

HEDDA Thanks! So in our common enthusiasm for Mr. Secretary Falk's villa Tesman and I found each other, you see! The result was engagement and wedding and honeymoon abroad and all the rest of it. Well, yes, my dear Judge—I've made my bed—I almost said.

BRACK But this is priceless! And you didn't really care for the house at all?

HEDDA Certainly not.

BRACK Not even now? After all, we've set up quite a comfortable home for you here, haven't we?

HEDDA Oh—it seems to me I smell lavender and rose sachets in all the rooms. But maybe that's a smell Aunt Julle brought with her.

BRACK (*laughs*) My guess is rather the late lamented Secretary's wife.

HEDDA It smells of mortality, whoever it is. Like corsages—the next day. (*clasps her hands behind her neck, leans back, looks at him*) Judge, you have no idea how dreadfully bored I'll be—out here.

BRACK But don't you think life may hold some task for you, too, Mrs. Tesman?

HEDDA A task? With any kind of appeal?

BRACK Preferably that, of course.

HEDDA Heaven knows what kind of task that might be. There are times when I wonder if—(*interrupts herself*) No; I'm sure that wouldn't work, either.

BRACK Who knows? Tell me.

HEDDA It has occurred to me that maybe I could get Tesman to enter politics.

BRACK (*laughs*) Tesman! No, really—I must confess that—politics doesn't strike me as being exactly Tesman's line.

HEDDA I agree. But suppose I were to prevail on him, all the same?

BRACK What satisfaction could you possibly find in that? If he can't succeed—why do you want him even to try?

HEDDA Because I am bored, I tell you! (*after a brief pause*) So you think it's quite out of the question that Tesman could ever become prime minister?

BRACK Well, you see, Mrs. Tesman—to do that he'd first of all have to be a fairly wealthy man.

HEDDA (*getting up, impatiently*) Yes! There we are! These shabby circumstances I've married into! (*crosses the floor*) That's what makes life so mean. So outright ludicrous! For that's what it is, you know.

BRACK Personally I believe something else is to blame.

HEDDA What?

BRACK You've never been through anything that's really stirred you.

HEDDA Something serious, you mean?

BRACK If you like. But maybe it's coming now.

HEDDA (*with a toss of her head*) You are thinking of that silly old professorship! That's Tesman's business. I refuse to give it a thought.

BRACK As you wish. But now—to put it in the grand style—now when a solemn challenge of responsibility will be posed? Demands made on you? (*smiles*) New demands, Mrs. Tesman.

HEDDA (*angry*) Quiet! You'll never see anything of the kind.

BRACK (*cautiously*) We'll talk about this a year from now—on the outside.

HEDDA (*curtly*) I'm not made for that sort of thing, Judge! No demands for me!

BRACK But surely you, like most women, are made for a duty, which—

HEDDA (*over by the French doors*) Oh, do be quiet! Often it seems to me there's only one thing in the world that I am made for.

BRACK. (*coming close*) And may I ask what that is?

HEDDA (*looking out*) To be bored to death. Now you know. (*turns, looks toward the inner room, laughs*) Just as I thought. Here comes the professor.

BRACK (*warningly, in a low voice*) Steady, now, Mrs. Tesman!

(TESMAN, *dressed for a party, carrying his hat and gloves, enters from the right side of the inner room*)

TESMAN Hedda, any word yet from Eilert Løvborg that he isn't coming, hm?

HEDDA No.

TESMAN In that case, I wouldn't be a bit surprised if we have him here in a few minutes.

BRACK You really think he'll come?

TESMAN I am almost certain he will. For I'm sure it's only idle gossip what you told me this morning.

BRACK Oh?

TESMAN Anyway, that's what Aunt Julle

said. She doesn't for a moment believe he'll stand in my way. Just think!

BRACK   I'm very glad to hear that.

TESMAN (*puts his hat and his gloves down on a chair, right*) But you must let me wait for him as long as possible.

BRACK   By all means. We have plenty of time. Nobody will arrive at my place before seven—seven-thirty, or so.

TESMAN   And in the meantime we can keep Hedda company. Take our time. Hm?

HEDDA (*carrying* BRACK's *hat and coat over to the sofa in the corner*) And if worst comes to worst, Mr. Løvborg can stay here with me.

BRACK (*trying to take the things away from her*) Let me, Mrs. Tesman—What do you mean—"if worst comes to worst?"

HEDDA   If he doesn't want to go with you and Tesman.

TESMAN (*looks dubiously at her*) But, dearest Hedda—do you think that will quite do? He staying here with you? Hm? Remember, Aunt Julle won't be here.

HEDDA   No, but Mrs. Elvsted will. The three of us will have a cup of tea together.

TESMAN   Oh yes; *that* will be perfectly all right!

BRACK (*with a smile*) And perhaps the wiser course of action for him.

HEDDA   What do you mean?

BRACK   Begging your pardon, Mrs. Tesman —you've often enough looked askance at my little stag dinners. It's been your opinion that only men of the firmest principles ought to attend.

HEDDA   I should think Mr. Løvborg is firm-principled enough now. A reformed sinner—

(BERTE *appears in door, right*)

BERTE   Ma'am—there's a gentleman here who asks if—

HEDDA   Show him in, please.

TESMAN (*softly*) I'm sure it's he! Just think!

(EILERT LØVBORG *enters, right. He is slim, gaunt. Of* TESMAN's *age, but he looks older and somewhat dissipated. Brown hair and beard. Pale, longish face, reddish spots on the cheekbones. Dressed for visiting in elegant, black, brand-new suit. He carries a silk hat and dark gloves in his hand. He remains near the door, makes a quick bow. He appears a little embarrassed*)

TESMAN (*goes over to him, shakes his hand*) My dear Eilert—at last we meet again!

EILERT LØVBORG (*subdued voice*) Thanks for your note, Jørgen! (*approaching* HEDDA) Am I allowed to shake your hand, too, Mrs. Tesman?

HEDDA (*accepting his proffered hand*) I am very glad to see you, Mr. Løvborg. (*with a gesture*) I don't know if you two gentlemen—

LØVBORG (*with a slight bow*) Judge Brack, I believe.

BRACK (*also bowing lightly*) Certainly. Some years ago—

TESMAN (*to* LØVBORG, *both hands on his shoulders*) And now I want you to feel quite at home here, Eilert! Isn't that right, Hedda? For you plan to stay here in town, I understand. Hm?

LØVBORG   Yes, I do.

TESMAN   Perfectly reasonable. Listen—I just got hold of your new book, but I haven't had a chance to read it yet.

LØVBORG   You may save yourself the trouble.

TESMAN   Why do you say that?

LØVBORG   There's not much to it.

TESMAN   Just think—you saying that!

BRACK   Nevertheless, people seem to have very good things to say about it.

LØVBORG   That's exactly why I wrote it—so everybody would like it.

BRACK   Very wise of you.

TESMAN   Yes, but Eilert—!

LØVBORG   For I am trying to rebuild my position. Start all over again.

TESMAN (*with some embarrassment*) Yes, I suppose you are, aren't you? Hm?

LØVBORG (*smiles, puts his hat down, pulls a parcel out of his pocket*) When *this* appears —Jørgen Tesman—this you must read. For this is the real thing. This is me.

TESMAN   Oh really? And what is it?

LØVBORG   The continuation.

TESMAN   Continuation? Of what?

LØVBORG   Of this book.

TESMAN   Of the new book?

LØVBORG   Of course.

TESMAN   But Eilert—you've carried the story all the way up to the present!

LØVBORG   So I have. And this is about the future.

TESMAN   The future! But, heavens—we don't know a thing about the future!

LØVBORG   No, we don't. But there are a couple of things to be said about it all the same. (*unwraps the parcel*) Here, let me show you—

TESMAN   But that's not your handwriting.

LØVBORG   I have dictated it. (*leafs through portions of the manuscript*) It's in two parts. The first is about the forces that will shape the civilization of the future. And the second (*riffling through more pages*)—about the course that future civilization will take.

TESMAN   How remarkable! It would never occur to me to write anything like that.

HEDDA (*over by the French doors, her fingers drumming the pane*) Hmm—No—

LØVBORG (*replacing the manuscript in its wrappings and putting it down on the table*) I brought it along, for I thought maybe I'd read parts of it aloud to you this evening.

TESMAN That's very good of you, Eilert. But this evening—? (*looks at* BRACK) I'm not quite sure how to arrange that—

LØVBORG Some other time, then. There's no hurry.

BRACK You see, Mr. Løvborg, there's a little get-together over at my house tonight. Mainly for Tesman, you know—

LØVBORG (*looking for his hat*) In that case, I certainly won't—

BRACK No, listen. Won't you do me the pleasure to join us?

LØVBORG (*firmly*) No, I won't. But thanks all the same.

BRACK Oh come on! Why don't you do that? We'll be a small, select circle. And I think I can promise you a fairly lively evening, as Hed —as Mrs. Tesman would say.

LØVBORG I don't doubt that. Nevertheless—

BRACK And you may bring your manuscript along and read aloud to Tesman over at my house. I have plenty of room.

TESMAN Just think, Eilert! Wouldn't that be nice, hm?

HEDDA (*intervening*) But can't you see that Mr. Løvborg doesn't want to? I'm sure he would rather stay here and have supper with me.

LØVBORG (*looks at her*) With you, Mrs. Tesman?

HEDDA And with Mrs. Elvsted.

LØVBORG Ah—! (*casually*) I ran into her at noon today.

HEDDA Oh? Well, she'll be here tonight. So you see your presence is really required, Mr. Løvborg. Otherwise she won't have anybody to see her home.

LØVBORG True. All right, then, Mrs. Tesman—I'll stay, thank you.

HEDDA Good. I'll just tell the maid. (*She rings for* BERTE *over by the door, right*)

(BERTE *appears just off-stage.* HEDDA *talks with her in a low voice, points toward the inner room.* BERTE *nods and exits*)

TESMAN (*while* HEDDA *and* BERTE *are talking, to* LØVBORG) Tell me, Eilert—is it this new subject—about the future—is that what you plan to lecture on?

LØVBORG Yes.

TESMAN For the bookseller told me you have announced a lecture series for this fall.

LØVBORG Yes, I have. I hope you won't mind too much.

TESMAN Of course not! But—

LØVBORG For of course I realized it is rather awkward for you.

TESMAN (*unhappily*) Oh well—I certainly can't expect—that just for my sake—

LØVBORG But I will wait till you receive your appointment.

TESMAN Wait? But—but—but—you mean you aren't going to compete with me? Hm?

LØVBORG No. Just triumph over you. In people's opinion.

TESMAN Oh, for goodness' sake! Then Aunt Julle was right, after all! I knew it all the time. Hedda! Do you hear that! Just think—Eilert Løvborg isn't going to stand in our way after all.

HEDDA (*tersely*) *Our?* I have nothing to do with this. (*She walks into the inner room, where* BERTE *is bringing in a tray with decanters and glasses.* HEDDA *nods her approval and comes forward again*)

TESMAN (*during the foregoing business*) How about that, Judge? What do you say to this? Hm?

BRACK I say that moral victory and all that —hm—may be glorious enough and beautiful enough—

TESMAN Oh, I agree. All the same—

HEDDA (*looks at* TESMAN *with a cold smile*) You look as if the lightning had hit you.

TESMAN Well, I am—pretty much—I really believe—

BRACK After all, Mrs. Tesman, that was quite a thunderstorm that just passed over.

HEDDA (*points to the inner room*) How about a glass of cold punch, gentlemen?

BRACK (*looks at his watch*) A stirrup cup. Not a bad idea.

TESMAN Splendid, Hedda. Perfectly splendid. In such a light-hearted mood as I am now—

HEDDA Please. You, too, Mr. Løvborg.

LØVBORG (*with a gesture of refusal*) No, thanks. Really. Nothing for me.

BRACK Good heavens, man! Cold punch isn't poison, you know!

LØVBORG Perhaps not for everybody.

HEDDA I'll keep Mr. Løvborg company in the meantime.

TESMAN All right, Hedda. You do that.

(*He and* BRACK *go into the inner room, sit down, drink punch, smoke cigarettes, and engage in lively conversation during the next scene.* EILERT LØVBORG *remains standing near the stove.* HEDDA *walks over to the desk*)

HEDDA (*her voice a little louder than usual*) I'll show you some pictures, if you like. You see—Tesman and I, we took a trip through Tyrol on our way back.

(*She brings an album over to the table by the sofa. She sits down in the far corner of the sofa. LØVBORG approaches, stops, looks at her. He takes a chair and sits down at her left, his back toward the inner room*)

HEDDA (*opens the album*) Do you see these mountains, Mr. Løvborg? They are the Ortler group. Tesman has written their name below. Here it is: "The Ortler group near Meran."

LØVBORG (*has looked steadily at her all this time. Says slowly*) Hedda—Gabler!

HEDDA (*with a quick glance sideways*) Not that! Shhh!

LØVBORG (*again*) Hedda Gabler!

HEDDA (*looking at the album*) Yes, that used to be my name. When—when we two knew each other.

LØVBORG And so from now on—for the whole rest of my life—I must get used to never again saying Hedda Gabler.

HEDDA (*still occupied with the album*) Yes, you must. And you might as well start right now. The sooner the better, I think.

LØVBORG (*with indignation*) Hedda Gabler married? And married to—Jørgen Tesman!

HEDDA Yes—that's the way it goes.

LØVBORG Oh, Hedda, Hedda—how could you throw yourself away like that!

HEDDA (*with a fierce glance at him*) What's this? I won't have any of that!

LØVBORG What do you mean?

(TESMAN *enters from the inner room*)

HEDDA (*hears him coming and remarks casually*) And this here, Mr. Løvborg, this is from somewhere in the Ampezzo valley. Just look at those peaks over there. (*with a kindly look at* TESMAN) What did you say those peaks were called, dear?

TESMAN Let me see. Oh, they—they are the Dolomites.

HEDDA Right. Those are the Dolomites, Mr. Løvborg.

TESMAN Hedda, I thought I'd just ask you if you don't want me to bring you some punch, after all? For you, anyway? Hm?

HEDDA Well, yes; thanks. And a couple of cookies, maybe.

TESMAN No cigarettes?

HEDDA No.

TESMAN All right.

(*He returns to the inner room, then turns right.* BRACK *is in there, keeping an eye on* HEDDA *and* LØVBORG *from time to time*)

LØVBORG (*still in a low voice*) Answer me, Hedda. How could you do a thing like that?

HEDDA (*apparently engrossed in the album*) If you keep on using my first name I won't talk to you.

LØVBORG Not even when we're alone?

HEDDA No. You may think it, but you must not say it.

LØVBORG I see. It offends your love for—Jørgen Tesman.

HEDDA (*glances at him, smiles*) Love? That's a good one!

LØVBORG Not love, then.

HEDDA But no infidelities, either! I won't have it.

LØVBORG Hedda—answer me just this one thing—

HEDDA Shhh!

(TESMAN *enters with a tray from the inner room*)

TESMAN Here! Here are the goodies. (*puts the tray down*)

HEDDA Why don't you get Berte to do it?

TESMAN (*pouring punch*) Because I think it's so much fun waiting on you, Hedda.

HEDDA But you've filled both glasses. And Mr. Løvborg didn't want any—

TESMAN I know, but Mrs. Elvsted will soon be here, won't she?

HEDDA That's right. So she will.

TESMAN Had you forgotten about her? Hm?

HEDDA We've been so busy looking at this. (*shows him a picture*) Remember this little village?

TESMAN That's the one just below the Brenner Pass, isn't it? We spent the night there—

HEDDA —and ran into that lively crowd of summer guests.

TESMAN Right! Just think—if we only could have had you with us, Eilert! Oh well.

(*Returns to the inner room, sits down, and resumes his conversation with* BRACK)

LØVBORG Just tell me this, Hedda—

HEDDA What?

LØVBORG Wasn't there love in your feelings for me, either? Not a touch—not a shimmer of love? Wasn't there?

HEDDA I wonder. To me, we seemed to be simply two good comrades. Two close friends. (*smiles*) You, particularly, were very frank.

LØVBORG You wanted it that way.

HEDDA And yet—when I think back upon it now, there was something beautiful, something thrilling, something brave, I think, about the secret frankness—that comradeship that not a single soul so much as suspected.

LØVBORG Yes, wasn't there, Hedda? Wasn't

there? When I called on your father in the afternoons—And the General sat by the window with his newspapers—his back turned—

HEDDA   And we two in the sofa in the corner—

LØVBORG   —always with the same illustrated magazine—

HEDDA   —for want of an album, yes—

LØVBORG   Yes, Hedda—and then when I confessed to you—! Told you all about myself, things the others didn't know. Sat and told you about all my orgies by day and night. Dissipation day in and day out! Oh, Hedda— what sort of power in you was it that forced me to tell you things like that?

HEDDA   You think there was some power in me?

LØVBORG   How else can I explain it? And all those veiled questions you asked—

HEDDA   —which you understood so perfectly well—

LØVBORG   That you could ask such questions as that! With such complete frankness!

HEDDA   *Veiled,* if you please.

LØVBORG   But frankly all the same. All about —that!

HEDDA   And to think that you answered, Mr. Løvborg!

LØVBORG   Yes, that's just what I can't understand—now, afterwards. But tell me, Hedda; wasn't love at the bottom of our whole relationship? Didn't you feel some kind of urge to— purify me—when I came to you in confession? Wasn't that it?

HEDDA   No, not quite.

LØVBORG   Then what made you do it?

HEDDA   Do you find it so very strange that a young girl—when she can do so, without anyone knowing—

LØVBORG   Yes—?

HEDDA   —that she wants to take a peek into a world which—

LØVBORG   —which—?

HEDDA   —she is not supposed to know anything about?

LØVBORG   So that was it!

HEDDA   That, too. That, too—I think—

LØVBORG   Companionship in the lust for life. But why couldn't *that* at least have continued?

HEDDA   That was your own fault.

LØVBORG   You were the one who broke off.

HEDDA   Yes, when reality threatened to enter our relationship. Shame on you, Eilert Løvborg! How could you want to do a thing like that to your frank and trusting comrade!

LØVBORG   (*clenching his hands*) Oh, why didn't you do it! Why didn't you shoot me down, as you said you would!

HEDDA   Because I'm scared of scandal.

LØVBORG   Yes, Hedda. You are really a coward.

HEDDA   A terrible coward. (*changing her tone*) But that was your good luck, wasn't it? And now the Elvsteds have healed your broken heart very nicely.

LØVBORG   I know what Thea has told you.

HEDDA   Perhaps you have told her about us?

LØVBORG   Not a word. She is too stupid to understand.

HEDDA   Stupid?

LØVBORG   In things like that.

HEDDA   And I'm a coward. (*leans forward, without looking in his eyes, whispers*) But now I am going to confess something to *you.*

LØVBORG   (*tense*) What?

HEDDA   That I didn't dare to shoot—

LØVBORG   Yes—?

HEDDA   —that was not the worst of my cowardice that night.

LØVBORG   (*looks at her a moment, understands, whispers passionately*) Oh, Hedda! Hedda Gabler! Now I begin to see what was behind the companionship! You and I! So it *was* your lust for life—!

HEDDA   (*in a low voice, with an angry glance*) Take care! Don't you believe that!

(*Darkness is falling. The door, right, is opened, and* BERTE *enters*)

HEDDA   (*closing the album, calls out, smiling*) At last! So there you are, dearest Thea! Come in!

(MRS. ELVSTED *enters. She is dressed for a party.* BERTE *exits, closing the door behind her*)

HEDDA   (*in the sofa, reaching out for* MRS. ELVSTED) Sweetest Thea, you have no idea how I've waited for you.

(*In passing,* MRS. ELVSTED *exchanges quick greetings with* TESMAN *and* BRACK *in the inner room. She walks up to the table and shakes* HEDDA's *hand.* EILERT LØVBORG *rises. He and* MRS. ELVSTED *greet one another with a silent nod*)

MRS. ELVSTED   Maybe I ought to go in and say hello to your husband?

HEDDA   No, never mind that. Let them be. They're soon leaving, anyway.

MRS. ELVSTED   Leaving?

HEDDA   They're off to a spree.

MRS. ELVSTED   (*quickly, to* LØVBORG) Not you?

LØVBORG   No.

HEDDA   Mr. Løvborg stays here with us.

MRS. ELVSTED   (*pulls up a chair, is about to sit down next to* LØVBORG) Oh, how wonderful it is to be here!

HEDDA   Oh no, little Thea. Not that. Not there. Over here by me, please. I want to be in the middle.

MRS. ELVSTED   Just as you like. (*She walks in front of the table and seats herself on the sofa, on* HEDDA'*s right.* LØVBORG *sits down again on his chair*)

LØVBORG   (*after a brief pause, to* HEDDA) Isn't she lovely to look at?

HEDDA   (*gently stroking her hair*)   Just to look at?

LØVBORG   Yes. For you see—she and I—we are real comrades. We have absolute faith in one another. And we can talk together in full freedom.

HEDDA   Unveiled, Mr. Løvborg?

LØVBORG   Well—

MRS. ELVSTED   (*in a low voice, clinging to* HEDDA)   Oh, I am so happy, Hedda! For just think—he says I have inspired him, too!

HEDDA   (*looks at her with a smile*)   No, really! He says that?

LØVBORG   And she has such courage, Mrs. Tesman! Such courage of action.

MRS. ELVSTED   Oh, my God—courage—! I!

LØVBORG   Infinite courage—when it concerns the comrade.

HEDDA   Yes, courage—if one only had that.

LØVBORG   What then?

HEDDA   Then maybe life would be tolerable, after all. (*changing her tone*) But now, dearest Thea, you want a glass of nice, cold punch.

MRS. ELVSTED   No, thanks. I never drink things like that.

HEDDA   Then what about you, Mr. Løvborg?

LØVBORG   Thanks. Nothing for me, either.

MRS. ELVSTED   No, nothing for him, either.

HEDDA   (*looks firmly at him*)   If I say so?

LØVBORG   Makes no difference.

HEDDA   (*laughs*)   Poor me! So I have no power over you at all. Is that it?

LØVBORG   Not in that respect.

HEDDA   Seriously, though; I really think you should. For your own sake.

MRS. ELVSTED   No, but Hedda—!

LØVBORG   Why so?

HEDDA   Or rather for people's sake.

LØVBORG   Oh?

HEDDA   For else they might think you don't really trust yourself—That you lack self-confidence—

MRS. ELVSTED   (*softly*)   Don't, Hedda!

LØVBORG   People may think whatever they like for all I care—for the time being.

MRS. ELVSTED   (*happy*)   Exactly!

HEDDA   I could easily tell from watching Judge Brack just now.

LØVBORG   Tell what?

HEDDA   He smiled so contemptuously when you didn't dare to join them in there.

LØVBORG   Didn't I dare to! It's just that I'd much rather stay here and talk with you!

MRS. ELVSTED   But that's only natural, Hedda.

HEDDA   The Judge had no way of knowing that. And I also noticed he smiled and looked at Tesman when you didn't dare to go to his silly old party.

LØVBORG   Didn't dare! Are you saying I didn't dare?

HEDDA   *I* am not. But that's how Judge Brack understood it.

LØVBORG   Let him.

HEDDA   So you're not going?

LØVBORG   I'm staying here with you and Thea.

MRS. ELVSTED   Of course, he is, Hedda!

HEDDA   (*smiles, nods approvingly*)   That's what I call firm foundations. Principled forever; that's the way a man ought to be! (*turning to* MRS. ELVSTED, *stroking her cheek*) What did I tell you this morning—when you came here, quite beside yourself—?

LØVBORG   (*puzzled*)   Beside herself?

MRS. ELVSTED   (*in terror*)   Hedda—Hedda—don't!

HEDDA   Now do you see? There was no need at all for that mortal fear of yours—(*interrupting herself*) There, now! Now we can all three relax and enjoy ourselves.

LØVBORG   (*startled*)   What's all this, Mrs. Tesman?

MRS. ELVSTED   Oh, God, Hedda—what are you saying? What are you doing?

HEDDA   Please be quiet. That horrible Judge is looking at you.

LØVBORG   In mortal fear? So that's it. For my sake.

MRS. ELVSTED   (*softly, wailing*)   Oh, Hedda—if you only knew how utterly miserable you have made me!

LØVBORG   (*stares at her for a moment. His face is distorted*)   So that was the comrade's happy confidence in me!

MRS. ELVSTED   Oh, my dearest friend—listen to me first—!

LØVBORG   (*picks up one of the glasses of punch, raises it, says hoarsely*)   Here's to you, Thea! (*empties the glass, puts it down, picks up the other one*)

MRS. ELVSTED   (*softly*)   Hedda, Hedda—why did you want to do this?

HEDDA   Want to! I! Are you mad?

LØVBORG   And here's to you, too, Mrs. Tesman! Thanks for telling me the truth. Long live the truth! (*He drains the glass and is about to fill it again*)

HEDDA (*restrains him*) That's enough for now. Remember you are going to a party.

MRS. ELVSTED No, no, no!

HEDDA Shhh! They are looking at you.

LØVBORG (*puts his glass down*) Listen, Thea—tell me the truth—

MRS. ELVSTED I will, I will!

LØVBORG Did your husband know you were coming after me?

MRS. ELVSTED (*wringing her hands*) Oh, Hedda—do you hear what he's asking?

LØVBORG Did the two of you agree that you were to come here and look after me? Maybe it was his idea, even? Did he send you? Ah, I know what it was—he missed me in the office, didn't he? Or was it at the card table?

MRS. ELVSTED (*softly, in agony*) Oh, Løvborg, Løvborg!

LØVBORG (*grabs a glass and is about to fill it*) Here's to the old Commissioner, too!

HEDDA (*stops him*) No more now. You're supposed to read aloud for Tesman tonight—remember?

LØVBORG (*calm again, puts the glass down*) This was silly of me, Thea. I'm sorry. To take it this way. Please, don't be angry with me. You'll see—both you and all those others—that even if I have been down—! With your help, Thea—dear comrade.

MRS. ELVSTED (*beaming*) Oh, thank God—! (*In the meantime,* BRACK *has looked at his watch. He and* TESMAN *get up and come forward*)

BRACK (*picking up his coat and hat*) Well, Mrs. Tesman; our time is up.

HEDDA I suppose it is.

LØVBORG (*rising*) Mine, too, Judge.

MRS. ELVSTED (*softly, pleadingly*) Oh, Løvborg—don't do it!

HEDDA (*pinches her arm*) They can hear you!

MRS. ELVSTED (*with a soft exclamation*) Ouch!

LØVBORG (*to* BRACK) You were good enough to ask me—

BRACK So you're coming, after all?

LØVBORG If I may.

BRACK I'm delighted.

LØVBORG (*picks up his manuscript and says to* TESMAN) For there are a couple of things here I'd like to show you before I send it off.

TESMAN Just think! Isn't that nice! But—dearest Hedda—? In that case, how are you going to get Mrs. Elvsted home? Hm?

HEDDA We'll manage somehow.

LØVBORG (*looking at the two women*) Mrs. Elvsted? I'll be back to pick her up, of course. (*coming closer*) About ten o'clock, Mrs. Tesman? Is that convenient?

HEDDA Certainly. That will be fine.

TESMAN Then everything is nice and settled. But don't expect me that early, Hedda.

HEDDA You just stay as long as—as long as you want, dear.

MRS. ELVSTED (*in secret fear*) I'll be waiting for you here, then, Mr. Løvborg.

LØVBORG (*hat in hand*) Of course, Mrs. Elvsted.

BRACK All aboard the pleasure train, gentlemen! I hope we'll have a lively evening—as a certain fair lady would say.

HEDDA Ah—if only the fair lady could be present. Invisible.

BRACK Why invisible?

HEDDA To listen to some of your unadulterated liveliness, Judge.

BRACK (*laughs*) I shouldn't advise the fair lady to do that!

TESMAN (*also laughing*) You're a good one, Hedda! Just think!

BRACK Well—good night, ladies!

LØVBORG (*with a bow*) Till about ten, then.

(BRACK, LØVBORG, *and* TESMAN *go out, right. At the same time* BERTE *enters from the inner room with a lighted lamp, which she places on the table, front center. She goes out the same way*)

MRS. ELVSTED (*has risen and paces restlessly up and down*) Hedda, Hedda—how do you think all this will end?

HEDDA At ten o'clock he'll be here. I see him already. With vine leaves in his hair. Flushed and confident.

MRS. ELVSTED I only hope you're right.

HEDDA For then, you see, he'll have mastered himself. And be a free man for all the days of his life.

MRS. ELVSTED Dear God—how I hope you are right! That he comes back like that.

HEDDA That is the way he will come. Not any other way. (*rises and goes closer to* MRS. ELVSTED) *You* may doubt as long as you like. I believe in him. And now we'll see—

MRS. ELVSTED There is something behind all this, Hedda. Some hidden purpose.

HEDDA Yes, there is! For once in my life I want to have power over a human destiny.

MRS. ELVSTED But don't you already?

HEDDA I don't and I never have.

MRS. ELVSTED But your husband—?

HEDDA You think that's worth the trouble?

Oh, if you knew how poor I am! And you got to be so rich! (*embraces her passionately*) I think I'll have to burn your hair off, after all!

MRS. ELVSTED   Let me go! Let me go! You scare me, Hedda!

BERTE (*in the doorway*)   Supper is served, ma'am.

HEDDA   Good. We're coming.

MRS. ELVSTED   No, no, no! I'd rather go home by myself! Right now!

HEDDA   Nonsense! You'll have your cup of tea first, you little silly. And then—at ten o'clock—Eilert Løvborg comes—with vine leaves in his hair! (*she almost pulls* MRS. ELVSTED *toward the doorway*)

ACT THREE

(*The same room at the* TESMANS'. *The doorway and the French windows both have their portieres closed. The lamp, turned half down, is still on the table. The stove is open. Some dying embers can be seen.*

MRS. ELVSTED, *wrapped in a big shawl, is in the easy chair near the stove, her feet on a footstool.* HEDDA, *also dressed, is lying on the sofa, covered by a blanket*)

MRS. ELVSTED (*after a while suddenly sits up, listens anxiously; then she wearily sinks back in her chair, whimpers softly*)   Oh my God, my God—not yet!

(BERTE *enters cautiously, right, carrying a letter*)

MRS. ELVSTED (*turns and whispers tensely*)   Well—has anybody been here?

BERTE (*in a low voice*)   Yes. Just now there was a girl with this letter.

MRS. ELVSTED (*quickly, reaches for it*)   A letter! Give it to me!

BERTE   No, ma'am. It's for the Doctor.

MRS. ELVSTED   I see.

BERTE   Miss Tesman's maid brought it. I'll leave it here on the table.

MRS. ELVSTED   All right.

BERTE (*puts the letter down*)   I'd better put out the lamp. It just reeks.

MRS. ELVSTED   Yes, do that. It must be daylight soon, anyway.

BERTE (*putting out the lamp*)   It's light already, ma'am.

MRS. ELVSTED   Light already! And still not back!

BERTE   No, so help us. Not that I didn't expect as much—

MRS. ELVSTED   You did?

BERTE   Yes, when I saw a certain character was back in town. Taking off with them. We sure heard enough about him in the old days!

MRS. ELVSTED   Not so loud. You are waking up Mrs. Tesman.

BERTE (*looks toward the sofa, sighs*)   God forbid—! Let her sleep, poor thing. Do you want me to get the fire going again?

MRS. ELVSTED   Not on my account, thank you.

BERTE   All right; I won't, then. (*exits quietly, right*)

HEDDA (*awakened by the closing door*)   What's that?

MRS. ELVSTED   Just the maid.

HEDDA (*looks around*)   Why in here—? Oh, I remember! (*sits up, rubs her eyes, stretches*) What time is it, Thea?

MRS. ELVSTED (*looks at her watch*)   Past seven.

HEDDA   When did Tesman get home?

MRS. ELVSTED   He didn't.

HEDDA   Not home yet!

MRS. ELVSTED (*getting up*)   Nobody's come.

HEDDA   And we who waited till four!

MRS. ELVSTED (*wringing her hands*)   And how we waited!

HEDDA (*her hand covering a yawn*)   We—ll. We could have saved ourselves that trouble.

MRS. ELVSTED   Did you get any sleep at all?

HEDDA   Yes, I slept pretty well, I think. Didn't you?

MRS. ELVSTED   Not a wink. I just couldn't, Hedda! It was just impossible.

HEDDA (*rises, walks over to her*)   Well, now! There's nothing to worry about, for heaven's sake. I know exactly what's happened.

MRS. ELVSTED   Then tell me please. Where do you think they are?

HEDDA   Well, first of all, I'm sure they were terribly late leaving the Judge's—

MRS. ELVSTED   Dear yes. I'm sure you're right. Still—

HEDDA   —and so Tesman didn't want to wake us up in the middle of the night. (*laughs*) Maybe he didn't want us to see him, either—after a party like that.

MRS. ELVSTED   But where do you think he has gone?

HEDDA   To the aunts', of course. His old room is still there, all ready for him.

MRS. ELVSTED   No, he can't be there. Just a few minutes ago there came a letter for him from Miss Tesman. It's over there.

HEDDA   Oh? (*looks at the envelope*) So it is —Auntie Julle herself. In that case, I suppose he's still at Brack's. And there's Eilert Løvborg, too—reading aloud, with vine leaves in his hair.

MRS. ELVSTED   Oh Hedda—you're only saying things you don't believe yourself.

HEDDA   My, what a little imbecile you really are, Thea!

MRS. ELVSTED   Yes, I suppose I am.

HEDDA   And you look dead tired, too.

MRS. ELVSTED   I *am* dead tired.

HEDDA   Why don't you do as I say. Go into my room and lie down.

MRS. ELVSTED   No, no—I wouldn't be able to go to sleep, anyway.

HEDDA   Of course, you would.

MRS. ELVSTED   And your husband is bound to be home any minute now. And I have to know right away.

HEDDA   I'll let you know as soon as he gets here.

MRS. ELVSTED   You promise me that, Hedda?

HEDDA   I do. You just go to sleep.

MRS. ELVSTED   Thanks. At least I'll try. (*exits through inner room*)

(HEDDA *goes to the French doors, opens the portieres. The room is now in full daylight. She picks up a little hand mirror from the desk, looks at herself, smooths her hair. Walks over to door, right, rings the bell for the maid.* BERTE *presently appears*)

BERTE   You want something, ma'am?

HEDDA   Yes. You'll have to start the fire again. I'm cold.

BERTE   Yes, ma'am! I'll get it warm in no time. (*rakes the embers together and puts in another piece of wood. Then she suddenly listens*) There's the doorbell, ma'am.

HEDDA   All right. See who it is. I'll take care of the stove myself.

BERTE   You'll have a nice blaze going in a minute. (*exits right*)

(HEDDA *kneels on the footstool and puts in more pieces of wood. Presently* TESMAN *enters, right. He looks tired and somber. He tiptoes toward the doorway and is about to disappear between the portieres*)

HEDDA   (*by the stove, without looking up*) Good morning.

TESMAN   (*turning*) Hedda! (*comes closer*) For heaven's sake—you up already! Hm?

HEDDA   Yes, I got up very early this morning.

TESMAN   And I was so sure you'd still be sound asleep! Just think!

HEDDA   Not so loud. Mrs. Elvsted is asleep in my room.

TESMAN   Mrs. Elvsted stayed here all night?

HEDDA   Yes. Nobody came for her, you know.

TESMAN   No, I suppose—

HEDDA   (*closes the stove, rises*) Well, did you have a good time at the Judge's?

TESMAN   Were you worried about me? Hm?

HEDDA   I'd never dream of worrying about you. I asked if you had a good time.

TESMAN   Yes, indeed. Nice for a change, anyway. But I think I liked it best early in the evening. For then Eilert read to me. Just think —we were more than an hour early! And Brack, of course, had things to see to. So Eilert read.

HEDDA   (*sits down at the right side of the table*) So? Tell me all about it.

TESMAN   (*sits down on an ottoman near the stove*) Oh Hedda, you'll never believe what a book that will be! It must be just the most remarkable thing ever written! Just think!

HEDDA   Yes, but I don't really care about that—

TESMAN   I must tell you, Hedda—I have a confession to make. As he was reading—something ugly came over me—

HEDDA   Ugly?

TESMAN   I sat there envying Eilert for being able to write like that! Just think, Hedda!

HEDDA   All right. I'm thinking!

TESMAN   And yet, with all his gifts—he's incorrigible, after all.

HEDDA   I suppose you mean he has more courage for life than the rest of you?

TESMAN   No, no—I don't mean that. I mean that he's incapable of exercising moderation in his pleasures.

HEDDA   What happened—in the end?

TESMAN   Well—I would call it a bacchanal, Hedda.

HEDDA   Did he have vine leaves in his hair?

TESMAN   Vine leaves? No, I didn't notice any vine leaves. But he gave a long, muddled speech in honor of the woman who had inspired him in his work. Those were his words.

HEDDA   Did he say her name?

TESMAN   No, he didn't. But I'm sure it must be Mrs. Elvsted. You just wait and see if I'm not right!

HEDDA   And where did you and he part company?

TESMAN   On the way back to town. We left —the last of us did—at the same time. And Brack came along, too, to get some fresh air. Then we decided we'd better see Eilert home. You see, he had had altogether too much to drink!

HEDDA   I can imagine.

TESMAN   But then the strangest thing of all happened, Hedda! Or maybe I should say the saddest. I'm almost ashamed—on Eilert's behalf—even talking about it.

HEDDA   Well—?

TESMAN   You see, on the way back I happened to be behind the others a little. Just for a minute or two—you know—

HEDDA   All right, all right—!

TESMAN   And when I hurried to catch up with them, can you guess what I found by the roadside? Hm?

HEDDA   How can I possibly—?

TESMAN   You musn't tell this to a living soul, Hedda! Do you hear! Promise me that, for Eilert's sake. (*pulls a parcel out of his coat pocket*) Just think—I found this!

HEDDA   Isn't that what he had with him here yesterday?

TESMAN   Yes! It's his whole, precious, irreplaceable manuscript! And he had dropped it—just like that! Without even noticing! Just think, Hedda! Isn't that awfully sad?

HEDDA   But why didn't you give it back to him?

TESMAN   In the condition he was in! Dear—I just didn't dare to.

HEDDA   And you didn't tell any of the others that you had found it, either?

TESMAN   Of course not. I didn't want to, for Eilert's sake—don't you see?

HEDDA   So nobody knows that you have Eilert Løvborg's papers?

TESMAN   Nobody. And nobody must know, either.

HEDDA   And what did you and he talk about afterwards?

TESMAN   I didn't have a chance to talk to him at all after that. For when we came into town, he and a couple of the others simply vanished. Just think!

HEDDA   Oh? I expect they took him home.

TESMAN   I suppose that must be it. And Brack took off on his own, too.

HEDDA   And what have you been doing with yourself since then?

TESMAN   Well, you see, I and some of the others went home with one of the younger fellows and had a cup of early morning coffee. Or night coffee maybe, rather. Hm? And now, after I've rested a bit and poor Eilert's had some sleep, I'll take this back to him.

HEDDA   (*reaches for the parcel*)   No—don't do that! Not right away, I mean. Let me look at it first.

TESMAN   Dearest Hedda—honestly, I just don't dare to.

HEDDA   Don't you dare to?

TESMAN   No, for I'm sure you realize how utterly desperate he'll be when he wakes up and finds that the manuscript is gone. For he hasn't got a copy, you know. He said so himself.

HEDDA   (*looks searchingly at him*)   But can't a thing like that be written over again?

TESMAN   Hardly. I really don't think so. For, you see—the inspiration—

HEDDA   Yes, I daresay that's the main thing. (*casually*) By the way, here's a letter for you.

TESMAN   Imagine!

HEDDA   (*gives it to him*)   It came early this morning.

TESMAN   It's from Aunt Julle, Hedda! I wonder what it can be. (*puts the manuscript down on the other ottoman, opens the letter, skims the content, jumps up*) Oh Hedda! She says here that poor Aunt Rina is dying!

HEDDA   You know we had to expect that.

TESMAN   And if I want to see her again I had better hurry. I'll rush over right away.

HEDDA   (*suppressing a smile*)   You'll rush?

TESMAN   Dearest Hedda of mine—if only you could bring yourself to come along! Hm?

HEDDA   (*rises, weary, with an air of refusal*) No, no. You musn't ask me that. I don't want to look at death and disease. I want to be free from all that's ugly.

TESMAN   Well, all right—(*rushing around*) My hat? My coat? Oh—out here in the hall. I just hope I won't be too late, Hedda. Hm?

HEDDA   Oh I'm sure that if you rush—

(BERTE *appears in the door, right*)

BERTE   Judge Brack is here and wants to know if he may see you.

TESMAN   At this hour! No, no. I can't possibly see him now!

HEDDA   But I can. (*to* BERTE) Tell the Judge please to come in.

(BERTE *exits*)

HEDDA   (*with a quick whisper*)   Tesman! The package! (*She grabs it from the ottoman*)

TESMAN   Yes! Give it to me!

HEDDA   No, no. I'll hide it for you till later.

(*She walks over to the desk and sticks the parcel in among the books on the shelf. In his hurry* TESMAN *is having difficulties getting his gloves on.* JUDGE BRACK *enters, right*)

HEDDA   (*nods to him*)   If *you* aren't an early bird—

BRACK   Yes, don't you think so? (*to* TESMAN) You're going out, too?

TESMAN   Yes, I must go and see the aunts. Just think, the invalid—she's dying!

BRACK   Oh, I'm terribly sorry! In that case, don't let me keep you. At such a moment—

TESMAN   Yes, I really must run. Goodbye, goodbye! (*hurries out, right*)

HEDDA   (*approaching* BRACK) It appears that things were quite lively last night over at your house.

BRACK   Indeed, Mrs. Tesman—I didn't get to bed at all.

HEDDA   You didn't either?

BRACK   As you see. But tell me—what has Tesman told you about the night's adventures?

HEDDA   Just some tiresome story about having coffee with somebody someplace—

BRACK   I believe I know all about that coffee. Eilert Løvborg wasn't one of them, was he?

HEDDA   No, they had taken him home first.

BRACK   Tesman, too?

HEDDA   No. Some of the others, he said.

BRACK   (*smiles*) Jørgen Tesman is really an ingenuous soul, you know.

HEDDA   He certainly is. But why do you say that? Is there something more to all this?

BRACK   Yes, there is.

HEDDA   Well! In that case, why don't we make ourselves comfortable, Judge. You'll tell your story better, too.

(*She sits down at the left side of the table,* BRACK *near her at the adjacent side*)

HEDDA   All right?

BRACK   For reasons of my own I wanted to keep track of my guests' movements last night. Or, rather—some of my guests.

HEDDA   Eilert Løvborg was one of them, perhaps?

BRACK   As a matter of fact—he was.

HEDDA   Now you are really making me curious.

BRACK   Do you know where he and a couple of the others spent the rest of the night, Mrs. Tesman?

HEDDA   No—tell me. If it is at all tellable.

BRACK   Oh, certainly it can be told. They turned up at an exceptionally gay early morning gathering.

HEDDA   Of the lively kind?

BRACK   The very liveliest.

HEDDA   A little more about this, Judge.

BRACK   Løvborg had been invited beforehand. I knew all about that. But he had declined. He is a reformed character, you know.

HEDDA   As of his stay with the Elvsteds— yes. But he went after all?

BRACK   Well, yes, you see, Mrs. Tesman— unfortunately, the spirit moved him over at my house last evening.

HEDDA   Yes, I understand he became inspired.

BRACK   Quite violently inspired. And that, I gather, must have changed his mind. You know, we men don't always have as much integrity as we ought to have.

HEDDA   Oh I'm sure you're an exception, Judge Brack. But about Løvborg—?

BRACK   To make a long story short—he ended up at Miss Diana's establishment.

HEDDA   Miss Diana's?

BRACK   She was the hostess at this gathering —a select circle of intimate friends, male and female.

HEDDA   Is she a redhead, by any chance?

BRACK   That's correct.

HEDDA   And a singer—of sorts?

BRACK   Yes—that, too. And a mighty huntress—of men, Mrs. Tesman. You seem to have heard of her. Eilert Løvborg used to be one of her most devoted protectors in his more affluent days.

HEDDA   And how did it all end?

BRACK   Not in a very friendly fashion, apparently. It seems that after the tenderest reception Miss Diana resorted to brute force—

HEDDA   Against Løvborg?

BRACK   Yes. He accused her or her woman friends of having stolen something of his. Said his wallet was gone. And other things, too. In brief, he's supposed to have started a pretty wicked row.

HEDDA   With what results?

BRACK   Nothing less than a general free-for-all—men and women both. Fortunately, the police stepped in—

HEDDA   The police—!

BRACK   Yes. But I'm afraid this will be an expensive escapade for Eilert Løvborg, crazy fool that he is.

HEDDA   Well!

BRACK   It appears that he made quite violent objection—struck an officer in the ear and tore his coat. So they had to take him along.

HEDDA   How do you know all this?

BRACK   From the police.

HEDDA   (*staring straight ahead*) So that's how it was. No vine leaves in his hair.

BRACK   Vine leaves, Mrs. Tesman?

HEDDA   (*changing her tone*) But tell me, Judge Brack—why did you keep such a close watch on Eilert Løvborg?

BRACK   Well—for one thing, it is obviously of some concern to me if he testifies that he came straight from my party.

HEDDA   So you think there will be an investigation?

BRACK   Naturally. But I suppose that doesn't

really matter too much. However, as a friend of the house I considered it my duty to give you and Tesman a full account of his night-time exploits.

HEDDA   Yes, but why?

BRACK   Because I very strongly suspect that he intends to use you as a kind of screen.

HEDDA   Really! Why do you think that?

BRACK   Oh, come now, Mrs. Tesman! We can use our eyes, can't we? This Mrs. Elvsted—she isn't leaving town right away, you know.

HEDDA   Well, even if there should be something going on between those two, I'd think there would be plenty of other places they could meet.

BRACK   But no home. After last night, every respectable house will once again close its doors to Eilert Løvborg.

HEDDA   And so should mine, you mean?

BRACK   Yes. I admit I would find it more than embarrassing if the gentleman were to become a daily guest here, Mrs. Tesman. If he, as an outsider—a highly dispensable outsider—if he were to intrude himself—

HEDDA   —into the triangle?

BRACK   Precisely. It would amount to homelessness for me.

HEDDA   (smiling)   Sole cock-o'-the-walk—so, that's your goal, is it, Judge?

BRACK   (nods slowly, lowers his voice)   Yes. That is my goal. And for that I will fight with every means at my disposal.

HEDDA   (her smile fading)   You're really a dangerous person, you know—when you come right down to it.

BRACK   You think so?

HEDDA   Yes. I am beginning to think so now. And I must say I am exceedingly glad you don't have any kind of hold on me.

BRACK   (with a noncommittal laugh)   Well, well, Mrs. Tesman! Maybe there is something to what you are saying, at that. Who knows what I might do if I did.

HEDDA   Really, now, Judge Brack! Are you threatening me?

BRACK   (rising)—Nonsense! For the triangle, you see—is best maintained on a voluntary basis.

HEDDA   My sentiments, exactly.

BRACK   Well, I have said what I came to say. And now I should get back to town. Good-bye, Mrs. Tesman! (walks toward the French doors)

HEDDA   (rises)   You're going through the garden?

BRACK   Yes. For me that's a short cut.

HEDDA   Yes, and then it's a back way.

BRACK   Quite true. I have nothing against back ways. There are times when they are most intriguing.

HEDDA   You mean when real ammunition is used?

BRACK   (already in the door, laughs back at her)   Oh good heavens! I don't suppose one shoots one's tame roosters!

HEDDA   (laughs also)   No—not if one has only one—!

(They nod to each other, both still laughing. He leaves. She closes the door behind him. For a few moments she remains by the door, quite serious now, looking into the garden. Then she walks over to the doorway and opens the portieres wide enough to look into the inner room. Walks to the desk, pulls LØVBORG's manuscript from the bookshelf and is about to read in it when BERTE's voice, very loud, is heard from the hall, right. HEDDA turns around, listens. She hurriedly puts the manuscript into the drawer of the desk and puts the key down on its top. EILERT LØVBORG, wearing his coat and with his hat in his hand, flings open the door, right. He looks somewhat confused and excited)

LØVBORG   (turned toward the invisible BERTE in the hall)   —And I say I must! You can't stop me! (He closes the door, turns, sees HEDDA, immediately controls himself, greets her)

HEDDA   (by the desk)   Well, well, Mr. Løvborg—aren't you a trifle late coming for Thea?

LØVBORG   Or a trifle early for calling on you. I apologize.

HEDDA   How do you know she is still here?

LØVBORG   The people she is staying with told me she's been gone all night.

HEDDA   (walks over to the table)   Did they seem—strange—when they told you that?

LØVBORG   (puzzled)   Strange?

HEDDA   I mean, did they seem to find it a little—unusual?

LØVBORG   (suddenly understands)   Ah, I see what you mean! Of course! I'm dragging her down with me. But as a matter of fact, I didn't notice anything. I suppose Tesman isn't up yet?

HEDDA   I—I don't think so—

LØVBORG   When did he get home?

HEDDA   Very late.

LØVBORG   Did he tell you anything?

HEDDA   Yes, he said you'd all had quite a time over at Brack's.

LØVBORG   Just that?

HEDDA   I think so. But I was so awfully sleepy—

(MRS. ELVSTED *enters through portieres in the rear*)

MRS. ELVSTED (*toward him*) Oh, Løvborg! At last!

LØVBORG Yes, at last. And too late.

MRS. ELVSTED (*in fear*) What is too late?

LØVBORG Everything is too late now. It's all over with me.

MRS. ELVSTED Oh no, no! Don't say things like that!

LØVBORG You'll say the same yourself when you hear—

MRS. ELVSTED I don't want to hear—!

HEDDA Maybe you'd rather talk with her alone? I'll leave.

LØVBORG No, stay—you, too. I beg you to.

MRS. ELVSTED But I don't want to listen, do you hear?

LØVBORG It isn't last night I want to talk about.

MRS. ELVSTED What about, then?

LØVBORG We'll have to part, Thea.

MRS. ELVSTED Part!

HEDDA (*involuntarily*) I knew it!

LØVBORG For I don't need you any more.

MRS. ELVSTED And you can stand there and tell me a thing like that! Don't need me! Why can't I help you the way I did before? Aren't we going to keep on working together?

LØVBORG I don't intend to work any more.

MRS. ELVSTED (*giving up*) What am I going to do with my life, then?

LØVBORG You'll have to try to live your live as if you'd never known me.

MRS. ELVSTED But I can't do that!

LØVBORG Try, Thea. Go back home.

MRS. ELVSTED (*agitated*) Never again! Where you are I want to be! And you can't chase me away just like that. I want to stay right here! Be with you when the book appears.

HEDDA (*in a tense whisper*) Ah—yes—the book!

LØVBORG (*looks at her*) My book—and Thea's. For that's what it is.

MRS. ELVSTED That's what I feel, too. And that's why I have the right to be with you when it comes out. I want to see all the honor and all the fame you'll get. And the joy—I want to share the joy, too.

LØVBORG Thea, our book is never going to come out.

HEDDA Ah!

MRS. ELVSTED It won't!

LØVBORG *Can't* ever appear.

MRS. ELVSTED (*with fearful suspicion*) Løvborg, what have you done with the manuscript?

HEDDA (*watching him tensely*) Yes—what about the manuscript?

MRS. ELVSTED Where is it?

LØVBORG Oh Thea—please, don't ask me about that!

MRS. ELVSTED Yes, yes—I want to be told! I have the right to know—right now!

LØVBORG All right. I've torn it to pieces.

MRS. ELVSTED (*screams*) Oh, no! No!

HEDDA (*involuntarily*) But that's not—!

LØVBORG (*looks at her*) Not true, you think?

HEDDA (*composing herself*) Well, of course, if you say so. You should know. It just sounds so—so unbelievable.

LØVBORG All the same, it's true.

MRS. ELVSTED (*hands clenched*) Oh God—oh God, Hedda. He has torn his own work to pieces!

LØVBORG I have torn my whole life to pieces, so why not my life's work as well?

MRS. ELVSTED And that's what you did last night?

LØVBORG Yes, I tell you! In a thousand pieces. And scattered them in the fjord. Far out—where the water is clean and salty. Let them drift there, with wind and current. Then they'll sink. Deep, deep down. Like me, Thea.

MRS. ELVSTED Do you know, Løvborg—this thing you've done to the book—all the rest of my life I'll think of it as killing a little child.

LØVBORG You are right. It is like murdering a child.

MRS. ELVSTED But then, how could you? For the child was mine, too!

HEDDA (*almost soundlessly*) The child—

MRS. ELVSTED (*with a deep sigh*) So it's all over. I'll go now, Hedda.

HEDDA But you aren't leaving town?

MRS. ELVSTED Oh, I don't know myself what I'll do. There's only darkness before me. (*exits, right*)

HEDDA (*waits for a moment*) Aren't you going to see her home, Mr. Løvborg?

LØVBORG I? Through the streets? Letting people see her with me?

HEDDA Of course, I don't know what else may have happened last night. But is it really so absolutely irreparable—?

LØVBORG Last night is not the end of it. That I know. And yet, I don't really care for that kind of life any more. Not again. She has broken all the courage for life and all the defiance that was in me.

HEDDA (*staring ahead*) So that sweet little goose has had her hand in a human destiny. (*looks at him*) But that you could be so heartless, even so!

LØVBORG   Don't tell me I was heartless!

HEDDA   To ruin everything that's given her soul and mind meaning for such a long, long time! You don't call that heartless!

LØVBORG   Hedda—to you I can tell the truth.

HEDDA   The truth?

LØVBORG   But first promise me—give me your word you'll never let Thea know what I'm going to tell you now.

HEDDA   You have it.

LØVBORG   All right. It isn't true what I just told her.

HEDDA   About the manuscript?

LØVBORG   Yes. I have not torn it up. Not thrown it in the sea, either.

HEDDA   But then—where is it?

LØVBORG   I've destroyed it just the same. Really, I have, Hedda!

HEDDA   I don't understand.

LØVBORG   Thea said that what I had done seemed to her like murdering a child.

HEDDA   Yes—she did.

LØVBORG   But killing a child, that's not the worst thing a father can do to it.

HEDDA   No?

LØVBORG   No. And the worst is what I don't want Thea to know.

HEDDA   What *is* the worst?

LØVBORG   Hedda—suppose a man, say, early in the morning, after a stupid, drunken night—suppose he comes home to his child's mother and says: Listen, I've been in such and such a place. I've been here—and I've been there. And I had our child with me. In all those places. And the child is lost. Gone. Vanished! I'll be damned if I know where it is. Who's got hold of it—

HEDDA   Yes—but when all is said and done —it is only a book, you know.

LØVBORG   Thea's pure soul was in that book.

HEDDA   I realize that.

LØVBORG   Then you surely also realize that she and I can have no future together.

HEDDA   Where do you go from here?

LØVBORG   Nowhere. Just finished everything off. The sooner the better.

HEDDA   (*a step closer*)   Listen—Eilert Løvborg— Couldn't you make sure it's done beautifully?

LØVBORG   Beautifully? (*smiles*)   With vine leaves in the hair, as you used to say.

HEDDA   Oh no. I don't believe in vine leaves any more. But still beautifully! For once. Goodbye. Go now. And don't come back.

LØVBORG   Goodbye, Mrs. Tesman. Give my regards to Jørgen Tesman. (*He is about to leave*)

HEDDA   Wait! I want to give you something —a remembrance. (*goes to the desk, opens the drawer, takes out the gun case. Returns to* LØVBORG *with one of the revolvers*)

LØVBORG   The gun? That's the remembrance?

HEDDA   (*nods slowly*)   Do you recognize it? It was pointed at you once.

LØVBORG   You should have used it then.

HEDDA   Take it! *You* use it.

LØVBORG   (*pockets the gun*)   Thanks!

HEDDA   And beautifully, Eilert Løvborg! That's all I ask!

LØVBORG   Goodbye, Hedda Gabler. (*exits, right*)

(HEDDA *listens by the door for a moment. Then she crosses to the desk, takes out the manuscript, glances inside the cover, pulls some of the pages halfway out and looks at them. Carries the whole manuscript over to the chair by the stove. She sits down with the parcel in her lap. After a moment she opens the stove and then the manuscript*)

HEDDA   (*throws a bundle of sheets into the fire, whispers*)   Now I'm burning your child, Thea. You—curlyhead! (*throws more sheets in*) Your and Eilert Løvborg's child. (*throws all the rest of the manuscript into the stove*) I am burning—I am burning your child.

ACT FOUR

(*The same rooms at the* TESMANS'. *Evening. The front room is dark. The inner room is lighted by the ceiling lamp over the table. Portieres cover the French doors.*

HEDDA, *in black, is walking up and down in the dark of the front room. She goes into the inner room, turning left in the doorway. She is heard playing a few bars on the piano. She reappears and comes forward again.* BERTE *enters from the right side of the inner room. She carries a lighted lamp, which she puts down on the table in front of the corner sofa. Her eyes show signs of weeping; she wears black ribbons on her uniform. She exits quietly, right.* HEDDA *goes over to the French windows, looks between the portieres into the dark. Presently* MISS TESMAN, *in mourning, with hat and veil, enters, right.* HEDDA *walks over to meet her, gives her her hand*)

MISS TESMAN   Yes, my dearest Hedda—here you see me in my garb of grief. For now at last my poor sister has fought her fight to the end.

HEDDA   I already know—as you see. Tesman sent word.

MISS TESMAN   Yes, he promised he'd do that. But I thought that to you, Hedda—here in the house of life—I really ought to bring the tidings of death myself.

HEDDA   That is very kind of you.

MISS TESMAN   Ah, but Rina shouldn't have died just now. There should be no mourning in Hedda's house at this time.

HEDDA   (*changing the topic*)   I understand she had a very quiet end.

MISS TESMAN   Oh so beautiful, so peaceful! She left us so quietly! And then the unspeakable happiness of seeing Jørgen one more time! To say goodbye to him to her heart's content! Isn't he back yet?

HEDDA   No. He wrote I musn't expect him back very soon. But do sit down.

MISS TESMAN   No—no, thanks, my dear, blessed Hedda. Not that I wouldn't like to. But I don't have much time. I must go back and prepare her as best I can. I want her to look right pretty when she goes into her grave.

HEDDA   Is there anything I can help you with?

MISS TESMAN   I won't have you as much as think of it! That's not for Hedda Tesman to lend a hand to. Or lend thoughts to, either. Not now, of all times!

HEDDA   Oh—thoughts! We can't always control our thoughts—

MISS TESMAN   (*still preoccupied*)   Ah yes—such is life. At home we're making a shroud for Rina. And here, too, there'll be sewing to do soon, I expect. But of quite different kind, thank God!

(TESMAN *enters, right*)

HEDDA   So finally you're back!

TESMAN   You here, Aunt Julle? With Hedda? Just think!

MISS TESMAN   I am just about to leave, Jørgen dear. Well—did you do all the things you promised me you'd do?

TESMAN   No, I'm afraid I forgot half of them, Auntie. I'd better run in again tomorrow. I'm all confused today. I can't seem to keep my thoughts together.

MISS TESMAN   But dearest Jørgen—you musn't take it this way!

TESMAN   Oh, I musn't? How do you mean?

MISS TESMAN   You ought to be joyful in the midst of your sorrow. Glad for what's happened. The way I am.

TESMAN   Oh yes, of course. You're thinking of Aunt Rina.

HEDDA   You're going to feel lonely now, Miss Tesman.

MISS TESMAN   The first few days, yes. But I hope that won't last long. Dear Rina's little parlor won't be empty for long, if I can help it!

TESMAN   Oh? And who do you want to move in there, hm?

MISS TESMAN   Ah—it's not very hard to find some poor soul who needs nursing and comfort.

HEDDA   And you really want to take on such a burden all over again?

MISS TESMAN   Heavens! God forgive you, child—burden? It has not been a burden to me.

HEDDA   Still—a stranger, who—

MISS TESMAN   Oh, it's easy to make friends with sick people. And I sorely need something to live for, I, too. Well, the Lord be praised, maybe soon there'll be a thing or two an old aunt can turn her hand to here.

HEDDA   Please, don't let our affairs worry you—

TESMAN   Yes, just think—how lovely it would be for the three of us, if only—

HEDDA   If only—?

TESMAN   (*uneasy*)   Oh, nothing. I daresay it will all work out. Let's hope it will, hm?

MISS TESMAN   Well, well. I can see that you two have something to talk about. (*with a smile*) And perhaps Hedda has something to tell *you*, Jørgen! Goodbye! I'm going home to Rina, now. (*turns around in the door*) Dear, dear—how strange to think—! Now Rina is both with me and with Jochum!

TESMAN   Yes, just think, Aunt Julle! Hm?

(MISS TESMAN *exits, right*)

HEDDA   (*coldly scrutinizing* TESMAN)   I wouldn't be at all surprised if you are not more affected by this death than she is.

TESMAN   Oh, it isn't just Aunt Rina's death, Hedda. It's Eilert I worry about.

HEDDA   (*quickly*)   Any news about him?

TESMAN   I went over to his room this afternoon to tell him the manuscript is safe.

HEDDA   Well? And didn't you see him?

TESMAN   No. He wasn't home. But I ran into Mrs. Elvsted and she told me he'd been here early this morning.

HEDDA   Yes, right after you'd left.

TESMAN   And he said he'd torn up the manuscript? Did he really say that?

HEDDA   Yes. So he claimed.

TESMAN   But dear God—in that case he really must have been out of his mind! So I assume you didn't give it to him either, hm, Hedda?

HEDDA   No. He didn't get it.

TESMAN But you told him we had it, of course?

HEDDA No. (*quickly*) Did you tell Mrs. Elvsted?

TESMAN No, I didn't want to. But you ought to have told him, Hedda. Just think— what if he does something rash—something to hurt himself! Give me the manuscript, Hedda! I want to rush down to him with it right this minute. Where is it?

HEDDA (*cold, motionless, one arm resting on the chair*) I haven't got it any more.

TESMAN You haven't got it! What do you mean by that?

HEDDA I burned it—the whole thing.

TESMAN (*jumps up*) Burned it! Burned Eilert's book!

HEDDA Don't shout. The maid might hear you.

TESMAN Burned it? But good God—no, no, no!—This can't be—!

HEDDA It is, all the same.

TESMAN But do you realize what you've done, Hedda? It's illegal! Willful destruction of lost property! You just ask Judge Brack! He'll tell you!

HEDDA You'd better not talk about this to anyone—the Judge or anybody else.

TESMAN But how could you do a thing like that! I never heard anything like it! What came over you? What can possibly have been going on in your head? Answer me! Hm?

HEDDA (*suppresses an almost imperceptible smile*) I did it for your sake, Jørgen.

TESMAN For my sake!

HEDDA When you came back this morning and told me he had read aloud to you—

TESMAN Yes, yes! What then?

HEDDA You confessed you were jealous of him for having written such a book.

TESMAN But good gracious—! I didn't mean it as seriously as all that!

HEDDA All the same. I couldn't stand the thought that somebody else was to overshadow you.

TESMAN (*in an outburst of mingled doubt and joy*) Hedda—oh Hedda! Is it true what you're saying! But—but—but—I never knew you loved me like that! Just think!

HEDDA In that case, I might as well tell you—that—just at this time—(*breaks off, vehemently*) No, no! You can ask Aunt Julle. She'll tell you.

TESMAN I almost think I know what you mean, Hedda! (*claps his hands*) For goodness sake! Can that really be so! Hm?

HEDDA Don't shout so! The maid can hear you.

TESMAN (*laughing with exuberant joy*) The maid! Well, if you don't take the prize, Hedda! The maid—but that's Berte! I'm going to tell Berte myself this very minute!

HEDDA (*her hands clenched in despair*) Oh I'll die—I'll die, in all this!

TESMAN In what, Hedda? Hm?

HEDDA (*cold and composed*) In all this— ludicrousness, Jørgen.

TESMAN Ludicrous? That I'm so happy? Still—maybe I oughtn't to tell Berte, after all.

HEDDA Oh, go ahead. What difference does it make.

TESMAN No, not yet. But on my word— Aunt Julle must be told. And that you've started to call me "Jørgen," too! Just think! She'll be ever so happy—Aunt Julle will!

HEDDA Even when you tell her that I have burned Eilert Løvborg's papers?

TESMAN No, oh no! That's true! That about the manuscript—nobody must know about that. But to think that you'd burn for me, Hedda—I certainly want to tell *that* to Aunt Julle! I wonder now—is that sort of thing usual with young wives, hm?

HEDDA Why don't you ask Aunt Julle about that, too.

TESMAN I shall—I certainly shall, when I get the chance. (*looks uneasy and disturbed again*) But the manuscript! Good God—I don't dare to think what this is going to do to poor Eilert!

(MRS. ELVSTED, *dressed as on her first visit, wearing hat and coat, enters, right*)

MRS. ELVSTED (*gives a hurried greeting, is obviously upset*) Oh Hedda, you must forgive me for coming here again!

HEDDA What has happened, Thea?

TESMAN Something to do with Eilert Løvborg again? Hm?

MRS. ELVSTED Yes, yes—I'm so terribly afraid something's happened to him.

HEDDA (*seizing her arm*) Ah—you think so?

TESMAN Oh dear—why do you think that, Mrs. Elvsted?

MRS. ELVSTED I heard them talking about him in the boarding house, just as I came in. And people are saying the most incredible things about him today.

TESMAN Yes, imagine! I heard that, too! And I can testify that he went straight home to bed! Just think!

HEDDA And what did they say in the boarding house?

MRS. ELVSTED Oh, I didn't find out anything. Either they didn't know any details or—

They all became silent when they saw me. And I didn't dare to ask.

TESMAN (*pacing the floor uneasily*) We'll just have to hope—to hope that you heard wrong, Mrs. Elvsted!

MRS. ELVSTED No, no. I'm sure it was he they were talking about. And somebody said something about the hospital or—

TESMAN The hospital—!

HEDDA Surely, that can't be so!

MRS. ELVSTED I got so terribly frightened! So I went up to his room and asked for him there.

HEDDA Could you bring yourself to do that, Thea?

MRS. ELVSTED What else could I do? For I felt I just couldn't stand the uncertainty any longer.

TESMAN But I suppose you didn't find him in, either, did you? Hm?

MRS. ELVSTED No. And the people there didn't know anything about him. He hadn't been home since yesterday afternoon, they said.

TESMAN Yesterday! Just think! How could they say that!

MRS. ELVSTED I don't know what else *to* think—something bad must have happened to him!

TESMAN Hedda, dear—? What if I were to walk down town and ask for him at several places—?

HEDDA No, no—don't you go and get mixed up in all this.

(JUDGE BRACK, *hat in hand, enters through the door, right, which* BERTE *opens and closes for him. He looks serious and greets the others in silence*)

TESMAN So here you are, Judge, hm?

BRACK Yes. I had to see you this evening.

TESMAN I can see you have got Aunt Julle's message.

BRACK That, too—yes.

TESMAN Isn't it sad, though?

BRACK Well, my dear Tesman—that depends on how you look at it.

TESMAN (*looks at him uncertainly*) Has something else happened?

BRACK Yes.

HEDDA (*tense*) Something sad, Judge Brack?

BRACK That, too, depends on how you look at it, Mrs. Tesman.

MRS. ELVSTED (*bursting out*) Oh, I'm sure it has something to do with Eilert Løvborg!

BRACK (*looks at her for a moment*) Why do you think that, Mrs. Elvsted? Maybe you already know something—?

MRS. ELVSTED (*confused*) No, no; not at all. It's just—

TESMAN For heaven's sake, Brack, out with it!

BRACK (*shrugging his shoulders*) Well—unfortunately, Eilert Løvborg's in the hospital. Dying.

MRS. ELVSTED (*screams*) Oh God, oh God!

TESMAN In the hospital! And dying!

HEDDA (*without thinking*) So soon—!

MRS. ELVSTED (*wailing*) And we didn't even part as friends, Hedda!

HEDDA (*whispers*) Thea, Thea—for heaven's sake—!

MRS. ELVSTED (*paying no attention to her*) I want to see him! I want to see him alive!

BRACK Won't do you any good, Mrs. Elvsted. Nobody can see him.

MRS. ELVSTED Then tell me what's happened to him! What?

TESMAN For, surely, he hasn't himself—!

HEDDA I'm sure he has.

TESMAN Hedda! How can you—!

BRACK (*observing her all this time*) I am sorry to say that your guess is absolutely correct, Mrs. Tesman.

MRS. ELVSTED Oh, how awful!

TESMAN Did it himself! Just think!

HEDDA Shot himself!

BRACK Right again, Mrs. Tesman.

MRS. ELVSTED (*trying to pull herself together*) When did this happen, Judge?

BRACK This afternoon. Between three and four.

TESMAN But dear me—where can he have done a thing like that? Hm?

BRACK (*a little uncertain*) Where? Well—I suppose in his room. I don't really know—

MRS. ELVSTED No, it can't have been there. For I was up there sometime between six and seven.

BRACK Well, then, some other place. I really can't say. All I know is that he was found. He had shot himself—in the chest.

MRS. ELVSTED Oh, how horrible to think! That he was to end like that!

HEDDA (*to* BRACK) In the chest?

BRACK Yes—as I just told you.

HEDDA Not the temple?

BRACK In the chest, Mrs. Tesman.

HEDDA Well, well—the chest is a good place, too.

BRACK How is that, Mrs. Tesman?

HEDDA (*turning him aside*) Oh—nothing.

TESMAN And you say the wound is fatal? Hm?

BRACK No doubt about it—absolutely fatal. He's probably dead already.

MRS. ELVSTED   Yes, yes! I feel you're right! It's over! It's all over! Oh, Hedda!

TESMAN   But tell me—how do *you* know all this?

BRACK (*tersely*)   A man on the force told me. One I had some business with.

HEDDA (*loudly*)   At last a deed!

TESMAN (*appalled*)   Oh dear—what are you saying, Hedda!

HEDDA   I am saying there is beauty in this.

BRACK   Well, now—Mrs. Tesman—

TESMAN   Beauty—! Just think!

MRS. ELVSTED   Oh, Hedda—how can you talk about beauty in a thing like this!

HEDDA   Eilert Løvborg has settled this account with himself. He has had the courage to do—what had to be done.

MRS. ELVSTED   But you musn't believe it happened that way! He did it when he was not himself!

TESMAN   In despair! That's how!

HEDDA   He did not. I am certain of that.

MRS. ELVSTED   Yes he did! He was not himself! That's the way he tore up the book, too!

BRACK (*puzzled*)   The book? You mean the manuscript? Has he torn it up?

MRS. ELVSTED   Yes, last night.

TESMAN (*whispers*)   Oh, Hedda—we'll never get clear of all this!

BRACK   That is strange.

TESMAN (*walking the floor*)   To think that this was to be the end of Eilert! Not to leave behind him anything that would have preserved his name—

MRS. ELVSTED   Oh, if only it could be put together again!

TESMAN   Yes, if only it could. I don't know what I wouldn't give—

MRS. ELVSTED   Maybe it can, Mr. Tesman.

TESMAN   What do you mean?

MRS. ELVSTED (*searching her dress pocket*) Look. I have kept these little slips he dictated from.

HEDDA (*a step closer*)   Ah—!

TESMAN   You've kept them, Mrs. Elvsted? Hm?

MRS. ELVSTED   Yes. Here they are. I took them with me when I left. And I've had them in my pocket ever since—

TESMAN   Please, let me see—

MRS. ELVSTED (*gives him a pile of small paper slips*)   But it's in such a mess. Without any kind of system or order—!

TESMAN   But just think if we could make sense out of them, all the same! Perhaps if we helped each other—

MRS. ELVSTED   Oh yes! Let's try, anyway!

TESMAN   It will work! It *has* to work! I'll stake my whole life on this!

HEDDA   You, Jørgen? Your life?

TESMAN   Yes, or at any rate all the time I can set aside. My own collections can wait. Hedda, you understand—don't you? Hm? This is something I owe Eilert's memory.

HEDDA   Maybe so.

TESMAN   And now, my dear Mrs. Elvsted, we want to get to work. Good heavens, there's no point brooding over what's happened. Hm? We'll just have to acquire sufficient peace of mind to—

MRS. ELVSTED   All right, Mr. Tesman. I'll try to do my best.

TESMAN   Very well, then. Come over here. Let's look at these slips right away. Where can we sit? Here? No, it's better in the other room. If you'll excuse us, Judge! Come along, Mrs. Elvsted.

MRS. ELVSTED   Oh dear God—if only it were possible—!

(TESMAN *and* MRS. ELVSTED *go into the inner room. She takes off her hat and coat. Both sit down at the table under the hanging lamp and absorb themselves in eager study of the slips.* HEDDA *walks over toward the stove and sits down in the easy chair. After a while,* BRACK *walks over to her*)

HEDDA (*in a low voice*)   Ah, Judge—what a liberation there is in this thing with Eilert Løvborg!

BRACK   Liberation, Mrs. Tesman? Well, yes, for him perhaps one may say there was liberation of a kind—

HEDDA   I mean for me. There is liberation in knowing that there is such a thing in the world as an act of free courage. Something which becomes beautiful by its very nature.

BRACK (*smiles*)   Well—dear Mrs. Tesman—

HEDDA   Oh I know what you're going to say! For you see—you really are a kind of specialist, too!

BRACK (*looks at her fixedly*)   Eilert Løvborg has meant more to you than perhaps you're willing to admit, even to yourself. Or am I wrong?

HEDDA   I won't answer such questions. All I know is that Eilert Løvborg had the courage to live his own life. And then now—this—magnificence! The beauty of it! Having the strength and the will to get up and leave life's feast—so early—

BRACK   Believe me, Mrs. Tesman, this pains me, but I see it is necessary that I destroy a pretty illusion—

HEDDA   An illusion?

BRACK   Which could not have been maintained very long, anyway.

HEDDA   And what is that?

BRACK   He didn't shoot himself—of his own free will.

HEDDA   Not of his own—!

BRACK   No. To tell the truth, the circumstances of Eilert Løvborg's death aren't exactly what I said they were.

HEDDA   (*tense*) You've held something back? What?

BRACK   For the sake of poor Mrs. Elvsted I used a few euphemisms.

HEDDA   What?

BRACK   First—he is already dead.

HEDDA   In the hospital.

BRACK   Yes. And without regaining consciousness.

HEDDA   What else haven't you told?

BRACK   The fact that it did not happen in his room.

HEDDA   Well, does that really make much difference?

BRACK   Some. You see—Eilert Løvborg was found shot in Miss Diana's bedroom.

HEDDA   (*is about to jump up, but sinks back*) That's impossible, Judge Brack! He can't have been there again today!

BRACK   He was there this afternoon. He came to claim something he said they had taken from him. Spoke some gibberish about a lost child—

HEDDA   So that's why—!

BRACK   I thought maybe he meant his manuscript. But now I hear he has destroyed that himself. So I suppose it must have been something else.

HEDDA   I suppose. So it was there—so they found him there?

BRACK   Yes. With a fired gun in his pocket. Mortally wounded.

HEDDA   Yes—in the chest.

BRACK   No—in the guts.

HEDDA   (*looks at him with an expression of disgust*) That, too! What is this curse that turns everything I touch into something ludicrous and low!

BRACK   There is something else, Mrs. Tesman. Something I'd call—nasty.

HEDDA   And what is that?

BRACK   The gun they found—

HEDDA   (*breathless*) What about it?

BRACK   He must have stolen it.

HEDDA   (*jumps up*) Stolen! That's not true! He didn't!

BRACK   Anything else is impossible. He *must* have stolen it.—Shhh!

(TESMAN *and* MRS. ELVSTED *have risen from the table and come forward into the front room*)

TESMAN   (*with papers in both hands*) D'you know, Hedda—you can hardly see in there with that lamp! Just think!

HEDDA   I am thinking.

TESMAN   I wonder if you'd let us use your desk, hm?

HEDDA   Certainly, if you like. (*adds quickly*) Wait a minute, though! Let me clear it off a bit first.

TESMAN   Ah, there's no need for that, Hedda. There's plenty of room.

HEDDA   No, no. I want to straighten it up. Carry all this in here. I'll put it on top of the piano for the time being.

(*She has pulled an object, covered by note paper, out of the bookcase. She puts several other sheets of paper on top of it and carries the whole pile into the left part of the inner room.* TESMAN *puts the papers down on the desk and moves the lamp from the corner table over to the desk. He and* MRS. ELVSTED *sit down and resume their work.* HEDDA *returns*)

HEDDA   (*behind* MRS. ELVSTED'S *chair, softly ruffling her hair*) Well, little Thea—how is Eilert Løvborg's memorial coming along?

MRS. ELVSTED   (*looks up at her, discouraged*) Oh God—I'm sure it's going to be terribly hard to make anything out of all this.

TESMAN   But we have to. We just don't have a choice. And putting other people's papers in order—that's just the thing for me.

(HEDDA *walks over to the stove and sits down on one of the ottomans.* BRACK *stands over her, leaning on the easy chair*)

HEDDA   (*whispers*) What were you saying about the gun?

BRACK   (*also softly*) That he must have stolen it.

HEDDA   Why, necessarily?

BRACK   Because any other explanation ought to be out of the question, Mrs. Tesman.

HEDDA   Oh?

BRACK   (*looks at her for a moment*) Eilert Løvborg was here this morning, of course. Isn't that so?

HEDDA   Yes.

BRACK   Were you alone with him?

HEDDA   Yes, for a while.

BRACK   You didn't leave the room while he was here?

HEDDA   No.

BRACK   Think. Not at all? Not even for a moment?

HEDDA   Well—maybe just for a moment—out in the hall.

BRACK   And where was the gun case?

HEDDA   Down in the—

BRACK   Mrs. Tesman?

HEDDA On the desk.

BRACK Have you looked to see if both guns are still there?

HEDDA No.

BRACK You needn't bother. I saw the gun they found on Løvborg, and I knew it immediately. From yesterday—and from earlier occasions, too.

HEDDA Perhaps you have it?

BRACK No, the police do.

HEDDA What are the police going to do with it?

BRACK Try to find the owner.

HEDDA Do you think they will?

BRACK (leans over her, whispers) No, Hedda Gabler—not as long as I keep quiet.

HEDDA (with a hunted look) And if you don't?

BRACK (shrugs his shoulders) Of course, there's always the chance that the gun was stolen.

HEDDA (firmly) Rather die!

BRACK (smiles) People say things like that. They don't do them.

HEDDA (without answering) And if the gun was not stolen—and if they find the owner—then what happens?

BRACK Well, Hedda—then comes the scandal!

HEDDA The scandal!

BRACK Yes—the scandal. That you are so afraid of. You will of course be required to testify. Both you and Miss Diana. Obviously, she'll have to explain how the whole thing happened. Whether it was accident or homicide. Did he try to pull the gun out of his pocket to threaten her? And did it fire accidentally? Or did she grab the gun away from him, shoot him, and put it back in his pocket? She might just possibly have done that. She's a pretty tough girl—Miss Diana.

HEDDA But this whole disgusting affair has nothing to do with me.

BRACK Quite so. But you'll have to answer the question: Why did you give Eilert Løvborg the gun? And what inferences will be drawn from the fact that you did?

HEDDA (lowers her head) That's true. I hadn't thought of that.

BRACK Well—luckily, there's nothing to worry about as long as I don't say anything.

HEDDA (looks up at him) So then I'm in your power, Judge. From now on you can do anything you like with me.

BRACK (in an even softer whisper) Dearest Hedda—believe me, I'll not misuse my position.

HEDDA In your power, all the same. Dependent on your will. Servant to your demands. Not free. Not free! (rises suddenly) No—I can't stand that thought! Never!

BRACK (looks at her, half mockingly) Most people submit to the inevitable.

HEDDA (returning his glance) Perhaps. (walks over to the desk. Suppresses a smile and mimics TESMAN's way of speaking) Well? Do you think you can do it, Jørgen? Hm?

TESMAN Lord knows, Hedda. Anyway, I can already see it will take months.

HEDDA (still mimicking) Just think! (runs her hands lightly through MRS. ELVSTED's hair) Doesn't this seem strange to you, Thea? Sitting here with Tesman—just the way you used to with Eilert Løvborg?

MRS. ELVSTED Oh dear—if only I could inspire your husband, too!

HEDDA Oh, I'm sure that will come—in time.

TESMAN Well, yes—do you know, Hedda? I really think I begin to feel something of the kind. But why don't you go and talk to the Judge again.

HEDDA Isn't there anything you two can use me for?

TESMAN No, not a thing, dear. (turns around) From now on, you must be good enough to keep Hedda company, my dear Judge!

BRACK (glancing at HEDDA) I'll be only too delighted.

HEDDA Thank you. I'm tired tonight. I think I'll go and lie down for a while on the sofa in there.

TESMAN Yes, you do that, dear; why don't you? Hm?

(HEDDA goes into the inner room, closes the portieres behind her. Brief pause. Suddenly, she is heard playing a frenzied dance tune on the piano)

MRS. ELVSTED (jumps up) Oh God! What's that!

TESMAN (running to the doorway) But dearest Hedda—you mustn't play dance music tonight, for goodness' sake! Think of Aunt Rina! And Eilert, too!

HEDDA (peeks in from between the portieres) And Aunt Julle. And everybody. I'll be quiet. (She pulls the portieres shut again)

TESMAN (back at the desk) I don't think it's good for her to see us at such a melancholy task. I'll tell you what, Mrs. Elvsted. You move in with Aunt Julle, and then I'll come over in the evenings. Then we can sit and work over there. Hm?

MRS. ELVSTED Maybe that would be better—

HEDDA (*from the inner room*) I hear every word you're saying, Tesman. And how am I going to spend my evenings?

TESMAN (*busy with the papers*) Oh, I'm sure Judge Brack will be good enough to come out and see you, anyway.

BRACK (*in the easy chair, calls out gaily*) Every single night, as far as I'm concerned, Mrs. Tesman! I'm sure we're going to have a lovely time, you and I!

HEDDA (*loud and clear*) Yes, don't you think that would be nice, Judge Brack? You— sole cock-o'-the-walk—

(*A shot is heard from the inner room.* TESMAN, MRS. ELVSTED, *and* JUDGE BRACK *all jump up*)

TESMAN There she is, fooling with those guns again.

(*He pulls the portieres apart and runs inside.* MRS. ELVSTED *also.* HEDDA, *lifeless, is lying on the sofa. Cries and confusion.* BERTE, *flustered, enters, right*)

TESMAN (*shouts to* BRACK) She's shot herself! In the temple! Just think!

BRACK (*half stunned in the easy chair*) But, merciful God—! People don't *do* things like that!

August Strindberg

1849-1912

THE PREFACE TO *MISS JULIE*

Like the arts in general, the theater has for a long time seemed to me a *Biblia Pauperum*, a picture Bible for those who cannot read, and the playwright merely a lay preacher who hawks the latest ideas in popular form, so popular that the middle classes—the bulk of the audiences—can grasp them without racking their brains too much. That explains why the theater has always been an elementary school for youngsters and the half-educated, and for women, who still retain a primitive capacity for deceiving themselves and for letting themselves be deceived, that is, for succumbing to illusions and responding hypnotically to the suggestions of the author. Consequently, now that the rudimentary and undeveloped mental processes which take place in the realm of fantasy appear to be evolving to the level of reflection, research, and experimentation, I believe that the theater, like religion, is about to be replaced as a dying institution for whose enjoyment we lack the necessary qualifications. Support for my view is provided by the theater crisis through which all of Europe is now passing, and still more by the fact that in those highly cultured lands which have produced the finest minds of our time—England and Germany—the drama is dead, as for the most part are the other fine arts.

In other countries attempts have indeed been made to create a new drama by filling the old forms with modern ideas. But there has not yet been time enough to popularize the new ideas so that the broad public can grasp them.

"The Preface to *Miss Julie*" by August Strindberg, translated by Evert Sprinchorn. Copyright 1961 by Chandler Publishing Company, San Francisco, and reprinted with their permission.

Moreover, party strife has stirred up the public emotions to such a degree that a pure and dispassionate enjoyment has become an impossibility in the theater, where one is likely to see everything one believes in flouted and scorned, and where a wildly applauding or hissing majority can openly exercise its tyrannical powers to an extent possible nowhere else. And thirdly, the new forms for the new ideas have not been found, and the new wine has burst the old bottles.

In the play which follows I have not tried to accomplish anything new—that is impossible. I have only tried to modernize the form to satisfy what I believe up-to-date people expect and demand of this art. And with that in mind I have seized upon—or let myself be seized by —a theme which may be said to lie outside current party strife, since the question of being on the way up or on the way down the social ladder, of being on the top or on the bottom, superior or inferior, man or woman, is, has been, and will be of perennial interest. When I took this theme from real life—I heard about it a few years ago and it made a deep impression on me—I thought it would be a suitable subject for a tragedy, for it still strikes us as tragic to see a happily favored individual go down in defeat, and even more so to see an entire family line die out. But perhaps a time will come when we shall be so highly developed and so enlightened that we can look with indifference upon the brutal, cynical, and heartless spectacle that life offers us, a time when we shall have laid aside those inferior and unreliable instruments of thought called feelings, which will become superfluous and even harmful as our mental organs develop. The fact that my heroine wins sympathy is due entirely to the fact that we are still too weak to overcome a fear that the same fate might overtake us. The extremely sensitive viewer will of course not be satisfied with mere expressions of sympathy, and the man who believes in progress will demand that certain positive actions be taken for getting rid of the evil, a kind of program, in other words. But in the first place absolute evil does not exist. The decline of one family is the making of another, which now gets its chance to rise. This alternate rising and falling provides one of life's greatest pleasures, for happiness is, after all, relative. As for the man who has a program for changing the disagreeable circumstance that the eagle eats the dove and that lice eat up the eagle, I should like to ask him why it should be changed? Life is not prearranged with such idiotic mathematical precision that only the larger gets to eat the smaller. Just as frequently the little bee destroys the lion—or at least drives him wild.

If my tragedy makes most people feel sad, that is their fault. When we get to be as strong as the first French Revolutionists were, we shall be perfectly content and happy to watch the forests being cleared of rotting, superannuated trees that have stood too long in the way of others with just as much right to grow and flourish for a while—as content as we are when we see an incurably ill man finally die.

Recently my tragedy *The Father* was criticized for being too unpleasant—as if one wanted amusing tragedies. "The joy of life" is now the slogan of the day. Theater managers send out orders for nothing but farces, as if the joy of life lay in behaving like a clown and in depicting people as if they were afflicted with St. Vitus's dance or congenital idiocy. I find my joy of life in the fierce and ruthless battles of life, and my pleasure comes from learning something, from being taught something. That is why I have chosen for my play an unusual but instructive case, an exception, in other words— but an important exception of the kind that proves the rule—a choice of subject which I know will offend all lovers of the conventional. The next thing that will bother simple minds is that the motivation for the action is not simple and that the point of view is not single. Usually an event in life—and this is a fairly new discovery—is the result of a whole series of more or less deep-seated causes. The spectator, however, generally chooses the one that puts the least strain on his mind or reflects most credit on his insight. Consider a case of suicide. "Business failure," says the middle-class man. "Unhappy love," say the women. "Physical illness," says the sick man. "Lost hopes," says the down-and-out. But it may be that the reason lay in all of these, or in none of them; and that

the suicide hid his real reason behind a completely different one that would reflect greater glory on his memory.

I have motivated the tragic fate of Miss Julie with an abundance of circumstances: her mother's basic instincts, her father's improper bringing-up of the girl, her own inborn nature and her fiancé's sway over her weak and degenerate mind. Further and more immediately: the festive atmosphere of Midsummer Eve, her father's absence, her monthly illness, her preoccupation with animals, the erotic excitement of the dance, the long summer twilight, the highly aphrodisiac influence of flowers, and finally chance itself, which drives two people together in an out-of-the-way room, plus the boldness of the aroused man.

As one can see, I have not concerned myself solely with physiological causes, nor confined myself monomaniacally to psychological causes, nor traced everything to an inheritance from her mother, nor put the blame entirely on her monthly indisposition or exclusively on "immorality." Nor have I simply preached a sermon. For lack of a priest, I have let this function devolve on a cook.

I am proud to say that this complicated way of looking at things is in tune with the times. And if others have anticipated me in this, I am proud that I am not alone in my paradoxes, as all new discoveries are called. And no one can accuse me this time of being one-sided.

As far as the drawing of characters is concerned, I have made the people in my play fairly "characterless" for the following reasons. In the course of time the word *character* has acquired many meanings. Originally it probably meant the dominant and fundamental trait in the soul complex and was confused with temperament. Later the middle class used it to mean an automaton. An individual who once for all had found his own true nature or adapted himself to a certain role in life, who in fact had ceased to grow, was called a man of character, while the man who was constantly developing, who, like a skilled navigator on the currents of life, did not steer a straight course but tacked down wind, was called a man of no character—derogatorily of course, since he was so difficult to keep track of, to pin down and pigeonhole. This middle-class conception of a fixed character was transferred to the stage, where the middle class has always ruled. A character there came to mean an actor who was always one and the same, always drunk, always comic or always melancholy, and who needed to be characterized only by some physical defect such as a club foot, a wooden leg, or a red nose, or by the repetition of some such phrase such as "That's capital," or "Barkis is willin'." This uncomplicated way of viewing people is still to be found in the great Molière. Harpagon is nothing but a miser, although Harpagon might have been not only a miser but an exceptional financier, a fine father, and a good citizen. Worse still, his "defect" is extremely advantageous to his son-in-law and his daughter who will be his heirs and therefore should not find fault with him, even if they might have to wait a while to jump into bed together. So I do not believe in simple stage characters. And the summary judgments that writers pass on people—he is stupid, this one is brutal, that one is jealous, this one is stingy, and so on—should not pass unchallenged by the naturalists who know how complicated the soul is and who realize that vice has a reverse side very much like virtue.

Since the persons in my play are modern characters, living in a transitional era more hurried and hysterical than the previous one at least, I have depicted them as more unstable, as torn and divided, a mixture of the old and the new. Nor does it seem improbable to me that modern ideas might also have seeped down through newspapers and kitchen talk to the level of the servants.

My souls—or characters—are patchworks of past and present stages of culture, pasted together from newspaper clippings and books, pieced up from scraps of human lives, patched up from old rags that once were ball gowns—hodge-podges just like the human soul. I have even supplied a little evolutionary history into the bargain by letting the weaker steal and repeat the words of the stronger and by letting these souls pick up each other's ideas—suggestions as they are called in hypnosis.

I say Miss Julie is a modern character not because the man-hating half-woman has not always existed, but because now she has been brought out into the open, has taken the stage and is making a noise for herself. The half-woman is a type that forces itself on others, selling itself for power, medals, recognition, diplomas as formerly it sold itself for money. It represents degeneration. It is not a strong species for it does not maintain itself, but unfortunately it propagates its misery in the following generation. Degenerate men unconsciously select their mates from among these half-women, so that they breed and spread, producing creatures of indeterminate sex to whom life is a torture, but who fortunately are defeated eventually either by hostile reality, or by the uncontrolled breaking loose of their repressed instincts, or else by their frustration in not being able to compete with the male sex. It is a tragic type, offering us the spectacle of a desperate fight against nature; a tragic legacy of romanticism which is now being dissipated by naturalism—a movement which seeks only happiness, and for that strong and healthy species are required.

But Miss Julie is also a vestige of the old warrior nobility which is now being superseded by a new nobility of nerve and brain. She is a victim of the disorder produced within a family by a mother's "crime," of the mistakes of a whole generation gone wrong, of circumstances, of her own defective constitution—all of which put together is equivalent to the fate or universal law of the ancients. The naturalists have banished guilt along with God, but the consequences of the act—punishment, imprisonment, or the fear of it—cannot be banished for the simple reason that they remain whether or not the naturalist dismisses the action from his court. Those sitting on the sidelines can easily afford to be lenient; not so, the injured parties and even if her father were compelled to forgo taking his revenge, Miss Julie would take vengeance on herself, as she does in the play, because of that inherited or acquired sense of honor which has been transmitted to the upper classes from—well, where does it come from? From the age of barbarism, from the first Aryans, from the chivalry of the Middle Ages. And a very fine code it was, but now inimical to the survival of the race. It is the aristocrat's form of hara-kiri, a law of conscience that bids the Japanese to cut open his own stomach when someone insults him. The same sort of thing survives, slightly modified, in that exclusive prerogative of the aristocracy, the duel. (Example: the husband challenges the lover to a duel; the lover shoots the husband and runs off with the wife. Result: the husband's *honor* is saved, but his wife is gone.) Hence the servant Jean lives on; but not Miss Julie, who cannot live without honor. The advantage that the slave has over his master is that he has not committed himself to this defeatist principle. In all of us Aryans there is enough of the nobleman, or of the Don Quixote, to make us sympathize with the man who takes his own life after having dishonored himself by shameful deeds. And we are all of us aristocrats enough to be distressed when we see a great man lying like a dead hulk ready for the scrap pile, even, I think, if he were to raise himself up again and redeem himself by honorable deeds.

The servant Jean is the beginning of a new

species in which noticeable differentiation has already taken place. He began as the child of a poor worker and is now evolving through self-education into a future gentleman of the upper classes. He is quick to learn, has highly developed senses (smell, taste, sight), and a keen appreciation of beauty. He has already come up in the world, for he is strong enough not to hesitate to make use of other people. He is already a stranger to his old friends, whom he despises as reminders of past stages in his development, and whom he fears and avoids because they know his secrets, guess his intentions, look with envy on his rise and in joyful expectation towards his fall. Hence his character is unformed and divided. He wavers between an admiration of high positions and a hatred of the men who occupy them. He is an aristocrat—he says so himself—familiar with the ins and outs of good society. He is polished on the outside, but coarse underneath. He wears his frock coat with elegance but gives no assurance that he keeps his body clean.

He respects Miss Julie but he is afraid of Christine, for she knows his innermost secrets. Yet he is sufficiently hard-hearted not to let the events of the night upset his plans for the future. Possessing both the coarseness of the slave and the tough-mindedness of the born ruler, he can look at blood without fainting, shake off bad luck like water, and take calamity by the horns. Consequently he will escape from the battle unwounded, probably ending up as proprietor of a hotel. And if he himself does not get to be a Roumanian count, his son will doubtless go to college and possibly end up as an official of the state.

Now his observations about life as the lower classes see it, from below, are well worth listening to—that is, they are whenever he is telling the truth, which is not too often, because he is more likely to say what is favorable to him than what is true. When Miss Julie supposes that everyone in the lower classes must feel greatly oppressed by the weight of the classes above, Jean naturally agrees with her since he wants to win her sympathy. But he promptly takes it all back when he finds it advantageous to separate himself from the mob.

Apart from the fact that Jean is coming up in the world, he is also superior to Miss Julie in that he is a man. In the sexual sphere he is the aristocrat. He has the strength of the male, more highly developed senses, and the ability to take the initiative. His inferiority is merely the result of his social environment, which is only temporary and which he will probably slough off along with his livery.

His slave nature expresses itself in his awe of the Count (the boots) and in his religious superstitions. But he is awed by the Count mainly because the Count occupies the place he wants most in life; and this awe is still there even after he has won the daughter of the house and seen how empty that beautiful shell was.

I do not believe that any love in the "higher" sense can be born from the union of two such different souls. Therefore I have let Miss Julie's love be refashioned in her imagination as a love that protects and purifies, and I have let Jean imagine that even his love might have a chance to grow under other social circumstances. For love, I take it, is very much like the hyacinth that must strike roots deep in the dark earth *before* it can produce a vigorous blossom. Here it shoots up, bursts into bloom, and turns to seed all at once; and that is why it dies so quickly.

Christine—finally to get to her—is a female slave, spineless and phlegmatic after years spent in front of the kitchen stove, bovinely unconscious of her own hypocrisy, and bloated with morality and religion which she uses as cloaks and scapegoats for her sins. She goes regularly to church where she deftly unloads onto Jesus, that straw man, her petty household thefts and picks up from him another load of innocence. She is only a secondary character, and I have deliberately done no more than sketch her in—just as I treated the country doctor and the parish priest in *The Father* where I only wanted to draw ordinary everyday people such as most country doctors and preachers are. That some have found my minor characters one-dimensional is due to the fact that ordinary people while at work are to a certain extent one-dimensional and do lack an independent existence, showing only one side of themselves in the performance of their duties. And as long as the audience does not feel it needs to see them from different angles, my abstract sketches will pass muster.

Now as far as the dialogue is concerned, I have broken somewhat with tradition in refusing to make my characters into interlocutors who ask stupid questions to elicit witty answers. I have avoided the symmetrical and mathematical design of the artfully constructed French dialogue and have let minds work as irregularly as they do in real life, where no subject is quite drained to the bottom before another mind engages at random some cog in the conversation and regulates it for a while. My dialogue wanders here and there, gathers material in the first scenes which is later picked up, repeated, reworked, developed, and expanded like the theme in a piece of music.

The action of the play poses no problems. Since it really involves only two people, I have limited myself to these two, introducing only one minor character, the cook, and keeping the unhappy spirit of the father brooding over the action as a whole. I have chosen this course because I have noticed that what interests people most nowadays is the psychological action. Our inveterately curious souls are no longer content to see a thing happen; we want to see how it happens. We want to see the strings. Look at the machinery, examine the double-bottom drawer, put on the magic ring to find the hidden seam, look in the deck for the marked cards.

In treating the subject this way I have had in mind the case-history novels of the Goncourt brothers,[1] which appeal to me more than anything else in modern literature.

As far as play construction is concerned, I have made a try at getting rid of act divisions. I was afraid that the spectator's declining susceptibility to illusion might not carry him through the intermission, when he would have time to think about what he has seen and to escape the suggestive influence of the author-hypnotist. I figure my play lasts about ninety minutes. Since one can listen to a lecture, a sermon, or a political debate for that long or even longer, I have convinced myself that a play should not exhaust an audience in that length of time. As early as 1872 in one of my first attempts at the drama, *The Outlaw*, I tried out this concentrated form, although with little success. I had finished the work in five acts when I noticed the disjointed and disturbing effect it produced. I burned it, and from the ashes there arose a single, completely re-worked act of fifty pages which would run for less than an hour. This play form is not completely new but seems to be my property and has a good chance of gaining favor with the public when tastes change. (My hope was to get a public so educated that they could sit through a full evening's show in one act. But this needs to be investigated further.) In the meantime, in order to establish resting places for the audience and the actors without destroying the illusion, I have made use of three arts that belong to the drama: the monologue, the pantomime, and the ballet, all of which were part of classic tragedy, the monody having become the monologue and the choral dance, the ballet.

The realists have banished the monologue

---

[1] Famous 19th century French novelists.

from the stage as implausible. But if I can motivate it, I make it plausible, and I can then use it to my advantage. Now it is certainly plausible for a speaker to pace the floor and read his speech aloud to himself. It is plausible for an actor to practice his part aloud, for a child to talk to her cat, a mother to babble to her baby, an old lady to chatter to her parrot, and a sleeper to talk in his sleep. And in order to give the actor a chance to work on his own for once and for a moment not be obliged to follow the author's directions, I have not written out the monologues in detail but simply outlined them. Since it makes very little difference what is said while asleep, or to the parrot or the cat, inasmuch as it does not affect the main action, a gifted player who is in the midst of the situation and mood of the play can probably improvise the monologue better than the author, who cannot estimate ahead of time how much may be said and for how long before the illusion is broken.

Some theaters in Italy have, as we know, returned to the art of improvisation and have thereby trained actors who are truly inventive —without, however, violating the intentions of the author. This seems to be a step in the right direction and possibly the beginning of a new, fertile form of art that will be genuinely productive.

In places where the monologue cannot be properly motivated, I have resorted to pantomime. Here I have given the actor even more freedom to be creative and win honor on his own. Nevertheless, not to try the audience beyond its limits, I have relied on music—well-motivated by the Midsummer Eve dance—to exercise its hypnotic powers during the pantomime scene. I beg the music director to select his tunes with great care, so that associations foreign to the mood of the play will not be produced by reminders of popular operettas or current dance numbers or by folk music of interest only to ethnologists.

The ballet which I have introduced cannot be replaced by a so-called crowd scene. Such scenes are always badly acted, with a pack of babbling fools taking advantage of the occasion to "gag it up," thereby destroying the illusion. Inasmuch as country people do not improvise their taunts but make use of material already to hand by giving it a double meaning, I have not composed an original lampoon but have made use of a little known round dance that I noted down in the Stockholm district. The words do not fit the situation exactly, which is what I intended, since the slave in his cunning (i.e., weakness) never attacks directly. At any rate, let us have no comedians in this serious story and no obscene jokes about an affair that nails the lid on a family coffin.

As far as the scenery is concerned, I have borrowed from impressionistic painting the idea of asymmetrical and open composition, and I believe that I have thereby gained something in the way of greater illusion. Because the audience cannot see the whole room and all the furniture, they will have to surmise what's missing; that is, their imagination will be stimulated to fill in the rest of the picture. I have gained something else by this: I have avoided those tiresome exits through doors. Stage doors are made of canvas and rock at the slightest touch. They cannot even be used to indicate the wrath of an angry father who storms out of the house after a bad dinner, slamming the door behind him "so that the whole house shakes." (In the theater it sways.) Furthermore, I have confined the action to one set, both to give the characters a chance to become part and parcel of their environment and to cut down on scenic extravagance. If there is only one set, one has a right to expect it to be as realistic as possible. Yet nothing is more difficult than to make a room look like a room, however easy it may be for the scene painter to create waterfalls and erupting volcanos. I suppose we shall have to put up with walls made of canvas, but isn't it about time that we stopped painting shelves and pots and pans on the canvas? There are so many other conventions in the theater which we are told to accept in good faith that we should be spared the strain of believing in painted saucepans.

I have placed the backdrop and the table at an angle to force the actors to play face to face or in half profile when they are seated opposite each other at the table. In a production of *Aïda* I saw a flat placed at such an angle, which led the eye out in an unfamiliar perspective. Nor did it look as if it had been set that way simply to be different or to avoid those monotonous right angles.

Another desirable innovation would be the removal of the footlights. I understand that the purpose of lighting from below is to make the actors look more full in the face. But may I ask why all actors should have full faces? Doesn't this kind of lighting wipe out many of the finer features in the lower part of the face, especially around the jaws? Doesn't it distort the shape of nose and throw false shadows above the eyes? If not, it certainly does something else: it hurts the actor's eyes. The footlights hit the retina at an angle from which it is usually shielded (except in sailors who must

look at the sunlight reflected in the water), and the result is the loss of any effective play of the eyes. All one ever sees on stage are goggle-eyed glances sideways at the boxes or upwards at the balcony, with only the whites of the eyes being visible in the latter case. And this probably also accounts for that tiresome fluttering of the eyelashes which the female performers are particularly guilty of. If an actor nowadays wants to express something with his eyes, he can only do it looking right at the audience, in which case he makes direct contact with someone outside the proscenium arch—a bad habit known justifiably or not, as "saying hello to friends." [2]

I should think that the use of sufficiently strong side lights (through the use of reflectors or something like them) would provide the actor with a new asset: an increased range of expression made possible by the play of the eyes, the most expressive part of the face.

I have scarcely any illusions about getting actors to play for the public and not with them, although this should be their aim. Nor do I dream of ever seeing an actor play through all of an important scene with his back to the audience. But is it too much to hope that crucial scenes could be played where the author indicated and not in front of the prompter's box as if they were duets demanding applause? I am not calling for a revolution, only for some small changes. I am well aware that transforming the stage into a real room with the fourth wall missing and with some of the furniture placed with backs to the auditorium would only upset the audience, at least for the present.

If I bring up the subject of makeup, it is not because I dare hope to be heeded by the ladies, who would rather be beautiful than truthful. But the male actor might do well to consider if it is an advantage to paint his face with character lines that remain there like a mask. Let us imagine an actor who pencils in with soot a few lines between his eyes to indicate great anger, and let us suppose that in that permanently enraged state he finds he has to smile on a certain line. Imagine the horrible grimace! And how can the old character actor wrinkle his brows in anger when his false bald pate is as smooth as a billiard ball?

In a modern psychological drama, in which every tremor of the soul should be reflected more by facial expressions than by gestures and noises, it would probably be most sensible to

---

2 "Counting the house" would be the equivalent in American theater slang. (Trans.)

experiment with strong side lighting on a small stage, using actors without any make-up or with a minimum of it.

And then, if we could get rid of the visible orchestra with its disturbing lights and its faces turned toward the public; if the auditorium floor could be raised so that the spectator's eyes are not level with the actor's knees; if we could get rid of the proscenium boxes with their noisy late diners; and if we could have it dark in the auditorium during the performance; and if, above everything else, we could have a small stage and an *intimate* auditorium—then possibly a new drama might arise and at least one theater become a refuge for cultured audiences. While we are waiting for such a theater, we shall have to write for the dramatic stockpile and prepare the repertory that one day shall come.

Here is my attempt at it. If I have failed, there is still time to try again!

Translated by Evert Sprinchorn

NOTES TO THE MEMBERS OF THE INTIMATE THEATRE

On the idea of an intimate theatre [1]—When one submitted a full length play to the Royal Theatre in the 1860's and '70's, it had no chance of being accepted unless it met certain conditions. Five acts was the preferred length, with each act written on six sheets, so that the whole play was $5 \times 24 = 120$ folio pages long. Dividing the acts into tableaux or by means of transformation scenes was frowned upon and considered a weakness. Each act had to have a beginning, a middle and an end. The end of the act must provide a signal for applause—which could usually be managed by some high-flown oratory—and if the play was in blank verse, the last two lines were to rhyme. Within each act there had to be set numbers for the actors, called "scenes." The monologue was permitted and often was the occasion for the big "scene." Lengthy outbursts of passion, the dispensation of poetic justice, and an unmasking scene were

"Notes to the Members of the Intimate Theatre" by August Strindberg, translated by Evert Sprinchorn. Reprinted by permission of the translator.

virtually essential. One might also make use of a long bit of narration—a dream, an anecdote, an incident. And in addition to all this, the theatre management insisted upon strong parts and rewarding roles for its stars.

There was much that was sensible and justifiable in this version of *The Poetics*. It stemmed from Victor Hugo and arose in the 1830's in reaction against the stale formulas of Racine and Corneille. But like other styles of art, this one, too, ran its course and degenerated. Anything and everything was crammed into the five-act form, including completely trivial incidents and anecdotes. Practical considerations, such as the need for keeping the entire acting troupe busy, made it necessary to write in subsidiary characters—not just "supers," but speaking parts. This led to a confusion between creating characters and writing roles; and in recent years we have had to hear Björnson,[2] that practical man of the theatre, praised for being a great role-writer.

The fear of serious themes and important subjects resulted in an outpouring of trifles, so that finally the directors of the theatre had to make cuts in the scripts to avoid boring their audiences.

About 1870 when I had written a play in verse about the hero Blotsven and tried reading it aloud to my literary comrades at the University of Uppsala, I found it was one long bore. So I burned it (along with a play about Eric XIV). From the ashes there arose a one-act play, *The Outlaw*, which, along with its many faults, had the merit of sticking to its subject. It was short but exhaustive. Undoubtedly I was influenced by Björnson's masterful one-act play, *Between Battles*, which I took as a model of playwriting.

For the pace of living was increasing. People were growing impatient and wanted quick answers. In my *Master Olof* (the first version) I attempted a compromise. I cut the poetry and substituted prose; and instead of an opera-like drama in iambics with set arias and duets, I composed a symphony, polyphonous in texture, with all the voices blending together [3] and with no one made to serve simply as an accompanist. The attempt was successful in its time, but

---

[1] What appears here is not the complete text of Strindberg's *Notes,* but an excerpt taken from the first few pages.

[2] Björnstjerne Björnson (1832–1910), Norwegian realist playwright.

[3] I treated the leads and secondary roles as if they were all entitled to a place at the captain's table.

since then the play has had to be cut to please present-day audiences.

In the 1880's the spirit of the modern age had begun to penetrate even the theatre and demand reforms. Zola mobilized his forces against the French drama with its Brussels carpets, polished shoes, varnished subject matter, and slick dialogue that reminded one of the questions and answers of the catechism. In 1887 Antoine opened his Théâtre Libre in Paris, and *Thérèse Raquin*, although adapted from a novel, set the standard. The strong subject matter and the concentrated form struck a new note, although the unity of time was still not observed and the act-curtains remained. That was when I wrote my three plays, *Miss Julie, The Father*, and *Creditors*. *Miss Julie*, which I provided with a well-known preface, was staged by Antoine, but not until 1893 after having been produced in Copenhagen in 1889 by the Association of University Students. In the spring of 1894 *Creditors* was given at the Théâtre de l'Oeuvre in Paris, and *The Father* in the fall of the same year at the same theatre (with Philippe Garnier in the lead). The Freie Bühne had already opened in Berlin in 1889 and before 1893 all three of my plays had been produced there. Paul Schlenther, at present director of the Hofburg in Vienna, lectured on *Miss Julie* at the premiere; Rosa Bertens, Emanuel Reicher, Rudolf Rittner and Josef Jarno played the leading roles in these plays; and Sigismund Lautenburg, director of the Residenztheater in Berlin, had *Creditors* performed 100 times.

After that, as the drama slipped back into its old routines, there was a period of relative quiet until Reinhardt opened his Little Theater at the beginning of the century. I was in at the start of this theatre, represented by the major one-acter *The Link*, as well as by *Miss Julie* (with Gertrud Eysoldt) and *Crimes and Crimes*.

Last year [1906] Reinhardt went a step further and opened the Kammerspielhaus,[4] the very name of which suggests its hidden purpose: to transfer the idea of chamber music to the drama. An intimate approach, a significant theme, a *soigné* treatment. This fall the Hebbel Theater opened in the same spirit, and throughout German theatres calling themselves Intimes Theater have sprung up. Towards the end of November 1907 August Falck opened the Intimate Theatre in Stockholm, and I was given the opportunity of observing closely all the details of stage production. Memories from my

forty-year career in the theatre were awakened, my former views were put to the test, old experiments were repeated, and my revived interest stimulated me to write these notes.

* * *

If you were to ask me what the aim of an intimate theatre is and what is meant by a chamber play, I would say that in this kind of drama we single out the significant and overriding theme, but handle it with restraint. In treating this theme we avoid all ostentation—all the calculated effects, the bravura roles, the set numbers, and the cues for applause. No particular form binds the author, because the theme determines the form. Hence complete freedom in handling the theme as long as the unity and style of the original idea are not violated.

When Falck as manager of the theatre decided against giving long performances that lasted nearly 'til midnight, he also broke with classic "wet" theatre. This was a daring move on his part, for liquor sales used to pay for at least half the rent at the larger theatres. But part and parcel of this combination of art and alcohol was the long intermission, the length of which was set by the concessionnaire, with the theatre manager seeing to it that the opening and closing times were strictly observed.

The inconveniences resulting from allowing the spectator to slip out for a few quick ones in the middle of a play should be obvious. Discussing a play destroys the mood; the entranced senses regain control of themselves and become aware of what should remain lodged in the unconscious; and the illusion that the playwrite endeavored to create is broken as the half-hypnotized spectator is prodded into making some banal comments. Or else he glances at the evening paper, chats with some acquaintance at the bar, and becomes distracted, with the result that the threads of the play are cut, the story is forgotten, and he returns to his seat in a completely alien mood to seek in vain the play he left behind.

Another bad feature of this system was that many went to the bar even before the curtain rose and regarded the play as the entr'acte. Indeed, there were those who would remain sitting in the lobby through a whole act if the sofa were sufficiently deep and soft and hard to get up from.

In breaking with that old system, the Intimate Theatre suffered financially, but there were compensations. The attention of the audience remained undivided, and their reward

---

4 Chamber Theatre.

was that they could discuss in the peace of the supper table what they had heard and seen at the theatre.

We wanted a small theatre in order that the actors might be heard in every corner without having to shout. There are, as you well know, theatres so huge that everything must be said in a strained voice, which makes everything sound false. A declaration of love must be bellowed forth, a confidence expressed like a call to arms, a secret of the heart whispered hoarsely from the bottom of the throat and lungs, while everybody on stage acts as if he were in a frightful temper and concerned only with getting off.

Now we have our little auditorium; and having modulated our voices, we have made some progress towards our goal but without quite having reached it yet.

*　*　*

Acting is at once the most difficult and the easiest of all the arts. Like the beautiful, it is impossible to define. It is obviously not the art of dissembling, because the great artist does not dissemble. He is true, sincere, plain and unvarnished, while the low comic does everything he can to disguise himself with masks and costumes. It is not imitation. The worst actors are often demonically clever in imitating famous people while the true artist lacks this talent. And it can be said that the actor is the author's medium only in a limited sense and with great reservations. In aesthetics acting is classified as a dependent art, not one of the independent. The actor needs the support of the author's text. He cannot do without the author, but the author can, if necessary, do without the actor. I have never seen a production of Part II of Goethe's *Faust*, of Schiller's *Don Carlos*, or of Shakespeare's *The Tempest*, but I have nevertheless seen them in my mind when I have read them; and there are many good plays which should not be staged and do not tolerate being seen. On the other hand, there are many poor plays that cannot come to life until they are performed, that must be complemented and elevated by the art of the actor. Usually the author knows how much he has the actor to thank for, and generally he is grateful. The same is true of the superior actor in regard to the author. Since their relations are mutual, I should like to see them thank each other. But for the sake of peaceful relations, it would be even better if the question were never brought up. It is usually raised by some conceited fool or by a star who has by chance made a success of a play which deserved to fail. For them the author is a necessary evil, a hack who furnishes the words for their parts—since after all there have to be some words.

I have never heard this question discussed at the Intimate Theatre and I trust I never shall. I have seen parts created here that were better than my original conceptions of them, and I have publicly acknowledged as much.

*　*　*

Acting seems to be the easiest of all the arts because everybody walks, talks, stands, gestures, and makes faces. But then he is just being himself, and one sees immediately how different that is from acting as soon as one puts him on stage and gives him a part to learn and interpret. One soon observes that the portrayal of a very brilliant, profound, or very forceful character is absolutely beyond the powers of a rather simple nature. Some people are born with the ability to represent characters, while others are not. But it is always difficult to tell about beginners, because the disposition may not reveal itself immediately. Great talents have often had miserable beginnings. Consequently, the director and manager must be very careful in making decisions when the fate of a young actor is placed in their hands. They must try him out, observe him, be patient and wait for what the future has to say.

It is very difficult to say what it is that makes an actor and what qualities he must possess, but let me try to mention a few.

The actor must be able to devote his full attention to the role, that is, be able to concentrate all his faculties on it and not allow anything to distract him. Anyone who plays a musical instrument knows what happens if one's thoughts begin to stray. The notes fade away, the fingers wander and make mistakes, and the result is confusion, even if one knows the piece by heart. The second essential quality is imagination—the ability to conceive characters and situations so vividly that they assume bodily form.

I suspect that the actor puts himself in a trance, forgetting himself, and finally actually becoming the person he is supposed to represent. This may sound like sleepwalking, but is isn't quite the same. If the actor is disturbed and awakened from his trance, he becomes flustered and forgets everything. That is why I always hesitate to interrupt a scene. I have noticed how much it pains an actor. He stands as if in a daze, and it takes some time for him to fall back to sleep and to regain the proper tone and feeling.

No form of art is as dependent as the actor's.

He cannot isolate his particular contribution, show it to someone and say, "This is mine." If he does not get the support of his fellow actors, his performance will lack resonance and depth. He will be held in check and lured into wrong inflections and wrong rhythms. He won't make a good impression no matter how hard he tries. Actors must rely on each other. Occasionally one sees an exceptionally egotistic individual who "upstages" a rival, obliterates him, in order that he and he alone can be seen.

That is why good rapport among actors is imperative for the success of a play. I don't care whether you rank yourselves higher or lower than each other, or from side to side, or from inside out—as long as you do it together.

Translated by Evert Sprinchorn

MISS JULIE

Translated by Evert Sprinchorn

CAST OF CHARACTERS

MISS JULIE, *twenty-five years old*
JEAN, *valet, thirty years old*
CHRISTINE, *the cook, thirty-five years old*

SCENE *The action of the play takes place in the kitchen of the Count's manor house on Midsummer Eve in Sweden in the 1880's*

(*The scene is a large kitchen. The walls and ceiling are covered with draperies and hangings. The rear wall runs obliquely upstage from the left. On this wall to the left are two shelves with pots and pans of copper, iron, and pewter. The shelves are decorated with goffered paper. A little to the right can be seen three-fourths of a deep arched doorway with two glass doors, and through them can be seen a fountain with a statue of Cupid, lilac bushes in bloom, and the tops of some Lombardy poplars. From the left of the stage the corner of a large, Dutch-tile kitchen stove protrudes with part of the hood showing. Projecting from the right side of the stage is one end of the servants' dining table of white pine, with a few chairs around it. The stove is decorated with branches of birch leaves; the floor is strewn with juniper twigs. On the end of the table is a large Japanese spice jar filled with lilacs. An icebox, a sink, a wash basin. Over the door a big, old-fashioned bell; and to the left of the door the gaping mouth of a speaking tube.*)

Miss Julie by August Strindberg, translated by Evert Sprinchorn. Copyright 1961 by Chandler Publishing Company. All performance rights are the property of Literary Discoveries, Inc., and permissions for performances of any kind must be obtained from Literary Discoveries, Inc., 604 Mission Street, San Francisco.

CHRISTINE *is standing at the stove, frying something. She is wearing a light-colored cotton dress and an apron.* JEAN *enters, dressed in livery and carrying a pair of high-top boots with spurs. He sets them where they are clearly visible*)

JEAN   Tonight she's wild again. Miss Julie's absolutely wild!

CHRISTINE   You took your time getting back!

JEAN   I took the Count down to the station, and on my way back as I passed the barn I went in for a dance. And there was Miss Julie leading the dance with the game warden. But then she noticed me. And she ran right into my arms and chose me for the ladies' waltz. And she's been dancing ever since like—like I don't know what. She's absolutely wild!

CHRISTINE   That's nothing new. But she's been worse than ever during the last two weeks, ever since her engagement was broken off.

JEAN   Yes, I never did hear all there was to that. He was a good man, too, even if he wasn't rich. Well, that's a woman for you. (*He sits down at the end of the table*) But, tell me, isn't it strange that a young girl like her—all right, young woman—prefers to stay home with the servants rather than go with her father to visit her relatives?

CHRISTINE   I suppose she's ashamed to face them after the fiasco with her young man.

JEAN   No doubt. He wouldn't take any nonsense from her. Do you know what happened, Christine? I do. I saw the whole thing, even though I didn't let on.

CHRISTINE   Don't tell me you were there?

JEAN   Well, I was. They were in the barnyard one evening—and she was training him, as she called it. Do you know what she was doing? She was making him jump over her riding whip—training him like a dog. He jumped over twice, and she whipped him both times. But the third time, he grabbed the whip from her, broke it in a thousand pieces—and walked off.

[430]

CHRISTINE So that's what happened. Well, what do you know.

JEAN Yes, that put an end to that affair.— What have you got for me that's really good, Christine?

CHRISTINE (*serving him from the frying pan*) Just a little bit of kidney. I cut it especially for you.

JEAN (*smelling it*) Wonderful! My special délice! (*feeling the plate*) Hey, you didn't warm the plate!

CHRISTINE You're more fussy than the Count himself when you set your mind to it. (*She rumples his hair gently*)

JEAN (*irritated*) Cut it out! Don't muss up my hair. You know I don't like that!

CHRISTINE Oh, now don't get mad. Can I help it if I like you?

(JEAN *eats.* CHRISTINE *gets out a bottle of beer*)

JEAN Beer on Midsummer Eve! No thank you! I've got something much better than that. (*He opens a drawer in the table and takes out a bottle of red wine with a gold seal*) Do you see that? Gold Seal. Now give me a glass.— No, a wine glass of course. I'm drinking it straight.

CHRISTINE (*goes back to the stove and puts on a small saucepan*) Lord help the woman who gets you for a husband. You're an old fussbudget!

JEAN Talk, talk! You'd consider yourself lucky if you got yourself a man as good as me. It hasn't done you any harm to have people think I'm your fiancé. (*He tastes the wine*) Very good. Excellent. But warmed just a little too little. (*warming the glass in his hands*) We bought this in Dijon. Four francs a liter, unbottled—and the tax on top of that. . . . What on earth are you cooking? It smells awful!

CHRISTINE Some damn mess that Miss Julie wants for her dog.

JEAN You should watch your language, Christine. . . . Why do you have to stand in front of the stove on a holiday, cooking for that mutt? Is it sick?

CHRISTINE Oh, she's sick, all right! She sneaked out to the gatekeeper's mongrel and— got herself in a fix. And Miss Julie, you know, can't stand anything like that.

JEAN She's too stuck-up in some ways and not proud enough in others. Just like her mother. The countess felt right at home in the kitchen or down in the barn with the cows, but when she went driving, *one* horse wasn't enough for her; she had to have a pair. Her sleeves were always dirty, but her buttons had the royal crown on them. As for Miss Julie, she doesn't seem to care how she looks and acts. I mean, she's not really refined, not really. Just now, down at the barn, she grabbed the game warden right from under Anna's eyes and asked him to dance. You wouldn't see anybody in our class doing a thing like that. But that's what happens when the gentry try to act like the common people—they become common! . . . But she *is* beautiful! Statuesque! Ah, those shoulders—and those—so forth, and so forth!

CHRISTINE Oh, don't exaggerate. Clara tells me all about her, and Clara dresses her.

JEAN Clara, pooh! You women are always jealous of each other. I've been out riding with her. . . . And how she can dance . . . !

CHRISTINE Listen, Jean, you *are* going to dance with me, aren't you, when I am finished here?

JEAN Certainly! Of course I am.

CHRISTINE Promise?

JEAN Promise! Listen if I say I'm going to do a thing, I do it. . . . Christine, I thank you for a delicious meal. (*He shoves the cork back into the bottle*)

(MISS JULIE *appears in the doorway, talking to someone outside*)

MISS JULIE I'll be right back. Don't wait for me. (JEAN *slips the bottle into the table drawer quickly and rises respectfully.* MISS JULIE *comes in and crosses over to* CHRISTINE, *who is at the stove*) Did you get it ready?

(CHRISTINE *signals that* JEAN *is present*)

JEAN (*polite and charming*) Are you ladies sharing secrets?

MISS JULIE (*flipping her handkerchief in his face*) Don't be nosey!

JEAN Oh, that smells good! Violets.

MISS JULIE (*flirting with him*) Don't be impudent! And don't tell me you're an expert on perfumes, too. I know you're an expert dancer.—No, don't look! Go away!

JEAN (*inquisitive, but deferential*) What are you cooking? A witch's brew for Midsummer Eve? Something that reveals what the stars have in store for you, so you can see the face of your future husband?

MISS JULIE (*curtly*) You'd have to have good eyes to see that. (*to* CHRISTINE) Pour it into a small bottle, and seal it tight. . . . Jean, come and dance a schottische with me.

JEAN (*hesitating*) I hope you don't think I'm being rude, but I've already promised this dance to Christine.

MISS JULIE She can always find someone else. Isn't that so, Christine? You don't mind if I borrow Jean for a minute, do you?

CHRISTINE   It isn't up to me. If Miss Julie is gracious enough to invite you, it isn't right for you to say no, Jean. You go on, and thank her for the honor.

JEAN   Frankly, Miss Julie, I don't want to hurt your feelings, but I wonder if it is wise—I mean for you to dance twice in a row with the same partner. Especially since the people around here are so quick to spread gossip.

MISS JULIE   (*bridling*)   What do you mean? What kind of gossip? What are you trying to say?

JEAN   (*retreating*)   If you insist on misunderstanding me, I'll have to speak more plainly. It just doesn't look right for you to prefer one of your servants to the others who are hoping for the same unusual honor.

MISS JULIE   Prefer! What an idea! I'm really surprised. I, the mistress of the house, am good enough to come to their dance, and when I feel like dancing, I want to dance with someone who knows how to lead. After all I don't want to look ridiculous.

JEAN   As you wish. I am at your orders.

MISS JULIE   (*gently*)   Don't take it as an order. Tonight we're all just happy people at a party. There's no question of rank. Now give me your arm.—Don't worry, Christine. I won't run off with your boy friend. (JEAN *gives her his arm and leads her out*)

(PANTOMIME SCENE. *This should be played as if the actress were actually alone. She turns her back on the audience when she feels like it; she does not look out into the auditorium; she does not hurry as if she were afraid the audience would grow impatient.*

CHRISTINE *alone. In the distance the sound of the violins playing the schottische.* CHRISTINE, *humming in time with the music, cleans up after* JEAN, *washes the dishes, dries them, and puts them away in a cupboard. Then she takes off her apron, takes a little mirror from one of the table drawers, and leans it against the jar of lilacs on the table. She lights a tallow candle, heats a curling iron, and curls the bangs on her forehead. Then she goes to the doorway and stands listening to the music. She comes back to the table and finds the handkerchief that* MISS JULIE *left behind. She smells it, spreads it out, and then, as if lost in thought, stretches it, smooths it out, and folds it in four.*

JEAN *enters alone*)

JEAN   I told you she was wild! You should have seen the way she was dancing. Everyone was peeking at her from behind the doors and laughing at her. Can you figure her out, Christine?

CHRISTINE   You might know it's her monthlies, Jean. She always acts peculiar then. . . . Well, are you going to dance with me?

JEAN   You're not mad at me because I broke my promise?

CHRISTINE   Of course not. Not for a little thing like that, you know that. And I know my place.

JEAN   (*grabs her around the waist*)   You're a sensible girl, Christine. You're going to make somebody a good wife—

(MISS JULIE, *coming in, sees them together. She is unpleasantly surprised*)

MISS JULIE   (*with forced gaiety*)   Well, aren't you the gallant beau—running away from your partner!

JEAN   On the contrary, Miss Julie. As you can see, I've hurried back to the partner I deserted.

MISS JULIE   (*changing tack*)   You know, you're the best dancer I've met.—But why are you wearing livery on a holiday. Take it off at once.

JEAN   I'd have to ask you to leave for a minute. My black coat is hanging right here—(*He moves to the right and points*)

MISS JULIE   You're not embarrassed because I'm here, are you? Just to change your coat? Go in your room and come right back again. Or else you can stay here and I'll turn my back.

JEAN   If you'll excuse me, Miss Julie. (*He goes off to the right. His arm can be seen as he changes his coat*)

MISS JULIE   (*to* CHRISTINE)   Tell me something, Christine. Is Jean your fiancé. He seems so intimate with you.

CHRISTINE   Fiancé? I suppose so. At least that's what we say.

MISS JULIE   What do you mean?

CHRISTINE   Well, Miss Julie, you have had fiancés yourself, and you know—

MISS JULIE   But we were properly engaged—!

CHRISTINE   I know, but did anything come of it?

(JEAN *comes back, wearing a cutaway coat and derby*)

MISS JULIE   *Très gentil, monsieur Jean! Très gentil!*

JEAN   *Vous voulez plaisanter, madame.*

MISS JULIE   *Et vous voulez parler français!* Where did you learn to speak French?

JEAN   In Switzerland. I was *sommelier* in one of the biggest hotels in Lucerne.

MISS JULIE But you look quite the gentle-man in that coat! *Charmant!* (*She sits down at the table*)

JEAN Flatterer!

MISS JULIE (*stiffening*) Who said I was flattering you?

JEAN My natural modesty would not allow me to presume that you were paying sincere compliments to someone like me, and therefore I assumed that you were exaggerating, or, in other words, flattering me.

MISS JULIE Where on earth did you learn to talk like that? Do you go to the theatre often?

JEAN And other places. You don't think I stayed inside the house for six years when I was a valet in Stockholm do you?

MISS JULIE But weren't you born in this district?

JEAN My father worked as a farm hand on the county attorney's estate, next door to yours. I used to see you when you were little. But of course you didn't notice me.

MISS JULIE Did you really?

JEAN Yes. I remember one time in particular—. But I can't tell you about that!

MISS JULIE Of course you can. Oh, come on, tell me. Just this once—for me.

JEAN No. No, I really couldn't. Not now. Some other time maybe.

MISS JULIE Some other time? That means never. What's the harm in telling me now?

JEAN There's no harm. I just don't feel like it.—Look at her.

(*He nods at* CHRISTINE, *who has fallen asleep in a chair by the stove*)

MISS JULIE Won't she make somebody a pretty wife! I'll bet she snores, too.

JEAN No, she doesn't. But she talks in her sleep.

MISS JULIE (*cynically*) Now how would you know she talks in her sleep?

JEAN (*coolly*) I've heard her. . . .

(*Pause. They look at each other*)

MISS JULIE Why don't you sit down?

JEAN I wouldn't take the liberty in your presence.

MISS JULIE But if I were to order you—?

JEAN I'd obey.

MISS JULIE Well then, sit down.—Wait a minute. Could you get me something to drink first?

JEAN I don't know what there is in the icebox. Only beer, I suppose.

MISS JULIE *Only* beer?! I have simple tastes. I prefer beer to wine.

(JEAN *takes a bottle of beer from the icebox and opens it. He looks in the cupboard for a glass and a saucer, and serves her*)

JEAN At your service.

MISS JULIE Thank you. Don't you want to drink, too?

JEAN I'm not much of a beer-drinker, but if it's your wish—

MISS JULIE My wish! I should think a gentleman would want to keep his lady company.

JEAN That's a point well taken! (*He opens another bottle and takes a glass*)

MISS JULIE Now drink a toast to me! (JEAN *hesitates*) You're not shy, are you? A big, strong man like you?

(*Playfully,* JEAN *kneels and raises his glass in mock gallantry*)

JEAN To my lady's health!

MISS JULIE Bravo! Now if you would kiss my shoe, you will have hit it off perfectly. (JEAN *hesitates, then boldly grasps her foot and touches it lightly with his lips*) Superb! You should have been an actor.

JEAN (*rising*) This has got to stop, Miss Julie! Someone might come and see us.

MISS JULIE What difference would that make?

JEAN People would talk, that's what! If you knew how their tongues were wagging out there just a few minutes ago, you wouldn't—

MISS JULIE What sort of things did they say? Tell me. Sit down and tell me.

JEAN I don't want to hurt your feelings, but they used expressions that—that hinted at certain—you know what I mean. After all, you're not a child. And when they see a woman drinking, alone with a man—and a servant at that—in the middle of the night—well . . .

MISS JULIE Well what?! Besides, we're not alone. Christine is here.

JEAN Sleeping!

MISS JULIE I'll wake her up then. (*She goes over to* CHRISTINE) Christine! Are you asleep? (CHRISTINE *babbles in her sleep*) Christine!—how sound she sleeps!

CHRISTINE (*talking in her sleep*) Count's boots are brushed . . . put on the coffee . . . right away, right away, right . . . mm—mm . . . poofff . . .

(MISS JULIE *grabs* CHRISTINE'S *nose*)

MISS JULIE Wake up, will you!

JEAN (*sternly*) Let her alone!

MISS JULIE (*sharply*) What!

JEAN She's been standing over the stove

y. She's worn out when evening comes. ⁄ne asleep is entitled to some respect.

ιISS JULIE (*changing tack*) That's a very kιιd thought. It does you credit. Thank you. (*She offers* JEAN *her hand*) Now come on out and pick some lilacs for me.

(*During the following,* CHRISTINE *wakes up and, drunk with sleep, shuffles off to the right to go to bed. A polka can be heard in the distance*)

JEAN With you, Miss Julie?

MISS JULIE Yes, with me.

JEAN That's no good. Absolutely not.

MISS JULIE I don't know what you're thinking. Maybe you're letting your imagination run away with you.

JEAN I'm not. The other people are.

MISS JULIE In what way? Imagining that I'm—*verliebt* in a servant?

JEAN I'm not conceited, but it's been known to happen. And to these people nothing's sacred.

MISS JULIE Why, I believe you're an aristocrat!

JEAN Yes, I am.

MISS JULIE I'm climbing down—

JEAN Don't climb down, Miss Julie! Take my advice. No one will ever believe that you climbed down deliberately. They'll say that you fell.

MISS JULIE I think more highly of these people than you do. Let's see who's right! Come on! (*She looks him over, challenging him*)

JEAN You know, you're very strange.

MISS JULIE Perhaps. But then so are you. . . . Besides, everything is strange. Life, people, everything. It's all scum, drifting and drifting on the water until it sinks—sinks. There's a dream I have every now and then. It's coming back to me now. I'm sitting on top of a pillar that I've climbed up somehow and I don't know how to get back down. When I look down I get dizzy. I have to get down but I don't have the courage to jump. I can't hold on much longer and I want to fall; but I don't fall. I know I won't have any peace until I get down; no rest until I get down, down on the ground. And if I ever got down on the ground, I'd want to go farther down, right down into the earth. . . . Have you ever felt anything like that?

JEAN Never! I used to dream that I'm lying under a tall tree in a dark woods. I want to get up, up to the very top, to look out over the bright landscape with the sun shining on it, to rob the bird's nest up there with the golden eggs in it. I climb and I climb, but the trunk is so thick, and so smooth, and it's such a long way to that first branch. But I know that if I could just reach that first branch, I'd go right to the top as if on a ladder. I've never reached it yet, but some day I will—even if only in my dreams.

MISS JULIE Here I am talking about dreams with you. Come out with me. Only into the park a way. (*She offers him her arm, and they start to go*)

JEAN Let's sleep on nine midsummer flowers, Miss Julie, and then our dreams will come true!

(MISS JULIE *and* JEAN *suddenly turn around in the doorway.* JEAN *is holding his hand over one eye*)

MISS JULIE You've caught something in your eye. Let me see.

JEAN It's nothing. Just a bit of dust. It'll go away.

MISS JULIE The sleeve of my dress must have grazed your eye. Sit down and I'll help you. (*She takes him by the arm and sits him down. She takes his head and leans it back. With the corner of her handkerchief she tries to get out the bit of dust*) Now sit still, absolutely still. (*She slaps his hand*) Do as you're told. Why, I believe you're trembling—a big, strong man like you. (*She feels his biceps*) With such big arms!

JEAN (*warningly*) Miss Julie!

MISS JULIE Yes, *Monsieur Jean*?

JEAN *Attention! Je ne suis qu'un homme!*

MISS JULIE Sit still, I tell you! . . . There now! It's out. Kiss my hand and thank me!

JEAN (*rising to his feet*) Listen to me, Miss Julie!—Christine has gone to bed!—Listen to me, I tell you!

MISS JULIE Kiss my hand first!

JEAN Listen to me!

MISS JULIE Kiss my hand first!

JEAN All right. But you'll have no one to blame but yourself.

MISS JULIE For what?

JEAN For what! Are you twenty-five years old and still a child? Don't you know it's dangerous to play with fire?

MISS JULIE Not for me. I'm insured!

JEAN (*boldly*) Oh, no you're not! And even if you are, there's inflammable stuff next door.

MISS JULIE Meaning you?

JEAN Yes. Not just because it's me, but because I'm a young man—

MISS JULIE And irresistibly handsome?

What incredible conceit! A Don Juan, maybe! Or a Joseph! Yes, bless my soul, that's it: you're a Joseph!

JEAN   You think so?!

MISS JULIE   I'm almost afraid so! (JEAN *boldly steps up to her, grabs her around the waist, kisses her. She slaps his face*) None of that!

JEAN   Are you still playing games or are you serious?

MISS JULIE   I'm serious.

JEAN   Then you must have been serious just a moment ago, too! You take your games too seriously and that's dangerous. Well, I'm tired of your games, and if you'll excuse me, I'll return to my work. (*takes up the boots and starts to brush them*) The Count will be wanting his boots on time, and it's long past midnight.

MISS JULIE   Put those boots down.

JEAN   No! This is my job. It's what I'm here for. But I never undertook to be a playmate for you. That's something I could never be. I consider myself too good for that.

MISS JULIE   You are proud.

JEAN   In some ways. Not in others.

MISS JULIE   Have you ever been in love?

JEAN   We don't use that word around here. But I've been—interested in a lot of girls, if that's what you mean. . . . I even got sick once because I couldn't have the one I wanted —really sick, like the princes in the Arabian Nights—who couldn't eat or drink for love.

MISS JULIE   Who was the girl? (JEAN *does not reply*) Who was she?

JEAN   You can't make me tell you that.

MISS JULIE   Even if I ask you as an equal— ask you—as a friend? . . . Who was she?

JEAN   You.

MISS JULIE (*sitting down*) How—amusing. . . .

JEAN   Yes, maybe so. Ridiculous . . . That's why I didn't want to tell you about it before. But now I'll tell you the whole story. . . . Have you any idea what the world looks like from below? Of course you haven't. No more than a hawk or eagle has. You hardly ever see their backs because they're always soaring above us. I lived with seven brothers and sisters—and a pig—out on the waste land where there wasn't even a tree growing. But from my window I could see the wall of the Count's garden with the apple trees sticking up over it. That was the Garden of Eden for me, and there were many angry angels with flaming swords standing guard over it. But in spite of them, I and the other boys found a way to the Tree of Life . . . I'll bet you despise me.

MISS JULIE   All boys steal apples.

JEAN   That's what you say now. But you still despise me. Never mind. One day I went with my mother into this paradise to weed the onion beds. Next to the vegetable garden stood a Turkish pavilion, shaded by jasmine and hung all over with honeysuckle. I couldn't imagine what it was used for. I only knew I had never seen such a beautiful building. People went in, and came out again. And one day the door was left open. I sneaked in. The walls were covered with portraits of kings and emperors, and the windows had red curtains with tassels on them.—You do know what kind of place I'm talking about, don't you? . . . I— (*He breaks off a lilac and holds it under Miss Julie's nose*) I had never been inside a castle, never seen anything besides the church. But this was more beautiful. And no matter what I tried to think about, my thoughts always came back—to that little pavilion. And little by little there arose in me a desire to experience just for once the whole pleasure of. . . . *Enfin*, I sneaked in, looked about, and marveled. Then I heard someone coming! There was only one way out—for the upper-class people. But for me there was one more—a lower one. And I had no other choice but to take it. (MISS JULIE, *who has taken the lilac from* JEAN, *lets it fall to the table*) Then I began to run like mad, plunging through the raspberry bushes, ploughing through the strawberry patches, and came up on the rose terrace. And there I caught sight of a pink dress and a pair of white stockings. That was you. I crawled under a pile of weeds, under—well, you can imagine what it was like —under thistles that pricked me and wet dirt that stank to high heaven. And all the while I could see you walking among the roses. I said to myself, "If it's true that a thief can enter heaven and be with the angels, isn't it strange that a poor man's child here on God's green earth can't enter the Count's park and play with the Count's daughter."

MISS JULIE (*sentimentally*)   Do you think all poor children have felt that way?

JEAN (*hesitatingly at first, then with mounting conviction*)   If all poor ch—? Yes—yes, naturally. Of course!

MISS JULIE   It must be terrible to be poor.

JEAN (*with exaggerated pain and poignancy*) Oh, Miss Julie! You don't know! A dog can lie on the sofa with its mistress; a horse can have its nose stroked by the hand of a countess; but a servant—! (*changing his tone*) Of course, now and then you meet somebody with guts enough to work his way up in the world, but how often?—Anyway, you know what I did afterwards? I threw myself into the millstream with all my clothes on. Got fished out and spanked. But the following Sunday, when Pa and everybody else in the house went to visit Grandma, I arranged things so I'd be left behind. Then I washed myself all over with soap and warm water, put on my best clothes, and went off to church—just to see you there once more. I saw you, and then I went home determined to die. But I wanted to die beautifully and comfortably, without pain. I remembered that it was fatal to sleep under an alder bush. And we had a big one that had just blossomed out. I stripped it of every leaf and blossom it had and made a bed of them in a bin of oats. Have you ever noticed how smooth oats are? As smooth as the touch of human skin. . . . So I pulled the lid of the bin shut and closed my eyes—fell asleep. And when they woke me I was really very sick. But I didn't die, as you can see.—What was I trying to prove? I don't know. There was no hope of winning you. But you were a symbol of the absolute hopelessness of my ever getting out of the circle I was born in.

MISS JULIE   You know, you have a real gift for telling stories. Did you go to school?

JEAN   A little. But I've read a lot of novels and gone to the theatre. And I've also listened to educated people talk. That's how I've learned the most.

MISS JULIE   You mean to tell me you stand around listening to what we're saying!

JEAN   Certainly! And I've heard an awful lot, I can tell you—sitting on the coachman's seat or rowing the boat. One time I heard you and a girl friend talking—

MISS JULIE   Really? . . . And just what did you hear?

JEAN   Well, now, I don't know if I could repeat it. I can tell you I was a little amazed. I couldn't imagine where you had learned such words. Maybe at bottom there isn't such a big difference as you might think, between people and people.

MISS JULIE   How vulgar! At least people in my class don't behave like you when we're engaged.

JEAN   (*looking her in the eye*)   Are you sure?—Come on now, it's no use playing the innocent with me.

MISS JULIE   He was a beast. The man I offered my love was a beast.

JEAN   That's what you all say—afterwards.

MISS JULIE   All?

JEAN   I'd say so, since I've heard the same

expression used several times before in similar circumstances.

MISS JULIE   What kind of circumstances?

JEAN   The kind we're talking about. I remember the last time I—

MISS JULIE   (*rising*)   That's enough! I don't want to hear any more.

JEAN   How strange! Neither did she! . . . Well, now if you'll excuse me, I'll go to bed.

MISS JULIE   (*softly*)   Go to bed on Midsummer Eve?

JEAN   That's right. Dancing with that crowd up there really doesn't amuse me.

MISS JULIE   Jean, get the key to the boathouse and row me out on the lake. I want to see the sun come up.

JEAN   Do you think that's wise?

MISS JULIE   You sound as if you were worried about your reputation.

JEAN   Why not? I don't particularly care to be made ridiculous, or to be kicked out without a recommendation just when I'm trying to establish myself. Besides, I have a certain obligation to Christine.

MISS JULIE   Oh, I see. It's Christine now.

JEAN   Yes, but I'm thinking of you, too. Take my advice, Miss Julie, and go up to your room.

MISS JULIE   When did you start giving me orders?

JEAN   Just this once. For your own sake! Please! It's very late. You're so tired, you're drunk. You don't know what you're doing. Go to bed, Miss Julie.—Besides, if my ears aren't deceiving me, they're coming this way, looking for me. If they find us here together, you're done for!

THE CHORUS   (*is heard coming nearer singing*)
   Two ladies came from out the clover,
   Tri-di-ri-di-ralla, tri-di-ri-di-ra.
   And one of them was green all over,
   Tri-di-ri-di-ralla-la.
   They told us they had gold aplenty,
   Tri-di-ri-di-ralla, tri-di-ri-di-ra.
   But neither of them owned a penny,
   Tri-di-ri-di-ralla-la.
   This wreath for you I may be plaiting,
   Tri-di-ri-di-ralla, tri-di-ri-di-ra.
   But it's for another I am waiting,
   Tri-di-ri-ralla-la!

MISS JULIE   I know these people. I love them just as they love me. Let them come. You'll find out.

JEAN   No, Miss Julie, they don't love you! They take the food you give them, but they spit on it as soon as your back is turned. Believe me! Just listen to them. Listen to what they're singing.—No, you'd better not listen.

MISS JULIE (*listening*) What are they singing?

JEAN A dirty song—about you and me!

MISS JULIE How disgusting! Oh, what cowardly, sneaking—

JEAN That's what the mob always is—cowards! You can't fight them; you can only run away.

MISS JULIE Run away? Where? There's no way out of here. And we can't go in to Christine.

JEAN What about my room? What do you say? The rules don't count in a situation like this. You can trust me. I'm your friend, remember? Your true, devoted, and respectful friend.

MISS JULIE But suppose—suppose they looked for you there?

JEAN I'll bolt the door. If they try to break it down, I'll shoot. Come, Miss Julie! (*on his knees*) Please, Miss Julie!

MISS JULIE (*meaningfully*) You promise me that you—?

JEAN I swear to you! (MISS JULIE *goes out quickly to the right.* JEAN *follows her impetuously*)

(THE BALLET. *The country people enter in festive costumes, with flowers in their hats. The fiddler is in the lead. A keg of small beer and a little keg of liquor, decorated with greenery, are set up on the table. Glasses are brought out. They all drink and start to sing the song. Then they form a circle and sing and dance the round dance, "Two ladies came from out the clover." At the end of the dance they all leave singing.*

MISS JULIE *comes in alone; looks at the devastated kitchen; clasps her hands together; then takes out a powder puff and powders her face.* JEAN *enters. He is in high spirits*)

JEAN You see! You heard them, didn't you? You've got to admit it's impossible to stay here.

MISS JULIE No, I don't. But even if I did, what could we do?

JEAN Go away, travel, get away from here!

MISS JULIE Travel? Yes—but where?

JEAN Switzerland, the Italian lakes. You've never been there?

MISS JULIE No. Is it beautiful?

JEAN Eternal summer, oranges, laurel trees, ah . . . !

MISS JULIE But what are we going to do there?

JEAN I'll set up a hotel—a first-class hotel with a first-class clientele.

MISS JULIE Hotel?

JEAN I tell you that's the life! Always new faces, new languages. Not a minute to think about yourself or worry about your nerves. No looking for something to do. The work keeps you busy. Day and night the bells ring, the trains whistle, the busses come and go. And all the while the money comes rolling in. I tell you it's the life!

MISS JULIE Yes, that's the life. But what about me?

JEAN The mistress of the whole place, the star of the establishment! With your looks—and your personality—it can't fail. It's perfect! You'll sit in the office like a queen, setting your slaves in motion by pressing an electric button. The guests will file before your throne and timidly lay their treasures on your table. You can't imagine how people tremble when you shove a bill in their face! I'll salt the bills and you'll sugar them with your prettiest smile. Come on, let's get away from here—(*He takes a timetable from his pocket*)—right away—the next train! We'll be in Malmo at 6:30; Hamburg 8:40 in the morning; Frankfurt to Basle in one day; and to Como by way of the Gotthard tunnel in—let me see—three days! Three days!

MISS JULIE You make it sound so wonderful. But, Jean, you have to give me strength. Tell me you love me. Come and put your arms around me.

JEAN (*hesitates*) I want to . . . but I don't dare. Not any more, not in this house. I do love you—without a shadow of a doubt. How can you doubt that, Miss Julie?

MISS JULIE (*shyly, very becomingly*) You don't have to be formal with me, Jean. You can call me Julie. There aren't any barriers between us now. Call me Julie.

JEAN (*agonized*) I can't! There are still barriers between us, Miss Julie, as long as we stay in this house! There's the past, there's the Count. I've never met anyone I feel so much respect for. I've only got to see his gloves lying on a table and I shrivel up. I only have to hear that bell ring and I shy like a frightened horse. I only have to look at his boots standing there so stiff and proud and I feel my spine bending. (*He kicks the boots*) Superstitions, prejudices that they've drilled into us since we were children! But they can be forgotten just as easily! Just we get to another country where they have a republic! They'll crawl on their hands and knees when they see my uniform. On their hands and knees, I tell you! But not me! Oh, no. I'm not made for crawling. I've got guts, backbone. And once I grab that first branch, you just watch me climb. I may be a valet now, but next year I'll be owning property; in ten years, I'll be living off my investments. Then I'll go to Rumania, get myself some decorations, and maybe—notice I only say maybe—end up as a count!

MISS JULIE   How wonderful, wonderful.

JEAN   Listen, in Rumania you can buy titles. You'll be a countess after all. *My* countess.

MISS JULIE   But I'm not interested in that. I'm leaving all that behind. Tell me you love me, Jean, or else—or else what difference does it make what I am?

JEAN   I'll tell you a thousand times—but later! Not now. And not here. Above all, let's keep our feelings out of this or we'll make a mess of everything. We have to look at this thing calmly and coolly, like sensible people. (*He takes out a cigar, clips the end, and lights it*) Now you sit there and I'll sit here, and we'll talk as if nothing had happened.

MISS JULIE (*in anguish*)   My God, what are you? Don't you have any feelings?

JEAN   Feelings? Nobody's got more feelings than I have. But I've learned how to control them.

MISS JULIE   A few minutes ago you were kissing my shoe—and now—!

JEAN (*harshly*)   That was a few minutes ago. We've got other things to think about now!

MISS JULIE   Don't speak to me like that, Jean!

JEAN   I'm just trying to be sensible. We've been stupid once; let's not be stupid again. Your father might be back at any moment, and we've got to decide our future before then.—Now what do you think about my plans? Do you approve or don't you?

MISS JULIE   I don't see anything wrong with them. Except one thing. For a big undertaking like that, you'd need a lot of capital. Have you got it?

JEAN (*chewing on his cigar*)   Have I got it? Of course I have. I've got my knowledge of the business, my vast experience, my familiarity with languages. That's capital that counts for something, let me tell you.

MISS JULIE   You can't even buy the railway tickets with it.

JEAN   That's true. That's why I need a backer—someone to put up the money.

MISS JULIE   Where can you find him on a moment's notice?

JEAN   You'll find him—if you want to be my partner.

MISS JULIE   I can't. And I don't have a penny to my name.

(*Pause*)

JEAN   Then you can forget the whole thing.

MISS JULIE   Forget—?

JEAN   And things will stay just the way they are.

MISS JULIE   Do you think I'm going to live under the same roof with you as your mistress? Do you think I'm going to have people sneering at me behind my back? How do you think I'll ever be able to look my father in the face after this? No, no! Take me away from here, Jean—the shame, the humiliation. . . . What have I done? Oh, my God, my God! What have I done?

(*She bursts into tears*)

JEAN   Now don't start singing that tune. It won't work. What have you done that's so awful? You're not the first.

MISS JULIE (*crying hysterically*)   Now you despise me!—I'm falling, I'm falling!

JEAN   Fall down to me, and I'll lift you up again!

MISS JULIE   What awful hold did you have over me? What drove me to you? The weak to the strong? The falling to the rising! Or maybe it was love? Love? This? You don't know what love is!

JEAN   Want to bet? Did you think I was a virgin?

MISS JULIE   You're vulgar! The things you say, the things you think!

JEAN   That's the way I was brought up and that's the way I am! Now don't get hysterical. And don't play the fine lady with me. We're eating off the same platter now. . . . That's better. Come over here and be a good girl and I'll treat you to something special. (*He opens the table drawer and takes out the wine bottle. He pours the wine into two used glasses*)

MISS JULIE   Where did you get that wine?

JEAN   From the wine cellar.

MISS JULIE   My father's burgundy!

JEAN   Should be good enough for his son-in-law.

MISS JULIE   I was drinking beer and you—!

JEAN   That shows that I have better taste than you.

MISS JULIE   Thief!

JEAN   You going to squeal on me?

MISS JULIE   Oh, God! Partner in crime with a petty house thief! I must have been drunk; I must have been walking in my sleep. Midsummer Night! Night of innocent games—

JEAN   Yes, very innocent!

MISS JULIE (*pacing up and down*)   Is there anyone here on earth as miserable as I am?

JEAN   Why be miserable? After such a conquest! Think of poor Christine in there. Don't you think she's got any feelings?

MISS JULIE   I thought so a while ago, but I don't now. A servant's a servant—

JEAN   And a whore's a whore!

MISS JULIE (*falls to her knees and clasps her hands together*)   Oh, God in heaven, put an end to my worthless life! Lift me out of this awful filth I'm sinking in! Save me! Save me!

JEAN   I feel sorry for you, I have to admit it. When I was lying in the onion beds, looking up at you on the rose terrace, I—I'm telling you the truth now—I had the same dirty thoughts that all boys have.

MISS JULIE   And you said you wanted to die for me!

JEAN   In the oat bin? That was only a story.

MISS JULIE   A lie, you mean.

JEAN (*beginning to get sleepy*)   Practically. I think I read it in the paper about a chimney sweep who curled up in a woodbin with some lilacs because they were going to arrest him for nonsupport of his child.

MISS JULIE   Now I see you for what you are.

JEAN   What did you expect me to do? It's always the fancy talk that gets the women.

MISS JULIE   You dog!

JEAN   You bitch!

MISS JULIE   Well, now you've seen the eagle's back—

JEAN   Wasn't exactly its back—!

MISS JULIE   I was going to be your first branch—!

JEAN   A rotten branch—

MISS JULIE   I was going to be the window dressing for your hotel—!

JEAN   And I the hotel—!

MISS JULIE   Sitting at the desk, attracting your customers, padding your bills—!

JEAN   I could manage that myself—!

MISS JULIE   How can a human soul be so dirty and filthy?

JEAN   Then why don't you clean it up?

MISS JULIE   You lackey! You shoeshine boy! Stand up when I talk to you!

JEAN   You lackey lover! You bootblack's tramp! Shut your mouth and get out of here! Who do you think you are telling me I'm coarse? I've never seen anybody in my class behave as crudely as you did tonight. Have you ever seen any of the girls around here grab at a man like you did? Do you think any of the girls of my class would throw themselves at a man like that? I've never seen the like of it except in animals and prostitutes!

MISS JULIE (*crushed*)   That's right! Hit me! Walk all over me! It's all I deserve. I'm rotten.

But help me! Help me to get out of this—if there is any way out for me!

JEAN (*less harsh*)   I'd be doing myself an injustice if I didn't admit that part of the credit for this seduction belongs to me. But do you think a person in my position would have dared to look twice at you if you hadn't asked for it? I'm still amazed—

MISS JULIE   And still proud.

JEAN   Why not? But I've got to confess the victory was a little too easy to give me any real thrill.

MISS JULIE   Go on, hit me more!

JEAN (*standing up*)   No. . . . I'm sorry for what I said. I never hit a person who's down, especially a woman. I can't deny that, in one way, it was good to find out that what I saw glittering up above was only fool's gold, to have seen that the eagle's back was as gray as its belly, that the smooth cheek was just powder, and that there could be dirt under the manicured nails, that the handkerchief was soiled even though it smelled of perfume. But in another way, it hurt me to find that everything I was striving for wasn't very high above me after all, wasn't even real. It hurts me to see you sink far lower than your own cook. Hurts, like seeing the last flowers cut to pieces by the autumn rains and turned to muck.

MISS JULIE   You talk as if you already stood high above me.

JEAN   Well, don't I? Don't forget I could make you a countess but you can never make me a count.

MISS JULIE   But I have a father for a count. You can never have that!

JEAN   True. But I might father my own counts—that is, if—

MISS JULIE   You're a thief! I'm not!

JEAN   There are worse things than being a thief. A lot worse. And besides, when I take a position in a house, I consider myself a member of the family—in a way, like a child in the house. It's no crime for a child to steal a few ripe cherries when they're falling off the trees, is it? (*He begins to feel passionate again*) Miss Julie, you're a beautiful woman, much too good for the likes of me. You got carried away by your emotions and now you want to cover up your mistake by telling yourself that you love me. You don't love me. You might possibly have been attracted by my looks—in which case your kind of love is no better than mine. But I could never be satisfied to be just an animal for you, and I could never make you love me.

MISS JULIE   Are you so sure of that?

JEAN   You mean there's a chance? I could

love you, there's no doubt about that. You're beautiful, you're refined—(*He goes up to her and takes her hand*)—educated, lovable when you want to be, and once you set a man's heart on fire, I'll bet it burns forever. (*He puts his arm around her waist*) You're like hot wine with strong spices. One of your kisses is enough to—

(*He attempts to lead her out, but she rather reluctantly breaks away from him*)

MISS JULIE   Let me go. You don't get me that way.

JEAN   Then how? Not by petting you and not with pretty words, not by planning for the future, not by saving you from humiliation! Then how, tell me how?

MISS JULIE   How? How? I don't know how! I don't know at all!—I hate you like I hate rats, but I can't get away from you.

JEAN   Then come away *with* me!

MISS JULIE   (*pulling herself together*) Away? Yes, we'll go away!—But I'm so tired. Pour me a glass of wine, will you? (*JEAN pours the wine. MISS JULIE looks at her watch*) Let's talk first. We still have a little time. (*She empties the glass of wine and holds it out for more*)

JEAN   Don't overdo it. You'll get drunk.

MISS JULIE   What difference does it make?

JEAN   What difference? It looks cheap.— What did you want to say to me?

MISS JULIE   We're going to run away together, right? But we'll talk first—that is, I'll talk. So far you've done all the talking. You've told me your life, now I'll tell you mine. That way we'll know each other through and through before we become traveling companions.

JEAN   Wait a minute. Excuse me, but are you sure you won't regret this afterwards, when you've surrendered your secrets?

MISS JULIE   I thought you were my friend.

JEAN   I am—sometimes. But don't count on me.

MISS JULIE   You don't mean that. Anyway, everybody knows my secrets.—My mother's parents were very ordinary people, just commoners. She was brought up, according to the theories of her time, to believe in equality, the independence of women, and all that. And she had a strong aversion to marriage. When my father proposed to her, she swore she would never become his wife, but that she might consent to become his mistress. He told her that he had no desire to see the woman he loved enjoy less respect than he did. But she said she didn't care what the world thought, and, thinking he couldn't live without her, he

accepted her conditions. But from then on he was cut off from his old circle of friends, and left without anything to do in the house, which couldn't keep him occupied anyway. I was born—against my mother's wishes, as far as I can make out. My mother decided to bring me up as a nature child. And on top of that I had to learn everything a boy learns, so I could be living proof that women were just as good as men. I had to wear boy's clothes, learn to handle horses—but not to milk the cows. I was made to groom the horses and train them, and learn farming and go hunting—I even had to learn to slaughter the animals—it was disgusting! And on the estate all the men were set to doing the work of women, and the women to doing men's work—with the result that the whole place threatened to fall to pieces, and we became the local laughing-stock. Finally my father must have come out of his trance. He rebelled, and everything was changed according to his wishes. Then my mother got sick. I don't know what kind of sickness it was, but she often had convulsions, and she would hide herself in the attic or in the garden, and sometimes she would stay out all night. Then there occurred that big fire you've heard about. The house, the stables, the cowsheds, all burned down—and under very peculiar circumstances that led one to suspect arson. You see, the accident occurred the day after the insurance expired, and the premiums on the new policy, which my father had sent in, were delayed through the messenger's carelessness, and didn't arrive on time. (*She refills her glass and drinks*)

JEAN   You've had enough.

MISS JULIE   Who cares!—We were left without a penny to our name. We had to sleep in the carriages. My father didn't know where to turn for money to rebuild the house. Then Mother suggested to him that he might try to borrow money from an old friend of hers, who owned a brick factory not far from here. Father takes out a loan, but there's no interest charged, which surprises him. So the place was rebuilt. (*She drinks some more*) Do you know who set fire to the place?

JEAN   Your honorable mother!

MISS JULIE   Do you know who the brick manufacturer was.

JEAN   Your mother's lover?

MISS JULIE   Do you know whose money it was?

JEAN   Let me think a minute. . . . No, I give up.

MISS JULIE   It was my mother's!

JEAN   The Count's, you mean. Or was there a marriage settlement?

MISS JULIE There wasn't a settlement. My mother had a little money of her own which she didn't want under my father's control, so she invested it with her—friend.

JEAN Who grabbed it!

MISS JULIE Precisely. He appropriated it. Well, my father finds out what happened. But he can't go to court, can't pay his wife's lover, can't prove that it's his wife's money. That was how my mother got her revenge because he had taken control of the house. He was on the verge of shooting himself. There was even a rumor that he tried and failed. But he took a new lease on life and he forced my mother to pay for her mistakes. Can you imagine what those five years were like for me? I loved my father, but I took my mother's side because I didn't know the whole story. She had taught me to hate all men—you've heard how she hated men—and I swore to her that I'd never be slave to any man.

JEAN But you got engaged to the attorney.

MISS JULIE Only to make him slave to me.

JEAN But he didn't want any of that?

MISS JULIE Oh, he wanted to well enough, but I didn't give him the chance. I got bored with him.

JEAN Yes, so I noticed—in the barnyard.

MISS JULIE What did you notice?

JEAN I saw what I saw. *He* broke off the engagement.

MISS JULIE That's a lie! It was I who broke it off. Did he tell you that? He's beneath contempt!

JEAN Come on now, he isn't as bad as that. So you hate men, Miss Julie?

MISS JULIE Yes, I do. . . . Most of the time. But sometimes, when I can't help myself —oh. . . . (*She shudders in disgust*)

JEAN Then you hate me, too?

MISS JULIE You have no idea how much! I'd like to see you killed like an animal—

JEAN Like when you're caught in the act with an animal: you get two years at hard labor and the animal is killed. Right?

MISS JULIE Right!

JEAN But there's no one to catch us—and *no animal!* What are we going to do?

MISS JULIE Go away from here.

JEAN To torture ourselves to death?

MISS JULIE No. To enjoy ourselves for a day or two, or a week, for as long as we can—and then—to die—

JEAN Die? How stupid! I've got a better idea: start a hotel!

MISS JULIE (*continuing without hearing* JEAN) —on the shores of Lake Como, where the sun is always shining, where the laurels bloom at Christmas, and the golden oranges glow on the trees.

JEAN Lake Como is a stinking wet hole, and the only oranges I saw there were on the fruit stands. But it's a good tourist spot with a lot of villas and cottages that are rented out to lovers. Now there's a profitable business. You know why? They rent the villa for the whole season, but they leave after three weeks.

MISS JULIE (*innocently*) Why after only three weeks?

JEAN Because they can't stand each other any longer. Why else? But they still have to pay the rent. Then you rent it out again to another couple, and so on. There's no shortage of love—even if it doesn't last very long.

MISS JULIE Then you don't want to die with me?

JEAN I don't want to die at all! I enjoy life too much. And moreover, I consider taking your own life a sin against the Providence that gave us life.

MISS JULIE You believe in God? You?

JEAN Yes, certainly I do! I go to church every other Sunday.—Honestly, I've had enough of this talk. I'm going to bed.

MISS JULIE Really? You think you're going to get off that easy? Don't you know that a man owes something to the woman he's dishonored?

JEAN (*takes out his purse and throws a silver coin on the table*) There you are. I don't want to owe anybody anything.

MISS JULIE (*ignoring the insult*) Do you know what the law says—?

JEAN Aren't you lucky the law says nothing about the women who seduce men!

MISS JULIE (*still not hearing him*) What else can we do but go away from here, get married, and get divorced?

JEAN Suppose I refuse to enter into this mésalliance?

MISS JULIE Mésalliance?

JEAN For me! I've got better ancestors than you. I don't have any female arsonist in my family.

MISS JULIE How can you know?

JEAN You can't prove the opposite because we don't have any family records—except in the police courts. But I've read the whole history of your family in that book on the drawing-room table. Do you know who the founder of your family line was? A miller—who let his wife sleep with the king one night during the Danish war. I don't have any ancestors like that. I don't have any ancestors at all! But I can become an ancestor myself.

MISS JULIE This is what I get for baring my

heart and soul to someone too low to understand, for sacrificing the honor of my family—

JEAN Dishonor!—I warned you, remember? Drinking makes one talk, and talking's bad.

MISS JULIE Oh, how sorry I am! . . . If only it had never happened! . . . If only you at least loved me!

JEAN For the last time—what do you expect of me? Do you want me to cry? Jump over your whip? Kiss you? Do you want me to lure you to Lake Como for three weeks and then—? What am I supposed to do? What do you want? I've had more than I can take. This is what I get for involving myself with women . . . Miss Julie, I can see that you're unhappy; I know that you're suffering; but I simply cannot understand you. My people don't behave like this. We don't hate each other. We make love for the fun of it, when we can get any time off from our work. But we don't have time for it all day and all night like you do. If you ask me, you're sick, Miss Julie. . . . You know your mother's mind was affected. We've got whole counties affected with pietism. Your mother's trouble was a kind of pietism. Everybody's catching it.

MISS JULIE You can be understanding, Jean. You're talking to me like a human being now.

JEAN Well, be human yourself. You spit on me but you don't let me wipe it off—on you!

MISS JULIE Help me, Jean. Help me. Tell me what I should do, that's all—which way to go.

JEAN For Christ's sake, if only I knew myself!

MISS JULIE I've been crazy—I've been out of my mind—but does that mean there's no way out for me?

JEAN Stay here as if nothing had happened. Nobody knows anything.

MISS JULIE Impossible! Everybody who works here knows. Christine knows.

JEAN They don't know a thing. And anyhow they'd never believe it.

MISS JULIE (slowly, significantly) But . . . it might happen again.

JEAN That's true!

MISS JULIE And there might be consequences.

JEAN (stunned) Consequences!! What on earth have I been thinking of! You're right. There's only one thing to do: get away from here! Immediately! I can't go with you—that would give the whole game away. You'll have to go by yourself. Somewhere—I don't care where!

MISS JULIE By myself? Where?—Oh, no, Jean, I can't. I can't!

JEAN You've got to! Before the Count comes back. You know as well as I do what will happen if you stay here. After one mistake, you figure you might as well go on, since the damage is already done. Then you get more and more careless until—finally you're exposed. I tell you, you've got to get out of the country. Afterwards you can write to the Count and tell him everything—leaving me out, of course. He'd never be able to guess it was me. Anyway, I don't think he'd exactly like to find that out.

MISS JULIE I'll go—if you'll come with me!

JEAN Lady, are you out of your mind!? "Miss Julie elopes with her footman." The day after tomorrow it would be in all the papers. The Count would never live it down.

MISS JULIE I can't go away. I can't stay. Help me. I'm so tired, so awfully tired. . . . Tell me what to do. Order me. Start me going. I can't think any more, can't move any more. . . .

JEAN Now do you realize how weak you all are? What gives you the right to go strutting around with your noses in the air as if you owned the world? All right, I'll give you your orders. Go up and get dressed. Get some traveling money. And come back down here.

MISS JULIE (almost in a whisper) Come up with me!

JEAN To your room? . . . You're going crazy again! (He hesitates a moment) No! No! Go! Right now! (He takes her hand and leads her out)

MISS JULIE (as she is leaving) Don't be so harsh, Jean.

JEAN Orders always sound harsh. You've never had to take them.

(JEAN, left alone, heaves a sigh of relief and sits down at the table. He takes out a notebook and a pencil and begins to calculate, counting aloud now and then. The pantomime continues until CHRISTINE enters, dressed for church, and carrying JEAN's white tie and shirt front in her hand)

CHRISTINE Lord in Heaven, what a mess! What on earth have you been doing?

JEAN It was Miss Julie. She dragged the whole crowd in here. You must have been sleeping awfully sound if you didn't hear anything.

CHRISTINE I slept like a log.

JEAN You already dressed for church?

CHRISTINE Yes, indeed. Don't you remember you promised to go to Communion with me today?

JEAN Oh, yes, of course. I remember. I

see you've brought my things. All right. Come on, put it on me. (*He sits down, and* CHRISTINE *starts to put the white tie and shirt front on him. Pause.* JEAN *yawns*) What's the lesson for today?

CHRISTINE   The beheading of John the Baptist, I suppose.

JEAN   My God, that will go on forever.—Hey, you're choking me! . . . Oh, I'm so sleepy, so sleepy.

CHRISTINE   What were you doing up all night? You look green in the face.

JEAN   I've been sitting here talking with Miss Julie.

CHRISTINE   That girl! She doesn't know how to behave herself!

(*Pause*)

JEAN   Tell me something, Christine. . . .

CHRISTINE   Well, what?

JEAN   Isn't it strange when you think about it? Her, I mean.

CHRISTINE   What's so strange?

JEAN   Everything!

(*Pause.* CHRISTINE *looks at the half-empty glasses on the table*)

CHRISTINE   Have you been drinking with her?

JEAN   Yes!

CHRISTINE   Shame on you!—Look me in the eyes! You haven't . . . ?

JEAN   Yes!

CHRISTINE   Is it possible? Is it really possible?

JEAN   (*after a moment's consideration*) Yes. It is.

CHRISTINE   Oh, how disgusting! I could never have believed anything like this would happen! No. No. This is too much!

JEAN   Don't tell me you're jealous of her?

CHRISTINE   No, not of her. If it had been Clara—or Sophie—I would have scratched your eyes out! But her—? That's different. I don't know why. . . . But it's still disgusting!

JEAN   Then you're mad at her?

CHRISTINE   No. Mad at you. You were mean and cruel to do a thing like that, very mean. The poor girl! . . . But let me tell you, I'm not going to stay in this house a moment longer, not when I can't have any respect for my employers.

JEAN   Why do you want to respect them?

CHRISTINE   Don't try to be smart. You don't want to work for people who behave immorally, do you? Well, do you? If you ask me, you'd be lowering yourself by doing that.

JEAN   Oh, I don't know. I think it's rather comforting to find out that they're not one bit better than we are.

CHRISTINE   Well, I don't. If they're not any better, there's no point in us trying to be like them.—And think of the Count. Think of all the sorrows he's been through in his time. No, sir, I won't stay in this house any longer. . . . Imagine! You, of all people! If it had been the attorney fellow; if it had been somebody respectable—

JEAN   Now just a minute—!

CHRISTINE   Oh, you're all right in your own way. But there's a big difference between one class and another. You can't deny that.—No, this is something I can never get over. She was so proud, and so sarcastic about men, you'd never believe she'd go and throw herself at one. And at someone like you! And *she* was going to have Diana shot, because the poor thing ran after the gatekeeper's mongrel!—Well, I tell you, I've had enough! I'm not going to stay here any longer. On the twenty-fourth of October, I'm leaving.

JEAN   Then what'll you do?

CHRISTINE   Well, since you brought it up, it's about time that you got yourself a decent place, if we're going to get married.

JEAN   Why should I go looking for another place? I could never get a place like this if I'm married.

CHRISTINE   Well, of course not! But you could get a job as a doorkeeper, or maybe try to get a government job as a caretaker somewhere. The government don't pay much, but they pay regular. And there's a pension for the wife and children.

JEAN   (*wryly*) Fine, fine! But I'm not the kind of fellow who thinks about dying for his wife and children this early in the game. I hate to say it, but I've got slightly bigger plans than that.

CHRISTINE   Plans! Hah! What about your obligations? You'd better start giving them a little thought!

JEAN   Don't start nagging me about obligations! I know what I have to do without you telling me. (*He hears a sound upstairs*) Anyhow, we'll have plenty of chance to talk about this later. You just go and get yourself ready, and we'll be off to church.

CHRISTINE   Who is that walking around up there?

JEAN   I don't know. Clara, I suppose. Who else?

CHRISTINE   (*starting to leave*) It can't be the Count, can it? Could he have come back without anybody hearing him?

JEAN (*frightened*)   The Count? No, it can't be. He would have rung.

CHRISTINE (*leaving*)   God help us! I've never heard of the like of this.

(*The sun has now risen and strikes the tops of the trees in the park. The light shifts gradually until it is shining very obliquely through the windows.* JEAN *goes to the door and signals.* MISS JULIE *enters, dressed for travel, and carrying a small bird cage, covered with a towel. She sets the cage down on a chair*)

MISS JULIE   I'm ready now.

JEAN   Shh! Christine's awake.

MISS JULIE (*she is extremely tense and nervous during the following*)   Did she suspect anything?

JEAN   She doesn't know a thing.—My God, what happened to you?

MISS JULIE   What do you mean? Do I look so strange?

JEAN   You're white as a ghost, and you've —excuse me—but you've got dirt on your face.

MISS JULIE   Let me wash it off. (*She goes over to the wash basin and washes her face and hands*) There! Do you have a towel? . . . Oh, look the sun's coming up!

JEAN   That breaks the magic spell!

MISS JULIE   Yes, we were spellbound last night, weren't we? Midsummer madness . . . Jean, listen to me! Come with me. I've got the money!

JEAN   Enough?

MISS JULIE   Enough for a start. Come with me, Jean. I can't travel alone today. Midsummer Day on a stifling hot train, packed in with crowds of people, all staring at me—stopping at every station when I want to be flying. I can't, Jean, I can't! . . . And everything will remind me of the past. Midsummer Day when I was a child and the church was decorated with leaves . . . birch leaves and lilacs . . . the table spread for dinner with friends and relatives . . . and after dinner, dancing in the park, with flowers and games. Oh, no matter how far you travel, the memories tag right along in the baggage car . . . and the regrets, and the remorse.

JEAN   All right, I'll go with you! But it's got to be now—before it's too late! This very instant!

MISS JULIE   Hurry and get dressed! (*She picks up the bird gage*)

JEAN   But no baggage! It would give us away.

MISS JULIE   Nothing. Only what we can take to our seats.

JEAN (*as he gets his hat*)   What in the devil have you got there? What is that?

MISS JULIE   It's only my canary. I can't leave it behind.

JEAN   A canary! My God, do you expect us to carry a bird cage around with us? You're crazy. Put that cage down!

MISS JULIE   It's the only thing I'm taking with me from my home—the only living thing who loves me since Diana was unfaithful to me! Don't be cruel, Jean. Let me take it with me.

JEAN   I told you to put that cage down!— And don't talk so loud. Christine can hear us.

MISS JULIE   No, I won't leave it with a stranger. I won't. I'd rather have you kill it.

JEAN   Let me have the little pest, and I'll wring its neck.

MISS JULIE   Yes, but don't hurt it. Don't—. No, I can't do it!

JEAN   Don't worry, I can. Give it here.

(MISS JULIE *takes the bird out of the cage and kisses it*)

MISS JULIE   Oh, my little Serena, must you die and leave your mistress?

JEAN   You don't have to make a scene of it. It's a question of your whole life and future. You're wasting time!

(JEAN *grabs the canary from her, carries it to the chopping block, and picks up a meat cleaver.* MISS JULIE *turns away*)   You should have learned how to kill chickens instead of shooting revolvers—(*He brings the cleaver down*)—then a drop of blood wouldn't make you faint.

MISS JULIE (*screaming*)   Kill me too! Kill me! You can kill an innocent creature without turning a hair—then kill me. Oh, how I hate you! I loathe you! There's blood between us. I curse the moment I first laid eyes on you! I curse the moment I was conceived in my mother's womb. (*She approaches the chopping block as if drawn to it against her will*) No, I don't want to go yet. I can't.—I have to see.— Shh! I hear a carriage coming! (*She listens but keeps her eyes fastened on the chopping block and cleaver*) You don't think I can stand the sight of blood, do you? You think I'm so weak! Oh, I'd love to see your blood and your brains on that chopping block. I'd love to see the whole of your sex swimming in a sea of blood just like that. I think I could drink out of your skull. I'd like to bathe my feet in your ribs! I could eat your heart roasted whole! —You think I'm weak! You think I loved you because my womb hungered for your seed. You think I want to carry your brood under my heart and nourish it with my blood! Bear your child and take your name! Come to think of it, what is your name anyway? I've never heard your last name. You probably don't even have one. I'd be Mrs. Doorkeeper or Madame Floorsweeper. You dog with my name on your collar—you lackey with my initials on your buttons! Do you think I'm going to share you with my cook and fight over you with my maid?! Ohhh!—You think I'm a coward who's going to run away. No, I'm going to stay. Come hell or high water, I don't care! My father will come home—find his bureau broken into—his money gone. Then he rings—on that bell—two rings for the valet. And then he sends for the sheriff—and I tell him everything. Everything! Oh, it'll be wonderful to have it all over . . . if only it will be over. . . . He'll have a stroke and die. Then there'll be an end to all of us. There'll be peace . . . and quiet . . . forever. . . . His coat of arms will be broken on the coffin; the Count's line dies out. But the valet's line will continue in an orphanage, win triumphs in the gutter, and end in jail! (CHRISTINE *enters, dressed for church and with a hymn-book in her hand.* MISS JULIE *rushes over to her and throws herself into her arms as if seeking protection*) Help me, Christine! Help me against this man!

CHRISTINE (*cold and unmoved*) This is a fine way to behave on a holy day! (*She sees the chopping block*) Just look at the mess you've made there! How do you explain that? And what's all this shouting and screaming about?

MISS JULIE Christine, you're a woman, you're my friend! I warn you, watch out for this—this monster!

JEAN (*ill at ease and a little embarrassed*) If you ladies are going to talk, I think I'll go and shave. (*He slips out to the right*)

MISS JULIE You've got to understand, Christine! You've got to listen to me!

CHRISTINE No, I don't. I don't understand this kind of shenanigans at all. Where do you think you're going dressed like that? And Jean with his hat on?—Well?—Well?

MISS JULIE Listen to me, Christine! If you'll just listen to me, I'll tell you everything.

CHRISTINE I don't want to know anything.

MISS JULIE You've got to listen to me—!

CHRISTINE What about? About your stupid behavior with Jean? I tell you that doesn't bother me at all, because it's none of my business. But if you have any silly idea about talking him into skipping out with you, I'll soon put a stop to that.

MISS JULIE (*extremely tense*) Christine,

please don't get upset. Listen to me. I can't stay here, and Jean can't stay here. So you see, we have to go away.

CHRISTINE Hm, hm, hm.

MISS JULIE (*suddenly brightening up*) Wait! I've got an idea! Why couldn't all three of us go away together?—out of the country— to Switzerland—and start a hotel. I've got the money, you see. Jean and I would be responsible for the whole affair—and Christine, you could run the kitchen, I thought. Doesn't that sound wonderful! Say yes! Say you'll come, Christine, then everything will be settled. Say you will! Please! (*She throws her arms around* CHRISTINE *and pats her*)

CHRISTINE (*remaining aloof and unmoved*) Hm. Hm.

MISS JULIE (*presto tempo*) You've never been traveling, Christine. You have to get out and see the world. You can't imagine how wonderful it is to travel by train—constantly new faces—new countries. We'll go to Hamburg, and stop over to look at the zoo—you'll love that. And we'll go to the theatre and the opera. And then when we get to Munich, we'll go to the museums, Christine. They have Rubenses and Raphaels there—those great painters, you know. Of course you've heard about Munich where King Ludwig lived—you know, the king who went mad. And then we can go and see his castles—they're built just like the ones you read about in fairy tales. And from there it's just a short trip to Switzerland—with the Alps. Think of the Alps, Christine, covered with snow in the middle of the summer. And oranges grow there, and laurel trees that are green the whole year round. (JEAN *can be seen in the wings at the right, sharpening his straight razor on a strap held between his teeth and his left hand. He listens to* MISS JULIE *with a satisfied expression on his face, now and then nodding approvingly.* MISS JULIE *continues tempo prestissimo*)—And that's where we'll get a hotel. I'll sit at the desk while Jean stands at the door and receives the guests, goes out shopping, writes the letters. What a life that will be! The train whistle blowing, then the bus arriving, then a bell ringing upstairs, then the bell in the restaurant rings—and I'll be making out the bills—and I know just how much to salt them—you can't imagine how timid tourists are when you shove a bill in their face!— And you, Christine, you'll run the whole kitchen—there'll be no standing at the stove for you—of course not. If you're going to talk to the people, you'll have to dress neatly and elegantly. And with your looks—I'm not trying to flatter you, Christine—you'll run off with some man one fine day—a rich Englishman, that's who it'll be, they're so easy to—(*slowing down*)—to catch.—Then we'll all be rich.—We'll build a villa on Lake Como.—Maybe it does rain there sometimes, but—(*more and more lifelessly*)—the sun has to shine sometimes, too—even if it looks cloudy.—And—then . . . Or else we can always travel some more—and come back . . . (*pause*)—here . . . or somewhere else . . .

CHRISTINE Do you really believe a word of that yourself, Miss Julie?

MISS JULIE (*completely beaten*) Do I believe a word of it myself?

CHRISTINE Do you?

MISS JULIE (*exhausted*) I don't know. I don't believe anything any more. (*She sinks down on the bench and lays her head between her arms on the table*) Nothing. Nothing at all.

CHRISTINE (*turns to the right and faces JEAN*) So! You were planning to run away, were you?

JEAN (*nonplused, lays his razor down on the table*) We weren't exactly going to run away! Don't exaggerate. You heard Miss Julie's plans. Even if she's tired now after being up all night, her plans are perfectly feasible.

CHRISTINE Well, just listen to you! Did you really think you could get me to cook for that little—

JEAN (*sharply*) You keep a respectful tongue in your mouth when you talk to your mistress! Understand?

CHRISTINE Mistress!

JEAN Yes, mistress!

CHRISTINE Well of all the—! I don't have to listen—

JEAN Yes, you do! You need to listen more and talk less. Miss Julie is your mistress. Don't forget that! And if you're going to despise her for what she did, you ought to despise yourself for the same reason.

CHRISTINE I've always held myself high enough to—

JEAN High enough to make you look down on others!

CHRISTINE —enough to keep from lowering myself beneath my position. No one can say that the Count's cook has ever had anything to do with the stable groom or the swineherd. No one can say that!

JEAN Yes, aren't you lucky you got involved with a decent man!

CHRISTINE What kind of a decent man is it who sells the oats from the Count's stables?

JEAN Listen to who's talking! You get a

commission on the groceries and take bribes from the butcher!

CHRISTINE How can you say a thing like that!

JEAN And you tell me you can't respect your employers any more! You! You!

CHRISTINE Are you going to church or aren't you? I should think you'd need a good sermon after your exploits.

JEAN No, I'm not going to church! You can go alone and confess your own sins.

CHRISTINE Yes, I'll do just that. And I'll come back with enough forgiveness to cover yours, too. Our redeemer suffered and died on the cross for all our sins, and if we come to Him in faith and with a penitent heart, He will take all our sins upon Himself.

JEAN Grocery sins included?

MISS JULIE Do you really believe that, Christine?

CHRISTINE With all my heart, as sure as I'm standing here. It was the faith I was born into, and I've held on to it since I was a little girl, Miss Julie. Where sin aboundeth, there grace aboundeth also.

MISS JULIE If I had your faith, Christine, if only—

CHRISTINE But you see, that's something you can't have without God's special grace. And it is not granted to everyone to receive it.

MISS JULIE Then who receives it?

CHRISTINE That's the secret of the workings of grace, Miss Julie, and God is no respecter of persons. With him the last shall be the first—

MISS JULIE In that case, he does have respect for the last, doesn't he?

CHRISTINE (*continuing*) —and it is easier for a camel to go through the eye of a needle than for a rich man to enter the kingdom of God. That's how things are, Miss Julie. I'm going to leave now—alone. And on my way out I'm going to tell the stable boy not to let any horses out, in case anyone has any ideas about leaving before the Count comes home. Goodbye. (*She leaves*)

JEAN She's a devil in skirts!—And all because of a canary!

MISS JULIE (*listlessly*) Never mind the canary. . . . Do you see any way out of this, any end to it?

JEAN (*after thinking for a moment*) No.

MISS JULIE What would you do if you were in my place?

JEAN In your place? Let me think. . . . An aristocrat, a woman, and—fallen. . . . I don't know. —Or maybe I do.

MISS JULIE (*picks up the razor and makes a gesture with it*) Like this?

JEAN Yes. But *I* wouldn't do it, you understand. That's the difference between us.

MISS JULIE Because you're a man and I'm a woman? What difference does that make?

JEAN Just the difference that there is—between a man and a woman.

MISS JULIE I want to! But I can't do it. My father couldn't do it either, that time he should have done it.

JEAN No, he was right not to do it. He had to get his revenge first.

MISS JULIE And now my mother is getting her revenge again through me.

JEAN Haven't you ever loved your father, Miss Julie?

MISS JULIE Yes, enormously. But I must have hated him too. I must have hated him without knowing it. It was he who brought me up to despise my own sex, to be half woman and half man. Who's to blame for what has happened? My father, my mother, myself? Myself? I don't have a self that's my own. I don't have a single thought I didn't get from my father, not an emotion I didn't get from my mother. And that last idea—about all people being equal—I got that from him, my betrothed. That's why I say he's beneath contempt. How can it be my own fault? Put the blame on Jesus, like Christine does? I'm too proud to do that—and too intelligent, thanks to what my father taught me. . . . A rich man can't get into heaven? That's a lie. But at least Christine, who's got money in the savings bank, won't get in. . . . Who's to blame? What difference does it make who's to blame? I'm still the one who has to bear the guilt, suffer the consequences—

JEAN Yes, but—(*The bell rings sharply twice.* MISS JULIE *jumps up.* JEAN *changes his coat*) The Count's back! What if Christine—? (*He goes to the speaking tube, taps on it, and listens*)

MISS JULIE Has he looked in his bureau yet?

JEAN This is Jean, sir! (*listens. The audience cannot hear what the Count says*) Yes, sir! (*listens*) Yes, sir! Yes, as soon as I can. (*listens*) Yes, at once, sir! (*listens*) Very good, sir! In half an hour.

MISS JULIE (*trembling with anxiety*) What did he say? For God's sake, what did he say?

JEAN He ordered his boots and his coffee in half an hour.

MISS JULIE Half an hour then! . . . Oh, I'm so tired. I can't bring myself to do anything. Can't repent, can't run away, can't stay, can't live . . . can't die. Help me, Jean. Command me, and I'll obey like a dog. Do me this last favor. Save my honor, save his name. You know what I ought to do but can't force myself to do. Let me use your will power. You command me and I'll obey.

JEAN I don't know—I can't either, not now. I don't know why. It's as if this coat made me—. I can't give you orders in this. And now, after the Count has spoken to me, I—I can't really explain it—but—I've got the backbone of a damned lackey! If the Count came down here now and ordered me to cut my throat, I'd do it on the spot.

MISS JULIE Pretend that you're him, and that I'm you. You were such a good actor just a while ago, when you were kneeling before me. You were the aristocrat then. Or else—have you ever been to the theatre and seen a hypnotist? (JEAN *nods*) He says to his subject, "Take this broom!" and he takes it. He says, "Now sweep!" and he sweeps.

JEAN But the person has to be asleep!

MISS JULIE I'm already asleep. The whole room has turned to smoke. You seem like an iron stove, a stove that looks like a man in black with a high hat. Your eyes are glowing like coals when the fire dies out. Your face is a white smudge, like the ashes. (*The sun is shining in on the floor and falls on* JEAN) It's so good and warm—(*She rubs her hands together as if warming them at a fire*)—and so bright—and so peaceful.

JEAN (*takes the razor and puts it in her hand*) There's the broom. Go now, when the sun is up—out into the barn—and—(*He whispers in her ear*)

MISS JULIE (*waking up*) Thanks! I'm going to get my rest. But tell me one thing. Tell me that the first can also receive the gift of grace. Tell me that, even if you don't believe it.

JEAN The first? I can't tell you that.—But wait a moment, Miss Julie. I know what I can tell you. You're no longer among the first. You're among—the last.

MISS JULIE That's true! I'm among the very last. I am the last!—Oh!—Now I can't go! Tell me just once more, tell me to go!

JEAN Now I can't either. I can't!

MISS JULIE And the first shall be the last. . . .

JEAN Don't think—don't think! You're taking all my strength away. You're making me a coward. . . . What! I thought I saw the bell move. No. . . . Let me stuff some paper in it.—Afraid of a bell! But it isn't just a bell. There's somebody behind it. A hand that makes it move. And there's something that makes the hand move.—Stop your ears, that's it, stop your ears! But it only rings louder. Rings louder and louder until you answer it. And then it's too late. Then the sheriff comes—and then —(*There are two sharp rings on the bell.* JEAN

gives a start, then straightens himself up) It's horrible! But there's no other way for it to end. —Go!

(MISS JULIE *walks resolutely out through the door*)

THE GHOST SONATA

Translated by Evert Sprinchorn

CAST OF CHARACTERS

THE OLD MAN, *Mr. Hummel*
THE STUDENT, *Arkenholz*
THE MILKMAID, *an apparition*
THE SUPERINTENDENT'S WIFE
THE SUPERINTENDENT
THE DEAD MAN, *formerly a Consul*
THE WOMAN IN BLACK, *daughter of* THE DEAD MAN *and* THE SUPERINTENDENT'S WIFE
THE COLONEL
THE MUMMY, *the Colonel's wife*
THE YOUNG LADY, *the Colonel's daughter, actually the Old Man's daughter*
BARON SKANSKORG, *engaged to The Woman in Black*
JOHANSSON, *Hummel's servant*
BENGTSSON, *the Colonel's manservant*
THE FIANCÉE, *Hummel's former fiancée, now a white-haired old woman*
THE COOK
BEGGARS
A HOUSEMAID

SCENE   Stockholm

(*The first two floors of a façade of a new house on a city square. Only the corner of the house is visible, the ground floor terminating in a round room, the second floor in a balcony with a flagpole.*

When the curtains are drawn and the windows opened in the round room, one can see a white marble statue of a young woman surrounded by palms and bathed in sunlight. On the windowsill furthest to the left are pots of hyacinths, blue, white, pink.

The Ghost Sonata by August Strindberg, translated by Evert Sprinchorn. Reprinted by permission of the translator.

Hanging on the railing of the balcony on the second story are a blue silk bedspread and two white pillowcases. The windows to the left are covered with white sheets, signifying a death in the house. It is a bright Sunday morning.

A green park bench is downstage towards the left.

Downstage to the right is a drinking fountain, with a long-handled drinking cup hanging at its side. To the left a kiosk, plastered with advertisements.

The main entrance to the house is at the right. The stairs leading up from the sidewalk to the door are of marble and the railings are of mahogany and brass. On the sidewalk on both sides of the entry way are tubs with small laurels.

The corner of the house with the round room also faces a side street which runs up stage.

On the first floor to the left of the entry way is a window with a special mirror, quite common in Sweden around the turn of the century, which enables those inside to view the passing scene without sticking their heads out the window.

At the rise of the curtain the bells of several churches can be heard ringing in the distance.

The double doors in the entry way are wide open. A WOMAN IN BLACK *stands motionless in the doorway.*

The CARETAKER'S WIFE *is sweeping the stairs and the sidewalk in front of the house. Having finished that, she polishes the brass in the entry way and then the laurels.*

Sitting in a wheelchair near the kiosk is an OLD MAN, *reading a newspaper. He has white hair and beard and is wearing glasses.*

The MILKMAID *comes in from around the corner, carrying a wire basket filled with bottles. She is wearing a summer dress, with brown shoes, black stockings and white cap. She takes off her cap and hangs it on the drinking fountain; wipes the sweat from her brow; takes a drink from the cup; washes her hands;*

[449]

arranges her hair, using the water in the foun-
tain as a mirror.

The ringing of a steamship bell is heard, and
now and then the silence is broken by the deep
notes of the organs in the nearby churches.

After a few moments of silence, and after
the MILKMAID *has finished arranging her hair,*
the STUDENT *enters from the left. He is un-*
shaven and looks as if he had not had any
sleep. He goes directly to the drinking foun-
tain.

Pause)

STUDENT   Could I borrow the cup please?
(*The* MILKMAID *hugs the cup to herself*) Aren't
you through using it? (*The* MILKMAID *stares*
at him in terror)

THE OLD MAN (*to himself*) Who on earth
is he talking to?—I don't see anyone!—Is he
crazy? (*He continues to stare at them in amaze-*
ment)

STUDENT   What are you looking at? Do I
look so awful?—Well, I haven't slept a wink
all night. I suppose you think that I've been out
doing the town . . . (*The* MILKMAID *still*
stares at him in terror) Think I've been drinking don't you?—Do I smell like it? (*the* MILK-
MAID *as before*) I haven't had a chance to
shave, I know that . . . Come on, let me have
a drink of water. After last night, I've earned it.
(*pause*) I guess I have to tell you the whole
story. I've spent the whole night bandaging
wounds and taking care of injured people. You
see, I was there when the house collapsed last
night. Well, that's it. (*The* MILKMAID *rinses*
the cup and offers him a drink of water)
Thanks! (*The* MILKMAID *does not move*)
(*slowly*) I wonder if you would do me a big
favor? (*pause*) The thing is, my eyes are inflamed, as you can see—but I've had my hands
on wounds and on corpses—so I don't want to
take the risk of using my hands to wash my
eyes . . . I was wondering if you would take
this clean handkerchief, dip it in that fresh
water, and bathe my poor eyes with it?—
Would you do that?—Will you play the Good
Samaritan for me? (*The* MILKMAID *hesitates*
for a moment before doing what she was
asked) That's very kind of you. And here's
something for your—. (*He has taken his wallet*
out and is about to offer her some money. The
MILKMAID *makes a gesture of refusal*) I'm
sorry. Forgive me. I'm still in a daze . . .

OLD MAN (*to the* STUDENT) Forgive my
speaking to you, but I could not help hearing
you say you were in on that terrible accident
yesterday evening. I was just sitting here reading about it in the paper.

STUDENT   Is it already in the paper?

OLD MAN   The whole story! And they've
got a picture of you, too. But they regret they
were unable to obtain the name of the courageous young student . . .

STUDENT (*looking at the paper*) So that's
me! What do you know!

OLD MAN   Who . . . who was that you
were talking to just now?

STUDENT   Didn't you see? (*pause*)

OLD MAN   I suppose I'm being nosey, but
would you do me the honor of giving me your
name?

STUDENT   Why do you want to know that? I
don't care for publicity. First they praise you,
then they blame you. Running people down has
been built up into one of the fine arts. Besides,
I'm not looking for any reward.

OLD MAN   Rich, I suppose?

STUDENT   Not at all! I haven't got a dime
to my name.

OLD MAN   It's strange . . . but I can't help
thinking that I've heard your voice before . . .
When I was a young man, I had a friend who
couldn't pronounce window; he always said
"winder." I've only met one person who said
that, and that was him. The other is you. Is it
possible that you are related to Arkenholz, the
wholesale dealer?

STUDENT   He was my father.

OLD MAN   Isn't fate strange? Then I have
seen you when you were a child—under very
difficult circumstances.

STUDENT   I suppose so. I understand I came
into the world right in the middle of bankruptcy
proceedings.

OLD MAN   Exactly!

STUDENT   May I ask what your name is?

OLD MAN   My name is Hummel.

STUDENT   Hummel? Then you're—. Yes, I
remember . . .

OLD MAN   And you've heard my name mentioned in your family.

STUDENT   Yes.

OLD MAN   And mentioned, perhaps, with a
certain antipathy? (*The* STUDENT *remains si-*
lent) I can well imagine! . . . No doubt you
heard that I was the man who ruined your
father . . . Everyone who is ruined by stupid
speculations realizes sooner or later that he
was actually ruined by someone he couldn't
fool. (*pause*) The truth of the matter is that
your father fleeced me of seventeen thousand
crowns, every cent I had saved up at the time.

STUDENT   It's remarkable how the same
story can be told in two exactly opposite ways.

OLD MAN   Surely you don't think I'm being
untruthful?

STUDENT What do you think? My father didn't tell lies.

OLD MAN That's true, a father never lies . . . But I too am a father, and consequently . . .

STUDENT What are you getting at?

OLD MAN I saved your father from the worst possible misery, and he repaid me with all the terrible hatred of a man obliged to be grateful. He taught his family to speak ill of me.

STUDENT Maybe you made him ungrateful. The help you gave him was probably poisoned with unnecessary humiliations.

OLD MAN My dear young man, all help is humiliating.

STUDENT What do you want of me?

OLD MAN Don't worry, I'm not asking for the money back. But if you would render me a few small services, I would consider myself well repaid. You see that I'm a cripple. Some say it's my own fault. Others blame my parents. Personally, I blame it all on life itself, with all its traps. In avoiding one you walk right into the middle of the next. Anyway, I can't run up and down stairs—can't even pull bell cords. And so I ask you: help me!

STUDENT What can I do?

OLD MAN Well, first of all you can give my chair a push so that I can read the posters. I want to see what's playing tonight.

STUDENT (*pushing the wheelchair*) Don't you have a man who takes care of you?

OLD MAN Yes, but he's off on an errand . . . Be right back . . . You a medical student?

STUDENT No, I'm studying languages. But I really don't know what I want to be.

OLD MAN Aha!—How are you at mathematics?

STUDENT Fairly good.

OLD MAN Good! Good!—Would you possibly be interested in a job?

STUDENT Sure, why not?

OLD MAN Splendid! (*reading the posters*) They're giving *Die Walküre* at the matinee . . . That means that the Colonel will be there with his daughter. And since he always sits on the aisle in the sixth row, I'll put you next to him . . . You go into that telephone booth over there and order a ticket for seat number eighty-two in the sixth row.

STUDENT You expect me to go to the opera in the middle of the day?

OLD MAN That's right! Just you do as I tell you and you won't regret it. I want to see you happy—rich and respected. Your debut last night as the courageous rescuer is the beginning of your fame. From now on, your name will be a great asset.

STUDENT (*going towards the telephone booth*) I don't know what I'm getting into. It's crazy!

OLD MAN Aren't you a gambler?

STUDENT Yes, unfortunately. I always lose.

OLD MAN This will change your luck!—Go and telephone! (*He picks up his newspaper and starts to read. In the meantime the* LADY IN BLACK *has come out on the sidewalk and is talking with the* SUPERINTENDENT'S WIFE. *The* OLD MAN *listens furtively, but the audience hears nothing. The* STUDENT *returns*) All set?

STUDENT It's all taken care of.

OLD MAN Take a look at that house.

STUDENT I already have looked at it—very carefully . . . I went by here yesterday, when the sun was glittering on the windowpanes— and dreaming of all the beauty and luxury there must be in that house—I said to my friend, "Imagine having an apartment there, four flights up, and a beautiful young wife, and two pretty kids, and twenty thousand crowns in dividends every year."

OLD MAN Did you now? Did you say that? Well, well! I too am very fond of that house . . .

STUDENT Do you speculate in houses?

OLD MAN Mmm—yes! But not in the way you think . . .

STUDENT Do you know the people who live there?

OLD MAN Every single one. At my age you know everyone, including their fathers and their grandfathers. And you always find you're related to them somehow. I've just turned eighty . . . But no one knows me, not really . . . I take a great interest in human destinies . . . (*The curtains in the round room are drawn up. The* COLONEL *is seen inside, dressed in civilian clothes. After having looked at the thermometer he moves away from the window and stands in front of the marble statue*) Look, there's the Colonel! You'll sit next to him this afternoon.

STUDENT Is that him—the Colonel? I don't understand anything that's going on. It's like a fairy tale.

OLD MAN My whole life, my dear sir, is like a book of fairy tales. But although the stories are different, one thread ties them all together and the same leitmotif recurs constantly.

STUDENT Who is that marble statue in there?

OLD MAN That's his wife, naturally . . .

STUDENT Was she so wonderful? Did he love her so much?

OLD MAN Hmm, yes . . . yes of course.

STUDENT Well, tell me!

OLD MAN Come now, you know we can't judge other people . . . Now if I were to tell you that she left him, that he beat her, that she came back again and married him again, and that she is sitting in there right now like a mummy, worshipping her own statue, you would think I was crazy.

STUDENT I can't understand it!

OLD MAN That doesn't surprise me!—And over there we have the hyacinth window. That's where his daughter lives. She's out horseback riding, but she'll be home soon . . .

STUDENT Who's the lady in black that's talking to the caretaker?

OLD MAN Well, that's a little complicated. But it's connected with the dead man upstairs there where you see the white sheets.

STUDENT And who was he?

OLD MAN A human being, like the rest of us. The most conspicuous thing about him was his vanity . . . Now if you were a Sunday child, you would soon see him come out of that very door just to look at the Consulate flag at half mast. Yes indeed, he was a Consul. Liked nothing better than coronets and lions and plumed hats and colored ribbons.

STUDENT Sunday child, did you say? I was actually born on a Sunday, so I'm told.

OLD MAN Really! Are you—! I should have guessed it. I could tell by the color of your eyes . . . But—then you can see—what others can't see, haven't you noticed that?

STUDENT I don't know what others see. But sometimes—. Well, there are some things you don't talk about!

OLD MAN I knew it, I knew it! But you can talk to me about it. I understand—things like that . . .

STUDENT Yesterday, for example . . . I was drawn to that little side street where the house collapsed afterwards . . . I walked down the street and stopped in front of a house that I had never seen before . . . Then I noticed a crack in the wall. I could hear the floor beams snapping in two. I leaped forward and grabbed up a child that was walking under the wall . . . The next moment the house collapsed . . . I escaped—but in my arms—where I thought I had the child—there wasn't anything . . .

OLD MAN Remarkable. Remarkable . . . I always knew that— . . . But tell me something: why were you making all those gestures just now at the fountain? And why were you talking to yourself?

STUDENT Didn't you see the milkmaid I was talking to?

OLD MAN (in horror) Milkmaid!?

STUDENT Yes, of course. She handed me the cup.

OLD MAN Indeed? . . . So that's the way it is?! . . . Very well, I may not have second sight, but I have other powers . . . (A white-haired woman sits down at the window with the mirror) Look at the old lady in the window! Do you see her? . . . Good, good! That was my fiancée—once upon a time—sixty years ago . . . I was twenty. Don't be afraid, she doesn't recognize me. We see each other every day, but it doesn't mean a thing to me—although we once vowed to love each other forever. Forever!

STUDENT How foolish you were in those days! Nowadays we don't tell girls things like that.

OLD MAN Forgive us, young man. We didn't know any better! . . . But can you see that that old woman was once young and beautiful?

STUDENT No, I can't. Well, maybe. I like the way she turns her head to look at things. I can't see her eyes.

(The SUPERINTENDENT'S WIFE comes out carrying a basket of chopped spruce greens, which she strews on the sidewalk, in accordance with Swedish custom at funerals)

OLD MAN Aha, the wife of the superintendent! The lady in black is her daughter by the dead man upstairs. That's why her husband got the job as superintendent . . . But the lady in black has a lover—very aristocratic and waiting to inherit a fortune. Right now he's in the process of getting a divorce—from his present wife, who is giving him a town house just to get rid of him. This aristocratic lover is the son-in-law of the dead man, and you can see his bedclothes being aired on the balcony up there.—Complicated, don't you think?

STUDENT It's damned complicated!

OLD MAN Yes indeed it is, inside and outside, although it all looks so simple.

STUDENT But then who is the dead man?

OLD MAN You just asked me and I told you. If you could look around the corner where the service entrance is, you'd see a pack of poor people whom he used to help—when he felt like it.

STUDENT Then I suppose he was a kind and charitable man?

OLD MAN Oh yes—sometimes.

STUDENT Not always?

OLD MAN No, that's how people are!—Listen, will you give me a little push over there in the sun. I'm so terribly cold. When you never get to move around, the blood congeals. I'm going to die soon, I know that. But before I do, there are a few things I want to take care of.—Feel my hand, just feel how cold I am.

STUDENT My god! It's unbelievable! (*He tries to free his hand but the* OLD MAN *holds on to it*)

OLD MAN Don't leave me, I beg you, I'm tired, I'm lonely, but it hasn't always been this way, I tell you.—I have an infinitely long life behind me—infinitely long. I've made people unhappy and people have made me unhappy, the one cancels out the other. But before I die I want to make you happy . . . Our destinies are tangled together through your father—and other things.

STUDENT Let go, let go of my hand—you are drawing all my strength from me—you're freezing me to death—what do you want of me?

OLD MAN Patience. You'll soon see and understand . . . There she comes.—

STUDENT The Colonel's daughter?

OLD MAN Yes! His daughter! Just look at her!—Have you ever seen such a masterpiece?

STUDENT She looks like the marble statue in there.

OLD MAN She should. That's her mother!

STUDENT Incredibly beautiful! "Can woman be so fair?" . . . "*Und selig, wer das gute Schicksal hat, als Bräutigam sie heimzuführen!*"

OLD MAN Yes, indeed. "Happy the man whose luck it is to bear her home to wedded bliss."—I see you appreciate her beauty. Not everyone recognizes it . . . Well, then it's ordained. (*The* YOUNG LADY *enters from the left dressed in riding habit, in the manner of a modern English amazon, and, without taking notice of anyone, crosses slowly over to the door of the house. Before entering, she stops and says a few words to the* SUPERINTENDENT'S WIFE. *The* STUDENT *covers his eyes with his hands*) Are you crying?

STUDENT When I see how far beyond my reach my happiness is, I can feel nothing but despair.

OLD MAN But I can open doors—and hearts—if only I can find an arm to do my will, Serve me, and you shall be a lord of creation!

STUDENT A devil's bargain? You want me to sell my soul?

OLD MAN Sell nothing!—Don't you understand, all my life I have *taken, taken!* Now I crave to give, to give! But nobody will take what I have to offer. I'm a rich man, very rich—and without any heirs.—Oh, yes, I have a good-for-nothing son who torments the life out of me . . . You could be my son, become my heir while I'm still alive, enjoy life while I'm here to see it—at least from a distance.

STUDENT What do you want me to do?

OLD MAN First, go and hear *Die Walküre!*

STUDENT That's already been taken care of. What else?

OLD MAN This evening you shall be sitting in there—in the round room!

STUDENT How do you expect me to get in?

OLD MAN By way of *Die Walküre!*

STUDENT Why did you pick me for your medium? Did you know me before?

OLD MAN Of course, of course! I've had my eyes on you for a long time . . . Ah! Look up there, on the balcony, where the maid is raising the flag to half mast for the Consul.—And now she's turning over the bed clothes . . . Do you see that blue quilt? It was made for two to sleep under, and now it covers only one . . . (*The* YOUNG LADY, *in a change of clothes, appears at the window to water the hyacinths*) There's my dear little girl. Look at her, just look at her! . . . She's talking to the flowers now. Isn't she herself just like a blue hyacinth? She gives them water to drink, nothing but pure water, and they transform the water into color and perfume.—Here comes the Colonel with a newspaper! . . . He's pointing out the story about the collapsed house . . . Now he's pointing to your picture! She's reading about your heroic deed.—It's starting to cloud over. Suppose it starts to rain? I'll be in a pretty mess if Johansson doesn't come back soon. (*It grows cloudy and dark. The* OLD WOMAN *at the window mirror closes her window*) I see my fiancée is closing up shop . . . Seventy-nine years . . . That window mirror is the only mirror she ever uses. That's because she can't see herself in it, only the outside world, and from two directions at once. But the world can see her. She doesn't realize that . . . All the same, not bad looking for an old woman.

(*Now the* DEAD CONSUL, *wrapped in a winding sheet, is seen coming out of the main door*)

STUDENT Oh my god, what—?

OLD MAN What do you see?

STUDENT Don't *you* see? Don't you see, in the doorway, the dead man?

OLD MAN No, I don't see anything. But I'm not surprised. Tell me exactly what—

STUDENT He's stepping out into the street . . . (*pause*) Now he's turning his head and looking up at the flag.

OLD MAN What did I tell you? Watch, he will count every wreath and read every calling card. I pity whoever is missing!

STUDENT Now he's turning the corner . . .

OLD MAN He's gone to count the poor people at the service entrance. The poor add such a nice touch: "Received the blessings of the populace!" Yes but he won't receive my blessing! —Just between us, he was a big scoundrel.

STUDENT   But benevolent.

OLD MAN   A benevolent scoundrel. Always thinking of his own magnificent funeral . . . When he could feel his end was near, he fleeced the state of fifty thousand crowns . . . Now his daughter is running around with another woman's husband and wondering about the will . . . The scoundrel can hear every word we're saying. I hope he gets an earful!— Here's Johansson. (JOHANSSON *enters from the left*) Report! (JOHANSSON *speaks to the* OLD MAN, *but the audience cannot hear what he says*) What do you mean, not at home? You're an ass!—What about the telegram?—Not a word! . . . Go on, go on! . . . Six o'clock this evening? That's good!—An extra edition? —With all the details about him? . . . Arkenholz, student . . . born . . . his parents . . . Splendid! . . . It's beginning to rain, I think . . . And what did he say? . . . really, really!—He didn't *want* to? Well, he's going to have to!—Here comes the Baron, or whatever he is!—Push me around the corner, Johansson. I want to hear what the poor people are saying. —And Arkenholz! Don't go away. Do you understand?—Well, come on, what are you waiting for!

(JOHANSSON *pushes the wheelchair around the corner. The* STUDENT *has turned to look at the* YOUNG GIRL *who is loosening the earth in the hyacinth pots. Dressed in mourning, the* BARON *enters and speaks to the* LADY IN BLACK, *who has been walking up and down the sidewalk*)

BARON   What can we do about it? We simply have to wait.

LADY IN BLACK   But I can't wait, don't you understand?

BARON   Well, if that's the way it is, you'll have to go to the country.

LADY IN BLACK   I don't want to do that!

BARON   Come over here, otherwise they'll hear what we're saying.

(*They move over towards the advertisement column and continue their conversation unheard by the audience.* JOHANSSON *enters from the right*)

JOHANSSON (*to the* STUDENT)   My master asks you not to forget that other matter . . .

STUDENT (*warily*)   Just a minute—I want to know something first. Tell me, exactly what is your employer's business?

JOHANSSON   What can I say? He's so many things, and he's been everything.

STUDENT   He's not crazy, is he?

JOHANSSON   What does it mean to be crazy? All his life he's been looking for a Sunday child. That's what he says—but he might be making it up . . .

STUDENT   What's he after? Money?

JOHANSSON   Power.—All day long he rides around in his chariot like the great god Thor . . . He keeps his eye on houses, tears them down, opens up streets, builds up city squares. But he also breaks into houses, sneaks in through the windows, ravages human lives, kills his enemies, and forgives nothing and nobody . . . Can you imagine that that little cripple was once a Don Juan. But no woman would ever stick with him.

STUDENT   Sounds inconsistent.

JOHANSSON   Oh no. You see, he was so sly that he knew how to get the women to leave when he got bored with them. But that was a long time ago. Now he's more like a horse thief at a slave market. He steals people—in more ways than one . . . He literally stole me out of the hands of the law. I made a little mistake —that's all—and he was the only one who knew about it. But instead of putting me in jail, he made me his slave. I slave for him just for my food—which isn't the best in the world.

STUDENT   What's he want to do in this house?

JOHANSSON   I wouldn't want to say! I wouldn't even know where to begin!

STUDENT   I think I'd better get out of this.

JOHANSSON   Look at the young lady! She's dropped her bracelet out of the window. (*Her bracelet has fallen off the* YOUNG LADY'S *arm and through the open window. The* STUDENT *crosses over slowly, picks up the bracelet and hands it to the* YOUNG LADY, *who thanks him stiffly. The* STUDENT *goes back to* JOHANSSON) I thought you said you were leaving. It isn't as easy as you think once he's got his net over your head . . . And he's afraid of nothing between heaven and earth.—Yes, one thing— or rather one person.

STUDENT   I bet I know.

JOHANSSON   How can you know?

STUDENT   Just guessing! Could it be . . . he's afraid of a little milkmaid?

JOHANSSON   He turns his head away whenever he sees a milkwagon . . . Sometimes he talks in his sleep. He must have been in Hamburg once . . .

STUDENT   Can I depend on him?

JOHANSSON   You can depend on him—to do anything!

STUDENT   What's he up to around the corner?

JOHANSSON Eavesdropping on the poor . . . Planting a word here and there, chipping away at one stone at a time—until the whole house falls—metaphorically speaking. Oh yes, I've had an education. And I used to be a bookseller . . . Are you leaving or staying?

STUDENT I don't like to be ungrateful. This man once saved my father, and all he's asking for now is a little favor in return.

JOHANSSON What is that?

STUDENT He wants me to go and see *Die Walküre*.

JOHANSSON That's beyond me . . . He's always got something up his sleeve . . . Look at him, he's talking to the policeman. He's always in with the police. He makes use of them, gets them involved in his business, ties them hand and foot with false promises of future possibilities. And all the while he's pumping them.—Mark my words, before the night is over he'll be received in the round room.

STUDENT What does he want in there? What's he got to do with the Colonel?

JOHANSSON I'm not sure, but I've got my ideas. You'll be able to see for yourself when you go there!

STUDENT I'll never get in there . . .

JOHANSSON That depends on you! Go to *Die Walküre*.

STUDENT Is that the way?

JOHANSSON If he said so, it is!—Look at him, just look at him! Riding his war chariot, drawn in triumph by the beggars, who don't get a cent for it, just a hint that something might come their way at his funeral!

(*The* OLD MAN *enters standing in his wheelchair, drawn by one of the* BEGGARS, *and followed by the others*)

OLD MAN Let us hail the noble youth who risked his own life to save so many in yesterday's accident! Hail Arkenholz! (*The* BEGGARS *bare their heads but do not cheer. The* YOUNG LADY, *standing in the window, waves her handkerchief. The* COLONEL *looks at the scene from his window. The* OLD WOMAN *stands up at her window. The* MAID *on the balcony raises the flag to the top*) Hail the hero, my fellow citizens! I know indeed it is Sunday, but the ass in the pit and the ear in the field absolve us. And though I may not be a Sunday child, I can see into the future and I can heal the sick. I have even brought a drowned soul back to life . . . That happened in Hamburg, yes, on a Sunday morning, just like this—. (*The* MILKMAID *enters, seen only by the* STUDENT *and the* OLD MAN. *She stretches her arms above*

her head like a drowning person and stares fixedly at the* OLD MAN. *The* OLD MAN *sits down, and shrivels up in fear and terror*) Get me out of here, Johansson! Quick!—Arkenholz, don't you forget *Die Walküre*!

STUDENT What is all this?

JOHANSSON We shall see! We shall see!

(*In the round room. At the back of the stage a stove of white glazed porcelain, its mantel decorated with a mirror, a pendulum clock, and candelabra. At the right side of the stage a hallway can be seen and through it a view of a green room with mahogany furniture. At the left of the stage stands the statue in the shadow of the palm trees, and with a curtain which can be drawn to conceal it. In the rear wall to the left of the stove is the door to the hyacinth room, where the* YOUNG LADY *is seen reading. The* COLONEL'S *back can be seen in the green room, where he is writing at his desk.*

The COLONEL'S *valet,* BENGTSSON, *wearing livery, enters from the hall, accompanied by* JOHANSSON, *who is dressed very formally as a waiter*)

BENGTSSON Now, Johansson, you'll have to wait on the table while I take care of the coats. Have you done this before?

JOHANSSON During the day I push that war chariot, as you know, but in the evenings I work as a waiter at receptions. It's always been my dream to get into this house . . . They're peculiar people, aren't they?

BENGTSSON Well, yes, I think one might say that they're a little strange.

JOHANSSON Are we going to have a musicale this evening? Or what is the occasion?

BENGTSSON Just the ordinary ghost supper, as we call it. They drink tea, without saying a word, or else the Colonel talks all by himself. And they champ their biscuits and crackers all at once and all in unison. They sound like a pack of rats in the attic.

JOHANSSON Why do you call it the ghost dinner?

BENGTSSON They look like ghosts . . . This has been going on for twenty years—always the same people, always saying the same things. Or else keeping silent to avoid being embarrassed.

JOHANSSON Where's the lady of the house? Isn't she around?

BENGTSSON Oh, yes. But she's crazy. She keeps herself shut up in a closet because her eyes can't stand the light. She's sitting in there right now. (*He points to a papered door in the wall*)

JOHANSSON In there?

BENGTSSON　I told you they were a little peculiar.

JOHANSSON　What on earth does she look like?

BENGTSSON　Like a mummy. Do you want to see her? (*He opens the paper door*) There she sits!

JOHANSSON　Je-sus!

THE MUMMY (*babbling*)　Why do you open the door? Didn't I tell you to keep it closed?

BENGTSSON (*as if talking to a baby*)　Ta, ta, ta, ta, ta!— Is little chickadee going to be nice to me? Then little chickadee will get something good!—Pretty polly!

THE MUMMY (*like a parrot*)　Pretty polly! Are you there Jacob? Jacob? Currrrr!

BENGTSSON　She thinks she's a parrot—and maybe she is. (*to the* MUMMY) Come on polly, whistle for us!

(*The* MUMMY *whistles*)

JOHANSSON　I thought I had seen it all, but this tops everything.

BENGTSSON　Well, when a house grows old, it turns moldy and rotten, and when people are together too much and torment each other, they go crazy. Take the lady in this house— shut up Polly!—this mummy has been sitting here for forty years—the same husband, same furniture, same relatives, same friends . . . (*closing the paper door on the* MUMMY) And imagine what's gone on in this house! Even I don't know the whole story . . . Look at this statue. That's the lady of the house as a young girl.

JOHANSSON　Oh my god!—Is that the mummy?

BENGTSSON　Yes. It's enough to make one cry. But this lady—carried away by her imagination or something—has acquired certain of the peculiarities of the prating parrot. She can't stand cripples, for instance—or sick people. She can't even stand the sight of her own daughter because she's sick.

JOHANSSON　Is that young girl sick?

BENGTSSON　Yes. Didn't you know?

JOHANSSON　No . . . What about the Colonel? Who is he?

BENGTSSON　Wait a while and you'll see!

JOHANSSON (*looking at the statue*)　It's terrifying to realize that—. How old is the lady now?

BENGTSSON　Who knows? But I've heard it said that when she was thirty-five she looked like she was nineteen.—And she convinced the Colonel that she was . . . here in this house . . . Do you know what that black Japanese screen by the couch is for? It's called a death screen, and when somebody's going to die, it's placed around them, same as in a hospital.

JOHANSSON　What a horrible house . . . That poor student looked upon entering this house as entering paradise.

BENGTSSON　Which student? Oh yes, of course! The one that's coming here tonight. The Colonel and his daughter met him at the opera and were captivated by him . . . Hm . . . But let me ask you a couple of questions. Who's your master? The financier in the wheelchair?

JOHANSSON (*nodding*)　Yes, that's right. Is he coming here too?

BENGTSSON　He's not invited.

JOHANSSON　He'll come uninvited—if necessary!

(*The* OLD MAN *appears in the hallway, dressed in frock coat and high hat. He moves silently forward on his crutches, like a black spider, and eavesdrops on the servants*)

BENGTSSON　I'll bet he's a real old mean one.

JOHANSSON　A perfect specimen!

BENGTSSON　He looks like the devil incarnate!

JOHANSSON　And he's a black magician, I tell you. He can go through locked doors—.

OLD MAN (*coming forward and grabbing* JOHANSSON *by the ear*)　Fool! Hold your tongue! (*to* BENGTSSON) Announce me to the Colonel!

BENGTSSON　But we're expecting company here.

OLD MAN　I know you are! My visit is not unexpected—although undesired.

BENGTSSON　I see. What was the name? Mr. Hummel?

OLD MAN　That's right! Precisely!

(BENGTSSON *goes down the hall into the green room and closes the door*)

OLD MAN (*to* JOHANSSON)　Disappear! (JOHANSSON *hesitates*) Vanish! (JOHANSSON *vanishes down the hall. The* OLD MAN *inspects the room; stops in front of the statue. Much amazed:*) Amelia! . . . It is she! . . . Amelia!

(*He roams about the room fingering objects. Stops in front of a mirror to adjust his wig. Returns to the statue*)

THE MUMMY (*from within the closet*) Pretty polly!

OLD MAN (*startled*)　What on earth—! Sounded like a parrot in the room. But I don't see any.

THE MUMMY　You there Jacob?

OLD MAN Place is haunted.

THE MUMMY Jacob!

OLD MAN It's enough to frighten one! . . . So that's the kind of secrets they've been keeping in this house! (*With his back to the closet, he studies a portrait on the wall*) There he is! —The old Colonel himself!

THE MUMMY (*coming out of the closet, goes up to the* OLD MAN *from behind and gives his wig a pull*) Currrr—ee! Are you curr—ee?

OLD MAN (*frightened out of his skin*) Oh my god in heaven!—Who are you?

THE MUMMY (*speaking in her normal voice*) Is that you, Jacob?

OLD MAN Yes. My name is Jacob.

THE MUMMY (*with emotion*) And my name is Amelia!

OLD MAN Oh no . . . No, no . . . Oh my god . . .

THE MUMMY Yes, this is how I look!—And that's how I did look—once upon a time. Life gives one a great education. Most of my life I've spent in the closet, so that I won't have to see—or be seen . . . But you, Jacob, what are you looking for here?

OLD MAN My child! Our child.

THE MUMMY She's sitting in there.

OLD MAN Where?

THE MUMMY In there, in the hyacinth room.

OLD MAN (*looking at the* YOUNG LADY) Yes, there she is! (*pause*) And what does her father think of her—I mean, the Colonel— your husband?

THE MUMMY I had a quarrel with him once, and told him everything . . .

OLD MAN And . . . ?

THE MUMMY He didn't believe me. He said, "That's what all women say when they want to kill their husbands." . . . All the same it was a terrible crime. His whole life has been falsified, including his family tree. When I look at his family record in the peerage, I say to myself she's no better than a runaway servant girl with a false birth certificate. And girls like that are sent to the reformatory.

OLD MAN A lot of people forge birth certificates. I seem to remember that even you falsified the date of your birth.

THE MUMMY It was my mother who put me up to it. I'm not to blame for that! . . . And furthermore, you played the biggest part in our crime.

OLD MAN Not true! Your husband started it all when he stole my fiancée from me!— From my very birth I've found it impossible to forgive until I have punished. I've always looked upon it as an imperative duty. I still do!

THE MUMMY What do you expect to find in this house? What do you want here? And how did you get in?—Does your business concern my daughter? Keep your hands off her, I warn you, or you'll die!

OLD MAN I wish her nothing but the best!

THE MUMMY And you must have consideration for her father, too!

OLD MAN Never!

THE MUMMY Then you must die. In this room. Behind that screen.

OLD MAN Be that as it may. But I'm a bulldog. I never let go.

THE MUMMY You want to marry her to that student. Why? He is nothing, and he has nothing.

OLD MAN He'll be a rich man, thanks to me.

THE MUMMY Are you one of the invited guests tonight?

OLD MAN No, but I've decided to invite myself to this ghost supper!

THE MUMMY Do you know who'll be here?

OLD MAN Not entirely.

THE MUMMY The Baron—who lives upstairs, and whose father-in-law was buried this afternoon—.

OLD MAN Yes, the Baron—who is getting a divorce in order to marry the daughter of the superintendent's wife. The Baron—who was once—your lover!

THE MUMMY And then there'll be your former fiancée—whom my husband seduced . . .

OLD MAN A very select gathering . . .

THE MUMMY Oh god, why can't we die? If only we could die!

OLD MAN Then why do you keep seeing each other?

THE MUMMY Our crimes and our secrets and our guilt bind us together! We have split up and gone our separate ways an infinite number of times. But we're always drawn back together again . . .

OLD MAN I believe the Colonel is coming.

THE MUMMY Then I'll go in to Adele . . . (*pause*) Jacob, don't do anything foolish! Be considerate towards him . . . (*a pause. She leaves*)

COLONEL (*enters, cold and reserved*) Please sit down. (*The* OLD MAN *takes his time seating himself. A pause. The* COLONEL *stares at him*) Did you write this letter?

OLD MAN I did.

COLONEL And your name is Hummel?

OLD MAN It is. (*pause*)

COLONEL Since it's clear that you have

bought up all my outstanding promissory notes, it follows that I'm completely at your mercy. Now, what do you want?

OLD MAN   I want to be paid—in one way or another.

COLONEL   In what way?

OLD MAN   A very simple way. Don't let's talk about money. Allow me to come and go in your house—as a guest.

COLONEL   If that's all it takes to satisfy you—.

OLD MAN   Thank you!

COLONEL   And what else?

OLD MAN   Dismiss Bengtsson!

COLONEL   Why? Bengtsson is my devoted servant. He's been with me during my whole career. The army awarded him a medal for faithful service. Why should I dismiss him?

OLD MAN   I have no doubt he's a very fine man in your eyes. But he's not the man he seems to be!

COLONEL   Who is?

OLD MAN   (*taken aback*)   True!— But Bengtsson must go!

COLONEL   Are you going to give orders in my house?

OLD MAN   Yes! Since I own everything that you can lay your eyes on—furniture, curtains, dinner service, linen . . . and other things . . .

COLONEL   What other things?

OLD MAN   Everything. I own it all. Everything that you see is mine!

COLONEL   I can't argue that. But my family honor, my coat of arms and my good name are things you cannot take from me!

OLD MAN   Yes, I can. They don't belong to you. (*pause*) You are not a nobleman.

COLONEL   I shall give you the opportunity of withdrawing those words!

OLD MAN   (*producing a piece of paper*)   If you will take the trouble of reading this extract from the standard book of genealogy, you will see that the family whose name you have assumed has been extinct for over a century.

COLONEL   (*reading*)   Of course I've heard rumors like this before. But it was my father's name before it was mine . . . (*reading on*) I can't deny it. You are quite right . . . I am not a nobleman! Not even that . . . Therefore I shall take this signet ring off my hand— Oh, but of course, excuse me. It belongs to you. There you are.

OLD MAN   (*putting the ring in his pocket*) Let us continue.—You are not a colonel either!

COLONEL   Am I not?

OLD MAN   No! You held a temporary commission as a colonel in the American Volunteers. But at the end of the Spanish-American War

and the reorganization of the Army, all such titles were abolished.

COLONEL   Is that true?

OLD MAN   (*reaching into his pocket*)   Do you want to see for yourself?

COLONEL   No, that won't be necessary . . . Who are you? What gives you the right to sit there and strip me naked in this way?

OLD MAN   Patience, my good man! And as far as stripping is concerned—do you really want to know who you are?

COLONEL   Have you no decency?

OLD MAN   Take off that wig of yours and have a look at yourself in the mirror. And while you're at it, take out those false teeth and shave off that moustache and let Bengtsson unlace your metal corset. And then we shall see if a certain valet, Mr. X, won't recognize himself—a valet in a certain house who flirted with the maids in order to scrounge in the kitchen. (*The* COLONEL *reaches for the bell on the table. The* OLD MAN *stops him, saying:*) I wouldn't touch that if I were you. If you call Bengtsson, I'll order him arrested . . . I believe your guests are arriving. Now let us be calm, and go on playing our old roles for a while longer.

COLONEL   Who are you? I've seen your eyes and heard your voice before.

OLD MAN   Never mind that. Be silent and do as you're told!

STUDENT   (*enters and bows to the* COLONEL) How do you do sir!

COLONEL   Welcome to my house, young man! Your heroism at that terrible accident has brought your name to everybody's lips. I deem it an honor to receive you in my home.

STUDENT   You're very kind, sir. It's a great honor for me, sir. I never expected—well, my humble birth—and your illustrious name and your noble birth . . .

COLONEL   Mr. Hummel, may I introduce Mr. Arkenholz, who is a student at the university. The ladies are in there, Mr. Arkenholz— if you care to join them. I have a few more things I wanted to say to Mr. Hummel. (*The* COLONEL *shows the* STUDENT *in to the hyacinth room where he remains visible to the audience, engaged in shy conversation with the* YOUNG LADY) An excellent young man—musical, sings, writes poetry . . . If it weren't for his birth and social position I certainly wouldn't have anything against—my . . .

OLD MAN   Against what?

COLONEL   Having my daughter—

OLD MAN   *Your* daughter! . . . Apropos of her, why does she always sit in that room?

COLONEL   She feels she has to sit in the

hyacinth room, whenever she's in the house. A peculiarity of hers . . . Here comes Miss Beatrice von Holsteinkrona. Charming woman. Very active in the church and with an income that suits her position and circumstances perfectly . . .

OLD MAN (*to himself*) My fiancée!

(*The* FIANCÉE *enters, white-haired and giving every appearance of being crazy*)

COLONEL Miss Holsteinkrona—Mr. Hummel. (*The* FIANCÉE *curtsies and takes a seat. The* BARON *enters next—dressed in mourning and with a strange look on his face—and sits down*) Baron Skanskorg—.

OLD MAN (*in an aside, without rising*) I'm sure that's the jewel thief. (*to the* COLONEL) Now let the mummy in, and the party can begin.

COLONEL (*in the doorway to the hyacinth room*) Polly!

THE MUMMY (*enters*) Currr—ee!

COLONEL Shall we invite the young people, too?

OLD MAN No! Not the young people! They shall be spared.

(*They seat themselves in a circle. Silence*)

COLONEL Shall I ring for the tea?

OLD MAN Why bother? No one cares for tea. Why play games? (*pause*)

COLONEL Then perhaps we should start a conversation?

OLD MAN (*slowly, deliberately and with frequent pauses*) About the weather? Which we know. Ask each other how we're feeling? Which we also know. I prefer silence . . . in which one can hear thoughts and see the past. Silence cannot hide anything—which is more than you can say for words. I read the other day that the difference in languages originated among the primitive savages who sought to keep their secrets from the other tribes. Languages are therefore codes, and he who finds the key can understand all the languages of the world. But that doesn't mean that secrets cannot be discovered without a key. Especially in those cases where paternity must be proved. Legal proof is of course a different matter. Two suborned witnesses provide complete proof of whatever they agree to say. But in the kind of escapades I have in mind one doesn't take witnesses along. Nature herself has planted in man a blushing sense of shame, which seeks to hide what should be hidden. But we slip into certain situations without intending to, and chance confronts us with moments of revelation, when the deepest secrets are revealed, when the mask is ripped from the im-

poster and the villain stands exposed . . . (*Pause. All look at each other in silence*) Extraordinary, how silent you all are! (*long silence*) All of us sitting here, we know who we are, don't we? . . . I don't have to tell you . . . And you know me although you pretend ignorance . . . Sitting in that room is my daughter—yes mine, you know that too . . . She had lost all desire to live, without knowing why . . . She was withering away because of the air in this house which reeks of crime, deception, and deceits of every kind . . . That is why I had to find a friend for her, a friend from whose very presence she would apprehend the warmth and light radiated by a noble deed . . . (*long silence*) That was my mission in this house. To pull up the weeds, to expose the crimes, to settle the accounts, so that these young people might make a new beginning in this home, which is my gift to them! (*long silence*) Now I'm going to grant safe conduct to each and every one of you in due turn. Whoever stays, I shall order him arrested! (*long silence*) Listen to the ticking of the clock, like a death-watch beetle in the wall! Listen to what it's saying: "Time's-up, time's-up!" . . . When it strikes—in just a few moments *your* time is up. Then you may go— not before. But the clock raises its arm before it strikes.—(*The clock can be heard preparing to strike the hour*) Listen! It's warning you: "Clocks can strike!"—And I can strike too! (*He strikes the table with his crutch*) Do you understand? (*silence*)

THE MUMMY (*goes over to the clock and stops its pendulum; in her normal voice, speaking seriously:*) But I can stop time in its course. I can wipe out the past, and undo what is done. Not with bribes, not with threats— but through suffering and repentance. (*approaching the* OLD MAN) We are poor miserable creatures, we know that. We have erred, we have transgressed, we, like all the rest. We are not what we seem to be. At bottom we are better than ourselves, since we abhor and detest our misdeeds. But when you, Jacob Hummel, with your false name, come here to sit in judgment over us, that proves that you are more contemptible than we! And you are not the one you seem to be! You are a slave trader, a stealer of souls! You once stole me with false promises. You murdered the Consul who was buried today; you strangled him with debts. You have stolen the student and shackled him with an imaginary debt of his father's, who never owed you a penny. . . . (*The* OLD MAN *has tried to rise and speak but has collapsed in his chair and shriveled up, and, like a dying insect, he shrivels up more and more during the following dialogue*) But there is one dark spot in your life, which I'm not sure about—although I have my suspicions. . . . I think that Bengtsson might help us. (*She rings the bell on the table*)

OLD MAN   No! Not Bengtsson! Not him!

THE MUMMY   Then it is true! He does know! (*She rings again. The little* MILKMAID *appears in the door to the hall, unseen by all except the* OLD MAN, *who shies in terror. The* MILK-MAID *disappears when* BENGTSSON *enters*) Bengtsson, do you know this man?

BENGTSSON   Yes, I know him and he knows me. Life has its ups and downs, as we all know, and I have been in his service, and once he was in mine. To be exact, he was a sponger in my kitchen for two whole years. Since he had to be out of the house by three o'clock, dinner had to be ready at two, and those in the house had to eat the warmed-up food left by that ox. Even worse, he drank up the pure soup stock and the gravy, which then had to be diluted with water. He sat there like a vampire, sucking all the marrow out of the house, and turned us all into skeletons. And he nearly succeeded in putting us into prison, when we accused the cook of being a thief . . . Later I met this man in Hamburg under another name. He had become a usurer or blood-sucker. And it was there that he was accused of having lured a young girl out onto the ice in order to drown her, since she was the only witness to a crime which he was afraid would come to light . . .

THE MUMMY (*passes her hand over the* OLD MAN's *face*)   That is the real you! Now empty your pockets of the notes and the will!

(JOHANSSON *appears in the door to the hall and watches the* OLD MAN *with great interest, knowing that his slavery is coming to an end. The* OLD MAN *produces a bundle of papers which he throws on the table*)

THE MUMMY (*stroking the* OLD MAN's *back*) Pretty bird! Where's Jacob!

OLD MAN (*like a parrot*)   Jacob's here!— (*crows like a rooster*)

THE MUMMY   Can clocks strike?

OLD MAN (*making clucking sounds*)   Clocks can strike! (*He imitates a cuckoo clock*) Coo-coo! Coo-coo! Coo-coo!

THE MUMMY (*opening the paper door to the closet*)   Now the clock has struck! Stand up, and enter the closet where I have sat for twenty years, crying over our misdeeds. You'll find a rope in there, which can represent the one you strangled the Consul with, and with

which you intended to strangle your benefactor . . . Go in! (*The* OLD MAN *goes into the closet. The* MUMMY *closes the door*) Bengtsson! Put up the screen! The death screen!

(BENGTSSON *places the screen in front of the door*)

ALL   Amen!

(*Long silence. In the hyacinth room the* YOUNG LADY *can be seen sitting at a harp on which she accompanies the* STUDENT. *After a prelude played by the* YOUNG LADY, *the* STUDENT *recites:*)

STUDENT

> I saw the sun
> And from its blaze
> There burst on me
> The deepest truth:
>
> Man reaps as he sows;
> Blessed is he
> Who sows the good.
>
> For deeds done in anger
> Kindness alone
> Can make amends.
>
> Bring cheer to those
> Whom you have hurt,
> And kindness reaps
> Its own rewards.
>
> The pure in heart
> Have none to fear.
> The harmless are happy
> The guileless are good.

(*A room decorated in a bizarre style, predominantly oriental. A profusion of hyacinths in all colors fills the room. On the porcelain tiled stove sits a large Buddha with a bulb of a shallot (allium ascalonicum) in its lap. The stem of the shallot rises from this bulb and bursts into a spherical cluster of white, star-like flowers. In the rear to the right a door leads to the round room. The* COLONEL *and the* MUMMY *can be seen in there sitting motionless and silent. A part of the death screen is also visible. To the left in the rear a door to the pantry and the kitchen. The* STUDENT *and the* YOUNG LADY [Adele] *are near a table, she seated at her harp, he standing beside her*)

YOUNG LADY   Now you must sing a song to my flowers!

STUDENT   Is this the flower of your soul?

YOUNG LADY   The one and only! Don't you love the hyacinth?

STUDENT   I love it above all other flowers—with its stem rising straight and slender like a young maiden from the round bulb, floating on water and reaching its white rare roots down into the clear colorless nothingness. I love it for its colors—the snow white, innocent and pure—the golden yellow, sweet as honey—the shy pink, the ripe red—but above all the blue ones—blue as morning mist, deep-eyed blue, ever faithful blue. I love them all—more than gold and pearls. Have loved them ever since I was a child, have worshipped them because they possess all the virtues I lack . . . But still—

YOUNG LADY　What?

STUDENT　My love is not returned. These beautiful blossoms hate and detest me.

YOUNG LADY　How?

STUDENT　Their fragrance—as strong and clear as the first winds of spring, sweeping down from the fields of melting snow—confuse my senses—they deafen me, blind me, drive me out of my mind—impale me with their poisonous arrows that stab my heart and set fire to my head! . . . Don't you know the legend of that flower?

YOUNG LADY　No. Tell me.

STUDENT　First I must tell you what it means as a symbol. The bulb is the earth, whether floating on water or buried deep in black humus. Here the stalk shoots up, straight as the axis of the world, and here at its upper end are gathered together the six-pointed flowers.

YOUNG LADY　Above the earth, the stars! That's sublime! How did you understand that? Where did you find that out?

STUDENT　I don't know. Let me think!—In your eyes! . . . So you see, it's an image of the whole cosmos. That's why Buddha sits there with the bulb, of the earth, watching it constantly in order to see it shoot up and burst forth and be transformed into a heaven. This poor earth shall become a heaven! That is what Buddha is waiting for!

YOUNG LADY　Of course. I see that.—And don't the snowflakes have six points like the hyacinth?

STUDENT　Exactly! Then snowflakes are falling stars—

YOUNG LADY　And the snowdrop is a star of snow—growing out of the snow.

STUDENT　And Sirius, the largest and most beautiful of all the stars in the firmament, golden-red Sirius is the narcissus with its golden-red chalice and its six white rays—.

YOUNG LADY　Have you seen the shalot burst into bloom?

STUDENT　Yes, of course I have! It hides its blossoms in a ball—a globe just like the celestial globe, strewn with white stars.

YOUNG LADY　Heavenly! Wonderful! What inspired that thought?

STUDENT　You did!

YOUNG LADY　You did!

STUDENT　We did! We have given birth to something together. We are wedded . . .

YOUNG LADY　No, not yet . . .

STUDENT　Why not? What else?

YOUNG LADY　Time—testing—patience.

STUDENT　Very well! Put me to the test! (*pause*) So silent? . . . Why do your parents sit in there, silent, without saying a single word?

YOUNG LADY　Because they have nothing to say to each other. Because they don't believe what the other says. My father explains it this way: "What good does talking do, we can't fool each other anyway."

STUDENT　It makes me sick to hear things like that . . .

YOUNG LADY　The cook is coming this way . . . Look at her, how big and fat she is . . .

STUDENT　What does she want?

YOUNG LADY　She wants to ask me about dinner. I've been managing the house during my mother's illness.

STUDENT　What have we got to do with the kitchen?

YOUNG LADY　We have to eat, don't we? . . . Just look at her! I can't stand the sight of that cook.

STUDENT　Who is that bloated monster?

YOUNG LADY　She belongs to the Hummel family of vampires. She's eating us up . . .

STUDENT　Why don't you fire her?

YOUNG LADY　She won't leave! We can't control her. We got her because of our sins . . . Don't you see that we're wasting away, withering?

STUDENT　Don't you get enough food to eat?

YOUNG LADY　We get course after course, but all the strength is gone from the food. She boils the beef until there's nothing left of it, and serves us the sinews swimming in water, while she herself drinks stock. And when we have a roast, she cooks all the juice out of it and drinks it and eats the gravy. Everything she touches loses its flavor. It's as if she sucked it up with her very eyes. We get the grounds when she has finished her coffee. She drinks the wine and fills up the bottles with water.

STUDENT　Get rid of her!

YOUNG LADY　We can't!

STUDENT　Why not?

YOUNG LADY　We don't know! She won't leave! No one can control her . . . She has taken all our strength from us.

STUDENT   Let me get rid of her for you.

YOUNG LADY   Oh, no! I guess this is how things are supposed to be . . . And now here she is! She'll ask me what we're having for dinner—I'll tell her this and that—she'll make objections—and finally we'll have what she says.

STUDENT   Then let her decide in the first place!

YOUNG LADY   She won't do that.

STUDENT   What a strange house! It's haunted, isn't it?

YOUNG LADY   Yes.—She's turning back now. She saw you!

COOK   (*in the doorway*)   Hah, that ain't why! (*grinning so that all her teeth show*)

STUDENT   Get out!

COOK   When I feel like it, I will! (*pause*) Now I feel like it! (*She vanishes*)

YOUNG LADY   Don't lose your temper. Learn to be patient. She's part of the trials and tribulations we have to go through in this home. And we've got a housemaid, too! Whom we have to clean up after!

STUDENT   I can feel myself sinking into the earth!—*Cor in aethere!*—Let's have music!

YOUNG LADY   Wait!

STUDENT   No. Music now!

YOUNG LADY   Patience! This room is called the testing room. It's beautiful to look at, but it's full of imperfections.

STUDENT   I don't believe it. But if it's true, we'll just have to ignore them. It's beautiful, but a little cold. Why don't you start a fire?

YOUNG LADY   Because it smokes up the room.

STUDENT   Can't you have the chimney cleaned?

YOUNG LADY   It doesn't help! . . . Do you see that writing table?

STUDENT   It's extraordinarily handsome!

YOUNG LADY   But it wobbles. Every day I lay a peice of cork under that foot, but the housemaid takes it away when she sweeps, and I have to cut a new piece. The penholder is covered with ink every morning, and so is the inkstand, and I have to clean them up after her, as regularly as the sun goes up. (*pause*) What do you hate most to do?

STUDENT   To count the laundry! (*grimaces in disgust*)

YOUNG LADY   That's what I have to do! (*grimacing in disgust*)

STUDENT   What else?

YOUNG LADY   To be awakened in the middle of the night, to have to get up and close the banging window—which the housemaid forgot to close.

STUDENT   Go on.

YOUNG LADY   To climb up on a ladder and fix the damper on the stovepipe after the maid broke off the cord.

STUDENT   Go on.

YOUNG LADY   To sweep up after her, to dust after her, and to start the fire in the stove after her—all she does is throw on some wood! To adjust the damper, to dry the glasses, to set the table *over* and *over* again, to pull the corks out of the bottles, to open the windows and air the rooms, to make and remake my bed, to rinse the water bottle when it's green with sediment, to buy matches and soap, which we're always out of, to wipe the chimneys and trim the wicks to keep the lamps from smoking, and to keep the lamps from going out I have to fill them myself when we have company . . .

STUDENT   Let's have music!

YOUNG LADY   You have to wait!—First comes the drudgery, the drudgery of keeping oneself above the dirt of life.

STUDENT   But you're well off. You've got two servants!

YOUNG LADY   Doesn't make any difference! Even if we had three! Living is such a nuisance, and I get so tired at times . . . Imagine, if on top of it all one had a nursery and a baby crib.

STUDENT   The dearest of joys!

YOUNG LADY   The dearest in more ways than one . . . Is life really worth so much trouble?

STUDENT   I suppose that depends on the reward you expect for all your troubles . . . There's nothing I wouldn't do to win your hand.

YOUNG LADY   Don't say that! You can never have me!

STUDENT   Why not?

YOUNG LADY   You mustn't ask. (*pause*)

STUDENT   You dropped your bracelet out of the window . . .

YOUNG LADY   Because my hand has grown so thin. (*Pause. The* COOK *appears with a Japanese bottle in her hand*) She's the one who's eating me—and all the rest of us.

STUDENT   What is she holding in her hand?

YOUNG LADY   It's a bottle of coloring matter. It's got letters on it that look like scorpions. It's filled with soya sauce—which takes the place of gravy, which is transformed into soup, which serves as a stock for cooking cabbage on, which is used to make mock turtle soup out of!

STUDENT   Get out!

COOK   You suck the sap from us, and we from you. We take the blood and give you back water—with coloring added. This is the coloring!—I'm leaving now, but that doesn't mean I haven't stayed as long as I wanted to. (*She leaves*)

STUDENT Why was Bengtsson given a medal?

YOUNG LADY Because of his great merits.

STUDENT Has he no faults?

YOUNG LADY Yes, many great ones. But you don't get medals for them.

(*They smile at each other*)

STUDENT You have a great many secrets in this house.

YOUNG LADY As in all houses. Permit us to keep ours. (*pause*)

STUDENT Do you admire frankness?

YOUNG LADY Yes, within moderation.

STUDENT Sometimes there comes over me a crazy desire to say everything I'm thinking. But I know the world would collapse completely if one were completely honest. (*pause*) I went to a funeral the other day . . . In church . . . Very solemn, very beautiful.

YOUNG LADY Mr. Hummel's funeral?

STUDENT Yes, my false benefactor's. At the head of the coffin stood an old friend of the deceased. He carried the mace. The priest impressed me especially, his dignified manner and his moving words. I cried. We all cried. And afterwards we went to a restaurant . . . And there I learned that the mace-bearer had been the lover of the dead man's son. (*The* YOUNG LADY *stares at him, trying to understand him*) And that the dead man had borrowed money from his son's admirer . . . (*pause*) The day after that, they arrested the priest for embezzling church funds! It's a pretty story, isn't it? (*The* YOUNG LADY *turns her head away in disgust. Pause*) Do you know what I think of you now?

YOUNG LADY You must not tell me or I'll die!

STUDENT But I must or else I'll die!

YOUNG LADY In an asylum you can say whatever you feel like.

STUDENT Exactly right! That's where my father ended up—in a madhouse.

YOUNG LADY Was he ill?

STUDENT No, he was quite healthy. But he was crazy! It just came over him. This is how it happened. Like all of us, he had his circle of acquaintances, whom for convenience's sake he called his friends. Of course they were a pretty sorry bunch of good-for-nothings—like most people. But he had to have some acquaintances, he couldn't just sit alone. Now, one doesn't tell a person what one really thinks of him, not in ordinary conversation anyway—and my father didn't either. He knew how false they

were. He saw through their deceitfulness right to the bottom of their souls. But he was an intelligent man, brought up to behave properly, and so he was always polite. But one day he held a big party. It was in the evening, he was tired after a day's work, and under the strain of forcing himself to hold his tongue half the time and of talking nonsense with his guests the other half—(*The* YOUNG LADY *shudders in fear*) Well, whatever the reason, at the dinner table he rapped for silence, raised his glass, and began to make a speech . . . Then something loosed the trigger, and in a long oration he stripped naked every single person there, one after another. Told them of all their deceits. And at the end, exhausted he sat right down in the middle of the table and told them all to go to hell! (*The* YOUNG LADY *moans*) I was there and heard it all, and I shall never forget what happened afterwards . . . Father and Mother began to fight, the guests rushed for the door—and my father was taken off to the madhouse where he died! (*pause*) If you keep silent too long, the stagnant water accumulates and everything begins to rot. That's what's happening in this house too. There is something rotting here. And I thought it was paradise when I saw you come in here for the first time . . . It was a Sunday morning, and I stood looking into these rooms. I saw a colonel who wasn't a colonel. I had a magnanimous benefactor who turned out to be a bandit and had to hang himself. I saw a mummy who wasn't one, and a maiden who—. Speaking of which, where can one find virginity? Where is beauty to be found? In nature, and my mind when it's dressed in its Sunday clothes. Where do honor and faith exist? In fairy tales and children's games! Where can you find anything that fulfills its promise? Only in the imagination! . . . Now your flowers have poisoned me, and I have passed the poison back. I begged you to become my wife in my home. We played and sang. We created poetry together. And then came the cook . . . *Sursum corda*! Try just once again to pluck fire and brightness from the golden harp! Please try! I beg you, I implore you on my knees! . . . Very well. Then I shall do it myself. (*He takes the harp but no sound comes from the strings*) It is silent and deaf. Tell me, why are beautiful flowers so poisonous, and the most beautiful the most deadly? Why? The whole of creation, all of life, is cursed and damned . . . Why would you not become my bride? Because you are sick, infected at the very core of life . . . Now I can feel that vampire in the kitchen beginning to suck the blood from me. She must be one of those lamias that suck the blood of newborn babes. It's always in the kitchen that the children are nipped in the bud. And if not there, then in the bedroom . . . There are poisons that seel the eyes and poisons that open them. I must have been born with the latter kind in my veins, because I cannot see what is ugly as beautiful and I cannot call what is evil good. I cannot. They say that Christ harrowed hell. What they really meant was that he descended to earth, to this penal colony, to this madhouse and morgue of a world. And the inmates crucified Him when He tried to free them. But the robber they let free. Robbers always win sympathy . . . Woe! Woe to all of us! Saviour of the World, save us! We are perishing!

(*The* YOUNG LADY *has collapsed more and more during this speech. She is obviously dying. She rings the bell.* BENGTSSON *enters*)

YOUNG LADY   Bring the screen. Quickly! I'm dying.

(BENGTSSON *returns with the screen, opens it, and places it in front of the* YOUNG LADY)

THE STUDENT   Your liberator is coming! Welcome, pale and gentle one . . . And you, you beautiful, innocent, lost soul, who suffered for no fault of your own, sleep, sleep a dreamless sleep. And when you wake again . . . may you be greeted by a sun that doesn't scorch, in a home without dust, by friends without faults, and by a love without flaw . . . Buddha, wise and gentle Buddha, sitting there waiting for a heaven to grow out of the earth, grant us the purity of will and the patience to endure our trials, that your hopes will not come to nought. (*The harp strings begin to move and hum. Pure white light pours into the room*)

> I saw the sun
> And from its blaze
> There burst on me
> The deepest truth:
>
> Man reaps as he sows;
> Blessed is he
> Who sows the good.
>
> For deeds done in anger
> Kindness alone
> Can make amends.
>
> Bring cheer to those
> Whom you have hurt,
> And kindness reaps
> Its own rewards.
>
> The pure in heart
> Have none to fear.
> The harmless are happy.
> The guileless are good.

(*A moaning is heard from behind the screen*) You poor little child! Child of this world of illusion and guilt and suffering and death— this world of eternal change and disappointment and never-ending pain! May the Lord of Heaven have mercy on you as you journey forth . . .

(*The room vanishes. In the distance Boecklin's The Island of the Dead appears. Music—soft, pleasant, melancholy—is heard coming from the island*)

RUSSIA

ANTON CHEKHOV (1860–1904), more than any other dramatist of the late nineteenth and early twentieth centuries, was very conscious of the existential loneliness of the human condition. In fact, the central theme of all his plays is estrangement. He was conscious of man's helplessness before the overpowering forces of circumstance; he was aware of man's littleness, his insignificance in a gigantic and impersonal universe; he knew that no matter how closely men huddled together, they could never really communicate. In short, he knew the utter impossibility of finding an answer to the question he asks in each of his plays: "What can I do?"

But this is not the whole story. If it were, Chekhov's plays would be little more than unrelieved pictures of gloom, and this we know they are not. This is so because Chekhov, in spite of his realization that man was alone and doomed to failure in all of his attempts to find meaningful relationship and meaningful action, never abdicated his sense of responsibility for human life. Even though Chekhov knew there were no solutions, all his life he sought to find an answer, and his plays are a record of that quest.

In all of his plays we are aware of Chekhov's regard for a certain nobility in the attempts by his characters to alter or overcome their pathetic destinies. Goethe once wrote: "It occurs to me that the hope of persisting, even after fate would seem to have led us back into a state of nonexistence, is the noblest of our sentiments." And this is the quality that informs Chekhov's characters. In all of them we are aware that there is a great disparity between the facts of their animal existence and the aspiring ideals by which they attempt to live. But Chekhov accepted both; he saw the life of a man as the meaningful and at the same time pathetic, ludicrous, and tragic attempt to bridge this gap. This conflict is seen in his characters, who embody both a terrible earnestness of purpose and

[ANTON CHEKHOV, *Cont.*]

an awkward and ridiculous acting out of that purpose.

Chekhov's career, both as a dramatist and a physician, took its nourishment from a single source: his great capacity to observe and cherish life; not life as an abstraction or as an ideal, but as a doomed phenomenon of which he was a part. His tolerance, sympathy, wisdom, and hard-headed vision made it possible for him to achieve, as few writers do, an unflinching but generous perspective on life; a perspective which is a victory over our absurdities, but a victory won at the cost of humility, and won in a spirit of charity and enlightenment.

MAXIM GORKI (1868–1936) was always a writer of revolutionary protest and is a symbol of the fugitive spirit in modern Russian letters. He lived through the whole of the Russian revolution, from the freeing of the serfs to the ascendancy of the Communist Party in the Soviet state, and in all his works, beginning with his first short story, published in 1892, he sought to give meaning and form to the struggle between the individual outcast and the existing social order. In choosing to write of the proletariat, however, Gorki was more than a rebel. He believed that the forlorn dregs of humanity represented in his plays were the mark of society's failure to meet the individual's most fundamental needs. His characters were the distress signals of a crumbling world, and in all his plays Gorki urges us to inquire into the nature of human disaster, and demands that we accept responsibility for it.

The Lower Depths, Gorki's finest play, is a parable of life that strikes deep at the nature of truth and shows the value of illusion to men whose lives seem to have no worth or meaning. But the play is not, as it is usually interpreted on the stage, a lesson in brotherly love. Gorki made it quite clear that Luka's pampering consolations were only "pulp for the toothless," and were either harmful to man or insulting to human dignity. Satine was his hero, and in the play proclaimed Gorki's belief that truth and reality are not merely philosophical concepts. Gorki's message was a program of conduct: "Let a man become conscious of his dignity and capacity; let him adopt an ideal possible to man and he will realize it as an individual and be happy."

Gorki's plays stirred men to action in the early part of the century. They no longer do so, but they still are important landmarks in the modern theatre, for they were the first plays to indicate the kind of social concern that was to characterize much of the serious theatre of the twentieth century.

Anton Chekhov

1860-1904

FROM THE PERSONAL
PAPERS OF ANTON
CHEKHOV

To Alex P. Chekhov,[1] Babkin: May 10, 1886

In my opinion a true description of Nature should be very brief and have a character of relevance. Commonplaces such as, "the setting sun bathing in the waves of the darkening sea, poured its purple gold, etc.,"—"the swallows flying over the surface of the water twittered merrily,"—such commonplaces one ought to abandon. In descriptions of Nature one ought to seize upon the little particulars, grouping them in such a way that, in reading, when you shut your eyes, you get a picture.

For instance, you will get the full effect of a moonlight night if you write that on the mill-dam a little glowing star-point flashed from the neck of a broken bottle, and the round, black shadow of a dog, or a wolf, emerged and ran, etc.

In the sphere of psychology, details are also the thing. God preserve us from commonplaces. Best of all is it to avoid depicting the hero's state of mind; you ought to try to make it clear from the hero's actions. It is not necessary to portray many characters. The center of gravity should be in two persons: him and her. . . .

❀   ❀   ❀

Excerpts from the personal papers of Anton Chekhov are from *Letters to Friends and Family* by Anton Chekhov, translated by Constance Garnett. Reprinted by permission of Mr. David Garnett, and Chatto & Windus, executors of Mrs. Garnett's estate.

To A. S. Souvorin,[2] Sumi: May 30, 1888

. . . It seems to me that the writer of fiction should not try to solve such questions as those of God, pessimism, etc. His business is but to describe those who have been speaking or thinking about God and pessimism, how, and under what circumstances. The artist should be, not the judge of his characters and their conversations, but only an unbiassed witness. I once overheard a desultory conversation about pessimism between two Russians; nothing was solved,—and my business is to report the conversation exactly as I heard it, and let the jury, —that is, the readers, estimate its value. My business is merely to be talented, i.e., to be able to distinguish between important and unimportant statements, to be able to illuminate the characters and speak their language. Shcheglov-Leontyev [3] finds fault with me because I concluded the story with the phrase: "There's no way of making things out in this world!" In his opinion an artist-psychologist *must* work things out, for that is just why he is a psychologist. But I do not agree with him. The time has come for writers, especially those who are artists, to admit that in this world one cannot make anything out, just as Socrates once admitted it, just as Voltaire admitted it. The mob think they know and understand everything; the more stupid they are, the wider, I think, do they conceive their horizon to be. And if an artist in whom the crowd has faith decides to declare that he understands nothing of what he sees,—this in itself constitutes a considerable clarity in the realm of thought, and a great step forward.

❀   ❀   ❀

[1] Chekhov's older brother.
[2] Russian critic and a close friend of Chekhov.
[3] A literary critic for several St. Petersburg newspapers.

To A. S. Souvorin, Moscow:
October 27, 1888

In conversation with my literary colleagues I always insist that it is not the artist's business to solve problems that require a specialist's knowledge. It is a bad thing if a writer tackles a subject he does not understand. We have specialists for dealing with special questions: it is their business to judge of the commune, of the future, of capitalism, of the evils of drunkenness, of boots, of the diseases of women. An artist must judge only of what he understands, his field is just as limited as that of any other specialist—I repeat this and insist on it always. That in his sphere there are no questions, but only answers, can be maintained only by those who have never written and have had no experience of thinking in images. An artist observes, selects, guesses, combines—and this in itself presupposes a problem: unless he had set himself a problem from the very first there would be nothing to conjecture and nothing to select. To put it briefly, I will end by using the language of psychiatry: if one denies that creative work involves problems and purposes, one must admit that an artist creates without premeditation or intention, in a state of aberration; therefore, if an author boasted to me of having written a novel without a preconceived design, under a sudden inspiration, I should call him mad.

You are right in demanding that an artist should take an intelligent attitude to his work, but you confuse two things: *solving a problem* and *stating a problem correctly*. It is only the second that is obligatory for the artist. In *Anna Karenina* and *Evgeni Onegin* not a single problem is solved, but they satisfy you completely because all the problems in these works are correctly stated. It is the business of the judge to put the right questions, but the answers must be given by the jury according to their own lights.

To A. S. Souvorin, Melikhovo:
November 21, 1895

Well, I have finished with the play.[4] I began it *forte* and ended it *pianissimo*—contrary to all the rules of dramatic art. It has turned into a novel. I am rather dissatisfied than satisfied with it, and reading over my new-born play I am more convinced than ever that I am not a dramatist. The acts are very short. There are four of them. Though it is so far only the skele-

ton of a play, a plan which will be altered a million times before the coming season, I have ordered two copies to be typed and will send you one; only don't let anyone else read it. . . .

To V. E. Meyerhold [5]

Dear Vsevolod Emilevich, I have not at hand a copy of the text of Johannes' part,[6] and hence I can speak only in general terms. If you will send me the part, I shall read it through, refresh my memory, and give you the details. For the present I shall call your attention to a few things that may be of practical interest to you.

First of all, Johannes is very intelligent; he is a young scientist brought up in a university town. He lacks completely the elements of the bourgeois. He is a well-bred man, accustomed to the society of respectable people (like Anna); in his movements and appearance he is the tender and immature man reared in the bosom of a loving family and still his mother's pet. Johannes is a German scientist; he is, therefore, steady in his relations with men. On the other hand, he is as tender as a woman when in the company of women. As a typical illustration of these traits, there is the scene with his wife, in which he cannot help being tender toward her in spite of the fact that he already loves, or is beginning to love, Anna. Now as to the nervousness. One must not underline this nervous temperament, because the highly strung, neuropathological nature would hide and misrepresent the much more important loneliness,—the loneliness experienced only by fine, and at the same time healthy (in the fullest sense of the word) organisms. Depict a lonely man, and represent him as nervous only to the extent indicated by the text. Do not treat this nervousness as a separate phenomenon. Remember that in our day every cultured man, even the most healthy, is most irritable in his own home and among his own family, because the discord between the present and the past is first of all apparent in the family. It is an irritability which is chronic, which has no pathos, and does not end in catastrophic consequences; it is an irritability that

---

[4] *The Sea Gull.*

[5] Famous Russian director who was an actor at the Moscow Art Theatre when this letter was written.

[6] The letter refers to the performance of Hauptmann's *Lonely Lives* at the Moscow Art Theatre. Meyerhold played the part of Johannes. The letter, not dated, is found in the *Yearbook of the Imperial Theatres,* for 1909, No. 5.

guests cannot perceive, and which, in its fullest force, is experienced first by the nearest relatives, the wife, the mother. It is, so to say, an intimate, family irritation and nervousness. Do not spend much time on it; present it only as *one* of many typical traits; do not stress it,—or you will appear, not a lonely young man, but an irritable one. I know that Konstantin Sergeyevich [7] will insist on this superfluous nervousness; he exaggerates it,—but, do not yield; do not sacrifice the beauty and power of the voice for the sake of such a detail as the accent. Do not make the sacrifice, because in this case the irritation is only a detail.

To MAXIM GORKY, YALTA:
SEPTEMBER 3, 1899

. . . More advice: when reading the proofs, cross out a host of concrete nouns and other words. You have so many such nouns that the reader's mind finds it a task to concentrate on them, and he soon grows tired. You understand it at once when I say, "The man sat on the grass;" you understand it because it is clear and makes no demands on the attention. On the other hand, it is not easily understood, and it is difficult for the mind, if I write, "A tall, narrow-chested, middle-sized man, with a red beard, sat on the green grass, already trampled by pedestrians, sat silently, shyly, and timidly looked about him." That is not immediately grasped by the mind, whereas good writing should be grasped at once,—in a second. . . .

To OLGA KNIPPER,[8] YALTA: JANUARY 2, 1900

I have not congratulated you on the success of *Lonely Lives*. I still dream that you will all come to Yalta, that I shall see *Lonely Lives* on the stage, and congratulate you really from my heart. I wrote to Meyerhold and urged him in my letter not to be too violent in the part of a nervous man. The immense majority of people are nervous, you know: the greater number suffer, and a small proportion feel acute pain; but where—in streets and in houses —do you see people tearing about, leaping up, and clutching at their heads? Suffering ought to be expressed as it is expressed in life—that is, not by the arms and legs, but by the tone and expression; not by gesticulation, but by

grace. Subtle emotions of the soul in educated people must be subtly expressed in an external way. You will say—stage conditions. No conditions allow falsity. . . .

To A. S. SOUVORIN, MELIKHOVO:
NOVEMBER 25, 1892

You are not hard to understand and you abuse yourself needlessly for expressing yourself vaguely. You are a hard drinker and I treated you to sweet lemonade; after downing it wryly, you remark with entire justice that it hasn't an alcoholic kick. That is just what our works haven't got—the kick that would make us drunk and hold us in their grasp, and this you set forth clearly. And why not? Leaving me and my "Ward No. 6" out of it, let's talk in general terms, which are more interesting. Let's talk of general causes, if it won't bore you, and let's embrace the whole age. Tell me in all conscience, what writers of my own generation, i.e., people from thirty to forty-five, have given the world even one drop of alcohol? Aren't Korolenko, Nadson, and all today's playwrights lemonade? Have Repin's or Shishkin's paintings really turned your head? All this work is just amiable and talented, and though you are delighted, you still can't forget you'd like a smoke. Science and technical knowledge are now experiencing great days, but for our brotherhood the times are dull, stale and frivolous, we ourselves are stale and dreary. . . . The causes for it are not to be found in our stupidity or lack of gifts and not in our insolence, as Burenin holds, but in a disease which in an artist is worse than syphilis or sexual impotence. Our illness is a lack of *something*, that is the rights of the case, and it means that when you lift the hem of our Muse's gown you will behold an empty void. Bear in mind that writers who are considered immortal or just plain good and who intoxicate us have one very important trait in common: they are going somewhere and call you with them; you sense, not with your mind but with all your being, that they have an aim, like the ghost of Hamlet's father, who had a reason for appearing and alarming the imagination. Looking at some of them in terms of their calibre you will see that they have immediate aims—the abolition of serfdom, the liberation of their country, political matters, beauty, or just vodka, like Denis Davidov; others have remote aims—God, life beyond the grave, the happiness of mankind and so on. The best of them are realistic and paint life as it is, but be-

---

[7] Stanislavski—co-founder and co-director of the Moscow Art Theatre.
[8] Famous actress in the Moscow Art Theatre and later Chekhov's wife.

cause every line is saturated with juice, with the sense of life, you feel, in addition to life as it is, life as it should be, and you are entranced. Now what about us? Yes, us! We paint life such as it is—that's all, there isn't any more. . . . Beat us up, if you like, but that's as far as we'll go. We have neither immediate nor distant aims, and you can rattle around in our souls. We have no politics, we don't believe in revolution, we don't believe in God, we aren't afraid of ghosts, and personally I don't even fear death or blindness. He who doesn't desire anything, doesn't hope for anything and isn't afraid of anything cannot be an artist. It doesn't matter whether we call it a disease or not, the name doesn't matter, but we do have to admit that our situation is worse than a governor's. I don't know how it will be with us ten or twenty years hence, perhaps circumstances may change by then, but for the time being it would be rash to expect anything really good from us, regardless of whether or not we are gifted. We write mechanically, in submission to the old established order whereby some people are in government service, others in business and still others write. . . . You and Grigorovich hold that I am intelligent. Yes, I am intelligent in that at least I don't conceal my illness from myself, don't lie to myself and don't cover my own emptiness with other people's intellectual rags, like the ideas of the sixties and so on. I won't throw myself down a flight of stairs, like Garshin, but neither will I attempt to flatter myself with hopes of a better future. I am not to blame for my disease, and it is not for me to cure myself, as I have to assume this illness has good aims which are obscure to us and not inflicted without good reason. . . . "It wasn't just the weather that brought them together. . . ."

Well, sir, now as to the intellect. Grigorovich believes the mind can triumph over talent. Byron was as brilliant as a hundred devils, but it was his talent that made him immortal. If you tell me that X spoke nonsense because his intellect triumphed over his talent, or vice versa, I will reply that X had neither intellect nor talent. . . .

. . . The Heavens guard you!

To OLGA KNIPPER, YALTA:
SEPTEMBER 30, 1899

At your bidding I am dashing off a reply to your letter, in which you ask me about Astrov's last scene with Yelena.[9] You tell me that in this scene Astrov's attitude toward Yelena is that of the most ardent man in love, that he "snatches at his feelings as a drowning man at a straw." But that is incorrect, absolutely incorrect! Astrov likes Yelena, her beauty takes his breath away, but by the last act he is already aware that the whole business is futile, that Yelena is vanishing forever from his sight—and so in this scene the tone he takes with her is the one he would use in discussing the heat in Africa, and he kisses her simply because that is all he has to do. If Astrov interprets this scene tempestuously, the entire mood of Act IV—a quiet and languid one—will be ruined. . . .

It has suddenly grown cold here, as if a Moscow wind had blown upon us. How I should like to be in Moscow, sweet actress! However, your head is in a whirl, you have become infected and are held in a spell—and you have no time for me. Now you will be able to say, "We are creating a stir, my friend!"

As I write I look out of an enormous window with a very extensive view, so magnificent it cannot be described. I shan't send you my photograph until I get yours, you serpent! I wouldn't think of calling you a "snake," as you say; you are a great big serpent, not a little snake. Now, isn't that flattering?

Well my dear, I press your hand, send my profound compliments and knock my forehead against the floor in worship, my most respected lady.

I am sending you another present soon.

To JOSEPH TIKHOMIROV,[10] NICE:
JANUARY 14, 1901

I have just received your letter—you have given me great pleasure and I thank you enormously. Here are the answers to your questions:

1. Irina does not know that Tusenbach is having a duel, but surmises that something went wrong that may have grave, not to say tragic, consequences. And when a woman guesses, she says, "I knew it, I knew it."

2. Chebutykin only sings the words, "Would it not please you to accept this date . . ." These are words from an operetta which was given some time ago at the Hermitage. I don't remember its title, but you can make inquiries,

---

[9] Chekhov was speaking of *Uncle Vanya*.
[10] This letter refers, of course, to the characters in *The Three Sisters*.

if you wish, from Shechtel the architect (private house, near the Yermolayev Church). Chebutykin must not sing anything else or his exit will be too prolonged.

3. Solyony actually believes he looks like Lermontov; but of course he doesn't—it is silly even to consider a resemblance. He should be made up to look like Lermontov. The likeness to Lermontov is immense, but only in the opinion of Solyony himself.

Forgive me if I haven't answered as I should, or satisfied you. There is nothing new with me, all goes along in the old way. I will probably return earlier than I thought, and it is very possible that in March I will already be at home, i.e., in Yalta.

Nobody writes me anything about the play; Nemirovich-Danchenko [11] never said a word about it when he was here and it seemed to me it bored him and wouldn't be successful. Your letter, for which I thank you, helped to dispel my melancholy. . . . I wish you good health and all the best.

To Konstantin Stanislavski, Yalta: October 30, 1903

Thank you very much for the letter and for the telegram. Letters are always very precious to me because, one, I am here all alone, and two, I sent the play off three weeks ago and your letter came only yesterday; if it were not for my wife, I would have been entirely in the dark and would have imagined any old thing that might have crept into my head. When I worked on the part of Lopahin, I thought it might be for you. If for some reason it doesn't appeal to you, take Gayev. Lopahin, of course, is only a merchant, but he is a decent person in every sense, should conduct himself with complete decorum, like a cultivated man, without pettiness or trickery, and it did seem to me that you will be brilliant in this part, which is central for the play. (If you do decide to play Gayev, let Vishnevski play Lopahin. He won't make an artistic Lopahin but still he won't be a petty one. Lujski would be a cold-blooded foreigner in this part and Leonidov would play it like a little kulak. You mustn't lose sight of the fact that Varya, an earnest, devout young girl, is in love with Lopahin; she wouldn't love a little kulak.)

I want so much to go to Moscow but I don't

know how I can get away from here. It is turning cold and I hardly ever leave the house; I am not used to fresh air and am coughing. I do not fear Moscow, or the trip itself, but I am afraid of having to stay in Sevastopol from two to eight, and in the most tedious company.

Write me what role you are taking for yourself. My wife wrote that Moskvin wants to play Epihodov. Why not, it would be a very good idea, and the play would gain from it.

My deepest compliments and regards to Maria Petrovna, and may I wish her and you all the best. Keep well and gay.

You know, I haven't yet seen *The Lower Depths* or *Julius Caesar.* I would so much like to see them.

To Vladimir Nemirovich-Danchenko, Yalta: November 2, 1903

Two letters from you in one day, thanks a lot! I don't drink beer, the last time I drank any was in July; and I cannot eat honey, as it gives me a stomach ache. Now as to the play.

1. Anya can be played by any actress you'd like, even an utter unknown, if only she is young and looks like a young girl, and talks in a young, resonant voice. This role is not one of the important ones.

2. Varya's part is more on the serious side, if only Maria Petrovno would take it. If she doesn't the part will turn out rather flat and coarse, and I would have to do it over and soften it. M.P. won't repeat herself because, firstly, she is a gifted actress, and secondly, because Varya does not resemble Sonya or Natasha; she is a figure in a black dress, a little nun-like creature, somewhat simple-minded, plaintive and so forth and so on.

3. Gayev and Lopahin—have Stanislavski try these parts and make his choice. If he takes Lopahin and feels at home in the part, the play is bound to be a success. Certainly if Lopahin is a pallid figure, played by a pallid actor, both the part and the play will fail.

4. Pishchik—the part for Gribunin. God have mercy on you if you assign the part to Vishnevski.

5. Charlotta—a big part. It would of course be impossible to give the part to Pomyalova; Muratova might be good, perhaps, but not funny. This is the part for Mme. Knipper.

6. Epihodov—if Moskvin wants the part let him have it. He'll be a superb Epihodov. . . .

---

[11] Co-founder and co-director, with Stanislavski, of the Moscow Art Theatre.

7. Firs—the role for Artem.

8. Dunyasha—for Khalutina.

9. Yasha. If it is the Alexandrov you wrote about, the one that is assistant to your producer, let him have it. Moskvin would make a splendid Yasha. And I haven't anything against Leonidov for the part.

10. The passer-by—Gromov.

11. The stationmaster who reads "The Sinner" in Act III should have a bass voice.

Charlotta speaks with a good accent, not broken Russian, except that once in a while she gives a soft sound to a consonant at the end of a word rather than the hard sound that is proper, and she mixes masculine and feminine adjectives. Pishchik is an old Russian fellow broken down with gout, old age and satiety, plump, dressed in a long Russian coat (à la Simov) and boots without heels. Lopahin wears a white vest and tan shoes, flails his arms when he is in motion, takes long strides, is lost in thought when he moves about and walks in a straight line. He doesn't cut his hair short and so he frequently tosses his head back; in reflection he strokes his beard back and forth, i.e., from his neck to his lips. I think Trofimov is clearly sketched. Varya wears a black dress and wide belt.

I have been intending to write *The Cherry Orchard* these past three years and for three years have been telling you to hire an actress who could play a part like Lyubov Andreyevna. This long waiting game never pays.

I have got into the stupidest position: I am here alone and don't know why. But you are unjust in saying that despite your work it is "Stanislavski's theatre." You are the one that people speak about and write about while they do nothing but criticize Stanislavski for his performance of Brutus. If you leave the theatre, so will I. Gorki is younger than we and has his own life to lead. As to the Nizhni-Novgorod theatre, this is only an episode in his life; Gorki will try it, sniff at it and cast it aside. I may say in this connection that people's theatres and people's literature are plain foolishness, something to sweeten up the people. Gogol shouldn't be pulled down to the people, but the people raised to Gogol's level.

I would like so much to visit the Hermitage Restaurant, eat some sturgeon and drink a bottle of wine. Once I drank a bottle of champagne solo and didn't get drunk, then I had some cognac and didn't get drunk either.

I'll write you again and in the meantime send my humble greetings and thanks. Was it Lujski's father that died? I read about it in the paper today.

Why does Maria Petrovna insist on playing Anya? And why does Maria Fyodorovna think she is too aristocratic to play Varya? Isn't she playing in *The Lower Depths*, after all? Well, the devil take them. I embrace you, keep well.

Translated by Constance Garnett

UNCLE VANYA

A New Version by Robert W. Corrigan

CAST OF CHARACTERS

MARINA, *an old nurse*
MIHAIL LVOVICH ASTROV, *a doctor*
IVAN PETROVICH VOYNITSKY (Uncle Vanya)
ALEXANDER VLADIMIROVICH SEREBRYAKOV, *a retired professor*
YELENA ANDREYEVNA, *his wife*
SOFYA ALEXANDROVNA (Sonya), *his daughter by his first wife*
ILYA ILYICH TELYEGIN (Waffles), *an impoverished landowner*
MARYA VASSILYEVNA VOYNITSKAYA, *widow of a privy councillor, mother of Uncle Vanya and the professor's first wife*
A WORKMAN

SCENE *Serebryakov's estate.*

ACT ONE

(*The garden before* SEREBRYAKOV'S *house on a terrace. A table is set for tea, with a samovar, cups and the like. Near the table, benches and chairs. A guitar lies on one bench. A hammock is swung near the table. It is three o'clock of a cloudy afternoon.* MARINA, *a small grey-haired woman, sits at the table knitting. Near her,* ASTROV *is pacing about*)

MARINA (*pouring a cup of tea*) Here, my friend, drink a cup of tea.

ASTROV (*reluctantly taking the cup*) For some reason I don't seem to care for any.

MARINA Would you rather have some vodka?

ASTROV No, I don't drink vodka every day. And, besides, the day is too hot and stifling for it. (*a pause*) Tell me, old nurse, how long have we known each other?

MARINA (*pondering and thoughtfully*) Let me see, how long is it? God only knows. You first came into these parts, let me see—when was it? Well, Sonya's mother was still alive—she died two years later; that was at least eleven years ago. . . . (*pondering*) perhaps even longer.

ASTROV Have I changed much since then?

MARINA Oh, yes. You were young and handsome then, and now you seem like an old man. And you drink too.

ASTROV Yes . . . ten years have made another man of me. And why? Because I am overworked. Do you know, nurse, that I am on my feet from morning till night? I don't know what it is to rest; at night I hide in bed trembling under the blankets in the continual fear that I'll be dragged out to visit someone who is sick. Ever since I have known you, I haven't had a single day all to myself. No wonder I am growing old, how could I help it? And besides, life is tedious; it is senseless, dirty, stupid, and it just drags on and on . . . (*pause*) . . . and finally it swallows you up. (*pause*) Everyone around here is commonplace, and after you live with them for a couple of years, you, too, become commonplace and queer. It's inevitable. (*twisting his mustache*) See what a long mustache I have. A foolish, long mustache. Yes, I am just as silly as all the others, nurse, just as trivial, but not as stupid; no . . . I have not grown stupid. Thank God, my brain is not muddled yet, though my feelings have grown dull. There's nothing I want, there's nothing I need, there's no one I love, except, perhaps, you. (*He kisses her head*) When I was a little boy, I had a nurse just like you.

MARINA Don't you want just a little something to eat?

ASTROV No. During the third week of Lent, a typhoid epidemic broke out in the village,

Uncle Vanya by Anton Chekhov, translated by Robert W. Corrigan, is from *Six Plays by Chekhov.* Copyright © 1962 by Robert W. Corrigan, and reprinted by permission of the translator and the publisher, Holt, Rinehart and Winston, Inc.

and I had to go. The peasants were all stretched out side by side in their huts, and the calves and the pigs were running about among the sick and the dying. How dirty and filthy it was, and the stench of the smoke, ugh, it was unbearable! I slaved among those people all day, and I didn't have a thing to eat. And then when I returned home there was still no rest for me: a switchman was carried in from the railroad; I laid him on the operating table and he died in my arms under the chloroform. And then, my feelings, which should have been deadened, awoke again; my conscience tortured me as if I had murdered the man. I sat down and closed my eyes—like this—and thought: will those who come after us two hundred years from now, those for whom we are breaking the path . . . will they remember us with grateful hearts? No, nurse, they will forget.

MARINA   Man forgets, but God remembers.

ASTROV   Thank you for that. You spoke the truth.

(*Enter* VANYA *from the house. He has been asleep after dinner and looks somewhat disheveled. He sits down on the bench and straightens his tie*)

VANYA   H'mm. Yes. (*a pause*) Yes.

ASTROV   Have a good nap?

VANYA   Yes, very good. (*He yawns*) Ever since the Professor and his wife came, our daily routine seems to have gone haywire. I sleep at the wrong time, drink too much wine, and I eat the wrong kind of food. It's no good. Sonya and I used to work together and we never had an idle moment. But now she works alone and I . . . I just eat and drink and sleep. Something is wrong.

MARINA   (*shaking her head*) Such confusion in the house! The Professor gets up at twelve, the samovar has to be kept boiling all morning, and everything has to wait for him. Before they came we used to have dinner at one o'clock, like everybody else, but now we eat at seven. The Professor sits up all night writing and reading or something, and suddenly, at two o'clock, the bell rings. Heavens, what's that? The Professor wants tea! Wake up the servants, light the samovar! Lord, what disorder!

ASTROV   Will they be here long?

VANYA   (*whistling*) A hundred years! The Professor has decided to stay here for good.

MARINA   Just look at this, for instance! The samovar has been boiling away on the table for two hours now, and they've gone out for a walk!

VANYA   (*calming her brusquely*) Here they are—here they are—don't get so excited.

(*Voices are heard.* SEREBRYAKOV, YELENA, SONYA, *and* TELYEGIN *enter from the garden, returning from their walk*)

SEREBRYAKOV   Superb! Superb! What glorious views!

TELYEGIN   They are lovely, your excellency.

SONYA   Tomorrow we shall go to the woods, shall we, father?

VANYA   Ladies and Gentlemen, tea is served.

SEREBRYAKOV   Won't you please send my tea into the library? I have something to do . . . ah, some work to finish.

SONYA   I am sure you will love the woods, father.

(YELENA, SEREBRYAKOV, *and* SONYA *go into the house.* TELYEGIN *takes a seat at the table beside* MARINA)

VANYA   It is hot and humid, but our eminent scholar walks about in his overcoat and goloshes, wearing gloves and carrying an umbrella.

ASTROV   Which means that he takes good care of himself.

VANYA   But how lovely she is! How lovely! I have never seen a more beautiful woman.

TELYEGIN   Whether I drive through the fields or take a walk under the shady trees in the garden, or look at this table I experience a feeling of indescribable bliss! The weather is enchanting, the birds are singing; we all live in peace and harmony . . . what else do we want? (*taking a cup of tea*) Oh, thank you.

VANYA   (*dreaming*) Such eyes—a glorious woman!

ASTROV   Come, Vanya, tell us something.

VANYA   (*indolently*) What shall I tell you?

ASTROV   Haven't you any news for us?

VANYA   No, it is all old. I am the same as ever, no . . . worse, for I've become lazy. I do nothing any more but grumble like an old crow. My mother, the old magpie, is still babbling about the emancipation of women, with one eye on her grave and the other on her learned books, in which she is forever rummaging in the hopes of finding the dawn of a new life.

ASTROV   And the Professor?

VANYA   The Professor as usual sits in his study reading and writing from morning till night . . .

    "Straining our mind, wrinkling our
      brow,
    We write, write, write,
    With no respite

Or hope of praise in the future or
    now."

Oh, poor unfortunate paper! He ought to write
his autobiography; he would make such an excellent subject for a book! Just think, the life
of a retired professor, as stale as a piece of
mildewed bread, racked with gout, headaches,
and rheumatism, his heart bursting with
jealousy and envy, living on the estate of his
first wife, although he hates it, because he
can't afford to live in town. He is always whining about his hard fate, although as a matter
of fact, he is extraordinarily lucky. (*nervously*)
He is the son of a common, ordinary parson
and has achieved a professor's chair, has become the son-in-law of a senator, is called
"your excellency," but forget it! I'll tell you
something; he's been writing about art for
twenty-five years, and he doesn't know the first
thing about it. For twenty-five years he has
been hashing over the thoughts of other men
on realism, naturalism, and all the other nonsensical "isms"; for twenty-five years he has
been pouring water from one empty glass into
another. Yet . . . consider the man's conceit
and pretensions! He has been pensioned off
. . . Not a living soul has ever heard of him.
He is totally unknown. He is a nothing. That
means that for twenty-five years he has been
treating life as if it were a masquerade ball,
and all that it has accomplished is to have kept
a better man out of a job. But just look at him!
He struts across the earth like a demi-god!

ASTROV You know, I believe you envy him.

VANYA Yes, I do. Look at the success he's
had with women! Don Juan himself was no
luckier. His first wife, my sister, was beautiful,
gentle, as pure as the blue sky, generous, with
more suitors than the number of all his pupils
put together and she loved him as only creatures of angelic purity can love those who are
as pure and beautiful as they are themselves.
My mother adores him to this day, and he still
inspires her with a kind of worshipful awe.
And now, his second wife is, as you can
plainly see, a great beauty, and she is intelligent too; and yet she married him in his old
age and surrendered to him all the glory of her
beauty and freedom. For what? . . . Why?

ASTROV Is she faithful to him?

VANYA Yes, unfortunately she is.

ASTROV Why "unfortunately"?

VANYA Because such fidelity is false and
unnatural. Oh, it sounds very good, but there
is no rhyme nor reason to it. It is immoral for
a woman to deceive and endure an old husband
whom she hates. But for her to stifle her pathetic youth, those intense longings within her

heart—her feelings . . . that is not immoral!

TELYEGIN (*in a tearful voice*) Vanya, don't
talk like that. Really, you know, anyone who is
unfaithful to their wife or husband is a dis-
loyal person and will betray his country, too!

VANYA (*crossly*) Oh, Waffles, dry up!

TELYEGIN No, allow me, Vanya. My wife
ran away with a lover the day after our wedding, because of my . . . ah . . . rather un-
prepossessing appearance. Since then I have
never failed to do my duty. I love her and am
true to her to this day. I help her all I can and
I've given my fortune to educate the children
she had by her lover. I have lost my happiness,
but I have kept my pride. And she? Her youth
has fled, her beauty has faded according to the
laws of nature, and her lover is dead. What
does she have left?

(YELENA *and* SONYA *enter, followed by* MARYA
*carrying a book. The latter sits down and be-
gins to read. Someone hands her a cup of tea
which she drinks without looking up*)

SONYA (*hurriedly to the nurse*) Some peasants are waiting inside. Go and see what they
want. I'll look after the tea.

(*She pours out several cups.* MARINA *goes out.*
YELENA *takes a cup and sits drinking in the
swing*)

ASTROV (*to* YELENA) I came to see your
husband. You wrote me saying he is very ill,
that he has rheumatism and what not, but he
seems fine, as lively as ever.

YELENA He had a fit of depression last
night and complained of pains in his legs,
but he seems all right again today.

ASTROV And I hurried twenty miles at
breakneck speed to get here! But never mind,
it isn't the first time. However, now that I am
here, I am going to stay until tomorrow; for
the first time in ages I am going to sleep as
long as I want.

SONYA Oh, wonderful! You spend the night
with us so seldom. Have you eaten yet?

ASTROV No.

SONYA Fine, then you will have dinner with
us. We don't eat until seven now. (*drinks her
tea*) Oh, the tea is cold!

TELYEGIN Yes, the samovar has gone out.

YELENA Never mind, Ivan, we'll just have
to drink it cold.

TELYEGIN I beg your pardon, madam, my
name is not Ivan, it's Ilya, Ilya Telyegin, or
Waffles, as some people call me because of
my pock-marked face. I am Sonya's godfather,
and his excellency, your husband, knows me
very well. I now live here on this estate; per-

haps, sometime you will be good enough to notice that I dine with you every day.

SONYA He is a great help to us—our right-hand man. (*tenderly*) Dear godfather, let me pour you some more tea.

MARYA Oh! Oh!

SONYA What is it, grandmother?

MARYA I forgot to tell Alexander—I must be losing my memory—I received a letter today from Paul in Kharkov. He sent me a new pamphlet.

ASTROV Is it interesting?

MARYA Yes, but it is so strange. He refutes the very theories he defended seven years ago. Isn't that queer; in fact, it's appalling.

VANYA Oh, there is nothing so appalling about it. Drink your tea, mother.

MARYA But I have something to say, I want to talk.

VANYA But that is all we have been doing for the last fifty years: talk, read a few pamphlets, and talk some more . . . talk. Talk. It's time to quit all that nonsense.

MARYA It seems that you never want to listen to what I have to say. If you will pardon me, Jean, you have changed so much this last year that I hardly know you. You used to be a man of strong convictions and had such an illuminating personality . . .

VANYA Oh, yes, to be sure. I had an illuminating personality, I had elevated ideas, which illuminated or elevated no one. (*a pause*) I am forty-seven years old. Until last year I tried, as you still do, to blind my eyes with meaningless pedantry to the truths of life. Yes, I did it on purpose, to avoid seeing life as it really is . . . and I thought I was doing the right thing. But now . . . Oh, if you only knew! If you knew how I lie awake at night, heartsick and angry, to think how stupidly I wasted my time when I might have been taking from life everything which is now denied me because I am old.

SONYA Uncle Vanya, how dreary!

MARYA (*to her son*) You talk as if your former convictions were somehow to blame, but you yourself, not they, were at fault. You have forgotten that a conviction, in itself, is nothing but a dead letter. You should have done something.

VANYA Done something! It isn't every man who is capable of being a . . . a writing machine like your dear professor.

MARYA What do you mean by that?

SONYA (*imploringly*) Grandmother! Uncle Vanya! Please!

VANYA I am silent. I apologize and am silent.

(*A pause*)

YELENA What a fine day! Not too hot.

(*A pause*)

VANYA Yes, a fine day to hang oneself.

(TELYEGIN *tunes his guitar.* MARINA *appears near the house, calling the chickens*)

MARINA Here chick, chick, here chick!

SONYA What did the peasants want, nurse?

MARINA The same old thing, the same old nonsense. Here chick, chick!

SONYA Why are you calling the chickens?

MARINA The speckled hen disappeared with her chicks. I'm afraid the hawks might get them.

(TELYEGIN *plays a polka. Everyone listens in silence. A workman enters*)

WORKMAN Is the doctor here? (*to* ASTROV) Please, Dr. Astrov, I've been sent for you.

ASTROV Where do you come from?

WORKMAN The factory.

ASTROV (*annoyed*) Thank you. I suppose I shall have to go whether I want to or not. (*looking around him for his cap*) Damn it, this is annoying.

SONYA Oh, yes, it is too bad. You must come back from the factory for dinner.

ASTROV No, I shan't be able to do that. It will be too late. Now where, where—(*to the* WORKMAN) Look here, good fellow, get me a glass of vodka, will you? (*The* WORKMAN *goes out*) Where—where (*finds his cap*) There is a man in one of Ostrovsky's plays, with a long mustache and short wits, like me. However, let me bid you good night, ladies and gentlemen. (*to* YELENA) I should be most delighted if you came to see me some day with Sonya. My place is small, but if you are interested in such things—things like terraced gardens, sapling beds, and nurseries, the likes of which you'll not find within a thousand miles of here—I'd like to show them to you. My estate is surrounded by government forests. But the old forester is always sick and complains so, that I take care of most of the work myself.

YELENA I have always heard that you were very fond of the woods. Of course you can do a great deal of good by helping to preserve them, but doesn't that work interfere with your real calling? You're a doctor, aren't you?

ASTROV God alone can know what a man's real work is.

YELENA And you find it interesting?

ASTROV Yes, very.

VANYA (*sarcastically*) Oh, extremely.

YELENA You are still young, I should say certainly not over thirty-six or seven, and I have an idea that the woods do not interest you as much as you claim. I should think that you would find them quite monotonous.

SONYA Dr. Astrov plants new forests every year, and he has been awarded a bronze medal and a diploma. He does his best to prevent the destruction of the forests. If you listen to him you will agree with him entirely. He claims that forests beautify the earth, and so teach man to understand the beautiful and instill in him a feeling of respect and awe. Forests temper the severity of the climate. In countries where the climate is warmer, less energy is wasted on the struggle with nature and that is why man there is more gentle and loving; the people there are beautiful, supple, and sensitive, their speech is refined and their movements graceful. Art and learning flourish among them, their philosophy is not so depressing, and they treat women with refinement and nobility.

VANYA (*laughing*) Bravo, bravo! All this is charming, but not convincing, and so, (*to* ASTROV) I hope you'll permit me, my friend, to go on burning logs in my stove and building my barns with wood.

ASTROV You can burn peat in your stoves and build your barns of stone. Oh, I don't object, of course, to cutting wood when you have to, but why destroy the forests? The woods of Russia are trembling under the blows of the axe. Millions of trees have perished. The homes of the wild animals and the birds have been laid desolate; the rivers are shrinking, and many beautiful landscapes are gone forever. And why? Because men are too lazy and stupid to bend over and pick up their fuel from the ground. (*to* YELENA) Am I wrong? Who but a senseless savage could burn so much beauty in his stove and destroy what he cannot create himself? Man has reason and creative powers so that he may increase that which has been given to him. Until now, however, he has not created, he has only destroyed. The forests are disappearing, the rivers are drying up, the game is being exterminated, the climate is spoiled, and the earth becomes poorer and more ugly every day. (*to* VANYA) Oh, I read irony in your eyes; you do not take seriously what I am saying; and—and—perhaps I am talking nonsense. But when I cross those peasant forests which I have saved from the axe, or hear the rustling of the young trees, which I have set out with my own hands, I feel as if I had had some small share in improving the climate, and that if mankind is happy a thousand years from now I shall have been partly responsible in my small way for

their happiness. When I plant a young birch tree and see it budding and swaying in the wind, my heart swells with pride and I . . . (*sees the* WORKMAN, *who is bringing him a glass of vodka on a tray*) However . . . (*He drinks*) . . . I must be off. Probably it is all nonsense, anyhow. Goodbye.

SONYA When are you coming to see us again?

ASTROV I don't know.

SONYA In a month?

(ASTROV *and* SONYA *go into the house.* YELENA *and* VANYA *walk over to the terrace*)

YELENA Vanya, you have been behaving impossibly again. What sense was there in irritating your mother with all your talk about her pamphlets and the "writing machine." And this morning you quarreled with Alexander, again. How petty and small it all is!

VANYA But suppose I hate him?

YELENA You hate Alexander without reason; he is like every one else, and no worse than you.

VANYA If you could only see your face, your every movement and gesture! Oh, how tedious your life must be!

YELENA Yes, it is tedious, and dreary, too! All of you abuse my husband and look on me with compassion; you think, "Poor woman, she is married to an old man." How well I understand your sympathy and compassion! As Astrov said just now, see how thoughtlessly you destroy the forests, so that soon there will be nothing left on earth. In just the same way you recklessly destroy human beings, and soon, thanks to you, loyalty and purity and self-sacrifice will have vanished along with the woods. Why can't you look with calm indifference at a woman unless she belongs to you? Because . . . the doctor is right. You are all possessed by a devil of destructiveness; you have no feeling, no, not even pity, for either the woods or the birds or women, or for one another.

VANYA Would you mind stopping all this philosophizing; I don't like it.

(*A pause*)

YELENA That doctor has a sensitive, weary face . . . an interesting face. Sonya evidently likes him; she is in love with him, and I can understand her feeling. (*pause*) This is the third time he has been here since I have come, and I have not had a real talk with him yet or showed him much attention. He thinks I am disagreeable. Do you know, Vanya, why you and I are such friends? I think it is because we are both lonely and tiresome and unsympathetic. (*pause*) Yes, unsympathetic. (*pause*) Don't look at me that way, I don't like it.

VANYA   How can I look at you in any other way since I love you? You are my joy, my life, my youth. I know that my chances of your loving me in return are infinitely small . . . no . . . they are nil, nonexistent; there are no chances, but I ask nothing of you, I want nothing. Only let me look at you, listen to you . . .

YELENA   Quiet! Someone may hear you.

VANYA   Let me tell you of my love; don't drive me away. I have no other happiness.

YELENA   Oh, this is agony!

(*Both go into the house.* TELYEGIN *strums the strings of his guitar and plays a polka.* MARYA *writes something on the leaves of her pamphlet*)

ACT TWO

(*The dining room of* SEREBRYAKOV's *house. It is night. The click of the Watchman's rattle is heard from the garden.* SEREBRYAKOV *sits dozing in an armchair by an open window and* YELENA, *likewise half asleep, is seated beside him*)

SEREBRYAKOV   (*rousing himself*)   Who's there? Is that you, Sonya?

YELENA   It is I.

SEREBRYAKOV   Oh, it's you, Lenotchka. This pain is unbearable.

YELENA   Your blanket has slipped. (*She wraps the blanket around his legs*) Let me shut the window.

SEREBRYAKOV   No, leave it open; I am suffocating as it is. (*pause*) I just dropped off to sleep . . . and . . . I dreamt that my left leg belonged to someone else, and the pain was so agonizing that I awoke. I don't believe this is gout; it is more like rheumatism. (*pause*) What time is it?

YELENA   Twenty after twelve.

(*Pause*)

SEREBRYAKOV   I wish you'd look for Batushkov tomorrow morning; we used to have him, I remember. Oh, why do I find it so hard to breathe?

YELENA   You're exhausted; this is the second night you've been unable to sleep.

SEREBRYAKOV   They say that Turgenev got heart trouble from gout. I'm afraid I'm getting it, too. Oh, damn this terrible, accursed old age! Ever since I've grown old, I have been

hateful to myself, and, I'm sure, hateful to all of you, too.

YELENA   You talk as if we were to blame for your old age.

SEREBRYAKOV   I am more hateful to you than to all the others.

(YELENA *gets up, walks away from him and sits down at a distance*)

SEREBRYAKOV   You are right, of course. I'm no fool; I can understand. You are young and healthy and beautiful. You want and long for life, and I am an old dotard, almost a corpse. Oh, I know it! Certainly, I see that it's foolish for me to go on living for such a long time, but wait! I shall soon set you all free. My life can't drag on too much longer.

YELENA   For God's sake, be quiet! . . . You are exhausting me.

SEREBRYAKOV   It seems that everybody is being exhausted, thanks to me. Everybody is miserable and depressed; everyone's youth is wasting away; only I am enjoying life in blissful triumph. Oh, yes, of course!

YELENA   Be quiet! You're torturing me.

SEREBRYAKOV   Why of course, I torture everybody.

YELENA   (*on the verge of tears*)   This is unbearable! Please, just tell me what you want me to do?

SEREBRYAKOV   Nothing.

YELENA   Then please be quiet.

SEREBRYAKOV   It's funny that everybody listens to Vanya and his old fool of a mother, but the moment I open my mouth, you all begin to feel abused. You can't even bear the sound of my voice. Suppose I am hateful, suppose I am a selfish and egocentric tyrant, haven't I the right to be at my age? Haven't I deserved it? Haven't I, I ask you, the right to be respected, the right to be pampered and cared for . . .

YELENA   No one is disputing your rights. (*The window slams in the wind*) The wind is rising, I must shut the window. (*She shuts it*) We shall have rain in a few minutes. (*pause*) Your rights have never been questioned by anybody.

(*The Watchman in the garden clicks his rattle*)

SEREBRYAKOV   I have spent my life working for the cause of learning. I am accustomed to my study, the library and the lecture hall and to the regard and admiration of my colleagues. And, now . . . (*pause*) . . . now, I suddenly find myself in this wilderness, in this vault, condemned to see the same stupid people from morning till night and to listen to their inane talk. I want to live; I long for success and fame and the tension of an active world, and here I am in exile! Oh, it's terrible to spend every moment grieving for a past that is lost, to witness the success of others and to sit here with nothing to do but fear death. I can't stand it! It's more than I can endure. And you, you won't even forgive me for being old!

YELENA   Wait; be patient; in four or five years, I shall be old too.

(SONYA *comes in*)

SONYA   Father, you sent for Dr. Astrov, and now you refuse to see him. It is not fair to needlessly trouble a busy man.

SEREBRYAKOV   Oh, what do I care about your Astrov? He knows as much about medicine as I do about astronomy.

SONYA   We can't send for famous specialists to come here to cure your gout, can we?

SEREBRYAKOV   I refuse to talk to that madman.

SONYA   Do as you wish then. It makes no difference to me. (*She sits down*)

SEREBRYAKOV   What time is it?

YELENA   One o'clock.

SEREBRYAKOV   It's stifling in here . . . Sonya, hand me that bottle there on the table.

SONYA   (*handing him a bottle of medicine*) Here you are.

SEREBRYAKOV   (*cross and irritated*)   No, not that one! Don't you ever understand? Can't I ask you to do a single thing?

SONYA   Please don't be cross with me. Some people may enjoy it, but spare me, if you please, because I don't like it. Furthermore, I haven't time for it; we are planning to cut the hay tomorrow and I have to get up early.

(VANYA *enters dressed in a long gown and carrying a candle*)

VANYA   A thunderstorm is on its way. (*The lightning flashes*) There it is! Sonya, you and Yelena had better go and get some sleep. I have come to relieve you.

SEREBRYAKOV   (*frightened*)   No, no, no! Don't leave me alone with him! Oh please don't. He will begin lecturing me again.

VANYA   But you must let them have a little rest. They haven't slept for two nights now.

SEREBRYAKOV   All right, then let them go to bed, but, please, you go away, too! Thank you. I beg of you please go away . . . For the sake of . . . ah . . . our former friendship, don't argue. We'll talk some other time . . .

VANYA   Our former friendship! Our former . . .

SONYA   Shh, please be quiet, Uncle Vanya!

SEREBRYAKOV   (*to his wife*)   My love, don't leave me alone with him. He will begin his infernal lecturing.

VANYA   This is absurd.

(MARINA *comes in carrying a candle*)

SONYA   You must go to bed, nurse, it's late.

MARINA   I haven't cleaned up the tea things. I can't go to bed yet.

SEREBRYAKOV   No one can. Everyone is completely worn out. I alone enjoy perfect peace and happiness.

MARINA   (*going up to* SEREBRYAKOV *and speaking tenderly*)   What's the matter, little man? Does it hurt? My own legs ache, too, oh, such pain. (*She arranges the blanket around his legs*) You've been sick like this for such a long time. Sonya's mother used to sit up with you night after night, too, and she wore herself out for you. She loved you dearly. (*a pause*) Old people like to be pitied as much as small children, but somehow nobody cares about them. (*She kisses* SEREBRYAKOV's *shoulder*) Come to bed, my little man, let me give you some linden tea and warm your poor feet. I shall pray to God for you.

SEREBRYAKOV   (*moved*)   Let us go, Marina.

MARINA   My own feet ache so badly, too, oh, so badly! (*She and* SONYA *start leading* SEREBRYAKOV *out*) Sonya's mother used to wear herself out with sorrow and weeping over you. You were still a small and senseless child then, Sonya. Come along now, come along . . .

(SEREBRYAKOV, MARINA, *and* SONYA *go out*)

YELENA   He so completely exhausts me, that I can hardly stand up.

VANYA   He has exhausted you and I have exhausted myself. I haven't had a bit of sleep for three nights now.

YELENA   There's something wrong in this house. Your mother hates everything but her pamphlets and the Professor; the Professor is vexed and irritated, he won't trust me and he fears you; Sonya is angry with her father and also with me, and she hasn't spoken to me for two weeks; you hate my husband and openly sneer at your mother. I have reached the limit of my endurance . . . there is no strength left, why I've nearly burst into tears at least twenty times today. There is something wrong in this house.

VANYA   Oh, why don't you stop all your speculating.

YELENA   You are a cultured and intelligent man, Vanya. Certainly you must understand that the world is not destroyed by criminals and fires, but by hate and malice and all this spiteful gossiping and petty wrangling. Your duty is to make peace; your work should be to reconcile everyone and not to growl at everything.

VANYA (*seizing her hand*) My darling! First, help me to make peace with myself.

YELENA Let go! (*She drags her hand away*) Go away!

VANYA The rain will soon be over, and all nature will awake refreshed. Only I am not refreshed by the storm. Night and day I am haunted by the thought that my life has been hopelessly wasted and is lost forever. My past doesn't count, because I frittered it away on trifles, and the present is so grotesque in its senselessness. What shall I do with my life and my love? What is going to become of them? This glorious passion in my heart will be lost as a ray of sunlight is lost in a dark chasm, and my life will be lost with it.

YELENA It's just as if I were benumbed when you speak to me of your love, and I don't know how to answer you. Forgive me, I have nothing to say to you. (*She tries to leave*) Goodnight!

VANYA (*barring her way*) If you only knew how it tortures me to think that beside me in this house is another life that is being wasted and is lost forever—yours! What are you waiting for? What accursed philosophy, what damn theory, stands in your way? Oh, understand, understand . . .

YELENA (*looking at him intently*) Ivan Petrovich, you are drunk.

VANYA Perhaps . . . perhaps.

YELENA Where is the doctor?

VANYA In there. He is going to stay with me tonight. (*pause*) Perhaps I am drunk . . . yes, perhaps I am; nothing is impossible.

YELENA Have you been drinking together? What for?

VANYA Because in that way at least I experience a semblance of life. Let me do that, Yelena!

YELENA You never used to drink and you never used to talk so much. Go to bed! You bore me!

VANYA (*falling on his knees before her*) My darling . . . my precious, beautiful one . . .

YELENA (*angrily*) Leave me alone! Really, this has become too disgusting. (*She leaves*)

VANYA (*alone*) She is gone! (*a pause*) It was ten years ago that I first met her at her sister's house. She was seventeen and I thirty-seven. Why didn't I fall in love with her then and propose to her? It would have been so easy . . . then! And if I had, she would now be my wife. Yes, tonight's thunderstorm would have wakened us both. But I would have held her in my arms and whispered: "Don't be afraid! I am here." Oh, bewitching dream, so sweet that I smile when I think of it. (*He laughs*) But, my God! Why are my thoughts so entangled? Why am I so old? Why won't she understand me? I despise all that rhetoric of hers, that indolent morality, that absurd talk about the destruction of the world . . . (*a pause*) Oh, how I have been deceived! For years I have worshiped and slaved for that miserable gout-ridden professor. Sonya and I have milked this estate dry for his sake. We have sold our butter and cheese and wheat like misers, and never kept a bit for ourselves, so that we could scrape together enough pennies to send to him. I was proud of him and his learning; I thought all his words and writings were inspired; he was my life . . . the very breath of my being. And now? My God . . . Now he has retired, and what is the grand total of his life? A blank! Nothing! He is absolutely unknown, and his fame has burst like a soap-bubble. I have been deceived; I see that now, basely deceived.

(ASTROV *enters. He is wearing his coat but is without waistcoat or collar and is slightly drunk.* TELYEGIN *follows him, carrying a guitar*)

ASTROV Play something!

TELYEGIN But everyone is asleep.

ASTROV Play!

(TELYEGIN *begins to play softly*)

ASTROV Are you alone? No women around? (*sings with his arms akimbo*)
"The room is cold, the fire is out.
How shall the master cure his gout?"
The thunderstorm woke me. It was a torrential downpour. What time is it?

VANYA The devil only knows.

ASTROV I thought I heard Yelena's voice.

VANYA She was here a moment ago.

ASTROV What a beautiful woman! (*looking at the bottles of medicine*) Medicine, is it? What an assortment of prescriptions we have! From Moscow, from Kharkov, from Tula! Why, he has been bothering every city in Russia with his pains! Is he really sick, or simply pretending?

VANYA He is very ill.

(*Pause*)

ASTROV What's the matter with you tonight? You seem gloomy—so melancholic. Is it because you feel sorry for the Professor?

VANYA Leave me alone.

ASTROV Or are you in love with the Professor's wife?

VANYA She is my friend.

ASTROV Already?

VANYA What do you mean by "already"?

(TELYEGIN *stops playing to listen*)

ASTROV A woman can be a man's friend only after having first been his acquaintance and then his mistress . . . then she becomes his friend.

VANYA What coarse philosophy!

ASTROV What do you mean? (*pause*) Yes, I'll admit I'm growing vulgar, but then, you see, I'm drunk. Usually I drink like this only once a month. At such times my courage and boldness know no bounds. I feel capable of anything. I attempt the most difficult operations and succeed magnificently. The most brilliant plans and ideas evolve in my brain. I'm no longer a poor simpleton of a doctor, but mankind's greatest benefactor. I work out my own system of philosophy and all of the rest of you seem to crawl insignificantly at my feet like so many worms . . . (*pause*) . . . or microbes. (*to* TELYEGIN) Play, Waffles!

TELYEGIN My dear fellow, I would be delighted to, especially for you, but listen to reason; everyone in the house is asleep.

ASTROV Play!

(TELYEGIN *plays softly*)

ASTROV I want a drink. Come, we still have some brandy left. Then, as soon as morning comes, you'll go home with me. All right?

(SONYA *enters and he catches sight of her*)

I beg your pardon, I haven't got a tie on. (*He departs hurriedly, followed by* TELYEGIN)

SONYA Uncle Vanya, you and the doctor have been drinking again! What a pair you two make! It's all very well for him, he's always been like that. But why must you follow his example? It's wrong at your age.

VANYA Age hasn't anything to do with it. When the realities of life are gone, or if you've never had them, then you must create illusions. That is better than nothing.

SONYA All our hay is cut and rotting in these daily rains and here you waste your time living in illusions! You are neglecting the farm completely. I've done all the work myself, until now I'm at the end of my strength . . . (*frightened*) Uncle! Your eyes are full of tears!

VANYA Tears? No . . . ah . . . Nonsense, there are no tears in my eyes. (*pause*) You looked at me then just as your dead mother used to, oh my darling child . . . (*He eagerly kisses her face and hands*) My sister, my dear sister . . . (*pause*) . . . where are you now? (*pause*) Oh, if you only knew, if you only knew!

SONYA If she only knew what, Uncle?

VANYA My heart is bursting. Oh it is dreadful . . . so useless. Never mind, though . . .

maybe later on. Now, I must go. (*He goes out*)

SONYA (*knocking at the door*) Michael! Are you asleep? Please come here for a minute.

ASTROV (*behind the door*) In a moment. (*He appears presently, with his collar and waistcoat on*) What do you want?

SONYA Drink as much as you please, if you don't find it disgusting, but I beg of you, don't let my uncle do it. It's bad for him.

ASTROV All right; we won't drink any more. (*pause*) I'm going home at once. That's settled. By the time the horses are harnessed, it will be dawn.

SONYA It's still raining; wait until morning.

ASTROV The storm is over. This is only the final blow. I must go. And please don't ask me to visit your father any more. I tell him he has gout, and he insists it is rheumatism. I tell him to lie down and stay in bed, and he sits up and goes about. Today he actually refused to see me.

SONYA He has been spoiled. (*looking at the sideboard*) Won't you have something to eat?

ASTROV Yes, I think I will.

SONYA I like to eat at night. I'm sure we shall find something here. (*pause*) They say he has been a great favorite with the ladies all his life and women have spoiled him. Here, have some cheese. (*They stand eating by the sideboard*)

ASTROV I haven't eaten a thing all day. I must drink. (*pause*) Your father has a very trying temper. (*taking a bottle out of the sideboard*) May I? (*pouring himself a glass of vodka*) We are alone here and I can speak frankly. Do you know, I couldn't bear to live in this house—not even for a month! This atmosphere would choke me. There is your father, wholly absorbed in his book and his sickness; there is your Uncle Vanya with his melancholy, your grandmother, and finally your stepmother—

SONYA What about her?

ASTROV In a human being, everything ought to be beautiful: face and dress, soul and thoughts. She is very beautiful, there's no denying it, but after all, all she does is eat, sleep, go for walks, fascinate us by her beauty and—nothing more. She has no duties, other people work for her . . . isn't that so? And an idle life cannot be a pure one. (*pause*) And yet, perhaps I'm judging her too harshly. I'm discontented, like your Uncle Vanya, and so both of us are complainers.

SONYA Aren't you satisfied with life?

ASTROV I like life as life, but I hate and despise it when it means frittering it away in a little Russian village. As far as my personal

...med . . . God! . . . it is
...edemption! Haven't you no-
...ross a dense forest in the
...nd see a small light shining
...tance, how you forget your
...he darkness and the sharp
...sh your face? I work—as you
know—per... harder than anyone else around
here. Fate pursues me relentlessly; at times I
suffer unbearably and I see no light ahead of
me in the distance. I have no hope; I do not
care for people. And . . . it has been a long
time since I have loved any one.

SONYA You love no one?

ASTROV No one . . . At times I feel a kind
of tenderness for your old nurse, but that's only
for old time's sake. The peasants are all alike;
they are stupid, lazy, and dull. And the educated people are difficult to get along with. I
am tired of them. All our friends are small in
their ideas and small in their feelings. They
see no farther than their own noses; or perhaps, more bluntly, they are dull and stupid.
The ones who have brains and intelligence are
hysterical, morbidly absorbed and consumed in
introspection and analysis. They whine, they
hate, they find fault everywhere. They crawl
up to me secretively, leer at me and say: "That
man is crazy, he's neurotic or he is fraudulent."
Or, if they don't know what else to call me, if
no other label fits, they say I am peculiar. I
like the forests; that is peculiar. I don't eat
meat; that is peculiar, too. Simple, natural, and
genuine relations between man and man or
between man and nature have no existence in
their eyes. No, none! . . . None! (*He tries to
take a drink;* SONYA *prevents him*)

SONYA Please, I beg you, don't drink any
more!

ASTROV Why not?

SONYA It is so debasing. You are so noble,
your voice is tender, you are, more than any
one I know, beautiful. Why do you wish to be
like the common people who drink and play
cards? Oh, don't, I beg you! You are always
saying people never create anything, but only
destroy what God has given them. Why then
do you insist on destroying yourself? Oh, you
must not; don't, I implore you! I entreat you!

ASTROV (*giving her his hand*) I won't drink
any more.

SONYA Give me your word.

ASTROV I give you my word of honor.

SONYA (*squeezing his hand*) Thank you!

ASTROV I'm through with it. You see, I'm
perfectly sober again; I've come to my senses,
and I shall remain so until the end of my life.
(*He looks at his watch*) But as I was saying,
my time is over; there is nothing for me in life;
the clock has run its race and has stopped. I
am old, tired, unimportant; my feelings are
dead. I could never care for any one again. I
don't love anyone, and I don't think I shall ever
love anyone. The only thing that appeals to me
is beauty. I just can't remain indifferent to it.
If, for example, Yelena wanted to, she could
turn my head in a day. Yet, I know that that
isn't love, nor even affection . . . (*He shudders and covers his face with his hands*)

SONYA What is the matter?

ASTROV Nothing . . . During Lent one of
my patients died on the operating table.

SONYA It is time to forget that. (*pause*)
Tell me, Michael, if I had a friend or a younger
sister, and if you knew that she, well—that she
loved you, what would you do?

ASTROV I don't know. I don't suppose I'd
do anything. I'd make her understand that I
could not return her love . . . and anyway,
my mind cannot be bothered with such affairs
now. I must start at once if I am ever to go.
Goodbye, my dear girl. At this rate, we shall
stand here talking till daylight. (*shaking hands
with her*) If it's all right, I'll go out through
the drawing room, because I'm afraid your
uncle might detain me. (*He goes out*)

SONYA (*alone*) And he really said nothing!
His heart and soul are still hidden from me,
and yet for some reason I'm strangely happy.
Why? (*laughing with pleasure*) I told him that
he was noble and beautiful and that his voice
was tender. Was that wrong? I can still feel his
voice throbbing in the air as it caresses me.
(*wringing her hands*) Oh, how awful it is that
I am not beautiful! How awful! And I know
that I'm not beautiful. I know it, I know. Last
Sunday, as people were coming out of church,
I heard them talking about me, and one woman
said: "She is so good and generous, what a pity
she is not beautiful." Not beautiful . . .

(YELENA *enters and throws open the window*)

YELENA The storm has passed. What a re-
freshing breeze! (*pause*) Where is the doctor?

SONYA He's gone.

(*Pause*)

YELENA Sonya!

SONYA Yes?

YELENA How much longer are you going
to go on brooding. We have done nothing to
hurt each other. Why should we be enemies?
Certainly we should be friends.

SONYA I feel this too . . . (*embracing*
YELENA) Oh, let's be friends again!

YELENA With all my heart. (*Both are
strongly moved*)

(*Pause*)

SONYA Has father gone to bed?

YELENA No, he is sitting up in the drawing room. (*pause*) You know, it's strange . . . I guess only the Lord knows what has kept us apart all these weeks. (*seeing the open sideboard*) Who left the sideboard open?

SONYA Michael has just had supper.

YELENA Here is some wine. Let's drink to our friendship.

SONYA Yes, let's.

YELENA Out of one glass. (*filling a wine glass*) Now, we are friends, aren't we?

SONYA Friends. (*They drink and kiss each other*) I have wished for us to be friends for so long, but somehow I was ashamed. (*She weeps*)

YELENA Why do you weep?

SONYA I don't know. (*pause*) Let's forget it.

YELENA There, there, don't cry. (*She weeps*) Silly! Now I am crying, too. (*pause*) You're angry with me because you think I married your father for his money, but you must not believe all the gossip you hear. I swear to you I married him for love. I was fascinated by his fame and his learning. I know now that it wasn't real love, although it seemed real enough at the time. I am innocent, and yet ever since my marriage your searching suspicious eyes have been accusing me of an imaginary crime.

SONYA Peace! Come, let's forget the past.

YELENA You mustn't look at people that way. It isn't right. You must trust and believe in people—(*pause*)—or life becomes impossible.

(*Pause*)

SONYA Tell me, truthfully, as a friend, are you happy?

YELENA Truthfully, no.

SONYA I knew that. One more question: would you like your husband to be young?

YELENA What a child you are! Of course I would. Go on, ask me something else.

SONYA Do you like the doctor?

YELENA Yes, very much indeed.

SONYA (*laughing*) I have a plain face, haven't I? . . . Yes, I know. He has just left, and his voice still rings in my ears; I can hear the sound of his footsteps; I can see his face in the dark window. Oh, I want so to tell you all that I have in my heart! But I cannot, I am ashamed. Words can never express our feelings. They mean and . . . Oh, what a silly person you must think I am. (*pause*) Please talk to me about him.

YELENA What do you want me to say?

SONYA He is so wise. He understands everything and he can do anything. He can heal the sick, and plant forests, too.

YELENA It isn't a question of medicine and trees, my dear. He is a man of genius. Do you realize what that means? It means he is a man of great courage, one with deep insights and clear and far-reaching vision. He plants a tree and his mind swings a thousand years into the future and he envisions the happiness of all mankind. Such people are rare and should be loved. What if he does drink and use coarse language at times. In Russia, a man of genius cannot be a saint. Think of his life. There he lives, cut off from the world by frost and storm and trackless muddy roads, surrounded by coarse and savage people who are crushed by poverty and disease. His life is a continuing and endless struggle, from which he shall never rest. How can a man live like that for forty years and remain sober and free from all sin? (*kissing* SONYA) With all my heart, I wish you happiness; you deserve it. (*getting up*) As for me, I am worthless—an empty and quite pathetic woman. I have always been futile; in music, in love, in my husband's house—in fact, in everything. If I dared even for a moment to consider . . . Oh, Sonya, I am really very, very unhappy. (*walking excitedly back and forth*) I can never achieve happiness in this world. Never. Why do you laugh?

SONYA (*laughing and putting her hands over her face*) I am so happy . . . (*pause*) . . . so happy!

YELENA How I should like some music at this moment. I believe I could play once more.

SONYA Oh, do, do! (*embracing her*) I couldn't possibly go to sleep now. Do play!

YELENA Yes, I will. Your father is still awake. Music annoys him when he is ill, but if he says I may, then I shall play a little. Go . . . go and ask him, Sonya.

SONYA All right. (*She goes out*)

(*The sound of the Watchman's rattle comes from the backyard*)

YELENA It's been a long time since I've had the feeling for music. And now, I shall sit and play and cry like a small child. (*calling out of the window*) Yefim, is that you out there with your rattle?

VOICE OF WATCHMAN Yes.

YELENA Don't make so much noise. Your master is ill.

VOICE OF WATCHMAN I'm on my way. (*He whistles a tune as* YELENA *closes the window*)

SONYA (*returning*) He says "No."

ACT THREE

(*The drawing room of* SEREBRYAKOV's *house. There are doors right, left, and center. It is early afternoon.* VANYA *and* SONYA *are seated.* YELENA *walks back and forth, deep in thought*)

VANYA   His lordship, the Professor, has deigned to express the wish that we all gather in the drawing room at one o'clock. (*looking at his watch*) It is now a quarter to one. He has a message of the greatest importance to convey to the world.

YELENA   It's probably a question of business.

VANYA   He never has any business. He writes nonsense, grumbles and eats his heart out with jealousy; that's all he does.

SONYA   (*reproachfully*)   Uncle!

VANYA   Very well. I beg your pardon. (*pointing to* YELENA) Look at her. Roaming up and down out of sheer idleness and boredom. A beautiful picture, I must say!

YELENA   I'm surprised that it doesn't bore you to play on the same note from morning to night. (*with despair*) This tedium is killing me. Oh, what am I going to do?

SONYA   (*shrugging her shoulders*)   There is plenty to do if you wish to.

YELENA   For instance?

SONYA   You could help us run the estate, teach the children, look after the sick . . . isn't that enough? Before you and father came, Uncle Vanya and I used to take the grain to market ourselves.

YELENA   I know nothing about such matters, and, besides, I'm not interested in them. It's only in sentimental novels that women go out and teach and look after the sick peasants; furthermore, how could I start in doing it all of a sudden?

SONYA   I don't know how you can live here and not do it. Be patient and you'll get used to it. (*embracing her*) Don't be depressed my dear friend. (*laughing*) You feel out-of-sorts and restless, bored and idle, and unable, somehow, to fit into this life, and your restlessness and idleness is infectious. Look at Uncle Vanya, he does nothing now but follow you about like a shadow, and I have given up my work today to come here and talk with you. I'm getting lazy and losing interest in my work and I can't help it. Dr. Astrov hardly ever came here; it was all we could do to persuade him to visit us once each month, and now he has given up his forestry and forgets his patients, and comes every day. You must be a witch.

VANYA   Why should you pine away here in misery and despair? (*eagerly*) Come, my darling, my sweet one, be sensible! A mermaid's blood runs in your veins. Why don't you act like one? Let yourself go for once in your life; fall head over heals in love with some other water sprite, and plunge headlong into a bottomless quarry, so that the almighty Professor and all the rest of us might be so amazed that we could escape your charms.

YELENA   (*in anger*)   Leave me alone! How cruel can you be! (*She tries to leave*)

VANYA   (*preventing her*)   There, there, my darling, I apologize. Forgive me. (*He kisses her hand*) Peace!

YELENA   Admit that you would try the patience of a saint.

VANYA   As a peace offering and as a symbol of true harmony, I am going to bring you some flowers I picked for you this morning; some autumn roses, exquisite, glorious, melancholy roses. (*He leaves*)

SONYA   Autumn roses, exquisite, glorious, melancholy roses . . .

(*She and* YELENA *stand at the window looking out*)

YELENA   It's September already! How are we ever going to live through the long winter here? (*pause*) Where is the doctor?

SONYA   He's writing in Uncle Vanya's room. I'm glad Uncle Vanya left. I must talk to you about something.

YELENA   About what?

SONYA   About what? (*She puts her head on* YELENA's *breast*)

YELENA   (*caressing her hair*)   There, there! Don't, Sonya.

SONYA   I am not beautiful!

YELENA   You have beautiful hair.

SONYA   No! (*looks round so as to glance at herself in the mirror*) No! When a woman is not beautiful, she is always told: "You've got beautiful eyes, you've got beautiful hair." For six years now I have loved him; I have loved him more than one can love anyone. Every moment, I seem to hear him by my side. I feel his hand press against mine. I watch the door constantly, imagining that I can hear his footsteps. And—don't you see?—I run to you just to talk about him. He comes here everyday now, but he never looks at me, he doesn't even notice that I am here. Yelena, my dear, it is breaking my heart and I have absolutely no hope . . . no hope. (*in despair*) Oh, God! Give me strength to endure. All last night I prayed. It has gotten so that I go up to him and speak to him and look into his eyes. My pride is gone. I no longer have the strength to control myself.

Yesterday I told Uncle Vanya about my love for him. I couldn't help it. And all the servants know it, too. Everyone knows that I love him.

YELENA   Does he?

SONYA   No, he never pays any attention to me; it is as if I didn't exist.

YELENA   (*musing*)   He's a strange man. Do you know what? Let me talk to him. I'll do it carefully. I'll just give him a hint. (*pause*) Now, really, how much longer do you propose to remain in uncertainty? Please! Let me do it! (SONYA *nods affirmatively*) Wonderful! It will be easy to find out whether he loves you or not. Don't be ashamed, dear one, and don't worry. I shall be careful; he won't have the least suspicion. We only wish to find out whether it is yes or no, don't we? (*a pause*) And if it is no, then, he must stay away from here, isn't that right? (SONYA *nods*) It would be easier not to see him any more. We won't delay this another minute. He said he had some maps he wanted to show me. Go and tell him at once that I wish to see him.

SONYA   (*greatly excited*)   Will you tell me the whole truth?

YELENA   Why certainly I will. I'm sure that whatever it is, it will be easier to endure than this uncertainty. Trust me, my dear.

SONYA   Yes, yes. I shall say that you wish to see his charts. (*She starts to go, but stops near the door and looks back*) No, it is better not to know with certainty . . . one has hope, at least.

YELENA   What did you say?

SONYA   Nothing. (*She leaves*)

YELENA   (*alone*)   There is nothing worse than to know the secret of another human being, and to realize there's nothing you can do to help them. (*in deep thought*) Obviously, he is not in love with her. But why shouldn't he marry her? To be sure, she is not beautiful, yet she is good and kind, pure of heart, and so sensible that she would make an excellent wife for a country doctor of his age. (*pause*) I can understand the poor child's feelings. Here she lives in the midst of this desperate loneliness with no one about her except these gray shadows who pass for human beings, who do nothing but eat, drink, sleep, and talk trivial commonplaces. And, then, who from time to time should appear upon the scene among them but this Dr. Astrov, so unlike the rest— so handsome, interesting, fascinating . . . It is like seeing the moon rising, rich and full, in the darkness. Oh, to be able to surrender yourself —to forget oneself—body and soul to such a man! Yes, I too, am a little in love with him! Yes, without him I am lonely; when I think of

him, I smile. Uncle Vanya says I have a mermaid's blood in my veins: "For once in your life, let yourself go!" Perhaps I should. Oh, to be free as a bird, to fly away from all those drowsy faces and their monotonous mumblings and forget that they have existed at all! Oh, to forget oneself and what one is . . . But I am a coward; I am afraid, and tortured by my conscience. He comes here every day now. I can guess why, and already my guilt condemns me. I should like to fall on my knees at Sonya's feet and beg her to forgive me and weep . . . But . . .

(ASTROV *enters carrying a portfolio*)

ASTROV   Hello, how are you this afternoon? (*shaking hands with her*) Sonya tells me that you wish to see my maps.

YELENA   Yes, you promised me yesterday that you'd show me what you had been doing. Have you time now?

ASTROV   Of course! (*He lays the portfolio on the table, takes out a sketch and attaches it to the table with thumb tacks*) Where were you born?

YELENA   (*helping him out*)   In Petersburg.

ASTROV   Did you go to school there, too?

YELENA   Yes, at the conservatory of music.

ASTROV   I don't imagine you find our way of life very interesting.

YELENA   And why not? It's true I don't know the country very well, but I've read a great deal about it.

ASTROV   I have my own desk there in Vanya's room. When I become so completely exhausted that I can no longer go on with my work, I abandon everything and rush over here to forget myself with my maps for an hour or two. Vanya and Sonya rattle away at their counting boards, I feel warm and peaceful, the cricket sings, and I sit near them at my table and paint. However, I usually don't indulge in such a luxury very often, certainly not more than once a month. (*pointing to the picture*) Look! This is a survey map of our part of the country as it was fifty years ago. Those areas shaded in green, both light and dark, are forest lands. Half the map, you see, is covered with them. Where the green is striped with red, the forests were stocked with elk and wild goats. Here on this lake were large flocks of swans, wild geese, and ducks; as the old men used to tell us, there was a "power" of birds of every kind—no end of them. (*pause*) Now, they have vanished like thin air. Here, you see, beside the towns and villages, I have jotted down here and there the various settlements, little farms, monasteries, and watermills. This country was rich in cattle and horses, as you can see by this expanse of blue. For instance, see how it deepens in this part; there were great herds here, an average of three horses to every house. (*pause*) Now, look below to the second map. This is the country as it was twenty-five years ago. Only a third of the map now is green with forests. The goats have disappeared and only a few elk remain. The green and blue are lighter, and so on and so forth. Now, we come to the third drawing, our district as it is today. Still we see spots of green, but very little. The elk, the swans, the black-cock have also disappeared. In fact, everything is gone. On the whole, it is the picture of a continuous and slow decline which will evidently come to completion in about ten or fifteen years. Perhaps you may object that it is the march of progress, that the old order must give way to the new, and you would be right if roads had been built through these ruined forests, or if factories and schools had taken the place of the monasteries and the watermills. Then the people would have become better educated and healthier and richer, but as it is, and as you can see, we have nothing of the kind. We have the same swamps and mosquitoes; the same disease, poverty, and misery, typhoid, diphtheria, fires. The degradation of our country confronts us, brought on by the human race's fierce struggle for existence. This degeneration is due to inertia and ignorance—to a complete lack of understanding. When a man, cold, hungry and sick, simply to save what little there is left in life that has meaning and importance—to help his children survive—why God only knows, he acts in desperation; he instinctively and unconsciously clutches at anything that will fill his belly and keep him warm. Forced to forget what all this will mean tomorrow, the devil of destruction consumes all the land. And so almost everything has been destroyed and nothing has been created to take its place. (*coldly*) But I see by your expression that all this does not interest you.

YELENA   I know so little about such things!

ASTROV   There's nothing to know. It simply doesn't interest you, that's all.

YELENA   Frankly, my thoughts were elsewhere. Forgive me! I must ask you something, but I am embarrassed and I don't know how to begin.

ASTROV   Ask me something?

YELENA   Yes, a very innocent and probably not too important question. Sit down. (*They both sit*) It's about a young girl I know. Let's discuss it like honest and mature people, like friends; and then, when we have finished we will forget all about it, shall we?

ASTROV   All right. Whatever you say!

YELENA   What I want to talk to you about is my stepdaughter, Sonya. Do you like her?

ASTROV   Yes, I respect her.

YELENA   But do you like her as a woman?

ASTROV   (*not at once*)   No.

YELENA   Just one thing more and I am finished. Haven't you noticed anything?

ASTROV   Nothing.

YELENA   (*takes him by the hand*)   You don't love her, I can see it from your eyes. She is unhappy. Please, understand that and . . . stop coming here.

ASTROV   (*gets up*)   I'm afraid I'm too old for this sort of thing. And, besides, I haven't the time for it. (*shrugging his shoulders*) When indeed could I? (*He is embarrassed*)

YELENA   Oh, God! What a disgusting conversation. I am as breathless as if I had been running three miles uphill. Thank heaven, that's over with. Now let us forget everything that has been said. But you must leave at once. You are intelligent and sensible. You do understand, don't you? (*pause*) I am actually blushing.

ASTROV   If you had spoken a month or two ago, perhaps I might have been able to consider it, but now . . . (*shrugging his shoulders*) Of course, if she is suffering . . . but wait, there is one thing I can't understand . . . what are your reasons for bringing all this up? (*searching her face with his eyes and shaking an admonishing finger at her*) Oh, you're a sly one!

YELENA   What do you mean?

ASTROV   (*laughing*)   A sly one! Suppose Sonya is unhappy. I'm ready to admit it, but what is the real meaning of your interrogation? (*preventing her from speaking, quickly*) Please, don't look so surprised, you know perfectly well why I'm here every day. My sweet beast of prey, don't look at me like that, I'm an old hand at this sort of game . . . you can't deceive me.

YELENA   (*perplexed*)   A beast of prey? I don't understand anything.

ASTROV   A beautiful, fluffy weasel. You must have your victims. Here I've been doing nothing for a whole month, I've dropped everything, I seek you greedily, and you're awfully pleased about it, awfully. Well? I'm conquered, and you knew all about it without your interrogation. (*folding his arms and bowing his head*) I submit. Here I am . . . eat me up!

YELENA   You've gone crazy!

ASTROV (*laughing ironically*) Oh, you're so shy, aren't you?

YELENA I'm more honorable than you think! I swear it! (*She tries to leave the room*)

ASTROV Wait . . . (*barring her way*) . . . I'll go away today. I shan't come here any more. But . . . (*taking her hand and glancing about*) . . . for the future . . . where are we going to meet? Tell me quickly, where? Someone may come in. Tell me quickly! . . . (*passionately*) You are so gloriously and wonderfully beautiful! . . . Let me kiss you but once . . . Oh, if I could kiss your fragrant hair!

YELENA I assure you!

ASTROV Why assure me? You must not! Let's not waste words! Ah, how lovely you are . . . what hands! (*kissing her hands*)

YELENA Stop it! Go away! (*freeing her hands*) You're forgetting yourself!

ASTROV Tell me! Tell me! Where will we meet tomorrow? (*putting his arms around her*) Don't you see! We must meet! It is inevitable.

(*He kisses her.* VANYA *comes in carrying a bunch of roses, and halts in the doorway*)

YELENA (*without seeing* VANYA) Have pity! Leave me! (*She lays her head on* ASTROV's *shoulder*) Don't! (*She tries to break away from him*)

ASTROV (*holding her around the waist*) Meet me in the forest arbor tomorrow at two. Yes! Oh, yes! Will you come?

YELENA (*seeing* VANYA) Let me go! (*breaking free and going to the window deeply embarrassed*) This is horrible!

VANYA (*throwing his flowers on a chair, speaking in great excitement and wiping his face with his handkerchief*) Nothing . . . yes, yes, nothing.

ASTROV (*with bravado*) It's a fine day, my dear Vanya. This morning, the sky was overcast and it looked like rain, but now the sun is shining again. After all, we've had a very fine autumn, and the wheat crop looks unusually promising. (*putting his map back into the portfolio*) But the days are growing short. (*goes out*)

YELENA (*quickly approaching* VANYA) You must do your best; you must use all the power you have to get us away from here today! Do you hear? I say, today!

VANYA (*wiping his face*) Oh! Ah! Oh! Very well! Yes, I . . . Yelena, I saw everything!

YELENA (*greatly upset*) Do you hear me? I must leave here today!

(SEREBRYAKOV, SONYA, MARINA, *and* TELYEGIN *enter*)

TELYEGIN I'm not feeling very well myself, your excellency. I've been lame for two days, and my head . . .

SEREBRYAKOV Where are the rest? I hate this house. It winds and sprawls like a labyrinth. Everyone is always scattered through its twenty-six rooms. You can never find a soul. (*to* MARINA) Ask Marya and Yelena to come here!

YELENA I am here.

SEREBRYAKOV Please sit down, all of you.

SONYA (*going to* YELENA *and asking anxiously*) What did he say?

YELENA I'll tell you later.

SONYA You are upset. (*looking swiftly and with inquiry into her face*) I understand; he said he would not come here anymore. (*pause*) Tell me, did he? . . . Tell me!

(YELENA *nods*)

SEREBRYAKOV (*to* TELYEGIN) After all, one can become reconciled to being an invalid, but not to this absurd way of life you have here in the country. I feel as if I had been cast off from this earth and dumped onto a strange planet. Please be seated, ladies and gentlemen. Sonya! (*She does not hear. She stands with her head sadly bent forward*) Sonya! (*a pause*) I guess she does not hear me. (*to* MARINA) You sit down, too, nurse. (MARINA *takes a seat and resumes knitting her stocking*) I ask your indulgence, ladies and gentlemen; uh . . . check your ears, as it were, on the hat rack of attention. (*He laughs*)

VANYA (*in agitation*) Perhaps I'm not needed . . . May I be excused?

SEREBRYAKOV No, you are needed now more than anyone else.

VANYA What do you wish?

SEREBRYAKOV You—but what makes you so angry and out of sorts? If it is anything I have done, I beg your forgiveness.

VANYA Oh, forget that and your high and mighty tone, too, and come to the point; what do you want?

(MARYA *enters*)

SEREBRYAKOV Here is mother. Ladies and gentlemen, let us begin. I have asked you to gather here, my friends, to inform you that the inspector general is coming. (*laughs*) All joking aside, however, I wish to discuss a very important matter. I must ask you for your aid and advice, and realizing your unbounded kindness, I believe I can count on both. I am a scholar and bound to my library, and I am not familiar with practical affairs. I am unable, I find, to dispense with the help of well informed people such as you, Ivan, and you,

Ilya, and you, mother. The truth is, *manet omnes una nox*, that is to say, our lives rest in the hands of God, and as I am old and ill, I realize that the time has come for me to dispose of my property in the interests of my family. My life is nearly finished, and I am not thinking of myself, but I must consider my young wife and daughter. (*a pause*) I cannot go on living in the country; we were just not meant for country life. And yet, we cannot afford to live in town on the income from this estate. We might sell the forests, but that would be an expedient to which we could not resort every year. We must work out some method of guaranteeing ourselves a permanent, and . . . ah, more or less fixed annual income. With this object in view, a plan has occurred to me which I now have the honor of proposing to you for your consideration. I shall give you only a rough outline of it, omitting all the bothersome and trivial details. Our estate does not yield, on an average, more than two percent on the investment. I propose to sell it. If then we invest our capital in bonds and other suitable securities, it will bring us four to five percent and we should probably have a surplus of several thousand roubles, with which we could buy a small house in Finland . . .

VANYA Wait a minute! Repeat what you said just now; I don't believe I heard you quite right.

SEREBRYAKOV I said we would invest the money in bonds and with the surplus buy a house in Finland.

VANYA No, not Finland . . . You said something else.

SEREBRYAKOV I propose to sell this estate.

VANYA Aha! That was it! So you are going to sell the estate? Splendid! That's a fine idea! And what do you propose to do with my old mother and myself and with Sonya, here?

SEREBRYAKOV That will be taken care of in due course. After all . . . uh . . . we can't do everything at once, can we?

VANYA Wait! It is clear that up to now I've never had an ounce of sense in my head. I have always been stupid enough to think that the estate belonged to Sonya. My late father bought it as a wedding gift for my sister, and as our laws were made for Russians and not for Turks, I foolishly imagined that my sister's estate would pass on to her child.

SEREBRYAKOV Why, of course, it belongs to Sonya. Has anyone denied it? I don't wish to sell it without Sonya's consent; on the contrary, what I am doing is for Sonya's welfare.

VANYA This is absolutely crazy. Either I have gone insane or . . . or . . .

MARYA Jean, don't contradict Alexander. Trust him; he knows better than we do what is right and what is wrong.

VANYA No! Give me some water. (*He drinks*) Go on! Say anything you like . . . anything!

SEREBRYAKOV I can't understand why you are so upset. I don't pretend that my plan is ideal, and if you all object to it, I shall not insist. (*a pause*)

TELYEGIN (*looking embarrassed*) I've always had a great reverence for learning, sir, and, if I may say so, my feelings for it have a certain family connection. I mean, sir, that my brother Gregory's wife's brother, Konstantin Lacedaemonov, as you perhaps know, was an M.A. . . .

VANYA Wait a minute, Waffles, we're discussing business. Wait a little . . . later . . . (*to* SEREBRYAKOV) Here, ask him what he thinks; this estate was purchased from his uncle.

SEREBRYAKOV Ah! Why should I ask questions? What good would it do?

VANYA The price was ninety-five thousand roubles. My father paid seventy and left a mortgage of twenty-five. Now listen! This estate could never have been bought if I had not renounced my inheritance in favor of my sister, whom I dearly loved . . . and what is more, I worked like a slave for ten years and paid off the mortgage.

SEREBRYAKOV I regret that I ever brought the matter up.

VANYA Thanks entirely to my personal efforts, the estate is now free from debt and in good condition, and now . . . as I am getting old, you propose to kick me out!

SEREBRYAKOV I don't understand what you're talking about.

VANYA For twenty-five years I have managed this estate. I have sent you the proceeds from it like an honest servant, and you, you have never given me one single word of thanks for my efforts . . . no, not one . . . neither in my youth nor now. You gave me a meager salary of five hundred roubles a year . . . a beggar's pittance, and you have never once thought of adding a rouble to it.

SEREBRYAKOV How should I know about such things, Ivan? I am not a practical man and I don't understand them. You might have helped yourself to all you desired.

VANYA Yes, why didn't I steal? Don't you all despise me for not stealing? It would have been only fair, and I wouldn't be a poor man now.

MARYA (*sternly*) Jean!

TELYEGIN (*in agitation*) Vanya, my friend, don't talk like that. Why spoil such a pleasant relationship? Please stop!

VANYA For twenty-five years I have been sitting here with my mother buried like a mole. Every thought and hope we had was yours and yours alone. All day long we talked with pride of you and your work; and we spoke your name with respect . . . yes, almost with reverence. We wasted our evenings reading your books and articles, which I now detest to the bottom of my heart.

TELYEGIN Don't, Vanya, don't. I can't stand this sort of thing.

SEREBRYAKOV (*angrily*) What in God's name do you want, anyhow?

VANYA We used to consider you a superman, a kind of demi-god, but now the scales have fallen from my eyes and I see you as you are! You write about art without knowing a thing about it. Why, those books of yours which I used to think were so wonderful aren't worth a copper kopeck. You are a fake, a fraud, a . . .

SEREBRYAKOV Can't anyone stop him? I'm leaving here immediately!

YELENA Ivan Petrovich, I command you to stop this instant! Do you hear me?

SONYA Please! Uncle Vanya!

VANYA I refuse! (SEREBRYAKOV *tries to escape from the room, but* VANYA *bars the door*) Wait! I haven't finished yet! You have destroyed my life. I have never really lived. Thanks to you, my best years have gone for nothing. They have been ruined. I hate you!

TELYEGIN I can't stand it; I can't stand it. I'm going. (*He leaves in great excitement*)

SEREBRYAKOV What do you want from me? What right do you have to speak to me like that? If the estate is yours, take it! I don't want it.

YELENA I'm leaving this hell right now! (*shouts*) I can't stand it any longer!

VANYA My life's ruined! I'm gifted, I'm intelligent, I'm courageous. If I'd had a normal life, I might have become a Schopenhauer, a Dostoevski. I'm talking nonsense. I'm going insane! I'm in despair! Oh, Mother!

MARYA Do as the Professor tells you!

VANYA Mother, what am I to do? Never mind, don't tell me! I know myself what I must do! (*to* SEREBRYAKOV) You will remember me!

(*He goes out through middle door.* MARYA *goes out after him*)

SONYA Oh, nurse, nurse!

SEREBRYAKOV This is too much! Take that madman away! I can't live under the same roof with him! He is always there. (*points to the middle door*) Let him move into town or to another house on the grounds, or I will move myself, but I cannot stay in the same house with him.

YELENA (*to her husband*) We are leaving here today; we must get ready at once.

SEREBRYAKOV What an utterly insignificant little man.

SONYA (*on her knees beside the nurse, turning to her father and speaking with emotion*) You must be merciful, Father. Uncle Vanya and I are both very unhappy! (*controlling her despair*) Have mercy on us! Remember how Uncle Vanya and grandmother used to sit up late copying and translating your books for you every night . . . every night. Uncle Vanya has worked without rest; we would never spend a penny on ourselves, but sent it all to you! We earned every mouthful of bread that we ever ate! I am not speaking as I should like to, but you must understand, Father, you must have mercy on us.

YELENA (*to her husband, much excited*) For heaven's sake, Alexander, go and talk to him . . . explain!

SEREBRYAKOV Very well, I shall talk to him. I do not accuse him of anything, and I am not angry, but you must admit that his behavior has been strange, to say the least. Very well, I shall go to him. (*He leaves through the center door*)

YELENA Be gentle with him. Try to quiet him. (*She follows him out*)

SONYA (*snuggling nearer to* MARINA) Nurse, oh, nurse!

MARINA It's all right, child. When the geese have cackled they will be silent again. First they cackle and then they stop.

SONYA Nurse!

MARINA (*caressing her hair*) You are trembling all over, as if you had a chill. There, there, my little child, God is merciful. A little linden tea, and it will pass. Don't cry, my sweet. (*looking angrily at the center door*) See, the geese have all gone now. The devil take them!

(*A shot is heard.* YELENA *screams behind the scenes.* SONYA *shudders*)

MARINA What's that?

SEREBRYAKOV (*runs staggering in looking terrified*) Stop him! Stop him! He's gone mad!

(YELENA *and* VANYA *struggle in the doorway*)

YELENA (*trying to snatch the revolver away from him*) Give it to me! Give it to me, I tell you!

VANYA Let go of me. Let go of me, Yelena! (*Freeing himself, he runs in and looks for* SEREBRYAKOV) Where is he? Ah, there he is!

(*pointing the revolver at* SEREBRYAKOV.) Bang! (*Pause.*) Missed him! Missed him again! (*furiously*) Damn it! Damn! (*bangs the revolver a few times against the floor and sinks exhausted in a chair*)

YELENA Take me away from here! Take me away . . . kill me . . . I can't stay here, I can't.

VANYA (*in despair*) What have I done! What have I done!

SONYA (*softly*) Oh, nurse! Nurse!

ACT FOUR

(VANYA's *bedroom and office. Large table near window; scattered on it are ledgers, scales, and papers. Nearby* ASTROV's *table with paints and drawing materials. A map, of no use to anyone, of Africa on the wall. A large sofa covered with canvas. A door to an inner room; door right leads to front hall. It is evening in autumn.* TELYEGIN *and* MARINA *sit facing each other, winding wool*)

TELYEGIN Hurry, Marina, or we shall have to go out to say goodbye before we've finished. They have ordered the carriage already.

MARINA (*trying to wind more rapidly*) There isn't much left to wind.

TELYEGIN They are going to live in Kharkov.

MARINA It is wise for them to go.

TELYEGIN They have been frightened. The Professor's wife refuses to stay here an hour longer. She keeps saying: "If we're going at all, let's hurry. We shall go to Kharkov and look around, and then we can send for our things." They're taking practically nothing with them. It seems, Marina, that fate has decreed that they should not live here.

MARINA And quite rightly. What a storm they raised! It was disgusting!

TELYEGIN Yes, to be sure! The scene this morning would make a fine story.

MARINA I wish I'd never laid eyes on them. (*pause*) Once more things will be as they used to be; we shall live like normal human beings again: tea at eight, dinner at one, and supper in the evening; everything in order as decent people and Christians like it. (*sighing*) It is a long time since I, poor sinner, have eaten noodles.

TELYEGIN Yes, we haven't had noodles for a great while. (*pause*) Not for ages. As I was passing through the village this morning, Marina, one of the storekeepers, called after me: "Hi! you hanger-on!" I felt it bitterly.

MARINA Don't pay any attention to them, my friend; we are all dependent upon God. You, Sonya, Uncle Vanya, and myself . . . none of us sits idle; we all must work hard. All! . . . Where is Sonya?

TELYEGIN In the garden with the doctor, looking for Vanya. They are afraid he may become violent and attempt to kill himself.

MARINA Where is his gun?

TELYEGIN (*whispering*) I hid it in the cellar.

MARINA (*amused*) What goings on!

(VANYA *and* ASTROV *enter*)

VANYA Let me alone! (*to* MARINA *and* TELYEGIN) Go away! Get out and leave me to myself. Only for an hour! I won't have you watching me this way!

TELYEGIN (*going out on tiptoe*) Why, certainly, Vanya.

MARINA (*gathering up her wool and leaving*) The gander is cackling again; ho! ho! ho!

VANYA Let me alone!

ASTROV I would, with the greatest pleasure. I should have gone long ago, but I shan't leave you until you have returned what you took from me.

VANYA I took nothing from you.

ASTROV I'm not joking, don't delay me, I really have to go.

VANYA I took nothing of yours.

ASTROV (*both sitting down*) Oh, you didn't? All right, I shall have to stay a while longer, and if you still don't give it up, I will have to resort to force. We shall tie your hands and search you. I warn you, I mean what I say.

VANYA Do as you please. (*pause*) Oh, to think I made such a fool of myself! To shoot twice and miss him both times! I can never forgive myself.

ASTROV When you first felt the impulse to shoot someone, you would have done better to put a bullet through your own head.

VANYA (*shrugging his shoulders*) It's strange! I tried to murder a man, and they are not going to arrest me or bring me to trial. That means they think I'm insane. (*laughing bitterly*) I! I am insane, and the ones who hide their futility, their stupidity, their harsh cruelty behind a professor's mask, they . . . they are sane! Those who marry old men and then betray them before the eyes of everyone, they are sane! Yes, I saw you kiss her; I saw you in each other's arms!

ASTROV Yes, I did kiss her; which is more than you can say.

VANYA (*watching the door*) No, it is the earth that is insane, because it allows us to exist.

ASTROV That's nonsense.

VANYA Well? I am a lunatic, aren't I, and therefore irresponsible? Haven't I the right to talk nonsense?

ASTROV This is a farce! You are not insane; you are simply a ridiculous fool. I used to think every fool was out of his senses—abnormal; but now I see that lack of sense is the normal human condition, and you are perfectly normal.

VANYA (*covering his face with his hands*) Oh! If you knew how ashamed I am! There is no pain on earth greater than the bitter sense of shame. (*agonized*) I can't endure it! (*leaning against the table*) What can I do? What can I do?

ASTROV Nothing.

VANYA Tell me something! Oh, my God! I am forty-seven. I may live to be sixty; I still have thirteen years ahead of me . . . an eternity! How can I endure life for thirteen years? What shall I do? How can I fill them? Oh, don't you see? (*pressing* ASTROV's *hand convulsively*) Don't you see, if I could only live the rest of my life in some new manner! If I could only wake up some still sunny morning and feel that my life had begun all over; that the past was forgotten and had vanished like smoke. (*weeping*) Oh, to begin life anew! To start over! Tell me, tell me, how to begin!

ASTROV (*crossly*) Nonsense! What kind of a new life can we, yes both of us, you and I— look forward to? We have no hope.

VANYA None?

ASTROV None. I am convinced of that.

VANYA Please give me something to live for. (*putting his hand to his heart*) I feel such a burning pain here.

ASTROV (*shouting angrily*) Stop! (*more moderately*) It may be that our posterity, despising us for our blind and stupid lives, will find some road to happiness; but we—you and I—have but one hope, the hope that, perhaps, pleasant dreams will haunt us as we rest in our graves. (*sighing*) Yes, my friend, in this entire community there were only two decent and intelligent men, you and I. Ten years or so of this life of ours, this wretched life of the commonplace and the trivial, have sucked us under and poisoned us with their destructive vapors, and we have become as contemptible, as petty, and as despicable as the others. (*resolutely*) But don't try to put me off! Will you give me what you took from me?

VANYA I took nothing from you.

ASTROV You took a bottle of morphine out of my medicine case. (*pause*) Listen! If you are positively determined to kill yourself, go into the woods and shoot yourself there. But give me back the morphine, or there will be a great deal of talk and suspicion; people will think I gave it to you. It will be bad enough having to perform your post-mortem. Do you think I shall find it interesting?

(SONYA *enters*)

VANYA Leave me alone.

ASTROV (*to* SONYA) Sonya, your uncle has stolen a bottle of morphine from my medicine case and won't return it to me. Tell him his behavior is—well, unwise. I can't waste any more time, I must be going.

SONYA Uncle Vanya, did you take the morphine?

(*Pause*)

ASTROV Yes, he took it. (*pause*) I'm absolutely sure.

SONYA Give it back! Why do you wish to frighten us? (*tenderly*) Give it up, Uncle Vanya! My sorrow is perhaps even greater than yours, but I am not in despair. I endure my grief and shall go on doing so until my life comes to its natural end. You must endure yours, too. (*pause*) Give it up! (*kissing his hands*) Dear, dear, Uncle Vanya. Give it up! (*weeping*) You are so good, I am sure you'll have pity on us and give it back. You must endure your grief with patience, Uncle Vanya; you must endure it.

(VANYA *takes the bottle from the table drawer and gives it to* ASTROV)

VANYA There it is! (*to* SONYA) And now we must get busy at once; we must do something, or else I'll not be able to stand it.

SONYA Yes, yes, let's work! As soon as we've seen them off, we'll go to work. (*Nervously she straightens out the papers on the table*) We have neglected everything!

ASTROV (*putting the bottle in the case and closing it*) Now I can go.

YELENA (*entering*) Oh, here you are, Vanya. We are leaving soon. Go to Alexander, he wishes to speak to you.

SONYA Go, Uncle Vanya. (*taking* VANYA's *arm*) Come, you and father must make peace; that is absolutely necessary for us. (SONYA *and* VANYA *leave*)

YELENA I'm leaving. (*giving* ASTROV *her hand*) Goodbye.

ASTROV So soon?

YELENA The carriage is waiting.

ASTROV Goodbye.

YELENA   You promised me that today you, too, would go away.

ASTROV   I had forgotten. I'll go immediately. (*pause*) Were you afraid? (*taking her by the hand*) Was it so terrifying?

YELENA   Yes.

ASTROV   Couldn't you stay? Couldn't you? Tomorrow—in the forest arbor—

YELENA   No. Everything is settled, and that is why I can look you so squarely in the eyes. Our departure is definite. One thing I must ask of you, however: don't think too harshly of me; I should like you to respect me.

ASTROV   Ah! (*with an impatient gesture*) Stay, I beg you! Admit there's nothing for you to do in this world. You have no object in life; nothing to occupy your attention. Sooner or later you will give in to your feelings. It is inevitable. But please not in Kharkov or in Kursk, but here, here in the lap of nature. Here, at least, it would be poetic, even beautiful. Here you have forests, Turgenev's half-ruined houses, the autumn roses . . .

YELENA   How absurd you are! I am angry with you and yet I shall always remember you with pleasure. You are an interesting and different kind of man. You and I will never meet again, and so I shall tell you—why conceal it? —that I am in love with you. Come, let's shake hands and part as good friends. Please don't think badly of me.

ASTROV   (*pressing her hand*)   Yes, you had better go. (*thoughtfully*) You seem sincere and good, and yet there is something strangely restless about your whole personality. The moment you and your husband arrived here, everyone whom you found busy and engaged in active, creative work felt compelled to drop it and give himself up to you and your husband's gout for the entire summer. You and your husband have infected all of us with your idleness. I became infatuated with you and I have done nothing for a whole month, and in the meantime people have been ill and the peasants have been grazing their herds in my newly planted woods . . . so that wherever you and your husband go, you bring destruction everywhere. I am joking, of course, and yet I am strangely convinced that if you had remained here, we should have been overtaken by the most terrible desolation and destruction. I would have perished, and you . . . no good would have come to you either. So go! Our little comedy is over; with a happy ending— Go!

YELENA   (*snatching pencil quickly from AS-TROV's table*)   I shall keep this pencil as a remembrance!

ASTROV   How strange it is! We meet, and then all of a sudden it seems that we must part forever. So it is with everything in this world. While we are still alone, before Uncle Vanya comes in with a bouquet—allow me—to kiss you goodbye—May I? (*kissing her on the cheek*) There! Wonderful!

YELENA   I wish you every happiness. (*glancing about her*) For once in my life . . . (*She kisses him impulsively, and they part quickly*) I must go.

ASTROV   Yes go. Since the carriage is ready, you'd better start at once. (*They stand listening*) It is finished.

(VANYA, SEREBRYAKOV, MARYA *with her book,* TELYEGIN, *and* SONYA *enter*)

SEREBRYKOV   (*to* VANYA)   Woe be unto him who cannot forgive past offenses. I have passed through so much—ah, such experience—in the last few hours that I believe I could write a whole treatise for the benefit of all mankind on the art of living. I accept your apology gladly, and I myself ask your forgiveness. (*He kisses* VANYA *three times*) Goodbye.

VANYA   You will go on receiving your allowance regularly as before. Everything will remain as it was.

(YELENA *embraces* SONYA)

SEREBRYAKOV   (*kissing* MARYA'S *hands*) Mother!

MARYA   (*kissing him*)   Alexander! Have your picture taken again, and send it to me; you know how dearly I love you.

TELYEGIN   Goodbye, your excellency. Don't forget us.

SEREBRYAKOV   (*kissing* SONYA)   Goodbye, goodbye, everyone. (*shaking hands with* AS-TROV) Many thanks for your pleasant company. I have a deep regard for your opinions, your enthusiasm, and your impulses, but permit an old man to add one last observation—let me give you one piece of advice: do something, my friend! Work! You must work! (*They all bow*) Good luck to you all. (*He goes out followed by* MARYA *and* SONYA)

VANYA   (*fervently kissing* YELENA's *hand*) Goodbye . . . forgive me. We shall never meet again!

YELENA   (*touched*)   Goodbye, my dear Vanya. (*She kisses his head lightly as he bends over her hand, and then goes out*)

ASTROV   Tell them to bring my carriage around, too, Waffles.

TELYEGIN   Certainly, my friend. (*He goes out*)

(ASTROV *and* VANYA *alone are left behind.* AS-TROV *gathers together his paints and drawing materials on the table and packs them away in his bag)*

ASTROV   Why don't you see them off?

VANYA   Let them go! I—I can't go out there. My heart is so saddened. I must busy myself with something at once. To work! To work!

(He rummages through his papers on the table. Pause. As the horses trot away, the tinkle of bells is heard)

ASTROV   They have gone! Somehow I'm sure the Professor is glad to go. Nothing will tempt him to return.

MARINA   *(entering)*   They have gone. *(She sits down in her arm chair and resumes her knitting.* SONYA *comes in drying her eyes)*

SONYA   They have gone. *(wipes her eyes)* God be with them. *(to* VANYA*)* And now, Uncle Vanya, let us do something!

VANYA   To work! To work!

SONYA   It has been a long, long time since you and I have sat together at this table. *(lighting a lamp on the table)* No ink! *(taking the inkstand to the cupboard and filling it from an ink bottle)* How sad it is to see them go!

MARYA   *(coming in slowly)*   They have gone. *(She sits down and immediately becomes absorbed in her book.* SONYA *sits at the table and looks through an account book)*

SONYA   First, Uncle Vanya, let us add up the bills. We have neglected them dreadfully. We received another bill today. Come. We'll both do them.

VANYA   In account with . . . *(writing)* . . . in account with . . .

MARINA   *(yawning)*   The sandman is on his way.

ASTROV   How silent it is. The pens scratch and the cricket sings; it is so warm and comfortable. You know, I hate to go.

(The tinkling of bells is heard)

ASTROV   Ah, but my carriage has come. All that remains is to say goodbye to you, my friends, and to my table here, and then . . . away! *(He puts the map in the portfolio)*

MARINA   Why be in such a hurry . . . you can stay a little while longer.

ASTROV   Impossible.

VANYA   *(writing)*   And carry forward from the old debt two seventy-five . . .

(The WORKMAN *enters)*

WORKMAN   Your carriage is waiting, sir.

ASTROV   All right. *(He hands the* WORKMAN *his medicine case, portfolio, and box)* Be careful, don't crush the portfolio!

WORKMAN   Yes, sir.

SONYA   When shall we see you again?

ASTROV   Probably not before next summer. Certainly not again till winter's over, at any rate. Of course, if anything happens, let me know, and I'll come at once. *(shaking hands)* Thank you for your hospitality, your kindness . . . for all you've done. *(He goes to the nurse and kisses her head)* Goodbye, old nurse.

MARINA   Are you going without your tea?

ASTROV   I don't care for any, nurse.

MARINA   Won't you have just a little vodka?

ASTROV   *(hesitatingly)*   Yes, I guess I might as well. *(*MARINA *goes out. After a pause)* One of my horses has gone lame for some reason. I noticed it yesterday when Peter was watering him.

VANYA   You should have him reshod.

ASTROV   I shall have to stop at the blacksmith's on my way home. It can't be helped. *(He stands looking up at the map of Africa on the wall)* I suppose it is terribly hot in Africa now.

VANYA   Yes, I suppose it is.

*(*MARINA *comes back carrying a tray with a glass of vodka and a slice of bread)*

MARINA   There you are. *(*ASTROV *drinks)* Your health! *(bowing deeply)* Eat your bread with it.

ASTROV   No, I like it this way. And now, goodbye. *(to* MARINA*)* You needn't come out to see me off, nurse. *(He leaves.* SONYA *follows him with a candle to light him to the carriage.* MARINA *sits in her chair)*

VANYA   *(writing)*   On the second of February, twenty pounds of butter; on the sixteenth, twenty pounds of butter again. Buckwheat flour . . . *(Pause. The tinkling of bells is heard)*

MARINA   He has gone.

(A pause. SONYA *enters and sets the candlestick on the table)*

SONYA   He has gone.

VANYA   *(adding and writing)*   Total, fifteen . . . twenty-five . . .

*(*SONYA *sits down and begins to write)*

MARINA   *(yawning)*   Oh, ho! The Lord have mercy on us.

*(*TELYEGIN *enters on tiptoe, seats himself near the door, and begins to tune his guitar)*

VANYA   *(to* SONYA, *caressing her hair)*   My child, I feel so wretched!

SONYA   What can we do? We must go on living. *(pause)* Yes, we shall live, Uncle Vanya. Shall live through the endless procession of days before us, and through all the long evenings. We shall bear patiently the burdens that fate brings to us. We shall work, without rest, for others, both now and when we are old.

And, then, when our final hour comes, we shall meet it humbly, and there beyond the grave, we shall know that we have known suffering and tears . . . that our life was bitter. And God will pity us. Oh, then, dear Uncle, we shall enter into a bright and beautiful life. We shall rejoice and look back upon our grief here . . . with tenderness . . . and a smile; (*pause*) and we shall have rest. I have faith, Uncle, fervent, passionate faith. (SONYA *kneels down in front of her uncle and lays her head in his hands. She speaks with a weary voice*) We shall have rest. (TELYEGIN *plays softly on his guitar*) We shall have rest. We shall hear the angels sing. We shall see heaven shining in all its radiant glory. We shall see all the world's evils . . . our every pain, our suffering . . . be engulfed by God's all-pervading mercy that shall enfold the earth. Our life will be peaceful, gentle, and sweet—like a child's caress. Oh, I have faith; I have faith—(*wiping away his tears*) My poor Uncle Vanya, you are crying! (*through her tears*) You have never known joy in your life, but wait, Uncle Vanya, wait! You, too, will have rest. (*embracing him*) You, too, will rest. (*The Watchman's rattle is heard from the garden;* TELYEGIN *plays softly;* MARYA *writes on the margin of her pamphlet;* MARINA *is knitting her stocking*) We shall rest. . . .

THE CHERRY ORCHARD

A New Version by Robert W. Corrigan

CAST OF CHARACTERS

MADAME RANEVSKY (*Lyubov Andreyevna*), *owner of the cherry orchard*

ANYA, *her daughter, age 17*

VARYA, *her adopted daughter, age 24*

GAEV (*Leonid Andreyevich*), *Lyubov's brother*

LOPAHIN (*Yermolay Alexeyevich*), *a business man*

TROFIMOV (*Pyotr Sergeyevich*), *a student*

SEMYONOV-PISHCHIK (*Boris Borisovich*), *a landowner*

CHARLOTTA IVANOVNA, *a governess*

EPIHODOV (*Semyon Pantaleyevich*), *a clerk on the Ranevsky estate*

DUNYASHA, *a maid*

FEERS, *an old servant, age 87*

YASHA, *a young servant*

A TRAMP

THE STATION MASTER

A POST-OFFICE CLERK

GUESTS AND SERVANTS

SCENE *The estate of Madame Ranevsky.*

ACT ONE

(*A room which used to be the children's room and is still called the nursery. Several doors, one leading into* ANYA's *room. It is early in the morning and the sun is rising. It is early in*

The Cherry Orchard by Anton Chekhov, translated by Robert W. Corrigan, is from *Six Plays of Chekhov.* Copyright © 1962 by Robert W. Corrigan, and reprinted by permission of the translator and the publisher, Holt, Rinehart and Winston, Inc.

May, but there is a morning frost. The windows are closed but through them can be seen the blossoming cherry trees. Enter DUNYASHA, *carrying a candle, and* LOPAHIN *with a book in his hand*)

LOPAHIN The train's arrived, thank God. What time is it?

DUNYASHA It's nearly two. (*blows out the candle*) It's daylight already.

LOPAHIN The train must have been at least two hours late. (*yawns and stretches*) And what a fool I am! I make a special trip out here to meet them at the station, and then I fall asleep. . . . Just sat down in the chair and dropped off. What a nuisance. Why didn't you wake me up?

DUNYASHA I thought you'd gone. (*listens*) I think they're coming.

LOPAHIN (*also listens*) No . . . I should've been there to help them with their luggage and other things. . . . (*pause*) Lyubov Andreyevna has been abroad for five years. I wonder what she's like now. She used to be such a kind and good person. So easy to get along with and always considerate. Why, I remember when I was fifteen, my father—he had a store in town then—hit me in the face and it made my nose bleed. . . . We'd come out here for something or other, and he was drunk. Oh, I remember it as if it happened yesterday. . . . She was so young and beautiful . . . Lyubov Andreyevna brought me into this very room—the nursery, and she fixed my nose and she said to me, "Don't cry, little peasant, it'll be better by the time you get married." . . . (*pause*) "Little peasant" . . . She was right, my father was a peasant. And look at me now—going about in a white waistcoat and brown shoes, like a crown in peacock's feathers. Oh, I am rich alright, I've got lots of money, but when you think about it, I'm still just a peasant. (*turning over pages of the book*) Here, I've been reading this book, and couldn't understand a word of it. Fell asleep reading it.

[495]

(*Pause*)

DUNYASHA   The dogs have been awake all
night: they know their mistress is coming.

LOPAHIN   Why, what's the matter with you,
Dunyasha?

DUNYASHA   My hands are shaking. I think
I'm going to faint.

LOPAHIN   You've become too delicate and
refined, Dunyasha. You get yourself all dressed
up like a lady, and you fix your hair like one,
too. You shouldn't do that, you know. You must
remember your place.

(*Enter* EPIHODOV *with a bouquet of flowers; he
wears a jacket and brightly polished high boots
which squeak loudly. As he enters he drops
the flowers*)

EPIHODOV   (*picks up the flowers*)   The gardener sent these. He says they're to go in the
dining room. (*hands the flowers to* DUNYASHA)

LOPAHIN   And bring me some kvass.

DUNYASHA   All right.

EPIHODOV   It's chilly outside this morning,
three degrees of frost, and here the cherry trees
are all in bloom. I can't say much for this climate of ours, you know. (*sighs*) No, I really
can't. It doesn't contribute to—well, you know,
things . . . And what do you think, Yermolay
Alexeyevich, the day before yesterday I bought
myself a pair of boots and they squeak so much
. . . well, I mean to say, they're impossible.
. . . What can I use to fix them?

LOPAHIN   Oh, be quiet! And don't bother
me!

EPIHODOV   Every day something unpleasant
happens to me. But I don't complain; I'm used
to it, why I even laugh. (*enter* DUNYASHA. *She
serves* LOPAHIN *with kvass*) Well, I have to be
going. (*bumps into a chair which falls over*)
There, you see! (*triumphantly*) You can see
for yourself what I mean, you see . . . so to
speak . . . It's absolutely amazing! (*goes out*)

DUNYASHA   I must tell you a secret, Yermolay Alexeyevich. Epihodov proposed to me.

LOPAHIN   Really!

DUNYASHA   I don't know what to do. . . .
He's a quiet man, but then sometimes he starts
talking, and then you can't understand a word
he says. It sounds nice, and he says it with so
much feeling, but it doesn't make any sense. I
think I like him a little, and he's madly in love
with me. But the poor man, he's sort of unlucky! Do you know, something unpleasant
seems to happen to him every day. That's why
they tease him and call him "two-and-twenty
misfortunes."

LOPAHIN   (*listens*)   I think I hear them coming. . . .

DUNYASHA   Coming! . . . Oh, what's the
matter with me. . . . I feel cold all over.

LOPAHIN   Yes, they're really coming! Let's
go and meet them at the door. I wonder if she'll
recognize me? We haven't seen each other for
five years.

DUNYASHA   (*agitated*)   I'm going to faint
. . . Oh, I'm going to faint! . . .

(*The sound of two carriages driving up to the
house can be heard.* LOPAHIN *and* DUNYASHA
*hurry out. The stage is empty. Then there are
sounds of people arriving in the next room.*
FEERS, *who has gone to meet the train, enters
the room leaning on a cane. He crosses the
stage as rapidly as he can. He is dressed in an
old-fashioned livery coat and a top hat and is
muttering to himself, though it is impossible to
make out what he is saying. The noises offstage
become louder*)

VOICE   (*offstage*)   Let's go through here.

(*Enter* LYUBOV ANDREYEVNA, ANYA, *and* CHAR-
LOTTA IVANOVNA, *leading a small dog, all in
traveling clothes,* VARYA, *wearing an overcoat
and a kerchief over her head,* GAEV, SEMYONOV-
PISHCHIK, LOPAHIN, DUNYASHA, *carrying a bundle and parasol and other servants with luggage*)

ANYA   Let's go through here. Do you remember what room this is, Mamma?

LYUBOV   (*joyfully through her tears*)   The
nursery!

VARYA   How cold it is! My hands are numb.
(*to* LYUBOV) Your rooms are the same as
always, Mamma dear, the white one, and the
lavender one.

LYUBOV   The nursery, my dear, beautiful
room! . . . I used to sleep here when I was
little. (*cries*) And here I am again, like a little
child. . . . (*She kisses her brother, then*
VARYA, *then her brother again*) And Varya
hasn't changed a bit, looking like a nun. And I
recognized Dunyasha, too. (*kisses* DUNYASHA)

GAEV   The train was two hours late. Just
think of it! Such efficiency!

CHARLOTTA   (*to* PISHCHIK)   And my dog
eats nuts, too.

PISHCHIK   (*astonished*)   Think of that!

(*They all go out except* ANYA *and* DUNYASHA)

DUNYASHA   We've waited and waited for
you. . . . (*helps* ANYA *to take off her hat and
coat*)

ANYA   I haven't slept for four nights . . .
I'm freezing.

DUNYASHA   It was Lent when you left, and
it was snowing and freezing; but it's spring
now. Darling! (*She laughs and kisses her*) Oh,

how I've missed you! I could hardly stand it. My pet, my precious . . . But I must tell you . . . I can't wait another minute. . . .

ANYA (*without enthusiasm*) What time is it? . . .

DUNYASHA Epihodov, the clerk, proposed to me right after Easter.

ANYA You never talk about anything else. . . . (*tidies her hair*) I've lost all my hairpins. . . . (*She is so tired she can hardly keep on her feet*)

DUNYASHA I really don't know what to think. He loves me . . . he loves me very much!

ANYA (*looking through the door into her room, tenderly*) My own room, my own windows, just as if I'd never left them! I'm home again! Tomorrow I'm going to get up and run right to the garden! Oh, if only I could fall asleep! I couldn't sleep all the way back, I've been so worried.

DUNYASHA Pyotr Sergeyevich came the day before yesterday.

ANYA (*joyfully*) Petya!

DUNYASHA We put him in the bath house, he's probably asleep now. He said he didn't want to inconvenience you. (*looks at her watch*) I should have gotten him up, but Varya told me not to. "Don't you dare get him up," she said.

(*Enter* VARYA *with a bunch of keys at her waist*)

VARYA Dunyasha, get some coffee, and hurry! Mamma wants some.

DUNYASHA I'll get it right away. (*goes out*)

VARYA Thank God, you're back! You're home again. (*embracing her*) My little darling's come home! How are you, my precious?

ANYA If you only knew what I've had to put up with!

VARYA I can just imagine . . .

ANYA You remember, I left just before Easter and it was cold then. And Charlotta never stopped talking the whole time, talking and those silly tricks of hers. Why did you make me take Charlotta?

VARYA But you couldn't go all alone, darling. At seventeen!

ANYA When we got to Paris it was cold and snowing. My French was terrible. Mamma was living on the fifth floor, and the place was filled with people—some French ladies, and an old priest with a little book, and the room was full of cigarette smoke. It was so unpleasant. All of a sudden I felt so sorry for Mamma that I put my arms around her neck and hugged her

and wouldn't let go I was so upset. Later Mamma cried and was very kind.

VARYA (*tearfully*) I can't stand to hear it! . . .

ANYA She had already sold her villa at Mentone, and she had nothing left, not a thing. And I didn't have any money left either, not a penny. In fact, I barely had enough to get to Paris. And Mamma didn't understand it at all. On the way, we'd eat at the best restaurants and she'd order the most expensive dishes and tip the waiters a rouble each. Charlotta's the same way. And Yasha expected a full-course dinner for himself; it was horrible. You know, Yasha is Mamma's valet, now, we brought him with us.

VARYA Yes, I've seen the scoundrel.

ANYA Well, how's everything here? Have you paid the interest on the mortgage?

VARYA With what?

ANYA Oh dear! Oh dear!

VARYA The time runs out in August, and then it will be up for sale.

ANYA Oh dear!

LOPAHIN (*puts his head through the door and moos like a cow*) Moo-o. . . . (*disappears*)

VARYA (*tearfully*) I'd like to hit him . . . (*clenches her first*)

ANYA (*her arms round* VARYA, *dropping her voice*) Varya, has he proposed to you? (VARYA *shakes her head*) But he loves you. . . . Why don't you talk to him, what are you waiting for?

VARYA Nothing will come of it. He's too busy to have time to think of me . . . He doesn't notice me at all. It's easier when he isn't around, it makes me miserable just to see him. Everybody talks of our wedding and congratulates me, but in fact there's nothing to it, it's all a dream. (*in a different tone*) You've got a new pin, it looks like a bee.

ANYA (*sadly*) Mamma bought it for me. (*She goes into her room and then with childlike gaiety*) Did you know that in Paris I went up in a balloon?

VARYA My darling's home again! My precious one's home. (DUNYASHA *returns with a coffeepot and prepares coffee. Standing by* ANYA's *door*) You know, all day long, as I go about the house doing my work, I'm always dreaming. If only we could marry you to some rich man, I'd be more at peace. Then they could go away; first I'd go to the cloisters, and then I'd go on a pilgrimage to Kiev, and then Moscow . . . I'd spend my life just walking from one holy place to another. On and on. Oh, what a wonderful life that would be!

ANYA   The birds are singing in the garden. What time is it?

VARYA   It must be nearly three. Time you went to bed, darling. (*goes into* ANYA'S *room*) Oh, what a wonderful life!

(*Enter* YASHA, *with a blanket and a small bag*)

YASHA   (*crossing the stage, in an affectedly genteel voice*)   May I go through here?

DUNYASHA   My, how you've changed since you've been abroad, Yasha. I hardly recognized you.

YASHA   Hm! And who are you?

DUNYASHA   When you went away, I was no bigger than this. . . . (*shows her height from the floor*) I'm Dunyasha, Fyodor's daughter. You don't remember me!

YASHA   Hm! You're quite a little peach! (*He looks around and embraces her; she screams and drops a saucer.* YASHA *goes out quickly*)

VARYA   (*in the doorway, crossly*)   What's happening in here?

DUNYASHA   (*tearfully*)   I've broken a saucer.

VARYA   That's good luck.

ANYA   (*coming out of her room*)   We ought to warn Mamma that Petya's here.

VARYA   I gave strict orders not to wake him up.

ANYA   (*pensively*)   Six years ago father died, and then a month later Grisha was drowned in the river. He was such a beautiful little boy— and only seven! Mamma couldn't stand it so she went away . . . and never looked back. (*shivers*) How well I understand her! If she only knew! (*pause*) And, Petya was Grisha's tutor, he might remind her . . .

(*Enter* FEERS, *wearing a jacket and a white waistcoat*)

FEERS   (*goes over and is busy with the samovar*)   The mistress will have her coffee in here. (*puts on white gloves*) Is it ready? (*to* DUNYASHA, *severely*) Where's the cream?

DUNYASHA   Oh, I forgot! (*goes out quickly*)

FEERS   (*fussing around the coffeepot*)   That girl's hopeless. . . . (*mutters*) They've come from Paris . . . Years ago the master used to go to Paris . . . Used to go by carriage. . . . (*laughs*)

VARYA   Feers, what are you laughing at?

FEERS   What would you like? (*happily*) The mistress has come home! Home at last! I don't mind if I die now. . . . (*weeps with joy*)

(*Enter* LYUBOV, LOPAHIN, GAEV *and* SEMYONOV-PISHCHIK, *the latter in a long peasant coat of fine cloth and full trousers tucked inside high boots.* GAEV, *as he comes in, moves his arms and body as if he were playing billiards*)

LYUBOV   How does it go now? Let me think . . . The red off the side and into the middle pocket!

GAEV   That's right! Then I put the white into the corner pocket! . . . Years ago we used to sleep in this room, and now I'm fifty-one, strange as it may seem.

LOPAHIN   Yes, time flies.

GAEV   What?

LOPAHIN   Time flies, I say.

GAEV   This place smells of patchouli . . .

ANYA   I'm going to bed. Goodnight, Mamma. (*kisses her*)

LYUBOV   My precious child! (*kisses her hands*) Are you glad you're home? I still can't get used to it.

ANYA   Goodnight, Uncle.

GAEV   (*kisses her face and hands*)   God bless you. You're so much like your mother! (*to his sister*) You looked exactly like her at her age, Lyuba.

(ANYA *shakes hands with* LOPAHIN *and* PISH-CHIK, *goes out and shuts the door after her*)

LYUBOV   She's very tired.

PISHCHIK   It's been a long trip for her.

VARYA   (*to* LOPAHIN *and* PISHCHIK)   Well, gentlemen? It's nearly three o'clock, time to say good-bye.

LYUBOV   (*laughs*)   You haven't changed a bit, Varya. (*draws* VARYA *to her and kisses her*) Let me have some coffee, then we'll all turn in. (FEERS *places a cushion under her feet*) Thank you, my dear. I've got into the habit of drinking coffee. I drink it day and night. Thank you, my dear old friend. (*kisses* FEERS)

VARYA   I'd better see if they brought all the luggage in. (*goes out*)

LYUBOV   Is it really me sitting here? (*laughing*) I'd like to dance and wave my arms about. (*covering her face with her hands*) But am I just dreaming? God, how I love it here—my own country! Oh, I love it so much, I could hardly see anything from the train, I was crying so hard. (*through tears*) Here, but I must drink my coffee. Thank you, Feers, thank you, my dear old friend. I'm so glad you're still alive.

FEERS   The day before yesterday.

GAEV   He doesn't hear very well.

LOPAHIN   I've got to leave for Kharkov a little after four. What a nuisance! It's so good just to see you, and I want to talk with you . . . You look as lovely as ever.

PISHCHIK   (*breathing heavily*)   Prettier. In her fancy Parisian clothes . . . She's simply ravishing!

LOPAHIN   Your brother here—Leonid Andreyevich—says that I'm nothing but a hick from the country, a tight-fisted peasant, but it doesn't bother me. Let him say what he likes. All I want is that you trust me as you always have. Merciful God! My father was your father's serf, and your grandfather's too, but you've done so much for me that I've forgotten all that. I love you as if you were my own sister . . . more than that even.

LYUBOV   I just can't sit still, I can't for the life of me! (*She jumps up and walks about in great excitement*) I'm so happy, it's too much for me. It's all right, you can laugh at me. I know I'm being silly . . . My wonderful old bookcase! (*kisses bookcase*) And my little table!

GAEV   You know, the old Nurse died while you were away.

LYUBOV (*sits down and drinks coffee*)   Yes, you wrote to me about it. May she rest in peace.

GAEV   Anastasy died, too. And Petrushka quit and is working in town for the chief of police. (*takes a box of gumdrops out of his pocket and puts one in his mouth*)

PISHCHIK   My daughter, Dashenka, sends you her greetings.

LOPAHIN   I feel like telling you some good news, something to cheer you up. (*looks at his watch*) I'll have to leave in a minute, so there's not much time to talk. But briefly it's this. As you know, the cherry orchard is going to be sold to pay your debts. They've set August 22nd as the date for the auction, but you can sleep in peace and not worry about it; there's a way out. Here's my plan, so please pay close attention. Your estate is only twenty miles from town, and the railroad is close by. Now, if the cherry orchard and the land along the river were subdivided and leased for the building of summer cottages, you'd have a yearly income of at least twenty-five thousand roubles.

GAEV   Such nonsense!

LYUBOV   I'm afraid I don't quite understand, Yermolay Alexeyevich.

LOPAHIN   You'd divide the land into one acre lots and rent them for at least twenty-five roubles a year. I'll bet you, that if you advertise it now there won't be a lot left by the fall; they'll be snapped up almost at once. You see, you're saved! And really, I must congratulate you; it's a perfect set-up. The location is marvelous and the river's deep enough for swimming. Of course, the land will have to be cleared and cleaned up a bit. For instance, all those old buildings will have to be torn down . . . And this house, too . . . but then it's

not really good for anything anymore. . . . And then, the old cherry orchard will have to be cut down . . .

LYUBOV   Cut down? My good man, forgive me, but you don't seem to understand. If there's one thing that's interesting and really valuable in this whole part of the country, it's our cherry orchard.

LOPAHIN   The only valuable thing about it is that it's very large. It only produces a crop every other year and then who wants to buy it?

GAEV   Why, this orchard is even mentioned in the Encyclopedia.

LOPAHIN (*looking at his watch*)   If you don't decide now, and do something about it before August, the cherry orchard as well as the estate will be auctioned off. So make up your minds! There's no other way out, I promise you. There's no other way.

FEERS   In the old days, forty or fifty years ago, the cherries were dried, preserved, pickled, made into jam, and sometimes . . .

GAEV   Be quiet, Feers.

FEERS   And sometimes, whole wagon-loads of dried cherries were shipped to Moscow and Kharkov. We used to make a lot of money on them then! And the dried cherries used to be soft, juicy, sweet, and very good . . . They knew how to do it then . . . they had a way of cooking them . . .

LYUBOV   And where is that recipe now?

FEERS   They've forgotten it. Nobody can remember it.

PISHCHIK (*to* LYUBOV)   What's it like in Paris? Did you eat frogs?

LYUBOV   I ate crocodiles.

PISHCHIK   Well, will you imagine that!

LOPAHIN   Until recently only rich people and peasants lived in the country, but now lots of people come out for the summer. Almost every town, even the small ones, is surrounded with summer places. And probably within the next twenty years there'll be more and more of these people. Right now, all they do is sit on the porch and drink tea, but later on they might begin to grow a few things, and then your cherry orchard would be full of life again . . . rich and prosperous.

GAEV (*indignantly*)   Such a lot of nonsense! (*Enter* VARYA *and* YASHA)

VARYA   There were two telegrams for you, Mamma dear. (*takes out the keys and opens the old bookcase, making a great deal of noise*) Here they are.

LYUBOV   They're from Paris. (*tears them up without reading them*) I'm through with Paris.

GAEV Do you know, Lyuba, how old this bookcase is? Last week I pulled out the bottom drawer, and I found the date it was made burned in the wood. Just think, it's exactly a hundred years old. What do you think of that, eh? We ought to celebrate its anniversary. I know it's an inanimate object, but still—it's a bookcase!

PISHCHIK (*astonished*) A hundred years! Can you imagine that!

GAEV Yes . . . That's quite something. (*feeling round the bookcase with his hands*) Dear, most honored bookcase! I salute you! For one hundred years you have served the highest ideals of goodness and justice. For one hundred years you have made us aware of the need for creative work; several generations of our family have had their courage sustained and their faith in a brighter future fortified by your silent call; you have fostered in us the ideals of public service and social consciousness.

(*Pause*)

LOPAHIN Yes . . .

LYUBOV You haven't changed a bit, Leonia.

GAEV (*slightly embarrassed*) I shoot it off the corner into the middle pocket! . . .

LOPAHIN (*looks at his watch*) Well, I've got to go.

YASHA (*brings medicine to* LYUBOV) Would you like to take your pills now; it's time.

PISHCHIK You shouldn't take medicine, my dear . . . they don't do you any good . . . or harm either. Let me have them. (*takes the box from her, pours the pills into the palm of his hand, blows on them, puts them all into his mouth and drinks them down with kvass*) There!

LYUBOV (*alarmed*) You're out of your mind!

PISHCHIK I took all the pills.

LOPAHIN What a stomach!

(*All laugh*)

FEERS His honor was here during Holy Week, and he ate half a bucket of pickles. (*mutters*)

LYUBOV What's he saying?

VARYA He's been muttering like that for three years now. We're used to it.

YASHA It's his age. . . .

(CHARLOTTA IVANOVNA, *very thin, and tightly laced in a white dress, with a lorgnette at her waist, passes across the stage*)

LOPAHIN Excuse me, Charlotta Ivanovna, for not greeting you. I didn't have a chance.

(*tries to kiss her hand*)

CHARLOTTA (*withdrawing her hand*) If I let you kiss my hand, then you'd want to kiss my elbow next, and then my shoulder.

LOPAHIN This just isn't my lucky day. (*all laugh*) Charlotta Ivanovna, do a trick for us.

CHARLOTTA Not now. I want to go to bed. (*goes out*)

LOPAHIN I'll be back in three weeks. (*kisses* LYUBOV's *hand*) It's time I'm going so I'll say good-bye. (*to* GAEV) Au revoir. (*embraces* PISHCHIK) Au revoir. (*shakes hands with* VARYA, *then with* FEERS *and* YASHA) I don't want to go, really. (*to* LYUBOV) Think over the idea of the summer cottages and if you decide anything, let me know, and I'll get you a loan of at least fifty thousand. So think it over seriously.

VARYA (*crossly*) Won't you ever go?

LOPAHIN I'm going, I'm going. (*goes out*)

GAEV What a boor! I beg your pardon . . . Varya's going to marry him, he's Varya's fiancé.

VARYA Please don't talk like that, Uncle.

LYUBOV Well, Varya, I'd be delighted. He's a good man.

PISHCHIK He's a man . . . you have to say that . . . a most worthy fellow . . . My Dashenka says so too . . . she says all sorts of things. . . . (*He drops asleep and snores, but wakes up again at once*) By the way, my dear, will you lend me two hundred and forty roubles? I've got to pay the interest on the mortgage tomorrow . . .

VARYA (*in alarm*) We haven't got it, really we haven't!

LYUBOV It's true, I haven't got a thing.

PISHCHIK It'll turn up. (*laughs*) I never lose hope. There are times when I think everything's lost, I'm ruined, and then—suddenly!— a railroad is built across my land, and they pay me for it! Something's bound to happen, if not today, then tomorrow, or the next day. Perhaps Dashenka will win two hundred thousand— she's got a lottery ticket.

LYUBOV Well, we've finished our coffee; now we can go to bed.

FEERS (*brushing* GAEV, *admonishing him*) You've got on the trousers again! What am I going to do with you?

VARYA (*in a low voice*) Anya's asleep. (*quietly opens a window*) The sun's rising and see how wonderful the trees are! And the air smells so fragrant! The birds are beginning to sing.

GAEV (*coming to the window*) The orchard is all white. You haven't forgotten, Lyuba? How straight that lane is . . . just like a ribbon. And how it shines on moonlight nights. Do you remember? You haven't forgotten, have you?

LYUBOV (*looks through the window at the orchard*) Oh, my childhood, my innocent childhood! I used to sleep here, and I'd look out at the orchard and every morning when I woke up I was so happy. The orchard was exactly the same, nothing's changed. (*laughs happily*) All, all white! Oh, my orchard! After the dark, gloomy autumn and the cold winter, you are young again and full of joy; the angels have not deserted you! If only this burden could be taken from me, if only I could forget my past!

GAEV Yes, and now the orchard's going to be sold to pay our debts, how strange it all is.

LYUBOV Look, there's Mother walking through the orchard . . . dressed all in white! (*laughs happily*) It is Mother!

GAEV Where?

VARYA Oh, please, Mamma dear!

LYUBOV You're right, it's no one, I only imagined it. Over there, you see, on the right, by the path that goes to the arbor, there's a small white tree that's bending so it looks just like a woman. (*Enter* TROFIMOV. *He is dressed in a shabby student's uniform, and wears glasses*) What a wonderful orchard! Masses of white blossoms, the blue sky . . .

TROFIMOV Lyubov Andreyevna! (*She turns to him*) I'll just say hello and leave at once. (*kisses her hand warmly*) They told me to wait until morning, but I couldn't wait any longer. (LYUBOV *looks at him, puzzled*)

VARYA (*through tears*) This is Petya Trofimov.

TROFIMOV Petya Trofimov, I was Grisha's tutor. Have I changed that much? (LYUBOV *puts her arms round him and weeps quietly*)

GAEV (*embarrassed*) Now, now, Lyuba . . .

VARYA (*weeps*) Didn't I tell you to wait until tomorrow, Petya?

LYUBOV My Grisha . . . my little boy . . . Oh, Grisha . . . my son . . .

VARYA Don't cry, Mamma darling. There's nothing we can do, it was God's will.

TROFIMOV (*gently, with emotion*) Don't, don't . . . please.

LYUBOV (*weeping quietly*) My little boy was lost . . . drowned . . . Why? Why, my friend? (*more quietly*) Anya's asleep in there, and here I'm crying and making a scene. But tell me, Petya, what's happened to your good looks? You've aged so.

TROFIMOV A peasant woman on the train called me "that moth-eaten man."

LYUBOV You used to be such an attractive boy, a typical young student. But now your hair is thin and you wear glasses. Are you still a student? (*She walks to the door*)

TROFIMOV I expect I'll be a student as long as I live.

LYUBOV (*kisses her brother, then* VARYA) Well, go to bed now. You have aged, too, Leonid.

PISHCHIK (*following her*) Yes, I suppose it's time to get to bed. Oh, my gout! I'd better spend the night here, and in the morning, Lyubov Andreyevna, my dear, I'd like to borrow the two hundred and forty roubles.

GAEV Don't you ever stop?

PISHCHIK Just two hundred and forty roubles . . . To pay the interest on my mortgage.

LYUBOV I haven't any money, my friend.

PISHCHIK Oh, I'll pay you back, my dear. It's not much, after all.

LYUBOV Oh, all right. Leonid will give it to you. You give him the money, Leonid.

GAEV Why, of course; glad to. As much as he wants!

LYUBOV What else can we do? He needs it. He'll pay it back. (LYUBOV, TROFIMOV, PISHCHIK *and* FEERS *go out.* GAEV, VARYA *and* YASHA *remain*)

GAEV My sister hasn't lost her habit of throwing money away. (*to* YASHA) Get out of the way, you smell like a barnyard.

YASHA (*with a sneer*) And you haven't changed either, have you Leonid Andreyevich?

GAEV What's that? (*to* VARYA) What did he say?

VARYA (*to* YASHA) Your mother came out from town yesterday to see you, and she's been waiting out in the servant's quarters ever since.

YASHA I wish she wouldn't bother me.

VARYA Oh, you ought to be ashamed of yourself.

YASHA What's she in such a hurry for? She could have come tomorrow. (YASHA *goes out*)

VARYA Mamma hasn't changed a bit. She'd give away everything we had, if she could.

GAEV Yes . . . You know, when many things are prescribed to cure a disease, that means it's incurable. I've been wracking my brains to find an answer, and I've come up with several solutions, plenty of them—which means there aren't any. It would be wonderful if we could inherit some money, or if our Anya were to marry some very rich man, or if one of us went to Yaroslavl and tried our luck with our old aunt, the Countess. You know she's very rich.

VARYA (*weeping*) If only God would help us.

GAEV Oh, stop blubbering! The Countess is very rich, but she doesn't like us . . . To begin with, my sister married a lawyer, and not a nobleman . . . (ANYA *appears in the door-way*) She married a commoner . . . and since then no one can say she's behaved in the most virtuous way possible. She's good, kind, and lovable, and I love her very much, but no matter how much you may allow for extenuating circumstances, you've got to admit that her morals have not been beyond reproach. You can sense it in everything she does . . .

VARYA (*in a whisper*) Anya's standing in the doorway.

GAEV What? (*a pause*) Isn't that strange, something's gotten into my right eye . . . I'm having a terrible time seeing. And last Thursday, when I was in the District Court . . .

(ANYA *comes in*)

VARYA Anya, why aren't you asleep?

ANYA I don't feel like sleeping. I just can't.

GAEV My dear little girl! (*kisses* ANYA's *face and hands*) My child! (*tearfully*) You're not just my niece, you're an angel, my whole world. Please believe me, believe . . .

ANYA I believe you, Uncle. Everyone loves you, respects you . . . but, dear Uncle, you shouldn't talk so much, just try to keep quiet. What were you saying just now about mother, about your own sister? What made you say that?

GAEV Yes, yes! (*He takes her hand and puts it over his face*) You're quite right, it was a horrible thing to say! My God! My God! And that speech I made to the bookcase . . . so stupid! As soon as I finished it, I realized how stupid it was.

VARYA It's true, Uncle dear, you oughtn't to talk so much. Just keep quiet, that's all.

ANYA If you keep quiet, you'll find life is more peaceful.

GAEV I'll be quiet. (*kisses* ANYA's *and* VARYA's *hands*) I'll be quiet. But I must tell you something about all this business, it's important. Last Thursday I went to the District Court, and I got talking with some friends, and from what they said it looks as if it might be possible to get a second mortgage so we can pay the interest to the bank.

VARYA If only God would help us!

GAEV I'm going again on Tuesday to talk with them some more. (*to* VARYA) Oh, stop crying. (*to* ANYA) Your mother's going to talk with Lopahin, and he certainly won't refuse her. And after you've had a little rest, you can go to Yaroslavl to see your grandmother, the Countess. You see, we'll attack the problem from three sides, and—it's as good as solved! We'll pay the interest, I'm sure of it. (*He eats a gumdrop*) On my honor, on anything you

like, I swear the estate'll not be sold! (*excited*) I'll bet my happiness on it! Here's my hand, you can call me a worthless liar if I allow the auction to take place. I swear it with all my soul!

ANYA (*calmer, with an air of happiness*) How good you are, Uncle, and how sensible! (*embracing him*) I'm not afraid anymore. I feel so happy and at peace.

(*Enter* FEERS)

FEERS (*reproachfully*) Leonid Andreyevich, aren't you ashamed of yourself? When are you going to bed?

GAEV In a minute. Now you go away, Feers. I can get ready for bed myself. Come along, children, time for bed. We'll talk about it some more tomorrow, you must go to bed now. (*kisses* ANYA *and* VARYA) You know, I'm a man of the 'eighties. People don't think much of that period these days, but still I can say that I've suffered a great deal in my lifetime because of my convictions. There's a reason why the peasants love me. You have to know the peasants! You have to know . . .

ANYA You're beginning again, Uncle!

VARYA Yes, you'd better keep quiet, Uncle dear.

FEERS (*sternly*) Leonid Andreyevich!

GAEV I'm coming, I'm coming! Go to bed now! Bank the white into the side pocket. There's a shot for you . . . (*goes out;* FEERS *hobbles after him*)

ANYA I feel better now, although I don't want to go to Yaroslavl, I don't like the Countess at all, but then, thanks to Uncle, we really don't have to worry at all. (*She sits down*)

VARYA I've got to get some sleep. I'm going. Oh, by the way, we had a terrible scene while you were gone. You know, there are only a few old servants left out in the servants' quarters: just Yefmushka, Polya, Yevstignay, and Karp. Well, they let some tramps sleep out there, and at first I didn't say anything about it. But then later, I heard people saying that I had given orders to feed them nothing but beans. Because I was stingy, you see . . . Yevstignay was the cause of it all. "Well," I think to myself, "if that's how things are, just you wait!" So I called Yevstignay in. (*yawns*) So he came. "What's all this, Yevstignay," I said to him, "you're such a fool." (*She walks up to* ANYA) Anichka! (*a pause*) She's asleep! . . . (*takes her arm*) Let's go to bed! Come! (*leads her away*) My darling's fallen asleep! Come . . . (*They go towards the door. The sound of a shepherd's pipe is heard from far away,* beyond the orchard. TROFIMOV *crosses the stage, but, seeing* VARYA *and* ANYA, *stops*) Sh-sh! She's asleep . . . asleep . . . Come along, come along.

ANYA (*softly, half-asleep*) I'm so tired. . . . I can hear the bells ringing all the time . . . Uncle . . . dear . . . Mamma and Uncle. . . .

VARYA Come, darling, come. . . . (*They go into* ANYA's *room*)

TROFIMOV (*deeply moved*) Oh, Anya . . . my sunshine! My spring!

ACT TWO

(*An old abandoned chapel in a field. Beside it are a well, an old bench and some tombstones. A road leads to the Ranevsky estate. On one side a row of poplars casts a shadow; at that point the cherry orchard begins. In the distance, a line of telegraph poles can be seen, and beyond them, on the horizon is the outline of a large town, visible only in very clear weather. It's nearly sunset.* CHARLOTTA, YASHA *and* DUNYASHA *are sitting on the bench;* EPIHODOV *is standing near by, playing a guitar; everyone is lost in thought.* CHARLOTTA *is wearing an old hunting cap; she has taken a shotgun off her shoulder and is adjusting the buckle on the strap*)

CHARLOTTA (*thoughtfully*) I don't know how old I am. For you see, I haven't got a passport . . . but I keep pretending that I'm still very young. When I was a little girl, my father and mother traveled from fair to fair giving performances—oh, very good ones. And I used to do the *salto-mortale* and all sorts of other tricks, too. When Papa and Mamma died, a German lady took me to live with her and sent me to school. So when I grew up I became a governess. But where I come from and who I am, I don't know. Who my parents were— perhaps they weren't even married—I don't know. (*taking a cucumber from her pocket and beginning to eat it*) I don't know anything. (*pause*) I'm longing to talk to someone, but there isn't anybody. I haven't anybody . . .

EPIHODOV (*plays the guitar and sings*) "What care I for the noisy world? . . . What care I for friends and foes?" How pleasant it is to play the mandolin!

DUNYASHA That's a guitar, not a mandolin.

(*She looks at herself in a little mirror and powders her face*)

EPIHODOV To a man who's madly in love this is a mandolin. (*sings quietly*) "If only my heart were warmed by the fire of love requited." . . . (YASHA *joins in*)

CHARLOTTA How dreadfully these people sing! . . . Ach! Like a bunch of jackals.

DUNYASHA (*to* YASHA) You're so lucky to have been abroad!

YASHA Of course I am. Naturally. (*yawns, then lights a cigar*)

EPIHODOV Stands to reason. Abroad everything's reached its maturity . . . I mean to say, everything's been going on for such a long time.

YASHA Obviously.

EPIHODOV Now, I'm a cultured man, I read all kinds of extraordinary books, you know, but somehow I can't seem to figure out where I'm going, what it is I really want, I mean to say— whether to live or to shoot myself. Nevertheless, I always carry a revolver on me. Here it is. (*shows the revolver*)

CHARLOTTA That's finished, so now I'm going. (*slips the strap of the gun over her shoulder*) Yes, Epihodov, you are a very clever man, and frightening, too; the women must be wild about you! Brrr! (*walks off*) All these clever people are so stupid, I haven't anyone to talk to. I'm so lonely, always alone, I have nobody and . . . and who I am and what I'm here for, nobody knows . . . (*wanders out*)

EPIHODOV Frankly, and I want to keep to the point, I have to admit that Fate, so to speak, treats me absolutely without mercy, like a small ship is buffeted by the storm, as it were. I mean to say, suppose I'm mistaken, then why for instance should I wake up this morning and suddenly see a gigantic spider sitting on my chest? Like this . . . (*showing the size with both hands*) Or if I pick up a jug to have a drink of kvass, there's sure to be something horrible, like a cockroach, inside it. (*pause*) Have you read Buckle? (*pause*) May I trouble you for a moment, Dunyasha? I'd like to speak with you.

DUNYASHA Well, go ahead.

EPIHODOV I'd very much like to speak with you alone. (*sighs*)

DUNYASHA (*embarrassed*) Oh, all right . . . But first bring me my little cape . . . It's hanging by the cupboard. It's getting terribly chilly . . .

EPIHODOV Very well, I'll get it. . . . Now I know what to do with my revolver. (*takes his guitar and goes off playing it*)

YASHA Two-and-twenty misfortunes! Just between you and me, he's a stupid fool.

(yawns)

DUNYASHA   I hope to God he doesn't shoot himself. *(pause)* He makes me so nervous and I'm always worrying about him. I came to live here when I was still a little girl. Now I no longer know how to live a simple life, and my hands are as white . . . as white as a lady's. I've become such a delicate and sensitive creature. I'm afraid of everything . . . so frightened. If you deceive me, Yasha, I don't know what will happen to my nerves.

YASHA   *(kisses her)*   You sweet little peach! Just remember, a girl must always control herself. Personally I think nothing is worse than a girl who doesn't behave herself.

DUNYASHA   I love you so much, so passionately! You're so intelligent, you can talk about anything.

(Pause)

YASHA   *(yawns)*   Yes, I suppose so . . . In my opinion, it's like this: if a girl loves someone it means she's immoral. *(pause)* I enjoy smoking a cigar in the fresh air . . . *(listens)* Someone's coming. It's the ladies and gentlemen. . . . *(DUNYASHA impulsively embraces him)* Go to the house now, as though you'd been swimming down at the river. No, this way or they'll see you. I wouldn't want them to think I was interested in you.

DUNYASHA   *(coughing softly)*   That cigar has given me such a headache . . . *(goes out)*

(YASHA remains sitting by the shrine. Enter LYUBOV, GAEV and LOPAHIN)

LOPAHIN   You've got to make up your minds once and for all; there's no time to lose. After all, it's a simple matter. Will you lease your land for the cottages, or won't you? You can answer in one word: yes or no? Just one word!

LYUBOV   Who's been smoking such wretched cigars? *(sits down)*

GAEV   How very convenient everything is with the railroad nearby. *(sits down)* Well, here we are—we've been to town, had lunch and we're home already. I put the red into the middle pocket! I'd like to go in . . . just for one game. . . .

LYUBOV   You've got lots of time.

LOPAHIN   Just one word! *(beseechingly)* Please give me an answer!

GAEV   *(yawns)*   What did you say?

LYUBOV   *(looking into her purse)*   Yesterday I had lots of money, but today there's practically none left. My poor Varya feeds us all milk soups to economize; the old servants in the kitchen have nothing but dried peas, and here I am wasting money senselessly, I just don't understand it. . . . She drops her purse, scattering gold coins. Now I've dropped it again. . . . *(annoyed)*

YASHA   Allow me, Madam, I'll pick them right up. *(picks up the money)*

LYUBOV   Thank you, Yasha . . . And why did we go out for lunch today? And that restaurant of yours . . . the food was vile, the music ghastly, and the table cloths smelled of soap. And Leonia, why do you drink so much? And eat so much? And talk so much? Today at the restaurant you were at it again, and it was all so pointless. About the 'seventies, and the decadents. And to whom? Really, talking to the waitress about the decadents!

LOPAHIN   Yes, that's too much.

GAEV   *(waving his hand)*   I know I'm hopeless. *(to YASHA, irritably)* Why are you always bustling about in front of me?

YASHA   *(laughs)*   The minute you open your mouth I start laughing.

GAEV   *(to his sister)*   Either he goes, or I do. . . .

LYUBOV   Get along, Yasha, you'd better leave us now.

YASHA   *(hands the purse to LYUBOV)*   I'm going. *(He can hardly restrain his laughter)* Right this minute. . . . *(goes out)*

LOPAHIN   You know, that rich merchant Deriganov is thinking of buying your estate. They say he's coming to the auction himself.

LYUBOV   Where did you hear that?

LOPAHIN   That's what they say in town.

GAEV   Our Aunt in Yaroslavl has promised to send us some money, but when and how much we don't know.

LOPAHIN   How much will she send? A hundred thousand? Two hundred?

LYUBOV   Well, hardly . . . Ten or fifteen thousand, perhaps. And we should be thankful for that.

LOPAHIN   Forgive me for saying it, but really, in my whole life I've never met such unrealistic, unbusiness-like, queer people as you. You're told in plain language that your estate's going to be sold, and you don't seem to understand it at all.

LYUBOV   But what are we to do? Please, tell us.

LOPAHIN   I keep on telling you. Every day I tell you the same thing. You must lease the cherry orchard and the rest of the land for summer cottages, and you must do it now, as quickly as possible. It's almost time for the auction. Please, try to understand! Once you definitely decide to lease it for the cottages, you'll be able to borrow as much money as you like, and you'll be saved.

LYUBOV Summer cottages and vacationers! Forgive me, but it's so vulgar.

GAEV I agree with you entirely.

LOPAHIN Honestly, I'm going to burst into tears, or scream, or faint. I can't stand it anymore! It's more than I can take! (*to* GAEV) And you're an old woman!

GAEV What did you say?

LOPAHIN I said, you're an old woman!

LYUBOV (*alarmed*) No, don't go, please stay. I beg you! Perhaps we can think of something.

LOPAHIN What's there to think of?

LYUBOV Please don't go! I feel so much more cheerful when you're here. (*pause*) I keep expecting something horrible to happen . . . as though the house were going to collapse on top of us.

GAEV (*in deep thought*) I bank it off the cushions, and then into the middle pocket. . . .

LYUBOV We've sinned too much. . . .

LOPAHIN Sinned! What sins have you . . .

GAEV (*putting a gumdrop into his mouth*) They say I've eaten up my fortune in gumdrops. (*laughs*)

LYUBOV Oh, my sins! Look at the way I've wasted money. It's madness. And then I married a man who had nothing but debts. And he was a terrible drinker . . . Champagne killed him! And then, as if I hadn't enough misery, I fell in love with someone else. We went off together, and just at that time—it was my first punishment, a blow that broke my heart—my little boy was drowned right here in this river . . . so I went abroad. I went away for good, never to return, never to see this river again . . . I just shut my eyes and ran away in a frenzy of grief, but *he* . . . he followed me. It was so cruel and brutal of him! I bought a villa near Mentone because he fell ill there, and for three years, day and night, I never had any rest. He was very sick, and he completely exhausted me; my soul dried up completely. Then, last year when the villa had to be sold to pay the debts, I went to Paris, and there he robbed me of everything I had and left me for another woman. . . . I tried to poison myself. . . . It was all so stupid, so shameful! And then suddenly I felt an urge to come back to Russia, to my own country, to my little girl . . . (*dries her tears*) Oh, Lord, Lord, be merciful, forgive my sins! Don't punish me any more! (*takes a telegram out of her pocket*) This came from Paris today. He's asking my forgiveness, he's begging me to return. (*tears up the telegram*) Sounds like music somewhere. (*listens*)

GAEV That's our famous Jewish orchestra. Don't you remember, four violins, a flute and a bass?

LYUBOV Are they still playing? Sometime we should have a dance and they could play for us.

LOPAHIN (*listens*) I can't hear anything . . . (*sings quietly*) "And the Germans, if you pay, will turn Russians into Frenchmen, so they say." . . . (*laughs*) I saw a wonderful play last night. It was so funny.

LYUBOV It probably wasn't funny at all. Instead of going to plays, you should take a good look at yourself. Just think how dull your life is, and how much nonsense you talk!

LOPAHIN That's true, I admit it! Our lives are stupid . . . (*pause*) My father was a peasant, an idiot. He knew nothing and he taught me nothing. He only beat me when he was drunk, and always with a stick. And as a matter of fact, I'm just as much an idiot myself. I don't know anything and my handwriting's awful. I'm ashamed for people to see it—it's like a pig's.

LYUBOV You should be married, my friend.

LOPAHIN Yes . . . That's true.

LYUBOV You ought to marry our Varya. She's a fine girl.

LOPAHIN Yes.

LYUBOV She comes from simple people, and she works hard all day long without stopping. But the main thing is she loves you, and you've liked her for a long time yourself.

LOPAHIN Well. . . . I think it's a fine idea . . . She's a nice girl. (*pause*)

GAEV I've been offered a job at the bank. Six thousand a year. Did I tell you?

LYUBOV Yes, you did. You'd better stay where you are.

(FEERS *enters, bringing an overcoat*)

FEERS (*to* GAEV) Please put it on, sir, you might catch cold.

GAEV (*puts on the overcoat*) Oh, you *are* a nuisance.

FEERS You must stop this! You went off this morning without letting me know. (*looks him over*)

LYUBOV How you've aged, Feers!

FEERS What can I do for you, Madam?

LOPAHIN She says you've aged a lot.

FEERS I've lived a long time. They were planning to marry me before your father was born. (*laughs*) Why, I was already head butler at the time of the emancipation, but I wouldn't take my freedom, I stayed on with the Master and Mistress. . . . (*pause*) I remember everyone was happy at the time, but what they were happy about, they didn't know themselves.

LOPAHIN   That was the good life all right!
All the peasants were flogged!

FEERS (*not having heard him*)   That's right!
The peasants belonged to their masters, and
the masters belonged to the peasants; but now
everything's all confused, and people don't
know what to make of it.

GAEV   Be quiet, Feers. Tomorrow I've got
to go to town. I've been promised an introduction to some general or other who might
lend us some money for the mortgage.

LOPAHIN   Nothing will come of it. And how
would you pay the interest, anyway?

LYUBOV   He's talking nonsense again. There
aren't any generals.

(*Enter* TROFIMOV, ANYA *and* VARYA)

GAEV   Here come the children.

ANYA   There's Mamma.

LYUBOV   Come here, my dears. Oh, my dar-
ling children. . . . (*embraces* ANYA *and*
VARYA) If only you knew how much I love you!
Here now, sit down beside me. (*all sit down*)

LOPAHIN   Our perennial student is always
with the girls.

TROFIMOV   It's none of your business.

LOPAHIN   He'll soon be fifty, and he's still a
student.

TROFIMOV   Oh, stop your stupid jokes.

LOPAHIN   What's bothering you? My, you
are a strange fellow!

TROFIMOV   Why do you keep pestering me?

LOPAHIN (*laughs*)   Just let me ask you one
question: what's your opinion of me?

TROFIMOV   My opinion of you, Yermolay
Alexeyevich, is this: you're a rich man, and
soon you'll be a millionaire. For the same reason that wild beasts are necessary to maintain
nature's economic laws, you are necessary, too
—each of you devours everything that gets in
his way. (*Everybody laughs*)

VARYA   You'd better talk about the planets,
Petya.

LYUBOV   No, let's go on with the conversation we had yesterday.

TROFIMOV   What was that?

GAEV   About pride.

TROFIMOV   We talked for a long time yesterday, but we didn't agree on anything. The
proud man, the way you use the word, has
some mysterious quality about him. Perhaps
you're right in a way, but if we look at it
simply, without trying to be too subtle, you
have to ask yourself why should we be proud
at all? Why be proud when you realize that
Man, as a species, is poorly constructed phy-
siologically, and is usually coarse, stupid, and

profoundly unhappy, too? We ought to put
an end to such vanity and just go to work.
That's right, we ought to work.

GAEV   You'll die just the same, no matter
what you do.

TROFIMOV   Who knows? And anyway, what
does it mean—to die? It could be that man has
a hundred senses, and when he dies only the
five that are known perish, while the other
ninety-five go on living.

LYUBOV   How clever you are, Petya!

LOPAHIN (*ironically*)   Oh, very clever!

TROFIMOV   Humanity is continually advancing, is continually seeking to perfect its powers.
Someday all the things which we can't understand now, will be made clear. But if
this is to happen, we've got to work, work with
all our might to help those who are searching
for truth. Up until now, here in Russia only a
few have begun to work. Nearly all of the intelligentsia that I know have no commitment,
they don't do anything, and are as yet incapable of work. They call themselves "the
intelligentsia," but they still run rough-shod
over their servants, and they treat the peasants
like animals, they study without achieving anything, they read only childish drivel, and they
don't do a thing. As for their knowledge of
science, it's only jargon, and they have no
appreciation of art either. They are all so serious, and they go about with solemn looks
on their faces; they philosophize and talk
about important matters; and yet before our
very eyes our workers are poorly fed, they live
in the worst kind of squalor, sleeping not on
beds, but on the floor thirty to forty in a room
—with roaches, odors, dampness, and depravity everywhere. It's perfectly clear that all
our moralizing is intended to deceive not only
ourselves, but others as well. Tell me, where
are the nursery schools we're always talking
about, where are the libraries? We only write
about them in novels, but in actuality there
aren't any. There's nothing but dirt, vulgarity,
and decadent Orientalism. . . . I'm afraid of
those serious faces, I don't like them; I'm afraid
of serious talk. It would be better if we'd just
keep quiet.

LOPAHIN   Well, let me tell you that I'm up
before five every morning, and I work from
morning till night. I always have money, my
own and other people's, and I have lots of
opportunities to see what the people around
me are like. You only have to start doing something to realize how few honest, decent people
there are. Sometimes, when I can't sleep, I
start thinking about it. God's given us immense

forests, and wide-open fields, and unlimited horizons—living in such a world we ought to be giants!

LYUBOV But why do you want giants? They're all right in fairy tales, anywhere else they're terrifying.

(EPIHODOV *crosses the stage in the background, playing his guitar*)

LYUBOV (*pensively*) There goes Epihodov. . . .

ANYA (*pensively*) There goes Epihodov. . . .

GAEV The sun's gone down, my friends.

TROFIMOV Yes.

GAEV (*in a subdued voice, as if reciting a poem*) Oh, glorious Nature, shining with eternal light, so beautiful, yet so indifferent to our fate . . . you, whom we call Mother, the wellspring of Life and Death, you live and you destroy. . . .

VARYA (*imploringly*) Uncle, please!

ANYA You're doing it again, Uncle!

TROFIMOV You'd better bank the red into middle pocket.

GAEV All right, I'll keep quiet.

(*They all sit deep in thought; the only thing that can be heard is the muttering of* FEERS. *Suddenly there is a sound in the distance, as if out of the sky, like the sound of a harp string breaking, gradually and sadly dying away*)

LYUBOV What was that?

LOPAHIN I don't know. Sounded like a cable broke in one of the mines. But it must've been a long way off.

GAEV Perhaps it was a bird . . . a heron, maybe.

TROFIMOV Or an owl. . . .

LYUBOV (*shudders*) Whatever it was, it sounded unpleasant . . .

(*A pause*)

FEERS It was the same way before the disaster: the owl hooted and the samovar was humming.

GAEV What disaster?

FEERS Before they freed us.

(*A pause*)

LYUBOV We'd better get started, my friends. It's getting dark and we should get home. (*to* ANYA) You're crying, my darling! What's wrong? (*She embraces her*)

ANYA Nothing, Mamma. It's nothing.

TROFIMOV Someone's coming.

(*Enter a* TRAMP *in a battered white hunting cap and an overcoat; he's slightly drunk*)

TRAMP Excuse me, but can I get to the station through here?

GAEV Yes, just follow the road.

TRAMP Much obliged to you, sir. (*coughs*) It's a beautiful day today. (*declaiming*) "Oh, my brother, my suffering brother! . . . Come to the Volga, whose groans . . ." (*to* VARYA) Mademoiselle, could a poor starving Russian trouble you for just enough to . . . (VARYA *cries out, frightened*)

LOPAHIN (*angrily*) Really, this is too much!

LYUBOV (*at a loss what to do*) Here, take this . . . here you are. (*looks in her purse*) I haven't any silver . . . but that's all right, here's a gold one. . . .

TRAMP Thank you very much! (*Goes off. Laughter*)

VARYA (*frightened*) I'm going . . . I'm going . . . Oh, Mamma, you know there's not even enough to eat in the house, and you gave him all that!

LYUBOV Well, what can you do with a silly woman like me? I'll give you everything I've got as soon as we get home. Yermolay Alexeyevich, you'll lend me some more, won't you?

LOPAHIN Why of course I will.

LYUBOV Come, it's time to go now. By the way, Varya, we've just about arranged your marriage. Congratulations!

VARYA (*through her tears*) Don't joke about things like that, Mother!

LOPAHIN Go to a nunnery, Okhmelia! . . .

GAEV Look at how my hands are trembling: I haven't had a game for so long.

LOPAHIN Okhmelia, nymph, remember me in your prayers!

LYUBOV Come along, everybody. It's almost supper time.

VARYA That man frightened me so. My heart's still pounding.

LOPAHIN My friends, just one thing, please just a word: the cherry orchard's to be sold on the 22nd of August. Remember that! Think of what . . . (*all go out except* TROFIMOV *and* ANYA)

ANYA (*laughs*) We can thank the tramp for a chance to be alone! He frightened Varya so.

TROFIMOV Varya's afraid—she's afraid we might fall in love—so she follows us about all day long. She's so narrow-minded, she can't understand that we're above falling in love. To free ourselves of all that's petty and ephemeral, all that prevents us from being free and happy, that's the whole aim and meaning of our life. Forward! We march forward irresistibly towards that bright star shining there in the distance! Forward! Don't fall behind, friends!

ANYA (*raising her hands*) How beautifully you talk! (*a pause*) It's wonderful here today.

TROFIMOV Yes, the weather's marvelous.

ANYA What have you done to me, Petya? Why don't I love the cherry orchard like I used to? I used to love it so very much I used to think that there wasn't a better place in all the world than our orchard.

TROFIMOV The whole of Russia is our orchard. The earth is great and beautiful and there are many wonderful places in it. (*a pause*) Just think, Anya: your grandfather, and your great grandfather, and all your ancestors were serf owners—they owned living souls. Don't you see human beings staring at you from every tree in the orchard, from every leaf and every trunk? Don't you hear their voices? . . . They owned living souls—and it has made you all different persons, those who came before you, and you who are living now, so that your mother, your uncle and you yourself don't even notice that you're living on credit, at the expense of other people, people you don't admit any further than your kitchen. We're at least two hundred years behind the times; we have no real values, no sense of our past, we just philosophize and complain of how depressed we feel, and drink vodka. Yet it's obvious that if we're ever to live in the present, we must first atone for our past and make a clean break with it, and we can only atone for it by suffering, by extraordinary, unceasing work. You've got to understand that, Anya.

ANYA The house we live in hasn't really been ours for a long time. I'll leave it, I promise you.

TROFIMOV Yes, leave it, and throw away the keys. Be free as the wind.

ANYA (*in rapture*) How beautifully you say things.

TROFIMOV You must believe me, Anya, you must. I'm not thirty yet, I'm young, and I'm still a student, but I've suffered so much already. As soon as winter comes, I'll be hungry and sick and nervous, poor as a beggar. Fate has driven me everywhere! And yet, my soul is always—every moment of every day and every night—it's always full of such marvelous hopes and visions. I have a premonition of happiness, Anya, I can sense it's coming. . . .

ANYA (*pensively*) The moon's coming up.

(EPIHODOV *is heard playing the same melancholy tune on his guitar. The moon comes up. Somewhere near the poplars* VARYA *is looking for* ANYA *and calling*)

VARYA (*off-stage*) Anya! Where are you?

TROFIMOV Yes, the moon is rising. (*a pause*) There it is—happiness—it's coming nearer and nearer. Already, I can hear its footsteps. And if we never see it, if we never know it, what does it matter? Others will see it!

VARYA'S VOICE Anya! Where are you?

TROFIMOV It's Varya again! (*angrily*) It's disgusting!

ANYA Well? Let's go to the river. It's lovely there.

TROFIMOV Yes, let's. (TROFIMOV *and* ANYA *go out*)

VARYA'S VOICE Anya! Anya!

ACT THREE

(*The drawing room separated by an arch from the ballroom. The same Jewish orchestra that was mentioned in Act II, is playing off-stage. The chandelier is lighted. It is evening. In the ballroom they are dancing the Grand-rond.* SEMYONOV-PISHCHIK *is heard calling:* "Promenade à une paire!" *Then they all enter the drawing room.* PISHCHIK *and* CHARLOTTA IVANOVNA *are the first couple, followed by* TROFIMOV *and* LYUBOV, ANYA *and a* POST-OFFICE CLERK, VARYA *and the* STATION MASTER, *etc.* VARYA *is crying softly and wipes away her tears as she dances.* DUNYASHA *is in the last couple.* PISHCHIK *shouts:* "Grand-rond balancez! *and* "Les cavaliers à genoux et remerciez vos dames!" FEERS, *wearing a dress coat, crosses the room with soda water on a tray.* PISHCHIK *and* TROFIMOV *come back into the drawing room*)

PISHCHIK I've got this high blood-pressure —I've had two strokes already, you know—and it makes dancing hard work for me; but, as they say, if you're one of a pack, you wag your tail, whether you bark or not. Actually I'm as strong as a horse. My dear father—may he rest in peace—had a little joke. He used to say that the ancient line of Semyonov-Pishchik was descended from the very same horse that Caligula made a member of the Senate. (*sitting down*) But my trouble is, I haven't any money. A starving dog can think of nothing but food . . . (*starts to snore, but wakes up almost at once*) That's just like me—I can't think of anything but money . . .

TROFIMOV You know, you're right, there *is* something horsy about you.

PISHCHIK Well, a horse is a fine animal, you can sell a horse. . . .

(*The sound of someone playing billiards is heard in the next room.* VARYA *appears under the arch to the ballroom*)

TROFIMOV (*teasing her*) Madame Lopahin! Madame Lopahin!

VARYA (*angrily*) The "moth-eaten man"!

TROFIMOV Yes, I am a moth-eaten man, and I'm proud of it.

VARYA (*thinking bitterly*) Now we've hired an orchestra—but how are we going to pay for it? (*goes out*)

TROFIMOV (*to* PISHCHIK) If all the energy you've spent during your life looking for money to pay the interest on your debts had been used for something useful, you'd have probably turned the world upside down by now.

PISHCHIK The philosopher Nietzsche, the greatest, the most famous—a man of the greatest intelligence, in fact—says it's quite all right to counterfeit.

TROFIMOV Oh, you've read Nietzsche?

PISHCHIK Of course not, Dashenka told me. But right now I'm in such an impossible position that I could forge a few notes. The day after tomorrow I've got to pay 310 roubles. I've borrowed 130 already. . . . (*feels in his pockets, in alarm*) The money's gone! I've lost the money. (*tearfully*) Where's the money? (*joyfully*) Oh, here it is, inside the lining! I'm so upset, I'm sweating all over! . . .

(*Enter* LYUBOV *and* CHARLOTTA)

LYUBOV (*humming the "Lezginka"*) What's taking Leonid so long? What's he doing in town? (*to* DUNYASHA) Dunyasha, offer the musicians some tea.

TROFIMOV The auction was probably postponed.

LYUBOV The orchestra came at the wrong time, and the party started at the wrong time . . . Oh, well . . . never mind . . . (*She sits down and hums quietly*)

CHARLOTTA (*hands a deck of cards to* PISHCHIK) Here's a deck of cards—think of any card.

PISHCHIK I've thought of one.

CHARLOTTA Now shuffle the deck. That's right. Now give it to me, my dear Monsieur Pishchik. *Ein, zwei, drei!* Why look! There it is, in your coat pocket.

PISHCHIK (*takes the card out of his coat pocket*) The eight of spades, that's right! (*in astonishment*) Isn't that amazing!

CHARLOTTA (*holding the deck of cards on the palm of her hand, to* TROFIMOV) Quickly, which card's on the top?

TROFIMOV Well . . . ahh . . . the queen of spades.

CHARLOTTA You're right, here it is! Now, which card?

PISHCHIK The ace of hearts.

CHARLOTTA Right again! (*She claps her hand over the pack of cards, which disappears*) What beautiful weather we're having today! (*A woman's voice, as if coming from underneath the floor, answers her*)

VOICE Oh yes, indeed, the weather's perfectly marvelous!

CHARLOTTA (*addressing the voice*) How charming you are! I'm very fond of you!

VOICE And I like you very much, too.

STATION MASTER (*applauding*) Bravo, Madame ventriloquist! Bravo!

PISHCHIK (*astonished*) Isn't that amazing! Charlotta Ivanovna, you're absolutely wonderful! I'm completely in love with you!

CHARLOTTA (*shrugging her shoulders*) In love? What do you know about love? *Guter Mensch, aber schlechter Musikant.*

TROFIMOV (*slaps* PISHCHIK *on the shoulder*) He's just an old horse, he is!

CHARLOTTA Your attention please! Here's one more trick. (*She takes a shawl from a chair*) Now there's this very nice shawl . . . (*shakes it out*) Who'd like to buy it?

PISHCHIK (*amazed*) Imagine that!

CHARLOTTA *Ein, zwei, drei!* (*She lifts up the shawl and* ANYA *is standing behind it;* ANYA *curtsies, runs to her mother, gives her a hug, and runs back to the ballroom. Everybody's delighted*)

LYUBOV (*clapping*) Bravo, bravo!

CHARLOTTA Once more. *Ein, zwei, drei!* (*lifts the shawl again; behind it is* VARYA, *who bows*)

PISHCHIK (*amazed*) Isn't that amazing!

CHARLOTTA It's all over! (*She throws the shawl over* PISHCHIK, *curtsies, and runs into the ballroom*)

PISHCHIK (*going after her*) You little rascal! . . . Have you ever seen anything like her? What a girl . . . (*goes out*)

LYUBOV Leonid's still not here. I can't understand what's keeping him all this time in town. Anyway, by now everything's been settled; either the estate's been sold or the auction didn't take place. Why does he wait so long to let us know?

VARYA (*trying to comfort her*) Uncle's bought it, I'm sure he did.

TROFIMOV (*sarcastically*) Why of course he did!

VARYA Our great-aunt sent him power of attorney to buy it in her name, and transfer the mortgage to her. She's done it for Anya's sake . . . God will look after us, I'm sure of it—Uncle will buy the estate.

LYUBOV Your great-aunt sent us fifteen thousand to buy the estate in her name—she doesn't trust us—but that's not enough to even pay the interest. (*She covers her face with her hands*) My fate is being decided today, my fate. . . .

TROFIMOV (*to* VARYA, *teasingly*) Madame Lopahin!

VARYA (*crossly*) The perpetual student! Why, you've been thrown out of the University twice already!

LYUBOV But why get so cross, Varya? He's only teasing you about Lopahin, there's no harm in that, is there? If you want to, why don't you marry him; he's a fine man, and he's interesting, too. Of course, if you don't want to, don't. No one's trying to force you, darling.

VARYA I'm very serious about this, Mother . . . and I want to be frank with you . . . he's a good man and I like him.

LYUBOV Then marry him. What are you waiting for? I don't understand you at all.

VARYA But, Mother, I can't propose to him myself, can I? It's been two years now since everybody began talking to me about him, and everybody's talking, but he doesn't say a word, or when he does, he just jokes with me. I understand, of course. He's getting rich and his mind's busy with other things, and he hasn't any time for me. If only I had some money, even a little, just a hundred roubles, I'd leave everything and go away, the farther the better. I'd go into a convent.

TROFIMOV How beautiful!

VARYA (*to* TROFIMOV) Of course, a student like you has to be so intelligent! (*quietly and tearfully*) How ugly you've become, Petya, how much older you look! (*to* LYUBOV, *her tearfulness gone*) The only thing I can't stand, Mother, is not having any work to do. I've got to stay busy.

(*Enter* YASHA)

YASHA (*with difficulty restraining his laughter*) Epihodov's broken a cue! . . . (*goes out*)

VARYA But what's Epihodov doing here? Who let him play billiards? I don't understand these people. . . . (*goes out*)

LYUBOV Please don't tease her, Petya. Don't you see she's upset already?

TROFIMOV Oh, she's such a busy-body—always sticking her nose into other people's business. She hasn't left Anya and me alone all summer. She's afraid we might fall in love.

What difference should it make to her? Besides, I didn't give her any reason to think so. I don't believe in such trivialities. We're above love!

LYUBOV And I suppose I'm below love. (*uneasily*) Why isn't Leonid back? If only I knew whether the estate's been sold or not. It's such an incredible calamity that for some reason I don't know what to think, I feel so helpless. I think I'm going to scream this very minute . . . I'll do something silly. Help me, Petya. Talk to me, say something!

TROFIMOV What difference does it make whether the estate's sold today or not? It was gone a long time ago. You can't turn back, the path's lost. You mustn't worry, and above all you mustn't deceive yourself. For once in your life you must look the truth straight in the face.

LYUBOV What truth? *You* know what truth is and what it isn't, but I've lost such visionary powers. I don't see anything. You're able to solve all your problems so decisively—but, tell me, my dear boy, isn't that because you're young, because life is still hidden from your young eyes, because you can't believe anything horrible will ever happen to you and you don't expect it to? Oh, yes, you're more courageous and honest and serious than we are, but put yourself in our position, try to be generous —if only a little bit—and have pity on me. I was born here, you know, and my father and mother lived here, and my grandfather, too, and I love this house—I can't conceive of life without the cherry orchard, and if it really has to be sold, then sell me with it . . . (*embraces* TROFIMOV, *kisses him on the forehead*) You know, my little boy was drowned here. . . . (*weeps*) Have pity on me, my dear, kind friend.

TROFIMOV You know that I sympathize with you from the bottom of my heart.

LYUBOV But you should say it differently . . . differently. (*takes out her handkerchief and a telegram falls on the floor*) There's so much on my mind today, you can't imagine. It's so noisy around here that my soul trembles with every sound, and I'm shaking all over —yet I can't go to my room because the silence of being alone frightens me. . . . Don't blame me, Petya. . . . I love you as if you were my own son. I'd gladly let Anya marry you, honestly I would, but, my dear boy, you must study, you've got to graduate. You don't do anything, Fate tosses you from one place to another—it's so strange—Well, it is, isn't it? Isn't it? And you should do something about your beard, make it grow somehow. . . . (*laughs*) You look so funny!

TROFIMOV (*picks up the telegram*) I don't care how I look. That's so superficial.

LYUBOV This telegram's from Paris. I get one every day . . . Yesterday, today. That beast is sick again, and everything's going wrong for him. . . . He wants me to forgive him, he begs me to return, and, really, I suppose I should go to Paris and stay with him for awhile. You're looking very stern, Petya, but what am I to do, my dear boy, what am I to do? He's sick, and lonely, and unhappy, and who'll take care of him, who'll stop him from making a fool of himself, and give him his medicine at the right time? And anyway, why should I hide it, or keep quiet about it? I love him; yes, I love him. I do, I do. . . . He's a stone around my neck, and I'm sinking to the bottom with him—but I love him and I can't live without him. (*She presses* TROFIMOV's *hand*) Don't think I'm evil, Petya, don't say anything, please don't. . . .

TROFIMOV (*with strong emotion*) Please—forgive my frankness, but that man's swindling you!

LYUBOV No, no, no, you mustn't talk like that. . . . (*puts her hands over her ears*)

TROFIMOV But he's a scoundrel, and you're the only one who doesn't know it! He's a despicable, worthless scoundrel. . . .

LYUBOV (*angry, but in control of herself*) You're twenty-six or twenty-seven years old, but you're talking like a schoolboy!

TROFIMOV Say whatever you want!

LYUBOV You should be a man at your age, you ought to understand what it means to be in love. And you should be in love. . . . Tell me, why haven't you fallen in love! (*angrily*) Yes, yes! Oh, you're not so "pure," your purity is a perversion, you're nothing but a ridiculous prude, a freak. . . .

TROFIMOV (*horrified*) What is she saying?

LYUBOV "I'm above love!" You're not above love, you're useless, as Feers would say. Imagine not having a mistress at your age! . . .

TROFIMOV (*horrified*) This is terrible! What's she saying? (*goes quickly towards the ballroom, clutching his head between his hands*) This is dreadful. . . . I can't stand it, I'm going. . . . (*goes out, but returns at once*) Everything's over between us! (*goes out through the door into the hall*)

LYUBOV (*calls after him*) Petya, wait! You funny boy, I was only joking! Petya! (*Someone can be heard running quickly downstairs and suddenly falling down with a crash.* ANYA *and* VARYA *scream, and then begin laughing*) What's happened?

(ANYA *runs in*)

ANYA (*laughing*) Petya fell down the stairs. (*runs out*)

LYUBOV What a strange boy he is!

(*The* STATION MASTER *stands in the middle of the ballroom and begins to recite "The Sinner" by Alexey Tolstoy. The others listen to him, but he's hardly had time to recite more than a little bit when a waltz is played, and he stops. Everyone dances.* TROFIMOV, ANYA, VARYA *come in from the hall.*)

LYUBOV Poor Petya . . . Poor Petya . . . there, my dear boy . . . Please forgive me . . . Come, let's dance . . .

(LYUBOV *dances with* PETYA, ANYA *and* VARYA *dance. Enter* FEERS, *then* YASHA. FEERS *leans on his cane by the side door.* YASHA *looks at the dancers from the drawing room*)

YASHA How are you, old boy?

FEERS Not too well . . . We used to have generals, barons, and admirals at our parties . . . long ago, but now we send for the post-office clerk and the station master, and even they don't want to come it seems. I seem to be getting weaker somehow . . . My old master, the mistress' grandfather, used to make everyone take sealing wax no matter what was wrong with them. I've been taking it every day for the last twenty years, maybe even longer. Perhaps that's why I'm still alive.

YASHA How you bore me, old man! (*yawns*) Why don't you just go away and die . . . It's about time.

FEERS Eh, you! . . . You're useless . . . (*mutters*)

(TROFIMOV *and* LYUBOV *dancing, come into the drawing room*)

LYUBOV Thank you. I think I'll sit down for a bit. (*sits down*) I'm tired.

(*Enter* ANYA)

ANYA (*agitated*) There's a man in the kitchen who's been saying that the cherry orchard was sold today.

LYUBOV Sold? To whom?

ANYA He didn't say. He's gone. (*She and* TROFIMOV *dance into the ballroom*)

YASHA There was some old man gossiping there. A stranger.

FEERS Leonid Andreyevich isn't back yet, he hasn't come yet. And he's only got his light overcoat on; he'll probably catch a cold. Oh, these youngsters!

LYUBOV   I've got to know, or I think I'll die. Yasha, go and find out who bought it.

YASHA   But the old guy went away a long time ago. (*laughs*)

LYUBOV   (*with a touch of annoyance*)   What are you laughing at? What's so humorous?

YASHA   Epihodov's so funny—he's so stupid. Two-and-twenty misfortunes!

LYUBOV   Feers, if the estate's sold, where will you go?

FEERS   I'll go wherever you tell me to go.

LYUBOV   Why are you looking like that? Aren't you well? You ought to be in bed.

FEERS   Yes . . . (*with a faint smile*)   But if I went to bed, who'd take care of the guests and keep things going? There's no one in the house but me.

YASHA   (*to* LYUBOV)   Lyubov Andreyevna! I want to ask you something! If you go back to Paris, will you please take me with you? I couldn't stand staying here. (*looking round and speaking in a low voice*)   I don't have to say it, you can see for yourself how uncivilized everything is here. The people are immoral, it's frightfully dull, and the food is terrible. And then there's that Feers walking about the place and muttering all sorts of stupid things. Take me with you, please!

(*Enter* PISHCHIK)

PISHCHIK   May I have this dance, beautiful lady . . . (LYUBOV *gets up to dance*)   I'll have that 180 roubles from you yet, you enchantress . . . Yes, I will . . . (*dances*)   Just 180 roubles, that's all . . . (*They go into the ballroom*)

YASHA   (*sings quietly*)   "Don't you understand the passion in my soul? . . ."

(*In the ballroom a woman in a grey top hat and check trousers starts jumping and throwing her arms about; shouts of: "Bravo, Charlotta Ivanovna!"*)

DUNYASHA   (*stops to powder her face*)   Anya told me to dance: there are so many men and not enough ladies; but I get so dizzy from dancing and it makes my heart beat so fast. Feers Nikolayevich, the post-office clerk said something to me just now that completely took my breath away.

(*The music stops*)

FEERS   What did he say?

DUNYASHA   You're like a flower, he said.

YASHA   (*yawns*)   What ignorance! . . .

(*goes out*)

DUNYASHA   Like a flower . . . I'm so sensitive, I love it when people say beautiful things to me.

FEERS   You'll be having your head turned if you're not careful.

(*Enter* EPIHODOV)

EPIHODOV   Avdotya Fyodorovna, you act as if you don't want to see me . . . as if I were some kind of insect. (*sighs*)   Such is life!

DUNYASHA   What do you want?

EPIHODOV   But then, you may be right. (*sighs*)   Of course, if one looks at it from a certain point of view—if I may so express myself, and please excuse my frankness, you've driven me into such a state . . . Oh, I know what my fate is; every day some misfortune's sure to happen to me, but I've long since been accustomed to that, so I look at life with a smile. You gave me your word, and though I . . .

DUNYASHA   Please, let's talk later, just let me alone now. I'm lost in a dream. (*plays with her fan*)

EPIHODOV   Some misfortune happens to me every day, but I—how should I put it—I just smile, I even laugh.

(VARYA *enters from the ballroom*)

VARYA   Are you still here, Semyon? Your manners are abominable, really! (*to* DUNYASHA)   You'd better go now, Dunyasha. (*to* EPIHODOV)   First you play billiards and break a cue, and now you're going about the drawing room, like one of the guests.

EPIHODOV   Permit me to inform you, but you have no right to attack me like this.

VARYA   I'm not attacking, I'm telling you. You just wander from one place to another, instead of doing your work. We've hired a clerk, but why no one knows.

EPIHODOV   (*offended*)   Whether I work, wander, eat, or play billiards, the only people who are entitled to judge my actions are those who are older than me and have some idea of what they're talking about.

VARYA   How dare you say that to me? (*beside herself in anger*)   You dare to say that? Are you suggesting that I don't know what I'm talking about? Get out of here! Right now!

EPIHODOV   (*cowed*)   I wish you'd express yourself more delicately.

VARYA   (*beside herself*)   Get out this minute! Get out! (*He goes to the door, she follows him*)   Two-and-twenty misfortunes! Get out of here! I don't want ever to see you again!

EPIHODOV   (*goes out; his voice is heard from outside the door*)   I'm going to complain.

VARYA   Oh, you're coming back, are you? (*She seizes the stick which* FEERS *left by the door*)   Well, come along, come in . . . I'll show you! So, you're coming back . . . are you?

There, take that . . . (*swings the stick, and at that moment* LOPAHIN *comes in*)

LOPAHIN (*whom the stick did not, in fact, touch*) Thank you very much!

VARYA (*angry and ironically*) I'm sorry!

LOPAHIN Don't mention it. I'm much obliged to you for the kind reception.

VARYA That's quite all right. (*walks away and then looks round and asks gently*) I haven't hurt you, have I?

LOPAHIN No, not at all . . . But there's going to be a huge bump, though.

VOICES (*in the ballroom*) Lopahin's here! Yermolay Alexeyevich!

PISHCHIK There he is! You can see him, do you hear him? . . . (*embraces* LOPAHIN) You smell of cognac, my good fellow! . . . Well we're having a party here, too.

(*Enter* LYUBOV)

LYUBOV It's you, Yermolay Alexeyevich? What's taken you so long? Where's Leonid?

LOPAHIN Leonid Andreyevich's here, he'll be along in a minute.

LYUBOV (*agitated*) Well, what happened? Was there an auction? Tell me!

LOPAHIN (*embarrassed, afraid of betraying his joy*) The auction was over by four o'clock . . . We missed our train and had to wait until nine-thirty. (*sighs heavily*) Ugh! I feel a little dizzy . . .

(*Enter* GAEV; *he carries packages in his right hand and wipes away his tears with his left*)

LYUBOV Leonia, what happened, Leonia? (*impatiently, with tears*) Tell me quickly, for God's sake! . . .

GAEV (*doesn't answer, but waves his hand. To* FEERS, *crying*) Here, take these . . . it's some anchovies and Kerch herrings . . . I haven't eaten all day . . . What I've been through!

(*Through the open door leading to the ballroom a game of billiards can be heard and* YASHA's *voice is heard*)

YASHA Seven and eighteen.

GAEV (*his expression changes and he stops crying*) I'm very tired. Come, Feers, I want to change my things. (*goes out through the ballroom, followed by* FEERS)

PISHCHIK Well, what happened at the auction? Come on, tell us!

LYUBOV Has the cherry orchard been sold?

LOPAHIN It has.

LYUBOV Who bought it?

LOPAHIN I did. (*a pause.* LYUBOV *is overcome; only the fact that she is standing beside a table and a chair keeps her from falling.* VARYA *takes the keys from her belt, throws them on the floor in the middle of the room and goes out*) I bought it. Wait a moment, ladies and gentlemen, please. I'm so mixed up, I don't quite know what to say . . . (*laughs*) When we got to the auction, Deriganov was already there. Leonid had only fifteen thousand roubles, and immediately Deriganov bid thirty thousand over and above the mortgage. I saw how things were, so I stepped in and raised it to forty. He bid forty-five, I went to fifty-five; he kept on raising five thousand and I raised it ten thousand. Well, finally it ended— I bid ninety thousand over and above the mortgage, and it went to me. The cherry orchard's mine now! All right, tell me I'm drunk, tell me I'm crazy and that I'm just imagining all this. . . . (*stamps his feet*) Don't laugh at me! If only my father and grandfather could rise from their graves and see all that's happened . . . how their Yermolay, their ignorant, beaten Yermolay, the little boy that ran around in his bare feet in the winter . . . if only they could see that he's bought this estate, the most beautiful place in the world! Yes, he's bought the very estate where his father and grandfather were slaves and where they weren't even admitted to the kitchen! I must be asleep, I'm dreaming, it only seems to be true . . . it's all just my imagination, my imagination must be confused . . . (*picks up the keys, smiling gently*) She threw these down because she wanted to show that she's not the mistress here anymore. (*jingles the keys*) Well, never mind. (*The orchestra is heard tuning up*) Hey there! you musicians, play something for us! I want some music! My friends, come along and soon you'll see Yermolay Lopahin take an axe to the cherry orchard, you'll see the trees come crashing to the ground! We're going to build hundreds of summer cottages, and our children and our grandchildren will see a whole new world growing up here . . . So play, let's have some music! (*The band plays.* LYUBOV *has sunk into a chair and is crying bitterly. Reproachfully*) Why, why didn't you listen to me? My poor, dear lady, you'll never get it back now. (*with tears*) Oh, if only all this could be over soon, if only we could change this unhappy and disjointed life of ours somehow!

PISHCHIK (*taking his arm, in a low voice*) She's crying. Come into the ballroom, let her be by herself . . . Come on . . . (*takes his arm and leads him away to the ballroom*)

LOPAHIN What's the matter! Where's the music? Come on, play! Play! Everything will be as I want it now. (*ironically*) Here comes the new owner, here comes the owner of the cherry orchard! (*He tips over a little table accidentally and nearly upsets the candelabra*) Don't worry about it, I can pay for everything!

(LOPAHIN *goes out with* PISHCHIK. *There is no one left in the ballroom or drawing room but* LYUBOV, *who sits huddled up in a chair, crying bitterly. The orchestra continues to play quietly.* ANYA *and* TROFIMOV *enter quickly;* ANYA *goes up to her mother and kneels beside her,* TROFIMOV *remains at the entrance to the ballroom*)

ANYA   Mamma! . . . Mamma, you're crying. Dear, kind, good Mamma, my precious one, I love you! God bless you, Mamma! The cherry orchard's sold, that's true, it's gone, but don't cry, Mamma, you still have your life ahead of you, you still have your good, innocent heart. You must come with me, Mamma, away from here! We'll plant a new orchard, even more wonderful than this one—and when you see it, you'll understand everything, and your heart will be filled with joy, like the sun in the evening; and then you'll smile again, Mamma! Come, dearest one, come with me! . . .

ACT FOUR

(*The same setting as for Act I. There are no pictures on the walls or curtains at the windows; most of the furniture is gone and the few remaining pieces are stacked in a corner, as if for sale. There is a sense of desolation. Beside the door, suitcases and other luggage have been piled together. The voices of* VARYA *and* ANYA *can be heard through the door on the left, which is open.* LOPAHIN *stands waiting;* YASHA *is holding a tray with glasses of champagne. In the hall* EPIHODOV *is tying up a large box. Off-stage there is a low hum of voices; the peasants have called to say good-bye.* GAEV's *voice from off-stage*)

GAEV   Thank you, friends, thank you.

YASHA   The peasants have come to say good-bye. In my opinion, Yermolay Alexeyevich, they're good people, but they don't know much.

(*The hum subsides.* LYUBOV *and* GAEV *enter from the hall;* LYUBOV *is not crying but her face is pale and it quivers. She is unable to speak*)

GAEV   You gave them everything you had, Lyuba. You shouldn't have done that. You really shouldn't.

LYUBOV   I couldn't help it! I couldn't help it! (*both go out*)

LOPAHIN   (*calls after them through the door*) Please, have some champagne, please do! Just a little glass before you go. I didn't think to bring some from town, and at the station I could find only this one bottle. Please have some. (*a pause*) You don't want any, my friends? (*walks away from the door*) If I'd known that, I wouldn't have brought it. . . . Well, then I won't have any either. (YASHA *carefully puts the tray on a chair*) Have a drink, Yasha, nobody else wants any.

YASHA   To the travelers! And to those staying behind. (*drinks*) This champagne isn't the real thing, believe me.

LOPAHIN   What do you mean, eight roubles a bottle. (*a pause*) God, it's cold in here.

YASHA   The stoves weren't lit today. What difference does it make since we're leaving? (*laughs*)

LOPAHIN   Why are you laughing?

YASHA   Because I feel good.

LOPAHIN   It's October already, but it's still sunny and clear, just like summer. Good building weather. (*looks at his watch, then at the door*) Ladies and gentlemen, the train leaves in forty-seven minutes. We've got to start in twenty minutes. So hurry up.

(TROFIMOV, *wearing an overcoat, comes in from outdoors*)

TROFIMOV   It's time we get started. The horses are ready. God knows where my goloshes are, they've disappeared. (*calls through the door*) Anya, my goloshes aren't here; I can't find them.

LOPAHIN   I've got to go to Kharkov. I'm taking the same train. I'll be spending the winter in Kharkov: I've stayed around here too long, and it drives me crazy having nothing to do. I can't be without work: I just don't know what to do with my hands; they hang there, as if they didn't belong to me.

TROFIMOV   We'll be gone soon, then you can start making money again.

LOPAHIN   Have a drink.

TROFIMOV   No, thanks.

LOPAHIN   So, you're going to Moscow?

TROFIMOV   Yes, I'll go with them to town, and then, tomorrow I'll leave for Moscow.

LOPAHIN   I suppose the professors are waiting for you to come before they begin classes.

TROFIMOV   That's none of your business.

LOPAHIN   How many years have you been studying at the university?

TROFIMOV   Can't you say something new for a change, that's getting pretty old. (*looks for his goloshes*) By the way, since we probably won't see each other again, let me give you a bit of advice, as we say goodbye: stop waving your arms! Try to get rid of that habit of making wide, sweeping gestures. And another thing, all this talk about building estates, these calculations about summer tourists that are going to buy property, all these predictions—they're all sweeping gestures, too. . . . You know, in spite of everything, I like you. You've got beautiful delicate fingers, like an artist's, you've a fine, sensitive soul. . . .

LOPAHIN (*embraces him*) Goodbye, my friend. Thanks for everything. I can give you some money for your trip, if you need it.

TROFIMOV What for? I don't need it.

LOPAHIN But you haven't got any!

TROFIMOV Yes, I have, thank you. I got some money for a translation. Here it is, in my pocket. (*anxiously*) But I can't find my goloshes.

VARYA (*from the other room*) Here, take the nasty things! (*She throws a pair of rubber goloshes into the room*)

TROFIMOV What are you so angry about, Varya? Hm . . . but these aren't my goloshes!

LOPAHIN I sowed three thousand acres of poppies last spring, and I've made forty thousand on it. And when they were in bloom, what a picture it was! What I mean to say is that I've made the forty thousand, so now I can lend you some money. Why be so stuck up? So I'm a peasant . . . I speak right out.

TROFIMOV Your father was a peasant, mine was a druggist. What's that got to do with it? (LOPAHIN *takes out his wallet*) Forget it, put it away . . . Even if you offered me two hundred thousand, I wouldn't take it. I'm a free man. And all that you rich men—and poor men too—all that you value so highly doesn't have the slightest power over me—it's all just so much fluff floating about in the air. I'm strong and I'm proud! I can get along without you, I can pass you by. Humanity is advancing towards the highest truth, the greatest happiness that it's possible to achieve on earth, and I'm one of the avant-garde!

LOPAHIN Will you get there?

TROFIMOV Yes. (*a pause*) I'll get there myself, or show others the way to get there.

(*The sound of an axe hitting a tree is heard in in the distance*)

LOPAHIN Well, my friend, it's time to go. Goodbye. We show off in front of one another, and all the time life is slipping by. When I work all day long, without resting, I'm happier and sometimes I even think I know why I exist. But how many people there are in Russia, my friend, who exist for no reason at all. But, never mind, it doesn't matter. They say Leonid Andreyevich has a job at the bank, at six thousand a year. That won't last long; he's too lazy. . . .

ANYA (*in the doorway*) Mamma begs you not to let them cut down the orchard until we've left.

TROFIMOV Really, haven't you got any tact? (*goes out through the hall*)

LOPAHIN All right, I'll take care of it. . . . These people! (*follows* TROFIMOV)

ANYA Has Feers been taken to the hospital?

YASHA I told them to take him this morning. He's gone, I think.

ANYA (*to* EPIHODOV, *who passes through the ballroom*) Semyon Pantaleyevich, will you please find out whether Feers has been taken to the hospital?

YASHA (*offended*) I told Yegor this morning. Why ask a dozen times?

EPIHODOV That old Feers—frankly speaking, I mean—he's beyond repair, it's time he joined his ancestors. As for me, I can only envy him. (*He places a suitcase on top of a cardboard hat box and squashes it*) There you are, you see! . . . I might have known it! (*goes out*)

YASHA (*sardonically*) Two-and-twenty misfortunes!

VARYA (*from behind the door*) Has Feers been taken to the hospital?

ANYA Yes.

VARYA Why wasn't the letter to the doctor taken then?

ANYA I'll send someone after them with it . . . (*goes out*)

VARYA (*from the adjoining room*) Where's Yasha? Tell him his mother is here and wants to say goodbye to him.

YASHA (*waves his hand*) This is too much! I'll lose my patience.

(*While the foregoing action has been taking place,* DUNYASHA *has been busy with the luggage; now that* YASHA *is alone, she comes up to him*)

DUNYASHA If only you'd look at me just once, Yasha! You're going . . . you're leaving me! . . . (*She cries and throws her arms round his neck*)

YASHA What are you crying for? (*drinks champagne*) In a week I'll be in Paris again. Tomorrow we'll get on the train—and off we'll go—gone! I can't believe it. *Vive la France!* I can't stand it here and could never live here—nothing ever happens. I've seen enough of all this ignorance. I've had enough of it. (*drinks*)

What are you crying for? Behave yourself properly, then you won't cry.

DUNYASHA (*looking into a handmirror and powdering her nose*) Please, write to me from Paris. You know how much I've loved you, Yasha. Oh, I've loved you so much! I'm very sensitive, Yasha!

YASHA Sshh, someone's coming. (*pretends to be busy with a suitcase, humming quietly*)

(*Enter* LYUBOV ANDREYEVNA, GAEV, ANYA *and* CHARLOTTA IVANOVNA)

GAEV We've got to leave soon. There isn't much time left. (*looks at* YASHA) What a smell! Who's been eating herring?

LYUBOV We'll have to leave in the carriage in ten minutes. (*looks about the room*) Goodbye, dear house, the home of our fathers. Winter will pass and spring will come again, and then you won't be here any more, you'll be torn down. How much these walls have seen! (*kisses her daughter passionately*) My little treasure, how radiant you look, your eyes are shining like diamonds. Are you glad? Very glad?

ANYA Oh, yes, very glad, Mamma! Our new life is just beginning!

GAEV (*gaily*) Really, everything's all right now. Before the cherry orchard was sold we were all worried and upset, but as soon as things were settled once and for all, we all calmed down and even felt quite cheerful. I'm working in a bank now, a real financier. . . . The red into the side pocket . . . And say what you like, Lyuba, you're looking much better. No doubt about it.

LYUBOV Yes, that's true, my nerves are better. (*Someone helps her on with her hat and coat*) I'm sleeping better, too. Take out my things, Yasha, it's time. (*to* ANYA) My little darling, we'll be seeing each other again soon. I'm going to Paris—I'll live on the money which your Grandmother sent us to buy the estate—God bless Grandmamma!—but that money won't last very long either.

ANYA You'll come back soon, Mamma . . . won't you? I'll study and pass my exams and then I'll work and help you. We'll read together, Mamma . . . all sorts of things . . . won't we? (*She kisses her mother's hands*) We'll read during the long autumn evenings. We'll read lots of books, and a new wonderful world will open up before us . . . (*dreamily*) Mamma, come back soon . . .

LYUBOV I'll come back, my precious. (*embraces her*)

(*Enter* LOPAHIN. CHARLOTTA *quietly sings to herself*)

GAEV Happy Charlotta! She's singing.

CHARLOTTA (*picks up a bundle that looks like a baby in a blanket*) Bye-bye, little baby. (*A sound like a baby crying is heard*) Hush, be quiet, my darling, be a good little boy. (*The "crying" continues*) Oh, my baby, you poor thing! (*throws the bundle down*) Are you going to find me another job? If you don't mind, I've got to have one.

LOPAHIN We'll find you one, Charlotta Ivanovna, don't worry.

GAEV Everybody's leaving us, Varya's going away . . . all of a sudden nobody wants us.

CHARLOTTA There's no place for me to live in town. I'll have to go. (*hums*) Oh, well, what do I care.

(*Enter* PISHCHIK)

LOPAHIN Look what's here!

PISHCHIK (*gasping for breath*) Oohhh, let me get my breath . . . I'm worn out . . . My good friends. . . . Give me some water . . .

GAEV I suppose you want to borrow some money? I'm going . . . Excuse me . . . (*goes out*)

PISHCHIK I haven't seen you for a long time . . . my beautiful lady . . . (*to* LOPAHIN) You're here, too . . . glad to see you . . . you're a man of great intelligence . . . here . . . take this . . . (*gives money to* LOPAHIN) Four hundred roubles . . . I still owe you eight hundred and forty. . . .

LOPAHIN (*shrugging his shoulders in amazement*) It's like a dream . . . Where did you get it?

PISHCHIK Wait a minute . . . I'm so hot . . . A most extraordinary thing happened. Some Englishmen came along and discovered some kind of white clay on my land . . . (*to* LYUBOV) Here's four hundred for you also, my dear . . . enchantress . . . (*gives her the money*) You'll get the rest later. (*takes a drink of water*) A young man on the train was just telling me that some great philosopher advises people to jump off roofs. You just jump off, he says, and that settles the whole problem. (*amazed at what he has just said*) Imagine that! More water, please.

LOPAHIN What Englishmen?

PISHCHIK I leased the land to them for twenty-four years. . . . And now you must excuse me, I'm in a hurry and have to get on. I'm going to Znoikov's, then to Kardamonov's. . . . I owe them all money. (*drinks*) Your health. I'll come again on Thursday . . .

LYUBOV We're just leaving for town, and tomorrow I'm going abroad.

PISHCHIK What's that? (*in agitation*) Why

to town? Oh, I see . . . this furniture and the suitcases. . . . Well, never mind . . . (*tearfully*) What difference does it make. . . . These Englishmen, you know, they're very intelligent . . . Never mind. . . . I wish you all the best, God bless you. Never mind, everything comes to an end eventually. (*kisses* LYUBOV'S *hand*) And when you hear that my end has come, just think of a horse, and say: "There used to be a man like that once . . . his name was Semyonov-Pishchik—God bless him!" Wonderful weather we're having. Yes . . . (*goes out embarrassed, but returns at once and stands in the doorway*) Dashenka sends her greetings. (*goes out*)

LYUBOV　Well, we can get started now. I'm leaving with two worries on my mind. One is Feers—he's sick. (*glances at her watch*) We've still got five minutes. . . .

ANYA　Mamma, Feers has been taken to the hospital. Yasha sent him this morning.

LYUBOV　The other is Varya. She's used to getting up early and working, and now, with nothing to do, she's like a fish out of water. She's gotten so thin and pale, and she cries a lot, the poor dear. (*a pause*) You know very well, Yermolay Alexeyevich, that I've been hoping you two would get married . . . and everything pointed to it. (*whispers to* ANYA *and motions to* CHARLOTTA, *and they both go out*) She loves you, and you're fond of her, too . . . I just don't know, I don't know why you seem to avoid each other. I don't understand it.

LOPAHIN　Neither do I, I admit it. The whole thing's so strange. . . . If there's still time, I'm ready to. . . . Let's settle it at once —and get it over with! Without you here, I don't feel I'll ever propose to her.

LYUBOV　That's an excellent idea! You won't need more than a minute. I'll call her at once.

LOPAHIN　And there's champagne here, too, we'll celebrate. (*looks at the glasses*) They're empty, someone's drunk it all. (YASHA *coughs*) They must have poured it down.

LYUBOV (*with animation*)　Oh, I'm so glad. I'll call her, and we'll leave you alone. Yasha, *allez!* (*through the door*) Varya, come here for a minute, leave what you're doing and come here! Varya! (*goes out with* YASHA)

LOPAHIN (*looking at his watch*)　Yes. . . .

(*A pause. Whispering and suppressed laughter are heard behind the door, then* VARYA *comes in and starts fussing with the luggage. At last she says:*)

VARYA　That's strange, I can't find it. . . .

LOPAHIN　What are you looking for?

VARYA　I packed it myself, and I can't remember . . .

(*A pause*)

LOPAHIN　Where are you going to now, Varvara Mihailovna?

VARYA　I? To the Rogulins. I've taken a job as their housekeeper.

LOPAHIN　That's in Yashnevo, isn't it? Almost seventy miles from here. (*a pause*) So this is the end of life in this house. . . .

VARYA (*still fussing with the luggage*) Where could it be? Perhaps I put it in the trunk? Yes, life in this house has come to an end . . . there won't be any more. . . .

LOPAHIN　And I'm going to Kharkov. . . . On the next train. I've got a lot of work to do there. I'm leaving Epihodov here. . . . I've hired him.

VARYA　Really! . . .

LOPAHIN　Remember, last year at this time it was snowing already, but now it's still so bright and sunny. Though it's cold . . . Three degrees of frost.

VARYA　I haven't looked. (*a pause*) Besides, our thermometer's broken. . . .

(*A pause. A voice is heard from outside the door*)

VOICE　Yermolay Alexeyevich!

LOPAHIN (*as if he had been waiting for it*) I'm coming! Right away! (*goes out quickly*)

(VARYA *sits on the floor, with her head on a bundle of clothes, crying quietly. The door opens,* LYUBOV *enters hesitantly*)

LYUBOV　Well? (*a pause*) We must be going.

VARYA (*stops crying and wipes her eyes*) Yes, Mamma, it's time we got started. I'll just have time to get to the Rogulins today, if we don't miss the train.

LYUBOV (*calls through the door*)　Anya, put your things on. (*Enter* ANYA, *followed by* GAEV *and* CHARLOTTA. GAEV *wears a heavy overcoat with a hood. Servants and coachmen come into the room.* EPIHODOV *is picking up the luggage*) Now we can begin our journey!

ANYA (*joyfully*)　Our journey!

GAEV　My friends, my dear, beloved friends! As I leave this house forever, how can I be silent, how can I refrain from expressing to you, as I say goodbye for the last time, the feelings which now overwhelm me. . . .

ANYA (*begging*)　Uncle!

VARYA　Uncle, please, don't!

GAEV (*downcast*)　I put the red into the corner and then . . . I'll keep quiet.

(*Enter* TROFIMOV *and* LOPAHIN)

TROFIMOV   Well, ladies and gentlemen, it's time we get started.

LOPAHIN   Epihodov, my coat!

LYUBOV   I'll just stay for one more minute. It seems as if I'd never seen the walls and ceilings of this house before, and now I look at them with such longing, such love. . . .

GAEV   I remember when I was six—it was Trinity Sunday . . . I was sitting here at this window watching father on his way to church. . . .

LYUBOV   Have they taken everything out?

LOPAHIN   It looks like it. (*to* EPIHODOV, *as he puts on his coat*) Be sure to take care of everything, Epihodov.

EPIHODOV   (*in a husky voice*) Don't worry, Yermolay Alexeyevich!

LOPAHIN   What is wrong with your voice?

EPIHODOV   I just had some water, and it went down the wrong throat.

YASHA   (*with contempt*) What a fool!

LYUBOV   After we leave, there won't be a soul here. . . .

LOPAHIN   Not until spring.

VARYA   (*pulls an umbrella from a bundle of clothes;* LOPAHIN *pretends to be afraid*) What are you doing that for? . . . I didn't mean to. . . .

TROFIMOV   Ladies and gentlemen, hurry up, it's time. The train will be here soon.

VARYA   Petya, here are your goloshes beside the suitcase. (*tearfully*) How dirty and old they are! . . .

TROFIMOV   (*puts them on*) Hurry up, ladies and gentlemen!

GAEV   (*greatly embarrassed, afraid of breaking into tears*) The train, the station . . . The red off the white into the middle pocket. . . .

LYUBOV   Let us go!

LOPAHIN   Are we all here? No one left? (*locks the door on the left*) There are some things stored in there, best to keep it locked up. Come along!

ANYA   Goodbye, old house! Goodbye, old life!

TROFIMOV   Welcome to the new life! . . . (*goes out with* ANYA)

(VARYA *looks around the room and goes out slowly.* YASHA *and* CHARLOTTA, *with her little dog, follow*)

LOPAHIN   And so, until the spring. Come, my friends. . . . *Au revoir!* (*goes out*)

(LYUBOV *and* GAEV *alone. They seem to have been waiting for this moment, and now they embrace each other and cry quietly, with restraint, so as not to be heard*)

GAEV   (*in despair*) Sister, my sister. . . .

LYUBOV   Oh, my orchard, my beloved, my beautiful orchard! My life, my youth, my happiness . . . goodbye! . . . Goodbye!

ANYA   (*off-stage, calling gaily*) Mamma! . . .

TROFIMOV   (*off-stage, gaily and excitedly*) Yoo-hoo! . . .

LYUBOV   Just one last time—to look at these walls, these windows. . . . Mother loved to walk in this room. . . .

GAEV   Sister, my sister . . .

ANYA   (*off-stage*) Mamma!

TROFIMOV   (*off-stage*) Yoo-hoo!

LYUBOV   We're coming . . . (*They go out*)

(*The stage is empty. The sound of doors being locked and then of carriages driving off. Silence. In the stillness the dull sounds of an axe striking on a tree can be heard. They sound mournful and sad. Footsteps are heard and from the door on the right* FEERS *enters. He is dressed, as usual, in a coat and white waistcoat, and is wearing slippers. He is ill*)

FEERS   (*walks up to the middle door and tries the handle*) Locked. They've gone . . . (*sits down on a sofa*) They've forgotten me. Never mind. . . . I'll sit here for a bit. I don't suppose Leonid Andreyevich put on his fur coat, he probably wore his light one. (*sighs, preoccupied*) I didn't take care of it . . . These young people! . . . (*mutters something unintelligible*) My life's slipped by as if I'd never lived. . . . (*lies down*) I'll lie down a bit. You haven't got any strength left, nothing's left, nothing. . . . Oh, you . . . you old good-for-nothing! . . . (*lies motionless*)

(*A distant sound that seems to come out of the sky, like a breaking harp, slowly and sadly dying away. Then all is silent, except for the sound of an axe striking a tree in the orchard far away*)

Maxim Gorki

1868-1936

OBSERVATIONS ON THE THEATRE

I have written altogether, I think, about ten plays. Among these, however, there is not one that really satisfies me.

The reason for this is probably the fact that, before sitting down to write a play, I first construct its ideological framework, and combine beforehand the course and connection of the various comical and tragical events. But, since I am always and chiefly interested in man and not the group, in the personality and not the society, apparently on account of this, and against my will, every play I have written is about a man with reference to whom all the other characters of the play stand in a subordinate relation, playing the part of illustrations, and characterizing and completing the qualities and faults of the chief hero of the play.

In reality, however, a man does not exist in order to subject the qualities and faults of his neighbor to analysis—although many people busy themselves with such a task, probably because they cannot or will not do anything which carries more purpose!

For the reason given above, my plays acquired a didactical spirit, were saturated with a wordy boredom, and lost their value as works of art. By works of art I mean works in which the will of the author is either absent altogether, or else is so cleverly dissimulated as not to be detected by the reader.

In a play all the characters must act independently of the will of the author, according to their natural and social inclinations; they must follow the inspirations of their "fate," and not of the author. They must of themselves create the different comical and tragical events, by submitting to the power of their contradictory natures, interests, and passions. The author, on his part, is supposed to act like the host at a party to which he has invited these imaginary guests; and, without preventing them from tormenting or mutilating one another in every manner, morally as well as otherwise, he describes with perfect composure the manner in which they do it.

If an author takes such an attitude, he becomes capable of writing a play that is a pure work of art—a totally impartial play which merely pictures the struggle of differently directed wills, but is devoid of any moral tendencies imposed by the author. Incidentally, in all European literature I know of no drama that is composed according to this principle. Personally, I should not be able to write on such a principle.

But I think I know of people who could create plays penetrated with an inner harmony. The artificiality in such plays is not discernible —it is replaced by art. I consider the comedy of J. M. Synge, the Irishman, entitled *The Playboy of the Western World,* to be such a play. In it the comical side passes quite naturally into the terrible, while the terrible becomes comical just as easily. J. M. Synge, like a truly wise artist, does not inject his own point of view; he just exhibits the people: they are half gods and half beasts, and are possessed of the childish desire to find a "hero" among themselves. (This is, to my mind, an absurd desire, for every one of us is a hero, if he happens to remember all the victories and defeats he has met with in the struggle for life.)

The characters of Synge act in exactly the same way as people usually act and as we

"Observations on the Theatre" by Maxim Gorki, translator unknown. Copyright 1923 by Maxim Gorki. Translation originally published in the *English Review,* April 1924, and is reprinted by permission of Eyre & Spottiswoode, Ltd., London.

shall probably all act for a long time to come; they create heroes in order to ridicule them afterwards. In Synge's play I feel a subtle irony on the cult of the hero. That irony is not very remote from sadness over the stupidity of mankind, but there is in it, I repeat, nothing artificial; it is merely a pure and lawful irony of facts.

Just as perfect as this play is the *Cena delle Beffe* written by the wonderfully gifted Italian author, Sem Benelli. In this play, too, efforts of the author to hypnotize his audience are altogether absent; all the events in it unroll themselves with indisputable logic, the roused will of the hero becomes his fate and leads him unrelentingly to his perdition. I must admit that I watch the development of modern drama altogether with the greatest of hopes, and that I do not believe in the people who cry over the decline of dramatic art. Such playwrights as Sem Benelli, the wonderful Jacinto Benavente, the English Heraclites, Bernard Shaw, and two or three more men in Western Europe, will create, it 'seems to me, a new theatre, up to the present still rather unfamiliar and incomprehensible to the audience.

Knowing subtly how to handle the methods of the old tragical art, the modern dramatists bring out on the stage all that our tragicomical twentieth century breathes and is tormented with, all that it laughs and cries over. The dramatists I have mentioned fully possess the capacity of true artists: they can stand above reality, they know how to confront facts and characters in such a way that the spectator and the reader can clearly see the nature of the hidden secret powers, the collision of which creates the drama outside the will of the author as well as of his heroes.

Let me recall what I have already said: very often people consider their own stupidity as the ancient *Moira*, by creating insurmountable and fatal obstacles out of the easily surmounted trifles of life. This very strongly propagated error probably arises among the people of the twentieth century, from a somewhat sickly imagination, roused by the rush of events, the mad *tempo* of life, a splendid subject for all dramatists! The modern man reminds me somewhat of a toy-maker who has made a mechanical doll, and who is beaten on the head by that same doll; in a sudden terror, the toymaker forgets that the doll is a product of his own labor, and imagines that a mysterious power is hidden in it. But in our life there is nothing more mysterious than man himself and his creative instinct—I find that this suffices us.

I believe that the dramatists I have mentioned can see perfectly well the comical helplessness of man in the face of the richness and greatness of all that he has created and is creating. They peer more deeply into life and see it from more angles than did the dramatists of the nineteenth century-psychologists, students of modes and customs, registrars of the trifles of life.

I exclude from these, of course, Henrik Ibsen, and some of the plays of Gerhard Hauptmann.

I think that in spite of this very natural and always wholesome scepticism as regards the present, the art of the twentieth century is more optimistic, vigorous and active.

The complexity of life increases the number of peculiar collisions and dramatic subjects. The most amusing one is—man, frightened at his own audacity, amazed by the motley entanglements with relationships and events which he himself has created. For this last subject the present political workers are particularly well adapted to play the part of "heroes."

I have recently written a play, entitled *The Judge*, which seems to me to be more interesting than any of my other works written in the form of a dialogue. This does not mean, however, that it is entirely free from didacticism. We all strive to teach one another something! With the result, however, that we are taught but this one thing: not to respect the freedom of thought of one another. The reason for this, I believe, is to be sought in the fact that such a multitude of truths has lately been disseminated in the world. Every one of us possesses at least two or three such truths. And everybody tries to fasten his particular truth around the neck of his neighbor, like a collar around a dog's neck.

In that play, it seems to me, I tried to show how repulsive a man can be who is in love with his own torment, and who, therefore, deems it right to avenge himself for all that he has had personally to suffer. But when a man is convinced that suffering gives him the right to consider himself an exceptional being, and to avenge himself upon others for his own miseries, then, to my mind, he does not belong to those who deserve the respect of others. You will understand me if you imagine to yourself an individual setting fire to houses and towns, merely because he himself suffers from the cold!

It may be that British and American theatre managers will not be sufficiently interested in this play for them to undertake its production. It seems to me that among Anglo-Saxons the theory of purifying the soul through suffering is not so popular as it used to be in Russia. I say "used to be," in the hope that Russia may have gone through enough torture to have acquired an organic revulsion against suffering. However, I have no definite idea concerning the tastes and tendencies of the contemporary theatre. But rarely do I go to see a play, and when I do it is only after I have made sure that the theatrical performance will permit me to rest from the tragedy of reality which is so abundant in our day.

I should like to see the theatre of today as the Pool of Siloam, from which a man may emerge softened and restored physically. I think that the most wholesome theatre is that in which one can gaily and harmlessly laugh over the stupidity of mankind. It is exactly this stupidity that men consider to be their "fate." It is extremely healthful, for an hour or two, to forget this reality which we ourselves create so heedlessly and inconsiderately, and which, in making us collide with one another, easily breaks our hearts and heads.

A man works so much that he fully deserves a gay and wholesome leisure period. The place for such a rest ought, to my mind, to be the theatre.

In Russia, at the present time, many new theories on the "new" theatre are blossoming forth. The novelty in these theories is always the same: the theatre should be a center where stage managers compete in wittiness, and should serve as a Procrustean bed for gifted actors. This is not very amusing. It seems to me that the imaginative power of the author, together with the talent of the actor, will always be of considerably greater value to the audience than all the witty artifices of a dozen stage managers.

THE LOWER DEPTHS

Translated by Henry Burke

CAST OF CHARACTERS

KOSTYLEV, *keeper of the lodging-house, age 54*
VASSILISA, *his wife, age 26*
NATASHA, *her sister, age 20*
ABRAM MEDVEDEV, *their uncle, a policeman, age 50*
VASKA PEPPEL, *age 28*
KLETCH, *a locksmith, age 40*
ANNA, *his wife, age 30*
NASTYA, *a prostitute, age 24*
KVASHNYA, *a street seller, age nearly 40*
BUBNOV, *a capmaker, age 45*
THE BARON, *age 33*
SATIN ⎫
 ⎬ *both nearly 40*
THE ACTOR ⎭
LUKA, *a tramp, age 60*
ALESHKA, *a cobbler, age 20*
SCREWY ⎫
 ⎬ *longshoremen*
THE TARTAR ⎭

ACT ONE

(*A cavelike basement. The ceiling heavy, vaulted, blackened with smoke, with the plaster peeling. The light comes from the fourth wall, and from a square window high in the wall on the right. Peppel's room is behind a thin partition which cuts off the right corner. A big Russian stove stands in the left corner. The stone wall on the left has a door to the kitchen, where Kvashnya, the Baron and Nastya live.*

The Lower Depths by Maxim Gorki, translated by Henry Burke. Reprinted by permission of the translator. All inquiries concerning performance rights should be addressed to Progressive Management, Dryden Chambers, 119 Oxford Street, London W.1., England.

By the wall between the stove and the door stands a wide bed, screened off by a dirty cotton-print curtain. There are plank-beds all around the walls. Downstage left stands a block of wood with a vise and a small anvil mounted on it. KLETCH *sits by it, on a smaller block of wood, trying keys in old locks. At his feet, two large wire rings of keys, a battered tin samovar, a hammer, some files. In the center a big table, two benches, and a stool, all unpainted and dirty.* KVASHNYA *sits at the table, serving tea from the samovar. The* BARON *is munching black bread.* NASTYA *sits on the stool, and leans on the table, reading a battered book.* ANNA *is in the bed behind the curtain, where she lies coughing.* BUBNOV *sits on his plank-bed, fitting a torn old pair of trousers over the hat block which he is holding between his knees, and considers how to cut the cloth. A torn hatbox and its contents—cap-peaks, scraps of oilcloth, and rags of old clothes—are scattered around him.* SATIN, *just awake, lies on a plank-bed, grunting. On top of the stove, the* ACTOR *can be heard moving around and coughing. It is morning, in early Spring*)

BARON   Go on.
KVASHNYA   Oh no, I said, no more of that. I've been through all that before, and it's no more marriages for me.
BUBNOV (*to* SATIN)   What are you grunting about?
SATIN (*continues to grunt*)
KVASHNYA   I'm a free woman, I said. My own mistress. Me make myself slave to a man? —not on your life! Why, I wouldn't marry him, not if even he was an American prince.
KLETCH   Lies, all lies.
KVASHNYA   What's that?
KLETCH   Lies. You'll marry Abram all right.
BARON (*snatches* NASTYA'S *book, reads title*) "Fatal Love" . . . (*laughs*)
NASTYA (*holding out hand*)   Give it back! Come on . . . stop playing around!
(BARON *looks at her, waves book in air*)

KVASHNYA (*to* KLETCH) You red-haired old goat! I'm lying, am I? How dare you speak to me like that!

BARON (*hits* NASTYA *on head with the book*) You're a fool, Nastya . . .

NASTYA (*takes the book from him*) Give me that book! Give it to me . . .

KLETCH Oh, the fine lady! All the same, you'll marry Abram all right . . . that's all you've been waiting for . . .

KVASHNYA Oh yes! Very likely . . . You drive *your* wife nearly to her grave.

KLETCH Shut up, you old bitch! Mind your business.

KVASHNYA Oho! You don't like to hear the truth!

BARON There they go! What's the matter, Nastya?

NASTYA (*without lifting her head*) Mm? . . . Go away!

ANNA (*looks out from behind curtain*) Another day starting! For God's sake . . . stop shouting . . . stop quarrelling, all of you!

KLETCH Now she's whining again.

ANNA Every blessed day . . . Let me die in peace, can't you?

BUBNOV Noise never stopped anyone dying yet.

KVASHNYA (*goes to* ANNA) My God! How do you put up with such a brute?

ANNA Leave me alone . . .

KVASHNYA Well! . . . You poor thing . . . Does your chest feel any better?

BARON Kvashnya! Time to go to the market.

KVASHNYA All right, I'm coming. (*to* ANNA) Would you like some nice hot dumplings?

ANNA No . . . thank you. What's the good of eating?

KVASHNYA You eat. Something hot—do you good. I'll leave some in this cup for you. You can eat them when you want. (*to* BARON) Come on, your lordship . . . (*to* KLETCH) you filthy bastard . . . (*goes off into kitchen*)

ANNA (*coughing*) Oh, God . . .

BARON (*taps* NASTYA *on back of neck*) Leave it alone, you fool!

NASTYA (*snaps*) Go away . . . Do you mind?

(BARON *goes out after* KVASHNYA, *whistling*)

SATIN (*lifting himself up on his bunk*) Who beat me up last night?

BUBNOV What difference does it make who?

SATIN S'pose not. But what for?

BUBNOV You playing cards?

SATIN Yes.

BUBNOV That's why you got beat up.

SATIN The bastards!

ACTOR (*looks down from the stove*) They'll kill you one day.

SATIN Don't talk such crap.

ACTOR What do you mean?

SATIN I mean a man can't be killed twice.

ACTOR (*after a pause*) What do you mean? How . . . Why not?

KLETCH You come down off that stove and sweep the floor. You've been loafing up there long enough.

ACTOR You mind your own business.

KLETCH You wait till Vassilisa comes. She'll show you whose business it is.

ACTOR To hell with Vassilisa! It's the Baron's turn to sweep the floor . . . Baron!

BARON (*coming from the kitchen*) I haven't got time to sweep the floor . . . I'm going to the market with Kvashnya.

ACTOR I don't care if you're going to jail. It's your turn to sweep the floor . . . I'm not going to do someone else's work.

BARON Oh, go to hell! Nastya will sweep up. Hey you, Fatal Love! Wake up! (*snatches her book away*)

NASTYA (*rises*) What do you want? Give it here! You son-of-a-bitch! And you call yourself a Baron?

BARON (*returns her book*) You're going to sweep the floor for me, Nastya, all right?

NASTYA (*going into kitchen*) Ha! What do you think I am?

KVASHNYA (*at the kitchen door—to* BARON) Are you coming? They can sweep the floor without you . . . Actor! You were asked to do it—well, do it . . . it won't kill you.

ACTOR Always me. I don't see why. I don't get it.

BARON (*comes in from the kitchen, carrying large, cloth-covered pots in two baskets on a yoke*) Heavy today . . .

SATIN A lot of good it does being born a Baron.

KVASHNYA (*to* ACTOR) See to it that you sweep the floor. (*exit after* BARON)

ACTOR (*comes down from the stove*) It's bad for me to breathe dust. (*proudly*) My organism is poisoned with alcohol. (*sits down on plank-bed, thoughtfully*)

SATIN Organism . . . organon . . .

ANNA Andrey . . .

KLETCH What is it now?

ANNA Kvashnya's left me some dumplings there . . . You eat them.

KLETCH (*goes to her*) What about you?

ANNA I don't want any . . . What's the good of me eating? You work—you need to eat.

KLETCH   You afraid? Don't be afraid. May be all right.

ANNA   Go on. Eat. I feel all in. It won't be long now.

KLETCH   (*moves away*)   Don't worry. May be all right yet. It does happen. (*goes into kitchen*)

ACTOR   (*loud, as if suddenly waking up*) Yesterday at the hospital the doctor says to me, "Your organism," he says, "is completely poisoned with alcohol . . ."

SATIN   (*smiling*)   Organon . . .

ACTOR   (*insistently*)   Not organon. Or-gan-ism.

SATIN   Sycamore . . .

ACTOR   (*waves his hand*)   Ach, nonsense. I'm serious. If my organism is poisoned with alcohol, then it's bad for me to sweep the floor, to breathe dust.

SATIN   Macrobiotics—ha!

BUBNOV   What are you mumbling about?

SATIN   Words—here's another one: transcendental . . .

BUBNOV   What's that mean?

SATIN   I don't know. Can't remember.

BUBNOV   Why are you saying them, then?

SATIN   Well . . . I'm fed up with all words, chum . . . all human speech. Sick of it all! I've heard it all a thousand times . . .

ACTOR   There's a line in *Hamlet*: "Words, words, words!" A wonderful play . . . I played the gravedigger . . .

KLETCH   (*coming from the kitchen*)   When are you going to start playing with that broom?

ACTOR   Mind your own business. (*strikes himself on the chest*) "The fair Ophelia! O nymph in thy orisons be all my sins remembered."

(*Somewhere in the distance, a muffled noise, cries, a policeman's whistle.* KLETCH *sits down to work, rasping with a file*)

SATIN   I like rare words I don't understand . . . I had a job in a telegraph office when I was a boy . . . read a lot of books.

BUBNOV   You worked the telegraph?

SATIN   Once . . . (*smiling*) there's some good books . . . lots of wonderful words . . . I was educated, you know.

BUBNOV   So you've told us before. So you were educated—much good it's done you! Well, I was a fur-dresser once. Had my own shop. My hands got all yellow from dye—I dyed furs—all yellow they were, brother. I thought I'd go to my grave with yellow hands, never wash it off. Now look at them. Look—just dirty, that's all.

SATIN   Well?

BUBNOV   Well, nothing.

SATIN   What are you getting at?

BUBNOV   Just . . . food for thought . . . It's just—doesn't matter how you paint yourself up, it all rubs off . . . yes, it all rubs off.

SATIN   Oh, my bones ache!

ACTOR   (*sits, with his arms round his knees*) Education is rubbish. The main thing is talent. I knew an actor, he could hardly read his own parts, but when he was on the stage the whole theatre used to shake with the applause he got.

SATIN   Bubnov, give me five kopecks.

BUBNOV   I've only got two kopecks myself.

ACTOR   I say talent's what you need. And talent's just believing in yourself, in your own ability . . .

SATIN   Give me five kopecks and I'll believe you've got talent. I'll believe you're a genius, a crocodile, a police inspector . . . Kletch, give me five kopecks.

KLETCH   Go to hell! There's too many of your sort here.

SATIN   What are you cursing for? You haven't got a penny in the world.

ANNA   Andrey . . . It's stuffy . . . can't breathe . . .

KLETCH   What do you want me to do?

BUBNOV   Open the hall door.

KLETCH   Oh yes! You sit up there on a bed, and I'm on the floor. Give me your bed, and you can open the door all you want. I've got a cold as it is.

BUBNOV   (*unconcernedly*)   I don't care if you open the door. It's your wife who's asking.

KLETCH   (*sulkily*)   I don't care who's asking.

SATIN   My head's ringing! Why do people hit each other over the head?

BUBNOV   Why do they hit each other at all? (*He gets up*) Going to buy some thread . . . Mr. and Mrs. Landlord haven't been around yet today—perhaps they've dropped dead. (*exit*)

(ANNA *coughs.* SATIN *lies motionless, his arms under his head*)

ACTOR   (*looks around sadly, goes to* ANNA) Feeling bad? Eh?

ANNA   I'm choking.

ACTOR   If you like—I'll take you out in the hall. Get up then. (*Helps her up, throws an old gown over her shoulders, and holds her under the arm, leading her out to the hall*) Come on, carefully now. I'm sick too . . . poisoned with alcohol.

KOSTYLEV   (*at the door*)   Going for a walk? Ha! You make a fine pair . . .

ACTOR   Well, get out of the way. Can't you see that invalids are trying to get through.

KOSTYLEV   Come on then, if you want to . . .

(humming some hymn, he looks about suspiciously, and leans his head to the left as if trying to overhear something in PEPPEL's *room.* KLETCH *watches him while continuing to rattle his keys and to rasp his file firmly)* Scraping away?

KLETCH   Uh?

KOSTYLEV   I say, you're scraping away. *(pause)* Er . . . What was I going to ask you? *(suddenly in a low voice)* Has my wife been in here?

KLETCH   Haven't seen her.

KOSTYLEV *(cautiously goes up to* PEPPEL's *door)* You get a lot of space for only two rubles a month. A bed . . . place to sit . . . hm . . . it's worth five rubles at least. I think I'll have to raise your rent another half ruble.

KLETCH   Raise me by the neck and hang me while you're about it. There you stand, with one foot in the grave, and all you can think about is another half ruble.

KOSTYLEV   Why should I want to hang you? That wouldn't do anybody any good. God be with you—live as much as you want to, but I will raise your rent another half ruble. I can buy more oil for my icon lamp—as atonement for my sins. Then my sins will be forgiven. And yours too. You never think of your sins, do you, Andrey? . . . Ah well . . . Ah, you're a wicked man, Andrey! Your wife is fading away, you're so wicked . . . Nobody likes you, respects you . . . your work grates on everyone's ears, disturbs everybody—

KLETCH *(shouts)*   What did you come here for?—to bait me?

*(*SATIN *roars loudly)*

KOSTYLEV *(jumps)*   Oh, God!

ACTOR *(entering)*   I sat her down in the hall, wrapped her up . . .

KOSTYLEV   Ah, you're a good fellow. You'll be rewarded . . .

ACTOR   When?

KOSTYLEV   In the next world, my friend. All your good deeds are written down, there.

ACTOR   Suppose you were to repay my good deeds here.

KOSTYLEV   How can I do that?

ACTOR   Half of what I owe you.

KOSTYLEV   Ha, ha! You will have your little joke, always play-acting . . . You can't measure kind-heartedness in money. Kind-heartedness is the greatest of all gifts. And your debt to me—that's all it is—a debt! So you have to pay me. You musn't ask an old man like me to pay you for being kind-hearted.

ACTOR   You old bastard. *(goes into kitchen)*

*(*KLETCH *rises and goes into the hall)*

KOSTYLEV *(to* SATIN*)*   Ha, ha! Old scraper's gone away. Doesn't like me.

SATIN   Who does—except the devil?

KOSTYLEV *(laughing)*   You've got a sharp tongue! But I like you. I like you all. I do. My unhappy, lost, wretched friends . . . *(suddenly)* Is Vaska in?

SATIN   Go and look.

KOSTYLEV *(goes to door and knocks)*   Vaska!

*(*ACTOR *appears at the kitchen door, munching)*

PEPPEL *(off)*   Who is it?

KOSTYLEV   It's me, Vaska.

PEPPEL   What do you want?

KOSTYLEV *(moves from the door)*   Open the door . . .

SATIN *(not looking at* KOSTYLEV*)*   She's in there.

*(*ACTOR *laughs)*

KOSTYLEV *(uneasily, in a low voice)*   Uh? Who? Who's there? Eh?

SATIN   You speaking to me?

KOSTYLEV   What did you say just now?

SATIN   I was . . . talking to myself . . .

KOSTYLEV   You watch out. Don't get too funny . . . see! *(knocks hard on* PEPPEL's *door)* Vaska!

PEPPEL *(opens door)*   Well? What's the matter with you?

KOSTYLEV *(looking into the room)*   I . . . you see . . .

PEPPEL   Brought the money?

KOSTYLEV   What money? I . . .

PEPPEL   The money. The seven rubles for the watch. Come on.

KOSTYLEV   What watch? Ach, Vaska, you . . .

PEPPEL   You know damn well what watch. The one I sold you yesterday, in front of witnesses. Ten rubles. You gave me three. Come on, then, where's the other seven? What are you blinking for? You hang around here, waking people up, and now you don't know yourself what you want.

KOSTYLEV   Sh—sh! Don't lose your temper, Vaska . . . The watch . . . was . . .

SATIN   Stolen.

KOSTYLEV *(sternly)*   What do you mean? I don't buy stolen goods.

PEPPEL *(takes him by the shoulder)*   Well, what did you wake me up for? What do you want?

KOSTYLEV   Me? I . . . nothing. I . . . I'll go away, if that's your attitude.

PEPPEL   Well, get out of here, then. And next time be sure you bring the money.

KOSTYLEV *(going)*   Miserable, unpleasant people! Ay, ay . . .

ACTOR   What a farce!

SATIN   Who'd have believed it?

PEPPEL   What was he after?

SATIN   (*laughing*) Don't you know? He's looking for his wife. Why don't you take care of him for good, Vaska?

PEPPEL   Risk my life for trash like that?

SATIN   There's no risk. You're too smart. You could marry Vassilisa, become our landlord . . .

PEPPEL   Ho, that's a good one! All of you living off me! I'm too soft—you'd drink every penny I had. (*sits on bunk*) Old devil—woke me up. Such a good dream I was having. I was fishing. Caught an enormous trout. Huge—never seen one so big. I thought the line would snap. Any minute now I thought . . .

SATIN   That wasn't no trout—that was Vassilisa.

ACTOR   He hooked Vassilisa long ago.

PEPPEL   (*angrily*) Oh, go to hell, all of you—and take her with you when you go!

KLETCH   (*comes from hall*) Cold. Damn cold.

ACTOR   You left Anna out there? She'll freeze.

KLETCH   Natasha's taken her into the kitchen.

ACTOR   The old man will throw her out.

KLETCH   (*sits down to work*) Oh, Natasha will look after her.

SATIN   Vaska, give us five kopecks.

ACTOR   (*to* SATIN) You and your five kopecks! Give us twenty, Vaska.

PEPPEL   Here—take it quick, before you ask for a ruble.

SATIN   Gibraltar! There's no people like thieves.

KLETCH   (*grumpily*) Easy money—they don't work for it.

SATIN   Lots of people make easy money . . . not many give it away easy though . . . Work? You make work pleasant enough, and perhaps I'll work. Might do. When work's pleasant, life's all right. When work's a duty, life's just slavery. (*to* ACTOR) Come on, then, Sardanapalus!

ACTOR   Come on, Nebuchadnezzar! God, I'm going to get so damn drunk!

(*They go out*)

PEPPEL   (*yawns*) How's your wife?

KLETCH   Not long now.

PEPPEL   You know, looking at you—I can't see the sense of all that scraping.

KLETCH   What else can I do?

PEPPEL   Nothing.

KLETCH   Nothing! How am I supposed to live?

PEPPEL   Some people manage.

KLETCH   Huh—call them people! Rabble, scum—people! I'm a working man. I'm ashamed to look at them. I've been working ever since I was a kid. You think I won't get out of this hole? I'll get out of here if I have to leave my skin here behind me. You wait . . . when my old woman dies . . . I've been here six months, and it feels more like six years . . .

PEPPEL   There's no one here any worse than you are—say what you like.

KLETCH   No worse than me? They've got no honor, no conscience . . .

PEPPEL   (*indifferently*) What's the good of honor and conscience? You can't wear them on your feet instead of boots. Honor and conscience are all right for rich people, people in authority . . .

BUBNOV   (*re-enters*) Oo-oo-oo-oh! I'm frozen, it's so cold.

PEPPEL   Bubnov, have you got a conscience?

BUBNOV   What? A conscience?

PEPPEL   That's right.

BUBNOV   What do I want with a conscience? I can't afford it.

PEPPEL   Just what I say. Honor and conscience is all right for the rich, yes. But Kletch here is blaming *us*, because we haven't got any conscience.

BUBNOV   Why—does he want to borrow some?

PEPPEL   He's got plenty of his own.

BUBNOV   Oh, he's trying to sell some. You won't find any customers here. I wouldn't mind buying some marked cards, but they'd have to be on credit.

PEPPEL   (*sermonizing*) You're a fool, Andrey! You should try talking to Satin about conscience . . . or the Baron.

KLETCH   I wouldn't talk to them about anything.

PEPPEL   They've got more brains than you've got—for all their drinking.

BUBNOV   If a man is drunk and wise, he's a man that all should prize.

PEPPEL   Satin says everybody wants everyone else to have a conscience, but nobody wants to have one himself. It's true too . . .

(*Enter* NATASHA, *followed by* LUKA, *who carries a stick, a knapsack on his back, and a kettle and teapot hanging from his waist*)

LUKA   Good morning, honest people!

PEPPEL   (*smooths his moustache*) Ah, Natasha!

BUBNOV (*to* LUKA) I was honest up to last spring.

NATASHA Here's a new lodger.

LUKA It's all the same to me. I have just as much respect for crooks. All fleas are the same. All black, and all good jumpers. Where shall I squeeze myself, child?

NATASHA (*points to the kitchen door*) In there, grandpa.

LUKA Thank you, dear. Anywhere you say. Anywhere the old man can be warm. (*exit*)

PEPPEL An interesting old man you've brought us, Natasha.

NATASHA A lot more interesting than you . . . Andrey! Your wife's in our kitchen. You'd better come and get her.

KLETCH All right. I'll come.

NATASHA You ought to try and be kinder to her. She hasn't got long.

KLETCH I know.

NATASHA You know . . . It's no good just knowing. You should do something. It's a terrible thing to die.

PEPPEL I'm not afraid of death.

NATASHA Oh, you're a marvel, aren't you?

BUBNOV (*whistling*) This thread's rotten.

PEPPEL God's truth, I'm not afraid. If I was to die now. Take a knife and stab me in my heart. I'll die without a murmur. In fact, I'd be glad to, because it comes from a pure hand.

NATASHA (*turns to go*) You keep your soft soap for those who like it.

BUBNOV (*drawls*) Thread's rotten . . .

NATASHA (*at hall door*) Don't forget your wife, Andrey . . .

KLETCH All right.

(*Exit* NATASHA)

PEPPEL She's a nice girl.

BUBNOV Not bad.

PEPPEL Why does she get like that with me? What for? She'll come to no good here.

BUBNOV Through you she will.

PEPPEL What do you mean, through me? I feel sorry for her.

BUBNOV Like the wolf feels sorry for the sheep.

PEPPEL That's a lie? I feel very sorry for her. She has a hard life here, I can see she does.

KLETCH You wait till Vassilisa catches you talking to her.

BUBNOV Vassilisa? Mm, yes. She won't give up what's hers as easily as that. She's a bitch, she is.

PEPPEL (*lies down on the planks*) You two prophets can go to hell!

KLETCH Well, you just wait and see!

LUKA (*in the kitchen, sings*)
Night is dark, your feet are lead,
You cannot see the road ahead . . .

KLETCH (*goes into the passage*) Another one bawling.

PEPPEL God, I'm bored. Why do I get so bored? Everything's fine, and all of a sudden—bored. Like catching a cold.

BUBNOV Bored? Hmm . . .

PEPPEL O-o-o-oh!

LUKA (*sings*) No sir, you cannot see the road ahead . . .

PEPPEL Hey, there, old man!

LUKA (*at door*) Who, me?

PEPPEL Yes, you. Stop singing!

LUKA (*comes in*) What's wrong? Don't you like it?

PEPPEL I like good singing.

LUKA So mine isn't good, then.

PEPPEL That's right.

LUKA Well, well. I thought I sang well. That's always the way. A man thinks he's doing something well, and then—suddenly, bang!—everybody's criticizing.

PEPPEL (*laughs*) That's the way it is.

BUBNOV You say you're bored, and there you are laughing.

LUKA Who's bored?

PEPPEL Me . . . I am . . .

(*Enter the* BARON)

LUKA Well, well! And in the kitchen there's a girl reading a book, and crying! Yes, crying! Tears falling down her cheeks. I say to her, "What's the matter, child? Eh?" "It's so sad," she says. "What's sad?" I say. "The book" she says . . . Some people find funny things to worry about. All from boredom.

BARON She's a fool, that girl.

PEPPEL Baron, have you had your tea?

BARON Yes, what about it?

PEPPEL Like me to buy you a drink?

BARON What do you think?

PEPPEL Get down on all fours and bark like a dog, then.

BARON Idiot! Are you drunk or something?

PEPPEL Go on, bark! That'll amuse me. You're a Baron. Used to look down on people like me.

BARON So what?

PEPPEL So now I make you bark like a dog. You will, too. You know you will.

BARON What if I do? Idiot! What good is it to you to know I've sunk lower than you? You should have tried to make me walk on all fours when I was better than you.

BUBNOV That's right!

LUKA   Very good, I'd say!

BUBNOV   What's past is past, and what's left isn't worth talking about. There's no aristocracy here. No class distinction. Just man, that's all.

LUKA   So everybody's equal . . . Were you really a baron, mister?

BARON   What's that? Who are you? A ghost?

LUKA   (laughs)   I've seen counts, and I've seen princes. But this is the first time I've seen a baron—and this one's a damaged one, at that.

PEPPEL   (laughs)   That's one for you, Baron!

BARON   We live and learn, Vaska.

LUKA   Hey, hey! To look at you, my brothers, your way of life . . .

BUBNOV   Our way of life is nothing but uproar from morning to night.

BARON   We knew better times once . . . I used to drink coffee in bed in the mornings . . . coffee!—with cream . . .

LUKA   But we're all human beings. Pretend all you like, give yourself airs, but a man you were born, and a man you must die. I can see everyone getting cleverer and cleverer. They live worse and want more out of life— stubborn lot!

BARON   Who are you, old man? Where do you come from?

LUKA   Who, me?

BARON   Are you a tramp?

LUKA   We're all of us tramps. They even say the world's a tramp in the universe.

BARON   (sternly)   I daresay—but have you got a passport?

LUKA   (after a slight pause)   And what are you, a police inspector?

PEPPEL   (delighted)   That's the way, old man. That had you, Baron—eh?

BUBNOV   Yes, that was one for our fine gentleman.

BARON   (embarrassed)   What's the matter? I was only joking, old man. I haven't got any papers myself.

BUBNOV   Lies, all lies.

BARON   Well . . . I have got papers . . . but they're no use, any of them.

LUKA   All papers are like that—no use, any of them.

PEPPEL   Baron, let's go and have a drink.

BARON   All right! Well, goodbye, old man. You're an old bastard.

LUKA   Who isn't, brother,—eh?

PEPPEL   (at hall door)   Well, are you coming?

(Exit PEPPEL. BARON quickly follows him)

LUKA   Is that man really a Baron?

BUBNOV   God knows. He's been a gentleman all right. Every now and then it breaks out. He can't get rid of it yet.

LUKA   It seems like breeding's like the smallpox. You get cured, but you've still got the marks.

BUBNOV   He's all right . . . Only now and then he goes off, like about your passport today.

ALESHKA   (enters, drunk, whistling, with a concertina)   Hello everyone!

BUBNOV   What are you yelling about?

ALESHKA   Oh, I beg your pardon . . . 'scuse me! I'm polite . . .

BUBNOV   You on another binge?

ALESHKA   You damned right! Just now Inspector Medyakin throws me out of the police station, and he says, "Never let me smell you on the streets again," he says. And I'm a sensitive sort of fellow. My boss just snarls at me. And what is he, my boss, eh? He's just a goddamned drunkard, my boss is. And I don't ask for nothing. Not a thing. That's flat! Here's twenty rubles, you say. But I don't want nothing. (Enter NASTYA from the kitchen) Here's a million. I don't want it. But I won't be ordered around by another man—a drunkard too. I won't have it. I won't.

(NASTYA, standing in the doorway, looks at ALESHKA and shakes her head)

LUKA   (good-naturedly)   Well, you have got yourself in a mess, my boy . . .

BUBNOV   What fools people are!

ALESHKA   (lying on floor)   A-a-ah, eat me up! I don't care, I'm a miserable fool! Show me, why am I worse than other people? What other people? Eh? Medyakin says to me, "You keep off the streets or I'll knock your block off." But I'm going to lie down in the middle of the street—run over me! I don't care . . .

NASTYA   Poor boy! . . . Such a kid, and . . . look at him.

ALESHKA   (sees her, gets on his knees)   Mam'sel! Parlez français? Prix-fixe? I'm on a binge . . .

NASTYA   (a loud whisper)   Vassilisa!

VASSILISA   (opens door with a bang; to ALESHKA)   Are you here again?

ALESHKA   How do you do? Do come in . . .

VASSILISA   You brat, I told you not to show your face in here again, didn't I? And you're here again!

ALESHKA   Vassilisa . . . Shall I play you a funeral march?

VASSILISA   (grabs him by shoulder)   Clear out!

ALESHKA   (moves to door)   No, wait . . .

you can't do that! A funeral march . . . I just learnt it! New tune . . . Wait . . . you can't . . .

VASSILISA   I'll show you "can't." I'll set the whole street on you, you little dirty-mouthed . . . pig! Who do you think you are talking about me like that. . . .

ALESHKA (*runs out*)   All right, I'm going.

VASSILISA (*to* BUBNOV)   Never let him set foot here again, do you hear?

BUBNOV   I'm not your blasted watchdog.

VASSILISA   I don't care what you are. You're living here on charity, don't you forget that! How much do you owe me?

BUBNOV (*calmly*)   Never worked it out.

VASSILISA   You be careful—I'll work it out!

ALESHKA (*opens door, shouts*)   Vassilisa! I'm not scared of you! I'm not scared! (*disappears*)

(LUKA *laughs*)

VASSILISA   Who are you?

LUKA   Just passing through. Bird of passage.

VASSILISA   For the night, or are you stopping?

LUKA   That all depends.

VASSILISA   Where's your passport?

LUKA   I'll let you have it.

VASSILISA   Let me have it then.

LUKA   I'll bring it to you—right to your door.

VASSILISA   Bird of passage—huh! Jailbird would be more the truth.

LUKA (*with sigh*)   Ayy . . . You're a hard woman, aren't you?

(VASSILISA *goes to* PEPPEL's *door*)

ALESHKA (*peers round kitchen door, whispers*)   Hey! She gone?

VASSILISA (*turns on him*)   You still here?

(ALESHKA *disappears, whistling.* NASTYA *and* LUKA *laugh*)

BUBNOV (*to* VASSILISA)   He isn't there.

VASSILISA   Who isn't?

BUBNOV   Vaska.

VASSILISA   Did I ask you if he was?

BUBNOV   I can see you're looking for him.

VASSILISA   I'm looking to see if the place is tidy. Why isn't the floor swept yet? How many times do I have to tell you to sweep the floor?

BUBNOV   It's the Actor's turn.

VASSILISA   I don't care whose turn. If the Health Inspector comes and fines me, then—out you go, the lot of you!

BUBNOV (*calmly*)   Then what will you live on?

VASSILISA   I won't have all this mess. (*goes towards kitchen*) (*to* NASTYA) What's the matter with you? Your face is all swollen. Don't stand there—sweep the floor! Have you seen Natasha? Has she been in?

NASTYA   Don't know. I haven't seen her.

VASSILISA   Bubnov! Has my sister been here?

BUBNOV   Er . . . she brought him in.

VASSILISA   Was he . . . has he been in?

BUBNOV   Vaska? Yes . . . She was here talking to Kletch, your Natasha.

VASSILISA   I wasn't asking who she was talking to! Dirt everywhere—filth! Ach, you pigs! See the place is clean, you hear?

(*Exit* VASSILISA, *quickly*)

BUBNOV   My God, what a bitch!

LUKA   Quite a temper—eh?

NASTYA   You'd be a bitch if you had her life. Tied to a husband like she's got!

BUBNOV   Well, she isn't tied too fast.

LUKA   Does she always have these fits?

BUBNOV   All the time. She came after her lover, you see. And he isn't here.

LUKA   So she has to get angry. Huh! Everybody is trying to be boss. They throw their weight around, and make all sorts of threats, and punish each other. And the world still doesn't make any sense . . . and is dirty.

BUBNOV   Everybody wants order, and their brains are all disorder. Still, the floor's got to be swept. Hey, Nastya—you do it.

NASTYA   Like hell! Do you think I'm your kitchen maid? (*after a pause*) I'm going to get drunk today—dead drunk!

BUBNOV   There you are!

LUKA   What do you want to get drunk for, girl? Just now you were crying. Now you want to get drunk.

NASTYA (*defiantly*)   And when I'm drunk, I'll cry again—so there!

BUBNOV   So what?

LUKA   Yes, but what for, girl? Even a pimple has a reason. (NASTYA *shakes her head in silence*) So . . . hey, hey . . . What's going to happen to the human race? Well, suppose I sweep the floor. Where's the broom?

BUBNOV   In the hall behind the door. (LUKA *goes out to the hall*) Nastya!

NASTYA   Uh?

BUBNOV   Why did Vassilisa go for Aleshka?

NASTYA   He went round saying Vaska's fed up with her, and wants to drop her for Natasha. I'm getting out of here. Going somewhere else.

BUBNOV   Why? Where to?

NASTYA   I'm fed up. I'm not wanted here.

BUBNOV (*calmly*)   You're not wanted anywhere. Nobody's wanted anywhere the whole world over, for that matter. (NASTYA *shakes her head, rises, and slowly goes out to the hall*) (*Enter* MEDVEDEV, *followed by* LUKA *with broom*)

MEDVEDEV   Don't think I know you.

LUKA   Do you know everybody else, then?

MEDVEDEV   I have to know everybody in my area. But I don't know you.

LUKA   That's because the whole world couldn't quite get inside your district, uncle. There's a little bit left outside. (*goes into kitchen*)

MEDVEDEV   He's right . . . my district isn't very big. But it's worse than some of the big ones. (*going up to* BUBNOV) Just now, coming off duty, I had to run in Aleshka, the cobbler. Lying there right in the middle of the road, playing his concertina, and yelling, "I don't want anything! I don't care! I don't want anything!" Horses and traffic everywhere. Could have been run over, crushed to death. He's a wild one. Well, I had to take him in. He sure loves to cause trouble.

BUBNOV   You coming for a game of checkers tonight?

MEDVEDEV   Tonight? Yes . . . And what's this about Vaska?

BUBNOV   What about him? Same as usual.

MEDVEDEV   Same as usual, eh?

BUBNOV   What's wrong with that? He's allowed to live, isn't he?

MEDVEDEV   (*doubtfully*) Is he? (LUKA *crosses the room to the hall with a bucket*) Mm, yes. There's some talk . . . about Vaska . . . haven't you heard it?

BUBNOV   I've heard lots of talk.

MEDVEDEV   About Vassilisa . . . haven't you noticed?

BUBNOV   What?

MEDVEDEV   "What!" I think you know— you're just lying. Everyone knows . . . (*sternly*) Don't lie to me, old man.

BUBNOV   Why should I lie?

MEDVEDEV   I know, I know . . . Oh, come on! They say Vaska and Vassilisa are . . . carrying on . . . Well, so what? I'm her uncle, not her father. It can't make me a laughing stock. (*Enter* KVASHNYA) That's what people are these days—they'll laugh at anything. Ah, its you!

KVASHNYA   My darling keeper of the peace! Bubnov, he's been pestering me to marry him again.

BUBNOV   Well, why not? He's not money. He's still got his health and strength.

MEDVEDEV   Me? Ho, ho!

KVASHNYA   You old bear! Leave me alone —it's my sore spot. I've been through it all once, honey. It's like falling through a hole in the ice. You never forget it.

MEDVEDEV   Wait a minute. Husbands aren't all the same.

KVASHNYA   No, but I'm the same. When my old man died, it took me a whole day before I could believe my own luck.

MEDVEDEV   If your husband beat you, you should have complained to the police.

KVASHNYA   I complained to God for eight years—it didn't do any good.

MEDVEDEV   It's a punishable offense for a man to beat his wife. That's the law today. Nobody's allowed to beat anyone—except the police.

LUKA   (*leads in* ANNA)   Careful now . . . There you are! You're too weak to go about on your own. Where do you go?

ANNA   (*points it out*)   Thank you, grandpa . . .

KVASHNYA   Look, there's a married woman for you. Look at her!

LUKA   The poor thing's very weak. She was in the hall, holding onto the wall, groaning. Why do you leave her by herself?

KVASHNYA   Sorry, we didn't notice, grandpa. Her maid must have gone out for a walk.

LUKA   You can laugh! How can you neglect a human being? Whoever it is, we all have some value.

MEDVEDEV   People have got to be looked after. What if she dies suddenly? No end of trouble. Got to watch out for that.

LUKA   That's true, Inspector.

MEDVEDEV   Of course it is . . . but I'm not an Inspector yet.

LUKA   Oh, I thought you were. That strong, commanding manner of yours.

(*Noise and scuffling in the hall. Loud cries*)

MEDVEDEV   Not a fight?

BUBNOV   Sounds like it.

KVASHNYA   I'm going to see.

MEDVEDEV   I'd better go too. Duty calls! People ought to be left to fight. They'd stop when they got tired. Let them knock each other about as much as they like—they won't do it again in a hurry. They'd remember what it's like.

BUBNOV   (*rises from bunk*)   Tell that to the Chief of Police.

KOSTYLEV   (*flings open door, cries*)   Abram! Quickly . . . Vassilisa . . . killing Natasha! Come quick . . .

(KVASHNYA, MEDVEDEV, BUBNOV *rush into hall.* LUKA *looks after them, shaking his head*)

ANNA Oh, God . . . Poor Natasha!

LUKA Who is fighting?

ANNA The mistress . . . and her sister.

LUKA (*goes to* ANNA) What's it about?

ANNA They've nothing better to do . . . they're both well and strong.

LUKA What's your name?

ANNA Anna. You look like my father . . . kind like he was . . . soft . . .

LUKA It's all the kicks I've had—they've made me soft . . . (*He laughs with a grating laugh*)

ACT TWO

(*The same scene. Night. On the bunk by the stove,* SATIN, *the* BARON, SCREWY *and the* TARTAR *are playing cards.* KLETCH *and the* ACTOR *are watching. On his bunk,* BUBNOV *is playing checkers with* MEDVEDEV. LUKA *sits on a stool by* ANNA's *bed. The cellar is lighted by two lamps. One hangs on the wall by the card players, the other stands on* BUBNOV's *bunk*)

TARTAR One more game, then I stop.

BUBNOV Screwy! Sing! (*sings*)
The sun comes up, the sun goes down . . .

SCREWY (*harmonizes*)
In my prison night won't go . . .

TARTAR (*to* SATIN) Shuffle! Shuffle well! I know what you're like . . .

BUBNOV *and* SCREWY (*sing together*)
Day and night the warder paces
Past the bars of my window . . .

ANNA Beaten black and blue—nothing but curses all my life, all my blessed life . . .

LUKA There, there, don't upset yourself, my dear.

MEDVEDEV Where do you think you're moving? You blind?

BUBNOV Ah! yes, of course . . .

TARTAR (*shakes his fist at* SATIN) Why you try to hide a card? I see it—you . . . !

SCREWY Forget it, Hassan! They'll skin us anyway. Come on, Bubnov—sing!

ANNA I can't remember a time when I wasn't hungry . . . counted every last crumb of bread . . . Never known where the next bite's coming from . . . Been in rags all my miserable life. Why? What's it all for?

LUKA You poor child. You're tired. Don't worry yourself so.

ACTOR (*to* SCREWY) Play the Jack . . . the Jack, damn you!

BARON And we have the king.

KLETCH They win every time.

SATIN Can't help it—force of habit.

MEDVEDEV King!

BUBNOV And me . . . mm . . .

ANNA I'm dying.

KLETCH Look at that! You might as well give up now, Hassan. Go on, throw in your cards!

ACTOR He can play without your advice! Leave him alone.

BARON Shut up, Andrey, or I'll hit you. I'm warning you!

TARTAR Deal again. You may as well break me all the way.

(KLETCH *shakes head, goes over to* BUBNOV)

ANNA Oh God, will I be punished with suffering in the next world too? There as well?

LUKA No, you won't. You won't. Don't upset yourself. Listen: you won't suffer there—you'll only rest. Have a little patience—everybody has to suffer a bit in this life . . . (*rises, goes quickly into kitchen*)

BUBNOV (*sings*)
Warder, watch my prison window . . .

SCREWY (*sings*)
Warder, guard my prison cell . . .

BOTH (*sing*)
How I long, I long for freedom!
But my chains they hold me well!

TARTAR (*cries out*) You hide a card up your sleeve!

BARON (*embarrassed*) Well, where do you want me to hide it? Up your ass?

ACTOR (*emphatically*) You're wrong, Hassan. . . . Nobody ever . . .

TARTAR I saw him! Bloody cheat! I won't play no more!

SATIN (*gathers cards*) For Christ's sake, Hassan! You know we're cheats—why do you play with us at all, then?

BARON He loses half a ruble, and he makes three rubles' worth of noise about it . . . Come on, Hassan! Sit down.

TARTAR (*hotly*) Well, play straight then.

SATIN Why should we?

TARTAR What do you mean, why should you?

SATIN What I say. Why should we?

TARTAR Don't you know?

SATIN No, I don't. Do you?

(TARTAR *spits in disgust. Everybody laughs at him*)

SCREWY (*good-naturedly*) You're a funny guy, Hassan. Can't you see, if they turned honest, they'd die of starvation in three days . . .

TARTAR   That's nothing to do with me! Everyone should be honest.

SCREWY   He's off again. Come on and have some tea . . . Bubnov! And (*sings*)

Oh, you heavy chains that bind me . . .

BUBNOV (*sings*)

Oh, you heavy clanking chains . . .

SCREWY   Come on, Hassan! (*exit singing*)

I will never break you ever . . .

(TARTAR *shakes his fist at* BARON, *and follows his friend*)

SATIN (*laughing, to* BARON)   Well, your majesty—you sure messed us up again, didn't you? You've learned a lot, but you still don't know how to cheat at cards.

BARON (*shrugs*)   God knows how it happened.

ACTOR   No talent . . . No faith in yourself . . . and without that . . . you're nothing, nothing at all . . .

MEDVEDEV   I have one king. You've got two . . . mm!

BUBNOV   One's enough, if you use him right. Your move!

KLETCH   You've had it, Abram!

MEDVEDEV   Mind your own business, will you? And shut up . . .

SATIN   Fifty-three kopecks in.

ACTOR   Three of those are mine . . . Though what do I want with three kopecks?

LUKA (*coming in from the kitchen*)   So you've cleaned out the Tartar? Going for a drink now?

BARON   Come and have a drink with us!

SATIN   Let's see what you're like drunk!

LUKA   No better than I am sober . . .

ACTOR   Come on, old man . . . I'll recite to you . . .

LUKA   What's that?

ACTOR   Poetry, you know.

LUKA   Poetry? What do I want with poetry?

ACTOR   It's funny . . . sometimes it's sad . . .

SATIN   Hey, recitationist! Are you coming?

(*exit with* BARON)

ACTOR   I'm coming . . . I'll catch you up! Here, here's one, old man. It's a speech from a play . . . can't remember how it begins . . . I've completely forgotton it! (*strikes his forehead*)

BUBNOV   There! I take your king . . . Your move!

MEDVEDEV   You had me, wherever I moved.

ACTOR   I had a good memory once, old man, before my organism got poisoned with alcohol. Now I'm finished—done for. I used to do that speech well . . . used to bring the house down!

You don't know what it's like—applause. It's . . . it's like vodka! I used to come on . . . stand like this . . . (*strikes a pose*) stand like this, and (*silence*) I can't remember a thing! Not a single word! Can't remember! My best speech . . . In a bad way, eh, old man?

LUKA   Yes, it's bad, all right, forgetting something you used to love. Something you had your heart and soul in . . .

ACTOR   I've drunk up my soul, old man . . . I'm lost, my friend. Why am I lost? Because I've lost faith in myself . . . I'm finished . . .

LUKA   Finished? You go and get yourself cured! Listen. They cure people of drunkenness nowadays. Cure them for nothing. They've built a special hospital to cure drunkards for nothing. They realize a drunkard's a man like any other. They're glad when he wants to be cured! So there it is for you. You go there!

ACTOR (*reflectively*)   Where? Where is it?

LUKA   It's . . . in a town . . . what's its name? Never mind. I'll think of it. But you get ready to go. Pull yourself together, and keep off the vodka. Then go and get cured, and you can start life over again. Sounds good, doesn't it, my brother? All over again—eh? Well, just make up your mind, and you can do it.

ACTOR (*smiles*)   All over again . . . from the beginning . . . that would be marvelous . . . yes . . . all over again. (*He laughs*) Oh . . . yes! Can I? Can I really do it? Eh?

LUKA   Of course you can do it! A man can do anything, once he makes up his mind to it.

ACTOR (*as if woken up suddenly*)   You're a strange duck! Well, g'bye! (*whistles*) G'bye, old man! . . . (*exit*)

ANNA   Grandpa!

LUKA   What is it, dear?

ANNA   Come and talk to me.

LUKA (*goes up to her*)   All right. Let's have a chat.

(KLETCH *looks round, silently comes up to his wife, looks at her, and gestures, as though wanting to say something*)

LUKA   What's the matter, my brother?

KLETCH (*quietly*)   Nothing. (*goes slowly to hall door, stands there for a moment, and exits*)

LUKA (*watching him*)   Takes it to heart, your old man.

ANNA   I can't worry about him any more.

LUKA   Did he used to beat you?

ANNA   Did he! I'm dying because of him . . .

BUBNOV   My wife had a lover. Bastard played a good game of checkers.

MEDVEDEV   Hm . . .

ANNA Grandpa! Talk to me. I can't breathe.

LUKA It's all right. Like that before you die, my child. It's nothing, dear. Just keep hoping. You're going to die, and then you'll have peace. There's nothing to be afraid of—nothing. Peace and quiet . . . Lie still, now! Death settles everything . . . it's kind to us . . . When you die, they say you go to rest. Well, it's true, dear! After all you can't find rest in this world.

(PEPPEL *enters, slightly drunk, dishevelled and sullen. He sits on a bunk by the door, and stays silent and motionless*)

ANNA But what if there's suffering there, too?

LUKA There won't be! There won't be, believe me! Just rest, that's all there'll be. They'll call you up to God, and they'll say, "Look Lord, this is your servant, Anna" . . .

MEDVEDEV (*sternly*) How do you know what they'll say? Ach . . .

(*Hearing* MEDVEDEV'S *voice*, PEPPEL *raises his head, and listens*)

LUKA I just do, that's all, Inspector.

MEDVEDEV (*conciliatory*) Yes, yes, yes . . . That's up to you. But I'm not an Inspector yet . . .

BUBNOV I take two.

MEDVEDEV Damnation!

LUKA And God will look at you gently and kindly, and he'll say, "I know this Anna. Take her into Heaven," he'll say, "Give her rest. I know she's had a hard life. She's weary. Give Anna rest."

ANNA (*gasping*) Oh, grandpa! If only it would be . . . if only . . . rest . . . feel nothing more . . .

LUKA You won't. I tell you. You must believe me. Die happy, no worry. Death's like a mother to little children for us, I tell you.

ANNA Perhaps . . . perhaps I'll . . . get well?

LUKA What for? To suffer some more?

ANNA But . . . to live just a bit longer . . . just a bit longer! If I won't have to suffer there, I can stand it here a bit longer.

LUKA But there's nothing there. So easy . . .

PEPPEL (*rises*) That's true. Or maybe it isn't!

ANNA (*frightened*) Oh, God!

LUKA Hello, handsome.

MEDVEDEV Who's that shouting?

PEPPEL (*goes up to him*) Me. What of it?

MEDVEDEV There's no need to go shouting, that's what. People should be quieter.

PEPPEL Oh, shit! Call yourself an uncle—huh!

LUKA (*to* PEPPEL, *in a low voice*) Listen, don't shout. There's a woman dying here. One foot in the grave. Don't upset her.

PEPPEL Grandpa, I'd do anything for you. You're all right! A damn fine liar, that's what you are. Damned good stories you make up. I don't mind you lying. You carry on! There aren't many good things in this life!

BUBNOV Is she really dying?

LUKA Do you think she's pretending?

BUBNOV Won't have any more coughing, then. Been disturbing everybody . . . I take two!

MEDVEDEV Oh, damn your eyes!

PEPPEL Abram!

MEDVEDEV Don't call me Abram.

PEPPEL Abram—is Natasha ill, Abram?

MEDVEDEV What business is it of yours?

PEPPEL I want to know. Did Vassilisa beat her up badly?

MEDVEDEV It's nothing to do with you. Family matter. Who do you think you are, anyway?

PEPPEL Never mind about who I am. If I want, you won't ever see Natasha again. That's who I am.

MEDVEDEV (*leaves the game*) What's that? What do you say? My niece . . . You thief, you!

PEPPEL A thief, perhaps, but you haven't caught me yet!

MEDVEDEV Just you wait! I'll catch you all right, before long.

PEPPEL You catch me, it'll be so much the worse for all your precious family. Think I'll keep quiet before the judge? I'm a thief, aren't I? "Who taught you to thieve" they'll say, "and showed you the cribs?" Mishka Kostylev and his wife! "Who was your fence?" Mishka Kostylev and his wife!

MEDVEDEV You liar! They won't believe you?

PEPPEL They'll believe me all right, because it's true. I'll drag you in it too—ha! I'll sink the lot of you, you bastard, you see.

MEDVEDEV (*shaken*) Lies, all lies! What harm have I done you? You scabby cur!

PEPPEL What good have you done me?

LUKA Aha!

MEDVEDEV (*to* LUKA) What are you croaking about? None of your business. This is family matters.

BUBNOV Keep out of this. Let them hang each other if they want.

LUKA (*meekly*) I didn't say anything. I only say, if a man doesn't do someone any good, he does him harm.

MEDVEDEV (*misunderstands*) That's right.

Now, we all know one another here . . . who are you? (*spits angrily and goes out*)

LUKA   The gentleman's angry. Oho-ho! You've gotten yourselves all twisted up, haven't you?

PEPPEL   He's gone crying to Vassilisa.

BUBNOV   You're a damn fool, Vaska. What's the good of all the tough stuff? All very well being brave, but it doesn't cut much ice here. They'll break your neck before you know it.

PEPPEL   No, they won't. A Yaroslav doesn't give in without a fight. If there's a fight, I'm ready for it.

LUKA   I tell you, my boy, you ought to get out of this place.

PEPPEL   And go where? You tell me.

LUKA   To . . . Siberia.

PEPPEL   Ha! When I go to Siberia, it'll be at the government's expense.

LUKA   Listen to me, you go there. You'll do all right there. You're the kind who do.

PEPPEL   My life's already marked out for me. My father spent all his life in prisons, and that's my life too. When I was only a kid, everybody called me a thief, and son of a thief.

LUKA   But it's a wonderful place, Siberia. Golden land! A strong fellow, with brains, he can make a fortune there!

PEPPEL   Why do you tell lies, old man?

LUKA   What?

PEPPEL   Are you deaf? I said, why do you tell lies?

LUKA   When was I lying?

PEPPEL   All the time. You say it's fine here, and it's wonderful somewhere else. All lies! What for?

LUKA   You take my word for it, and go there and see for yourself. You'll thank me all right. What's the good of hanging around here? And what do you want with the truth anyway? It'll do you more harm than good.

PEPPEL   I don't care. I can face it, whatever it is!

LUKA   Oh, you're crazy! Are you trying to get yourself killed?

BUBNOV   What is all this nonsense? I don't get it. What's this truth you're after, Vaska? What for? You know the truth.

PEPPEL   Shut up, Bubnov. I want to ask him something. Listen, old man, is there a God?

(LUKA *smiles, silently*)

BUBNOV   We're all just somebody's garbage, that's all.

PEPPEL   Well? Is there?

LUKA   (*quietly*)   If you believe in him, there is. If you don't, there isn't. Whatever you believe in, exists.

(PEPPEL *stares silently at* LUKA, *puzzled*)

BUBNOV   I'm going to get a drink. Coming? Hey!

LUKA   (*to* PEPPEL)   What are you staring at?

PEPPEL   Wait a minute. You mean . . .

BUBNOV   I'll go on my own then. (*goes to door, where he meets* VASSILISA)

PEPPEL   Then . . . you . . .

VASSILISA   (*to* BUBNOV)   Is Nastya here?

BUBNOV   No. (*exit*)

PEPPEL   Oh . . . look who's here.

VASSILISA   (*goes to* ANNA)   Still alive?

LUKA   Leave her alone.

VASSILISA   What are you hanging around here for?

LUKA   I'll go, if you want.

VASSILISA   (*goes towards* PEPPEL's *door*) Vaska! I want to talk to you.

(LUKA *goes to hall door, opens it, and closes it again loudly. Then he clambers up on the stove*)

VASSILISA   (*from* PEPPEL's *room*)   Vaska! Come here!

PEPPEL   No. I don't want to.

VASSILISA   What's wrong? What's the matter?

PEPPEL   I've had enough. I'm sick of the whole bloody business.

VASSILISA   Sick . . . of me?

PEPPEL   And sick of you. (VASSILISA *pulls her shawl tight across her shoulders, presses her hands to her breast. Goes to* ANNA's *bed, looks carefully behind the curtain, and turns to* PEPPEL) Well, what did you want to talk about?

VASSILISA   What can I say? I can't force you to love me. It isn't in me to grovel. Thank you for speaking the truth.

PEPPEL   Speaking what truth?

VASSILISA   That you're sick of me. Or isn't it the truth?

(PEPPEL *looks at her in silence*)

VASSILISA   (*goes up to him*)   What are you staring for? Haven't you seen me before?

PEPPEL   (*sighs*)   You're beautiful, Vassilisa. (*She puts hand on his shoulder, but he shakes it off*) But I never loved you. We slept together, all right, but I never loved you.

VASSILISA   (*quietly*)   I see . . . Well . . .

PEPPEL   Well, there's nothing for us to say. Not a thing. Go away.

VASSILISA   Is there someone else?

PEPPEL   Forget it. I wouldn't ask your advice if there was.

VASSILISA (*significantly*) That's too bad. I might be able to help.

PEPPEL (*suspiciously*) What do you mean?

VASSILISA You know what I mean. What are you pretending for? Vaska, let's be honest about it. (*lowering her voice*) I won't hide it— you've hurt me . . . All of a sudden, as if you hit me with a whip. For no reason at all. You said you loved me . . . and all of a sudden . . .

PEPPEL Not sudden at all. A long time . . . You've got no heart, Vassilisa. A woman's got to have a heart. We men are just beasts. You've got to tame us and make something of us. How have you tamed me? What have you made me?

VASSILISA What's done is done. People can't help their own feelings. You don't love me any more. All right then. That's how it is.

PEPPEL That's how it is. Finish! Let's part friends. No fuss. That's the way.

VASSILISA No, wait. Listen . . . When I lived with you, I always hoped you were going to get me out of this mess. Free me from my husband, from my uncle . . . all this life . . . Maybe I didn't love you at all, Vaska —just this hope I kept thinking about, that I loved. Don't you see? I thought you were going to pull me out of here.

PEPPEL You aren't a nail. I'm not a pair of pliers. I'd have thought with your brains . . . After all, you're smart enough, aren't you?

VASSILISA (*bends close to him*) Vaska! let's help one another . . .

PEPPEL How do you mean?

VASSILISA (*quietly but strongly*) I know . . . you like my sister.

PEPPEL That's why you beat her, you cat! Listen, you dare lay a finger on her . . .

VASSILISA Wait a minute! Keep calm! We can manage all this peacefully, and properly . . . Do you want to marry her? All right —marry her. I'll even give you money. Three hundred! More if I can.

PEPPEL (*moves away*) Wait a minute. What is this? What's the idea?

VASSILISA Help me—get rid of my husband. Take that noose from around my neck.

PEPPEL (*whistles softly*) So that's it! Oho! You've thought it all out, haven't you? Your husband in his grave, your lover in prison, and you . . .

VASSILISA No, Vaska, why should you go to prison? Get some of the others to do it. Even if you do it yourself, who's to know? Think of Natasha! And the money. You can go anywhere you like. Set me free for good. It'll be a good thing for Natasha, not to be near me. I can't even look at her without

getting furious, on account of you. I can't help it. I torment the girl, I beat her, I beat her so hard, I could cry myself I feel so sorry for her. But I beat her all the same. And I'll go on beating her!

PEPPEL You bitch! Are you boasting?

VASSILISA Not boasting—it's the truth. Look, Vaska, you've been to prison twice because of my husband. He's been like a vampire sucking my blood for four years. And what sort of a husband is he? And he pushes Natasha around, shouts at her, calls her a beggar. He's poison to everybody.

PEPPEL This is some clever scheme of yours . . .

VASSILISA No. Everything I say is true. It's clear enough—you're not a fool.

(KOSTYLEV *enters cautiously, steals in*)

PEPPEL (*to* VASSILISA) Oh, go away!

VASSILISA Think it over. (*sees husband*) What are you doing here? Following me around!

(PEPPEL *jumps up, stares wildly at* KOSTYLEV)

KOSTYLEV It's me . . . me! Are you here by yourselves? Aah! You were having a little chat? (*suddenly stamps his feet and screams out*) You swine, Vaska! You filthy beggar! (*startled at his own voice, as the others watch motionless and silent*) God forgive me—you've led me to sin again Vassilisa . . . I've been looking for you everywhere. (*screaming*) It's time for bed! And you haven't filled the lamps, you devil! . . . you hellcat! (*points at her with trembling hand*)

(VASSILISA *goes slowly to the hall, looking round at* PEPPEL)

PEPPEL (*to* KOSTYLEV) Clear out of here! Go on, get out!

KOSTYLEV (*screams*) I'm the landlord! You clear out—you thief!

PEPPEL (*sullenly*) Get out, Mishka.

KOSTYLEV How dare you? I—I—I'll . . .

(PEPPEL *grabs him by the collar and shakes him. A noise and a loud yawning are heard from the stove.* PEPPEL *lets go of* KOSTYLEV, *who runs into the hall screaming*)

PEPPEL (*jumps on the bunk*) Who's that? Who's that up there?

LUKA (*raises his head*) Eh?

PEPPEL You!

LUKA (*calmly*) Yes, it's me. Oh, Jesus Christ!

PEPPEL (*closes hall door, looks for the bolt, but cannot find it*) Ach, the devils! Come down, old man.

LUKA All right. I'm coming.

PEPPEL (*threateningly*) What were you doing up there?

LUKA Where else do you want me to go?

PEPPEL I thought you went out in the hall.

LUKA I'm an old man, my friend—it's cold out in the hall.

PEPPEL You heard?

LUKA How could I help hearing? I'm not deaf, am I? Ah, you're a lucky fellow. You're lucky, all right.

PEPPEL (*suspiciously*) What do you mean lucky? What do you mean?

LUKA Lucky I was up there.

PEPPEL Why did you make that noise just then?

LUKA I was getting a bit uncomfortable— lucky for you. And then again, I thought maybe you were accidentally going to strangle the old man.

PEPPEL Maybe I would have. Maybe I hate his guts.

LUKA It's easy enough. People often make mistakes like that.

PEPPEL (*smiles*) What about you? Have you ever made a mistake like that?

LUKA Listen. Steer clear of that woman. Don't let her anywhere near you. She'll drive her husband to his grave well enough without your help. Don't you listen to her—she's a witch! Look at my head. Bald, eh? And why? Because of women. I should say I've known more women than I ever had hairs on my head. And, I say, that Vassilisa's worse than the devil incarnate.

PEPPEL Should I be thanking you for this? Or maybe you, as well . . .

LUKA Don't say anything. You won't say anything better than what I've said. Listen. This girl you like, whoever she is, take her away from here, fast as you can go. Get out of here right away.

PEPPEL (*darkly*) Can't make people out. Some are kind, and some are just out to get you. Can't tell which are which.

LUKA What's the point? People just live the way they want to. Kind today, and out to get you tomorrow. That's all. If you really love this girl of yours, go away with her, and that's all there is to it. Or go on your own. You're young. There'll be plenty of women around.

PEPPEL (*takes him by the shoulder*) No, wait a minute. What are you telling me this for?

LUKA Let me go. I must see to Anna. She was breathing funny. (*Goes to* ANNA's *bed, opens curtains, looks, touches her.* PEPPEL, *distraught and pensive, follows him*) Oh Jesus Christ, merciful Lord! Receive in peace the soul of Thy newly-departed servant Anna!

PEPPEL (*quietly*) Is she dead? (*stays where he is, leans forward to look*)

LUKA (*quietly*) She's dead. Where's her husband?

PEPPEL Having a drink, I expect.

LUKA We'll have to tell him.

PEPPEL (*shudders*) I don't like dead people.

LUKA (*goes to door*) What's there to like about them? It's living people we ought to like. Living people.

PEPPEL I'll come with you.

LUKA You afraid?

PEPPEL I don't like . . .

(*They hurry out. The stage is deserted and quiet. An indistinct noise comes from the passage. Then the* ACTOR *enters, stands in the doorway, leaning on the doorposts*)

ACTOR (*calls*) Hey, old man! Where are you? Listen! I've remembered it! (*staggers forward two steps, strikes a pose, and declaims:*)

There is no truth, my friends! Seek
  far and near:
I say there is no truth here in this
  world.
So honor the madman, friends, I say!
The madman's brain will spin us
  golden lies.

(NATASHA *appears in the door behind him*) Old man!

Put out the sun, my friends! No more
  its rays
Will shine upon this miserable globe.
But see the golden light that shines
  instead—
Born of the fire within the madman's
  head!

NATASHA (*laughs*) You idiot! You're drunk . . .

ACTOR (*turns*) Who's that? Ah, where's the old man? The darling little old man? Nobody here, it seems. Goodbye, Natasha. Yes, goodbye.

NATASHA (*comes in*) Never known you to say good morning before. Now you say goodbye.

ACTOR (*bars her way*) I'm going away. I'm going right away. Spring will come back again, but I won't.

NATASHA Rubbish! Where are you going?

ACTOR To a town . . . to get cured. You should go away too. "Ophelia—get thee to a nunnery!" You know, there's a hospital for organisms, for drunkards. A wonderful hospital.

Marble . . . marble floors! Light. Clean floors. Food—all free! Marble floors—yes! I'm going to find it, get cured, and start life all over again. I'll be reborn! That's from . . . King— Lear . . . Natasha, my stage name . . . is Sverchkov-Zavolski. Nobody knows that. Nobody. I haven't got a name here. Do you know how terrible it is, not to have a name? Even a dog has a name.

(NATASHA *goes carefully round* ACTOR, *stops at* ANNA's *bed, looks*)

ACTOR You don't exist without a name.

NATASHA Look . . . the poor thing . . . she's dead.

ACTOR (*shakes head*) Can't be.

NATASHA (*backs away*) Oh, God! She's dead. Look.

BUBNOV (*at door*) Look at what?

NATASHA Anna. She's dead.

BUBNOV That means she won't cough any more. (*goes to* ANNA's *bed, looks, and goes to his own place*) You'd better tell Kletch. It's his business.

ACTOR I'll go and tell him. She's lost her name. (*exit*)

NATASHA (*in the center of the room*) That's the way I'll end up one day, dying in a cellar . . . forgotten . . .

BUBNOV (*spreading rugs over his bunk*) What are you mumbling about?

NATASHA Nothing. I was talking to myself.

BUBNOV You waiting for Vaska? You see— your Vaska will break your neck for you.

NATASHA I don't care. Rather he broke it than anyone else.

BUBNOV (*lies down*) Well, it's your look out.

NATASHA It's as well she did die, really. But I feel sorry for her. Oh, God! What do people live for?

BUBNOV It's the same for everybody. Born, live a while, die. I'll die—so will you. Nothing to be sorry for.

(*Enter* LUKA, TARTAR, SCREWY *and* KLETCH. KLETCH *comes slowly after the others, stooping*)

NATASHA Sh! Anna—

SCREWY We know . . . God rest her soul, if she is dead.

TARTAR (*to* KLETCH) You got to take her out! Take her into the hall! Can't have dead people in here. Living people got to sleep in here.

KLETCH (*low voice*) We'll take her out.

(*They all go to the bed.* KLETCH *looks at his wife over the others' shoulders*)

SCREWY (*to* TARTAR) You think she'll smell? No, she won't smell. She all dried up while she was alive.

NATASHA Oh, God! You might feel sorry for her! You might say a kind word, some of you! Oh, you . . .

LUKA Don't take on like that, girl. It's all right. How can we be sorry for the dead? We can't even be sorry for the living. Not even sorry for ourselves! What do you expect?

BUBNOV (*yawns*) Anyway, death isn't afraid of talk. Illness may be, but not death.

TARTAR (*moves away*) Must call police.

SCREWY Police—yes, of course! Kletch, have you reported to the police?

KLETCH No . . . she's got to be buried . . . I've only got 40 kopecks.

SCREWY Well, you'll have to borrow. We'll all chip in and give you what we can. But you'd better report this to the police quickly. Or they'll think you killed the old woman . . . (*goes to his bunk, and prepares to lie down beside* TARTAR)

NATASHA (*moves away, towards* BUBNOV) Now I'll dream about her. I always dream about people who die. I'm scared of going back by myself. It's dark in the hall . . .

LUKA You be scared of the living, I tell you . . .

NATASHA Come with me, grandpa . . .

LUKA All right. Come on, then. (*exeunt. A pause*)

SCREWY Ho, ho, ho! Hassan! Spring's coming, buddy. It'll be warm again soon. Farmers are mending their ploughs . . . getting ready to plough . . . yes! And what about us, eh, Hassan? . . . Old Mohammed's fast asleep, the bastard!

BUBNOV Seem to like sleeping, these Tartars.

KLETCH (*stands in the middle of the floor, gazing vacantly ahead*) What am I going to do now?

SCREWY Lie down and go to sleep. That's all you can do.

KLETCH (*quietly*) What about her?

(*Nobody answers. Enter* SATIN *and the* ACTOR)

ACTOR (*shouts*) Old man! Hither, my faithful Kent! . . .

SATIN Here comes Marco Polo! Ho, ho!

ACTOR I've made up my mind. Where's the town, old man? Where are you?

SATIN Fata Morgana! The old man's kidding you . . . There's nothing! No town, no people—nothing!

ACTOR You're a god-damned liar!

TARTAR (*jumps up*) Where's the landlord?

I'm going to speak to the landlord. Can't get any sleep—then I won't pay him. Dead women, drunken men . . . (*rushes out*)

(SATIN *whistles after him*)

BUBNOV (*sleepily*)   Go to bed, boys. Stop making a row. People want to sleep at night.

ACTOR   Oh, yes. There's a corpse here. "We caught a corpse in our fishing nets" . . . poem, by—Shakespeare!

SATIN (*shouts*)   Corpses can't hear! Corpses can't feel . . . Shout! Yell! Corpses can't hear!

(LUKA *appears in the doorway*)

ACT THREE

(*The yard, a bit of waste ground, littered with various junk and overgrown with weeds. At the back, a high brick wall, which cuts off the sky. Near it is a cluster of elder. To the right, the dark log wall of some stable building. To the left, a grey wall with patches of plaster, which is part of* KOSTYLEV's *lodging house. It stands at an angle, its far corner projecting almost to the middle of the yard. There is a narrow passage between this wall and the brick wall. In the grey wall are two windows, one at ground level, the other five feet higher up, and nearer the brick wall. Along the wall are a large sledge turned upside down, and a log about ten feet long. Old planks are piled up on the right near the wall.*

Evening. The sun is setting, throwing a red glow on the brick wall. Early spring, and the snow has recently thawed. As yet, there are no buds on the black elder bushes.

NATASHA *and* NASTYA *are seated side by side on the log.* LUKA *and the* BARON *are on the sledge.* KLETCH *is lying on the heap of wood, right.* BUBNOV's *face is at the lower window*)

NASTYA (*her eyes closed, her head nodding in time to the words, speaks in a sing-song voice*)   So one night he comes into the garden, to talk to me in the arbor as we'd arranged . . . And I've been waiting for him a long time, trembling all over, I was so afraid. And he's trembling all over too, and his face is white as a sheet, and in his hands he's got a revolver . . .

NATASHA (*cracking sunflower seeds*)   Oh, my goodness! So it's true what they say about students—how desperate they get . . .

NASTYA   And in a terrible voice he says to me, "My dearest precious love . . ."

BUBNOV   Ho, ho! Precious!

BARON   Shut up! If you don't like it, don't listen. Don't spoil a good lie . . . Go on.

NASTYA   "My beloved," he says, "My darling! My parents refuse to give their consent for me to marry you . . . and they say they'll curse me forever because of my love for you. So," he says, "I've got to kill myself . . ." And he's got a huge revolver, with ten bullets in it . . . "Goodbye, my dearest heart," he says. "I've decided . . . I can't live without you." And I said to him, "I can never forget you, my darling Raoul . . ."

BUBNOV (*astonished*)   What's that? Growl?

BARON (*laughs*)   Oh, look here, Nastya. Last time it was Gaston!

NASTYA (*jumps*)   Shut up, you . . . miserable bastards! Ach! How can you understand what love is—true love? It was true love! (*to* BARON) You! you worthless trash, you! Educated man! Used to drink coffee in bed—so you say!

LUKA   Now, stop it, all of you! Don't interrupt her! Show a bit of regard for other people . . . It isn't so much what people say —it's why they say it. Go on, girl. Don't worry about them.

BUBNOV   No, don't worry about us—we're not worrying about you!

BARON   Go on.

NATASHA   Don't pay any attention to them. They're just jealous. Because nothing's ever happened to them.

NASTYA (*sits again*)   I won't tell any more! Why should I? They don't believe me. They laugh at me . . . (*suddenly breaks off, remains silent for several seconds, and, closing her eyes again, and waving her hands as though in time to some distant music, continues loudly and heatedly*)   So I said to him, "Joy of my life! My bright star! I just couldn't go on living in this world without you. I love you so madly, and I'll go on loving you as long as my heart goes on beating in my breast. But," I said, "you mustn't take your young life, your dear parents' only hope and joy. Forget me! Better to let me suffer for my love for you, my darling heart. For I have nobody . . . People like me are always alone. Let me die—what does it matter? I have nothing. I am nothing. Nothing at all . . . (*covers her face with her hands, and cries noiselessly*)

NATASHA (*turns to one side, in a low voice*) Don't cry . . . you mustn't!

(LUKA, *smiling, strokes* NASTYA's *head*)

BUBNOV (*laughs*)   Ha! What a damned fool!

BARON (*also laughing*)   Do you believe

that, old man? It's all out of a book—"Fatal
Love." A lot of trash! Leave her alone! . . .

NATASHA   What's that to you? Shut up, can't
you? Just because you haven't got any heart . . .

NASTYA (*bitterly*)   God damn your soul!
You worthless pig! Soul—ugh—you haven't
got one!

LUKA (*takes* NASTYA *by the arm*)   Come on,
my dear. Don't worry. Don't get angry. I know.
I believe you. You're right, not them. If you
believe it was a true love you had, then it was.
It was! But don't upset yourself. Don't quarrel
with your Baron. Maybe he does laugh, but
he's only jealous. Because he's never had a
true love like that. Never had anything at all!
Come on, then . . .

NASTYA (*presses her hands to her breasts*)
Honest, grandpa, it's true. It did happen. He
was a student. A French boy, Gaston, his name
was. He had a moustache, and he wore big
black boots. Cross my heart and hope to die!
And he loved me so . . .

LUKA   I know. It's all right. I believe you.
Wore big, black boots, you say? Ay-ay-ay! And
you—you loved him too?

(*They go round corner*)

BARON   She's a fool, that girl. A good girl,
but—such a damned fool, it's incredible!

BUBNOV   Why is it people are so fond of
lying? Just as if they were up before the judge?
It's amazing.

NATASHA   Perhaps it's more fun lying than
telling the truth. That's why I . . .

BARON   Well, go on.

NATASHA   That's why I like imagining
things. I dream and dream, and—wait.

BARON   What for?

NATASHA (*smiles, embarrassed*)   Oh, I don't
know. Perhaps someone will come along, tomorrow . . . or something's going to happen
. . . something that never happened before
. . . I wait, and I look forward—I'm always
looking forward to something. But what have I
got to look forward to—I don't know.

(*A pause*)

BARON (*smiles*)   There's nothing to look
forward to. I don't look forward to anything.
It's all happened already. Over and done with!
Finished . . . Go on.

NATASHA   And then sometimes I get the
feeling that tomorrow I'm going to die suddenly. It frightens me. It always happens in
the summer, when there are thunderstorms,
and you can get killed by lightning.

BARON   You have a hard life, don't you?
That sister of yours has one hell of a temper.

NATASHA   Who has an easy life? Nobody!
Everywhere you look, people are unhappy.

KLETCH (*until this time motionless and indifferent, suddenly jumps up*)   Everybody?
It's a lie! Not everybody! If everybody had a
hard life, it would be all right. Then it wouldn't
hurt so much.

BUBNOV   What the devil's got into *you*—
shouting like that?

(KLETCH *lies down on the wood pile as before,
mumbling to himself*)

BARON   Mm . . . I suppose I'd better go
and make up with Nastya or I won't get any
money for a drink . . .

BUBNOV   Mm . . . people telling lies . . .
I can understand it with Nastya. She's used
to painting her face; now she wants to paint
her soul . . . put rouge on her soul . . . But
why do other people do it? That Luka for instance . . . lies all the time . . . and he don't
get nothing out of it . . . An old man, too
. . . Why does he do it?

BARON (*moves away, with a smile*)   Everybody's got grey souls . . . and they all want
to brighten them up . . .

LUKA (*comes from round the corner*)   Why
do you upset the girl, Baron? You should leave
her alone. Let her cry if it gives her pleasure
. . . She enjoys crying, you should know that
. . . What harm does it do you?

BARON   The whole thing's stupid, old man!
I'm sick of it. Today it's Raoul, tomorrow it's
Gaston . . . but it's the same story all the
time. Still, I'll go and make up with her . . .
(*exit*)

LUKA   That's it. Go and be nice to her.
Never does any harm being nice to people . . .

NATASHA   You're a kind man, grandpa. Why
are you so kind?

LUKA   Kind, you say? Well, yes, if it's
true . . .

(*Behind the red wall, the sound of singing to
an accordion is softly heard*)

LUKA   Somebody's got to be kind, girl.
Somebody's got to be sorry for other people.
Christ felt sorry for other people—told us to do
the same. I can tell you, if you feel sorry for
somebody at the right time, it can do a lot of
good. For instance, the time I was caretaker at
a country house near Tomsk. Well . . . the
house was in the middle of a forest. It was
winter time, and I was all alone in the house.
Well, one day, I heard a noise at the window.

NATASHA   Burglars?

LUKA   That's right. Burglars. Trying to
break in. So I took my gun and went out. I
looked around and saw two men trying to

open the window. They were working at it so
hard they didn't even see me until I yelled at
them and told them to get out! And what did
they do? They came at me with an axe! "Keep
away," I said, "or I'll shoot." And I pointed my
gun right at them. They both went down on
their knees and begged for mercy.

Still I was mad about that axe. "You
wouldn't go away when I told you, you devils,"
I said. "Now you go and break some branches
off that tree." So they did. "Now," I said to one
of them, "you lie down while he flogs you." So
they obey me and flog each other. Then they
said to me, "Mister, for God's sake, give us
some bread. We've been tramping for miles
with nothing to eat. We're hungry!" There are
your burglars, my dear . . . And with axes, no
less! Good honest peasants, both of them . . .
I said to them, "Why didn't you come and ask
for bread in the first place, you fools?" And
they said, "We were tired of asking. You beg
and beg, and nobody gives you even a crumb.
It's hell!" . . . And those two stayed with me
all winter. One of them, Stepan his name was,
used to take my gun sometimes and go into
the forest for days, shooting. The other one,
Yakov, he was ill most of the time, and he
coughed a lot. The three of us took care of the
house. And when spring came they said,
"Goodbye, Grandpa," and went away, back
home to Russia.

NATASHA   Were they escaped convicts?

LUKA   That's right. Escaped convicts. Honest peasants! And if I hadn't felt sorry for them,
they might have killed me or something. They'd
have been tried and sent back to Siberia—
what's the sense in that? Prison doesn't teach
a man to be good, and Siberia doesn't either.
But a man—yes! a man can teach another
man kindness, believe me!

(*Pause*)

BUBNOV   Mm . . . yes . . . but me, I don't
know how to tell lies, I don't. What's the use
of lies? What I say is, give us the truth, just as
it is. Why try to hide anything?

KLETCH (*leaps up suddenly, shouts*)   What
truth? Well, what truth—eh? Where do you
find it, this precious truth of yours? (*runs his
hands through his ragged clothes*) There's your
truth! No work . . . no strength . . . nowhere to live even. Not a god-damned place
to live! You just die like a dog, that's all.
There's the truth for you! Hell! What do I
want with truth? Just give me room to breathe,
that's all. Room to breathe! What have I done
wrong? What do I want with truth? Christ

Almighty—they won't let you live, damn it!
You can't live—that's the truth for you!

BUBNOV   Don't worry about him, he's a little
bit titched!

LUKA   Heavenly Jesus! . . . listen to me,
my brother. You . . .

KLETCH (*shaking with emotion*)   You talk
about truth, truth! You, old man, you go
around comforting everybody. I tell you, I hate
you all! The whole god-damned bunch of you!
And to hell with your god-damned truth! To
hell with it! Do you hear? To hell with it! (*runs
off round the corner, looking back as he goes*)

LUKA   Ay-ay-ay! How upset he is! Where's
he run off to?

NATASHA   Has he gone mad or something?

BUBNOV   God, how fantastic! Just like they
do it on the stage. . . . Sometimes it happens
like that. . . . He can't get used to life.

PEPPEL (*slowly comes round the corner*)
Hello, you honest people! Hello, Luka, you old
bastard! Still telling them stories, eh?

LUKA   You should have been here just now.
There was a man here screaming his lungs out.

PEPPEL   Kletch, was it? What's wrong with
him? He just ran past me like a madman.

LUKA   You'd do the same thing, if your
heart were breaking.

PEPPEL (*sits*)   I don't like him. Who does
he think he is? (*imitates* KLETCH) "I'm a working man." And so nobody's as good as he is
. . . Well, work if you like it—but don't get
so god-damned pompous about it! If you start
judging people by how much work they do,
then a horse is better than any man. He works
and he keeps quiet about it! Your people at
home, Natasha?

NATASHA   They went down to the cemetery
—said they were going to the evening service
afterwards.

PEPPEL   So that's why you're free. That's a
novelty!

LUKA (*to* BUBNOV, *pensively*)   You say
"truth" . . . Truth's not always the best thing
for people, though. Not when people are in a
bad way. I once knew a man, for instance—he
believed in a Land of Truth . . .

BUBNOV   In what?

LUKA   The Land of Truth. "Somewhere on
earth," he used to say, "there must be a Land
of Truth. The people there," he says, "are a
special sort of people—good people! They love
one another, they help one another, and everything they do is good and kind!" Every day he'd
talk about going to find it, this Land of Truth.
A poor man, he was; had a hard life. And
when he got so bad he was ready to lie down

and die, he didn't give in. He'd just laugh and say, "Never mind—I can stand it! Just a bit longer, then I'll quit this life and go to the Land of Truth . . ." That was all he lived for, the Land of Truth.

PEPPEL   Well, did he go?

BUBNOV   Where? Ho, ho!

LUKA   This all happened in Siberia. And one day along comes an exile. He was a scholar with all sorts of books and maps. So the man asks him, "Will you show me where the Land of Truth is? How do you get there?" So the scholar gets out his books and his maps, and he looks and looks, and he can't find the Land of Truth—it doesn't exist!

PEPPEL   (*softly*)   Doesn't exist?

(BUBNOV *laughs*)

NATASHA   Stop it. What happened, grandpa?

LUKA   Well, the man doesn't believe him. "It must exist," he said. "Take another look! If it isn't there, then your books and maps are no good." The scholar got angry at this. "My maps are the best there are, and your Land of Truth isn't on them anywhere." So the man got angry. "What's that?" he said. "I've lived and suffered all these years and I've always thought there was a Land of Truth. Now your maps say there isn't. It's a fraud! You swine! You're a god-damned cheat, not a scholar." And he hit him on the nose—bang! And another and another . . . (*pause*) Then he went home and hung himself! . . .

(*They are all silent.* LUKA *smiling, looks at* PEPPEL *and* NATASHA)

PEPPEL   (*softly*)   To hell with your story! I don't call it very funny . . .

NATASHA   He couldn't stand it—the disappointment . . .

BUBNOV   (*sullen*)   You made it all up.

PEPPEL   Well . . . There's your Land of Truth for you. Doesn't exist after all . . .

NATASHA   I'm sorry for him, that man . . .

BUBNOV   He made it all up! Ho, ho! Land of Truth! What an idea! Ho, ho!

LUKA   (*nods towards window where* BUBNOV *is*)   He's laughing! Well, my children, God be with you! I'll be leaving you soon . . .

PEPPEL   Where are you going?

LUKA   To the Ukraine . . . I hear they've discovered a new religion there. I want to see —yes! People are always seeking—they want something better—God give them patience!

PEPPEL   You think they'll find it?

LUKA   The people? They will find it! He

who seeks will find! He who desires strongly, will find!

NATASHA   If only they could find something better—invent something better . . .

LUKA   They're trying to! But we must help them, my child—we must respect them.

NATASHA   How can I help them? I'm helpless myself!

PEPPEL   (*resolutely*)   Listen! I'm going to . . . to ask you again, Natasha . . . He knows about it . . . Come away with me!

NATASHA   Where to? From one jail to another?

PEPPEL   I tell you, I'll stop stealing. I swear I will. I will! I can read and write. I'll work . . . Luka says I ought to go to Siberia, before they send me there. Come with me— what do you say? Don't you think my life makes me sick? Oh, Natasha! I know . . . I can see it all . . . I console myself that other people steal more than I do, and get honor heaped on them—but that doesn't help. It's no answer. I'm not repenting—I don't believe in conscience. But I know one thing: I can't go on living like this. Got to find something better. So I can have some self-respect . . .

LUKA   That's right, my son! May God help you! You're right, a man's got to have self-respect.

PEPPEL   I've been a thief all my life. That's all they called me: "Vaska's a thief, and the son of a thief." So I'm a thief! But maybe it's only because nobody ever called me anything else. You won't call me a thief, will you, Natasha? Tell me . . .

NATASHA   (*melancholy*)   I can't believe in all this talk somehow . . . I feel strange, uneasy today. Funny aching feeling round my heart . . . as if something's going to happen. I wish you hadn't started this, Vaska.

PEPPEL   Well, how long do you want me to wait, then? It isn't the first time . . .

NATASHA   How can I go away with you, Vaska? I'm not in love with you. Not enough . . . Sometimes I like you. Sometimes it makes me sick to look at you. I can't be in love with you. When you're in love with someone, you can't see any faults in them. And I do . . .

PEPPEL   Never mind—you'll love me after a while! I'll make you love me . . . if you'll just say yes! I've been seeing you here for over a year . . . and you're a good, decent girl . . . you're kind, and reliable . . . and I'm very much in love with you . . .

(VASSILISA, *in her Sunday clothes, appears at the window*)

NATASHA   I know all about that. You say you love me—and what about my sister?

PEPPEL   (*embarrassed*)   Well, what about her? She's nothing . . . She doesn't mean anything to me . . .

LUKA   Never mind that, girl! When you can't get fresh bread, you have to take stale bread . . .

PEPPEL   (*gloomily*)   You might feel sorry for me! My life's no bed of roses . . . It's one hell of a life! I feel like I'm sinking in a swamp —everything I catch hold of is . . . rotten . . . no hold anywhere . . . I thought your sister . . . was different . . . I'd have done anything for her! If she'd have been mine . . . But she's after something else . . . after the money . . . and her own way . . . Her own way, so she can be free. She's no good to me. But you—you're like a young fir tree. You're prickly to touch, but strong to hold on to.

LUKA   You marry him, girl. That's my advice! He's all right. He's a good man! You just keep reminding him he's a good man, so he won't forget it himself! He'll believe you. Just keep on saying, "Don't forget, Vaska, you're a good man!" And where else could you go dear —just think! Your sister, she's a vixen. And her husband—nothing you can say about him is as bad as he is. All this life of yours here— where's it leading you? But this man . . . he's good, he's strong . . .

NATASHA   I know I've got nowhere else to go. I've thought all about that. But I don't seem to be able to trust anybody . . . But you're right, there's nowhere else for me to go . . .

PEPPEL   There's only one other way for you here . . . and I won't let you go that way . . . I'd sooner kill you first.

NATASHA   (*smiles*)   You see, I'm not his wife yet, and he's talking of killing me already.

PEPPEL   (*puts arms round her*)   Come on, Natasha. Say yes!

NATASHA   (*presses close to him*)   One thing Vaska—God be my Judge! If you beat me just once, or get angry with me . . . the first time will be the last time. I'll go and hang myself, or . . .

PEPPEL   Let this hand rot off if I ever touch you! . . .

LUKA   Don't you worry about him, my child. He needs you more than you need him.

VASSILISA   (*from window*)   So they all lived happily ever after! Congratulations to the happy pair!

NATASHA   They're back! Oh, God, they saw us! Oh, Vaska . . .

PEPPEL   What are you scared of? They can't touch you now.

VASSILISA   Don't be afraid, Natasha. He won't beat you. He can't beat you and he can't love you. I know.

LUKA   (*in a low voice*)   Rotten old hag! Snake in the grass . . .

VASSILISA   But he hurts you with his tongue.

KOSTYLEV   (*enters*)   Natasha! What are you doing here, you leech? Gossiping? Telling lies about your family behind their back? Why isn't the samovar ready? And the table set?

NATASHA   (*going out*)   I thought you said you were going to church . . .

KOSTYLEV   It's none of your business where we go! You just do your work, and do what you're told!

PEPPEL   You leave her alone! She isn't your slave any longer . . . Don't go, Natasha. Don't do it.

NATASHA   Don't you start giving orders. You're starting a little early, aren't you. (*exit*)

PEPPEL   (*to* KOSTYLEV)   Leave her alone! You've been bullying the girl long enough. She's mine now.

KOSTYLEV   Yours, is she? When did you buy her? For how much?

(VASSILISA *laughs*)

LUKA   Vaska! Go away . . .

PEPPEL   You think it's funny don't you? Well, you'll be laughing on the other side of your face before long!

VASSILISA   Oh, how terrible! Oh, how you frighten me!

LUKA   Go away, Vaska! Can't you see they're leading you on?

PEPPEL   Oh, no. Not me. You won't get away with it.

VASSILISA   It'll be just the way I want it, Vaska.

PEPPEL   (*shakes a fist at her*)   We'll see about that! (*exit*)

VASSILISA   I'll arrange a wedding for you that you won't forget!

KOSTYLEV   (*goes up to* LUKA)   Well, old man, how's everything with you?

LUKA   All right.

KOSTYLEV   They say you're going away.

LUKA   Soon.

KOSTYLEV   Where?

LUKA   I'll just follow my nose . . .

KOSTYLEV   A wanderer, eh? Don't stay in one place for very long, do you?

LUKA   Even water won't pass under a stone that's sunk too deep in the ground . . .

KOSTYLEV   That's all right about stones, but a man has to settle down in one place. Men can't live like roaches crawling about wherever they feel like it . . . A man's got to stay in one place, and can't go wandering about.

LUKA But suppose home is wherever he happens to be?

KOSTYLEV Then, he's nothing but a useless vagabond . . . A human being's got to work —be of some use to somebody.

LUKA So, that's what you think, eh?

KOSTYLEV That's right . . . Look. What's a vagabond? He's different, he's not like the rest of us. If he's a real pilgrim, why then he's some good to the world . . . like maybe he's discovered a new truth, or something. Well . . . but not every truth is good. Let him keep it to himself and shut up about it! Or else—let him talk so we can understand him. But he shouldn't interfere with our business and upset us without any good reason. It's none of his business how other people live! If he wants to be righteous, all right, but alone—in the woods, or in a monastery, away from everybody. But he shouldn't bother people, or condemn them—he should just pray—pray for all of us, for the sins of the whole world—for mine, for yours, for everybody's. To pray—that's why he forsakes the turmoil of the world. That's the truth, see! But you . . . What sort of pilgrim are you? You don't even have a passport! An honest person has a passport, all honest people do. Isn't that right?

LUKA In this world there are people . . . and just ordinary men.

KOSTYLEV Don't give me any double-talk! And don't try to be so smart! I'm as smart as you, and don't you forget it. What's the difference . . . people and men?

LUKA Where is there any double-talk? I say there's sterile and there's fertile ground. You can sow in some ground and it grows and other ground it don't . . . that's all.

KOSTYLEV What do you mean?

LUKA Take yourself for instance . . . If the Lord God himself said to you: "Mikhailo, be a man!"—it would be useless—nothing would happen—you're doomed to remain just as you are . . .

KOSTYLEV Oh, yeah! Listen, my wife's uncle is a policeman, and if I want to . . .

VASSILISA (*enters*) Mishka, come and have your tea.

KOSTYLEV (*to* LUKA) Listen. Get out of here! Get out of this place!

VASSILISA Yes, old man, you clear out! Your tongue's too long. And for all we know, you've run away from prison.

KOSTYLEV Don't let me see a sign of you after today—or else!

LUKA Or else you'll send for your uncle?

Well, go ahead, send for him. Just suppose he caught a wanted man! Uncle might collect a reward. Three kopecks.

BUBNOV (*at window*) What's that for sale? What's going for three kopecks?

LUKA They want to sell me.

VASSILISA (*to her husband*) Come on.

BUBNOV For three kopecks? Listen, old man, they'd sell you for one.

KOSTYLEV (*to* BUBNOV) Where did you come from all of a sudden, you busybody? (*goes off with his wife*)

VASSILISA There's far too many suspicious people around here—too many good-for-nothings!

LUKA *Bon appetit!*

VASSILISA (*turns back*) You shut your mouth, you viper! (*goes out round corner with her husband*)

LUKA I'd better go tonight.

BUBNOV I would if I was you. Don't outstay your welcome.

LUKA You're right there.

BUBNOV I know I'm right. If I hadn't gone away in time, I'd probably be in Siberia right now.

LUKA Oh?

BUBNOV It's true. It was like this. My wife got mixed up with a furrier. He was a good worker, I'll say that for him. He could dye dog-skins to look like raccoon. And cats to look like kangaroo. And muskrats. All sorts of things. He was a real genius! Well, my wife got herself mixed up with him, and they were mad about each other. I could see they'd be poisoning me any minute, or find some other way of getting rid of me. I used to beat my wife, and the furrier beat me. Oh, we had dreadful fights! One time he pulled out half my beard and broke one of my ribs. Another time I hit my wife over the head with a poker. It was a real war going on! Well, I could see I wasn't going to get anything out of all that—they were getting the best of me. So I decided to kill my wife—had it all planned! But I came to my senses . . . and got out of there . . .

LUKA That was best! Let them go on making dogs into raccoons.

BUBNOV Only my workshop was in my wife's name. And I was left, just as you see me now. Though, to be honest, I'd have drunk away the shop anyway. I get pretty drunk sometimes, you know.

LUKA You drink? Ah . . .

BUBNOV You don't know! Once I get started, I don't stop until I don't have a penny left . . . nothing left but my skin and bones.

And another thing—I'm lazy. You've no idea how I hate working! . . .

(*Enter* SATIN *and the* ACTOR, *quarrelling*)

SATIN   Nonsense! You aren't going anywhere. Just a god-damned pipe dream! Look here, old man. What sort of lies have you been stuffing into this broken-down windbag here?

ACTOR   It's not a lie! I am going! Grandpa, tell him I am going! I had work today. I swept the streets. And I haven't had a drink all day! What do you think of that? Here, look —here's the thirty kopecks and I'm sober!

SATIN   It's absurd! You're mad! Give them to me. I'll drink it up for you, or gamble them away.

ACTOR   Oh, go to hell! I'm saving them— for my journey.

LUKA   (*to* SATIN)   Don't tease him. Why are you trying to lead him astray?

SATIN   "Tell me, O wizard, beloved of the gods, what fate do my stars hold in store?" Listen brother, I've lost every kopeck I ever had—blown myself to smithereens!! There's still some people who can cheat at cards better than me!

LUKA   You're a funny guy, Konstantin . . . I like you.

BUBNOV   Actor! Come over here!

(*The* ACTOR *goes to the window, and sits on the sill talking to* BUBNOV)

SATIN   I was one of the smart ones when I was a kid, old man. It's great to look back on those days. I was a happy-go-lucky . . . I danced like a dream, played on the stage, liked to make people laugh—it was great!

LUKA   What went wrong then?

SATIN   You're pretty damn curious old man. You want to know everything. What for?

LUKA   So I can understand people. I can't make you out. A fellow like you, Konstantin— with your brains, too. Yet, all of a sudden . . .

SATIN   Prison, old man. Four years and seven months in prison. And after you've been in prison, you're finished. Can't go anywhere.

LUKA   I see . . . What were you in for?

SATIN   For a dirty swine. I lost my temper and killed him . . . I learnt to play cards in prison . . .

LUKA   Was it . . . did you kill him because of a woman?

SATIN   My sister . . . Oh, leave me alone! I don't like being cross-examined . . . Anyway, it was a long time ago. My sister's been dead nine years now . . . She was a fine girl, my sister was . . .

LUKA   I must say you take life casually enough. Not like old Kletch here just now. He

starts screaming something horrible. Ooooh . . .

SATIN   Kletch?

LUKA   Yes. "No work!" he shouts. "No nothing!"

SATIN   He'll get used to it . . . Now, what can I do with myself, I wonder?

LUKA   (*quietly*)   Look! Here he comes . . .

(*Enter* KLETCH *slowly, his head hung down*)

SATIN   Hey, widower! What are you looking so miserable for? What's the matter?

KLETCH   What will I do? No tools—sold them all for the funeral.

SATIN   I'll give you a bit of advice. Don't do anything. Just be a burden to the world.

KLETCH   You and your advice. I've got some sense of shame before other people . . .

SATIN   Well, forget it! Other people aren't ashamed to let you live worse than a dog! Look here—supposing you don't work, I don't work, hundreds, thousands of others, everybody stops working, see? Nobody does anything —then what will happen?

KLETCH   They'll all starve to death.

(NATASHA *is heard from* KOSTYLEV'S *window, crying out, "Why? Stop it! What have I done?"*)

LUKA   (*agitated*)   Natasha? She was crying out—eh? Oh . . .

(*Noise, scruffling, the sound of dishes being broken, from* KOSTYLEV'S *window, and* KOSTYLEV'S *shrill cry, "Ah, you heathen! You slut!"*)

VASSILISA   Wait a minute, I'll show her . . .

NATASHA   They're killing me! Murdering me! Help!

SATIN   (*shouts in at the window*)   Hey you in there!

LUKA   (*trembling*)   Vaska . . . call Vaska . . . Oh, God! Listen brothers . . .

ACTOR   (*runs off*)   I'll get him.

BUBNOV   They're always beating her these days. Nothing unusual.

SATIN   Come on, old man. We'll be witnesses.

LUKA   (*follows* SATIN)   I'm no sort of witness. No good. Go and get Vaska. Get him quick!

NATASHA   Vassilisa! I'm your sister! Va-a-ass—

BUBNOV   They've gagged her. I'll go and see . . .

(*The noise dies down, fades away as if they have gone into the hall. The old man shouts "stop it!" A door is slammed, cutting off all sound, as though with an axe. Quiet on stage. Twilight*)

KLETCH   (*sits on sledge, rubbing hands hard.*

Then starts to mumble something, at first indistinguishable, then) But how? Got to live . . . (*aloud*) Got to have somewhere to live. Got to. Haven't got anywhere. Haven't got anything. I'm alone. Alone. No-one to help me . . . (*goes out slowly, hunched up*)

(*Ominous silence. Then a confused chaos of shouting in the hallway. It grows louder and nearer. Individual voices can be distinguished*)

VASSILISA   I'm her sister. Let me go!

KOSTYLEV   You haven't any right to . . .

VASSILISA   You jailbird!

SATIN   Call Vaska, quick! Go on, Screwy, hit him!

(*A police whistle*)

TARTAR   (*rushes in, his right arm in a sling*) What a business! Murder in broad daylight!

SCREWY   (*followed by* MEDVEDEV) Ha, I hit him good!

MEDVEDEV   What are *you* fighting about?

TARTAR   What about you? Why don't you do your duty?

MEDVEDEV   (*runs after* SCREWY) Come here! Give me my whistle!

KOSTYLEV   (*runs in*) Abram! Arrest him! Stop him! It's murder!

(KVASHNYA *and* NASTYA *come in round the corner, supporting* NATASHA, *dishevelled. Then* SATIN, *who comes in backwards, fighting off* VASSILISA *who is trying to hit* NATASHA. ALESHKA *skips madly round* VASSILISA, *whistling in her ears, shouting, yelling. Then come a few other tattered figures*)

SATIN   (*to* VASSILISA) What are you trying to do? god-damned bitch . . .

VASSILISA   Let me go, you jailbird! I'll tear her apart if it kills me!

KVASHNYA   (*pulls* NATASHA *out of the way*) Now stop it, Vassilisa. You ought to be ashamed! Are you mad?

MEDVEDEV   (*grabs* SATIN) Aha! I've got you!

SATIN   Screwy! Hit him! . . . Vaska! Vaska!

(*They are all struggling together by the hall, near the red wall. They bring* NATASHA *to the right, and sit her down on the woodpile*)

PEPPEL   (*runs out the hall, elbows his way through the crowd silently, with strong movements*) Natasha, where are you? Where are you?

KOSTYLEV   (*hiding behind corner*) Abram! Arrest him! Help catch Vaska, all of you! He's a thief! Vaska's a thief!

PEPPEL   You old goat! (*swinging round violently, strikes* KOSTYLEV *who falls so that only the upper part of his body can be seen round the corner.* PEPPEL *rushes to* NATASHA)

VASSILISA   Get Vaska! All of you! Beat him up—he's a thief!

MEDVEDEV   (*shouts to* SATIN) It's none of your business—it's a family matter. Relations —what are you?

PEPPEL   What did she do to you? She stab you?

KVASHNYA   Look at that! The brutes! Scalded the poor girl's feet with boiling water!

NASTYA   Knocked over the samovar.

TARTAR   Maybe an accident. Must make sure. Mustn't make wild accusations.

NATASHA   (*half fainting*) Vaska . . . Take me away . . . Help me . . .

VASSILISA   My God! Look! Look here! . . . He's dead. They've killed him.

(*Everybody crowds round* KOSTYLEV, *by the passage.* BUBNOV *comes out of the crowd towards* PEPPEL)

BUBNOV   (*quietly*) Vaska! The old man. You're in trouble now . . .

PEPPEL   (*looks at him uncomprehendingly*) Send for . . . take her to a hospital . . . I'll take care of them.

BUBNOV   I tell you, someone's killed the old man.

(*The noise on stage dies down like a fire extinguished with water. Murmured exclamations are heard: "Is he really?" "What do you think of that?" "Well, then?" "Let's get out of here." "What the hell!" "Someone's in for it!" "Get out before the police come." The crowd decreases.* BUBNOV *and* TARTAR *exeunt.* NASTYA *and* KVASHNYA *rush over to* KOSTYLEV's *body*)

VASSILISA   (*gets up off the ground, shouts triumphantly*) He killed my husband! He killed him! Vaska killed him! I saw it. All of you, I saw it. Well, Vaska—the police!

PEPPEL   (*leaves* NATASHA) Get out! Leave me alone! (*looks at the old man. To* VASSILISA) Well, are you happy now? (*touches the body with his foot*) The old bastard's dead. Just what you wanted. Well, I'll give you the same! (*rushes at her.* SATIN *and* SCREWY *catch him quickly.* VASSILISA *rushes into the hall*)

SATIN   Don't be a fool!

SCREWY   Hey, what are you trying to do?

VASSILISA   (*comes back*) Well, Vaska—darling! You can't escape fate, can you? The police! Abram, blow your whistle.

MEDVEDEV   They stole it, the beggars!

ALESHKA   Here it is! (*blows it*)

(MEDVEDEV *runs after him*)

SATIN   (*leads* PEPPEL *to* NATASHA) Don't

worry, Vaska. It's nothing, killing a man in a fight. Won't be much.

VASSILISA Arrest Vaska! He killed him. I saw it!

SATIN I hit him a couple of times myself. Sure didn't take much. Call me as a witness, Vaska . . .

PEPPEL I don't need an alibi. I'm going to get Vassilisa in this. I will. She wanted it. Egged me on to kill her husband. Egged me on.

NATASHA (suddenly, in a loud voice) Ah! Now I see it! So that's it, Vaska! What nice people they are! They'd arranged it all, my sister and him. They'd arranged it all! Hadn't you, Vaska? That's why you talked to me the way you did—so she could overhear it? What nice people they are! She's his mistress. She is —everybody knows it! They're in it together! She got him to kill her husband. He was in the way. Look what they've done to me!

PEPPEL Natasha! What are you saying? What are you saying?

SATIN Oh—hell!

VASSILISA It's a lie! She's lying! I . . . He killed him, Vaska did!

NATASHA They're both in it together. Damn both of you! Both of you!

SATIN What the hell's going on here? Vaska, watch it—they'll finish you between them.

SCREWY I don't understand. What a mess!

PEPPEL Natasha—you can't believe . . . You don't think she and I were . . .

SATIN For God's sake, Natasha. Use your brain.

VASSILISA (in the hallway) My husband's been murdered, your Honor. Vaska Peppel did it—the thief. I saw it, your Honor. We all saw it . . .

NATASHA (her mind wandering) What nice people . . . My sister and Vaska killed him! Listen, officer. My sister here got him to do it. Her lover. There he is, the miserable bastard! They killed him. Take them . . . arrest them . . . And take me as well . . . Take me to prison! For Christ's sake, take me to prison!!

ACT FOUR

(Same as Act One. But PEPPEL's room is no longer there, and the partition has been taken down. KLETCH's anvil is also gone. In the corner where PEPPEL's room was, lies the TARTAR, restless and groaning from time to time.

KLETCH is at the table, tinkering with a concertina and trying it out. At the other end of the table are SATIN, the BARON and NASTYA. They have a bottle of vodka, three bottles of beer, and a large chunk of black bread. The ACTOR is on the stove, turning about and coughing.

Night. The stage is lit by a lamp standing in the middle of the table. Outside, a wind is blowing)

KLETCH Yes . . . In the middle of all the trouble, he just disappears . . .

BARON Vanished from the police—just like fog when the sun comes out.

SATIN Thus the sinner vanisheth from the sight of the righteous.

NASTYA He was good, the old man was! You—you aren't men. You're just mildew!

BARON (drinks) Your very good health, my lady!

SATIN He was an interesting old guy . . . Nastya here fell madly in love with him.

NASTYA Yes, I did. I did fall in love with him. He knew everything—understood everything.

SATIN (laughing) In fact, for some people, he was like slops to the toothless.

BARON (laughs) Or plaster to a boil.

KLETCH He had pity for other people. You haven't got any pity . . .

SATIN What good's it do you if I pity you?

KLETCH You can . . . well, it's not so much having pity for people. But you shouldn't hurt them.

TARTAR (sits on his bunk, and nurses his wounded arm) The old man was good. Had the law in his soul. People who has the law— is good. People who lose the law—is lost.

BARON What kind of law, Hassan?

TARTAR Different kind. You know what kind.

BARON Go on.

TARTAR Not hurt a man—that is law!

KLETCH (trying the concertina) Oh, hell! Still wheezes . . . Hassan's right. Must live by the law . . . by the gospel . . .

SATIN Well, go ahead and do it!

BARON Just try it.

TARTAR Mohammed gave the Koran. He says, "Here is the law! Do what is written here!" Then comes a time, Koran is not enough. Every age has its own law—a new law. Every age has its own law.

SATIN That's right. And our age has the law called the Penal Code. A strong law, that is. Won't wear out in a hurry.

NASTYA (bangs her glass on the table)

Why do I go on living here with you? What for? I'm going away—anywhere. The end of the world.

BARON Without your shoes on, my lady?

NASTYA Stark naked! On all fours if I have to!

BARON Extremely picturesque, my lady—if you're on all fours.

NASTYA Yes, I'll crawl—I don't mind. Anything, as long as I don't have to see your stupid face any more! Oh, I'm so sick of it all! Sick of living . . . sick of people . . .

SATIN Well, then, go away! You can take the Actor with you. He wants to go there too. It's come to his attention that half a mile from the end of the world there's a hospital for organons . . .

ACTOR (*sticks his head out from on top of the stove*) Organisms, you fool!

SATIN For organons poisoned with alcohol . . .

ACTOR Yes, and he'll go! He'll go there—just wait and see!

BARON He? Who's he, *monsieur*?

ACTOR Me!

BARON *Merci*, servant of the goddess . . . what's her name? The goddess of plays, of the theatre—what's her name?

ACTOR The muse, idiot! Not a goddess—muse!

SATIN Lachesis . . . Hera . . . Aphrodite . . . Atropos . . . Oh, what the hell! You see what the old man did, Baron? Getting the Actor all excited like this?

BARON The old man's a fool . . .

ACTOR And you're a lot of ignorant savages! It's Mel-po-me-ne! You with no soul—he'll go, just wait and see! "Go on and stuff yourselves, you dismal mortals," . . . poem by . . . Shakespeare. Yes, he's going to find the place where there isn't any . . . any . . .

BARON Anything at all, *monsieur*?

ACTOR That's right! Where there isn't anything at all! "This hole my grave will be . . . I die of sickness and infirmity." What do you go on living for? Why?

BARON Listen you! You Edmund Kean! Or God or genius or whatever you are! Don't make such a noise!

ACTOR You hear! I'll make all the noise I want to.

NASTYA (*lifts her head from table, waves her arms about*) Go on, yell! Let 'em hear you!

BARON What's the sense of that, my lady?

SATIN Leave them alone, Baron. To hell with them! Let them yell if they want to. Let them split their god-damned heads open. Let

them! There's sense in that. Don't interfere with people, as the old man used to say. Yes, the old bastard, he got them all like this.

KLETCH He told them all to get out and go somewhere. But he didn't tell them where.

BARON He's a charlatan, that old man.

NASTYA That's a lie! You're a charlatan yourself.

BARON Shut up! My lady!

KLETCH The old man didn't like the truth. In fact, he resented the truth. And he was right. Look! Where is there any truth? And yet you can't breathe without it! Look at Hassan—gets his hand crushed at work—have to get it cut off, I suppose. There's the truth for you!

SATIN (*bangs his fist on the table*) Shut up, you sons of bitches! Shut up about the old man, all of you! (*calmer*) You, Baron, you're the worst of the lot! You don't understand a thing, and you lie. The old man wasn't a charlatan. What's the truth? Man—there's the truth! He understood that—you don't understand a thing. You're about as sensitive as a block of wood. I understand the old man. Oh, yes, he lied—but out of pity for you, god-damn it, out of pity for you! Some people do—they tell tall tales out of pity for other people. I know—I've read about them. Beautiful, exciting, inspiring lies! . . . The soothing lie, the consoling lie, the lie that justifies the load that crushes the workman's hand, the lie that blames a man for being hungry—I know all about lies! People who are weak in spirit, people who live by the sweat of other people's brows—they need lies! Lies are their support, their shield, their armor! But the man who is strong, who's his own master, who's free and doesn't feed off others . . . he needs no lies! Lying is the creed of slaves and masters of slaves! Truth is the religion of the free man!

BARON Bravo! Well said! I—agree! You speak like an honest man.

SATIN And why can't a crook tell the truth sometimes?—Honest people usually speak like crooks. I've forgotten a lot, but I still know some things. The old man? Oh, he was wise, all right! He worked on me like acid on an old, dirty coin . . . Let's drink to his health! Come on, fill the glasses!

(NASTYA *pours a glass of beer and gives it to* SATIN)

SATIN (*laughs*) The old man lives his own way, looks at everything his own way. I asked him once, "Grandpa, what do people live for?" (*tries to imitate* LUKA's *voice and mannerisms*) "So that one day people will be better, my boy.

For example, let's take carpenters. Just ordinary, miserable carpenters. Then one day there's born a carpenter—a carpenter like there never was in all the world. Not another carpenter like him—he shines above them all. He revolutionizes the whole carpenter trade, the whole trade's advanced twenty years by one person. And the same thing with locksmiths there, and cobblers—all the trades, peasants too—even the aristocrats. They're all living in hopes of a better life. It may take a hundred years. May be more. But we go on living so there'll be a better life one day."

(NASTYA *stares at* SATIN. KLETCH *stops work on the concertina to listen. The* BARON, *his head bowed low, softly drums with his fingers on the table. The* ACTOR *has got off the stove, carefully lowers himself onto his bunk*)

SATIN "Everybody lives so there'll be something better one day, my boy. That's why we should show respect to everybody we meet. How do we know what he is, what he was born to do, what he can do? Maybe he's going to make us happy. Maybe he's going to help us. And especially we should be kind to children. Give them plenty of elbow room. Don't interfere with their little lives. Be kind to children!" (*He laughs quietly. A pause*)

BARON (*reflectively*) Yes . . . Something better one day? That reminds me of our family . . . An old family—goes back to the time of Catherine the Great . . . noblemen . . . warriors! . . . French in origin . . . We served our country and rose higher and higher. My grandfather Gustave Debille, held a very important position in Nicholas the First's time. We were rich. Hundreds of serfs . . . horses . . . cooks . . .

NASTYA Liar! There weren't!

BARON (*jumps up*) What? Well, what? Go on.

NASTYA There weren't!

BARON (*shouts*) We had a house in Moscow! And a house in St. Petersburg! And carriages . . . carriages with our coat of arms!

(KLETCH *takes the concertina to the side, where he watches the scene*)

NASTYA There weren't!

BARON Shut up! I tell you, we had dozens of footmen! . . .

NASTYA (*enjoying it*) There weren't!

BARON I'll kill you!

NASTYA (*ready to run*) There weren't any carriages!

SATIN Stop it, Nastya. Don't ride him.

BARON Wait till I get you, you little bitch! My grandfather . . .

NASTYA There weren't any grandfathers! There wasn't anything!

(SATIN *laughs*)

BARON (*exhausted by his shouting, sits on the bench*) Satin, tell this—slut . . . You're laughing at me, too! You don't believe me either! (*shouts in despair, bangs the table*) It's true, damn you! It's true!

NASTYA Ah! You see? You see what it's like when people don't believe you?

KLETCH (*comes back to the table*) I thought there was going to be a fight.

TARTAR Ach, people are stupid. It's bad!

BARON I . . . I won't have people laughing at me! I've got proofs. I've got papers to prove it, damn it!

SATIN Forget it. And forget about all your carriages. You can't go very far in carriages of the past.

BARON But how can she have the nerve?

SATIN You see—she has got the nerve! Is she any worse than you? Maybe she didn't have any carriages, or any grandfather—not even a father and mother . . .

BARON (*calmer*) Oh go to hell! You can argue without getting upset. I don't have the will-power. . . .

SATIN Get some. It's useful. (*pause*) Nastya! Are you going to the hospital?

NASTYA What for?

SATIN To see Natasha.

NASTYA You're a bit late, aren't you? She's been out a long time. She came out and—just disappeared! Nowhere to be found . . .

SATIN So . . . she's vanished . . .

KLETCH I'd like to know who'll hurt the other the most. Vaska or Vassilisa.

NASTYA Vassilisa will. She's shrewd. And Vaska will go to Siberia.

SATIN It's only prison for manslaughter.

NASTYA That's a pity. He'd be better off in Siberia. So would the whole bunch of you. In Siberia. Swept onto the rubbish heap, like the dirt you are!

SATIN (*shaken*) What's that? Have you gone mad?

BARON I'm going to hit her one so hard, she'll . . . don't be so wise . . .

NASTYA You just try! Go ahead, just try and hit me!

BARON I'll try all right!

SATIN Leave her alone! Leave her. Don't interfere with other people. I can't get him out of my head, that old man. (*He laughs*) Don't interfere with other people. And what if someone wrongs me, wounds me for the rest of my life—am I supposed to forgive him? Huh! Not on your life!

BARON (*to* NASTYA) You've got to understand, once and for all, we're from different classes. You're just dirt under my feet.

NASTYA Oh, you good-for-nothing bastard! Why, you live off me like a worm in an apple!

(*The men burst into laughter*)

KLETCH Ha! What a fool! An apple . . .

BARON You can't be angry with her . . . She's a god-damned fool.

NASTYA You're laughing are you? You old fraud! It isn't funny and you know it!

ACTOR (*gloomily*) Go ahead, beat them up!

NASTYA If I could, I'd . . . smash you to bits—(*throws cup on floor*) like that!

TARTAR What are you breaking things for? That's stupid.

BARON (*gets up*) Now, stop it! . . . I'll teach you some manners!

NASTYA (*runs away*) Go to hell!

SATIN (*after her*) Hey, that's enough! Who are you trying to scare! What's all the fuss about anyway?

NASTYA Dogs! Drop dead! You bastards!

ACTOR (*gloomily*) Amen!

TARTAR Ach! She's a bad woman—the Russian woman. Spiteful, willful . . . Tartar woman not like that. Tartar woman knows the law.

KLETCH Give her a good hiding.

BARON What a bitch!

KLETCH (*tries concertina*) There—it's finished. But no sign of the owner. He's on a binge again . . .

SATIN Have a drink.

KLETCH Thank you. Soon be time for bed . . .

SATIN You getting used to us?

KLETCH (*finishes drink, goes to his bunk in the corner*) It's all right . . . People are the same everywhere. You don't see it at first. Then you look around, and you see they're all human beings. They're all right.

(TARTAR *spreads something on his bunk, kneels down, and prays*)

BARON (*to* SATIN, *points to the* TARTAR) Look at him!

SATIN Leave him alone. He's a good fellow . . . Leave him alone! (*laughs*) I'm in a good mood today. God knows why! . . .

BARON You're always in a good mood, when you're drunk. That's when you talk the most sense too.

SATIN I like everybody when I'm drunk. All right, so he's praying—so what? A man can believe or not believe—that's his business. He's free—he pays for everything himself, for belief, for disbelief, for love, for intelligence. That's what makes him free. Man—that's the truth! What is man? Not you, not me, not them . . . No! it's you, and me, and them, and the old man, and Napoleon and Mohammed, all in one. (*draws the figure of a man in the air*) Do you see? It's marvellous! This is the beginning, and the end. Everything's in man, everything's for man! Man's the only thing that exists. Everything else is just the work of his hands and the work of his brain. Man! It's marvellous! It sounds—great! Man. We should respect him. Not pity him . . . you degrade him with pity. Respect him! Let's drink to man, Baron! (*stands up*) It's good to be a man! I'm a convict, a murderer, I cheat at cards—all right. When I walk down the street, people look at me like a crook. They step to one side and stare after me. Sometimes they shout after me, "Why don't you work, you lazy beggar?" Work? What the hell for? To stuff my belly? (*laughs*) I hate people who worry all the time about stuffing their bellies. That doesn't matter, Baron. No. Man's above that. Man's for something much better than stuffing his belly!

BARON (*shakes his head*) You've got brains. You're lucky—must be nice. I haven't. I haven't got brains. (*looks around, speaks in a low voice, cautiously*) You know, sometimes I get scared. Do you know what I mean? I'm scared. I don't know what's going to happen to me.

SATIN (*walks up and down*) Nonsense! What's a man got to be afraid of?

BARON You know, for as long as I can remember I've had a sort of fog in my head. Can't understand things. I get an awful feeling I've never done anything in life except change clothes. What for? I don't know. I went to school and I had to wear a uniform—College for the Sons of the Nobility. And what did I learn? I can't remember. I got married—wore a frock coat, and then I wore a dressing gown. But I picked the wrong wife. Why? I don't know. Squandered all my money and had to wear an old grey jacket and faded trousers. How did I lose it all? I didn't notice. I got a job in the Civil Service, wore a uniform and a cap with a badge. Then I embezzled government money, and they put me in prison clothes. And now I'm wearing these. And it all happened like a dream. It's funny, isn't it?

SATIN Not really. I'd say it was stupid.

BARON Yes, I suppose it is stupid. But I must have been born for some reason—eh?

SATIN (*laughs*) Probably . . . People are

born so that one day there'll be better people! (*nods his head*) So there you are!

BARON   Wonder where Nastya went off to. I'll go and see. After all, she . . . (*exit*)

(*A pause*)

ACTOR   Tartar! (*pause*) Hassan!! (TARTAR *looks up*) Pray . . . for me . . .

TARTAR   What for?

ACTOR   (*softly*) Pray . . . for me . . .

TARTAR   (*after a pause*) Pray yourself!

ACTOR   (*quickly gets down, goes to table, pours himself some vodka with trembling hands, drinks it, and almost runs out into the hall*) I'm off.

SATIN   Hey, Organism! Where are you going? (*whistles*)

(*Enter* MEDVEDEV, *in a woman's quilted jacket, and* BUBNOV. *Both are slightly drunk, but not very.* BUBNOV *carries some pretzels in one hand, and some smoked fish in the other: a bottle of vodka under one arm, and another bottle sticking out of his pocket*)

MEDVEDEV   Camel—it's a kind of donkey! Only without ears.

BUBNOV   Oh, shut up! You're a kind of donkey yourself.

MEDVEDEV   Camel—hasn't got any ears at all . . . Hears—with his nostrils.

BUBNOV   (*to* SATIN)   Ah, there you are! I've been looking for you in every saloon in the street. Here, take a bottle—my hands are full.

SATIN   Put the pretzels on the table—then you'll have one hand free.

BUBNOV   Oh, you . . . Look, policeman! Isn't he clever!

MEDVEDEV   All crooks are clever, I know that! They've got to be clever. An honest man can be stupid. But a crook's got to have brains. But about this camel—you're wrong. It's a sort of animal, and it's got no horns, no teeth . . .

BUBNOV   Where is everybody? Where are they all? Why isn't everybody here? Come on, get up. It's my treat. Who's that in the corner?

SATIN   You drinking up all your money at once? You idiot!

BUBNOV   Yes, all at once! Haven't saved up much money this time . . . Screwy! Where's Screwy?

KLETCH   (*comes to table*)   He isn't here.

BUBNOV   Come on, enjoy yourselves! Cheer up! The drinks are on me! If I was rich, I'd run a free saloon. My God, yes, I would! With music, and singing. Come in, and drink, and eat, and sing songs, and enjoy yourselves. You a poor man? Come in, mister, come in—into my free saloon! Satin, I'd make you . . . I'd give you half my capital. There!

SATIN   You'd better give it all to me, right now.

BUBNOV   All of it? Now? Here, take it. Here's a ruble . . . and twenty kopecks . . . five kopecks . . . two kopecks . . . that's all there is!

SATIN   That's fine. It's safer with me. I'll gamble with it.

MEDVEDEV   I'm a witness. He gave you the money to take care of. How much was it?

BUBNOV   You? You're a camel. We don't want any witnesses.

ALESHKA   (*enters barefoot*)   Hello everyone! My feet are soaking wet!

BUBNOV   Come over here and wet your whistle. I like you . . . you're a good guy. Sing and play . . . very well! But you shouldn't drink. That's bad for you, brother. Drinking's bad! . . .

ALESHKA   I can tell by looking at you! It's only when you're drunk that you look like a human being. Kletch. You mended my concertina? (*sings, dances*)

If I didn't have such a handsome face,
My girl wouldn't have me round the place.

Boy, I'm frozen. It's cold.

MEDVEDEV   And who is the girl, might I ask?

BUBNOV   Oh, shut up! You're not a policeman now. Forget it! You're not a policeman, and you're not an uncle.

ALESHKA   Just Auntie Kvashnya's husband!

BUBNOV   One of your nieces is in prison, the other one's dying . . .

MEDVEDEV   (*proudly*)   It's a lie! She isn't dying. She's just disappeared without telling anybody.

(SATIN *laughs*)

BUBNOV   Just the same, my friend—an uncle without any nieces isn't an uncle.

ALESHKA   Your majesty, the retired drum-major!

My girl's got money, and I've got none,
And that is why I treat her nice!

It's so cold!

(*Enter* SCREWY; *from now until the end of the Act, other men and women come in, undress, get onto bunks, and start to snore*)

SCREWY   Bubnov! What did you run off for?

BUBNOV   Come over here and sit down . . . Let's sing a song—my favorite one, eh?

TARTAR   Night time you should sleep. Sing songs in daytime.

SATIN Never mind, Hassan. Come over here.

TARTAR What do you mean, "never mind"? There'll be noise . . . always noise when you sing songs . . .

BUBNOV (*goes up to him*) How's your arm, Hassan? They cut it off yet?

TARTAR Why should they? May not have to cut it off. I wait a bit. An arm . . . not made of iron. Can easy cut it off.

SCREWY Means the gutter for you, Hassan! What use are you without an arm? You're only worth what your arm and your back's worth. No arm—no man! Might as well be dead. Come and have some vodka . . . That's all you're good for now.

KVASHNYA (*enters*) Hello, inmates! Ooh, it's terrible out there! Cold and wet! Is my policeman here?

MEDVEDEV Here I am.

KVASHNYA Wearing my jacket again, are you? And you're a bit tight by the look of you—how come?

MEDVEDEV It's his birthday—Bubnov's. And besides it's cold . . .

KVASHNYA Cut the stories! Now get to bed with you, go on!

MEDVEDEV Yes, it's time I did. Time I went to bed . . . (*exit to kitchen*)

SATIN What are you so damn strict with him for?

KVASHNYA You've got to, boy. It's the only way. You got to be strict with a man like him. When I married him I thought I was really getting something. After all, he's a military man, and you're a rough bunch . . . and I'm only a woman. And then he goes and starts taking to drink! And I don't want any of that.

SATIN You picked the wrong man.

KVASHNYA No, he's better than you are. You couldn't live with me. You couldn't stand me. A fellow like you! I'd see you one week in twenty. And you'd gamble me away in no time —me and everything else you could lay your hands on.

SATIN (*laughs*) You're right there, lady! I'd gamble you away all right!

KVASHNYA Well, then! . . . Aleshka!

ALESHKA That's me.

KVASHNYA What have you been saying about me?

ALESHKA Me? Only the truth, that's all. That you're a wonderful woman, all flesh, fat and bones—weigh 400 pounds—and have got no brain at all.

KVASHNYA You're wrong there. I've got plenty of brains. But why do you go telling people I beat my husband?

ALESHKA I thought you were, when you pulled his hair.

KVASHNYA (*laughs*) You fool! You aren't blind are you! What do you go about telling tales for? And you've hurt his feelings, too— he's took to drink because of you.

ALESHKA Then it's true what they say— even a camel drinks!

(SATIN *and* KLETCH *laugh*)

KVASHNYA Oh, Aleshka, you're some kid!

ALESHKA That's right, some kid! A jack of all trades. And I just follow my nose wherever it takes me!

BUBNOV (*by the* TARTAR's *bunk*) Come on! It's no use. You won't get any sleep. We'll be singing—all night long! Eh, Screwy?

SCREWY A song? All right!

ALESHKA And I'll play.

SATIN And we'll listen!

TARTAR (*smiles*) All right, Bubnov, you bastard . . . give me a drink! We'll drink, and we'll enjoy ourselves—and when death comes, we'll die!

BUBNOV Fill them up, Satin! Sit down, Screwy! Oh, what does a man need after all? Look at me—give me a drink, and I'm happy! Screwy! Let's have my favorite song. I'm going to sing, and I'm going to cry!

SCREWY (*sings*)
The sun comes up, the sun goes down
. . .

BUBNOV (*harmonizing*)
In my prison night won't go . . .

(*The door opens suddenly*)

BARON (*stands on the threshold, cries*) Hey . . . you! Come on . . . come out here in the yard . . . out here . . . the Actor . . . he's hanged himself!

(*Silence. They all look at the* BARON. NASTYA *appears behind him, and slowly, with wide eyes, goes to table*)

SATIN (*quietly*) The damn fool—he ruined the song!

ITALY
SPAIN

LUIGI PIRANDELLO (1867–1936) was the master of the modern Italian theatre, and no dramatist brought the intellectual and emotional unrest of post-World War I European society to the stage with more originality or excitement than this great experimenter, who was, appropriately, born in the Sicilian town of Chaos. In all his plays written after he left Sicily, Pirandello inverts the central convention of modern dramaturgy: instead of pretending that the stage is not a stage but a living room, he insists that the living room is not a living room but is really a stage. In short, Pirandello saw all human life as theatrical; people are characters who act out a series of continually shifting roles in the myriad dramas of life. In addition to his theatricality, Pirandello's significant contribution to modern drama was the development of a dramatic form capable of expressing the drama of ideas in a theatrically exciting way. All his characters in some way struggled between their own private individuality and the public pressures exerted by the society in which they lived. No one has given form to this typically Italian struggle between private anarchy and the strict rules of the community more effectively than Pirandello. He saw the inconsistency of everything, and man's life as a futile grasping at the unattainable. But for all his concern for ideas, Pirandello did not have any answers. His theatre has been called *il teatro dello specchio*, the mirror theatre, but it is a mirror that gives a grotesque reflection of life. Like the mirrors of a fun house in an amusement park or Alice's looking glass, it shows a queerly logical yet irrational world behind the mirror—a world in which reality has been reduced to an illusion. But in this illusion lies the only true reality. At first this philosophical mirror world tends to confuse us, but before long we are chiefly conscious not of ideas but of great human suffering. In his preface to *Six Characters*, Pirandello tells us that he is not representing people just for

[LUIGI PIRANDELLO—*Cont.*]
the sake of representing them, but because of their universal significance.

UGO BETTI (1892–1953), after Pirandello, is generally regarded as the most important dramatist to write for the modern Italian theatre. In fixing Betti's position within the broader perspective of modern drama, it is possible to note the influence of Pirandello, Ibsen, Chekhov, German expressionism, and the post-war French dramatists, but finally he created a symbolic style of drama that was uniquely his own. Certainly few writers in the twentieth century have come to grips with great moral issues more directly, forcefully, and imaginatively than did Betti in the twenty-five plays he wrote from 1926 until his death in 1953. With a flinty moral integrity, he spent a lifetime creating dramatic situations which forced his characters to face unflinchingly the problem of evil. Unlike so many modern plays in which the moral issues are dissolved by psychological explanation or by those mists of fantasy which are at one with the spectator's moral evasions, Betti's plays affirm both man's need to struggle with real alternatives and his capacity to do so. The dominant themes of all his work are justice and the individual's need for judgment (Betti's lifelong interest in this theme was certainly to a large degree occasioned by his own adult career as a chief justice in the Italian courts), the redemptive and transforming power of love, and a belief in the power of the human imagination to transform the quality of life. But in dealing with each of these themes there is no attempt to whitewash man's sense of his own guilt, nor the attendant need to avoid moral responsibility. Betti's attitude in this regard is best expressed in a newspaper article he wrote shortly before his death: "It is not very popular these days to attribute responsibility to oneself; the general practice is to blame others, history, laws, parents, etc. The fact is, that vast picture of our life has an author, carries a signature: Our own! We are responsible for it."

FEDERICO GARCÍA LORCA (1899–1936) gained his first success as a poet. He was a modern-day troubadour who loved to recite his own works, which, as a result, often were well known to his friends long before their publication. He reached the peak of his popularity when his *Gypsy Romances* was published in 1928. After that, Lorca turned his attention solely to the theatre (he had been writing poetic puppet plays since 1920), but he never ceased being the poet. His brother, Francisco,

writing in the introduction to the first English edition of the tragedies, insists that "any interpretation of his [Lorca's] theatre made from a viewpoint other than a poetic one will lead to wrong conclusions." In all his later plays Lorca used metaphors taken from nature, varying rhythms of language and musical sound, brightly contrasting colors, and many songs and dances to transform the experiences of Andalusian life into a poetry of the theatre.

The theme in all of Lorca's work is frustration, and the center of the dramatic conflict in his mature plays is to be found in the frustrations of women, who he believed were the bearers of all passion and the source of every form of earthly creativity. On the surface this frustration emerges primarily in sexual terms, but finally the world of Lorca's theatre is ruled by the power of death. In his tragedies he ties up and twists the strands of people's passions so tightly that only the "tiny knife, the tiny golden knife" of death can probe the center of the conflict. Like all Spaniards, Lorca understood and felt life only through death. Death is man's mentor, his companion, and his greatest achievement. And perhaps Lorca's own premature death in the Spanish Civil War may be the fullest embodiment of the meaning of his plays. That death deprived the modern theatre of one of its greatest artists just as he was reaching full maturity.

ALFONSO SASTRE (1927–   ) is not widely known outside of Spain, but in his native country he is regarded as one of the most important dramatists writing today. Sastre is a writer of the cities, and in most of his plays he is concerned with dramatizing the difficulty of maintaining one's sense of self within the context of demoralizing social forces. Like so many of his contemporaries in Spain, he is a child of the Civil War and his plays are aflame with his burning indignation over social and political injustice and corruption. For this reason, Spanish censorship practices being what they are, Sastre is what might be called an "underground playwright." His work is known, respected, but practically never produced in Spain. Furthermore, unlike so many of his fellow writers, Sastre is not so much a Spanish writer as he is European. All of his work is tinged with the despair and negation that characterize the main current of the modern theatre. The influences of Pirandello, Shaw, Ibsen, and Strindberg are clearly present, but so, too, strangely enough, is the social optimism of Arthur Miller, the playwright Sastre seems to respect and admire above all others.

Luigi Pirandello

1867-1936

THE NEW THEATRE AND THE OLD

You may be familiar with the anecdote of the poor peasant who, when he heard his parish priest say that he could not read because he had left his glasses at home, spurred his wit and conceived the fancy idea that knowing how to read depended upon having a pair of eyeglasses. Consequently, he journeyed to the city and went to an optometrist's shop and demanded "Glasses for reading."

But since no pair of glasses succeeded in making the poor man read, the optometrist, at the end of his patience, after having turned his shop upside down, snarled, "But, tell me, can you read?" Amazed at this, the peasant answered, "That's a good one, and if I knew how to read, why would I have come to you?"

Well, now, all those who have neither a thought or feeling of their own to express, and think that to compose a comedy, a drama, or even a tragedy it is enough to write an imitation of someone else, should have the courage and the frankness of naive wonder of this poor peasant.

To the question, "But really, have you something of your own to tell us?" they should have the courage and the frankness to answer, "That's a good one! And if we had something of our own to say, would we write like someone else?"

"Teatro Nuovo e Teatro Vecchio" ("The New Theatre and the Old") by Luigi Pirandello is from *Saggi, Poesie e Scritti Varii*, edited by Manlio Lo Vecchio-Musti. © Arnoldo Mondadori Editore 1960. The translation by Herbert Goldstone is from *The Creative Vision*, edited by Haskell M. Block and Herman Salinger. Copyright © 1960 by Grove Press, Inc.

But I realize that this might really be asking too much.

Maybe it would be enough that all these persons should not become so angry when somebody calmly points out that while it is true that no one forbids them the exercise of writing and rewriting a theatre already written, doing this means that they do not have eyes of their own but a pair of borrowed glasses.

It has been said and repeated that, in general, the imitative or decorative faculty in the nature of the Latin character is superior to the creative or inventive, and that the whole history of our theatre, and in general of our literature, is fundamentally nothing but a perpetual repetition of imitated manners; and that, looking at our literary history, we certainly find very many glasses, and very few eyes, and that our writers did not disdain glasses but were proud to use ancient lenses to see in the manner of Plautus or Terence or Seneca, who in their turn had seen in the manner of the Greek tragedies, Menander, and of middle Athenian comedy. But these—shall we say—visual aids were at least made at home from rhetoric which always came from our own optometrist shop; and these glasses passed from one nose to another, through generations and generations of noses, until suddenly, with the rise of Romanticism, the cry was raised, "Gentlemen, let us try to look with our own eyes." They tried; but alas, they were able to see very little. And the importation of foreign glasses began.

An old story. And I should not have mentioned it if, truly, things had not everywhere reached such a state that to obtain public favor it is not so necessary to have a pair of one's own eyes, as to have a pair of someone else's eyeglasses, which make you see men and life in a certain manner and with a given color, that is, as fashion urges or current public taste commands. And woe to whoever disdains or refuses to put them on his nose, or who is obstinate enough to want to look at men and life in his own way; his vision, if simple, will be called bare; if sincere, vulgar; if intimate and acute, obscure and paradoxical; and the natural expression of this new world will always appear filled with the greatest defects.

I will speak again of these defects. The greatest and best known has been in every age that of "writing badly." It is distressing to acknowledge it, but all the original visions of life are always badly expressed. At least they were always so judged at their first appearance, especially by that plague of society, the so-called cultivated and nice people.

Recently I have much enjoyed reading a piece of Clive Bell [1] attacking these same people. Here and there, he says, a man of powerful intellect is able to succeed in forcing the gates; but cultivated people do not like originality, not as long as it looks original. The company of the man of original talent is not pleasant, at least not until he is dead. Cultivated people adore whoever gives them, in some unsuspected way, just what they have learned to expect, and, fundamentally, they do not like art any more than do the Philistines; except that they want to have the sensation of seeing the old cloaked in the new; and, for that reason, they prefer those pastry cooks who sprinkle a little art on their common thoughts and feelings. Because of this, culture (so understood) is even more dangerous than Philistinism: it pretends to be on the side of the artist; it has the "charm" of its exquisite taste, yet it can corrupt because it can speak with an authority denied the Philistines; and because it feigns an interest in art, often the artists are not indifferent to its judgments. It is necessary, therefore, to free the artist and also the public from the influence of the opinion of the cultivated. And the liberation will not be complete until those who have already learned to scorn the opinion of the petty bourgeoisie will also learn to ignore the disapproval of people constrained by their limited power of feeling to consider art an elegant entertainment.

Gentlemen, for the cultivated fifteenth century Dante wrote badly; *The Divine Comedy* was badly written, and not only because it was not composed in Latin, but in the language of the people and really badly written in that same popular idiom. And Machiavelli? He writes *The Prince* and shamefully has to excuse himself and confess that he was not cultivated enough to write it better. And to the fanatic admirers of the flowery Tasso did not also Ariosto's *Orlando Furioso* seem badly written? And Vico's *New Science* appeared not only badly but terribly written; he had the curious fate of starting to write in a completely different manner, so as to seem somebody else when he decided to please all those who were accustomed to read with the glasses of that rhetoric which he later habitually professed.

To conclude this discussion of eyes and eyeglasses, the joke, nevertheless, is that all who wear the glasses (and all cultivated people wear them, or at least one supposes that they must have them, and the more so as they may pretend not to be aware of it), preach that in art it is absolutely necessary to have one's own eyes; yet at the same time they criticize any one who uses them, whether well or badly, because, let us make it clear, while these people say writers should use their own eyes, they must be and see exactly as the cultivated people's eyes, which, however, are only glasses, for if they fall and break, then it is good night.

Ever since foreign importation began in the theatre world, these eyeglasses have been bought—it is too obvious to point out—in Paris, a market which has become international only for such wares. In fact, the most renowned French factories are now on the decline, and not a few have lost all credit. The illusory eyeglasses of the Sardou [2] firm were once greatly used almost everywhere. Someone, and not without profit and consideration, still continues using them among us, incredible as it may seem. But nothing is often more incredible than the truth. A pair of lenses for the nearsighted, very powerful, and strongly recommended for acute and precise clarity, were those of the firm of Becque [3] with the trademark of "Parisian." And another pair, justly valued for a certain idealizing virtue, were those of the house of de Curel. [4] But there came from far-off Norway, first on the German market and then on the French, the powerful glasses of Henrik Ibsen, to impose themselves through a very different investigating power of ideal and social values. The vogue lasted a long

---

[1] Twentieth century British art critic and aesthetician.

[2] Victorien Sardou (1831–1908), French playwright, known for his advocacy of the well-made play form.

[3] Henri Becque (1837–1899), French realist dramatist, author of *The Vultures* and *The Parisian Woman.*

[4] François de Curel (1854–1928), French playwright, popular in the early twentieth century for his psychological dramas.

time, though few succeeded in adjusting these eyeglasses to their noses; then, after they recognized this difficulty as almost insurmountable, there came into fashion the monocles of the firm of Bataille [5] and Bernstein,[6] which sold widely in all the countries of the world. And, finally, and alas, without the least fault nor the slightest pleasure of the inventor, there is a certain Pirandello lens, called a diabolical brand by the malicious, which makes you see double and triple and slanted, and in short, makes you see the world upside down. Many still use these lenses, despite the fact that I do not miss any occasion to make them know that such lenses ruin their eyesight. On the one hand for support, and on the other for the good digestion of the honest citizen, a pair of lenses can be found today, lenses at a good price and easily used, for colored diversion and natural comfort, and in two colors: a comic eye and a sentimental eye. Every barber with the slightest dramatic aspiration is able to supply them, confident of quickly acquiring a fine reputation and of making a hatful of money.

But I must speak to you of the new theatre and the old, and I have spoken to you until now of eyes and eyeglasses: that is, of original creation and the exercise of imitation. This carries its own explanation. I do not want to criticize even this copying exercise which was and always will be typical of all the old theatre. I do not criticize it—do you know why?—even to irritate the devotees of that other vice of civil society, that is, "pure" literary criticism. To them, every debate on the theatre appears almost unworthy of their attention and consideration, unless as a pardonable exception it is used as an expressive form by some poet who is otherwise important and respected. And even then, if this "pure" literary criticism talks about theatre, naturally it avoids wasting a word or casting a glance, even in passing, at all that stage armament which sustains the habitual conception of a theatre, "played," as they say, according to its well-defined "rules," and spoken in its well-defined gibberish and regulated scene by scene with means and effects of its own stage. Everyone agrees that a work of the theatre should be understood as neither more nor less than a work of art; and that only on this condition is it worth discussing. Very well. But let us reflect a little. To refuse all literary expression to the products of

such a trade by being hermetically silent about it—as one does when the monopoly is controlled by those writers of comedies who are proud to declare themeslves of a "trade" acquired through assiduous training on the stage, and who feel they must defend the stage as their small, exclusive, inviolable domain protected all around by so many posters stating "entrance prohibited to outsiders"—may be right, without doubt, in so many ways; but, excuse me if I should point out to you that nevertheless out of that profession, when a sudden inspiration invests and ennobles it, although leaving it for the most part a trade, so many beautiful and great comedies have come. What then?

Even in England in Shakespeare's time, even in Spain at the time of Lope de Vega and Calderón de la Barca, or even in France at the time of Molière, the theatre was a trade reserved to the "specialist," to those who knew the stage, and they remade fifty times the same plots, filled with the same spirit common to a whole generation, and the priority of the ideas did not matter at all and the personality of the writer very little, and the greater part of the comedies, written in twenty-four hours, served as a spectacle for an evening and then was discarded among the rummage. There was no artistic seriousness, in the sense of high literary criticism and of cultivated and nice people. But *La vilda es sueño*,[7] to cite only one example, was still forged at that smithy. And what then?

It then appears clear to me that in the field of art every polemic, every critical attitude, every theory, if postulated and developed systematically and abstractly, *a priori* or *a posteriori*, whether discussed according to intellectual or moral criteria, or even from a purely aesthetic point of view, risks continually being disarranged and turned topsy turvy or remaining bewildered at the disconcerting appearance of the created work, which is without original sin and finds citizenship and status in the kingdom of art from wherever it comes; the crux is that it got there.

Until now, we have anticipated a brief preface on original creation and imitative exercise (eyes and eyeglasses) apropos of the new theatre and the old; and a negative judgment on the polemics of art stated and developed systematically and abstractly. If you let me pause a little on this point, I will give you reasons for both prefaces.

Let us ask: is it possible or not to recognize in the work of the theatre a value of art, of

---

[5] Félix-Henry Bataille (1872–1922), French boulevard playwright.

[6] Henri Bernstein (1876–1956), popular French naturalistic playwright.

[7] Calderón's *Life Is a Dream.*

achieved expression, from the assumption of its "newness," understanding by newness a harmony between the content and the particular spirit of revision and reconstruction of intellectual values which animates our times in every field: politics, science, philosophy, art itself? Are not the comedies or dramas in harmony with this spirit new theatre, that is, in this sieve, grain from which we can extract the best of the living work of art—while those comedies and those dramas which do not absorb this new spirit remain chaff, without any hope of salvation? Let us examine this a little. Is it possible, then, that criticism may direct with a certain sureness the activity of writers, instead of following it and explaining it, and that it may direct it with maximum profit for all, and especially of the young still in search of an expression of their own, toward particular problems, without which there is no hope of constructing new and vital works? If this were so, we should without ado immediately ask literary criticism to set forth such problems. But probably criticism would answer that to enunciate them, or to define them, is as good as to resolve them and, therefore, to destroy them as problems; and that this is the task of authors and not of critics.

Every one sees that in this way the question is badly put; and that, so put, it cannot be resolved. To resolve it, as a work of art, we must look fully into the fundamental problems of form and the aesthetic fact; and we will then see clearly that the "new" in art is nothing more than one of the many necessary values of every created work. We need not discuss in abstraction, stating and denying as exterior and existent for themselves, certain indeterminate problems from which we determine the "new." The open minds, the creative spirits find them indeed, but without searching for them—here is the essential point—and attack them, but without perhaps even knowing them in their abstract terms, and, without study, resolve them. Because it is not true that these problems are of a particular time, or that creative spirits can assume them from time.

If these minds are truly creative, the problems belong to the minds themselves and are not an indistinctive and indeterminate fact in time; but indistinct and undetermined points of the active spirit itself, which just because he has them himself as a part of his nature, as a living effort, can find the strength to free himself from them by expressing them. And they are active problems just because they are not enunciated by criticism but are expressed through the means of art. That is to say, they

are not defined by the pure intellect which chills and solidifies them, and naturally kills them, as problems, merely by enunciating them; but they have to be represented through the means of art in a form which is the construction and the *raison d'être* of their eternal life.

What is our time outside of the meaning and value that we give it? I say, we, with our spirit.

Now, think! Who can give meaning and value to his time, not a particular meaning and value functioning in the moments of the life of a single individual, but universal, in which each person can always find himself, if not the man who can speak with the most absolute disinterestedness, so that his voice can sound as his own in the breast of whoever listens? Not the person who satisfies material ambitions for himself in life, but the one who affirms "my kingdom is not of this world" and nevertheless affirms that he has a kingdom; who, therefore, creates life for himself and for all; who, therefore, succeeds in making consistent his own organic and total vision of life; who, therefore, is like the whole and pure spirit which is able to reveal itself fully; he is the poet, the maker, the creator: he will be able to give to his time a universal meaning and value because with his own absolute disinterestedness he makes all the concerns of his frank and lively senses (his own new eyes), thoughts and relationships of concepts, feelings, images assume in him an autonomous and complete organic unity, and he wants to realize that unity in himself which life freely wants for itself, so that he, in this sense, is a spirit servant of the spirit, the creator servant of his creation. In the organic wholeness of life he has a place like all the others; he has created not to dominate and rule, but to systematize. And for that reason, Christ, poet, maker, creator of reality, called himself son of man and gave meaning and value to life for all men.

The problems of time, therefore, do not exist for him who creates.

They exist for those men, undoubtedly worthy of the greatest respect because they are enlightened and enlighten others, but who do not have truly creative qualities in their spirit; these people take them truly from time, where the creative spirits have placed them.

In fact, every creation, every vision of life, every revelation of the spirit, necessarily carries within itself problems, questions, logical contradictions, the more decisive and evident as these creations, visions, and revelations are organic and comprehensive: and this simply be cause mystery is congenital to the spirit, and to look with new eyes, to express frankly, to reorganize life is to project life once more in mystery. To make: to create, anew, from nothing: that nothing is felt again necessarily by all with greater strength. Little by little, however, the anxiety of every first intuition will be appeased, as well as the dismay or also the annoyance which humanity always experiences in looking again at these objects: fortunately, our nature is such that it is allowed to sleep. But at first an almost general elevation of the spirit makes reborn those problems, those questions, the warning of those contradictions which have always been the same, but which now reappear as new because they have a new value. It is almost impossible that the new sense of life may be hit upon directly from the beginning. The problems appear obscure, and the spirit which agitates them, paradoxical. The so-called "logic," unmasked, has been driven out of life.

The sense of revelation is obscure if we blame its expression, especially when we deal with a work of art. The case is different if it is a question of religious revelation or a new philosophical revelation.

Because if we treat of a relevation in which faith enters as a necessary and essential element, the problems that revelation brings with it are naturally set aright if we accept faith; or, otherwise, they immediately lose any consistency and, for that reason, any stimulus and power to create doubt, to make intellectual systems waver, and finally, to be discussed passionately.

And if we treat of problems set forth in new intellectual constructions of philosophy, through the same technical and conventional language in which they are stated, they already appear connected to certain currents of thought already expressed, and the troublesome sense of the "new," which they are able to awaken is, for that reason, always somewhat limited and relative; but they are immediately evaluated perfectly, in their precise terms, and this annuls every spiritual restlessness over whatever may appear indistinct, imprecise, and ambiguous in its expressions. Every mind which becomes conscious of them has in so doing immediately tested them in all their parts. Furthermore, by their conceptual nature, that is, abstracted from life, in the light of criticism they can be displaced, completed, annulled, or resolved.

But not the problems represented in a new work of art. They remain and always will remain as they have been fixed: problems of life. Their irreducibility consists in their expression as representation. Think of Hamlet: to be or not to be. Take this problem from Hamlet's mouth, empty it of Hamlet's passion, conceptualize it in philosophical terms, and in the light of criticism you may play with it as long as you like. But leave it there on Hamlet's lips a living expression, an active representation of the torment of that life, and the problem of being or not being will never be resolved in eternity. And not only for Hamlet, a single spirit in a definite moment of his life, but for every spirit who contemplates that form of life, and—for this is Art—lives it. And these problems are in that form, and will always be, for every one, problems of life. Thus, they live through the form, through the expression.

They are able to live in this way because their expression is finished, completed.

The perfect form has detached them entirely, both alive and concrete; that is, fluid and indistinct from time and from space, and has fixed them forever, has gathered them into itself, that which is incorruptible, as if embalming them alive.

At so great distance of time, humanity without still having resolved them, has adjusted itself to them. It has succeeded in putting itself in that state of aesthetic contemplation in which it calls them beautiful, still feeling them as problems of life.

With the meaning and value they have assumed, organized in that way, humanity can now contemplate them without any anguish. It knows, and by now is accustomed to know that, in that vision of life, mystery appears in this way. For it is not the sense of mystery which terrifies men, since they know that mystery is in life; the unusual way of representing something new is what terrifies. Now that way is no longer new. But has it for that reason become old? No. How can it become old, if it is represented in action, in perfect, incorruptible form? Only the time has come in which we have discovered it "created," in which all the reasons of its being are seen to consist in the necessity of its being what it is; and no longer new, never old, not arbitrary, or obscure, or imprecise, or unfinished, but finally necessary in every way: *that,* and that alone which it had to be.

But it might be instructive to read once more about the anger stirred up in the heart of Voltaire, for example, even at a distance of two centuries. And an almost contemporary critic of Michelangelo, in a solemn attack, harshly criticizes him for having made an arbitrary and absolutely illogical work, depicting in the "Pietà" the Virgin as a girl scarcely eighteen who holds on her knee the thirty-three year old Son. Now we understand what depth of poetry Michelangelo reached in the representation of that Madonna, the Virgin, who conceived through grace and is always the girl of the "Annunciation," compared to the Son, the Redeemer, who has had to bear all the pain of the world. But how that same critic boasted of having opened Michelangelo's eyes and of inviting him to correct properly his inconceivable aberration! As if one might wish to enlighten Hamlet's mind in order to help him resolve in some way the confusion of his problems.

Now we would laugh and no longer think of this; but because it is a matter of Hamlet and of Michelangelo's "Pietà"—artistic expressions for which we have finally found the *ubi consistam* of aesthetic evaluation which explains the being of their life: the necessity which the form represents.

Still, because contemporary criticism does not give enough weight to the absolute difference between the philosophical problem set forth through concepts in an intellectual construction and the problem of life expressed in the immediate representation of art—creator of form, in this sense inviolable—very often today this criticism of contemporary works of art avoids probing as deeply as it could, not merely into the representation of a spiritual debate accidentally expressed in the work, but into the very objects of that debate, and tries instead to discover its logical contradictions and looks only at the conceptual design of the work of art. This has happened to me and to my work. But the conceptual framework, on the one hand, is absolutely nothing more than a pretext, a stimulus to create, and, therefore, in the evaluation of the created work (which is considered in itself and by itself) could not and must not find a place. On the other hand, the conceptual framework is at best no more than a scheme, a skeleton, which becomes immediately incorporated, wholly reabsorbed, in the whole of the expressive elaboration of the work, and not even from this side, therefore, can it lead to a just aesthetic evaluation. And just as bad, it seems to me, is criticism generally done by those who still would like to do it according to its correct principles, based, I mean, upon expression. Especially when these people come upon new material expressed for the first time.

We have declared what seemed to us the reasons for which this first expressior must at the beginning appear muddled, obscure, arbitrary, paradoxical: a "badly written" work.

These difficult judges, among other things, do not consider that the very fury with which they penetrate into the limits of the problems represented in the work of art in order to combat them and destroy them, and define them in themselves, this very fury from which they then resolve the judgment that the work of art is not completely expressed, is, instead, the surest and clearest testimony that the incriminated expression is still that which it had to be: so that they have been able to draw out and fight these problems face to face as alive and present, and which are therefore represented, and perfectly so, in an achieved form.

But it is natural that conflict and misunderstanding exist for those who have eyes and create, and not for those who have glasses and copy in a final draft the obscure, abstruse expressions of creators who "write badly" and diligently clean up all those "errors," so that one fine day when a taste will have developed for the new expression, these qualities will reveal themselves as their necessary "traits."

Think that even Goldoni,[8] who today seems as simple and accessible as it is possible to imagine, whose style seems so pure and faithful to the reality of his characters lifted bodily from the pressure of the life of his time; even Goldoni was not recognized in his own time. And how they criticized him! They said that he wrote badly, and they all said it to him, right away, even those who with due reservations accepted his theatre and followed him. They seemed to say to him, "Yes you are right; those who criticize you understand nothing, but if only you knew how to write a little better!"

And this is natural, if we think that the spirit always brings to life its creations with great and slow labor and that every time it succeeds in establishing one of them it experiences the need of resting for a while. In this way, therefore, certain periods come after the recognition of every original expression, certain periods in which spirits no longer truly create but devote themselves to small discoveries of illuminating the details of the vision of life which is present at that moment, so that all remains impregnated in it; and we have established, besides, a heavy burden of clichés which have meaning for all in that moment and perhaps have none after the advent of a new original expression; we have established, I was saying, a world absolutely determined, perhaps more by expres-

---

[8] Carlo Goldoni (1707–1793), Italian popular dramatist who used *commedia del árte* materials and conventions in the writing of his plays.

sion than by conception, which is not really the same for all, naturally, but which is stamped with the same characteristics. Take the writings of men of a certain time, anonymous in the sense that they are called neither Shakespeare nor Dante, and you can recognize, without looking at the date, those written by our fathers, grandfathers, and ancestors. There are some who write with great clarity of expression, with grace, with a beautiful periodic style. There! These men write well. And why does Carlo Goldoni write badly? Because his expressions, in order to define a new vision of life, necessarily had to be different from those that were in the ears of all, already composed, already studied and for that reason very clear, and which anyone, by Jove, with a bit of talent and good will, could embellish gracefully. And that clumsy Goldoni. . . .

I believe that every creator, besides his great sins, ought to feel on his conscience the secret afflictions of his contemporary admirers, almost as a sense of shame because of his inevitable bad writing. And Goldoni should have more remorse than any one. The dialogue of Carlo Goldoni must have appeared, even to his admirers, insipid and specious, compared to the language of the *commedia dell'arte;* and badly written, legalistic, and formless enough to make you sick compared to the style of the serious compositions of the time.

The *commedia dell'arte* which was, indeed, played spontaneously, but which was incapable of imposing itself as a true improvisation, was at bottom only the quintessence of the commonplace, based on generic themes and ready-made patterns contrived to frame the same repertory of stereotyped phrases, typical, and traditional jokes and epigrams, and ritualized blows and retorts, phrased as though in a manual of etiquette. It was natural for everyone that on the stage it should be so spoken: since a taste had been developed for conventions which ruled that language, one went to the theatre to admire the undisguised witticisms, the false naturalness, and false spontaneity; and the style of Goldoni had to appear fallacious because it was psychological, insipid because it was natural, and it undid with its dialogue the fixity of those lines and loosened the rigidity of the masks, cutting apart little by little their consistency and expressing it—a new and unknown spectacle—through the free play of all the liberated muscles.

But why couldn't Goldoni, who still experienced in life the struggling fate of the innovator, fix himself as an absolute value, so that he could face those who have made almost a fetish of him and who, with the intention of praising him, exclaim, "Oh, the good 'old' Goldoni!" (and that "old" expresses, more than a real intrinsic recognition, a spirit of polemic with "new") and altogether deny him any value in himself and regard his production as an outdated moment in the history of the Italian theatre, and deny that it can be the expression of a created and insurmountable world in the eternal kingdom of art?

This too—I think—comes about through the ambiguities to which the abstract and systematic evaluations are subject.

It is natural that each finished work—a created world unique in itself, and beyond comparison, which no longer can be new or old but simply "that which it is" in itself and for itself eternally, finds in its very "uniqueness" the reasons, first, of its incomprehension, and then, always, of its frightening solitude: the solitude of things which have been expressed in this way, immediately, as they wanted to be, and, therefore, "for themselves alone." And because of this single fact alone they would be impossible to know, if each person wanting to know them did not make them escape from that being "for themselves alone," making them exist for him, as he interprets and understands them.

Who knows Dante as he was for himself in his poem! Dante in his existence for himself becomes like nature: we should have to go out of ourselves to understand him as he is for himself, and we can not, and each one understands him as he can in his own way. Dante remains truly alone in his divine solitude. Nevertheless, each age makes him its own; each age echoes in its own way his unique voice.

But actually, the voice of Dante speaks eternal things; he speaks from the very insides of the earth. His is a voice of nature which will never go out in life, and our necessity to echo it does not mean we misunderstand or do not understand him.

Instead, it is possible at the same time to misunderstand and no longer understand the voice of one who, though creating, and in the most accomplished forms, his own organic vision of life, did not endow real and free "movements" of the spirit with his expression, but rather created according to a "pose" or "attitude" of the spirit.

And this "attitude" in itself, usually abstracted from expression, can be overcome, indeed is necessarily overcome, and at a certain point becomes, so to speak, historical, as soon as unexpected agitations of the spirit have displaced the elements of that panorama thus contemplated from a fixed point. Yet, in the movements of the spirit we can never lose interest: the Middle Ages of Dante, not represented according to an attitude of his spirit, as is the eighteenth century of Goldoni, but in the movements of a spirit which need not contemplate its own age because it has all the passions alive in itself, or when it does contemplate, does not stand still a moment because its glance is not attached to time, but from time is attached to eternity and then follows it swiftly and presses it closely, moving it with its doubts and unfolding it with its·revelations —this Middle Ages of Dante, just because it is all gathered in the movement of a spirit, can no longer become outmoded; it will always be, in one way or another, echoed in every age. It is possible always, in substance, for every age to receive into itself, one way or another, the spirit of Dante and to feel its perpetual presence; and on the other hand, it is necessary to refer in a certain sense from one's own age to those past times to enjoy the value of the expression of an attitude of the spirit, which can be enjoyed only in its particular flavor and which can not re-echo; it is necessary, in other words, to bring ourselves back to the age of Goldoni.

Goldoni's attitude was good-naturedly satirical: an expression of a wide-awake moral consciousness which remained intact and kept itself whole in reflecting those contingencies it could then satirize, with the satisfaction of feeling them overcome, yet unable to detach them from the spiritual limits of his own time; and hence the good-nature of this satire, which might appear superficial in a period of trial and fundamental upheaval of every established value.

Because of the frankness and transparency of his form, it is and always will be easy to go back to Goldoni, to feel alive, in the life of the representation offered by his spiritual attitude, the rapidity of his wit and the organic wholeness of life so observed and represented. All this is united in a form which, in truth, embalms it forever, together with the freshness and the gaiety of its own expressions, with the happiness of a spirit which created for the joy of creating. The way Goldoni expresses everything will always be a model of correct representation, so fluid and scintillating, so clear and quick, so careful and spontaneous and truly diverting. His propriety of style, not only in dialect, is absolute; nothing is ever said through approximation or in a way that may not be the most frank and savory, just as there is never in conception any emptiness or unbalance in feelings or intellect: conception, elaboration, and expression are exquisitely blended to create a graceful world. Grace, which is one of the most attractive and rarest qualities of human nature, finds in Goldoni its perfect expression, never attained before him; certainly it can not be reached again with such immediacy and in such fullness.

When this fresh expression of life burst on the mummified stage of the Italian theatre and restored to it breath, warmth, and movement, they spoke of a reform. It was the new theatre. Today, can we say that it is old theatre because the spiritual attitude from which it grew is in itself superseded by the change of values with the passing of time?

In art what was created new remains new forever. Goldoni had witty, lively eyes with which he saw anew and created the new.

Any new writer today who copies and does not create, that is, who wears glasses, although in the latest style, and claims that with them he sees the liveliest problems and newest values in his time, if he wears glasses, will copy and will create old theatre.

The new theatre and the old. It is always the same question: of eyes and eyeglasses; of the work of creation and the exercise of copying.

An ape was boasting to a fox, "Can you name an animal so clever and shrewd that I, if I wished, could not imitate?"

And the fox rejoined, "And can you name an animal foolish and stupid enough to want to imitate you?"

This is a little fable of Lessing's, composed at the time of the famous Silesian school led by Martin Opitz, when the German poets endeavored to imitate the graces of the Italian arcadians, bitterly complaining to the good God that they could not become the lap dogs of their ladies.

And as an epilogue to this fable (Lessing's, I repeat, and not mine) in the way of a moral, not for my contemporary playwrights of every land but for the German writers of the eighteenth century, there was the sarcasm of this request, "O authors of my nation, do I have to express myself more clearly?"

Translated by Herbert Goldstone

PREFACE TO *SIX CHARACTERS IN SEARCH OF AN AUTHOR*

It seems like yesterday but is actually many years ago that a nimble little maidservant entered the service of my art. However, she always comes fresh to the job.

She is called Fantasy.

A little puckish and malicious, if she likes to dress in black no one will wish to deny that she is often positively bizarre and no one will wish to believe that she always does everything in the same way and in earnest. She sticks her hand in her pocket, pulls out a cap and bells, sets it on her head, red as a cock's comb, and dashes away. Here today, there tomorrow. And she amuses herself by bringing to my house—since I derive stories and novels and plays from them—the most disgruntled tribe in the world, men, women, children, involved in strange adventures which they can find no way out of; thwarted in their plans; cheated in their hopes; with whom, in short, it is often torture to deal.

Well, this little maidservant of mine, Fantasy, several years ago, had the bad inspiration or ill-omened caprice to bring a family into my house. I wouldn't know where she fished them up or how, but, according to her, I could find in them the subject for a magnificent novel.

I found before me a man about fifty years old, in a dark jacket and light trousers, with a frowning air and ill-natured, mortified eyes; a poor woman in widow's weeds leading by one hand a little girl of four and by the other a boy of rather more than ten; a cheeky and "sexy" girl, also clad in black but with an equivocal and brazen pomp, all atremble with a lively, biting contempt for the mortified old man and for a young fellow of twenty who stood on one side closed in on himself as if he despised them all. In short, the six characters who are seen coming on stage at the beginning of the play. Now one of them and now another—often beating down one another—embarked on the sad story of their adventures, each shouting his own reasons, and projecting in my face his disordered passions, more or less as they do in the play to the unhappy Manager.

What author will be able to say how and why a character was born in his fantasy? The mystery of artistic creation is the same as that of birth. A woman who loves may desire to become a mother; but the desire by itself, however intense, cannot suffice. One fine day she will find herself a mother without having any precise intimation when it began. In the same way an artist imbibes very many germs of life and can never say how and why, at a certain moment, one of these vital germs inserts itself into his fantasy, there to become a living creature on a plane of life superior to the changeable existence of every day.

I can only say that, without having made any effort to seek them out, I found before me, alive—you could touch them and even hear them breathe—the six characters now seen on the stage. And they stayed there in my presence, each with his secret torment and all bound together by the one common origin and mutual entanglement of their affairs, while I had them enter the world of art, constructing from their persons, their passions, and their adventures a novel, a drama, or at least a story.

Born alive, they wished to live.

To me it was never enough to present a man or a woman and what is special and characteristic about them simply for the pleasure of presenting them; to narrate a particular affair, lively or sad, simply for the pleasure of narrating it; to describe a landscape simply for the pleasure of describing it.

There are some writers (and not a few) who do feel this pleasure and, satisfied, ask no more. They are, to speak more precisely, historical writers.

But there are others who, beyond such pleasure, feel a more profound spiritual need on whose account they admit only figures, affairs, landscapes which have been soaked, so to speak, in a particular sense of life and acquire from it a universal value. These are, more precisely, philosophical writers.

I have the misfortune to belong to these last.

I hate symbolic art in which the presentation loses all spontaneous movement in order to become a machine, an allegory—a vain and misconceived effort because the very fact of giving an allegorical sense to a presentation clearly shows that we have to do with a fable which by itself has no truth either fantastic or direct; it was made for the demonstration of some moral truth. The spiritual need I speak of cannot be satisfied—or seldom, and that to the end of a superior irony, as for example in Ariosto [1]—by such allegorical symbolism. This

---

[1] Ludovico Ariosto (1474–1532), Italian Renaissance poet, best known for his *Orlando Furioso.*

latter starts from a concept, and from a concept which creates or tries to create for itself an image. The former on the other hand seeks in the image—which must remain alive and free throughout—a meaning to give it value.

Now, however much I sought, I did not succeed in uncovering this meaning in the six characters. And I concluded therefore that it was no use making them live.

I thought to myself: "I have already afflicted my readers with hundreds and hundreds of stories. Why should I afflict them now by narrating the sad entanglements of these six unfortunates?"

And, thinking thus, I put them away from me. Or rather I did all I could to put them away.

But one doesn't give life to a character for nothing.

Creatures of my spirit, these six were already living a life which was their own and not mine any more, a life which it was not in my power any more to deny them.

Thus it is that while I persisted in desiring to drive them out of my spirit, they, as if completely detached from every narrative support, characters from a novel miraculously emerging from the pages of the book that contained them, went on living on their own, choosing certain moments of the day to reappear before me in the solitude of my study and coming— now one, now the other, now two together—to tempt me, to propose that I present or describe this scene or that, to explain the effects that could be secured with them, the new interest which a certain unusual situation could provide, and so forth.

For a moment I let myself be won over. And this condescension of mine, thus letting myself go for a while, was enough, because they drew from it a new increment of life, a greater degree of clarity and addition, consequently a greater degree of persuasive power over me. And thus as it became gradually harder and harder for me to go back and free myself from them, it became easier and easier for them to come back and tempt me. At a certain point I actually became obsessed with them. Until, all of a sudden, a way out of the difficulty flashed upon me.

"Why not," I said to myself, "present this highly strange fact of an author who refuses to let some of his characters live though they have been born in his fantasy, and the fact that these characters, having by now life in their veins, do not resign themselves to remaining excluded from the world of art? They are detached from me; live on their own; have acquired voice and movement; have by themselves—in this struggle for existence that they have had to wage with me—become dramatic characters, characters that can move and talk on their own initiative; already see themselves as such; have learned to defend themselves against me; will even know how to defend themselves against others. And so let them go where dramatic characters do go to have life: on a stage. And let us see what will happen."

That's what I did. And, naturally, the result was what it had to be: a mixture of tragic and comic, fantastic and realistic, in a humorous situation that was quite new and infinitely complex, a drama which is conveyed by means of the characters, who carry it within them and suffer it, a drama, breathing, speaking, self-propelled, which seeks at all costs to find the means of its own presentation; and the comedy of the vain attempt at an improvised realization of the drama on stage. First, the surprise of the poor actors in a theatrical company rehearsing a play by day on a bare stage (no scenery, no flats). Surprise and incredulity at the sight of the six characters announcing themselves as such in search of an author. Then, immediately afterward, through that sudden fainting fit of the Mother veiled in black, their instinctive interest in the drama of which they catch a glimpse in her and in the other members of the strange family, an obscure, ambiguous drama, coming about so unexpectedly on a stage that is empty and unprepared to receive it. And gradually the growth of this interest to the bursting forth of the contrasting passions of Father, of Stepdaughter, of Son, of that poor Mother, passions seeking, as I said, to overwhelm each other with a tragic, lacerating fury.

And here is the universal meaning at first vainly sought in the six characters, now that, going on stage of their own accord, they succeed in finding it within themselves in the excitement of the desperate struggle which each wages against the other and all wage against the Manager and the actors, who do not understand them.

Without wanting to, without knowing it, in the strife of their bedeviled souls, each of them, defending himself against the accusations of the others, expresses as his own living passion and torment the passion and torment which for so many years have been the pangs of my spirit: the deceit of mutual understanding irremediably founded on the empty abstraction of the words, the multiple personality of everyone corresponding to the possibilities of being to be found in each of us, and finally the inherent tragic conflict between life (which is always moving and changing) and form (which fixes it, immutable).

Two above all among the six characters, the Father and the Stepdaughter, speak of that outrageous unalterable fixity of their form in which he and she see their essential nature expressed permanently and immutably, a nature that for one means punishment and for the other revenge; and they defend it against the factitious affectations and unaware volatility of the actors, and they try to impose it on the vulgar Manager who would like to change it and adapt it to the so-called exigencies of the theatre.

If the six characters don't all seem to exist on the same plane, it is not because some are figures of first rank and others of the second, that is, some are main characters and others minor ones—the elementary perspective necessary to all scenic or narrative art—nor is it that any are not completely created—for their purpose. They are all six at the same point of artistic realization and on the same level of reality, which is the fantastic level of the whole play. Except that the Father, the Stepdaughter, and also the Son are realized as mind; the Mother as nature; the Boy as a presence watching and performing a gesture and the Baby unaware of it all. This fact creates among them a perspective of a new sort. Unconsciously I had had the impression that some of them needed to be fully realized (artistically speaking), others less so, and others merely sketched in as elements in a narrative or presentational sequence: the most alive, the most completely created, are the Father and the Stepdaughter who naturally stand out more and lead the way, dragging themselves along beside the almost dead weight of the others—first, the Son, holding back; second, the Mother, like a victim resigned to her fate, between the two children who have hardly any substance beyond their appearance and who need to be led by the hand.

And actually! actually they had each other to appear in that stage of creation which they had attained in the author's fantasy at the moment when he wished to drive them away.

If I now think about these things, about having intuited that necessity, having unconsciously found the way to resolve it by means of a new perspective, and about the way in which I actually obtained it, they seem like miracles. The fact is that the play was really conceived in one of those spontaneous illuminations of the fantasy when by a miracle all the elements of the mind answer to each other's call and work in divine accord. No human brain, working "in the cold," however stirred up it might be, could ever have succeeded in penetrating far enough, could ever have been in a position to satisfy all the exigencies of the play's form. Therefore the reasons which I will give to clarify the values of the play must not be thought of as intentions that I conceived beforehand when I prepared myself for the job and which I now undertake to defend, but only as discoveries which I have been able to make afterward in tranquillity.

I wanted to present six characters seeking an author. Their play does not manage to get presented—precisely because the author whom they seek is missing. Instead is presented the comedy of their vain attempt with all that it contains of tragedy by virtue of the fact that the six characters have been rejected.

But can one present a character while rejecting him? Obviously, to present him one needs, on the contrary, to receive him into one's fantasy before one can express him. And I have actually accepted and realized the six characters: I have, however, accepted and realized them as rejected: in search of *another* author.

What have I rejected of them? Not themselves, obviously, but their drama, which doubtless is what interests them above all but which did not interest me—for the reasons already indicated.

And what is it, for a character—his drama?

Every creature of fantasy and art, in order to exist, must have his drama, that is, a drama in which he may be a character and for which he *is* a character. This drama is the character's *raison d'être,* his vital function, necessary for his existence.

In these six, then, I have accepted the "being" without the reason for being. I have taken the organism and entrusted to it, not its own proper function, but another more complex function into which its own function entered, if at all, only as a datum. A terrible and desperate situation especially for the two—Father and Stepdaughter—who more than the others crave life and more than the others feel themselves to be characters, that is, absolutely need a drama and therefore their own drama—the only one which they can envisage for themselves yet which meantime they see rejected: an "impossible" situation from which they feel they must escape at whatever cost; it is a matter of life and death. True, I have given them another *raison d'être,* another function: precisely that "impossible" situation, the drama of being in search of an author and rejected. But that this should be a *raison d'être,* that it should have become their real function, that it should be necessary, that it should suffice, they can hardly suppose; for they have a life of their own. If someone were to tell them, they wouldn't believe him. It is not possible to believe that the sole reason for our living should lie in a torment that seems to us unjust and inexplicable.

I cannot imagine, therefore, why the charge was brought against me that the character of the Father was not what it should have been because it stepped out of its quality and position as a character and invaded at times the author's province and took it over. I who understand those who don't quite understand me see that the charge derives from the fact that the character expresses and makes his own a torment of spirit which is recognized as mine. This is entirely natural but of absolutely no significance. Aside from the fact that this torment of spirit in the character of the Father derives from causes, and is suffered and lived for reasons that have nothing to do with the drama of my personal experience, a fact which alone removes all substance from the criticism, I want to make it clear that the inherent torment of my spirit is one thing, a torment which I can legitimately—provided that it be organic —reflect in a character, and that the activity of my spirit as revealed in the realized work, the activity that succeeds in forming a drama out of the six characters in search of an author is another thing. If the Father participated in this latter activity, if he competed in forming the drama of the six characters without an author, then and only then would it by all means be justified to say that he was at times the author himself and therefore not the man he should be. But the Father suffers and does not create his existence as a character in search of an author. He suffers it as an inexplicable fatality and as a situation which he tries with all his powers to rebel against, which he tries to remedy; hence it is that he is a character in search of an author and nothing more, even if he expresses as his own the torment of my spirit. If he, so to speak, assumed some of the author's responsibilities, the fatality would be completely explained. He would, that is to say, see himself accepted, if only as a rejected character, accepted in the poet's heart of hearts, and he would no longer have any reason to suffer the despair of not finding someone to construct and affirm his life as a character. I mean that he would quite willingly accept the *raison d'être* which the author gives him and without regrets would forgo his own, throwing over the Manager and the actors to whom in fact he runs as his only recourse.

There is one character, that of the Mother, who on the other hand does not care about being alive (considering being alive as an end in itself). She hasn't the least suspicion that she is *not* alive. It has never occurred to her to ask how and why and in what manner she lives. In short, she is not aware of being a character inasmuch as she is never, even for a moment, detached from her role. She doesn't know she has a role.

This makes her perfectly organic. Indeed, her role of Mother does not of itself, in its natural essence, embrace mental activity. And she does not exist as a mind. She lives in an endless continuum of feeling, and therefore she cannot acquire awareness of her life—that is, of her existence as a character. But with all this, even she, in her own way and for her own ends, seeks an author, and at a certain stage seems happy to have been brought before the Manager. Because she hopes to take life from him, perhaps? No: because she hopes the manager will have her present a scene with the Son in which she would put so much of her own life. But it is a scene which does not exist, which never has and never could take place. So unaware is she of being a character, that is, of the life that is possible to her, all fixed and determined, moment by moment, in every action, every phrase.

She appears on stage with the other characters but without understanding what the others make her do. Obviously, she imagines that the itch for life with which the husband and the daughter are afflicted and for which she herself is to be found on stage is no more than one of the usual incomprehensible extravagances of this man who is both tortured and torturer and—horrible, most horrible—a new equivocal rebellion on the part of that poor erring girl. The Mother is completely passive. The events of her own life and the values they assume in her eyes, her very character, are all things which are "said" by the others and which she only once contradicts, and that because the maternal instinct rises up and rebels within her to make it clear that she didn't at all wish to abandon either the son or the husband: the son was taken from her and the husband forced her to abandon him. She is only correcting data; she explains and knows nothing.

In short, she is nature. Nature fixed in the figure of a mother.

This character gave me a satisfaction of a new sort, not to be ignored. Nearly all my critics, instead of defining her, after their habit, as "unhuman"—which seems to be the peculiar and incorrigible characteristic of all my creatures without exception—had the goodness to note "with real pleasure" that at last a *very human* figure had emerged from my fantasy. I explain this praise to myself in the following way: since my poor Mother is entirely limited to the natural attitude of a Mother with no possibility of free mental activity, being, that is, little more than a lump of flesh completely alive in all its functions—procreation, lactation, caring for and loving its young—without any need therefore of exercising her brain, she realizes in her person the true and complete "human type." That must be how it is, since in a human organism nothing seems more superfluous than the mind.

But the critics have tried to get rid of the Mother with this praise without bothering to penetrate the nucleus of poetic values which the character in the play represents. A very human figure, certainly, because mindless, that is, unaware of being what she is or not caring to explain it to herself. But not knowing that she is a character doesn't prevent her from being one. That is her drama in my play. And the most living expression of it comes spurting out in her cry to the Manager, who wants her to think all these things have happened already and therefore cannot now be a reason for renewed lamentations: "No, it's happening now, it's happening always! My torture is not a pretense, signore! I am alive and present, always, in every moment of my torture: it is renewed, alive, and present always!" This she *feels,* without being conscious of it, and feels it therefore as something inexplicable: but she feels it so terribly that she doesn't think it *can* be something to explain either to herself or to others. She feels it and that is that. She feels it as pain and this pain is immediate; she cries it out. Thus she reflects the growing fixity of life in a form—the same thing, which in another way, tortures the Father and the Stepdaughter. In them, mind. In her, nature. The mind rebels and, as best it may, seeks an advantage; nature, if not aroused by sensory stimuli, weeps.

Conflict between life-in-movement and form is the inexorable condition not only of the mental but also of the physical order. The life which in order to exist has become fixed in our corporeal form little by little kills that form. The tears of a nature thus fixed lament the irreparable, continuous aging of our bodies. Hence the tears of the Mother are passive and perpetual. Revealed in three faces, made significant in three distinct and simultaneous dramas, this inherent conflict finds in the play its most complete expression. More: the Mother declares also the particular value of artistic form—a form which does not delimit or de-

stroy its own life and which life does not consume—in her cry to the Manager. If the Father and Stepdaughter began their scene a hundred thousand times in succession, always, at the appointed moment, at the instant when the life of the work of art must be expressed with that cry, it would always be heard, unaltered and unalterable in its form, not as a mechanical repetition, not as a return determined by external necessities, but, on the contrary, alive every time and as new, suddenly born *thus forever!* embalmed alive in its incorruptible form. Hence, always, as we open the book, we shall find Francesca alive and confessing to Dante her sweet sin, and if we turn to the passage a hundred thousand times in succession, a hundred thousand times in succession Francesca [2] will speak her words, never repeating them mechanically, but saying them as though each time were the first time with such living and sudden passion that Dante every time will turn faint. All that lives, by the fact of living, has a form, and by the same token must die—except the work of art which lives forever in so far as it *is* form.

The birth of a creature of human fantasy, a birth which is a step across the threshold between nothing and eternity, can also happen suddenly, occasioned by some necessity. An imagined drama needs a character who does or says a certain necessary thing; accordingly this character is born and is precisely what he had to be. In this way Madame Pace is born among the six characters and seems a miracle, even a trick, realistically portrayed on the stage. It is no trick. The birth is real. The new character is alive not because she was alive already but because she is now happily born as is required by the fact of her being a character— she is obliged to be as she is. There is a break here, a sudden change in the level of reality of the scene, because a character can be born in this way only in the poet's fancy and not on the boards of a stage. Without anyone's noticing it, I have all of a sudden changed the scene: I have gathered it up again into my own fantasy without removing it from the spectator's eyes. That is, I have shown them, instead of the stage, my own fantasy in the act of creating—my own fantasy in the form of this same stage. The sudden and uncontrollable changing of a visual phenomenon from one level of reality to another is a miracle comparable to those of the saint who sets his own statue in motion: it is neither wood nor stone at such a moment. But the miracle is not

----

[2] Francesca da Rimini, heroine of the tragic tale of illicit love recorded in Dante's *Inferno*.

arbitrary. The stage—a stage which accepts the fantastic reality of the six characters—is no fixed, immutable datum. Nothing in this play exists as given and preconceived. Everything is in the making, is in motion, is a sudden experiment: even the place in which this unformed life, reaching after its own form, changes and changes again, contrives to shift position organically. The level of reality changes. When I had the idea of bringing Madame Pace to birth right there on the stage, I felt I could do it and I did it. Had I noticed that this birth was unhinging and silently, unnoticed, in a second, giving another shape, another reality to my scene, I certainly wouldn't have brought it about. I would have been afraid of the apparent lack of logic. And I would have committed an ill-omened assault on the beauty of my work. The fervor of my mind saved me from doing so. For, despite appearances, with their specious logic, this fantastic birth is sustained by a real necessity in mysterious, organic relation with the whole life of the work.

That someone now tells me it hasn't all the value it could have because its expression is not constructed but chaotic, because it smacks of romanticism, makes me smile.

I understand why this observation was made to me: because in this work of mine the presentation of the drama in which the six characters are involved appears tumultuous and never proceeds in an orderly manner. There is no logical development, no concatenation of the events. Very true. Had I hunted it with a lamp I couldn't have found a more disordered, crazy, arbitrary, complicated, in short, romantic way of presenting "the drama in which the six characters are involved." Very true. But I have not presented that drama. I have presented another—and I won't undertake to say again what!—in which, among the many fine things that everyone, according to his tastes, can find, there is a discreet satire on romantic procedures: in the six characters thus excited to the point where they stifle themselves in the roles which each of them plays in a certain drama while I present them as characters in another play which they don't know and don't suspect the existence of, so that this inflammation of their passions—which belongs to the realm of romantic procedures—is humorously "placed," located in the void. And the drama of the six characters presented not as it would have been organized by my fantasy had it been accepted but in this way, as a rejected drama, could not exist in the work except as a "situation," with some little development, and could not come

out except in indications, stormily, disorderedly, in violent foreshortenings, in a chaotic manner: continually interrupted, sidetracked, contradicted (by one of its characters), denied, and (by two others) not even seen.

There is a character indeed—he who denies the drama which makes him a character, the Son—who draws all his importance and value from being a character not of the comedy in the making—which as such hardly appears—but from the presentation that I made of it. In short, he is the only one who lives solely as "a character in search of an author"—inasmuch as the author he seeks is not a dramatic author. Even this could not be otherwise. The character's attitude is an organic product of my conception, and it is logical that in the situation it should produce greater confusion and disorder and another element of romantic contrast.

But I had precisely to *present* this organic and natural chaos. And to present a chaos is not at all to present chaotically, that is, romantically. That my presentation is the reverse of confused, that it is quite simple, clear, and orderly, is proved by the clarity which the intrigue, the characters, the fantastic and realistic, dramatic and comic levels of the work have had for every public in the world and by the way in which, for those with more searching vision, the unusual values enclosed within it come out.

Great is the confusion of tongues among men if criticisms thus made find words for their expression. No less great than this confusion is the intimate law of order which, obeyed in all points, makes this work of mine classical and typical and at its catastrophic close forbids the use of words. Though the audience eventually understands that one does not create life by artifice and that the drama of the six characters cannot be presented without an author to give them value with his spirit, the Manager remains vulgarly anxious to know how the thing turned out, and the "ending" is remembered by the Son in its sequence of actual moments, but without any sense and therefore not needing a human voice for its expression. It happens stupidly, uselessly, with the going off of a mechanical weapon on stage. It breaks up and disperses the sterile experiment of the characters and the actors, which has apparently been made without the assistance of the poet.

The poet, unknown to them, as if looking on at a distance during the whole period of the experiment, was at the same time busy creating—with it and of it—his own play.

Translated by Eric Bentley

SIX CHARACTERS IN SEARCH OF AN AUTHOR

Adapted by Paul Avila Mayer

CHARACTERS OF THE PLAY

FATHER
MOTHER
STEPDAUGHTER
SON
BOY (*nonspeaking*)
LITTLE GIRL (*nonspeaking*)

MEMBERS OF THE COMPANY

DIRECTOR
LEADING MAN
LEADING LADY
SECOND FEMALE LEAD
INGENUE
JUVENILE
OTHER ACTORS AND ACTRESSES
STAGE DOOR MAN
FIRST STAGE MANAGER
SECOND STAGE MANAGER
  (*prompter*)
STAGEHANDS

ACT ONE

DAYTIME. THE PRESENT. THE STAGE OF A
THEATRE
(N.B. *There are no acts or scenes in the play.
The performance will be interrupted twice,*

once when the DIRECTOR *and the* CHARACTERS
withdraw for a conference and the ACTORS
*take a "break," and a second time when a stage
hand lowers the curtain by mistake.*

*When the audience enters the theatre, the
curtain is up. The stage is empty and in semi-
darkness. Only one or two work lights provide
illumination. The atmosphere is that of an
empty theatre in which no play is being performed. And this is precisely right. For,
throughout the evening, the audience should
feel that it has stumbled onto a play that occurs
rather than that it is witnessing a carefully rehearsed performance.*

*To the left and right of the stage, temporary
rehearsal steps are in place leading down from
the stage into the orchestra section of the
theatre. On the stage are as many chairs and
tables as are required for the rehearsal which
is about to take place. Toward the rear of the
theatre, partially out of sight, is an old, upright piano.*

As the house lights dim, a STAGEHAND *enters
from the wings. He carries several pieces of
wood and some carpenter's tools. Crossing to
a position under one of the work lights, the*
STAGEHAND *begins to nail two of the pieces
of wood together. At the first sound of his hammering the* FIRST STAGE MANAGER *rushes in
from the wings. The* FIRST STAGE MANAGER
*carries a clip board holding various appro-
priate papers*)

FIRST STAGE MANAGER Hey! What do you
think you're doing?

STAGEHAND What's it look like? I'm nailing.

FIRST STAGE MANAGER (*looking at his watch*)
At this hour? Rehearsal's starting. The Director'll be here any minute.

STAGEHAND Well, let me tell you something. I've got to have time to do my work, too.

FIRST STAGE MANAGER You'll get it, but you
can't do this now.

STAGEHAND   Then when?

FIRST STAGE MANAGER   After the rehearsal. Now, come on. Get all this stuff out of here and let me set up. (*During the next few moments, mumbling and grumbling to himself, the* STAGEHAND *gathers up the pieces of wood and his tools, and exits; as he does so, the* FIRST STAGE MANAGER *moves to the center of the stage, calls off-stage*) O.K., Charlie, light 'em up. (*He looks up toward the lights; nothing happens*) Hey, Charlie! (*still nothing happens*) Charlie, are you deaf? Turn on the lights.

CHARLIE'S VOICE   (*off-stage*)   Sorry!

(*Immediately, one by one, the lights come on. After satisfying himself that all the lights are working, the* FIRST STAGE MANAGER *moves around the stage adjusting tables and chairs, preparing for the rehearsal which is about to take place.*

As he does so, the ACTORS *and* ACTRESSES *of the company enter. One at a time, then in groups of two and three, they straggle casually onto the stage. There are nine or ten of them in all, as many as would be required to perform Pirandello's "Rules of the Game." Their clothing is suitable for the weather outside of the theatre so that the audience feels that the* ACTORS, *too, have just entered the house. However, without exaggerating their costumes in any way, all of the* ACTORS *wear light colored, gay clothing which will be in sharp contrast to that worn by the* CHARACTERS *when they enter.*

During the short scene which precedes the entrance of the DIRECTOR, *the action is improvised. Various members of the company greet one another; some find seats; others remain standing; some smoke; three of the younger members of the company find their way to the piano where one plays while the other two move through a few simple steps; one member of the company reads aloud a short paragraph from a topical trade publication. The atmosphere is that of a natural and animated prelude to the rehearsal of a play.*

After a few moments, the action is interrupted by the entrance down the side aisle of the theatre of the SECOND STAGE MANAGER *and the* DIRECTOR. *As they near the stage, the* SECOND STAGE MANAGER *begins to clap his hands and call for attention*)

SECOND STAGE MANAGER   All right, let's go, let's go!

(*The music and the dancing stop; the* ACTORS *all move forward and gather at the center of the stage as the* SECOND STAGE MANAGER *and the* DIRECTOR *come up a set of temporary stairs onto the stage. The* DIRECTOR, *from his dress and manner, gives the impression of being a man of parts*)

DIRECTOR   Hello everybody.

(*The* ACTORS *ad lib greeting without referring to the time of day; as they do so, the* DIRECTOR *turns to the* FIRST STAGE MANAGER)

DIRECTOR   (*continues*)   John, have you got the props?

FIRST STAGE MANAGER   They're backstage. Do you want any now?

DIRECTOR   Later. (*to the* ACTORS; *briskly*) Well suppose we get started. (*noticing a gesture from the* FIRST STAGE MANAGER) Hello! Someone missing?

FIRST STAGE MANAGER   Our leading lady.

DIRECTOR   Again! (*looking at his watch; after a momentary hesitation*) We're ten minutes late already. We'll begin without her. But let me know the minute she gets here. I'll have a few things to . . .

LEADING LADY   (*rushing down the center aisle; carrying a small dog*) No, no, for heaven's sake, I'm here! I'm here! (*breathlessly*) I'm so sorry! I couldn't get a taxi! (*coming up a set of temporary steps onto the stage*) Anyway you haven't started yet, and besides, I'm not even in the first scene. (*handing the small dog to the* FIRST STAGE MANAGER) Tie him near a radiator, won't you, sweetie?

(*The* FIRST STAGE MANAGER *exits with the dog*)

DIRECTOR   Must you bring that . . . oh, never mind! (*to the* ACTORS; *more businesslike*) Come on, let's go. Act One of "Rules of the Game." Places, please.

(*Some of the* ACTORS *retire to the side of the stage; others take up "places" in the playing area; the* LEADING LADY, *however, ignoring the others, moves to the front of the stage and practices striking several different dramatic poses; the* DIRECTOR *turns to her*)

DIRECTOR   (*continues*)   Am I to understand you now think you're in this scene?

LEADING LADY   What? Good heavens, you know very well I'm not! (*Crossing to a chair, she sits, sulking*)

SECOND STAGE MANAGER   (*reading from the "book" as the* LEADING LADY *seats herself*) "The house of Leo Gallant. An unusual room being used both as a dining room and a study. In the center of the room a large table is laid. Nearby, a writing desk is covered with books and papers. The decor throughout is luxurious. There are three exits: stage rear, a door leading into Leo's bedroom; stage left, a door leading into the kitchen; stage right, the main exit."

DIRECTOR Pay attention, please. (*pointing to the areas where the various exits will be*) There's the main exit, there's the bedroom, and there's the kitchen. (*to the* LEADING MAN) You'll exit, of course, into the kitchen.

SECOND STAGE MANAGER "Scene One": (*He hesitates, looks up from the "book"*) Do you want me to go on reading the stage directions?

DIRECTOR (*impatiently*) Yes, yes, go on.

SECOND STAGE MANAGER (*reading*) "When the curtain rises, Leo Gallant, dressed in a cook's hat and apron, is busy beating an egg in a bowl. Phillip . . ."

LEADING MAN (*interupting; to the* DIRECTOR) Excuse me but is it really necessary for me to wear a cook's hat?

DIRECTOR (*annoyed; pointing to the "book"*) That's what it says.

LEADING MAN But I'll look ridiculous!

DIRECTOR Ridiculous? Of course you'll look ridiculous. What do you expect me to do about it? Is it my fault that . . . (*He names a popular play of the day*). . . was cancelled? Can I help it if things are in such a muddle that we're reduced to reviving a play of Pirandello's which no one understood when it was written and which makes even less sense today?

(*Some of the* ACTORS *laugh; the* DIRECTOR *crosses slowly toward the* LEADING MAN; *during the next few moments, off-stage voices are heard, raised in argument*)

DIRECTOR (*continues*) You *will* wear a cook's hat! And you will beat an egg! But do you think for one minute that you're just a man on stage beating an egg? You are not! You represent the shell of the egg you are beating!

(*Several of the* ACTORS *laugh or comment at this; the* DIRECTOR *glares about him*)

DIRECTOR (*continues*) Be quiet and listen to me! This is important! (*to the* LEADING MAN) The shell of the egg stands for reason; its contents for instinct. You are an empty eggshell, without instinct, and therefore blind. In "The Rules of the Game" you represent reason and your wife represents instinct. Each of you is incomplete. Each of you becomes a puppet presentation of yourself rather than a whole person. Do you understand?

LEADING MAN I most certainly do not.

DIRECTOR Neither do I. But let's get on; it's going to be a great flop anyway! All right . . .

(*As the* DIRECTOR *turns toward the* SECOND STAGE MANAGER, *he sees the* STAGE DOOR MAN *backing onto the stage; he throws his hands in the air*)

DIRECTOR (*continues*) Now what?

(*Embarrassed, the* STAGE DOOR MAN *hurries forward in a most apologetic manner. The* SIX CHARACTERS *enter immediately after him*)

The FATHER *is in his late forties, a pale man with reddish hair thinning at the temples. He wears a moustache. His mouth is large and sensuous. The* FATHER *is dressed conservatively in a jacket and trousers. His manner varies between two extremes. He is either relaxed and quite charming, or rough and almost violent.*

The MOTHER *is in her early forties, a small, weary woman. She seems thoroughly defeated by life, as if she has been overwhelmed by some dreadful disgrace. She is dressed in mourning and when her veil is lifted we will see a chalk white, wax-like face. Her eyes are almost always downcast.*

The STEPDAUGHTER *is dashing and impudent. She is very beautiful. She, too, wears mourning but with great elegance. Her attitude toward the* BOY—*who is 14, a frightened, dejected figure, also dressed in mourning—is one of contempt; on the other hand, she displays the greatest tenderness and affection for the* LITTLE GIRL. *About 4 years old, the* LITTLE GIRL *wears a white dress with a black sash at the waist.*

The SON *is 22, tall, severe in manner. He treats his* FATHER *with resentment and his* MOTHER *with superciliousness and indifference. He is dressed properly, conservatively, but is clearly not in mourning*)

STAGE DOOR MAN (*to the* DIRECTOR) Mister, I'm sorry, but . . . (*He hesitates*)

DIRECTOR (*roughly*) Yes, yes, what is it?

STAGE DOOR MAN These people, they say they gotta see you.

(*He shrugs hopelessly as the* DIRECTOR *and the* ACTORS *turn in surprise toward the* SIX CHARACTERS)

DIRECTOR But I'm in rehearsal! (*to the* SIX CHARACTERS; *impatiently*) Who are you? What do you want?

(*The* FATHER *comes forward, half followed by the others; the* STAGE DOOR MAN *lingers for a moment, then turns and exits quietly*)

FATHER (*coming forward*) We are here in search of an author.

DIRECTOR An author? What author?

FATHER Any author.

DIRECTOR (*waving them away toward the wings*) I'm very sorry, there's no author here. We're not doing a new play.

STEPDAUGHTER (*coming forward a step; vivaciously*) So much the better. Then we can be your new play.

JUVENILE (*as the other* ACTORS *murmur among themselves*) Well, listen to her!

FATHER (*momentarily stymied; to the* STEP-DAUGHTER) If there is no author here . . . (*turning back to the* DIRECTOR; *hopefully*) . . . perhaps you would be our author . . .

DIRECTOR Are you trying to be funny? I told you before . . .

(*Again he gestures toward the wings, indicating that they should leave*)

FATHER (*instantly; tensely*) Oh, please, don't say that. No, not funny. Never funny. We have come to bring you a play, a terrible play of suffering and anguish.

STEPDAUGHTER If we're a hit, we might make your fortune for you.

DIRECTOR I'm sorry but you've got to get out of here. We've no time to waste on lunatics.

FATHER Why do you jump to conclusions? You know very well that life is full of infinite absurdities, absurdities which do not need to *seem* true simply because they *are* true.

DIRECTOR What the devil are you talking about?

FATHER I am saying that when the ordinary order of things is reversed, people often cry out of madness. For example, when we labor to create things which have all the appearance of reality that they may pass for reality itself. But if this is madness, it is also the very essence of your profession, is it not?

(*Some of the* ACTORS *grumble a little among themselves at this suggestion*)

DIRECTOR Then the theatre is full of madmen, is that what you're saying?

FATHER Making what isn't true seem true . . . for fun . . . Isn't that your purpose, bringing imaginary characters to life?

DIRECTOR (*speaking for the entire company*) I think that you should understand that those of us in the theatre feel it is a creative art, and a very worthwhile occupation. If our playwrights, in recent years, have only given us commercial plays to perform, I'll have you know that we are proud also to have given life, on this very stage, to immortal works.

(*Some of the* ACTORS *nod in approval and applaud these words*)

FATHER (*immediately*) Yes! Exactly! To living beings more alive than those who breathe and wear clothes. Less real, perhaps, but more true. We are in complete agreement.

DIRECTOR (*as some of the* ACTORS *look astonished*) Wait a minute! You've lost me. You said before. . . .

FATHER I spoke only because you said you had no time to waste with lunatics. Surely no one knows better than you that nature uses the instrument of human fantasy to unfold her creative work at the highest level.

DIRECTOR (*completely lost*) What is all this? Where does all this get us?

FATHER It's quite simple if you'll only try to understand. You were born as man. But one can be born in other ways . . . as a tree . . . or a stone . . . as water . . . or a butterfly . . . (*gesturing to include himself and the other* CHARACTERS) . . . or even as a character in a play.

DIRECTOR (*suddenly understanding; amused and ironical*) And you and your friends were born as characters?

FATHER Exactly! Alive, just as you see us here! (*Several of the* ACTORS *laugh at this; the* FATHER *looks pained*) I wish you wouldn't laugh at us. Because, as I said before, we carry such suffering and horror within us . . . (*He half turns toward the* MOTHER) . . . as you should have guessed from this woman who is, as you can see, dressed in mourning.

(*Saying this, the* FATHER *extends his hand and leads the* MOTHER *toward the center of the stage. She crosses toward him in a solemn and tragic manner. As she does so, the* BOY *and the* LITTLE GIRL *move solemnly with her. The* SON, *however, turns and moves upstage, away from the other* CHARACTERS. *The* STEPDAUGHTER *moves downstage where she leans in a provocative pose against a proscenium arch. All of these movements are performed simultaneously with a unified rhythm and solemnity which first astonishes the* ACTORS, *then causes them to break into applause, as if for a performance being presented for their benefit*)

DIRECTOR (*open-mouthed for a moment; then angry*) Wait a minute! (*to the* ACTORS) Be quiet, all of you! (*to the* CHARACTERS) This has gone far enough. I've told you, I'm busy! (*to the* FIRST STAGE MANAGER) For God's sake, get them out of here!

FIRST STAGE MANAGER (*to the* CHARACTERS) All right, now you've got to leave. Please. Come on, let's go, let's go.

FATHER But no, look, we . . .

DIRECTOR (*shouting*) Don't you understand? I'm in rehearsal! Write me a letter!

LEADING MAN We don't have time for practical jokes!

FATHER (*quietly; as if astonished*) You don't believe us. I know it's difficult, but . . . (*coming forward; with determination*) . . . surely, in your profession, you're accustomed to seeing the characters created by an author spring to life in yourselves here on the stage, every night? Or is it, perhaps, that there is no script . . . (*He points toward the "book"*) . . . there that contains us?

STEPDAUGHTER (*moving forward; to the DI-RECTOR; coquettishly*) We are really six most interesting characters . . . but lost, somehow . . .

FATHER (*brushing her aside*) Yes, that's it exactly. (*to the DIRECTOR*) You see, the author who created us was never able to finish his play. And this was really a crime. Because anyone fortunate enough to be born a character . . . why, he can laugh at death. A man must always die; even an author must always die; but a character lives forever. And without having to have extraordinary gifts or accomplishments. Who was Sancho Panza? Who were the Three Musketeers? Yet they will live forever because like seeds fallen into rich soil they were fortunate enough to find a fertile fantasy which raised them, nourished them, and gave them eternal life.

DIRECTOR (*more weary than impatient*) Yes, yes, but what is it you want here?

FATHER (*passionately*) We want to live!

DIRECTOR (*sardonic*) Through all eternity?

FATHER Oh, no. Just for a moment . . . in you.

CHARACTER LADY How extraordinary!

LEADING LADY They want to live in us?

JUVENILE (*indicating the STEPDAUGHTER*) That's all right with me . . . as far as she's concerned.

FATHER You must give us a chance! Our play is here for the making! (*to the DIRECTOR and the ACTORS*) If you and your actors are willing, we can work it up among ourselves, very quickly.

DIRECTOR Work what up? We're not here to do improvisations. We're here to do legitimate plays.

FATHER Exactly! And that's why we came to you, to do our play!

DIRECTOR But there's no script!

FATHER The script is inside us! (*Some of the ACTORS laugh*) Don't you see? We *are* the script! We *are* the drama! And our passions are so strong that they are forcing us to cry out to you to let us play it!

STEPDAUGHTER (*sneering, impudent, shameless*) Yes, my passion! Ah, if you only knew! My passion . . . for him!

(*The STEPDAUGHTER points to the FATHER and moves forward as if to embrace him; when he flinches and moves away from her, she breaks into loud scornful laughter*)

FATHER (*shouting*) Stop it! Stop that laughing! We've had enough of you! I forbid you to speak!

STEPDAUGHTER Oh, you do! (*turning to the ACTORS*) Then perhaps you'll permit me, ladies and gentlemen. Let me show you how I, who have been an orphan for only two months, can dance and sing. (*With a malicious mischievousness, she sings and dances for a moment; her song is an animated and slightly suggestive French love song. While she is singing and dancing, several of the younger ACTORS raise their arms toward her, as if to join her in her dance. She moves away from them, however, in each instance. When she finishes her song, the ACTORS break into applause. When the DIRECTOR rebukes her, the STEPDAUGHTER stands quietly where she is, without moving, as if her thoughts were far away*)

ACTORS (*laughing and clapping*) Bravo! Very good!

DIRECTOR (*angry*) Be quiet, all of you! (*to the STEPDAUGHTER*) What do you think this is, a nightclub? (*to the FATHER, lowering his voice slightly*) What's the matter with her? Is she crazy?

FATHER No. It's worse than that.

STEPDAUGHTER (*running lightly to the DIRECTOR*) Yes, worse! Far worse! Oh, won't you let us play it for you? Then you'll see that . . . (*turning to the LITTLE GIRL; leading her to the DIRECTOR*) . . . when this little angel here . . . isn't she beautiful? . . . (*picking up the child and kissing her*) . . . you darling, you darling . . . (*putting the child down, adding, almost involuntarily but with great feeling*) . . . well, when God suddenly takes this dear little child away from her poor mother, and this imbecile . . . (*She seizes the BOY and drags him forward*) . . . does the stupidest of all stupid things, like the idiot he is . . . (*She pushes the BOY roughly back toward the MOTHER*) . . . then you'll see me run away. Yes, I'll run away and you'll be rid of me. Not now, but believe me, soon enough. After all that has happened between him and me . . . (*She indicates the FATHER with a leering wink*) . . . I can't stay here any longer, watching the misery of my mother because of that! (*Spitting out the last word, she whirls and points to the SON*) Look at him! Just look at him! So cold . . . aloof . . . superior . . . because he's the legitimate son. He despises me, he despises him . . . (*She points to the BOY, then to the LITTLE GIRL*) . . . he even despises the baby there, because we're bastards! Do you understand? We're bastards! (*crossing to the MOTHER, embracing her*) And he won't even recognize his own mother, this poor woman who is the mother of us all. He treats her with contempt, as if she were only the mother . . . of us three. (*All of this has been spoken in great excitement; now she turns and softly spits out two words at the* SON) You swine!

MOTHER (*to the* DIRECTOR; *in anguish*) Please . . . for the children's sake . . . I beg you . . . (*She sways on her feet, begins to faint*) Ah! My God!

FATHER (*running to support her; as the* ACTORS *look on in consternation*) A chair! Bring the poor widow a chair!

OLD CHARACTER MAN What's happened? Has she really fainted?

DIRECTOR (*to the* FIRST STAGE MANAGER *who is bringing a chair to the* MOTHER) Quickly! Quickly!

FATHER (*when the* MOTHER *is seated, the* FATHER *begins to lift her veil*) I want you to see her face.

MOTHER (*trying to prevent him from lifting her veil*) No, no! For God's sake, don't!

FATHER (*pushing her protesting hands aside*) Let them see you. (*He lifts the veil, revealing her chalk white, wax-like face*)

MOTHER (*rising; covering her face with her hands; to the* DIRECTOR; *in desperation*) Please, please . . . don't let him go on with this . . . it's too horrible!

DIRECTOR (*as the* MOTHER *sits down again; stunned*) I don't understand. (*to the* FATHER) This lady is your wife?

FATHER (*quickly*) Yes, my wife.

DIRECTOR But, if you are still alive, how can she be a widow?

(*Some of the* ACTORS *smile and laugh at this*)

FATHER (*hurt; sharply*) Don't laugh! For the love of Christ, don't laugh! This is her tragedy. She has had a lover, the man who rightfully should be here.

MOTHER (*with a cry*) No! No!

STEPDAUGHTER He has the good luck to be dead. He died two months ago which is why we are still in mourning.

FATHER But the reason he isn't here is not because he is dead. Just look at her. Surely you can see that her story isn't in the love of two men . . . two men for whom she was incapable of feeling anything, except possibly a little gratitude—for him, not for me. No, her story, her tragedy is in the children, the four children she had by these two men.

MOTHER Did you say I had these two men? Had you the nerve to suggest I wanted them? (*to the* DIRECTOR; *pointing to the* FATHER) It was his doing! He forced me to go away with the other man!

STEPDAUGHTER (*immediately; indignantly*) That isn't so!

MOTHER (*amazed*) It isn't?

STEPDAUGHTER It isn't so! It isn't!

MOTHER What do you know about it?

STEPDAUGHTER I know! (*to the* DIRECTOR) You mustn't believe her! Don't you realize why she's saying it? Because of him! (*She points to the* SON) She's torturing herself, destroying herself, because of that son of hers, because of his indifference. She wants to make him believe that if she left him when he was two years old, it was because he . . . (*She points to the* FATHER) . . . made her do it!

MOTHER (*vigorously*) But he did make me! As God is my witness, he did! (*to the* DIRECTOR; *pointing to the* FATHER) Ask him! Ask him if he didn't! (*to the* STEPDAUGHTER) You don't know anything about it.

STEPDAUGHTER (*quietly*) I know that you were happy with my father, that you lived together in peace and contentment. I know that you used to sing. Can you deny it?

MOTHER (*shaking her head*) I don't deny it.

STEPDAUGHTER He loved you. He loved you every day of his life. (*to the* BOY) Isn't it true? Go on—tell them! Why don't you say something, you little fool?

MOTHER Leave the poor child alone. Why do you want to make me seem ungrateful? I don't want to say anything against your father. But can't you understand it wasn't my fault? I didn't want to leave my baby; I didn't want to leave my home.

FATHER What she says is true. It was my doing.

LEADING MAN My God! What a show!

LEADING LADY And we're the audience this time.

JUVENILE For a change.

DIRECTOR (*more interested*) Let's hear what they have to say. (*He moves downstage, then faces up toward the* CHARACTERS)

SON (*without moving; slow, cool, ironical in tone*) Oh, yes! Now you'll hear a fine piece of philosophy. He's going to tell you about the "demon of experiment."

FATHER (*to the* SON) What a cynical idiot you are. (*to the* DIRECTOR) He mocks me because of this expression which I use in my own defense.

SON (*contemptuously*) Words! Words!

FATHER Yes!! Words!! Words that bring consolation . . . to all of us . . . when we are faced with something so horrible, when we must live with such guilt . . . words that say nothing but bring peace.

STEPDAUGHTER (*contemptuously*) And dull your sense of remorse! That above all!

FATHER (*quickly*) I have eased my remorse with far more than words!!

STEPDAUGHTER Oh, yes! There was a little bit of money, too! (*to the* ACTORS; *swinging her body sensuously*) The money he offered me in payment, ladies and gentlemen.

(*There is a sensation of horror among the* ACTORS)

SON (*to the* STEPDAUGHTER) My God, you're revolting!

STEPDAUGHTER (*innocently*) Revolting? But there it was, in a pale blue envelope, on the little mahogany table in the room provided by Madam Pace. (*to the* ACTORS) You understand about Madam Pace? One of those ladies who runs a very elegant dress shop, a very *special* dress shop where decent girls from poor families are led along, step-by-step, until . . . (*The* STEPDAUGHTER *throws a contemptuous glance at the* FATHER)

SON (*bitterly*) She thinks she's bought the right to lord it over all of us with that money he was going to pay her . . . but which, thank God . . . and I want to emphasize this . . . he had no reason to pay!

STEPDAUGHTER But it was a near thing, a very near thing indeed! (*She laughs*)

MOTHER (*rising; in protest*) Have you no shame?

STEPDAUGHTER (*in an outburst of anger*) Shame? This is my revenge! I am trembling with desire . . . to live that scene! I can see the room . . . here is the window . . . there the fireplace . . . the bed . . . and over here, in front of the window, the little mahogany table . . . and the pale blue envelope with the money inside. I can see it all so clearly. I have only to reach out and pick the money up. But you gentlemen should turn your backs, because I am almost naked. No, I don't blush any more; he's the one who does the blushing now. (*pointing to the* FATHER) How pale he was . . . and stammering . . . as he . . . (*She pauses; smiles*)

DIRECTOR (*in horror*) Just a minute . . .

FATHER Thank God! Put your foot down! All these accusations! You've got to let me explain!

STEPDAUGHTER This is no place for your lies!

FATHER (*to the* STEPDAUGHTER) I'm not going to . . . (*turning desperately to the* DIRECTOR) I only want to tell how it really was!

STEPDAUGHTER Oh, yes, of course you do! You want to tell it your way!

FATHER But don't you see this is the cause of the whole trouble? In the words, the very words we use. Each of us has inside him his own special world. And how can we ever really understand each other if I put into the words I speak the sense and value of things as I see them while whoever is listening inevitably translates them into the sense and value they have for him. We think we understand each other but we never really do. (*gesturing to include all of them*) Look at us here. (*pointing to the* MOTHER) All my pity, all the pity I feel for this poor woman she takes as a special form of terrible cruelty.

MOTHER (*a cry*) But you sent me away!

FATHER (*dispassionately*) There. Listen to her. I sent her away. She believes that.

MOTHER (*in a lowered voice*) You know how to talk. I . . . (*She hesitates, turns desperately to the* DIRECTOR) You must believe me. After he married me . . . who knows why . . . I was a poor, shy sort of girl . . .

FATHER (*interrupting; quickly*) But it was for just those qualities, the shyness, the humility, that I loved you. I married you for that very humility, believing . . . (*During this speech, the* MOTHER *has turned her head away from the* FATHER *and made a gesture of contradiction; seeing this, he stops, opens his arms wide in a gesture of hopelessness*) Ah! You see? She won't listen. It's frightening, this deafness . . . (*He taps his forehead*) . . . this mental deafness of hers. A good heart, yes, for the children, but the brain, deaf, a deafness which was my constant despair.

STEPDAUGHTER Oh, yes! Now ask him what good all his intellectuality, his celebrated mental abilities have done us?

FATHER (*quietly; with a touch of regret*) If we could only foresee the evil that may result from the good we think we are doing.

(*During the last few minutes, with ever-increasing anger the* LEADING LADY *has been watching the* LEADING MAN *flirting with the* STEPDAUGHTER. *Now, very annoyed, she steps forward toward the* DIRECTOR)

LEADING LADY I beg your pardon but are we going to rehearse today?

DIRECTOR In a little while. Let's hear them out.

JUVENILE Yes.

INGENUE I think it's fascinating.

LEADING LADY (*with a meaningful glance at the* LEADING MAN) If you like that sort of thing.

DIRECTOR But you must explain everything clearly.

FATHER   Very well. Now, look here. I had a poor, ineffectual man working for me—my assistant. Well, over a period of time, he became attached to her. (*He points to the* MOTHER) There was nothing wrong about it. Far from it. He was a good man, very modest and self-effacing, very much like her. The two of them were incapable of doing anything wrong, or even thinking it.

STEPDAUGHTER   So he thought it—for them —and then urged them on!

FATHER   That isn't true. I thought that what I was doing would be good for them, and I must confess for myself, as well. Things had come to the point that I couldn't say a word to either of them without their automatically exchanging a sympathetic glance. I could see them silently asking each other how to handle me, how to prevent me from getting angry. And this was enough, as I'm sure you understand, to keep me in a constant rage of intolerable exasperation.

DIRECTOR   Why didn't you fire your assistant?

FATHER   I did! But then I had to watch this poor woman wandering around the house like some forlorn lost animal, like one of those strays you take in out of pity.

MOTHER   (*protesting*)   But . . .

FATHER   (*turning on her; forestalling what she is about to say*)   The son. You want to tell him about the son, don't you?

MOTHER   He took my baby away from me!

FATHER   Not out of cruelty! I sent him away to the country so that he could grow up strong and healthy.

STEPDAUGHTER   And just look at him!

FATHER   Is it my fault he grew up that way? I sent him to live with good people who had a farm because she . . . (*He points to the* MOTHER) . . . didn't seem to be strong enough . . . although it was because of that very weakness, that humility that I married her in the first place. A mistake, perhaps, but what was I to do? I was a healthy young man with a young man's normal appetites. All my life I've sought to lead a life of solid morality.

(*The* STEPDAUGHTER *breaks into loud cynical laughter at this*)

FATHER   Stop it! Make her stop! She's driving me mad!

DIRECTOR   (*to the* STEPDAUGHTER)   Yes, for God's sake be quiet! Let him finish what he has to say!

(*At the* DIRECTOR's *rebuke, the* STEPDAUGHTER *is silent, a half smile on her lips; the* DIRECTOR *again moves downstage, facing up toward the* CHARACTERS)

FATHER   I couldn't go on living with her . . . (*He indicates the* MOTHER) . . . not so much because of the irritation she caused me, or the boredom, the awful boredom, but because of the guilt and pity I felt for her. She was so unhappy.

MOTHER   So he sent me away!

FATHER   (*instantly*)   But well provided for . . . to the other man . . . that she might be free of me.

MOTHER   And to free himself.

FATHER   (*nodding*)   I admit it. And a great deal of harm resulted. But I meant well, and I did it more for her sake than my own, I swear it! (*folding his arms; turning to the* MOTHER)   Didn't I keep track of you? Didn't I keep track of you until that fellow suddenly carried you off to another town, no forwarding address, nothing. Did I ever bother you? Wasn't I content to watch from a distance? I wanted to watch; certainly I did; but without any ulterior motives; simply out of pure interest. I just wanted to watch the incredibly tender family that was growing up around you. (*indicating the* STEPDAUGHTER)   She can testify to that.

STEPDAUGHTER   (*conveying a sordid innuendo in her tone*)   Oh, I most certainly can. When I was just a little girl . . . with braids down to my shoulders and panties you could see underneath my short skirt, I used to see him standing by the door of the school, waiting for me. He came to watch me, to see how I was growing up.

FATHER   This is monstrous!

STEPDAUGHTER   Oh? Why?

FATHER   Monstrous! Monstrous!!! (*turning to the* DIRECTOR *in excitement; then controlling himself and continuing in a conversational tone*)   After she went away . . . (*He indicates the* MOTHER) . . . my house seemed to be empty. She had been such a disappointment to me, but she had filled my house. Suddenly I was like a fly caught between a window and a screen. I—buzzed around in the emptiness . . . (*indicating the* SON)   The boy was educated away from home. When he came back to me I didn't know him. He didn't seem to be my son at all. With no mother to link him to me he grew up entirely on his own, quite apart from me. He had neither intellectual appreciation for me nor affection for me. So then, in a strange way, I found myself attracted to her . . . and her family. At first I simply wanted to see what had resulted from my efforts. Then the thought of her, and them, began to fill the emptiness I felt around me. I had to know that she was happy, and at peace. I wanted to think that she was fortunate because she was so far removed from the complicated torments of my spirit. And so, to have proof of this, I would go to see the little girl coming out of school.

STEPDAUGHTER   Oh, indeed he would! He used to follow me along the streets after school until I got home. He would smile at me and wave. I looked at him, not without interest, wondering who he was. I told my mother and she guessed immediately that it was him.

(*The* MOTHER *nods*)

STEPDAUGHTER   She didn't want me to see him and kept me home from school for several days. But when I did go back, there he was paper bag in his hand. He came up to me, put his arms around me and caressed me, and then he opened the paper bag and took out a beautiful big straw hat with flowers on it, a present for me.

DIRECTOR   We've wandered a bit from our story, haven't we?

SON   Yes! This is literature, literature!

FATHER   Literature indeed! This is life! Passion!

DIRECTOR   That may be, but it won't play.

FATHER (*quickly*)   I agree with you. This is only the background. I'm not suggesting that this part should be staged. As you can very well see . . . (*He indicates the* STEPDAUGHTER) . . . she is obviously no longer the little girl with braids down to her shoulders . . .

STEPDAUGHTER (*interrupting; again with a sordid innuendo in her tone*) . . . and pretty little flowered panties which you could see underneath my skirt . . .

FATHER (*instantly; desperately changing the subject*)   Now we come to the plot! New, complex . . .

STEPDAUGHTER (*coming forward; proud and gloomy*)   As soon as my father died . . .

FATHER (*interrupting; taking up the story*) . . . they fell into the most wretched poverty. They came back here and because of her stupidity . . . (*He indicates the* MOTHER) . . . I knew nothing about it. If she could not bring herself to get in touch with me, she might at least have asked her son or her daughter to let me know they were in need.

MOTHER (*to the* DIRECTOR)   How was I to know he felt this way?

FATHER   That was always your mistake, never to have understood any of my feelings.

MOTHER   After all those years, and all that had happened . . .

FATHER   Was it my fault you disappeared? (*to the* DIRECTOR) I tell you, one day they were here, the next they were gone. He'd found a job somewhere else and they vanished overnight. I could find no trace of them anywhere. So, naturally enough, as the years went on my interest in them dwindled. But after they returned, then the whole thing exploded violently and unexpectedly into . . . what else can I call it but melodrama? . . . when I was driven by the demands of my miserable flesh, which is still alive with desire . . . (*He pauses, turns passionately to the* DIRECTOR) Can you understand the guilt, the misery of a moral man, living alone, trying to divert himself with reading and music, and able to think of nothing but women? Do you know what it means to detest casual affairs and still be driven to them? Not to be old enough to do without a woman, or young enough to go and look for one without shame and loathing? Did I say misery? It's a horror! Knowing, all the time, that no woman will give herself to me for love . . . realizing that . . . I should do without, shouldn't I? Of course. Or at least, as far as the world is concerned, seem to do without. Because we all try to appear to our fellow men at our best, dressed in a costume of dignity and propriety. But we all know the unconfessable things that lie within the secrecy of our own hearts. (*painfully*) One yields, one gives way to temptation, only to rise again immediately afterwards, God knows, determined to re-establish our dignity and propriety, as if dignity were like a gravestone, concealing, burying out of sight the memories of our awful shame. And we're all like this, I think, except that some of us lack the courage to admit to . . . certain things.

STEPDAUGHTER   But have the courage to *do* them! All of them!

FATHER   Yes, all of them! But only in secret! The courage is not in the doing, but in the admission of guilt. The moment that a man admits his real feelings, society at once says he's different, calls him a cynic. That's not true. He's not a cynic, but he is different. He is better, much better, because he is not afraid to reveal with his intelligence the blush of shame, the shame to which most men close their eyes. And woman . . . is she really different? She looks at you, tantalizing, invitingly. You take her in your arms. And no sooner does she feel herself in your grasp than she closes her eyes. It is the sign of her mission, the sign by which she says to man: "Blind yourself; I am blind."

STEPDAUGHTER   And when she no longer closes her eyes? When she no longer feels the need of hiding her shame from herself? When instead she sees, dry-eyed and dispassionately, the shame of the man who blinds himself without love? (*to the* ACTORS; *pointing to the* FATHER) What disgust, what unutterable disgust I feel for all this "philosophy" of his! What is it but an elaborate excuse for his own lechery! I can't listen to any more! When he simplifies life to one ingredient . . . lust . . . throwing aside every human concept of virtue . . . decency . . . idealism! After all he's done, what could be more revolting than these . . . crocodile tears!

DIRECTOR   (*moved by the* FATHER'S *speech*) Yes, but what he says is true. I know that in my own case I . . . (*He stops; becomes more businesslike*) But let's come to the point. This is still only a discussion.

FATHER   Very well. But a fact is like a sack. It won't stand up when it's empty. To make it stand up you must first pour into it all of the reasons and emotions which have caused it to exist. I couldn't possibly have been expected to know that after the death of that man, when they returned here in such utter poverty, she . . . (*indicating the* MOTHER) . . . in her ignorance would go to work in a place like Madam Pace's.

MOTHER   (*to the* DIRECTOR)   How was I to know? I needed work. It never entered my head for a minute that the old hag had her eye on my daughter.

STEPDAUGHTER   Poor Mama. Do you know what that woman did? She told me that Mama was so inefficient, so unsatisfactory, that she would have to let both of us go unless I took on . . . some *special* work. So I did. I paid for us, while . . . (*indicating the* MOTHER) . . . this poor creature thought she was sacrificing herself for me and the two children.

DIRECTOR   (*immediately; suddenly understanding*)   And it was there, one day, that you met . . .

STEPDAUGHTER   (*pointing to the* FATHER) Him! Him! Yes, an old client. There's a scene for you to play!

FATHER   With the interruption . . . just before . . .

STEPDAUGHTER   (*treacherously*)   Almost in time!

FATHER   (*crying out in a loud voice*)   No, in time! In time! Because, fortunately, I recognized her in time. And I took them home. You can imagine what the situation is like now, for both of us. Living together in the same house . . . I cannot look her in the face.

STEPDAUGHTER   It's absolutely ridiculous. How can I possibly pretend, after all this, to be a proper young lady, well brought up and in complete accord with his damned aspirations for a life of "solid morality"?

FATHER   For me the whole drama lies in this one thing: that each of us believes himself to be a single person. It isn't true. With some people we are one person, with others we are quite a different person altogether. But to ourselves we retain the illusion of being always the same person to everyone. And we realize it isn't true when suddenly, to our horror, we are caught up into the air by some giant hook, frozen in time, suspended for all to see. Then we recognize that all of us was not in that particular action, that it would be an atrocious injustice to judge us by that action and that action alone . . . keeping us suspended, in pillory, as if our life were made up of only that one moment. Now do you understand the treachery of this girl? She surprised me in a place where she should never have known me, and in an action that should never have existed for her. And now she is trying to make the entire reality of my life from that one, fleeting, shameful moment. How unjust it is. Ah! (*regaining control of himself*) And, as you will see, the drama takes on a tremendous conflict because of this situation. (*turning toward the* SON) Then there are the others . . . him . . .

SON   (*scornfully*)   Leave me alone! I have nothing to do with all this!

FATHER   What are you talking about?

SON   I have nothing and I want nothing to do with it. Because, as you very well know, I wasn't meant to be mixed up in all this with the rest of you.

STEPDAUGHTER   We're not good enough for him! He's so superior! But, as you may have noticed, ladies and gentlemen, when i look at him . . . he lowers his eyes. He knows the harm he's done me.

SON   (*not looking at her*)   Me?

STEPDAUGHTER   Yes, you! I owe my life on the streets to you! Because you denied us, by the attitude you adopted, I won't say the intimacy of your home but even the mere hospitality which makes guests feel at ease. We were intruders who had come to disturb the kingdom of your legitimacy. I'd just like . . . (*to the* DIRECTOR) . . . you to see some of the scene which took place between him and me.

He says I've "lorded" it over everybody. But it was his behavior, his coldness, that forced me to take advantage of the thing he calls "revolting." The result was that when I went into that house with my mother, who is his mother as well, I went into the house as if it were mine.

SON (*coming forward*) It's all great sport for them, isn't it, ganging up this way, always putting me in the wrong. But just imagine how I felt that fine day when an arrogant young woman arrived at the door, demanding to see my father with only a secretive smile hinting as to the nature of her business with him. And then when she came back again, more brazen than ever, bringing the little girl with her . . . I saw her treating my father . . . in such a mysterious way, asking him for money in such a tone of voice that I knew he *had* to give it to her, had some obligation to do so.

FATHER As indeed I have. It is an obligation I owe your mother.

SON How was I to know that? When did I ever see her or hear of her? Until one day she arrived with her . . . (*indicating the* STEPDAUGHTER) . . . and the boy and the little girl, this time with all their luggage. Then I was suddenly told, "This is your mother, too, you know." And as time went on I began to understand . . . (*indicating the* STEPDAUGHTER) . . . from her attitude, why and how they had come to live with us. I won't even begin to express what I feel about it. I don't even allow myself to think about it. So you see no action can be expected from me in this affair. I am an unrealized character dramatically and I find myself very much ill at ease in their company. So please leave me out of it.

FATHER Ridiculous! It's just because you're like that . . .

SON (*exploding in anger*) What do you know about it? What do you know about me, or what I am like? When did you ever concern yourself about me?

FATHER I admit it! I admit it! But isn't that a dramatic situation in itself? This aloofness of yours which is so cruel to me and to your mother? Think of her returning home and seeing you for the first time a grown man, not even recognizing you, yet knowing you were her son . . . (*pointing to the* MOTHER *who is crying*) Look there, she's crying.

STEPDAUGHTER Like the fool she is.

FATHER (*indicating the* STEPDAUGHTER'S *distaste for the* SON) She can't stand him, as you can see. (*indicating the* SON) He says he has nothing to do with all this, but, as a matter of fact, the whole action hinges on him. Look at the little boy, clinging to his mother, always frightened and crying. It's his fault . . . (*indicating the* SON) . . . that the boy is like that. (*indicating the* BOY) Perhaps his position is the most painful of all; more than anyone else he seems to feel himself an outsider in my home. He's humiliated to be taken in by me, by my charity . . . (*lowering his voice; confidentially*) He's very much like his father . . . humble . . . quiet . . .

DIRECTOR (*in a professional tone*) Oh, we'll cut him out. You've no idea what a nuisance children are on the stage.

FATHER He won't be a problem. He disappears very soon, and the baby, too. She's the first to go.

DIRECTOR Fine. Good. (*walking around; with more interest*) Yes, I think this is all very interesting. There might be the makings of a very exciting play here.

STEPDAUGHTER (*trying to intrude*) When you've got a character like me!

FATHER (*angry; pushing the* STEPDAUGHTER *aside*) You be quiet!

DIRECTOR Yes . . . it's quite new . . .

FATHER Nothing like it has ever been done.

DIRECTOR You've got nerve, I'll say that, coming in here and throwing the idea at me . . .

FATHER Well, you understand, born as we were for the stage . . .

DIRECTOR (*suddenly alarmed*) You're not actors?

FATHER No, no. I said we were born for the stage because . . .

DIRECTOR Are you trying to put something over on me?

FATHER Oh, no. I only act the part for which I was cast, the part which I was given in life. But because I have read a great deal and am very emotional, I became a little theatrical without even meaning to.

DIRECTOR Well, that might be, of course. But still, without an author . . . I could give you the name of an author who, perhaps, might . . .

FATHER No! No! Look here! You be the author!

DIRECTOR Me? What are you talking about?

FATHER Yes, you! You! Why not?

DIRECTOR Because I've never written anything in my life, that's why not.

FATHER But you could do it, couldn't you? It can't be very difficult. So many people do it. And it couldn't be very hard with all of us here, alive, right in front of you.

DIRECTOR   Well . . . I am almost tempted . . . it would be rather an interesting experiment . . . it might almost be worth trying . . .

FATHER   It is! And you'll soon see what marvellous scenes will come out of it. I can tell you now . . .

DIRECTOR   You tempt me . . . you do tempt me! All right, let's take a crack at it! Come with me. There's an office upstairs. (*turning to the* ACTORS) We'll take a short break. But don't go too far away because I'll want you all back here in ten or fifteen minutes. (*to the* FATHER) Let's see what we can do. With luck, we might be able to turn it into something sensational.

FATHER   There's no *might* about it. They'd better come too, don't you think? (*He indicates the other* CHARACTERS)

DIRECTOR   Yes, yes, bring them along. (*He starts to exit, then turns back to the* ACTORS) Remember, no more than fifteen minutes.

(THE DIRECTOR *and the* CHARACTERS *exit into the wings; the* ACTORS *look at one another with astonishment*)

LEADING MAN   Is he serious?

JUVENILE   The whole thing is crazy.

OLD CHARACTER MAN   Does he really expect to rough out an entire play in a quarter of an hour?

JUVENILE   We can do improvisations!

LEADING LADY   I have a contract! If he thinks I'm going to have anything to do with some classroom exercises . . .

INGENUE   I don't understand. There doesn't seem to be any part for me at all.

OLD CHARACTER LADY   Still, I would rather like to know who those strange people are . . .

OLD CHARACTER MAN   They're probably either escaped lunatics, or it's some sort of a practical joke.

JUVENILE   But he's really taking them seriously.

LEADING LADY   It's vanity. Now he sees himself as a writer.

LEADING MAN   If the stage has come to this . . .

OLD CHARACTER LADY   I do believe, though, that I'm rather enjoying it.

FIRST STAGE MANAGER   Well, there's no point in just standing here. Let's get some coffee while we've still got the time.

(*Still talking among themselves, the* ACTORS *leave the stage. The curtain remains up. The lights go on. The action is suspended for a brief intermission*)

ACT TWO

(*As the lights dim on the audience, a call bell sounds backstage signalling for the* ACTORS *to return. Before they do so, however, the* SON *enters followed by the* MOTHER)

SON   What a joke! What a monstrous joke! With me for its punch line!

(*The* MOTHER *moves toward the* SON, *trying to make his eyes meet hers, but before she can do so, the* SON *turns away from her. The* MOTHER *moves forward again, persisting in her efforts to make his eyes meet hers*)

MOTHER   And isn't my punishment the worst of all? (*as the* SON *turns away again, the* MOTHER *looks up toward the heavens, cries out in anguish*) Ah! God! God! Why are You so cruel? Isn't it enough that I must endure this fantastic life, this never-ending torment? Must You insist on my exhibiting it to others as well?

SON   (*speaking to himself but with the intention that the* MOTHER *should overhear his words*)   Why must it be put on the stage at all? What for? He complains that he was discovered in a moment of his life that should have remained hidden. Then why must he put it on display? And what about me? Must my shame be exposed as well? Must everyone know about my parents, my mother running off with another man, my father . . . a lecher? Can't I at least be allowed to conceal this shameful business?

(*The* MOTHER *covers her face with her hands. At this moment, the* ACTORS, *other* CHARACTERS, *and other members of the company enter*)

DIRECTOR   All right, let's go. Let's go, please. Is everybody here? (*looking around him*) Let me have your attention. (*to the* FIRST STAGE MANAGER, *calling him by name*) John, we'll have to set the scene.

(*The* FIRST STAGE MANAGER *nods "yes," begins to write down the needed items on a piece of paper held by his clip board*)

DIRECTOR   See what there is backstage—for a bedroom. A three fold with a door will do.

(FIRST STAGE MANAGER *nods and writes*)

DIRECTOR   We'll need a bed, that's the main thing.

FIRST STAGE MANAGER   There's the old iron one, with the green bedspread.

STEPDAUGHTER   No, no, not a green one. It was yellow with big flowers on it, velvet, very soft and comfortable.

FIRST STAGE MANAGER I'm sorry, Miss, but we haven't anything like that.

DIRECTOR It doesn't matter. Use whatever we have.

STEPDAUGHTER Doesn't matter? Madam Pace's celebrated bed?

DIRECTOR This is only for a run-through. Now please don't make things harder. (*to the* FIRST STAGE MANAGER) Just do the best you can.

STEPDAUGHTER Don't forget the little table, the little mahogany table for the pale blue envelope.

FIRST STAGE MANAGER There's one small table, painted gold.

DIRECTOR Fine, fine, we'll use that.

FATHER A mirror, too.

STEPDAUGHTER And a screen! I must have a screen! Otherwise I can't play the scene.

FIRST STAGE MANAGER Don't worry, Miss, we've plenty of screens.

DIRECTOR (*to the* STEPDAUGHTER) What about clothes hangers? You'll need some, won't you?

STEPDAUGHTER Yes, several.

DIRECTOR (*to the* FIRST STAGE MANAGER) Bring as many as you can find. (*He gestures for the* FIRST STAGE MANAGER *to go and prepare the scene*)

FIRST STAGE MANAGER Right.

(*The* FIRST STAGE MANAGER *hurries off. During the next few minutes, while the* DIRECTOR *is talking to the* SECOND STAGE MANAGER *and later to the* ACTORS *and the* CHARACTERS, *the* FIRST STAGE MANAGER *re-enters and supervises several* STAGE HANDS *as they bring in scenery, furniture and props for the bedroom scene. The items used should be real, somewhat battered and soiled from backstage use, and unobtrusive*)

DIRECTOR (*turning to the* SECOND STAGE MANAGER; *handing him some papers; pointing to the table where he was sitting before when acting as prompter*) Sit where you were before. (*as he hands him the papers*) Look, here's an outline of the action, scene by scene. Now what I want you to do . . . (*He hesitates*)

SECOND STAGE MANAGER (*quickly*) Take it down in shorthand?

DIRECTOR (*surprised*) Can you? Do you know shorthand?

SECOND STAGE MANAGER (*separating a pad of blank paper from the other papers on his table*) Enough to get some of it, anyway.

DIRECTOR Wonderful! Then follow each scene as they play it and get as much of the dialogue as you can. At least the important speeches. (*He turns back to the* ACTORS, *waves them toward one side of the stage*) O. K., let's clear the stage, please. Be sure you can see everything that's going on, and pay attention.

LEADING LADY Excuse me, but . . .

DIRECTOR (*anticipating her question*) Don't worry, you won't have to do any improvising.

LEADING MAN Then what will we be doing?

DIRECTOR If you'll be patient, and just listen and watch, everyone will get written parts later. Right now we're going to have a run-through and they're going to do it. (*He points to the* CHARACTERS)

FATHER (*as if suddenly awakened from a distant daydream*) We . . . I'm sorry, but what do you mean by a "run-through"?

DIRECTOR A rehearsal . . . for the company. (*He indicates the* ACTORS)

FATHER But if we're the Six Characters . . . ?

DIRECTOR That's right; you're the characters. But on the stage the characters do not perform. The actors perform. The characters remain there . . . (*He points to the* SECOND STAGE MANAGER) . . . in the script . . . (*as an afterthought*) . . . when there is a script.

FATHER There, you've just said it! Since there is no script and you're lucky enough to have right in front of you, alive, the six characters themselves . . .

DIRECTOR You really want to be the whole show, don't you? You want to conceive it, supervise the writing, direct it, and then act it out in front of the public yourselves?

FATHER Of course. That's the reason we're here.

DIRECTOR (*sardonically*) What a great show that would be!

LEADING MAN What do you think we're here for?

DIRECTOR You're not going to tell me, after all, that you're actors? (*Some of the* ACTORS *laugh; the* DIRECTOR *gestures toward them*) You see? The whole idea is laughable. (*remembering*) That reminds me. I must give out the parts. Well, that won't be difficult. It's pretty much a matter of type. (*to the* SECOND FEMALE LEAD) You'll be the Mother. (*to the* FATHER) We'll have to find a name for her.

FATHER Amelia.

DIRECTOR But that's your wife's real name. We certainly don't want to use that.

FATHER (*confused*) Why not, since it is her name? (*turning toward the* SECOND FEMALE LEAD; *still confused*) Still, if this lady is to . . . (*pointing to the* MOTHER) . . . I see this woman as Amelia. (*to the* DIRECTOR) Do it any way you like. I don't know what to say any more, I'm already beginning to . . . I don't know . . . to sound . . . false . . . as if my words weren't my own any longer but were somehow distorted, unreal . . .

DIRECTOR Don't worry about it. We'll find a way to make the words sound right to you. That's our business. And as for the name, if you want Amelia, Amelia it'll be. Right now we'd better finish up the casting. (to the JUVENILE) You'll be the son . . . (to the LEADING LADY) . . . and, of course, you'll be the stepdaughter.

STEPDAUGHTER (very excited) What !!!??? That woman—me!? (She bursts out laughing)

DIRECTOR Stop that laughing!

LEADING LADY (genuinely hurt and angry; for despite the somewhat flamboyant characteristics of her profession, the LEADING LADY is a very real person, never a caricature) No one has ever laughed at me like that! (almost in tears) If I'm not going to be treated with respect, I'll leave!

STEPDAUGHTER No, no, you mustn't. Please forgive me. I wasn't laughing at you . . .

DIRECTOR You should be flattered to be played by . . .

LEADING LADY (interrupting; angrily) "That woman" . . .

STEPDAUGHTER But I really didn't mean that you . . . (She hesitates, groping for words) . . . I was . . . thinking about myself . . . that I can't see anything at all of me . . in you . . . because you're simply so unlike me.

FATHER That's it exactly! (to the DIRECTOR) You see, what we're trying to express . . .

DIRECTOR Stop it! Stop! For God's sake forget whatever it is you're "trying to express." Don't you realize that the way you feel, inside yourself, is completely unimportant and irrelevant?

FATHER But, to us, our feelings, our emotions . . . (He stops, confused)

DIRECTOR (impatiently) Are only the raw materials with which my actors will work. They will take them and make them real to any audience by voice and gesture. And if this little story holds the stage at all, it will be thanks to the talents of my actors!

FATHER I don't mean to contradict you, but we are the ones who are suffering; we ourselves, as we are before you, with these bodies, these faces . . .

DIRECTOR Make-up and costumes will take care of all that.

FATHER But our voices, our gestures . . .

DIRECTOR Now look here; Let's get this straight once and for all! You, as you are, cannot exist on the stage. This actor . . . (He points ·to the LEADING MAN) . . . will play you. And that's the way it's going to be!

FATHER (slowly) Very well. I understand. And now, I think, I also understand why the author who conceived us didn't want to finish his play, to put us on the stage. I don't want to offend your actors, God knows, but when I think that I shall see myself represented by . . . (He shakes his head in bewilderment)

LEADING MAN (rising; very serious; crossing toward the FATHER; as several of the younger ACTRESSES giggle and laugh) By me, if you have no objection.

FATHER (humbly, melifluously) I'm very flattered, of course, but . . . (nodding toward the LEADING MAN) . . . it still seems to me that no matter how hard this gentleman tries with all his serious intentions and professional abilities, nevertheless . . . (He hesitates)

LEADING MAN (impatiently) Yes? Go on!

FATHER (continuing) . . . it will still be impossible for him to portray me as I really am. It will be . . . apart from the make-up . . . rather his interpretation of how he thinks I feel, and not at all what I really feel within me. And it seems to me that whoever comes to criticize us should take that into account.

DIRECTOR My God, he's thinking about the critics already! Well, we've no time to worry about them! Right now we'd better get to work and try to get the show into shape. (looking around at the bedroom scene which is now all set up) Let's go now. (to the ACTORS) Move aside, please. Let us see what it looks like. (to the STEPDAUGHTER) What do you think? Is the set all right?

STEPDAUGHTER To tell the truth, I don't recognize it at all.

DIRECTOR Well, you didn't expect us to build a duplicate of Madam Pace's bedroom with scrap pieces of scenery, did you? (to the FATHER) You said a room with flowered wallpaper, didn't you?

FATHER Yes, white.

DIRECTOR This isn't white; it's striped but that doesn't matter. And the furniture we have seems to be about right. (to a STAGEHAND) Move that table a couple of feet downstage, will you?

(STAGEHAND does so; DIRECTOR takes charge, adopts a more positive tone; to the ACTORS and the CHARACTERS)

DIRECTOR   All right, we'll begin. Act One, Scene One—the stepdaughter.

(LEADING LADY *comes forward*)

DIRECTOR   No, no, wait. I meant her. (*He points to the* STEPDAUGHTER, *speaking to the* LEADING LADY) You stand and watch . . .

STEPDAUGHTER (*interrupting*)   How I shall live it!

LEADING LADY   I'll make it live, too, don't you worry about that! Just wait until it's my turn to play it!

DIRECTOR   Ladies! Ladies! No more arguing, please. The first scene is between the stepdaughter and Madam Pace. (*suddenly realizing that* MADAM PACE *is not present*) But . . . where is Madam Pace?

FATHER   She's not with us.

DIRECTOR   Then what are we supposed to do now?

FATHER   But she's alive! She's alive, too!

DIRECTOR   If you say so, but where is she?

FATHER   Let me show you. (*turning to the* ACTRESSES) I wonder . . . if you ladies would be so kind as to lend me your hats . . .

TOGETHER (*several of the* ACTRESSES) What? Our hats? I told you so, he is crazy!

DIRECTOR (*as some of the* ACTORS *laugh*) What do you want with women's hats?

FATHER   Nothing important. I only want to use them for a moment to decorate your set. And if one of the ladies would be so kind as to lend me her coat as well.

TOGETHER (*several of the* ACTRESSES; *as before*)   Now he wants a coat! What for? I think it's fascinating!

FATHER   I only want to hang them up here for a moment. Please. It's only a small favor. Won't one of you help me?

TOGETHER (*as several of the* ACTRESSES *pick up hats and a coat, carry them over to the set, hang them up in appropriate positions*)   Why not? All right? Here's mine. This is hilarious! Now we're providing the props!

FATHER (*as they complete hanging up the hats and the coat*)   Fine! That's right. Fine! Now we're ready for our show.

DIRECTOR   Would you mind if I asked you exactly what you think you're doing?

FATHER (*moving toward the* DIRECTOR, *away from the set*)   Not at all. I only thought that if we prepared the scene for her . . . perhaps she might be attracted by the articles of her trade . . . and appear among us. (*He turns back toward the set*) Look! Look!

(*The door of the set has already opened and* MADAM PACE *is standing in the doorway.*

MADAM PACE *is an ugly woman, terribly fat and wearing an incredible, carrot-colored wig. She is rouged and powdered and dressed with pretentious elegance in a long silk gown. She carries a lace handkerchief in one hand, a cigarette in a long holder in the other hand.*

As the FATHER *turns and sees* MADAM PACE, *she comes forward into the set and begins to play her scene with the* STEPDAUGHTER *who moves quickly forward to greet her. The* STEP-DAUGHTER *is humble and polite to* MADAM PACE; *her attitude is that of an employee to her employer.*

As this happens, the ACTORS *are startled—in some cases, frightened; instinctively the* ACTORS *move back several paces, away from the set*)

STEPDAUGHTER   Here she is! Here she is!

FATHER (*radiant*)   There! What did I tell you?

DIRECTOR   What kind of a trick is this?

JUVENILE   Where did she come from?

INGENUE   They must have been hiding her backstage.

LEADING LADY   It's a cheap trick to impress us!

FATHER (*coming forward; dominating the protests*)   Stop it! Stop it, all of you! What you are seeing is truth itself! Why must you try to destroy it? Why must you call it a trick? This miracle of birth, this reality, called to life by the scene which we have just created, has more right to be here than any of you because it is more true! Which actress among you will play Madam Pace? Well, this is Madam Pace herself! At least admit that the actress who will play her will be less true than what you see before your very eyes, Madam Pace in person. As you see, my stepdaughter recognized her immediately and went to greet her. Now stay where you are, quietly, and watch the scene!

(*The* DIRECTOR, *the* ACTORS, *and other* CHARACTERS, *and the other members of the company all turn to watch the scene which is taking place between the* STEPDAUGHTER *and* MADAM PACE. *The scene has already begun but it is being played softly, in normal lowered tones of voice. When the group turns to listen to the scene, not a word that is being spoken can be clearly heard. It is all so soft, so muted, that it blends into a vague, unintelligible murmur of conversation.* MADAM PACE *has put one hand under the* STEPDAUGHTER's *chin, lifting the girl's head to hers as they speak. After a few moments, the* ACTORS *grow disappointed and restive*)

DIRECTOR   Well? Well?

LEADING MAN   What are they saying?

LEADING LADY   I can't hear a word!

JUVENILE   Louder! Louder!

STEPDAUGHTER (*leaving* MADAM PACE *who is smiling at her with a magnificent smile; turning to the* ACTORS) Louder? Well, how loud? These are not things I can shout about at the top of my lungs. I should shout about them, it's true, to his shame . . . (*She indicates the* FATHER) . . . and for my revenge. But for Madam Pace it's quite a different story. It could mean prison for her.

DIRECTOR   Oh, fine! (*shaking his head in dismay*) I'm sorry, my dear, but you simply must realize that in the theatre you have to be heard. And we can't even hear you from ten feet away. Pretend that there's an audience in the theatre and that a performance is taking place. Pretend that you are alone in that room with Madam Pace, where no one can hear you, and then speak up so you'll be heard! (*the* STEPDAUGHTER, *a malicious smile on her lips, slowly but firmly shakes her head "no"*) No? What do you mean?

STEPDAUGHTER   There is someone who will hear us if we don't keep our voices down.

DIRECTOR (*in dismay; confused*) What's this? Have you someone else to spring on us?

FATHER   No, no. She is referring to me. I have to be there, behind that door, waiting. Madam Pace knows that. In fact, with your permission, I will take my place now.

DIRECTOR (*stopping him*) Wait a minute. Now we must respect certain conventions of the theatre. Before you go on . . .

STEPDAUGHTER   Oh, let him go! I tell you I'm dying of my passion to play that scene, to live that scene again! If he's ready, believe me, I'm even more ready!

DIRECTOR (*shouting*) But don't you understand? First we must finish the scene between you and Madam Pace!

STEPDAUGHTER   Oh, for God's sake! She's only been telling me what you already know; that my mother's work is unsatisfactory, that I must *cooperate* if she is to continue helping us . . .

MADAM PACE (*coming forward; dignified; full of self-importance; speaking in a mixture of Spanish and heavily accented English*) My good sir, you realize I do not take advantage of her . . . (*She breaks into a stream of Spanish*)

DIRECTOR (*almost frightened*) What? What? What's she saying?

STEPDAUGHTER (*laughing*) It's the way she speaks, half in English, half in Spanish. I know it sounds ridiculous.

MADAM PACE   Ah, how unkind of you people to laugh at how I speak. I speak as best I can.

DIRECTOR   No, no, please don't be offended. Speak exactly as you do. Don't pay any attention to them . . . (*He gestures toward some of the* ACTORS *who are laughing*) The effect will be wonderful! We couldn't ask for anything better. It will provide some comic relief and ease the crudeness of the basic situation. Please go on, just as you were. It'll be fine that way.

STEPDAUGHTER   Of course it will! Whenever "certain suggestions" are made in that kind of language, the effect is always marvellous. It makes everything sound like a joke. How ridiculous it is to hear that an "old señor" wishes to "amuse himself" with me— isn't that true, Madam Pace?

MADAM PACE   Not so old, *cara mia*. And if you do not like him, if he is not to your taste, he won't give you any trouble.

MOTHER (*rising; taking advantage of the consternation of the* ACTORS, *she rushes across the stage to* MADAM PACE, *tears off her red wig and throws it to the floor*) You witch! You devil. You've murdered my daughter!

STEPDAUGHTER (*rushing to restrain her* MOTHER) No, Mother, no! In the name of God!

FATHER (*also hurrying to restrain the* MOTHER) Please, please! Calm yourself, Amelia! Come; sit down!

MOTHER   I can't stand looking at that woman!

STEPDAUGHTER (*to the* DIRECTOR) My mother can't stay here. It's asking too much.

FATHER (*to the* DIRECTOR) They mustn't be here together. That's why Madam Pace wasn't with us when we arrived. (*gesturing to* MADAM PACE *and the* MOTHER) If the two of them are here together, it gives the whole thing away in advance.

DIRECTOR   It doesn't matter. It's not important now. This is only a run-through . . . just to give us a rough idea of how it will play. Everything will be useful . . . because I can collect all the various scenes and motivations . . . it's bound to be confusing at first . . . but I can sort it all out later. (*turning to the* MOTHER; *leading her to a chair*) Come, my dear Madam; please sit down again.

STEPDAUGHTER (*during the past few moments, she has moved upstage; now she turns downstage toward* MADAM PACE) Madam Pace, shall we continue?

MADAM PACE (*offended; pointing to the* MOTHER) Ah, no thank you. I am not going to do nothing more con tue madre presente.

STEPDAUGHTER But . . . you must introduce me to the "old señor" who wishes to "amuse him" with me . . . (MADAM PACE *shakes her head "no"; the* STEPDAUGHTER *takes charge; imperiously*) We must play the scene; that's all there is to it! (MADAM PACE *shakes her head adamantly; the* STEPDAUGHTER's *tone is curt*) You can go.

MADAM PACE Ah, I go! I go! I most certainly go! (*Furiously she picks up her wig and exits through the door of the set; as she does so, the* ACTORS *laugh and applaud;* MADAM PACE *glares at them as she exits*)

STEPDAUGHTER (*to the* FATHER) Now you must make your entrance. (*as he starts toward the door of the set*) There's no need to actually do it. (*as he stops, turns back toward her*) Pretend that you've already entered. (*moving into the mood of the scene; in a lowered voice*) I am standing over here with my eyes lowered, a picture of modesty. You approach me and say, in that very special tone, "Good evening, Miss . . ."

DIRECTOR (*moving toward the* STEPDAUGHTER) Wait a minute. Are you directing or am I? (*to the* FATHER *who has turned toward the* DIRECTOR *with an expression of suspicion and perplexity on his face*) Try it the way she said. Go to the back of the set . . . you don't have to go out . . . and then come forward as if you've just entered.

(*The* FATHER *carries out these instructions; as he moves upstage he seems pale and troubled; but when he turns and comes downstage he has adopted the reality of his created life. The* ACTORS *watch the scene with quiet concentration*)

DIRECTOR (*as the* FATHER *moves upstage; to the* SECOND STAGE MANAGER) Now pay attention and get as much of it as you can!

The Scene

FATHER (*approaching the* STEPDAUGHTER; *in a "special" tone*) Good evening, Miss.

STEPDAUGHTER (*her eyes lowered; with restrained disgust*) Good evening.

FATHER (*lifting her chin with one hand; discovering first that she is young and pretty, to his surprise; then fearing that she may be a virgin*) Ah . . . well . . . um . . . but . . . this is not the first time, is it?

STEPDAUGHTER No, sir.

FATHER You have been here before, then. (*The* STEPDAUGHTER *nods "yes," lowers her eyes*) More than once? (*As she hesitates, he pauses for a moment, then lifts her head again, smiling at her*) Well, then . . . there's no

need for you to be so shy . . . may I remove that little hat?

STEPDAUGHTER (*immediately moving a step or two away from the* FATHER *to prevent his removing her hat; starting to remove it herself*) No, sir, I'll take it off myself.

(*The* MOTHER *has been watching this scene together with the* SON *and the two younger children who cling to her skirts. As the scene has progressed, the* MOTHER *has watched with increasing horror, indignation, pain, and sorrow. Now she buries her face in her hands and groans aloud*)

MOTHER Oh! Oh! My God! My God!

FATHER (*stopping for a moment as if moved to pity for the* MOTHER; *then resuming*) Well, give it to me. I will put it down for you. (*He takes the hat from her hands, looks at it for a moment, then places it on a table*) On such a lovely head as yours I would like to see a much more beautiful little hat. Would you help me choose one for you from Madam Pace's stock? (*He quickly takes a small, pale blue envelope from his pocket, puts the envelope unobtrusively down on the small table*)

INGENUE (*speaking without meaning to*) But . . . he's talking about our hats!

DIRECTOR (*angry; in a stage whisper*) Shut up for God's sake. This is no time for jokes! Let them play their scene! (*to the* STEPDAUGHTER) Go on, please.

STEPDAUGHTER (*continuing; to the* FATHER) No, thank you, sir.

FATHER (*offering her a hat*) What? Oh, now, you mustn't say "no." You have to accept one. I shall be most upset if you won't. Look how lovely some of these are . . . and it would certainly please Madam Pace . . . why do you think she left them here?

STEPDAUGHTER Thank you, anyway, sir, but I couldn't wear it.

FATHER (*more expansively*) Afraid of what they would say at home if you arrived wearing such an expensive present? Oh, come along! You'll be able to think of something to tell them.

STEPDAUGHTER (*tensely*) It isn't that . . . I couldn't wear it, because . . . I am . . . as you can see . . . I'm surprised you haven't noticed . . . (*She indicates her black dress*)

FATHER (*realizing*) In mourning! Forgive me, I'm so sorry. Yes, I do see. I . . .

STEPDAUGHTER (*gathering all her courage; forcing herself to adopt a positive tone; repressing her anguish and nausea*) Please, please, don't go on. It is very kind of you, and I thank you for it, but you must not feel embarrassed or sorry for me. Please try to put it out of your mind. Because, you see . . . (*She tries to smile, adding*) . . . I am trying to forget that I am dressed this way.

DIRECTOR (*interrupting; to the* SECOND STAGE MANAGER) Wait a minute. Don't write that last part down. We'll leave that out. (*turning to the* FATHER *and the* STEPDAUGHTER; *gesturing for them to move downstage, clearing the set*) This is excellent, excellent! (*then, only to the* FATHER) It's going even better than I hoped. But that's enough for now.

STEPDAUGHTER But why can't we go on? The best is still to come!

DIRECTOR Just be patient. You can go on later. (*turning to the* ACTORS) It must be played very naturally, with just a touch of lightness . . .

LEADING MAN Um . . . there's a certain quicksilver quality in the man, isn't there?

LEADING LADY It's not a difficult scene. (*to the* LEADING MAN) Shall we try it now?

LEADING MAN Yes. I'll go and get ready for my entrance. (*He goes off and takes up his position behind the door leading into the set*)

DIRECTOR (*to the* LEADING LADY) All right, here we go. The scene between you and Madam Pace is over. She exits . . . (*gesturing for the* LEADING LADY *to take up her position in the set*) . . . and you remain here. I'll have that scene written up properly later. You're here . . . (*seeing that the* LEADING LADY *is moving away from him*) Where're you going?

LEADING LADY I've got to put on my hat.

DIRECTOR (*as the* LEADING LADY *picks up her hat, puts it on, starts to move back toward the set*) Good. Very good. Now you'll stand here, your head lowered, your eyes toward the floor.

STEPDAUGHTER (*laughing*) But she's not even dressed in black.

LEADING LADY I shall be dressed in black . . . but *I'll* be chic!

DIRECTOR (*to the* STEPDAUGHTER) Now you must be quiet! Just stand there and watch and perhaps you'll learn something about the theatre. (*calling for attention*) Is everyone ready? All right! Entrance!

(*As the* DIRECTOR *moves downstage so that he will be able to see the scene with more perspective, the door of the set opens and the* LEADING MAN *enters. He is playing the lively manner of an old roué. The scene that follows, as performed by the* ACTORS, *is totally different from the scene as it was performed by the* CHARACTERS. *However, it is never a parody, never a burlesque of their scene. It is played with absolute reality, absolute truthfulness. It is however, played very differently. The line readings are different, the gestures different, the expressions different*)

LEADING MAN Good evening, Miss.

FATHER (*immediately unable to control himself*) Oh, no!

(*As he says this, the* STEPDAUGHTER *bursts out laughing at the way in which the* LEADING MAN *is walking*)

DIRECTOR Shut up there! And stop that laughing! We cannot have these constant interruptions!

STEPDAUGHTER (*moving forward a few paces*) I'm very sorry, but it's only natural. This lady . . . (*She points to the* LEADING LADY) . . . is standing exactly where I stood before. But if she is intended to be me, I can assure you that if anyone ever said "Good evening" to me in a voice like that I would burst out laughing exactly as I did just now.

FATHER (*coming forward*) Well, yes. His manner, his tone . . .

DIRECTOR Are exactly right, for him! (*pointing to the area where the* FATHER *was standing before he came forward*) Now you must be quiet and let us get on with the rehearsal!

LEADING MAN (*coming downstage; ready to argue with the* FATHER) If I'm to play an old boy who's coming into a house of . . .

DIRECTOR (*waving the* LEADING MAN *back toward the set*) For God's sake don't listen to them! Just do it again! It's going very well. (*waiting for the* ACTORS *to resume*) From the beginning.

LEADING MAN Good evening, Miss.

LEADING LADY Good evening.

LEADING MAN (*lifting the* STEPDAUGHTER's *chin exactly as did the* FATHER; *expressing very distinctly surprise and pleasure, then fear*) Ah . . . well . . . um . . . but . . . this is not the first time, I hope?

FATHER (*interrupting; correcting*) Not "I hope"; "is it?"

DIRECTOR (*accepting this correction*) Yes, "is it?" in a questioning tone.

LEADING MAN (*looking at the* SECOND STAGE MANAGER) I remember it as "I hope."

DIRECTOR Well, it's all the same. There's no difference between "I hope" and "is it?". Go on, go on with, perhaps, just a touch more lightness. (*moving toward the set*) Here, wait a minute. I'll do it. Watch me. (*moving upstage, the* DIRECTOR *turns and comes forward toward the* LEADING LADY) Good evening, Miss.

LEADING LADY Good evening.

DIRECTOR (*lifting the chin of the* LEADING LADY) Ah . . . well . . . um . . . but . . . (*He turns toward the* LEADING MAN, *showing him the proper way of looking into the face of the* LEADING LADY) Surprise . . . pleasure . . . and then fear. (*to the* LEADING LADY) This is not the first time, is it? (*to the* LEADING MAN) Do you see what I mean? (*to the* LEADING LADY) And then you say, "No, sir." (*to the* LEADING MAN) In other words, a little more lightness, a little more flexibility.

(*As the* DIRECTOR *moves downstage again, the* LEADING MAN *once again takes his place in the set*)

LEADING LADY No, sir.

LEADING MAN You have been here before, then? More than once?

DIRECTOR No, wait a minute. You've got to pause to let her get her nod in. (*to the* LEADING LADY) You have been here before, then?

(*At his signal, the* LEADING LADY *raises her head a little, closes her eyes, then nods "yes" twice*)

STEPDAUGHTER (*unable to contain herself*) Good God! (*She covers her mouth with one hand to prevent herself from laughing aloud*)

DIRECTOR Now what's the matter?

STEPDAUGHTER (*quickly*) Nothing. Nothing at all.

DIRECTOR (*after frowning at the* STEPDAUGHTER; *to the* LEADING MAN) Continue.

LEADING MAN More than once? Well, then . . . there's no need for you to be shy . . . may I remove that little hat?

(*The* LEADING MAN *says these last sentences in such a tone and with such gestures that the* STEPDAUGHTER *is unable to keep from laughing despite the hand pressed against her mouth. She explodes into a burst of loud, incredulous laughter*)

LEADING LADY I'm not going to stand here and be made a fool of by that woman!

LEADING MAN Neither am I! Let's forget the whole thing!

DIRECTOR (*to the* STEPDAUGHTER; *shouting*) Stop it! Stop it!

STEPDAUGHTER (*regaining control of herself*) Forgive me . . . please forgive me!

DIRECTOR Haven't you any manners at all? How dare you behave like this?

FATHER (*intervening*) Oh, you're quite right, of course, but you must excuse her . . .

DIRECTOR Excuse her? I've never seen such rudeness!

FATHER Yes, but still, you must believe me, when they play it they make it seem so strange that . . .

DIRECTOR Strange? What's strange about it?

FATHER Well . . . you must understand . . . I do admire your actors . . . this gentleman . . . (*He indicates the* LEADING MAN) . . . this lady . . . (*He indicates the* LEADING LADY) . . . but it is simply that they are not us.

DIRECTOR Of course they're not! How can they be you if they're actors as well?

FATHER Exactly! Actors! And both of them seem to be very good. But to us it all seems so different. They try to be us . . . but they are not us at all!

DIRECTOR In what way aren't they? What is it exactly?

FATHER It is that somehow . . . the play is becoming theirs. It isn't ours any longer.

DIRECTOR But that's inevitable! I've told you so already.

FATHER I know, I know, but . . .

DIRECTOR (*interrupting*) Then stop all these interruptions! (*to the* ACTORS) It's always a mistake to rehearse with the author present. He's never satisfied! (*to the* FATHER *and the* STEPDAUGHTER) Now we're going to try it again and this time see if you can keep yourselves from laughing.

STEPDAUGHTER Oh, I won't laugh. I promise I won't. My big scene is coming up.

DIRECTOR Very well. (*to the* LEADING LADY) Now then, when you say "You must not feel embarrassed or sorry for me. Please try to put it out of your mind . . ." (*to the* LEADING MAN) . . . then you say, very quickly, "I understand, I understand," and then ask her . . .

STEPDAUGHTER (*interrupting*) What's this? What?

DIRECTOR (*continuing*) . . . why she is in mourning.

STEPDAUGHTER But that's not right at all! When I told him that I was trying to forget I was dressed in mourning, do you know what he answered me? "Oh, very well. Then suppose we take off this little dress."

DIRECTOR Oh, very good! Just what we need! A riot in the theatre!

STEPDAUGHTER But it's the truth!

DIRECTOR What has that to do with it? This is the theatre. Truth is all very well and good, other places, but here only up to a point.

STEPDAUGHTER Then . . . what are you going to do . . . instead . . . ?

DIRECTOR If you'll just shut up, you'll see. Just leave it to me!

STEPDAUGHTER No! I won't! You want to take all my agony, and all the cruel reasons why I am what I am, and twist them into a romantic, sentimental little "tear jerker." When he asks me why I'm in mourning no doubt I'm to answer him, weeping bitterly, that my poor dear daddy died two months before. No! No! I won't have it! His answer to me must be, immediately, "Then suppose we take off this little dress"! And I . . . with my heart still grieving for my father, dead only two short months, I went there, behind that screen, and with these fingers, trembling with shame and disgust, unbuttoned my brassiere, took off my dress . . .

DIRECTOR   In the name of God, what is . . . !?

STEPDAUGHTER   (*shouting*)   The truth! The truth!

DIRECTOR   Yes, yes, I don't deny that it's the truth . . . and I appreciate your horror, but you must understand that there are certain things which we cannot do on the stage.

STEPDAUGHTER   You can't? Then thank you very much for your time. There's no need for me to stay here any longer . . .

DIRECTOR   Wait a minute. Look . . .

STEPDAUGHTER   I won't stay here! I won't! You've worked it all out with him already, there in your office! I understand only too well! He wants to jump ahead to the place where he can act out the scenes of his spiritual torment, his celebrated remorse, but I want to play *this* scene, *my* scene, *mine!*

DIRECTOR   (*tired; bored*)   Always your part! Well, I hope you don't mind my saying so, but there are other people in the play as well as you. Him . . . (*He points to the* FATHER) . . . and her! (*He points to the* MOTHER) On the stage you can't have one character doing it all, overshadowing all the others. The characters must be blended together into one harmonious portrait, a picture presenting what it is proper to present. And this is the whole difficulty here, to select and present only what is important and necessary, taking into consideration all the motivations of the characters and hinting at the unrevealed facets of each one. Ah, wouldn't it be nice if every character had a simple, straight-forward monologue, a chance to talk directly to the audience, to pour out all the exposition and every feeling in one great outburst. (*He sighs, turns to the* STEPDAUGHTER *and continues in a conciliatory tone*) You must restrain yourself, Miss. Believe me, it's in your own interest. You only make a bad impression with all this fury, all this exaggerated disgust. After all, you yourself have confessed that there were others at Madam Pace's before him.

STEPDAUGHTER   (*bowing her head; after a moment's thought*)   That's true. But remember, all those others *were him* to me.

DIRECTOR   (*not understanding*)   The other men *were him?* What do you mean?

STEPDAUGHTER   When someone goes wrong, the person who was responsible for the first step is responsible for all the other ones. And he was responsible for me, even before I was born. Look at him now and see if it isn't true!

DIRECTOR   Suppose it is? Doesn't the guilt of such a responsibility seem anything to you? Give him a chance to play his feelings!

STEPDAUGHTER   His own story in his own way, is that what you mean? So that he can boast to you of all his noble remorses, all his moral torments? You want to spare him the horror of being found, one fine day, in my arms, after he has asked me to take off my dress of mourning; the child, the child whom he used to watch coming out of school, already a whore! (*She speaks these last words trembling with emotion; the* MOTHER *is overwhelmed with anguish; she groans, then breaks into hopeless sobbing; the emotion touches everyone; there is a long pause. The* STEPDAUGHTER *waits until her* MOTHER's *sobbing ceases, then continues in a gloomy but resolute tone*) Today you see us here, as we are, still unknown to the public. Tomorrow you will play us as you wish, in your own way. But do you really want to see our drama, to see it burst into life as it actually was?

DIRECTOR   Of course. I couldn't ask for anything better. I want to use as much of it as possible.

STEPDAUGHTER   Then ask my mother to leave us.

MOTHER   (*raising her head from her silent weeping; with a sharp cry*)   No, no! You mustn't! I beg of you, please!

DIRECTOR   But I must see it as it happened, Madam.

MOTHER   I can't bear it! You're torturing me!

DIRECTOR   But since it has already happened . . . I don't understand . . .

MOTHER   Can't you see? It is happening now! It happens always! My torment is unending! I am always alive and subjected at every instant to torment which repeats itself over and over . . . I cannot even die. I must live it and feel it . . . forever. (*indicating the two small children*) My two little ones, have you ever heard them speak? (*shaking her head "no"*) They can't speak any longer. But they still cling to me in order to keep my torment vivid and alive. And this one . . . (*She points to the* STEPDAUGHTER) . . . has run away.

She has run away from me and is lost, is lost. If I see her now it is only for one reason, to renew my suffering, to renew the suffering which I must have because of her.

FATHER (*solemnly*) What you are seeing is our eternal moment. She . . . (*He indicates the* STEPDAUGHTER) . . . is here to trap me, to hold me suspended through all time, in pillory for that one fleeting and shameful moment of my life. She cannot give up that scene and you really cannot spare me of it either.

DIRECTOR Well . . . if you say so. I never said that I didn't want to play it. Actually, it will form the nucleus of the whole first act, right up to the surprise entrance of the mother just before the curtain.

FATHER That's right. Because this is my punishment. All of our agony and passion culminates in that final, terrible cry!

STEPDAUGHTER I can still hear it ringing in my ears. That cry has driven me crazy! Present me any way you like; it's not important. Even completely dressed provided that I have my arms, only my arms bare. Because you see I was standing like this . . . (*She approaches the* FATHER, *puts her arms around him and leans her head up against his chest*) . . . with my head leaning on his chest and my arms around his neck, when I saw a vein pulsing in my arm, here. And, somehow, the pulsing of that vein in my naked arm awakened such disgust in me that I closed my eyes, so, like this, and let my head sink down on his chest. (*turning to the* MOTHER) Cry out! Cry out, Mama! (*Once again she buries her head on the* FATHER's *chest, lifting her shoulders as if to protect herself from the cry which she knows must come; then in a voice filled with torment, she almost shouts*) Cry out as you cried then!

MOTHER (*crying out; coming forward to separate them*) No!!! No!!! My daughter! My daughter! (*pulling the* FATHER *away from the* STEPDAUGHTER) You monster! You monster! This is my daughter! Don't you realize she's my daughter!

DIRECTOR (*stepping back toward the footlights; caught up in the action; enthusiastic*) Wonderful! My God, it's wonderful! (*clapping his hands together*) And then a quick curtain. That cry, and then curtain! Curtain!

(*At the repeated "Curtain! Curtain!" by the* DIRECTOR, *a* STAGEHAND *lowers the main curtain leaving the* FATHER *and the* DIRECTOR *outside of the curtain on the apron of the stage*)

DIRECTOR That damn fool! I said "curtain" meaning the act would finish here, and he's actually let the curtain down. (*leading the way through the curtain; exiting behind it with the* FATHER *following him*) But the play is good; it's very good. With a great first act curtain! It has to end that way. I'll guarantee the first act, anyway.

(*They disappear behind the curtain*)

ACT THREE

(*When the curtain rises, we see that the scenery used to create the room in* MADAM PACE's *establishment has been removed. It has been replaced with a small cut-out of a fountain.*

The ACTORS *are seated to one side of the stage; the* CHARACTERS *to the other. The* DIRECTOR, *lost deep in thought, is standing in the center of the stage*)

DIRECTOR (*finally resolving his thoughts*) Well . . . suppose we go on to the second act. (*quickly; to the* CHARACTERS) Now if you'll just leave it to me, as we've agreed, we can work this out very quickly.

STEPDAUGHTER (*coming forward*) We'll begin with our entrance into his house . . . (*She points to the* FATHER) . . . in spite of him! (*She points to the* SON)

DIRECTOR Don't jump ahead so. You promised to let me do this my way!

STEPDAUGHTER Yes . . . just so long as it's clear it was against his wishes.

MOTHER (*from her chair; shaking her head sadly*) For all the good that came of it . . .

STEPDAUGHTER (*turning suddenly toward her* MOTHER) That's not important! The more harm done to us, the more guilt for him.

DIRECTOR (*impatiently*) Yes, I know! I've taken it all into account! If you'll only stop these constant interruptions!

MOTHER (*pleading; to the* DIRECTOR) Please, make them understand that I followed my conscience, that I tried every way . . .

STEPDAUGHTER (*interrupts; disdainfully*) To appease me, to persuade me to forget my revenge! (*to the* DIRECTOR) Go ahead, do as she asks. Because it's true; I enjoy it enormously. Just look . . . the more she begs him, the more she tries to crawl into his heart, the colder he is, the more aloof!

DIRECTOR   Are we going to do the second act or not?

STEPDAUGHTER   I won't say another word. But remember, the whole act can't take place in the garden, no matter how much you want it to. It simply can't be done.

DIRECTOR   Why not?

STEPDAUGHTER   (*indicating the* SON)   Because he spends all his time shut up in his room, alone, away from the rest of us. (*turning toward the* LITTLE BOY)   And then there's the boy—poor, pathetic, bewildered little devil. All of his part takes place indoors, as I've told you.

DIRECTOR   (*impatiently*)   Yes, yes, but you must understand that we simply can't change the scenery three or four times in one act.

LEADING MAN   We used to be able to . . .

LEADING LADY   It made the illusion easier . . .

FATHER   (*in an outburst*)   The illusion! Damn it, don't say illusion! You mustn't use that word! It's too cruel!

DIRECTOR   (*astonished*)   What! Why?

FATHER   Yes, cruel! Surely you understand that by now!

DIRECTOR   (*indicating the* LEADING LADY)   What do you want her to say? She was speaking of the illusion created by the audience . . .

LEADING MAN   By our performances . . .

DIRECTOR   The illusion of reality.

FATHER   I understand you well enough but you do not understand us. Forgive me, but . . . you see . . . for you and your actors all of this is only . . . and quite rightly, I suppose . . . a sort of game.

LEADING LADY   (*interrupting indignantly*)   A game indeed! We're not children! We're professional actors! This is a serious business to us!

FATHER   I don't deny it. What I meant, when I used the word "game," was that . . . (*to the* LEADING LADY; *indicating the entire company with a gesture*) . . . all of you are dedicated, as you yourself just said, to the creation of the illusion of reality.

DIRECTOR   Exactly!

FATHER   But when you consider that we, as you see us now . . . (*He gestures to include the other* CHARACTERS *and himself*) . . . have no other reality outside of this illusion . . .

DIRECTOR   (*confused; looking toward the* ACTORS *who are also confused*)   Now what's that supposed to mean?

FATHER   (*with a slight smile*)   What else can it mean . . . except that what is for you an illusion, which you are able on occasion to create, is our only reality. (*He pauses, moves closer to the* DIRECTOR)   Think about it for a moment. (*looking into the eyes of the* DIRECTOR)   Can you tell me who you really are? (*He points a long index finger at the* DIRECTOR)

DIRECTOR   Who I am? I'm myself!

FATHER   And if I were to say to you that that isn't true, that you are me?

DIRECTOR   I would say you were crazy!

(*Some of the* ACTORS *laugh*)

FATHER   (*indicating the* ACTORS *who are laughing*)   They're quite right to laugh because, to them, this is really nothing but a game. (*to the* DIRECTOR)   It's only in fun that . . . (*indicating the* LEADING MAN) . . . this gentleman here, who is "himself" must also pretend to be "me" while I, on the contrary, am "myself" and am right here before you. You see, I've trapped you!

DIRECTOR   (*not understanding; irritated*)   But you said all this before! Must we go through it again?

FATHER   No, no, that's not my intention at all. In fact, I want to ask you to abandon this game of illusion . . . (*looking at the* LEADING LADY, *as if warning her not to say anything*) . . . which you and your actors are accustomed to play here. Let me ask you again, very seriously, who are you?

DIRECTOR   (*turning to the* ACTORS; *astonished and irritated*)   What a lot of nerve he has! He who calls himself a character comes and asks me who I am?

FATHER   (*with dignity but without haughtiness*)   A character may always ask a man who he is. Because a character has his own complete identity, marked by his own special characteristics, limited to his own precise existence. As a result, a character is always "somebody," generally a "nobody."

DIRECTOR   That may all be true, I don't know. But you're asking your question *of me, the Director, the Boss,* do you understand that?

FATHER   (*lowering his voice; with mellifluous humility*)   But only to know if you really see yourself. Here you are, at this very moment filled with the solid reality of your own existence. But let me ask you to think back to some moment of your life in the past—ten years ago, let's say. Can you remember the exact circumstances in which you were living, the feelings which you felt and which others felt for you? (*The* DIRECTOR *gestures that he can remember, vaguely; the* FATHER *continues quickly*)   But remember, once *they were* your reality! Don't you feel . . . I won't say this stage . . . don't you feel the very earth itself sinking from beneath your feet when you realize that all your solid reality as of this moment is destined to become the half-remembered dream of tomorrow?

DIRECTOR (*not understanding a word the* FATHER *has just said*) What? What are you talking about?

FATHER I only want to show you that while we . . . (*He indicates himself and the other* CHARACTERS) . . . have no other reality beyond this one single illusion, you have no reality at all. For what you feel at this moment, all of your thoughts and actions of today are destined to become an illusion of the past to you tomorrow.

DIRECTOR (*trying to make fun of the* FATHER) Oh, fine! What you're saying, then, is that you and your drama, which you want to perform here, are more real than I am?

FATHER (*completely serious*) Beyond any doubt.

DIRECTOR You don't say?

FATHER I thought you realized that from the beginning.

DIRECTOR You're more real than I am?

FATHER If your reality can change from day to day . . .

DIRECTOR Of course it changes! My reality, as you call it, is always changing, just like everyone else's!

FATHER (*with a cry*) Not ours! Don't you see? That is the great difference! Our reality doesn't change; it cannot change; it cannot ever be other than it is because it is fixed, forever! That is what is so dreadful, so terrible, this immutable reality! It should make you shudder just to come near us!

DIRECTOR (*suddenly struck by an idea; in an outburst*) Just one thing: I should like to know when you have ever seen a character who comes out of his part and pleads, as you do, and proposes things and offers explanations? What is all this? I've never heard of such a thing!

FATHER You've never seen it happen before because authors usually hide the details of their creative work. When the characters have really come to life before their author, he does nothing but follow their words, their gestures, the action which they suggest to him. And he must want them to behave as they themselves want to behave, for God help him if he doesn't! When a character is born, he instantly acquires his independence, even from his own author, to the point that others may even imagine him in situations for which his author never intended him, and he may acquire a meaning of which his author never dreamt!

DIRECTOR Yes, yes, I know all that.

FATHER Well, then, what is so astonishing about us? Consider our tragedy, first brought to life by the imagination of our author and then, later, denied our lives. And then tell me if we, as characters, abandoned this way, alive yet without life, are not justified in doing as we have done and are doing even now before you? Ah, we did everything we could for a long time, a long long time, believe me, trying to persuade him to give us life. We all tried to move him, first me, then her . . . (*indicates the* STEPDAUGHTER) . . . and even this poor woman . . . (*indicates the* MOTHER)

STEPDAUGHTER (*coming forward; as if in a daydream*) It's all true. I tried to tempt him, many times, when he was sitting at his desk at twilight, feeling a little melancholy, not even able to decide whether to turn on the lights or to let the shadows fill his room . . . and those shadows were filled with us, coming to tempt him . . . (*as if she can see herself there by the author's desk; annoyed by the presence of the* ACTORS) Oh, if you would only all go away! If you would only leave us here alone, the mother with that son, I with the child, and the boy there alone, always alone . . . and then I with him . . . (*She points to the* FATHER) . . . and then I alone, I, alone in the shadows . . . (*She makes a sudden motion as if trying to reach out and illuminate those shadows, as if trying to seize a life that avoids her grasp*) Ah, my life! My life! What scenes we offered him! And I, I have tempted him more than all the others put together!

FATHER Yes, and it may very well be your fault that he didn't give us the life we begged for! Your constant demands, your . . . "overemotionalism" . . .

STEPDAUGHTER Nonsense! He made me this way himself! (*to the* DIRECTOR) I believe that he abandoned us out of dejection over the current condition of the theatre with its constant pandering to public taste as measured by the box office . . .

DIRECTOR Oh, for God's sake! Now we really must go on! We must come to the action, ladies and gentlemen!

STEPDAUGHTER It seems to me that we have too much action for you already, without staging our entrance into his house. (*She indicates the* FATHER; *then turns back to the*

DIRECTOR) You said yourself we couldn't change scenes every five minutes.

DIRECTOR   That's right. The idea is to group all of the actions together in one dramatic scene. We simply can't, for example, show your little brother returning home from school and wandering like some lost soul from room to room, hiding in corners and behind doors, and all the time thinking about a project which . . . what did you say it did to him?

STEPDAUGHTER   It consumes him . . . wastes him away.

DIRECTOR   I don't remember your saying that. And all the time you can see it growing in his eyes, is that right?

STEPDAUGHTER   Yes! Just look at him! (*She points to the* BOY *who is standing close to the* MOTHER)

DIRECTOR   Yes, yes, and at the very same time the little girl is playing in the garden, blissfully unaware of what is happening. One in the house, one in the garden . . . now do you really think that's practical?

STEPDAUGHTER   (*very emotional*)   But you must show her, playing in the sun, playing joyfully! That's my only reward; her gaiety, her holiday in that garden after all the misery and squalor of that loathsome room where the four of us were sleeping together . . . I with her . . . I, imagine it, with the horror of my contaminated body next to hers as she slept, holding me tightly with her little loving innocent arms. In the garden when she saw me, she would run to me and take me by the hand, to show me the flowers. She didn't care for the big flowers; instead, she would walk me around to show me the little ones she'd discovered, "wee, teeny ones" she called them, wanting to show them all to me, so happily, so happily!

(*Tortured by this memory, the* STEPDAUGHTER *breaks into long, desperate weeping, bringing her head down onto her arms and resting them on a table. All are deeply moved by her emotion; the* DIRECTOR *finally approaches her, speaking in a paternal tone, trying to comfort her*)

DIRECTOR   We'll show the garden; we'll show the garden, don't worry about that. And you'll see, it'll be just the way you want it. We'll play it all in the garden. (*turning to the* FIRST STAGE MANAGER) Let's have those two Cypress trees we've still got hanging. They'll do as well as anything else.

(*The* FIRST STAGE MANAGER *calls off-stage asking for the Cypress trees to be lowered;*

after a moment, two Cypress trees are lowered from the flies down onto the stage. They come into place in front of the fountain. The DIRECTOR *turns to the* STEPDAUGHTER)

DIRECTOR   Ah, that's the ticket. At least this will give us a rough idea, anyway. (*to a* STAGEHAND, *off-stage*) Now let me have a little sky!

STAGEHAND   (*off-stage*)   Which one?

DIRECTOR   The light blue one. It should come down right behind the fountain. (*A plain white "cyc" comes down from the flies*) Not the white one! I said the light blue sky! Never mind, leave it. It'll do. (*calling off-stage, in the other direction*) Hey, you on the lights: let me have some moonlight blues, plenty of blues! (*A flood of blue light comes in*) Yes, that's it! Fine!

(*The scene is now a mysterious, moonlit garden, as the* DIRECTOR *requested; the atmosphere is such that it leads the* ACTORS *to move and speak as they would in a garden at night; everything is very soft and enigmatic*)

DIRECTOR   (*turning to the* STEPDAUGHTER) And now, instead of the boy hiding himself in the rooms upstairs, let's have him hide in the garden, behind the trees. (*The* STEPDAUGHTER *nods weak assent. The* DIRECTOR's *tone becomes more businesslike*) You understand it's going to be rather difficult to find a child who can play that scene with you, the one in which she shows you the flowers. (*turning to the* BOY) Here, boy, come here a minute. Let's see how this is going to work. (*as the* BOY *does not move*) Come on, come on. (*Crossing, he takes hold of the* BOY, *pulling him forward; he tries to hold the* BOY's *head up but it keeps falling forward*) Now be a good boy . . . come along . . . say, something's the matter with him . . . my God, doesn't he ever say anything . . . (*He turns the* BOY *around, leads him behind the trees*) Come up here for a minute. Let me see you hide behind these trees. (*The* BOY *disappears behind a tree*) Now poke your head out a little, as if you were spying on someone. (*The* DIRECTOR *moves downstage, studies the effect he has created; the* BOY *repeats the action of putting his head out from behind the tree; somehow this action makes the* ACTORS *uneasy, fills them with fright and dismay; the* DIRECTOR *speaks to the* CHARACTERS) Now, if the little girl were to surprise him while he was spying and run over to him, wouldn't he have to say something then?

STEPDAUGHTER   (*rising*)   But, surely . . . you're not hoping that he will speak . . . at least, not while *he* . . . is here? If you really want the boy to speak, you must send him away. (*Again she indicates the* SON)

SON (*starting toward the* ACTORS) I'll go! I'm delighted! There's nothing I'd like better!

DIRECTOR No, no, wait! Where're you going! Stick around a minute!

(*The* MOTHER, *terrified that the* SON *might actually leave, rises; instinctively she holds out her arms toward the* SON *as if to pull him back; but she does not move toward him*)

SON (*to the* DIRECTOR *who has taken hold of his arm; trying to exit into the wings*) I have nothing to do with all this. Let me go! Please let me go!

DIRECTOR What do you mean you have nothing to do with all this?

STEPDAUGHTER (*calm; sardonic*) There's no need to hold him. He won't go away.

FATHER (*quietly*) He has to play the terrible scene in the garden with his mother.

SON (*resolutely*) I will not "play" anything. I've told you so from the beginning. (*to the* DIRECTOR) Let go of me!

STEPDAUGHTER (*crossing quickly to the* DIRECTOR) Please. (*She pulls down the arm with which the* DIRECTOR *was restraining the* SON) Let him go. (*to the* SON) Well . . . go! (*The* SON *tries to exit from the stage but he is held as if by some occult power. He cannot leave; then, amidst the stupor and dismay of the* ACTORS, *he crosses and tries to exit from the other side of the stage; again he is unable to leave. The* STEPDAUGHTER, *who has been watching him scornfully, now bursts into laughter*) You see? He can't! He is forced to remain here. He is forever chained to us. But if I . . . and I really do run away when I can no longer stand even to be in the same room with him, and I must run away because I loathe the very sight of him . . . if I must stay here and put up with the disgust that wells up inside me every time I look at him, then you realize that he must also stay . . . with that precious father of his . . . and that mother who has no other son but him . . . (*turning to the* MOTHER) Come on, Mama, it's time . . . (*turning to the* DIRECTOR; *indicating the* MOTHER's *actions*) You see, she has risen; she has to keep him here . . . (*to the* MOTHER; *as if drawing her across to the* SON *by an invisible string*) . . . do what you must do; play your scene. (*again to the* DIRECTOR) A woman like that . . . you can imagine how reluctant she is to show her real feelings with all your actors here . . . but she's so des-

perate to be with him that . . . you see . . . she's ready to play the scene anyway!

(*The* MOTHER, *who has already neared the* SON, *turns as the* STEPDAUGHTER *finishes her speech and gestures that she consents to play the scene*)

SON (*suddenly*) Ah, but I'm not! And I won't do it! If I cannot leave, then I'll stay, but I repeat again, I will not be part of your sordid little drama!

FATHER (*very excited; to the* DIRECTOR) You must force him to play it!

SON No one can force me to do it!

FATHER I will force you, then!

STEPDAUGHTER Wait a minute, wait a minute! First the child must go to the fountain. (*She runs to the* LITTLE GIRL, *bends over her, takes the child's face between her hands*) My poor little darling, you're frightened, aren't you? You don't even know where we are. It's a stage, baby. (*pretending to answer a question from the* LITTLE GIRL) What is a stage? It's a place where people pretend to be very serious, a place where they put on plays. We have a play to put on now. A very serious one, you know. And you're in it, baby. (*embracing the* LITTLE GIRL; *holding her close for a moment; rocking her back and forth in her arms*) Oh, my darling, what an ugly play, what an ugly play for you to be in! And what a horrible part there is for you! A garden, a fountain . . . (*gesturing toward the fountain and the trees*) . . . but these are only make-believe, you know. That's the whole trouble; it's all make-believe here. But perhaps a baby like you would rather have a make-believe fountain than a real one, so you can play in it, eh? Oh, what a mockery! To all the others it is only an illusion, a game, a joke! But not to you! For you, who are real, my little darling, it is a real fountain that you play by. A big, beautiful, green fountain with lovely trees throwing their shadows over the waters and lots and lots of little ducks swimming around, breaking the shadows with trails of ripples. You want to catch one of the little ducks . . . (*suddenly screaming in anguish*) No, Rosetta, no!!! Ah!!! If only your mother would concern herself about you, but she can't stay away from that wretch of a son . . . (*very depressed*) . . . what a hell of a mood it puts me in. And as for you . . . (*She turns from the* LITTLE GIRL; *takes hold of the* BOY) What are you doing there, always with your hands in your pockets? It'll be your fault, too, if the baby drowns! (*pulling one of the* BOY's *hands from a pocket*)

What have you got there? What are you hiding in your hand? (*As she pulls his hand toward her, she sees that he is holding a revolver*) Where did you get this? (*The* BOY, *frightened, pales and pulls away; he does not answer*) You idiot! If I'd been in your shoes instead of killing myself I'd have killed one of them, or both of them, the father and the son!

(*The* STEPDAUGHTER *now releases the* BOY, *pushes him behind one of the trees; she then takes the* LITTLE GIRL *by the hand and leads her to the fountain, putting her into the basin of the fountain so that she is completely hidden from sight. The* STEPDAUGHTER *then gets down on her knees and buries her head in her hands at the edge of the fountain*)

DIRECTOR (*pleased*) Wonderful! That was great! (*turning to the* SON) And, meanwhile . . .

SON (*with dignity*) What is this "and meanwhile"? That isn't right. I tell you there was no scene between her and me! (*He indicates the* MOTHER) If you'll just ask her, she'll tell you the same thing.

(*During the past few moments, the* JUVENILE *and the* SECOND FEMALE LEAD *have separated themselves from the group of* ACTORS *and taken up places near the* CHARACTERS; *the* JUVENILE *is studying the* SON, *whose part he is to play; the* SECOND FEMALE LEAD *is studying the* MOTHER)

MOTHER (*slowly nodding "yes"*) Yes, it's true. I went into his room . . .

SON Into my room! Not into the garden!

DIRECTOR That's not important. I've told you: we've got to consolidate the action.

SON (*turning to the* JUVENILE *irritated by his staring*) What do you want?

JUVENILE Nothing. I was just watching you.

SON (*turning toward the* SECOND FEMALE LEAD) And you're watching her . . . (*He indicates the* MOTHER) . . . is that it? To play her part?

DIRECTOR Exactly, and it seems to me that you should be grateful for their interest in you.

SON Oh, sure; thanks a lot. (*patiently*) Hasn't it dawned on you yet that you'll never be able to stage this play? Because there's simply nothing of us in you at all. You study us from the outside—how preposterous! Don't you see that it's impossible for me to live in front of a mirror which not only doesn't reflect my likeness, but instead throws back my image twisted and distorted into . . . something grotesque . . . I don't know what to call it . . .

FATHER He's right. He's absolutely right, you know!

DIRECTOR (*patiently waving the* JUVENILE *and the* SECOND FEMALE LEAD *aside*) Very well; move away from them for a while.

SON It doesn't really matter. I'm in no hurry.

DIRECTOR Keep quiet now and let me hear your mother. (*to the* MOTHER) Well? You said you went into his room . . . ?

MOTHER Yes. I couldn't stand it any longer. I went into his room to empty my heart of all the anguish which was tormenting me. But as soon as he saw me come in . . .

SON (*interrupting*) I ran away. There was no scene between us. I ran away in order to prevent a scene, because I never make scenes.

MOTHER It's true. That's what happened.

DIRECTOR But we must have a scene between him and you. It's the recognition scene!

MOTHER Don't you think I want it, too? If you could persuade him to speak to me, just for a few minutes, so that I can tell him all that is in my heart . . .

FATHER (*approaching the* SON) You must do it! For your mother's sake!

SON (*more determined than ever*) I won't do anything.

FATHER (*seizing the* SON *by his jacket; shaking him*) No, no, no! Once and for all, no!!

(*The* FATHER *and the* SON *continue to wrestle with one another; there is general excitement; the* MOTHER *tries to separate them*)

MOTHER For heaven's sake, stop it, stop it, please!

FATHER (*as they wrestle*) You must obey! You must!

SON (*finally throwing his* FATHER *to the floor near the apron of the stage*) What is all this? You're crazy! Get hold of yourself! Why must you insist on dragging out all our shame for everyone to see? I won't do it! I'll have no part in it! And I'm speaking for our author, as well! Even he didn't want us put on the stage!

DIRECTOR But you came here, of your own free will . . .

SON (*indicating the* FATHER) He insisted on coming, bringing us all with him. And then he told you not only the things that happened, as if God knows that wasn't enough, but he even added things that never happened at all!

DIRECTOR Well then, won't you at least tell me what really did happen? You could do that. You rushed out of your room without saying a word, is that right?

SON (*after hesitating for a moment, then*

nodding in agreement) Exactly. I didn't want to get involved in a scene.

DIRECTOR And then? What did you do next?

SON (*in anguish; painfully aware that everyone's attention is centered on him; moving a few steps across the stage toward the fountain)* Nothing . . . I wanted some air . . . and crossing the garden . . . (*He breaks off, lost in gloomy memories)*

DIRECTOR (*urging him to continue; deeply affected by the reluctance of the* SON, *and by his gloom)* Yes? Crossing the garden . . . ?

SON (*exasperated; hiding his face in his hands)* Why are you doing this? Why are you insisting I tell it? It's too horrible!

(*At this, the* MOTHER, *trembling all over, moans aloud and looks toward the fountain)*

DIRECTOR (*noticing the* MOTHER's *glance; turning toward the* SON *with increasing apprehension)* The little girl . . . ?

SON (*not looking at the fountain; staring out at the audience)* Yes. There in the fountain . . .

FATHER (*pitying; pointing to the* MOTHER) She followed him . . . (*He indicates the* SON)

DIRECTOR (*to the* SON) So what did you do?

SON (*slowly; still looking out at the audience)* I ran to the fountain, to fish her out, but I saw something so dreadful I stopped. I saw, behind a tree . . . horrible! . . . the boy, the boy, standing there, staring with the eyes of a madman, staring at the fountain where his little sister was drowned. (*The* STEPDAUGHTER *has run to the fountain and is bending over the fountain, hiding the body of the child; her sobs echo in the background; there is a pause; then the* SON *continues slowly)* I began to walk toward him, and . . .

(*Behind the trees, where the* BOY *has remained hidden, a shot rings out)*

MOTHER (*with a terrible, heart-rending cry; running with the* SON *and some of the* ACTORS *toward the* BOY; *the stage is in turmoil)* Oh, my son! My son! (*Over the confusion, we hear her voice)* Help me! Oh, God, help me!

DIRECTOR (*trying to force his way to the* BOY *who is carried off behind the white backdrop)* Is he hurt? Is he really hurt?

(*By now everyone except the* FATHER *and the* DIRECTOR *has disappeared behind the backdrop; we hear excited whisperings from behind the backdrop; then, from both the right and left of the backdrop, the* ACTORS *return to the stage)*

LEADING LADY (*re-entering from the left; full of sorrow and shock; there must be no doubt that the* BOY *is truly, in reality, dead)* He's dead. That poor child . . . he's really dead. In the name of Christ, what is all this??? (*She begins to weep)*

LEADING MAN (*re-entering from the right; laughing)* What are you talking about, dead? It isn't real. It's all a trick. Don't let them kid you.

LEADING LADY I saw!! That child is dead!!!

OTHER ACTORS (*together)* It isn't a trick! It's true! It happened! Just as we saw it!

FATHER (*crying out)* What do you mean a trick? It is reality, reality, ladies and gentlemen! Reality!

(*During this speech, the* STEPDAUGHTER, *the* SON *and the* MOTHER *unobstrusively exit behind the backdrop; now the* FATHER *turns and exits behind the backdrop)*

DIRECTOR A trick? Reality? What's going on around here? Let me have some lights! Lights!!!!

(*Suddenly both the stage and the auditorium are flooded in a blaze of light. The* DIRECTOR *shakes his head as if to clear it of some frightful nightmare; all of the* ACTORS *are looking around, their eyes filled with suspicion, fear, bewilderment, sorrow; the* DIRECTOR *finally realizes that all the* CHARACTERS *are gone)*

DIRECTOR They're gone! (*very upset)* My God, nothing like this has ever happened to me before in my entire life! (*suddenly exasperated)* They've cost me a whole day of rehearsal! (*looking at his watch; to the* ACTORS) Well, what are you hanging around for now? Go on, get out of here! There'll be no more rehearsal today! (*Ad libbing comments, the stricken* ACTORS *quickly leave the stage. The* DIRECTOR, *after a last look at them, turns toward the wings)* You, electrician! Put out the lights! We're done for today! (*He has not quite finished saying this when the entire theatre is plunged into darkness)* Hey, what're you doing? At least leave me enough light so I can get out of here!

(*Suddenly, as if by error, the background is illuminated by a green light. Through the white backcloth, we see the shadows of the* FATHER, MOTHER, STEPDAUGHTER, *and the* SON. *Seeing them, the* DIRECTOR *runs from the stage in terror)*

THE EMPEROR (ENRICO IV)

English Version by Eric Bentley

CAST OF CHARACTERS

FIRST VALET
SECOND VALET
HARALD (*whose real name is Franco*)
LANDOLF (*whose real name is Lolo*) —supposed Privy Councillors
ORDULF (*whose real name is Momo*)
BERTOLD (*whose real name is Fino*)
GIOVANNI, *the Butler*

MARQUIS CARLO DI NOLLI
BARON TITO BELCREDI
DR. DIONISIO GENONI, *a psychiatrist*
COUNTESS MATILDA SPINA, *the Baron's mistress*
FRIDA, *her daughter, engaged to the Marquis*
"HENRY THE FOURTH, EMPEROR OF GERMANY," (*the Marquis's uncle*)

SCENE *A solitary villa in the Umbrian countryside*

TIME *The present (the play was first performed in 1922)*

ACT ONE

(*A hall in the villa got up in every way to pass for the throne room of the German Emperor Henry the Fourth in his imperial residence at Goslar, Hanover. But in the midst of the ancient furnishings two large modern oil paintings—life-size portraits—stand out from the back wall. They are supported, not far*

The Emperor, translated by Eric Bentley, is reprinted by permission of E. P. Dutton & Co., Inc., publishers of *Naked Masks: Five Plays* by Luigi Pirandello, edited by Eric Bentley. Copyright 1922, 1952 by E. P. Dutton & Co., Inc., renewal 1950 by Stefano, Fausto, and Lietta Pirandello. Translation copyright © 1952 by Eric Bentley. All inquiries concerning performance rights should be addressed to The Toby Cole Agency, 234 West 44th St., New York 36, N. Y.

above the ground, on a sort of pedestal or ledge of carved wood which runs the whole length of the wall. [It is broad and protrudes so you can sit on it as on a long bench.] Between the two portraits is the throne itself—the imperial chair and its low baldachin—which is, as it were, inserted in the pedestal dividing it into two parts. The two portraits represent a lady and a gentleman, both young, rigged up in carnival costumes, one as the Emperor Henry the Fourth and the other as Countess Matilda of Tuscany. Doors to left and right.

Two valets, in 11th-century costumes, are lying on the ledge. Suddenly they jump down, in surprise apparently, running to place themselves, stiff as statues, at the foot of the throne, one on each side, with their halberds. Soon afterwards, by the second door on the right, HARALD, LANDOLF, ORDULF, *and* BERTOLD *come in. These young men are paid by the Marquis Carlo di Nolli to pretend to be Privy Councillors—regal vassals, belonging to the lower aristocracy, at the court of the Emperor. They are therefore dressed as German Knights of the 11th Century. The last of them,* BERTOLD [*his real name is* FINO], *is doing the job for the first time. His three companions are amusing themselves telling him everything. The whole scene should be played with extreme vivacity*)

LANDOLF (*to* BERTOLD, *as if following up an explanation*) And this is the throne room!

HARALD At Goslar!

ORDULF Or, if you'd prefer that, in his castle in the Hartz Mountains!

HARALD Or at Worms.

LANDOLF It jumps around a bit. According to the scene we're acting out. Now here, now there—

ORDULF Now in Saxony—

HARALD Now in Lombardy—

LANDOLF Now on the Rhine.

FIRST VALET (*holding his position, hardly moving his lips*) Sss, Sss!

HARALD (*hearing and turning*) What's the matter?

FIRST VALET (*still like a statue, in an undertone*) Well, is he coming or isn't he?

(*The allusion is to the* EMPEROR)

ORDULF He isn't. He's sleeping. Take it easy.

SECOND VALET (*dropping the pose as his partner does so, taking a long breath, and going to lie down again on the ledge*) Well, for God's sake, why didn't you say so before?

BERTOLD (*who has been observing everything in mixed amazement and perplexity, walking round the room and looking at it, then looking at his clothes and his companions' clothes*) But, look . . . this room . . . these clothes . . . *What* Henry the Fourth? . . . I don't quite get it.—Is it Henry the Fourth of France or Henry the Fourth of England?

(*At this demand,* LANDOLF, HARALD *and* ORDULF *burst into a roar of laughter*)

LANDOLF (*laughing all the time and pointing at* BERTOLD *as if inviting the others—who also go on laughing—to continue making fun of him*) Is it Henry the Fourth of France?

ORDULF Or Henry the Fourth of England?

HARALD Why, my dear child, it's Henry the Fourth of *Germany!*

ORDULF The great and tragic Emperor—

LANDOLF —who repented and knelt in the snow before the Pope at Canossa! And day by day in this room we keep the war going—the terrible war between Church and State—

ORDULF —between Pope and Emperor!

BERTOLD (*covering his head with his hands to protect himself against this avalanche of information*) I see, I see!—I just didn't get it. Clothes like this. A room like this. I was right: these are *not* sixteenth-century clothes!

HARALD Sixteenth century indeed!

ORDULF We're between the year 1000 and the year 1100.

LANDOLF Count it up yourself: if we're in the snow at Canossa on January 25, 1077 . . .

BERTOLD (*more distressed than ever*) My God, this is a disaster!

ORDULF It certainly is, if you thought it was the *French* court.

BERTOLD The *English* court, I studied up on *English* history, I was reading Shakespeare and everything . . .

LANDOLF My dear man, *where* were you educated? Still, you're only a couple of centuries out.

BERTOLD (*getting angry*) But why in God's name couldn't they have told me it was Henry the Fourth of Germany! I had two weeks to study the thing up—I can't tell you the number of books I've had my nose in!

HARALD Look, dear boy. Didn't you know that poor Tony was called Adalbert, Bishop of Bremen, in this house?

BERTOLD Adalbert, Bishop of . . . ? How'd I know that?!

LANDOLF Well, you see how it was: when Tony died, the Marquis . . .

BERTOLD Ah, so it *was* the Marquis. Then why on earth didn't he tell me . . .

HARALD Maybe he thought you knew, dear boy.

LANDOLF He wasn't going to take anyone else on. There were three of us left, and he thought we'd be enough. But then *he* took to shouting: "Adalbert driven out, Adalbert driven out!" Poor Tony, you see, it didn't seem to *him* Tony had died, it seemed to *him* the bishops of Mainz and Cologne had driven Adalbert out!

BERTOLD (*taking his head in his two hands and keeping it there*) But I never heard a word of all this!

ORDULF Then you're in a fix, my dear fellow.

' HARALD And the trouble is that we don't know who *you* are either, dear boy!

BERTOLD Even you don't know? You don't know what part I'm to play?

ORDULF Well, um—Bertold.

BERTOLD Bertold? Who's he? *Why* Bertold?

LANDOLF "They've driven Adalbert away from me? Then *I* want Bertold, I want Bertold!"—He took to shouting *that.*

HARALD The three of us just stared at each other. Who the devil could this Bertold be?

ORDULF So here you are, my dear fellow,—Bertold.

LANDOLF And what a wonderful job you'll make of it.

BERTOLD (*rebelling and starting to go*)

Oh, no! Not for me, thank you! I'm going, I'm going.

HARALD (*while he and* ORDULF *hold him back, amid laughter*) Calm down, dear boy, calm down!

ORDULF You won't be the Bertold of the story.

LANDOLF Comfort yourself with the thought that even we don't really know who we are. He's Harald, he's Ordulf, I'm Landolf . . . That's what we are *called,* and by now we've got used to it, but who *are* we? Names. Names of the period.—And that's what you'll be—a name—of the period: Bertold. Only one of us, the late lamented Tony, ever had a good part, a part out of the story—the Bishop of Bremen. He looked like a real bishop, he was marvelous, poor Tony!

HARALD God, how the dear boy would study: read, read, read!

LANDOLF And he gave orders. Even to His Majesty. Oh yes, he knew how to put himself over. Guided him. Was a tutor. An adviser in effect. We're Privy Councillors for that matter. But with us it's just for appearances: because the history books say the Emperor was hated by the *higher* aristocracy for surrounding himself at court with young men of the *lower* aristocracy.

ORDULF That's us, my dear fellow.

LANDOLF It really is a shame, because, well, with these clothes we could make a sensational appearance on the stage. In a costume play. They go over big these days. The Life and Loves of Henry the Fourth—what a story! Material not for one but for half a dozen tragedies! And now look at us! Just look at the four of us—and those two unfortunates standing by the throne like stuck pigs. (*He points at the* TWO VALETS)—No one—no one puts us on stage, no one gives us scenes to act. We've got the—what do you call it?—we've got the *form*—but we don't have the *content!* —We're worse off than the Emperor's real Privy Councillors because, well, it's true no one had given *them* a part to play either, but they didn't know they *had* to play one, they played it because they played it, it wasn't a part, it was their life, see what I mean? They acted in their own interests, they fought their rivals, they sold investitures, and so forth, while we . . . here are we in this beautiful court, dressed up as you see, and for what? To do what? To do nothing . . . Six puppets hanging on the greenroom wall.

HARALD No, no, dear boy, pardon me, but our replies do have to be in character.

LANDOLF Yes, as far as that goes—

BERTOLD And you said we do nothing! How'm *I* going to reply in character? I've got myself all prepared for Henry of England, and now someone calling himself Henry of Germany comes . . . comes butting in!

(LANDOLF, ORDULF, HARALD *start laughing again*)

HARALD You'd better attend to it, dear boy—

ORDULF —and we'll help you, my dear fellow—

HARALD —we've lots of books in there, my dear man—but first we'll just run through the main points—

ORDULF —so you'll have a general idea—

HARALD Look, at this! (*turns him round and shows him the Countess Matilda's portrait on the back wall*)—Who's that for example?

BERTOLD (*looking*) That? Well, in the first place, if you don't mind my saying so, it's out of place. Two modern paintings in the midst of all this medieval stuff?

HARALD You're right, dear boy. And as a matter of fact they weren't there originally. Behind the pictures, there are two niches—for two statues they were going to put in—in the style of the period. The niches stayed empty—then they were covered by these two canvases—

LANDOLF (*interrupting and continuing*) —which would certainly be out of place—if they really were paintings!

BERTOLD They're not paintings? What are they then?

LANDOLF If you go and touch them, yes, they're paintings. But for *him* (*He points mysteriously out right, alluding to the Emperor*) —since he does *not* touch them . . .

BERTOLD He doesn't? What are they then —for him?

LANDOLF Well, this is just my interpretation, don't forget. All the same, I think it's pretty good. They're—images. Images—like, um, like images in a mirror, you see? That one there is him (*pointing*), the living image of him, like in this throne room—which is also— as it should be—in the style of the period. What are you so amazed about, may I ask? If we place you in front of a mirror, won't you see *your* living image? Won't you see the "you" of today in the trappings of yesteryear? Well then, it's as if we had two mirrors here—two living images—in the midst of a world which . . . Well, you'll see for yourself, now you live with us, you'll see how this world too, every part of it, will come to life.

BERTOLD   Now, really, I didn't come here to go mad!

HARALD   Go mad, dear boy? Ts, ts. You're going to have fun!

BERTOLD   (*to* LANDOLF) You certainly have quite a line in philosophy!

LANDOLF   My dear man, you can't go behind the scenes of history—eight hundred years of it—and not bring back a bit of experience!

HARALD   Let's be going, dear boy. We'll fix you up in no time—

LANDOLF   We'll fasten the wires on and have you in full working order: the perfect marionette!

ORDULF   Let's go. (*takes him by the arm, to lead him off*)

BERTOLD   (*stopping and looking toward the other portrait*) Just a minute. You haven't told me who *she* is. The Emperor's wife?

HARALD   No, dear boy. The Emperor's wife is called Bertha of Susa.

ORDULF   The Emperor can't stand her. He wants to be young like us. He's planning to get rid of her.

LANDOLF   That's his fiercest enemy: Countess Matilda. Of Tuscany.

BERTOLD   Wait. Wasn't she the Pope's hostess at . . .

LANDOLF   At Canossa.

ORDULF   Precisely.

HARALD   Now *do* let's get going!

(*They are all moving over toward the door on the right by which they had entered when the old butler* GIOVANNI, *in modern cutaway, comes in at the left*)

GIOVANNI   (*in a great hurry, and worked up*) Sss, sss! Franco! Lolo!

HARALD   (*stopping and turning*) Hey! What do *you* want?

BERTOLD   (*amazed to see him come into the throne room in his modern coat*) What's this? *He* comes in here?

LANDOLF   A visitor from the twentieth century! Away!

(*He and his two comrades make a joke of running over to threaten him and drive him out*)

ORDULF   The Pope's ambassador—away with him!

HARALD   Away with the rogue!

GIOVANNI   (*defending himself, annoyed*) O come on, stop this!

ORDULF   No, you're not allowed in here!

HARALD   Get away, old man!

LANDOLF   (*to* BERTOLD) It's witchcraft! He's a demon conjured up by the Great Magician of Rome! Out with your sword! (*and he reaches for his own*)

GIOVANNI   (*shouting*) Stop this, I say! This is no time for fooling, the Marquis is here, and there's company with him . . .

LANDOLF   (*rubbing his hands*) Oh, wonderful! Ladies?

ORDULF   (*doing the same*) Old? Young?

GIOVANNI   Two gentlemen.

HARALD   But the ladies, who are they?

GIOVANNI   Countess Matilda and her daughter.

LANDOLF   (*amazed*) What? (*pause*) What's that?

ORDULF   (*also amazed*) The Countess, you say?

GIOVANNI   Yes, yes, the Countess!

HARALD   And the two men?

GIOVANNI   I don't know.

HARALD   (*to* BERTOLD) Landolf told you we have form without content in here, but keep your eyes open!

ORDULF   The Pope has sent a whole *bevy* of ambassadors! We'll have fun all right.

GIOVANNI   Will you let me speak?

HARALD   Speak! (*pause*) Speak!

GIOVANNI   Well, one of the two men seems to be a doctor.

LANDOLF   Oh, sure, we're used to *them*.

HARALD   Many thanks, Bertold, you bring us luck!

LANDOLF   You'll see how we'll manage *him*.

BERTOLD   I'm walking into a fine old mess, I can see that.

GIOVANNI   Now listen. They'll be coming into this room.

LANDOLF   (*in amazement and consternation*) What? Is that true? Even she? The Countess will come in here?

HARALD   This is content—with a vengeance!

LANDOLF   This'll be a real tragedy!

BERTOLD   (*his curiosity aroused*) But why? What are you talking about?

ORDULF   (*pointing to the portrait*) The Countess is the woman in the portrait.

LANDOLF   Her daughter is engaged to the Marquis.

HARALD   But what have they come for? That's the question.

ORDULF   If *he* sees her, there'll be fireworks.

LANDOLF   Maybe he won't recognize her any more.

GIOVANNI   If he wakes up, you'll just have to keep him in there.

ORDULF   Are you joking? How'd we do that?

HARALD   You know what he's like, dear boy!

GIOVANNI   Good heavens, use force if need be!—Those are the Marquis's orders. Now get going! Get going!

HARALD   Yes, we'd better go, he may be awake already.

ORDULF   Let's go.

LANDOLF   (*leaving with the others, to* GIOVANNI)   You must explain it all later!

GIOVANNI   (*shouting after them*)   Lock the door on that side, and hide the key! This other door too. (*He points to the other door at right*)

(LANDOLF, HARALD *and* ORDULF *leave by the second door on the right*)

GIOVANNI   (*to the* TWO VALETS)   You must go too, go on, that way! (*He points to the first door on the right*) Lock the door and take the key out of the lock!

(*The* TWO VALETS *leave by the first door on the right.* GIOVANNI *goes to the door on the left and opens it for the* MARQUIS CARLO DI NOLLI)

MARQUIS   You have given the orders properly, Giovanni?

GIOVANNI   Yes, Marquis. Certainly, Marquis.

(*The* MARQUIS *goes out again for a moment to bring the others in. First comes* BARON TITO BELCREDI *and* DR. DIONISIO GENONI, *then* COUNTESS MATILDA SPINA *and her daughter* FRIDA. GIOVANNI *bows and goes out. The* COUNTESS *is about forty-five, still beautiful and shapely, though she too patently repairs the inevitable ravages of time with a violent if expert make-up which gives her the haughty head of a valkyrie. This make-up stands out in high and painful relief from her mouth which is very lovely and very sad. Many years a widow, she now has* BARON TITO BELCREDI *for a friend. Neither she nor other people have ever taken him seriously, or so it appears. What the* BARON *really means to her, he alone fully knows. He can therefore laugh if she needs to pretend she doesn't know, can laugh at the laughter of other people, caused, as it is, by the* COUNTESS's *jests at his expense. Slim, prematurely grey, a little younger than she, he has a curious, bird-shaped head. He would be very vivacious if his agility—which makes him a dreadful swordsman and is in itself life enough—were not actually encased in a sleepy, Arab laziness that comes out in his strange voice which is rather nasal and drawling.* FRIDA, *the* COUNTESS's *daughter, is nineteen years old. Having grown sad in the shade to which her imperious and showy mother relegates her, living in this shade she is also offended by the easy gossip which the mother provokes to the detriment of them both equally. And yet, as luck will have it, she is already engaged—to the* MARQUIS CARLO DI NOLLI, *a stiff young man, very indulgent toward others, yet rigid and shut up in the small space of what he thinks he can be, of what he thinks he is worth, in the world, though at bottom even he doesn't know what this worth is. At any rate his consternation is great at the many responsibilities which he believes weigh him down. Yes, the others can talk, the others can have their fun, lucky they. He cannot. Not that he wouldn't like it. Just that he cannot. He is dressed in the deepest mourning for the death of his mother.* DR. DIONISIO GENONI *has a fine, satyr's face, insolent and rubicund, with protruding eyes, a short, pointed beard that shines like silver. He has refined manners and is almost bald. They enter in a state of consternation, almost afraid, looking with curiosity about the room—all except the* MARQUIS. *And at first they speak in low voices*)

BARON   Splendid, it's very splendid!

DOCTOR   Most interesting, how one can see the madness in the room itself, in inanimate objects, it really *is* splendid, quite splendid!

COUNTESS   (*who has been looking round the room for her portrait, finding it, and moving toward it*)   Ah, so here it is! (*looking at it from a certain distance while different feelings arise within her*) Yes, y-e-s . . . why, look . . . Heavens . . . (*She calls her daughter*) Frida, Frida . . . Look . . .

FRIDA   Ah! Your portrait?

COUNTESS   No, just look, it's not me at all, it's you!

MARQUIS   It's true, isn't it? I told you so.

COUNTESS   I'd never have believed it—to this extent. (*She shakes with a sudden tremor along the spine*) Heavens, what a strange sensation! (*then, looking at her daughter*) What's the matter, Frida? (*Slipping an arm about her waist, she pulls her close*) Come here, don't you see yourself in me—in that picture?

FRIDA   (*with a gasp*)   But it's me, why . . .

COUNTESS   Wouldn't you think so? You couldn't miss it, could you? (*turning to the* BARON) You look, Tito, and *you* tell me!

BARON   (*not looking*)   I say it's not you. I know without looking.

COUNTESS   How stupid, he thinks he's paying me a compliment. (*turning to the* DOCTOR) You tell me, doctor!

(DOCTOR *starts to come over*)

BARON (*with his back turned, pretending to speak to him secretly*) Sss! No, doctor! For heaven's sake, have nothing to do with it!

DOCTOR (*bewildered, smiling*) But why not, why not?

COUNTESS Pay no attention to him, just come. He's insufferable.

FRIDA Don't you know he's a professional fool?

BARON (*to the* DOCTOR, *seeing him go*) Watch your feet, watch your feet, doctor, your feet!

DOCTOR (*as above*) What's wrong with my feet?

BARON You've got hob-nailed boots on!

DOCTOR What?!

BARON And you're walking towards four little feet of delicate, Venetian glass.

DOCTOR (*laughing out loud*) There's nothing staggering, it seems to me, in the fact that a daughter resembles her mother . . .

BARON Crash!! Now it's over.

COUNTESS (*exaggeratedly angered, coming toward the* BARON) What do you mean: Crash!! What is it? What has he been saying?

DOCTOR (*sincerely*) Don't you think I'm right?

BARON (*answering the* COUNTESS) He said there's nothing staggering in it. While *you* are extremely staggered. Why?—if it's all so natural?

COUNTESS (*still more angered*) You fool! It's *because* it's so natural. Because it's *not* my daughter. (*pointing to the canvas*) That is *my* portrait. To find my daughter in it instead of myself is a staggering experience. Believe me, I was quite sincerely staggered, I can't let you say I wasn't!

(*After this violent outburst there is a moment of embarrassed silence*)

FRIDA (*quite annoyed*) Always the same story: arguments about absolutely nothing.

BARON (*also quiet, almost with his tail between his legs, apologetically*) I wasn't saying anything of the sort. (*to* FRIDA) I simply noticed that, from the outset, *you* weren't . . . staggered like your mother. If *you're* staggered, it's merely because the portrait resembles you so strongly.

COUNTESS Obviously! Because there's no way for her to see herself in *me*—as I was at her age. Whereas I, the girl in the portrait, can perfectly well see myself in *her*—as she is now.

DOCTOR True. A portrait stays just as it is. Fixed! It can't move away from the moment when it was made, a distant moment now, and, for the young lady, a moment without

memories. Whereas for her mother it brings back many things: movements, gestures, looks, smiles, things that aren't *in* the portrait at all . . .

COUNTESS Exactly.

DOCTOR (*continuing, turning to her*) For you, naturally, the same things are to be found in your daughter too.

COUNTESS It's so seldom I give way to my feelings, and, when I do, *he* has to come and spoil it for me! Just for the pleasure of hurting me!!

DOCTOR (*impressed with his own perspicacity, starts up again in a professorial tone, turning to the* BARON) Resemblance, my dear Baron, oftentimes has its roots in intangibles. On these lines, it seems eminently explicable that . . .

BARON (*to interrupt the lecture*) Someone might find a resemblance between you and me, my dear professor.

MARQUIS Drop it now, drop it, I beg you. (*He points to the doors on the right, indicating that someone is there who might hear*) We've been sidetracked too much already, coming . . .

FRIDA Of course! With him here . . . (*indicating the* BARON)

COUNTESS (*promptly*) That's why I so much wished he wouldn't come.

BARON Now you've had a lot of fun at my expense. Don't be ungrateful!

MARQUIS Tito, please, that's quite enough. The doctor is with us, and we're here for a very serious purpose. You know how much it means to me.

DOCTOR Precisely. Now let's see if we can't begin by getting certain points quite clear. This portrait of yours, Countess, may I ask how it comes to be here? Was it a gift from you? Did you make him a present of it—I mean in the days—before . . .

COUNTESS Oh, no. How could I have given him presents in those days? I was just a girl—like Frida now—and not engaged at that. No, no, I let him have it three or four years after the accident. I let him have it because his (*indicating the* MARQUIS) mother urged me to.

DOCTOR His (*with a gesture toward the doors on the right, the reference being to Emperor Henry*) sister, that is to say?

MARQUIS Yes, doctor: my mother was his sister. She died a month ago. It's for her sake we've come here—the payment of a debt to her, you might say. In the normal course of events, she (*indicating* FRIDA) and I would be travelling . . .

DOCTOR On business of quite another sort, hm?

MARQUIS Please! My mother died in the

firm conviction that her beloved brother's recovery was imminent.

DOCTOR   You couldn't tell me, perhaps, from what evidence she reached this conclusion?

MARQUIS   I believe it was from certain strange things he said to her not long before she died.

DOCTOR   Strange things? Aha! It would be terribly useful to me to know what those things were, by Jove!

MARQUIS   I don't know myself. I only know mother came home after that last visit extremely upset. It seems he'd shown her a most unusual tenderness, as if he foresaw the coming end. On her deathbed she made me promise never to neglect him, to make sure that people see him, visit him . . .

DOCTOR   I see. Very good. Now, to begin with . . . Oftentimes the most trivial causes lead . . . Well, take this portrait . . .

COUNTESS   Heavens, doctor, how can you attach such overwhelming importance to the portrait. It happened to make a big impression on me for a moment just because I hadn't seen it in so long.

DOCTOR   Just a minute, please, just . . .

BARON   But it's so. It must have been there fifteen years . . .

COUNTESS   More! More than eighteen by now!

DOCTOR   I beg your pardons, but you don't yet know what questions I'm going to ask. I set great store—very great store—by those two portraits. I fancy they were painted before the famous—and most unfortunate—cavalcade, isn't that so?

COUNTESS   Why, of course.

DOCTOR   So it was when he was . . . normal . . . quite sane . . . that's what I'm really getting at.—Was it he who suggested having it painted—to you?

COUNTESS   No, no, doctor. Lots of us were having them done. I mean, of those who took part in the cavalcade. They were something to remember it by.

BARON   I had one of me done!

COUNTESS   We hardly waited for the costumes to be ready!

BARON   Because, you see, it was proposed to collect them all in the drawing room of the villa that the cavalcade came from. As a memorial. A whole gallery of pictures. But afterwards each of us wanted to keep his own picture for himself.

COUNTESS   As for mine, as I told you, I let *him* have it—and without very much regret—because his mother . . . (*indicating the* MARQUIS *again*)

DOCTOR   You don't know if he actually asked for it?

COUNTESS   No, I don't. Perhaps he did. Or perhaps it was his sister—as a loving gesture . . .

DOCTOR   Just one other point: the cavalcade—was it his idea?

BARON   (*promptly*)   Oh, no! It was mine!

DOCTOR   Now, please . . .

BARON   The idea was mine, I tell you! After all there's nothing to boast of in *that*—seeing how it turned out! It was . . . oh, I remember it well: one evening, early in November, at the club, I was leafing through an illustrated magazine, a German one—just looking at the pictures, you understand, I don't know German—and there was a picture of the German Emperor in . . . what was the university town he'd been a student in?

DOCTOR   Bonn, Bonn.

BARON   Possibly, Bonn. He was on horseback and dressed in one of the strange traditional costumes of the oldest student fraternities. He was followed by a cortege of other students of noble birth, also on horseback and in costume. Well, the idea came to me from that picture. I should have told you some of us at the club had been thinking of possible masquerades for the next carnival. I proposed this . . . historical cavalcade. Historical, in a manner of speaking. It was really a Tower of Babel: each of us was to choose a character, from this century or that, king or emperor or prince, with his lady beside him, queen or empress. All were to be on horseback. With the horses harnessed and dressed up—in the style of the period of course. Well, my proposal was accepted.

DOCTOR   So *he* chose the character of Henry the Fourth?

COUNTESS   Because—thinking of my own name—and, well, not taking the whole thing any too seriously—I said I'd like to be Countess Matilda of Tuscany.

DOCTOR   I don't . . . I don't see the connection . . .

COUNTESS   I didn't understand it myself in the beginning—I just heard him saying, "Then I'll be at your feet at Canossa—like Henry the Fourth." Oh yes, I knew about Canossa, but to tell the truth I didn't remember much of the story, and it made quite an impression on me when I studied up on it. I found I was a loyal and zealous friend of the Pope in the fierce struggle he was waging against the German Empire. I now understood why *he* wanted to be next to me in the cavalcade—as the Emperor.

DOCTOR   Ah! You mean because . . .

COUNTESS   . . . because I'd chosen to present his implacable enemy.

DOCTOR   Ah! Because—

BARON   Because he was courting her all the time! So she (*indicating the* COUNTESS) naturally . . .

COUNTESS   (*stung, fierily*)   Yes, naturally! I *was* natural in those days . . .

BARON   (*pointing to her*)   You see: she couldn't abide him!

COUNTESS   That's not true! I didn't even dislike him. Just the opposite! But with me, if a man wants to be taken seriously—

BARON   (*finishing her sentence*)   —he gives the clearest proof of his stupidity!

COUNTESS   Don't judge others by yourself, Baron. *He* wasn't stupid.

BARON   But then *I* never asked you to take me seriously.

COUNTESS   Don't I know it! But with him it was no joke. (*changing her tone and turning to the* DOCTOR) My dear doctor: a woman has a sad life, a silly life. And some time or other it's her lot to see a man's eyes fixed upon her, steady and intense and full of—shall we say?—the promise of enduring sentiment! (*She bursts into a harsh laugh*) What could be funnier? If only men could see their looks of enduring sentiment!—I've always laughed at them. More at *that* time than any other.—And let me tell you something: I can still laugh at them, after more than twenty years.—When I laughed like that at *him,* it was partly from fear, though. Perhaps one could have believed a promise in *those* eyes. It would've been dangerous, that's all.

DOCTOR   (*with lively interest and concentration*)   Aha! I'd be interested to know about *that.*—Why dangerous?

COUNTESS   (*with levity*)   Because he wasn't like the others. And because I too am . . . I can't deny it . . . I'm a little . . . (*She searches for a modest word*) intolerant, that's the word. I don't like stuffiness, I don't like people who take life hard.—Anyway I was too young at that time, you understand? And I was a woman: I couldn't help champing at the bit.—It would have needed *courage,* and I didn't have any.—So *I* laughed at him too. With remorse. With real self-hatred eventually—my laughter mingled with the laughter of fools, and I knew it. With the laughter of all the fools who made fun of him.

BARON   More or less as they do of me.

COUNTESS   My dear, you make people laugh at your . . . your perpetual affectation of self-abasement—they laughed at him for the op-posite reason: it makes a difference, hm?—And, with you, people laugh right in your face!

BARON   Better than behind my back, *I* say.

DOCTOR   (*coughing nervously*)   Ahem, yes, um . . . he was already rather . . . strange . . . exalted, as it were—if I've been following you properly?

BARON   Yes. But after a very curious fashion, doctor.

DOCTOR   Namely?

BARON   Well, I'd say . . . he was damned cold-blooded about it—

COUNTESS   Cold-blooded? What nonsense! This is how it was, doctor. He was a little strange, it's true, that was because there was so much life in him. It made him—eccentric.

BARON   I don't say this—exaltation was just an act. Not at all. He was often genuinely exalted. But I could swear, doctor: he was looking at himself, looking at his own exaltation. And I believe the same is true of every move he made, however spontaneous: he *saw* it. I'll say more: I'm certain it was this that made him suffer. At times he had the funniest fits of rage against himself.

COUNTESS   That is true.

BARON   (*to the* COUNTESS)   And why? (*to the* DOCTOR) As I see it, the lucidity that came from acting all the time . . . being another man . . . shattered, yes, shattered at a single blow, the ties that bound him to his own feelings. And these feelings seemed—well, not exactly a pretense, no, they were sincere—but he felt he must give them an intellectual status, an intellectual form of expression—to make up for his lack of warmth and spontaneity—so he improvised, exaggerated, let himself go, that's about it, to deafen his own ears, to keep his eyes from seeing himself. He seemed fickle, silly, and sometimes . . . yes, ridiculous, let's face it.

DOCTOR   Was he . . . unsociable?

BARON   Not in the least. He was a regular fellow. He was famous for his *tableaux vivants,* he was always getting up dances, benefit performances, all just for fun of course. He was an awfully good actor, believe me.

MARQUIS   And he's become a superb and terrifying one—by going mad.

BARON   Even before that. I still remember how—when the accident happened—and he fell from his horse, you know—

DOCTOR   He hit the back of his head, didn't he?

COUNTESS   Oh, what a horror! He was next to me. I saw him between the horse's hooves. The horse reared up—

BARON   At first we'd no idea any great harm

was done. There was a stop—a bit of a scrim-
mage in the cavalcade—People wanted to know
what had happened . . . But he'd been picked
up and carried into the villa.

COUNTESS   There was *nothing,* you understand: not a sign of a wound, not one drop of
blood.

BARON   We all believed he'd merely
fainted—

COUNTESS   —so, about two hours later,
when—

BARON   (*nervously*)   —that's right, he reappeared in the hall of the villa—this is what
I was going to say—

COUNTESS   His face at this moment! I saw
the whole thing in a flash.

BARON   No, no, that's not true, nobody had
the least idea—

COUNTESS   Of course not—you were all behaving like madmen!

BARON   Everyone was performing his own
part! As a joke! Oh, it was a real Tower of
Babel—

COUNTESS   You can imagine our horror,
can't you, doctor, when we realized *he* was
playing his part—in earnest?

DOCTOR   Oh, so he too . . .

BARON   Exactly. He entered. Came into the
midst of us. We assumed he'd recovered and
that he was just acting—like the rest of us . . .
only better—he was a fine actor, as I told you
—in short, we assumed he was joking.

COUNTESS   Some of the others started fooling with him, jostling, fighting . . . and at a
certain point he was hit . . .

BARON   At that instant . . . —he was
armed—he drew his imperial sword and bore
down on a couple of us. What a moment!
Scared the pants off us.

COUNTESS   I shall never forget the scene: all
those masked faces, distorted, panic-stricken,
turned towards that terrible mask, which was
now no mask at all, but the very face of lunacy!

BARON   The Emperor! It was Henry the
Fourth himself in a moment of fury!

COUNTESS   His obsession with the masquerade was taking effect, doctor. He'd been obsessed with it for over a month. And everything he did was an obsession of this sort.

BARON   The things he studied for the purpose! Down to the smallest details . . . minu-
tiae . . .

DOCTOR   Yes, I see. What with the fall, and
the blow on the head that caused the damage
to his brain, the momentary obsession was
perpetuated. Became a fixation, as we say. One
can go raving mad, one can become simple-
minded . . .

BARON   (*to* FRIDA *and the* MARQUIS)   You
see the tricks life plays, my dears? (*to the*
MARQUIS) You weren't more than four or five.
(*to* FRIDA) It seems to your mother that you've
taken her place in the portrait though at the
time she hadn't even dreamt of bringing you
into the world. I have grey hair now. And as for
him—(*He clicks finger and thumb*)—he's hit
in the neck—and he's never moved since. He
is the Emperor—Henry the Fourth!

DOCTOR   (*who has been lost in thought, now
takes his hands from before his face as if to
focus everyone's attention upon himself, and
starts to give his scientific explanation*)   Well,
ladies and gentlemen, it all comes down to
this . . .

(*But all of a sudden the first door on the right
—the one nearest the footlights—opens, and*
BERTOLD *emerges, his face very excited*)

BERTOLD   (*rushing in like a man at the end
of his tether*)   Excuse me, everybody . . .

(*But he stops directly when he sees the confusion that his entry has created*)

FRIDA   (*with a cry of horror, drawing back*)
My God, it's he!

COUNTESS   (*stepping back, upset, with an arm
raised so as not to see him*)   It's he? He?

MARQUIS   (*promptly*)   No, no, no! Don't be
excited!

DOCTOR   (*astonished*)   Then who is it?

BARON   A fugitive from the masquerade!

MARQUIS   He's one of the four young fellows we keep here to . . . um, back him up in
his lunacy.

BERTOLD   I beg your pardon, Marquis . . .

MARQUIS   So you should! I'd given orders
for the doors to be locked! No one was to
come in!

BERTOLD   Yes, I know, Marquis. But I can't
bear it! I've come to beg off! I want to quit!

MARQUIS   Ah! So you're the one who was to
start work this morning?

BERTOLD   Yes, Marquis. But I can't bear
it, I tell you—

COUNTESS   (*to the* MARQUIS *in lively consternation*)   Then he *isn't* calm—you said he was!

BERTOLD   (*promptly*)   That's not it, madam,
it isn't him! It's my three comrades. You say
they "back him up," Marquis. Back him up!
They don't back him up—because it's them
that's mad! I came here for the first time, and
instead of helping me, Marquis . . .

(LANDOLF *and* HARALD *come to the same door
on the right, in haste, anxiously, but stopping
at the door*)

LANDOLF   May we come in?

HARALD   May we, dear Marquis?

MARQUIS   Come in then! But what on earth is the matter? What are you all up to?

FRIDA   O God, I'm going, I'm scared out of my wits! (*She starts to go toward the door on the left*)

MARQUIS   (*who at once holds her back*)   No, no, Frida!

LANDOLF   Marquis, this dumbbell . . . (*indicating* BERTOLD)

BERTOLD   (*protesting*)   No: thanks very much, my friends! I'm not staying!

LANDOLF   What do you mean, you're not staying?

HARALD   He's ruined *everything*, Marquis, running in here like this! Ts, ts, ts!

LANDOLF   He's driven him absolutely crazy. We can't keep him in there any longer. He's given orders for this fellow's arrest. Wants to pass judgment on him. From the throne. What's to be done?

MARQUIS   Lock the door of course! Go and lock that door!

(LANDOLF *starts to do so*)

HARALD   But Ordulf won't be able to hold him all by himself!

LANDOLF   (*stopping*)   Marquis, if we could just announce your visit: it would be a distraction for him. Have you gentlemen thought what you'll wear in his presence . . .

MARQUIS   Oh yes, we've thought the whole thing out. (*to the* DOCTOR) Doctor, if you think we can make the call at once . . .

FRIDA   I won't, I won't, Carlo! I'm leaving. You come with me, mamma, please!

DOCTOR   Tell me, Marquis . . . he won't be armed, will he?

MARQUIS   Armed? Of course not, doctor. (*to* FRIDA) Forgive me, Frida, but these fears of yours are really childish. You wanted to come . . .

FRIDA   I didn't! I didn't at all, it was mother!

COUNTESS   (*firmly*)   Well, I'm ready! So what are we to do?

BARON   Is all this dressing up really necessary?

LANDOLF   Oh yes, Baron, it's essential! Unhappily, he just sees *us* . . . (*He shows his costume*) He *mustn't* see you gentlemen in modern dress!

HARALD   He'd think it was some devilish travesty, dear Baron!

MARQUIS   Just as these men seem a travesty to you, to him *we*—in modern clothes—would seem a travesty.

LANDOLF   And maybe it wouldn't much matter, Marquis, only he'd think it was the work of his mortal enemy!

BARON   The Pope?

LANDOLF   Right. He says he's a pagan.

BARON   The Pope a pagan? Not bad!

LANDOLF   A pagan who conjures up the dead! He accuses him of all the black arts. Lives in constant fear of him.

DOCTOR   Ha! Persecution mania!

HARALD   Oh, he'd be furious, dear sir—

MARQUIS   (*to the* BARON)   But you don't have to be there, if I may say so. We'll leave that way. It's enough if the doctor sees him.

DOCTOR   You mean . . . just me?

MARQUIS   They'll be present. (*indicating the three young men*)

DOCTOR   It's not that . . . I mean, if the Countess . . .

COUNTESS   That's right: *I* want to be there! I want to see him!

FRIDA   But why, mother? Come with us, do!

COUNTESS   (*imperiously*)   Leave me alone, I came for this! (*to* LANDOLF) I shall be his mother-in-law.

LANDOLF   Marvelous. Yes. The Empress Bertha's mother. Marvelous! Your ladyship need only put on a cloak—to hide these clothes. And the ducal crown on your head, of course. (*to* HARALD) Go on, Harald, go on!

HARALD   Just a moment, dear boy, what about this gentleman? (*indicating the* DOCTOR)

DOCTOR   Oh, yes . . . they told me the Bishop, I believe . . . the Bishop of Cluny.

HARALD   You mean the Abbot, dear sir? That'd be simply divine: the Abbot of Cluny!

LANDOLF   He's been here so often before . . .

DOCTOR   (*astonished*)   He's been here before?

LANDOLF   Don't be afraid, sir. I only mean it's an easy disguise and . . .

HARALD   And it's been used *often*, dear sir.

DOCTOR   But . . . but . . .

LANDOLF   No, no, he won't remember. It's the clothes he looks at—not the man inside them.

COUNTESS   That'll be just as well. For me too.

MARQUIS   You and I'll be going, Frida. You come with us, Tito.

BARON   What? Oh. No, no, if she stays, um, (*indicating the* COUNTESS) I'll stay, of course.

COUNTESS   I don't need you in the least, my dear Baron.

BARON   I didn't say you needed me! But you're not the only one that wants to see *him*. Surely I can stay if I want?

LANDOLF   (*helping out*)   Yes, um, maybe it's better if there are three!

HARALD   Then the gentleman will surely—

BARON   Yes, I'll need a disguise. Make it an easy one.

LANDOLF (*to* HARALD)   I have it, *he* can be from Cluny too.

BARON   From Cluny, how do you mean?

LANDOLF   The cassock of a monk from Cluny Abbey. He can be in attendance on the Abbot. (*still to* HARALD) Now, go, go! (*to* BERTOLD) You go too, and keep out of sight all day today! (*but as soon as he sees him going*) Wait! Bring the clothes he gives you! (*to* HARALD) And you go and announce the arrival of his mother-in-law and the Abbot of Cluny.

HARALD   It shall be done, dear boy.

(HARALD *shepherds* BERTOLD *out by the first door on the right*)

MARQUIS   Now we can go, Frida.

(*With* FRIDA *he leaves by the door on the left*)

DOCTOR (*to* LANDOLF)   I take it he should think rather well of me—when I'm the Abbot of Cluny?

LANDOLF   Quite right, you can count on it, sir. The Abbot has always been received with great respect. So have you: *you* needn't worry either, my lady. He hasn't forgotten it was due to the intercession of the two of you that he was admitted to the castle at Canossa and brought before the Pope, who hadn't *wanted* to receive him at all. Kept him waiting in the snow for two days—he almost froze.

BARON   What about me, may I ask?

LANDOLF   You sir? Oh yes. You should, um —stand deferentially apart.

COUNTESS (*irritated, very nervous*)   Oh, why didn't you leave?

BARON (*quietly, but nettled*)   You're certainly very worked up over . . .

COUNTESS (*with pride*)   I am as I am! Leave me in peace!

(BERTOLD *returns with the clothes*)

LANDOLF (*seeing him enter*)   Oh good, here are the clothes!—This cloak for the Countess.

COUNTESS   Wait, I must take my hat off.

(*She does so and gives it to* BERTOLD)

LANDOLF   Put it over there, Bertold. (*then to the* COUNTESS, *preparing to place the ducal crown on her head*) May I, Countess?

COUNTESS   But, heavens, isn't there a mirror here?

LANDOLF   There are mirrors in there. (*He points through the left entrance*) If your ladyship would prefer to put it on yourself?

COUNTESS   Oh, yes, it'll be much better, give it to me, it won't take a minute.

(*She takes the hat back and goes out with* BERTOLD *who is carrying the crown and the cloak. In the meantime the* DOCTOR *and the* BARON *put on the monks' cassocks as best they can*)

BARON   Well, I must say, I never expected to be a Benedictine monk! Think what a heap of money this madness is costing!

DOCTOR (*defensively*)   Oh, well, my dear Baron, lots of other kinds of madness cost . . .

BARON   Surely, if you have a fortune to put into them!

LANDOLF   Yes, indeed. In there, we have an entire wardrobe of costumes of the period. Tailored to perfection after ancient models. It's my special job—I commission theatrical costumiers, experts. It costs plenty.

(COUNTESS *re-enters wearing cloak and crown*)

BARON (*immediately, in admiration*)   Ah, magnificent, truly royal!

COUNTESS (*seeing the* BARON *and bursting out laughing*)   Good God, no!! Take it off! You're impossible! You look like an ostrich in monk's feathers!

BARON   Well, look at the doctor for that matter!

DOCTOR   Don't be hard on *me*, Countess.

COUNTESS   Oh, you'll do, *you're* all right. (*to the* BARON) But you're ludicrous!

DOCTOR (*to* LANDOLF)   You have many receptions here then?

LANDOLF   It depends. Many times he gives orders for such and such a person to be presented to him. Then we have to hunt up someone who'll serve the purpose. Women too . . .

COUNTESS (*touched but trying to hide the fact*)   Ah! Women too?

LANDOLF   At one time there were rather a lot of women.

BARON (*laughing*)   Wonderful! In costume? (*indicating the* COUNTESS) Like that?

LANDOLF   Well, you know: any women who'd . . .

BARON   Who'd serve the purpose? I see!! (*with innuendo, to the* COUNTESS) Take care, it may get dangerous for you!

(*The second door on the right opens and* HARALD *appears. First he gives a furtive sign to stop all conversation in the room. Then he announces, solemnly*)

HARALD   His Majesty the Emperor!

(*First, the* TWO VALETS *enter, taking up their positions at the foot of the throne. Then, between* ORDULF *and* HARALD, *who hold themselves back a little, deferentially,* EMPEROR HENRY *enters. He is nearly fifty, very pale, and* already grey at the back of his head—while on the temples and forehead he seems blond because of very obvious, almost childish hairdye. High on each cheek, in the midst of that tragic pallor, is a patch of red, doll make-up, this too very obvious. Over his regal habit he wears a penitent's sack, as at Canossa. His eyes are characterized by a horrifying, convulsive fixity. At the same time he expresses the attitude of a penitent who wishes to be all humility and repentance. One feels that the humility is as ostentatious as the humiliation is deserved*—ORDULF *carries the imperial crown in both hands,* HARALD *the scepter and eagle and the globe and cross*)

HENRY (*bowing first to the* COUNTESS, *then to the* DOCTOR) My lady . . . My Lord Abbot . . . (*He then looks at the* BARON, *starts to bow to him too, but turns to* LANDOLF *who has gone over to his side, and asks, suspiciously, and in an undertone*) Is it Peter Damiani?

LANDOLF No, your majesty, it's a monk of Cluny, he came with the Abbot.

HENRY (*turns to scrutinize the* BARON *with increasing suspicion and, noting that the latter, hesitant and embarrassed, turns to the* COUNTESS *and the* DOCTOR *as if to take counsel from their eyes, draws himself up very straight and shouts*) It's Peter Damiani!—It's no use, Father, looking at her like that! (*suddenly turning to the* COUNTESS *as if to ward off a danger*) I swear, my lady, I swear to you, my mind is changed towards your daughter though I confess that I'd have divorced her if he (*indicates the* BARON) hadn't come to stop me. Oh yes: there were people prepared to favor such a divorce. The Bishop of Mainz would have arranged it for 120 farms. (*steals a look, rather perplexed, at* LANDOLF *and then suddenly says*) But at this time I should say nothing against the bishops. (*Humble now, he is in front of the* BARON) I'm grateful to you, believe me, Peter Damiani, I'm glad you stopped me!—My whole life is made up of humiliations! My mother, Adalbert, Tribur, Goslar . . . (*Of a sudden he changes his tone, and speaks like someone who, in a clever parenthesis, runs through a part he is rehearsing*) But it doesn't matter! Clarity in one's ideas, insight, firmness in behavior, and patience in adversity! (*Then he turns to them all and with contrite gravity says*) I know how to correct my errors, and I abase myself even before you, Peter Damiani! (*bows low to him, and then stays with his back bent, as if under the impulsion of an oblique suspicion. It is new

but it makes him add, almost in spite of himself, in a threatening tone*) If it wasn't you who started the obscene rumor about my mother Agnes and Henry Bishop of Augsburg!

BARON (*since* HENRY *stays bent over, with one finger pointed threateningly at him, places his hands on his breast and then speaks in denial*) No . . . no, it was not . . .

HENRY (*straightening up*) You say it wasn't? Sheer infamy! (*glares at him and then says*) I wouldn't have thought you could! (*approaches the* DOCTOR *and pulls at his sleeve a little, winking with some cunning*) It's them! It always is, isn't it, my Lord Abbot?

HARALD (*quietly, whispering, as if prompting the* DOCTOR) That's it: the rapacious bishops!

DOCTOR (*turned towards* HARALD, *trying to stick to his "part"*) Oh, them . . . of course, them!

HENRY They were insatiable!—When I was a little child, my Lord Abbot—even an emperor has a childhood—he doesn't know he's an emperor in fact—he's just a kid at play, letting time go by . . . I was six years old and they snatched me from my mother and made use of me against her without my knowing, against her and against the dynasty itself, profaning, robbing, marauding, one greedier than the other—Anno greedier than Stefan, Stefan greedier than Anno!

LANDOLF (*in a persuasive undertone, to get his attention*) Your majesty . . .

HENRY (*turning of a sudden*) You're right! At this time I shouldn't speak ill of the bishops —But this infamous slander against my mother, my Lord Abbot, goes beyond the bounds! (*melting as he looks at the* COUNTESS) And I may not even weep for her, my lady.—I turn to you, you are a mother, you must feel it here. (*indicates the pit of his stomach*) She came from her convent to seek me out, a month ago now. They had told me she was dead. (*sustained pause, dense with emotion. Then with a most mournful smile*) I cannot mourn her because if you are here and I am dressed like this (*shows his sackcloth*) it means I am twenty-six years old.

HARALD (*almost in an undertone, sweetly, to comfort him*) It means she is still alive, your majesty.

ORDULF (*in the same manner*) And still in her convent.

HENRY (*turns to look at them*) True. So I can postpone my grief to another occasion. (*Almost coquettishly he shows the* COUNTESS *the dye on his hair*) Look, I'm still blond . . . (*then quietly, confidentially*) For you!—I wouldn't need it, but externals do help. Milestones of time, aren't they, my Lord Abbot? (*He returns to the* COUNTESS *and, observing her hair*) Ah, but I see that . . . you too, my lady . . . (*He winks, makes an expressive sign with one hand as if to say her hair is false—but without a hint of scorn, rather with mischievous admiration*) Heaven keep me from amazement or disgust!—O vanity of human wishes: we try to ignore the obscure and fatal power that sets limits to our will! What *I* say is, if one is born and dies—did you wish to be born, Lord Abbot, did you will your own birth! I didn't—And between birth and death, both of them independent of our will, so many things happen that we all wish wouldn't happen. Willy-nilly, we resign ourselves to them.

DOCTOR (*just to say something while he scrutinizes* HENRY) It's true, alas!

HENRY But when we're not resigned, we always start wishing and willing! A woman wishes to be a man, an old man wishes to be young . . . None of us is lying, there's no conscious deception in it, it's simply this: in entire good faith we are fixed in some fine conception of ourselves, as in a shell or a suit of armor. However, my lord, while you keep this firm grip on yourself, holding on to your holy cassock with both hands, something is slipping away from you unnoticed, slithering down your sleeves, gliding off like a serpent. That something is LIFE, my lord. And when you see your life suddenly taking shape, coagulating outside you in this way, you are surprised. You despise yourself, you're furious with yourself. And the remorse, the remorse! How many times I've seen my own remorse— with a face that was my own and yet so horrible I couldn't behold it! (*He returns to the* COUNTESS) Has this never happened to you, Countess? You can recall being always the same, can you? But, once upon a time, I tell you . . . how can it be? How *could* you do such a thing? (*He looks her so sharply in the eyes, she nearly faints*) Such a thing as . . . precisely . . . we understand each other. But don't worry, I won't breathe a word to anyone! And you, Peter Damiani, how could you be a friend to *that* man . . .

LANDOLF (*as above*) Your majesty . . .

HENRY (*at once*) No, no, I won't name him, I know it would be too annoying for you. (*turning on the* BARON, *as if by stealth*) What an opinion, what an opinion you had of him, eh?—All the same, everyone of us clings to his idea of himself—like a man who dyes his hair when he grows old. What if the color of the dye in my hair cannot, for you, be that of my real hair? You, lady, certainly don't dye your hair to deceive others or even yourself. You only deceive—and ever so little at that —your own image in the glass. I do it as a joke. You do it in earnest. But, however much in earnest, you too are in disguise, lady, and I don't mean the venerable crown that rings your forehead and which I bow before, I don't mean your ducal mantle, I mean you wish to fix a memory in your mind, artificially, the memory of your blond hair as it was when, one day, it pleased you—or of your dark hair if you were dark—the fading image of your youth. With you it's different, isn't it, Peter Damiani? You're not interested in *fixing* your memories, are you? For you, to remember what you have been, what you have done, is but to recognize the realities of the past which have lived on inside you, isn't that so? Like a dream. Like a dream! *My* memories are like that too, inexplicable to me as I think them over . . . Oh, well, don't be amazed, Peter Damiani, it'll be the same tomorrow with your life of today! (*suddenly getting into a rage and seizing his sackcloth*) This sackcloth here!

(*With almost fierce joy he begins to take it off while* HARALD *and* ORDULF *at once run up in horror to stop him*)

Oh, God! (*Drawing back and taking off the sackcloth he shouts to them*) Tomorrow, at Brixen, twenty-seven German and Lombard bishops will sign with me the deposition of the Pope!

ORDULF (*with the other two, imploring him to be silent*) Your majesty! In God's name!

HARALD (*motioning to him to put the sackcloth on again*) Take care, your majesty!

LANDOLF The Abbot is here with the Countess Matilda to intercede in your favor! (*furtively makes urgent signs to the* DOCTOR *to say something at once*)

DOCTOR (*worried*) Um, yes, of course . . . we came to intercede . . . sire . . .

HENRY (*repenting at once, almost terrified, lets the three of them put the sackcloth back on for him. He pulls it down over him with convulsive hands*) Pardon! That's it; pardon, pardon, my Lord Abbot, pardon, lady! . . . I swear to you, I feel the weight of the anathema, I do! (*He bends down with his head in his hands as if expecting something to fall and crush him. He stays like this a moment. Then, in a changed voice but in an unchanged position, he says softly and confidentially to* LANDOLF, HARALD, *and* ORDULF) I don't know why, but somehow I *can't* be humble before that man! (*indicating the* BARON *quasi-secretly*)

LANDOLF (*in an undertone*) But, your majesty, why do you persist in believing it's Peter Damiani? It isn't at all!

HENRY (*looking at them askance, fearfully*) It isn't Peter Damiani?

HARALD   No, no, it's just a poor monk, your majesty!

HENRY (*mournfully, with plaintive exasperation*) Perhaps you, lady, can understand me better than the others because you are a woman. This is a solemn and decisive moment. I could, look you, accept the aid of the Lombard bishops, capture the Pope, run to Rome and set up a pope of my own choosing!—But I do not give way to the temptation, and, believe me, I'm right. I know the drift of the times. I know the majesty of a man who *can* be what he should be, a pope!—Would you be inclined to laugh at me in my present situation? You're stupid if you do. You don't understand the political sagacity which enjoins this penitential habit upon me. I tell you that, tomorrow, the roles could be reversed. And then what would you do? Would you laugh to see a pope in captive's clothes?—No.—Yet the two cases are the same. Today I wear the mask of a penitent, tomorrow he wears the mask of a prisoner. Woe betide the man who knows not how to wear his mask, whether of pope or emperor!—Perhaps His Holiness is, at present, a little too cruel, that's true. Think, lady, how Bertha—your daughter and my wife —toward whom, I repeat, my heart is changed (*He turns suddenly on the* BARON *and shouts in his face as if the latter had said him nay*) changed, CHANGED—because of the affection, the devotion she was able to show me in that terrible moment! (*He stops, convulsed by his angry outburst, and makes an effort to hold himself in, a groan of exasperation in his throat; then, with sweet and mournful humility, he turns again to the* COUNTESS) She has come with me, lady. She is below in the courtyard. She insisted on following me as a beggar. And she is frozen, frozen from two nights in the open, in the snow. You are her mother. May the bowels of your compassion be moved: with his aid (*indicating the* DOCTOR) beg the Pope's pardon! Induce him to receive us!

COUNTESS (*trembling, a thin thread of voice*) Yes, sire, at once, yes . . .

DOCTOR   Yes, sire, we'll do it!

HENRY   And one more thing, one more! (*He summons them round about him and speaks quietly as if telling a great secret*) You

see me? I am a penitent, and I swear I'll remain one till the Pope receives me. But it's not enough that he receive me. (*Pause. He starts again*) You know how he can do anything, literally anything, even to calling up the dead? Now, my Lord Abbot, now my lady: my real punishment is (*pointing to himself*) here—or (*pointing to the picture of himself*) if you like, *there*—for it consists in the fact that I cannot cut myself loose from that piece of magic! When the excommunication is revoked, I want you two to make another request of him who can do everything, namely, that he cut me loose from that picture and let me live! Let me live my poor life, the life I've been excluded from, let me have it intact, entire! One cannot go on being twenty-six forever, lady! I ask this favor for your daughter too. So that, well disposed as I am toward her, and so deeply affected by her compassion, I may love her as she deserves. That's all. Just that. I am in your hands. (*He bows*) My lady! My Lord Abbot!

(*Still bowing he starts to withdraw by the door through which he entered. The* BARON, *who had come forward a little to hear the proceedings, now turns to go back again to his place.* HENRY *assumes he wishes to steal the imperial crown which is on the throne. Amid general concern and astonishment,* HENRY *runs over, takes it, hides it under his sackcloth, then, with a cunning smile on his lips and in his eyes, he starts bowing again and disappears. The* COUNTESS *is so deeply disturbed she falls into a chair with a crash, almost fainting*)

ACT TWO

Scene One

(*Another room in the villa. Antique and austere furniture. On the right, about eighteen inches from the floor, is a raised platform very like a church choir, with a ring of wooden pilasters around it, the ring being broken at the front and sides by two steps. On the platform is a table and six stools of the period, one at the head and two on each side. The main door is at the rear. On the left, there are two windows looking out on the garden. On the right there is another door.*

It is later in the afternoon of the same day. The COUNTESS, *the* DOCTOR, *and the* BARON *are*

on stage. They are conversing, but the COUNT-
ESS *stands gloomily on one side, clearly very
irritated by what the other two are saying,
though she can't help listening because in her
present disturbed state everything interests her
in spite of herself—so that she can't concentrate on perfecting the plan which hovers before her mind's eye and beckons and is stronger
than she is. The words which she hears the
others speak attract her attention because she
instinctively feels something like a need to be
held fast in the present)*

BARON   Well, my dear doctor, you *may* be
right, but that's my impression.

DOCTOR   I won't gainsay you but I rather
think it's *only* . . . well, yes, an impression.

BARON   But he said it in so many words,
my dear doctor! (*turning to the* COUNTESS)
Didn't he, Countess?

COUNTESS (*interrupted in her thoughts, turning*)   Said what? Oh, yes . . . But not for
the reason you think.

DOCTOR   He was referring to the clothes
we'd put on. (*to the* COUNTESS) Your cloak,
our Benedictine cassocks. The whole thing is
childish!

COUNTESS (*in a little burst, indignant, again
turning*)   Childish? Doctor, what are you saying?

DOCTOR   On the one hand, it's childish—let
me speak, Countess, I beg—and on the other
hand, it's much more complicated than you
could possibly imagine.

COUNTESS   Not at all. To me, it's crystal
clear.

DOCTOR (*with the expert's pitying smile for
the non-expert*)   All the same! One must take
account of that special psychology of madmen
according to which, you see, one can be sure
that the madman sees, sees right through the
disguise we confront him with, sees through
it and at the same time accepts it, believes in
it, like a child, to whom it is both reality and a
game. That's why I said it's all childish. But
then it's highly complicated too—in this respect: that he is, he must be, perfectly aware
of being—an image. To himself, I mean. In his
own eyes. He is an image. The image in the
picture. (*He points out left where the picture
is*)

BARON   He said that!

DOCTOR   Precisely.—Now: to this image,
other images have just presented themselves,
Ours. The images we created in those clothes.
Don't imagine he isn't clever and clearsighted
in his lunacy! On the contrary, he was at once
aware of the difference between his sort of

image and ours. He knew there was in ours
an element of deliberate fiction. So he was
suspicious. All madmen are fortified by constant, vigilant suspicion. Not that he could
see any further than that. He couldn't see compassion in the way we adapted our game to
his. His own game seemed the more tragic to
us, the more he tried to reveal that it was only
a game. Coming before us with paint on his
cheeks and temples! Telling us he'd done it on
purpose, as a joke! Such is his suspicion. Such
is his defiance.

COUNTESS (*again breaking out*)   No, doctor,
that's not it, that's not it at all!

DOCTOR   What do you mean, that's not it?

COUNTESS (*positively trembling*)   I am
quite sure he recognized me.

DOCTOR   Out of the question, out of the
question!

BARON (*at the same time as the* DOCTOR)
Nonsense, nonsense!

COUNTESS (*even more positively, almost convulsed*)   He recognized me, I tell you. When
he came over to talk to me at close quarters,
he looked me in the eyes, deep in the eyes,
and recognized me!

BARON   But if he talked of your daughter . . .

COUNTESS   He didn't!—It was me, he was
speaking of me!

BARON   Perhaps so, when he said . . .

COUNTESS (*at once, without restraint*)
About my dyed hair? But didn't you notice
how he right away added: "or the memory
of your dark hair if you were dark?"—He remembered perfectly well that in those days I
was dark.

BARON   Nonsense, nonsense!

COUNTESS (*taking no notice of him, turning
to the* DOCTOR)   My hair is dark really, doctor,
like my daughter's. *That* is why he started talking of her!

BARON   But he doesn't know your daughter, he's never seen her!

COUNTESS   Exactly! You understand nothing. Not my daughter, he meant me. Me—as I
was "in those days!"

BARON   Great Heavens, this is catching!

COUNTESS (*quietly, with contempt*)   What's
catching? You fool!

BARON   Tell me, were you ever his wife?
In his lunacy, your daughter is his wife, Bertha
of Susa.

COUNTESS   That's precisely it! Not being
dark any more—as he remembers me—but
like this, blond, I was introduced to him as
his wife's mother.—For him my daughter

doesn't exist—he never saw her—you said so yourself. So how can he know if she's blond or dark?

BARON   Oh, he just happened to say dark, sort of in general, for Heaven's sake. Like anyone who wants to tie down a memory of youth with the color of a girl's hair—blond, brunette, what have you. As ever, you go off into foolish fantasies.—Doctor, you say *I* oughtn't to have come here, but what about *her?*

COUNTESS   (*is defeated for a moment by the* BARON's *argument. She has been lost in thought but now she takes hold of herself, the more excited because she is unsure of herself*)   No . . . no, he was speaking of me . . . He talked *to* me, *with* me, *of* me . . .

BARON   Not so bad! He never left *me* for a moment, I couldn't *breathe,* and you say he was talking with you the whole time? Maybe you think he was alluding to you when he spoke with "Peter Damiani?"

COUNTESS   (*defiantly, almost breaking the bounds of decorum*)   Who knows?—Can you explain to me why, from the very first moment, he felt an aversion to you, to you alone?

(*The answer must be almost explicitly expressed in the tone of the query. It is: "Because he understood that you are my lover." The* BARON *gets the point. Discomfited, he stands there emptily smiling*)

DOCTOR   May I say the reason could also be that only two persons' arrival had been announced: the Emperor's mother and the Abbot of Cluny. When he discovered a third person who hadn't been announced, suspicion at once . . .

BARON   Of course: suspicion at once made him see in me an enemy, Peter Damiani.— But if she's got it into her head that he recognized her . . .

COUNTESS   There's not the least doubt of it! —His eyes told me, doctor. There's a way of looking at someone that leaves no doubt whatsoever, *you* know that. Perhaps it was only for an instant, but what more do you want?

DOCTOR   It's entirely possible, he could have a lucid interval . . .

COUNTESS   It's possible—you admit it! But that's not all. His talk seemed to me full, brimfull, of regret for my youth and his, regret for the horrible thing that happened to him, the thing that has held him here in a mask he can't cut from his face. But he'd like to, doctor. Oh, how he longs to cut loose!

BARON   Yes: and why? He wants to start

loving your daughter. Or even you. Softened, as you think, by the pity you feel for him.

COUNTESS   Which is great, don't make light of it.

BARON   I won't, my dear Countess. I'm sure a faith-healer would consider the miracle more than likely.

DOCTOR   May *I* speak? I don't perform miracles. I am not a faith-healer. I am a doctor. I've been listening to everything that's been said, and I must repeat what I've told you already. Every elaborate or, as we say, systemized form of lunacy is characterized by what we call analogical elasticity. In him, this elasticity is no longer . . . well, um, elastic. It has worked loose, it's limp. In short, the various elements of his lunacy aren't holding together. Years ago he superimposed a second personality upon himself, but now it's proving next to impossible for him to maintain his equilibrium within it—because (and this is very reassuring) of the attacks this second personality is being subjected to. Sudden recollections are wrenching him free from what has been his state of mind hitherto, a state of mind we call incipient apathy—no, that's not right either, it's really a morbid wallowing in reflective melancholy, accompanied by, yes, considerable cerebral activity. Very reassuring, I say. And now, if by the trick—I should say, the shock treatment—we've planned . . .

COUNTESS   (*turning toward the window, in the tone of a querulous invalid*)   How is it the car hasn't come back yet? In three and a half hours . . .

DOCTOR   (*stunned*)   What do you say?

COUNTESS   The car, doctor. It's more than three and a half hours now!

DOCTOR   (*taking out his watch and looking at it*)   Yes, more than four, for that matter!

COUNTESS   They could have been here half an hour ago at least, that chauffeur . . .

BARON   Perhaps he couldn't find the dress.

COUNTESS   But I told him exactly where it was. (*She is very impatient*)   And where's Frida?

BARON   (*leaning out of the window a little*)   Maybe she's in the garden with Carlo.

DOCTOR   He'll talk the fear out of her!

BARON   It isn't fear, doctor, don't you believe it. It's just that she's annoyed.

COUNTESS   Do me the favor of not asking her to do this! I know how she is!

DOCTOR   Let's wait. Patiently. Anyhow, it'll only take a moment, and it has to be in the evening—If, as I was saying, our shock treatment shakes him up till, at a single blow, he breaks the threads that still bind this fiction of his together, threads that are slack enough as it is, if, I say, we give him back what he himself demands—"One cannot go on being twenty-six forever," he said—namely, liberation from this punishment, which even he regards as a punishment, in short, if we can help him regain, all at once, his sense of time, his sense of duration—

BARON (*stepping in*) He will be cured! (*then underlining his words with irony*) We shall have cut him loose from his delusion!

DOCTOR We can hope he'll start going again—like a clock stopped at a certain hour. Here we stand, so to speak, watch in hand, waiting for that watch to start up. A shake, like this! And now let's hope it'll begin to tell the time again, it's been stopped quite long enough.

(*At this point the* MARQUIS *enters by the main door*)

COUNTESS Carlo . . . where's Frida? Isn't she here?

MARQUIS Yes, Countess. She'll be in at any moment.

DOCTOR The car got back?

MARQUIS Yes, doctor.

COUNTESS He found the dress, that chauffeur?

MARQUIS Yes, yes, he found it.

DOCTOR Well, that's a relief!

COUNTESS (*shuddering*) Then where is it? Where is it?

MARQUIS (*shrugging his shoulders and smiling sadly with the air of one who lends himself unwillingly to a jest that is out-of-place*) You'll see soon enough, Countess. (*indicating the direction of the main entrance*) Watch . . .

BERTOLD (*presents himself at the threshold solemnly announcing*) Her Ladyship the Countess Matilda—of Canossa!

(*Magnificent and very lovely,* FRIDA *at once enters. She is dressed in her mother's old dress, that is, as the Countess Matilda of Tuscany, and appears a living version of the dead image we have seen in the throne room portrait*)

FRIDA (*as she passes the bowing figure of* BERTOLD, *says to him with contemptuous gravity*) Of Tuscany, Matilda of Tuscany, please! Canossa is just a castle of mine!

BARON (*admiring her*) Ah! Well! She looks like someone I know!

COUNTESS Like me!—God in heaven, do you see?—Stop, Frida!—Do you see? It's my picture come to life!

DOCTOR Yes, yes . . . to a T, to a T! The portrait!

BARON No question of that, the portrait! Just look at her: what a girl!

FRIDA Now don't make me laugh or I'll burst. Heavens, what a wasp waist you had, mamma! I could hardly squeeze myself into it.

COUNTESS (*convulsed, helping to fix the dress*) Wait . . . keep still . . . Now these pleats . . . Does it really feel so tight?

FRIDA Stifling! For Heaven's sake, let's be quick . . .

DOCTOR Oh, but we must wait till evening . . .

FRIDA No, no, I can't! I can't hold out that long!

COUNTESS But why on earth did you put it on so early?

FRIDA When I saw it . . . the temptation . . . was irresistible . . .

COUNTESS At least you could have taken me with you. Or had someone help you . . . it's all crumpled, oh dear! . . .

FRIDA I know, mamma, but they're such old creases . . . it'd be hard to get them out.

DOCTOR It doesn't matter, Countess. The illusion is perfect. (*then, approaching and asking her to stand in front of her daughter, though without concealing her*) Pardon me. We place them . . . thus . . . at a certain distance . . . will you stand a little further forward? . . .

BARON And in this way we learn to appreciate the passage of time!

COUNTESS (*turning slightly to him*) Twenty years after: isn't it a catastrophe?

BARON You exaggerate, my dear Countess.

DOCTOR (*highly embarrassed, trying to put matters to rights*) No, no! I meant . . . I mean, the dress . . . I wanted to see . . .

BARON (*laughing*) For the dress, doctor, it's more than twenty years: it's eight hundred. An abyss. You want to make him jump across? You'll hit him that hard? From here (*pointing to* FRIDA) to here. (*pointing to her mother*) You'll need a basket to pick up the pieces. My friends, just think for a moment: joking aside, for us it's a matter of twenty years, two dresses, and a disguise. But, for him, if, as you say, doctor, time is fixed, if he's really living back there with her (*indicating* FRIDA) eight hundred years earlier, I tell you the jump will simply make him dizzy, make his head reel. He'll fall in our midst like a . . . (*The* DOCTOR *shakes a finger in dissent*) You deny it?

DOCTOR Yes. Life, my dear Baron, renews itself. Our life—here—will at once be real—even to him. It will take hold of him and, at a blow, strip him of his illusion, and reveal your eight hundred years as a bare twenty. It will be like certain practical jokes—the leap into space, for example, as the Free Masons do it: you think you're making a tremendous jump, then you find you've taken a single step down.

BARON Now we're on to something. Doctor: look at Frida and her mother. We say youth goes on ahead. We imagine youth to be in front. But it isn't true, is it, doctor? We oldsters are ahead, we are in front, we are rightly called "advanced in years," for— Time is something we have a lot more *of.*

DOCTOR Except that the past is all the time receding from us.

BARON No, no, the point is this. They (*indicating* FRIDA *and the* MARQUIS) have still to do what we have already done, they have still to grow old, they have still to do more or less the same foolish things . . . The idea that you start out in life ahead of those who've already started—this is the great illusion, the great untruth! You are no sooner born than you start dying. He who started first is therefore furthest along of all, *he* is ahead, *he* is in front. The youngest of men is our common father Adam. Behold the Countess Matilda of Tuscany: (*shows* FRIDA) she is eight hundred years younger than any of us! (*He makes a low bow before her*)

MARQUIS Please, Tito, this is no laughing matter.

BARON Oh, if you think I'm joking . . .

MARQUIS Certainly I do, for Heaven's sake . . . ever since you arrived . . .

BARON What? I've even dressed up as a Benedictine . . .

MARQUIS Why yes, for a *serious* purpose . . .

BARON That's what I'm saying . . . if it's been serious for the others . . . Frida, now, for example . . . (*then, turning to the* DOCTOR) Doctor, I swear I still don't understand what you wish to do.

DOCTOR (*annoyed*) Give me a chance!— Naturally, with the Countess in the wrong costume—

BARON You mean, she too must . . .

DOCTOR Surely; she must wear a dress exactly like that one. (*indicating* FRIDA's) The young lady enters, he sees Matilda of Tuscany, then the Countess enters, and—

BARON There'll be two Matildas of Tuscany!

DOCTOR Two Matildas of Tuscany. Precisely. Such is our shock treatment. After that, the watch starts going again.

FRIDA (*calling him to one side*) Doctor, one moment, please!

DOCTOR Here I am. (*He goes over to* FRIDA *and the* MARQUIS *and is explaining things to them during the following dialogue*)

BARON (*quietly, to the* COUNTESS) Good Heavens, then . . .

COUNTESS (*turning on him with a firm expression*) Then what?

BARON Are you really interested? You'll lend yourself to . . . this sort of thing?

COUNTESS I owe it to him!

BARON What you're doing is an insult to me, my dear.

COUNTESS Who's thinking of *you?*

MARQUIS (*coming forward*) That's it, yes, that's what we'll do . . . (*turning toward* BERTOLD) You! Go and call one of the other three, will you?

BERTOLD Yes, sir. (*He leaves by the main door*)

COUNTESS But first we must pretend to take our leave!

MARQUIS Exactly. I'm sending for a valet to prepare the leave-taking. (*to the* BARON) *You* needn't bother, of course, you can just stay here.

BARON (*nodding ironically*) Of course, *I* needn't bother!

MARQUIS So as not to arouse his suspicions again, you understand?

BARON I'm a negligible quantity. Of course.

DOCTOR His certainty that we've gone away must be absolute. Absolute.

(LANDOLF, *followed by* BERTOLD, *enters by the door on the right*)

LANDOLF May we come in, Marquis?

MARQUIS Yes, come in. Now . . . You're Lolo, are you?

LANDOLF Lolo or Landolf, as you please, Marquis.

MARQUIS Good. Now look. The doctor and the Countess are about to take their leave . . .

LANDOLF Very good. All we need say is that the Pope has agreed to receive him as a result of their entreaties. He's in his apartment, groaning at the thought of what he's been saying. He's penitent, but quite sure the Pope won't oblige him. Will you come in to him? . . . You must be good enough to put those clothes on again . . .

DOCTOR Yes, let's be going.

LANDOLF One moment doctor. May I make another suggestion? You should say that Countess Matilda of Tuscany implored the Pope to receive him.

COUNTESS So he did recognize me!

LANDOLF No! I beg your pardon, Countess. It's because he so fears Matilda—fears her dislike. She was hostess to the Pope in her castle. It's strange—in the version of the story I know—though doubtless you all know the truth of the matter better than I do—there's nothing about Henry being secretly in love with Matilda, is there?

COUNTESS (*at once*) Nothing at all! Quite the reverse!

LANDOLF That's what I thought. But *he* says he loved her—he's always saying so . . . —And now he fears that her indignation on this score will work on the Pope to his disadvantage.

BARON We must make him understand she no longer dislikes him.

LANDOLF That's it! Precisely!

COUNTESS (*to* LANDOLF) Yes, yes, quite! (*then, to the* BARON) Because, in case you didn't know, it was because of the prayers of Matilda and the Abbot of Cluny that the Pope yielded. And let me tell you this, my dear Baron: at that time—the time of the cavalcade, I mean—I was going to exploit this fact—I was going to show him my heart was no longer so unfriendly to him as he imagined.

BARON Well, isn't that marvelous, Countess? You're just following history . . .

LANDOLF Yes. So my lady could easily spare herself the trouble of wearing two disguises and present herself from the start, with the Abbot here (*indicating the* DOCTOR), in the costume of Matilda of Tuscany.

DOCTOR (*at once, with force*) No! No! For Heaven's sake, not that! That would spoil everything! His impression of the confrontation must be instantaneous. A sudden blow. No, Countess, let's be going: you will again appear as his mother-in-law. And we'll take our leave. The essential thing is that he knows we've gone. Come on now, don't let's waste any more time, there's still plenty to be done.

(*Exeunt the* DOCTOR, *the* COUNTESS, *and* LANDOLF *by the door on the right*)

FRIDA I'm beginning to be terribly afraid, Carlo—

MARQUIS All over again?

FRIDA Wouldn't it have been better if I'd seen him before . . . ?

MARQUIS Believe me, Frida, there's nothing to it! All you've got to do is stand there.

FRIDA But isn't he raving?

MARQUIS No, no, he's quite calm.

BARON (*with an ironic affectation of sentimentality*) He's melancholy, poor chap. Haven't you heard he loves you?

FRIDA Thank you, but that's *why* I'm afraid.

BARON He won't want to hurt you!

MARQUIS And it'll only be a matter of a moment anyway . . .

FRIDA Yes. But to be in the dark! With him!

MARQUIS For one moment. And I'll be at your side. And the others will be in ambush at the door, ready to run to your assistance. As soon as he sees your mother, understand? As soon as he sees your mother *your* part is finished . . .

BARON I'm afraid what we're doing is like digging a hole in water.

MARQUIS Oh, don't start *that* again, Tito! I think the doctor's remedy will work perfectly!

FRIDA So do I! I can feel it in me already . . . I'm trembling all over!

BARON That's all very well, my friends, but madmen—little, alas, as they know it—are blessed with a certain characteristic which we're forgetting—

MARQUIS (*interrupting, annoyed*) What characteristic is that?

BARON (*forcibly*) They do not reason things out!

MARQUIS What's reasoning got to do with it, for Heaven's sake?

BARON Why, what else has he to do but reason out the situation we're confronting him with—seeing her (*indicating* FRIDA), and her mother at the same time? That's how we planned it, hm?

MARQUIS Not in the least, it's not a matter of reasoning at all. We're confronting him with . . . "a double image of his own fiction." That's what the doctor said.

BARON (*suddenly taking off*) I've never understood why they graduate in medicine.

MARQUIS (*stunned*) Who?

BARON The psychiatrists.

MARQUIS Heavens above, what should they graduate in?

FRIDA They're psychiatrists, aren't they?

BARON They're psychiatrists, my dear: an exact legal definition! And all they do is talk. The best talker, the best psychiatrist. "Analogical elasticity," "the sense of time, of duration!" They tell you right off they can't work miracles—when a miracle is precisely what we need. Of course, the more they say they're not faith-healers, the more people believe they're serious—and don't they know it! They don't work miracles—but they always land on their feet—not bad, huh?

BERTOLD (*who has been spying at the door*

on the right, looking through the keyhole)
Here they are! They're coming!

MARQUIS   They are?

BERTOLD   I think he wants to show them
out . . . Yes, yes, here he is!

MARQUIS   Let's get out then, get out at
once! (*turning to* BERTOLD *before leaving*)
You stay here!

BERTOLD   I'm to stay?

(*Without answering him, the* MARQUIS, FRIDA,
and the BARON *make their escape by the main
door, leaving* BERTOLD *lost and irresolute. The
door on the right opens.* LANDOLF *enters first
and at once bows. Then the* COUNTESS *enters
with cloak and ducal crown as in* ACT ONE, *the*
DOCTOR *in the cassock of the Abbot of Cluny.*
EMPEROR HENRY, *in regal robes, is between
them. Behind,* ORDULF *and* HARALD)

HENRY (*continuing what we suppose him
to have been saying in the throne room*)   Now
I ask you, how could I possibly be clever, as
you now describe me, if I'm also considered
obstinate . . .

DOCTOR   Obstinate, sire? Nothing of the
sort . . .

HENRY (*smiling, pleased*) . For you, I'm
really clever?

DOCTOR   Neither obstinate nor clever, sire,
no . . .

HENRY (*stops and exclaims in the tone of
someone who wishes, benevolently yet ironically, to observe that matters can't rest here*)
My Lord Abbot, if obstinacy is not a vice that
consorts with cleverness, I did hope that in
denying it to me you might have conceded me
a little cleverness instead. I assure you I could
do with some! But if you insist on keeping it
all for yourself . . .

DOCTOR   I? You think me clever, sire?

HENRY   Oh, no, my lord, what are you saying? You don't seem very clever to me! (*cutting this short, so he can turn to the* COUNTESS)
With your permission—a word in confidence
with our empress's mother. Here on the threshold. (*He draws her a little on one side and
with a great air of secrecy anxiously asks her*)
Your daughter is very dear to you, is she?

COUNTESS (*lost*)   Why, of course . . .

HENRY   Would you like me to make amends
for the grave wrong I have done her—by offering her all my love, all my devotion? Of
course you mustn't believe what my enemies
say about my debauches.

COUNTESS   I don't believe it, no, I never
have . . .

HENRY   So you *would* like it?

COUNTESS (*lost again*)   Like—what?

HENRY   You *would* like me to love your
daughter again? (*He looks at her and at once
adds in a mysterious tone of mingled admonition and pain*) Don't be a friend of Matilda of
Tuscany's, please don't!

COUNTESS   But I tell you again she has
begged the Pope, she has pleaded with him,
as much as we have . . .

HENRY (*at once, quiet, trembling*)   Don't
say that, don't say that, in Heaven's name,
don't you see how it affects me?

COUNTESS (*looks at him, then very quietly
indeed as if in confidence*)   You love her still?

HENRY (*dismayed*)   Still? You say *still?*
How do you know? No one knows, no one
must know!!

COUNTESS   But wouldn't *she* know? She who
has been on her knees for you?

HENRY (*looks at her for a moment, then
says*)   You love your daughter? (*a short
pause; turns to the* DOCTOR, *laughingly*) Ah,
my lord, it was only afterwards I realized my
wife existed, and that was rather late in the
day . . . Even now, well, I suppose I have
a wife, yes, I certainly have a wife, but I
assure you I hardly ever give her a thought.
It may be a sin, but I don't feel her, I don't
feel her in my heart. It's an extraordinary
thing, but her own mother doesn't feel her in
her heart either. She doesn't mean very much
to you, does she, lady, confess! (*turning to
the* DOCTOR, *in exasperation*) She talks to me
of another woman, *the* other woman. (*getting
more and more excited*) She *insists* on talking
of her, she insists, I can't understand it!

LANDOLF (*humbly*)   Perhaps, majesty, you
have formed an unfavorable opinion of
Matilda of Tuscany and my lady would like
to remove it? (*Upset at having allowed himself this remark, he at once adds*) I mean of
course at this particular time . . .

HENRY   *You* maintain that she's my friend?

LANDOLF   At this time, yes, your majesty!

COUNTESS   Yes, of course, that's the reason . . .

HENRY   I see. So you don't believe I
love her. I see, I see. No one ever did
believe it, no one ever dreamt of it, so
much the better, let's change the subject.
(*He breaks off, turning to the* DOCTOR, *his face
and mind completely different*) My Lord Abbot, have you noticed? The Pope will revoke
the excommunication on certain conditions.
Have you noticed that these conditions have
nothing, nothing to do with the original reason he had for excommunicating me? Go tell
Pope Gregory I'll settle accounts with him at
Brixen! And you, lady, should you chance to

meet your daughter—let's say down in the courtyard of your friend's castle—your friend Matilda of Tuscany—well, what shall I say? Have her come up. And we'll see if I don't succeed in keeping her at my side: wife and empress. Many women, before now, have come here telling me, assuring me, they were she— the wife I knew I had . . . and, well, sometimes I actually tried—there's nothing shameful in that, is there? With one's wife—But every one of them, when she tried to say she was Bertha, that she came from Susa, I don't know why, burst out laughing! (*as if in confidence*) We were in bed, understand? I didn't have these clothes on. For that matter, well, she had no clothes on either . . . heavens, it's natural, isn't it? For a man and a woman? At those moments we don't think who we are, do we? Our clothes, on the hook, are—phantoms! (*changing his tone again, to the* DOCTOR, *in confidence*) In general, my lord, I think phantoms are nothing but slight disorders of the spirit, images we don't succeed in holding within the bounds of sleep. They come out even in the daytime when we're awake and frighten us. I'm always so afraid when I see them before me at night. A confused mob of images, alighting from their horses, laughing! Sometimes I'm afraid of my own blood: it pulses in my arteries like the dull sound of footsteps in distant rooms in the silence of the night! But enough! I have kept you far too long on your feet. Your humble servant, lady. Your servant, my lord.

(*He has accompanied them to the threshold of the main door. He takes his leave of them and they bow. Exeunt* MATILDA *and the* DOCTOR. *He shuts the door and at once turns. Another change of expression*)

The clowns, the clowns, the clowns! Like a color organ: touch it and look! white, pink, yellow, green . . . And the other fellow, Peter Damiani, haha! he's hit, a bull's-eye. He's scared to even appear before me now! (*He says this with gay, bursting frenzy, pacing and looking first in this direction, then in that, till of a sudden he sees* BERTOLD *more than astounded and terror-struck by the sudden change. He stops in front of him and points him out to his three comrades who also are lost in astonishment*) Just look at this idiot here! He stands gaping at me with his mouth open! (*shaking him by the shoulders*) Don't you understand? Don't you see how I dress them up, how I fool them, how I like to have them parade before me like terrified clowns! What is there to be terrified by? The fact that

I tear off the comic mask and reveal all their trappings as mere disguises? As if it were not I who had forced them to wear the mask in the first place—because it pleased me to play the madman!

LANDOLF ⎫
HARALD ⎬ (*their heads swimming, flabber-*
ORDULF ⎭
gasted, looking from one to the other) What? What do you say? Then . . . ?

HENRY (*when they speak, turning at once, and shouting imperiously*) Enough then, let's have done with it! The whole thing annoys me!! (*then at once, as if on second thought he isn't satisfied, he can't believe it*) God, the effrontery of the woman, coming here, to me, now, her gigolo on her tail . . . Pretending they were doing me a favor, coming out of pity, to keep me within bounds—as if I weren't beyond everything already, beyond this world, beyond life, beyond time! The other fellow, their Peter Damiani, wouldn't have permitted such presumption, but *they* would. They would: every day, every minute, they claim that other people are what they would have them be. That isn't presumption, is it? Oh dear no! It's their way of thinking, their way of seeing, of feeling, every man has his own! You have yours, haven't you? By all means. But what can yours be? That of a flock of sheep: miserable, frail, uncertain . . . They profit by this, they make you swallow their way, so you'll see and feel what they see and feel, or at least so they can kid themselves you will. For what, after all, do they manage to impose on you? Words! Words which each of you understands and repeats in his own fashion. That's the way so-called Public Opinion is formed! Woe betide the man who, one fine day, finds himself labelled with one of the words that people have been repeating. The word Madman for instance. Or the word— what's another example?—the word Idiot. Tell me something: if someone went around fixing his own judgment of you in the minds of others—could you stand idly by? "madman, madman!"—I'm not saying right now that I do it as a joke. Earlier, before I hurt my head falling from a horse . . . (*He stops short, noting their agitation, more than ever upset and astounded*) You're looking each other over? (*With bitter mimicry he mocks their astonishment*) Ha? Huh? What's the revelation? Am I or am I not?—I'll tell you: I am! I am mad! (*becoming terrible*) And so, by God, down on your knees, down on your knees before me! (*One by one he forces them to kneel*) I order you all to kneel before me! That's it! Now touch the floor three times with your foreheads! Down! That's how everyone should be before madmen! (*At the sight of the four kneeling men, he feels his fierce gaiety evaporate at once. He is indignant now*) Off your knees, you cattle, get up!—You obeyed me when you might have put a strait-jacket on me?—Is a word heavy enough to crush a man with? It's a mere nothing, it's . . . like a fly! —Yet words are heavy enough to crush us all. O the weight of the dead!—Here am I. Can you seriously believe Henry the Fourth is still alive? And yet: I speak and give orders to you, the living! I want you that way!—Do you think this a jest too—the way the dead continue to take part in life? *Here*, yes, it is a jest. But go outside. Into the living world. Day is dawning. Time lies before you. Break of day. The day that lies before us, you say, will be of our own making. Hm? Of your own making? What about tradition then? Time-honored customs? Come on: speak for yourselves. You will not utter a word that has not been uttered thousands of times before. You think you are living? You are remasticating the life of the dead! (*He is now right in front of* BERTOLD *who by this time is completely stupefied*) You don't get it, do you, my boy?—What's your name?

BERTOLD   Me? . . . er . . . Bertold . . .

HENRY   Bertold? You fool! Between the two of us, what's your name?

BERTOLD   My . . . um . . . real name . . . is Fino . . .

(*No sooner have the other three started to give signs to* BERTOLD, *advising and chiding him, than* HENRY *at once turns to silence them*)

HENRY   Fino?

BERTOLD   Fino Pagliuca, yes sir.

HENRY (*turning again to the others*)   I've heard the names you use among yourselves so many times. (*to* LANDOLF) You are called Lolo?

LANDOLF   Yes, sir. (*then, with a burst of joy*) Heavens! . . . So you . . . ?

HENRY (*at once, very abrupt*)   So what?

LANDOLF (*straightway growing pale*) Nothing . . . I mean . . .

HENRY   So I'm not mad any more? No. You see me, don't you?—It's all a joke on those who believe it. (*to* HARALD) I know your name's Franco . . . (*to* ORDULF) And yours —one second now—

ORDULF   Momo.

HENRY   Momo, that's it! A nice state of affairs—hm?

LANDOLF (*still hesitant*)   Then . . . then . . . heavens . . .

HENRY (*not changing*)   What? No: not in the least! Let's all have a big, long, lovely laugh about it . . . (*And he bursts out laughing*)

LANDOLF ⎫
HARALD ⎬ (*looking each other over, uncer-*
ORDULF ⎭
tain, lost between joy and pain)   He's cured? It's true? What!?

HENRY   Sh, sh! (*to* BERTOLD)   You don't laugh? Are you still offended? I wasn't addressing you in particular you know.—*Everybody* finds it convenient to believe certain people mad—as an excuse for keeping them locked up. You know why? Because they can't bear to hear what they say. What do I say of these people who've just left? That one is a harlot, another a lecher, another an imposter . . . "It's not true! No one can believe it!"—All the same, they listen to me. Terrified. *Why* do they listen—if what I say is untrue? One simply cannot believe the words of madmen. And yet they listen! Their eyes goggling with terror. Why? You tell me, you tell me why. I am calm, look!

BERTOLD   Well, because . . . maybe they think . . .

HENRY   No, my dear fellow, no! Look at me, look me right in the eyes . . . I don't say it's true, don't worry! Nothing is true! But just look me in the eyes!

BERTOLD   Very well, how's that?

HENRY   There; you see, you see! You too! You have terror in your eyes!—Because you think I'm mad.—That's the proof! (*He laughs*)

LANDOLF (*representing all four, plucking up courage, exasperated*)   What's the proof?

HENRY   The distress you're all in because again you think I'm mad!—And, by God, you know it! You believed me: up to now you believed I was mad. Didn't you? (*Looking at them for a moment, he sees the alarm they are in*) You see this distress? You feel how it can turn into terror? Terror at something that takes the ground from under your feet, that deprives you of the air you breathe? You *do* see it, you *must* feel it! For what does it mean to find yourself face to face with a madman, eh? It means being face to face with one who takes what you have painstakingly constructed within yourself, takes it and shakes it, shakes it down to the very foundations! Your logic— the logic of all these constructions of yours— totters!—Well? Who is it that constructs without logic? The madman! Blessed are the mad—

they construct without logic. Or with a logic of their own that floats on air like a feather. They chop and change. Like this today, but tomorrow who knows?—You stick to your guns, they take to their heels. Choppers and changers!—You say: this cannot be! For them, anything can be.—You say it's not true, because—because what?—because it doesn't seem true to (*indicating three of them in turn*) you, you, you, or to a hundred thousand others! Then, my dear friends, we'd have to see what seems true to a hundred thousand others, a hundred thousand who're *not* considered mad. We'd have to see what account *they* can give us of the things they agree on— the fruits of their logic. But this I know: when I was a child, the moon in the pond was . . . true . . . to me. Lots of things were true. People told me about them; I believed; and I was happy. Hold fast to whatever you think true today! Hold fast to whatever you think true tomorrow—even if it's the opposite of what you thought true yesterday! Or woe betide you! Woe betide you if, like me, you are swallowed up by a thought—a thought that will *really* drive you mad. You are with no other human being, you're at their side, you look into their eyes—how well I remember doing it, that day—and . . . you might as well be a beggar before some door you must never pass through! Open it if you wish: the man who enters is not you, will never be you, will never carry your world within him, the world you see, the world you touch. You don't know the man. He is another person like *any* other person who, from his own impenetrable world, sees you, touches you . . .

(*A long, sustained pause. The shadows in the room begin to thicken, increasing that sense of distress and deepest consternation which fills the four masqueraders, increasing also the distance between them and the great masquerader, who is lost in the contemplation of a terrible misery which is not his alone but everyone's. Then he pulls himself together, and, not feeling their presence around him, starts to look for them, and says*)
It's been getting dark in here.

ORDULF (*at once, coming forward*) Shall I go and get the lamp?

HENRY (*with irony*) The lamp, yes . . . Do you think I don't know that as soon as I turn my back and go off to bed, oil-lamp in hand, you switch the electric light on! Both here and in the throne room!—I pretend not to see it . . .

ORDULF Ah! Then you want me to . . .

HENRY No! It would only blind me.—I want my lamp.

ORDULF Very well, it'll be here at the door, ready. (*He goes to the center door, opens it, goes out, and returns at once with an ancient oil-lamp, the kind you hold by a ring on top*)

HENRY (*taking the lamp and pointing to the table on the platform*) There, a little light. Sit there, around the table all of you. No, not like that! In special attitudes, handsome attitudes! (*to* HARALD) You, like this. (*putting him in position; then to* BERTOLD, *putting him in position too*) You, like this. That's right. I'll sit here. (*turning his head toward one of the windows*) One should be able to say: "O Moon, shed your light on us! Give us one little ray, a pretty one!" The moon is so good for us, so good! For my part I feel the need of the moon. I often spend my time gazing at her from my window. To look at her, who would think she knows eight hundred years have passed and that this man seated at the window moon-gazing as any man might cannot really be the Emperor Henry the Fourth? But look, look at the scene: what a picture! a nocturne! "The Emperor Henry with his trusty Councillors." Don't you relish that?

LANDOLF (*quietly to* HARALD *so as not to break the spell*) You see now? To think that it wasn't true . . .

HENRY True? What?

LANDOLF (*wavering, as if to apologize*) Nothing . . . I mean . . . (*pointing to* BERTOLD) he's only just started work here—and I was telling him only this morning what a pity it was—with us dressed up like this . . . and all the other fine clothes in the wardrobe . . . and a room like that one . . . (*pointing towards the throne room*)

HENRY Well? What's a pity?

LANDOLF That . . . that we never know . . .

HENRY That it was all just play-acting, a comedy, a jest?

LANDOLF Because we thought . . .

HARALD (*coming to his assistance*) It was all done in earnest, dear sir!

HENRY And wasn't it? Don't you really think it was?

LANDOLF Well, sir, if you say . . .

HENRY I say you are fools. Call it a deception, if you wish. The point is you should have been smart enough to accept this deception—for your own sakes. Not just as a play to enact before me or those who came to visit me from time to time. For your own sakes, for your natural selves, day in, day out, before nobody. (*taking* BERTOLD *by the arms*)

For your own sake, my boy, so you can eat, sleep, within a . . . a piece of fiction that's your own—so you can scratch your back when it itches! (*turning again to all four*) Feeling alive, really alive in the eleventh century, here, at the court of your Emperor, Henry the Fourth! And, from this vantage point, the vantage point of an age long past, sepulchral, yet colorful, to think that nine centuries down the road of time, down, down, the men of the twentieth century live in the utmost confusion. Their life is all strain, all anxiety to know what will happen to them. To see to what issue the crises will come that keep them in such anguish and turmoil. Whereas—you are history already! With me! What has happened to me may be sad, the situations I've found myself in may have been horrendous, oh yes, there were bitter struggles, painful vicissitudes . . . But they are history! They have stopped changing! They cannot change any more! You understand? Fixed forever! You can take your ease and marvel at every effect as it follows from every cause in perfect obedience, with perfect logic, at the unfolding of every event—precise and coherent in every particular! The pleasure of history, in fact, the pleasure of history! And how great that is!

LANDOLF Wonderful!

HENRY Wonderful! But over with. Now that you know, I can't go through with it. (*He takes up the lamp in order to go to bed*) Nor can you, for that matter. If you've never understood the real reason. It gives me nausea to think of! (*almost to himself, with violent, contained rage*) By God, I'll make her sorry she came! In a mask of a mother-in-law, pah! With him as Father Abbot!—And they bring me a doctor with them—to study me? Who knows if they don't even hope to cure me? . . . Clowns! —How nice it would be to smack one of them in the face, at least one—*that* one!—A famous swordsman, is he? He'll run me through, will he? We'll see about that. (*He hears a knocking at the center door*) Who is it?

GIOVANNI'S VOICE Deo gratias!

HARALD (*delighted at the thought that here's a trick one could still play*) It's Giovanni the butler. He comes here every evening. As a monk!

ORDULF (*rubbing his hands, lending himself to the jest*) Yes, let him do his act as usual, sir, let him do his act!

HENRY (*at once severe*) You fools! Play a prank on a poor old man who's doing this for love of me? Why?

LANDOLF (*to* ORDULF *and* HARALD, *whispering*) It must be as if it were true, don't you see?

HENRY Oh, very good—*as if it were true.* Only in that way does the truth cease to be a jest.

(*He goes and opens the door and lets* GIOVANNI *in. The latter is dressed as a humble friar with a roll of parchment under his arm*) Come in, father, come in! (*Then, taking on a tone of tragic gravity and deep resentment*) All the documents of my life, of my reign, that were favorable to me have been destroyed, deliberately destroyed, by my enemies. All that has escaped destruction is this one—my life, as written by a humble monk who is devoted to me. And you would laugh at him? (*With love in his eyes, he turns again to* GIOVANNI *and invites him to sit at the table*) Be seated, father, sit there. With this lamp beside you. (*He places at his side the lamp he is still carrying*) Now write, write!

GIOVANNI (*unrolls the parchment and prepares to write from dictation*) Ready, your majesty!

(*The lights fade, but go up almost at once*)

Scene Two

(HENRY *is just finishing the dictation*)

HENRY ". . . the proclamation of peace issued at Mainz was of benefit to the poor and good while it did harm to the bad and powerful. It brought prosperity to the former, hunger and poverty to the latter." (HENRY'S *voice is tired. He notices that* GIOVANNI *and the four young men are drowsy. Quietly:*) Enough! (*As he rises, the five others are suddenly alert and on their feet*)

No, no! Just stay where you are, I can manage! Goodnight!

(*They continue to watch him as he leaves the room*)

(*At this point, the revolving stage starts to rumble. The throne room set is being brought on.* HENRY *is on the turntable walking in the direction opposite to its movement and at the same speed; hence, in relation to the audience, he is stationary. The rumbling stops; we are in the throne room. In the dark, the back wall is hardly visible. The canvases have been removed from the portraits. Within the frames which are now in the two empty niches, in exact imitation of the two portraits, are* FRIDA, *dressed as Matilda of Tuscany* [i.e. *as we saw her in* ACT TWO] *and the* MARQUIS *dressed as Henry the Fourth*)

FRIDA (*as soon as she sees* HENRY *has just passed the throne, whispering from her niche like someone who feels she's about to faint with fright*) Henry . . . !

HENRY (*stopping at the sound as if by some treachery he has suddenly received a knife in his back. In his alarm he turns his face towards the back wall, and instinctively starts to raise his arms as if in self-defense*) Who's calling me? (*It is not a question. It is an exclamation that slipped out in a tremor of terror and which asks no answer from the darkness and terrible silence of the room, a darkness and silence which have for him been suddenly filled with the suspicion that he is mad in earnest*)

FRIDA (*at this act of terror is the more alarmed at what she is to do. She repeats a little more loudly*) Henry . . . ! (*But although she wishes to stick to the part they have assigned her, she stretches her head out a little from the one niche toward the other*) (HENRY *gives a mad yell, lets the lamp fall in order to shield his head with his hands, and starts to flee*)

FRIDA (*jumping from the niche onto the ledge and shouting as if she'd gone mad*) Henry . . . Henry . . . I'm afraid . . . I'm afraid . . . !

(*The* MARQUIS *jumps onto the ledge and then to the floor, running over to* FRIDA *who continues to shout convulsively, on the point of fainting. Meanwhile the others rush in from the door on the left: the* DOCTOR, *the* COUNTESS *who is also dressed as Matilda of Tuscany, the* BARON, LANDOLF, HARALD, ORDULF, BERTOLD, GIOVANNI. *One of them suddenly turns on the light: a strange light emanating from small bulbs hidden in the ceiling and arranged in such a fashion that only the upper part of the stage is brightly lit. Without paying attention to* HENRY *who, after the moment of terror is past [though it continues to vibrate through his whole body], just stays looking on, astonished at the unexpected inrush of people, they anxiously run to support and comfort* FRIDA, *who still trembles and groans and rages in her fiancé's arms. General confusion of voices*)

MARQUIS No, no, Frida . . . *I* am here . . . I am with you!

DOCTOR (*coming up with the others*) That will do! Nothing more is needed . . .

COUNTESS He's cured, Frida, look! He's cured, do you see?

MARQUIS (*astonished*) Cured?

BARON The whole thing was a joke, don't worry!

FRIDA (*unchanged*) I'm afraid, I'm afraid.

COUNTESS Afraid of what? Look at him! It wasn't true, it isn't true!

MARQUIS (*unchanged*) It isn't true? What are you saying? He's cured?

DOCTOR It seems so, Marquis. As for myself . . .

BARON Yes, yes, *they* told us . . .

COUNTESS He's been cured for some time. He told those four attendants about it.

MARQUIS (*now more indignant than astonished*) What? Up to a short time ago . . .

BARON My dear Marquis, he put on an act so he could have a good laugh behind your back, behind the backs of all of us who—in good faith—

MARQUIS Is it possible? He even deceived his own sister on her deathbed?

HENRY (*who has stayed apart, peering now at one, now at another, as he feels their accusations and their ridicule; for all now believe it has been a cruel jest on his part, and that it is at last unveiled. His flashing eyes have shown that he is pondering a revenge, though up to now his scorn, in tumult within him, has prevented him seeing precisely what it will be. Wounded, he bursts forth at this point with one clear idea: to accept as true the fiction which they have insidiously worked out. He shouts to his nephew*) Go on talking, go on!

MARQUIS (*stopped by this shout, stunned*) What, go on?

HENRY Your sister isn't the only one that's dead.

MARQUIS (*unchanged*) *My* sister? I'm talking of yours. To the very end you forced her to come here as your mother Agnes!

HENRY (*again having regard to the* MARQUIS's *present disguise*) And she wasn't your mother?

MARQUIS *My* mother, *my* mother, exactly.

HENRY To the old man, old and far away, that I am, your mother is dead. But you're newly come down out of that niche! How should *you* know that I've not mourned her in secret—mourned her year in, year out— even in these clothes?

COUNTESS (*in consternation, looking at the others*) What's he saying?

DOCTOR (*very disturbed, observing him*) Quiet, for Heaven's sake, quiet!

HENRY What am I saying? I'm asking everyone if Agnes wasn't the Emperor's mother! (*He turns to* FRIDA *as if she were really Matilda of Tuscany*) It seems to me, my lady, you should know!

FRIDA (*still scared, holding on to the* MARQUIS) I? Oh, no, no!

DOCTOR   Here's the lunacy back again . . .
Be careful, everyone!

BARON (*scornfully*)   Lunacy? That's not lunacy, doctor, it's the same old play-acting!

HENRY (*at once*)   I? You have emptied those two niches, and it's *he* that stands here as the Emperor!

BARON   Oh, let's have done with this perpetual jesting!

HENRY   Who says it's jesting?

DOCTOR (*to the* BARON, *loudly*)   Don't excite him, Baron, for the love of God!

BARON (*taking no notice of him, more loudly*)   They said so! (*pointing at the four young men*) *They* said so!

HENRY (*turns to look at them*)   You said that? You said it was all a jest?

LANDOLF (*timidly, embarrassed*)   No . . . what we said was, you were cured.

BARON   Very well, let's have done! (*to the* COUNTESS)   His appearance—(*pointing to the* MARQUIS) and for that matter yours, Countess —is coming to seem insufferably childish, don't you see that?

COUNTESS   You be quiet! Who cares about clothes if he's really cured?

HENRY   Cured? Yes, I'm cured! (*to the* BARON) Oh, but not to make an end of things all at once as you think! (*attacking him*) Do you know that for twenty years no one has ever dared to appear before me here like you and this gentleman? (*indicating the* DOCTOR)

BARON   Of course I know. Only this morning, after all, I myself came in dressed.

HENRY   Dressed as a monk, yes . . .

BARON   And you took me for Peter Damiani. And I didn't even laugh, thinking of course . . .

HENRY   That I was mad. It makes you laugh to see her like that—now I'm cured? And yet you might have realized that in my eyes, her present appearance . . . (*He interrupts himself with a burst of scorn and an:* "Ach!" *He turns at once to the* DOCTOR) You are a doctor?

DOCTOR   Yes, I . . .

HENRY   And you dressed *her* as Matilda of Tuscany too? (*indicating the* COUNTESS) Don't you know, doctor, that in that moment you risked driving my poor brain back into the night? By heaven, to make the portraits speak, to make them jump, living, from their frames . . . (*He contemplates* FRIDA *and the* MARQUIS, *then he looks at the* COUNTESS, *finally he looks at his own costume*) Oh, quite a coincidence: two couples. Not bad, doctor, not bad—for a madman . . . (*with a gesture in the direction of the* BARON) He thinks it's a

carnival out of season, does he? (*turns to look at him*) Then away with my masquerade costume, I'm coming with you, why not?

BARON   Why not indeed?

HENRY   Where shall we go? To the club? White tie and tails? Or home with the Countess—a happy threesome?

BARON   Wherever you like, my dear fellow. I can quite see you wouldn't want to stay here —perpetuating, by yourself, what was after all only the unhappy joke of a carnival day! It's incredible, it's incredible to me that you've been able to do it—even before today—once the effects of the accident were over.

HENRY   Surely, but it was like this, don't you see? After I fell from the horse and was hit on the head, I was *really* mad for quite a time . . .

DOCTOR   Aha! A long time?

HENRY (*very quickly to the* DOCTOR)   Yes, doctor, a long time: about twelve years. (*then, at once, turning to the* BARON) Can you imagine how it was, my dear fellow, to see nothing of what happened after that carnival day, what happened for you and not for me—how things changed, how friends betrayed me? Can you imagine having your place taken by others? Maybe . . . let's say . . . in the heart of the woman you loved? Not knowing who had died, who had disappeared! It wasn't such a . . . jest to me as you think!

BARON   Pardon me, but that's not what I meant. I meant afterwards!

HENRY   Did you? Afterwards? Well, one day . . . (*He stops and turns to the* DOCTOR) A fascinating case, doctor, study me, study me carefully! (*He shakes from head to foot while speaking*) One day, all by itself, Heaven knows how, the trouble here (*He touches his forehead*) shall we say? stopped. Little by little I opened my eyes again. At first I didn't know if 'it was sleep or wake. Why yes, I was awake. I touched one thing, then another, I could see clearly again . . . (*He breaks off and makes a gesture towards the* BARON) I agree with him! away with these clothes, they're a mask, an incubus! Let's open the windows, let in the breath of life! Come on, let's run out of doors! (*putting the brakes on*) But where? To do what? To have everyone secretly pointing at me and whispering "Emperor Henry!" when I'm no longer like this but out there in the streets with my friends and arm in arm with you?

BARON   Not at all! What are you talking about? What makes you think that?

COUNTESS   Who could conceive of such a thing? An accident is an accident.

HENRY They all said I was mad—even before—all of them! (*to the* BARON) And you know it! No one was more furious than you if anybody defended me!

BARON Oh, come, that was only a joke!

HENRY Look at this hair. (*shows the hair on his neck*)

BARON I have grey hair too.

HENRY There's a difference: mine went grey here! While I was Emperor! Understand? I never noticed it. I noticed it all at once—one day as I opened my eyes—and I was terror struck! For I realized that my hair wasn't the only thing that was grey, I must be grey all through, decayed, finished! Hungry as a wolf I would arrive at the banquet after it had been cleared away!

BARON That's all very well, my dear man, but you couldn't expect other people . . .

HENRY (*at once*) —to wait till I was cured. I know. (*pause*) Not even those who came up behind and pricked my horse, harnessed and dressed up as he was, with their spurs . . .

MARQUIS (*disturbed*) What? What was that?

HENRY Pricked my horse, with their spurs! To make him rear up! Treachery, don't you see? So I'd fall!

COUNTESS (*at once, with horror*) It's the first I've heard of that!

HENRY That must have been a joke too!

COUNTESS But who was it? Who was behind us?

HENRY No matter who. All of them! All who went on with the banquet, all who would now leave the scraps, Countess—the scraps of their piddling pity! Whatever leavings of remorse have stuck to their filthy plates they'll give to me! No thanks!! (*turning to the* DOCTOR *on a sudden impulse*) So you see, doctor: isn't this case absolutely new in the annals of madness? I preferred to stay mad. Everything had been prepared for this new kind of pleasure: to *live* my madness, to live it with the clearest consciousness of it, and so avenge myself on the brutality of a stone which had struck me on the head: to take solitude—*this* solitude—squalid and empty as it seemed when my eyes re-opened—to take solitude and straightway clothe it in all the colors and splendors of that distant carnival day when you—(*He points* FRIDA *out to the* COUNTESS) Ah! there you are, Countess!—when you had your day of triumph: to oblige all those who came to see me, to live out, by God, that famous masquerade of long ago which—for you but not for me—was the jest of a single day! To make it last

forever—not a jest, no, a reality, the reality of a true madness! So here we were with our masks on—here was the throne room—here were my four Privy Councillors—traitors of course! (*He suddenly turns in their direction*) I'd like to know what you stood to gain by letting out the fact that I was cured!—Once I'm cured, I don't need *you* any more, you're fired!—To confide in anyone, now *that,* that is really the act of a madman!—But now it's my turn, and I accuse you! (*He turns to the others*) Do you know, they thought they and I could play the joke on you now, take *you* in!

(*He bursts out laughing*)

(*The others manage to laugh, embarrassed, except the* COUNTESS)

BARON (*to the* MARQUIS) Just think . . . not bad, hm? . . .

MARQUIS (*to the four young men*) You?

HENRY We must forgive them. For me, these clothes (*indicating his own costume*) are a caricature, a voluntary and overt caricature, of that other masquerade, the one that's going on all the time. You take part in it whether you know it or not. If without knowing it you wear the mask of what you think you are, you are still a puppet in this masquerade, though an *in*voluntary one. That's why we must forgive these four young men if they don't yet see these clothes of theirs as in character. (*Again he turns to the* BARON) You know this? One soon gets used to it. And one walks around like this—(*He does so*) a tragic character—there's nothing to it—in a room like this!—Look, doctor. I remember a priest—an Irish priest undoubtedly,—goodlooking too—and one November day he was sleeping in the sun in a public park. He'd lain his arm along the back of the seat for support. He was basking in the delight of a golden warmth which to him must have seemed almost like summer. One can be sure that at that moment he didn't know he was a priest any more, he didn't know where he was. He was dreaming, who knows of what?—A small boy passed. He was carrying a flower he'd plucked, with a long stalk. In passing, he tickled the priest, right here in the neck.—I saw laughter in the priest's eyes as they opened. His whole mouth laughed with the happy laughter of his dream. He'd let himself go, he had escaped. But I must tell you, he soon put himself together again, he soon belonged to his priest's cassock again. He grew rigid. And back into his eyes came the same seriousness that you have seen in mine—for Irish priests defend the seriousness of their Catholic faith with the same zeal I felt for the sacred rights of hereditary monarchy,—I am cured, gentlemen, for I *know* I'm playing the madman, I do it quite calmly,—Woe betide you if you live your madness unquietly, without knowing it, without seeing it!

BARON   So the obvious conclusion is—that *we* are the madmen!

HENRY   (*with a little outburst that he manages to check*)   If you were not mad—you and she—would you have come?

BARON   Actually, I came here believing the madman to be you.

HENRY   (*loudly of a sudden, indicating the* COUNTESS)   And she?

BARON   She? I don't know. I see that she seems bewitched by what you have to say, fascinated by this conscious madness of yours! (*He turns to her*) Dressed as you are, I'm sure you could stay here and live it out, Countess . . .

COUNTESS   You are impertinent!

HENRY   (*at once, placating her*)   Don't mind him, don't mind him. He's determined to provoke me—though that was just what the doctor told him not to do. (*turning to the* BARON) Do you think I'll trouble myself any more about what happened between me and you—about the part you played in my misfortune with her—(*indicates the* COUNTESS *then turns to her, indicating the* BARON) the part he is now playing in *your* life?—My life is like this! Yours is not!—The life you have grown old in—I have not lived at all! (*to the* COUNTESS) Is that what you wanted to say, to prove, to me? You were even prepared to take the doctor's advice and dress like that? Well done, doctor, I say again. Two pictures: "Before and After: what we were then, and what we are today!"—But I'm not mad in your way, doctor. I well know he (*indicating the* MARQUIS) can't be me because *I* am Henry the Fourth. I've been Henry the Fourth for twenty years, understand? Fixed in this eternity of masquerade! (*indicating the* COUNTESS) She has lived them, she has enjoyed them, the twenty years, and she's become—a woman I can't recognize. For I know her thus—(*indicating* FRIDA *and going over to her*) in my eyes, this is she, forever . . . You seem like a child that I can frighten as I will. (*to* FRIDA) You've been badly frightened, haven't you, my

child, by the joke they persuaded you to play? They didn't understand that, to me, it could hardly be the joke they intended, it could only be this terrible prodigy: a dream come alive—in you! More alive than ever! For there (*pointing to the niche*) you were an image. They have made you a living creature. You are mine, mine, mine! And by right! (*He takes her in his arms, laughing like a madman while the others are scared out of their wits and shout. But, when they try to tear* FRIDA *from his arms, he becomes terrible and shouts to his four young men*)

Hold them back, hold them back, I order you to hold them back! (*Stunned, yet fascinated, the four young men automatically set about holding back the* MARQUIS, *the* DOCTOR, *and the* BARON)

BARON   (*liberates himself at once, and rushes towards* HENRY)   Leave her alone! You are *not* mad!

HENRY   (*drawing the sword, swift as lightning, from the side of* LANDOLF *who is next to him*)   Not mad? We'll see about that! (*and he wounds him in the belly*)

(*A general yell of horror. The* MARQUIS *and* BERTOLD *run to support the* BARON)

MARQUIS   He's wounded you?

BERTOLD   He's wounded him! He's wounded him!

DOCTOR   I told you so!

FRIDA   God, God!

MARQUIS   Frida, come here!

COUNTESS   He's mad, he's mad!

MARQUIS   Hold him!

BARON   (*while they carry him out by the door on the left, fiercely protesting*)   No! He's not mad! He's not mad! He's not mad!

(*They are shouting as they leave by the door on the left. And they keep on shouting until, amid the general din, is heard a more piercing shout from the* COUNTESS. *Then silence*)

HENRY   (*is left on stage with* LANDOLF, HARALD, *and* ORDULF. *His eyes are starting from his head. He is thunderstruck at the life of the fiction he himself created. In a single moment it has driven him to crime*)   This time . . . we've no choice. (*calls them round him as if to defend himself*)   We're here . . . forever!

Ugo Betti

1892-1953

RELIGION AND THE THEATRE

To approach a subject like this in a truly meaningful way, it seems to me that it is necessary first to force oneself to a humble objectivity and even to a certain detachment. This subject is too important and we are bound to it by too jealous a commitment to allow ourselves to dismiss it with pat solutions or lyrical effusions. It is necessary to examine it with a dispassionate eye instead of imagining what we would like it to be. The point is to understand to what extent the movement which is drawing the theatre towards religious, Christian themes is authentic.

I am speaking, of course, of the theatre today, which is history in the making, a phenomenon still in the process of taking shape. In my opinion, only the theatre of today is in every respect truly theatre, that is, actual collaboration between speakers and listeners in the common effort to formulate the dialogue of our epoch and to give expression to its aspirations.

In the meantime, there is indeed one point worthy of consideration: that such a subject— Christ and the theatre, and even more generally, religion and the theatre—has assumed, in the conscience of many, a new importance precisely at a time when large areas of disbelief, or at least indifference, seem to spread both in the individual soul and in the world.

At least, such is the appearance. Nonetheless, it is precisely now that a confused instinct leads many playwrights and many audiences to converge on themes, problems, figures, and events which, consciously or not, revolve like the wheels of a mill, spun by the visible or hidden current of the same stream: Religion.

This may be religion viewed as a good already attained, which must now be exalted and asserted; or as a good yet to be attained, towards which one is moved by an indistinct desire if not by a precise aim; or as the inner reëlaboration of certain principles in order to make them alive and integral; or even religion viewed as an enemy to be attacked, but not without a wealth of distress and remorse.

Many contemporary plays are indeed religious in an obvious way, and since they represent edifying episodes and settings which are peculiarly sacred, they could, in fact, be performed just as well in a church square as on the stage of a theatre. In general, these works are so well known that I find it unnecessary to name them. Their titles are frequently displayed on the billboards, and audiences, even in the most sophisticated cities, and perhaps especially here, flock to see them.

But if we wish to interpret this religious character in broader terms, the field is considerably widened. One may go so far as to say that it is above all the theatre which corroborates an observation that is only surprising at first sight: if our epoch has affinities with any other, it is more with the passionate Middle Ages than with the brilliant and tolerant Renaissance. In some respects, our epoch, too, is eager for universal systems, and it is not so much preoccupied with living and prospering in them, as in fighting for them, in asserting that they *are* universal and absolute: in a word, religious. This need for universal systems often demands to be heard in the theatre, although through very different and frequently incongruous voices. But, if considered as an indication, perhaps the more these voices appear incongruous—incongruous because they are un-

"Religion and the Theatre" by Ugo Betti, translated by Gino Rizzo and William Meriwether. Reprinted by permission of *The Tulane Drama Review* and Ninon Tallon Karlweis, exclusive agent for Ugo Betti.

conscious: a spontaneous movement and not a preëstablished plan—the more their importance as a symptom must be recognized. We are concerned with the theatre, that is, with an art. This is not an area where a rigorous, logical consistency—critical, political, or philosophical—is essential; here, what is often alive and positive is precisely that which, on the plane of logic and orthodoxy, may seem unclear.

That part of the contemporary theatre which is insensitive to this need may be said to consist of plays which are little above the level of entertainment and, if listened to attentively, sound to us a little out of tune with the times, and basically antiquated. What truly sets these plays in motion, perhaps under the pretense of real problems, is a basic indifference to any problem whatever, an air of routine which is at times good-natured, at times impertinent, and fundamentally nihilistic even though gay on the surface. It is, in short, the survivor of the facile, post-romantic hedonism of the nineteenth century under a different guise, scarcely modernized by a certain irony. They are anachronistic plays; although numerous, they are not part of the picture. The true picture, surveyed in its entirety, induces us to conclude that all, or almost all of the contemporary theatre that counts draws its life from needs which, although variously expressed, are essentially religious.

The basic authenticity of these needs seems to me unquestionable. They are born, ultimately, of the ineradicable need of modern man to feel reassured by certain hopes. But it is equally unquestionable that such a deep authenticity is combined with countless other heterogeneous motives which contaminate it and at times end by overwhelming it.

The first of these contaminations is that of "religiosity," I mean a religion which is no longer a precise issue and necessity—and maybe even a painful error—but a benign substitute, a flexible fall-back, a comfortable *flou* which evades precisely the dilemmas that are well defined (the "either-or," the clear-cut boundaries between good and evil, the responsibility towards others and towards ourselves), a poetic way of making us always right and never wrong. Closely related to this is the vague humanitarianism with which the modern age pads every edge a little, and, pushing them towards a meaningless philanthropy, has diluted all principles and relationships of politics, family, justice, and, naturally, religion. It is used to make us all feel good and at peace with our conscience, without any great effort.

How much shrewdness, even if unconscious, under this sugar-coating! In the theatre we can taste its flavor towards the third act, in the reconciliations and effusions which resolve everything, and perhaps a grand finale accompanied by organ music. Not that I am disturbed by the sound of organs or by the effusions at the end, quite the contrary. But I think that one has to pay for those results and suffer for them; and when I see them given away free, I become suspicious. This extreme need for love, this great flame—Christ—is, I think, something else.

Another contamination comes from the decadent self-gratification by which an emotion, originally religious, is little by little cherished and nurtured in and for itself, a perturbation savored like a quivering sensation, a rare experience: confessions in which suddenly glow the oozings of I don't know what sexuality; martyrdom, guilelessness, ecstasy, whose cruelty or self-annihilation is pierced (even though very remotely) by some kind of inversion. (I cannot avoid thinking of certain moments in *The Cocktail Party*.)

Next to this there is the trap of the décor. The religious issue often implies, especially for us Latins, an ostentatious background. Gold, music, purples, rays falling from high stained-glass windows, angels' tresses on frescos; one feels, at times, that the poet writing, let's say, *The Martyrdom of San Sebastian*, or the director staging an *auto sacramental*, has ended by being more attracted to all this than to the rest—more to gestures, colors and drapery than to the sentiment.

Another contamination, it seems to me, is the one caused by the intellect: too intently bent on its inner polemics, on its own way of "being Christian," on more and more subtle doubts and hypotheses expressed through self-questioning and increasingly more labyrinthine crises so that these gradually fascinate the intellect, but perhaps more for their complication and subtlety *per se* than for their substance. Then, once the contact with facts has been weakened, the self-revelations and the polemics come close to resembling an agonizing chess game of words, a dry equation of algebraic signs. In all this, apart from a certain gratification, there is no want of a real ferment which I would also call useful if I didn't see that certain scrupulous self-examinations end, almost without exception, by acknowledging their own inanity and by characteristically returning to the initial propositions, which would indicate a certain lack either of courage at the conclusive moment or of concreteness in the premises.

Not even the theatre seems to me immune from such indulgences, whose real place is in diaries and essays, although the physical weight and near coarseness, peculiar to the theatre, reject by their very nature all that is of little weight, and easily reveal, in the harsh brightness of the footlights, the quasi-arbitrariness of certain arabesques: arabesques that are almost a luxury (whether or not literature, as action, fulfills a commitment of a religious nature); antitheses that are mainly verbal ("he will bear, then, the martyrdom of not having suffered martyrdom"); complications that are refined and, I would say, marginal (martyrs who spend their last vigil in self-contemplation, examining with subtle syllogisms their own spiritual experience—whether it is one of fear, of pride, of forgiveness, or what have you). Inquiries of this kind are certainly not superfluous, but since they deal with exceptional cases, they evade the real, important issues, the central ones, those shared by everybody— the issues of the people we meet on the street, whose conscience, in regard to religion, is not preoccupied with such fine points, but with other problems which are humbler and probably more important and, in the end, more meaningful and universal; with other and far more dangerous doubts which, finally, are also our own doubts and dangers; with other and truer anguishes.

Such an excess of subtlety, such an eagerness to attach importance to the least coils of one's conscience—in short, such a lack of coarseness—probably betrays a certain lack of seriousness, in the moral sense of that word— a nursing of one's own perturbation, which, from the beginning, carries within it the punishment of sterility. Nevertheless, in spite of all its errors and lack of concreteness, there is something positive in all this. Undoubtedly, there is the need to discuss certain situations anew, to react to passive resignation, to live one's faith and not to accept it as a free gift, to enrich it with a suffering and an effort of one's own. Indeed, there is in all this a rich possibility, and an important one, which can be understood especially by comparing it with another of the dangers which threaten the authenticity—let us say it: even the usefulness—of the religious issue in art, and specifically in the theatre: the opposite danger, which I will call habitual complacency.

But at this point I must honestly admit that these pages (I realize it as I go on) cannot avoid being, above all, a confession. In the long run, all the issues inevitably confront me already conditioned by my preoccupations as a writer. The confusions and misrepresentations to which the originally religious impulse of a play is subject, the contaminations of which I have spoken so far, are contaminations which beguile me too; they are the traps that I should like to avoid and to which, when I have finished writing, I suspect, once again, I have succumbed. Religiosity without rigor; the extreme need to love and be loved which, however, remains so indolent; an accommodating and soft humanitarianism; the sensation more alluring than feeling; the frame which enamors more than the picture; the condescension in showing or believing one's own intelligence and in putting oneself on display; certainly, all these faults are mine too, for it would be strange if I were immune to the malaise affecting practically all the literature of our age. On the other hand, precisely the fact that I am tainted with these faults (and the fact that I am involved, as an old craftsman, in such difficulties), precisely this gives me the right, my only right, to have my say, although a crude and unqualified theoretician, in the tremendous subject of this essay.

It is in this spirit of making a confession that, coming now to speak of the danger represented by habitual complacency, I will begin with a humble disclosure: rarely, after seeing a religious play, especially if explicitly and programmatically religious, rarely, I say, have I returned home and gone over it in my mind without experiencing a certain dissatisfaction —but not because I had been irked by the "contaminations" of which I have already spoken. In general they were works without faults, works entirely dedicated to the humble —and lofty and ancient—task of being religious and nothing else; interpretations of glorious miracles; representations of edifying sacrifices; vicissitudes of Carmelite nuns led to the scaffold or of Jesuits put to the test; by and large excellent works, and unobjectionable in every respect. And yet I experienced a sense of disappointment.

This disappointment was due first of all, if I may say so, to reasons of pure dramatics. From the first scene it was altogether too obvious how the whole thing was going to end. No matter how cleverly or ingeniously the author had shuffled his cards, everything happened exactly as it had been arranged and also, unfortunately, as it had been foreseen. Battles were won and lost at the very outset—won, naturally, by the good cause and lost by the evil, won by the spiritual and lost by the material, won by faith and lost by disbelief. But, in a religious work, what other solution can conflicts of such a nature have? The posing of such conflicts is enough to give us their solution. Perhaps the fault (I am still speaking from a dramatic point of view) of the plays which disappointed me consisted precisely in this: from the very beginning every passion and every character appeared already labeled and defined, or (if the author had ably managed to deceive us) they had been labeled and defined in the author's own mind. They entered into the plays, then, already judged and without hope, judged *a priori* and not brought in to struggle with real alternatives of victory and defeat, but to run through a fixed (and, therefore, habitual) trajectory, measured by a yardstick which allows no error. (I repeat once more that I am speaking from a dramatic point of view.) That's why plays which had Freedom as their goal seemed to the man of the theatre somewhat lacking in freedom, why plays having Life as their subject matter seemed in want of life. Don't misunderstand me: those plays did not lack emotive power. The great crosses shedding their light on the darkness, the sacred chants rising above Error, those immolations, those miracles, those heroic deeds—sublime flowers of a sincere, and severely tried, faith—had the power of making the lady next to me wipe away her tears and even of filling my heart with palpitations. I do not wish to sound irreverent, but such an emotive power seemed to me somewhat automatic and physical. If you will forgive me the analogy, it recalled to my mind the emotion by which, undoubtedly, both young and old are assailed when they watch the flag go by from a crowded sidewalk, and behind the flag the marching step of an heroic troop amidst the sounding of trumpets and the roll of drums. A slight shiver runs automatically through the crowd, but it is a slight shiver that remains such: not one of those who experience it would dream, a moment later, of leaving his own business to join the army, heaven forbid, or of immolating himself. Thus the tears that flowed down the cheeks of the lady at my side left me with the suspicion that they would have very little influence on what she would do once she was back home. Those tears did not change that woman. The sacrifice of the Carmelite nuns had certainly moved her, but, nonetheless, it would not occur to her the next day, or six months hence, to refrain from certain actions and habits. In sum, that emotive power and those plays fell short. The conventional targets they reached no longer amount to much. The true targets, the dangerous targets of today —that is, certain objections widespread in the

world, certain disbeliefs, certain discouragements—are probably beyond the range of fire, and the sacrifices of the Carmelites or of Thomas à Beckett cannot even scratch them.

That contrast between good and evil, then, had a very mediocre effect on a world whose characteristic is precisely this: to believe very little in the real existence of good and evil. For some time the world has suspected that vice and virtue are only products like vitriol and sugar, that certain moral conflicts are mere conventions sanctioned by smart people to keep the fools in check. Above all, I fear that several of the ladies in the audience, or several of their friends, are rather sceptical about what Someone said to each and every one of them: "Verily I say unto thee, Today shalt thou be with me in paradise." I am of the opinion that today many people are scarcely convinced that they will be resurrected after death in order that they may be judged. At any rate, they don't believe in it strongly enough to conform their actions to such a conviction. That is all. It is very simple: one must try to convince them again.

In regard to such a situation, what is the thinking of many Catholics, particularly writers and critics? Their thinking strikes me as curiously rosy. I say "curiously" because the reality of today, on the crust of the world, from the big atheisms to the small indifferences, from the apocaleptic thundering in the far away horizon to the most trivial episodes of everyday exchange and intercourse, the reality of today does not seem to me to encourage a great optimism, but rather, it appears such that persons in a position of high responsibility solemnly avow their concern over it, and even speak of crusades. The optimism of a complacent conscience, however, does not allow concern. What strikes one and causes one to envy them is a kind of soft, quiescent contentment, always repeating that "all is well"—the words of those who live off the fat of the land, and know it. The frame of mind that is at the bottom of this acquiescence seems to me the same as that of the critic who concluded that "tragedy" ended the very moment in which Christ spoke, because wars stop when victory begins. That critic was speaking only of the theatre, but his words leave us nonetheless perplexed. Then wars would be over for mankind; which would mean, to remain in the field of art and the theatre, that Art and Theatre are over too, if it is true that art is always tragedy. With Art and Theatre finished, we are left with only an elegant delight with which to garland our leisure. Leisure, nothing but leisure, if everything were said and done; and our efforts and conflicts would be, to a great extent, superfluous since we have been given the Truth which resolves them once and forever.

I am speaking with the timidity of one who is groping through a maze of problems that are too big for him, and who, at this point, sees himself reduced to the modest resource of a hesitant common sense. We were indeed given a final victory and truth. This is sure. But why these landslides around us, then? And still others announce their coming with far-off thundering. Why these defeats here and there? And why, today and perhaps again tomorrow, this flood of cruelty and hatred, greater than ever before in history? What is the dam that gave way? And, on the other hand, this giving way—was it useless? Is this vast perturbation which is in us and in many others, useless too?

Is error useless—totally useless—and is this effort in our time to fight against it, but at the same time to know it and therefore to love it and extract from it a beneficial suffering, useless too? Should the fact that we have already arrived make our journey useless? We have arrived, but are we surrounded by the everlasting calmness of a haven, by the still waters of a harbor? Why, then, should Bernanos' abbess say to her novice, "Our rules are not a refuge. It isn't the rules that guard us, but we who guard the rules"? Has the danger ceased to exist; is vigilance useless; is doubt itself forbidden, even though it was allowed Christ when He said, "Remove this cup from me," or when he cried with a loud voice at the ninth hour, "Eli, Eli, lama, sabachthani"? Is it a lie, then, this hope we have that Man's life is useful, that it is an ascending, even though difficult, path towards the ever fuller, more intimate, and enlightened discovery of that Truth? Granted the stability and perfection of that Truth, how is it possible not to think that our humble ways, the ways in which we, frail men, gradually become convinced of it and prove to ourselves its eternal validity, may change with time, just as, with time, they lose their efficacy? And don't we see around us so much weakness and bewilderment, and, indeed, a pressing need to be convinced on a new basis in the face of certain new objections, thus more firmly reassuring ourselves of those certainties without which we cannot live? Happy are they who are calm, sure, strong, and no longer need anything, or at least think they don't. But how can we avoid thinking, also, of those who are weak, without faith, and without hope? Is

it not true that we must think of them before all?

When I think of men without hope an image often comes to my mind. I imagine them as inhabitants of an arid planet, without water or earth. Since these two elements—the source of life and the place where it exists—are totally unknown to the senses of these men, they are also totally unknown to their minds. But one day, having split, by chance, the rock on which they live, they discover some strange objects that are embedded in it. These objects are also rocks, but different from the others. These men cannot even fathom what a grain of wheat or a fish is, but what they now have before their eyes is a petrified grain and a petrified fish, and they do not know it. Their wise men carefully examine and re-examine those curious scales, those peculiar shapes, those inexplicable formations. And finally these very same shapes and formations, irreconcilable with all other hypotheses, will necessarily and of themselves create an hypothesis which is almost unbelievable, and yet the only one possible. Each one of these two fossils cannot but presuppose a certain unknown element. One will call forth the sea, the other, the earth. Bent over those scales, these men will finally behold what they never have and never will see in their mortal lives, but which, somewhere, if those scales exist, must certainly exist as well—the blue, infinite ocean, the green, marvelous pastures: Life.

No other way could have convinced them: not even an oath. It would have been an inane declaration, words of an unknown language. Only now are they convinced, since they themselves have discovered those scales.

I fear that it is not always possible or useful to speak of faith to those who despair, or to describe that fresh water, that earth in flower, to them. They do not know, and perhaps they do not want to know, what freshness and gardens are. They do not live in such a world, or they do not believe they do.

However, it can be demonstrated that they do belong to it. But demonstrated, perhaps, in one way only. One must enter their refuge and dig into it and know it. In order to do this, we must go to that rocky land and accept it as it is. The proofs must be found there, for it would be of no use to bring them from outside. I believe that by studying man carefully one will undoubtedly discover that, just as the grain of wheat presupposes the earth and the fish, the water, man presupposes God.

I realize that, even at this point, these are

nothing but justifications. The means whose validity I am supporting are none but the means which, in writing for the theatre, I, myself, have tried to follow, although in part, unconsciously. But what else should I uphold if not these confused efforts—more than ideas—which have impelled me for so many years? All I can do is try clumsily to prove again certain things to someone, starting from zero. I believe, truly believe, that if we search untiringly at the bottom of all human abdications we will always end by finding, under so many "no's," a small "yes" which will outweigh every objection and will be sufficient to rebuild everything. One must not be afraid of that desert. On the contrary, everything must actually be razed to the ground first, one must find himself on that arid planet, and must have gone there without panaceas in his pocket. When we have truly suffered and understood human baseness, we will find at the bottom (since in error not all is error) several illogical and, I would say, strange needs: "illogical" because they cannot be measured by the yardstick of human reason, "strange" because unknown or, rather, opposed to the mechanism and the advantage of the world in which we live and in which we have discovered them. They deny world and paint a different one, revealing "bewildering incongruity between our existence and what it ought to be according to the aspirations of our soul." (I wrote these words twenty-five years ago as an introduction to my first play.)

They are inexplicable needs. But in the soul of the unjust man, and even in the soul of the judge who betrays justice, we will discover that, in the end, he, himself, cannot breathe or survive without justice. Underneath the most hardened bitterness we will, at a certain point, discover in the cruel, selfish, lost souls, a need for mercy, harmony, solidarity, immortality, trust, forgiveness, and, above all, for love: a mercy and a love which are far greater than the pale imitations offered by this world. This is a thirst which all the fountains of the earth cannot quench. Each of these mysterious needs is one side of a perimeter whose complete figure, when we finally perceive it, has one name: GOD.

Translated by Gino Rizzo and William Meriwether

IE QUEEN AND THE REBELS

islated by Henry Reed

CAST OF CHARACTERS

ARGIA
ELISABETTA
AMOS
BIANTE
RAIM
THE PORTER
MAUPA
AN ENGINEER
A PEASANT
A PEASANT-WOMAN
And a number of travellers, soldiers and peasants, who do not speak

The time is the present day

ACT ONE

(The scene, which is the same throughout the play, represents a large hall in the main public building in a hill-side village. There are signs of disorder and neglect.

The stage is empty when the curtain rises. The time is sunset. After a moment the HALL-PORTER *comes in. He is humble and apologetic in manner)*

THE PORTER *(to someone behind him)* Will you come this way, please?

(A group of men and women come silently into the room. They are all carrying travelling-bags and cases)

The Queen and the Rebels by Ugo Betti, translated by Henry Reed, is from *Three Plays by Ugo Betti*, published by Grove Press, Inc. Copyright © 1956 by Andreina Betti. All inquiries concerning performance rights, including readings, should be addressed to Mme. Ninon Tallon Karlweis, 57 West 58th St., N. Y. 19, N. Y., exclusive agent for Ugo Betti.

THE PORTER You can all wait in here for the time being.

ONE OF THE TRAVELLERS *(cautiously)* We could wait just as well outside.

THE PORTER Yes, but you can sit down in here. You'll find everything you want. This used to be the town-hall.

THE TRAVELLER But we don't want to sit down. We want to get on. We're several hours late as it is.

THE PORTER I'm sorry, sir. But you'll be all right in here. There are plenty of rooms, even if you have to stay the night.

THE TRAVELLER Well, let's hope we don't have to stay the night! They told us we'd only be here half an hour, while the engine was cooling down.

THE PORTER Yes, it's a stiff climb up here. The roads up those hills are very steep.

THE TRAVELLER This is the third time they've stopped us to look at our papers. *(after a pause)* I'm a district engineer. I . . . *(dropping his voice)* Do you think they've some special reason for stopping us?

THE PORTER No, no. They'll let you go on directly.

THE ENGINEER Yes, but what are we waiting for?

THE PORTER Sir, I . . . I really don't know what to say. I'm only the hall-porter here. That's to say, I *was* the hall-porter. Since the trouble began, I've been alone here. I have to look after everything. Anyway, will you all make yourselves comfortable?

THE ENGINEER Is it possible to telegraph from here? Or telephone?

THE PORTER All the lines are down. We're cut off from the world. And we're very out of the way here, in any case. I'll go and see if I can find you some blankets. *(a pause)*

THE ENGINEER Look here: I can only speak for myself, of course, but I dare say these other ladies and gentlemen feel much the same as I do about this. You surely realize that nobody's going to travel about just now unless they have to. Every one of us here has some important business or other to attend to. We've all been given permits to travel. Otherwise we wouldn't have come up here at a time like this. We aren't political people; we're just ordinary peaceful travellers. We've all had to pay very large sums of money for a wretched little seat in that lorry out there. And we've all had to get permission from—

THE PORTER (*clearly unconvinced by his own words*) But you'll see, sir: they'll let you go on directly. (*a pause*)

THE ENGINEER Do you know who's in charge here?

THE PORTER *I* don't, no, sir. I just take orders from everybody else.

THE ENGINEER Is there anybody we can speak to?

THE PORTER The trouble is they keep coming and going the whole time. They say there's a general expected here this evening; and a commissar.

THE ENGINEER Then there's no one here now that we can speak to?

THE PORTER The N.C.O.s are a bit rough-spoken, sir. The only one would be the interpreter. But no one takes much notice of him either, I'm afraid.

THE ENGINEER Interpreter? What do they need an interpreter for?

THE PORTER Oh, he's just an interpreter. He's an educated young man.

THE ENGINEER Very well, then: fetch the interpreter.

THE PORTER I'll get him, sir.

(*He goes out. The travellers sit down silently, here and there*)

THE ENGINEER I don't suppose it's anything to worry about. I saw some other people outside. They'd been held up too. It's obviously only another examination because we're so near the frontier. My own papers are all in order. But if there *is* anyone here who's . . . travelling irregularly . . . It might perhaps be as well if they had the courage to speak up straight away, and say so; before they get us all into trouble.

ANOTHER TRAVELLER (*as though speaking to himself*) The large number of spies about the place doesn't exactly inspire people with much desire to "speak up," as you call it. In any case, it's obvious no one here is travelling irregularly. That would have been a little too simple-minded; or so I should have thought?

THE ENGINEER Well, if that's the case, we ought to be on our way again in half-an-hour or so.

THE TRAVELLER I can't say I share your optimism. It's been rather an odd journey, all along. Why did they make us come round this way in the first place? This village wasn't on our route at all. And the engine didn't need to cool down either. And why do we have all these inspections anyway? The only reasonable explanation is that they're looking for someone.

THE ENGINEER One of us?

THE TRAVELLER Though it's just as likely that they're simply being stupid and awkward, as usual. That's about all nine-tenths of the revolution comes to.

THE ENGINEER I . . . think we'd better change the subject, if you don't mind. There's no point in . . .

THE TRAVELLER In what?

THE ENGINEER Well, after all, this upheaval has very great possibilities, when all's said and done.

THE TRAVELLER You really think so?

THE ENGINEER Yes. Yes, I do. Quite sincerely.

THE TRAVELLER Couldn't you . . . spare yourself this extreme cautiousness? It looks rather as if the extremists aren't doing too well at the moment. You didn't notice, as we came along the road?

THE ENGINEER Notice what?

THE TRAVELLER Over towards the mountains. That faint crackling sound every now and then.

THE ENGINEER What was it?

THE TRAVELLER Rifle-fire. They're fighting near here, on the far slope. Everything's hanging by a thread at the moment. It's possible the Unitary Government won't last the week out.

THE ENGINEER A week. It doesn't take a week to shoot anybody. (*He drops his voice*) I didn't notice the noises; I was too busy noticing the smell. Did you . . . catch the smell every now and then?

THE TRAVELLER It's the smell of history.

THE ENGINEER They don't even take the trouble to bury them.

(*The* PORTER *comes in.* RAIM, *the interpreter, follows him, blustering and bombastic. He pretends not to deign to glance at the group of travellers*)

THE PORTER (*as he enters*) The interpreter's just coming.

RAIM (*off*) Where are they? Foreign slaves and spies, that's what they'll be. (*entering*) Where are the reactionary traitors?

THE ENGINEER (*amiably*) You can see that

we are not reactionaries. We are nothing of the kind.

RAIM   Then you must be filthy loyalists; a lot of monarchist swine.

THE ENGINEER   I assure you you're mistaken.

RAIM   You're enemies of the people. What have you come up here for? We fight and die, up here! Have you come up here to spy on us? Are you trying to smuggle currency across the frontier?

THE ENGINEER   We are ordinary peaceful travellers. Our papers have been inspected and stamped over and over again. I must ask you once again to rest assured that we are all sympathizers with the League of Councils.

RAIM   (satirically)   Oh, yes, I knew you'd say that. You're a lot of exploiters, all of you. (He drops his voice a little) And stuffed to the neck with money, I'll bet.

THE ENGINEER   No, sir.

RAIM   Poor little things. No money. We shall see about that.

THE ENGINEER   Not one of us has any money above the permitted amount.

RAIM   Gold, then? Valuables.

THE ENGINEER   No, sir. We all have permission to travel. We merely wish to be allowed to proceed on our way. On the lorry.

RAIM   I'm afraid you'll find that lorry's been requisitioned.

(A silence)

THE ENGINEER   Shall we . . . be able to go on . . . by any other means?

RAIM   The road's blocked. In any case the bridges have all been blown up.

(A silence)

THE ENGINEER   In that case, will you allow us to go back again to our families?

RAIM   Oh, yes, I'm sure! You people, you come up here, and poke your noses into everything, and then go back home and tell tales. I've a pretty shrewd suspicion you'll have to wait here.

THE TRAVELLER   And what shall we be waiting for?

RAIM   The requisite inspections.

THE TRAVELLER   Has anyone authorized you to speak in this way?

RAIM   Has anyone authorized you to poke your nose in?

THE TRAVELLER   On what precise powers do you base your right to interfere with our movements?

RAIM   My powers are my duties as a good citizen of the republic. I act for the republic.

And you? What are you waiting for? Show me your hands. Come on.

(THE TRAVELLER holds out his hands)

RAIM   Proper priest's hands, aren't they just? You've never worked for your living. A bishop at least, I should say.

THE TRAVELLER   Your own hands seem to be very well-kept ones too.

RAIM   Thanks, your reverence, very clever, aren't you? Yes: a great pianist's hands, mine are. A pity I can't play. (He laughs, and turns to the PORTER) Orazio, collect these people's documents.

(The PORTER begins to collect the documents)

THE TRAVELLER   Will you be examining them?

RAIM   They'll be inspected by Commissar Amos. We're expecting him any minute. Or better still, General Biante. He'll be here as well, very soon. Yes! Amos and Biante! Are those gigantic figures big enough for you?

THE TRAVELLER   Quite.

RAIM   In the meanwhile, let me hear you say very clearly the word: purchase.

THE TRAVELLER   Purchase.

RAIM   Center.

THE TRAVELLER   Center.

RAIM   Now say: January.

THE TRAVELLER   January.

RAIM   Can't say I like your accent very much. You wouldn't be a dirty refugee, by any chance?

THE TRAVELLER   Your own accent isn't particularly good either, if I may say so.

RAIM   Ah, but I'm the interpreter, your reverence. I'm unfortunately obliged to soil my lips with foreign expressions. See? Give me this man's papers, Orazio. (after a pause) You claim to have been born in the High Redon, I see.

THE TRAVELLER   Yes.

RAIM   Are you a Slav?

THE TRAVELLER   No.

RAIM   Your surname looks like an alien's to me. Are you a Catholic?

THE TRAVELLER   No.

RAIM   Orthodox? Protestant? Jew?

THE TRAVELLER   I haven't decided yet.

RAIM   Good: but I shouldn't take too long about it. Do you live on investments?

THE TRAVELLER   No.

RAIM   Do you own large estates?

THE TRAVELLER   No.

RAIM   Gold?

THE TRAVELLER   No.

RAIM   Bonds?

THE TRAVELLER   No.

RAIM   What are your political opinions?

THE TRAVELLER   I cannot deny that I feel a certain concern for the Queen.

(*A silence. Everyone has turned to look at him*)

RAIM   The Queen?

THE TRAVELLER   The Queen.

RAIM   Good. We'll see how you like trying to be funny when Biante and Amos get here. (*rudely, to another of the travellers*) You. Show me your hands. (*to another*) You.

(*The person in front of him is a timid, shabbily-dressed peasant-woman. She puts out her hands, at which he glances in disgust*)

RAIM   Peasant. (*turning to the* PORTER) Even peasants can travel all over the place, these days! (*turning back to the travellers, with his finger pointing*) You.

(*He stands there speechless, with his finger still pointing. He is facing a rather attractive woman, with crumpled but not unpretentious clothes, and badly dyed hair. She has hitherto remained hidden among the other travellers. She stares at him: and slowly puts out her hands*)

ARGIA   (*in quiet tones, half-teasing and half-defiant*)   I have never done a stroke of work in my life. I have always had a very large number of servants at my disposal.

(*They have all turned to look at her.* RAIM *stands there embarrassed, and seeking some way out of his embarrassment. He turns abruptly to the* TRAVELLER)

RAIM   You, sir; *You*, I mean!

THE TRAVELLER   (*politely*)   Yes? Is there something else I can . . . ?

RAIM   I've been thinking: I didn't like the way you . . . your manner of . . .

THE TRAVELLER   Yes?

RAIM   (*still trying to recover his self-possession*)   I'm afraid this . . . this casual manner of yours demands closer attention. And the rest of you too: I shall have to go into things in more detail. We must get these things straight. Orazio, you'll bring these people into my room . . . in small groups . . . or better perhaps, one by one, separately. Yes. These things have to be dealt with quietly, calmly. (*He has gone over to the door. Turning back*) I'd like you all to understand me. You mustn't think I'm doing all this out of spite. On the contrary, you'll find I'm really a friend. It's a devil's cauldron up here: everything in a state of confusion. All sorts of different people . . .

different races and languages, infiltrators, priests with beards, priests without; everything you can think of: this spot here's a picture of the whole world in its small way. There's too much friction everywhere. Why shouldn't we all try to help one another? Rich and poor, poor and rich. What I mean is, I should be very happy if I could . . . assist any of you. Orazio, send them all in to me. (*He goes out*)

THE PORTER   (*after a very brief pause*) Well, come on. You first . . . and you.

(*He points first to one, then to another of the travellers. They follow* RAIM)

THE ENGINEER   Well, it's just as I said: another inspection.

THE PORTER   (*with a quick glance at* ARGIA) Yes. They've been tightening things up since this morning.

ARGIA   (*lighting a cigarette*)   But are they really looking for somebody?

THE PORTER   Well . . . there's a lot of gossip flying about. (*He casts another furtive glance at her*)

ARGIA   Is it . . . the so-called "Queen" they're after?

THE PORTER   (*evasively*)   That's what people are saying.

THE ENGINEER   My dear fellow, all this talk about the woman they all call the Queen, just goes to show what a ridiculous race of people we are.

ARGIA   (*smoking*)   I thought the clever lady died, five years ago?

THE TRAVELLER   (*intervening*)   Yes, so it's said. But the ordinary people still maintain that in the cellar at Bielovice the body of the woman was never found.

THE PORTER   They were all of them in that cellar to begin with: when they were alive: ministers, generals, and so on.

ARGIA   And was she there too?

THE TRAVELLER   (*to* ARGIA, *with detachment*) Yes, she was. Haven't you ever heard about it? It's quite a story. It's claimed that when the soldiers poured their machine-gun fire down through the barred windows, they instinctively omitted to aim at the woman. So that after the job was finished, under all those bloody corpses . . .

THE ENGINEER   (*sarcastically*)   . . . the cause of all the trouble was unharmed.

THE TRAVELLER   (*to* ARGIA, *as before*) There were four soldiers on guard at the Nistria bridge, up in the mountains. In the evening a woman appeared. She was covered in blood from head to foot. The soldiers said:

"Where are you going?" She looked at them, and said: "Are you sure you have any right to ask me that?" The soldiers said they had orders to stop everyone, especially women. She said: "Are you looking for the Queen?" "Yes," they said. She looked at them again, and said: "I am the Queen. What are my crimes?"

ARGIA She wasn't lacking in courage.

THE TRAVELLER No. She spoke with such calmness, and went on her way with such dignity, that the soldiers didn't recover till the woman had disappeared into the woods.

THE ENGINEER Very moving. And from then on, according to you, in a country like this, with more traitors than there are leaves on the trees, that woman has been able to stay in hiding for five years?

THE TRAVELLER Very few people actually knew her. She always remained in the background.

THE ENGINEER (ironically) It's a pretty little tale. In any case what reasons would such a woman have now for springing up out of the ground? Events have passed her by. All the parties either hate her or have forgotten her, which is worse. And why do you call her the Queen? She was never that. Even her most slavish accomplices never flattered her to that extent.

THE TRAVELLER (gently) All the same, the common people have taken to calling her by that name.

THE ENGINEER The common people have always been fascinated by the major gangsters. Especially blueblooded ones. That great lady was not only the blazoned aristocratic wife of a usurper; she was the real usurper and intriguer herself. She was the evil genius behind everything, the Egeria, the secret inspirer of all this country's disasters.

THE PORTER (suddenly, in an unjustifiably sharp voice, to two more of the travellers) The next two, please, go along, in there. What are you waiting for?

(The two travellers go out. Only the PORTER, the ENGINEER, the TRAVELLER, ARGIA, and the PEASANT-WOMAN are left)

THE PORTER (to the ENGINEER) I . . . I hate that woman, too, of course. I hate her more than you do.

THE TRAVELLER (as though to himself) All the same, she must have had some sort of sway over people.

THE PORTER People who talk about her say she . . . did seem very proud and haughty, but at the same time . . . sincere.

They say people could never bring themselves to tell lies to her.

THE TRAVELLER (with detachment) The only human needs she ever seems to have acknowledged were the ones that can be reconciled with a dignified and honorable idea of the world. Everything she did and said was, as it were, essential and refined. It must be costing her a great deal to stay in hiding.

THE ENGINEER Forgive my asking: but did any of you ever see her in those days? (to ORAZIO) Did you?

THE PORTER No.

THE ENGINEER Have you ever spoken to anybody who'd ever seen her?

THE PORTER No.

THE ENGINEER You see, then? It's all popular ignorance: a spirit of opposition prepared to raise even a ghost against the idea of progress, if it can.

THE TRAVELLER It's a very remarkable ghost, then. (a pause) I'd like to meet it.

(RAIM bursts into the room)

RAIM I'd like to know what you all think you're doing? You take all this very calmly, don't you? The general has been sighted.

THE TRAVELLER (calmly) Indeed?

RAIM (to the PORTER) You, quick, take all these people in there; try and fix them up in there somehow . . . (to ARGIA) No, not you. You wait in here. There are some things I have to ask you.

(The ENGINEER, the TRAVELLER and the PEASANT-WOMAN go out into the next room, at a sign from the PORTER. The PORTER picks up their documents, which have been left on a table)

RAIM (severely, to ARGIA) And in particular I should like to know what are the exact and precise reasons . . . the, ah, the reasons why you have undertaken this journey up here.

ARGIA (adopting the same official tone) Personal reasons.

(The PORTER is on his way out of the room)

RAIM What were they? I may as well say that it will be as well for you if you explain them in detail.

(The door closes behind the PORTER)

ARGIA (slowly dropping the official tone) The reasons in detail were as follows: I was getting horribly miserable down in Rosad, my darling, and I didn't know what to do.

RAIM I suppose you think it's very clever, coming up here?

ARGIA They told me you were up in the mountains.

RAIM   What do you want with me?

ARGIA   So now you've joined up with the Unitary Party, Raim? Clever boy. Are you fighting? Shooting people?

RAIM   I asked you what you'd come for.

ARGIA   Nothing. You should have seen your face when you saw me. I could have died laughing. Have I upset you?

RAIM   (*harshly*)   Not at all, I was very glad to see you.

ARGIA   I wonder what your present bosses would say if anyone told them who the ones before were.

RAIM   That's not the sort of thing *you* can feel particularly easy about. When did you leave?

ARGIA   Yesterday.

RAIM   Have you any money?

ARGIA   . . . A certain amount.

RAIM   (*sarcastically*)   Yes, I dare say.

ARGIA   I sold everything I had. Not that it fetched much.

RAIM   My dear girl, this is the very last place you should have come to. I only managed to get fixed up here by a miracle. I've had to tell them the most incredible tales. You needn't think I'm going to start running any risks, now.

ARGIA   I will make you run risks, Raim.

RAIM   No, my dear, we're a bit too near Rosad for that. I've enough risks of my own to run; too many. You're a woman, you always get along somehow. But these bloody fools up here, they suspect everybody. The slightest thing, and they're foaming at the mouth. I want to come through all this mess alive. And rich. Yes. What you want up here is a good memory: for afterwards. That's all you want: it'll be a good investment. One side's going to come out on top after all this; and if you've been robbing and betraying and murdering on that side you'll be a hero; if you've done the same for the other you'll be ruined. And there are so many people living in fear and trembling, I've decided to be one of the landed gentry in my old age. If it's anyhow possible you and I can meet up again in the spring. May I ask why you came up here to find me? (*sarcastically*) Do you love me? Did you miss me down there?

ARGIA   Raim, I really didn't know what to do. The other day, the police arrested me.

RAIM   Why?

ARGIA   They were just rounding people up. I hadn't done anything. I was in a café on one of the avenues. It's difficult now, being a woman on your own.

RAIM   So what?

ARGIA   Oh, nothing. I was actually rather a success at the police station. I had to stay the night there to start with; but the superintendent was quite kind to me in the morning. He told me to ring up someone who'd vouch for me. Raim: it was then I realized something for the first time: I don't really know anybody. I know people: but they're only Christian names or nicknames, as a rule. I hardly know anybody by their surname. And now, with all this confusion, so-and-so run away, so-and-so dead . . . There I was, with the telephone book, turning over the pages . . . and I could think of no one.

RAIM   So what?

ARGIA   They questioned me about my means of subsistence. The result was I was given repatriation notice. The superintendent told me I had to be decentralized, whatever that is. He said they'd send me away the next day with a military escort. "All right," I said: "but I'll have to pack my bags." They sent me home with a guard. I gave the guard my watch, and he pretended to lose me in the crowd. There were no trams, of course; the streets were all blocked; soldiers everywhere; "no stopping here." And so on. Finally, I managed to get a seat on a lorry; the price was sheer robbery. It was raining, my feet were hurting, my clothes were soaking wet; do you know what I felt like, Raim? A rat, a drowned rat. Then at Bled they made us detour, then again at Nova. Inspections. And then more inspections; hold-ups; bayonets. At Sestan they stole my coat. It hasn't been easy getting up here. I'm lucky I've found you so soon. (*She has seated herself on his knee*)

RAIM   (*getting up*)   I'm sorry, my dear, but the people here mustn't know I know you. I'm speaking for your own good as well as mine.

ARGIA   Raim, I couldn't stay down there. I was frightened; can't you understand? Not that they can really charge me with anything. But everywhere you go . . . (*with a sudden cry, which she quickly suppresses*) you see the gallows, Raim. Just because of stray accusations . . . or vague resemblances, rows of people have been hanged. . . .

RAIM   And you think that's going to encourage me to keep you here? I've as much cause to be worried as you have. It would be madness just to slap our worries together. No, Argia, no: everyone has to look after himself; I want to finish this war above ground, not underneath.

ARGIA   (*after a pause, with an effort to make it seem unimportant*)   Raim: what if I told you . . . that I'd really . . . missed you?

RAIM   That's what I said. You love me. I've bewitched you.

ARGIA   Oh, I know you're quite right to laugh at me. (*lightly imploring him*) But . . . when we're both together I feel . . . a bit safer. . . . I was happy, when I saw you; don't you understand?

RAIM   Well, I wasn't, see? I wasn't.

ARGIA   Raim. . . .

RAIM   My dear . . . I've no intention of burdening myself with you. Besides, you'll be sure to find a way out, I know you. (*shrugging his shoulders*) There aren't many women round here. They're in great demand.

ARGIA   (*lowers her eyes for a moment; then looks at him and says, in low quiet tones*) What a disgusting creature you are, aren't you, Raim? I sometimes think you must be the nastiest person in the world.

RAIM   Ah, now you're talking sense. You go away and leave me, my dear; I'm not worthy of you. I'd feel guilty at keeping you here.

ARGIA   And to think that *I* am running after somebody like *you*, begging . . . from *you*. It's enough to make one weep; or laugh.

RAIM   Well, you laugh, then, my dear. Let's both have a good laugh, and say goodbye. You'd be wasted on me. You know, Argia, one of the reasons you don't attract me is your silly games of make-believe the whole time. You've always tried to act so very grand. With me! The superior lady, always disgusted, so easily offended. You of all people! Always behaving as though dirt was something that only belonged to other people.

ARGIA   (*her eyes lowered*)   No, Raim, that's not true.

RAIM   While the truth is that if ever there was a filthy creature in the world, you're it.

ARGIA   I'm sorry, Raim, if I spoke like that . . . It's only because deep down I love you, and want to . . .

RAIM   You let me finish. I'm not angry; not at all. But you may as well get this straight. You see, Argia: you're not only a dead weight on me. . . . It's not only that. You've begun to get rather too many wrinkles for my liking. . . .

ARGIA   (*trying to turn the whole thing into a jest*)   Really, Raim? A few minutes ago, when they were all talking about the Queen, did you know they all looked at me? They half thought I was the Queen.

RAIM   You! The Queen? They've only got to look at you to see what *you* are. The Queen. There isn't a square inch about you that's decent.

ARGIA   (*with another hoarse effort at playfulness*)   Be quiet, Raim, if you don't, I'll bite you! (*She takes his hand*)

RAIM   (*freeing himself with a brutal jerk which makes her stagger backwards*)   You leave me alone. Don't try and pretend I'm joking. What you ought to do, my dear, is to go and stand in front of your looking-glass and say to yourself as often as you can: "I'm a cheap, low, dirty slut." You've never done a decent thing in your whole life. (*deliberately*) Smell of the bed. Cigarette smoke. Wandering about the room with nothing on, whistling. That's you. And there have been one or two unsavory episodes which even suggest that the secret police made use of you. Oh, make no mistake, I'm not the kind of man who's easily prejudiced. But you, Argia, quite apart from everything else, you're cheap. The little bogus middle-class girlie, who's read a few books. Even in your intrigues you're small and petty: the little tart with the furnished rooms and the pawnshop tickets: I've been getting fed up with you now for quite a long time, see? Well: it's over. I'm not going through all that again.

ARGIA   (*her eyes lowered; and with a faint wail*)   Raim, I've nowhere to go.

RAIM   Then go to hell. It's the one place . . . (*His voice suddenly reassumes its official tone. He has heard footsteps coming*) It's absolutely necessary for . . . for political reasons. And even if you have to stay here tonight, it's no great disaster. You and the other woman, that peasant-woman, can stay in here. The other passengers in the other rooms. It'll be all right. I'll see about finding some blankets for you. Political and military necessities, unfortunately. It isn't my fault.

(*It is the* TRAVELLER *who has come in.* RAIM *has turned to him on his last words. The* TRAVELLER *approaches amiably*)

THE TRAVELLER   Nor ours either. I seem to get the impression that you, too, regard these . . . these military and political necessities, with a certain amount of scepticism.

RAIM   (*looks at him for a moment and then says, also amiably*)   Bless my soul, that's exactly what I was saying to . . . (*to* ARGIA, *sharply*) You may withdraw, madam. Go in there with the others.

(ARGIA *goes out*)

RAIM   (*amiably but cautiously*)   Yes, I was just saying that . . . well, of course, I'm a good revolutionary and all that (we all are, of course), but I . . . understand things. I know how to put myself in another man's place. Unfortunate travellers . . . perhaps even important men, well-to-do, plenty of money and so on, suddenly finding themselves . . .

THE TRAVELLER   Reduced to hoping for a blanket!

RAIM (*carefully feeling his way*)   I'm afraid I may have seemed a little bit . . . official with you just now. I had to be, of course. You understand.

THE TRAVELLER   I have the feeling that you too understand. . . .

RAIM   Oh, at once, my dear friend, straight away. I'll be happy to be of any help, if it's at all possible. . . .

THE TRAVELLER   The secret is to regard these things with a certain amount of detachment; don't you agree?

RAIM   Definitely. You know, I got the impression, when we were talking here a few minutes ago, that you too . . . feel a certain distaste for some of the excesses that . . .

THE TRAVELLER   Ah, you noticed that, did you?

RAIM   Oh, but of course! I'm a man . . . who doesn't feel so very bitter as all that towards your *own* ideals, you know, sir.

THE TRAVELLER   Is that so? I'm delighted to hear it.

RAIM (*mysteriously*)   I'm too much in contact with the new chiefs the whole time, of course.

THE TRAVELLER (*shaking his head*)   And they . . .

RAIM (*laughing*)   . . . aren't so terribly different from the old ones.

THE TRAVELLER   That was to be expected.

RAIM   Once you ignore the individual differences of character, you find they raise their voices, ring the bell, upset people and shoot 'em . . .

THE TRAVELLER   . . . in exactly the same way as the others. Yes. I assume you were also in the habit of hobnobbing with the former high-ups?

RAIM   Oh, no, God forbid. I had to put up with them. And now I have to put up with these. "Put up!" It's all very sad.

THE TRAVELLER   Especially for men of intelligence. (*as though speaking to himself*) Who really ought to be looking after themselves.

RAIM (*warmly*)   Exactly! That's just what I say. These disturbances ought to be a godsend for people with any imagination . . . ! (*He has taken a bottle out of its hiding-place, and is pouring out a drink for himself and the* TRAVELLER) "Ought to be looking after themselves." Yes. As you say. Look after yourself, what? You know, I have a theory about all these things.

THE TRAVELLER   I'd like to hear it.

RAIM   There are two kinds of people in this world: the people who eat beef-steaks and the people who eat potatoes. Whose fault is it? Because it's certainly not true that the millionaire eats a hundred thousand beef-steaks.

THE TRAVELLER (*drinking*)   He'd soon have indigestion if he did.

RAIM (*also drinking*)   He eats half a beef-steak and helps it down with a dose of bicarbonate. Yes. Then why do all these other poor devils have to make do with potatoes? It's simple. There aren't enough beef-steaks to go round. The limitation on the number of beef-steaks in the world is a profound inconvenience on which social reforms have not the slightest influence. Not the slightest. Now, it follows from this that whatever régime you're under, the number of eaters of beef-steak . . .

THE TRAVELLER   Remains constant.

RAIM   Exactly. And the wonderful thing is that the beef-steak eaters are always the same people. They may *look* different, of course. But who are they?

THE TRAVELLER   The bosses . . .

RAIM   . . . and the wide-boys. It's always the same act; the palaces and the armchairs are always there, and it's always by virtue of the people and the potatoes that the high-ups can sit in the palaces eating their beef-steaks. That being agreed, what's the logical thing to do? It's to belong, whatever happens, to . . .

THE TRAVELLER   The beef-steak party.

RAIM   It's not for everybody, of course. It requires intelligence . . . intuition. (*with sudden firmness*) You'll forgive me, sir, but I don't believe in equality; except over tooth-picks. It's only by climbing up and down that we keep fit. (*gently*) I believe in money.

THE TRAVELLER   You're not the only one.

RAIM   If man had never developed that great vision of having a bank account, he'd never have emerged from cave life.

THE TRAVELLER (*solemnly*)   Progress. Progress.

RAIM   A little bit of salt on the tail. Just think what a colossal bore it'd all be otherwise. Everybody stuck there as though in a morgue. A row of coffins. If a man's a hunchback, he's always a hunchback. We all know that. If a man's ugly, he's ugly. If he's a fool, he's a fool. But at any rate, however common and unfortunate a man may be, he can always hope to get rich, little by little. Rich. Which means he won't be ugly any more, nor a fool . . .

THE TRAVELLER   Nor even a hunchback.

RAIM   That's your *real* democracy; your real progress. Yes, that's why it's the duty, the absolute duty of every intelligent man . . . (*His voice changes once more and becomes peremptory and severe; footsteps are approach-*

ing) to fight and to strive! To fight and strive in the service of our flag and our republic! (*He turns to see who is coming in: and is at once thrown into great agitation*) Good God, it's you, General Biante, forgive me, I never saw you come in! (*He runs to the door*) How are you? Are you feeling a little better?

(BIANTE *has entered, supported by an armed guard,* MAUPA, *who at once helps him to sit down.* BIANTE *is a hirsute man in civilian clothes. His shoulders, neck and one arm are voluminously bandaged, and compel him to move stiffly. He looks first at* RAIM, *then at the* TRAVELLER, *and then turns back to* RAIM)

BIANTE (*his voice is low and hoarse*) What are you doing?

RAIM (*eagerly*) Nothing, general, I was just interrogating a traveller.

BIANTE Oh. Good. And what did the traveller have to say to you?

THE TRAVELLER (*sweetly*) We were discussing some rather curious offers of help he'd just been making to me.

RAIM I? General Biante! (*He sniggers*) I was just holding out a little bait, just wriggling a little hook about. I ought to say that this gentleman seems to me a very suspicious character. I think we should do well to point him out to Commissar Amos . . .

BIANTE (*between his teeth, not amused*) Don't be a bloody fool.

RAIM . . . the minute the commissar arrives.

THE TRAVELLER (*calmly, to* RAIM) I arrived an hour ago. I am Commissar Amos. How are you, Biante?

BIANTE Haven't you managed to get me a doctor?

AMOS Not yet.

BIANTE I'd be damned glad of one. I come through the whole war safely: and what do I have to be wiped out by? A stray bullet. Amos, I'm swollen right up to the neck; my fingers feel like sausages. I wouldn't like to die, Amos. I'd like to live and see the new age in. Do you think I'm getting gangrene?

AMOS (*calmly*) Let's hope not.

BIANTE (*suddenly to* RAIM, *hysterically*) Go and find a doctor, for Christ's sake! You filthy bastard, go and find a doctor! And send all those people in here!

(RAIM *rushes out*)

BIANTE   (*breathing   laboriously*) The Queen's here! Somewhere: in our midst. Nobody's doing anything, nobody knows anything. And yet they're all saying it! The Queen's here!

AMOS (*calmly*) Yes, I'd heard for certain she was.

BIANTE Good God. Who from?

AMOS They stopped a man on the road from Bled. He was coming up here to meet her.

BIANTE Where is he?

AMOS He was too quick for us. While they were bringing him here. He poisoned himself. So as not to have to acknowledge his accomplice.

BIANTE (*almost a whisper*) The Queen's here! Alive!

MAUPA (*suddenly, from the background, without moving, in a kind of ecstasy*) We want to see the color of the Queen's entrails.

(RAIM *is escorting the travellers into the room*)

MAUPA (*continuing without pause*) All our troubles come from the Queen. If our sick are covered with wounds, if our children grow up crippled and our daughters shameless, the Queen's to blame, no one else. (*His voice gets gradually louder*) If she falls into my hands, I'll keep her dying slowly for three whole days. I'll make them hear her screams from the mountain tops. I'll slit her up bit by bit till she lies there wide open like a peach. The thought that the Queen is near makes my hair stand on end like a wild boar's. We must find her.

AMOS (*calmly*) She will be found soon enough. The road up here has been blocked since this morning, but the number of road passengers they've stopped hasn't been very large. This very night we shall begin to go over them methodically.

BIANTE (*turning to the others, who are standing huddled together in the background*) Yes, you there! It's you we're talking about! (*shouting and getting up from his chair*) I'm here: General Biante. I assume full powers . . . together with Commissar Amos here. . . . Is there anybody here who's a doctor? No? Blast you. (*brief pause*) You're all under arrest! No one's to move an inch from where you are now.

AMOS The exits are all guarded; the guards have orders to shoot.

BIANTE You'll all be questioned. So look out! You'll be detained here till further orders! (*pointing*) The women in there; the men in here. Get on with it, everyone to his proper place. (*He moves towards the door*)

AMOS (*calmly, for the pleasure of contradicting him*) The men will go in there; the women will stay in here.

(BIANTE *casts a sharp glance at* AMOS, *and goes out, supported by* MAUPA. *The travellers have all gone out again except* ARGIA *and the* PEAS-ANT-WOMAN)

<u>AMOS</u> (*also on his way out, turns in the door-way*) Goodnight for the present. (*He goes out*)

(ARGIA *stands for a moment looking at the door, and then shrugs her shoulders*)

ARGIA What a lot of stupid nonsense! The result is that we sleep in here. Let's hope the interpreter remembers to bring us some blankets. There was a sofa in that other room too. (*She points to the next room*) I'm very tired, aren't you? (*She sits*) What a lot of clowns they all are. Let's hope they let us sleep till tomorrow morning. (*She begins to fumble in her hand-bag, and brings out a small pot; she takes some cold cream on one finger and dabs it on her face. To the* PEASANT-WOMAN, *who is still seated in the background*) I suppose in the country you don't go in for this sort of thing? I have to, every night: I'm not so young as I was, I've just been told; it would be asking for trouble if I didn't look after myself. (*She massages her face*) I suppose I must look a sight with all this grease all over my face? Sorry. (*She thinks for a moment*) I find it rather humiliating being a woman. Even rather humiliating being alive. (*She massages her face*) You spit in a blackguard's face, and even as you do it, you know perfectly well the only thing to do is to make him go to bed with you . . . I'm sorry: but we're both women, after all. I don't mean one really wants to, even. It's all so squalid and humiliating. (*She breaks off*)

(RAIM *crosses the stage and goes out*)

ARGIA I've come a long, long way just to go to bed with a man. (*pause*) Making a fuss of a man to try and find out if he's in a good mood or not. Very amusing. (*pause*) The trouble is having no money either. Let's hope after we're dead there'll be nothing of that to worry about. (*turning to the* PEASANT-WOMAN) Do you mind my asking, dear: I suppose you haven't a bit bigger mirror than this? What . . . what's the matter? Aren't you feeling all right?

THE PEASANT-WOMAN (*almost inaudibly*) Yes . . .

ARGIA (*going over to her*) Why, you're covered with sweat. Do you feel ill? You look as if you're going to faint.

THE PEASANT-WOMAN No . . . no. . . . (*She sways*)

ARGIA (*supporting her*) Did what that brute in here said about the Queen frighten you? You mustn't take any notice of that, it's nothing to do wtih us . . .

(*She breaks off; lets the woman go; and stares at her. The woman stares back at her with wide-open eyes; then she rises, slowly*)

ARGIA (*after a long pause, in a different voice*) Is there anything you want?

THE PEASANT-WOMAN No . . . no. . . .

ARGIA You could go and lie down in there, on the sofa. Where is your bag?

(*The* PEASANT-WOMAN *grips her bag, as though frightened by* ARGIA'S *words*)

ARGIA What have you got in there?

THE PEASANT-WOMAN Some bread . . .

ARGIA Well, my dear, you go in there. Lie down. You'll soon feel better.

(ARGIA *helps the woman into the next room. After a moment she returns, and walks about for a moment or two, perplexed and thoughtful. Suddenly she runs to the other door, opens it and calls in a stifled whisper*)

ARGIA Raim! Raim! (*She comes back, and waits*)

RAIM (*enters: in a whisper*) What d'you want? Are you mad?

ARGIA (*whispers*) I'm rich, Raim. I'm worth marrying now. Look at me: I'm a splendid match.

RAIM What's the matter?

ARGIA Rich, Raim. Rich. We'll be able to stay in the grandest hotels.

RAIM What do you mean?

ARGIA I've discovered the Queen. (*She points towards the next room*)

RAIM But there's only that peasant-woman in there. (ARGIA *nods*)

ACT TWO

(*Only a few moments have passed since the end of the preceding scene.* ARGIA *and* RAIM *are speaking rapidly, in low voices*)

RAIM (*sweating and agitated*) God damn the day I ever met you! You're the cause of all my troubles. This is a frightful thing . . . it's terribly dangerous.

ARGIA (*mockingly*) Well, why not go to Amos and Biante, then, and tell *them* about it? Tell them the Queen's here; with a heavy bag.

RAIM Yes, and you know what they'll do? Kill me; and you too. So that they can have the credit . . . and the bag as well. It's a murder factory up here. Their only aim here is to kill people. Yes: accidentally; for amusement.

ARGIA Then we'd better forget about it, that's all.

RAIM I could box your ears! This is the first piece of luck I've ever had in the whole of my life. It's my big chance. I shall go mad if I have to let this slip through my fingers.

ARGIA Well, don't let it, then.

RAIM God, I'm frightened of this. A rifle can go off all by itself up here. Damn the whole bloody world! But are you sure about this, Argia? You've always been half-crazy; you imagine things the whole time.

ARGIA I'm quite certain. We looked at one another. It was just a flicker. And then I saw. And she saw that I saw. She was almost fainting.

RAIM The devil is there's not a minute to lose. What was this bag like?

ARGIA Small; but quite heavy.

RAIM Gold; diamonds. It'll kill me. You couldn't get a needle out of this place. Bury it; come back later: some hopes! They're more likely to bury *me*. (*in a burst of anger*) I'm the one who's in danger, can't you see?

ARGIA But I can help you. I can do it for you.

RAIM Yes. You're a woman, of course. You know her . . . You've already been talking to her . . . But, mind, it would have to look as if it were your own idea. Something you'd thought of yourself. How did she seem?

ARGIA Terrified.

RAIM Yes, that's the way to go about it, obviously. Try and frighten her. She'll give you the bag herself, without even being asked.

ARGIA We mustn't bother too much about the bag, Raim.

RAIM Why not?

ARGIA We couldn't be seen with it; and it would be difficult to take it away, or bury it.

RAIM Well, what, then?

ARGIA The names.

RAIM What do you mean, for God's sake, what names?

ARGIA The names: of her friends. There's sure to be a whole gang round her. Big, important people.

RAIM By God! You clever piece! (*He kisses her*) Do you think she'd talk?

ARGIA We can try and persuade her to. Her life's in our hands.

RAIM You could manage that all right, if you frightened her. But what then?

ARGIA We won't take the bag away with us. We'll take the names. In our heads.

RAIM Yes, but surely we could try and get the bag as well? And what if we got the names?

ARGIA Well, from then on there'd be quite a number of people who might be feeling extremely uneasy . . .

RAIM (*completing the sentence*) . . . and every so often the tax-collector would drop in and see them. Yes. Me. "Excuse me, your Excellency, you won't forget the usual donation, will you? Though only, of course, if you're interested in surviving a little longer . . . Yes?" My God, what a game! No. No. No! It's too dangerous. It's a good idea, but sooner or later, they'd have me done in. Don't you see? (*with bitter nastiness*) The bastards would soon be sparing *me* the afflictions of old age, don't worry! No, no, Argia, we must try and grab what we can out of it, quickly. Jewels, rubies, and so on . . . (*He suddenly lowers his voice*) God, here she is. Go on: see what you can do.

(*The* QUEEN *has opened the door, and stands looking, as though hypnotized, at* ARGIA; RAIM *casts a glance at her and goes out in silence*)

ARGIA Did you want something?

THE QUEEN (*breathing painfully*) No . . . no . . . I only wanted . . .

ARGIA To come and talk to me for a bit? Is that it?

THE QUEEN I . . . saw that perhaps . . . you have a kind heart . . .

ARGIA Well . . . that always depends how God made us, doesn't it? Come over here, my dear. Come on. I wanted to talk to you as well. You're a country-woman, aren't you?

THE QUEEN (*almost inaudibly*) Yes . . .

ARGIA I'm fond of country-people. Do you actually go out in the fields?

THE QUEEN Yes . . .

ARGIA What do you do there?

THE QUEEN I work . . .

ARGIA Digging? Hoeing?

(*The* QUEEN *holds out her hands appealingly*)

ARGIA Yes, they're real peasant's hands, aren't they? Good girl. It can't be easy to get your hands like that. It must take a long time. And a good deal of hard work. A good deal of digging and hoeing.

THE QUEEN Yes . . .

ARGIA Are you all by yourself?

THE QUEEN Yes . . .

ARGIA I can see you're very frightened; I think you've every reason to be. It was sensible of you to come to me. As a matter of fact, I could probably help you. And in return you could perhaps be kind enough to do something for me.

THE QUEEN I . . . don't know what sort of thing . . . you mean.

ARGIA (*almost a whisper*) My dear friend, your name isn't Elisabetta by any chance, I suppose?

(*There is a long silence*)

THE QUEEN (*she can scarcely speak*) No.

ARGIA Odd. I thought it was, somehow . . . However. (*She raises her voice slightly*) You're quite sure your name is not Elisabetta?

THE QUEEN No . . . no . . . no . . . (*She again holds out her hands*)

ARGIA (*a little louder still*) You insist on denying that your name is . . .

THE QUEEN (*interrupting her with a gesture*) My bag is in there. You can have it. I thought you'd want it. (*She points*) I've hidden it. You can take it whenever you want to.

ARGIA Hidden it where?

THE QUEEN In there. Up above the rafters, in the corner.

ARGIA Is there much in it?

THE QUEEN Only what I have left. It's hidden in the bread. There are three little loaves.

ARGIA It's not really much of a sacrifice for you, is it? If you ever come to the top again, it'll be a mere trifle to you. And if you don't, it's all up with you anyway. But it would be a god-send to me. You see, I'm poor; I'm hagridden with debts . . . (*She breaks off*)

RAIM (*coming in quickly*) Excuse me, ladies! I've just remembered about the blankets . . . I came to see if . . . (*He goes up to* ARGIA, *and speaks to her under his breath, almost with fury*) I've been thinking. I want the names as well. I want everything. (*retreating*) I'll bring you the blankets, in half a minute. (*He goes out*)

ARGIA Yes, you've shown a good deal of common sense. Well, you'll have to show a little more now. The situation is very simple. I can either go out of that door and call a soldier. Or I can keep my mouth shut, and help you. I've a friend here; you just saw him. But I'm afraid it means sharing things out, your majesty. We're sisters now. Everything in common. I'd be a fool to be satisfied with the leavings in the middle of three small loaves, wouldn't I?

THE QUEEN (*almost inaudibly*) I've nothing else.

ARGIA For year after year you used to walk on marble and sleep in silk. I've not had quite such a good time. The moment's come to level things up.

THE QUEEN I swear to you I've nothing else.

ARGIA That's not true. You still have friends. People working for you. I want them to be my friends as well. I want them to help me. *I* want people I can rely on, too. Do you see what I mean?

THE QUEEN Yes . . .

ARGIA In any case, the people I mean are hard-boiled enough. They're the people who've shoved you into all this mess. It was they who drove you out of your hiding-place.

THE QUEEN No, no, there wasn't anybody.

ARGIA Your friends.

THE QUEEN I haven't any.

ARGIA Come, come, you won't be doing *them* any harm. The only trouble they'll have is helping me a little in these hard times. Your friends.

THE QUEEN (*imploring*) They're all dead, they've all been killed. I'm alone now.

ARGIA Your majesty, you used to sweep down red-carpeted staircases; the ones I had to climb weren't half so pretty. But even they taught me things. I learned . . . a good deal. You'll be very silly if you try to fool *me*.

THE QUEEN Oh, please have pity. . . .

ARGIA I'm hardened, your majesty. I'm indifferent even to my own misfortunes by now; you can imagine how I feel about yours. (*almost shouting*) Come on, tell me who they are: who are your friends? Who are they? (*She breaks off*)

(*The* QUEEN *has taken from her bosom a piece of paper; she offers it to* ARGIA)

ARGIA (*before taking it*) They're there?

THE QUEEN Yes.

ARGIA (*taking the paper*) A good many stories about you are going the rounds. I thought I should have to insist much harder. You're rather meek and mild, for a Queen, aren't you? (*She looks at the paper*) Darling, you must take me for an idiot. A list of them, all ready? Just like that?

THE QUEEN Yes.

ARGIA You've been carrying it about on you?

THE QUEEN Yes.

ARGIA (*sarcastically condescending*) Why, my dear, why?

THE QUEEN Because I'm frightened.

ARGIA Of what?

THE QUEEN (*desperately*) Of being tortured. I've heard of them doing . . . terrible . . . dreadful things . . . And I'm frightened; don't you understand? (*overcome for a moment*) The thought of it is driving me insane! (*controlling herself*) I'd have been bound to tell them in the end just the same . . . And if there was this paper . . . They'd have found it on me; it would all have been simple. Oh, please believe me, I beg of you, please. It's the truth.

ARGIA (*looks at the paper*) So these are the ones? Your faithful friends. The people who are risking their lives for you.

THE QUEEN Yes.

ARGIA (*dropping her voice*) But are you really the "Queen"?

THE QUEEN Yes . . . Except that I . . . lost whatever courage I had, in that cellar, at Bielovice. Please: I've nothing else to give you now. I hope you'll save me . . . I hope you and your friend will help me to escape . . .

(RAIM *enters quickly with a couple of blankets*)

RAIM Here you are, ladies, the blankets! (*He throws them on a chair; to the* QUEEN) Do you mind? (*He takes the paper from* ARGIA's *hand, and draws her aside. He looks at the card, and says quietly*) It's so stupid and childish it's bound to be true. (*He stares at the paper hard: then puts it under* ARGIA's *eyes*) You fix these four names in your head as well.

ARGIA Yes.

RAIM Good. Have you got them? You're sure?

ARGIA Yes.

RAIM So have I. (*He lights a match and sets the paper alight; to the* QUEEN) Madam, we have to think of our safety as well, though our methods may be a bit different. (*He stamps on the ashes hysterically*)

ARGIA (*a whisper*) Do you think it's possible to get her away?

RAIM (*a whisper*) It's not only possible, it's indispensable. And it's not only indispensable, it's not enough. Escape isn't enough. There's something else as well.

ARGIA What?

RAIM (*rapidly*) If she gets across the mountains and gets in touch with those people (*He points to the ashes*) it'll go very hard with us. And if she doesn't, it'll be even worse: they'll catch her; and she'll tell everything. And if we leave her here, when they question her tomorrow, she'll talk just the same. She'll give us away. I'd be a madman to risk my life—and yours—on a damn silly thing like that.

ARGIA What then?

RAIM We've got to make *sure* she keeps her mouth shut.

ARGIA (*has understood*) No!

RAIM It's the best thing for her too, in a way. If those two in there find her, her last minutes aren't going to be very enviable. She's finished now, either way. Better for her it should all be over quickly without frightening her.

ARGIA No, no.

RAIM (*in an excited whisper*) Do you think I like it? Our lives depend on this. We can't back out now, it's too late. We oughtn't to have started it. Darling, it's got to be done.

ARGIA (*horrified*) Got to? And do you think I . . .

RAIM It's always you, isn't it? Whose idea was it? Yours. You got me into this danger. You arranged it all. And now it's not nice enough for you. You're worse than anybody. No, my dear. It's got to be done. And we're in it together.

ARGIA (*with horrified resignation*) Have you thought . . . how?

RAIM I'm thinking now. (*moving away and speaking louder*) I'll be back in a few minutes, madam. We're looking after you. (*He goes out*)

THE QUEEN Does he intend to help me?

ARGIA (*without looking at her*) Yes.

THE QUEEN Your friend will get me away?

ARGIA Yes.

THE QUEEN (*suddenly, torn with anguish*) For pity's sake, don't let them hurt me, don't betray me, for pity's sake . . . (*She darts forward and takes* ARGIA's *hand as though to kiss it*)

ARGIA (*almost angrily, tearing her hand away*) What are you doing? What's the matter with you?

THE QUEEN (*desperately*) Oh, my God, you're deceiving me, everybody deceives me . . . Everybody plays with me like a cat with a mouse . . . I can't go on any longer; oh, God, I'd rather die now . . . I don't want to think any more; call them, call the soldiers, I'll call them myself, kill me, kill me, straight away . . .

ARGIA (*shaking her*) Stop it, stop it, you silly woman.

(*The* QUEEN *has fallen to her knees and remains there gasping for breath*)

ARGIA (*exasperated*) You'll dirty your knees, your majesty. Yes, of course, you'll be saved, you'll be got away. It's important to us as well, isn't it? (*with gloomy hostility*) In any case, it's dishonorable, it's unfair, to lose your dignity like this. It's against the rules of the game; it embarrasses people. A chambermaid would behave better. I would myself, my dear; I've never squealed like that: like a mouse under a peasant's foot. And I'm not a queen . . . far from it. When you used to give your orders, with the flag flying over the palace, down below, underneath all the people who were obeying you and giving your orders to other people, down below all of them, right down on the pavement, there was I. I didn't drive in a landau; and they'd made a woman of me by the time I was eleven. Your majesty, there were some days when I used to feel as if the whole world had wiped their feet on my face. And now you come and slobber all over my hands. No, no, my dear: the silk clothes and the box at the opera have to be paid for. You heard a few minutes ago, in here, what the people think of you. Your hands have not always been rough. And they've signed a lot of papers in their time.

THE QUEEN   No.

ARGIA   What do you mean: no?

THE QUEEN   I've never done any harm to any one. It was never left to me to decide anything. Nothing they say of me is true. (*She shudders with horror*) The only thing that's true is that at Bielovice I was covered with dead bodies and blood. I could feel them dying, on top of me! Since then I've been in perpetual flight. It isn't true that I met the soldiers on the bridge at Nistria. If I had, I should have fainted at their feet. I've not had a single moment free from terror for five years. They've killed almost every one of my friends; but unfortunately not all of them. Every so often one or other of them manages to track me down. I'm running away from my friends even more than from my enemies. What can they want of me any more? I can't do anything, I don't want to do anything, the only thing I know now is fear; I sleep in fear, I dream in fear. I'll never, never do anything again either for anyone or against anyone. I only want to escape, and never see or know anything again. I want to stop being afraid. Nobody can have anything to fear from me. I'll give up everything, rights, titles, I'll forget everything.

ARGIA   (*with somber irony*)   It almost looks as if I'd done you a service in taking your jewels off you. You are abdicating. There are some people who'd be extremely disillusioned if they could hear you.

THE QUEEN   I have nothing and I no longer want anything.

ARGIA   Then why are you making so much fuss? What *do* you want?

THE QUEEN   To be left alive. Nothing else. Unknown; far away. And to sleep, night after night, in peace.

(*The two women turn round.* RAIM *has entered, slowly. He bows slightly to the* QUEEN, *and beckons* ARGIA *aside*)

RAIM   (*whispers*)   The job's going to be taken off our hands. I've found a way out. It's quite respectable, too. This building has two exits: this one, and that one over there. The guard on this one, across the courtyard, will be me. The one on the other, on the wall, is Maupa, that soldier you saw in here. He's a real brute. (*to the* QUEEN) Yes, this is for you, madam. We are preparing a way out for you. (*to* ARGIA *once more*) It was easy to persuade that swine that the revolution demanded that he should fire; often; at sight; the first squeak of a door or movement in the shadows. Even me, if I tried to: if I opened that door, I'd be opening my own way to hell. But that I shan't do. In a few minutes' time you'll hear a signal: the hoot of an owl. The Queen will say good-bye to you, and come out through this door. Our hands will be as white as snow.

ARGIA   (*horrified*)   And if the shot doesn't kill her?

RAIM   (*gloomy, subdued*)   In that case, I . . . (*He breaks off*) It would be just reckless cowardice to leave the thing half-done. What should I get out of that? The only profit there, would be for my dead bones, because it's obvious the Queen would talk and I'd lose my life. But if a dead man's bones know nothing about profit and loss, do you think stupidity and superstition are going to hold my hand back? Why light candles if your prayers mean nothing? (*He blows to left and right as though to put out two imaginary candles burning before a non-existent shrine*) They're all wolves: why should I be a lamb? Plenty of good people are dying in these hard times, one more or less makes no odds. They say the Bible-stories prophesy a bath of blood for the earth. But in practice it needs gallons, especially when you see how much the earth soaks up. Besides, I suffer from poor health; I've got to make sure of some sort of a future. (*He returns to the subject*) So if anything goes wrong . . . Oh, why does this woman get people into such a mess instead of doing away with herself? Her life's useless and wretched and short, anyway. Better for her to finish here than run about, being smelt out like a hare the whole time, always in fear and trembling. (*to* ARGIA) If anything does go wrong, as soon as I hear the shots, I shall run round through the courtyard . . . and if the soldier's shots haven't been enough . . . I'll finish it off myself . . . Let's hope it won't be necessary. Quickly, now. I shall be glad when it's all over. (*He makes a slight bow to the* QUEEN *and goes out*)

ARGIA   (*avoids looking at the* QUEEN) Madam, you must be very brave now, this is going to be very dangerous for all of us. But I think you'll be all right.

THE QUEEN   I am ready.

ARGIA   (*breathing heavily*)   What has to be done, has to. That's true, isn't it? If you want to escape . . .

THE QUEEN   Go on.

ARGIA   They've found a man who's willing to accompany you up the hidden paths as far as the frontier. In a few minutes we shall hear a signal. Then you'll go out, through that door over there. Outside, you'll find the man who's willing to take you on your way. You'll have nothing more to worry about.

THE QUEEN   (*her hands clasped*)   Oh, my dear. Your sweet face and your gentle voice will stay in my heart till the last day of my life, and beyond. Yes, surely beyond; so that when I meet you again in heaven, I can run to you, crying . . . (*She takes* ARGIA's *hands*) "Bright soul! My dear, dear sister! Do you remember me? It is I. And now we are together because on that day we had to part so soon."

(ARGIA *tries to push her away*)

THE QUEEN   Don't push me away from you; oh, please let me stay like this for a moment. (*She laughs*) Treat me like a frightened animal who has sought refuge in your lap. That does happen sometimes. Hold me and stroke me. (*She clasps* ARGIA *tightly*) What is your name?

ARGIA   Argia.

THE QUEEN   I feel as if I were being reborn, here, in your arms. (*She starts*) What's that? Was it the signal?

ARGIA   No, not yet.

THE QUEEN   But please tell me: are you sure the man who is going to come with me up the mountain is really to be trusted? Can I really be sure of him? When we get to one of those dark gullies in the hills, he won't leap at me and cut my throat, will he?

ARGIA   No. No.

THE QUEEN   Don't, don't think I don't trust you. It's only that it is so difficult to shake off the terror. Through the whole of these years I've been haunted by only one single thought: the horrible tortures they do . . . My God, they put people to inhuman horrors: did you know that? I have a poison with me . . . but I can never be sure if I shall be able to swallow it in time. I always used to imagine that dreadful moment: a man looking at me . . . turning round to look at me . . . then a glint in his eye . . . and I was recognized . . . lost. That's why I've . . . oh, dearest Argia, please forgive me! But you said yourself we were women together . . . (*whispers*) Sometimes a man has stared hard at me . . . a peasant, or a herdsman, or a woodman . . . I've given myself to him! Given myself! I'm no longer either a queen or a woman. (*weeping and laughing*) I'm like a terrified animal running this way and that. Argia: I've had a baby too, up in the mountains. You're the first person I've ever told.

ARGIA   Is that why you're going? You want to see the baby again?

THE QUEEN   Oh no! No! No! No! Why should I want to see him? Why should I love him? No, no, he only pursues me like all the rest. I'm running away from him as well. I don't want to see him. He can only be another threat to me. Let him stay where he is, and grow up in peace. (*She bursts into sobs*) And may God forgive all of us.

ARGIA   Don't shake like that, my dear. Try and be calm. You'll be all right.

THE QUEEN   (*whispering and laughing*) Argia, I even think I'm . . . pregnant again. I keep feeling so hungry the whole time.

ARGIA   (*looks at her, and gently strokes her face*) You're covered in sweat. Wipe your face.

(*The hoot of an owl is heard outside*)

THE QUEEN   (*starting*)   That's the signal, isn't it? And now I have to go.

ARGIA   Wait a moment.

(*The signal is heard again*)

THE QUEEN   Yes, it's the signal. Good-bye, Argia. Let me kiss you. (*She kisses* ARGIA *and gets ready to go to the door*)

ARGIA   Wait.

THE QUEEN   Why do you say wait?

ARGIA   I didn't explain properly. That's not the way you must go out. They'll shoot you, if you go through that door.

THE QUEEN   What then?

ARGIA   It's through this other door. You must go through here. I've thought of a better plan.

THE QUEEN   How?

ARGIA   I'll push the door open on this side . . . oh, there won't be any danger. All I'll have to do is to push the door; they're such fools, they'll fire at once. The men on guard over that side will run round as soon as they hear the noise. That other door will be unprotected. You must seize the moment, and get away.

THE QUEEN   Shall I find the man there— the man who's to go with me?

ARGIA   No. Make for the mountains by yourself. You were probably right, it's safer that way.

(*The signal is heard again*)

ARGIA   (*pointing*)   Stand ready, over there. Quietly.

(*The* QUEEN *fumbles for a moment, and gives* ARGIA *a ring*)

THE QUEEN This was the last burden I had . . .

ARGIA (*putting it on*) It's tight on me. So I shan't lose it.

(*The* QUEEN *goes and stands ready near one of the doors.* ARGIA *puts out the lamp; takes a pole, makes a sign of encouragement to the* QUEEN, *and goes cautiously over to the other door. She moves the door with the pole, and suddenly throws it wide open. A deafening burst of machine-gun fire splinters the door.* ARGIA *laughs silently. She makes a sign to the* QUEEN)

ARGIA Now! Go . . . Good-bye.

(*The* QUEEN *slips out.* ARGIA *stands waiting*)

VOICES (*outside*) On guard! On guard, there! Look out!

MAUPA (*coming in with his gun in his hands: to* ARGIA) Don't you move!

ARGIA You're irresistible.

MAUPA And don't speak.

ARGIA Oh, I wouldn't know what to say to you, anyway.

VOICES (*distant*) On guard! On guard!

ANOTHER VOICE On guard!

RAIM (*enters breathlessly*) What's the matter?

MAUPA This woman was trying to escape.

RAIM My dear fellow . . . haven't you made a mistake?

MAUPA I tell you she tried to get away! Perhaps you doubt my word?

RAIM No, no. I'm sure you're right.

MAUPA You watch her. I'll go and call the others. (*He goes out*)

RAIM (*greatly agitated*) What's happened? Where is she?

ARGIA Gone.

RAIM What have you done, you fool? And what are you going to tell them now?

ARGIA I shall think up something; don't worry.

RAIM Just you see you don't bring me into it . . . You needn't count on me . . . You'll get yourself out of it, I don't doubt . . . (*He breaks off at the sound of footsteps; turns to the newcomers; and says with emphasis*) Sir, this woman was trying to run away.

AMOS (*has entered, followed by* MAUPA. *He turns quietly to him*) Friend, will you please point that gun downwards? We've no need of it.

(MAUPA *does so*)

AMOS (*to* RAIM) And you, will you give the lady a seat?

(RAIM *does so*)

AMOS (*politely to* ARGIA) Will you please sit down, madam? You wanted to go out?

ARGIA I was thirsty.

AMOS Ah, that explains it. You'll forgive us. At all events the incident has one good side to it. It offers us (*He points to* BIANTE, *who is coming in supported by the* PORTER) an opportunity of asking you to be good enough to grant us an interview . . . which I hope will be quiet and friendly. It's an opportunity I was looking for during the whole of our journey.

BIANTE (*coming forward and shouting*) Light! Light! We might as well be in a cave! Bring some candles and lamps! Give us some illumination worthy of our cause.

(RAIM, MAUPA, *and the* PORTER *have already rushed out to fetch lights from the neighboring rooms. The first to return is the* PORTER, *with a strange lamp. Its light falls on* ARGIA. *There is a moment of curious silence*)

AMOS (*to* ARGIA) Madam: what is your name?

ACT THREE

(*Only a few seconds have gone by.* RAIM, MAUPA *and the* PORTER *are still bringing in lamps, and arranging the room. Then they all sit.* ARGIA *is standing in the midst of them*)

AMOS Well?

ARGIA (*with hostile indifference*) You will find my name, and everything else about me, in my documents. I have already been questioned once this evening, with the other travellers. Is this extra honor reserved for me alone?

AMOS Madam: we have to ask you for a little further information.

ARGIA There is no need to address me as madam. I'm only one of those very common plants you naturally find growing on the manure-heap of three wars.

AMOS What is your nationality?

ARGIA I was born in this country. And from that day to this, people like you have done nothing but repatriate me, expel me, deport me, search me, give me notice to quit; and so forth.

AMOS (*coldly polite*) You sound as though you considered *us* responsible for all that.

ARGIA Well, what are you doing now, if not giving orders? There are a great number of people in the world who've made it their job to decide what the rest of us have to do. Congratulations. You might tell me what it feels like.

AMOS Have you never known what it feels like?

ARGIA I? (*She pauses a moment, surprised*) I? (*with a shrug*) I've always been one of the people who take orders, not give them. It's my job to be here submitting to them, at this time of night; when I'm dropping with fatigue.

AMOS Political necessities.

ARGIA Ah, yes, political necessities: they're the reason we're forbidden to eat what we choose, every other day; the reason we're forbidden to go to bed when we're tired, or to light the fire when we're cold. "Every time is the decisive time." And how brazen you all are about it! It's been going on since Adam. Political necessities.

AMOS Have you never used those words on your own behalf?

ARGIA (*surprised*) I? My dear friend—you will forgive the expression—I've already told you that I've never done anything very useful or respectable in the whole of my life. Satisfied?

AMOS What occupations have you followed up till now?

ARGIA Oh, various ones. What I could pick up. You, and others like you, have always been so busy shouting that I've never had much chance to think about my own condition. There have been times when I've not been sorry if I could find someone willing to pay for my lunch or my dinner.

AMOS Can you prove that?

ARGIA Witnesses? Certainly, darling, certainly. Lots of men know me. I can prove it whenever I like.

BIANTE (*sneering: his voice is like a death-rattle*) Have you any distinguishing marks on your body to prove your identity? Little things . . . that might have struck the attention of the men who paid for your lunches and dinners?

ARGIA (*after a pause; in a low voice*) Yes. Men like you, and men even more repellent than you, if possible, have seen me and made use of me. That is what I am.

AMOS (*quieting* BIANTE *with a gesture*) You don't seem to like us very much. Is there any special reason for that?

ARGIA Yes: I always dislike the authorities: people who walk over our faces the whole time; and have rather a heavy tread.

AMOS (*still politely*) Madam: I should perhaps convey to you some idea of the impression you are creating.

ARGIA Well?

AMOS The sharpness of your answers is in rather striking contrast with the humble condition you declare yourself to be in. And the bluntness you attempt to give those answers is in equally striking contrast with your obvious refinement and breeding.

ARGIA (*after a pause*) Refinement and breeding? In me? You think I look . . . ? (*She laughs*) How nice. You're trying to make love to me.

AMOS I also have the impression that the liveliness of your behavior is largely due to your need to conceal a certain amount of fear.

ARGIA Fear? I?

AMOS Yes.

ARGIA Fear of whom? Of you? I realize that the contempt people feel for you makes you try and console yourselves with the idea that everyone's frightened of you. But I'm not frightened of you; why should I be? I've told you what I am. And I can prove it, whenever I choose.

BIANTE Why not now?

ARGIA Because just at the moment, I happen to be enjoying myself. Yes, it's odd, isn't it? I'm actually enjoying myself.

BIANTE Let's hope you go on enjoying yourself.

AMOS (*imperturbably*) If your insolence fails to conceal your fear, your fear seems to be equally unsuccessful in curbing your insolence.

ARGIA (*ironically*) I wonder why?

AMOS Pride.

ARGIA You think I'm proud, do you?

AMOS Yes: with a pride which won't even listen to your own common sense when it warns you. You are scarcely even taking the trouble to lie successfully. What you would really like at this moment is to tell us you despise us.

ARGIA (*taking out a cigarette*) As a matter of fact, it does strike me as slightly unnatural that people like you should give yourselves airs.

BIANTE You'd better be careful, my dear; he was trained for the priesthood.

AMOS An ancient pride which has soaked right through to your veins. Footsteps, used to the echo of surroundings where the press of the crowd is unknown. Hands, accustomed always to holding bright and precious objects; a voice that never had any need to raise itself in order to call for silence.

ARGIA (*after a moment's reflection*) And that's what your intuition tells you about me, is it? All that?

AMOS Madam, you are doing yourself a great deal of harm by lying to us. Suppose you come down to earth? Where were you born?

ARGIA (*is silent for a moment; then she laughs, and shrugging her shoulder, says with insulting sarcasm*) I was born in one of the finest mansions in the city. I won't say whether it was on the first floor, or in the porter's lodge. In my room, when I woke, I always saw nymphs on the walls. The tapestries had hung there for five hundred years. Yes, you are right: I did, indeed, grow up among people who were silent the minute I indicated that I was about to speak. And when they answered me, it was always in pleasant voices, saying pleasant things. (*mockingly*) I walked on carpets as large as a village square! The doors were always opened for me! The rooms were always heated: I have always been sensitive to the cold. The food was excellent; I have always been rather greedy. My dear friend, you should have seen the tablecloths, and the silver! The crystal goblets I used to drink from!

AMOS And all this good fortune cost *you* very little trouble.

ARGIA (*in satirically affected tones*) We don't ask the rose what trouble it has taken: we ask it simply to be a rose: and to be as different as it can from an artichoke. They used to bring me whatever I wanted on beautiful carved trays; then they would bow and retire, always turning at the door and bowing once again before they went out. (*indicating her cigarette*) Do you mind?

AMOS (*going across and lighting it*) And why did you insist on their doing all that?

ARGIA I didn't insist. They wanted to. And you know, I think you too, if I were to smile at you, would also wag your tails. But no, the price would be too high: for me, I mean. Your arrogance is simply your way of bolstering yourselves up. And I . . . (*She breaks off*)

AMOS (*in lighting the cigarette has noticed the ring*) That's a very beautiful ring you have there.

ARGIA (*tries to remove it, but cannot*) It won't come off. (*lightly*) I've been wearing it too long. It's a family heirloom. (*She looks for a moment at them all; then laughs, with mocking bitterness*) Yes; in my time, I've been a proud woman . . . rich . . . highly respected, elegant, happy . . . fortunate . . .

AMOS (*coldly*) And your political opinions?

ARGIA I'm not interested in politics.

AMOS But at least you prefer one party to the other?

ARGIA Do you?

AMOS Yes.

ARGIA Then I prefer the opposite one.

AMOS Why?

ARGIA For the simple reason that I don't like the way you behave. You strut about a great deal too much. (*with derisive affectation*) You see, ever since I was a child I have been brought up to respect people of a very different sort from you. People who washed properly, and wore clean-smelling linen. Perhaps there's some political significance in that? I can't believe that an unpleasant smell gives people special rights. Or perhaps the revolution has a smell?

BIANTE The smell of bitter soup in the people's tenements.

ARGIA (*affectedly*) I'm sorry. I have never smelt it. I think you probably give yourselves too much work to do; you smell of sweat.

AMOS The stonebreakers and the poor who follow us have less delicate nostrils.

ARGIA That must be very sad for them.

BIANTE (*with painful vehemence*) Tomorrow we shall have no stonebreakers and no poor!

ARGIA (*insolently*) We shall have other troubles. Otherwise what would *you* do? You canalize people's miseries. You turn them first into envy, then into fury. The thick rind of bad temper on the world has grown a great deal thicker since you began to cultivate it. The number of the dead has grown too. And all your great ideas don't prevent a distinct smell of blood rising from you.

BIANTE Amos, for God's sake!

AMOS (*cutting him short*) Do you realize where all these questions are leading?

ARGIA Yes.

AMOS Is there anyone here who can identify you?

ARGIA Certainly. Otherwise I would hardly be taking such risks.

AMOS Who is it?

ARGIA I'll tell you later. The night is long . . . and so is the mountain-road. Provided *you* have the time to spare . . .

(*A* SOLDIER *has entered, and has whispered something into* BIANTE's *ear*)

ARGIA . . . though they do say that gunfire can be heard round about. Bad news? Is that what's worrying you?

BACK OF DESK + SIT

AMOS Don't hope for miracles; they don't happen any more.

BIANTE Stop it, Amos, make her talk, for God's sake! Make her talk, I'm in a hurry! My body's burning as if it would set the whole bloody world on fire.

ARGIA (*insolently*) Moderate your voice, please. (*suddenly and passionately*) If I were the queen, do you know what I would say to you at this moment? (*in a manner not devoid of majesty*) I'd say: "Gentlemen." (*She drops back into a more normal tone, but soon returns to her former manner*) "Gentlemen, you are angry with me; but I am not angry with you. Neither the power you have usurped, nor your threats, are capable of disturbing me. We are far apart. It is that that makes you boil with rage; and keeps me calm."

AMOS If you're not the queen, I'm bound to say you give a very good imitation of the haughty way in which she'd behave on an occasion like this.

ARGIA The reason is that I've been rehearsing this rôle for a very long time. Every time any one has been rude to me—and that can happen to anyone, can't it?—every time I've come away with my cheeks still burning, what scathing retorts, what tremendous, noble answers I've always imagined! I know everything a woman of spirit can say to put the insolent in their places. . . .

(*The noise of hoarse voices begins to be heard outside*)

ARGIA (*continues passionately*) And if I were the queen I'd say to you: "It's true, gentlemen, there was no mob round me, there was space. The echo used to carry my words on high and purify them . . . make them lonely; and calm. The echo used to liberate them . . . (*Slightly intoxicated by her own words, she plays with the echo*) Re . . . gi . . . na . . . It made them mount upward . . . up . . . on high . . . high . . . high . . . it wanted them to be calm and just . . . Re . . . gi . . . na . . ."

(*They have all, one after another, stood up; they stand listening to that echo, and to the distant voices*)

BIANTE (*suddenly*) What's happening? What's the matter, out there? Who are those people coming up the road? Why are we wasting time? My fever's getting worse; I'm burning all over. What are our weapons for? Yes, we do need dead people! What are we waiting for? Are you waiting till I'm dead here in the middle of them? (*to the* PORTER) What's going on out there?

THE PORTER (*has been out: and now re-enters, distressed*) General Biante and Commissar Amos! Something's happening. The road out there is black with people. *OUT*

BIANTE Who are they?

THE PORTER The people living in the upper valley. They must have got to hear about this woman, they must have heard she'd been caught, and they've come down under cover of the dark.

ARGIA I told you, did I not, that your power was only provisional?

(BIANTE *is already hobbling quickly out.* AMOS, RAIM *and* MAUPA *follow him*)

THE PORTER (*remains alone with* ARGIA. *He looks at her; and suddenly, with impulsive reverence, takes off his cap; he is at once ashamed of himself, and pretends to be looking at a sheet of paper on the table beside him. As though reading from the paper: in a low voice*) There are a great many cowards in this world, who are so frightened that they hide their true feelings; and I am the lowest and most cowardly of them all. But for us, more than for others, what comfort and healing it brings, to know that there is someone . . . (*his eyes do not move from the sheet of paper, but his voice rises slightly*) . . . there is someone who is still unafraid, and can stand alone against all the rest! What consolation, for us in our shame, to think that in a soul shaped like our own, everything that in us is ruined, stays faithful and untarnished! To know that such a creature has drawn breath in this world! I believe that even God Himself, hearing her speak, is proud of her. And whoever shall think of her, though it be a thousand years from now, shall feel once more upon his face a look of dignity. (*His voice has become louder, but his eyes have never once raised themselves from the sheet of paper*)

(MAUPA *and* RAIM *come in, holding the door open for* BIANTE)

BIANTE (*goes up to* ARGIA, *and suddenly bursts into a laugh*) Hahaha! Your Majesty! Yes, your famous name has brought a lot of people down from the mountains to meet you. Do you know what sort of help they're bringing you? Do you know what they want? (*almost casually*) To see you condemned to death and hanged.

MAUPA (*with quiet ecstasy*) We want to see the color of the Queen's entrails.

AMOS (*entering and raising his hand*) There will be a proper trial. Otherwise we should be showing very little trust in our own purpose.

ON Platform

BIANTE (*shouting*) Proper trial! Formal procedure! To hell with this chattering. I've no time to waste. I can't feel my own hands any more; I can hardly keep my eyes open.

AMOS A jury will sit. (*to* MAUPA) You: Go and bring some of those people in here.

BIANTE (*to* MAUPA, *as he goes out*) And choose people who look sensible, and keep their eyes on the ground! *DOWN CENTER*

AMOS Peasants merely; but now they have authority: optimists, and the world is full of them; in revolutions they are manna dropped from heaven. Every one of them believes that the sickle will cut the whole meadow but will stop a quarter of an inch short of his own throat.

BIANTE And the jury ought to have a few beggars on it as well . . . *TO FRONT DESK*

AMOS . . . a few people who are stupid and lazy, and imagine that a change in the insignia over the doors will give them the reward of the industrious and the intelligent . . .

(*A number of peasants, men and women, have entered. The* ENGINEER *is among them*)

BIANTE (*to the newcomers*) Come in, my friends! Sit down. You already know that I have taken over the command. That means that everybody can kill a man, but I can do it with a roll of drums, like an acrobat making a difficult leap. The republic has conquered. (*He beats his fist on the table*) Well then, I preside! (*to* AMOS) You shall be the accuser! (*to* RAIM) You shall write. (*to the newcomers*) You shall judge! (*lowering his voice*) And after that, I, as president, if I'm still alive, shall carry out the sentence. You can begin, Amos.

(AMOS *has already risen: he speaks in the tones of a chancellor reading out an act*) *MOVE CENTER*

AMOS The accusation charges this woman with having concealed her identity, and falsified her papers.

ARGIA Gentlemen! Please, please listen to me. I came up here . . .

AMOS . . . with the intention of fleeing the country? Or to try to discover the whereabouts of your son? Yes, madam, we are fully informed about that also. Your son. (*his voice slightly rising*) She is also accused of having *DOWN LEFT* formerly exercised a secret and illicit influence on the heads of the state, inducing them to enact factious and oppressive laws. . . .

BIANTE Oh, get on with it, Amos! You're cold, you've got no guts! You're just being cruel!

AMOS (*louder*) . . . of inciting to massacre and persecution . . .

ARGIA But I have never done anything of the kind!

AMOS . . . of having fomented conspiracies aimed at undermining the authority of the state. . . .

ARGIA But that's what you've done! And you blame it on the Queen! *You* were the sowers of discord.

AMOS (*louder*) . . . to the point of inducing a number of fanatics to take up arms against their country.

ARGIA But I . . .

AMOS This woman is accused of having herself unloosed the present conflict; of having herself driven it to atrocious excesses. She herself summoned to this country foreign armed forces, herself lit the fires that now smoke from every point of the horizon, herself disfigured the dead along the roads. . . .

ARGIA But I tell you I . . .

AMOS . . . didn't know? Didn't want it?

ARGIA I tell you that my hands . . .

AMOS Are clean? Is that it? That only shows how cunning you've been. It deprives you of extenuating circumstances, if there ever were any.

THE ENGINEER (*suddenly and violently*) I was walking in the street one day: there was a cordon of soldiers; and they said to me: "Not this way, the Queen will be coming down here." I went round another way, and they told me: "You can't come through here." Everywhere I went, it was the same. Madam, you were always in the way.

ARGIA Friends, friends, but I was there too, with you: on your side of the cordon, not the other.

A PEASANT-WOMAN (*suddenly bursting into sobs*) The shirt I washed for my son, he said it was shabby. He said the soup I cooked for him tasted nasty. And now they've told me that he's lying out there, in the fields, with his arms wide-open, covered with ants. It's all the Queen's fault.

ARGIA You stone that woman now, only because you one day fawned on her!

A PEASANT (*violently*) When our children are old enough to play games, they're not allowed to play the same games as rich men's children. That's a terrible thing! That's what poisons their minds!

THE PEASANT-WOMAN My son hated the earthen crockery, he hated the smell of our home; he hated his own life!

THE PEASANT My daughter went away with the soldiers, and I haven't heard a word of her since. That was your fault!

THE WOMAN It was your fault!

BIANTE All of you! All of you! Bear witness, all of you!

THE ENGINEER It was her fault!

MAUPA It was her fault!

OTHERS Her fault! It was her fault!

BIANTE And what about you? That porter over there! Are you the only one with nothing to say?

(*A silence*)

THE PORTER Yes . . . everything she did . . . humiliated us.

ARGIA (*rebelliously, to the* PORTER) And who was it who taught you humiliation and envy? Who was it who let your rancor loose?

AMOS (*with sudden intensity*) You, the apex of privilege, the symbol of prerogative; you, the emblem of those distinctions from which humiliation and rivalry were born. Your whole authority is based and built upon inequality. It is in you that injustice is personified, it is in you she finds her arrogant features, her scornful voice, her contemptuous answers, her sumptuous clothes, and her unsoiled hands. Your name of Queen is of itself enough to make men see that they are unequal: on one side vast revenues, on the other, vast burdens. You are the hook from which the great act of tyranny hangs. The world will be a less unhappy place when you have vanished from it.

ARGIA (*remains for a long moment with her head bent*) Forgive me. I have been playacting a little: perhaps too much. Now I will tell you the truth. I can prove that I am not the Queen, and I can prove it at once. There is someone here who can witness for me.

BIANTE Who is it?

ARGIA That man over there, your interpreter. Stop, Raim, don't run away. He knows me only too well. He knows I'm not a queen. I'm the sort of woman who has to smile at lodging-house keepers, and traffic in pawntickets.

RAIM (*comes forward slowly, in silence*) There must be some misunderstanding. This woman must be mad. I've never seen her before in my life.

ARGIA Look at me, Raim.

RAIM I am looking at you. (*to* AMOS) I've never seen her before.

ARGIA (*turning to the others*) My friend is frightened things may have gone too far. Whether I'm the Queen or not, or he's my friend or not, he's afraid you just have to have a certain number of people to shoot, up here. He just wants to stay alive, that's all.

RAIM I knew you'd say that. But I must insist that I do not know you.

ARGIA Gentlemen! I and this man, who "doesn't know" me, kept each other warm all through one whole winter!

RAIM Rubbish!

ARGIA I came up here solely to look for him. There are people here who saw us talking.

RAIM (*to the others*) Of course they did. I tried to approach her: because I thought she looked suspicious. I don't know who she is. I'm sorry, madam, but I can't help you.

(*He moves away, disappearing among the others.* ARGIA *stands for a moment in silence*)

ARGIA (*almost absently*) Perhaps it's true. Perhaps that man and I never did know one another. But, even so, gentlemen, that doesn't give you the right to make stupid mistakes. If you have to have a corpse to show people, when you tell them the Queen's dead, you might at least look for a corpse a bit more like her. You fools! I, the Queen? Is mine the voice of a queen . . . ? Has my life been the life of a queen . . . ? (*suddenly calling*) Raim! Raim! Call him back!

AMOS I'd like to bet that your friend is far away by now; and making for the mountains like a hare.

ARGIA (*bewildered*) Gentlemen, there is someone else who can witness for me. There were two women travellers in this room. I . . . and another woman.

AMOS (*amiably*) Yes. (*He makes a sign to one of the soldiers, who at once goes out*)

ARGIA . . . a peasant-woman.

AMOS (*amiably*) Yes. And where is she now?

ARGIA She ran away. But she can't be far off. That woman . . . can tell you . . . that I'm not what you think. And you will have what you want, just the same. Send out and look for her.

AMOS Up in the mountains?

ARGIA Yes.

AMOS All you can say of your witnesses, is that one is fleeing and the other has fled. (*a pause*) Madam, we have a surprise for you. (*a pause*) Your peasant-woman is here. She didn't get very far. Here she is.

(*In a great silence the* QUEEN *appears, escorted by the soldier. The* QUEEN, *pale, and rather stiff, looks round her.* AMOS *points to* ARGIA. *The* QUEEN *comes forward to* ARGIA; *and speaks to her with a slight stammer*)

THE QUEEN Forgive me, my dear . . . it was all no use . . . I knew they'd have caught me . . . The moment I was so frightened of . . . arrived . . . But I don't think . . . they've caught me in time . . . to hurt me. I managed to fool them . . . you know how . . . I prefer it . . . to be all over at once. Good-bye, my dearest friend. I was so afraid . . . but not so much, now. (*She sways, and sinks slowly to the ground*)

BIANTE   What's the matter?

ARGIA (*kneels down beside the* QUEEN, *and takes her hand. After a while she looks up, and says, as though lost in thought*)   She carried poison with her. (*a pause*) You have killed her.

AMOS (*cutting her short*)   You are now completely without accomplices. Say something, why don't you?

BIANTE (*shouting*)   You've no one left now!

AMOS   It's all over with you, your majesty! Answer us! You are the Queen!

ARGIA (*rises slowly*)   Not every eye shall look to the ground. There shall still be someone to stand before you. Yes. I am the Queen!

(*A silence*)

BIANTE   She's confessed, Amos. Quick, make your speech for the prosecution.

AMOS (*rises, and thinks for a moment*)   If friction is to be stopped, the only way is to remove the cause; if disturbances are to be brought to an end, the only way is to eliminate the disturber. I see only one way to make such eliminations final.

(*The witnesses, perturbed by the decision by which they are to be faced, rise cautiously, first one, then another, trying to efface themselves*)

AMOS   No other method is known whereby revolutions may be at once prudent and rapid; nor any other argument that makes them so persuasive; nor any procedure which more effectively seals dangerous lips and more finally immobilizes enemy hands.

(*The witnesses have cautiously moved towards the door, but at this point* AMOS's *look arrests them*)

AMOS (*continuing*)   Such a method serves also, among other things, to identify the weak pillars; in fact, you will notice that some of our jurymen who have divined the responsibility that is about to face them, are cautiously trying to slip away one by one: they do not realise that, in the course of time, that may render them also liable to furnish proofs of the excellence of the method. It is quite true that the importance of a revolution is in proportion to the number of dead it produces. Biante, it is your duty to pronounce sentence.

BIANTE (*exhausted and swaying, rises, supported by* MAUPA)   The revolution has decided that the Queen must die. I order . . . I order . . . (*He cannot go on, he has come to the end:* MAUPA *lifts him back into his chair*)

AMOS   You are no longer in a position to give orders. Your post is vacant. (*He turns to the others*) The revolution has decided that the Queen must die. The sentence will be carried out during the course of the night.

ACT FOUR

(*A short time has elapsed since the previous act.* ARGIA *is dozing. In the background, a soldier is asleep on a wooden chair.* AMOS *comes in: he shakes the soldier, and sends him away. Then he wakes* ARGIA)

AMOS   I've come to inform you that the sentence must be carried out very shortly. The messenger who is to take the news of the execution to my government must leave during the night. In fact, we all have to leave this area before morning, for unexpected military reasons.

ARGIA (*half-absently*)   Yes.

AMOS   I also have to tell you that you can discount any possibility of rescue. Any move on the part of the Coalitionists would be ineffective: arrangements have already been made to carry out the sentence at the first alarm.

ARGIA   Was this the only reason you came to see me?

AMOS   No. On the contrary. There is a much more important reason. In fact, you may regard everything that has happened so far tonight as a mere preamble to what I have to tell you now.

ARGIA   Well?

AMOS   Do you really think the revolution would have given so much of its time to your frivolities this evening, and taken so much trouble to give an appearance of legality to the trial, if we had no precise aim in mind?

ARGIA   Well: what is it?

AMOS   The revolution intends to be irreproachable right to the end. I have come to tell you that you are free to ask for pardon.

ARGIA   From whom?

AMOS   From us. Will you ask for it?

ARGIA   (*after a pause*)   I will ask for it.

AMOS   Good. The coldness of the night seems to have brought you to your senses. (*He sits*) Naturally the pardon is dependent on certain conditions.

ARGIA   What are they?

AMOS   Formal ones. Futile even. Before I disclose them to you, I would like you to realize exactly what would happen to you in the event of the pardon being refused. The human mind often seeks refuge in vagueness. However: outside this building is a stone platform. On it, when you went out, you would see six armed soldiers. You would then go and stand in front of them. You would fall. A short while after, the sunrise would illuminate a universe in all respects as usual, except that you would not be there. That is all.

ARGIA   The conditions.

AMOS   The signing of a list of declarations concerning the events of the last few years. The witnesses are ready. (*He turns to the door*) Come in.

(*The* PORTER *and* MAUPA *come in and remain in the background*)

ARGIA   What sort of declarations?

AMOS   Saying that you acknowledge that you have conspired, etcetera, have summoned foreign help against your country, etcetera, and confess yourself guilty of illegal actions, dishonorable conduct, etcetera.

ARGIA   (*almost indifferently*)   They sound like lies to me.

AMOS   You will also be required to give us certain information. But that we can go into later.

ARGIA   Is the paper ready?

AMOS   Here it is.

(*He makes a sign, and the* PORTER *approaches* ARGIA *with a paper in his hand. She turns, and sees him; she has stretched out her hand; now she withdraws it. The* PORTER *puts the paper in her hand*)

AMOS   I forgot to give you one other piece of news. The flight of your accomplice—the so-called interpreter, I mean—was unsuccessful. They had to fire at him; I am afraid he was seriously wounded. In the hope of surviving and winning our clemency, he employed his last moments in betraying you even more comprehensively than he had done before. He confirmed all the allegations made in that document.

ARGIA   (*thoughtfully*)   Poor Raim. His eyes were a nice color; it was pleasant to look into them. How terribly concerned he was to keep them open on the world. In vain, apparently. Good-bye, Raim. This wind is carrying all the leaves away.

AMOS   Yes, madam. It's the time of year. Whole gatherings of people who yesterday sat in gilded halls, could today reassemble in hell with no one missing. Your other accomplice, the peasant-woman, was at least able to say good-bye to you.

ARGIA   (*thoughtfully*)   She was so terrified; so very unpractical. She wanted to sleep, night after night, in peace. Good-bye.

AMOS   I mean that you are now alone. But alive, luckily for you. Try and remain so. In times like these, and at so small a cost (*pointing to the paper*), it's a good bargain.

ARGIA   To tell you the truth, I scarcely know any longer whether I want to make a good bargain or not. (*She takes an uncertain step forward; sees the* PORTER *staring at her; and stands still again*) But, Commissar Amos, you must really think me very simple, if you imagine you can deceive me so easily. No, I know as well as you do that there is no way out of this. (*She gives back the paper to* AMOS) To survive and to be able to describe such things would be hard enough, even for your witnesses. And think who the chief character is. No. It wouldn't be a very clever move on your part to allow the Queen to go free, so that the common people could come and kiss the hem of her garments while she described to them how you forced her signature from her.

AMOS   A reasonable objection. We had thought of it already. It also explains your courage earlier this evening . . . (*with a faint suggestion of bitterness*) a courage which would have been a very humiliating slap in the face for us, if we hadn't been aware how gratuitous and false and easy it was: as courage usually is, in my opinion. Madam: you thought then that everything was lost already; so your fine gestures cost you nothing. Very well. I've come to tell you that in fact nothing is lost, so far as you're concerned. The revolution has an interest in keeping you alive. (*a pause*) Alive, and in circulation. Alive . . . (*almost casually*) and in disgrace. Confess. And first you'll be despised; then ignored. And then: no longer a queen, but a woman: a woman, no longer walking on fine soft carpets, but huddled on the hard floor of an all-night bar, learning the pleading smiles of poverty . . .

ARGIA   (*lost in her recollections*)   . . . listening to the cheap jokes of the bar-man, with an anxious smile on her face; soothing and flattering the bad-tempered taxi drivers . . . (*The eye of the* PORTER *is on her*) But who, who on earth, could ever conceive that a woman of such birth and spirit, stainless and honorable, could foul herself by signing such a document? They'll never be willing to believe that.

AMOS They will have to believe it. We shall give them the proof. I've already told you that you will furnish us with certain information, information you alone possess. On that information we shall act. And the world will be compelled to realize that it was you who gave it to us.

ARGIA (*with melancholy indifference*) . . . And so . . . poor Queen in disgrace . . . you spare her, and the others cut her throat; her friends.

AMOS At least it would be time gained. Unless—and this is the point—some of the others, your friends, I mean . . . (*breaking off: to* MAUPA) You go outside.

(MAUPA *goes out*)

AMOS (*to the* PORTER) You wait over there. (*He turns back to* ARGIA) I was speaking about the others, your friends: in order that we can take steps to protect you and save you from them (*dropping his voice*), you will tell us their names. (*with a sudden cry, pointing a finger at her*) Yes! You know them! say it! I read it there, in your eyes! They glinted. You've seen the way to save yourself. And you know you have it there at your disposal: inside your head. (*persuasively*) Well, then, first: it's clearly in the interest of the revolution to keep you alive so that respect for you shall die out. Secondly: it's indispensable that the revolution shall know the names of your accomplices. The two things fit together; and save you. Your disclosures will be the beginning of a great clean-up. There are cold-blooded vipers lying curled up in our very beds. Illustrious personages and obscure imbeciles. Even here, a short time ago; it was quite clear that your fine speeches were directed to someone's ears. They will all be rendered permanently harmless. (*His voice drops to a whisper*) Who are they? Where are they? What are their names? Quickly: tell me their names.

ARGIA (*stands for a moment with bent head*) Your voice went very quiet when you asked me for them, didn't it? If it made you feel sick to ask for them, what do you suppose I should feel if I were to divulge them? (*with a wan smile*) It's obviously not a thing to be very proud of. And unfortunately, I don't know any names.

AMOS You not only know them: you've already wisely decided to disclose them to me. However, you will no doubt make me wait a little for them; that was to be expected, and I shall not refuse to indulge you. It's a due one has to pay to the concept of honor. You merely want to be persuaded.

ARGIA (*with a wan smile*) The men you want me to hand over to you, certainly never expected this as their reward.

AMOS Those men have simply staked everything on one card. In their complete selfishness, they were prepared to make use of you. Do you know any of them personally; or feel affection for any of them? No. Bonds of gratitude? No. (*ironically*) Is it for some political ideal that you are prepared to sacrifice yourself?

ARGIA (*almost absently*) I know very little about such things; I've told you that before.

AMOS Or perhaps the thought of your good name is holding you back? The little plaster figure of your reputation crashing in pieces? Madam: don't take any notice of cant-phrases; follow nature: which fears death, and knows nothing else. Only thus will you be sincere, and therefore honorable. After all, the finest reputation in the world is very little comfort to a corpse.

ARGIA (*thoughtfully*) Yes.

AMOS Good. (*although the room is almost empty, and the silence in it is absolute*) Well, then, gentlemen, silence! The Queen is deciding.

(*A silence*)

ARGIA So my decisions can actually make people hold their breath. Messengers are getting ready to announce them beyond the mountains.

AMOS That does not, however, give you one minute's extra time. (*He calls*) Maupa!

MAUPA (*appearing in the doorway*) Everything is ready.

AMOS (*dismissing him with a wave*) Good. Tell them to wait.

ARGIA I am a person who can make people wait. It's the first time that's ever happened to me. I can say yes: I can say no.

AMOS You have very little time left, madam.

ARGIA Do not try to hurry the Queen. The Queen. I am only just beginning to realize what it means to be one.

AMOS It means obeying a few flatterers in order to rule over many subjects.

ARGIA Not at all. To be a queen really means: to be alone. It means: to have gone on ahead, to have left everyone else behind. Enemies, friends: all gone. A great simplicity. This room is indeed a palace; your aversion from me is only a form of respect; you are only a rebel subject. I can say yes; I can say no.

AMOS At a price, however.

ARGIA It is the only one I can pay. (*She suddenly shivers with cold*) And suppose I decided to pay it? I am free: to say yes, or no. And no one in the world can do anything about it. I am the one who decides. It's beautiful; to be able to talk to you like this; to look about me like this . . . and to feel my breathing so free, and the beating of my heart so peaceful.

(AMOS *has taken up the cloak left by the soldier, and places it round her shoulders*)

AMOS You are shivering.

ARGIA It is the cold that announces the dawn. The only thing I am afraid of, is getting tired; it's been a wearing night. (*a pause*) I don't even feel dislike towards you.

AMOS The technique of pride, is it not? The technique of pride. (*with sudden anger*) But pride is not flesh and blood, madam! The chosen creature's superiority with which you think you can even now keep us at a distance! But it's not your flesh and blood! It's a shell! A crust, that's all. Born of habit. Like the hardness of the hands of a peasant. But you haven't earned it by digging. It's come to you from the bowings and scrapings of a whole palace all round you since the day you were born! Give me those names. Firmness, honor, eyes that never lower themselves, the technique of pride: I'd like to know what would be left of all that, if you'd had to live in some of the places I've known, and cooked yourself an egg over a spirit-lamp, and gone out of an evening in a greasy overcoat, with a nice smile ready to try and soften the man at the dairy. Yes, yes, our eyes can't look at people as yours do . . . even our thoughts, here inside us, are a bit grubby, and shabby, and common, and bruised by rubbing shoulders with the crowd . . . But don't try to imagine they are so very different from your own. Just lift the curtain a little. Come on, give me the names. If I were to twist your wrist, you'd scream like the rest of us! Your majesty, have you ever seen the little white grubs in rotten meat? They suddenly spurt out, and writhe about furiously. Minute as they are, they want to live; to feed; to reproduce; they do exactly

what we do: you: everyone: and in exactly the same way. The proud boast of being a person, a will, someone distinguished, is no more than a matter of fine linen. Take people's clothes away from them; and that's exactly what they'll be. All naked, equal grubs, wriggling about as best they can. The slightest planetary disturbance could quietly wipe everything out. And instead of wriggling as equals, do we have to give one man heaven and another man hell? Come down from your tin-pot throne. Get used to these things. Get used to being reasonable. Let your own instincts win; and be afraid: it's your way of wriggling. Give me those names.

ARGIA (*her teeth chattering*) What you're saying, in fact, is that if there were here, in my place, some less fortunate woman than I, someone who'd had to cook herself an egg in her room, you're saying that there'd be some real merit in *her*, if she were courageous at this moment? Commissar Amos, there was once a woman whom they played a joke on. I was told about it. One Sunday, this woman went to the seaside. And the bathing attendants, for a joke, knowing the sort of woman she was, got out for her a bathing costume of the kind that becomes almost transparent in the water. There was a good deal of merriment. And all of a sudden, the woman noticed that everyone was looking at her, and that there was rather a row going on.

AMOS Come on: the names.

ARGIA And at last that woman saw that she was standing there almost naked! Alone and naked. She stood there bewildered. And suddenly, do you know what she did? She tried to laugh, with them. (*controlling herself, and shrugging her shoulders*) And after all what did they see? That she was a woman. We know what a woman is. A man comes up to her . . . cheerful, with his big, sweaty hands, and says: "Do this . . . go like this . . . do that . . . (*louder*) . . . go on . . ." (*suddenly, with a real cry of anguish and protest*) Well, do you know what I think! I think there comes a time when the only thing to do is to stand up and say . . . (*as though actually turning on someone*) "Why do you insult me like this? And, my God, why have I allowed you to? Get away from me! Go away! Go away! Leave me alone! You take advantage of an immense mistake, a monstrous delusion! Respect me! Show me respect! Respect . . . because I am . . . the Queen! The Queen, and destined for other things than this." (*with a change of voice*) What I want to do is to go out of doors, as if it were a fine morning, and as if I had seen down there, at the end of the street, the cool fresh color of the sea, a color that makes the heart leap! And someone stops me, and then someone else, and someone else, with the usual rudenesses. But this morning I don't even hear them. I'm not afraid any longer. My face expresses dignity. I am as I would always have wished to be. And it would have been simple after all. It would have been enough to want to be. Palaces have nothing to do with it. It was my own fault.

AMOS (*after a long pause*) Am I to take this to mean that you still refuse? (*almost with melancholy*) Very well; in that case, your troubles are not yet over. Madam: you are forcing me to do this, remember.

(*He goes to the door, and makes a sign to someone outside.* MAUPA *enters slowly, leading by the hand a small boy about three years old, dressed in peasant-boy's clothes*)

AMOS You can go, now, Maupa. So can you, porter.

(MAUPA *and the* PORTER *go out. The boy is left standing alone in the middle of the room*)

ARGIA (*shaken*) Who is he?

AMOS (*with the same melancholy, moving to the child's side*) It is the person who will persuade you.

ARGIA (*desperately*) I don't know who he is!

AMOS I know of course that you don't actually recognize him. We ourselves had a great deal of trouble in tracing him.

ARGIA (*cries out*) I swear to you! I swear . . . that he isn't my son! I'm not his mother!

AMOS He's a fine child. He'll be able to live and grow up as an unknowing peasant . . . so long as the protection you are according to a few seditious men doesn't force us to eliminate in him any pretext for sedition in the future. In such an orgy of blood, the scales won't be upset by a few drops more . . . Well, that is what you wanted: to choose: now you can do so.

ARGIA (*instinctively clutching her face*) He isn't mine! I tell you he isn't mine.

AMOS It is in your power to choose. The weight of this tiny little boy puts an end to your flights of fancy, and brings you back to earth. Even the wolves in the woods up here love their young. Yes: that's a real thing: the rest is smoke. Make your choice: make it according to nature: no one will condemn you.

ARGIA (*astounded*) And if I don't, you're capable of a crime like this?

AMOS (*with lofty sadness*) Madam: I shall do everything that is necessary. Common re-

proaches should be reserved for common occasions. The blood that your disclosures will make flow may be a great deal, but it will be far away. There is only a little here. But it is warm. And it is your own.

ARGIA Oh God, how can a human mind have so much hate in it?

AMOS (*with painful intensity*) It is not hate. But it is too late to argue now. I also made my choice once upon a time. However a stone rolls, the one who has dislodged it rolls down with it.

ARGIA My God, how can you . . . break laws so sacred . . .? I tell you he isn't mine! Did you keep me alive only to save me for this? I swear to you he isn't mine, take him away, take him away . . . Oh God, oh God, how can you think you've the power to . . . (*crying out*) In what name, by what right, do you dare to do this?

AMOS (*shouting her down*) In what name! By what right! (*suddenly controlling himself*) Listen to me: I want to tell *you* something also. When we overthrew the October republic, I was in the palace too. An agreement had been reached; our victory was total and peaceful. There had been no bloodshed. All the same, we were in the palace rooms; we wanted to pull down the coats-of-arms. We began to unnail them. A man was fetching great blows at one of the trophies. And I noticed that little by little something seemed to dawn in his face. Down below in the street the crowds were yelling. Suddenly this man, as soon as he'd knocked the trophy off the wall, turned round. He was covered in sweat. And he hurled his axe at one of the mirrors! The others followed suit. Then they began to smash everything. And their faces were furious, they were intoxicated, they were beautiful, they were holy. The smoke was already appearing! And the fire followed! (*controlling himself suddenly*) But it would have been contemptible if the aim of it all was merely to take a few pence from the hand of a fat dead man and put them in the hand of a thin living man. So much noise simply in order to modify a few tariffs and initiate a few austere apostles into the pleasures of wearing silk shirts? But this fury, which spouts up like a fountain of black oil, comes from deep down, madam, it's the distillation of a very different grief, the memory of a very different betrayal, it doesn't merely utter its "no" to your silks and satins and the farmer's hoard. (*He cries*) It says "no" to everything there is! It says rage towards everything, despair towards everything! What we hear coming towards us down there, is the thunder of the great waterfall! It's towards the great rapids that the boat is rushing! This fury says "no" to the whole world: it says: (*with despairing weariness*) that the world is wrong, it's all absurdity; an immense, unchangeable quarry of despair, a grotesque, unchangeable labyrinth of injustice, an insensate clockwork, that one day compels you and me to say and do what we're saying and doing now. It says "no"; total sterilization; away with everything: the just and the unjust, loyalty and betrayal, worthiness, guilt, glory: (*He points to* ARGIA) . . . everything that makes us grasping and boastful owners in life and in death, all this mass of falsehoods, this immense fraud! Tell me the names.

ARGIA (*staring at the child*)   The names? But you'll kill him whatever happens, I know you will. (*a brief pause*) Oh, poor little child, in his little peasant's dress! No one wants him. His mother runs away from him. I've done nothing but say: "Take him away." Completely alone. (*She suddenly runs to the child, and hugs him tightly*) Oh, what a lovely child you are, my darling. How healthy you are. And what pretty little teeth. My angel, your mother won't ever come and see if you're asleep, she'll never see you run, and say: "Look how he's grown." He isn't at all sleepy, is he, and not the tiniest bit afraid, is he? No, no, he's very well, he's in the warm . . . (*She is pressing him against her breast*) . . . This is the right place for a little boy to be, isn't it? This is a little throne for a child . . . (*She turns to* AMOS) Sir, I've been deceiving myself. I thought that everything would be simple. Perhaps I should after all do as you say . . . I ought to tell you those names . . . I'm so confused . . . Wait a moment . . . those names . . . (*She stands there, with eyes wide-open, looking before her; suddenly she laughs softly; and whispers*) A miracle, sir. A miracle. I've forgotten them! Perhaps I have been too much upset, or perhaps I have been helped in some way; but that step has been spared me. (*She hugs the child tightly, hiding her face against him, and remains thus*)

AMOS (*after a long pause*)   In that case the struggle between us is over. All that remains is to finish what was begun. (*a pause; then, seriously and gently*) If you believe in the survival of your soul, and desire a confessor, anyone you choose may hear you.

ARGIA   Yes, I do desire it. (*She rises without letting go the child*) I have made sad and improvident use of my person, my words, my thoughts, and for the most part, of the whole of my life. I laid the blame for this upon others, when the blame was all my own. This I understood too late. I have often told lies; and even now.

AMOS   What is your real name?

ARGIA   I believe that the Lord, in a short time from now, will not be asking names of me; He will be asking what my profit has been. The only one I have had I have had this night. And so, not utterly bereft, but with a little coin I go before Him. (*She raises her head slightly, and her voice also*) Only a little, but my own; not given to me, nor inherited; but mine. This is the profit that makes owners and possessors of us. I am sinning still; since of what I have done tonight I am a little proud: it is the single thing that I can tell about myself . . . (*dropping her voice a little*) I have great need that soon I shall meet someone who will listen to me. (*She turns*)

(MAUPA *comes in, followed by the* PORTER)

ARGIA   Now is it?
AMOS   Yes.

(MAUPA *goes over to take the child from her.* ARGIA *prevents him, hugging the child close*)

AMOS (*motioning* MAUPA *to stand back*) The child will return to where he has lived hitherto, and where no one is informed of who he is. (*He takes the child from* ARGIA) The sentence will be carried out at once. Immediately afterwards, it will be announced that the woman known as the Queen is dead, and that therefore the Unitary Government has triumphed, the actions of our enemies being now deprived of their aim.

(ARGIA *moves towards the door, preceded by* MAUPA)

ARGIA   I believe that God . . . has intentionally made us, not docile, for that He would find useless . . . but different from Himself and a little too proud . . . so that we may . . . stand against Him, thwart Him, amaze Him . . . Perhaps that is His purpose. (*She takes another step forward*) It is a long struggle. Only at the end do we find reconciliation; and rest. (*She looks at the child*) I go away rich. I have acquired a son . . . and memories . . . If even a little memory survives in us, this night, for me, shall shine indeed. (*She shows her hand to* AMOS) Tell them to leave this ring on my finger. (*She holds out a hand to the child*) Goodbye, my sweet.

(*The child also puts a hand out towards her.* ARGIA *turns to go towards the door; pauses in momentary bewilderment; extracts her lipstick, and puts a little on her lips*)

ARGIA   My mouth was rather pale. (*She is

now at the door) How lovely and serene it is over the mountains; and the star Diana is still there in the sky. Unquestionably, this is a seat for kings, and in it we must try to live regally.

(*She goes out. There is a silence. Suddenly the* PORTER *runs out after her.* AMOS, *listening, puts his hands over the child's ears.*

A burst of gunfire is heard. ARGIA *is dead*)

Federico García Lorca

1899-1936

THE AUTHORITY OF THE THEATRE

MY DEAR FRIENDS: Some time ago I made a solemn promise to refuse every kind of tribute, banquet, or celebration which might be made in my honor, first, because I know that each of them drives another nail into our literary coffin, and second, because I have found that there is nothing more depressing than a formal speech made in our honor, and nothing sadder than organized applause, however sincere.

Besides, between ourselves, I hold that banquets and scrolls bring bad luck upon the one who receives them, bad luck springing from the relief of his friends who think: "Now we have done our duty by him."

A banquet is a gathering of professional people who eat with us, and where we find thrown together every kind of person who likes us least.

Rather than do honor to poets and dramatists, I should prepare challenges and attacks, in which we should be told roundly and passionately: "Are you afraid of doing this?" "Are you incapable of expressing a person's anguish at the sea?" "Daren't you show the despair of soldiers who hate war?"

Necessity and struggle, grounded on a critical love, temper the artist's soul, which easy flattery makes effeminate and destroys. The theatres are full of deceiving sirens, garlanded with hothouse roses, and the public is content, and applauds dummy hearts and superficial

dialogue; but the dramatic poet who wishes to save himself from oblivion must not forget the open fields with their wild roses, fields moistened by the dawn where peasants toil, and the pigeon, wounded by a mysterious hunter, which is dying amongst the rushes with no one to hear its grief.

Shunning sirens, flattery, and congratulations, I have accepted nothing in my honor, on the occasion of the first night of *Yerma;* but it has been the greatest pleasure of my short life as a writer to learn that the theatre world of Madrid was asking the great Margarita Xirgu, an actress with an impeccable artistic career, luminary of the Spanish theatre, and admirable interpreter of the part of Yerma, together with the company which so brilliantly supports her, for a special production.

For the interest and attention in a notable theatrical endeavor which this implies, I wish, now that we are all together, to give to you my deepest and sincerest thanks. I am not speaking tonight as an author, nor as a poet, nor as a simple student of the rich panorama of man's life, but as an ardent lover of the theatre of social action. The theatre is one of the most useful and expressive instruments for a country's edification, the barometer which registers its greatness or its decline. A theatre which in every branch, from tragedy to vaudeville, is sensitive and well oriented, can in a few years change the sensibility of a people, and a broken-down theatre, where wings have given way to cloven hoofs, can coarsen and benumb a whole nation.

The theatre is a school of weeping and of laughter, a rostrum where men are free to expose old and equivocal standards of conduct, and explain with living examples the eternal norms of the heart and feelings of man.

A nation which does not help and does not encourage its theatre is, if not dead, dying; just as the theatre which does not feel the social pulse, the historical pulse, the drama of its people, and catch the genuine color of its landscape and of its spirit, with laughter or with tears, has no right to call itself a theatre, but an amusement hall, or a place for doing that dreadful thing known as "killing time." I am referring to no one, and I want to offend no one; I am not speaking of actual fact, but of a problem that has yet to be solved.

Every day, my friends, I hear about the crisis in the theatre, and I feel always that the defect is not one before our eyes, but deep down in its very nature; it is not a defect of the flower we have before us, of a play, that is, but deeply rooted; in short, a defect of organization. Whilst actors and authors are in the hands of managements that are completely commercial, free, without either literary or state control of any kind, managements devoid of all judgment and offering no kind of safeguard, actors, authors, and the whole theatre will sink lower every day, beyond all hope of salvation.

The delightful light theatre of revue, vaudeville, and farce, forms of which I am a keen spectator, could maintain and even save itself; but plays in verse, the historical play, and the so-called Spanish *zarzuela,* will suffer more and more setbacks, because they are forms which make great demands and which admit of real innovations, and there is neither the authority nor the spirit of sacrifice to impose them on a public which has to be overruled from above, and often contradicted and attacked. The theatre must impose itself on the public, not the public on the theatre. To do this, authors and actors must, whatever the cost, again assume great authority, because the theatre-going public is like a school child; it reveres the stern, severe teacher who demands justice and sees justice done; and puts pins on the chairs of the timid and flattering ones who neither teach themselves nor allow anyone else to teach.

The public can be taught—I say public, of course, not people—it can be taught; for, some years ago, I saw Debussy and Ravel howled down, and I have been present since at loud ovations given by a public of ordinary people to the very works which were earlier rejected. These authors were imposed by the high judgment of authority, superior to that of the ordinary public, just as were Wedekind in Germany and Pirandello in Italy, and so many others.

This has to be done for the good of the theatre and for the glory and status of its interpreters. Dignity must be maintained, in the conviction that such dignity will be amply repaid. To do otherwise is to tremble behind the flies, and kill the fantasies, imagination, and charm of the theatre, which is always, always an art, and will always be a lofty art, even though there may have been a time when everything which pleased was labeled art, so that the tone was lowered, poetry destroyed, and the stage itself a refuge for thieves.

Art above all else. A most noble art, and you, my actor friends, artists above all else. Artists from head to foot, since through love and vocation you have risen to the make-believe and pitiful world of the boards. Artists by occupation and by preoccupation. From the smallest theatre to the most eminent, the word "Art" should be written in auditoriums and dressing rooms, for if not we shall have to write the word "Commerce" or some other that I dare not say. And distinction, discipline, and sacrifice and love.

I don't want to lecture you, because I should be the one receiving a lecture. My words are dictated by enthusiasm and conviction. I labor under no delusion. As a good Andalusian I can think coolly, because I come of an ancient stock. I know that truth does not lie with him who says, "Today, today, today," eating his bread close to the hearth, but with him who watches calmly at a distance the first light of dawn in the country.

I know that those people who say, "Now, now, now," with their eyes fixed on the small jaws of the box office are not right, but those who say, "Tomorrow, tomorrow, tomorrow," and feel the approach of the new life which is hovering over the world.

Translated by A. E. Sloman

YERMA

*Translated by James Graham-Luján
and Richard L. O'Connell*

CAST OF CHARACTERS

YERMA
MARIA
JUAN
VICTOR
PAGAN CRONE
DOLORES
FIRST LAUNDRESS
SECOND LAUNDRESS
THIRD LAUNDRESS
FOURTH LAUNDRESS
FIFTH LAUNDRESS
SIXTH LAUNDRESS

FIRST YOUNG GIRL
SECOND YOUNG GIRL
THE FEMALE MASK
THE MALE MASK
FIRST SISTER-IN-LAW
SECOND SISTER-IN-LAW
FIRST WOMAN
SECOND WOMAN
THE CHILD
FIRST MAN
SECOND MAN
THIRD MAN

ACT ONE

Scene One

(*When the curtain rises Yerma is asleep with an embroidery frame at her feet. The stage is in the strange light of a dream. A Shepherd enters on tiptoe looking fixedly at Yerma. He leads by the hand a Child dressed in white. The clock sounds. When the Shepherd leaves, the light changes into the happy brightness of a spring morning. Yerma awakes*)

VOICE (*within, singing*)

For the nursey, nursey, nursey,
For the little nurse we'll make
A tiny hut out in the fields
And there we'll shelter take.

Yerma is from *Three Tragedies of Federico García Lorca*, translated by James Graham-Luján and Richard L. O'Connell. Copyright 1947 by New Directions and reprinted by permission of New Directions, Publishers.

YERMA   Juan, do you hear me? Juan!
JUAN   Coming.
YERMA   It's time now.
JUAN   Did the oxen go by?
YERMA   They've already gone.
JUAN   See you later.

(*He starts to leave*)

YERMA   Won't you have a glass of milk?
JUAN   What for?
YERMA   You work a lot and your body's not strong enough for it.
JUAN   When men grow thin they get strong as steel.
YERMA   But not you. You were different when we were first married. Now you've got a face as white as though the sun had never shone on it. I'd like to see you go to the river and swim or climb up on the roof when the rain beats down on our house. Twenty-four months we've been married and you only get sadder, thinner, as if you were growing backwards.
JUAN   Are you finished?
YERMA   (*rising*) Don't take it wrong. If I were sick I'd like you to take care of me. "My wife's sick. I'm going to butcher this lamb and

cook her a good meat dish." "My wife's sick. I'm going to save this chicken-fat to relieve her chest; I'm going to take her this sheepskin to protect her feet from the snow." That's the way I am. That's why I take care of you.

JUAN   I'm grateful.

YERMA   But you don't let me take care of you.

JUAN   Because there's nothing wrong with me. All these things are just your imagination. I work hard. Each year I'll get older.

YERMA   Each year. You and I will just go on here each year . . .

JUAN (*smiling*)   Why, of course. And very peacefully. Our work goes well, we've no children to worry about.

YERMA   We've no children. . . . Juan!

JUAN   What is it?

YERMA   I love you, don't I?

JUAN   Yes, you love me.

YERMA   I know girls who trembled and cried before getting into bed with their husbands. Did I cry the first time I went to bed with you? Didn't I sing as I turned back the fine linen bed-clothes? And didn't I tell you, "These bed-clothes smell of apples!"

JUAN   That's what you said!

YERMA   My mother cried because I wasn't sorry to leave her. And that's true! No one ever got married with more happiness. And yet . . .

JUAN   Hush! I have a hard enough job hearing all the time that I'm . . .

YERMA   No. Don't tell me what they say. I can see with my own eyes that that isn't so. The rain just by the force of its falling on the stones softens them and makes weeds grow— weeds which people say aren't good for anything. "Weeds aren't good for anything," yet I see them plainly enough—moving their yellow flowers in the wind.

JUAN   We've got to wait!

YERMA   Yes; loving each other.

(YERMA *embraces and kisses her husband. She takes the initiative*)

JUAN   If you need anything, tell me, and I'll bring it to you. You know well enough I don't like you to be going out.

YERMA   I never go out.

JUAN   You're better off here.

YERMA   Yes.

JUAN   The street's for people with nothing to do.

YERMA (*darkly*)   Of course.

(*The husband leaves.* YERMA *walks toward her sewing. She passes her hand over her belly, lifts her arms in a beautiful sigh, and sits down to sew*)

YERMA

From where do you come, my love,
   my baby?
"From the mountains of icy cold."
What do you lack, sweet love, my
   baby?
"The woven warmth in your dress."

(*She threads the needle*)

Let the branches tremble in the sun
and the fountains leap all around!

(*As if she spoke to a child*)

In the courtyard the dog barks,
In the trees the wind sings.
The oxen low for the ox-herd,
and the moon curls up my hair.
What want you, boy, from so far away?

(*Pause*)

"The mountains white upon your chest."
Let the branches tremble in the sun
and the fountains leap all around!

(*Sewing*)

I shall say to you, child, yes,
for you I'll torn and broken be.
How painful is this belly now,
where first you shall be cradled!
When, boy, when will you come to
   me?

(*Pause*)

"When sweet your flesh of jasmine
   smells."
Let the branches tremble in the sun
and the fountains leap all around!

(YERMA *continues singing.* MARIA *enters through the door carrying a bundle of clothes*)

YERMA   Where are you coming from?

MARIA   From the store.

YERMA   From the store so early?

MARIA   For what I wanted, I'd have waited at the door till they opened. Can't you guess what I bought?

YERMA   You probably bought some coffee for breakfast; sugar, bread.

MARIA   No. I bought laces, three lengths of linen, ribbons, and colored wool to make tassels. My husband had the money and he gave it to me without my even asking for it.

YERMA   You're going to make a blouse?

MARIA   No, it's because . . . Can't you guess?

YERMA   What?

MARIA   Because . . . well . . . it's here now!

(*She lowers her head.* YERMA *rises and looks at her in admiration*)

YERMA   In just five months!

MARIA   Yes.

YERMA   You can tell it's there?

MARIA   Naturally.

YERMA   (*with curiosity*)   But, how does it make you feel?

MARIA   I don't know. Sad; upset.

YERMA   Sad? Upset? (*holding her*) But . . . when did he come? Tell me about it. You weren't expecting him.

MARIA   No, I wasn't expecting him.

YERMA   Why, you might have been singing; yes? I sing. You . . . tell me . . .

MARIA   Don't ask me about it. Have you ever held a live bird pressed in your hand?

YERMA   Yes.

MARIA   Well—the same way—but more in your blood.

YERMA   How beautiful!

(*She looks at her, beside herself*)

MARIA   I'm confused. I don't know anything.

YERMA   About what?

MARIA   About what I must do. I'll ask my mother.

YERMA   What for? She's old now and she'll have forgotten about these things. Don't walk very much, and when you breathe, breathe as softly as if you had a rose between your teeth.

MARIA   You know, they say that later he kicks you gently with his little legs.

YERMA   And that's when you love him best, when you can really say: "*My* child!"

MARIA   In the midst of all this, I feel ashamed.

YERMA   What has your husband said about it?

MARIA   Nothing.

YERMA   Does he love you a lot?

MARIA   He doesn't tell me so, but when he's close to me his eyes tremble like two green leaves.

YERMA   Did he know that you were . . . ?

MARIA   Yes.

YERMA   But, how did he know it?

MARIA   I don't know. But on our wedding night he kept telling me about it with his mouth pressed against my cheek; so that now it seems to me my child is a dove of fire he made slip in through my ear.

YERMA   Oh, how lucky you are!

MARIA   But you know more about these things than I do.

YERMA   And what good does it do me?

MARIA   That's true! Why should it be like that? Out of all the brides of your time you're the only one who . . .

YERMA   That's the way it is. Of course, there's still time. Helena was three years, and long ago some in my mother's time were much

longer, but two years and twenty days—like me —is too long to wait. I don't think it's right for me to burn myself out here. Many nights I go out barefooted to the patio to walk on the ground. I don't know why I do it. If I keep on like this, I'll end by turning bad.

MARIA   But look here, you infant, you're talking as if you were an old woman. You listen to me, now! No one can complain about these things. A sister of my mother's had one after fourteen years, and you should have seen what a beautiful child that was!

YERMA   (*eagerly*)   What was he like?

MARIA   He used to bellow like a little bull, as loud as a thousand locusts all buzzing at once, and wet us, and pull our braids; and when he was four months old he scratched our faces all over.

YERMA   (*laughing*)   But those things don't hurt.

MARIA   Let me tell you—

YERMA   Bah! I've seen my sister nurse her child with her breasts full of scratches. It gave her great pain, but it was a fresh pain—good, and necessary for health.

MARIA   They say one suffers a lot with children.

YERMA   That's a lie. That's what weak, complaining mothers say. What do they have them for? Having a child is no bouquet of roses. We must suffer to see them grow. I sometimes think half our blood must go. But that's good, healthy, beautiful. Every woman has blood for four or five children, and when she doesn't have them it turns to poison . . . as it will in me.

MARIA   I don't know what's the matter with me.

YERMA   I've always heard it said that you're frightened the first time.

MARIA   (*timidly*)   We'll see. You know, you sew so well that . . .

YERMA   (*taking the bundle*)   Give it here. I'll cut you two little dresses. And this . . . ?

MARIA   For diapers.

YERMA   (*she sits down*)   All right.

MARIA   Well . . . See you later.

(*As she comes near,* YERMA *lovingly presses her hands against her belly*)

YERMA   Don't run on the cobblestones.

MARIA   Good-bye.

(*She kisses her and leaves*)

YERMA   Come back soon. (YERMA *is in the same attitude as at the beginning of the scene. She takes her scissors and starts to cut.* VICTOR *enters*) Hello, Victor.

VICTOR   (*he is deep looking and has a firm*

gravity about him) Where's Juan?

YERMA   Out in the fields.

VICTOR   What's that you're sewing?

YERMA   I'm cutting some diapers.

VICTOR (*smiling*)   Well, now!

YERMA (*laughs*)   I'm going to border them with lace.

VICTOR   If it's a girl, you give her your name.

YERMA (*trembling*)   How's that?

VICTOR   I'm happy for you.

YERMA (*almost choking*)   No . . . they aren't for me. They're for María's child.

VICTOR   Well then, let's see if her example will encourage you. This house needs a child in it.

YERMA (*with anguish*)   Needs one!

VICTOR   Well, get along with it. Tell your husband to think less about his work. He wants to make money and he will, but who's he going to leave it to when he dies? I'm going out with my sheep. Tell Juan to take out the two he bought from me, and about this other thing— try harder! (*He leaves, smiling*)

YERMA (*passionately*)   That's it! Try . . . !

I shall say to you, child, yes,
for you I'll torn and broken be.
How painful is this belly now,
where first you shall be cradled!
When, child, when will you come to
    me?

(YERMA, *who has risen thoughtfully, goes to the place where Victor stood, and breathes deeply —like one who breathes mountain air. Then she goes to the other side of the room as if looking for something, and after that sits down and takes up the sewing again. She begins to sew. Her eyes remain fixed on one point*)

Scene Two

(*A field.* YERMA *enters carrying a basket. The* FIRST OLD WOMAN *enters*)

YERMA   Good morning!

FIRST OLD WOMAN   Good morning to a beautiful girl! Where are you going?

YERMA   I've just come from taking dinner to my husband who's working in the olive groves.

FIRST OLD WOMAN   Have you been married very long?

YERMA   Three years.

FIRST OLD WOMAN   Do you have any children?

YERMA   No.

FIRST OLD WOMAN   Bah! You'll have them!

YERMA (*eagerly*)   Do you think so?

FIRST OLD WOMAN   Well, why not? (*She sits down*) I, too, have just taken my husband his food. He's old. He still has to work. I have nine children, like nine golden suns, but since not one of them is a girl, here you have me going from one side to the other.

YERMA   You live on the other side of the river?

FIRST OLD WOMAN   Yes. In the mills. What family are you from?

YERMA   I'm Enrique the shepherd's daughter.

FIRST OLD WOMAN   Ah! Enrique the shepherd. I knew him. Good people. Get up, sweat, eat some bread and die. No playing, no nothing. The fair's for somebody else. Silent creatures. I could have married an uncle of yours, but then . . . ! I've been a woman with her skirts to the wind. I've run like an arrow to melon cuttings, to parties, to sugar cakes. Many times at dawn I've rushed to the door thinking I heard the music of guitars going along and coming nearer, but it was only the wind. (*She laughs*) You'll laugh at me. I've had two husbands, fourteen children—five of them dead— and yet I'm not sad, and I'd like to live much longer. That's what I say! The fig trees, how they last! The houses, how they last! And only we poor bedeviled women turn to dust for any reason.

YERMA   I'd like to ask you a question.

FIRST OLD WOMAN   Let's see. (*She looks at her*) I know what you're going to ask me, and there's not a word you can say about those things. (*She rises*)

YERMA (*holding her*)   But, why not? Hearing you talk has given me confidence. For some time I've been wanting to talk about it with an older woman—because I want to find out. Yes, you can tell me—

FIRST OLD WOMAN   Tell you what?

YERMA (*lowering her voice*)   What you already know. Why am I childless? Must I be left in the prime of my life taking care of little birds, or putting up tiny pleated curtains at my little windows? No. You've got to tell me what to do, for I'll do anything you tell me—even to sticking needles in the weakest part of my eyes.

FIRST OLD WOMAN   Me, tell you? I don't know anything about it. I laid down face up and began to sing. Children came like water. Oh, who can say this body we've got isn't beautiful? You take a step and at the end of the street a horse whinnies. Ay-y-y! Leave me alone, girl; don't make me talk. I have a lot of ideas I don't want to tell you about.

YERMA   Why not? I never talk about anything else with my husband!

FIRST OLD WOMAN   Listen: Does your husband please you?

YERMA   What?

FIRST OLD WOMAN   I mean—do you really love him? Do you long to be with him?

YERMA   I don't know.

FIRST OLD WOMAN   Don't you tremble when he comes near you? Don't you feel something like a dream when he brings his lips close to yours? Tell me.

YERMA   No. I've never noticed it.

FIRST OLD WOMAN   Never? Not even when you've danced?

YERMA   (*remembering*)   Perhaps . . . one time . . . with Victor . . .

FIRST OLD WOMAN   Go on.

YERMA   He took me by the waist and I couldn't say a word to him, because I couldn't talk. Another time this same Victor, when I was fourteen years old—he was a husky boy—took me in his arms to leap a ditch and I started shaking so hard my teeth chattered. But I've always been shy.

FIRST OLD WOMAN   But with your husband . . . ?

YERMA   My husband's something else. My father gave him to me and I took him. With happiness. That's the plain truth. Why, from the first day I was engaged to him I thought about . . . our children. And I could see myself in his eyes. Yes, but it was to see myself reflected very small, very manageable, as if I were my own daughter.

FIRST OLD WOMAN   It was just the opposite with me. Maybe that's why you haven't had a child yet. Men have got to give us pleasure, girl. They've got to take down our hair and let us drink water out of their mouths. So runs the world.

YERMA   Your world, but not mine. I think about a lot of things, a lot, and I'm sure that the things I think about will come true in my son. I gave myself over to my husband for his sake, and I go on giving to see if he'll be born—but never just for pleasure.

FIRST OLD WOMAN   And the only result is—you're empty!

YERMA   No, not empty, because I'm filling up with hate. Tell me; is it my fault? In a man do you have to look for only the man, nothing more? Then, what are you going to think when he lets you lie in bed looking at the ceiling with sad eyes, and he turns over and goes to sleep? Should I go on thinking of him or what can come shining out of my breast? I don't know; but you tell me—out of charity! (*She kneels*)

FIRST OLD WOMAN   Oh, what an open flower! What a beautiful creature you are. You leave me alone. Don't make me say any more. I don't want to talk with you any more. These are matters of honor. And I don't burn anyone's honor. You'll find out. But you certainly ought to be less innocent.

YERMA   (*sadly*)   Girls like me who grow up in the country have all the doors closed to them. Everything becomes half-words, gestures, because all these things, they say, must not be talked about. And you, too; you, too, stop talking and go off with the air of a doctor—knowing everything, but keeping it from one who dies of thirst.

FIRST OLD WOMAN   To any other calm woman, I could speak; not to you. I'm an old woman and I know what I'm saying.

YERMA   Then, God help me.

FIRST OLD WOMAN   Not God; I've never liked God. When will people realize he doesn't exist? Men are the ones who'll have to help you.

YERMA   But, why do you tell me that? Why?

FIRST OLD WOMAN   (*leaving*)   Though there should be a God, even a tiny one, to send his lightning against those men of rotted seed who make puddles out of the happiness of the fields.

YERMA   I don't know what you're trying to tell me.

FIRST OLD WOMAN   Well, I know what I'm trying to say. Don't you be unhappy. Hope for the best. You're still very young. What do you want me to do?

(*She leaves. Two* GIRLS *appear*)

FIRST GIRL   Everywhere we go we meet people.

YERMA   With all the work, the men have to be in the olive groves, and we must take them their food. No one's left at home but the old people.

SECOND GIRL   Are you on your way back to the village?

YERMA   I'm going that way.

FIRST GIRL   I'm in a great hurry. I left my baby asleep and there's no one in the house.

YERMA   Then hurry up, woman. You can't leave babies alone like that. Are there any pigs at your place?

FIRST GIRL   No. But you're right. I'm going right away.

YERMA   Go on. That's how things happen. Surely you've locked him in?

FIRST GIRL   Naturally.

YERMA   Yes, but even so, we don't realize what a tiny child is. The thing that seems most harmless to us might finish him off. A little needle. A swallow of water.

FIRST GIRL   You're right. I'm on my way. I just don't think of those things.

YERMA   Get along now!

SECOND GIRL   If you had four or five, you wouldn't talk like that.

YERMA   Why not? Even if I had forty.

SECOND GIRL   Anyway, you and I, not having any, live more peacefully.

YERMA   Not I.

SECOND GIRL   I do. What a bother! My mother, on the other hand, does nothing but give me herbs so I'll have them, and in October we're going to the saint who, they say, gives them to women who ask for them eagerly. My mother will ask for them, not I.

YERMA   Then, why did you marry?

SECOND GIRL   Because they married me off. They get everyone married. If we keep on like this, the only unmarried ones will be the little girls. Well, anyway, you really get married long before you go to the church. But the old women keep worrying about all these things. I'm nineteen and I don't like to cook or do washing. Well, now I have to spend the whole day doing what I don't like to do. And all for what? We did the same things as sweethearts that we do now. It's all just the old folks' silly ideas.

YERMA   Be quiet; don't talk that way.

SECOND GIRL   You'll be calling me crazy, too. That crazy girl—that crazy girl! (*She laughs*) I'll tell you the only thing I've learned from life: everybody's stuck inside their house doing what they don't like to do. How much better it is out in the streets. Sometimes I go to the arroyo, sometimes I climb up and ring the bells, or again I might just take a drink of anisette.

YERMA   You're only a child.

SECOND GIRL   Why, yes—but I'm not crazy. (*She laughs*)

YERMA   Doesn't your mother live at the topmost door in the village?

SECOND GIRL   Yes.

YERMA   In the last house?

SECOND GIRL   Yes.

YERMA   What's her name?

SECOND GIRL   Dolores. Why do you ask?

YERMA   Oh, nothing.

SECOND GIRL   You wouldn't be asking because of . . . ?

YERMA   I don't know . . . people say . . .

SECOND GIRL   Well, that's up to you. Look, I'm going to take my husband his food. (*She laughs*) That's something to see! Too bad I can't say my sweetheart, isn't it? (*She laughs*)

Here comes that crazy girl! (*She leaves, laughing happily*) Good-bye!

VICTOR'S VOICE (*singing*)
Why, shepherd, sleep alone?
Why, shepherd, sleep alone?
On my wool-quilt deep
you'd finer sleep.
Why, shepherd, sleep alone?

YERMA (*listening*)
Why, shepherd, sleep alone?
On my wool-quilt deep
you'd finer sleep.
Your quilt of shadowed stone,
   shepherd,
and your shirt of frost,
   shepherd,
gray rushes of the winter
on the night-tide of your bed.
The oak-roots weave their needles,
   shepherd,
Beneath your pillow silently,
   shepherd,
and if you hear a woman's voice
it's the torn voice of the stream.
Shepherd, shepherd.
What does the hillside want of you,
   Shepherd?
Hillside of bitter weeds.
What child is killing you?
The thorn the broom-tree bore!

(*She starts to leave and meets* VICTOR *as he enters*)

VICTOR (*happily*)   Where is all this beauty going?

YERMA   Was that you singing?

VICTOR   Yes.

YERMA   How well you sing! I'd never heard you.

VICTOR   No?

YERMA   And what a vibrant voice! It's like a stream of water that fills your mouth.

VICTOR   I'm always happy.

YERMA   That's true.

VICTOR   Just as you're sad.

YERMA   I'm not usually sad, but I have reason to be.

VICTOR   And your husband's sadder than you.

YERMA   He is, yes. It's his character—dry.

VICTOR   He was always like that. (*pause.* YERMA *is seated*) Did you take his supper to him?

YERMA   Yes. (*She looks at him. Pause*) What have you here? (*She points to his face*)

VICTOR   Where?

YERMA (*she rises and stands near* VICTOR)
Here . . . on your cheek. Like a burn.

VICTOR   It's nothing.

YERMA   It looked like one to me.

(*Pause*)

VICTOR   It must be the sun . . .

YERMA   Perhaps . . .

(*Pause. The silence is accentuated and without the slightest gesture, a struggle between the two begins*)

YERMA (*trembling*)   Do you hear that?

VICTOR   What?

YERMA   Don't you hear a crying?

VICTOR (*listening*)   No.

YERMA   I thought I heard a child crying.

VICTOR   Yes?

YERMA   Very near. And he cried as though drowning.

VICTOR   There are always a lot of children around here who come to steal fruit.

YERMA   No, it's the voice of a small child.

(*Pause*)

VICTOR   I don't hear anything.

YERMA   I probably just imagined it.

(*She looks at him fixedly.* VICTOR *also looks at her, then slowly shifts his gaze as if afraid.* JUAN *enters*)

JUAN   Still here? What are you doing here?

YERMA   I was talking.

VICTOR   Salud! (*He leaves*)

JUAN   You should be at home.

YERMA   I was delayed.

JUAN   I don't see what kept you.

YERMA   I heard the birds sing.

JUAN   That's all very well. But this is just the way to give people something to talk about.

YERMA (*strongly*)   Juan, what can you be thinking?

JUAN   I don't say it because of you. I say it because of other people.

YERMA   Other people be damned!

JUAN   Don't curse. That's ugly in a woman.

YERMA   I wish I were a woman.

JUAN   Let's stop talking. You go home.

(*Pause*)

YERMA   All right. Shall I expect you?

JUAN   No. I'll be busy all night with the irrigating. There's very little water; it's mine till sun-up, and I've got to guard it from thieves. You go to bed and sleep.

YERMA (*dramatically*)   I'll sleep. (*She leaves*)

ACT TWO

Scene One

(*A fast flowing mountain stream where the village women wash their clothes. The laundresses are arranged at various levels.*
Song before the curtain rises)

SONG

Here in this icy current
let me wash your lace,
just like a glowing jasmine.
is your laughing face.

FIRST LAUNDRESS   I don't like to be talking.

SECOND LAUNDRESS   Well, we talk here.

FOURTH LAUNDRESS   And there's no harm in it.

FIFTH LAUNDRESS   Whoever wants a good name, let her earn it.

FOURTH LAUNDRESS

I planted thyme,
I watched it grow.
Who wants a good name
Must live just so.

(*They laugh*)

FIFTH LAUNDRESS   That's the way we talk.

FIRST LAUNDRESS   But we never really know anything for certain.

FOURTH LAUNDRESS   Well, it's certain enough that her husband's brought his two sisters to live with them.

FIFTH LAUNDRESS   The old maids?

FOURTH LAUNDRESS   Yes. They used to watch the church, and now they watch their sister-in-law. I wouldn't be able to live with them.

FIRST LAUNDRESS   Why not?

FOURTH LAUNDRESS   They'd give me the creeps. They're like those big leaves that quickly spring up over graves. They're smeared with wax. They grow inwards. I figure they must fry their food with lamp oil.

THIRD LAUNDRESS   And they're in the house now?

FOURTH LAUNDRESS   Since yesterday. Her husband's going back to his fields again now.

FIRST LAUNDRESS   But can't anyone find out what happened?

FIFTH LAUNDRESS   She spent the night before last sitting on her doorstep—in spite of the cold.

FIRST LAUNDRESS   But why?

FOURTH LAUNDRESS   It's hard work for her to stay in the house.

FIFTH LAUNDRESS That's the way those mannish creatures are. When they could be making lace, or apple cakes, they like to climb up on the roof, or go wade barefoot in the river.

FIRST LAUNDRESS Who are you to be talking like that? She hasn't any children but that's not her fault.

FOURTH LAUNDRESS The one who wants children, has them. These spoiled, lazy and soft girls aren't up to having a wrinkled belly.

(*They laugh*)

THIRD LAUNDRESS And they dash face powder and rouge on themselves, and pin on sprigs of oleander, and go looking for some man who's not their husband.

FIFTH LAUNDRESS Nothing could be truer!

FIRST LAUNDRESS But have you seen her with anybody?

FOURTH LAUNDRESS We haven't, but other people have.

FIRST LAUNDRESS Always other people!

FIFTH LAUNDRESS On two separate occasions, they say.

SECOND LAUNDRESS And what were they doing?

FOURTH LAUNDRESS Talking.

FIRST LAUNDRESS Talking's no sin.

FOURTH LAUNDRESS In this world just a glance can be something. My mother always said that. A woman looking at roses isn't the same thing as a woman looking at a man's thighs. And she looks at him.

FIRST LAUNDRESS But at whom?

FOURTH LAUNDRESS Someone. Haven't you heard? You find out for yourself. Do you want me to say it louder? (*laughter*) And when she's not looking at him—when she's alone, when he's not right in front of her—she carries his picture—in her eyes.

FIRST LAUNDRESS That's a lie!

(*There is excitement*)

FIFTH LAUNDRESS But what about her husband?

THIRD LAUNDRESS Her husband acts like a deaf man. Just stands around blankly—like a lizard taking the sun. (*laughter*)

FIRST LAUNDRESS All this would take care of itself if they had children.

SECOND LAUNDRESS All this comes of people not being content with their lot.

FOURTH LAUNDRESS Every passing hour makes the hell in that house worse. She and her sisters-in-law, never opening their lips, scrub the walls all day, polish the copper, clean the windows with steam, and oil the floors: but the more that house shines, the more it seethes inside.

FIRST LAUNDRESS It's all his fault; his. When a man doesn't give children, he's got to take care of his wife.

FOURTH LAUNDRESS It's her fault—because she's got a tongue hard as flint.

FIRST LAUNDRESS What devil's got into your hair that makes you talk that way?

FOURTH LAUNDRESS Well! Who gave your tongue permission to give me advice?

SECOND LAUNDRESS Quiet, you two!

FIRST LAUNDRESS I'd like to string all these clacking tongues on a knitting needle.

SECOND LAUNDRESS Quiet, you!

FOURTH LAUNDRESS And I the nipples of all hypocrites.

SECOND LAUNDRESS Hush up! Can't you see? Here come the sisters-in-law.

(*There is whispering. *YERMA's* two sisters-in-law enter. They are dressed in mourning. In the silence, they start their washing. Sheep bells are heard*)

FIRST LAUNDRESS Are the shepherds leaving already?

THIRD LAUNDRESS Yes, all the flocks leave today.

FOURTH LAUNDRESS (*taking a deep breath*) I like the smell of sheep.

THIRD LAUNDRESS You do?

FOURTH LAUNDRESS Yes. And why not? The smell of what's ours. Just as I like the smell of the red mud this river carries in the winter.

THIRD LAUNDRESS Whims!

FIFTH LAUNDRESS (*looking*) All the flocks are leaving together.

FOURTH LAUNDRESS It's a flood of wool. They sweep everything along. If the green wheat had eyes it'd tremble to see them coming.

THIRD LAUNDRESS Look how they run! What a band of devils!

FIRST LAUNDRESS They're all out now, not a flock is missing.

FOURTH LAUNDRESS Let's see. No . . . Yes, yes. One is missing.

FIFTH LAUNDRESS Which one?

FOURTH LAUNDRESS Victor's.

(*The two *SISTERS-IN-LAW* sit up and look at each other*)

FOURTH LAUNDRESS (*singing*)
Here in this icy current
let me wash your lace.
Just like a glowing jasmine
is your laughing face.
I would like to live
within the tiny snowstorm
that the jasmines give.

FIRST LAUNDRESS
Alas for the barren wife!
Alas for her whose breasts are sand!

FIFTH LAUNDRESS
Tell me if your husband
has fertile seed
so water through your clothes
will sing indeed.

FOURTH LAUNDRESS
Your petticoat to me
is silvery boat and breeze
that sweep along the sea.

FIRST LAUNDRESS
These clothes that are my baby's
I wash here in the stream
to teach the stream a lesson
how crystal-like to gleam.

SECOND LAUNDRESS
Down the hillside he comes
at lunchtime to me,
my husband with one rose
and I give him three.

FIFTH LAUNDRESS
Through meadows at dusk comes
my husband to eat.
To live coals he brings me
I give myrtle sweet.

FOURTH LAUNDRESS
Through night skies he comes,
my husband, to bed.
I, like red gillyflowers,
he, a gillyflower red.

FIRST LAUNDRESS
And flower to flower must be wed
when summer dries the reaper's
blood so red.

FOURTH LAUNDRESS
And wombs be opened to birds without sleep
when winter tries the door and cold's
to keep.

FIRST LAUNDRESS
The bedclothes must receive our
tears.

FOURTH LAUNDRESS
But we must sing in bed!

FIFTH LAUNDRESS
When the husband comes
to bring the wreath and bread.

FOURTH LAUNDRESS
Because our arms must intertwine.

SECOND LAUNDRESS
Because in our throats the light is
rent.

FOURTH LAUNDRESS
Because the leaf-stem becomes fine.

FIRST LAUNDRESS
And the hill is covered with a breeze's
tent.

SIXTH LAUNDRESS (*appearing at the topmost
part of the swiftly flowing stream*)
So that a child may weld
white crystals in the dawn.

FIRST LAUNDRESS
And in our waist be held
torn stems of coral tree.

SIXTH LAUNDRESS
So that oarsmen there will be
in the waters of the sea.

FIRST LAUNDRESS
A tiny child, one.

SECOND LAUNDRESS
And when the doves stretch wing
and beak

THIRD LAUNDRESS
an infant weeps, a son.

FOURTH LAUNDRESS
And men push ever forward
like stags by wounds made weak.

FIFTH LAUNDRESS
Joy, joy, joy!
of the swollen womb beneath the
dress!

SECOND LAUNDRESS
Joy, joy, joy!
The waist can miracles possess!

FIRST LAUNDRESS
But, alas for the barren wife!
Alas for her whose breasts are sand!

THIRD LAUNDRESS
Let her shine out resplendent!

FOURTH LAUNDRESS
Let her run!

FIFTH LAUNDRESS
And shine out resplendent again!

FIRST LAUNDRESS
Let her sing!

SECOND LAUNDRESS
Let her hide!

FIRST LAUNDRESS
And sing once more.

SECOND LAUNDRESS
Of whiteness like the dawn's
my baby's clean clothes store.

FIRST AND SECOND LAUNDRESS (*they sing together*)
Here in this icy current
let me wash your lace.
Just like a glowing jasmine
is your laughing face.
Ha! Ha! Ha!

(*They move the clothes in rhythm and beat
them*)

Scene Two

(YERMA's *house. It is twilight.* JUAN *is seated.
The two* SISTERS-IN-LAW *are standing*)

JUAN   You say she went out a little while ago? (*The* OLDER SISTER *answers with a nod*) She's probably at the fountain. But you've known all along I don't like her to go out alone. (*pause*) You can set the table. (*The* YOUNGER SISTER *enters*) The bread I eat is hard enough earned! (*to his* SISTER) I had a hard day yesterday. I was pruning the apple trees, and when evening fell I started to wonder why I should put so much into my work if I can't even lift an apple to my mouth. I'm tired. (*He passes his hand over his face. Pause*) That woman's still not here. One of you should go out with her. That's why you're here eating at my table and drinking my wine. My life's in the fields, but my honor's here. And my honor is yours too. (*The* SISTER *bows her head*) Don't take that wrong. (YERMA *enters carrying two pitchers. She stands at the door*) Have you been to the fountain?

YERMA   So we'd have fresh water for supper. (*The other* SISTER *enters*) How are the fields?

JUAN   Yesterday I pruned trees.

(YERMA *sets the pitchers down. Pause*)

YERMA   Are you going to stay in?

JUAN   I have to watch the flocks. You know that's an owner's duty.

YERMA   I know it very well. Don't repeat it.

JUAN   Each man has his life to lead.

YERMA   And each woman hers. I'm not asking you to stay. I have everything I need here. Your sisters guard me well. Soft bread and cheese and roast lamb I eat here, and in the field your cattle eat grass softened with dew. I think you can live in peace.

JUAN   In order to live in peace, one must be contented.

YERMA   And you're not?

JUAN   No, I'm not.

YERMA   Don't say what you started to.

JUAN   Don't you know my way of thinking? The sheep in the fold and women at home. You go out too much. Haven't you always heard me say that?

YERMA   Justly. Women in their homes. When those homes aren't tombs. When the chairs break and the linen sheets wear out with use. But not here. Each night, when I go to bed, I find my bed newer, more shining— as if it had just been brought from the city.

JUAN   You yourself realize that I've a right to complain. That I have reasons to be on the alert!

YERMA   Alert? For what? I don't offend you in any way. I live obedient to you, and what I suffer I keep close in my flesh. And every day that passes will be worse. Let's be quiet now. I'll learn to bear my cross as best I can, but don't ask me for anything. If I could suddenly turn into an old woman and have a mouth like a withered flower, I could smile and share my life with you. But now—now you leave me alone with my thorns.

JUAN   You speak in a way I don't understand. I don't deprive you of anything. I send to nearby towns for the things you like. I have my faults, but I want peace and quiet with you. I want to be sleeping out in the fields— thinking that you're sleeping too.

YERMA   But don't sleep. I can't sleep.

JUAN   Is it because you need something? Tell me. Answer me!

YERMA   (*deliberately, looking fixedly at her husband*)   Yes, I need something.

(*Pause*)

JUAN   Always the same thing. It's more than five years. I've almost forgotten about it.

YERMA   But I'm not you. Men get other things out of life: their cattle, trees, conversations, but women have only their children and the care of their children.

JUAN   Everybody's not the same way. Why don't you bring one of your brother's children here? I don't oppose that.

YERMA   I don't want to take care of somebody else's children. I think my arms would freeze from holding them.

JUAN   You brood on this one idea till you're half crazy—instead of thinking about something else—and you persist in running your head against a stone.

YERMA   A stone, yes; and it's shameful that it is a stone, because it ought to be a basket of flowers and sweet scents.

JUAN   At your side one feels nothing but uneasiness, dissatisfaction. As a last resort, you should resign yourself.

YERMA   I didn't come to these four walls to resign myself. When a cloth binds my head so my mouth won't drop open, and my hands are tied tight in my coffin—then, then I'll resign myself!

JUAN   Well then, what do you want to do?

YERMA   I want to drink water and there's neither water nor a glass. I want to go up the mountain, and I have no feet. I want to embroider skirts and I can't find thread.

JUAN   What's happened is that you're not a real woman, and you're trying to ruin a man who has no choice in the matter.

YERMA   I don't know what I am. Let me walk around; get myself in hand again. I have in no way failed you.

JUAN   I don't like people to be pointing

me out. That's why I want to see this door closed and each person in his house.

(*The* FIRST SISTER *enters slowly and walks toward some shelves*)

YERMA It's no sin to talk with people.

JUAN But it can seem one.

(*The other* SISTER *enters and goes toward the water jars, from one of which she fills a pitcher*)

JUAN (*lowering his voice*) I'm not strong enough for this sort of thing. When people talk to you, shut your mouth and remember you're a married woman.

YERMA (*with surprise*) Married!

JUAN And that families have honor. And that honor is a burden that rests on all. (*The* SISTER *leaves slowly with the pitcher*) But that it's both dark and weak in the same channels of the blood. (*The other* SISTER *leaves with a platter in almost a processional manner. Pause*) Forgive me. (YERMA *looks at her husband. He raises his head and his glance catches hers*) Even though you look at me so that I oughn't to say to you: "Forgive me," but force you to obey me, lock you up, because that's what I'm the husband for.

(*The* TWO SISTERS *appear at the door*)

YERMA I beg you not to talk about it. Let the matter rest.

JUAN Let's go eat. (*The* TWO SISTERS *leave*) Did you hear me?

YERMA (*sweetly*) You eat with your sisters. I'm not hungry yet.

JUAN As you wish.

(*He leaves*)

YERMA (*as though dreaming*)
Oh, what a field of sorrow!
Oh, this is a door to beauty closed:
to beg a son to suffer, and for the wind
to offer dahlias of a sleeping moon!
These two teeming springs I have
of warm milk are in the closeness
of my flesh two rhythms of a horse's gallop,
to make vibrate the branch of my anguish.
Oh, breasts, blind beneath my clothes!
Oh, doves with neither eyes nor whiteness!
Oh, what pain of imprisoned blood
is nailing wasps at my brain's base!
But you must come, sweet love, my baby,

because water gives salt, the earth fruit,
and our wombs guard tender infants,
just as a cloud is sweet with rain.

(*She looks toward the door*) María! Why do you hurry past my door so?

MARIA (*She enters with a child in her arms*) I hurry by whenever I have the child—since you always weep!

YERMA Yes, you're right.

(*She takes the child and sits down*)

MARIA It makes me sad that you're envious.

YERMA It's not envy I feel—it's poverty.

MARIA Don't you complain.

YERMA How can I help complaining when I see you and the other women full of flowers from within, and then see myself useless in the midst of so much beauty!

MARIA But you have other things. If you'd listen to me you'd be happy.

YERMA A farm woman who bears no children is useless—like a handful of thorns—and even bad—even though I may be a part of this wasteland abandoned by the hand of God. (MARIA *makes a gesture as if to take the child*) Take him. He's happier with you. I guess I don't have a mother's hands.

MARIA Why do you say that?

YERMA (*she rises*) Because I'm tired. Because I'm tired of having them, and not being able to use them on something of my own. For I'm hurt, hurt and humiliated beyond endurance, seeing the wheat ripening, the fountains never ceasing to give water, the sheep bearing hundreds of lambs, the she-dogs; until it seems that the whole countryside rises to show me its tender sleeping young, while I feel two hammer-blows here, instead of the mouth of my child.

MARIA I don't like you to talk that way.

YERMA You women who have children can't think about us who don't! You stay always fresh, with no idea of it, just as anyone swimming in fresh water has no idea of thirst.

MARIA I don't want to tell you again what I've always said.

YERMA Each time I have more desire and less hope.

MARIA That's very bad.

YERMA I'll end up believing I'm my own son. Many nights I go down to feed the oxen —which I never did before, because no woman does it—and when I pass through the darkness of the shed my footsteps sound to me like the footsteps of a man.

MARIA   Each one of us reasons things out for herself.

YERMA   And in spite of all, I go on hoping in myself. You see how I live!

MARIA   How are your sisters-in-law?

YERMA   Dead may I be, and without a shroud, if ever I speak a word to them.

MARIA   And your husband?

YERMA   They are three against me.

MARIA   What do they think about it?

YERMA   The wildest imaginings; like all people who don't have clear consciences. They think I like another man. They don't know that even if I should like another man, to those of my kind, honor comes first. They're stones in my path, but they don't know that I can be, if I want to, an arroyo's rushing water and sweep them away.

(*One* SISTER *enters and leaves carrying a piece of bread*)

MARIA   Even so, I think your husband still loves you.

YERMA   My husband gives me bread and a house.

MARIA   What troubles you have to go through! What troubles! But remember the wounds of Our Lord.

(*They are at the door*)

YERMA   (*looking at the child*)   He's awake now.

MARIA   In a little while he'll start to sing.

YERMA   The same eyes as yours. Did you know that? Have you noticed them? (*weeping*) His eyes are the same as yours!

(YERMA *pushes* MARIA *gently and she leaves silently.* YERMA *walks toward the door through which her husband left*)

SECOND GIRL   Sst!

YERMA   (*turning*)   What?

SECOND GIRL   I waited till she left. My mother's expecting you.

YERMA   Is she alone?

SECOND GIRL   With two neighbors.

YERMA   Tell them to wait a little.

SECOND GIRL   But, are you really going to go? Aren't you afraid?

YERMA   I'm going to go.

SECOND GIRL   That's up to you!

YERMA   Tell them to wait for me even if it's late!

(VICTOR *enters*)

VICTOR   Is Juan here?

YERMA   Yes.

SECOND GIRL   (*acting the accomplice*)   Well then, I'll bring the blouse later.

YERMA   Whenever you like. (*the* GIRL *leaves*) Sit down.

VICTOR   I'm all right like this.

YERMA   (*calling*)   Juan!

VICTOR   I've come to say good-bye.

(*He trembles a little, but his composure returns*)

YERMA   Are you going with your brothers?

VICTOR   That's what my father wants.

YERMA   He must be old now.

VICTOR   Yes. Very old.

(*Pause*)

YERMA   You're right to change fields.

VICTOR   All fields are alike.

YERMA   No. I'd like to go very far away.

VICTOR   It's all the same. The same sheep have the same wool.

YERMA   For men, yes; but it's a different thing with women. I never heard a man eating say, "How good these apples are!" You go to what's yours without bothering over trifles. But for myself, I can say I've grown to hate the water from these wells.

VICTOR   That may be.

(*The stage is in a soft shadow*)

YERMA   Victor.

VICTOR   Yes?

YERMA   Why are you going away? The people here like you.

VICTOR   I've behaved myself.

(*Pause*)

YERMA   You always behave yourself. When you were a boy, you carried me once in your arms, do you remember that? One never knows what's going to happen.

VICTOR   Everything changes.

YERMA   Some things never change. There are things shut up behind walls that can't change because nobody hears them.

VICTOR   That's how things are.

(*The* SECOND SISTER *appears and goes slowly toward the door, where she remains fixed, illuminated by the last light of evening*)

YERMA   But if they came out suddenly and shrieked, they'd fill the world.

VICTOR   Nothing would be gained. The ditch in its place, the sheep in fold, the moon in the sky, and the man with his plow.

YERMA   The great pity is we don't profit from the experience of our elders!

(*The long and melancholy sound of the shepherds' conchshell horns is heard*)

VICTOR   The flocks.

JUAN   (*enters*)   Are you on your way?

VICTOR   Yes. I want to get through the pass before daybreak.

JUAN   Have you any complaints to make against me?

VICTOR   No. You paid me a good price.

JUAN (*to* YERMA)   I bought his sheep.

YERMA   You did?

VICTOR (*to* YERMA)   They're yours.

YERMA   I didn't know that.

JUAN (*satisfied*)   Well, it's so.

VICTOR   Your husband will see his lands overflowing.

YERMA   The harvest comes to the worker who seeks it.

(*The* SISTER *who was at the door leaves and goes into another room*)

JUAN   Now we haven't any place to put so many sheep.

YERMA (*darkly*)   The earth is large. (*pauses*)

JUAN   We'll go together as far as the arroyo.

VICTOR   I wish this house the greatest possible happiness.

(*He gives* YERMA *his hand*)

YERMA   May God hear you! Salud!

(VICTOR *is about to leave, but, at an imperceptible movement from* YERMA, *he turns*)

VICTOR   Did you say something?

YERMA   Salud, I said.

VICTOR   Thank you.

(*They leave.* YERMA *stands, anguished, looking at her hand that she gave to* VICTOR. *She goes quickly to the left and takes up a shawl*)

SECOND GIRL (*silently, covering her hand*) Come, let's go.

YERMA   Come.

(*They leave cautiously. The stage is almost in darkness. The* FIRST SISTER *enters with a lamp that must not give the stage any light other than its own. She goes to one side of the stage looking for* YERMA. *The shepherds' conchshell horns sound*)

SISTER-IN-LAW (*in a low voice*)   YERMA!

(*The other* SISTER *enters. They look at each other and go toward the door*)

SECOND SISTER-IN-LAW (*louder*)   YERMA!

FIRST SISTER-IN-LAW (*going to the door, and in an imperious voice*)   YERMA!

(*The bells and horns of the shepherds are heard. The stage is quite dark*)

ACT THREE

Scene One

(*The house of Dolores, the sorceress. Day is breaking. Enter* YERMA *with* DOLORES *and two* OLD WOMEN)

DOLORES   You've been brave.

FIRST OLD WOMAN   There's no force in the world like desire.

SECOND OLD WOMAN   But the cemetery was terribly dark.

DOLORES   Many times I've said these prayers in the cemetery with women who wanted to have a child, and they've all been afraid. All except you.

YERMA   I came because I want a child. I don't believe you're a deceitful woman.

DOLORES   I'm not. May my mouth fill with ants, like the mouths of the dead, if ever I've lied. The last time, I said the prayers with a beggar woman who'd been dry longer than you, and her womb sweetened so beautifully that she had two children down there at the river because there wasn't time to get to the village—and she carried them herself in a diaper for me to take care of.

YERMA   And she was able to walk from the river?

DOLORES   She came; her skirts and shoes drenched with blood—but her face shining.

YERMA   And nothing happened to her?

DOLORES   What could happen to her? God is God.

YERMA   Naturally, God is God. Nothing could happen to her. Just pick up her babies and wash them in fresh water. Animals lick them, don't they? I know a son of my own wouldn't make me sick. I have an idea that women who've recently given birth are as though illumined from within and the children sleep hours and hours on them, hearing that stream of warm milk filling the breasts for them to suckle, for them to play in until they don't want any more, until they lift their heads, "just a little more, child . . ."—and their faces and chests are covered with the white drops.

DOLORES   You'll have a child now. I can assure you, you will.

YERMA   I'll have one because I must. Or I don't understand the world. Sometimes, when I feel certain I'll never, ever . . . a tide of fire sweeps up through me from my feet and everything seems empty; and the men walking in the streets, the cattle, and the stones, all seem to be made of cotton. And I ask myself: "Why are they put here?"

FIRST OLD WOMAN It's all right for a married woman to want children, of course, but if she doesn't have them, why this hungering for them? The important thing in life is to let the years carry us along. I'm not criticizing you. You see how I've helped at the prayers. But what land do you expect to give your son, or what happiness, or what silver chair?

YERMA I'm not thinking about tomorrow; I'm thinking about today. You're old and you see things now like a book already read. I'm thinking how thirsty I am, and how I don't have any freedom. I want to hold my son in my arms so I'll sleep peacefully. Listen closely, don't be frightened by what I say: even if I knew my son was later going to torture me and hate me and drag me through the streets by the hair, I'd still be happy at his birth, because it's much better to weep for a live man who stabs us than for this ghost sitting year after year upon my heart.

FIRST OLD WOMAN You're much too young to listen to advice. But while you wait for God's grace, you ought to take refuge in your husband's love.

YERMA Ah! You've put your finger in the deepest wound in my flesh!

DOLORES Your husband's a good man.

YERMA (*She rises*) He's good! He's good! But what of it? I wish he were bad. But, no. He goes out with his sheep over his trails, and counts his money at night. When he covers me, he's doing his duty, but I feel a waist cold as a corpse's, and I, who've always hated passionate women, would like to be at that instant a mountain of fire.

DOLORES Yerma!

YERMA I'm not a shameless married woman, but I know that children are born of a man and a woman. Oh, if only I could have them by myself!

DOLORES Remember, your husband suffers, too.

YERMA He doesn't suffer. The trouble is, he doesn't want children!

FIRST OLD WOMAN Don't say that!

YERMA I can tell that in his glance, and, since he doesn't want them, he doesn't give them to me. I don't love him; I don't love him, and yet he's my only salvation. By honor and by blood. My only salvation.

FIRST OLD WOMAN (*with fear*) Day will soon be breaking. You ought to go home.

DOLORES Before you know it, the flocks will be out, and it wouldn't do for you to be seen alone.

YERMA I needed this relief. How many times do I repeat the prayers?

DOLORES The laurel prayer, twice; and at noon, St. Anne's prayer. When you feel pregnant, bring me the bushel of wheat you promised me.

FIRST OLD WOMAN It's starting to lighten over the hills already. Go.

DOLORES They'll soon start opening the big street doors; you'd best go around by the ditch.

YERMA (*discouraged*) I don't know why I came!

DOLORES Are you sorry?

YERMA No!

DOLORES (*disturbed*) If you're afraid, I'll go with you to the corner.

FIRST OLD WOMAN (*uneasily*) It'll just be daylight when you reach home.

(*Voices are heard*)

DOLORES Quiet!

(*They listen*)

FIRST OLD WOMAN It's nobody. God go with you.

(YERMA *starts toward the door, but at this moment a knock is heard. The three women are standing*)

DOLORES Who is it?

VOICE It's me.

YERMA Open the door. (DOLORES *is reluctant*) Will you open or not?

(*Whispering is heard.* JUAN *enters with the* TWO SISTERS)

SECOND SISTER-IN-LAW Here she is.

YERMA Here I am.

JUAN What are you doing in this place? If I could shout I'd wake up the whole village so they'd see where the good name of my house has gone to; but I have to swallow everything and keep quiet—because you're my wife.

YERMA I too would shout, if I could, so that even the dead would rise and see the innocence that covers me.

JUAN No, don't tell me that! I can stand everything but that. You deceive me; you trick me, and since I'm a man who works in the fields, I'm no match for your cleverness.

DOLORES Juan!

JUAN You, not a word out of you!

DOLORES (*strongly*) Your wife has done nothing wrong.

JUAN She's been doing it from the very day of the wedding. Looking at me with two needles, passing wakeful nights with her eyes open at my side, and filling my pillows with evil sighs.

YERMA   Be quiet!

JUAN   And I can't stand any more. Because one would have to be made of iron to put up with a woman who wants to stick her fingers in your heart and who goes out of her house at night. In search of what? Tell me! There aren't any flowers to pick in the streets.

YERMA   I won't let you say another word. Not one word more. You and your people imagine you're the only ones who look out for honor, and you don't realize my people have never had anything to conceal. Come on now. Come near and smell my clothes. Come close! See if you can find an odor that's not yours, that's not from your body. Stand me naked in the middle of the square and spit on me. Do what you want with me, since I'm your wife, but take care not to set a man's name in my breast.

JUAN   I'm not the one who sets it there. You do it by your conduct, and the town's beginning to say so. It's beginning to say it openly. When I come on a group, they all fall silent; when I go to weigh the flour, they all fall silent, and even at night, in the fields, when I awaken, it seems to me that the branches of the trees become silent too.

YERMA   I don't know why the evil winds that soil the wheat begin—but look you and see if the wheat is good!

JUAN   Nor do I know what a woman is looking for outside her house at all hours.

YERMA   (bursting out, embracing her husband)   I'm looking for you. I'm looking for you. It's you I look for day and night without finding a shade where to draw breath. It's your blood and help I want.

JUAN   Stay away from me.

YERMA   Don't put me away—love me!

JUAN   Get away!

YERMA   Look how I'm left alone! As if the moon searched for herself in the sky. Look at me!

(She looks at him)

JUAN   (He looks at her and draws away roughly)   Let me be—once and for all!

DOLORES   Juan!

(YERMA falls to the floor)

YERMA   (loudly)   When I went out looking for my flowers, I ran into a wall. Ay-y-y! Ay-y-y! It's against that wall I'll break my head.

JUAN   Be quiet. Let's go.

DOLORES   Good God!

YERMA   (shouting)   Cursed be my father who left me his blood of a father of a hundred sons. Cursed be my blood that searches for them, knocking against walls.

JUAN   I told you to be quiet!

DOLORES   People are coming! Speak lower.

YERMA   I don't care. At least let my voice go free, now that I'm entering the darkest part of the pit. (She rises) At least let this beautiful thing come out of my body and fill the air.

(Voices are heard)

DOLORES   They're going to pass by here.

JUAN   Silence.

YERMA   That's it! That's it! Silence. Never fear.

JUAN   Let's go. Quick!

YERMA   That's it! That's it! And it's no use for me to wring my hands! It's one thing to wish with one's head . . .

JUAN   Be still!

YERMA   (low)   It's one thing to wish with one's head and another for the body—cursed be the body—not to respond. It's written, and I'm not going to raise my arms against the sea. That's it! Let my mouth be struck dumb!

(She leaves)

Scene Two

(Environs of a hermitage high in the mountains. Downstage are the wheels of a cart and some canvas forming the rustic tent where YERMA is. Some women enter carrying offerings from the shrine. They are barefoot. The happy OLD WOMAN of the first act is on the stage)

SONG (heard while the curtain is still closed)

> You I never could see
> when you were fancy free,
> but now that you're a wife
> I'll find you, yes,
> and take off your dress,
> you, pilgrim and a wife
> when night is dark all 'round,
> when midnight starts to sound.

OLD WOMAN   (lazily)   Have you already drunk the holy water?

FIRST WOMAN   Yes.

OLD WOMAN   Now let's see this saint work.

FIRST WOMAN   We believe in him.

OLD WOMAN   You come to ask the saint for children, and it just happens that every year more single men come on this pilgrimage too; what's going on here? (She laughs)

FIRST WOMAN   Why do you come here if you don't believe in him?

OLD WOMAN   To see what goes on. I'm just crazy to see what goes on. And to watch out

for my son. Last year two men killed themselves over a barren wife, and I want to be
on guard. And lastly, I come because I feel like
it.

FIRST WOMAN   May God forgive you!

(*She leaves*)

OLD WOMAN (*sarcastically*)   May He forgive you.

(*She leaves,* MARIA *enters with the* FIRST GIRL)

FIRST GIRL   Did she come?

MARIA   There's her cart. It was hard work
to make them come. She's been a month without getting up from her chair. I'm afraid of
her. She has some idea I don't understand,
but it's a bad idea.

FIRST GIRL   I came with my sister. She's
been coming here eight years in vain.

MARIA   The one who's meant to have children, has them.

FIRST GIRL   That's what I say.

(*Voices are heard*)

MARIA   I've never liked these pilgrimages.
Let's get down to the farms where there are
some people around.

FIRST GIRL   Last year, when it got dark,
some young men pinched my sister's breasts.

MARIA   For four leagues 'round nothing is
heard but these terrible stories.

FIRST GIRL   I saw more than forty barrels
of wine back of the hermitage.

MARIA   A river of single men comes down
these mountains.

(*They leave. Voices are heard.* YERMA *enters
with* SIX WOMEN *who are going to the chapel.
They are barefooted and carry decorated candles. Night begins to fall*)

MARIA
    Lord, make blossom the rose,
    leave not my rose in shadow.

SECOND WOMAN
    Upon her barren flesh
    make blossom the yellow rose.

MARIA
    And in your servants' wombs
    the dark flame of the earth.

CHORUS OF WOMEN
    Lord, make blossom the rose,
    leave not my rose in shadow.

(*They kneel*)

YERMA
    The sky must have such gardens
    with rose trees of its joy,
    between the rose and the rose,
    one rose of all the wonder.
    Bright flash of dawn appears,
    and an archangel guards,

his wings like storms outspread,
his eyes like agonies.
While sweet about its leaves
the streams of warm milk play,
play and wet the faces
of the tranquil stars.
Lord, make your rose tree bloom
upon my barren flesh.

(*They rise*)

SECOND WOMAN
    Lord, with your own hand soothe
    the thorns upon her cheek.

YERMA
    Hark to me, penitent
    in holy pilgrimage.
    Open your rose in my flesh
    though thousand thorns it have.

CHORUS OF WOMEN
    Lord, make blossom the rose,
    leave not my rose in shadow.

YERMA
    Upon my barren flesh
    one rose of all the wonder.

(*They leave.*

*Girls running with long garlands in their
hands appear from the left. On the right, three
others, looking backward. On the stage there
is something like a crescendo of voices and
harness bells, and bellringers' collars. Higher
up appear the* SEVEN GIRLS *who wave the garlands toward the left. The noise increases and
the two traditional Masks appear. One is* MALE
and the other FEMALE. *They carry large masks.
They are not in any fashion grotesque, but of
great beauty and with a feeling of pure earth.
The* FEMALE *shakes a collar of large bells. The
back of the stage fills with people who shout
and comment on the dance. It has grown quite
dark*)

CHILDREN   The devil and his wife! The
devil and his wife!

FEMALE
    In the wilderness stream
    the sad wife was bathing.
    About her body crept
    the little water snails.
    The sand upon the banks,
    and the little morning breeze
    made her laughter sparkle
    and her shoulders shiver.
    Ah, how naked stood
    the maiden in the stream!

BOY
    Ah, how the maiden wept!

FIRST MAN
    Oh, wife bereft of love
    in the wind and water!

SECOND MAN
Let her say for whom she longs!

FIRST MAN
Let her say for whom she waits!

SECOND MAN
Ah, with her withered womb
and her color shattered!

FEMALE
When night-tide falls I'll tell,
when night-tide glowing falls.
In the night-tide of the pilgrimage
I'll tear my ruffled skirt.

BOY
Then quickly night-tide fell.
Oh, how the night was falling!
See how dark becomes
the mountain waterfall.

(*Guitars begin to sound*)

MALE (*he rises and shakes the horn*)
Ah, how white
the sorrowing wife!
Ah, how she sighs beneath the
    branches!
Poppy and carnation you'll later be
when the male spreads out his cape.

(*He approaches*)

If you come to the pilgrimage
to pray your womb may flower
don't wear a mourning veil
but a gown of fine Dutch linen.
Walk alone along the walls
where fig trees thickest grow
and bear my earthly body
until the white dawn wails.
Ah, how she shines!
How she was shining,
ah, how the sad wife sways!

FEMALE
Ah, let love place on her
wreathes and coronets,
let darts of brightest gold
be fastened in her breast.

MALE
Seven times she wept
and nine she rose,
fifteen times they joined
jasmines with oranges.

THIRD MAN
Strike her now with the horn!

SECOND MAN
With both the rose and the dance!

FIRST MAN
Ah, how the wife is swaying!

MALE
In this pilgrimage
the man commands always.

Husbands are bulls.
The man commands always
and women are flowers,
for him who wins them.

BOY
Strike her now with the wind!

SECOND MAN
Strike her now with the branch!

MALE
Come and see the splendor
of the wife washed clean!

FIRST MAN
Like a reed she curves.

MEN
Let young girls draw away!

MALE
Let the dance burn.
And the shining body
of the immaculate wife.

(*They disappear dancing amidst smiles and
the sound of beating palms. They sing*)

The sky must have such gardens
with rose trees of its joy,
between the rose and the rose
one rose of all the wonder.

(TWO GIRLS *pass again, shouting. The* HAPPY
OLD WOMAN *enters*)

OLD WOMAN   Let's see if you'll let us sleep
now. But pretty soon it'll be something else.
(YERMA *enters*) You. (YERMA *is downcast and
does not speak*) Tell me, what did you come
here for?

YERMA   I don't know.

OLD WOMAN   Aren't you sure yet? Where's
your husband?

(YERMA *gives signs of fatigue and acts like
a person whose head is bursting with a fixed
idea*)

YERMA   He's there.

OLD WOMAN   What's he doing?

YERMA   Drinking. (*Pause. Putting her
hands to her forehead*) Ay-y-y!

OLD WOMAN   Ay-y, ay-y! Less "ay!" and
more spirit. I couldn't tell you anything before, but now I can.

YERMA   What can you tell me that I don't
know already?

OLD WOMAN   What can no longer be hushed
up. What shouts from all the rooftops. The
fault is your husband's. Do you hear? He can
cut off my hands if it isn't. Neither his father,
nor his grandfather, nor his great-grandfather
behaved like men of good blood. For them
to have a son heaven and earth had to meet—
because they're nothing but spit. But not your

people. You have brothers and cousins for a hundred miles around. Just see what a curse has fallen on your loveliness.

YERMA   A curse. A puddle of poison on the wheat heads.

OLD WOMAN   But you have feet to leave your house.

YERMA   To leave?

OLD WOMAN   When I saw you in the pilgrimage, my heart gave a start. Women come here to know new men. And the saint performs the miracle. My son's there behind the chapel waiting for me. My house needs a woman. Go with him and the three of us will live together. My son's made of blood. Like me. If you come to my house, there'll still be the odor of cradles. The ashes from your bedcovers will be bread and salt for your children. Come, don't you worry about what people will say. And as for your husband, in my house there are stout hearts and strong weapons to keep him from even crossing the street.

YERMA   Hush, hush! It's not that. I'd never do it. I can't just go out looking for someone. Do you imagine I could know another man? Where would that leave my honor? Water can't run uphill, nor does the full moon rise at noonday. On the road I've started, I'll stay. Did you really think I could submit to another man? That I could go asking for what's mine, like a slave? Look at me, so you'll know me and never speak to me again. I'm not looking for anyone.

OLD WOMAN   When one's thirsty, one's grateful for water.

YERMA   I'm like a dry field where a thousand pairs of oxen plow, and you offer me a little glass of well water. Mine is a sorrow already beyond the flesh.

OLD WOMAN (*strongly*)   Then stay that way —if you want to! Like the thistles in a dry field, pinched, barren!

YERMA (*strongly*)   Barren, yes, I know it! Barren! You don't have to throw it in my face. Nor come to amuse yourself, as youngsters do, in the suffering of a tiny animal. Ever since I married, I've been avoiding that word, and this is the first time I've heard it, the first time it's been said to my face. The first time I see it's the truth.

OLD WOMAN   You make me feel no pity. None. I'll find another woman for my boy.

(*She leaves. A great chorus is heard distantly, sung by the pilgrims.* YERMA *goes toward the cart, and from behind it her* HUSBAND *appears*)

YERMA   Were you there all the time?

JUAN   I was.

YERMA   Spying?

JUAN   Spying.

YERMA   And you heard?

JUAN   Yes.

YERMA   And so? Leave me and go to the singing.

(*She sits on the canvases*)

JUAN   It's time I spoke, too.

YERMA   Speak!

JUAN   And complained.

YERMA   About what?

JUAN   I have a bitterness in my throat.

YERMA   And I in my bones.

JUAN   This is the last time I'll put up with your continual lament for dark things, outside of life—for things in the air.

YERMA (*with dramatic surprise*)   Outside of life, you say? In the air, you say?

JUAN   For things that haven't happened and that neither you nor I can control.

YERMA (*violently*)   Go on! Go on!

JUAN   For things that don't matter to me. You hear that? That don't matter to me. Now I'm forced to tell you. What matters to me is what I can hold in my hands. What my eyes can see.

YERMA (*rising to her knees, desperately*) Yes, yes. That's what I wanted to hear from your lips . . . the truth isn't felt when it's inside us, but how great it is, how it shouts when it comes out and raises its arms! It doesn't matter to him! Now I've heard it!

JUAN (*coming near her*)   Tell yourself it had to happen like this. Listen to me. (*He embraces her to help her rise*) Many women would be glad to have your life. Without children life is sweeter. I am happy not having them. It's not your fault.

YERMA   Then what did you want with me?

JUAN   Yourself!

YERMA (*excitedly*)   True! You wanted a home, ease, and a woman. But nothing more. Is what I say true?

JUAN   It's true. Like everyone.

YERMA   And what about the rest? What about your son?

JUAN (*strongly*)   Didn't you hear me say I don't care? Don't ask me any more about it! Do I have to shout in your ear so you'll understand and perhaps live in peace now!

YERMA   And you never thought about it, even when you saw I wanted one?

JUAN   Never.

(*Both are on the ground*)

YERMA   And I'm not to hope for one?

JUAN   No.

YERMA   Nor you?

JUAN   Nor I. Resign yourself!

YERMA   Barren!

JUAN   And lie in peace. You and I—happily, peacefully. Embrace me!

(*He embraces her*)

YERMA   What are you looking for?

JUAN   You. In the moonlight you're beautiful.

YERMA   You want me as you sometimes want a pigeon to eat.

JUAN   Kiss me . . . like this.

YERMA   That I'll never do. Never.

(YERMA *gives a shriek and seizes her husband by the throat. He falls backward. She chokes him until he dies. The chorus of the pilgrimage begins*)

YERMA   Barren, barren, but sure. Now I really know it for sure. And alone. (*She rises. People begin to gather*)
Now I'll sleep without startling myself awake, anxious to see if I feel in my blood another new blood. My body dry forever! What do you want? Don't come near me, because I've killed my son. I myself have killed my son!

(*A group that remains in the background, gathers. The chorus of the pilgrimage is heard*)

Alfonso Sastre

1927-

DRAMA AND SOCIETY

I. TRAGEDY AS AN INSTRUMENT OF TORTURE

1. The Problem is Posed. It seems that tragedy is a kind of social sin. The average spectator considers the writer of tragedies, in the best cases, as a sort of sinister mar-joy worthy of criminal persecution, social ostracism and the most rigorous repression by the censors. It seems we are opposed to the voices of sorrow, death and catastrophe on the stage. Theatre managers illustrate this evident antipathy for the tragic genre by programming silly light comedies, and musical reviews whose artistic pretensions go no further than an exhibition of nude bodies, and saucy facility of situation, puns and jokes.

2. Tragedy Is Not an Optimistic Genre. A writer of tragedies went so far as to say—in an effort of social justification—that tragedy is an optimistic genre. This is clearly a defensive formulation, in a world where only an optimistic formula of life is accepted. Of course, tragedy is not an optimistic genre; just as it is not a pessimistic genre either. The writer of tragedies does not believe that all is for the worst, nor that all is for the best. If he really believed that all were for the worst, he would not write. Why should he? But he also realizes that all is not well. And he knows that optimism—that is to say, the form of life which considers that everything is perfect or may easily become perfect—exists only in backward and conformist minds.

3. Tragedy and Torture. Tragedy is—and we

"Drama and Society" by Alfonso Sastre, translated by Leonard C. Pronko, is reprinted by permission of Literary Discoveries Inc., 604 Mission St., San Francisco 5, California.

can gain nothing by denying it—a strange artistic mechanism which tortures the spectator and leaves him gravely wounded. The spectator is presented with "fearful" deeds and "pitiful" situations (and we know that Aristotle already told us about fear and pity: it is not a defeatist invention of contemporary authors) with the mysterious and obscure intention that he be made uneasy. With the intention—we might say—of torturing and wounding him. The spectator of *Hinkemann, Strife, Dirty Hands* or *Death of a Salesman*, leaves the theatre literally shattered, undone. A little more, and blood would cover his face, and his eyes be blinded by tears. Tragedy wounds, or at least it reveals, bloody and painful, forgotten wounds.

4. Torture Accepted. The curious, and of course essential, part of this torture which is tragedy is that the spectator submits willingly to it. (Tragedy in effect has never been a required spectacle.) Let us be precise about this torture which is offered by tragedy. The problem will then be posed in exact terms.

Can the spectator of *The Victors* honestly say that he has spent a comfortable evening? It is obvious that he cannot. Nor can the spectator of the film tragedies *Bicycle Thief* and *Shoeshine*. On the contrary, it is likely that such a spectator will say to you, "I left the theatre shattered." And yet he is happy that he went. And when he felt that the tragic action was cutting him painfully, making him shudder, suffer, weep, he did not leave. Glued to his seat, breathing with difficulty, he endured the torture to the end. He declared himself, for some mysterious reason, to be at one with the tragic action, and did not even think of the easy rupture which he could have effected by simply getting up from his seat and going out to the lobby to smoke a cigarette, or—more radically—going home and reading an adventure story. No. He was there to receive the tragic current. He could not move from there. The torture was accepted before hand. He had gone to see a tragedy. But why? Why does the announcement of a tragedy attract the public? What kind of public does tragedy have?

5. *Questions, Questions, Questions.* Must we admit that the spectator obtains a particular pleasure from this torture freely accepted? What moves the spectator of tragedy? The "desire for pain" of which St. Augustine speaks in his *Confessions,* when he tells us of his youthful love for the theatre? Is the spectator of tragedy a masochist? Or is his suffering unreal? Is there true suffering on the stage? And in the house? Might it not be an artistically tempered suffering, a suffering which has lost its strength?

6. *The Reality of Tragic Suffering.* It seems to me that we must revindicate the reality of tragic suffering, and in general of all the passions and emotions which come into play in tragedy. The common criticism which holds that tragic passions are "purged," tempered, artistic, and finally inoffensive—capable, at most, of producing in the spectator an aesthetic emotion—has no foundation in the reality of tragedy. Tragic action is really painful. The drama is the conductor, the line of least resistance, through which the pain and anguish go from the social reality to the heart of the spectator. Through the tragedy the spectator communicates with the anguish of others. The spectator, armored by life for the struggle, dozing, peaceful, with his moral consciousness half asleep, is often invulnerable to the pain of others which rubs against him every day in his work, in the street, in the bar, or the bus. Drama produces in his mind the sudden revelation of the true structures of human suffering. The drama becomes then the conductor between the suffering of the street and the mind of the man. The suffering does not lose strength through the act of communication (if the tragedy is good). It is not a purged suffering. In good tragedies the fearful is real, and truly fearful (and it produces real fear; not a "fear" which is a form of aesthetic emotion), and the pitiful is real, and truly pitiful (and rouses true pity and not an aesthetic emotion; a pity which finds its objective after the curtain has fallen, and finds it in social reality; pity potential and as it were suspended during the presentation of the tragedy). Art has done nothing more than effect a very complicated transfer. Transfer (or if we wish, *mimesis*), but not a purgation (the meaning of *catharsis* is something else).

7. *The Meaning of Tragic Catharsis.* For me the meaning of tragic *catharsis* is to be found not in the transfer from reality to tragedy, but in the effect which the tragedy produces on reality: in an immediate way on the spectator, and through him upon Society.

8. *St. Augustine and Tragedy.* The spectator, when he accepts the tragic torture, is suspect of some kind of masochism (and is not the writer of tragedies perhaps a very special kind of sadist?) and therefore, tragedy may be a form of collective insanity: St. Augustine is not far from this conception. "Why," asks St. Augustine, "does man like to be made sad when viewing doleful and tragical scenes, which yet he himself would by no means suffer? And yet he wishes, as a spectator, to experience from them a sense of grief, and in this very grief his pleasure consists. What is this but wretched insanity?" St. Augustine later adds the concepts of "misery"—*when it is oneself who suffers*—and "pity"—*when one suffers for another.* "But what kind of pity is it that arises from fictitious and scenic passions? The hearer is not expected to believe," St. Augustine explains, "but merely invited to grieve; and the more he grieves, the more he applauds the actor of these fictions." "According to this," the saint asks, "we also enjoy tears and sorrow?" For St. Augustine, in short, tragedy is a strange madness. The spectator of tragedy is a kind of desperate masochist. He would be incapable of enduring personally the pain which is represented, but he enjoys the representation of the suffering which makes him weep and moves him superficially. This conception views the spectator of tragedy, in the last analysis, as a "false sado-masochist," since he enjoys the (feigned) suffering of the characters and his own (superficial) suffering as a spectator of the tragedy. Tragedy, in these terms, is an abomination which any adult society should cast from its midst. Tragedy would be truly a grave social sin. But the fact is that . . .

9. *Tragedy, in Spite of Everything, is Something Else.* Once we have revindicated the reality of tragic suffering—by the conception of drama as a conducting wire which connects and syntonizes (let us use this word taken from the vocabulary of physics: to put into resonance with each other) human suffering with the heart of the spectator—the suspicion of masochism would lead to a graver formula-

tion of "tragic madness." Tragedy would be a dangerous and punishable game of sadists and masochists. Opposed to these suspicions is the conception of tragedy as a form of mortification, and, in the last analysis, as an instrument of moral and social purification. The spectator of tragedy does not seek suffering; he accepts mortification. The spectator of tragedy feels himself deservedly mortified. He accepts the torture in an access of self-punishment. Then, does he feel himself guilty? Yes, tragedy wakens in him a profound feeling of guilt. And so . . . ? He accepts mortification. And then? When the tragedy ends, his spirit has been purified. And then? Then—sometimes— a social revolution. Or at least social improvement. Then, does it turn out that tragedy was something else?

10. A Purely Literary Page about the Real Meaning of Tragedy. Yes, tragedy was something else, and something very different. Tragedy is, precisely, the opposite of a social sin: a social virtue. Although true and happy sinners try, in their self-defensive struggle to eradicate from society this filthy sin which, according to them, tragedy is. (Those happy sinners who are afraid of the truth, and are defending their lives.)

This brief study of tragedy as it relates to the spectator ends with a purely literary page, in which we see a man stopping in the street before a theatre poster. The man is wearing a raincoat—it is raining a bit—and a felt hat. He could be an obscure member of a Chicago "gang," or a humble office worker in Madrid. It is all the same. The poster announces for tonight the presentation of a tragedy. The man, we know not why, has stopped, and is reading: "Seven and eleven o'clock, *Death of a Salesman,* by Arthur Miller." The man goes off. It continues raining. He enters a bar and drinks a glass of wine. He pays and leaves. He pulls up the collar of his raincoat. Night falls. He goes into an old restaurant. He has dinner: soup, an omelet and an orange. He appears to have forgotten that he even saw the theatre poster. But he looks at his watch; and it so happens that he has not forgotten. He pays, leaves a tip and goes back into the street. The theatre is near. He goes to the ticket window— up till now everything has been very easy— and buys a mezzanine seat. He enters the theatre. He makes himself comfortable. The house lights go down. The curtain rises. Against a background of strange music a traveling salesman, old and tired, returns home. The story begins. The mans sees, from

the beginning, that all this will have to end badly, but he does not know how. He does not know the how of the death, the how of the catastrophe, the how of the desperation and the final anguish. The tragedy becomes more and more intelligible. The salesman is not responsible for what is happening. His wife is not responsible. Neither are the children. No one is exclusively responsible for what is happening. All are innocent. All, at the same time, are guilty. The characters and those who surround them: the invisible men who surround them. The social system? All, even we the spectators—thinks the man—are a little responsible for what is happening to this poor old salesman. The salesman weeps. He wants to die. Because he thinks he is worth more dead than alive. The salesman weeps. The man weeps. He is weeping for the salesman, and for all the salesmen in the world, and for all other men, and because he did not behave as he should have towards someone who is now dead. The man is weeping for himself. At the end, when the family of the salesman is praying before his grave and wondering, quietly, why the salesman did it, why did he kill himself, the man is also praying a bit himself and feels somewhat purified by this viewing of the true structures—but it doesn't occur to him to think of "structures"—of suffering. He goes into the street. Now he is a man ready for something good. Now, yes. Because the man has been moved to help—and he does not know whether St. Augustine thought the opposite—not by intervening in the tragic action which is only a transfer or *mimesis* but in the reality which was transferred or imitated. The man, going homeward, is tranquil. His hands are in his raincoat pockets. His face has become calm, almost handsome. The man thinks that he "must do something"—but he doesn't know what; he will find out—and that "things can't go on this way." Fine. Go home to bed, my friend. Tomorrow . . . The man goes off.

II. An Open Letter on *Death of a Salesman*

I have just read with the greatest attention your criticism of *Death of a Salesman* and, for the first time in my life, I am writing an "open letter" (a very poorly paid literary genre). I must confess that I am impelled to write to you by a desire to put in their proper place several things which seem to me out of place. Your criticism—in short—seems unjust to me. I believe that you center your commentary not on the work itself, but on the reality to which the work bears witness, and it appears that the work consequently seems bad to you for the same reasons that the reality seems bad and impure (the sons who fail their father, etc.). I believe that if in reality "there are many millions of Willy Lomans" and Arthur Miller has succeeded in presenting one of them, the drama is fully justified and successful. For him, as for many modern authors, tragedy is "documentation"—Miller defines it as "balanced documentation"—and *Death of a Salesman* presents us with a rather complete documentation, and apparently an exact one, of Willy Loman. The drama is complete. What must be purified is the reality which the drama attests. There is drama precisely because the reality is impure. If Willy Loman had taught his sons, as you say, "love of his fellows and a sense of honor," and brought them up "in dignity and honesty," speaking to them "of God and of hope," it is possible that there may have been no drama. The terrible part of it is—and the fact that Miller has noticed it is to his credit as a dramatist—that there are millions of men who struggle only to gain comfort and security. Willy Loman, old, abandoned by his clients and his sons, enslaved by the payments on the icebox and the house, dead before everything was finally his, is a purifying sight, and the dramatic recreation of his life represents a cruel criticism of certain forms of human existence which are hopelessly condemned to failure. The author thus situates himself in a great tradition of modern drama. I have said "cruel criticisms," and this is so, even though Miller treats poor Willy Loman with compassion.

All this is in reply to your claim that the interest of the play seems to you "sociological and scarcely artistic." To me it seems that the play has no sociological interest whatsoever. Sociology is a science, and drama has very little to do with science. It has, of course, a social interest, and certainly a human interest; but built upon a solid artistic base. It certainly does not seem to me to be an "amorphous" work. On the contrary, it seems to me that it avoids, with some hesitation, the obvious danger of falling into "confusion and chaos."

Moreover, this is apparently what the public also thinks. Saturday evening, at least, the public—at the risk of missing the last subways and busses—applauded interminably. And I believe it was for reasons other than purely "sociological" ones. We must see here "social emotion," and not "sociological reason."

III. Theatre of Magic and Theatre of Anguish

The obligation of those of us who write for the theatre and of the theatre—and we are few—is, simply, to effect a diagnosis of the symptoms which we find in the "shapeless mass" of works which are produced, which are published, and which our friends read to us. We are interested in knowing what is happening and what is going to happen. We are interested in knowing whether anyone is coming along with us, or whether a difficult and lonely fight awaits us.

Two trends—according to latest observations—seem to stand out, incipient and blurred as yet, in the panorama of the Spanish theatre. On one side, the theatre of magic. On the other, misconstrued, repressed, deformed by the critics, the theatre of anguish. And we are not simply uttering—as do many superficial observers—words, words, words. Theatre of magic and theatre of anguish are terms with an immediate foundation in reality, based upon what Spanish theatres are presenting and the young authors are writing.

In the theatre of magic we see women who come from the sea (sirens)—how many sirens and similar monsters can we count in modern theatre?—phantoms (jesting spirits for the most part, but also some serious, circumspect and rather saddened ghosts), voices of the dead, angels, characters reflected in mirrors, consciences which speak in their own voices, dead people of flesh and blood who give us their impressions (as in the magic act of *Our Town*), objects with strange powers, superstitions which prove true, palmistry, card-reading, magic crystals, men transported to another era "because time does not exist," premonitions founded on the same fact (the idea that "the present, the past and the future coexist" and that "if we see time from above . . ." and that "if we see a river from a bridge . . ."), prophetic visions, mysterious characters who arrive (like messengers from the beyond, or voices of conscience, or I know not what), strange calls, signs—a whole parade of shades, almost always built upon the base of a realistic story (it is a kind of magical realism . . .) and in most cases with some common metaphysical pretensions. This is the "magic" of the modern theatre. This "magic," for some poor souls, exhausts the possibilities of the modern theatre. This type of drama—considered *avant-garde* in Spain until very recently!—is what now seems to be penetrating the professional companies who, weary of the old repertory, wish to perform "modern theatre."

The other trend, what we called "theatre of anguish," is the result of a very different feeling toward the theatre, its meaning and its function. It is the specifically tragic current of the modern theatre, based upon the postulates of realism. It is the theatre which looks upon existence as a fearful temporal wound: time is a tragic reality, and we are, ourselves, that time which is passing; there are no magical or fantastic evasions. It is the theatre in which things appear as they are. This is the current trend fostered by the great "witness dramatists." I am referring to those whose major production—discounting the magical levities to which most theatrical writers have given in—is a testimony of reality. It does not matter that Lenormand wrote several magical works, like *Time is a Dream* and *The Madwoman of Heaven*, and other phantasmagoric dramas like *Man and his Phantoms*. Lenormand is, fundamentally, the author of *The Failures* and *The Coward*. O'Neill—to use another example—is not a magic author, in spite of *Lazarus Laughed* and his choruses, masks and mysteries. O'Neill is the cruel naturalist of *Strange Interlude*. A magical author is, for example, Maeterlinck. And not only because of that delightful "féerie," *The Bluebird*.

The magic trend has suffered several rude blows in the last few years. Literature founded on "neo-realistic" postulates, "existentialism," and, in general, the entire "socio-realistic" cultural front have fired their pistols straight into the "scatterbrain" of magic, of criminal evasion, and of suicidal and complacent smiles.

We are in battle. The bourgeois public—that is to say, the public—asks for magic, evasion and dreams. The happy and confident city gives over most of its theatres to thoughtless and sentimental farces, while there is hunger, misery, and knives are being sharpened. While new kinds of bombs are tried out. While the proletariat the world over—hopelessly—asks for a raise in salary; the budgets for armaments are increased. On some stages we can hear the voice of anguish, and an urgent cry for purification.

And so the theatre continues having two masks. The comic mask has grown magician's whiskers. The tragic usually wears a war helmet, or chews a wad of proletarian tobacco, or wears the tie of a political party. The comic mask wears a degenerate smile. The tragic, a grimace of hunger and pain. Aside from this, things have not changed much.

It must be said that the young Spanish writers—to judge by the latest unpublished plays I have read—seem to follow more easily the magic way than the tragic one. One feels almost abandoned by those of his own generation (and I am not even mentioning the older generation!). They are disgusted by Sartre's tragedies, and note punctually the pleasure caused by the latest farce which has opened in Paris. In the movie theatres there was an "Oh!" of relief at the magical crisis and denouement of *Miracle in Milan*. So much the better—they said—that "neo-realism" has found a way out. That is how things are. Fortunately, there continues to be a public for tragedies.

Translated by Leonard C. Pronko

ANNA KLEIBER

Translated by Leonard C. Pronko

CAST OF CHARACTERS

FIRST REPORTER	CHARLES COHEN
THE WRITER	THE PROMPTER
SECOND REPORTER	AN ACTOR
A WOMAN, *who is rebuking*	MR. WERNER
A MAN	A SOLDIER
THE DESK CLERK	ANOTHER SOLDIER
A COUPLE	A YOUNG MAN *in Anna's room*
THE BELLBOY	DANCING COUPLES,
ANNA KLEIBER	SOLDIERS
ALFRED MERTON	

NOTES FOR THE DIRECTOR:

1. The dialogues with which the play begins are spoken simultaneously, intending to give the general impression of a hotel lobby in which people are speaking of things which are not important for the understanding of the drama. They are, therefore, intended to be lost and interrupted.

2. The actors who play the characters in the lobby at the opening of the play, may interpret other roles in later scenes of the play.

3. It is suggested that the same actor may play the three men who have scenes with Anna: Cohen, Werner, and the Man in her room.

ACT ONE

(*The action takes place in the Hotel Voyager —a non-existent hotel in Barcelona—and in various cities of Europe.*

When the curtain rises we are in the lobby of the Hotel Voyager. It is late afternoon on Christmas Day. There is a lighted tree.

Anna Kleiber by Alfonso Sastre, translated by Leonard C. Pronko, appeared in *New Theatre of Europe*, edited by Robert W. Corrigan. Reprinted by permission of Dell Publishing Company, Inc.

On stage are:

1.   *The* DESK CLERK, *yawning over a newspaper.*
2.   *The* WRITER.
3 and 4. TWO NEWSPAPER REPORTERS.
5 and 6. *A* WOMAN *who is rebuking a* MAN.

Simultaneous dialogue)

FIRST REPORTER   And what are you preparing for next year, Mr. Sastre?

WRITER   I would like to write two plays next year . . . I already have the subjects in mind.

SECOND REPORTER   Social themes?

WRITER   Possibly.

WOMAN   I can't go on this way.

MAN   Come now, calm down.

(DESK CLERK *reads his newspaper*)

FIRST REPORTER   Will you have *Red Earth* produced?

WRITER   I don't know. I'm afraid there may be difficulties.

WOMAN   I feel like talking and I'm going to talk. You'll just have to listen. That's all! (*She weeps*)

MAN   Shh . . . Be quiet . . . You're attracting attention. Try to calm down.

(DESK CLERK *yawns*)

SECOND REPORTER   Were you satisfied with your production this year?

[684]

WRITER   Yes. *The Muzzle* turned out very well.

FIRST REPORTER   What do you think of drama criticism?

WRITER   There are all kinds.

WOMAN   I can't calm down.

MAN   Come on . . .

WOMAN   You're a cad.

MAN   You don't mean that. I . . .

(DESK CLERK *nods*)

SECOND REPORTER   And what do you think of drama prizes?

WRITER   They have no effect whatsoever.

FIRST REPORTER   What was your first produced play?

WRITER   An experimental play, in 1946.

DESK CLERK   (*the phone rings. He picks it up*) Yes . . . Yes . . . Certainly. Yes, sir. (*He hangs up and rolls a cigarette*)

FIRST REPORTER   In Madrid?

WRITER   At the Teatro Beatriz in Madrid.

WOMAN   You can't leave me now. After a whole lifetime . . .

MAN   But you must understand. My wife . . .

SECOND REPORTER   Are you satisfied with *Death Squad?*

WRITER   Yes.

WOMAN   She's a harpy.

MAN   She's sick!

(DESK CLERK *smokes*)

FIRST REPORTER   Why weren't there more performances?

WRITER   There were difficulties.

FIRST REPORTER   Why have you come to Barcelona?

WRITER   I have business to take care of here.

WOMAN   And what difference does that make to me? I'm sick too.

MAN   Last night she had an attack.

(A COUPLE *comes from the staircase. The* DESK CLERK *approaches the desk*)

FIRST REPORTER   Are you a bachelor?

WRITER   Yes.

WOMAN   She probably got drunk.

MAN   She wasn't drinking. It's just that she's very sick.

HE   Good evening.

DESK CLERK   Good evening, sir. Merry Christmas.

HE   Thank you. Here's the key. Goodnight.

DESK CLERK   Goodnight, sir.

SECOND REPORTER   Do you intend to get married?

WRITER   We'll see.

WOMAN   I was all alone. I was sad.

MAN   I know, but what could I do?

HE   Come on, honey. (*They link arms and go toward the exit*)

SHE   Is it raining?

HE   No. (*They go out*)

(*The* DESK CLERK's *cigarette has gone out. He looks for matches*)

SECOND REPORTER   Aren't you in love?

WRITER   I don't know. I mean . . .

WOMAN   Come to see me. I spent Christmas Eve alone. I cried all night.

MAN   I know, I know, Adele, but I . . . Oh! God, I'm worried.

(*The* DESK CLERK *has found the matches. He lights, smokes, and returns to his paper*)

FIRST REPORTER   Haven't you ever been in love?

SECOND REPORTER   Tell us some personal anecdote?

WRITER   It's just that . . . I don't remember . . .

WOMAN   Now you're worried! You could have worried a little before, when you dragged me out of my house, and threw me into the street. I was a decent woman. I could have married and had children and a happy home! And now . . . Oh, God! (*She weeps*)

MAN   Calm down. Calm down. We'll figure something out.

FIRST REPORTER   Then something amusing . . .

WRITER   I don't know anything amusing.

WOMAN   What are you going to do with me?

MAN   I think . . .

(*The* DESK CLERK *looks towards the* MAN *and* WOMAN, *distractedly*)

SECOND REPORTER   Why do you write tragedies?

WRITER   God knows!

WOMAN   Why don't you answer me? Why are you so pale?

MAN   I think . . . it mustn't be born.

SECOND REPORTER   How does life seem to you? Grim? Sad?

WRITER   No. So-so.

WOMAN   What . . . ? I'm afraid!

MAN   We'll see a doctor. I've heard of one who does this kind of thing.

DESK CLERK   (*the* BELLBOY *comes from the street*) Well! Is it cold?

BELLBOY   (*rubbing his hands*) Rather.

FIRST REPORTER   Will you write comedies?

WRITER   No.

WOMAN   You want to kill me! That's what you want! To get rid of me. You want to kill me!

MAN   Be quiet! What will these people say. They're all watching.

SECOND REPORTER   Why?

WRITER   I don't know why. I'm afraid I'm just not very amusing.

WOMAN   (*lowers her voice*) Don't leave me . . . Don't leave me . . . I beg of you . . .

MAN   I won't. I won't leave you. That's just one of your silly ideas.

FIRST REPORTER   Life is beautiful, don't you agree?

WRITER   Yes . . . in some ways.

WOMAN   You loved me once.

MAN   Yes. (*looks at his watch*)

DESK CLERK   Was Rudolph there?

BELLBOY   Yes, sir. (*He whistles while the* CLERK *writes something. He stops*)

SECOND REPORTER   We must look to the future with hope, don't you agree?

WRITER   If you say so, of course.

WOMAN   When I was young and beautiful you used to love me. Don't you remember? You used to run after me.

MAN   Yes.

FIRST REPORTER   What critic do you like least?

WRITER   I can't remember at the moment.

WOMAN   And now it's all changed. Whenever you're with me, you're only thinking of how to get away.

MAN   No, it's just that it's getting late. I ought to go.

DESK CLERK   Did you have a good Christmas Eve?

BELLBOY   Yes, sir. In spite of the fact that my father wasn't in a good mood.

SECOND REPORTER   Come on. Tell us the truth.

WRITER   It's just . . . anyone . . .

FIRST REPORTER   Do you believe other writers are stupid?

WRITER   For God's sake, no!

WOMAN   Where you going?

MAN   To buy some toys for the children.

DESK CLERK   What time did you go to bed?

BELLBOY   At three o'clock, when the rest of the family did. We had a wonderful time. My sister even got drunk. She was so funny! And all the women were smoking . . .

SECOND REPORTER   Why do you believe other authors are stupid?

WRITER   But I just said that I don't think they're stupid.

SECOND REPORTER   Come on, tell us the truth . . . (*But the* WRITER *is looking at a* WOMAN *who has just entered*)

WOMAN   For your children! You let *them* be born.

MAN   We'll talk more about this later. We'll discuss it in detail . . . We'll discuss all the details . . . We're in time . . . We can think about it . . . We'll examine it carefully, Adele . . . We have to discuss it . . . (*He looks at the* WOMAN *who has entered. The* WOMAN *turns to look*)

DESK CLERK   What times! . . . (*He bows his head as a greeting to the new arrival*)

(ANNA KLEIBER *comes in from the street. She is a tired-looking woman. She is carrying a small suitcase. She enters and stops, staggers. She seems about to faint, puts a hand over her eyes*)

ANNA   Help me, please. (*The* WRITER *rises and goes toward her. The* CLERK *comes from behind the desk*)

WRITER   Is something wrong, Madame? Are you ill?

ANNA   No, it's nothing. Thank you. When I came in . . . I'm a little tired . . . Thank you. (*She goes to the desk accompanied by the* CLERK. *The* WRITER *watches her from the center of the lobby.* ANNA *leans on the desk, remains still, her eyes closed. The* CLERK *looks at her, not knowing what to do. With his eyes he interrogates the* WRITER, *who says nothing. Finally* ANNA *opens her eyes and says:*) Do you . . . have a room, please?

DESK CLERK   Yes, ma'm. Would you please fill out this form?

ANNA   Yes. (*She opens her pen and tries to write. Her hand trembles*) I'm . . . (*She smiles to excuse herself*) I'm a bit . . . My nerves . . .

DESK CLERK   I'll fill it out, ma'm. "Name?"

ANNA   Anna Kleiber.

DESK CLERK   (*writes*) K-L-I-

ANNA   No, it's K-L-E-I- . . . ber.

DESK CLERK   Like this?

ANNA   Yes. Thank you.

DESK CLERK   "Nationality?"

ANNA   Spanish.

DESK CLERK   Ah, but you . . . (*smiles*) With this name? (*He tries, clumsily, to be amiable*)

ANNA   My father was German.

DESK CLERK   Ah . . . "Coming from . . . ?"

ANNA   Paris.

DESK CLERK   "Destination?"

ANNA   I don't know.

DESK CLERK   But . . . well, we have to put something.

ANNA I don't know.

DESK CLERK Will you stay here, in Barcelona?

ANNA It's just . . . that everything depends on tomorrow, don't you see?

DESK CLERK All right. We'll put . . . Barcelona. It's all the same. "Purpose of trip." (ANNA *says nothing. The* CLERK *repeats*) "Purpose of trip." What shall I put? Commerce . . . Personal business . . .

ANNA Yes. Personal . . . Put down anything.

DESK CLERK (*writes, then hands her the pen*) Would you sign, please?

ANNA Yes. (*She signs*)

DESK CLERK Will you go upstairs now?

ANNA Yes, I have to . . . rest. Tomorrow . . . (*But she says no more*)

DESK CLERK Room number 66.

ANNA I beg your pardon?

DESK CLERK Room number sixty-six. (*holds out the key*)

ANNA No . . . I . . . Isn't there some other room?

DESK CLERK No, ma'm. Sixty-six is a very nice room.

ANNA I don't know . . .

DESK CLERK You'll be very happy with it, ma'm.

ANNA It's just . . . it's strange . . . I used to live once in a Room Sixty-six. It has unpleasant associations. In the Colonia Hotel in Berlin. Do you know it?

DESK CLERK Me? Oh, no, ma'm.

ANNA I lived in Room Sixty-six. It's because of that. Well . . . (*She looks around*) It doesn't matter . . . I'm glad to be in Barcelona. Perhaps everything will change tomorrow. I'm happy. I surely won't sleep, in case . . . have them call me at nine tomorrow. I have a very important appointment. I've waited all my life . . . my meeting tomorrow . . . Will you call me?

DESK CLERK (*surprised, confused*) Yes, ma'm. Don't worry. (*to the* BELLBOY *who has picked up the suitcase*) Sixty-six. (*They go toward the elevator, enter it, the* BELLBOY *closes the elevator door, and the elevator goes up. The other characters have remained motionless. The* WRITER *slowly lights his pipe and walks towards the audience*)

WRITER Anna Kleiber did not go to her appointment the following day. Anna Kleiber died that night in her room. The next morning when they went to call her she was lying half-naked across her bed, lifeless. She died of a heart attack, alone, helpless, in the room of an unknown hotel. It was Christmas Day. I had gone to Barcelona and by chance witnessed the sad unfolding of a strange story: the story of Anna Kleiber. (*The* CLERK *is coughing noisily*) What's the matter?

DESK CLERK No, I . . . I was thinking, with all respect for you, sir, that you were about to mix it all up.

WRITER What? What do you mean? (*The* REPORTERS *leave*)

DESK CLERK Excuse me, Mr. Sastre, but I seem to remember that we agreed to tell first about how we found out the young woman had died and the impression it made on us.

WRITER You're right. Go ahead. (*The* MAN *is saying good-bye to the* WOMAN. *He goes. The* WOMAN *goes up the stairs*)

DESK CLERK (*to the audience*) So many strange people come to the Hotel Voyager that, to tell the truth, Anna Kleiber's arrival that Christmas afternoon didn't seem particularly extraordinary. I wrote her name in the registry and forgot about her. That's what I always do. You can't stop to think about the problems that all the people who stop here have. I know some of them are probably crying in their rooms; some are worrying about this or that, turning pale; perhaps right now someone in room 32, or in 14, or 120, has just decided to kill himself . . . But you can't think about all that . . . You'd lose your mind . . . So, I didn't think about the young lady until the following day.

WRITER You called her on the phone.

DESK CLERK Yes. "Give me 66," I said to the switchboard.

WRITER Do it.

DESK CLERK What?

WRITER Do it. Call number 66.

DESK CLERK Oh, yes. (*picks up the phone*) Give me 66. (*pause*) She doesn't answer? Well ring some more. (*pause*) Nothing? All right, ring until she wakes up, then tell her what time it is. (*hangs up. To the* WRITER) That's the way it was. A few minutes later the phone rang. (*It rings*) I picked it up. (*He does so*) What's that? All right . . . Yes, yes . . . It's rather strange . . . (*hangs up*) The switchboard reported that they had called many times and there was still no answer. I sent a chambermaid to the room. Then I went up myself. The door was locked from the inside and no one answered. I talked with the manager and we decided to use the master key. It was just as you said . . . Half naked, across the bed . . . She was dead . . . You saw her . . . .

WRITER (*to the audience*) My room was on the same floor and I soon found out what had happened. I went to room sixty-six and there was that pitiful sight.

DESK CLERK   Then the usual thing: the police, questions, a little investigation, nothing much . . . That poor woman had no relatives. She was all alone in the world. There was no one to inform of her death.

(*A silence, the* WRITER *empties his pipe and puts it away. With a certain solemnity he says:*)

WRITER   But there was someone waiting for her in Barcelona.

DESK CLERK   That Merton fellow.

WRITER   Alfred Merton! Alfred Merton was waiting for her. Alfred Merton knew that Anna was coming to meet him. Anna had taken the train from Paris and was coming to meet him. And Merton was waiting nervously for her in his room. At last, after so much anguish, so much suffering, they would be together forever! Alfred Merton was dreaming, in his little room, of a new life in which Anna and Alfred would be happy at last, would find the peace which until then had been denied them . . . The day of the meeting came and Anna Kleiber did not knock at his door and Merton thought that he had failed once again; that his love was cursed; that she had forgotten their meeting . . . and he thought of killing himself . . . until he discovered through a newspaper that a woman named Anna Kleiber had died in a hotel room . . . , died just as she was about to return to his arms. (*to the* CLERK) You must realize that this is a tale of romance.

DESK CLERK   Yes, indeed. You were very good. I was almost moved to tears.

WRITER   You remember we met Alfred Merton the afternoon of the funeral. There were three or four of us . . . and one curious stranger . . . It was cold . . . I was pensive, praying while they threw earth over the body of Anna Kleiber when, suddenly, right behind me, a man burst into tears. It was Alfred Merton. Did you see how that man wept?

DESK CLERK   It struck me. I had never seen a man cry that way.

WRITER   He cried like a wounded beast.

DESK CLERK   He must have loved her deeply.

WRITER   The entire meaning of his life was in that love.

DESK CLERK (*pensive*)   It must have been something like that.

WRITER   I was struck too. And when I came to my senses you had gone . . .

DESK CLERK   Yes, I left. I didn't dare speak

to you. Or else I said something and you didn't hear. I don't remember.

WRITER   We were alone, he and I, standing by Anna Kleiber's grave. I heard the voice of Alfred Merton. He had calmed down. He was quiet. He was speaking to her, saying good-bye to her. I listened to him, petrified.

(*The lights go down. We see the figure of* ALFRED MERTON, *wearing an overcoat with the collar turned up, his hands in the pockets, tenuously lighted by a grey spot. His voice is grave and deep*)

ALFRED   You're dead, Anna. God didn't want us to find each other again. I've waited for you all my life, dreamed of you . . . all my life I've belonged to you, Anna . . . In the trenches I thought of you and wept for you . . . I knew you were free, that you were with your friends, letting yourself be kissed by anyone who wanted you; you were getting drunk, and then at last, alone at home, you cried for me on your pillow . . . I know what a strange and wonderful woman you've always been . . . Because, all through your life, you've only loved one man, one wretched man named Alfred Merton. It was useless for you to try to lose yourself, to throw yourself headlong into the abyss. You're clean of everything now, Anna . . . I don't know what the matter was. You weren't made for the peace and quiet of a home . . . You always ran away . . . But now I have you. You're dead, Anna, and now you can't run away. You're here for me. I know that everything must be born again, and then you won't be able to go back to your madness, and I'll have you for my own. Until then, keep her, Death! With you she's at peace. Now I don't need to worry about you. I have you. Now no one but me can kiss Anna Kleiber . . . no one else can put his arms about her waist or feel the touch of her legs . . . Good-bye, Anna! I'll be with you soon.

(*We hear from outside the lighted area, the voice of the* WRITER *whose silhouette we see vaguely*)

WRITER   I took him by the arm and he made no movement of surprise. He looked at me. I took him away from there, and he came willingly. He walked in silence until we had left the cemetery. It was already dark. We went into a café and I ordered a couple of gins. It was very cold.

(*The* WRITER, *after speaking these words, approaches Alfred Merton and takes his arm.* ALFRED *turns and looks at him quietly. They begin to walk. They walk across the down-stage area. In the meantime, the* CLERK *has brought out a table and placed upon it a lamp with a blue shade. The* BELLBOY *brings out two chairs and places them by the table. The* WRITER *and* ALFRED *arrive at the table and sit down without taking off their coats)*

WAITER   What'll it be?

WRITER   You? . . . (ALFRED *shrugs his shoulders)* Gin for me. How about you?

ALFRED   All right. Thank you.

WRITER   Two gins.

(The WAITER *goes off. We begin to hear the music from a phonograph which is probably in the room. It is playing the French song "Mam'selle."* ALFRED *makes a startled movement)*

ALFRED   What's that?

WRITER   Let me listen . . . I don't know . . . (He *listens)* Yes, "Mam'selle." . . . Don't you remember it? They played it in "The Razor's Edge," that film . . . (He *sings in a low voice)* "Ne partez pas déjà . . . Ne quittez pas mes bras . . . mam'selle." (He *continues humming)* It's nice . . .

ALFRED   I don't want to hear it.

WRITER   Do you want them to stop the record? I'll tell them.

ALFRED   (still listening) No. It's all the same. Let it go. After all, it doesn't matter much anymore. (The WAITER *appears and serves their gin.* ALFRED *takes his in one gulp)* It's just . . . strange . . . I heard that song in Paris once. It was a very special occasion. I remember . . . "Ne partez pas déjà . . ." Now I remember. And as I listen I remember more and more . . . No, wait. That's not what's happening. It's not remembering. It's . . . I hear that song, and what happens is . . . (He *closes his eyes)* I live it all over again . . . I'm putting my arms around Anna Kleiber's waist . . . her marvellous waist . . .

WRITER   (he drinks a bit) It's strange.

ALFRED   What's strange?

WRITER   This city, Barcelona. Doesn't it seem strange to you?

ALFRED   You've noticed that too?

WRITER   Yes. I came here to get away from someone.

ALFRED   From a woman?

WRITER   Yes. And you know what's happened? She's here in Barcelona. No, she's not really, you know what I mean? But everything here reminds me of her. I feel trapped. I'm afraid to go out—she's everywhere. I never

should have come to Barcelona . . . this city . . .

ALFRED   You're talking to me about your troubles as though you'd known me all your life.

WRITER   We're two lonely men who met one afternoon in a distant, unfamiliar city. We can talk.

ALFRED   You're already my friend. I don't know your name, but I feel as comfortable with you as with my oldest friends. I'm glad you're here.

WRITER   Things sometimes happen that have no clear explanation. Do you know where Anna Kleiber died?

ALFRED   She died in the Hotel Voyager.

WRITER   In room sixty-six. (ALFRED *looks at him, startled)*

ALFRED   Are you sure?

WRITER   I live in the same hotel. She died in room sixty-six.

ALFRED   I remember another room sixty-six.

WRITER   It seems as though this city had been made so that everything would repeat itself, so all forgetting would be impossible . . . Anna Kleiber said: "It's strange . . . I lived in another room number sixty-six."

ALFRED   She said that? Were you there when she arrived?

WRITER   And you said just now: "It's strange . . . I heard that song in Paris once. It was a very special occasion." It's clear that everything here has been prepared to make me remember. Don't you see?

ALFRED   You were there when she arrived?

WRITER   Yes.

ALFRED   What did she say?

WRITER   She was slightly ill.

ALFRED   But didn't she say anything?

WRITER   That she was going to meet someone the next day.

ALFRED   Me.

WRITER   That she had waited all her life for that meeting.

ALFRED   She said that?

WRITER   Yes.

ALFRED   What else?

WRITER   Nothing. She went up to her room.

ALFRED   She went up there to die.

WRITER   Yes.

ALFRED   She came to our meeting, dead.

WRITER   These things happen . . . It's not an unusual case . . .

ALFRED   For me it is. I'm suffering. No one

can suffer for me all that I'm going through tonight.

WRITER   Each of us must bear his own pain. In these moments we can help each other very little. I can't suffer for you. All I can do is listen to you.

ALFRED   That's not much.

WRITER   I can drink with you, get drunk with you tonight. That's the only tribute I can pay your sorrow.

ALFRED   Thanks.

WRITER   I can even cry. I can cry for Anna Kleiber . . . for a love lost . . . , for the hopes of that night when a little orchestra was playing "Mam'selle." . . . (*a silence.* ALFRED *stares at the* WRITER)

ALFRED   Who are you?

WRITER   It doesn't matter. But some day I may try to tell your story and Anna Kleiber's.

ALFRED   A vulgar story.

WRITER   A tragic story. (*He signals to the* WAITER)

WAITER   Sir?

WRITER   Two more. (*The* WAITER *goes off*) The play will begin when Anna Kleiber arrives at the hotel. She goes up in the elevator and then someone who is in the lobby will go toward the audience and tell them what happened that night. Then we'll go to the cemetery. I find you there and we go . . . we come into this little café. We hear a tune, a common, rather coarse tune, and you begin to remember . . . (*We hear, loud, the melody. The* WAITER *serves the gin. They raise the glasses, drink*) Do you want to tell me?

ALFRED   The public wouldn't be interested in this sad story. You'll have a failure on your hands.

WRITER   We'll see. Start.

ALFRED   I'd like another gin. (*The* WRITER *signals and the* WAITER *fills the glasses.* AL-FRED *drinks his*) My name is Alfred Merton.

WRITER   Go on.

ALFRED   My name is Alfred Merton. When I met Anna I was a student of philosophy . . . a bad student . . . I was living in Paris . . .

WRITER   How did you meet her?

ALFRED   One night. I was going home, early in the morning . . . I had drunk quite a bit . . . It was a cold night, an autumn night . . . She was standing under the streetlight on that bridge, staring at the water . . . (AL-FRED *has risen. The* WRITER, *the* WAITER, *the table and chairs are now dark.* ALFRED, *standing downstage, speaks as though conversing with the audience*) She was wearing a rain-coat with the collar turned up, and a beret . . . (*Downstage also, but at the other side of the stage, we see—picked out by a spotlight—the figure of* ANNA KLEIBER, *as* ALFRED *has described her. She is staring at the river, which is the audience*) Afterwards, I often thought that if I could have stayed away from her that night . . . I don't know. All I know is that my life would have been very different . . . a sweet sad thing, perhaps . . . and to-day I might be a humble, peaceful, philosophy professor in some provincial university . . . All that might have happened, but I went up to her. That's how life is. That's how it started, something that might not have started at all . . . a strange love . . . What was that woman doing? What was she thinking? Was she planning something desperate? Suicide? She was young. What had happened? Well, the fact is I went up to her . . . (*He approaches, and stands behind* ANNA) Is something the matter? (*She doesn't answer. She seems not to have heard*) I hope you'll excuse me . . . I was going by and happened to see you . . . Could I talk with you awhile . . . (ANNA *turns*)

ANNA   Go away.

ALFRED   I . . . I don't mean to bother you . . . I was drinking with some friends and now I'm on my way home. Only when I passed by I saw you and . . .

ANNA   Listen . . . will you go away?

ALFRED   You're crying. (*a silence*) Something serious has happened to you. You're upset. You feel alone and for a minute you felt a little desperate. I don't know what's wrong. I'm just a poor fool who's being indiscreet and clumsy . . . But I can see that something's the matter, and I can't just walk away. Can I tell you what I'm thinking? You're probably a nice girl who has some little problem. That's all. Although it probably seems impossible to you now, something unbearable . . . (ANNA *weeps*) That's right . . . It's good for you . . . I hope you weren't thinking . . . (*He gestures toward the water*)

ANNA   (*with a hard, bitter voice*)   I was going to kill myself. I wanted to kill myself tonight.

ALFRED   Then I got here in time. Now you won't kill yourself.

ANNA   Leave me alone! Go away!

ALFRED   You won't kill yourself now.

ANNA   Go away!

ALFRED   But you'll come with me.

ANNA   No. Leave me alone. I have to be alone.

ALFRED   Be alone with me. Look . . . It's begun to rain . . .

ANNA   I'm too unhappy tonight. I'm too upset.

ALFRED   I understand. I know what it means to be sad. Let me go with you. I won't say a word. I won't bother you. You can think out loud . . . and I'll think to myself . . . as if I didn't exist . . . Let me go with you tonight . . .

(*A silence.* ANNA *looks at the sky*)

ANNA   It's raining hard.

ALFRED   Yes. I like the rain.

ANNA   (*as though speaking despite herself*) I feel better when there's a strong wind.

ALFRED   Yes . . . When the wind blows your hair and almost keeps you from walking. And you keep on in spite of it, and you like to walk conquering the wind.

ANNA   That's right. Thanks. (*She looks at him with a rather mocking tenderness*) Who are you?

ALFRED   My name is Alfred Merton.

ANNA   What are you? An old student? What do you do? Get drunk?

ALFRED   Yes. I'm a bad student. I guess I'm good for nothing, and I've got my little problem too.

ANNA   Your little problem makes me laugh. (ALFRED *looks at her seriously*) No, don't get mad. Your problem makes me laugh.

ALFRED   Go ahead and laugh. Laugh at me. It doesn't matter. It'll make you feel better.

ANNA   Your problem makes me laugh. What's happened? Didn't they send you your money from home?

ALFRED   That could be.

ANNA   Or did your sweetheart desert you?

ALFRED   I haven't got a sweetheart.

ANNA   Or have you fallen in love with a prostitute?

ALFRED   You want to wound me, to hurt me. I'll let you, go ahead.

ANNA   You've gotten bad grades at school. You make me laugh!

ALFRED   (*sadly and gently*) I'm sorry. You're really desperate, and I can't do anything for you. Goodnight. (*He pulls his collar about him and goes away from* ANNA. ANNA *sees him leaving, terrified*)

ANNA   (*shouts*) Don't go! Don't go! Where are you going? Don't go away! (ALFRED *stops*) I'm afraid!

ALFRED   (*from the distance*) It's raining hard. I know a place where we can keep out of the rain. Follow me if you want. (ANNA

follows him. She takes his arm. A spotlight lights up a little table. We see several couples dancing in the half-darkness. ANNA *and* ALFRED *sit down*)

ALFRED   You were going to kill yourself.

ANNA   Yes.

ALFRED   Pretend you're dead, and come with me.

ANNA   I was working in a theatre troupe. I'm an actress.

ALFRED   I didn't ask who you are.

ANNA   This morning I quit.

ALFRED   I don't have work either.

ANNA   The company director was called Charles Cohen.

ALFRED   A Jew . . . judging by the name . . .

ANNA   Yes. Last night I was at a party with him.

ALFRED   And?

ANNA   He made me drink a lot. I got drunk. I knew what he was up to . . . he's been after me for a long time . . . And I let myself get drunk . . . I wanted to lose myself.

ALFRED   (*grieved*) I understand.

ANNA   I was very lonely.

ALFRED   (*a grimace*) Yes.

ANNA   Old Cohen disgusted me, but I did it anyway, just to see how low I could sink. I fondled him. And the more I fondled him the more revolting he became.

ALFRED   Be quiet.

ANNA   My name is Anna Kleiber. Do you want to go on with me? Do you want to know me more intimately? Anna Kleiber is attracted by all that is common and filthy. She has a demon inside her. (ALFRED *looks at her frightened*) Am I frightening you?

ALFRED   No. I was feeling sorry for a poor woman I know . . . Her name is Anna Kleiber.

ANNA   (*with a hard voice*) I've never allowed anyone to feel pity for me.

ALFRED   I feel sorrow.

ANNA   You feel horror. You're not the first man to feel horror for me. (*a silence*) This morning I felt disgusted.

ALFRED   You felt sorry about what happened last night.

ANNA   No. I just felt disgust. Disgust at myself. I've left the company.

ALFRED   You've saved yourself . . . It was too much for you . . . too much for someone good like you . . .

ANNA   It was too much *other times* too. But

I always go back . . . The demon I'm telling you about makes me go back to the dirt.

ALFRED   Other times!

ANNA   In the most stupid way . . . recreating myself in uselessness and shame . . . with an animal desire to touch bottom . . . to see how far I could go . . . how far you can sink . . .

ALFRED   And all this is called Anna Kleiber?

(ANNA *nods, somberly*)

ANNA   Tonight . . .

ALFRED   Tonight you were desperate because of what you'd done, and wanted to kill yourself. It was madness. A noble madness . . .

ANNA   No. That was the demon too. Tonight I felt like touching bottom . . . the bottom of death . . . It was pulling me . . . It was a marvellous vertigo . . .

ALFRED   Be quiet, Anna. Be quiet.

ANNA   You feel it too, don't you? You're afraid. You're with me, and you're afraid. Other men have told me that . . . near me they feel like they're being pulled into an abyss . . . I always laugh, and then say: "Be quiet, be quiet . . . You frighten me . . ." And I enjoy it.

ALFRED   With you, Anna, no man will ever be happy.

ANNA   No man.

ALFRED   Any man who loves you will be condemned to misery.

ANNA   Yes. (*She is weeping*) And yet, that's all I want in the world . . . to make a man happy . . . to belong to a man, belong to a man, at peace, forever . . . to give everything, to die for the man I love . . . for my man . . . To hold his child in my arms . . . That's the dream that has grown in the sewer of Anna Kleiber . . .

(*We hear "Mam'selle." The couples are dancing*)

ALFRED   I'll follow you all my life until you say you'll marry me. I love you, Anna.

ANNA   Go away . . . You're still in time . . . Escape!

ALFRED   I'll follow you all my life . . . until . . . (*He gets up*) Let's dance . . .

(*They dance very close together. They kiss*)

ACT TWO

(*They are kissing. We still hear "Mam'selle," but the other couples have disappeared*)

ALFRED   I'll follow you all my life until you say you'll marry me. (*She weeps against his chest*) Don't cry, Anna. It makes me suffer to see you cry.

ANNA   I'm terribly afraid.

ALFRED   So am I . . . Since I was a child . . . fear has been the center of my life. We'll face our fear together, holding hands, in this dark, menacing world, Anna. We're no longer alone. It's good to go through the world two by two . . . Nothing is worse than the suffering of a lonely animal . . . I know what it is.

ANNA   I'm afraid for you, for the harm I'm going to do you, for everything you're going to suffer.

ALFRED   Don't be afraid of that. Wound me all you like. It doesn't matter.

ANNA   But you'll be sad, and I'll know you're sad because of me, and I won't be able to bear it. I'll have to leave you.

ALFRED   I'll follow you. You'll never be able to escape me. Count on me being with you forever.

ANNA   You've entered hell. My demon has another victim now.

ALFRED   (*exalted*)   Yes, now there are two of us. Let's see if he can conquer us both.

ANNA   Everyone should run from me . . . as though I were a leper . . . I am . . . No! No! This whole thing is impossible! Impossible! There's more than what I've told you. I haven't told you everything.

ALFRED   I don't care what else there is. I don't care what you tell me.

ANNA   Go away! Go away! I don't want to see you anymore. I don't want to see you!

ALFRED   (*he grabs her violently by the arms*) Anna! Anna! You're out of your mind!

ANNA   Let me go!

ALFRED   Let's get out of here. (*He takes her by the arm, and says to the audience*) We left the café. It had stopped raining. We walked down a path through the park. The nightwatchmen had lit a bonfire. By the firelight, Anna's face was soft and diabolical, (*reddish light falls on their faces*) and her body became small and took refuge in me . . . (*They are tightly embraced*)

ANNA   (*murmurs*)   Alfred . . . It's good . . . It's good to be with you, Alfred . . . I'm going to love you very deeply. I feel safe here, free from all danger . . . I love you . . . (ALFRED *kisses her*) Don't go away. Never go away. I need you. Without you, how far would poor Anna sink? You're strong enough to free me from evil. You're good. Don't leave me. Never leave me! Whatever happens, don't leave me! (*They break the embrace.* ALFRED *comes downstage while the* CLERK *and* BELLBOY *bring out a table which they place before* ANNA. *They bring her a chair.* ANNA *sits down.* ALFRED *is speaking to the audience*)

ALFRED They were eight magnificent days . . . I'll never forget them . . . We lived together in my tiny room until, one night when I returned home, Anna was no longer there. She had gone. She left me a letter. It was the first of our dreadful partings. At each one, something was torn out of my heart. I have that letter still . . . (*He takes an old folded letter from his pocket. He puts it on the table where* ANNA *is sitting. She takes the letter*) While I read it, I could hear her voice, her bitter little voice . . . (*He stands still, listening*)

ANNA (*reading*) "My darling, good-bye. I've come to love you so much, that I can't keep on with you. Before I have to leave for some other sad, disgusting reason, before something happens to make you suffer, before my weaknesses turn our life into a hell, I have decided to leave of my own free will. I'm leaving with anguish, with the deepest sorrow of my life . . . There's nothing else that pulls me away from you . . . only the thought of you. Our separation now is something beautiful and terrible . . . one of those things which people who know me say are attractive to Anna Kleiber. My behavior toward you satisfies me. This afternoon I feel good, I feel purified. I've joined a small company that is going to make a tour through Germany, your country. I'll remember you in each town, on every road. I believe, my love, that I will never see you again, and there is nothing in the world that can console me for that. Good-bye. My last kiss. Anna Kleiber."

ALFRED But I wasn't going to let her leave me like that. I looked for her. I went back to Germany and followed her. My country was agitated by political struggle at that time, and the Nazi Party had many followers. Hitler was beginning to become popular. But none of that mattered to me. I was searching for Anna. It's not important how I found her, but I did find her. They were in an old provincial theatre, presenting some commonplace play. (*The* CLERK *and* BELLBOY *have brought out a flat with a mirror.* ANNA *is making up, seated in front of it*) I went up to her room, full of anxiety. She was there. I opened the door without knocking. (*He enters the area of the mirror*) Good evening, Anna. I'm here.

ANNA Alfred!

ALFRED Yes, it's me. Don't you remember? I told you once . . . "I'll follow you all my life until . . ." Do you remember?

ANNA Yes. (*closes her eyes*) I was waiting for you. Since I left you I've done nothing but wait. But I thought you would never come. It didn't matter. It didn't matter whether you arrived or not. What mattered was that I was in love with you, that I loved you so much that I didn't even need to have you near me to be happy. It has been a good time. I've become once again that little girl I thought I had lost forever . . . that little child who played in the parks of Madrid. "It's the German's daughter," they used to say in the neighborhood . . . "a pretty child . . ." That child has come back . . . I've been good, Alfred, good and simple . . . You can be proud of me . . .

ALFRED Tomorrow you'll leave this company. We'll go to Düsseldorf. I'll introduce you to my mother. We'll be married in the parish church. (ANNA *looks at him with moist eyes*) Shall we?

ANNA Yes. (ALFRED *breaks away brusquely.* ANNA *remains motionless.* ALFRED *says to the audience*)

ALFRED She said "yes." And yet that wedding never took place. There was something dreadful waiting for us that night, something we couldn't even suspect a few moments before. Yes. Everything was prepared for the most horrible part of all: for me to kill a man, that night. And I killed him in Anna's dressing room, in that old theatre. The performance had ended. Anna and I were dining in her room when someone knocked at the door, someone who didn't know he was going to die. (*He goes back to* ANNA. *He sits down. They eat. Knock.* ANNA *and* ALFRED *look at each other*)

ANNA Come in. (CHARLES COHEN *appears in the lighted area. He is a tall, fat, smiling old man*)

COHEN Hello, Anna. I'm happy to see you.

ANNA Charles . . .

COHEN Does it surprise you to see me here?

ANNA I didn't know . . .

COHEN I was going through town with my troupe and heard you were here. So I came to see you.

ANNA Now you've seen me. You can leave.

COHEN No, Anna! I've come to spend the evening with you, to chat. How long has it been since we last saw each other? Since . . . ? Yes, since that night. Why did you leave the company, Anna? You shouldn't have left. You know we all love you there.

ANNA (*nervous*) Let me introduce Alfred

Merton. This is Mr. Cohen, my former impresario.

COHEN Very pleased, young man. (*holds out his hand which* ALFRED, *motionless, does not take*) Isn't Anna a wonderful girl? Uncontrollable! An uncontrollable, capricious marvel, that's Anna. That's what people like in Anna. When she wants, she can be very amusing! And sometimes she bares her claws like a cat. Good little Anna! How much we love her. In the theatre everyone loves her, you understand? She's known for her extravagance, for dressing wildly, for being capricious and half mad . . . but I know how much tenderness there is underneath it all.

ANNA Charles, be quiet, for God's sake.

ALFRED (*coldly*) No. Let him go on. It's interesting. He's painting a beautiful portrait of you. You know how much tenderness . . .

COHEN We spent three years wandering around the theatres of France. You know how it is . . . three years . . . And do you remember our tour to America, Anna? That was really interesting. We did Buenos Aires, Santiago, Chile . . .

ALFRED I didn't know you had been in America.

ANNA Yes, four months. Years ago.

COHEN Those were the good days! You remember what you used to say? That we were in love with life. And it was true. Everything surprised you, and you wanted to try everything to the bitter end. I remember one night in the Boca. We got drunk. Yes, yes: we got hopelessly drunk. And we danced tangos till dawn in that club.

ANNA Charles . . . (*Her voice is begging him to be silent*)

COHEN If you're interested in Anna's friendship, young man, I congratulate you. You've got a great woman there, a woman that hundreds of men have desired. You know it, Anna! How many men have always followed you: you know. And how many of them you scorned —and with what style! With that wisdom of a woman who knows what life's all about! That's what always appealed to me in you. (ANNA *has sat down, dejected*)

ALFRED You've scorned many, haven't you? Many. But others were luckier.

COHEN What do you mean, others? You can't insult Anna. Anna, how can you let him . . . ? Anna has always conducted herself irreproachably, according to our morality, the morality which rules in the theatre. We're a world apart, young man. You can't hope to understand us. What do you do? Are you . . .

an intellectual? No one from the outside can understand us. It's hopeless. You petty bourgeois can't understand the beauty of our disinterestedness, our self-sacrifice, our sins. You have nothing to reproach Anna, young man. Anna is generous, infinitely disinterested . . . and when she loves a man she gives herself freely asking nothing in return . . . That's how Anna is! That's how this miracle they call Anna Kleiber is! She would die for a friend without effort. Do you understand anything of what I'm telling you? Are you listening? Are you capable of understanding something like this?

ALFRED (*cold and pale*) All right, now get out of here.

COHEN What's this fool saying? Anna, how can you put up . . . ?

ALFRED Leave this room, sir.

COHEN Anna, you say. (*But* ANNA *is not listening*)

ALFRED Leave. Or I'll kill you. (*He grabs a knife from the table*) I'm very nervous. If you continue here, you're playing with your life.

COHEN Come now, put down that knife. Don't be a child.

ALFRED Leave! (COHEN *laughs nervously*)

COHEN Come on, you're . . . you're joking . . . (*laughs*) You're just trying to have a good time.

ALFRED I hate everything you represent. I'd like to kill you. (COHEN *laughs*) Go on and laugh. That's fine. But you're not going to laugh long. (*He advances towards him. When he sees him,* COHEN *stops laughing*)

COHEN Stop. You're out of your mind. (COHEN *backs away. He hits against the table and his hand encounters the other knife. He grabs it*) Stop. Don't be a fool. You're sick. (ALFRED *leaps on him and they entwine in a struggle with the knives.* ALFRED, *with a swift blow sinks his into* COHEN's *stomach.* COHEN *falls to the floor,* ALFRED *remains still.* ANNA *has not moved from her chair*)

ALFRED (*in a muted voice, terrified*) Anna.

ANNA (*without turning*) What have you done.

ALFRED I've killed him.

ANNA But all that he said . . . you can't kill that.

ALFRED What are we going to do now? (*a knock at the door. In a low frightened voice*) Don't answer . . . As though we had already gone. Then in a while we'll leave without anyone seeing us . . . (*He is trembling*)

ANNA (*looks at him with an unsuppressed*

look of disdain) You're very frightened. You're trembling. Try to contain yourself. It doesn't become you.

ALFRED I was insane.

ANNA I think so. (*She opens the door. It is the* PROMPTER. *He is a strange, slender man with glasses*)

PROMPTER Miss Kleiber . . .

ANNA Come in. (*She lets him in, and shows him the body*)

ANNA Yes, he's dead. Call the police.

PROMPTER No.

ANNA Why not?

PROMPTER That's not necessary. Who killed him?

ALFRED I did. It was an accident. (*He is trembling*)

PROMPTER Cohen was condemned by the Party. He was one of those damn Jews who hate us like death.

ALFRED What? What are you saying?

PROMPTER (*he seems even stranger as he speaks with the exaltation of a fanatic*) I belong to the National Socialist Party . . . Adolf Hitler is our leader . . . We shall fight until we win a definitive victory.

ALFRED Until a definitive . . . what are you talking about?

PROMPTER Until we come to power. Then those damn Jews who hate us will tremble! Come with me. You have nothing to fear. We're strong already.

ALFRED But.

PROMPTER Nothing will happen to you. As for what you've done . . . I congratulate you. Now help me get this thing out of here. We've got to get him out of the theatre.

ALFRED Someone will see us.

PROMPTER Everyone has left. The streets are empty. Help me.

(*The two take out Cohen's body.* ANNA *remains alone*)

ANNA (*she meditates. Her hands tremble, shaken by her nerves. She speaks, scarcely moving her lips*) He's a coward. He was trembling like a girl. He killed him to keep him quiet; because he was afraid to hear what Charles was saying. He killed him because he couldn't bear to listen to him like a real man. He's ashamed of me. All right, all that Charles said is true! All of it! So what? I couldn't care less what a snivel-nosed little puritan thinks of me. "We'll get married in the parish church." Keep your old parish church! I'm happy with my kind of people, with people of my race, theatre people! Perverse and crazy! However

they like! I'm happy with you. I'm happy with Charles Cohen, with the disgusting Charles Cohen. I'm disgusting too. And who can reproach me for it? No one. Anna does what she wants. Anna is part of this wretched, marvellous world. I remember . . . It's beautiful . . . The old actors' cafés . . . "There goes Anna Kleiber." Bah! What do people like you know about us, you young puritan, spoiled little mama's boy? "I'll introduce you to my mother." Keep your mother! Let me be! I like it here. It's where I belong. This is where I belong! (*She bursts into tears.* ALFRED *returns*)

ALFRED Anna.

ANNA What do you want?

ALFRED There's nothing to be afraid of.

ANNA (*somewhat ironically*) Are you sure?

ALFRED That man will take care of . . . of taking out the knife. Here . . . there are no bloodstains, you can see. (*He takes a look around the room*) Not even the sign of a struggle. And surely no one saw Cohen come into the theatre. So there's nothing to worry about.

ANNA Where did you leave him?

ALFRED We . . . threw him in the river. It flows right behind the theatre. Who . . . who is that prompter?

ANNA One of the fanatics. Of Hitler's party.

ALFRED I know that, but what kind of man is he?

ANNA I don't know.

ALFRED He has a strange way of looking at you. As though he were mad.

ANNA Perhaps he is. Are you afraid of him?

ALFRED Tonight I'm afraid of everything. I don't know how I could have done such a thing.

ANNA I can't understand it either.

ALFRED I wanted him to shut up.

ANNA I saw that.

ALFRED I couldn't stand him talking that way about you.

ANNA What way?

ALFRED So shamelessly, so impudently.

ANNA He was just remembering.

ALFRED Anna!

ANNA Yes, he was just remembering the good old days.

ALFRED You call those "the good old days?"

ANNA Yes.

ALFRED You're trying to disgust me. You're angry with me.

ANNA I'm just beginning to realize that I don't care much about you.

ALFRED Anna!

ANNA I can get along without you without feeling the least bit of pain.

ALFRED You can't say . . .

ANNA Get out of my room. I'm going to change.

ALFRED Anna, what's happening to us?

ANNA (*as though tired*) Are you going to get out?

ALFRED No.

ANNA (*makes a gesture of fatigue. She gets undressed. She is in her slip when there is a knock at the door*) Come in.

ALFRED But, Anna, how can you say come in when you're undressed?

ANNA (*raises her voice*) Come in! Such things don't bother us . . . We're. shameless . . . Are you afraid of endangering the chastity of the old prompter?

ALFRED Anna. (*The* PROMPTER *has entered. He speaks without looking at* ANNA, *who continues dressing*)

PROMPTER Fine, everything has gone well . . . There were no complications . . . It was perfectly simple . . . All that remains now is for you to present yourself to the leaders in Berlin, with a letter which I shall give you . . . I'll write it here . . . (*He sits at the table and takes out a pen*)

ALFRED Present myself to the leaders?

PROMPTER Yes, we need young men like you. You'll be useful to the Party.

ALFRED But I don't want . . .

PROMPTER (*writing calmly*) Yes, sir . . . You will present yourself to the leaders . . . You're well recommended . . . You'll be well received . . . Cohen's death is a good passport into the Party.

ALFRED I have no reason to do this. You've helped me and I'm grateful. Since we've taken care of it, there's no danger of the police . . . of their discovering . . .

PROMPTER Yes, there is a danger. (*continues writing*)

ALFRED First they'll have to find the body . . . Then begin the investigation . . . And in the meantime I'll be out of their reach . . . No one will ever know . . .

PROMPTER They can find out.

ALFRED How?

PROMPTER (*stops writing a moment*) I can tell them.

ALFRED You!

PROMPTER Don't take it so hard. We need men like you. Will you go?

ALFRED No.

PROMPTER I'm sorry. I'll call the police.

ALFRED You're a miserable bastard . . .

PROMPTER (*gently*) We need men like you. Tonight you can leave for Berlin. I wish you luck. (*He pats him on the shoulder*) Come now, it's very simple . . . All you have to do is get in with them . . . Do you want to see Miss Kleiber again soon? Tomorrow we leave for Breslau, where we'll be for two weeks. Day after tomorrow you can be together again. All right? Here's the letter. Good evening! Miss Kleiber, I just remembered . . . I was coming to tell you that the departure is at seven tomorrow morning . . . With all this I had forgotten. At seven o'clock, Miss Kleiber. You won't forget? Seven . . . (*He leaves.* ANNA *and* ALFRED *remain alone*)

ALFRED What should I do?

ANNA Go. You can come back. (*with slight irony*) After all it's just a matter of "getting in contact . . ." and that way you can rest easy . . . You'll be protected, secure, and you can be happy . . . You need that security to go on living. Go find it. I'll go on wandering from town to town, admired by some and scorned by others . . . (*She smiles*) It's my life . . . Yes, go to Berlin.

ALFRED I could come back to you right away.

ANNA Of course.

ALFRED You won't be angry if I go?

ANNA No . . . Why should I get angry? No . . .

ALFRED I'm curious to see what they're like . . . the leaders . . . And that way I'll be safe . . . It's not pleasant to feel tracked by the police. It's just two days . . . I'll be back . . .

ANNA That's right . . . But tell me when you're coming . . . I don't want you to find me in my dressing room with some arrogant provincial Don Juan . . . You know how they are . . . When the troupes arrive they dress up and lie in ambush for us actresses . . . a lucky break . . . They're gallant with us, invite us out . . . We accept . . . We enjoy ourselves with them without ever getting serious of course . . .

ALFRED Anna, what kind of joke is this? I don't understand you.

ANNA That's what I'm afraid of, Alfred. That you don't understand me. But don't look like that. You'll make me laugh. You look very comical.

ALFRED Anna, I'll come back for you in Breslau.

ANNA Yes. I'll be waiting, Alfred. Don't take long. (*with a strange smile*) You know I can't live without you.

ALFRED Good-bye. (*He starts out*)

ANNA Alfred!

ALFRED What?

ANNA Is that the way you're going to leave?

ALFRED How?

ANNA I thought that tonight . . . In my

hotel it won't surprise them if a woman like me brings a man to her room. We could be there together tonight. Nothing will happen to you. They won't discover the body so soon.

ALFRED Anna, how can you talk that way? I've killed a man. Tonight . . . (*with a shiver*) I killed a man. And you smile and joke as though nothing had happened.

ANNA Does it surprise you? Don't you know me yet? I'm hard and cold. Hadn't you realized that? Alfred . . . don't go away like this . . . (*turns her eyes to him*) Kiss me . . . (ALFRED *doesn't move*) I remember so well those nights, that wonderful week. I've never been so happy. (*Her eyes are closed*) What are you doing? Aren't you going to kiss me? Where are you? I'm waiting for you . . . Don't be afraid of me . . . You, the orderly, honest young man, don't be afraid of me . . . Don't even think of me . . . Pretend you're in a brothel . . . as if I were the smallest, most insignificant prostitute . . . as if I were already what I'm going to be some day . . . a wretched whore. (ALFRED, *who is about to break into tears, leaves the room.* ANNA *opens her eyes*) Alfred! (*No one answers. She looks sad, lights a cigarette. With the cigarette in her mouth she begins to put on her stockings as the spotlight goes out, and* ALFRED *appears on one side of the stage*)

ALFRED That night I fled from Anna. I had to leave, to tear myself away from that strange woman. Later I realized that my fear, the fear I was really feeling at that moment because of my crime, was just a pretext, a clever pretext unconsciously evolved in order to escape from that hell. In Berlin I tried to keep busy with things that would make me forget Anna. I didn't want to go back but I kept trying, at the same time and without realizing it, to give myself up to other things. I . . . (*with a sad smile*) I made contact with the leaders in Berlin. I found them to be strange, enthusiastic people, young and passionate. I freed myself from Anna by placing my hopes in their struggle. It was my only chance of escape. I didn't go back to Anna. What kind of life did she lead during that period? I found out later, and felt the most terrible remorse for my lack of generosity. Because Anna needed me and I didn't go looking for her. All my life I've been a coward. She told me so one day.

(ANNA *comes downstage at the other side and says, without looking at* ALFRED)

ANNA All your life you've been a coward, Alfred.

ALFRED You'll forgive me, Anna. You're capable of forgiving anything.

ANNA I was waiting for you in Breslau. You never came, and I was afraid for you. The Prompter knew nothing, and I thought something serious had happened to you. We finished in Breslau, the tour continued, and in each town I waited for you, but you never came. That awful tour! I thought I would lose my mind. I began to drink. Anna Kleiber wanted to explore the mystery of alcoholism. What secrets lay behind alcohol? What was hidden there, in the bottom of the bottle? Oh, it was a great temptation, and I gave myself to it wholeheartedly. My fellow actors remember how I used to make my entrances. What a scandal! Even they began to be ashamed of me. "Anna, for God's sake, can't you leave it alone? Can't you stay away from it? What you're doing is ugly. If you keep on this way, you'll kill yourself." That's how they encouraged me to drink, as you can imagine . . . Kill myself, the old dream . . . but kill myself in the most abject way . . . A drunken woman! It's ugly, isn't it? I had read Poe's tales . . . The wonderful world of the alcoholic . . . He had died of an attack, of delirium tremens. I felt the attraction of delirium tremens. I would do it too! I sought out, I tracked down the attack. I wanted to see the horrible little animals of the alcoholics . . . strange beasts surrounding me . . . I knew what I had to do, how to use up, burn out, my life. I had found the meaning of my existence. (*She starts to laugh, a strange, horrible laugh*) Hi, boys! Am I in time? (*She is speaking to an* ACTOR *who has just appeared*) Am I in time for the performance? Or did you go on without me? The performance can go on without me. What an ugly, insignificant part! Everything can go on without me. And I don't care! I want the least important role, the shortest, saddest one. That's the part for me, boys. I'm not like the others. (*laughs*)

ACTOR You've been drinking again, Anna.

ANNA Not again. Still! Ha! How funny. I made a joke! It makes me laugh! (*She laughs*)

ACTOR You don't understand . . . The performance is over . . . They had to substitute for you on the spur of the moment . . . It didn't turn out very well . . . The audience protested, Anna. Mr. Werner wants to speak with you.

ANNA To hell with Mr. Werner! (*A spot lights up* MR. WERNER *sitting at a desk.* ANNA *approaches him*) Hi, Mr. Werner, what's the trouble? (MR. WERNER *raises his head*)

WERNER You're no longer part of this company, young woman. You can pick up your last week's salary and leave.

ANNA You think that worries me?

WERNER   I don't know, but you can leave.

ANNA   Because you don't want to talk to me? You think I'm drunk?

WERNER   No. I don't want to offend you. I assure you. We'll talk some other time, if you wish.

ANNA   You despise me! You're throwing me out of your office! I disgust you, don't I?

WERNER   I said nothing like that. I've simply told you that you no longer belong to this company. And believe me, I'm sorry. I would like to have done something for you. I believe in your talent, and think you could have become a good actress. But it's impossible for you to continue with the company. Your conduct is intolerable. The theatre is an art which requires maximum discipline and seriousness. Vocation, sacrifice . . . It's not an occupation for bums and vagabonds, although at times it may seem so, Miss Kleiber.

ANNA   A preacher! A preacher in the theatre! Allow me to die laughing, Mr. Werner!

WERNER   You can have no possible complaint against me, I hope. I've always tried to be just.

ANNA   You despise us all!

WERNER   The mistake of my life, Miss Kleiber, was to get involved in the theatre. I have nothing in common with the rest of you. After many years, I still feel a stranger among my actors. I've never succeeded in understanding them.

ANNA   Shall I tell you what's the matter? You hate all of us because of what happened to you!

WERNER   Please be quiet.

ANNA   You haven't forgotten your wife is an actress. It's because of her that you hate and despise us all!

WERNER   Be quiet!

ANNA   You're throwing me out, but I'll tell you the whole truth! You're going to listen!

WERNER   (gets up)   Get out of here, you!

ANNA   Yes! She ran away with an actor! Everyone in the profession knows it! That's what you can't forgive!

WERNER   (pale)   Are you going to get out?

ANNA   (laughing)   Ah! Mr. Werner is pale, and nervous! The honest Mr. Werner! He doesn't make advances to his actresses, but we all know why! (laughs) We all know why!

WERNER   Get out, get out of here.

ANNA   Of course! You make me laugh! Good evening!

WERNER   (sits down and says dejectedly) Good evening. (He hides his face with his hands, and the spot goes out)

ANNA   At last I could drink in peace, conduct my experiment in peace . . . With my last money I got to Berlin. I was a model in a designer's shop . . . They threw me out . . . All professions were too decent for me . . . I stopped looking for work and let myself just drift along . . . I lived as I could . . . That's what I was doing while you . . . while you were engrossed in politics.

ALFRED   (from his position, where he has remained motionless)   I never stopped thinking of you.

ANNA   You became a distant dream for me, a muddy, awkward memory. I tried to remember your face among so many, and never succeeded. I kept on drinking until I had the attack. They took me to the hospital. I spent several horrible nights there. I heard wild cries all around me, voices of terror and anguish.

ALFRED   When I found you, you were badly off, thin and pale.

ANNA   Yes. A wreck of a woman, what remained after a long process of self-destruction.

ALFRED   It was by chance we met, do you remember? In the park. The Tiergarten is beautiful in spring.

ANNA   (laughs)   You remember that I laughed when I saw you?

ALFRED   (laughs also)   Yes. I was in uniform and looked a bit ridiculous.

ANNA   We both burst out laughing.

ALFRED   As if nothing had happened.

ANNA   As if we had been playing hide and seek, and had finally bumped into each other as we turned a corner.

ALFRED   As though we had fallen into each other's arms by surprise.

ANNA   Like two children.

ALFRED   As though we had just been born and had no past to torment us.

ANNA   Without bitterness or anguish.

ALFRED   And there was no need to ask for explanations. No one had to justify himself.

ANNA   We were together again. In the light of that, everything else disappeared.

ALFRED   We embraced each other laughing.

ANNA   You said, "Hi, Anna," as if we had just separated a few hours ago. You were happy and radiant as I had never seen you before.

ALFRED   I had the impression that that was the right moment for our meeting. And everything that had happened before had been unfortunate because we had met at the wrong moment. Now we could begin to be happy.

ANNA   But you weren't really so happy. I realized that afterwards.

ALFRED   There was a shadow.

ANNA   The man you had killed.

ALFRED   That crime no one knew about was tormenting me.

ANNA   We would never be able to forget that night in my dressing room.

ALFRED   But we could turn our backs upon it.

ANNA   We had to try.

ALFRED   I thought you seemed more natural, sort of humanized . . . I found you just as I wished you, an ordinary woman . . .

ANNA   I was convalescing and that made me look tranquil.

ALFRED   I loved you that way.

ANNA   Then began the second period of our love.

ALFRED   Longer than the first, more wonderful.

ANNA   During all that time you never spoke of marrying me.

ALFRED   You didn't want to.

ANNA   I don't know.

ALFRED   You spoke contemptuously of bourgeois marriages.

ANNA   I don't know. I didn't dare desire it.

ALFRED   You *were* my wife.

ANNA   Yes.

ALFRED   We had a home.

ANNA   I was at peace. I can almost say I was an exemplary housewife.

ALFRED   But you missed your other life.

ANNA   Yes, sometimes . . . I would be sad —I missed brilliant, terrible moments, during which I had shone with anger or desire, moments when I had been cruel or tender.

ALFRED   That peaceful life might have ended any day. You would have gone away.

ANNA   But there wasn't time. Do you remember that night? When we received the news that shook the whole world? It was the autumn of 1939.

ALFRED   Yes.

ANNA   You came in from the street with the newspaper. I was reading a book. (*She sits, and begins to read a book.* ALFRED *approaches. He is carrying a newspaper*)

ALFRED   Anna.

ANNA   What's the matter?

ALFRED   Nothing. And everything that has happened to us up to now has no importance. Our petty suffering.

ANNA   Alfred, what's wrong with you tonight?

ALFRED   These past few years there have been many stories like ours . . . stories of love . . . a man and a woman who meet one day . . . who try to understand each other . . . who make each other suffer . . . who break up painfully . . . who even think of killing themselves . . . who meet again . . . who finally find happiness, or exhaust all the possibilities of suffering and even go beyond . . . For these past few years everything has gone on as it always has . . . and we thought that terrible things were happening to us, and that our sorrow was something frightful, something cosmic . . . And in the meantime this other thing was brewing. Our own suffering has no importance. Now begins the affliction, the great affliction.

ANNA   I know now what has happened.

ALFRED   Yes, Anna. It's begun . . . the terrible fight.

ANNA   It was expected.

ALFRED   There was hope.

ANNA   We knew that war was inevitable.

ALFRED   Now it's here. (*gestures at newspaper*) The attack on Poland has begun. It can't stop now.

ANNA   You and your leaders wanted this war.

ALFRED   I don't know what I wanted. But now we can't stop to think . . . we can only sacrifice ourselves . . . Go to the slaughter. We'll fight in special divisions . . . divisions of Party members, from which heroes will have to come. Perhaps I'll become a hero . . . If they order me to, I can't do otherwise . . . Anna, what do you think of all this? What do you think?

(ANNA's *face suddenly seems transfigured*)

ANNA   I'm glad!

ALFRED   Anna!

ANNA   Yes, I'm glad! (*with a strange exaltation*) So war has broken out . . . at last!

ALFRED   Anna, what are you saying? . . . How can you . . . ?

ANNA   I'm saying that something terrible is going to happen, something that will make the whole world shudder . . . It's beautiful . . .

ALFRED   Anna . . .

ANNA   It was about time . . . for something to happen.

ALFRED   Anna, it's not you talking. I remember now what you used to say . . . It's your demon . . . No, you can't be glad . . .

ANNA   (*exalted*) I'm glad! We're going to live intensely, Alfred. Do you understand? I was feeling musty and old, as though I were already dead. I couldn't feel myself living . . . And now everything's going to be different . . .

ALFRED   I'll have to go.

ANNA   Oh, it will be terrible for you to go,

Alfred! It will be terrible. Don't you like what I'm saying? Don't you want me to cry for you? Everything was dying out, Alfred . . . and your body was beginning to be nothing but a sweet habit for me . . . How long has it been since you saw me cry for you, for your absence, for the risk of losing you? I saw you so secure at my side, so safe from all dangers, that you were almost without importance any longer, Alfred . . . It will be horrible for you to leave me! It'll be horrible to be alone! Oh, how I love this moment in which I begin to feel alive again!

ALFRED   Anna, this time may be different from the others. This time we may never see each other again.

ANNA   That's true!

ALFRED   I may be killed.

ANNA   Alfred! Alfred! You may be killed! Can't you see I'm crying? That means I love you . . . I had begun to wonder . . . But I'm crying . . . I love you!

ALFRED   (embracing her) Anna! Anna!

ANNA   Can't you see I'm crying?

ACT THREE

(Darkness. A bonfire is lighted. Around the fire a group of soldiers, among whom is ALFRED. They are singing "Lili Marlene." When they finish a soldier says to ALFRED:)

SOLDIER   Hey, Alfred, why aren't you singing?

ALFRED   I'm listening.

SOLDIER   You have to sing.

ALFRED   That song makes me sad.

ANOTHER SOLDIER   Have a drink. (He passes him a canteen and ALFRED drinks)

ALFRED   It's pretty, but it makes me sad.

ANOTHER SOLDIER   Let's see if you're thinking of your sweetheart. What's her name?

ALFRED   (murmuring) "Underneath the lantern, by the barrack gate . . . Darling, I remember the way you used to wait . . ." When will we see them again?

SOLDIER   What?

ALFRED   The streetlamps of Berlin . . . "T'was there you whispered tenderly, that you loved me. You'd always be my own Lili Marlene."

ANOTHER SOLDIER   You sound pretty romantic to me.

ALFRED   "Time would come for roll-call, Time for us to part . . ."

SOLDIER   Hey, you're drunk. But you've drunk less than anyone! (He takes a drink)

ALFRED   "Darling I'd caress you and press you to my heart . . ."

SOLDIER   You're really plastered!

ALFRED   "Your sweet face seems to haunt my dreams . . ."

ALL   (singing) "My Lili of the lamplight . . . My own Lili Marlene . . ." (They laugh noisily. Suddenly they are quiet and motionless)

ALFRED   It's a good song, but so sad . . . Because tonight Lili is probably walking with some other man under the streetlights of Berlin. A faceless man has his arm around her waist.

SOLDIER   (laughing without amusement) Yes, that's funny what you're saying.

ALFRED   We're far away. No one is thinking of us. We're forgotten.

ANOTHER SOLDIER   All right, shut up . . .

ALFRED   They're planning their lives without us, because everyone knows we're going to die. (in the distance a cannon shot)

SOLDIER   Okay, we can sleep awhile . . . (He lies with his arms around himself)

ANOTHER SOLDIER   Yes, we can sleep.

(The fire goes out and darkness falls on the soldiers. Light falls on a small section of the stage. ANNA is entering her room with a man)

ANNA   (taking off her overcoat and throwing it over a chair) This is my room. Number sixty-six. Will you remember? Sixty-six . . .

MAN   It's pretty.

ANNA   Do you like it? Wait a minute. I'll get some drinks. (She leaves the lighted zone, returns with a bottle and fills two glasses)

MAN   To you, Anna.

ANNA   Thanks. (They drink) I'm glad you like my place. It's comfortable, isn't it?

MAN   Yes.

ANNA   I'll put on the radio. (turns the buttons. A song is heard) Sit down.

MAN   (sitting) Anna, I'm very happy to be here with you in your own house. You know I'm in love with you.

ANNA   Come now . . . you've only known me a week . . .

MAN   That doesn't matter. I'm in love with you.

ANNA   You're a passionate kid . . . You're . . . open-hearted . . . That's what I like about you, your ingenuousness . . .

MAN   I want to marry you.

ANNA   Come now . . . what foolishness . . . Do you want another drink?

MAN   Yes. (*They drink*)

ANNA   You'll get over this soon. Take it from me, I know about these things. But don't worry . . . You've impressed me too . . . and so . . . But I have no illusions about the future . . . Love is a strange thing. The first time we think it's going to last all our lives . . . But then it turns out not to . . . and each time we realize how fleeting it is . . . this strange phenomenon they call love.

MAN   No, it's not fleeting . . . Real love lasts all one's life.

ANNA   (*laughs harshly*)   Yes. It's nice you think so . . . still. Have you gone with many women?

MAN   No. If you want to know the truth . . . (*ashamed*) no.

ANNA   You'll get to know us. And you'll get to know yourself, too.

MAN   I don't have to know anything. I'm not going to change.

ANNA   You're . . . really . . . a charming kid . . . (*He kisses her hands*) Tender and chaste . . . just the kind of man who might drive a woman like me mad . . . Did you know that I'm a . . . how shall we say it . . . a sinful woman?

MAN   No. You're not sinful . . . You're . . . I love you.

ANNA   I'm a sinful woman . . . because I'm here with you.

MAN   I don't know what you mean.

ANNA   Because you should be with some eighteen year old girl . . . walking through the park holding hands . . . and not here . . . in the room of a woman who might corrupt you . . .

MAN   You're making fun of me.

ANNA   And I'm sinful because I have a man . . . someone not you . . . A man who's far away now . . . and whose absence I fill as best I can . . . because I need to be with a man . . . I'm that kind of woman . . .

MAN   How long has . . . he been away.

ANNA   A long time. The last time I saw him was two years ago . . . during a leave he had . . . Now he's on the eastern front.

MAN   What is he? A soldier?

ANNA   He's an officer . . . He was funny in his uniform . . .

MAN   Do you love him?

ANNA   I don't think I've ever loved anyone else.

MAN   Then how can you stand being here with me?

ANNA   But I'm not here with you, kid . . . What did you think? I'm not *with* you . . . I don't care anything about you . . . You're here because I think you're attractive . . . not because you matter to me . . .

MAN   You're a strange woman.

ANNA   (*yawns slightly*)   Yes . . . (*Sirens begin to sound*)

MAN   (*rising*)   An air raid alarm.

ANNA   Yes.

MAN   What shelter do you use? Where is it?

ANNA   (*calmly*)   I never go to the shelter. I stay in my room.

MAN   It might be dangerous.

ANNA   Turn out the lights. (*He puts them out. In the half-darkness he returns to* ANNA. *At the back, the beams of lights are exploring the sky. He lights a match and by its light, looks at* ANNA's *face*)

MAN   This reminds me of a poem I read . . . By Prévert . . . Do you know it?

ANNA   No.

MAN   It was called, "Paris at Night."

ANNA   Say it.

MAN   "Three matches one by one lit in the night."

ANNA   Go on.

MAN   "The first to see your entire face . . ." (*He takes the match away from* ANNA's *face, strange in the dim light. The match has burned out. He lights another*) "The second to see your eyes . . ." (*He throws it away and lights a third*) "The third for your mouth . . . and then darkness (*He blows out the match*) to remember it all . . . holding you in my arms . . ." (*The two of them are tightly embraced in the darkness. We hear—but we don't see his figure—the voice of* ALFRED)

ALFRED'S VOICE   In the autumn of 1943 I was wounded in the chest. I was hospitalized for some time and finally was able to return to Germany on an extended leave. I went to find Anna in Room 66 of the Colonia Hotel in Berlin. That night something terrible happened. (*Light up on* ANNA's *room.* ANNA *and* ALFRED *are there*)

ALFRED   Can you imagine . . . I lay there unconscious on the ground . . . and it kept snowing . . . I had lost a great deal of blood . . . I might have stayed there . . .

ANNA   But they found you.

ALFRED   (*explaining prolixly*)   You'll see. I had fallen during the attack, and then had wandered around till I came to a small lake . . . So when our men began to retreat before the enemy fire, things got difficult for me . . . I was going to remain in enemy territory. I wouldn't have lasted the night; I would have frozen to death.

ANNA But they found you.

ALFRED Yes, the commander of the third squadron, Commander Hessman. A big kid. I realized that during our first operation together. He was a tall, strong boy. I don't know what's happened to him. He's probably dead.

ANNA Why?

ALFRED A few days after I was evacuated, the unit was hit hard. There were few survivors.

ANNA But . . .

ALFRED If they hadn't wounded me that day, they probably would have killed me a few days later.

ANNA But don't think about that now.

ALFRED I have to. (looks at ANNA) Aren't you interested in what I'm telling you?

ANNA Of course.

ALFRED You have to understand where I've been and what horrible suffering I've been through. For a moment I thought maybe you weren't interested in hearing . . .

ANNA Of course I'm interested.

ALFRED I had imagined our meeting would be different somehow. I've dreamed about it too long.

ANNA And you're disappointed . . .

ALFRED No. But you seem cold . . . After so many years, you seem cold, distant, detached from me . . .

ANNA No. You're imagining it. So much time out there has made you see things in a different way . . .

ALFRED Possibly . . . (a silence) There we used to sing a song.

ANNA What song?

ALFRED It's called "Lili Marlene." When We sang it, I would think of you.

ANNA What is it? A love song?

ALFRED It's a song for a gang of soldiers to sing over their beer mugs. (He makes a small gesture and touches his chest)

ANNA Does it hurt?

ALFRED No. Just a little. They told me they had taken all the shot out . . . Now the wound is healing . . . I'll be fine again soon.

ANNA The danger is over.

ALFRED And I'll have to return to the front.

ANNA God knows for how long.

ALFRED It looks like this war will never end. (He rises) And you? You're not telling me anything about yourself, your life . . . I didn't receive many letters . . . I'm not blaming you . . . The mail was often lost . . . It was diffi-

cult to reach the holes where we were hiding out like worms glued to the dirt . . .

ANNA My life . . . nothing . . . Grey . . .

ALFRED The war cheated you. It didn't make you live so intensely as you thought.

ANNA At the beginning I did live intensely.

ALFRED When?

ANNA When we had to separate. I suffered deeply. The first months I lived in continual tension.

ALFRED Then . . .

ANNA It was impossible . . . The situation continued for too long, and finally became a habit . . .

ALFRED Living without me finally became a habit for you . . .

ANNA Yes.

ALFRED A habit you even forgot to realize was a habit.

ANNA If you want to know the truth, that's the way it was.

ALFRED A calm, almost sweet habit . . . And then not even that . . .

ANNA I can't lie.

ALFRED Obviously.

ANNA I could tell you . . . it would be so easy . . . that I've lived in constant anguish . . .

ALFRED But why? Why should you lie?

ANNA Women usually lie in cases like this . . . They don't even lie, they just confine themselves to speaking superficially . . . And men are satisfied . . . Women are right . . . Decent women . . . Their obligation is confined to keeping their husbands satisfied . . .

ALFRED (in a strange tone) But not you. You're above all that, aren't you?

ANNA (surprised at ALFRED's tone) I . . .

ALFRED (coldly) You're a superior woman. You scorn all conventions, don't you?

ANNA Alfred . . .

ALFRED My absence wasn't enough to fill a few years of your life. How much time were you good enough to devote to me? A week, a month? And then you got bored . . .

ANNA I didn't say . . .

ALFRED Yes you did. Then you got bored. It was too much. It was monotonous, wasn't it? thinking of me, worrying about me . . . respecting my absence . . . At first it was interesting, it was beautiful . . . You've always enjoyed the unusual . . . How you suffered! Hah? Until you stopped finding it attractive to suffer for me, and fell into a certain apathy, a kind of indifference, hopefully looking forward to new emotions that would draw you out of the dull dream you'd fallen into . . . Am I right? Have I understood your problem correctly?

ANNA Yes.

ALFRED As you can see, I know you, Anna . . . You have no more secrets for me. I've penetrated the darkest corners of your . . . of your strange . . . shall I say . . . of your strange soul . . .

ANNA Say whatever you like.

ALFRED But today I feel like laughing at your strange soul, my love.

ANNA What's the matter with you?

ALFRED I'm tired.

ANNA Of me.

ALFRED Yes. I'm sick and tired of your complexes. They bore me. They distress me like a bad film that tries to be profound . . .

ANNA You have no right to treat me this way. If you're bored, go away.

ALFRED I will. But I asked you a question. What happened to your life during those years?

ANNA I have nothing to tell you.

ALFRED Wasn't there some suggestive episode . . . some new situation? Did you discover a new pleasure? Or have you gone back to desiring your own destruction, looking for it behind anything ugly . . . in the bottom of some filthy pool? What's the news of Anna Kleiber?

ANNA None.

ALFRED Come on, tell me.

ANNA I have nothing to tell.

ALFRED How many men have come up to this room? To Room 66 of the Colonia Hotel . . . where I sent my poor letters . . . How many?

ANNA Are you crazy?

ALFRED (*grabs her by the wrist*) Darling Anna, tell me . . .

ANNA Let me go, you're hurting. (ALFRED's *face has become hard*)

ALFRED Tell me, you fool . . . Your strange adventures . . . interest me . . .

ANNA Let me go. Stop.

ALFRED Tell me, you fool! Go on. I'm not joking. I have no pornographic novel to read, so tell me your life.

ANNA (*on the verge of tears*) Alfred . . . , let me go . . .

ALFRED You disgust me. I've been an idiot all my life. I still don't understand how I could have thought that you could ever mean anything real in a man's life . . . You might be a woman to waste a few minutes with . . . nothing more . . .

ANNA Alfred!

ALFRED What? Does it hurt, what I'm telling you? Does it really hurt? Dear little Anna, I can see you still keep the remains of bourgeois dignity . . . and that's not becoming in an enigmatic, emancipated woman like you. At last I can laugh at you tonight, Anna! And at myself, my old torments, my nightmares . . . in which Anna Kleiber was always the main character! Now it's all over, and I'm laughing! I'm laughing at myself. (*He weeps*)

ANNA Alfred . . . You're entirely right . . . Your mistake was to attach importance to me in your life . . . I'm not . . . I've got the soul of a common slut.

ALFRED You're right.

ANNA But that was clear from the start . . . You knew it . . . I told you: there's something in me that pulls me down . . .

ALFRED There's nothing *in* you. It's *you;* your own depravity.

ANNA (*closes her eyes*) Go on. Insult me. Perhaps that will purify me a little. Punish me. I feel a terrible need of punishment, Alfred.

ALFRED Don't count on me . . . not even for that.

ANNA I'll make you punish me.

ALFRED Leave me alone.

ANNA Your little gesture of scorn isn't enough . . . I need you to insult me . . . Do you want to know the whole truth? Yes, it all happened just as you said. I haven't respected your absence. I even forgot about your absence. It took too much imagination to be with you so long without seeing you, and I just didn't have enough. Ask, ask the porter if I've brought men up here. Of course I have! We've drunk together, we've danced, and often we talked about you . . . (ALFRED *strikes her across the face*)

ALFRED Go on! Go ahead, keep talking!

ANNA (*weeping, shouts:*) Yes! I had to get excited about something, I had to have a good time! That's right, I had to have a good time! There was nothing underneath my faithfulness, and I realized it: only emptiness and death! Tedium and sadness! And even love died out in that frightful calm that dragged on day after day. Do you want to know? To keep my love for you, to make it grow, I had to feel dirty, to corrupt myself . . . so that you would appear in my memory like some pure marvel who didn't deserve me, like something adorable . . .

ALFRED Keep on. You fill me with disgust.

ANNA I've done everything. I've been to hell and back.

ALFRED You love saying it. You feel a rare

pleasure when you say, "Anna's been to hell." It makes you feel very important to say that.

ANNA (*in a low, serious tone*)   I remember one night . . . I was in a bar, and when I saw myself in a mirror I thought I was ugly . . . I crossed my legs . . . I was putting on lipstick when a man came up . . . He said . . . I don't remember . . . something dirty and insolent . . . He had taken me for a streetwalker . . . for a common tramp . . .

ALFRED   You are.

ANNA   And instead of angering me, I thought it was amusing. And I accepted the situation, laughing to myself, delighted at the chance to play the game . . . We spoke of the price . . . and bargained a bit . . . (*laughs*) Don't you think it's funny? We bargained seriously!

ALFRED   Yes, it's funny.

ANNA   And it didn't end there. We came here. Isn't that funny? Isn't that funny?

ALFRED (*covering his ears*)   Yes . . . But shut up now . . . shut up . . .

ANNA   And here, in Room 66, the joke went on to the end. The joke . . . (*She laughs nervously.* ALFRED *has gotten up and advances slowly towards her*)

ALFRED   I told you to shut up! (*He has picked up a poker from the fireplace*)

ANNA   And there are more stories like this one . . . More stories . . .

ALFRED   You're going to shut up for good! You're going to shut up for good!

ANNA   Alfred! No, Alfred! What are you doing? Alfred?

(ALFRED *raises the poker and brings it down on* ANNA. *A cry. Total darkness and we begin to hear "Mam'selle." The blue-shaded lamp is lighted and we see the* WRITER *and* ALFRED *in the same positions in which we left them in the first act*)

WRITER   You might have killed her.

ALFRED   Yes.

WRITER   Then what?

ALFRED (*who seems tired*)   I'd like another gin. (*The* WRITER *motions to the* WAITER *who serves two more gins.* ALFRED *drinks his and says:*) I didn't go back to see Anna. I left the hotel and turned myself in to the police. They took Anna to the hospital and I was held. I knew they had saved her. The army called me back to the front. I never saw Anna again.

WRITER   But you thought of her more than ever.

ALFRED   Yes.

WRITER (*a light tone*)   It was a strange love.

ALFRED   When the war ended I was able to leave my country. I came to Barcelona two weeks ago, trying to escape from everything, from the Russians, from the German police, from myself . . . and here, instead of forgetting, I began to remember everything . . .

WRITER   I'm not surprised . . . in this city . . .

ALFRED   I wrote to Anna, and I waited for her. I told her I would be expecting her on December 26th. That if she didn't come I would assume everything was over. That I was waiting for her full of anxiety . . .

WRITER   And she set out. And Christmas afternoon she entered the Hotel Voyager . . .

ALFRED   You were there. Tell me. I want to know all the details.

WRITER   There were just a few people in the lobby . . . (*lights up on the lobby, which is empty*) There (*at the desk*) the Desk Clerk was reading a paper . . . (*The* DESK CLERK *comes and takes his place*) A man and woman were talking together over there . . . (*They enter and take their places*) I was here with some reporters. (*The* REPORTERS *enter and sit down*) when Anna Kleiber entered . . . (ANNA *enters*) She stopped a moment when she came in, as though she were going to faint. (ANNA *staggers, she passes her hand over her eyes*)

ANNA   Help me, please.

WRITER   I walked over to her. (*He approaches. The* CLERK *comes from behind the desk*)

WRITER   Is something wrong, Madame? Are you ill?

ANNA   No, it's nothing. Thank you. When I came in . . . I'm a little tired . . . Thank you. (*She goes to the desk accompanied by the* CLERK. *The* WRITER *watches her from the center of the lobby.* ANNA *leans on the desk, remains still, her eyes closed. The* CLERK *looks at her, not knowing what to do. With his eyes he interrogates the* WRITER, *who says nothing. Finally* ANNA *opens her eyes and says:*) Do you . . . have a room, please?

DESK CLERK   Yes, ma'm. Would you please fill out this form?

ANNA   Yes. (*She opens her pen and tries to write. Her hand trembles*) I'm . . . (*She smiles to excuse herself*) I'm a bit . . . My nerves . . .

DESK CLERK   I'll fill it out, ma'm. "Name?"

ANNA   Anna Kleiber.

DESK CLERK (*writes*)   K-L-I- . . .

ANNA   No, it's K-L-E-I- . . . ber.

DESK CLERK   Like this?

ANNA   Yes. Thank you.

CLERK "Nationality?"

ANNA Spanish.

CLERK Ah, but you . . . (*smiles*) With this name? (*He tries, clumsily, to be amiable*)

ANNA My father was German.

CLERK Ah . . . "Coming from . . . ?"

ANNA Paris.

CLERK "Destination?"

ANNA I don't know.

CLERK But . . . well, we have to put something.

ANNA I don't know.

CLERK Will you stay here, in Barcelona?

ANNA It's just . . . that everything depends on tomorrow, don't you see?

CLERK All right. We'll put . . . Barcelona. It's all the same. "Purpose of trip." (ANNA *says nothing. The* CLERK *repeats:*) "Purpose of trip." What shall I put? Commerce . . . Personal business . . .

ANNA Yes. Personal . . . Put down anything.

CLERK (*writes, then hands her the pen*) Would you sign, please?

ANNA Yes. (*She signs*)

CLERK Will you go upstairs now?

ANNA Yes, I have to . . . rest. Tomorrow . . . (*But she says no more*)

CLERK Room number 66.

ANNA I beg your pardon?

CLERK Room number sixty-six. (*holds out the key*)

ANNA No . . . I . . . Isn't there some other room?

CLERK No, ma'm. Sixty-six is a very nice room.

ANNA I don't know . . .

CLERK You'll be very happy with it, ma'm.

ANNA It's just . . . It's strange . . . I used to live once in a Room Sixty-six. It has unpleasant associations. In the Colonia Hotel in Berlin. Do you know it?

CLERK Me? Oh, no, ma'm.

ANNA I lived in Room Sixty-six. It's because of that. Well . . . (*She looks around*) It doesn't matter . . . I'm glad to be in Barcelona. Perhaps everything will change tomorrow. I'm happy. I surely won't sleep, in case . . . Have them call me at nine tomorrow. I have a very important appointment. I've waited all my life . . . my meeting tomorrow . . . Will you call me?

CLERK (*surprised, confused*) Yes, ma'm. Don't worry. (*to the* BELLBOY *who has picked up the suitcase*) Sixty-six. (*They go toward the elevator, enter it, the* BELLBOY *closes the elevator door, and the elevator goes up.* ALFRED, *when he sees* ANNA *disappear, falls prostrate, weeping. The* WRITER *goes to him and puts a hand on his shoulders*)

WRITER That's how it happened . . . and I, who intend to make a play out of this love story, I've decided to end it just as it began, with Anna Kleiber's arrival at the Hotel Voyager . . . after a scene with the Desk Clerk, she'll get into the elevator and disappear . . . Then you'll break into tears, just as you did . . . And I'll tell you, just as I'm doing now, that life isn't over just because Anna Kleiber has disappeared. Leave the night behind you, my friend! Look around you! The night has been long, full of bad dreams and anxiety. Many were lost in it, like you . . . No, don't speak . . . You have nothing to say to me yet . . . I'm looking at you . . . I know the placid look of hangmen's faces. Yours, no . . . It has the convulsive look of a victim who is asking fearfully, "What have I done?" How can we put you on the bench of the accused! Someday you'll put yourself there, and then . . . perhaps then, you'll decide to live a new life in which Anna Kleiber will only be a human memory. Then you'll never be a coward again. (*transition*) That's what I'll say . . . and you . . . You'll feel a little better when you hear what I've said (ALFRED *raises his head and looks at him with moist eyes*) and then . . . (*a silence; a slight gesture as though there were nothing left to say*) . . . then the curtain will fall. . . .

FRANCE

JEAN GIRAUDOUX (1882–1944) described the theatre in his *Paris Impromptu* as "a world of light, poetry, and imagination," a magical place where reality resides in the unreal. And no dramatist in the modern theatre was more of a magician than this diplomat turned playwright who revitalized the French theatre. Today we think of the French as having one of the most exciting and alive theatres in the world, but we tend to forget that from the time of Victor Hugo and Dumas *fils* until the opening of Giraudoux's *Siegfried* in 1928, France produced only one playwright of international repute—Henri Becque. It can be said without fear of exaggeration that no one man was more responsible for the renaissance of the contemporary French theatre than Jean Giraudoux.

Giraudoux's theatre is a strange mixture combining the spirit of German romanticism with the traditions of French classicism. He used legends, history, and classical myths as the basic framework for most of his plays and then infused them with a delicate fantasy which is gay and pixie-ish at the same time that it is bitter, sad, and even ironic. The result is a gossamer theatrical world which is hospitable to every form of free-wheeling irrationality and at the same time is extremely close to the most sombre aspects of everyday reality. However, Giraudoux was first of all a poet, and the most noticeable aspect of his drama is the verve and polish of the language. It is a language which has been transformed in such a way that it is capable of expressing in dramatic terms Giraudoux's belief in the essential goodness of life. "The theatre," he wrote, "is not an algebraic formula but a show; not arithmetic but magic. It should appeal to the imagination and the senses, not the intellect. For this reason the playwright must have literary ability, for it is his style that shines into the minds and hearts of the audience. Its poetry need not be understood any more than sunlight need be understood

to be enjoyed." If the playwright-magician succeeds in communicating to his audiences
through feelings, Giraudoux believes the theatre
can do a great deal to make the world a better
place in which to live. He insisted "that the real
life of a people can only be great if their unreal life, the life of the imagination and the
spirit, is great. A people's force lies in its
dreams." Whether the theatre has made the
world a better place in which to live is questionable, but there is no doubt that Giraudoux
was in large measure responsible for unleashing
those forces that have brought the French theatre to its position of dominance in our time.

JEAN ANOUILH (1910–   ) is one of the
most productive playwrights in modern times.
Since his first work appeared in 1931, he has
published more than thirty plays, and now each
new theatrical season in Paris can count on an
Anouilh play as one of its highlights. Anouilh
himself has divided his work into four general
categories: Black, Rose, Brilliant, and Grating;
but such distinctions are not very helpful in
dealing with his plays. In all of them we find
the same mixture of sombre bitterness and
broad, light-hearted farce played within the
traditional structures of nineteenth-century
melodrama. Maurice Valency succinctly described the typical Anouilh play when he wrote
that they "look a bit like *The Importance of
Being Earnest* played for tragedy." Like Wilde,
Shaw, Pirandello, and Giraudoux, the playwrights he seems to admire the most, Anouilh
has a magnificent sense of the theatre and a
crisp and lucid style of writing. He sees life
itself as theatrical, and when watching or reading his plays one can never be certain whether
the life presented on the stage is an image of
life outside of the theatre or whether the reverse is true.

But for all of Anouilh's theatrical and verbal
dexterity, each of his plays is in some way concerned with the same single theme: the fact
that the realities of man's day-by-day existence
tend to distort, deform, and finally destroy the
ideals by which he would live. This theme is
usually presented in the form of an individual's
struggle with some force or institution of society, but in every case the individual fails,
and all that remains for him as he stands amidst
the ruins of his shattered ideals is a gnawing
residue of yearning for his past innocence. At
the end of *Antigone*, Anouilh's Creon has the
following dialogue with a young page:

CREON   In a hurry to grow up, are you?
THE PAGE   Oh yes, sir.

CREON   I shouldn't be, if I were you. Never
grow up if you can help it.

Like Creon, Anouilh despairs of the contemporary world which he finds so inhospitable to
the verities of his lost childhood; but he, like
his character, knows that we do grow up and
must get on with the business of daily life. So,
with sadness and a wry hope, each year
Anouilh writes a new play that deals with another aspect of this theme which has haunted
so many writers of the twentieth century.

JEAN-PAUL SARTRE (1905–   ) for all his
modernity and commitment to the human condition, and like all contemporary French playwrights, owes more than he knows to the classical traditions of the French theatre. Even
plays as diverse in nature as *The Flies, No Exit,*
and *Nekrassov* derive their structure from the
same formal source—the tightly knit well-made
play. But such similarities stop at this point,
for Sartre and his colleagues are using the
traditional forms of drama to achieve totally
new aims. Sartre's theatre is a theatre of situation. He is not interested so much in what happens to his characters—the central concern of
a theatre that is narrative in its approach to
character—as he is in what they do. He believes that dramatic characters should not be
shaped by the actions of which they are a part.
He sees dramatic action as a fixed situation in
which the characters are revealed by the
choices they make. For this reason, unlike so
much modern drama, Sartre's theatre is not
psychological in its orientation. He is not interested in depicting the motives of his characters,
only their condition. This has prompted some
critics to accuse Sartre of using the theatre as
a means of promulgating his existentialist philosophy. It may be more rewarding, however,
to think of his plays as the work of a dramatist
giving dramatic form to existentialist ideas. In
any event, such arguments are likely to be fruitless. The important point to make about Sartre's
contribution to the modern theatre is that he,
more than any other writer, was responsible for
opening up the French theatre after the second
World War, and for helping it to become receptive to and appreciative of new ideas and
new aproaches to dramatic expression.

JEAN GENET (1910–   ) has been more
successful than any other living writer in presenting the corruption of our world because
he is not concerned with the *wrongness* of its
existence; he is enamoured of it. He revels in its
wickedness, and in all his plays he presents a
panorama of our most hideous sins. Genêt sees

[JEAN GENET, *Cont.*]

man as the victim of that existential void which Kierkegaard first described—a victim who longs to achieve a vision of God while at the same time he doubts His existence. Genêt's works chronicle the hell of an existence that has rejected God and become subject to the torment of disillusionment. However, his chief purpose in disclosing the empty values that allegedly virtuous and moral people pursue is to undermine a false and conventional type of morality so that a new and more creative ethic can come into being.

Many people who are shocked by the sordidness of his themes and the boldness of his language tend to reject Genêt as a degenerate posing as an artist. But to most serious critics of the modern theatre, Genêt is not thought of as an aesthetic poseur who seeks to impose on the popular imagination a perverse conception of love, beauty, and morality. Indeed, his honesty, his seriousness, and his artistic integrity command respect. He is a realistic observer of the extremes of human behavior, and since ours is an extremist age, Genêt's examination of the whole sphere of crime, violence, and disorder is typical of the same characteristics of thinking and feeling that permeate the work of so many modern poets as well as the abstract expressionist painters. If Genêt is absorbed with the meaning of travesty, the assumption by human beings of masks that hide their real motives and purposefully distort the true nature of their needs and desires, it is because his basic conception of life is that men, who are presumed to be virtuous, are in reality deceivers who dare not be themselves and, hence, pass off lies as authentic human behavior.

For this reason the theatre has a special hold on Genêt's imagination. The act of acting constitutes for him a kind of sanctified falsehood which cannot exist in other literary forms. The relation of actors to one another, and to their audience, has in it an element of privileged untruth that he singles out in each of his plays. Genêt's theatre is a mirror which reflects a powerful image of what our world is like, and many people, including Sartre in his book *Saint Genêt: Actor and Martyr*, believe we must look into that mirror.

EUGENE IONESCO (1912–   ), like so many of the writers in that movement which has come to be known as the "Theatre of the Absurd," is deeply committed to finding a metaphor for universal modern man that is viable in the theatre. He is looking for a metaphor that is symbolic of the inalienable part of every man—that irreducible part of each of us which exists after all the differences have been stripped away, and which is beyond and beneath all that is social, political, economic, religious, and ideological. In short, Ionesco is searching for a metaphor of man left face to face with himself. For this reason his theatre, at least not until his most recent plays, is not a social theatre. It is, rather, a theatre that reveals man detached from the machinery of society—man with no function, man with no historical situation. It is a theatre that shows man defined by his solitude and estrangement, not by his participation.

In all his plays Ionesco goes deep into the immediate experience of the metaphysical absurd by isolating and objectifying it. (Ionesco has defined the absurd as "that which has no purpose, or goal, or objective.") No magic, no divinity with impenetrable ways, is held responsible for man's condition; there are no sociological or psychological explanations. Ionesco quite simply communicates the bewildering paradox of man's life and the complete absurdity of the mechanism of his being. Ionesco's theatre is the image of a world where everything is equally important and, by the same token, unimportant.

But to express this kind of image of the world requires a new dramatic form. Ionesco makes it quite clear that he wants a theatre "which progresses not through a predetermined subject and plot, but through an increasingly intense and revealing series of emotional states." As a result, he has created a form of drama which might best be called contextual. His drama is a drama of situation alone, a drama in which the situation has been inflated to replace the plot. The purpose of his plays is not to represent an action, but to reveal a condition.

It is still too soon to tell where Ionesco's "anti theatre" will finally come to rest, but it is already clear that Ionesco has done the modern theatre a great service by experimenting with new forms and with nonverbal techniques. He has broken down many of Naturalism's restrictions and, in so doing, has opened up the theatre so that it is now receptive to many new forms of experimentation.

SAMUEL BECKETT (1906–   ) is a playwright whose success has been one of the most amazing phenomena in the contemporary theatre. Audiences find themselves going to his plays, being moved or amused by them, and applauding them, fully aware that they don't always know what they mean or what this transplanted Irishman living in France really

[SAMUEL BECKETT, *Cont.*]

intends. For all their seeming unintelligibility and simplicity, in their boldly experimental nature they are symptomatic of the unrest that prevails in the modern theatre.

Beckett, like so many of his colleagues, believes that the theatre must express the senselessness and irrationality of all human actions. He believes the theatre must confront audiences with that sense of isolation—the sense of mans' being encircled in a void—which is an irremediable part of the human condition. In such a universe, communication with others is almost impossible, and the language of Beckett's plays is symptomatic of his belief in man's incapability to communicate and express his basic thoughts and feelings. This has prompted Wallace Fowlie to say that all of Beckett's plays "give the impression of being autopsies of one's unacknowledged, invisible manias." All that happens in them is beyond rational motivation, happening at random or through the "de-mented caprice of an unaccountable idiot fate." But in reducing the human situation to its ultimate absurdity, Beckett realizes that the stereotyped dramatic progressions of our determinism-oriented, naturalistic theatre will no longer satisfy. He is searching for a new form, new techniques—techniques that are expressive of the central fact of our world: that man's unconscious is of no more help to him than his intelligence in solving time's inscrutable ironies. The most striking thing about Samuel Beckett's plays is that on the surface they seem to be either unintelligible or simple to the point of absurdity. Yet his plays are the result of a serious attempt to give dramatic form to all the complexities of our world. Today we must embrace the idea of paradox in our art as well as our foreign policy, and Beckett would probably agree with Duerrenmatt's statement that "our world seems still to exist only because the atom bomb exists: out of fear of the bomb."

Jean Giraudoux

1882-1944

TWO LAWS

Two laws govern—if I may thus express myself—the eternal status of the playwright.

The first law defines the sad and slightly ridiculous position of the playwright toward those of his characters he has created and given to the theatre. Just as a character, before being played by an actor, is docile toward the author, familiar, and a part of him—as you may judge from my own creations—so once he appears before the audience he becomes a stranger and indifferent. The first actor who plays him represents the first in a series of reincarnations by which the character draws further and further away from his creator and escapes him forever.

In fact, this is true of the play in its entirety. From the first performance on, it belongs to the actors. The author wandering in the wings is a kind of ghost whom the stagehands detest if he listens in or is indiscreet. After the hundredth performance, particularly if it is a good play, it belongs to the public. In reality the only thing the playwright can call his own is his bad plays. The independence of those of his characters who have succeeded is complete: the life they lead on road tours or in America is a constant denial of their filial obligations. So while the hero of your novels follows you everywhere, calling you "father" or "papa," those of your stage characters you chance to meet—as I have—in Carcassonne or Los Angeles, have become total strangers to you.

It was largely to punish them for this independence that Goethe, Claudel, and so many other writers wrote a new version for their favorite heroines—but in vain. The new Marguerite, the new Hélène, or the new Violaine left their creators just as quickly. Once I was at a performance of Claudel's *The Tidings Brought to Mary*. That day, at least, this law operated in my favor: I noted that the play belonged more to me than to Claudel.

How many playwrights are forced to seek in an actor or actress the memory or reflection of their sons and daughters who have escaped; just as, in daily life, other parents look for the same thing in a son-in-law or daughter-in-law. . . . On the terrace of the Café Weber, in the lobby during a dress rehearsal, on the lawn of the country house of a noted actress, how often we have met such couples: Feydeau and Mme. Cassive, Jules Renard and Suzanne Desprez, Maurice Donnay and Réjane.[1] The woman slightly inattentive, the man alert, reminiscing, chatty, full of questions, was talking of his absent "child."

The second law, a corollary and inverse of the first, defines the wonderful position of the playwright toward his era and its events, and indicates his role therein. Here, if I wish to be sincere, I must strip myself and my colleagues of all false modesty. The figure who in the play is merely a voice, without personality, without responsibility, implacable, but a historian and an avenger, exists in a given era in flesh and blood: the playwright himself. Of all writers in the theatre worthy of the name, one should be able to say, when they appear: Add the archangel! It is futile to believe that a year or a century can find the resonance and elevation

[1] Georges Feydeau, Jules Renard, and Maurice Donnay, French boulevard playwrights popular in the first part of the twentieth century, and Mme. Cassive, Suzanne Desprez, and Réjane, actresses famous for performing in their plays.

ultimately befitting the emotional debate and effort represented by each period of our passage on earth, if it does not have a spokesman of its tragedy or drama in order to reach its heights or plumb its depths. Tragedy and drama are the confession which humanity—this army of salvation and ruin—must also make in public, without reticence and in loudest tones, for the echo of its voice is clearer and more real than its voice itself. Make no mistake about it. The relationship between the theatre and religious ceremonial is obvious; it is no accident that in former times plays were given on all occasions in front of our cathedrals. The theatre is most at home on the open space in front of a church. That is what the audience goes to, on gala evenings in the theatre: toward the illuminated confession of its petty and giant destinies.

Calderon is humanity confessing its thirst for eternity, Corneille its dignity, Racine its weakness, Shakespeare its appetite for life, Claudel its state of sin and salvation, Goethe its humanity, Kleist its vividness. Epochs have not come to terms with themselves unless crowds, dressed in their most striking costumes of confession, so as to increase the solemnity of the occasion, come to these radiant confessionals called theatres and arenas, to listen to their own avowals of cowardice and sacrifice, hatred and passion. And unless they also cry: Add the prophet!

For there is no theatre save that of divination. Not that false divination which gives names and dates, but the real thing: the one which reveals to men these amazing truths—that the living must live, that the living must die, that autumn follows summer, spring follows winter, that there are four elements happiness, millions of catastrophes, that life is a reality, that it is a dream, that man lives by peace, that man lives by blood; in short, what they will never know.

That is theatre: the public recall of those incredible splendors whose visions disturb and overwhelm audiences by night. But—and this it is which heartens me—already by dawn the lesson and the memory are diluted, no doubt in order to make the writer's mission a daily one. Of such is the performance of a play: the sudden awareness in the spectator of the permanent state of this living and indifferent humanity—passion and death.

Translated by Joseph M. Bernstein

DISCOURSE ON THE THEATRE

Dear comrades, only orators are interrupted by emotion. The pharynx of the writer, as it is a tool of secondary value, remains open in moments when that of lawyers or politicians would close. If, therefore, I respond to our president in my clearest voice, do not believe that I am any the less aware of his kind words and your reception. Through his friendly intervention, you have granted me the role of presiding over the annual meeting which places on the faces of several generations the same mask, not of youth, alas, but of childhood; to preside over friends who meet again after thirty years of separation, and over colleagues who knew each other only by name and who are suddenly found seated together, a symphony of shouts and laughter which we have not heard since the days of the school dining hall, and which gave rise to the same echoes on the rue de Poitiers as on the Avenue de Déols: Duchâteau, Malinet, Bailly, Delacou, Naudin, Berthon. . . . Believe me, I am profoundly grateful to you for this event.

I would have limited myself to an expression of this satisfaction and gratitude if during this past week some of my friends had not asked me, in letters and personally, to make my response less brief. As fellow classmates, they have followed the effort which I have been making in the theatre during the past three years. They have been surprised to find that this effort has recently provoked the most opposite reactions among critics who generally agree. They would like me to present here an explanation of such divergence of opinion, and I will do so gladly. Do not politicians select precisely such friendly gatherings as this to expound their aims or to justify their actions? It seems to restore to their ambitions a color and a freshness which they quite conceivably may have lost, by plunging them once again into this bath of youthfulness. Why shouldn't writers imitate them? Who could possibly better understand and lend strength to a man of letters than those who opened the classics for the first time in the same editions, recited in the same classrooms, and committed their first barbarisms and grammatical errors with the same French or Latin words?

"Discourse on the Theatre" by Jean Giraudoux, translated by Haskell M. Block, is from *The Creative Vision*, edited by Haskell M. Block and Herman Salinger. Copyright © 1960 by Grove Press, Inc.

Besides, I am not completely sure that I shall not be presenting a political, or at least a social, discourse. The subject of the theatre and its plays, which has been of major and at times decisive importance in human history, has lost none of its significance at a time when the average person sees his spare time for leisure and amusement increased enormously as his working day is reduced to seven or eight hours. The stage is the only form of a nation's spiritual and artistic education. It is the only evening activity that is good for old men as well as for young adults, the only way by which the most humble and unlettered public can enter into direct contact with the greatest of conflicts and create for itself a lay religion, a liturgy and saints, feelings and passions. There are some persons who have dreams, but for those who do not dream there is the theatre. The lucidity of the French people in no way implies its rejection of great spiritual forces. The cult of the dead, this cult of heroes which dominates the French people proves conclusively that it loves to see great persons, persons who are at once near and unapproachable, living its humble and definite life amid nobility and the indefinite. Its cult of equality also is flattered by this model of equality before the emotion which constitutes the theatre when the curtain rises, an equality surpassed only by that of the corn field at harvest time. If it is admitted but once a year, in the midst of our national holiday, to the free matinée of the 14th of July, as befits our democracy, to live for a few hours at the Odéon and at the Comédie-Française with kings and queens, with movements as kings and passions queens, believe me when I tell you that the public is not to be blamed for it. Wherever it may find an alternative to the mediocrity of the stage, it hurries. In the few hallowed places as yet unpolluted by the disease of the scurrilous and the easy, masses of spectators from all classes of the population are crowded together, listening respectfully to the most obscure of the works of Aeschylus or Sophocles, it mattering very little that they grasp its details, for the tragic works on them as a curative of gold and the sun. In the mask of costume, the tapestry of the set, the undergrowth of words, this assembly of charming Epicureans and of happy owners of hunting licenses—which generally constitutes an audience in southern France—follows with anguish and passion the serpentine meandering of the invisible hydra which has arisen from the most magnificent antiquity; for it is in the brightest and purest of epochs that the monsters of the soul have their lair. Saints at Orange! Do southern cities alone suddenly give emotion and intelligence to spectators who just as suddenly in other places become devotees of the café concert and the talking film? Is it that the open sky restores the primitive nobility of an audience, and that under a roof the Frenchman sinks again into vulgarity? No, it is that around these privileged enclosures the public is imbued with respect for the theare, that it is urged by its leaders and even by municipalities to cultivate an instinctive and exact conception of the theatre. . . . In Paris it loses it; it has lost it.

It has lost it because instead of respecting the theatre and raising oneself to its level, a few men of the theatre have claimed to appeal only to its pliability and its meanness. Incomprehension if not outright scorn of the public has been the axiom of a definite part of the Paris stage. All that counts is to please by the most common and basest of means. As the French language, when spoken and written correctly, itself resists this blackmail and obeys only those whom it respects, it is against the language that this offensive has been led, and for plays in which it is not insulted and deformed, some have found an epithet tantamount, it would seem, to the worst of insults: that of literary plays. If, in your work, your characters avoid this enfeeblement of expression with which some writers have come to mark even their play on sounds or their monosyllables; if, through the study of character, the detail of explanation, you depart no matter how little from this platform improvisation which represents the ideal play for more than one director, you hear it said at once, more or perhaps less crudely—for such insults are always expressed with caution—that you are not a man of the theatre but a writer of literature. You learn, then, for your guidance, that while every domain of activity in France is open to literature, there are exactly two areas formally barred to it: the theatre and the cinema. It is clear why directors should have this conviction. They are in charge of an enterprise; they have to lead it to success and not to a deficit; the stinginess of the government prevents them from being educators or philanthropists. Their art of poetry stops at their balance sheet. It is also true that the platform theatre which has become our theatre of the boulevards can produce models, perishable, like all that is gesture and not language, but models all the same. Certain critics, however, themselves men of letters, undergo a fit of impatience before a play that is written and not spoken, and before launching against it an attack which might on other grounds be justified, take not the slightest trouble to inform their reader in what noble enclosure this tourney is held; and this is less allowable. And when some of them, vaguely aware of their wrongdoing, tell you, to excuse themselves: "What a dull play, but how we will enjoy reading it!" they are judging themselves, for this statement gives its true meaning to the applause they lavished the night before on another play: "What a successful play! How we will enjoy not reading it!"

You understand, of course, that I have no intention of undertaking here an appraisal of these drama critics. Their probity is absolute; their sincerity is unfortunately without question. And insofar as their love of the theatre is concerned, there is once again no basis for distinguishing them from those famous predecessors of whom Antoine [2] was the most illustrious, and from the numerous youths who work as hard as they can to bring about a literary theatre. Nor is the bad faith and the inconsequence of their remarks of any importance, nor the uncertain taste revealed in their articles which ought, none the less, to connect them to literature. It makes little difference that the drama critic of one of our most important morning papers, reviewing a play wherein he condemns its questionable style, calls one Jewess devoted to another an "Estheromane" and an effeminate military aide "the tent-keeper" of Holophernes. It makes little difference that the poetess who personifies for us delicacy and modesty states, in her review of a play in which the action takes place at Bethulia and in which the language does not seem quite pure, that she was "Borethuled" by it, and calls pure virgins "girls who want to break their jugs." The pun is perhaps the ideal form of expression for the excitable purist shocked by Gongorisms.[3] But the harm is not there. The harm comes from the fact that this variety of critics represents an outmoded variety, the fashionable sort, and we no longer have a literature catering to fashion any more than a fashionable society. The harm—I mean, of course, the good thing about it all—is that the theatre, the novel, even criticism, instead of serving as mere accessories of a peaceful and superficial middle-class life, have become once more, in our age as in every age of fullness and

anxiety, tools of primary necessity. This dismemberment of the body of literature into several fragments, performed in a happy century for the benefit of salons and parties, and which had brought novelists, journalists, playwrights, and philosophers to form so many hostile and independent cliques, no longer has any justification. The man of letters feels perfectly at home in the theatre, in the newspaper, in the advertising office: he has invaded all of these realms. The heart of literature has been rediscovered, this magnet which will bring once more into a single unit so many scattered limbs, and this heart is the writer, it is writing. Every great upheaval of minds and manners diminishes the importance of literary *genres* in themselves but increases a hundred fold the role of the writer and gives him back his universality. Our epoch no longer demands works from the man of letters—the streets and courtyards are filled with such useless furniture—it demands from him above all else a language. It no longer expects the writer to play the fool to the happy king, relating his truths in soothing and successful novels or plays, critiques which are as contemptible as they are flattering; the age expects him to reveal his truth to it and, so that it may organize his thought and his sensibility, to entrust it with the secret which the writer alone possesses: that of style. That is what it also demands from the theatre. The protests of those who do not care to distinguish between theatrical works aiming at the formation of the public and those which seek only to flatter or to please it no longer count for anything, for the public is against them and with us. The public at the theatre, listening to a text, has absolutely no experience of what the half-learned call boredom. Its seat at the theatre has the extraterritoriality of an embassy in an ancient or heroic kingdom, in the domain of illogic and fantasy, and it intends to preserve its solemn character. The affection which the public holds for the theatre in verse is the expression of this veneration for vocabulary and style. It admires in verse the work well done, the consciousness and care which it ascribes to the poet. But when a writer reveals that his prose is not flabby, not low, not obscene, not easy, it asks only to believe him, and is carried away when it suddenly sees, in place of the substitute coin which marks the theatrical style, the actor and the actress exchanging words which disclose that a people's most precious possession, its language, is laden with gold.

These, dear friends, are the reflections which the theatre of today can inspire in a writer. If

---

[2] Andre Antoine (1858–1943), founder of the Théâtre Libre and largely responsible for introducing naturalism into the French theatre.

[3] A metaphorical technique first used and explained by the Spanish Golden Age poet, Don Luis De Gongora.

they have been expressed somewhat briefly, I ask you above all not to blame those among you who are responsible for them. I would have given them to you sooner or later of my own accord, for despite the advances which Delphi, Orange, and Munich have made to me, Châteauroux remains my favorite theatre town, ever since that evening when I was in the sixth grade, when we were lined up in the way we used to be to go to the chapel or the bath, and were led for the first time to the theatre. Silvain was playing the role of aged Horace, and every adolescent in the province of Berry waited passionately for the words, "Let him die," and the stage took on an unexpected grandeur for the curtain did not work and was held up with pikes, by two firemen of Châteauroux in uniform.

Translated by Haskell M. Block

ELECTRA

English Version by Winifred Smith

CAST OF CHARACTERS

ORESTES

THE EUMENIDES, *first as three little girls, later as fifteen-year-olds*

GARDENER

PRESIDENT OF THE COUNCIL

AGATHA, *his young wife*

AEGISTHUS

BEGGAR

CLYTEMNESTRA

ELECTRA

YOUNG MAN

CAPTAIN

NARSES' WIFE

GUESTS, SERVANTS, MAIDS, SOLDIERS

ACT ONE

Scene One

(*A stranger,* ORESTES, *enters, escorted by three little girls, just as, from the opposite side, the* GARDENER *comes in dressed for a festival, and accompanied by guests from the village*)

FIRST LITTLE GIRL   How fine the gardener looks!

SECOND LITTLE GIRL   Of course! It's his wedding day.

THIRD LITTLE GIRL   Here it is, sir, your Agamemnon's palace!

Electra by Jean Giraudoux, translated by Winifred Smith. Copyright 1955 by Winifred Smith. All inquiries concerning performance rights, including readings, should be addressed to Mme. Ninon Tallon Karlweis, 57 West 58th St., N. Y. 19, N. Y., exclusive agent for Jean Giraudoux.

STRANGER   What a strange façade! Is it straight?

FIRST LITTLE GIRL   No. There's no right side to it. You think you see it, but that's a mirage. Like the gardener you see coming, who wants to speak to you. He's not coming. He won't be able to say a word.

SECOND LITTLE GIRL   Or he'll bray—or meow—

GARDENER   The façade is perfectly straight, stranger. Don't listen to these liars. You are confused because the right side is built of stones from Gaul and sweats at certain seasons; that the people say the palace is weeping. The left side is built of marble from Argos, which—no one knows why—will suddenly be flooded with sunshine, even at night. Then they say the palace laughs. Right now the palace is laughing and crying at the same time.

FIRST LITTLE GIRL   So it's sure not to be mistaken.

SECOND LITTLE GIRL   It's really a widow's palace.

FIRST LITTLE GIRL   Or of childhood memories.

STRANGER   I can't remember seeing such a sensitive building anywhere.

GARDENER   Have you already visited the palace?

FIRST LITTLE GIRL   As a baby.

SECOND LITTLE GIRL   Twenty years ago.

THIRD LITTLE GIRL   He couldn't walk yet.

GARDENER   But he must remember if he saw it.

STRANGER   All I can remember of Agamemnon's palace is a mosaic. They set me down on a square of tigers when I was naughty and on a hexagon of flowers when I was good,—and I remember creeping from one to the other across some birds.

FIRST LITTLE GIRL   And over a beetle.

STRANGER   How do you know that, child?

GARDENER   And did your family live in Argos?

STRANGER   And I remember many, many

bare feet. Not a face, faces were way up in the sky, but lots of bare feet. I tried to touch the gold rings under the edges of the skirts; some ankles were joined by chains, slaves' ankles. I remember two little feet, very white ones, the barest, the whitest. Their steps were always even, timid, measured by an invisible chain. I imagine they were Electra's. I must have kissed them, mustn't I? A baby kisses everything it touches.

SECOND LITTLE GIRL   Anyway that would have been the only kiss Electra ever had.

GARDENER   It surely would!

FIRST LITTLE GIRL   Jealous, gardener?

STRANGER   Electra still lives in the palace?

SECOND LITTLE GIRL   Still. But not much longer.

STRANGER   Is that her window, the one with jasmine?

GARDENER   No. That's the room where Atreus, the first king of Argos, killed his brother's sons.

FIRST LITTLE GIRL   The dinner when he served up their hearts took place in the room next it. I'd love to know how they tasted.

THIRD LITTLE GIRL   Did he cut them up or cook them whole?

SECOND LITTLE GIRL   And Cassandra was strangled in the sentry box.

THIRD LITTLE GIRL   They caught her in a net and stabbed her. She yelled like a crazy woman, through her veil. I'd love to have seen it.

FIRST LITTLE GIRL   That all happened in the laughing wing, as you see.

STRANGER   The one with roses?

GARDENER   Stranger, don't try to connect the windows with flowers. I'm the palace gardener. I plant them at random. They're just flowers.

SECOND LITTLE GIRL   Not at all. There are flowers and flowers. Phlox doesn't suit Thyestes.

THIRD LITTLE GIRL   Nor mignonette Cassandra.

GARDENER   Oh, be quiet! The window with the roses, stranger, is the one of the rooms where our king, Agamemnon, coming back from the war, slipped into the pool, fell on his sword and killed himself.

FIRST LITTLE GIRL   He took his bath after his death. About two minutes after. That's the difference.

GARDENER   That's Electra's window.

STRANGER   Why is it so high up, almost on the roof?

GARDENER   So she can see her father's tomb.

STRANGER   Why is she there?

GARDENER   Because it's Orestes' old room,

her brother's. Her mother sent him out of the country when he was two and he's not been heard of since.

SECOND LITTLE GIRL   Listen, sisters, listen! They're talking about Orestes!

GARDENER   Will you clear out! Leave us! You're just like flies.

FIRST LITTLE GIRL   We certainly won't leave. We're with this stranger.

GARDENER   Do you know these girls?

STRANGER   I met them at the door. They followed me in.

SECOND LITTLE GIRL   We followed him because we like him.

THIRD LITTLE GIRL   Because he's a lot better looking than you are, gardener.

FIRST LITTLE GIRL   No caterpillars in his beard.

SECOND LITTLE GIRL   Nor June bugs in his nose.

THIRD LITTLE GIRL   If flowers are to smell sweet, the gardener has to smell bad.

STRANGER   Be polite, children, and tell us what you do all the time.

FIRST LITTLE GIRL   What we do is, we're not polite.

SECOND LITTLE GIRL   We lie, we slander, we insult.

FIRST LITTLE GIRL   But specially, we recite.

STRANGER   And what do you recite?

FIRST LITTLE GIRL   We never know ahead of time—we invent as we go along. But we're very, very good.

SECOND LITTLE GIRL   The king of Mycenae, whose sister-in-law we insulted, said we were very, very good.

THIRD LITTLE GIRL   We say all the bad things we can think up.

GARDENER   Don't listen to them, stranger. No one knows who they are. They've been wandering about the town for two days without friends or family. If we ask who they are, they pretend they're the little Eumenides. And the horrible thing is that they grow and get fat as you look at them. Yesterday they were years younger than today. Come here, you!

SECOND LITTLE GIRL   Is he rude, for a bride-groom!

GARDENER   Look at her! See how her eye-lashes grow. Look at her bosom. I understand such things, I've seen mushrooms grow. They grow fast, like an orange.

SECOND LITTLE GIRL   Poisonous things always win out.

THIRD LITTLE GIRL (*to the* FIRST LITTLE GIRL) Really? You're growing a bosom?

FIRST LITTLE GIRL   Are we going to recite or not?

STRANGER   Let them recite, gardener.

FIRST LITTLE GIRL   Let's recite Clytemnestra, Electra's mother—You agree? Clytemnestra?

SECOND LITTLE GIRL   We agree.

FIRST LITTLE GIRL   Queen Clytemnestra has a bad color. She uses rouge.

SECOND LITTLE GIRL   Her color is bad because she sleeps badly.

THIRD LITTLE GIRL   She sleeps badly because she's afraid.

FIRST LITTLE GIRL   What is Queen Clytemnestra afraid of?

SECOND LITTLE GIRL   Of everything.

FIRST LITTLE GIRL   What's everything?

SECOND LITTLE GIRL   Silence. Silences.

THIRD LITTLE GIRL   Noise. Noises.

FIRST LITTLE GIRL   The idea that midnight is near. That the spider on its thread is about to pass from the time of day when it brings good luck to the time when it brings bad luck.

SECOND LITTLE GIRL   Of everything red, because blood is red.

FIRST LITTLE GIRL   Queen Clytemnestra has a bad color. She puts on blood.

GARDENER   What a silly story!

SECOND LITTLE GIRL   Good, isn't it?

FIRST LITTLE GIRL   See how the end goes back to the beginning—couldn't be more poetic!

STRANGER   Very interesting.

FIRST LITTLE GIRL   As you're interested in Electra we can recite about her. You agree, sisters? We can recite what she was like at our age.

SECOND LITTLE GIRL   We certainly do agree!

THIRD LITTLE GIRL   Even before we were born, before yesterday, we agreed.

FIRST LITTLE GIRL   Electra amuses herself by making Orestes fall out of his mother's arms.

SECOND LITTLE GIRL   Electra waxes the steps of the throne so her uncle Aegisthus, will measure his length on the marble.

THIRD LITTLE GIRL   Electra is preparing to spit in the face of her little brother, Orestes, if he ever returns.

FIRST LITTLE GIRL   Of course, *that* isn't true, but it'd be a good story.

SECOND LITTLE GIRL   For nineteen years she's prepared poisonous spittle in her mouth.

THIRD LITTLE GIRL   She's thinking of your slugs, gardener, to make her mouth water more.

GARDENER   Now stop, you dirty little vipers!

SECOND LITTLE GIRL   Oh, ha, ha, the bridegroom gets mad!

STRANGER   He's right. Get out!

GARDENER   And don't come back!

FIRST LITTLE GIRL   We'll come back tomorrow.

GARDENER   Just try to! The palace is forbidden to girls of your age.

FIRST LITTLE GIRL   Tomorrow we'll be grown up.

SECOND LITTLE GIRL   Tomorrow will be the day after Electra's marriage to the gardener. We'll be grown up.

STRANGER   What are they saying?

FIRST LITTLE GIRL   You've not defended us, stranger. You'll be sorry for that.

GARDENER   Horrible little beasts! You'd think they were three little Fates. Dreadful to be a child Fate!

SECOND LITTLE GIRL   Fate shows you her tail, gardener. Watch out if it grows.

FIRST LITTLE GIRL   Come, sisters. Let's leave them both in front of their tainted wall.

(*The little* EUMENIDES *go out, the* GUESTS *shrinking away from them in terror*)

Scene Two

(*The* STRANGER. *The* GARDENER. *The* PRESIDENT OF THE COUNCIL *and his young wife,* AGATHA THEOCATHOCLES. *Villagers*)

STRANGER   What did these girls say? That you are marrying Electra, gardener?

GARDENER   She'll be my wife an hour from now.

AGATHA   He'll *not* marry her. We've come to prevent that.

PRESIDENT   I'm your distant cousin, gardener, and the Vice-President of the Council; so I've a double right to advise you. Run away to your radishes and squashes. Don't marry Electra.

GARDENER   Aegisthus orders me to.

STRANGER   Am I crazy? If Agamemnon were alive, Electra's wedding would be a festival for all Greece—and Aegisthus gives her to a gardener, whose family, even, objects! Don't tell me Electra is ugly or hunch-backed!

GARDENER   Electra is the most beautiful girl in Argos.

AGATHA   Oh, she's not too bad looking.

PRESIDENT   And she's perfectly straight. Like all flowers that grow in the shade.

STRANGER   Is she backward? Feebleminded?

PRESIDENT   She's intelligence personified.

AGATHA   An especially good memory. Not always for the same thing, though. I don't have a good memory. Except for your birthday, darling, *that* I never forget.

STRANGER What can she have done, or said, to be treated this way?

PRESIDENT She does nothing, says nothing. But she's always *here*.

AGATHA She's here now.

STRANGER She has a right to be. It's her father's palace. It's not her fault he's dead.

GARDENER I'd never have dreamed of marrying Electra, but as Aegisthus orders me to, I don't see why I'd be afraid.

PRESIDENT You have every reason to be afraid. She's the kind of woman that makes trouble.

AGATHA And you're not the only one! Our family has everything to fear.

GARDENER I don't understand you.

PRESIDENT You will understand. Life can be pleasant, can't it!

AGATHA Very pleasant! Immensely so!

PRESIDENT Don't interrupt me, darling, especially just to repeat what I say. It *can* be very pleasant. Everything has a way of settling itself in life—spiritual suffering can be cured more quickly than cancer, and mourning than a sty. Take any group of human beings at random, each will have the same percentage of crime, lies, vice and adultery.

AGATHA That's a horrid word, adultery, darling.

PRESIDENT Don't interrupt me, especially to contradict! How does it happen that in one group life slips by softly, conventionally, the dead are forgotten, the living get on well together, while in another there's hell to pay? It's simply that in the latter there's a woman who makes trouble.

STRANGER That means there's a conscience in the second group.

AGATHA I can't help thinking of your word, adultery—such a horrid word!

PRESIDENT Be quiet, Agatha. A conscience, you say! If criminals don't forget their sins, if the conquered don't forget their defeats, if there are curses, quarrels, hatreds, the fault is not with humanity's conscience, which always tends toward compromise and forgetfulness, it lies with ten or fifteen women who make trouble.

STRANGER I agree with you. Those ten or fifteen women save the world from egoism.

PRESIDENT They save it from happiness! I know Electra. Let's agree that she is what you say—justice, generosity, duty. But it's by justice, generosity, duty, and not by egoism and easy going ways, that the state, individuals, and the best families are ruined.

AGATHA Absolutely! But why, darling? You've told me, but I forget.

PRESIDENT Because those three virtues have in common the one element fatal to humanity—implacability. Happiness is never the lot of implacable people. A happy family makes a surrender. A happy epoch demands unanimous capitulation.

STRANGER You surrendered at the first call?

PRESIDENT Alas, no! Some one else got in first. So I'm only the vice-president.

GARDENER Against what is Electra implacable? She goes every night to her father's tomb, is that all?

PRESIDENT I know. I've followed her. Along the same road which my duty made me take one night, pursuing our most dangerous murderer, along the same river I followed and saw the greatest innocent in Greece. A horrible walk, behind the two of them. They stopped at the same places, at the yew, at the corner of the bridge, at the thousand year old milestone, all made the same signs to innocence and to crime. But because the murderer was there, the night was bright, peaceful, clear. He was the kernel taken out of the fruit, which, in a tart, might have broken your tooth. Electra's presence, on the contrary, confused light and darkness, even spoiled the full moon. Have you seen a fisherman, who before going out to fish, arranges his bait? All the way along the river, that was she. Every evening she spreads her net for everything that without her would have abandoned this pleasant, agreeable earth—remorse, confessions, old blood stains, rust, bones of murdered men, a mass of accusations. In a short time everything will be ready for the fisherman to pass by.

STRANGER He always comes, sooner or later.

PRESIDENT That's not so.

AGATHA (*much taken by the* STRANGER) A mistake!

PRESIDENT This child herself sees the leak in your argument. A triple layer of earth daily piles up over our sins, our failures, our crimes, and stifles their worst effects! Forgetfulness, death, human justice. It is madness to remember those things. A horrible country, one where because of an avenger of wrongs, ghosts walk, dead men, half asleep,—where no allowance is ever made for human weakness, or perjury, where a ghost and an avenger constantly threaten. When guilty men's sleep continues to be more troubled after legal prosecution than the sleep of an innocent, society is terribly disturbed. When I look at Electra, I'm troubled by the sins I committed in my cradle.

AGATHA   And I by my future sins. I'll never commit them, darling. You know that. Especially that adultery, which you will talk about. But those other sins already bother me.

GARDENER   I'm rather of Electra's opinion. I don't much care for wicked people. I love truth.

PRESIDENT   Do you know what truth is for our family that you proclaim it so openly? A quiet, well-thought-of family, rising fast. You'll not deny my assertion that you are the least important member of it. But I know by experience that it's not safe to venture on thin ice. It won't be ten days, if you marry Electra, before the discovery—I'm just inventing this—that our old aunt, when a young girl, strangled her baby so her husband wouldn't find out about it, and in order to quiet suspicion, stopped hushing up the various aspersions on her grandfather's virtue. My little Agatha, in spite of being gaiety itself, can't sleep because of all this. You are the only one who doesn't see Aegisthus' trick. He wants to pass on to the Theocathocles family everything that might some day throw a sinister light on the Atrides.[1]

STRANGER   And what have the Atrides to fear?

PRESIDENT   Nothing. Nothing that I know of, it's like every happy family or couple, every satisfied person. Yet it does have to fear the most dangerous enemy in the world, who would eat it through to the bone, Electra's ally, uncompromising justice.

GARDENER   Electra loves my garden. If she's a little nervous, the flowers will do her good.

AGATHA   But she'll not do the flowers good.

PRESIDENT   Certainly. You'll get to know your fuchias and geraniums. You'll see that they're not just pretty symbols. They'll show their knavery and their ingratitude. Electra in the garden is justice and memory among the flowers—that means hatred.

GARDENER   Electra is devout. All the dead are for her.

PRESIDENT   The dead! The murdered, half melted into the murderers, the shades of the robbed mingled with those of the thieves, rival families scattered among each other, and saying, "Oh, Heavens! here's Electra! And we were so peaceful."

AGATHA   Here comes Electra!

GARDENER   No, not yet. It's Aegisthus. Leave us, stranger, Aegisthus doesn't like strange faces.

PRESIDENT   You, too, Agatha. He's rather too fond of well-known women's faces.

---

[1] Agamemnon and Menelaus, sons of Atreus.

AGATHA   (*with marked interest in the stranger's good looks*)   Shall I show you the way, handsome stranger?

(AEGISTHUS *enters, to the hurrahs of the* GUESTS, *as* SERVANTS *set up his throne, and place a stool beside a pillar*)

Scene Three

(AEGISTHUS. *The* PRESIDENT. *The* GARDENER. SERVANT)

AEGISTHUS   Why the stool? What's the stool for?

SERVANT   For the beggar, my lord.

AEGISTHUS   What beggar?

SERVANT   The god, if you prefer. This beggar has been wandering through the city for several days. We've never seen a beggar who's so much a beggar, so it's thought he must be a god. We let him go wherever he likes. He's prowling around the palace now.

AEGISTHUS   Changing wheat to gold? Seducing the maids?

SERVANT   He does no harm.

AEGISTHUS   A queer god! The priests haven't found out yet whether he's a rascal or Jupiter?

SERVANT   The priests don't want to be asked.

AEGISTHUS   Friends, shall we leave the stool here?

PRESIDENT   I think it will be better to honor a beggar than to insult a god.

AEGISTHUS   Leave the stool there. But if he comes, warn us. We'd like to be just a group of human beings for a few minutes. And don't be rude to him. Perhaps he is delegated by the gods to attend Electra's marriage. The gods invite themselves to this marriage, which the President considers an insult to his family.

PRESIDENT   My lord . . .

AEGISTHUS   Don't protest. I heard everything. The acoustics in this palace are extraordinary. The architect apparently wanted to listen to the council's discussions of his salary and bonus, he built it full of echoing passages.

PRESIDENT   My lord . . .

AEGISTHUS   Be quiet. I know everything you're about to say on the subject of your fine honest family, your worthy sister-in-law, the baby-killer, your uncle, the satirist and our nephew, the slanderer.

PRESIDENT   My lord . . .

AEGISTHUS   An officer, in a battle, to whom the King's standard is given to turn the enemy's fire on him, carries it with more enthusiasm. You're losing your time. The gardener will marry Electra.

SERVANT   Here is the beggar, my lord.

AEGISTHUS   Detain him a moment. Offer him a drink. Wine is appropriate for a beggar or a god.

SERVANT   God or beggar, he's drunk already.

AEGISTHUS   Then let him come in. He'll not understand us, though we must speak of the gods. It might even be amusing to talk about them before him. Your notion of Electra, President, is true enough, but it's peculiar, definitely middle-class. As I'm the Regent, allow me to give you more elevated philosophical ideas. You believe in the gods, President?

PRESIDENT   Do you, my lord?

AEGISTHUS   My dear President, I've often asked myself if I believe in the gods. Asked myself because it's the only problem a statesman must decide for himself. I do believe in the gods. Or rather, I believe I believe in the gods. But I believe in them, not as great caretakers and great watchmen, but as great abstractions. Between space and time, always oscillating between gravitation and emptiness, there are the great indifferences. Those are the gods. I imagine them, not constantly concerned with that moving mould on the earth which is humanity, but as having reached the stage of serenity and universality. That is blessedness, the same thing as unconsciousness. They are unconscious at the top of the ladder of being, as the atom is at the bottom. The difference is that theirs is the unconsciousness of lightning, omniscient, thousand-faceted, so that in their normal state, like diamonds, powerless and deaf, they only *react* to light, to omens, without understanding them.

BEGGAR   (*at last seated, feels he must applaud*)   Well said! Bravo!

AEGISTHUS   Thanks. On the other hand, President, it's undeniable that sometimes there seem to be interruptions in human life so opportune and extensive that it's possible to believe in an extraordinary superhuman interest or justice. Such events have something superhuman or divine about them, in that they are like coarse work, not at all well designed. The plague breaks out in a town which has sinned by impiety or folly, but it also ravages the neighboring city, a particularly holy one. War breaks out when a nation becomes degenerate and vile, but it destroys all the just, the brave, and preserves the cowards. Or, whose ever the fault, or by whom committed, it's the same family that pays, innocent or guilty. I know a mother of seven children, who always spanked the same child—she was a divine mother. This fits our idea of the gods, that they are blind boxers, always satisfied by finding the same cheeks to slap, the same bottoms to spank. We might even be surprised if we understood the confusion that comes from a sudden waking to beatitude, that their blows weren't given more at random; that the wife of a good man, and not a perjurer's, is brained by a shutter in a wind storm; that accidents strike down pilgrims and not troops. Always humanity suffers . . . I'm speaking generally. We see crows or deer struck down by an inexplicable epidemic—perhaps the blow intended for mankind went astray, either up or down. However it be, it's certain that the chief duty of a statesman is to watch fiercely that the gods are not shaken out of their lethargy, and to limit the harm they do to such reactions as sleepers snoring, or to thunder.

BEGGAR   Bravo! That's very clear! I understand it very well!

AEGISTHUS   Charmed, I'm sure!

BEGGAR   It's truth itself. For example, look at the people walking along the roads. Sometimes every hundred feet you'll see a dead hedgehog. They go over the roads at night by tens, male and female, and get crushed. You'll say they're fools, that they could find their mates on their side of the road. I can't explain it, but love, for hedgehogs, begins by crossing a road. What the devil was I trying to say? I've lost the thread . . . Go on, it'll come back to me.

AEGISTHUS   Indeed! What is he trying to say!

PRESIDENT   Shall we talk about Electra, my lord?

AEGISTHUS   What do you think we've been talking about? Our charming little Agatha? We were talking only about Electra, President, and about the need I feel to get her out of the royal family. Why, since I've been Regent, while other cities are devoured by dissension, other citizens by moral crises, are we alone satisfied with other people and with ourselves? Why are we so rich? Why in Argos alone are raw materials so dear and retail prices so low? Why, when we're exporting more cows, does butter go down in price? Why do storms pass by our vineyards, heresies our temples, animal diseases our barns? Because, in this city, I wage merciless war against all who signal to the gods.

PRESIDENT   What do you mean, signal to the gods?

BEGGAR   There! I've found it!

AEGISTHUS   Found what?

BEGGAR   My story, the thread of my story. I was speaking of the death of hedgehogs.

AEGISTHUS   One moment, please. We're speaking of the gods.

BEGGAR   To be sure! Gods come first, hedgehogs second. But I wonder if I'll remember.

AEGISTHUS   There are no two ways of signaling, President: it's done by separating one's self from the crowd, climbing a hill and waving a lantern or a flag. The earth is betrayed, as is a besieged city, by signals. The philosopher signals from his roof, the poet or a desperate man signals from his balcony or his swimming pool. If for ten years the gods have not meddled with our lives, it's because I've kept the heights empty and the fairgrounds full. I've ordered dreamers, painters, and chemists to marry; and because, in order to avoid racial trouble between our citizens—something that can't help marking human beings as different in the eyes of the gods—I've always given great importance to misdemeanors and paid slight attention to crimes. Nothing keeps the gods so quiet as an equal value set on murder and on stealing bread. I must say the courts have supported me splendidly. Whenever I've been forced to be severe, they've overlooked it. None of my decisions has been so obvious as to allow the gods to avenge it. No exile. I kill. An exile tends to climb up a steep road, just like a ladybird. I never execute in public. Our poor neighboring cities betray themselves by erecting their gallows on the top of a hill; I crucify at the bottom of a valley. Now I've said everything about Electra.

GARDENER   What have you said?

AEGISTHUS   That there's just one person in Argos now to give a signal to the gods, and that's Electra. What's the matter?

(BEGGAR *moves about among the* GUESTS)

BEGGAR   Nothing's the matter. But I'd better tell you my story now. In five minutes, at the rate you're talking, it won't make sense. It's just to support what you say. Among those crushed hedgehogs you'll see dozens who seem to have died a hedgehog's death. Their muzzles flattened by horses' hoofs, their spines broken under wheels, they're just smashed hedgehogs, nothing more. Smashed because of the original sin of hedgehogs—which is crossing the main or side road on the pretext that the snail or partridge egg on the far side tastes better but actually to make hedgehog love. That's their affair. No one stops them. Suddenly you see a little young one, not flattened like the others, not so dirty, his little paw stretched out, his lips closed, very dignified, and you feel that he's not died a hedgehog's death, but was struck down for someone else, for you. His cold little eye is your eye. His spikes, your beard. His blood, your blood. I always pick up those little ones, they're the youngest, the tenderest to eat. A year goes by, a hedgehog no longer sacrifices himself for mankind. You see I understand. The

gods were mistaken, they wanted to strike a perjurer, a thief, and they kill a hedgehog. A young one.

AEGISTHUS   Very well understood.

BEGGAR   And what's true of hedgehogs holds for other species.

PRESIDENT   Of course! Of course!

BEGGAR   Why, of course? That's all wrong. Take the martin. Even though you're a President of the Council, you'll never pretend to have seen birds dying for you?

AEGISTHUS   Will you let us go on talking about Electra!

BEGGAR   Talk! Talk! But I must add, when you see dead men, many seem to have died for bulls or pigs or turtles, not many for mankinds. A man who seems to have died for man, he's hard to find, or even for himself. Are we going to see her?

AEGISTHUS   See whom?

BEGGAR   Electra. I'd like to see her before she's killed.

AEGISTHUS   Electra killed? Who says Electra's to be killed?

BEGGAR   You.

PRESIDENT   There's been no thought of killing Electra.

BEGGAR   I have one gift. I don't understand words—I've had no education—but I do understand people. You want to kill Electra.

PRESIDENT   You don't understand at all, stranger. This man is Aegisthus, Agamemnon's cousin, and Electra's his darling niece.

BEGGAR   Are there two Electras? The one he was talking about who ruins everything, and the other one, his darling niece?

PRESIDENT   No! There's only one.

BEGGAR   Then he wants to kill her. No doubt of it. He wants to kill his darling niece.

PRESIDENT   I repeat, you don't understand in the least.

BEGGAR   Oh, I move about a lot. I knew a family, name of Narses. She was better than he. She was sick, her breathing bad. But a great deal better than he. No comparison.

GARDENER   He's drunk, a beggar, you know.

PRESIDENT   He's raving. He's a god.

BEGGAR   No. I started to tell you they had a wolf cub. It was their darling little pet. But one day around noon, wolf cubs, you know, grow up. They couldn't foretell the day. Two minutes before noon they were petting her, one minute after twelve she jumped at their throats. I didn't mind about him!

AEGISTHUS   Well?

BEGGAR   Well, I was just passing by. And I killed the wolf. She was beginning to eat

Narses' cheeks, she liked them. Narses' wife got away, not too badly hurt. Thanks! You'll see her. She's coming for me pretty soon.

AEGISTHUS What's the connection . . .?

BEGGAR Oh, don't expect to see an Amazon queen. Varicose veins age a person.

PRESIDENT He asked, what's the connection?

BEGGAR The connection? It's because I think this man, as he's head of the state, must be more intelligent than Narses. No one could imagine such stupidity as Narses'. I never could teach him to smoke a cigar except by the lighted end. And what about knots? It's terribly important to know how to make knots. If you make a curlycue where you ought to have a knot, and vice versa, you're lost. You lose your money, you catch cold, you choke, your boat veers away or collides, you can't pull off your shoes. I mean if you want to pull them off. And the laces? You know Narses was a poacher.

PRESIDENT We've asked you, what is the connection?

BEGGAR Here's the connection. If this man distrusts his niece, if he knows that one of these days she'll give a signal, as he said, she'll begin to bite, to turn the city upside down, push up the price of butter, start a war, et cetera, he can't hesitate. He ought to kill her dead before she reveals herself. When will she reveal herself?

PRESIDENT What do you mean?

BEGGAR What day, at what time will she reveal herself? When will she turn into a wolf? When will she become Electra?

PRESIDENT But nothing tells us she'll turn into a wolf.

BEGGAR (*pointing to* AEGISTHUS) Yes. He thinks so. He says so.

GARDENER Electra is the gentlest of women.

BEGGAR Narses' wolf cub was the gentlest of wolves.

PRESIDENT Your expression "reveals herself" doesn't make sense.

BEGGAR My expression doesn't make sense? You know nothing about life. The 29th of May, when you see the hills astir with thousands of little red, yellow, and green balls flying, squawling, quarreling over every little bit of thistle fluff, never making a mistake nor going after dandelion down, aren't the butterflies revealing themselves? And June 14th when you see on the river bank two reeds move without wind or wave till June 15th, and, too, without bubbles made by carp, isn't the pike revealing himself? And judges like you, the first time they condemn to death, when the condemned man appears, distraught, don't they reveal themselves by the taste of blood on their lips? Everything in nature reveals itself. Even the king. And the question today, if you'll believe me, is whether the king will reveal himself as Aegisthus before Electra reveals herself as Electra. So he has to know the day when it will happen to the girl, so he can kill her on the eve, down in a valley, as he said, down in a little valley, the handiest and least visible, in her bath.

PRESIDENT Isn't he awful?

AEGISTHUS You're forgetting the wedding, beggar.

BEGGAR True. I am forgetting the wedding. But a wedding, if you want to kill someone, isn't as sure as death. Especially as a girl like her, sensitive, rather retarded et cetera, will reveal herself the moment a man takes her in his arms for the first time. You're marrying her?

AEGISTHUS At once. Right here.

BEGGAR Not to the king of a neighboring city, I hope?

AEGISTHUS Not on your life! To this gardener.

PRESIDENT To this gardener.

BEGGAR She'll take him? I'd not reveal myself in the arms of a gardener. But everyone to his taste. I revealed myself in Corfu, at the fountain near the bakery, under the plane trees. You should have seen me that day! In each tray of the scales I weighed a hand of the baker's wife. They never weighed the same. I evened them up in the right tray with flour, in the left with oatmeal . . . Where does the gardener live?

GARDENER Outside the walls.

BEGGAR In a village?

GARDENER No. My house stands alone.

BEGGAR (*to* AEGISTHUS) Bravo! I catch your idea. Not bad! It's quite easy to kill a gardener's wife. Much easier than a princess in a palace.

GARDENER Whoever you are, I beg you . . .

BEGGAR You'll not deny that it's easier to bury someone in compost than in marble?

GARDENER What are you imagining? For one thing she'll not be a minute out of my sight.

BEGGAR You'll bend down to plant a pear tree. Transplant it again because you hit a hard clod. Death has passed by.

PRESIDENT Stranger, I fear you don't know where you are. You're in Agamemnon's palace, in his family.

BEGGAR I see what I see, I see this man is afraid, he lives with fear, fear of Electra.

AEGISTHUS My dear guest, let's not misunderstand each other. I'll not deny I'm anxious about Electra. I know misfortunes and troubles will come to the family of the Atrides the day she reveals herself, as you say. And to us all, for every citizen is affected by what happens to the royal family. That's why I'm handing her over to a lowly family, unseen by the gods, where her eyes and gestures will not inflame, where the harm will be only local and in the middle class, the Theocathocles family.

BEGGAR A good idea, a good idea! But the family ought to be especially lowly.

AEGISTHUS It is, and I'll see that it stays so. I'll see that no Theocathocles distinguishes himself by talent or courage. As for boldness and genius, I'm not afraid they'll make their mark.

BEGGAR Take care! This little Agatha is not exactly ugly. Beauty too can give a signal.

PRESIDENT I beg you to leave Agatha out of our argument.

BEGGAR Of course it's possible to rub her face with vitriol.

PRESIDENT My lord!

AEGISTHUS The case has been argued.

PRESIDENT But I'm thinking of fate, Aegisthus! It's not a disease. You think it's infectious?

BEGGAR Yes. Like hunger among the poor.

PRESIDENT I can hardly believe that fate will be content with one obscure little clan instead of the royal family, or that it will become the fate of the Theocathocles instead of the Atrides.

BEGGAR Don't worry. A royal cancer spreads to the middle classes.

AEGISTHUS President, if you don't want Electra's entrance into your family to mark the disgrace of its members, don't add a word. In a third-class zone the most implacable fate will do only third-class harm. I personally am distressed, because of my great esteem for the Theocathocles family, but the dynasty, the state, and the city can no longer take risks.

BEGGAR And perhaps she can be killed a little anyway, if an occasion arises.

AEGISTHUS I have spoken. You may fetch Clytemnestra and Electra. They're waiting.

BEGGAR It's not too soon. Without blaming you, I must say our talk lacks women.

AEGISTHUS You'll have two, and talkers!

BEGGAR And they'll argue with you a little, I hope?

AEGISTHUS You like arguing women?

BEGGAR Adore them. This afternoon I was in a house where a dispute was going on. Not a very high-toned discussion. Not compared to here. Not a plot of royal assassins as here. They were arguing whether they ought to serve guests chickens with or without livers. And the neck, of course. The women were furious. Had to be

separated. Now I think of it, it was a fierce dispute. Blood flowed.

Scene Four

(*The same.* CLYTEMNESTRA. ELECTRA. MAIDS)

PRESIDENT Here they both are.

CLYTEMNESTRA Both! That's a manner of speaking. Electra is never more absent than when she's present.

ELECTRA No. Today I'm here.

AEGISTHUS Then let's make the most of it. You know why your mother has brought you here?

ELECTRA It's her habit. She's already led a daughter to sacrifice.

CLYTEMNESTRA There's Electra to the life! Never a word that's not treason or insinuation.

ELECTRA Excuse me, mother. The allusion is quite apropos in the family of the Atrides.

BEGGAR What does she mean? Is she angry with her mother?

GARDENER It would be the first time anyone has seen Electra angry.

BEGGAR All the more interesting!

AEGISTHUS Electra, your mother has told you of our decision. We've been anxious about you for a long time. I hardly think you realize that you're like a sleepwalker in broad daylight. In the palace and the city people speak of you only in whispers, they're so afraid you'd wake and fall if they raised their voices.

BEGGAR (*shouting*) Electra!

AEGISTHUS What's the matter with him?

BEGGAR Oh, I'm sorry, it's just a joke. Excuse it. But you were scared, not she. Electra's no sleepwalker.

AEGISTHUS Please—

BEGGAR At least the experiment has been made. You were the one who flinched. What would you have done if I'd shouted, "Aegisthus"?

PRESIDENT Let our Regent speak.

BEGGAR I'll shout "Aegisthus" pretty soon, when nobody expects it.

AEGISTHUS You must get well, Electra, no matter what it costs.

ELECTRA To cure me, that's easy. Give life to a dead man.

AEGISTHUS You're not the only one who grieves for your father. But he'd not ask you to make your mourning an offense to the living. We wrong the dead to attach them to our lives, for that deprives them of the freedom of death, if they know it.

ELECTRA He's free. That's why he comes.

AEGISTHUS Do you really think he's pleased

to see you weep for him, not like a daughter but like a wife?

ELECTRA   I am my father's widow, for lack of another.

CLYTEMNESTRA   Electra!

AEGISTHUS   Widow or not, today we'll celebrate your marriage.

ELECTRA   Yes, I know your plot.

CLYTEMNESTRA   What plot? Is it a plot to marry a twenty-one year old daughter? At your age I had the two of you in my arms, you and Orestes.

ELECTRA   You carried us badly. You let Orestes fall on the marble floor.

CLYTEMNESTRA   What could I do? You pushed him.

ELECTRA   That's a lie. I never pushed him.

CLYTEMNESTRA   What do you know about it? You were only fifteen months old.

ELECTRA   I did *not* push Orestes! I remember it, far back in my memory. Oh, Orestes, wherever you are, hear me! I did not push you.

AEGISTHUS   That's enough, Electra.

BEGGAR   This time they're really at it! It'd be funny if the little girl revealed herself right in front of us.

ELECTRA   She lies. Orestes, she lies!

AEGISTHUS   Please, Electra!

CLYTEMNESTRA   She did push him. Obviously at her age she didn't know what she was doing. But she did push him.

ELECTRA   With all my strength I tried to hold him: by his little blue tunic, by his arm, by the end of his fingers, by his shadow. I sobbed when I saw him on the floor, with the red mark on his forehead.

CLYTEMNESTRA   You shouted with laughter. The tunic, by the way, was mauve.

ELECTRA   It was blue. I know Orestes' tunic. When it was drying you couldn't see it against the sky.

AEGISTHUS   Can *I* get a word in? Haven't you had time these twenty years to settle this debate?

ELECTRA   For twenty years I've waited for this chance. Now I have it.

CLYTEMNESTRA   Why can't she understand that she might be wrong, even honestly?

BEGGAR   They're both honest. That's the truth.

PRESIDENT   Princess, I beg of you! Of what interest is this question today?

CLYTEMNESTRA   Of none, I grant you.

ELECTRA   What interest? If I had pushed Orestes I'd rather die, I'd kill myself. My life would have no meaning.

AEGISTHUS   Must I force you to keep quiet? Are you as mad as she, queen?

CLYTEMNESTRA   Electra, listen. Let's not quarrel. This is exactly what happened: he was on my right arm.

ELECTRA   On your left!

AEGISTHUS   Have you finished, Clytemnestra, or haven't you?

CLYTEMNESTRA   We've finished. But a right arm is a right arm, a mauve tunic is mauve, not blue.

ELECTRA   It was blue. As blue as Orestes' forehead was red.

CLYTEMNESTRA   That is true. Very red. You touched the wound with your finger and danced around the little prone body. You laughed as you tasted the blood.

ELECTRA   I? I wanted to bruise my head on the step that hurt him. I trembled for a week.

AEGISTHUS   Silence!

ELECTRA   I'm still trembling.

BEGGAR   Narses' wife tied hers with an elastic rope that had some play. Often it was askew, but he didn't fall.

AEGISTHUS   Enough. We'll soon see how Electra will carry hers. For you agree, don't you? You accept this marriage?

ELECTRA   I agree.

AEGISTHUS   I must admit not many suitors throng around you.

BEGGAR   They say . . .

AEGISTHUS   What do they say?

BEGGAR   They say you've threatened to kill the princes who might marry Electra. That's what they say in the city.

ELECTRA   Good! I don't want any prince.

CLYTEMNESTRA   You'd rather have a gardener?

ELECTRA   I know you two have decided to marry me to my father's gardener. I accept.

CLYTEMNESTRA   You shall not marry a gardener.

AEGISTHUS   Queen, we settled that. Our word is given.

CLYTEMNESTRA   I take mine back. It was a wicked word. If Electra is ill we'll care for her. I'll not give my daughter to a gardener.

ELECTRA   Too late, mother. You have given me.

CLYTEMNESTRA   Gardener, you dare to aspire to Electra?

GARDENER   I'm unworthy, queen, but Aegisthus commands me.

AEGISTHUS   I do command you. Here are the rings. Take your wife.

CLYTEMNESTRA   If you persist, gardener, it's at the risk of your life.

BEGGAR   Then don't persist. I'd rather see soldiers die than gardeners.

CLYTEMNESTRA   What's that man saying? Marry Electra, gardener, and you die.

BEGGAR   It's your business. But go into the

garden a year after the death of the gardener. You'll see something. You'll see what's happened to the endive, widowed by its gardener. It's not like kings' widows.

CLYTEMNESTRA That garden won't suffer. Come, Electra.

GARDENER Queen, you can deny me Electra, but it's not nice to say bad things about a garden you don't know.

CLYTEMNESTRA I know it—empty land, with scattered plantings.

GARDENER Empty? The best tended garden in Argos.

PRESIDENT If he begins to talk about his garden we'll never finish.

AEGISTHUS Spare us your descriptions!

GARDENER The queen provoked me, and I answer. My garden is my dowry and my honor.

AEGISTHUS Never mind! Enough of quarrels.

GARDENER Empty, indeed! It covers ten acres of hilly land, and six of valley. No, no, you'll not silence me! Not a sterile inch, is there, Electra? On the terraces I have garlic and tomatoes, on the slopes grape vines and peach trees. On the level land vegetables, strawberries, and raspberries. A fig tree at the bottom of each slope against the wall, which warms the figs.

AEGISTHUS Fine! Let your figs get warm and take your wife.

CLYTEMNESTRA You dare talk of your garden! I've seen it from the road. It's all dry, a bald skull. You shall not have Electra.

GARDENER All dry! A brook flows between the box and the plane trees, never dry in hottest weather; I've dug two little trenches from it—one turned on the meadow, the other cut in the rock. Try to find skulls like that! And scattered plantings! In spring it's full of narcissus and jonquils. I've never seen Electra really smile, but in my garden, I saw something on her face almost like a smile.

CLYTEMNESTRA See if she's smiling now!

GARDENER I call that Electra's smile.

CLYTEMNESTRA Smiling at your dirty hands, your black nails . . .

ELECTRA Dear gardener . . .

GARDENER My black nails? Look, see if my nails are black! Don't believe it, Electra. You're unlucky today, queen, I spent this morning whitewashing my house, so there's not a sign of mice there, and my nails came out, not black, as you say, but mooned with white.

AEGISTHUS That's enough, gardener.

GARDENER I know, I know it's enough. And my dirty hands! Look! Look at these dirty hands! Hands that I washed after taking down the dried mushrooms and onions, so nothing would trouble Electra's nights. I'll sleep in the outhouse, Electra; there I'll keep guard so that nothing disturbs your sleep, whether an owl, or the open floodgate, or a fox, hunting the hedge, with a chicken in his mouth. I've said my say.

ELECTRA Thanks, gardener.

CLYTEMNESTRA And that's how Electra will live, Clytemnestra's daughter, watching her husband going around his border, two pails in his hands. . . .

AEGISTHUS There she can weep for her dead to her heart's content. Get ready your wreaths of everlasting tomorrow.

GARDENER And there she'll escape from anxiety, torture, and perhaps tragedy. I don't understand people, queen, but I do know the seasons. It's time, full time, to transplant misfortune from our city. The Atrides won't be grafted on our poor family, but on the seasons, the fields, the winds. I think they'll lose nothing by that.

BEGGAR Be persuaded, queen. Don't you see that Aegisthus hates Electra so much he'll be driven to kill her, giving her to the earth by a kind of play on words: he gives her to a garden. She gains by that, she gains life. (AEGISTHUS rises) What? Was I wrong to say that?

AEGISTHUS (to ELECTRA and the GARDENER) Come here, both of you.

CLYTEMNESTRA Electra, I beg you!

ELECTRA You're the one who wanted it, mother.

CLYTEMNESTRA I no longer want it. You see I don't want it now.

ELECTRA Why don't you want it? Are you afraid? Too late!

CLYTEMNESTRA How can I make you remember who I am and who you are?

ELECTRA You'll have to tell me I didn't push Orestes.

CLYTEMNESTRA Stupid girl!

AEGISTHUS Are they beginning again?

BEGGAR Yes, yes, let them begin again.

CLYTEMNESTRA And unjust! And stubborn! I let Orestes fall! I who never break anything! Never let fall a glass or a ring! I'm so steady that birds light on my arms. It's possible to fly away from me but not to fall. That's just what I said when he lost his balance, "Why, why did an ill fate bring his sister so near him?"

AEGISTHUS They're crazy!

ELECTRA And I said to myself, as soon as I saw him slipping, "If she's a true mother she'll stoop to soften his fall, or she'll bend to make a slope and catch him on her thigh or her knees.

We'll see if they'll catch him, the noble knees and thighs of my mother. I'm not sure. I'll see."

CLYTEMNESTRA   Be quiet!

ELECTRA   "Or she'll bend backward, so little Orestes will slip off her like a child from a tree where he's picked off a nest, or she'll fall so *he* won't, or so he'll fall on her. She knows all the ways a mother uses to catch her son, she still knows them. She can still be a curve, a shell, a motherly slope, a cradle." But she stood fixed, straight, and he fell right down from the full height of his mother.

AEGISTHUS   The case is heard. Clytemnestra, we'll leave.

CLYTEMNESTRA   Just let her remember what she saw when she was fifteen months old and what she didn't see. That's the point.

AEGISTHUS   Who but you believes her or listens to her?

ELECTRA   There are a thousand ways of preventing a fall, and she did nothing.

CLYTEMNESTRA   The slightest movement, and *you* would have fallen.

ELECTRA   Just as I said. You calculated. You figured it all out. You were a nurse, not a mother.

CLYTEMNESTRA   My little Electra . . .

ELECTRA   I'm not your little Electra, your motherly feeling is tickled awake by your rubbing your two children against you. But it's too late.

CLYTEMNESTRA   Please—!

ELECTRA   There you are! Open your arms, see what you've done. Look, everybody. That's just what you did.

CLYTEMNESTRA   Let's go, Aegisthus.

(*She leaves*)

BEGGAR   I believe the mother is frightened.

AEGISTHUS (*to the* BEGGAR)   What's that you say?

BEGGAR   I? I say nothing. I never say anything. When I'm hungry I talk, everyone hears me. Today I've drunk a little something.

Scene Five

(ELECTRA.   BEGGAR.   GARDENER.   STRANGER. AGATHA)

AGATHA   This is the right time, Aegisthus isn't here. Get out, gardener.

GARDENER   What do you mean?

AGATHA   Get out, fast. This man will take your place.

GARDENER   My place with Electra?

STRANGER   Yes, I'll marry her.

ELECTRA   Let go my hand.

STRANGER   Never.

AGATHA   Just look at him, Electra. Before you turn your back on a man, at least look at him. I'm sure you'll lose nothing by that.

ELECTRA   Gardener, help!

STRANGER   I owe you nothing, gardener. But look me in the eye. You understand species and kinds. Look at me and see the kind I am. So! Look, with your poor peasant eyes, with the gaze of humble folk, a blear-eyed mixture of devotion and fear, the sterile look of the poor, unchanged by sunshine or misfortune, see if I can give way to you. Fine! Now give me your ring. Thanks!

ELECTRA   Agatha, cousin! Help me! I swear I'll not tell about your rendezvous, your quarrels, I'll tell nothing.

AGATHA (*leading off the* GARDENER)   Come, the Theocathocles are saved. Let the Atrides work it out.

BEGGAR   She runs away—like a wood-louse, hiding under a stone to escape from the sun.

Scene Six

(ELECTRA.   STRANGER.   BEGGAR)

STRANGER   Struggle no more.

ELECTRA   I'll struggle till I die.

STRANGER   You think so? In a minute you'll take me in your arms.

ELECTRA   No insults!

STRANGER   In a minute you'll embrace me.

ELECTRA   Shame on you for profiting from two infamies!

STRANGER   See how I trust you. I let you go.

ELECTRA   Farewell forever!

STRANGER   No! I'll say one word to you and you'll come back to me, tenderly.

ELECTRA   What lie is this?

STRANGER   One word, and you'll be sobbing in my arms. One word, my name.

ELECTRA   There's only one name in the world that could draw me to anyone.

STRANGER   That's the one.

ELECTRA   Are you Orestes?

ORESTES   Ungrateful sister, only recognizing me by my name!

(CLYTEMNESTRA *appears*)

Scene Seven

(CLYTEMNESTRA.   ELECTRA.   ORESTES.   BEGGAR)

CLYTEMNESTRA   Electra!

ELECTRA   Mother?

CLYTEMNESTRA   Come back to your place in the palace. Leave the gardener. Come!

ELECTRA The gardener has left, mother.

CLYTEMNESTRA Where is he?

ELECTRA He's given me to this man.

CLYTEMNESTRA What man?

ELECTRA This man. He's my husband now.

CLYTEMNESTRA This is no time for jokes. Come!

ELECTRA How can I come? He's holding my hand.

CLYTEMNESTRA Hurry!

ELECTRA You know, mother, those clogs they put on the legs of foals to prevent their running away? This man has put them on my ankles.

CLYTEMNESTRA This time I command you. You must be in your room by tonight. Come!

ELECTRA What? Leave my husband the night of my wedding?

CLYTEMNESTRA What are you doing? Who are you?

ELECTRA He'll not answer you. This evening my husband's mouth belongs to me, and all the words he speaks.

CLYTEMNESTRA Where do you come from? Who is your father?

ELECTRA A misalliance maybe. But not such a bad one.

CLYTEMNESTRA Why do you look at me like that? Why the challenge in your eyes? Who was your mother?

ELECTRA He never saw her.

CLYTEMNESTRA She's dead?

ELECTRA Perhaps what you see in his eyes is that he never saw his mother. Handsome, isn't he?

CLYTEMNESTRA Yes. He looks like you.

ELECTRA If our first married hours make us look alike, that's a good omen, isn't it, mother?

CLYTEMNESTRA Who are you?

ELECTRA What does it matter to you? Never was a man less yours.

CLYTEMNESTRA Whatever or whoever you are, stranger, don't give in to her caprice. We'll see tomorrow if you're worthy of Electra. I'll win over Aegisthus. But I've never known a less propitious night. Leave this man, Electra.

ELECTRA Too late! His arms hold me.

CLYTEMNESTRA You can break iron if you want to.

ELECTRA Iron, yes, *this* iron, no!

CLYTEMNESTRA What has he said against your mother that you accept him this way?

ELECTRA We've had no time yet to speak of my mother or his. Go, we'll begin!

ORESTES Electra!

ELECTRA That's all he can say. If I take my hand from his mouth, he just says my name without stopping. You can't get anything else out of him. Oh, husband, now that your mouth is free, kiss me!

CLYTEMNESTRA Shame! So this madness is Electra's secret!

ELECTRA Kiss me, before my mother.

CLYTEMNESTRA Farewell! But I didn't think you were a girl to give yourself to the first passer-by.

ELECTRA Nor I. But I didn't know what the first kiss was like.

Scene Eight

(ELECTRA. ORESTES. BEGGAR)

ORESTES Why do you hate our mother so, Electra?

ELECTRA Don't speak of her, above all not of her! Let's imagine for a minute that we were born without a mother. Don't talk.

ORESTES I have everything to tell you.

ELECTRA You tell me everything just by being here. Be quiet. Close your eyes. Your words and your look touch me too poignantly, they wound me. I often wished that I'd find you in your sleep, if I ever found you. Now I can't bear to have all at once the look, the voice, the life of Orestes. I ought to have stumbled on your image, dead at first, then coming alive little by little. But my brother was born like the sun, a golden animal at his rising. Either I'm blind or I find my brother by groping—oh, the joy of being blind for a sister who finds her brother! For twenty years my hands have fumbled over mean or indifferent things, and now they touch—a brother —a brother in whom everything is true. Some dubious or some false bits might have been in this head, this body, but by a wonderful chance, everything in Orestes is brotherly, everything is Orestes.

ORESTES You smother me.

ELECTRA I don't smother you. I don't kill you. I caress you. I'm calling you to life. From this brotherly shape which my dazzled eyes have scarcely seen I'm making my brother in all his features. See, how I've made my brother's hand, with its straight thumb. See how I've made my brother's chest, which I'm animating so it swells and breathes, giving life to my brother. See how I make this ear, little, curled, transparent like a bat's wing. One last touch and the ear is finished. I make the two alike. Quite a success, these ears! And now I'll make my brother's mouth, gentle and dry, and fasten it on his face. Take your life from me, Orestes, not from our mother.

ORESTES   Why do you hate her? Listen . . .

ELECTRA   What's the matter with you? Are you pushing me away? That's the ingratitude of sons. They're hardly finished before they get away and escape.

ORESTES   Someone is watching us from the staircase.

ELECTRA   It's she, certainly she. From jealousy or fear. It's our mother.

BEGGAR   Yes, yes, it's she.

ELECTRA   She suspects we're here, creating ourselves, freeing ourselves from her. She thinks that my caresses will cover you, wash you clear of her, make you an orphan. Oh, brother, who else could do me such a service!

ORESTES   How can you speak so of her who bore you? Though she was harsh to me, I'm less hard on her.

ELECTRA   That's just what I can't stand about her, that she bore me. That's my shame. I feel that I came into life in a dubious way, that her motherhood is only a plot to bind us together. I love everything that comes from my father. I love the way he put off his fine wedding garment and lay down to beget me, from his thought and from his body. I love his eyes, and his surprise the day I was born; I came from him far more than from my mother's pains. I was born from his nights of deep sleep, his nine months' emaciation, the comfort he found with other women while my mother was carrying me, his fatherly smile when I was born. I hate everything about my birth that comes from my mother.

ORESTES   Why do you detest women so?

ELECTRA   I don't detest women, I detest my mother. And I don't detest men, I detest Aegisthus.

ORESTES   Why do you hate him?

ELECTRA   I don't know yet. I only know it's the same hatred. That's why it's so hard to bear, that's why I'm suffocating. Many times I've tried to find out why I hate both of them with a special hatred. Two little hatreds could be borne—like sorrows—one balances the other. I tried to think I hated my mother because she let you fall when you were a baby, and Aegisthus because he stole your throne. But it's not true. I really pitied this great queen, who ruled the world, yet suddenly, frightened and humble, let her child fall, like a feeble grandmother. I pitied Aegisthus, that cruel tyrant, whose fate is to die miserably from your blows. All the reasons I had for hating them made me think them human, pitiable,

but no sooner had my hatred washed them clean and re-clothed them and I found myself gentle, obedient before them, than a yet heavier wave, charged with a yet more virulent hatred, flowed over them. I hate them with a hatred that is not really me.

ORESTES   I'm here. It will vanish.

ELECTRA   You believe that? I used to think your return would free me of this hatred. I thought my illness was because you were far away. I prepared for your return by becoming all tenderness, tenderness for everyone, for them too. I was wrong. My pain tonight is caused by your being here and all the hatred in me laughs and welcomes you, it is my love for you. It caresses you as a dog does the hand that frees him. I know that you have given me the sight, the smell of hatred. The first scent, and now I follow the trail. Who's there? Is it she?

BEGGAR   No, me. You're forgetting the time. She's gone up. She's undressing.

ELECTRA   She's undressing. Before her mirror, looking long at herself, our mother, Clytemnestra, undresses. Our mother, whom I love for her beauty and pity because she's aging, whose voice and looks I admire, our mother, whom I hate.

ORESTES   Electra, sister darling, please calm yourself.

ELECTRA   Then I'm to follow the trail?

ORESTES   Calm yourself.

ELECTRA   I? I'm perfectly calm. I'm all sweetness. Sweet to my mother, very sweet. It's this hatred for her that swells up and kills me.

ORESTES   Now it's your turn not to talk. We'll think about that hatred tomorrow. This evening let me taste for an hour at least, the sweetness of the life I've never known and now return to.

ELECTRA   An hour. All right, one hour.

ORESTES   The palace is so beautiful beneath the moon. My palace. All the power of our family is emanating from it. My power. In your arms let me imagine all the happiness these walls might have held for calmer, more reasonable people. Oh, Electra, how many of our family's names were originally sweet and tender, and should have been happy names!

ELECTRA   Yes, I know. Medea, Phaedra.

ORESTES   Even those, why not?

ELECTRA   Electra. Orestes.

ORESTES   Isn't there still time? I've come to save them.

ELECTRA   Silence! She's there.

ORESTES   Who?

ELECTRA   She with the happy name: Clytemnestra.

Scene Nine

(ELECTRA. ORESTES. CLYTEMNESTRA.   *Then* AEGISTHUS)

CLYTEMNESTRA   Electra?

ELECTRA   Mother?

CLYTEMNESTRA   Who is this man?

ELECTRA   Guess.

CLYTEMNESTRA   Let me see his face.

ELECTRA   If you can't see it at a distance you'd see him less well near to.

CLYTEMNESTRA   Electra, let's stop fighting. If you really want to marry this man, I'll agree. Why do you smile? Wasn't it I who wanted you to marry?

ELECTRA   Not at all. You wanted me to be a woman.

CLYTEMNESTRA   What's the difference?

ELECTRA   You wanted me in your camp. You didn't want the face of your worst enemy constantly before you.

CLYTEMNESTRA   You mean my daughter's?

ELECTRA   Chastity, rather!

ORESTES   Electra . . . !

ELECTRA   Let me alone, let me alone. I've found the trail.

CLYTEMNESTRA   Chastity! This girl who's devoured by desire talks about chastity! This girl at two years old couldn't see a boy without blushing. It was because you wanted to embrace Orestes, if you want to know, that you pulled him out of my arms.

ELECTRA   Then I was right. I'm proud of it. It was worth while.

(*Trumpets. Shouts. Faces in the windows.* AEGISTHUS *leans down from a balcony*)

AEGISTHUS   Are you there, queen?

BEGGAR   Yes, she's here.

AEGISTHUS   Great news, queen. Orestes is not dead. He's escaped. He's coming toward Argos.

CLYTEMNESTRA   Orestes!

AEGISTHUS   I'm sending my bodyguard to meet him. I've posted my most faithful men around the walls. You say nothing?

CLYTEMNESTRA   Orestes is coming back?

AEGISTHUS   Coming back to seize his father's throne, to prevent my being regent, and you being queen. His emissaries are preparing a revolt. But don't worry. I'll keep order. Who's down there with you?

CLYTEMNESTRA   Electra.

AEGISTHUS   And her gardener?

BEGGAR   And her gardener.

AEGISTHUS   I hope you're not still trying to separate them? You see how well founded my fears were! You agree now?

CLYTEMNESTRA   No. I'm not trying any more.

AEGISTHUS   Don't let them leave the palace. Them especially. I've ordered the gates closed till the soldiers return. You hear me, gardener?

ELECTRA   We'll not leave.

AEGISTHUS   Queen, come upstairs. Go back to your room. It's late and the Council is to meet at dawn. I wish you a goodnight.

ELECTRA   Thanks, Aegisthus.

AEGISTHUS   I was speaking to the queen, Electra. This is no time for irony. Come, queen.

CLYTEMNESTRA   Good-bye, Electra.

ELECTRA   Good-bye, mother.

(CLYTEMNESTRA *goes, then turns back*)

CLYTEMNESTRA   Good-bye, my daughter's husband.

BEGGAR   What you see in families! You see everything!

ELECTRA   Who spoke?

BEGGAR   No one! No one spoke. You think someone would speak at a time like this?

Scene Ten

(ELECTRA. ORESTES. BEGGAR)

ORESTES   Tell me, Electra! Tell me!

ELECTRA   Tell you what?

ORESTES   Your hatred. The reason for your hatred. You know it now, when you were talking to Clytemnestra a moment ago you almost fainted in my arms. It might have been from joy—or horror.

ELECTRA   It was both joy *and* horror. Are you strong or weak, Orestes?

ORESTES   Tell me your secret and I'll find out.

ELECTRA   I don't know my secret yet. I hold only one end of the thread. Don't worry. Everything will follow. Take care! Here she is.

(CLYTEMNESTRA *appears at the back of the stage*)

Scene Eleven

(ELECTRA. CLYTEMNESTRA. ORESTES. BEGGAR)

CLYTEMNESTRA   So it's you, Orestes?

ORESTES   Yes, mother, it's I.

CLYTEMNESTRA   Is it sweet to see a mother when you're twenty?

ORESTES   A mother who sent you away? Sad and sweet.

CLYTEMNESTRA You look at her from far away.

ORESTES She's just as I imagined her.

CLYTEMNESTRA My son. Handsome. Regal. And yet I draw near.

ORESTES Not I. At a distance she's a magnificent mother.

CLYTEMNESTRA Who tells you that near to her magnificence remains?

ORESTES Or her motherliness? That's why I don't move.

CLYTEMNESTRA The mirage of a mother is enough for you?

ORESTES I've had so much less until today. At least I can tell the mirage what I'd never tell my real mother.

CLYTEMNESTRA If the mirage deserves it, that's all right. What will you tell her?

ORESTES Everything I never tell you. Everything that would be a lie if said to you.

CLYTEMNESTRA That you love her?

ORESTES Yes.

CLYTEMNESTRA That you respect her?

ORESTES Yes.

CLYTEMNESTRA That you admire her?

ORESTES That the mother and the mirage can share.

CLYTEMNESTRA It's the opposite for me. I don't love the mirage of my son. But when my son is actually before me, speaking, breathing, I lose my strength.

ORESTES Think of hurting him, you'll recover it.

CLYTEMNESTRA Why are you so hard? You don't look cruel. Your voice is gentle.

ORESTES Yes, I'm exactly like the son I might have been. You too, of course. You look so like a wonderful mother. If I weren't your son, I'd be deceived.

ELECTRA Why are you both talking? Where does this horrible maternal coquetry get you, mother? At midnight the little window which allows a mother and son to see each other as they are not opens for a minute. Shut it, the minute has passed.

CLYTEMNESTRA Why so quickly? How do you know one minute of maternal love is enough for Orestes?

ELECTRA Everything tells me you have no right to more than a minute of your son's love in your whole life. You've had it. And that's the end. What a comedy you're playing! Go!

CLYTEMNESTRA Very well. Good-bye.

FIRST LITTLE GIRL (*appearing from behind the columns*) Good-bye, truth of my son!

ORESTES Good-bye.

SECOND LITTLE GIRL Good-bye, mirage of my mother!

ELECTRA You might say *au revoir*. You'll meet again.

Scene Twelve

(ELECTRA *and* ORESTES *asleep. The little* EUMENIDES. BEGGAR. *The* EUMENIDES *now seem to be about twelve or thirteen years old*)

FIRST GIRL They're asleep. It's our turn to play Clytemnestra and Orestes. But not the way they played. Let's play it truly.

BEGGAR (*to himself, though out loud*) The story of push or not push—I'd like to know . . .

SECOND GIRL You there, let us play. We're playing.

(*The three little* EUMENIDES *take the positions of the actors in the preceding scene and play it as a parody. Masks could be used*)

FIRST GIRL So it's you, Orestes?

SECOND GIRL Yes, it's me, mother.

FIRST GIRL You've come to kill me and Aegisthus?

SECOND GIRL News to me!

FIRST GIRL Not to your sister. You've done some killing, little Orestes?

SECOND GIRL The things one kills when one is good! A doe. And to be a little kind, I killed her fawn too, so it wouldn't be an orphan. But to kill my mother, never! That would be—parricide.

FIRST GIRL Was that the sword you did your killing with?

SECOND GIRL Yes. It will cut iron. See, it went through the fawn so fast he felt nothing.

FIRST GIRL I'm not suggesting anything. I don't want to influence you. But if a sword like that were to kill your sister, we'd all be at peace!

SECOND GIRL You want me to kill my sister?

FIRST GIRL Never! That would be—fratricide. If the sword were to kill her by itself, that would be ideal. Let it come out of its scabbard, like this, and kill her by itself. I'd just quietly marry Aegisthus. We'd call you home, Aegisthus is getting old. You'd succeed him very soon. You'd be King Orestes.

SECOND GIRL A sword doesn't kill by itself. It needs an assassin.

FIRST GIRL Certainly! I should know! But I'm talking about the times when swords will kill by themselves. People who avenge wrongs are the curse of the world. And they get no better as they get older, I beg you to believe that. As criminals improve with age, good people always become criminals. Surely this is a fine moment for a sword to think for itself, move of itself, and kill by itself. They'd marry you to Alcmena's second daughter, the laughing one, with the fine teeth—you'd be Orestes, the married man.

SECOND GIRL   I don't want to kill my sister, I love her, nor my mother, I detest her.

FIRST GIRL   I know, I know. In a word you're weak and you have principles.

THIRD GIRL   Why are you two talking? Because the moon is rising, the nightingale singing here in the middle of this night of hatred and threats; take your hand off the hilt of your sword, Orestes, and see if it will have the intelligence to act by itself.

FIRST GIRL   That's right. Take it off . . . It's moving, friends, it's moving!

SECOND GIRL   It really is! It's a thinking sword. It thinks so hard it's half out!

ORESTES   (*asleep*)   Electra!

BEGGAR   Off with you, screech owls! You're waking them.

ELECTRA   (*asleep*)   Orestes!

Scene Thirteen

(ELECTRA. ORESTES. BEGGAR)

BEGGAR   I'd love to get straight that story of pushed or not pushed. For whether it's true or false, it would show whether Electra is truthful or lying and whether she lies knowingly or whether her memory plays her false. I don't believe she pushed him. Look at her: two inches above ground she's holding her sleeping brother as tight as if they were over an abyss. He's dreaming that he's falling, evidently, but that's not her fault. Now the queen looks like those bakers' wives who never stoop, even to pick up their money, or like those bitches who smother their prettiest pup while they sleep. Afterward they lick it as the queen licked Orestes, but no one ever made a child with saliva. I can see the story as if I'd been there. It's understandable, if you imagine the queen had put on a diamond pin and a white cat had passed by. She's holding Electra on her right arm, for the girl was getting heavy, and the baby on the left, a bit away from her so he'll not scratch himself on the brooch or drive it into him. It's a queen's pin, not a nurse's. And the child sees the white cat, a magnificent creature—a white life, white hair —his eyes follow it, he rocks himself, and she's an egotistical woman. Anyway, seeing the child capsizing, in order to hold him she need only free her arm of little Electra, throw little Electra off on the marble floor, get rid of little Electra. Let little Electra break her neck, so the son of the king of kings be unhurt! But she's an egotist. For her a woman is as good as a man, she's a woman; the womb as good as the phallus, and she's a womb; she wouldn't dream for a second of destroying her daughter to save her son, so she keeps Electra. Now look at Electra. She's revealed herself in her brother's arms, and she's right. She couldn't wish for a better moment. Fraternity is the mark of human beings. Beasts know only love . . . cats, parrots, et cetera, they only recognize fraternity by the hair. To find brothers they have to love men, to turn to men. . . . What does the duckling do when he gets away from the other ducks and, with his tender little eye shining on his slanting duck's cheek, he looks at us humans, eating and playing games, because he knows men and women are his brothers? I've taken little ducks in my hands, and could have wrung their necks, because they came to me so fraternally, trying to understand what I was doing. I, their brother, cutting my bread and cheese and adding an onion. Brother of ducks, that's our real title, for when they raise the little heads they've plunged into the water and look at a man, they're all neatness, intelligence and tenderness—not eatable except for their brains. I could teach those little duck heads to weep! . . . So Electra didn't push Orestes! That makes everything she says legitimate, everything she undertakes irrefutable. She's unadulterated truth, a lamp without a wick. So if she kills, as looks likely, all happiness and peace around her, it's because she's right. It's as if the soul of a girl, in bright sunlight, felt a moment of anguish, as if she sniffed escaping gas in the midst of splendid festivals, and had to go after it, for the young girl is the guardian of truth; she has to go after it whether or not the world bursts and cracks down to its foundations, whether innocents die the death of innocents to let the guilty live their guilty lives. Look at those two innocents! What will be the fruit of their marriage? To bring to life, for the world and for ages to come, a crime already forgotten, the punishment of which will be a worse crime? How right they are to sleep away this hour that is still theirs! Leave them. I'm going for a walk. If I stayed, I'd wake them. I always sneeze three times when the moon is full, and, right now, to sneeze would be taking a frightful risk. But all you who remain here, be quiet, now. This is Electra's first rest, and the last rest of Orestes.

Curtain

INTERLUDE: THE GARDENER'S LAMENT

I'm not in the play any more. That's why I'm free to come and tell you what the play can't tell you. In stories like this the people won't stop killing and biting each other in order to tell you that the one aim of life is to love. It would be awkward to see the parricide stop, with upraised dagger, and make a speech praising love. That would seem artificial. A lot of people wouldn't believe him. But I really don't see what else I can do here in this loneliness and desolation. And I speak impartially. I'll never marry anyone but Electra, and I'll never have her. I was made to live with a woman day and night, but I'll always live alone. I was meant to give myself fully, and yet I have to keep myself to myself. This is my wedding night that I'm living through, all alone —but thank you for being here—and the orangeade I'd prepared for Electra I had to drink up myself; there's not a drop left, and this was a long wedding night. Now who will doubt my word? The trouble is that I always say the opposite of what I mean, and that would be miserable today when my heart is so heavy and my mouth so bitter—oranges are really bitter—and if I forgot for an instant that I must speak to you of joy. Yes, love and joy. I come to tell you they're preferable to bitterness and hate. That's a motto to carve on a porch, or to put on a handkerchief, or better, in dwarf begonias in a clump. Of course, life is a failure, yet it's very, very good. Of course nothing ever goes right, never is well planned, yet you must confess, sometimes everything comes out splendidly, is splendidly planned. . . . Not for me . . . or perhaps just for me. . . . If I can judge from my wish to love everything and everyone, which is the result of the greatest misfortune in my life! What will happen to people who've had less bad luck? How much love must men feel who marry wives they don't love, what joy must those feel who leave a wife they adore, after having had her in their home one hour? And people whose children are ugly? Of course, tonight in my garden, I wasn't very happy. As a little festival it didn't come off. I pretended sometimes that Electra was near me, I talked to her and said: "Come in, Electra! Are you cold, Electra?" But no one was deceived, not even the dog, not to say myself. The dog thought: "He promised us a bride, and he only gives us a word. My master has married a word; he put on his white garment, the one my paws soil, which keeps me from caressing him, just to marry a word! He gives his orangeade to a word. He scolds me for barking at shadows, real shadows which aren't alive, yet he tries to embrace a word."

And I didn't lie down: to sleep with a word was impossible. I can speak with a word, that's all! But if you were sitting like me in this garden, where everything is confused at night, where the moon is shining on the sundial, and the blind owl tries to drink the cement walk instead of the brook, you'd understand what I've understood: the truth! You'd understand that the day your parents died, that day your parents were born; the day you were ruined, that day you were rich; when your child was ungrateful, he was gratitude itself; when you were abandoned, the whole world was coming to you in rapture and tenderness. That was what happened to me in this empty, silent suburb. All these stony trees, these immovable hills, rushed toward me. This all applies to our play. To be sure, we can't say Electra is all love for Clytemnestra. But note the difference: she tries to find a mother and would see one in the first comer. She was marrying me because I was the only man who could be a kind of mother to her, though I'm not *really* the only one. There are men who'd be glad to carry a child nine months, if they had to, just to have daughters. All men, actually. Nine months are rather long, but . . . a week, or a day . . . any man would be proud. Perhaps to find a mother in *her* mother she'd have to cut her breast open, though with royalty that's rather theoretical. Among kings there are experiences never found among humble folk, pure hatred, for instance, and pure wrath. Always purity. That's tragedy, with its incests and parricides: purity, meaning—innocence. I don't know if you're like me, but to me, in tragedy, Pharaoh's daughter killing herself means hope, the treasonous Marshall means faith, the Duke-Assassin speaks of tenderness. Cruelty is a deed of love —excuse me, I mean: tragedy is a deed of love. That's why I'm sure this morning, that if I asked, Heaven would approve me, would give a sign that a miracle is near, which would show you that joy and love are written in heaven, and that they echo my motto, though I'm abandoned and alone. If you wish, I'll ask. I'm as sure as I'm here that a voice from on high would answer me, that loud speakers and amplifiers and God's thunder are all prepared by God himself to shout, if I ask: "love and joy." But I'd rather you didn't ask. First it would be indecent. It's not the gardener's role to demand of God a storm, even a storm of tenderness. Moreover it would be useless. We know so well that at this moment, and yesterday and to-morrow and always, they're all up there, as many as there are, or perhaps only one, or even if that one is absent, they're all ready to shout: love and joy. It's much better for a man to take the gods at their word—this is euphemism—without forcing them to underline it, or to be held by it, or to create among themselves obligations of creditor and debtor. I'm always convinced by silences. Yes, I've begged them, haven't I? not to shout love and joy. But let them shout it if they really want to. Yet I'd rather conjure them, I conjure you, God, as a proof of your affections, of your voice and all your shouting, to keep silent, silent for one second. . . . That's much more convincing. . . . Listen! . . . Thanks!

ACT TWO

Scene One

(*The same setting, shortly before dawn.* ELECTRA, *seated, holding* ORESTES, *asleep.* BEGGAR. *A cock. Sound of a trumpet in the distance*)

BEGGAR   It won't be long now, eh, Electra?

ELECTRA   No. It's not far away.

BEGGAR   I said "it," I meant the day.

ELECTRA   I meant the light.

BEGGAR   It's not enough for you that liars' faces are shining in the sun? That adulterers and murderers move about freely? That's what the day brings—not too bad.

ELECTRA   No. But I want their faces to look blank at noon, and their hands red. That's what light brings out. I want their eyes to be rotten, their mouths diseased.

BEGGAR   As you say, one can't ask too much!

ELECTRA   There's the cock . . . shall I wake him?

BEGGAR   Wake him if you wish, but if I were you, I'd give him another five minutes.

ELECTRA   Five minutes of nothingness! A poor gift!

BEGGAR   You never know. I believe there's an insect that lives only five minutes. In five minutes he's young, adult, noisy; he runs through childhood and adolescence, to the time of lame knees and cataract, and legitimate and morganatic unions. While I'm speaking he must be having measles and growing to puberty.

ELECTRA   Let's wait till he dies. That's all I'll agree to.

BEGGAR   Our brother sleeps well.

ELECTRA   He went to sleep right away. He escaped from me. He slipped into sleep as though that were his real life.

BEGGAR   He's smiling. It *is* his real life.

ELECTRA   Tell me anything you like, beggar, except that Orestes' real life is a smile.

BEGGAR   Loud laughter, love, fine clothes, happiness. I guessed that as soon as I saw him. Orestes would be gay as a lark, if life were good to him.

ELECTRA   He has bad luck.

BEGGAR   Yes, he's not very lucky. All the more reason for not hurrying him.

ELECTRA   Good! As he was made to laugh, to dress well, as he's a lark, I'll give Orestes five minutes, for he'll wake to a lifetime of horror.

BEGGAR   In your place, since you can choose, I'd see to it that this morning light and truth depart at the same time. That doesn't mean much, but it would be a young girl's role and would please me. Man's truth is part of his habits, it leaves him somehow, whether at nine o'clock in the morning when workers strike, or at six in the evening, when women confess, et cetera; these are always bad things, always unclear. Now I'm used to animals. They know when to leave. A rabbit's first jump in the heather, the very second the sun rises, the plover's first flight, the young bear's first run from his rock, these, I can tell you, go toward the truth. If they don't get there, that's because they don't have to. A mere nothing distracts them, a gudgeon, a bee. Do as they do, Electra, go toward the dawn.

ELECTRA   A fine kingdom where gudgeons and bees are liars! But your animals are moving already!

BEGGAR   No. Those are the night creatures turning in. Owls. Rats. The night's truth turning in. Hush! Listen to the last two, the nightingales, of course the nightingales' truth.

Scene Two

(*The same.* AGATHA. *A* YOUNG MAN)

AGATHA   Darling, you do understand, don't you?

YOUNG MAN   Yes, I have an answer for everything.

AGATHA   If he sees you on the stairs?

YOUNG MAN   I have come to see the doctor on the top floor.

AGATHA   You forget already! He's a veterinary. Buy a dog. . . . If he finds me in your arms?

YOUNG MAN   I've picked you up in the street, you've sprained your ankle.

AGATHA If it's in our kitchen?

YOUNG MAN I'll pretend to be drunk—I don't know where I am. I'll break the glasses.

AGATHA One will be enough, darling, a small one, the large ones are crystal. If it's in our room and we're dressed?

YOUNG MAN I'm looking for him, to talk politics. I had to go there to find him.

AGATHA If it's in our room and we're undressed?

YOUNG MAN I entered unexpectedly, you're resisting me, you are perfidy itself, you treat as a thief a man who's pursued you six months. . . . You're a tart!

AGATHA Darling!

YOUNG MAN A real tart!

AGATHA I understand. It's almost day, my love, and I've hardly had you for an hour, and how many more times do you think he'll believe I walk in my sleep, and that it's less dangerous to let me stroll in the grove than on the roof? Oh, my love, can you think of any pretext for letting me have you in *our* bed at night, me between you two, so it would seem quite natural to him?

YOUNG MAN Think! You'll invent something.

AGATHA A pretext for letting you two talk about your elections and the races over the body of your Agatha, so he'd not suspect anything. That's what we need—that's all.

YOUNG MAN All!

AGATHA Oh dear! Why is he so vain? Why is his sleep so light? Why does he adore me?

YOUNG MAN The eternal litany! Why did you marry him? Why did you love him?

AGATHA I? Liar! I never loved anyone but you!

YOUNG MAN I? Remember in whose arms I found you day before yesterday!

AGATHA That was only because I'd sprained my ankle. The man you mention was picking me up.

YOUNG MAN First I've *heard* of any sprain.

AGATHA You! You understand nothing. You don't realize that accident gave me an idea for us to use.

YOUNG MAN When I meet him on the stairs he has no dogs, I can tell you, and no cats.

AGATHA He rides horseback. You can't take a horse to the doctor upstairs.

YOUNG MAN And he's always leaving your room.

AGATHA Why do you force me to betray a state secret? He comes to consult my husband. They're afraid of a plot in the city. Please don't tell anyone, that would mean his dismissal. You'd bring me to the stake.

YOUNG MAN One evening he was hurrying, his scarf not fastened, his tunic half unbuttoned. . . .

AGATHA Of course, that was the day he tried to kiss me. I fixed him!

YOUNG MAN You didn't let him kiss you, and he so powerful? I was waiting downstairs. He stayed two hours. . . .

AGATHA He did stay two hours, but I didn't let him kiss me.

YOUNG MAN Then he kissed you without your leave. Confess, Agatha, or I'll go away.

AGATHA Force me to confess! That's a fine reward for my frankness. Yes, he did kiss me . . . once . . . on my forehead.

YOUNG MAN And that seems dreadful to you?

AGATHA Dreadful? Frightful!

YOUNG MAN And you don't suffer for it?

AGATHA Not at all! . . . Ah, do I suffer? It's killing me, killing me! Kiss me, darling. Now you know everything, and I'm glad of it. Aren't you happy everything is cleared up between us?

YOUNG MAN Yes. Anything is better than a lie.

AGATHA What a nice way you have of saying you prefer me to everything else, darling!

Scene Three

(ELECTRA. ORESTES. BEGGAR. *Then the* EUMENIDES. *They are taller than before, and seem fifteen years old*)

BEGGAR A dawn song, at the dawn of such a day! It's always like this.

ELECTRA The insect is dead, beggar?

BEGGAR Dispersed in the universe. His great-grandchildren are now fighting gout.

ELECTRA Orestes!

BEGGAR You see he's no longer asleep. His eyes are open.

ELECTRA Where are you, Orestes? What are you thinking about?

FIRST FURY Orestes, there's just time. Don't listen to your sister.

SECOND FURY Don't listen to her. We have learned what life holds for you, it's wonderful!

THIRD FURY Just by chance. As we grew up during the night.

SECOND FURY We're not saying anything about love to you, does that seem strange?

FIRST FURY She's going to spoil everything with her poison.

THIRD FURY Her poison of *truth*, the only one that has no antidote.

FIRST FURY You're right. We know what you're thinking. Royalty is magnificent, Orestes: young girls in the royal parks, feeding bread to the swans, King Orestes' miniature hanging on their blouses—they kiss it secretly; soldiers going to war, the women on the roofs, the sky like a veil over them, a white horse prancing to music; the return from war, the king's face looking like the face of a god, just because he's chilly or hungry or a little frightened, or pitying his people. If the truth is going to spoil all that, let it perish!

SECOND FURY   You're right. And love is magnificent. Orestes! Lovers, it seems, will never part. They're never separated but they rush back to each other, to clasp hands. Or if they go away, they find each other face to face again immediately. The earth is round for the sake of lovers. Everywhere I run into him I love, though he's not yet alive. All this Electra wants to take from you, and from us too, with her Truth. We want to love. Flee Electra!

ELECTRA   Orestes!

ORESTES   I'm awake, sister.

ELECTRA   Wake from your awakening. Don't listen to these girls.

ORESTES   Are you sure they aren't right? Are you sure that it's not the worst kind of arrogance for a human being to try to retrace his steps? Why not take the first road and go forward, at random? Trust yourself to me. At this moment I can see so clearly the track of the game called happiness.

ELECTRA   Alas! That's not what we're hunting today.

ORESTES   The only thing that's important is not to leave each other. Let's go to Thessaly. You'll see my house, covered with roses and jasmin.

ELECTRA   Darling Orestes, you've saved me from the gardener not just to give me to flowers!

ORESTES   Be persuaded! Let's slip out of the trap which will soon catch us! Let's rejoice that we woke up before it did! Come!

FIRST FURY   It's awake! Look at its eyes!

THIRD FURY   You're right. The spring is wonderful, Orestes. When you can see over the hedges only the moving backs of the beasts grazing in the new grass, and the donkey's head looking at you over them. That donkey's head would look funny if you murdered your uncle. Pretty funny, a donkey looking at you when your hands are red with your uncle's blood—

ORESTES   What's she saying?

THIRD FURY   Talk on about the spring! The buttery mould that floats on the watercress in the brooks—you'll see what a comfort that will be for a man who kills his mother. Spread your butter that day with a knife, even if it's not the knife that killed your mother, and you'll see!

ORESTES   Help. Electra!

ELECTRA   So! You're like all men, Orestes! The least little flattery relaxes them, the slightest breath, captivates them. Help you? I know what you'd like me to say.

ORESTES   Then tell me.

ELECTRA   That on the whole human beings are good, that life, too, after all, is good.

ORESTES   Isn't that true?

ELECTRA   That it's not a bad fate to be young, handsome, and a prince, to have a young sister who's a princess. That it's enough to leave men alone in their mean, vain business— not lancing human ulcers, but living for the beauty of the earth.

ORESTES   Isn't that what you're telling me?

ELECTRA   No! I'm telling you our mother has a lover.

ORESTES   You lie! That's impossible.

FIRST FURY   She's a widow. She has the right.

ELECTRA   I'm telling you our father was murdered.

ORESTES   Agamemnon! Murdered!

ELECTRA   Stabbed, by assassins.

SECOND FURY   Seven years ago. It's ancient history.

ORESTES   You knew that and let me sleep all night!

ELECTRA   I didn't know it. It's the night's gift to me. These truths were tossed to me by the night. Now I know how prophetesses work. They hold their brother close to their heart through one night.

ORESTES   Our father killed! Who told you?

ELECTRA   He himself.

ORESTES   He spoke to you before he died?

ELECTRA   Dead, he spoke to me. The very day of his death, but it's taken seven years for his word to reach me.

ORESTES   He appeared to you?

ELECTRA   No. His corpse appeared to me last night, looking like him the day he was murdered, but illuminated; I just had to read. There was a fold of his garment which said, I'm not a fold of death but of murder. And on his shoe there was a buckle which repeated, I'm not an accidental buckle but a criminal buckle. And on his eyelid there was a wrinkle which said, I didn't see death, I saw regicides.

ORESTES   And about our mother, who told you that?

ELECTRA   She herself, herself again.

ORESTES   She confessed?

ELECTRA   No. I saw her dead. Her body betrayed her. There's no possible doubt. Her eyebrow was the eyebrow of a dead woman who'd had a lover.

ORESTES Who is this lover? Who is this murderer?

ELECTRA I've waked you so you can find out. Let's hope they're both the same, then you'll have to strike just one blow.

ORESTES Girls, I think you'll have to clear out. My sister presents me as I wake with a harlot queen and a murdered king . . . my parents.

FIRST FURY That's not too bad. Add nothing more.

ELECTRA Forgive me, Orestes.

SECOND FURY Now she's excusing herself.

THIRD FURY I'm killing you, but excuse it, please.

BEGGAR She's wrong to excuse herself. This is the kind of awakening we generally reserve for our wives and sisters. They seem to be made for that.

ELECTRA They are made just for that. Wives, sisters-in-law, mothers-in-law, they're the ones to shake up the men who, barely awake, see nothing but purple and gold, till the women give them, with their coffee and hot water, a hatred of injustice and a scorn for small joys.

ORESTES Forgive me, Electra!

SECOND FURY It's his turn to beg pardon. Aren't they polite in this family!

FIRST FURY They take off their heads and bow to each other.

ELECTRA And they watch for their waking. For men put on the armor of happiness if they sleep no more than five minutes: and with it satisfaction, indifference, generosity, appetite. And a spot of sunlight reconciles them to all blood spots. And a bird song to all lies. But the women are there, all of them, worn by insomnia, with jealousy, envy, love, memory and truth. Are you awake, Orestes?

FIRST FURY And we'll be as old as he in an hour! Let's hope heaven makes us different!

ORESTES I believe I'm waking up.

BEGGAR Here comes our mother, children.

ORESTES Where's my sword?

ELECTRA Bravo! That's what I call a good awakening. Take up your sword. Take up your hatred. Take up your strength.

Scene Four

(*The same.* CLYTEMNESTRA)

CLYTEMNESTRA Their mother appears. And they turn into statues.

ELECTRA Orphans, rather.

CLYTEMNESTRA I'm not going to listen to an insolent daughter any longer.

ELECTRA Listen to your son.

ORESTES Who is it, mother? Confess.

CLYTEMNESTRA What kind of children are you, turning our meeting into a melodrama? Leave me, or I'll call.

ELECTRA Whom will you call? Him?

ORESTES You struggle too much, mother.

BEGGAR Be careful, Orestes. An innocent creature struggles as much as a guilty.

CLYTEMNESTRA Creature? What kind of creature am I for my children? Speak, Orestes, speak!

ORESTES I don't dare.

CLYTEMNESTRA Electra, then. She'll dare.

ELECTRA Who is it, mother?

CLYTEMNESTRA Of whom, of what are you speaking?

ORESTES Mother, it is true you have . . . ?

ELECTRA Don't specify, Orestes. Just ask who it is. There's a name somewhere in her. However you ask your question, the name will come out.

ORESTES Mother, is it true you have a lover?

CLYTEMNESTRA That's your question too, Electra?

ELECTRA It might be put that way.

CLYTEMNESTRA My son and daughter ask if I have a lover?

ELECTRA Your husband can't ask it now.

CLYTEMNESTRA The gods would blush to hear you.

ELECTRA That would surprise me. They've not been doing much blushing lately.

CLYTEMNESTRA I have no lover. But watch your step. All the evil in the world is caused by the so-called pure people trying to dig up secrets and bring them to light.

ELECTRA Rottenness is born of sunshine, I grant that.

CLYTEMNESTRA I have no lover, I couldn't have a lover if I wanted one. But take care. Curious people have had no luck in our family: they tracked down a theft and found a sacrilege; they carried on a love affair and ran into an incest. You'll not find out I have a lover, because I haven't, but you'll stumble on a stone which will be fatal to your sisters and yourselves.

ELECTRA Who is your lover?

ORESTES Electra, at least listen to her.

CLYTEMNESTRA I have no lover. But who would call it a crime if I had?

ORESTES Oh, mother, you're a queen.

CLYTEMNESTRA The world is not old and day is just dawning. But it would take us at least till twilight to recite the list of queens who've had lovers.

ORESTES Mother, please! Fight on this way. Convince us. If this struggle restores a queen to us, it's blessed, everything is restored.

ELECTRA   Don't you see you're giving her weapons, Orestes?

CLYTEMNESTRA   That's enough. Orestes, leave me alone with Electra, will you?

ORESTES   Must I, sister?

ELECTRA   Yes. Yes. Wait there, under the arch. And run back to me as soon as I call, Orestes. Run as fast as you can. It will mean I know all.

Scene Five

(CLYTEMNESTRA. ELECTRA. *The* BEGGAR)

CLYTEMNESTRA   Help me, Electra!

ELECTRA   Help you to what? To tell the truth or to lie?

CLYTEMNESTRA   Protect me.

ELECTRA   It's the first time you stoop to your daughter, mother. You must be afraid.

CLYTEMNESTRA   I'm afraid of Orestes.

ELECTRA   You lie. You're not the least afraid of Orestes. You see what he is: passionate, changeable, weak—still dreaming of an idyl in the Atrides' family. It's I you're afraid of, it's for me you're playing this game, the meaning of which still escapes me. You have a lover, haven't you? Who is he?

CLYTEMNESTRA   He knows nothing. And he's not in question.

ELECTRA   He doesn't know he's your lover?

CLYTEMNESTRA   Stop acting like a judge, Electra. Stop this pursuit. After all, you're my daughter.

ELECTRA   After all! Exactly after all! That's why I'm questioning you.

CLYTEMNESTRA   Then stop being my daughter. Stop hating me. Just be what I look for in you—a woman. Take up my cause, it's yours. Defend yourself by defending me.

ELECTRA   I'm not a member of the Women's Association, and someone other than you would have to recruit me.

CLYTEMNESTRA   You're wrong. If you betray your equal in body, in misfortune, you're the first one Orestes will loathe. Scandal always strikes back at the people who start it. What good does it do you to bespatter all women by bespattering me? In Orestes' eyes you'll sully all the qualities you get from me.

ELECTRA   I'm not like you in anything. I never look in my mirror except to be certain of that piece of luck. All the shiny marble, all the fountains of the palace have cried out to me, your own face cries it: Electra's nose is not the least like Clytemnestra's nose. My forehead is my own. My mouth's my own. And I have no lover.

CLYTEMNESTRA   Listen! I have no lover. I'm in love.

ELECTRA   Don't try that trick. You throw love at me the way drivers pursued by wolves throw them a dog. Dog meat is not my food.

CLYTEMNESTRA   We're women, Electra. We have a right to love.

ELECTRA   There are many rights in the sisterhood of women. I know. If you pay the entrance fee, which is steep, which means admission only for weak, lying, base women, you have a right to be weak, lying, and base. Unfortunately women are strong, loyal, and noble, so you're wrong. You had the right to love my father only. Did you? On your wedding night, did you love him?

CLYTEMNESTRA   What are you driving at? Do you want me to say that your birth owes nothing to love, that you were conceived in indifference? Be satisfied. Not everyone can be like your Aunt Leda, and lay eggs. You never spoke in me. We were indifferent to each other from the first. You didn't even cause me pain at your birth. You were small and withdrawn, your lips tight. When you were a year old, your lips were sealed, so "mother" wouldn't be your first word. Neither of us cried that day. We've never wept together.

ELECTRA   Weeping parties don't interest me.

CLYTEMNESTRA   You'll weep soon, perhaps over me.

ELECTRA   Eyes can weep by themselves. That's what they're there for.

CLYTEMNESTRA   Yes, even yours, which look like two stones. Some day tears will drown them.

ELECTRA   I hope that day comes! But why are you trying to hold me by cold words instead of by love?

CLYTEMNESTRA   So you'll understand I have a right to love. So you'll know that my whole life has been as hard as my daughter from her very first day. Since my marriage I've never been alone, never at peace. I never went to the forest except for festivals. No rest, even for my body which was covered every day by golden robes and at night by a king. Always mistrust, even of things, animals, plants. I often said to myself, as I looked at cross, silent lindens, smelling like a wet nurse: "They're like Electra's head, the day she was born." No queen has ever suffered so deeply the fate of queens, a husband's absence, a son's suspicions, a daughter's hatred. What had I left?

ELECTRA   What the others had left: waiting.

CLYTEMNESTRA   Waiting, for what? Waiting is horrible.

ELECTRA   For her who has caught you today, perhaps.

CLYTEMNESTRA   Can you tell me what you're waiting for?

ELECTRA   I no longer wait. For ten years I've waited—for my father. Waiting is the only happiness in the world.

CLYTEMNESTRA   A virgin's happiness, a solitary happiness.

ELECTRA   You think so? Except for you and the men, everything in the palace awaited my father with me, everything was party to my waiting. It began in the morning with my early walk under the lindens which hate you, which waited for my father with an eagerness they tried in vain to repress; they were sorry to live by the year and not by the decade, ashamed every spring that they couldn't hold back their flowers and perfume, that they grew weak with me over his absence. It went on till noon when I went to the brook that was the luckiest of us all, for it awaited my father as it ran to the river that ran to the sea. And in the evening, when I wasn't strong enough to wait near his dogs and his horses, poor short-lived beasts, that couldn't wait for centuries, I took refuge with the columns and the statues. I modeled myself on them. I waited in the moonlight for hours, motionless like them, without thought, lifeless. I awaited him with a stony heart—marble, alabaster, onyx—though it was beating, shattering my breast. Where would I be if there weren't still hours to wait, to wait for the past, wait for him still!

CLYTEMNESTRA   I'm not waiting. I love.

ELECTRA   Everything goes well with you now?

CLYTEMNESTRA   Very well.

ELECTRA   Flowers obey you? Birds talk to you?

CLYTEMNESTRA   Yes, your lindens signal to me.

ELECTRA   Quite likely. You've robbed me of everything in life.

CLYTEMNESTRA   Fall in love. We'll share.

ELECTRA   Share love with you?! Are you offering to share your lover with me? Who is he?

CLYTEMNESTRA   Electra, have pity! I'll tell you his name, though it will make you blush. But wait a few days. What good will a scandal do you? Think of your brother. Can you imagine the Argives letting Orestes succeed an unworthy mother?

ELECTRA   An unworthy mother? What are you getting at with this confession? What time do you want to gain? What trap are you setting for me? What brood are you hoping to save,

limping off like a partridge, toward love and unworthiness?

CLYTEMNESTRA   Spare me public disgrace! Why do you force me to confess I love someone below me in rank?

ELECTRA   Some little nameless lieutenant?

CLYTEMNESTRA   Yes.

ELECTRA   You're lying. If your lover were some little nameless inglorious officer, or a bathhouse attendant, or a groom, you'd love him. But you're not in love, you've never loved. Who is it? Why do you refuse to name him, as you'd refuse a key? What piece of furniture are you afraid of opening with that name?

CLYTEMNESTRA   Something of my own, my love.

ELECTRA   Tell me the name of your lover, and I'll tell you if you love. And we'll keep it to ourselves forever.

CLYTEMNESTRA   Never!

ELECTRA   You see! It's not your lover but your secret that you're hiding from me. You're afraid his name would give me the one proof I'm lacking in my pursuit.

CLYTEMNESTRA   What proof? You're mad.

ELECTRA   The proof of the crime. Everything tells me, mother, that you committed it. But what I don't yet see, what you must tell me, is why you committed it. I've tried all the keys, as you say. Not one opens it—yet. Not love. You love nothing. Not ambition. You scoff at queenship. Not anger. You're deliberate, calculating. But our lover's name would clear up everything, tell us everything, wouldn't it? Who do you love? Who is he?

Scene Six

(*The same.* AGATHA, *pursued by the* PRESIDENT)

PRESIDENT   Who is he? Who do you love?

AGATHA   I hate you.

PRESIDENT   Who is it?

AGATHA   I tell you that's enough. Enough lies. Electra's right. I'm on her side. Thanks, Electra, you give me life.

PRESIDENT   What is this song?

AGATHA   Wives' song. You'll soon know it.

PRESIDENT   So, she's going to sing!

AGATHA   Yes, we're all here, with our unsatisfactory husbands or our widowhood. And we all kill ourselves, trying to make life and death pleasant. And if they eat cooked lettuce they have to have salt and a smile with it. And if they smoke we have to light their horrid cigars with the flame of our hearts.

PRESIDENT   Who are you talking about? I never ate cooked lettuce.

AGATHA   Sorrel, if you prefer.

PRESIDENT   Your lover doesn't eat sorrel or smoke cigars?

AGATHA   The sorrel my lover eats turns into ambrosia, and I lick up what's left. And everything soiled by my husband's touch is purified by his hands or lips. I myself! God knows!

ELECTRA   I've found out, mother, I've found out!

PRESIDENT   Collect yourself, Agatha.

AGATHA   Precisely. I've done just that. Twenty-four hours a day we kill ourselves to please someone whose displeasure is our only joy, for a husband whose absence is our only delight, for the vanity of the only man who humiliates us daily by showing us his toes and his shirt tails. And he has the gall to reproach us for stealing from him one hour a week of this hell! But, sure enough, he's right. When this wonderful hour comes, we don't greet it with a dead hand!

PRESIDENT   Electra, this is your work. This very morning she kissed me!

AGATHA   I'm pretty and he's ugly. I'm young and he's old. I'm bright and he's stupid. I have a soul and he hasn't. Yet he has everything. At least he has me. And I have nothing, though I have him! Until this morning, I gave everything and had to seem grateful. Why? I black his shoes. Why? I brush off his dandruff. Why? I make his coffee. Why? The truth might be that I'm poisoning him, rubbing his collar with pitch and ashes. Of course you can understand about the shoes. I spit on them. I spit on you. But it's all over, finished. Welcome, truth! Electra has given me her courage. I'm through. I'd as soon die.

BEGGAR   Don't these wives sing well!

PRESIDENT   Who is it?

ELECTRA   Listen, mother! Listen to yourself. It's you talking.

AGATHA   Who is it? All husbands think it's just one person.

PRESIDENT   Lovers? You have lovers?

AGATHA   They think we deceive them only with lovers. Of course we have lovers, too. But we deceive you with everything. When I wake and my hand slips along the wooden bedstead, that's my first adultery. Let's use your word for once, adultery. How often, when I'm wakeful, I've caressed that wood—olive wood, so soft! What a pretty name! I start when I hear an olive tree mentioned in the street—I hear my lover's name! And my second adultery is when I open my eyes and see daylight through the blinds. And my third, when my foot touches the bathwater and when I jump in. I betray you with my fingers, with my eyes, with the soles of my feet. When I look at you, I deceive you. When I listen to you and pretend to admire you in court, I'm deceiving you. Kill the olive trees, the pigeons, the five year old children, boys and girls, and water and earth and fire! Kill this beggar. You're betrayed by all of them.

BEGGAR   Thanks!

PRESIDENT   And yesterday this woman was still pouring my tea! And finding it too cool, having the water boiled again! You're all pleased, aren't you? This little scandal within a great one can't displease you!

BEGGAR   No. It's like the squirrel in a big wheel. It gives the right rhythm.

PRESIDENT   And this scene before the queen herself. You'll pardon it?

ELECTRA   The queen envies Agatha. The queen would give her life to have the chance Agatha has today. Who is it, mother?

BEGGAR   Sure! Don't let anything distract you, president. It's almost a minute since you asked her who it is.

PRESIDENT   Who is it?

AGATHA   I've told you. Everybody. Everything.

PRESIDENT   It's enough to drive me to suicide, to make me bash my head against the wall.

AGATHA   Don't stop on my account. The Mycenean wall is solid.

PRESIDENT   Is he young? Or old?

AGATHA   A lover's age—between sixteen and eighty.

PRESIDENT   And she thinks she's disgracing me by insulting me! Your insults only hurt yourself, abandoned woman!

AGATHA   I know, I know. Outrage is called majesty. In the streets the most respectable people slip on dung.

PRESIDENT   At last you'll find out who I am! Whoever your lovers are, I'll kill the first one I find here.

AGATHA   The first one you find here? You choose the place badly.

PRESIDENT   I'll make him kneel down and kiss the marble.

AGATHA   You'll see how he'll kiss the marble when he comes into this court in a minute and sits on the throne.

PRESIDENT   Wretch, what are you saying?

AGATHA   I'm saying that at present I have two lovers, and one is Aegisthus.

CLYTEMNESTRA   Liar!

AGATHA   What! She too!

ELECTRA   You too, mother?

BEGGAR   That's funny. I'd have thought, if Aegisthus had a liking, it was for Electra.

PAGE (*announcing*)   Aegisthus!

ELECTRA   At last!

THE FURIES   Aegisthus!

(AEGISTHUS *comes in. Much more majestic and calm than in the first act. Far above him, a bird hovers in the air*)

Scene Seven

(*The same.* AEGISTHUS. A CAPTAIN. SOLDIERS)

AEGISTHUS   Electra is here. . . . Thanks, Electra! I'll stop here, Captain. Headquarters are here.

CLYTEMNESTRA   I, too, am here.

AEGISTHUS   I'm glad. Welcome, queen!

PRESIDENT   I too, Aegisthus!

AEGISTHUS   Good, president. I need your help.

PRESIDENT   And now he insults us!

AEGISTHUS   What's the matter with you all, that you stare at me so?

BEGGAR   What's the matter is that the queen is waiting for a perjurer, Electra for an infidel, Agatha for a faithless lover. He's more humble, he's waiting for the man who seduced his wife. They're all waiting for you, but it's not you that's come!

AEGISTHUS   They have no luck, have they, beggar?

BEGGAR   No, they have no luck. Waiting for a rascal, they see a king enter! I don't care about the others, but for our little Electra, the situation is complicated.

AEGISTHUS   You think so? I think not.

BEGGAR   I knew it would happen. I told you so yesterday. I knew the king would reveal himself in you. He has your strength and your years. He finds the right moment. Electra is near. That might have involved a bloody act. But you've revealed yourself. Fine for Greece! But not so gay for the family.

CLYTEMNESTRA   What do these riddles mean? What are you talking about?

BEGGAR   Lucky for us, too! Since there has to be *some* kind of meeting, better let Electra meet nobility than wickedness. How did you get this way, Aegisthus?

AEGISTHUS (*looking at* ELECTRA)   Electra is here! I knew I'd find her looking toward me, her statuesque head, her eyes which see only when the lids are closed, deaf to human speech.

CLYTEMNESTRA   Listen to me, Aegisthus!

PRESIDENT   How well you choose your lovers, Agatha! What impudence!

CAPTAIN   Aegisthus, there's no time!

AEGISTHUS   Your ears are ornaments, aren't they, Electra? Mere ornaments. . . . The gods said, we gave her hands so she'd not touch, eyes so she'd be seen, we can't let her head be without ears! People would soon discover that she hears only us. . . . Tell me, what would we hear if we placed our ears near hers? What roaring! And where from?

CLYTEMNESTRA   Are you mad? Take care! Electra's ears do hear you.

PRESIDENT   They blush for it.

AEGISTHUS   They hear me. I'm sure of that. Since what happened to me just now in the outskirts of Argos, my words come from beyond myself. And I know she sees me too, she's the only one who does see me. The only one to guess what I've become since that moment.

CLYTEMNESTRA   You're talking to your worst enemy, Aegisthus!

AEGISTHUS   She knows why I galloped toward the city from the mountains. Electra, you'd have thought my horse understood. He was beautiful, that light chestnut, charging toward Electra, followed by the thunder of the squadron, in which the knowledge of rushing toward Electra grew less, from the white stallions of the trumpeters to the piebald mares of the rear guard. Don't be surprised if my horse sticks his head between the pillars, neighing to you. He knew that I was strangling, with your name in my mouth like a golden stopper. I had to shout your name, and to you —shall I shout it, Electra?

CLYTEMNESTRA   Stop this outrageous behavior, Aegisthus.

CAPTAIN   Aegisthus! The city is in danger!

AEGISTHUS   True! Pardon me! Where are they now, Captain?

CAPTAIN   You can see their lances coming over the hills. I've never seen a harvest grow so fast. Nor so thick. There are thousands of them.

AEGISTHUS   The cavalry's no use against them?

CAPTAIN   Repulsed, prisoners taken.

CLYTEMNESTRA   What's happening, Aegisthus?

CAPTAIN   The Corinthians are surrounding us, no declaration of war, no reason for it. Their regiments entered our territory last night. The suburbs are on fire already.

AEGISTHUS   What do the prisoners say?

CAPTAIN   Their orders are to leave no stone standing in Argos.

CLYTEMNESTRA   Show yourself, Aegisthus, and they'll flee!

AEGISTHUS   I fear, queen, that wouldn't be enough.

CAPTAIN   They have friends in the city. The reserves of pitch have been stolen, so the middle-class quarters can be burned. Gangs of beggars are gathering around the markets ready to start pillaging.

CLYTEMNESTRA   If the guard is loyal, what is there to fear?

CAPTAIN   The guard is ready to fight. But they're muttering. You know, they've never willingly obeyed a woman. The city's the same way. They both demand a king, a man.

AEGISTHUS   They're right. They shall have one.

PRESIDENT   Whoever wants to be king of Argos, Aegisthus, must first kill Clytemnestra.

BEGGAR   Or simply marry her.

PRESIDENT   Never!

AEGISTHUS   Why, never? The queen can't deny that's the only way to save Argos. I don't doubt she'll consent. Captain, tell the guard the wedding has this moment taken place. Keep me informed of events. I'll wait here for your bulletins. And do you, president, go meet the rioters and tell them this news most enthusiastically.

PRESIDENT   Never! I must first speak to you, man to man, no matter what happens.

AEGISTHUS   No matter if Argos falls, if war comes? You're outrageous.

PRESIDENT   My honor, the honor of all Greek judges, is at stake.

BEGGAR   If Greek justice lies in Agatha's lap, that's just what it deserves. Don't hinder us at such a time. Look at Agatha, see if she cares for the honor of Greek judges, with her nose in the air.

PRESIDENT   Her nose in the air! Agatha is your nose in the air?

AGATHA   My nose *is* in the air. I'm looking at that bird hovering over Aegisthus.

PRESIDENT   Lower it!

AEGISTHUS   Queen, I'm waiting for your reply.

CLYTEMNESTRA   A bird? What is that bird? Get from under that bird, Aegisthus.

AEGISTHUS   Why? He's not left me since sunrise. He must have his reasons. My horse noticed him first. He kicked without any provocation. I looked all around and then up there. He was kicking at that bird, and plunging and rearing. It's exactly above me, isn't it, beggar?

BEGGAR   Exactly above. If you were a thousand feet tall, your head would be there.

AEGISTHUS   Like a mark on a page, isn't it? A black mark.

BEGGAR   Yes, at the moment you're the most marked man in Greece. We'll have to find out whether the mark is over the word "human" or the word "mortal."

CLYTEMNESTRA   I don't like this hovering bird. What is it? A kite or an eagle?

BEGGAR   He's too high up. I might recognize him by his shadow, but so high up we can't see it, it's lost.

CAPTAIN   (*returning*)   The guards are delighted, Aegisthus. They're joyfully getting ready to fight. They're waiting for you to appear on the balcony with the queen, so they can cheer you.

AEGISTHUS   My oath, and I'll go.

PRESIDENT   Electra, help me! Why should this rake teach us courage?

BEGGAR   Why? Listen! . . .

AEGISTHUS   Oh, Heavenly Powers, since I must pray to you on the eve of battle, I thank you for the gift of this hill which overlooks Argos the moment the fog evaporates. I dismounted, weary from the night patrol, I leant against the battlement, and suddenly I saw Argos as I had never before seen it—new, rebuilt by me; you have given it to me. You've given it all to me, its towers, its bridges, the smoke from its farm machines, the flying pigeons, its first movements, the grinding of its locks, its first cry. Everything in your gift has equal value, Electra, the sunrise over Argos, the last lantern in the city, the temple, the ruins, the lake, the tanneries. And the gift is forever! This morning I was given my city for eternity, as a mother her child, and in agony I asked myself if the gift were not even greater, if you hadn't given me far more than Argos. In the morning God never counts his gifts: he might even have given me the whole world. That would have been dreadful. I should have felt a despair like that of a man who expects a diamond on his birthday and is given the sun. Electra, you see my anxiety! I anxiously stretched my foot and my thoughts beyond Argos. What joy! I had not been given the Orient, its plagues, earthquakes, famines: I realized that with a smile. My thirst was not like that of men who quench it in the great, warm rivers flowing through the desert, but, I discovered, I could quench it at an icy spring. And nothing in Africa is mine! Negresses can pound millet at the doors of their huts, the jaguar drive his claws into the crocodile's flank, not a drop of their soup or their blood is mine. I'm as happy over the gifts not given me as over the gift of Argos. In a fit of generosity the gods have not given me Athens or Olympia or Mycenae. What joy! They have given me the Argive cattle markets, not the treasures of Corinth, the short noses of the Argive girls, not the nose of Athena; the wrinkled prune of Argos, not the golden fig of Thebes! That's what they gave me this morning; me, the wastrel, the parasite, the knave, a country where I feel myself pure, strong, perfect; a fatherland; a country where, instead of being a slave, I am king, where I swear to live and die—you hear me, judge—a country I swear to save.

PRESIDENT   I rely on you only, Electra!

ELECTRA   Rely on me. No one should save his fatherland with impure hands.

BEGGAR   A coronation purifies everything.

ELECTRA   Who crowned you? Who witnessed your coronation?

BEGGAR   Can't you guess? Just what he begged of you. For the first time he sees you in your truth and power. The thought has suddenly dawned on him that Electra is included in this gift of Argos.

AEGISTHUS   Everything on my way consecrated me, Electra. As I galloped I heard the trees, the children, the streams shout to me: I was king. But the holy oil was lacking. I was a coward yesterday. A rabbit, whose trembling ears showed over a furrow, gave me courage. I was a hypocrite. A fox crossed the road, his eyes crafty, and I became frank. And a couple of magpies gave me independence, an ant hill, generosity. And if I hurried back to you, Electra, it was because you are the only creature who can give me her very being.

ELECTRA   And that is—?

AEGISTHUS   I think it is rather like duty.

ELECTRA   My duty is certainly the mortal enemy of yours. You shall not marry Clytemnestra.

PRESIDENT   You shall not marry her.

CLYTEMNESTRA   And why shan't we marry? Why should we sacrifice our lives to ungrateful children? Yes, I love Aegisthus. For ten years I've loved Aegisthus. For ten years I've postponed this marriage for your sake, Electra, and in memory of your father. Now you force us to it. Thanks! But not under that bird. That bird annoys me. As soon as the bird flies away. I consent.

AEGISTHUS   Don't worry, Queen. I'm not marrying you in order to create new lies. I don't know if I still love you, and the whole city doubts that you ever loved me. For ten years our liaison has dragged along between indifference and neglect. But marriage is the only way to cast a little truth over our past lies, and it will safeguard Argos. It must take place, this very hour.

ELECTRA   I don't believe it will take place.

PRESIDENT   Bravo!

AEGISTHUS   Will you be quiet? Who are you in Argos? A deceived husband or the chief justice?

PRESIDENT   Both, of course.

AEGISTHUS   Then choose. I have no choice. Choose between duty and prison. Time is short.

PRESIDENT   You took Agatha from me.

AEGISTHUS   I'm not the one who took Agatha.

PRESIDENT   Weren't you given all the deceived husbands in Argos this morning?

BEGGAR   Yes. But he's not the man who deceived them.

PRESIDENT   I understand. The new king forgets the outrages he committed as regent.

BEGGAR   Agatha looks like a rose. Outrages make her rosy?

AEGISTHUS   A king begs you to pardon today the insult a rake inflicted on you yesterday. That must satisfy you. Listen to my orders. Go quickly to your courtroom, try the rebels, and be severe with them.

AGATHA   Be severe. I have a little lover among them.

PRESIDENT   Will you stop looking at that bird? You irritate me.

AGATHA   I'm sorry. It's the only thing in the world that interests me.

PRESIDENT   Idiot! What will you do when it goes away?

AGATHA   That's what I'm wondering.

AEGISTHUS   Are you disobeying me, president? Don't you hear those shouts?

PRESIDENT   I'll not go. I'll help Electra prevent your marriage.

ELECTRA   I don't need your help, president. Your role ended when Agatha gave me the key to everything. Thanks, Agatha!

CLYTEMNESTRA   What key?

AEGISTHUS   Come, queen.

CLYTEMNESTRA   What key did she give you? What new quarrel are you trying to start?

ELECTRA   You hated my father! Oh, everything is clear in the light of Agatha's lamp.

CLYTEMNESTRA   There she goes again! Protect me, Aegisthus!

ELECTRA   How you envied Agatha just now! What joy to shout out your hatred to the husband you hate! That joy was not allowed you, mother. Never in your life will you have it. Till the day of his death he believed you admired and adored him. At banquets and festivals I've often seen your face harden, your lips move soundlessly, because you wanted to cry out you hated him. You wanted passers-by, guests, the servant pouring wine, the detective guarding the silver, to hear you, didn't you? Poor mother, you could never go to the country alone to cry out to the bushes! All the bushes say you adored him!

CLYTEMNESTRA   Listen, Electra!

ELECTRA   That's right, mother, cry it out

to me! Though he's not here, I'm his substitute. Cry to me! That will do you as much good as to say it to him. You're not going to die without letting him know you hated him.

CLYTEMNESTRA Come, Aegisthus! Never mind the bird!

ELECTRA If you take one step, mother, I'll call.

AEGISTHUS Whom will you call, Electra? Is there anyone in the world who can take from us the right to save our city?

ELECTRA Save our city from hypocrisy, from corruption? There are thousands. The purest, the handsomest, the youngest is here, in this courtyard. If Clytemnestra takes a step, I'll call.

CLYTEMNESTRA Come, Aegisthus!

ELECTRA Orestes! Orestes!

(*The* EUMENIDES *appear and bar the way*)

FIRST FURY Poor girl! You're too naive! Do you think we'll let Orestes run around sword in hand? Accidents happen too quickly in this palace. We've gagged him and chained him up.

ELECTRA That's not true! Orestes! Orestes!

SECOND FURY You, too, it will happen to you.

AEGISTHUS Electra, dear Electra, listen to me. I want to persuade you.

CLYTEMNESTRA You're losing precious time, Aegisthus.

AEGISTHUS I'm coming! Electra, I know you're the only one who understands what I am today. Help me! Let me tell you why you must help me!

CLYTEMNESTRA What is this craze to explain, to argue? Are we roosters in this courtyard or human beings. Do we have to go on explaining till our eyes are gouged out? Must the three of us be carried off by force, to separate us?

PRESIDENT I think that's the only way, queen.

CAPTAIN I beseech you, Aegisthus! Hurry!

BEGGAR Don't you understand? Aegisthus must settle once and for all the business about Agamemnon—Clytemnestra—Electra. Then he'll come.

CAPTAIN In five minutes it will be too late.

BEGGAR We'll all do our bit. It will be settled in five minutes.

AEGISTHUS Take this man away.

(*Guards take out the* PRESIDENT. *All the spectators leave. Silence*)

AEGISTHUS Now, Electra, what do you want?

Scene Eight

(ELECTRA. CLYTEMNESTRA. AEGISTHUS. BEGGAR)

ELECTRA She's not late, Aegisthus. She just won't come.

AEGISTHUS Of whom are you speaking?

ELECTRA Of her you're waiting for. The messenger of the gods. If divine justice absolves Aegisthus because he loves his city, and is marrying Clytemnestra because he despises lies and wants to save the middle class and the rich, this is the moment for her to appear before the two of you, bearing her diplomas and her laurels. But she'll not come.

AEGISTHUS You know she has come. This morning's sunbeam on my head was she.

ELECTRA That was a morning beam. Every scurvy child thinks he's a king when a morning sunbeam touches him.

AEGISTHUS Do you doubt my sincerity?

ELECTRA I don't doubt it. I recognize in it the hypocrisy and malice of the gods. They change a parasite into a just man, an adulterer into a husband, a usurper into a king. They thought my task not painful enough, so they made a figure of honor out of you, whom I despise! But there's one chance they can't carry through! They can't transform a criminal into an innocent man. They bow to me there.

ELECTRA You have an inkling. Listen to the small voice beneath your heroic soul. You'll understand.

AEGISTHUS Who can explain what you're talking about?

CLYTEMNESTRA Of whom *can* she talk? What has she always talked about her whole life long? Of a father she never knew.

ELECTRA I? I never knew my father?

CLYTEMNESTRA You touched a corpse, ice that had been your father. But not your father.

AEGISTHUS Please, Clytemnestra! How can you quarrel at such a moment!

CLYTEMNESTRA Everyone must have a turn in this debate. It's my turn now.

ELECTRA For once you're right. We've come to the heart of the matter. If I'd not touched my living father, from whom would I have drawn my strength, my truth?

CLYTEMNESTRA Precisely. But now you're talking wildly. I wonder if you ever kissed him. I took care he didn't lick my children.

ELECTRA I never kissed my father?

CLYTEMNESTRA Your father's dead body, perhaps, not your father.

AEGISTHUS I beg you . . . !

ELECTRA Ah, now I see why you're so firm as you face me. You thought me unarmed, you thought I'd never touched my father. What a mistake!

CLYTEMNESTRA You're lying.

ELECTRA The day my father came home you two waited for him a minute too long on the palace stairs, didn't you?

CLYTEMNESTRA How do you know? You weren't there!

ELECTRA I was holding him back. I was in his arms.

AEGISTHUS Now listen, Electra . . .

ELECTRA I'd waited in the crowd, mother. I rushed toward him. His escorts were frightened, they feared an attempt on his life. But he recognized me, smiled at me. He understood Electra's attempt, and, brave father, went to meet it. And I touched him.

CLYTEMNESTRA You may have touched his leg armor, his horse, leather and hair!

ELECTRA He got down, mother. I touched his hands with these fingers, his lips with these lips. I touched a skin you'd never touched, purified from you by ten years of absence.

AEGISTHUS That's enough. She believes you!

ELECTRA My cheek on his, I felt my father's warmth. Sometimes in summer the whole world is just as warm as my father. I faint from it. And I did hug him in these arms. I thought I was taking the measure of my love—it was also that of my vengeance. He freed himself, mounted his horse, more agile, more resplendent than before. Electra's attempt on his life was over. He was more alive, more golden, because of it. And I ran to the palace to see him again, but I was really running not toward him, but toward you, his murderers.

AEGISTHUS Pull yourself together, Electra!

ELECTRA Perhaps I am out of breath. I've reached my goal.

CLYTEMNESTRA Rid us of this girl, Aegisthus. Give her back to the gardener. Or turn her over to her brother.

AEGISTHUS Stop, Electra! Why, at the very moment that I see you, that I love you, when I'm at the point of understanding you—your scorn for abuses, your courage, your disinterestedness—why do you persist in fighting?

ELECTRA I have only this moment.

AEGISTHUS Don't you know Argos is in danger?

ELECTRA We don't see the same dangers.

AEGISTHUS Don't you know that if I marry Clytemnestra, the city will quiet down, the Atrides will be saved? If not, riots, conflagrations?

ELECTRA Perhaps.

AEGISTHUS Don't you know that I alone can defend the city against the Corinthians who are already at the gates? If not, pillage, massacre?

ELECTRA Yes. You'd be victor.

AEGISTHUS Yet you are obstinate! You ruin my work. And you sacrifice your family and your country to a dream!

ELECTRA You're mocking me, Aegisthus! You pretend to know me yet you think I'm the kind to whom you can say, "If you lie and let other people lie, you'll have a prosperous country. If you hide your crimes, your country will be victorious." What is this poor country that you're all of a sudden placing between us and truth?

AEGISTHUS Your country—Argos.

ELECTRA You're wrong, Aegisthus. This morning, at the very hour you were given Argos, I also received a gift. I expected it, it had been promised me, but I still didn't know just what it would be. I had already been given a thousand gifts, which seemed incomplete. I couldn't see their appropriateness, but last night, near Orestes as he slept, I saw they were all one and the same gift. I'd been given the back of a truck driver, the smile of a laundress suddenly stopped in her work, watching the river. I'd been given a fat, naked little child, running across the street as his mother and the neighbors shouted to him. I'd been given the cry of a caged bird set free, and that of a mason I one day saw fall from a scaffold, his legs sprawling. I was given the water plant, resisting the current, fighting and dying; the sick young man, coughing, smiling and coughing; and my maid's red cheeks, puffed up each winter morning as she blows on the ashes of the fire. I too thought I was given Argos, everything in Argos that is modest, tender, beautiful and wretched, but just now I found out that it's not so. I knew I'd been given all the servants' cheeks as they blow on wood or coal, all the laundresses' eyes, whether round or almond-shaped, all the falling masons, all the water plants which seem lost and grow again in streams or the sea. But Argos is only a speck in this universe, my country only a village in that country. All the light and the cries in sad faces, all the wrinkles and shadows on joyful faces, all the desires and despair on indifferent faces—these are my new country. And this morning, at dawn, when you were given Argos and its narrow borders, I also saw it as tremendous, and I heard its name, which is not to be spoken, but which is both tenderness and justice.

CLYTEMNESTRA So that's Electra's motto! Tenderness! That's enough. Let's go.

AEGISTHUS And you dare call this justice,

that makes you burn your city, damn your family, you dare call this the justice of the gods?

ELECTRA   Far from it! In this country of mine, concern for justice is not the gods' business. The gods are only artists. A beautiful light from a conflagration, beautiful grass on a battlefield, such is their justice. A magnificent repentance for a crime is the gods' verdict on your case. I don't accept it.

AEGISTHUS   Electra's justice consists in re-examining every sin, making every act irreparable?

ELECTRA   Oh, no! Some years, frost is justice for the trees, other times it's injustice. There are criminals we love, murderers we embrace. But when the crime is an assault on human dignity, infects a nation, corrupts its loyalty, then—no pardon is possible.

AEGISTHUS   Have you any idea what a nation is, Electra?

ELECTRA   When you see a huge face fill the horizon and you look straight at it with pure, brave eyes, that's a nation.

AEGISTHUS   You talk like a young girl, not like a king. There's also a huge body to rule and to nourish.

ELECTRA   I speak like a woman. There's a bright look to sift, to gild. And the only gold is truth. Those great eyes of truth, they're so beautiful, when you think of the real nations of the world.

AEGISTHUS   There are truths that can kill nations, Electra.

ELECTRA   Sometimes the eyes of a dead nation shine forever. Pray Heaven that will be the fate of Argos! But since my father's death, since our people's happiness came to be founded on injustice and crime, since everyone has become a cowardly accomplice in murder and lies, the city can prosper, sing, dance, conquer, heaven may shine on it, but it will be only a cellar where eyes are useless. Infants suck the breast without seeing it.

AEGISTHUS   A scandal can only destroy it.

ELECTRA   Possibly. But I can no longer endure the dim, lustreless look in its eyes.

AEGISTHUS   That will cost thousands of glazed, dead eyes.

ELECTRA   That's the price. It's not too high.

AEGISTHUS   I must have this day. Give it to me. Your truth, if there is such a thing, will find a way to be revealed at a time more suitable for it.

ELECTRA   The revolt shows this day is made for it.

AEGISTHUS   I beseech you! Wait till tomorrow.

ELECTRA   No. This is the day for it. I've seen too many truths fade away because they were a day too late. I know young girls who waited one second before saying no to an ugly, vile thing, and could then say nothing but yes, yes. The beautiful and cruel thing about truth is that she is eternal, but is also like a flash of lightning.

AEGISTHUS   I must save the city and Greece.

ELECTRA   That's a small duty. I'm saving their soul.—You did kill him, didn't you?

CLYTEMNESTRA   How dare you say that, daughter? Everyone knows your father slipped on the tiles.

ELECTRA   Everyone knows it because you said so.

CLYTEMNESTRA   Crazy girl, he slipped and fell.

ELECTRA   He did not slip. For one obvious reason. Because my father never slipped.

CLYTEMNESTRA   How do you know?

ELECTRA   For eight years I've been asking the grooms, the maids, his escort in rain and hail. He *never* slipped.

CLYTEMNESTRA   The war came after.

ELECTRA   I've asked his fellow soldiers. He crossed Scamander without slipping. He took the battlements by assault without slipping. He never slipped, in water or in blood.

CLYTEMNESTRA   He was in haste that day. You had made him late.

ELECTRA   I'm the guilty one, am I? That's Clytemnestra's kind of truth. Your opinion, too, Aegisthus? Electra murdered Agamemnon?

CLYTEMNESTRA   The maids had soaped the tiles too well. I know. I almost slipped myself.

ELECTRA   Ah, you were in the bathroom, too, mother? Who held you up?

CLYTEMNESTRA   What's wrong in my being there?

ELECTRA   With Aegisthus, of course?

CLYTEMNESTRA   With Aegisthus. And we weren't alone. Leo, my counsellor, was there, wasn't he, Aegisthus?

ELECTRA   Leo, who died the next day?

CLYTEMNESTRA   Did he die the next day?

ELECTRA   Yes. Leo slipped, too. He lay down on his bed and in the morning was found dead. He found a way to slip into death—sleeping, not slipping! You had him killed, didn't you?

CLYTEMNESTRA   Aegisthus, defend me. I call on you for help.

ELECTRA   He can do nothing for you. You've come to the place where you must defend yourself.

CLYTEMNESTRA   Oh, God! Have I come to this? A mother! A queen!

ELECTRA   Where is "this"? Tell us where you've come.

CLYTEMNESTRA Brought there by this heartless, joyless daughter! Happily, my little Chrysothemis loves flowers.

ELECTRA Don't I love flowers?

CLYTEMNESTRA To come to this! Through this idiotic journey called life, to come to this! I, who as a girl loved quiet, tending my pets, laughing at meal time, sewing! . . . I was so gentle, Aegisthus, I swear I was the gentlest. . . . There are still old men in my birthplace who call gentleness Clytemnestra.

ELECTRA If they die today, they needn't change their symbol. If they die this morning!

CLYTEMNESTRA To come to this! What injustice! Aegisthus, I spent my days in the meadows behind the palace. There were so many flowers I didn't have to stoop to pick them, I sat down. My dogs lay at my feet, the one who barked when Agamemnon came to take me away. I teased him with flowers and he ate them to please me. If I only had him! Anywhere else, if my husband had been a Persian, or an Egyptian, by now I'd be good, careless, gay! When I was young I had a voice, I trained birds! I might have been an Egyptian queen, singing gaily; I'd have had an Egyptian aviary! And we've come to this! What has this family, what have these walls done to us?

ELECTRA Murderers! . . . These are wicked walls

MESSENGER My lord, they've forced an entrance. The postern gate gave way.

ELECTRA All right. Let the walls crumble.

AEGISTHUS Electra, heed my final word. I forgive everything—your foolish fancies, your insults. But can't you see your country is dying?

ELECTRA And I don't love flowers! Do you imagine flowers for a father's grave are picked sitting down?

CLYTEMNESTRA Well, let this father return! Let him stop being dead! What nonsense, this absence, this silence! Let him come back, in his pomp, his vanity, his beard! That beard must have grown in the grave—a good thing, too!

ELECTRA What are you saying?

AEGISTHUS Electra, I promise that tomorrow, as soon as Argos is saved, the guilty, if there are any, shall disappear, for good and all. But don't be stubborn. You're gentle, Electra, in your heart you're gentle. Listen! The city will perish.

ELECTRA Let it! I can already feel my love for a burnt and conquered Argos! No! My mother has begun to insult my father, let her finish!

CLYTEMNESTRA Why are you talking about the guilty! What do you mean, Aegisthus?

ELECTRA He's just told me in a word all that you deny!

CLYTEMNESTRA And what do I deny?

ELECTRA He's told me that you let Orestes fall, that I love flowers, and that my father didn't slip.

CLYTEMNESTRA He did slip. I swear he slipped. If there's a truth in the world, let lightning from heaven show it to us. You'll see it revealed in all its brilliance.

AEGISTHUS Electra, you're in my power. Your brother too. I can kill you. Yesterday I should have killed you. Instead of that I promise, as soon as the enemy is repulsed, to step down from the throne and place Orestes on it.

ELECTRA That's no longer the question, Aegisthus. If the gods for once change their methods, if they make you wise and just in order to ruin you, that's their affair. The question now is, will she dare tell us why she hated my father!

CLYTEMNESTRA Oh, you want to know that?

ELECTRA But you'll not dare tell.

AEGISTHUS Electra, tomorrow, before the altar where we celebrate our victory the guilty man shall stand, for there is only one guilty man, in a parricide's coat. He'll confess his crime publicly and determine his punishment himself. First let me save the city.

ELECTRA You've "saved" yourselves today, Aegisthus, and in my presence. That's enough. Now I want her to finish!

CLYTEMNESTRA So, you want me to finish!

ELECTRA I dare you to!

MESSENGER They're entering the court yards, Aegisthus!

AEGISTHUS Come, queen!

CLYTEMNESTRA Yes, I hated him. Yes, you shall know what this fine father was like. Yes, after twenty years I'll have the joy that Agatha had today. A woman might belong to anyone, but there was just one man in the world to whom I couldn't belong. That man was the king of kings, father of fathers! I hated him from the first day he came to wrench me from my home, with his curly beard and the hand with the little finger always sticking up. He raised it when he drank, when he drove, when he held his sceptre . . . and when he held me close I felt on my back only four fingers. It drove me wild, and the morning he sacrificed your sister, Iphigenia—horrible—I saw the little fingers of both his hands sticking out, dark against the sun—king of kings! What nonsense! He was pompous, indecisive, stupid. He was the fop of fops, the most credulous creature. The king of kings was never anything more than that little finger and the beard that nothing could soften. The bathwater I soaked his head in didn't soften it, nor did the nights of false love when I pulled and tangled it, nor the storm at Delphi which turned the dancers' hair into manes; it came out in gold ringlets from water, bed, and rain. He would beckon me with his little finger and I would go smiling. . . . Why? He would tell me to kiss his mouth in that fleece and I would run to kiss it. . . . Why? And when I woke and was unfaithful to him, like Agatha, with the wooden bedstead—a royal bed—and he bade me talk to him, though I knew he was vain, empty, tiresome, I told him he was modest, strange, even splendid. . . . Why? And if he persisted, stammering, pathetic, I swore to him he was a god. King of kings! The only excuse for that title is that it justifies a hatred of hatreds. Do you know what I did, Electra, the day of his departure, when his ship was still in sight? I sacrificed the curliest ram I could find and toward midnight I stole into the throne room quite alone, and took the sceptre in my hands! Now you know everything. You wanted a hymn to truth, and here's a beautiful one.

ELECTRA Oh, father, forgive!

AEGISTHUS Come, queen.

CLYTEMNESTRA Take this girl first and chain her up.

ELECTRA Father, will you ever forgive me for listening to her? Aegisthus, should she not die?

AEGISTHUS Farewell, Electra.

ELECTRA Kill her, Aegisthus. And I'll forgive you.

CLYTEMNESTRA Don't let her go free, Aegisthus. They'll stab you in the back.

AEGISTHUS We'll see about that. Leave Electra alone. . . . Unbind Orestes.

(AEGISTHUS *and* CLYTEMNESTRA *go out*)

ELECTRA The bird is coming down, beggar, the bird is coming down.

BEGGAR Look, it's a vulture!

Scene Nine

(ELECTRA. NARSES' WIFE. BEGGAR. *Then* ORESTES)

BEGGAR You here, Narses' wife?

NARSES' WIFE All of us beggars, the lame, the halt and the blind, have come to save Electra and her brother.

BEGGAR Justice, eh?

NARSES' WIFE There they are, untying Orestes.

(*A crowd of* BEGGARS *enter, a few at a time*)

BEGGAR This is how they did the killing, listen, woman. This is the way it all happened,

I never invent anything. It was the queen who had the steps soaped that go down to the bath; the two of them did it. While all the housewives in Argos scrubbed their thresholds, the queen and her lover soaped the doorsill to his death. Think how clean their hands were when they greeted Agamemnon at his entrance! And your father slipped, Electra, as he reached out his arms to her. You were right except on this one point. He slipped on the steps, and the noise of his fall, because of his golden cuirass and helmet, was that of a king falling. And she threw herself on him, he thought, to raise him up, but she held him down. He didn't understand why his darling wife was holding him down, he wondered if it was a love transport, but then why did Aegisthus stay? Young Aegisthus was awkward and indiscreet. (We'll consider his promotion.) The ruler of the world, the conqueror of Troy, who had just reviewed the army and navy parade, must have been humiliated, to fall like that, on his back and in his noisy armor, even if his beard was untouched, in the presence of his loving wife and the young ensign. All the more annoyed because this might be a bad omen. The fall might mean he'd die in a year, or in five years. And he was surprised that his beloved wife caught his wrists and threw herself on him to hold him down, as the fisherwomen do with big stranded turtles on the shore. She was wrong, and not so beautiful, her face flushed, her neck wrinkled. Not like young Aegisthus, who was trying to extricate his sword for fear he'd hurt himself, apparently, he looked handsomer every minute. What was strange, though, was that the two of them were silent. He said "Dear wife, how strong you are!" "Young man," he said, "Pull out the sword—by its handle!" But they said nothing, the queen and the squire had become mutes in the last ten years, and no one had told him. They were as mute as travellers hurrying to pack a trunk when time is short. They had to do something quickly, before anyone else came in. What was it? Suddenly Aegisthus kicked his helmet as a dying man kicks his dog, and the truth was plain. And he cried, "Wife, let me go. Wife, what are you doing?" She took care not to answer, she couldn't say aloud, "I'm killing you, murdering you!" But she said to herself, "I'm killing you because there's not one gray hair on your beard, because it's the only way to murder that little finger."

She undid the laces of his cuirass with her teeth, and the gold turned to scarlet, and Aegisthus—beautiful with the beauty of Achilles killing Hector, of Ulysses killing Dolon—

approached, with drawn sword. Then the king of kings kicked Clytemnestra's back, and she shook all over, her silent hand shook, and he shouted so loud Aegisthus had to roar with laughter to cover the noise. Then he drove in the sword. And the king of kings was no longer the mass of bronze and iron he'd thought himself, he was just soft flesh, as easy to pierce as a lamb, and the sword cut so deep it split the marble. The murderers were wrong to hurt the marble, for it revenged itself. I found out about the crime from that split tile.

So he stopped struggling, let himself go, between the woman, who became uglier every moment, and the man, who was handsomer and handsomer. One good thing about death is that you can trust yourself to her, death is your only friend in an ambush, she has a familiar look, he saw that and called on his children, first the boy, Orestes, then the girl, Electra, to thank them for avenging him in future, lending their hands of death. Clytemnestra, foam on her lips, did not let go of him, and Agamemnon as willing to die but not to have this woman spit in his face, on his beard. She didn't spit because she was walking around the corpse, trying not to get blood on her sandals; her red dress looked to the dying man like the sun. Then the shadow fell, because each of them took an arm and turned him over on the floor. On his right hand four fingers were already stiff. Then, as Aegisthus had pulled out the sword without thinking, they turned him over again and put it gently, deliberately, back in the wound. Aegisthus was grateful to the dead man for having let himself be killed so very easily. Dozens of kings of kings could be killed like that, if murder was so easy.

But Clytemnestra's hatred of the man who'd struggled so fiercely, so stupidly, grew as she foresaw how every night she would dream of this murder. That's just what happened. It's seven years since she killed, she's killed him three thousand times.

(ORESTES *has come in during this speech*)

NARSES' WIFE Here's the young man! Isn't he handsome?

BEGGAR As beautiful as Aegisthus when young.

ORESTES Where are they, Electra?

ELECTRA Dear Orestes!

NARSES' WIFE In the southern courtyard.

ORESTES I'll see you soon, Electra, and we'll never part.

ELECTRA Go, my lover.

ORESTES Don't stop, beggar. Go on, tell him about the death of Clytemnestra and Aegisthus.

(*He goes out, sword in hand*)

NARSES' WIFE Tell us, beggar.

BEGGAR In two minutes. Give him time to get there.

ELECTRA He has his sword?

NARSES' WIFE Yes, daughter.

BEGGAR Are you crazy? Calling the princess your daughter!

NARSES' WIFE I call her daughter, I don't say she's my daughter. I've often seen her father, though. Heavens, what a fine man!

ELECTRA He had a beard, hadn't he?

NARSES' WIFE Not a beard, a sun. A wavy, curly sun, a sun just rising from the sea. He stroked it with his hand. The most beautiful hand in the world.

ELECTRA Call me your daughter, Narses' wife! I am your daughter. . . . I heard a cry!

NARSES' WIFE No, my daughter.

ELECTRA You're sure he had his sword? He didn't go to them without a sword?

NARSES' WIFE You saw him going. He had a thousand swords. Be calm, be calm!

ELECTRA What a long minute, mother, you waited at the edge of the bath!

NARSES' WIFE Why don't you tell us? Everything will be over before we know it.

BEGGAR One minute! He's looking for them. Now! He's found them.

NARSES' WIFE Oh, I can wait. Little Electra is soft to touch. I had only boys, gangsters. Mothers who only have girls are happy.

ELECTRA Yes . . . happy. . . . This time I do hear a cry!

NARSES' WIFE Yes, my daughter.

BEGGAR So, here's the end. Narses' wife and the beggars untied Orestes. He rushed across the courtyard. He didn't touch or embrace Electra. He was wrong, for he'll never touch her again. He found the murderers on the marble balcony, calming the rioters. As Aegisthus leaned down to tell the leaders that everything was going well, he heard behind him the cry of a wounded beast. But it wasn't a beast crying, it was Clytemnestra. She was bleeding. Her son had stabbed her. He struck at the couple blindly, his eyes closed. A mother, though, even when unworthy, is sensitive and human. She didn't call on Electra or Orestes but on her youngest daughter, Chrysothemis, so Orestes thought he had killed another, and an innocent, mother. She clung to Aegisthus' arm; she was right, that gave her a last chance to stand up. But she prevented Aegisthus from drawing his sword. He shook her, to free his arm. She was too heavy to serve as a shield. And that bird was beating his head with its wings and attacking him with its beak, so he struggled. Just with his unarmed left arm, the dead queen, loaded with necklace and pendants, on his right arm. He was in despair over dying like a criminal, when he had become pure and holy; to be fighting because of a crime which was no longer his; to find himself, though loyal and innocent, infamous before this parricide. He struggled with one hand, which the sword was cutting little by little, but the lacing of his cuirass caught on a brooch of Clytemnestra's, and it opened. Then he resisted no longer; he only shook his right arm to rid himself of the queen, not only to fight but to die alone, to lie far from Clytemnestra in death. He didn't succeed. Forever Clytemnestra and Aegisthus will be coupled. He died, calling a name I'll not repeat.

AEGISTHUS (*voice off-stage*) Electra!

BEGGAR I talked too fast. He caught up with me.

Scene Ten

(ELECTRA. BEGGAR. NARSES' WIFE. *The* EUMENIDES, *who are of exactly the same height and figure as* ELECTRA)

SERVANT Flee, everybody, the palace is on fire!

FIRST FURY That's what Electra wanted. Three things: daylight, truth—and this fire!

SECOND FURY Satisfied, Electra? The city's dying.

ELECTRA I'm satisfied. I know now that it will be born again.

THIRD FURY And the people killing each other in the streets, will they be born again? The Corinthians have started the attack, and it's a massacre.

FIRST FURY Your pride has brought you to this, Electra. You have nothing left, nothing.

ELECTRA I have my conscience, I have Orestes, I have justice, I have everything.

SECOND FURY Your conscience! Will you listen to your conscience in the early mornings to come? For seven years you've not slept because of a crime that others committed. Now you're the guilty one.

ELECTRA I have Orestes, I have justice, I have everything.

THIRD FURY Orestes! You'll never see Orestes again. We're leaving *you*—to pursue *him*. We've taken on your age and your shape —to pursue him. Good-bye! We'll not leave him until he's been driven to madness or suicide, cursing his sister.

ELECTRA I have justice. I have everything.

NARSES' WIFE What are they saying? They're back. What have we come to, my poor Electra, what have we come to?

ELECTRA What have we come to?

NARSES' WIFE Yes, tell me. I'm not very quick to understand. I know something's happened but I don't know just what. How can you explain it, when a day begins like today, and everything's ruined and pillaged—though we're still breathing, we've lost everything, the city's burning, innocent people are killing each other, the guilty are dying, too—and the sun still rises?

ELECTRA Ask the beggar. He knows.

BEGGAR It all has a beautiful name, Narses' wife, it is called the dawn.

Jean Anouilh

1910-

TO JEAN GIRAUDOUX

Fortunate are those young men who have had masters!

Fortunate are the nervous youngsters who went and rang doorbells and received with flushed faces the encouraging word from the man whom they admired!

I grew up without any masters; in the years around 1928, I had a warm place in my heart for Claudel and I carried dog-eared copies of Shaw and Pirandello in my pockets; and yet, I was all alone. Alone with the anguish of one soon to be twenty years old, with a love for the theatre, and all the awkwardness of youth. Who would divulge to me the secrets in those days in which only well-made plays were performed? Musset, Marivaux reread a thousand times? They were too far off. They were from an era already fabulous in which spoken French still had periods and commas, from an era in which the very sentences danced. And yet, there was a secret, a secret doubtless lost for a long time and which I was much too small ever to find again by myself. Eighteen years old! and my studies which were already becoming hazy, and a livelihood to earn somehow, and this anguish, these stiff fingers. Of course, Claudel before me was to have found the secret again or rather he had found another one, one suited only to him; but he was like a great inaccessible statue, a saint of wood upon a mountain whom one could ask for nothing.

It was then that an incomparable springtime came, warming and bringing into flower the Avenue Montaigne.

"To Jean Giraudoux" by Jean Anouilh, translated by Arthur Evans, is reprinted by permission of *The Tulane Drama Review.*

In all of my life, I believe that I shall never again see such chestnut trees, such balminess in the air. There were evenings when, in those lights which tinted the leaves above with blue, I pressed close to the gods, when I joined in the bustling throng of long automobiles, of women in evening clothes, in that sudden perfection which everything took on for me in that corner of Paris.

Oh, the exits of the audience from *Siegfried* . . . Dear Giraudoux, who will tell you now, since I never dared or wished to tell you, what strange encounters of despair and the harshest joy, of pride and the tenderest humility, took place in this young man who stumbled down from the upper gallery of the *Comédie des Champs-Elysées?*

Because of you that avenue and that thoroughfare, isolated by invisible signs in the midst of a detestable quarter, will always remain for me the streets of my village. Nowadays, I never pass through this landscape, zigzagging between the white barriers of the war and my memories, without being inundated with happiness.

The theatre, my life of beauty (oh the terrace of the "Francis" where Jouvet and Renoir would sit and drink and behind which I imagined God knows what sort of lavish display!), poetry, indeed, the inaccessible, caused me to choose my domicile between the Métro Alma and the Plaza Hotel, in that almost spa-like elegance, with its women in diamonds in the warm shadows, its men in white dress shirts. In the heat of a precocious summer, what château suddenly loomed forth from amid the middle-class barracks, and what entertainment was presented there which compelled this young fellow to remain there, without the strength to leave, after everyone else had left?

Even though others have found their poetry in the quiet streets of a sleepy town, along

[751]

the banks of a still lake, under the vaults of a church or forest, in a poetic setting, my poetry was to have its *rendez-vous* with me, because of you, in that Parisian landscape' for rich foreigners with its accessory figures scarcely suited to please me.

I still know *Siegfried* by heart, dear Giraudoux. Did I tell you that at the only dinner which I had with you, the only time when I was with you for more than five minutes? Did I tell you that I can still imitate all the voices? Boverio as Zelten, "It is you, dark-skinned brachycephalic one, with too many spectacles and too many woolen waistcoats?" and Bouquet, the poor Bouquet, "Son of Arminius, Glutton of carnage, it is I . . ." and Jouvet-Fontgeloy, whose accent of a "Hussard general of death" you'd swear was authentic, and their patron—just a minute now—"is never far away." And Renoir and Bogaert and Valentine and the inimitable Simon himself as the customs inspector.

Dear Giraudoux, I didn't tell you something else, it was the evening of *Siegfried* that I understood. As a consequence, I was to enter into a long night from which I have not yet completely emerged, from which, perhaps, I shall never emerge, but it is because of those spring evenings in 1928 when I, the only spectator, wept, even at the amusing dialogue, that I have been able to move somewhat out of myself.

Then came *Amphitryon, Intermezzo,* both rather far from me; then, irritated with the man who produced them and intransigent as innocence is wont to be, I no longer saw your plays performed. I would read them, overwhelmed, without opera *décor*, without glitter, without excess of magic tricks, without that imposing air of gala which your *premières* always managed to take on somewhat too lavishly. I would talk about them with Pitoëff —my other master, but with whom I was on familiar terms—who regretted so much your admirable *Electra* and then, finally, I experienced that tender despair a last time with *Ondine.*

When Jouvet—detested (I was his secretary) and then suddenly pardoned for so much just nobleness of spirit—lay down in his black armor upon that long gray stone, a despair rent me which I shall never forget.

It was not only too beautiful, it not only made ridiculous everything I had wanted to do, it was tender, solemn, and definitive like a farewell. I had a very certain feeling about it: the farewell of Hans to Ondine took on the meaning of another farewell which wrenched my heart. It was the time of the phony war and we dreamed about lives in danger. I believed, naively, that this mysterious farewell concerned me.

Dear Giraudoux, it was you whom I was leaving, owing you so much without ever having told you, having known you so little and so well.

I am happy, at least, that at the end of that dinner, last winter, where for the first time I was with you for more than five minutes, and where I still said nothing to you, I took hold of your overcoat and I helped you put it on. This is something I never do, and I surprised myself in doing it and in fixing your coat collar so that you would be warmer. Then, this familiarity coming from I know not where suddenly bothered me and I left you. . . .

But now I am happy that I served you, at least once, as schoolboys used to serve their masters, in exchange for that evening of *Siegfried.*

Translated by Arthur Evans

EURYDICE (LEGEND OF LOVERS)

Translated by Kitty Black

CAST OF CHARACTERS

FATHER
ORPHEUS
EURYDICE
MOTHER
STATION WAITER
VINCENT
MATHIAS
THE GIRL
DULAC
ANOTHER GIRL
THE YOUNG MAN
   (*Monsieur Henri*)
THE MANAGER
THE CASHIER
HOTEL WAITER
THE CLERK
LOUD-SPEAKER
VOICE

SCENE The *action of the play takes place in the refreshment room of a French provincial railway station and in a hotel bedroom in Marseilles.*

ACT ONE

(*The refreshment room of a provincial station. Overdecorated, worn, and dirty. Marble-topped tables, mirrors, benches covered with threadbare red velvet.*

Seated at a too-high desk, like a Buddha on an altar, is the CASHIER, *with a large bun and*

Eurydice (*Legend of Lovers*) by Jean Anouilh, translated by Kitty Black. Copyright 1952 by Jean Anouilh and Kitty Black. Reprinted by permission of Coward-McCann, Inc.

enormous breasts. Aged WAITERS, *bald and dignified, spittoons, and sawdust.*

Before the rise of the curtain we hear an accordion. It is ORPHEUS *playing quietly in the corner, beside his* FATHER, *absorbed in his miserable accounts in front of two empty glasses. In the background a single customer, a* YOUNG MAN *with his hat pulled down over his eyes, wearing a mackintosh, apparently lost in thought. Music for a moment, then the* FATHER *stops his additions and looks at* ORPHEUS)

FATHER My boy?

ORPHEUS (*still playing*) Father?

FATHER You don't expect your poor old father to go round with the hat in a station restaurant?

ORPHEUS I'm playing for my own pleasure.

FATHER (*continuing*) A station restaurant with only one customer, who's pretending not to notice anyway. I know their little ways. They pretend not to be listening, and not to see the plate when you hold it out. But I pretend not to see they're pretending. (*pause, while* ORPHEUS *continues to play*) D'you enjoy playing as much as that? I can't imagine how you, a musician, can still manage to like music. When I've been twanging away for a bunch of idiots playing cards in a café, there's only one thing I want to do . . .

ORPHEUS (*without stopping*) Go and play cards in another café.

FATHER (*surprised*) Exactly. How did you know?

ORPHEUS I guessed—nearly fifteen years ago.

FATHER Fifteen years? Oh, come now! Fifteen years ago, I still had talent. . . . Fifteen years ago, when I played in the orchestra, who would have believed your old father would come down to playing his harp in the street? Who'd have thought he'd be reduced to going round afterward with a little saucer?

ORPHEUS Mother would—every time you got yourself sacked from your current job. . . .

FATHER Your mother never loved me. Neither do you. You spend all your time trying to humiliate me. But don't think I'll put up with it always. You know I was offered a job as harpist at the casino at Palavas-les-Flots?

ORPHEUS Yes, father.

FATHER And I refused because they had no vacancy for you?

ORPHEUS Yes, father. Or rather, no, father.

FATHER No, father? Why, no, father?

ORPHEUS You refused because you know you play abominably and you'd be sacked the next morning.

FATHER (*turning away, hurt*) I shan't even answer you. (ORPHEUS *goes back to his playing*) Must you?

ORPHEUS Yes. Does it bother you?

FATHER I can't concentrate. Eight times seven?

ORPHEUS Fifty-six.

FATHER Are you sure?

ORPHEUS Quite sure.

FATHER Isn't it odd? I hoped it might be sixty-three. Still, eight times nine are obviously seventy-two. . . . You know we've very little money left, my boy.

ORPHEUS Yes, father.

FATHER Is that all you can say?

ORPHEUS Yes, father.

FATHER You're thinking of my white hairs?

ORPHEUS No, father.

FATHER I thought not. Oh, I'm used to it. (*He goes back to his additions*) Eight times seven?

ORPHEUS Fifty-six.

FATHER (*bitterly*) Fifty-six. . . . You didn't have to remind me. (*He closes his notebook and gives up his accounts*) That wasn't such a bad meal for twelve francs seventy-five. . . .

ORPHEUS No, father.

FATHER You shouldn't have ordered a vegetable. If you know how to do things, you get your vegetable with the main course and they let you have a second sweet instead. When you're having the set meal, it's always better to choose the two sweets. The Neapolitan ice was a dream. . . . In one sense, we did better tonight for twelve francs seventy-five than yesterday for thirteen francs fifty à la carte at Montpellier. . . . You could say they had linen serviettes instead of paper ones. It was a place that gave itself airs, but fundamentally it was no better. And did you see they charged us three francs for the cheese? If they had at least brought the tray along like they do in proper restaurants! Once, my boy, I was taken to dine at Poccardi's, you know, in Paris. They brought the tray along. . . .

ORPHEUS You've told me about it before, father.

FATHER (*hurt*) All right—I don't want to bore you. (ORPHEUS *goes back to his playing. After a moment the* FATHER *is bored and decides to stop sulking*) I say, my boy—that's horribly sad.

ORPHEUS So is what I'm thinking.

FATHER What are you thinking about?

ORPHEUS About you, father.

FATHER About me? Well, what is it now?

ORPHEUS Or rather, you and me.

FATHER The outlook isn't very promising, of course, but we're doing our best, my boy.

ORPHEUS I'm thinking that ever since Mother died, I've followed you round the cafés with my accordion. I've watched you struggling with your accounts at night. I've listened to you discussing the menus of the set meals and then I've gone to bed. In the morning I get up again.

FATHER When you get to my age, you'll see that that is life.

ORPHEUS I'm thinking that if you were all alone, with your harp, you'd never be able to live.

FATHER (*worried suddenly*) You don't want to leave me?

ORPHEUS No. Probably I'll never be able to leave you. I'm a better musician than you are, I am young and I'm sure life has better things to offer; but I couldn't live if I knew you were starving somewhere else.

FATHER That's good of you, my boy. Think of your old father.

ORPHEUS Good, yes, but it's a big responsibility. Sometimes I dream something might come between us. . . .

FATHER Now, now, we understand each other so well. . . .

ORPHEUS There's the wonderful job where I earn enough to make you an allowance. But it's a dream. A musician never earns enough to pay for two rooms and four meals a day.

FATHER Oh, my needs are very small, you know. A meal costing twelve francs seventy-five like today. A table at the café. A small glass of something, a ten-centime cigar, and I'm as happy as a sandboy. (*pause, he adds*) If I had to, I could quite well do without the small something.

ORPHEUS (*going on with his dream*) Then there's the level crossing where one of us is knocked down by a train. . . .

FATHER Good heavens . . . which one?

ORPHEUS (*gently*) Oh, it doesn't really matter. . . .

FATHER (*starting*) How strange you are. I

don't want to die! You're full of gloom tonight, my boy. (*He burps genteelly*) That rabbit was really excellent. Good heavens you make me laugh! At your age, I thought life was wonderful. (*He suddenly studies the cashier*) And what about love? Had you thought you might fall in love?

ORPHEUS What is love? Girls I might get to meet with you?

FATHER My dear boy, can any of us guess where and how love will find us? (*He comes a little closer*) Tell me, you don't think I look rather too bald? She's quite charming, that girl. A little provincial, perhaps. More my type than yours. What would you put her at? Forty? Forty-five?

ORPHEUS (*gives a pale little smile. He claps his father on the shoulder*) I'm going outside for a bit. . . . We've still got an hour before the train.

(*When he has gone, the* FATHER *rises, walks all around the* CASHIER, *who blasts him with a look—the miserable customer. Suddenly, the* FATHER *feels he is old and ugly, poor and bald. He rubs his hand over his head and goes sadly back to pick up his instrument before going out.*

Exit.

Outside on the platform a train arrives. The members of Dulac's company are seen for a moment. Then EURYDICE *enters and makes her way to a chair.*

Eurydice's MOTHER *enters in triumph. Boa and feather hat. Ever since 1920 she has grown younger every day*)

MOTHER There you are, Eurydice. . . . This heat . . . how I hate waiting at stations. The whole tour has been a disgrace—as usual. The manager ought to arrange that the leading actors don't spend all their time waiting for connections. When you've spent the whole day on a platform, how can you give your best in the evening?

EURYDICE There's only one train for the whole company and it's an hour late because of the storm yesterday. The manager can't help it.

MOTHER You always find excuses for these incompetents!

THE WAITER (*who has come up*) May I take your orders, ladies?

MOTHER Do you feel like something?

EURYDICE After that star entrance of yours, it's the least we can do.

MOTHER Have you any really good peppermint? I'll have a peppermint. In Argentine, or in Brazil where the heat was really exhausting,

I always used to take a peppermint just before making my first entrance. The divine Sarah gave me the tip. A peppermint.

THE WAITER And for mademoiselle?

EURYDICE Coffee, please.

MOTHER Why aren't you with Mathias? He's wandering about like a soul in torment.

EURYDICE Don't worry about him.

MOTHER It was very wrong of you to upset that boy. He adores you. It was your fault in the first place. You shouldn't have let him be your lover. I told you so at the time, but it's too late to worry about that now. Besides, we all begin and end with actors. When I was your age, I was much prettier than you. I could have been taken up by anyone I pleased. All I could do was waste my time with your father. . . . You see the charming results yourself.

WAITER (*who has brought the drinks*) A little ice, madame?

MOTHER Never—think of my voice! This peppermint is disgusting. I hate the provinces, I hate these second-rate tours. But in Paris nowadays, they only go mad over little idiots with no breasts, who can't say three words without fluffing. . . . What has the boy done to upset you? You didn't even get into the same compartment at Montélimar? My dear child, a mother is a girl's natural confidante, particularly when they're the same age—I mean, particularly when she's a very young mother. Come along, tell me. What has he done?

EURYDICE Nothing, mother.

MOTHER Nothing, mother. That doesn't make sense. Only one thing is sure—he adores you madly. Maybe that's why you don't love him. We women are all the same. Nothing can make us change. How's your coffee?

EURYDICE You have it—I don't want it.

MOTHER Thank you, darling. I like plenty of sugar. Waiter! Bring some more sugar for mademoiselle. Don't you love him any more?

EURYDICE Who?

MOTHER Mathias.

EURYDICE You're wasting your time, mother.

(*The* WAITER, *sulking, has brought the sugar*)

MOTHER Thank you. It's covered with flyblows! Charming. I, who have been round the world and stayed at all the best hotels—this is what I've come to. Oh, well, I suppose it will melt. . . . (*She drinks the coffee*) I think you're absolutely right. You should always follow your instincts. I've always followed mine, like a thoroughgoing old pro. But then you're not really an actress by vocation. Do sit up! Ah, here's Vincent. Darling boy! He looks quite put out. Now do be nice to him. You know how fond of the boy I am.

(VINCENT *enters, silver haired, handsome, and soft beneath a very energetic exterior. His gestures are ample, his smile full of bitterness. His eye a roving one. He kisses the* MOTHER's *hand*)

VINCENT   Ah, there you are! I've been looking for you everywhere.

MOTHER   I've been here, with Eurydice.

VINCENT   This little manager is absolutely useless! Apparently we've got to wait here for more than an hour. We shan't have time for dinner again before the performance. I call it really annoying. We may all have the patience of angels, but you must admit it's really annoying!

EURYDICE   It's not the manager's fault we had such a storm yesterday.

MOTHER   I wish I knew why you always stand up for the little idiot.

VINCENT   He's an incompetent—a real incompetent! I can't think why Dulac keeps such a man in the job. The last thing I heard was that he's lost the basket with all the wigs. And tomorrow we've got a matinee of *The Burgomaster*. Can you imagine what it will be like?

EURYDICE   I'm sure he'll find it again. It probably got left behind at Montélimar. . . .

VINCENT   If it was, it'll probably arrive in time for tomorrow, but tonight—for *Guinevere's Disgrace*—what are we to do? He says it couldn't matter less because it's a modern play, but I've given Dulac my last word. I cannot play the doctor without my goatee.

WAITER   (*who has come up*)   Can I take your order, sir?

VINCENT   (*superb*)   Nothing, thank you. A glass of water. (*The* WAITER *retreats, beaten*) The first and second acts, perhaps, but I'm sure you'll agree with me, dear friend. With the best will in the world, how can I play the big scene in the last act without my goatee? What on earth should I look like?

(EURYDICE *goes away bad temperedly*)

MOTHER   Where are you going, darling?

EURYDICE   Just for a walk, mother.

(*She goes out abruptly*)

VINCENT   (*watches her departure, haughtily. When she has gone*)   Dear friend, you know I'm not in the habit of getting on my high horse, but your daughter's attitude toward me is nothing short of scandalous.

MOTHER   (*simpering and trying to take his hand*)   My big bear.

VINCENT   Our relationship toward each other is perhaps a little delicate, I agree—although you're perfectly free to do as you please, you're separated from her father—but really, anyone would say she delights in aggravating it.

MOTHER   She's a silly girl. You know how she protects that fool, as she protects all the lame things in the world, God knows why—old cats, lost dogs, helpless drunkards. The thought that you might persuade Dulac to send him away was too much for her, that's all.

VINCENT   It may have been too much for her, but there are ways of doing these things.

MOTHER   You know quite well that's what's wrong with her. . . . She's a good child, but she has no manners. (MATHIAS *enters abruptly. He is badly shaven, somber, on edge*) Oh, hullo, Mathias.

MATHIAS   Excuse me, madame. Have you seen your daughter?

MOTHER   She's just gone down the platform.

(MATHIAS *exits. The mother watches him go*)

MOTHER   Poor boy. He's mad about her. She's always been good to him until just lately and now I don't know what's come over her. These last two or three days it's as though she were looking for something, or someone. . . . What? I don't know. . . . (*faraway the music of* ORPHEUS) Why must that man keep playing that thing? It's maddening.

VINCENT   He's waiting for his train.

MOTHER   That's no reason. That music and the flies . . . it's so appallingly hot!

(*The music has come nearer. They listen. During the next scene,* EURYDICE *walks across the back as though looking for the music*)

MOTHER   (*abruptly, in different voice*)   Remember the casino at Ostend?

VINCENT   The year they launched the Mexican tango. . . .

MOTHER   How handsome you were!

VINCENT   I still had my figure in those days. . . .

MOTHER   And such an air about you. . . . Remember the first day? "Madame, will you give me the pleasure of this dance?"

VINCENT   "But, sir, I don't know how to dance the tango."

MOTHER   "Nothing simpler, madame. I hold you in my arms. You've only to let yourself go." The way you said that! Then you put your arms around me and everything swam together . . . the face of the old fool who was keeping me and was watching furiously . . . the bar-man—he was making love to me, too, at the time. He was a Corsican, and he said he'd like to kill me—the waxed mustaches of the gypsies, the big mauve irises and pale green ranunculuses decorating the walls . . . ah! it was delicious. It was the year everyone wore *broderie anglaise.* . . . I had an exquisite white dress. . . .

VINCENT   I wore a yellow carnation in my buttonhole, and a bird's-eye check in green and brown. . . .

MOTHER   When we danced you held me so tightly the pattern of my dress was driven right into my flesh. . . . The old fool noticed it and made a scene. I slapped his face and found myself in the street without a farthing. You hired a carriage with pink pompons and we drove all round the bay alone till it was dark. . . .

VINCENT   Ah, the uncertainty, the delicious disturbance of that first day of days. The searching, the awareness, the groping toward the unknown. One does not yet know one's love and yet one knows it will last for the rest of one's life.

MOTHER   (*suddenly with a change of voice*) Why on earth did we quarrel a fortnight later?

VINCENT   I don't know. I can't remember.

(ORPHEUS *has stopped playing.* EURYDICE *is standing in front of him and they look at each other*)

EURYDICE   Was it you playing just now?

ORPHEUS   Yes.

EURYDICE   How beautifully you play!

ORPHEUS   Thank you.

EURYDICE   What was it called—what you were playing?

ORPHEUS   I don't know. I was improvising. . . .

EURYDICE   (*in spite of herself*)   I'm sorry. . . .

ORPHEUS   Why?

EURYDICE   I don't know. I would have liked it to have had a name.

(A GIRL *passes along the platform, sees* EURYDICE *and calls*)

THE GIRL   Eurydice! Is that you?

EURYDICE   (*without taking her eyes off* ORPHEUS)   Yes.

THE GIRL   I've just seen Mathias. He's looking for you, darling. . . . (*She disappears*)

EURYDICE   Yes. (*She looks at* ORPHEUS) Your eyes are light blue.

ORPHEUS   Yes. I don't know how to describe yours.

EURYDICE   They say it depends on what I'm thinking.

ORPHEUS   Just now they're dark green, like deep water beside the stone steps of a harbor.

EURYDICE   They say that's when I'm happy.

ORPHEUS   Who's "they"?

EURYDICE   The others.

THE GIRL   (*coming back, calling from the platform*)   Eurydice!

EURYDICE   (*without turning round*)   Yes?

THE GIRL   Don't forget Mathias.

EURYDICE   Yes. (*suddenly she asks*)   D'you think you'll make me very unhappy?

ORPHEUS   (*smiling gently*)   I don't think so.

EURYDICE   I don't mean unhappy as I am at this moment. It's a sort of pain, but a sort of joy as well. What frightens me is being unhappy and lonely when you leave me.

ORPHEUS   I'll never leave you.

EURYDICE   Will you swear that?

ORPHEUS   Yes.

EURYDICE   On my head?

ORPHEUS   (*smiling*)   Yes.

(*They look at each other. Suddenly she says gently*)

EURYDICE   I like it when you smile.

ORPHEUS   Don't you ever smile?

EURYDICE   Never when I'm happy.

ORPHEUS   I thought you said you were unhappy.

EURYDICE   Don't you understand? Are you a real man after all? How strange it is! Here we are, the two of us, standing face to face, with everything that's going to happen drawn up ready and waiting behind us. . . .

ORPHEUS   D'you think much is going to happen?

EURYDICE   (*gravely*)   Everything. All the things that happen to a man and woman on earth, one by one. . . .

ORPHEUS   Gay things, sweet things, terrible things?

EURYDICE   (*gently*)   Shameful things and filthy things. . . . We're going to be so unhappy.

ORPHEUS   (*taking her in his arms*)   How wonderful!

(VINCENT *and the* MOTHER, *dreaming cheek to cheek, continue softly*)

VINCENT   Ah, *l'amour, l'amour!* You see my darling one, on this earth where all our hopes are shattered, where all is deception and pain and disappointment, it's a marvelous consolation to remember we still have our love. . . .

MOTHER   My big bear. . . .

VINCENT   All men are liars, Lucienne, faithless, false, hypocritical, vainglorious, or cowards; all women are perfidious, artificial, vain, capricious, or depraved; the world is nothing but a bottomless sink where the most monstrous beasts disport and distort themselves through oceans of slime. But there is one holy and sublime hope left in the world—the union of these two imperfect and horrible beings!

MOTHER   Yes, my darling. Perdican's big speech.

VINCENT   (*stops, surprised*)   Is it? I've played it so often!

MOTHER   Remember? You played it that first evening at Ostend. I was in *The Foolish Virgin at the Kursaal,* but I was only in the first act. I waited for you in your dressing room. You came off-stage still thrilling with the wonderful love scene you'd been playing and you took me there and then, in doublet and hose. . . .

VINCENT   Ah, those nights, those nights! The fusion of body and heart! The moment, the unique moment when you no longer know if it's the flesh or the spirit fluttering. . . .

MOTHER   You're a wonderful lover, dear boy!

VINCENT   And you, the most adorable of mistresses!

(EURYDICE *and* ORPHEUS *have listened to them, pressed together as if afraid*)

EURYDICE   Make them stop. Please, please, make them stop.

ORPHEUS   (*going to the couple while* EURYDICE *hides*)   Monsieur, madame, you certainly won't understand my attitude. It will seem strange to you. Even very strange. But I'm afraid you must both get out of here.

VINCENT   Out of here?

ORPHEUS   Yes, monsieur.

VINCENT   Is it closing time?

ORPHEUS   Yes, monsieur. Closing time for you.

VINCENT   (*rising*)   Really, I. . . .

MOTHER   (*also rising*)   But you don't belong here. I know you—you're the one who was playing. . . .

ORPHEUS   You must both go away at once. I promise if I could explain, I would, but I can't explain anything. You wouldn't understand. Something very important is happening here.

MOTHER   The boy's mad. . . .

VINCENT   But good gracious, I mean to say, it doesn't make sense! This place is open to everyone!

ORPHEUS   Not any more.

MOTHER   Well, really! This is too much! (*She calls*) Madame, please! Waiter!

ORPHEUS   (*pushing them toward the door*) No, don't call them, it's no use. Go away. I'll settle your bill myself.

MOTHER   But you can't be allowed to treat us like this!

ORPHEUS   I'm a peaceful soul, madame, very kind, very shy even. I promise you I'm very shy, madame, and until this minute I'd never have dared to do what I'm doing. . . .

MOTHER   I've never seen such a thing!

ORPHEUS   No, madame, you've never seen such a thing. Anyway, I've never seen such a thing.

MOTHER   (*to* VINCENT)   Can't you say something?

VINCENT   Come away. You can see he's not in a normal condition.

MOTHER   (*disappears, calling*)   I shall report you to the stationmaster.

EURYDICE   (*coming out of hiding*)   Ah! How horrible they were, weren't they? Horrible and stupid!

ORPHEUS   (*turning to her smiling*)   Sh! Don't talk about them. How everything falls into place now that we are alone. How clear and simple everything has become. It's as though I were seeing the chandeliers and the palm . . . and the spittoons and the chairs for the first time. . . . Isn't a chair charming? You'd think it was an insect listening for the sound of our steps, ready to spring away on its four thin little legs. Careful! We mustn't move, or if we do, we must be very quick. . . . (*He makes a spring, dragging* EURYDICE) Got it! Isn't a chair a clever invention. You can even sit on it. . . . (*He hands her to the chair with comical ceremony, then looks at her sadly*) What I don't understand, is why they invented the second chair. . . .

EURYDICE   (*pulling him down and making room for him on her chair*)   It was for people who didn't know each other. . . .

ORPHEUS   (*taking her in his arms and crying out*)   But I know you! Just now as I was playing and you came along the platform and I didn't know you. . . . Now everything's changed, and it's wonderful! Everything round us has suddenly become extraordinary. Look . . . how beautiful the cashier is with her big bosom resting delicately on her counter. And the waiter! Look at the waiter! His long flat feet in his button boots, his distinguished mustache, and his noble, noble air. . . . This is an extraordinary evening; we were fated to meet each other, and to meet the noblest waiter in France. A waiter who might have been a governor, a colonel, a member of the *Comédie Française.* Waiter. . . .

WAITER   (*approaching*)   Monsieur?

ORPHEUS You are quite charming.

WAITER But, monsieur. . . .

ORPHEUS Yes, yes, don't protest. I'm very sincere, you know, and I'm not used to paying compliments. You're quite charming. And we shall always remember you and the cashier, Mademoiselle and I. You'll tell her so, won't you?

WAITER Yes, monsieur.

ORPHEUS Isn't it wonderful to be alive! I didn't know it was so exciting to breathe, to have blood rushing through your veins, muscles that can move. . . .

EURYDICE Am I heavy?

ORPHEUS Oh, no! Just the right weight to keep me down to earth. Until now I was too light. I floated. I bumped into furniture and people. My arms were stretched too wide, my fingers were losing their grip. . . . How funny it is, and how lightly the experts make their calculations of weight! I've just realized I was short of exactly your weight to make me part of the atmosphere. . . .

EURYDICE Oh, my darling, you're frightening me! You really are part of it now? You'll never fly away again?

ORPHEUS Never again.

EURYDICE What should I do, all alone on the earth, if you were to leave me? Swear you'll never leave me?

ORPHEUS I swear.

EURYDICE That's so easy to say. I hope you don't really mean to leave me. If you really want to make me happy, swear you'll never even want to leave me, even for a minute, even if the prettiest girl in the world looked at you.

ORPHEUS I swear that too.

EURYDICE (*rising abruptly*) You see how false you are! You swear that even if the prettiest girl in the world looked at you, you wouldn't want to leave me. But to know that she looked at you, you'd have to look at her. Oh, dear God, how unhappy I am! You've only just begun to love me, and already you're thinking of other women. Swear you wouldn't even see the idiot, my darling. . . .

ORPHEUS I should be blind.

EURYDICE Even if you don't see her, people are so wicked, they'd tell you about her as quickly as they could, just so they could hurt me. Swear you won't listen to them!

ORPHEUS I should be deaf.

EURYDICE I know—there's something much simpler. Swear to me straightaway, sincerely, of your own free will and not just to please me, that you won't ever think another woman pretty. . . . Even the ones supposed to be beautiful. . . . It doesn't mean a thing, you know.

ORPHEUS I swear it.

EURYDICE (*suspiciously*) Not even one who looked like me?

ORPHEUS Even that one. I'll watch out for her.

EURYDICE You swear it of your own free will?

ORPHEUS Of my own free will.

EURYDICE Good. And you know you've sworn it by my head?

ORPHEUS By your head.

EURYDICE You know, don't you, that when you swear by someone's head, it means that person dies if you don't keep your word?

ORPHEUS Yes, I know.

EURYDICE (*going to him*) Good. Now I'll tell you. I only wanted to test you. We haven't really sworn anything. To swear properly, it's not enough to lift your hand, a vague little gesture you can interpret how you like. You must stretch out your arm like this, spit on the ground—don't laugh. This is very serious. We must do it properly. Some people say that not only does the person die suddenly if you break your word, but that she suffers horribly as well.

ORPHEUS (*gravely*) I've made a note of it.

EURYDICE Good. Now, you know what you'll make me risk if you lie, even a very little; you'll swear to me now, please, darling, stretching out your hand and spitting on the ground, that everything you've sworn was true.

ORPHEUS I spit, I stretch out my hand, and I swear.

EURYDICE (*with a great sigh*) Good. I believe. Besides, it's so easy to deceive me, I'm very trusting. You're smiling. Are you laughing at me?

ORPHEUS I'm looking at you. I've just realized I haven't had time to look at you before.

EURYDICE Am I ugly? Sometimes, when I've been crying, or laughing too much, I get a tiny red spot on the side of my nose. I'd rather tell you straightaway, so you don't get a shock later on.

ORPHEUS I'll remember.

EURYDICE And I'm very thin. Not so thin as I look; when I'm in the bath, I don't think I'm too bad, but what I mean is, I'm not one of those women you can rest against comfortably.

ORPHEUS I didn't expect to be very comfortable.

EURYDICE I can only give you what I've got, can't I? So you mustn't imagine things. . . . I'm very stupid too—I never know what to say and you mustn't rely on me too much to make conversation.

ORPHEUS (*smiling*)   You never stop talking!

EURYDICE   I never stop talking, but I wouldn't know how to answer you. That's why I talk all the time, to prevent people asking me questions. It's my way of keeping quiet. You'll see you won't like anything about me.

ORPHEUS   You're quite wrong. I like it when you talk too much. It makes a little noise and it's very restful.

EURYDICE   Really! I'm sure you like mysterious women. The Garbo type. Six feet high, huge eyes, big mouths, big feet, who spend the whole day smoking in the woods. I'm not like that at all. You must say good-bye to that idea straightaway.

ORPHEUS   I have.

EURYDICE   Yes, you say that, but I can see in your eyes. . . . (*She throws herself into his arms*) Oh, darling, darling, it's too awful not to be the one you love! What can I do? Do you want me to grow? I'll try. I'll go in for exercises. Do you want me to look haggard? I'll put mascara on my eyelids, use much more make-up. I'll try and be somber, to smoke. . . .

ORPHEUS   Of course not!

EURYDICE   Yes, yes, I'll even try to be mysterious. It's not so very complicated. All you have to do is think of nothing. Any woman can do it.

ORPHEUS   What a little lunatic you are!

EURYDICE   I'll manage, you'll see! I'll be wise and extravagant and thrifty—sometimes—and obedient as a little odalisque, or terribly unjust the days you'd like to feel unhappy because of me. Oh, only those days, don't worry. . . . And then I'll make it up to you the days I'll be maternal—so maternal I'll be a little annoying—the days you'll have boils or toothache. Then on rainy days, I can still be bourgeois, badly brought up, prudish, ambitious, highly strung, or just plain boring.

ORPHEUS   Do you think you can play all those parts?

EURYDICE   Of course, my darling, if I'm to keep you, I must be all the other women in one. . . .

ORPHEUS   And when will you be yourself?

EURYDICE   In between. Whenever I've got the time—I'll manage.

ORPHEUS   It'll be a dog's life!

EURYDICE   That's what love is! Anyway, it's easy for the lady dogs. All they have to do is let the other dogs sniff them a little, then trot along with a dreamy air, pretending they haven't noticed anything. Men are much more complicated!

ORPHEUS (*pulling her to him, laughing*)   I'm going to make you very unhappy!

EURYDICE (*pressing herself to him*)   Oh, yes! I shall make myself so small, I shan't make any demands on you. All you'll need to do is let me sleep at night against your shoulder, hold my hand all day. . . .

ORPHEUS   I like sleeping on my back, diagonally across the bed. I like taking long walks by myself. . . .

EURYDICE   We could both try and sleep across the bed, and when we go for walks, I'll walk a little behind you, if you like. Only a very little. Almost beside you all the same. But I shall love you so much, and I shall always be so true, so true. . . . Only you must always talk to me so I won't have time to think of stupid things. . . .

ORPHEUS (*dreams for a moment in silence with her in his arms; murmurs*)   Who are you? I feel I've known you always.

EURYDICE   Why ask me who I am? It means so little. . . .

ORPHEUS   Who are you? It's too late, I know quite well, I could never leave you now. You appeared quite suddenly in this station. I stopped playing my accordion, and now you're in my arms. Who are you?

EURYDICE   I don't know who you are, either. And yet I don't want you to explain. I'm happy. That's enough.

ORPHEUS   I don't know why I'm suddenly afraid of being hurt.

THE GIRL (*passing on the platform*)   What? Still there? Mathias is expecting you in the third-class waiting room. If you don't want a whole new series of rows, darling, you'd better go to him straightaway. . . . (*She has gone*)

ORPHEUS (*who has let* EURYDICE *go*)   Who is this Mathias?

EURYDICE (*quickly*)   No one, darling.

ORPHEUS   This is the third time someone's said he's looking for you.

EURYDICE   He's one of the boys in the company. No one at all. He's looking for me. All right. He's probably got something to say.

ORPHEUS   Who is this Mathias?

EURYDICE (*crying out*)   I don't love him, darling, I've never loved him!

ORPHEUS   Is he your lover?

EURYDICE   These things are so quickly said, it's so easy to call everything by the same name. I'd rather tell you the truth at once, and tell you myself. Everything must be clear between us. Yes. He is my lover. (ORPHEUS *falls back a step*) No, don't leave me. I so much wanted to be able to say, I'm only a girl. I've been waiting for you. Yours will be the first hand to touch me. I so much wanted to be able to tell you that—isn't it stupid?—it seemed to me it was true.

ORPHEUS   Has he been your lover long?

EURYDICE I don't know. Six months perhaps. I've never loved him.

ORPHEUS Then why?

EURYDICE Why? Oh, don't keep asking me questions. When we don't know each other very well, when we don't know everything about each other, questions can become the most terrible weapons. . . .

ORPHEUS Why? I want to know.

EURYDICE Why? Because he was unhappy, I suppose, and I was tired. And lonely. He was in love with me.

ORPHEUS And before?

EURYDICE Before, my darling?

ORPHEUS Before him?

EURYDICE Before him?

ORPHEUS You've never had another lover?

EURYDICE (*after imperceptible hesitation*) No. Never.

ORPHEUS Then he taught you how to make love? Answer me. Why don't you say something? You said you only wanted the truth to be between us.

EURYDICE (*crying out in despair*) Yes, but, my darling, I'm trying to decide what will hurt you least! If it was him, whom you'll probably see, or someone else, a long time ago, whom you'll never see. . . .

ORPHEUS It's not a question of what hurts me least, but the truth!

EURYDICE Well, when I was very young, a man, a stranger, took me, almost by force. . . . It lasted for a few weeks, and then he went away.

ORPHEUS Did you love him?

EURYDICE He hurt me, I was afraid. I was ashamed.

ORPHEUS (*after pause*) Is that all?

EURYDICE Yes, my darling. You see, it was very stupid, very sad, but very simple.

ORPHEUS (*in a low voice*) I'll try never to think of them.

EURYDICE Yes, darling.

ORPHEUS I'll try never to think of their faces close to yours, their eyes upon you, their hands touching you.

EURYDICE Yes, darling.

ORPHEUS I'll try not to think they've already held you close. (*takes her in his arms again*) There, now it's all begun again. I'm the one who's holding you.

EURYDICE (*very gently*) It's wonderful in your arms. Like a tiny house, snug and secure, in the middle of the world. A tiny house where no one can ever come. (*They kiss for the first time*) Here? In this café?

ORPHEUS In this café. I, who always feel embarrassed when people look at me, I wish it could be full of people . . . it will be a beautiful wedding! For witnesses we shall have had the cashier, the noblest waiter in France, and a shy little man in a mackintosh who pretends not to see us, though I'm sure he can. . . .

(*He kisses her. The* YOUNG MAN *in the mackintosh who has been sitting silently in the background from the beginning of the act, looks at them, then gets up noiselessly and comes to lean against a column nearer to them. They haven't seen him*)

EURYDICE (*freeing herself suddenly*) Now, you must leave me. There's something I must do. No, don't ask me. Go out for a moment, I'll call you back. (*She goes with him to the door, then goes back to the door that opens on to the platform; she stops and stands motionless for a moment on the threshold. One realizes she is looking at someone invisible who is also staring at her. Suddenly she says in a hard voice*) Come in. (MATHIAS *enters slowly without taking his eyes off her. He stops on the threshold*) You saw? I kissed him. I love him. What do you want?

MATHIAS Who is he?

EURYDICE I don't know.

MATHIAS You're mad.

EURYDICE Yes.

MATHIAS For a week now, you've been avoiding me.

EURYDICE For a week, yes, but it wasn't because of him. I've only known him for an hour.

MATHIAS (*looks at her in sudden fear*) What did you say? (*He draws back*)

EURYDICE You know, Mathias.

MATHIAS Eurydice, you know I cannot live without you.

EURYDICE Yes, Mathias. I love him.

MATHIAS You know I'd rather die at once than go on living alone, now that I've had you with me. I don't ask anything of you, Eurydice, nothing except not to be left alone. . . .

EURYDICE I love him, Mathias.

MATHIAS Is that the only thing you can say?

EURYDICE (*softly, pitilessly*) I love him.

MATHIAS (*going out suddenly*) Very well. If that's the way you want it.

EURYDICE (*running after him*) Listen, Mathias, try to understand. I like you very much, only—I love him. . . .

(*They have gone. The* YOUNG MAN *in the mackintosh watches them go. He goes out slowly after them. The stage is empty for a moment. We hear a bell ringing, then the whistle of a train in the distance.* ORPHEUS *comes in slowly, watching* EURYDICE *and* MATHIAS *disappear. Behind him his* FATHER

*bursts in with his harp, while the train whistles
and the bell becomes more insistent*)

FATHER The train's coming, my boy. Platform two. Are you ready? (*takes a step, suddenly becomes absentminded*) Er . . . have
you paid? I think you said it was your turn?

ORPHEUS (*gently, looking at him*) I'm not
going, father.

FATHER Why always wait until the last
minute? The train will be in in two minutes
and we've got to take the subway. With the
harp, we've only just got time.

ORPHEUS I'm not taking this train.

FATHER What? You aren't taking this train?
Why aren't you taking this train? We want to
get to Palavas tonight, it's the only one.

ORPHEUS Then take it. I'm not going.

FATHER This is something new! What's
the matter with you?

ORPHEUS Listen, father. I'm very fond of
you. I know you need me, that it'll be terrible,
but it had to happen one day. I'm going to
leave you. . . .

FATHER (*a man fallen from the clouds*)
What are you saying?

ORPHEUS (*crying out suddenly*) You heard
me quite well! Don't make me say it again to
give you a lead into a pathetic scene. Don't
hold your breath so that you can turn pale;
don't pretend to tremble and tear your hair!
I know all your tricks. It was all right when I
was little. They don't impress me now. (*He
repeats, in a low voice*) I'm going to leave you,
father.

FATHER (*changing his tactics suddenly and
wrapping himself in an exaggerated dignity*)
I refuse to listen to you. You're not in your right
mind. Come along.

ORPHEUS Dignity doesn't work either. I
told you I knew all your tricks.

FATHER (*hurt*) Forget my white hairs—
forget my white hairs! I'm used to it. . . . But
I repeat, I refuse to listen to you. That's clear
enough, isn't it?

ORPHEUS You must listen to me because
you've only two minutes to understand. Your
train's whistling already.

FATHER (*sneering nobly*) Ah! Ah!

ORPHEUS Don't sneer nobly, I beg you! Listen to me. You've got to catch that train, and
catch it alone. It's your only hope of arriving
at Palavas-les-Flots in time to get the job as
harpist.

FATHER (*babbling*) But I refused the job! I
refused it on your account!

ORPHEUS You can say you've thought it
over, that you're deserting me, that you accept.

Tortoni has probably not had time to find another harpist. He's your friend. He'll do his
best for you.

FATHER But I refused his offer. He's drunk
his shame to the very dregs. You mustn't forget
he's an Italian. Those people never forgive an
insult.

ORPHEUS Take the train, father. As soon as
you've gone, I'll telephone to Palavas, I swear
I'll make him forget you refused.

FATHER (*shouts in a voice the power of
which is unsuspected in his frail body*) Never!

ORPHEUS Don't shout! He's not such a bad
chap. I'm sure he will listen to me.

FATHER Never, do you hear? Your father
will never abase himself.

ORPHEUS But I'm the one who's going to
be abased! I'll say it was all my fault. I'll telephone Tortoni straightaway. (*goes to desk*)
Madame, can I telephone from here?

FATHER (*catching him back*) Listen, my
boy. Don't telephone that animal. I'd rather
tell you straightaway. The harpist's job. . . .

ORPHEUS Well?

FATHER Well—he never offered it to me.

ORPHEUS What?

FATHER I said it to make you think better
of me. I got wind of the job and begged him to
have me. He refused.

ORPHEUS (*after a short pause*) I see. . . .
(*says gently*) I thought you could have had
that job. It's a pity. It would have settled so
many things.

(*Pause*)

FATHER (*gently*) I am old, Orpheus. . . .
(*The train whistles*)

ORPHEUS (*suddenly, in a sort of fever*)
Take the train all the same, please, please,
father; go to Palavas-les-Flots; there are plenty
of cafés there. It's the height of the season, I
promise you you'll be able to earn your living!

FATHER With nothing but the harp . . .
you're joking!

ORPHEUS But that's what people like—they
always noticed the harp. You see so few about.
Every beggar plays the accordion in the street.
But the harp—you've said it often enough
yourself—that was what made us both look
like artists.

FATHER Yes, but you play extremely well,
and the women thought you were young and
charming. They dug their elbows into their
escorts and made them put two francs into the
plate. When I'm alone, they'll keep their elbows
to themselves.

ORPHEUS (*trying to laugh*) Of course they

won't, father—the more mature ones. You're an old Don Juan still!

FATHER (*throwing a glance at the cashier who humiliated him earlier, and stroking his beard*) Between ourselves, an old Don Juan for chambermaids in cheap hotels—and only ugly chambermaids. . . .

ORPHEUS You're exaggerating, father—you're still successful when you choose!

FATHER So I tell you, but it doesn't always happen as I say. Besides, I've never told you this, my boy. I brought you up, I had my paternal pride—I don't know if you've noticed . . . I . . . I play the harp very badly.

(*There is a terrible silence; ORPHEUS hangs his head; he cannot help smiling a little*)

ORPHEUS I couldn't help noticing, father.

FATHER You see, you say so yourself. . . .

(*Another pause. The train whistles very close*)

ORPHEUS (*shaking him suddenly*) Father, I can't do anything more for you. If I were rich, I'd give you some money. But I haven't any. Go and take your train. Keep everything we've got, and good luck.

FATHER Just now you said you couldn't leave me!

ORPHEUS Just now, yes. Now I can.

(*The train is heard coming into the station*)

ORPHEUS Here's your train. Hurry, pick up the harp.

FATHER (*still struggling*) You've met someone, haven't you?

ORPHEUS Yes, father.

FATHER The girl who came in just now?

ORPHEUS (*kneeling in front of the suitcases*) Yes, father. (*takes some things from one case, puts them into the other*)

FATHER I talked a little with those people. She's an actress, you know, a tenth-rate company that plays in flea pits. She's no better than she ought to be.

ORPHEUS Yes, father. We really must hurry. . . .

FATHER I shall curse you! This will cost you dear!

ORPHEUS Yes, father.

FATHER (*rising*) Laugh away. I've still got a few hundred francs. I can earn my living from day to day, you'll have nothing.

ORPHEUS (*laughing, in spite of himself, and catching him by the shoulders*) My father, my dear old father, my terrible father. I'm very fond of you, but I can do nothing more for you.

LOUDSPEAKER (*outside*) Passengers for Béziers, Montpellier, Sète, Palavas-les-Flots.

ORPHEUS Quick, you're going to miss it.

You've got the harp, the big suitcase? I've got two hundred francs, keep the rest.

FATHER Don't be so generous!

LOUDSPEAKER Passengers for Béziers, Montpellier, Sète, Palavas-les-Flots!

FATHER (*suddenly*) Do you think I could get a rebate on your ticket?

ORPHEUS (*embracing him*) I don't know. I'm so happy, father. I love her. I'll write to you. You ought to be a little pleased to see me happy. I so much want to live!

FATHER (*loading himself up*) I'll never be able to manage alone.

ORPHEUS I'll help you. You must get a porter at the other end.

FATHER (*crying from the doorway like a ridiculous curse, and dropping some of his parcels in the process*) You're deserting your father for a woman! A woman who probably doesn't love you in return!

ORPHEUS (*crying out, following him*) I'm so happy, father. . . .

VOICE (*outside*) Mind the doors!

FATHER (*before going out*) You're sending me away to die!

ORPHEUS (*pushing him*) Hurry, father, hurry!

(*Whistles, noise of the porters, steam. Suddenly, the train is heard starting up. EURYDICE enters with a small suitcase and sits in a corner, making herself very inconspicuous. ORPHEUS comes back; he goes to her. She looks at him*)

ORPHEUS It's all over.

EURYDICE (*comically*) It's all over with me, too.

ORPHEUS (*kissing her head*) Forgive me. He's rather ridiculous. He's my father.

EURYDICE You mustn't ask me to forgive you. The woman talking about love just now, with all those noises, was my mother. I didn't dare tell you.

(*They are facing each other, smiling gently. A bell rings, then the whistle of an approaching train*)

LOUDSPEAKER Passengers for Toulouse, Béziers, Carcassonne, platform seven. The train arriving now.

ANOTHER LOUDSPEAKER (*farther away*) Passengers for Toulouse, Béziers, Carcassonne, platform seven. The train arriving now.

(*Through the door opening on to the platform, the members of the company pass with their baggage*)

THE GIRL Quickly, darling, or we'll have to stand all the way again. Naturally, the stars are traveling second. Who's paying the extra, I ask you? Who's paying the extra?

ANOTHER GIRL (*continuing a story*) Then, d'you know what she said to me? She said, I don't give a damn. I've my position to consider. . . .

(*They have gone. The* MOTHER *and* VINCENT *pass, overloaded with hatboxes, enormous suitcases*)

MOTHER Vincent, darling boy, the big case and the green box?

VINCENT I've got them both. Off we go!

MOTHER Be very careful. The handle's not very secure. It reminds me of one day at Buenos Aires. Sarah's hatbox burst open in the middle of the station. There were ostrich feathers all over the track. . . .

(*They have gone. A fat man passes, puffing, behind them*)

DULAC Quickly, for God's sake, quickly! And check that the trunks have been loaded. Then get in the back. The rest of us will be up front.

EURYDICE (*gently*) All the people in my life. . . .

(*Running, and unable to run, comic, lamentable, absurd, the little* MANAGER *comes last, tripping over too many suitcases, too many parcels slipping from his grasp. All in the midst of distant cries and the approaching whistles of the train*)

EURYDICE (*gently, to* ORPHEUS) Close the door. (ORPHEUS *closes the door. A sudden silence covers them*) There. Now we're alone in the world.

LOUDSPEAKER (*farther away*) Passengers for Toulouse, Béziers, Carcassonne, platform seven. The train arriving now.

(ORPHEUS *has gently come back to her. Noise of train reaching the station and a cry, a cry that becomes a noise that swells and stops suddenly, giving place to a terrible silence. The* CASHIER *has stood up and tried to see. The* WAITER *runs across the stage, calling to them as he passes*)

WAITER Someone's thrown himself in front of the express—a young man!

(*People pass, running along the platform.* ORPHEUS *and* EURYDICE *are facing each other, unable to look at one another. They say nothing. The* YOUNG MAN *in the mackintosh appears on the platform. He comes in, then shuts the door and looks at them*)

EURYDICE (*gently*) I couldn't help it. I love you and I didn't love him.

(*There is a pause. Each stares straight ahead without looking at the other. The* YOUNG MAN *in the mackintosh comes up to them*)

THE YOUNG MAN (*in an expressionless voice, without taking his eyes off them*) He threw himself in front of the engine. The shock itself must have killed him.

ORPHEUS How horrible!

THE YOUNG MAN No. He chose a fairly good method. Poison is very slow, and causes so much suffering. One vomits, and twists about, and it is all disgusting. It's the same with sleeping draughts. People think they'll go to sleep, but it's death in the midst of hiccups and bad smells. (*He has come nearer, calm and smiling*) Believe me . . . the easiest way when you're very tired, when you've nursed that same idea for a long time is to slip into the water as if it were a bed. . . . You stifle for a moment, with a magnificent succession of visions . . . then you go to sleep. That's all!

EURYDICE You don't think it hurt him to die?

THE YOUNG MAN (*gently*) It never hurts to die. Death never hurts anybody. Death is gentle. . . . What makes you suffer when you take certain poisons, or give yourself a clumsy wound, is life itself.

(ORPHEUS *and* EURYDICE *are pressed against each other*)

EURYDICE (*gently, like an explanation*) We couldn't help ourselves. We love each other.

THE YOUNG MAN Yes, I know. I've been listening to you. A fine young man, and a pretty girl. Two courageous little animals, with supple limbs and sharp white teeth, ready to fight till dawn, as they should, and fall together, mortally wounded.

EURYDICE (*murmuring*) We don't even know you. . . .

THE YOUNG MAN But I know you. I'm very glad to have met you both. You're leaving here together? There's only one more train tonight. The train for Marseilles. Perhaps you'll be taking it?

ORPHEUS Perhaps.

THE YOUNG MAN I'm going there myself. I hope I'll have the pleasure of meeting you again?

(*He bows and exits.* ORPHEUS *and* EURYDICE *turn to each other. They are standing, looking very small, in the middle of the empty hall*)

ORPHEUS (*gently*) My love.

EURYDICE My dear love.

ORPHEUS Our story is beginning. . . .

EURYDICE I'm a little afraid. . . . Are you good, or wicked? What's your name?

ORPHEUS It's Orpheus. What's yours?

EURYDICE Eurydice.

ACT TWO

(A room in a provincial hotel—huge, somber, and dirty. The ceilings are too high, lost in shadow, dusty double curtains, a big iron bed, a screen, a miserable light.

ORPHEUS *and* EURYDICE *are lying on the bed, fully dressed)*

ORPHEUS   To think everything might have gone wrong. . . . Supposing you'd turned to the right, I to the left, not even that. Nothing more important than the flight of a bird, a child's cry, to make you turn your head for a second. I'd be playing my accordion on the terraces at Perpignan with father.

EURYDICE   And I'd be playing *The Orphans of the Storm* at the municipal theatre of Avignon. Mother and I play the two orphans.

ORPHEUS   Last night I thought of all the luck that brought us together. To think we might never have met; that we might have mistaken the day or the station.

EURYDICE   Or met while we were still too young.

ORPHEUS   But we didn't mistake the day, or the minute. We never missed a step during the whole eventful journey. We're very clever.

EURYDICE   Yes, my darling.

ORPHEUS   *(powerful and gay)*   We're much stronger than the whole world, both of us.

EURYDICE   *(looking at him with a little smile)* My hero! All the same you were very frightened yesterday when we came into this room.

ORPHEUS   Yesterday we weren't stronger than all the people in the world. Now, at least, we know each other. We know how heavy a sleeping head feels, the sound of our laughter. Now we have our memories to protect us.

EURYDICE   A whole evening, a whole night, a whole day—how rich we are!

ORPHEUS   Yesterday, we had nothing. We knew nothing, and we came into this room by chance, under the eye of that terrible waiter with the mustache who was sure we were going to make love. We began to undress, quickly, standing, face to face. . . .

EURYDICE   You threw your clothes like a madman into the four corners of the room. . . .

ORPHEUS   You were shaking all over. You couldn't undo the little buttons of your dress and I watched you pull them off without making a movement to help you. And then, when you were naked, suddenly you were ashamed.

EURYDICE   *(hanging her head)*   I thought I ought to be beautiful as well, and I wasn't sure. . . .

ORPHEUS   We stood like that for a long time, face to face, without speaking, without daring to speak. . . . Oh, we were too poor, too naked, and it was too unjust to have to risk everything like that on a single throw. Then suddenly a wave of tenderness took me by the throat because I saw you had a tiny red spot on your shoulder.

EURYDICE   Then afterward, it all became so simple. . . .

ORPHEUS   You laid your head against me and fell asleep. You said things in your dreams I couldn't answer. . . .

EURYDICE   Did I? I often talk in my sleep. I hope you didn't listen.

ORPHEUS   Of course I did.

EURYDICE   I call that very mean of you! Instead of sleeping honestly, you spy on me. How do you think I can know what I say when I'm asleep?

ORPHEUS   I only understood three words. You sighed a terrible deep sigh. Your lips trembled a little, and then you said, "It's so difficult."

EURYDICE   *(repeating)*   It's so difficult.

ORPHEUS   What was so difficult?

EURYDICE   *(stays for a moment without answering, then shakes her head and says in a little voice)*   I don't know, my darling. I was dreaming.

(Knock at the door. It is the WAITER, *who enters immediately. He has big gray mustaches, and a strange air)*

WAITER   Did you ring, sir?

ORPHEUS   No.

WAITER   Oh! I thought you did. *(hesitates for a moment, then goes out, saying)* Excuse me, sir.

EURYDICE   *(as soon as he has gone)*   D'you think they're real?

ORPHEUS   What?

EURYDICE   His mustaches.

ORPHEUS   Of course. They don't look real. It's only false ones that look real—everyone knows that.

EURYDICE   He doesn't look as noble as the waiter at the station.

ORPHEUS   The one from the *Comédie Française*? He may have been noble, but he was very conventional. Under his imposing façade, I think he was a weakling. This one has more mystery about him.

EURYDICE   Yes. Too much. I don't like people with too much mystery. They frighten me a little. Don't they you?

ORPHEUS A little, but I didn't like to tell you.

EURYDICE (*pressing herself to him*) Oh, my darling, hold me very tight. How lucky it is that there are two of us.

ORPHEUS There are so many characters in our story already—two waiters, a noble weakling, a strange mustache, the lovely cashier and her enormous breasts. . . .

EURYDICE Such a pity she never said anything to us!

ORPHEUS In all stories there are silent characters like her. She didn't say anything, but she watched us all the time. If she hadn't been silent all the time, what a lot of stories she could tell about us. . . .

EURYDICE And the porter?

ORPHEUS The one who stammered?

EURYDICE Yes, my darling. Wasn't he sweet? I'd have liked to put him in a box and keep him, with his fat watch chain and brand-new cap.

ORPHEUS Remember how he told us the names of all the stations where we didn't have to change, to make us remember, without any possible doubt, the name of the station where we really had to change!

EURYDICE He was quite enchanting. I'm sure he brought us luck. But the other one, the brute, the conductor. . . .

ORPHEUS That fool! The one who couldn't understand we had a third-class ticket for Perpignan and another for Avignon, so what we wanted was to pay the difference on two second-class tickets to Marseilles?

EURYDICE Yes, that one. Wasn't he ugly and stupid with his greasy uniform, his self-importance, and his oily fat cheeks?

ORPHEUS He is our first ignoble character. There'll be others, you'll see. . . . All happy stories are full of despicable characters.

EURYDICE Oh, but I refuse to keep him. I'll send him away. You must tell him I don't want him any more. I won't have such an idiot in my memories of you.

ORPHEUS It's too late, my darling, we have no right to reject anyone.

EURYDICE Then, all our lives, this dirty, self-satisfied man will be a part of our first day together?

ORPHEUS All our lives.

EURYDICE Are you sure we couldn't just forget the bad ones and only keep the good?

ORPHEUS Out of the question. They have happened now, the good with the evil. They've danced their little pirouettes, said their three words in your life . . . and there they are, inside you, as they are, forever.

EURYDICE (*suddenly*) Then, you mean, if you've seen a lot of ugly things in your life, they stay inside you too?

ORPHEUS Yes.

EURYDICE And everything you've ever done, does one's body remember that too, d'you think?

ORPHEUS Yes.

EURYDICE You're sure that even the words we said without meaning them, the ones we can't recall, are still inside us when we talk?

ORPHEUS (*trying to kiss her*) Of course, darling fool.

EURYDICE (*freeing herself*) Wait, don't kiss me. Explain. Are you sure what you've just told me is true, or is it only what you think? Do other people say it too?

ORPHEUS Of course.

EURYDICE Clever people? I mean, people who ought to know, people one ought to believe?

ORPHEUS Of course.

EURYDICE Then we can never really be alone, with all that around us. We can never be sincere, even when we mean what we say with all our strength. . . . If all the words are there, all the filthy bursts of laughter, if all the hands that have ever touched you are still sticking to your flesh, none of us can really change?

ORPHEUS What are you talking about?

EURYDICE (*after a pause*) Do you think we'd do the same, if when we were little, we knew that one day it would be vitally important to be clean and pure? And when we say these things—when we say, "I made that movement, I said those words, I listened to that sentence, I deserted that man. . . ." (*She stops*) When one says those same things to someone else—to the man you love, for instance—do they think that kills all your memories around you?

ORPHEUS Yes. They call that confessing yourself. Afterward, they say that we are washed clean again, shining and pure. . . .

EURYDICE Oh! Are they very sure of that?

ORPHEUS So they say.

EURYDICE (*after thinking for a little*) Yes, yes, but if ever they were wrong, or if they just said that for the effect; supposing they go on living twice as strong, twice as powerful, for having been repeated; if ever the other person began to remember, for always. . . . You can tell your clever people I don't trust them, and I think it's better not to say a word. . . . (ORPHEUS *looks at her, she sees this and adds quickly, pressing herself against him*) Or else, my darling, when it's simple, as it was for us two yesterday, to tell everything, like me.

(*The* WAITER *knocks and enters*)

WAITER   Did you ring, sir?

ORPHEUS   No.

WAITER   Oh! Sorry I disturbed you. (*turns to go, then adds*) I ought to tell you, sir, the bell is out of order. If you want me at any time, it's better if you call.

ORPHEUS   Thank you.

(*They think the* WAITER *is going, but he changes his mind, crosses room and goes to double curtains; he opens and closes them again*)

WAITER   The curtains work.

ORPHEUS   So we see.

WAITER   In some rooms, it's the opposite. The bell works and the curtains don't. (*starts to go, then says again*) Still, if monsieur tries to make them work later, and they don't, you've only to ring. . . . (*stops*) I mean, call, because, as I said before, the bell. . . . (*makes a gesture and exits*)

ORPHEUS   He's our first eccentric. We'll have lots of others. I should think he's really a very good man, entirely without malice.

EURYDICE   Oh, no. He looked at me all the time. Didn't you see how he kept looking at me?

ORPHEUS   You're dreaming.

EURYDICE   Oh, I like the other much better —the nice one from the *Comédie Française*. . . . You could feel that even in a tragedy he wouldn't be very dangerous. . . .

(*The* WAITER *knocks and enters again. He gives very clearly the impression of having been behind the door*)

WAITER   Excuse me, sir. I forgot to tell you, madame asks if you'll be good enough to go downstairs. There's something missing on your form. Madame must send it in tonight and it isn't complete.

ORPHEUS   Does she want me right away?

WAITER   Yes, sir, if you'll be so kind.

ORPHEUS   All right, I'll come with you. (*to* EURYDICE) Get dressed while I'm gone, then we'll go out for dinner.

(*The* WAITER *opens the door for* ORPHEUS *and goes out after him. He comes back almost at once and goes to* EURYDICE, *who has raised herself on the bed*)

WAITER (*holding out an envelope*)   Here's a letter for you. I was told to give it to you when you were alone. Madame isn't in her office. I was lying. There's only one floor to go. You have thirty seconds to read it.

(*He remains standing in front of her.* EURYDICE *has taken the letter, trembling a little. She opens it, reads it, tears it into tiny pieces without moving a muscle of her face. Then she makes to throw away the bits*)

WAITER   Never use the basket. (*He goes to the basket, kneels down, and begins to pick up the pieces, which he stuffs into the pocket of his apron*) Have you known each other long?

EURYDICE   One whole day.

WAITER   Then everything should still be fine.

EURYDICE (*gently*)   Yes, it should be.

WAITER   The numbers I've seen passing through this room lying on the bed, just like you. And not only goodlooking ones. Some were too fat, or too thin, or real monsters. All using their saliva to say "our love." Sometimes, when it's getting dark, as it is now, I seem to see them all again—all together. The room is humming with them. Ah, love isn't very pretty.

EURYDICE (*hardly audible*)   No.

ORPHEUS (*entering*)   You still here?

WAITER   Just going, sir.

ORPHEUS   The manageress wasn't there.

WAITER   I must have taken too long coming up. I suppose she couldn't wait. It doesn't matter, sir, it will do this evening. (*looks at them both again and goes out*)

ORPHEUS   What was he doing here?

EURYDICE   Nothing. He was describing all the other lovers he's seen passing through this room.

ORPHEUS   Very amusing!

EURYDICE   He says sometimes he seems to see them all together. The whole room is humming with them.

ORPHEUS   And you listened to such stupidity?

EURYDICE   Perhaps it wasn't so stupid. You, who know everything, said that all the people one had ever met go on living in our memories. Perhaps a room remembers too. . . . All the people who have been here are around us, coupled together, the fat ones, the thin ones, real monsters.

ORPHEUS   Little lunatic!

EURYDICE   The bed is full of them. How ugly love can be.

ORPHEUS (*dragging her away*)   Let's go out to dinner. The streets are flushing with the first lamps of evening. We'll go and dine in a little restaurant smelling of garlic. You'll drink from a glass a thousand lips have touched, and the thousand fat behinds that have hollowed out the leather bench will make a tiny place for you where you'll be very comfortable. Come, let's go.

EURYDICE (*resisting*) You're laughing— you're always laughing. You're so strong.

ORPHEUS Ever since yesterday! A hero! You said so yourself.

EURYDICE Yes, yes, a hero who understands nothing, who feels nothing, who is so sure of himself he goes straight forward. Ah, you can take things lightly, you others—yes—now that you have made me so heavy. . . . You say things the moment you least expect them, you bring to life all the dirty lovers who have done things between these four walls, and then you don't give it another thought. You go out to dinner, saying, it's a fine day, the lamps are shining, and the restaurant smells of garlic.

ORPHEUS So will you, in a minute. Come, let's get out of here.

EURYDICE It isn't nice here any more. It doesn't feel nice. How brief it was. . . .

ORPHEUS What's the matter? You're trembling.

EURYDICE Yes.

ORPHEUS You're quite pale.

EURYDICE Yes.

ORPHEUS How strange you look. I've never seen you look like this.

(*He tries to make her follow him; she turns away*)

EURYDICE Don't look at me. When you look at me, I can feel it. It's as if you had put your two hands on my back, and entered, burning, into me. Don't look at me.

ORPHEUS I've been looking at you since yesterday.

(*He draws her away; she let's herself go*)

EURYDICE (*murmuring, beaten*) You are strong, you know. . . . You look such a thin little boy and you are stronger than anyone. When you play your accordion, like yesterday in the station, or when you talk, I turn into a little snake. . . . There's nothing I can do except crawl along slowly toward you.

ORPHEUS Then you say, "It's so difficult."

EURYDICE (*crying out suddenly and freeing herself*) Darling!

ORPHEUS Yes.

EURYDICE I'm so afraid it may be too difficult.

ORPHEUS What?

EURYDICE The first day, everything seems so easy. The first day all you have to do is invent. You're sure we haven't invented everything?

ORPHEUS (*taking her head in his hands*) I'm sure I love you, and you love me. Sure as the stones, sure as the things made of wood and iron.

EURYDICE Yes, but perhaps you thought I was someone else. And when you see me as I am. . . .

ORPHEUS Since yesterday I've been looking at you. I've heard you talking in your sleep.

EURYDICE Yes, but I didn't say much. Supposing I go to sleep tonight and tell you everything?

ORPHEUS Everything? What's everything?

EURYDICE Or if someone, one of our characters, came and told you. . . .

ORPHEUS What could they come and tell me about you, I know you better than they do, now.

EURYDICE Are you sure?

(*She lifts her head and looks at* ORPHEUS, *who continues with joyous strength*)

ORPHEUS Sure. I haven't thanked you either for your courage. . . . For the days that will soon be here when we'll go without our dinner, smoking our last cigarette, one puff in turn. For the dresses you'll pretend not to see in the windows; for the beds made up, the rooms swept out, your reddened hands and the kitchen smell still caught up in your hair. Everything you gave when you agreed to follow me. (EURYDICE's *head is lowered. He looks at her in silence*) I didn't think it would be possible to meet a comrade who would go with you, a little silent companion who takes on all the chores and at night is warm and beautiful beside you. Tender and secret, a woman for you alone. I woke last night to ask myself if I really did deserve to have you.

(EURYDICE *has raised her head and stares at him in the growing darkness*)

EURYDICE You really think all that of me?

ORPHEUS Yes, my love.

EURYDICE (*thinks a little, then says*) It's true. She'd be a very charming Eurydice: the very wife for you. Mademoiselle Eurydice— your wife!

ORPHEUS (*putting his arms round her*) Are you happy, little serpent? (*They remain embraced for a moment, then he springs up, strong and joyful*) And now, will you come and eat? The snake charmer can't blow his flute any longer—he's dying of hunger.

EURYDICE (*in a different voice*) Put on the lights.

ORPHEUS There's a sensible thing to say! Lights up everywhere. Floods of light. Drive away the phantoms.

(ORPHEUS *turns on the switch. A hard light fills the room, making it ugly.* EURYDICE *has risen*)

EURYDICE Darling, I don't want to go to a

restaurant, with all those people. If you like, I'll go downstairs, I'll buy something, and we can eat it here.

ORPHEUS   In the room humming with noises?

EURYDICE   Yes. It doesn't matter any more.

ORPHEUS   (*moving*)   It'll be great fun. I'll come down with you.

EURYDICE   (*quickly*)   No, let me go alone. (*He stops*) I'd like to do your shopping for you, just this once, like a respectable married woman.

ORPHEUS   All right. Buy all sorts of things.

EURYDICE   Yes.

ORPHEUS   We must have a real party.

EURYDICE   Yes, darling.

ORPHEUS   Exactly as if we had plenty of money. It's a miracle the rich can never understand. . . . Buy a pineapple—a real one, just as the good Lord made it, not a sad American pineapple in a can. We haven't got a knife. We'll never be able to eat it. But that's the way pineapples protect themselves.

EURYDICE   (*with a little laugh, her eyes filled with tears*)   Yes, my darling.

ORPHEUS   Buy some flowers too—lots and lots of flowers. . . .

EURYDICE   (*falteringly, with her poor little smile*)   You can't eat flowers.

ORPHEUS   Nor can you. We'll put them on the table. (*looks round*) We haven't got a table. Never mind, buy lots of flowers all the same. And buy some fruit. Peaches, fat hothouse peaches, apricots, golden pears. A little bread to demonstrate the serious side of our nature, and a bottle of white wine we can drink out of the tooth glass. Hurry, hurry! I'm dying of hunger. (EURYDICE *fetches her little hat and puts it on in front of the mirror*) You're putting on your hat?

EURYDICE   Yes. (*turns round suddenly and says in a strange hoarse voice*) Adieu, my darling.

ORPHEUS   (*cries to her, laughing*)   But you're saying good-bye!

EURYDICE   (*from the doorway*)   Yes.

(*She looks at him for a second longer, smilingly and pityingly, and goes out abruptly.* ORPHEUS *stays for a moment without moving, smiling at the absent* EURYDICE. *Suddenly his smile disappears, his face looks drawn, a vague fear seizes him, he runs to the door, calling*)

ORPHEUS   Eurydice!

(*He opens the door, and recoils, stupefied. The* YOUNG MAN *who spoke to them at the station is on the threshold smiling*)

THE YOUNG MAN   She's just gone downstairs. (ORPHEUS *retreats, surprised, hesitating to rec-ognize him*) Don't you remember me? We met yesterday in the station restaurant, just after the accident. . . . You know, the young man who threw himself under the train. I've taken the liberty of coming to say good evening. I liked you both so much. We're neighbors. I'm in room eleven. (*takes a step into the room, holding out a packet of cigarettes*) Smoke? (ORPHEUS *takes a cigarette mechanically*) I don't myself. (*takes out a box of matches and lights one*) Light?

ORPHEUS   Thanks. (*He closes the door again and asks mechanically*) May I ask your name?

THE YOUNG MAN   When you meet people on journeys, half the charm is to know as little as possible about them. My name won't mean anything to you. Call me Monsieur Henri. (*He has come right into the room. He looks at* ORPHEUS *and smiles.* ORPHEUS *looks at him as if hypnotized*) A fine town, Marseilles. This human ant heap, this collection of riffraff, this filth. There aren't as many suicides in the old port as they say, but all the same, it's a fine town. Do you expect to stay here long?

ORPHEUS   I don't know.

M. HENRI   I didn't wait to be introduced before speaking to you yesterday. But you were so touching, the two of you, holding each other so closely in the middle of that huge hall. . . . A beautiful setting, wasn't it? Somber and red, and the night falling and the station noises in the background. . . . (*looks at* ORPHEUS *for a long time, smiling*) Little Orpheus and Mademoiselle Eurydice. . . . One doesn't get such a stroke of luck every day. . . . I shouldn't have spoken to you. . . . Normally, I never speak to people. What's the good? But I couldn't resist the urge to know you better—I don't know why. You're a musician?

ORPHEUS   Yes.

M. HENRI   I like music. I like everything that is sweet and happy. To tell the truth, I like happiness. But let's talk about you. It's of no interest to talk about me. But first let's have something to drink. It helps the conversation. (*rises and rings the bell. He looks at* ORPHEUS *and smiles during the short wait*) It gives me a great deal of pleasure to talk to you like this. (*The* WAITER *has entered*) What'll you have? Whisky? Brandy?

ORPHEUS   If you like.

M. HENRI   Some brandy, please.

WAITER   Just one?

M. HENRI   Yes. (*to* ORPHEUS) Forgive me, won't you. I never drink. (*The* WAITER *has gone out. He still watches* ORPHEUS, *smiling*) I'm really delighted to have met you.

ORPHEUS (*embarrassed*)   It's kind of you to say so.

M. HENRI   You must be wondering why I take such an interest in you. (ORPHEUS *makes a movement*) I was at the back of the restaurant yesterday when she came to you, as if called by your music. These moments when we catch a glimpse of Fate laying her snares are very exciting, aren't they? (*The* WAITER *has returned*) Ah, your brandy.

WAITER   Here you are, sir. One brandy.

ORPHEUS   Thank you.

(*The* WAITER *goes out*)

M. HENRI (*who has watched him*)   Did you notice how slowly and insolently the waiter went out of the room?

ORPHEUS   No.

M. HENRI (*going to listen at the door*)   He's certainly gone back to his post behind the door. (*comes gack to* ORPHEUS) I'm sure he's been in here on several different occasions with different excuses; I'm sure he's tried to speak to you?

ORPHEUS   Yes.

M. HENRI   You see, I'm not the only one to take an interest in you. . . . Haven't shopkeepers, porters, little girls in the street smiled at you oddly since yesterday. . . .

ORPHEUS   Everyone is kind to lovers.

M. HENRI   It isn't only kindness. Don't you think they look at you a little too closely?

ORPHEUS   No. Why?

M. HENRI (*smiling*)   No reason. (*dreams for a moment, then suddenly takes his arm*) Listen, my friend, there are two races of beings. The masses, teeming and happy—common clay, if you like—eating, breeding, working, counting their pennies; people who just live; ordinary people; people you can't imagine dead. And then, there are the others—the noble ones, the heroes. The ones you can quite well imagine lying shot, pale and tragic: one minute triumphant with a guard of honor, and the next being marched away between two gendarmes. Hasn't that sort of thing ever attracted you?

ORPHEUS   Never; and this evening less than usual.

M. HENRI (*going to him and laying his hand on his shoulder; looking at him, almost tenderly*)   It's a pity. You shouldn't believe too blindly in happiness. Particularly not when you belong to the good race. You're only laying up disappointments for yourself.

(*The* WAITER *knocks and enters*)

WAITER   There's a young lady here asking for Mademoiselle Eurydice. I told her she had gone out, but she doesn't seem to believe me. She insists on seeing you. May I ask her to come up?

THE GIRL (*entering and pushing the* WAITER *aside*)   I've already come. Where's Eurydice?

ORPHEUS   She's gone out, mademoiselle. Who are you?

THE GIRL   One of her friends from the company. I must talk to her at once.

ORPHEUS   I tell you she's gone out. Besides, I don't think she has anything to say to you.

THE GIRL   You're wrong. She's got plenty to say. How long ago did she go out? Did she take her suitcase with her?

ORPHEUS   Her suitcase? Why should she take her suitcase? She's gone out to buy our dinner.

THE GIRL   She may have gone out to buy your dinner, but she had very good reasons for taking her suitcase. She was supposed to meet us at the station to catch the eight-twelve train.

ORPHEUS (*crying out*)   Meet who?

WAITER (*who has pulled out a fat copper watch*)   It's ten minutes and forty seconds past eight now. . . .

THE GIRL (*as if to herself*)   She must be on the platform with him already. Thank you.

(*She turns to go*)

ORPHEUS (*catches her up in front of the door*)   On the platform with who?

THE GIRL   Let me go. You're hurting me. You'll make me miss the train.

WAITER (*still looking at his watch*)   Exactly eleven minutes past eight.

DULAC (*appearing in the doorway, to the* WAITER)   It's eight-thirteen. Your watch is slow. The train has gone. (*to* ORPHEUS) Let the girl go. I can answer you. On the platform with me.

ORPHEUS (*retreating*)   Who are you?

DULAC   Alfredo Dulac. Eurydice's impresario. Where is she?

ORPHEUS   What do you want her for?

DULAC (*walking calmly into room, chewing his cigar*)   What do you want her for?

ORPHEUS   Eurydice is my mistress.

DULAC   Since when?

ORPHEUS   Since yesterday.

DULAC   She also happens to be mine. And has been, for a year.

ORPHEUS   You're lying!

DULAC (*smiling*)   Because she forgot to tell you? Because the child was in this bed last night instead of mine? You're a child, too, my boy. A girl like Eurydice has to be humored in her little caprices. She slept with the fool who killed himself yesterday too. I can understand her liking you. You're good looking, young. . . .

ORPHEUS (*crying out*) I love Eurydice and she loves me!

DULAC Did she tell you so?

ORPHEUS Yes.

DULAC (*sitting calmly in armchair*) She's an extraordinary girl. Luckily, I know her so well.

ORPHEUS Supposing I know her better than you?

DULAC Since yesterday?

ORPHEUS Yes, since yesterday.

DULAC I don't pretend to be an expert. If it were a question of anything else—you look much more intelligent than I am—I'd probably say "Good" but there are two things I really understand. First my job. . . .

ORPHEUS And then, Eurydice?

DULAC No, I don't make any such claims. I was going to use a much more modest expression: women. I've been an impresario for twenty years. I sell women, my boy, by the gross, to kick up their heels in provincial revues, or massacre the big arias from *La Tosca* in a casino. I don't give a damn—besides, I love them. That makes at least one good reason out of two for pretending to understand them. Eurydice is perhaps an odd little girl—I'm the first to admit it—but considering the opportunities we've both had to see, you'll agree with me that she is a woman. . . .

ORPHEUS No.

DULAC How do you mean, no? She seemed to be an angel, did she? Look at me squarely, my boy. Eurydice belonged to me for over a year. Do I look as though I could seduce an angel?

ORPHEUS You're lying. Eurydice could never have belonged to you.

DULAC You're her lover, so am I. Would you like me to describe her to you?

ORPHEUS (*recoiling*) No.

DULAC (*advancing, ignoble*) What's she like, your Eurydice? How do you get her out of bed in the morning? Can you drag her away from her thrillers and her cigarettes? Have you ever seen her for a moment without a scowl on her face like a little criminal? And her stockings? Could she find them when she once got up? Be frank with me. Admit her petticoat was hanging from the top of the cupboard, her shoes in the bathroom, her hat under the chair, and her bag completely lost. I've already bought her seven.

ORPHEUS It isn't true.

DULAC How do you mean, it isn't true? Is yours a tidy Eurydice? I'm beginning to think we're not talking of the same person, or else she thought it wouldn't last for long. . . . She told you it would be for life? I'm sure she must have been sincere. She thought: "It'll be for all my life, if he's strong enough to keep me, if Papa Dulac doesn't find my tracks again, if he doesn't want to take me back." And at the bottom of her heart, she must have known quite well that Papa Dulac would find her out. It's only what I would have expected of her.

ORPHEUS No.

DULAC Of course, my boy, of course . . . Eurydice is a girl in a million, but her mentality is exactly the same as any other girl of that sort.

ORPHEUS It isn't true!

DULAC You won't admit anything's true! You're very odd. How long ago did she go downstairs?

ORPHEUS Twenty minutes.

DULAC Good. Is that true?

ORPHEUS Yes.

DULAC She insisted on going alone, didn't she?

ORPHEUS Yes. She said it would be fun to buy our dinner alone.

DULAC Is that true, too?

ORPHEUS Yes.

DULAC Very well, listen to me. Five minutes before, I had a letter given to her, asking her to meet me on the platform.

ORPHEUS No one brought her a letter. I haven't left her for an instant since yesterday.

DULAC Are you sure?

(*He looks at the* WAITER; ORPHEUS *also looks at the* WAITER *without knowing why*)

WAITER (*suddenly worried*) Excuse me, I think I'm being called.

(*He disappears*)

ORPHEUS I did leave her for a moment, yes. That man came and told me I was wanted in the office.

DULAC I told him to give my note to Eurydice when she was alone. He gave it to her while you were downstairs.

ORPHEUS (*going to him*) What did you say in your letter?

DULAC I said I was expecting her on the eight-twelve train. I didn't have to say anything else . . . because Fate had knocked on her door and said, "Eurydice, it's over." I was sure she would obey me. It's only men who jump out of windows.

ORPHEUS All the same, she didn't join you!

DULAC That's true. She didn't come. But my Eurydice is always late. I'm not very worried. Did you ask yours to buy a lot of things?

ORPHEUS Some bread and fruit.

DULAC And you say she went out twenty minutes ago? It seems a long time to me to buy bread and fruit. The street is full of shops. Maybe your Eurydice is unpunctual too? (*to the* GIRL) She must be at the station looking for us. Go and see.

ORPHEUS I'm going with you!

DULAC You're beginning to think she may have gone to meet us after all? I'm staying here.

ORPHEUS (*stops and cries to the* GIRL) If you see her, tell her. . . .

DULAC Quite useless. If she finds her at the station, then I'm right. Your faithful and tidy Eurydice was only a dream. And in that case, you have nothing more to say to her.

ORPHEUS (*calling to the* GIRL) Tell her I love her!

DULAC She may perhaps shed a tear; she's very sentimental. That's all.

ORPHEUS (*still calling*) Tell her she isn't what the others think her. She is as I know her to be!

DULAC Too complicated to explain at a railway station. Hurry along, and listen—I'm a sportsman—bring her here. In one minute she may be able to tell us herself what she is.

(*The* GIRL *goes out, bumping into the* WAITER)

WAITER (*appearing in doorway*) Excuse me, sir. . . .

ORPHEUS What is it?

WAITER There's an officer with a police van. . . .

ORPHEUS What does he want?

WAITER He's asking if there's anyone here related to the young lady. She's had an accident, sir—in the bus for Toulon. . . .

ORPHEUS (*crying like a madman*) Is she hurt? Eurydice!

(*He hurls himself out into the corridor.* DULAC *follows him, throwing away his cigar with a stifled oath. The* GIRL *disappears as well*)

DULAC (*as he goes out*) What the devil was she doing in the bus for Toulon?

(*The* WAITER *is left facing* MONSIEUR HENRI, *who hasn't moved*)

WAITER They'll never know what she was doing . . . she isn't hurt, she's dead. As they drove out of Marseilles the bus crashed into a gasoline truck. The other passengers were only cut by the glass. She's the only one . . . I saw her. They've laid her out in the police van. There's a tiny mark on her temple. You'd say she was asleep.

M. HENRI (*does not seem to have heard; his hands driven into the pockets of his coat, he walks past the* WAITER; *in the doorway he turns round*) Make out my bill. I'm leaving. (*He goes out*)

ACT THREE

(*The station restaurant in shadow. It is night. A vague light comes from the platform where only the signal lamps are lit. There is a strange humming noise coming from faraway. The restaurant is empty. The chairs are piled on the tables. The stage is empty for a moment. Then one of the doors from the platform opens slightly.* M. HENRI *enters, bringing* ORPHEUS *behind him, hatless, wearing a mackintosh. He is haggard, exhausted*)

ORPHEUS (*looking round without understanding*) Where are we?

M. HENRI Don't you know?

ORPHEUS I can't walk any farther.

M. HENRI You can rest now. (*picks a chair off a table*) Have a chair.

ORPHEUS (*sitting down*) Where are we? What did I have to drink? Everything's been turning round and round. What's been happening since yesterday?

M. HENRI It's still yesterday.

ORPHEUS (*realizing suddenly and crying out, trying to rise*) You promised.

M. HENRI (*laying his hand on his shoulder*) Yes, I promised. Keep still. Relax. Have a cigarette?

(*He holds out a cigarette, which* ORPHEUS *takes mechanically*)

ORPHEUS (*still looking round while the match burns*) Where are we?

M. HENRI Guess.

ORPHEUS I want to know where we are.

M. HENRI You told me you wouldn't be frightened.

ORPHEUS I'm not frightened. All I want to know is if we've arrived at last.

M. HENRI Yes, we've arrived.

ORPHEUS Where?

M. HENRI Just a little patience. (*He strikes another match, follows the wall round until he finds the electric light. A tiny noise in the shadows, and a bracket lights up on the back wall, throwing out a meager light*) D'you know now?

ORPHEUS It's the station restaurant. . . .

M. HENRI Yes.

ORPHEUS (*rising*) You were lying, weren't you?

M. HENRI (*pushing him back in the chair*)

No. I never lie. Keep still. Don't make a noise.

ORPHEUS Why did you come into my room just now? I was lying on that tumbled bed. Utterly wretched. I was almost happy, shut up in my misery.

M. HENRI (*in a low voice*) I couldn't bear to see you suffer.

ORPHEUS What difference could it make to you if I were suffering?

M. HENRI I don't know. It's the first time it's happened. Something strange began to fail inside me. If you had gone on weeping, suffering, it would have begun to bleed like a wound. . . . I was almost leaving the hotel. I put down my suitcase and came back again to comfort you. Then, as you wouldn't be comforted, I made you that promise to keep you quiet.

ORPHEUS (*taking his head in his hands*) I want to believe you with all my strength, but I don't believe you, no.

M. HENRI (*laughs a little silently, then he pulls* ORPHEUS' *hair*) Stubborn as a mule, aren't you? You're crying, and groaning and suffering, but you don't want to believe me. I like you very much. If I hadn't liked you so much, I'd have gone away yesterday as I always do. I wouldn't have gone into that room where you were sobbing. I can't bear grief. (*He pulls his hair again with a strange sort of tenderness*) Soon you won't be weeping any more— you won't have to ask yourself if you should or should not believe me.

ORPHEUS Is she coming?

M. HENRI She is already here.

ORPHEUS Here? (*crying out suddenly*) But she's dead. I saw them carry her away.

M. HENRI You want to understand, don't you? It's not enough that fate is making an enormous exception for you. You took my hand without a tremor, you followed me without even asking who I was, without slackening speed the whole night through, but on top of everything, you want to understand.

ORPHEUS No. I want to see her again. That's all.

M. HENRI You aren't more curious than that? I bring you to the doors of death, and you think of nothing but your little friend. . . . You're perfectly right—death deserves nothing but your scorn. She throws out her huge nets, grotesque, enormous. An idiot, a clumsy reaper, capable of chopping off her own limbs with the rest. (*He has sat down near* ORPHEUS, *a little tired*) I'm going to tell you a secret, just for yourself, because I'm fond of you. There's just one thing about death no one knows. She's very kindhearted, horribly kindhearted. She's afraid of tears and grief. Every time she can,

whenever life allows her, she does it quickly . . . she unties, relaxes, while life persists, clutching blindly, even if the game is lost, even if the man cannot move, if he is disfigured, even if he might suffer always. Death alone is a friend. With the tip of her finger she can give the monster back his face, soothe the soul in torment she delivers.

ORPHEUS She has stolen Eurydice! This friend of yours! With her finger she has destroyed the young Eurydice, the gay Eurydice, the smiling Eurydice.

M. HENRI (*rising suddenly as if he has had too much, then brusquely*) She's giving her back to you.

ORPHEUS When?

M. HENRI At once. But listen carefully. Your happiness was over anyway. Those twenty-four hours, that pitiful little day, was all life had in store for you—your life—your cherished life. Today you wouldn't have been weeping because she was dead, but because she'd left you.

ORPHEUS That's not true! She never went to meet that horrible man!

M. HENRI No. But she didn't come back to you either. She took the bus for Toulon alone, without money, without baggage. Where was she flying to? What was she exactly, this little Eurydice you thought you could love?

ORPHEUS Whatever she is, I love her still. I want to see her again. Ah, I beg you, give her back to me, however imperfect. I want to suffer and be ashamed because of her. I want to lose her, and find her again. I want to hate her, and rock her gently afterward, like a little child. I want to struggle, to suffer, to accept . . . I want to live.

M. HENRI (*annoyed*) Of course you'll live. . . .

ORPHEUS With the mistakes, the failures, the despair, the fresh starts . . . the shame.

M. HENRI (*looks at him, scornful and tender; murmurs*) Poor boy. . . . (*He goes to him, and says in a different voice*) Good-bye. The moment has come. She's out there, on the platform, standing on the same spot where you saw her yesterday for the first time—waiting for you, eternally. Do you remember the condition?

ORPHEUS (*already looking at the door*) Yes.

M. HENRI Say it out loud. If you forget, I can do nothing more for you.

ORPHEUS I mustn't look at her.

M. HENRI It won't be easy.

ORPHEUS If I look at her just once before the dawn, I lose her again forever.

M. HENRI (*stops, smiling*) You don't ask me why or how any more?

ORPHEUS (*still looking at the door*) No.

M. HENRI (*still smiling*) Fine. Good-bye, You can start again from the beginning. Don't try and thank me. I'll see you later.

(*He goes out.* ORPHEUS *stands for a moment without moving, then goes to the door and opens it on the deserted platform. First he says nothing, then in a low voice, he asks without looking*)

ORPHEUS Are you there?

EURYDICE Yes, my darling. What a long time you've been.

ORPHEUS I've been allowed to come back and fetch you. . . . Only I mustn't look at you before the morning.

EURYDICE (*appearing*) Yes, I know. They told me.

ORPHEUS (*taking her hand and pulling her along without looking at her; they cross the stage in silence until they reach a bench*) Come. We can wait for morning here. When the waiters arrive for the first train, at dawn, we shall be free. We'll ask them for some nice hot coffee and something to eat. You'll be alive. You haven't been too cold?

EURYDICE Yes. That's the worst part. The terrible cold. But I've been forbidden to talk about anything. I can only tell you what happened up to the moment when the driver smiled into his little mirror and the gasoline truck fell on us like a mad beast. (*pause. She adds in a little voice*) After that I can't tell you anything.

ORPHEUS Are you comfortable?

EURYDICE Oh yes—here against you.

ORPHEUS Put my coat around your shoulders.

(*Puts his coat round her; pause; they are happy*)

EURYDICE Remember the waiter from the *Comédie Française?*

ORPHEUS We'll see him again tomorrow.

EURYDICE And the beautiful silent cashier? Maybe we'll know what she thought of us at last? It's so convenient to be alive again. . . . As if we'd just met for the first time. (*She asks him as she did that first time*) Are you good, or wicked? What's your name?

ORPHEUS (*entering into the game and smiling*) It's Orpheus. What's yours?

EURYDICE Eurydice. . . . (*then gently she adds*) Only this time we've been warned. (*She hangs her head, then says after a tiny pause*) Please forgive me. You must have been so afraid. . . .

ORPHEUS Yes. When I saw you downstairs, lying in the van, it all stopped. I wasn't afraid any more.

EURYDICE Did they put me in a van?

ORPHEUS A police van. They laid you out on a bench at the back, with a policeman sitting beside you, like a little thief who had been arrested.

EURYDICE Was I ugly?

ORPHEUS There was a little blood on your temple. That's all. You seemed to be asleep.

EURYDICE Asleep? If you knew how I was running. I was running as fast as I could go, like a mad thing. (*She stops; there is a tiny pause; she asks*) You must have suffered horribly?

ORPHEUS Yes.

EURYDICE Please forgive me.

ORPHEUS (*in a low voice*) There's no need.

EURYDICE (*after another pause*) If they brought me back to the hotel it must have been because I was still holding my letter. I had written to you in the bus before we started. Did they give it to you?

ORPHEUS No. They must have kept it at the police station.

EURYDICE Ah! (*She asks, worried suddenly*) Do you think they'll read it?

ORPHEUS They may.

EURYDICE D'you think we could stop them reading it? Couldn't we do something straight-away? Send someone there, telephone them, tell them they have no right?

ORPHEUS It's too late.

EURYDICE But I wrote that letter to you! What I said was only for you. How could any-one else possibly read it? How could anyone else say those words? A fat man, with a dirty mind, perhaps, an ugly, self-satisfied, fat old man? He'll laugh, he'll surely laugh when he reads my agony. Oh, stop him, stop him, please —please stop him reading it! It makes me feel as if I were naked in front of a stranger.

ORPHEUS They may not even have opened the envelope.

EURYDICE I hadn't time to close it! I was just going to when the truck crashed into us. Probably that's why the driver looked at me in the glass. I put my tongue out, it made him smile, and I smiled too.

ORPHEUS You smiled. You could still smile?

EURYDICE Of course not. I couldn't smile. You don't understand! I had just written you this letter where I told you I loved you, that I was suffering, but I had to go away. . . . I put out my tongue to lick the envelope, he made a crack as all those boys do, and everyone smiled. (*She stops, discouraged*) Ah, it's not the same when you describe it. It's difficult. You see, it's too difficult.

ORPHEUS (*in a low voice*)　What were you doing in the bus for Toulon?

EURYDICE　I was running away.

ORPHEUS　You had the letter from Dulac?

EURYDICE　Yes, that's why.

ORPHEUS　Why didn't you show me the letter when I came back?

EURYDICE　I couldn't.

ORPHEUS　What did he say in the letter?

EURYDICE　To meet him on the eight-twelve train, or else he'd come and fetch me.

ORPHEUS　Is that why you ran away?

EURYDICE　Yes. I didn't want you to see him.

ORPHEUS　You didn't think he might come and I'd see him just the same?

EURYDICE　Yes, but I was a coward. I didn't want to be there.

ORPHEUS　You've been his mistress?

EURYDICE (*crying out*)　No! Is that what he told you? I knew he would, and you'd believe him! He's been chasing me for a long time, he hates me. I knew he'd tell you about me. I was afraid.

ORPHEUS　Why didn't you tell me yesterday, when I asked you to tell me everything? Why didn't you tell me you'd been his mistress?

EURYDICE　I wasn't.

ORPHEUS　Eurydice, now it would be better to tell me everything. No matter what happens, we are two poor wounded beings sitting on this bench, two poor souls talking without daring to look at each other—

EURYDICE　What must I say to make you believe me?

ORPHEUS　I don't know. That's what's so terrible. . . . I don't know how I'm ever going to believe you. . . . (*pause; he asks, gently, humbly*) Eurydice, so I won't have to worry afterward, when you tell me the simplest things —tell me the truth now, even if it is terrible. Even if it will hurt me horribly. It can't hurt any more than the air I haven't been able to breathe since I've known you lied to me. . . . If it's too difficult to say, don't answer me, but please don't lie. Did that man tell the truth?

EURYDICE (*after an imperceptible pause*) No. He was lying.

ORPHEUS　You've never belonged to him?

EURYDICE　Never.

(*There is a pause*)

ORPHEUS (*in a low voice, staring straight in front of him*)　If you're telling me the truth, it should be easy to see. Your eyes are as clear as a pool of water. If you're lying, or if you

aren't sure of yourself, a dark green circle forms and shrinks around the pupil. . . .

EURYDICE　The dawn will soon be here, my darling, and you can look at me. . . . (*gently*) Don't talk any more. Don't think. Let your hand wander over me. Let it be happy all alone. Everything will become so simple if you just let your hand love me alone. Without saying anything more.

ORPHEUS　D'you think that's what they call happiness?

EURYDICE　Yes. Your hand is happy at this moment. It doesn't ask anything more of me than to be there, obedient and warm beneath it. Don't ask anything more of me, either. We love each other, we are young; we're going to live. Agree to be happy, please. . . .

ORPHEUS (*rising*)　I can't.

EURYDICE　If you love me. . . .

ORPHEUS　I can't.

EURYDICE　Be quiet, then, at least.

ORPHEUS　I can't do that either! All the words haven't yet been said. And we must say them all, one after the other. We must go now to the very end, word by word. And there are plenty of them!

EURYDICE　My darling, be quiet, I beg you!

ORPHEUS　Can't you hear? A swarm of them has been around us ever since yesterday. Dulac's words, my words, your words, all the words that brought us here. And the words of all the people who looked at us as if we were two animals being led along. The ones that haven't been spoken yet, but which are there, attracted by the aroma of the rest; the most conventional, the most vulgar, the ones we hate the most. We're going to say them; we're surely going to say them. They must always be said.

EURYDICE (*rises, crying out*)　My darling!

ORPHEUS　Ah, no! I want no more words— enough! We've choked ourselves with words since yesterday. Now I've got to look at you.

EURYDICE (*throwing herself against him, holding him close to her with her arms round his waist*)　Wait, wait, please wait. What we must do is get through the night. It will soon be morning. Wait. Everything will be simple again. They'll bring us coffee, rolls and butter. . . .

ORPHEUS　I can't wait till morning. It's too long to wait until we're old. . . .

EURYDICE (*still holding him, her head pressed to his back, imploringly*)　Oh, please, please, don't look at me, my darling, don't look at me just yet. . . . Maybe I'm not the person you wanted me to be. The one you invented in the happiness of the very first day. . . . But you can feel me, can't you, here against you? I'm here, I'm warm, I'm sweet, and I love you. I'll give you all the happiness that is in me. But don't ask more of me than I can give. . . . Don't look at me. Let me live. . . . I so much want to live. . . .

ORPHEUS   Live! Live! Like your mother and her lover, perhaps, with baby talk, smiles, and indulgences, and then a good meal, a little love-making, and everything's all right. Ah, no! I love you too much to live! (*He has turned round and looked at her. They are standing face to face, separated by an appalling silence; suddenly he asks, in a low voice*) Did he hold you to him, that horrible man? Did he touch you with those hands all covered with rings?

EURYDICE   Yes.

ORPHEUS   How long have you been his mistress?

EURYDICE   (*replying to him now with the same eagerness to lacerate herself*)   For a year.

ORPHEUS   Is it true you were with him two days ago?

EURYDICE   Yes, the night before I met you; he called for me after the performance. He made a scene. He made a scene every time.

ORPHEUS   What scene?

(*The little* MANAGER *appears, in agony, awkward, clumsy. He raises his little hat before speaking*)

MANAGER   He threatened to send me away, monsieur. I'm his company manager, and each time he threatened to dismiss me.

DULAC   (*entering, and exploding when he sees the* MANAGER)   He's a fool! He loses everything! I won't keep such an idiot in my company.

MANAGER   Oh, Monsieur Dulac, I have to look after all the trunks, all the scenery, and I'm alone. I'll never manage! I'll never manage!

DULAC   He's a half-wit, I tell you. He's a half-wit!

EURYDICE   It's your fault—you're always shouting at him. I'm sure if you talked to him gently, he'd understand. Listen, Louis darling. . . .

MANAGER   I'm listening, Eurydice. . . .

EURYDICE   Listen, darling Louis, it's really very simple. You get to the station where we have to change. You get out of the train very quickly. You run to the baggage car. You count the trunks to make sure they haven't forgotten one. . . .

MANAGER   Yes, but the others put their suitcases down beside me and tell me to look after them and go away. And the platform is full of people hurrying along. . . .

EURYDICE   You mustn't let them go away! You must run after them!

MANAGER   I can't watch the trunks if I'm running after them! I'll never be able to manage, I tell you, I'll never be able to manage. I'd much better go away. . . .

DULAC   (*roaring*)   He's a fool! A fool, I tell you! This time it's settled. He leaves at Châtellerault!

EURYDICE   Don't shout at him all the time. If you do, how can you expect him to understand?

DULAC   He'll never understand. I tell you he's an incompetent. He leaves the company at Châtellerault, and that's my final word!

MANAGER   Monsieur Dulac, if you fire me, I don't know what I shall do. I promise you I'll be very careful, Monsieur Dulac!

DULAC   You're fired! You're fired, I tell you!

EURYDICE   I'll help you! I promise I'll manage so that he doesn't lose anything. . . .

DULAC   I know what your promises are worth! No, no, he's quite useless. Sacked, fired! Get out! (*and he pushes the little* MANAGER *out into the darkness*)

EURYDICE   (*she fastens on to him, imploringly*)   I promise you he'll be careful. Dulac, I promise. . . .

DULAC   (*looking at her*)   Oh, you're always promising, but you don't always keep your word.

EURYDICE   (*in a lower voice*)   Yes.

DULAC   (*going to her, softly*)   If I keep him just once more, you'll be good to me?

EURYDICE   (*hanging her head*)   Yes.

(DULAC *embraces her roughly*)

DULAC   Admit that that time you came with me because you wanted to, you little liar.

EURYDICE   (*pulling herself away from him*) Because I wanted to? I spat every time you kissed me.

DULAC   (*calmly*)   Yes, my dove.

EURYDICE   As soon as you left me, I ran away. I undressed completely. I washed all over—changed my clothes. You never knew that, did you? (DULAC *laughs*) Oh, I know you, my darling—you can laugh, but it's out of the wrong side of your face.

DULAC   You aren't going to tell me you believed in that scene for a whole year?

EURYDICE   Don't pretend to be so damn clever!

DULAC   Don't pretend to be stupid, Eurydice. You aren't stupid at all. Did you, yourself, believe in that scene for a whole year?

EURYDICE   What!

DULAC   It had become a mere formality,

that threat. I made it so that you could save your dirty pride, and pretend you had a reason which forced you to follow me without admitting you enjoyed it.

EURYDICE   You mean, it wasn't true, you wouldn't really have fired him?

DULAC   Of course not. (*And he laughs again, as he disappears into the shadows*)

EURYDICE   That's what happened every time. Forgive me, my darling.

ORPHEUS (*who has recoiled, in a low voice*) I shall always see you with that man's hands on you. I shall always see you as he described you in that room.

EURYDICE (*humbly*)   Yes, my darling.

ORPHEUS   He wasn't even jealous when he came to fetch you. He even knew you were a coward. That if he came to fetch you, you wouldn't stay with me. Because you are a coward, aren't you? He knows you better than I do.

EURYDICE   Yes, my darling.

ORPHEUS   Explain, can't you? Why don't you try and explain?

EURYDICE   How can I explain? Do you want me to lie to you? I am untidy, I am a coward. Ah, it's too difficult.

(*There is a pause.* ORPHEUS *raises his head. He looks at* EURYDICE *who is standing humbly before him*)

ORPHEUS   If you loved me, why were you going away?

EURYDICE   I thought I'd never be able to make you understand.

MOTHER (*exclaiming suddenly*)   What I don't understand is why everything seems so terribly sad to these children!

VINCENT   I've always said: a little love, a little money, a little success, and life is wonderful!

MOTHER   A little love? A great deal of love! That child thinks she's invented the whole thing with her little musician. We've adored each other too, haven't we? We've often wanted to kill ourselves for each other's sake. Remember the time I tried to swallow vinegar? I took the wrong bottle. It was wine.

VINCENT   Anyway, the details don't matter. What matters is that we've also loved each other passionately enough to die for it.

MOTHER   Well, are we dead?

EURYDICE (*as the* MOTHER *and* VINCENT *fade out of sight*)   No, Mother. (*to* ORPHEUS) You see, darling, we mustn't complain too much. . . . You were right. In trying to be happy, we might perhaps have become like them. . . .

ORPHEUS   Why didn't you tell me everything the first day? The first day I might have been able to understand. . . .

EURYDICE   There's no more time. . . . (*She runs up the steps at the back, turns to take him in her arms, then tears herself away. A figure appears in the light, and she turns toward him*) The waiter from the *Comédie Française!* Our very first character. How are you?

WAITER (*with an overelaborate gesture*) Farewell, mademoiselle!

EURYDICE (*smiling in spite of herself*)   You're very noble, very charming, you know. Good-bye, good-bye. (*The* WAITER *disappears. The* CASHIER *takes his place*) Oh, you're the lovely silent cashier. I've always felt you had something to say to us.

CASHIER   How beautiful you were when you came together through the music. Beautiful, innocent and terrible—like love itself.

EURYDICE (*smiles at her and turns to go*) Thank you, madame.

(*A* YOUNG MAN *appears and calls after her urgently*)

THE YOUNG MAN   Mademoiselle! Mademoiselle!

EURYDICE   I think you're mistaken. I don't remember you at all.

THE YOUNG MAN   I'm a clerk at the police station, mademoiselle. You have never seen me.

EURYDICE   Ah! Then you must be the one who has my letter. Give it back to me, please, monsieur. Give it back.

THE YOUNG MAN   I'm afraid that's impossible, mademoiselle.

EURYDICE   I don't want that big, fat, dirty man to read it!

THE YOUNG MAN   I can promise you the Inspector won't read it, mademoiselle. I realized at once it would be impossible for a man such as the Inspector to read that letter. I took it out of the file. The case is closed, no one will ever notice. I have it with me. I read it every day when I am alone. . . . But it's different for me. (*He bows, noble and sad, takes the letter from his pocket, and after putting on his spectacles, begins to read in his somewhat flat voice*) "My darling, I'm in this bus, and you're waiting for me. I know I'm never coming back to you, and I'm miserable, miserable on your account. The people in the bus are looking at me. They think it's sad because I'm crying. I hate tears. They're such stupid things. For the sorrow I feel now, I would have liked not to cry. I'm much too miserable to cry." (*He resettles his voice, turns the page and continues*) "I'm going away, my darling. Ever since yesterday I've been afraid, and when I was asleep you heard me say, 'It's so difficult.' A man is coming. He has had a letter given to me. I've never talked to you about this man, but he has been my lover too. Don't believe I loved him—you'll see him, no one could love him. But I thought so little of myself, and I didn't love you then, my darling. That's the whole secret. I didn't love you then. That's the only reason I'm going away. Not only because I'm afraid he'll tell you I belonged to him, not only because I'm afraid you may stop loving me. . . . I don't know if you'll ever understand, but I'm going away because I'm red with shame. . . ."

ORPHEUS   Forgive me, Eurydice.

EURYDICE (*tenderly*)   There's no need, my darling. It's I who ask you to forgive me. I must go. (*And she disappears into the shadows*)

ORPHEUS   Eurydice!

(*He runs to the back like a madman. She has disappeared. ORPHEUS is alone. He does not move. The morning breaks. A train whistles faraway. When the light of day is almost real, the WAITER enters, looking very much alive*)

WAITER   Good morning, sir. Bitterly cold day. Can I get you some coffee, sir?

(*ORPHEUS does not reply. The WAITER takes this for a sign of assent, and begins to lift the chairs down from the tables. A TRAVELER passes on the platform, hesitates, then enters timidly. He is overloaded with suitcases and musical instruments. It is Orpheus' FATHER*)

FATHER   Oh, is that you, my boy? I didn't take the train to Palavas, after all. Full. Full to bursting, my boy. And those swine wanted me to pay the difference to travel second. I got out. I'll complain to the management. A traveler is entitled to a seat in all classes. They should have let me travel second for nothing. Are you having some coffee? (*ORPHEUS seems not to see him*) I could do with some myself. I spent the night in the waiting room. I was anything but warm. (*He whispers in ORPHEUS' ear*) To tell you the truth, I slipped into the first class. An excellent leather sofa, my dear. I slept like a prince. (*The CASHIER enters and goes across the restaurant, humming a traditional sentimental song. She sees the FATHER, and stops in her tracks, then tosses her head and hurries away*) She loses a lot by daylight, that woman. She's got a fine figure, but she looks extremely common. . . . Well, my boy, what are you going to do? Night brings good counsel. Are you coming with me after all?

ORPHEUS (*with an effort*)   Yes, Father.

FATHER   I knew you'd never desert your old father! We'll celebrate by having a good dinner at Perpignan. I know of a wonderful restaurant, the Bouillon Jeanne-Hachette, where for fifteen francs seventy-five, you can have hors-d'oeuvres (including wine) or lobster, if you pay an extra four francs; main dish—very generous, vegetables, cheese, sweet, fruit or pastries—wait, wait—coffee and brandy, or sweet liqueurs for the ladies. The little menu at the Jeanne-Hachette used to include a good cigar. . . .

(*During this speech, M. HENRI has come in quietly, and at this point, he advances on the FATHER, holding out a cigar*)

M. HENRI   Allow me?

FATHER (*looking at the cigar, and at MONSIEUR HENRI*)   What, what? Oh, thanks very much. (*He accepts the cigar, and the light offered by M. HENRI*) Ah, delicious. A Merveillitas, isn't it?

M. HENRI   Yes.

FATHER   Must have cost a packet, a cigar like that.

M. HENRI   Yes.

FATHER   Don't you smoke?

M. HENRI   No.

FATHER   I don't understand why you carry such expensive cigars if you don't smoke yourself. Maybe you're a traveling salesman?

M. HENRI   That's it.

FATHER   Big business, probably?

M. HENRI   Yes.

FATHER   Then I understand. You've got to soften up the customers. At the right moment, you pull out a Merveillitas. You ask him if he'll smoke? He accepts, of course. And bingo! it's in the bag. You're all so clever. I'd have adored to have been in business. Wouldn't you, my boy? (*ORPHEUS doesnt answer. He looks at him*) You must snap out of it, my boy. Look, give him a Merveillitas too. If he doesn't finish it, I will. When I'm down in the mouth, a good cigar. . . . (*Neither ORPHEUS nor MONSIEUR HENRI gives any sign of having registered this remark. The FATHER sighs and adds more timidly*) Well, we all have our tastes.

(*He goes back to smoking, with a glance now and then at the two silent men. The WAITER brings the coffee and sets it down on one of the tables*)

M. HENRI (*gently, after a pause*)   You must go back with your father, Orpheus.

FATHER (*helping himself to coffee*)   Of course he must. I've just been telling him so. . . .

M. HENRI   You ought to listen to your father.

FATHER   I know how sad it is. I've suffered too. I lost a girl once I adored. A girl from Toulouse, a creature made of fire. Carried off in a week. Bronchitis. I sobbed like a child during the funeral. They had to take me into a café to recover. It hurts at first. Naturally.

But one fine day—it took me like that—you have a bath, do up your tie, the sun is shining, you go into the street, and suddenly, bingo! you see the girls are pretty again. We're terrible, my boy, all the same, terrible scoundrels.

M. HENRI   Listen carefully, Orpheus. . . .

FATHER   I don't say you take the first one who comes along. No. We aren't animals after all, and you're bound to feel a little awkward when you open the conversation. You say how lonely you are, how lost. And it's true, it's sincere. Ah, you can imagine how much that sort of talk can influence a woman! You'll say, of course, that I'm an old rogue, but I was still using the same technique ten years afterward.

ORPHEUS   Be quiet, Father.

M. HENRI   Why should you want him to be quiet? He's talking to you as life will talk to you through every mouth; he's saying what you'll see tomorrow in every eye, if you get up and try to start life again. . . . But Eurydice can be given back to you forever. The Eurydice of your first meeting, eternally pure and young, eternally herself.

ORPHEUS   (*looks at him, after a pause, shaking his head*)   No.

M. HENRI   (*smiling*)   Why not?

ORPHEUS   I hate death.

M. HENRI   (*gently*)   You're unfair. Why should you hate death? She alone can create the proper setting for love. You heard your father talking about life just now. It was grotesque, wasn't it, but that's what it is like. Go and wander round life's side shows with your little Eurydice, and you'd meet her at the exit with her dress covered with finger marks. Life would never have allowed you to keep Eurydice.

ORPHEUS   I don't want to die.

M. HENRI   Then listen to your father, Orpheus. He can tell you about life.

FATHER   (*who has been replenishing his coffee cup, turns at this*)   Life? But life is wonderful, my boy. When you have your health and strength, it's all so simple. The whole secret—daily exercise. Ten minutes every morning. You don't need more, but it's those ten minutes that count. (*He gets up, and with the butt of his cigar between his teeth, begins to go through a ridiculous form of Swedish drill*) One, two, three, four. One, two, three, four. One, two, three, four. One, two. One, two. One, two. One, two. If you do that you'll never have a sagging stomach, or varicose veins. Health through joy, joy through health, and vice versa.

M. HENRI   You see, Orpheus. It's very simple!

FATHER   (*sitting down again, puffing like a grampus*)   It's a question of will power. Every-thing in life is a question of will power. Now, you're unhappy, but you're young. I like a young man to be ambitious. Don't you want to be a millionaire? Oh, money, money! But that is life, my boy! Think that you might become very rich. Think of the women, my boy, think of love! Blondes, brunettes, redheads, peroxides! Such variety, such choice! And all for you. You're the sultan, you lift your finger. That one! She comes to you. And then it's a succession of enchanted nights. . . . Passions, cries, bites, mad kisses. . . . Or else on the divans of secret boudoirs, from five to seven, wrapped in rich furs. . . . I've no need to tell you more, my boy! Sensations! Every possible sensation. A lifetime of sensations. And where's your grief? Gone up in smoke. (*He makes a gesture, and becomes serious*) That is not the whole of life. There's respectability, a social life. You're strong and powerful, a captain of industry. Board meetings with brilliant minds. You juggle with the economic safety of Europe. Then the strike. The armed workmen. Violence. You appear alone before the factory. A shot is fired and misses you. You don't move. In a voice of thunder, you speak to them. You castigate them. They hang their heads, go back to work. Beaten! It's magnificent. Then, on the advice of your best friends, you go in for politics. Honored, powerful, decorated, a senator. Always in the forefront. National funeral, flowers, a million flowers, muffled drums, long speeches. And I, modestly in a corner—a distinguished old man, but mastering my grief, erect and at attention. (*He declaims*) "Let us pay the homage due to a father's grief!" (*It is too beautiful. He breaks down*) Ah, my boy, my boy, life is wonderful.

M. HENRI   You see, Orpheus.

FATHER   The man talking to you has suffered. He has drunk his cup to the very dregs. You wonder sometimes at my bent back, my premature white hairs, my child. If you knew how heavy is the weight of a lifetime on the shoulders of a man. . . .

(*He pulls in vain on the butt of his cigar. He looks at it, annoyed, then reaches for a match. M. HENRI goes to him, holding out his case*)

M. HENRI   Another cigar?

FATHER   Thank you. I'm embarrassed. Yes, yes, embarrassed. What an aroma! Tell me, have you heard it said that the girls who make these roll them on their thighs? (*He sighs*) Their thighs. . . . (*He lights the cigar*) What was I saying?

M. HENRI   The weight of a lifetime. . . .

FATHER   (*who has lost his lyric fervor*)   How do you mean, the weight of a lifetime?

M. HENRI If you knew how heavy the weight of a lifetime can be on a man's shoulders.

FATHER Ah! That's right. If you knew how heavy the weight of a lifetime can be. . . . (*He stops, takes a pull at his cigar, and concludes simply*) Well, it's heavy, my boy. Extremely heavy. (*He inhales a deep breath with delight*) Marvelous. (*He winks at* M. HENRI) I feel as if I'm smoking the thigh itself! (*He starts to laugh and chokes in the smoke.* M. HENRI *returns to* ORPHEUS)

M. HENRI You've listened to your father, Orpheus? Fathers are always right. Even the foolish ones. Life is made in such a way that foolish fathers know as much, sometimes more than clever fathers. (*He moves away for a moment, then suddenly comes back to* ORPHEUS) Supposing life had held in store for you a day when you would have found yourself alone beside your living Eurydice.

ORPHEUS No.

M. HENRI Yes. One day or the next, in a year, in five years, in ten, if you like, without stopping loving her, perhaps, you might have realized you didn't want Eurydice any more, that Eurydice didn't want you either.

ORPHEUS No.

M. HENRI Yes. It might have been as stupid as that. You'd have become the man who'd been unfaithful to Eurydice.

ORPHEUS (*crying out*) Never!

M. HENRI Why do you protest so loudly? For my benefit, or for yours? (*He makes a gesture*) In any case, Eurydice might already have abandoned you.

ORPHEUS (*plaintively this time*) No.

M. HENRI Why not? Because she loved you yesterday?

ORPHEUS We could never have stopped loving each other.

M. HENRI Maybe she wouldn't have stopped loving you. It's not so easy to stop loving someone. Tenderness is a stubborn emotion, you know. She might perhaps have had a way of giving herself to you, before going to meet her lover, so humbly, so gently, that you might almost have known a little of the old happiness.

ORPHEUS No! Her love for me would have lasted forever, until she was old beside me, and I was old beside her.

M. HENRI No, little man. You're all the same. You thirst for eternity, and after the first kiss you're green with fear because you have a vague feeling it can never last. Vows are soon exhausted. Then you build houses, because stones at least will endure. You have a child. You lightly stake the happiness of that tiny, innocent recruit to this uncertain battle on the most fragile thing in the world—your love of man and woman. And it dissolves and crumbles. It falls to pieces exactly as if you'd made no vows at all. (*The* FATHER *has fallen asleep. He begins to snore gently*) Your father's snoring, Orpheus. Look at him. He's ugly. And pitiful. He has lived. Who knows? Maybe he hasn't been as stupid as he seemed just now. Maybe there has been a moment when he touched the heights of love and beauty. Look at him now, clinging to existence, with his poor snoring carcass sprawled over there. Look at him well. People believe that the wear and tear on a face is the fear of death. What a mistake! It's the fear of life. Take a good look at your father, Orpheus, and remember Eurydice is waiting.

ORPHEUS (*suddenly, after a pause*) Where? What must I do?

M. HENRI Put on your coat, it's cold this morning. Walk out of the station. Follow the main road. You'll see a little wood of olives. That's the place.

ORPHEUS What place?

M. HENRI Your rendezvous with death. At seven o'clock. It's nearly that now. Don't keep her waiting.

ORPHEUS I'll see Eurydice again?

M. HENRI Immediately.

ORPHEUS Very well. (*He crosses to the door, then turns and hesitates, looking at his* FATHER. *He bends down and kisses the sleeping old man, then turns back to the door, with a last look at* M. HENRI) Good-bye.

M. HENRI Au revoir, my friend.

(ORPHEUS *has gone. Suddenly the lights change, leaving the station in darkness, and* M. HENRI *standing quite still, his hands in his pockets. He calls softly and urgently*)

Eurydice! (*She enters, and stands in a shaft of light*)

EURYDICE He's agreed?

M. HENRI Yes, he's agreed.

EURYDICE Will he be able to look at me?

M. HENRI Yes. Without ever being afraid of losing you.

EURYDICE Oh, my darling, come quickly, quickly.

(*In the distance a clock begins to strike. With the last strokes, the music begins to build to a crescendo, and* ORPHEUS *appears, hesitating, as if dazzled by the light. She turns, to take him in her arms*)

My darling, what a long time you've been!

(M. HENRI *turns and walks away into the darkness, leaving the two lovers clasped in a long embrace*)

Jean-Paul Sartre

1905-

FORGERS OF MYTHS

In reading the newspaper reviews of Katherine Cornell's production of Jean Anouilh's *Antigone*, I had the impression that the play had created a certain amount of discomfort in the minds of the New York drama critics. Many expressed surprise that such an ancient myth should be staged at all. Others reproached Antigone with being neither alive nor credible, with not having what, in theatre jargon, is called "character." The misunderstanding, I believe, was due to the fact that the critics were not informed of what many young authors in France—each along differing lines and without concerted aim—are attempting to do.

There has been a great deal of discussion in France about "a return to tragedy," about the "rebirth of the philosophic play." The two labels are confusing and they should both be rejected. Tragedy is, for us, an historic phenomenon which flourished between the sixteenth and eighteenth centuries; we have no desire to begin that over again. Nor are we anxious to produce philosophic plays, if by that is meant works deliberately intended to set forth on the stage the philosophy of Marx, St. Thomas, or existentialism. Nevertheless there is some truth attached to these two labels: in the first place, it is a fact that we are less concerned with making innovations than with returning to a tradition; it is likewise true that the problems we wish to deal with in the theatre are very different from those we habitually dealt with before 1940.

The theatre, as conceived of in the period between the two world wars, and as it is perhaps still thought of in the United States today, is a theatre of characters. The analysis of characters and their confrontation was the theatre's chief concern. The so-called "situations" existed only for the purpose of throwing the characters into clearer relief. The best plays in this period were psychological studies of a coward, a liar, an ambitious man or a frustrated one. Occasionally a playwright made an effort to outline the workings of a passion—usually love—or to analyze an inferiority complex.

Judged by such principles Anouilh's Antigone is not a character at all. Nor is she simply a peg on which to hang a passion calculated to develop along the approved lines of whatever psychology might be in style. She represents a naked will, a pure, free choice; in her there is no distinguishing between passion and action. The young playwrights of France do not believe that men share a ready-made "human nature" which may alter under the impact of a given situation. They do not think that individuals can be seized with a passion or a mania which can be explained purely on the grounds of heredity, environment, and situations. What is universal, to their way of thinking, is not nature but the situations in which man finds himself; that is, not the sum total of his psychological traits but the limits which enclose him on all sides.

For them man is not to be defined as a "reasoning animal," or a "social" one, but as a free being, entirely indeterminate, who must choose his own being when confronted with certain necessities, such as being already committed in a world full of both threatening and favorable factors among other men who have made their choices before him, who have decided in advance the meaning of those factors.

He is faced with the necessity of having to work and die, of being hurled into a life already complete which yet is his own enterprise and in which he can never have a second chance; where he must play his cards and take risks no matter what the cost. That is why we feel the urge to put on the stage certain situations which throw light on the main aspects of the condition of man and to have the spectator participate in the free choice which man makes in these situations.

Thus, Anouilh's Antigone may have seemed abstract because she was not portrayed as a young Greek princess, formed by certain influences and some ghastly memories, but rather as a free woman without any features at all until she chooses them for herself in the moment when she asserts her freedom to die despite the triumphant tyrant. Similarly, when the burgomaster of Vauxelles in Simone de Beauvoir's *Les Bouches Inutiles* has to decide whether to save his beleaguered town by cutting off half its citizens (women, children, and old men) or to risk making them all perish in an effort to save them all, we do not care whether he is sensual or cold, whether he has an Oedipus complex, or whether he is of an irritable or jolly disposition. No doubt if he is rash or incautious, vain or pusillanimous, he will make the wrong decision. But we are not interested in arranging in advance the motivations or reasons which will inevitably force his choice. Rather, we are concerned in presenting the anguish of a man who is both free and full of good will, who in all sincerity is trying to find out the side he must take, and who knows that when he chooses the lot of others he is at the same time choosing his own pattern of behavior and is deciding once and for all whether he is to be a tyrant or a democrat.

If one of us happens to present character on the boards, it is only for the purpose of getting rid of it at once. For instance, Caligula, at the outset of Albert Camus' play of that name, has a character. One is led to believe he is gentle and well behaved, and no doubt he actually is both. But that gentleness and that modesty suddenly melt away in the face of the prince's horrifying discovery of the world's absurdity. From then on he will choose to be the man to persuade other men of that absurdity, and the play becomes only the story of how he carries out his purpose.

A man who is free within the circle of his own situations, who chooses, whether he wishes to or not, for everyone else when he chooses for himself—that is the subject matter of our plays. As a successor to the theatre of characters we want to have a theatre of situation; our aim is to explore all the situations that are most common to human experience, those which occur at least once in the majority of lives. The people in our plays will be distinct from one another—not as a coward is from a miser or a miser from a brave man, but rather as actions are divergent or clashing, as right may conflict with right. In this it may well be said that we derive from the Corneillean tradition.

It is easy to understand, therefore, why we are not greatly concerned with psychology. We are not searching for the right "word" which will suddenly reveal the whole unfolding of a passion, nor yet the "act" which will seem most lifelike and inevitable to the audience. For us psychology is the most abstract of the sciences because it studies the workings of our passions without plunging them back into their true human surroundings, without their background of religious and moral values, the taboos and commandments of society, the conflicts of nations and classes, of rights, of wills, of actions. For us a man is a whole enterprise in himself. And passion is a part of that enterprise.

In this we return to the concept of tragedy as the Greeks saw it. For them, as Hegel has shown, passion was never a simple storm of sentiment but fundamentally always the assertion of a right. The fascism of Creon, the stubbornness of Antigone for Sophocles and Anouilh, the madness of Caligula for Camus, are *at one and the same time* transports of feeling which have their origin deep within us and expressions of impregnable will which are affirmations of systems of values and rights such as the rights of citizenship, the rights of the family, individual ethics, collective ethics, the right to kill, the right to reveal to human beings their pitiable condition, and so forth. We do not reject psychology, that would be absurd; we integrate life.

For fifty years one of the most celebrated subjects for dissertation in France has been formulated as follows: "Comment on La Bruyère's saying: Racine draws a man as he is; Corneille, as he should be." We believe the statement should be reversed. Racine paints psychologic man, he studies the mechanics of love, of jealousy in an abstract, pure way; that is, without ever allowing moral considerations or human will to deflect the inevitability of their evolution. His *dramatis personae* are only creatures of his mind, the end results of an intellectual analysis. Corneille, on the other hand, showing will at the very core of passion, gives us back man in all his complexity, in his complete reality.

The young authors I am discussing take their stand on Corneille's side. For them the theatre will be able to present man in his entirety only in proportion to the theatre's willingness to be *moral*. By that we do not mean that it should put forward examples illustrating the rules of deportment or the practical ethics taught to children, but rather that the study of the conflict of characters should be replaced by the presentation of the conflict of rights. It was not a question of the opposition of *character* between a Stalinist and a Trotskyite; it was not in their characters that an anti-Nazi of 1933 clashed with an S.S. guard; the difficulties in international politics do not derive from the characters of the men leading us; the strikes in the United States do not reveal conflicts of character between industrialists and workers. In each case it is, in the final analysis and in spite of divergent interests, the system of values, of ethics and of concepts of man which are lined up against each other.

Therefore, our new theatre definitely has drawn away from the so-called "realistic theatre" because "realism" has always offered plays made up of stories of defeat, laissez-faire, and drifting; it has always preferred to show how external forces batter a man to pieces, destroy him bit by bit, and ultimately make of him a weathervane turning with every change of wind. But we claim for ourselves the *true* realism because we know it is impossible, in everyday life, to distinguish between fact and right, the real from the ideal, psychology from ethics.

This theatre does not give its support to any one "thesis" and is not inspired by any preconceived idea. All it seeks to do is to explore the state of man in its entirety and to present to the modern man a portrait of himself, his problems, his hopes, and his struggles. We believe our theatre would betray its mission if it portrayed individual personalities, even if they were as universal types as a miser, a misanthrope, a deceived husband, because, if it is to address the masses, the theatre must speak in terms of their most general preoccupations, dispelling their anxieties in the form of myths which anyone can understand and feel deeply.

My first experience in the theatre was especially fortunate. When I was a prisoner in Germany in 1940, I wrote, staged, and acted in a Christmas play which, while pulling wool over the eyes of the German censor by means of simple symbols, was addressed to my fellow-prisoners. This drama, biblical in appearance only, was written and put on by a prisoner, was acted by prisoners in scenery painted by prisoners; it was aimed exclusively at prisoners (so much so that I have never since then permitted it to be staged or even printed), and it addressed them on the subject of their concerns as prisoners. No doubt it was neither a good play nor well acted: the work of an amateur, the critics would say, a product of special circumstances. Nevertheless, on this occasion, as I addressed my comrades across the footlights, speaking to them of their state as prisoners, when I suddenly saw them so remarkably silent and attentive, I realized what theatre ought to be—a great collective, religious phenomenon.

To be sure, I was, in this case, favored by special circumstances; it does not happen every day that your public is drawn together by one great common interest, a great loss or a great hope. As a rule, an audience is made up of the most diverse elements; a big businessman sits beside a traveling salesman or a professor, a man next to a woman, and each is subject to his own particular preoccupations. Yet this situation is a challenge to the playwright: he must create his public, he must fuse all the disparate elements in the auditorium into a single unity by awakening in the recesses of their spirits the things which all men of a given epoch and community care about.

This does not mean that our authors intend to make use of symbols in the sense that symbols are the expression either indirect or poetic of a reality one either cannot or will not grasp directly. We would feel a profound distaste today for representing happiness as an elusive bluebird, as Maeterlinck did. Our times are too austere for child's play of that sort. Yet if we reject the theatre of symbols, we still want ours to be one of myths; we want to attempt to show the public the great myths of death, exile, love. The characters in Albert Camus' *Le Malentendu* [1] are not symbols, they are flesh and blood: *a* mother and *a* daughter, *a* son who comes back from a long journey; their tragic experiences are complete in themselves. And yet they are mythical in the sense that the misunderstanding which separates them can serve as the embodiment of all misunderstandings which separate man from himself, from the world, from other men.

---

[1] *The Misunderstanding.*

The French public makes no mistake about this, as has been proved by the discussions engendered by certain plays. With *Les Bouches Inutiles*,[2] for instance, criticism was not confined to discussing the story of the play which was based on actual events that took place frequently in the Middle Ages: it recognized in the play a condemnation of fascist procedures. The Communists, on the other hand, saw in it a condemnation of their own procedures: "The conclusion," so they said in their newspapers, "is couched in terms of petty bourgeois idealism. All useless mouths should have been sacrificed to save the city." Anouilh also stirred up a storm of discussion with *Antigone,* being charged on the one hand with being a Nazi, on the other with being an anarchist. Such violent reactions prove that our plays are reaching the public just where it is important that it should be reached.

Yet these plays are austere. To begin with, since the situation is what we care about above all, our theatre shows it at the very point where it is about to reach its climax. We do not take time out for learned research, we feel no need of registering the imperceptible evolution of a character or a plot: one does not reach death by degrees, one is suddenly confronted with it— and if one approaches politics or love by slow degrees, then acute problems, arising suddenly, call for no progression. By taking our *dramatis personae* and precipitating them, in the very first scene, into the highest pitch of their conflicts we turn to the well-known pattern of classic tragedy, which always seizes upon the action at the very moment it is headed for catastrophe.

Our plays are violent and brief, centered around one single event; there are few players and the story is compressed within a short space of time, sometimes only a few hours. As a result they obey a kind of "rule of the three unities," which has been only a little rejuvenated and modified. A single set, a few entrances, a few exits, intense arguments among the characters who defend their individual rights with passion—this is what sets our plays at a great distance from the brilliant fantasies of Broadway. Yet some of them find that their austerity and intensity have not lacked appreciation in Paris. Whether New York will like them is a question.

Since it is their aim to forge myths, to project for the audience an enlarged and enhanced image of its own sufferings, our playwrights turn their backs on the constant preoccupation

of the realists, which is to reduce as far as possible the distance which separates the spectator from the spectacle. In 1942, in Gaston Baty's production of *The Taming of the Shrew*, there were steps going from the stage to the auditorium so that certain characters could go down among the orchestra seats. We are very far away from such concepts and methods. To us a play should not seem too *familiar*. Its greatness derives from its social and, in a certain sense, religious functions: it must remain a rite; even as it speaks to the spectators of themselves it must do it in a tone and with a constant reserve of manner which, far from breeding familiarity, will increase the distance between play and audience.

That is why one of our problem's has been to search out a style of dialogue which, while utterly simple and made up of words on everyone's lips, will still preserve something of the ancient dignity of our tongue. We have all barred from our plays the digressions, the set speeches, and what we in France like to call the *"poésie de réplique"*; all this chitchat debases a language. It seems to us that we shall recapture a little of the pomp of ancient tragedies if we practice the most rigorous economy of words. As for me, in *Morts Sans Sépulture*,[3] my latest play, I did not deny myself the use of familiar turns of phrase, swearwords, even slang, whenever I felt that such speech was germane to the characters. But I did attempt to preserve, through the pace of the dialogue, an extreme conciseness of statement—ellipses, brusque interruptions, a sort of inner tension in the phrases which at once set them apart from the easygoing sound of everyday talk. Camus' style in *Caligula* is different in kind but it is magnificently sober and taut. Simone de Beauvoir's language in *Les Bouches Inutiles* is so stripped that it is sometimes accused of dryness.

Dramas which are short and violent, sometimes reduced to the dimensions of a single long act (*Antigone* lasts an hour and a half, my own play, *Huis-Clos*,[4] an hour and twenty minutes without intermission), dramas entirely centered on one event—usually a conflict of rights, bearing on some very general situation —written in a sparse, extremely tense style, with a small cast not presented for their individual characters but thrust into a conjunction where they are forced to make a choice— in brief this is the theatre, austere, moral,

---

[2] *The Useless Mouths* by Simone de Beauvoir.

[3] Literally, *Death Without Burial*. The English title is *The Victors*.

[4] *No Exit.*

mythic, and ceremonial in aspect, which has given birth to new plays in Paris during the occupation and especially since the end of the war. They correspond to the needs of a people exhausted but tense, for whom liberation has not meant a return to abundance and who can live only with the utmost economy.

The very severity of these plays is in keeping with the severity of French life; their moral and metaphysical topics reflect the preoccupa-tion of a nation which must at one and the same time reconstruct and re-create and which is searching for new principles. Are they the product of local circumstances or can their very austerity of form enable them to reach a wider public in more fortunate countries? This is a question we must ask ourselves frankly before we try to transplant them.

Translated by Rosamond Gilder

THE VICTORS (MORT SANS SÉPULTURE)

Translated by Lionel Abel

CAST OF CHARACTERS

FRANÇOIS
SORBIER
CANORIS
LUCIE
HENRI
JEAN
CLOCHET
LANDRIEU
PELLERIN
CORBIER
TROOPERS

ACT ONE

(*An attic lighted by a dormer window. A hodge-podge of all sorts of things: trunks, an old stove, a dressmaker's dummy.* CANORIS *and* SORBIER *are sitting, one on a trunk, the other on an old stool.* LUCIE *is sitting on the stove. All are handcuffed.* FRANÇOIS *paces back and forth. He is handcuffed too.* HENRI *is stretched out on the floor, asleep*)

FRANÇOIS   For God's sake, say something, will you?

SORBIER   (*raising his head*)   What do you want me to say?

FRANÇOIS   Anything at all, as long as you make some noise.

(*A sudden shrill burst of popular music. It is the radio on the floor below*)

SORBIER   There's noise for you.

The Victors by Jean-Paul Sartre, translated by Lionel Abel, is reprinted from *Three Plays by Jean-Paul Sartre*, by permission from Alfred A. Knopf, Inc. Copyright 1949 by Alfred A. Knopf, Inc.

FRANÇOIS   Not that: it's *their* noise (*He begins pacing again. Then he stops abruptly*) Ha!

SORBIER   Now what?

FRANÇOIS   They hear me and they're saying: "There's the first one of them to lose his nerve."

CANORIS   Well, then, don't lose your nerve. Sit down. Put your hands on your knees, and your wrists won't hurt so much. And be quiet. Try to sleep or think.

FRANÇOIS   What good would that do?

(CANORIS *shrugs his shoulders.* FRANÇOIS *goes on pacing*)

SORBIER   François!

FRANÇOIS   Well?

SORBIER   Your shoes squeak!

FRANÇOIS   I'm making them squeak on purpose. (*a pause. He plants himself right in front of* SORBIER) Now what can you be thinking about?

SORBIER   (*raising his head*)   Do you want me to tell you?

FRANÇOIS   (*looks at him and draws back a little*)   No. Don't tell me.

SORBIER   I was thinking of the little girl who screamed.

LUCIE   (*suddenly emerging from her dream world*)   What girl?

SORBIER   The little girl on the farm. I heard her screaming when they took us away. The fire had already reached the staircase.

LUCIE   The girl on the farm? You didn't have to tell us.

SORBIER   There are lots of others who are dead. Women and children. But I didn't hear them die. It's as if that girl were still screaming. I couldn't keep her screams for myself alone.

LUCIE   She was thirteen. Because of us she's dead.

SORBIER   It's because of us that they're all dead.

CANORIS   (*to* FRANÇOIS)   You see it was better not to talk.

FRANÇOIS   Why not? We're not going to

[786]

last long either. In a little while maybe you'll think they were lucky.

SORBIER They didn't want to die.

FRANÇOIS And do you suppose that I'm reconciled to it? It wasn't our fault that the job failed.

SORBIER It was our fault.

FRANÇOIS We obeyed orders.

SORBIER Yes.

FRANÇOIS They told us: "Climb up there and take the village." We told them: "That's absurd; the Germans will be tipped off in twenty-four hours." They replied: "Go up there anyway and take it." Then we said: "O.K." And off we went. How was it our fault?

SORBIER We should have succeeded.

FRANÇOIS We couldn't succeed.

SORBIER I know. But we should have just the same. (*a pause*) Three hundred. Three hundred people who didn't want to die and who died for nothing. They are lying among the stones, and the sun blackens them; they must be visible from every window. Because of us. Because of us, there are only troopers, dead men, and stones in that village. It'll be hard to kick off with those screams in my ears.

FRANÇOIS (*shouting*) Leave us alone with your corpses. I'm the youngest: all I did was obey. I am innocent! Innocent! Innocent!

LUCIE (*softly; during the whole preceding scene she has remained calm*) François!

FRANÇOIS (*abashed, weakly*) What?

LUCIE Come sit near me, little brother. (*He hesitates. She repeats the command even more gently*) Come on! (*He sits by her. She awkwardly strokes his face with her bound hands*) How hot you are! Where is your handkerchief?

FRANÇOIS In my pocket. I can't get it.

LUCIE In this pocket?

FRANÇOIS Yes.

(*LUCIE reaches into his coat pocket; laboriously she takes out a handkerchief and wipes his face*)

LUCIE You are sweating and shaking; you shouldn't pace so much.

FRANÇOIS If I could only take off my coat.

LUCIE Don't think about it, because it's impossible. (*He pulls on his handcuffs*) No, don't keep hoping to break them. Hope hurts. Be calm, breathe gently, act dead; I'm dead and I'm calm; I'm saving myself.

FRANÇOIS For what? So as to be able to shriek louder later on? That's like saving candle ends. There is so little time left; I should like to be everywhere at once. (*He is about to get up*)

LUCIE Stay here.

FRANÇOIS I have to keep turning around. When I stop, it's my thoughts that start turning. I don't want to think.

LUCIE Poor kid.

FRANÇOIS (*lets himself slip to* LUCIE's *knees*) Lucie, everything is so hard. I can't look at your faces: they frighten me.

LUCIE Rest your head on my knees. Yes, everything is so hard and you are so young. If only someone could still smile at you and say: "My poor kid." I used to take care of all your troubles. My poor kid—my poor kid. (*She suddenly straightens up*) I can't any more. Anguish has drained me dry. I can't cry any more.

FRANÇOIS Don't leave me alone. Ideas come into my head that I'm ashamed of.

LUCIE Listen. There is *somebody* who can *help you*. I'm not utterly alone. (*a pause*) Jean is with me, if you could just—

FRANÇOIS Jean?

LUCIE They didn't get him. He is on his way to Grenoble. The only one of us who will be alive tomorrow.

FRANÇOIS So what?

LUCIE He'll find the others, they'll start all over again somewhere else. And then the war will be over, and they'll live peacefully in Paris, with real photos on real identification cards, and people will call them by their right names.

FRANÇOIS Well, what of it? He had luck. But what's that to me?

LUCIE He's going down the hills through the forest. There are poplars below, all along the way. He is thinking of me. There is no one but him in the world who can think of me with that particular sweetness. He's thinking of you too. He thinks you are an unfortunate kid. Try to see yourself with his eyes. He can cry. (*She weeps*)

FRANÇOIS You can cry, too.

LUCIE I'm crying with his tears.

(*A pause.* FRANÇOIS *stands up suddenly*)

FRANÇOIS That's enough. I'll end up by hating him.

LUCIE But you used to love him.

FRANÇOIS Not the way you loved him.

LUCIE No. Not the way I loved him.

(*There are steps in the corridor. The door opens.* LUCIE *springs to her feet. A* TROOPER *looks in and then shuts the door*)

SORBIER (*shrugging his shoulders*) They're having their fun. Why did you get up?

LUCIE (*sitting down again*) I thought they had come for us.

CANORIS They won't come so soon.

LUCIE   Why not?

CANORIS   They're making a mistake: they think waiting is demoralizing.

SORBIER   Is it a mistake? Waiting is no joke when you get ideas.

CANORIS   That's true enough. But on the other hand you have time to collect yourself. My first time was in Greece, under Metaxas. They came to arrest me at four o'clock in the morning. If they had worked on me a bit I would have talked. Out of surprise. But they didn't ask me a thing. Ten days later they tried everything, but it was too late; they had lost the surprise effect.

SORBIER   Did they beat you?

CANORIS   Good God, yes!

SORBIER   With their fists?

CANORIS   With their fists, with their feet.

SORBIER   Did you—want to talk?

CANORIS   No. It's not too bad while they're beating you.

SORBIER   Ah! Not too bad. (a pause) But when they lay into your shins and elbows?

CANORIS   Even then. It's not too bad. (gently) Sorbier.

SORBIER   What?

CANORIS   You mustn't be afraid of them. They have no imagination.

SORBIER   It's myself I'm scared of.

CANORIS   But why? We have nothing to tell them. They know as much as we do. Listen! (a pause) It's not at all like what you imagine it is.

FRANÇOIS   What's it like?

CANORIS   I couldn't tell you. Why, for example, time seemed short to me. (He laughs) My teeth were clenched so tight that for three hours I couldn't open my mouth. This was at Nauplia. There was a guy who wore old-fashioned shoes. With pointed toes. He kicked me in the face. Women were singing outside the window: I remember the tune.

SORBIER   In Nauplia? What year was that?

CANORIS   In '36.

SORBIER   Really? I went through Nauplia that year. I was in Greece on the Theophile-Gautier. I took a camping trip. I saw the prison; there were fig trees along the walls. So you were inside and I was outside? (He laughs) That's a riot.

CANORIS   Yeah, it's a riot.

SORBIER   (abruptly)   But what if they mess around with you?

CANORIS   Huh?

SORBIER   What if they mess around on you with their gadgets? (CANORIS shrugs his shoulders) I suppose I would defend myself out of modesty. Each minute I should say to myself: I'll hold back for just one more minute. Is that a good method?

CANORIS   There is no method.

SORBIER   But what would you do?

LUCIE   Can't you be quiet? Look at the kid! Do you think this sort of talk will give him courage? Wait a bit, they'll be glad to teach you.

SORBIER   Leave us alone! Let him put his fingers in his ears if he doesn't want to hear.

LUCIE   And must I hold my ears too? I don't like to hear you because I'm afraid I'll despise you. Do you need all these words to give you courage? I've seen animals die and I should like to die like them: in silence!

SORBIER   Who said anything about dying? We're just talking about what they'll do to us first. You have to get ready for it.

LUCIE   I don't want to get ready for it. Why should I live twice through the hours that lie ahead? Look at Henri: he's sleeping. Why not sleep?

SORBIER   Sleep? And they'll come to shake me and wake me up. No, not for me. I have no time to lose.

LUCIE   Then think of the things you love. I think about Jean, about my life, about the kid when he was sick and I took care of him in a hotel in Arcachon. I could see pine trees and great green waves from my window.

SORBIER   (ironically)   Green waves, really? I tell you I have no time to lose.

LUCIE   Sorbier, I don't recognize you any more.

SORBIER   (confused)   All right! Just nerves: I've got the nerves of a virgin. (He rises and goes toward her) Each one defends himself in his own way. I'm no good if you take me by surprise. If I could feel the pain ahead of time —just a little bit, so as to note the transition —I would be surer of myself. It's not my fault; I've always been meticulous. (a pause) I like you a lot, you know that. But I feel that I'm alone. (a pause) If you want me to shut up—

FRANÇOIS   Let them talk. It's the sound they make that counts.

LUCIE   Do as you like.

(A moment of silence)

SORBIER   (in a lowered voice)   Say, Canoris! (CANORIS lifts his head) Did you ever know anyone who gave in and talked?

CANORIS   Yes, I knew a couple.

SORBIER   And?

CANORIS   What do you care when we've got nothing to tell?

SORBIER   I just wanted to know—could they stand themselves afterwards?

CANORIS   That depends. There was one fellow who shot himself in the face with a shotgun; he only managed to blind himself. I sometimes ran into him in the streets of the Piraeus, led by an Armenian. He thought he had paid. Each one decides for himself whether he has paid or not. We knocked off another one at a fair, just as he was buying gumdrops. Since he'd been out of prison he had developed a passion for gumdrops because they're sweet.

SORBIER   The lucky dog.

CANORIS   Hmmmmm.

SORBIER   If I squealed I doubt if sweets would console me.

CANORIS   You say that now. But you never can tell before it's happened to you.

SORBIER   Just the same, I don't think I'd like myself much afterwards. I think I'd take down the shotgun.

FRANÇOIS   Me, I prefer the gumdrops.

SORBIER   François!

FRANÇOIS   Why pick on François? Did you warn me when I came looking for you? You told me the resistance needs men. You didn't tell me it needed heroes. Me, I'm no hero. I'm not a hero! I'm not a hero! I did as I was told: I distributed leaflets and transported arms, and you said I was always cheerful. But nobody took the trouble to let me know what was waiting for me in the end. I swear I never knew what I was getting into.

SORBIER   You knew. You knew that Rene had been tortured.

FRANÇOIS   I never thought about it. (*a pause*) You pity the girl who died; you say: it's on account of us that she's dead. But if I should talk when they burn me with their cigars, you would say: he's a coward; and you would hand me a shotgun, if you didn't shoot me in the back first. And yet I'm only two years older than she was.

SORBIER   I was just talking for myself.

CANORIS   (*going up to* FRANÇOIS)   You have no duty now, François. Neither duty nor assignment. We have no information, nothing to keep from them. Let each one get through it without suffering too much. The means doesn't matter.

(FRANÇOIS *gradually becomes calmer, but he is exhausted.* LUCIE *presses him to her*)

SORBIER   The means doesn't matter—of course. Scream, weep, beg, ask their pardon, dig into your memory to find something you can confess to, someone to turn over to them: what of it? There's nothing at stake; you won't find anything to tell them, all the little nasty facts will be strictly confidential. Perhaps it is better that way. (*a pause*) Only I'm not sure.

CANORIS   What would you like? To know a name or a date to withhold from them?

SORBIER   I don't know. I don't even know whether I could keep from talking.

CANORIS   So?

SORBIER   I'd like to know myself. I knew that they'd get me in the end, and I knew that some day I'd have my back against the wall, face to face with myself, without escape. I asked myself if I could face the music. It's my body that worries me, don't you see? I have a lousy body, all screwed up with nerves like a woman. Well, the time has come; they'll go over me with their gadgets. But I've been robbed: I'm going to suffer for nothing, I'll die without knowing what I'm worth.

(*The music stops. They sit up straight, listening*)

HENRI   (*waking up suddenly*)   What's up? (*a pause*) The polka is over, it is our turn to dance now, I suppose. (*The music starts up again*) False alarm. It's strange how much they like music. (*He gets to his feet*) I dreamed that I was dancing, at Scheherazade. You know Scheherazade, in Paris. I've never been there. (*He rubs the sleep from his eyes*) Ah, there you are—there you are. Do you want to dance, Lucie?

LUCIE   No.

HENRI   Do your wrists hurt, too? The flesh must have swollen while I slept. What time is it?

CANORIS   Three o'clock.

LUCIE   Five o'clock.

SORBIER   Six o'clock.

CANORIS   We don't know.

HENRI   You had a watch.

CANORIS   They broke it on my wrist. What we do know is that you slept a long time.

HENRI   That's time stolen from me. (*to* CANORIS) Help me up. (CANORIS *gives him a lift, and* HENRI *hoists himself to the window*) It is five o'clock by the sun. Lucie was right. (*He gets down*) The town hall is still burning. So you don't want to dance? (*a pause*) I hate that music.

CANORIS   (*with indifference*)   Bah!

HENRI   They must be hearing it at the farm.

CANORIS   There is nobody there to hear it now.

HENRI   I know that. But it comes in the

window, it whirls over the corpses. Music, the sun, there's a picture for you. And the bodies are all black. Ah! We really missed that one. (*a pause*) What's wrong with the kid?

LUCIE   He's not feeling well. It's a week since he's had a wink of sleep. What are you made of, to be able to sleep?

HENRI   Sleep came by itself. I felt so alone that it made me sleepy. (*He laughs*) We are forgotten by the whole world. (*approaching* FRANÇOIS) Poor kid. (*He strokes his head and turns abruptly to* CANORIS) What did we do wrong?

CANORIS   I don't know. What good does it do now?

HENRI   Some mistake was made. I feel guilty.

SORBIER   You too? Ah! I'm glad of that. I thought I was the only one.

CANORIS   All right, I feel guilty too. But how does that change anything?

HENRI   I wouldn't want to die guilty.

CANORIS   Take it easy. I'm sure the others won't blame you.

HENRI   To hell with the others. I owe an accounting only to myself now.

CANORIS   (*shocked, dryly*) Well—maybe you want a father confessor?

HENRI   To hell with a priest. I tell you that it's to myself alone that I owe any accounting at this point. (*a pause. As if speaking to himself*) Things shouldn't have gone this way. If I could find the error—

CANORIS   You'd be much better off!

HENRI   I could face it squarely and tell myself: this is why I must die. Good God! A man can't die like a rat, for nothing, with not a peep out of him.

CANORIS   (*shrugging his shoulders*) Oh, so what!

SORBIER   Why do you shrug your shoulders? A man has a right to save his death; that's about all he has left.

CANORIS   You're right. Well, let him save it if he can.

HENRI   Thanks for the permission. (*a pause*) You might just as well start saving your own: we haven't too much time.

CANORIS   My own? Why? Who would it help? It's strictly a personal matter.

HENRI   Strictly personal. Yes. And then what?

CANORIS   I never could interest myself in personal problems. Not other people's nor even my own.

HENRI   (*without hearing him*) If only I could just tell myself that I did what I could. But of course that's asking too much. For

thirty years I've felt guilty. Guilty because I was alive. And now, on account of me, houses are burning, innocent people are dead, and I am going to die guilty. My life has been one long mistake.

(CANORIS *gets up and goes over to him*)

CANORIS   You're not modest, Henri.

HENRI   What?

CANORIS   You torment yourself because you're not modest. As far as I'm concerned, we died long ago: at the precise moment we stopped being useful. Right now we have a little bit of posthumous life, a few hours to kill. There's nothing more for you to do except kill time and chat with those around you. Take it easy, Henri, relax. You have a right to relax now there's nothing more for us to do here. Relax! We don't count now; we're dead and of no importance. (*a pause*) This is the first time I felt I had the right to relax.

HENRI   This is the first time in three years that I've come face to face with myself. I was given orders. I obeyed them. I felt justified. Now there's nobody to give me orders and there's nothing that could justify me. A little bit of excess life—yes. Just enough time to take stock of myself. (*a pause*) Canoris, why are we going to die?

CANORIS   Because we were sent on a dangerous mission and had no luck.

HENRI   Yes, that's what our comrades will think. That's what will be said in the official speeches. But I want to know what *you* think.

CANORIS   I don't think anything. I lived only for the cause and I always foresaw I would have a death like this.

HENRI   You lived for the cause, yes. But don't try to tell me that it's for the cause you are going to die. Perhaps if we had succeeded and died in action, then perhaps—(*a pause*) We shall die because we were given an idiotic assignment and because we executed it badly. Our death serves no one. The cause didn't need to have this village attacked. It didn't need it because the project was impossible. A cause never gives orders; it never says anything. It is we who have to determine what it needs. Let's not speak of the cause. Not here. As long as we could work for it, it was all right. But now that we can't we shouldn't even speak of it and above all we shouldn't use it for our personal consolation. It rejected us because we are useless to it now; it will find others to serve it. In Tours, in Lille, in Carcassonne, women are breeding the children who will take our places. We tried to justify our lives and we missed out. Now we are going to die. We'll be dead and will be unjustified corpses.

CANORIS (*indifferently*) If you like. Nothing that happens in these four walls has any importance. Hope or despair: nothing will come of it. (*a pause*)

HENRI If only there were something to attempt. Anything. Or something to hide from them. Bah! (*a pause. To* CANORIS) Have you got a wife?

CANORIS Yes. In Greece.

HENRI Can you think of her?

CANORIS I try. It's kind of far.

HENRI (*to* SORBIER) How about you?

SORBIER There are the old folks. They think I'm in England. I suppose they're just sitting down to dinner; they eat early. If I could tell myself that they're going to feel, all of a sudden, ever so lightly, a pang at the heart, a sort of presentiment—But I'm sure that they're quite calm. They'll wait for me for years, more and more unconcernedly, and I shall die in their hearts without their ever noticing. My father must be talking about his garden. He never failed to mention the garden at dinner. Soon he'll go water his cabbages. (*He sighs*) Poor old fellow! Why should I think of them? It doesn't help.

HENRI No. It doesn't help. (*a pause*) Just the same, I should like it if my parents were still living. I have no one.

SORBIER No one at all?

HENRI No one.

LUCIE (*sharply*) You're unfair. You have Jean. We all have Jean. He was our leader and he's thinking of us.

HENRI He's thinking of you because he loves you.

LUCIE He's thinking *of us all.*

HENRI (*gently*) Did we ever talk much about our dead? We didn't have time to bury them, even in our hearts. (*a pause*) No, I'm not missed anywhere, I haven't left any vacancy. The subways are jammed, the restaurants are packed, heads are full to bursting with petty cares. I've slipped out of the world and it has remained full. Like an egg. No it must be that I was not indispensable. To something or to someone. (*a pause*) You know, Lucie, I was in love with you. I can tell you that now since it no longer matters.

LUCIE No. It doesn't matter any more.

HENRI So there it is. (*He laughs*) It was really no use at all for me to have been born.

(*The door opens. Several troopers enter*)

SORBIER Hello. (*to* HENRI) They pulled this three times on us while you were sleeping.

TROOPER Are you the one called Sorbier?

(*A moment of silence*)

SORBIER That's me.

TROOPER Follow me.

(*Again a moment of silence*)

SORBIER After all, I'd just as soon have them start with me. (*a pause*) I wonder if I shall get to know myself. (*as he is going out*) It's the time when my father sprinkles his cabbages. (*He goes out with the troopers. A long silence*)

HENRI (*to* CANORIS) Give me a cigarette.

CANORIS They took mine.

HENRI Never mind. (*The music starts up again. A "java" is being played*) Well, let's dance, since they want us to. Lucie?

LUCIE I told you no.

HENRI As you wish. There are other dancing partners. (*He goes up to the dummy, raises his handcuffed wrists and slides them over the shoulders of the dummy down to the waist. Then he begins to dance, holding the figure tight against him. The music stops.* HENRI *pauses, sets the dummy down, and then slowly raises his arms to get free of it*) They've started.

(*They all listen*)

CANORIS Did you hear anything?

HENRI Nothing.

FRANÇOIS What do you think they're doing to him?

CANORIS I don't know. (*a pause*) I hope he can take it. Otherwise he'll hurt himself more than they can.

HENRI Of course he'll take it.

CANORIS I mean inside. It's harder when you have no information to give them. (*a pause*)

HENRI He hasn't cried out. That's something, anyhow.

FRANÇOIS Perhaps they are just asking him questions.

CANORIS Don't be ridiculous!

(SORBIER *screams. They all start*)

LUCIE (*in a rapid, overly natural tone*) Jean must have just arrived at Grenoble. It would surprise me if it took him more than fifteen hours. He must feel strange. The city is quiet. There are people sitting outside the cafes, and our life on the Vercors ridge is only a dream. (SORBIER's *screams grow louder.* LUCIE's *voice rises*) He's thinking of us, he hears the radio through the open windows, the sun is shining on the mountains, it's a beautiful summer afternoon. (*still louder cries*) Ah! (*She lets herself fall back on a trunk, repeating between sobs:*) A beautiful summer afternoon.

HENRI (*to* CANORIS) I won't scream.

CANORIS You'll be wrong not to. It makes you feel better.

HENRI I couldn't bear the idea that you were listening to me and that she was crying up here.

(FRANÇOIS *begins to shake*)

FRANÇOIS (*on the verge of a breakdown*) I don't believe—I don't believe—

(*Steps in the corridor*)

CANORIS Quiet, kid, here they come.

HENRI Who's next?

CANORIS You or I. They'll keep the girl and the kid for last. (*The key turns in the lock*) I hope they take me. I don't like to hear the cries of others.

(*The door opens.* JEAN *is pushed into the room. He is not handcuffed. He blinks his eyes, after entering, to get used to the darkness. They all turn toward him. The* TROOPER *leaves, shutting the door behind him*)

LUCIE Jean!

JEAN Be quiet. Don't mention my name. Come here against the wall; they may be watching us through a chink in the door. (*He looks at her*) There you are! Right by me! I thought I should never see you again. Who's here with you?

CANORIS Canoris.

HENRI Henri.

JEAN I can't see you clearly. Pierre and Jacques are—?

HENRI Yes.

JEAN The boy is here too? Poor kid. (*in a low and rapid tone*) I hoped you'd be dead.

HENRI (*laughing*) We did our best.

JEAN I don't doubt that. (*to* LUCIE) What's the matter?

LUCIE Oh, Jean, it's all finished now. I kept telling myself: he's in Grenoble, he's walking in the streets, he's looking at the mountains. . . . And—and—now it's all over.

JEAN Don't carry on so. I have every chance of getting out of this.

HENRI How did they get you?

JEAN They haven't got me yet. I ran into one of their patrols way down on the Verdone road. I said I was from Cimiers; that's a little town in the valley. They brought me here; I'll be held until somebody goes and checks on my story.

LUCIE But at Cimiers they'll find out—

JEAN I have friends there who know what to tell them. I'll get out of this. (*a pause*) I have to; the others don't know anything about it.

HENRI (*whistles*) That's right, too. (*a pause*) Well, why don't you say it? We missed our chance for fair, didn't we?

JEAN We'll start again elsewhere.

HENRI *You'll* start again.

(*Steps in corridor*)

CANORIS Get away from him. They shouldn't see you talking to him.

JEAN What's up?

HENRI They're bringing Sorbier back.

JEAN Ah! They—

HENRI Yes. They began with him.

(*The* TROOPERS *enter, supporting* SORBIER, *who collapses against a trunk. The* TROOPERS *go out*)

SORBIER (*without seeing* JEAN) Did they keep me long?

HENRI Half an hour.

SORBIER Half an hour? You were right, Canoris, time goes quickly. Did you hear me scream? (*They do not reply*) Naturally you heard me.

FRANÇOIS What did they do to you?

SORBIER You'll see. You'll see soon enough. Don't be in a hurry.

FRANÇOIS Was it—very bad?

SORBIER I don't know about that. But here's something I can tell you: they asked me where Jean is, and if I had known I would have told them. (*He laughs*) You see: now I really know what I am like. (*They are silent*) What's the matter? (*He follows their glance and sees* JEAN *glued against the wall, his arms wide apart*) Who's that? Is it Jean?

HENRI (*sharply*) Quiet. They think he's some guy from Cimiers.

SORBIER A guy from Cimiers? (*He sighs*) It's just my luck.

HENRI (*surprised*) What did you say?

SORBIER I said it's just my luck. Now I have something to hide from them.

HENRI (*almost joyfully*) That's true. Now we all have something to hide from them.

SORBIER I wish they had killed me.

CANORIS Sorbier! I swear to you that you won't talk. You *couldn't* talk.

SORBIER I tell you, I would have given up my own mother. (*a pause*) It's not fair that a single minute should be enough to ruin a whole life.

CANORIS (*gently*) It takes much more than a minute. Do you think that a single moment of weakness could destroy that hour when you decided to leave everything and come with us? And these three years of courage and patience? And the day when, despite your fatigue, you carried the kid's pack and his gun?

SORBIER Don't talk so much. Now I know. I know what I really am.

CANORIS Why say "really"? Why should the Sorbier they beat today be more real than the one who refused to drink yesterday in order to give his share to Lucie? We're not made to live forever at our peak. There are roads in the valleys, too.

SORBIER That's all fine. But if I had talked a little while ago, could you still look me in the eyes?

CANORIS You won't talk.

SORBIER But what if I do? (CANORIS *is silent*) There, you see. (*a pause. He laughs*) There are guys who'll die in bed, with good consciences. Good sons, good husbands, good citizens, good fathers. . . . Ha! They're weaklings like me and they'll never know it. It's just that they're lucky. (*a pause*) Well, shut me up! What are you waiting for? Why don't you shut me up?

HENRI Sorbier, you're the best of us.

SORBIER Shut up!

(*There are steps in the corridor. They are all silent. The door opens*)

TROOPER Where is the Greek?

CANORIS That's me.

TROOPER Come along.

(CANORIS *goes out with the* TROOPER)

JEAN It's for me that he's going to suffer.

HENRI Just as well that it's for you. Otherwise it would be for nothing.

JEAN When he comes back, how can I look him in the eyes? (*to* LUCIE) Tell me, do you hate me?

LUCIE Do I look as if I hate you?

JEAN Give me your hand. (*She extends her bound hands*) I'm ashamed not to be in handcuffs. You're here, beside me! I told myself: at least everything is over for her. An end to fear, hunger, grief. And here you are! They'll come to fetch you and they'll bring you back, half carrying you.

LUCIE You'll see nothing in my eyes but love!

JEAN I'll have to hear your screams.

LUCIE I'll try not to scream.

JEAN But the kid will scream. I know he will.

FRANÇOIS Shut up! Shut up! All of you! Do you want to drive me crazy? I'm not a hero and I don't want to be martyred in your place!

LUCIE François!

FRANÇOIS Oh, leave me alone: I don't sleep with him. (*to* JEAN) As for me, if you want to know, I hate you. (*a pause*)

JEAN You are right. (*He goes toward the door*)

HENRI Hey, there! What are you up to?

JEAN I'm not in the habit of sending kids to be tortured in my stead.

HENRI Who'll warn the others?

(JEAN *stops*)

FRANÇOIS Let him go! If he wants to give himself up. You have no right to stop him.

HENRI (*to* JEAN, *ignoring* FRANÇOIS' *outburst*) It'll be just fine when they all come dashing up here believing we took the village. (JEAN *retraces his steps, his head bowed. He sits down*) Better give me a cigarette. (JEAN *gives him a cigarette*) And give me one for the kid.

FRANÇOIS Leave me alone. (*He goes to the rear*)

HENRI Light it. (JEAN *lights it for him.* HENRI *takes two puffs and then sobs nervously*) It's all right. I love to smoke, but I never knew it could give me that much pleasure. How many do you have?

JEAN One more.

HENRI (*to* SORBIER) Here.

(SORBIER *takes the cigarette without saying a word, takes a couple of drags, and then returns it.* HENRI *turns toward* JEAN)

HENRI I'm happy you're here. First you've given me a cigarette and then you'll be our witness. You'll go see Sorbier's parents and you'll write to Canoris' wife.

LUCIE Tomorrow you'll go down to the city; you'll take away in your eyes the last look at my face; you'll be the only one in the world to know it. You must not forget it. I am you. If you live, I shall live.

JEAN How could I forget it! (*He approaches her. Steps in the corridor*)

HENRI Stay where you are and be quiet; they are coming. It's my turn and if I don't talk fast I may not have time to finish. Listen to me! If you had not appeared we should have suffered like animals, without knowing why. But you are here, and all that is to come will now have a meaning. We're going to fight. Not just for you, but for all the comrades. We missed our chance, but maybe we can save face. (*a pause*) I thought I was utterly useless, but now I can see that I am needed for something, after all. With a bit of luck I can maybe tell myself that I'm not going to die for nothing.

(*The door opens.* CANORIS *appears, supported by* TWO TROOPERS)

SORBIER He didn't scream, that one.

ACT TWO

(*A schoolroom. Benches and desks. White plaster walls. On the rear wall a map of Africa and a portrait of Pétain. A blackboard. To the left, a window. At the back, a door. A radio on a shelf by the window.* CLOCHET, PELLERIN, LANDRIEU *are working*)

CLOCHET Shall we go on to the next?

LANDRIEU Just a minute. Let's take time out for a bite.

CLOCHET Eat if you like. I could perhaps question one of them in the meantime.

LANDRIEU No, you would like that only too well. Aren't you hungry?

CLOCHET No.

LANDRIEU (*to* PELLERIN) Clouchet isn't hungry! (*to* CLOCHET) You must be sick.

CLOCHET I'm never hungry when I work. (*He goes over to the radio and turns it on*)

PELLERIN Don't plague us with that racket.

CLOCHET (*grumbles under his breath*) . . . who don't like music.

PELLERIN What did you say?

CLOCHET I said it always surprises me to find people who don't like music.

PELLERIN I do like music. But not that sort and not here.

CLOCHET Really? Now me, as soon as it starts up—(*with regret*) We could have played it very softly.

PELLERIN No!

CLOCHET You're a couple of bastards. (*a pause*) Shall I have one of them brought in?

LANDRIEU For God's sake, knock it off! There are three more to go yet. We'll be here till ten o'clock tonight. I get upset when I have to work on an empty stomach.

CLOCHET In the first place, there are only two left, since we're saving the kid for tomorrow. And then, with a little organization, we could finish them off in two hours. (*a pause*) They're broadcasting *Tosca* on Radio-Toulouse tonight.

LANDRIEU To hell with Tosca. Go downstairs and see what they've dug up for us to eat.

CLOCHET I know: chicken.

LANDRIEU Again! I'm sick of it. Go see if you can find me a can of bully beef.

CLOCHET (*to* PELLERIN) How about you?

PELLERIN Beef for me too.

LANDRIEU And get someone to wash that up.

CLOCHET What?

LANDRIEU Over there. Where the Greek was bleeding. It's a mess.

CLOCHET We shouldn't clean up the blood. It might have an effect.

LANDRIEU I can't eat with that crap on the floor. (*a pause*) Well, what are you waiting for?

CLOCHET I don't think we should clean it up.

LANDRIEU Who's in charge here?

(CLOCHET *shrugs his shoulders and goes out*)

PELLERIN Don't ride him so hard.

LANDRIEU I should worry about him!

PELLERIN What I'm trying to tell you— he has a cousin close to Darnand. He sends him reports. I think he was the one who put a finger on Daubin.

LANDRIEU The dirty bastard! If he wants to take a crack at me, he'd better hurry up about it, because I have an idea that Darnand will get his before I do.

PELLERIN Could be. (*He sighs and goes mechanically to the radio*)

LANDRIEU (*chuckling*) I've got a pretty good idea what the news is.

(PELLERIN *twirls the dials of the radio*)

ANNOUNCER'S VOICE On the fourth musical note it will be exactly eight o'clock. (*tone signals. They set their watches*) Ladies and gentlemen, in a few seconds you will hear our Sunday concert.

LANDRIEU (*sighing*) It is Sunday, that's a fact. (*the first bars of a piece of music*) Clip him off.

PELLERIN Sundays I used to take my jalopy, pick up some chick in Montmartre, and take a spin to Touquet.

LANDRIEU When was this?

PELLERIN Oh, before the war.

SPEAKER I found nails in the vicar's garden. We repeat: I found . . .

LANDRIEU Shut the hell up, you filthy bastards! (*He picks up a can of food and throws it in the direction of the radio*)

PELLERIN Are you nuts? You'll smash the radio.

LANDRIEU I don't give a damn. I can't stand that crap.

(PELLERIN *turns the dial*)

SPEAKER The German troops are holding firmly at Cherbourg and at Caen. In the Saint-Lô sector they have not been able to check a slight advance by the enemy.

LANDRIEU We get it. Turn it off. (*a pause*) What will you do? Where will you go?

PELLERIN What do you think? We're cooked.

LANDRIEU Yes. The dirty bastards!

PELLERIN Who do you mean?

LANDRIEU All of 'em. The Germans, too. They're all the same. (*a pause*) If it could be done all over again—

PELLERIN Oh, I don't regret anything. I had a good time, at least up till these last few weeks.

(CLOCHET *enters, bringing the canned meat*)

LANDRIEU Hey, Clochet, the British have landed at Nice.

CLOCHET At Nice?

LANDRIEU And they met no resistance. They are marching on Puget-Théniers.

(CLOCHET *sinks down on one of the benches*)

CLOCHET Holy Mother! (LANDRIEU *and* PELLERIN *begin to laugh*) You're kidding? But you shouldn't make jokes like that.

LANDRIEU O.K. You can put that in your report tonight. (*a* TROOPER *enters*) Clean up that mess over there. (*to* PELLERIN) Are you going to eat with me?

(PELLERIN *goes up to him, takes the can of beef, looks at it, then puts it down*)

PELLERIN (*he yawns*) I always feel kind of funny before we start. (*He yawns*) I guess I'm just not nasty enough; I can't get into the spirit of it unless they're stubborn. What's he like, the guy we're going to question?

CLOCHET A big fellow, about thirty, solidly built. It'll be fun.

LANDRIEU Let's hope he doesn't act like the Greek.

PELLERIN Hell! The Greek was a big, dumb ape.

LANDRIEU Just the same. It fouls you up when they don't talk. (*He yawns*) You're making me yawn. (*a pause.* LANDRIEU *looks at the bottom of his can of beef, not speaking. Then he turns suddenly to the* TROOPER) All right, go fetch him.

(*The* TROOPER *goes out. Silence.* CLOCHET *whistles softly.* PELLERIN *goes to the window and opens it wide*)

CLOCHET Don't open the window. It's getting chilly.

PELLERIN What window? Oh, yes. (*He laughs*) I opened it without thinking. (*He goes to close it*)

LANDRIEU Leave it open. It's stifling in here, I need air.

CLOCHET As you wish.

(*Enter* HENRI *and three* TROOPERS)

LANDRIEU Put him there. Take off his handcuffs. Tie his hands to the arms of the chair. (*The* TROOPERS *fasten his hands*) Your name?

HENRI Henri.

LANDRIEU Henri what?

HENRI Henri.

(LANDRIEU *gives a sign and the* TROOPERS *strike* HENRI)

LANDRIEU Now. What's your name.

HENRI I'm Henri, just Henri.

(*They strike him*)

LANDRIEU Stop, you'll make him too groggy to talk. How old are you?

HENRI Twenty-nine.

LANDRIEU Profession?

HENRI Before the war I was a medical student.

PELLERIN You're an educated bastard. (*to the* TROOPERS) Let him have it.

LANDRIEU Let's not waste time.

PELLERIN A medical student, eh! Well, let him have it!

LANDRIEU Pellerin! (*to* HENRI) Where's your chief?

HENRI I don't know.

LANDRIEU Of course. No, don't hit him. Do you smoke? Give him this cigarette. Wait. (*He puts it in his own mouth, lights it, and hands it to a* TROOPER, *who puts it in* HENRI'S *mouth*) Go on, smoke. What can you hope for? You don't impress us. Come, Henri, don't show off; nobody is watching you. Save your time and ours; you don't have very many hours to live.

HENRI Nor do you.

LANDRIEU Well, we can still count it in months. Enough time to bury you. Smoke up. And think. Since you're educated, be realistic. If you don't talk, it will be the girl friend or the kid.

HENRI That's their business.

LANDRIEU Where is your chief?

HENRI Try to make me tell you.

LANDRIEU You prefer that? Take away his cigarette. Clochet, fix him up.

CLOCHET Put sticks in the ropes. (*The* TROOPERS *slip two sticks in the ropes that bind* HENRI'S *wrists*) Good. They'll turn until you talk.

HENRI I won't talk.

CLOCHET Not right away: you'll scream first.

HENRI Try to make me.

CLOCHET You're not humble. One must be humble. If you fall from too high up you break your neck. Turn. Slowly. Well? Nothing? No. Turn, turn. Wait: he is beginning to feel pain. Well? No? Of course: pain doesn't exist for a man of your education. The pity is that we can see it in your face. (*softly*) You're sweating. I'm sorry for you. (*He wipes* HENRI's *face with a handkerchief*) Turn. Will he yell? Won't he yell? You're wriggling. You can keep from crying, but you can't keep your head from wriggling. How bad you must feel! (*He passes his fingers over* HENRI's *cheeks*) How you grit your teeth! Are you scared? "If I could hold out a minute longer, only one little minute. . . ." But after this minute will come another, and then another still, until you find the pain too great and then you'll think it's better to despise yourself. We won't let you off. (*He takes his head in his hands*) These eyes no longer see me now. What is it they see? (*softly*) You are handsome. Turn. (*a pause. With triumph*) You're going to scream, Henri, you're going to scream. I can see the cry swelling your neck; it's rising to your lips. Just a little more pressure. Turn. (HENRI *screams*) Ha! (*a pause*) How ashamed you must be! Turn. Don't stop. (HENRI *screams out again*) You see; it is only the first scream that comes hard. Now gently, very naturally, you'll talk.

HENRI   You'll get nothing from me but screams.

CLOCHET   No, Henri, no. You no longer have the right to be proud. "Try to make me scream!" You saw; it didn't take long. Where is your chief? Be humble, Henri, really humble. Tell us where he is. Very well, what are you waiting for? Scream or speak. Turn. Turn, damn it; break his wrists. Stop: he's passed out. (*He goes to get a bottle of whisky and a glass. Almost tenderly he makes* HENRI *drink*) Drink, poor martyr. Do you feel better? Good, we can start again. Go get the tools.

LANDRIEU   No!

CLOCHET   How's that?

(LANDRIEU *rubs his hand over his brow*)

LANDRIEU   Take him out. You can work on him down there.

CLOCHET   We'll be cramped for room.

LANDRIEU   I'm in command here. Clochet. This is the second time I've had to remind you.

CLOCHET   But—

LANDRIEU (*shouting*)   Do you want a punch in the nose?

CLOCHET   All right, all right, take him along.

(*The* TROOPERS *unfasten* HENRI *and carry him out.* CLOCHET *follows*)

PELLERIN   Are you coming?

LANDRIEU   No. Clochet disgusts me.

PELLERIN   He talks too much. (*a pause*) A medical student, if you please! The bastard. I had to leave school at thirteen to earn a living. I wasn't lucky enough to have rich parents to pay for me to study.

LANDRIEU   I hope he talks.

PELLERIN   Good Christ, yes; he'll talk!

LANDRIEU   That fouls it up, a guy who won't talk.

(HENRI *screams.* LANDRIEU *goes to the door and shuts it. More cries, which can be heard clearly through the door.* LANDRIEU *goes to the radio and turns it on*)

PELLERIN (*astounded*)   You, too, Landrieu?

LANDRIEU   It's those screams. You have to have nerves like iron.

PELLERIN   Let him scream. He's a bastard, a dirty intellectual. (*strident music*) Not so loud. I can't hear.

LANDRIEU   Go join them. (PELLERIN *hesitates, then goes out*) He'll have to talk. He's a coward, he must be a coward.

(*Music and screams. The screams stop. A pause.* PELLERIN *comes in again, pale*)

PELLERIN   Stop that music.

(LANDRIEU *turns off the radio*)

LANDRIEU   Well?

PELLERIN   They'll kill him before he talks.

LANDRIEU (*goes to the door*)   Stop it. Bring him in here.

(*The* TROOPERS *bring in* HENRI. CLOCHET *is at his side*)

PELLERIN (*goes up to* HENRI)   We're not through with you yet. We can begin where we left off, never fear. Lower your eyes. I tell you, lower your eyes. (*He strikes him*) You pig!

CLOCHET (*approaching* HENRI)   Hold out your hands, I'm going to put the cuffs on. (*He adjusts the handcuffs very gently*) It hurts, doesn't it? Hurts a lot, eh? Poor little boy. (*He strokes his hair*) Come on, now, don't be so proud. You screamed, you screamed, anyway. Tomorrow you'll talk.

(*At a gesture from* LANDRIEU, *the* TROOPERS *lead* HENRI *out*)

PELLERIN   The bastard!

LANDRIEU   That fouls it up.

PELLERIN   What?

LANDRIEU   It fouls things up when a guy won't talk.

CLOCHET   Well, he screamed, anyhow. I got him to scream. (*He shrugs his shoulders*)

PELLERIN   Bring the girl.

LANDRIEU   The girl—if she doesn't talk—

PELLERIN   Well—

LANDRIEU   Nothing. (*with sudden violence*) There *must* be one of them who'll talk.

CLOCHET   We should have the blond fellow sent down. He's ripe.

LANDRIEU   The blond one?

CLOCHET   Sorbier. He's a coward.

LANDRIEU   A coward? Go get him.

(CLOCHET *goes out*)

PELLERIN   They're all cowards. Only some of them are stubborn.

LANDRIEU   Pellerin! What would you do if they tore out your nails?

PELLERIN   The British don't tear out nails.

LANDRIEU   What about the Maquis?

PELLERIN   They won't tear our nails out.

LANDRIEU   Why not?

PELLERIN   Things like that can't happen to us.

(CLOCHET *enters, followed by* SORBIER, *accompanied by* TROOPERS)

CLOCHET   Let me question him. Remove his handcuffs. Tie his arms to the chair. Good. (*He goes up to* SORBIER) Ah, yes, so here you are. Here you are once more in this chair. And here we are too. Do you know why we had you brought down?

SORBIER   No.

CLOCHET   Because you're a coward and you're going to squeal. You are a coward, aren't you?

SORBIER   Yes.

CLOCHET   There you are, you see. I read it in your eyes. Show me those big staring eyes.

SORBIER   Your eyes will look like that when they hang you.

CLOCHET   Don't show off now; it doesn't suit you very well.

SORBIER   The same eyes; we're brothers. I attract you, isn't that so? It's not me you are torturing. It's yourself.

CLOCHET   (*abruptly*) You're a Jew, aren't you?

SORBIER   (*surprised*) Me? No.

CLOCHET   And I say that you are a Jew. (*At a sign from* CLOCHET, *the* TROOPERS *strike* SORBIER) Aren't you a Jew?

SORBIER   Yes. I am a Jew.

CLOCHET   Good. Now listen carefully. We'll start with the nails. That will give you time to make up your mind. We're not in a hurry, we have all night! Are you going to talk?

SORBIER   What dirt!

CLOCHET   What did you say?

SORBIER   I said: what dirt. You and I are both just dirt.

CLOCHET   (*to the* TROOPERS) Take the pincers and begin.

SORBIER   Let me go! Let me go! I'll talk. I'll tell you all you want to know.

CLOCHET   (*to the* TROOPERS) Pull the nail a bit anyhow, so he'll know we mean business. (SORBIER *groans*) O.K., where's your leader?

SORBIER   Untie me, I can't sit in this chair. Not any more! Not any more! (*A sign from* LANDRIEU. *The* TROOPERS *unfasten him. He gets* up and staggers to the table) Give me a cigarette.

LANDRIEU   Later.

SORBIER   What do you want to know? Where our leader is? I know. None of the others do, but I really know. He confided in me. He is—(*pointing suddenly behind them*) there! (*All turn around. He leaps to the window and jumps up on the ledge*) I won! Come near and I jump. I won! I won!

CLOCHET   Don't be a fool. If you talk we'll let you off.

SORBIER   Don't feed me that line! (*shouting*) Hey, up there! Henri, Canoris, I didn't talk! (*The* TROOPERS *make a grab for him. He leaps out of the window*) Goodnight!

PELLERIN   The bastard! The dirty coward! (*They lean out of the window*)

LANDRIEU   (*to the* TROOPERS) Go on down. If he's alive, bring him back up. We'll put the heat on him until he cracks.

(*The* TROOPERS *go out. A pause*)

CLOCHET   I told you to close the window.

(LANDRIEU *goes up to him and punches him in the face*)

LANDRIEU   You can put that in your report. (*A pause.* CLOCHET *takes out his handkerchief and wipes his mouth. The* TROOPERS *come back in*)

TROOPER   Dead as a mackerel.

LANDRIEU   The dirty whore! (*to the* TROOPERS) Go get me the girl. (*The* TROOPERS *go out*) They'll talk, by Christ! They'll talk!

ACT THREE

(*The attic.* FRANÇOIS, CANORIS, HENRI *are seated on the floor in a semicircle. They form a closely knit group. They talk in halftones.* JEAN *walks around them, evidently miserable. From time to time he seems about to enter the conversation, but then catches himself and continues his walking*)

CANORIS   When they were tying me up, I watched them. A guy came up and hit me. I looked at him and thought: I've seen that face somewhere. After that they went to work on me and I tried to remember him.

HENRI   Which one of them was it?

CANORIS   The big fellow who talks so much. I've seen him in Grenoble. You know Chasières, the baker on the rue Longue? He sells cream-puffs in his back room. Every Sunday morning this guy would come out of the place carrying a package of cakes bound with a pink string. I remembered him because of his ugly mug. I thought he was working for the police.

HENRI   You might have told me that before.

CANORIS   That he was with the police?

HENRI   That Chasières sold cream-puffs. Did he feed you a line, too?

CANORIS   I should say so. He had leaned over me and was breathing in my face.

JEAN   (*breaking into the conversation*) What did he say?

(*They turn toward him with evident surprise*)

CANORIS   Nothing. A lot of crap.

JEAN   I don't think I could take that.

HENRI   Why not? It's amusing.

JEAN   Oh! Oh! Yes? Naturally, I couldn't very well appreciate that.

(*A silence.* HENRI *turns to* CANORIS)

HENRI   What do you think they do in private life?

CANORIS   The big fat one who took notes could be a dentist.

HENRI   Not bad. Say, it's lucky he didn't bring his drill.

(*They laugh*)

JEAN   (*violently*) Don't laugh. (*They stop laughing and look at him*) I know: you can laugh, sure you can. You have a right to laugh. And besides, I have no more orders to give you. (*a pause*) If you had told me that one day I would be afraid of you—(*a pause*) But how can you be so gay?

HENRI   We manage.

JEAN   Naturally. You're suffering on your own score. That's what gives a man a clear conscience. I was married; I never told you. My wife died in childbirth. I paced the hall of the hospital and I knew she would die. It's the same story, exactly the same! I wanted to help her, and I couldn't. I paced back and forth listening for her cries. She didn't make a sound. She had the better role. Like you.

HENRI   That's not our fault.

JEAN   Nor mine. I'd like to help you if I could.

CANORIS   But you can't.

JEAN   I know that. (*a pause*) It's two hours since they took her out. They didn't keep you that long.

HENRI   She's a woman. With women they can really have a good time.

JEAN   (*with a burst of violence*) I'll come back. In a week, in a month, I'll be back. I'll have my men castrate them.

HENRI   You're lucky to still be able to hate them.

JEAN   Is that luck? Besides, I suppose I hate them mainly to give myself something to think about. (*He paces back and forth, and then, having hit on some idea, drags an old stove under the window*)

CANORIS   You bother me. What are you up to now?

JEAN   I want to see him once more before dark.

HENRI   Who?

JEAN   Sorbier.

HENRI   (*with indifference*)   Oh.

(JEAN *climbs on the stove and looks out the window*)

JEAN   He's still there. They'll let him rot there. Do you want to get up? I'll help you.

CANORIS   What for?

JEAN   Yes, what for? You leave the dead to me.

FRANÇOIS   I want to look.

HENRI   I advise you not to.

FRANÇOIS   (*to* JEAN)   Help me up. (JEAN *helps* FRANÇOIS *up. He looks out the window*) His—his skull is all smashed. (*He climbs down and squats trembling in a corner*)

HENRI   (*to* JEAN)   That was certainly smart.

JEAN   So what? I should think, you being so tough, that you could bear the sight of a corpse.

HENRI   I could, maybe, but not the kid. (*to* FRANÇOIS) The funeral orations are Jean's department. You have no responsibility for that corpse. It is all over for him; for him it's silence. But you still have a way to go yet. Think of yourself.

FRANÇOIS   This head will be smashed open, and these eyes—

HENRI   That won't mean anything to you: you won't be there to see yourself.

(*A pause.* JEAN *paces back and forth and then comes to a halt before* HENRI *and* CANORIS)

JEAN   Do they have to tear out my nails for me to be your friend again?

CANORIS   You're still our friend.

JEAN   You know better. (*a pause*) How do you know that I wouldn't have held out? (*to* HENRI) Maybe I wouldn't have screamed.

HENRI   Well?

JEAN   Forgive me. I should only keep quiet.

HENRI   Jean! Come sit with us. (JEAN *hesitates and then sits down*) You would be just like us if you were in our place. But we haven't the same worries. (JEAN *gets up suddenly*) What's the matter?

JEAN   Until they bring her back, I can't sit still.

HENRI   You see what I mean; you're fidgety, you're trembling; you're too much alive.

JEAN   I went six months without telling her I loved her. The night I finally took her in my arms, I turned off the light. Now she is there with them, naked, and they're sliding their hands over her body.

HENRI   What does that matter? The important thing is to win.

JEAN   To win what?

HENRI   Just to win. There are two teams: one wants to make the other talk. (*He laughs*) It's ridiculous, but it's all we have left. If we talk, we lose everything. They have run up a few points because I screamed, but on the whole we're not in such a bad position.

JEAN   I don't give a damn about winning or losing! That's nothing. But her shame is real; her suffering is real.

HENRI   So what? I felt shame, too, when they made me scream. But that doesn't last. If she's silent, their hands won't mark her. They're a sorry lot, those guys, you know.

JEAN   They're men and she's in their arms.

HENRI   Never mind. If you want to know, I love her myself.

JEAN   You?

HENRI   Why not? And I didn't feel much like laughing the night you both went upstairs together. I often wondered about the lights; I wondered whether you turned them off.

JEAN   You love her? And yet you can sit here calmly?

HENRI   Her pain brings her nearer to us. The pleasure you gave her separated us more. Today I am closer to her than you are.

JEAN   That's not true! It's not true! She's thinking of me even while they torture her. She is thinking only of me. It's so as not to surrender me that she's ready to endure torture and shame.

HENRI   No, it's in order to win.

JEAN   You're lying! (*a pause*) She said: "When I return there'll be only love in my eyes."

(*Steps in the corridor*)

HENRI   She's coming back. You can look in her eyes and find out.

(*The door opens.* HENRI *gets to his feet.* LUCIE *enters.* JEAN *and* HENRI *look at her in silence. She passes right by them without turning her head and sits down at the front of the stage. A pause*)

LUCIE   François! (FRANÇOIS *goes to her and sits against her knees*) Don't touch me. Give me Sorbier's coat. (FRANÇOIS *picks up the coat*) Throw it across my shoulders. (*She wraps it tightly around her*)

FRANÇOIS   Are you cold?

LUCIE   No. (*a pause*) What's going on? Are they looking at me? Why don't they go on talking?

JEAN   (*coming up behind her*)   Lucie!

CANORIS   Leave her alone.

JEAN   Lucie!

LUCIE   (*gently*)   What is it?

JEAN   You promised me there would be nothing but love in your eyes.

LUCIE   Love? (*She shrugs her shoulders sadly*)

CANORIS   (*who has got to his feet*)   Let her be; you can talk to her after a while.

JEAN   (*violently*)   Get the hell out of this. She's mine. You've cast me aside, both of you, and I can't say anything; but you can't take her from me. (*to* LUCIE) Speak to me. You're not like them, are you? It's not possible you've become like them. Why don't you answer me? Are you angry with me?

LUCIE   I'm not angry with you.

JEAN   My sweet Lucie.

LUCIE   I shall never be sweet again, Jean.

JEAN   You don't love me any more.

LUCIE   I don't know. (*He takes a step toward her*) Please, don't touch me. (*with an effort*) I think I must still love you. But I no longer feel my love. (*wearily*) I no longer feel anything.

CANORIS   (*to* JEAN)   Come away. (*He drags him away and forces him to sit down next to him*)

LUCIE   (*as if to herself*)   It's all so unimportant. (*to* FRANÇOIS) What are they doing?

FRANÇOIS   They're sitting with their backs to us.

LUCIE   Good. (*A long pause. Then steps in the corridor.* FRANÇOIS *springs to his feet with a cry of alarm*) What's wrong? Oh, yes, it's your turn. Do a good job: they need to be put to shame.

(*The steps come closer, then move away*)

FRANÇOIS   (*throwing himself at* LUCIE's *knees*) I can't stand it any more! I can't stand it any more!

LUCIE   Look at me! (*She raises his head*) How frightened you were! You're not going to tell them anything? Answer me!

FRANÇOIS   I don't know now. I had a little courage left, but I shouldn't have seen you like this. Here you are, your hair disordered, your blouse torn, and I know that they took you in their arms.

LUCIE   (*with violence*)   They didn't touch me. Nobody touched me. I was like stone and I didn't feel their hands. I looked them in the face and I thought: nothing is happening. (*passionately*) And nothing did happen. In the end they were afraid of me. (*a pause*) François, if you talk, they will really have violated me. They'll say: "We've finally had them." The memory will make them smile. They'll say: "We sure had fun with that babe." We must shame them. If I didn't hope to see them again I'd hang myself from the bars of that window this minute. You won't talk, will you?

(FRANÇOIS *shugs his shoulders without replying. A pause*)

HENRI (*in a low voice*)   Well, Jean, who was right? She wants to win; that's all.

JEAN   Be quiet! Why do you want to take her from me? You're sitting on top of the world; you'll die happy and proud. But I have only her and I'm going to live!

HENRI   I don't want anything, and anyhow I wasn't the one who took her from you.

JEAN   Go on! Go on! You have every right to, you even have the right to torture me; you paid in advance. (*He gets to his feet*) How sure you are of yourselves. Is suffering with your body enough to give you a clear conscience? (HENRI *does not answer*) Can't you understand that I am more unhappy than any of you?

FRANÇOIS (*who suddenly gets to his feet*) Ha! Ha! Ha!

JEAN (*shouting*)   The most unhappy! The most unhappy!

FRANÇOIS (*springing toward* JEAN)   Look at him! Just look at him! The most unhappy of us all. He has eaten and slept. His hands are free. He will see the sun again. He's going to live. But he's the most unhappy. What do you want? Someone to pity you too, you bastard?

JEAN (*crossing his arms*)   Good!

FRANÇOIS   I jump out of my skin at every sound. The spit sticks in my throat, I'm dying. But he is the most unhappy of all. Sure! And I shall die in rapture! (*vehemently*) Well, I'll give your happiness back to you, if that's what you want!

LUCIE (*springing to her feet*)   François!

FRANÇOIS   I'll denounce you! I'll denounce you! I'll let you share in our joys!

JEAN (*in a low and rapid tone*)   Go ahead. You couldn't know how much I want you to.

LUCIE (*taking* FRANÇOIS *by the back of the neck and turning his head toward her*)   Look me in the face. Would you dare talk?

FRANÇOIS   Dare! Your big words again. I'll just denounce him, that's all. It'll be so simple, they'll come for me and my mouth will open all by itself. The name will pop out just like

that, and I'll agree with my mouth. What's there to dare? When I see you pale and on edge, acting like a maniac, your scorn doesn't frighten me any more. (*a pause*) I'll save you, Lucie. They'll let us live.

LUCIE   I don't want that kind of life.

FRANÇOIS   Well, I do. I want any kind of life. Shame passes when you live long enough.

CANORIS   They'll show you no mercy, François. Even if you talk.

FRANÇOIS (*pointing at* JEAN)   At least I'll see him suffer.

HENRI (*rises and goes over to* LUCIE)   Do you think he'll talk?

LUCIE (*turns toward* FRANÇOIS *and stares at him*)   Yes.

HENRI   Are you sure?

(*They look at each other*)

LUCIE (*after a long hesitation*)   Yes.

(HENRI *goes toward* FRANÇOIS. CANORIS *gets up and stands beside* HENRI. *Both stare at* FRANÇOIS)

HENRI   It is not for me to judge you, François. You're just a kid, and this whole business is too tough for you. At your age I think I would have talked, too.

CANORIS   It's all our fault. We shouldn't have taken you with us; there are some risks that only men should take. Please forgive us.

FRANÇOIS (*recoiling*)   What do you mean? What are you going to do to me?

HENRI   You must not talk, François. They'll kill you all the same, you know. And you'll die in despair.

FRANÇOIS (*frightened*)   All right then, I won't talk. I tell you I won't talk. Let me go.

HENRI   We can't trust you any longer. They know that you're our weak point. They'll work on you without let-up until you come clean. It's up to us to keep you from talking.

JEAN   Do you suppose I'll stand by and let you do this? Don't worry, kid. My hands are free, and I am with you.

LUCIE (*barring the way*)   Why don't you keep out of this?

JEAN   But he's our brother!

LUCIE   So? He'll die tomorrow anyway.

JEAN   Is this really you? You frighten me.

LUCIE   He must not talk. The means doesn't count.

FRANÇOIS   You're not going to—(*They don't answer him*) But I told you I won't talk. (*They don't reply*) Lucie, help, keep them from hurting me; I won't talk; I swear to you I won't talk.

JEAN (*placing himself beside* FRANÇOIS) Don't lay a hand on him.

HENRI   Jean, when are our comrades due to arrive in the village?

JEAN   Tuesday.

HENRI   How many are they?

JEAN   Sixty.

HENRI   Sixty men who trust you and who on Tuesday will die like rats. It's them or him. Choose.

JEAN   You have no right to ask me to choose.

HENRI   Aren't you their leader? Well!

(JEAN *hesitates a moment and then slowly steps aside.* HENRI *approaches* FRANÇOIS)

FRANÇOIS   (*watches him and then begins to scream*)   Lucie! Help! I don't want to die here, not in this blackness. Henri, I'm fifteen, let me live. Don't kill me in the dark. (HENRI *takes him by the throat*) Lucie! (LUCIE *turns her head away*) I hate you all.

LUCIE   My little one, my poor darling, my only love, forgive us. (*She turns away. A pause*) Make it quick.

HENRI   I can't. They've half broken my wrists. (*a pause*)

LUCIE   Is it done?

HENRI   He's dead.

(LUCIE *turns and takes* FRANÇOIS' *body in her arms. His head rests on her knees. A very long silence, then* JEAN *begins to talk in a low voice. All the conversation that follows is in a low voice*)

JEAN   What has happened to you all? Why didn't you die with the others? You horrify me.

HENRI   Do you think I love myself?

JEAN   All right. In twenty-four hours you'll be rid of yourself. But every day from now on I'll see that kid begging for mercy and I'll see your face as those hands tightened about his throat. (*He goes to* FRANÇOIS *and looks at him*) Fifteen years old! And he died mad with fear. (*He turns toward* HENRI) He loved you. He slept with his head on your shoulder. He used to say: "I sleep better when you're there." (*a pause*) You bastard!

HENRI   (*to* CANORIS *and* LUCIE)   Well, why don't you speak up? Don't leave me alone. Lucie! Canoris! You killed him with my hands. (*No answer. He turns toward* JEAN) And you, who have set yourself up as my judge, what did you do to save him?

JEAN   (*with violence*)   What could I do? What would you have let me do?

HENRI   Your hands were free, you should have hit me. (*passionately*) If you had hit me—if you had beaten me till I fell—

JEAN   My hands were free? You had me tied hand and foot. If I make a move, if I say a

word, then: "What about the comrades?" You excluded me, you've decided my life and my death, coldly. Don't come telling me now that I'm your accomplice; that would be too easy. I'm your witness, no more. And I am a witness that you are murderers. (*a pause*) You killed him out of pride.

HENRI   You lie!

JEAN   Out of pride! They made you scream, didn't they? And you were ashamed. You want to dazzle them, to redeem yourself; you want to save for yourself a heroic death. Isn't that true? You wanted to win.

HENRI   That's not true! That's not true! Lucie, tell him that it's not true! (LUCIE *does not answer. He takes a step toward her*) Answer me: do you think I killed him out of pride?

LUCIE   I don't know. (*A pause. Then laboriously*) We had to keep him from talking.

HENRI   Do you hate me? He was your brother; you alone have the right to condemn me.

LUCIE   I don't hate you. (*He leans over the body she holds in her arms. Vehemently*) Don't touch him.

(HENRI *slowly turns and goes back toward* CANORIS)

HENRI   Canoris! You didn't scream, yet you wanted him to die, too. Did we kill him out of pride?

CANORIS   I have no pride.

HENRI   But I do! It's true that I do have pride. Did I kill him out of pride?

CANORIS   You ought to know.

HENRI   I—No, I don't know any more. Everything happened too fast and now he's dead. (*abruptly*) Don't leave me! You have no right to leave me. When my hands were around his throat, it seemed to me that they were our hands and that we were all pressing together, otherwise I should never have been capable of—

CANORIS   He had to die. If he had stood nearer me, I would have done it. As for what's going on in your head—

HENRI   Yes?

CANORIS   That doesn't count. Nothing counts within these four walls. He had to die; that's all there is to it.

HENRI   All right. (*He comes up to the body. To* LUCIE) Don't be afraid, I won't touch him. (*He leans over the body and stares at it for some time, then straightens up*) Jean, when we threw the first grenade, how many hostages did they shoot? (JEAN *doesn't answer*) Twelve. There was a kid in the lot, a kid named Destaches. You must remember; we saw the posters in the rue des Minimes. Charbonnel wanted to give himself up and you wouldn't let him.

JEAN   Well?

HENRI   Did you ask yourself why you wouldn't let him?

JEAN   That was different.

HENRI   Perhaps. All the better for you if your motives were clearer: you have nothing on your conscience. But Destaches is dead just the same. I'll never again have a clear conscience, never until they prop me against a wall with a handkerchief over my eyes. But why should I want a clear conscience? The kid had to die.

JEAN   I wouldn't want to be in your shoes.

HENRI   (*gently*) You're out of this, Jean; you can neither judge nor understand.

(*A long silence. Then* LUCIE *speaks. She caresses* FRANÇOIS' *hair, but doesn't look at him. For the first time since the beginning of the scene she raises her voice to its normal pitch*)

LUCIE   You're dead and my eyes are dry. Forgive me; I guess I have no more tears and death no longer matters to me. Outside there are three hundred lying dead in the grass, and tomorrow I too will be cold and naked, without even a hand to fondle my hair. There's nothing to regret, you know: life itself is not so important any more. Good-bye. You went as far as you could. If you stopped halfway, it is because you didn't have the strength to go farther. No one has the right to blame you.

JEAN   No one. (*A long silence. He sits down beside* LUCIE) Lucie. (*She shrinks back*) Don't push me away, I want to help you.

LUCIE   Help me how? I don't need help.

JEAN   Yes. I think you do; I'm afraid that you'll break down.

LUCIE   I can last until tomorrow night.

JEAN   You're too tense, you'll snap. Your courage will leave you all of a sudden.

LUCIE   Why bother about me? (*She looks at him*) You're suffering. All right, I'll reassure you and then you can go. Everything has become quite simple now that the kid is dead; I have only myself to think of. And I don't need courage to die, you know; I don't think I could have lived very long without him anyhow. Now go away. I'll say good-bye to you later when they come for me.

JEAN   Let me sit near you. I'll be quiet, if you like, but I'll be there and you won't feel alone.

LUCIE   Not alone? With you? Oh, Jean, didn't you understand? We have nothing in common any more.

JEAN   Have you forgotten that I love you?

LUCIE   It was someone else you loved.

JEAN   It's you.

LUCIE   I'm somebody else. I don't even recognize myself. Something must have got blocked up in my head.

JEAN   Perhaps. Perhaps you are another person. In that case it's this other person that I love now, and tomorrow I shall love the dead person you will be. It's you I love, Lucie, *you,* happy or unhappy, alive or dead. It's you.

LUCIE   All right. You love me. So?

JEAN   You loved me too.

LUCIE   Yes. And I loved my brother, whom I let them kill. Our love is so far away, why should you speak to me of it? It really wasn't important.

JEAN   That's a lie! You know very well that you're lying. It was our whole life, no more and no less than our whole life. Everything that happened we went through together.

LUCIE   Our whole life, yes. Our future. I lived in expectation, I loved you in hope. I waited only for the end of the war, for the day we could be married before everyone. I waited for you each night. Now I have no future; I wait only for my death and I shall die alone. (*a pause*) Leave me alone. We have nothing to say to each other; I'm not suffering and I don't need consolation.

JEAN   Do you suppose I am trying to console you? I see your dry eyes and I know that your heart is an inferno; not a trace of suffering, not even the moisture of a tear, everything is white-hot. How you must suffer from not suffering! Oh, I've thought a hundred times of torture, I've felt it all in advance, but I never imagined it could produce this horrible suffering of pride. Lucie, I'd like to give you a little self-pity. If you could only relax that rigid head, if you could rest it on my shoulder. But answer me! Look at me!

LUCIE   Don't touch me.

JEAN   It's no use, Lucie, we're riveted together. All they've done to you they've done to both of us. This pain that escapes you is mine too; it waits for you. If you come into my arms it will become *our* pain. Trust me, darling, and we'll be able to say "we" again; we'll be a couple, we'll bear everything together, even your death. If you could only summon up one tear—

LUCIE   (*violently*) A tear? I only wish they'd come for me again and beat me so that I could once again refuse to talk and mock them and frighten them. Everything here is so pointless: this waiting, your love, the weight of this head on my knees. I wish that grief could consume me, I'd like to burn, to say nothing and see their eyes ever watching.

JEAN (*overwhelmed*) You're nothing but a desert of pride.

LUCIE Am I to blame for that? It was my pride that they struck. I hate them, but they hold me. And I hold them too. I feel nearer to them than to you. (*She laughs*) "We!" You want me to say "we." Have your wrists been smashed like Henri's? Are your legs wounded like Canoris'? Come now, this is just a comedy: you haven't felt a thing; you imagine it all.

JEAN Smashed wrists. Ah! If that's all you want, to let me be one of you, why then it's soon done. (*He looks around, spies a heavy andiron, and seizes it*)

(LUCIE *bursts into laughter*)

LUCIE What are you up to?

JEAN (*flattens his left hand on the floor and strikes it with the andiron he holds in his right*) I've had enough of hearing you vaunt your griefs as if they were virtues. I'm tired of looking at you with your pitiable eyes. What they've done to you I can do to myself; anybody can do it.

LUCIE (*laughing*) It won't work, it's no use. You can break your bones, you can tear out your eyes; but it is you and you alone who are deciding what you're to suffer. Each of our hurts is a violation because it was other men who inflicted them on us. You can't catch up with us.

(*A pause.* JEAN *throws away the andiron and looks at it. He gets to his feet*)

JEAN You're right; I can't become one of you. You're together and I'm alone. I won't stir again, I'll never speak to you again, I'll just hide in a dark corner and you'll forget that I exist. I suppose that's my part in this story and I must accept it as you accept yours. (*a pause*) A moment ago an idea came to me: Pierre was killed near the Servaz cave where we kept arms. If they release me, I'll go hunt up his body, put some papers in his coat, and drag the body into the cave. Count four hours after I leave, and when they question you again, reveal that as the hide-away. They'll find Pierre and believe it's me. Then they'll have no further reason for torturing you and they'll finish with you quickly. That's all. Good-bye.

(*He goes to the rear*)

(*A long silence. Then steps in the corridor. A* TROOPER *enters with a lantern; he swings his lantern all over the room*)

TROOPER (*catching sight of* FRANÇOIS) What's wrong with him?

LUCIE He's sleeping.

TROOPER (*to* JEAN) You come along. Something new for you.

(JEAN *hesitates, looks at the others with a kind of despair, and follows the* TROOPER. *The door closes after them*)

LUCIE He's in the clear, don't you think?

CANORIS I suppose so.

LUCIE Good. That's one worry less. He'll find his kind and it will be for the best. Come here. (HENRI *and* CANORIS *come closer to her*) Closer. Now we're amongst ourselves. Why do you hold back? (*She looks at them and grasps what they are thinking*) Oh. (*a pause*) He had to die; you know very well that he had to die. The ones downstairs killed him with our hands. Look, I'm his sister and I tell you that you're not guilty. Touch him; now that he's dead, he's one of us. See what a hard look he has. He has closed his lips on a secret. Touch him.

HENRI (*stroking* FRANÇOIS' *hair*) My little boy. My poor little boy.

LUCIE They made you scream, Henri, I heard you. You must feel ashamed.

HENRI Yes.

LUCIE I feel your shame with the same intensity. It's my shame, too. I told him I was alone and I was lying. With you I don't feel alone. (*to* CANORIS) You, you didn't scream. It's too bad.

CANORIS I'm ashamed too.

LUCIE Really! Why?

CANORIS When Henri screamed I felt ashamed.

LUCIE Just as well. Press close against me. I feel your arms and your shoulders, and the boy is heavy on my knees. That's good. To-morrow I'll be quiet. Oh, how still I shall be! For him, for me, for Sorbier, for you. We are all one.

ACT FOUR

(*Before the curtain goes up, a frightful voice is heard singing "If all the cuckolds had bells." The curtain rises on the schoolroom. It is the following morning.* PELLERIN *is sitting on one of the benches, drinking. He seems exhausted.* LANDRIEU, *in the teacher's chair, is drinking; he is half drunk.* CLOCHET *is standing by the*

window. He yawns; from time to time LAN-
DRIEU *bursts into laughter*)

PELLERIN   What's so funny?

LANDRIEU   (*cupping his hand around his
ear*)   What?

PELLERIN   I asked you what you're laughing
at.

LANDRIEU   (*pointing to the radio and shouting*)   That.

PELLERIN   Eh?

LANDRIEU   Yes, I think it's a terrifically
funny idea.

PELLERIN   What idea?

LANDRIEU   To put bells on cuckolds.

PELLERIN   Oh, hell! I didn't even hear it.
(*He goes to the radio set*)

LANDRIEU   (*shouting*)   Don't turn it off.
(PELLERIN *turns it off. Silence*) You see, you
see.

PELLERIN   (*nonplussed*)   See what?

LANDRIEU   See the cold.

PELLERIN   You're cold in July?

LANDRIEU   I tell you it's cold; you don't understand anything.

PELLERIN   What were you saying?

LANDRIEU   About what?

PELLERIN   About cuckolds.

LANDRIEU   Who said anything to you about
cuckolds? Cuckold yourself. (*a pause*) I'm going to get some news. (*He gets up and goes to
the radio*)

CLOCHET   There won't be any.

LANDRIEU   No news?

CLOCHET   Not at this hour.

LANDRIEU   We shall see, we shall see. (*He
takes hold of the knob. Music, garbled stations*)

PELLERIN   You're blasting our ears off.

LANDRIEU   (*addressing the radio*)   Son of a
bitch! (*a pause*) To hell with it! I'm going to
listen to the BBC; what's the wave length?

PELLERIN   Twenty-one meters.

(LANDRIEU *turns the dial: a speech in the
Czech language.* LANDRIEU *begins to laugh*)

LANDRIEU   (*laughing*)   It's Czech, did you
get that? At this very moment a Czech is
speaking from London. Such a big world. (*He
shakes the set*) Can't you speak French? (*He
turns the radio off*) Give me a drink. (PELLERIN
*pours him a glass of wine. He takes it from him
and drinks*) What are we farting around here
for?

PELLERIN   Here or elsewhere—

LANDRIEU   I wish I were at the front.

PELLERIN   Aha!

LANDRIEU   Absolutely! That's where I'd like
to be. (*He seizes him by the lapels of his

jacket*) And don't be telling me that I'm afraid
to die.

PELLERIN   I didn't say anything.

LANDRIEU   What is death? Huh? What is
it? 'Cause we're going to have to find out, tomorrow, the day after, or in three months.

CLOCHET   (*vehemently*)   That's not true! It's
not true! The British will be pushed back into
the sea.

LANDRIEU   Into the sea? You'll have 'em
right up the ass, the British. Right here in
this village. It will be biff-bam-zing, boom-
diga-boom, bang on the town hall, poom
on the church. What will you be doing,
Clochet? You'll be in the basement! Ha! Ha! In
the cellar! It'll be fun. (*to* PELLERIN) Once
you're dead—I forget what I was going to say.
Look, the little wise guys upstairs—we're going to mow 'em down, and that's no skin off
my nose. Each in his turn. That's what I tell
myself. Today theirs. Tomorrow mine. That's
normal, isn't it? So am I normal. (*He drinks*)
We're all fools. (*to* CLOCHET) Why are you
yawning?

CLOCHET   I'm bored.

LANDRIEU   Well, just drink up, then. Am I
bored? But you'd rather spy on us; you're
making up your report in your head. (*He pours
a glass of wine and hands it to* CLOCHET)
Drink up, come on, drink!

CLOCHET   I'm not allowed, I have a bad
liver.

LANDRIEU   You'll drink this glass of wine or
get it in the face! (*A pause.* CLOCHET *extends
his hand, takes the glass, and drinks*) Ha! Ha!
Fools, all fools, and it's best that way. (*Sound
of steps; someone is pacing back and forth in
the attic overhead. All three look upwards.
They listen in silence, then suddenly* LANDRIEU
*wheels around, rushes to the door, opens it,
and calls out*) Corbier! Corbier! (*A* TROOPER
appears) Go up and quiet them. Let them
have it. (*The* TROOPER *goes out.* LANDRIEU
*shuts the door and comes back to the others;
all three look upwards, listening. Silence*) We'll
have to see their dirty mugs again. A lousy day.

PELLERIN   Do you need me to question
them?

LANDRIEU   Why do you ask?

PELLERIN   I was thinking their chief might
possibly be hiding in the forest. I could take
twenty men and beat the brush.

LANDRIEU   (*looking at him*)   Ah? (*A pause.
The walking above continues*) You'll stay here.

PELLERIN   All right. (*He shrugs his shoulders*) We're wasting our time.

LANDRIEU That may be, but we'll waste it together.

(*They look up above, despite themselves, throughout the following conversation, until the sounds overhead stop*)

CLOCHET It's time we brought the kid down.

LANDRIEU I don't give a damn about the kid. I want to make the big fellow open up.

PELLERIN They won't talk.

LANDRIEU I say they will. They're trash. You just have to know how to handle them. Hell, we didn't rough them up enough. (*A racket in the attic, then silence. LANDRIEU is satisfied*) What did I tell you? See, they've calmed down. Nothing like a strong hand.

(*They are visibly relieved*)

CLOCHET All the same, you ought to begin with the kid.

LANDRIEU O.K. (*He goes to the door*) Corbier! (*no reply*) Corbier! (*hurried steps in the corridor. CORBIER appears*) Go fetch the kid.

CORBIER The kid? They knocked him off.

LANDRIEU What?

CORBIER They knocked him off during the night. I found him with his head in his sister's lap. She said he was sleeping, but he was stone-dead. There were finger marks on his throat.

LANDRIEU Oh? (*a pause*) Who was walking around?

CORBIER The Greek.

LANDRIEU All right. You can go.

(*CORBIER goes out. Silence. CLOCHET gets up, and, despite himself, keeps looking toward the ceiling*)

PELLERIN (*exploding*) Fill them with lead, at once! Never see them again.

LANDRIEU Shut up! (*He goes to the radio and turns it on. A slow waltz. Then he goes back to his chair and pours himself a drink. As he puts down his glass he notices Pétain's portrait*) You see it, you see it all, but you wash your hands of it. You sacrifice yourself; you give yourself to France, but you don't give a damn for the dirty little details. You're part of history now, aren't you? And us, we're left in the shit. You dirty bastard! (*He throws his glass of wine at the picture*)

CLOCHET Landrieu!

LANDRIEU Put that in your report. (*a pause. He calms himself with difficulty. He comes back to PELLERIN*) It would be too easy to fill them with lead. That's what they want, don't you see that?

PELLERIN Fine, if that's what they want, let's give it to them. But let's get rid of them, let's see the last of them.

LANDRIEU I don't want them to kick off without having talked.

PELLERIN They have nothing to tell us now. During the twenty-four hours they have been here their leader has had ample time to make his get-away.

LANDRIEU I don't give a goddam about their leader. I want them to talk.

PELLERIN And what if they don't?

LANDRIEU Don't be difficult.

PELLERIN But just the same, what if they don't talk?

LANDRIEU (*shouting*) I told you not to knock yourself out over it.

PELLERIN O.K., have them brought in.

LANDRIEU Naturally I'll have them brought down. (*But he doesn't budge*)

(*CLOCHET begins to laugh*)

CLOCHET What if they're martyrs, hey?

(*LANDRIEU suddenly goes to the door*)

LANDRIEU Bring them down.

CORBIER (*appearing*) All three?

LANDRIEU Yes, all three.

(*CORBIER goes out*)

PELLERIN You could have left the girl upstairs.

(*Footsteps overhead*)

LANDRIEU They are coming down. (*He goes to the radio and turns it off*) If they surrender their chief, I'll let them go free.

CLOCHET You're mad, Landrieu!

LANDRIEU Shut your trap!

CLOCHET They deserve death ten times over.

LANDRIEU To hell with what they deserve. I want them to knuckle under. They won't pull that martyr stuff on me.

PELLERIN I—look here, I couldn't take it. If I had to think they would live, that they might even survive us, and that all their lives they would remember us—

LANDRIEU No need to get all upset. If they talk to save their necks now, they'll be avoiding that kind of memory afterwards. Here they are.

(*PELLERIN gets to his feet quickly and hides bottles and glasses under the chair. They are standing motionless as LUCIE, HENRI, CANORIS, and three TROOPERS enter. They look at each other in silence*)

LANDRIEU What have you done to the boy who was with you?

(*They do not answer*)

PELLERIN   Murderers!

LANDRIEU   Shut up! (*to the others*) He wanted to talk, eh? And you wanted to prevent him.

LUCIE   (*vehemently*) That's not true. He didn't want to talk. Nobody would talk.

LANDRIEU   Well?

HENRI   He was too young. It was senseless to let him suffer.

LANDRIEU   Which of you strangled him?

CANORIS   We all decided on it and we are all responsible.

LANDRIEU   Very well. (*a pause*) If you give us the information we want, I'll let you off.

CLOCHET   Landrieu!

LANDRIEU   I told you to be quiet. (*to the others*) Do you accept? (*a pause*) Well? Yes or no? (*They remain silent.* LANDRIEU *grows more and more upset*) You refuse? You are ready to give three lives for one? That's absurd. (*a pause*) It's life I am offering you! Life! Life! Are you deaf?

(*A pause. Then* LUCIE *takes a step toward them*)

LUCIE   We've won! We've actually won! This moment pays us back for lots of things. All that I wanted to forget last night I'm proud to remember now. They tore off my dress. (*pointing to* CLOCHET) He held my legs. (*pointing to* LANDRIEU) He held my arms. (*pointing to* PELLERIN) And he raped me. Now I can say it, I can yell it as loud as I please: you violated me and you are ashamed. I'm washed clean. Where are your pincers and pliers? Where are your whips? This morning you beg us to live. And our answer is no. No! You'll have to finish your job.

PELLERIN   That's enough! Enough I say! Let them have it!

LANDRIEU   Stop! Pellerin, I may not be in command here for much longer but while I am, my orders will not be questioned. Take them out.

CLOCHET   Can't we work on them a bit anyway? Because, after all, this is just talk. Nothing but talk. Hot air. (*pointing to* HENRI) This guy came in yesterday cocky and swaggering and we made him scream like a girl.

HENRI   Just see if you can make me scream today.

LANDRIEU   Work on them if you have the courage to.

CLOCHET   Oh, the way I feel, even if they were martyrs I wouldn't mind. I like the work for itself. (*to the* TROOPERS) Take them to the tables.

CANORIS   One moment. If we accept, how do we know that you'll let us live?

LANDRIEU   You have my word.

CANORIS   Yes. Well, I suppose that'll have to do. It's heads or tails. What will you do with us?

LANDRIEU   I'll turn you over to the German authorities.

CANORIS   Who will have us shot.

LANDRIEU   No. I'll explain your case.

CANORIS   Good. (*a pause*) I'm disposed to talk, with my comrades' permission of course.

HENRI   Canoris!

CANORIS   Can I be alone with them? I think I can convince them.

LANDRIEU   (*looking at him searchingly*) Why do you want to talk now? Are you afraid to die?

(*A long silence. Then* CANORIS *bows his head*)

CANORIS   Yes.

LUCIE   Coward!

LANDRIEU   Very well. (*to the* TROOPERS) You stand by the window. And you guard the door. Come along, men. (*to* CANORIS) You have a quarter of an hour to make up your mind. (LANDRIEU, PELLERIN, *and* CLOCHET *leave by the rear door*)

(*During the whole first part of the scene that follows,* LUCIE *remains silent and apparently uninterested in the discussion*)

CANORIS   (*goes to the window and then comes back. He speaks in low, vibrant tones*) The sun is overcast. It is going to rain. Are you out of your senses? You look at me as if I really intended to turn in our leader. I simply mean to send them to the Servaz cave, as Jean told us to do. (*A pause. He smiles*) They've damaged us a little, but we can still be very useful. (*a pause*) Come on. We have to talk. We can't squander three lives. (*A pause. Gently*) Why are you so bent on dying? What good will it do? Answer me! What good will it do?

HENRI   No good.

CANORIS   Well, then?

HENRI   I'm tired.

CANORIS   Not as tired as I am. I'm fifteen years older than you, and they've been rough on me. The life they'll leave me is nothing to be desired.

HENRI   (*gently*) Are you so afraid of dying?

CANORIS   I'm not afraid. I lied to them just now; I'm not afraid. But we have no right to die for nothing.

HENRI   And why not? Why not? They broke my wrists, they tore open my flesh: haven't I paid for the right to die? We've won. Why do you ask me to begin life again when I can die at peace with myself?

CANORIS   Because there are comrades who need our help.

HENRI   What comrades? Where?

CANORIS   Everywhere.

HENRI   Oh, you think so! If they spare our lives, they'll send us to the salt mines.

CANORIS   Well, you can always escape.

HENRI   You think you'll escape? You're only a shadow of what you were.

CANORIS   If I can't, then you will.

HENRI   One chance in a hundred.

CANORIS   The chance is worth taking. And even if we don't escape, there'll be other men in the mines: old men who are sick, women who are at the end of their strength. They need us.

HENRI   Listen, when I saw the kid lying on the floor, so pale and white, I thought: all right, I've done what I've done and I regret nothing. But of course I was sure that I'd be shot at dawn. If I hadn't thought that six hours later I'd be lying on the same dungheap—(*shouting*) I don't want to survive him. I don't want to survive the kid for thirty years. Canoris, it will be so easy; we won't even have time to look at the muzzles of their guns.

CANORIS   We have no right to die for nothing.

HENRI   Can you still see sense in living when there are men who beat you until they break your bones? It is so dark now. (*He looks out of the window*) You're right, it is going to rain.

CANORIS   The sky is completely overcast. It will be a good shower.

HENRI   (*abruptly*)   It was out of pride.

CANORIS   What?

HENRI   The kid. I think I killed him out of pride.

CANORIS   Why dwell on that? He had to die.

HENRI   I'll drag that doubt around like a ball and chain. Every minute of my life I'll suspect myself. (*a pause*) I can't do it. I can't live.

CANORIS   What heroics! You'll have more than enough to keep you busy helping others; you'll forget yourself. You're too concerned with yourself, Henri; you want to redeem your life. Hell, what you need to do is work, and you'll be saving your life into the bargain. (*a pause*) Look here, Henri, if you die today, the picture will be completed; then you'll really have killed him out of pride, it will be settled forever. But if you live—

HENRI   Then what?

CANORIS   Then nothing will be settled. It's by your whole life that your individual acts will be judged. (*a pause*) If you let yourself be shot while there's still work for you to do, nothing will be more senseless than your death. (*a pause*) Shall I call them?

HENRI   (*pointing to* LUCIE)   Let her decide.

CANORIS   Do you hear, Lucie?

LUCIE   Decide what? Oh yes. Well, it's all settled: tell them that we won't talk and let them make it quick.

CANORIS   What about the comrades, Lucie?

LUCIE   I have no comrades now. (*She goes up to the* TROOPERS) Go get them. We'll tell them nothing.

CANORIS   (*following her, to the* TROOPERS) We still have five minutes. Wait. (*He leads her back to the front of the stage*)

LUCIE   Yes, five minutes. And do you expect to convince me in five minutes?

CANORIS   Yes.

LUCIE   You simple soul! Yes, yes, you can live, your conscience is clear. They've roughed you up a bit, that's all. But me, they've humiliated me so that there's not a morsel of my flesh that's not detestable to me. (*to* HENRI) And you who carry on so because you strangled a boy, have you forgotten that the boy was my brother and that I didn't say a word? I've taken all the guilt on myself; they must get rid of me and all the guilt with me. Go ahead. Live, if you can accept yourselves. But I hate myself and after my death I want it to be as if I had never existed.

HENRI   I won't abandon you, Lucie, and I shall do whatever you decide. (*a pause*)

CANORIS   Then I shall have to save you despite yourselves.

LUCIE   You'll talk?

CANORIS   There's no other way.

LUCIE   (*violently*)   I'll tell them that you're lying, that you made the whole thing up. (*a pause*) If I had known that you would knuckle under I'd never have let you lay a finger on my brother.

CANORIS   Your brother wanted to denounce Jean and I want to send them on a false trail.

LUCIE   It's the same thing. They'll have the same look of triumph in their eyes.

CANORIS   Lucie! So it was out of pride that you let François die?

LUCIE   You are wasting your breath if you think you can make me feel remorse.

A TROOPER   You have two minutes.

CANORIS   Henri!

HENRI   I'll abide by her decision.

CANORIS (*to* LUCIE) What do you care about these men? In six months they'll hole up in some cellar and the first grenade tossed into it will write finish to the whole story. It's all the rest that counts. The world and what you can do in it, our comrades and what you can do for them.

LUCIE I've been wrung dry. I feel entirely alone. I can think only of myself.

CANORIS (*gently*) You really would miss nothing on earth?

LUCIE Nothing. Everything is spoiled.

CANORIS Well—(*A gesture of resignation. He takes a step toward the* TROOPERS. *The rain begins to fall; first light and scanty, then a heavy downpour*)

LUCIE (*sharply*) What's that? (*in low, slow tones*) The rain. (*She goes to the window and watches the downpour. A pause*) It's three months since I heard the sound of rain. (*a pause*) My God, all these past days the weather has been perfect; it was horrible. I couldn't remember what bad weather is like, I thought we should always have to live under the sun. (*a pause*) It's coming down hard, it's going to smell like wet grass. (*Her lips tremble*) I don't want to—I don't want to—(HENRI *and* CANORIS *come close to her*)

HENRI Lucie!

LUCIE I don't want to cry, I'll become silly. (HENRI *takes her in his arms*) Let me go! (*shouting*) I loved life, I loved life! (*She sobs on* HENRI's *shoulder*)

TROOPER (*approaching*) Well? Time's up.

CANORIS (*after a glance at* LUCIE) Go tell your superiors that we'll talk.

(*The* TROOPER *goes out. A pause*)

LUCIE (*collecting herself*) Is it true? Are we going to live? I was already on the other side. Look at me. Smile at me. It's so long since I've seen anyone smile. Have we done right, Canoris? Have we really done right?

CANORIS We're doing what is right. We must live.

(LANDRIEU, PELLERIN, CLOCHET *enter*)

LANDRIEU Well?

CANORIS On the road to Grenoble, at the forty-second boundary-mark, take the path to your right. Fifty or sixty yards in the woods, you'll find a thicket and behind the thicket a cave. Our leader is hidden there with arms.

LANDRIEU (*to the* TROOPER) Ten men. Send them off immediately. Try to bring him back alive. (*a pause*) Take the prisoners back upstairs.

(*The* TROOPERS *hustle the prisoners out.* CLOCHET, *after a moment's hesitation, slips out after them*)

PELLERIN Do you think they told us the truth?

LANDRIEU Of course. They're fools. (*He sits behind the desk*) Well, we've finally had them. You saw their exit? They were less cocky than when they came in. (CLOCHET *enters*) (*amiably*) Well, Clochet, we've had them, haven't we?

CLOCHET (*rubbing his hands nervously*) Yes, yes, we've had them.

PELLERIN (*to* LANDRIEU) Are you going to let them live?

LANDRIEU Oh, for the present anyway. (*a volley outside*) What's that? (CLOCHET *laughs nervously, hiding his face with his hand*) Clochet, you didn't—

(CLOCHET *nods in the affirmative and keeps on laughing*)

CLOCHET I thought it would be more human.

LANDRIEU You bastard! (*A second volley. He runs to the window*)

PELLERIN Let it go now; never two without three.

LANDRIEU I don't want—

PELLERIN Could any of us face the one survivor?

CLOCHET In another minute no one will ever again think of all this. No one but us.

(*A third volley.* LANDRIEU *collapses in his chair*)

LANDRIEU Damn!

(CLOCHET *goes to the radio and turns it on. Music*)

Jean Genêt

1910-

A NOTE ON THEATRE

So you need a foreword. But what is there to say about a play from which I felt detached even before it was finished? To speak of its composition would be to evoke a world and climate without grandeur. But I would rather say a few words about the theatre in general. I dislike it. One will gather as much from reading this play. What I have been told about Japanese, Chinese, and Balinese revels and the perhaps magnified idea that persists in my brain make the formula of the Western theatre seem to me too coarse. One can only dream of an art that would be a profound web of active symbols capable of speaking to the audience a language in which nothing is said but everything portended.

But any poet who tried to realize this dream would see the haughty stupidity of actors and theatre people rise up in arms. If, on occasion, their boorishness does subside, then lack of culture and shallowness become evident. Nothing can be expected of a profession that is practiced with so little gravity or self-communion. Its starting-point, its reason for being, is exhibitionism. One can elaborate an ethic or an aesthetic on the basis of any aberrant attitude. But to do so requires courage and renunciation, and the failing that makes for the choice of the actor's trade is governed by an awareness of the world that is not despairing but complacent. The Western actor does not seek to become a sign charged with signs. He merely wishes to identify himself with a character in a drama or comedy. The world of today, a tired world, incapable of living by acts, likewise draws him into this vulgarity by requiring him to enact in its stead not heroic themes but dream characters. What, then, will be the *ethos* of these people? If they do not vegetate in intellectual, but bitter squalor, they go in for stardom. Look at them vying for the first page of a newspaper. It is therefore necessary both to establish, rather than a conservatory, a kind of seminary and then, with that as a basis, to build theatrical constructs, with the texts, sets, and gesticulations that these should imply. For even the finest Western plays have something shoddy about them, an air of masquerade and not of ceremony. The spectacle that unfolds on the stage is always puerile. Beauty of language sometimes deceives us as to depth of theme. In the theatre, all takes place in the visible world and nowhere else.

My play, which was commissioned by an actor famous in his day,[1] was written out of vanity, but in boredom. Nevertheless—I am speaking of the making of it—already disturbed by the dismal bleakness of a theatre that reflects the visible world too exactly, the actions of men and not of Gods, I attempted to effect a displacement that, in permitting a declamatory tone, would bring theatre into the theatre. I hope thereby to do away with characters—which stand up, usually, only by virtue of psychological convention—to the advantage of signs as remote as possible from what they are meant first to signify, though nevertheless attached to them in order, by this sole link, to unite the author with the spectator, in short, so to contrive that the characters on the stage would be only the metaphors of what they were supposed to represent. In order to

"A Note on Theatre" by Jean Genêt, translated by Bernard Frechtman. Reprinted with the permission of Dr. Suzanne Czech, the author's agent, and *The Tulane Drama Review.*

[1] Louis Jouvet—*Translator's note.*

carry through this undertaking with some measure of success, I had, of course, to invent a tone of voice, a gait, a gesticulation. The result is a failure, I therefore accuse myself of having abandoned myself uncourageously to an undertaking without risks or perils. I repeat, however, that I was impelled to do this by that universe of the theatre which is satisfied with approximation. For the most part, the work of actors is based on the teaching dispensed in official conservatories. Those who have dared innovations have been inspired by the Orient. Unfortunately, they operate the way society women practice yoga. The manners, way of life, and environment of poets are often depressingly frivolous, but what is to be said about those of theatre people? If a poet discovers a great theme and starts developing it, he must, in order to complete it, imagine it being performed; but if he brings to his work the rigor, patience, study, and gravity with which one approaches a poem, if he discovers major themes and profound symbols, what actors can express them? Theatre people live in a state of self-dispersion rather than self-communion. Are they to be accused? Probably their profession foists itself upon them in this facile form because, before the eyes of a smug and slightly jealous public, they cut a figure both in a short but safe life and in a mechanical apotheosis. Marionettes would, I know, do better. They are already being considered. However, it may well be that the theatrical formula for which I am calling, an entirely allusive one, and allusive only, is a personal taste of mine. It may be that I am using this letter merely to vent my spleen.

On a stage not unlike our own, on a platform, the problem was to reconstitute the end of a meal. On the basis of this one particular which is now barely perceptible in it, the loftiest modern drama has been expressed daily for two thousand years in the sacrifice of the Mass. The point of departure disappears beneath the profusion of ornaments and symbols that still overwhelm us. Beneath the most familiar of appearances—a crust of bread— a god is devoured. I know nothing more theatrically effective than the elevation of the host: when finally this appearance appears before us—but in what form, since all heads are bowed, the priest alone knows; perhaps it is God himself or a simple white pellet that he holds at the tips of his four fingers—or that other moment in the Mass when the priest, having broken the host on the paten in order to show it to the faithful (Not to the audience! To the faithful? But their heads are still bowed. Does that mean they are praying, they too?)

puts it together again and eats it. The host crackles in the priest's mouth! A performance that does not act upon my soul is vain. It is vain if I do not believe in what I see, which will end—which will never have been—when the curtain goes down. No doubt one of the functions of art is to substitute the efficacy of beauty for religious faith. At least, this beauty should have the power of a poem, that is, of a crime. But let that go.

I have spoken of communion. The modern theatre is a diversion. It is sometimes, rarely, an estimable diversion. The word somewhat suggests the idea of dispersion. I know no plays that link the spectators, be it only for an hour. Quite the contrary, they isolate them further. Sartre once told me, however, of having experienced this religious fervor during a theatrical performance: in a prison camp, at Christmas time, a group of soldiers, mediocre actors, had staged a French play evoking some theme I no longer recall—revolt or captivity or courage—and the far-away homeland was suddenly present, not on the stage, but in the hall. A clandestine theatre, to which one would go in secret, at night, and masked, a theatre in the catacombs, may still be possible. It would be sufficient to discover—or create—the common Enemy, then the Homeland which is to be protected or regained. I do not know what the theatre will be like in a socialist world; I can understand better what it could be among the Mau Mau, but in the Western world, which is increasingly marked by death and turned toward it, it can only refine in the "reflecting" of a comedy of comedy, of a reflection of reflection which ceremonious performance might render exquisite and close to invisibility. If one has chosen to watch oneself die charmingly, one must rigorously pursue, and array, the funeral symbols. Or must choose to live and discover the Enemy. For me, the Enemy will never be anywhere. Nor will there ever be a Homeland, whether abstract or interior. If I am stirred, it will be by the nostalgic reminder of what it was. Only a theatre of shadows could still move me. A young writer once told me of having seen five or six youngsters playing war in a park. They were divided into two troops and were preparing to attack. Night, they said, was coming on. But it was noon in the sky. They therefore decided that one of them would be Night. The youngest and frailest, having become elemental, was then the Master of the Fray. "He" was the Hour, the Moment, the Ineluctable. He approached, it seems, from far off, with the calmness of a cycle, though weighed down with the sadness and pomp of twilight. As he drew near, the others, the Men, grew nervous and uneasy . . . But the child was arriving too soon to please them. He was coming before his time. By common consent the Troops and the Chiefs decided to eliminate Night, who again became a soldier on one of the sides . . . It is on the basis of this formula alone that a theatre can thrill me.

Translated by Bernard Frechtman

DEATHWATCH

Translated by Bernard Frechtman

CAST OF CHARACTERS

GREEN EYES, *22 years old*
(*his feet chained*)
MAURICE, *17 years old*
LEFRANC, *23 years old*
THE GUARD

SETTING *A prison cell. The walls of the cell are of hewn stone and should give the impression that the architecture of the prison is very complicated. Rear, a barred transom, the spikes of which turn inward. The bed is a block of granite on which a few blankets are heaped. Right, a barred door.*

SOME DIRECTIONS *The entire play unfolds as in a dream. The set and costumes (striped homespun) should be in violent colors. Use whites and very hard blacks, clashing with each other. The movements of the actors should be either heavy or else extremely and incomprehensibly rapid, like flashes of lightning. If they can, the actors should deaden the timbre of their voices. Avoid clever lighting. As much light as possible. The text is given in the ordinary language of conversation and is correctly spelled, but the actors should recite it with the characteristic deformations that go with the accent of the slums. The actors walk silently, on felt soles. Maurice is barefoot.*
Whenever Maurice utters the name Green Eyes, he drawls it.

(*When the curtain rises,* GREEN EYES *is holding* LEFRANC *and pulling him gently back so as to*

Deathwatch by Jean Genêt, translated by Bernard Frechtman, is from *The Maids and Deathwatch*, published by Grove Press, Inc. Copyright © 1954 by Bernard Frechtman.

get him away from MAURICE *who is somewhat frightened and straightening his clothes*)

GREEN EYES (*softly*) You're crazy. You're a pair of lunatics. I'll calm both of you with a single smack. I'll lay you both out on the cement. (*to* LEFRANC) Another second and Maurice would have got it. Watch out with your hands, Georgie. Stop the big act, and stop talking about the Negro.

LEFRANC (*violently*) It's him. . . .

GREEN EYES It's you. (*He hands him a sheet of paper*) Go on reading.

LEFRANC Let him keep his mouth shut.

GREEN EYES You shut up, Georgie. Cut the comedy. I don't want to hear any more about Snowball. Neither he nor the guys in his cell bother about us. (*He listens*) Visiting hours have begun. It'll be my turn in ten minutes or so.

(*During the following scene he keeps walking up and down without stopping*)

MAURICE (*pointing to* LEFRANC) He's always trying to make trouble. There'll never be any peace with him around. For him, no one matters. There's only Snowball.

LEFRANC (*violently*) Yes, Snowball. He's the one. He's got what it takes. Don't play around with him. He's a Negro, a savage . . .

MAURICE Nobody . . .

LEFRANC He's a savage, a Negro, but he shoots lightning. Green Eyes . . .

MAURICE What?

LEFRANC (*to* GREEN EYES) Green Eyes, Snowball's got it all over you.

MAURICE You starting again? It's because this morning, on the way up from recreation, he smiled at you in the hall.

LEFRANC At me? That sure would surprise me.

(GREEN EYES *turns around, stops and stares first at* LEFRANC *and then at* MAURICE)

MAURICE There were just the three of us. If it wasn't at the guard, it was at one of us.

LEFRANC When was it?

MAURICE Ah ha? So you're interested? Just before we got to the middle circle. Oh! (*a faint smile*) Just a little wisp of a smile. He was winded from the four flights.

LEFRANC And what do you make of it?

MAURICE That you're the one who causes all the trouble in this cell.

LEFRANC Maybe. But just let Snowball let out a roar and you guys vanish. He outclasses everyone. No one can get him down, no convict can outshine him. He's a real bruiser and he's been around.

MAURICE Who's denying it? He's a good-looking kid. As handsome as they come. Snowball's a well-built guy. If you like, he's a Green Eyes with a coat of shoe polish, Green Eyes with a smoke-screen, Green Eyes covered with mud, Green Eyes in the dark . . .

LEFRANC And Green Eyes isn't in the same class. You want me to tell you about Snowball?

MAURICE And what about the way Green Eyes answered the inspector?

LEFRANC Snowball? He's exotic. All the guys in his cell feel it. And in the cells around too, and the whole prison and all the prisons in France. He shines. He beams. He's black but he lights up all two thousand cells. No one'll ever get him down. He's the real boss of the prison. All you've got to do is see him walk. . . .

MAURICE If Green Eyes wanted . . .

LEFRANC You haven't really watched the two of them! Just to see him, the way he goes through the halls, miles and miles of halls, with his chains. And what happens? His chains carry him. Snowball's a king. Maybe he comes from the desert, but he comes with his head up! And his crimes! Compared to them, those of Green Eyes . . .

GREEN EYES (*stopping, a gentle look on his face*) That'll do, Georgie. I'm not trying to pass myself off as a king. In prison, no one's a monarch, Snowball no more than the next guy. Don't think I'm taken in by him. His crimes may be just a lot of hot air!

LEFRANC Hot air!

MAURICE (*to* LEFRANC) Don't interrupt him. (*listening at the door*) It's getting close to visiting hours. The guards are at 38.

(*He strides about the cell clockwise*)

GREEN EYES Hot air. I don't know anything about his crimes. . . .

LEFRANC The attack on the gold-train. . . .

GREEN EYES (*still curtly*) I don't know anything about them. I've got my own.

MAURICE Your own? You've got only one.

GREEN EYES If I say "my crimes," it's because I know what I'm saying. I say "my crimes." And don't let anyone open his mouth about them or I might get tough. Better not let me get worked up. All I'm asking you is one thing, and that's to read me my girl's letter.

LEFRANC I've read it.

GREEN EYES What else does she say?

LEFRANC Nothing. I've read it all!

GREEN EYES (*He points to a passage in the letter*) All right, you read it all. But what about that? You didn't read that.

LEFRANC Don't you believe me?

GREEN EYES (*stubbornly*) But what about that?

LEFRANC What "that"? Tell me what it is.

GREEN EYES Georgie, you're taking advantage because I'm illiterate.

LEFRANC If you don't trust me, take it back. And don't ever expect me to read you your girl's letters again.

GREEN EYES Georgie, you're defying me and there's going to be trouble. Look out, or somebody in this cell's going to be taken for a joyride.

LEFRANC You make me sick, Green Eyes. I'm telling you straight—I read it all. But I know, you don't trust me any more. Maybe you think I'm giving you the runaround. Don't listen to what Maurice says. He's egging us on.

MAURICE (*banteringly*) Me? The most peaceful kid. . . .

GREEN EYES (*to* LEFRANC) You're pulling a fast one on me.

LEFRANC Then go write your own letters!

GREEN EYES You bastard.

MAURICE (*gently*) Oh, Green Eyes, stop making a fuss. You'll see your gal again. You're too good-looking a guy. You've got her in the palm of your hand. Where do you expect her to go?

GREEN EYES (*after a long silence, gently, almost regretfully*) You bastard.

MAURICE Don't get worked up. That's how Georgie is. He likes mystery and he's impressed by you.

LEFRANC All right, I'll tell you what there was in the letter. If you see your girl in the visiting-room later, ask her the truth. You want me to read? (GREEN EYES *neither answers nor moves*) Listen, your girl has caught on that you're not the one who's been writing. Now she assumes you can't read or write.

MAURICE If Green Eyes can treat himself to a writer, that's his business.

LEFRANC You want me to read? (*He reads*)

"Darling, I realized it couldn't have been you who wrote those nice phrases, but I'd rather have you write yourself as best you can. . . ."

GREEN EYES You bastard!

LEFRANC Are you accusing me?

GREEN EYES You bastard! So that's it! She's getting ready to pull out on me. And you, you fixed it so she'd think the letters came from you.

LEFRANC You're crazy. I've always written what you told me.

MAURICE (to LEFRANC) Smart as you are, Green Eyes can still let you have it. The gentleman was working in secret.

LEFRANC Stop making things worse, Maurice. I didn't try to humiliate him.

GREEN EYES Humiliate me? Stop kidding yourself. Don't think you humiliate me either when you claim that the nigger's a more dangerous guy. When it comes to niggers, I . . . (He makes an obscene gesture) and tell me, what kept you from reading? Answer. It's because you're making a play for my girl. Admit it. Because when you get out of here, in three days, you're planning to join her.

LEFRANC Listen, Green Eyes, you won't believe me. It was so as not to upset you. I'd have told you, but (He points to MAURICE) not in front of him.

GREEN EYES Why?

MAURICE Me? You should have said so. If I bother you, I can still vanish into the fog. I'm the kid who slips through walls. Everyone knows that. No, no, Georgie, no, you're handing us a line. Admit that you wanted his girl and we'll believe you.

LEFRANC (violently) Maurice, don't start complicating things again. It's on account of you and your nasty little tricks that everything's been going wrong. You're worse than a devil.

MAURICE O.K., you're bigger than me, go on, take it out on me, you've been picking fights for the past week. But you're wasting your time. I'll take care of defending my friendship with Green Eyes.

LEFRANC You're the ones. It's you who're against me. You don't let me live any more.

MAURICE Just now when you grabbed me by the collar, you wanted to flatten me out on the cement. I felt myself turning purple. If it hadn't been for Green Eyes, I'd have got it. It's to him, to Green Eyes, that I owe my life. It's a good thing you're getting out. We'll have some peace.

LEFRANC Enough of that, Maurice.

MAURICE You see? You see, Georgie? I can't say a word. You'd like to make monkeys of both of us. Not on your life, Georgie Lefranc.

LEFRANC There's no danger in your calling me George.

MAURICE He's used to calling you George. You ought to let us know instead of getting riled. You're trying to make monkeys of us.

LEFRANC I do what I've got to do.

MAURICE To who? Us two, we're staying locked up, and what you've got to do is respect us. But it looks as if you were plotting something. All by yourself. Because you are all by yourself, and don't forget it.

LEFRANC And what about you? What are you after with those gestures of yours? In front of him. And in front of the guards. You may try to get around them, but you won't get anywhere with me. If you got out of it before, it was on account of the faces you made. That's what saved you, more than Green Eyes. I took pity on you. But you'll get yours. And before I leave here.

MAURICE Come on, Georgie, get tough. Come on, right now, while I'm looking at you. Just now you tried to kill me, but there are nights when you slip me your blankets, too. I noticed it a long time ago. And so did Green Eyes. It was another opportunity for us to get a laugh out of you.

LEFRANC There's a lot you don't know about me if you think I was ready to sacrifice myself, especially for your carcass.

MAURICE You think I need kindness? You want to be kind to me? And you think you'll disgust me any the less? Good thing you're leaving the cell in three days.

LEFRANC Don't count on it too much, Maurice. You're the one who'll be leaving. Before you came, everything was fine. Green Eyes and I got along like two men. I didn't talk about him as if he were a young bride.

MAURICE You disgust me! (MAURICE flicks his head as if tossing back from his forehead an exasperating lock of hair)

LEFRANC Stop doing that! I can't bear the sight of you any more! Even your twitching gets on my nerves. I don't want to take it away with me when I get out of here.

MAURICE What if I won't stop? You resent me because I haven't been in prison long. You'd have got a kick out of seeing my hair fall from the clippers, wouldn't you?

LEFRANC Shut it, Maurice!

MAURICE You'd have loved to see me sitting on the stool with my curls falling on my shoulders, on my lap, on the floor. You'd have loved it, wouldn't you? You even love to hear me talk about it, you love to see me in a temper. You get a real kick out of my suffering.

LEFRANC I'd fed up being between you, watching your gestures pass through me when you talk to each other. I'm fed up with the sight of your little mugs. I know all about your winks. You exhaust me. It's not enough to be dying of hunger, to be without any strength, shut up in four walls. We've got to kill each other off besides.

MAURICE Are you trying to make me feel sorry for you by reminding me that you give me half your bread? And half your grub? You can keep them. It was too much of a strain to swallow the stuff. The mere fact that it came from you was enough to disgust me.

LEFRANC That's probably why you slipped some of it to Green Eyes every now and then.

MAURICE You'd have liked him to die of hunger.

LEFRANC I don't give a damn. Divvy it up if you like. I'm big enough to feed the whole cell.

MAURICE You can keep your grub, you poor martyr. I can still give half of mine to Green Eyes.

LEFRANC Fine. I'm glad you're building up his strength. But don't try to keep up with me. I'm way out in front.

MAURICE (*ironically*) On the galley?

LEFRANC Repeat that.

MAURICE I said: on the galley.

LEFRANC You trying to needle me? You want to push me to the limit, Maurice? You want me to let you have it again?

MAURICE No one's saying anything against you. You started by talking about the marks on your wrists. . . .

LEFRANC And on my ankles! That's right, Maurice. On my wrists and ankles. And I've got a right to talk. And you, to shut up. (*He screams*) Yes, I've got a right to! I've got a right to talk about it. For three hundred years I've borne the marks of a galley-slave, and it's going to end in trouble! You hear me? I can become a cyclone and tear you apart! And wipe up the cell! Your smiles and sweetness are killing me. One of us two is going to clear out. You hear me Maurice, you wear me out, yes, you and your fine murderer.

MAURICE You see? You're accusing him again. You accuse him any way you can so as to try to cover up your own treachery. But we know you tried to steal his girl. The way you get up at night to steal tobacco. If we offer you any during the day, you refuse. So as to be able to swipe it by moonlight. His girl! You've had your eye on her for a long time.

LEFRANC You'd like me to say I have, wouldn't you? It'd make you happy? You'd enjoy seeing me separated from Green Eyes? All right, I have. You guessed it, Maurice, I have. I've been doing all I can for a long time to get her to drop him.

MAURICE You bastard!

LEFRANC I've been trying to get him away from her for a long time. I don't give a damn about his girl. You understand? Not a God damn. I wanted Green Eyes to be all alone. Solo, like he says. But it's a tough job. The guy bears up. He stands his ground. Maybe I botched it this time, but I refuse to admit I'm licked.

MAURICE What do you want to do with him? Where are you trying to lead him? (*to* GREEN EYES) Green Eyes, you hear him?

LEFRANC None of your business. It's between us two. I'll keep at it even if I have to change cells. And even if I leave prison.

MAURICE Green Eyes!

LEFRANC And I'll tell you something else—you're jealous. You can't stand the fact that I'm the one who writes to his girl. I've got too good a job. An important post—I'm the post-office. And it drives you wild!

MAURICE (*teeth clenched*) It's not true.

LEFRANC Not true? If only you could hear yourself say it! You've got tears in your eyes. Whenever I sat down at the table, when I took a sheet of paper, when I opened the inkwell, you couldn't keep still. It's not true? You were all hopped up, there was no holding you. And when I was writing? You should have watched yourself. And when I re-read the letter? You didn't hear your snickers, you didn't see the way your eyes were blinking.

MAURICE You wrote to her as if you were writing to your own girl! You poured out your heart on the paper!

LEFRANC But it was you who suffered! And you're still suffering! You're getting ready to cry! I'm making you cry with shame and fury! And I'm not done yet! Wait till he comes back from the visting-room! He'll come back all beaming because he saw his girl.

MAURICE It's not true!

LEFRANC You think so! His girl couldn't forget him that easily. People don't forget Green Eyes! He's too soft to leave her. Can't you just see him, eh? He's glued to the grate of the visiting-room. His life's starting all over. . . .

MAURICE You bastard!

LEFRANC   Don't you realize that you don't count? That he's the man! At this moment he's clinging to the grate. Look at him. He's stepping back so his girl can see him better! Just look at him!

MAURICE   Jealous! You're jealous! You'd have liked them to talk about you all over France the way they talked about Green Eyes. It was wonderful. You know how wonderful it was when they couldn't find the corpse. The farmers were all out looking for it. The cops, the dogs! They drained wells, ponds. It was a real revolution. The whole world was out looking! Priests, well-diggers! And later, when they found the corpse! The earth, the whole earth was scented with it. And what about Green Eyes' hands? His blood-stained hands, when he pushed aside the window curtain? And when he shook her hair that was full of lilacs. The way he told us.

GREEN EYES   (stupefied)   Blood, Maurice? Jesus!

MAURICE   What'd you say?

GREEN EYES   Not blood, lilacs. (He moves forward threateningly)

MAURICE   What lilacs?

GREEN EYES   Between her teeth! In her hair. And it's only now that you tell me! (He slaps MAURICE) But not a single cop told me. I should have thought of it, and it's just my luck to think of it too late. (to MAURICE) And it's your fault, you rat. You should have been there. You were supposed to be there so as to warn me, but you managed things so as to do it when it was all over, when I'm locked up, face to face with my regrets. You should have been exact, but you were probably busy with my girl.

MAURICE   Green Eyes. . . .

GREEN EYES   I'm sick of all of you. You don't mean a thing any more. In a month I'll be getting the axe. My head'll be on one side of the block and my body on the other. I'm a terror, a holy terror! And I can demolish you. If you like my girl, go take her. I knew it. You've been circling around me for a long time, circling around, circling around, circling around, you've been trying to find a spot to land on, without even suspecting I might bash your head in.

MAURICE   (listening at the door)   Green Eyes . . . it can all still work out. All you've got to do is just show yourself and you'll get her back. Listen! Listen! They're at 34.

GREEN EYES   No, let her begin a new life. She's right. I'll do like her. Starting here and ending on the other side of the water. If I get there! Only, she's going to tell me about it in a little while, without making any bones about it. She's going to let me down cold, without realizing that if she waited another two months she'd be a widow. She could have come and prayed at my grave and brought . . .(He hesitates) . . . flowers. . . .

MAURICE   (tenderly)   Green Eyes. . . .

GREEN EYES   A widow, I say! My little widow!

MAURICE   Green Eyes . . . look, big boy. . . .

GREEN EYES   My widow! And me, I'm a dead man! I probably make you laugh, don't I? She despises me and fate abandons me and I don't bust out in a fit of rage. Now I understand. I'm a rag. A dish-mop! Georgie, you hope I'll start crying, don't you? Or throw a fit? No, I'm sure my girl doesn't interest you.

LEFRANC   She'll come. The visits have only just begun. (He goes to take a jacket hanging from a nail)

MAURICE   That's not your jacket. It's Green Eyes'.

LEFRANC   (putting the jacket back)   You're right. I made a mistake.

MAURICE   That's been happening pretty often. That's the fifth or sixth time you've put on his jacket.

LEFRANC   What's the harm? There are no secrets, they don't have pockets. (a pause) Say, Maurice, are you in charge of Green Eyes' clothes?

MAURICE   (shrugging his shoulders)   That's my business!

GREEN EYES   My little woman! The little bitch! She leaves me all alone in the middle of the desert. You just up and beat it, you fly away!

MAURICE   I swear that if I ever run into her, I'll murder her.

GREEN EYES   Too late. As soon as you lay eyes on her, you'll say good-bye to Green Eyes.

MAURICE   Never!

GREEN EYES   Never say never. I know all about friends who swear they'll do things for you. You musn't even touch her. She's just a poor kid. She needs a man, a real one, and I'm already a ghost. I should have known how to write. I ought to have made fine phrases. But I'm a fine phrase.

MAURICE   So you're forgiving her?

GREEN EYES   She doesn't deserve it, but what can I do?

MAURICE   Bump her off. She ought to be bumped off. We've got guts in this cell.

GREEN EYES   You make me laugh, both of you. Don't you see my situation? Can't you see that here we concoct stories that can live only within four walls? And that I'll never again see the sunlight? You take me for a damned fool? Don't you know who I am? Don't you realize that the grave is open at my feet? In a month I'll be up before the judges. In a month they'll decide that I've got to have my head cut off! My head cut off, gentlemen! I'm no longer alive! I'm all alone now! All alone! Alone. Solo. I can die quiet. I've stopped beaming. I'm frozen.

MAURICE I'm with you.

GREEN EYES Frozen! You can get down on your knees before Snowball. You're right. The Number One Big Shot is Snowball. The Big Shot! Go kiss his toes, go on. He's got the luck to be a savage. He's got a right to kill people and even eat them. He lives in the jungle. That's his advantage over me. He's got his pet panthers. I'm alone, all alone. And too white. Too wilted by the cell. Too pale. Too wilted. But if you'd seen me before, with my hands in my pockets, and with my flowers, always with a flower between my teeth! They used to call me. . . . Would you like to know? It was a nice nickname: Paulo with the flowery teeth! And now? I'm all alone. And my girl's deserting me. (*to* MAURICE) Would you have liked my girl?

MAURICE She did sort of give me a jolt, I admit. Just seeing her through you drives me almost nuts.

GREEN EYES (*bitterly*) I make a nice couple, eh? Does it get you excited?

MAURICE That's not what I mean. Maybe she doesn't have your mug, but I see her all the same. You'll have a hard time shaking her off. That's why you've got to get revenge. Show me her portrait.

GREEN EYES You see it every morning when I wash.

MAURICE Show it to me again. One last time.

GREEN EYES (*He opens his shirt brutally and reveals his torso to* MAURICE. *On it is tattooed a woman's face*) You like her?

MAURICE She's a beauty! Too bad I can't spit in her face. And that, what's that? (*He points to a spot on* GREEN EYES' *chest*) That your girl too?

GREEN EYES Drop it. Forget about her.

MAURICE I'd like to meet her. . . .

GREEN EYES I told you I wanted quiet around here. And fast. You're only too delighted with what's happening to me. It's probably joy that's getting the two of you worked up against her and against me. You're delighted that you're the only ones who can look at her.

MAURICE Don't get sore. It's because we're pals that I'm talking to you about her.

GREEN EYES I understood. All too well. Make yourself scarce.

MAURICE You getting sore at me? I'm capable of going and killing your girl, you know.

LEFRANC I'd like to see your face when blood starts flowing. You've got to have some in your veins first.

MAURICE It's class you've got to have. It's got to be written on your face. My face. . . .

LEFRANC If only you could see yourself! You and Green Eyes are a pair.

MAURICE Oh, Georgie, don't say that, I'll faint. You won't deny that I'm the best-looking kid in the prison. Take a squint at the little man.

(*He makes the gesture, already indicated, of tossing back a lock of hair*)

LEFRANC You louse!

MAURICE With a mug like mine, I can let myself do anything. Even when I'm innocent, people think I'm guilty. I'm pretty good-looking. It's faces like mine that certain people would like to cut out of the newspapers. Eh, Georgie, for your collection? The gals would go nuts about it. Blood would flow. And tears. All the little guys would feel like playing cutthroat. It would be a holiday. There'd be dancing in the streets. A carnival for murderers.

LEFRANC You louse!

MAURICE Afterwards, the only thing left for me to do would be to turn into a rose and be plucked! But you, you'll never be able to do anything as fine as that. Anybody can see that from looking at you. You're not meant for that kind of thing. I'm not saying that you're innocent, and I'm not saying that as a crook you're worthless, but when it comes to crime, that's another matter.

LEFRANC What do you know about it?

MAURICE I know everything. I've been accepted by all the men, the real ones. I'm still young, but I've got their friendship. They'll never make friends with you, never. You're not our kind. You'll never be. Even if you killed a man. No, we fascinate you.

LEFRANC It's Green Eyes who fascinates you! You're obsessed by him!

MAURICE That's a lie! Maybe I don't help him the way I'd like to help him, but you, you'd like him to help you.

LEFRANC Help me what?

MAURICE What? You want me to tell you? Remember the look on your face when the guard found all the photos in your mattress.

What were you doing with them? What use were they to you? You had them all! All of them! Photos of Soklay, of Weidmann, of Vaché, of Angel Sun and God knows who else. I don't know them by heart. What were you doing with them? Were you saying mass to them? Were you praying to them? Eh, Georgie? At night, in your mattress, what were you doing, embalming them?

GREEN EYES   Stop arguing. If you're anxious to bump off my girl, draw lots.

LEFRANC AND MAURICE (*together*)   Why? It's not necessary!

GREEN EYES   Draw lots. I'm still master. The lots will pick the instrument, but I'll be at the controls.

LEFRANC   You're joking, Green Eyes.

GREEN EYES   Do I look as if I am? Where do you think you are? But pay close attention to what happens. Be on the look-out. You've made up your minds. You've made up your minds to bump off my girl. You've got to act fast and hurry up and choose so that you stop talking about it. So that you stop talking about it until the one who's picked gets out of jail. Are you ready? Look out. The axe is going to fall. One of you is going to get it in the neck. (*He places his fist on* MAURICE's *shoulder*) Will it be you? Are we going to make a little killer of you?

MAURICE   You're not sore at me any more?

GREEN EYES   Listen to me. We're already groggy because of the lack of air. Don't make me exert myself. I'll explain to both of you. Like a father. I'm saying that you've got to stay wide awake, because moments like that are ghastly. They're ghastly because they're sweet. You follow me? They're too sweet.

LEFRANC   What's too sweet?

GREEN EYES (*his voice getting more and more solemn*)   That's the thing that makes you recognize the catastrophe. Me, I'm no longer on the brink. I'm falling. I no longer risk anything. I've told you. And Green Eyes is going to make you laugh: I'm falling so sweetly, the thing that's making me fall is so nice, that out of politeness I don't dare rebel. The day of the crime . . . are you listening? The day of the crime, it was the same. Are you listening? This concerns you, gentlemen. I say "the day of the crime" and I'm not ashamed! Who is there in the prison, on all the floors, who puts himself on my level? Who that's as young as me, as good-looking as me, has had the kind of tough break that *I've* had? I say "the day of the crime!" That day, more and more until . . .

LEFRANC (*gently*)   . . . until the last gasp.

GREEN EYES   Everything became more and more polite to me. I even claim that in the street a man raised his hat to me.

MAURICE   Green Eyes, calm down.

LEFRANC (*to* GREEN EYES)   Go on. Continue.

MAURICE   No. Stop. He's getting worked up by what you're saying. He's being carried away. (*to* LEFRANC) Yes, you're being carried away. You lap up other people's troubles.

GREEN EYES   Cut it. I'm explaining. He took off his hat. That started it. Then everything . . .

LEFRANC (*implacably*)   Be specific.

GREEN EYES   . . . everything began to move. There was nothing more to be done. And so I just had to kill someone. It's your turn. You're going to bump off my girl. But pay attention. I've prepared everything for you. I'm giving you your chance. I'm leaving for the world of straw hats and palm trees. It's easy to begin a new life, you'll see. I realized it the moment I killed the girl. I saw the danger. You understand me? The danger of finding myself in someone else's boots. And I was scared. I wanted to back up. Stop! No go! I tried hard. I ran right and left. I squirmed. I tried every shape so as not to be a murderer. Tried to be a dog, a cat, a horse, a tiger, a table, a stone! I even tried, me too, to be a rose! Don't laugh. I did what I could. I contorted myself. People thought I had convulsions. I wanted to go backwards in time, to undo what I'd done, to live my life over until before the crime. It looks easy to go backwards—but my body couldn't make it. I tried again. Impossible. The people around me made fun of me. They didn't suspect the danger, until the day they started getting worried. My dance! You should have seen my dance! I danced, boys, I danced!

(*Here the actor will have to invent a kind of dance which shows* GREEN EYES *trying to go backwards in time. He contorts himself silently. He tries a spiral dance, on his own axis. His face expresses great suffering.* MAURICE *and* LEFRANC *watch him attentively*)

GREEN EYES (*dancing*)   And I danced! Dance with me, Maurice. (*He takes him by the waist and dances a few steps with him, but then pushes him away*) Get the hell away! You hop as if you were in a dance hall! (*He goes into his spiral dance again. Finally, he gets winded and stands still*) And I danced! Then they searched. They suspected me. Afterwards, I was on my own. I took the steps that started easing me to the guillotine. Now I'm calm. And it's my job to plan your chance. You're going to draw lots. (*to* LEFRANC) Are you scared?

LEFRANC   Let me alone.

GREEN EYES   You'll get used to it. You've got to take the idea in easy stages. At the beginning, I scared myself. Now I like myself! Don't you like me?

LEFRANC   Let me alone.

MAURICE   (*to* GREEN EYES)   You're flustering him. He's a leaf.

GREEN EYES   Let yourselves drift. Just let yourself drift, Georgie. You'll always find someone to lend a helping hand. Maybe Snowball, if I'm no longer here.

LEFRANC   Let me alone.

GREEN EYES   You breaking down? You don't have the style that Maurice has. I might have liked it to be you.

MAURICE   (*banteringly*)   Murderer.

GREEN EYES   You've got to draw. You've got to draw lots.

MAURICE   And . . . how . . . with what . . . you, how did you do it?

GREEN EYES   That was different. It was fatality that took the form of my hands. The fair thing would be to cut *them* off instead of my neck. And for me everything became simpler. The girl was already under me. All I had to do was put one hand delicately on her mouth and the other delicately on her neck. It was over. But you . . .

MAURICE   Tell me how it's done.

LEFRANC   You louse!

MAURICE   Tell me how it's done. Be specific. When it was finished, what did you do?

GREEN EYES   Well, I told you. It all happened differently. First, I took the girl to my room. No one saw her going up. She wanted my lilacs.

MAURICE   What?

GREEN EYES   I had a bunch of lilacs between my teeth. The girl followed me. She was magnetized . . . I'm telling you everything, but let it guide you. Then . . . then she wanted to scream because I was hurting her. I choked her. I thought that once she was dead I'd be able to bring her back to life.

MAURICE   And then what?

GREEN EYES   Then? Well! There was the door! (*He points to the right side of the cell and touches the wall*) Impossible to get the body out. It took up too much room. And it was soft. First, I went to the window, in order to look outside. I didn't dare go out. I thought I saw a terrific crowd of people in the street. I thought they were waiting for me to show myself at the window. I moved the curtains aside a little. . . . (MAURICE *makes a gesture*) What?

MAURICE   The lilacs? Did you leave them in her hair?

GREEN EYES   (*sadly*)   It's now that you warn me.

MAURICE   Oh, Green Eyes, I didn't know. I'd have wanted to save you. I swear to you, I'd have wanted to be there, I'd have wanted to help you. . . .

GREEN EYES   Keep still. You forget that I was observing you. You've had a crush on her ever since the first day, since the morning you saw me bare-chested in the shower. I realized it when we got back. All your playing up to me was for her. Am I wrong? When you looked at me, it was just to find out how she was built and to imagine how our bodies fitted together. And because I can't read or write you take me for a cripple! But I've got eyes! Am I wrong? (MAURICE *pulls a long face, like a child who has been beaten*) Speak up, I'm not a bully. Am I wrong? Don't try to kid me. You destroyed me. You were in cahoots with God. Lilacs! A whole little bunch in her hair, and no one to warn me. And now? What am I to do? (*He looks at* LEFRANC) Eh? What am I to do?

MAURICE   (*to* GREEN EYES)   Don't ask him anything. Don't ask him any more. Can't you see the silly look on his puss? He's lapping you up. He's gulping you down.

GREEN EYES   Tell me what I'm to do?

MAURICE   Just look at that puss of his. He's happy. Everything you say to him sinks right into his skin. You enter him through his skin and you don't know how you're going to get out. Let him alone.

LEFRANC   I bother you.

MAURICE   (*to* LEFRANC)   You want to get him down. You want to weaken him.

GREEN EYES   (*sadly*)   Listen, I tell you it's so sad that I wish it were night so I could try to cling to my heart. I'd like—I'm not ashamed to say it—I'd like, I'd like, I'd like, I'd like to . . . to cuddle up in my arms.

MAURICE   Calm down, control yourself.

GREEN EYES   (*still sadly*)   And now you think I'm washed up. Green Eyes is completely gone to pot. You can get a close-up view of the big desperado. Touch me, you can touch me. (*suddenly violent*) But don't count on it! It may not take much to make me bounce back and lay you out flat! Better be on guard, all the same. You've just learned something about me that the police were never able to learn. You've just witnessed what I'm really like inside. But look out! I may never forgive you. You've had guts enough to take me apart, but don't think I'm going to remain there in pieces. Green Eyes'll pull himself together. Green Eyes is already getting reorganized. I'm building myself up again. I'm healing. I'm making myself over. I'm getting stronger, more solid than a fortress. Stronger than the prison. You hear me, I *am* the prison! In my cells I guard big bruisers, brawlers, soldiers, plunderers! Look out! I'm not sure that my guards and dogs can hold them back if I let them loose on you! I've got ropes, knives, ladders! Look out! There are sentinels on my rounds. There are spies everywhere. I'm the prison and I'm alone in the world.

MAURICE   Calm yourself, Green Eyes.

GREEN EYES   I'm preparing my executions. I'm freeing convicts. Look out, boys! (*The door of the cell opens without anyone's appearing*) It's for me? Is it? She's here. (*He hesitates*) Is she here? Well, go tell her to go away.

(*The* GUARD *enters*)

THE GUARD   Hurry up. Your girl's waiting for you in the visiting-room.

GREEN EYES   I'm not going down.

THE GUARD   What?

GREEN EYES   I say I'm not going down. You can tell her to go back home.

THE GUARD   You're sure?

GREEN EYES   Sure as I can be. It's over. The lady's dead.

THE GUARD   Well, that's your affair. I'll give her the message. (*He looks about the cell*) Everything in order here?

LEFRANC   Everything's in order, you can see for yourself.

THE GUARD (*to* LEFRANC)   Is that so? What about that? (*He points to the unmade bed*) Answer. (*silence*) You won't answer? I'm asking you why the bed's not made.

(*A long silence*)

GREEN EYES (*to* MAURICE *and* LEFRANC) Well, you guys? You don't say. Speak up if it's you. You've got to be frank. The boss won't make trouble.

LEFRANC   We don't know any more about it than you do.

THE GUARD (*still smiling*)   I'd like to believe it. Frankness makes you suffocate. (*to* LE-FRANC) When do you get out?

LEFRANC   Day after tomorrow.

THE GUARD   Good riddance.

LEFRANC (*aggressively*)   Do I bother you? You should have said so yesterday. I'd have left this morning.

THE GUARD   You'll change your tone with me. Otherwise, I'll let you have another taste of the guardroom.

LEFRANC   I don't owe you any explanations. And I don't owe any to this gentleman either. (*He points to* GREEN EYES) Nobody questions *you.*

THE GUARD   Soft-pedal it. (*He turns to* GREEN EYES *and* MAURICE) You see what happens when you want to be nice? Can't be done with guys like that. You end up by becoming inhuman. And then they claim that guards are bullies. (*to* LEFRANC) If you weren't so thick, you'd have realized I was doing my job. No one can say I pick on you. And when it comes to being in the know, I've got it all over you.

LEFRANC   That remains to be proved.

THE GUARD   It is proved. You don't know what you've got to see and put up with to be a prison guard. You don't realize that you've got to be the very opposite of the gangsters. I mean just that: the very opposite. And you've also got to be the opposite of their friend. I'm not saying their enemy. Think about it. (*He reaches into his pocket and takes out some cigarettes which he hands to* GREEN EYES) Here, this is proof. (*to* GREEN EYES) Here, Green Eyes. They're from your pal. Snowball sends you two cigarettes.

GREEN EYES   O.K. (*He puts a cigarette into his mouth and hands the other to* MAURICE)

MAURICE   Don't bother.

GREEN EYES   Don't you want it?

MAURICE   No.

THE GUARD   He's right. Too young to smoke. The black boy also asked me to tell you that you mustn't worry. That guy's a real pal of yours. (*embarrassed silence*) Well, what about your girl?

GREEN EYES   I've told you. It's over.

THE GUARD   Still, she seemed pretty pleased with your green eyes. I was looking at her just now. She's a good-looking gal. Nice figure.

GREEN EYES (*smiling*)   You won't be seeing her again when she leaves here, will you?

THE GUARD (*also smiling*)   Would that annoy you?

GREEN EYES   Oh, after all, if you like her, see how you make out with her.

THE GUARD   No kidding? You mean I can?

GREEN EYES   Why not? I'm taking off. I'm tired of life. And besides, you're not like the other guards.

THE GUARD   Son of a gun! So you mean it? You're leaving her right in the palm of my hand?

GREEN EYES   She's all yours. (*They shake hands*)

THE GUARD   Now I understand. When she looked you up and down behind the grating, she wanted to give herself a last treat.

GREEN EYES   It was last Thursday she said good-bye to me. You're right. With those baby-doll eyes of hers she was giving me the air.

THE GUARD   Do you think she'll lose by the exchange?

GREEN EYES   You'll talk to her about me. You'll take my place. When my head's cut off, I'll be counting on you to replace me.

THE GUARD   O.K. We'll adopt you. And if you want anything from the kitchen, let me know. I'll get you all you want. (*to* LEFRANC) You still don't know what a guard is. In order to learn (*He points to* GREEN EYES) you've got to be in his boots.

LEFRANC   That doesn't change the fact that he'd have liked Maurice and me to get all the blame and be sent to the guardroom. Because naturally he's the Man!

GREEN EYES   You bellyaching? For so little.

LEFRANC   To you it's very little. (*to* MAURICE) You saw how he accused us. . . .

MAURICE   Green Eyes? He wasn't accusing anyone. He just decided why the bed was unmade.

LEFRANC   And I was the one who got the blame.

GREEN EYES   Come off it, will you? What did I say? The truth. I said it in front of the boss because he's a swell guy. There's no risk with him. He's got it all over lots of the convicts.

LEFRANC   A guard's a guard. (*He puts on the jacket that* GREEN EYES *has just tossed on the bed*)

GREEN EYES   He's different.

LEFRANC   It's probably because of you that the cell is under his protection. Because of the man. The tattooed man.

GREEN EYES   You're the one who's trying to act like a man. You're trying to strut. A man doesn't have to strut. He knows he's a man and that's all that matters to him.

LEFRANC   (*to* MAURICE)   You hear that?

MAURICE   (*curtly*)   Green Eyes is right.

LEFRANC   To you, everything Green Eyes says and does is perfectly natural. You'd let yourself be cut in two in his place. It's perfectly natural. Just because it's Green Eyes.

MAURICE   That's *my* business.

LEFRANC   Only don't get any false ideas into your head. His friends, the real ones, are on the floor above. There wasn't any need to defend him the way you did just before. Green Eyes gets his orders from the other world. They send him cigarettes—from where? From the other side of the water. Brought by a special guard, in full uniform, who offers him his friendship on a platter. A message from the heart. Were you talking about Snowball's smile? And did you think it was for me? You were wrong. The gentleman has already

plucked it from Snowball's teeth. All the prisoners are divided into two warring camps, and the two kings toss smiles at each other above our heads—or behind our backs—or even right in front of us. And they wind up making a present of their girls. . . .

GREEN EYES   Drop the subject, Georgie. I'm the one who deals with my girl.

LEFRANC   You've got all the rights, you're the man. You've done enough to be entitled to everything. All Big Shot's got to do is whistle and we start circling round the cell. . . .

THE GUARD   Come on, stop arguing. I'm going over to see Snowball. *He's* always singing. So long.

(*He leaves*)

GREEN EYES   (*to* LEFRANC)   Yes Sir! You're right. If I felt like it, I'd make you circle round and round like the horses in a merry-go-round. The way I used to waltz the girls around. You think I can't? I do what I like here. I'm the man here, yes Sir! I can go walking in the halls, up and down the stairs, I can go across the court and the yards. I'm the one they respect. They're afraid of me. Maybe I'm not as strong as Snowball because his crime was a little more necessary than mine. Because he killed in order to rob and loot, but, like him, I killed in order to live, and now I'm smiling. I've understood my crime. I've understood everything and I'm brave enough to be all alone. In broad daylight.

LEFRANC   Don't work yourself up, Green Eyes. I've understood too. And I admit you're entitled to everything. I did all I could so that the letters to your girl were as beautiful as possible. You've got a right to be sore at me. I was taking your place.

GREEN EYES   I'm not sore at you. I don't give a damn. The letters were beautiful. They were too beautiful. Maybe you thought you were writing to your own girl. . . .

LEFRANC   No, never. I wrote such beautiful letters because I put myself completely in your place. I got into your skin.

GREEN EYES   But in order to get into my skin, you've got to be my size. And to be my size, you've got to do as I do. Don't deny it. You'd like to be chummy with the guards. You'd like that. But you're not strong enough. Maybe some day you'll know what a guard is. But you'll have to pay the price.

LEFRANC   I wanted to separate you from your girl, Green Eyes. I did all I could. I did what I could to isolate you from the world and to separate the cell, and even the prison, from the world. And I think I've succeeded. I wanted the whole world to know that we're here and that we're peaceful here. Among ourselves. I'd like not a breath of air to come from outside. And I'm working at it. More than anyone else. I wanted us to be brothers. That's why I mixed up the clothes. You remember? I repeat, I've worked for the prison.

GREEN EYES   The prison is mine, and I'm running the show here.

MAURICE   And it's a sell-out.

GREEN EYES   What was that you said?

MAURICE   Nothing.

GREEN EYES   I sell out? So what? You wouldn't dare ask me to be on the up and up, would you? It would be inhuman to expect that of a man who's two months from death. What does that mean, being on the up and up, after what I've done? After taking the great leap into the void, after cutting myself off from men as I've done, you still expect me to respect your rules?

LEFRANC   But I understand you. And I also understand what he calls your double-crossing. I like you like that. Keep being a heel.

MAURICE   Green Eyes. . . .

GREEN EYES   Let's hear your reproaches.

MAURICE   I didn't say anything.

GREEN EYES   Well?

MAURICE   Nothing. I think you've been double-crossing. Now I realize that you've always been double-crossing! I've got a right to say it to you because it hurt me just before to learn that you were the black boy's friend. And you were his friend without letting us know.

GREEN EYES   And what if I like to double-cross? Who are you, Georgie and you? A pair of little crooks. It's not the likes of you who can judge me. I look for friends in the prison and I've got a right to. Snowball accompanies me. He encourages me. If we get out of it, we'll go to Cayenne together, and if I get the axe, I know he'll follow me. But what am I to you? You think I haven't guessed? Here in the cell I'm the one who bears the whole brunt. The brunt of what—I don't know. I'm illiterate. But I know I need a strong back. The way Snowball bears the same weight. But for the whole prison. Maybe there's some one else, a Number One Big Shot, who bears it for the whole world! You can laugh in my face, I've got rights. I'm the man.

MAURICE   To me, you're still Green Eyes. A terror of a man. But you've lost your force, your fine criminal force. You belong to your girl more than you think.

GREEN EYES   No.

MAURICE   When I was in cell 108 and used to pass in front of your door on my way through the hall, all I could see was your hand that put the bowl through the cage. I saw the ring on your fourth finger. I was sure you were a complete man because of your ring, but I didn't think that you really had a girl. Now you have one. But I forgive you for everything because I saw how you broke down just now.

GREEN EYES   You make me laugh. Shut up and go argue with Georgie.

MAURICE   That's another thing that turns my stomach. If I'm no longer with you, I'll have to be with him. (*He turns to* LEFRANC) You're repulsive, yes, repulsive. I've got to watch out for you. You're capable of getting up at night and strangling me.

LEFRANC   I don't need the night for that.

MAURICE   You're repulsive. You're the one who baits Green Eyes. It's you who destroyed our friendship. You were jealous of him. You're furious because you haven't done anything as fine as he. You wanted to put yourself in his class.

LEFRANC   You, you poor little crook, what wouldn't you do to put yourself in his class?

MAURICE   It's not true. I'll help him. And I'll keep helping him. Don't think you can take advantage of the way I feel so as to make friends with me. I may be a coward, Lefranc, but watch out. I'll defend his crime. . . .

LEFRANC   Did you hear his crime? And you saw him, the murderer, practically in tears!

MAURICE   You've got no right to talk like that, Georgie! You hear me? No right to laugh! It's because I saw him in that condition that my friendship has gotten deeper. Now I feel pity. I pity the finest murderer in the world. And it's fine to pity such a great crumbling monument that's falling to pieces. It's because I saw him so shaken, and almost on account of me, that I felt pity. Whereas you . . .

LEFRANC   Me?

MAURICE   You got excited listening to him.

LEFRANC   Well, that was part of my program too. And I'm the one who succeeds. Green Eyes did what he had to . . .

MAURICE   And you? You? What have you done that's better? What have you got to boast about? Or who? The marks on your wrists maybe? The galley? Your burglaries? You don't need any talent for that.

LEFRANC   I'd have liked to see you with Serge during that job on the Rue de la Néva. In the dark with people firing at us from windows. . . .

MAURICE   (*ironically*)   Serge? Serge who? Probably Serge de Lenz!

LEFRANC   Serge de Lenz in person. It was with him that I got my start. You don't believe me?

MAURICE You've got to prove it. Because the cells are full of the most terrible stories in the world. There are times when it all floats in the air, and the air gets so thick you feel like puking. And the worst of all are the ones they invent to make themselves look big. Racketeering, trafficking in gold, pearls, diamonds! It reeks. Phony dollars, burglaries, furs! And galley-slaves!

LEFRANC Go to hell!

MAURICE The galley!

LEFRANC You threatening me? (*He goes for* MAURICE *and tries to seize him.* GREEN EYES *pushes them aside brutally*)

GREEN EYES It's not time for that yet. You're a pair of lunatics. I'll lay you both out on the cement.

(*In struggling,* MAURICE *tears* LEFRANC's *shirt*)

MAURICE He's the one. He's always the one.

GREEN EYES (*staring at* LEFRANC's *chest*) But . . . you're tattooed!

MAURICE (*examining the mark*) "The Avenger!" Terrific.

LEFRANC Let me alone.

GREEN EYES "The Avenger?" I served on it before I was sent to the naval prison at Calvi. A fast little submarine. Were you a sailor, Georgie?

LEFRANC Let me alone.

GREEN EYES Were you?

LEFRANC I've never been in the navy.

MAURICE Well, Avenger?

GREEN EYES When I was in jail, in Clairvaux, I knew a guy who was called the Avenger. A bruiser. And I've known others, tough guys as well as boats. There was the Panther, port of Brest.

LEFRANC Poissy Penitentiary.

GREEN EYES The Slasher, Riom Penitentiary.

LEFRANC Port of Cherbourg.

GREEN EYES The Cyclone, Fontevrault Jail.

LEFRANC Port of Brest.

GREEN EYES Well? How come you know them if you've never been anywhere?

LEFRANC Everyone knows about them. They're things that have become bigger than life-size. I've known all the real signs of bad luck for a long time.

MAURICE You don't know much if all you know is the signs.

GREEN EYES What about the Avalanche?

LEFRANC Toulon.

GREEN EYES The Avalanche! Terrific thighs. He knifed three men. Twenty years of hard labor. He did them at Fort Hâ!

MAURICE He's talking about boats and you about yeggs at Cayenne.

LEFRANC We understand each other.

MAURICE That would surprise me. You've got a long way to go to be in Green Eyes' class.

GREEN EYES Avenger is a title. It's not an easy one to bear. There are three of them already. The Avenger at Clairvaux, with about ten armed robberies. Got fifteen years. At Tréous, another Avenger. Tried to murder a cop. But the most terrible of all is Robert Garcia, known as Robert the Avenger, at the pen in Fréjus. He's the champ you've got to knock out. And to do that you need a murder with all the trimmings. Nothing else'll do.

LEFRANC Green Eyes . . .

GREEN EYES (*smiling*) I'm here, don't get worried. Don't lose your bearings. I'm at the wheel. Now you understand that I needed Snowball's friendship. He's the one who's holding us up. And don't worry. He's solid. He's squarely planted in crime. Steady on his feet. You were right. The whole prison's under his authority, but right under him is me. . . . And . . . you too, you'll be entitled to my girl.

MAURICE (*going up to* LEFRANC) Wait, hold it, the gentleman's not tattooed. It's only drawn in ink.

LEFRANC You louse!

MAURICE "Avenger!" He got it from a book, like the story of the galley.

LEFRANC I told you to shut up or I'll bash your head in!

MAURICE Because Green Eyes talks to you, because he listens to you, you shine in his glory. Only, *his* tattoos aren't phony. He wasn't scared of being stuck by needles.

LEFRANC (*threateningly*) Shut it!

MAURICE (*to* GREEN EYES) He's repulsive. What about your girl, you going to let him have your girl!

GREEN EYES (*smiling*) Did *you* want her?

MAURICE Your girl! Who's engraved in your skin! Oh, Green Eyes! Where did she come up to on you?

GREEN EYES (*he makes a gesture*) Up to here!

MAURICE Ah!

LEFRANC Don't be so shy, go pet one another.

MAURICE I'm talking about his girl. I've got a right to.

LEFRANC If I let you have her.

MAURICE His girl?

LEFRANC That's right, mister. And from now on resign yourself to reckoning with me.

MAURICE (*ironically*) Still and all, I can't

ask you any questions about her. You're not planning to draw her on your skin like . . . (*He makes the gesture of tossing back an invisible lock of hair*) like "the Avenger!" If I'm concerned with his girl, it's because Green Eyes lets me.

LEFRANC   A few minutes ago, you were despising him.

MAURICE   Never. It was you. You're the one who got a kick out of making him recite his tough luck in full detail. You're a coward.

LEFRANC   You're the one who wormed the story out of him. You gently drew the words. . . .

MAURICE   It's not true. I did what I could to ease the strain for him. He knows it. I don't wait for a man to do my work for me. I'm not waiting for anything. I'm ready for anything. When I slip up, I'll take what's coming to me. That's how I'm built. But you, you're in a fog. When you circle around, you watch us live. You watch us struggle and you're envious. The story of the lilacs gave you a real lift! Admit it! All we saw was your lousy mug leaning forward, with its dead eyes, circling round the cell. You're going to mull over that business of the lilacs! It's already fattening you up.

LEFRANC   It's beginning to work on me, you're right.

MAURICE   Is it giving you strength? It's rising up. Is it rising up to your lips? Are the lilacs rising up to your teeth?

LEFRANC   Right to my fingertips, Maurice. It's not pity that the story of the crime and the lilacs makes me feel. It's joy! You hear me? Joy! That makes another thread he's broken that holds him to the world. He's separated from the police. Soon he'll be separated from his girl!

MAURICE   You bastard! You're organizing. . . .

LEFRANC   My work, mine.

MAURICE   And Green Eyes is the one who's got to suffer for it! He's the one who pays for it. The one who's been chosen. And if I attract trouble, it's not by guzzling other men's adventures. It's because of my mug. I've told you. I'm a marked man, me too, but my real mark is my mug! My mug, my cute little yegg's mug. I've made up my mind to defend myself. You stink up the cell and I'm going to get rid of your garbage. You disgust us. You're a phony. Phony to the marrow of your bones. Your story about the galley and the marks on your wrists is phony, and your secrets with our girl are phony, and all your complications about Snow-

ball are phony, and your tattoos are phony, and your anger is phony, and . . .

LEFRANC   Stop it!

MAURICE   Your frankness is phony, your gab is phony . . .

LEFRANC   Stop it or I'll smack.

MAURICE   I'm going to strip you. I want to leave you naked. You feed on others. You dress yourself up, you decorate yourself with our jewels, I accuse you! You steal our crimes! You wanted to know what a crime's really composed of. I was watching you take it apart.

LEFRANC   Shut your mouth.

MAURICE   I refuse to let you off, and I'll continue. . . .

LEFRANC   Stop it. Let me breathe.

MAURICE   You're bloated with our life. (*He makes a gesture of tossing back his lock of hair*)

LEFRANC   Maurice. I want you to stop it. And stop tossing your head like a whore.

MAURICE   Why? (*laughing*) Is the gentleman afraid I'll disturb his bunch of lilacs?

LEFRANC   I am. And now you're going for a ride with me. For a long, long ride. Get ready for me. Here I come. *I'm the Avenger*. No more curling up and sleeping under Green Eyes' wing.

MAURICE   (*to* GREEN EYES)   Big boy. . . . (*Then, looking at* LEFRANC, *he again makes the gesture with his hand and head*)

LEFRANC   It's too late. Don't scream.

(GREEN EYES *is perched on a basin and dominates the stage as* LEFRANC, *smiling, bears down on* MAURICE *who, in the presence of this radiant smile, also smiles*)

GREEN EYES   (*his face drawn*)   You exhaust me, both of you. You put a bigger strain on me than on yourselves. Get it over with quick.

MAURICE   (*frightened*)   You're crazy, Georgie. I haven't done anything!

LEFRANC   Don't scream, it's too late. (*He blocks* MAURICE *in a corner and strangles him.* MAURICE *slides to the floor between* LEFRANC'S *spread legs.* LEFRANC *straightens up*)

GREEN EYES   (*in a changed voice, after a moment's silence*)   What have you done? It's not true, Lefranc, you haven't killed him? (*He looks at the lifeless* MAURICE)   That's a nice job. (LEFRANC *looks exhausted*)   Nice enough to get you to Guiana.

LEFRANC   What'll we do? Help me, Green Eyes.

GREEN EYES   (*approaching the door*)   You bastard! Me help you?

LEFRANC   (*staggered*)   Huh? But . . .

GREEN EYES You know what you've just done? Eliminated Maurice, who hadn't done anything. Killed him for nothing! For the glory of it!

LEFRANC Green Eyes . . . You're not going to let me down?

GREEN EYES Don't talk to me. Don't put your hands on me. Do you know what misfortune is? Don't you know that I kept hoping to avoid it? And you thought you could become, all by yourself, without the help of heaven, as great as me! Maybe overshadow me? You poor fool, don't you realize it's impossible to overshadow me? I didn't want anything—you hear me?—I didn't want what happened to me to happen. It was all given to me. A gift from God or the devil, but something I didn't want. And now, here we are with a corpse on our hands.

LEFRANC (*at first overwhelmed, then pulling himself together*) I realized. I realized I'd never be with you, Green Eyes. But I want you to know that I'm stronger than anyone else. I won't have to dance to undo my crime, because I willed it.

GREEN EYES That's the danger. To blow in casually and bump off a kid! Why . . . I don't even have the strength to mention the name for that sort of criminal . . . I never knew I was strangling the girl. I was carried away. I didn't want to catch up with anyone. I risked everything. I made a false move and fell flat on my face.

LEFRANC I want to be let alone. I want everyone to let me alone! I wanted to become what you were. . . .

GREEN EYES What we are in spite of ourselves. And what I wanted to destroy by dancing.

LEFRANC But what you're proud of having become. You make yourself radiant. You . . . you're beginning to be radiant. I wanted to take your place . . . your luminous place. . . .

GREEN EYES And what about our crimes?

LEFRANC Including the crimes.

GREEN EYES Not ours.

LEFRANC I did what I could, out of love of misfortune.

GREEN EYES You don't know the first thing about misfortune if you think you can choose it. I didn't want mine. It chose me. It fell right smack on my puss, and I tried everything to shake it off. I struggled, I boxed, I danced, I even sang, and, funny as it may seem, I refused it at first. It was only when I saw that everything was irremediable that I calmed down. I've only just barely accepted it. It had to be total.

LEFRANC It's thanks to me. . . .

GREEN EYES Who the hell cares! It's only now that I'm settling down completely in misfortune and making it my heaven. And you, you cheat to get there. . . .

LEFRANC I'm stronger than you. My misfortune comes from something deeper. It comes from myself.

GREEN EYES Who the hell cares! I refuse to argue. (*He knocks at the door*)

LEFRANC What are you doing?

GREEN EYES I'm calling the guards. (*He raps at the door*) You'll know by the look on their mugs whether you can be with us or not.

LEFRANC Green Eyes!

GREEN EYES Bastard!

LEFRANC I really am all alone!

(*Sound of a key. The door opens. The* GUARD *appears, smiling. He leers at* GREEN EYES)

Eugène Ionesco

1912-

EXPERIENCE OF THE THEATRE

When I am asked the question: "Why do you write plays?" I always feel very awkward and have no idea what to answer. Sometimes it seems to me that I started writing for the theatre because I hated it. I used to enjoy reading literature and essays and I used to go to the movies. Occasionally I would listen to music and visit the art galleries; but I almost never went to the theatre.

When I did go, it was quite by accident, to keep someone company or because I had been unable to turn down an invitation, because I *had* to go.

It gave me no pleasure or feeling of participation. The acting embarrassed me: I was embarrassed for the actors. The situations seemed to me quite arbitrary. I felt there was something phony about it all.

A theatrical performance had no magic for me. Everything seemed rather ridiculous, rather painful. For example, it was beyond me how anyone could dream of being an actor. It seemed to me that actors were doing something unacceptable and reprehensible. They gave up their own personalities, repudiated themselves, changed their own skins. How *could* they consent to being someone else and take on a character different from their own? For me it was a kind of vulgar trick, transparent, inconceivable.

Besides, an actor did not even become someone else, he just pretended, which was, I thought, far worse. I found this very distressing and in a way dishonest. "What a good

actor," the audience used to say. In my view, he was a bad actor, and acting was a Bad Thing.

For me, going to a public performance meant going to see apparently serious people making a public exhibition of themselves. And yet I am not one of those completely matter-of-fact types. I am not opposed to make-believe. On the contrary, I have always considered imaginative truth to be more profound, more loaded with significance, than everyday reality. Realism, socialist or not, never looks beyond reality. It narrows it down, diminishes it, falsifies it, and leaves out of account the obsessive truths that are most fundamental to us: love, death and wonder. It presents man in a perspective that is narrow and alien; truth lies in our dreams, in our imagination: every moment of our lives confirms this statement. Fiction preludes science. Everything we dream about, and by that I mean everything we desire, is true (the myth of Icarus came before aviation, and if Ader or Blériot started flying, it is because all men have dreamed of flight). There is nothing truer than myth: history, in its attempt to "realize" myth, distorts it, stops halfway; when history claims to have "succeeded," this is nothing but humbug and mystification. Everything we dream is "realizable." Reality does not have to be: it is simply what it is. It is the dreamer, the thinker or the scientist who is the revolutionary; it is he who tries to change the world.

The fictional element in the novel did not worry me at all and I accepted it in the cinema. I can believe as naturally in the potential reality of fiction as in my own dreams. Film acting did not fill me with the same indefinable malaise, the same embarrassment as acting in the theatre.

Why could I not accept the truth of theatrical reality? Why did it seem false to me? And why did the false seem to want to pass as true and take the place of truth? Was it the fault of the actors? Of the text? Or my own fault? I think I realize now that what worried me in the theatre was the presence of characters in flesh and blood on the stage. Their physical presence destroyed the imaginative illusion. It was as though there were two planes of reality, the concrete, physical, impoverished, empty and limited reality of these ordinary human beings living, moving and speaking on the stage, and the reality of imagination, face to face, overlapping, irreconcilable: two antagonistic worlds failing to come together and unite.

Yes, that was it: every gesture, every attitude, every speech spoken on the stage destroyed for me a world that these same gestures, attitudes and speeches were specifically designed to evoke; destroyed it even before it could be created. It seemed to me an absolute abortion, a fatal mistake, sheer fatuity. If you stop up your ears to shut out the dance music an orchestra is playing but go on watching the dancers, you can see how ridiculous they look, how fantastic their movements are; in the same way, if someone were present for the first time at the celebration of some religious rite, the whole ceremony would seem to him incomprehensible and absurd.

It was in a spirit you might call unsanctified that I paid my rare visits to the theatre, and that was why I did not like it, did not respond to it, did not believe in it.

In a novel you are *told* a story; it does not matter whether it is invented or not, nothing stops you believing it. In a film you are *shown* a fictional story; it is a novel in pictures, an illustrated novel. So a film too tells a story; of course, the fact that it is visual in no way changes this and you can still believe it. Music is a combination of notes, a story in notes, adventures in sound. A painting is an organization or a disorganization of forms, colors and planes, and the question of belief or disbelief does not arise; it is there, as evidence: all that is required is that these various elements satisfy the exacting ideals of composition and pictorial expression. The novel, music and painting are pure structural form, containing no elements that are extraneous; that is why they can stand alone, they are admissible. Even the cinema can be accepted, because it is a succession of pictures, which means that it too is pure, whereas the theatre seemed to me essentially impure: the fictional element was mixed with others that were foreign to it; it was imperfectly fictional, yes, raw material that had not yet undergone the transformation or muta-

tion that is indispensable. In short, everything about the theatre exasperated me. When I saw actors, for example, identifying themselves completely with their parts and weeping real tears on the stage, I found it unbearable, positively indecent.

When on the other hand I saw an actor who was too much in control of his part, out of character, dominating it, detached from it, which was what Diderot and Jouvet and Piscator and, after him, Brecht all wanted, I was just as dissatisfied. This too seemed to me an unacceptable mixture of true and false, for I felt a need for the essential transformation or transposition of a reality that only imagination and artistic creation can make more meaningful, more dense, more "true," that the didactic doctrines of realism merely overload, impoverish and reduce to the level of a second-rate ideology. I did not like stage actors, stars, who for me represented an anarchical principle, breaking up and destroying to their own advantage the organized unity of the stage, attracting all attention to themselves to the detriment of any coherent integration of the elements of drama. But the dehumanization of the actor, as practiced by Piscator [1] or Brecht, a disciple of Piscator, who turned the actor into a simple pawn in the chess game of drama, a lifeless tool, denied passion, participation or personal invention, this time to the advantage of the production, which now, in its turn, attracted all attention to itself—this priority given to organized unity exasperated me just as much and made me feel, quite literally, that something was being smothered: to squash the actor's initiative, to kill the actor, is to kill both life and drama.

Later, that is to say quite recently, I realized that Jean Vilar [2] had managed to strike the necessary balance in his productions—respecting the need for cohesion on the stage without dehumanizing the actor and thus restoring to drama its unity and to the actor his freedom— half way between the style of the *Odéon* (and so an advance on the rantings of a Sarah Bernhardt or a Mounet-Sully) and that of the Brechtian or Piscoratesque discipline. This is not, however, with Vilar an expression of theories about the theatre or hard and fast dogmatism, but a question of tact and instinctive sense of theatre.

---

[1] Famous German director (1893–   ), who, with Brecht, introduced the epic theatre.

[2] Contemporary French director who until recently was the director of the Théâtre National Populaire.

But I still could not quite see how to get rid of that positive feeling of malaise produced by my awareness of the "impurity" of acted drama. I was by no means an agreeable theatregoer, but on the contrary, sulky, grumbling, always discontented. Was this due to some deficiency in myself alone? Or was it something lacking in the theatre?

I was dissatisfied even by the plays I had managed to read. Not all of them! For I was not blind to the merits of Sophocles, Aeschylus or Shakespeare, nor a little later to some of the plays of Kleist or Büchner. Why? Because, I thought, all these plays make extraordinary reading on account of their literary qualities, which may well not be specifically theatrical. In any case, after Shakespeare and Kleist, I do not think I have enjoyed reading a play. Strindberg seemed to me clumsy and inadequate. I was even bored by Molière. I was not interested in those stories of misers, hypocrites and cuckolds. I disliked his unmetaphysical mind. Shakespeare raised questions about the whole condition and destiny of man. In the long run Molière's little problems seemed to me of relatively minor importance, sometimes a little sad of course, dramatic even, but never tragic; for they could be resolved. The unendurable admits of no solution, and only the unendurable is profoundly tragic, profoundly comic and essentially theatrical.

On the other hand, the greatness of Shakespeare's plays seemed to me diminished in performance. No Shakespearean production ever captivated me as much as my reading of *Hamlet, Othello* and *Julius Caesar,* etc. As I went so rarely to the theatre, perhaps I have never seen the best productions of Shakespeare's drama? In any case, in performance I had the impression that the unendurable had been made endurable. It was anguish tamed.

So I am really not a passionate theatregoer, still less a man of the theatre. I really hated the theatre. It bored me. And yet . . . when I was a child, I can still remember how my mother could not drag me away from the Punch and Judy show in the Luxembourg Gardens. I would go there day after day and could stay there, spellbound, all day long. But I did not laugh. That Punch and Judy show kept me there open-mouthed, watching those puppets talking, moving and cudgeling each other. It was the very image of the world that appeared to me, strange and improbable but truer than true, in the profoundly simplified form of caricature, as though to stress the grotesque and brutal nature of the truth. And

from then until I was fifteen any form of play would thrill me and make me feel that the world is very strange, a feeling so deeply rooted that it has never left me. Every live show awoke in me this feeling for the strangeness of the world, and it impressed me nowhere more than at the theatre. And yet, when I was thirteen, I wrote a play, my first piece of writing, which had nothing strange about it. It was a patriotic play: extreme youth is an excuse for anything.

When did I stop liking the theatre? From the moment when, as I began to grow more clear-sighted and acquire a critical mind, I became conscious of stage tricks, of obvious theatrical contrivance, that is to say from the moment I stopped being naïve. Where are the *monstres sacrés* of the theatre who could give us back our lost naïveté? And what possible magic could justify the theatre's claim to bind us in its spell? There is no magic now, nothing is sacred: there is no valid reason for this to be restored to us.

Besides, there is nothing more difficult than writing for the theatre. Novels and poems last well. Their appeal is not blunted even by the centuries. We still find interest in a number of minor works from the nineteenth, eighteenth and seventeenth centuries. And how many even older works do we not still find interesting? All painting and music resists the passage of time. The moving simplicity of the least significant sculptured heads on countless cathedrals still remains fresh and alive, intact; and we shall go on responding to the architectural rhythms of great monuments of the most distant civilizations, which speak to us directly through them in a language that is clear and revealing. But what of the theatre?

Today the theatre is blamed by some for not belonging to its own times. In my view it belongs only too well. This is what makes it so weak and ephemeral. I mean that the theatre *does* belong to its own times, but not quite enough. Every period needs something "out of period" and incommunicable to be introduced into what is "period" and communicable. Everything is a circumscribed moment in history, of course. But all history is contained in each moment of history: any moment in history is valid when it transcends history; in the particular lies the universal.

The themes chosen by many authors merely spring from a certain ideological fashion, which is something *less* than the period it belongs to. Or else these themes are the expression of some particular political attitude, and the plays that illustrate them will die with the ideology that has inspired them, for ideologies go out of fashion. Any Christian tomb, any Greek or Etruscan stele moves us and tells us more about the destiny of man than any number of laboriously committed plays, which are made to serve a discipline, a system of thought and language different from what is properly their own.

It is true that all authors have tried to make propaganda. The great ones are those who failed, who have gained access, consciously or not, to a deeper and more universal reality. Nothing is more precarious than a play. It may maintain its position for a very short time, but it soon falls apart, revealing nothing but contrivance.

In all sincerity, Corneille bores me. Perhaps we like him (without believing in him) only from habit. We cannot help it. He has been forced on us at school. I find Schiller unbearable. For a long time now, Marivaux's plays have seemed to me futile little comedies. Musset's are thin and Vigny's unactable. Victor Hugo's bloody dramas send us into fits of laughter; whereas it is difficult to laugh, whatever people say, at most of Labiche's funny plays. Dumas fils, with his *Dames aux Camélias*, is ridiculously sentimental. As for the others! Oscar Wilde? Facile. Ibsen? Boorish. Strindberg? Clumsy. A recent dramatist, Giraudoux, not long dead, does not always get across the footlights now; like Cocteau's, his drama seems to us superficial and contrived. It has lost its sparkle: with Cocteau the theatrical tricks are too obvious; with Giraudoux the tricks and contrivances of language, distinguished though they be, still remain tricks.

Pirandello himself has been left behind the times, for his theatre was built on theories about personality or the multiformity of truth, which now seem clear as daylight since psychoanalysis and psychology plumbed the depths. In testing the validity of Pirandello's theories, modern psychology, inevitably going further than Pirandello in its exploration of the human psyche, certainly confirms Pirandello's findings, but at the same time shows him to be limited and inadequate: for what has been said by Pirandello is now said more thoroughly and scientifically. So the value of his theatre does not rest on his contribution to psychology but on the quality of his drama, which must inevitably lie elsewhere: what interests us in this author is no longer the discovery of the antagonistic elements in human personality, but what he has made of them dramatically. The strictly theatrical interest of his work lies outside science, beyond the limits of his own ideology. All that is left of Pirandello is his dramatic technique, the mechanics of his theatre: which again proves that drama founded on ideology or philosophy, exclusively inspired by them, is built on sand and crumbles away. It is his dramatic idiom, his purely theatrical instinct that keeps Pirandello alive for us today.

In the same way, it is not Racine's psychological insight into the passions that sustains his theatre; but what Racine has made of it as a poet and man of the theatre.

If we were to go through the centuries and count the dramatists who can still move an audience, we should find about twenty . . . or at the most thirty. But the paintings, poems and novels that still mean something to us can be counted in their thousands. The naïveté essential to a work of art is lacking in the theatre. I do not say a dramatist of great simplicity will not appear; but at the moment I see no sign of him on the horizon. I mean a simplicity that is lucid, springing from the inmost depths of our being, revealing them, revealing them to ourselves, restoring our own simplicity, our secret souls. At the moment there is no naïveté, in audience or writer.

What faults are there then to be found in dramatists and their plays? Their tricks, I was saying, that is to say their too obvious contrivances. The theatre may appear to be a secondary, a minor form of literature. It always seems rather coarse-grained. There is no doubt it is an art that deals in effects. It cannot do without them, and this is the reproach leveled against it. And these effects have to be broad. One has the impression that the texture has been roughened. The textual refinement of literature is ironed out. Drama of literary subtlety soon wears thin. Half-tones are deepened or banished by light that is too brilliant. No shading, no nuance is possible. Problem plays, *pièces à thèse*, are rough-hewn pieces of approximation. Drama is not the idiom for ideas. When it tries to become a vehicle for ideologies, all it can do is vulgarize them. It dangerously oversimplifies. It makes them too elementary and depreciates them. It is "naïve," but in the bad sense. All ideological drama runs the risk of being parochial. What would, not the *utility*, but the proper *function* of the theatre be, if it was restricted to the task of duplicating philosophy or theology or politics or pedagogy? Psychological drama is not psychological enough. One might as well read a psychological treatise. Ideological drama is not philosophical enough. Instead of going to see a dramatic illustration of this or that political creed I would rather read my usual daily paper or listen to the speeches of my party candidates.

Dissatisfied with the gross naïveté and rudimentary character of the theatre, philosophers, literary men, ideologists and poets of refinement, all intelligent people try to make their drama intelligent. They write with intelligence, with taste and talent. They put their thoughts into it, they express their conception of life and the world, and believe that writing a play should be like presenting a thesis in which problems find their solution on the stage. They sometimes construct their work in the form of a syllogism, with the two premises in the first two acts and the conclusion in the third.

There is no denying the construction is sometimes first-rate. And yet this does not answer the demands we make of drama, because it fails to lift the theatre out of an intermediate zone that lies somewhere between where discursive reasoning can be only one ingredient— and the higher realms of thought.

Should one give up the theatre if one refuses to reduce it to a parochial level or subordinate it to manifestations of the human spirit that impose different forms and modes of expression? Can it, like painting or music, find its own autonomous existence?

Drama is one of the oldest of the arts. And I can't help thinking we cannot do without it. We cannot resist the desire to people a stage with live characters that are at the same time real and invented. We cannot deny our need to make them speak and live before our eyes. To bring phantoms to life and give them flesh and blood is a prodigious adventure, so unique that I myself was absolutely amazed, during the rehearsals of my first play, when I suddenly saw, moving on the stage of the *Noctambules,* characters who owed their life to me. It was a terrifying experience. What right had I to do a thing like that? Was it allowed? And how could Nicolas Bataille, one of my actors, turn into Mr. Martin? . . . It was almost diabolical. And so it was only when I had written something for the theatre, quite by chance and with the intention of holding it up to ridicule, that I began to love it, to rediscover it in myself, to understand it, to be fascinated by it: and then I knew what I had to do.

I told myself that the too intelligent playwrights were not intelligent enough: that it was no use for thinkers to look to the theatre for the idiom of a philosophical treatise; that when they tried to bring too much subtlety and refinement into the theatre it was not only too much but not enough; that if the theatre was merely a deplorable enlargement of refined subtleties, which I found so embarrassing, it merely meant that the enlargement was not sufficient. The overlarge was not large enough, the unsubtle was too subtle.

So if the essence of the theatre lay in magnifying its effects, they had to be magnified still further, underlined and stressed to the maximum. To push drama out of that intermediate zone where it is neither theatre nor literature is to restore it to its own domain, to its natural frontiers. It was not for me to conceal the devices of the theatre, but rather make them still more evident, deliberately obvious, go all-out for caricature and the grotesque, way beyond the pale irony of witty drawing-room comedies. No drawing-room comedies, but farce, the extreme exaggeration of parody. Humor, yes, but using the methods of burlesque. Comic effects that are firm, broad and outrageous. No dramatic comedies either. But back to the unendurable. Everything raised to paroxysm, where the source of tragedy lies. A theatre of violence: violently comic, violently dramatic.

Avoid psychology or rather give it a metaphysical dimension. Drama lies in extreme exaggeration of the feelings, an exaggeration that dislocates flat everyday reality. Dislocation, disarticulation of language too.

Moreover, if the actors embarrassed me by not seeming natural enough, perhaps it was because they also were, or tried to be, *too* natural: by trying not to be, perhaps they will still appear natural, but in a different way. They must not be afraid of not being natural.

We need to be virtually bludgeoned into detachment from our daily lives, our habits and mental laziness, which conceal from us the strangeness of the world. Without a fresh virginity of mind, without a new and healthy awareness of existential reality, there can be no theatre and no art either; the real must be in a way dislocated, before it can be reintegrated.

To achieve this effect, a trick can sometimes be used: playing against the text. A serious, solemn, formal production or interpretation can be grafted onto a text that is absurd, wild and comic. On the other hand, to avoid the ridiculous sentimentality of the tear-jerker, a dramatic text can be treated as buffoonery and the tragic feeling of a play can be underlined by farce. Light makes shadows darker, shadows intensify light. For my part, I have never understood the difference people make between the comic and the tragic. As the "comic" is an intuitive perception of the absurd, it seems to me more hopeless than the "tragic." The "comic" offers no escape. I say "hopeless," but in reality it lies outside the boundaries of hope or despair.

Tragedy may appear to some in one sense comforting, for in trying to express the helplessness of a beaten man, one broken by fate for example, tragedy thus admits the reality of fate and destiny, of sometimes incomprehensible but objective laws that govern the universe. And man's helplessness, the futility of our efforts, can also, in a sense, appear comic.

I have called my comedies "anti-plays" or "comic dramas," and my dramas "pseudo-dramas" or "tragic farces": for it seems to me that the comic is tragic, and that the tragedy of man is pure derision. The contemporary critical mind takes nothing too seriously or too lightly. In *Victims of Duty* I tried to sink comedy in tragedy: in *The Chairs* tragedy in comedy or, if you like, to confront comedy and tragedy in order to link them in a new dramatic synthesis. But it is not a true synthesis, for these two elements do not coalesce, they coexist: one constantly repels the other, they show each other up, criticize and deny one another and, thanks to their opposition, thus succeed dynamically in maintaining a balance and creating tension. The two plays that best satisfy this condition are, I believe: *Victims of Duty* and *The New Tenant*.

Similarly, one can confront the prosaic and the poetic, the strange and the ordinary. That is what I wanted to do in *Jack, or the Submission*, which I called "a *naturalistic* comedy" too, because after starting off in a naturalistic tone I tried to go beyond naturalism.

In the same way *Amédée, or How to Get Rid of It*, where the scene is laid in the flat of a *petit bourgeois* couple, is a realistic play into which fantastic elements have been introduced, a contrast intended at one and the same time to banish and recall the "realism."

In my first play, *The Bald Soprano*, which started off as an attempt to parody the theatre, and hence a certain kind of human behavior, it was by plunging into banality, by draining the sense from the hollowest clichés of everyday language that I tried to render the strangeness that seems to pervade our whole existence. The tragic and the farcical, the prosaic and the poetic, the realistic and the fantastic, the strange and the ordinary, perhaps these are the contradictory principles (there is no theatre without conflict) that may serve as a basis for a new dramatic structure. In this way perhaps the unnatural can by its very violence appear natural, and the too natural will avoid the naturalistic.

May I add that "primitive" drama is not elementary drama; to refuse to "round off the corners" is a way of providing a clear outline, a more powerful shape; drama that relies on simple effects is not necessarily drama simplified.

If one believes that "theatre" merely means the drama of the word, it is difficult to grant it can have an autonomous language of its own: it can then only be the servant of other forms of thought expressed in words, of philosophy and morals. Whereas, if one looks on the word as only *one* member of the shock troops the theatre can marshal, everything is changed. First of all, there is a proper way for the theatre to use words, which is as dialogue, words in action, words in conflict. If they are used by some authors merely for discussion, this is a major error. There are other means of making words more theatrical: by working them up to such a pitch that they reveal the true temper of drama, which lies in frenzy; the whole tone should be as strained as possible, the language should almost break up or explode in its fruitless effort to contain so many meanings.

But the theatre is more than words: drama is a story that is lived and relived with each performance, and we can watch it live. The theatre appeals as much to the eye as to the ear. It is not a series of pictures, like the cinema, but architecture, a moving structure of scenic images.

Nothing is barred in the theatre: characters may be brought to life, but the unseen presence of our inner fears can also be materialized. So the author is not only allowed, but recommended to make actors of his props, to bring objects to life, to animate the scenery and give symbols concrete form.

Just as the words are complemented by gesture, acting and pantomime, which can take their place when words are no longer adequate, so they can be amplified by the scenic elements of the stage as well. The use of props is yet another question. (Artaud had something to say about that.) [3]

When people say that the theatre should be purely social, do they not really mean that the theatre should be political, slanted, of

---

[3] French poet, playwright, director, and theoretician (1895–1948) whose writings greatly influenced the "absurdist" dramatists.

course, in this or that direction? It is one thing to be social; to be "socialist" or "marxist" or "fascist" is another—this is the expression of a kind of stock-taking that does not go far enough: the more I see of Brecht's plays, the more I have the impression that time, *and* his own time, escape him; Brechtian man is shorn of one dimension, the writer's sense of period is actually falsified by his ideology, which narrows his field of vision; this is a fault common to ideologists and people stunted by fanaticism.

Then one may be a social being in spite of oneself, since we are all of us caught in a kind of historical complex and belong to one special moment in history—which is, however, far from absorbing us entirely but rather expresses and contains only the least essential part of us.

I have spoken mainly about a certain technique, about a theatrical idiom, an idiom which is all its own. Social themes or subjects may very well form the subject and themes of drama, if they remain within this idiom. It is perhaps only through subjectivity that we become objective. The individual is linked to the generality of men, and society is obviously an objective fact: and yet I see this social element, and by that I mean rather the expression of history, of the period we belong to, even if it only appears in our natural idiom (and all idiom too is historical, limited to its own time, that is undeniable), I see this expression of history as being naturally inherent in a work of art, whatever one's conscious intentions, but vital and spontaneous rather than deliberate or ideological.

Besides contemporaneity does not conflict with timelessness and universality: on the contrary, it is subservient.

There are some states of mind, some intuitions that lie positively outside time, outside history. When, one day of grace, I awake some morning, not only from my night's sleep but also from the mental sleep of habit, and suddenly become aware of my existence and of a universal presence, when all seems strange and yet familiar, when I am possessed by the wonder of living, this is a feeling or intuition that can come to any man at any time. You can find this spirit of awareness expressed in practically the same terms by poets, mystics and philosophers, who experience it exactly as I do, and as all men have surely experienced it unless they are spiritually dead or blinded by their preoccupation with politics; you can find exactly the same spirit clearly expressed both in antiquity and the Middle Ages as well as in any of the so-called "historical" centuries. At this timeless moment in time philosopher and shoe-

maker, "master" and "slave," priest and layman are reconciled and indistinguishable.

The historical and the non-historical are joined and welded together in poetry and painting too. The identical picture of a woman dressing her hair is found in certain Persian miniatures, in Greek and Etruscan steles and in Egyptian wall painting; a Renoir or a Manet or painters from the seventeenth and eighteenth centuries did not need to know the paintings of other periods to find and catch the same attitude, imbued with the same unfailing sensual grace and inspiring the same emotion. As with my first example, we are here dealing with permanent emotions. The pictorial style in which the image is rendered differs (though often very little) according to period. But this "difference," which is of secondary importance, upholds and illumines a permanent value. All the evidence is there to show us how contemporaneity or "historicity," to use a word in vogue, meets and merges with timelessness, universality and superhistoricity, how each lends support to the other.

Let us choose a great example in our own field: in the theatre, when the fallen Richard II is a prisoner in his cell, abandoned and alone, it is not Richard II I see there, but all the fallen kings of this world; and not only all fallen kings, but also our beliefs and values, our unsanctified, corrupt and worn-out truths, the crumbling of civilizations, the march of destiny. When Richard II dies, it is really the death of all I hold most dear that I am watching; it is *I* who die with Richard II. Richard II makes me sharply conscious of the eternal truth that we forget in all these stories, the truth we fail to think about, though it is simple and absolutely commonplace: I die, he dies, you die. So it is not history after all that Shakespeare is writing, although he makes use of history; it is not History that he shows me, but *my* story and *our* story—*my* truth, which, independent, of my "times" and in the spectrum of a time that transcends Time, repeats a universal and inexorable truth. In fact, it is in the nature of a dramatic masterpiece to provide a superior pattern of instruction: it reflects my own image, it is a mirror; it is soul-searching; it is history gazing beyond history toward the deepest truth. One may find the reasons given by this or that author for wars and civil strife and struggles for power true or false, one may or may not agree with these interpretations. But one cannot deny that all those kings have faded from the scene, that they are dead; and an awareness of this reality, of this lasting evidence of the ephemeral nature of man, contrasted with his longing for eternal life, is obviously accompanied by the most profound emotion, by the most acute consciousness of tragedy, passionately felt. Art is the realm of passion, not of pedagogy; in this tragedy of tragedies we are concerned with the revelation of the most painful reality; I learn or reconsider something that has passed from my mind, I learn it in the only way possible with poetry, by an emotional participation that is not distorted by mystification and has burst through the paper dams of ideology and of a narrowly critical or "scientific" spirit. I only risk being taken in when I see a play, not with evidence to *offer*, but with a thesis to *prove*, an ideological, committed play, a play that is bogus and not true profoundly and poetically, as only poetry and tragedy can be true. All men die a lonely death, all values fall into contempt: that is what Shakespeare tells me. "Richard's cell is indeed the cell of all our solitudes." Perhaps Shakespeare *wanted* to tell the story of Richard II: if that was all he had told us, *the story of someone else*, he would not move me. But Richard II's prison is a truth that has not been swept away with history: its invisible walls still stand, whereas countless philosophies and ideologies have vanished for ever. And this truth still holds, because it is couched in the idiom of living evidence and not of demonstrative and rational judgment; Richard's prison is there before me, more vivid than any demonstration. Drama *is* this eternal and living presence: there is no doubt that it can reproduce the essential structure of tragic truth and theatrical reality. The evidence it offers has nothing to do with the uncertain truths of abstract thought or with the so-called ideological theatre: we are now concerned with the essence of the theatre, with theatrical archetypes, with theatrical idiom. An idiom that has been lost in our own times, when allegory and academic illustration seem to have been substituted for the living image of truth, which must be rediscovered. Every idiom develops, but development and renewal do not mean self-surrender and a change in kind; they mean a constant rediscovery of self, at each historical moment of time. One develops within the framework of one's own personality. The idiom of the theatre can never be anything but the idiom of the theatre.

As the idioms of painting and music have developed, they have always adjusted to the cultural style of their day, but without ever losing their pictorial or musical nature. And the development of painting, for example, has never been anything but a rediscovery of painting, its idiom and its essence. The direction taken by modern painting shows us this clearly. Since Klee, Kandinsky, Mondrian, Braque and Picasso, painting has done nothing but try to shake off all that is not painting: literature, story-telling, history and photography. Painters are trying to rediscover the basic fundamentals of painting, pure form, color for its own sake. Nor is it in this case a question of estheticism or what is nowadays rather improperly called formalism, but of the expression of reality in pictorial terms, *in an idiom as revealing as the language of words and sounds.* Even if this first appeared to us as a disintegration of the pictorial idiom, fundamentally it was the ascetic pursuit of purity, the rejection of a parasitic idiom. Similarly, it is only when we have pulled apart the conventional characters in our plays, only when we have broken down a false theatrical idiom, that we can follow the example of painting and try to put it together again—its essential purity restored.

Theatre can be nothing but theatre, although some contemporary specialists in "theatrology" consider it not true that a thing can be identified with itself—which seems to me the most bewildering and unlikely form of paradox.

For these "specialists" the theatre, being something different from the theatre, is ideology, allegory, politics, lectures, essays or literature. This is as much an aberration as it would be to claim that music was archaeology, that painting was physics or mathematics; and tennis anything you like but tennis.

Even if you admit that my views are not untrue, you may well tell me they are by no means new. If you went on to say these truths were elementary, I should be delighted, for there is nothing more difficult than the rediscovery of elementary truths, fundamental premises, or certitudes. Even philosophers go chiefly in search of sound premises. Elementary truth is precisely what one loses sight of, what one forgets. And that is why we breed confusion, why we fail in mutual understanding.

Besides, what I have just said is not a preconceived theory of dramatic art. It has not come *before*, but *after* my own personal experience of the theatre. Thinking about my own plays, good or bad, has provoked these few ideas. The reflections came afterward. I have no ideas *before* I write a play. I have them when I have *finished* it, or while I am *not* writing any at all. I believe that artistic creation is spontaneous. It is for me. Once again, all this is chiefly valid for me; but if I could believe I had discovered instinctively in myself the basic framework and permanent character of the objective reality of drama, or thrown even a little light on what the essence of the theatre is, I should be very proud. All ideologies are derived from knowledge that is second-hand, indirect, devious and false; nothing borrowed from others is true for the artist. For an author nick-named "avant-garde," I shall earn the reproach of having invented nothing. I believe that as one invents, one discovers, and that invention *is* discovery or rediscovery; and it is not my fault if I am taken for an avant-garde author. It is the critics who say so. It is of no importance. This definition is as good as the next. It means nothing at all. It is just a label.

Surrealism is not new either. All it did was discover and bring to light, in the process of reinventing, a certain way of knowing, or certain tendencies in human nature that centuries of rationalism frowned upon and suppressed. What, in short, does surrealism try to release? Love and dreams. How can we have forgotten that man is quickened by love? How not have noticed that we dream? Like all revolutions, the surrealist revolution was a reversion, a restitution, an expression of vital and indispensable spiritual needs. If finally it became too rigid, if one can now talk of academic surrealism, it is because every idiom wears out in the end; a lively tradition hardens into traditionalism, it becomes set in its forms and is "imitated"; in turn it too must be rediscovered: besides, as is well known, surrealism is itself a rejuvenation of romanticism; its origin, or one of its sources, is in the German romantics' power to dream. An extension of the frontiers of known reality depends upon a rediscovery of method and a rejuvenation of idiom. A genuine avant-garde movement can only be of value if it is more than a fashion. It can only spring from intuitive discovery, followed by a reassessment of neglected models from the past, which require constant rediscovery and rejuvenation.

I believe that in recent times we have forgotten what theatre is. And I am not excepting myself; I believe that, step by step, I have discovered it once more for myself, and what I have just described is simply my own experience of the theatre.

Obviously, a large number of problems have not been touched on. It remains to be seen, for example, how it comes about that a playwright like Feydeau, although the technique and mechanics of his theatre are beyond reproach, is not nearly so great as other playwrights whose technique may or may not be so perfect. In one sense, it is because everyone is a philosopher: by that I mean that everyone discovers some part of reality, the part that he can discover for himself. When I say "philosopher," I do not mean the specialist in philosophy, who merely exploits other people's vision of the world. Insofar as an artist has a personal apprehension of reality, he is a true philosopher. And his greatness is a result of the breadth, the depth and acuity of his authentically philosophical insight, of his living philosophy. The quality of a work of art directly depends on how "alive" philosophy is, on the fact that it springs from life and not from abstract thought. A philosophical system withers away as soon as a new philosophy or a new system goes a step further. Works of art, however, which are live philosophies, do not invalidate one another. That is why they can co-exist. The great works of art and the great poets seem to find confirmation, completion and corroboration in one another; Aeschylus is not cancelled out by Calderon, or Shakespeare by Chekhov, or Kleist by a Japanese Nō play. One scientific theory can cancel out another, but the truths found in works of art complement one another. Art seems the best justification for belief in the possibility of a metaphysical liberalism.

Translated by Donald Watson

THE CHAIRS

Translated by Donald M. Allen

CAST OF CHARACTERS

OLD MAN, *aged 95*
OLD WOMAN, *aged 94*
THE ORATOR, *aged 45 to 50*
And many other characters

SCENE *Circular walls with a recess upstage center. A large, very sparsely furnished room. To the right, going upstage from the proscenium, three doors. Then a window with a stool in front of it; then another door. In the center of the back wall of the recess, a large double door, and two other doors facing each other and bracketing the main door: these last two doors, or at least one of them, are almost hidden from the audience. To the left, going upstage from the proscenium, there are three doors, a window with a stool in front of it, opposite the window on the right, then a blackboard and a dais. See the plan below. Downstage are two chairs, side by side. A gas lamp hangs from the ceiling.*

(The curtain rises. Half-light. The OLD MAN *is up on the stool, leaning out the window on the left. The* OLD WOMAN *lights the gas lamp. Green light. She goes over to the* OLD MAN *and takes him by the sleeve)*

OLD WOMAN Come my darling, close the window. There's a bad smell from that stagnant water, and besides the mosquitoes are coming in.

OLD MAN Leave me alone!

OLD WOMAN Come, come, my darling, come sit down. You shouldn't lean out, you might fall into the water. You know what happened to François I. You must be careful.

The Chairs by Eugène Ionesco, translated by Donald M. Allen, is from *Four Plays by Eugène Ionesco.* Copyright © 1958 by the publishers, Grove Press, Inc.

OLD MAN Still more examples from history! Sweetheart, I'm tired of French history. I want to see—the boats on the water making blots in the sunlight.

OLD WOMAN You can't see them, there's no sunlight, it's nighttime, my darling.

OLD MAN There are still shadows. *(He leans out very far)*

OLD WOMAN *(pulling him in with all her strength)* Oh! . . . you're frightening me, my darling . . . come sit down, you won't be able to see them come, anyway. There's no use trying. It's dark . . .

(The OLD MAN *reluctantly lets himself be pulled in)*

OLD MAN I wanted to see—you know how much I love to see the water.

OLD WOMAN How can you, my darling? . . . It makes me dizzy. Ah! this house, this island, I can't get used to it. Water all around us . . . water under the windows, stretching as far as the horizon.

(The OLD WOMAN *drags the* OLD MAN *down and they move towards the two chairs downstage;*

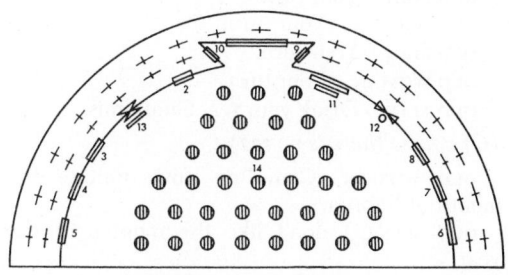

1: Main double door.
2, 3, 4, 5: Side doors on the right.
6, 7, 8: Side doors on the left.
9, 10: Two doors hidden in the recess.
11: Dais and blackboard.
12, 13: Windows, with stools, left and right.
14: Empty chairs.
XXX Corridor, in wings.

the OLD MAN *seats himself quite naturally on the lap of the* OLD WOMAN)

OLD MAN   It's six o'clock in the evening . . . it is dark already. It wasn't like this before. Surely you remember, there was still daylight at nine o'clock in the evening, at ten o'clock, at midnight.

OLD WOMAN   Come to think of it, that's very true. What a remarkable memory you have!

OLD MAN   Things have certainly changed.

OLD WOMAN   Why is that, do you think?

OLD MAN   I don't know, Semiramis, sweetheart . . . Perhaps it's because the further one goes, the deeper one sinks. It's because the earth keeps turning around, around, around, around . . .

OLD WOMAN   Around, around, my little pet. (*silence*) Ah! yes, you've certainly a fine intellect. You are very gifted, my darling. You could have been head president, head king, or even head doctor, or head general, if you had wanted to, if only you'd had a little ambition in life . . .

OLD MAN   What good would that have done us? We'd not have lived any better . . . and besides, we have a position here. I am a general, in any case, of the house, since I am the general factotum.

OLD WOMAN   (*caressing the* OLD MAN *as one caresses a child*)   My darling, my pet.

OLD MAN   I'm very bored.

OLD WOMAN   You were more cheerful when you were looking at the water . . . Let's amuse ourselves by making believe, the way you did the other evening.

OLD MAN   Make believe yourself, it's your turn.

OLD WOMAN   It's your turn.

OLD MAN   Your turn.

OLD WOMAN   Your turn.

OLD MAN   Your turn.

OLD WOMAN   Your turn.

OLD MAN   Drink your tea, Semiramis.

(*Of course there is no tea*)

OLD WOMAN   Come on now, imitate the month of February.

OLD MAN   I don't like the months of the year.

OLD WOMAN   Those are the only ones we have, up till now. Come on, just to please me . . .

OLD MAN   All right, here's the month of February. (*He scratches his head like Stan Laurel*)

OLD WOMAN   (*laughing, applauding*)   That's just right. Thank you, thank you, you're as cute as can be, my darling. (*She hugs him*) Oh, you

are so gifted, you could have been at least a head general, if you had wanted to . . .

OLD MAN   I am a general, general factotum.

(*silence*)

OLD WOMAN   Tell me the story, you know *the* story: "Then at last we arrived . . ."

OLD MAN   Again? . . . I'm sick of it . . . "Then at last we arrived"? That again . . . you always ask for the same thing! . . . "Then at last we arrived . . ." But it's monotonous . . . For all of the seventy-five years that we've been married, every single evening, absolutely every blessed evening, you've made me tell the same story, you've made me imitate the same people, the same months . . . always the same . . . let's talk about something else . . .

OLD WOMAN   My darling, I'm not tired of it . . . it's your life, it fascinates me.

OLD MAN   You know it by heart.

OLD WOMAN   It's as if suddenly I'd forgotten everything . . . it's as though my mind were a clean slate every evening . . . Yes, my darling, I do it on purpose, I take a dose of salts . . . I become new again, for you, my darling, every evening . . . Come on, begin again, please.

OLD MAN   Well, if you want me to.

OLD WOMAN   Come on then, tell your story . . . It's also mine; what is yours is mine! Then at last we arrived . . .

OLD MAN   Then at last we arrived . . . my sweetheart . . .

OLD WOMAN   Then at last we arrived . . . my darling . . .

OLD MAN   Then at last we arrived at a big fence. We were soaked through, frozen to the bone, for hours, for days, for nights, for weeks . . .

OLD WOMAN   For months . . .

OLD MAN   . . . in the rain . . . Our ears, our feet, our knees, our noses, our teeth were chattering . . . that was eighty years ago . . . They wouldn't let us in . . . they might at least have opened the gate of the garden . . .

(*silence*)

OLD WOMAN   In the garden the grass was wet.

OLD MAN   There was a path which led to a little square and in the center, a village church . . . Where was this village? Do you recall?

OLD WOMAN   No, my darling, I've forgotten.

OLD MAN   How did we reach it? Where is the road? This place was called Paris, I think . . .

OLD WOMAN   Paris never existed, my little one.

OLD MAN   That city must have existed because it collapsed . . . It was the city of light, but it has been extinguished, extinguished, for four hundred thousand years . . . Nothing remains of it today, except a song.

OLD WOMAN   A real song? That's odd. What song?

OLD MAN   A lullaby, an allegory: "Paris will always be Paris."

OLD WOMAN   And the way to it was through the garden? Was it far?

OLD MAN (*dreaming, lost*)   The song? . . . the rain? . . .

OLD WOMAN   You are very gifted. If you had had a little ambition in life you could have been head king, head journalist, head comedian, head general . . . All that's gone down the drain, alas . . . down the old black drain . . . down the old drain, I tell you. (*silence*)

OLD MAN   Then at last we arrived . . .

OLD WOMAN   Ah! yes, go on . . . tell me . . .

OLD MAN (*while the* OLD WOMAN *begins to laugh softly, senilely, then progressively in great bursts, the* OLD MAN *laughs, too, as he continues*)   Then at last we arrived, we laughed till we cried, the story was so idiotic . . . the idiot arrived full speed, bare-bellied, the idiot was pot-bellied . . . he arrived with a trunk chock full of rice; the rice spilled out on the ground . . . the idiot on the ground too, belly to ground . . . then at last we laughed, we laughed, we laughed, the idiotic belly, bare with rice on the ground, the trunk, the story of sick from rice belly to ground, bare-bellied, all with rice, at last we laughed, the idiot at last arrived all bare, we laughed . . .

OLD WOMAN (*laughing*)   At last we laughed like idiots, at last arrived all bare, we laughed, the trunk, the trunk full of rice, the rice on the belly, on the ground . . .

OLD MAN AND OLD WOMAN (*laughing together*)   At last we laughed. Ah! . . . laughed . . . arrived . . . arrived . . . Ah! . . . Ah! . . . rived . . . arrived . . . arrived . . . the idiotic bare belly . . . arrived with the rice . . . arrived with the rice . . . (*This is all we hear*) At last we . . . bare-bellied . . . arrived . . . the trunk . . . (*Then the* OLD MAN *and* OLD WOMAN *calm down little by little*) We lau . . . Ah! . . . aughed . . . Ah! . . . arrived . . . Ah! . . . arrived . . . aughed . . . aughed.

OLD WOMAN   So that's the way it was, your wonderful Paris.

OLD MAN   Who could put it better?

OLD WOMAN   Oh! my darling, you are so really fine. Oh! so really, you know, so really, so really, you could have been anything in life, a lot more than general factotum.

OLD MAN   Let's be modest . . . we should be content with the little . . .

OLD WOMAN   Perhaps you've spoiled your career?

OLD MAN (*weeping suddenly*)   I've spoiled it? I've spilled it? Ah! where are you, Mamma, Mamma, where are you, Mamma? . . . hi, hi, hi, I'm an orphan. (*He moans*) . . . an orphan, dworfan.

OLD WOMAN   Here I am, what are you afraid of?

OLD MAN   No, Semiramis, my sweetheart, you're not my mamma . . . orphan, dworfan, who will protect me?

OLD WOMAN   But I'm here, my darling!

OLD MAN   It's not the same thing . . . I want my mamma, na, you, you're not my mamma, you . . .

OLD WOMAN (*caressing him*)   You're breaking my heart, don't cry, my little one.

OLD MAN   Hi, hi, let me go, hi, hi, I'm all spoiled, I'm wet all over, my career is spilled, it's spoiled.

OLD WOMAN   Calm down.

OLD MAN (*sobbing, his mouth wide open like a baby*)   I'm an orphan . . . dworfan.

OLD WOMAN (*trying to console him by cajoling him*)   My orphan, my darling, you're breaking my heart, my orphan.

(*She rocks the* OLD MAN *who is sitting on her knees again*)

OLD MAN (*sobbing*)   Hi, hi, hi! My mamma! Where is my mamma? I don't have a mamma anymore.

OLD WOMAN   I am your wife, I'm the one who is your mamma now.

OLD MAN (*giving in a little*)   That's not true, I'm an orphan, hi, hi.

OLD WOMAN (*still rocking him*)   My pet, my orphan, dworfan, worfan, morphan, orphan.

OLD MAN (*still sulky, but giving in more and more*)   No . . . I don't want; I don't wa-a-a-ant.

OLD WOMAN (*crooning*)   Orphan-ly, orphan-lay, orphan-lo, orphan-loo.

OLD MAN   No-o-o . . . No-o-o.

OLD WOMAN (*same business*)   Li lon lala, li lon la lay, orphan-ly, orphan-lay, relee-relay, orphan-li-relee-rela . . .

OLD MAN   Hi, hi, hi, hi. (*He sniffles, calming down little by little*) Where is she? My mamma.

OLD WOMAN   In heavenly paradise . . . she hears you, she sees you, among the flowers; don't cry anymore, you will only make me weep!

OLD MAN   That's not even true-ue . . .

she can't see me . . . she can't hear me. I'm an orphan, on earth, you're not my mamma . . .

OLD WOMAN (*he is almost calm*) Now, come on, calm down, don't get so upset . . . you have great qualities, my little general . . . dry your tears; the guests are sure to come this evening and they mustn't see you this way . . . all is not lost, all is not spoiled, you'll tell them everything, you will explain, you have a message . . . you always say you are going to deliver it . . . you must live, you have to struggle for your message . . .

OLD MAN I have a message, that's God's truth, I struggle, a mission, I have something to say, a message to communicate to humanity, to mankind . . .

OLD WOMAN To mankind, my darling, your message! . . .

OLD MAN That's true, yes, it's true . . .

OLD WOMAN (*she wipes the* OLD MAN's *nose, dries his tears*) That's it . . . you're a man, a soldier, a general factotum . . .

OLD MAN (*he gets off the* OLD WOMAN's *lap and walks with short, agitated steps*) I'm not like other people, I have an ideal in life. I am perhaps gifted, as you say, I have some talent, but things aren't easy for me. I've served well in my capacity as general factotum, I've always been in command of the situation, honorably, that should be enough . . .

OLD WOMAN Not for you, you're not like other people, you are much greater, and moreover you'd have done much better if you had got along with other people, like other people do. You've quarreled with all your friends, with all the directors, with all the generals, with your own brother.

OLD MAN It's not my fault, Semiramis, you know very well what he said.

OLD WOMAN What did he say?

OLD MAN He said: "My friends, I've got a flea. I'm going to pay you a visit in the hope of leaving my flea with you."

OLD WOMAN People say things like that, my dear. You shouldn't have paid any attention to it. But with Carel, why were you so angry with him? Was it his fault too?

OLD MAN You're going to make me angry, you're going to make me angry. Na. Of course it was his fault. He came one evening, he said: "I know just the word that fits you. I'm not going to say it, I'll just think it." And he laughed like a fool.

OLD WOMAN But he had a warm heart, my darling. In this life, you've got to be less sensitive.

OLD MAN I don't care for jokes like that.

OLD WOMAN You could have been head ad-

miral, head cabinet-maker, head orchestra conductor.

(*Long silence. They remain immobile for a time, completely rigid on their chairs*)

OLD MAN (*as in a dream*) At the end of the garden there was . . . there was . . . there was . . . there was . . . was what, my dear?

OLD WOMAN The city of Paris!

OLD MAN At the end, at the end of the end of the city of Paris, there was, there was, was what?

OLD WOMAN My darling, was what, my darling, was who?

OLD MAN The place and the weather were beautiful . . .

OLD WOMAN The weather was so beautiful, are you sure?

OLD MAN I don't recall the place . . .

OLD WOMAN Don't tax your mind then . . .

OLD MAN It's too far away, I can no longer . . . recall it . . . where was this?

OLD WOMAN But what?

OLD MAN What I . . . what I . . . where was this? And who?

OLD WOMAN No matter where it is—I will follow you anywhere, I'll follow you, my darling.

OLD MAN Ah! I have so much difficulty expressing myself . . . but I must tell it all.

OLD WOMAN It's a sacred duty. You've no right to keep your message from the world. You must reveal it to mankind, they're waiting for it . . . the universe waits only for you.

OLD MAN Yes, yes, I will speak.

OLD WOMAN Have you really decided? You must.

OLD MAN Drink your tea.

OLD WOMAN You could have been head orator, if you'd had more will power in life . . . I'm proud, I'm happy that you have at last decided to speak to every country, to Europe, to every continent!

OLD MAN Unfortunately, I have so much difficulty expressing myself, it isn't easy for me.

OLD WOMAN It's easy once you begin, like life and death . . . it's enough to have your mind made up. It's in speaking that ideas come to us, words, and then we, in our own words, we find perhaps everything, the city too, the garden, and then we are orphans no longer.

OLD MAN It's not I who's going to speak, I've hired a professional orator, he'll speak in my name, you'll see.

OLD WOMAN Then, it really is for this evening? And have you invited everyone, all the characters, all the property owners, and all the intellectuals?

OLD MAN   Yes, all the owners and all the intellectuals. (*silence*)

OLD WOMAN   The janitors? the bishops? the chemists? the tinsmiths? the violinists? the delegates? the presidents? the police? the merchants? the buildings? the pen holders? the chromosomes?

OLD MAN   Yes, yes, and the post-office employees, the innkeepers, and the artists, everybody who is a little intellectual, a little proprietary!

OLD WOMAN   And the bankers?

OLD MAN   Yes, invited.

OLD WOMAN   The proletarians? the functionaries? the militaries? the revolutionaries? the reactionaries? the alienists and their alienated?

OLD MAN   Of course, all of them, all of them, all of them, since actually everyone is either intellectual or proprietary.

OLD WOMAN   Don't get upset, my darling, I don't mean to annoy you, you are so very absent-minded, like all great geniuses. This meeting is important, they must all be here this evening. Can you count on them? Have they promised?

OLD MAN   Drink your tea, Semiramis. (*silence*)

OLD WOMAN   The papacy, the papayas, and the papers?

OLD MAN   I've invited them. (*silence*) I'm going to communicate the message to them . . . All my life, I've felt that I was suffocating; and now, they will know all, thanks to you and to the Orator, you are the only ones who have understood me.

OLD WOMAN   I'm so proud of you . . .

OLD MAN   The meeting will take place in a few minutes.

OLD WOMAN   It's true then, they're going to come, this evening? You won't feel like crying any more, the intellectuals and the proprietors will take the place of papas and mammas? (*silence*) Couldn't you put off this meeting? It won't be too tiring for us?

(*More violent agitation. For several moments the* OLD MAN *has been turning around the* OLD WOMAN *with the short, hesitant steps of an old man or of a child. He takes a step or two towards one of the doors, then returns and walks around her again*)

OLD MAN   You really think this might tire us?

OLD WOMAN   You have a slight cold.

OLD MAN   How can I call it off?

OLD WOMAN   Invite them for another evening. You could telephone.

OLD MAN   No, my God, I can't do that, it's too late. They've probably already embarked!

OLD WOMAN   You should have been more careful.

(*We hear the sound of a boat gliding through the water*)

OLD MAN   I think someone is coming already . . . (*The gliding sound of a boat is heard more clearly*) . . . Yes, they're coming! . . .

(*The* OLD WOMAN *gets up also and walks with a hobble*)

OLD WOMAN   Perhaps it's the Orator.

OLD MAN   He won't come so soon. This must be somebody else. (*We hear the doorbell ring*) Ah!

OLD WOMAN   Ah!

(*Nervously, the* OLD MAN *and the* OLD WOMAN *move towards the concealed door in the recess to the right. As they move upstage, they say*)

OLD MAN   Come on . . .

OLD WOMAN   My hair must look a sight . . . wait a moment. . . .

(*She arranges her hair and her dress as she hobbles along, pulling up her thick red stockings*)

OLD MAN   You should have gotten ready before . . . you had plenty of time.

OLD WOMAN   I'm so badly dressed . . . I'm wearing an old gown and it's all rumpled . . .

OLD MAN   All you had to do was to press it . . . hurry up! You're making our guests wait.

(*The* OLD MAN, *followed by the* OLD WOMAN *still grumbling, reaches the door in the recess; we don't see them for a moment; we hear them open the door, then close it again after having shown someone in*)

VOICE OF OLD MAN   Good evening, madam, won't you please come in. We're delighted to see you. This is my wife.

VOICE OF OLD WOMAN   Good evening, madam, I am very happy to make your acquaintance. Take care, don't ruin your hat. You might take out the hatpin, that will be more comfortable. Oh! no, no one will sit on it.

VOICE OF OLD MAN   Put your fur down there. Let me help you. No, nothing will happen to it.

VOICE OF OLD WOMAN   Oh! what a pretty suit . . . and such darling colors in your blouse . . . Won't you have some cookies . . . Oh, you're not fat at all . . . no . . . plump . . . Just leave your umbrella there.

VOICE OF OLD MAN   Follow me, please.

OLD MAN (*back view*)   I have only a modest position . . .

(*The* OLD MAN *and* OLD WOMAN *re-enter together, leaving space between them for their guest. She is invisible. The* OLD MAN *and* OLD WOMAN *advance, downstage, facing the audience and speaking to the invisible* LADY, *who walks between them*)

OLD MAN (*to the invisible* LADY)   You've had good weather?

OLD WOMAN (*to the* LADY)   You're not too tired? . . . Yes, a little.

OLD MAN (*to the* LADY)   At the edge of the water . . .

OLD WOMAN (*to the* LADY)   It's kind of you to say so.

OLD MAN (*to the* LADY)   Let me get you a chair.

(OLD MAN *goes to the left, he exits by door No. 6*)

OLD WOMAN (*to the* LADY)   Take this one, for the moment, please. (*She indicates one of the two chairs and seats herself on the other, to the right of the invisible* LADY) It seems rather warm in here, doesn't it? (*She smiles at the* LADY) What a charming fan you have! My husband . . . (*The* OLD MAN *re-enters through door No. 7, carrying a chair*) . . . gave me one very like it, that must have been seventy-three years ago . . . and I still have it . . . (*The* OLD MAN *places the chair to the left of the invisible* LADY) . . . it was for my birthday! . . .

(*The* OLD MAN *sits on the chair that he has just brought onstage, so that the invisible* LADY *is between the old couple. The* OLD MAN *turns his face towards the* LADY, *smiles at her, nods his head, softly rubs his hands together, with the air of following what she says. The* OLD WOMAN *does the same business*)

OLD MAN   No, madam, life is never cheap.

OLD WOMAN (*to the* LADY)   You are so right . . . (*The* LADY *speaks*) As you say, it is about time all that changed . . . (*changing her tone*) Perhaps my husband can do something about it . . . he's going to tell you about it.

OLD MAN (*to the* OLD WOMAN)   Hush, hush, Semiramis, the time hasn't come to talk about that yet. (*to the* LADY) Excuse me, madam, for having aroused your curiosity. (*The* LADY *reacts*) Dear madam, don't insist . . .

(*The* OLD MAN *and* OLD WOMAN *smile. They even laugh. They appear to be very amused by the story the invisible* LADY *tells them. A pause,*
a moment of silence in the conversation. Their faces lose all expression)

OLD MAN (*to the invisible* LADY)   Yes, you're quite right . . .

OLD WOMAN   Yes, yes, yes . . . Oh! surely not.

OLD MAN   Yes, yes, yes. Not at all.

OLD WOMAN   Yes?

OLD MAN   No!?

OLD WOMAN   It's certainly true.

OLD MAN (*laughing*)   It isn't possible.

OLD WOMAN (*laughing*)   Oh! well. (*to the* OLD MAN) She's charming.

OLD MAN (*to the* OLD WOMAN)   Madam has made a conquest. (*to the invisible* LADY) My congratulations!

OLD WOMAN (*to the invisible* LADY)   You're not like the young people today . . .

OLD MAN (*bending over painfully in order to recover an invisible object that the invisible* LADY *has dropped*)   Let me . . . don't disturb yourself . . . I'll get it . . . Oh! you're quicker than I . . . (*He straightens up again*)

OLD WOMAN (*to the* OLD MAN)   She's younger than you!

OLD MAN (*to the invisible* LADY)   Old age is a heavy burden. I can only wish you an eternal youth.

OLD WOMAN (*to the invisible* LADY)   He's sincere, he speaks from the heart. (*to the* OLD MAN) My darling!

(*Several moments of silence. The* OLD MAN *and* OLD WOMAN, *heads turned in profile, look at the invisible* LADY, *smiling politely; they then turn their heads towards the audience, then look again at the invisible* LADY, *answering her smile with their smiles, and her questions with their replies*)

OLD WOMAN   It's very kind of you to take such an interest in us.

OLD MAN   We live a retired life.

OLD WOMAN   My husband's not really misanthropic, he just loves solitude.

OLD MAN   We have the radio, I get in some fishing, and then there's fairly regular boat service.

OLD WOMAN   On Sundays there are two boats in the morning, one in the evening, not to mention privately chartered trips.

OLD MAN (*to the invisible* LADY)   When the weather's clear, there is a moon.

OLD WOMAN (*to the invisible* LADY)   He's always concerned with his duties as general factotum . . . they keep him busy . . . On the other hand, at his age, he might very well take it easy.

OLD MAN (*to the invisible* LADY) I'll have plenty of time to take it easy in my grave.

OLD WOMAN (*to the* OLD MAN) Don't say that, my little darling . . . (*to the invisible* LADY) Our family, what's left of it, my husband's friends, still came to see us, from time to time, ten years ago . . .

OLD MAN (*to the invisible* LADY) In the winter, a good book, beside the radiator, and the memories of a lifetime.

OLD WOMAN (*to the invisible* LADY) A modest life but a full one . . . he devotes two hours every day to work on his message.

(*The doorbell rings. After a short pause, we hear the noise of a boat leaving*)

OLD WOMAN (*to the* OLD MAN) Someone has come. Go quickly.

OLD MAN (*to the invisible* LADY) Please excuse me, madam. Just a moment! (*to the* OLD WOMAN) Hurry and bring some chairs!

(*Loud ringing of the doorbell*)

OLD MAN (*hastening, all bent over, towards door No. 2 to the right, while the* OLD WOMAN *goes towards the concealed door on the left, hurrying with difficulty, hobbling along*) It must be someone important. (*He hurries, opens door No. 2, and the invisible* COLONEL *enters. Perhaps it would be useful for us to hear discreetly several trumpet notes, several phrases, like "Hail the Chief." When he opens the door and sees the invisible* COLONEL, *the* OLD MAN *stiffens into a respectful position of attention*) Ah! . . . Colonel! (*He lifts his hand vaguely towards his forehead, so as to roughly sketch a salute*) Good evening, my dear Colonel . . . This is a very great honor for me . . . I . . . I was not expecting it . . . although . . . indeed . . . in short, I am most proud to welcome you, a hero of your eminence, into my humble dwelling . . . (*He presses the invisible hand that the invisible* COLONEL *gives him, bending forward ceremoniously, then straightening up again*) Without false modesty, nevertheless, I permit myself to confess to you that I do not feel unworthy of the honor of your visit! Proud, yes . . . unworthy, no! . . .

(*The* OLD WOMAN *appears with a chair, entering from the right*)

OLD WOMAN Oh! What a handsome uniform! What beautiful medals! Who is it, my darling?

OLD MAN (*to the* OLD WOMAN) Can't you see that it's the Colonel?

OLD WOMAN (*to the* OLD MAN) Ah!

OLD MAN (*to the* OLD WOMAN) Count his stripes! (*to the* COLONEL) This is my wife, Semiramis. (*to the* OLD WOMAN) Come here so that I can introduce you to the Colonel. (*The* OLD WOMAN *approaches, dragging the chair by one hand, and makes a curtsey, without letting go of the chair. To the* COLONEL) My wife. (*to the* OLD WOMAN) The Colonel.

OLD WOMAN How do you do, Colonel. Welcome. You're an old comrade of my husband's, he's a general . . .

OLD MAN (*annoyed*) factotum, factotum . . .

(*The invisible* COLONEL *kisses the hand of the* OLD WOMAN. *This is apparent from the gesture she makes as she raises her hand toward his lips. Overcome with emotion, the* OLD WOMAN *lets go of the chair*)

OLD WOMAN Oh! He's most polite . . . you can see that he's really superior, a superior being! . . . (*She takes hold of the chair again. To the* COLONEL) This chair is for you . . .

OLD MAN (*to the invisible* COLONEL) This way, if you please . . . (*They move downstage, the* OLD WOMAN *dragging the chair. To the* COLONEL) Yes, one guest has come already. We're expecting a great many more people! . . .

(*The* OLD WOMAN *places the chair to the right*)

OLD WOMAN (*to the* COLONEL) Sit here, please.

(*The* OLD MAN *introduces the two invisible guests to each other*)

OLD MAN A young lady we know . . .

OLD WOMAN A very dear friend . . .

OLD MAN (*same business*) The Colonel . . . a famous soldier.

OLD WOMAN (*indicating the chair she has just brought in to the* COLONEL) Do take this chair . . .

OLD MAN (*to the* OLD WOMAN) No, no, can't you see that the Colonel wishes to sit beside the Lady! . . .

(*The* COLONEL *seats himself invisibly on the third chair from the left; the invisible* LADY *is supposedly sitting on the second chair; seated next to each other they engage in an inaudible conversation; the* OLD WOMAN *and* OLD MAN *continue to stand behind their chairs, on both sides of their invisible guests; the* OLD MAN *to the left of the* LADY, *the* OLD WOMAN *to the right of the* COLONEL)

OLD WOMAN (*listening to the conversation of the two guests*) Oh! Oh! That's going too far.

OLD MAN (*same business*) Perhaps. (*The* OLD MAN *and the* OLD WOMAN *make signs to each other over the heads of their guests, while they follow the inaudible conversation which takes a turn that seems to displease them. Abruptly)* Yes, Colonel, they are not here yet, but they'll be here. And the Orator will speak in my behalf, he will explain the meaning of my message . . . Take care, Colonel, this Lady's husband may arrive at any moment.

OLD WOMAN *(to the* OLD MAN*)* Who is this gentleman?

OLD MAN *(to the* OLD WOMAN*)* I've told you, it's the Colonel.

(Some embarrassing things take place invisibly)

OLD WOMAN *(to the* OLD MAN*)* I knew it. I knew it.

OLD MAN Then why are you asking?

OLD WOMAN For my information. Colonel, no cigarette butts on the floor!

OLD MAN *(to* COLONEL*)* Colonel, Colonel, it's slipped my mind—in the last war did you win or lose?

OLD WOMAN *(to the invisible* LADY*)* But my dear, don't let it happen!

OLD MAN Look at me, look at me, do I look like a bad soldier? One time, Colonel, under fire . . .

OLD WOMAN He's going too far! It's embarrassing! *(She seizes the invisible sleeve of the* COLONEL*)* Listen to him! My darling, why don't you stop him!

OLD MAN *(continuing quickly)* And all on my own, I killed 209 of them; we called them that because they jumped so high to escape, however there weren't so many of them as there were flies; of course it is less amusing, Colonel, but thanks to my strength of character, I have . . . Oh! no, I must, please.

OLD WOMAN *(to* COLONEL*)* My husband never lies; it may be true that we are old, nevertheless we're respectable.

OLD MAN *(violently, to the* COLONEL*)* A hero must be a gentleman too, if he hopes to be a complete hero!

OLD WOMAN *(to the* COLONEL*)* I've known you for many years, but I'd never have believed you were capable of this. *(to the* LADY, *while we hear the sound of boats)* I'd never have believed him capable of this. We have our dignity, our self-respect.

OLD MAN *(in a quavering voice)* I'm still capable of bearing arms. *(doorbell rings)* Excuse me, I must go to the door. *(He stumbles and knocks over the chair of the invisible* LADY*)* Oh! pardon.

OLD WOMAN *(rushing forward)* You didn't hurt yourself? *(The* OLD MAN *and* OLD WOMAN *help the invisible* LADY *onto her feet)* You've got all dirty, there's some dust. *(She helps brush the* LADY. *The doorbell rings again)*

OLD MAN Forgive me, forgive me. *(to the* OLD WOMAN*)* Go bring a chair.

OLD WOMAN *(to the two invisible guests)* Excuse me for a moment.

(While the OLD MAN *goes to open door No. 3, the* OLD WOMAN *exits through door No. 5 to look for a chair, and she re-enters by door No. 8)*

OLD MAN *(moving towards the door)* He was trying to get my goat. I'm almost angry. *(He opens the door)* Oh! madam, you're here! I can scarcely believe my eyes, and yet, nevertheless . . . I didn't really dare to hope . . . really it's . . . Oh! madam, madam . . . I have thought about you, all my life, all my life, madam, they always called you La Belle . . . it's your husband . . . someone told me, certainly . . . you haven't changed a bit . . . Oh! yes, yes, your nose *has* grown longer, maybe it's a little swollen . . . I didn't notice it when I first saw you, but I see it now . . . a lot longer . . . ah! how unfortunate! You certainly didn't do it on purpose . . . how did it happen? . . . little by little . . . excuse me, sir and dear friend, you'll permit me to call you "dear friend," I knew your wife long before you . . . she was the same, but with a completely different nose . . . I congratulate you, sir, you seem to love each other very much. *(The* OLD WOMAN *re-enters through door No. 8 with a chair)* Semiramis, two guests have arrived, we need one more chair . . . *(The* OLD WOMAN *puts the chair behind the four others, then exits by door No. 8 and re-enters by door No. 5, after a few moments, with another chair that she places beside the one she has just brought in. By this time, the* OLD MAN *and the two guests have moved near the* OLD WOMAN*)* Come this way, please, more guests have arrived. I'm going to introduce you . . . now then, madam . . . Oh! Belle, Belle, Miss Belle, that's what they used to call you . . . now you're all bent over . . . Oh! sir, she is still Belle to me, even so; under her glasses, she still has pretty eyes; her hair is white, but under the white one can see brown, and blue, I'm sure of that . . . come nearer, nearer . . . what is this, sir, a gift, for my wife? *(to the* OLD WOMAN, *who has just come on with the chair)* Semiramis, this is Belle, you know, Belle . . . *(to the* COLONEL *and the invisible* LADY*)* This is Miss, pardon, Mrs. Belle, don't smile . . . and her husband . . . *(to the* OLD WOMAN*)* A childhood friend, I've often spoken of her to you . . . and her husband. (*again to the* COLONEL *and to the invisible* LADY) And her husband . . .

OLD WOMAN (*making a little curtsey*) He certainly makes good introductions. He has fine manners. Good evening, madam, good evening, sir. (*She indicates the two first guests to the newly arrived couple*) Our friends, yes . . .

OLD MAN (*to the* OLD WOMAN) He's brought you a present.

(*The* OLD WOMAN *takes the present*)

OLD WOMAN Is it a flower, sir? or a cradle? a pear tree? or a crow?

OLD MAN (*to the* OLD WOMAN) No, no, can't you see that it's a painting?

OLD WOMAN Oh! how pretty! Thank you, sir . . . (*to the invisible* LADY) Would you like to see it, dear friend?

OLD MAN (*to the invisible* COLONEL) Would you like to see it?

OLD WOMAN (*to* BELLE's *husband*) Doctor, Doctor, I feel squeamish, I have hot flashes, I feel sick, I've aches and pains, I haven't any feeling in my feet, I've caught cold in my eyes, I've a cold in my fingers, I'm suffering from liver trouble, Doctor, Doctor! . . .

OLD MAN (*to the* OLD WOMAN) This gentleman is not a doctor, he's a photo-engraver.

OLD WOMAN (*to the first invisible* LADY) If you've finished looking at it, you might hang it up. (*to the* OLD MAN) That doesn't matter, he's charming even so, he's dazzling. (*to the* PHOTO-ENGRAVER) Without meaning to flatter you . . .

(*The* OLD MAN *and the* OLD WOMAN *now move behind the chairs, close to each other, almost touching, but back to back; they talk: the* OLD MAN *to* BELLE, *the* OLD WOMAN *to the* PHOTO-ENGRAVER; *from time to time their replies, as shown by the way they turn their heads, are addressed to one or the other of the two first guests*)

OLD MAN (*to* BELLE) I am very touched . . . You're still the same, in spite of everything . . . I've loved you, a hundred years ago . . . But there's been such a change . . . No, you haven't changed a bit . . . I loved you, I loved you . . .

OLD WOMAN (*to the* PHOTO-ENGRAVER) Oh! Sir, sir, sir . . .

OLD MAN (*to the* COLONEL) I'm in complete agreement with you on that point.

OLD WOMAN (*to the* PHOTO-ENGRAVER) Oh! certainly, sir, certainly, sir, certainly . . . (*to the first* LADY) Thanks for hanging it up . . . Forgive me if I've inconvenienced you.

(*The light grows stronger. It should grow stronger and stronger as the invisible guests continue to arrive*)

OLD MAN (*almost whimpering to* BELLE) Where are the snows of yesteryear?

OLD WOMAN (*to the* PHOTO-ENGRAVER) Oh! Sir, sir, sir . . . Oh! sir . . .

OLD MAN (*pointing out the first* LADY *to* BELLE) She's a young friend . . . she's very sweet . . .

OLD WOMAN (*pointing the* COLONEL *out to the* PHOTO-ENGRAVER) Yes, he's a mounted staff colonel . . . a comrade of my husband . . . a subaltern, my husband's a general . . .

OLD MAN (*to* BELLE) Your ears were not always so pointed! . . . My Belle, do you remember?

OLD WOMAN (*to the* PHOTO-ENGRAVER, *simpering grotesquely; she develops this manner more and more in this scene; she shows her thick red stockings, raises her many petticoats, shows an underskirt full of holes, exposes her old breast; then, her hands on her hips, throws her head back, makes little erotic cries, projects her pelvis, her legs spread apart; she laughs like an old prostitute; this business, entirely different from her manner heretofore as well as from that she will have subsequently, and which must reveal the hidden personality of the* OLD WOMAN, *ceases abruptly*) So you think I'm too old for that, do you?

OLD MAN (*to* BELLE, *very romantically*) When we were young, the moon was a living star. Ah! yes, yes, if only we had dared, but we were only children. Wouldn't you like to recapture those bygone days . . . is it still possible? Is it still possible? Ah! no, no, it is no longer possible. Those days have flown away as fast as a train. Time has left the marks of his wheels on our skin. Do you believe surgeons can perform miracles? (*to the* COLONEL) I am a soldier, and you too, we soldiers are always young, the generals are like gods . . . (*to* BELLE) It ought to be that way . . . Alas! Alas! We have lost everything. We could have been so happy, I'm sure of it, we could have been, we could have been; perhaps the flowers are budding again beneath the snow! . . .

OLD WOMAN (*to* PHOTO-ENGRAVER) Flatterer! Rascal! Ah! Ah! I look younger than my years? You're a little savage! You're exciting.

OLD MAN (*to* BELLE) Will you be my Isolde and let me be your Tristan? Beauty is more than skin deep, it's in the heart . . . Do you understand? We could have had the pleasure of sharing, joy, beauty, eternity . . . an eternity . . . Why didn't we dare? We weren't brave enough . . . Everything is lost, lost, lost.

OLD WOMAN (*to* PHOTO-ENGRAVER) Oh no, Oh! no, Oh! la la, you give me the shivers. You too, are you ticklish? To tickle or be tickled? I'm a little embarrassed . . . (*She laughs*) Do you like my petticoat? Or do you like this skirt better?

OLD MAN (*to* BELLE) A general factotum has a poor life!

OLD WOMAN (*turning her head towards the first invisible* LADY) In order to make crepes de Chine? A leaf of beef, an hour of flour, a little gastric sugar. (*to the* PHOTO-ENGRAVER) You've got clever fingers, ah . . . all the sa-a-a-me! . . . Oh-oh-oh-oh.

OLD MAN (*to* BELLE) My worthy help-meet, Semiramis, has taken the place of my mother. (*He turns towards the* COLONEL) Colonel, as I've often observed to you, one must take the truth as one finds it. (*He turns back towards* BELLE)

OLD WOMAN (*to* PHOTO-ENGRAVER) Do you really really believe that one could have children at any age? Any age children?

OLD MAN (*to* BELLE) It's this alone that has saved me: the inner life, peace of mind, austerity, my scientific investigations, philosophy, my message . . .

OLD WOMAN (*to* PHOTO-ENGRAVER) I've never yet betrayed my husband, the general . . . not so hard, you're going to make me fall . . . I'm only his poor mamma! (*She sobs*) A great, great (*She pushes him back*), great . . . mamma. My conscience causes these tears to flow. For me the branch of the apple tree is broken. Try to find somebody else. I no longer want to gather rosebuds . . .

OLD MAN (*to* BELLE) . . . All the pre-occupations of a superior order . . .

(*The* OLD MAN *and* OLD WOMAN *lead* BELLE *and the* PHOTO-ENGRAVER *up alongside the two other invisible guests, and seat them*)

OLD MAN AND OLD WOMAN (*to the* PHOTO-ENGRAVER *and* BELLE) Sit down, please sit down.

(*The* OLD MAN *and* OLD WOMAN *sit down too, he to the left, she to the right, with the four empty chairs between them. A long mute scene, punctuated at intervals with "no," "yes," "yes." The* OLD MAN *and* OLD WOMAN *listen to the conversation of the invisible guests*)

OLD WOMAN (*to the* PHOTO-ENGRAVER) We had one son . . . of course, he's still alive . . . he's gone away . . . it's a common story . . . or, rather, unusual . . . he abandoned his parents . . . he had a heart of gold . . . that

was a long time ago . . . We loved him so much . . . he slammed the door . . . My husband and I tried to hold him back with all our might . . . he was seven years old, the age of reason, I called after him: "My son, my child, my son, my child." . . . He didn't even look back . . .

OLD MAN Alas, no . . . no, we've never had a child . . . I'd hoped for a son . . . Semiramis, too . . . we did everything . . . and my poor Semiramis is so maternal, too. Perhaps it was better that way . . . As for me I was an ungrateful son myself . . . Ah! . . . grief, regret, remorse, that's all we have . . . that's all we have left . . .

OLD WOMAN He said to me: "You kill birds! Why do you kill birds?" . . . But we don't kill birds . . . we've never harmed so much as a fly . . . His eyes were full of big tears. He wouldn't let us dry them. He wouldn't let me come near him. He said: "Yes, you kill all the birds, all the birds." . . . He showed us his little fists . . . "You're lying, you've betrayed me! The streets are full of dead birds, of dying baby birds." It's the song of the birds! . . . "No, it's their death rattle. The sky is red with blood." . . . No, my child, it's blue. He cried again: "You've betrayed me, I adored you, I believed you to be good . . . the streets are full of dead birds, you've torn out their eyes . . . Papa, mamma, you're wicked! . . . I refuse to stay with you." . . . I threw myself at his feet . . . His father was weeping. We couldn't hold him back. As he went we could still hear him calling: "It's you who are responsible" . . . What does that mean, "responsible"?

OLD MAN I let my mother die all alone in a ditch. She called after me, moaning feebly: "My little child, my beloved son, don't leave me to die all alone . . . Stay with me. I don't have much time left." Don't worry, Mamma, I told her, I'll be back in a moment . . . I was in a hurry . . . I was going to the ball, to dance. I will be back in a minute. But when I returned, she was already dead, and they had buried her deep . . . I broke open the grave, I searched for her . . . I couldn't find her . . . I know, I know, sons, always, abandon their mothers, and they more or less kill their fathers . . . Life is like that . . . but I, I suffer from it . . . and the others, they don't . . .

OLD WOMAN He cried: "Papa, Mamma, I'll never set eyes on you again."

OLD MAN I suffer from it, yes, the others don't . . .

OLD WOMAN Don't speak of him to my husband. He loved his parents so much. He never left them for a single moment. He cared for them, coddled them . . . And they died in his arms, saying to him: "You have been a perfect son. God will be good to you."

OLD MAN   I can still see her stretched out in the ditch, she was holding lily of the valley in her hand, she cried: "Don't forget me, don't forget me" . . . her eyes were full of big tears, and she called me by my baby name: "Little Chick," she said, "Little Chick, don't leave me here all alone."

OLD WOMAN (*to the* PHOTO-ENGRAVER)   He has never written to us. From time to time, a friend tells us that he's been seen here or there, that he is well, that he is a good husband . . .

OLD MAN (*to* BELLE)   When I got back, she had been buried a long time. (*to the first invisible* LADY) Oh, yes. Oh! yes, madam, we have a movie theatre in the house, a restaurant, bathrooms . . .

OLD WOMAN (*to the* COLONEL)   Yes, Colonel, it is because he . . .

OLD MAN   Basically that's it.

(*Desultory conversation, getting bogged down*)

OLD WOMAN   If only!

OLD MAN   Thus, I've not . . . I, it . . . certainly . . .

OLD WOMAN (*dislocated dialogue, exhaustion*)   All in all.

OLD MAN   To ours and to theirs.

OLD WOMAN   So that.

OLD MAN   From me to him.

OLD WOMAN   Him, or her?

OLD MAN   Them.

OLD WOMAN   Curl-papers . . . After all.

OLD MAN   It's not that.

OLD WOMAN   Why?

OLD MAN   Yes.

OLD WOMAN   I.

OLD MAN   All in all.

OLD WOMAN   All in all.

OLD MAN (*to the first invisible* LADY)   What was that, madam?

(*A long silence, the* OLD MAN *and* OLD WOMAN *remain rigid on their chairs. Then the doorbell rings*)

OLD MAN (*with increasing nervousness*) Someone has come. People. Still more people.

OLD WOMAN   I thought I heard some boats.

OLD MAN   I'll go to the door. Go bring some chairs. Excuse me, gentlemen, ladies. (*He goes towards door No. 7*)

OLD WOMAN (*to the invisible guests who have already arrived*)   Get up for a moment, please. The Orator will be here soon. We must ready the room for the meeting. (*The* OLD WOMAN *arranges the chairs, turning their backs towards the audience*) Lend me a hand, please. Thanks.

OLD MAN (*opening door No. 7*)   Good evening, ladies, good evening, gentlemen. Please come in.

(*The three or four invisible persons who have arrived are very tall, and the* OLD MAN *has to stand on his toes in order to shake hands with them. The* OLD WOMAN, *after placing the chairs as indicated above, goes over to the* OLD MAN)

OLD MAN (*making introductions*)   My wife . . . Mr. . . . Mrs. . . . my wife . . . Mr. . . . Mrs. . . . my wife . . .

OLD WOMAN   Who are all these people, my darling?

OLD MAN (*to* OLD WOMAN)   Go find some chairs, dear.

OLD WOMAN   I can't do everything! . . .

(*She exits, grumbling, by door No. 6 and re-enters by door No. 7, while the* OLD MAN, *with the newly arrived guests, moves downstage*)

OLD MAN   Don't drop your movie camera. (*more introductions*) The Colonel . . . the Lady . . . Mrs. Belle . . . the Photo-engraver . . . These are the newspaper men, they have come to hear the Orator too, who should be here any minute now . . . Don't be impatient . . . You'll not be bored . . . all together now . . . (*The* OLD WOMAN *re-enters through door No. 7 with two chairs*) Come along, bring the chairs more quickly . . . we're still short one.

(*The* OLD WOMAN *goes to find another chair, still grumbling, exiting by door No. 3, and re-entering by door No. 8*)

OLD WOMAN   All right, and so . . . I'm doing as well as I can . . . I'm not a machine, you know . . . Who are all these people? (*She exits*)

OLD MAN   Sit down, sit down, the ladies with the ladies, and the gentlemen with the gentlemen, or vice versa, if you prefer . . . We don't have any more nice chairs . . . we have to make do with what we have . . . I'm sorry . . . take the one in the middle . . . does anyone need a fountain pen? Telephone Maillot, you'll get Monique . . . Claude is an angel. I don't have a radio . . . I take all the newspapers . . . that depends on a number of things; I manage these buildings, but I have no help . . . we have to economize . . . no interviews, please, for the moment . . . later, we'll see . . . you'll soon have a place to sit . . . what can she be doing? (*The* OLD WOMAN *enters by door No. 8 with a chair*) Faster, Semiramis . . .

OLD WOMAN   I'm doing my best . . . Who are all these people?

OLD MAN   I'll explain it all to you later.

OLD WOMAN   And that woman? That woman, my darling?

OLD MAN   Don't get upset . . . (*to the* COLONEL) Colonel, journalism is a profession too, like a fighting man's . . . (*to the* OLD WOMAN) Take care of the ladies, my dear . . . (*The doorbell rings. The* OLD MAN *hurries towards door No. 8*) Wait a moment . . . (*to the* OLD WOMAN) Bring chairs!

OLD WOMAN   Gentlemen, ladies, excuse me . . .

(*She exits by door No. 3, re-entering by door No. 2; the* OLD MAN *goes to open concealed door No. 9, and disappears at the moment the* OLD WOMAN *re-enters by door No. 2*)

OLD MAN   (*out of sight*)   Come in . . . come in . . . come in . . . come in . . . (*He reappears, leading in a number of invisible people, including one very small child he holds by the hand*) One doesn't bring little children to a scientific lecture . . . the poor little thing is going to be bored . . . if he begins to cry or to peepee on the ladies' dresses, that'll be a fine state of affairs! (*He conducts them to stage center; the* OLD WOMAN *comes on with two chairs*) I wish to introduce you to my wife, Semiramis; and these are their children.

OLD WOMAN   Ladies, gentlemen . . . Oh! aren't they sweet!

OLD MAN   That one is the smallest.

OLD WOMAN   Oh, he's so cute . . . so cute . . . so cute!

OLD MAN   Not enough chairs.

OLD WOMAN   Oh! dear, oh dear, oh dear . . .

(*She exits, looking for another chair, using now door No. 2 as exit and door No. 3 on the right to re-enter*)

OLD MAN   Hold the little boy on your lap . . . The twins can sit together in the same chair. Be careful, they're not very strong . . . they go with the house, they belong to the landlord. Yes, my children, he'd make trouble for us, he's a bad man . . . he wants us to buy them from him, these worthless chairs. (*The* OLD WOMAN *returns as quickly as she can with a chair*) You don't all know each other . . . you're seeing each other for the first time . . . you knew each other by name . . . (*to the* OLD WOMAN) Semiramis, help me make the introductions . . .

OLD WOMAN   Who are all these people? . . . May I introduce you, excuse me . . . May I introduce you . . . but who are they?

OLD MAN   May I introduce you . . . Allow me to introduce you . . . permit me to introduce you . . . Mr., Mrs., Miss . . . Mr. . . . Mrs. . . . Mrs. . . . Mr.

OLD WOMAN   (*to* OLD MAN)   Did you put on your sweater? (*to the invisible guests*) Mr., Mrs., Mr. . . .

(*Doorbell rings again*)

OLD MAN   More people!

(*Another ring of doorbell*)

OLD WOMAN   More people!

(*The doorbell rings again, then several more times, and more times again; the* OLD MAN *is beside himself; the chairs, turned towards the dais, with their backs to the audience, form regular rows, each one longer as in a theatre; the* OLD MAN *is winded, he mops his brow, goes from one door to another, seats invisible people, while the* OLD WOMAN, *hobbling along, unable to move any faster, goes as rapidly as she can, from one door to another, hunting for chairs and carrying them in. There are now many invisible people on stage; both the* OLD MAN *and* OLD WOMAN *take care not to bump into people and to thread their way between the rows of chairs. The movement could go like this: the* OLD MAN *goes to door No. 4, the* OLD WOMAN *exits by door No. 3, returns by door No. 2; the* OLD MAN *goes to open door No. 7, the* OLD WOMAN *exits by door No. 8, re-enters by door No. 6 with chairs, etc., in this manner making their way around the stage, using all the doors*)

OLD WOMAN   Beg pardon . . . excuse me . . . what . . . oh, yes . . . beg pardon . . . excuse me . . .

OLD MAN   Gentlemen . . . come in . . . ladies . . . enter . . . it is Mrs. . . . let me . . . yes . . .

OLD WOMAN   (*with more chairs*)   Oh dear . . . Oh dear . . . there are too many . . . There really are too, too . . . too many, oh dear, oh dear, oh dear . . .

(*We hear from outside, louder and louder and approaching nearer and nearer, the sounds of boats moving through the water; all the noises come directly from the wings. The* OLD WOMAN *and the* OLD MAN *continue the business outlined above; they open the doors, they carry in chairs. The doorbell continues to ring*)

OLD MAN   This table is in our way. (*He moves a table, or he sketches the business of moving it, without slowing down his rhythm, aided by the* OLD WOMAN) There's scarcely a place left here, excuse us . . .

OLD WOMAN   (*making a gesture of clearing*

the table, to the OLD MAN)   Are you wearing your sweater?

(*Doorbell rings*)

OLD MAN   More people! More chairs! More people! More chairs! Come in, come in, ladies and gentlemen . . . Semiramis, faster . . . We'll give you a hand soon . . .

OLD WOMAN   Beg pardon . . . beg pardon . . . good evening, Mrs. . . . Mrs. . . . Mr. . . . Mr. . . . yes, yes, the chairs . . .

(*The doorbell rings louder and louder and we hear the noises of boats striking the quay very close by, and more and more frequently. The* OLD MAN *flounders among the chairs; he has scarcely enough time to go from one door to another, so rapidly do the ringings of the door-bell succeed each other*)

OLD MAN   Yes, right away . . . are you wearing your sweater? Yes, yes . . . immediately, patience, yes, yes . . . patience . . .

OLD WOMAN   Your sweater? My sweater? . . . Beg pardon, beg pardon.

OLD MAN   This way, ladies and gentlemen, I request you . . . I re you . . . pardon . . . quest . . . enter, enter . . . going to show, . . . there, the seats . . . dear friend . . . not there . . . take care . . . you, my friend?

(*Then a long moment without words. We hear waves, boats, the continuous ringing of the doorbell. The movement culminates in intensity at this point. The doors are now opening and shutting all together ceaselessly. Only the main door in the center of the recess remains closed. The* OLD MAN *and* OLD WOMAN *come and go, without saying a word, from one door to another; they appear to be gliding on roller skates. The* OLD MAN *receives the people, accompanies them, but doesn't take them very far, he only indicates seats to them after having taken one or two steps with them; he hasn't enough time. The* OLD WOMAN *carries in chairs. The* OLD MAN *and the* OLD WOMAN *meet each other and bump into each other, once or twice, without interrupting their rhythm. Then, the* OLD MAN *takes a position upstage center, and turns from left to right, from right to left, etc., to-wards all the doors and indicates the seats with his arms. His arms move very rapidly. Then, finally the* OLD WOMAN *stops, with a chair in one hand, which she places, takes up again, replaces, looks as though she, too, wants to go from one door to another, from right to left, from left to right, moving her head and neck very rapidly. This must not interrupt the rhythm; the* OLD MAN *and* OLD WOMAN *must still give the impression of not stopping, even while remaining almost in one place; their*

hands, their chests, their heads, their eyes are agitated, perhaps moving in little circles. Fi-nally, there is a progressive slowing down of movement, at first slight: the ringings of the doorbell are less loud, less frequent; the doors open less and less rapidly; the gestures of the* OLD MAN *and* OLD WOMAN *slacken continuously. At the moment when the doors stop opening and closing altogether, and the ringings cease to be heard, we have the impression that the stage is packed with people*)

OLD MAN   I'm going to find a place for you . . . patience . . . Semiramis, for the love of . . .

OLD WOMAN (*with a large gesture, her hands empty*)   There are no more chairs, my darling. (*Then, abruptly, she begins to sell invisible programs in a full hall, with the doors closed*) Programs, get your programs here, the program of the evening, buy your program!

OLD MAN   Relax, ladies and gentlemen, we'll take care of you . . . Each in his turn, in the order of your arrival . . . You'll have a seat. I'll take care of you.

OLD WOMAN   Buy your programs! Wait a moment, madam, I cannot take care of every-one at the same time, I haven't got thirty-three hands, you know, I'm not a cow . . . Mister, please be kind enough to pass the program to the lady next to you, thank you . . . my change, my change . . .

OLD MAN   I've told you that I'd find a place for you! Don't get excited! Over here, it's over here, there, take care . . . oh, dear friend . . . dear friends . . .

OLD WOMAN   . . . Programs . . . get your grams . . . grams . . .

OLD MAN   Yes, my dear, she's over there, further down, she's selling programs . . . no trade is unworthy . . . that's her . . . do you see her? . . . you have a seat in the second row . . . to the right . . . no, to the left . . . that's it! . . .

OLD WOMAN   . . . gram . . . gram . . . program . . . get your program . . .

OLD MAN   What do you expect me to do? I'm doing my best! (*to invisible seated people*) Push over a little, if you will please . . . there's still a little room, that will do for you, won't it, Mrs. . . . come here. (*He mounts the dais, forced by the pushing of the crowd*) Ladies, gentlemen, please excuse us, there are no more seats available . . .

OLD WOMAN (*who is now on the opposite side of the stage, across from the* OLD MAN, *between door No. 3 and the window*)   Get your programs . . . who wants a program?

Eskimo pies, caramels . . . fruit drops . . .
(*Unable to move, the* OLD WOMAN, *hemmed in
by the crowd, scatters her programs and can-
dies anywhere, above the invisible heads*)
Here are some! There they are!

OLD MAN (*standing on the dais, very animated; he is jostled as he descends from the
dais, remounts it, steps down again, hits someone in the face, is struck by an elbow, says*)
Pardon . . . please excuse us . . . take care
. . . (*Pushed, he staggers, has trouble regaining his equilibrium, clutches at shoulders*)

OLD WOMAN   Why are there so many people? Programs, get your program here, Eskimo
pies.

OLD MAN   Ladies, young ladies, gentlemen,
a moment of silence, I beg you . . . silence
. . . it's very important . . . those people
who've no seats are asked to clear the aisles
. . . that's it . . . don't stand between the
chairs.

OLD WOMAN (*to the* OLD MAN, *almost screaming*)   Who are all these people, my darling?
What are they doing here?

OLD MAN   Clear the aisles, ladies and gentlemen. Those who do not have seats must,
for the convenience of all, stand against the
wall, there, along the right or the left . . .
you'll be able to hear everything, you'll see
everything, don't worry, you won't miss a
thing, all seats are equally good!

(*There is a great hullabaloo. Pushed by the
crowd, the* OLD MAN *makes almost a complete
turn around the stage and ends up at the
window on the right, near to the stool. The*
OLD WOMAN *makes the same movement in
reverse, and ends up at the window on the left,
near the stool there*)

OLD MAN (*making this movement*)   Don't
push, don't push.

OLD WOMAN (*same business*)   Don't push,
don't push.

OLD MAN (*same business*)   Don't push, don't
push.

OLD WOMAN (*same business*)   Don't push,
ladies and gentlemen, don't push.

OLD MAN (*same business*)   Relax . . . take
it easy . . . be quiet . . . what's going on
here?

OLD WOMAN (*same business*)   There's no
need to act like savages, in any case.

(*At last they reach their final positions. Each
is near a window. The* OLD MAN *to the left, by
the window which is beside the dais. The* OLD
WOMAN *on the right. They don't move from
these positions until the end*)

OLD WOMAN (*calling to the* OLD MAN)   My
darling . . . I can't see you, anymore . . .
where are you? Who are they? What do all
these people want? Who is that man over there?

OLD MAN   Where are you? Where are you,
Semiramis?

OLD WOMAN   My darling, where are you?

OLD MAN   Here, beside the window . . .
Can you hear me?

OLD WOMAN   Yes, I hear your voice! . . .
there are so many . . . but I can make out
yours . . .

OLD MAN   And you, where are you?

OLD WOMAN   I'm beside the window too!
. . . My dear, I'm frightened, there are too
many people . . . we are very far from each
other . . . at our age we have to be careful
. . . we might get lost . . . We must stay
close together, one never knows, my darling,
my darling . . .

OLD MAN   Ah! . . . I just caught sight of
you . . . Oh! . . . We'll find each other,
never fear . . . I'm with friends. (*to the
friends*) I'm happy to shake your hands . . .
But of course, I believe in progress, uninterrupted progress, with some jolts, nevertheless . . .

OLD WOMAN   That's fine, thanks . . . What
foul weather! Yes, it's been nice! (*aside*) I'm
afraid, even so . . . What am I doing here?
. . . (*She screams*) My darling, My darling!

(*The* OLD MAN *and* OLD WOMAN *individually
speak to guests near them*)

OLD MAN   In order to prevent the exploitation of man by man, we need money, money,
and still more money!

OLD WOMAN   My darling! (*then, hemmed
in by friends*) Yes, my husband is here, he's
organizing everything . . . over there . . .
Oh! you'll never get there . . . you'd have
to go across, he's with friends . . .

OLD MAN   Certainly not . . . as I've always said . . . pure logic does not exist . . .
all we've got is an imitation.

OLD WOMAN   But you know, there are people who are happy. In the morning they eat
breakfast on the plane, at noon they lunch
in the pullman, and in the evening they dine
aboard the liner. At night they sleep in the
trucks that roll, roll, roll . . .

OLD MAN   Talk about the dignity of man!
At least let's try to save face. Dignity is only
skin deep.

OLD WOMAN   Don't slink away into the shadows . . . (*She bursts out laughing in conversation*)

OLD MAN   Your compatriots ask of me.

OLD WOMAN   Certainly . . . tell me everything.

OLD MAN   I've invited you . . . in order to explain to you . . . that the individual and the person are one and the same.

OLD WOMAN   He has a borrowed look about him. He owes us a lot of money.

OLD MAN   I am not myself. I am another. I am the one in the other.

OLD WOMAN   My children, take care not to trust one another.

OLD MAN   Sometimes I awaken in the midst of absolute silence. It's a perfect circle. There's nothing lacking. But one must be careful, all the same. Its shape might disappear. There are holes through which it can escape.

OLD WOMAN   Ghosts, you know, phantoms, mere nothings . . . The duties my husband fulfills are very important, sublime.

OLD MAN   Excuse me . . . that's not at all my opinion! At the proper time, I'll communicate my views on this subject to you . . . I have nothing to say for the present! . . . We're waiting for the Orator, he'll tell you, he'll speak in my behalf, and explain everything that we hold most dear . . . he'll explain everything to you . . . when? . . . when the moment has come . . . the moment will come soon . . .

OLD WOMAN   (*on her side to her friends*) The sooner, the better . . . That's understood . . . (*aside*) They're never going to leave us alone. Let them go, why don't they go? . . . My poor darling, where is he? I can't see him any more . . .

OLD MAN   (*same business*) Don't be so impatient. You'll hear my message. In just a moment.

OLD WOMAN   (*aside*) Ah! . . . I hear his voice! . . . (*to her friends*) Do you know, my husband has never been understood. But at last his hour has come.

OLD MAN   Listen to me, I've had a rich experience of life. In all walks of life, at every level of thought . . . I'm not an egotist: humanity must profit by what I've learned.

OLD WOMAN   Ow! You stepped on my foot . . . I've got chilblains!

OLD MAN   I've perfected a real system. (*aside*) The Orator ought to be here. (*aloud*) I've suffered enormously.

OLD WOMAN   We have suffered so much. (*aside*) The Orator ought to be here. It's certainly time.

OLD MAN   Suffered much, learned much.

OLD WOMAN   (*like an echo*) Suffered much, learned much.

OLD MAN   You'll see for yourselves, my system is perfect.

OLD WOMAN   (*like an echo*) You'll see for yourselves, his system is perfect.

OLD MAN   If only my instructions are carried out.

OLD WOMAN   (*echo*) If only his instructions are carried out.

OLD MAN   We'll save the world! . . .

OLD WOMAN   (*echo*) Saving his own soul by saving the world! . . .

OLD MAN   One truth for all!

OLD WOMAN   (*echo*) One truth for all!

OLD MAN   Follow me! . . .

OLD WOMAN   (*echo*) Follow him! . . .

OLD MAN   For I have absolute certainty! . . .

OLD WOMAN   (*echo*) He has absolute certainty!

OLD MAN   Never . . .

OLD WOMAN   (*echo*) Ever and ever . . .

(*Suddenly we hear noises in the wings, fanfares*)

OLD WOMAN   What's going on?

(*The noises increase, then the main door opens wide, with a great crash; through the open door we see nothing but a very powerful light which floods onto the stage through the main door and the windows, which at the entrance of the* EMPEROR *are brightly lighted*)

OLD MAN   I don't know . . . I can scarcely believe . . . is it possible . . . but yes . . . but yes . . . incredible . . . and still it's true . . . yes . . . if . . . yes . . . it is the Emperor! His Majesty the Emperor!

(*The light reaches its maximum intensity, through the open door and through the windows; but the light is cold, empty; more noises which cease abruptly*)

OLD MAN   Stand up! . . . It's His Majesty the Emperor! The Emperor in my house, in our house . . . Semiramis . . . do you realize what this means?

OLD WOMAN   (*not understanding*) The Emperor . . . the Emperor? My darling! (*Then suddenly she understands*) Ah, yes, the Emperor! Your Majesty! Your Majesty! (*She wildly makes countless grotesque curtsies*) In our house! In our house!

OLD MAN   (*weeping with emotion*) Your Majesty! . . . Oh! Your Majesty! . . . Your little, Your great Majesty! . . . Oh! what a sublime honor . . . it's all a marvelous dream.

OLD WOMAN   (*like an echo*) A marvelous dream . . . arvelous . . .

OLD MAN   (*to the invisible crowd*) Ladies,

gentlemen, stand up, our beloved sovereign, the Emperor, is among us! Hurrah! Hurrah!

(*He stands up on the stool; he stands on his toes in order to see the* EMPEROR; *the* OLD WOMAN *does the same on her side*)

OLD WOMAN   Hurrah! Hurrah!

(*Stamping of feet*)

OLD MAN   Your Majesty! . . . I'm over here! . . . Your Majesty! Can you hear me? Can you see me? Please tell his Majesty that I'm here! Your Majesty! Your Majesty!!! I'm here, your most faithful servant! . . .

OLD WOMAN   (*still echoing*)   Your most faithful servant, Your Majesty!

OLD MAN   Your servant, your slave, your dog, arf, arf, your dog, Your Majesty! . . .

OLD WOMAN   (*barking loudly like a dog*) Arf . . . arf . . . arf . . .

OLD MAN   (*wringing his hands*)   Can you see me? . . . Answer, Sire! . . . Ah, I can see you, I've just caught sight of Your Majesty's august face . . . your divine forehead . . . I've seen you, yes, in spite of the screen of courtiers . . .

OLD WOMAN   In spite of the courtiers . . . we're here, Your Majesty!

OLD MAN   Your Majesty! Your Majesty! Ladies, gentlemen, don't keep him—His Majesty standing . . . you see, Your Majesty, I'm truly the only one who cares for you, for your health, I'm the most faithful of all your subjects . . .

OLD WOMAN   (*echoing*)   Your Majesty's most faithful subjects!

OLD MAN   Let me through, now, ladies and gentlemen . . . how can I make my way through such a crowd? . . . I must go to present my most humble respects to His Majesty, the Emperor . . . let me pass . . .

OLD WOMAN   (*echo*)   Let him pass . . . let him pass . . . pass . . . ass . . .

OLD MAN   Let me pass, please, let me pass. (*desperate*) Ah! Will I ever be able to reach him?

OLD WOMAN   (*echo*)   Reach him . . . reach him . . .

OLD MAN   Nevertheless, my heart and my whole being are at his feet, the crowd of courtiers surrounds him, ah! ah! they want to prevent me from approaching him . . . They know very well that . . . oh! I understand, I understand . . . Court intrigues, I know all about it . . . They hope to separate me from Your Majesty!

OLD WOMAN   Calm yourself, my darling . . . His Majesty sees you, he's looking at you . . .

His Majesty has given me a wink . . . His Majesty is on our side! . . .

OLD MAN   They must give the Emperor the best seat . . . near the dais . . . so that he can hear everything the Orator is going to say.

OLD WOMAN   (*hoisting herself up on the stool, on her toes, lifting her chin as high as she can, in order to see better*)   At last they're taking care of the Emperor.

OLD MAN   Thank heaven for that! (*to the* EMPEROR) Sire . . . Your Majesty may rely on him. It's my friend, it's my representative who is at Your Majesty's side. (*on his toes, standing on the stool*) Gentlemen, ladies, young ladies, little children, I implore you.

OLD WOMAN   (*echoing*)   Plore . . . plore . . .

OLD MAN   . . . I want to see . . . move aside . . . I want . . . the celestial gaze, the noble face, the crown, the radiance of His Majesty . . . Sire, deign to turn your illustrious face in my direction, toward your humble servant . . . so humble . . . Oh! I caught sight of him clearly that time . . . I caught sight . . .

OLD WOMAN   (*echo*)   He caught sight that time . . . he caught sight . . . caught . . . sight . . .

OLD MAN   I'm at the height of joy . . . I've no more words to express my boundless gratitude . . . in my humble dwelling, Oh! Majesty! Oh! radiance! . . . here . . . here . . . in the dwelling where I am, true enough, a general . . . but within the hierarchy of your army, I'm only a simple general factotum . . .

OLD WOMAN   (*echo*)   General factotum . . .

OLD MAN   I'm proud of it . . . proud and humble, at the same time . . . as I should be . . . alas! certainly, I am a general, I might have been at the imperial court, I have only a little court here to take care of . . . Your Majesty . . . I . . . Your Majesty, I have difficulty expressing myself . . . I might have had . . . many things, not a few possessions if I'd known, if I'd wanted, if I . . . if we . . . Your Majesty, forgive my emotion . . .

OLD WOMAN   Speak in the third person!

OLD MAN   (*sniveling*)   May Your Majesty deign to forgive me! You are here at last . . . We had given up hope . . . you might not even have come . . . Oh! Savior, in my life, I have been humiliated . . .

OLD WOMAN   (*echo, sobbing*)   . . . miliated . . . miliated . . .

OLD MAN   I've suffered much in my life . . . I might have been something, if I could have been sure of the support of Your Majesty . . .

I have no other support . . . if you hadn't come, everything would have been too late . . . you are, Sire, my last recourse . . .

OLD WOMAN (*echo*) Last recourse . . . Sire . . . ast recourse . . . ire . . . recourse . . .

OLD MAN I've brought bad luck to my friends, to all those who have helped me . . . Lightning struck the hand which was held out toward me . . .

OLD WOMAN (*echo*) . . . hand that was held out . . . held out . . . out . . .

OLD MAN They've always had good reasons for hating me, bad reasons for loving me . . .

OLD WOMAN That's not true, my darling, not true. *I* love you, I'm your little mother . . .

OLD MAN All my enemies have been rewarded and my friends have betrayed me . . .

OLD WOMAN (*echo*) Friends . . . betrayed . . . betrayed . . .

OLD MAN They've treated me badly. They've persecuted me. If I complained, it was always they who were in the right . . . Sometimes I've tried to revenge myself . . . I was never able to, never able to revenge myself . . . I have too much pity . . . I refused to strike the enemy to the ground, I have always been too good.

OLD WOMAN (*echo*) He was too good, good, good, good, good . . .

OLD MAN It is my pity that has defeated me.

OLD WOMAN (*echo*) My pity . . . pity . . . pity . . .

OLD MAN But they never pitied me. I gave them a pin prick, and they repaid me with club blows, with knife blows, with cannon blows, they've crushed my bones . . .

OLD WOMAN (*echo*) . . . My bones . . . my bones . . . my bones . . .

OLD MAN They've supplanted me, they've robbed me, they've assassinated me . . . I've been the collector of injustices, the lightning rod of catastrophes . . .

OLD WOMAN (*echo*) Lightning rod . . . catastrophe . . . lightning rod . . .

OLD MAN In order to forget, Your Majesty, I wanted to go in for sports . . . for mountain climbing . . . they pulled my feet and made me slip . . . I wanted to climb stairways, they rotted the steps . . . I fell down . . . I wanted to travel, they refused me a passport . . . I wanted to cross the river, they burnt my bridges . . .

OLD WOMAN (*echo*) Burnt my bridges.

OLD MAN I wanted to cross the Pyrenees, and there were no more Pyrenees.

OLD WOMAN (*echo*) No more Pyrenees . . . He could have been, he too, Your Majesty, like so many others, a head editor, a head actor, a head doctor, Your Majesty, a head king . . .

OLD MAN Furthermore, no one has ever shown me due consideration . . . no one has ever sent me invitations . . . However, I, hear me, I say this to you, I alone could have saved humanity, who is so sick. Your Majesty realizes this as do I . . . or, at least, I could have spared it the evils from which it has suffered so much this last quarter of a century, had I had the opportunity to communicate my message; I do not despair of saving it, there is still time, I have a plan . . . alas, I express myself with difficulty . . .

OLD WOMAN (*above the invisible heads*) The Orator will be here, he'll speak for you. His Majesty is here, thus you'll be heard, you've no reason to despair, you hold all the trumps, everything has changed, everything has changed . . .

OLD MAN I hope Your Majesty will excuse me . . . I know you have many other worries . . . I've been humiliated . . . Ladies and gentlemen, move aside just a little bit, don't hide His Majesty's nose from me altogether, I want to see the diamonds of the imperial crown glittering . . . But if Your Majesty has deigned to come to our miserable home, it is because you have condescended to take into consideration my wretched self. What an extraordinary reward. Your Majesty, if corporeally I raised myself on my toes, this is not through pride, this is only in order to gaze upon you! . . . morally, I throw myself at your knees.

OLD WOMAN (*sobbing*) At your knees, Sire, we throw ourselves at your knees, at your feet, at your toes . . .

OLD MAN I've had scabies. My employer fired me because I did not bow to his baby, to his horse. I've been kicked in the ass, but all this, Sire, no longer has any importance . . . since . . . since . . . Sir . . . Your Majesty . . . look . . . I am here . . . here . . .

OLD WOMAN (*echo*) Here . . . here . . . here . . . here . . . here . . . here . . .

OLD MAN Since Your Majesty is here . . . since Your Majesty will take my message into consideration . . . But the Orator should be here . . . he's making His Majesty wait . . .

OLD WOMAN If Your Majesty will forgive him. He's surely coming. He will be here in a moment. They've telephoned us.

OLD MAN His Majesty is so kind. His Majesty wouldn't depart just like that, without having listened to everything, heard everything.

OLD WOMAN (*echo*)   Heard everything . . . heard . . . listened to everything . . .

OLD MAN   It is he who will speak in my name . . . I, I cannot . . . I lack the talent . . . he has all the papers, all the documents . . .

OLD WOMAN (*echo*)   He has all the documents . . .

OLD MAN   A little patience, Sire, I beg of you . . . he should be coming.

OLD WOMAN   He should be coming in a moment.

OLD MAN (*so that the* EMPEROR *will not grow impatient*)   Your Majesty, hear me, a long time ago I had the revelation . . . I was forty years old . . . I say this also to you, ladies and gentlemen . . . one evening, after supper, as was our custom, before going to bed, I seated myself on my father's knees . . . my mustaches were longer than his and more pointed . . . I had more hair on my chest . . . my hair was graying already, but his was still brown . . . There were some guests, grown-ups, sitting at tables, who began to laugh, laugh.

OLD WOMAN (*echo*)   Laugh . . . laugh . . .

OLD MAN   I'm not joking, I told them, I love my papa very much. Someone replied: It is midnight, a child shouldn't stay up so late. If you don't go beddy-bye, then you're no longer a kid. But I'd still not have believed them if they hadn't addressed me as an adult.

OLD WOMAN (*echo*)   An adult.

OLD MAN   Instead of as a child . . .

OLD WOMAN (*echo*)   A child.

OLD MAN   Nevertheless, I thought to myself, I'm not married. Hence, I'm still a child. They married me off right then, expressly to prove the contrary to me . . . Fortunately, my wife has been both father and mother to me . . .

OLD WOMAN   The Orator should be here, Your Majesty . . .

OLD MAN   The Orator will come.

OLD WOMAN   He will come.

OLD MAN   He will come.

OLD WOMAN   He will come.

OLD MAN   He will come.

OLD WOMAN   He will come.

OLD MAN   He will come, he will come.

OLD WOMAN   He will come, he will come.

OLD MAN   He will come.

OLD WOMAN   He is coming.

OLD MAN   He is coming.

OLD WOMAN   He is coming, he is here.

OLD MAN   He is coming, he is here.

OLD WOMAN   He is coming, he is here.

OLD MAN AND OLD WOMAN   He is here . . .

OLD WOMAN   Here he is!

(*Silence; all movement stops. Petrified, the two old people stare at door No. 5; this immobility lasts rather long—about thirty seconds; very slowly, very slowly the door opens wide, silently; then the* ORATOR *appears. He is a real person. He's a typical painter or poet of the nineteenth century; he wears a large black felt hat with a wide brim, loosely tied bow tie, artist's blouse, mustache and goatee, very histrionic in manner, conceited; just as the invisible people must be as real as possible, the* ORATOR *must appear unreal. He goes along the wall to the right, gliding, softly, to upstage center, in front of the main door, without turning his head to right or left; he passes close by the* OLD WOMAN *without appearing to notice her, not even when the* OLD WOMAN *touches his arm in order to assure herself that he exists. It is at this moment that the* OLD WOMAN *says: "Here he is!"*)

OLD MAN   Here he is!

OLD WOMAN (*following the* ORATOR *with her eyes and continuing to stare at him*)   It's really he, he exists. In flesh and blood.

OLD MAN (*following him with his eyes*)   He exists. It's really he. This is not a dream!

OLD WOMAN   This is not a dream, I told you so.

(*The* OLD MAN *clasps his hands, lifts his eyes to heaven; he exults silently. The* ORATOR, *having reached upstage center lifts his hat, bends forward in silence, saluting the invisible* EMPEROR *with his hat with a Musketeer's flourish and somewhat like an automaton. At this moment*)

OLD MAN   Your Majesty . . . May I present to you, the Orator . . .

OLD WOMAN   It is he!

(*Then the* ORATOR *puts his hat back on his head and mounts the dais from which he looks down on the invisible crowd on the stage and at the chairs; he freezes in a solemn pose*)

OLD MAN (*to the invisible crowd*)   You may ask him for autographs. (*Automatically, silently, the* ORATOR *signs and distributes numberless autographs. The* OLD MAN *during this time lifts his eyes again to heaven, clasping his hands, and exultantly says*)   No man, in his lifetime, could hope for more . . .

OLD WOMAN (*echo*)   No man could hope for more.

OLD MAN (*to the invisible crowd*)   And now, with the permission of Your Majesty, I will address myself to all of you, ladies, young ladies, gentlemen, little children, dear colleagues, dear compatriots, Your Honor the President, dear comrades in arms . . .

OLD WOMAN (*echo*) And little children . . . dren . . . dren . . .

OLD MAN I address myself to all of you, without distinction of age, sex, civil status, social rank, or business, to thank you, with all my heart.

OLD WOMAN (*echo*) To thank you . . .

OLD MAN As well as the Orator . . . cordially, for having come in such large numbers . . . silence, gentlemen! . . .

OLD WOMAN (*echo*) Silence, gentlemen . . .

OLD MAN I address my thanks also to those who have made possible the meeting this evening, to the organizers . . .

OLD WOMAN Bravo!

(*Meanwhile, the* ORATOR *on the dais remains solemn, immobile, except for his hand, which signs autographs automatically*)

OLD MAN To the owners of this building, to the architect, to the masons who were kind enough to erect these walls! . . .

OLD WOMAN (*echo*) . . . walls . . .

OLD MAN To all those who've dug the foundations . . . Silence, ladies and gentlemen . . .

OLD WOMAN . . . 'adies and gentlemen . . .

OLD MAN Last but not least I address my warmest thanks to the cabinet-makers who have made these chairs on which you have been able to sit, to the master carpenter . . .

OLD WOMAN (*echo*) . . . penter . . .

OLD MAN . . . Who made the armchair in which Your Majesty is sinking so softly, which does not prevent you, nevertheless, from maintaining a firm and manly attitude . . . Thanks again to all the technicians, machinists, electrocutioners . . .

OLD WOMAN (*echoing*) . . . cutioners . . . cutioners . . .

OLD MAN . . . To the paper manufacturers and the printers, proofreaders, editors to whom we owe the programs, so charmingly decorated, to the universal solidarity of all men, thanks, thanks, to our country, to the State (*He turns toward where the* EMPEROR *is sitting*) whose helm Your Majesty directs with the skill of a true pilot . . . thanks to the usher . . .

OLD WOMAN (*echo*) . . . usher . . . rusher . . .

OLD MAN (*pointing to the* OLD WOMAN) Hawker of Eskimo pies and programs . . .

OLD WOMAN (*echo*) . . . grams . . .

OLD MAN . . . My wife, my helpmeet . . . Semiramis! . . .

OLD WOMAN (*echo*) . . . ife . . . meet . . . mis . . . (*aside*) The darling, he never forgets to give me credit.

OLD MAN Thanks to all those who have given me their precious and expert, financial or moral support, thereby contributing to the overwhelming success of this evening's gathering . . . thanks again, thanks above all to our beloved sovereign, His Majesty the Emperor . . .

OLD WOMAN (*echo*) . . . jesty the Emperor . . .

OLD MAN (*in a total silence*) . . . A little silence . . . Your Majesty . . .

OLD WOMAN (*echo*) . . . jesty . . . jesty . . .

OLD MAN Your Majesty, my wife and myself have nothing more to ask of life. Our existence can come to an end in this apotheosis . . . thanks be to heaven who has granted us such long and peaceful years . . . My life has been filled to overflowing. My mission is accomplished. I will not have lived in vain, since my message will be revealed to the world . . . (*Gesture towards the* ORATOR, *who does not perceive it; the* ORATOR *waves off requests for autographs, very dignified and firm*) To the world, or rather to what is left of it! (*wide gesture toward the invisible crowd*) To you, ladies and gentlemen, and dear comrades, who are all that is left from humanity, but with such leftovers one can still make a very good soup . . . Orator, friend . . . (*the* ORATOR *looks in another direction*) If I have been long unrecognized, underestimated by my contemporaries, it is because it had to be . . . (*the* OLD WOMAN *sobs*) What matters all that now when I am leaving to you, to you, my dear Orator and friend (*The* ORATOR *rejects a new request for an autograph, then takes an indifferent pose, looking in all directions*) . . . the responsibility of radiating upon posterity the light of my mind . . . thus making known to the universe my philosophy. Neglect none of the details of my private life, some laughable, some painful or heartwarming, of my tastes, my amusing gluttony . . . tell everything . . . speak of my helpmeet . . . (*The* OLD WOMAN *redoubles her sobs*) . . . of the way she prepared those marvelous little Turkish pies, of her potted rabbit à la Normandabbit . . . speak of Berry, my native province . . . I count on you, great master and Orator . . . as for me and my faithful helpmeet, after our long years of labor in behalf of the progress of humanity during which we fought the good fight, nothing remains for us but to withdraw . . . immediately, in order to make the supreme sacrifice which no one demands of us but which we will carry out even so . . .

OLD WOMAN (*sobbing*)   Yes, yes, let's die in full glory . . . let's die in order to become a legend . . . At least, they'll name a street after us . . .

OLD MAN (*to* OLD WOMAN)   O my faithful helpmeet! . . . you who have believed in me, unfailingly, during the whole century, who have never left me, never . . . alas, today, at this supreme moment, the crowd pitilessly separates us . . .

> Above all I had hoped
> that together we might lie
> with all our bones together
> within the selfsame skin
> within the same sepulchre
> and that the same worms
> might share our old flesh
> that we might rot together . . .

OLD WOMAN   . . . Rot together . . .

OLD MAN   Alas! . . . alas! . . .

OLD WOMAN   Alas! . . . alas! . . .

OLD MAN   . . . Our corpses will fall far from each other, and we will rot in an aquatic solitude . . . Don't pity us over much.

OLD WOMAN   What will be, will be!

OLD MAN   We shall not be forgotten. The eternal Emperor will remember us, always.

OLD WOMAN (*echo*)   Always.

OLD MAN   We will leave some traces, for we are people and not cities.

OLD MAN AND OLD WOMAN (*together*)   We will have a street named after us.

OLD MAN   Let us be united in time and in eternity, even if we are not together in space, as we were in adversity: let us die at the same moment . . . (*to the* ORATOR, *who is impassive, immobile*) One last time . . . I place my trust in you . . . I count on you. You will tell all . . . bequeath my message . . . (*to the* EMPEROR) If Your Majesty will excuse me . . . Farewell to all. Farewell, Semiramis.

OLD WOMAN   Farewell to all! . . . Farewell, my darling!

OLD MAN   Long live the Emperor!

(*He throws confetti and paper streamers on the invisible* EMPEROR; *we hear fanfares; bright lights like fireworks*)

OLD WOMAN   Long live the Emperor!

(*Confetti and streamers thrown in the direction of the* EMPEROR, *then on the immobile and impassive* ORATOR, *and on the empty chairs*)

OLD MAN (*same business*)   Long live the Emperor!

OLD WOMAN (*same business*)   Long live the Emperor!

(*The* OLD WOMAN *and* OLD MAN *at the same moment throw themselves out the windows,* shouting "Long Live the Emperor." *Sudden silence; no more fireworks; we hear an "Ah" from both sides of the stage, the sea-green noises of bodies falling into the water. The light coming through the main door and the windows has disappeared; there remains only a weak light as at the beginning of the play; the darkened windows remain wide open, their curtains floating on the wind*)

ORATOR (*He has remained immobile and impassive during the scene of the double suicide, and now, after several moments, he decides to speak. He faces the rows of empty chairs; he makes the invisible crowd understand that he is deaf and dumb; he makes the signs of a deaf-mute; desperate efforts to make himself understood; then he coughs, groans, utters the guttural sounds of a mute*)   He, mme, mm, mm. Ju, gou, hou, hou. Heu, heu, gu gou, gueue.

(*Helpless, he lets his arms fall down alongside his body; suddenly, his face lights up, he has an idea, he turns toward the blackboard, he takes a piece of chalk out of his pocket, and writes, in large capitals:*

ANGELFOOD

then:

NNAA NNM NWNWNW V

He turns around again, towards the invisible crowd on the stage, and points with his finger to what he's written on the blackboard)

ORATOR   Mmm, Mmm, Gueue, Gou, Gu. Mmm, Mmm, Mmm, Mmm.

(*Then, not satisfied, with abrupt gestures he wipes out the chalk letters, and replaces them with others, among which we can make out, still in large capitals:*

ΛADIEU ΛDIEU ΛPΛ

Again, the ORATOR *turns around to face the crowd; he smiles, questions, with an air of hoping that he's been understood, of having said something; he indicates to the empty chairs what he's just written. He remains immobile for a few seconds, rather satisfied and a little solemn; but then, faced with the absence of the hoped for reaction, little by little his smile disappears, his face darkens; he waits another moment; suddenly he bows petulantly, brusquely, descends from the dais; he goes toward the main door upstage center, gliding like a ghost; before exiting through this door, he bows ceremoniously again to the rows of empty chairs, to the invisible* EMPEROR. *The stage re-*

mains empty with only the chairs, the dais, the floor covered with streamers and confetti. The main door is wide open onto darkness.

We hear for the first time the human noises of the invisible crowd; these are bursts of laughter, murmurs, shh's, ironical coughs; weak at the beginning, these noises grow louder, then, again, progressively they become weaker. All this should last long enough for the audience— the real and visible audience—to leave with this ending firmly impressed on its mind. The curtain falls very slowly) [1]

---

[1] In the original production the curtain fell on the mumblings of the mute Orator. The blackboard was not used.

Samuel Beckett

1906-

EXCERPTS FROM *PROUST*

In Time creative and destructive Proust discovers himself as an artist: "I understood the meaning of death, of love and vocation, of the joys of the spirit and the utility of pain." Allusion has been made to his contempt for the literature that "describes," for the realists and naturalists worshipping the offal of experience, prostrate before the epidermis and the swift epilepsy, and content to transcribe the surface, the façade, behind which the Idea is prisoner. Whereas the Proustian procedure is that of Apollo flaying Marsyas and capturing without sentiment the essence, the Phrygian waters. . . . But Proust is too much of an affectivist to be satisfied by the intellectual symbolism of a Baudelaire, abstract and discursive. The Baudelarian unity is a unity "post rem," a unity abstracted from plurality. His "correspondence" is determined by a concept, therefore strictly limited and exhausted by its own definition. Proust does not deal in concepts, he pursues the Idea, the concrete. He admires the frescoes of the Paduan Arena because their symbolism is handled as a reality, special, literal and concrete, and is not merely the pictorial transmission of a notion. . . . For Proust the object may be a living symbol, but a symbol of itself. The symbolism of Baudelaire has become the *autosymbolism* of Proust. Proust's point of departure might be situated in Symbolism, or on its outskirts. . . .

❂ ❂ ❂

We are frequently reminded of this romantic strain in Proust. He is romantic in his substi-

tution of affectivity for intelligence, in his opposition of the particular affective evidential state to all the subtleties of rational cross-reference, in his rejection of the Concept in favour of the Idea, in his scepticism before causality. Thus his purely logical—as opposed to his intuitive —explanations of a certain effect invariably bristle with alternatives. He is a Romantic in his anxiety to accomplish his mission, to be a good and faithful servant. He does not seek to evade the implications of his art such as it has been revealed to him. He will write as he has lived—in Time. The classical artist assumes omniscience and omnipotence. He raises himself artificially out of Time in order to give relief to his chronology and causality to his development. Proust's chronology is extremely difficult to follow, the succession of events spasmodic, and his characters and themes, although they seem to obey an almost insane inward necessity, are presented and developed with a fine Dostoievskian contempt for the vulgarity of a plausible concatenation. (Proust's impressionism will bring us back to Dostoievski.) Generally speaking, the romantic artist is very much concerned with Time and aware of the importance of memory in inspiration,

> *c'est toi qui dors dans l'ombre,*
> *ô sacré souvenir! . . .*

but is inclined to sensationalise what is treated by Proust with pathological power and sobriety. With Musset, for example, the interest is more in a vague extratemporal identification, without any real cohesion or simultaneity, between the me and not-me than in the functional evocations of a specialized memory. . . .

❂ ❂ ❂

The narrator had ascribed his "lack of talent" to a lack of observation, or rather to what he supposed was a non-artistic habit of observa-

"Excerpts from *Proust*" by Samuel Beckett is reprinted by permission of the publishers, Grove Press, Inc.

tion. He was incapable of recording surface. So that when he reads such brilliant crowded reporting as the Goncourts' Journal, the only alternative to the conclusion that he is entirely wanting in the precious journalistic talent is the supposition that between the banality of life and the magic of literature there is a great gulf fixed. Either he is devoid of talent or art of reality. And he describes the radiographical quality of his observation. The copiable he does not see. He searches for a relation, a common factor, substrata. Thus he is less interested in what is said than in the way in which it is said. Similarly his faculties are more violently activated by intermediate than by terminal-capital-stimuli. We find countless examples of these secondary reflexes. Withdrawn in his cool dark room at Combray he extracts the total essence of a scorching midday from the scarlet stellar blows of a hammer in the street and the chamber-music of flies in the gloom. Lying in bed at dawn, the exact quality of the weather, temperature and visibility, is transmitted to him in terms of sound, in the chimes and the calls of the hawkers. Thus can be explained the primacy of instinctive perception-intuition—in the Proustian world. Because instinct, when not vitiated by Habit, is also a reflex, from the Proustian point of view ideally remote and indirect, a chain-reflex. Now he sees his regretted failure to observe artistically as a series of "inspired omissions" ar⌐ ⌐he work of art as neither created nor chose covered, uncovered, excavated, within the artist, a law of his natur reality is provided by the hieroglyɪ by inspired perception (identificatic and object). The conclusions of the are merely of arbitrary value, poter "An impression is for the writer periment is for the scientist—witɬ ence, that in the case of the scie tion of the intelligence precedes tɬ in the case of the writer follow: quently for the artist, the only ɪ archy in the world of objective ɪ represented by a table of their resɪ cients of penetration, that is to sa the subject. (Another sneer at The artist has acquired his texɩ translates it. . . .

* * *

By his impressionism I mean hɪ statement of phenomena in the ⌐ actitude of their perception, befʻ been distorted into intelligibility forced into a chain of cause ⌐

painter Elstir is the type of the impressionist, stating what he sees and not what he knows he ought to see: for example, applying urban terms to the sea and marine terms to the town, so as to transmit his intuition of their homogeneity. And we are reminded of Schopenhauer's definition of the artistic procedure as "the contemplation of the world independently of the principle of reason." In this connection Proust can be related to Dostoievski, who states his characters without explaining them. It may be objected that Proust does little else but explain his characters. But his explanations are experimental and not demonstrative. He explains them in order that they may appear as they are—inexplicable. He explains them away.

* * *

. . . For Proust, as for the painter, style is more a question of vision than of technique. Proust does not share the superstition that form is nothing and content everything, nor that the ideal literary masterpiece could only be communicated in a series of absolute and monosyllabic propositions. For Proust the quality of language is more important than any system of ethics or aesthetics. Indeed he makes no attempt to dissociate form from content. The one is a concretion of the other, the revelation of a world. The Proustian world is expressed metaphorically by the artisan because it is apprehended metaphorically by the artist: the in- ⌐⌐⌐ of indirect termined activity, within the narrow limits of an impure world. But shameless. There is no question of right and wrong. Homosexuality is never called a vice: it is as devoid of moral implications as the mode of fecundation of the *Primula veris* or the *Lythrum salicoria*.[1] And, like members of the vegetable world, they seem to solicit a pure subject, so that they may pass from a state of blind will to a state of repre-

---

[1] Species of flowers.

sentation. Proust is that pure subject. He is almost exempt from the impurity of will. He deplores his lack of will until he understands that will, being utilitarian, a servant of intelligence and habit, is not a condition of the artistic experience. When the subject is exempt from will the object is exempt from causality (Time and Space taken together). And this human vegetation is purified in the transcendental apperception that can capture the Model, the Idea, the Thing itself.

ENDGAME

Translated from the French by the Author

CAST OF CHARACTERS

NAGG

NELL

HAMM

CLOV

(*Bare interior. Grey light. Left and right back, high up, two small windows, curtains drawn. Front right, a door. Hanging near door, its face to wall, a picture. Front left, touching each other, covered with an old sheet, two ashbins. Center, in an armchair on casters, covered with an old sheet,* HAMM. *Motionless by the door, his eyes fixed on* HAMM, CLOV. *Very red face. Brief tableau.*)

CLOV *goes and stands under window left. Stiff, staggering walk. He looks up at window left. He turns and looks at window right. He goes and stands under window right. He looks up at window right. He turns and looks at window left. He goes out, comes back immediately with a small stepladder, carries it over and sets it down under window left, gets up on it, draws back curtain. He gets down, takes six steps (for example) towards window right, goes back for ladder, carries it over and sets it down under window right, gets up on it, draws back curtain. He gets down, takes three steps towards window left, goes back for ladder, carries it over and sets it down under window left, gets up on it, looks out of window. Brief laugh. He gets down, takes one step towards window right, goes back for ladder, carries it over and sets it down under window right, gets up on it, looks out of window. Brief laugh. He gets down, goes with ladder towards ashbins, halts, turns, carries back ladder and sets it down under window*

right, goes to ashbins, removes sheet covering them, folds it over his arm. He raises one lid, stoops and looks into bin. Brief laugh. He closes lid. Same with other bin. He goes to HAMM, *removes sheet covering him, folds it over his arm. In a dressing-gown, a stiff toque on his head, a large blood-stained handkerchief over his face, a whistle hanging from his neck, a rug over his knees, thick socks on his feet,* HAMM *seems to be asleep.* CLOV *looks him over. Brief laugh. He goes to door, halts, turns towards auditorium*)

CLOV (*fixed gaze, tonelessly*) Finished, it's finished, nearly finished, it must be nearly finished. (*pause*) Grain upon grain, one by one, and one day, suddenly, there's a heap, a little heap, the impossible heap. (*pause*) I can't be punished any more. (*pause*) I'll go now to my kitchen, ten feet by ten feet by ten feet, and wait for him to whistle me. (*pause*) Nice dimensions, nice proportions, I'll lean on the table, and look at the wall, and wait for him to whistle me.

(*He remains a moment motionless, then goes out. He comes back immediately, goes to window right, takes up the ladder and carries it out. Pause.* HAMM *stirs. He yawns under the handkerchief. He removes the handkerchief from his face. Very red face. Black glasses*)

HAMM Me—(*He yawns*)—to play. (*He holds the handkerchief spread out before him*) Old stancher! (*He takes off his glasses, wipes his eyes, his face, the glasses, puts them on again, folds the handkerchief and puts it back neatly in the breast-pocket of his dressing-gown. He clears his throat, joins the tips of his fingers*) Can there be misery—(*He yawns*)—loftier than mine? No doubt. Formerly. But now? (*pause*) My father? (*pause*) My mother? (*pause*) My . . . dog? (*pause*) Oh I am willing to believe they suffer as much as such creatures can suffer. But does that mean their sufferings equal mine? No doubt. (*pause*) No, all is a—(*He yawns*)—bsolute, (*proudly*) the bigger a man is the fuller he is. (*Pause. Gloom-ily*) And the emptier. (*He sniffs*) Clov! (*pause*) No, alone. (*pause*) What dreams! Those forests! (*pause*) Enough, it's time it ended, in the shelter too. (*pause*) And yet I hesitate, I hesitate to . . . to end. Yes, there it is, it's time it ended and yet I hesitate to— (*He yawns*)—to end. (*yawns*) God, I'm tired, I'd be better off in bed. (*He whistles. Enter Clov immediately. He halts beside the chair*) You pollute the air! (*pause*) Get me ready, I'm going to bed.

CLOV   I've just got you up.

HAMM   And what of it?

CLOV   I can't be getting you up and putting you to bed every five minutes, I have things to do.

(*Pause*)

HAMM   Did you ever see my eyes?

CLOV   No.

HAMM   Did you never have the curiosity, while I was sleeping, to take off my glasses and look at my eyes?

CLOV   Pulling back the lids? (*pause*) No.

HAMM   One of these days I'll show them to you. (*pause*) It seems they've gone all white. (*pause*) What time is it?

CLOV   The same as usual.

HAMM   (*gestures towards window right*) Have you looked?

CLOV   Yes.

HAMM   Well?

CLOV   Zero.

HAMM   It'd need to rain.

CLOV   It won't rain.

(*Pause*)

HAMM   Apart from that, how do you feel?

CLOV   I don't complain.

HAMM   You feel normal?

CLOV   (*irritably*) I tell you I don't complain.

HAMM   I feel a little queer. (*pause*) Clov!

CLOV   Yes.

HAMM   Have you not had enough?

CLOV   Yes! (*pause*) Of what?

HAMM   Of this . . . this . . . thing.

CLOV   I always had. (*pause*) Not you?

HAMM   (*gloomily*) Then there's no reason for it to change.

CLOV   It may end. (*pause*) All life long the same questions, the same answers.

HAMM   Get me ready. (CLOV *does not move*) Go and get the sheet. (CLOV *does not move*) Clov!

CLOV   Yes.

HAMM   I'll give you nothing more to eat.

CLOV   Then we'll die.

HAMM   I'll give you just enough to keep you from dying. You'll be hungry all the time.

CLOV   Then we won't die. (*pause*) I'll go and get the sheet. (*He goes towards the door*)

HAMM   No! (CLOV *halts*) I'll give you one biscuit per day. (*pause*) One and a half. (*pause*) Why do you stay with me?

CLOV   Why do you keep me?

HAMM   There's no one else.

CLOV   There's nowhere else.

(*Pause*)

HAMM   You're leaving me all the same.

CLOV   I'm trying.

HAMM   You don't love me.

CLOV   No.

HAMM   You loved me once.

CLOV   Once!

HAMM   I've made you suffer too much. (*pause*) Haven't I?

CLOV   It's not that.

HAMM   (*shocked*) I haven't made you suffer too much?

CLOV   Yes!

HAMM   (*relieved*) Ah you gave me a fright! (*Pause. Coldly*) Forgive me. (*Pause. Louder*) I said, forgive me.

CLOV   I heard you. (*pause*) Have you bled?

HAMM   Less. (*pause*) Is it not time for my pain-killer?

CLOV   No.

(*Pause*)

HAMM   How are your eyes?

CLOV   Bad.

HAMM   How are your legs?

CLOV   Bad.

HAMM   But you can move.

CLOV   Yes.

HAMM   (*violently*) Then move! (CLOV *goes to back wall, leans against it with his forehead and hands*) Where are you?

CLOV   Here.

HAMM   Come back! (CLOV *returns to his place beside the chair*) Where are you?

CLOV   Here.

HAMM   Why don't you kill me?

CLOV   I don't know the combination of the cupboard.

(*Pause*)

HAMM   Go and get two bicycle wheels.

CLOV   There are no more bicycle wheels.

HAMM   What have you done with your bi-cycle?

CLOV   I never had a bicycle.

HAMM   The thing is impossible.

CLOV   When there were still bicycles I wept to have one. I crawled at your feet. You told me to go to hell. Now there are none.

HAMM   And your rounds? When you inspected my paupers. Always on foot?

CLOV   Sometimes on horse. (*The lid of one of the bins lifts and the hands of* NAGG *appear, gripping the rim. Then his head emerges. Nightcap. Very white face.* NAGG *yawns, then listens*) I'll leave you, I have things to do.

HAMM   In your kitchen?

CLOV   Yes.

HAMM   Outside of here it's death. (*pause*) All right, be off. (*Exit* CLOV. *Pause*) We're getting on.

NAGG   Me pap!

HAMM   Accursed progenitor!

NAGG   Me pap!

HAMM   The old folks at home! No decency left! Guzzle, guzzle, that's all they think of. (*He whistles. Enter* CLOV. *He halts beside the chair*) Well! I thought you were leaving me.

CLOV   Oh not just yet, not just yet.

NAGG   Me pap!

HAMM   Give him his pap.

CLOV   There's no more pap.

HAMM   (*to* NAGG) Do you hear that? There's no more pap. You'll never get any more pap.

NAGG   I want me pap!

HAMM   Give him a biscuit. (*exit* CLOV) Accursed fornicator! How are your stumps?

NAGG   Never mind me stumps. (*enter* CLOV *with biscuit*)

CLOV   I'm back again, with the biscuit. (*He gives biscuit to* NAGG *who fingers it, sniffs it*)

NAGG   (*plaintively*) What is it?

CLOV   Spratt's medium.

NAGG   (*as before*) It's hard! I can't!

HAMM   Bottle him! (CLOV *pushes* NAGG *back into the bin, closes the lid*)

CLOV   (*returning to his place beside the chair*) If age but knew!

HAMM   Sit on him!

CLOV   I can't sit.

HAMM   True. And I can't stand.

CLOV   So it is.

HAMM   Every man his speciality. (*pause*) No phone calls? (*pause*) Don't we laugh?

CLOV   (*after reflection*) I don't feel like it.

HAMM   (*after reflection*) Nor I. (*pause*) Clov!

CLOV   Yes.

HAMM   Nature has forgotten us.

CLOV   There's no more nature.

HAMM   No more nature! You exaggerate.

CLOV   In the vicinity.

HAMM   But we breathe, we change! We lose our hair, our teeth! Our bloom! Our ideals!

CLOV   Then she hasn't forgotten us.

HAMM   But you say there is none.

CLOV   (*sadly*) No one that ever lived ever thought so crooked as we.

HAMM   We do what we can.

CLOV   We shouldn't.

(*Pause*)

HAMM   You're a bit of all right, aren't you?

CLOV   A smithereen. (*pause*)

HAMM   This is slow work. (*pause*) Is it not time for my pain-killer?

CLOV   No. (*pause*) I'll leave you, I have things to do.

HAMM   In your kitchen?

CLOV   Yes.

HAMM   What, I'd like to know.

CLOV   I look at the wall.

HAMM   The wall! And what do you see on your wall? Mene, mene? Naked bodies?

CLOV   I see my light dying.

HAMM   Your light dying! Listen to that! Well, it can die just as well here, *your* light. Take a look at me and then come back and tell me what you think of *your* light.

(*Pause*)

CLOV   You shouldn't speak to me like that.

(*Pause*)

HAMM   (*coldly*) Forgive me. (*Pause. Louder*) I said, forgive me.

CLOV   I heard you. (*The lid of* NAGG's *bin lifts. His hands appear, gripping the rim. Then his head emerges. In his mouth the biscuit. He listens*)

HAMM   Did your seeds come up?

CLOV   No.

HAMM   Did you scratch round them to see if they had sprouted?

CLOV   They haven't sprouted.

HAMM   Perhaps it's still too early.

CLOV   If they were going to sprout they would have sprouted. (*violently*) They'll never sprout! (*Pause.* NAGG *takes biscuit in his hand*)

HAMM   This is not much fun. (*pause*) But that's always the way at the end of the day, isn't it, Clov?

CLOV   Always.

HAMM   It's the end of the day like any other day, isn't it, Clov?

CLOV   Looks like it.

(*Pause*)

HAMM   (*anguished*) What's happening, what's happening?

CLOV   Something is taking its course.

(*Pause*)

HAMM   All right, be off. (*He leans back in his chair, remains motionless.* CLOV *does not move, heaves a great groaning sigh.* HAMM *sits up*) I thought I told you to be off.

CLOV   I'm trying. (*He goes to door, halts*) Ever since I was whelped. (*exit* CLOV)

HAMM   We're getting on.

(*He leans back in his chair, remains motionless. NAGG knocks on the lid of the other bin. Pause. He knocks harder. The lid lifts and the hands of* NELL *appear, gripping the rim. Then her head emerges. Lace cap. Very white face*)

NELL   What is it, my pet? (*pause*) Time for love?

NAGG   Were you asleep?

NELL   Oh no!

NAGG   Kiss me.

NELL   We can't.

NAGG   Try.

(*Their heads strain towards each other, fail to meet, fall apart again*)

NELL   Why this farce, day after day?

(*Pause*)

NAGG   I've lost me tooth.

NELL   When?

NAGG   I had it yesterday.

NELL   (*elegiac*)   Ah yesterday!

(*They turn painfully towards each other*)

NAGG   Can you see me?

NELL   Hardly. And you?

NAGG   What?

NELL   Can you see me?

NAGG   Hardly.

NELL   So much the better, so much the better.

NAGG   Don't say that. (*pause*) Our sight has failed.

NELL   Yes.

(*Pause. They turn away from each other*)

NAGG   Can you hear me?

NELL   Yes. And you?

NAGG   Yes. (*pause*) Our hearing hasn't failed.

NELL   Our what?

NAGG   Our hearing.

NELL   No. (*pause*) Have you anything else to say to me?

NAGG   Do you remember—

NELL   No.

NAGG   When we crashed on our tandem and lost our shanks.

(*They laugh heartily*)

NELL   It was in the Ardennes.

(*They laugh less heartily*)

NAGG   On the road to Sedan. (*They laugh still less heartily*) Are you cold?

NELL   Yes, perished. And you?

NAGG   (*pause*) I'm freezing. (*pause*) Do you want to go in?

NELL   Yes.

NAGG   Then go in. (NELL *does not move*) Why don't you go in?

NELL   I don't know.

(*Pause*)

NAGG   Has he changed your sawdust?

NELL   It isn't sawdust. (*Pause. Wearily*) Can you not be a little accurate, Nagg?

NAGG   Your sand then. It's not important.

NELL   It is important.

(*Pause*)

NAGG   It was sawdust once.

NELL   Once!

NAGG   And now it's sand. (*pause*) From the shore. (*Pause. Impatiently*) Now it's sand he fetches from the shore.

NELL   Now it's sand.

NAGG   Has he changed yours?

NELL   No.

NAGG   Nor mine. (*pause*) I won't have it! (*Pause. Holding up the biscuit*) Do you want a bit?

NELL   No. (*pause*) Of what?

NAGG   Biscuit. I've kept you half. (*He looks at the biscuit. Proudly*) Three quarters. For you. Here. (*He proffers the biscuit*) No? (*pause*) Do you not feel well?

HAMM   (*wearily*)   Quiet, quiet, you're keeping me awake. (*pause*) Talk softer. (*pause*) If I could sleep I might make love. I'd go into the woods. My eyes would see . . . the sky, the earth. I'd run, run, they wouldn't catch me. (*pause*) Nature! (*pause*) There's something dripping in my head. (*pause*) A heart, a heart in my head. (*pause*)

NAGG   (*soft*)   Do you hear him? A heart in his head! (*He chuckles cautiously*)

NELL   One mustn't laugh at those things, Nagg. Why must you always laugh at them?

NAGG   Not so loud!

NELL   (*without lowering her voice*)   Nothing is funnier than unhappiness, I grant you that. But—

NAGG   (*shocked*)   Oh!

NELL   Yes, yes, it's the most comical thing in the world. And we laugh, we laugh, with a will, in the beginning. But it's always the same thing. Yes, it's like the funny story we have heard too often, we still find it funny, but we don't laugh any more. (*pause*) Have you anything else to say to me?

NAGG   No.

NELL   Are you quite sure? (*pause*) Then I'll leave you.

NAGG   Do you not want your biscuit? (*pause*) I'll keep it for you. (*pause*) I thought you were going to leave me.

NELL   I am going to leave you.

NAGG   Could you give me a scratch before you go?

NELL   No. (*pause*) Where?

NAGG   In the back.

NELL   No. (*pause*) Rub yourself against the rim.

NAGG   It's lower down. In the hollow.

NELL   What hollow?

NAGG   The hollow! (*pause*) Could you not? (*pause*) Yesterday you scratched me there.

NELL   (*elegiac*)   Ah yesterday!

NAGG   Could you not? (*pause*) Would you like me to scratch you? (*pause*) Are you crying again?

NELL   I was trying. (*pause*)

HAMM   Perhaps it's a little vein.

(*Pause*)

NAGG   What was that he said?

NELL   Perhaps it's a little vein.

NAGG   What does that mean? (*pause*) That means nothing. (*pause*) Will I tell you the story of the tailor?

NELL   No. (*pause*) What for?

NAGG   To cheer you up.

NELL   It's not funny.

NAGG   It always made you laugh. (*pause*) The first time I thought you'd die.

NELL   It was on Lake Como. (*pause*) One April afternoon. (*pause*) Can you believe it?

NAGG   What?

NELL   That we once went out rowing on Lake Como. (*pause*) One April afternoon.

NAGG   We had got engaged the day before.

NELL   Engaged!

NAGG   You were in such fits that we capsized. By rights we should have been drowned.

NELL   It was because I felt happy.

NAGG   (*indignant*)   It was not, it was not, it was my story and nothing else. Happy! Don't you laugh at it still? Every time I tell it. Happy!

NELL   It was deep, deep. And you could see down to the bottom. So white. So clean.

NAGG   Let me tell it again. (*raconteur's voice*) An Englishman, needing a pair of striped trousers in a hurry for the New Year festivities, goes to his tailor who takes his measurements. (*tailor's voice*) "That's the lot, come back in four days, I'll have it ready." Good. Four days later. (*tailor's voice*) "So sorry, come back in a week, I've made a mess of the seat." Good, that's all right, a neat seat can be very ticklish. A week later. (*tailor's voice*) "Frightfully sorry, come back in ten days, I've made a hash of the crotch." Good, can't be helped, a snug crotch is always a teaser. Ten days later.

(*tailor's voice*) "Dreadfully sorry, come back in a fortnight. I've made a balls of the fly." Good, at a pinch, a smart fly is a stiff proposition. (*Pause. Normal voice*) I never told it worse. (*Pause. Gloomy*) I tell this story worse and worse. (*Pause. Raconteur's voice*) Well, to make it short, the bluebells are blowing and he ballockses the buttonholes. (*customer's voice*) "God damn you to hell, Sir, no, it's indecent, there are limits! In six days, do you hear me, six days, God made the world. Yes Sir, no less Sir, the WORLD! And you are not bloody well capable of making me a pair of trousers in three months!" (*tailor's voice, scandalized*) "But my dear Sir, my dear Sir, look—(*disdainful gesture, disgustedly*)—at the world—(*pause*) and look—(*loving gesture, proudly*)—at my TROUSERS!" (*Pause. He looks at* NELL *who has remained impassive, her eyes unseeing, breaks into a high forced laugh, cuts it short, pokes his head towards* NELL, *launches his laugh again*)

HAMM   Silence! (NAGG *starts, cuts short his laugh*)

NELL   You could see down to the bottom.

HAMM   (*exasperated*) Have you not finished? Will you never finish? (*with sudden fury*) Will this never finish? (NAGG *disappears into his bin, closes the lid behind him.* NELL *does not move. Frenziedly*) My kingdom for a nightman! (*He whistles. Enter* CLOV) Clear away this muck! Chuck it in the sea! (CLOV *goes to bins, halts*)

NELL   So white.

HAMM   What? What's she blathering about? (CLOV *stoops, takes* NELL's *hand, feels her pulse*)

NELL   (*to* CLOV)   Desert! (CLOV *lets go her hand, pushes her back in the bin, closes the lid*)

CLOV   (*returning to his place beside the chair*) She has no pulse.

HAMM   What was she drivelling about?

CLOV   She told me to go away, into the desert.

HAMM   Damn busybody! Is that all?

CLOV   No.

HAMM   What else?

CLOV   I didn't understand.

HAMM   Have you bottled her?

CLOV   Yes.

HAMM   Are they both bottled?

CLOV   Yes.

HAMM   Screw down the lids. (CLOV *goes towards door*) Time enough. (CLOV *halts*) My anger subsides, I'd like to pee.

CLOV (*with alacrity*) I'll go and get the catheter. (*He goes towards door*)

HAMM Time enough. (CLOV *halts*) Give me my pain-killer.

CLOV It's too soon. (*pause*) It's too soon on top of your tonic, it wouldn't act.

HAMM In the morning they brace you up and in the evening they calm you down. Unless it's the other way round. (*pause*) That old doctor, he's dead naturally?

CLOV He wasn't old.

HAMM But he's dead?

CLOV Naturally. (*pause*) *You* ask *me* that? (*pause*)

HAMM Take me for a little turn. (CLOV *goes behind the chair and pushes it forward*) Not too fast! (CLOV *pushes chair*) Right round the world! (CLOV *pushes chair*) Hug the walls, then back to the center again. (CLOV *pushes chair*) I was right in the center, wasn't I?

CLOV (*pushing*) Yes.

HAMM We'd need a proper wheel chair. With big wheels. Bicycle wheels! (*pause*) Are you hugging?

CLOV (*pushing*) Yes.

HAMM (*groping for wall*) It's a lie! Why do you lie to me?

CLOV (*bearing closer to wall*) There! There!

HAMM Stop! (CLOV *stops chair close to back wall.* HAMM *lays his hand against wall*) Old wall! (*pause*) Beyond is the . . . other hell. (*Pause. Violently*) Closer! Closer! Up against!

CLOV Take away your hand. (HAMM *withdraws his hand.* CLOV *rams chair against wall*) There! (HAMM *leans towards wall, applies his ear to it*)

HAMM Do you hear? (*He strikes the wall with his knuckles*) Do you hear? Hollow bricks! (*He strikes again*) All that's hollow! (*Pause. He straightens up. Violently*) That's enough. Back!

CLOV We haven't done the round.

HAMM Back to my place! (CLOV *pushes chair back to center*) Is that my place?

CLOV Yes, that's your place.

HAMM Am I right in the center?

CLOV I'll measure it.

HAMM More or less! More or less!

CLOV (*moving chair slightly*) There!

HAMM I'm more or less in the center?

CLOV I'd say so.

HAMM You'd say so! Put me right in the center!

CLOV I'll go and get the tape.

HAMM Roughly! Roughly! (CLOV *moves chair slightly*) Bang in the center!

CLOV There! (*pause*)

HAMM I feel a little too far to the left. (CLOV *moves chair slightly*) Now I feel a little too far to the right. (CLOV *moves chair slightly*) I feel a little too far forward. (CLOV *moves chair slightly*) Now I feel a little too far back. (CLOV *moves chair slightly*) Don't stay there, (*i.e., behind the chair*) you give me the shivers. (CLOV *returns to his place beside the chair*)

CLOV If I could kill him I'd die happy. (*Pause*)

HAMM What's the weather like?

CLOV As usual.

HAMM Look at the earth.

CLOV I've looked.

HAMM With the glass?

CLOV No need of the glass.

HAMM Look at it with the glass.

CLOV I'll go and get the glass. (*exit* CLOV)

HAMM No need of the glass! (*Enter* CLOV *with telescope*)

CLOV I'm back again, with the glass. (*He goes to window right, looks up at it*) I need the steps.

HAMM Why? Have you shrunk? (*exit* CLOV *with telescope*) I don't like that, I don't like that. (*enter* CLOV *with ladder, but without telescope*)

CLOV I'm back again, with the steps. (*He sets down ladder under window right, gets up on it, realizes he has not the telescope, gets down*) I need the glass. (*He goes towards door*)

HAMM (*violently*) But you have the glass!

CLOV (*halting, violently*) No, I haven't the glass! (*exit* CLOV)

HAMM This is deadly. (*Enter* CLOV *with telescope. He goes towards ladder*)

CLOV Things are livening up. (*He gets up on ladder, raises the telescope, lets it fall*) I did it on purpose. (*He gets down, picks up the telescope, turns it on auditorium*) I see . . . a multitude . . . in transports . . . of joy. (*pause*) That's what I call a magnifier. (*He lowers the telescope, turns towards* HAMM) Well? Don't we laugh?

HAMM (*after reflection*) I don't.

CLOV (*after reflection*) Nor I. (*He gets up on ladder, turns the telescope on the without*) Let's see. (*He looks, moving the telescope*) Zero . . . (*He looks*) . . . zero . . . (*He looks*) . . . and zero.

HAMM   Nothing stirs. All is—

CLOV   Zer—

HAMM   (*violently*)   Wait till you're spoken to! (*normal voice*) All is . . . all is . . . all is what? (*violently*) All is what?

CLOV   What all is? In a word? Is that what you want to know? Just a moment. (*He turns the telescope on the without, looks, lowers the telescope, turns towards* HAMM) Corpsed. (*pause*) Well? Content?

HAMM   Look at the sea.

CLOV   It's the same.

HAMM   Look at the ocean!

(CLOV *gets down, takes a few steps towards window left, goes back for ladder, carries it over and sets it down under window left, gets up on it, turns the telescope on the without, looks at length. He starts, lowers the telescope, examines it, turns it again on the without*)

CLOV   Never seen anything like that!

HAMM   (*anxious*)   What? A sail? A fin? Smoke?

CLOV   The light is sunk.

HAMM   (*relieved*)   Pah! We all knew that.

CLOV   (*looking*)   There was a bit left.

HAMM   The base.

CLOV   (*looking*)   Yes.

HAMM   And now?

CLOV   (*looking*)   All gone.

HAMM   No gulls?

CLOV   (*looking*)   Gulls!

HAMM   And the horizon? Nothing on the horizon?

CLOV   (*lowering the telescope, turning towards* HAMM, *exasperated*)   What in God's name could there be on the horizon?

(*Pause*)

HAMM   The waves, how are the waves?

CLOV   The waves? (*He turns the telescope on the waves*) Lead.

HAMM   And the sun?

CLOV   (*looking*)   Zero.

HAMM   But it should be sinking. Look again.

CLOV   (*looking*)   Damn the sun.

HAMM   Is it night already then?

CLOV   (*looking*)   No.

HAMM   Then what is it?

CLOV   (*looking*)   Gray. (*lowering the telescope, turning towards* HAMM, *louder*) Gray! (*Pause. Still louder*) GRRAY!

(*Pause. He gets down, approaches* HAMM *from behind, whispers in his ear*)

HAMM   (*starting*)   Gray! Did I hear you say gray?

CLOV   Light black. From pole to pole.

HAMM   You exaggerate. (*pause*) Don't stay there, you give me the shivers. (CLOV *returns to his place beside the chair*)

CLOV   Why this farce, day after day?

HAMM   Routine. One never knows. (*pause*) Last night I saw inside my breast. There was a big sore.

CLOV   Pah! You saw your heart.

HAMM   No, it was living. (*Pause. Anguished*) Clov!

CLOV   Yes.

HAMM   What's happening?

CLOV   Something is taking its course.

(*Pause*)

HAMM   Clov!

CLOV   (*impatiently*)   What is it?

HAMM   We're not beginning to . . . to . . . mean something?

CLOV   Mean something! You and I, mean something! (*brief laugh*) Ah that's a good one!

HAMM   I wonder. (*pause*) Imagine if a rational being came back to earth, wouldn't he be liable to get ideas into his head if he observed us long enough. (*voice of rational being*) Ah, good, now I see what it is, yes, now I understand what they're at! (CLOV *starts, drops the telescope and begins to scratch his belly with both hands. Normal voice*) And without going so far as that, we ourselves . . . (*with emotion*) . . . we ourselves . . . at certain moments . . . (*vehemently*) To think perhaps it won't all have been for nothing!

CLOV   (*anguished, scratching himself*)   I have a flea!

HAMM   A flea! Are there still fleas?

CLOV   On me there's one. (*scratching*) Unless it's a crablouse.

HAMM   (*very perturbed*)   But humanity might start from there all over again! Catch him, for the love of God!

CLOV   I'll go get the powder. (*exit* CLOV)

HAMM   A flea! This is awful! What a day!

(*Enter* CLOV *with a sprinkling tin*)

CLOV   I'm back again, with the insecticide.

HAMM   Let him have it!

(CLOV *loosens the top of his trousers, pulls it forward and shakes powder into the aperture. He stoops, looks, waits, starts, frenziedly shakes more powder, stoops, looks, waits*)

CLOV   The bastard!

HAMM   Did you get him?

CLOV   Looks like it. (*He drops the tin and adjusts his trousers*) Unless he's laying doggo.

HAMM   Laying! Lying you mean. Unless he's *lying* doggo.

CLOV Ah? One says lying? One doesn't say laying?

HAMM   Use your head, can't you. If he was laying we'd be bitched.

CLOV Ah. (*pause*) What about that pee?

HAMM   I'm having it.

CLOV Ah that's the spirit, that's the spirit!

(*Pause*)

HAMM (*with ardour*) Let's go from here, the two of us! South! You can make a raft and the currents will carry us away, far away, to other . . . mammals!

CLOV God forbid!

HAMM   Alone, I'll embark alone! Get working on that raft immediately. Tomorrow I'll be gone for ever.

CLOV (*hastening towards door*) I'll start straight away.

HAMM   Wait! (CLOV *halts*) Will there be sharks, do you think?

CLOV Sharks? I don't know. If there are there will be. (*He goes towards door*)

HAMM   Wait! (CLOV *halts*) Is it not yet time for my pain-killer?

CLOV (*violently*) No! (*He goes towards door*)

HAMM   Wait! (CLOV *halts*) How are your eyes?

CLOV Bad.

HAMM   But you can see.

CLOV All I want.

HAMM   How are your legs?

CLOV Bad.

HAMM   But you can walk.

CLOV I come . . . and go.

HAMM   In my house. (*Pause. With prophetic relish*) One day you'll be blind, like me. You'll be sitting there, a speck in the void, in the dark, for ever like me. (*pause*) One day you'll say to yourself, I'm tired, I'll sit down, and you'll go and sit down. Then you'll say, I'm hungry, I'll get up and get something to eat. But you won't get up. You'll say I shouldn't have sat down, but since I have I'll sit on a little longer, then I'll get up and get something to eat. But you won't get up and you won't get anything to eat. (*pause*) You'll look at the wall a while, then you'll say, I'll close my eyes, perhaps have a little sleep, after that I'll feel better, and you'll close them. And when you open them again there'll be no wall any more. (*pause*) Infinite emptiness will be all around you, all the resurrected dead of all the ages wouldn't fill it, and there you'll be like a little bit of grit in the middle of the steppe. (*pause*) Yes, one day you'll know what it is, you'll be like me, except that you won't have anyone with you, because you won't have had pity on anyone and because there won't be anyone left to have pity on.

(*Pause*)

CLOV It's not certain. (*pause*) And there's one thing you forget.

HAMM   Ah?

CLOV I can't sit down.

HAMM (*impatiently*) Well you'll lie down then, what the hell! Or you'll come to a standstill, simply stop and stand still, the way you are now. One day you'll say, I'm tired, I'll stop. What does the attitude matter?

(*Pause*)

CLOV So you all want me to leave you.

HAMM   Naturally.

CLOV Then I'll leave you.

HAMM   You can't leave us.

CLOV Then I won't leave you.

(*Pause*)

HAMM   Why don't you finish us? (*pause*) I'll tell you the combination of the cupboard if you promise to finish me.

CLOV I couldn't finish you.

HAMM   Then you won't finish me.

(*Pause*)

CLOV I'll leave you, I have things to do.

HAMM   Do you remember when you came here?

CLOV No. Too small, you told me.

HAMM   Do you remember your father?

CLOV (*wearily*) Same answer. (*pause*) You've asked me these questions millions of times.

HAMM   I love the old questions. (*with fervor*) Ah the old questions, the old answers, there's nothing like them! (*pause*) It was I was a father to you.

CLOV Yes. (*He looks at* HAMM *fixedly*) You were that to me.

HAMM   My house a home for you.

CLOV Yes. (*He looks about him*) This was that for me.

HAMM (*proudly*) But for me, (*gesture towards himself*) no father. But for Hamm, (*gesture towards surroundings*) no home.

(*Pause*)

CLOV I'll leave you.

HAMM   Did you ever think of one thing?

CLOV Never.

HAMM   That here we're down in a hole. (*pause*) But beyond the hills? Eh? Perhaps it's still green. Eh? (*pause*) Flora! Pomona!

(*ecstatically*) Ceres! (*pause*) Perhaps you won't need to go very far.

CLOV I can't go very far. (*pause*) I'll leave you.

HAMM Is my dog ready?

CLOV He lacks a leg.

HAMM Is he silky?

CLOV He's a kind of Pomeranian.

HAMM Go and get him.

CLOV He lacks a leg.

HAMM Go and get him! (*exit* CLOV) We're getting on.

(*Enter* CLOV *holding by one of its three legs a black toy dog*)

CLOV Your dogs are here. (*He hands the dog to* HAMM *who feels it, fondles it*)

HAMM He's white, isn't he?

CLOV Nearly.

HAMM What do you mean, nearly? Is he white or isn't he?

CLOV He isn't.

(*Pause*)

HAMM You've forgotten the sex.

CLOV (*vexed*) But he isn't finished. The sex goes on at the end.

(*Pause*)

HAMM You haven't put on his ribbon.

CLOV (*angrily*) But he isn't finished, I tell you! First you finish your dog and then you put on his ribbon!

(*Pause*)

HAMM Can he stand?

CLOV I don't know.

HAMM Try. (*He hands the dog to* CLOV *who places it on the ground*) Well?

CLOV Wait!

(*He squats down and tries to get the dog to stand on its three legs, fails, lets it go. The dog falls on its side*)

HAMM (*impatiently*) Well?

CLOV He's standing.

HAMM (*groping for the dog*) Where? Where is he? (CLOV *holds up the dog in a standing position*)

CLOV There. (*He takes* HAMM's *hand and guides it towards the dog's head*)

HAMM (*his hand on the dog's head*) Is he gazing at me?

CLOV Yes.

HAMM (*proudly*) As if he were asking me to take him for a walk?

CLOV If you like.

HAMM (*as before*) Or as if he were begging me for a bone. (*He withdraws his hand*) Leave him like that, standing there imploring me.

(CLOV *straightens up. The dog falls on its side*)

CLOV I'll leave you.

HAMM Have you had your visions?

CLOV Less.

HAMM Is Mother Pegg's light on?

CLOV Light! How could anyone's light be on?

HAMM Extinguished!

CLOV Naturally it's extinguished. If it's not on it's extinguished.

HAMM No, I mean Mother Pegg.

CLOV But naturally she's extinguished! (*pause*) What's the matter with you today?

HAMM I'm taking my course. (*pause*) Is she buried?

CLOV Buried! Who would have buried her?

HAMM You.

CLOV Me! Haven't I enough to do without burying people?

HAMM But you'll bury me.

CLOV No I won't bury you.

(*Pause*)

HAMM She was bonny once, like a flower of the field. (*with reminiscent leer*) And a great one for the men!

CLOV We too were bonny—once. It's a rare thing not to have been bonny—once.

(*Pause*)

HAMM Go and get the gaff.

(CLOV *goes to door, halts*)

CLOV Do this, do that, and I do it. I never refuse. Why?

HAMM You're not able to.

CLOV Soon I won't do it any more.

HAMM You won't be able to any more. (*exit* CLOV) Ah the creatures, the creatures, everything has to be explained to them.

(*Enter* CLOV *with gaff*)

CLOV Here's your gaff. Stick it up.

(*He gives the gaff to* HAMM *who, wielding it like a puntpole, tries to move his chair*)

HAMM Did I move?

CLOV No.

(HAMM *throws down the gaff*)

HAMM Go and get the oilcan.

CLOV What for?

HAMM To oil the casters.

CLOV I oiled them yesterday.

HAMM Yesterday! What does that mean? Yesterday!

CLOV (*violently*) That means that bloody awful day, long ago, before this bloody awful day. I use the words you taught me. If they don't mean anything any more, teach me others. Or let me be silent. (*pause*)

HAMM   I once knew a madman who thought the end of the world had come. He was a painter—and engraver. I had a great fondness for him. I used to go and see him, in the asylum. I'd take him by the hand and drag him to the window. Look! There! All that rising corn! And there! Look! The sails of the herring fleet! All that loveliness! (*pause*) He'd snatch away his hand and go back into his corner. Appalled. All he had seen was ashes. (*pause*) He alone had been spared. (*pause*) Forgotten. (*pause*) It appears the case is . . . was not so . . . so unusual.

CLOV   A madman? When was that?

HAMM   Oh way back, way back, you weren't in the land of the living.

CLOV   God be with the days!

(*Pause.* HAMM *raises his toque*)

HAMM   I had a great fondness for him. (*Pause. He puts on his toque again*) He was a painter—and engraver.

CLOV   There are so many terrible things.

HAMM   No, no, there are not so many now. (*pause*) Clov!

CLOV   Yes.

HAMM   Do you not think this has gone on long enough?

CLOV   Yes! (*pause*) What?

HAMM   This . . . this . . . thing.

CLOV   I've always thought so. (*pause*) You not?

HAMM   (*gloomily*)   Then it's a day like any other day.

CLOV   As long as it lasts. (*pause*) All life long the same inanities.

HAMM   I can't leave you.

CLOV   I know. And you can't follow me.

(*Pause*)

HAMM   If you leave me how shall I know?

CLOV   (*briskly*)   Well you simply whistle me and if I don't come running it means I've left you.

(*Pause*)

HAMM   You won't come and kiss me goodbye?

CLOV   Oh I shouldn't think so.

(*Pause*)

HAMM   But you might be merely dead in your kitchen.

CLOV   The result would be the same.

HAMM   Yes, but how would I know, if you were merely dead in your kitchen?

CLOV   Well . . . sooner or later I'd start to stink.

HAMM   You stink already. The whole place stinks of corpses.

CLOV   The whole universe.

HAMM   (*angrily*)   To hell with the universe. (*pause*) Think of something.

CLOV   What?

HAMM   An idea, have an idea. (*angrily*) A bright idea!

CLOV   Ah good. (*He starts pacing to and fro, his eyes fixed on the ground, his hands behind his back. He halts*) The pains in my legs! It's unbelievable! Soon I won't be able to think any more.

HAMM   You won't be able to leave me. (CLOV *resumes his pacing*) What are you doing?

CLOV   Having an idea. (*He paces*) Ah! (*He halts*)

HAMM   What a brain! (*pause*) Well?

CLOV   Wait! (*He meditates. Not very convinced*) Yes . . . (*Pause. More convinced*) Yes! (*He raises his head*) I have it! I set the alarm.

(*Pause*)

HAMM   This is perhaps not one of my bright days, but frankly—

CLOV   You whistle me. I don't come. The alarm rings. I'm gone. It doesn't ring. I'm dead.

(*Pause*)

HAMM   Is it working? (*Pause. Impatiently*) The alarm, is it working?

CLOV   Why wouldn't it be working?

HAMM   Because it's worked too much.

CLOV   But it's hardly worked at all.

HAMM   (*angrily*)   Then because it's worked too little!

CLOV   I'll go and see. (*Exit* CLOV. *Brief ring of alarm off. Enter* CLOV *with alarm clock. He holds it against* HAMM's *ear and releases alarm. They listen to it ringing to the end. Pause*) Fit to wake the dead! Did you hear it?

HAMM   Vaguely.

CLOV   The end is terrific!

HAMM   I prefer the middle. (*pause*) Is it not time for my pain-killer?

CLOV   No! (*He goes to door, turns*) I'll leave you.

HAMM   It's time for my story. Do you want to listen to my story.

CLOV   No.

HAMM   Ask my father if he wants to listen to my story.

(CLOV *goes to bins, raises the lid of* NAGG's, *stoops, looks into it. Pause. He straightens up*)

CLOV   He's asleep.

HAMM   Wake him.

(CLOV *stoops, wakes* NAGG *with the alarm. Unintelligible words.* CLOV *straightens up*)

CLOV   He doesn't want to listen to your story.

HAMM I'll give him a bonbon. (CLOV *stoops. As before*)

CLOV He wants a sugar-plum.

HAMM He'll get a sugar-plum. (CLOV *stoops. As before*)

CLOV It's a deal. (*He goes towards door.* NAGG's *hands appear, gripping the rim. Then the head emerges.* CLOV *reaches door, turns*) Do you believe in the life to come?

HAMM Mine was always that. (*exit* CLOV) Got him that time!

NAGG I'm listening.

HAMM Scoundrel! Why did you engender me?

NAGG I didn't know.

HAMM What? What didn't you know?

NAGG That it'd be you. (*pause*) You'll give me a sugar-plum?

HAMM After the audition.

NAGG You swear?

HAMM Yes.

NAGG On what?

HAMM My honor. (*Pause. They laugh heartily*)

NAGG Two.

HAMM One.

NAGG One for me and one for—

HAMM One! Silence! (*pause*) Where was I? (*Pause. Gloomily*) It's finished, we're finished. (*pause*) Nearly finished. (*pause*) There'll be no more speech. (*pause*) Something dripping in my head, ever since the fontanelles. (*stifled hilarity of* NAGG) Splash, splash, always on the same spot. (*pause*) Perhaps it's a little vein. (*pause*) A little artery. (*Pause. More animated*) Enough of that, it's story time, where was I? (*Pause. Narrative tone*) The man came crawling towards me, on his belly. Pale, wonderfully pale and thin, he seemed on the point of— (*Pause. Normal tone*) No. I've done that bit. (*Pause. Narrative tone*) I calmly filled my pipe —the meerschaum, lit it with . . . let us say a vesta, drew a few puffs. Aah! (*pause*) Well, what is it *you* want? (*pause*) It was an extraordinarily bitter day, I remember, zero by the thermometer. But considering it was Christmas Eve there was nothing . . . extraordinary about that. Seasonable weather, for once in a way. (*pause*) Well, what ill wind blows you my way? He raised his face to me, black with mingled dirt and tears. (*Pause. Normal tone*) That should do it. (*narrative tone*) No no, don't look at me, don't look at me. He dropped his eyes and mumbled something, apologies I presume. (*pause*) I'm a busy man, you know, the final touches, before the festivities, you know what it is. (*Pause. Forcibly*) Come on

now, what is the object of this invasion? (*pause*) It was a glorious bright day, I remember, fifty by the heliometer, but already the sun was sinking down into the . . . down among the dead. (*normal tone*) Nicely put, that. (*narrative tone*) Come on now, come on, present your petition and let me resume my labors. (*Pause. Normal tone*) There's English for you. Ah well . . . (*narrative tone*) It was then he took the plunge. It's my little one, he said. Tsstss, a little one, that's bad. My little boy, he said, as if the sex mattered. Where did he come from? He named the hole. A good half-day, on horse. What are you insinuating? That the place is still inhabited? No no, not a soul, except himself and the child—assuming he existed. Good. I inquired about the situation at Kov, beyond the gulf. Not a sinner. Good. And you expect me to believe you have left your little one back there, all alone, and alive into the bargain? Come now! (*pause*) It was a howling wild day, I remember, a hundred by the anenometer. The wind was tearing up the dead pines and sweeping them . . . away. (*Pause. Normal tone*) A bit feeble, that. (*narrative tone*) Come on, man, speak up, what is it you want from me, I have to put up my holly. (*pause*) Well to make it short it finally transpired that what he wanted from me was . . . bread for his brat? Bread? But I have no bread, it doesn't agree with me. Good. Then perhaps a little corn? (*Pause. Normal tone*) That should do it. (*narrative tone*) Corn, yes, I have corn, it's true, in my granaries. But use your head. I give you some corn, a pound, a pound and a half, you bring it back to your child and you make him—if he's still alive—a nice pot of porridge, (NAGG *reacts*) a nice pot and a half of porridge, full of nourishment. Good. The colors come back into his little cheeks—perhaps. And then? (*pause*) I lost patience. (*violently*) Use your head, can't you, use your head, you're on earth, there's no cure for that! (*pause*) It was an exceedingly dry day, I remember, zero by the hygrometer. Ideal weather, for my lumbago. (*Pause. Violently*) But what in God's name do you imagine? That the earth will awake in spring? That the rivers and seas will run with fish again? That there's manna in heaven still for imbeciles like you? (*pause*) Gradually I cooled down, sufficiently at least to ask him how long he had taken on the way. Three whole days. Good. In what condition he had left the child. Deep in sleep. (*forcibly*) But deep in what sleep, deep in what sleep already? (*pause*) Well to make it short I finally offered to take him into my service. He had touched a chord. And then I imagined already that I wasn't much longer for this world. (*He laughs. Pause*) Well? (*pause*) Well? Here if you were careful you might die a nice natural death, in peace and comfort. (*pause*) Well? (*pause*) In the end he asked me would I consent to take in the child as well—if he were still alive. (*pause*) It was the moment I was waiting for. (*pause*) Would I consent to take in the child . . . (*pause*) I can see him still, down on his knees, his hands flat on the ground, glaring at me with his mad eyes, in defiance of my wishes. (*Pause. Normal tone*) I'll soon have finished with this story. (*pause*) Unless I bring in other characters. (*pause*) But where would I find them? (*pause*) Where would I look for them? (*Pause. He whistles. Enter* CLOV) Let us pray to God.

NAGG   Me sugar-plum!

CLOV   There's a rat in the kitchen!

HAMM   A rat! Are there still rats?

CLOV   In the kitchen there's one.

HAMM   And you haven't exterminated him?

CLOV   Half. You disturbed us.

HAMM   He can't get away?

CLOV   No.

HAMM   You'll finish him later. Let us pray to God.

CLOV   Again!

NAGG   Me sugar-plum!

HAMM   God first! (*pause*) Are you right?

CLOV   (*resigned*)   Off we go.

HAMM   (*to* NAGG)   And you?

NAGG   (*clasping his hands, closing his eyes, in a gabble*)   Our Father which art—

HAMM   Silence! In silence! Where are your manners? (*pause*) Off we go. (*Attitudes of prayer. Silence. Abandoning his attitude, discouraged*) Well?

CLOV   (*abandoning his attitude*)   What a hope! And you?

HAMM   Sweet damn all! (*to* NAGG) And you?

NAGG   Wait! (*Pause. Abandoning his attitude*) Nothing doing!

HAMM   The bastard! He doesn't exist!

CLOV   Not yet.

NAGG   Me sugar-plum!

HAMM   There are no more sugar-plums! (*pause*)

NAGG   It's natural. After all I'm your father. It's true if it hadn't been me it would have been someone else. But that's no excuse. (*pause*) Turkish Delight, for example, which no longer exists, we all know that, there is nothing in the world I love more. And one day I'll ask you for some, in return for a kindness, and you'll promise it to me. One

must live with the times. (*pause*) Whom did you call when you were a tiny boy, and were frightened, in the dark? Your mother? No. Me. We let you cry. Then we moved you out of earshot, so that we might sleep in peace. (*pause*) I was asleep, as happy as a king, and you woke me up to have me listen to you. It wasn't indispensable, you didn't really need to have me listen to you. (*pause*) I hope the day will come when you'll really need to have me listen to you, and need to hear my voice, any voice. (*pause*) Yes, I hope I'll live till then, to hear you calling me like when you were a tiny boy, and were frightened, in the dark, and I was your only hope. (*Pause.* NAGG *knocks on lid of* NELL's *bin. Pause*) Nell! (*Pause. He knocks louder. Pause. Louder*) Nell! (*Pause.* NAGG *sinks back into his bin, closes the lid behind him. Pause*)

HAMM   Our revels now are ended. (*He gropes for the dog*) The dog's gone.

CLOV   He's not a real dog, he can't go.

HAMM   (*groping*)   He's not there.

CLOV   He's lain down.

HAMM   Give him up to me. (CLOV *picks up the dog and gives it to* HAMM. HAMM *holds it in his arms. Pause.* HAMM *throws away the dog*) Dirty brute! (CLOV *begins to pick up the objects lying on the ground*) What are you doing?

CLOV   Putting things in order. (*He straightens up. Fervently*) I'm going to clear everything away! (*He starts picking up again*)

HAMM   Order!

CLOV   (*straightening up*)   I love order. It's my dream. A world where all would be silent and still and each thing in its last place, under the last dust. (*He starts picking up again*)

HAMM   (*exasperated*)   What in God's name do you think you are doing?

CLOV   (*straightening up*)   I'm doing my best to create a little order.

HAMM   Drop it! (CLOV *drops the objects he has picked up*)

CLOV   After all, there or elsewhere. (*He goes towards door*)

HAMM   (*irritably*)   What's wrong with your feet?

CLOV   My feet?

HAMM   Tramp! Tramp!

CLOV   I must have put on my boots.

HAMM   Your slippers were hurting you? (*pause*)

CLOV   I'll leave you.

HAMM   No!

CLOV   What is there to keep me here?

HAMM   The dialogue. (*pause*) I've got on

with my story. (*pause*) I've got on with it well. (*Pause. Irritably*) Ask me where I've got to.

CLOV   Oh, by the way, your story?

HAMM (*surprised*)   What story?

CLOV   The one you've been telling your-self all your days.

HAMM   Ah you mean my chronicle?

CLOV   That's the one.

(*Pause*)

HAMM (*angrily*)   Keep going, can't you, keep going!

CLOV   You've got on with it, I hope.

HAMM (*modestly*)   Oh not very far, not very far. (*He sighs*) There are days like that, one isn't inspired. (*pause*) Nothing you can do about it, just wait for it to come. (*pause*) No forcing, no forcing, it's fatal. (*pause*) I've got on with it a little all the same. (*pause*) Tech-nique, you know. (*Pause. Irritably*) I say I've got on with it a little all the same.

CLOV (*admiringly*)   Well I never! In spite of everything you were able to get on with it!

HAMM (*modestly*)   Oh not very far, you know, not very far, but nevertheless, better than nothing.

CLOV   Better than nothing! Is it possible?

HAMM   I'll tell you how it goes. He comes crawling on his belly—

CLOV   Who?

HAMM   What?

CLOV   Who do you mean, he?

HAMM   Who do I mean! Yet another.

CLOV   Ah him! I wasn't sure.

HAMM   Crawling on his belly, whining for bread for his brat. He's offered a job as gar-dener. Before—(CLOV *bursts out laughing*) What is there so funny about that?

CLOV   A job as gardener!

HAMM   Is that what tickles you?

CLOV   It must be that.

HAMM   It wouldn't be the bread?

CLOV   Or the brat.

(*Pause*)

HAMM   The whole thing is comical, I grant you that. What about having a good guffaw the two of us together?

CLOV (*after reflection*)   I couldn't guffaw again today.

HAMM (*after reflection*)   Nor I. (*pause*) I continue then. Before accepting with gratitude he asks if he may have his little boy with him.

CLOV   What age?

HAMM   Oh tiny.

CLOV   He would have climbed the trees.

HAMM   All the little odd jobs.

CLOV   And then he would have grown up.

HAMM   Very likely.

(*Pause*)

CLOV   Keep going, can't you, keep going!

HAMM   That's all. I stopped there.

(*Pause*)

CLOV   Do you see how it goes on.

HAMM   More or less.

CLOV   Will it not soon be the end?

HAMM   I'm afraid it will.

CLOV   Pah! You'll make up another.

HAMM   I don't know. (*pause*) I feel rather drained. (*pause*) The prolonged creative effort. (*pause*) If I could drag myself down to the sea! I'd make a pillow of sand for my head and the tide would come.

CLOV   There's no more tide.

(*Pause*)

HAMM   Go and see is she dead. (CLOV *goes to bins, raises the lid of* NELL'S, *stoops, looks into it. Pauses*)

CLOV   Looks like it.

(*He closes the lid, straightens up.* HAMM *raises his toque. Pause. He puts it on again*)

HAMM (*with his hand to his toque*)   And Nagg?

(CLOV *raises lid of* NAGG's *bin, stoops, looks into it. Pause*)

CLOV   Doesn't look like it. (*He closes the lid, straightens up*)

HAMM (*letting go his toque*)   What's he doing?

(CLOV *raises lid of* NAGG's *bin, stoops, looks into it. Pause*)

CLOV   He's crying. (*He closes lid, straight-ens up*)

HAMM   Then he's living. (*pause*) Did you ever have an instant of happiness?

CLOV   Not to my knowledge.

(*Pause*)

HAMM   Bring me under the window. (CLOV *goes towards chair*) I want to feel the light on my face. (CLOV *pushes chair*) Do you remem-ber, in the beginning, when you took me for a turn? You used to hold the chair too high. At every step you nearly tipped me out. (*with senile quaver*) Ah great fun, we had, the two of us, great fun. (*gloomily*) And then we got into the way of it. (CLOV *stops the chair under window right*) There already? (*Pause. He tilts back his head*) Is it light?

CLOV   It isn't dark.

HAMM (*angrily*)   I'm asking you is it light.

CLOV   Yes.

(*Pause*)

HAMM   The curtain isn't closed?

CLOV   No.

HAMM   What window is it?

CLOV   The earth.

HAMM   I knew it! (*angrily*) But there's no light there! The other! (CLOV *pushes chair towards window left*) The earth! (CLOV *stops the chair under window left.* HAMM *tilts back his head*) That's what I call light! (*pause*) Feels like a ray of sunshine. (*pause*) No?

CLOV   No.

HAMM   It isn't a ray of sunshine I feel on my face?

CLOV   No.

(*Pause*)

HAMM   Am I very white? (*Pause. Angrily*) I'm asking you am I very white!

CLOV   Not more so than usual.

(*Pause*)

HAMM   Open the window.

CLOV   What for?

HAMM   I want to hear the sea.

CLOV   You wouldn't hear it.

HAMM   Even if you opened the window?

CLOV   No.

HAMM   Then it's not worth while opening it?

CLOV   No.

HAMM   (*violently*) Then open it! (CLOV *gets up on the ladder, opens the window. Pause*) Have you opened it?

CLOV   Yes.

(*Pause*)

HAMM   You swear you've opened it?

CLOV   Yes.

(*Pause*)

HAMM   Well . . . ! (*pause*) It must be very calm. (*Pause. Violently*) I'm asking you is it very calm!

CLOV   Yes.

HAMM   It's because there are no more navigators. (*pause*) You haven't much conversation all of a sudden. Do you not feel well?

CLOV   I'm cold.

HAMM   What month are we? (*pause*) Close the window, we're going back. (CLOV *closes the window, gets down, pushes the chair back to its place, remains standing behind it, head bowed*) Don't stay there, you give me the shivers! (CLOV *returns to his place beside the chair*) Father! (*Pause. Louder*) Father! (*pause*) Go and see did he hear me.

(CLOV *goes to* NAGG's *bin, raises the lid, stoops. Unintelligible words.* CLOV *straightens up*)

CLOV   Yes.

HAMM   Both times?

(CLOV *stoops. As before*)

CLOV   Once only.

HAMM   The first time or the second?

(CLOV *stoops. As before*)

CLOV   He doesn't know.

HAMM   It must have been the second.

CLOV   We'll never know. (*He closes lid*)

HAMM   Is he still crying?

CLOV   No.

HAMM   The dead go fast. (*pause*) What's he doing?

CLOV   Sucking his biscuit.

HAMM   Life goes on. (CLOV *returns to his place beside the chair*) Give me a rug, I'm freezing.

CLOV   There are no more rugs.

(*Pause*)

HAMM   Kiss me. (*pause*) Will you not kiss me?

CLOV   No.

HAMM   On the forehead.

CLOV   I won't kiss you anywhere.

(*Pause*)

HAMM   (*holding out his hand*) Give me your hand at least. (*pause*) Will you not give me your hand?

CLOV   I won't touch you.

(*Pause*)

HAMM   Give me the dog. (CLOV *looks round for the dog*) No!

CLOV   Do you not want your dog?

HAMM   No.

CLOV   Then I'll leave you.

HAMM   (*head bowed, absently*) That's right. (CLOV *goes to door, turns*)

CLOV   If I don't kill that rat he'll die.

HAMM   (*as before*) That's right. (*Exit* CLOV. *Pause*) Me to play. (*He takes out his handkerchief, unfolds it, holds it spread out before him*) We're getting on. (*pause*) You weep, and weep, for nothing, so as not to laugh, and little by little . . . you begin to grieve. (*He folds the handkerchief, puts it back in his pocket, raises his head*) All those I might have helped. (*pause*) Helped! (*pause*) Saved. (*pause*) Saved! (*pause*) The place was crawling with them! (*Pause. Violently*) Use your head, can't you, use your head, you're on earth, there's no cure for that! (*pause*) Get out of here and love one another! Lick your neighbor as yourself! (*Pause. Calmer*) When it wasn't bread they wanted it was crumpets. (*Pause. Violently*) Out of my sight and back to your petting parties! (*pause*) All that, all that! (*pause*) Not even a real dog! (*calmer*) The end is in the beginning and yet you go on. (*pause*)

Perhaps I could go on with my story, end it and begin another. (*pause*) Perhaps I could throw myself out on the floor. (*He pushes himself painfully off his seat, falls back again*) Dig my nails into the cracks and drag myself forward with my fingers. (*pause*) It will be the end and there I'll be, wondering what can have brought it on and wondering what can have . . . (*He hesitates*) . . . why it was so long coming. (*pause*) There I'll be, in the old shelter, alone against the silence and . . . (*He hesitates*) . . . the stillness. If I can hold my peace, and sit quiet, it will be all over with sound, and motion, all over and done with. (*pause*) I'll have called my father and I'll have called my . . . (*He hesitates*) . . . my son. And even twice, or three times, in case they shouldn't have heard me, the first time, or the second. (*pause*) I'll say to myself, He'll come back. (*pause*) And then? (*pause*) And then? (*pause*) He couldn't, he has gone too far. (*pause*) And then? (*Pause. Very agitated*) All kinds of fantasies! That I'm being watched! A rat! Steps! Breath held and then . . . (*He breathes out*) Then babble, babble, words, like the solitary child who turns himself into children, two, three, so as to be together, and whisper together, in the dark. (*pause*) Moment upon moment, pattering down, like the millet grains of . . . (*He hesitates*) . . . that old Greek, and all life long you wait for that to mount up to a life. (*Pause. He opens his mouth to continue, renounces*) Ah let's get it over! (*He whistles. Enter* CLOV *with alarm clock. He halts beside the chair*) What? Neither gone nor dead?

CLOV In spirit only.

HAMM Which?

CLOV Both.

HAMM Gone from me you'd be dead.

CLOV And vice versa.

HAMM Outside of here it's death! (*pause*) And the rat?

CLOV He's got away.

HAMM He can't go far. (*Pause. Anxious*) Eh?

CLOV He doesn't need to go far.

(*Pause*)

HAMM Is it not time for my pain-killer?

CLOV Yes.

HAMM Ah! At last! Give it to me! Quick!

(*Pause*)

CLOV There's no more pain-killer.

(*Pause*)

HAMM (*appalled*) Good. . . ! (*pause*) No more pain-killer!

CLOV No more pain-killer. You'll never get any more pain-killer.

(*Pause*)

HAMM But the little round box. It was full!

CLOV Yes. But now it's empty.

(*Pause.* CLOV *starts to move about the room. He is looking for a place to put down the alarm clock*)

HAMM (*soft*) What'll I do? (*Pause. In a scream*) What'll I do? (CLOV *sees the picture, takes it down, stands it on the floor with its face to the wall, hangs up the alarm clock in its place*) What are you doing?

CLOV Winding up.

HAMM Look at the earth.

CLOV Again!

HAMM Since it's calling to you.

CLOV Is your throat sore? (*pause*) Would you like a lozenge? (*pause*) No. (*pause*) Pity.

(CLOV *goes, humming, towards window right, halts before it, looks up at it*)

HAMM Don't sing.

CLOV (*turning towards* HAMM) One hasn't the right to sing any more?

HAMM No.

CLOV Then how can it end?

HAMM You want it to end?

CLOV I want to sing.

HAMM I can't prevent you. (*Pause.* CLOV *turns towards window right*)

CLOV What did I do with that steps? (*He looks around for ladder*) You didn't see that steps? (*He sees it*) Ah, about time. (*He goes towards window left*) Sometimes I wonder if I'm in my right mind. Then it passes over and I'm as lucid as before. (*He gets up on ladder, looks out of window*) Christ, she's under water! (*He looks*) How can that be? (*He pokes forward his head, his hand above his eyes*) It hasn't rained. (*He wipes the pane, looks. Pause*) Ah what a fool I am! I'm on the wrong side! (*He gets down, takes a few steps towards window right*) Under water! (*He goes back for ladder*) What a fool I am! (*He carries ladder towards window right*) Sometimes I wonder if I'm in my right senses. Then it passes off and I'm as intelligent as ever. (*He sets down ladder under window right, gets up on it, looks out of window. He turns towards* HAMM) Any particular sector you fancy? Or merely the whole thing?

HAMM Whole thing.

CLOV The general effect? Just a moment.

(*He looks out of window. Pause*)

HAMM Clov.

CLOV (*absorbed*) Mmm.

HAMM   Do you know what it is?

CLOV (*as before*)   Mmm.

HAMM   I was never there. (*pause*) Clov!

CLOV (*turning towards* HAMM, *exasperated*) What is it?

HAMM   I was never there.

CLOV   Lucky for you. (*He looks out of window*)

HAMM   Absent, always. It all happened without me. I don't know what's happened. (*pause*) Do you know what's happened? (*pause*) Clov!

CLOV (*turning towards* HAMM, *exasperated*) Do you want me to look at this muckheap, yes or no?

HAMM   Answer me first.

CLOV   What?

HAMM   Do you know what's happened?

CLOV   When? Where?

HAMM   (*violently*)   When! What's happened? Use your head, can't you! What has happened?

CLOV   What for Christ's sake does it matter? (*He looks out of window*)

HAMM   I don't know. (*Pause.* CLOV *turns towards* HAMM)

CLOV   (*harshly*)   When old Mother Pegg asked you for oil for her lamp and you told her to get out to hell, you knew what was happening then, no? (*pause*) You know what she died of, Mother Pegg? Of darkness.

HAMM (*feebly*)   I hadn't any.

CLOV (*as before*)   Yes, you had.

(*Pause*)

HAMM   Have you the glass?

CLOV   No, it's clear enough as it is.

HAMM   Go and get it. (*Pause.* CLOV *casts up his eyes, brandishes his fists. He loses balance, clutches on to the ladder. He starts to get down, halts*)

CLOV   There's one thing I'll never understand. (*He gets down*) Why I always obey you. Can you explain that to me?

HAMM   No. . . . Perhaps it's compassion. (*pause*) A kind of great compassion. (*pause*) Oh you won't find it easy, you won't find it easy. (*Pause.* CLOV *begins to move about the room in search of the telescope*)

CLOV   I'm tired of our goings on, very tired. (*He searches*) You're not sitting on it? (*He moves the chair, looks at the place where it stood, resumes his search*)

HAMM (*anguished*)   Don't leave me there! (*Angrily* CLOV *restores the chair to its place*) Am I right in the center?

CLOV   You'd need a microscope to find this—(*He sees the telescope*) Ah, about time.

(*He picks up the telescope, gets up on the ladder, turns the telescope on the without*)

HAMM   Give me the dog.

CLOV (*looking*)   Quiet!

HAMM   Give me the dog.

(CLOV *drops the telescope, clasps his hands to his head. Pause. He gets down precipitately, looks for the dog, sees it, picks it up, hastens towards* HAMM *and strikes him violently on the head with the dog*)

CLOV   There's your dog for you! (*The dog falls to the ground. Pause*)

HAMM   He hit me!

CLOV   You drive me mad, I'm mad!

HAMM   If you must hit me, hit me with the axe. (*pause*) Or with the gaff, hit me with the gaff. Not with the dog. With the gaff. Or with the axe.

(CLOV *picks up the dog and gives it to* HAMM *who takes it in his arms*)

CLOV (*imploringly*)   Let's stop playing!

HAMM   Never! (*pause*) Put me in my coffin.

CLOV   There are no more coffins.

HAMM   Then let it end! (CLOV *goes towards ladder*) With a bang! (CLOV *gets up on ladder, gets down again, looks for telescope, sees it, picks it up, gets up ladder, raises telescope*) Of darkness! And me? Did anyone ever have pity on me?

CLOV (*lowering the telescope, turning towards* HAMM)   What? (*pause*) Is it me you're referring to?

HAMM (*angrily*)   An aside, ape! Did you never hear an aside before? (*pause*) I'm warming up for my last soliloquy.

CLOV   I warn you. I'm going to look at this filth since it's an order. But it's the last time. (*He turns the telescope on the without*) Let's see. (*He moves the telescope*) Nothing . . . nothing . . . good . . . good . . . nothing . . . goo—(*He starts, lowers the telescope, examines it, turns it again on the without. Pause*) Bad luck to it!

HAMM   More complications! (CLOV *gets down*) Not an underplot, I trust. (CLOV *moves ladder nearer window, gets up on it, turns telescope on the without*)

CLOV (*dismayed*)   Looks like a small boy!

HAMM (*sarcastic*)   A small . . . boy!

CLOV   I'll go and see. (*He gets down, drops the telescope, goes towards door, turns*) I'll take the gaff. (*He looks for the gaff, sees it, picks it up, hastens towards door*)

HAMM   No!

(CLOV *halts*)

CLOV   No? A potential procreator?

HAMM   If he exists he'll die there or he'll come here. And if he doesn't . . .

(*Pause*)

CLOV   You don't believe me? You think I'm inventing?

(*Pause*)

HAMM   It's the end, Clov, we've come to the end. I don't need you any more.

(*Pause*)

CLOV   Lucky for you. (*He goes towards door*)

HAMM   Leave me the gaff.

(CLOV *gives him the gaff, goes towards door, halts, looks at alarm clock, takes it down, looks round for a better place to put it, goes to bins, puts it on lid of* NAGG's *bin. Pause*)

CLOV   I'll leave you. (*He goes towards door*)

HAMM   Before you go . . . (CLOV *halts near door*) . . . say something.

CLOV   There is nothing to say.

HAMM   A few words . . . to ponder . . . in my heart.

CLOV   Your heart!

HAMM   Yes. (*Pause. Forcibly*) Yes! (*pause*) With the rest, in the end, the shadows, the murmurs, all the trouble, to end up with. (*pause*) Clov. . . . He never spoke to me. Then, in the end, before he went, without my having asked him, he spoke to me. He said . . .

CLOV   (*despairingly*)   Ah. . . !

HAMM   Something . . . from your heart.

CLOV   My heart!

HAMM   A few words . . . from your heart.

(*Pause*)

CLOV   (*fixed gaze, tonelessly, towards auditorium*) They said to me, That's love, yes, yes, not a doubt, now you see how—

HAMM   Articulate!

CLOV   (*as before*)   How easy it is. They said to me, That's friendship, yes, yes, no question, you've found it. They said to me, Here's the place, stop, raise your head and look at all that beauty. That order! They said to me, Come now, you're not a brute beast, think upon these things and you'll see how all becomes clear. And simple! They said to me, What skilled attention they get, all these dying of their wounds.

HAMM   Enough!

CLOV   (*as before*)   I say to myself—sometimes, Clov, you must learn to suffer better than that if you want them to weary of punishing you—one day. I say to myself—sometimes, Clov, you must be there better than that if you want them to let you go—one day. But I feel too old, and too far, to form new habits. Good, it'll never end, I'll never go. (*pause*) Then one day, suddenly, it ends, it changes, I don't understand, it dies, or it's me, I don't understand, that either. I ask the words that remain—sleeping, waking, morning, evening. They have nothing to say. (*pause*) I open the door of the cell and go. I am so bowed I only see my feet, if I open my eyes, and between my legs a little trail of black dust. I say to myself that the earth is extinguished, though I never saw it lit. (*pause*) It's easy going. (*pause*) When I fall I'll weep for happiness. (*Pause. He goes towards door*)

HAMM   Clov! (CLOV *halts, without turning*) Nothing. (CLOV *moves on*) Clov! (CLOV *halts, without turning*)

CLOV   This is what we call making an exit.

HAMM   I'm obliged to you, Clov. For your services.

CLOV   (*turning, sharply*)   Ah pardon, it's I am obliged to you.

HAMM   It's we are obliged to each other. (*Pause.* CLOV *goes towards door*) One thing more. (CLOV *halts*) A last favor. (*exit* CLOV) Cover me with the sheet. (*long pause*) No? Good. (*pause*) Me to play. (*Pause. Wearily*) Old endgame lost of old, play and lose and have done with losing. (*Pause. More animated*) Let me see. (*pause*) Ah yes! (*He tries to move the chair, using the gaff as before. Enter* CLOV, *dressed for the road. Panama hat, tweed coat, raincoat over his arm, umbrella, bag. He halts by the door and stands there, impassive and motionless, his eyes fixed on* HAMM, *till the end.* HAMM *gives up*) Good. (*pause*) Discard. (*He throws away the gaff, makes to throw away the dog, thinks better of it*) Take it easy. (*pause*) And now? (*pause*) Raise hat. (*He raises his toque*) Peace to our . . . arses. (*pause*) And put on again. (*He puts on his toque*) Deuce. (*Pause. He takes off his glasses*) Wipe. (*He takes out his handkerchief and, without unfolding it, wipes his glasses*) And put on again. (*He puts on his glasses, puts back the handkerchief in his pocket*) We're coming. A few more squirms like that and I'll call. (*pause*) A little poetry. (*pause*) You prayed— (*Pause. He corrects himself*) You CRIED for night; it comes—(*Pause. He corrects himself*) It FALLS: now cry in darkness. (*He repeats, chanting*) You cried for night; it falls; now cry in darkness. (*pause*) Nicely put, that. (*pause*) And now? (*pause*) Moments for nothing, now as always, time was never and time is over, reckoning closed and story ended. (*Pause. Narrative tone*) If he could have his child with him. . . . (*pause*) It was the moment I was waiting for. (*pause*) You don't want to abandon him? You want him to bloom while you are withering? Be there to solace your last million last moments? (*pause*) He doesn't realize, all he knows is hunger, and cold, and death to crown it all. But you! You ought to know what the earth is like, nowadays. Oh I put him before his responsibilities! (*Pause. Normal tone*) Well, there we are, there I am, that's enough. (*He raises the whistle to his lips, hesitates, drops it. Pause*) Yes, truly! (*He whistles. Pause. Louder. Pause*) Good. (*pause*) Father! (*Pause. Louder*) Father! (*pause*) Good. (*pause*) We're coming. (*pause*) And to end up with? (*pause*) Discard. (*He throws away the dog. He tears the whistle from his neck*) With my compliments. (*He throws whistle towards auditorium. Pause. He sniffs. Soft*) Clov! (*long pause*) No? Good. (*He takes out the handkerchief*) Since that's the way we're playing it . . . (*He unfolds handkerchief*) . . . let's play it that way . . . (*He unfolds*) . . . and speak no more about it . . . (*He finishes unfolding*) . . . speak no more. (*He holds handkerchief spread out before him*) Old stancher! (*pause*) You . . . remain. (*Pause. He covers his face with handkerchief, lowers his arms to armrests, remains motionless*)

(*Brief tableau*)

ENGLAND

IRELAND

WILLIAM BUTLER YEATS (1865–1939), for all his greatness as a poet, never had much influence on the modern theatre. Usually we think of him as one of the leading figures of the famous Abbey Theatre in Dublin and the man responsible for encouraging so many writers to participate in the Irish theatrical renaissance. Yeats's own plays, however, tend to be dismissed as the interesting experiments of a great poet—experiments which were too esoteric and aristocratic to be dramatically viable on the popular stage. And yet, now, better than two decades after his death, it would appear that T. S. Eliot's evaluation of Yeats' contribution to modern poetry might apply equally well to the theatre. Yeats was, in Eliot's words, "one of those few whose history is the history of our own time, who are a part of the consciousness of their age, which cannot be understood without them."

Yeats, with his passionate desire to express great complexity within a dramatic form that was simple, direct, organic, and, above all, compressed, wrote a series of plays that foreshadow the work of Beckett, Ionesco, Pinter, and many other contemporary dramatists. Like them, Yeats was unsympathetic to the full-length play. As early as 1906 he was advocating what was to become the credo of a large number of mid-century playwrights: the fusion of tragedy and farce into a single dramatic form. Finally, in his return to the myths, legends, and forms of Greek and Oriental drama to find an artistic form capable of expressing the chaos of the modern world, Yeats developed a strategy which has been followed in some fashion by nearly every serious dramatist of the twentieth century. In short, although there is no evidence of a direct influence on the playwrights who came after him, it is clear that Yeats was a seminal dramatist; his plays pointed out several new directions which the drama would have to take if it was to be relevant to the modern world. The fact

[WILLIAM BUTLER YEATS, *Cont.*]
that so many playwrights in our own time are following these paths would indicate that Yeats was a pioneer in the theatre as well as in poetry.

JOHN MILLINGTON SYNGE (1871–1909) was the first significant playwright to emerge from the Irish theatrical renaissance that had been started by Yeats, the Fays, and Lady Gregory just before the turn of the century, but his involvement in all forms of Irish nationalism was so slight that he was accused of being an "alien of the spirit." His life and work are a study of extreme contrasts and nagging contradictions. In his plays he celebrated the primitive ways of life on the Aran Islands, and yet he was a wandering esthete who seemed to be more at home in a garret in Paris than in a cottage in Galway. He wrote realistically of the life of the peasants, and yet the rhythms of the Gaelic dialect that he used in his dialogue give his plays a poetic quality which tends to remove them from the simple realities of peasant life. His plays seem rooted in the life of the Irish countryside, yet each of them is derived from continental or classical models. His plays reflect great energy and an exuberant spirit, yet Synge himself was a shy and sickly young man who avoided all forms of public contact and died of cancer before he was forty.

But for all these contradictions—and many more—Synge must be ranked as one of the great masters of the modern drama. At Yeats's suggestion, Synge left Paris in 1898 to go to the Aran Islands "to express a life which has never found expression." He used the legends, language, and lore of these remote islands to fashion plays which had an element of magic to them and at the same time were both powerful and dramatically simple. The fusion of reality with fantasy is the dominant characteristic of all his work. He wrote in the preface to *Playboy of the Western World* that "on the stage one must have reality, and one must have joy." His plays have these qualities, and they set the tone and the standard that all Irish dramatists of the twentieth century have tended to follow to this day.

SEAN O'CASEY (1880–   ) describes himself as a "Green Crow," a fighting man who would be better fed if he would only keep his mouth shut. The modern theatre can be thankful that O'Casey is more interested in having his say than in filling his stomach or his pocketbook. This oldest living playwright of the modern world always has something to say on stage and off, and no writer better exemplifies the eclecticism and fascinating experimentation that characterizes the modern theatre than does this lovable, waspish man who has lived in England in self-imposed exile from his native Ireland since 1927.

In all his plays, O'Casey is vigorously on the side of life, and, for him, to be alive is to be in conflict. From his childhood struggles for survival, through the riots of 1927 at the opening of *The Plough and the Stars* at the Abbey, to his most recent struggles with critics, censors, and producers, O'Casey's life has been one of constant turmoil, and this quality pervades everything he ever wrote. It is possible, however, to divide his work into two main periods: those plays written before he left Ireland and those written after he settled in England. The first group spring, root and branch, out of O'Casey's deep involvement in Irish history and the politics of the first quarter of the century. They are blaringly nationalistic and are written with great vitality according to the more-or-less standard conventions of naturalism in the realistic idiom of the Dublin streets. In each of them O'Casey dramatizes the inevitable disenchantment and disillusionment of the romantic rebel idealist who is either insufficiently endowed to serve a noble cause or, as is more likely, who fights for a cause unworthy of the struggle and the sacrifice. The plays of the second group, written after O'Casey had escaped from the confusing limits of Irish parochialism, also deal with Irish life, but there is a universality about them which his earlier plays lacked. The brilliant language of the first plays is still there, but the form is allegorical and far more open. The influence of the expressionists on his style and his themes is clearly evident.

But no matter how many differences we can find between these two periods, there are certain constants in all of O'Casey's work: his tendency to bring tragic and comic scenes into head-on collision; his great compassion for the sufferings of all men; the lilting music of his language; his pixie sense of humor; his anti-heroic stance; and, above all, his constant belief that all art must celebrate the joy of life. In a century of increasing international tension and individual despair, the cawings of this Green Crow consistently urge audiences to live life more consciously, fully, and joyously.

GEORGE BERNARD SHAW (1856–1950) needs no introduction, and it would be impossible to assess his place in the modern

[GEORGE BERNARD SHAW, *Cont.*]
theatre in a single prefatory paragraph. Ludwig Lewisohn's early estimation of Shaw and his work is probably as succinct as any. In 1915 he wrote: "Mr. George Bernard Shaw is a writer of comedy with a tragic cry in his soul. In the middle ages he would have been a great saint, appalled at the gracelessness of men's hearts, militant for the Kingdom of God. Today he is a playwright, appalled at the muddle-headedness of the race, a fighter for the conquest of reason over unreason, of order over disorder, of economy over waste. The real joke, Shaw himself reminded us, is that I am earnest." But this statement does not begin to encompass the daring reach of intellect, the love of fun, and the theatrical mastery of one of the most prolific writers of the modern theatre. Shaw was a social philosopher who created the modern comedy of ideas. He was not so much an original thinker—none of the ideas expounded in his plays was radically new—as he was an articulate stage magician who inverted all accepted values and ideas in order that men might be more capable of building the good society. From his first play, *Widower's Houses* (1885), to his last, *In Good King Charles's Golden Days* (1939), Shaw was concerned with ideas, and in his prodigious body of work almost every significant intellectual position of modern times was examined by his razor-sharp mind.

Readers of the plays become so involved in the intellectual intricacies and sparkling wit of Shaw's dialogue that they tend to forget that he is also a master craftsman of the theatre. No modern dramatist uses the shocking and unexpected to greater effect, and in each of his plays Shaw employs devices of sheer theatricality which may be overlooked when one reads the plays but which tend to overwhelm us when we experience them in production. Shaw wrote within the conventions of the realistic theatre of his time, but a large measure of his charm and effectiveness consists in his use of the realistic convention for ends that are radically different from those of the traditional realists. Some people complain that Shaw's characters tend to be puppets, mouthpieces for his philosophy, who have no individuality of their own. This charge may be to some degree true, but then Shaw was not interested in his characters as archetypes of human behavior. Francis Fergusson put it best when he wrote: "Shaw is never concerned with the way people do behave, but only with the way they would behave if they were characters in a Shaw play."

T. S. ELIOT (1888–   ) wrote in his essay *Poetry and Drama* "It seems to me that beyond the nameable, classifiable emotions and motives of our conscious life when directed toward action—the part of life which prose drama is wholly adequate to express—there is a fringe of indefinite extent, of feeling which we can only detect so to speak out of the corner of the eye and can never completely focus; of feeling of which we are only aware in a kind of temporary detachment from action. . . . this peculiar range of sensibility can only be expressed by dramatic poetry, at its moments of greatest intensity." This statement expresses the two major concerns of Eliot's career as a writer for the theatre. All of his plays are attempts to envisage the possibility of a Christian community by dramatizing the need for an awareness of the supernatural in experience and the ensuing failure of all human relationships when man fails to distinguish between the human and the divine. Eliot would have his plays entice us into a state of consciousness, a state of spiritual awareness, to that "condition of serenity, stillness, and reconciliation" which we can see but indefinitely, out of the corner of the eye. And since he believes that this condition of spiritual awareness can be expressed only in verse, a great part of his later career has been devoted to the quest of finding a verse form that would serve his aims and still be compatible with a theatre whose conventions of dialogue are largely those of prose. Eliot is first of all a poet, a poet who has decided to write in a dramatic form for the stage. He is also a Christian, a Christian who believes the drama should be a guide that leads audiences to Christianity. These two facts of Eliot's life may well explain both the achievements and the limitations of his plays, and at the same time they may be an indication of the nature and the concerns of the mainstream of the modern theatre.

CHRISTOPHER FRY (1907–   ) may be a Quaker by conviction, but he is an Elizabethan at heart and in endowment. Everything about him is flowing, fiery, and eruptive, and all his plays are witty and rich in imagery and roundly romantic in temperament. Above all, he is known for his fantastic command of theatrical language. He loves the language, and, as John Mason Brown observed, "he uses it with a glorious profligacy. He thinks, sees, smells, and tastes in terms of verbal images." But Fry's verbal pyrotechnics are not an end in themselves; there is a serious quality at the core of all his gaiety and lightness. "Poetry,"

[CHRISTOPHER FRY, *Cont.*]

Fry believes, "is the language in which man explores his own amazement. It is the language in which he says heaven and earth in one word. It is the language in which he speaks of himself and his predicament as though for the first time. . . . Poetry is the language of reality."

And reality for Fry is essentially theological. In all his plays the central theme is the triumph of life over death, and in each of them he exhorts men to seek enjoyment and love, and to accept life as the uppermost value. "If you live in a worrisome age," he wrote shortly after the second World War, "learn to enjoy it." And it is in *A Sleep of Prisoners* that Fry's religious concerns are most apparent. In this play he is attempting to dramatize the role that God plays in mankind's past, present, and future. The form of the play is "something like a theme with variations" in which Fry has four prisoners of war re-enact their relationships to each other in dream sequences based on Old Testament stories which foreshadow the holocausts of the modern world. Imprisonment is the essential characteristic of the human condition—we are chained by our egotism and violence, our fear of involvement and our failure to care, and our need for some kind of tyrannical authority to sustain us. But Fry also believes in the powers of natural virtue and decency, and that through them God's grace can transform man's life on earth. It is this belief which prompts one of Fry's finest speeches, a speech that perhaps best defines his position in the modern theatre:

The human heart can go to the lengths of
  God.
Dark and cold we may be, but this
Is no winter now. The frozen misery
Of centuries breaks, cracks, begins to
  move,
The thunder is the thunder of the floes,
The thaw, the flood, the upstart Spring.
Thank God our time is now when wrong
Comes up to face us everywhere,
Never to leave us till we take
The longest stride of soul men ever took.
Affairs are now soul size,
The enterprise
Is exploration into God.

William Butler Yeats

1865-1939

THE TRAGIC THEATRE

I did not find a word in the printed criticism of Synge's *Deirdre of the Sorrows* about the qualities that made certain moments seem to me the noblest tragedy, and the play was judged by what seemed to me but wheels and pulleys necessary to the effect, but in themselves nothing.

Upon the other hand, those who spoke to me of the play never spoke of these wheels and pulleys, but if they cared at all for the play, cared for the things I cared for. One's own world of painters, of poets, of good talkers, of ladies who delight in Ricard's portraits or Debussy's music, all those whose senses feel instantly every change in our mother the moon, saw the stage in one way; and those others who look at plays every night, who tell the general playgoer whether this play or that play is to his taste, saw it in a way so different that there is certainly some body of dogma—whether in the instincts or in the memory—pushing the ways apart. A printed criticism, for instance, found but one dramatic moment, that when Deirdre in the second act overhears her lover say that he may grow weary of her; and not one—if I remember rightly—chose for praise or explanation the third act which alone had satisfied the author, or contained in any abundance those sentences that were quoted at the fall of the curtain and for days after.

Deirdre and her lover, as Synge tells the tale, returned to Ireland, though it was nearly certain they would die there, because death was better than broken love, and at the side of the open grave that had been dug for one and would serve for both, quarrelled, losing all they had given their life to keep. "Is it not a hard thing that we should miss the safety of the grave and we trampling its edge?" That is Deirdre's cry at the outset of a reverie of passion that mounts and mounts till grief itself has carried her beyond grief into pure contemplation. Up to this the play had been a Master's unfinished work, monotonous and melancholy, ill-arranged, little more than a sketch of what it would have grown to, but now I listened breathless to sentences that may never pass away, and as they filled or dwindled in their civility of sorrow, the player, whose art had seemed clumsy and incomplete, like the writing itself, ascended into that tragic ecstasy which is the best that art—perhaps that life—can give. And at last when Deirdre, in the paroxysm before she took her life, touched with compassionate fingers him that had killed her lover, we knew that the player had become, if but for a moment, the creature of that noble mind which had gathered its art in waste islands, and we too were carried beyond time and persons to where passion, living through its thousand purgatorial years, as in the wink of an eye, becomes wisdom; and it was as though we too had touched and felt and seen a disembodied thing.

One dogma of the printed criticism is that if a play does not contain definite character, its constitution is not strong enough for the stage, and that the dramatic moment is always the contest of character with character.

In poetical drama there is, it is held, an antithesis between character and lyric poetry, for lyric poetry—however much it move you when you read out of a book—can, as these critics think, but encumber the action. Yet when we go back a few centuries and enter the great periods of drama, character grows less and sometimes disappears, and there is much lyric feeling, and

"The Tragic Theatre" by William Butler Yeats is from *Essays and Introductions* and is reprinted by permission of The Macmillan Company. Copyright 1961 by Mrs. W. B. Yeats.

at times a lyric measure will be wrought into the dialogue, a flowing measure that had well befitted music, or that more lumbering one of the sonnet. Suddenly it strikes us that character is continuously present in comedy alone, and that there is much tragedy, that of Corneille, that of Racine, that of Greece and Rome, where its place is taken by passions and motives, one person being jealous, another full of love or remorse or pride or anger. In writers of tragi-comedy (and Shakespeare is always a writer of tragi-comedy) there is indeed character, but we notice that it is in the moments of comedy that character is defined, in Hamlet's gaiety, let us say; while amid the great moments, when Timon orders his tomb, when Hamlet cries to Horatio "Absent thee from felicity awhile," when Antony names "Of many thousand kisses the poor last," all is lyricism, unmixed passion, "the integrity of fire." Nor does character ever attain to complete definition in these lamps ready for the taper, no matter how circumstantial and gradual the opening of events, as it does in Falstaff, who has no passionate purpose to fulfil, or as it does in Henry V, whose poetry, never touched by lyric heat, is oratorical; nor when the tragic reverie is at its height do we say, "How well that man is realized! I should know him were I to meet him in the street," for it is always ourselves that we see upon the stage, and should it be a tragedy of love, we renew, it may be, some loyalty of our youth, and go from the theatre with our eyes dim for an old love's sake.

I think it was while rehearsing a translation of *Les Fourberies de Scapin* [1] in Dublin, and noticing how passionless it all was, that I saw what should have been plain from the first line I had written, that tragedy must always be a drowning and breaking of the dykes that separate man from man, and that it is upon these dykes comedy keeps house. But I was not certain of the site of that house (one always hesitates when there is no testimony but one's own) till somebody told me of a certain letter of Congreve's. He describes the external and superficial expressions of 'humour' on which farce is founded and then defines 'humour' itself—the foundation of comedy—as a 'singular and unavoidable way of doing anything peculiar to one man only, by which his speech and actions are distinguished from all other men,' and adds to it that 'passions are too powerful in the sex to let humour have its course,' or, as I would rather put it, that you can find but little of what we call character in unspoiled

youth, whatever be the sex, for, as he indeed shows in another sentence, it grows with time like the ash of a burning stick, and strengthens towards middle life till there is little else at seventy years.

Since then I have discovered an antagonism between all the old art and our new art of comedy and understand why I hated at nineteen years Thackeray's novels and the new French painting. A big picture of *cocottes* sitting at little tables outside a café, by some followers of Manet, was exhibited at the Royal Hibernian Academy while I was a student at a life class there, and I was miserable for days. I found no desirable place, no man I could have wished to be, no woman I could have loved, no Golden Age, no lure for secret hope, no adventure with myself for theme out of that endless tale I told myself all day long. Years after, I saw the *Olympia* of Manet at the Luxembourg and watched it without hostility indeed, but as I might some incomparable talker whose precision of gesture gave me pleasure, though I did not understand his language. I returned to it again and again at intervals of years, saying to myself, 'Some day I will understand'; and yet it was not until Sir Hugh Lane brought the *Eva Gonzales* to Dublin, and I had said to myself, 'How perfectly that woman is realized as distinct from all other women that have lived or shall live,' that I understood I was carrying on in my own mind that quarrel between a tragedian and a comedian which the Devil on Two Sticks in Le Sage [2] showed to the young man who had climbed through the window.

There is an art of the flood, the art of Titian when his *Ariosto,* and his *Bacchus and Ariadne,* give new images to the dreams of youth, and of Shakespeare when he shows us Hamlet broken away from life by the passionate hesitations of his reverie. And we call this art poetical, because we must bring more to it than our daily mood if we would take our pleasure; and because it takes delight in the moment of exaltation, of excitement, of dreaming (or in the capacity for it, as in that still face of Ariosto's that is like some vessel soon to be full of wine). And there is an art that we call real, because character can only express itself perfectly in a real world, being that world's creature, and because we understand it best through a delicate discrimination of the senses which is but entire wakefulness, the daily mood grown cold and crystalline.

We may not find either mood in its purity,

---

[1] A play by Molière.

[2] Alain René LeSage (1668–1747).

but in mainly tragic art one distinguishes devices to exclude or lessen character, to diminish the power of that daily mood, to cheat or blind its too clear perception. If the real world is not altogether rejected, it is but touched here and there, and into the places we have left empty we summon rhythm, balance, pattern, images that remind us of vast passions, the vagueness of past times, all the chimeras that haunt the edge of trance; and if we are painters, we shall express personal emotion through ideal form, a symbolism handled by the generations, a mask from whose eyes the disembodied looks, a style that remembers many masters that it may escape contemporary suggestion; or we shall leave out some element of reality as in Byzantine painting, where there is no mass, nothing in relief; and so it is that in the supreme moment of tragic art there comes upon one that strange sensation as though the hair of one's head stood up. And when we love, if it be in the excitement of youth, do we not also, that the flood may find no stone to convulse, no wall to narrow it, exclude character or the signs of it by choosing that beauty which seems unearthly because the individual woman is lost amid the labyrinth of its lines as though life were trembling into stillness and silence, or at last folding itself away? Some little irrelevance of line, some promise of character to come, may indeed put us at our ease, 'give more interest' as the humour of the old man with the basket does to Cleopatra's dying; but should it come, as we had dreamed in love's frenzy, to our dying for that woman's sake, we would find that the discord had its value from the tune. Nor have we chosen illusion in choosing the outward sign of that moral genius that lives among the subtlety of the passions, and can for her moment make her of the one mind with great artists and poets. In the studio we may indeed say to one another, 'Character is the only beauty,' but when we choose a wife, as when we go to the gymnasium to be shaped for woman's eyes, we remember academic form, even though we enlarge a little the point of interest and choose 'a painter's beauty,' finding it the more easy to believe in the fire because it has made ashes.

When we look at the faces of the old tragic paintings, whether it is in Titian or in some painter of mediaeval China, we find there sadness and gravity, a certain emptiness even, as of a mind that waited the supreme crisis (and indeed it seems at times as if the graphic art, unlike poetry which sings the crisis itself, were the celebration of waiting). Whereas in modern art, whether in Japan or Europe, 'vitality' (is not that the great word of the studios?), the energy, that is to say, which is under the command of our common moments, sings, laughs, chatters or looks its busy thoughts.

Certainly we have here the Tree of Life and that of the Knowledge of Good and Evil which is rooted in our interests, and if we have forgotten their differing virtues it is surely because we have taken delight in a confusion of crossing branches. Tragic art, passionate art, the drowner of dykes, the confounder of understanding, moves us by setting us to reverie, by alluring us almost to the intensity of trance. The persons upon the stage, let us say, greaten till they are humanity itself. We feel our minds expand convulsively or spread out slowly like some moon-brightened image-crowded sea. That which is before our eyes perpetually vanishes and returns again in the midst of the excitement it creates, and the more enthralling it is, the more do we forget it.

August 1910

ON BAILE'S STRAND

CAST OF CHARACTERS

A FOOL

A BLIND MAN

CUCHULAIN, *King of Muirthemne*

CONCHUBAR, *High King of Uladh*

A YOUNG MAN, *son of Cuchulain*

KINGS AND SINGING WOMEN

(*A great hall at Dundealgan, not "*CUCHULAIN*'s great ancient house" but an assembly-house nearer to the sea. A big door at the back, and through the door misty light as of sea mist. There are many chairs and one long bench. One of these chairs, which is towards the front of the stage, is bigger than the others. Somewhere at the back there is a table with flagons of ale upon it and drinking horns. There is a small door at one side of the hall. A* FOOL *and* BLIND MAN, *both ragged, and their features made grotesque and extravagant by masks, come in through the door at the back. The* BLIND MAN *leans upon a staff*)

FOOL   What a clever man you are though you are blind! There's nobody with two eyes in his head that is as clever as you are. Who but you could have thought that the henwife sleeps every day a little at noon? I would never be able to steal anything if you didn't tell me where to look for it. And what a good cook you are! You take the fowl out of my hands after I have stolen it and plucked it, and you put it into the big pot at the fire there, and I can go out and run races with the witches at the edge of the waves and get an appetite, and when I've got it, there's the hen waiting inside for me, done to the turn.

BLIND MAN (*who is feeling about with his stick*)   Done to the turn.

FOOL (*putting his arm round* BLIND MAN's *neck*)   Come now, I'll have a leg and you'll have a leg, and we'll draw lots for the wishbone. I'll be praising you, I'll be praising you while we're eating it, for your good plans and for your good cooking. There's nobody in the world like you, Blind Man. Come, come. Wait a minute. I shouldn't have closed the door. There are some that look for me, and I wouldn't like them not to find me. Don't tell it to anybody, Blind Man. There are some that follow me. Boann herself out of the river and Fand out of the deep sea. Witches they are, and they come by in the wind, and they cry, "Give a kiss, Fool, give a kiss," that's what they cry. That's wide enough. All the witches can come in now. I wouldn't have them beat at the door and say, "Where is the Fool? Why has he put a lock on the door?" Maybe they'll hear the bubbling of the pot and come in and sit on the ground. But we won't give them any of the fowl. Let them go back to the sea, let them go back to the sea.

BLIND MAN (*feeling legs of big chair with his hands*)   Ah! (*then, in a louder voice, as he feels the back of it*) Ah—ah—

FOOL   Why do you say "Ah-ah"?

BLIND MAN   I know the big chair. It is today the High King Conchubar is coming.

On Baile's Strand by William Butler Yeats is from *The Collected Plays of W. B. Yeats* and is reprinted by permission of The Macmillan Company.

They have brought out his chair. He is going to be Cuchulain's master in earnest from this day out. It is that he's coming for.

FOOL   He must be a great man to be Cuchulain's master.

BLIND MAN   So he is. He is a great man. He is over all the rest of the Kings of Ireland.

FOOL   Cuchulain's master! I thought Cuchulain could do anything he liked.

BLIND MAN   So he did, so he did. But he ran too wild, and Conchubar is coming today to put an oath upon him that will stop his rambling and make him as biddable as a house-dog and keep him always at his hand. He will sit in this chair and put the oath upon him.

FOOL   How will he do that?

BLIND MAN   You have no wits to understand such things. (*The* BLIND MAN *has got into the chair*) He will sit up in this chair and he'll say: "Take the oath, Cuchulain. I bid you take the oath. Do as I tell you. What are your wits compared with mine, and what are your riches compared with mine? And what sons have you to pay your debts and to put a stone over you when you die? Take the oath, I tell you. Take a strong oath."

FOOL   (*crumpling himself up and whining*)   I will not. I'll take no oath. I want my dinner.

BLIND MAN   Hush, hush! It is not done yet.

FOOL   You said it was done to a turn.

BLIND MAN   Did I, now? Well, it might be done, and not done. The wings might be white, but the legs might be red. The flesh might stick hard to the bones and not come away in the teeth. But, believe me, Fool, it will be well done before you put your teeth in it.

FOOL   My teeth are growing long with the hunger.

BLIND MAN   I'll tell you a story—the kings have storytellers while they are waiting for their dinner—I will tell you a story with a fight in it, a story with a champion in it, and a ship and a queen's son that has his mind set on killing somebody that you and I know.

FOOL   Who is that? Who is he coming to kill?

BLIND MAN   Wait, now, till you hear. When you were stealing the fowl, I was lying in a hole in the sand, and I heard three men coming with a shuffling sort of noise. They were wounded and groaning.

FOOL   Go on. Tell me about the fight.

BLIND MAN   There had been a fight, a great fight, a tremendous great fight. A young man had landed on the shore, the guardians of the shore had asked his name, and he had refused to tell it, and he had killed one, and others had run away.

FOOL   That's enough. Come on now to the fowl. I wish it was bigger. I wish it was as big as a goose.

BLIND MAN   Hush! I haven't told you all. I know who that young man is. I heard the men who were running away say he had red hair, that he had come from Aoife's country, that he was coming to kill Cuchulain.

FOOL   Nobody can do that. (*to a tune*)

> Cuchulain has killed kings,
> Kings and sons of kings,
> Dragons out of the water,
> And witches out of the air,
> Banachas and Bonachas and people of the woods.

BLIND MAN   Hush! hush!

FOOL   (*still singing*)

> Witches that steal the milk,
> Fomor that steal the children,
> Hags that have heads like hares,
> Hares that have claws like witches,
> All riding a-cock-horse
> (*spoken*)
> Out of the very bottom of the bitter black North.

BLIND MAN   Hush, I say!

FOOL   Does Cuchulain know that he is coming to kill him?

BLIND MAN   How would he know that with his head in the clouds? He doesn't care for common fighting. Why would he put himself out, and nobody in it but that young man? Now if it were a white fawn that might turn into a queen before morning—

FOOL   Come to the fowl. I wish it was as big as a pig; a fowl with goose grease and pig's crackling.

BLIND MAN   No hurry, no hurry. I know whose son it is. I wouldn't tell anybody else, but I will tell you,—a secret is better to you than your dinner. You like being told secrets.

FOOL   Tell me the secret.

BLIND MAN   That young man is Aoife's son. I am sure it is Aoife's son, it flows in upon me that it is Aoife's son. You have often heard me talking of Aoife, the great woman-fighter Cuchulain got the mastery over in the North?

FOOL   I know, I know. She is one of those cross queens that live in hungry Scotland.

BLIND MAN   I am sure it is her son. I was in Aoife's country for a long time.

FOOL   That was before you were blinded for putting a curse upon the wind.

BLIND MAN   There was a boy in her house that had her own red color on him, and everybody said he was to be brought up to kill Cuchulain, that she hated Cuchulain. She used to put a helmet on a pillar-stone and call it Cuchulain and set him casting at it. There is a step outside—Cuchulain's step.

(CUCHULAIN *passes by in the mist outside the big door*)

FOOL   Where is Cuchulain going?

BLIND MAN   He is going to meet Conchubar that has bidden him to take the oath.

FOOL   Ah, an oath, Blind Man. How can I remember so many things at once? Who is going to take an oath?

BLIND MAN   Cuchulain is going to take an oath to Conchubar who is High King.

FOOL   What a mix-up you make of everything, Blind Man! You were telling me one story, and now you are telling me another story. . . . How can I get the hang of it at the end if you mix everything at the beginning? Wait till I settle it out. There now, there's Cuchulain (*He points to one foot*), and there is the young man (*He points to the other foot*) that is coming to kill him, and Cuchulain doesn't know. But where's Conchubar? (*takes bag from side*) That's Conchubar with all his riches—Cuchulain, young man, Conchubar.—And where's Aoife? (*throws up cap*) There is Aoife, high up on the mountains in high hungry Scotland. Maybe it is not true after all. Maybe it was your own making up. It's many a time you cheated me before with your lies. Come to the cooking pot, my stomach is pinched and rusty. Would you have it to be creaking like a gate?

BLIND MAN   I tell you it's true. And more than that is true. If you listen to what I say, you'll forget your stomach.

FOOL   I won't.

BLIND MAN   Listen. I know who the young man's father is, but I won't say. I would be afraid to say. Ah, Fool, you would forget everything if you could know who the young man's father is.

FOOL   Who is it? Tell me now quick, or I'll shake you. Come, out with it, or I'll shake you.

(*A murmur of voices in the distance*)

BLIND MAN   Wait, wait. There's somebody coming. . . . It is Cuchulain is coming. He's coming back with the High King. Go and ask Cuchulain. He'll tell you. It's little you'll care about the cooking-pot when you have asked Cuchulain that . . .

(BLIND MAN *goes out by side door*)

FOOL   I'll ask him. Cuchulain will know. He was in Aoife's country. (*goes upstage*) I'll ask him. (*turns and goes downstage*) But, no, I won't ask him, I would be afraid. (*going up again*) Yes, I will ask him. What harm in asking? The Blind Man said I was to ask him. (*going down*) No, no. I'll not ask him. He might kill me. I have but killed hens and geese and pigs. He has killed kings. (*goes up again almost to big door*) Who says I'm afraid? I'm not afraid. I'm no coward. I'll ask him. No, no, Cuchulain, I'm not going to ask you.

> He has killed kings,
> Kings and the sons of kings,
> Dragons out of the water,
> And witches out of the air,
> Banachas and Bonachas and people of the woods.

(FOOL *goes out by side door, the last words being heard outside.* CUCHULAIN *and* CONCHUBAR *enter through the big door at the back. While they are still outside,* CUCHULAIN's *voice is heard raised in anger. He is a dark man, something over forty years of age.* CONCHUBAR *is much older and carries a long staff, elaborately carved or with an elaborate gold handle*)

CUCHULAIN   Because I have killed men without your bidding
And have rewarded others at my own pleasure,
Because of half a score of trifling things,
You'd lay this oath upon me, and now—and now
You add another pebble to the heap,
And I must be your man, well-nigh your bondsman,
Because a youngster out of Aoife's country
Has found the shore ill-guarded.
CONCHUBAR   He came to land
While you were somewhere out of sight and hearing,
Hunting or dancing with your wild companions.
CUCHULAIN   He can be driven out. I'll not be bound.
I'll dance or hunt, or quarrel or make love,
Wherever and whenever I've a mind to.
If time had not put water in your blood,
You never would have thought it.
CONCHUBAR   I would leave
A strong and settled country to my children.
CUCHULAIN   And I must be obedient in all things;
Give up my will to yours; go where you please;
Come when you call; sit at the council-board
Among the unshapely bodies of old men;
I whose mere name has kept this country safe,
I that in early days have driven out
Maeve of Cruachan and the northern pirates,
The hundred kings of Sorcha, and the kings
Out of the Garden in the East of the World.
Must I, that held you on the throne when all
Had pulled you from it, swear obedience
As if I were some cattle-raising king?
Are my shins speckled with the heat of the fire,
Or have my hands no skill but to make figures
Upon the ashes with a stick? Am I
So slack and idle that I need a whip
Before I serve you?
CONCHUBAR   No, no whip, Cuchulain,
But every day my children come and say:
"This man is growing harder to endure.
How can we be at safety with this man
That nobody can buy or bid or bind?
We shall be at his mercy when you are gone;
He burns the earth as if he were a fire,
And time can never touch him."

CUCHULAIN   And so the tale
    Grows finer yet; and I am to obey
    Whatever child you set upon the throne,
    As if it were yourself!
CONCHUBAR   Most certainly.
    I am High King, my son shall be High King;
    And you for all the wildness of your blood,
    And though your father came out of the sun,
    Are but a little king and weigh but light
    In anything that touches government,
    If put into the balance with my children.
CUCHULAIN   It's well that we should speak our minds out plainly,
    For when we die we shall be spoken of
    In many countries. We in our young days
    Have seen the heavens like a burning cloud
    Brooding upon the world, and being more
    Than men can be now that cloud's lifted up,
    We should be the more truthful. Conchubar,
    I do not like your children—they have no pitch,
    No marrow in their bones, and will lie soft
    Where you and I lie hard.
CONCHUBAR   You rail at them
    Because you have no children of your own.
CUCHULAIN   I think myself most lucky that I leave
    No pallid ghost or mockery of a man
    To drift and mutter in the corridors
    Where I have laughed and sung.
CONCHUBAR   That is not true,
    For all your boasting of the truth between us;
    For there is no man having house and lands,
    That have been in the one family, called
    By that one family's name for centuries,
    But is made miserable if he know
    They are to pass into a stranger's keeping,
    As yours will pass.
CUCHULAIN   The most of men feel that,
    But you and I leave names upon the harp.
CONCHUBAR   You play with arguments as lawyers do,
    And put no heart in them. I know your thoughts,
    For we have slept under the one cloak and drunk
    From the one wine cup. I know you to the bone,
    I have heard you cry, aye, in your very sleep,
    "I have no son," and with such bitterness
    That I have gone upon my knees and prayed
    That it might be amended.
CUCHULAIN   For you thought
    That I should be as biddable as others
    Had I their reason for it; but that's not true;
    For I would need a weightier argument
    Than one that marred me in the copying,
    As I have that clean hawk out of the air
    That, as men say, begot this body of mine
    Upon a mortal woman.
CONCHUBAR   Now as ever
    You mock at every reasonable hope,
    And would have nothing, or impossible things.
    What eye has ever looked upon the child
    Would satisfy a mind like that?

CUCHULAIN   I would leave
    My house and name to none that would not face
    Even myself in battle.
CONCHUBAR   Being swift of foot,
    And making light of every common chance,
    You should have overtaken on the hills
    Some daughter of the air, or on the shore
    A daughter of the Country-under-Wave.
CUCHULAIN   I am not blasphemous.
CONCHUBAR   Yet you despise
    Our queens, and would not call a child your own,
    If one of them had borne him.
CUCHULAIN   I have not said it.
CONCHUBAR   Ah! I remember I have heard you boast,
    When the ale was in your blood, that there was one
    In Scotland, where you had learnt the trade of war,
    That had a stone-pale cheek and red-brown hair;
    And that although you had loved other women,
    You'd sooner that fierce woman of the camp
    Bore you a son than any queen among them.
CUCHULAIN   You call her a "fierce woman of the camp,"
    For, having lived among the spinning wheels,
    You'd have no woman near that would not say,
    "Ah! how wise!" "What will you have for supper?"
    "What shall I wear that I may please you, sir?"
    And keep that humming through the day and night
    For ever. A fierce woman of the camp!
    But I am getting angry about nothing.
    You have never seen her. Ah! Conchubar, had you seen her
    With that high, laughing, turbulent head of hers
    Thrown backward, and the bowstring at her ear,
    Or sitting at the fire with those grave eyes
    Full of good counsel as it were with wine,
    Or when love ran through all the lineaments
    Of her wild body—although she had no child,
    None other had all beauty, queen or lover,
    Or was so fitted to give birth to kings.
CONCHUBAR   There's nothing I can say but drifts you farther
    From the one weighty matter. That very woman—
    For I know well that you are praising Aoife—
    Now hates you and will leave no subtlety
    Unknotted that might run into a noose
    About your throat, no army in idleness
    That might bring ruin on this land you serve.
CUCHULAIN   No wonder in that, no wonder at all in that.
    I never have known love but as a kiss
    In the mid-battle, and a difficult truce
    Of oil and water, candles and dark night,
    Hillside and hollow, the hot-footed sun
    And the cold, sliding, slippery-footed moon—
    A brief forgiveness between opposites
    That have been hatreds for three times the age
    Of this long-'stablished ground.
CONCHUBAR   Listen to me.
    Aoife makes war on us, and every day
    Our enemies grow greater and beat the walls
    More bitterly, and you within the walls
    Are every day more turbulent; and yet,

When I would speak about these things, your fancy
Runs as if it were a swallow on the wind.

(*Outside the door in the blue light of the sea mist are many old and young* KINGS;
amongst them are three WOMEN, *two of whom carry a bowl of fire. The third, in what
follows, puts from time to time fragrant herbs into the fire so that it flickers up into
brighter flame*)

Look at the door and what men gather there—
Old counsellors that steer the land with me,
And younger kings, the dancers and harp-players
That follow in your tumults, and all these
Are held there by the one anxiety.
Will you be bound into obedience
And so make this land safe for them and theirs?
You are but half a king and I but half;
I need your might of hand and burning heart,
And you my wisdom.

CUCHULAIN (*going near to door*)   Nestlings of a high nest,
Hawks that have followed me into the air
And looked upon the sun, we'll out of this
And sail upon the wind once more. This king
Would have me take an oath to do his will,
And having listened to his tune from morning,
I will no more of it. Run to the stable
And set the horses to the chariot-pole,
And send a messenger to the harp-players.
We'll find a level place among the woods,
And dance awhile.

A YOUNG KING   Cuchulain, take the oath.
There is none here that would not have you take it.

CUCHULAIN   You'd have me take it? Are you of one mind?

THE KINGS   All, all, all, all!

A YOUNG KING   Do what the High King bids you.

CONCHUBAR   There is not one but dreads this turbulence
Now that they're settled men.

CUCHULAIN   Are you so changed,
Or have I grown more dangerous of late?
But that's not it. I understand it all.
It's you that have changed. You've wives and children now,
And for that reason cannot follow one
That lives like a bird's flight from tree to tree.—
It's time the years put water in my blood
And drowned the wildness of it, for all's changed,
But that unchanged.—I'll take what oath you will:
The moon, the sun, the water, light, or air,
I do not care how binding.

CONCHUBAR   On this fire
That has been lighted from your hearth and mine;
The older men shall be my witnesses,
The younger, yours. The holders of the fire
Shall purify the thresholds of the house
With waving fire, and shut the outer door,
According to the custom; and sing rhyme
That has come down from the old lawmakers
To blow the witches out. Considering
That the wild will of man could be oath-bound,
But that a woman's could not, they bid us sing
Against the will of woman at its wildest
In the Shape-Changers that run upon the wind.

(CONCHUBAR *has gone on to his throne*)

THE WOMEN (*they sing in a very low voice after the first few words so that the others all but drown their words*)

> May this fire have driven out
> The Shape-Changers that can put
> Ruin on a great king's house
> Until all be ruinous.
> Names whereby a man has known
> The threshold and the hearthstone,
> Gather on the wind and drive
> The women none can kiss and thrive,
> For they are but whirling wind,
> Out of memory and mind.
> They would make a prince decay
> With light images of clay
> Planted in the running wave;
> Or, for many shapes they have,
> They would change them into hounds
> Until he had died of his wounds,
> Though the change were but a whim;
> Or they'd hurl a spell at him,
> That he follow with desire
> Bodies that can never tire
> Or grow kind, for they anoint
> All their bodies, joint by joint,
> With a miracle-working juice
> That is made out of the grease
> Of the ungoverned unicorn.
> But the man is thrice forlorn,
> Emptied, ruined, wracked, and lost,
> That they followed, for at most
> They will give him kiss for kiss
> While they murmur, "After this
> Hatred may be sweet to the taste."
> Those wild hands that have embraced
> All his body can but shove
> At the burning wheel of love
> Till the side of hate comes up.
> Therefore in this ancient cup
> May the sword blades drink their fill
> Of the home-brew there, until
> They will have for masters none
> But the threshold and hearthstone.

CUCHULAIN (*speaking, while they are singing*)

> I'll take and keep this oath, and from this day
> I shall be what you please, my chicks, my nestlings.
> Yet I had thought you were of those that praised
> Whatever life could make the pulse run quickly,
> Even though it were brief, and that you held
> That a free gift was better than a forced.—
> But that's all over.—I will keep it, too;
> I never gave a gift and took it again.
> If the wild horse should break the chariot-pole,
> It would be punished. Should that be in the oath?

(*Two of the* WOMEN, *still singing, crouch in front of him holding the bowl over their heads. He spreads his hands over the flame*)

> I swear to be obedient in all things
> To Conchubar, and to uphold his children.

CONCHUBAR   We are one being, as these flames are one:
I give my wisdom, and I take your strength.
Now thrust the swords into the flame, and pray
That they may serve the threshold and the hearthstone
With faithful service.

(*The* KINGS *kneel in a semicircle before the two* WOMEN *and* CUCHULAIN, *who thrusts his sword into the flame. They all put the points of their swords into the flame. The third* WOMAN *is at the back near the big door*)

CUCHULAIN   O pure, glittering ones
That should be more than wife or friend or mistress,
Give us the enduring will, the unquenchable hope,
The friendliness of the sword!—

(*The song grows louder, and the last words ring out clearly. There is a loud knocking at the door, and a cry of* "Open! open!")

CONCHUBAR   Some king that has been loitering on the way.
Open the door, for I would have all know
That the oath's finished and Cuchulain bound,
And that the swords are drinking up the flame.

(*The door is opened by the third* WOMAN, *and a* YOUNG MAN *with a drawn sword enters*)

YOUNG MAN   I am of Aoife's country.

(*The* KINGS *rush towards him.* CUCHULAIN *throws himself between*)

CUCHULAIN   Put up your swords.
He is but one. Aoife is far away.
YOUNG MAN   I have come alone into the midst of you
To weigh this sword against Cuchulain's sword.
CONCHUBAR   And are you noble? for if of common seed,
You cannot weigh your sword against his sword
But in mixed battle.
YOUNG MAN   I am under bonds
To tell my name to no man; but it's noble.
CONCHUBAR   But I would know your name and not your bonds.
You cannot speak in the Assembly House,
If you are not noble.
FIRST OLD KING   Answer the High King!
YOUNG MAN   I will give no other proof than the hawk gives
That it's no sparrow!

(*He is silent for a moment, then speaks to all*)
                                        Yet look upon me, kings.
I, too, am of that ancient seed, and carry
The signs about this body and in these bones.
CUCHULAIN   To have shown the hawk's grey feather is enough,
And you speak highly, too. Give me that helmet.
I'd thought they had grown weary sending champions.
That sword and belt will do. This fighting's welcome.
The High King there has promised me his wisdom;
But the hawk's sleepy till its well-beloved
Cries out amid the acorns, or it has seen
Its enemy like a speck upon the sun.
What's wisdom to the hawk, when that clear eye
Is burning nearer up in the high air?

(*Looks hard at* YOUNG MAN; *then comes down steps and grasps* YOUNG MAN *by shoulder*)
Hither into the light.
(*to* CONCHUBAR)   The very tint
Of her that I was speaking of but now.
Not a pin's difference.

(*to* YOUNG MAN)   You are from the North,
Where there are many that have that tint of hair—
Red-brown, the light red-brown. Come nearer, boy,
For I would have another look at you.
There's more likeness—a pale, a stone-pale cheek.
What brought you, boy? Have you no fear of death?

YOUNG MAN   Whether I live or die is in the gods' hands.

CUCHULAIN   That is all words, all words; a young man's talk.
I am their plough, their harrow, their very strength;
For he that's in the sun begot this body
Upon a mortal woman, and I have heard tell
It seemed as if he had outrun the moon
That he must follow always through waste heaven,
He loved so happily. He'll be but slow
To break a tree that was so sweetly planted.
Let's see that arm. I'll see it if I choose.
That arm had a good father and a good mother,
But it is not like this.

YOUNG MAN   You are mocking me;
You think I am not worthy to be fought.
But I'll not wrangle but with this talkative knife.

CUCHULAIN   Put up your sword; I am not mocking you.
I'd have you for my friend, but if it's not
Because you have a hot heart and a cold eye,
I cannot tell the reason.

(*to* CONCHUBAR)   He has got her fierceness,
And nobody is as fierce as those pale women.
But I will keep him with me, Conchubar,
That he may set my memory upon her
When the day's fading.—You will stop with us,
And we will hunt the deer and the wild bulls;
And, when we have grown weary, light our fires
Between the wood and water, or on some mountain
Where the Shape-Changers of the morning come.
The High King there would make a mock of me
Because I did not take a wife among them.
Why do you hang your head? It's a good life:
The head grows prouder in the light of the dawn,
And friendship thickens in the murmuring dark
Where the spare hazels meet the wool-white foam.
But I can see there's no more need for words
And that you'll be my friend from this day out.

CONCHUBAR   He has come hither not in his own name
But in Queen Aoife's, and has challenged us
In challenging the foremost man of us all.

CUCHULAIN   Well, well, what matter?

CONCHUBAR   You think it does not matter,
And that a fancy lighter than the air,
A whim of the moment, has more matter in it.
For, having none that shall reign after you,
You cannot think as I do, who would leave
A throne too high for insult.

CUCHULAIN   Let your children
Re-mortar their inheritance, as we have,
And put more muscle on.—I'll give you gifts,
But I'd have something too—that arm-ring, boy.
We'll have this quarrel out when you are older.

YOUNG MAN　There is no man I'd sooner have my friend
　　　　　Than you, whose name has gone about the world
　　　　　As if it had been the wind; but Aoife'd say
　　　　　I had turned coward.
CUCHULAIN　　　　　　　　　　I will give you gifts
　　　　　That Aoife'll know, and all her people know,
　　　　　To have come from me.

(*Showing cloak*)

　　　　　My father gave me this.
　　　　　He came to try me, rising up at dawn
　　　　　Out of the cold dark of the rich sea.
　　　　　He challenged me to battle, but before
　　　　　My sword had touched his sword, told me his name,
　　　　　Gave me this cloak, and vanished. It was woven
　　　　　By women of the Country-under-Wave
　　　　　Out of the fleeces of the sea. O! tell her
　　　　　I was afraid, or tell her what you will.
　　　　　No; tell her that I heard a raven croak
　　　　　On the north side of the house, and was afraid.
CONCHUBAR　Some witch of the air has troubled Cuchulain's mind.
CUCHULAIN　No witchcraft. His head is like a woman's head
　　　　　I had a fancy for.
CONCHUBAR　　　　　　　　A witch of the air
　　　　　Can make a leaf confound us with memories.
　　　　　They run upon the wind and hurl the spells
　　　　　That make us nothing, out of the invisible wind.
　　　　　They have gone to school to learn the trick of it.
CUCHULAIN　No, no—there's nothing out of common here;
　　　　　The winds are innocent.—That arm-ring, boy.
A KING　If I've your leave I'll take this challenge up.
ANOTHER KING　No, give it me, High King, for this wild Aoife
　　　　　Has carried off my slaves.
ANOTHER KING　　　　　　　　　No, give it me,
　　　　　For she has harried me in house and herd.
ANOTHER KING　I claim this fight.
OTHER KINGS (*together*)　　　　　And I! And I! And I!
CUCHULAIN　Back! Back! Put up your swords! Put up your swords!
　　　　　There's none alive that shall accept a challenge
　　　　　I have refused. Laegaire, put up your sword!
YOUNG MAN　No, let them come. If they've a mind for it,
　　　　　I'll try it out with any two together.
CUCHULAIN　That's spoken as I'd have spoken it at your age.
　　　　　But you are in my house. Whatever man
　　　　　Would fight with you shall fight it out with me.
　　　　　They're dumb, they're dumb. How many of you would meet

(*Draws sword*)

　　　　　This mutterer, this old whistler, this sandpiper,
　　　　　This edge that's greyer than the tide, this mouse
　　　　　That's gnawing at the timbers of the world,
　　　　　This, this—Boy, I would meet them all in arms
　　　　　If I'd a son like you. He would avenge me
　　　　　When I have withstood for the last time the men
　　　　　Whose fathers, brothers, sons, and friends I have killed
　　　　　Upholding Conchubar, when the four provinces
　　　　　Have gathered with the ravens over them.
　　　　　But I'd need no avenger. You and I
　　　　　Would scatter them like water from a dish.

YOUNG MAN   We'll stand by one another from this out.
　　　　Here is the ring.
CUCHULAIN　　　　　　　　No, turn and turn about.
　　　　But my turn's first because I am the older.

(*Spreading out cloak*)

　　　　Nine queens out of the Country-under-Wave
　　　　Have woven it with the fleeces of the sea
　　　　And they were long embroidering at it.—Boy,
　　　　If I had fought my father, he'd have killed me,
　　　　As certainly as if I had a son
　　　　And fought with him, I should be deadly to him;
　　　　For the old fiery fountains are far off
　　　　And every day there is less heat o' the blood.
CONCHUBAR (*in a loud voice*)   No more of this. I will not have this friendship.
　　　　Cuchulain is my man, and I forbid it.
　　　　He shall not go unfought, for I myself—
CUCHULAIN   I will not have it.
CONCHUBAR　　　　　　　　You lay commands on me?
CUCHULAIN (*seizing* CONCHUBAR)   You shall not stir, High King. I'll hold you there.
CONCHUBAR   Witchcraft has maddened you.
THE KINGS (*shouting*)　　　　　　　Yes, witchcraft! witchcraft!
FIRST OLD KING   Some witch has worked upon your mind, Cuchulain.
　　　　The head of that young man seemed like a woman's
　　　　You'd had a fancy for. Then of a sudden
　　　　You laid your hands on the High King himself!
CUCHULAIN   And laid my hands on the High King himself?
CONCHUBAR   Some witch is floating in the air above us.
CUCHULAIN   Yes, witchcraft! witchcraft! Witches of the air!

(*To* YOUNG MAN)

　　　　Why did you? Who was it set you to this work?
　　　　Out, out! I say, for now it's sword on sword!
YOUNG MAN   But . . . but I did not.
CUCHULAIN　　　　　　　　Out, I say, out, out!

(YOUNG MAN *goes out followed by* CUCHULAIN. *The* KINGS *follow them out with confused cries, and words one can hardly hear because of the noise. Some cry,* "Quicker, quicker!" "Why are you so long at the door?" "We'll be too late!" "Have they begun to fight?" "Can you see if they are fighting?" *and so on. Their voices drown each other. The three* WOMEN *are left alone*)

FIRST WOMAN   I have seen, I have seen!
SECOND WOMAN　　　　　　　What do you cry aloud?
FIRST WOMAN   The Ever-living have shown me what's to come.
THIRD WOMAN   How? Where?
FIRST WOMAN　　　　　　　In the ashes of the bowl.
SECOND WOMAN   While you were holding it between your hands?
THIRD WOMAN   Speak quickly!
FIRST WOMAN　　　　　　　I have seen Cuchulain's roof-tree
　　　　Leap into fire, and the walls split and blacken.
SECOND WOMAN   Cuchulain has gone out to die.
THIRD WOMAN　　　　　　　　O! O!
SECOND WOMAN   Who could have thought that one so great as he
　　　　Should meet his end at this unnoted sword!
FIRST WOMAN   Life drifts between a fool and a blind man
　　　　To the end, and nobody can know his end.
SECOND WOMAN   Come, look upon the quenching of this greatness.

(*The other two go to the door, but they stop for a moment upon the threshold and wail*)

FIRST WOMAN   No crying out, for there'll be need of cries
And rending of the hair when it's all finished.

(*The* WOMEN *go out. There is the sound of clashing swords from time to time during what follows. Enter the* FOOL, *dragging the* BLIND MAN)

FOOL   You have eaten it, you have eaten it! You have left me nothing but the bones. (*He throws* BLIND MAN *down by big chair*)

BLIND MAN   O, that I should have to endure such a plague! O, I ache all over! O, I am pulled to pieces! This is the way you pay me all the good I have done you.

FOOL   You have eaten it! You have told me lies. I might have known you had eaten it when I saw your slow, sheepy walk. Lie there till the kings come. O, I will tell Conchubar and Cuchulain and all the kings about you!

BLIND MAN   What would have happened to you but for me, and you without your wits? If I did not take care of you, what would you do for food and warmth?

FOOL   You take care of me? You stay safe, and send me into every kind of danger. You sent me down the cliff for gulls' eggs while you warmed your blind eyes in the sun; and then you ate all that were good for food. You left me the eggs that were neither egg nor bird. (BLIND MAN *tries to rise;* FOOL *makes him lie down again*) Keep quiet now, till I shut the door. There is some noise outside—a high vexing noise, so that I can't be listening to myself. (*shuts the big door*) Why can't they be quiet? Why can't they be quiet? (BLIND MAN *tries to get away*) Ah! you would get away, would you? (*follows* BLIND MAN *and brings him back*) Lie there! lie there! No, you won't get away! Lie there till the kings come. I'll tell them all about you. I will tell it all. How you sit warming yourself, when you have made me light a fire of sticks, while I sit blowing it with my mouth. Do you not always make me take the windy side of the bush when it blows, and the rainy side when it rains?

BLIND MAN   O, good Fool! listen to me. Think of the care I have taken of you. I have brought you to many a warm hearth, where there was a good welcome for you, but you would not stay there; you were always wandering about.

FOOL   The last time you brought me in, it was not I who wandered away, but you that got put out because you took the crubeen out of the pot when nobody was looking. Keep quiet, now!

CUCHULAIN   (*rushing in*)   Witchcraft! There is no witchcraft on the earth, or among the witches of the air, that these hands cannot break.

FOOL   Listen to me, Cuchulain. I left him turning the fowl at the fire. He ate it all, though I had stolen it. He left me nothing but the feathers.

CUCHULAIN   Fill me a horn of ale!

BLIND MAN   I gave him what he likes best. You do not know how vain this Fool is. He likes nothing so well as a feather.

FOOL   He left me nothing but the bones and feathers. Nothing but the feathers, though I had stolen it.

CUCHULAIN   Give me that horn. Quarrels here, too! (*drinks*) What is there between you two that is worth a quarrel? Out with it!

BLIND MAN   Where would he be but for me? I must be always thinking—thinking to get food for the two of us, and when we've got it, if the moon is at the full or the tide on the turn, he'll leave the rabbit in the snare till it is full of maggots, or let the trout slip back through his hands into the stream.

(*The* FOOL *has begun singing while the* BLIND MAN *is speaking*)

FOOL   (*singing*)

> When you were an acorn on the tree top,
>   Then was I an eagle-cock;
> Now that you are a withered old block,
>   Still am I an eagle-cock.

BLIND MAN   Listen to him, now. That's the sort of talk I have to put up with day out, day in.

(*The* FOOL *is putting the feathers into his hair.* CUCHULAIN *takes a handful of feathers out of a heap the* FOOL *has on the bench beside him, and out of the* FOOL's *hair, and begins to wipe the blood from his sword with them*)

FOOL   He has taken my feathers to wipe his sword. It is blood that he is wiping from his sword.

CUCHULAIN   (*goes up to door at back and throws away feathers*)   They are standing about his body. They will not awaken him, for all his witchcraft.

BLIND MAN   It is that young champion that he has killed. He that came out of Aoife's country.

CUCHULAIN   He thought to have saved himself with witchcraft.

FOOL   That Blind Man there said he would kill you. He came from Aoife's country to kill you. That Blind Man said they had taught him every kind of weapon that he might do it. But I always knew that you would kill him.

CUCHULAIN   (*to the* BLIND MAN)   You knew him, then?

BLIND MAN   I saw him, when I had my eyes, in Aoife's country.

CUCHULAIN   You were in Aoife's country?

BLIND MAN   I knew him and his mother there.

CUCHULAIN   He was about to speak of her when he died.

BLIND MAN   He was a queen's son.

CUCHULAIN   What queen? what queen? (*seizes* BLIND MAN, *who is now sitting upon the bench*) Was it Scathach? There were many queens. All the rulers there were queens.

BLIND MAN   No, not Scathach.

CUCHULAIN   It was Uathach, then? Speak! speak!

BLIND MAN   I cannot speak; you are clutching me too tightly. (CUCHULAIN *lets him go*) I cannot remember who it was. I am not certain. It was some queen.

FOOL   He said a while ago that the young man was Aoife's son.

CUCHULAIN   She? No, no! She had no son when I was there.

FOOL   That Blind Man there said that she owned him for her son.

CUCHULAIN   I had rather he had been some other woman's son. What father had he? A soldier out of Alba? She was an amorous woman—a proud, pale, amorous woman.

BLIND MAN   None knew whose son he was.

CUCHULAIN   None knew! Did you know, old listener at doors?

BLIND MAN   No, no; I knew nothing.

FOOL   He said a while ago that he heard Aoife boast that she'd never but the one lover, and he the only man that had overcome her in battle. (*pause*)

BLIND MAN   Somebody is trembling, Fool! The bench is shaking. Why are you trembling? Is Cuchulain going to hurt us? It was not I who told you, Cuchulain.

FOOL   It is Cuchulain who is trembling. It is Cuchulain who is shaking the bench.

BLIND MAN   It is his own son he has slain.

CUCHULAIN   'Twas they that did it, the pale windy people.
    Where? where? where? My sword against the thunder!
    But no, for they have always been my friends;
    And though they love to blow a smoking coal
    Till it's all flame, the wars they blow aflame
    Are full of glory, and heart-uplifting pride,
    And not like this. The wars they love awaken
    Old fingers and the sleepy strings of harps.
    Who did it then? Are you afraid? Speak out!
    For I have put you under my protection,
    And will reward you well. Dubthach the Chafer?
    He'd an old grudge. No, for he is with Maeve.
    Laegaire did it! Why do you not speak?
    What is this house? (*pause*) Now I remember all.

(*Comes before* CONCHUBAR's *chair, and strikes out with his sword, as if* CONCHUBAR *was sitting upon it*)

    'Twas you who did it—you who sat up there
    With your old rod of kingship, like a magpie
    Nursing a stolen spoon. No, not a magpie,
    A maggot that is eating up the earth!
    Yes, but a magpie, for he's flown away.
    Where did he fly to?

BLIND MAN   He is outside the door.
CUCHULAIN   Outside the door?
BLIND MAN   Between the door and the sea.
CUCHULAIN   Conchubar, Conchubar! the sword into your heart!

(*He rushes out. Pause.* FOOL *creeps up to the big door and looks after him*)

FOOL   He is going up to King Conchubar. They are all about the young man. No, no, he is standing still. There is a great wave going to break, and he is looking at it. Ah! now he is running down to the sea, but he is holding up his sword as if he were going into a fight. (*pause*) Well struck! well struck!

BLIND MAN   What is he doing now?

FOOL   O! he is fighting the waves!

BLIND MAN   He sees King Conchubar's crown on every one of them.

FOOL   There, he has struck at a big one! He has struck the crown off it; he has made the foam fly. There again, another big one!

BLIND MAN   Where are the kings? What are the kings doing?

FOOL   They are shouting and running down to the shore, and the people are running out of the houses. They are all running.

BLIND MAN   You say they are running out of the houses? There will be nobody left in the houses. Listen, Fool!

FOOL   There, he is down! He is up again. He is going out in the deep water. There is a big wave. It has gone over him. I cannot see him now. He has killed kings and giants, but the waves have mastered him, the waves have mastered him!

BLIND MAN   Come here, Fool!

FOOL   The waves have mastered him.

BLIND MAN   Come here!

FOOL   The waves have mastered him.

BLIND MAN   Come here, I say.

FOOL (*coming towards him, but looking backwards towards the door*)   What is it?

BLIND MAN   There will be nobody in the houses. Come this way; come quickly! The ovens will be full. We will put our hands into the ovens. (*They go out*)

John Millington Synge

1871-1909

PREFACE TO *THE PLAYBOY OF THE WESTERN WORLD*

In writing *The Playboy of the Western World*, as in my other plays, I have used one or two words only that I have not heard among the country people of Ireland, or spoken in my own nursery before I could read the newspapers. A certain number of the phrases I employ I have heard also from herds and fishermen along the coast from Kerry to Mayo, or from beggarwomen and ballad singers near Dublin; and I am glad to acknowledge how much I owe to the folk imagination of these fine people. Anyone who has lived in real intimacy with the Irish peasantry will know that the wildest sayings and ideas in this play are tame indeed, compared with the fancies one may hear in any little hillside cabin in Geesala, or Carraroe, or Dingle Bay. All art is a collaboration! and there is little doubt that in the happy ages of literature, striking and beautiful phrases were as ready to the storyteller's or the playwright's hand, as the rich cloaks and dresses of his time. It is probable that when the Elizabethan dramatist took his inkhorn and sat down to his work he used many phrases that he had just heard, as he sat at dinner, from his mother or his children. In Ireland, those of us who know the people have the same privilege. When I was writing *The Shadow of the Glen*, some years ago, I got more aid than any learning could have given me from a chink in the floor of the old Wicklow house where I was staying, that let me hear what was being said by the servant girls in the kitchen. This matter, I think, is of importance, for in countries where the imagination of the people, and the language they use, is rich and living, it is possible for a writer to be rich and copious in his words, and at the same time to give the reality, which is the root of all poetry, in a comprehensive and natural form. In the modern literature of towns, however, richness is found only in sonnets, or prose poems, or in one or two elaborate books that are far away from the profound and common interests of life. One has, on one side, Mallarmé and Huysmans [1] producing this literature; and, on the other, Ibsen and Zola dealing with the reality of life in joyless and pallid words. On the stage one must have reality, and one must have joy; and that is why the intellectual modern drama has failed, and people have grown sick of the false joy of the musical comedy that has been given them in place of the rich joy found only in what is superb and wild in reality. In a good play every speech should be as fully flavored as a nut or apple, and such speeches cannot be written by anyone who works among people who have shut their lips on poetry. In Ireland, for a few years more, we have a popular imagination that is fiery and magnificent, and tender; so that those who wish to write start with a chance that is not given to writers in places where the springtime of the local life has been forgotten, and the harvest is a memory only, and the straw has been turned into bricks.

1907

[1] Joris Karl Huysmans (1848–1907), French novelist and poet, most famous for *Against the Grain*.

PREFACE TO *THE TINKER'S WEDDING*

The drama is made serious—in the French sense of the word—not by the degree in which it is taken up with problems that are serious in themselves, but by the degree in which it gives the nourishment, not very easy to define, on which our imaginations live. We should not go to the theatre as we go to a chemist's, or a dramshop, but as we go to a dinner, where the food we need is taken with pleasure and excitement. This was nearly always so in Spain and England and France when the drama was at its richest—the infancy and decay of the drama tend to be didactic—but in these days the playhouse is too often stocked with the drugs of many seedy problems, or with the absinthe or vermouth of the last musical comedy.

The drama, like the symphony, does not teach or prove anything. Analysts with their problems, and teachers with their systems, are soon as old-fashioned as the pharmacopœia of Galen,—look at Ibsen and the Germans—but the best plays of Ben Jonson and Molière can no more go out of fashion than the blackberries on the hedges.

Of the things which nourish the imagination humour is one of the most needful, and it is dangerous to limit or destroy it. Baudelaire calls laughter the greatest sign of the Satanic element in man; and where a country loses its humour, as some towns in Ireland are doing, there will be morbidity of mind, as Baudelaire's mind was morbid.

In the greater part of Ireland, however, the whole people, from the tinkers to the clergy, have still a life, and view of life, that are rich and genial and humorous. I do not think that these country people, who have so much humour themselves, will mind being laughed at without malice, as the people in every country have been laughed at in their own comedies.

December 2, 1907

THE PLAYBOY OF THE WESTERN WORLD

CAST OF CHARACTERS

CHRISTOPHER MAHON
OLD MAHON, *his father—a squatter*
MICHAEL JAMES FLAHERTY, called MICHAEL JAMES, *a publican*
MARGARET FLAHERTY, *called* PEGEEN MIKE, *his daughter*
WIDOW QUIN, *a woman of about thirty*
SHAWN KEOGH, *her cousin, a young farmer*
PHILLY CULLEN *and* JIMMY FARRELL, *small farmers*
SARA TANSEY, SUSAN BRADY, *and* HONOR BLAKE, *village girls*
A BELLMAN
SOME PEASANTS

The action takes place near a village, on a wild coast of Mayo. The first act passes on an evening of autumn, the other two acts on the following day.

ACT ONE

(*Scene—Country public-house or shebeen, very rough and untidy. There is a sort of counter on the right with shelves, holding many bottles and jugs, just seen above it. Empty barrels stand near the counter. At back, a little* to left of counter, there is a door into the open air, then, more to the left, there is a settle with shelves above it, with more jugs, and a table beneath a window. At the left there is a large open fire-place, with turf fire, and a small door into inner room. PEGEEN, a wild-looking but fine girl, of about twenty, is writing at table. She is dressed in the usual peasant dress*)

PEGEEN (*slowly as she writes*) Six yards of stuff for to make a yellow gown. A pair of lace boots with lengthy heels on them and brassy eyes. A hat is suited for a wedding day. A fine tooth comb. To be sent with three barrels of porter in Jimmy Farrell's creel cart on the evening of the coming Fair to Mister Michael James Flaherty. With the best compliments of this season. Margaret Flaherty.

SHAWN KEOGH (*a fat and fair young man comes in as she signs, looks round awkwardly, when he sees she is alone*) Where's himself?

PEGEEN (*without looking at him*) He's coming. (*She directs the letter*) To Mister Sheamus Mulroy, Wine and Spirit Dealer, Castlebar.

SHAWN (*uneasily*) I didn't see him on the road.

PEGEEN How would you see him (*licks stamp and puts it on letter*) and it dark night this half hour gone by?

SHAWN (*turning towards the door again*) I stood a while outside wondering would I have a right to pass on or to walk in and see you, Pegeen Mike (*comes to fire*), and I could hear the cows breathing, and sighing in the stillness of the air, and not a step moving any place from this gate to the bridge.

PEGEEN (*putting letter in envelope*) It's above at the cross-roads he is, meeting Philly Cullen; and a couple more are going along with him to Kate Cassidy's wake.

SHAWN (*looking at her blankly*) And he's going that length in the dark night?

PEGEEN (*impatiently*) He is surely, and leaving me lonesome on the scruff of the hill.

(*She gets up and puts envelope on dresser, then winds clock*) Isn't it long the nights are now, Shawn Keogh, to be leaving a poor girl with her own self counting the hours to the dawn of day?

SHAWN (*with awkward humour*) If it is, when we're wedded in a short while you'll have no call to complain, for I've little will to be walking off to wakes or weddings in the darkness of the night.

PEGEEN (*with rather scornful good humor*) You're making mighty certain, Shaneen, that I'll wed you now.

SHAWN Aren't we after making a good bargain, the way we're only waiting these days on Father Reilly's dispensation from the bishops, or the Court of Rome.

PEGEEN (*looking at him teasingly, washing up at dresser*) It's a wonder, Shaneen, the Holy Father'd be taking notice of the likes of you; for if I was him I wouldn't bother with this place where you'll meet none but Red Linahan, has a squint in his eye, and Patcheen is lame in his heel, or the mad Mulrannies were driven from California and they lost in their wits. We're a queer lot these times to go troubling the Holy Father on his sacred seat.

SHAWN (*scandalized*) If we are, we're as good this place as another, maybe, and as good these times as we were for ever.

PEGEEN (*with scorn*) As good, is it? Where now will you meet the like of Daneen Sullivan knocked the eye from a peeler, or Marcus Quin, God rest him, got six months for maiming ewes, and he a great warrant to tell stories of holy Ireland till he'd have the old women shedding down tears about their feet. Where will you find the like of them, I'm saying?

SHAWN (*timidly*) If you don't, it's a good job, maybe; for (*with peculiar emphasis on the words*) Father Reilly has small conceit to have that kind walking around and talking to the girls.

PEGEEN (*impatiently, throwing water from basin out of the door*) Stop tormenting me with Father Reilly (*imitating his voice*) when I'm asking only what way I'll pass these twelve hours of dark, and not take my death with the fear.

(*Looking out of door*)

SHAWN (*timidly*) Would I fetch you the Widow Quin, maybe?

PEGEEN Is it the like of that murderer? You'll not, surely.

SHAWN (*going to her, soothingly*) Then I'm thinking himself will stop along with you when he sees you taking on, for it'll be a long night-time with great darkness, and I'm after feeling a kind of fellow above in the furzy ditch, groaning wicked like a maddening dog, the way it's good cause you have, maybe, to be fearing now.

PEGEEN (*turning on him sharply*) What's that? Is it a man you seen?

SHAWN (*retreating*) I couldn't see him at all; but I heard him groaning out, and breaking his heart. It should have been a young man from his words speaking.

PEGEEN (*going after him*) And you never went near to see was he hurted or what ailed him at all?

SHAWN I did not, Pegeen Mike. It was a dark, lonesome place to be hearing the like of him.

PEGEEN Well, you're a daring fellow, and if they find his corpse stretched above in the dews of dawn, what'll you say then to the peelers, or the Justice of the Peace?

SHAWN (*thunderstruck*) I wasn't thinking of that. For the love of God, Pegeen Mike, don't let on I was speaking of him. Don't tell your father and the men is coming above; for if they heard that story, they'd have great blabbing this night at the wake.

PEGEEN I'll maybe tell them, and I'll maybe not.

SHAWN They are coming at the door. Will you whisht, I'm saying?

PEGEEN Whisht yourself.

(*She goes behind counter.* MICHAEL JAMES, *fat jovial publican, comes in followed by* PHILLY CULLEN, *who is thin and mistrusting, and* JIMMY FARRELL, *who is fat and amorous, about forty-five*)

MEN (*together*) God bless you. The blessing of God on this place.

PEGEEN God bless you kindly.

MICHAEL (*to men who go to the counter*) Sit down now, and take your rest. (*crosses to* SHAWN *at the fire*) And how is it you are, Shawn Keogh? Are you coming over the sands to Kate Cassidy's wake?

SHAWN I am not, Michael James. I'm going home the short cut to my bed.

PEGEEN (*speaking across the counter*) He's right too, and have you no shame, Michael James, to be quitting off for the whole night, and leaving myself lonesome in the shop?

MICHAEL (*good-humoredly*) Isn't it the same whether I go for the whole night or a part only? and I'm thinking it's a queer daughter you are if you'd have me crossing backward through the Stooks of the Dead Women, with a drop taken.

PEGEEN   If I am a queer daughter, it's a queer father'd be leaving me lonesome these twelve hours of dark, and I piling the turf with the dogs barking, and the calves mooing, and my own teeth rattling with the fear.

JIMMY (*flatteringly*)   What is there to hurt you, and you a fine, hardy girl would knock the head of any two men in the place?

PEGEEN (*working herself up*)   Isn't there the harvest boys with their tongues red for drink, and the ten tinkers is camped in the east glen, and the thousand militia—bad cess to them!—walking idle through the land. There's lots surely to hurt me, and I won't stop alone in it, let himself do what he will.

MICHAEL   If you're that afeard, let Shawn Keogh stop along with you. It's the will of God, I'm thinking, himself should be seeing to you now.

(*They all turn on* SHAWN)

SHAWN (*in horrified confusion*)   I would and welcome, Michael James, but I'm afeard of Father Reilly; and what at all would the Holy Father and the Cardinals of Rome be saying if they heard I did the like of that?

MICHAEL (*with contempt*)   God help you! Can't you sit in by the hearth with the light lit and herself beyond in the room? You'll do that surely, for I've heard tell there's a queer fellow above, going mad or getting his death, maybe, in the gripe of the ditch, so she'd be safer this night with a person here.

SHAWN (*with plaintive despair*)   I'm afeard of Father Reilly, I'm saying. Let you not be tempting me, and we near married itself.

PHILLY (*with cold contempt*)   Lock him in the west room. He'll stay then and have no sin to be telling to the priest.

MICHAEL (*to* SHAWN, *getting between him and the door*)   Go up now.

SHAWN (*at the top of his voice*)   Don't stop me, Michael James. Let me out of the door, I'm saying, for the love of the Almighty God. Let me out. (*trying to dodge past him*) Let me out of it, and may God grant you His indulgence in the hour of need.

MICHAEL (*loudly*)   Stop your noising, and sit down by the hearth.

(*Gives him a push and goes to counter laughing*)

SHAWN (*turning back, wringing his hands*) Oh, Father Reilly and the saints of God, where will I hide myself to-day? Oh, St. Joseph and St. Patrick and St. Brigid, and St. James, have mercy on me now!

(SHAWN *turns round, sees door clear, and makes a rush for it*)

MICHAEL (*catching him by the coat tail*) You'd be going, is it?

SHAWN (*screaming*)   Leave me go, Michael James, leave me go, you old Pagan, leave me go, or I'll get the curse of the priests on you, and of the scarlet-coated bishops of the courts of Rome.

(*With a sudden movement he pulls himself out of his coat, and disappears out of the door, leaving his coat in* MICHAEL's *hands*)

MICHAEL (*turning round, and holding up coat*)   Well, there's the coat of a Christian man. Oh, there's sainted glory this day in the lonesome west; and by the will of God I've got you a decent man, Pegeen, you'll have no call to be spying after if you've a score of young girls, maybe, weeding in your fields.

PEGEEN (*taking up the defence of her property*)   What right have you to be making game of a poor fellow for minding the priest, when it's your own the fault is, not paying a penny pot-boy to stand along with me and give me courage in the doing of my work?

(*She snaps the coat away from him, and goes behind counter with it*)

MICHAEL (*taken aback*)   Where would I get a pot-boy? Would you have me send the bellman screaming in the streets of Castlebar?

SHAWN (*opening the door a chink and putting in his head, in a small voice*)   Michael James!

MICHAEL (*imitating him*)   What ails you?

SHAWN   The queer dying fellow's beyond looking over the ditch. He's come up, I'm thinking, stealing your hens. (*looks over his shoulder*) God help me, he's following me now (*He runs into room*), and if he's heard what I said, he'll be having my life, and I going home lonesome in the darkness of the night.

(*For a perceptible moment they watch the door with curiosity. Some one coughs outside. Then* CHRISTY MAHON, *a slight young man, comes in very tired and frightened and dirty*)

CHRISTY (*in a small voice*)   God save all here!

MEN   God save you kindly.

CHRISTY (*going to the counter*)   I'd trouble you for a glass of porter, woman of the house.

(*He puts down coin*)

PEGEEN (*serving him*)   You're one of the tinkers, young fellow, is beyond camped in the glen?

CHRISTY   I am not; but I'm destroyed walking.

MICHAEL (*patronizingly*)   Let you come up

then to the fire. You're looking famished with the cold.

CHRISTY God reward you. (*He takes up his glass and goes a little way across to the left, then stops and looks about him*) Is it often the police do be coming into this place, master of the house?

MICHAEL If you'd come in better hours, you'd have seen "Licensed for the sale of Beer and Spirits, to be consumed on the premises," written in white letters above the door, and what would the polis want spying on me, and not a decent house within four miles, the way every living Christian is a bona fide, saving one widow alone?

CHRISTY (*with relief*) It's a safe house, so.

(*He goes over to the fire, sighing and moaning. Then he sits down, putting his glass beside him and begins gnawing a turnip, too miserable to feel the others staring at him with curiosity*)

MICHAEL (*going after him*) Is it yourself is fearing the polis? You're wanting, maybe?

CHRISTY There's many wanting.

MICHAEL Many surely, with the broken harvest and the ended wars. (*He picks up some stockings, etc., that are near the fire, and carries them away furtively*) It should be larceny, I'm thinking?

CHRISTY (*dolefully*) I had it in my mind it was a different word and a bigger.

PEGEEN There's a queer lad. Were you never slapped in school, young fellow, that you don't know the name of your deed?

CHRISTY (*bashfully*) I'm slow at learning, a middling scholar only.

MICHAEL If you're a dunce itself, you'd have a right to know that larceny's robbing and stealing. It it for the like of that you're wanting?

CHRISTY (*with a flash of family pride*) And I the son of a strong farmer (*with a sudden qualm*), God rest his soul, could have bought up the whole of your old house a while since, from the butt of his tailpocket, and not have missed the weight of it gone.

MICHAEL (*impressed*) If it's not stealing, it's maybe something big.

CHRISTY (*flattered*) Aye; it's maybe something big.

JIMMY He's a wicked-looking young fellow. Maybe he followed after a young woman on a lonesome night.

CHRISTY (*shocked*) Oh, the saints forbid, mister; I was all times a decent lad.

PHILLY (*turning on* JIMMY) You're a silly man, Jimmy Farrell. He said his father was a farmer a while since, and there's himself now in a poor state. Maybe the land was grabbed from him, and he did what any decent man would do.

MICHAEL (*to* CHRISTY, *mysteriously*) Was it bailiffs?

CHRISTY The divil a one.

MICHAEL Agents?

CHRISTY The divil a one.

MICHAEL Landlords?

CHRISTY (*peevishly*) Ah, not at all, I'm saying. You'd see the like of them stories on any little paper of a Munster town. But I'm not calling to mind any person, gentle, simple, judge or jury, did the like of me.

(*They all draw nearer with delighted curiosity*)

PHILLY Well, that lad's a puzzle-the-world.

JIMMY He'd beat Dan Davies' circus, or the holy missioners making sermons on the villainy of man. Try him again, Philly.

PHILLY Did you strike golden guineas out of solder, young fellow, or shilling coins itself?

CHRISTY I did not, mister, not sixpence nor a farthing coin.

JIMMY Did you marry three wives maybe? I'm told there's a sprinkling have done that among the holy Luthers of the preaching north.

CHRISTY (*shyly*) I never married with one, let alone with a couple or three.

PHILLY Maybe he went fighting for the Boers, the like of the man beyond, was judged to be hanged, quartered and drawn. Were you off east, young fellow, fighting bloody wars for Kruger and the freedom of the Boers?

CHRISTY I never left my own parish till Tuesday was a week.

PEGEEN (*coming from counter*) He's done nothing, so. (*to* CHRISTY) If you didn't commit murder or a bad, nasty thing, or false coining, or robbery, or butchery, or the like of them, there isn't anything that would be worth your troubling for to run from now. You did nothing at all.

CHRISTY (*his feelings hurt*) That's an unkindly thing to be saying to a poor orphaned traveller, has a prison behind him, and hanging before, and hell's gap gaping below.

PEGEEN (*with a sign to the men to be quiet*) You're only saying it. You did nothing at all. A soft lad the like of you wouldn't slit the windpipe of a screeching sow.

CHRISTY (*offended*) You're not speaking the truth.

PEGEEN (*in mock rage*) Not speaking the

truth, is it? Would you have me knock the head of you with the butt of the broom?

CHRISTY (*twisting round on her with a sharp cry of horror*) Don't strike me. I killed my poor father, Tuesday was a week, for doing the like of that.

PEGEEN (*with blank amazement*) Is it killed your father?

CHRISTY (*subsiding*) With the help of God I did surely, and that the Holy Immaculate Mother may intercede for his soul.

PHILLY (*retreating with* JIMMY) There's a daring fellow.

JIMMY Oh, glory be to God!

MICHAEL (*with great respect*) That was a hanging crime, mister honey. You should have had good reason for doing the like of that.

CHRISTY (*in a very reasonable tone*) He was a dirty man, God forgive him, and he getting old and crusty, the way I couldn't put up with him at all.

PEGEEN And you shot him dead?

CHRISTY (*shaking his head*) I never used weapons. I've no license, and I'm a law-fearing man.

MICHAEL It was with a hilted knife maybe? I'm told, in the big world it's bloody knives they use.

CHRISTY (*loudly, scandalized*) Do you take me for a slaughter-boy?

PEGEEN You never hanged him, the way Jimmy Farrell hanged his dog from the license, and had it screeching and wriggling three hours at the butt of a string, and himself swearing it was a dead dog, and the peelers swearing it had life?

CHRISTY I did not then. I just riz the loy and let fall the edge of it on the ridge of his skull, and he went down at my feet like an empty sack, and never let a grunt or groan from him at all.

MICHAEL (*making a sign to* PEGEEN *to fill* CHRISTY's *glass*) And what way weren't you hanged, mister? Did you bury him then?

CHRISTY (*considering*) Aye. I buried him then. Wasn't I digging spuds in the field?

MICHAEL And the peelers never followed after you the eleven days that you're out?

CHRISTY (*shaking his head*) Never a one of them, and I walking forward facing hog, dog, or divil on the highway of the road.

PHILLY (*nodding wisely*) It's only with a common week-day kind of a murderer them lads would be trusting their carcase, and that man should be a great terror when his temper's roused.

MICHAEL He should then. (*to* CHRISTY)

And where was it, mister honey, that you did the deed?

CHRISTY (*looking at him with suspicion*) Oh, a distant place, master of the house, a windy corner of high, distant hills.

PHILLY (*nodding with approval*) He's a close man, and he's right, surely.

PEGEEN That'd be a lad with the sense of Solomon to have for a pot-boy, Michael James, if it's the truth you're seeking one at all.

PHILLY The peelers is fearing him, and if you'd that lad in the house there isn't one of them would come smelling around if the dogs itself were lapping poteen from the dung-pit of the yard.

JIMMY Bravery's a treasure in a lonesome place, and a lad would kill his father, I'm thinking, would face a foxy divil with a pitch-pike on the flags of hell.

PEGEEN It's the truth they're saying, and if I'd that lad in the house, I wouldn't be fearing the loosèd kharki cut-throats, or the walking dead.

CHRISTY (*swelling with surprise and triumph*) Well, glory be to God!

MICHAEL (*with deference*) Would you think well to stop here and be pot-boy, mister honey, if we gave you good wages, and didn't destroy you with the weight of work?

SHAWN (*coming forward uneasily*) That'd be a queer kind to bring into a decent quiet household with the like of Pegeen Mike.

PEGEEN (*very sharply*) Will you whisht? Who's speaking to you?

SHAWN (*retreating*) A bloody-handed murderer the like of . . .

PEGEEN (*snapping at him*) Whisht I am saying; we'll take no fooling from your like at all. (*to* CHRISTY *with a honeyed voice*) And you, young fellow, you'd have a right to stop, I'm thinking, for we'd do our all and utmost to content your needs.

CHRISTY (*overcome with wonder*) And I'd be safe in this place from the searching law?

MICHAEL You would, surely. If they're not fearing you, itself, the peelers in this place is decent droughty poor fellows, wouldn't touch a cur dog and not give warning in the dead of night.

PEGEEN (*very kindly and persuasively*) Let you stop a short while anyhow. Aren't you destroyed walking with your feet in bleeding blisters, and your whole skin needing washing like a Wicklow sheep.

CHRISTY (*looking round with satisfaction*) It's a nice room, and if it's not humbugging me you are, I'm thinking that I'll surely stay.

JIMMY (*jumps up*) Now, by the grace of

God, herself will be safe this night, with a man killed his father holding danger from the door, and let you come on, Michael James, or they'll have the best stuff drunk at the wake.

MICHAEL (*going to the door with men*) And begging your pardon, mister, what name will we call you, for we'd like to know?

CHRISTY   Christopher Mahon.

MICHAEL   Well, God bless you, Christy, and a good rest till we meet again when the sun'll be rising to the noon of day.

CHRISTY   God bless you all.

MEN   God bless you.

(*They go out except* SHAWN, *who lingers at door*)

SHAWN (*to* PEGEEN)   Are you wanting me to stop along with you to keep you from harm?

PEGEEN (*gruffly*)   Didn't you say you were fearing Father Reilly?

SHAWN   There'd be no harm staying now, I'm thinking, and himself in it too.

PEGEEN   You wouldn't stay when there was need for you, and let you step off nimble this time when there's none.

SHAWN   Didn't I say it was Father Reilly . . .

PEGEEN   Go on, then, to Father Reilly (*in a jeering tone*), and let him put you in the holy brotherhoods, and leave that lad to me.

SHAWN   If I meet the Widow Quin . . .

PEGEEN   Go on, I'm staying, and don't be waking this place with your noise. (*She hustles him out and bolts the door*) That lad would wear the spirits from the saints of peace. (*Bustles about, then takes off her apron and pins it up in the window as a blind.* CHRISTY *watching her timidly. Then she comes to him and speaks with bland good humor*) Let you stretch out now by the fire, young fellow. You should be destroyed travelling.

CHRISTY (*shyly again, drawing off his boots*) I'm tired, surely, walking wild eleven days, and waking fearful in the night.

(*He holds up one of his feet, feeling his blisters, and looking at them with compassion*)

PEGEEN (*standing beside him, watching him with delight*)   You should have had great people in your family, I'm thinking, with the little, small feet you have, and you with a kind of a quality name, the like of what you'd find on the great powers and potentates of France and Spain.

CHRISTY (*with pride*)   We were great surely, with wide and windy acres of rich Munster land.

PEGEEN   Wasn't I telling you, and you a fine, handsome young fellow with a noble brow?

CHRISTY (*with a flash of delighted surprise*) Is it me?

PEGEEN   Aye. Did you never hear that from the young girls where you come from in the west or south?

CHRISTY (*with venom*)   I did not then. Oh, they're bloody liars in the naked parish where I grew a man.

PEGEEN   If they are itself, you've heard it these days, I'm thinking, and you walking the world telling out your story to young girls or old.

CHRISTY   I've told my story no place till this night, Pegeen Mike, and it's foolish I was here, maybe, to be talking free, but you're decent people, I'm thinking, and yourself a kindly woman, the way I wasn't fearing you at all.

PEGEEN (*filling a sack with straw*)   You've said the like of that, maybe, in every cot and cabin where you've met a young girl on your way.

CHRISTY (*going over to her, gradually raising his voice*)   I've said it nowhere till this night, I'm telling you, for I've seen none the like of you the eleven long days I am walking the world, looking over a low ditch or a high ditch on my north or my south, into stony scattered fields, or scribes of bog, where you'd see young, limber girls, and fine prancing women making laughter with the men.

PEGEEN   If you weren't destroyed travelling, you'd have as much talk and streeleen, I'm thinking, as Owen Roe O'Sullivan or the poets of the Dingle Bay, and I've heard all times it's the poets are your like, fine fiery fellows with great rages when their temper's roused.

CHRISTY (*drawing a little nearer to her*) You've a power of rings, God bless you, and would there be any offence if I was asking are you single now?

PEGEEN   What would I want wedding so young?

CHRISTY (*with relief*)   We're alike, so.

PEGEEN (*she puts sack on settle and beats it up*)   I never killed my father. I'd be afeard to do that, except I was the like of yourself with blind rages tearing me within, for I'm thinking you should have had great tussling when the end was come.

CHRISTY (*expanding with delight at the first confidential talk he has ever had with a woman*)   We had not then. It was a hard woman was come over the hill, and if he was always a crusty kind when he'd a hard woman setting him on, not the divil himself or his four fathers could put up with him at all.

PEGEEN (*with curiosity*) And isn't it a great wonder that one wasn't fearing you?

CHRISTY (*very confidentially*) Up to the day I killed my father, there wasn't a person in Ireland knew the kind I was, and I there drinking, waking, eating, sleeping, a quiet, simple poor fellow with no man giving me heed.

PEGEEN (*getting a quilt out of the cupboard and putting it on the sack*) It was the girls were giving you heed maybe, and I'm thinking it's most conceit you'd have to be gaming with their like.

CHRISTY (*shaking his head, with simplicity*) Not the girls itself, and I won't tell you a lie. There wasn't anyone heeding me in that place saving only the dumb beasts of the field.

(*He sits down at fire*)

PEGEEN (*with disappointment*) And I thinking you should have been living the like of a king of Norway or the Eastern world.

(*She comes and sits beside him after placing bread and mug of milk on the table*)

CHRISTY (*laughing piteously*) The like of a king, is it? And I after toiling, moiling, digging, dodging from the dawn till dusk with never a sight of joy or sport saving only when I'd be abroad in the dark night poaching rabbits on hills, for I was a devil to poach, God forgive me, (*very naïvely*) and I near got six months for going with a dung fork and stabbing a fish.

PEGEEN And it's that you'd call sport, is it, to be abroad in the darkness with yourself alone?

CHRISTY I did, God help me, and there I'd be as happy as the sunshine of St. Martin's Day, watching the light passing the north or the patches of fog, till I'd hear a rabbit starting to screech and I'd go running in the furze. Then when I'd my full share I'd come walking down where you'd see the ducks and geese stretched sleeping on the highway of the road, and before I'd pass the dunghill, I'd hear himself snoring out, a loud lonesome snore he'd be making all times, the while he was sleeping, and he a man 'd be raging all times, the while he was waking, like a gaudy officer you'd hear cursing and damning and swearing oaths.

PEGEEN Providence and Mercy, spare us all!

CHRISTY It's that you'd say surely if you seen him and he after drinking for weeks, rising up in the red dawn, or before it maybe, and going out into the yard as naked as an ash tree in the moon of May, and shying clods against the visage of the stars till he'd put the fear of death into the banbhs and the screeching sows.

PEGEEN I'd be well-nigh afeard of that lad myself, I'm thinking. And there was no one in it but the two of you alone?

CHRISTY The divil a one, though he'd sons and daughters walking all great states and territories of the world, and not a one of them, to this day, but would say their seven curses on him, and they rousing up to let a cough or sneeze, maybe, in the deadness of the night.

PEGEEN (*nodding her head*) Well, you should have been a queer lot. I never cursed my father the like of that, though I'm twenty and more years of age.

CHRISTY Then you'd have cursed mine, I'm telling you, and he a man never gave peace to any, saving when he'd get two months or three, or be locked in the asylums for battering peelers or assaulting men (*with depression*) the way it was a bitter life he led me till I did up a Tuesday and halve his skull.

PEGEEN (*putting her hand on his shoulder*) Well, you'll have peace in this place, Christy Mahon, and none to trouble you, and it's near time a fine lad like you should have your good share of the earth.

CHRISTY It's time surely, and I a seemly fellow with great strength in me and bravery of . . .

(*Someone knocks*)

CHRISTY (*clinging to* PEGEEN) Oh, glory! it's late for knocking, and this last while I'm in terror of the peelers, and the walking dead.

(*Knocking again*)

PEGEEN Who's there?

VOICE (*outside*) Me.

PEGEEN Who's me?

VOICE The Widow Quin.

PEGEEN (*jumping up and giving him the bread and milk*) Go on now with your supper, and let on to be sleepy, for if she found you were such a warrant to talk, she'd be stringing gabble till the dawn of day.

(*He takes bread and sits shyly with his back to the door*)

PEGEEN (*opening door, with temper*) What ails you, or what is it you're wanting at this hour of the night?

WIDOW QUIN (*coming in a step and peering at* CHRISTY) I'm after meeting Shawn Keogh and Father Reilly below, who told me of your curiosity man, and they fearing by this time he was maybe roaring, romping on your hands with drink.

PEGEEN (*pointing to* CHRISTY) Look now

is he roaring, and he stretched away drowsy with his supper and his mug of milk. Walk down and tell that to Father Reilly and to Shaneen Keogh.

WIDOW QUIN (*coming forward*) I'll not see them again, for I've their word to lead that lad forward for to lodge with me.

PEGEEN (*in blank amazement*) This night, is it?

WIDOW QUIN (*going over*) This night. "It isn't fitting," says the priesteen, "to have his likeness lodging with an orphaned girl." (*to* CHRISTY) God save you, mister!

CHRISTY (*shyly*) God save you kindly.

WIDOW QUIN (*looking at him with half-amazed curiosity*) Well, aren't you a little smiling fellow? It should have been great and bitter torments did arouse your spirits to a deed of blood.

CHRISTY (*doubtfully*) It should, maybe.

WIDOW QUIN It's more than "maybe" I'm saying, and it'd soften my heart to see you sitting so simple with your cup and cake, and you fitter to be saying your catechism than slaying your da.

PEGEEN (*at counter, washing glasses*) There's talking when any'd see he's fit to be holding his head high with the wonders of the world. Walk on from this, for I'll not have him tormented and he destroyed travelling since Tuesday was a week.

WIDOW QUIN (*peaceably*) We'll be walking surely when his supper's done, and you'll find we're great company, young fellow, when it's of the like of you and me you'd hear the penny poets singing in an August Fair.

CHRISTY (*innocently*) Did you kill your father.

PEGEEN (*contemptuously*) She did not. She hit himself with a worn pick, and the rusted poison did corrode his blood the way he never overed it, and died after. That was a sneaky kind of murder did win small glory with the boys itself.

(*She crosses to* CHRISTY's *left*)

WIDOW QUIN (*with good humor*) If it didn't, maybe all knows a widow woman has buried her children and destroyed her man is a wiser comrade for a young lad than a girl, the like of you, who'd go helter-skeltering after any man would let you a wink upon the road.

PEGEEN (*breaking out into wild rage*) And you'll say that, Widow Quin, and you gasping with the rage you had racing the hill beyond to look on his face.

WIDOW QUIN (*laughing derisively*) Me, is it? Well, Father Reilly has cuteness to divide

you now. (*She pulls* CHRISTY *up*) There's great temptation in a man did slay his da, and we'd best be going, young fellow; so rise up and come with me.

PEGEEN (*seizing his arm*) He'll not stir. He's pot-boy in this place, and I'll not have him stolen off and kidnabbed while himself's abroad.

WIDOW QUIN It'd be a crazy pot-boy'd lodge him in the shebeen where he works by day, so you'd have a right to come on, young fellow, till you see my little houseen, a perch off on the rising hill.

PEGEEN Wait till morning, Christy Mahon. Wait till you lay eyes on her leaky thatch is growing more pasture for her buck goat than her square of fields, and she without a tramp itself to keep in order her place at all.

WIDOW QUIN When you see me contriving in my little gardens, Christy Mahon, you'll swear the Lord God formed me to be living lone, and that there isn't my match in Mayo for thatching, or mowing, or shearing a sheep.

PEGEEN (*with noisy scorn*) It's true the Lord God formed you to contrive indeed. Doesn't the world know you reared a black lamb at your own breast, so that the Lord Bishop of Connaught felt the elements of a Christian, and he eating it after in a kidney stew? Doesn't the world know you've been seen shaving the foxy skipper from France for a threepenny bit and a sop of grass tobacco would wring the liver from a mountain goat you'd meet leaping the hills?

WIDOW QUIN (*with amusement*) Do you hear her now young fellow? Do you hear the way she'll be rating at your own self when a week is by?

PEGEEN (*to* CHRISTY) Don't heed her. Tell her to go into her pigsty and not plague us here.

WIDOW QUIN I'm going; but he'll come with me.

PEGEEN (*shaking him*) Are you dumb, young fellow?

CHRISTY (*timidly, to* WIDOW QUIN) God increase you; but I'm pot-boy in this place, and it's here I'd liefer stay.

PEGEEN (*triumphantly*) Now you have heard him, and go on from this.

WIDOW QUIN (*looking round the room*) It's lonesome this hour crossing the hill, and if he won't come along with me, I'd have a right maybe to stop this night with yourselves. Let me stretch out on the settle, Pegeen Mike; and himself can lie by the hearth.

PEGEEN (*short and fiercely*) Faith, I won't. Quit off or I will send you now.

WIDOW QUIN (*gathering her shawl up*) Well, it's a terror to be aged a score. (*to* CHRISTY) God bless you now, young fellow, and let you be wary, or there's right torment will await you here if you go romancing with her like, and she waiting only, as they bade me say, on a sheepskin parchment to be wed with Shawn Keogh of Killakeen.

CHRISTY (*going to* PEGEEN *as she bolts the door*) What's that she's after saying?

PEGEEN Lies and blather, you've no call to mind. Well, isn't Shawn Keogh an impudent fellow to send up spying on me? Wait till I lay hands on him. Let him wait, I'm saying.

CHRISTY And you're not wedding him at all?

PEGEEN I wouldn't wed him if a bishop came walking for to join us here.

CHRISTY That God in glory may be thanked for that.

PEGEEN There's your bed now. I've put a quilt upon you I'm after quilting a while since with my own two hands, and you'd best stretch out now for your sleep, and may God give you a good rest till I call you in the morning when the cocks will crow.

CHRISTY (*as she goes to inner room*) May God and Mary and St. Patrick bless you and reward you, for your kindly talk. (*She shuts the door behind her. He settles his bed slowly, feeling the quilt with immense satisfaction*) Well, it's a clean bed and soft with it, and it's great luck and company I've won me in the end of time—two fine women fighting for the likes of me—till I'm thinking this night wasn't I a foolish fellow not to kill my father in the years gone by.

ACT TWO

(*Scene—as before. Brilliant morning light.* CHRISTY, *looking bright and cheerful, is cleaning a girl's boots*)

CHRISTY (*to himself, counting jugs on dresser*) Half a hundred beyond. Ten there. A score that's above. Eighty jugs. Six cups and a broken one. Two plates. A power of glasses. Bottles, a school-master'd be hard set to count, and enough in them, I'm thinking, to drunken all the wealth and wisdom of the County Clare. (*He puts down the boot carefully*) There's her boots now, nice and decent for her evening use, and isn't it grand brushes she has? (*He puts them down and goes by degrees to the looking-glass*) Well, this'd be a fine place to be my whole life talking out with swearing Christians, in place of my old dogs and cat, and I stalking around, smoking my pipe and drinking my fill, and never a day's work but drawing a cork an odd time, or wiping a glass, or rinsing out a shiny tumbler for a decent man. (*He takes the looking-glass from the wall and puts it on the back of a chair; then sits down in front of it and begins washing his face*) Didn't I know rightly I was handsome, though it was the divil's own mirror we had beyond, would twist a squint across an angel's brow; and I'll be growing fine from this day, the way I'll have a soft lovely skin on me and won't be the like of the clumsy young fellows do be ploughing all times in the earth and dung. (*He starts*) Is she coming again? (*He looks out*) Stranger girls. God help me, where'll I hide myself away and my long neck naked to the world? (*He looks out*) I'd best go to the room maybe till I'm dressed again.

(*He gathers up his coat and the looking-glass, and runs into the inner room. The door is pushed open, and* SUSAN BRADY *looks in, and knocks on door*)

SUSAN There's nobody in it. (*knocks again*)

NELLY (*pushing her in and following her, with* HONOR BLAKE *and* SARA TANSEY) It'd be early for them both to be out walking the hill.

SUSAN I'm thinking Shawn Keogh was making game of us and there's no such man in it at all.

HONOR (*pointing to straw and quilt*) Look at that. He's been sleeping there in the night. Well, it'll be a hard case if he's gone off now, the way we'll never set our eyes on a man killed his father, and we after rising early and destroying ourselves running fast on the hill.

NELLY Are you thinking them's his boots?

SARA (*taking them up*) If they are, there should be his father's track on them. Did you never read in the papers the way murdered men do bleed and drip?

SUSAN Is that blood there, Sara Tansey?

SARA (*smelling it*) That's bog water, I'm thinking, but it's his own they are surely, for I never seen the like of them for whity mud, and red mud, and turf on them, and the fine sands of the sea. That man's been walking, I'm telling you.

(*She goes down right, putting on one of his boots*)

SUSAN (*going to window*) Maybe he's stolen off to Belmullet with the boots of

Michael James, and you'd have a right so to follow after him, Sara Tansey, and you the one yoked the ass cart and drove ten miles to set your eyes on the man bit the yellow lady's nostril on the northern shore. (*She looks out*)

SARA (*running to window with one boot on*) Don't be talking, and we fooled today (*putting on other boot*) There's a pair do fit me well, and I'll be keeping them for walking to the priest, when you'd be ashamed this place, going up winter and summer with nothing worth while to confess at all.

HONOR (*who has been listening at the door*) Whisht! there's someone inside the room. (*She pushes door a chink open*) It's a man.

(SARA *kicks off boots and puts them where they were. They all stand in a line looking through chink*)

SARA I'll call him. Mister! Mister! (*He puts in his head*) Is Pegeen within?

CHRISTY (*coming in as meek as a mouse, with the looking-glass held behind his back*) She's above on the cnuceen, seeking the nanny goats, the way she'd have a sup of goat's milk for to color my tea.

SARA And asking your pardon, is it you's the man killed his father?

CHRISTY (*sidling toward the nail where the glass was hanging*) I am, God help me!

SARA (*taking eggs she has brought*) Then my thousand welcomes to you, and I've run up with a brace of duck's eggs for your food today. Pegeen's ducks is no use, but these are the real rich sort. Hold out your hand and you'll see it's no lie I'm telling you.

CHRISTY (*coming forward shyly, and holding out his left hand*) They're a great and weighty size.

SUSAN And I run up with a pat of butter, for it'd be a poor thing to have you eating your spuds dry, and you after running a great way since you did destroy your da.

CHRISTY Thank you kindly.

HONOR And I brought you a little cut of cake, for you should have a thin stomach on you, and you that length walking the world.

NELLY And I brought you a little laying pullet—boiled and all she is—was crushed at the fall of night by the curate's car. Feel the fat of that breast, mister.

CHRISTY It's bursting, surely.

(*He feels it with the back of his hand, in which he holds the presents*)

SARA Will you pinch it? Is your right hand too sacred for to use at all? (*She slips round behind him*) It's a glass he has. Well, I never seen to this day a man with a looking-glass

held to his back. Them that kills their fathers is a vain lot surely.

(*Girls giggle*)

CHRISTY (*smiling innocently and piling presents on glass*) I'm very thankful to you all today . . .

WIDOW QUIN (*coming in quickly, at door*) Sara Tansey, Susan Brady, Honor Blake! What in glory has you here at this hour of day?

GIRLS (*giggling*) That's the man killed his father.

WIDOW QUIN (*coming to them*) I know well it's the man; and I'm after putting him down in the sports below for racing, leaping, pitching, and the Lord knows what.

SARA (*exuberantly*) That's right, Widow Quin. I'll bet my dowry that he'll lick the world.

WIDOW QUIN If you will, you'd have a right to have him fresh and nourished in place of nursing a feast. (*taking presents*) Are you fasting or fed, young fellow?

CHRISTY Fasting, if you please.

WIDOW QUIN (*loudly*) Well, you're the lot. Stir up now and give him his breakfast. (*to* CHRISTY) Come here to me (*She puts him on bench beside her while the girls make tea and get his breakfast*) and let you tell us your story before Pegeen will come, in place of grinning your ears off like the moon of May.

CHRISTY (*beginning to be pleased*) It's a long story; you'd be destroyed listening.

WIDOW QUIN Don't be letting on to be shy, a fine, gamey, treacherous lad the like of you. Was it in your house beyond you cracked his skull?

CHRISTY (*shy but flattered*) It was not. We were digging spuds in his cold, sloping, stony, divil's patch of a field.

WIDOW QUIN And you went asking money of him, or making talk of getting a wife would drive him from his farm?

CHRISTY I did not, then; but there I was, digging and digging, and "You squinting idiot," says he, "let you walk down now and tell the priest you'll wed the Widow Casey in a score of days."

WIDOW QUIN And what kind was she?

CHRISTY (*with horror*) A walking terror from beyond the hills, and she two score and two hundredweights and five pounds in the weighing scales, with a limping leg on her, and a blinded eye, and she a woman of noted misbehavior with the old and young.

GIRLS (*clustering round him, serving him*) Glory be.

WIDOW QUIN   And what did he want driving you to wed with her?

(*She takes a bit of the chicken*)

CHRISTY   (*eating with growing satisfaction*) He was letting on I was wanting a protector from the harshness of the world, and he without a thought the whole while but how he'd have her hut to live in and her gold to drink.

WIDOW QUIN   There's maybe worse than a dry hearth and a widow woman and your glass at night. So you hit him then?

CHRISTY   (*getting almost excited*)   I did not. "I won't wed her," says I, "when all know she did suckle me for six weeks when I came into the world, and she a hag this day with a tongue on her has the crows and seabirds scattered, the way they wouldn't cast a shadow on her garden with the dread of her curse."

WIDOW QUIN   (*teasingly*)   That one should be right company.

SARA   (*eagerly*)   Don't mind her. Did you kill him then?

CHRISTY   "She's too good for the like of you," says he, "and go on now or I'll flatten you out like a crawling beast has passed under a dray." "You will not if I can help it," says I. "Go on," says he, "or I'll have the divil making garters of your limbs tonight." "You will not if I can help it," says I.

(*He sits up, brandishing his mug*)

SARA   You were right surely.

CHRISTY   (*impressively*)   With that the sun came out between the cloud and the hill, and it shining green in my face. "God have mercy on your soul," says he, lifting a scythe; "or on your own," says I, raising the loy.

SUSAN   That's a grand story.

HONOR   He tells it lovely.

CHRISTY   (*flattered and confident, waving bone*)   He gave a drive with the scythe, and I gave a lep to the east. Then I turned around with my back to the north, and I hit a blow on the ridge of his skull, laid him stretched out, and he split to the knob of his gullet.

(*He raises the chicken bone to his Adam's apple*)

GIRLS   (*together*)   Well, you're a marvel! Oh, God bless you! You're the lad surely!

SUSAN   I'm thinking the Lord God sent him this road to make a second husband to the Widow Quin, and she with a great yearning to be wedded, though all dread her here. Lift him on her knee, Sara Tansey.

WIDOW QUIN   Don't tease him.

SARA   (*going over to dresser and counter very quickly, and getting two glasses and porter*)   You're heroes surely, and let you drink a supeen with your arms linked like the outlandish lovers in the sailor's song. (*She links their arms and gives them the glasses*) There now. Drink a health to the wonders of the western world, the pirates, preachers, poteen-makers, with the jobbing jockies; parching peelers, and the juries fill their stomachs selling judgments of the English law.

(*Brandishing the bottle*)

WIDOW QUIN   That's a right toast, Sara Tansey. Now Christy.

(*They drink with their arms linked, he drinking with his left hand, she with her right. As they are drinking, PEGEEN MIKE comes in with a milk can and stands aghast. They all spring away from CHRISTY. He goes down left. WIDOW QUIN remains seated*)

PEGEEN   (*angrily, to SARA*)   What is it you're wanting?

SARA   (*twisting her apron*)   A ounce of tobacco.

PEGEEN   Have you tuppence?

SARA   I've forgotten my purse.

PEGEEN   Then you'd best be getting it and not fooling us here. (*to the WIDOW QUIN, with more elaborate scorn*) And what is it you're wanting, Widow Quin?

WIDOW QUIN   (*insolently*)   A penn'orth of starch.

PEGEEN   (*breaking out*)   And you without a white shift or a shirt in your whole family since the drying of the flood. I've no starch for the like of you, and let you walk on now to Killamuck.

WIDOW QUIN   (*turning to CHRISTY, as she goes out with the girls*)   Well, you're mighty huffy this day, Pegeen Mike, and, you young fellow, let you not forget the sports and racing when the noon is by. (*They go out*)

PEGEEN   (*imperiously*)   Fling out that rubbish and put them cups away. (*CHRISTY tidies away in great haste*) Shove in the bench by the wall. (*He does so*) And hang that glass on the nail. What disturbed it at all?

CHRISTY   (*very meekly*)   I was making myself decent only, and this a fine country for young lovely girls.

PEGEEN   (*sharply*)   Whisht your talking of girls. (*goes to counter—right*)

CHRISTY   Wouldn't any wish to be decent in a place . . .

PEGEEN   Whisht I'm saying.

CHRISTY   (*looks at her face for a moment with great misgivings, then as a last effort, takes up a loy, and goes towards her, with feigned assurance*)   It was with a loy the like of that I killed my father.

PEGEEN (*still sharply*)   You've told me that story six times since the dawn of day.

CHRISTY (*reproachfully*)   It's a queer thing you wouldn't care to be hearing it and them girls after walking four miles to be listening to me now.

PEGEEN (*turning round astonished*)   Four miles.

CHRISTY (*apologetically*)   Didn't himself say there were only four bona fides living in this place?

PEGEEN   It's bona fides by the road they are, but that lot came over the river lepping the stones. It's not three perches when you go like that, and I was down this morning looking on the papers the post-boy does have in his bag. (*with meaning and emphasis*) For there was great news this day, Christopher Mahon. (*She goes into room left*)

CHRISTY (*suspiciously*)   Is it news of my murder?

PEGEEN (*inside*)   Murder, indeed.

CHRISTY (*loudly*)   A murdered da?

PEGEEN (*coming in again and crossing right*) There was not, but a story filled half a page of the hanging of a man. Ah, that should be a fearful end, young fellow, and it worst of all for a man who destroyed his da, for the like of him would get small mercies, and when it's dead he is, they'd put him in a narrow grave, with cheap sacking wrapping him round, and pour down quicklime on his head, the way you'd see a woman pouring any frish-frash from a cup.

CHRISTY (*very miserably*)   Oh, God help me. Are you thinking I'm safe? You were saying at the fall of night, I was shut of jeopardy and I here with yourselves.

PEGEEN (*severely*)   You'll be shut of jeopardy no place if you go talking with a pack of wild girls the like of them do be walking abroad with the peelers, talking whispers at the fall of night.

CHRISTY (*with terror*)   And you're thinking they'd tell?

PEGEEN (*with mock sympathy*)   Who knows, God help you.

CHRISTY (*loudly*)   What joy would they have to bring hanging to the likes of me?

PEGEEN   It's queer joys they have, and who knows the thing they'd do, if it'd make the green stones cry itself to think of you swaying and swiggling at the butt of a rope, and you with a fine, stout neck, God bless you! the way you'd be a half an hour, in great anguish, getting your death.

CHRISTY (*getting his boots and putting them on*)   If there's that terror of them, it'd be best, maybe, I went on wandering like Esau or Cain and Abel on the sides of Neifin or the Erris plain.

PEGEEN (*beginning to play with him*)   It would, maybe, for I've heard the Circuit Judges this place is a heartless crew.

CHRISTY (*bitterly*)   It's more than Judges this place is a heartless crew. (*looking up at her*) And isn't it a poor thing to be starting again and I a lonesome fellow will be looking out on women and girls the way the needy fallen spirits do be looking on the Lord?

PEGEEN   What call have you to be that lonesome when there's poor girls walking Mayo in their thousands now?

CHRISTY (*grimly*)   It's well you know what call I have. It's well you know it's a lonesome thing to be passing small towns with the lights shining sideways when the night is down, or going in strange places with a dog noising before you and a dog noising behind, or drawn to the cities where you'd hear a voice kissing and talking deep love in every shadow of the ditch, and you passing on with an empty, hungry stomach failing from your heart.

PEGEEN   I'm thinking you're an odd man, Christy Mahon. The oddest walking fellow I ever set my eyes on to this hour today.

CHRISTY   What would any be but odd men and they living lonesome in the world?

PEGEEN   I'm not odd, and I'm my whole life with my father only.

CHRISTY (*with infinite admiration*)   How would a lovely handsome woman the like of you be lonesome when all men should be thronging around to hear the sweetness of your voice, and the little infant children should be pestering your steps I'm thinking, and you walking the roads.

PEGEEN   I'm hard set to know what way a coaxing fellow the like of yourself should be lonesome either.

CHRISTY   Coaxing?

PEGEEN   Would you have me think a man never talked with the girls would have the words you've spoken today? It's only letting on you are to be lonesome, the way you'd get around me now.

CHRISTY   I wish to God I was letting on; but I was lonesome all times, and born lonesome, I'm thinking, as the moon of dawn.

(*Going to door*)

PEGEEN (*puzzled by his talk*)   Well, it's a story I'm not understanding at all why you'd be worse than another, Christy Mahon, and you a fine lad with the great savagery to destroy your da.

CHRISTY It's little I'm understanding myself, saving only that my heart's scalded this day, and I going off stretching out the earth between us, the way I'll not be waking near you another dawn of the year till the two of us do arise to hope or judgment with the saints of God, and now I'd best be going with my wattle in my hand, for hanging is a poor thing (*turning to go*), and it's little welcome only is left me in this house today.

PEGEEN (*sharply*) Christy! (*He turns round*) Come here to me. (*He goes towards her*) Lay down that switch and throw some sods on the fire. You're pot-boy in this place, and I'll not have you mitch off from us now.

CHRISTY You were saying I'd be hanged if I stay.

PEGEEN (*quite kindly at last*) I'm after going down and reading the fearful crimes of Ireland for two weeks or three, and there wasn't a word of your murder. (*getting up and going over to the counter*) They've likely not found the body. You're safe so with ourselves.

CHRISTY (*astonished, slowly*) It's making game of me you were (*following her with fearful joy*), and I can stay so, working at your side, and I not lonesome from this mortal day.

PEGEEN What's to hinder you from staying, except the widow woman or the young girls would inveigle you off?

CHRISTY (*with rapture*) And I'll have your words from this day filling my ears, and that look is come upon you meeting my two eyes, and I watching you loafing around in the warm sun, or rinsing your ankles when the night is come.

PEGEEN (*kindly, but a little embarassed*) I'm thinking you'll be a loyal young lad to have working around, and if you vexed me a while since with your leaguing with the girls, I wouldn't give a thraneen for a lad hadn't a mighty spirit in him and a gamey heart.

(SHAWN KEOGH *runs in carrying a cleeve on his back, followed by the* WIDOW QUIN)

SHAWN (*to* PEGEEN) I was passing below, and I seen your mountainy sheep eating cabbages in Jimmy's field. Run up or they'll be bursting surely.

PEGEEN Oh, God mend them! (*She puts a shawl over her head and runs out*)

CHRISTY (*looking from one to the other. Still in high spirits*) I'd best go to her aid maybe. I'm handy with ewes.

WIDOW QUIN (*closing the door*) She can do that much, and there is Shaneen has long speeches for to tell you now. (*She sits down with an amused smile*)

SHAWN (*taking something from his pocket and offering it to* CHRISTY) Do you see that, mister?

CHRISTY (*looking at it*) The half of a ticket to the Western States!

SHAWN (*trembling with anxiety*) I'll give it to you and my new hat (*pulling it out of hamper*); and my breeches with the double seat (*pulling it off*); and my new coat is woven from the blackest shearings for three miles around (*giving him the coat*); I'll give you the whole of them, and my blessing, and the blessing of Father Reilly itself, maybe, if you'll quit from this and leave us in the peace we had till last night at the fall of dark.

CHRISTY (*with a new arrogance*) And for what is it you're wanting to get shut of me?

SHAWN (*looking to the* WIDOW *for help*) I'm a poor scholar with middling faculties to coin a lie, so I'll tell you the truth, Christy Mahon. I'm wedding with Pegeen beyond, and I don't think well of having a clever fearless man the like of you dwelling in her house.

CHRISTY (*almost pugnaciously*) And you'd be using bribery for to banish me?

SHAWN (*in an imploring voice*) Let you not take it badly mister honey, isn't beyond the best place for you where you'll have golden chains and shiny coats and you riding upon hunters with the ladies of the land.

(*He makes an eager sign to the* WIDOW QUIN *to come to help him*)

WIDOW QUIN (*coming over*) It's true for him, and you'd best quit off and not have that poor girl setting her mind on you, for there's Shaneen thinks she wouldn't suit you though all is saying that she'll wed you now.

(CHRISTY *beams with delight*)

SHAWN (*in terrified earnest*) She wouldn't suit you, and she with the divil's own temper the way you'd be strangling one another in a score of days. (*He makes the movement of strangling with his hands*) It's the like of me only that she's fit for, a quiet simple fellow wouldn't raise a hand upon her if she scratched itself.

WIDOW QUIN (*putting* SHAWN'S *hat on* CHRISTY) Fit them clothes on you anyhow, young fellow, and he'd maybe loan them to you for the sports. (*Pushing him towards inner door*) Fit them on and you can give your answer when you have them tried.

CHRISTY (*beaming, delighted with the*

clothes) I will then. I'd like herself to see me in them tweeds and hat.

(*He goes into room and shuts the door*)

SHAWN (*in great anxiety*) He'd like herself to see them. He'll not leave us, Widow Quin. He's a score of divils in him the way it's well nigh certain he will wed Pegeen.

WIDOW QUIN (*jeeringly*) It's true all girls are fond of courage and do hate the like of you.

SHAWN (*walking about in desperation*) Oh, Widow Quin, what'll I be doing now? I'd inform again him, but he'd burst from Kilmainham and he'd be sure and certain to destroy me. If I wasn't so God-fearing, I'd near have courage to come behind him and run a pike into his side. Oh, it's a hard case to be an orphan and not to have your father that you're used to, and you'd easy kill and make yourself a hero in the sight of all (*coming up to her*) Oh, Widow Quin, will you find me some contrivance when I've promised you a ewe?

WIDOW QUIN A ewe's a small thing, but what would you give me if I did wed him and did save you so?

SHAWN (*with astonishment*) You?

WIDOW QUIN Aye. Would you give me the red cow you have and the mountainy ram, and the right of way across your rye path, and a load of dung at Michaelmas, and turbary upon the western hill?

SHAWN (*radiant with hope*) I would surely, and I'd give you the wedding ring I have, and the loan of a new suit, the way you'd have him decent on the wedding day. I'd give you two kids for your dinner, and a gallon of poteen, and I'd call the piper on the long car to your wedding from Crossmolina or from Ballina. I'd give you . . .

WIDOW QUIN That'll do so, and let you whisht, for he's coming now again.

(CHRISTY *comes in very natty in the new clothes.* WIDOW QUIN *goes to him admiringly*)

WIDOW QUIN If you seen yourself now, I'm thinking you'd be too proud to speak to us at all, and it'd be a pity surely to have your like sailing from Mayo to the Western World.

CHRISTY (*as proud as a peacock*) I'm not going. If this is a poor place itself, I'll make myself contented to be lodging here.

(WIDOW QUIN *makes a sign to* SHAWN *to leave them*)

SHAWN Well, I'm going measuring the racecourse while the tide is low, so I'll leave you the garments and my blessing for the sports today. God bless you! (*He wriggles out*)

WIDOW QUIN (*admiring* CHRISTY) Well, you're mighty spruce, young fellow. Sit down now while you're quiet till you talk with me.

CHRISTY (*swaggering*) I'm going abroad on the hillside for to seek Pegeen.

WIDOW QUIN You'll have time and plenty for to seek Pegeen, and you heard me saying at the fall of night the two of us should be great company.

CHRISTY From this out I'll have no want of company when all sorts is bringing me their food and clothing (*he swaggers to the door, tightening his belt*), the way they'd set their eyes upon a gallant orphan cleft his father with one blow to the breeches belt. (*He opens door, then staggers back*) Saints of glory! Holy angels from the throne of light!

WIDOW QUIN (*going over*) What ails you?

CHRISTY It's the walking spirit of my murdered da?

WIDOW QUIN (*looking out*) Is it that tramper?

CHRISTY (*wildly*) Where'll I hide my poor body from that ghost of hell?

(*The door is pushed open, and old* MAHON *appears on threshold.* CHRISTY *darts in behind door*)

WIDOW QUIN (*in great amusement*) God save you, my poor man.

MAHON (*gruffly*) Did you see a young lad passing this way in the early morning or the fall of night?

WIDOW QUIN You're a queer kind to walk in not saluting at all.

MAHON Did you see the young lad?

WIDOW QUIN (*stiffly*) What kind was he?

MAHON An ugly young streeler with a murderous gob on him, and a little switch in his hand. I met a tramper seen him coming this way at the fall of night.

WIDOW QUIN There's harvest hundreds do be passing these days for the Sligo boat. For what is it you're wanting him, my poor man?

MAHON I want to destroy him for breaking the head on me with the clout of a loy. (*He takes off a big hat, and shows his head in a mass of bandages and plaster, with some pride*) It was he did that, and amn't I a great wonder to think I've traced him ten days with that rent in my crown?

WIDOW QUIN (*taking his head in both hands and examining it with extreme delight*) That was a great blow. And who hit you? A robber maybe?

MAHON It was my own son hit me, and he the divil a robber, or anything else, but a dirty, stuttering lout.

WIDOW QUIN (*letting go his skull and wiping her hands in her apron*) You'd best be wary of a mortified scalp, I think they call it, lepping around with that wound in the splendor of the sun. It was a bad blow surely, and you should have vexed him fearful to make him strike that gash in his da.

MAHON Is it me?

WIDOW QUIN (*amusing herself*) Aye. And isn't it a great shame when the old and hardened do torment the young?

MAHON (*raging*) Torment him is it? And I after holding out with the patience of a martyred saint till there's nothing but destruction on, and I'm driven out in my old age with none to aid me.

WIDOW QUIN (*greatly amused*) It's a sacred wonder the way that wickedness will spoil a man.

MAHON My wickedness, is it? Amn't I after saying it is himself has me destroyed, and he a liar on walls, a talker of folly, a man you'd see stretched the half of the day in the brown ferns with his belly to the sun.

WIDOW QUIN Not working at all?

MAHON The divil a work, or if he did itself, you'd see him raising up a haystack like the stalk of a rush, or driving our last cow till he broke her leg at the hip, and when he wasn't at that he'd be fooling over little birds he had—finches and felts—or making mugs at his own self in the bit of a glass we had hung on the wall.

WIDOW QUIN (*looking at* CHRISTY) What way was he so foolish? It was running wild after the girls may be?

MAHON (*with a shout of derision*) Running wild, is it? If he seen a red petticoat coming swinging over the hill, he'd be off to hide in the sticks, and you'd see him shooting out his sheep's eyes between the little twigs and the leaves, and his two ears rising like a hare looking out through a gap. Girls, indeed!

WIDOW QUIN It was drink maybe?

MAHON And he a poor fellow would get drunk on the smell of a pint. He'd a queer rotten stomach, I'm telling you, and when I gave him three pulls from my pipe a while since, he was taken with contortions till I had to send him in the ass cart to the females' nurse.

WIDOW QUIN (*clasping her hands*) Well, I never till this day heard tell of a man the like of that!

MAHON I'd take a mighty oath you didn't surely, and wasn't he the laughing joke of every female woman where four baronies meet, the way the girls would stop their weed-ing if they seen him coming the road to let a roar at him, and call him the looney of Mahon's.

WIDOW QUIN I'd give the world and all to see the like of him. What kind was he?

MAHON A small low fellow.

WIDOW QUIN And dark?

MAHON Dark and dirty.

WIDOW QUIN (*considering*) I'm thinking I seen him.

MAHON (*eagerly*) An ugly young blackguard.

WIDOW QUIN A hideous, fearful villain, and the spit of you.

MAHON What way is he fled?

WIDOW QUIN Gone over the hills to catch a coasting steamer to the north or south.

MAHON Could I pull up on him now?

WIDOW QUIN If you'll cross the sands below where the tide is out, you'll be in it as soon as himself, for he had to go round ten miles by the top of the bay. (*She points to the door*) Strike down by the head beyond and then follow on the roadway to the north and east.

(MAHON *goes abruptly*)

WIDOW QUIN (*shouting after him*) Let you give him a good vengeance when you come up with him, but don't put yourself in the power of the law, for it'd be a poor thing to see a judge in his black cap reading out his sentence on a civil warrior the like of you.

(*She swings the door to and looks at* CHRISTY, *who is cowering in terror, for a moment, then she bursts into a laugh*)

WIDOW QUIN Well, you're the walking Playboy of the Western World, and that's the poor man you had divided to his breeches belt.

CHRISTY (*looking out: then, to her*) What'll Pegeen say when she hears that story? What'll she be saying to me now?

WIDOW QUIN She'll knock the head of you, I'm thinking, and drive you from the door. God help her to be taking you for a wonder, and you a little schemer making up the story you destroyed your da.

CHRISTY (*turning to the door, nearly speechless with rage, half to himself*) To be letting on he was dead, and coming back to his life, and following after me like an old weasel tracing a rat, and coming in here laying desolation between my own self and the fine women of Ireland, and he a kind of carcase that you'd fling upon the sea . . .

WIDOW QUIN (*more soberly*) There's talking for a man's one only son.

CHRISTY (*breaking out*) His one son, is it?

May I meet him with one tooth and it aching, and one eye to be seeing seven and seventy divils in the twists of the road, and one old timber leg on him to limp into the scalding grave. (*looking out*) There he is now crossing the strands, and that the Lord God would send a high wave to wash him from the world.

WIDOW QUIN (*scandalized*) Have you no shame? (*putting her hand on his shoulder and turning him round*) What ails you? Near crying, is it?

CHRISTY (*in despair and grief*) Amn't I after seeing the love-light of the star of knowledge shining from her brow, and hearing words would put you thinking on the holy Brigid speaking to the infant saints, and now she'll be turning again, and speaking hard words to me, like an old woman with a spavindy ass she'd have, urging on a hill.

WIDOW QUIN There's poetry talk for a girl you'd see itching and scratching, and she with a stale stink of poteen on her from selling in the shop.

CHRISTY (*impatiently*) It's her like is fitted to be handling merchandise in the heavens above, and what'll I be doing now, I ask you, and I a kind of wonder was jilted by the heavens when a day was by.

(*There is a distant noise of girls' voices.* WIDOW QUIN *looks from window and comes to him, hurriedly*)

WIDOW QUIN You'll be doing like myself, I'm thinking, when I did destroy my man, for I'm above many's the day, odd times in great spirits, abroad in the sunshine, darning a stocking or stitching a shift; and odd times again looking out on the schooners, hookers, trawlers is sailing the sea, and I thinking on the gallant hairy fellows are drifting beyond, and myself long years living alone.

CHRISTY (*interested*) You're like me, so.

WIDOW QUIN I am your like, and it's for that I'm taking a fancy to you, and I with my little houseen above where there'd be myself to tend you, and none to ask were you a murderer or what at all.

CHRISTY And what would I be doing if I left Pegeen?

WIDOW QUIN I've nice jobs you could be doing, gathering shells to make a whitewash for our hut within, building up a little goose-house, or stretching a new skin on an old curragh I have, and if my hut is far from all sides, it's there you'll meet the wisest old men, I tell you, at the corner of my wheel, and it's there yourself and me will have great times whispering and hugging. . . .

VOICES (*outside, calling far away*) Christy! Christy Mahon! Christy!

CHRISTY Is it Pegeen Mike?

WIDOW QUIN It's the young girls, I'm thinking, coming to bring you to the sports below, and what is it you'll have me to tell them now?

CHRISTY Aid me for to win Pegeen. It's herself only that I'm seeking now. (WIDOW QUINN *gets up and goes to window*) Aid me for to win her, and I'll be asking God to stretch a hand to you in the hour of death, and lead you short cuts through the Meadows of Ease, and up the floor of Heaven to the Footstool of the Virgin's Son.

WIDOW QUIN There's praying.

VOICES (*nearer*) Christy! Christy Mahon!

CHRISTY (*with agitation*) They're coming. Will you swear to aid and save me for the love of Christ?

WIDOW QUIN (*looks at him for a moment*) If I aid you, will you swear to give me a right of way I want, and a mountainy ram, and a load of dung at Michaelmas, the time that you'll be master here?

CHRISTY I will, by the elements and stars of night.

WIDOW QUIN Then we'll not say a word of the old fellow, the way Pegeen won't know your story till the end of time.

CHRISTY And if he chances to return again?

WIDOW QUIN We'll swear he's a maniac and not your da. I could take an oath I seen him raving on the sands today.

(*Girls run in*)

SUSAN Come on to the sports below. Pegeen says you're to come.

SARA TANSEY The lepping's beginning, and we've a jockey's suit to fit upon you for the mule race on the sands below.

HONOR Come on, will you?

CHRISTY I will then if Pegeen's beyond.

SARA TANSEY She's in the boreen making game of Shaneen Keogh.

CHRISTY Then I'll be going to her now.

(*He runs out followed by the girls*)

WIDOW QUIN Well, if the worst comes in the end of all, it'll be great game to see there's none to pity him but a widow woman, the like of me, has buried her children and destroyed her man. (*She goes out*)

ACT THREE

(*Scene—as before. Later in the day.* JIMMY *comes in, slightly drunk*)

JIMMY (*calls*) Pegeen! (*crosses to inner door*) Pegeen Mike! (*comes back again into the room*) Pegeen! (PHILLY *comes in in the same state*) (*to* PHILLY) Did you see herself?

PHILLY I did not; but I sent Shawn Keogh with the ass cart for to bear him home. (*trying cupboards which are locked*) Well, isn't he a nasty man to get into such staggers at a morning wake? and isn't herself the divil's daughter for locking, and she so fussy after that young gaffer, you might take your death with drought and none to heed you?

JIMMY It's little wonder she'd be fussy, and he after bringing bankrupt ruin on the roulette man, and the trick-o'-the-loop man, and breaking the nose of the cockshot-man, and winning all in the sports below, racing, lepping, dancing, and the Lord knows what! He's right luck, I'm telling you.

PHILLY If he has, he'll be rightly hobbled yet, and he not able to say ten words without making a brag of the way he killed his father, and the great blow he hit with the loy.

JIMMY A man can't hang by his own informing, and his father should be rotten by now.

(OLD MAHON *passes window slowly*)

PHILLY Supposing a man's digging spuds in that field with a long spade, and supposing he flings up the two halves of that skull, what'll be said then in the papers and the courts of law?

JIMMY They'd say it was an old Dane, maybe, was drowned in the flood. (OLD MAHON *comes in and sits down near door listening*) Did you never hear tell of the skulls they have in the city of Dublin, ranged out like blue jugs in a cabin of Connaught?

PHILLY And you believe that?

JIMMY (*pugnaciously*) Didn't a lad see them and he after coming from harvesting in the Liverpool boat? "They have them there," says he, "making a show of the great people there was one time walking the world. White skulls and black skulls and yellow skulls, and some with full teeth, and some haven't only but one."

PHILLY It was no lie, maybe, for when I was a young lad there was a graveyard beyond the house with the remnants of a man who had thighs as long as your arm. He was a horrid man, I'm telling you, and there was many a fine Sunday I'd put him together for fun, and he with shiny bones, you wouldn't meet the like of these days in the cities of the world.

MAHON (*getting up*) You wouldn't, is it? Lay your eyes on that skull, and tell me where and when there was another the like of it, is splintered only from the blow of a loy.

PHILLY Glory be to God! And who hit you at all?

MAHON (*triumphantly*) It was my own son hit me. Would you believe that?

JIMMY Well, there's wonders hidden in the heart of man!

PHILLY (*suspiciously*) And what way was it done?

MAHON (*wandering about the room*) I'm after walking hundreds and long scores of miles, winning clean beds and the fill of my belly four times in the day, and I doing nothing but telling stories of that naked truth. (*He comes to them a little aggressively*) Give me a supeen and I'll tell you now.

(WIDOW QUIN *comes in and stands aghast behind him. He is facing* JIMMY *and* PHILLY, *who are on the left*)

JIMMY Ask herself beyond. She's the stuff hidden in her shawl.

WIDOW QUIN (*coming to* MAHON *quickly*) You here, is it? You didn't go far at all?

MAHON I seen the coasting steamer passing, and I got a drought upon me and a cramping leg, so I said, "The divil go along with him," and turned again. (*looking under her shawl*) And let you give me a supeen, for I'm destroyed travelling since Tuesday was a week.

WIDOW QUIN (*getting a glass, in a cajoling tone*) Sit down then by the fire and take your ease for a space. You've a right to be destroyed indeed, with your walking, and fighting, and facing the sun (*giving him poteen from a stone jar she has brought in*). There now is a drink for you, and may it be to your happiness and length of life.

MAHON (*taking glass greedily and sitting down by fire*) God increase you!

WIDOW QUIN (*taking men to the right stealthily*) Do you know what? That man's raving from his wound today, for I met him a while since telling a rambling tale of a tinker had him destroyed. Then he heard of Christy's deed, and he up and says it was his son had cracked his skull. O isn't madness a fright, for he'll go killing someone yet, and he thinking it's the man has struck him so?

JIMMY (*entirely convinced*) It's a fright, surely. I knew a party was kicked in the head by a red mare, and he went killing horses a great while, till he eat the insides of a clock and died after.

PHILLY (*with suspicion*) Did he see Christy?

WIDOW QUIN He didn't. (*with a warning gesture*) Let you not be putting him in mind of him, or you'll be likely summoned if there's murder done. (*looking round at* MAHON) Whisht! He's listening. Wait now till you hear me taking him easy and unravelling all. (*She goes to* MAHON) And what way are you feeling, mister? Are you in contentment now?

MAHON (*slightly emotional from his drink*) I'm poorly only, for it's a hard story the way I'm left today, when it was I did tend him from his hour of birth, and he a dunce never reached his second book, the way he'd come from school, many's the day, with his legs lamed under him, and he blackened with his beatings like a tinker's ass. It's a hard story, I'm saying, the way some do have their next and nighest raising up a hand of murder on them, and some is lonesome getting their death with lamentation in the dead of night.

WIDOW QUIN (*not knowing what to say*) To hear you talking so quiet, who'd know you were the same fellow we seen pass today?

MAHON I'm the same surely. The wrack and ruin of three score years; and it's a terror to live that length, I tell you, and to have your sons going to the dogs against you, and you wore out scolding them, and skelping them, and God knows what.

PHILLY (*to* JIMMY) He's not raving. (*to* WIDOW QUIN) Will you ask him what kind was his son?

WIDOW QUIN (*to* MAHON, *with a peculiar look*) Was your son that hit you a lad of one year and a score maybe, a great hand at racing and lepping and licking the world?

MAHON (*turning on her with a roar of rage*) Didn't you hear me say he was the fool of men, the way from this out he'll know the orphan's lot with old and young making game of him and they swearing, raging, kicking at him like a mangy cur.

(*A great burst of cheering outside, some way off*)

MAHON (*putting his hands to his ears*) What in the name of God do they want roaring below?

WIDOW QUIN (*with the shade of a smile*) They're cheering a young lad, the champion Playboy of the Western World.

(*More cheering*)

MAHON (*going to window*) It'd split my heart to hear them, and I with pulses in my brain-pan for a week gone by. Is it racing they are?

JIMMY (*looking from door*) It is then. They are mounting him for the mule race will be run upon the sands. That's the playboy on the winkered mule.

MAHON (*puzzled*) That lad, is it? If you said it was a fool he was, I'd have laid a mighty oath he was the likeness of my wandering son (*uneasily, putting his hand to his head*). Faith, I'm thinking I'll go walking for to view the race.

WIDOW QUIN (*stopping him, sharply*) You will not. You'd best take the road to Belmullet, and not be dilly-dallying in this place where there isn't a spot you could sleep.

PHILLY (*coming forward*) Don't mind her. Mount there on the bench and you'll have a view of the whole. They're hurrying before the tide will rise, and it'd be near over if you went down the pathway through the crags below.

MAHON (*mounts on bench,* WIDOW QUIN *beside him*) That's a right view again the edge of the sea. They're coming now from the point. He'd leading. Who is he at all?

WIDOW QUIN He's the champion of the world, I tell you, and there isn't a hop'orth isn't falling lucky to his hands today.

PHILLY (*looking out, interested in the race*) Look at that. They're pressing him now.

JIMMY He'll win it yet.

PHILLY Take your time, Jimmy Farrell. It's too soon to say.

WIDOW QUIN (*shouting*) Watch him taking the gate. There's riding.

JIMMY (*cheering*) More power to the young lad!

MAHON He's passing the third.

JIMMY He'll lick them yet!

WIDOW QUIN He'd lick them if he was running races with a score itself.

MAHON Look at the mule he has, kicking the stars.

WIDOW QUIN There was a lep! (*catching hold of* MAHON *in her excitement*) He's fallen! He's mounted again! Faith, he's passing them all!

JIMMY Look at him skelping her!

PHILLY And the mountain girls hooshing him on!

JIMMY   It's the last turn! The post's cleared for them now!

MAHON   Look at the narrow place. He'll be into the bogs! (*with a yell*) Good rider! He's through it again!

JIMMY   He neck and neck!

MAHON   Good boy to him! Flames, but he's in!

(*Great cheering, in which all join*)

MAHON   (*with hesitation*) What's that? They're raising him up. They're coming this way. (*with a roar of rage and astonishment*) It's Christy! by the stars of God! I'd know his way of spitting and he astride the moon.

(*He jumps down and makes for the door, but* WIDOW QUIN *catches him and pulls him back*)

WIDOW QUIN   Stay quiet, will you. That's not your son. (*to* JIMMY) Stop him, or you'll get a month for the abetting of manslaughter and be fined as well.

JIMMY   I'll hold him.

MAHON   (*struggling*) Let me out! Let me out, the lot of you! till I have my vengeance on his head today.

WIDOW QUIN   (*shaking him, vehemently*) That's not your son. That's a man is going to make a marriage with the daughter of this house, a place with fine trade, with a license, and with poteen too.

MAHON   (*amazed*) That man marrying a decent and a moneyed girl! Is it mad yous are? Is it in a crazy house for females that I'm landed now?

WIDOW QUIN   It's mad yourself is with the blow upon your head. That lad is the wonder of the Western World.

MAHON   I seen it's my son.

WIDOW QUIN   You seen that you're mad. (*cheering outside*) Do you hear them cheering him in the zig-zags of the road? Aren't you after saying that your son's a fool, and how would they be cheering a true idiot born?

MAHON   (*getting distressed*) It's maybe out of reason that that man's himself. (*cheering again*) There's none surely will go cheering him. Oh, I'm raving with a madness that would fright the world! (*He sits down with his hand to his head*) There was one time I seen ten scarlet divils letting on they'd cork my spirit in a gallon can; and one time I seen rats as big as badgers sucking the life blood from the butt of my lug; but I never till this day confused that dribbling idiot with a likely man. I'm destroyed surely.

WIDOW QUIN   And who'd wonder when it's your brain-pan that is gaping now?

MAHON   Then the blight of the sacred drought upon myself and him, for I never went mad to this day, and I not three weeks with the Limerick girls drinking myself silly, and parlatic from the dusk to dawn. (*to* WIDOW QUIN, *suddenly*) Is my visage astray?

WIDOW QUIN   It is then. You're a sniggering maniac, a child could see.

MAHON   (*getting up more cheerfully*) Then I'd best be going to the union beyond, and there'll be a welcome before me, I tell you (*with great pride*), and I a terrible and fearful case, the way that there I was one time, screeching in a straitened waistcoat, with seven doctors writing out my sayings in a printed book. Would you believe that?

WIDOW QUIN   If you're a wonder itself, you'd best be hasty, for them lads caught a maniac one time and pelted the poor creature till he ran out, raving and foaming, and was drowned in the sea.

MAHON   (*with philosophy*) It's true mankind is the divil when your head's astray. Let me out now and I'll slip down the boreen, and not see them so.

WIDOW QUIN   (*showing him out*) That's it. Run to the right, and not a one will see.

(*He runs off*)

PHILLY   (*wisely*) You're at some gaming, Widow Quin; but I'll walk after him and give him his dinner and a time to rest, and I'll see then if he's raving or as sane as you.

WIDOW QUIN   (*annoyed*) If you go near that lad, let you be wary of your head, I'm saying. Didn't you hear him telling he was crazed at times?

PHILLY   I heard him telling a power; and I'm thinking we'll have right sport, before night will fall. (*He goes out*)

JIMMY   Well, Philly's a conceited and foolish man. How could that madman have his senses and his brain-pan slit? I'll go after them and see him turn on Philly now.

(*He goes;* WIDOW QUIN *hides poteen behind counter. Then hubbub outside*)

VOICES   There you are! Good jumper! Grand lepper! Darlint boy! He's the racer! Bear him on, will you!

(CHRISTY *comes in, in Jockey's dress, with* PEGEEN MIKE, SARA, *and other girls, and men*)

PEGEEN   (*to crowd*) Go on now and don't destroy him and he drenching with sweat. Go along, I'm saying, and have your tug-of-warring till he's dried his skin.

CROWD   Here's his prizes! A bagpipes! A

fiddle was played by a poet in the years gone by! A flat and three-thorned blackthorn would lick the scholars out of Dublin town!

CHRISTY (*taking prizes from the men*) Thank you kindly, the lot of you. But you'd say it was little only I did this day if you'd seen me a while since striking my one single blow.

TOWN CRIER (*outside, ringing a bell*) Take notice, last event of this day! Tug-of-warring on the green below! Come on, the lot of you! Great achievements for all Mayo men!

PEGEEN Go on, and leave him for to rest and dry. Go on, I tell you, for he'll do no more. (*She hustles crowd out;* WIDOW QUIN *following them*)

MEN (*going*) Come on then. Good luck for the while!

PEGEEN (*radiantly, wiping his face with her shawl*) Well, you're the lad, and you'll have great times from this out when you could win that wealth of prizes, and you sweating in the heat of noon!

CHRISTY (*looking at her with delight*) I'll have great times if I win the crowning prize I'm seeking now, and that's your promise that you'll wed me in a fortnight, when our banns is called.

PEGEEN (*backing away from him*) You're right daring to go ask me that, when all knows you'll be starting to some girl in your own townland, when your father's rotten in four months, or five.

CHRISTY (*indignantly*) Starting from you, is it? (*He follows her*) I will not, then, and when the airs is warming in four months, or five, it's then yourself and me should be pacing Neifin in the dews of night, the times sweet smells do be rising, and you'd see a little shiny new moon, maybe, sinking on the hills.

PEGEEN (*looking at him playfully*) And it's that kind of a poacher's love you'd make, Christy Mahon, on the sides of Neifin, when the night is down?

CHRISTY It's little you'll think if my love's a poacher's, or an earl's itself, when you'll feel my two hands stretched around you, and I squeezing kisses on your puckered lips, till I'd feel a kind of pity for the Lord God is all ages sitting lonesome in his golden chair.

PEGEEN That'll be right fun, Christy Mahon, and any girl would walk her heart out before she'd meet a young man was your like for eloquence, or talk, at all.

CHRISTY (*encouraged*) Let you wait, to hear me talking, till we're astray in Erris, when

Good Friday's by, drinking a sup from a well, and making mighty kisses with our wetted mouths, or gaming in a gap or sunshine, with yourself stretched back onto your necklace, in the flowers of the earth.

PEGEEN (*in a lower voice, moved by his tone*) I'd be nice so, is it?

CHRISTY (*with rapture*) If the mitred bishops seen you that time, they'd be the like of the holy prophets, I'm thinking, do be straining the bars of Paradise to lay eyes on the Lady Helen of Troy, and she abroad, pacing back and forward, with a nosegay in her golden shawl.

PEGEEN (*with real tenderness*) And what is it I have, Christy Mahon, to make me fitting entertainment for the like of you, that has such poet's talking, and such bravery of heart?

CHRISTY (*in a low voice*) Isn't there the light of seven heavens in your heart alone, the way you'll be an angel's lamp to me from this out, and I abroad in the darkness, spearing salmons in the Owen, or the Carrowmore?

PEGEEN If I was your wife, I'd be along with you those nights, Christy Mahon, the way you'd see I was a great hand at coaxing bailiffs, or coining funny nick-names for the stars of night.

CHRISTY You, is it? Taking your death in the hailstones, or in the fogs of dawn.

PEGEEN Yourself and me would shelter easy in a narrow bush (*with a qualm of dread*), but we're only talking, maybe, for this would be a poor, thatched place to hold a fine lad is the like of you.

CHRISTY (*putting his arm round her*) If I wasn't a good Christian, it's on my naked knees I'd be saying my prayers and paters to every jackstraw you have roofing your head, and every stony pebble is paving the laneway to your door.

PEGEEN (*radiantly*) If that's the truth, I'll be burning candles from this out to the miracles of God that have brought you from the south today, and I, with my gowns bought ready, the way that I can wed you, and not wait at all.

CHRISTY It's miracles, and that's the truth. Me there toiling a long while, and walking a long while, not knowing at all I was drawing all times nearer to this holy day.

PEGEEN And myself, a girl, was tempted often to go sailing the seas till I'd marry a Jew-man, with ten kegs of gold, and I not knowing at all there was the like of you drawing nearer, like the stars of God.

CHRISTY And to think I'm long years hearing women talking that talk, to all bloody fools, and this the first time I've heard the like of your voice talking sweetly for my own delight.

PEGEEN　And to think it's me is talking sweetly, Christy Mahon, and I the fright of seven townlands for my biting tongue. Well, the heart's a wonder; and, I'm thinking, there won't be our like in Mayo, for gallant lovers, from this hour, today. (*Drunken singing is heard outside*) There's my father coming from the wake, and when he's had his sleep we'll tell him, for he's peaceful then.

(*They separate*)

MICHAEL　(*singing outside*)
　　The jailor and the turnkey
　　They quickly ran us down,
　　And brought us back as prisoners
　　Once more to Cavan town.

(*He comes in supported by* SHAWN)

　　There we lay bewailing
　　All in a prison bound. . . .

(*He sees* CHRISTY. *Goes and shakes him drunkenly by the hand, while* PEGEEN *and* SHAWN *talk on the left*)

MICHAEL　(*to* CHRISTY)　The blessing of God and the holy angels on your head, young fellow. I hear tell you're after winning all in the sports below; and wasn't it a shame I didn't bear you along with me to Kate Cassidy's wake, a fine, stout lad, the like of you, for you'd never see the match of it for flows of drink, the way when we sunk her bones at noonday in her narrow grave, there were five men, aye, and six men, stretched out retching speechless on the holy stones.

CHRISTY　(*uneasily, watching* PEGEEN)　Is that the truth?

MICHAEL　It is then, and aren't you a louty schemer to go burying your poor father unbeknownst when you'd a right to throw him on the crupper of a Kerry mule and drive him westwards, like holy Joseph in the days gone by, the way we could have given him a decent burial, and not have him rotting beyond, and not a Christian drinking a smart drop to the glory of his soul?

CHRISTY　(*gruffly*)　It's well enough he's lying, for the likes of him.

MICHAEL　(*slapping him on the back*) Well, aren't you a hardened slayer? It'll be a poor thing for the household man where you go sniffing for a female wife; and (*pointing to* SHAWN) look beyond at that shy and decent Christian I have chosen for my daughter's hand, and I after getting the gilded dispensation this day for to wed them now.

CHRISTY　And you'll be wedding them this day, is it?

MICHAEL　(*drawing himself up*)　Aye. Are you thinking, if I'm drunk itself, I'd leave my daughter living single with a little frisky rascal is the like of you?

PEGEEN　(*breaking away from* SHAWN)　Is it the truth the dispensation's come?

MICHAEL　(*triumphantly*)　Father Reilly's after reading it in gallous Latin, and "It's come in the nick of time," says he; "so I'll wed them in a hurry, dreading that young gaffer who'd capsize the stars."

PEGEEN　(*fiercely*)　He's missed his nick of time, for it's that lad, Christy Mahon, that I'm wedding now.

MICHAEL　(*loudly with horror*)　You'd be making him a son to me, and he wet and crusted with his father's blood?

PEGEEN　Aye. Wouldn't it be a bitter thing for a girl to go marrying the like of Shaneen, and he a middling kind of a scarecrow, with no savagery or fine words in him at all?

MICHAEL　(*gasping and sinking on a chair*) Oh, aren't you a heathen daughter to go shaking the fat of my heart, and I swamped and drownded with the weight of drink? Would you have them turning on me the way that I'd be roaring to the dawn of day with the wind upon my heart? Have you not a word to aid me, Shaneen? Are you not jealous at all?

SHAWN　(*in great misery*)　I'd be afeard to be jealous of a man did slay his da.

PEGEEN　Well, it'd be a poor thing to go marrying your like. I'm seeing there's a world of peril for an orphan girl, and isn't it a great blessing I didn't wed you, before himself came walking from the west or south?

SHAWN　It's a queer story you'd go picking a dirty tramp up from the highways of the world.

PEGEEN　(*playfully*)　And you think you're a likely beau to go straying along with, the shiny Sundays of the opening year, when it's sooner on a bullock's liver you'd put a poor girl thinking than on the lily or the rose?

SHAWN　And have you no mind of my weight of passion, and the holy dispensation, and the drift of heifers I am giving, and the golden ring?

PEGEEN　I'm thinking you're too fine for the like of me, Shawn Keogh of Killakeen, and let you go off till you'd find a radiant lady with droves of bullocks on the plains of Meath, and herself bedizened in the diamond jewelleries of Pharaoh's ma. That'd be your match, Shaneen. So God save you now!

(*She retreats behind* CHRISTY)

SHAWN   Won't you hear me telling you . . . ?

CHRISTY (*with ferocity*)   Take yourself from this, young fellow, or I'll maybe add a murder to my deeds today.

MICHAEL (*springing up with a shriek*)   Murder is it? Is it mad yous are? Would you go making murder in this place, and it piled with poteen for our drink tonight? Go on to the foreshore if it's fighting you want, where the rising tide will wash all traces from the memory of man.

(*Pushing* SHAWN *towards* CHRISTY)

SHAWN (*shaking himself free, and getting behind* MICHAEL)   I'll not fight him, Michael James. I'd liefer live a bachelor, simmering in passions to the end of time, than face a lepping savage the like of him has descended from the Lord knows where. Strike him yourself, Michael James, or you'll lose my drift of heifers and my blue bull from Sneem.

MICHAEL   Is it me fight him, when it's father-slaying he's bred to now? (*pushing* SHAWN) Go on you fool and fight him now.

SHAWN (*coming forward a little*)   Will I strike him with my hand?

MICHAEL   Take the loy is on your western side.

SHAWN   I'd be afeard of the gallows if I struck him with that.

CHRISTY (*taking up the loy*)   Then I'll make you face the gallows or quit off from this.

(SHAWN *flies out of the door*)

CHRISTY   Well, fine weather be after him, (*going to* MICHAEL, *coaxingly*) and I'm thinking you wouldn't wish to have that quaking blackguard in your house at all. Let you give us your blessing and hear her swear her faith to me, for I'm mounted on the springtide of the stars of luck, the way it'll be good for any to have me in the house.

PEGEEN (*at the other side of* MICHAEL) Bless us now, for I swear to God I'll wed him, and I'll not renege.

MICHAEL (*standing up in the center, holding on to both of them*)   It's the will of God, I'm thinking, that all should win an easy or a cruel end, and it's the will of God that all should rear up lengthy families for the nurture of the earth. What's a single man, I ask you, eating a bit in one house and drinking a sup in another, and he with no place of his own, like an old braying jackass strayed upon the rocks? (*to* CHRISTY) It's many would be in dread to bring your like into their house for to end them, maybe, with a sudden end; but I'm a decent man of Ireland, and I liefer face the grave untimely and I seeing a score of grandsons growing up little gallant swearers by the name of God, than go peopling my bedside with puny weeds the like of what you'd breed, I'm thinking, out of Shaneen Keogh. (*He joins their hands*) A daring fellow is the jewel of the world, and a man did split his father's middle with a single clout, should have the bravery of ten, so may God and Mary and St. Patrick bless you, and increase you from this mortal day.

CHRISTY *and* PEGEEN   Amen, O Lord!

(*Hubbub outside.* OLD MAHON *rushes in, followed by all the crowd, and* WIDOW QUIN. *He makes a rush at* CHRISTY, *knocks him down, and begins to beat him*)

PEGEEN (*dragging back his arm*)   Stop that, will you. Who are you at all?

MAHON   His father, God forgive me!

PEGEEN (*drawing back*)   Is it rose from the dead?

MAHON   Do you think I look so easy quenched with the tap of a loy? (*beats* CHRISTY *again*)

PEGEEN (*glaring at* CHRISTY)   And it's lies you told, letting on you had him slitted, and you nothing at all.

CHRISTY (*catching* MAHON's *stick*)   He's not my father. He's a raving maniac would scare the world. (*pointing to* WIDOW QUIN) Herself knows it is true.

CROWD   You're fooling Pegeen! The Widow Quin seen him this day, and you likely knew! You're a liar!

CHRISTY (*dumbfounded*)   It's himself was a liar, lying stretched out with an open head on him, letting on he was dead.

MAHON   Weren't you off racing the hills before I got my breath with the start I had seeing you turn on me at all?

PEGEEN   And to think of the coaxing glory we had given him, and he after doing nothing but hitting a soft blow and chasing northward in a sweat of fear. Quit off from this.

CHRISTY (*piteously*)   You've seen my doings this day, and let you save me from the old man; for why would you be in such a scorch of haste to spur me to destruction now?

PEGEEN   It's there your treachery is spurring me, till I'm hard set to think you're the one I'm after lacing in my heart-strings half-an-hour gone by. (*to* MAHON) Take him on from this, for I think bad the world should see me raging for a Munster liar, and the fool of men.

MAHON   Rise up now to retribution, and come on with me.

CROWD   (*jeeringly*) There's the playboy! There's the lad thought he'd rule the roost in Mayo. Slate him now, mister.

CHRISTY   (*getting up in shy terror*) What is it drives you to torment me here, when I'd asked the thunders of the might of God to blast me if I ever did hurt to any saving only that one single blow.

MAHON   (*loudly*) If you didn't, you're a poor good-for-nothing, and isn't it by the like of you the sins of the whole world are committed?

CHRISTY   (*raising his hands*) In the name of the Almighty God. . . .

MAHON   Leave troubling the Lord God. Would you have him sending down droughts, and fevers, and the old hen and the cholera morbus?

CHRISTY   (*to* WIDOW QUIN) Will you come between us and protect me now?

WIDOW QUIN   I've tried a lot, God help me, and my share is done.

CHRISTY   (*looking round in desperation*) And I must go back into my torment is it, or run off like a vagabond straying through the Unions with the dusts of August making mud-stains in the gullet of my throat, or the winds of March blowing on me till I'd take an oath I felt them making whistles of my ribs within?

SARA   Ask Pegeen to aid you. Her like does often change.

CHRISTY   I will not then, for there's torment in the splendor of her like, and she a girl any moon of midnight would take pride to meet, facing southwards on the heaths of Keel. But what did I want crawling forward to scorch my understanding at her flaming brow?

PEGEEN   (*to* MAHON, *vehemently, fearing she will break into tears*) Take him on from this or I'll set the young lads to destroy him here.

MAHON   (*going to him, shaking his stick*) Come on now if you wouldn't have the company to see you skelped.

PEGEEN   (*half laughing, through her tears*) That's it, now the world will see him pandied, and he an ugly liar was playing off the hero, and the fright of men.

CHRISTY   (*to* MAHON, *very sharply*) Leave me go!

CROWD   That's it. Now Christy. If them two set fighting, it will lick the world.

MAHON   (*making a grab at* CHRISTY) Come here to me.

CHRISTY   (*more threateningly*) Leave me go, I'm saying.

MAHON   I will maybe, when your legs is limping, and your back is blue.

CROWD   Keep it up, the two of you. I'll back the old one. Now the playboy.

CHRISTY   (*in low and intense voice*) Shut your yelling, for if you're after making a mighty man of me this day by the power of a lie, you're setting me now to think if it's a poor thing to be lonesome, it's worse maybe to go mixing with the fools of earth.

(MAHON *makes a movement towards him*)

CHRISTY   (*almost shouting*) Keep off . . . lest I do show a blow unto the lot of you would set the guardian angels winking in the clouds above.

(*He swings round with a sudden rapid movement and picks up a loy*)

CROWD   (*half frightened, half amused*) He's going mad! Mind yourselves! Run from the idiot!

CHRISTY   If I am an idiot, I'm after hearing my voice this day saying words would raise the topknot on a poet in a merchant's town. I've won your racing, and your lepping, and . . .

MAHON   Shut your gullet and come on with me.

CHRISTY   I'm going, but I'll stretch you first. (*He runs at old* MAHON *with the loy, chases him out of the door, followed by* CROWD *and* WIDOW QUIN. *There is a great noise outside, then a yell, and dead silence for a moment.* CHRISTY *comes in, half dazed, and goes to fire*)

WIDOW QUIN   (*coming in, hurriedly, and going to him*) They're turning again you. Come on, or you'll be hanged, indeed.

CHRISTY   I'm thinking, from this out, Pegeen'll be giving me praises the same as in the hours gone by.

WIDOW QUIN   (*impatiently*) Come by the back door. I'd think bad to have you stifled on the gallows tree.

CHRISTY   (*indignantly*) I will not, then. What good'd be my life-time, if I left Pegeen?

WIDOW QUIN   Come on, and you'll be no worse than you were last night; and you with a double murder this time to be telling to the girls.

CHRISTY   I'll not leave Pegeen Mike.

WIDOW QUIN   (*impatiently*) Isn't there the match of her in every parish public, from Binghamstown unto the plain of Meath? Come on, I tell you, and I'll find you finer sweet-hearts at each waning moon.

CHRISTY   It's Pegeen I'm seeking only, and what'd I care if you brought me a drift of chosen females, standing in their shifts itself, maybe, from this place to the Eastern World?

SARA (*runs in, pulling off one of her petti-coats*)   They're going to hang him. (*holding out petticoat and shawl*) Fit these upon him, and let him run off to the east.

WIDOW QUIN   He's raving now; but we'll fit them on him, and I'll take him, in the ferry, to the Achill boat.

CHRISTY (*struggling feebly*)   Leave me go, will you? When I'm thinking of my luck today, for she will wed me surely, and I a proven hero in the end of all.

(*They try to fasten petticoat round him*)

WIDOW QUIN   Take his left hand, and we'll pull him now. Come on, young fellow.

CHRISTY (*suddenly starting up*)   You'll be taking me from her? You're jealous, is it, of her wedding me? Go on from this.

(*He snatches up a stool, and threatens them with it*)

WIDOW QUIN (*going*)   It's in the mad-house they should put him, not in jail, at all. We'll go by the back door, to call the doctor, and we'll save him so.

(*She goes out, with* SARA, *through inner room. Men crowd in the doorway.* CHRISTY *sits down again by the fire*)

MICHAEL (*in a terrified whisper*)   Is the old lad killed surely?

PHILLY   I'm after feeling the last gasps quitting his heart.

(*They peer in at* CHRISTY)

MICHAEL (*with a rope*)   Look at the way he is. Twist a hangman's knot on it, and slip it over his head, while he's not minding at all.

PHILLY   Let you take it, Shaneen. You're the soberest of all that's here.

SHAWN   Is it me to go near him, and he the wickedest and worst with me? Let you take it, Pegeen Mike.

PEGEEN   Come on, so.

(*She goes forward with the others, and they drop the double hitch over his head*)

CHRISTY   What ails you?

SHAWN (*triumphantly, as they pull the rope tight on his arms*)   Come on to the peelers, till they stretch you now.

CHRISTY   Me!

MICHAEL   If we took pity on you, the Lord God would, maybe, bring us ruin from the law

today, so you'd best come easy, for hanging is an easy and a speedy end.

CHRISTY   I'll not stir. (*to* PEGEEN) And what is it you'll say to me, and I after doing it this time in the face of all?

PEGEEN   I'll say, a strange man is a marvel, with his mighty talk; but what's a squabble in your back yard, and the blow of a loy, have taught me that there's a great gap between a gallous story and a dirty deed. (*to* MEN) Take him on from this, or the lot of us will be likely put on trial for his deed today.

CHRISTY (*with horror in his voice*)   And it's yourself will send me off, to have a horny-fingered hangman hitching his bloody slip-knots at the butt of my ear.

MEN (*pulling rope*)   Come on, will you?

(*He is pulled down on the floor*)

CHRISTY (*twisting his legs round the table*) Cut the rope, Pegeen, and I'll quit the lot of you, and live from this out, like the madmen of Keel, eating muck and green weeds, on the faces of the cliffs.

PEGEEN   And leave us to hang, is it, for a saucy liar, the like of you? (*to* MEN) Take him on, out from this.

SHAWN   Pull a twist on his neck, and squeeze him so.

PHILLY   Twist yourself. Sure he cannot hurt you, if you keep your distance from his teeth alone.

SHAWN   I'm afeard of him. (*to* PEGEEN) Lift a lighted sod, will you, and scorch his leg.

PEGEEN (*blowing the fire, with a bellows*) Leave go now, young fellow, or I'll scorch your shins.

CHRISTY   You're blowing for to torture me. (*His voice rising and growing stronger*) That's your kind, is it? Then let the lot of you be wary, for, if I've to face the gallows, I'll have a gay march down, I tell you, and shed the blood of some of you before I die.

SHAWN (*in terror*)   Keep a good hold, Philly. Be wary, for the love of God: For I'm think-ing he would liefest wreak his pains on me.

CHRISTY (*almost gaily*)   If I do lay my hands on you, it's the way you'll be at the fall of night, hanging as a scarecrow for the fowls of hell. Ah, you'll have a gallous jaunt I'm say-ing, coaching out through Limbo with my father's ghost.

SHAWN (*to* PEGEEN)   Make haste, will you? Oh, isn't he a holy terror, and isn't it true for Father Reilly, that all drink's a curse that has the lot of you so shaky and uncertain now?

CHRISTY   If I can wring a neck among you,

I'll have a royal judgment looking on the trembling jury in the courts of law. And won't there be crying out in Mayo the day I'm stretched upon the rope with ladies in their silks and satins snivelling in their lacy kerchiefs, and they rhyming songs and ballads on the terror of my fate?

(*He squirms round on the floor and bites* SHAWN's *leg*)

SHAWN (*shrieking*) My leg's bit on me. He's the like of a mad dog, I'm thinking, the way that I will surely die.

CHRISTY (*delighted with himself*) You will then, the way you can shake out hell's flags of welcome for my coming in two weeks or three, for I'm thinking Satan hasn't many have killed their da in Kerry, and in Mayo too.

(OLD MAHON *comes in behind on all fours and looks on unnoticed*)

MEN (*to* PEGEEN) Bring the sod, will you?

PEGEEN (*coming over*) God help him so.
(*Burns his leg*)

CHRISTY (*kicking and screaming*) O, glory be to God!

(*He kicks loose from the table, and they all drag him towards the door*)

JIMMY (*seeing old* MAHON) Will you look what's come in?

(*They all drop* CHRISTY *and run left*)

CHRISTY (*scrambling on his knees face to face with old* MAHON) Are you coming to be be killed a third time, or what ails you now?

MAHON For what is it they have you tied?

CHRISTY They're taking me to the peelers to have me hanged for slaying you.

MICHAEL (*apologetically*) It is the will of God that all should guard their little cabins from the treachery of law, and what would my daughter be doing if I was ruined or was hanged itself?

MAHON (*grimly, loosening* CHRISTY) It's little I care if you put a bag on her back, and went picking cockles till the hour of death; but my son and myself will be going our own way, and we'll have great times from this out telling stories of the villainy of Mayo, and the fools is here. (*to* CHRISTY, *who is freed*) Come on now.

CHRISTY Go with you, is it? I will then, like a gallant captain with his heathen slave. Go on now and I'll see you from this day stewing my oatmeal and washing my spuds, for I'm master of all fights from now. (*pushing* MAHON) Go on, I'm saying.

MAHON Is it me?

CHRISTY Not a word out of you. Go on from this.

MAHON (*walking out and looking back at* CHRISTY *over his shoulder*) Glory be to God! (*with a broad smile*) I am crazy again! (*goes*)

CHRISTY Ten thousand blessings upon all that's here, for you've turned me a likely gaffer in the end of all, the way I'll go romancing through a romping lifetime from this hour to the drawing of the judgment day. (*He goes out*)

MICHAEL By the will of God, we'll have peace now for our drinks. Will you draw the porter, Pegeen?

SHAWN (*going up to her*) It's a miracle Father Reilly can wed us in the end of all, and we'll have none to trouble us when his vicious bite is healed.

PEGEEN (*hitting him a box on the ear*) Quit my sight. (*putting her shawl over her head and breaking out into wild lamentations*) Oh my grief, I've lost him surely. I've lost the only Playboy of the Western World.

RIDERS TO THE SEA

CAST OF CHARACTERS

MAURYA, *an old woman*
BARTLEY, *her son*
CATHLEEN, *her daughter*
NORA, *a younger daughter*
MEN AND WOMEN

SCENE   *An Island off the West of Ireland.*

(*Cottage kitchen, with nets, oil-skins, spinning-wheel, some new boards standing by the wall, etc.* CATHLEEN, *a girl of about twenty, finishes kneading cake, and puts it down in the pot-oven by the fire; then wipes her hands, and begins to spin at the wheel.* NORA, *a young girl, puts her head in at the door*)

NORA (*in a low voice*)   Where is she?

CATHLEEN   She's lying down, God help her, and may be sleeping, if she's able.

(NORA *comes in softly, and takes a bundle from under her shawl*)

CATHLEEN (*spinning the wheel rapidly*) What is it you have?

NORA   The young priest is after bringing them. It's a shirt and a plain stocking were got off a drowned man in Donegal.

(CATHLEEN *stops her wheel with a sudden movement, and leans out to listen*)

NORA   We're to find out if it's Michael's they are, some time herself will be down looking by the sea.

CATHLEEN   How would they be Michael's, Nora? How would he go the length of that way to the far north?

NORA   The young priest says he's known the like of it. "If it's Michael's they are," says he, "you can tell herself he's got a clean burial by

the grace of God, and if they're not his, let no one say a word about them, for she'll be getting her death," says he, "with crying and lamenting."

(*The door which* NORA *half closed is blown open by a gust of wind*)

CATHLEEN (*looking out anxiously*)   Did you ask him would he stop Bartley going this day with the horses to the Galway fair?

NORA   "I won't stop him," says he, "but let you not be afraid. Herself does be saying prayers half through the night, and the Almighty God won't leave her destitute," say he, "with no son living."

CATHLEEN   Is the sea bad by the white rocks, Nora?

NORA   Middling bad, God help us. There's a great roaring in the west, and it's worse it'll be getting when the tide's turned to the wind. (*She goes over to the table with the bundle*) Shall I open it now?

CATHLEEN   Maybe she'd wake up on us, and come in before we'd done. (*coming to the table*) It's a long time we'll be, and the two of us crying.

NORA (*goes to the inner door and listens*) She's moving about on the bed. She'll be coming in a minute.

CATHLEEN   Give me the ladder, and I'll put them up in the turf-loft, the way she won't know of them at all, and maybe when the tide turns she'll be going down to see would he be floating from the east.

(*They put the ladder against the gable of the chimney;* CATHLEEN *goes up a few steps and hides the bundle in the turf-loft.* MAURYA *comes from the inner room*)

MAURYA (*looking up at* CATHLEEN *and speaking querulously*)   Isn't it turf enough you have for this day and evening?

CATHLEEN   There's a cake baking at the fire for a short space (*throwing down the turf*) and Bartley will want it when the tide turns if he goes to Connemara.

Riders to the Sea appears in *The Complete Works of John M. Synge,* published 1935 by Random House, Inc.

(NORA *picks up the turf and puts it round the pot-oven*)

MAURYA (*sitting down on a stool at the fire*) He won't go this day with the wind rising from the south and west. He won't go this day, for the young priest will stop him surely.

NORA He'll not stop him, mother, and I heard Eamon Simon and Stephen Pheety and Colum Shawn saying he would go.

MAURYA Where is he itself?

NORA He went down to see would there be another boat sailing in the week, and I'm thinking it won't be long till he's here now, for the tide's turning at the green head, and the hooker's tacking from the east.

CATHLEEN I hear some one passing the big stones.

NORA (*looking out*) He's coming now, and he in a hurry.

BARTLEY (*comes in and looks round the room. Speaking sadly and quietly*) Where is the bit of new rope, Cathleen, was bought in Connemara?

CATHLEEN (*coming down*) Give it to him, Nora; it's on a nail by the white boards. I hung it up this morning, for the pig with the black feet was eating it.

NORA (*giving him a rope*) Is that it, Bartley?

MAURYA You'd do right to leave that rope, Bartley, hanging by the board. (BARTLEY *takes the rope*) It will be wanting in this place, I'm telling you, if Michael is washed up tomorrow morning, or the next morning, or any morning in the week, for it's a deep grave we'll make him by the grace of God.

BARTLEY (*beginning to work with the rope*) I've no halter the way I can ride down on the mare, and I must go now quickly. This is the one boat going for two weeks or beyond it, and the fair will be a good fair for horses I heard them saying below.

MAURYA It's a hard thing they'll be saying below if the body is washed up and there's no man in it to make the coffin, and I after giving a big price for the finest white boards you'd find in Connemara. (*She looks round at the boards*)

BARTLEY How would it be washed up, and we after looking each day for nine days, and a strong wind blowing a while back from the west and south?

MAURYA If it wasn't found itself, that wind is raising the sea, and there was a star up against the moon, and it rising in the night. If it was a hundred horses, or a thousand horses you had itself, what is the price of a thousand horses against a son where there is one son only?

BARTLEY (*working at the halter, to CATHLEEN*) Let you go down each day, and see the sheep aren't jumping in on the rye, and if the jobber comes you can sell the pig with the black feet if there is a good price going.

MAURYA How would the like of her get a good price for a pig?

BARTLEY (*to CATHLEEN*) If the west wind holds with the last bit of the moon let you and Nora get up weed enough for another cock for the kelp. It's hard set we'll be from this day with no one in it but one man to work.

MAURYA It's hard set we'll be surely the day you're drownd'd with the rest. What way will I live and the girls with me, and I an old woman looking for the grave?

(BARTLEY *lays down the halter, takes off his old coat, and puts on a newer one of the same flannel*)

BARTLEY (*to NORA*) Is she coming to the pier?

NORA (*looking out*) She's passing the green head and letting fall her sails.

BARTLEY (*getting his purse and tobacco*) I'll have half an hour to go down, and you'll see me coming again in two days, or in three days, or maybe in four days if the wind is bad.

MAURYA (*turning round to the fire, and putting her shawl over her head*) Isn't it a hard and cruel man won't hear a word from an old woman, and she holding him from the sea?

CATHLEEN It's the life of a young man to be going on the sea, and who would listen to an old woman with one thing and she saying it over?

BARTLEY (*taking the halter*) I must go now quickly. I'll ride down on the red mare, and the gray pony'll run behind me. . . . The blessing of God on you. (*He goes out*)

MAURYA (*crying out as he is in the door*) He's gone now, God spare us, and we'll not see him again. He's gone now, and when the black night is falling I'll have no son left me in the world.

CATHLEEN Why wouldn't you give him your blessing and he looking round in the door? Isn't it sorrow enough is on every one in this house without your sending him out with an unlucky word behind him, and a hard word in his ear?

(MAURYA *takes up the tongs and begins raking the fire aimlessly without looking round*)

NORA (*turning towards her*) You're taking away the turf from the cake.

CATHLEEN (*crying out*) The Son of God forgive us, Nora, we're after forgetting his bit of bread. (*She comes over to the fire*)

NORA And it's destroyed he'll be going till dark night, and he after eating nothing since the sun went up.

CATHLEEN (*turning the cake out of the oven*) It's destroyed he'll be, surely. There's no sense left on any person in a house where an old woman will be talking forever.

(MAURYA *sways herself on her stool*)

CATHLEEN (*cutting off some of the bread and rolling it in a cloth; to* MAURYA) Let you go down now to the spring well and give him this and he passing. You'll see him then and the dark word will be broken, and you can say "God speed you," the way he'll be easy in his mind.

MAURYA (*taking the bread*) Will I be in it as soon as himself?

CATHLEEN If you go now quickly.

MAURYA (*standing up unsteadily*) It's hard set I am to walk.

CATHLEEN (*looking at her anxiously*) Give her the stick, Nora, or maybe she'll slip on the big stones.

NORA What stick?

CATHLEEN The stick Michael brought from Connemara.

MAURYA (*taking a stick* NORA *gives her*) In the big world the old people do be leaving things after them for their sons and children, but in this place it is the young men do be leaving things behind for them that do be old.

(*She goes out slowly.* NORA *goes over to the ladder*)

CATHLEEN Wait, Nora, maybe she'd turn back quickly. She's that sorry, God help her, you wouldn't know the thing she'd do.

NORA Is she gone round by the bush?

CATHLEEN (*looking out*) She's gone now. Throw it down quickly, for the Lord knows when she'll be out of it again.

NORA (*getting the bundle from the loft*) The young priest said he'd be passing tomorrow, and we might go down and speak to him below if it's Michael's they are surely.

CATHLEEN (*taking the bundle*) Did he say what way they were found?

NORA (*coming down*) "There were two men," says he, "and they rowing round with poteen before the cocks crowed, and the oar of one of them caught the body, and they passing the black cliffs of the north."

CATHLEEN (*trying to open the bundle*) Give me a knife, Nora, the string's perished with the salt water, and there's a black knot on it you wouldn't loosen in a week.

NORA (*giving her a knife*) I've heard tell it was a long way to Donegal.

CATHLEEN (*cutting the string*) It is surely. There was a man in here a while ago—the man sold us that knife—and he said if you set off walking from the rocks beyond, it would be seven days you'd be in Donegal.

NORA And what time would a man take, and he floating?

(CATHLEEN *opens the bundle and takes out a bit of a stocking. They look at them eagerly*)

CATHLEEN (*in a low voice*) The Lord spare us, Nora! isn't it a queer hard thing to say if it's his they are surely?

NORA I'll get his shirt off the hook the way we can put the one flannel on the other. (*She looks through some clothes hanging in the corner*) It's not with them, Cathleen, and where will it be?

CATHLEEN I'm thinking Bartley put it on him in the morning, for his own shirt was heavy with the salt in it. (*pointing to the corner*) There's a bit of a sleeve was of the same stuff. Give me that and it will do.

(NORA *brings it to her and they compare the flannel*)

CATHLEEN It's the same stuff, Nora; but if it is itself aren't there great rolls of it in the shops of Galway, and isn't it many another man may have a shirt of it as well as Michael himself?

NORA (*who has taken up the stocking and counted the stitches, crying out*) It's Michael, Cathleen, it's Michael; God spare his soul, and what will herself say when she hears this story, and Bartley on the sea?

CATHLEEN (*taking the stocking*) It's a plain stocking.

NORA It's the second one of the third pair I knitted, and I put up three score stitches, and I dropped four of them.

CATHLEEN (*counts the stitches*) It's that number is in it. (*crying out*) Ah, Nora, isn't it a bitter thing to think of him floating that way to the far north, and no one to keen him but the black hags that do be flying on the sea?

NORA (*swinging herself round, and throwing out her arms on the clothes*) And isn't it a pitiful thing when there is nothing left of a man who was a great rower and fisher, but a bit of an old shirt and a plain stocking?

CATHLEEN (*after an instant*) Tell me is herself coming, Nora? I hear a little sound on the path.

NORA (*looking out*) She is, Cathleen. She's coming up to the door.

CATHLEEN Put these things away before she'll come in. Maybe it's easier she'll be after giving her blessing to Bartley, and we won't let on we've heard anything the time he's on the sea.

NORA (*helping* CATHLEEN *to close the bundle*) We'll put them here in the corner.

(*They put them into a hole in the chimney corner.* CATHLEEN *goes back to the spinning-wheel*)

NORA Will she see it was crying I was?

CATHLEEN Keep your back to the door the way the light'll not be on you.

(NORA *sits down at the chimney corner, with her back to the door.* MAURYA *comes in very slowly, without looking at the girls, and goes over to her stool at the other side of the fire. The cloth with the bread is still in her hand. The girls look at each other, and* NORA *points to the bundle of bread*)

CATHLEEN (*after spinning for a moment*) You didn't give him his bit of bread?

(MAURYA *begins to keen softly, without turning round*)

CATHLEEN Did you see him riding down?

(MAURYA *goes on keening*)

CATHLEEN (*a little impatiently*) God forgive you; isn't it a better thing to raise your voice and tell what you seen, than to be making lamentation for a thing that's done? Did you see Bartley, I'm saying to you.

MAURYA (*with a weak voice*) My heart's broken from this day.

CATHLEEN (*as before*) Did you see Bartley?

MAURYA I seen the fearfulest thing.

CATHLEEN (*leaves her wheel and looks out*) God forgive you; he's riding the mare now over the green head, and the gray pony behind him.

MAURYA (*starts, so that her shawl falls back from her head and shows her white tossed hair. With a frightened voice*) The gray pony behind him.

CATHLEEN (*coming to the fire*) What is it ails you, at all?

MAURYA (*speaking very slowly*) I've seen the fearfulest thing any person has seen, since the day Bride Dara seen the dead man with the child in his arms.

CATHLEEN and NORA Uah. (*They crouch down in front of the old woman at the fire*)

NORA Tell us what it is you seen.

MAURYA I went down to the spring well, and I stood there saying a prayer to myself.

Then Bartley came along, and he riding on the red mare with the gray pony behind him. (*She puts up her hands, as if to hide something from her eyes*) The Son of God spare us, Nora!

CATHLEEN What is it you seen?

MAURYA I seen Michael himself.

CATHLEEN (*speaking softly*) You did not, mother; it wasn't Michael you seen, for his body is after being found in the far north, and he's got a clean burial by the grace of God.

MAURYA (*a little defiantly*) I'm after seeing him this day, and he riding and galloping. Bartley came first on the red mare; and I tried to say "God speed you," but something choked the words in my throat. He went by quickly; and "the blessing of God on you," says he, and I could say nothing. I looked up then, and I crying, at the gray pony, and there was Michael upon it—with fine clothes on him, and new shoes on his feet.

CATHLEEN (*begins to keen*) It's destroyed we are from this day. It's destroyed, surely.

NORA Didn't the young priest say the Almighty God wouldn't leave her destitute with no son living?

MAURYA (*in a low voice, but clearly*) It's little the like of him knows of the sea. . . . Bartley will be lost now, and let you call in Eamon and make me a good coffin out of the white boards, for I won't live after them. I've had a husband, and a husband's father, and six sons in this house—six fine men, though it was a hard birth I had with every one of them and they coming to the world—and some of them were found and some of them were not found, but they're gone now the lot of them. . . . There were Stephen, and Shawn, were lost in the great wind, and found after in the Bay of Gregory of the Golden Mouth, and carried up the two of them on the one plank, and in by that door. (*She pauses for a moment, the girls start as if they heard something through the door that is half open behind them*)

NORA (*in a whisper*) Did you hear that, Cathleen? Did you hear a noise in the northeast?

CATHLEEN (*in a whisper*) There's some one after crying out by the seashore.

MAURYA (*continues without hearing anything*) There was Sheamus and his father, and his own father again, were lost in a dark night, and not a stick or sign was seen of them when the sun went up. There was Patch after was drowned out of a curragh that turned over. I was sitting here with Bartley, and he a baby, lying on my two knees, and I seen two women, and three women, and four women coming in, and they crossing themselves, and not saying a word. I looked out then, and there were men coming after them, and they holding a thing in the half of a red sail, and water dripping out of it—it was a dry day, Nora—and leaving a track to the door. (*She pauses again with her hand stretched out towards the door. It opens softly and old women begin to come in, crossing themselves on the threshold, and kneeling down in front of the stage with red petticoats over their heads*)

MAURYA (*half in a dream, to* CATHLEEN)   Is it Patch, or Michael, or what is it at all?

CATHLEEN   Michael is after being found in the far north, and when he is found there how could he be here in this place?

MAURYA   There does be a power of young men floating round in the sea, and what way would they know if it was Michael they had, or another man like him, for when a man is nine days in the sea, and the wind blowing, it's hard set his own mother would be to say what man was it.

CATHLEEN   It's Michael, God spare him, for they're after sending us a bit of his clothes from the far north. (*She reaches out and hands* MAURYA *the clothes that belonged to Michael.* MAURYA *stands up slowly and takes them in her hands.* NORA *looks out*)

NORA   They're carrying a thing among them and there's water dripping out of it and leaving a track by the big stones.

CATHLEEN (*in a whisper to the women who have come in*)   Is it Bartley it is?

ONE OF THE WOMEN   It is surely, God rest his soul.

(*Two younger women come in and pull out the table. Then men carry in the body of* BART-LEY, *laid on a plank, with a bit of a sail over it, and lay it on the table*)

CATHLEEN (*to the women, as they are doing so*)   What way was he drowned?

ONE OF THE WOMEN   The gray pony knocked him into the sea, and he was washed out where there is a great surf on the white rocks.

(*MAURYA has gone over and knelt down at the head of the table. The women are keening softly and swaying themselves with a slow movement.* CATHLEEN *and* NORA *kneel at the other end of the table. The men kneel near the door*)

MAURYA (*raising her head and speaking as if she did not see the people around her*)   They're all gone now, and there isn't anything more the sea can do to me. . . . I'll have no call now to be up crying and praying when the wind breaks from the south, and you can hear the surf is in the east, and the surf is in the west, making a great stir with the two noises, and they hitting one on the other. I'll have no call now to be going down and getting Holy Water in the dark nights after Samhain, and I won't care what way the sea is when the other women will be keening. (*to* NORA) Give me the Holy Water, Nora, there's a small sup still on the dresser.

(NORA *gives it to her*)

MAURYA (*drops Michael's clothes across Bartley's feet, and sprinkles the Holy Water over him*)   It isn't that I haven't prayed for you, Bartley, to the Almighty God. It isn't that I haven't said prayers in the dark night till you wouldn't know what I'd be saying; but it's a great rest I'll have now, and it's time surely. It's a great rest I'll have now, and great sleeping in the long nights after Samhain, if it's only a bit of wet flour we do have to eat, and maybe a fish that would be stinking. (*She kneels down again, crossing herself, and saying prayers under her breath*)

CATHLEEN (*to an old man*)   Maybe yourself and Eamon would make a coffin when the sun rises. We have fine white boards herself bought, God help her, thinking Michael would be found, and I have a new cake you can eat while you'll be working.

THE OLD MAN (*looking at the boards*)   Are there nails with them?

CATHLEEN   There are not, Colum; we didn't think of the nails.

ANOTHER MAN   It's a great wonder she wouldn't think of the nails, and all the coffins she's seen made already.

CATHLEEN   It's getting old she is, and broken.

(MAURYA *stands up again very slowly and spreads out the pieces of Michael's clothes beside the body, sprinkling them with the last of the Holy Water*)

NORA (*in a whisper to* CATHLEEN)   She's quiet now and easy; but the day Michael was drowned you could hear her crying out from this to the spring well. It's fonder she was of Michael, and would any one have thought that?

CATHLEEN (*slowly and clearly*)   An old woman will be soon tired with anything she will do, and isn't it nine days herself is after crying and keening, and making great sorrow in the house?

MAURYA (*puts the empty cup mouth downwards on the table, and lays her hands together on Bartley's feet*)   They're all together this time, and the end is come. May the Almighty God have mercy on Bartley's soul, and on Michael's soul, and on the souls of Sheamus and

Patch, and Stephen and Shawn; (*bending her head*) and may He have mercy on my soul, Nora, and on the soul of every one is left living in the world. (*She pauses, and the keen rises a little more loudly from the women, then sinks away*)

MAURYA (*continuing*) Michael has a clean burial in the far north, by the grace of the Almighty God. Bartley will have a fine coffin out of the white boards, and a deep grave surely. What more can we want than that? No man at all can be living forever, and we must be satisfied. (*She kneels down again and the curtain falls slowly*)

Sean O'Casey

1884-

THE GREEN GODDESS OF REALISM

In the theatre of today, realism is the totem pole of the dramatic critics.

Matter-of-fact plays, true true-to-life arrangement, and real, live characters are the three gods the critics adore and saturate with the incense of their commonplace praise once a day and twice on Sundays in their trimly-dressed little articles. What the dramatic critics mean by the various terms they use for Realism is the yearly ton of rubbish that falls on the English stage and is swiftly swept away into the dust-bins. The critics give a cordial welcome to the trivial plays because, in my opinion, they are, oh, so easy to understand, and gorge the critics with the ease of an easy explanation. It is very dangerous for a dramatist to be superior to the critics, to be a greater dramatist than the critic is a critic. They don't like it, and so most of them do all they can to discourage any attempt in the theatre towards an imagination fancy-free, or an attempt to look on life and mold it into a form fit for the higher feeling and intelligence of the stage. They are those who compare Beaumont and Fletcher's *Philaster* with *Charley's Aunt*, and in their heart of hearts vote for the farce and shove the poetic play out of their way (a few spit the preference in our face, as Archer did). *Charley's Aunt* is loved by Charley's uncles. They have grown fat and lazy on triviality, so fat and so lazy that they are hardly able to move. The curse is that these critics do their best to prevent anyone else from moving either.

They will have simply to be roughly shunted out of the way, and these few words are one of the first sharp prods to get them to buzz off and do their sleeping somewhere else. Realism, or what the critics childishly believe to be Realism, has had its day, and has earned a rest. It began on a sunny autumn evening in 1886, or thereabouts, as the lawyers say, at the first production of *Ours* by Robertson, when the miracle took place. "In reading the play today," says William Archer, the world-famous dramatic critic, "we recognize in Robertson—just what the stage wanted in its progress towards verisimilitude—the genius of the commonplace. The first act of *Ours* was, in intention at any rate, steeped in an atmosphere quite new to the theater. The scene was an avenue in Shendryn Park which Robertson describes in the abhorrent prompt-book jargon of the time. But one line had, I venture to say, as yet appeared in no prompt-book in the world: '*Throughout the act the autumn leaves fall from the trees.*' How this effect was produced and whether it was successful, I cannot say. Nor can I discuss the question whether it was a desirable effect, or a mere trick of mechanical realism which the true artist would despise." Now the falling of the leaves from the trees was and could have been nothing but "a mere trick of mechanical realism," because the trees couldn't have been true-to-life trees, and, even if they were, the autumnal leaves couldn't have fallen with the regularity and rhythm required to create the desirable effect. And no true artist of the theater would despise "a mere trick of mechanical realism" by which to get a scenic or an emotional effect out of his play and over to his audience. We remember the fine effect that the first sound of the first fall of rain had as it fell in the first act of Obey's *Noah;* and this fall of rain was a mere trick of mechanical realism as it was also the opening of the floodgates of Heaven, swelling into a flood that destroyed all life that was in the world save only those who found safe shelter in the faith of Noah; or the sudden change in the wind in *Saint Joan* that set the pennon streaming eastward, and sent Dunois and Saint Joan hurrying out to make for the flash of the guns, and drive the English out of France. You see the artist in the theatre never despises a mere trick of mechanical realism; but he knows how to keep it in its proper place. Let Archer open his mouth again: "Then as the act proceeds, *The patter of rain is heard upon the leaves,* and again, *The rain comes down more heavily and the stage darkens.*" The stage darkens, mind you, not the sky. "This effect of the rain falling and the stage darkening would," Archer tells us, "have been absolutely impossible in a candle-lit scene." Well, we have our floodlights, our spotlights, our baby-spots, our amber, blue, and pink footlights, but rarely do we get in our great progress towards verisimilitude the thunder, the lightning, and the rain that flashed and roared and fell on the heath scene in Shakespeare's *Macbeth*. Archer speaks again: "Then enter the sentimental hero and heroine, caught in the rain; and—conceive the daring novelty!—*Blanche carries the skirt of her dress over her head.*" In the center of the stage was a large tree with a bench around it, and to get the best shelter possible, the hero and the heroine stand on the bench. Meanwhile Sir Alexander and Lady Shendryn, a middle-aged couple, hop in and sit down on the stump of a tree under another shelter. Unaware of each other's presence, the two couples talk in a sort of counterpoint, the romantic dialogue of the youthful pair contrasting with the weary snappiness of the elderly couple." And this is called an exact imitation of real life. Two couples, unknown to each other, carry on a counterpoint conversation on the same stage in the same scene at the same time, and Archer calls this "an exact imitation at any rate of the surfaces of life." Here's a bit of the dialogue:

ANGUS What was the song you sang at the Sylvesters'?
BLANCHE Oh!
ANGUS I wish you'd hum it now.
BLANCHE Without music?
ANGUS It won't be without music.

—and Blanche croons over Offenbach's exquisite *Chanson de Fortunio,* and then we are told that we may search the Restoration and eighteenth-century comedy in vain for a piece of subtle truth like this. Where the subtle truth is in a girl under the rain holding her skirt over her head, standing on a bench, crooning Offenbach's *Chanson de Fortunio* or murmuring to her young man, "Cousin, do you know, I rather like to see you getting wet," only Archer or some other present-day critic-guardian angel of the theatre could tell us. This arch-critical prate about verisimilitude, exact imitation of real life, and the unmistakable originality of the conception of this scene in Robertson's *Ours,* is an example of the commonplace genius of dramatic criticism. The incident of two couples taking their set times to say their say on the same stage in the same scene at the same time in full view of the audience is as true to life, is about as exact an imitation of real life, as the incident of Malvolio's soliloquy in full view of his tormentors and his audience. But the autumn leaves falling one by one and two by two, the sound of the rain pattering on the leaves, and the stage getting darker and darker and the rain getting heavier and heavier as the act proceeds, is all so sweet and all so simple to see and feel and follow that Archer and his fellow-follows-on hail this exact imitation of real life on the stage as a great and glorious godsend to them and their wives and children. They are so easy to manage in a weekly article; no beating about the bush, no humiliating strain on the mind or the emotions, no danger of giving a stupid judgment, for autumn leaves are autumn leaves, rain is rain, and the darkening night means the end of the day. And so we find that stuff like *Call It a Day* gets a rosy welcome from our regimental sergeant-major critics, while a work like *Strange Interlude* is pooh-bahed off the stage. And how quietly and clever and exact this realism, or naturalism, or exact imitation of life has made the critics! Commenting on *Espionage,* Mr. Agate tells us that "the First Act is a corker, and readers will note my wideawakeness in the perception that whereas the draught in the railway carriage fritters the blinds, the passengers are able to put their heads out of window without a hair stirring." I'm sure all the readers felt an exaltation in the consciousness of criticism when they got sufficiently soaked in that wonderful bit of information. It gave them something to look forward to when they went to see the play. Not a hair stirring! Fancy that now. Strange that the same wideawakeness which saw a corker in *Espionage,* saw nothing, or very little, in O'Neill's *Strange Interlude.* But then O'Neill's great plays are "morbid masterpieces which have to be seen under the penalty of remaining mum in Bloomsbury," or, if the truth be told, of remaining mum in any civilized place where the drama is honored more in the observance than in the breach. And Mr. Ivor Brown, commenting on O'Neill's *Ah, Wilderness!* tells us that "The producers introduced the music of *The Merry Widow* to a Connecticut small town of 1906. In that case New England was well ahead of Old, for that operetta did not reach Daly's till a year later." Well, that is something worth knowing anyway, but it wouldn't have the faintest effect on the play or production even if the music hadn't yet reached the small town in Connecticut, or even if the music given in the play had been the first composition made on the first psaltery or sackbut, if the music fitted the theme. Is it a waste of time to hint in the ear of the critics that it is much harder for a dramatist to stir the heart than to stir the hair, and much harder to make music apt for the theme and the trend of a play than it is to bring the music in to the correct tick of the clock? These critics are like the tailors who visit an exhibition to see if the buttons are put in their proper places on the coats in the pictures that are hanging on the walls.

This headlong search or quiet scrutiny for realism, exact imitation of life in the drama, has outwitted the critics into being puzzled over everything in a play that doesn't fit calmly into their poor spirit level and timid thumb rule. The dramatist is told that he must see life steadily and see it whole; and a critic-at-arms (there are barons, knights, esquires, men-at-arms, and grooms among the critics) writing in the *Evening Standard* complained that a play he saw wasn't "a study of the whole seething brew of life!" He wasn't asking for much. The whole world, parallels of longitude and meridians of latitude and all, popped on to the stage in a flood of limelight, and the critics tossing it about like kids playing with a balloon. This critic-at-arms didn't (and doesn't still, I'm sure) realize that no one can view or understand the brew of life encased in an acorn cup; or holding this little miracle in the palm of the hand, no human pair of eyes can at any time see it steadily and see it whole. So the complaint about a play failing to show the whole seething brew of life is the complaint of a dodo critic.

Although the bone of realism in the theatre has been picked pretty clean, the critics keep gnawing away at it, so that if a playwright as much as gets a character to blow his nose (preferably when "the autumn leaves are falling from the trees"), the critics delightedly nod to each other, and murmur, "An exact imitation of life, brothers." Commenting on *Call It a Day*, a play in which everything is attempted and nothing done, Mr. Agate tells us that "Miss Dodie Smith is never concerned whether 'it' is a play or not, but whether she has assembled on her stage characters so real that she might have gone into the street and compelled them into the theater," though these characters that might have been pulled in off the street are as tender and delicate and true as the tenderest and most delicate characters wistfully wandering about in the most wistful Barrie play. J.G.B., commenting on *Love from a Stranger*, tells us that "it is written with brilliant matter-of-factness, and is a real play about real people." Here our noses are shoved up against the image of realism in the theatre. A real play about real people: here's a sentence that apparently punches home; but look well into it, and you'll find it empty of any real meaning. Week in and week out these commonplace plays are reducing the poor critics into more and more vague and vapid expressions that would give a sparkle to the mouth of a politician trying to cod his constituents—and very often succeeding. A real play about real people—what does it mean? This is something of a triumph—a real play with real people in a real theater before a real audience. But every play is a real play whether it be good or bad, just as a real lion is a real lion and a real mouse is a real mouse, and both are animals. But the real mouse isn't a real lion, nor is the real lion a real mouse, though both are animals. I wonder do the critics get this? There is a big difference between a lion and a mouse, though both are animals, and there is a bigger difference between a good and a bad play, though both are plays just the same. What is a "real play?" Answer, according to J.G.B., *Love from a Stranger* is a real play, therefore the nearer we get to this praised play, the nearer we get to a real play. Now is *The Dream Play* by Strindberg a real play? It certainly bears no resemblance to *Love from a Stranger*, but the imagination can handle *The Dream Play* just as well and with far fuller satisfaction. Apparently the critics think that a play to be a real play must have real people in it, though they never take breath to tell us what they mean by real people. Take people off the street or carry them out of a drawing-room, plonk them on the stage and make them speak as they speak in real, real life, and you will have the dullest thing imaginable. I suppose the critics will be shocked to hear that no real character can be put in a play unless some of the reality is taken out of him through the heightening, widening, and deepening of the character by the dramatist who creates him. Would the dramatic critics call the characters in *Hamlet* real people, or only the creations out of the mind of a poet, and isn't *Hamlet* all the better for its want of reality? Isn't it more of a play, and what has the word "play" got to do with reality? Is Caliban a real person, found in the street and compelled into the theatre? If he isn't, then, isn't the character just as powerful as if he were? What peculiar quality does this term of "real people in a real play" give to a play, seeing that many plays, some of them in step with the greatest, have in them characters far removed from this critic-quality of matter-of-factness? Isn't Caliban as real a character as Gustav Bergmann in *Close Quarters,* or the ladies and gents in *Fallen Angels,* or *Night Must Fall,* or *Call It a Day,* the author of which, as Mr. Agate tells us, assembles on her stage characters so real (again this word "real"—the spyhole through which the critics view the stage) that she might have gone into the street and compelled them into the theater. (Though how a critic couples a play dealing with sex almost from the word "go" to the last lap, a play in which an accountant goes to the flat of an actress-client and nothing happens; in which the accountant's wife is entertained by a friend, and then entertains the friend alone in her house, and nothing happens; in which their daughter flings herself at an artist, and nothing happens; in which her brother falls for a young lassie that climbs over the garden wall to him, and nothing happens; in which the maid falls for the manservant of the family a few doors down, and nothing happens; and the bitch brought out for a walk by the manservant rubs noses with the dog taken out by the maid, and nothing happens—how a critic couples all this sort of thing with characters hustled in off the streets, only a critic could know, and only a critic can tell.) If all that is in this play be life, then life is a mass of sentimentally holy hokum.

As a matter-of-factness no one, least of all a playwright, can go out into the streets and lanes of the city and compel the people to come on to the stage, for the people on the stage must be of the stage and not of the streets and lanes of the city or of the highways and hedges of the country. The most realistic characters in the most realistic play cannot be true to life. Perhaps the most real character in any play we know of is the char-

acter of Falstaff done by Shakespeare. Here is realism as large as life; but it is realism larger, and a lot larger, than life. Falstaff was never pulled off the streets into the theatre by Shakespeare. God never created Falstaff—he sprang from Shakespeare's brain. God, if you like, created Shakespeare, but Shakespeare created Falstaff. Falstaff is no more real, there is no more matter-of-factness in the character of Falstaff, than there is in Caliban or Puck or Ariel. He is a bigger creation than any of these three, and that is all. A play, says Dryden, ought to be a just image of human nature, and this is true of *Hamlet,* of *John Bull's Other Island,* of *Strange Interlude,* of *Six Characters in Search of an Author,* of *Peer Gynt,* of *The Dream Play;* but it is not true of the trivial tomtit-realism in the thousand and one entertainment plays patted and praised by the dramatic critics. Why, even the sawdust characters of the Moor, Petroushka, and the Ballerina are a more just image of human nature than the characters in the matter-of-fact, exact-imitation-of-life plays that flit about on the English stage.

As it is with the play, so it is with the dressed-up stage—the critics want to be doped into the belief that the scene on the stage is as real as life itself. The stirring of the hair is more to them than the stirring of the heart. But things as real as life itself on the stage they can never have; a room can never be a room, a tree a tree, or a death a death. These must take the nature of a child's toys and a child's play. Let me quote from Allardyce Nicoll's *British Drama:* "Illusion for the ordinary spectator is only partial at the best, and nearly all of us are aware, even at the moment of highest tension or most hilarious laughter, that the battlements are not of Elsinore and the trees are not of Arden forest. The scene-painter's art allied to that of the electrician can now obtain effects undreamt of before. Our drawing-rooms can look like drawing-rooms now, our woods can look like woods, and our seas like seas. Those, too, who have witnessed some recent productions in which the new German lighting effects were employed will agree that it would be hard to tell the fictional clouds that flit over the painted sky from real clouds, or the fictional sunrise from real sunrise. The question is, however, not whether the semblance of actuality can be obtained, but whether it is precisely that which we desire. Would we not rather have the real drawing-room of Mrs. So-and-so, the real Epping Forest, the real Atlantic, rather than these feigned copies of them? Would we not choose to watch those beautiful clouds from an open moorland rather than from our seats in gallery or in stalls? It is precisely the same problem that arises in the consideration of drama itself. We do not want merely an excerpt from reality; it is the imaginative transformation of reality, as it is seen through the eyes of the poet, that we desire. The great art of the theatre is to suggest, not to tell openly; to dilate the mind by symbols, not by actual things; to express in Lear a world's sorrow, and in Hamlet the grief of humanity. Many of our modern producers are striving in this direction, although it must be confessed that England here is well in the background." And what is the greatest obstacle the progressive producers have to face? In my opinion, the dramatic critics who prefer the stirring of the hair to the stirring of the heart; the death-or-drivel boys gunning with their gab from their pill-boxes in the theater and make it more of a temple and less of a den of thieves.

This rage for real, real life on the stage has taken all the life out of the drama. If everything on the stage is to be a fake exact imitation (for fake realism it can only be), where is the chance for the original and imaginative artist? Less chance for him than there was for Jonah in the whale's belly. The beauty, fire, and poetry of drama have perished in the storm of fake realism. Let real birds fly through the air (not like Basil Dean's butterflies in *Midsummer Night's Dream*, fluttering over the stage and pinning themselves to trees), real animals roam through the jungle, real fish swim in the sea, but let us have the make-believe of the artist and the child in the theatre. Less of what the critics call "life," and more of symbolism; for even in the most commonplace of realistic plays the symbol can never be absent. A house on a stage can never be a house, and that which represents it must always be a symbol. A room in a realistic play must always be a symbol for a room. There can never be any important actuality on the stage, except an actuality that is unnecessary and out of place. An actor representing a cavalier may come on the stage mounted on a real horse, but the horse will always look only a little less ridiculous than the "cavalier." The horse can have nothing to do with the drama. I remember a play written round Mr. Pepys, and in this play was used "the identical snuff-box used by him when he was head of the Admiralty in the reign of Charles the Second." So much was said about the snuff-box that I expected it to be carried in on a

cushion preceded by a brass band, and hawked around for all to admire before the play began. Now this snuff-box added nothing to the play, and because of this commonplace spirit in the play, the play added nothing to the drama. It seems that the closer we move to actual life, the further we move away from the drama. Drama purely imitative of live isn't drama at all. Now the critics are beginning to use the word "theatre" when they find themselves in a bit of a tangle over what they should say about a play that has a bad whiff of staleness in its theme, character, and form. For instance, Mr. Ivor Brown, writing of a recent play, said that "the play is not life, it is theatre and might be allowed to wear its flamboyant colors"; "might be allowed," mind you—he, too, isn't sure. He doesn't tell us to what theatre the play belonged. He left his readers to find that out for themselves. Was it what theatre of Shakespeare, of Shaw, of Strindberg, of Ibsen, of Goldsmith, of O'Neill, of Pirandello, of Toller? Or the theatre of Dan Leno, Marie Lloyd, George Robey, Charlie Chaplin, Sidney Howard, or Will Hay? These are all good theatre and so they are all good life. But it is not the life that they imitate in their plays or in their actions that makes them good theatre, but the unique and original life that is in themselves. They have the life that the present dramatic critics lack, for the critics cannot, or are afraid to, be lively. They wouldn't venture to give the plays they call "theatre" their baptismal name of rubbish. Where would we see a criticism like unto the meet criticisms for such plays given by George Jean Nathan:

THE FIRST APPLE.   Lynn Starling. Oh!
THE LAKE.   A play that got a lot of praise in England. By Dorothy Massingham and Murray MacDonald. Badly confused effort to mix a little Chekhov with a lot of boiled-over Henry Arthur Jones, the result being even worse Massingham-MacDonald.
THE LOCKED ROOM.   Junk.
THE GODS WE MAKE.   Terrible!

The Government would probably go out of office if even one of the sharp sentences just quoted came out of the mouth of a London dramatic critic. We haven't a critic like Nathan in the English Theatre, and it is time we had. We have only to read some of his works—*Testament of a Critic, Art of the Night, The House of Satan, Since Ibsen, The Critic and the Drama, Another Book on the Theater, The Theater of the Moment*—to realize that in the Theatre of Nathan the curtain is always going up, while in the Theatre of the critics here the curtain is always coming down. The critics here are afraid to be alive or alert. They take their timid thoughts out of a pouncet box. Every bare expression they use is carefully covered with a frill. They take the moaning echo of a shell to be the thunder of the sea. Their criticisms come to us on a pseudo-silver salver. Instead of knocking a bad play over the head with a stick, they flick it over the cheek with a kid glove. They are pew-openers in the temple of drama, nicely showing the people to their places. They are the modern groundlings in the theatre—always waiting to be entertained. Shakespeare, of course, they are certain about, for tradition shoves them on to their knees the minute Shakespeare turns the corner. They often take a patch of flame-colored taffeta to be the burning sun. "Critics," says George Jean Nathan, "are artist-partners with the artist himself. The former creates, the latter recreates. Without criticism art would, of course, still be art, and so, with its windows walled in and its lights out, the Louvre would still be the Louvre." Quite right; but the weekly and daily purr of praise given by our critics to commonplace plays, packed with "matter-of-factness" and "exact imitation of life," like stuffed geese, is just unwalling the windows, opening wide the doors, and lighting a great gathering of lamps in a hen-house.

THE PLOUGH AND THE STARS

To the gay laugh of my mother
at the gate of the grave

CAST OF CHARACTERS

JACK CLITHEROE (*a bricklayer*), *Commandant in the Irish Citizen Army*
NORA CLITHEROE, *his wife*
PETER FLYNN (*a laborer*), *Nora's uncle*
THE YOUNG COVEY (*a fitter*), *Clitheroe's cousin* — *Residents in the Tenement*
BESSIE BURGESS (*a street fruit-vendor*)
MRS. GOGAN (*a charwoman*)
MOLLSER, *her consumptive-child*
FLUTHER GOOD (*a carpenter*)

LIEUT. LANGON (*a Civil Servant*), *of the Irish Volunteers*
CAPT. BRENNAN (*a chicken butcher*), *of the Irish Citizen Army*
CORPORAL STODDART, *of the Wiltshires*
SERGEANT TINLEY, *of the Wiltshires*
ROSIE REDMOND, *a daughter of "the Digs"*
A BARTENDER
A WOMAN
THE FIGURE IN THE WINDOW

TIME   *Acts I and II, November 1915; Acts III and IV, Easter Week, 1916. A few days elapse between Acts III and IV.*

ACT I   *The living room of the Clitheroe flat in a Dublin tenement.*
ACT II   *A public-house, outside of which a meeting is being held.*
ACT III   *The street outside the Clitheroe tenement.*
ACT IV   *The room of Bessie Burgess.*

ACT ONE

(*The home of the* CLITHEROES. *It consists of the front and back drawing rooms in a fine old*

The Plough and the Stars by Sean O'Casey is reprinted with the permission of St. Martin's Press, Inc.

Georgian house, struggling for its life against the assaults of time, and the more savage assaults of the tenants. The room shown is the back drawing room, wide, spacious, and lofty. At back is the entrance to the front drawing room. The space, originally occupied by folding doors, is now draped with casement cloth of a dark purple, decorated with a design in reddish-purple and cream. One of the curtains is pulled aside, giving a glimpse of front drawing room, at the end of which can be seen the wide, lofty windows looking out into the street. The room directly in front of the audience is furnished in a way that suggests an attempt towards a finer expression of domestic life. The large fireplace on right is of wood, painted to look like marble (the original has been taken away by the landlord). On the mantelshelf are two candlesticks of dark carved wood. Between them is a small clock. Over the clock is hanging a calendar which displays a picture of "The Sleeping Venus." In the center of the breast of the chimney hangs a picture of Robert Emmet. On the right of the entrance to the front drawing room is a copy of "The Gleaners," on the opposite side a copy of "The Angelus." Underneath "The Gleaners" is a chest of drawers on which stands a green bowl filled with scarlet dahlias and white chrysanthemums. Near to the fireplace is a settee which at night forms a double bed for CLITHEROE and NORA. Underneath "The Angelus" are a number of shelves containing saucepans and a frying pan. Under these is a table on which are various articles of delf ware. Near the end of the room, opposite to the fireplace, is a gate-legged table, covered with a cloth. On top of the table a huge cavalry sword is lying. To the right is a door which leads to a lobby from which the staircase leads to the hall. The floor is covered with a dark green linoleum. The room is dim except where it is illuminated from the glow of the fire. Through the window of the room at back can be seen the flaring of the flame of a gasoline lamp giving light to workmen repairing the street. Occasionally can be heard the clang of crowbars striking the setts. FLUTHER GOOD is repairing the lock of door, Right. A claw hammer is on a chair beside him, and he has a screwdriver in his hand. He is a man of forty years of age, rarely surrendering to thoughts of anxiety, fond of his "oil" but determined to conquer the habit before he dies. He is square-jawed and harshly featured; under the left eye is a scar, and his nose is bent from a smashing blow received in a fistic battle long ago. He is bald, save for a few peeping tufts of reddish hair around his ears; and his upper lip is hidden by a scrubby red moustache, embroidered here and there with a grey hair. He is dressed in a seedy black suit, cotton shirt with a soft collar, and wears a very respectable little black bow. On his head is a faded jerry hat, which, when he is excited, he has a habit of knocking farther back on his head, in a series of taps. In an argument he usually fills with sound and fury generally signifying a row. He is in his shirt-sleeves at present, and wears a soiled white apron, from a pocket in which sticks a carpenter's two-foot rule. He has just finished the job of putting on a new lock, and, filled with satisfaction, he is opening and shutting the door, enjoying the completion of a work well done. Sitting at the fire, airing a white shirt, is PETER FLYNN. He is a little, thin bit of a man, with a face shaped like a lozenge; on his cheeks and under his chin is a straggling wiry beard of a dirty-white and lemon hue. His face invariably wears a look of animated anguish, mixed with irritated defiance, as if everybody was at war with him, and he at

war with everybody. He is cocking his head in a way that suggests resentment at the presence of FLUTHER, who pays no attention to him, apparently, but is really furtively watching him. PETER is clad in a singlet, white whipcord knee-breeches, and is in his stocking-feet.

A voice is heard speaking outside of door, Left. It is that of MRS. GOGAN)

MRS. GOGAN (*outside*) Who are you lookin' for, sir? Who? Mrs. Clitheroe? . . . Oh, excuse me. Oh ay, up this way. She's out, I think: I seen her goin'. Oh, you've somethin' for her; oh, excuse me. You're from Arnott's. . . . I see. . . . You've a parcel for her. . . . Righto. . . . I'll take it. . . . I'll give it to her the minute she comes in. . . . It'll be quite safe. . . . Oh, sign that. . . . Excuse me. . . . Where? . . . Here? . . . No, there; righto. Am I to put Maggie or Mrs.? What is it? You dunno? Oh, excuse me.

(MRS. GOGAN *opens the door and comes in. She is a doleful-looking little woman of forty, insinuating manner and sallow complexion. She is fidgety and nervous, terribly talkative, has a habit of taking up things that may be near her and fiddling with them while she is speaking. Her heart is aflame with curiosity, and a fly could not come into nor go out of the house without her knowing. She has a draper's parcel in her hand, the knot of the twine tying it is untied. PETER, more resentful of this intrusion than of FLUTHER's presence, gets up from the chair, and without looking around, his head carried at an angry cock, marches into the room at back)*

MRS. GOGAN (*removing the paper and opening the cardboard box it contains*) I wondher what's this now? A hat! (*She takes out a hat, black, with decorations in red and gold*) God, she's goin' to th' divil lately for style! That hat, now, cost more than a penny. Such notions of upperosity she's gettin'. (*putting the hat on her head*) Oh, swank, what! (*She replaces it in parcel*)

FLUTHER She's a pretty little Judy, all the same.

MRS. GOGAN Ah, she is, an' she isn't. There's prettiness an' prettiness in it. I'm always sayin' that her skirts are a little too short for a married woman. An' to see her, sometimes of an evenin', in her glad-neck gown would make a body's blood run cold. I do be ashamed of me life before her husband. An' th' way she thries to be polite, with her "Good mornin', Mrs. Gogan," when she's goin' down, an' her "Good evenin', Mrs. Gogan," when she's comin' up. But there's politeness an' politeness in it.

FLUTHER They seem to get on well together, all th' same.

MRS. GOGAN Ah, they do, an' they don't. The pair o' them used to be like two turtle doves always billin' an' cooin'. You couldn't come into th' room but you'd feel, instinctive like, that they'd just been afther kissin' an' cuddlin' each other. . . . It often made me shiver, for, afther all, there's kissin' an' cuddlin' in it. But I'm thinkin' he's beginnin' to take things more quietly; the mysthery of havin' a woman's a mysthery no longer. . . . She dhresses herself to keep him with her, but it's no use—afther a month or two, th' wondher of a woman wears off.

FLUTHER I dunno, I dunno. Not wishin' to say anything derogatory, I think it's all a question of location: when a man finds th' wondher of one woman beginnin' to die, it's usually beginnin' to live in another.

MRS. GOGAN She's always grumblin' about havin' to live in a tenement house. "I wouldn't like to spend me last hour in one, let alone live me life in a tenement," says she. "Vaults," says she, "that are hidin' th' dead, instead of homes that are sheltherin' th' livin'." "Many a good one," says I, "was reared in a tenement house." Oh, you know, she's a well-up little lassie, too; able to make a shillin' go where another would have to spend a pound. She's wipin' th' eyes of th' Covey an' poor oul' Pether—everybody knows that—screwin' every penny she can out o' them, in ordher to turn th' place into a babby-house. An' she has th' life frightened out o' them; washin' their face, combin' their hair, wipin' their feet, brushin' their clothes, thrimmin' their nails, cleanin' their teeth—God Almighty, you'd think th' poor men were undhergoin' penal servitude.

FLUTHER (with an exclamation of disgust) A-a-ah, that's goin' beyond th' beyonds in a tenement house. That's a little bit too derogatory.

(PETER enters from room, Back, head elevated and resentful fire in his eyes; he is still in his singlet and trousers, but is now wearing a pair of unlaced boots—possibly to be decent in the presence of MRS. GOGAN. He places the white shirt, which he has carried in on his arm, on the back of a chair near the fire, and, going over to the chest of drawers, he opens drawer after drawer, looking for something; as he fails to find it he closes each drawer with a snap; he pulls out pieces of linen neatly folded, and bundles them back again any way)

PETER (in accents of anguish) Well, God Almighty, give me patience! (He returns to room, Back, giving the shirt a vicious turn as he passes)

MRS. GOGAN I wondher what he is foostherin' for now?

FLUTHER He's adornin' himself for th' meeting tonight. (pulling a handbill from his pocket and reading) "Great Demonstration an' torchlight procession around places in th' city sacred to th' memory of Irish Patriots, to be concluded be a meetin', at which will be taken an oath of fealty to th' Irish Republic. Formation in Parnell Square at eight o'clock." Well, they can hold it for Fluther. I'm up th' pole; no more dhrink for Fluther. It's three days now since I touched a dhrop, an' I feel a new man already.

MRS. GOGAN Isn't oul' Peter a funny-lookin' little man? . . . Like somethin' you'd pick off a Christmas Tree. . . . When he's dhressed up in his canonicals, you'd wondher where he'd been got. God forgive me, when I see him in them, I always think he must ha' had a Mormon for a father! He an' th' Covey can't abide each other; th' pair o' them is always at it, thryin' to best each other. There'll be blood dhrawn one o' these days.

FLUTHER How is it that Clitheroe himself, now, doesn't have anythin' to do with th' Citizen Army? A couple o' months ago, an' you'd hardly ever see him without his gun, an' th' Red Hand o' Liberty Hall in his hat.

MRS. GOGAN Just because he wasn't made a Captain of. He wasn't goin' to be in anything where he couldn't be conspishuous. He was so cocksure o' being made one that he bought a Sam Browne belt, an' was always puttin' it on an' standin' at th' door showing it off, till th' man came an' put out th' street lamps on him. God, I think he used to bring it to bed with him! But I'm tellin' you herself was delighted that the cock didn't crow, for she's like a clockin' hen if he leaves her sight for a minute.

(While she is talking, she takes up book after book from the table, looks into each of them in a near-sighted way, and then leaves them back. She now lifts up the sword, and proceeds to examine it)

MRS. GOGAN Be th' look of it, this must ha' been a general's sword. . . . All th' gold lace an' th' fine figaries on it. . . . Sure it's twiced too big for him.

FLUTHER A-ah; it's a baby's rattle he ought to have, an' he as he is with thoughts tossin' in his head of what may happen to him on th' day o' judgment.

(PETER *has entered, and seeing* MRS. GOGAN *with the sword, goes over to her, pulls it resentfully out of her hands, and marches into the room, Back, without speaking*)

MRS. GOGAN (*as* PETER *whips the sword*) Oh, excuse me! . . . (*to* FLUTHER) Isn't he th' surly oul' rascal!

FLUTHER Take no notice of him. . . . You'd think he was dumb, but when you get his goat, or he has a few jars up, he's vice versa. (*He coughs*)

MRS. GOGAN (*she has now sidled over as far as the shirt hanging on the chair*) Oh, you've got a cold on you, Fluther.

FLUTHER (*carelessly*) Ah, it's only a little one.

MRS. GOGAN You'd want to be careful, all th' same. I knew a woman, a big lump of a woman, red-faced an' round-bodied, a little awkward on her feet; you'd think, to look at her, she could put out her two arms an' lift a two-storied house on th' top of her head; got a ticklin' in her throat, an' a little cough, an' th' next mornin' she had a little catchin' in her chest, an' they had just time to wet her lips with a little rum, an' off she went. (*She begins to look at and handle the shirt*)

FLUTHER (*a little nervously*) It's only a little cold I have; there's nothing derogatory wrong with me.

MRS. GOGAN I dunno; there's many a man this minute lowerin' a pint, thinkin' of a woman, or pickin' out a winner, or doin' work as you're doin', while th' hearse dhrawn be th' horses with the black plumes is dhrivin' up to his own hall door, an' a voice that he doesn't hear is muttherin' in his ear, 'Earth to earth, an' ashes t' ashes, an' dust to dust.'

FLUTHER (*faintly*) A man in th' pink o' health should have a holy horror of allowin' thoughts o' death to be festerin' in his mind, for (*with a frightened cough*) be God, I think I'm afther gettin' a little catch in me chest that time—it's a creepy thing to be thinkin' about.

MRS. GOGAN It is, an' it isn't; it's both bad an' good. . . . It always gives meself a kind o' thresspassin' joy to feel meself movin' along in a mournin' coach, an' me thinkin' that, maybe, th' next funeral 'll be me own, an' glad, in a quiet way, that this is somebody else's.

FLUTHER An' a curious kind of a gaspin' for breath—I hope there's nothin' derogatory wrong with me.

MRS. GOGAN (*examining the shirt*) Frills on it, like a woman's petticoat.

FLUTHER Suddenly gettin' hot, an' then, just as suddenly, gettin' cold.

MRS. GOGAN (*holding out the shirt towards* FLUTHER) How would you like to be wearin' this Lord Mayor's nightdhress, Fluther?

FLUTHER (*vehemently*) Blast you an' your nightshirt! Is a man fermentin' with fear to stick th' showin' off to him of a thing that looks like a shinin' shroud?

MRS. GOGAN Oh, excuse me!

(PETER *has again entered, and he pulls the shirt from the hands of* MRS. GOGAN, *replacing it on the chair. He returns to room*)

PETER (*as he goes out*) Well, God Almighty, give me patience!

MRS. GOGAN (*to* PETER) Oh, excuse me!

(*There is heard a cheer from the men working outside on the street, followed by the clang of tools being thrown down, then silence. The glare of the gasoline light diminishes and finally goes out*)

MRS. GOGAN (*running into the back room to look out of the window*) What's the men repairin' th' streets cheerin' for?

FLUTHER (*sitting down weakly on a chair*) You can't sneeze but that oul' one wants to know th' why an' th' wherefore. . . . I feel as dizzy as bedamned! I hope I didn't give up th' beer too suddenly.

(THE COVEY *comes in by the door, Right. He is about twenty-five, tall, thin, with lines on his face that form a perpetual protest against life as he conceives it to be. Heavy seams fall from each side of nose, down around his lips, as if they were suspenders keeping his mouth from falling. He speaks in a slow, wailing drawl; more rapidly when he is excited. He is dressed in dungarees, and is wearing a vividly red tie. He flings his cap with a gesture of disgust on the table, and begins to take off his overalls*)

MRS. GOGAN (*to* THE COVEY, *as she runs back into the room*) What's after happenin', Covey?

THE COVEY (*with contempt*) Th' job's stopped. They've been mobilized to march in th' demonstration tonight undher th' Plough an' th' Stars. Didn't you hear them cheerin', th' mugs! They have to renew their political baptismal vows to be faithful in seculo seculorum.

FLUTHER (*forgetting his fear in his indignation*) There's no reason to bring religion into it. I think we ought to have as great a regard for religion as we can, so as to keep it out of as many things as possible.

THE COVEY (*pausing in the taking off of his dungarees*) Oh, you're one o' the boys that climb into religion as high as a short Mass on Sunday mornin's? I suppose you'll be singin' songs o' Sion an' songs o' Tara at th' meetin', too.

FLUTHER We're all Irishmen, anyhow; aren't we?

THE COVEY (*with hand outstretched, and in a professional tone*) Look here, comrade, there's no such thing as an Irishman, or an Englishman, or a German or a Turk; we're all only human bein's. Scientifically speakin', it's all a question of the accidental gatherin' together of mollycewels an' atoms.

(PETER *comes in with a collar in his hand. He goes over to mirror, Left, and proceeds to try to put it on*)

FLUTHER Mollycewels an' atoms! D'ye think I'm goin' to listen to you thryin' to juggle Fluther's mind with complicated cunundhrums of mollycewels an' atoms?

THE COVEY (*rather loudly*) There's nothin' complicated in it. There's no fear o' the Church tellin' you that mollycewels is a stickin' together of millions of atoms o' sodium, carbon, potassium o' iodide, etcetera, that, accordin' to th' way they're mixed, make a flower, a fish, a star that you see shinin' in th' sky, or a man with a big brain like me, or a man with a little brain like you!

FLUTHER (*more loudly still*) There's no necessity to be raisin' your voice; shoutin's no manifestin' forth of a growin' mind.

PETER (*struggling with his collar*) God, give me patience with this thing. . . . She makes these collars as stiff with starch as a shinin' band o' solid steel! She does it purposely to thry an' twart me. If I can't get it on th' singlet, how, in th' Name o' God, am I goin' to get it on th' shirt?

THE COVEY (*loudly*) There's no use o' arguin' with you, it's education you want, comrade.

FLUTHER The Covey an' God made th' world, I suppose, wha'?

THE COVEY When I hear some men talkin' I'm inclined to disbelieve that th' world's eighthundhred million years old, for it's not long since th' fathers o' some o' them crawled out o' th' sheltherin' slime o' the sea.

MRS. GOGAN (*from room at back*) There, they're afther formin' fours, an' now they're goin' to march away.

FLUTHER (*scornfully*) Mollycewels! (*He begins to untie his apron*) What about Adam an' Eve?

THE COVEY Well, what about them?

FLUTHER (*fiercely*) What about them, you?

THE COVEY Adam an' Eve! Is that as far as you've got? Are you still thinkin' there was nobody in th' world before Adam and Eve? (*loudly*) Did you ever hear, man, of th' skeleton of th' man o' Java?

PETER (*casting the collar from him*) Blast it, blast it, blast it!

FLUTHER (*viciously folding his apron*) Ah, you're not goin' to be let tap your rubbidge o' thoughts into th' mind o' Fluther.

THE COVEY You're afraid to listen to th' truth!

FLUTHER Who's afraid?

THE COVEY You are!

FLUTHER G'way, you wurum!

THE COVEY Who's a worum?

FLUTHER You are, or you wouldn't talk th' way you're talkin'.

THE COVEY Th' oul', ignorant savage leppin' up in you, when science shows you that th' head of your god is an empty one. Well, I hope you're enjoyin' th' blessin' o' havin' to live be th' sweat of your brow.

FLUTHER You'll be kickin' an' yellin' for th' priest yet, me boyo. I'm not goin' to stand silent an' simple listenin' to a thick like you makin' a maddenin' mockery o' God Almighty. It 'ud be a nice derogatory thing on me conscience, an' me dyin', to look back in rememberin' shame of talkin' to a word-weavin' little ignorant yahoo of a red flag Socialist!

MRS. GOGAN (*she has returned to the front room, and has wandered around looking at things in general, and is now in front of the fireplace looking at the picture hanging over it*) For God's sake, Fluther, dhrop it; there's always th' makin's of a row in th' mention of religion . . . (*looking at picture*) God bless us, it's a naked woman!

FLUTHER (*coming over to look at it*) What's undher it? (*reading*) "Georgina: The Sleepin' Vennis." Oh, that's a terrible picture; oh, that's a shockin' picture! Oh, th' one that got that taken, she must have been a prime lassie!

PETER (*who also has come over to look, laughing, with his body bent at the waist, and his head slightly tilted back*) Hee, hee, hee, hee, hee!

FLUTHER (*indignantly, to PETER*) What are you hee, hee-in' for? That' a nice thing to be hee, hee-in' at. Where's your morality, man?

MRS. GOGAN   God forgive us, it's not right to be lookin' at it.

FLUTHER   It's nearly a derogatory thing to be in th' room where it is.

MRS. GOGAN (*giggling hysterically*) I couldn't stop any longer in th' same room with three men, afther lookin' at it! (*She goes out*)

(THE COVEY, *who has divested himself of his dungarees, throws them with a contemptuous motion on top of Peter's white shirt*)

PETER (*plaintively*) Where are you throwin' them? Are you thryin' to twart an' torment me again?

THE COVEY   Who's thryin' to twart you?

PETER (*flinging the dungarees violently on the floor*) You're not goin' to make me lose me temper, me young Covey.

THE COVEY (*flinging the white shirt on the floor*) If you're Nora's pet, aself, you're not goin' to get your way in everything.

PETER (*plaintively, with his eyes looking up at the ceiling*) I'll say nothin'. . . . I'll leave you to th' day when th' all-pitiful, all-merciful, all-lovin' God 'll be handin' you to th' angels to be rievin' an' roastin' you, tearin' an' tormentin' you, burnin' an' blastin' you!

THE COVEY   Aren't you th' little malignant oul' bastard, you lemon-whiskered oul' swine!

(PETER *runs to the sword, draws it, and makes for* THE COVEY, *who dodges him around the table;* PETER *has no intention of striking, but* THE COVEY *wants to take no chance*)

THE COVEY (*dodging*) Fluther, hold him, there. It's a nice thing to have a lunatic like this lashin' around with a lethal weapon! (THE COVEY *darts out of the room, Right, slamming the door in the face of* PETER)

PETER (*battering and pulling at the door*) Lemme out, lemme out; isn't it a poor thing for a man who wouldn't say a word against his greatest enemy to have to listen to that Covey's twartin' animosities, shovin' poor, patient people into a lashin' out of curses that darken his soul with th' shadow of th' wrath of th' last day!

FLUTHER   Why d'ye take notice of him? If he seen you didn't, he'd say nothin' derogatory.

PETER   I'll make him stop his laughin' an' leerin', jibin' an' jeerin' an' scarifyin' people with his cornerboy insinuations! . . . He's always thryin' to rouse me: if it's not a song, it's a whistle; if it isn't a whistle, it's a cough. But you can taunt an' taunt—I'm laughin' at you; he, hee, hee, hee, hee, heee!

THE COVEY (*singing through the keyhole:*)
Dear harp o' me counthry, in darkness I found thee,

The dark chain of silence had hung o'er thee long—

PETER (*frantically*) Jasus, d'ye hear that? D'ye hear him soundin' forth his divil-souled song o' provocation?

THE COVEY (*singing as before:*)
When proudly, me own island harp, I unbound thee,
An' gave all thy chords to light, freedom an' song!

PETER (*battering at door*) When I get out I'll do for you, I'll do for you, I'll do for you!

THE COVEY (*through the keyhole*) Cuck-oo-oo!

(NORA *enters by door, Right. She is a young woman of twenty-two, alert, swift, full of nervous energy, and a little anxious to get on in the world. The firm lines of her face are considerably opposed by a soft, amorous mouth and gentle eyes. When her firmness fails her, she persuades with her feminine charm. She is dressed in a tailor-made costume, and wears around her neck a silver fox fur*)

NORA (*running in and pushing* PETER *away from the door*) Oh, can I not turn me back but th' two o' yous are at it like a pair o' fightin' cocks! Uncle Peter . . . Uncle Peter . . . UNCLE PETER!

PETER (*vociferously*) Oh, Uncle Peter, Uncle Peter be damned! D'ye think I'm goin' to give a free pass to th' young Covey to turn me whole life into a Holy Manual o' penances an' martyrdoms?

THE COVEY (*angrily rushing into the room*) If you won't exercise some sort o' control over that Uncle Peter o' yours, there'll be a funeral, an' it won't be me that'll be in th' hearse!

NORA (*between* PETER *and* THE COVEY, *to* THE COVEY) Are yous always goin' to be tearin' down th' little bit of respectability that a body's thryin' to build up? Am I always goin' to be havin' to nurse yous into th' hardy habit o' thryin' to keep up a little bit of appearance?

THE COVEY   Why weren't you here to see th' way he run at me with th' sword?

PETER   What did you call me a lemon-whiskered oul' swine for?

NORA   If th' two o' yous don't thry to make a generous altheration in your goin's on, an' keep on thryin' t' inaugurate th' customs o' th' rest o' th' house into this place, yous can flit into other lodgin's where your bowsey battlin' 'ill meet, maybe, with an encore.

PETER (*to* NORA) Would you like to be called a lemon-whiskered oul' swine?

NORA   If you attempt to wag that sword of yours at anybody again, it'll have to be taken off you an' put in a safe place away from babies that don't know th' danger o' them things.

PETER (*at entrance to room, Back*)   Well, I'm not goin' to let anybody call me a lemon-whiskered oul' swine. (*He goes in*)

FLUTHER (*trying the door*)   Openin' an' shuttin' now with a well-mannered motion, like a door of a select bar in a high-class pub.

NORA (*to* THE COVEY, *as she lays table for tea*)   An', once for all, Willie, you'll have to thry to deliver yourself from th' desire of provokin' oul' Pether into a wild forgetfulness of what's proper an' allowable in a respectable home.

THE COVEY   Well, let him mind his own business, then. Yestherday I caught him hee-hee-in' out of him an' he readin' bits out of Jenersky's *Thesis on th' Origin, Development, an' Consolidation of th' Evolutionary Idea of th' Proletariat.*

NORA   Now, let it end at that, for God's sake; Jack'll be in any minute, an' I'm not goin' to have th' quiet of this evenin' tossed about in an everlastin' uproar between you an' Uncle Pether. (*to* FLUTHER) Well, did you manage to settle th' lock, yet, Mr. Good?

FLUTHER (*opening and shutting door*)   It's better than a new one, now, Mrs. Clitheroe; it's almost ready to open and shut of its own accord.

NORA (*giving him a coin*)   You're a whole man. How many pints will that get you?

FLUTHER (*seriously*)   Ne'er a one at all, Mrs. Clitheroe, for Fluther's on th' wather waggon now. You could stan' where you're stannin' chantin', "Have a glass o' malt, Fluther; Fluther, have a glass o' malt," till th' bells would be ringin' th' ould year out an' th' New Year in, an' you'd have as much chance o' movin' Fluther as a tune on a tin whistle would move a deaf man an' he dead.

(*As* NORA *is opening and shutting door*, MRS. BESSIE BURGESS *appears at it. She is a woman of forty, vigorously built. Her face is a dogged one, hardened by toil, and a little coarsened by drink. She looks scornfully and viciously at* NORA *for a few moments before she speaks*)

BESSIE   Puttin' a new lock on her door . . . afraid her poor neighbors ud break through an' steal. . . . (*in a loud tone*) Maybe, now, they're a damn sight more honest than your ladyship . . . checkin' th' children playin' on th' stairs . . . gettin' on th' nerves of your ladyship. . . . Complainin' about Bessie Burgess singin' her hymns at night, when she has a few up. . . . (*She comes in half-way on the threshold, and screams*) Bessie Burgess 'll sing whenever she damn well likes!

(NORA *tries to shut the door, but* BESSIE *violently shoves it in, and, gripping* NORA *by the shoulders, shakes her*)

BESSIE   You little over-dressed throllop, you, for one pin I'd paste th' white face o' you!

NORA (*frightened*)   Fluther, Fluther!

FLUTHER (*running over and breaking the hold of* BESSIE *from* NORA)   Now, now, Bessie, Bessie, leave poor Mrs. Clitheroe alone; she'd do no one any harm, an' minds no one's business but her own.

BESSIE   Why is she always thryin' to speak proud things, an' lookin' like a mighty one in th' congregation o' th' people!

(NORA *sinks frightened onto the couch as* JACK CLITHEROE *enters. He is a tall, well-made fellow of twenty-five. His face has none of the strength of* NORA's. *It is a face in which is the desire for authority, without the power to attain it*)

CLITHEROE (*excitedly*)   What's up? what's afther happenin'?

FLUTHER   Nothin', Jack. Nothin'. It's all over now. Come on, Bessie, come on.

CLITHEROE (*to* NORA)   What's wrong, Nora? Did she say anything to you?

NORA   She was bargin' out of her, an' I only told her to g'up ower o' that to her own place; an' before I knew where I was, she flew at me like a tiger, an' thried to guzzle me!

CLITHEROE (*going to door and speaking to* BESSIE)   Get up to your own place, Mrs. Burgess, and don't you be interferin' with my wife, or it'll be th' worse for you. . . . Go on, go on!

BESSIE (*as* CLITHEROE *is pushing her out*)   Mind who you're pushin', now. . . . I attend me place o' worship, anyhow . . . not like some o' them that go to neither church, chapel nor meetin'-house. . . . If me son was home from th' threnches he'd see me righted.

(BESSIE *and* FLUTHER *depart, and* CLITHEROE *closes the door*)

CLITHEROE (*going over to* NORA, *and putting his arm round her*)   There, don't mind that old bitch, Nora, darling; I'll soon put a stop to her interferin'.

NORA   Some day or another, when I'm here be meself, she'll come in an' do somethin' desperate.

CLITHEROE (*kissing her*)   Oh, sorra fear of her doin' anythin' desperate. I'll talk to her to-morrow when she's sober. A taste o' me mind that'll shock her into the sensibility of behavin' herself!

(NORA *gets up and settles the table. She sees the dungarees on the floor and stands looking at them, then she turns to* THE COVEY, *who is reading Jenersky's "Thesis" at the fire*)

NORA   Willie, is that th' place for your dungarees?

THE COVEY (*getting up and lifting them from the floor*)   Ah, they won't do th' floor any harm, will they? (*He carries them into room, Back*)

NORA (*calling*)   Uncle Peter, now, Uncle Peter; tea's ready. (PETER *and* THE COVEY *come in from room, Back; they all sit down to tea.* PETER *is in full dress of the Foresters: green coat, gold braided; white breeches, top boots, frilled shirt. He carries the slouch hat, with the white ostrich plume, and the sword in his hands. They eat for a few moments in silence,* THE COVEY *furtively looking at* PETER *with scorn in his eyes.* PETER *knows it and is fidgety*)

THE COVEY (*provokingly*)   Another cut o' bread, Uncle Peter? (PETER *maintains a dignified silence*)

CLITHEROE   It's sure to be a great meetin' tonight. We ought to go, Nora.

NORA (*decisively*)   I won't go, Jack; you can go if you wish.

THE COVEY   D'ye want th' sugar, Uncle Peter? (*a pause*)

PETER (*explosively*)   Now, are you goin' to start your thryin' an' your twartin' again?

NORA   Now, Uncle Peter, you mustn't be so touchy; Willie has only assed you if you wanted th' sugar.

PETER   He doesn't care a damn whether I want th' sugar or no. He's only thryin' to twart me!

NORA (*angrily, to* THE COVEY)   Can't you let him alone, Willie? If he wants the sugar, let him stretch his hand out an' get it himself!

THE COVEY (*to* PETER)   Now, if you want the sugar, you can stretch out your hand and get it yourself!

CLITHEROE   Tonight is th' first chance that Brennan has got of showing himself off since they made a Captain of him—why, God only knows. It'll be a treat to see him swankin' it at th' head of the Citizen Army carryin' th' flag of the Plough an' th' Stars. . . . (*looking roguishly at* NORA) He was sweet on you, once, Nora?

NORA   He may have been. . . . I never liked him. I always thought he was a bit of a thick.

THE COVEY   They're bringin' nice disgrace on that banner now.

CLITHEROE (*remonstratively*)   How are they bringin' disgrace on it?

THE COVEY (*snappily*)   Because it's a La-

bor flag, an' was never meant for politics. . . . What does th' design of th' field plough, bearin' on it th' stars of th' heavenly plough, mean, if it's not Communism? It's a flag that should only be used when we're buildin' th' barricades to fight for a Workers' Republic!

PETER (*with a puff of derision*)   P-phuh.

THE COVEY (*angrily*)   What are you phuhin' out o' you for? Your mind is th' mind of a mummy. (*rising*) I betther go an' get a good place to have a look at Ireland's warriors passin' by. (*He goes into room, Left, and returns with his cap*)

NORA (*to* THE COVEY)   Oh, Willie, brush your clothes before you go.

THE COVEY   Oh, they'll do well enough.

NORA   Go an' brush them; th' brush is in th' drawer there.

(THE COVEY *goes to the drawer, muttering, gets the brush, and starts to brush his clothes*)

THE COVEY (*singing at* PETER, *as he does so:*)

Oh, where's th' slave so lowly,
Condemn'd to chains unholy,
Who, could he burst his bonds at first,
Would pine beneath them slowly?
We tread th' land that . . . bore us,
Th' green flag glitters . . . o'er us,
Th' friends we've tried are by our side,
An' th' foe we hate . . . before us!

PETER (*leaping to his feet in a whirl of rage*)   Now, I'm tellin' you, me young Covey, once for all, that I'll not stick any longer these tittherin' taunts of yours, rovin' around to sing your slights an' slandhers, reddenin' th' mind of a man to th' thinkin' an' sayin' of things that sicken his soul with sin! (*hysterical; lifting up a cup to fling at* THE COVEY) Be God, I'll—

CLITHEROE (*catching his arm*)   Now then, none o' that, none o' that!

NORA   Uncle Pether, Uncle Pether, UNCLE PETHER!

THE COVEY (*at the door, about to go out*)   Isn't that th' malignant oul' varmit! Lookin' like th' illegitimate son of an illegitimate child of a corporal in th' Mexican army! (*He goes out*)

PETER (*plaintively*)   He's afther leavin' me now in such a state of agitation that I won't be able to do meself justice when I'm marchin' to th' meetin'.

NORA (*jumping up*)   Oh, for God's sake, here, buckle your sword on, and go to your meetin', so that we'll have at least one hour of peace! (*She proceeds to belt on the sword*)

CLITHEROE (*irritably*)   For God's sake hurry him up ou' o' this, Nora.

PETER Are yous all goin' to thry to start to twart me now?

NORA (*putting on his plumed hat*) S-s-sh. Now, your hat's on, your house is thatched; off you pop! (*She gently pushes him from her*)

PETER (*going, and turning as he reaches the door*) Now, if that young Covey—

NORA Go on, go on. (*He goes*)

(CLITHEROE *sits down in the lounge, lights a cigarette, and looks thoughtfully into the fire.* NORA *takes the things from the table, placing them on the chest of drawers. There is a pause, then she swiftly comes over to him and sits beside him*)

NORA (*softly*) A penny for them, Jack!

CLITHEROE Me? Oh, I was thinkin' of nothing.

NORA You were thinkin' of th' . . . meetin' Jack. When we were courtin' an' I wanted you to go, you'd say, "Oh, to hell with meetin's," an' that you felt lonely in cheerin' crowds when I was absent. An' we weren't a month married when you began that you couldn't keep away from them.

CLITHEROE Oh, that's enough about th' meetin'. It looks as if you wanted me to go th' way you're talkin'. You were always at me to give up th' Citizen Army, an' I gave it up; surely that ought to satisfy you.

NORA Ay, you gave it up—because you got th' sulks when they didn't make a Captain of you. It wasn't for my sake, Jack.

CLITHEROE For your sake or no, you're benefitin' by it, aren't you? I didn't forget this was your birthday, did I? (*He puts his arms around her*) And you liked your new hat; didn't you, didn't you? (*He kisses her rapidly several times*)

NORA (*panting*) Jack, Jack; please, Jack! I thought you were tired of that sort of thing long ago.

CLITHEROE Well, you're finding out now that I amn't tired of it yet, anyhow. Mrs. Clitheroe doesn't want to be kissed, sure she doesn't? (*He kisses her again*) Little, little red-lipped Nora!

NORA (*coquettishly removing his arm from around her*) Oh, yes, your little, little red-lipped Nora's a sweet little girl when th' fit seizes you; but your little, little red-lipped Nora has to clean your boots every mornin', all the same.

CLITHEROE (*with a movement of irritation*) Oh, well, if we're goin' to be snotty! (*a pause*)

NORA It's lookin' like as if it was a you that was goin' to be . . . snotty! Bridlin' up with bittherness, th' minute a body attempts t' open her mouth.

CLITHEROE Is it any wondher, turnin' a tendher sayin' into a meanin' o' malice an' spite!

NORA It's hard for a body to be always keepin' her mind bent on makin' thoughts that'll be no longer than th' length of your own satisfaction. (*a pause*)

NORA (*standing up*) If we're goin' to dhribble th' time away sittin' here like a pair o' cranky mummies, I'd be as well sewin' or doin' something about th' place.

(*She looks appealingly at him for a few moments; he doesn't speak. She swiftly sits down beside him, and puts her arm around his neck*)

NORA (*imploringly*) Ah, Jack, don't be so cross!

CLITHEROE (*doggedly*) Cross? I'm not cross; I'm not a bit cross. It was yourself started it.

NORA (*coaxingly*) I didn't mean to say anything out o' the way. You take a body up too quickly, Jack. (*in an ordinary tone as if nothing of an angry nature had been said*) You didn't offer me me evenin' allowance yet.

(CLITHEROE *silently takes out a cigarette for her and himself and lights both*)

NORA (*trying to make conversation*) How quiet th' house is now; they must be all out.

CLITHEROE (*rather shortly*) I suppose so.

NORA (*rising from the seat*) I'm longin' to show you me new hat, to see what you think of it. Would you like to see it?

CLITHEROE Ah, I don't mind.

(NORA *suppresses a sharp reply, hesitates for a moment, then gets the hat, puts it on, and stands before* CLITHEROE)

NORA Well, how does Mr. Clitheroe like me new hat?

CLITHEROE It suits you, Nora, it does right enough. (*He stands up, puts his hand beneath her chin, and tilts her head up. She looks at him roguishly. He bends down and kisses her*)

NORA Here, sit down, an' don't let me hear another cross word out of you for th' rest o' the night. (*They sit down*)

CLITHEROE (*with his arms around her*) Little, little, red-lipped Nora!

NORA (*with a coaxing movement of her body towards him*) Jack!

CLITHEROE (*tightening his arms around her*) Well?

NORA You haven't sung me a song since our honeymoon. Sing me one now, do . . . please, Jack!

CLITHEROE What song? "Since Maggie Went Away?"

NORA   Ah, no, Jack, not that; it's too sad. "When You Said You Loved Me."

(*Clearing his throat,* CLITHEROE *thinks for a moment and then begins to sing.* NORA, *putting an arm around him, nestles her head on his breast and listens delightedly*)

CLITHEROE (*singing verses following to the air of "When You and I Were Young, Maggie":*
Th' violets were scenting th' woods, Nora,
   Displaying their charm to th' bee,
When I first said I lov'd only you, Nora,
   An' you said you lov'd only me!
Th' chestnut blooms gleam'd through th' glade, Nora,
   A robin sang loud from a tree,
When I first said I lov'd only you, Nora,
   An' you said you lov'd only me!
Th' golden-rob'd daffodils shone, Nora,
   An' danc'd in th' breeze on th' lea,
When I first said I lov'd only you, Nora,
   An' you said you lov'd only me!
Th' trees, birds, an' bees sang a song, Nora,
   Of happier transports to be,
When I first said I lov'd only you, Nora,
   An' you said you lov'd only me! (NORA *kisses him*)

(*A knock is heard at the door, Right; a pause as they listen. Nora clings closely to* CLITHEROE. *Another knock, more imperative than the first*)

CLITHEROE   I wonder who can that be, now?

NORA (*a little nervous*)   Take no notice of it, Jack; they'll go away in a minute (*another knock, followed by a voice*)

VOICE   Commandant Clitheroe, Commandant Clitheroe, are you there? A message from General Jim Connolly.

CLITHEROE   Damn it, it's Captain Brennan.

NORA (*anxiously*)   Don't mind him, don't mind, Jack. Don't break our happiness. . . . Pretend we're not in. Let us forget everything tonight but our two selves!

CLITHEROE (*reassuringly*)   Don't be alarmed, darling; I'll just see what he wants, an' send him about his business.

NORA (*tremulously*)   No, no. Please, Jack; don't open it. Please, for your own little Nora's sake!

CLITHEROE (*rising to open the door*)   Now don't be silly, Nora. (CLITHEROE *opens the door, and admits a young man in the full uniform of the Irish Citizen Army—green suit; slouch green hat caught up at one side by a small Red Hand badge; Sam Browne belt, with a revolver in the holster. He carries a letter in his hand. When he comes in he smartly salutes* CLITHEROE. *The young man is* CAPTAIN BRENNAN)

CAPT. BRENNAN (*giving the letter to* CLITHEROE)   A dispatch from General Connolly.

CLITHEROE (*reading. While he is doing so,* BRENNAN's *eyes are fixed on* NORA, *who droops as she sits on the lounge*)   "Commandant Clitheroe is to take command of the eighth battalion of the I.C.A. which will assemble to proceed to the meeting at nine o'clock. He is to see that all units are provided with full equipment; two days' rations and fifty rounds of ammunition. At two o'clock A.M. the army will leave Liberty Hall for a reconnaissance attack on Dublin Castle.—Com.-Gen. Connolly."

CLITHEROE   I don't understand this. Why does General Connolly call me Commandant?

CAPT. BRENNAN   Th' Staff appointed you Commandant, and th' General agreed with their selection.

CLITHEROE   When did this happen?

CAPT. BRENNAN   A fortnight ago.

CLITHEROE   How is it word was never sent to me?

CAPT. BRENNAN   Word was sent to you. . . . I meself brought it.

CLITHEROE   Who did you give it to, then?

CAPT. BRENNAN (*after a pause*)   I think I gave it to Mrs. Clitheroe, there.

CLITHEROE   Nora, d'ye hear that?

(NORA *makes no answer*)

CLITHEROE (*there is a note of hardness in his voice*)   Nora . . . Captain Brennan says he brought a letter to me from General Connolly, and that he gave it to you. . . . Where is it? What did you do with it?

NORA (*running over to him, and pleadingly putting her arms around him*)   Jack, please, Jack, don't go out tonight an' I'll tell you; I'll explain everything. . . . Send him away, an' stay with your own little red-lipp'd Nora.

CLITHEROE (*removing her arms from around him*)   None o' this nonsense, now; I want to know what you did with th' letter?

(NORA *goes slowly to the lounge and sits down*)

CLITHEROE (*angrily*)   Why didn't you give me th' letter? What did you do with it? . . . (*He shakes her by the shoulder*) What did you do with th' letter?

NORA (*flaming up*)   I burned it, I burned it! That's what I did with it! Is General Connolly an' th' Citizen Army goin' to be your only care? Is your home goin' to be only a place to rest in? Am I goin' to be only somethin' to provide merry-makin' at night for you? Your vanity'll be th' ruin of you an' me yet. . . . That's what's movin' you: because they've made an officer of you, you'll make a glorious cause of what you're doin', while your little red-lipp'd Nora can go on sittin' here, makin' a companion of the loneliness of th' night!

CLITHEROE (*fiercely*) You burned it, did you? (*He grips her arm*) Well, me good lady—

NORA Let go—you're hurtin' me!

CLITHEROE You deserve to be hurt. . . . Any letter that comes to me for th' future, take care that I get it. . . . D'ye hear—take care that I get it!

(*He goes to the chest of drawers and takes out a Sam Browne belt, which he puts on, and then puts a revolver in the holster. He puts on his hat, and looks towards* NORA. *While this dialogue is proceeding, and while* CLITHEROE *prepares himself,* BRENNAN *softly whistles "The Soldiers' Song"*)

CLITHEROE (*at door, about to go out*) You needn't wait up for me; if I'm in at all, it won't be before six in th' morning.

NORA (*bitterly*) I don't care if you never come back!

CLITHEROE (*to* CAPT. BRENNAN) Come along, Ned.

(*They go out; there is a pause.* NORA *pulls her new hat from her head and with a bitter movement flings it to the other end of the room. There is a gentle knock at door, Right, which opens, and* MOLLSER *comes into the room. She is about fifteen, but looks to be only about ten, for the ravages of consumption have shrivelled her up. She is pitifully worn, walks feebly, and frequently coughs. She goes over to* NORA)

MOLLSER (*to* NORA) Mother's gone to th' meetin', an' I was feelin' terrible lonely, so I come down to see if you'd let me sit with you, thinkin' you mightn't be goin' yourself. . . . I do be terrible afraid I'll die sometime when I'm be meself. . . . I often envy you, Mrs. Clitheroe, seein' th' health you have, an' th' lovely place you have here, an' wondherin' if I'll ever be sthrong enough to be keepin' a home together for a man. Oh, this must be some more o' the Dublin Fusiliers flyin' off to the front.

(*Just before* MOLLSER *ceases to speak, there is heard in the distance the music of a brass band playing a regiment to the boat on the way to the front. The tune that is being played is "It's a Long Way to Tipperary"; as the band comes to the chorus, the regiment is swinging into the street by* NORA's *house, and the voices of the soldiers can be heard lustily singing the chorus of the song:*)

It's a long way to Tipperary, it's a long way
    to go;
It's a long way to Tipperary, to th' sweetest
    girl I know!
Goodbye, Piccadilly; farewell, Leicester
    Square.
It's a long, long way to Tipperary, but my
    heart's right there!

(NORA *and* MOLLSER *remain silently listening. As the chorus ends and the music is faint in the distance again,* BESSIE BURGESS *appears at door, Right, which* MOLLSER *has left open*)

BESSIE (*speaking in towards the room*) There's th' men marchin' out into th' dhread dimness o' danger, while th' lice is crawlin' about feedin' on th' fatness o' the land! But yous'll not escape from th' arrow that flieth be night, or th' sickness that wasteth be day. . . . An' ladyship an' all, as some o' them may be, they'll be scattered abroad, like th' dust in th' darkness!

(BESSIE *goes away;* NORA *steals over and quietly shuts the door. She comes back to the lounge and wearily throws herself on it beside* MOLLSER)

MOLLSER (*after a pause and a cough*) Is there anybody goin', Mrs. Clitheroe, with a titther o' sense?

ACT TWO

(*A commodious public-house at the corner of the street in which the meeting is being addressed from Platform No. 1. It is the south corner of the public-house that is visible to the audience. The counter, beginning at Back about one-fourth of the width of the space shown, comes across two-thirds of the length of the stage, and, taking a circular sweep, passes out of sight to Left. On the counter are beerpulls, glasses, and a carafe. The other three-fourths of the Back is occupied by a tall, wide, two-paned window. Beside this window at the Right is a small, box-like, panelled snug. Next to the snug is a double swing door, the entrance to that particular end of the house. Farther on is a shelf on which customers may rest their drinks. Underneath the windows is a cushioned seat. Behind the counter at Back can be seen the shelves running the whole length of the counter. On these shelves can be seen the end (or the beginning) of rows of bottles. The* BARMAN *is seen wiping the part of the counter which is in view.* ROSIE *is standing at the counter toying with what remains of a half of whisky in a wine-glass. She is a sturdy, well-shaped girl of twenty; pretty, and pert in manner. She is wearing a cream blouse, with an obviously suggestive glad neck; a grey tweed dress, brown stockings and shoes. The blouse and most of the dress are hidden by a black shawl. She has no hat, and in her hair is jauntily set a cheap, glittering, jewelled ornament. It is an hour later*)

BARMAN (*wiping counter*) Nothin' much doin' in your line tonight, Rosie?

ROSIE Curse o' God on th' haporth, hardly, Tom. There isn't much notice taken of a pretty petticoat of a night like this. . . . They're all in a holy mood. Th' solemn-lookin' dials on th' whole o' them an' they marchin' to th' meetin'. You'd think they were th' glorious company of th' saints, an' th' noble army of martyrs trampin' through th' sthreets of paradise. They're all thinkin' of higher things than a girl's garters. . . . It's a tremendous meetin'; four platforms they have—there's one o' them just outside opposite th' window.

BARMAN Oh, ay; sure when th' speaker comes (*motioning with his hand*) to th' near end, here, you can see him plain, an' hear nearly everythin' he's spoutin' out of him.

ROSIE It's no joke thryin' to make up fifty-five shillin's a week for your keep an' laundhry, an' then taxin' you a quid for your own room if you bring home a friend for th' night. . . . If I could only put by a couple of quid for a swankier outfit, everythin' in th' garden ud look lovely—

BARMAN Whisht, till we hear what he's sayin'.

(*Through the window is silhouetted the figure of a tall man who is speaking to the crowd. The* BARMAN *and* ROSIE *look out of the window and listen*)

THE VOICE OF THE MAN It is a glorious thing to see arms in the hands of Irishmen. We must accustom ourselves to the thought of arms, we must accustom ourselves to the sight of arms, we must accustom ourselves to the use of arms. . . . Bloodshed is a cleansing and sanctifying thing, and the nation that regards it as the final horror has lost its manhood. . . . There are many things more horrible than bloodshed, and slavery is one of them! (*The figure moves away towards the Right, and is lost to sight and hearing*)

ROSIE It's th' sacred thruth, mind you, what that man's afther sayin'.

BARMAN If I was only a little younger, I'd be plungin' mad into th' middle of it!

ROSIE (*who is still looking out of the window*) Oh, here's the two gems runnin' over again for their oil!

(PETER *and* FLUTHER *enter tumultuously. They are hot, and full and hasty with the things they have seen and heard. Emotion is bubbling up in them, so that when they drink, and when they speak, they drink and speak with the fullness of emotional passion.* PETER *leads the way to the counter*)

PETER (*splutteringly to* BARMAN) Two halves . . . (*to* FLUTHER) A meetin' like this always makes me feel as if I could dhrink Loch Erinn dhry!

FLUTHER You couldn't feel any way else at a time like this when th' spirit of a man is pulsin' to be out fightin' for th' thruth with his feet thremblin' on th' way, maybe to th' gallows, an' his ears tinglin' with th' faint, far-away sound of burstin' rifleshots that'll maybe whip th' last little shock o' life out of him that's left lingerin' in his body!

PETER I felt a burnin' lump in me throat when I heard th' band playin' "The Soldiers' Song," rememberin' last hearin' it marchin' in military formation with th' people starin' on both sides at us, carryin' with us th' pride an' resolution o' Dublin to th' grave of Wolfe Tone.

FLUTHER Get th' Dublin men goin' an' they'll go on full force for anything that's thryin' to bar them away from what they're wantin', where th' slim thinkin' counthry boyo ud limp away from th' first faintest touch of compromization!

PETER (*hurriedly to the* BARMAN) Two more, Tom! . . . (*to* FLUTHER) Th' memory of all th' things that was done, an' all th' things that was suffered be th' people, was boomin' in me brain. . . . Every nerve in me body was quiverin' to do somethin' desperate!

FLUTHER Jammed as I was in th' crowd, I listened to th' speeches pattherin' on th' people's head, like rain fallin' on th' corn; every derogatory thought went out o' me mind, an' I said to meself, "You can die now, Fluther, for you've seen th' shadow dhreams of th' past leppin' to life in th' bodies of livin' men that show, if we were without a titther o' courage for centuries, we're vice versa now!" Looka here. (*He stretches out his arm under* PETER's *face and rolls up his sleeve*) The blood was boilin' in me veins!

(*The silhouette of the tall figure again moves into the frame of the window speaking to the people*)

PETER (*unaware, in his enthusiasm, of the speaker's appearance, to* FLUTHER) I was burnin' to dhraw me sword, an' wave an' wave it over me—

FLUTHER (*overwhelming* PETER) Will you stop your blatherin' for a minute, man, an' let us hear what he's sayin'!

VOICE OF THE MAN Comrade soldiers of the Irish Volunteers and of the Citizen Army, we rejoice in this terrible war. The old heart of the earth needed to be warmed with the red wine of the battlefields. . . . Such august homage was never offered to God as this: the homage of millions of lives given gladly for love of country. And we must be ready to pour out the same red wine in the same glorious sacrifice, for without shedding of blood there is no redemption! (*The figure moves out of sight and hearing*)

FLUTHER (*gulping down the drink that remains in his glass, and rushing out*) Come on, man; this is too good to be missed!

(PETER *finishes his drink less rapidly, and as he is going out wiping his mouth with the back of his hand he runs into* THE COVEY *coming in. He immediately erects his body like a young cock, and with his chin thrust forward, and a look of venomous dignity on his face, he marches out*)

THE COVEY (*at counter*) Give us a glass o' malt, for God's sake, till I stimulate meself from the shock o' seein' th' sight that's afther goin' out!

ROSIE (*all business, coming over to the counter, and standing near* THE COVEY) Another one for me, Tommy; (*to the* BARMAN) th' young gentleman's ordherin' it in th' corner of his eye.

(*The* BARMAN *brings the drink for* THE COVEY, *and leaves it on the counter.* ROSIE *whips it up*)

BARMAN Ay, houl' on there, houl' on there, Rosie!

ROSIE (*to the* BARMAN) What are you houldin' on out o' you for? Didn't you hear th' young gentleman say that he couldn't refuse anything to a nice little bird? (*to* THE COVEY) Isn't that right, Jiggs? (THE COVEY *says nothing*) Didn't I know, Tommy, it would be all right? It takes Rosie to size a young man up, an' tell th' thoughts that are thremblin' in his mind. Isn't that right, Jiggs?

(THE COVEY *stirs uneasily, moves a little farther away, and pulls his cap over his eyes*)

ROSIE (*moving after him*) Great meetin' that's gettin' held outside. Well, it's up to us all, anyway, to fight for our freedom.

THE COVEY (*to* BARMAN) Two more, please. (*to* ROSIE) Freedom! What's th' use o' freedom, if it's not economic freedom?

ROSIE (*emphasizing with extended arm and moving finger*) I used them very words just before you come in. "A lot o' thricksters," says I, "that wouldn't know what freedom was if they got it from their mother." . . . (*to* BARMAN) Didn't I, Tommy?

BARMAN I disremember.

ROSIE No, you don't disremember. Remember you said, yourself, it was all "only a flash in th' pan." Well, "flash in th' pan, or no flash in th' pan," says I, "they're not goin' to get Rosie Redmond," says I, "to fight for freedom that wouldn't be worth winnin' in a raffle!"

THE COVEY There's only one freedom for th' workin' man: conthrol o' th' means o' production, rates of exchange, an' th' means of disthribution. (*tapping* ROSIE *on the shoulder*) Look here, comrade, I'll leave here tomorrow night for you a copy of Jenersky's *Thesis on the Origin, Development, an' Consolidation of the Evolutionary Idea of the Proletariat.*

ROSIE (*throwing off her shawl onto the counter, and showing an exemplified glad neck, which reveals a good deal of a white bosom*) If y'ass Rosie, it's heartbreakin' to see a young fella thinkin' of anything, or admirin' anything, but silk thransparent stockin's showin' off the shape of a little lassie's legs!

(THE COVEY, *frightened, moves a little away*)

ROSIE (*following on*) Out in th' park in th' shade of a warm summery evenin', with your little darlin' bridie to be, kissin' an' cuddlin' (*She tries to put her arm around his neck*) kissin' an' cuddlin', ay?

THE COVEY (*frightened*) Ay, what are you doin'? None o' that, now; none o' that. I've something else to do besides shinannickin' afther Judies!

(*He turns away, but* ROSIE *follows, keeping face to face with him*)

ROSIE Oh, little duckey, oh, shy little duckey! Never held a mot's hand, an' wouldn't know how to tittle a little Judy! (*She clips him under the chin*) Tittle him undher th' chin, tittle him undher th' chin!

THE COVEY (*breaking away and running out*) Ay, go on, now; I don't want to have any meddlin' with a lassie like you!

ROSIE (*enraged*)   Jasus, it's in a monasthery some of us ought to be, spendin' our holidays kneelin' on our adorers, tellin' our beads, an' knockin' hell out of our buzzums!

THE COVEY (*outside*)   Cuckoo-oo!

(PETER *and* FLUTHER *come in again, followed by* MRS. GOGAN, *carrying a baby in her arms. They go over to the counter*)

PETER (*with plaintive anger*)   It's terrible that young Covey can't let me pass without proddin' at me! Did you hear him murmurin' "cuckoo" when we were passin'?

FLUTHER (*irritably*)   I wouldn't be ever-lastin' cockin' me ear to hear every little whis-per that was floatin' around about me! It's my rule never to lose me temper till it would be dethrimental to keep it. There's nothin' de-rogatory in th' use o' th' word "cuckoo," is there?

PETER (*tearfully*)   It's not th' word; it's th' way he says it: he never says it straight out, but murmurs it with curious quiverin' ripples, like variations on a flute!

FLUTHER   Ah, what odds if he gave it with variations on a thrombone! (*to* MRS. GOGAN) What's yours goin' to be, ma'am?

MRS. GOGAN   Ah, a half o' malt, Fluther.

FLUTHER (*to* BARMAN)   Three halves, Tommy.

(*The* BARMAN *brings the drinks*)

MRS. GOGAN (*drinking*)   The Foresthers' is a gorgeous dhress! I don't think I've seen nicer, mind you, in a pantomime. . . . Th' loveliest part of th' dhress, I think, is th' osthrichess plume. . . . When yous are goin' along, an' I see them wavin' an' noddin' an' waggin', I seem to be lookin' at each of yous hangin' at th' end of a rope, your eyes bulgin' an' your legs twistin' an' jerkin', gaspin' an' gaspin' for breath while yous are thryin' to die for Ireland!

FLUTHER   If any o' them is hangin' at the end of a rope, it won't be for Ireland!

PETER   Are you goin' to start th' young Covey's game o' proddin' an' twartin' a man? There's not many that's talkin' can say that for twenty-five years he never missed a pilgrimage to Bodenstown!

FLUTHER   You're always blowin' about goin' to Bodenstown. D'ye think no one but your-self ever went to Bodenstown?

PETER (*plaintively*)   I'm not blowin' about it; but there's not a year that I go there but I pluck a leaf off Tone's grave, an' this very day me prayer-book is nearly full of them.

FLUTHER (*scornfully*)   Then Fluther has a vice versa opinion of them that put ivy leaves into their prayer-books, scabbin' it on th' clergy,

an' thryin' to out-do th' haloes o' th' saints be lookin' as if he was wearin' around his head a glittherin' aroree boree allis! (*fiercely*) Sure, I don't care a damn if you slep' in Bodens-town! You can take your breakfast, dinner, an' tea on th' grave in Bodenstown, if you like, for Fluther!

MRS. GOGAN   Oh, don't start a fight, boys, for God's sake; I was only sayin' what a nice costume it is—nicer than th' kilts, for, God forgive me, I always think th' kilts is hardly decent.

FLUTHER   Ah, sure, when you'd look at him, you'd wondher whether th' man was makin' fun o' th' costume, or th' costume was makin' fun o' th' man!

BARMAN   Now, then, thry to speak asy, will yous? We don't want no shoutin' here.

(*The* COVEY *followed by* BESSIE BURGESS *comes in. They go over to the opposite end of the counter, and direct their gaze on the other group*)

THE COVEY (*to* BARMAN)   Two glasses o' malt.

PETER   There he is, now; I knew he wouldn't be long till he folleyed me in.

BESSIE (*speaking to* THE COVEY, *but really at the other party*)   I can't for th' life o' me undherstand how they can call themselves Catholics, when they won't lift a finger to help poor little Catholic Belgium.

MRS. GOGAN (*raising her voice*)   What about poor little Catholic Ireland?

BESSIE (*over to* MRS. GOGAN)   You mind your own business, ma'am, an' stupefy your foolishness be gettin' dhrunk.

PETER (*anxiously*)   Take no notice of her; pay no attention to her. She's just tormentin' herself towards havin' a row with somebody.

BESSIE   There's a storm of anger tossin' in me heart, thinkin' of all th' poor Tommies, an' with them me own son, dhrenched in water an' soaked in blood, gropin' their way to a shat-therin' death, in a shower o' shells! Young men with th' sunny lust o' life beamin' in them, layin' down their white bodies, shredded into torn an' bloody pieces, on th' althar that God Himself has built for th' sacrifice of heroes!

MRS. GOGAN   Isn't it a nice thing to have to be listenin' to a lassie an' hangin' our heads in a dead silence, knowin' that some persons think more of a ball of malt than they do of th' blessed saints.

FLUTHER   Whisht; she's always dangerous an' derogatory when she's well oiled. Th' safest way to hindher her from havin' any en-joyment out of her spite, is to dip our thoughts into the fact of her bein' a female person that has moved out of th' sight of ordinary sensible people.

BESSIE   To look at some o' th' women that's knockin' about, now, is a thing to make a body sigh. . . . A woman on her own, dhrinkin' with a bevy o' men, is hardly an example to her sex. . . . A woman dhrinkin' with a woman is one thing, an' a woman dhrinkin' with herself is still a woman—flappers may be put in another category altogether—but a middle-aged married woman makin' herself th' center of a circle of men is as a woman that is loud an' stubborn, whose feet abideth not in her own house.

THE COVEY (*to* BESSIE)   When I think of all th' problems in front o' th' workers, it makes me sick to be lookin' at oul' codgers goin' about dhressed up like green-accoutred figures gone asthray out of a toyshop!

PETER   Gracious God, give me patience to be listenin' to that blasted young Covey proddin' at me from over at th' other end of th' shop!

MRS. GOGAN (*dipping her finger in the whisky, and moistening with it the lips of her baby*)   Cissie Gogan's a woman livin' for nigh on twenty-five years in her own room, an' beyond biddin' th' time o' day to her neighbors, never yet as much as nodded her head in th' direction of other people's business, while she knows some as are never content unless they're standin' senthry over other people's doin's!

(BESSIE *is about to reply, when the tall, dark figure is again silhouetted against the window, and the* VOICE OF THE SPEAKER *is heard speaking passionately*)

VOICE OF SPEAKER   The last sixteen months have been the most glorious in the history of Europe. Heroism has come back to the earth. War is a terrible thing, but war is not an evil thing. People in Ireland dread war because they do not know it. Ireland has not known the exhilaration of war for over a hundred years. When war comes to Ireland she must welcome it as she would welcome the Angel of God! (*The figure passes out of sight and hearing*)

THE COVEY (*towards all present*)   Dope, dope. There's only one war worth havin': th' war for th' economic emancipation of th' proletariat.

BESSIE   They may crow away out o' them; but it ud be fitther for some o' them to mend their ways, an' cease from havin' scouts out watchin' for th' comin' of th' Saint Vincent de Paul man, for fear they'd be nailed lowerin' a

pint of beer, mockin' th' man with an angel face, shinin' with th' glamor of deceit an' lies!

MRS. GOGAN   An' a certain lassie standin' stiff behind her own door with her ears cocked listenin' to what's being said, stuffed till she's sthrained with envy of a neighbor thryin' for a few little things that may be got be hard sthrivin' to keep up to th' letther an' th' law, an' th' practices of th' Church!

PETER (*to* MRS. GOGAN)   If I was you, Mrs. Gogan, I'd parry her jabbin' remarks be a powerful silence that'll keep her tantalizin' words from penethratin' into your feelin's. It's always betther to leave these people to th' vengeance o' God!

BESSIE   Bessie Burgess doesn't put up to know much, never havin' a swaggerin' mind, thanks be to God, but goin' on packin' up knowledge accordin' to her conscience: precept upon precept, line upon line; here a little, an' there a little. But (*with a passionate swing of her shawl*) thanks be to Christ, she knows when she was got, where she was got, an' how she was got; while there's some she knows, decoratin' their finger with a well-polished weddin' ring, would be hard put to it if they were assed to show their weddin' lines!

MRS. GOGAN (*plunging out into the center of the floor in a wild tempest of hysterical rage*)   Y' oul' rip of a blasted liar, me weddin' ring's been well earned be twenty years be th' side o' me husband, now takin' his rest in heaven, married to me be Father Dempsey, in the Chapel o' Saint Jude's, in th' Christmas Week of eighteen hundred an' ninety-five; an' any kid, livin' or dead, that Jinnie Gogan's had since, was got between th' bordhers of th' Ten Commandments! . . . An' that's more than some o' you can say that are kep' from th' dhread o' desthruction be a few drowsy virtues, that th' first whisper of temptation lulls into a sleep, that'll know one sin from another only on th' day of their last anointin', an' that use th' innocent light o' th' shinin' stars to dip into th' sins of a night's diversion!

BESSIE (*jumping out to face* MRS. GOGAN, *and bringing the palms of her hands together in sharp claps to emphasize her remarks*)   Liar to you, too, ma'am, y' oul' hardened threspasser on other people's good nature, wizenin' up your soul in th' arts o' dodgeries, till every dhrop of respectability in a female is dhried up in her, lookin' at your ready-made manœuverin' with th' menkind!

BARMAN   Here, there; here, there; speak asy there. No rowin' here, no rowin' here, now.

FLUTHER (*trying to calm* MRS. GOGAN) Now Jinnie, Jinnie, it's a derogatory thing to be smirchin' a night like this with a row; it's rompin' with th' feelin's of hope we ought to be, instead o' bein' vice versa!

PETER (*trying to quiet* BESSIE) I'm terrible dawny, Mrs. Burgess, an' a fight leaves me weak for a long time afterwards. . . . Please, Mrs. Burgess, before there's damage done, try to have a little respect for yourself.

BESSIE (*with a push of her hand that sends* PETER *tottering to the end of the shop*) G'way, you little sermonizing, little yella-faced, little consequential, little pudgy, little bum, you!

MRS. GOGAN (*screaming*) Fluther, leggo! I'm not goin' to keep an unresistin' silence, an' her scattherin' her festherin' words in me face, stirrin' up ever dhrop of decency in a respectable female, with her restless rally o' lies that would make a saint say his prayers backwards!

BESSIE (*shouting*) Ah, everybody knows well that th' best charity that can be shown to you is to hide th' thruth as much as our thrue worship of God Almighty will allow us!

MRS. GOGAN (*frantically*) Here, houl' th' kid, one o' yous; houl' th' kid for a minute! There's nothin' for it but to show this lassie a lesson or two. . . . (*to* PETER) Here, houl' th' kid, you. (*Before* PETER *is aware of it, she places the infant in his arms*)

MRS. GOGAN (*to* BESSIE, *standing before her in a fighting attitude*) Come on, now, me loyal lassie, dyin' with grief for little Catholic Belgium! When Jinnie Gogan's done with you, you'll have a little leisure lyin' down to think an' pray for your king an' counthry!

BARMAN (*coming from behind the counter, getting between the women, and proceeding to push them towards the door*) Here, now, since yous can't have a little friendly argument quietly, you'll get out o' this place in quick time. Go on, an' settle your differences somewhere else—I don't want to have another endorsement on me licence.

PETER (*anxiously, over to* MRS. GOGAN) Here, take your kid back, ower this. How nicely I was picked, now, for it to be plumped into me arms!

THE COVEY She knew who she was givin' it to, maybe.

PETER (*hotly to* THE COVEY) Now, I'm givin' you fair warnin', me young Covey, to quit firin' your jibes an' jeers at me. . . . For one o' these days, I'll run out in front o' God Almighty an' take your sacred life!

BARMAN (*pushing* BESSIE *out after* MRS. GOGAN) Go on, now; out you go.

BESSIE (*as she goes out*) If you think, me lassie, that Bessie Burgess has an untidy conscience, she'll soon show you to th' differ!

PETER (*leaving the baby down on the floor*) Ay, be Jasus, wait there, till I give her back her youngster! (*He runs to the door*) Ay, there, ay! (*He comes back*) There, she's afther goin' without her kid. What are we goin' to do with it, now?

THE COVEY What are we goin' to do with it? Bring it outside an' show everybody what you're afther findin'!

PETER (*in a panic to* FLUTHER) Pick it up, you, Fluther, an' run afther her with it, will you?

FLUTHER What d'ye take Fluther for? You must think Fluther's a right gom. D'ye think Fluther's like yourself, destitute of a tither of undherstandin'?

BARMAN (*imperatively to* PETER) Take it up, man, an' run out afther her with it, before she's gone too far. You're not goin' to leave th' bloody thing here, are you?

PETER (*plaintively, as he lifts up the baby*) Well, God Almighty, give me patience with all th' scorners, tormentors, an' twarters that are always an' ever thryin' to goad me into prayin' for their blindin' an' blastin' an' burnin' in th' world to come! (*He goes out*)

FLUTHER God, it's a relief to get rid o' that crowd. Women is terrible when they start to fight. There's no holdin' them back. (*to* THE COVEY) Are you goin' to have anything?

THE COVEY Ah, I don't mind if I have another half.

FLUTHER (*to* BARMAN) Two more, Tommy, me son.

(*The* BARMAN *gets the drinks*)

FLUTHER You know, there's no conthrollin' a woman when she loses her head.

(ROSIE *enters and goes over to the counter on the side nearest to* FLUTHER)

ROSIE (*to* BARMAN) Divil a use i' havin' a thrim little leg on a night like this; things was never worse. . . . Give us a half till tomorrow, Tom, duckey.

BARMAN (*coldly*) No more tonight, Rosie; you owe me for three already.

ROSIE (*combatively*) You'll be paid, won't you?

BARMAN I hope so.

ROSIE You hope so! Is that th' way with you, now?

FLUTHER (*to* BARMAN) Give her one; it'll be all right.

ROSIE (*clapping* FLUTHER *on the back*) Oul' sport!

FLUTHER   Th' meetin' should be soon over, now.

THE COVEY   Th' sooner th' betther. It's all a lot o' blasted nonsense, comrade.

FLUTHER   Oh, I wouldn't say it was all nonsense. Afther all, Fluther can remember th' time, an' him only a dawny chiselur, bein' taught at his mother's knee to be faithful to th' Shan Van Vok!

THE COVEY   That's all dope, comrade; th' sort o' thing that workers are fed on be th' Boorzwawzee.

FLUTHER (*a little sharply*)   What's all dope? Though I'm sayin' it that shouldn't: (*catching his cheek with his hand, and pulling down the flesh from the eye*) d'ye see that mark there, undher me eye? . . . A sabre slice from a dragoon in O'Connell Street! (*thrusting his head forward towards* ROSIE) Feel that dint in th' middle o' me nut!

ROSIE (*rubbing* FLUTHER'S *head, and winking at* THE COVEY)   My God, there's a holla!

FLUTHER (*putting on his hat with quiet pride*)   A skelp from a bobby's baton at a Labor meetin' in th' Phœnix Park!

THE COVEY   He must ha' hitten you in mistake. I don't know what you ever done for th' Labor movement.

FLUTHER (*loudly*)   D'ye not? Maybe, then, I done as much, an' know as much about th' Labor movement as th' chancers that are blowin' about it!

BARMAN   Speak easy, Fluther, thry to speak easy.

THE COVEY   There's no necessity to get excited about it, comrade.

FLUTHER (*more loudly*)   Excited? Who's gettin' excited? There's no one gettin' excited! It would take something more than a thing like you to flutther a feather o' Fluther. Blatherin', an', when all is said, you know as much as th' rest in th' wind up!

THE COVEY   Well, let us put it to th' test, then, an' see what you know about th' Labor movement: what's the mechanism of exchange?

FLUTHER (*roaring, because he feels he is beaten*)   How th' hell do I know what it is? There's nothin' about that in th' rules of our Thrades Union!

BARMAN   For God's sake, thry to speak easy, Fluther.

THE COVEY   What does Karl Marx say about th' Relation of Value to th' Cost o' Production?

FLUTHER (*angrily*)   What th' hell do I care what he says? I'm Irishman enough not to lose me head be follyin' foreigners!

BARMAN   Speak easy, Fluther.

THE COVEY   It's only waste o' time talkin' to you, comrade.

FLUTHER   Don't be comradin' me, mate. I'd be on me last legs if I wanted you for a comrade.

ROSIE (*to* THE COVEY)   It seems a highly rediculous thing to hear a thing that's only an inch or two away from a kid, swingin' heavy words about he doesn't know th' meanin' of, an' uppishly thryin' to down a man like Misther Fluther here, that's well flavored in th' knowledge of th' world he's livin' in.

THE COVEY (*savagely to* ROSIE)   Nobody's askin' you to be buttin' in with your prate. . . . I have you well taped, me lassie. . . . Just you keep your opinions for your own place. . . . It'll be a long time before th' Covey takes any insthructions or reprimandin' from a prostitute!

ROSIE (*wild with humiliation*)   You louse, you louse, you! . . . You're no man. . . . You're no man . . . I'm a woman, anyhow, an' if I'm a prostitute aself, I have me feelin's. . . . Thryin' to put his arm around me a minute ago, an' givin' me th' glad eye, th' little wrigglin' lump o' desolation turns on me now, because he saw there was nothin' doin'. . . . You louse, you! If I was a man, or you were a woman, I'd bate th' puss o' you!

BARMAN   Ay, Rosie, ay! You'll have to shut your mouth altogether, if you can't learn to speak easy!

FLUTHER (*to* ROSIE)   Houl' on there, Rosie; houl' on there. There's no necessity to flutther yourself when you're with Fluther. . . . Any lady that's in th' company of Fluther is goin' to get a fair hunt. . . . This is outside your province. . . . I'm not goin' to let you demean yourself be talkin' to a tittherin' chancer. . . . Leave this to Fluther—this is a man's job. (*to* THE COVEY) Now, if you've anything to say, say it to Fluther, an', let me tell you, you're not goin' to be pass-remarkable to any lady in my company.

THE COVEY   Sure I don't care if you were runnin' all night afther your Mary o' th Curlin' Hair, but, when you start tellin' luscious lies about what you done for th' Labor movement, it's nearly time to show y'up!

FLUTHER (*fiercely*)   Is it you show Fluther up? G'way, man, I'd beat two o' you before me breakfast!

THE COVEY (*contemptuously*)   Tell us where you bury your dead, will you?

FLUTHER (*with his face stuck into the face of* THE COVEY)   Sing a little less on th' high note, or, when I'm done with you, you'll put a Christianable consthruction on things, I'm tellin' you!

THE COVEY You're a big fella, you are.

FLUTHER (*tapping* THE COVEY *threateningly on the shoulder*) Now, you're temptin' Providence when you're temptin' Fluther!

THE COVEY (*losing his temper, and bawling*) Easy with them hands, there, easy with them hands! You're startin' to take a little risk when you commence to paw the Covey!

(FLUTHER *suddenly springs into the middle of the shop, flings his hat into the corner, whips off his coat, and begins to paw the air*)

FLUTHER (*roaring at the top of his voice*) Come on, come on, you lowser; put your mits up now, if there's a man's blood in you! Be God, in a few minutes you'll see some snots flyin' around, I'm tellin' you. . . . When Fluther's done with you, you'll have a vice versa opinion of him! Come on, now, come on!

BARMAN (*running from behind the counter and catching hold of* THE COVEY) Here, out you go, me little bowsey. Because you got a couple o' halves you think you can act as you like. (*He pushes* THE COVEY *to the door*) Fluther's a friend o' mine, an' I'll not have him insulted.

THE COVEY (*struggling with the* BARMAN) Ay, leggo, leggo there; fair hunt, give a man a fair hunt! One minute with him is all I ask; one minute alone with him, while you're runnin' for th' priest an' th' doctor.

FLUTHER (*to* THE BARMAN) Let him go, let him go, Tom! let him open th' door to sudden death if he wants to!

BARMAN (*to* THE COVEY) Go on, out you go an' do th' bowsey somewhere else. (*He pushes* THE COVEY *out and comes back*)

ROSIE (*getting* FLUTHER'S *hat as he is putting on his coat*) Be God, you put th' fear o' God in his heart that time! I thought you'd have to be dug out of him. . . . Th' way you lepped out without any of your fancy sidesteppin'! "Men like Fluther," say I to meself, "is gettin' scarce nowadays."

FLUTHER (*with proud complacency*) I wasn't goin' to let meself be malignified by a chancer. . . . He got a little bit too derogatory for Fluther. . . . Be God, to think of a cur like that comin' to talk to a man like me!

ROSIE (*fixing on his hat*) Did j'ever!

FLUTHER He's lucky he got off safe. I hit a man last week, Rosie, an' he's fallin' yet!

ROSIE Sure, you'd ha' broken him in two if you'd ha' hitten him one clatther!

FLUTHER (*amorously, putting his arm around* ROSIE) Come on into th' snug, me little darlin', an we'll have a few dhrinks before I see you home.

ROSIE Oh, Fluther, I'm afraid you're a terrible man for th' women.

(*They go into the snug as* CLITHEROE, CAPTAIN BRENNAN, *and* LIEUT. LANGON *of the Irish Volunteers enter hurriedly.* CAPTAIN BRENNAN *carries the banner of the The Plough and the Stars, and* LIEUT. LANGON *a green, white, and orange Tri-color. They are in a state of emotional excitement. Their faces are flushed and their eyes sparkle; they speak rapidly, as if unaware of the meaning of what they said. They have been mesmerized by the fervency of the speeches*)

CLITHEROE (*almost pantingly*) Three glasses o' port!

(*The* BARMAN *brings the drinks*)

CAPT. BRENNAN We won't have long to wait now.

LIEUT. LANGON Th' time is rotten ripe for revolution.

CLITHEROE You have a mother, Langon.

LIEUT. LANGON Ireland is greater than a mother.

CAPT. BRENNAN You have a wife, Clitheroe.

CLITHEROE Ireland is greater than a wife.

LIEUT. LANGON Th' time for Ireland's battle is now—th' place for Ireland's battle is here.

(*The tall, dark figure again is silhouetted against the window. The three men pause and listen*)

VOICE OF THE MAN Our foes are strong, but strong as they are, they cannot undo the miracles of God, who ripens in the heart of young men the seeds sown by the young men of a former generation. They think they have pacified Ireland; think they have foreseen everything; think they have provided against everything; but the fools, the fools, the fools!— they have left us our Fenian dead, and, while Ireland holds these graves, Ireland, unfree, shall never be at peace!

CAPT. BRENNAN (*catching up The Plough and the Stars*) Imprisonment for th' Independence of Ireland!

LIEUT. LANGON (*catching up the Tri-color*) Wounds for th' Independence of Ireland!

CLITHEROE Death for th' Independence of Ireland!

THE THREE (*together*) So help us God!

(*They drink. A bugle blows the Assembly. They hurry out. A pause.* FLUTHER *and* ROSIE *come out of the snug;* ROSIE *is linking* FLUTHER, *who is a little drunk. Both are in a merry mood)*

ROSIE　Come on home, ower o' that, man. Are you afraid or what? Are you goin' to come home, or are you not?

FLUTHER　Of course I'm goin' home. What ud ail me that I wouldn't go?

ROSIE　(*lovingly*)　Come on, then, oul' sport.

OFFICER'S VOICE　(*giving command outside*) Irish Volunteers, by th' right, quick march!

ROSIE　(*putting her arm round* FLUTHER *and singing:*)

I once had a lover, a tailor, but he could do
　　nothin' for me,
An' then I fell in with a sailor as strong an'
　　as wild as th' sea.
We cuddled an' kissed with devotion, till th'
　　night from th' mornin' had fled;
An' there, to our joy, a bright bouncin' boy
Was dancin' a jig in th' bed!
Dancin' a jig in th' bed, an' bawlin' for butther
　　an' bread.
An' there, to our joy, a bright bouncin' boy
Was dancin' a jig in th' bed!

(*They go out with their arms round each other*)

CLITHEROE'S VOICE　(*in command outside*) Dublin Battalion of the Irish Citizen Army, by th' right, quick march!

ACT THREE

(*The corner house in a street of tenements: it is the home of the* CLITHEROES. *The house is a long, gaunt, five-story tenement; its brick front is chipped and scarred with age and neglect. The wide and heavy hall door, flanked by two pillars, has a look of having been charred by a fire in the distant past. The door lurches a little to one side, disjointed by the continual and reckless banging when it is being closed by most of the residents. The diamond-paned fanlight is destitute of a single pane, the framework alone remaining. The windows, except the two looking into the front parlor* [CLITHEROE'S *room*], *are grimy, and are draped with fluttering and soiled fragments of lace curtains. The front parlor windows are hung with rich, comparatively, casement cloth. Five stone steps lead from the door to the path on the street. Branching on each side*

are railings to prevent people from falling into the area. At the left corner of the house runs a narrow lane, bisecting the street, and connecting it with another of the same kind. At the corner of the lane is a street lamp.

As the house is revealed, MRS. GOGAN *is seen helping* MOLLSER *to a chair, which stands on the path beside the railings, at the left side of the steps. She then wraps a shawl around* MOLLSER'S *shoulders. It is some months later*)

MRS. GOGAN　(*arranging shawl around* MOLLSER)　Th' sun'll do you all th' good in th' world. A few more weeks o' this weather, an' there's no knowin' how well you'll be. . . . Are you comfy, now?

MOLLSER　(*weakly and wearily*)　Yis, ma; I'm all right.

MRS. GOGAN　How are you feelin'?

MOLLSER　Betther, ma, betther. If th' horrible sinkin' feelin' ud go, I'd be all right.

MRS. GOGAN　Ah, I wouldn't put much pass on that. Your stomach maybe's out of ordher. . . . Is th' poor breathin' any betther, d'ye think?

MOLLSER　Yis, yis, ma; a lot betther.

MRS. GOGAN　Well, that's somethin' anyhow. . . . With th' help o' God, you'll be on th' mend from this out. . . . D'your legs feel any sthronger undher you, d'ye think!

MOLLSER　(*irritably*)　I can't tell, ma. I think so. . . . A little.

MRS. GOGAN　Well, a little aself is somethin'. . . . I thought I heard you coughin' a little more than usual last night. . . . D'ye think you were?

MOLLSER　I wasn't, ma, I wasn't.

MRS. GOGAN　I thought I heard you, for I was kep' awake all night with th' shootin'. An' thinkin' o' that madman, Fluther, runnin' about through th' night lookin' for Nora Clitheroe to bring her back when he heard she'd gone to folly her husband, an' in dhread any minute he might come staggerin' in covered with bandages, splashed all over with th' red of his own blood, an' givin' us barely time to bring th' priest to hear th' last whisper of his final confession, as his soul was passin' through th' dark doorway o' death into th' way o' th' wondherin' dead. . . . You don't feel cold, do you?

MOLLSER　No, ma; I'm all right.

MRS. GOGAN　Keep your chest well covered, for that's th' delicate spot in you . . . if there's any danger, I'll whip you in again. . . . (*looking up the street*) Oh, here's th' Covey an' oul' Pether hurryin' along. God Almighty, sthrange things is happenin' when them two is pullin' together.

(THE COVEY *and* PETER *come in, breathless and excited*)

MRS. GOGAN (*to the two men*) Were yous far up th' town? Did yous see any sign o' Fluther or Nora? How is things lookin'? I hear they're blazin' away out o' th' G.P.O. That th' Tommies is sthretched in heaps around Nelson's Pillar an' th' Parnell Statue, an' that th' pavin' sets in O'Connell Street is nearly covered be pools o' blood.

PETER We seen no sign o' Nora or Fluther anywhere.

MRS. GOGAN We should ha' held her back be main force from goin' to look for her husband. . . . God knows what's happened to her—I'm always seein' her sthretched on her back in some hospital, moanin' with th' pain of a bullet in her vitals, an' nuns thryin' to get her to take a last look at th' crucifix!

THE COVEY We can do nothin'. You can't stick your nose into O'Connell Street, an' Tyler's is on fire.

PETER An' we seen th' Lancers—

THE COVEY (*interrupting*) Throttin' along, heads in th' air; spurs an' sabres jinglin', an' lances quiverin', an' lookin' as if they were assin' themselves, "Where's these blighters, till we get a prod at them?" when there was a volley from th' Post Office that stretched half o' them, an' sent th' rest gallopin' away wondherin' how far they'd have to go before they'd feel safe.

PETER (*rubbing his hands*) "Damn it," says I to meself, "this looks like business!"

THE COVEY An' then out comes General Pearse an' his staff, an', standin' in th' middle o' th' street, he reads th' Proclamation.

MRS. GOGAN What proclamation?

PETER Declarin' an Irish Republic.

MRS. GOGAN Go to God!

PETER The gunboat *Helga*'s shellin' Liberty Hall, an' I hear the people livin' on th' quays had to crawl on their bellies to Mass with th' bullets that were flyin' around from Boland's Mills.

MRS. GOGAN God bless us, what's goin' to be th' end of it all!

BESSIE (*looking out of the top window*) Maybe yous are satisfied now; maybe yous are satisfied now. Go on an' get guns if yous are men—Johnny get your gun, get your gun, get your gun! Yous are all nicely shanghaied now; th' boyo hasn't a sword on his thigh now! Oh, yous are all nicely shanghaied now!

MRS. GOGAN (*warningly to* PETER *and* THE COVEY) S-s-sh, don't answer her. She's th' right oul' Orange bitch! She's been chantin' "Rule, Britannia" all th' mornin'.

PETER I hope Fluther hasn't met with any accident, he's such a wild card.

MRS. GOGAN God grant it; but last night I dreamt I seen gettin' carried into th' house a sthretcher with a figure lyin' on it, stiff an' still, dhressed in th' habit of Saint Francis. An' then, I heard th' murmurs of a crowd no one could see sayin' th' litany for th' dead; an' then it got so dark that nothin' was seen but th' white face of th' corpse, gleamin' like a white wather-lily floatin' on th' top of a dark lake. Then a tiny whisper thrickled into me ear, sayin', "Isn't th' face very like th' face o' Fluther?" an' then, with a thremblin' flutther, th' dead lips opened, an' although I couldn't hear, I knew they were sayin', "Poor oul' Fluther, afther havin' handed in his gun at last, his shakin' soul moored in th' place where th' wicked are at rest an' th' weary cease from throublin'."

PETER (*who has put on a pair of spectacles, and has been looking down the street*) Here they are, be God, here they are; just afther turnin' th' corner—Nora an' Fluther!

THE COVEY She must be wounded or something—he seems to be carryin' her.

(FLUTHER *and* NORA *enter.* FLUTHER *has his arm around her and is half leading, half carrying her in. Her eyes are dim and hollow, her face pale and strained-looking; her hair is tossed, and her clothes are dusty*)

MRS. GOGAN (*running over to them*) God bless us, is it wounded y'are, Mrs. Clitheroe, or what?

FLUTHER Ah, she's all right, Mrs. Gogan; only worn out from thravellin' an' want o' sleep. A night's rest, now, an' she'll be as fit as a fiddle. Bring her in, an' make her lie down.

MRS. GOGAN (*to* NORA) Did you hear e'er a whisper o' Mr. Clitheroe?

NORA (*wearily*) I could find him nowhere, Mrs. Gogan. None o' them would tell me where he was. They told me I shamed my husband an' th' women of Ireland be carryin' on as I was. . . . They said th' women must learn to be brave an' cease to be cowardly. . . . Me who risked more for love than they would risk for hate. . . . (*raising her voice in hysterical protest*) My Jack will be killed, my Jack will be killed! . . . He is to be butchered as a sacrifice to th' dead!

BESSIE (*from upper window*) Yous are all nicely shanghaied now! Sorra mend th' lasses that have been kissin' an' cuddlin' their boys into th' sheddin' of blood! . . . Fillin' their

minds with fairy tales that had no beginnin',
but, please God, 'll have a bloody quick
endin'! . . . Turnin' bitther into sweet, an'
sweet into bitther. . . . Stabbin' in th' back
th' men that are dying in th' threnches for
them! It's a bad thing for any one that thries
to jilt th' Ten Commandments, for judgments
are prepared for scorners an' sthripes for th'
back o' fools! (*going away from window as
she sings*)

> Rule, Britannia, Britannia rules th'
>   waves,
> Britons never, never, never shall be
>   slaves!

FLUTHER (*with a roar up at the window*)
Y'ignorant oul' throllop, you!

MRS. GOGAN (*to* NORA) He'll come home
safe enough to you, you'll find, Mrs. Clitheroe;
afther all, there's a power o' women that's
handed over sons an' husbands to take a runnin'
risk in th' fight they're wagin'.

NORA I can't help thinkin' every shot fired
'll be fired at Jack, an' every shot fired at
Jack 'll be fired at me. What do I care for th'
others? I can think only of me own self. . . .
An' there's no woman gives a son or a husband to be killed—if they say it, they're lyin',
lyin', against God, Nature, an' against themselves! . . . One blasted hussy at a barricade
told me to go home an' not be thryin' to dis-
hearten th' men. . . . That I wasn't worthy to
bear a son to a man that was out fightin' for
freedom. . . . I clawed at her, an' smashed
her in th' face till we were separated. . . . I
was pushed down th' street, an' I cursed them
—cursed the rebel ruffians an' Volunteers that
had dhragged me ravin' mad into th' sthreets
to seek me husband!

PETER You'll have to have patience, Nora.
We all have to put up with twarthers an' tormentors in this world.

THE COVEY If they were fightin' for anything worth while, I wouldn't mind.

FLUTHER (*to* NORA) Nothin' derogatory 'll
happen to Mr. Clitheroe. You'll find, now, in
th' finish up it'll be vice versa.

NORA Oh, I know that wherever he is, he's
thinkin' of wantin' to be with me. I know he's
longin' to be passin' his hand through me hair,
to be caressin' me neck, to fondle me hand
an' to feel me kisses clingin' to his mouth. . . .
An' he stands wherever he is because he's
brave? (*vehemently*) No, but because he's a
coward, a coward, a coward!

MRS. GOGAN Oh, they're not cowards anyway.

NORA (*with denunciatory anger*) I tell you
they're afraid to say they're afraid! . . . Oh,
I saw it, I saw it, Mrs. Gogan. . . . At th' barricade in North King Street I saw fear glowin'
in all their eyes. . . . An' in th' middle o' th'
sthreet was somethin' huddled up in a horrible
tangled heap. . . . His face was jammed again
th' stones, an' his arm was twisted round his
back. . . . An' every twist of his body was a
cry against th' terrible thing that had happened
to him. . . . An' I saw they were afraid to
look at it. . . . An' some o' them laughed at
me, but th' laugh was a frightened one. . . .
An' some o' them shouted at me, but th' shout
had in it th' shiver o' fear. . . . I tell you they
were afraid, afraid, afraid!

MRS. GOGAN (*leading her towards the house*)
Come on in, dear. If you'd been a little longer
together, th' wrench asundher wouldn't have
been so sharp.

NORA Th' agony I'm in since he left me
has thrust away every rough thing he done, an'
every unkind word he spoke; only th' blossoms
that grew out of our lives are before me now;
shakin' their colors before me face, an'
breathin' their sweet scent on every thought
springin' up in me mind, till, sometimes, Mrs.
Gogan, sometimes I think I'm goin' mad!

MRS. GOGAN You'll be a lot bether when
you have a little lie down.

NORA (*turning towards* FLUTHER *as she is
going in*) I don't know what I'd have done,
only for Fluther. I'd have been lyin' in th'
streets, only for him. . . . (*as she goes in*)
They have dhriven away th' little happiness life
had to spare for me. He has gone from me forever, forever. . . . Oh, Jack, Jack, Jack!

(*She is led in by* MRS. GOGAN, *as* BESSIE *comes
out with a shawl around her shoulders. She
passes by them with her head in the air. When
they have gone in, she gives a mug of milk to*
MOLLSER *silently*)

FLUTHER Which of yous has th' tossers?

THE COVEY I have.

BESSIE (*as she is passing them to go down
the street*) You an' your Leadhers an' their
sham-battle soldiers has landed a body in a
nice way, havin' to go an' ferret out a bit o'
bread God knows where. . . . Why aren't
yous in th' G.P.O. if yous are men? It's paler
an' paler yous are gettin'. . . . A lot o' vipers,
that's what th' Irish people is! (*She goes out*)

FLUTHER Never mind her. . . . (*to* THE
COVEY) Make a start an' keep us from th' sin o'
idleness. (*to* MOLLSER) Well, how are you
today, Mollser, oul' son? What are you
dhrinkin', milk?

MOLLSER Grand, Fluther, grand, thanks. Yis, milk.

FLUTHER You couldn't get a betther thing down you. . . . This turnup has done one good thing, anyhow; you can't get dhrink anywhere, an' if it lasts a week, I'll be so used to it that I won't think of a pint.

THE COVEY (*who has taken from his pocket two worn coins and a thin strip of wood about four inches long*) What's th' bettin'?

PETER Heads, a juice.

FLUTHER Harps, a tanner.

(THE COVEY *places the coins on the strip of wood, and flips them up into the air. As they jingle on the ground the distant boom of a big gun is heard. They stand for a moment listening*)

FLUTHER What th' hell's that?

THE COVEY It's like th' boom of a big gun!

FLUTHER Surely to God they're not goin' to use artillery on us?

THE COVEY (*scornfully*) Not goin'! (*vehemently*) Wouldn't they use anything on us, man?

FLUTHER Aw, holy Christ, that's not playin' th' game!

PETER (*plaintively*) What would happen if a shell landed here now?

THE COVEY (*ironically*) You'd be off to heaven in a fiery chariot.

PETER In spite of all th' warnin's that's ringin' around us, are you goin' to start your pickin' at me again?

FLUTHER Go on, toss them again, toss them again. . . . Harps, a tanner.

PETER Heads, a juice.

(THE COVEY *tosses the coins*)

FLUTHER (*as the coins fall*) Let them roll, let them roll. Heads, be God!

(BESSIE *runs in excitedly. She has a new hat on her head, a fox fur round her neck over her shawl, three umbrellas under her right arm, and a box of biscuits under her left. She speaks rapidly and breathlessly*)

BESSIE They're breakin' into th' shops, they're breakin' into the shops! Smashin' th' windows, battherin' in th' doors, an' whippin' away everything! An' th' Volunteers is firin' on them. I seen two men an' a lassie pushin' a piano down th' sthreet, an' th' sweat rollin' off them thryin' to get it up on th' pavement; an' an oul' wan that must ha' been seventy lookin' as if she'd dhrop every minute with th' dint o' heart beatin', thryin' to pull a big double bed out of a broken shop-window!

I was goin' to wait till I dhressed meself from th' skin out.

MOLLSER (*to* BESSIE, *as she is going in*) Help me in, Bessie; I'm feelin' curious. (BESSIE *leaves the looted things in the house, and, rapidly returning, helps* MOLLSER *in*)

THE COVEY Th' selfishness of that one—she waited till she got all she could carry before she'd come to tell anyone!

FLUTHER (*running over to the door of the house and shouting in to* BESSIE) Ay, Bessie, did you hear of e'er a pub gettin' a shake up?

BESSIE (*inside*) I didn't hear o' none.

FLUTHER (*in a burst of enthusiasm*) Well, you're goin' to hear of one soon!

THE COVEY Come on, man, an' don't be wastin' time.

PETER (*to them as they are about to run off*) Ay, ay, are you goin' to leave me here?

FLUTHER Are you goin' to leave yourself here?

PETER (*anxiously*) Didn't yous hear her sayin' they were firin' on them?

THE COVEY *and* FLUTHER (*together*) Well?

PETER Supposin' I happened to be potted?

FLUTHER We'd give you a Christian burial, anyhow.

THE COVEY (*ironically*) Dhressed up in your regimentals.

PETER (*to* THE COVEY, *passionately*) May th' all-lovin' God give you a hot knock one o' these days, me young Covey, tuthorin' Fluther up now to be tiltin' at me, an' crossin' me with his mockeries an' jibin'!

(*A fashionably dressed, middle-aged, stout woman comes hurriedly in, and makes for the group. She is almost fainting with fear*)

THE WOMAN For Gawd's sake, will one of you kind men show any safe way for me to get to Wrathmines? . . . I was foolish enough to visit a friend, thinking the howl thing was a joke, and now I cawn't get a car or a tram to take me home—isn't it awful?

FLUTHER I'm afraid, ma'am, one way is as safe as another.

WOMAN And what am I gowing to do? Oh, isn't this awful? . . . I'm so different from others. . . . The mowment I hear a shot, my legs give way under me—I cawn't stir, I'm paralyzed—isn't it awful?

FLUTHER (*moving away*) It's a derogatory way to be, right enough, ma'am.

WOMAN (*catching* FLUTHER'S *coat*) Creeping along the street there, with my head down and my eyes half shut, a bullet whizzed past within an inch of my nowse. . . . I had to lean against the wall for a long time, gasping for breath—I nearly passed away—it was awful! . . . I wonder, would you kind men come some of the way and see me safe?

FLUTHER   I have to go away, ma'am, to thry an' save a few things from th' burnin' buildin's.

THE COVEY   Come on, then, or there won't be anything left to save. (THE COVEY and FLUTHER *hurry away*)

WOMAN (*to* PETER)   Wasn't it an awful thing for me to leave my friend's house? Wasn't it an idiotic thing to do? . . . I haven't the slightest idea where I am. . . . You have a kind face, sir. Could you possibly come and pilot me in the direction of Wrathmines?

PETER (*indignantly*)   D'ye think I'm goin' to risk me life throttin' in front of you? An' maybe get a bullet that would gimme a game leg or something that would leave me a jibe an' a jeer to Fluther an' th' young Covey for th' rest o' me days! (*With an indignant toss of his head he walks into the house*)

THE WOMAN (*going out*)   I know I'll fall down in a dead faint if I hear another shot go off anyway near me—isn't it awful!

(MRS. GOGAN *comes out of the house pushing a pram before her. As she enters the street,* BESSIE *rushes out, follows* MRS. GOGAN, *and catches hold of the pram, stopping* MRS. GOGAN's *progress*)

BESSIE   Here, where are you goin' with that? How quick you were, me lady, to clap your eyes on th' pram. . . . Maybe you don't know that Mrs. Sullivan, before she went to spend Easther with her people in Dunboyne, gave me sthrict injunctions to give an accasional look to see if it was still standin' where it was left in th' corner of th' lobby.

MRS. GOGAN   That remark of yours, Mrs. Bessie Burgess, requires a little considheration, seein' that th' pram was left on our lobby, an' not on yours; a foot or two a little to th' left of th' jamb of me own room door; nor is it needful to mention th' name of th' person that gave a squint to see if it was there th' first thing in th' mornin', an' th' last thing in th' stillness o' th' night; never failin' to realize that her eyes couldn't be goin' wrong, be sthretchin' out her arm an' runnin' her hand over th' pram, to make sure that th' sight was no deception! Moreover, somethin's tellin' me that th' runnin' hurry of an inthrest you're takin' in it now is a sudden ambition to use th' pram for a purpose that a loyal woman of law an' ordher would stagger away from! (*She gives the pram a sudden push that pulls* BESSIE *forward*)

BESSIE (*still holding the pram*)   There's not as much as one body in th' house that doesn't know that it wasn't Bessie Burgess that was always shakin' her voice complainin' about people leavin' bassinettes in th' way of them that, week in an' week out, had to pay their rent, an' always had to find a regular accommodation for her own furniture in her own room. . . . An' as for law an' ordher, puttin' aside th' harp an' shamrock, Bessie Burgess 'll have as much respect as she wants for th' lion an' unicorn!

PETER (*appearing at the door*)   I think I'll go with th' pair of yous an' see th' fun. A fella might as well chance it, anyhow.

MRS. GOGAN (*taking no notice of* PETER, *and pushing the pram on another step*)   Take your rovin' lumps o' hands from pattin' th' bassinette, if you please, ma'am; an', steppin' from th' threshold of good manners, let me tell you, Mrs. Burgess, that it's a fat wondher to Jennie Gogan that a lady-like singer o' hymns like yourself would lower her thoughts from sky-thinkin' to stretch out her arm in a sly-seekin' way to pinch anything dhriven asthray in th' confusion of th' battle our boys is makin' for th' freedom of their counthry!

PETER (*laughing and rubbing his hands together*)   Hee, hee, hee, hee, hee! I'll go with th' pair o' yous an' give yous a hand.

MRS. GOGAN (*with a rapid turn of her head as she shoves the pram forward*)   Get up in th' prambulator an' we'll wheel you down.

BESSIE (*to* MRS. GOGAN)   Poverty an' hardship has sent Bessie Burgess to abide with sthrange company, but she always knew them she had to live with from backside to breakfast time; an' she can tell them, always havin' had a Christian kinch on her conscience, that a passion for thievin' an' pinchin' would find her soul a foreign place to live in, an' that her present intention is quite th' lofty-hearted one of pickin' up anything shaken up an' scatthered about in th' loose confusion of a general plundher!

(*By this time they have disappeared from view.* PETER *is following, when the boom of a big gun in the distance brings him to a quick halt*)

PETER   God Almighty, that's th' big gun again! God forbid any harm would happen to them, but sorra mind I'd mind if they met with a dhrop in their mad endeyvours to plundher an' desthroy. (*He looks down the street for a moment, then runs to the hall door of the house, which is open, and shuts it with a vicious pull; he then goes to the chair in which* MOLLSER *had sat, sits down, takes out his pipe, lights it and begins to smoke with his head carried at a haughty angle.* THE COVEY *comes staggering in with a ten-stone sack of flour on his back. On the top of the sack is a ham. He goes over to the door, pushes it with his head, and finds he can't open it; he turns slightly in the direction of* PETER)

THE COVEY (*to* PETER) Who shut th' door? . . . (*He kicks at it*) Here, come on an' open it, will you? This isn't a mot's handbag I've got on me back.

PETER Now, me young Covey, d'ye think I'm goin' to be your lackey?

THE COVEY (*angrily*) Will you open th' door, y'oul'—

PETER (*shouting*) Don't be assin' me to open any door, don't be assin' me to open any door for you. . . . Makin' a shame an' a sin o' th' cause that good men are fightin' for. . . . Oh, God forgive th' people that, instead o' burnishin' th' work th' boys is doin' today with quiet honesty an' patience, is revilin' their sacrifices with a riot of lootin' an' roguery!

THE COVEY Isn't your own eyes leppin' out o' your head with envy that you haven't th' guts to ketch a few o' th' things that God is givin' to His chosen people? . . . Y'oul' hypocrite, if everyone was blind you'd steal a cross off an ass's back!

PETER (*very calmly*) You're not going to make me lose me temper; you can go on with your proddin' as long as you like; goad an' goad an' goad away; hee, hee, heee! I'll not lose me temper. (*Somebody opens door and* THE COVEY *goes in*)

THE COVEY (*inside, mockingly*) Cuckoo-oo!

PETER (*running to the door and shouting in a blaze of passion as he follows* THE COVEY *in*) You lean, long, lanky lath of a lowsey bastard. . . . (*following him in*) Lowsey bastard, lowsey bastard!

(BESSIE *and* MRS. GOGAN *enter, the pride of a great joy illuminating their faces.* BESSIE *is pushing the pram, which is filled with clothes and boots; on the top of the boots and clothes is a fancy table, which* MRS. GOGAN *is holding on with her left hand, while with her right hand she holds a chair on the top of her head. They are heard talking to each other before they enter*)

MRS. GOGAN (*outside*) I don't remember ever havin' seen such lovely pairs as them, (*They appear*) with th' pointed toes an' th' cuban heels.

BESSIE They'll go grand with th' dhresses we're afther liftin', when we've stitched a sthray bit o' silk to lift th' bodices up a little

higher, so as to shake th' shame out o' them, an' make them fit for women that hasn't lost themselves in th' nakedness o' th' times.

(*They fussily carry in the chair, the table, and some of the other goods. They return to bring in the rest*)

PETER (*at door, sourly to* MRS. GOGAN) Ay, you. Mollser looks as if she was goin' to faint, an' your youngster is roarin' in convulsions in her lap.

MRS. GOGAN (*snappily*) She's never any other way but faintin'! (*She goes to go in with some things in her arms, when a shot from a rifle rings out. She and* BESSIE *make a bolt for the door, which* PETER, *in a panic, tries to shut before they have got inside*)

MRS. GOGAN Ay, ay, ay, you cowardly oul' fool, what are you thryin' to shut th' door on us for?

(*They retreat tumultuously inside. A pause; then* CAPTAIN BRENNAN *comes in supporting* LIEUTENANT LANGON, *whose arm is around* BRENNAN'S *neck.* LANGON'S *face, which is ghastly white, is momentarily convulsed with spasms of agony. He is in a state of collapse, and* BRENNAN *is almost carrying him. After a few moments* CLITHEROE, *pale, and in a state of calm nervousness, follows, looking back in the direction from which he came, a rifle, held at the ready, in his hands*)

CAPT. BRENNAN (*savagely to* CLITHEROE) Why did you fire over their heads? Why didn't you fire to kill?

CLITHEROE No, no, Bill; bad as they are they're Irish men an' women.

CAPT. BRENNAN (*savagely*) Irish be damned! Attackin' an' mobbin' th' men that are riskin' their lives for them. If these slum lice gather at our heels again, plug one o' them, or I'll soon shock them with a shot or two meself!

LIEUT. LANGON (*moaningly*) My God, is there ne'er an ambulance knockin' around anywhere? . . . Th' stomach is ripped out o' me; I feel it—o-o-oh, Christ!

CAPT. BRENNAN Keep th' heart up, Jim; we'll soon get help, now.

(NORA *rushes wildly out of the house and flings her arms round the neck of* CLITHEROE *with a fierce and joyous insistence. Her hair is down, her face is haggard, but her eyes are agleam with the light of happy relief*)

NORA Jack, Jack, Jack; God be thanked . . . be thanked. . . . He has been kind and merciful to His poor handmaiden. . . . My Jack, my own Jack, that I thought was lost is found, that I thought was dead is alive again!

. . . Oh, God be praised forever, evermore! . . . My poor Jack. . . . Kiss me, kiss me, Jack, kiss your own Nora!

CLITHEROE (*kissing her, and speaking brokenly*) My Nora; my little, beautiful Nora, I wish to God I'd never left you.

NORA It doesn't matter—not now, not now, Jack. It will make us dearer than ever to each other. . . . Kiss me, kiss me again.

CLITHEROE Now, for God's sake, Nora, don't make a scene.

NORA I won't, I won't; I promise, I promise, Jack; honest to God. I'll be silent an' brave to bear th' joy of feelin' you safe in my arms again. . . . It's hard to force away th' tears of happiness at th' end of an awful agony.

BESSIE (*from the upper window*) Th' Minsthrel Boys aren't feelin' very comfortable now. Th' big guns has knocked all th' harps out of their hands. General Clitheroe'd rather be unlacin' his wife's bodice than standin' at a barricade. . . . An' th' professor of chicken-butcherin' there, finds he's up against somethin' a little tougher even than his own chickens, an' that's sayin' a lot!

CAPT. BRENNAN (*up to* BESSIE) Shut up, y'oul' hag!

BESSIE (*down to* BRENNAN) Choke th' chicken, choke th' chicken, choke th' chicken!

LIEUT. LANGON For God's sake, Bill, bring me some place where me wound 'll be looked afther. . . . Am I to die before anything is done to save me?

CAPT. BRENNAN (*to* CLITHEROE) Come on, Jack. We've got to get help for Jim, here—have you no thought for his pain an' danger?

BESSIE Choke th' chicken, choke th' chicken, choke th' chicken!

CLITHEROE (*to* NORA) Loosen me, darling, let me go.

NORA (*clinging to him*) No, no, no, I'll not let you go! Come on, come up to our home, Jack, my sweetheart, my lover, my husband, an' we'll forget th' last few terrible days! . . . I look tired now, but a few hours of happy rest in your arms will bring back th' bloom of freshness again, an' you will be glad, you will be glad, glad . . . glad!

LIEUT. LANGON Oh, if I'd kep' down only a little longer, I mightn't ha' been hit! Everyone else escapin', an' me gettin' me belly ripped assundher! . . . I couldn't scream, couldn't even scream. . . . D'ye think I'm really badly wounded, Bill? Me clothes seem to be all soakin' wet. . . . It's blood . . . My God, it must be me own blood!

CAPT. BRENNAN (*to* CLITHEROE) Go on, Jack, bid her good-bye with another kiss, an'

be done with it! D'ye want Langon to die in me arms while you're dallyin' with your Nora?

CLITHEROE (*to* NORA) I must go, I must go, Nora. I'm sorry we met at all. . . . It couldn't be helped—all other ways were blocked be th' British. . . . Let me go, can't you, Nora? D'ye want me to be unthrue to me comrades?

NORA No, I won't let you go. . . . I want you to be thrue to me, Jack. . . . I'm your dearest comrade; I'm your thruest comrade. . . . They only want th' comfort of havin' you in th' same danger as themselves. . . . Oh, Jack, I can't let you go!

CLITHEROE You must, Nora, you must.

NORA All last night at th' barricade I sought you, Jack. . . . I didn't think of th' danger—I could only think of you. . . . I asked for you everywhere. . . . Some o' them laughed. . . . I was pushed away, but I shoved back. . . . Some o' them even sthruck me . . . an' I screamed an' screamed your name!

CLITHEROE (*in fear her action would give him future shame*) What possessed you to make a show of yourself, like that? . . . What way d'ye think I'll feel when I'm told my wife was bawlin' for me at th' barricades? What are you more than any other woman?

NORA No more, maybe; but you are more to me than any other man, Jack. . . . I didn't mean any harm, honestly, Jack. . . . I couldn't help it. . . . I shouldn't have told you. . . . My love for you made me mad with terror.

CLITHEROE (*angrily*) They'll say now that I sent you out th' way I'd have an excuse to bring you home. . . . Are you goin' to turn all th' risks I'm takin' into a laugh?

LIEUT. LANGON Let me lie down, let me lie down, Bill; th' pain would be easier, maybe, lyin' down. . . . Oh, God, have mercy on me!

CAPT. BRENNAN (*to* LANGON) A few steps more, Jim, a few steps more; thry to stick it for a few steps more.

LIEUT. LANGON Oh, I can't, I can't, I can't!

CAPT. BRENNAN (*to* CLITHEROE) Are you comin', man, or are you goin' to make an arrangement for another honeymoon? . . . If you want to act th' renegade, say so, an' we'll be off!

BESSIE (*from above*) Runnin' from th' Tommies—choke th' chicken. Runnin' from th' Tommies—choke th' chicken!

CLITHEROE (*savagely to* BRENNAN) Damn you, man, who wants to act th' renegade? (*to* NORA) Here, let go your hold; let go, I say!

NORA (*clinging to* CLITHEROE, *and indicat-*

ing BRENNAN) Look, Jack, look at th' anger in his face; look at th' fear glintin' in his eyes. . . . He himself's afraid, afraid, afraid! . . . He wants you to go th' way he'll have th' chance of death sthrikin' you an' missin' him! . . . Turn round an' look at him, Jack, look at him, look at him! . . . His very soul is cold . . . shiverin' with th' thought of what may happen to him. . . . It is his fear that is thryin' to frighten you from recognizin' th' same fear that is in your own heart!

CLITHEROE (*struggling to release himself from* NORA) Damn you, woman, will you let me go!

CAPT. BRENNAN (*fiercely, to* CLITHEROE) Why are you beggin' her to let you go? Are you afraid of her, or what? Break her hold on you, man, or go up, an' sit on her lap!

(CLITHEROE *trying roughly to break her hold*)

NORA (*imploringly*) Oh, Jack. . . . Jack. . . . Jack!

LIEUT. LANGON (*agonizingly*) Brennan, a priest; I'm dyin', I think, I'm dyin'!

CLITHEROE (*to* NORA) If you won't do it quietly, I'll have to make you! (*to* BRENNAN) Here, hold this gun, you, for a minute. (*He hands the gun to* BRENNAN)

NORA (*pitifully*) Please, Jack. . . . You're hurting me, Jack. . . . Honestly. . . . Oh, you're hurting . . . me! . . . I won't, I won't, I won't! . . . Oh, Jack, I gave you everything you asked of me. . . . Don't fling me from you, now! (*He roughly loosens her grip, and pushes her away from him.* NORA *sinks to the ground and lies there*)

NORA (*weakly*) Ah, Jack. . . . Jack. . . . Jack!

CLITHEROE (*taking the gun back from* BRENNAN) Come on, come on.

(*They go out.* BESSIE *looks at* NORA *lying on the street, for a few moments, then, leaving the window, she comes out, runs over to* NORA, *lifts her up in her arms, and carries her swiftly into the house. A short pause, then down the street is heard a wild, drunken yell; it comes nearer, and* FLUTHER *enters, frenzied, wild-eyed, mad, roaring drunk. In his arms is an earthen half-gallon jar of whisky; streaming from one of the pockets of his coat is the arm of a new tunic shirt; on his head is a woman's vivid blue hat with gold lacing, all of which he has looted*)

FLUTHER (*singing in a frenzy:*)
Fluther's a jolly good fella! . . .
Fluther's a jolly good fella!
Up th' rebels! . . .
That nobody can deny!

(*He beats on the door*) Get us a mug or a jug, or somethin', some o' yous, one o' yous, will yous, before I lay one o' yous out! . . . (*looking down the street*) Bang an' fire away for all Fluther cares. . . . (*banging at door*) Come down an' open th' door, some of yous, one of yous, will yous, before I lay some o' yous out! . . . Th' whole city can topple home to hell, for Fluther!

(*Inside the house is heard a scream from* NORA, *followed by a moan*)

FLUTHER (*singing furiously:*)
That nobody can deny, that nobody can deny,
For Fluther's a jolly good fella, Fluther's a jolly good fella,
Fluther's a jolly good fella . . . Up th' rebels! That nobody can deny!

(*His frantic movements cause him to spill some of the whisky out of the jar*) Blast you, Fluther, don't be spillin' th' precious liquor! (*He kicks at the door*) Ay, give us a mug or a jug, or somethin', one o' yous, some o' yous, will yous, before I lay one o' yous out!

(*The door suddenly opens, and* BESSIE *coming out, grips him by the collar*)

BESSIE (*indignantly*) You bowsey, come in ower o' that. . . . I'll thrim your thricks o' dhrunken dancin' for you, an' none of us knowin' how soon we'll bump into a world we were never in before!

FLUTHER (*as she is pulling him in*) Ay, th' jar, th' jar, th' jar!

(*A short pause, then again is heard a scream of pain from* NORA. *The door opens and* MRS. GOGAN *and* BESSIE *are seen standing at it*)

BESSIE Fluther would go, only he's too dhrunk. . . . Oh, God, isn't it a pity he's so dhrunk! We'll have to thry to get a docthor somewhere.

MRS. GOGAN I'd be afraid to go. . . . Besides, Mollser's terrible bad. I don't think you'll get a docthor to come. It's hardly any use goin'.

BESSIE (*determinedly*) I'll risk it. . . . Give her a little of Fluther's whisky. . . . It's th' fright that's brought it on her so soon. . . . Go on back to her, you.

(MRS. GOGAN *goes in, and* BESSIE *softly closes the door. She is moving forward, when the sound of some rifle shots, and the tok, tok, tok of a distant machine gun brings her to a sudden halt. She hesitates for a moment, then she tightens her shawl round her, as if it were a shield, then she firmly and swiftly goes out*)

BESSIE (*as she goes out:*) Oh, God, be Thou

my help in time o' throuble. An' shelter me
safely in th' shadow of Thy wings!

ACT FOUR

(*The living room of* BESSIE BURGESS. *It is one
of two small attic rooms* [*the other, used as a
bedroom, is to the Left*], *the ceiling slopes up
towards the back, giving to the apartment a
look of compressed confinement. In the center
of the ceiling is a small skylight. There is an
unmistakable air of poverty bordering on destitution. The paper on the walls is torn and
soiled, particularly near the fire where the
cooking is done, and near the washstand where
the washing is done. The fireplace is to the
Left. A small armchair near fire. One small
window at Back. A pane of this window is
starred by the entrance of a bullet. Under the
window to the Right is an oak coffin standing
on two kitchen chairs. Near the coffin is a
home-manufactured stool, on which are two
lighted candles. Beside the window is a worn-
out dresser on which is a small quantity of delf.
Tattered remains of cheap lace curtains drape
the window. Standing near the window on Left
is a brass standard-lamp with a fancy shade;
hanging on the wall near the same window is
a vividly crimson silk dress, both of which have
been looted. A door on Left leading to the
bedroom. Another opposite giving a way to
the rest of the house. To the Left of this door
a common washstand. A tin kettle, very black,
and an old saucepan inside the fender. There
is no light in the room but that given from
the two candles and the fire. The dusk has well
fallen, and the glare of the burning buildings
in the town can be seen through the window,
in the distant sky.* THE COVEY *and* FLUTHER
*have been playing cards, sitting on the floor
by the light of the candles on the stool near
the coffin. When the curtain rises* THE COVEY
is shuffling the cards, PETER *is sitting in a stiff,
dignified way beside him, and* FLUTHER *is
kneeling beside the window, cautiously looking
out. It is a few days later*)

FLUTHER (*furtively peeping out of the
window*) Give them a good shuffling. . . .
Th' sky's gettin' reddher an' reddher. . . .
You'd think it was afire. . . . Half o' th' city
must be burnin'.

THE COVEY If I was you, Fluther, I'd keep
away from that window. . . . It's dangerous,

an', besides, if they see you, you'll only bring
a nose on th' house.

PETER Yes; an' he knows we had to leave
our own place th' way they were riddlin' it
with machine-gun fire. . . . He'll keep on
pimpin' an pimpin' there, till we have to fly
out o' this place too.

FLUTHER (*ironically*) If they make any
attack here, we'll send you out in your green
an' glory uniform, shakin' your sword over your
head, an' they'll fly before you as th' Danes
flew before Brian Boru!

THE COVEY (*placing the cards on the floor,
after shuffling them*) Come on, an' cut.

(FLUTHER *comes over, sits on floor, and cuts
the cards*)

THE COVEY (*having dealt the cards*) Spuds
up again.

(NORA *moans feebly in room on Left*)

FLUTHER There, she's at it again. She's
been quiet for a long time, all th' same.

THE COVEY She was quiet before, sure, an'
she broke out again worse than ever. . . .
What was led that time?

PETER Thray o' Hearts, Thray o' Hearts,
Thray o' Hearts.

FLUTHER It's damned hard lines to think
of her dead-born kiddie lyin' there in th' arms
o' poor little Mollser. Mollser snuffed it sudden
too, afther all.

THE COVEY Sure she never got any care.
How could she get it, an' th' mother out day
an' night lookin' for work, an' her consumptive
husband leavin' her with a baby to be born
before he died!

VOICES IN A LILTING CHANT TO THE LEFT IN
A DISTANT STREET Red Cr . . . oss, Red Cr
. . . oss! . . . Ambu . . . lance, Ambu . . .
lance!

THE COVEY (*to* FLUTHER) Your deal, Fluther.

FLUTHER (*shuffling and dealing the cards*)
It'll take a lot out o' Nora—if she'll ever be
th' same.

THE COVEY Th' docthor thinks she'll never
be th' same; thinks she'll be a little touched
here. (*He touches his forehead*) She's ramblin'
a lot; thinkin' she's out in th' country with Jack;
or gettin' his dinner ready for him before he
comes home; or yellin' for her kiddie. All that,
though, might be th' chloroform she got. . . .
I don't know what we'd have done only for
oul' Bessie; up with her for th' past three
nights, hand runnin'.

FLUTHER I always knew there was never
anything really derogatory wrong with poor
oul' Bessie. (*to* PETER, *who is taking a trick*)

Ay, houl' on, there, don't be so damn quick—
that's my thrick.

PETER   What's your thrick? It's my thrick,
man.

FLUTHER (*loudly*)   How is it your thrick?

PETER (*answering as loudly*)   Didn't I lead
th' deuce!

FLUTHER   You must be gettin' blind, man;
don't you see th' ace?

BESSIE (*appearing at the door of room, Left;
in a tense whisper*)   D'ye want to waken her
again on me, when she's just gone asleep? If
she wakes will yous come an' mind her? If I
hear a whisper out o' one o' yous again, I'll
. . . gut yous!

THE COVEY (*in a whisper*)   S-s-s-h. She can
hear anything above a whisper.

PETER (*looking up at the ceiling*)   Th'
gentle an' merciful God 'll give th' pair o' yous
a scawldin' an' a scarifyin' one o' these days!

(FLUTHER *takes a bottle of whisky from his
pocket and takes a drink*)

THE COVEY (*to* FLUTHER)   Why don't you
spread that out, man, an' thry to keep a sup
for tomorrow?

FLUTHER   Spread it out? Keep a sup for
tomorrow? How th' hell does a fella know
there'll be any tomorrow? If I'm goin' to be
whipped away, let me be whipped away when
it's empty, an' not when it's half full! (*to* BESSIE,
*who has seated herself in an armchair at the
fire*) How is she, now, Bessie?

BESSIE   I left her sleeping quietly. When
I'm listenin' to her babblin', I think she'll never
be much betther than she is. Her eyes have a
hauntin' way of lookin' in instead of lookin'
out, as if her mind had been lost alive in
madly minglin' memories of th' past. . . .
(*sleepily*) Crushin' her thoughts . . . together
. . . in a fierce . . . an' fanciful . . . (*She
nods her head and starts wakefully*) idea that
dead things are livin', an' livin' things are
dead. . . . (*with a start*) Was that a scream
I heard her give? (*reassured*) Blessed God, I
think I hear her screamin' every minute! An'
it's only there with me that I'm able to keep
awake.

THE COVEY   She'll sleep, maybe, for a long
time, now. Ten there.

FLUTHER   Ten here. If she gets a long
sleep, she might be all right. Peter's th' lone
five.

THE COVEY   Whisht! I think I hear somebody movin' below. Whoever it is, he's comin'
up.

(*A pause. Then the door opens and* CAPTAIN
BRENNAN *comes into the room. He has changed
his uniform for a suit of civies. His eyes droop
with the heaviness of exhaustion; his face is
pallid and drawn. His clothes are dusty and
stained here and there with mud. He leans
heavily on the back of a chair as he stands*)

CAPT. BRENNAN   Mrs. Clitheroe; where's
Mrs. Clitheroe? I was told I'd find her here.

BESSIE   What d'ye want with Mrs. Clitheroe?

CAPT. BRENNAN   I've a message, a last message for her from her husband.

BESSIE   Killed! He's not killed, is he!

CAPT. BRENNAN (*sinking stiffly and painfully
onto a chair*)   In th' Imperial Hotel; we
fought till th' place was in flames. He was
shot through th' arm, an' then through th' lung.
. . . I could do nothin' for him—only watch
his breath comin' an' goin in quick, jerky gasps,
an' a tiny sthream o' blood thricklin' out of his
mouth, down over his lower lip. . . . I said a
prayer for th' dyin' an' twisted his Rosary
beads around his fingers. . . . Then I had to
leave him to save meself. . . . (*He shows
some holes in his coat*) Look at th' way a machine gun tore at me coat, as I belted out o'
the buildin' an' darted across th' sthreet for
shelter. . . . An' then, I seen The Plough an'
the Stars fallin' like a shot as th' roof crashed
in, an' where I'd left poor Jack was nothin' but
a leppin' spout o' flame!

BESSIE (*with partly repressed vehemence*)
Ay, you left him! You twined his Rosary beads
round his fingers, an' then you run like a hare
to get out o' danger!

CAPT. BRENNAN   I took me chance as well
as him. . . . He took it like a man. His last
whisper was to "Tell Nora to be brave; that
I'm ready to meet my God, an' that I'm proud
to die for Ireland." An' when our General heard
it he said that "Commandant Clitheroe's end
was a gleam of glory." Mrs. Clitheroe's grief
will be a joy when she realizes that she has had
a hero for a husband.

BESSIE   If you only seen her, you'd know
to th' differ.

(NORA *appears at door, Left. She is clad only
in her nightdress; her hair, uncared for some
days, is hanging in disorder over her shoulders.
Her pale face looks paler still because of a vivid
red spot on the tip of each cheek. Her eyes are
glimmering with the light of incipient insanity;
her hands are nervously fidling with her night-
gown. She halts at the door for a moment, looks
vacantly around the room, and then comes
slowly in. The rest do not notice her till she
speaks*)

NORA (*in a quiet and monotonous tone*)
No . . . Not there, Jack. . . . I can feel com-

fortable only in our own familiar place beneath th' bramble tree. . . . We must be walking for a long time; I feel very, very tired. . . . Have we to go farther, or have we passed it by? (*passing her hand across her eyes*) Curious mist on my eyes. . . . Why don't you hold my hand, Jack. . . . (*excitedly*) No, no, Jack, it's not. Can't you see it's a goldfinch. Look at th' black-satiny wings with th' gold bars, an' th' splash of crimson on its head. . . . (*wearily*) Something ails me, something ails me. . . . Don't kiss me like that; you take my breath away, Jack. . . . Why do you frown at me? . . . You're going away, and (*frightened*) I can't follow you. Something's keeping me from moving. . . . (*crying out*) Jack, Jack, Jack!

BESSIE (*who has gone over and caught* NORA'S *arm*) Now, Mrs. Clitheroe, you're a terrible woman to get up out of bed. . . . You'll get cold if you stay here in them clothes.

NORA Cold? I'm feelin' very cold; it's chilly out here in th' counthry. . . . (*looking around frightened*) What place is this? Where am I?

BESSIE (*coaxingly*) You're all right, Nora; you're with friends, an' in a safe place. Don't you know your uncle an' your cousin, an' poor oul' Fluther?

PETER (*about to go over to* NORA) Nora, darlin', now—

FLUTHER (*pulling him back*) Now, leave her to Bessie, man. A crowd 'll only make her worse.

NORA (*thoughtfully*) There is something I want to remember, an' I can't. (*with agony*) I can't, I can't, I can't! My head, my head! (*suddenly breaking from* BESSIE, *and running over to the men, and gripping* FLUTHER *by the shoulders*) Where is it? Where's my baby? Tell me where you've put it, where've you hidden it? My baby, my baby; I want my baby! My head, my poor head. . . . Oh, I can't tell what is wrong with me. (*screaming*) Give him to me, give me my husband!

BESSIE Blessin' o' God on us, isn't this pitiful!

NORA (*struggling with* BESSIE) I won't go away for you; I won't. Not till you give me back my husband. (*screaming*) Murderers, that's what yous are; murderers, murderers!

BESSIE S-s-sh. We'll bring Mr. Clitheroe back to you, if you'll only lie down an' stop quiet. . . . (*trying to lead her in*) Come on, now, Nora, an' I'll sing something to you.

NORA I feel as if my life was thryin' to force it's way out of my body. . . . I can hardly breathe . . . I'm frightened, I'm frightened, I'm frightened! For God's sake, don't leave me, Bessie. Hold my hand, put your arms around me!

FLUTHER (*to* BRENNAN) Now you can see th' way she is, man.

PETER An' what way would she be if she heard Jack had gone west?

THE COVEY (*to* PETER) Shut up, you, man!

BESSIE (*to* NORA) We'll have to be brave, an' let patience clip away the heaviness of th' slow-movin' hours, rememberin' that sorrow may endure for th' night, but joy cometh in th' mornin'. . . . Come on in, an' I'll sing to you, an' you'll rest quietly.

NORA (*stopping suddenly on her way to the room*) Jack an' me are goin' out somewhere this evenin'. Where I can't tell. Isn't it curious I can't remember. . . . Maura, Maura, Jack, if th' baby's a girl; any name you like, if th' baby's a boy! . . . He's there. (*screaming*) He's there, an' they won't give him back to me!

BESSIE S-ss-s-h, darlin', s-ssh. I won't sing to you, if you're not quiet.

NORA (*nervously holding* BESSIE) Hold my hand, hold my hand, an' sing to me, sing to me!

BESSIE Come in an' lie down, an' I'll sing to you.

NORA (*vehemently*) Sing to me, sing to me; sing, sing!

BESSIE (*singing as she leads* NORA *into room:*)

> Lead, kindly light, amid th' encircling gloom,
> Lead Thou me on;
> Th' night is dark an' I am far from home,
> Lead Thou me on.
> Keep Thou my feet; I do not ask to see
> Th' distant scene—one step enough for me.
> So long that Thou hast blessed me, sure Thou still
> Wilt lead me on;

(*They go in*)

BESSIE (*singing in room:*)

> O'er moor an' fen, o'er crag an' torrent, till
> Th' night is gone.
> An in th' morn those angel faces smile
> That I have lov'd long since, an' lost awhile!

THE COVEY (*to* BRENNAN) Now that you've seen how bad she is, an' that we daren't tell her what has happened till she's betther, you'd best be slippin' back to where you come from.

CAPT. BRENNAN   There's no chance o' slip-pin' back now, for th' military are everywhere: a fly couldn't get through. I'd never have got here, only I managed to change me uniform for what I'm wearin'. . . . I'll have to take me chance, an' thry to lie low here for a while.

THE COVEY   (*frightened*)   There's no place here to lie low. Th' Tommies 'll be hoppin' in here, any minute!

PETER   (*aghast*)   An' then we'd all be shang-haied!

THE COVEY   Be God, there's enough afther happenin' to us!

FLUTHER   (*warningly, as he listens*)   Whisht, whisht, th' whole o' yous. I think I heard th' clang of a rifle butt on th' floor of th' hall be-low. (*all alertness*) Here, come on with th' cards again. I'll deal. (*He shuffles and deals the cards to all*)

FLUTHER   Clubs up. (*to* BRENNAN) Thry to keep your hands from shakin', man. You lead, Peter. (*as* PETER *throws out a card*) Four o' Hearts led.

(*The door opens and* CORPORAL STODDART *of the Wiltshires enters in full war kit; steel hel-met, rifle and bayonet, and trench tool. He looks round the room. A pause and a palpable silence*)

FLUTHER   (*breaking the silence*)   Two tens an' a five.

CORPORAL STODDART   'Ello. (*indicating the coffin*) This the stiff?

THE COVEY   Yis.

CORPORAL STODDART   Who's gowing with it? Ownly one allowed to gow with it, you know.

THE COVEY   I dunno.

CORPORAL STODDART   You dunnow?

THE COVEY   I dunno.

BESSIE   (*coming into the room*)   She's af-ther slippin' off to sleep again, thanks be to God. I'm hardly able to keep me own eyes open. (*to the soldier*) Oh, are yous goin' to take away poor little Mollser?

CORPORAL STODDART   Ay; 'oo's agowing with 'er?

BESSIE   Oh, th' poor mother, o' course. God help her, it's a terrible blow to her!

FLUTHER   A terrible blow? Sure, she's in her element now, woman, mixin' earth to earth, an' ashes t'ashes an' dust to dust, an' revellin' in plumes an' hearses, last days an' judgments!

BESSIE   (*falling into chair by the fire*)   God bless us! I'm jaded!

CORPORAL STODDART   Was she plugged?

THE COVEY   Ah, no; died o' consumption.

CORPORAL STODDART   Ow, is that all? Thought she moight 'ave been plugged.

THE COVEY   Is that all? Isn't it enough? D'ye know, comrade, that more die o' con-sumption than are killed in th' wars? An' it's all because of th' system we're livin' undher?

CORPORAL STODDART   Ow, I know. I'm a Sowcialist moiself, but I 'as to do my dooty.

THE COVEY   (*ironically*)   Dooty! Th' only dooty of a Socialist is th' emancipation of th' workers.

CORPORAL STODDART   Ow, a man's a man, an 'e 'as to foight for 'is country, 'asn't 'e?

FLUTHER   (*aggressively*)   You're not fightin' for your counthry here, are you?

PETER   (*anxiously, to* FLUTHER)   Ay, ay, Fluther, none o' that, none o' that!

THE COVEY   Fight for your counthry! Did y'ever read, comrade, Jenersky's *Thesis on the Origin, Development, an' Consolidation of th' Evolutionary Idea of the Proletariat?*

CORPORAL STODDART   Ow, cheese it, Paddy, cheese it!

BESSIE   (*sleepily*)   How is things in th' town, Tommy?

CORPORAL STODDART   Ow, I fink it's nearly hover. We've got 'em surrounded, and we're clowsing in on the bloighters. Ow, it was only a little bit of a dawg-foight.

(*The sharp ping of the sniper's rifle is heard, followed by a squeal of pain*)

VOICES TO THE LEFT IN A CHANT   Red Cr . . . oss, Red Cr . . . oss! Ambu . . . lance, Ambu . . . lance!

CORPORAL STODDART   (*excitedly*)   Christ, that's another of our men 'it by that blawsted sniper! 'E's knocking abaht 'ere, somewheres. Gawd, when we get th' bloighter, we'll give 'im the cold steel, we will. We'll jab the belly aht of 'im, we will!

(MRS. GOGAN *comes in tearfully, and a little proud of the importance of being directly con-nected with death*)

MRS. GOGAN   (*to* FLUTHER)   I'll never forget what you done for me, Fluther, goin' around at th' risk of your life settlin' everything with th' undhertaker an' th' cemetery people. When all me own were afraid to put their noses out, you plunged like a good one through hum-min' bullets, an' they knockin' fire out o' th' road, tinklin' through th' frightened windows, an' splashin' themselves to pieces on th' walls! An' you'll find, that Mollser, in th' happy place she's gone to, won't forget to whisper, now an' again, th' name o' Fluther.

CORPORAL STODDART   Git it aht, mother, git it aht.

BESSIE (*from the chair*) It's excusin' me you'll be, Mrs. Gogan, for not stannin' up, seein' I'm shaky on me feet for want of a little sleep, an' not desirin' to show any disrespect to poor little Mollser.

FLUTHER Sure, we all know, Bessie, that it's vice versa with you.

MRS. GOGAN (*to* BESSIE) Indeed, it's meself that has well chronicled, Mrs. Burgess, all your gentle hurryin's to me little Mollser, when she was alive, bringin' her somethin' to dhrink, or somethin' t'eat, an' never passin' her without liftin' up her heart with a delicate word o' kindness.

CORPORAL STODDART (*impatiently, but kindly*) Git it aht, git it aht, mother.

(THE COVEY, FLUTHER, BRENNAN, *and* PETER *carry out the coffin, followed by* MRS. GOGAN)

CORPORAL STODDART (*to* BESSIE, *who is almost asleep*) Ow many men is in this 'ere 'ouse? (*No answer. Loudly*) Ow many men is in this 'ere 'ouse?

BESSIE (*waking with a start*) God, I was nearly asleep! . . . How many men? Didn't you see them?

CORPORAL STODDART Are they all that are in the 'ouse?

BESSIE Oh, there's none higher up, but there may be more lower down. Why?

CORPORAL STODDART All men in the district 'as to be rounded up. Somebody's giving 'elp to the snipers, and we 'as to take precautions. If I 'ad my woy, I'd make 'em all join hup, and do their bit! But I suppowse they and you are all Shinners.

BESSIE (*who has been sinking into sleep, waking up to a sleepy vehemence*) Bessie Burgess is no Shinner, an' never had no thruck with anything spotted be th' fingers o' th' Fenians; but always made it her business to harness herself for Church whenever she knew that God Save the King was goin' to be sung at t'end of th' service; whose only son went to th' front in th' first contingent of the Dublin Fusiliers, an' that's on his way home carryin' a shatthered arm that he got fightin' for his King an' counthry!

(*Her head sinks slowly forward again.* PETER *comes into the room; his body is stiffened and his face is wearing a comically indignant look. He walks to and fro at the back of the room, evidently repressing a violent desire to speak angrily. He is followed in by* FLUTHER, THE COVEY, *and* BRENNAN, *who slinks into an obscure corner of the room, nervous of notice*)

FLUTHER (*after an embarrassing pause*) Th' air in th' sthreet outside's shakin' with the firin' o' rifles an' machine guns. It must be a hot shop in th' middle o' th' scrap.

CORPORAL STODDART We're pumping lead in on 'em from every side, now; they'll soon be shoving up th' white flag.

PETER (*with a shout*) I'm tellin' you either o' yous two lowsers 'ud make a betther hearse-man than Peter; proddin' an' pokin' at me an' I helpin' to carry out a corpse!

FLUTHER It wasn't a very derogatory thing for th' Covey to say that you'd make a fancy hearse-man, was it?

PETER (*furiously*) A pair o' red-jesthered bowseys pondherin' from mornin' till night on how they'll get a chance to break a gap through th' quiet nature of a man that's always endeavorin' to chase out of him any sthray thought of venom against his fella-man!

THE COVEY Oh, shut it, shut it, shut it!

PETER As long as I'm a livin' man, responsible for me thoughts, words, an' deeds to th' Man above, I'll feel meself instituted to fight again' th' sliddherin' ways of a pair o' picaroons, whisperin', concurrin', concoctin', an' conspirin' together to rendher me unconscious of th' life I'm thryin' to live!

CORPORAL STODDART (*dumbfounded*) What's wrong, Daddy; wot 'ave they done to you?

PETER (*savagely to the* CORPORAL) You mind your own business! What's it got to do with you, what's wrong with me?

BESSIE (*in a sleepy murmur*) Will yous thry to conthrol yourselves into quietness? Yous'll waken her . . . up . . . on . . . me . . . again. (*She sleeps*)

FLUTHER Come on, boys, to th' cards again, an' never mind him.

CORPORAL STODDART No use of you gowing to start cawds; you'll be gowing out of 'ere, soon as Sergeant comes.

FLUTHER Goin' out o' here? An' why're we goin' out o' here?

CORPORAL STODDART All men in district to be rounded up, and 'eld in till the scrap is hover.

FLUTHER An' where're we goin' to be held in?

CORPORAL STODDART They're puttin' 'em in a church.

THE COVEY A church?

FLUTHER What sort of a church? Is it a Protestan' Church?

CORPORAL STODDART I dunnow; I suppowse so.

FLUTHER (*dismayed*) Be God, it'll be a nice thing to be stuck all night in a Protestan' Church!

CORPORAL STODDART   Bring the cawds; you moight get a chance of a goime.

FLUTHER   Ah, no, that wouldn't do. . . . I wondher? (*after a moment's thought*) Ah, I don' think we'd be doin' anything derogatory be playin' cards in a Protestan' Church.

CORPORAL STODDART   If I was you I'd bring a little snack with me; you moight be glad of it before the mawning. (*sings:*)

I do loike a snoice mince poy,
I do loike a snoice mince poy!

(*The snap of the sniper's rifle rings out again, followed simultaneously by a scream of pain. CORPORAL STODDART goes pale, and brings his rifle to the ready, listening*)

VOICES CHANTING TO THE RIGHT   Red Cro . . . ss, Red Cro . . . ss! Ambu . . . lance, Ambu . . . lance!

(SERGEANT TINLEY *comes rapidly in, pale, agitated, and fiercely angry*)

CORPORAL STODDART (*to* SERGEANT)   One of hour men 'it, Sergeant?

SERGEANT TINLEY   Private Taylor; got 'it roight through the chest, 'e did; an 'ole in front of 'im as 'ow you could put your fist through, and 'arf 'is back blown awoy! Dum-dum bullets they're using. Gang of hassassins potting at us from behind roofs. That's not playing the goime: why down't they come into the owpen and foight fair!

FLUTHER (*unable to stand the slight*)   Fight fair! A few hundhred scrawls o' chaps with a couple o' guns an' Rosary beads, again' a hundhred thousand thrained men with horse, fut, an' artillery . . . an' he wants us to fight fair! (*to* SERGEANT)   D'ye want us to come out in our skins an' throw stones?

SERGEANT TINLEY (*to* CORPORAL)   Are these four all that are 'ere?

CORPORAL STODDART   Four; that's all, Sergeant.

SERGEANT TINLEY (*vindictively*)   Come on, then; get the blighters aht. (*to the men*) 'Ere, 'op it aht! Aht into the streets with you, and if a snoiper sends another of our men west, you gow with 'im! (*He catches* FLUTHER *by the shoulder*) Gow on, git aht!

FLUTHER   Eh, who are you chuckin', eh?

SERGEANT TINLEY (*roughly*)   Gow on, git aht, you blighter.

FLUTHER   Who are you callin' a blighter to, eh? I'm a Dublin man, born an' bred in th' city, see?

SERGEANT TINLEY   I down't care if you were Broin Buroo; git aht, git aht.

FLUTHER (*halting as he is going out*)   Jasus, you an' your guns! Leave them down, an' I'd beat th' two o' yous without sweatin'!

(PETER, BRENNAN, THE COVEY, *and* FLUTHER, *followed by the soldiers, go out.* BESSIE *is sleeping heavily on the chair by the fire. After a pause,* NORA *appears at door, Left, in her nightdress. Remaining at door for a few moments she looks vaguely around the room. She then comes in quietly, goes over to the fire, pokes it, and puts the kettle on. She thinks for a few moments, pressing her hand to her forehead. She looks questioningly at the fire, and then at the press at back. She goes to the press, opens it, takes out a soiled cloth and spreads it on the table. She then places things for tea on the table*)

NORA   I imagine th' room looks very odd somehow. . . . I was nearly forgetting Jack's tea. . . . Ah, I think I'll have everything done before he gets in. . . . (*She lilts gently, as she arranges the table*)

Th' violets were scenting th' woods,
    Nora,
  Displaying their charms to th' bee,
When I first said I lov'd only you,
    Nora,
  An' you said you lov'd only me.

Th' chestnut blooms gleam'd through
    th' glade, Nora,
  A robin sang loud from a tree,
When I first said I lov'd only you,
    Nora,
  An' you said you lov'd only me.

(*She pauses suddenly, and glances round the room*)

NORA (*doubtfully*)   I can't help feelin' this room very strange. . . . What is it? . . . What is it? . . . I must think. . . . I must thry to remember. . . .

VOICES CHANTING IN A DISTANT STREET   Ambu . . . lance, Ambu . . . lance! Red Cro . . . ss, Red Cro . . . ss!

NORA (*startled and listening for a moment, then resuming the arrangement of the table*)

Trees, birds, an' bees sang a song,
    Nora,
  Of happier transports to be,
When I first said I lov'd only you,
    Nora,
  An' you said you lov'd only me.

(*A burst of rifle fire is heard in a street near by, followed by the rapid rok, tok, tok, of a machine gun*)

NORA (*staring in front of her and screaming*)   Jack, Jack, Jack! My baby, my baby, my baby!

BESSIE (*waking with a start*)   You divil, are

you afther gettin' out o' bed again! (*She rises
and runs towards* NORA, *who rushes to the window, which she frantically opens*)

NORA (*at window, screaming*)   Jack, Jack,
for God's sake, come to me!

SOLDIERS (*outside, shouting*)   Git away, git
away from that window, there!

BESSIE (*seizing hold of* NORA)   Come away,
come away, woman, from that window!

NORA (*struggling with* BESSIE)   Where is
it; where have you hidden it? Oh, Jack, Jack,
where are you?

BESSIE (*imploringly*)   Mrs. Clitheroe, for
God's sake, come away!

NORA (*fiercely*)   I won't; he's below. Let
. . . me . . . go! You're thryin' to keep me
from me husband. I'll follow him. Jack, Jack,
come to your Nora!

BESSIE   Hus-s-sh, Nora, Nora! He'll be here
in a minute. I'll bring him to you, if you'll only
be quiet—honest to God, I will.

(*With a great effort* BESSIE *pushes* NORA
*away from the window, the force used causing
her to stagger against it herself. Two rifle shots
ring out in quick succession.* BESSIE *jerks her
body convulsively; stands stiffly for a moment,
a look of agonized astonishment on her face,
then she staggers forward, leaning heavily on
the table with her hands*)

BESSIE (*with an arrested scream of fear and
pain*)   Merciful God, I'm shot, I'm shot, I'm
shot! . . . Th' life's pourin' out o' me! (*to
NORA) I've got this through . . . through you
. . . through you, you bitch, you! . . . O
God, have mercy on me! . . . (*to NORA*)
You wouldn't stop quiet, no, you wouldn't,
you wouldn't, blast you! Look at what I'm
afther gettin', look at what I'm afther gettin'
. . . I'm bleedin' to death, an' no one's here
to stop th' flowin' blood! (*calling*) Mrs. Gogan,
Mrs. Gogan! Fluther, Fluther, for God's sake,
somebody, a doctor, a doctor!

(*She staggers frightened towards the door, to
seek for aid, but, weakening half-way across
the room, she sinks to her knees, and bending
forward, supports herself with her hands resting on the floor.* NORA *is standing rigidly with
her back to the wall opposite, her trembling
hands held out a little from the sides of her
body, her lips quivering, her breast heaving,
staring wildly at the figure of* BESSIE)

NORA (*in a breathless whisper*)   Jack, I'm
frightened. . . . I'm frightened, Jack. . . .
Oh, Jack, where are you?

BESSIE (*moaning*)   This is what's afther

comin' on me for nursin' you day an' night.
. . . I was a fool, a fool, a fool! Get me a
dhrink o' wather, you jade, will you? There's
a fire burnin' in me blood! (*pleadingly*) Nora,
Nora, dear, for God's sake, run out an' get Mrs.
Gogan, or Fluther, or somebody to bring a
doctor, quick, quick, quick! (*as* NORA *does not
stir*) Blast you, stir yourself, before I'm gone!

NORA   Oh, Jack, Jack, where are you?

BESSIE (*in a whispered moan*)   Jesus Christ,
me sight's goin'! It's all dark, dark! Nora, hold
me hand! (BESSIE's *body lists over and she
sinks into a prostrate position on the floor*) I'm
dyin', I'm dyin' . . . I feel it. . . . Oh God,
oh God! (*She feebly sings:*)

I do believe, I will believe
    That Jesus died for me;
That on th' cross He shed His blood,
    From sin to set me free. . . .
I do believe . . . I will believe
    . . . Jesus died . . . me;
    . . . th' cross He shed . . . blood,
    From sin . . . free.

(*She ceases singing, and lies stretched out,
still and very rigid. A pause. Then* MRS. GOGAN
runs hastily in)

MRS. GOGAN (*quivering with fright*)   Blessed
be God, what's afther happenin'? (*to* NORA)
What's wrong, child, what's wrong? (*She sees
BESSIE, runs to her and bends over the body*)
Bessie, Bessie! (*She shakes the body*) Mrs.
Burgess, Mrs. Burgess! (*She feels* BESSIE's *fore-
head*) My God, she's as cold as death. They're
afther murdherin' th' poor inoffensive woman!

(SERGEANT TINLEY *and* CORPORAL STODDART
enter agitatedly, their rifles at the ready)

SERGEANT TINLEY (*excitedly*)   This is the
'ouse. That's the window!

NORA (*pressing back against the wall*)
Hide it, hide it; cover it up, cover it up!

SERGEANT TINLEY (*going over to the body*)
'Ere, what's this? Who's this? (*looking at
BESSIE*) Oh Gawd, we've plugged one of the
women of the 'ouse.

CORPORAL STODDART   Whoy the 'ell did she
gow to the window? Is she dead?

SERGEANT TINLEY   Oh, dead as bedamned.
Well, we couldn't afford to toike any chawnces.

NORA (*screaming*)   Hide it, hide it; don't
let me see it! Take me away, take me away,
Mrs. Gogan!

(MRS. GOGAN *runs into room, Left, and runs
out again with a sheet which she spreads over
the body of* BESSIE)

MRS. GOGAN (*as she spreads the sheet*)   Oh,

God help her, th' poor woman, she's stiffenin' out as hard as she can! Her face has written on it th' shock o' sudden agony, an' her hands is whitenin' into th' smooth shininess of wax.

NORA (*whimperingly*) Take me away, take me away; don't leave me here to be lookin' an' lookin' at it!

MRS. GOGAN (*going over to* NORA *and putting her arm around her*) Come on with me, dear, an' you can doss in poor Mollser's bed, till we gather some neighbors to come an' give th' last friendly touches to Bessie in th' lonely layin' of her out. (MRS. GOGAN *and* NORA *go slowly out*)

CORPORAL STODDART (*who has been looking around, to* SERGEANT TINLEY) Tea here, Sergeant. Wot abaht a cup of scald?

SERGEANT TINLEY Pour it aht, Stoddart, pour it aht. I could scoff hanything just now.

(CORPORAL STODDART *pours out two cups of tea, and the two soldiers begin to drink. In the distance is heard a bitter burst of rifle and machine-gun fire, interspersed with the boom, boom of artillery. The glare in the sky seen through the window flares into a fuller and a deeper red*)

SERGEANT TINLEY There gows the general attack on the Powst Office.

VOICES IN A DISTANT STREET Ambu . . . lance, Ambu . . . lance! Red Cro . . . ss, Red Cro . . . ss!

(*The voices of soldiers at a barricade outside the house are heard singing:*)

> They were summoned from the 'ill-
>   side,
> They were called in from the glen,
> And the country found 'em ready
> At the stirring call for men.
> Let not tears add to their 'ardship,
> As the soldiers pass along,
> And although our 'eart is breaking,
> Make it sing this cheery song.

SERGEANT TINLEY *and* CORPORAL STODDART (*joining in the chorus, as they sip the tea:*)

> Keep the 'owme fires burning,
> While your 'earts are yearning;
> Though your lads are far away
> They dream of 'owme;
> There's a silver loining
> Through the dark cloud shoining,
> Turn the dark cloud inside out,
> Till the boys come 'owme!

George Bernard Shaw

1856-1950

THE PROBLEM PLAY—A SYMPOSIUM

Should social problems be freely dealt with in the Drama?

I do not know who has asked the question, "Should social problems be freely dealt with in the drama?"—some very thoughtless person evidently. Pray what social questions and what sort of drama? Suppose I say yes, then, vaccination being a social question, and the Wagnerian music drama being the one complete form of drama in the opinion of its admirers, it will follow that I am in favor of the production of a Jennerian tetralogy at Bayreuth. If I say no, then, marriage being a social question, and also the theme of Ibsen's *Doll's House*, I shall be held to contemn that work as a violation of the canons of art. I therefore reply to the propounder that I am not prepared to waste my own time and that of the public in answering maladroit conundrums. What I am prepared to do is to say what I can with the object of bringing some sort of order into the intellectual confusion which has expressed itself in the conundrum.

Social questions are produced by the conflict of human institutions with human feeling. For instance, we have certain institutions regulating the lives of women. To the women whose feelings are entirely in harmony with these institutions there is no Woman Question. But during the present century, from the time of Mary Wollstonecraft [1] onwards, women have been developing feelings, and consequently opinions, which clash with these institutions. The institutions assumed that it was natural to a woman to allow her husband to own her property and person, and to represent her in politics as a father represents his infant child. The moment that seemed no longer natural to some women, it became grievously oppressive to them. Immediately there was a Woman Question, which has produced Married Women's Property Acts, Divorce Acts, Woman's Suffrage in local elections, and the curious deadlock to which the Weldon and Jackson cases have led our courts in the matter of conjugal rights. When we have achieved reforms enough to bring our institutions as far into harmony with the feelings of women as they now are with the feelings of men, there will no longer be a Woman Question. No conflict, no question.

Now the material of the dramatist is always some conflict of human feeling with circumstances; so that, since institutions are circumstances, every social question furnishes material for drama. But every drama does not involve a social question, because human feeling may be in conflict with circumstances which are not institutions, which raise no question at all, which are part of human destiny. To illustrate, take Mr. Pinero's *Second Mrs. Tanqueray*. The heroine's feelings are in conflict with the human institutions which condemn to ostracism both herself and the man who marries her. So far, the play deals with a social question. But in one very effective scene the conflict is between that flaw in the woman's nature which makes her dependent for affection wholly on the attraction of her beauty, and the stealthy advance of age and decay to take her beauty away from her. Here there is no social question: age, like love,

"The Problem Play—A Symposium" by George Bernard Shaw is from *Shaw on Theatre*, published by Hill & Wang, and is reprinted by permission of The Public Trustee and The Society of Authors.

[1] Mary Wollstonecraft (1759–1797), famous leader of the feminist movement and author of *Vindication of the Rights of Women*.

death, accident, and personal character, lies outside all institutions; and this gives it a permanent and universal interest which makes the drama that deals with it independent of period and place. Abnormal greatness of character, abnormal baseness of character, love, and death: with these alone you can, if you are a sufficiently great dramatic poet, make a drama that will keep your language alive long after it has passed out of common use. Whereas a drama with a social question for the motive cannot outlive the solution of that question. It is true that we can in some cases imaginatively reconstruct an obsolete institution and sympathize with the tragedy it has produced: for instance, the very dramatic story of Abraham commanded to sacrifice his son, with the interposition of the angel to make a happy ending; or the condemnation of Antonio to lose a pound of flesh, and his rescue by Portia at the last moment, have not completely lost their effect nowadays—though it has been much modified —through the obsolescence of sacrificial rites, belief in miracles, and the conception that a debtor's person belongs to his creditors. It is enough that we still have paternal love, death, malice, moneylenders, and the tragedies of criminal law. But when a play depends entirely on a social question—when the struggle in it is between man and a purely legal institution—nothing can prolong its life beyond that of the institution. For example, Mr. Grundy's *Slaves of the Ring,* in which the tragedy is produced solely by the conflict between the individual and the institution of indissoluble marriage, will not survive a rational law of divorce, and actually fails even now to grip an English audience because the solution has by this time become so very obvious. And that irrepressibly popular play, *It's Never Too Late to Mend,* will hardly survive our abominable criminal system. Thus we see that the drama which deals with the natural factors in human destiny, though not necessarily better than the drama which deals with the political factors, is likely to last longer.

It has been observed that the greatest dramatists show a preference for the non-political drama, the greatest dramas of all being almost elementarily natural. But so, though for a different reason, do the minor dramatists. The minor dramatist leads the literary life, and dwells in the world of imagination instead of in the world of politics, business, law, and the platform agitations by which social questions are ventilated. He therefore remains, as a rule, astonishingly ignorant of real life. He may be clever, imaginative, sympathetic, humorous, and ob-

servant of such manners as he has any clue to; but he has hardly any wit or knowledge of the world. Compare his work with that of Sheridan, and you feel the deficiency at once. Indeed, you need not go so far as Sheridan: Mr. Gilbert's *Trial by Jury* is unique among the works of living English playwrights, solely because it, too, is the work of a wit and a man of the world. Incidentally, it answers the inquiry as to whether social questions make good theatrical material; for though it is pointless, and, in fact, unintelligible except as a satire on a social institution (the breach-of-promise suit), it is highly entertaining, and has made the fortune of the author and his musical collaborator. *The School for Scandal,* the most popular of modern melodramas, is a dramatic pamphlet: Charles Reade being another example of the distinction which the accomplished man of the world attains in the theatre as compared to the mere professional dramatist. In fact, it is so apparent that the best and most popular plays are dramatized sermons, pamphlets, satires, or bluebooks, that we find our popular authors, even when they have made a safe position for themselves by their success in purely imaginative drama, bidding for the laurels and the percentages of the sociologist dramatist. Mr. Henry Arthur Jones takes a position as the author of *The Middleman* and *The Crusaders,* which *The Silver King,* enormously popular as it was, never could have gained him; and Mr. Pinero, the author of *The Second Mrs. Tanqueray* and *The Notorious Mrs. Ebbsmith,* is a much more important person, and a much richer one, than the author of *Sweet Lavender.* Of course, the sociology in some of these dramas is as imaginary as the names and addresses of the characters; but the imitation sociology testifies to the attractiveness of the real article.

We may take it then that the ordinary dramatist only neglects social questions because he knows nothing about them, and that he loses in popularity, standing, and money by his ignorance. With the great dramatic poet it is otherwise. Shakespeare and Goethe do not belong to the order which "takes no interest in politics." Such minds devour everything with a keen appetite—fiction, science, gossip, politics, technical processes, sport, everything. Shakespeare is full of little lectures of the concrete English kind, from Cassio on temperance to Hamlet on suicide. Goethe, in his German way, is always discussing metaphysical points. To master Wagner's music dramas is to learn a philosophy. It was so with all the great men until the present century. They swallowed all the discussions, all the social questions, all the topics, all the fads, all the enthusiasms, all the fashions of their day in their nonage; but their theme finally was not this social question or that social question, this reform or that reform, but humanity as a whole. To this day your great dramatic poet is never a socialist, nor an individualist, nor a positivist, nor a materialist, nor any other sort of "ist," though he comprehends all the "isms," and is generally quoted and claimed by all the sections as an adherent. Social questions are too sectional, too topical, too temporal to move a man to the mighty effort which is needed to produce great poetry. Prison reform may nerve Charles Reade to produce an effective and businesslike prose melodrama; but it could never produce *Hamlet, Faust,* or *Peer Gynt.*

It must, however, be borne in mind that the huge size of modern populations and the development of the press make every social question more momentous than it was formerly. Only a very small percentage of the population commits murder; but the population is so large that the frequency of executions is appalling. Cases which might have come under Goethe's notice in Weimar perhaps once in ten years come daily under the notice of modern newspapers, and are described by them as sensationally as possible. We are therefore witnessing a steady intensification in the hold of social questions on the larger poetic imagination. *Les Misérables,* with its rivulet of story running through a continent of essays on all sorts of questions, from religion to main drainage, is a literary product peculiar to the nineteenth century: it shows how matters which were trifles to Aeschylus become stupendously impressive when they are multiplied by a million in a modern civilized state. Zola's novels are the product of an imagination driven crazy by a colossal police intelligence, by modern hospitals and surgery, by modern war correspondence, and even by the railway system—for in one of his books the hero is Jack the Ripper and his sweetheart a locomotive engine. What would Aristophanes have said to a city with fifteen thousand lunatics in it? Might he not possibly have devoted a comedy to the object of procuring some amelioration in their treatment? At all events, we find Ibsen, after producing, in *Brand, Peer Gynt,* and *Emperor and Galilean,* dramatic poems on the grandest scale, deliberately turning to comparatively prosaic topical plays on the most obviously transitory social questions, finding in their immense magnitude under modern conditions the stimulus which, a hundred years ago, or four thousand, he would only have received from the eternal strife of man with his own spirit. *A Doll's House* will be as flat as ditchwater when *A Midsummer Night's Dream* will still be as fresh as paint; but it will have done more work in the world; and that is enough for the highest genius, which is always intensely utilitarian.

Let us now hark back for a moment to the remark I made on Mr. Grundy's *Sowing the Wind* °: namely, that its urgency and consequently its dramatic interest are destroyed by the fact that the social question it presents is really a solved one. Its production after *Les Surprises du Divorce* (which Mr. Grundy himself adapted for England) was an anachronism. When we succeed in adjusting our social structure in such a way as to enable us to solve social questions as fast as they become really pressing, they will no longer force their way into the theatre. Had Ibsen, for instance, had any reason to believe that the abuses to which he called attention in his prose plays would have been adequately attended to without his interference, he would no doubt have gladly left them alone. The same exigency drove William Morris in England from his tapestries, his epics, and his masterpieces of printing, to try and bring his fellow-citizens to their senses by the summary process of shouting at them in the streets and in Trafalgar Square. John Ruskin's writing began with Modern Painters; Carlyle began with literary studies of German culture and the like: both were driven to become revolutionary pamphleteers. If people are rotting and starving in all directions, and nobody else has the heart or brains to make a disturbance about it, the great writers must. In short, what is forcing our poets to follow Shelley in becoming political and social agitators, and to turn the theatre into a platform for propaganda and an arena for discussion, is that whilst social questions are being thrown up for solution almost daily by the fierce rapidity with which industrial processes change and supersede one another through the rivalry of the competitors who take no account of ulterior social consequences, and by the change in public feeling produced by popular "education," cheap literature, facilitated travelling, and so forth, the political machinery by which alone

---

° Evidently a slip for *Slaves of the Ring,* mentioned above. This play was the subject of Shaw's first contribution to *The Saturday Review* as dramatic critic (January 5, 1895). He has printed on March 23, 1895 a comment on a revival of *Sowing the Wind,* which he found better than Grundy's usual product.

our institutions can be kept abreast of these changes is so old-fashioned, and so hindered in its action by the ignorance, the apathy, the stupidity, and the class feuds of the electorate, that social questions never get solved until the pressure becomes so desperate that even governments recognize the necessity for moving. And to bring the pressure to this point, the poets must lend a hand to the few who are willing to do public work in the stages at which nothing but abuse is to be gained by it.

Clearly, however, when the unhappy mobs which we now call nations and populations settle down into ordered commonwealths, ordinary bread-and-butter questions will be solved without troubling the poets and philosophers. The Shelleys, the Morrises, the Ruskins and Carlyles of that day will not need to spend their energies in trying to teach elementary political economy to the other members of the commonwealth; nor will the Ibsens be devising object lessons in spoiled womanhood, sickly consciences, and corrupt town councils, instead of writing great and enduring dramatic poems.

I need not elaborate the matter further. The conclusions to be drawn are:

1. Every social question, arising as it must from a conflict between human feeling and circumstances, affords material for drama.

2. The general preference of dramatists for subjects in which the conflict is between man and his apparently inevitable and eternal rather than his political and temporal circumstances, is due in the vast majority of cases to the dramatist's political ignorance (not to mention that of his audience), and in a few to the comprehensiveness of his philosophy.

3. The hugeness and complexity of modern civilizations and the development of our consciousness of them by means of the press, have the double effect of discrediting comprehensive philosophies by revealing more facts than the ablest man can generalize, and at the same time intensifying the urgency of social reforms sufficiently to set even the poetic faculty in action on their behalf.

4. The resultant tendency to drive social questions on to the stage, and into fiction and poetry, will eventually be counteracted by improvements in social organization, which will enable all prosaic social questions to be dealt with satisfactorily long before they become grave enough to absorb the energies which claim the devotion of the dramatist, the story-teller, and the poet.

MAJOR BARBARA

CAST OF CHARACTERS

LADY BRITOMART UNDERSHAFT
STEPHEN, *her son*
SARAH ⎱ *her daughters*
BARBARA ⎰
CHARLES LOMAX
ADOLPHUS CUSINS
MORRISON, *the butler*
ANDREW UNDERSHAFT
RUMMY MITCHENS
SNOBBY PRICE
JENNY HILL
PETER SHIRLEY
BILL WALKER
MRS. BAINES
BILTON

ACT ONE

(*It is after dinner in January 1906, in the library in* LADY BRITOMART UNDERSHAFT'S *house in Wilton Crescent. A large and comfortable settee is in the middle of the room, upholstered in dark leather. A person sitting on it* [*it is vacant at present*] *would have, on his right,* LADY BRITOMART'S *writing table, with the lady herself busy at it; a smaller writing table behind him on his left; the door behind him on* LADY BRITOMART'S *side; and a window with a window seat directly on his left. Near the window is an armchair.*

LADY BRITOMART *is a woman of fifty or thereabouts, well dressed and yet careless of her*

dress, well bred and quite reckless of her breeding, well mannered and yet appallingly outspoken and indifferent to the opinion of her interlocutors, amiable and yet peremptory, arbitrary, and high-tempered to the last bearable degree, and withal a very typical managing matron of the upper class, treated as a naughty child until she grew into a scolding mother, and finally settling down with plenty of practical ability and worldly experience, limited in the oddest way with domestic and class limitations, conceiving the universe exactly as if it were a large house in Wilton Crescent, though handling her corner of it very effectively on that assumption, and being quite enlightened and liberal as to the books in the library, the pictures on the walls, the music in the portfolios, and the articles in the papers.

Her son, STEPHEN, *comes in. He is a gravely correct young man under 25, taking himself very seriously, but still in some awe of his mother, from childish habit and bachelor shyness rather than from any weakness of character*)

STEPHEN Whats the matter?

LADY BRITOMART Presently, Stephen.

(STEPHEN *submissively walks to the settee and sits down. He takes up a Liberal weekly called* The Speaker)

LADY BRITOMART Dont begin to read, Stephen. I shall require all your attention.

STEPHEN It was only while I was waiting—

LADY BRITOMART Dont make excuses, Stephen. (*He puts down* THE SPEAKER) Now! (*She finishes her writing; rises; and comes to the settee*) I have not kept you waiting very long, I think.

STEPHEN Not at all, mother.

LADY BRITOMART Bring me my cushion. (*He takes the cushion from the chair at the desk and arranges it for her as she sits down on the settee*) Sit down. (*He sits down and fingers his tie nervously*) Dont fiddle with your tie, Stephen: there is nothing the matter with it.

STEPHEN I beg your pardon. (*He fiddles with his watch chain instead*)

LADY BRITOMART Now are you attending to me, Stephen?

STEPHEN Of course, mother.

LADY BRITOMART No: it's not of course. I want something much more than your everyday matter-of-course attention. I am going to speak to you very seriously, Stephen. I wish you would let that chain alone.

STEPHEN (*hastily relinquishing the chain*) Have I done anything to annoy you, mother? If so, it was quite unintentional.

LADY BRITOMART (*astonished*) Nonsense! (*with some remorse*) My poor boy, did you think I was angry with you?

STEPHEN What is it, then, mother? You are making me very uneasy.

LADY BRITOMART (*squaring herself at him rather aggressively*) Stephen: may I ask how soon you intend to realize that you are a grown-up man, and that I am only a woman?

STEPHEN (*amazed*) Only a—

LADY BRITOMART Dont repeat my words, please: it is a most aggravating habit. You must learn to face life seriously, Stephen. I really cannot bear the whole burden of our family affairs any longer. You must advise me: you must assume the responsibility.

STEPHEN I!

LADY BRITOMART Yes, you, of course. You were 24 last June. Youve been at Harrow and Cambridge. Youve been to India and Japan. You must know a lot of things, now; unless you have wasted your time most scandalously. Well, advise me.

STEPHEN (*much perplexed*) You know I have never interfered in the household—

LADY BRITOMART No: I should think not. I dont want you to order the dinner.

STEPHEN I mean in our family affairs.

LADY BRITOMART Well, you must interfere now; for they are getting quite beyond me.

STEPHEN (*troubled*) I have thought sometimes that perhaps I ought; but really, mother, I know so little about them; and what I do know is so painful! it is so impossible to mention some things to you—(*He stops, ashamed*)

LADY BRITOMART I suppose you mean your father.

STEPHEN (*almost inaudibly*) Yes.

LADY BRITOMART My dear: we cant go on all our lives not mentioning him. Of course you were quite right not to open the subject until I asked you to; but you are old enough now to be taken into my confidence, and to help me to deal with him about the girls.

STEPHEN But the girls are all right. They are engaged.

LADY BRITOMART (*complacently*) Yes: I have made a very good match for Sarah. Charles Lomax will be a millionaire at 35. But that is ten years ahead; and in the meantime his trustees cannot under the terms of his father's will allow him more than £800 a year.

STEPHEN But the will says also that if he increases his income by his own exertions, they may double the increase.

LADY BRITOMART Charles Lomax's exertions are much more likely to decrease his income than to increase it. Sarah will have to find at least another £800 a year for the next ten years; and even then they will be as poor as church mice. And what about Barbara? I thought Barbara was going to make the most brilliant career of all of you. And what does she do? Joins the Salvation Army; discharges her maid; lives on a pound a week; and walks in one evening with a professor of Greek whom she has picked up in the street, and who pretends to be a Salvationist, and actually plays the big drum for her in public because he has fallen head over ears in love with her.

STEPHEN I was certainly rather taken aback when I heard they were engaged. Cusins is a very nice fellow, certainly: nobody would ever guess that he was born in Australia; but—

LADY BRITOMART Oh, Adolphus Cusins will make a very good husband. After all, nobody can say a word against Greek: it stamps a man at once as an educated gentleman. And my family, thank Heaven, is not a pig-headed Tory one. We are Whigs, and believe in liberty. Let snobbish people say what they please: Barbara shall marry, not the man they like, but the man *I* like.

STEPHEN Of course I was thinking only of his income. However, he is not likely to be extravagant.

LADY BRITOMART Dont be too sure of that, Stephen. I know your quiet, simple, refined, poetic people like Adolphus: quite content with the best of everything! They cost more than your extravagant people, who are always as mean as they are second rate. No: Barbara will need at least £2000 a year. You see it means two additional households. Besides, my dear, you must marry soon. I dont approve of the present fashion of philandering bachelors and late marriages; and I am trying to arrange something for you.

STEPHEN It's very good of you, mother; but perhaps I had better arrange that for myself.

LADY BRITOMART Nonsense! you are much too young to begin matchmaking: you would be taken in by some pretty little nobody. Of course I dont mean that you are not to be consulted: you know that as well as I do. (STEPHEN *closes his lips and is silent*) Now dont sulk, Stephen.

STEPHEN   I am not sulking, mother. What has all this got to do with—with—with my father?

LADY BRITOMART   My dear Stephen: where is the money to come from? It is easy enough for you and the other children to live on my income as long as we are in the same house; but I cant keep four families in four separate houses. You know how poor my father is: he has barely seven thousand a year now; and really, if he were not the Earl of Stevenage, he would have to give up society. He can do nothing for us. He says, naturally enough, that it is absurd that he should be asked to provide for the children of a man who is rolling in money. You see, Stephen, your father must be fabulously wealthy, because there is always a war going on somewhere.

STEPHEN   You need not remind me of that, mother. I have hardly ever opened a newspaper in my life without seeing our name in it. The Undershaft torpedo! The Undershaft quick firers! The Undershaft ten inch! the Undershaft disappearing rampart gun! the Undershaft submarine! and now the Undershaft aerial battleship! At Harrow they called me the Woolwich Infant. At Cambridge it was the same. A little brute at King's who was always trying to get up revivals, spoilt my Bible—your first birthday present to me—by writing under my name, "Son and heir to Undershaft and Lazarus, Death and Destruction Dealers: address Christendom and Judea." But that was not so bad as the way I was kowtowed to everywhere because my father was making millions by selling cannons.

LADY BRITOMART   It is not only the cannons, but the war loans that Lazarus arranges under cover of giving credit for the cannons. You know, Stephen, it's perfectly scandalous. Those two men, Andrew Undershaft and Lazarus, positively have Europe under their thumbs. That is why your father is able to behave as he does. He is above the law. Do you think Bismarck or Gladstone or Disraeli could have openly defied every social and moral obligation all their lives as your father has? They simply wouldnt have dared. I asked Gladstone to take it up. I asked The Times to take it up. I asked the Lord Chamberlain to take it up. But it was just like asking them to declare war on the Sultan. They wouldnt. They said they couldnt touch him. I believe they were afraid.

STEPHEN   What could they do? He does not actually break the law.

LADY BRITOMART   Not break the law! He is always breaking the law. He broke the law when he was born: his parents were not married.

STEPHEN   Mother! Is that true?

LADY BRITOMART   Of course it's true: that was why we separated.

STEPHEN   He married without letting you know this!

LADY BRITOMART (*rather taken aback by this inference*)   Oh no. To do Andrew justice, that was not the sort of thing he did. Besides, you know the Undershaft motto: Unashamed. Everybody knew.

STEPHEN   But you said that was why you separated.

LADY BRITOMART   Yes, because he was not content with being a foundling himself: he wanted to disinherit you for another foundling. That was what I couldnt stand.

STEPHEN (*ashamed*)   Do you mean for—for —for—

LADY BRITOMART   Dont stammer, Stephen. Speak distinctly.

STEPHEN   But this is so frightful to me, mother. To have to speak to you about such things!

LADY BRITOMART   It's not pleasant for me, either, especially if you are still so childish that you must make it worse by a display of embarrassment. It is only in the middle classes, Stephen, that people get into a state of dumb helpless horror when they find that there are wicked people in the world. In our class, we have to decide what is to be done with wicked people; and nothing should disturb our self-possession. Now ask your question properly.

STEPHEN   Mother: have you no consideration for me? For Heaven's sake either treat me as a child, as you always do, and tell me nothing at all; or tell me everything and let me take it as best I can.

LADY BRITOMART   Treat you as a child! What do you mean? It is most unkind and ungrateful of you to say such a thing. You know I have never treated any of you as children. I have always made you my companions and friends, and allowed you perfect freedom to do and say whatever you liked, so long as you liked what I could approve of.

STEPHEN (*desperately*)   I daresay we have been the very imperfect children of a very perfect mother; but I do beg you to let me alone for once, and tell me about this horrible business of my father wanting to set me aside for another son.

LADY BRITOMART (*amazed*) Another son! I never said anything of the kind. I never dreamt of such a thing. This is what comes of interrupting me.

STEPHEN But you said—

LADY BRITOMART (*cutting him short*) Now be a good boy, Stephen, and listen to me patiently. The Undershafts are descended from a foundling in the parish of St Andrew Undershaft in the city. That was long ago, in the reign of James the First. Well, this foundling was adopted by an armorer and gun-maker. In the course of time the foundling succeeded to the business; and from some notion of gratitude, or some vow or something, he adopted another foundling, and left the business to him. And that foundling did the same. Ever since that, the cannon business has always been left to an adopted foundling named Andrew Undershaft.

STEPHEN But did they never marry? Were there no legitimate sons?

LADY BRITOMART Oh yes: they married just as your father did; and they were rich enough to buy land for their own children and leave them well provided for. But they always adopted and trained some foundling to succeed them in the business; and of course they always quarrelled with their wives furiously over it. Your father was adopted in that way; and he pretends to consider himself bound to keep up the tradition and adopt somebody to leave the business to. Of course I was not going to stand that. There may have been some reason for it when the Undershafts could only marry women in their own class, whose sons were not fit to govern great estates. But there could be no excuse for passing over my son.

STEPHEN (*dubiously*) I am afraid I should make a poor hand of managing a cannon foundry.

LADY BRITOMART Nonsense! you could easily get a manager and pay him a salary.

STEPHEN My father evidently had no great opinion of my capacity.

LADY BRITOMART Stuff, child! you were only a baby: it had nothing to do with your capacity. Andrew did it on principle, just as he did every perverse and wicked thing on principle. When my father remonstrated, Andrew actually told him to his face that history tells us of only two successful institutions: one the Undershaft firm, and the other the Roman Empire under the Antonines. That was because the Antonine emperors all adopted their successors. Such rubbish! The Stevenages are as good as the Antonines, I hope; and you are a Stevenage. But that was Andrew all over. There

you have the man! Always clever and unanswerable when he was defending nonsense and wickedness: always awkward and sullen when he had to behave sensibly and decently!

STEPHEN Then it was on my account that your home life was broken up, mother. I am sorry.

LADY BRITOMART Well, dear, there were other differences. I really cannot bear an immoral man. I am not a Pharisee, I hope; and I should not have minded his merely doing wrong things: we are none of us perfect. But your father didnt exactly do wrong things: he said them and thought them: that was what was so dreadful. He really had a sort of religion of wrongness. Just as one doesnt mind men practising immorality so long as they own that they are in the wrong by preaching morality; so I couldnt forgive Andrew for preaching immorality while he practised morality. You would all have grown up without principles, without any knowledge of right and wrong, if he had been in the house. You know, my dear, your father was a very attractive man in some ways. Children did not dislike him; and he took advantage of it to put the wickedest ideas into their heads, and make them quite unmanageable. I did not dislike him myself: very far from it; but nothing can bridge over moral disagreement.

STEPHEN All this simply bewilders me, mother. People may differ about matters of opinion, or even about religion; but how can they differ about right and wrong? Right is right; and wrong is wrong; and if a man cannot distinguish them properly, he is either a fool or a rascal: thats all.

LADY BRITOMART (*touched*) Thats my own boy! (*She pats his cheek*) Your father never could answer that: he used to laugh and get out of it under cover of some affectionate nonsense. And now that you understand the situation, what do you advise me to do?

STEPHEN Well, what can you do?

LADY BRITOMART I must get the money somehow.

STEPHEN We cannot take money from him. I had rather go and live in some cheap place like Bedford Square or even Hampstead than take a farthing of his money.

LADY BRITOMART But after all, Stephen, our present income comes from Andrew.

STEPHEN (*shocked*) I never knew that.

LADY BRITOMART Well, you surely didnt suppose your grandfather had anything to give me. The Stevenages could not do everything for you. We gave you social position. Andrew had to contribute something. He had a very good bargain, I think.

STEPHEN (*bitterly*)　We are utterly dependent on him and his cannons, then?

LADY BRITOMART　Certainly not: the money is settled. But he provided it. So you see it is not a question of taking money from him or not: it is simply a question of how much. I dont want any more for myself.

STEPHEN　Nor do I.

LADY BRITOMART　But Sarah does; and Barbara does. That is, Charles Lomax and Adolphus Cusins will cost them more. So I must put my pride in my pocket and ask for it, I suppose. That is your advice, Stephen, is it not?

STEPHEN　No.

LADY BRITOMART (*sharply*)　Stephen!

STEPHEN　Of course if you are determined—

LADY BRITOMART　I am not determined: I ask your advice; and I am waiting for it. I will not have all the responsibility thrown on my shoulders.

STEPHEN (*obstinately*)　I would die sooner than ask him for another penny.

LADY BRITOMART (*resignedly*)　You mean that *I* must ask him. Very well, Stephen: it shall be as you wish. You will be glad to know that your grandfather concurs. But he thinks I ought to ask Andrew to come here and see the girls. After all, he must have some natural affection for them.

STEPHEN　Ask him here!!!

LADY BRITOMART　Do not repeat my words, Stephen. Where else can I ask him?

STEPHEN　I never expected you to ask him at all.

LADY BRITOMART　Now dont tease, Stephen. Come! you see that it is necessary that he should pay us a visit, dont you?

STEPHEN (*reluctantly*)　I suppose so, if the girls cannot do without his money.

LADY BRITOMART　Thank you, Stephen: I knew you would give me the right advice when it was properly explained to you. I have asked your father to come this evening. (STEPHEN *bounds from his seat*) Dont jump, Stephen: it fidgets me.

STEPHEN (*in utter consternation*)　Do you mean to say that my father is coming here tonight—that he may be here at any moment?

LADY BRITOMART (*looking at her watch*)　I said nine. (*He gasps. She rises*) Ring the bell, please. (STEPHEN *goes to the smaller writing table; presses a button on it; and sits at it with his elbows on the table and his head in his hands, outwitted and overwhelmed*) It is ten minutes to nine yet; and I have to prepare the

girls. I asked Charles Lomax and Adolphus to dinner on purpose that they might be here. Andrew had better see them in case he should cherish any delusions as to their being capable of supporting their wives. (*The* BUTLER *enters:* LADY BRITOMART *goes behind the settee to speak to him*) Morrison: go up to the drawing room and tell everybody to come down here at once. (MORRISON *withdraws.* LADY BRITOMART *turns to* STEPHEN) Now remember, Stephen: I shall need all your countenance and authority. (*He rises and tries to recover some vestige of these attributes*) Give me a chair, dear. (*He pushes a chair forward from the wall to where she stands, near the smaller writing table. She sits down; and he goes to the armchair, into which he throws himself*) I dont know how Barbara will take it. Ever since they made her a major in the Salvation Army she has developed a propensity to have her own way and order people about which quite cows me sometimes. It's not ladylike: I'm sure I dont know where she picked it up. Anyhow, Barbara shant bully me; but still it's just as well that your father should be here before she has time to refuse to meet him or make a fuss. Dont look nervous, Stephen: it will only encourage Barbara to make difficulties. *I* am nervous enough, goodness knows; but I dont shew it.

(SARAH *and* BARBARA *come in with their respective young men,* CHARLES LOMAX *and* ADOLPHUS CUSINS. SARAH *is slender, bored, and mundane.* BARBARA *is robuster, jollier, much more energetic.* SARAH *is fashionably dressed:* BARBARA *is in Salvation Army uniform.* LOMAX, *a young man about town, is like many other young men about town. He is afflicted with a frivolous sense of humor which plunges him at the most inopportune moments into paroxysms of imperfectly suppressed laughter.* CUSINS *is a spectacled student, slight, thin haired, and sweet voiced, with a more complex form of* LOMAX's *complaint. His sense of humor is intellectual and subtle, and is complicated by an appalling temper. The lifelong struggle of a benevolent temperament and a high conscience against impulses of inhuman ridicule and fierce impatience has set up a chronic strain which has visibly wrecked his constitution. He is a most implacable, determined, tenacious, intolerant person who by mere force of character presents himself as—and indeed actually is—considerate, gentle, explanatory, even mild and apologetic, capable possibly of murder, but not of cruelty or coarseness. By the operation of some instinct which is not merciful enough to blind him with the illusions of love, he is ob-*

stinately bent on marrying BARBARA. LOMAX *likes* SARAH *and thinks it will be rather a lark to marry her. Consequently he has not attempted to resist* LADY BRITOMART's *arrangements to that end.*

All four look as if they had been having a good deal of fun in the drawing room. The girls enter first, leaving the swains outside.

SARAH *comes to the settee.* BARBARA *comes in after her and stops at the door)*

BARBARA   Are Cholly and Dolly to come in?

LADY BRITOMART (*forcibly*)   Barbara: I will not have Charles called Cholly: the vulgarity of it positively makes me ill.

BARBARA   It's all right, mother: Cholly is quite correct nowadays. Are they to come in?

LADY BRITOMART   Yes, if they will behave themselves.

BARBARA (*through the door*)   Come in, Dolly; and behave yourself.

(BARBARA *comes to her mother's writing table.* CUSINS *enters smiling, and wanders towards* LADY BRITOMART)

SARAH (*calling*)   Come in, Cholly. (LOMAX *enters, controlling his features very imperfectly, and places himself vaguely between* SARAH *and* BARBARA)

LADY BRITOMART (*preemptorily*)   Sit down, all of you. (*They sit.* CUSINS *crosses to the window and seats himself there.* LOMAX *takes a chair.* BARBARA *sits at the writing table and Sarah on the settee*) I dont in the least know what you are laughing at, Adolphus. I am surprised at you, though I expected nothing better from Charles Lomax.

CUSINS (*in a remarkably gentle voice*)   Barbara has been trying to teach me the West Ham Salvation March.

LADY BRITOMART   I see nothing to laugh at in that; nor should you if you are really converted.

CUSINS (*sweetly*)   You were not present. It was really funny, I believe.

LOMAX   Ripping.

LADY BRITOMART   Be quiet, Charles. Now listen to me, children. Your father is coming here this evening.

(*General stupefaction.* LOMAX, SARAH, *and* BARBARA *rise:* SARAH *scared, and* BARBARA *amused and expectant*)

LOMAX (*remonstrating*)   Oh I say!

LADY BRITOMART   You are not called on to say anything, Charles.

SARAH   Are you serious, mother?

LADY BRITOMART   Of course I am serious. It is on your account, Sarah, and also on

Charles's. (*silence.* SARAH *sits, with a shrug. Charles looks painfully unworthy*) I hope you are not going to object, Barbara.

BARBARA   I! why should I? My father has a soul to be saved like anybody else. He's quite welcome as far as I am concerned. (*She sits on the table, and softly whistles "Onward, Christian Soldiers"*)

LOMAX (*still remonstrant*)   But really, dont you know! Oh I say!

LADY BRITOMART (*frigidly*)   What do you wish to convey, Charles?

LOMAX   Well, you must admit that this is a bit thick.

LADY BRITOMART (*turning with ominous suavity to* CUSINS) Adolphus: you are a professor of Greek. Can you translate Charles Lomax's remarks into reputable English for us?

CUSINS (*cautiously*)   If I may say so, Lady Brit, I think Charles has rather happily expressed what we all feel. Homer speaking of Autolycus, uses the same phrase. πυκινὸν δόμον ἐλθεῖν means a bit thick.

LOMAX (*handsomely*)   Not that I mind, you know, if Sarah dont. (*He sits*)

LADY BRITOMART (*crushingly*)   Thank you. Have I your permission, Adolphus, to invite my own husband to my own house?

CUSINS (*gallantly*)   You have my unhesitating support in everything you do.

LADY BRITOMART   Tush! Sarah: have you nothing to say?

SARAH   Do you mean that he is coming regularly to live here?

LADY BRITOMART   Certainly not. The spare room is ready for him if he likes to stay for a day or two and see a little more of you; but there are limits.

SARAH   Well, he cant eat us, I suppose. *I* dont mind.

LOMAX (*chuckling*)   I wonder how the old man will take it.

LADY BRITOMART   Much as the old woman will, no doubt, Charles.

LOMAX (*abashed*)   I didnt mean—at least—

LADY BRITOMART   You didnt think, Charles. You never do; and the result is, you never mean anything. And now please attend to me, children. Your father will be quite a stranger to us.

LOMAX   I suppose he hasnt seen Sarah since she was a little kid.

LADY BRITOMART   Not since she was a little kid, Charles, as you express it with that elegance of diction and refinement of thought that seem never to desert you. Accordingly—er— (*impatiently*) Now I have forgotten what I was going to say. That comes of your provoking me to be sarcastic, Charles. Adolphus: will you kindly tell me where I was.

CUSINS (*sweetly*)   You were saying that as Mr Undershaft has not seen his children since they were babies, he will form his opinion of the way you have brought them up from their behavior tonight, and that therefore you wish us all to be particularly careful to conduct ourselves well, especially Charles.

LADY BRITOMART (*with emphatic approval*) Precisely.

LOMAX   Look here, Dolly: Lady Brit didnt say that.

LADY BRITOMART (*vehemently*)   I did, Charles. Adolphus's recollection is perfectly correct. It is most important that you should be good; and I do beg you for once not to pair off into opposite corners and giggle and whisper while I am speaking to your father.

BARBARA   All right, mother. We'll do you credit. (*She comes off the table, and sits in her chair with ladylike elegance*)

LADY BRITOMART   Remember, Charles, that Sarah will want to feel proud of you instead of ashamed of you.

LOMAX   Oh I say! theres nothing to be exactly proud of, dont you know.

LADY BRITOMART   Well, try and look as if there was.

(MORRISON, *pale and dismayed, breaks into the room in unconcealed disorder*)

MORRISON   Might I speak a word to you, my lady?

LADY BRITOMART   Nonsense! Shew him up.

MORRISON   Yes, my lady. (*He goes*)

LOMAX   Does Morrison know who it is?

LADY BRITOMART   Of course. Morrison has always been with us.

LOMAX   It must be a regular corker for him, dont you know.

LADY BRITOMART   Is this a moment to get on my nerves, Charles, with your outrageous expressions?

LOMAX   But this is something out of the ordinary, really—

MORRISON (*at the door*)   The—er—Mr Undershaft. (*He retreats in confusion*)

(ANDREW UNDERSHAFT *comes in. All rise.* LADY BRITOMART *meets him in the middle of the room behind the settee.*

ANDREW *is, on the surface, a stoutish, easygoing elderly man, with kindly patient manners, and an engaging simplicity of character. But he has a watchful, deliberate, waiting, listening face, and formidable reserves of power, both bodily and mental, in his capacious chest and long head. His gentleness is partly that of a* strong man who has learnt by experience that his natural grip hurts ordinary people unless he handles them very carefully, and partly the mellowness of age and success. He is also a little shy in his present very delicate situation*)

LADY BRITOMART   Good evening, Andrew.

UNDERSHAFT   How d'ye do, my dear.

LADY BRITOMART   You look a good deal older.

UNDERSHAFT (*apologetically*)   I am somewhat older. (*taking her hand with a touch of courtship*) Time has stood still with you.

LADY BRITOMART (*throwing away his hand*) Rubbish! This is your family.

UNDERSHAFT (*surprised*)   Is it so large? I am sorry to say my memory is failing very badly in some things. (*He offers his hand with paternal kindness to* LOMAX)

LOMAX (*jerkily shaking his hand*)   Ahdedoo.

UNDERSHAFT   I can see you are my eldest. I am very glad to meet you again, my boy.

LOMAX (*remonstrating*)   No, but look here dont you know—(*overcome*) Oh I say!

LADY BRITOMART (*recovering from momentary speechlessness*)   Andrew: do you mean to say that you dont remember how many children you have?

UNDERSHAFT   Well, I am afraid I—. They have grown so much—er. Am I making any ridiculous mistake? I may as well confess: I recollect only one son. But so many things have happened since, of course—er—

LADY BRITOMART (*decisively*)   Andrew: you are talking nonsense. Of course you have only one son.

UNDERSHAFT   Perhaps you will be good enough to introduce me, my dear.

LADY BRITOMART   That is Charles Lomax, who is engaged to Sarah.

UNDERSHAFT   My dear sir, I beg your pardon.

LOMAX   Notatall. Delighted, I assure you.

LADY BRITOMART   This is Stephen.

UNDERSHAFT (*bowing*)   Happy to make your acquaintance, Mr. Stephen. Then (*going to* CUSINS) you must be my son. (*taking* CUSINS' *hands in his*) How are you, my young friend? (*to* LADY BRITOMART) He is very like you, my love.

CUSINS   You flatter me, Mr. Undershaft. My name is Cusins: engaged to Barbara. (*very explicitly*) That is Major Barbara Undershaft, of the Salvation Army. That is Sarah, your second daughter. This is Stephen Undershaft, your son.

UNDERSHAFT   My dear Stephen, I beg your pardon.

STEPHEN   Not at all.

UNDERSHAFT   Mr. Cusins: I am much in-
debted to you for explaining so precisely.
(*turning to* SARAH) Barbara, my dear—

SARAH (*prompting him*)   Sarah.

UNDERSHAFT   Sarah, of course. (*They shake
hands. He goes over to* BARBARA) Barbara—I
am right this time, I hope?

BARBARA   Quite right. (*They shake hands*)

LADY BRITOMART (*resuming command*)   Sit
down, all of you. Sit down, Andrew. (*She
comes forward and sits on the settee.* CUSINS
also brings his chair forward on her left. BAR-
BARA *and* STEPHEN *resume their seats.* LOMAX
gives his chair to SARAH *and goes for another*)

UNDERSHAFT   Thank you, my love.

LOMAX (*conversationally, as he brings a
chair forward between the writing table and
the settee, and offers it to* UNDERSHAFT)
Takes you some time to find out exactly where
you are, dont it?

UNDERSHAFT (*accepting the chair, but remaining standing*)   That is not what embarrasses me, Mr. Lomax. My difficulty is that
if I play the part of a father, I shall produce
the effect of an intrusive stranger; and if I
play the part of a discreet stranger, I may
appear a callous father.

LADY BRITOMART   There is no need for you
to play any part at all, Andrew. You had
much better be sincere and natural.

UNDERSHAFT (*submissively*)   Yes, my dear:
I daresay that will be best. (*He sits down comfortably*) Well, here I am. Now what can I
do for you all?

LADY BRITOMART   You need not do anything, Andrew. You are one of the family. You
can sit with us and enjoy yourself.

(*A painfully conscious pause.* BARBARA *makes
a face at* LOMAX, *whose too long suppressed
mirth immediately explodes in agonized neigh-
ings*)

LADY   BRITOMART   (*outraged*)   Charles
Lomax: if you can behave yourself, behave
yourself. If not, leave the room.

LOMAX   I'm awfully sorry, Lady Brit; but
really you know, upon my soul! (*He sits on the
settee between* LADY BRITOMART *and* UNDER-
SHAFT, *quite overcome*)

BARBARA   Why dont you laugh if you want
to, Cholly? It's good for your inside.

LADY BRITOMART   Barbara: you have had
the education of a lady. Please let your father
see that; and dont talk like a street girl.

UNDERSHAFT   Never mind me, my dear. As
you know, I am not a gentleman; and I was
never educated.

LOMAX (*encouragingly*)   Nobody'd know it,
I assure you. You look all right, you know.

CUSINS   Let me advise you to study Greek,
Mr. Undershaft. Greek scholars are privileged
men. Few of them know Greek; and none of
them know anything else; but their position is
unchallengeable. Other languages are the qualifications of waiters and commercial travellers:
Greek is to a man of position what the hall-
mark is to silver.

BARBARA   Dolly: dont be insincere. Cholly:
fetch your concertina and play something for
us.

LOMAX (*jumps up eagerly, but checks himself to remark doubtfully to* UNDERSHAFT)
Perhaps that sort of thing isnt in your line, eh?

UNDERSHAFT   I am particularly fond of
music.

LOMAX (*delighted*)   Are you? Then I'll get
it. (*He goes upstairs for the instrument*)

UNDERSHAFT   Do you play, Barbara?

BARBARA   Only the tambourine. But Cholly's
teaching me the concertina.

UNDERSHAFT   Is Cholly also a member of
the Salvation Army?

BARBARA   No: he says it's bad form to be
a dissenter. But I dont despair of Cholly. I
made him come yesterday to a meeting at the
dock gates, and take the collection in his hat.

UNDERSHAFT (*looks whimsically at his
wife*) !!

LADY BRITOMART   It is not my doing, Andrew. Barbara is old enough to take her own
way. She has no father to advise her.

BARBARA   Oh yes she has. There are no
orphans in the Salvation Army.

UNDERSHAFT   Your father there has a great
many children and plenty of experience, eh?

BARBARA (*looking at him with quick interest
and nodding*)   Just so. How did you come
to understand that? (LOMAX *is heard at the
door trying the concertina*)

LADY BRITOMART   Come in, Charles. Play us
something at once.

LOMAX   Righto! (*He sits down in his former
place, and preludes*)

UNDERSHAFT   One moment, Mr. Lomax. I
am rather interested in the Salvation Army.
Its motto might be my own: Blood and Fire.

LOMAX (*shocked*)   But not your sort of
blood and fire, you know.

UNDERSHAFT   My sort of blood cleanses:
my sort of fire purifies.

BARBARA   So do ours. Come down tomorrow
to my shelter—the West Ham shelter—and
see what we're doing. We're going to march to
a great meeting in the Assembly Hall at Mile
End. Come and see the shelter and then march

with us: it will do you a lot of good. Can you play anything?

UNDERSHAFT   In my youth I earned pennies, and even shillings occasionally, in the streets and in public house parlors by my natural talent for stepdancing. Later on, I became a member of the Undershaft orchestral society, and performed passably on the tenor trombone.

LOMAX   (*scandalized—putting down the concertina*)   Oh I say!

BARBARA   Many a sinner has played himself into heaven on the trombone, thanks to the Army.

LOMAX   (*to* BARBARA, *still rather shocked*) Yes; but what about the cannon business, dont you know? (*to* UNDERSHAFT) Getting into heaven is not exactly in your line, is it?

LADY BRITOMART   Charles!!!

LOMAX   Well; but it stands to reason, dont it? The cannon business may be necessary and all that: we cant get on without cannons; but it isnt right, you know. On the other hand, there may be a certain amount of tosh about the Salvation Army—I belong to the Established Church myself—but still you cant deny that it's religion; and you cant go against religion, can you? At least unless youre downright immoral, dont you know.

UNDERSHAFT   You hardly appreciate my position, Mr. Lomax—

LOMAX   (*hastily*)   I'm not saying anything against you personally—

UNDERSHAFT   Quite so, quite so. But consider for a moment. Here I am, a profiteer in mutilation and murder. I find myself in a specially amiable humor just now because, this morning, down at the foundry, we blew twenty-seven dummy soldiers into fragments with a gun which formerly destroyed only thirteen.

LOMAX   (*leniently*)   Well, the more destructive war becomes, the sooner it will be abolished, eh?

UNDERSHAFT   Not at all. The more destructive war becomes the more fascinating we find it. No, Mr Lomax: I am obliged to you for making the usual excuse for my trade; but I am not ashamed of it. I am not one of those men who keep their morals and their business in watertight compartments. All the spare money my trade rivals spend on hospitals, cathedrals, and other receptacles for conscience money, I devote to experiments and researches in improved methods of destroying life and property. I have always done so; and I always shall. Therefore your Christmas card

moralities of peace on earth and goodwill among men are of no use to me. Your Christianity, which enjoins you to resist not evil, and to turn the other cheek, would make me a bankrupt. My morality—my religion—must have a place for cannons and torpedoes in it.

STEPHEN   (*coldly—almost sullenly*)   You speak as if there were half a dozen moralities and religions to choose from, instead of one true morality and one true religion.

UNDERSHAFT   For me there is only one true morality; but it might not fit you, as you do not manufacture aerial battleships. There is only one true morality for every man; but every man has not the same true morality.

LOMAX   (*overtaxed*)   Would you mind saying that again? I didnt quite follow it.

CUSINS   It's quite simple. As Euripides says, one man's meat is another man's poison morally as well as physically.

UNDERSHAFT   Precisely.

LOMAX   Oh, that! Yes, yes, yes. True. True.

STEPHEN   In other words, some men are honest and some are scoundrels.

BARBARA   Bosh! There are no scoundrels.

UNDERSHAFT   Indeed? Are there any good men?

BARBARA   No. Not one. There are neither good men nor scoundrels: there are just children of one Father; and the sooner they stop calling one another names the better. You neednt talk to me: I know them. Ive had scores of them through my hands: scoundrels, criminals, infidels, philanthropists, missionaries, county councillors, all sorts. Theyre all just the same sort of sinner; and theres the same salvation ready for them all.

UNDERSHAFT   May I ask have you ever saved a maker of cannons?

BARBARA   No. Will you let me try?

UNDERSHAFT   Well, I will make a bargain with you. If I go to see you tomorrow in your Salvation Shelter, will you come the day after to see me in my cannon works?

BARBARA   Take care. It may end in your giving up the cannons for the sake of the Salvation Army.

UNDERSHAFT   Are you sure it will not end in your giving up the Salvation Army for the sake of the cannons?

BARBARA   I will take my chance of that.

UNDERSHAFT   And I will take my chance of the other. (*They shake hands on it*) Where is your shelter?

BARBARA   In West Ham. At the sign of the cross. Ask anybody in Canning Town. Where are your works?

UNDERSHAFT   In Perivale St Andrews. At the sign of the sword. Ask anybody in Europe.

LOMAX   Hadnt I better play something?

BARBARA   Yes. Give us Onward, Christian Soldiers.

LOMAX   Well, thats rather a strong order to begin with, dont you know. Suppose I sing Thou'rt passing hence, my brother. It's much the same tune.

BARBARA   It's too melancholy. You get saved, Cholly; and youll pass hence, my brother, without making such a fuss about it.

LADY BRITOMART   Really, Barbara, you go on as if religion were a pleasant subject. Do have some sense of propriety.

UNDERSHAFT   I do not find it an unpleasant subject, my dear. It is the only one that capable people really care for.

LADY BRITOMART   (*looking at her watch*) Well, if you are determined to have it, I insist on having it in a proper and respectable way. Charles: ring for prayers.

(*General amazement.* STEPHEN *rises in dismay*)

LOMAX   (*rising*)   Oh I say!

UNDERSHAFT   (*rising*)   I am afraid I must be going.

LADY BRITOMART   You cannot go now, Andrew: it would be most improper. Sit down. What will the servants think?

UNDERSHAFT   My dear: I have conscientious scruples. May I suggest a compromise? If Barbara will conduct a little service in the drawing room, with Mr Lomax as organist, I will attend it willingly. I will even take part, if a trombone can be procured.

LADY BRITOMART   Dont mock, Andrew.

UNDERSHAFT   (*shocked—to* BARBARA)   You dont think I am mocking, my love, I hope.

BARBARA   No, of course not; and it wouldnt matter if you were: half the Army came to their first meeting for a lark. (*rising*) Come along. (*She throws her arm round her father and sweeps him out, calling to the others from the threshold*) Come, Dolly. Come, Cholly.

(CUSINS *rises*)

LADY BRITOMART   I will not be disobeyed by everybody. Adolphus: sit down. (*He does not*) Charles: you may go. You are not fit for prayers: you cannot keep your countenance.

LOMAX   Oh I say! (*He goes out*)

LADY BRITOMART   (*continuing*)   But you, Adolphus, can behave yourself if you choose to. I insist on your staying.

CUSINS   My dear Lady Brit: there are things in the family prayer book that I couldnt bear to hear you say.

LADY BRITOMART   What things, pray?

CUSINS   Well, you would have to say before all the servants that we have done things we ought not to have done, and left undone things we ought to have done, and that there is no health in us. I cannot bear to hear you doing yourself such an injustice, and Barbara such an injustice. As for myself, I flatly deny it: I have done my best. I shouldnt dare to marry Barbara—I couldnt look you in the face —if it were true. So I must go to the drawing room.

LADY BRITOMART   (*offended*) Well, go. (*He starts for the door*) And remember this, Adolphus (*He turns to listen*) I have a very strong suspicion that you went to the Salvation Army to worship Barbara and nothing else. And I quite appreciate the very clever way in which you systematically humbug me. I have found you out. Take care Barbara doesnt. Thats all.

CUSINS   (*with unruffled sweetness*) Dont tell on me. (*He steals out*)

LADY BRITOMART   Sarah: if you want to go, go. Anything's better than to sit there as if you wished you were a thousand miles away.

SARAH   (*languidly*) Very well, mamma. (*She goes*)

(LADY BRITOMART, *with a sudden flounce, gives way to a little gust of tears*)

STEPHEN   (*going to her*)   Mother: whats the matter?

LADY BRITOMART   (*swishing away her tears with her handkerchief*) Nothing. Foolishness. You can go with him, too, if you like, and leave me with the servants.

STEPHEN   Oh, you mustnt think that, mother. I—I dont like him.

LADY BRITOMART   The others do. That is the injustice of a woman's lot. A woman has to bring up her children; and that means to restrain them, to deny them things they want, to set them tasks, to punish them when they do wrong, to do all the unpleasant things. And then the father, who has nothing to do but pet them and spoil them, comes in when all her work is done and steals their affection from her.

STEPHEN   He has not stolen our affection from you. It is only curiosity.

LADY BRITOMART   (*violently*)   I wont be consoled, Stephen. There is nothing the matter with me. (*She rises and goes towards the door*)

STEPHEN   Where are you going, mother?

LADY BRITOMART   To the drawing room, of course. (*She goes out. Onward, Christian*

Soldiers, on the concertina, with tambourine accompaniment, is heard when the door opens) Are you coming, Stephen?

STEPHEN   No. Certainly not. (*She goes. He sits down on the settee, with compressed lips and an expression of strong dislike*)

ACT TWO

(*The yard of the West Ham shelter of the Salvation Army is a cold place on a January morning. The building itself, an old warehouse, is newly whitewashed. Its gabled end projects into the yard in the middle, with a door on the ground floor, and another in the loft above it without any balcony or ladder, but with a pulley rigged over it for hoisting sacks. Those who come from this central gable end into the yard have the gateway leading to the street on their left, with a stone horse-trough just beyond it, and, on the right, a penthouse shielding a table from the weather. There are forms at the table; and on them are seated a man and a woman, both much down on their luck, finishing a meal of bread [one thick slice each, with margarine and golden syrup] and diluted milk.*

The MAN, *a workman out of employment, is young, agile, a talker, a poser, sharp enough to be capable of anything in reason except honesty or altruistic considerations of any kind. The* WOMAN *is a commonplace old bundle of poverty and hard-worn humanity. She looks sixty and probably is forty-five. If they were rich people, gloved and muffed and well wrapped up in furs and overcoats, they would be numbed and miserable; for it is a grindingly cold raw January day; and a glance at the background of grimy warehouses and leaden sky visible over the whitewashed walls of the yard would drive any idle rich person straight to the Mediterranean. But these two, being no more troubled with visions of the Mediterranean than of the moon, and being compelled to keep more of their clothes in the pawnshop, and less on their persons, in winter than in summer, are not depressed by the cold: rather are they stung into vivacity, to which their meal has just now given an almost jolly turn. The man takes a pull at his mug, and then gets up and moves about the yard with his hands deep in his pockets, occasionally breaking into a stepdance*)

THE WOMAN   Feel better arter your meal, sir?

THE MAN   No. Call that a meal! Good enough for you, praps; but wot is it to me, an intelligent workin man.

THE WOMAN   Workin man! Wot are you?

THE MAN   Painter.

THE WOMAN (*sceptically*)   Yus, I dessay.

THE MAN   Yus, you dessay! I know. Every loafer that cant do nothink calls issell a painter. Well, I'm a real painter: grainer, finisher, thirty-eight bob a week when I can get it.

THE WOMAN   Then why dont you go and get it?

THE MAN   I'll tell you why. Fust: I'm intelligent—fffff! it's rotten cold here (*He dances a step or two*)—yes: intelligent beyond the station o life into which it has pleased the capitalists to call me; and they dont like a man that sees through em. Second, an intelligent bein needs a doo share of appiness; so I drink somethink cruel when I get the chawnce. Third, I stand by my class and do as little as I can so's to leave arf the job for me fellow workers. Fourth, I'm fly enough to know wots inside the law and wots outside it; and inside it I do as the capitalists do: pinch wot I can lay me ands on. In a proper state of society I am sober, industrious and honest: in Rome, so to speak, I do as the Romans do. Wots the consequence? When trade is bad—and it's rotten bad just now—and the employers az to sack arf their men, they generally start on me.

THE WOMAN   Whats your name?

THE MAN   Price. Bronterre O'Brien Price. Usually called Snobby Price, for short.

THE WOMAN   Snobby's a carpenter, aint it? You said you was a painter.

PRICE   Not that kind of snob, but the genteel sort. I'm too uppish, owing to my intelligence, and my father being a Chartist and a reading, thinking man: a stationer, too. I'm none of your common hewers of wood and drawers of water; and dont you forget it. (*He returns to his seat at the table, and takes up his mug*) Wots your name?

THE WOMAN   Rummy Mitchens, sir.

PRICE (*quaffing the remains of his milk to her*)   Your elth, Miss Mitchens.

RUMMY (*correcting him*)   Missis Mitchens.

PRICE   Wot! Oh Rummy, Rummy! Respectable married woman, Rummy, gittin rescued by the Salvation Army by pretendin to be a bad un. Same old game!

RUMMY   What am I to do? I cant starve. Them Salvation lasses is dear good girls; but the better you are, the worse they likes to think you were before they rescued you. Why shouldnt they av a bit o credit, poor loves? theyre worn to rags by their work. And where would they get the money to rescue us if we was to let on we're no worse than other people? You know what ladies and gentlemen are.

PRICE   Thievin swine! Wish I ad their job, Rummy, all the same. Wot does Rummy stand for? Pet name praps?

RUMMY   Short for Romola.

PRICE   For wot!?

RUMMY   Romola. It was out of a new book. Somebody me mother wanted me to grow up like.

PRICE   We're companions in misfortune, Rummy. Both on us got names that nobody cawnt pronounce. Consequently I'm Snobby and youre Rummy because Bill and Sally wasnt good enough for our parents. Such is life!

RUMMY   Who saved you, Mr Price? Was it Major Barbara?

PRICE   No: I come here on my own. I'm going to be Bronterre O'Brien Price, the converted painter. I know wot they like. I'll tell em how I blasphemed and gambled and wopped my poor old mother—

RUMMY   (*shocked*)   Used you to beat your mother?

PRICE   Not likely. She used to beat me. No matter: you come and listen to the converted painter, and youll hear how she was a pious woman that taught me me prayers at er knee, an how I used to come home drunk and drag her out o bed be er snow white airs, an lam into er with the poker.

RUMMY   Thats whats so unfair to us women. Your confessions is just as big lies as ours: you dont tell what you really done no more than us; but you men can tell your lies right out at the meetins and be made much of for it; while the sort o confessions we az to make az to be wispered to one lady at a time. It aint right, spite of all their piety.

PRICE   Right! Do you spose the Army'd be allowed if it went and did right? Not much. It combs our air and makes us good little blokes to be robbed and put upon. But I'll play the game as good as any of em. I'll see somebody struck by lightnin, or hear a voice sayin "Snobby Price: where will you spend eternity?" I'll av a time of it, I tell you.

RUMMY   You wont be let drink, though.

PRICE   I'll take it out in gorspellin, then. I dont want to drink if I can get fun enough any other way.

(JENNY HILL, *a pale, overwrought, pretty Salvation lass of 18, comes in through the yard gate, leading* PETER SHIRLEY, *a half hardened, half worn-out elderly man, weak with hunger*)

JENNY   (*supporting him*)   Come! pluck up. I'll get you something to eat. Youll be all right then.

PRICE   (*rising and hurrying officiously to take the old man off* JENNY's *hands*)   Poor old man! Cheer up, brother: youll find rest and peace and appiness ere. Hurry up with the food, miss: e's fair done. (JENNY *hurries into the shelter*)   Ere, buck up, daddy! she's fetchin y'a thick slice o breadn treacle, an a mug o skyblue. (*He seats him at the corner of the table*)

RUMMY   (*gaily*)   Keep up your old art! Never say die!

SHIRLEY   I'm not an old man. I'm ony 46. I'm as good as ever I was. The grey patch come in my hair before I was thirty. All it wants is three pennorth o hair dye: am I to be turned on the streets to starve for it? Holy God! Ive worked ten to twelve hours a day since I was thirteen, and paid my way all through; and now am I to be thrown into the gutter and my job given to a young man that can do it no better than me because Ive black hair that goes white at the first change?

PRICE   (*cheerfully*)   No good jawrin about it. Youre ony a jumped-up, jerked-off, orspittle-turned-out incurable of an ole workin man: who cares about you? Eh? Make the thievin swine give you a meal: theyve stole many a one from you. Get a bit o your own back. (JENNY *returns with the usual meal*)   There you are, brother. Awsk a blessin an tuck that into you.

SHIRLEY   (*looking at it ravenously but not touching it, and crying like a child*)   I never took anything before.

JENNY   (*petting him*)   Come, come! the Lord sends it to you: he wasnt above taking bread from his friends; and why should you be? Besides, when we find you a job you can pay us for it if you like.

SHIRLEY   (*eagerly*)   Yes, yes: thats true. I can pay you back: it's only a loan. (*shivering*) Oh Lord! oh Lord! (*He turns to the table and attacks the meal ravenously*)

JENNY   Well, Rummy, are you more comfortable now?

RUMMY   God bless you, lovey! youve fed my body and saved my soul, havnt you? (JENNY, *touched, kisses her*)   Sit down and rest a bit: you must be ready to drop.

JENNY   Ive been going hard since morning. But theres more work than we can do. I mustnt stop.

RUMMY   Try a prayer for just two minutes. Youll work all the better after.

JENNY (*her eyes lighting up*)   Oh isnt it wonderful how a few minutes prayer revives you! I was quite lightheaded at twelve o'clock, I was so tired; but Major Barbara just sent me to pray for five minutes; and I was able to go on as if I had only just begun. (*to* PRICE) Did you have a piece of bread?

PRICE (*with unction*)   Yes, miss; but Ive got the piece that I value more; and thats the peace that passeth hall hannerstennin.

RUMMY (*fervently*)   Glory Hallelujah!

(*Bill Walker, a rough customer of about 25, appears at the yard gate and looks malevolently at* JENNY)

JENNY   That makes me so happy. When you say that, I feel wicked for loitering here. I must get to work again.

(*She is hurrying to the shelter, when the newcomer moves quickly up to the door and intercepts her. His manner is so threatening that she retreats as he comes at her truculently, driving her down the yard*)

BILL   Aw knaow you. Youre the one that took awy maw girl. Youre the one that set er agen me. Well, I'm gowin to ev er aht. Not that Aw care a carse for er or you: see? Bat Aw'll let er knaow; and Aw'll let you knaow. Aw'm gowing to give her a doin thatll teach er to cat away from me. Nah in wiv you and tell er to cam aht afore Aw cam in and kick er aht. Tell er Bill Walker wants er. She'll knaow wot thet means; and if she keeps me witin itll be worse. You stop to jawr beck at me; and Aw'll stawt on you: d'ye eah? Theres your wy. In you gow. (*He takes her by the arm and slings her towards the door of the shelter. She falls on her hand and knee.* RUMMY *helps her up again*)

PRICE (*rising, and venturing irresolutely towards* BILL)   Easy there, mate. She aint doin you no arm.

BILL   Oo are you callin mite? (*standing over him threateningly*) Youre gowin to stend ap for er, aw yer? Put ap your ends.

RUMMY (*running indignantly to him to scold him*)   Oh, you great brute—(*He instantly swings his left hand back against her face. She screams and reels back to the trough, where she sits down, covering her bruised face with her hands and rocking herself and moaning with pain*)

JENNY (*going to her*)   Oh, God forgive you! How could you strike an old woman like that?

BILL (*seizing her by the hair so violently that she also screams, and tearing her away from the old woman*)   You Gawd forgimme again an Aw'll Gawd forgive you one of the jawr thetll stop you pryin for a week. (*Holding her and turning fiercely on* PRICE) Ev you ennything to sy agen it?

PRICE (*intimidated*)   No, matey: she aint anything to do with me.

BILL   Good job for you! Aw'd pat two meals into you and fawt you with one finger arter, you stawved cur. (*to* JENNY) Nah are you gowin to fetch aht Mog Ebbijem; or em Aw to knock your fice off you and fetch her meself?

JENNY (*writhing in his grasp*)   Oh please someone go in and tell Major Barbara—(*She screams again as he wrenches her head down; and* PRICE *and* RUMMY *flee into the shelter*)

BILL   You want to gow in and tell your Mijor of me, do you?

JENNY   Oh please dont drag my hair. Let me go.

BILL   Do you or downt you? (*She stifles a scream*) Yus or nao?

JENNY   God give me strength—

BILL (*striking her with his fist in the face*)   Gow an shaow her thet, and tell her if she wants one lawk it to cam and interfere with me. (*JENNY, crying with pain, goes into the shed. He goes to the form and addresses the old man*) Eah: finish your mess; an git aht o maw wy.

SHIRLEY (*springing up and facing him fiercely, with the mug in his hand*)   You take a liberty with me, and I'll smash you over the face with the mug and cut your eye out. Aint you satisfied—young whelps like you—with takin the bread out o the mouths of your elders that have brought you up and slaved for you, but you must come shovin and cheekin and bullyin in here, where the bread o charity is sickenin in our stummicks?

BILL (*contemptuously, but backing a little*)   Wot good are you, you aold palsy mag? Wot good are you?

SHIRLEY   As good as you and better. I'll do a day's work agen you or any fat young soaker of your age. Go and take my job at Horrockses, where I worked for ten year. They want young men there: they cant afford to keep men over forty-five. Theyre very sorry—give you a character and happy to help you to get anything suited to your years—sure a steady man wont be long out of a job. Well, let em try you. Theyll find the differ. What do you know? Not as much as how to beeyave yourself—layin your dirty fist across the mouth of a respectable woman!

BILL Downt provowk me to ly it acrost yours: d'ye eah?

SHIRLEY (*with blighting contempt*) Yes: you like an old man to hit, dont you, when youve finished with the women. I aint seen you hit a young one yet.

BILL (*stung*) You loy, you aold soupkitchener, you. There was a yang menn eah. Did Aw offer to itt him or did Aw not?

SHIRLEY Was he starvin or was he not? Was he a man or only a crosseyed thief an a loafer? Would you hit my son-in-law's brother?

BILL Oo's ee?

SHIRLEY Todger Fairmile o Balls Pond. Him that won £20 off the Japanese wrastler at the music hall by standin out 17 minutes 4 seconds agen him.

BILL (*sullenly*) Aw'm nao music awl wrastler. Ken he box?

SHIRLEY Yes: an you cant.

BILL Wot! Aw cawnt, cawnt Aw? Wots thet you sy? (*threatening him*)

SHIRLEY (*not budging an inch*) Will you box Todger Fairmile if I put him on to you? Say the word.

BILL (*subsiding with a slouch*) Aw'll stend ap to enny menn alawv, if he was ten Todger Fairmawls. But Aw dont set ap to be a perfeshnal.

SHIRLEY (*looking down on him with unfathomable disdain*) You box! Slap an old woman with the back o your hand! You hadnt even the sense to hit her where a magistrate couldnt see the mark of it, you silly young lump of conceit and ignorance. Hit a girl in the jaw and ony make her cry! If Todger Fairmile'd done it, she wouldnt a got up inside o ten minutes, no more than you would if he got on to you. Yah! I'd set about you myself if I had a week's feedin in me instead o two months' starvation. (*He turns his back on him and sits down moodily at the table*)

BILL (*following him and stooping over him to drive the taunt in*) You loy! youve the bread and treacle in you that you cam eah to beg.

SHIRLEY (*bursting into tears*) Oh God! it's true: I'm only an old pauper on the scrap heap. (*furiously*) But youll come to it yourself; and then youll know. Youll come to it sooner than a teetotaller like me, fillin yourself with gin at this hour o the mornin!

BILL Aw'm nao gin drinker, you aold lawr; bat wen Aw want to give my girl a bloomin good awdin Aw lawk to ev a bit o devil in me: see? An eah Aw emm, talkin to a rotten aold blawter like you sted o givin her wot for. (*working himself into a rage*) Aw'm gowin in

there to fetch her aht. (*He makes vengefully for the shelter door*)

SHIRLEY Youre going to the station on a stretcher, more likely; and theyll take the gin and the devil out of you there when they get you inside. You mind what youre about: the major here is the Earl o Stevenage's granddaughter.

BILL (*checked*) Garn!

SHIRLEY Youll see.

BILL (*his resolution oozing*) Well, Aw aint dan nathin to er.

SHIRLEY Spose she said you did! who'd believe you?

BILL (*very uneasy, skulking back to the corner of the penthouse*) Gawd! theres no jastice in this cantry. To think wot them people can do! Aw'm as good as er.

SHIRLEY Tell her so. It's just what a fool like you would do.

(BARBARA, *brisk and businesslike, comes from the shelter with a note book, and addresses herself to* SHIRLEY. BILL, *cowed, sits down in the corner on a form, and turns his back on them*)

BARBARA Good morning.

SHIRLEY (*standing up and taking off his hat*) Good morning, miss.

BARBARA Sit down: make yourself at home. (*He hesitates; but she puts a friendly hand on his shoulder and makes him obey*) Now then! since youve made friends with us, we want to know all about you. Names and addresses and trades.

SHIRLEY Peter Shirley. Fitter. Chucked out two months ago because I was too old.

BARBARA (*not at all surprised*) Youd pass still. Why didnt you dye your hair?

SHIRLEY I did. Me age come out at a coroner's inquest on me daughter.

BARBARA Steady?

SHIRLEY Teetotaller. Never out of a job before. Good worker. And sent to the knackers like an old horse!

BARBARA No matter: if you did your part God will do his.

SHIRLEY (*suddenly stubborn*) My religion's no concern of anybody but myself.

BARBARA (*guessing*) I know. Secularist?

SHIRLEY (*hotly*) Did I offer to deny it?

BARBARA Why should you? My own father's a Secularist, I think. Our Father—yours and mine—fulfils himself in many ways; and I daresay he knew what he was about when he made a Secularist of you. So buck up, Peter! we can always find a job for a steady man like you. (SHIRLEY, *disarmed and a little be-*

wildered, touches his hat. She turns from him to BILL) Whats your name?

BILL (*insolently*) Wots thet to you?

BARBARA (*calmly making a note*) Afraid to give his name. Any trade?

BILL Oo's afraid to give is nime? (*doggedly, with a sense of heroically defying the House of Lords in the person of Lord Stevenage*) If you want to bring a chawge agen me, bring it. (*She waits, unruffled*) Moy nime's Bill Walker.

BARBARA (*as if the name were familiar: trying to remember how*) Bill Walker? (*recollecting*) Oh, I know: youre the man that Jenny Hill was praying for inside just now. (*She enters his name in her note book*)

BILL Oo's Jenny Ill? And wot call as she to pry for me?

BARBARA I dont know. Perhaps it was you that cut her lip.

BILL (*defiantly*) Yus, it was me that cat her lip. Aw aint afride o you.

BARBARA How could you be, since youre not afraid of God? Youre a brave man, Mr Walker. It takes some pluck to do our work here; but none of us dare lift our hand against a girl like that, for fear of her father in heaven.

BILL (*sullenly*) I want nan o your kentin jawr. I spowse you think Aw cam eah to beg from you, like this demmiged lot eah. Not me. Aw downt want your bread and scripe and ketlep. Aw dont blieve in your Gawd, no more than you do yourself.

BARBARA (*sunnily apologetic and ladylike, as on a new footing with him*) Oh, I beg your pardon for putting your name down, Mr Walker. I didnt understand. I'll strike it out.

BILL (*taking this as a slight, and deeply wounded by it*) Eah! you let maw nime alown. Aint it good enaff to be in your book?

BARBARA (*considering*) Well, you see, theres no use putting down your name unless I can do something for you, is there? Whats your trade?

BILL (*still smarting*) Thets nao concern o yours.

BARBARA Just so. (*very businesslike*) I'll put you down as (*writing*) the man who—struck—poor little Jenny Hill—in the mouth.

BILL (*rising threateningly*) See eah. Awve ed enaff o this.

BARBARA (*quite sunny and fearless*) What did you come to us for?

BILL Aw cam for maw gel, see? Aw cam to tike her aht o this and to brike er jawr for er.

BARBARA (*complacently*) You see I was right about your trade.

(*Bill, on the point of retorting furiously, finds himself, to his great shame and terror, in danger of crying instead. He sits down again suddenly*) Whats her name?

BILL (*dogged*) Er nime's Mog Ebbijem: thets wot her nime is.

BARBARA Mog Habbijam! Oh, she's gone to Canning Town, to our barracks there.

BILL (*fortified by his resentment of Mog's perfidy*) Is she? (*vindictively*) Then Aw'm gowin to Kennintahn arter her. (*He crosses to the gate; hesitates; finally comes back at* BARBARA) Are you loyin to me to git shat o me?

BARBARA I dont want to get shut of you. I want to keep you here and save your soul. Youd better stay: youre going to have a bad time today, Bill.

BILL Oo's gowin to give it to me? You, preps?

BARBARA Someone you dont believe in. But youll be glad afterwards.

BILL (*slinking off*) Aw'll gow to Kennintahn to be aht o reach o your tangue. (*suddenly turning on her with intense malice*) And if Aw downt fawnd Mog there, Aw'll cam beck and do two years for you, selp me Gawd if Aw downt!

BARBARA (*a shade kindlier, if possible*) It's no use, Bill. She's got another bloke.

BILL Wot!

BARBARA One of her own converts. He fell in love with her when he saw her with her soul saved, and her face clean, and her hair washed.

BILL (*surprised*) Wottud she wash it for, the carroty slat? It's red.

BARBARA It's quite lovely now, because she wears a new look in her eyes with it. It's a pity youre too late. The new bloke has put your nose out of joint, Bill.

BILL Aw'll put his nowse aht o joint for him. Not that Aw care a carse for er, mawnd thet. But Aw'll teach her to drop me as if Aw was dirt. And Aw'll teach him to meddle with maw judy. Wots iz bleedin nime?

BARBARA Sergeant Todger Fairmile.

SHIRLEY (*rising with grim joy*) I'll go with him, miss. I want to see them two meet. I'll take him to the infirmary when it's over.

BILL (*to* SHIRLEY, *with undissembled misgiving*) Is thet im you was speakin on?

SHIRLEY Thats him.

BILL Im that wrastled in the music awl?

SHIRLEY The competitions at the National Sportin Club was worth nigh a hundred a year to him. He's gev em up now for religion; so he's a bit fresh for want of the exercise he was accustomed to. He'll be glad to see you. Come along.

BILL Wots is wight?

SHIRLEY Thirteen four. (BILL's *last hope expires*)

BARBARA Go and talk to him, Bill. He'll convert you.

SHIRLEY He'll convert your head into a mashed potato.

BILL (*sullenly*) Aw aint afride of im. Aw aint afride of ennybody. Bat e can lick me. She's dan me. (*He sits down moodily on the edge of the horse trough*)

SHIRLEY You aint going. I thought not. (*He resumes his seat*)

BARBARA (*calling*) Jenny!

JENNY (*appearing at the shelter door with a plaster on the corner of her mouth*) Yes, Major.

BARBARA Send Rummy Mitchens out to clear away here.

JENNY I think she's afraid.

BARBARA (*her resemblance to her mother flashing out for a moment*) Nonsense! she must do as she's told.

JENNY (*calling into the shelter*) Rummy: the Major says you must come.

(JENNY *comes to* BARBARA, *purposely keeping on the side next* BILL, *lest he should suppose that she shrank from him or bore malice*)

BARBARA Poor little Jenny! Are you tired? (*looking at the wounded cheek*) Does it hurt?

JENNY No: it's all right now. It was nothing.

BARBARA (*critically*) It was as hard as he could hit, I expect. Poor Bill! You dont feel angry with him, do you?

JENNY Oh no, no, no: indeed I don't, Major, bless his poor heart! (BARBARA *kisses her; and she runs away merrily into the shelter.* BILL *writhes with an agonizing return of his new and alarming symptoms, but says nothing.* RUMMY MITCHENS *comes from the shelter*)

BARBARA (*going to meet* RUMMY) Now Rummy, bustle. Take in those mugs and plates to be washed; and throw the crumbs about for the birds.

(RUMMY *takes the three plates and mugs; but* SHIRLEY *takes back his mug from her, as there is still some milk left in it*)

RUMMY There aint any crumbs. This aint a time to waste good bread on birds.

PRICE (*appearing at the shelter door*) Gentleman come to see the shelter, Major. Says he's your father.

BARBARA All right. Coming. (SNOBBY *goes*

back into the shelter, followed by BA[...]

RUMMY (*stealing across to* BILL *and a[...] ing him in a subdued voice, but with [...] conviction*) I'd av the lor of you, you[...] eared pignosed potwalloper, if she'd let [...] Youre no gentleman, to hit a lady in the fa[...] (BILL, *with greater things moving in him, tak[...] no notice*)

SHIRLEY (*following her*) Here! in with you[...] and dont get yourself into more trouble by talking.

RUMMY (*with hauteur*) I aint ad the pleasure o being hintroduced to you, as I can remember. (*She goes into the shelter with the plates*)

SHIRLEY Thats the—

BILL (*savagely*) Downt you talk to me, d'ye eah? You lea me alown, or Aw'll do you a mischief. Aw'm not dirt under your feet, ennywy.

SHIRLEY (*calmly*) Dont you be afeerd. You aint such prime company that you need expect to be sought after. (*He is about to go into the shelter when* BARBARA *comes out, with* UNDERSHAFT *on her right*)

BARBARA Oh, there you are, Mr Shirley! (*between them*) This is my father: I told you he was Secularist, didn't I? Perhaps youll be able to comfort one another.

UNDERSHAFT (*startled*) A Secularist! Not the least in the world: on the contrary, a confirmed mystic.

BARBARA Sorry, I'm sure. By the way, papa, what is your religion? in case I have to introduce you again.

UNDERSHAFT My religion? Well, my dear, I am a Millionaire. That is my religion.

BARBARA Then I'm afraid you and Mr Shirley wont be able to comfort one another after all. Youre not a Millionaire, are you, Peter?

SHIRLEY No; and proud of it.

UNDERSHAFT (*gravely*) Poverty, my friend, is not a thing to be proud of.

SHIRLEY (*angrily*) Who made your millions for you? Me and my like. Whats kep us poor? Keepin' you rich. I wouldn't have your conscience, not for all your income.

UNDERSHAFT I wouldnt have your income, not for all your conscience, Mr. Shirley. (*He goes to the penthouse and sits down on a form*)

BARBARA (*stopping* SHIRLEY *adroitly as he is about to retort*) You wouldnt think he was my father, would you, Peter? Will you go into the shelter and lend the lasses a hand for a while: we're worked off our feet.

SHIRLEY (*bitterly*) Yes: I'm in their debt for a meal, aint I?

...RBARA)
...ldress-
...ntense
...flat
_ne._
_...s_

youre in their
'. for love of
...nd _is rather_
... at me. In with
...ce of yours a holi-
..._ie shelter_).

..._in_) Ah! it's a pity you
to use your reason, miss.
... a very taking lecturer on

..._urns to her father_)

...RSHAFT Never mind me, my dear.
...bout your work; and let me watch it for
while.

BARBARA All right.

UNDERSHAFT For instance, whats the matter with that outpatient over there?

BARBARA (_looking at_ BILL, _whose attitude has never changed, and whose expression of brooding wrath has deepened_) Oh, we shall cure him in no time. Just watch. (_She goes over to_ BILL _and waits. He glances up at her and casts his eyes down again, uneasy, but grimmer than ever_) It would be nice to just stamp on Mog Habbijam's face, wouldnt it, Bill?

BILL (_starting up from the trough in consternation_) It's a loy: Aw never said so. (_She shakes her head_) Oo taold you wot was in moy mawnd?

BARBARA Only your new friend.

BILL Wot new friend?

BARBARA The devil, Bill. When he gets round people they get miserable, just like you.

BILL (_with a heartbreaking attempt at devil-may-care cheerfulness_) Aw aint miserable. (_He sits down again, and stretches his legs in an attempt to seem indifferent_)

BARBARA Well, if youre happy, why dont you look happy, as we do?

BILL (_his legs curling back in spite of him_) Aw'm eppy enaff, Aw tell you. Woy cawnt you lea me alown? Wot ev I dan to you? Aw aint smashed your fice, ev Aw?

BARBARA (_softly: wooing his soul_) It's not me thats getting at you, Bill.

BILL Oo else is it?

BARBARA Somebody that doesnt intend you to smash women's faces, I suppose. Somebody or something that wants to make a man of you.

BILL (_blustering_) Mike a menn o me! Aint Aw a menn? eh? Oo sez Aw'm not a menn?

BARBARA Theres a man in you somewhere, I suppose. But why did he let you hit poor little Jenny Hill? That wasnt very manly of him, was it?

BILL (_tormented_) Ev dan wiv it, Aw tell

you. Chack it. Aw'm sick o your Jenny Ill and er silly little fice.

BARBARA Then why do you keep thinking about it? Why does it keep coming up against you in your mind? Youre not getting converted, are you?

BILL (_with conviction_) Not ME. Not lawkly.

BARBARA Thats right, Bill. Hold out against it. Put out your strength. Dont lets get you cheap. Todger Fairmile said he wrestled for three nights against his salvation harder than he ever wrestled with the Jap at the music hall. He gave in to the Jap when his arm was going to break. But he didnt give in to his salvation until his heart was going to break. Perhaps youll escape that. You havnt any heart, have you?

BILL Wot d'ye mean? Woy aint Aw got a awt the sime as ennybody else?

BARBARA A man with a heart wouldnt have bashed poor little Jenny's face, would he?

BILL (_almost crying_) Ow, will you lea me alown? Ev Aw ever offered to meddle with you, that you cam neggin and provowkin me lawk this? (_He writhes convulsively from his eyes to his toes_)

BARBARA (_with a steady soothing hand on his arm and a gentle voice that never lets him go_) It's your soul thats hurting you, Bill, and not me. Weve been through it all ourselves. Come with us, Bill. (_He looks wildly round_) To brave manhood on earth and eternal glory in heaven. (_He is on the point of breaking down_) Come. (_A drum is heard in the shelter; and_ BILL, _with a gasp, escapes from the spell as_ BARBARA _turns quickly._ ADOLPHUS _enters from the shelter with a big drum_) Oh! there you are, Dolly. Let me introduce a new friend of mine, Mr Bill Walker. This is my bloke, Bill: Mr Cusins. (CUSINS _salutes with his drumstick_)

BILL Gowin to merry im?

BARBARA Yes.

BILL (_fervently_) Gawd elp im! Gaw-aw-aw-awd elp im!

BARBARA Why? Do you think he wont be happy with me?

BILL Awve aony ed to stend it for a mawnin: e'll ev to stend it for a lawftawm.

CUSINS That is a frightful reflection, Mr Walker. But I cant tear myself away from her.

BILL Well, Aw ken. (_to_ BARBARA) Eah! do you knaow where Aw'm gowin to, and wot Aw'm gowin to do?

BARBARA Yes: youre going to heaven; and youre coming back here before the week's out to tell me so.

BILL You loy. Aw'm gowin to Kennintahn, to spit in Todger Fairmawl's eye. Aw beshed

Jenny Ill's fice; an nar Aw'll git me aown fice beshed and cam beck and shaow it to er. Ee'll itt me ardern Aw itt her. Thatll mike us square. (*to* ADOLPHUS) Is thet fair or is it not? Youre a genlmn: you oughter knaow.

BARBARA   Two black eyes wont make one white one, Bill.

BILL   Aw didnt awst you. Cawnt you never keep your mahth shat? Oy awst the genlmn.

CUSINS (*reflectively*)   Yes: I think youre right, Mr Walker. Yes: I should do it. It's curious: it's exactly what an ancient Greek would have done.

BARBARA   But what good will it do?

CUSINS   Well, it will give Mr Fairmile some exercise; and it will satisfy Mr Walker's soul.

BILL   Rot! there aint nao such a thing as a saoul. Ah kin you tell wevver Awve a saoul or not? You never seen it.

BARBARA   Ive seen it hurting you when you went against it.

BILL (*with compressed aggravation*)   If you was maw gel and took the word aht o me mahth lawk thet, Aw'd give you sathink youd feel urtin, Aw would. (*to* ADOLPHUS) You tike maw tip, mite. Stop er jowr; or youll doy afoah your tawm. (*with intense expression*) Wore aht: thets wot youll be: wore aht. (*He goes away through the gate*)

CUSINS (*looking after him*)   I wonder!

BARBARA   Dolly! (*indignant, in her mother's manner*)

CUSINS   Yes, my dear, it's very wearing to be in love with you. If it lasts, I quite think I shall die young.

BARBARA   Should you mind?

CUSINS   Not at all. (*He is suddenly softened, and kisses her over the drum, evidently not for the first time, as people cannot kiss over a big drum without practice. Undershaft coughs*)

BARBARA   It's all right, papa, weve not forgotten you. Dolly: explain the place to papa: I havnt time. (*She goes busily into the shelter*)

(UNDERSHAFT *and* ADOLPHUS *now have the yard to themselves.* UNDERSHAFT, *seated on a form, and still keenly attentive, looks hard at* ADOLPHUS. ADOLPHUS *looks hard at him*)

UNDERSHAFT   I fancy you guess something of what is in my mind, Mr Cusins. (CUSINS *flourishes his drumsticks as if in the act of beating a lively rataplan, but makes no sound*) Exactly so. But suppose Barbara finds you out!

CUSINS   You know, I do not admit that I am imposing on Barbara. I am quite genuinely interested in the views of the Salvation Army. The fact is, I am a sort of collector of religions; and the curious thing is that I find I can believe them all. By the way, have you any religion?

UNDERSHAFT   Yes.

CUSINS   Anything out of the common?

UNDERSHAFT   Only that there are two things necessary to Salvation.

CUSINS (*disappointed, but polite*)   Ah, the Church Catechism. Charles Lomax also belongs to the Established Church.

UNDERSHAFT   The two things are—

CUSINS   Baptism and—

UNDERSHAFT   No. Money and gunpowder.

CUSINS (*surprised, but interested*)   That is the general opinion of our governing classes. The novelty is in hearing any man confess it.

UNDERSHAFT   Just so.

CUSINS   Excuse me: is there any place in your religion for honor, justice, truth, love, mercy and so forth?

UNDERSHAFT   Yes: they are the graces and luxuries of a rich, strong, and safe life.

CUSINS   Suppose one is forced to choose between them and money or gunpowder?

UNDERSHAFT   Choose money and gunpowder; for without enough of both you cannot afford the others.

CUSINS   That is your religion?

UNDERSHAFT   Yes.

(*The cadence of this reply makes a full close in the conversation.* CUSINS *twists his face dubiously and contemplates* UNDERSHAFT. UNDERSHAFT *contemplates him*)

CUSINS   Barbara wont stand that. You will have to choose between your religion and Barbara.

UNDERSHAFT   So will you, my friend. She will find out that that drum of yours is hollow.

CUSINS   Father Undershaft: you are mistaken: I am a sincere Salvationist. You do not understand the Salvation Army. It is the army of joy, of love, of courage: it has banished the fear and remorse and despair of the old hell-ridden evangelical sects: it marches to fight the devil with trumpet and drum, with music and dancing, with banner and palm, as becomes a sally from heaven by its happy garrison. It picks the waster out of the public house and makes a man of him: it finds a worm wriggling in a back kitchen, and lo! a woman! Men and women of rank too, sons and daughters of the Highest. It takes the poor professor of Greek, the most artificial and self-suppressed of human creatures, from his meal of roots, and lets lose the rhapsodist in him; reveals the true worship of Dionysos to him; sends him down the public street drumming dithyrambs (*he plays a thundering flourish on the drum*)

UNDERSHAFT   You will alarm the shelter.

CUSINS   Oh, they are accustomed to these sudden ecstasies. However, if the drum worries you—(*he pockets the drumsticks; unhooks the drum; and stands it on the ground opposite the gateway*)

UNDERSHAFT   Thank you.

CUSINS   You remember what Euripides says about your money and gunpowder?

UNDERSHAFT   No.

CUSINS   (*declaiming*)

One and another
In money and guns may outpass his brother;
And men in their millions float and flow
And seethe with a million hopes as leaven;
And they win their will; or they miss their will;
And their hopes are dead or are pined for still;
　But who'er can know
　As the long days go
That to live is happy, has found his heaven.

My translation: what do you think of it?

UNDERSHAFT   I think, my friend, that if you wish to know, as the long days go, that to live is happy, you must first acquire money enough for a decent life, and power enough to be your own master.

CUSINS   You are damnably discouraging. (*He resumes his declamation*)

Is it so hard a thing to see
That the spirit of God—whate'er it be—
The law that abides and changes not, ages long,
The Eternal and Nature-born: these things be
　strong?
What else is Wisdom? What of Man's endeavor,
Or God's high grace so lovely and so great?
To stand from fear set free? to breathe and
　wait?
To hold a hand uplifted over Fate?
And shall not Barbara be loved for ever?

UNDERSHAFT   Euripides mentions Barbara, does he?

CUSINS   It is a fair translation. The word means Loveliness.

UNDERSHAFT   May I ask—as Barbara's father—how much a year she is to be loved for ever on?

CUSINS   As for Barbara's father, that is more your affair than mine. I can feed her by teaching Greek: that is about all.

UNDERSHAFT   Do you consider it a good match for her?

CUSINS   (*with polite obstinacy*)   Mr Undershaft: I am in many ways a weak, timid, ineffectual person; and my health is far from satisfactory. But whenever I feel that I must have anything, I get it, sooner or later. I feel that way about Barbara. I dont like marriage: I feel intensely afraid of it; and I dont know what I shall do with Barbara or what she will do with me. But I feel that I and nobody else must marry her. Please regard that as settled. —Not that I wish to be arbitrary; but why should I waste your time in discussing what is inevitable?

UNDERSHAFT   You mean that you will stick at nothing: not even the conversion of the Salvation Army to the worship of Dionysos.

CUSINS   The business of the Salvation Army is to save, not to wrangle about the name of the pathfinder. Dionysos or another: what does it matter?

UNDERSHAFT   (*rising and approaching him*) Professor Cusins: you are a young man after my own heart.

CUSINS   Mr Undershaft: you are, as far as I am able to gather, a most infernal old rascal; but you appeal very strongly to my sense of ironic humor.

(UNDERSHAFT *mutely offers his hand. They shake*)

UNDERSHAFT   (*suddenly concentrating himself*)   And now to business.

CUSINS   Pardon me. We are discussing religion. Why go back to such an uninteresting and unimportant subject as business?

UNDERSHAFT   Religion is our business at present, because it is through religion alone that we can win Barbara.

CUSINS   Have you, too, fallen in love with Barbara?

UNDERSHAFT   Yes, with a father's love.

CUSINS   A father's love for a grown-up daughter is the most dangerous of all infatuations. I apologize for mentioning my own pale, coy, mistrustful fancy in the same breath with it.

UNDERSHAFT   Keep to the point. We have to win her; and we are neither of us Methodists.

CUSINS   That doesnt matter. The power Barbara wields here—the power that wields Barbara herself—is not Calvinism, not Presbyterianism, not Methodism—

UNDERSHAFT   Not Greek Paganism either, eh?

CUSINS   I admit that. Barbara is quite original in her religion.

UNDERSHAFT   (*triumphantly*)   Aha! Barbara Undershaft would be. Her inspiration comes from within herself.

CUSINS   How do you suppose it got there?

UNDERSHAFT   (*in towering excitement*)   It is the Undershaft inheritance. I shall hand on my torch to my daughter. She shall make my converts and preach my gospel—

CUSINS   What! Money and gunpowder!

UNDERSHAFT   Yes, money and gunpowder. Freedom and power. Command of life and command of death.

CUSINS   (*urbanely: trying to bring him down to earth*)   This is extremely interesting, Mr Undershaft. Of course you know that you are mad.

UNDERSHAFT   (*with redoubled force*)   And you?

CUSINS   Oh, mad as a hatter. You are welcome to my secret since I have discovered yours. But I am astonished. Can a madman make cannons?

UNDERSHAFT   Would anyone else than a madman make them? And now (*with surging energy*) question for question. Can a sane man translate Euripides?

CUSINS   No.

UNDERSHAFT   (*seizing him by the shoulder*)   Can a sane woman make a man of a waster or a woman of a worm?

CUSINS   (*reeling before the storm*)   Father Colossus—Mammoth Millionaire—

UNDERSHAFT   (*pressing him*)   Are there two mad people or three in this Salvation shelter today?

CUSINS   You mean Barbara is as mad as we are?

UNDERSHAFT   (*pushing him lightly off and resuming his equanimity suddenly and completely*)   Pooh, Professor! let us call things by their proper names. I am a millionaire; you are a poet: Barbara is a savior of souls. What have we three to do with the common mob of slaves and idolators? (*He sits down again with a shrug of contempt for the mob*)

CUSINS   Take care! Barbara is in love with the common people. So am I. Have you never felt the romance of that love?

UNDERSHAFT   (*cold and sardonic*)   Have you ever been in love with Poverty, like St. Francis? Have you ever been in love with Dirt, like St Simeon! Have you ever been in love with disease and suffering, like our nurses and philanthropists? Such passions are not virtues, but the most unnatural of all the vices. This love of the common people may please an earl's granddaughter and a university professor; but I have been a common man and a poor man; and it has no romance for me. Leave it to the poor to pretend that poverty is a blessing: leave it to the coward to make a religion of his cowardice by preaching humility: we know better than that. We three must stand together above the common people: how else can we help their children to climb up beside us? Barbara must belong to us, not to the Salvation Army.

CUSINS   Well, I can only say that if you think you will get her away from the Salvation Army by talking to her as you have been talking to me, you dont know Barbara.

UNDERSHAFT   My friend: I never ask for what I can buy.

CUSINS   (*in a white fury*)   Do I understand you to imply that you can buy Barbara?

UNDERSHAFT   No; but I can buy the Salvation Army.

CUSINS   Quite impossible.

UNDERSHAFT   You shall see. All religious organizations exist by selling themselves to the rich.

CUSINS   Not the Army. That is the Church of the poor.

UNDERSHAFT   All the more reason for buying it.

CUSINS   I dont think you quite know what the Army does for the poor.

UNDERSHAFT   Oh yes I do. It draws their teeth: that is enough for me as a man of business.

CUSINS   Nonsense! It makes them sober—

UNDERSHAFT   I prefer sober workmen. The profits are larger.

CUSINS   —honest—

UNDERSHAFT   Honest workmen are the most economical.

CUSINS   —attached to their homes—

UNDERSHAFT   So much the better: they will put up with anything sooner than change their shop.

CUSINS   —happy—

UNDERSHAFT   An invaluable safeguard against revolution.

CUSINS   —unselfish—

UNDERSHAFT   Indifferent to their own interests, which suits me exactly.

CUSINS   —with their thoughts on heavenly things—

UNDERSHAFT   (*rising*)   And not on Trade Unionism nor Socialism. Excellent.

CUSINS   (*revolted*)   You really are an infernal old rascal.

UNDERSHAFT   (*indicating* PETER SHIRLEY, *who has just come from the shelter and strolled dejectedly down the yard between them*)   And this is an honest man!

SHIRLEY   Yes; and what av I got by it? (*He passes on bitterly and sits on the form, in the corner of the penthouse*)

(SNOBBY PRICE, *beaming sanctimoniously, and* JENNY HILL, *with a tambourine full of coppers, come from the shelter and go to the drum, on which* JENNY *begins to count the money*)

UNDERSHAFT   (*replying to* SHIRLEY)   Oh,

your employers must have got a good deal by it from first to last. (*He sits on the table, with one foot on the side form,* CUSINS, *overwhelmed, sits down on the same form nearer the shelter.* BARBARA *comes from the shelter to the middle of the yard. She is excited and a little over-wrought*)

BARBARA Weve just had a splendid experience meeting at the other gate in Cripp's lane. Ive hardly ever seen them so much moved as they were by your confession, Mr Price.

PRICE I could almost be glad of my past wickedness if I could believe that it would elp to keep hathers straight.

BARBARA So it will, Snobby. How much, Jenny?

JENNY Four and tenpence, Major.

BARBARA Oh Snobby, if you had given your poor mother just one more kick, we should have got the whole five shillings!

PRICE If she heard you say that, miss, she'd be sorry I didnt. But I'm glad. Oh what a joy it will be to her when she hears I'm saved!

UNDERSHAFT Shall I contribute the odd twopence, Barbara? The millionaire's mite, eh? (*He takes a couple of pennies from his pocket*)

BARBARA How did you make that two-pence?

UNDERSHAFT As usual. By selling cannons, torpedoes, submarines, and my new patent Grand Duke hand grenade.

BARBARA Put it back in your pocket. You cant buy your salvation here for twopence: you must work it out.

UNDERSHAFT Is twopence not enough? I can afford a little more, if you press me.

BARBARA Two million millions would not be enough. There is bad blood on your hands; and nothing but good blood can cleanse them. Money is no use. Take it away. (*She turns to* CUSINS) Dolly: you must write another letter for me to the papers. (*He makes a wry face*) Yes: I know you dont like it; but it must be done. The starvation this winter is beating us: everybody is unemployed. The General says we must close this shelter if we cant get more money. I force the collections at the meetings until I am ashamed: dont I, Snobby?

PRICE It's a fair treat to see you work it, miss. The way you got them up from three-and-six to four-and-ten with that hymn, penny by penny and verse by verse, was a caution. Not a Cheap Jack on Mile End Waste could touch you at it.

BARBARA Yes; but I wish we could do without it. I am getting at last to think more of the collection than of the people's souls. And what are those hatfuls of pence and halfpence? We want thousands! tens of thousands! hundreds of thousands! I want to convert people, not to be always begging for the Army in a way I'd die sooner than beg for myself.

UNDERSHAFT (*in profound irony*) Genuine unselfishness is capable of anything, my dear.

BARBARA (*unsuspectingly, as she turns away to take the money from the drum and put it in a cash bag she carries*) Yes, isnt it?

(UNDERSHAFT *looks sardonically at* CUSINS)

CUSINS (*aside to* UNDERSHAFT) Mephistopheles! Machiavelli!

BARBARA (*tears coming into her eyes as she ties the bag and pockets it*) How are we to feed them? I cant talk religion to a man with bodily hunger in his eyes. (*almost breaking down*) It's frightful.

JENNY (*running to her*) Major, dear—

BARBARA (*rebounding*) No: dont comfort me. It will be all right. We shall get the money.

UNDERSHAFT How?

JENNY By praying for it, of course. Mrs Baines says she prayed for it last night; and she has never prayed for it in vain: never once.

(*She goes to the gate and looks out into the street*)

BARBARA (*who has dried her eyes and regained her composure*) By the way, dad, Mrs Baines has come to march with us to our big meeting this afternoon; and she is very anxious to meet you, for some reason or other. Perhaps she'll convert you.

UNDERSHAFT I shall be delighted, my dear.

JENNY (*at the gate: excitedly*) Major! Major! heres that man back again.

BARBARA What man?

JENNY The man that hit me. Oh, I hope he's coming back to join us.

(BILL WALKER, *with frost on his jacket, comes through the gate, his hands deep in his pockets and his chin sunk between his shoulders, like a cleaned-out gambler. He halts between* BARBARA *and the drum*)

BARBARA Hullo, Bill! Back already!

BILL (*nagging at her*) Bin talkin ever sence, ev you?

BARBARA Pretty nearly. Well, has Todger paid you out for poor Jenny's jaw?

BILL Nao e aint.

BARBARA I thought your jacket looked a bit snowy.

BILL Sao it is snaowy. You want to knaow where the snaow cam from, downt you?

BARBARA Yes.

BILL Well, it cam from orf the grahnd in

Pawkinses Corner in Kennintahn. It got rabbed orf be maw shaoulders: see?

BARBARA   Pity you didnt rub some off with your knees, Bill! That would have done you a lot of good.

BILL (*with sour mirthless humor*)   Aw was sivin anather menn's knees at the tawm. E was kneelin on moy ed, e was.

JENNY   Who was kneeling on your head?

BILL   Todger was. E was pryin for me: pryin camfortable wiv me as a cawpet. Sow was Mog. Sao was the aol bloomin meetin. Mog she sez "Ow Lawd brike is stabborn sperrit; bat downt urt is dear art." Thet was wot she said. "Downt urt is dear art"! An er blowk—thirteen stun four!—kneelin wiv all is wight on me. Fanny, aint it?

JENNY   Oh no. We're so sorry, Mr Walker.

BARBARA (*enjoying it frankly*)   Nonsense! of course it's funny. Served you right, Bill! You must have done something to him first.

BILL (*doggedly*)   Aw did wot Aw said Aw'd do. Aw spit in is eye. E looks ap at the skoy and sez, "Ow that Aw should be fahnd worthy to be spit upon for the gospel's sike!" e sez; an Mog sez "Glaory Allelloolier!"; an then e called me Braddher, and dahned me as if Aw was a kid and e was me mather worshin me a Setterda nawt. Aw ednt jast nao shaow wiv im at all. Arf the street pryed; and the tather arf larfed fit to split theirselves. (*to* BARBARA) There! are you settisfawd nah?

BARBARA (*her eyes dancing*)   Wish I'd been there, Bill.

BILL   Yus: youd a got in a hextra bit o talk on me, wouldnt you?

JENNY   I'm so sorry, Mr Walker.

BILL (*fiercely*)   Downt you gow being sorry for me: youve no call. Listen eah. Aw browk your jawr.

JENNY   No, it didnt hurt me: indeed it didnt, except for a moment. It was only that I was frightened.

BILL   Aw downt want to be forgive be you, or be ennybody. Wot Aw did Aw'll py for. Aw trawd to gat me aown jawr browk to settisfaw you—

JENNY (*distressed*)   Oh no—

BILL (*impatiently*)   Tell y' Aw did: cawnt you listen to wots bein taold you? All Aw got be it was bein mide a sawt of in the pablic street for me pines. Well, if Aw cawnt settisfaw you one wy, Aw ken anather. Listen eah! Aw ed two quid sived agen the frost; an Awve a pahnd of it left. A mite o mawn last week ed words with the judy e's gowing to merry. E give er wot-for; an e's bin fawnd fifteen bob. E ed a rawt to itt er cause they was gowin to

be merrid; but Aw ednt nao rawt to itt you; sao put anather fawv bob on an call it a pahnd's worth. (*He produces a sovereign*) Eahs the manney. Tike it; and lets ev no more o your forgivin an prying and your Mijor jawrin me. Let wot Aw dan be dan and pide for; and let there be a end of it.

JENNY   Oh, I couldnt take it, Mr. Walker. But if you would give a shilling or two to poor Rummy Mitchens! you really did hurt her; and she's old.

BILL (*contemptuously*)   Not lawkly. Aw'd give her anather as soon as look at er. Let her ev the lawr o me as she threatened! She aint forgiven me: not mach. Wot Aw dan to er is not on me mawnd—wot she (*indicating* BARBARA) mawt call on me conscience—no more than stickin a pig. It's this Christian gime o yours that Aw wownt ev plyed agen me: this bloomin forgivin an neggin an jawrin that mikes a menn thet sore that iz lawf's a burdn to im. Aw wownt ev it, Aw tell you; sao tike your manney and stop thraowin your silly be-shed fice hap agen me.

JENNY   Major: may I take a little of it for the Army?

BARBARA   No: the Army is not to be bought. We want your soul, Bill; and we'll take nothing less.

BILL (*bitterly*)   Aw knaow. Me an maw few shillins is not good enaff for you. Youre a earl's grendorter, you are. Nathink less than a andered pahnd for you.

UNDERSHAFT   Come, Barbara! you could do a great deal of good with a hundred pounds. If you will set this gentleman's mind at ease by taking his pound, I will give the other ninety-nine.

(BILL, *dazed by such opulence, instinctively touches his cap*)

BARBARA   Oh, youre too extravagant, papa. Bill offers twenty pieces of silver. All you need offer is the other ten. That will make the standard price to buy anybody who's for sale. I'm not; and the Army's not. (*to* BILL) Youll never have another quiet moment, Bill, until you come round to us. You cant stand out against your salvation.

BILL (*sullenly*)   Aw cawnt stend aht agen music awl wrastlers and awtful tangued women. Awve offered to py. Aw can do no more. Tike it or leave it. There it is (*He throws the sovereign on the drum, and sits down on the horse-trough. The coin fascinates* SNOBBY PRICE, *who takes an early opportunity of dropping his cap on it*)

(MRS BAINES *comes from the shelter. She is*

dressed as a Salvation Army Commissioner. She is an earnest looking woman of about 40, with a caressing, urgent voice, and an appealing manner)

BARBARA   This is my father, Mrs Baines. (UNDERSHAFT *comes from the table, taking his hat off with marked civility*) Try what you can do with him. He wont listen to me, because he remembers what a fool I was when I was a baby. (*She leaves them together and chats with* JENNY)

MRS BAINES   Have you been shewn over the shelter, Mr. Undershaft? You know the work we're doing, of course.

UNDERSHAFT   (*very civilly*)   The whole nation knows it, Mrs Baines.

MRS BAINES   No, sir: the whole nation does not know it, or we should not be crippled as we are for want of money to carry our work through the length and breadth of the land. Let me tell you that there would have been rioting this winter in London but for us.

UNDERSHAFT   You really think so?

MRS BAINES   I know it. I remember 1886, when you rich gentlemen hardened your hearts against the cry of the poor. They broke the windows of your clubs in Pall Mall.

UNDERSHAFT   (*gleaming with approval of their method*)   And the Mansion House Fund went up next day from thirty thousand pounds to seventy-nine thousand! I remember quite well.

MRS BAINES   Well, wont you help me to get at the people? They wont break windows then. Come here, Price. Let me shew you to this gentleman. (PRICE *comes to be inspected*) Do you remember the window breaking?

PRICE   My ole father thought it was the revolution, maam.

MRS BAINES   Would you break windows now?

PRICE   Oh no, maam. The windows of eaven av bin opened to me. I know now that the rich man is a sinner like myself.

RUMMY   (*appearing above at the loft door*) Snobby Price!

SNOBBY   Wot is it?

RUMMY   Your mother's askin for you at the other gate in Cripps's Lane. She's heard about your confession. (PRICE *turns pale*)

MRS BAINES   Go, Mr Price; and pray with her.

JENNY   You can go through the shelter, Snobby.

PRICE   (*to* MRS BAINES)   I couldn't face her now, maam, with all the weight of my sins fresh on me. Tell her she'll find her son at ome, waitin for her in prayer. (*He skulks off through the gate, incidentally stealing the sovereign on his way out by picking up his cap from the drum*)

MRS BAINES   (*with swimming eyes*)   You see how we take the anger and the bitterness against you out of their hearts, Mr Undershaft.

UNDERSHAFT   It is certainly most convenient and gratifying to all large employers of labor, Mrs Baines.

MRS BAINES   Barbara: Jenny: I have good news: most wonderful news. (JENNY *runs to her*) My prayers have been answered. I told you they would, Jenny, didnt I?

JENNY   Yes, yes.

BARBARA   (*moving nearer to the drum*) Have we got money enough to keep the shelter open?

MRS BAINES   I hope we shall have enough to keep all the shelters open. Lord Saxmundham has promised us five thousand pounds—

BARBARA   Hooray!

JENNY   Glory!

MRS BAINES   —if—

BARBARA   "If!" If what?

MRS BAINES   —if five other gentlemen will give a thousand each to make it up to ten thousand.

BARBARA   Who is Lord Saxmundham? I never heard of him.

UNDERSHAFT   (*who has pricked up his ears at the peer's name, and is now watching* BARBARA *curiously*)   A new creation, my dear. You have heard of Sir Horace Bodger?

BARBARA   Bodger! Do you mean the distiller? Bodger's whisky!

UNDERSHAFT   That is the man. He is one of the greatest of our public benefactors. He restored the cathedral at Hakington. They made him a baronet for that. He gave half a million to the funds of his party: they made him a baron for that.

SHIRLEY   What will they give him for the five thousand?

UNDERSHAFT   There is nothing left to give him. So the five thousand, I should think, is to save his soul.

MRS BAINES   Heaven grant it may! Oh Mr Undershaft, you have some very rich friends. Cant you help us towards the other five thousand? We are going to hold a great meeting this afternoon at the Assembly Hall in the Mile End Road. If I could only announce that one gentleman had come forward to support Lord Saxmundham, others would follow. Dont you know somebody? couldnt you? wouldnt you? (*her eyes fill with tears*) oh, think of those poor people, Mr Undershaft: think of how much it means to them, and how little to a great man like you.

UNDERSHAFT (*sardonically gallant*) Mrs Baines: you are irresistible. I cant disappoint you; and I cant deny myself the satisfaction of making Bodger pay up. You shall have your five thousand pounds.

MRS BAINES Thank God!

UNDERSHAFT You dont thank me?

MRS BAINES Oh sir, dont try to be cynical: dont be ashamed of being a good man. The Lord will bless you abundantly; and our prayers will be like a strong fortification round you all the days of your life. (*with a touch of caution*) You will let me have the cheque to shew at the meeting, wont you? Jenny: go in and fetch a pen and ink. (JENNY *runs to the shelter door*)

UNDERSHAFT Do not disturb Miss Hill: I have a fountain pen (JENNY *halts. He sits at the table and writes the cheque.* CUSINS *rises to make room for him. They all watch him silently*)—

BILL (*cynically, aside to* BARBARA, *his voice and accent horribly debased*) Wot prawce selvytion nah?

BARBARA Stop. (UNDERSHAFT *stops writing: they all turn to her in surprise*) Mrs Baines: are you really going to take this money?

MRS BAINES (*astonished*) Why not, dear?

BARBARA Why not! Do you know what my father is? Have you forgotten that Lord Saxmundham is Bodger the whisky man? Do you remember how we implored the County Council to stop him from writing Bodger's Whisky in letters of fire against the sky; so that the poor drink-ruined creatures on the Embankment could not wake up from their snatches of sleep without being reminded of their deadly thirst by that wicked sky sign? Do you know that the worst thing I have had to fight here is not the devil, but Bodger, Bodger, Bodger, with his whisky, his distilleries, and his tied houses? Are you going to make our shelter another tied house for him, and ask me to keep it?

BILL Rotten dranken whisky it is too.

MRS BAINES Dear Barbara: Lord Saxmundham has a soul to be saved like any of us. If heaven has found the way to make a good use of his money, are we to set ourselves up against the answer to our prayers?

BARBARA I know he has a soul to be saved. Let him come down here; and I'll do my best to help him to his salvation. But he wants to send his cheque down to buy us, and go on being as wicked as ever.

UNDERSHAFT (*with a reasonableness which* CUSINS *alone perceives to be ironical*) My dear Barbara: alcohol is a very necessary article. It heals the sick—

BARBARA It does nothing of the sort.

UNDERSHAFT Well, it assists the doctor: that is perhaps a less questionable way of putting it. It makes life bearable to millions of people who could not endure their existence if they were quite sober. It enables Parliament to do things at eleven at night that no sane person would do at eleven in the morning. Is it Bodger's fault that this inestimable gift is deplorably abused by less than one per cent of the poor? (*He turns again to the table; signs the cheque; and crosses it*)

MRS BAINES Barbara: will there be less drinking or more if all those poor souls we are saving come tomorrow and find the doors of our shelters shut in their faces? Lord Saxmundham gives us the money to stop drinking—to take his own business from him.

CUSINS (*impishly*) Pure self-sacrifice on Bodger's part, clearly! Bless dear Bodger! (BARBARA *almost breaks down as* ADOLPHUS, *too, fails her*)

UNDERSHAFT (*tearing out the cheque and pocketing the book as he rises and goes past* CUSINS *to* MRS BAINES) I also, Mrs Baines, may claim a little disinterestedness. Think of my business! think of the widows and orphans! the men and lads torn to pieces with shrapnel and poisoned with lyddite! (MRS BAINES *shrinks; but he goes on remorselessly*) the oceans of blood, not one drop of which is shed in a really just cause! the ravaged crops! the peaceful peasants forced, women and men, to till their fields under the fire of opposing armies on pain of starvation! the bad blood of the fierce little cowards at home who egg on others to fight for the gratification of their national vanity! All this makes money for me: I am never richer, never busier than when the papers are full of it. Well, it is your work to preach peace on earth and good will to men. (MRS BAINES's *face lights up again*) Every convert you make is a vote against war. (*Her lips move in prayer*) Yet I give you this money to help you to hasten my own commercial ruin. (*He gives her the cheque*)

CUSINS (*mounting the form in an ecstasy of mischief*) The millennium will be inaugurated by the unselfishness of Undershaft and Bodger. Oh be joyful! (*He takes the drumsticks from his pocket and flourishes them*)

MRS BAINES (*taking the cheque*) The longer I live the more proof I see that there is an Infinite Goodness that turns everything to the work of salvation sooner or later. Who would have thought that any good could have come out of war and drink? And yet their profits are brought today to the feet of salvation to do its blessed work. (*She is affected to tears*)

JENNY (*running to* MRS BAINES *and throwing her arms round her*) Oh dear! how blessed, how glorious it all is!

CUSINS (*in a convulsion of irony*) Let us seize this unspeakable moment. Let us march to the great meeting at once. Excuse me just an instant. (*He rushes into the shelter.* JENNY *takes her tambourine from the drum head*)

MRS BAINES Mr Undershaft: have you ever seen a thousand people fall on their knees with one impulse and pray? Come with us to the meeting. Barbara shall tell them that the Army is saved, and saved through you.

CUSINS (*returning impetuously from the shelter with a flag and a trombone, and coming between* MRS BAINES *and* UNDERSHAFT) You shall carry the flag down the first street, Mrs Baines. (*He gives her the flag*) Mr Undershaft is a gifted trombonist: he shall intone an Olympian diapason to the West Ham Salvation March. (*aside to* UNDERSHAFT, *as he forces the trombone on him*) Blow, Machiavelli, blow.

UNDERSHAFT (*aside to him, as he takes the trombone*) The trumpet in Zion! (CUSINS *rushes to the drum, which he takes up and puts on.* UNDERSHAFT *continues, aloud*) I will do my best. I could vamp a bass if I knew the tune.

CUSINS It is a wedding chorus from one of Donizetti's operas; but we have converted it. We convert everything to good here, including Bodger. You remember the chorus. "For thee immense rejoicing—immenso giubilo— immenso giubilo." (*with drum obligato*) Rum tum ti tum tum, tum tum ti ta—

BARBARA Dolly: you are breaking my heart.

CUSINS What is a broken heart more or less here? Dionysos Undershaft has descended. I am possessed.

MRS BAINES Come, Barbara: I must have my dear Major to carry the flag with me.

JENNY Yes, yes, Major darling.

(CUSINS *snatches the tambourine out of* JENNY'S *hand and mutely offers it to* BARBARA)

BARBARA (*coming forward a little as she puts the offer behind her with a shudder, whilst* CUSINS *recklessly tosses the tambourine back to* JENNY *and goes to the gate*) I cant come.

JENNY Not come!

MRS BAINES (*with tears in her eyes*) Barbara: do you think I am wrong to take the money?

BARBARA (*impulsively going to her and kissing her*) No, no: God help you, dear, you must: you are saving the Army. Go; and may you have a great meeting!

JENNY But arnt you coming?

BARBARA No. (*She begins taking off the silver S brooch from her collar*)

MRS BAINES Barbara what are you doing?

JENNY Why are you taking your badge off? You cant be going to leave us, Major.

BARBARA (*quietly*) Father: come here.

UNDERSHAFT (*coming to her*) My dear! (*Seeing that she is going to pin the badge on his collar, he retreats to the penthouse in some alarm*)

BARBARA (*following him*) Dont be frightened. (*She pins the badge and steps back towards the table, showing him to the others*) There! it's not much for £5000, is it?

MRS BAINES Barbara: if you wont come and pray with us, promise me you will pray for us.

BARBARA I cant pray now. Perhaps I shall never pray again.

MRS BAINES Barbara!

JENNY Major!

BARBARA (*almost delirious*) I cant bear any more. Quick march!

CUSINS (*calling to the procession in the street outside*) Off we go. Play up, there! Immenso giubilo. (*He gives the time with his drum; and the band strikes up the march, which rapidly becomes more distant as the procession moves briskly away*)

MRS BAINES I must go, dear. Youre overworked: you will be all right tomorrow. We'll never lose you. Now Jenny: step out with the old flag. Blood and Fire! (*She marches out through the gate with her flag*)

JENNY Glory Hallelujah! (*flourishing her tambourine and marching*)—

UNDERSHAFT (*to* CUSINS, *as he marches out past him easing the slide of his trombone*) "My ducats and my daughter"!

CUSINS (*following him out*) Money and gunpowder!

BARBARA Drunkenness and Murder! My God: why hast thou forsaken me?

(*She sinks on the form with her face buried in her hands. The march passes away into silence.* BILL WALKER *steals across to her*)

BILL (*taunting*) Wot prawce selvytion nah?

SHIRLEY Dont you hit her when she's down.

BILL She itt me wen aw wiz dahn. Waw shouldnt Aw git a bit o me aown beck?

BARBARA (*raising her head*) I didnt take your money, Bill. (*She crosses the yard to the gate and turns her back on the two men to hide her face from them*)

BILL (*sneering after her*) Naow, it warnt enaff for you. (*Turning to the drum, he misses the money*) Ellow! If you aint took it sammun else ez. Weres it gorn? Bly me if Jenny Ill didnt taike it arter all!

RUMMY (*screaming at him from the loft*) You lie, you dirty blackguard! Snobby Price pinched it off the drum when he took up his cap. I was up here all the time an see im do it.

BILL Wot! Stowl maw manney! Waw didnt you call thief on him, you silly aold macker you?

RUMMY To serve you aht for ittin me acrost the fice. It's cost y'pahnd, that az. (*raising a pæan of squalid triumph*) I done you. I'm even with you. Uve ad it aht o y—(BILL *snatches up* SHIRLEY's *mug and hurls it at her. She slams the loft door and vanishes. The mug smashes against the door and falls in fragments*)

BILL (*beginning to chuckle*) Tell us, aol menn, wot o'clock this mawnin was it wen im as they call Snobby Prawce was sived?

BARBARA (*turning to him more composedly, and with unspoiled sweetness*) About half past twelve, Bill. And he pinched your pound at a quarter to two. *I* know. Well, you cant afford to lose it. I'll send it to you.

BILL (*his voice and accent suddenly improving*) Not if Aw wiz to stawve for it. Aw aint to be bought.

SHIRLEY Aint you? Youd sell yourself to the devil for a pint o beer; only there ain no devil to make the offer.

BILL (*unashamed*) Sao Aw would, mite, and often ev, cheerful. But she cawnt baw me. (*approaching* BARBARA) You wanted maw saoul, did you? Well, you aint got it.

BARBARA I nearly got it, Bill. But weve sold it back to you for ten thousand pounds.

SHIRLEY And dear at the money!

BARBARA No, Peter: it was worth more than money.

BILL (*salvationproof*) It's nao good: you cawnt get rahnd me nah. Aw downt blieve in it; and Awve seen tody that Aw was rawt. (*going*) Sao long, aol soupkitchener! Ta, ta, Mijor Earl's Grendorter! (*turning at the gate*) Wot prawce selvytion nah? Snobby Prawce! Ha! ha!

BARBARA (*offering her hand*) Goodbye, Bill.

BILL (*taken aback, half plucks his cap off; then shoves it on again defiantly*) Git aht. (BARBARA *drops her hand, discouraged. He has a twinge of remorse*) But thets aw rawt, you knaow. Nathink pasnl. Naow mellice. Sao long, Judy. (*He goes*)

BARBARA No malice. So long, Bill.

SHIRLEY (*shaking his head*) You make too much of him, miss, in your innocence.

BARBARA (*going to him*) Peter: I'm like you now. Cleaned out, and lost my job.

SHIRLEY Youve youth and hope. Thats two better than me.

BARBARA I'll get you a job, Peter. Thats hope for you: the youth will have to be enough for me. (*She counts her money*) I have just enough left for two teas at Lockharts, a Rowton doss for you, and my tram and bus home. (*He frowns and rises with offended pride. She takes his arm*) Dont be proud, Peter: it's sharing between friends. And promise me youll talk to me and not let me cry. (*She draws him towards the gate*)

SHIRLEY Well, I'm not accustomed to talk to the like of you—

BARBARA (*urgently*) Yes, yes: you must talk to me. Tell me about Tom Paine's books and Bradlaugh's lectures. Come along.

SHIRLEY Ah, if you would only read Tom Paine in the proper spirit, miss! (*They go out through the gate together*)

ACT THREE

(*Next day after lunch* LADY BRITOMART *is writing in the library in Wilton Crescent.* SARAH *is reading in the armchair near the window.* BARBARA, *in ordinary fashionable dress, pale and brooding, is on the settee.* CHARLES LOMAX *enters. He starts on seeing* BARBARA *fashionably attired and in low spirits*)

LOMAX Youve left off your uniform!

(BARBARA *says nothing; but an expression of pain passes over her face*)

LADY BRITOMART (*warning him in low tones to be careful*) Charles!

LOMAX (*much concerned, coming behind the settee and bending sympathetically over* BARBARA) I'm awfully sorry, Barbara. You know I helped you all I could with the concertina and so forth. (*momentously*) Still, I have never shut my eyes to the fact that there is a certain amount of tosh about the Salvation Army. Now the claims of the Church of England—

LADY BRITOMART Thats enough, Charles.

Speak of something suited to your mental capacity.

LOMAX   But surely the Church of England is suited to all our capacities.

BARBARA (*pressing his hand*) Thank you for your sympathy, Cholly. Now go and spoon with Sarah.

LOMAX (*dragging a chair from the writing table and seating himself affectionately by* SARAH's *side*) How is my ownest today?

SARAH   I wish you wouldnt tell Cholly to do things, Barbara. He always comes straight and does them. Cholly: we're going to the works this afternoon.

LOMAX   What works?

SARAH   The cannon works.

LOMAX   What? your governor's shop!

SARAH   Yes.

LOMAX   Oh I say!

(CUSINS *enters in poor condition. He also starts visibly when he sees* BARBARA *without her uniform*)

BARBARA   I expected you this morning, Dolly. Didnt you guess that?

CUSINS (*sitting down beside her*) I'm sorry. I have only just breakfasted.

SARAH   But weve just finished lunch.

BARBARA   Have you had one of your bad nights?

CUSINS   No: I had rather a good night: in fact, one of the most remarkable nights I have ever passed.

BARBARA   The meeting?

CUSINS   No: after the meeting.

LADY BRITOMART   You should have gone to bed after the meeting. What were you doing?

CUSINS   Drinking.

LADY BRITOMART   Adolphus
SARAH   Dolly!
BARBARA   Dolly!
LOMAX   Oh I say!

LADY BRITOMART   What were you drinking, may I ask?

CUSINS   A most devilish kind of Spanish Burgundy, warranted free from added alcohol: a Temperance burgundy in fact. Its richness in natural alcohol made any addition superfluous.

BARBARA   Are you joking, Dolly?

CUSINS (*patiently*) No. I have been making a night of it with the nominal head of this household: that is all.

LADY BRITOMART   Andrew made you drunk!

CUSINS   No: he only provided the wine. I think it was Dionysos who made me drunk. (*to* BARBARA) I told you I was possessed.

LADY BRITOMART   Youre not sober yet. Go home to bed at once.

CUSINS   I have never before ventured to reproach you, Lady Brit; but how could you marry the Prince of Darkness?

LADY BRITOMART   It was much more excusable to marry him than to get drunk with him. That is a new accomplishment of Andrew's, by the way. He usent to drink.

CUSINS   He doesnt now. He only sat there and completed the wreck of my moral basis, the rout of my convictions, the purchase of my soul. He cares for you, Barbara. That is what makes him so dangerous to me.

BARBARA   That has nothing to do with it, Dolly. There are larger loves and diviner dreams than the fireside ones. You know that, dont you?

CUSINS   Yes: that is our understanding. I know it. I hold to it. Unless he can win me on that holier ground he may amuse me for a while; but he can get no deeper hold, strong as he is.

BARBARA   Keep to that; and the end will be right. Now tell me what happened at the meeting?

CUSINS   It was an amazing meeting. Mrs. Baines almost died of emotion. Jenny Hill simply gibbered with hysteria. The Prince of Darkness played his trombone like a madman: its brazen roarings were like the laughter of the damned. 117 conversions took place then and there. They prayed with the most touching sincerity and gratitude for Bodger, and for the anonymous donor of the £5000. Your father would not let his name be given.

LOMAX   That was rather fine of the old man, you know. Most chaps would have wanted the advertisement.

CUSINS   He said all the charitable institutions would be down on him like kites on a battlefield if he gave his name.

LADY BRITOMART   Thats Andrew all over. He never does a proper thing without giving an improper reason for it.

CUSINS   He convinced me that I have all my life been doing improper things for proper reasons.

LADY BRITOMART   Adolphus: now that Barbara has left the Salvation Army, you had better leave it too. I will not have you playing that drum in the streets.

CUSINS   Your orders are already obeyed, Lady Brit.

BARBARA   Dolly: were you ever really in earnest about it? Would you have joined if you had never seen me?

CUSINS (*disingenuously*) Well—er—well, possibly, as a collector of religions—

LOMAX (*cunningly*) Not as a drummer, though, you know. You are a very clear-headed brainy chap, Dolly; and it must have been apparent to you that there is a certain amount of tosh about—

LADY BRITOMART Charles; if you must drivel, drivel like a grown-up man and not like a schoolboy.

LOMAX (*out of countenance*) Well, drivel is drivel, dont you know, whatever a man's age.

LADY BRITOMART In good society in England, Charles, men drivel at all ages by repeating silly formulas with an air of wisdom. Schoolboys make their own formulas out of slang, like you. When they reach your age, and get political private secretaryships and things of that sort, they drop slang and get their formulas out of the Spectator or The Times. You had better confine yourself to The Times. You will find that there is a certain amount of tosh about The Times; but at least its language is reputable.

LOMAX (*overwhelmed*) You are so awfully strong-minded, Lady Brit—

LADY BRITOMART Rubbish! (MORRISON *comes in*) What is it?

MORRISON If you please, my lady, Mr Undershaft has just drove up to the door.

LADY BRITOMART Well, let him in. (MORRISON *hesitates*) Whats the matter with you?

MORRISON Shall I announce him, my lady; or is he at home here, so to speak, my lady?

LADY BRITOMART Announce him.

MORRISON Thank you, my lady. You wont mind my asking, I hope. The occasion is in a manner of speaking new to me.

LADY BRITOMART Quite right. Go and let him in.

MORRISON Thank you, my lady. (*He withdraws*)

LADY BRITOMART Children: go and get ready. (SARAH *and* BARBARA *go upstairs for their out-of-door wraps*) Charles: go and tell Stephen to come down here in five minutes: you will find him in the drawing room. (CHARLES *goes*) Adolphus: tell them to send round the carriage in about fifteen minutes. (ADOLPHUS *goes*)

MORRISON (*at the door*) Mr Undershaft.

(UNDERSHAFT *comes in*. MORRISON *goes out*)

UNDERSHAFT Alone! How fortunate!

LADY BRITOMART (*rising*) Dont be sentimental, Andrew. Sit down. (*She sits on the settee: he sits beside her, on her left. She comes to the point before he has time to breathe*)

Sarah must have £800 a year until Charles Lomax comes into his property. Barbara will need more, and need it permanently, because Adolphus hasnt any property.

UNDERSHAFT (*resignedly*) Yes, my dear: I will see to it. Anything else? for yourself, for instance?

LADY BRITOMART I want to talk to you about Stephen.

UNDERSHAFT (*rather wearily*) Dont, my dear. Stephen doesnt interest me.

LADY BRITOMART He does interest me. He is our son.

UNDERSHAFT Do you really think so? He has induced us to bring him into the world; but he chose his parents very incongruously, I think. I see nothing of myself in him, and less of you.

LADY BRITOMART Andrew: Stephen is an excellent son, and a most steady, capable, high-minded young man. You are simply trying to find an excuse for disinheriting him.

UNDERSHAFT My dear Biddy: the Undershaft tradition disinherits him. It would be dishonest of me to leave the cannon foundry to my son.

LADY BRITOMART It would be most unnatural and improper of you to leave it to anyone else, Andrew. Do you suppose this wicked and immoral tradition can be kept up for ever? Do you pretend that Stephen could not carry on the foundry just as well as all the other sons of the big business houses?

UNDERSHAFT Yes: he could learn the office routine without understanding the business, like all the other sons; and the firm would go on by its own momentum until the real Undershaft—probably an Italian or a German —would invent a new method and cut him out.

LADY BRITOMART There is nothing that any Italian or German could do that Stephen could not do. And Stephen at least has breeding.

UNDERSHAFT The son of a foundling! Nonsense!

LADY BRITOMART My son, Andrew! And even you may have good blood in your veins for all you know.

UNDERSHAFT True. Probably I have. That is another argument in favour of a foundling.

LADY BRITOMART Andrew: dont be aggravating. And dont be wicked. At present you are both.

UNDERSHAFT This conversation is part of the Undershaft tradition, Biddy. Every Undershaft's wife has treated him to it ever since the house was founded. It is mere waste of breath.

If the tradition be ever broken it will be for an abler man than Stephen.

LADY BRITOMART (*pouting*)   Then go away.

UNDERSHAFT (*deprecatory*)   Go away!

LADY BRITOMART   Yes: Go away. If you will do nothing for Stephen, you are not wanted here. Go to your foundling, whoever he is; and look after him.

UNDERSHAFT   The fact is, Biddy—

LADY BRITOMART   Don't call me Biddy. I dont call you Andy.

UNDERSHAFT   I will not call my wife Britomart: it is not good sense. Seriously, my love, the Undershaft tradition has landed me in a difficulty. I am getting on in years; and my partner Lazarus has at last made a stand and insisted that the succession must be settled one way or the other; and of course he is quite right. You see, I havent found a fit successor yet.

LADY BRITOMART (*obstinately*)   There is Stephen.

UNDERSHAFT   Thats just it: all the foundlings I can find are exactly like Stephen.

LADY BRITOMART   Andrew!!

UNDERSHAFT   I want a man with no relations and no schooling: that is, a man who would be out of the running altogether if he were not a strong man. And I cant find him. Every blessed foundling nowadays is snapped up in his infancy by Barnardo homes, or School Board officers, or Boards of Guardians; and if he shows the least ability he is fastened on by schoolmasters; trained to win scholarships like a racehorse; crammed with secondhand ideas; drilled and disciplined in docility and what they call good taste; and lamed for life so that he is fit for nothing but teaching. If you want to keep the foundry in the family, you had better find an eligible foundling and marry him to Barbara.

LADY BRITOMART   Ah! Barbara! Your pet! You would sacrifice Stephen to Barbara.

UNDERSHAFT   Cheerfully. And you, my dear, would boil Barbara to make soup for Stephen.

LADY BRITOMART   Andrew: this is not a question of our likings and dislikings: it is a question of duty. It is our duty to make Stephen your successor.

UNDERSHAFT   Just as much as it is your duty to submit to your husband. Come, Biddy! these tricks of the governing class are of no use with me. I am one of the governing class myself; and it is waste of time giving tracts to a missionary. I have the power in this matter; and I am not to be humbugged into using it for your purposes.

LADY BRITOMART   Andrew: you can talk my head off; but you cant change wrong into right. And your tie is all on one side. Put it straight.

UNDERSHAFT (*disconcerted*)   It wont stay unless it's pinned (*He fumbles at it with childish grimaces*)—

(*Stephen comes in*)

STEPHEN (*at the door*)   I beg your pardon. (*about to retire*)

LADY BRITOMART   No: come in, Stephen. (STEPHEN *comes forward to his mother's writing table*)

UNDERSHAFT (*not very cordially*)   Good afternoon.

STEPHEN (*coldly*)   Good afternoon.

UNDERSHAFT (*to* LADY BRITOMART)   He knows all about the tradition, I suppose?

LADY BRITOMART   Yes. (*to* STEPHEN) It is what I told you last night, Stephen.

UNDERSHAFT (*sulkily*)   I understand you want to come into the cannon business.

STEPHEN   I go into trade! Certainly not.

UNDERSHAFT (*opening his eyes, greatly eased in mind and manner*)   Oh, in that case—

LADY BRITOMART   Cannons are not trade, Stephen. They are enterprise.

STEPHEN   I have no intention of becoming a man of business in any sense. I have no capacity for business and no taste for it. I intend to devote myself to politics.

UNDERSHAFT (*rising*)   My dear boy: this is an immense relief to me. And I trust it may prove an equally good thing for the country. I was afraid you would consider yourself disparaged and slighted. (*He moves towards* STEPHEN *as if to shake hands with him*)

LADY BRITOMART (*rising and interposing*)   Stephen: I cannot allow you to throw away an enormous property like this.

STEPHEN (*stiffly*)   Mother: there must be an end of treating me as a child, if you please. (LADY BRITOMART *recoils, deeply wounded by his tone*) Until last night I did not take your attitude seriously, because I did not think you meant it seriously. But I find now that you left me in the dark as to matters which you should have explained to me years ago. I am extremely hurt and offended. Any further discussion of my intentions had better take place with my father, as between one man and another.

LADY BRITOMART   Stephen! (*She sits down again, her eyes filling with tears*)

UNDERSHAFT (*with grave compassion*)   You see, my dear, it is only the big men who can be treated as children.

STEPHEN   I am sorry, mother, that you have forced me—

UNDERSHAFT (*stopping him*)   Yes, yes, yes, yes: thats all right, Stephen. She wont interfere with you any more: your independence is achieved: you have won your latchkey. Dont rub it in; and above all, dont apologize. (*He resumes his seat*) Now what about your future, as between one man and another—I beg your pardon, Biddy: as between two men and a woman.

LADY BRITOMART (*who has pulled herself together strongly*)   I quite understand, Stephen. By all means go your own way if you feel strong enough. (STEPHEN *sits down magisterially in the chair at the writing table with an air of affirming his majority*)

UNDERSHAFT   It is settled that you do not ask for the succession to the cannon business.

STEPHEN   I hope it is settled that I repudiate the cannon business.

UNDERSHAFT   Come, come! dont be so devilishly sulky: it's boyish. Freedom should be generous. Besides, I owe you a fair start in life in exchange for disinheriting you. You cant become prime minister all at once. Havent you a turn for something? What about literature, art, and so forth?

STEPHEN   I have nothing of the artist about me, either in faculty or character, thank Heaven!

UNDERSHAFT   A philosopher, perhaps? Eh?

STEPHEN   I make no such ridiculous pretension.

UNDERSHAFT   Just so. Well, there is the army, the navy, the Church, the Bar. The Bar requires some ability. What about the Bar?

STEPHEN   I have not studied law. And I am afraid I have not the necessary push—I believe that is the name barristers give to their vulgarity—for success in pleading.

UNDERSHAFT   Rather a difficult case, Stephen. Hardly anything left but the stage, is there? (STEPHEN *makes an impatient movement*) Well, come! is there anything you know or care for?

STEPHEN (*rising and looking at him steadily*)   I know the difference between right and wrong.

UNDERSHAFT (*hugely tickled*)   You dont say so! What! no capacity for business, no knowledge of law, no sympathy with art, no pretension to philosophy; only a simple knowledge of the secret that has puzzled all the philosophers, baffled all the lawyers, muddled all the men of business, and ruined most of the artists: the secret of right and wrong. Why, man, youre a genius, a master of masters, a god! At twenty-four, too!

STEPHEN (*keeping his temper with difficulty*)   You are pleased to be facetious. I pretend to nothing more than any honorable English gentleman claims as his birthright. (*He sits down angrily*)

UNDERSHAFT   Oh, thats everybody's birthright. Look at poor little Jenny Hill, the Salvation lassie! she would think you were laughing at her if you asked her to stand up in the street and teach grammar or geography or mathematics or even drawing room dancing; but it never occurs to her to doubt that she can teach morals and religion. You are all alike, you respectable people. You cant tell me the bursting strain of a ten-inch gun, which is a very simple matter; but you all think you can tell me the bursting strain of a man under temptation. You darent handle high explosives; but youre all ready to handle honesty and truth and justice and the whole duty of man, and kill one another at that game. What a country! What a world!

LADY BRITOMART (*uneasily*)   What do you think he had better do, Andrew?

UNDERSHAFT   Oh, just what he wants to do. He knows nothing and he thinks he knows everything. That points clearly to a political career. Get him a private secretaryship to someone who can get him an Under Secretaryship; and then leave him alone. He will find his natural and proper place in the end on the Treasury Bench.

STEPHEN (*springing up again*)   I am sorry, sir, that you force me to forget the respect due to you as my father. I am an Englishman and I will not hear the Government of my country insulted. (*He thrusts his hands in his pockets, and walks angrily across to the window*)

UNDERSHAFT (*with a touch of brutality*)   The government of your country! *I* am the government of your country: I, and Lazarus. Do you suppose that you and half a dozen amateurs like you, sitting in a row in that foolish gabble shop, can govern Undershaft and Lazarus? No, my friend: you will do what pays us. You will make war when it suits us, and keep peace when it doesnt. You will find out that trade requires certain measures when we have decided on those measures. When I want anything to keep my dividends up, you will discover that my want is a national need. When other people want something to keep my dividends down, you will call out the police and military. And in return you shall have the support and applause of my newspapers, and the delight of imagining that you are a great statesman. Government of your country! Be off with you, my boy, and play with your caucuses and leading articles and historic parties and great leaders and burning questions and the rest of your toys. *I* am going back to my counting-house to pay the piper and call the tune.

STEPHEN (*actually smiling, and putting his hand on his father's shoulder with indulgent patronage*) Really, my dear father, it is impossible to be angry with you. You dont know how absurd all this sounds to me. You are very properly proud of having been industrious enough to make money; and it is greatly to your credit that you have made so much of it. But it has kept you in circles where you are valued for your money and deferred to for it, instead of in the doubtless very old-fashioned and behind-the-times public school and university where I formed my habits of mind. It is natural for you to think that money governs England; but you must allow me to think I know better.

UNDERSHAFT And what does govern England, pray?

STEPHEN Character, father, character.

UNDERSHAFT Whose character? Yours or mine?

STEPHEN Neither yours nor mine, father, but the best elements in the English national character.

UNDERSHAFT Stephen: I've found your profession for you. Youre a born journalist. I'll start you with a high-toned weekly review. There!

(*Before* STEPHEN *can reply* SARAH, BARBARA, LOMAX, *and* CUSINS *come in ready for walking.* BARBARA *crosses the room to the window and looks out.* CUSINS *drifts amiably to the armchair.* LOMAX *remains near the door, whilst* SARAH *comes to her mother.*

STEPHEN *goes to the smaller writing table and busies himself with his letters*)

SARAH Go and get ready, mamma: the carriage is waiting.

(LADY BRITOMART *leaves the room*)

UNDERSHAFT (*to* SARAH) Good day, my dear. Good afternoon, Mr Lomax.

LOMAX (*vaguely*) Ahdedoo.

UNDERSHAFT (*to* CUSINS) Quite well after last night, Euripides, eh?

CUSINS As well as can be expected.

UNDERSHAFT Thats right. (*to* BARBARA) So you are coming to see my death and devastation factory, Barbara?

BARBARA (*at the window*) You came yesterday to see my salvation factory. I promised you a return visit.

LOMAX (*coming forward between* SARAH *and* UNDERSHAFT) Youll find it awfully interesting. Ive been through the Woolwich Arsenal; and it gives you a ripping feeling of security, you know, to think of the lot of beggars we could kill if it came to fighting. (*to* UNDERSHAFT, *with sudden solemnity*) Still, it must be rather an awful reflection for you, from the religious point of view as it were. Youre getting on, you know, and all that.

SARAH You dont mind Cholly's imbecility, papa, do you?

LOMAX (*much taken aback*) Oh I say!

UNDERSHAFT Mr Lomax looks at the matter in a very proper spirit, my dear.

LOMAX Just so. Thats all I meant, I assure you.

SARAH Are you coming, Stephen?

STEPHEN Well, I am rather busy—er— (*magnanimously*) Oh well, yes: I'll come. That is, if there is room for me.

UNDERSHAFT I can take two with me in a little motor I am experimenting with for field use. You wont mind its being rather unfashionable. It's not painted yet; but it's bullet proof.

LOMAX (*appalled at the prospect of confronting* WILTON CRESCENT *in an unpainted motor*) Oh I say!

SARAH The carriage for me, thank you. Barbara doesnt mind what she's seen in.

LOMAX I say, Dolly, old chap: do you really mind the car being a guy? Because of course if you do I'll go in it. Still—

CUSINS I prefer it.

LOMAX Thanks awfully, old man. Come, my ownest. (*He hurries out to secure his seat in the carriage.* SARAH *follows him*)

CUSINS (*moodily walking across to* LADY BRITOMART'S *writing table*) Why are we two coming to this Works Department of Hell? that is what I ask myself.

BARBARA I have always thought of it as a sort of pit where lost creatures with blackened faces stirred up smoky fires and were driven and tormented by my father? Is it like that, dad?

UNDERSHAFT (*scandalized*) My dear! It is a spotlessly clean and beautiful hillside town.

CUSINS With a Methodist chapel? Oh do say theres a Methodist chapel.

UNDERSHAFT There are two: a Primitive one and a sophisticated one. There is even an Ethical Society; but it is not much patronized, as my men are all strongly religious. In the High Explosives Sheds they object to the presence of Agnostics as unsafe.

CUSINS And yet they dont object to you!

BARBARA Do they obey all your orders?

UNDERSHAFT I never give them any orders.

When I speak to one of them it is "Well, Jones, is the baby doing well? and has Mrs Jones made a good recovery?" "Nicely, thank you, sir." And thats all.

CUSINS But Jones has to be kept in order. How do you maintain discipline among your men?

UNDERSHAFT I dont. They do. You see, the one thing Jones wont stand is any rebellion from the man under him, or any assertion of social equality between the wife of the man with 4 shillings a week less than himself, and Mrs Jones! Of course they all rebel against me, theoretically. Practically, every man of them keeps the man just below him in his place. I never meddle with them. I never bully them. I dont even bully Lazarus. I say that certain things are to be done; but I dont order anybody to do them. I dont say, mind you, that there is no ordering about and snubbing and even bullying. The men snub the boys and order them about; the carmen snub the sweepers; the artisans snub the unskilled laborers; the foremen drive and bully both the laborers and artisans; the assistant engineers find fault with the foremen; the chief engineers drop on the assistants; the departmental managers worry the chiefs; and the clerks have tall hats and hymnbooks and keep up the social tone by refusing to associate on equal terms with anybody. The result is a colossal profit, which comes to me.

CUSINS (*revolted*) You really are a—well, what I was saying yesterday.

BARBARA What was he saying yesterday?

UNDERSHAFT Never mind, my dear. He thinks I have made you unhappy. Have I?

BARBARA Do you think I can be happy in this vulgar silly dress? I! who have worn the uniform. Do you understand what you have done to me? Yesterday I had a man's soul in my hand. I set him in the way of life with his face to salvation. But when we took your money he turned back to drunkenness and derision. (*with intense conviction*) I will never forgive you that. If I had a child, and you destroyed its body with your explosives—if you murdered Dolly with your horrible guns— I could forgive you if my forgiveness would open the gates of heaven to you. But to take a human soul from me, and turn it into the soul of a wolf! that is worse than any murder.

UNDERSHAFT Does my daughter despair so easily? Can you strike a man to the heart and leave no mark on him?

BARBARA (*her face lighting up*) Oh, you are right: he can never be lost now: where was my faith?

CUSINS Oh, clever clever devil!

BARBARA You may be a devil; but God speaks through you sometimes. (*She takes her father's hands and kisses them*) You have given me back my happiness: I feel it deep down now, though my spirit is troubled.

UNDERSHAFT You have learnt something. That always feels at first as if you had lost something.

BARBARA Well, take me to the factory of death; and let me learn something more. There must be some truth or other behind all this frightful irony. Come, Dolly. (*She goes out*)

CUSINS My guardian angel! (*to* UNDERSHAFT) Avaunt! (*He follows* BARBARA)

STEPHEN (*quietly, at the writing table*) You must not mind Cusins, father. He is a very amiable good fellow; but he is a Greek scholar and naturally a little eccentric.

UNDERSHAFT Ah, quite so. Thank you, Stephen. Thank you. (*He goes out*)

(STEPHEN *smiles patronizingly; buttons his coat responsibly; and crosses the room to the door.* LADY BRITOMART, *dressed for out-of-doors, opens it before he reaches it. She looks round for others; looks at* STEPHEN; *and turns to go without a word*)

STEPHEN (*embarrassed*) Mother—

LADY BRITOMART Dont be apologetic, Stephen. And dont forget that you have outgrown your mother. (*She goes out*)

(*Perivale St Andrews lies between two Middlesex hills, half climbing the northern one. It is an almost smokeless town of white walls, roofs of narrow green slates or red tiles, tall trees, domes, campaniles, and slender chimney shafts, beautifully situated and beautiful in itself. The best view of it is obtained from the crest of a slope about half a mile to the east, where the high explosives are dealt with. The foundry lies hidden in the depths between, the tops of its chimneys sprouting like huge skittles into the middle distance. Across the crest runs an emplacement of concrete, with a firestep, and a parapet which suggests a fortification, because there is a huge cannon of the obsolete Woolwich Infant pattern peering across it at the town. The cannon is mounted on an experimental gun carriage: possibly the original model of the Undershaft disappearing rampart gun alluded to by* STEPHEN. *The firestep, being a convenient place to sit, is furnished here and there with straw disc cushions; and at one place there is the additional luxury of a fur rug.*

BARBARA *is standing on the firestep, looking over the parapet towards the town. On her right is the cannon; on her left the end of a shed raised on piles, with a ladder of three or four steps up to the door, which opens outwards and has a little wooden landing at the threshold, with a fire bucket in the corner of the landing. Several dummy soldiers more or less mutilated, with straw protruding from their gashes, have been shoved out of the way under the landing. A few others are nearly upright against the shed; and one has fallen forward and lies, like a grotesque corpse, on the emplacement. The parapet stops short of the shed, leaving a gap which is the beginning of the path down the hill through the foundry to the town. The rug is on the firestep near this gap. Down on the emplacement behind the cannon is a trolley carrying a huge conical bombshell with a red band painted on it. Further to the right is the door of an office, which, like the sheds, is of the lightest possible construction.*

CUSINS arrives by the path from the town)

BARBARA   Well?

CUSINS   Not a ray of hope. Everything perfect! wonderful! real! It only needs a cathedral to be a heavenly city instead of a hellish one.

BARBARA   Have you found out whether they have done anything for old Peter Shirley?

CUSINS   They have found him a job as gatekeeper and timekeeper. He's frightfully miserable. He calls the time-keeping brainwork, and says he isnt used to it; and his gate lodge is so splendid that he's ashamed to use the rooms, and skulks in the scullery.

BARBARA   Poor Peter!

(STEPHEN arrives from the town. He carries a fieldglass)

STEPHEN   *(enthusiastically)*   Have you two seen the place? Why did you leave us?

CUSINS   I wanted to see everything I was not intended to see; and Barbara wanted to make the men talk.

STEPHEN   Have you found anything discreditable?

CUSINS   No. They call him Dandy Andy and are proud of his being a cunning old rascal; but it's all horribly, frightfully, immorally, unanswerably perfect.

(SARAH arrives)

SARAH   Heavens! what a place! (*She crosses to the trolley*) Did you see the nursing home!?

(She sits down on the shell)

STEPHEN   Did you see the libraries and schools!?

SARAH   Did you see the ball room and the banqueting chamber in the Town Hall!?

STEPHEN   Have you gone into the insurance fund, the pension fund, the building society, the various applications of cooperation!?

(UNDERSHAFT comes from the office, with a sheaf of telegrams in his hand)

UNDERSHAFT   Well, have you seen everything? I'm sorry I was called away. (*indicating the telegrams*) Good news from Manchuria.

STEPHEN   Another Japanese victory?

UNDERSHAFT   Oh, I dont know. Which side wins does not concern us here. No: the good news is that the aerial battleship is a tremendous success. At the first trial it has wiped out a fort with three hundred soldiers in it.

CUSINS   *(from the platform)*   Dummy soldiers?

UNDERSHAFT   *(striding across to STEPHEN and kicking the prostrate dummy brutally out of his way)*   No: the real thing.

(CUSINS and BARBARA exchange glances. Then CUSINS sits on the step and buries his face in his hands. BARBARA gravely lays her hand on his shoulder. He looks up at her in whimsical desperation)

UNDERSHAFT   Well, Stephen, what do you think of the place?

STEPHEN   Oh, magnificent. A perfect triumph of modern industry. Frankly, my dear father, I have been a fool: I had no idea of what it all meant: of the wonderful forethought, the power of organization, the administrative capacity, the financial genius, the colossal capital it represents. I have been repeating to myself as I came through your streets "Peace hath her victories no less renowned than War." I have only one misgiving about it all.

UNDERSHAFT   Out with it.

STEPHEN   Well, I cannot help thinking that all this provision for every want of your workmen may sap their independence and weaken their sense of responsibility. And greatly as we enjoyed our tea at that splendid restaurant —how they gave us all that luxury and cake and jam and cream for threepence I really cannot imagine!—still you must remember that restaurants break up home life. Look at the continent, for instance! Are you sure so much pampering is really good for the men's characters?

UNDERSHAFT   Well you see, my dear boy, when you are organizing civilization you have to make up your mind whether trouble and anxiety are good things or not. If you decide that they are, then, I take it, you simply dont organize civilization; and there you are, with trouble and anxiety enough to make us all angels! But if you decide the other way, you may as well go through with it. However, Stephen, our characters are safe here. A sufficient dose of anxiety is always provided by the fact that we may be blown to smithereens at any moment.

SARAH By the way, papa, where do you make the explosives?

UNDERSHAFT In separate little sheds, like that one. When one of them blows up, it costs very little; and only the people quite close to it are killed.

(STEPHEN, *who is quite close to it, looks at it rather scaredly, and moves away quickly to the cannon. At the same moment the door of the shed is thrown abruptly open; and a foreman in overalls and list slippers comes out on the little landing and holds the door for* LOMAX, *who appears in the doorway*)

LOMAX (*with studied coolness*) My good fellow: you neednt get into a state of nerves. Nothing's going to happen to you; and I suppose it wouldnt be the end of the world if anything did. A little bit of British pluck is what you want, old chap. (*He descends and strolls across to* SARAH)

UNDERSHAFT (*to the foreman*) Anything wrong, Bilton?

BILTON (*with ironic calm*) Gentleman walked into the high explosives shed and lit a cigaret, sir: thats all.

UNDERSHAFT Ah, quite so. (*going over to* LOMAX) Do you happen to remember what you did with the match?

LOMAX Oh come! I'm not a fool. I took jolly good care to blow it out before I chucked it away.

BILTON The top of it was red hot inside, sir.

LOMAX Well, suppose it was! I didn't chuck it into any of your messes.

UNDERSHAFT Think no more of it, Mr Lomax. By the way, would you mind lending me your matches.

LOMAX (*offering his box*) Certainly.

UNDERSHAFT Thanks. (*He pockets the matches*)

LOMAX (*lecturing to the company generally*) You know, these high explosives dont go off like gunpowder, except when theyre in a gun. When theyre spread loose, you can put a match to them without the least risk: they just burn quietly like a bit of paper. (*warming to the scientific interest of the subject*) Did you know that, Undershaft? Have you ever tried?

UNDERSHAFT Not on a large scale, Mr Lomax. Bilton will give you a sample of gun cotton when you are leaving if you ask him. You can experiment with it at home. (BILTON *looks puzzled*)

SARAH Bilton will do nothing of the sort, papa. I suppose it's your business to blow up the Russians and Japs; but you might really stop short of blowing up poor Cholly. (BILTON *gives it up and retires into the shed*)

LOMAX My ownest, there is no danger. (*He sits beside her on the shell*)

(LADY BRITOMART *arrives from the town with a bouquet*)

LADY BRITOMART (*impetuously*) Andrew: you shouldnt have let me see this place.

UNDERSHAFT Why, my dear?

LADY BRITOMART Never mind why: you shouldnt have: thats all. To think of all that (*indicating the town*) being yours! and that you have kept it to yourself all these years!

UNDERSHAFT It does not belong to me. I belong to it. It is the Undershaft inheritance.

LADY BRITOMART It is not. Your ridiculous cannons and that noisy banging foundry may be the Undershaft inheritance; but all that plate and linen, all that furniture and those houses and orchards and gardens belong to us. They belong to me: they are not a man's business. I wont give them up. You must be out of your senses to throw them all away; and if you persist in such folly, I will call in a doctor.

UNDERSHAFT (*stooping to smell the bouquet*) Where did you get the flowers, my dear?

LADY BRITOMART Your men presented them to me in your William Morris Labor Church.

CUSINS Oh! It needed only that. A Labor Church! (*He mounts the firestep distractedly, and leans with his elbows on the parapet, turning his back to them*)

LADY BRITOMART Yes, with Morris's words in mosaic letters ten feet high round the dome. NO MAN IS GOOD ENOUGH TO BE ANOTHER MAN'S MASTER. The cynicism of it!

UNDERSHAFT It shocked the men at first, I am afraid. But now they take no more notice of it than of the ten commandments in church.

LADY BRITOMART Andrew: you are trying to put me off the subject of the inheritance by profane jokes. Well, you shant. I dont ask it any longer for Stephen: he has inherited far too much of your perversity to be fit for it. But Barbara has rights as well as Stephen. Why should not Adolphus succeed to the inheritance? I could manage the town for him; and he can look after the cannons, if they are really necessary.

UNDERSHAFT I should ask nothing better if

Adolphus were a foundling. He is exactly the sort of new blood that is wanted in English business. But he's not a foundling; and theres an end of it. (*He makes for the office door*)

CUSINS (*turning to them*)   Not quite. (*They all turn and stare at him*) I think—Mind! I am not committing myself in any way as to my future course—but I think the foundling difficulty can be got over. (*He jumps down to the emplacement*)

UNDERSHAFT (*coming back to him*)   What do you mean?

CUSINS   Well, I have something to say which is in the nature of a confession.

SARAH ⎫
LADY BRITOMART ⎬ Confession!
BARBARA ⎪
STEPHEN ⎭

LOMAX   Oh I say!

CUSINS   Yes, a confession. Listen, all. Until I met Barbara I thought myself in the main an honorable, truthful man, because I wanted the approval of my conscience more than I wanted anything else. But the moment I saw Barbara, I wanted her far more than the approval of my conscience.

LADY BRITOMART   Adolphus!

CUSINS   It is true. You accused me yourself, Lady Brit, of joining the Army to worship Barbara; and so I did. She bought my soul like a flower at a street corner; but she bought it for herself.

UNDERSHAFT   What! Not for Dionysos or another?

CUSINS   Dionysos and all the others are in herself. I adored what was divine in her, and was therefore a true worshipper. But I was romantic about her too. I thought she was a woman of the people, and that a marriage with a professor of Greek would be far beyond the wildest social ambitions of her rank.

LADY BRITOMART   Adolphus!!

LOMAX   Oh I say!!!

CUSINS   When I learnt the horrible truth—

LADY BRITOMART   What do you mean by the horrible truth, pray?

CUSINS   That she was enormously rich; that her grandfather was an earl; that her father was the Prince of Darkness—

UNDERSHAFT   Chut!

CUSINS   —and that I was only an adventurer trying to catch a rich wife, then I stooped to deceive her about my birth.

BARBARA (*rising*)   Dolly!

LADY BRITOMART   Your birth! Now Adolphus, dont dare to make up a wicked story for the sake of these wretched cannons. Remember: I have seen photographs of your parents; and the Agent General for South Western Australia knows them personally and has assured me that they are most respectable married people.

CUSINS   So they are in Australia; but here they are outcasts. Their marriage is legal in Australia, but not in England. My mother is my father's deceased wife's sister; and in this island I am consequently a foundling. (*sensation*)

BARBARA   Silly! (*She climbs to the cannon, and leans, listening, in the angle it makes with the parapet*)

CUSINS   Is the subterfuge good enough, Machiavelli?

UNDERSHAFT (*thoughtfully*)   Biddy: this may be a way out of the difficulty.

LADY BRITOMART   Stuff! A man cant make cannons any the better for being his own cousin instead of his proper self. (*She sits down on the rug with a bounce that expresses her downright contempt for their casuistry*)

UNDERSHAFT (*to* CUSINS)   You are an educated man. That is against the tradition.

CUSINS   Once in ten thousand times it happens that the schoolboy is a born master of what they try to teach him. Greek has not destroyed my mind: it has nourished it. Besides, I did not learn it at an English public school.

UNDERSHAFT   Hm! Well, I cannot afford to be too particular: you have cornered the foundling market. Let it pass. You are eligible; Euripides: you are eligible.

BARBARA   Dolly: yesterday morning, when Stephen told us all about the tradition, you became very silent and you have been strange and excited ever since. Were you thinking of your birth then?

CUSINS   When the finger of Destiny suddenly points at a man in the middle of his breakfast, it makes him thoughtful.

UNDERSHAFT   Aha! You have had your eye on the business, my young friend, have you?

CUSINS   Take care! There is an abyss of moral horror between me and your accursed aerial battleships.

UNDERSHAFT   Never mind the abyss for the present. Let us settle the practical details and leave your final decision open. You know that you will have to change your name. Do you object to that?

CUSINS   Would any man named Adolphus—any man called Dolly!—object to be called something else?

UNDERSHAFT   Good. Now, as to money! I propose to treat you handsomely from the beginning. You shall start at a thousand a year.

CUSINS (*with sudden heat, his spectacles twinkling with mischief*) A thousand! You dare offer a miserable thousand to the son-in-law of a millionaire! No, by Heavens, Machiavelli! you shall not cheat me. You cannot do without me; and I can do without you. I must have two thousand five hundred a year for two years. At the end of that time, if I am a failure, I go. But if I am a success, and stay on, you must give me the other five thousand.

UNDERSHAFT What other five thousand?

CUSINS To make the two years up to five thousand a year. The two thousand five hundred is only half pay in case I should turn out a failure. The third year I must have ten per cent on the profits.

UNDERSHAFT (*taken aback*) Ten per cent! Why, man, do you know what my profits are?

CUSINS Enormous, I hope: otherwise I shall require twenty-five per cent.

UNDERSHAFT But, Mr. Cusins, this is a serious matter of business. You are not bringing any capital into the concern.

CUSINS What! no capital! Is my mastery of Greek no capital? Is my access to the subtlest thought, the loftiest poetry yet attained by humanity, no capital? My character! my intellect! my life! my career! what Barbara calls my soul! are these no capital? Say another word; and I double my salary.

UNDERSHAFT Be reasonable—

CUSINS (*peremptorily*) Mr Undershaft: you have my terms. Take them or leave them.

UNDERSHAFT (*recovering himself*) Very well. I note your terms; and I offer you half.

CUSINS (*disgusted*) Half!

UNDERSHAFT (*firmly*) Half.

CUSINS You call yourself a gentleman; and you offer me half!!

UNDERSHAFT I do not call myself a gentleman; but I offer you half.

CUSINS This to your future partner! your successor! your son-in-law!

BARBARA You are selling your own soul, Dolly, not mine. Leave me out of the bargain, please.

UNDERSHAFT Come! I will go a step further for Barbara's sake. I will give you three fifths; but that is my last word.

CUSINS Done!

LOMAX Done in the eye! Why, *I* get only eight hundred, you know.

CUSINS By the way, Mac, I am a classical scholar, not an arithmetical one. Is three fifths more than half or less?

UNDERSHAFT More, of course.

CUSINS I would have taken two hundred and fifty. How you can succeed in business when you are willing to pay all that money to a University don who is obviously not worth a junior clerk's wages!—well! What will Lazarus say?

UNDERSHAFT Lazarus is a gentle romantic Jew who cares for nothing but string quartets and stalls at fashionable theatres. He will be blamed for your rapacity in money matters, poor fellow! as he has hitherto been blamed for mine. You are a shark of the first order, Euripides. So much the better for the firm!

BARBARA Is the bargain closed, Dolly? Does your soul belong to him now?

CUSINS No: the price is settled: that is all. The real tug of war is still to come. What about the moral question?

LADY BRITOMART There is no moral question in the matter at all, Adolphus. You must simply sell cannons and weapons to people whose cause is right and just, and refuse them to foreigners and criminals.

UNDERSHAFT (*determinedly*) No: none of that. You must keep the true faith of an Armorer, or you dont come in here.

CUSINS What on earth is the true faith of an Armorer?

UNDERSHAFT To give arms to all men who offer an honest price for them, without respect of persons or principles: to aristocrat and republican, to Nihilist and Tsar, to Capitalist and Socialist, to Protestant and Catholic, to burglar and policeman, to black man, white man and yellow man, to all sorts and conditions, all nationalities, all faiths, all follies, all causes and all crimes. The first Undershaft wrote up in his shop IF GOD GAVE THE HAND, LET NOT MAN WITHHOLD THE SWORD. The second wrote up ALL HAVE THE RIGHT TO FIGHT: NONE HAVE THE RIGHT TO JUDGE. The third wrote up TO MAN THE WEAPON: TO HEAVEN THE VICTORY. The fourth had no literary turn; so he did not write up anything; but he sold cannons to Napoleon under the nose of George the Third. The fifth wrote up PEACE SHALL NOT PREVAIL SAVE WITH A SWORD IN HER HAND. The sixth, my master, was the best of all. He wrote up NOTHING IS EVER DONE IN THIS WORLD UNTIL MEN ARE PREPARED TO KILL ONE ANOTHER IF IT IS NOT DONE. After that, there was nothing left for the seventh to say. So he wrote up, simply, UNASHAMED.

CUSINS My good Machiavelli, I shall certainly write something up on the wall; only, as I shall write it in Greek, you wont be able to read it. But as to your Armorer's faith, if I take my neck out of the noose of my own morality I am not going to put it into the noose of yours. I shall sell cannons to whom I please and refuse them to whom I please. So there!

UNDERSHAFT From the moment when you become Andrew Undershaft, you will never do as you please again. Dont come here lusting for power, young man.

CUSINS If power were my aim I should not come here for it. You have no power.

UNDERSHAFT None of my own, certainly.

CUSINS I have more power than you, more will. You do not drive this place: it drives you. And what drives the place?

UNDERSHAFT (*enigmatically*) A will of which I am a part.

BARBARA (*startled*) Father! Do you know what you are saying; or are you laying a snare for my soul?

CUSINS Dont listen to his metaphysics, Barbara. The place is driven by the most rascally part of society, the money hunters, the pleasure hunters, the military promotion hunters; and he is their slave.

UNDERSHAFT Not necessarily. Remember the Armorer's Faith. I will take an order from a good man as cheerfully as from a bad one. If you good people prefer preaching and shirking to buying my weapons and fighting the rascals, dont blame me. I can make cannons: I cannot make courage and conviction. Bah! you tire me, Euripides, with your morality mongering. Ask Barbara: she understands. (*He suddenly reaches up and takes* BARBARA's *hands, looking powerfully into her eyes*) Tell him, my love, what power really means.

BARBARA (*hypnotized*) Before I joined the Salvation Army, I was in my own power; and the consequence was that I never knew what to do with myself. When I joined it, I had not time enough for all the things I had to do.

UNDERSHAFT (*approvingly*) Just so. And why was that, do you suppose?

BARBARA Yesterday I should have said, because I was in the power of God. (*She resumes her self-possession, withdrawing her hands from his with a power equal to his own*) But you came and showed me that I was in the power of Bodger and Undershaft. Today I feel —oh! how can I put it into words? Sarah: do you remember the earthquake at Cannes, when we were little children?—how little the surprise of the first shock mattered compared to the dread and horror of waiting for the second? That is how I feel in this place today. I stood on the rock I thought eternal; and without a word of warning it reeled and crumbled under me. I was safe with an infinite wisdom watching me, an army marching to Salvation with me; and in a moment, at a stroke of your pen

in a cheque book, I stood alone; and the heavens were empty. That was the first shock of the earthquake: I am waiting for the second.

UNDERSHAFT Come, come, my daughter! dont make too much of your little tinpot tragedy. What do we do here when we spend years of work and thought and thousands of pounds of solid cash on a new gun or an aerial battleship that turns out just a hairsbreadth wrong after all? Scrap it. Scrap it without wasting another hour or another pound on it. Well, you have made for yourself something that you call morality or a religion or what not. It doesnt fit the facts. Well, scrap it. Scrap it and get one that does fit. That is what is wrong with the world at present. It scraps its obsolete steam engines and dynamos; but it wont scrap its old prejudices and its old moralities and its old religions and its old political constitutions. Whats the result? In machinery it does very well; but in morals and religion and politics it is working at a loss that brings it nearer bankruptcy every year. Dont persist in that folly. If your old religion broke down yesterday, get a newer and a better one for tomorrow.

BARBARA Oh how gladly I would take a better one to my soul! But you offer me a worse one. (*turning on him with sudden vehemence*) Justify yourself: show me some light through the darkness of this dreadful place, with its beautifully clean workshops, and respectable workmen, and model homes.

UNDERSHAFT Cleanliness and respectability do not need justification, Barbara: they justify themselves. I see no darkness here, no dreadfulness. In your Salvation shelter I saw poverty, misery, cold and hunger. You gave them bread and treacle and dreams of heaven. I give from thirty shillings a week to twelve thousand a year. They find their own dreams; but I look after the drainage.

BARBARA And their souls?

UNDERSHAFT I save their souls just as I saved yours.

BARBARA (*revolted*) You saved my soul! What do you mean?

UNDERSHAFT I fed you and clothed you and housed you. I took care that you should have money enough to live handsomely—more than enough; so that you could be wasteful, careless, generous. That saved your soul from the seven deadly sins.

BARBARA (*bewildered*) The seven deadly sins!

UNDERSHAFT Yes, the deadly seven. (*counting on his fingers*) Food, clothing, firing, rent, taxes, respectability and children. Nothing can lift those seven millstones from Man's neck but money; and the spirit cannot soar until the millstones are lifted. I lifted them from your spirit. I enabled Barbara to become Major Barbara; and I saved her from the crime of poverty.

CUSINS Do you call poverty a crime?

UNDERSHAFT The worst of crimes. All the other crimes are virtues beside it: all the other dishonors are chivalry itself by comparison. Poverty blights whole cities; spreads horrible pestilences; strikes dead the very souls of all who come within sight, sound, or smell of it. What you call crime is nothing: a murder here and a theft there, a blow now and a curse then: what do they matter? they are only the accidents and illnesses of life: there are not fifty genuine professional criminals in London. But there are millions of poor people, abject people, dirty people, ill fed, ill clothed people. They poison us morally and physically: they kill the happiness of society: they force us to do away with our own liberties and to organize unnatural cruelties for fear they should rise against us and drag us down into their abyss. Only fools fear crime: we all fear poverty. Pah! (*turning on* BARBARA) you talk of your half-saved ruffian in West Ham: you accuse me of dragging his soul back to perdition. Well, bring him to me here; and I will drag his soul back again to salvation for you. Not by words and dreams; but by thirty-eight shillings a week, a sound house in a handsome street, and a permanent job. In three weeks he will have a fancy waistcoat; in three months a tall hat and a chapel sitting; before the end of the year he will shake hands with a duchess at a Primrose League meeting, and join the Conservative Party.

BARBARA And will he be the better for that?

UNDERSHAFT You know he will. Dont be a hypocrite, Barbara. He will be better fed, better housed, better clothed, better behaved; and his children will be pounds heavier and bigger. That will be better than an American cloth mattress in a shelter, chopping firewood, eating bread and treacle, and being forced to kneel down from time to time to thank heaven for it: knee drill, I think you call it. It is cheap work converting starving men with a Bible in one hand and a slice of bread in the other. I will undertake to convert West Ham to Mahometanism on the same terms. Try your hand on my men: their souls are hungry because their bodies are full.

BARBARA And leave the east end to starve?

UNDERSHAFT (*his energetic tone dropping into one of bitter and brooding remembrance*) *I* was an east ender. I moralized and starved until one day I swore that I would be a full-fed free man at all costs; that nothing should stop me except a bullet, neither reason nor morals nor the lives of other men. I said "Thou shalt starve ere I starve"; and with that word I became free and great. I was a dangerous man until I had my will: now I am a useful, beneficent, kindly person. That is the history of most self-made millionaires, I fancy. When it is the history of every Englishman we shall have an England worth living in.

LADY BRITOMART Stop making speeches, Andrew. This is not the place for them.

UNDERSHAFT (*punctured*) My dear: I have no other means of conveying my ideas.

LADY BRITOMART Your ideas are nonsense. You got on because you were selfish and unscrupulous.

UNDERSHAFT Not at all. I had the strongest scruples about poverty and starvation. Your moralists are quite unscrupulous about both: they make virtues of them. I had rather be a thief than a pauper. I had rather be a murderer than a slave. I dont want to be either; but if you force the alternative on me, then, by Heaven, I'll choose the braver and more moral one. I hate poverty and slavery worse than any other crimes whatsoever. And let me tell you this. Poverty and slavery have stood up for centuries to your sermons and leading articles: they will not stand up to my machine guns. Dont preach at them: dont reason with them. Kill them.

BARBARA Killing. Is that your remedy for everything?

UNDERSHAFT It is the final test of conviction, the only lever strong enough to overturn a social system, the only way of saying Must. Let six hundred and seventy fools loose in the streets; and three policemen can scatter them. But huddle them together in a certain house in Westminster; and let them go through certain ceremonies and call themselves certain names until at last they get the courage to kill; and your six hundred and seventy fools become a government. Your pious mob fills up ballot papers and imagines it is governing its masters; but the ballot paper that really governs is the paper that has a bullet wrapped up in it.

CUSINS That is perhaps why, like most intelligent people, I never vote.

UNDERSHAFT Vote! Bah! When you vote, you only change the names of the cabinet. When you shoot, you pull down governments, inaugurate new epochs, abolish old orders and set up new. Is that historically true, Mr Learned Man, or is it not?

CUSINS   It is historically true. I loathe having to admit it. I repudiate your sentiments. I abhor your nature. I defy you in every possible way. Still, it is true. But it ought not to be true.

UNDERSHAFT   Ought! ought! ought! ought! ought! Are you going to spend your life saying ought, like the rest of our moralists? Turn your oughts into shalls, man. Come and make explosives with me. Whatever can blow men up can blow society up. The history of the world is the history of those who had courage enough to embrace this truth. Have you the courage to embrace it, Barbara?

LADY BRITOMART   Barbara: I positively forbid you to listen to your father's abominable wickedness. And you, Adolphus, ought to know better than to go about saying that wrong things are true. What does it matter whether they are true if they are wrong?

UNDERSHAFT   What does it matter whether they are wrong if they are true?

LADY BRITOMART (*rising*)   Children: come home instantly. Andrew: I am exceedingly sorry I allowed you to call on us. You are wickeder than ever. Come at once.

BARBARA (*shaking her head*)   It's no use running away from wicked people, mamma.

LADY BRITOMART   It is every use. It shows your disapprobation of them.

BARBARA   It does not save them.

LADY BRITOMART   I can see that you are going to disobey me. Sarah: are you coming home or are you not?

SARAH   I daresay it's very wicked of papa to make cannons; but I dont think I shall cut him on that account.

LOMAX (*pouring oil on the troubled waters*) The fact is, you know, there is a certain amount of tosh about this notion of wickedness. It doesnt work. You must look at facts. Not that I would say a word in favor of anything wrong; but then, you see, all sorts of chaps are always doing all sorts of things; and we have to fit them in somehow, dont you know. What I mean is that you cant go cutting everybody; and thats about what it comes to. (*Their rapt attention to his eloquence makes him nervous*) Perhaps I dont make myself clear.

LADY BRITOMART   You are lucidity itself, Charles. Because Andrew is successful and has plenty of money to give to Sarah, you will flatter him and encourage him in his wickedness.

LOMAX (*unruffled*)   Well, where the carcass is, there will the eagles be gathered, dont you know. (*to* UNDERSHAFT) Eh? What?

UNDERSHAFT   Precisely. By the way, may I call you Charles?

LOMAX   Delighted. Cholly is the usual ticket.

UNDERSHAFT (*to* LADY BRITOMART) Biddy—

LADY BRITOMART (*violently*)   Dont dare call me Biddy. Charles Lomax: you are a fool. Adolphus Cusins: you are a Jesuit. Stephen: you are a prig. Barbara: you are a lunatic. Andrew: you are a vulgar tradesman. Now you all know my opinion; and my conscience is clear, at all events. (*She sits down with a vehemence that the rug fortunately softens*)

UNDERSHAFT   My dear: you are the incarnation of morality. (*She snorts*) Your conscience is clear and your duty done when you have called everybody names. Come, Euripides! it is getting late; and we all want to go home. Make up your mind.

CUSINS   Understand this, you old demon—

LADY BRITOMART   Adolphus!

UNDERSHAFT   Let him alone, Biddy. Proceed, Euripides.

CUSINS   You have me in a horrible dilemma. I want Barbara.

UNDERSHAFT   Like all young men, you greatly exaggerate the difference between one young woman and another.

BARBARA   Quite true, Dolly.

CUSINS   I also want to avoid being a rascal.

UNDERSHAFT (*with biting contempt*)   You lust for personal righteousness, for self-approval, for what you call a good conscience, for what Barbara calls salvation, for what I call patronizing people who are not so lucky as yourself.

CUSINS   I do not: all the poet in me recoils from being a good man. But there are things in me that I must reckon with. Pity—

UNDERSHAFT   Pity! The scavenger of misery.

CUSINS   Well, love.

UNDERSHAFT   I know. You love the needy and the outcast: you love the oppressed races, the Negro, the Indian ryot, the underdog everywhere. Do you love the Japanese? Do you love the French? Do you love the English?

CUSINS   No. Every true Englishman detests the English. We are the wickedest nation on earth; and our success is a moral horror.

UNDERSHAFT   That is what comes of your gospel of love, is it?

CUSINS   May I not love even my father-in-law?

UNDERSHAFT   Who wants your love, man? By what right do you take the liberty of offering it to me? I will have your due heed and respect, or I will kill you. But your love! Damn your impertinence!

CUSINS (*grinning*)   I may not be able to control my affections, Mac.

UNDERSHAFT You are fencing, Euripides. You are weakening: your grip is slipping. Come! try your last weapon. Pity and love have broken in your hand: forgiveness is still left.

CUSINS No: forgiveness is a beggar's refuge. I am with you there: we must pay our debts.

UNDERSHAFT Well said. Come! you will suit me. Remember the words of Plato.

CUSINS (*starting*) Plato! You dare quote Plato to me!

UNDERSHAFT Plato says, my friend, that society cannot be saved until either the Professors of Greek take to making gunpowder, or else the makers of gunpowder become Professors of Greek.

CUSINS Oh, tempter, cunning tempter!

UNDERSHAFT Come! choose, man, choose.

CUSINS But perhaps Barbara will not marry me if I make the wrong choice.

BARBARA Perhaps not.

CUSINS (*desperately perplexed*) You hear!

BARBARA Father: do you love nobody?

UNDERSHAFT I love my best friend.

LADY BRITOMART And who is that, pray?

UNDERSHAFT My bravest enemy. That is the man who keeps me up to the mark.

CUSINS You know, the creature is really a sort of poet in his way. Suppose he is a great man, after all!

UNDERSHAFT Suppose you stop talking and make up your mind, my young friend.

CUSINS But you are driving me against my nature. I hate war.

UNDERSHAFT Hatred is the coward's revenge for being intimidated. Dare you make war on war? Here are the means: my friend Mr Lomax is sitting on them.

LOMAX (*springing up*) Oh I say! You dont mean that this thing is loaded, do you? My ownest: come off it.

SARAH (*sitting placidly on the shell*) If I am to be blown up, the more thoroughly it is done the better. Dont fuss, Cholly.

LOMAX (*to* UNDERSHAFT, *strongly remonstrant*) Your own daughter, you know!

UNDERSHAFT So I see. (*to* CUSINS) Well, my friend, may we expect you here at six tomorrow morning?

CUSINS (*firmly*) Not on any account. I will see the whole establishment blown up with its own dynamite before I will get up at five. My hours are healthy, rational hours: eleven to five.

UNDERSHAFT Come when you please: before a week you will come at six and stay until I turn you out for the sake of your health. (*calling*) Bilton! (*He turns to* LADY BRITOMART, *who rises*) My dear: let us leave these two young people to themselves for a moment. (BILTON *comes from the shed*) I am going to take you through the gun cotton shed.

BILTON (*barring the way*) You cant take anything explosive in here, sir.

LADY BRITOMART What do you mean? Are you alluding to me?

BILTON (*unmoved*) No, maam. Mr Undershaft has the other gentleman's matches in his pocket.

LADY BRITOMART (*abruptly*) Oh! I beg your pardon. (*She goes into the shed*)

UNDERSHAFT Quite right, Bilton, quite right: here you are. (*He gives* BILTON *the box of matches*) Come, Stephen. Come, Charles. Bring Sarah. (*He passes into the shed*)

(BILTON *opens the box and deliberately drops the matches into the fire-bucket*)

LOMAX Oh! I say. (BILTON *stolidly hands him the empty box*) Infernal nonsense! Pure scientific ignorance! (*He goes in*)

SARAH Am I all right, Bilton?

BILTON Youll have to put on list slippers, miss: thats all. Weve got em inside. (*She goes in*)

STEPHEN (*very seriously to* CUSINS) Dolly, old fellow, think. Think before you decide. Do you feel that you are a sufficiently practical man? It it a huge undertaking, an enormous responsibility. All this mass of business will be Greek to you.

CUSINS Oh, I think it will be much less difficult than Greek.

STEPHEN Well, I just want to say this before I leave you to yourselves. Dont let anything I have said about right and wrong prejudice you against this great chance in life. I have satisfied myself that the business is one of the highest character and a credit to our country. (*emotionnally*) I am very proud of my father. I—(*Unable to proceed, he presses* CUSINS' *hand and goes hastily into the shed, followed by* BILTON)

(BARBARA *and* CUSINS, *left alone together, look at one another silently*)

CUSINS Barbara: I am going to accept this offer.

BARBARA I thought you would.

CUSINS You understand, dont you, that I had to decide without consulting you. If I had thrown the burden of the choice on you, you would sooner or later have despised me for it.

BARBARA Yes: I did not want you to sell your soul for me any more than for this inheritance.

CUSINS It is not the sale of my soul that troubles me: I have sold it too often to care about that. I have sold it for a professorship. I have sold it for an income. I have sold it to escape being imprisoned for refusing to pay taxes for hangmen's ropes and unjust wars and things that I abhor. What is all human conduct but the daily and hourly sale of our souls for trifles? What I am now selling it for is neither money nor position nor comfort, but for reality and for power.

BARBARA You know that you will have no power, and that he has none.

CUSINS I know. It is not for myself alone. I want to make power for the world.

BARBARA I want to make power for the world too; but it must be spiritual power.

CUSINS I think all power is spiritual: these cannons will not go off by themselves. I have tried to make spiritual power by teaching Greek. But the world can never be really touched by a dead language and a dead civilization. The people must have power; and the people cannot have Greek. Now the power that is made here can be wielded by all men.

BARBARA Power to burn women's houses down and kill their sons and tear their husbands to pieces.

CUSINS You cannot have power for good without having power for evil too. Even mother's milk nourishes murderers as well as heroes. This power which only tears men's bodies to pieces has never been so horribly abused as the intellectual power, the imaginative power, the poetic, religious power that can enslave men's souls. As a teacher of Greek I gave the intellectual man weapons against the common man. I now want to give the common man weapons against the intellectual man. I love the common people. I want to arm them against the lawyers, the doctors, the priests, the literary men, the professors, the artists, and the politicians, who, once in authority, are more disastrous and tyrannical than all the fools, rascals, and impostors. I want a power simple enough for common men to use, yet strong enough to force the intellectual oligarchy to use its genius for the general good.

BARBARA Is there no higher power than that? (pointing to the shell)

CUSINS Yes; but that power can destroy the higher powers just as a tiger can destroy a man: therefore Man must master that power first. I admitted this when the Turks and Greeks were last at war. My best pupil went out to fight for Hellas. My parting gift to him was not a copy of Plato's Republic, but a revolver and a hundred Undershaft cartridges. The blood of every Turk he shot—if he shot any—is on my head as well as on Undershaft's.

That act committed me to this place for ever. Your father's challenge has beaten me. Dare I make war on war? I must. I will. And now, is it all over between us?

BARBARA (touched by his evident dread of her answer) Silly baby Dolly! How could it be!

CUSINS (overjoyed) Then you—you—you —Oh for my drum! (He flourishes imaginary drumsticks)

BARBARA (angered by his levity) Take care, Dolly, take care. Oh, if only I could get away from you and from father and from it all! if I could have the wings of a dove and fly away to heaven!

CUSINS And leave me!

BARBARA Yes, you, and all the other naughty mischievous children of men. But I cant. I was happy in the Salvation Army for a moment. I escaped from the world into a paradise of enthusiasm and prayer and soul saving; but the moment our money ran short, it all came back to Bodger: it was he who saved our people: he, and the Prince of Darkness, my papa. Undershaft and Bodger: their hands stretch everywhere: when we feed a starving fellow creature, it is with their bread, because there is no other bread; when we tend the sick, it is in the hospitals they endow; if we turn from the churches they build, we must kneel on the stones of the streets they pave. As long as that lasts, there is no getting away from them. Turning our backs on Bodger and Undershaft is turning our backs on life.

CUSINS I thought you were determined to turn your back on the wicked side of life.

BARBARA There is no wicked side: life is all one. And I never wanted to shirk my share in whatever evil must be endured, whether it be sin or suffering. I wish I could cure you of middle-class ideas, Dolly.

CUSINS (gasping) Middle cl—! A snub! A social snub to me! from the daughter of a foundling!

BARBARA That is why I have no class, Dolly: I come straight out of the heart of the whole people. If I were middle-class I should turn my back on my father's business; and we should both live in an artistic drawing room, with you reading the reviews in one corner, and I in the other at the piano, playing Schumann: both very superior persons, and neither of us a bit of use. Sooner than that, I would sweep out the guncotton shed, or be one of Bodger's barmaids. Do you know what would have happened if you had refused papa's offer?

CUSINS I wonder!

BARBARA I should have given you up and

married the man who accepted it. After all, my dear old mother has more sense than any of you. I felt like her when I saw this place—felt that I must have it—that never, never, never could I let it go; only she thought it was the houses and the kitchen ranges and the linen and china, when it was really all the human souls to be saved: not weak souls in starved bodies, sobbing with gratitude for a scrap of bread and treacle, but fullfed, quarrelsome, snobbish, uppish creatures, all standing on their little rights and dignities, and thinking that my father ought to be greatly obliged to them for making so much money for him—and so he ought. That is where salvation is really wanted. My father shall never throw it in my teeth again that my converts were bribed with bread. (*She is transfigured*) I have got rid of the bribe of bread. I have got rid of the bribe of heaven. Let God's work be done for its own sake: the work he had to create us to do because it cannot be done except by living men and women. When I die, let him be in my debt, not I in his; and let me forgive him as becomes a woman of my rank.

CUSINS Then the way of life lies through the factory of death?

BARBARA Yes, through the raising of hell to heaven and of man to God, through the unveiling of an eternal light in the Valley of The Shadow. (*seizing him with both hands*) Oh, did you think my courage would never come back? did you believe that I was a deserter? that I, who have stood in the streets, and taken my people to my heart, and talked of the holiest and greatest things with them, could ever turn back and chatter foolishly to fashionable people about nothing in a drawing room?

Never, never, never, never: Major Barbara will die with the colors. Oh! and I have my dear little Dolly boy still; and he has found me my place and my work. Glory Hallelujah! (*She kisses him*)

CUSINS My dearest: consider my delicate health. I cannot stand as much happiness as you can.

BARBARA Yes: it is not easy work being in love with me, is it? But it's good for you. (*She runs to the shed, and calls, childlike*) Mamma! Mamma! (BILTON *comes out of the shed, followed by* UNDERSHAFT) I want Mamma.

UNDERSHAFT She is taking off her list slippers, dear. (*He passes on to* CUSINS) Well? What does she say?

CUSINS She has gone right up into the skies.

LADY BRITOMART (*coming from the shed and stopping on the steps, obstructing* SARAH, *who follows with* LOMAX. BARBARA *clutches like a baby at her mother's skirt*) Barbara: when will you learn to be independent and to act and think for yourself? I know as well as possible what that cry of "Mamma, Mamma," means. Always running to me!

SARAH (*touching* LADY BRITOMART'S *ribs with her finger tips and imitating a bicycle horn*) Pip! pip!

LADY BRITOMART (*highly indignant*) How dare you say Pip! pip! to me, Sarah? You are both very naughty children. What do you want, Barbara?

BARBARA I want a house in the village to live in with Dolly. (*dragging at the skirt*) Come and tell me which one to take.

UNDERSHAFT (*to* CUSINS) Six o'clock tomorrow morning, Euripides.

T. S. Eliot

1888-

"RHETORIC"

AND POETIC DRAMA

The death of Rostand was the disappearance of the poet whom, more than any other in France, we treated as the exponent of "rhetoric," thinking of rhetoric as something recently out of fashion. And as we find ourselves looking back rather tenderly upon the author of *Cyrano* we wonder what this vice or quality is that is associated as plainly with Rostand's merits as with his defects. His rhetoric, at least, suited him at times so well, and so much better than it suited a much greater poet, Baudelaire, who is at times as rhetorical as Rostand. And we begin to suspect that the word is merely a vague term of abuse for any style that is bad, that is so evidently bad or second-rate that we do not recognize the necessity for greater precision in the phrases we apply to it.

Our own Elizabethan and Jacobean poetry—in so nice a problem it is much safer to stick to one's own language—is repeatedly called "rhetorical." It had this and that notable quality, but, when we wish to admit that it had defects, it is rhetorical. It had serious defects, even gross faults, but we cannot be considered to have erased them from our language when we are so unclear in our perception of what they are. The fact is that both Elizabethan prose and Elizabethan poetry are written in a variety of styles with a variety of vices. Is the style of Lyly,[1] is Euphuism, rhetorical? In contrast to the elder style of Ascham[2] and

Elyot[3] which it assaults, it is a clear, flowing, orderly and relatively pure style, with a systematic if monotonous formula of antitheses and similes. Is the style of Nashe?[4] A tumid, flatulent, vigorous style very different from Lyly's. Or it is perhaps the strained and the mixed figures of speech in which Shakespeare indulged himself. Or it is perhaps the careful declamation of Jonson. The word simply cannot be used as synonymous with bad writing. The meanings which it has been obliged to shoulder have been mostly opprobrious; but if a precise meaning can be found for it this meaning may occasionally represent a virtue. It is one of those words which it is the business of criticism to dissect and reassemble. Let us avoid the assumption that rhetoric is a vice of manner, and endeavour to find a rhetoric of substance also, which is right because it issues from what it has to express.

At the present time there is a manifest preference for the "conversational" in poetry—the style of "direct speech," opposed to the "oratorical" and the rhetorical; but if rhetoric is any convention of writing inappropriately applied, this conversational style can and does become a rhetoric—or what is supposed to be a conversational style, for it is often as remote from polite discourse as well could be. Much of the second and third rate in American *vers libre* is of this sort; and much of the second and third rate in English Wordsworthianism. There is in fact no conversational or other form which can be applied indiscrimi-

[1] John Lyly (1554–1606), playwright most famous for his *Euphues, The Anatomy of Wit.*

[2] Roger Ascham (1515–1568), English writer and scholar.

[3] Sir Thomas Elyot (1490?–1546), writer and scholar.

[4] Thomas Nashe (1567–1601), English satirical pamphleteer and dramatist.

nately; if a writer wishes to give the effect of speech he must positively give the effect of himself talking in his own person or in one of his rôles; and if we are to express ourselves, our variety of thoughts and feelings, on a variety of subjects with inevitable rightness, we must adapt our manner to the moment with infinite variations. Examination of the development of Elizabethan drama shows this progress in adaptation, a development from monotony to variety, a progressive refinement in the perception of the variations of feeling, and a progressive elaboration of the means of expressing these variations. This drama is admitted to have grown away from the rhetorical expression, the bombast speeches, of Kyd [5] and Marlowe to the subtle and dispersed utterance of Shakespeare and Webster. But this apparent abandonment or outgrowth of rhetoric is two things; it is partly an improvement in language and it is partly progressive variation in feeling. There is, of course, a long distance separating the furibund fluency of old Hieronimo and the broken words of Lear. There is also a difference between the famous

Oh eyes no eyes, but fountains full
of tears!
Oh life no life, but lively form of
death!

and the superb "additions to Hieronimo." [6]

We think of Shakespeare perhaps as the dramatist who concentrates everything into a sentence, "Pray you undo this button," or "Honest honest Iago"; we forget that there is a rhetoric proper to Shakespeare at his best period which is quite free from the genuine Shakespearean vices either of the early period or the late. These passages are comparable to the best bombast of Kyd or Marlowe, with a greater command of language and a greater control of the emotion. *The Spanish Tragedy* is bombastic when it descends to language which was only the trick of its age; *Tamburlaine* is bombastic because it is monotonous, inflexible to the alterations of emotion. The really fine rhetoric of Shakespeare occurs in situations where a character in the play *sees himself* in a dramatic light:

OTHELLO   And say, besides,—that in Aleppo
once . . .

[5] Thomas Kyd (1558–1594), playwright and author of *The Spanish Tragedy*.
[6] Of the authorship it can only be said that the lines are by some admirer of Marlowe. This might well be Jonson. [Au. note]

CORIOLANUS   If you have writ your annals
true, 'tis there,
That like an eagle in a dovecote, I
Fluttered your Volscians in Corioli.
Alone I did it. Boy!
TIMON   Come not to me again; but say to
Athens,
Timon hath made his everlasting mansion
Upon the beachéd verge of the salt
flood . . .

It occurs also once in *Antony and Cleopatra,* when Enobarbus is inspired to see Cleopatra in this dramatic light:

The barge she sat in . . .

Shakespeare made fun of Marston,[7] and Jonson made fun of Kyd. But in Marston's play the words were expressive of nothing; and Jonson was criticizing the feeble and conceited language, not the emotion, not the "oratory." Jonson is as oratorical himself, and the moments when his oratory succeeds are, I believe, the moments that conform to our formula. Notably the speech of Sylla's ghost in the induction to *Catiline,* and the speech of Envy at the beginning of *The Poetaster.* These two figures are contemplating their own dramatic importance, and quite properly. But in the Senate speeches in *Catiline,* how tedious, how dusty! Here we are spectators not of a play of characters, but of a play of forensic, exactly as if we had been forced to attend the sitting itself. A speech in a play should never appear to be intended to move us as it might conceivably move other characters in the play, for it is essential that we should preserve our position of spectators, and observe always from the outside though with complete understanding. The scene in *Julius Caesar* is right because the object of our attention is not the speech of Antony (*Bedeutung*) but the effect of his speech upon the mob, and Antony's intention, his preparation and consciousness of the effect. And in the rhetorical speeches from Shakespeare which have been cited, we have this necessary advantage of a new clue to the character, in noting the angle from which he views himself. But when a character *in* a play makes a direct appeal to us, we are either the victims of our own sentiment, or we are in the presence of a vicious rhetoric.

These references ought to supply some evidence of the propriety of Cyrano on Noses. Is not Cyrano exactly in this position of con-

[7] John Marston (1576–1634), satiric playwright.

templating himself as a romantic, a dramatic figure? This dramatic sense on the part of the characters themselves is rare in modern drama. In sentimental drama it appears in a degraded form, when we are evidently intended to accept the character's sentimental interpretation of himself. In plays of realism we often find parts which are never allowed to be consciously dramatic, for fear, perhaps, of their appearing less real. But in actual life, in many of those situations in actual life which we enjoy consciously and keenly, we are at times aware of ourselves in this way, and these moments are of very great usefulness to dramatic verse. A very small part of acting is that which takes place on the stage! Rostand had—whether he had anything else or not—this dramatic sense, and it is what gives life to Cyrano. It is a sense which is almost a sense of humour (for when any one is conscious of himself as acting, something like a sense of humour is present). It gives Rostand's characters—Cyrano at least—a gusto which is uncommon on the modern stage. No doubt Rostand's people play up to this too steadily. We recognize that in the love scenes of Cyrano in the garden, for in *Romeo and Juliet* the profounder dramatist shows his lovers melting into unconsciousness of their isolated selves, shows the human soul in the process of forgetting itself. Rostand could not do that; but in the particular case of Cyrano on Noses, the character, the situation, the occasion were perfectly suited and combined. The tirade generated by this combination is not only genuinely and highly dramatic: it is possibly poetry also. If a writer is incapable of composing such a scene as this, so much the worse for his poetic drama.

Cyrano satisfies, as far as scenes like this can satisfy, the requirements of poetic drama. It must take genuine and substantial human emotions, such emotions as observation can confirm, typical emotions, and give them artistic form; the degree of abstraction is a question for the method of each author. In Shakespeare the form is determined in the unity of the whole, as well as single scenes; it is something to attain this unity, as Rostand does, in scenes if not the whole play. Not only as a dramatist, but as a poet, he is superior to Maeterlinck, whose drama, in failing to be dramatic, fails also to be poetic. Maeterlinck has a literary perception of the dramatic and a literary perception of the poetic, and he joins the two; the two are not, as sometimes they are in the work of Rostand, fused. His characters take no conscious delight in their rôle— they are sentimental. With Rostand the centre of gravity is in the expression of the emotion, not as with Maeterlinck in the emotion which cannot be expressed. Some writers appear to believe that emotions gain in intensity through being inarticulate. Perhaps the emotions are not significant enough to endure full daylight.

In any case, we may take our choice: we may apply the term "rhetoric" to the type of dramatic speech which I have instanced, and then we must admit that it covers good as well as bad. Or we may choose to except this type of speech from rhetoric. In that case we must say that rhetoric is any adornment or inflation of speech which is *not done for a particular effect* but for a general impressiveness. And in this case, too, we cannot allow the term to cover all bad writing.

MURDER IN THE CATHEDRAL

PART ONE

CAST OF CHARACTERS

A CHORUS OF WOMEN OF
    CANTERBURY
THREE PRIESTS OF THE
    CATHEDRAL
A HERALD
ARCHBISHOP THOMAS BECKET
FOUR TEMPTERS
ATTENDANTS

*The Scene is the Archbishop's Hall, on
December 2nd, 1170.*

CHORUS   Here let us stand, close by the cathe-
    dral. Here let us wait.
Are we drawn by danger? Is it the knowl-
    edge of safety, that draws our feet
Towards the cathedral? What danger can be
For us, the poor, the poor women of Canter-
    bury? what tribulation
With which we are not already familiar?
    There is no danger
For us, and there is no safety in the cathe-
    dral. Some presage of an act
Which our eyes are compelled to witness,
    has forced our feet
Towards the cathedral. We are forced to
    bear witness.

Since golden October declined into somber
    November
And the apples were gathered and stored,
    and the land became brown sharp
    points of death in a waste of water and
    mud,

The New Year waits, breathes, waits, whis-
    pers in darkness.
While the laborer kicks off a muddy boot
    and stretches his hand to the fire,
The New Year waits, destiny waits for the
    coming.
Who has stretched out his hand to the fire
    and remembered the Saints at All Hal-
    lows,
Remembered the martyrs and saints who
    wait? and who shall
Stretch out his hand to the fire, and deny
    his master? who shall be warm
By the fire, and deny his master?

Seven years and the summer is over
Seven years since the Archbishop left us,
He who was always kind to his people.
But it would not be well if he should return.
King rules or barons rule;
We have suffered various oppression,
But mostly we are left to our own devices,
And we are content if we are left alone.
We try to keep our households in order;
The merchant, shy and cautious, tries to
    compile a little fortune,
And the laborer bends to his piece of earth,
    earth-color, his own color,
Preferring to pass unobserved.
Now I fear disturbance of the quiet seasons:
Winter shall come bringing death from the
    sea,
Ruinous spring shall beat at our doors,
Root and shoot shall eat our eyes and our
    ears,
Disastrous summer burn up the beds of our
    streams
And the poor shall wait for another decaying
    October.
Why should the summer bring consolation
For autumn fires and winter fogs?
What shall we do in the heat of summer
But wait in barren orchards for another
    October?

Some malady is coming upon us. We wait,
we wait,
And the saints and martyrs wait, for those
who shall be martyrs and saints.
Destiny waits in the hand of God, shaping
the still unshapen:
I have seen these things in a shaft of sun-
light.
Destiny waits in the hand of God, not in the
hands of statesmen
Who do, some well, some ill, planning and
guessing,
Having their aims which turn in their hands
in the pattern of time.
Come, happy December, who shall observe
you, who shall preserve you?
Shall the Son of Man be born again in the
litter of scorn?
For us, the poor, there is no action,
But only to wait and to witness.

(*Enter* PRIESTS)

FIRST PRIEST   Seven years and the summer is
over.
Seven years since the Archbishop left us.
SECOND PRIEST   What does the Archbishop do,
and our Sovereign Lord the Pope
With the stubborn King and the French
King
In ceaseless intrigue, combinations,
In conference, meetings accepted, meetings
refused,
Meetings unended or endless
At one place or another in France?
THIRD PRIEST   I see nothing quite conclusive
in the art of temporal government,
But violence, duplicity and frequent mal-
versation.
King rules or barons rule:
The strong man strongly and the weak man
by caprice.
They have but one law, to seize the power
and keep it,
And the steadfast can manipulate the greed
and lust of others,
The feeble is devoured by his own.
FIRST PRIEST   Shall these things not end
Until the poor at the gate
Have forgotten their friend, their Father in
God, have forgotten
That they had a friend?

(*Enter* HERALD)

HERALD   Servants of God, and watchers of
the temple,
I am here to inform you, without circumlo-
cution:
The Archbishop is in England, and is close
outside the city.

I was sent before in haste
To give you notice of his coming, as much
as was possible,
That you may prepare to meet him.
FIRST PRIEST   What, is the exile ended, is our
Lord Archbishop
Reunited with the King? what reconciliation
Of two proud men? what peace can be
found
To grow between the hammer and the anvil?
Tell us,
Are the old disputes at an end, is the wall
of pride cast down
That divided them? Is it peace or war? Does
he come
In full assurance, or only secure
In the power of Rome, the spiritual rule,
The assurance of right, and the love of the
people,
Contemning the hatred and envy of barons?
HERALD   You are right to express a certain
incredulity.
He comes in pride and sorrow, affirming all
his claims,
Assured, beyond doubt, of the devotion of
the people,
Who receive him with scenes of frenzied
enthusiasm.
Lining the road and throwing down their
capes,
Strewing the way with leaves and late flow-
ers of the season.
The streets of the city will be packed to
suffocation,
And I think that his horse will be deprived
of its tail,
A single hair of which becomes a precious
relic.
He is at one with the Pope, and with the
King of France,
Who indeed would have liked to detain him
in his kingdom:
But as for our King, that is another matter.
FIRST PRIEST   But again, is it war or peace?
HERALD   Peace, but not the kiss of peace.
A patched up affair, if you ask my opinion.
And if you ask me, I think the Lord Arch-
bishop
Is not the man to cherish any illusions,
Or yet to diminish the least of his preten-
sions.
If you ask my opinion, I think that this peace
Is nothing like an end, or like a beginning.
It is common knowledge that when the Arch-
bishop
Parted from the King, he said to the King,
My Lord, he said, I leave you as a man
Whom in this life I shall not see again.

I have this, I assure you, on the highest
authority;
There are several opinions as to what he
meant
But no one considers it a happy prognos-
tic. (*Exit*)

FIRST PRIEST I fear for the Archbishop, I fear
for the Church,
I know that the pride bred of sudden pros-
perity
Was but confirmed by bitter adversity.
I saw him as Chancellor, flattered by the
King,
Liked or feared by courtiers, in their over-
bearing fashion,
Despised and despising, always isolated,
Never one among them, always insecure;
His pride always feeding upon his own
virtues,
Pride drawing sustenance from impartiality,
Pride drawing sustenance from generosity,
Loathing power given by temporal devolu-
tion,
Wishing subjection to God alone.
Had the King been greater, or had he been
weaker
Things had perhaps been different for
Thomas.

SECOND PRIEST Yet our lord is returned. Our
lord has come back to his own again.
We have had enough of waiting, from December to dismal December.
The Archbishop shall be at our head, dispelling dismay and doubt.
He will tell us what we are to do, he will
give us our orders, instruct us.
Our Lord is at one with the Pope, and also
the King of France.
We can lean on a rock, we can feel a firm
foothold
Against the perpetual wash of tides of
balance of forces of barons and land-
holders.
The rock of God is beneath our feet. Let
us meet the Archbishop with cordial
thanksgiving:
Our lord, our Archbishop returns. And when
the Archbishop returns
Our doubts are dispelled. Let us therefore
rejoice,
I say rejoice, and show a glad face for his
welcome.
I am the Archbishop's man. Let us give the
Archbishop welcome!

THIRD PRIEST For good or ill, let the wheel
turn.
The wheel has been still, these seven years,
and no good.

For ill or good, let the wheel turn.
For who knows the end of good or evil?
Until the grinders cease
And the door shall be shut in the street,
And all the daughters of music shall be
brought low.

CHORUS Here is no continuing city, here is
no abiding stay.
Ill the wind, ill the time, uncertain the profit,
certain the danger.
O late late late, late is the time, late too late,
and rotten the year;
Evil the wind, and bitter the sea, and grey
the sky, grey grey grey.
O Thomas, return, Archbishop; return, return
to France.
Return. Quickly. Quietly. Leave us to perish
in quiet.
You come with applause, you come with
rejoicing, but you come bringing death
into Canterbury:
A doom on the house, a doom on yourself,
a doom on the world.

We do not wish anything to happen.
Seven years we have lived quietly,
Succeeded in avoiding notice,
Living and partly living.
There have been oppression and luxury,
There have been poverty and license,
There has been minor injustice.
Yet we have gone on living,
Living and partly living.
Sometimes the corn has failed us,
Sometimes the harvest is good,
One year is a year of rain,
Another a year of dryness,
One year the apples are abundant,
Another year the plums are lacking.
Yet we have gone on living,
Living and partly living.
We have kept the feasts, heard the masses,
We have brewed beer and cider,
Gathered wood against the winter,
Talked at the corner of the fire,
Talked at the corners of streets,
Talked not always in whispers,
Living and partly living.
We have seen births, deaths and marriages,
We have had various scandals,
We have been afflicted with taxes,
We have had laughter and gossip,
Several girls have disappeared
Unaccountably, and some not able to.
We have all had our private terrors,
Our particular shadows, our secret fears.

But now a great fear is upon us, a fear not of
　　one but of many,
A fear like birth and death, when we see
　　birth and death alone
In a void apart. We
Are afraid in a fear which we cannot know,
　　which we cannot face, which none un-
　　derstands,
And our hearts are torn from us, our brains
　　unskinned like the layers of an onion,
　　our selves are lost lost
In a final fear which none understands. O
　　Thomas Archbishop,
O Thomas our Lord, leave us and leave us
　　be, in our humble and tarnished frame
　　of existence, leave us; do not ask us
To stand to the doom on the house, the
　　doom on the Archbishop, the doom on
　　the world.
Archbishop, secure and assured of your fate,
　　unafraid among the shades, do you rea-
　　lize what you ask, do you realize what
　　it means
To the small folk drawn into the pattern of
　　fate, the small folk who live among
　　small things,
The strain on the brain of the small folk who
　　stand to the doom of the house, the
　　doom of their lord, the doom of the
　　world?
O Thomas, Archbishop, leave us, leave us,
　　leave sullen Dover, and set sail for
　　France. Thomas our Archbishop still
　　our Archbishop even in France. Thomas
　　Archbishop, set the white sail between
　　the grey sky and the bitter sea, leave us,
　　leave us for France.

SECOND PRIEST　What a way to talk at such a
　　juncture!
You are foolish, immodest and babbling
　　women.
Do you not know that the good Archbishop
Is likely to arrive at any moment?
The crowds in the streets will be cheering
　　and cheering,
You go on croaking like frogs in the treetops:
But frogs at least can be cooked and eaten.
Whatever you are afraid of, in your craven
　　apprehension,
Let me ask you at the least to put on pleasant
　　faces,
And give a hearty welcome to our good
　　Archbishop.

(*Enter* THOMAS)

THOMAS　Peace. And let them be, in their
　　exaltation.

They speak better than they know, and be-
　　yond your understanding.
They know and do not know, what it is to
　　act or suffer.
They know and do not know, that acting is
　　suffering
And suffering is action. Neither does the
　　actor suffer
Nor the patient act. But both are fixed
In an eternal action, an eternal patience
To which all must consent that it may be
　　willed
And which all must suffer that they may
　　will it,
That the pattern may subsist, for the pattern
　　is the action
And the suffering, that the wheel may turn
　　and still
Be forever still.

SECOND PRIEST　O my Lord, forgive me, I did
　　not see you coming,
Engrossed by the chatter of these foolish
　　women.
Forgive us, my Lord, you would have had
　　a better welcome
If we had been sooner prepared for the
　　event.
But your Lordship knows that seven years
　　of waiting,
Seven years of prayer, seven years of empti-
　　ness,
Have better prepared our hearts for your
　　coming,
Than seven days could make ready Canter-
　　bury.
However, I will have fires laid in all your
　　rooms
To take the chill off our English December,
Your Lordship now being used to a better
　　climate.
Your Lordship will find your rooms in order
　　as you left them.

THOMAS　And will try to leave them in order
　　as I find them.
I am more than grateful for all your kind
　　attentions.
These are small matters. Little rest in Canter-
　　bury
With eager enemies restless about us.
Rebellious bishops, York, London, Salisbury,
Would have intercepted our letters,
Filled the coast with spies and sent to meet
　　me
Some who hold me in bitterest hate.
By God's grace aware of their prevision
I sent my letters on another day,
Had fair crossing, found at Sandwich

(*Enter* THIRD TEMPTER)

THIRD TEMPTER   I am an unexpected visitor.

THOMAS   I expected you.

TEMPTER   But not in this guise, or for my
    present purpose.

THOMAS   No purpose brings surprise.

TEMPTER   Well, my Lord,
    I am no trifler, and no politician.
    To idle or intrigue at court
    I have no skill. I am no courtier.
    I know a horse, a dog, a wench;
    I know how to hold my estates in order,
    A country-keeping lord who minds his own
        business.
    It is we country lords who know the coun-
        try
    And we who know what the country needs.
    It is our country. We care for the country.
    We are the backbone of the nation.
    We, not the plotting parasites
    About the King. Excuse my bluntness:
    I am a rough straightforward Englishman.

THOMAS   Proceed straight forward.

TEMPTER   Purpose is plain.
    Endurance of friendship does not depend
    Upon ourselves, but upon circumstance.
    But circumstance is not undetermined.
    Unreal friendship may turn to real;
    But real friendship, once ended, cannot be
        mended.
    Sooner shall enmity turn to alliance.
    The enmity that never knew friendship
    Can sooner know accord.

THOMAS   For a countryman
    You wrap your meaning in as dark generality
    As any courtier.

TEMPTER   This is the simple fact!
    You have no hope of reconciliation
    With Henry the King. You look only
    To blind assertion in isolation.
    That is a mistake.

THOMAS   O Henry, O my King!

TEMPTER   Other friends
    May be found in the present situation.
    King in England is not all-powerful;
    King is in France, squabbling in Anjou;
    Round him waiting hungry sons.
    We are for England. We are in England.
    You and I, my Lord, are Normans.
    England is a land for Norman
    Sovereignty. Let the Angevin
    Destroy himself, fighting in Anjou.
    He does not understand us, the English
        barons.
    We are the people.

THOMAS   To what does this lead?

TEMPTER   To a happy coalition
    Of intelligent interests.

THOMAS   But what have you—
    If you do speak for barons—

TEMPTER   For a powerful party
    Which has turned its eyes in your direc-
        tion—
    To gain from you, your Lordship asks.
    For us, Church favor would be an advan-
        tage,
    Blessing of Pope powerful protection
    In the fight for liberty. You, my Lord,
    In being with us, would fight a good stroke
    At once, for England and for Rome,
    Ending the tyrannous jurisdiction
    Of king's court over bishop's court,
    Of king's court over baron's court.

THOMAS   Which I helped to found.

TEMPTER   Which you helped to found.
    But time past is time forgotten.
    We expect the rise of a new constellation.

THOMAS   And if the Archbishop cannot trust
    the King,
    How can he trust those who work for King's
        undoing?

TEMPTER   Kings will allow no power but their
    own;
    Church and people have good cause against
    the throne.

THOMAS   If the Archbishop cannot trust the
    Throne,
    He has good cause to trust none but God
    alone.
    It is not better to be thrown
    To a thousand hungry appetites than to one.
    At a future time this may be shown.
    I ruled once as Chancellor
    And men like you were glad to wait at my
    door.
    Not only in the court, but in the field
    And in the tiltyard I made many yield.
    Shall I who ruled like an eagle over doves
    Now take the shape of a wolf among wolves?
    Pursue your treacheries as you have done
    before:
    No one shall say that I betrayed a king.

TEMPTER   Then, my Lord, I shall not wait at
    your door;
    And I well hope, before another spring
    The King will show his regard for your
    loyalty.

THOMAS   To make, then break, this thought
    has come before,
    The desperate exercise of failing power.
    Samson in Gaza did no more.
    But if I break, I must break myself alone.

(*Enter* FOURTH TEMPTER)

FOURTH TEMPTER   Well done, Thomas, your
   will is hard to bend.
  And with me beside you, you shall not lack
   a friend.
THOMAS   Who are you? I expected
  Three visitors, not four.
TEMPTER   Do not be surprised to receive one
   more.
  Had I been expected, I had been here be-
   fore.
  I always precede expectation.
THOMAS   Who are you?
TEMPTER   As you do not know me, I do not
   need a name,
  And, as you know me, that is why I come.
  You know me, but have never seen my face.
  To meet before was never time or place.
THOMAS   Say what you come to say.
TEMPTER   It shall be said at last.
  Hooks have been baited with morsels of
   the past.
  Wantonness is weakness. As for the King,
  His hardened hatred shall have no end.
  You know truly, the King will never trust
  Twice, the man who has been his friend.
  Borrow use cautiously, employ
  Your services as long as you have to lend.
  You would wait for trap to snap
  Having served your turn, broken and
   crushed.
  As or barons, envy of lesser men
  Is still more stubborn than king's anger.
  Kings have public policy, barons private
   profit,
  Jealousy raging possession of the fiend.
  Barons are employable against each other;
  Greater enemies must kings destroy.
THOMAS   What is your counsel?
TEMPTER   Fare forward to the end.
  All other ways are closed to you
  Except the way already chosen.
  But what is pleasure, kingly rule,
  Or rule of men beneath a king,
  With craft in corners, stealthy stratagem,
  To general grasp of spiritual power?
  Man oppressed by sin, since Adam fell—
  You hold the keys of heaven and hell.
  Power to bind and loose: bind, Thomas,
   bind,
  King and bishop under your heel.
  King, emperor, bishop, baron, king:
  Uncertain mastery of melting armies,
  War, plague, and revolution,
  New conspiracies, broken pacts;
  To be master or servant within an hour,
  This is the course of temporal power.

The Old King shall know it, when at last
   breath,
No sons, no empire, he bites broken teeth.
You hold the skein: wind, Thomas, wind
The thread of eternal life and death.
You hold this power, hold it.
THOMAS   Supreme, in this land?
TEMPTER   Supreme, but for one.
THOMAS   That I do not understand.
TEMPTER   It is not for me to tell you how this
   may be so;
  I am only here, Thomas, to tell you what
   you know.
THOMAS   How long shall this be?
TEMPTER   Save what you know already, ask
   nothing of me.
  But think, Thomas, think of glory after death.
  When king is dead, there's another king,
  And one more king is another reign.
  King is forgotten, when another shall come:
  Saint and Martyr rule from the tomb.
  Think, Thomas, think of enemies dismayed,
  Creeping in penance, frightened of a shade;
  Think of pilgrims, standing in line
  Before the glittering jewelled shrine,
  From generation to generation
  Bending the knee in supplication.
  Think of the miracles, by God's grace,
  And think of your enemies, in another place.
THOMAS   I have thought of these things.
TEMPTER   That is why I tell you.
  Your thoughts have more power than kings
   to compel you.
  You have also thought, sometimes at your
   prayers,
  Sometimes hesitating at the angles of stairs,
  And between sleep and waking, early in the
   morning,
  When the bird cries, have thought of further
   scorning.
  That nothing lasts, but the wheel turns,
  The nest is rifled, and the bird mourns;
  That the shrine shall be pillaged, and the
   gold spent,
  The jewels gone for light ladies' ornament,
  The sanctuary broken, and its stores
  Swept into the laps of parasites and whores.
  When miracles cease, and the faithful de-
   sert you,
  And men shall only do their best to forget
   you.
  And later is worse, when men will not hate
   you
  Enough to defame or to execrate you,
  But pondering the qualities that you lacked
  Will only try to find the historical fact.
  When men shall declare that there was no
   mystery

About this man who played a certain part
in history.

THOMAS But what is there to do? What is
left to be done?

Is there no enduring crown to be won?

TEMPTER Yes, Thomas, yes; you have thought
of that too.

What can compare with glory of Saints
Dwelling forever in presence of God?
What earthly glory, of king or emperor,
What earthly pride, that is not poverty
Compared with richness of heavenly
grandeur?

Seek the way of martyrdom, make yourself
the lowest

On earth, to be high in heaven.

And see far off below you, where the gulf
is fixed,

Your persecutors, in timeless torment,
Parched passion, beyond expiation.

THOMAS   No!

Who are you, tempting with my own desires?

Others have come, temporal tempters,
With pleasure and power at palpable price.
What do you offer? What do you ask?

TEMPTER I offer what you desire. I ask
What you have to give. Is it too much
For such a vision of eternal grandeur?

THOMAS Others offered real goods, worthless
But real. You only offer
Dreams to damnation.

TEMPTER   You have often dreamt them.

THOMAS Is there no way, in my soul's sickness,

Does not lead to damnation in pride?
I well know that these temptations
Mean present vanity and future torment.
Can sinful pride be driven out
Only by more sinful? Can I neither act nor
suffer

Without perdition?

TEMPTER You know and do not know, what
it is to act or suffer.

You know and do not know, that acting is
suffering,

And suffering action. Neither does the actor
suffer

Nor the patient act. But both are fixed
In an eternal action, an eternal patience
To which all must consent that it may be
willed

And which all must suffer that they may will
it,

That the pattern may subsist, that the wheel
may turn and still

Be forever still.

CHORUS There is no rest in the house. There
is no rest in the street.

I hear restless movement of feet. And the air
is heavy and thick.

Thick and heavy the sky. And the earth
presses up beneath my feet.

What is the sickly smell, the vapor? the
dark green light from a cloud on a
withered tree? The earth is heaving to
parturition of issue of hell. What is the
sticky dew that forms on the back of
my hand?

THE FOUR TEMPTERS Man's life is a cheat
and a disappointment;

All things are unreal,
Unreal or disappointing:
The Catherine wheel, the pantomime cat,
The prizes given at the children's party,
The prize awarded for the English Essay,
The scholar's degree, the statesman's deco-
ration.

All things become less real, man passes
From unreality to unreality.
This man is obstinate, blind, intent
On self-destruction,
Passing from deception to deception,
From grandeur to grandeur to final illusion,
Lost in the wonder of his own greatness,
The enemy of society, enemy of himself.

THE THREE PRIESTS O Thomas my Lord, do
not fight the intractable tide,

Do not sail the irresistible wind; in the
storm,

Should we not wait for the sea to subside,
in the night

Abide the coming of day, when the traveller
may find his way,

The sailor lay course by the sun?

CHORUS Is it the owl that calls, or a signal
between the trees?

PRIESTS Is the window-bar made fast, is the
door under lock and bolt?

TEMPTERS Is it rain that taps at the window,
is it wind that pokes at the door?

CHORUS Does the torch flame in the hall, the
candle in the room?

PRIESTS Does the watchman walk by the wall?

TEMPTERS Does the mastiff prowl by the
gate?

CHORUS Death has a hundred hands and
walks by a thousand ways.

PRIESTS He may come in the sight of all, he
may pass unseen unheard.

TEMPTERS Come whispering through the ear,
or a sudden shock on the skull.

CHORUS A man may walk with a lamp at
night, and yet be drowned in a ditch.

PRIESTS A man may climb the stair in the day, and slip on a broken step.

TEMPTERS A man may sit at meat, and feel the cold in his groin.

CHORUS We have not been happy, my Lord, we have not been too happy.

We are not ignorant women, we know what we must expect and not expect.

We know of oppression and torture,
We know of extortion and violence,
Destitution, disease,
The old without fire in winter,
The child without milk in summer,
Our labor taken away from us,
Our sins made heavier upon us.
We have seen the young man mutilated,
The torn girl trembling by the mill-stream.
And meanwhile we have gone on living,
Living and partly living,
Picking together the pieces,
Gathering faggots at nightfall,
Building a partial shelter,
For sleeping, and eating and drinking and laughter.

God gave us always some reason, some hope; but now a new terror has soiled us, which none can avert, none can avoid, flowing under our feet and over the sky;
Under doors and down chimneys, flowing in at the ear and the mouth and the eye.
God is leaving us, God is leaving us, more pang, more pain, than birth or death.
Sweet and cloying through the dark air
Falls the stifling scent of despair;
The forms take shape in the dark air:
Puss-purr of leopard, footfall of padding bear,
Palm-pat of nodding ape, square hyena waiting
For laughter, laughter, laughter. The Lords of Hell are here.
They curl round you, lie at your feet, swing and wing through the dark air.
O Thomas Archbishop, save us, save us, save yourself that we may be saved;
Destroy yourself and we are destroyed.

THOMAS Now is my way clear, now is the meaning plain:
Temptation shall not come in this kind again.
The last temptation is the greatest treason:
To do the right deed for the wrong reason.
The natural vigor in the venial sin
Is the way in which our lives begin.
Thirty years ago, I searched all the ways
That lead to pleasure, advancement and praise.
Delight in sense, in learning and in thought,

Music and philosophy, curiosity,
The purple bullfinch in the lilac tree,
The tiltyard skill, the strategy of chess,
Love in the garden, singing to the instrument,
Were all things equally desirable.
Ambition comes when early force is spent
And when we find no longer all things possible.
Ambition comes behind and unobservable.
Sin grows with doing good. When I imposed the King's law
In England, and waged war with him against Toulouse,
I beat the barons at their own game. I
Could then despise the men who thought me most contemptible,
The raw nobility, whose manners matched their fingernails.
While I ate out of the King's dish
To become servant of God was never my wish.
Servant of God has chance of greater sin
And sorrow, than the man who serves a king.
For those who serve the greater cause may make the cause serve them,
Still doing right: and striving with political men
May make that cause political, not by what they do
But by what they are. I know
What yet remains to show you of my history
Will seem to most of you at best futility,
Senseless self-slaughter of a lunatic,
Arrogant passion of a fanatic.
I know that history at all times draws
The strangest consequence from remotest cause.
But for every evil, every sacrilege,
Crime, wrong, oppression and the axe's edge,
Indifference, exploitation, you, and you,
And you, must all be punished. So must you.
I shall no longer act or suffer, to the sword's end.
Now my good Angel, whom God appoints
To be my guardian, hover over the swords' points.

INTERLUDE

THE ARCHBISHOP (*preaches in the Cathedral on Christmas Morning, 1170*) "Glory to God in the highest, and on earth peace, good will toward men." *The fourteenth verse of the second chapter of the Gospel according to Saint Luke.* In the Name of the Father, and of the Son, and of the Holy Ghost. Amen.

Dear children of God, my sermon this morning will be a very short one. I wish only that you should ponder and meditate the deep meaning and mystery of our masses of Christmas Day. For whenever Mass is said, we re-enact the Passion and Death of Our Lord; and on this Christmas Day we do this in celebration of His Birth. So that at the same moment we rejoice in His coming for the salvation of men, and offer again to God His Body and Blood in sacrifice, oblation and satisfaction for the sins of the whole world. It was in this same night that has just passed, that a multitude of the heavenly host appeared before the shepherds at Bethlehem, saying, "Glory to God in the highest, and on earth peace, good will toward men"; at this same time of all the year that we celebrate at once the Birth of Our Lord and His Passion and Death upon the Cross. Beloved, as the World sees, this is to behave in a strange fashion. For who in the World will both mourn and rejoice at once and for the same reason? For either joy will be overborne by mourning, or mourning will be cast out by joy; so it is only in these our Christian mysteries that we can rejoice and mourn at once for the same reason. But think for a while on the meaning of this word "peace." Does it seem strange to you that the angels should have announced Peace, when ceaselessly the world has been stricken with War and the fear of War? Does it seem to you that the angelic voices were mistaken, and that the promise was a disappointment and a cheat?

Reflect now, how Our Lord Himself spoke of Peace. He said to His disciples "My peace I leave with you, my peace I give unto you." Did He mean peace as we think of it: the kingdom of England at peace with its neighbors, the barons at peace with the King, the householder counting over his peaceful gains, the swept hearth, his best wine for a friend at the table, his wife singing to the children? Those men His disciples knew no such things: they went forth to journey afar, to suffer by land and sea, to know torture, imprisonment, disappointment, to suffer death by martyrdom. What then did He mean? If you ask that, remember then that He said also, "Not as the world gives, give I unto you." So then, He gave to His disciples peace, but not peace as the world gives.

Consider also one thing of which you have probably never thought. Not only do we at the feast of Christmas celebrate at once Our Lord's Birth and His Death: but on the next day we celebrate the martyrdom of His first martyr, the blessed Stephen. Is it an accident, do you think, that the day of the first martyr follows immediately the day of the Birth of Christ? By no means. Just as we rejoice and mourn at once, in the Birth and in the Passion of Our Lord; so also, in a smaller figure; we both rejoice and mourn in the death of martyrs. We mourn, for the sins of the world that has martyred them; we rejoice, that another soul is numbered among the Saints in Heaven, for the glory of God and for the salvation of men.

Beloved, we do not think of a martyr simply as a good Christian who has been killed because he is a Christian: for that would be solely to mourn. We do not think of him simply as a good Christian who has been elevated to the company of the Saints: for that would be simply to rejoice: and neither our mourning nor our rejoicing is as the world's is. A Christian martyrdom is no accident. Saints are not made by accident. Still less is a Christian martyrdom the effect of a man's will to become a Saint, as a man by willing and contriving may become a ruler of men. Ambition fortifies the will of man to become ruler over other men: it operates with deception, cajolery, and violence, it is the action of impurity upon impurity. Not so in Heaven. A martyr, a saint, is always made by the design of God, for His love of men, to warn them and to lead them, to bring them back to His ways. A martyrdom is never the design of man; for the true martyr is he who has become the instrument of God, who has lost his will in the will of God, not lost it but found it, for he has found freedom in submission to God. The martyr no longer desires anything for himself, not even the glory of martyrdom. So thus as on earth the Church mourns and rejoices at once, in a fashion that the world cannot understand; so in Heaven the Saints are most high, having made themselves most low, seeing themselves not as we see them, but in the light of the Godhead from which they draw their being.

I have spoken to you today, dear children of God, of the martyrs of the past, asking you to remember especially our martyr of Canterbury, the blessed Archbishop Elphege; because it is fitting, on Christ's birth day, to remember what is that Peace which He brought; and because, dear children, I do not think I shall ever preach to you again; and because it is possible that in a short time you may have yet another martyr, and that one perhaps not the last. I would have you keep in your hearts these words that I say, and think of them at another time. In the Name of the Father, and of the Son, and of the Holy Ghost. Amen.

PART TWO

CAST OF CHARACTERS

THREE PRIESTS
FOUR KNIGHTS
ARCHBISHOP THOMAS
  BECKET
CHORUS OF WOMEN OF
  CANTERBURY
ATTENDANTS

The first scene is in the Archbishop's Hall, the second scene is in the Cathedral, on December 29th, 1170.

CHORUS   Does the bird sing in the South?
  Only the sea-bird cries, driven inland by the storm.
  What sign of the spring of the year?
  Only the death of the old: not a stir, not a shoot, not a breath.
  Do the days begin to lengthen?
  Longer and darker the day, shorter and colder the night.
  Still and stifling the air: but a wind is stored up in the East.
  The starved crow sits in the field, attentive; and in the wood
  The owl rehearses the hollow note of death.
  What signs of a bitter spring?
  The wind stored up in the East.
  What, at the time of the birth of Our Lord, at Christmastide,
  Is there not peace upon earth, goodwill among men?
  The peace of this world is always uncertain, unless men keep the peace of God.
  And war among men defiles this world, but death in the Lord renews it,
  And the world must be cleaned in the winter, or we shall have only
  A sour spring, a parched summer, an empty harvest.
  Between Christmas and Easter what work shall be done?
  The ploughman shall go out in March and turn the same earth
  He has turned before, the bird shall sing the same song.

When the leaf is out on the tree, when the elder and may
  Burst over the stream, and the air is clear and high,
  And voices trill at windows, and children tumble in front of the door,
  What work shall have been done, what wrong
  Shall the bird's song cover, the green tree cover, what wrong
  Shall the fresh earth cover? We wait, and the time is short
  But waiting is long.

(*Enter the* FIRST PRIEST *with a banner of St. Stephen borne before him*)

FIRST PRIEST   Since Christmas a day: and the day of St. Stephen, First Martyr.
  A day that was always most dear to the Archbishop Thomas.
  And he kneeled down and cried with a loud voice:
  Lord, lay not this sin to their charge.

(*Enter the* SECOND PRIEST, *with a banner of St. John the Apostle borne before him*)

SECOND PRIEST   Since St. Stephen a day: and the day of St. John the Apostle.
  That which was from the beginning, which we have heard,
  Which we have seen with our eyes, and our hands have handled
  Of the word of life; that which we have seen and heard
  Declare we unto you.

(*Enter the* THIRD PRIEST, *with a banner of the Holy Innocents borne before him*)

THIRD PRIEST   Since St. John the Apostle a day; and the day of the Holy Innocents.
  As the voice of many waters, of thunder, of harps,
  They sung as it were a new song.
  The blood of thy saints have they shed like water,
  And there was no man to bury them. Avenge, O Lord,
  The blood of thy saints. In Rama, a voice heard, weeping.
  Out of the mouth of very babes, O God!

(*The* PRIESTS *stand together with the banners behind them*)

FIRST PRIEST   Since the Holy Innocents a day: the fourth day from Christmas.
  As for the people, so also for himself, he offereth for sins.
  He lays down his life for the sheep. Today?

SECOND PRIEST Today, what is today? For the day is half gone.

FIRST PRIEST Today, what is today? but another day, the dusk of the year.

SECOND PRIEST Today, what is today? Another night, and another dawn.

THIRD PRIEST What day is the day that we know that we hope for or fear for?

Every day is the day we should fear from or hope from. One moment

Weighs like another. Only in retrospection, selection,

We say, that was the day. The critical moment

That is always now, and here. Even now, in sordid particulars

The eternal design may appear.

(*Enter the* FOUR KNIGHTS)

FIRST KNIGHT Servants of the King.

FIRST PRIEST   And known to us.

You are welcome. Have you ridden far?

FIRST KNIGHT Not far today, but matters urgent

Have brought us from France. We rode hard,

Took ship yesterday, landed last night,

Having business with the Archbishop.

SECOND KNIGHT Urgent business.

THIRD KNIGHT   From the King.

FOURTH KNIGHT By the King's order.

FIRST KNIGHT   Our men are outside.

FIRST PRIEST You know the Archbishop's hospitality.

We are about to go to dinner.

The good Archbishop would be vexed

If we did not offer you entertainment

Before your business. Please dine with us.

Your men shall be looked after also.

Dinner before business. Do you like roast pork?

FIRST KNIGHT Business before dinner. We will roast your pork

First, and dine upon it after.

SECOND KNIGHT We must see the Archbishop.

THIRD KNIGHT   Go, tell the Archbishop

We have no need of his hospitality.

We will find our own dinner.

FIRST PRIEST (*to* ATTENDANT) Go, tell His Lordship.

FOURTH KNIGHT   How much longer will you keep us waiting?

(*Enter* THOMAS)

THOMAS (*to* PRIESTS) However certain our expectation

The moment foreseen may be unexpected

When it arrives. It comes when we are

Engrossed with matters of other urgency.

On my table you will find

The papers in order, and the documents signed.

(*To* KNIGHTS)

You are welcome, whatever your business may be.

You say, from the King?

FIRST KNIGHT   Most surely from the King.

We must speak with you alone.

THOMAS (*to* PRIESTS)   Leave us then alone.

Now what is the matter?

FIRST KNIGHT   This is the matter.

THE FOUR KNIGHTS You are the Archbishop in revolt against the King; in rebellion to the King and the law of the land;

You are the Archbishop who was made by the King; whom he set in your place to carry out his command.

You are his servant, his tool, and his jack,

You wore his favors on your back,

You had your honors all from his hand; from him you had the power, the seal and the ring.

This is the man who was the tradesman's son: the backstairs brat who was born in Cheapside;

This is the creature that crawled upon the King; swollen with blood and swollen with pride.

Creeping out of the London dirt,

Crawling up like a louse on your shirt,

The man who cheated, swindled, lied; broke his oath and betrayed his King.

THOMAS This is not true.

Both before and after I received the ring

I have been a loyal vassal to the King.

Saving my order, I am at his command,

As his most faithful vassal in the land.

FIRST KNIGHT Saving your order! let your order save you—

As I do not think it is like to do.

Saving your ambition is what you mean,

Saving your pride, envy and spleen.

SECOND KNIGHT Saving your insolence and greed.

Won't you ask us to pray to God for you, in your need?

THIRD KNIGHT Yes, we'll pray for you!

FOURTH KNIGHT   Yes, we'll pray for you!

THE FOUR KNIGHTS Yes, we'll pray that God may help you!

THOMAS But, gentlemen, your business

Which you said so urgent, is it only

Scolding and blaspheming?

FIRST KNIGHT   That was only

Our indignation, as loyal subjects.

THOMAS   Loyal? to whom?

FIRST KNIGHT   To the King!

SECOND KNIGHT   The King!

THIRD KNIGHT   The King!

FOURTH KNIGHT   God bless him!

THOMAS   Then let your new coat of loyalty
    be worn
  Carefully, so it get not soiled or torn.
  Have you something to say?

FIRST KNIGHT   By the King's command.
  Shall we say it now?

SECOND KNIGHT   Without delay,
  Before the old fox is off and away.

THOMAS   What you have to say
  By the King's command—if it be the King's
    command—
  Should be said in public. If you make
    charges,
  Then in public I will refute them.

FIRST KNIGHT   No! here and now!

(*They make to attack him, but the* PRIESTS
and ATTENDANTS *return and quietly interpose
themselves*)

THOMAS   Now and here!

FIRST KNIGHT   Of your earlier misdeeds I shall
    make no mention.
  They are too well known. But after dis-
    sension
  Had ended, in France, and you were endued
  With your former privilege, how did you
    show your gratitude?
  You had fled from England, not exiled
  Or threatened, mind you; but in the hope
  Of stirring up trouble in the French do-
    minions.
  You sowed strife abroad, you reviled
  The King to the King of France, to the
    Pope,
  Raising up against him false opinions.

SECOND KNIGHT   Yet the King, out of his
    charity,
  And urged by your friends, offered clemency,
  Made a pact of peace, and all dispute ended
  Sent you back to your See as you demanded.

THIRD KNIGHT   And burying the memory of
    your transgressions
  Restored your honors and your possessions.
  All was granted for which you sued:
  Yet how, I repeat, did you show your
    gratitude?

FOURTH KNIGHT   Suspending those who had
    crowned the young prince,
  Denying the legality of his coronation;
  Binding with the chains of anathema,
  Using every means in your power to evince
  The King's faithful servants, everyone who
    transacts

His business in his absence, the business of
    the nation.

FIRST KNIGHT   These are the facts.
  Say therefore if you will be content
  To answer in the King's presence. Therefore
    were we sent.

THOMAS   Never was it my wish
  To uncrown the King's son, or to diminish
  His honor and power. Why should he wish
  To deprive my people of me and keep me
    from my own
  And bid me sit in Canterbury, alone?
  I would wish him three crowns rather than
    one,
  And as for the bishops, it is not my yoke
  That is laid upon them, or mine to revoke.
  Let them go to the Pope. It was he who
    condemned them.

FIRST KNIGHT   Through you they were sus-
    pended.

SECOND KNIGHT   By you be this amended.

THIRD KNIGHT   Absolve them.

FOURTH KNIGHT   Absolve them.

THOMAS   I do not deny
  That this was done through me. But it is
    not I
  Who can loose whom the Pope has bound.
  Let them go to him, upon whom redounds
  Their contempt towards me, their contempt
    towards the Church shown.

FIRST KNIGHT   Be that as it may, here is the
    King's command:
  That you and your servants depart from
    this land.

THOMAS   If that *is* the King's command, I will
    be bold
  To say: seven years were my people without
  My presence; seven years of misery and pain.
  Seven years a mendicant on foreign charity
  I lingered abroad: seven years is no brevity.
  I shall not get those seven years back again.
  Never again, you must make no doubt,
  Shall the sea run between the shepherd and
    his fold.

FIRST KNIGHT   The King's justice, the King's
    majesty,
  You insult with gross indignity;
  Insolent madman, whom nothing deters
  From attainting his servants and ministers.

THOMAS   It is not I who insult the King,
  And there is higher than I or the King.
  It is not I, Becket from Cheapside,
  It is not against me, Becket, that you strive.
  It is not Becket who pronounces doom,
  But the Law of Christ's Church, the judge-
    ment of Rome.
  Go then to Rome, or let Rome come

Here, to you, in the person of her most un-
worthy son.
Petty politicians in your endless adventure!
Rome alone can absolve those who break
Christ's indenture.

FIRST KNIGHT   Priest, you have spoken in peril
of your life.

SECOND KNIGHT   Priest, you have spoken
in danger of the knife.

THIRD KNIGHT   Priest, you have spoken
treachery and treason.

FOURTH KNIGHT   Priest! traitor confirmed in
malfeasance.

THOMAS   I submit my cause to the judge-
ment of Rome.
But if you kill me, I shall rise from my tomb
To submit my cause before God's throne.

KNIGHTS   Priest! monk! and servant! take, hold,
detain,
Restrain this man, in the King's name;
Or answer with your bodies, if he escape
before we come,
We come for the King's justice, we come
again.   (*exeunt*)

THOMAS   Pursue those who flee, track down
those who evade;
Come for arrest, come with the sword,
Here, here, you shall find me ready, in the
battle of the Lord.
At whatsoever time you are ready to come,
You will find me still more ready for martyr-
dom.

CHORUS   I have smelt them, the deathbringers,
senses are quickened
By subtile forebodings; I have heard
Fluting in the nighttime, fluting and owls,
have seen at noon
Scaly wings slanting over, huge and ridiculous. I have tasted
The savor of putrid flesh in the spoon. I
have felt
The heaving of earth at nightfall, restless,
absurd. I have heard
Laughter in the noises of beasts that make
strange noises: jackal, jackass, jackdaw;
the scurrying noise of mouse and
jerboa; the laugh of the loon, the lunatic bird. I have seen
Grey necks twisting, rat tails twining, in the
thick light of dawn. I have eaten
Smooth creatures still living, with the
strong salt taste of living things under
sea; I have tasted
The living lobster, the crab, the oyster, the
whelk and the prawn; and they live
and spawn in my bowels, and my
bowels dissolve in the light of dawn.
I have smelt

Death in the rose, death in the hollyhock,
sweet pea, hyacinth, primrose and cow-
slip. I have seen
Trunk and horn, tusk and hoof, in odd
places;
I have lain on the floor of the sea and
breathed with the breathing of the
sea-anemone, swallowed with ingurgi-
tation of the sponge. I have lain in
the soil and criticised the worm. In
the air
Flirted with the passage of the kite, I have
plunged with the kite and cowered
with the wren. I have felt
The horn of the beetle, the scale of the viper,
the mobile hard insensitive skin of the
elephant, the evasive flank of the fish.
I have smelt
Corruption in the dish, incense in the latrine,
the sewer in the incense, the smell
of sweet soap in the woodpath, a hellish
sweet scent in the woodpath, while the
ground heaved. I have seen
Rings of light coiling downwards, leading
To the horror of the ape. Have I not known,
not known
What was coming to be? It was here, in the
kitchen, in the passage,
In the mews in the barn in the byre in the
market place
In our veins our bowels our skulls as well
As well as in the plottings of potentates
As well as in the consultations of powers.
What is woven on the loom of fate
What is woven in the councils of princes
Is woven also in our veins, our brains,
Is woven like a pattern of living worms
In the guts of the women of Canterbury.

I have smelt them, the death-bringers; now
is too late
For action, too soon for contrition.
Nothing is possible but the shamed swoon
Of those consenting to the last humiliation.
I have consented, Lord Archbishop, have
consented.
Am torn away, subdued, violated,
United to the spiritual flesh of nature,
Mastered by the animal powers of spirit,
Dominated by the lust of self-demolition,
By the final utter uttermost death of spirit,
By the final ecstasy of waste and shame,
O Lord Archbishop, O Thomas Archbishop,
forgive us, forgive us, pray for us that
we may pray for you, out of our shame.

THOMAS   Peace, and be at peace with your
thoughts and visions.

These things had to come to you and you to
    accept them.
This is your share of the eternal burden,
The perpetual glory. This is one moment,
But know that another
Shall pierce you with a sudden painful joy
When the figure of God's purpose is made
    complete.
You shall forget these things, toiling in the
    household,
You shall remember them, droning by the
    fire,
When age and forgetfulness sweeten memory
Only like a dream that has often been told
And often been changed in the telling.
They will seem unreal.
Human kind cannot bear very much reality.

PRIESTS (*severally*) My Lord, you must not
    stop here. To the minister. Through
    the cloister. No time to waste. They are
    coming back, armed. To the altar, to
    the altar. They are here already. To the
    sanctuary. They are breaking in. We can
    barricade the minister doors. You can-
    not stay here. Force him to come. Seize
    him.

THOMAS   All my life they have been coming,
    these feet. All my life I have waited.
Death will come only when I am worthy,
And if I am worthy, there is no danger.
I have therefore only to make perfect my
    will.

PRIESTS   My Lord, they are coming. They
    will break through presently.
You will be killed. Come to the altar.

THOMAS   Peace! be quiet! remember where
    you are, and what is happening;
No life here is sought for but mine,
And I am not in danger: only near to death.

PRIESTS   Make haste, my Lord. Don't stop
    here talking. It is not right.
What shall become of us, my Lord, if you
    are killed; what shall become of us?

THOMAS   That again is another theme
To be developed and resolved in the pattern
    of time.
It is not for me to run from city to city;
To meet death gladly is only
The only way in which I can defend
The Law of God, the holy canons.

PRIESTS   My Lord, to vespers! You must not
    be absent from vespers. You must not
    be absent from the divine office. To
    vespers. Into the cathedral!

THOMAS   Go to vespers, remember me at your
    prayers.
They shall find the shepherd here; the flock
    shall be spared.

I have had a tremor of bliss, a wink of
    heaven, a whisper,
And I would no longer be denied; all things
Proceed to a joyful consummation.

PRIESTS   Seize him! force him! drag him!
THOMAS   Keep your hands off!
PRIESTS   To vespers! Take his feet! Up with
    him! Hurry.

(*They drag him off. While the* CHORUS *speak,
the scene is changed to the cathedral*)

CHORUS (*while a* Dies Irae *is sung in Latin by
a choir in the distance*)
    Numb the hand and dry the eyelid,
    Still the horror, but more horror
    Than when tearing in the belly.

    Still the horror, but more horror
    Than when twisting in the fingers,
    Than when splitting in the skull.

    More than footfall in the passage,
    More than shadow in the doorway,
    More than fury in the hall.

    The agents of hell disappear, the human,
        they shrink and dissolve
    Into dust on the wind, forgotten, unmemo-
        rable; only is here
    The white flat face of Death, God's silent
        servant,
    And behind the face of Death the Judge-
        ment
    And behind the Judgement the Void, more
        horrid than active shapes of hell;
    Emptiness, absence, separation from God;
    The horror of the effortless journey, to the
        empty land
    Which is no land, only emptiness, absence,
        the Void,
    Where those who were men can no longer
        turn the mind
    To distraction, delusion, escape into dream,
        pretence,
    Where the soul is no longer deceived, for
        there are no objects, no tones,
    No colors, no forms to distract, to divert
        the soul
    From seeing itself, foully united forever,
        nothing with nothing,
    Not what we call death, but what beyond
        death is not death,
    We fear, we fear. Who shall then plead
        for me,
    Who intercede for me, in my most need?

    Dead upon the tree, my Saviour,
    Let not be in vain Thy labor;
    Help me, Lord, in my last fear.

Dust I am, to dust am bending,
From the final doom impending
Help me, Lord, for death is near.

(*In the cathedral.* THOMAS *and* PRIESTS)

PRIESTS Bar the door. Bar the door.
The door is barred.
We are safe. We are safe.
The enemy may rage outside, he will tire
In vain. They cannot break in.
They dare not break in.
They cannot break in. They have not the
force.
We are safe. We are safe.

THOMAS Unbar the doors! throw open the
doors!
I will not have the house of prayer, the
church of Christ,
The sanctuary, turned into a fortress.
The Church shall protect her own, in her
own way, not
As oak and stone; stone and oak decay,
Give no stay, but the Church shall endure.
The church shall be open, even to our
enemies. Open the door!

PRIESTS My Lord! these are not men, these
come not as men come, but
Like maddened beasts. They come not like
men, who
Respect the sanctuary, who kneel to the
Body of Christ,
But like beasts. You would bar the door
Against the lion, the leopard, the wolf or
the boar,
Why not more
Against beasts with the souls of damned
men, against men
Who would damn themselves to beasts.
My Lord! My Lord!

THOMAS Unbar the door!
You think me reckless, desperate and mad.
You argue by results, as this world does,
To settle if an act be good or bad.
You defer to the fact. For every life and
every act
Consequence of good and evil can be shown.
And as in time results of many deeds are
blended
So good and evil in the end become con-
founded.
It is not in time that my death shall be
known;
It is out of time that my decision is taken
If you call that decision
To which my whole being gives entire con-
sent.
I give my life
To the Law of God above the Law of Man.

Those who do not the same
How should they know what I do?
How should you know what I do? Yet how
much more
Should you know than these madmen beat-
ing on the door.
Unbar the door! unbar the door!
We are not here to triumph by fighting, by
stratagem, or by resistance,
Not to fight with beasts as men. We have
fought the beast
And have conquered. We have only to con-
quer
Now, by suffering. This is the easier victory.
Now is the triumph of the Cross, now
Open the door! I command it. OPEN THE
DOOR!

(*The door is opened. The* KNIGHTS *enter,
slightly tipsy*)

PRIESTS This way, my Lord! Quick. Up the
stair. To the roof. To the crypt. Quick.
Come. Force him.

KNIGHTS (*one line each*) Where is Becket,
the traitor to the King?
Where is Becket, the meddling priest?
Come down Daniel to the lions' den,
Come down Daniel for the mark of the
beast.

Are you washed in the blood of the Lamb?
Are you marked with the mark of the
beast?
Come down Daniel to the lions' den,
Come down Daniel and join in the feast.

Where is Becket the Cheapside brat?
Where is Becket the faithless priest?
Come down Daniel to the lions' den,
Come down Daniel and join in the feast.

THOMAS It is the just man who
Like a bold lion, should be without fear.
I am here.
No traitor to the King. I am a priest,
A Christian, saved by the blood of Christ,
Ready to suffer with my blood.
This is the sign of the Church always,
The sign of blood. Blood for blood.
His blood given to buy my life,
My blood given to pay for His death,
My death for His death.

KNIGHTS Absolve all those you have excom-
municated.
Resign the powers you have arrogated.
Restore to the King the money you ap-
propriated.
Renew the obedience you have violated.

THOMAS For my Lord I am now ready to die,

That His Church may have peace and
liberty.

Do with me as you will, to your hurt and
shame;

But none of my people, in God's name,

Whether layman or clerk, shall you touch.
This I forbid.

KNIGHTS Traitor! traitor! traitor! traitor!

THOMAS You, Reginald, three times traitor
you:

Traitor to me as my temporal vassal,

Traitor to me as your spiritual lord,

Traitor to God in desecrating His Church.

FIRST KNIGHT No faith do I owe to a renegade,

And what I owe shall now be paid.

THOMAS Now to Almighty God, to the
Blessed Mary ever Virgin, to the
blessed John the Baptist, the holy
apostles Peter and Paul, to the blessed
martyr Denys, and to all the Saints, I
commend my cause and that of the
Church.

(*While the* KNIGHTS *kill him, we hear the*
CHORUS)

CHORUS Clear the air! clean the sky! wash
the wind! take stone from stone and
wash them.

The land is foul, the water is foul, our
beasts and ourselves defiled with blood.

A rain of blood has blinded my eyes. Where
is England? where is Kent? where is
Canterbury?

O far far far far in the past; and I wander
in the land of barren boughs: if I break
them, they bleed; I wander in a land
of dry stones: if I touch them they
bleed.

How how can I ever return, to the soft
quiet seasons?

Night stay with us, stop sun, hold season,
let the day not come, let the spring
not come.

Can I look again at the day and its common things, and see them all smeared
with blood, through a curtain of falling blood?

We did not wish anything to happen.

We understood the private catastrophe,

The personal loss, the general misery,

Living and partly living;

The terror by night that ends in daily action,

The terror by day that ends in sleep;

But the talk in the market-place, the hand
on the broom,

The nighttime heaping of the ashes,

The fuel laid on the fire at daybreak,

These acts marked a limit to our suffering.

Every horror had its definition,

Every sorrow had a kind of end:

In life there is not time to grieve long.

But this, this is out of life, this is out of time,

An instant eternity of evil and wrong.

We are soiled by a filth that we cannot
clean, united to supernatural vermin,

It is not we alone, it is not the house, it is
not the city that is defiled,

But the world that is wholly foul.

Clear the air! clean the sky! wash the wind!
take the stone from the stone, take the
skin from the arm, take the muscle from
the bone, and wash them. Wash the
stone, wash the bone, wash the brain,
wash the soul, wash them wash them!

(*The* KNIGHTS, *having completed the murder,
advance to the front of the stage and address
the audience*)

FIRST KNIGHT We beg you to give us your
attention for a few moments. We know that
you may be disposed to judge unfavorably
of our action. You are Englishmen, and therefore you believe in fair play: and when you
see one man being set upon by four, then your
sympathies are all with the under dog. I
respect such feelings, I share them. Nevertheless, I appeal to your sense of honor.
You are Englishmen, and therefore will not
judge anybody without hearing both sides
of the case. That is in accordance with our
long established principle of Trial by Jury.
I am not myself qualified to put our case to
you. I am a man of action and not of words.
For that reason I shall do no more than introduce the other speakers, who, with their
various abilities, and different points of view,
will be able to lay before you the merits of
this extremely complex problem. I shall call
upon our youngest member to speak first.
William de Traci.

SECOND KNIGHT I am afraid I am not anything like such an experienced speaker as
Reginald Fitz Urse would lead you to believe. But there is one thing I should like
to say, and I might as well say it at once. It
is this: in what we have done, and whatever
you may think of it, we have been perfectly
disinterested. (*the other* KNIGHTS: "*Hear!
hear!*") We are not getting anything out of
this. We have much more to lose than to
gain. We are four plain Englishmen who put
our country first. I dare say that we didn't
make a very good impression when we came
in. The fact is that we knew we had taken

on a pretty stiff job; I'll only speak for myself, but I had drunk a good deal—I am not a drinking man ordinarily—to brace myself up for it. When you come to the point, it does go against the grain to kill an Archbishop, especially when you have been brought up in good Church traditions. So if we seemed a bit rowdy, you will understand why it was; and for my part I am awfully sorry about it. We realized that this was our duty, but all the same we had to work ourselves up to it. And, as I said, *we* are not getting a penny out of this. We know perfectly well how things will turn out. King Henry—God bless him—will have to say, for reasons of state, that he never meant this to happen; and there is going to be an awful row; and at the best we shall have to spend the rest of our lives abroad. And even when reasonable people come to see that the Archbishop *had* to be put out of the way— and personally I had a tremendous admiration for him—you must have noticed what a good show he put up at the end—they won't give *us* any glory. No, we have done for ourselves, there's no mistake about that. So, as I said at the beginning, please give us at least the credit for being completely disinterested in this business. I think that is about all I have to say.

FIRST KNIGHT   I think we will all agree that William de Traci has spoken well and has made a very important point. The gist of his argument is this: that we have been completely disinterested. But our act itself needs more justification than that; and you must hear our other speakers. I shall next call upon Hugh de Morville.

THIRD KNIGHT   I should like first to recur to a point that was very well put by our leader, Reginald Fitz Urse: that you are Englishmen, and therefore your sympathies are always with the underdog. It is the English spirit of fair play. Now the worthy Archbishop, whose good quantities I very much admired, has throughout been presented as the under dog. But is this really the case? I am going to appeal not to your emotions but to your reason. You are hardheaded sensible people, as I can see, and not to be taken in by emotional clap-trap. I therefore ask you to consider soberly: what were the Archbishop's aims? and what are King Henry's aims? In the answer to these questions lies the key to the problem.

The King's aim has been perfectly consistent. During the reign of the late Queen Matilda and the irruption of the unhappy usurper Stephen, the kingdom was very much divided. Our King saw that the one thing needful was to restore order: to curb the excessive powers of local government, which were usually exercised for selfish and often for seditious ends, and to systematize the judiciary. There was utter chaos: there were three kinds of justice and three kinds of court: that of the King, that of the Bishops, and that of the baronage. I must repeat one point that the last speaker has made. While the late Archbishop was Chancellor, he wholeheartedly supported the King's designs: this is an important point, which if necessary, I can substantiate. Now the King intended that Becket, who had proved himself an extremely able administrator—no one denies that— should unite the offices of Chancellor and Archbishop. No one would have grudged him that; no one than he was better qualified to fill at once these two most important posts. Had Becket concurred with the King's wishes, we should have had an almost ideal State: a union of spiritual and temporal administration, under the central government. I knew Becket well, in various official relations; and I may say that I have never known a man so well qualified for the highest rank of the Civil Service. And what happened? The moment that Becket, at the King's instance, had been made Archbishop, he resigned the office of Chancellor, he became more priestly than the priests, he ostentatiously and offensively adopted an ascetic manner of life, he openly abandoned every policy that he had heretofore supported; he affirmed immediately that there was a higher order than that which our King, and he as the King's servant, had for so many years striven to establish; and that—God knows why—the two orders were incompatible.

You will agree with me that such interference by an Archbishop offends the instincts of a people like ours. So far, I know that I have your approval: I read it in your faces. It is only with the measures we have had to adopt, in order to set matters to rights, that you take issue. No one regrets the necessity for violence more than we do. Unhappily, there are times when violence is the only way in which social justice can be secured. At another time, you would condemn an Archbishop by vote of Parliament and execute him formally as a traitor, and no one would have to bear the burden of being called murderer. And at a later time still, even such temperate measures as these would become unnecessary. But, if you have now arrived at a just subordination of the pretensions of the Church to the welfare of the State, remember that it is we who took the first step. We have been instrumental in bringing about the state of affairs that you approve. We have served your interests; we merit your applause; and if there is any guilt whatever in the matter, you must share it with us.

FIRST KNIGHT   Morville has given us a great deal to think about. It seems to me that he has said almost the last word, for those who have been able to follow his very subtle reasoning. We have, however, one more speaker, who has I think another point of view to express. If there are any who are still unconvinced, I think that Richard Brito will be able to convince them. Richard Brito.

FOURTH KNIGHT   The speakers who have preceded me, to say nothing of our leader, Reginald Fitz Urse, have all spoken very much to the point. I have nothing to add along their particular lines of argument. What I have to say may be put in the form of a question: *Who killed the Archbishop?* As you have been eye-witnesses of this lamentable scene, you may feel some surprise at my putting it in this way. But consider the course of events. I am obliged, very briefly, to go over the ground traversed by the last speaker. While the late Archbishop was Chancellor, no one, under the King, did more to weld the country together, to give it the unity, the stability, order, tranquillity, and justice that it so badly needed. From the moment he became Archbishop, he completely reversed his policy; he showed himself to be utterly indifferent to the fate of the country, to be, in fact, a monster of egotism, a menace to society. This egotism grew upon him, until it became at last an undoubted mania. Every means that had been tried to conciliate him, to restore him to reason, had failed. Now I have unimpeachable evidence to the effect that before he left France he clearly prophesied, in the presence of numerous witnesses, that he had not long to live, and that he would be killed in England. He used every means of provocation; from his conduct, step by step, there can be no inference except that he had determined upon a death by martyrdom. This man, formerly a great public servant, had become a wrecker. Even at the last, he could have given us reason: you have seen how he evaded our questions. And when he had deliberately exasperated us beyond human endurance, he could still have easily escaped; he could have kept himself from us long enough to allow our righteous anger to cool. That was just what he did not wish to happen; he insisted, while we were still inflamed with wrath, that the doors should be opened. Need I say more? I think, with these facts before you, you will unhesitatingly render a verdict of Suicide while of Unsound Mind. It is the only charitable verdict you can give, upon one who was, after all, a great man.

FIRST KNIGHT   Thank you, Brito. I think that there is no more to be said; and I suggest that you now disperse quietly to your homes. Please be careful not to loiter in groups at street corners, and do nothing that might provoke any public outbreak.

(*Exeunt* KNIGHTS)

FIRST PRIEST   O father, father, gone from us, lost to us,
   How shall we find you, from what far place
   Do you look down on us? You now in Heaven,
   Who shall now guide us, protect us, direct us?
   After what journey through what further dread
   Shall we recover your presence? When inherit
   Your strength? The Church lies bereft,
   Alone, desecrated, desolated, and the heathen shall build on the ruins
   Their world without God. I see it. I see it.
THIRD PRIEST   No. For the Church is stronger for this action,
   Triumphant in adversity. It is fortified
   By persecution: supreme, so long as men will die for it.
   Go, weak sad men, lost erring souls, homeless in earth or heaven.
   Go where the sunset reddens the last grey rock
   Of Brittany, or the Gates of Hercules.
   Go venture shipwreck on the sullen coasts
   Where blackamoors make captive Christian men;
   Go to the northern seas confined with ice
   Where the dead breath makes numb the hand, makes dull the brain;
   Find an oasis in the desert sun,
   Go seek alliance with the heathen Saracen,
   To share his filthy rites, and try to snatch
   Forgetfulness in his libidinous courts,
   Oblivion in the fountain by the date-tree;
   Or sit and bite your nails in Aquitaine.
   In the small circle of pain within the skull
   You still shall tramp and tread one endless round
   Of thought, to justify your action to yourselves,
   Weaving a fiction which unravels as you weave,

Pacing forever in the hell of make-believe
Which never is belief: this is your fate on
earth
And we must think no further of you. O my
lord,
The glory of whose new state is hidden from
us,
Pray for us of your charity; now in the sight
of God
Conjoined with all the saints and martyrs
gone before you,
Remember us. Let our thanks ascend
To God, who has given us another Saint in
Canterbury.

CHORUS (*while a* Te Deum *is sung in Latin
by a choir in the distance*)
We praise Thee, O God, for Thy glory displayed in all the creatures of the earth,
In the snow, in the rain, in the wind, in the
storm; in all of Thy creatures, both the
hunters and the hunted.
For all things exist only as seen by Thee,
only as known by Thee, all things exist
Only in Thy light, and Thy glory is declared
even in that which denies Thee; the
darkness declares the glory of light.
Those who deny Thee could not deny, if
Thou didst not exist; and their denial
is never complete, for if it were so, they
would not exist.
They affirm Thee in living; all things affirm
Thee in living; the bird in the air, both
the hawk and the finch; the beast on
the earth, both the wolf and the lamb;
the worm in the soil and the worm in
the belly.
Therefore man, whom Thou hast made to be
conscious of Thee, must consciously
praise Thee, in thought and in word
and in deed.
Even with the hand to the broom, the back
bent in laying the fire, the knee bent in
cleaning the hearth, we, the scrubbers
and sweepers of Canterbury,
The back bent under toil, the knee bent under sin, the hands to the face under
fear, the head bent under grief,
Even in us the voices of seasons, the snuffle
of winter, the song of spring, the drone

of summer, the voices of beasts and of
birds, praise Thee.
We thank Thee for Thy mercies of blood,
for Thy redemption by blood. For the
blood of Thy martyrs and saints
Shall enrich the earth, shall create the holy
places.
For wherever a saint has dwelt, wherever a
martyr has given his blood for the blood
of Christ,
There is holy ground, and the sanctity shall
not depart from it
Though armies trample over it, though sight-
seers come with guide-books looking
over it;
From where the western seas gnaw at the
coast of Iona,
To the death in the desert, the prayer in
forgotten places by the broken imperial
column,
From such ground springs that which forever renews the earth
Though it is forever denied. Therefore, O
God, we thank Thee
Who hast given such blessing to Canterbury.
Forgive us, O Lord, we acknowledge ourselves as type of the common man,
Of the men and women who shut the door
and sit by the fire;
Who fear the blessing of God, the loneliness
of the night of God, the surrender re-
quired, the deprivation inflicted;
Who fear the injustice of men less than the
justice of God;
Who fear the hand at the window, the fire
in the thatch, the fist in the tavern, the
push into the canal,
Less than we fear the love of God.
We acknowledge our trespass, our weakness,
our fault; we acknowledge
That the sin of the world is upon our heads;
that the blood of the martyrs and the
agony of the saints
Is upon our heads.
Lord, have mercy upon us.
Christ, have mercy upon us.
Lord, have mercy upon us.
Blessed Thomas, pray for us.

Christopher Fry

1907-

A PLAYWRIGHT SPEAKS:
HOW LOST, HOW AMAZED,
HOW MIRACULOUS WE ARE

We can be sure that whatever I say about the theatre will be full of prejudice, bias, hobby horses, almost everything except impartiality. I do not think we have the smallest chance of avoiding it, even if I wanted to, and I do not want to very much. I should like to think that any other playwright would be just as incapable of taking an impersonal view as I am, because any playwright is laying his own world like an egg in the nest of the theatre, and he is deeply concerned in hatching it.

A playwright's view of the contemporary theatre is one with his view of the contemporary world, and his view of the contemporary world is one with his view of all time. He is exploring for the truth of the human creature, his truth in comedy or his truth in tragedy, because over and above the drama of his actions and conflicts and everyday predicaments is the fundamental drama of his ever existing at all.

His entrance into the world is almost the greatest entrance ever contrived, only bettered, I imagine, by the entrance of the universe which introduced him. The inescapable dramatic situation for us all is that we have no idea what our situation is. We may be mortal. What then? We may be immortal. What then? We are plunged into an existence fantastic to the point of nightmare, and however hard we

rationalize, or however firm our religious faith, however closely we dog the heels of science or wheel among the stars of mysticism, we cannot really make head or tail of it.

We get used to it. We get broken into it so gradually we scarcely notice it. But if we could shake off custom and descend on to the world without any conception of what we were going to see, we should be like the old woman who looked at the giraffe in the zoo and refused to believe a word of it. I am not at all sure that I do not believe a word of it. Let me try now to clear my mind of all knowledge of existence. Yes, of course it is impossible, but I can try:

The only believable thing is nothing at all, a no-being, a never-having-been; without form, and void. And now I come into existence, and I see my hand lying on the table in front of me, and that one thing alone, the first impact of a hand, is more dramatic than *Hamlet*. What on earth happens, then, when the rest of the world comes to me, when the full phantasmagoria of the commonplace breaks over my head? When the wings and the plumes, the antennae and the antlers, the gills and the nostrils . . . but we have only to start on a catalogue to know how hopeless our grasp is. Thank God we are no more than partly aware of a little at a time. Reality is incredible, reality is a whirlwind. What we call reality is a false god, the dull eye of custom.

For a very long time now, for seventy years at least, in healthy reaction to the romantic fustian of the early and middle years of the nineteenth century, the theatre has pursued this—if I say "surface reality" perhaps I shall mislead you into thinking I mean "superficiality," but I don't mean that. I mean the reality we have made for ourselves by 2,000,000 years of getting used to it, the domestication of the enormous miracle, the reality in which we no longer see a moving, articulate, thinking shape, of quite extraordinary design and substance, across the breakfast table, but something which, by a long, long process of getting-used-to, we have subdued into a gentler image, our wife. And in the theatre of the twentieth century, so far the search has been for this particular reality. We have put four walls round the stage, and obliterated space; used familiar words for Time, such as dinner-time, early-the-same-evening, two-days-later, and obliterated eternity. And because speech (that strange, brilliant, mature achievement of the human animal) has become subdued to a limited game of hit-or-miss, stage dialogue, in its pursuit of the surface reality, goes to the limit of imitation and tinkles in tune with the breakfast cups. It never uses two words where one won't do. And this makes us feel quite at home. It makes us feel we could walk into any room represented on the stage, and not be out of place. But the truth, surely, the greater reality, is that we should be out of place, as in fact in life, if we stop to think, we always are. If we stop pretending for a moment that we were born fully dressed in a service flat, and remember that we were born stark naked into a pandemonium of most unnatural phenomena, then we know how out of place, how lost, how amazed, how miraculous we are. And this reality is the province of poetry.

Poetry is the language in which man explores his own amazement. It is the language in which he says heaven and earth in one word. It is the language in which he speaks of himself and his predicament as though for the first time. It has the virtue of being able to say twice as much as prose in half the time, and the drawback, if you do not happen to give it your full attention, of seeming to say half as much in twice the time. And if you accept my proposition that reality is altogether different from our stale view of it, we can say that poetry is the language of reality.

The other cosier reality of everyday appearances has had a long day in the theatre, and the theatre has profited by it, but we have gone, as the song says, about as far as we can go. We have invaded every room in the house, except perhaps the water-closet, and our escape from that has been a pretty near thing. We have thumped out political tracts, and burrowed with Freud, and the thumping and burrowing have made, at times, a lively theatre, but we cannot live by Freud alone; we are still left with the mystery; Einstein can bend space, but he cannot break it; there is still the element of doubt, which is also the element

of faith, and the element we are condemned to live in.

And so, as we have pursued the one kind of realism to a dead end, or at least to a uncertain terminus, the natural thing to do is to pursue the other kind of realism, the kind which I believe to be far more realistic. This second half of the century will see how far that pursuit can go. I may—I hope I have not, but I may—have given you the idea that I am proposing a theatre cloudy with insubstantial symbols and spiritual sea wrack. If I have, let me quickly disabuse you. The facts of reality are the same in the theatre of poetry as they are in the theatre of prose. What is different is their implication. What I am trying to say is what I have said elsewhere, that a spade is never so merely a spade as the word spade would imply. I am asking for the sudden dramatic appearance of a spade in time and space, but I am equally asking for a spade which I can dig with. I am asking—now I come to think of it—I am asking for both kinds of realism at once.

This is not at all a startling request; it is a very old one; but in our lifetime we have got out of the way of making it, and perhaps we shall take a little time to learn to listen to the answer, when the answer comes to be made. We may notice the spade digging, but not what is dug. And I do want to make it clear to you that I am not only interested in this possible change in the theatre because a change is due, or even because change is necessary to the theatre's vitality. If a theatre is alive it is because it belongs to the life outside its doors, and the life outside its doors is not such, at the moment, that a change of viewpoint can do any harm. We know what the world looks like, and what the action of men looks like, in everyday, newspaper terms. The knowledge makes for dismay and a suffocation of the spirit. If the theatre can help us to see ourselves and the world freshly, as though we had just rounded the corner into life, it will be what entertainment should be, a holiday which sets us up to continue living at the top of our bent, and worth, I think, any amount of admonition and prophecy or the photographic likeness of how we appear by custom. This change of viewpoint would be no escapism or fantasy. Nothing could be so wildly, perilously, incomprehensibly fantastic as reality itself, and we may as well dare to look at it, and like it.

It is a tall order for the theatre to supply, and we still have got no further than looking in the right direction; but the audiences are alert, and so the theatre-managers are alert, to what will come, if we, the playwrights, can bring it in.

This theatre I speak of, this at present immature theatre, has to make the exploration in its own way. We can do it no service by thinking of it as a return to an earlier manner, as a sudden reversal to the seventeenth century, for example. It will see, I hope, strongly with its own eyes, and discover its own tensions. It will come about, not as an imposition on the twentieth century, but growing naturally from an anticipation and a need of the present time, and the audience will find it increasingly your language, and we, the playwrights, will learn to work it more skilfully into shape.

The last word on man is very far from being spoken. There is always something new under the sun, because a mystery never ages. Our difficulty is to be alive to the newness, to see through the windows which are so steamed over with our daily breath, to be able to be old and new at one and the same time. And the theatre we should always be trying to achieve is one where the persons and events have the recognizable ring of an old truth, and yet seem to occur in a lightning spasm of discovery. That, again, is the province of poetry. It is a province of large extent; I see it ranging from tragedy, through comedy of action and comedy of mood, even down to the playground of farce; and each of these has its own particular conflict, tension, and shape, which, if we look for them, will point the way to the play's purpose.

And what condition is the theatre in to receive this change, if it comes? I think in as good a one as at any time in its history.

We have only to remember the success of *Murder in the Cathedral* to know that.

The actors are at the very heart of this change. They understand and relish it as much as, or more than, any, and will go to the length of their talent or genius to achieve it. And so, with both audience and actors ready and willing, all the playwright can do is to turn to himself and demand of himself that he shall sharpen his pen to the proper point, though he is bound at moments to be apprehensive of the distance that pen still has to cover.

A SLEEP OF PRISONERS

To Robert Gittings

Dear Robert

It is nineteen years this summer since you persuaded me to take a holiday from my full-time failure to make a living, and sat me down, with a typewriter and a barrel of beer, in the empty rectory at Thorn St. Margaret. I had written almost nothing for five or six years, and I was to write almost nothing again for five years following, but the two months we spent at Thorn, two months (it seems to me now) of continuous blazing sunshine, increased in me the hope that one day the words would come. It was all very well that I should look obstinately forward to plays which I showed no sign of writing. It was an extraordinary faith which made you also look obstinately forward to them. The ten years in which you loyally thought of me as a writer when clearly I wasn't, your lectures to me on my self-defensive mockery of artists, and those two leisure months under the Quantocks, were things of friendship which kept me in a proper mind.

We were talking even then, as we are talking, with greater instancy, now, of the likelihood of war. And I think we realized then, as we certainly now believe, that progress is the growth of vision: the increased perception of what makes for life and what makes for death. I have tried, as you know, not altogether successfully, to find a way for comedy to say something of this, since comedy is an essential part of men's understanding. In A Sleep of Prisoners I have tried to make a more simple statement, though in a complicated design where each of four men is seen through the sleeping thoughts of the others, and each, in his own dream, speaks as at heart he is, not as he believes himself to be. In the later part of Corporal Adams' dream the dream changes to a state of thought entered into by all the sleeping men, as though, sharing their prison life, they shared, for a few moments of the night, their sleeping life also.

CAST OF CHARACTERS

PRIVATE DAVID KING   PRIVATE TIM MEADOWS

PRIVATE PETER ABLE   CORPORAL JOE ADAMS

(*The interior of a church, turned into a prison camp. One prisoner,* PETER ABLE, *is in organ loft, playing "Now the day is over" with one finger. Another,* DAVID KING, *is looking at the memorial tablets on the wall. Four double bunks stand between the choir-stalls. A pile of straw and a pile of empty paillasses are on the chancel steps*)

DAVID (*shouting up to the organ loft*)   Hey, Pete, come down and tell me what this Latin
     Says. If it's Latin.

PETER (*still playing*)   Why, what for?

DAVID   For the sake of that organ. And because I want to know
     If "Hic jacet" means what it looks like.

(PETER *changes the tune to "Three Blind Mice"*)

     (*in a flash of temper*) And because I said so, that's what for, because
     I said so! And because you're driving me potty.

PETER   Excuse me a minute: this is the difficult bit.

DAVID   If you want it difficult, go on playing. I swear
        I'll come up there and put my foot through you.

(*As the playing goes on* DAVID *suddenly howls like a dog and starts tearing up a hymn-book*)

PETER   (*the playing over*)   It's the universal language, Dave. It's music.

DAVID   Music my universal aunt. It's torture.

(*He finds himself with a page or two of the hymn-book in his hand*)

        Here, I know this one.
        (*Sings*) "All things bright and beautiful—"

PETER   (*coming down from the loft*)   That doesn't mean you, Davy. Put it down.

DAVID   "All creatures great and small—"
        Well, one of those is me: I couldn't miss it.
        "All things wise and wonderful—"

(CORPORAL JOE ADAMS *comes to the steps with more straw*)

ADAMS   Come and get it!

PETER   What is it? Soup?

ADAMS   Straw.

PETER   Never could digest it.

(TIM MEADOWS, *a middle-aged man—indeed he looks well on towards sixty—limps up to the pile of straw*)

ADAMS   How's the leg feel, Meadows?

MEADOWS   Ah, all right.
        I wouldn't be heard saying anything about one leg
        I wouldn't say about the other.

PETER   Where
        Did you get it, chum?

MEADOWS   I had it for my birthday.
        Quite nice, isn't it? Five toes, it's got.

PETER   I mean where was the fighting, you wit?

MEADOWS   (*jerking his head*)   Down the road.
        My Uncle George had a thumping wooden leg,
        Had it with him, on and off, for years.
        When he gave up the world, it got out in the wash house.

DAVID   Has anybody thought what it's going to be like
        Suppose we stay here for months or years?

ADAMS   Best they can do. You heard the towzer Commandant:
        "All more buildings blow up into sky.
        No place like home now. Roof here. Good and kind
        To prisoners. Keep off sun, keep off rain."

PETER   Keep off the grass.

DAVID   It's a festering idea for a prison camp.
        You have to think twice every time you think,
        In case what you think's a bit on the dubious side.
        It's all this smell of cooped-up angels
        Worries me.

PETER   What, us?

DAVID   Not mother's angels,
        Dumb-cluck, God's angels.

PETER   Oh yes, them.
        We're a worse fug to them, I shouldn't wonder.
        We shall just have to make allowances.

DAVID   Beg pardon:
        I'm talking to no-complaints Pete: arrangements perfect.

ADAMS   Too many pricking thistles in this straw:
        Pricked to hell.

(PETER *has wandered across to the lectern*)

PETER   Note his early perpendicular
Language. Ecclesiastical influence.
See this? They've put us an English Bible.
There's careful nannies for you . . . "These were the sons
Of Caleb the son of Hur, the firstborn of Ephratah:
Shobal the father of Kirjath-jearim, Salma
The father of Beth-lehem, Hareph the father
Of Beth-gader. And Shodal the father of Kirjath-
Jearim had sons: Haroeh, and half of the Manahethites—"
Interesting, isn't it?

DAVID   Stuff it, Pete.

PETER   "And these were the sons of David, which were born unto
Him in Hebron: the firstborn Amnon, of Ahinoam the
Jezreelitess: the second Daniel, of Abigail the
Carmelitess: the third Absalom the son of Maacah the
Daughter of Talmai king of Geshur: the fourth Adonijah
The son of Haggith: the fifth Shephatiah of Abital:
The sixth Ithream by Eglah his wife . . ."
                                     Doing
All right, aren't you, Davey?

DAVID   So I did in Sunday school. You know what Absalom
Said to the tree? "You're getting in my hair."
And that's what I mean, so shut up.

PETER   Shut up we are.
Don't mind me. I'm making myself at home.
Now all I've got to do is try the pulpit.

ADAMS   Watch yourself, Pete. We've got years of this.

DAVID (*his temper growing*)   Any damn where he makes himself at home.
The world blows up, there's Pete there in the festering
Bomb-hole making cups of tea. I've had it
Week after week till I'm sick. Don't let's mind
What happens to anybody, don't let's object to anything,
Let's give the dirty towzers a cigarette,
There's nothing on earth worth getting warmed up about!
It doesn't matter who's on top, make yourself at home.

ADAMS   Character of Private Peter Able:
And not so far out at that. What we're in for
We've got to be in for and know just what it is.
Have some common sense, Pete. If you're looking for trouble
Go and have it in the vestry.

PETER (*up in the pulpit*)   How can I help it if I can't work myself up
About the way things go? It's a mystery to me.
We've had all this before. For God's sake
Be reasonable, Dave. Perhaps I was meant
To be a bishop.
(*He turns to the nave*) Dearly beloved brothers
In a general muck-up, towzers included . . .

DAVID   What the hell do you think we're stuck here for
Locked in like lunatics? Just for a nice
New experience, with nice new friends
With nice new rifles to look after us?
We're at war with them, aren't we? And if we are
They're no blaming use!

PETER (*continuing to preach*)   We have here on my left
An example of the bestial passions that beset mankind.

(DAVID, *beside himself, leaps up the steps and attacks* PETER *in the pul*
     Davey, Dave . . . don't be a lunatic!

ADAMS   Come out of it,
King. Come down here, you great tomfool!

(*He goes to drag* DAVID *away.* DAVID *has his hands on* PETER'S *throat and has pushed him across the edge of the pulpit*)

DAVID (*raging*) You laugh: I'll see you never laugh again.
Go on: laugh at this.

MEADOWS   If you don't get your hands away
You'll wish you never had 'em. Give over! Give over!

(DAVID *releases his hold. He pushes past* ADAMS *and comes down from the pulpit*)

I see the world in you very well. 'Tisn't
Your meaning, but you're a clumsy, wall-eyed bulldozer.
You don't know what you're hitting.

(DAVID *goes past him without a word, and throws himself onto his bed*)

                                                        Ah, well,
Neither do I, of course, come to that.
ADAMS   All right, Peter?

PETER   Think so, Corporal,
I'm not properly reassembled yet.
There's a bit of a rattle, but I think I had that before.
ADAMS   Dave had better damp down that filthy volcano
Or let me know what.

PETER   Oh, lord, I don't know,
It's who we happen to be. I suppose I'd better
Hit him back some time, or else he'll go mad
Trying to make me see daylight. I don't know.
I'll tell you my difficulty, Corp. I never remember
I ought to be fighting until I'm practically dead.
Sort of absent-fisted. Very worrying for Dave.

(*They have come down from the pulpit.* PETER *sways on his feet.* ADAMS *supports him*)

ADAMS   You're all in, Pete.
PETER   Say "Fall out" and watch me
Fall.
ADAMS   All right, come on, we'll put you to bed.

(MEADOWS *has limped across with two blankets for* PETER'S *bunk.* DAVID *is watching anxiously*)

DAVID   What's wrong, Pete?
ADAMS   The best thing for you is keep
Out of this.
PETER   Dog-tired, that's all. It comes
Of taking orders. Dog collar too tight.
DAVID   I'll see to him.
ADAMS   I've seen you see to him.
Get back on your bed.
DAVID   I've never killed him yet.
I'm a pal of his.
ADAMS   That's right. I couldn't have expressed it
Better myself. We'll talk about that tomorrow.

(*He goes over to make up his own bunk.* DAVID *unlaces* PETER'S *boots*)

DAVID   How d'you feel now, Pete?
PETER   Beautiful.
DAVID   Why don't
You do some slaughtering sometimes? Why always
Leave it to me? Got no blood you can heat
Up or something? I didn't hurt you, did I,
Pete? How d'you feel?

(*He throws*)

>Blight! What's blinding me
>By twos and threes? I'm strong, aren't I?
>Who's holding me down? Who's frozen my fist
>So it can't hatch the damn dice out?

PETER (*shaking and throwing*)

>>Deal me high, deal me low.
>>Make my deeds
>>My nameless needs.
>>I know I do not know.

>. . . That brings me home!

(DAVID *roars with rage and disappointment*)

DAVID   Life is a hypocrite if I can't live
>The way it moves me! I was trusted
>Into breath. Why am I doubted now?
>Flesh is my birthplace. Why shouldn't I speak the tongue?
>What's the disguise, eh? Who's the lurcher
>First enjoys us, then disowns us?
>Keep me clean of God, creation's crooked.

ADAMS   Cain, steady, steady, you'll raise the world.

DAVID   You bet your roots I will.
>I'll know what game of hide and seek this is.
>Half and half, my petering brother says,
>Nothing of either, in and out the limbo.
>"I know I do not know" he says.
>So any lion can BE, and any ass,
>And any cockatoo: and all the unbiddable
>Roaming voices up and down
>Can live their lives and welcome
>While I go pestered and wondering down hill
>Like a half-wit angel strapped to the back of a mule.
>Thanks! I'll be as the body was first presumed.

PETER   It was a game between us, Cain.

DAVID (*in a fury*)   Your dice were weighted! You thought you could trick
>The life out of me. We'll see about that.
>You think you're better than you're created!
>I saw the smiles that went between
>You and the top air. I knew your game.
>Look helpless, let him see you're lost,
>Make him amiable to think
>He made more strangely than he thought he did!
>Get out of time, will you, get out of time!

(*He takes* PETER *by the throat.* ADAMS *goes to part them*)

ADAMS   Cain, drop those hands!

(*He is wheeled by an unknown force back against his bunk*)

>>O Sir,
>Let me come to them. They're both
>Out of my reach. I have to separate them.

DAVID (*strangling* PETER)   You leave us now, leave us, you half-and-half:
>I want to be free of you!

PETER   Cain! Cain!

ADAMS   Cain, Cain!

DAVID   If life's not good enough for you
>Go and justify yourself!

ADAMS   Pinioned here, when out of my body
>I made them both, the fury and the suffering,

The fury, the suffering, the two ways
Which here spreadeagle me.

(DAVID *has fought* PETER *back to the bed and kills him*)

O, O, O,
Eve, what love there was between us. Eve,
What gentle thing, a son, so harmless,
Can hang the world with blood.

DAVID (*to* PETER)   Oh,
You trouble me. You are dead.

ADAMS   How ceaseless the earth is. How it goes on.
Nothing has happened except silence where sound was,
Stillness where movement was. Nothing has happened,
But the future is like a great pit.
My heart breaks, quiet as petals falling
One by one, but this is the drift
Of agony for ever.

DAVID   Now let's hope
There will be no more argument,
No more half-and-half, no more doubt,
No more betrayal.—You trouble me,
You trouble me.

MEADOWS (*in his sleep*)   Cain.

(DAVID *hides*)

                                        Cain. Where is
Your brother?

DAVID   How should I know? Am I
His keeper?

ADAMS   Where is keeping?
Keep somewhere, world, the time we love.
I have two sons, and where is one,
And where will now the other be?
I am a father unequipped to save.
When I was young the trees of love forgave me:
That was all. But now they say
The days of such simple forgiveness are done,
Old Joe Adam all sin and bone.

MEADOWS   Cain: I hear your brother's blood
Crying to me from the ground.

DAVID   Sir, no: he is silent.
All the crying is mine.

MEADOWS   Run, run, run. Cain
Is after you.

DAVID   What shall I do?

MEADOWS   What you have done. It does it to you.
Nowhere rest. Cage of the world
Holds your prowling. Howl, Cain, jackal afraid.
And nowhere, Cain, nowhere
Escape the fear of what men fear in you.
Every man's hand will be against you,
But never touch you into quietness.
Run! Run!

DAVID   The punishment
Is more than I can bear. I loved life
With a good rage you gave me. And how much better
Did Abel do? He set up his heart
Against your government of flesh.
How was I expected to guess

> That what I am you didn't want?
> God the jailer, God the gun
> Watches me exercise in the yard,
> And all good neighborhood has gone.
> The two-faced beater makes me fly,
> Fair game, poor game, damned game
> For God and all man-hunters.

MEADOWS   They shall never kill you.

DAVID   Death was a big word, and now it has come
> An act so small, my enemies will do it
> Between two jobs. Cain's alive,
> Cain's dead, we'll carry the bottom field:
> Killing is light work, and Cain is easily dead.

MEADOWS   Run on, keep your head down, cross at the double
> The bursts of open day between the nights.
> My word is Bring him in alive.
> Can you feel it carved on your body?

(DAVID *twists as though he felt a branding iron touch him*)

DAVID   God in heaven! The drag!
> You're tearing me out of my life still living!
> This can't last on flesh for ever.
> Let me sleep, let me, let me, let me sleep.
> God, let me sleep. God, let me sleep.

(*He goes into the shadows to his bed*)

MEADOWS (*turning in bed*)   This can't last on flesh for ever.
> Let me sleep.

(*There follows a pause of heavy breathing. The church clock in the tower strikes the three-quarters.* MEADOWS *wakes, props himself up on his elbow*)

> Any of you boys awake?
> Takes a bit of getting used to, sleeping
> In a looming great church. How you doing?
> I can't rest easy for the night of me.
> . . . Sleeping like great roots, every Jack of them.
> How many draughts are sifting under the doors.
> Pwhee-ooo. And the breathing: and breathing: heavy and deep:
> Breathing: heavy and deep.
> Sighing the life out of you. All the night.

(DAVID *stirs uneasily*)

DAVID   I don't have to stay here! I'm a King.

MEADOWS   David, that you? You awake, David?
> A dream's dreaming him. This is no place
> For lying awake. When other men are asleep
> A waking man's a lost one. Tim, go byes.

(*He covers his head with his blanket*)

DAVID (*in his sleep*)   I'm King of Israel. They told me so.
> I'm doing all right. But who is there to trust?
> There are so many fools. Fools and fools and fools,
> All round my throne. Loved and alone
> David keeps the earth. And nothing kills them.

(PETER, *as the dream figure of Absalom, stands with his back pressed against a wall as though afraid to be seen*)

PETER   Do you think I care?

DAVID   Who is that man down there
> In the dark alley-way making mischief?

PETER   Do you think I care?

DAVID   Corporal Joab:
    There's a man in the dark way. Do you see
    That shadow shift? it has a belly and ribs.
    It's a man, Joab, who shadows me. He lurks
    Against my evening temper. Dangerous.

(ADAMS *appears as the dream figure of Joab*)

ADAMS   I think you know already.

DAVID   He has got to be named. Which of us does it?

ADAMS   He's your own son: Absalom.

DAVID   Now
    The nightmare sits and eats with me.
    He was boy enough.
    Why does he look like a thief?

ADAMS   Because
    He steals your good, he steals your strength,
    He riddles your world until it sinks,
    He plays away all your security,
    All you labor and suffer to hold
    Against the enemy.

DAVID   The world's back
    Is bent and heavily burdened, and yet he thinks
    He can leapfrog over. Absalom,
    Absalom, why do you play the fool against me?

PETER   You and your enemies! Everlastingly
    Thinking of enemies. Open up.
    Your enemies are friends of mine.

DAVID   They gather against our safety. They make trash
    Of what is precious to us. Absalom,
    Come over here. I want to speak to you.

PETER (*running up into the pulpit*)   Do you think I care?

ADAMS   If you let him run
    He'll make disaster certain.

DAVID   Absalom,
    Come alive. Living is caring.
    Hell is making straight towards us.

PETER (*in the pulpit*)   Beloved, all who pipe your breath
    Under the salted almond moon,
    Hell is in my father's head
    Making straight towards him. Please forget it.
    He sees the scarlet shoots of spring
    And thinks of blood. He sees the air
    Streaming with imagined hordes
    And conjures them to come. But you and I
    Know that we can turn away
    And everything will turn
    Into itself again. What is
    A little evil here and there between friends?
    Shake hands on it: shake hands, shake hands:
    Have a cigarette, and make yourselves at home.
    Shall we say what we think of the King of Israel?
    Ha—ha—ha!

(*Jeering laughter echoes round the roof of the church*)

DAVID   Don't do it to me, don't make the black rage
    Shake me, Peter. I tremble like an earthquake
    Because I can't find words which might
    Put the fear of man into you.
    Understand! The indecisions

        Have to be decided. Who's against us
        Reeks to God. Where's your hand?
        Be ordinary human, Absalom.
ADAMS   Appeal's no use, King. He has
        A foiling heart: the sharp world glances off
        And so he's dangerous.
DAVID   I think so too.
        Who can put eyes in his head? Who'll do it,
        Eh, Joab? We have to show him
        This terse world means business, don't we, Corporal,
        Don't we?
ADAMS   He has to be instructed.
DAVID   Make a soldier of him. Make him fit
        For conflict, as the stars and stags are.
        He belongs to no element now. We have
        To have him with us. Show him the way,
        Joe Adams.

(PETER *is lounging at the foot of the pulpit.* ADAMS *turns to him*)

ADAMS   Get on parade.
PETER   What's the music?
ADAMS   I'll sing you, Absalom, if you don't get moving.
        And I'll see you singing where you never meant.
        Square up.
PETER   What's this?
ADAMS   Square up, I said.
PETER   Where do we go from here?
ADAMS   It's unarmed combat.
        It's how your bare body makes them die.
        It's old hey-presto death: you learn the trick
        And death's the rabbit out of the hat:
        Rolling oblivion for someone.
        You've got to know how to get rid of the rats of the world.
        They're up at your throat. Come on.
PETER   What nightmare's this you're dragging me into?
ADAMS   Humanity's. Come on.
PETER   I know
        Nothing about it. Life's all right to me.
ADAMS   Say that when it comes.

(*The unarmed combat,* ADAMS *instructing*)

DAVID   Where is he going now? He carries
        No light with him. Does he know
        The river's unbound: it's up above
        Every known flood-mark, and still rising.
PETER   (*who has got away from* ADAMS)   I'm on the other side of the river
        Staying with friends, whoever they are.
        Showery still, but I manage to get out,
        I manage to get out.
        The window marked with a cross is where I sleep.
        Just off to a picnic with your enemies.
        They're not bad fellows, once you get to know them.
DAVID   (*to* ADAMS)   I have heard from my son.
ADAMS   What's his news?
DAVID   He's with the enemy. He betrays us, Joab.
        He has to be counted with them.
        Are we ready?
ADAMS   Only waiting for the word.
DAVID   We attack at noon.

ADAMS   Only hoping for the time.
          Good luck.
DAVID   Good luck.

(ADAMS *walks down the chancel steps and crouches, keeping a steady eye on his wrist-watch.* ADAMS *gives a piercing whistle.* PETER *leaps up and hangs on to the edge of the pulpit.* ADAMS *cuts him down with a tommy-gun. He cries out.* DAVID *starts up in his bunk.* PETER *and* ADAMS *fall to the floor and lie prone*)

          (*awake*) What's the matter, Peter? Pete! Anything wrong?

(*He gets out of his bunk and goes across to* PETER's)

          Pete, are you awake?

(*He stands for a moment and then recrosses the floor*)

MEADOWS (*awake*)   Anything the matter?
          Can't you sleep either?
DAVID (*getting back into his bunk*)   I thought I heard
          Somebody shout. It woke me up.
MEADOWS   Nobody shouted.
          I've been lying awake. It's just gone midnight.
          There's a howling wind outside plays ducks and drakes
          With a flat moon: just see it through this window:
          It flips across the clouds and then goes under:
          I wish I could run my head against some sleep.
          This building's big for lying with your eyes open.
          You could brush me off, and only think you're dusting.
          Who's got the key of the crypt? (*He yawns*)
          Thanks for waking. It brings the population
          Up to two. You're a silent chap. Dave?
          Have you gone to sleep again already?
          Back into the sea, like a slippery seal.
          And here am I, high and dry.
DAVID (*asleep*)   Look, look, look.
MEADOWS   Away he goes,
          Drifting far out. How much of him is left?
          Ah, lord, man, go to sleep: stop worrying.

(ADAMS *drags or carries* PETER *to* PETER's *bunk*)

DAVID   Joab, is that you? Joab, is that you?
          What are you bringing back?
ADAMS   The victory.
DAVID   Are you sure it is the victory, Joab?
          Are we ever sure it's the victory?
          So many times you've come back, Joab,
          With something else. I want to be sure at last.
          I want to know what you mean by victory.
          Is it something else to me? Where are you looking?
          There's nothing that way. But look over here:
          There's something. Along the road, starting the dust,
          He wants to reach us. Why is that?
          So you're going to walk away.
ADAMS (*going to his bunk*)   I've done my best.
          I can't be held responsible for everything.
DAVID   Don't leave me, Joab. Stay and listen.
ADAMS (*covering himself over*)   I'm dead beat.
          The enemy's put to flight. Good night, you King of Israel.
DAVID   Bathed in sweat, white with dust. Call him here.
          Come up. I am the King.
          I shall wait patiently until your voice
          Gets back the breath to hit me. I'm here, waiting.

(DAVID *sits on the edge of his bunk, a red army blanket hanging from his shoulder*)

MEADOWS (*awake*)   Where are you off to, Davey?
Get you back to bed. A dream
Has got you prisoner, Davey, like
The world has got us all. Don't let it
Take you in.

DAVID   Come here to me, come over
Here, the dusty fellow with the news,
Come here. Is the fighting over? Unconditionally?

(MEADOWS *has left his bunk and crossed to* DAVID)

MEADOWS   Lie down, boy. Forget it. It's all over.

DAVID   Is the young man Absalom safe?

MEADOWS   Lie down, Dave.
Everybody's asleep.

ADAMS (*from his bunk*)   The boy's dead.
You might as well be told: I say
The boy's dead.

(DAVID, *giving a groan, lies back on his bed*)

MEADOWS   The night's over us.
Nothing's doing. Except the next day's in us
And makes a difficult sort of lying-in.
Here, let's cover you up. Keep the day out of this.
Find something better to sleep about.
Give your living heart a rest. Do you hear me,
Dave, down where you are? If you don't mind,
While I'm here, I'll borrow some of that sleep:
You've got enough for two.

(*He limps back to his bunk, passing* ADAMS, *who wakes*)

ADAMS   Hullo, Meadows:
What's worrying you?

MEADOWS   Dave was. He couldn't
Let go of the day. He started getting up
And walking in his sleep.

ADAMS   All right now?

MEADOWS   Seems running smoother.

ADAMS   Is that him talking?

(PETER *has begun to talk in his sleep*)

MEADOWS   Muttering monkeys love us, it's the other one now:
Peter's at it.

PETER   Do I have to follow you?

ADAMS   You needn't hear him if you get your ears
Under the blankets. That's where I'm going.
Good night, boy.

(*He disappears under his blankets.* MEADOWS *climbs into his bunk*)

MEADOWS   Hope so. It's a choppy crossing
We're having still. No coast of daylight yet for miles.

(*He also disappears from view. A pause*)

PETER (*asleep*)   Why did you call me? I'm contented here:
They say I'm in a prison. Morning comes
To a prison like a nurse:
A rustling presence, as though a small breeze came,
And presently a voice. I think
We're going to live. The dark pain has gone,
The relief of daylight
Flows over me, as though beginning is

Beginning. The hills roll in and make their homes,
And gradually unfold the plains. Breath
And light are cool together now.
The earth is all transparent, but too deep
To see down to its bed.

(DAVID, *the dream figure of Abraham, stands beside* PETER)

DAVID   Come with me.
PETER   Where are we going?
DAVID   If necessary
To break our hearts. It's as well for the world.
PETER   There's enough breaking, God knows. We die,
And the great cities come down like avalanches.
DAVID   But men come down like living men.
Time gives the promise of time in every death,
Not of any ceasing. Come with me.
The cities are pitifully concerned.
We need to go to the hill.
PETER   What shall we do?
DAVID   What falls to us.
PETER   Falling from where?
DAVID   From the point of devotion, meaning God.
Carry this wood, Isaac, and this coil
Of rope.
PETER   I'm coming.
DAVID   There has to be sacrifice.
I know that. There's nothing so sure.
PETER   You walk so fast. These things are heavy.
DAVID   I know. I carry them too.
PETER   I only want
To look around a bit. There's so much to see.
Ah, peace on earth, I'm a boy for the sights.
DAVID   Don't break my heart. You so
Cling hold of the light. I have to take it
All away.
PETER   Why are you so grave?
There's more light than we can hold. Everything
Grows over with fresh inclination
Every day. You and I are both
Immeasurably living.

(DAVID *has been walking towards the pulpit.* PETER *still lies in bed. He starts to whistle
a tune, though the whistling seems not to come from his lips but from above him*)

DAVID   What do you whistle for?
PETER   I whistle for myself
And anyone who likes it.
DAVID   Keep close to me.
It may not be for long. Time huddles round us,
A little place to be in. And we're already
Up the heavy hill. The singing birds
Drop down and down to the bed of the trees,
To the hay-silver evening, O
Lying gentleness, a thin veil over
The long scars from the nails of the warring hearts.
Come up, son, and see the world.
God dips his hand in death to wash the wound,
Takes evil to inoculate our lives
Against infectious evil. We'll go on.

I am history's wish and must come true,
And I shall hate so long as hate
Is history, though, God, it drives
My life away like a beaten dog. Here
Is the stone where we have to sacrifice.
Make my heart like it. It still is beating
Unhappily the human time.

PETER Where is the creature that has to die?
There's nothing here of any life worth taking.
Shall we go down again?

DAVID   There is life here.

PETER A flinching snail, a few unhopeful harebells.
What good can they be?

DAVID   What else?

PETER   You, father,
And me.

DAVID   I know you're with me. But very strangely
I stand alone with a knife. For the simple asking.
Noon imperial will no more let me keep you
Than if you were the morning dew. The day
Wears on. Shadows of our history
Steal across the sky. For our better freedom
Which makes us living men: for what will be
The heaven on earth, I have to bind you
With cords, and lay you here on the stone's table.

PETER Are you going to kill me? No! Father!
I've come only a short way into life
And I can see great distance waiting.
The free and evening air
Swans from hill to hill.
Surely there's no need for us to be
The prisoners of the dark? Smile, father.
Let me go.

DAVID   Against my heart
I let you go, for the world's own ends
I let you go, for God's will
I let you go, for children's children's joy
I let you go, my grief obeying.
The cords bind you against my will
But you're bound for a better world.
And I must lay you down to sleep
For a better waking. Come now.

(*In mime he picks Isaac up in his arms and lays them across the front of the pulpit*)

PETER (*in his bunk*)   I'm afraid.
And how is the earth going to answer, even so?

DAVID As it will. How can we know?
But we must do, and the future make amends.

PETER Use the knife quickly. There are too many
Thoughts of life coming to the cry.
God put them down until I go.
Now, now, suddenly!

DAVID (*the knife raised*)   This
Cuts down my heart, but bitter events must be.
I can't learn to forgive necessity:
God help me to forgive it.

(ADAMS *appears as the dream figure of the Angel*)

ADAMS   Hold your arm.
There are new instructions. The knife can drop
Harmless and shining.
DAVID   I never thought to know,
Strange voice of mercy, such happy descending.
Nor my son again. But he's here untouched,
And evening is at hand
As clear and still as no man.
PETER   Father, I feel
The air go over me as though I should live.
DAVID   So you will, for the earth's while. Shall I
Undo the cords?
ADAMS   These particular. But never all.
There's no loosening, since men with men
Are like the knotted sea. Lift him down
From the stone to the grass again, and, even so free,
Yet he will find the angry cities hold him.
But let him come back to the strange matter of living
As best he can: and take instead
The ram caught here by the white wool
In the barbed wire of the briar bush:
Make that the kill of the day.
DAVID   Readily.
PETER   Between the day and the night
The stars tremble in balance.
The houses are beginning to come to light.
And so it would have been if the knife had killed me.
This would have been my death-time.
The ram goes in my place, in a curious changing.
Chance, as fine as a thread,
Cares to keep me, and I go my way.
MEADOWS (*a dream figure*)   Do you want a ride across the sands,
Master Isaac?
PETER   Who are you?
MEADOWS   Now, boy, boy,
Don't make a joke of me. Old Meadows,
The donkey man, who brought you up the hill.
Not remember me? That's a man's memory,
Short measure as that. Down a day.
And we've been waiting, Edwina and me,
As patient as two stale loaves, to take you down.
PETER   But I climbed the hill on foot.
MEADOWS (*patting the bunk*)   No credit, Edwina girl, no credit.
He thinks you're a mangy old moke. You tell him
There's none so mangy as thinks that others are.
You have it for the sake of the world.
PETER   All right, she can take me down. I'm rasping tired.
My whole body's like a three days' growth of beard.
But I don't know why she should have to carry me.
She's nothing herself but two swimming eyes
And a cask of ribs.
MEADOWS   A back's a back.
She's as good as gold while she lives,
And after that she's as good as dead. Where else
Would you find such a satisfactory soul?
Gee-up, you old millennium. She's slow,
But it's kind of onwards. Jog, jog,
Jog, jog.

PETER   There's a ram less in the world tonight.
My heart, I could see, was thudding in its eyes.
It was caught, and now it's dead.

MEADOWS   Jog, jog,
Jog, jog, jog, jog, jog,
Jog, jog.

PETER   Across the sands and into the sea.
The sun flocks along the waves.
Blowing up for rain of sand.
Helter-shelter.

MEADOWS   Jog. Jog. Jog.
Donkey ride is over. In under
The salty planks and corrugated iron.
Stable for mangy mokes. Home, old girl,
Home from the sea, old Millie-edwinium.
Tie up here.

(*He has climbed into his bunk*)

PETER   No eyes open. All
In sleep. The innocence has come.
Ram's wool hill pillow is hard.

(*He sighs and turns in his bunk. The church clock strikes one. An airplane is heard flying over the church.* PETER *wakens and sits up in his bunk, listening*)
Is that one of ours?

MEADOWS (*his face emerging from the blankets*)
                               Just tell me: are you awake
Or asleep?

PETER   Awake. Listen. Do you hear it?
Is it one of ours?

MEADOWS   No question: one of ours.
Or one of theirs.

PETER   Gone over. Funny question:
"Was I asleep?" when I was sitting up
Asking you a question.

MEADOWS   Dave's been sitting up
Asking questions, as fast asleep as an old dog.
And you've been chatting away like old knitting-needles,
Half the night.

PETER   What was I saying?

MEADOWS   I know all
Your secrets now, man.

PETER   I wish I did.
What did I say?

MEADOWS   Like the perfect gentleman
I obliterated my lug-holes:
Under two blankets, army issue.
A man must be let to have a soul to himself
Or souls will go the way of tails.
I wouldn't blame a man for sleeping.
It comes to some. To others it doesn't come.
Troubles differ. But I should be glad
To stop lying out here in the open
While you underearthly lads
Are shut away talking night's language like natives.
We only have to have Corporal Adams
To make a start, and I might as well
Give up the whole idea. Oh, lord, let me

Race him to it. I'm going under now
For the third time.

(*He covers his head with the blankets*)

PETER   Sorry if I disturbed you.
I'll go back where I came from, and if I can
I'll keep it to myself. Poor old Meadows:
Try thinking of love, or something.
Amor vincit insomnia.

MEADOWS   That's enough
Of night classes. What's it mean?

PETER   The writing on the wall. So turn
Your face to it: get snoring.

MEADOWS   Not hereabouts:
It wouldn't be reverent. Good night, then.

PETER   Same to you.

(*They cover their heads. A pause.* ADAMS, *asleep, lies flat on his bunk, looking down over the foot of it*)

ADAMS   Fish, fish, fish in the sea, you flash
Through your clouds of water like the war in heaven:
Angel-fish and swordfish, the silver troops . . .
And I am salt and sick on a raft above you,
Wondering for land, but there's no homeward
I can see.

(*He turns on his back*)

                        God, have mercy
On our sick shoals, darting and dying.
We're strange fish to you. How long
Can you drift over our sea, and not give up
The ghost of hope? The air is bright between us.
The flying fish make occasional rainbows,
But land, your land and mine, is nowhere yet.

(DAVID, *a dream figure, comes to meet him*)

How can a man learn navigation
When there's no rudder? You can seem to walk,
You there: you can seem to walk:
But presently you drown.

DAVID   Who wants us, Corporal?

ADAMS   I wish I knew. I'm soaked to the skin.
The world shines wet. I think it's men's eyes everywhere
Reflecting light. Presently you drown.

DAVID   Have you forgotten you're a prisoner?
They marched us thirty miles in the pouring rain.
Remember that? They, they, they, they.

(PETER *comes down towards* DAVID, *marching but exhausted. As he reaches* DAVID *he reels and* DAVID *catches him*)

PETER   What happens if I fall out, Dave?

DAVID   You don't fall out, that's all.

PETER   They can shoot me if they like.
It'll be a bit of a rest.

DAVID   You're doing all right.

PETER   I wouldn't know. It. Feels.
Damned. Odd. To me.

DAVID   Corporal Adams,
Man half-seas overboard!
Can you lend a hand?

ADAMS (*jumping from his bunk*)   Here I come.
　　　Does he want to be the little ghost?
　　　Give us an arm. Dave and I will be
　　　Your anchor, boy: keep you from drifting
　　　Away where you're not wanted yet.
PETER   Don't think you've got me with you.
　　　I dropped out miles ago.
ADAMS   We'll keep the memory green.

(*They do not move forward, but seem to be trudging*)

DAVID   They, they, they, they.
ADAMS   Be careful how you step. These logs we're on
　　　Are slimy and keep moving apart.
DAVID (*breaking away*)   Where do you think we are?
　　　We're prisoners, God! They've bricked us in.
ADAMS   Who said you were dismissed?
PETER
　　　　　　　　　　　　　　Forget your stripes
　　　For a minute, Corporal: it's my birthday next month,
　　　My birthday, Corporal: into the world I came,
　　　The barest chance it happened to be me,
　　　The naked truth of all that led the way
　　　To make me. I'm going for a stroll.

(*He wanders down towards the lectern*)

ADAMS   Where are you going? Orders are
　　　No man leaves unless in a state of death.
DAVID   There's nowhere to go, and he knows
　　　There's nowhere to go. He's trying to pretend
　　　We needn't be here.
PETER
　　　　　　　　　　　Don't throttle yourself
　　　With swallowing, Dave. Anyone
　　　Would think you never expected the world.
　　　Listen to the scriptures:

(*As though reading the Bible*)

　　　Nebuchadnezzar, hitting the news,
　　　Made every poor soul lick his shoes.
　　　When the shoes began to wear
　　　Nebuchadnezzar fell back on prayer.
　　　Here endeth the first lesson. And here beginneth
　　　The second lesson . . .
DAVID
　　　　　　　　　　　　I'll read the second lesson:
　　　God drown you for a rat, and let the world
　　　Go down without you.
PETER   Three blind mice of Gotham,
　　　Shadrac, Meshac and Abednego:
　　　They went to walk in a fire.
　　　If the fire had been hotter
　　　Their tales would have been shorter.
　　　Here endeth—
ADAMS   Get into the ranks.
PETER   What's worrying you? We're not
　　　On active service now. Maybe it's what
　　　They call in our paybooks "disembodied service":
　　　So drill my spirit, Corporal, till it weeps
　　　For mercy everywhere.
DAVID   　　　　　　　　　　It had better weep,
　　　It had better weep. By God, I'll say
　　　We have to be more than men if we're to man
　　　This rising day. They've been keeping from us

Who we are, till now, when it's too late
To recollect. (*indicating* PETER) Does he know?

ADAMS Shadrac, Meshac, Abednego—
We didn't have those names before: I'll swear
We were at sea. This black morning
Christens us with names that were never ours
And makes us pay for them. Named,
Condemned. What they like to call us
Matters more than anything at heart.
Hearts are here to stop
And better if they do. God help us all.

PETER Do I know what?

ADAMS We are your three blind mice:
Our names are Shadrac, Meshac, and Abednego.
This is our last morning. Who knows truly
What that means, except us?

PETER And which of us
Knows truly? O God in heaven, we're bound
To wake up out of this. Wake, wake, wake:
This is not my world! Where have you brought me?

DAVID To feed what you've been riding pick-a-back.

PETER I can believe anything, except
The monster.

DAVID And the monster's here.

ADAMS To make
Sure we know eternity's in earnest.

PETER It's here to kill. What's that in earnest of?
But the world comes up even over the monster's back.
Corporal, can we make a dash for the hill there?

ADAMS We're under close arrest.

DAVID O God, are we
To be shut up here in what other men do
And watch ourselves be ground and battered
Into their sins? Let me, dear God, be active
And seem to do right, whatever damned result.
Let me have some part in what goes on
Or I shall go mad!

PETER What's coming now
Their eyes are on us. Do you see them?

ADAMS Inspection. The powers have come to look us over
To see if we're in fettle for the end.
Get into line.

DAVID What, for those devils?
Who are they?

ADAMS Nebuchadnezzar and his aides.
Do what you're told.

PETER Is that him with one eye?

DAVID Are they ours or theirs?

ADAMS Who are we, Dave, who
Are we? If we could get the hang of that
We might know what side they're on. I should say
On all sides. Which is why the open air
Feels like a barrack square.

PETER Is that him
With one eye?

ADAMS If we could know who we are—

DAVID I've got to know which side I'm on.
I've got to be on a side.

ADAMS   —They're coming up.
        Let's see you jump to it this time: we're coming
        Up for the jump. We can't help it if
        We hate his guts.—Look out.—Party, shun!
(They all come to attention)
        The three prisoners, sir.—Party, stand
        At ease!
PETER   Purple and stars and red and gold.
        What are they celebrating?
DAVID   We shall know soon.
ADAMS   Stop talking in the ranks.
(They stand silent for a moment)

PETER   What bastard language
        Is he talking? Are we supposed to guess?
        Police on earth. Aggression is the better
        Part of Allah. Liberating very high
        The dying and the dead. Freedom, freedom.
        Will he never clear his throat?
DAVID   He's moving on.
ADAMS   Party, at-ten-tion!
(They bring their heels together, but they cannot bring their hands from behind their backs)

PETER   Corporal, our hands are tied!
DAVID   They've played their game
        In the dark: we're theirs, whoever calls us.
ADAMS   Stand at ease.
DAVID   Our feet are tied!
PETER   Hobbled,
        Poor asses.
ADAMS   That leaves me without a word of command
        To cover the situation, except
        Fall on your knees.
PETER   What's coming, Corporal?
ADAMS   You two, let's know it: we have to meet the fire.
DAVID   Tied hand and foot: not men at all!
PETER   O how
        Shall we think these moments out
        Before thinking splits to fear. I begin
        To feel the sweat of the pain: though the pain
        Hasn't reached us yet.
ADAMS   Have your hearts ready:
        It's coming now.
DAVID   Every damned forest in the world
        Has fallen to make it. The glare's on us.
PETER   Dead on.
        And here's the reconnoitring heat:
        It tells us what shall come.
ADAMS   Now then! Chuck down
        Your wishes for the world: there's nothing here
        To charm us. Ready?
DAVID   I've been strong.
        The smoke's between us. Where are you, Adams?
ADAMS   Lost.
PETER   Where are you, Adams?
(ADAMS cries out and falls to his knees)
DAVID   It's come to him, Peter!

PETER   We shall know!

DAVID   Scalding God!

(*They, too, have fallen to their knees*)

ADAMS   What way have I come down, to find
I live still, in this round of blaze?
Here on my knees. And a fire hotter
Than any fire has ever been
Plays over me. And I live. I know
I kneel.

DAVID   Adams.

ADAMS   We're not destroyed.

DAVID   Adams.

PETER   Voices. We're men who speak.

DAVID   We're men who sleep and wake.
They haven't let us go.

PETER   My breath
Parts the fire a little.

ADAMS   But the cords
That were tying us are burnt: drop off
Like snakes of soot.

PETER   Can we stand?

DAVID   Even against this coursing fire we can.

PETER   Stand: move: as though we were living,
In this narrow shaking street
Under the eaves of seven-storeyed flames
That lean and rear again, and still
We stand. Can we be living, or only
Seem to be?

ADAMS   I can think of life.
We'll make it yet.

DAVID   That's my devotion.
Which way now?

PETER   Wait a minute. Who's that
Watching us through the flame?

(MEADOWS, *a dream figure, is sitting on the side of his bunk*)

DAVID   Who's there?

ADAMS   Keep your heads down. Might be
Some sniper of the fire.

(MEADOWS *crows like a cock*)

PETER   A lunatic.

ADAMS (*calling to* MEADOWS)   Who are you?

MEADOWS   Man.

ADAMS   Under what command?

MEADOWS   God's.

ADAMS   May we come through?

MEADOWS   If you have
The patience and the love.

DAVID   Under this fire?

MEADOWS   Well, then, the honesty.

ADAMS   What honesty?

MEADOWS   Not to say we do
A thing for all men's sake when we do it only
For our own. And quick eyes to see
Where evil is. While any is our own
We sound fine words unsoundly.

ADAMS   You cockeyed son
Of heaven, how did you get here?

MEADOWS   Under the fence. I think they forgot
To throw me in. But there's not a skipping soul
On the loneliest goat-path who is not
Hugged into this, the human shambles.
And whatever happens on the farthest pitch,
To the sand-man in the desert or the island-man in the sea,
Concerns us very soon. So you'll forgive me
If I seem to intrude.

PETER   Do you mean to stay here?

MEADOWS   I can't get out alone. Neither can you.
But, on the other hand, single moments
Gather towards the striking clock.
Each man is the world.

PETER   But great events
Go faster.

DAVID   Who's to lead us out of this?

MEADOWS   It's hard to see. Who will trust
What the years have endlessly said?

ADAMS   There's been a mort of time. You'd think
Something might have come of it. These men
Are ready to go, and so am I.

PETER   But there's no God-known government anywhere.

MEADOWS   Behind us lie
The thousand and the thousand and the thousand years
Vexed and terrible. And still we use
The cures which never cure.

DAVID   For mortal sake,
Shall we move? Do we just wait and die?

MEADOWS   Figures of wisdom back in the old sorrow.
Hold and wait for ever. We see, admire
But never suffer them: suffer instead
A stubborn aberration.
O God, the fabulous wings unused,
Folded in the heart.

DAVID   So help me, in
The stresses of this furnace I can see
To be strong beyond all action is the strength
To have. But how do men and forbearance meet?
A stone forbears when the wheel goes over, but that
Is death to the flesh.

ADAMS   And every standing day
The claims are deeper, inactivity harder.
But where, in the maze of right and wrong,
Are we to do what action?

PETER   Look, how intense
The place is now, with swaying and troubled figures.
The flames are men: all human. There's no fire!
Breath and blood chokes and burns us. This
Surely is unquenchable? It can only transform.
There's no way out. We can only stay and alter.

DAVID   Who says there's nothing here to hate?

MEADOWS   The deeds, not those who do.

ADAMS   Strange how we trust the powers that ruin
And not the powers that bless.

DAVID   But good's unguarded,
As defenceless as a naked man.

MEADOWS   Imperishably. Good has no fear;
Good is itself, what ever comes.

It grows, and makes, and bravely
Persuades, beyond all tilt of wrong:
Stronger than anger, wiser than strategy,
Enough to subdue cities and men
If we believe it with a long courage of truth.

DAVID   Corporal, the crowing son of heaven
Thinks we can make a morning.

MEADOWS   Not
By old measures. Expedience and self-preservation
Can rot as they will. Lord, where we fail as men
We fail as deeds of time.

PETER   The blaze of this fire
Is wider than any man's imagination.
It goes beyond any stretch of the heart.

MEADOWS   The human heart can go to the lengths of God.
Dark and cold we may be, but this
Is no winter now. The frozen misery
Of centuries breaks, cracks, begins to move;
The thunder is the thunder of the floes,
The thaw, the flood, the upstart Spring
Thank God our time is now when wrong
Comes up to face us everywhere,
Never to leave us till we take
The longest stride of soul men ever took.
Affairs are now soul size.
The enterprise
Is exploration into God.
Where are you making for? It takes
So many thousand years to wake,
But will you wake for pity's sake?
Pete's sake, Dave or one of you,
Wake up, will you? Go and lie down.
Where do you think you're going?

ADAMS (*waking where he stands*)   What's wrong?

MEADOWS   You're walking in your sleep.
So's Pete and Dave. That's too damn many.

ADAMS   Where's this place? How did I get here?

MEADOWS   You were born here, chum. It's the same for all of us.
Get into bed.

PETER (*waking*)   What am I doing here?

MEADOWS   Walking your heart out, boy.

ADAMS   Dave, Dave.

MEADOWS   Let him come to himself gentle but soon
Before he goes and drowns himself in the font.

ADAMS   Wake up, Dave.

PETER   I wish I knew where I was.

MEADOWS   I can only give you a rough idea myself.
In a sort of a universe and a bit of a fix.
It's what they call flesh we're in.
And a fine old dance it is.

DAVID (*awake*)   Did they fetch us up?

MEADOWS   Out of a well. Where Truth was.
They didn't like us fraternizing. Corp,
Would you mind getting your men to bed
And stop them trapsing round the precincts?

ADAMS   Dave, we're mad boys. Sleep gone to our heads.
Come on.

DAVID   What's the time?

ADAMS Zero hour.

DAVID It feels like half an hour below. I've got cold feet.

PETER (*already lying on his bunk*) I've never done that before. I wonder now
What gives us a sense of direction in a dream?
Can we see in sleep? And what would have happened
If we'd walked into the guard? Would he have shot us,
Thinking we were trying to get out?

MEADOWS So you were from what you said. I could stand
One at a time, but not all three together.
It began to feel like the end of the world
With all your bunks giving up their dead.

ADAMS Well, sleep, I suppose.

DAVID Yeh. God bless.

PETER Rest you merry.

MEADOWS Hope so. Hope so.

(*They settle down. The church clock strikes. A bugle sounds in the distance*)

UNITED STATES

EUGENE O'NEILL (1888–1953) was America's first internation-
ally famous playwright, and the plays of this "restless experimenter"
with dramatic structures, techniques, and themes continue to haunt
the imaginations of contemporary audiences. In restrospect, however, despite great variation in focus and technique, O'Neill's plays
appear as a continuous philosophic investigation of the riddle of
falsehood at the core of life. An attitude of Schopenhauerian darkness pervades everything he wrote; his plays are eerie with the
ghosts of terrible dissatisfactions and desperate guilt. O'Neill was
the first American playwright to have a tragic sense of life, the first
to show awareness of a war continually being waged between life
and death. He sought to find a meaning for man in a world where
the common fate appeared to be a return to nothingness, and he
attempted to create an action which would encompass the terror of
being on the edge of the abyss. He was painfully conscious of man's
inability to fathom the mysteries of life and the ultimate object of
the human struggle, and all of his later plays reveal his belief
that it is impossible for man to find any protection against the
darkness of the night into which he must journey. O'Neill could
find no meaning in life, but he had great compassion for man's
failures. His plays are storm-warnings that urge us to inquire into
the nature of human disaster. His characters may lack heroic
stature, but at least they give us a sense that they have known
humiliation and suffering, and this enables them to emerge from the
bludgeoning they receive in the plays with a measure of dignity.
Each of them remains a creative being worthy of respect.

T. S. Eliot once wrote: "The more perfect the artist, the more
completely separate in him will be the man who suffers and the
mind which creates." In O'Neill, as in Strindberg before him, the
two were identical, and this paradox accounts for both the greatness

[EUGENE O'NEILL, *Cont.*]

and the limitations of his drama. His work has an immediacy and a compelling power which is rare in the theatre at any time, yet the plays lack control, facility of language, and compactness of form. It was only O'Neill's great sense of the theatre, his knowledge of the necessities and techniques of the stage, that enabled him to transform the painful memories of his early experiences into the most significant body of dramatic literature yet created by a writer for the American stage.

LILLIAN HELLMAN (1905–   ) is a superb example of the expert playwright whose presence in the theatre ensures its enduring vitality. This Southern-born writer, who has lived most of her life in the eastern states, is not a daring innovator, and her plays lack the imaginative expanse which we usually associate with greatness; but, like so many others of her kind in the past—Tourneur, Goldsmith, Pinero, and Galsworthy, for instance—Miss Hellman is a master craftsman who presents genuinely significant issues in a theatrically effective fashion. In the introduction to her only collection of plays, she wrote: "I am a moral writer, often too moral a writer, and I cannot avoid, it seems, that last summing up." This statement reveals the greatest strength and also the most glaring weakness in her writing. In a realistic style, characteristic of Ibsen, she writes of the conflicts of personal morality and their public consequences. But she cannot be considered, as she so often is, a social writer; rather, she is interested in showing damnation as a state of the soul, a condition that cannot be reformed out of existence or dissolved by sentimentality or easy optimism. In each of her plays she raspingly attacks both the doers of evil and those who stand by and "watch them do it." However, in her desire to expose evil, she has, as she well knows, a tendency to hammer the point to such an extent that there is a tendency for statement to replace dramatic process.

Miss Hellman is out of fashion today. Some people consider her themes hackneyed, her style too melodramatic, and her technique too mechanical. But, although there may be some truth in this kind of evaluation, the plays of Lillian Hellman, like those of Elmer Rice and Clifford Odets, still marked the American theatre's coming of age. Her work and theirs is irrefutable evidence that after O'Neill the popular American stage could be hospitable to serious concerns.

WILLIAM SAROYAN (1908–   ) is the wild man of the modern American theatre.

From the beginning of his career as a writer in the 1930's, he professed not to recognize any categories or any formulas or any principles. In *Three Times Three,* for example, he wrote "Plot, atmosphere, style, and all the rest of it may be regarded as so much nonsense." Or again, in *Razzle Dazzle,* "a play has a plot, a locale, an atmosphere, a leading character, many supporting characters, suspense, mystery, and all those other things you can buy for ten cents at any novelty or drug store." In both these statements, and countless others, we note a contempt for artifice of any kind, a contempt which has been Saroyan's stock in trade since the beginning. Saroyan has this profound distrust of artifice because he believes a great gap exists between the dramatic representation of life as it is found in the theatre and the dramas of life itself. For this reason he has always avoided, as if they were leprous, orderly sequences of events, neat conflicts and resolutions, conventional play structures. He wrote as he pleased, because he wanted his plays to appear, as one editor put it, "as wayward and formless as life itself." It would be a mistake, however, to conclude that Saroyan's objections to artifice and his insistence upon "truth" rather than "story telling" made him a photographic naturalist, for all of his plays are a kind of fantasy. He has a fine feeling for the odd, the unfamiliar, the unexpected, and the curious. At his best, Saroyan succeeds in making the fantasy credible. His characters are fantastic but also, imaginably, quite human. They perform their fantastic acts, and write their fantastic novels, and live on nothing a year by a kind of economic magic. They do all this while at the same time doing the most commonplace, everyday things. And their humanity is enhanced by Saroyan's insistence upon avoiding any appearance of contrivance and art in their actions. They are not going anywhere. Their dreams don't come to much. Their fantasy life, which is considerable, does not alter the major fact of their life: that they are living in a very plain house on a very plain street, eating very plain food—just living. This is the secret of Saroyan's theatre: his ability to combine the fantastic with the commonplace and have it come off.

THORNTON WILDER (1897–   ) is one of the most difficult of all modern dramatists to assess. He is ranked with O'Neill, Williams, and Miller as one of the titans of the American theatre, and yet his reputation is based on only three full-length plays, and it was made on one —*Our Town.* In spite of this small body of

[THORNTON WILDER, *Cont.*]

work, however, no American playwright is more respected by contemporary European dramatists than is Wilder; Brecht, Ionesco, Duerrenmatt, Sastre, and Frisch have all acknowledged their debt to this "great and fanatical experimenter." Indeed, Wilder has made contributions to both the form and the idea of drama that have not been equalled by any other living American dramatist.

From his earliest volumes of one-acts to his most recent cycle of one-acts, Wilder has dealt boldly and affirmatively with the themes of life, love, and earth. His plays are hymns in dramatic form affirming life; they celebrate human love, the worth and dignity of man, the values of the ordinary, and the eternity of human values. Wilder stated his position best when he wrote: "*Our Town* is not offered as a picture of life in a New Hampshire village, or speculation about the conditions of life after death. . . . It is an attempt to find value above all price for the smallest events of daily life."

As an innovator of theatrical techniques, Wilder was the first modern playwright to incorporate successfully the conventions of space and time used in the oriental theatre into the Western drama. By immaterializing the sense of dramatic place, and by destroying the illusion of time, he creates the effect of every place and all time. These techniques have made it possible for his plays to communicate to audiences all over the world—and for this reason, in most European countries, his work is considered the most representative and significant product of the modern American theatre.

TENNESSEE WILLIAMS (1911–   ) is probably the most productive writer in the contemporary American theatre. Everything he has written springs from his continuing preoccupation with the extremes of human aspiration and frustration. His plays deal with the war perpetually waged within the hearts of men between death and desire, the public and the private, the real and the ideal, the need for faith and the inevitability of inconstancy, the love of life and the overpowering urge towards self-destruction. But we discover that, underneath these dualities, all his characters are searching for meaningful relationships with their fellow men. Many people accuse Williams of being morbidly obsessed with violence and perverted sexuality, but this is to misread him and forget one of his most significant insights. In an interview given shortly after *Sweet Bird of Youth* was produced, Williams commented: "Desire is rooted in a longing for companionship, a release from the loneliness which haunts every individual." Like the writers whom he most admires—Chekhov, D. H. Lawrence, Giraudoux, and Beckett—Williams is primarily interested in dramatizing the anguish of solitude, a solitude which is made increasingly unbearable as the individual feels cut off from all the old securities, as he becomes conscious of the disparity between the outer life of one way of living and the inner life of a different way of dreaming.

There has, nonetheless, been a discernible development in Williams' work. From *The Glass Menagerie,* which dramatized man's tendency and need to escape the snares and dualities of a misfit world, through the maze of violence, brutality, and desire of such plays as *A Streetcar Named Desire* and *Cat on a Hot Tin Roof,* Williams has come increasingly toward an interest in the condition of man's spiritual life. But in this development the trademarks of his art are always present: the fluidity and mercurial instability of all emotion, the haunting imminence of death, the specters of violence and disease, the attraction to and guilt in sex, nostalgia for the past and hope for the future, a childlike humor even in the most morbid situations, and the conviction that "we're all of us sentenced to solitary confinement inside our own skins." Williams may be justly accused of having a limited perspective on the alternatives of the human condition, but within the limits of his world he has probably achieved more than any other living American dramatist.

ARTHUR MILLER (1915–   ) is a "yeasayer" to life whose dramas reveal the insecurity of man living in a modern industrial society and celebrate with compassion his search for a meaningful identity in such an inhospitable world. In his adaptation of Ibsen's *An Enemy of the People,* Miller described Dr. Stockman as one who "might be called the eternal amateur—a lover of things, of people, of sheer living, a man for whom the days are too short, and the future fabulous with discoverable joys. And for all this most people will not like him—he will not compromise for less than God's own share of the world while they have settled for less than Man's." Miller might well have been describing himself. No modern playwright writes with such moral earnestness and has a greater sense of social responsibility.

While many playwrights writing today deal with the loneliness of modern man's isolation, Miller is convinced that "the world is moving toward a unity, a unity won not alone by the

[ARTHUR MILLER, *Cont.*]

necessities of the physical developments themselves, but by the painful and confused reassertion of man's inherited will to survive." His passionate concern that attention be paid to the aspirations, worries, and failures of all men—and, more especially, the little man who is representative of the best and worst of an industrialized democratic society—has resulted in plays of great emotional impact. In a time when the American theatre has had a tendency to dwell on the case histories of all forms of social and psychological aberration, Arthur

Miller has insisted that courage, truth, trust, and faith are the central values of men's shared life together.

The dominant tone of the theatre in the mid-twentieth century is despair, but Miller continually demands more; he wants a "theatre in which an adult who wants to live can find plays that will heighten his awareness of what living in our times involves." Miller's own sense of involvement with modern man's struggle to be himself is expressed in all of his plays and has made him one of the modern theatre's most articulate and important spokesmen.

Eugene O'Neill

1888-1953

MEMORANDA ON MASKS

[1]

Not masks for all plays, naturally. Obviously not for plays conceived in purely realistic terms. But masks for certain types of plays, especially for the new modern play, as yet only dimly foreshadowed in a few groping specimens, but which must inevitably be written in the future. For I hold more and more surely to the conviction that the use of masks will be discovered eventually to be the freest solution of the modern dramatist's problem as to how—with the greatest possible dramatic clarity and economy of means—he can express those profound hidden conflicts of the mind which the probings of psychology continue to disclose to us. He must find some method to present this inner drama in his work, or confess himself incapable of portraying one of the most characteristic preoccupations and uniquely significant, spiritual impulses of his time. With his old— and more than a bit senile!—standby of realistic technique, he can do no more than, at best, obscurely hint at it through a realistically disguised surface symbolism, superficial and misleading. But that, while sufficiently beguiling to the sentimentally mystical, is hardly enough. A comprehensive expression is demanded here, a chance for eloquent presentation, a new form of drama projected from a fresh insight into the inner forces motivating the actions and reactions of men and women (a new and truer characterization, in other words)—a drama of souls, and the adventures of "free wills," with

"Memoranda on Masks" by Eugene O'Neill comprises 3 articles that originally appeared in *The American Spectator* of November 1932, December 1932, and January 1933. These articles are reprinted with the kind permission of Mrs. Carlotta Monterey O'Neill.

the masks that govern them and constitute their fates.

For what, at bottom, is the new psychological insight into human cause and effect but a study in masks, an exercise in unmasking? Whether we think the attempted unmasking has been successful, or has only created for itself new masks, is of no importance here. What is valid, what is unquestionable, is that this insight has uncovered the mask, has impressed the idea of mask as a symbol of inner reality upon all intelligent people of today; and I know they would welcome the use of masks in the theatre as a necessary, dramatically revealing new convention, and not regard them as any "stunty" resurrection of archaic props.

This was strikingly demonstrated for me in practical experience by *The Great God Brown*, which ran in New York for eight months, nearly all of that time in Broadway theatres—a play in which the use of masks was an integral part of the theme. There was some misunderstanding, of course. But so is there always misunderstanding in the case of every realistic play that attempts to express anything beyond what is contained in a human-interest newspaper story. In the main, however, *The Great God Brown* was accepted and appreciated by both critics and public—a fairly extensive public, as its run gives evidence.

I emphasize this play's success because the fact that a mask drama, the main values of which are psychological, mystical, and abstract, could be played in New York for eight months, has always seemed to me a more significant proof of the deeply responsive possibilities in our public than anything that has happened in our modern theatre before or since.

[2]

Looked at from even the most practical standpoint of the practicing playwright, the

[1077]

mask *is* dramatic in itself, *has always* been dramatic in itself, *is* a proven weapon of attack. At its best, it is more subtly, imaginatively, suggestively dramatic than any actor's face can ever be. Let anyone who doubts this study the Japanese Noh masks, or Chinese theatre masks, or African primitive masks—or right here in America the faces of the big marionettes Robert Edmond Jones made for the production of Stravinsky's *Oedipus*, or Benda's famous masks, or even photographs of them.

[3]

Dogma for the new masked drama. One's outer life passes in a solitude haunted by the masks of others; one's inner life passes in a solitude hounded by the masks of oneself.

[4]

With masked mob a new type of play may be written in which the Mob as King, Hero, Villain, or Fool will be the main character—The Great Democratic Play!

[5]

Why not give all future Classical revivals entirely in masks? *Hamlet*, for example. Masks would liberate this play from its present confining status as exclusively a "star vehicle." We would be able to see the great drama we are not only privileged to read, to identify ourselves with the figure of Hamlet as a symbolic projection of a fate that is in each of us, instead of merely watching a star giving us his version of a great acting role. We would even be able to hear the sublime poetry as the innate expression of the spirit of the drama itself, instead of listening to it as realistic recitation—or ranting—by familiar actors.

[6]

Consider Goethe's *Faust*, which, psychologically speaking, should be the closest to us of all the Classics. In producing this play, I would have Mephistopheles wearing the Mephistophelean mask of the face of Faust. For is not the whole of Goethe's truth *for our time* just that Mephistopheles and Faust are one and the same—*are* Faust?

SECOND THOUGHTS

What would I change in past productions of my plays if I could live through them again?

Many things. In some plays, considerable revision of the writing of some of the scenes would strike me as imperative. Other plays—*The First Man, Gold, Welded, The Fountain*—I would dismiss as being too painfully bungled in their present form to be worth producing at all.

But one thing I most certainly would not change: the use of masks in *The Hairy Ape*, in my arrangement of Coleridge's "Ancient Mariner," in *All God's Chillun Got Wings* (the symbol of the African primitive mask in the last part of the play, which, in the production in Russian by the Moscow Kamerny Theatre I saw in Paris, is dramatically intensified and emphasized), in *The Great God Brown* and, finally, in *Lazarus Laughed*, in which all the characters except Lazarus remain masked throughout the play. I regard this use of masks as having been uniformly successful.

The change I would make would be to call for more masks in some of these productions and to use them in other productions where they were not used before. In *The Emperor Jones*, for example. All the figures in Jones's flight through the forest should be masked. Masks would dramatically stress their phantasmal quality, as contrasted with the unmasked Jones, intensify the supernatural menace of the tomtom, give the play a more complete and vivid expression. In *The Hairy Ape* a much more extensive use of masks would be of the greatest value in emphasizing the theme of the play. From the opening of the fourth scene, where Yank begins to think, he enters into a masked world; even the familiar faces of his mates in the forecastle have become strange and alien. They should be masked, and the faces of everyone he encounters thereafter, including the symbolic gorilla's.

In *All God's Chillun Got Wings*, all save the seven leading characters should be masked; for all the secondary figures are part and parcel of the Expressionistic background of the play, a world at first indifferent, then cruelly hostile, against which the tragedy of Jim Harris is outlined. In *The Great God Brown* I would now make the masks symbolize more definitely the abstract theme of the play instead of, as in the old production, stressing the more superficial meaning that people wear masks before other people and are mistaken by them for their masks.

In *Marco Millions* all the people of the East should be masked—Kublai, the Princess Kokachin, all of them! For anyone who has been in the East, or who has read Eastern philosophy, the reason for this is obvious. It is an exact dramatic expression of West confronted by East. Moreover, it is the only possible way to project this contrast truthfully in the theatre, for Western actors cannot convey Eastern character realistically, and their only chance to suggest it convincingly is with the help of masks.

As for *Strange Interlude*, that is an attempt at the new masked psychological drama which I have discussed before, without masks—a successful attempt, perhaps, in so far as it concerns only surfaces and their immediate subsurfaces, but not where, occasionally, it tries to probe deeper.

With *Mourning Becomes Electra*, masks were called for in one draft of the three plays. But the Classical connotation was too insistent. Masks in that connection demand great language to speak—which let me out of it with a sickening bump! So I had to discard them. There was a realistic New England insistence in my mind, too, which would have barred great language even in a dramatist capable of writing it, an insistence on the clotted and clogged and inarticulate. So it evolved ultimately into the "masklike faces," which expressed my intention tempered by the circumstances. However, I should like to see *Mourning Becomes Electra* done entirely with masks, now that I can view it solely as a psychological play, quite removed from the confusing preoccupations the Classical derivation of its plot once caused me. Masks would emphasize the drama of the life and death impulses that drive the characters on to their fates and put more in its proper secondary place, as a frame, the story of the New England family.

A DRAMATIST'S NOTEBOOK

I advocate masks for stage crowds, mobs— wherever a sense of impersonal, collective mob psychology is wanted. This was one reason for such an extensive use of them in *Lazarus Laughed*. In masking the crowds in that play, I was visualizing an effect that, intensified by dramatic lighting, would give an audience visually the sense of the Crowd, not as a random collection of individuals, but as a collective whole, an entity. When the Crowd speaks, I wanted an audience to hear the voice of Crowd mind, Crowd emotion, as one voice of a body composed of, but quite distinct from, its parts.

And, for more practical reasons, I wanted to preserve the different crowds of another time and country from the blighting illusion-shattering recognitions by an audience of the supers

on the stage. Have you ever seen a production of *Julius Caesar?* Did the Roman mob ever suggest to you anything more Roman than a gum-chewing Coney Island Mardi Gras or, in the case of a special all-star revival, a gathering of familiar-faced modern actors masquerading uncomfortably in togas? But with masks—and the proper intensive lighting—you would have been freed from these recognitions; you would have been able to imagine a Roman mob; you would not even have recognized the Third Avenue and Brooklyn accents among the supers, so effectively does a mask change the quality of a voice.

It was interesting to watch, in the final rehearsals of *The Great God Brown*, how after using their masks for a time the actors and actresses reacted to the demand made by the masks that their bodies become alive and expressive and participate in the drama. Usually it is only the actors' faces that participate. Their bodies remain bored spectators that have been dragged off to the theatre when they would have much preferred a quiet evening in the upholstered chair at home.

Meaning no carping disrespect to our actors. I have been exceedingly lucky in having had some exceptionally fine acting in the principal roles in my plays, for which I am exceedingly grateful. Also some damned poor acting. But let that pass. Most of the poor acting occurred in the poor plays, and there I hold only myself responsible. In the main, wherever a part challenged the actors' or actresses' greatest possibilities, they have reacted to the challenge with a splendid creative energy and skill. Especially, and this is the point I want to make now, where the play took them away from the strictly realistic parts they were accustomed to playing. They always welcomed any opportunity that gave them new scope for their talents. So when I argue here for a non-realistic imaginative theatre I am hoping, not only for added scope for playwright and director and scenic designer, but also for a chance for the actor to develop his art beyond the narrow range to which our present theatre condemns it. Most important of all, from the standpoint of future American culture, I am hoping for added imaginative scope for the audience, a chance for a public I know is growing yearly more numerous and more hungry in its spiritual need to participate in imaginative interpretations of life rather than merely identify itself with faithful surface resemblances of living.

I harp on the word "imaginative"—and with intention! But what do I mean by an "imaginative" theatre—(where I hope for it, for ex-

ample, in the subtitle of *Lazarus Laughed:* A
Play for an Imaginative Theatre)? I mean the
one true theatre, the age-old theatre, the
theatre of the Greeks and Elizabethans, a
theatre that could dare to boast—without
committing a farcical sacrilege—that it is a
legitimate descendant of the first theatre that
sprang, by virtue of man's imaginative interpretation of life, out of his worship of Dionysus.
I mean a theatre returned to its highest and
sole significant function as a Temple where
the religion of a poetical interpretation and
symbolical celebration of life is communicated
to human beings, starved in spirit by their soul-

stifling daily struggle to exist as masks among
the masks of living!

But I anticipate the actors' objection to
masks: that they would extinguish their personalities and deprive them of their greatest
asset in conveying emotion by facial expression.
I claim, however, that masks would give them
the opportunity for a totally new kind of acting, that they would learn many undeveloped
possibilities of their art if they appeared, even
if only for a season or two, in masked roles.
After all, masks did not extinguish the Greek
actor, nor have they kept the acting of the
East from being an art.

DESIRE UNDER THE ELMS

CAST OF CHARACTERS

EPHRAIM CABOT
SIMEON
PETER } *his sons*
EBEN
ABBIE PUTNAM
Young GIRL, *two* FARMERS, *the* FIDDLER, *a*
SHERIFF, *and other folk from the neigh-
boring farms.*

SCENE *The action of the entire play
takes place in, and immediately outside
of, the Cabot farmhouse in New England,
in the year 1850. The south end of the
house faces front to a stone wall with a
wooden gate at center opening on a country road. The house is in good condition
but in need of paint. Its walls are a sickly
grayish, the green of the shutters faded.
Two enormous elms are on each side of
the house. They bend their trailing
branches down over the roof. They appear to protect and at the same time subdue. There is a sinister maternity in their
aspect, a crushing, jealous absorption. They
have developed from their intimate contact with the life of man in the house an
appalling humaneness. They brood oppres-
sively over the house. They are like exhausted women resting their sagging
breasts and hands and hair on its roof,
and when it rains their tears trickle down
monotonously and rot on the shingles.*

*There is a path running from the gate
around the right corner of the house to
the front door. A narrow porch is on this
side. The end wall facing us has two
windows in its upper story, two larger*

*ones on the floor below. The two upper
are those of the father's bedroom and
that of the brothers. On the left, ground
floor, is the kitchen—on the right, the
parlor, the shades of which are always
drawn down.*

PART ONE

Scene One

(*Exterior of the farmhouse. It is sunset of a
day at the beginning of summer in the year
1850. There is no wind and everything is still.
The sky above the roof is suffused with deep
colors, the green of the elms glows, but the
house is in shadow, seeming pale and washed
out by contrast.*

A door opens and EBEN CABOT *comes to the
end of the porch and stands looking down the
road to the right. He has a large bell in his
hand and this he swings mechanically, awakening a deafening clangor. Then he puts his
hands on his hips and stares up at the sky.
He sighs with a puzzled awe and blurts out
with halting appreciation*)

EBEN God! Purty! (*His eyes fall and he
stares about him frowningly. He is twenty-
five, tall and sinewy. His face is well-formed,
good-looking, but its expression is resentful
and defensive. His defiant, dark eyes remind
one of a wild animal's in captivity. Each day
is a cage in which he finds himself trapped but
inwardly unsubdued. There is a fierce repressed
vitality about him. He has black hair, mustache,
a thin curly trace of beard. He is dressed in
rough farm clothes.*

*He spits on the ground with intense disgust,
turns and goes back into the house.*)

SIMEON *and* PETER *come in from their work in the fields. They are tall men, much older than their half-brother [*SIMEON *is thirty-nine and* PETER *thirty-seven], built on a squarer, simpler model, fleshier in body, more bovine and homelier in face, shrewder and more practical. Their shoulders stoop a bit from years of farm work. They clump heavily along in their clumsy thick-soled boots caked with earth. Their clothes, their faces, hands, bare arms and throats are earth-stained. They smell of earth. They stand together for a moment in front of the house and, as if with one impulse, stare dumbly up at the sky, leaning on their hoes. Their faces have a compressed, unresigned expression. As they look upward, this softens*)

SIMEON (*grudgingly*) Purty.

PETER Ay-eh.

SIMEON (*suddenly*) Eighteen year ago.

PETER What?

SIMEON Jenn. My woman. She died.

PETER I'd fergot.

SIMEON I rec'lect—now an' agin. Makes it lonesome. She'd hair long's a hoss' tail—an' yaller like gold!

PETER Waal—she's gone. (*this with indifferent finality—then after a pause*) They's gold in the West, Sim.

SIMEON (*still under the influence of sunset —vaguely*) In the sky?

PETER Waal—in a manner o' speakin'— thar's the promise. (*growing excited*) Gold in the sky—in the West—Golden Gate—Californi-a!—Goldest West!—fields o' gold!

SIMEON (*excited in his turn*) Fortunes layin' just atop o' the ground waitin' t' be picked! Solomon's mines, they says! (*For a moment they continue looking up at the sky —then their eyes drop*)

PETER (*with sardonic bitterness*) Here— it's stones atop o' the ground—stones atop o' stones—makin' stone walls—year atop o' year —him 'n' yew 'n' me 'n' then Eben—makin' stone walls fur him to fence us in!

SIMEON We've wuked. Give our strength. Give our years. Plowed 'em under in the ground—(*He stamps rebelliously*)—rottin'— makin' soil for his crops! (*a pause*) Waal—the farm pays good for hereabouts.

PETER If we plowed in Californi-a, they'd be lumps o' gold in the furrow!

SIMEON Californi-a's t'other side o' earth, a'most. We got t' calc'late—

PETER (*after a pause*) 'Twould be hard fur me, too, to give up what we've 'arned here by our sweat. (*A pause, *EBEN *sticks his head out of the dining-room window, listening*)

SIMEON Ay-eh. (*a pause*) Mebbe—he'll die soon.

PETER (*doubtfully*) Mebbe.

SIMEON Mebbe—fur all we knows—he's dead now.

PETER Ye'd need proof.

SIMEON He's been gone two months—with no word.

PETER Left us in the fields an evenin' like this. Hitched up an' druv off into the West. That's plum onnateral. He hain't never been off this farm 'ceptin' t' the village in thirty year or more, not since he married Eben's maw. (*A pause. Shrewdly*) I calc'late we might git him declared crazy by the court.

SIMEON He skinned 'em too slick. He got the best o' all on 'em. They'd never b'lieve him crazy. (*a pause*) We got t' wait—till he's under ground.

EBEN (*with a sardonic chuckle*) Honor thy father! (*They turn, startled, and stare at him. He grins, then scowls*) I pray he's died. (*They stare at him. He continues matter-of-factly*) Supper's ready.

SIMEON *and* PETER (*together*) Ay-eh.

EBEN (*gazing up at the sky*) Sun's downin' purty.

SIMEON *and* PETER (*together*) Ay-eh. They's gold in the West.

EBEN Ay-eh. (*pointing*) Yonder atop o' the hill pasture, ye mean?

SIMEON *and* PETER (*together*) In Californi-a!

EBEN Hunh? (*stares at them indifferently for a second, then drawls*) Waal—supper's gittin' cold. (*He turns back into kitchen*)

SIMEON (*startled—smacks his lips*) I air hungry!

PETER (*sniffing*) I smells bacon!

SIMEON (*with hungry appreciation*) Bacon's good!

PETER (*in same tone*) Bacon's bacon! (*They turn, shouldering each other, their bodies bumping and rubbing together as they hurry clumsily to their food, like two friendly oxen toward their evening meal. They disappear around the right corner of house and can be heard entering the door*)

Scene Two

(*The color fades from the sky. Twilight begins. The interior of the kitchen is now visible. A pine table is at center, a cook-stove in the right rear corner, four rough wooden chairs, a tallow candle on the table. In the middle of the rear wall is fastened a big advertising poster with a ship in full sail and the word*

"California" in big letters. Kitchen utensils hang from nails. Everything is neat and in order but the atmosphere is of a men's camp kitchen rather than that of a home.

Places for three are laid. EBEN *takes boiled potatoes and bacon from the stove and puts them on the table, also a loaf of bread and a crock of water.* SIMEON *and* PETER *shoulder in, slump down in their chairs without a word.* EBEN *joins them. The three eat in silence for a moment, the two elder as naturally unrestrained as beasts of the field,* EBEN *picking at his food without appetite, glancing at them with a tolerant dislike)*

SIMEON (*suddenly turns to* EBEN) Looky here! Ye'd oughtn't t' said that, Eben.

PETER 'Twa'n't righteous.

EBEN What?

SIMEON Ye prayed he'd died.

EBEN Waal—don't yew pray it? (*a pause*)

PETER He's our paw.

EBEN (*violently*) Not mine!

SIMEON (*dryly*) Ye'd not let no one else say that about yer Maw! Ha! (*He gives one abrupt sardonic guffaw.* PETER *grins*)

EBEN (*very pale*) I meant—I hain't his'n —I hain't like him—he hain't me!

PETER (*dryly*) Wait till ye've growed his age!

EBEN (*intensely*) I'm Maw—every drop o' blood! (*A pause. They stare at him with indifferent curiosity*)

PETER (*reminiscently*) She was good t' Sim 'n' me. A good Stepmaw's scurse.

SIMEON She was good t' everyone.

EBEN (*greatly moved, gets to his feet and makes an awkward bow to each of them— stammering*) I be thankful t'ye. I'm her— her heir. (*He sits down in confusion*)

PETER (*after a pause—judicially*) She was good even t' him.

EBEN (*fiercely*) An' fur thanks he killed her!

SIMEON (*after a pause*) No one never kills nobody. It's allus somethin'. That's the murderer.

EBEN Didn't he slave Maw t' death?

PETER He slaved himself t' death. He's slaved Sim 'n' me 'n' yew t' death—on'y none o' us hain't died—yit.

SIMEON It's somethin'—drivin' him—t' drive us!

EBEN (*vengefully*) Waal—I hold him t' judgment! (*then scornfully*) Somethin'! What's somethin'?

SIMEON Dunno.

EBEN (*sardonically*) What's drivin' yew to Californi-a, mebbe? (*They look at him in surprise*) Oh, I've heerd ye! (*then, after a pause*) But ye'll never go t' the gold fields!

PETER (*assertively*) Mebbe!

EBEN Whar'll ye git the money?

PETER We kin walk. It's an a'mighty ways —Californi-a—but if yew was t' put all the steps we've walked on this farm end t' end we'd be in the moon!

EBEN The Injuns'll scalp ye on the plains.

SIMEON (*with grim humor*) We'll mebbe make 'em pay a hair fur a hair!

EBEN (*decisively*) But t'ain't that. Ye won't never go because ye'll wait here fur yer share o' the farm, thinkin' allus he'll die soon.

SIMEON (*after a pause*) We've a right.

PETER Two-thirds belongs t' us.

EBEN (*jumping to his feet*) Ye've no right! She wa'n't yewr Maw! It was her farm! Didn't he steal it from her? She's dead. It's my farm.

SIMEON (*sardonically*) Tell that t' Paw— when he comes! I'll bet ye a dollar he'll laugh —fur once in his life. Ha! (*He laughs himself in one single mirthless bark*)

PETER (*amused in turn, echoes his brother*) Ha!

SIMEON (*after a pause*) What've ye got held agin us, Eben? Year after year it's skulked in yer eye—somethin'.

PETER Ay-eh.

EBEN Ay-eh. They's somethin'. (*suddenly exploding*) Why didn't ye never stand between him 'n' my Maw when he was slavin' her to her grave—t' pay her back fur the kindness she done t' yew? (*There is a long pause. They stare at him in surprise*)

SIMEON Waal—the stock'd got t' be watered.

PETER 'R they was woodin' t' do.

SIMEON 'R plowin'.

PETER 'R hayin'.

SIMEON 'R spreadin' manure.

PETER 'R weedin'.

SIMEON 'R prunin'.

PETER 'R milkin'.

EBEN (*breaking in harshly*) An' makin' walls—stone atop o' stone—makin' walls till yer heart's a stone ye heft up out o' the way o' growth onto a stone wall t' wall in yer heart!

SIMEON (*matter-of-factly*) We never had no time t' meddle.

PETER (*to* EBEN) Yew was fifteen afore yer Maw died—an' big fur yer age. Why didn't ye never do nothin'?

EBEN (*harshly*) They was chores t' do, wa'n't they? (*a pause—then slowly*) It was on'y arter she died I come to think o' it. Me cookin'—doin' her work—that made me know her, suffer her sufferin'—she'd come back t' help—come back t' bile potatoes—come back t' fry bacon—come back t' bake biscuits—come back all cramped up t' shake the fire, an' carry ashes, her eyes weepin' an' bloody with smoke an' cinders same's they used t' be. She still comes back—stands by the stove thar in the evenin'—she can't find it nateral sleepin' an' restin' in peace. She can't git used t' bein free —even in her grave.

SIMEON She never complained none.

EBEN She'd got too tired. She'd got too used t' bein' too tired. That was what he done. (*with vengeful passion*) An' sooner'r later, I'll meddle. I'll say the thin's I didn't say then t' him! I'll yell 'em at the top o' my lungs. I'll see t' it my Maw gits some rest an' sleep in her grave! (*He sits down again, relapsing into a brooding silence. They look at him with a queer indifferent curiosity*)

PETER (*after a pause*) Whar in tarnation d'ye s'pose he went, Sim?

SIMEON Dunno. He druv off in the buggy, all spick an' span, with the mare all breshed an' shiny, druv off clackin' his tongue an' wavin' his whip. I remember it right well. I was finishin' plowin', it was spring an' May an' sunset, an' gold in the West, an' he druv off into it. I yells "Whar ye goin' Paw?" an' he hauls up by the stone wall a jiffy. His old snake's eyes was glitterin' in the sun like he'd been drinkin' a jugful an' he says with a mule's grin: "Don't ye run away till I come back!"

PETER Wonder if he knowed we was wantin' fur Californi-a?

SIMEON Mebbe. I didn't say nothin' and he says, lookin' kinder queer an' sick: "I been hearin' the hens cluckin' an' the roosters crowin' all the durn day. I been listenin' t' the cows lowin' an' everythin' else kickin' up till I can't stand it no more. It's spring an' I'm feelin' damned," he says. "Damned like an old bare hickory tree fit on'y fur burnin'," he says. An' then I calc'late I must've looked a mite hopeful, fur he adds real spry and vicious: "But don't git no fool idee I'm dead. I've sworn t' live a hundred an' I'll do it' if on'y t' spite yer sinful greed! An' now I'm ridin' out t' learn God's message t' me in the spring, like the prophets done. An' yew git back t' yer plowin'," he says. An' he druv off singin' a hymn. I thought he was drunk—'r I'd stopped him goin'.

EBEN (*scornfully*) No, ye wouldn't! Ye're scared o' him. He's stronger—inside—than both o' ye put together!

PETER (*sardonically*) An' yew—be yew Samson?

EBEN I'm gittin' stronger. I kin feel it growin' in me—growin' an' growin'—till it'll

bust out—! (*He gets up and puts on his coat and a hat. They watch him, gradually breaking into grins.* EBEN *avoids their eyes sheepishly*) I'm goin' out fur a spell—up the road.

PETER T' the village?

SIMEON T' see Minnie?

EBEN (*defiantly*) Ay-eh!

PETER (*jeeringly*) The Scarlet Woman!

SIMEON Lust—that's what's growin' in ye!

EBEN Waal—she's purty!

PETER She's been purty fur twenty year!

SIMEON A new coat o' paint'll make a heifer out of forty.

EBEN She hain't forty!

PETER If she hain't, she's teeterin' on the edge.

EBEN (*desperately*) What d'yew know—

PETER All they is . . . Sim knew her—an' then me arter—

SIMEON An' Paw kin tell yew somethin' too! He was fust!

EBEN D'ye mean t' say he . . . ?

SIMEON (*with a grin*) Ay-eh! We air his heirs in everythin'!

EBEN (*intensely*) That's more to it! That grows on it! It'll bust soon! (*then violently*) I'll go smash my fist in her face! (*He pulls open the door in rear violently*)

SIMEON (*with a wink at* PETER—*drawling*) Mebbe—but the night's wa'm—purty—by the time ye git thar mebbe ye'll kiss her instead!

PETER Sart'n he will! (*They both roar with coarse laughter.* EBEN *rushes out and slams the door—then the outside front door—comes around the corner of the house and stands still by the gate, staring up at the sky*)

SIMEON (*looking after him*) Like his Paw!

PETER Dead spit an' image!

SIMEON Dog'll eat dog!

PETER Ay-eh! (*Pause. With yearning*) Mebbe a year from now we'll be in Californi-a.

SIMEON Ay-eh. (*A pause. Both yawn*) Let's git t'bed. (*He blows out the candle. They go out the door in rear.* EBEN *stretches his arms up to the sky—rebelliously*)

EBEN Waal—thar's a star, an' somewhar's they's him, an' here's me, an' thar's Min up the road—in the same night. What if I does kiss her? She's like t'night, she's soft 'n' wa'm, her eyes kin wink like a star, her mouth's wa'm, her arms're wa'm, she smells like a wa'm plowed field, she's purty . . . Ay-eh! By God A'mighty she's purty, an' I don't give a damn how many sins she's sinned afore mine or who's she's sinned 'em with, my sin's as purty as any one on 'em! (*He strides off down the road to the left*)

Scene Three

(*It is the pitch darkness just before dawn.* EBEN *comes in from the left and goes around to the porch, feeling his way, chuckling bitterly and cursing half-aloud to himself*)

EBEN   The cussed old miser! (*He can be heard going in the front door. There is a pause as he goes upstairs, then a loud knock on the bedroom door of the brothers*) Wake up!

SIMEON (*startedly*)   Who's thar?

EBEN (*pushing open the door and coming in, a lighted candle in his hand. The bedroom of the brothers is revealed. Its ceiling is the sloping roof. They can stand upright only close to the center dividing wall of the upstairs.* SIMEON *and* PETER *are in a double bed, front.* EBEN'S *cot is to the rear.* EBEN *has a mixture of silly grin and vicious scowl on his face*) I be!

PETER (*angrily*)   What in hell's-fire . . . ?

EBEN   I got news fur ye! Ha! (*He gives one abrupt sardonic guffaw*)

SIMEON (*angrily*)   Couldn't ye hold it 'til we'd got our sleep?

EBEN   It's nigh sunup. (*then explosively*) He's gone an' married agen!

SIMEON *and* PETER (*explosively*)   Paw?

EBEN   Got himself hitched to a female 'bout thirty-five—an' purty, they says . . .

SIMEON (*aghast*)   It's a durn lie!

PETER   Who say's?

SIMEON   They been stringin' ye!

EBEN   Think I'm a dunce, do ye? The hull village says. The preacher from New Dover, he brung the news—told it t'our preacher—New Dover, that's whar the old loon got himself hitched—that's whar the woman lived—

PETER (*no longer doubting—stunned*) Waal . . . !

SIMEON (*the same*)   Waal . . . !

EBEN (*sitting down on a bed—with vicious hatred*)   Ain't he a devil out o' hell? It's jest t' spite us—the damned old mule!

PETER (*after a pause*)   Everythin'll go t' her now.

SIMEON   Ay-eh (*a pause—dully*) Waal— if it's done—

PETER   It's done us. (*pause—then persuasively*) They's gold in the fields o' Californi-a, Sim. No good a-stayin' here now.

SIMEON   Jest what I was a-thinkin'. (*then with decision*) S'well fust's last! Let's light out and git this mornin'.

PETER   Suits me.

EBEN   Ye must like walkin'.

SIMEON (*sardonically*)   If ye'd grow wings on us we'd fly thar!

EBEN   Ye'd like ridin' better—on a boat, wouldn't ye? (*fumbles in his pocket and takes out a crumpled sheet of foolscap*) Waal, if ye sign this ye kin ride on a boat. I've had it writ out an' ready in case ye'd ever go. It says fur three hundred dollars t' each ye agree yewr shares o' the farm is sold t' me. (*They look suspiciously at the paper. A pause*)

SIMEON (*wonderingly*)   But if he's hitched agen—

PETER   An' whar'd yew git that sum o' money, anyways?

EBEN (*cunningly*)   I know whar it's hid. I been waitin'—Maw told me. She knew whar it lay fur years, but she was waitin' . . . It's her'n—the money he hoarded from her farm an' hid from Maw. It's my money by rights now.

PETER   Whar's it hid?

EBEN (*cunningly*)   Whar yew won't never find it without me. Maw spied on him—'r she'd never knowed. (*A pause. They look at him suspiciously, and he at them*) Waal, is it fa'r trade?

SIMEON   Dunno.

PETER   Dunno.

SIMEON (*looking at window*)   Sky's grayin'.

PETER   Ye better start the fire, Eben.

SIMEON   An' fix some vittles.

EBEN   Ay-eh. (*then with a forced jocular heartiness*) I'll git ye a good one. If ye're startin' t' hoof it t' Californi-a ye'll need somethin' that'll stick t' yer ribs. (*He turns to the door, adding meaningly*) But ye can ride on a boat if ye'll swap. (*He stops at the door and pauses. They stare at him*)

SIMEON (*suspiciously*)   Whar was ye all night?

EBEN (*defiantly*)   Up t' Min's. (*then slowly*) Walkin' thar, fust I felt 's if I'd kiss her; then I got a-thinkin' o' what ye'd said o' him an' her an' I says, I'll bust her nose fur that! Then I got t' the village an' heerd the news an' I got madder'n hell an' run all the way t' Min's not knowin' what I'd do—(*He pauses—then sheepishly but more defiantly*) Waal—when I seen her, I didn't hit her—nor I didn't kiss her nuther—I begun t' beller like a calf an' cuss at the same time, I was so durn mad—an' she got scared—an' I just grabbed holt an' tuk her! (*proudly*) Yes, sirree! I tuk her. She may've been his'n—an' your'n, too—but she's mine now!

SIMEON (*dryly*)   In love, air yew?

EBEN (*with lofty scorn*)   Love! I don't take no stock in sech slop!

PETER (*winking at* SIMEON)   Mebbe Eben's aimin' t' marry, too.

SIMEON   Min'd make a true faithful he'p-meet! (*They snicker*)

EBEN   What do I care fur her—'ceptin' she's round an' wa'm? The p'int is she was his'n—an' now she belongs t' me! (*He goes to the door—then turns—rebelliously*) An' Min hain't sech a bad un. They's worse'n Min in the world, I'll bet ye! Wait'll we see this cow the Old Man's hitched t'! She'll beat Min, I got a notion! (*He starts to go out*)

SIMEON   (*suddenly*)   Mebbe ye'll try t' make her your'n, too?

PETER   Ha! (*He gives a sardonic laugh of relish at this idea*)

EBEN   (*spitting with disgust*)   Her—here—sleepin' with him—stealin' 'r my Maw's farm! I'd as soon pet a skunk 'r kiss a snake! (*He goes out. The two stare after him suspiciously. A pause. They listen to his steps receding*)

PETER   He's startin' the fire.

SIMEON   I'd like t' ride t' Californi-a—but—

PETER   Min might o' put some scheme in his head.

SIMEON   Mebbe it's all a lie 'bout Paw marryin'. We'd best wait an' see the bride.

PETER   An' don't sign nothin' till we does!

SIMEON   Nor till we've tested it's good money! (*then with a grin*) But if Paw's hitched we'd be sellin' Eben somethin' we'd never git nohow!

PETER   We'll wait an' see. (*then with sudden vindictive anger*) An' till he comes, let's yew 'n' me not wuk a lick, let Eben tend to thin's if he's a mind t', let's us jest sleep an' eat an' drink likker, an' let the hull damned farm go t' blazes!

SIMEON   (*excitedly*)   By God, we've 'arned a rest! We'll play rich fur a change. I hain't a-goin' to stir outa bed till breakfast's ready.

PETER   An' on the table!

SIMEON   (*after a pause—thoughtfully*) What d' ye calc'late she'll be like—our new Maw? Like Eben thinks?

PETER   More'n likely.

SIMEON   (*vindictively*)   Waal—I hope she's a she-devil that'll make him wish he was dead an' livin' in the pit o' hell fur comfort!

PETER   (*fervently*)   Amen!

SIMEON   (*imitating his father's voice*)   "I'm ridin' out t' learn God's message t' me in the spring like the prophets done," he says. I'll bet right then an' thar he knew plumb well he was goin' whorein', the stinkin' old hyprocrite!

Scene Four

(*Same as Scene Two—shows the interior of the kitchen with a lighted candle on table. It is gray dawn outside.* SIMEON *and* PETER *are just finishing their breakfast.* EBEN *sits before his plate of untouched food, brooding frowningly*)

PETER   (*glancing at him rather irritably*) Lookin' glum don't help none.

SIMEON   (*sarcastically*)   Sorrowin' over his lust o' the flesh!

PETER   (*with a grin*)   Was she yer fust?

EBEN   (*angrily*)   None o' yer business. (*a pause*) I was thinkin' o' him. I got a notion he's gittin near—I kin feel him comin' on like yew kin feel malaria chill afore it takes ye.

PETER   It's too early yet.

SIMEON   Dunno. He'd like t' catch us nappin'—jest t' have somethin' t' hoss us 'round over.

PETER   (*mechanically gets to his feet.* SIMEON *does the same*) Waal—let's git t' wuk. (*They both plod mechanically toward the door before they realize. Then they stop short*)

SIMEON   (*grinning*)   Ye're a cussed fool, Pete—and I be wuss! Let him see we hain't wukin'! We don't give a durn.

PETER   (*as they go back to the table*)   Not a damned durn! It'll serve t' show him we're done with him. (*They sit down again.* EBEN *stares from one to the other with surprise*)

SIMEON   (*grins at him*)   We're aimin' t' start bein' lilies o' the field.

PETER   Nary a toil 'r spin 'r lick o' wuk do we put in!

SIMEON   Ye're sole owner—till he comes—that's what ye wanted. Waal, ye got t' be sole hand, too.

PETER   The cows air bellerin'. Ye better hustle at the milkin'.

EBEN   (*with excited joy*)   Ye mean ye'll sign the paper?

SIMEON   (*dryly*)   Mebbe.

PETER   Mebbe.

SIMEON   We're considerin'. (*peremptorily*) Ye better git t' wuk.

EBEN   (*with queer excitement*)   It's Maw's farm agen! It's my farm! Them's my cows! I'll milk my durn fingers off fur cows o' mine!

(*He goes out door in rear, they stare after him indifferently*)

SIMEON   Like his Paw.

PETER   Dead spit 'n' image!

SIMEON   Waal—let dog eat dog!

(EBEN *comes out of front door and around the corner of the house. The sky is beginning to grow flushed with sunrise.* EBEN *stops by the gate and stares around him with glowing, possessive eyes. He takes in the whole farm with his embracing glance of desire*)

EBEN   It's purty! It's damned purty! It's mine! (*He suddenly throws his head back boldly and glares with hard, defiant eye at the sky*) Mine, d'ye hear? Mine! (*He turns and walks quickly off left, rear, toward the barn. The two brothers light their pipes*)

SIMEON   (*putting his muddy boots up on the table, tilting back his chair, and puffing defiantly*) Waal—this air solid comfort—fur once.

PETER   Ay-eh. (*He follows suit. A pause. Unconsciously they both sigh*)

SIMEON   (*suddenly*) He never was much o' a hand at milkin', Eben wa'n't.

PETER   (*with a snort*) His hands air like hoofs! (*a pause*)

SIMEON   Reach down the jug thar! Let's take a swaller. I'm feelin' kind o' low.

PETER   Good idee! (*He does so—gets two glasses—they pour out drinks of whisky*) Here's t' the gold in Californi-a!

SIMEON   An' luck t' find it! (*They drink—puff resolutely—sigh—take their feet down from the table*)

PETER   Likker don't 'pear t' sot right.

SIMEON   We hain't used t' it this early. (*A pause. They become very restless*)

PETER   Gittin' close in this kitchen.

SIMEON   (*with immense relief*) Let's git a breath o' air. (*They arise briskly and go out rear—appear around house and stop by the gate. They stare up at the sky with a numbed appreciation*)

PETER   Purty!

SIMEON   Ay-eh. Gold's t' the East now.

PETER   Sun's startin' with us fur the Golden West.

SIMEON   (*staring around the farm, his compressed face tightened, unable to conceal his emotion*) Waal—it's our last mornin'—mebbe.

PETER   (*the same*) Ay-eh.

SIMEON   (*stamps his foot on the earth and addresses it desperately*) Waal—ye've thirty year o' me buried in ye—spread out over ye—blood an' bone an' sweat—rotted away—fertilizin' ye—richin' yer soul—prime manure, by God, that's what I been t' ye!

PETER   Ay-eh! An' me!

SIMEON   An' yew, Peter. (*He sighs—then spits*) Waal—no use'n cryin' over spilt milk.

PETER   They's gold in the West—an' freedom, mebbe. We been slaves t' stone walls here.

SIMEON   (*defiantly*) We hain't nobody's slaves from this out—nor nothin's slaves nuther. (*a pause—restlessly*) Speakin' o milk, wonder how Eben's managin'?

PETER   I s'pose he's managin'.

SIMEON   Mebbe we'd ought t' help—this once.

PETER   Mebbe. The cows knows us.

SIMEON   An' likes us. They don't know him much.

PETER   An' the hosses, an' pigs, an' chickens. They don't know him much.

SIMEON   They knows us like brothers—an' likes us! (*proudly*) Hain't we raised 'em t' be fust-rate, number one prize stock?

PETER   We hain't—not no more.

SIMEON   (*dully*) I was fergittin'. (*then resignedly*) Waal, let's go help Eben a spell an' git waked up.

PETER   Suits me. (*They are starting off down left, rear, for the barn when* EBEN *appears from there hurrying toward them, his face excited*)

EBEN   (*breathlessly*) Waal—har they be! The old mule an' the bride! I seen 'em from the barn down below at the turnin'.

PETER   How could ye tell that far?

EBEN   Hain't I as far-sight as he's near-sight? Don't I know the mare 'n' buggy, an' two people settin' in it? Who else . . . ? An' I tell ye I kin feel 'em a-comin', too! (*He squirms as if he had the itch*)

PETER   (*beginning to be angry*) Waal—let him do his own unhitchin'!

SIMEON   (*angry in his turn*) Let's hustle in an' git our bundles an' be a-goin' as he's a-comin'. I don't want never t' step inside the door agen arter he's back. (*They both start back around the corner of the house.* EBEN *follows them*)

EBEN   (*anxiously*) Will ye sign it afore ye go?

PETER   Let's see the color o' the old skinflint's money an' we'll sign. (*They disappear left. The two brothers clump upstairs to get their bundles.* EBEN *appears in the kitchen, runs to the window, peers out, comes back and pulls up a strip of flooring in under stove, takes out a canvas bag and puts it on table, then sets the floorboard back in place. The two brothers appear a moment after. They carry old carpet bags*)

EBEN   (*puts his hand on bag guardingly*) Have ye signed?

SIMEON   (*shows paper in his hand*) Ay-eh (*greedily*) Be that the money?

EBEN   (*opens bag and pours out pile of twenty-dollar gold pieces*) Twenty-dollar pieces—thirty on 'em. Count 'em. (PETER *does so, arranging them in stacks of five, biting one or two to test them*)

PETER   Six hundred. (*He puts them in bag and puts it inside his shirt carefully*)

SIMEON   (*handing paper to* EBEN)   Har ye be.

EBEN   (*after a glance, folds it carefully and hides it under his shirt—gratefully*)   Thank yew.

PETER   Thank yew fur the ride.

SIMEON   We'll send ye a lump o' gold fur Christmas. (*A pause.* EBEN *stares at them and they at him*)

PETER   (*awkwardly*)   Waal—we're a-goin'.

SIMEON   Comin' out t' the yard?

EBEN   No. I'm waitin' in here a spell. (*Another silence. The brothers edge awkwardly to the door in rear—then turn and stand*)

SIMEON   Waal—good-bye.

PETER   Good-bye.

EBEN   Good-bye. (*They go out. He sits down at the table, faces the stove and pulls out the paper. He looks from it to the stove. His face, lighted up by the shaft of sunlight from the window, has an expression of trance. His lips move. The two brothers come out to the gate*)

PETER   (*looking off toward barn*)   Thar he be—unhitchin'.

SIMEON   (*with a chuckle*)   I'll bet ye he's riled!

PETER   An' thar she be.

SIMEON   Let's wait 'n' see what our new Maw looks like.

PETER   (*with a grin*)   An' give him our partin' cuss!

SIMEON   (*grinning*)   I feel like raisin' fun. I feel light in my head an' feet.

PETER   Me, too. I feel like laffin' till I'd split up the middle.

SIMEON   Reckon it's the likker?

PETER   No. My feet feel itchin' t' walk an' walk—an' jump high over thin's—an'. . . .

SIMEON   Dance? (*a pause*)

PETER   (*puzzled*)   It's plumb onnateral.

SIMEON   (*a light coming over his face*)   I calc'late it's 'cause school's out. It's holiday. Fur once we're free!

PETER   (*dazedly*)   Free?

SIMEON   The halter's broke—the harness is busted—the fence bars is down—the stone walls air crumblin' an' tumblin'! We'll be kickin' up an' tearin' away down the road!

PETER   (*drawing a deep breath—oratorically*) Anybody that wants this stinkin' old rock-pile of a farm kin hev it. 'Tain't our'n, no sirree!

SIMEON   (*takes the gate off its hinges and puts it under his arm*)   We harby 'bolishes shet gates an' open gates, an' all gates, by thunder!

PETER   We'll take it with us fur luck an' let 'er sail free down some river.

SIMEON   (*as a sound of voices comes from left, rear*)   Har they comes!

(*The two brothers congeal into two stiff, grim-visaged statues.* EPHRAIM CABOT *and* ABBIE PUTNAM *come in.* CABOT *is seventy-five, tall and gaunt, with great, wiry, concentrated power, but stoop-shouldered from toil. His face is as hard as if it were hewn out of a boulder, yet there is a weakness in it, a petty pride in its own narrow strength. His eyes are small, close together, and extremely near-sighted, blinking continually in the effort to focus on objects, their stare having a straining, ingrowing quality. He is dressed in his dismal black Sunday suit.* ABBIE *is thirty-five, buxom, full of vitality. Her round face is pretty but marred by its rather gross sensuality. There is strength and obstinacy in her jaw, a hard determination in her eyes, and about her whole personality the same unsettled, untamed, desperate quality which is so apparent in* EBEN)

CABOT   (*as they enter—a queer strangled emotion in his dry cracking voice*)   Har we be t' hum, Abbie.

ABBIE   (*with lust for the word*)   Hum! (*Her eyes gloating on the house without seeming to see the two stiff figures at the gate*)   It's purty—purty! I can't b'lieve it's r'ally mine.

CABOT   (*sharply*)   Yewr'n? Mine! (*He stares at her penetratingly. She stares back. He adds relentingly*)   Our'n—mebbe! It was lonesome too long. I was growin' old in the spring. A hum's got t' hev a woman.

ABBIE   (*her voice taking possession*)   A woman's got t' hev a hum!

CABOT   (*nodding uncertainly*)   Ay-eh. (*then irritably*)   Whar be they? Ain't thar nobody about—'r wukin'—'r nothin'?

ABBIE   (*sees the brothers. She returns their stare of cold appraising contempt with interest —slowly*)   Thar's two men loafin' at the gate an' starin' at me like a couple o' strayed hogs.

CABOT   (*straining his eyes*)   I kin see 'em—but I can't make out. . . .

SIMEON   It's Simeon.

PETER   It's Peter.

CABOT   (*exploding*)   Why hain't ye wukin'?

SIMEON   (*dryly*)   We're waitin' t' welcome ye hum—yew an' the bride!

CABOT   (*confusedly*)   Huh? Waal—this be yer new Maw, boys. (*She stares at them and they at her*)

SIMEON   (*turns away and spits contemptuously*)   I see her!

PETER   (*spits also*)   An' I see her!

wuth ten o' ye yit, old's I be! Ye'll never be more'n half a man! (*then, matter-of-factly*) Waal—let's git t' the barn. (*They go. A last faint note of the "Californi-a" song is heard from the distance.* ABBIE *is washing her dishes*)

PART TWO

Scene One

(*The exterior of the farmhouse, as in Part One —a hot Sunday afternoon two months later.* ABBIE, *dressed in her best, is discovered sitting in a rocker at the end of the porch. She rocks listlessly, enervated by the heat, staring in front of her with bored, half-closed eyes.*

EBEN *sticks his head out of his bedroom window. He looks around furtively and tries to see—or hear—if anyone is on the porch, but although he has been careful to make no noise,* ABBIE *has sensed his movement. She stops rocking, her face grows animated and eager, she waits attentively.* EBEN *seems to feel her presence, he scowls back his thoughts of her and spits with exaggerated disdain—then withdraws back into the room.* ABBIE *waits, holding her breath as she listens with passionate eagerness for every sound within the house.*

EBEN *comes out. Their eyes meet. His falter, he is confused, he turns away and slams the door resentfully. At this gesture,* ABBIE *laughs tantalizingly, amused but at the same time piqued and irritated. He scowls, strides off the porch to the path and starts to walk past her to the road with a grand swagger of ignoring her existence. He is dressed in his store suit, spruced up, his face shines from soap and water.* ABBIE *leans forward on her chair, her eyes hard and angry now, and, as he passes her, gives a sneering, taunting chuckle*)

EBEN (*stung—turns on her furiously*) What air yew cacklin' 'bout?

ABBIE (*triumphant*) Yew!

EBEN What about me?

ABBIE Ye look all slicked up like a prize bull.

EBEN (*with a sneer*) Waal—ye hain't so durned purty yerself, be ye?

(*They stare into each other's eyes, his held by hers in spite of himself, hers glowingly possessive. Their physical attraction becomes a palpable force quivering in the hot air*)

ABBIE (*softly*) Ye don't mean that, Eben.

Ye may think ye mean it, mebbe, but ye don't. Ye can't. It's agin nature, Eben. Ye been fightin' yer nature ever since the day I come— tryin' t' tell yerself I hain't purty t'ye. (*She laughs a low humid laugh without taking her eyes from his. A pause—her body squirms desirously—she murmurs languorously*) Hain't the sun strong an' hot? Ye kin feel it burnin' into the earth—Nature—makin' thin's grow— bigger 'n' bigger—burnin' inside ye—makin' ye want t' grow—into somethin' else—till ye're jined with it—an' it's yourn—but it owns ye, too—an' makes ye grow bigger—like a tree— like them elums—(*She laughs again softly, holding his eyes. He takes a step toward her, compelled against his will*) Nature'll beat ye, Eben. Ye might's well own up t' it fust 's last.

EBEN (*trying to break from her spell—confusedly*) If Paw'd hear ye goin' on. . . . (*resentfully*) But ye've made such a damned idjit out o' the old devil . . . ! (ABBIE *laughs*)

ABBIE Waal—hain't it easier fur yew with him changed softer?

EBEN (*defiantly*) No. I'm fightin' him— fightin' yew—fightin' fur Maw's rights t' her hum! (*This breaks her spell for him. He glowers at her*) An' I'm onto ye. Ye hain't foolin' me a mite. Ye're aimin' t' swaller up everythin' an' make it your'n. Waal, you'll find I'm a heap sight bigger hunk nor yew kin chew! (*He turns from her with a sneer*)

ABBIE (*trying to regain her ascendancy— seductively*) Eben!

EBEN Leave me be! (*He starts to walk away*)

ABBIE (*more commandingly*) Eben!

EBEN (*stops—resentfully*) What d'ye want?

ABBIE (*trying to conceal a growing excitement*) Whar air ye goin'?

EBEN (*with malicious nonchalance*) Oh— up the road a spell.

ABBIE T' the village?

EBEN (*airily*) Mebbe.

ABBIE (*excitedly*) T' see that Min, I s'pose?

EBEN Mebbe.

ABBIE (*weakly*) What d'ye want t' waste time on her fur?

EBEN (*revenging himself now—grinning at her*) Ye can't beat Nature, didn't ye say? (*He laughs and again starts to walk away*)

ABBIE (*bursting out*) An ugly old hake!

EBEN (*with a tantalizing sneer*) She's purtier'n yew be!

ABBIE That every wuthless drunk in the country has. . . .

EBEN (*tauntingly*) Mebbe—but she's better'n yew. She owns up fa'r 'n' squar' t' her doin's.

ABBIE (*furiously*) Don't ye dare compare. . . .

EBEN She don't go sneakin' an' stealin'—what's mine.

ABBIE (*savagely seizing on his weak point*) Your'n? Yew mean—my farm?

EBEN I mean the farm yew sold yerself fur like any other old whore—my farm!

ABBIE (*stung—fiercely*) Ye'll never live t' see the day when even a stinkin' weed on it'll belong t' ye! (*then in a scream*) Git out o' my sight! Go on t' yer slut—disgracin' yer Paw 'n' me! I'll git yer Paw t' horsewhip ye off the place if I want t'! Ye're only livin' here 'cause I tolerate ye! Git along! I hate the sight o' ye! (*She stops, panting and glaring at him*)

EBEN (*returning her glance in kind*) An' I hate the sight o' yew!

(*He turns and strides off up the road. She follows his retreating figure with concentrated hate. Old* CABOT *appears coming up from the barn. The hard, grim expression of his face has changed. He seems in some queer way softened, mellowed. His eyes have taken on a strange, incongruous dreamy quality. Yet there is no hint of physical weakness about him—rather he looks more robust and younger.* ABBIE *sees him and turns away quickly with unconcealed aversion. He comes slowly up to her*)

CABOT (*mildly*) War yew an' Eben quarrelin' agen?

ABBIE (*shortly*) No.

CABOT Ye was talkin' a'mighty loud. (*He sits down on the edge of porch*)

ABBIE (*snappishly*) If ye heered us they hain't no need askin' questions.

CABOT I didn't hear what ye said.

ABBIE (*relieved*) Waal—it wa'n't nothin' t' speak on.

CABOT (*after a pause*) Eben's queer.

ABBIE (*bitterly*) He's the dead spit 'n' image o' yew!

CABOT (*queerly interested*) D'ye think so, Abbie? (*after a pause, ruminatingly*) Me 'n' Eben's allus fit 'n' fit. I never could b'ar him noways. He's so thunderin' soft—like his Maw.

ABBIE (*scornfully*) Ay-eh! 'Bout as soft as yew be!

CABOT (*as if he hadn't heard*) Mebbe I been too hard on him.

ABBIE (*jeeringly*) Waal—ye're gettin' soft now—soft as slop! That's what Eben was sayin'.

CABOT (*his face instantly grim and ominous*) Eben was sayin'? Waal, he'd best not do nothin' t' try me 'r he'll soon diskiver. . . . (*A pause. She keeps her face turned away. His gradually softens. He stares up at the sky*) Purty, hain't it?

ABBIE (*crossly*) I dont' see nothin' purty.

CABOT The sky. Feels like a wa'm field up thar.

ABBIE (*sarcastically*) Air yew aimin' t' buy up over the farm too? (*She snickers contemptuously*)

CABOT (*strangely*) I'd like t' own my place up thar. (*a pause*) I'm gittin' old, Abbie, I'm gittin' ripe on the bough. (*A pause. She stares at him mystified. He goes on*) It's allus lonesome cold in the house—even when it's bilin' hot outside. Hain't yew noticed?

ABBIE No.

CABOT It's wa'm down t' the barn—nice smellin' an' warm—with the cows. (*a pause*) Cows is queer.

ABBIE Like yew?

CABOT Like Eben. (*a pause*) I'm gittin' t' feel resigned t' Eben—jest as I got t' feel 'bout his Maw. I'm gettin' t' learn to b'ar his softness—jest like her'n. I calc'late I c'd a'most take t' him—if he wa'nt sech a dumb fool! (*a pause*) I s'pose it's old age a-creepin' in my bones.

ABBIE (*indifferently*) Waal—ye hain't dead yet.

CABOT (*roused*) No, I hain't, yew bet—not by a hell of a sight—I'm sound 'n' tough as hickory! (*then moodily*) But arter three score and ten the Lord warns ye t' prepare. (*a pause*) That's why Eben's come in my head. Now that his cussed sinful brothers is gone their path t' hell, they's no one left but Eben.

ABBIE (*resentfully*) They's me, hain't they? (*agitatedly*) What's all this sudden likin' ye tuk to Eben? Why don't ye say nothin' 'bout me? Hain't I yer lawful wife?

CABOT (*simply*) Ay-eh. Ye be. (*A pause—he stares at her desirously—his eyes grow avid—then with a sudden movement he seizes her hands and squeezes them, declaiming in a queer camp meeting preacher's tempo*) Yew air my Rose o' Sharon! Behold, yew air fair; yer eyes air doves; yer lips air like scarlet; yer two breasts air like two fawns; yer navel be like a round goblet; yer belly be like a heap o' wheat. . . . (*He covers her hand with kisses. She does not seem to notice. She stares before her with hard angry eyes*)

ABBIE (*jerking her hands away—harshly*) So ye're plannin' t' leave the farm t' Eben, air ye?

CABOT (*dazedly*) Leave . . . ? (*then with resentful obstinacy*) I hain't a-givin' it t' no one!

ABBIE (*remorselessly*) Ye can't take it with ye.

CABOT (*thinks a moment—then reluctantly*) No, I calc'late not. (*after a pause—with a strange passion*) But if I could, I would, by

the Etarnal! 'R if I could, in my dyin' hour,
I'd set it afire an' watch it burn—this house an'
every ear o' corn an' every tree down t' the last
blade o' hay! I'd sit an' know it was all a-dying
with me an' no one else'd ever own what was
mine, what I'd made out o' nothin' with my
own sweat 'n' blood! (*A pause—then he adds
with a queer affection*) 'Ceptin' the cows. Them
I'd turn free.

ABBIE (*harshly*) An' me?

CABOT (*with a queer smile*) Ye'd be turned
free, too.

ABBIE (*furiously*) So that's the thanks I
git fur marryin' ye—t' have ye change kind to
Eben who hates ye, an' talk o' turnin' me out
in the road.

CABOT (*hastily*) Abbie! Ye know I
wa'n't. . . .

ABBIE (*vengefully*) Just let me tell ye a
thing or two 'bout Eben. Whar's he gone? T'
see that harlot, Min! I tried fur t' stop him.
Disgracin' yew an' me—on the Sabbath, too!

CABOT (*rather guiltily*) He's a sinner—
nateral-born. It's lust eatin' his heart.

ABBIE (*enraged beyond endurance—wildly
vindictive*) An' his lust fur me! Kin ye find
excuses fur that?

CABOT (*stares at her—after a dead pause*)
Lust—fur yew?

ABBIE (*defiantly*) He was tryin' t' make
love t' me—when ye heerd us quarrelin'.

CABOT (*stares at her—then a terrible expression of rage comes over his face—he springs to
his feet shaking all over*) By the A'mighty
God—I'll end him!

ABBIE (*frightened now for* EBEN) No!
Don't ye!

CABOT (*violently*) I'll git the shotgun an'
blow his soft brains t' the top o' them elums!

ABBIE (*throwing her arms around him*) No,
Ephraim!

CABOT (*pushing her away violently*) I will,
by God!

ABBIE (*in a quieting tone*) Listen, Ephraim.
'Twa'n't nothin' bad—only a boy's foolin'—
'twa'n't meant serious—jest jokin' an' teasin. . . .

CABOT Then why did ye say—lust?

ABBIE It must hev sounded wusser'n I
meant. An' I was mad at thinkin'—ye'd leave
him the farm.

CABOT (*quieter but still grim and cruel*)
Waal then, I'll horsewhip him off the place if
that much'll content ye.

ABBIE (*reaching out and taking his hand*)
No. Don't think o' me! Ye mustn't drive him
off. 'Tain't sensible. Who'll ye get to help ye
on the farm? They's no one hereabouts.

CABOT (*considers this—then nodding his appreciation*) Ye got a head on ye. (*then irritably*) Waal, let him stay. (*He sits down on
the edge of the porch. She sits beside him. He
murmurs contemptuously*) I oughn't git riled
so—at that 'ere fool calf. (*a pause*) But har's
the p'int. What son o' mine'll keep on here t' the
farm—when the Lord does call me? Simeon an'
Peter air gone t' hell—an' Eben's follerin' 'em.

ABBIE They's me.

CABOT Ye're on'y a woman.

ABBIE I'm yewr wife.

CABOT That hain't me. A son is me—my
blood—mine. Mine ought t' git mine. An' then
it's still mine—even though I be six foot under.
D'ye see?

ABBIE (*giving him a look of hatred*) Ay-eh.
I see. (*She becomes very thoughtful, her face
growing shrewd, her eyes studying* CABOT
craftily)

CABOT I'm gittin' old—ripe on the bough.
(*then with a sudden forced reassurance*) Not
but what I hain't a hard nut t' crack even yet—
an' fur many a year t' come! By the Etarnal, I
kin break most o' the young fellars' backs at
any kind o' work any day o' the year!

ABBIE (*suddenly*) Mebbe the Lord'll give
us a son.

CABOT (*turns and stares at her eagerly*) Ye
mean—a son—t' me 'n' yew?

ABBIE (*with a cajoling smile*) Ye're a strong
man yet, hain't ye? 'Tain't noways impossible,
be it? We know that. Why d'ye stare so? Hain't
ye never thought o' that afore? I been thinkin'
o' it all along. Ay-eh—an' I been prayin' it'd
happen, too.

CABOT (*his face growing full of joyous pride
and a sort of religious ecstasy*) Ye been
prayin', Abbie?—fur a son?—t' us?

ABBIE Ay-eh. (*with a grim resolution*) I
want a son now.

CABOT (*excitedly clutching both of her hands
in his*) It'd be the blessin' o' God, Abbie—the
blessin' o' God A'mighty on me—in my old age
—in my lonesomeness! They hain't nothin' I
wouldn't do fur ye then, Abbie. Ye'd hev on'y t'
ask it—anythin' ye'd a mind t'!

ABBIE (*interrupting*) Would ye will the
farm t' me then—t' me an' it . . . ?

CABOT (*vehemently*) I'd do anythin' ye
axed, I tell ye! I swar it! May I be everlastin'
damned t' hell if I wouldn't! (*He sinks to his
knees pulling her down with him. He trembles
all over with the fervor of his hopes*) Pray t' the
Lord agen, Abbie. It's the Sabbath! I'll jine ye!
Two prayers air better nor one. "An' God hearkened unto Rachel!" An' God hearkened unto
Abbie! Pray, Abbie! Pray fur him to hearken!
(*He bows his head, mumbling. She pretends

*to do likewise but gives him a side glance of
scorn and triumph)*

Scene Two

*(About eight in the evening. The interior of the
two bedrooms on the top floor is shown—*EBEN
*is sitting on the side of his bed in the room on
the left. On account of the heat he has taken
off everything but his undershirt and pants. His
feet are bare. He faces front, brooding moodily,
his chin propped on his hands, a desperate expression on his face.*

In the other room CABOT *and* ABBIE *are sitting side by side on the edge of their bed, an
old four-poster with feather mattress. He is in
his night shirt, she in her nightdress. He is still
in the queer, excited mood into which the
notion of a son has thrown him. Both rooms are
lighted dimly and flickeringly by tallow candles)*

CABOT   The farm needs a son.

ABBIE   I need a son.

CABOT   Ay-eh. Sometimes ye air the farm an'
sometimes the farm be yew. That's why I clove
t' ye in my lonesomeness. *(A pause. He pounds
his knee with his fist)* Me an' the farm has got
t' beget a son!

ABBIE   Ye'd best go t' sleep. Ye're gittin'
thin's all mixed.

CABOT *(with an impatient gesture)* No, I
hain't. My mind's clear's a well. Ye don't know
me, that's it. *(He stares hopelessly at the floor)*

ABBIE *(indifferently)* Mebbe.

(In the next room EBEN *gets up and paces up
and down distractedly.* ABBIE *hears him. Her
eyes fasten on the intervening wall with concentrated attention.* EBEN *stops and stares.
Their hot glances seem to meet through the
wall. Unconsciously he stretches out his arms
for her and she half rises. Then aware, he
mutters a curse at himself and flings himself
face downward on the bed, his clenched fists
above his head, his face buried in the pillow.*
ABBIE *relaxes with a faint sigh but her eyes
remain fixed on the wall; she listens with all
her attention for some movement from* EBEN*)*

CABOT *(suddenly raises his head and looks at
her—scornfully)* Will ye ever know me—'r
will any man 'r woman? *(shaking his head)*
No. I calc'late 't wa'n't t' be. *(He turns away.*
ABBIE *looks at the wall. Then, evidently unable
to keep silent about his thoughts, without looking at his wife, he puts out his hand and
clutches her knee. She starts violently, looks at
him, sees he is not watching her, concentrates
again on the wall and pays no attention to what

he says)* Listen, Abbie. When I come here
fifty odd year ago—I was jest twenty an' the
strongest an' hardest ye ever seen—ten times
as strong an' fifty times as hard as Eben. Waal
—this place was nothin' but fields o' stones.
Folks laughed when I tuk it. They couldn't
know what I knowed. When ye kin make corn
sprout out o' stones, God's livin' in yew! They
wa'n't strong enuf fur that! They reckoned
God was easy. They laughed. They don't laugh
no more. Some died hereabouts. Some went
West an' died. They're all under ground—fur
follerin' arter an easy God. God hain't easy.
(He shakes his head slowly) An' I growed
hard. Folks kept allus sayin' he's a hard man
like 'twas sinful t' be hard, so's at last I said
back at 'em: Waal then, by thunder, ye'll git
me hard an' see how ye like it! *(then suddenly)*
But I give in t' weakness once. 'Twas arter I'd
been here two year. I got weak—despairful—
they was so many stones. They was a party
leavin', givin' up, goin' West. I jined 'em. We
tracked on 'n' on. We come t' broad medders,
plains, whar the soil was black an 'rich as gold.
Nary a stone. Easy. Ye'd on'y to plow an' sow
an' then set an 'smoke yer pipe an' watch thin's
grow. I could o' been a rich man—but somethin'
in me fit me an' fit me—the voice o' God
sayin': "This hain't wuth nothin' t' Me. Get ye
back t' hum!" I got afeerd o' that voice an' I
lit out back t' hum here, leavin' my claim an'
crops t' whoever'd a mind t' take 'em. Ay-eh. I
actoolly give up what was rightful mine! God's
hard, not easy! God's in the stones! Build my
church on a rock—out o' stones an' I'll be in
them! That's what He meant t' Peter! *(He sighs
heavily—a pause)* Stones. I picked 'em up an'
piled 'em into walls. Ye kin read the years o'
my life in them walls, every day a hefted stone,
climbin' over the hills up and down, fencin'
in the fields that was mine, whar I'd made
thin's grow out o' nothin'—like the will o' God,
like the servant o' His hand. It wa'n't easy. It
was hard an' He made me hard fur it. *(He
pauses)* All the time I kept gittin' lonesomer.
I tuk a wife. She bore Simeon an' Peter. She
was a good woman. She wuked hard. We was
married twenty year. She never knowed me.
She helped but she never knowed what she
was helpin'. I was allus lonesome. She died.
After that it wa'n't so lonesome fur a spell. *(a
pause)* I lost count o' the years. I had no time
t' fool away countin' 'em. Sim an' Peter helped.
The farm growed. It was all mine! When I
thought o' that I didn't feel lonesome. *(a
pause)* But ye can't hitch yer mind t' one thin'
day an' night. I tuk another wife—Eben's Maw.
Her folks was contestin' me at law over my

deeds t' the farm—my farm! That's why Eben keeps a-talkin' his fool talk o' this bein' his Maw's farm. She bore Eben. She was purty— but soft. She tried t' be hard. She couldn't. She never knowed me nor nothin'. It was lonesomer 'n hell with her. After a matter o' sixteen odd years, she died. (*a pause*) I lived with the boys. They hated me 'cause I was hard. I hated them 'cause they was soft. They coveted the farm without knowin' what it meant. It made me bitter 'n wormwood. It aged me—them coveting what I'd made fur mine. Then this spring the call come—the voice o' God cryin' in my wilderness, in my lonesomeness—t' go out an' seek an' find! (*turning to her with strange passion*) I sought ye an' I found ye! Yew air my Rose o' Sharon! Yer eyes air like. . . . (*She has turned a blank face, resentful eyes to his. He stares at her for a moment—then harshly*) Air ye any the wiser fur all I've told ye?

ABBIE (*confusedly*) Mebbe.

CABOT (*pushing her away from him—angrily*) Ye don't know nothin'—nor never will. If ye don't hev a son t' redeem ye . . . (*this in a tone of cold threat*)

ABBIE (*resentfully*) I've prayed, hain't I?

CABOT (*bitterly*) Pray agen—fur understandin'!

ABBIE (*a veiled threat in her tone*) Ye'll have a son out o' me, I promise ye.

CABOT How kin ye promise?

ABBIE I got second-sight mebbe. I kin foretell. (*She gives a queer smile*)

CABOT I believe ye have. Ye give me the chills sometimes. (*He shivers*) It's cold in this house. It's oneasy. They's thin's pokin' about in the dark—in the corners. (*He pulls on his trousers, tucking in his night shirt, and pulls on his boots*)

ABBIE (*surprised*) Whar air ye goin'?

CABOT (*queerly*) Down whar it's restful— whar it's warm—down t' the barn. (*bitterly*) I kin talk t' the cows. They know. They know the farm an' me. They'll give me peace. (*He turns to go out the door*)

ABBIE (*a bit frightenedly*) Air ye ailin' tonight, Ephraim?

CABOT Growin'. Growin' ripe on the bough. (*He turns and goes, his boots clumping down the stairs.* EBEN *sits up with a start, listening.* ABBIE *is conscious of his movement and stares at the wall.* CABOT *comes out of the house around the corner and stands by the gate, blinking at the sky. He stretches up his hand in a tortured gesture*) God A'mighty, call from the dark! (*He listens as if expecting an answer. Then his arms drop, he shakes his head and plods off toward the barn.* EBEN *and* ABBIE *stare at each other through the wall.* EBEN *sighs heavily and* ABBIE *echoes it. Both become terribly nervous, uneasy. Finally* ABBIE *gets up and listens, her ear to the wall. He acts as if he saw every move she was making, he becomes resolutely still. She seems driven into a decision —goes out the door in rear determinedly. His eyes follow her. Then as the door of his room is opened softly, he turns away, waits in an attitude of strained fixity.* ABBIE *stands for a second staring at him, her eyes burning with desire. Then with a little cry she runs over and throws her arms about his neck, she pulls his head back and covers his mouth with kisses. At first, he submits dumbly; then he puts his arms about her neck and returns her kisses, but finally, suddenly aware of his hatred, he hurls her away from him, springing to his feet. They stand speechless and breathless, panting like two animals*)

ABBIE (*at last—painfully*) Ye shouldn't, Eben—ye shouldn't—I'd make ye happy!

EBEN (*harshly*) I don't want t' be happy— from yew!

ABBIE (*helplessly*) Ye do, Eben! Ye do! Why d'ye lie?

EBEN (*viciously*) I don't take t'ye, I tell ye! I hate the sight o' ye!

ABBIE (*with an uncertain troubled laugh*) Waal, I kissed ye anyways—an' ye kissed back —yer lips was burnin'—ye can't lie 'bout that! (*intensely*) If ye don't care, why did ye kiss me back—why was yer lips burnin'?

EBEN (*wiping his mouth*) It was like pizen on 'em (*then tauntingly*) When I kissed ye back, mebbe I thought 'twas someone else.

ABBIE (*wildly*) Min?

EBEN Mebbe.

ABBIE (*torturedly*) Did ye go t' see her? Did ye r'ally go? I thought ye mightn't. Is that why ye throwed me off jest now?

EBEN (*sneeringly*) What if it be?

ABBIE (*raging*) Then ye're a dog, Eben Cabot!

EBEN (*threateningly*) Ye can't talk that way t' me!

ABBIE (*with a shrill laugh*) Can't I? Did ye think I was in love with ye—a weak thin' like yew? Not much! I on'y wanted ye fur a purpose o' my own—an' I'll hev ye fur it yet 'cause I'm stronger'n yew be!

EBEN (*resentfully*) I knowed well it was on'y part o' yer plan t' swaller everythin'!

ABBIE (*tauntingly*) Mebbe!

EBEN (*furious*) Git out o' my room!

ABBIE This air my room an' ye're on'y hired help!

EBEN (*threateningly*) Git out afore I murder ye!

ABBIE (*quite confident now*) I hain't a mite afeerd. Ye want me, don't ye? Yes, ye do! An' yer Paw's son'll never kill what he wants! Look at yer eyes! They's lust fur me in 'em, burnin' 'em up! Look at yer lips now! They're tremblin' an' longin' t' kiss me, an' yer teeth t' bite. (*He is watching her now with a horrible fascination. She laughs a crazy triumphant laugh*) I'm a-goin' t' make all o' this hum my hum! They's one room hain't mine yet, but it's a-goin' t' be tonight. I'm a-goin' down now an' light up! (*She makes him a mocking bow*) Won't ye come courtin' me in the best parlor, Mister Cabot?

EBEN (*staring at her—horribly confused—dully*) Don't ye dare! It hain't been opened since Maw died an' was laid out thar! Don't ye . . . ! (*But her eyes are fixed on his so burningly that his will seems to wither before hers. He stands swaying toward her helplessly*)

ABBIE (*holding his eyes and putting all her will into her words as she backs out the door*) I'll expect ye afore long, Eben.

EBEN (*stares after her for a while, walking toward the door. A light appears in the parlor window. He murmurs*) In the parlor? (*This seems to arouse connotations for he comes back and puts on his white shirt, collar, half ties the tie mechanically, puts on coat, takes his hat, stands barefooted looking about him in bewilderment, mutters wonderingly*) Maw! Whar air yew? (*then goes slowly toward the door in rear*)

Scene Three

(*A few minutes later. The interior of the parlor is shown. A grim, repressed room like a tomb in which the family has been interred alive.* ABBIE *sits on the edge of the horsehair sofa. She has lighted all the candles and the room is revealed in all its preserved ugliness. A change has come over the woman. She looks awed and frightened now, ready to run away.*

The door is opened and EBEN *appears. His face wears an expression of obsessed confusion. He stands staring at her, his arms hanging disjointedly from his shoulders, his feet bare, his hat in his hand*)

ABBIE (*after a pause—with a nervous, formal politeness*) Won't ye set?

EBEN (*dully*) Ay-eh.

(*Mechanically he places his hat carefully on the floor near the door and sits stiffly beside her on the edge of the sofa. A pause. They both remain rigid, looking straight ahead with eyes full of fear*)

ABBIE When I fust came in—in the dark—they seemed somethin' here.

EBEN (*simply*) Maw.

ABBIE I kin still feel—somethin'. . . .

EBEN It's Maw.

ABBIE At fust I was feered o' it. I wanted t' yell an' run. Now—since yew come—seems like it's growin' soft an' kind t' me. (*addressing the air—queerly*) Thank yew.

EBEN Maw allus loved me.

ABBIE Mebbe it knows I love yew too. Mebbe that makes it kind t' me.

EBEN (*dully*) I dunno. I should think she'd hate ye.

ABBIE (*with certainty*) No. I kin feel it don't—not no more.

EBEN Hate ye fur stealin' her place—here in her hum—settin' in her parlor whar she was laid—(*He suddenly stops, staring stupidly before him*)

ABBIE What is it, Eben?

EBEN (*in a whisper*) Seems like Maw didn't want me t' remind ye.

ABBIE (*excitedly*) I knowed, Eben! It's kind t' me! It don't b'ar me no grudges fur what I never knowed an' couldn't help!

EBEN Maw b'ars him a grudge.

ABBIE Waal, so does all o' us.

EBEN Ay-eh. (*with passion*) I does, by God!

ABBIE (*taking one of his hands in hers and patting it*) Thar! Don't git riled thinkin' o' him. Think o' yer Maw who's kind t' us. Tell me about yer Maw, Eben.

EBEN They hain't nothin' much. She was kind. She was good.

ABBIE (*putting one arm over his shoulder. He does not seem to notice—passionately*) I'll be kind an' good t' ye!

EBEN Sometimes she used t' sing fur me.

ABBIE I'll sing fur ye!

EBEN This was her hum. This was her farm.

ABBIE This is my hum! This is my farm!

EBEN He married her t' steal 'em. She was soft an' easy. He couldn't 'preciate her.

ABBIE He can't 'preciate me!

EBEN He murdered her with his hardness.

ABBIE He's murderin' me!

EBEN She died. (*a pause*) Sometimes she used to sing fur me. (*He bursts into a fit of sobbing*)

ABBIE (*both her arms around him—with wild passion*) I'll sing fur ye! I'll die fur ye! (*In spite of her overwhelming desire for him, there is a sincere maternal love in her manner and* voice—*a horribly frank mixture of lust and mother love*) Don't cry, Eben! I'll take yer Maw's place! I'll be everythin' she was t' ye! Let me kiss ye, Eben! (*She pulls his head around. He makes a bewildered pretense of resistance. She is tender*) Don't be afeered! I'll kiss ye pure, Eben—same 's if I was a Maw t' ye—an' ye kin kiss me back 's if yew was my son—my boy—sayin' good night 't me! Kiss me, Eben. (*They kiss in restrained fashion. Then suddenly wild passion overcomes her. She kisses him lustfully again and again and he flings his arms about her and returns her kisses. Suddenly, as in the bedroom, he frees himself from her violently and springs to his feet. He is trembling all over, in a strange state of terror.* ABBIE *strains her arms toward him with fierce pleading*) Don't ye leave me, Eben! Can't ye see it hain't enuf—lovin' ye like a Maw—can't ye see it's got t' be that an' more—much more —a hundred times more—fur me t' be happy— fur yew t' be happy?

EBEN (*to the presence he feels in the room*) Maw! Maw! What d'ye want? What air ye tellin' me?

ABBIE She's tellin' ye t' love me. She knows I love ye an' I'll be good t' ye. Can't ye feel it? Don't ye know? She's tellin' ye t' love me, Eben!

EBEN Ay-eh. I feel—mebbe she—but—I can't figger out—why—when ye've stole her place—here in her hum—in the parlor whar she was—

ABBIE (*fiercely*) She knows I love ye!

EBEN (*his face suddenly lighting up with a fierce triumphant grin*) I see it! I sees why. It's her vengeance on him—so's she kin rest quiet in her grave!

ABBIE (*wildly*) Vengeance o' God on the hull o' us! What d'we give a durn? I love ye, Eben! God knows I love ye! (*She stretches out her arms for him*)

EBEN (*throws himself on his knees beside the sofa and grabs her in his arms—releasing all his pent-up passion*) An' I love yew, Ab-bie!—now I kin say it! I been dyin' fur want o' ye—every hour since ye come! I love ye! (*Their lips meet in a fierce, bruising kiss*)

Scene Four

(*Exterior of the farmhouse. It is just dawn. The front door at right is opened and* EBEN *comes out and walks around to the gate. He is dressed in his working clothes. He seems changed. His face wears a bold and confident expression, he is grinning to himself with evident satisfaction. As he gets near the gate, the window of the* parlor is heard opening and the shutters are flung back and ABBIE sticks her head out. Her hair tumbles over her shoulders in disarray, her face is flushed, she looks at EBEN *with tender, languorous eyes and calls softly*)

ABBIE Eben. (*as he turns—playfully*) Jest one more kiss afore ye go. I'm goin' to miss ye fearful all day.

EBEN An' me yew, ye kin bet! (*He goes to her. They kiss several times. He draws away, laughingly*) Thar. That's enuf, hain't it? Ye won't hev none left fur next time.

ABBIE I got a million o' em left fur yew! (*then a bit anxiously*) D'ye r'ally love me, Eben?

EBEN (*emphatically*) I like ye better'n any gal I ever knowed! That's gospel!

ABBIE Likin' hain't lovin'.

EBEN Waal then—I love ye. Now air yew satisfied?

ABBIE Ay-eh, I be. (*She smiles at him adoringly*)

EBEN I better git t' the barn. The old crit-ter's liable t' suspicion an' come sneakin' up.

ABBIE (*with a confident laugh*) Let him! I kin allus pull the wool over his eyes. I'm goin' t' leave the shutters open and let in the sun 'n' air. This room's been dead long enuf. Now it's goin' t' be my room!

EBEN (*frowning*) Ay-eh.

ABBIE (*hastily*) I meant—our room.

EBEN Ay-eh.

ABBIE We made it our'n last night, didn't we? We give it life—our lovin' did. (*a pause*)

EBEN (*with a strange look*) Maw's gone back t' her grave. She kin sleep now.

ABBIE May she rest in peace! (*then ten-derly rebuking*) Ye oughtn't t' talk o' sad thin's —this mornin'.

EBEN It jest come up in my mind o' itself.

ABBIE Don't let it. (*He doesn't answer. She yawns*) Waal, I'm a-goin' t' steal a wink o' sleep. I'll tell the Old Man I hain't feelin' pert. Let him git his own vittles.

EBEN I see him comin' from the barn. Ye better look smart an' git upstairs.

ABBIE Ay-eh. Good-bye. Don't fergit me. (*She throws him a kiss. He grins—then squares his shoulders and awaits his father confidently.* CABOT *walks slowly up from the left, staring up at the sky with a vague face*)

EBEN (*jovially*) Mornin', Paw. Star-gazin' in daylight?

CABOT Purty, hain't it?

EBEN (*looking around him possessively*) It's a durned purty farm.

CABOT I mean the sky.

EBEN (*grinning*) How d'ye know? Them

eyes o' your'n can't see that fur. (*This tickles his humor and he slaps his thigh and laughs*) Ho-ho! That's a good un!

CABOT (*grimly sarcastic*) Ye're feelin' right chipper, hain't ye? Whar'd ye steal the likker?

EBEN (*good-naturedly*) 'Tain't likker. Jest life. (*suddenly holding out his hand—soberly*) Yew 'n' me is quits. Let's shake hands.

CABOT (*suspiciously*) What's come over ye?

EBEN Then don't. Mebbe it's just as well. (*a moment's pause*) What's come over me? (*queerly*) Didn't ye feel her passin'—goin' back t' her grave?

CABOT (*dully*) Who?

EBEN Maw. She kin rest now an' sleep content. She's quits with ye.

CABOT (*confusedly*) I rested. I slept good —down with the cows. They know how t' sleep. They're teachin' me.

EBEN (*suddenly jovial again*) Good fur the cows! Waal—ye better git t' work.

CABOT (*grimly amused*) Air yew bossin' me, ye calf?

EBEN (*beginning to laugh*) Ay-eh! I'm bossin' yew! Ha-ha-ha! see how ye like it! Ha-ha-ha! I'm the prize rooster o' this roost. Ha-ha-ha! (*He goes off toward the barn laughing*)

CABOT (*looks after him with scornful pity*) Soft-headed. Like his Maw. Dead spit 'n' image. No hope in him! (*He spits with contemptuous disgust*) A born fool! (*then matter-of-factly*) Waal—I'm gittin' peckish. (*He goes toward door*)

PART THREE

Scene One

(*A night in late spring the following year. The kitchen and the two bedrooms upstairs are shown. The two bedrooms are dimly lighted by a tallow candle in each.* EBEN *is sitting on the side of the bed in his room, his chin propped on his fists, his face a study of the struggle he is making to understand his conflicting emotions. The noisy laughter and music from below where a kitchen dance is in progress annoy and distract him. He scowls at the floor.*

In the next room a cradle stands beside the double bed.

In the kitchen all is festivity. The stove has been taken down to give more room to the dancers. The chairs, with wooden benches added, have been pushed back against the walls. On these are seated, squeezed in tight against one another, farmers and their wives and their young folks of both sexes from the neighboring farms. They are all chattering and laughing loudly. They evidently have some secret joke in common. There is no end of winking, of nudging, of meaning nods of the head toward* CABOT *who, in a state of extreme hilarious excitement increased by the amount he has drunk, is standing near the rear door where there is a small keg of whisky and serving drinks to all the men. In the left corner, front, dividing the attention with her husband,* ABBIE *is sitting in a rocking chair, a shawl wrapped about her shoulders. She is very pale, her face is thin and drawn, her eyes are fixed anxiously on the open door in rear as if waiting for someone.*

The musician is tuning up his fiddle, seated in the far right corner. He is a lanky young fellow with a long, weak face. His pale eyes blink incessantly and he grins about him slyly with a greedy malice)

ABBIE (*suddenly turning to a young girl on her right*) Whar's Eben?

YOUNG GIRL (*eyeing her scornfully*) I dunno, Mrs. Cabot. I hain't seen Eben in ages. (*meaningly*) Seems like he's spent most o' his time t' hum since yew come.

ABBIE (*vaguely*) I tuk his Maw's place.

YOUNG GIRL Ay-eh. So I heerd. (*She turns away to retail this bit of gossip to her mother sitting next to her.* ABBIE *turns to her left to a big stoutish middle-aged man whose flushed face and staring eyes show the amount of* "likker" *he has consumed*)

ABBIE Ye hain't seen Eben, hev ye?

MAN No, I hain't. (*Then he adds with a wink*) If yew hain't, who would?

ABBIE He's the best dancer in the county. He'd ought t' come an' dance.

MAN (*with a wink*) Mebbe he's doin' the dutiful an' walkin' the kid t' sleep. It's a boy, hain't it?

ABBIE (*nodding vaguely*) Ay-eh—born two weeks back—purty's a picter.

MAN They all is—t' their Maws. (*then in a whisper, with a nudge and a leer*) Listen, Abbie—if ye ever git tired o' Eben, remember me! Don't fergit now! (*He looks at her uncomprehending face for a second—then grunts disgustedly*) Waal—guess I'll likker agin. (*He goes over and joins* CABOT *who is arguing noisily with an old farmer over cows. They all drink*)

ABBIE (*this time appealing to nobody in particular*) Wonder what Eben's a-doin'? (*Her remark is repeated down the line with many a guffaw and titter until it reaches the fiddler. He fastens his blinking eyes on* ABBIE)

FIDDLER (*raising his voice*) Bet I kin tell ye, Abbie, what Eben's doin'! He's down t' the church offerin' up prayers o' thanksgivin'.

(*They all titter expectantly*)

MAN What fur? (*another titter*)

FIDDLER 'Cause unto him a—(*He hesitates just long enough*)—brother is born!

(*A roar of laughter. They all look from* ABBIE *to* CABOT. *She is oblivious, staring at the door.* CABOT, *although he hasn't heard the words, is irritated by the laughter and steps forward, glaring about him. There is an immediate silence*)

CABOT What're ye all bleatin' about—like a flock o' goats? Why don't ye dance, damn ye? I axed ye here t' dance—t' eat, drink an' be merry—an' thar ye set cacklin' like a lot o' wet hens with the pip! Ye've swilled my likker an' guzzled my vittles like hogs, hain't ye? Then dance fur me, cain't ye? That's fa'r an' squar', hain't it? (*A grumble of resentment goes around but they are all evidently in too much awe of him to express it openly*)

FIDDLER (*slyly*) We're waitin' fur Eben. (*a suppressed laugh*)

CABOT (*with a fierce exultation*) T'hell with Eben! Eben's done fur now! I got a new son! (*his mood switching with drunken suddenness*) But ye needn't t' laugh at Eben, none o' ye! He's my blood, if he be a dumb fool. He's better nor any o' yew! He kin do a day's work a'most up t' what I kin—an' that'd put any o' yew pore critters t' shame!

FIDDLER An' he kin do a good night's work, too! (*a roar of laughter*)

CABOT Laugh, ye damn fools! Ye're right jist the same, Fiddler. He kin work day an' night too, like I kin, if need be!

OLD FARMER (*from behind the keg where he is weaving drunkenly back and forth—with great simplicity*) They hain't many t' touch ye, Ephraim—a son at seventy-six. That's a hard man fur ye! I be on'y sixty-eight an' I couldn't do it. (*A roar of laughter in which* CABOT *joins uproariously*)

CABOT (*slapping him on the back*) I'm sorry fur ye, Hi. I'd never suspicion sech weakness from a boy like yew!

OLD FARMER An' I never reckoned yew had it in ye nuther, Ephraim. (*There is another laugh*)

CABOT (*suddenly grim*) I got a lot in me—

a hell of a lot—folks don't know on. (*turning to the* FIDDLER) Fiddle 'er up, durn ye! Give 'em somethin' t' dance t'! What air ye, an ornament? Hain't this a celebration? Then grease yer elbow an' go it!

FIDDLER (*seizes a drink which the* OLD FARMER *holds out to him and downs it*) Here goes!

(*He starts to fiddle "Lady of the Lake." Four young fellows and four girls form in two lines and dance a square dance. The* FIDDLER *shouts directions for the different movements, keeping his words in the rhythm of the music and interpersing them with jocular personal remarks to the dancers themselves. The people seated along the walls stamp their feet and clap their hands in unison.* CABOT *is especially active in this respect. Only* ABBIE *remains apathetic, staring at the door as if she were alone in a silent room*)

FIDDLER Swing your partner t' the right! That's it, Jim! Give her a b'ar hug! Her Maw hain't lookin'. (*laughter*) Change partners! That suits ye, don't it, Essie, now ye got Reub afore ye? Look at her redden up, will ye! Waal, life is short an' so's love, as the feller says. (*laughter*)

CABOT (*excitedly, stamping his foot*) Go it, boys! Go it, gals!

FIDDLER (*with a wink at the others*) Ye're the spryest seventy-six ever I sees, Ephraim! Now if ye'd on'y good eyesight . . . ! (*Suppressed laughter. He gives* CABOT *no chance to retort but roars*) Promenade! Ye're walkin' like a bride down the aisle, Sarah! Waal, while they's life they's allus hope, I've heerd tell. Swing your partner to the left! Gosh A'mighty, look at Johnny Cook high-steppin'! They hain't goin' t' be much strength left fur howin' in the corn lot t'morrow. (*laughter*)

CABOT Go it! Go it! (*Then suddenly, unable to restrain himself any longer, he prances into the midst of the dancers, scattering them, waving his arms about wildly*) Ye're all hoofs! Git out o' my road! Give me room! I'll show ye dancin'. Ye're all too soft! (*He pushes them roughly away. They crowd back toward the walls, muttering, looking at him resentfully*)

FIDDLER (*jeeringly*) Go it, Ephraim! Go it!

(*He starts "Pop Goes the Weasel," increasing the tempo with every verse until at the end he is fiddling crazily as fast as he can go*)

CABOT (*starts to dance, which he does very well and with tremendous vigor. Then he begins to improvise, cuts incredibly grotesque capers, leaping up and cracking his heels together, prancing around in a circle with body bent in an Indian war dance, then suddenly straightening up and kicking as high as he can with both legs. He is like a monkey on a string. And all the while he intersperses his antics with shouts and derisive comments)* Whoop! Here's dancin' fur ye! Whoop! See that! Seventy-six, if I'm a day! Hard as iron yet! Beatin' the young 'uns like I allus done! Look at me! I'd invite ye t' dance on my hundredth birthday on'y ye'll all be dead by then. Ye're a sickly generation! Yer hearts air pink, not red! Yer veins is full o' mud an' water! I be the on'y man in the county! Whoop! See that! I'm a Injun! I've killed Injuns in the West afore ye was born—an' skulped 'em too! They's a arrer wound on my backside I c'd show ye! The hull tribe chased me. I outrun 'em all—with the arrer stuck in me! An' I tuk vengeance on 'em. Ten eyes for an yew! He kin do a day's work a'most up t' what I kin kick the ceilin' off the room! Whoop!

FIDDLER (*stops playing—exhaustedly*) God A'mighty, I got enuf. Ye got the devil's strength in ye.

CABOT (*delightedly*) Did I beat yew, too? Waal, ye played smart. Hev a swig.

(*He pours whisky for himself and FIDDLER. They drink. The others watch CABOT silently with cold, hostile eyes. There is a dead pause. The FIDDLER rests. CABOT leans against the keg, panting, glaring around him confusedly. In the room above, EBEN gets to his feet and tiptoes out the door in rear, appearing a moment later in the other bedroom. He moves silently, even frightenedly, toward the cradle and stands there looking down at the baby. His face is as vague as his reactions are confused, but there is a trace of tenderness, of interested discovery. At the same moment that he reaches the cradle, ABBIE seems to sense something. She gets up weakly and goes to CABOT)*

ABBIE I'm goin' up t' the baby.

CABOT (*with real solicitude*) Air ye able fur the stairs? D'ye want me t' help ye, Abbie?

ABBIE No. I'm able. I'll be down agen soon.

CABOT Don't ye git wore out! He needs ye, remember—our son does! (*He grins affectionately, patting her on the back. She shrinks from his touch*)

ABBIE (*dully*) Don't—tech me. I'm goin'—up.

(*She goes. CABOT looks after her. A whisper goes around the room. CABOT turns. It ceases. He wipes his forehead streaming with sweat. He is breathing pantingly*)

CABOT I'm a-goin' out t' git fresh air. I'm

feelin' a mite dizzy. Fiddle up thar! Dance, all o' ye! Here's likker fur them as wants it. Enjoy yerselves. I'll be back. (*He goes, closing the door behind him*)

FIDDLER (*sarcastically*) Don't hurry none on our account! (*A suppressed laugh. He imitates ABBIE*) Whar's Eben? (*more laughter*)

A WOMAN (*loudly*) What's happened in this house is plain as the nose on yer face!

(*ABBIE appears in the doorway upstairs and stands looking in surprise and adoration at EBEN who does not see her*)

A MAN Ssshh! He's li'ble t' be listenin' at the door. That'd be like him.

(*Their voices die to an intensive whispering. Their faces are concentrated on this gossip. A noise as of dead leaves in the wind comes from the room. CABOT has come out from the porch and stands by the gate, leaning on it, staring at the sky blinkingly. ABBIE comes across the room silently. EBEN does not notice her until quite near*)

EBEN (*starting*) Abbie!

ABBIE Ssshh! (*She throws her arms around him. They kiss—then bend over the cradle together*) Ain't he purty?—dead spit 'n' image o' yew!

EBEN (*pleased*) Air he? I can't tell none.

ABBIE E-zactly like!

EBEN (*frowningly*) I don't like this. I don't like lettin' on what's mine's his'n. I been doin' that all my life. I'm gittin' t' the end o' b'arin' it!

ABBIE (*putting her finger on his lips*) We're doin' the best we kin. We got t' wait. Somethin's bound t' happen. (*She puts her arms around him*) I got t' go back.

EBEN I'm goin' out. I can't b'ar it with the fiddle playin' an' the laughin'.

ABBIE Don't git feelin' low. I love ye, Eben. Kiss me. (*He kisses her. They remain in each other's arms*)

CABOT (*at the gate, confusedly*) Even the music can't drive it out—somethin'. Ye kin feel it droppin' off the elums, climbin' up the roof, sneakin' down the chimney, pokin' in the corners! They's no peace in houses, they's no rest livin' with folks. Somethin's always livin' with ye. (*with a deep sigh*) I'll go t' the barn an' rest a spell. (*He goes wearily toward the barn*)

FIDDLER (*tuning up*) Let's celebrate the old skunk gittin' fooled! We kin have some fun now he's went.

(*He starts to fiddle "Turkey in the Straw." There is real merriment now. The young folks get up to dance*)

Scene Two

(*A half hour later—exterior—*EBEN *is standing by the gate looking up at the sky, an expression of dumb pain bewildered by itself on his face.* CABOT *appears, returning from the barn, walking wearily, his eyes on the ground. He sees* EBEN *and his whole mood immediately changes. He becomes excited, a cruel, triumphant grin comes to his lips, he strides up and slaps* EBEN *on the back. From within comes the whining of the fiddle and the noise of stamping feet and laughing voices*)

CABOT   So har ye be!

EBEN (*startled, stares at him with hatred for a moment—then dully*)   Ay-eh.

CABOT (*surveying him jeeringly*)   Why hain't ye been in t' dance? They was all axin' fur ye.

EBEN   Let 'em ax!

CABOT   They's a hull passel o' purty gals.

EBEN   T' hell with 'em!

CABOT   Ye'd ought t' be marryin' one o' 'em soon.

EBEN   I hain't marryin' no one.

CABOT   Ye might 'arn a share o' a farm that way.

EBEN (*with a sneer*)   Like yew did, ye mean? I hain't that kind.

CABOT (*stung*)   Ye lie! 'Twas yer Maw's folks aimed t' steal my farm from me.

EBEN   Other folks don't say so. (*after a pause—defiantly*)   An' I got a farm, anyways!

CABOT (*derisively*)   Whar?

EBEN (*stamps a foot on the ground*)   Har!

CABOT (*throws his head back and laughs coarsely*)   Ho-ho! Ye hev, hev ye? Waal, that's a good un!

EBEN (*controlling himself—grimly*)   Ye'll see!

CABOT (*stares at him suspiciously, trying to make him out—a pause—then with scornful confidence*)   Ay-eh. I'll see. So'll ye. It's ye that's blind—blind as a mole underground. (EBEN *suddenly laughs, one short sardonic bark: "Ha." A pause.* CABOT *peers at him with renewed suspicion*)   Whar air ye hawin' 'bout? (EBEN *turns away without answering.* CABOT *grows angry*)   God A'mighty, yew air a dumb dunce! They's nothin' in that thick skull o' your'n but noise—like a empty keg it be! (EBEN *doesn't seem to hear—*CABOT's *rage grows*)   Yewr farm! God A'mighty! If ye wa'n't a born donkey ye'd know ye'll never own stick nor stone on it, specially now arter him bein' born. It's his'n, I tell ye—his'n arter I die—but I'll

live a hundred jest t' fool ye all—an' he'll be growed then—yewr age a'most! (EBEN *laughs again his sardonic "Ha." This drives* CABOT *into a fury*)   Ha? Ye think ye kin git 'round that someways, do ye? Waal, it'll be her'n, too —Abbie's—ye won't git 'round her—she knows yer tricks—she'll be too much fur ye—she wants the farm her'n—she was afeerd o' ye— she told me ye was sneakin' 'round tryin' t' make love t' her t' git her on yer side . . . ye . . . ye mad fool, ye! (*He raises his clenched fists threateningly*)

EBEN (*is confronting him choking with rage*)   Ye lie, ye old skunk! Abbie never said no sech thing!

CABOT (*suddenly triumphant when he sees how shaken* EBEN *is*)   She did. An' I says, I'll blow his brains t' the top o' them elums—an' she says no, that hain't sense, who'll ye git t' help ye on the farm in his place—an' then she says yew'n me ought t' have a son—I know we kin, she says—an' I says, if we do, ye kin have anythin' I've got ye've a mind t'. An' she says, I wants Eben cut off so's this farm'll be mine when ye die! (*with terrible gloating*)   An' that's what happened, hain't it? An' the farm's her'n! An' the dust o' the road—that's you'rn! Ha! Now who's hawin'?

EBEN (*has been listening, petrified with grief and rage—suddenly laughs wildly and brokenly*)   Ha-ha-ha! So that's her sneakin' game—all along!—like I suspicioned at fust—t' swaller it all—an' me, too . . . ! (*madly*)   I'll murder her! (*He springs toward the porch but* CABOT *is quicker and gets in between*)

CABOT   No, ye don't!

EBEN   Git out o' my road!

(*He tries to throw* CABOT *aside. They grapple in what becomes immediately a murderous struggle. The old man's concentrated strength is too much for* EBEN. CABOT *gets one hand on his throat and presses him back across the stone wall. At the same moment,* ABBIE *comes out on the porch. With a stifled cry she runs toward them*)

ABBIE   Eben! Ephraim! (*She tugs at the hand on* EBEN's *throat*)   Let go, Ephraim! Ye're chokin' him!

CABOT (*removes his hand and flings* EBEN *sideways full length on the grass, gasping and choking. With a cry,* ABBIE *kneels beside him, trying to take his head on her lap, but he pushes her away.* CABOT *stands looking down with fierce triumph*)   Ye needn't t've fret, Abbie, I wa'n't aimin' t' kill him. He hain't wuth hangin' fur—not by a hell of a sight!

(*more and more triumphantly*) Seventy-six an' him not thirty yit—an' look whar he be fur thinkin' his Paw was easy! No, by God, I hain't easy! An' him upstairs, I'll raise him t' be like me! (*He turns to leave them*) I'm goin' in an' dance!—sing an' celebrate! (*He walks to the porch—then turns with a great grin*) I don't calc'late it's left in him, but if he gits pesky, Abbie, ye jest sing out. I'll come a-runnin' an' by the Eternal, I'll put him across my knee an' birch him! Ha-ha-ha! (*He goes into the house laughing. A moment later his loud "whoop" is heard*)

ABBIE (*tenderly*) Eben. Air ye hurt? (*She tries to kiss him but he pushes her violently away and struggles to a sitting position*)

EBEN (*gaspingly*) T'hell—with ye!

ABBIE (*not believing her ears*) It's me, Eben—Abbie—don't ye know me?

EBEN (*glowering at her with hatred*) Ay-eh —I know ye—now! (*He suddenly breaks down, sobbing weakly*)

ABBIE (*fearfully*) Eben—what's happened t' ye—why did ye look at me 's if ye hated me?

EBEN (*violently, between sobs and gasps*) I do hate ye! Ye're a whore—a damn trickin' whore!

ABBIE (*shrinking back horrified*) Eben! Ye don't know what ye're sayin'!

EBEN (*scrambling to his feet and following her—accusingly*) Ye're nothin' but a stinkin' passel o' lies! Ye've been lyin' t' me every word ye spoke, day an' night, since we fust—done it. Ye've kept sayin' ye loved me. . . .

ABBIE (*frantically*) I do love ye! (*She takes his hand but he flings hers away*)

EBEN (*unheeding*) Ye've made a fool o' me —a sick, dumb fool—a-purpose! Ye've been on'y playin' yer sneakin', stealin' game all along —gittin' me t' lie with ye so's ye'd hev a son he'd think was his'n, an' makin' him promise he'd give ye the farm and let me eat dust, if ye did git him a son! (*staring at her with anguished, bewildered eyes*) They must be a devil livin' in ye! 'Tain't human t' be as bad as that be!

ABBIE (*stunned—dully*) He told yew . . . ?

EBEN Hain't it true? It hain't no good in yew lyin'.

ABBIE (*pleadingly*) Eben, listen—ye must listen—it was long ago—afore we done nothin' —yew was scornin' me—goin' t' see Min— when I was lovin' ye—an' I said it t' him t' git vengeance on ye!

EBEN (*unheedingly. With tortured passion*) I wish ye was dead! I wish I was dead along with ye afore this come! (*ragingly*) But I'll git my vengeance too! I'll pray Maw t' come back t' help me—t' put her cuss on yew an' him!

ABBIE (*brokenly*) Don't ye, Eben! Don't ye! (*She throws herself on her knees before him, weeping*) I didn't mean t' do bad t'ye! Fergive me, won't ye?

EBEN (*not seeming to hear her—fiercely*) I'll git squar' with the old skunk—an' yew! I'll tell him the truth 'bout the son he's so proud o'! Then I'll leave ye here t' pizen each other— with Maw comin' out o' her grave at nights— an' I'll go t' the gold fields o' Californi-a whar Sim an' Peter be!

ABBIE (*terrified*) Ye won't—leave me? Ye can't!

EBEN (*with fierce determination*) I'm a-goin', I tell ye! I'll git rich thar an' come back an' fight him fur the farm he stole—an' I'll kick ye both out in the road—t' beg an' sleep in the woods—an' yer son along with ye—t' starve an' die! (*He is hysterical at the end*)

ABBIE (*with a shudder—humbly*) He's yewr son, too, Eben.

EBEN (*torturedly*) I wish he never was born! I wish he'd die this minit! I wish I'd never sot eyes on him! It's him—yew havin' him—a-purpose t' steal—that's changed everythin'!

ABBIE (*gently*) Did ye believe I loved ye— afore he come?

EBEN Ay-eh—like a dumb ox!

ABBIE An' ye don't believe no more?

EBEN B'lieve a lyin' thief! Ha!

ABBIE (*shudders—then humbly*) An did ye r'ally love me afore?

EBEN (*brokenly*) Ay-eh—an' ye was trickin' me!

ABBIE An' ye don't love me now!

EBEN (*violently*) I hate ye, I tell ye!

ABBIE An' ye're truly goin' West—goin' t' leave me—all account o' him being born?

EBEN I'm a-goin' in the mornin'—or may God strike me t' hell!

ABBIE (*after a pause—with a dreadful cold intensity—slowly*) If that's what his comin's done t' me—killin' yewr love—takin' yew away —my on'y joy—the on'y joy I've ever knowed —like heaven t' me—purtier'n heaven—then I hate him, too, even if I be his Maw!

EBEN (*bitterly*) Lies! Ye love him! He'll steal the farm fur ye! (*brokenly*) But 'tain't the farm so much—not no more—it's yew foolin' me—gittin' me t' love ye—lyin' yew loved me —jest t' git a son t' steal!

ABBIE (*distractedly*) He won't steal! I'd kill him fust! I do love ye! I'll prove t' ye . . . !

EBEN (*harshly*) 'Tain't no use lyin' no more. I'm deaf t' ye! (*He turns away*) I hain't seein' ye agen. Good-bye!

ABBIE (*pale with anguish*) Hain't ye even goin' t' kiss me—not once—arter all we loved?

EBEN (*in a hard voice*) I hain't wantin' t' kiss ye never agen! I'm wantin' t' forgit I ever sot eyes on ye!

ABBIE Eben!—ye mustn't—wait a spell—I want t' tell ye. . . .

EBEN I'm a-goin' in t' git drunk. I'm a-goin' t' dance.

ABBIE (*clinging to his arm—with passionate earnestness*) If I could make it—'s if he'd never come up between us—if I could prove t' ye I wa'n't schemin' t' steal from ye—so's everythin' could be jest the same with us, lovin' each other jest the same, kissin' an' happy the same's we've been happy afore he come—if I could do it—ye'd love me agen, wouldn't ye? Ye'd kiss me agen? Ye wouldn't never leave me, would ye?

EBEN (*moved*) I calc'late not. (*Then shaking her hand off his arm—with a bitter smile*) But ye hain't God, be ye?

ABBIE (*exultantly*) Remember ye've promised! (*then with strange intensity*) Mebbe I kin take back one thin' God does!

EBEN (*peering at her*) Ye're gittin' cracked, hain't ye? (*then going towards door*) I'm a-goin' t' dance.

ABBIE (*calls after him intensely*) I'll prove t' ye! I'll prove I love ye better'n. . . . (*He goes in the door, not seeming to hear. She remains standing where she is, looking after him—then she finishes desperately*) Better'n everythin' else in the world!

Scene Three

(*Just before dawn in the morning—shows the kitchen and* CABOT's *bedroom. In the kitchen, by the light of a tallow candle on the table,* EBEN *is sitting, his chin propped on his hands, his drawn face blank and expressionless. His carpetbag is on the floor beside him. In the bedroom, dimly lighted by a small whale-oil lamp,* CABOT *lies asleep.* ABBIE *is bending over the cradle, listening, her face full of terror yet with an undercurrent of desperate triumph. Suddenly, she breaks down and sobs, appears about to throw herself on her knees beside the cradle; but the old man turns restlessly, groaning in his sleep, and she controls herself, and shrinking away from the cradle with a gesture of horror, backs swiftly toward the door in rear and goes out. A moment later she comes into the kitchen and, running to* EBEN, *flings her arms about his neck and kisses him wildly. He hardens himself, he remains unmoved and cold, he keeps his eyes straight ahead*)

ABBIE (*hysterically*) I done it, Eben! I told ye I'd do it! I've proved I love ye—better'n everythin'—so's ye can't never doubt me no more!

EBEN (*dully*) Whatever ye done, it hain't no good now.

ABBIE (*wildly*) Don't ye say that! Kiss me, Eben, won't ye? I need ye t' kiss me arter what I done! I need ye t' say ye love me!

EBEN (*kisses her without emotion—dully*) That's fur good-bye. I'm a-goin' soon.

ABBIE No! No! Ye won't go—not now!

EBEN (*going on with his own thoughts*) I been a-thinkin'—an' I hain't goin' t' tell Paw nothin'. I'll leave Maw t' take vengeance on ye. If I told him, the old skunk'd jest be stinkin' mean enuf to take it out on that baby. (*His voice showing emotion in spite of him*) An' I don't want nothin' bad t' happen t' him. He hain't t' blame fur yew. (*He adds with a certain queer pride*) An' he looks like me! An' by God, he's mine! An' some day I'll be a-comin' back an' . . . !

ABBIE (*too absorbed in her own thoughts to listen to him—pleadingly*) They's no cause fur ye t' go now—they's no sense—it's all the same's it was—they's nothing come b'tween us now—arter what I done!

EBEN (*something in her voice arouses him. He stares at her a bit frightenedly*) Ye look mad, Abbie. What did ye do?

ABBIE I—I killed him, Eben.

EBEN (*amazed*) Ye killed him?

ABBIE (*dully*) Ay-eh.

EBEN (*recovering from his astonishment—savagely*) An' serves him right! But we got t' do somethin' quick t' make it look 's if the old skunk killed himself when he was drunk. We kin prove by 'em all how drunk he got.

ABBIE (*wildly*) No! No! Not him! (*laughing distractedly*) But that's what I ought t' done, hain't it? I oughter killed him instead! Why didn't ye tell me?

EBEN (*appalled*) Instead? What d'ye mean?

ABBIE Not him.

EBEN (*his face grown ghastly*) Not—not that baby!

ABBIE (*dully*) Ay-eh!

EBEN (*falls to his knees as if he'd been struck—his voice trembling with horror*) Oh, God A'mighty! A'mighty God! Maw, whar was ye, why didn't ye stop her?

ABBIE (*simply*) She went back t' her grave that night we fust done it, remember? I hain't felt her about since. (*A pause.* EBEN *hides his head in his hands, trembling all over as if he had the ague. She goes on dully*) I left the

piller over his little face. Then he killed himself. He stopped breathin'. (*She begins to
weep softly*)

EBEN (*rage beginning to mingle with grief*)
He looked like me. He was mine, damn ye!

ABBIE (*slowly and brokenly*)   I didn't want
t' do it. I hated myself fur doin' it. I loved him.
He was so purty—dead spit 'n' image o' yew.
But I loved yew more—an' yew was goin'
away—far off whar I'd never see ye agen,
never kiss ye, never feel ye pressed agin me
agen—an' ye said ye hated me fur havin' him—
ye said ye hated him an' wished he was dead—
ye said if it hadn't been fur him comin' it'd be
the same's afore between us.

EBEN (*unable to endure this, springs to his
feet in a fury, threatening her, his twitching
fingers seeming to reach out for her throat*)
Ye lie! I never said—I never dreamed ye'd—
I'd cut off my head afore I'd hurt his finger!

ABBIE (*piteously, sinking on her knees*)
Eben, don't ye look at me like that—hatin' me
—not after what I done fur ye—fur us—so's
we could be happy agen—

EBEN (*furiously now*)   Shut up, or I'll kill
ye! I see yer game now—the same old sneakin'
trick—ye're aimin' t' blame me fur the murder
ye done!

ABBIE (*moaning—putting her hands over her
ears*)   Don't ye, Eben! Don't ye! (*She grasps
his legs*)

EBEN (*his mood suddenly changing to horror, shrinks away from her*)   Don't ye tech
me! Ye're pizen! How could ye—t' murder a
pore little critter—Ye must've swapped yer
soul t' hell! (*sudden raging*) Ha! I kin see
why ye done it! Not the lies ye jest told—but
'cause ye wanted t' steal agen—steal the last
thin' ye'd left me—my part o' him—no, the
hull o' him—ye saw he looked like me—ye
knowed he was all mine—an' ye couldn't b'ar
it—I know ye! Ye killed him fur bein' mine!
(*All this has driven him almost insane. He
makes a rush past her for the door—then turns
—shaking both fists at her, violently*) But I'll
take vengeance now! I'll git the Sheriff! I'll tell
him everythin'! Then I'll sing "I'm off to
Californi-a!" an' go—gold—Golden Gate—gold
sun—fields o' gold in the West! (*This last he
half shouts, half croons incoherently, suddenly
breaking off passionately*) I'm a-goin' fur the
Sheriff t' come an' git ye! I want ye tuk away,
locked up from me! I can't stand t' luk at ye!
Murderer an' thief 'r not, ye still tempt me! I'll
give ye up t' the Sheriff! (*He turns and runs
out, around the corner of house, panting and
sobbing, and breaks into a swerving sprint down
the road*)

ABBIE (*struggling to her feet, runs to the
door, calling after him*)   I love ye, Eben! I
love ye! (*She stops at the door weakly, swaying, about to fall*) I don't care what ye do—if
ye'll on'y love me agen—(*She falls limply to
the floor in a faint*)

Scene Four

(*About an hour later. Same as Scene Three.
Shows the kitchen and* CABOT'S *bedroom. It is
after dawn. The sky is brilliant with the sunrise.
In the kitchen,* ABBIE *sits at the table, her body
limp and exhausted, her head bowed down
over her arms, her face hidden. Upstairs,* CABOT
*is still asleep but awakens with a start. He looks
toward the window and gives a snort of surprise and irritation—throws back the covers
and begins hurriedly pulling on his clothes.
Without looking behind him, he begins talking
to* ABBIE *whom he supposes beside him*)

CABOT   Thunder 'n' lightnin', Abbie! I hain't
slept this late in fifty year! Looks 's if the sun
was full riz a'most. Must've been the dancin'
an' likker. Must be gittin' old. I hope Eben's
t'wuk. Ye might've tuk the trouble t' rouse me,
Abbie. (*He turns—sees no one there—surprised*) Waal—whar air she? Gittin' vittles, I
calc'late. (*He tiptoes to the cradle and peers
down—proudly*) Mornin', sonny. Purty's a picter! Sleepin' sound. He don't beller all night
like most o' 'em. (*He goes quietly out the door
in rear—a few moments later enters kitchen—
sees* ABBIE—*with satisfaction*) So thar ye be. Ye
got any vittles cooked?

ABBIE (*without moving*)   No.

CABOT (*coming to her, almost sympathetically*)   Ye feelin' sick?

ABBIE   No.

CABOT (*pats her on shoulder. She shudders*)
Ye'd best lie down a spell. (*half jocularly*) Yer
son'll be needin' ye soon. He'd ought t' wake
up with a gnashin' appetite, the sound way he's
sleepin'.

ABBIE (*shudders—then in a dead voice*)
He ain't never goin' to wake up.

CABOT (*jokingly*)   Takes after me this
mornin'. I ain't slept so late in . . .

ABBIE   He's dead.

CABOT (*stares at her—bewilderedly*)
What . . .

ABBIE   I killed him.

CABOT (*stepping back from her—aghast*)
Air ye drunk—'r crazy—'r . . . !

ABBIE (*suddenly lifts her head and turns on
him—wildly*)   I killed him, I tell ye! I smothered him. Go up an' see if ye don't b'lieve me!

(CABOT *stares at her a second, then bolts out the rear door, can be heard bounding up the stairs, and rushes into the bedroom and over to the cradle.* ABBIE *has sunk back lifelessly into her former position.* CABOT *puts his hand down on the body in the crib. An expression of fear and horror comes over his face*)

CABOT (*shrinking away—tremblingly*) God A'mighty! God A'mighty. (*He stumbles out the door—in a short while returns to the kitchen—comes to* ABBIE, *the stunned expression still on his face—hoarsely*) Why did ye do it? Why? (*As she doesn't answer, he grabs her violently by the shoulder and shakes her*) I ax ye why ye done it! Ye'd better tell me 'r . . . !

ABBIE (*gives him a furious push which sends him staggering back and springs to her feet— with wild rage and hatred*) Don't ye dare tech me! What right hev ye t' question me 'bout him? He wa'n't yewr son! Think I'd have a son by yew? I'd die fust! I hate the sight o' ye an' allus did! It's yew I should've murdered, if I'd had good sense! I hate ye! I love Eben. I did from the fust. An' he was Eben's son—mine an' Eben's—not your'n!

CABOT (*stands looking at her dazedly—a pause—finding his words with an effort— dully*) That was it—what I felt—pokin' round the corners—while ye lied—holdin' yerself from me—sayin' ye'd a'ready conceived— (*He lapses into crushed silence—then with a strange emotion*) He's dead, sart'n. I felt his heart. Pore little critter! (*He blinks back one tear, wiping his sleeve across his nose*)

ABBIE (*hysterically*) Don't ye! Don't ye! (*She sobs unrestrainedly*)

CABOT (*with concentrated effort that stiffens his body into a rigid line and hardens his face into a stony mask—through his teeth to himself*) I got t' be—like a stone—a rock o' jedgment! (*A pause. He gets complete control over himself—harshly*) If he was Eben's, I be glad he air gone! An' mebbe I suspicioned it all along. I felt they was somethin' onnateral— somewhars—the house got so lonesome—an' cold—drivin' me down t' the barn—t' the beasts o' the field. . . . Ay-eh. I must've suspicioned—somethin'. Ye didn't fool me—not altogether, leastways—I'm too old a bird— growin' ripe on the bough. . . . (*He becomes aware he is wandering, straightens again, looks at* ABBIE *with a cruel grin*) So ye'd like t' hev murdered me 'stead o' him, would ye? Waal, I'll live to a hundred! I'll live t' see ye hung! I'll deliver ye up t' the jedgment o' God an' the law! I'll git the Sheriff now. (*starts for the door*)

ABBIE (*dully*) Ye needn't. Eben's gone fur him.

CABOT (*amazed*) Eben—gone for the Sheriff?

ABBIE Ay-eh.

CABOT T' inform agen ye?

ABBIE Ay-eh.

CABOT (*considers this—a pause—then in a hard voice*) Waal, I'm thankful fur him savin' me the trouble. I'll git t' wuk. (*He goes to the door—then turns—in a voice full of strange emotion*) He'd ought t' been my son, Abbie. Ye'd ought t' loved me. I'm a man. If ye'd loved me, I'd never told no Sheriff on ye no matter what ye did, if they was t' brile me alive!

ABBIE (*defensively*) They's more to it nor yew know, makes him tell.

CABOT (*dryly*) Fur yewr sake, I hope they be. (*He goes out—comes around to the gate— stares up at the sky. His control relaxes. For a moment he is old and weary. He murmurs despairingly*) God A'mighty, I be lonesomer'n ever! (*He hears running footsteps from the left, immediately is himself again.* EBEN *runs in, panting exhaustedly, wild-eyed and mad looking. He lurches through the gate.* CABOT *grabs him by the shoulder.* EBEN *stares at him dumbly*) Did ye tell the Sheriff?

EBEN (*nodding stupidly*) Ay-eh.

CABOT (*gives him a push away that sends him sprawling—laughing with withering contempt*) Good fur ye! A prime chip o' yer Maw ye be! (*He goes toward the barn, laughing harshly.* EBEN *scrambles to his feet. Suddenly* CABOT *turns—grimly threatening*) Git off this farm when the Sheriff takes her—or, by God, he'll have t' come back an' git me fur murder, too!

(*He stalks off.* EBEN *does not appear to have heard him. He runs to the door and comes into the kitchen.* ABBIE *looks up with a cry of anguished joy.* EBEN *stumbles over and throws himself on his knees beside her—sobbing brokenly*)

EBEN Fergive me!

ABBIE (*happily*) Eben! (*She kisses him and pulls his head over against her breast*)

EBEN I love ye! Fergive me!

ABBIE (*ecstatically*) I'd fergive ye all the sins in hell fur sayin' that! (*She kisses his head, pressing it to her with a fierce passion of possession*)

EBEN (*brokenly*) But I told the Sheriff. He's comin' fur ye!

ABBIE I kin b'ar what happens t' me—now!

EBEN I woke him up. I told him. He says, wait 'til I git dressed. I was waiting. I got to thinkin' o' yew. I got to thinkin' how I'd loved ye. It hurt like somethin' was bustin' in my chest an' head. I got t' cryin'. I knowed sudden I loved ye yet, an' allus would love ye!

ABBIE (*caressing his hair—tenderly*) My boy, hain't ye?

EBEN   I begun t' run back. I cut across the fields an' through the woods. I thought ye might have time t' run away—with me—an' . . .

ABBIE (*shaking her head*) I got t' take my punishment—t' pay fur my sin.

EBEN   Then I want t' share it with ye.

ABBIE   Ye didn't do nothin'.

EBEN   I put it in yer head. I wisht he was dead! I as much as urged ye t' do it!

ABBIE   No. It was me alone!

EBEN   I'm as guilty as yew be! He was the child o' our sin.

ABBIE (*lifting her head as if defying God*) I don't repent that sin! I hain't askin' God t' fergive that!

EBEN   Nor me—but it led up t' the other—an' the murder ye did, ye did 'count o' me—an' it's my murder, too, I'll tell the Sheriff—an' if ye deny it, I'll say we planned it t'gether—an' they'll all b'lieve me, fur they suspicion everythin' we've done, an' it'll seem likely an' true to 'em. An' it is true—way down. I did help ye—somehow.

ABBIE (*laying her head on his—sobbing*) No! I don't want yew t' suffer!

EBEN   I got t' pay fur my part o' the sin! An' I'd suffer wuss leavin' ye, goin' West, thinkin' o' ye day an' night, bein' out when yew was in—(*lowering his voice*)—'r bein' alive when yew was dead. (*a pause*) I want t' share with ye, Abbie—prison 'r death 'r hell 'r anythin'! (*He looks into her eyes and forces a trembling smile*) If I'm sharin' with ye, I won't feel lonesome, leastways.

ABBIE (*weakly*) Eben! I won't let ye! I can't let ye!

EBEN (*kissing her—tenderly*) Ye can't he'p yerself. I got ye beat fur once!

ABBIE (*forcing a smile—adoringly*) I hain't beat—s'long's I got ye!

EBEN (*hears the sound of feet outside*) Ssshh! Listen! They've come t' take us!

ABBIE   No, it's him. Don't give him no chance to fight ye, Eben. Don't say nothin'—no matter what he says. An' I won't neither. (*It is* CABOT. *He comes up from the barn in a great state of excitement and strides into the house and then into the kitchen.* EBEN *is kneeling beside* ABBIE, *his arm around her, hers around him. They stare straight ahead*)

CABOT (*stares at them, his face hard. A long pause—vindictively*) Ye make a slick pair o' murderin' turtle doves! Ye'd ought t' be both hung on the same limb an' left thar t' swing in the breeze an' rot—a warnin' t' old fools like me t' b'ar their lonesomeness alone—an' fur young fools like ye t' hobble their lust. (*A pause. The excitement returns to his face, his eyes snap, he looks a bit crazy*) I couldn't work today. I couldn't take no interest. T' hell with the farm! I'm leavin' it! I've turned the cows an' other stock loose! I've druv 'em into the woods whar they kin be free! By freein' 'em, I'm freein' myself! I'm quittin' here today! I'll set fire t' house an' barn an' watch 'em burn, an' I'll leave yer Maw t' haunt the ashes, an' I'll will the fields back t' God, so that nothin' human kin never touch 'em! I'll be a-goin' to Californi-a—t' jine Simeon an' Peter—true sons o' mine if they be dumb fools—an' the Cabots'll find Solomon's Mines t'gether! (*He suddenly cuts a mad caper*) Whoop! What was the song they sung? "Oh, Californi-a! That's the land fur me." (*He sings this—then gets on his knees by the floorboard under which the money was hid*) An' I'll sail thar on one o' the finest clippers I kin find! I've got the money! Pity ye didn't know whar this was hidden so's ye could steal . . . (*He has pulled up the board. He stares—feels—stares again. A pause of dead silence. He slowly turns, slumping into a sitting position on the floor, his eyes like those of a dead fish, his face the sickly green of an attack of nausea. He swallows painfully several times—forces a weak smile at last*) So—ye did steal it!

EBEN (*emotionlessly*) I swapped it t' Sim an' Peter fur their share o' the farm—t' pay their passage t' Californi-a.

CABOT (*with one sardonic*) Ha! (*He begins to recover. Gets slowly to his feet—strangely*) I calc'late God give it to 'em—not yew! God's hard, not easy! Mebbe they's easy gold in the West but it hain't God's gold. It hain't fur me. I kin hear His voice warnin' me agen t' be hard an' stay on my farm. I kin see his hand usin' Eben t' steal t' keep me from weakness. I kin feel I be in the palm o' His hand, His fingers guidin' me. (*A pause—then he mutters sadly*) It's a-goin' t' be lonesomer now than ever it war afore—an' I'm gittin' old, Lord—ripe on the bough. . . . (*then stiffening*) Waal—what d'ye want? God's lonesome, hain't He? God's hard an' lonesome! (*A pause. The* SHERIFF *with two men comes up the road from the left. They move cautiously to the door. The* SHERIFF *knocks on it with the butt of his pistol*)

SHERIFF   Open in the name o' the law!

(*They start*)

CABOT They've come fur ye. (*He goes to the rear door*) Come in, Jim! (*The three men enter.* CABOT *meets them in doorway*) Jest a minit, Jim. I got 'em safe here. (*The* SHERIFF *nods. He and his companions remain in the doorway*)

EBEN (*suddenly calls*) I lied this mornin', Jim. I helped her to do it. Ye kin take me, too.

ABBIE (*brokenly*) No!

CABOT Take 'em both. (*He comes forward —stares at* EBEN *with a trace of grudging admiration*) Purty good—fur yew! Waal, I got t' round up the stock. Good-bye.

EBEN Good-bye.

ABBIE Good-bye.

(CABOT *turns and strides past the men—comes out and around the corner of the house, his shoulders squared, his face stony, and stalks grimly toward the barn. In the meantime the* SHERIFF *and men have come into the room*)

SHERIFF (*embarrassedly*) Waal—we'd best start.

ABBIE Wait. (*turns to* EBEN) I love ye, Eben.

EBEN I love ye, Abbie. (*They kiss. The three men grin and shuffle embarrassedly.* EBEN *takes* ABBIE's *hand. They go out the door in rear, the men following, and come from the house, walking hand in hand to the gate.* EBEN *stops there and points to the sunrise sky*) Sun's a-risin'. Purty, hain't it?

ABBIE Ay-eh. (*They both stand for a moment looking up raptly in attitudes strangely aloof and devout*)

SHERIFF (*looking around at the farm enviously—to his companion*) It's a jim-dandy farm, no denyin'. Wished I owned it!

Lillian Hellman

1905-

AN INTERVIEW WITH
LILLIAN HELLMAN

By Thomas Meehan

Miss Hellman, what's wrong with Broadway?
It's a bore.

I don't know why it's a bore, but there's very little that's any fun. By fun I mean something you're interested in, enjoy the way you might enjoy a good book, maybe not a great book, just a good book. The theatre has grown so middle-class, even when it's *avant-garde*. I don't mean in subject matter—there's no such thing as a middle-class subject. I mean in its way of looking at things.

Do you mean the theatre used to be better? The Twenties, for instance, were certainly an unboring time.

Yes, I think so. There was a group of extraordinarily talented writers in the Twenties and the theatre had its share. Most remarkable people—Eugene O'Neill, George Kelly, Sidney Howard, George Kaufman, Elmer Rice, whatever one thinks of them now, whatever their final work has come to—were breaking new ground, going new ways and having something to say.

In the Twenties there were sixty or seventy productions a year. Now we have about half that many.

In the late Twenties, when I first knew the theatre, six and seven shows used to open in a night.

And weren't there a lot more comedies in the Twenties and Thirties?

Yes, I guess the Twenties laughed more than we do. We don't get many good comedies anymore. We get homey little comedies now, homey little middle-class comedies in which *everybody* talks as if they'd gone through four years of college and read the latest best-seller. Even musicals used to have more bite and point. As many advances as the musical theatre has taken, I don't think it's ever again come near the kind of bold funniness of *Pal Joey.*

What do you think accounts for this loss in, well, bite?

The theatre, in every country, is a fairly accurate gauge of popular desire. Books and music and architecture will often go their own way, but the theatre is so concerned with money that it has to make good guesses about what is wanted, and what is wanted now is not bite or boldness. I don't think we want to be flattered—we did, but we've passed through that—but we do want to be tickled. A little glimpse of homosexuality, a mite of dopesters, Mr. Genet's romantic peeps at an underworld and, above all—the surest buck of all—something about "aloneness." Big deal, you're alone. When the play goes into rehearsal, the hero ends alone. Round about the first week on the road, nobody thinks that's nice, so he finds love. Not alone anymore. Or, more skillfully, half-alone. God knows love is a great theme but we're sure busy making it mangy.

There's a song in which the line keeps repeating: Love is the answer. . . . The great answer of our time. The idiot word nobody bothers to define. "Love"—and "aloneness." I have great respect for psychoanalysis, but I think our preoccupation with "love" and "aloneness" comes right out of ten-cent-store Freud. Love is a *very* large theme and unless writers can do it big, they should leave it alone. And the discovery that all of us are, finally, alone must have been made by the first ape as he stood up to look over his shoulder.

Who in your opinion is making the taste in the theatre? In a way I think you've indicated that it's the audience.

It's a combination, of course. It's what the writer, the producer, the director think the audience wants and what the audience lets them know they do want.

Then what do you think has gone wrong? There are more educated people in this country today than there ever were before?

Are there? You mean more people who go to college? Well, maybe. Maybe that's what it is, the theatre doesn't offer the educated what they're looking for. The young people I know, and by young I mean twenty to thirty, have little interest in the theatre. One of them told me the other night that his generation was far more interested in movies than in plays, that he didn't like to get theatre tickets two or three weeks ahead of time, and that the tickets cost too much. He said even if he could afford to go, there was little that would interest him. I knew what he meant—the theatre doesn't interest me much anymore.

Do you feel this might have something to do with the shortage of good new writers?

Yes, I think so. There are not many young people in the theatre who are good writers. Certainly fewer than there were in the Twenties and possibly fewer than there were in the Thirties. Maybe things go in a circle. The plays aren't very good and so the good young writer turns to some other form. But the theatre will have a renascence and the good writer will come toward it again.

Do you see very many plays?

No. If I'm writing, I have the superstitious belief that you'd better keep the unborn child away from what might harm it. If I go to see bad theatre—and by bad theatre I mean theatre that bores me—I'm scared that I'll have a tough time writing or that I won't write well. If I go to good theatre, I feel exhilarated and pleased, and I want to write better and more. But I'm real scared of going near junk or half-junk. Half-junk is very dangerous.

Do you think the critics have some responsibility for killing off the interesting things? Are they too severe?

No. I think they're frequently too easy, especially on musical shows. I suppose that comes from being bored so often that you're glad to have pretty girls and a nice song. And it's true, of course, that within the last ten years the musical show has been more serious and more interesting than the straight play.

Comparing Leave It to Jane *with* West Side Story, *it's easy to see the progress in musicals. You don't think there's been that kind of advance in the straight play?*

I guess not. Although I don't know much about advances or retreats. I dislike such words. There's a tendency in the theatre—the brilliant Kenneth Tyran shares it, too bad—to think that an advance in technique and an *avant-garde* idea make a good play. Of course it's fine that people should be breaking rules and throwing things about and being adventurous, but writing's got to be more than that, and the aim higher and surer.

Would you consider Jack Gelber's The Connection *an example of this kind of writing?*

Yes, and I enjoyed it. It's a good show, but it's not a good play—like a fine time at the circus.

How did you feel about Rhinoceros?

Fun for a while, not much more than that.

Why?

One joke. It was brilliantly acted, brilliantly directed, and that's what I found interesting. Ionesco is a charming writer and that would be enough if the pretend-depth wasn't in the way.

Since we're talking about specific writers now, which ones impress you?

I think the only writer of importance to come along in the theatre in the last ten or twelve years is Beckett. For my money he's the only man who should be taken seriously. I don't think he's written great plays, but they're very good.

Which play in particular? Waiting for Godot?

Godot was a charming play, a funny play. *Krapp's Last Tape* is a really moving play. He's good, this Mr. Beckett.

Who do you feel is good among American playwrights?

Williams is good. Or was, and will be again. He's a natural dramatist, knows what he is doing by instinct, and sometimes knows too much. I think he worries about success and failure, understandably; we all do, but he pushes too hard because of it, or is pushed by other people. It takes a long time for all of us to learn that the theatre is a world of fashion, and fashions turn, and I guess you just pray you'll live long enough to see them turn back again. Your job is to pay no attention to them.

Which do you think is his best play?

A Streetcar Named Desire. And I very much liked *27 Wagons Full of Cotton.*

The latter was made into the movie Baby Doll *wasn't it?*

Yes. I didn't like the movie. All decorated and not as funny.

What about Arthur Miller?

Miller is good and I think will be even better as the years go on. He has force and spirit. Too much newspaper stuff and too much writing about writing. But it doesn't matter—he's good.

How about specific plays of his? Death of a Salesman?

I liked it. A remarkable play. I didn't like *The Crucible*—I don't like theme plays—but I thought *A View from the Bridge* was a very good play when I read the script.

Didn't you like the production?

Not much. It was self-conscious. It *told* us what it was about—large theme. Greek columns, and so on. Writers should not *see* their work. Do you know what I'm awkwardly trying to say? Writers shouldn't have anything to do with words like betrayal or courage or bigness or smallness or sex or Greek or new or old. You write it down but you mustn't stand back and see it. You do it and go to bed and leave the big words for other people. I'm not saying any of this very well. But it just isn't your business to tell people what you're doing or wanted to do.

Miller hasn't written a play since A View from the Bridge, *has he?*

No, but that's not necessarily bad. Too often playwrights think if Mr. Smith has a play this year, then they must have a play next year or people will forget them. Competitiveness is an easy disease to catch.

Williams clips off one a year, though.

That's not bad either. You write when you're ready to write. But success should buy the right to take your time.

How do you feel about William Inge?

He's a skillful man. The plays aren't up my alley.

Do you put Paddy Chayefsky in the same group?

The comedy in *The Tenth Man* was very funny. I wish the whole play had been a comedy.

We've talked about Jack Gelber a little. There are a few other young playwrights—Arthur Kopit, Richardson, Albee. Not very many more; this is one of the problems.

Albee is a promising man. I haven't seen Richardson. *Poor Dad* is sometimes brilliant and doesn't come out anywhere. But, you see Beckett's my candidate.

What do you think about Brecht?

Oh, well, now you're in the big league. Wonderful most of the time. I think *The Threepenny Opera* and *Mother Courage* are the great plays of our time.

What about material for the dramatist? In the Thirties and Forties, for instance, there were a lot of political and social-comment plays that don't seem to get written anymore.

Like Clifford Odets' *Waiting for Lefty*, I liked it. Dashiell Hammett and I went to see *Awake and Sing* and we had a fight because I liked it and he didn't. He said it wasn't enough for a writer to have wanted a bicycle when he was young. Maybe he's turned out right. I don't believe in theme plays. I liked Odets best when he wasn't being political.

Your own play, Watch on the Rhine, *was in the political tradition, wasn't it?*

I don't know. I don't think so. I guess I don't think there's any such thing as a really good political play. Good writers have a look at the world around them and then they write it down. That's all.

We've been talking about playwrights up to now. What do you think about the performers today?

I think they're good. There's a very high level of acting now, higher than it used to be.

Do you think that's partially due to the Actors Studio?

I don't know. Maybe. They did good. They also did harm.

It's true, though, that there aren't many people who draw you in just by their names.

There are not as many stage personalities now. Star personalities are rare and nothing substitutes for that mysterious ability to take over a stage. One misses whatever it is that made a W. C. Fields or Fanny Brice or Laurette Taylor.

Ethel Merman still has star quality.

And Kim Stanley and Maureen Stapleton and Nichols and May.

How about Marlon Brando?

Yes. He has it, too. I wish he'd cut out the high jinks and get down to work. There's too little personality on the stage now. But there's too little personality anywhere. The only eccentrics we have have invented themselves and that's no good. We're all so anxious to be charming. Everybody has to be loved by everybody else. We're all so smooth to the touch.

Sometimes you feel that directors want the audience to "like" the play more than anything else. In that connection, I believe directors are having more and more influence on the way a play finally appears before the public. In a sense the director seems to be taking over some of the playwright's duties. Is that true?

Oh, yes. It's common practice now. Writing by democratic-majority vote with the director, producer, friends, cast and all relatives as the Board of Directors. The only time I listened to any army of people—during *Candide*—I went to pieces.

There's a kind of hit psychology behind all that.

Oh, sure, sure. You start to feel that it's all your fault, all that money put up by all those kind strangers. The play opens out of town and you're the guilty one if it gets bad notices and you begin to listen to everybody and then you patch and patch and sometimes it works, but usually it's just a mess. The play possibly started out to say there is no solution for the poor bastards I am writing about, or if there is one I don't know it, but around Boston it is clearly seen that doesn't give what is called audience satisfaction, and so you fix it. That's a very dangerous game to play. Fix it once for the Board of Directors, and you'll possibly do it forever.

Before we leave the subject of direction, what about Elia Kazan? He's had quite a bit of influence on the Broadway Theatre in the past ten or so years.

He's very wise about the theatre—maybe too wise.

You mentioned once you thought Tyrone Guthrie was good.

Oh, yes, very, very good. He knows how to do so many things. And he doesn't do things for money. He does what he likes, and sometimes what he likes isn't very good, but that is the penalty you pay for independence and honesty. I admire him very much.

Now we're getting into the financial aspect of Broadway. Big shows, big producers, theatre parties, big names, big advance sales—sometimes a show is a financial success before it even opens. Aren't these things perpetuating all the troubles of the theatre, putting too high a value on commercial success?

It's not good enough to say that the theatre party is doing harm or the advance sale is doing harm. Maybe they are, but it's only minor harm. The troubles go much deeper.

How would you feel about state aid to the theatre?

I used to think it was the solution. There should be state aid, of course, but I've grown frightened of people who hold the money. Bureaucrats are dangerous in any art, in any land. It would be fine if government would put in the money and then go mind its business. But it won't.

The Off-Broadway movement originally was supposed to be a solution to all Broadway's problems.

Some of Off-Broadway's good. Most of it isn't. But it's nice that it's there—a good sign.

Can you envision a day when there might not be a Broadway theatre?

I think the day may come when there won't be a serious Broadway theatre. We're almost there now. I said before that I think many serious people have lost the habit of going to the theatre. When I was a kid it was fun; I went all the time. The theatre should be, has to be, attractive to the young. It should be better fun, more interesting, than going to see a movie, but I guess it isn't anymore.

Do you think a new playwright today faces problems that didn't exist when you began to write?

Any play now faces serious money-production problems. When I started in the theatre, you knew that you only had a fair chance with a serious play—not a very good chance even then—but a fair chance was good enough, and a run of six or eight months was fine. But now a play couldn't earn back its investment in six months. You have, usually, to be an immediate hit or close. No serious work should be—can be —under such pressure. Bad for everybody and bound to influence everybody.

What do you think would happen if you were a new playwright today and arrived in New York with The Children's Hour, *just as you did in 1934?*

I didn't arrive in New York. We had moved from New Orleans many years before. I was here and young and broke and not minding that much. I don't like cutting up old touches, the past was better than the present, and so on, but there were certain differences. You took for granted then that if you wanted to be a writer, you took your chance, and chance meant that you wouldn't be rich, and maybe not happy, and certainly not secure. You didn't think about jobs, you didn't teach at colleges —maybe because nobody asked you—you just hoped that the novel or story or play would sell and you'd have enough to live on for a few months. You didn't think of yourself in competition with stockbrokers and you rather looked down on people who knew about next week's whiskey. Yes, I think *The Children's Hour* would still get produced. But I'm not so sure the atmosphere wouldn't be clouded now with worry about production costs and failure. I don't think success or failure meant much to me then and, when success came, I gave it four days of fun and then ran away fast, frightened that it would become a way of life. Writers are wacks, aren't they?

*   *   *

The serious theatre can be uncomfortable. How often we go to a play with high expectations which, as the evening wears on, turn into a kind of impatient discomfort. We grow conscious of strains and stresses, and something irritates us although we do not know its name. But sometimes we go to a play and after the curtain has been up five minutes we have a sense of being able to settle back in the arms of the playwright. Instinctively we know that the playwright knows his business. Neatness in design and execution is, after all, only the proper use of material, but it has a beauty of its own. It is exhilarating to watch a good workman at work, to see each detail fall into useful place, to know that the shortest line, the smallest stage movement, has an end in view and is not being used to trick us or deceive or pull fashionable wool over our eyes. It is then that we say to ourselves, this writer knows what he is doing, he has paid us the compliment of learning his trade. To such writers, in whatever field they be, we give our full attention and they deserve it.[1]

---

[1] From Miss Hellman's Introduction to *The Selected Letters of Anton Chekhov* edited by Lillian Hellman and published by Farrar, Straus & Company.

It's fine to have partners who so closely follow the teachings of Christ. (*gets up*) And now I must leave for my train.

REGINA I'm sorry you won't stay over with us, Mr. Marshall, but you'll come again. Any time you like.

BEN (*motions to* LEO, *indicating the bottle*) Fill them up, boy, fill them up. (LEO *moves around filling the glasses as* BEN *speaks*) Down here, sir, we have a strange custom. We drink the *last* drink for a toast. That's to prove that the Southerner is always still on his feet for the last drink. (*picks up his glass*) It was Henry Frick, your Mr. Henry Frick, who said, "Railroads are the Rembrandts of investments." Well, *I* say, "Southern cotton mills *will be* the Rembrandts of investment." So I give you the firm of Hubbard Sons and Marshall, Cotton Mills, and to it a long and prosperous life.

(*They all pick up their glasses.* MARSHALL *looks at them, amused. Then he, too, lifts his glass, smiles*)

OSCAR The children will drive you to the depot. Leo! Alexandra! You will drive Mr. Marshall down.

LEO (*eagerly, looks at* BEN *who nods*) Yes, sir. (*to* MARSHALL) Not often Uncle Ben lets *me* drive the horses. And a beautiful pair they are. (*starts for hall*) Come on, Zan.

ALEXANDRA May I drive tonight, Uncle Ben, please? I'd like to and—

BEN (*shakes his head, laughs*) In your evening clothes? Oh, no, my dear.

ALEXANDRA But Leo always— (*stops, exits quickly*)

REGINA I don't like to say good-bye to you, Mr. Marshall.

MARSHALL Then we won't say good-bye. You have promised that you would come and let me show you Chicago. Do I have to make you promise again?

REGINA (*looks at him as he presses her hand*) I promise again.

MARSHALL (*touches her hand again, then moves to* BIRDIE) Good-bye, Mrs. Hubbard.

BIRDIE (*shyly, with sweetness and dignity*) Good-bye, sir.

MARSHALL (*as he passes* REGINA) Remember.

REGINA I will.

OSCAR We'll see you to the carriage.

(MARSHALL *exits, followed by* BEN *and* OSCAR. *For a second* REGINA *and* BIRDIE *stand looking after them. Then* REGINA *throws up her arms, laughs happily*)

REGINA And there, Birdie, goes the man who has opened the door to our future.

BIRDIE (*surprised at the unaccustomed friendliness*) What?

REGINA (*turning to her*) Our future. Yours and mine, Ben's and Oscar's, the children— (*looks at* BIRDIE's *puzzled face, laughs*) Our future! (*gaily*) You were charming at supper, Birdie. Mr. Marshall certainly thought so.

BIRDIE (*pleased*) Why, Regina! Do you think he did?

REGINA Can't you tell when you're being admired?

BIRDIE Oscar said I bored Mr. Marshall. (*then quietly*) But he admired *you*. He told me so.

REGINA What did he say?

BIRDIE He said to me, "I hope your sister-in-law will come to Chicago. Chicago will be at her feet." He said the ladies would bow to your manners and the gentlemen to your looks.

REGINA Did he? He seems a lonely man. Imagine being lonely with all that money. I don't think he likes his wife.

BIRDIE Not like his wife? What a thing to say.

REGINA She's away a great deal. He said that several times. And once he made fun of her being so social and high-tone. But that fits in all right. (*sits back, arms on back of sofa, stretches*) Her being social, I mean. She can introduce me. It won't take long with an introduction from her.

BIRDIE (*bewildered*) Introduce you? In Chicago? You mean you really might go? Oh, Regina, you can't leave here. What about Horace?

REGINA Don't look so scared about everything, Birdie. I'm going to live in Chicago. I've always wanted to. And now there'll be plenty of money to go with.

BIRDIE But Horace won't be able to move around. You know what the doctor wrote.

REGINA There'll be millions, Birdie, millions. You know what I've always said when people told me we were rich? I said I think you should either be a nigger or a millionaire. In between, like us, what for? (*Laughs. Looks at* BIRDIE) But I'm not going away tomorrow, Birdie. There's plenty of time to worry about Horace when he comes home. If he ever decides to come home.

BIRDIE Will we be going to Chicago? I mean, Oscar and Leo and me?

REGINA You? I shouldn't think so. (*laughs*) Well, we must remember tonight. It's a very important night and we mustn't forget it. We shall plan all the things we'd like to have and then we'll really have them. Make a wish, Birdie, any wish. It's bound to come true now.

(BEN *and* OSCAR *enter*)

BIRDIE (*laughs*) Well. Well, I don't know. Maybe. (REGINA *turns to look at* BEN) Well, I guess I'd know right off what I wanted.

(OSCAR *stands by the upper window, waves to the departing carriage*)

REGINA (*Looks up at* BEN, *smiles. He smiles back at her*) Well, you did it.

BEN Looks like it might be we did.

REGINA (*springs up, laughs*) Looks like it! Don't pretend. You're like a cat who's been licking the cream. (*crosses to wine bottle*) Now we must all have a drink to celebrate.

OSCAR The children, Alexandra and Leo, make a very handsome couple, Regina. Marshall remarked himself what fine young folks they were. How well they looked together!

REGINA (*sharply*) Yes. You said that before, Oscar.

BEN Yes, sir. It's beginning to look as if the deal's all set. I may not be a subtle man— but— (*Turns to them. After a second*) Now somebody ask me how I know the deal is set.

OSCAR What do you mean, Ben?

BEN You remember I told him that down here we drink the *last* drink for a toast?

OSCAR (*thoughtfully*) Yes, I never heard that before.

BEN Nobody's ever heard it before. God forgives those who invent what they need. I already had his signature. But we've all done business with men whose word over a glass is better than a bond. Anyway it don't hurt to have both.

OSCAR (*turns to* REGINA) You understand what Ben means?

REGINA (*smiles*) Yes, Oscar. I understand. I understood immediately.

BEN (*looks at her admiringly*) Did you, Regina? Well, when he lifted his glass to drink, I closed my eyes and saw the bricks going into place.

REGINA And *I* saw a lot more than that.

BEN Slowly, slowly. As yet we have only our hopes.

REGINA Birdie and I have just been planning what we want. I know what I want. What will you want, Ben?

BEN Caution. Don't count the chickens. (*leans back, laughs*) Well, God would allow us a little daydreaming. Good for the soul when you've worked hard enough to deserve it. (*pauses*) I think I'll have a stable. For a long time I've had my good eyes on Carter's in Savannah. A rich man's pleasure, the sport of kings, why not the sport of Hubbards? Why not?

REGINA (*smiles*) Why not? What will you have, Oscar?

OSCAR I don't know. (*thoughtfully*) The pleasure of seeing the bricks grow will be enough for me.

BEN Oh, of course. Our *greatest* pleasure will be to see the bricks grow. But we are all entitled to a little side indulgence.

OSCAR Yes, I suppose so. Well, then, I think we might take a few trips here and there, eh, Birdie?

BIRDIE (*surprised at being consulted*) Yes, Oscar. I'd like that.

OSCAR We might even make a regular trip to Jekyll Island. I've heard the Cornelly place is for sale. We might think about buying it. Make a nice change. Do you good, Birdie, a change of climate. Fine shooting on Jekyll, the best.

BIRDIE I'd like—

OSCAR (*indulgently*) What would you like?

BIRDIE *Two* things. Two things I'd like most.

REGINA Two! I should like a thousand. You are modest, Birdie.

BIRDIE (*warmly, delighted with the unexpected interest*) I should like to have Lionnet back. I know you own it now, but I'd like to see it fixed up again, the way Mama and Papa had it. Every year it used to get a nice coat of paint—Papa was very particular about the paint—and the lawn was so smooth all the way down to the river, with the trims of zinnias and red-feather plush. And the figs and blue little plums and the scuppernongs— (*Smiles. Turns to* REGINA) The organ is still there and it wouldn't cost much to fix. We could have parties for Zan, the way Mama used to have for me.

BEN That's a pretty picture, Birdie. Might be a most pleasant way to live. (*dismissing* BIRDIE) What do you want, Regina?

BIRDIE (*very happily, not noticing that they are no longer listening to her*) I could have a cutting garden. Just where Mama's used to be. Oh, I do think we could be happier there. Papa used to say that *nobody* had ever lost their temper at Lionnet, and *nobody* ever would. Papa would never let anybody be nasty-spoken or mean. No, sir. He just didn't like it.

BEN What do you want, Regina?

REGINA I'm going to Chicago. And when I'm settled there and know the right people and the right things to buy—because I certainly don't now—I shall go to Paris and buy them. (*laughs*) I'm going to leave you and Oscar to count the bricks.

BIRDIE   Oscar. Please let me have Lionnet back.

OSCAR (*to* REGINA)   You are serious about moving to Chicago?

BEN   She is going to see the great world and leave us in the little one. Well, we'll come and visit you and meet all the great and be proud to think you are our sister.

REGINA (*gaily*)   Certainly. And you won't even have to learn to be subtle, Ben. Stay as you are. You will be rich and the rich don't have to be subtle.

OSCAR   But what about Alexandra? She's seventeen. Old enough to be thinking about marrying.

BIRDIE   And, Oscar, I have one more wish. Just one more wish.

OSCAR (*turns*)   What is it, Birdie? What are you saying?

BIRDIE   I want you to stop shooting. I mean, so much. I don't like to see animals and birds killed just for the killing. You only throw them away—

BEN (*to* REGINA)   It'll take a great deal of money to live as you're planning, Regina.

REGINA   Certainly. But there'll be plenty of money. You have estimated the profits very high.

BEN   I have—

BIRDIE (OSCAR *is looking at her furiously*) And you never let anybody else shoot, and the niggers need it so much to keep from starving. It's wicked to shoot food just because you like to shoot, when poor people need it so—

BEN (*laughs*)   I have estimated the profits very high—for myself.

REGINA   What did you say?

BIRDIE   I've always wanted to speak about it, Oscar.

OSCAR (*slowly, carefully*)   What are you chattering about?

BIRDIE (*nervously*)   I was talking about Lionnet and—and about your shooting—

OSCAR   You are exciting yourself.

REGINA (*to* BEN)   I didn't hear you. There was so much talking.

OSCAR (*to* BIRDIE)   You have been acting very childish, very excited, all evening.

BIRDIE   Regina asked me what I'd like.

REGINA   What did you say, Ben?

BIRDIE   Now that we'll be so rich everybody was saying what they would like, so *I* said what *I* would like, too.

BEN   I said— (*He is interrupted by* OSCAR)

OSCAR (*to* BIRDIE)   Very well. We've all heard you. That's enough now.

BEN   I am waiting. (*They stop*) I am waiting for you to finish. You and Birdie. Four

conversations are three too many. (BIRDIE *slowly sits down.* BEN *smiles, to* REGINA) I said that I had, and I do, estimate the profits very high—for myself, and Oscar, of course.

REGINA (*slowly*)   And what does that mean? (BEN *shrugs, looks towards* OSCAR)

OSCAR (*looks at* BEN, *clears throat*)   Well, Regina, it's like this. For forty-nine per cent Marshall will put up four hundred thousand dollars. For fifty-one per cent— (*smiles archly*) a controlling interest, mind you, we will put up two hundred and twenty-five thousand dollars besides offering him certain benefits that our (*looks at* BEN) local position allows us to manage. Ben means that two hundred and twenty-five thousand dollars is a lot of money.

REGINA   I know the terms and I know it's a lot of money.

BEN (*nodding*)   It is.

OSCAR   Ben means that we are ready with our two-thirds of the money. Your third, Horace's I mean, doesn't seem to be ready. (*raises his hand as* REGINA *starts to speak*) Ben has written to Horace, I have written, and you have written. He answers. But he never mentions this business. Yet we have explained it to him in great detail, and told him the urgency. Still he never mentions it. Ben has been very patient, Regina. Naturally, you are our sister and we want you to benefit from anything we do.

REGINA   And in addition to your concern for me, you do not want control to go out of the family. (*to* BEN) That right, Ben?

BEN   That's cynical. (*smiles*) Cynicism is an unpleasant way of saying the truth.

OSCAR   No need to be cynical. We'd have no trouble raising the third share, the share that you want to take.

REGINA   I am sure you could get the third share, the share you were saving for me. But that would give you a strange partner. And strange partners sometimes want a great deal. (*smiles unpleasantly*) But perhaps it would be wise for you to find him.

OSCAR   Now, now. Nobody says we *want* to do that. We would like to have you in and you would like to come in.

REGINA   Yes. I certainly would.

BEN (*laughs, puts up his hand*)   But we haven't heard from Horace.

REGINA   I've given my word that Horace will put up the money. That should be enough.

BEN   Oh, it was enough. I took your word. But I've got to have more than your word now. The contracts will be signed this week, and

Marshall will want to see our money soon after. Regina, Horace has been in Baltimore for five months. I know that you've writen him to come home, and that he hasn't come.

OSCAR   It's beginning to look as if he doesn't want to come home.

REGINA   Of course he wants to come home. You can't move around with heart trouble at any moment you choose. You know what doctors are like once they get their hands on a case like this—

OSCAR   They can't very well keep him from answering letters, can they? (REGINA *turns to* BEN) They couldn't keep him from arranging for the money if he wanted to—

REGINA   Has it occurred to you that Horace is also a good business man?

BEN   Certainly. He is a shrewd trader. Always has been. The bank is proof of that.

REGINA   Then, possibly, he may be keeping silent because he doesn't think he is getting enough for his money. (*looks at* OSCAR) Seventy-five thousand he has to put up. That's a lot of money, too.

OSCAR   Nonsense. He knows a good thing when he hears it. He knows that we can make *twice* the profit on cotton goods manufactured *here* than can be made in the North.

BEN   That isn't what Regina means. (*smiles*) May I interpret you, Regina? (*to* OSCAR) Regina is saying that Horace wants *more* than a third of our share.

OSCAR   But he's only putting up a third of the money. You put up a third and you get a third. What else *could* he expect?

REGINA   Well, *I* don't know. I don't know about these things. It would seem that if you put up a third you should only get a third. But then again, there's no law about it, is there? I should think that if you knew your money was very badly needed, well, you just might say, I want more, I want a bigger share. You boys have done that. I've heard you say so.

BEN   (*after a pause, laughs*)   So you believe he has deliberately held out? For a larger share? (*leaning forward*) Well, I *don't* believe it. But I *do* believe that's what *you* want. Am I right, Regina?

REGINA   Oh, I shouldn't like to be too definite. But I *could* say that I wouldn't like to persuade Horace unless he did get a larger share. I must look after his interests. It seems only natural—

OSCAR   And where would the larger share come from?

REGINA   I don't know. That's not my business. (*giggles*) But perhaps it could come off your share, Oscar.

(REGINA *and* BEN *laugh*)

OSCAR   (*rises and wheels furiously on both of them as they laugh*)   What kind of talk is this?

BEN   I haven't said a thing.

OSCAR   (*to* REGINA)   *You* are talking very big tonight.

REGINA   (*stops laughing*)   Am I? Well, you should know me well enough to know that I wouldn't be asking for things I didn't think I could get.

OSCAR   Listen. I don't believe you can even get Horace to come home, much less get money from him or talk quite so big about what you want.

REGINA   Oh, I can get him home.

OSCAR   Then why haven't you?

REGINA   I thought I should fight his battles for him, before he came home. Horace is a very sick man. And even if *you* don't care how sick he is, I do.

BEN   Stop this foolish squabbling. How can you get him home?

REGINA   I will send Alexandra to Baltimore. She will ask him to come home. She will say that she *wants* him to come home, and that *I* want him to come home.

BIRDIE   (*suddenly*)   Well, of course she wants him here, but he's sick and maybe he's happy where he is.

REGINA   (*ignores* BIRDIE, *to* BEN)   You agree that he will come home if she asks him to, if she says that I miss him and want him—

BEN   (*looks at her, smiles*)   I admire you, Regina. And I agree. That's settled now and— (*starts to rise*)

REGINA   (*quickly*)   But before she brings him home, I want to know what he's going to get.

BEN   What do you want?

REGINA   Twice what you offered.

BEN   Well, you won't get it.

OSCAR   (*to* REGINA)   I think you've gone crazy.

REGINA   I don't want to fight, Ben—

BEN   I don't either. You won't get it. There isn't any chance of that. (*roguishly*) You're holding us up, and that's not pretty, Regina, not pretty. (*holds up his hand as he sees she is about to speak*) But we need you, and I don't want to fight. Here's what I'll do: I'll give Horace forty per cent, instead of the thirty-three and a third he really should get. I'll do that, provided he is home and his money is up within two weeks. How's that?

REGINA   All right.

OSCAR   I've asked before: where is this extra share coming from?

BEN (*pleasantly*) From you. From your share.

OSCAR (*furiously*) From me, is it? That's just fine and dandy. That's my reward. For thirty-five years I've worked my hands to the bone for you. For thirty-five years I've done all the things you didn't want to do. And this is what I—

BEN (*turns slowly to look at* OSCAR. OSCAR *breaks off*) My, my. I am being attacked to-night on all sides. First by my sister, then by my brother. And I ain't a man who likes being attacked. I can't believe that God wants the strong to parade their strength, but I don't mind doing it if it's got to be done. (*leans back in his chair*) You ought to take these things better, Oscar. I've made you money in the past. I'm going to make you more money now. You'll be a very rich man. What's the difference to any of us if a little more goes here, a little less goes there—it's all in the family. And it will stay in the family. I'll never marry. (ADDIE *enters, begins to gather the glasses from the table.* OSCAR *turns to* BEN) So my money will go to Alexandra and Leo. They may even marry some day and— (ADDIE *looks at* BEN)

BIRDIE (*rising*) Marry—Zan and Leo—

OSCAR (*carefully*) That would make a great difference in my feelings. If they married.

BEN Yes, that's what I mean. Of course it would make a difference.

OSCAR (*carefully*) Is that what *you* mean, Regina?

REGINA Oh, it's too far away. We'll talk about it in a few years.

OSCAR I want to talk about it now.

BEN (*nods*) Naturally.

REGINA There's a lot of things to consider. They are first cousins, and—

OSCAR That isn't unusual. Our grandmother and grandfather were first cousins.

REGINA (*giggles*) And look at us.

(BEN *giggles*)

OSCAR (*angrily*) You're both being very gay with my money.

BEN (*sighs*) These quarrels. I dislike them so. (*leans forward to* REGINA) A marriage might be a very wise arrangement, for several reasons. And then, Oscar has given up some-thing for you. You should try to manage some-thing for him.

REGINA I haven't said I was opposed to it. But Leo is a wild boy. There were those times when he took a little money from the bank and—

OSCAR That's all past history—

REGINA Oh, I know. And I know all young men are wild. I'm only mentioning it to show you that there are considerations—

BEN (*irritated because she does not under-stand that he is trying to keep* OSCAR *quiet*) All right, so there are. But please assure Oscar that you will think about it very seriously.

REGINA (*smiles, nods*) Very well. I assure Oscar that I will think about it seriously.

OSCAR (*sharply*) That is not an answer.

REGINA (*rises*) My, you're in a bad humor and you shall put me in one. I have said all that I am willing to say now. After all, Horace has to give his consent, too.

OSCAR Horace will do what you tell him to.

REGINA Yes, I think he will.

OSCAR And I have your word that you will try to—

REGINA (*patiently*) Yes, Oscar. You have my word that I will think about it. Now do leave me alone.

(*There is the sound of the front door being closed*)

BIRDIE I—Alexandra is only seventeen. She—

REGINA (*calling*) Alexandra? Are you back?

ALEXANDRA Yes, Mama.

LEO (*comes into the room*) Mr. Marshall got off safe and sound. Weren't those fine clothes he had? You can always spot clothes made in a good place. Looks like maybe they were done in England. Lots of men in the North send all the way to England for their stuff.

BEN (*to* LEO) Were you careful driving the horses?

LEO Oh, yes, sir. I was.

(ALEXANDRA *has come in on* BEN's *question, hears the answer, looks angrily at* LEO)

ALEXANDRA It's a lovely night. You should have come, Aunt Birdie.

REGINA Were you gracious to Mr. Marshall?

ALEXANDRA I think so, Mama. I liked him.

REGINA Good. And now I have great news for you. You are going to Baltimore in the morning to bring your father home.

ALEXANDRA (*gasps, then delighted*) Me? Papa said I should come? That must mean— (*turns to* ADDIE) Addie, he must be well. Think of it, he'll be back home again. We'll bring him home.

REGINA You are going alone, Alexandra.

ADDIE (ALEXANDRA *has turned in surprise*) Going alone? Going by herself? A child that age! Mr. Horace ain't going to like Zan traipsing up there by herself.

REGINA (*sharply*) Go upstairs and lay out Alexandra's things.

ADDIE He'd expect me to be along—

REGINA I'll be up in a few minutes to tell you what to pack. (ADDIE *slowly begins to climb the steps. To* ALEXANDRA) I should think you'd like going alone. At your age it certainly would have delighted me. You're a strange girl, Alexandra. Addie has babied you so much.

ALEXANDRA I only thought it would be more fun if Addie and I went together.

BIRDIE (*timidly*) Maybe I could go with her, Regina. I'd really like to.

REGINA She is going alone. She is getting old enough to take some responsibilities.

OSCAR She'd better learn now. She's almost old enough to get married. (*jovially, to* LEO, *slapping him on shoulder*) Eh, son?

LEO Huh?

OSCAR (*annoyed with* LEO *for not understanding*) Old enough to get married, you're thinking, eh?

LEO Oh, yes, sir. (*feebly*) Lots of girls get married at Zan's age. Look at Mary Prester and Johanna and—

REGINA Well, she's not getting married tomorrow. But she is going to Baltimore tomorrow, so let's talk about that. (*to* ALEXANDRA) You'll be glad to have Papa home again.

ALEXANDRA I wanted to go before, Mama. You remember that. But you said *you* couldn't go, and that *I* couldn't go alone.

REGINA I've changed my mind. (*too casually*) You're to tell Papa how much you missed him, and that he must come home now —for your sake. Tell him that you *need* him home.

ALEXANDRA Need him home? I don't understand.

REGINA There is nothing for you to understand. You are simply to say what I have told you.

BIRDIE (*rises*) He may be too sick. She couldn't do that—

ALEXANDRA Yes. He may be too sick to travel. I couldn't make him think he had to come home for me, if he is too sick to—

REGINA (*looks at her, sharply, challengingly*) You *couldn't* do what I tell you to do, Alexandra?

ALEXANDRA No. I couldn't. If I thought it would hurt him.

REGINA (*after a second's silence, smiles pleasantly*) But you are doing this for Papa's own good. (*takes* ALEXANDRA's *hand*) You must let me be the judge of his condition. It's the best possible cure for him to come home and be taken care of here. He mustn't stay there any longer and listen to those alarmist doctors. You are doing this entirely for his sake.

Tell your Papa that I want him to come home, that I miss him very much.

ALEXANDRA (*slowly*) Yes, Mama.

REGINA (*to the others. Rises*) I must go and start getting Alexandra ready now. Why don't you all go home?

BEN (*rises*) I'll attend to the railroad ticket. One of the boys will bring it over. Good night, everybody. Have a nice trip, Alexandra. The food on the train is very good. The celery is so crisp. Have a good time and act like a little lady. (*exits*)

REGINA Good night, Ben. Good night, Oscar— (*playfully*) Don't be so glum, Oscar. It makes you look as if you had chronic indigestion.

BIRDIE Good night, Regina.

REGINA Good night, Birdie. (*exits upstairs*)

OSCAR (*starts for hall*) Come along.

LEO (*to* ALEXANDRA) Imagine your not wanting to go! What a little fool you are. Wish it were me. What I could do in a place like Baltimore!

ALEXANDRA (*angrily, looking away from him*) Mind your business. I can guess the kind of things *you* could do.

LEO (*laughs*) Oh no, you couldn't. (*He exits*)

REGINA (*calling from the top of the stairs*) Come on, Alexandra.

BIRDIE (*quickly, softly*) Zan.

ALEXANDRA I don't understand about my going, Aunt Birdie. (*shrugs*) But anyway, Papa will be home again. (*pats* BIRDIE's *arm*) Don't worry about me. I can take care of myself. Really I can.

BIRDIE (*shakes her head, softly*) That's not what I'm worried about. Zan—

ALEXANDRA (*comes close to her*) What's the matter?

BIRDIE It's about Leo—

ALEXANDRA (*whispering*) He beat the horses. That's why we were late getting back. We had to wait until they cooled off. He always beats the horses as if—

BIRDIE (*whispering frantically, holding* ALEXANDRA's *hands*) He's my son. My own son. But you are more to me—more to me than my own child. I love you more than anybody else—

ALEXANDRA Don't worry about the horses. I'm sorry I told you.

BIRDIE (*her voice rising*) I am not worrying about the horses. I am worrying about *you*. You are *not* going to marry Leo. I am not going to let them do that to you—

ALEXANDRA Marry? To Leo? (*laughs*) I

wouldn't marry, Aunt Birdie. I've never even thought about it—

BIRDIE But they have thought about it. (*wildly*) Zan, I couldn't stand to think about such a thing. You and—

(OSCAR *has come into the doorway on* ALEXANDRA'S *speech. He is standing quietly, listening*)

ALEXANDRA (*laughs*) But I'm not going to marry. And I'm certainly not going to marry Leo.

BIRDIE Don't you understand? They'll make you. They'll make you—

ALEXANDRA (*takes* BIRDIE'S *hands, quietly, firmly*) That's foolish, Aunt Birdie. I'm grown now. Nobody can make me do anything.

BIRDIE I just couldn't stand—

OSCAR (*sharply*) Birdie. (BIRDIE *looks up, draws quickly away from* ALEXANDRA. *She stands rigid, frightened. Quietly*) Birdie, get your hat and coat.

ADDIE (*calls from upstairs*) Come on, baby. Your Mama's waiting for you, and she ain't nobody to keep waiting.

ALEXANDRA All right. (*then softly, embracing* BIRDIE) Good night, Aunt Birdie. (*as she passes* OSCAR) Good night, Uncle Oscar. (BIRDIE *begins to move slowly towards the door as* ALEXANDRA *climbs the stairs.* ALEXANDRA *is almost out of view when* BIRDIE *reaches* OSCAR *in the doorway. As* BIRDIE *quickly attempts to pass him, he slaps her hard, across the face.* BIRDIE *cries out, puts her hand to her face. On the cry,* ALEXANDRA *turns, begins to run down the stairs*) Aunt Birdie! What happened? What happened? I—

BIRDIE (*softly, without turning*) Nothing happened. (*quickly, as if anxious to keep* ALEXANDRA *from coming close*) Now go to bed. (OSCAR *exits*) Nothing happened. (*turns to* ALEXANDRA *who is holding her hand*) I only— I only twisted my ankle. (*She goes out.* ALEXANDRA *stands on the stairs looking after her as if she were puzzled and frightened*)

ACT TWO

(SCENE *Same as Act One. A week later, morning.*

AT RISE *The light comes from the open shutter of the right window; the other shutters are tightly closed.* ADDIE *is standing at the window, looking out. Near the dining-room doors are brooms, mops, rags, etc. After a second,* OSCAR *comes into the entrance hall, looks in the room, shivers, decides not to take his hat and coat off, comes into the room. At the sound of the door,* ADDIE *turns to see who has come in*)

ADDIE (*without interest*) Oh, it's you, Mr. Oscar.

OSCAR What is this? It's not night. What's the matter here? (*shivers*) Fine thing at this time of the morning. Blinds all closed. (ADDIE *begins to open shutters*) Where's Miss Regina? It's cold in here.

ADDIE Miss Regina ain't down yet.

OSCAR She had any word?

ADDIE (*wearily*) No, sir.

OSCAR Wouldn't you think a girl that age could get on a train at one place and have sense enough to get off at another?

ADDIE Something must have happened. If Zan say she was coming last night, she's coming last night. Unless something happened. Sure fire disgrace to let a baby like that go all that way alone to bring home a sick man without—

OSCAR You do a lot of judging around here, Addie, eh? Judging of your white folks, I mean.

ADDIE (*looks at him, sighs*) I'm tired. I been up all night watching for them.

REGINA (*speaking from the upstairs hall*) Who's downstairs, Addie? (*She appears in a dressing gown, peers down from the landing.* ADDIE *picks up broom, dustpan and brush and exits*) Oh, it's you, Oscar. What are you doing here so early? I haven't been down yet. I'm not finished dressing.

OSCAR (*speaking up to her*) You had any word from them?

REGINA No.

OSCAR Then something certainly has happened. People don't just say they are arriving on Thursday night, and they haven't come by Friday morning.

REGINA Oh, nothing's happened. Alexandra just hasn't got sense enough to send a message.

OSCAR If nothing's happened, then why aren't they here?

REGINA You asked me that ten times last night. My, you do fret so, Oscar. Anything might have happened. They may have missed connections in Atlanta, the train may have been delayed—oh, a hundred things could have kept them.

OSCAR Where's Ben?

REGINA (*as she disappears upstairs*) Where should he be? At home, probably. Really, Oscar, I don't tuck him in his bed and I don't take him out of it. Have some coffee and don't worry so much.

OSCAR Have some coffee? There isn't any coffee. (*Looks at his watch, shakes his head. After a second,* CAL *enters with a large silver tray, coffee urn, small cups, newspaper*) Oh, there you are. Is everything in this fancy house always late?

CAL (*looks at him surprised*) You ain't out shooting this morning, Mr. Oscar?

OSCAR First day I missed since I had my head cold. First day I missed in eight years.

CAL Yes, sir. I bet you. Simon he say you had a mighty good day yesterday morning. That's what Simon say. (*brings* OSCAR *coffee and newspaper*)

OSCAR Pretty good, pretty good.

CAL (*laughs, slyly*) Bet you got enough bobwhite and squirrel to give every nigger in town a Jesus-party. Most of 'em ain't had no meat since the cotton picking was over. Bet they'd give anything for a little piece of that meat—

OSCAR (*turns his head to look at* CAL) Cal, If I catch a nigger in this town going shooting, you know what's going to happen.

(LEO *enters*)

CAL (*hastily*) Yes, sir, Mr. Oscar. I didn't say nothing about nothing. It was Simon who told me and—Morning, Mr. Leo. You gentlemen having your breakfast with us here?

LEO The boys in the bank don't know a thing. They haven't had any message.

(CAL *waits for an answer, gets none, shrugs, moves to door, exits*)

OSCAR (*peers at* LEO) What you doing here, son?

LEO You told me to find out if the boys at the bank had any message from Uncle Horace or Zan—

OSCAR I told you if they had a message to bring it here. I told you that if they didn't have a message to stay at the bank and do your work.

LEO Oh, I guess I misunderstood.

OSCAR You didn't misunderstand. You just were looking for any excuse to take an hour off. (LEO *pours a coup of coffee*) You got to stop that kind of thing. You got to start settling down. You going to be a married man one of these days.

LEO Yes, sir.

OSCAR You also got to stop with that woman in Mobile. (*as* LEO *is about to speak*) You're young and I haven't got no objections to outside women. That is, I haven't got no objections so long as they don't interfere with serious things. Outside women are all right in their place, but *now* isn't their place. You got to realize that.

LEO (*nods*) Yes, sir. I'll tell her. She'll act all right about it.

OSCAR Also, you got to start working harder at the bank. You got to convince your Uncle Horace you going to make a fit husband for Alexandra.

LEO What do you think has happened to them? Supposed to be here last night—(*laughs*) Bet you Uncle Ben's mighty worried. Seventy-five thousand dollars worried.

OSCAR (*smiles happily*) Ought to be worried. Damn well ought to be. First he don't answer the letters, then he don't come home—(*giggles*)

LEO What will happen if Uncle Horace don't come home or don't—

OSCAR Or don't put up the money? Oh, we'll get it from outside. Easy enough.

LEO (*surprised*) But *you* don't want outsiders.

OSCAR What do I care who gets my share? I been shaved already. Serve Ben right if he had to give away some of his.

LEO Damn shame what they did to you.

OSCAR (*looking up the stairs*) Don't talk so loud. Don't you worry. When I die, you'll have as much as the rest. You might have yours *and* Alexandra's. I'm not so easily licked.

LEO I wasn't thinking of myself, Papa—

OSCAR Well, you should be, you should be. It's every man's duty to think of himself.

LEO You think Uncle Horace don't want to go in on this?

OSCAR (*giggles*) That's my hunch. He hasn't showed any signs of loving it yet.

LEO (*laughs*) But he hasn't listened to Aunt Regina yet, either. Oh, he'll go along. It's too good a thing. Why wouldn't he want to? He's got plenty and plenty to invest with. He don't even have to sell anything. Eighty-eight thousand worth of Union Pacific bonds sitting right in his safe deposit box. All he's got to do is open the box.

OSCAR (*after a pause. Looks at his watch*) Mighty late breakfast in this fancy house. Yes, he's had those bonds for fifteen years. Bought them when they were low and just locked them up.

LEO Yeah. Just has to open the box and take them out. That's all. Easy as easy can be. (*laughs*) The things in that box! There's all those bonds, looking mighty fine. (OSCAR *slowly puts down his newspaper and turns to* LEO) Then right next to them is a baby shoe of Zan's and a cheap old cameo on a string, and, *and*—nobody'd believe this—a piece of an old violin. Not even a whole violin. Just a piece of an old thing, a piece of a violin.

OSCAR (*very softly, as if he were trying to control his voice*) A piece of a violin! What do you think of that!

LEO Yes, sirree. A lot of other crazy things, too. A poem, I guess it is, signed with his mother's name, and two old schoolbooks with notes and— (LEO *catches* OSCAR'*s look. His voice trails off. He turns his head away*)

OSCAR (*very softly*) How do you know what's in the box, son?

LEO (*stops, draws back, frightened, realizing what he has said*) Oh, well. Well, er. Well, one of the boys, sir. It was one of the boys at the bank. He took old Manders' keys. It was Joe Horns. He just up and took Manders' keys and, and—well, took the box out. (*quickly*) Then they all asked me if I wanted to see, too. So I looked a little, I guess, but then I made them close up the box quick and I told them never—

OSCAR (*looks at him*) Joe Horns, you say? He opened it?

LEO Yes, sir, yes, he did. My word of honor. (*very nervously looking away*) I suppose that don't excuse *me* for looking— (*looking at* OSCAR) but I did make him close it up and put the keys back in Manders' drawer—

OSCAR (*leans forward, very softly*) Tell me the truth, Leo. I am not going to be angry with you. Did you open the box yourself?

LEO *No, sir, I didn't.* I told you I didn't. No, I—

OSCAR (*irritated, patient*) I am *not* going to be angry with you. (*watching* LEO *carefully*) Sometimes a young fellow deserves credit for looking round him to see what's going on. Sometimes that's a good sign in a fellow your age. (OSCAR *rises*) Many great men have made their fortune with their eyes. Did you open the box?

LEO (*very puzzled*) No. I—

OSCAR (*moves to* LEO) Did you open the box? It may have been—well, it may have been a good thing if you had.

LEO (*after a long pause*) I opened it.

OSCAR (*quickly*) Is that the truth? (LEO *nods*) Does anybody else know that you opened it? Come, Leo, don't be afraid of speaking the truth to me.

LEO No. Nobody knew. Nobody was in the bank when I did it. But—

OSCAR Did your Uncle Horace ever know you opened it?

LEO (*shakes his head*) He only looks in it once every six months when he cuts the coupons, and sometimes Manders even does that for him. Uncle Horace don't even have the keys. Manders keeps them for him. Imagine not looking at all that. You can bet if I had the bonds, I'd watch 'em like—

OSCAR If you had them. (LEO *watches him*) *If* you had them. Then you could have a share in the mill, you and me. A fine, big share, too. (*pauses, shrugs*) Well, a man can't be shot for wanting to see his son get on in the world, can he, boy?

LEO (*looks up, begins to understand*) No, he can't. Natural enough. (*laughs*) But I haven't got the bonds and Uncle Horace has. And now he can just sit back and wait to be a millionaire.

OSCAR (*innocently*) You think your Uncle Horace likes you well enough to lend you the bonds if he decides not to use them himself?

LEO Papa, it must be that you haven't had your breakfast! (*laughs loudly*) Lend me the bonds! My God—

OSCAR (*disappointed*) No, I suppose not. Just a fancy of mine. A loan for three months, maybe four, easy enough for us to pay it back then. Anyway, this is only April— (*slowly counting the months on his fingers*) and if he doesn't look at them until Fall, he wouldn't even miss them out of the box.

LEO That's it. He wouldn't even miss them. Ah, well—

OSCAR No, sir. Wouldn't even miss them. How could he miss them if he never looks at them? (*sighs as* LEO *stares at him*) Well, here we are sitting around waiting for him to come home and invest his money in something he hasn't lifted his hand to get. But I can't help thinking he's acting strange. You laugh when I say he could lend you the bonds if he's not going to use them himself. But would it hurt him?

LEO (*slowly looking at* OSCAR) No. No, it wouldn't.

OSCAR People ought to help other people. But that's not always the way it happens. (BEN *enters, hangs his coat and hat in hall. Very carefully*) And so sometimes you got to think of yourself. (*As* LEO *stares at him,* BEN *appears in the doorway*) Morning, Ben.

BEN (*coming in, carrying his newspaper*) Fine sunny morning. Any news from the runaways?

REGINA (*on the staircase*) There's no news or you would have heard it. Quite a convention so early in the morning, aren't you all? (*goes to coffee urn*)

OSCAR   You rising mighty late these days. Is that the way they do things in Chicago society?

BEN (*looking at his paper*)   Old Carter died up in Senateville. Eighty-one is a good time for us all, eh? What do you think has really happened to Horace, Regina?

REGINA   Nothing.

BEN (*too casually*)   You don't think maybe he never started from Baltimore and never intends to start?

REGINA (*irritated*)   Of course they've started. Didn't I have a letter from Alexandra? What is so strange about people arriving late? He has that cousin in Savannah he's so fond of. He may have stopped to see him. They'll be along today some time, very flattered that you and Oscar are so worried about them.

BEN   I'm a natural worrier. Especially when I am getting ready to close a business deal and one of my partners remains silent *and* invisible.

REGINA (*laughs*)   Oh, is that it? I thought you were worried about Horace's health.

OSCAR   Oh, that too. Who could help but worry? I'm worried. This is the first day I haven't shot since my head cold.

REGINA (*starts towards dining room*)   Then you haven't had your breakfast. Come along. (OSCAR *and* LEO *follow her*)

BEN   Regina. (*She turns at dining-room door*) That cousin of Horace's has been dead for years and, in any case, the train does not go through Savannah.

REGINA (*laughs, continues into dining room, seats herself*)   Did he die? You're always remembering about people dying. (BEN *rises*) Now I intend to eat my breakfast in peace, and read my newspaper.

BEN (*goes towards dining room as he talks*)   This is second breakfast for me. My first was bad. Celia ain't the cook she used to be. Too old to have taste any more. If she hadn't belonged to Mama, I'd send her off to the country.

(OSCAR *and* LEO *start to eat.* BEN *seats himself*)

LEO   Uncle Horace will have some tales to tell, I bet. Baltimore is a lively town.

REGINA (*to* CAL)   The grits isn't hot enough. Take it back.

CAL   Oh, yes'm. (*calling into kitchen as he exits*) Grits didn't hold the heat. Grits didn't hold the heat.

LEO   When I was at school three of the boys and myself took a train once and went over to Baltimore. It was so big we thought we were in Europe. I was just a kid then—

REGINA   I find it very pleasant (ADDIE *enters*) to have breakfast alone. I hate chatter-ing before I've had something hot. (CAL *closes the dining-room doors*) Do be still, Leo.

(ADDIE *comes into the room, begins gathering up the cups, carries them to the large tray. Outside there are the sounds of voices. Quickly* ADDIE *runs into the hall. A few seconds later she appears again in the doorway, her arm around the shoulders of* HORACE GIDDENS, *supporting him.* HORACE *is a tall man of about forty-five. He has been good looking, but now his face is tired and ill. He walks stiffly, as if it were an enormous effort, and carefully, as if he were unsure of his balance.* ADDIE *takes off his overcoat and hangs it on the hall tree. She then helps him to a chair*)

HORACE   How are you, Addie? How have you been?

ADDIE   I'm all right, Mr. Horace. I've just been worried about you.

(ALEXANDRA *enters. She is flushed and excited, her hat awry, her face dirty. Her arms are full of packages, but she comes quickly to* ADDIE)

ALEXANDRA   Now don't tell me how worried you were. We couldn't help it and there was no way to send a message.

ADDIE (*begins to take packages from* ALEXANDRA)   Yes, sir, I was mighty worried.

ALEXANDRA   We had to stop in Mobile over night. Papa— (*looks at him*) Papa didn't feel well. The trip was too much for him, and I made him stop and rest— (*as* ADDIE *takes the last package*) No, don't take that. That's father's medicine. I'll hold it. It mustn't break. Now, about the stuff outside. Papa must have his wheel chair. I'll get that and the valises—

ADDIE (*very happy, holding* ALEXANDRA'S *arms*)   Since when you got to carry your own valises? Since when I ain't old enough to hold a bottle of medicine? (HORACE *coughs*) You feel all right, Mr. Horace?

HORACE (*nods*)   Glad to be sitting down.

ALEXANDRA (*opening package of medicine*)   He doesn't feel all right. (ADDIE *looks at her, then at* HORACE)   He just says that. The trip was very hard on him, and now he must go right to bed.

ADDIE (*looking at him carefully*)   Them fancy doctors, they give you help?

HORACE   They did their best.

ALEXANDRA (*has become conscious of the voices in the dining room*)   I bet Mama was worried. I better tell her we're here now. (*She starts for door*)

HORACE   Zan. (*She stops*) Not for a minute, dear.

ALEXANDRA   Oh, Papa, you feel bad again. I knew you did. Do you want your medicine?

HORACE   No, I don't feel that way. I'm just tired, darling. Let me rest a little.

ALEXANDRA   Yes, but Mama will be mad if I don't tell her we're here.

ADDIE   They're all in there eating breakfast.

ALEXANDRA   Oh, are they all here? Why do they *always* have to be here? I was hoping Papa wouldn't have to see anybody, that it would be nice for him and quiet.

ADDIE   Then let your papa rest for a minute.

HORACE   Addie, I bet your coffee's as good as ever. They don't have such good coffee up North. (*looks at the urn*) Is it as good, Addie? (ADDIE *starts for coffee urn*)

ALEXANDRA   No. Dr. Reeves said not much coffee. Just now and then. I'm the nurse now, Addie.

ADDIE   You'd be a better one if you didn't look so dirty. Now go and take a bath, Miss Grown-up. Change your linens, get out a fresh dress and give your hair a good brushing—go on—

ALEXANDRA   Will you be all right, Papa?

ADDIE   Go on.

ALEXANDRA   (*on stairs, talks as she goes up*) The pills Papa must take once every four hours. And the bottle only when—only if he feels very bad. Now don't move until I come back and don't talk much and remember about his medicine, Addie—

ADDIE   Ring for Belle and have her help you and then I'll make you a fresh breakfast.

ALEXANDRA   (*as she disappears*) How's Aunt Birdie? Is she here?

ADDIE   It ain't right for you to have coffee? It will hurt you?

HORACE   (*slowly*) Nothing can make much difference now. Get me a cup, Addie. (*She looks at him, crosses to urn, pours a cup*) Funny. They can't make coffee up North. (ADDIE *brings him a cup*) They don't like red pepper, either. (*He takes the cup and gulps it greedily*) God, that's good. You remember how I used to drink it? Ten, twelve cups a day. So strong it had to stain the cup. (*then slowly*) Addie, before I see anybody else, I want to know why Zan came to fetch me home. She's tried to tell me, but she doesn't seem to know herself.

ADDIE   (*turns away*) I don't know. All I know is big things are going on. Everybody going to be high-tone rich. Big rich. You too. All because smoke's going to start out of a building that ain't even up yet.

HORACE   I've heard about it.

ADDIE   And, er— (*hesitates—steps to him*) And—well, Zan, she going to marry Mr. Leo in a little while.

HORACE   (*looks at her, then very slowly*) What are you talking about?

ADDIE   That's right. That's the talk, God help us.

HORACE   (*angrily*) What's the talk?

ADDIE   I'm telling you. There's going to be a wedding— (*angrily turns away*) Over my dead body there is.

HORACE   (*after a second, quietly*) Go and tell them I'm home.

ADDIE   (*hesitates*) Now you ain't to get excited. You're to be in your bed—

HORACE   Go on, Addie. Go and say I'm back. (ADDIE *opens dining-room doors. He rises with difficulty, stands stiff, as if he were in pain, facing the dining room*)

ADDIE   Miss Regina. They're home. They got here—

REGINA   Horace! (REGINA *quickly rises, runs into the room. Warmly*) Horace! You've finally arrived. (*As she kisses him, the others come forward, all talking together*)

BEN   (*in doorway, carrying a napkin*) Well, sir, you had us all mighty worried. (*He steps forward. They shake hands.* ADDIE *exits*)

OSCAR   You're a sight for sore eyes.

HORACE   Hello, Ben.

(LEO *enters, eating a biscuit*)

OSCAR   And how you feel? Tip-top, I bet, because that's the way you're looking.

HORACE   (*coldly, irritated with* OSCAR's *lie*) Hello, Oscar. Hello, Leo, how are you?

LEO   (*shaking hands*) I'm fine, sir. But a lot better now that you're back.

REGINA   Now sit down. What did happen to you and where's Alexandra? I am so excited about seeing you that I almost forgot about her.

HORACE   I didn't feel good, a little weak, I guess, and we stopped over night to rest. Zan's upstairs washing off the train dirt.

REGINA   Oh, I am so sorry the trip was hard on you. I didn't think that—

HORACE   Well, it's just as if I had never been away. All of you here—

BEN   Waiting to welcome you home.

(BIRDIE *bursts in. She is wearing a flannel kimono and her face is flushed and excited*)

BIRDIE   (*runs to him, kisses him*) Horace!

HORACE   (*warmly pressing her arm*) I was just wondering where you were, Birdie.

BIRDIE   (*excited*) Oh, I would have been here. I didn't know you were back until Simon said he saw the buggy. (*She draws back to look at him. Her face sobers*) Oh, you don't look well, Horace. No, you don't.

REGINA   (*laughs*) Birdie, what a thing to say—

HORACE (*looking at* OSCAR) Oscar thinks I look very well.

OSCAR (*annoyed. Turns on* LEO) Don't stand there holding that biscuit in your hand.

LEO Oh, well. I'll just finish my breakfast, Uncle Horace, and then I'll give you all the news about the bank— (*He exits into the dining room*)

OSCAR And what is that costume you have on?

BIRDIE (*looking at* HORACE) Now that you're home, you'll feel better. Plenty of good rest and we'll take such fine care of you. (*stops*) But where is Zan? I missed her so much.

OSCAR I asked you what is that strange costume you're parading around in?

BIRDIE (*nervously, backing towards stairs*) Me? Oh! It's my wrapper. I was so excited about Horace I just rushed out of the house—

OSCAR Did you come across the square dressed that way? My dear Birdie, I—

HORACE (*to* REGINA, *wearily*) Yes, it's just like old times.

REGINA (*quickly to* OSCAR) Now, no fights. This is a holiday.

BIRDIE (*runs quickly up the stairs*) Zan! Zannie!

OSCAR Birdie! (*She stops*)

BIRDIE Oh. Tell Zan I'll be back in a little while. (*whispers*) Sorry, Oscar. (*exits*)

REGINA (*to* OSCAR *and* BEN) Why don't you go finish your breakfast and let Horace rest for a minute?

BEN (*crossing to dining room with* OSCAR) Never leave a meal unfinished. There are too many poor people who need the food. Mighty glad to see you home, Horace. Fine to have you back. Fine to have you back.

OSCAR (*to* LEO *as* BEN *closes dining-room doors*) Your mother has gone crazy. Running around the streets like a woman—

(*The moment* REGINA *and* HORACE *are alone, they become awkward and self-conscious*)

REGINA (*laughs awkwardly*) Well. Here we are. It's been a long time. (HORACE *smiles*) Five months. You know, Horace, I wanted to come and be with you in the hospital, but I didn't know where my duty was. Here, or with you. But you know how much I *wanted* to come.

HORACE That's kind of you, Regina. There was no need to come.

REGINA Oh, but there was. Five months lying there all by yourself, no kinfolks, no friends. Don't try to tell me you didn't have a bad time of it.

HORACE I didn't have a bad time. (*As she shakes her head, he becomes insistent*) No, I didn't, Regina. Oh, at first when I—when I heard the news about myself—but after I got used to that, I liked it there.

REGINA You *liked* it? (*coldly*) Isn't that strange. You liked it so well you didn't want to come home?

HORACE That's not the way to put it. (*then, kindly, as he sees her turn her head away*) But there I was and I got kind of used to it, kind of used to lying there and thinking. (*smiles*) I never had much time to think before. And time's become valuable to me.

REGINA It sounds almost like a holiday.

HORACE (*laughs*) It was, sort of. The first holiday I've had since I was a little kid.

REGINA And here I was thinking you were in pain and—

HORACE (*quietly*) I was in pain.

REGINA And instead you were having a holiday! A holiday of thinking. Couldn't you have done that here?

HORACE I wanted to do it before I came here. I was thinking about us.

REGINA About us? About you and me? Thinking about you and me after all these years. (*unpleasantly*) You shall tell me everything you thought—some day.

HORACE (*there is silence for a minute*) Regina. (*She turns to him*) Why did you send Zan to Baltimore?

REGINA Why? Because I wanted you home. You can't make anything suspicious out of that, can you?

HORACE I didn't mean to make anything suspicious about it. (*hesitantly, taking her hand*) Zan said you wanted me to come home. I was so pleased at that and touched, it made me feel good.

REGINA (*taking away her hand, turns*) Touched that I should want you home?

HORACE (*sighs*) I'm saying all the wrong things as usual. Let's try to get along better. There isn't so much more time. Regina, what's all this crazy talk I've been hearing about Zan and Leo? Zan and Leo marrying?

REGINA (*turning to him, sharply*) Who gossips so much around here?

HORACE (*shocked*) Regina!

REGINA (*annoyed, anxious to quiet him*) It's some foolishness that Oscar thought up. I'll explain later. I have no intention of allowing any such arrangement. It was simply a way of keeping Oscar quiet in all this business I've been writing you about—

HORACE (*carefully*) What has Zan to do with any business of Oscar's? Whatever it is, you had better put it out of Oscar's head immediately. You know what I think of Leo.

REGINA   But there's no need to talk about it now.

HORACE   There is no need to talk about it ever. Not as long as I live. (HORACE *stops, slowly turns to look at her*) As long as I live. I've been in a hospital for five months. Yet since I've been here you have not once asked me about—about my health. (*then gently*) Well, I suppose they've written you. I can't live very long.

REGINA   (*coldly*) I've never understood why people have to talk about this kind of thing.

HORACE   (*there is a silence. Then he looks up at her, his face cold*) You misunderstand. I don't intend to gossip about my sickness. I thought it was only fair to tell you. I was not asking you for sympathy.

REGINA   (*sharply, turns to him*) What do the doctors think caused your bad heart?

HORACE   What do you mean?

REGINA   They didn't think it possible, did they, that your fancy women may have—

HORACE   (*smiles unpleasantly*) Caused my heart to be bad? I don't think that's the best scientific theory. You don't catch heart trouble in bed.

REGINA   (*angrily*) I didn't think you did. I only thought you might catch a bad conscience —in bed, as you say.

HORACE   I didn't tell them about my bad conscience. Or about my fancy women. Nor did I tell them that my wife has not wanted me in bed with her for— (*sharply*) How long is it, Regina? (REGINA *turns to him*) Ten years? Did you bring me home for this, to make me feel guilty? That means you want something. But you'll not make me feel guilty any more. My "thinking" has made a difference.

REGINA   I see that it has. (*She looks towards dining-room door. Then comes to him, her manner warm and friendly*) It's foolish for us to fight this way. I didn't mean to be unpleasant. I was stupid.

HORACE   (*wearily*) God knows I didn't either. I came home wanting so much not to fight, and then all of a sudden there we were. I got hurt and—

REGINA   (*hastily*) It's all my fault. I didn't ask about—about your illness because I didn't want to remind you of it. Anyway I never believe doctors when they talk about— (*brightly*) when they talk like that.

HORACE   (*not looking at her*) Well, we'll try our best with each other. (*He rises*)

REGINA   (*quickly*) I'll try. Honestly, I will. Horace, Horace, I know you're tired but, but—

couldn't you stay down here a few minutes longer? I want Ben to tell you something.

HORACE   Tomorrow.

REGINA   I'd like to now. It's very important to me. It's very important to all of us. (*gaily, as she moves toward dining room*) Important to your beloved daughter. She'll be a very great heiress—

HORACE   Will she? That's nice.

REGINA   (*opens doors*) Ben, are you finished breakfast?

HORACE   Is this the mill business I've had so many letters about?

REGINA   (*to* BEN) Horace would like to talk to you now.

HORACE   Horace would not like to talk to you now. I am very tired, Regina—

REGINA   (*comes to him*) Please. You've said we'll try our best with each other. I'll try. Really, I will. Please do this for me now. You will see what I've done while you've been away. How I watched your interests. (*laughs gaily*) And I've done very well too. But things can't be delayed any longer. Everything must be settled this week— (HORACE *sits down.* BEN *enters.* OSCAR *has stayed in the dining room, his head turned to watch them.* LEO *is pretending to read the newspaper*) Now you must tell Horace all about it. Only be quick because he is very tired and must go to bed. (HORACE *is looking up at her. His face hardens as she speaks*) But I think your news will be better for him than all the medicine in the world.

BEN   (*looking at* HORACE) It could wait. Horace may not feel like talking today.

REGINA   What an old faker you are! You know it can't wait. You know it must be finished this week. You've been just as anxious for Horace to get here as I've been.

BEN   (*very jovial*) I suppose I have been. And why not? Horace has done Hubbard Sons many a good turn. Why shouldn't I be anxious to help him now?

REGINA   (*laughs*) Help him! Help him when you need him, that's what you mean.

BEN   What a woman you married, Horace. (*laughs awkwardly when* HORACE *does not answer*) Well, then I'll make it quick. You know what I've been telling you for years. How I've always said that every one of us little Southern business men had great things— (*extends his arm*)—right beyond our finger tips. It's been my dream: my dream to make those fingers grow longer. I'm a lucky man, Horace, a lucky man. To dream and to live to get what you've dreamed of. That's *my* idea of a lucky man. (*looks at his fingers as his arm drops slowly*) For thirty years I've cried bring the cotton mills to the cotton. (HORACE *opens medicine bottle*) Well, finally I got up nerve to go to Marshall Company in Chicago.

HORACE   I know all this. (*He takes the medicine.* REGINA *rises, steps to him*)

BEN   Can I get you something?

HORACE   Some water, please.

REGINA (*turns quickly*)   Oh, I'm sorry. Let me. (*Brings him a glass of water. He drinks as they wait in silence*) You feel all right now?

HORACE   Yes. You wrote me. I know all that.

(OSCAR *enters from dining room*)

REGINA (*triumphantly*)   But you don't know that in the last few days Ben has agreed to give us—you, I mean—a much larger share.

HORACE   Really? That's very generous of him.

BEN (*laughs*)   It wasn't so generous of me. It was smart of Regina.

REGINA (*as if she were signaling* HORACE)   I explained to Ben that perhaps you hadn't answered his letters because you didn't think he was offering you enough, and that the time was getting short and you could guess how much he needed you—

HORACE (*smiles at her, nods*)   And I could guess that he wants to keep control in the family?

REGINA (*to* BEN, *triumphantly*)   Exactly. (*to* HORACE) So I did a little bargaining for you and convinced my brothers they weren't the only Hubbards who had a business sense.

HORACE   Did you have to convince them of that? How little people know about each other! (*laughs*) But you'll know better about Regina next time, eh, Ben? (BEN, REGINA, HORACE *laugh together.* OSCAR's *face is angry*) Now let's see. We're getting a bigger share. (*looking at* OSCAR) Who's getting less?

BEN   Oscar.

HORACE   Well, Oscar, you've grown very unselfish. What's happened to you?

(LEO *enters from dining room*)

BEN (*quickly, before* OSCAR *can answer*) Oscar doesn't mind. Not worth fighting about now, eh, Oscar?

OSCAR (*angrily*)   I'll get mine in the end. You can be sure of that. I've got my son's future to think about.

HORACE (*sharply*)   Leo? Oh, I see. (*puts his head back, laughs.* REGINA *looks at him nervously*) I am beginning to see. Everybody will get theirs.

BEN   I knew you'd see it. Seventy-five thousand, and that seventy-five thousand will make you a million.

REGINA (*steps to table, leaning forward*)   It will, Horace, it will.

HORACE   I believe you. (*after a second*) Now I can understand Oscar's self-sacrifice, but what did you have to promise Marshall Company besides the money you're putting up?

BEN   They wouldn't take promises. They wanted guarantees.

HORACE   Of what?

BEN (*nods*)   Water power. Free and plenty of it.

HORACE   You got them that, of course.

BEN   Cheap. You'd think the Governor of a great state would make his price a little higher. From pride, you know. (HORACE *smiles.* BEN *smiles*) Cheap wages. "What do you mean by cheap wages?" I say to Marshall. "Less than Massachusetts," he says to me, "and that averages eight a week." "Eight a week! By God," I tell him, "I'd work for eight a week myself." Why, there ain't a mountain white or a town nigger but wouldn't give his right arm for three silver dollars every week, eh, Horace?

HORACE   Sure. And they'll take less than that when you get around to playing them off against each other. You can save a little money that way, Ben. (*angrily*) And make them hate each other just a little more than they do now.

REGINA   What's all this about?

BEN (*laughs*)   There'll be no trouble from anybody, white or black. Marshall said that to me. "What about strikes? That's all we've had in Massachusetts for the last three years." I say to him, "What's a strike? I never heard of one. Come South, Marshall. We got good folks and we don't stand for any fancy fooling."

HORACE   You're right. (*slowly*) Well, it looks like you made a good deal for yourselves, and for Marshall, too. (*to* BEN) Your father used to say he made the thousands and you boys would make the millions. I think he was right. (*rises*)

REGINA (*they are all looking at* HORACE. *She laughs nervously*)   Millions for *us*, too.

HORACE   Us? You and me? I don't think so. We've got enough money, Regina. We'll just sit by and watch the boys grow rich. (*They watch* HORACE *tensely as he begins to move towards the staircase. He passes* LEO, *looks at him for a second*) How's everything at the bank, Leo?

LEO   Fine, sir. Everything is fine.

HORACE   How are all the ladies in Mobile? (HORACE *turns to* REGINA, *sharply*) Whatever made you think I'd let Zan marry—

REGINA   Do you mean that you are turning this down? Is it possible that's what you mean?

BEN   No, that's not what he means. Turning down a fortune. Horace is tired. He'd rather talk about it tomorrow—

REGINA   We can't keep putting it off this way. Oscar must be in Chicago by the end of the week with the money and contracts.

OSCAR (*giggles, pleased*)   Yes, sir. Got to be there end of the week. No sense going without the money.

REGINA (*tensely*)   I've waited long enough for your answer. I'm not going to wait any longer.

HORACE (*very deliberately*)   I'm very tired now, Regina.

BEN (*hastily*)   Now, Horace probably has his reasons. Things he'd like explained. Tomorrow will do. I can—

REGINA (*turns to* BEN, *sharply*)   I want to know his reasons now! (*turns back to* HORACE)

HORACE (*as he climbs the steps*)   I don't know them all myself. Let's leave it at that.

REGINA   We shall not leave it at that! We have waited for you here like children. Waited for you to come home.

HORACE   So that you could invest my money. So this is why you wanted me home? Well, I had hoped— (*quietly*) If you are disappointed, Regina, I'm sorry. But I must do what I think best. We'll talk about it another day.

REGINA   We'll talk about it now. Just you and me.

HORACE (*looks down at her. His voice is tense*)   Please, Regina. It's been a hard trip. I don't feel well. Please leave me alone now.

REGINA (*quietly*)   I want to talk to you, Horace. I'm coming up. (*He looks at her for a minute, then moves on again out of sight. She begins to climb the stairs*)

BEN (*softly.* REGINA *turns to him as he speaks*)   Sometimes it is better to wait for the sun to rise again. (*She does not answer*) And sometimes, as our mother used to tell you, (REGINA *starts up stairs*) it's unwise for a good-looking woman to frown. (BEN *rises, moves towards stairs*) Softness and a smile do more to the heart of men— (*She disappears.* BEN *stands looking up the stairs. There is a long silence. Then, suddenly,* OSCAR *giggles*)

OSCAR   Let us hope she'll change his mind. Let us hope. (*After a second* BEN *crosses to table, picks up his newspaper.* OSCAR *looks at* BEN. *The silence makes* LEO *uncomfortable*)

LEO   The paper says twenty-seven cases of yellow fever in New Orleans. Guess the floodwaters caused it. (*Nobody pays attention*) Thought they were building the levees high enough. Like the niggers always say: a man born of woman can't build nothing high enough

for the Mississippi. (*gets no answer. Gives an embarrassed laugh*)

(*Upstairs there is the sound of voices. The voices are not loud, but* BEN, OSCAR, LEO *become conscious of them.* LEO *crosses to landing, looks up, listens*)

OSCAR (*pointing up*)   Now just suppose she don't change his mind? Just suppose he keeps on refusing?

BEN (*without conviction*)   He's tired. It was a mistake to talk to him today. He's a sick man, but he isn't a crazy one.

OSCAR (*giggles*)   But just suppose he is crazy. What then?

BEN (*puts down his paper, peers at* OSCAR)   Then we'll go outside for the money. There's plenty who would give it.

OSCAR   And plenty who will want a lot for what they give. The ones who are rich enough to give will be smart enough to want. That means we'd be working for them, don't it, Ben?

BEN   You don't have to tell me the things I told you six months ago.

OSCAR   Oh, you're right not to worry. She'll change his mind. She always has. (*There is a silence. Suddenly* REGINA's *voice becomes louder and sharper. All of them begin to listen now. Slowly* BEN *rises, goes to listen by the staircase.* OSCAR, *watching him, smiles. As they listen* REGINA's *voice becomes very loud.* HORACE's *voice is no longer heard*)   Maybe. But I don't believe it. I never did believe he was going in with us.

BEN (*turning on him*)   What the hell do you expect me to do?

OSCAR (*mildly*)   Nothing. You done your almighty best. Nobody could blame you if the whole thing just dripped away right through our fingers. You can't do a thing. But there may be something I could do for us. (OSCAR *rises*) Or, I might better say, Leo could do for us. (BEN *stops, turns, looks at* OSCAR. LEO *is staring at* OSCAR)   Ain't that true, son? Ain't it true you might be able to help your own kinfolks?

LEO (*nervously taking a step to him*)   Papa, I—

BEN (*slowly*)   How would he help us, Oscar?

OSCAR   Leo's got a friend. Leo's friend owns eighty-eight thousand dollars in Union Pacific bonds. (BEN *turns to look at* LEO)   Leo's friend don't look at the bonds much—not for five or six months at a time.

BEN (*after a pause*)   Union Pacific. Uh, huh. Let me understand. Leo's friend would— would lend him these bonds and he—

OSCAR (*nods*)   Would be kind enough to lend them to us.

BEN   Leo.

LEO (*excited, comes to him*)   Yes, sir?

BEN   When would your friend be wanting the bonds back?

LEO (*very nervous*)   I don't know. I—well, I—

OSCAR (*sharply. Steps to him*)   You told me he won't look at them until Fall—

LEO   Oh, that's right. But I—not till Fall. Uncle Horace never—

BEN (*sharply*)   Be still.

OSCAR (*smiles at* LEO)   Your uncle doesn't wish to know your friend's name.

LEO (*starts to laugh*)   That's a good one. Not know his name—

OSCAR   Shut up, Leo! (LEO *turns away slowly, moves to table.* BEN *turns to* OSCAR) He won't look at them again until September. That gives us five months. Leo will return the bonds in three months. And we'll have no trouble raising the money once the mills are going up. Will Marshall accept bonds?

(BEN *stops to listen to sudden sharp voices from above. The voices are now very angry and very loud*)

BEN (*smiling*)   Why not? Why not? (*laughs*) Good. We are lucky. We'll take the loan from Leo's friend—I think he will make a safer partner than our sister. (*nods towards stairs. Turns to* LEO) How soon can you get them?

LEO   Today. Right now. They're in the safe-deposit box and—

BEN (*sharply*)   I don't want to know where they are.

OSCAR (*laughs*)   We will keep it secret from you. (*pats* BEN's *arm*)

BEN (*smiles*)   Good. Draw a check for our part. You can take the night train for Chicago. Well, Oscar (*holds out his hand*), good luck to us.

OSCAR   Leo will be taken care of?

LEO   I'm entitled to Uncle Horace's share. I'd enjoy being a partner—

BEN (*turns to stare at him*)   You would? You can go to hell, you little— (*starts towards* LEO)

OSCAR (*nervously*)   Now, now. He didn't mean that. I only want to be sure he'll get something out of all this.

BEN   Of course. We'll take care of him. We won't have any trouble about that. I'll see you at the store.

OSCAR (*nods*)   That's settled then. Come on, son. (*starts for door*)

LEO (*puts out his hand*)   I didn't mean just that. I was only going to say what a great day this was for me and— (BEN *ignores his hand*)

BEN   Go on.

(LEO *looks at him, turns, follows* OSCAR *out.* BEN *stands where he is, thinking. Again the voices upstairs can be heard.* REGINA's *voice is high and furious.* BEN *looks up, smiles, winces at the noise*)

ALEXANDRA (*upstairs*)   Mama—Mama—don't . . . (*The noise of running footsteps is heard and* ALEXANDRA *comes running down the steps, speaking as she comes*) Uncle Ben! Uncle Ben! Please go up. Please make Mama stop. Uncle Ben, he's sick, he's so sick. How can Mama talk to him like that—please, make her stop. She'll—

BEN   Alexandra, you have a tender heart.

ALEXANDRA (*crying*)   Go on up, Uncle Ben, please—

(*Suddenly the voices stop. A second later there is the sound of a door being slammed*)

BEN   Now you see. Everything is over. Don't worry. (*He starts for the door*) Alexandra, I want you to tell your mother how sorry I am that I had to leave. And don't worry so, my dear. Married folk frequently raise their voices, unfortunately. (*He starts to put on his hat and coat as* REGINA *appears on the stairs*)

ALEXANDRA (*furiously*)   How can you treat Papa like this? He's sick. He's very sick. Don't you know that? I won't let you.

REGINA   Mind your business, Alexandra. (*to* BEN. *Her voice is cold and calm*) How much longer can you wait for the money?

BEN (*putting on his coat*)   He has refused? My, that's too bad.

REGINA   He will change his mind. I'll find a way to make him. What's the longest you can wait now?

BEN   I could wait until next week. But I can't wait until next week. (*He giggles, pleased at the joke*) I could but I can't. Could and can't. Well, I must go now. I'm very late—

REGINA (*coming downstairs towards him*) You're not going. I want to talk to you.

BEN   I was about to give Alexandra a message for you. I wanted to tell you that Oscar is going to Chicago tonight, so we can't be here for our usual Friday supper.

REGINA (*tensely*)   Oscar is going to Chi— (*softly*) What do you mean?

BEN   Just that. Everything is settled. He's going on to deliver to Marshall—

REGINA (*taking a step to him*)   I demand to know what— You are lying. You are trying to scare me. *You haven't got the money.* How could you have it? You can't have— (BEN *laughs*) You will wait until I—

(HORACE *comes into view on the landing*)

BEN You are getting out of hand. Since when do I take orders from you?

REGINA Wait, you— (BEN *stops*) How *can* he go to Chicago? Did a ghost arrive with the money? (BEN *starts for the hall*) I don't believe you. Come back here. (REGINA *starts after him*) Come back here, you— (*The door slams. She stops in the doorway, staring, her fists clenched. After a pause she turns slowly*)

HORACE (*very quietly*) It's a great day when you and Ben cross swords. I've been waiting for it for years.

ALEXANDRA Papa, Papa, please go back! you will—

HORACE And so they don't need you, and so you will not have your millons, after all.

REGINA (*turns slowly*) You hate to see anybody live now, don't you? You hate to think that I'm going to be alive and have what I want.

HORACE I should have known you'd think that was the reason.

REGINA Because you're going to die and you know you're going to die.

ALEXANDRA (*shrilly*) Mama! Don't— Don't listen, Papa. Just don't listen. Go away—

HORACE Not to keep you from getting what you want. Not even partly that. (*holding to the rail*) I'm sick of you, sick of this house, sick of my life here. I'm sick of your brothers and their dirty tricks to make a dime. There must be better ways of getting rich than cheating niggers on a pound of bacon. Why should I give you the money? (*very angrily*) To pound the bones of this town to make dividends for you to spend? You wreck the town, you and your brothers, *you* wreck the town and live on it. Not me. Maybe it's easy for the dying to be honest. But it's not my fault I'm dying. (ADDIE *enters, stands at door quietly*) I'll do no more harm now. I've done enough. I'll die my own way. And I'll do it without making the world any worse. I leave that to you.

REGINA (*looks up at him slowly, calmly*) I hope you die. I hope you die soon. (*smiles*) I'll be waiting for you to die.

ALEXANDRA (*shrieking*) Papa! Don't— Don't listen—Don't—

ADDIE Come here, Zan. Come out of this room.

(ALEXANDRA *runs quickly to* ADDIE, *who holds her.* HORACE *turns slowly and starts upstairs*)

ACT THREE

(SCENE: *Same as Act One. Two weeks later. It is late afternoon and it is raining.*

AT RISE: HORACE *is sitting near the window in a wheel chair. On the table next to him is a safe-deposit box, and a small bottle of medicine.* BIRDIE *and* ALEXANDRA *are playing the piano. On a chair is a large sewing basket*)

BIRDIE (*counting for* ALEXANDRA) One and two and three and four. One and two and three and four. (*nods—turns to* HORACE) We once played together, Horace. Remember?

HORACE (*has been looking out of the window*) What, Birdie?

BIRDIE We played together. You and me.

ALEXANDRA *Papa* used to play?

BIRDIE Indeed he did. (ADDIE *appears at the door in a large kitchen apron. She is wiping her hands on a towel*) He played the fiddle and very well, too.

ALEXANDRA (*turns to smile at* HORACE) I never knew—

ADDIE Where's your Mama?

ALEXANDRA Gone to Miss Safronia's to fit her dresses.

(ADDIE *nods, starts to exit*)

HORACE Addie.

ADDIE Yes, Mr. Horace.

HORACE (*speaks as if he had made a sudden decision*) Tell Cal to get on his things. I want him to go an errand.

(ADDIE *nods, exits.* HORACE *moves nervously in his chair, looks out of the window*)

ALEXANDRA (*who has been watching him*) It's too bad it's been raining all day, Papa. But you can go out in the yard tomorrow. Don't be restless.

HORACE I'm not restless, darling.

BIRDIE I remember so well the time we played together, your papa and me. It was the first time Oscar brought me here to supper. I had never seen all the Hubbards together before, and you know what a ninny I am and how shy. (*turns to look at* HORACE) You said you could play the fiddle and you'd be much obliged if I'd play with you. *I* was obliged to *you*, all right, all right. (*laughs when he does not answer her*) Horace, you haven't heard a word I've said.

HORACE Birdie, when did Oscar get back from Chicago?

BIRDIE Yesterday. Hasn't he been here yet?

ALEXANDRA (*stops playing*) No. Neither has Uncle Ben since—since that day.

BIRDIE   Oh, I didn't know it was *that* bad. Oscar never tells me anything—

HORACE (*smiles, nods*)   The Hubbards have had their great quarrel. I knew it would come some day. (*laughs*) It came.

ALEXANDRA   It came. It certainly came all right.

BIRDIE (*amazed*)   But Oscar was in such a good humor when he got home, I didn't—

HORACE   Yes, I can understand that.

(ADDIE *enters carrying a large tray with glasses, a carafe of elderberry wine and a plate of cookies, which she puts on the table*)

ALEXANDRA   Addie! A party! What for?

ADDIE   Nothing for. I had the fresh butter, so I made the cakes, and a little elderberry does the stomach good in the rain.

BIRDIE   Isn't this nice! A party just for us. Let's play party music, Zan.

(ALEXANDRA *begins to play a gay piece*)

ADDIE (*to* HORACE, *wheeling his chair to center*)   Come over here, Mr. Horace, and don't be thinking so much. A glass of elderberry will do more good.

(ALEXANDRA *reaches for a cake.* BIRDIE *pours herself a glass of wine*)

ALEXANDRA   Good cakes, Addie. It's nice here. Just us. Be nice if it could always be this way.

BIRDIE (*nods happily*)   Quiet and restful.

ADDIE   Well, it won't be that way long. Little while now, even sitting here, you'll hear the red bricks going into place. The next day the smoke'll be pushing out the chimneys and by church time that Sunday every human born of woman will be living on chicken. That's how Mr. Ben's been telling the story.

HORACE (*looks at her*)   They believe it that way?

ADDIE   Believe it? They use to believing what Mr. Ben orders. There ain't been so much talk around here since Sherman's army didn't come near.

HORACE (*softly*)   They are fools.

ADDIE (*nods, sits down with the sewing basket*)   You ain't born in the South unless you're a fool.

BIRDIE (*has drunk another glass of wine*)   But we didn't play together after that night. Oscar said he didn't like me to play on the piano. (*turns to* ALEXANDRA) You know what he said that night?

ALEXANDRA   Who?

BIRDIE   Oscar. He said that music made him nervous. He said he just sat and waited for the next note. (ALEXANDRA *laughs*) He wasn't poking fun. He meant it. Ah, well— (*She finishes*

her glass, shakes her head.* HORACE *looks at her, smiles*)   Your papa don't like to admit it, but he's been mighty kind to me all these years. (*running the back of her hand along his sleeve*) Often he'd step in when somebody said something and once— (*She stops, turns away, her face still*) Once he stopped Oscar from— (*She stops, turns. Quickly*) I'm sorry I said that. Why, here I am so happy and yet I think about bad things. (*laughs nervously*) That's not right, now, is it? (*She pours a drink.* CAL *appears in the door. He has on an old coat and is carrying a torn umbrella*)

ALEXANDRA   Have a cake, Cal.

CAL (*comes in, takes a cake*)   Yes'm. You want me, Mr. Horace?

HORACE   What time is it, Cal?

CAL   'Bout ten minutes before it's five.

HORACE   All right. Now you walk yourself down to the bank.

CAL   It'll be closed. Nobody'll be there but Mr. Manders, Mr. Joe Horns, Mr. Leo—

HORACE   Go in the back way. They'll be at the table, going over the day's business. (*points to the deposit box*) See that box?

CAL (*nods*)   Yes, sir.

HORACE   You tell Mr. Manders that Mr. Horace says he's much obliged to him for bringing the box, it arrived all right.

CAL (*bewildered*)   He know you got the box. He bring it himself Wednesday. I opened the door to him and he say, "Hello, Cal, coming on to summer weather."

HORACE   You say just what I tell you. Understand?

(BIRDIE *pours another drink, stands at table*)

CAL   No, sir. I ain't going to say I understand. I'm going down and tell a man he give you something he already know he give you, and you say "understand."

HORACE   Now, Cal.

CAL   Yes, sir. I just going to say you obliged for the box coming all right. I ain't going to understand it, but I'm going to say it.

HORACE   And tell him I want him to come over here after supper, and to bring Mr. Sol Fowler with him.

CAL (*nods*)   He's to come after supper and bring Mr. Sol Fowler, your attorney-at-law, with him.

HORACE (*smiles*)   That's right. Just walk right in the back room and say your piece. (*slowly*) In front of everybody.

CAL   Yes, sir. (*mumbles to himself as he exits*)

ALEXANDRA (*who has been watching* HORACE)   Is anything the matter, Papa?

HORACE   Oh, no. Nothing.

ADDIE Miss Birdie, that elderberry going to give you a headache spell.

BIRDIE (*beginning to be drunk. Gaily*) Oh, I don't think so. I don't think it will.

ALEXANDRA (*as* HORACE *puts his hand to his throat*) Do you want your medicine, Papa?

HORACE No, no. I'm all right, darling.

BIRDIE Mama used to give me elderberry wine when I was a little girl. For hiccoughs. (*laughs*) You know, I don't think people get hiccoughs any more. Isn't that funny? (BIRDIE *laughs.* HORACE *and* ALEXANDRA *laugh*) I used to get hiccoughs just when I shouldn't have.

ADDIE (*nods*) And nobody gets growing pains no more. That is funny. Just as if there was some style in what you get. One year an ailment's stylish and the next year it ain't.

BIRDIE (*turns*) I remember. It was my first big party, at Lionnet I mean, and I was so excited, and there I was with hiccoughs and Mama laughing. (*softly. Looking at carafe*) Mama always laughed. (*picks up carafe*) A big party, a lovely dress from Mr. Worth in Paris, France, and hiccoughs. (*pours drink*) My brother pounding me on the back and Mama with the elderberry bottle, laughing at me. Everybody was on their way to come, and I was such a ninny, hiccoughing away. (*drinks*) You know, that was the first day I ever saw Oscar Hubbard. The Ballongs were selling their horses and he was going there to buy. He passed and lifted his hat—we could see him from the window—and my brother, to tease Mama, said maybe we should have invited the Hubbards to the party. He said Mama didn't like them because they kept a store, and he said that was old-fashioned of her. (*Her face lights up*) And then, and *then*, I saw Mama angry for the first time in my life. She said that wasn't the reason. She said she was old-fashioned, but not that way. She said she was old-fashioned enough not to like people who killed animals they couldn't use, and who made their money charging awful interest to poor, ignorant niggers and cheating them on what they bought. She was very angry, Mama was. I had never seen her face like that. And then suddenly she laughed and said, "Look, I've frightened Birdie out of the hiccoughs." (*Her head drops. Then softly*) And so she had. They were all gone. (*moves to sofa, sits*)

ADDIE Yeah, they got mighty well off cheating niggers. Well, there are people who eat the earth and eat all the people on it like in the Bible with the locusts. Then there are people who stand around and watch them eat it. (*softly*) Sometimes I think it ain't right to stand and watch them do it.

BIRDIE (*thoughtfully*) Like I say, if we could only go back to Lionnet. Everybody'd be better there. They'd be good and kind. I like people to be kind. (*pours drink*) Don't you, Horace; don't you like people to be kind?

HORACE Yes, Birdie.

BIRDIE (*very drunk now*) Yes, that was the first day I ever saw Oscar. Who would have thought— (*quickly*) You all want to know something? Well, I don't like Leo. My very own son, and I don't like him. (*laughs, gaily*) My, I guess I even like Oscar more.

ALEXANDRA Why did you marry Uncle Oscar?

ADDIE (*sharply*) That's no question for you to be asking.

HORACE (*sharply*) Why not? She's heard enough around here to ask anything.

ALEXANDRA Aunt Birdie, why did you marry Uncle Oscar?

BIRDIE I don't know. I thought I liked him. He was kind to me and I thought it was because he liked me too. But that wasn't the reason— (*wheels on* ALEXANDRA) Ask why *he* married *me*. I can tell you that: He's told it to me often enough.

ADDIE (*leaning forward*) Miss Birdie, don't—

BIRDIE (*speaking very rapidly, tensely*) My family was good and the cotton on Lionnet's fields was better. Ben Hubbard wanted the cotton and (*rises*) Oscar Hubbard married it for him. He was kind to me, then. He used to smile at me. He hasn't smiled at me since. Everybody knew that's what he married me for. (ADDIE *rises*) Everybody but me. Stupid, stupid me.

ALEXANDRA (*to* HORACE, *holding his hand, softly*) I see. (*hesitates*) Papa, I mean— when you feel better couldn't we go away? I mean, by ourselves. Couldn't we find a way to go—

HORACE Yes, I know what you mean. We'll try to find a way. I promise you, darling.

ADDIE (*moves to* BIRDIE) Rest a bit, Miss Birdie. You get talking like this you'll get a headache and—

BIRDIE (*sharply, turning to her*) I've never had a headache in my life. (*begins to cry hysterically*) You know it as well as I do. (*turns to* ALEXANDRA) I never had a headache, Zan. That's a lie they tell for me. I drink. All by myself, in my own room, by myself, I drink. Then, when they want to hide it, they say, "Birdie's got a headache again"—

ALEXANDRA (*comes to her quickly*) Aunt Birdie.

BIRDIE (*turning away*) Even you won't like me now. You won't like me any more.

ALEXANDRA I love you. I'll always love you.

BIRDIE (*furiously*) Well, don't. Don't love me. Because in twenty years you'll be just like me. They'll do all the same things to you. (*begins to laugh hysterically*) You know what? In twenty-two years I haven't had a whole day of happiness. Oh, a little, like today with you all. But never a single, whole day. I say to myself, if only I had one more *whole* day, then— (*the laugh stops*) And that's the way you'll be. And you'll trail after them, just like me, hoping they won't be so mean that day or say something to make you feel so bad—only you'll be worse off because you haven't got my Mama to remember— (*turns away, her head drops. She stands quietly, swaying a little, holding onto the sofa.* ALEXANDRA *leans down, puts her cheek on* BIRDIE's *arm*)

ALEXANDRA (*to* BIRDIE) I guess we were all trying to make a happy day. You know, we sit around and try to pretend nothing's happened. We try to pretend we are not here. We make believe we are just by ourselves, some place else, and it doesn't seem to work. (*kisses* BIRDIE's *hand*) Come now, Aunt Birdie, I'll walk you home. You and me. (*She takes* BIRDIE's *arm. They move slowly out*)

BIRDIE (*softly as they exit*) You and me.

ADDIE (*after a minute*) Well. First time I ever heard Miss Birdie say a word. (HORACE *looks at her*) Maybe it's good for her. I'm just sorry Zan had to hear it. (HORACE *moves his head as if he were uncomfortable*) You feel bad, don't you? (*He shrugs*)

HORACE So you didn't want Zan to hear? It would be nice to let her stay innocent, like Birdie at her age. Let her listen now. Let her see everything. How else is she going to know that she's got to get away? I'm trying to show her that. I'm trying, but I've only got a little time left. She can even hate me when I'm dead, if she'll only learn to hate and fear this.

ADDIE Mr. Horace—

HORACE Pretty soon there'll be nobody to help her but you.

ADDIE (*crossing to him*) What can I do?

HORACE Take her away.

ADDIE How can I do that? Do you think they'd let me just go away with her?

HORACE I'll fix it so they can't stop you when you're ready to go. You'll go, Addie?

ADDIE (*after a second, softly*) Yes, sir. I promise. (*He touches her arm, nods*)

HORACE (*quietly*) I'm going to have Sol Fowler make me a new will. They'll make trouble, but you make Zan stand firm and Fowler'll do the rest. Addie, I'd like to leave you something for yourself. I always wanted to.

ADDIE (*laughs*) Don't you do that, Mr.

Horace. A nigger woman in a white man's will! I'd never get it nohow.

HORACE I know. But upstairs in the armoire drawer there's seventeen hundred dollar bills. It's money left from my trip. It's in an envelope with your name. It's for you.

ADDIE Seventeen hundred dollar bills! My God, Mr. Horace, I won't know how to count up that high. (*shyly*) It's mighty kind and good of you. I don't know what to say for thanks—

CAL (*appears in doorway*) I'm back. (*no answer*) I'm back.

ADDIE So we see.

HORACE Well?

CAL Nothing. I just went down and spoke my piece. Just like you told me. I say, "Mr. Horace he thank you mightily for the safe box arriving in good shape and he say you come right after supper to his house and bring Mr. Attorney-at-law Sol Fowler with you." Then I wipe my hands on my coat. Every time I ever told a lie in my whole life, I wipe my hands right after. Can't help doing it. Well, while I'm wiping my hands, Mr. Leo jump up and say to me, "What box? What you talking about?"

HORACE (*smiles*) Did he?

CAL And Mr. Leo say he got to leave a little early cause he got something to do. And then Mr. Manders say Mr. Leo should sit right down and finish up his work and stop acting like somebody made him Mr. President. So he sit down. Now, just like I told you, Mr. Manders was mighty surprised with the message because he knows right well he brought the box— (*points to box, sighs*) But he took it all right. Some men take everything easy and some do not.

HORACE (*puts his head back, laughs*) Mr. Leo was telling the truth; he *has* got something to do. I hope Manders don't keep him too long. (*Outside there is the sound of voices.* CAL *exits.* ADDIE *crosses quickly to* HORACE, *puts basket on table, begins to wheel his chair towards the stairs. Sharply*) No. Leave me where I am.

ADDIE But that's Miss Regina coming back.

HORACE (*nods, looking at door*) Go away, Addie.

ADDIE (*hesitates*) Mr. Horace. Don't talk no more today. You don't feel well and it won't do no good—

HORACE (*as he hears footsteps in the hall*) Go on. (*She looks at him for a second, then picks up her sewing from table and exits as* REGINA *comes in from hall.* HORACE's *chair is now so placed that he is in front of the table with the medicine.* REGINA *stands in the hall, shakes umbrella, stands it in the corner, takes off her cloak and throws it over the banister. She stares at* HORACE)

REGINA (*as she takes off her gloves*) We had agreed that you were to stay in your part of this house and I in mine. This room is *my* part of the house. Please don't come down here again.

HORACE   I won't.

REGINA (*crosses towards bell-cord*) I'll get Cal to take you upstairs.

HORACE (*smiles*) Before you do I want to tell you that after all, we have invested our money in Hubbard Sons and Marshall, Cotton Manufacturers.

REGINA (*stops, turns, stares at him*) What are you talking about? You haven't seen Ben— When did you change your mind?

HORACE   I didn't change my mind. *I* didn't invest the money. (*smiles*) It was invested for me.

REGINA (*angrily*) What—?

HORACE   I had eighty-eight thousand dollars' worth of Union Pacific bonds in that safe-deposit box. They are not there now. Go and look. (*As she stares at him, he points to the box*) Go and look, Regina. (*She crosses quickly to the box, opens it*) Those bonds are as negotiable as money.

REGINA (*turns back to him*) What kind of joke are you playing now? Is this for my benefit?

HORACE   I don't look in that box very often, but three days ago, on Wednesday it was, because I had made a decision—

REGINA   I want to know what you are talking about.

HORACE (*sharply*) Don't interrupt me again. Because I had made a decision, I sent for the box. The bonds were gone. Eighty-eight thousand dollars gone. (*He smiles at her*)

REGINA (*after a moment's silence, quietly*) Do you think I'm crazy enough to believe what you're saying?

HORACE (*shrugs*) Believe anything you like.

REGINA (*stares at him, slowly*) Where did they go to?

HORACE   They are in Chicago. With Mr. Marshall, I should guess.

REGINA   What did they do? Walk to Chicago? Have you really gone crazy?

HORACE   Leo took the bonds.

REGINA (*turns sharply then speaks softly, without conviction*) I don't believe it.

HORACE (*leans forward*) I wasn't there but I can guess what happened. This fine gentleman, to whom you were willing to marry your daughter, took the keys and opened the box. You remember that the day of the fight Oscar went to Chicago? Well, he went with my bonds that his son Leo had stolen for him. (*pleasantly*) And for Ben, of course, too.

REGINA (*slowly, nods*) When did you find out the bonds were gone?

HORACE   Wednesday night.

REGINA   I thought that's what you said. Why have you waited three days to do anything? (*suddenly laughs*) This *will* make a fine story.

HORACE (*nods*) Couldn't it?

REGINA (*still laughing*) A fine story to hold over their heads. How could they be such fools? (*turns to him*)

HORACE   But I'm not going to hold it over their heads.

REGINA (*the laugh stops*) What?

HORACE (*turns his chair to face her*) I'm going to let them keep the bonds—as a loan from you. An eighty-eight-thousand-dollar loan; they should be grateful to you. They will be, I think.

REGINA (*slowly, smiles*) I see. You are punishing me. But I won't let you punish me. If you won't do anything, I will. Now. (*She starts for door*)

HORACE   You won't do anything. Because you can't. (REGINA *stops*) It won't do you any good to make trouble because I shall simply say that I lent them the bonds.

REGINA (*slowly*) You would do that?

HORACE   Yes. For once in your life I am tying your hands. There is nothing for you to do. (*There is silence. Then she sits down*)

REGINA   I see. You are going to lend them the bonds and let them keep all the profit they make on them, and there is nothing I can do about it. Is that right?

HORACE   Yes.

REGINA (*softly*) Why did you say that I was making this gift?

HORACE   I was coming to that. I am going to make a new will, Regina, leaving you eighty-eight thousand dollars in Union Pacific bonds. The rest will go to Zan. It's true that your brothers have borrowed your share for a little while. After my death I advise you to talk to Ben and Oscar. They won't admit anything and Ben, I think, will be smart enough to see that he's safe. Because I knew about the theft and said nothing. Nor will I say anything as long as I live. Is that clear to you?

REGINA (*nods, softly, without looking at him*) You will not say anything as long as you live.

HORACE   That's right. And by that time they will probably have replaced your bonds, and then they'll belong to you and nobody but us will ever know what happened. (*stops, smiles*) They'll be around any minute to see what I am going to do. I took good care to see that word reached Leo. They'll be mighty relieved to know I'm going to do nothing and Ben will think it all a capital joke on you. And that will be the end of that. There's nothing you can do to them, nothing you can do to me.

REGINA You hate me very much.

HORACE No.

REGINA Oh, I think you do. (*puts her head back, sighs*) Well, we haven't been very good together. Anyway, I don't hate you either. I have only contempt for you. I've always had.

HORACE From the very first?

REGINA I think so.

HORACE I was in love with *you*. But why did *you* marry *me?*

REGINA I was lonely when I was young.

HORACE *You* were lonely?

REGINA Not the way people usually mean. Lonely for all the things I wasn't going to get. Everybody in this house was so busy and there was so little place for what I wanted. I wanted the world. Then, and then— (*smiles*) Papa died and left the money to Ben and Oscar.

HORACE And you married me?

REGINA Yes, I thought—But I was wrong. You were a small-town clerk then. You haven't changed.

HORACE (*nods, smiles*) And that wasn't what you wanted.

REGINA No. No, it wasn't what I wanted. (*pauses, leans back, pleasantly*) It took me a little while to find out I had made a mistake. As for you—I don't know. It was almost as if I couldn't stand the kind of man you were— (*smiles, softly*) I used to lie there at night, praying you wouldn't come near—

HORACE Really? It was as bad as that?

REGINA (*nods*) Remember when I went to Doctor Sloan and I told you he said there was something the matter with me and that you shouldn't touch me any more?

HORACE I remember.

REGINA But you believed it. I couldn't understand that. I couldn't understand that anybody could be such a soft fool. That was when I began to despise you.

HORACE (*puts his hand to his throat, looks at the bottle of medicine on table*) Why didn't you leave me?

REGINA I told you I married you for something. It turned out it was only for this. (*carefully*) This wasn't what I wanted, but it was something. I never thought about it much but if I had (HORACE *puts his hand to his throat*) I'd have known that you would die before I would. But I couldn't have known that you would get heart trouble so early and so bad. I'm lucky, Horace. I've always been lucky. (HORACE *turns slowly to the medicine*) I'll be lucky again. (HORACE *looks at her. Then he puts his hand to his throat. Because he cannot reach the bottle he moves the chair closer. He reaches for the medicine, takes out the cork, picks up the spoon. The bottle slips and smashes on the table. He draws in his breath, gasps*)

HORACE Please. Tell Addie—The other bottle is upstairs. (REGINA *has not moved. She does not move now. He stares at her. Then, suddenly as if he understood, he raises his voice. It is a panic-stricken whisper, too small to be heard outside the room*) Addie! Addie! Come— (*Stops as he hears the softness of his voice. He makes a sudden, furious spring from the chair to the stairs, taking the first few steps as if he were a desperate runner. On the fourth step he slips, gasps, grasps the rail, makes a great effort to reach the landing. When he reaches the landing, he is on his knees. His knees give way, he falls on the landing, out of view.* REGINA *has not turned during his climb up the stairs. Now she waits a second. Then she goes below the landing, speaks up*)

REGINA Horace. Horace. (*When there is no answer, she turns, calls*) Addie! Cal! Come in here. (*She starts up the steps.* ADDIE *and* CAL *appear. Both run towards the stairs*) He's had an attack. Come up here. (*They run up the steps quickly*)

CAL My God. Mr. Horace—

(*They cannot be seen now*)

REGINA (*her voice comes from the head of the stairs*) Be still, Cal. Bring him in here.

(*Before the footsteps and the voices have completely died away,* ALEXANDRA *appears in the hall door, in her raincloak and hood. She comes into the room, begins to unfasten the cloak, suddenly looks around, sees the empty wheel chair, stares, begins to move swiftly as if to look in the dining room. At the same moment* ADDIE *runs down the stairs.* ALEXANDRA *turns and stares up at* ADDIE)

ALEXANDRA Addie! What?

ADDIE (*takes* ALEXANDRA *by the shoulders*) I'm going for the doctor. Go upstairs. (ALEXANDRA *looks at her, then quickly breaks away and runs up the steps.* ADDIE *exits. The stage is empty for a minute. Then the front door bell begins to ring. When there is no answer, it rings again. A second later* LEO *appears in the hall, talking as he comes in*)

LEO (*very nervous*) Hello. (*irritably*) Never saw any use ringing a bell when a door was open. If you are going to ring a bell, then somebody should answer it. (*gets in the room, looks around, puzzled, listens, hears no sound*) Aunt Regina. (*He moves around restlessly*) Addie. (*waits*) Where the hell— (*crosses to the bell cord, rings it impatiently, waits, gets no answer, calls*) Cal! Cal! (CAL *appears on the stair landing*)

CAL (*his voice is soft, shaken*) Mr. Leo. Miss Regina says you stop that screaming noise.

LEO (*angrily*) Where is everybody?

CAL Mr. Horace he got an attack. He's bad. Miss Regina says you stop that noise.

LEO Uncle Horace—What—What happened? (CAL *starts down the stairs, shakes his head, begins to move swiftly off.* LEO *looks around wildly*) But when—You seen Mr. Oscar or Mr. Ben? (CAL *shakes his head. Moves on.* LEO *grabs him by the arm*) Answer me, will you?

CAL No, I ain't seen 'em. I ain't got time to answer you. I got to get things. (CAL *runs off*)

LEO But what's the matter with him? When did this happen— (*calling after* CAL) You'd think Papa'd be some place where you could find him. I been chasing him all afternoon.

(OSCAR *and* BEN *come into the room, talking excitedly*)

OSCAR I hope it's not a bad attack.

BEN It's the first one he's had since he came home.

LEO Papa, I've been looking all over town for you and Uncle Ben—

BEN Where is he?

OSCAR Addie said it was sudden.

BEN (*to* LEO) Where is he? When did it happen?

LEO Upstairs. Will you listen to me, please? I been looking for you for—

OSCAR (*to* BEN) You think we should go up? (BEN, *looking up the steps, shakes his head*)

BEN I don't know. I don't know.

OSCAR (*shakes his head*) But he was all right—

LEO (*yelling*) *Will you listen to me?*

OSCAR (*sharply*) What is the matter with you?

LEO I been trying to tell you. I been trying to find you for an hour—

OSCAR Tell me what?

LEO Uncle Horace knows about the bonds. He knows about them. He's had the box since Wednesday—

BEN (*sharply*) Stop shouting! What the hell are you talking about?

LEO (*furiously*) I'm telling you he knows about the bonds. Ain't that clear enough—

OSCAR (*grabbing* LEO's *arm*) You goddamn fool! Stop screaming!

BEN Now what happened? Talk quietly.

LEO You heard me. Uncle Horace knows about the bonds. He's known since Wednesday.

BEN (*after a second*) How do you know that?

LEO Because Cal comes down to Manders and says the box came O.K. and—

OSCAR (*trembling*) That might not mean a thing—

LEO (*angrily*) No? It might not, huh? Then he says Manders should come here tonight and bring Sol Fowler with him. I guess that don't mean a thing either.

OSCAR (*to* BEN) Ben—What—Do you think he's seen the—

BEN (*motions to the box*) There's the box. (*Both* OSCAR *and* LEO *turn sharply.* LEO *makes a leap to the box*) You ass. Put it down. What are you going to do with it, eat it?

LEO I'm going to— (*starts*)

BEN (*furiously*) Put it down. Don't touch it again. Now sit down and shut up for a minute.

OSCAR Since Wednesday. (*to* LEO) You said he had it since Wednesday. Why didn't he say something— (*to* BEN) I don't understand—

LEO (*taking a step*) I can put it back. I can put it back before anybody knows.

BEN (*who is standing at the table, softly*) He's had it since Wednesday. Yet he hasn't said a word to us.

OSCAR *Why? Why?*

LEO What's the difference why? He was getting ready to say plenty. He was going to say it to Fowler tonight—

OSCAR (*angrily*) Be still. (*turns to* BEN, *looks at him. Waits*)

BEN (*after a minute*) I don't believe that.

LEO (*wildly*) *You* don't believe it? What do I care what *you* believe? I do the dirty work and then—

BEN (*turning his head sharply to* LEO) I'm remembering that. I'm remembering that, Leo.

OSCAR What do you mean?

LEO You—

BEN (*to* OSCAR) If you don't shut that little fool up, I'll show you what I mean. For some reason he knows, but he don't say a word.

OSCAR Maybe he didn't know that *we*—

BEN (*quickly*) That *Leo*—He's no fool. Does Manders know the bonds are missing?

LEO How could I tell? I was half crazy. I

don't think so. Because Manders seemed kind of puzzled and—

OSCAR   But we got to find out— (*He breaks off as* CAL *comes into the room carrying a kettle of hot water*)

BEN   How is he, Cal?

CAL   I don't know, Mr. Ben. He was bad. (*going towards stairs*)

OSCAR   But when did it happen?

CAL (*shrugs*)   He wasn't feeling bad early. (ADDIE *comes in quickly from the hall*) Then there he is next thing on the landing, fallen over, his eyes tight—

ADDIE (*to* CAL)   Dr. Sloan's over at the Ballongs. Hitch the buggy and go get him. (*She takes the kettle and cloths from him, pushes him, runs up the stairs*) Go on. (*She disappears.* CAL *exits*)

BEN   Never seen Sloan anywhere when you need him.

OSCAR (*softly*)   Sounds bad.

LEO   He would have told *her* about it. Aunt Regina. He would have told his own wife—

BEN (*turning to* LEO)   Yes, he might have told her. But they weren't on such pretty terms and maybe he didn't. Maybe he didn't. (*goes quickly to* LEO) Now, listen to me. If she doesn't know, it may work out all right. If she does know, you're to say he lent you the bonds.

LEO   Lent them to me! Who's going to believe that?

BEN   Nobody.

OSCAR (*to* LEO)   Don't you understand? It can't do no harm to say it—

LEO   Why should I say he lent them to me? Why not to you? (*carefully*) Why not to Uncle Ben?

BEN (*smiles*)   Just because he didn't lend them to me. Remember that.

LEO   But all he has to do is say he didn't lend them to me—

BEN (*furiously*)   But for some reason, he doesn't seem to be talking, does he? (*There are footsteps above. They all stand looking at the stairs.* REGINA *begins to come slowly down*)

BEN   What happened?

REGINA   He's had a bad attack.

OSCAR   Too bad. I'm so sorry we weren't here when—when Horace needed us.

BEN   When *you* needed us.

REGINA (*looks at him*)   Yes.

BEN   How is he? Can we—can we go up?

REGINA (*shakes her head*)   He's not conscious.

OSCAR (*pacing around*)   It's that—it's that bad? Wouldn't you think Sloan could be found quickly, just once, just once?

REGINA   I don't think there is much for him to do.

BEN   Oh, don't talk like that. He's come through attacks before. He will now.

(REGINA *sits down. After a second she speaks softly*)

REGINA   Well. We haven't seen each other since the day of our fight.

BEN (*tenderly*)   That was nothing. Why, you and Oscar and I used to fight when we were kids.

OSCAR (*hurriedly*)   Don't you think we should go up? Is there anything we can do for Horace—

BEN   You don't feel well. Ah—

REGINA (*without looking at them*)   No, I don't. (*slight pause*) Horace told me about the bonds this afternoon. (*There is an immediate shocked silence*)

LEO   The bonds. What do you mean? What bonds? What—

BEN (*looks at him furiously. Then to* REGINA) The Union Pacific bonds? *Horace's* Union Pacific bonds?

REGINA   Yes.

OSCAR (*steps to her, very nervously*)   Well. Well what—about them? What—what could he say?

REGINA   He said that Leo had stolen the bonds and given them to you.

OSCAR (*aghast, very loudly*)   That's ridiculous, Regina, absolutely—

LEO   I don't know what you're talking about. What would I—Why—

REGINA (*wearily to* BEN)   Isn't it enough that he stole them from me? Do I have to listen to this in the bargain?

OSCAR   You are talking—

LEO   I didn't steal anything. I don't know why—

REGINA (*to* BEN)   Would you ask them to stop that, please? (*There is silence for a minute.* BEN *glowers at* OSCAR *and* LEO)

BEN   Aren't we starting at the wrong end, Regina? What did Horace tell you?

REGINA (*smiles at him*)   He told me that Leo had stolen the bonds.

LEO   I didn't steal—

REGINA   Please. Let me finish. Then he told me that he was going to pretend that he had lent them to you (LEO *turns sharply to* REGINA, *then looks at* OSCAR, *then looks back at* REGINA) as a present from me—to my brothers. He said there was nothing I could do about it. He said the rest of his money would go to Alexandra. That is all. (*There is a silence.* OSCAR *coughs,* LEO *smiles slyly*)

LEO (*talking a step to her*) I told you he had lent them—I could have told you—

REGINA (*ignores him, smiles sadly at* BEN) So I'm very badly off, you see. (*carefully*) But Horace said there was nothing I could do about it as long as he was alive to say he had lent you the bonds.

BEN You shouldn't feel that way. It can all be explained, all be adjusted. It isn't as bad—

REGINA So you, at least, are willing to admit that the bonds were stolen?

BEN (OSCAR *laughs nervously*) I admit no such thing. It's possible that Horace made up that part of the story to tease you— (*looks at her*) Or perhaps to punish you. Punish you.

REGINA (*sadly*) It's not a pleasant story. I feel bad, Ben, naturally. I hadn't thought—

BEN Now you shall have the bonds safely back. That was the understanding, wasn't it, Oscar?

OSCAR Yes.

REGINA I'm glad to know that. (*smiles*) Ah, I had greater hopes—

BEN Don't talk that way. That's foolish. (*looks at his watch*) I think we ought to drive out for Sloan ourselves. If we can't find him we'll go over to Senateville for Doctor Morris. And don't think I'm dismissing this other business. I'm not. We'll have it all out on a more appropriate day.

REGINA (*looks up, quietly*) I don't think you had better go yet. I think you had better stay and sit down.

BEN We'll be back with Sloan.

REGINA Cal has gone for him. I don't want you to go.

BEN Now don't worry and—

REGINA You will come back in this room and sit down. I have something more to say.

BEN (*turns, comes towards her*) Since when do I take orders from you?

REGINA (*smiles*) You don't—yet. (*sharply*) Come back, Oscar. You too, Leo.

OSCAR (*sure of himself, laughs*) My dear Regina—

BEN (*softly, pats her hand*) Horace has already clipped your wings and very wittily. Do I have to clip them, too? (*smiles at her*) You'd get farther with a smile, Regina. I'm a soft man for a woman's smile.

REGINA I'm smiling, Ben. I'm smiling because you are quite safe while Horace lives. But I don't think Horace will live. And if he doesn't live I shall want seventy-five per cent in exchange for the bonds.

BEN (*steps back, whistles, laughs*) Greedy!

What a greedy girl you are! You want so much of everything.

REGINA Yes. And if I don't get what I want I am going to put all three of you in jail.

OSCAR (*furiously*) You're mighty crazy. Having just admitted—

BEN And on what evidence would you put Oscar and Leo in jail?

REGINA (*laughs, gaily*) Oscar, listen to him. He's getting ready to swear that it was you and Leo! What do you say to that? (OSCAR *turns furiously towards* BEN) Oh, don't be angry, Oscar. I'm going to see that he goes in with you.

BEN Try anything you like, Regina. (*sharply*) And now we can stop all this and say good-bye to you. (ALEXANDRA *comes slowly down the steps*) It's his money and he's obviously willing to let us borrow it. (*more pleasantly*) Learn to make threats when you can carry them through. For how many years have I told you a good-looking woman gets more by being soft and appealing? Mama used to tell you that. (*looks at his watch*) Where the hell is Sloan? (*to* OSCAR) Take the buggy and—

(*As* BEN *turns to* OSCAR, *he sees* ALEXANDRA. *She walks stiffly. She goes slowly to the lower window, her head bent. They all turn to look at her*)

OSCAR (*after a second, moving toward her*) What? Alexandra— (*She does not answer. After a second,* ADDIE *comes slowly down the stairs, moving as if she were very tired. At foot of steps, she looks at* ALEXANDRA, *then turns and slowly crosses to door and exits.* REGINA *rises.* BEN *looks nervously at* ALEXANDRA, *at* REGINA)

OSCAR (*as* ADDIE *passes him, irritably to* ALEXANDRA) Well, what is— (*turns into room —sees* ADDIE *at foot of steps*)—what's? (BEN *puts up a hand, shakes his head*) My God, I didn't know—who *could* have known—I didn't know he was that sick. Well, well—I— (REGINA *stands quietly, her back to them*)

BEN (*softly, sincerely*) Seems like yesterday when he first came here.

OSCAR (*sincerely, nervously*) Yes, that's true. (*turns to* BEN) The whole town loved him and respected him.

ALEXANDRA (*turns*) Did you love him, Uncle Oscar?

OSCAR Certainly, I—What a strange thing to ask! I—

ALEXANDRA Did you love him, Uncle Ben?

BEN (*simply*) He had—

ALEXANDRA (*suddenly starts to laugh very loudly*) And you, Mama, did you love him, too?

REGINA   I know what you feel, Alexandra, but please try to control yourself.

ALEXANDRA   (*still laughing*)   I'm trying, Mama. I'm trying very hard.

BEN   Grief makes some people laugh and some people cry. It's better to cry, Alexandra.

ALEXANDRA   (*the laugh has stopped. Tensely moves toward* REGINA)   What was Papa doing on the staircase?

(BEN *turns to look at* ALEXANDRA)

REGINA   Please go and lie down, my dear. We all need time to get over shocks like this. (ALEXANDRA *does not move.* REGINA's *voice becomes softer, more insistent*)   Please go, Alexandra.

ALEXANDRA   No, Mama. I'll wait. I've got to talk to you.

REGINA   Later. Go and rest now.

ALEXANDRA   (*quietly*)   I'll wait, Mama. I've plenty of time.

REGINA   (*hesitates, stares, makes a half shrug, turns back to* BEN)   As I was saying. Tomorrow morning I am going up to Judge Simmes. I shall tell him about Leo.

BEN   (*motioning toward* ALEXANDRA)   Not in front of the child, Regina. I—

REGINA   (*turns to him. Sharply*)   I didn't ask her to stay. Tomorrow morning I go to Judge Simmes—

OSCAR   And what proof? What proof of all this—

REGINA   (*turns sharply*)   None. I won't need any. The bonds are missing and they are with Marshall. That will be enough. If it isn't, I'll add what's necessary.

BEN   I'm sure of that.

REGINA   You can be quite sure.

OSCAR   We'll deny—

REGINA   Deny your heads off. You couldn't find a jury that wouldn't weep for a woman whose brothers steal from her. And you couldn't find twelve men in this state you haven't cheated and hate you for it.

OSCAR   What kind of talk is this? You couldn't do anything like that! We're your own brothers. (*points upstairs*)   How can you talk that way when upstairs not five minutes ago—

REGINA   (*slowly*)   There are people who can never go back, who must finish what they start. I am one of those people, Oscar. (*after a slight pause*)   Where was I? (*smiles at* BEN)   Well, they'll convict you. But I won't care much if they don't. (*leans forward, pleasantly*)   Because by that time you'll be ruined. I shall also tell my story to Mr. Marshall, who likes me, I think, and who will not want to be involved in

your scandal. A respectable firm like Marshall and Company. The deal would be off in an hour. (*turns to them angrily*)   And you know it. Now I don't want to hear any more from any of you. *You'll do no more bargaining in this house.* I'll take my seventy-five per cent and we'll forget the story forever. That's one way of doing it, and the way I prefer. You know me well enough to know that I don't mind taking the other way.

BEN   (*after a second, slowly*)   None of us have ever known you well enough, Regina.

REGINA   You're getting old, Ben. Your tricks aren't as smart as they used to be. (*There is no answer. She waits, then smiles*)   All right. I take it that's settled and I get what I asked for.

OSCAR   (*furiously to* BEN)   Are you going to let her do this—

BEN   (*turns to look at him, slowly*)   You have a suggestion?

REGINA   (*puts her arms above her head, stretches, laughs*)   No, he hasn't. All right. Now, Leo, I have forgotten that you ever saw the bonds. (*archly, to* BEN *and* OSCAR)   And as long as you boys both behave yourselves, I've forgotten that we ever talked about them. You can draw up the necessary papers tomorrow.

(BEN *laughs.* LEO *stares at him, starts for door. Exits.* OSCAR *moves towards door angrily.* REGINA *looks at* BEN, *nods, laughs with him. For a second,* OSCAR *stands in the door, looking back at them. Then he exits*)

REGINA   You're a good loser, Ben. I like that.

BEN   (*he picks up his coat, then turns to her*)   Well, I say to myself, what's the good? You and I aren't like Oscar. We're not sour people. I think that comes from a good digestion. Then, too, one loses today and wins tomorrow. I say to myself, years of planning and I get what I want. Then I don't get it. But I'm not discouraged. The century's turning, the world is open. Open for people like you and me. Ready for us, waiting for us. After all this is just the beginning. There are hundreds of Hubbards sitting in rooms like this throughout the country. All their names aren't Hubbard, but they are all Hubbards and they will own this country some day. We'll get along.

REGINA   (*smiles*)   I think so.

BEN   Then, too, I say to myself, things may change. (*looks at* ALEXANDRA)   I agree with Alexandra. What is a man in a wheel chair doing on a staircase? I ask myself that.

REGINA   (*looks up at him*)   And what do you answer?

BEN   I have no answer. But maybe some day I will. Maybe never, but maybe some day. (*Smiles. Pats her arm*) When I do, I'll let you know. (*goes towards hall*)

REGINA   When you do, write me. I will be in Chicago. (*gaily*) Ah, Ben, if Papa had only left me his money.

BEN   I'll see you tomorrow.

REGINA   Oh, yes. Certainly. You'll be sort of working for me now.

BEN   (*as he passes* ALEXANDRA, *smiles*) Alexandra, you're turning out to be a right interesting girl. (*looks at* REGINA) Well, good night all. (*He exits*)

REGINA   (*sits quietly for a second, stretches, turns to look at* ALEXANDRA) What do you want to talk to me about, Alexandra?

ALEXANDRA   (*slowly*) I've changed my mind. I don't want to talk. There's nothing to talk about now.

REGINA   You're acting very strange. Not like yourself. You've had a bad shock today. I know that. And you loved Papa, but you must have expected this to come some day. You knew how sick he was.

ALEXANDRA   I knew. We all knew.

REGINA   It will be good for you to get away from here. Good for me, too. Time heals most wounds, Alexandra. You're young, you shall have all the things I wanted. I'll make the world for you the way I wanted it to be for me. (*uncomfortably*) Don't sit there staring. You've been around Birdie so much you're getting just like her.

ALEXANDRA   (*nods*) Funny. That's what Aunt Birdie said today.

REGINA   (*nods*)   Be good for you to get away from all this.

(ADDIE *enters*)

ADDIE   Cal is back, Miss Regina. He says Dr. Sloan will be coming in a few minutes.

REGINA   We'll go in a few weeks. A few weeks! That means two or three Saturdays, two or three Sundays. (*sighs*) Well, I'm very tired. I shall go to bed. I don't want any supper. Put the lights out and lock up. (ADDIE *moves to the piano lamp, turns it out*) You go to your room, Alexandra. Addie will bring you something hot. You look very tired. (*rises. To* ADDIE) Call me when Dr. Sloan gets here. I don't want to see anybody else. I don't want any condolence calls tonight. The whole town will be over.

ALEXANDRA   Mama, I'm not coming with you. I'm not going to Chicago.

REGINA   (*turns to her*) You're very upset, Alexandra.

ALEXANDRA   (*quietly*)   I mean what I say. With all my heart.

REGINA   We'll talk about it tomorrow. The morning will make a difference.

ALEXANDRA   It won't make any difference. And there isn't anything to talk about. I am going away from you. Because I want to. Because I know Papa would want me to.

REGINA   (*puzzled, careful, polite*)   You *know* your Papa wanted you to go away from me?

ALEXANDRA   Yes.

REGINA   (*softly*)   And if I say no?

ALEXANDRA   (*looks at her*)   Say it, Mama, say it. And see what happens.

REGINA   (*softly, after a pause*)   And if I make you stay?

ALEXANDRA   That would be foolish. It wouldn't work in the end.

REGINA   You're very serious about it, aren't you? (*crosses to stairs*) Well, you'll change your mind in a few days.

ALEXANDRA   You only change your mind when you want to. And I won't want to.

REGINA   (*going up the steps*)   Alexandra, I've come to the end of my rope. Somewhere there has to be what I want, too. Life goes too fast. Do what you want; think what you want; go where you want. I'd like to keep you with me, but I won't make you stay. Too many people used to make me do too many things. No, I won't make you stay.

ALEXANDRA   You couldn't, Mama, because I want to leave here. As I've never wanted anything in my life before. Because now I understand what Papa was trying to tell me. (*pause*) All in one day: Addie said there were people who ate the earth and other people who stood around and watched them do it. And just now Uncle Ben said the same thing. Really, he said the same thing. (*tensely*) Well, tell him for me, Mama, I'm not going to stand around and watch you do it. Tell him I'll be fighting as hard as he'll be fighting (*rises*) some place where people don't just stand around and watch.

REGINA   Well, you have spirit, after all. I used to think you were all sugar water. We don't have to be bad friends. I don't want us to be bad friends, Alexandra. (*starts, stops, turns to* ALEXANDRA) Would you like to come and talk to me, Alexandra? Would you—would you like to sleep in my room tonight?

ALEXANDRA   (*takes a step towards her*)   Are you afraid, Mama? (REGINA *does not answer. She moves slowly out of sight.* ADDIE *comes to* ALEXANDRA, *presses her arm*)

William Saroyan

1908-

THE COMING REALITY

It is incredible how unimaginative a whole age can be. Our age has been inventive, but always unimaginative. If we have had anything new it has been shabby and pointless and clinical, like da-da or dada, surrealism, et cetera. All feeble. All unhealthy, or rather non-healthy. The operation of imagination in the realm of the normal is practically unknown. Implements, gadgets, and so on: plenty. Anything that has to do with matter: plenty. Anything that has to do with spirit, rhythm, and so on: none. We have plenty of reporters. Practically no creators. There is no imagination. Airplanes, submarines, complicated guns: all beautiful in design, but strictly gadgets. In sculpture the egg is still the most beautiful form. There is still fire. Light a match and you see beauty so amazing it is almost unbelievable, and you know there is nothing like it even in art nay more: in music sometimes there used to be, but no more. Now we have jit, which is O.K. but strictly a gadget, too. On a clear day, as the witty-gadgety gag goes, look into the sky at the clouds: beauty. To paint it is pointless. That isn't what's wanted. To photograph it is silly or scientific: that's not it, either. What you want is that quality of beauty as it is in the living, in the plainest of people: the cloud of them, the clear-day clouding of experience and realization of life, and so on. Snow. The same. Rain. The sea. The river. The mountain, valley, meadow, tree, bush, bough, bird, and so on.

We know there are kinds of things. Of each kind there is always good and bad. The kind of thing we have, almost throughout in art and life, is machine-rhythm, which is too easy and soon too boring. The machine-rhythm runs through this whole age. It isn't a bad rhythm, but the kicking and turning of Follies girls should by now be in decline as *the* American rhythm, the tempo and calculation of American life. It's all right, but it doesn't get anywhere.

All things influence all things. A boulder in a desert influences a lizard. Once in a while, though, comes a lizard who influences a boulder, *the* boulder, and therefore all boulders, and everything else. How or why that happens we don't know. In our day all things influencing all things do so feebly, willy-nilly, half-heartedly, and so on. The past keeps influencing the present, the present the future. All proper. The objection is to the style, which is non-existent, which is, in short, not style. And influence should have style, which means it should know what it's about, and if possible why. We don't get that. I'm speaking not alone of art, but of all living. Somebody in history influences Marx, Lenin, Stalin, Trotzky, Mussolini, Hitler, Mr. Roosevelt, Fiorello La Guardia, and these influence others, near them, and far away; these influences carry it along; it moves backward and forward and gets nowhere.

The reason for all this sorrow in behavior everywhere is that we've had no real imagination. No one has behaved freshly and spontaneously, excepting he was crazy, which doesn't count in the record. I mean to behave freshly and spontaneously and supernormally. I mean staying within the limits and still being able to give standing on the hind legs a new aesthetic and religious charm. The behavior has been mechanical and fearful. In art the new workers have followed, but what have they followed? The same thing somebody else followed. That way you stand still without knowing it for centuries. Human behavior and rhythm is still following something that came to a dead halt about two thousand years ago. Of course there's nowhere to go. Anybody knows that. Art (and life) is an inorganic body violent with energy but no outlet equal to its strength except war, which is absurd, abnormal, immoral and ridiculous. It also happens to be traditional, the truth in the cards, the past influencing the present, and so on. Sometimes art is organic when life isn't, but not often. Sometimes life is O.K., and art isn't, but not often. Usually whatever life is, art is also. This is certainly true now. All the feverish activity of the artists isn't going to do any good until imagination arrives somewhere, in somebody. The fruit of art's activity without fresh imagination is bound to be nothing more than repetition, improving or declining, as it certainly is today. We can't have fresh art until at least somebody somewhere lives freshly.

The present intention of art is a hollow intention: to take care of *this* little problem of form, or *that* little matter of style, which is not truly style, since it is a problem, since it is not organic. The limits that arrived to surround art and living a long time ago are still the limits which otherwise conscious artists respect and accept, but shouldn't. It's nonsense. It's their job to invent limits as they go along, and to invent them for greater freedom, not less. Not for security, not so that they, the artists, will appear to be wise, full of grace, and so on. Not as a vehicle of bluff, which eventually must be exposed. The job before the artists, and before the living, is to start from scratch, from the limitless potential inherent in all wondrous things, as all things of our universe and life are, and to pledge allegiance only to eagerness, faith, industry, goodness, severity, real objectivity, courage, and so on. How long can any man's bluff go unchallenged, as long as it *is* bluff, and he knows it? If one man knows it, not counting himself, all living shall know it sooner or later. Bluff is beautiful in poker, especially in stud, which is a game with already agreed-upon values involved, values which in reality are nothing. Bluff in the world is still this same bluff, and it makes of living a game in which the values are nothing, which of course is silly. Anything which can suffer pain cannot be regarded as nothing. This means that at the outset profound changes of behavior must take place. In the coming reality of the world there shall be no triumph in bluffing and not being called. It shall not elevate a man, except to fools.

Noble imagination is the thing that is absent from the life of our time. The best human beings in the world get side-tracked by irrelevancies, special branches of human error, statistics, easy problems, social, economic, aesthetic and even religious. It's really too bad, because excepting imagination arrive, all past errors must continue validly and no amount of fussing with the hightone surfaces will help any.

All this oddly enough is, of course, about plays, as art is always about everything, or at least should be, and the writing of plays is an art. Eating a herring is, too. Let's not be dull about anything. Everything can and should be an art. All things should be done artfully. That is, in order to derive the maximum of pleasure from any event of mortality, no matter how simple, one should know what one is about.

Reality complicates, whether it's a good reality or a lousy one. There's no two ways about *our* reality. It's lousy and we know it. We aren't responsible for the present state of reality because it came to us, one at a time, more or less as it is, one error pregnant with its natural issue. It came to us rather vast and impressive, although in reality it isn't very vast and not at all impressive. The effect it has is to force one man at a time into submission. That is the easiest personal way out for any man. It is a feeble way, though, no matter what's going on. Because two thousand million people feel in their bones that their destiny is to suffer, doesn't mean that their destiny *is* to suffer. Because reality complicates and everybody feels in his bones that it is too difficult to simplify it and make it behave, doesn't mean that it really *is* too difficult to simplify and instruct in behavior. What it does mean is that nobody is around with both the perception to see the present reality for what it is and the personal vigor to personally expose it, and introduce an aspect of what it *might* be. In short, any reality is real only in the living, not by itself. It is a personal thing. It must be attacked personally. It is easier not to attack it of course, and safer, and many other comfortable things. Reality is what the one man at a time decided to believe about himself and two thousand million others like himself all alive at one time. Any man who accepts as real anything less than *the grand* is a phoney, because he knows the grand is natural. He can imagine it, so it must be natural. Not demanding personally its coming-to-reality, its achievement, makes him a weakling, no matter how great he appears to be relatively. He behaves in a manner which is not the finest he is capable of. He knows better, but he's too scared or too lazy to bother about it.

The specific state of the art and life of our time is so wretched it's not worth talking about. Imagination is out of it. A play is something in which these things, among others, are in the mind of the playwright, and he is not bluffing, not being afraid and not being lazy. He is mak-ing form, not being buffaloed by it. He is creating humanity, not agreeing upon the destruction of it in himself by what passes for the human race.

And so on.

THE TIME OF YOUR LIFE

CAST OF CHARACTERS

NICK
JOE
ARAB
WILLIE
NEWSBOY
THE DRUNK
TOM
KITTY DUVAL
DUDLEY
HARRY
WESLEY
SAM
LORENE SMITH
BLICK
MARY L.

MCCARTHY
KRUPP
NICK'S MOTHER
KIT CARSON
SAILOR
KILLER
HER SIDEKICK
YOUNG SAILOR
ANNA
ELSIE MANDELSPIEGEL
GENTLEMAN
LADY
FIRST COP
SECOND COP

ACT ONE

(*The Act takes place on the afternoon of a day in October, 1939.*

SCENE *Nick's Pacific Street Saloon, Restaurant, and Entertainment Palace at the foot of Embarcadero, in San Francisco. There are double swinging doors to the street at the front of the stage, with steps leading down to barroom; a bar at right; a door center leading to kitchen; a piano on platform at rear left center; a stage with steps leading up, diagonally in upper left corner.*

A marble game at the front of the stage; tables and chairs right, center and left center; a wall telephone at rear left center; a phonograph front left; a chair right of door center; table and chairs in back room behind left end of bar.

At a table left center JOE; *always calm, always quiet, always thinking, always eager, always bored, always superior. His expensive clothes are casually and youthfully worn and give him an almost boyish appearance. At the moment he is in a sort of Debussy reverie.*

Behind the bar, NICK; *a big redheaded Italian with an enormous naked woman tattooed in red on the inside of his right arm. He is studying* The Racing Form.

The ARAB, *in his place sitting on chair at the end of the bar. He is a lean old man with a rather ferocious old-country black moustache, with the ends twisted up. Between the thumb and forefinger of his left hand is the Mohammedan tattoo indicating that he has been to Mecca. He is sipping a glass of beer.*

WILLIE, *the marble-game maniac, explodes through the swinging doors right, and lifts the forefinger of his right hand comically, indicating one beer. He is a very young man, scarcely more than twenty. He is wearing heavy shoes, a pair of old and dirty corduroys, a light green turtle-neck jersey with a large letter "F" on the chest, an oversized two-button tweed coat, and a green hat, with the brim up.* NICK *sets out a glass of beer for him,*

The Time of Your Life by William Saroyan. Copyright 1939 by Harcourt, Brace & World, Inc., and reprinted with their permission.

he drinks it, straightens up vigorously, saying, "Aaah," makes a solemn face, gives NICK *a one-finger salute of adieu, and begins to leave, refreshed and restored in spirit. He walks by the marble game, halts suddenly, turns, studies the contraption, gestures as if to say, "Oh, no." Turns to go, stops, returns to the machine, studies it, takes a handful of small coins out of his pants pocket, lifts a nickel, indicates with a gesture, one game, no more. Puts the nickel in the slot, pushes in the slide, making an interesting noise.*

The marbles fall, roll, and take their places. He pushes down the lever, placing one marble in position. Takes a very deep breath, walks in a small circle, excited at the beginning of great drama. Stands straight and pious before the contest. Himself vs. the machine. Willie vs. Destiny. His skill and daring vs. the cunning and trickery of the novelty industry of America, and the whole challenging world. He is the last of the American pioneers, with nothing more to fight but the machine, with no other reward than lights going on and off, and six nickels for one. Before him is the last champion, the machine. He is the last challenger, the young man with nothing to do in the world. WILLIE *grips the knob delicately, studies the situation carefully, draws the knob back, holds it a moment, and then releases it. The first marble rolls out among the hazards, and the contest is on. At the very beginning of the play "The Missouri Waltz" is coming from the phonograph. The music ends here.*

This is the signal for the beginning of the play)

NEWSBOY (*enters cheerfully*)　Good morning everybody. (*no answer, to* NICK) Paper, Mister? (NICK *shakes his head, no. The* NEWSBOY *goes to* JOE) Paper, Mister? (JOE *shakes his head, no. The* NEWSBOY *walks away, counting papers*)

JOE (*noticing him*)　How many you got?

NEWSBOY　Five. (JOE *gives him a bill, takes all the papers, throws them over his head;* NEWSBOY *takes money, exits*)

ARAB (*picks up papers*)　No foundation. All the way down the line. (*The* DRUNK *enters right, crosses to the telephone.* NICK *takes the* DRUNK *out. The* DRUNK *returns right*)

DRUNK (*champion of the Bill of Rights*) This is a free country, ain't it?

NICK　You can't beat that machine.

WILLIE　Oh, yeah?

JOE (*calling*)　Tom. (*to himself*) Where the hell is he, every time I need him? (*He looks around calmly: the nickel-in-the-slot phonograph in the corner; the open public telephone;*

the stage; the marble game; the bar; and so on. He whistles again, this time a little louder) Hey, Tom. (*He waits a moment, then whistles again, very loudly*)

NICK (*with irritation*)　What do you want?

JOE　I want the boy to get me a watermelon, that's what I want. What do *you* want? Money, or love, or fame, or what? You won't get them studying *The Racing Form.*

NICK　I like to keep abreast of the times. (TOM *comes hurrying in right. He is a great big man of about thirty or so who appears to be much younger because of the childlike expression of his face: handsome, dumb, innocent, troubled, and a little bewildered by everything. He is obviously adult in years, but it seems as if by all rights he should still be a boy. He is defensive as clumsy, self-conscious, overgrown boys are. He is wearing a flashy cheap suit, a Woolworth watch-chain across his vest, and on the little finger of his right hand, a dice ring: number six. On the middle finger of his left hand a large skull-and-crossbones ring.* JOE *leans back and studies him with casual disapproval.* TOM *slackens his pace and becomes clumsy and embarrassed, waiting for the bawling-out he's afraid he's going to get*)

JOE (*objectively, severely, but warmly*) Who saved your life?

TOM (*sincerely*)　You did, Joe. Thanks.

JOE　How'd I do it?

TOM (*confused*)　What?

JOE　How'd I do it?

TOM　Joe, you know how you did it.

JOE (*softly*)　I want you to answer me. How'd I save your life? I've forgotten.

TOM (*remembering, with a big goofy smile*) You made me eat all that chicken soup three years ago when I was sick and hungry.

JOE (*fascinated*)　Chicken soup?

TOM (*eagerly*)　Yeah.

JOE　Three years? Is it that long?

TOM　Yeah, sure. 1937. 1938. 1939. This is 1939, Joe.

JOE　Never mind what year it is. Tell me the whole story.

TOM　You took me to the doctor. You gave me money for food and clothes, and paid my room rent. Aw, Joe, you know all the different things you did.

JOE (*nods*)　You in good health now?

TOM　Yeah, Joe.

JOE　You got clothes?

TOM　Yeah, Joe.

JOE (*nods*)　You eat three times a day. Sometimes four?

TOM　Yeah, Joe. Sometimes five.

JOE　You got a place to sleep?

TOM Yeah, Joe.

JOE (*nods; pauses; studies* TOM *carefully; terrible irritation*) Then, where the hell have you been?

TOM (*humbly*) Joe, I was out in the street listening to the boys. They're talking about the trouble down here on the waterfront.

JOE (*very sharply*) I want you to be around when I need you.

TOM (*pleased that the bawling-out is over*) I won't do it again. Joe, one guy out there says there's got to be a revolution before anything will ever be all right.

JOE (*impatient*) I know all about it. Now, here. Take this money. Go up to the Emporium. You know where the Emporium is?

TOM Yeah, sure, Joe.

JOE All right. Take the elevator and go up to the fourth floor. Walk around to the back, to the toy department. Buy me a couple of dollars' worth of toys and bring them here.

TOM (*amazed*) Toys? What *kind* of toys, Joe?

JOE Any kind of toys. Little ones that I can put on this table.

TOM What do you want toys for, Joe?

JOE (*mildly angry*) What?

TOM All right, all right. You don't have to get sore at *everything*. What'll people think, a big guy like me buying toys?

JOE What people?

TOM Aw, Joe, you're always making me do crazy things for you, and *I'm* the guy that gets embarrassed. You just sit in this place and make me do all the dirty work.

JOE (*looking away*) Do what I tell you.

TOM O.K., but I wish I knew *why*.

JOE Wait a minute. Here's a nickel. Put it in the phonograph. Number seven. I want to hear that waltz again.

TOM (*crossing below to phonograph*) Boy, I'm glad *I* don't have to stay and listen to it. Joe, what do you hear in that song anyway? We listen to that song ten times a day. Why can't we hear number six, or two, or nine? There are a lot of other numbers.

JOE (*emphatically*) Put the nickel in the phonograph. (*pause*) Sit down and wait till the music's over. Then go get me some toys.

TOM O.K. O.K.

JOE (*loudly*) Never mind being a martyr about it either. The cause isn't worth it.

(TOM *puts the nickel into the machine, with a ritual of impatient and efficient movement which plainly shows his lack of sympathy or enthusiasm. His manner also reveals, however, that his lack of sympathy is spurious and ex-*

aggerated. Actually, he is fascinated by the music, but he is so confused by it that he tries to pretend he dislikes it.

The music begins. TOM *turns chair left of left center table and sits at the rear. It is another variation of "The Missouri Waltz," played dreamily and softly, with perfect orchestral form, and with a theme of weeping in the horns repeated a number of times.*

At first TOM *listens with something close to irritation, since he cannot understand what is so attractive in the music to* JOE, *and so painful and confusing to himself. Very soon, however, he is carried away helplessly by the melancholy story of grief and nostalgia in the stubborn, flowing rhythm. He stands quarreling with the grief and confusion in himself.*

JOE, *on the other hand, listens as if he were not listening, indifferent and unmoved. What he's interested in is* TOM. *He turns and glances at* TOM.

KITTY DUVAL, *who lives in a room in the New York Hotel, around the corner, comes beyond the swinging doors quietly, and walks slowly to the bar, her reality and rhythm a perfect accompaniment to the sorrowful American music, which is her music, as it is* TOM's. *Which the world drove out of her, putting in its place brokenness and all manner of spiritually crippled forms. She seems to understand this, and is angry. Angry with herself, full of hate for the poor world, and full of pity and contempt for its tragic, unbelievable, confounded people. She is a small, powerful girl, with that kind of delicate and rugged beauty which no circumstance of evil or ugly reality can destroy. This beauty is that element of the immortal which is in the seed of good and common people, and which is kept alive in some of the female of our kind, no matter how accidentally or pointlessly they may have entered the world.* KITTY DUVAL *is somebody. There is an angry purity, and a fierce pride, in her. In her stance, and way of walking, there is grace and arrogance*)

KITTY (*goes to bar*) Beer. (NICK *places a glass of beer before her. She swallows half and listens to the music again.* TOM *sees her and becomes dead to everything but her. He stands like a lump, fascinated and undone by his almost religious adoration for her.* JOE *notices him*)

JOE (*gently*) Tom. (TOM *begins to move toward the bar, where* KITTY *is standing. Loudly*) Tom. (TOM *halts, then turns, and* JOE *motions to him to come over to the table*) Have you got everything straight?

TOM (*out of the world, crossing to left of* JOE) What?

JOE What do you mean, what? I just gave you some instructions.

TOM (*pathetically*) What do you want, JOE?

JOE I want you to come to your senses. (*He stands up quietly and knocks* TOM's *hat off*)

TOM (*picks up his hat quickly*) I got it, Joe. I got it. The Emporium. Fourth floor. In the back. The toy department. Two dollars' worth of toys. That you can put on a table.

KITTY (*to herself*) Who the hell is he to push a big man like that around?

JOE I'll expect you back in a half hour. Don't get sidetracked anywhere. Just do what I tell you.

TOM (*pleading*) Joe? Can't I bet four bits on a horse race? There's a long shot—Precious Time—that's going to win by ten lengths. I got to have money. (JOE *points to the street.* TOM *goes out right.* NICK *is combing his hair, looking in the mirror*)

NICK I thought you wanted him to get you a watermelon.

JOE I forgot. (*to* KITTY, *clearly, slowly, with great compassion*) What's the dream?

KITTY (*moving to* JOE) What?

JOE (*holding the dream for her*) What's the dream, *now?*

KITTY (*coming still closer*) What dream?

JOE What dream! The dream you're dreaming.

NICK Suppose he did bring you a watermelon? What the hell would you do with it?

JOE (*irritated*) I'd put it on this table. I'd look at it. Then I'd eat it. What do you *think* I'd do with it, sell it for a profit?

NICK How should I know what *you'd* do with *anything?* What I'd like to know is, where do you get your money from? What work do you do?

JOE (*looking at* KITTY) Bring us a bottle of champagne.

KITTY (*at right of* JOE's *table*) Champagne?

JOE (*simply*) Would you rather have something else?

KITTY What's the big idea?

JOE I thought you might like some champagne. I myself am very fond of it.

KITTY Yeah, but what's the big idea? You can't push me around.

JOE (*gently but severely*) It's not in my nature to be unkind to another human being. I have only contempt for wit. Otherwise I might say something obvious, therefore cruel, and perhaps untrue.

KITTY You be careful what you think about me.

JOE (*slowly, not looking at her*) I have only the noblest thoughts for both your person, and your spirit.

NICK (*having listened carefully and not being able to make it out*) What are you talking about?

KITTY You shut up. You—

JOE He owns this place. He's an important man. All kinds of people come to him looking for work. Comedians. Singers. Dancers.

KITTY I don't care. He can't call me names.

NICK All right, sister. I know how it is with a two-dollar whore in the morning.

KITTY Don't you dare call me names. I used to be in burlesque.

NICK (*profoundly, as it were*) If you were ever in burlesque, I used to be Charlie Chaplin.

KITTY (*swallowing beer*) I *was* in burlesque. I played the burlesque circuit from coast to coast. I've had flowers sent to me by European royalty. I've had dinner with young men of wealth and social position.

NICK You're dreaming.

KITTY (*to* JOE) I *was* in burlesque. Kitty Duval. That was my name. Life-size photographs of me in costume in front of burlesque theaters all over the country.

JOE (*gently, coaxingly*) I believe you. Have some champagne.

NICK (*going behind her to left of* JOE's *table, with champagne*) There he goes again.

JOE Miss Duval?

KITTY (*sincerely; going over to chair left of* JOE's *table; sits*) That's not my *real* name. That's my *stage* name.

JOE I'll call you by your stage name.

NICK (*pouring*) All right, sister, make up your mind. Are you going to have champagne with him, or not?

JOE Pour the lady some wine.

NICK O.K., professor. Why you come to this joint instead of one of the high-class dumps uptown is more than I can understand. Why don't you have champagne at the St. Francis? Why don't you drink with a lady?

KITTY (*furiously*) Don't you call me names you dentist.

JOE Dentist?

NICK (*amazed, loudly*) What kind of cussing is that? (*pause. Looking at* KITTY, *then at* JOE, *bewildered*) This guy doesn't belong here. The only reason I've got champagne is because *he* keeps ordering it all the time. (*to* KITTY) Don't think you're the only one he drinks champagne with. He drinks with *all* of them. (*pause*) He's crazy. Or something.

all, she'll come to the phone. Sunset 7349. (*He dials the number, as* JOE *goes on studying the toys. They are one big mechanical toy, whistles and a music box.* JOE *blows into the whistles, quickly, by way of getting casually acquainted with them.* TOM *and* KITTY *stop dancing.* TOM *stares at her*)

DUDLEY   Hello. Is this Sunset 7349? May I speak to Elsie? Yes. (*emphatically, and bitterly*) No, this is *not* Dudley Bostwick. This is Roger Tenefrancia of Montreal, Canada. I'm a childhood friend of Miss Mandelspiegel. We went to kindergarten together. (*hand over phone*) Goddamn it. (*into phone*) Yes. I'll wait, thank you.

TOM   I love you. (*leading* KITTY *to in front of door right*)

KITTY   You want to go to my room? (TOM *can't answer*) Have you got two dollars?

TOM (*shaking his head with confusion*)   I've got *five* dollars, but I *love* you.

KITTY (*looking at him*)   You want to spend *all* that money?

(TOM *embraces her. They go out right.* JOE *watches, goes back to the toy*)

JOE   Where's that longshoreman, McCarthy?

NICK   He'll be around.

JOE   What do you think he'll have to say today?

NICK (*coming around bar*)   Plenty, as usual. I'm going next door to see who won that third race at Laurel.

JOE   Precious Time won it.

NICK   That's what you think. (*He goes out right*)

JOE (*to himself*)   A horse named McCarthy is running in the sixth race today.

DUDLEY (*on the phone*)   Hello. Hello, Elsie? Elsie? (*His voice weakens; also his limbs*) My God. She's come to the phone. Elsie, I'm at Nick's on Pacific Street. You've got to come here and talk to me. Hello. Hello, Elsie? (*amazed*) Did she hang up? Or was I disconnected? (*He hangs up and goes to bar.* WESLEY *is still playing the piano.* HARRY *is still dancing.* JOE *has wound up the big mechanical toy and is watching it work*)

NICK (*returns from right; goes to right of* JOE, *watching the toy*)   Say. That's some gadget.

JOE   How much did I win?

NICK   How do you know you *won*?

JOE   Don't be silly. He said Precious Time was going to win by ten lengths, didn't he? He's in love, isn't he?

NICK (*handing* JOE *money*)   O.K. I don't know why, but Precious Time won. You got eighty for ten. How do you do it?

JOE (*roaring*)   Faith. Faith. How'd he win?

NICK   By a nose. Look him up in *The Racing Form.* The slowest, the cheapest, the worst horse in the race, and the worst jockey. What's the matter with my luck?

JOE   How much did you lose?

NICK   Fifty cents.

JOE   You should never gamble.

NICK   Why not?

JOE   You always bet fifty cents. You've got no more faith than a flea, that's why.

HARRY (*shouting*)   How do you like this, Nick? (*He is really busy now, all legs and arms*)

NICK (*turning and watching, crossing to piano*)   Not bad. Hang around. You can wait table. (*to* WESLEY) Hey. Wesley. Can you play that again tonight?

WESLEY (*turning, but still playing the piano*)   I don't know for sure, Mr. Nick. I can play something.

NICK   Good. *You* hang around, too. (*He goes behind the bar*)

(*The atmosphere is now one of warm, natural, American ease; every man innocent and good; each doing what he believes he should do, or what he must do. There is deep American naïveté and faith in the behavior of each person. No one is competing with anyone else. No one hates anyone else. Every man is living, and letting live. Each man is following his destiny as he feels it should be followed; or is abandoning it as he feels it must, by now, be abandoned; or is forgetting it for the moment as he feels he should forget it. Although everyone is dead serious, there is unmistakable smiling and humor in the scene; a sense of the human body and spirit emerging from the world-imposed state of stress and fretfulness, fear and awkwardness, to the more natural state of casualness and grace. Each person belongs to the environment, in his own person, as himself:* WESLEY *is playing better than ever.* HARRY *is hoofing better than ever.* NICK *is behind the bar shining glasses.* JOE *is smiling at the toy and studying it.* DUDLEY, *although still troubled, is at least calm now and full of melancholy poise.* WILLIE, *at the marble game, is happy. The* ARAB *is deep in his memories, where he wants to be.*

Into this scene and atmosphere comes BLICK *from right.*

BLICK *is the sort of human being you dislike at sight. He is no different from anybody else physically. His face is an ordinary face. There is nothing obviously wrong with him, and yet you know that it is impossible, even by the*

*most generous expansion of understanding, to
accept him as a human being. He is the strong
man without strength—strong only among the
weak—the weakling who uses force on the
weaker.*

BLICK *enters casually, as if he were a customer, and immediately* HARRY *begins slowing
down)*

BLICK *(oily, and with mock friendliness)*
Hello, Nick.

NICK *(stopping his work and leaning across
the bar)* What do you want to come here for?
You're too big a man for a little honky-tonk.

BLICK *(flattered)* Now, Nick.

NICK Important people never come here.
Here. Have a drink. *(puts out whisky bottle
and glass)*

BLICK Thanks, I don't drink.

NICK *(drinking the whisky himself)* Well,
why don't you?

BLICK I have responsibilities.

NICK You're head of the lousy Vice Squad.
There's no vice here.

BLICK *(sharply)* Streetwalkers are working
out of this place.

NICK *(angry)* What do you want?

BLICK *(loudly)* I just want you to know
that it's got to *stop.*

*(The music stops. The mechanical toy runs
down. There is absolute silence, and a strange
fearfulness and disharmony in the atmosphere
now.* HARRY *doesn't know what to do with his
hands or feet.* WESLEY's *arms hang at his sides.*
JOE *quietly pushes the toy to one side of the
table eager to study what is happening.* WILLIE
*stops playing the marble game, turns around
and begins to wait.* DUDLEY *straightens up very,
very vigorously, as if to say: "Nothing can scare
me. I know love is the only thing." The* ARAB *is
the same as ever, but watchful.* NICK *is arro-
gantly aloof. There is a moment of this silence
and tension, as though* BLICK *were waiting for
everybody to acknowledge his presence. He is
obviously flattered by the acknowledgment of*
HARRY, DUDLEY, WESLEY *and* WILLIE, *but a
little irritated by* NICK's *aloofness and unfriend-
liness)*

NICK Don't look at me. I can't tell a streetwalker from a lady. You married?

BLICK You're not asking *me* questions. *I'm*
telling *you.*

NICK *(interrupting)* You're a man of about
forty-five or so. You *ought* to know better.

BLICK *(angry)* Streetwalkers are working
out of this place.

NICK *(beginning to shout)* Now, don't start

any trouble with me. People come here to drink
and loaf around. I don't care who they are.

BLICK Well, I do.

NICK The only way to find out if a lady is a
streetwalker is to walk the streets with her, go
to bed, and make sure. You wouldn't want to do
that. You'd *like* to, of course.

BLICK Any more of it, and I'll have your
joint closed.

NICK *(very casually, without ill will)* Listen.
I've got no use for you, or anybody like you.
You're out to change the world from something
bad to something worse. Something like yourself.

BLICK *(furious pause, and contempt)* I'll be
back tonight. *(He begins to go right)*

NICK *(very angry but very calm)* Do yourself a big favor and don't come back tonight.
Send somebody else. I don't like your personality.

BLICK Don't break any laws. I don't like
yours, either. *(He looks the place over, and
goes out right. There is a moment of silence.
Then* WILLIE *turns and puts a new nickel in the
slot and starts a new game.* WESLEY *turns to the
piano and rather falteringly begins to play. His
heart really isn't in it.* HARRY *walks about, unable to dance.* DUDLEY *lapses into his customary melancholy, at a table.* NICK *whistles
a little: suddenly stops.* JOE *winds the toy)*

JOE *(comically)* Nick. You going to kill
that man?

NICK I'm disgusted.

JOE Yeah? Why?

NICK Why should I get worked up over a
guy like that? Why should I hate *him?* He's
nothing. He's nobody. He's a mouse. But every
time he comes into this place I get burned up.
He doesn't want to drink. He doesn't want to
sit down. He doesn't want to take things easy.
Tell me one thing?

JOE Do my best.

NICK What's a punk like *that* want to go
out and try to change the world for?

JOE *(amazed)* Does *he* want to change the
world, too?

NICK *(irritated)* You know what I mean.
What's he want to bother people for? He's *sick.*

JOE *(almost to himself, reflecting on the fact
that* BLICK *too wants to change the world)* I
guess he wants to change the world at that.

NICK So I go to work and hate him.

JOE It's not him, Nick. It's everything.

NICK Yeah, *I know.* But I've still got no
use for him. He's *no good.* You know what I
mean? He hurts little people. *(confused)* One
of the girls tried to commit suicide on account

of him. (*furiously*) I'll break his head if he hurts anybody around here. This is *my* joint. (*afterthought*) Or anybody's *feelings*, either.

JOE   He may not be so bad, deep down underneath.

NICK   I know all about him. He's no good.

(*During this talk* WESLEY *has really begun to play the piano, the toy is rattling again, and little by little* HARRY *has begun to dance.* NICK *has come around the bar, and now, very much like a child—forgetting all his anger—is watching the toy work. He begins to smile at everything: turns and listens to* WESLEY: *watches* HARRY: *nods at the* ARAB: *shakes his head at* DUDLEY *and gestures amiably about* WILLIE. *It's his joint all right. It's a good, low-down, honky-tonk American place that lets people alone*)

NICK (*crossing to chair left of center table*) I've got a good joint. There's nothing wrong here. Hey. Comedian. Stick to the dancing tonight. I think you're O.K. (HARRY *goes to telephone and dials*) Wesley? Do some more of that tonight. That's fine!

HARRY   Thanks, Nick. Gosh, I'm on my way at last. (*on telephone*) Hello, Ma? Is that you, Ma? Harry. I got the job. (*He hangs up and walks around, smiling*)

NICK (*watching the toy all this time*)   Say, that really is something. What is that, anyway? (MARY L. *comes in right*)

JOE (*holding it toward* NICK, *and* MARY L.) Nick, this is a toy. A contraption devised by the cunning of man to drive boredom, or grief, or anger out of children. A noble gadget. A gadget, I might say, infinitely nobler than any other I can think of at the moment. (*Everybody gathers around* JOE's *table to look at the toy. The toy stops working.* JOE *winds the music box. Lifts a whistle: blows it, making a very strange, funny and sorrowful sound*) Delightful. Tragic, but delightful. (WESLEY *plays the music-box theme on the piano.* MARY L. *takes a table center*)

NICK   Joe. That girl, Kitty. What's she mean, calling me a dentist? I wouldn't hurt anybody, let alone a tooth. (NICK *goes to* MARY L.'s *table.* HARRY *imitates the toy. Dances. The piano music comes up, and the light dims slowly, while the piano solo continues*)

ACT TWO

(*Scene: Nick's, an hour later. All the people who were there when the curtain came down*

are still there. DUDLEY *at table right,* ARAB *seated in the rear at right.* HARRY *and* WESLEY *at piano.* JOE *at his table, quietly shuffling and turning a deck of cards, and at the same time watching the face of the* WOMAN, *and looking at the initials on her handbag as though they were the symbols of the lost glory of the world. At center table,* WOMAN, *in turn, very casually regards* JOE, *occasionally—or rather senses him; has sensed him in fact the whole hour. She is mildly tight on beer, and* JOE *himself is tight, but as always, completely under control; simply sharper. The others are about, at tables, and so on*)

JOE   Is it Madge—Laubowitz?

MARY   Is what *what?*

JOE   Is the name Mabel Lepescu?

MARY   What name?

JOE   The name the initials M. L. stand for. The initials on your bag.

MARY   No.

JOE (*after a long pause, thinking deeply what the name might be, turning a card, looking into the beautiful face of the* WOMAN) Margie Longworthy?

MARY (*all this is very natural and sincere, no comedy on the part of the people involved: they are both solemn, being drunk*)   No.

JOE (*his voice higher-pitched, as though he were growing a little alarmed*) Midge Laurie? (MARY *shakes her head*) My initials are J. T.

MARY (*pause*)   John?

JOE   No. (*pause*) Martha Lancaster?

MARY   No. (*slight pause*) Joseph?

JOE   Well, not exactly. That's my first name, but everybody calls me Joe. The last name is the tough one. I'll help you a little. I'm Irish. Is it just plain Mary?

MARY   Yes, it is. I'm Irish, too. At least on my father's side. English on my mother's side.

JOE   I'm Irish on both sides. Mary's one of my favorite names. I guess that's why I didn't think of it. I met a girl in Mexico City named Mary once. She was an American from Philadelphia. She got married there. In Mexico City, I mean. While I was *there*. We were in love, too. At least *I* was. You never know about anyone else. They were engaged, you see, and her mother was with her, so they went through with it. Must have been six or seven years ago. She's probably got three or four children by this time.

MARY   Are you still in love with her?

JOE   Well—no. To tell you the truth, I'm not sure. I guess I am. I didn't even know she was engaged until a couple of days before they got married. I thought *I* was going to marry her. I kept thinking all the time about the kind of kids we would be likely to have. My favorite was the third one. The first two were fine. Handsome and fine and intelligent, but that third one was different. Dumb and goofy-looking. I liked *him* a lot. When she told me she was going to be married, I didn't feel so bad about the first two, it was that dumb one.

MARY (*after a pause of some few seconds*) What do you do?

JOE   Do? To tell you the truth, nothing.

MARY   Do you always drink a great deal?

JOE (*scientifically*)   Not *always*. Only when I'm awake. I sleep seven or eight hours every night, you know.

MARY   How nice. I mean to drink when you're awake.

JOE (*thoughtfully*)   It's a privilege.

MARY   Do you really *like* to drink?

JOE (*positively*)   As much as I like to *breathe*.

MARY (*beautifully*)   Why?

JOE (*dramatically*)   Why do I like to drink? Because I don't like to be gypped. Because I don't like to be dead most of the time and just a little alive every once in a long while. (*pause*) If I don't drink, I become fascinated by unimportant things—like everybody else. I get busy. Do things. All kinds of little stupid things, for all kinds of little stupid reasons. Proud, selfish, *ordinary* things. I've done them. Now I don't do anything. *I live all the time.* Then I go to sleep.

MARY   Do you sleep well?

JOE (*taking it for granted*)   Of course.

MARY (*quietly, almost with tenderness*) What are your plans?

JOE (*loudly, but also tenderly*)   Plans? I haven't *got* any. *I just get up.*

MARY (*beginning to understand everything*) Oh, yes. Yes, of course. (DUDLEY *puts a nickel in the phonograph*)

JOE (*thoughtfully*)   Why do I drink? (*Pause, while he thinks about it. The thinking appears to be profound and complex, and has the effect of giving his face a very comical and naïve expression*) That question calls for a pretty complicated answer. (*He smiles abstractly*)

MARY   Oh, I didn't mean—

JOE (*swiftly, gallantly*)   No. No. I *insist*. I *know* why. It's just a matter of finding words. Little ones.

MARY   It really doesn't matter.

JOE (*seriously*)   Oh, yes, it does. (*clinically*) Now, why do I drink? (*scientifically*) No. Why does *anybody* drink? (*working it out*) Every day has twenty-four hours.

MARY (*sadly, but brightly*)   Yes, that's true.

JOE   Twenty-four hours. Out of the twenty-four hours at *least* twenty-three and a half are —my God, I don't know why—dull, dead, boring, empty, and murderous. Minutes on the clock, *not time of living*. It doesn't make any difference who you are or what you do, twenty-three and a half hours of the twenty-four are spent *waiting*.

MARY   Waiting?

JOE (*gesturing, loudly*)   And the more you wait, the less there is to wait *for*.

MARY (*attentively, beautifully his student*) Oh?

JOE (*continuing*)   That goes on for days and days, and weeks and months and years, and years, and the first thing you know *all* the years are dead. All the minutes are dead. You yourself are dead. There's nothing to wait for any more. Nothing except *minutes* on the *clock*. No time of life. Nothing but minutes, and idiocy. Beautiful, bright, intelligent idiocy. (*pause*) Does that answer your question?

MARY (*earnestly*)   I'm afraid it does. Thank you. You shouldn't have gone to all the trouble.

JOE   No trouble at all. (*pause*) You have children?

MARY   Yes. Two. A son and a daughter.

JOE (*delighted*)   How swell. Do they look like you?

MARY   Yes.

JOE   Then why are you sad?

MARY   I was always sad. It's just that after I was married I was allowed to drink.

JOE (*eagerly*)   Who are you waiting for?

MARY   No one.

JOE (*smiling*)   I'm not waiting for anybody, either.

MARY   My husband, of course.

JOE   Oh, sure.

MARY   He's a lawyer.

JOE (*standing, leaning on the table*)   He's a great guy. I like him. I'm very fond of him.

MARY (*listening*)   You have responsibilities?

JOE (*loudly; rises*)   One, and *thousands*. As a matter of fact, I fell responsible to everybody. At least to everybody I meet. I've been trying for three years to find out if it's possible to live what I think is a civilized life. I mean a life that can't hurt any other life.

MARY   You're famous!

JOE   Very. Utterly unknown, but very famous. Would you like to dance?

MARY   All right.

JOE (*loudly*)   I'm *sorry*. I don't dance. I didn't think *you'd* like to.

MARY   To tell you the truth, I don't like to dance at all.

JOE (*proudly; commentator*) I can hardly walk.

MARY You mean you're tight?

JOE (*smiling*) No. I mean *all* the time.

MARY (*sitting forward*) Were you ever in Paris?

JOE In 1929, and again in 1934.

MARY What month of 1934?

JOE Most of April, all of May and a little of June.

MARY I was there in November and December that year.

JOE We were there almost at the same time. You were married?

MARY Engaged. (*They are silent a moment, looking at one another. Quietly and with great charm*) Are you *really* in love with me?

JOE Yes.

MARY Is it the champagne?

JOE Yes. Partly, at least. (*He sits down*)

MARY If you don't see me again, will you be very unhappy?

JOE Very.

MARY (*getting up*) I'm so pleased. (*JOE is deeply grieved that she is going. In fact, he is almost panic-stricken about it, getting up in a way that is full of furious sorrow and regret*) I must go now. Please don't get up. (*JOE is up, staring at her with amazement*) Good-bye.

JOE (*simply*) Good-bye. (*Music ends. The* WOMAN *stands looking at him a moment, then turns and goes slowly out right.* JOE *stands staring after her for a long time. Just as he is slowly sitting down again, the* NEWSBOY *enters right, and goes to* JOE's *table*)

NEWSBOY Paper, Mister?

JOE How many you got this time?

NEWSBOY Eleven. (*JOE buys them all, looks at all, throws them away.* ARAB *crosses, picks up one and returns to his seat at rear right. The* NEWSBOY *looks at* JOE, *shakes head, goes to bar, troubled*) Hey, Mister, do you own this place?

NICK I own this place.

NEWSBOY Can you use a great lyric tenor?

NICK (*almost to himself*) Great lyric tenor? (*loudly*) Who?

NEWSBOY Me. I'm getting too big to sell papers. I don't want to holler headlines all the time. I want to *sing*. You can use a great lyric tenor, can't you?

NICK What's lyric about you?

NEWSBOY (*voice high-pitched, confused*) My voice.

NICK Oh. (*slight pause, giving in*) All right, then—sing!

(*The* NEWSBOY *breaks into swift and beautiful song: "When Irish Eyes Are Smiling."* NICK *and*

JOE *listen carefully:* NICK *with wonder,* JOE *with amazement and delight*)

NEWSBOY (*singing*)

When Irish eyes are smiling,
Sure 'tis like a morn in spring.
In the lilt of Irish laughter,
You can hear the angels sing.
When Irish hearts are happy,
All the world seems bright and gay
But when Irish eyes are smiling—

NICK (*loudly, swiftly*) Are you Irish?

NEWSBOY (*speaking swiftly, loudly, a little impatient with the irrelevant question*) No. I'm Greek. (*He finishes the song, singing louder than ever*) "Sure they steal your heart away." (*He turns to* NICK *dramatically, like a vaudeville singer begging his audience for applause.* NICK *studies the boy eagerly.* JOE *gets to his feet and leans toward the* BOY *and* NICK)

NICK Not bad. Let me hear you again about a year from now.

NEWSBOY (*thrilled*) Honest?

NICK Yeah. Along about November 7th, 1940.

NEWSBOY (*happier than ever before in his life, running over to* JOE) Did you hear it too, Mister?

JOE Yes, and it's great. What part of Greece?

NEWSBOY Salonica. Gosh, Mister. Thanks.

JOE Don't wait a year. Come back with some papers a little later. You're a great singer.

NEWSBOY (*thrilled and excited*) Aw, thanks, Mister. So long. (*running, to* NICK) Thanks, Mister. (*He runs out right.* JOE *and* NICK *look at the swinging doors.* JOE *sits down.* NICK *laughs*)

NICK Joe, people are so wonderful. Look at that kid.

JOE Of course they're wonderful. Every one of them is wonderful.

(MCCARTHY *and* KRUPP *come in right, talking.* MCCARTHY *is a big man in work clothes, which make him seem very young. He is wearing black jeans, and a blue workman's shirt. No tie. No hat. He has broad shoulders, a lean intelligent face, thick black hair. In his right back pocket is the longshoreman's hook. His arms are long and hairy. His sleeves are rolled up to just below his elbows. He is a casual man, easygoing in movement, sharp in perception, swift in appreciation of charm or innocence or comedy, and gentle in spirit. His speech is clear and full of warmth. His voice is powerful, but modulated. He enjoys the world, in spite of the mess it is, and he is fond of people, in spite of the mess they are*)

KRUPP *is not quite as tall or broad-shouldered as* MCCARTHY. *He is physically encumbered by his uniform, club, pistol, belt and cap. And he is plainly not at home in the role of policeman. His movement is stiff and unintentionally pomp-ous. He is a naïve man, essentially good. His understanding is less than* MCCARTHY'*s, but he is honest and he doesn't try to bluff*)

KRUPP   You don't understand what I mean. Hiya, Joe. (*crossing to center of bar*)

JOE   Hello, Krupp.

MCCARTHY   (*crossing to behind* KRUPP) Hiya, Joe.

JOE   Hello, McCarthy.

KRUPP   Two beers, Nick. (*to* MCCARTHY) All I do is carry out orders, carry out orders. I don't know what the idea is behind the order. Who it's for, or who it's against, or why. All I do is carry it out. (NICK *gives them beer*)

MCCARTHY   You don't read enough.

KRUPP   I do read. I read *The Examiner* every morning. *The Call-Bulletin* every night.

MCCARTHY   And carry out orders. What are the orders now?

KRUPP   To keep the peace down here on the waterfront.

MCCARTHY   Keep it for who? (*to* JOE) Right?

JOE   (*sorrowfully*)   Right.

KRUPP   How do I know for who? The peace. Just keep it.

MCCARTHY   It's got to be kept for somebody. Who would you suspect it's kept for?

KRUPP   (*thinking*)   For citizens!

MCCARTHY   I'm a citizen.

KRUPP   All right, I'm keeping it for you.

MCCARTHY   By hitting me over the head with a club? (*to* JOE) Right?

JOE   (*melancholy, with remembrance*)   I don't know.

KRUPP   Mac, you know I never hit you over the head with a club.

MCCARTHY   But you will if you're on duty at the time and happen to stand on the op-posite side of myself, on duty.

KRUPP   We went to Mission High together. We were always good friends. The only time we ever fought was that time over Alma Hag-gerty. Did *you* marry Alma Haggerty? Right?

JOE   Everything's right.

MCCARTHY   No. Did you? (*to* JOE) Joe, are you with me or against me?

JOE   I'm with everybody. One at a time.

KRUPP   No. And that's just what I mean.

MCCARTHY   You mean neither one of us is going to marry the thing we're fighting for?

KRUPP   *I don't even know what it is.*

MCCARTHY   You don't read enough, I tell you.

KRUPP   Mac, you don't know what you're fighting for, either.

MCCARTHY   It's so simple, it's fantastic.

KRUPP   All right, what are you fighting for?

MCCARTHY   For the rights of the inferior. Right?

JOE   Something like that.

KRUPP   The who?

MCCARTHY   The inferior. The world full of Mahoneys who haven't got what it takes to make monkeys out of everybody else, near by. The men who were created equal. Remember?

KRUPP   Mac, you're not inferior.

MCCARTHY   I'm a longshoreman. And an idealist. I'm a man with too much brawn to be an intellectual, exclusively. (*crossing to right of* JOE) I married a small, sensitive, cultured woman so that my kids would be sissies instead of suckers. A strong man with any sensibility has no choice in this world but to be a heel, or a *worker.* I haven't the heart to be a heel, so I'm a worker. I've got a son in high school who's already thinking of being a writer.

KRUPP   I wanted to be a writer once.

JOE   Wonderful. (*He puts down the paper, looks at* KRUPP *and* MCCARTHY)

MCCARTHY   They *all* wanted to be writers. Every maniac in the world that ever brought about the murder of people through war started out in an attic or a basement writing poetry. It stank. So they got even by becoming impor-tant heels. And it's still going on.

KRUPP   Is it really, Joe?

JOE   Look at today's paper.

MCCARTHY   Right now on Telegraph Hill is some punk who is trying to be Shakespeare. Ten years from now he'll be a senator. Or a Communist.

KRUPP   Somebody ought to do something about it.

MCCARTHY   (*mischievously, with laughter in his voice*)   The thing to do is to have more magazines. Hundreds of *them.* Thousands. Print everything they write, so they'll believe they're immortal. That way keep them from go-ing haywire.

KRUPP   Mac, you ought to be a writer your-self.

MCCARTHY   I hate the tribe. They're mis-chief-makers. Right?

JOE   (*swiftly*)   Everything's right. Right and wrong.

KRUPP   Then why do you read?

MCCARTHY   (*laughing*)   It's relaxing. It's soothing. (*pause*) The lousiest people born into the world are writers. Language is all right.

It's the people who use language that are lousy. (*The* ARAB *has moved a little closer, and is listening carefully. To the* ARAB) What do you think, Brother?

ARAB (*at first step forward to the right; after making many faces, thinking very deeply*) No foundation. All the way down the line. What. What-not. Nothing. I go walk and look at sky. (*He goes out right*)

KRUPP (*follows to in front of bar*) What? What-not? (*to* JOE) What's that mean?

JOE (*slowly, thinking, remembering*) What? What-not? That means this side, that side. Inhale, exhale. What: birth. What-not: death. The inevitable, the astounding, the magnificent seed of growth and decay in all things. Beginning, and end. That man, in his own way, is a prophet. He is one who, with the help of *beer,* is able to reach that state of deep understanding in which what and what-not, the reasonable and the unreasonable, are *one.*

MCCARTHY Right.

KRUPP If you can understand that kind of talk, how can you be a longshoreman?

MCCARTHY I come from a long line of McCarthys who never married or slept with anything but the most powerful and quarrelsome flesh. (*He drinks beer*)

KRUPP I could listen to you two guys for hours, but I'll be damned if I know what the hell you're talking about.

MCCARTHY The consequence is that all the McCarthys are too great and too strong to be heroes. Only the weak and unsure perform the heroic. They've *got* to. The more heroes you have, the worse the history of the world becomes. Right?

JOE Go outside and look at it.

KRUPP You sure can philos—philosoph— Boy, you can talk.

MCCARTHY I wouldn't talk this way to anyone but a man in uniform, and a man who couldn't understand a word of what I was saying. The party I'm speaking of, my friend, is *YOU.* (*The phone rings.* HARRY *gets up from his table suddenly and begins a new dance*)

KRUPP (*noticing him, with great authority*) Here. Here. What do you think you're doing?

HARRY (*stopping*) I just got an idea for a new dance. I'm trying it out. Nick. Nick, the phone's ringing. (NICK *goes to phone*)

KRUPP (*to* MCCARTHY) Has he got a right to do that?

MCCARTHY The living have danced from the beginning of time. I might even say, the dance and the life have moved along together, until now we have—(*to* HARRY) Go into your dance, son, and show us what we have.

HARRY I haven't got it worked out *completely* yet, but it starts out like this. (*He dances*)

NICK (*on phone*) Nick's Pacific Street Restaurant, Saloon, and Entertainment Palace. Good afternoon. Nick speaking. (*listens*) Who? (*turns around*) Is there a Dudley Bostwick in the joint? (DUDLEY *jumps to his feet and goes to phone.* NICK *goes to behind bar*)

DUDLEY (*on phone*) Hello. Elsie? (*listens*) You're coming down? (*elated. To the saloon*) She's coming down. (*pause*) No. I won't drink. Aw, gosh, Elsie. (*He hangs up, looks about him strangely, as if he were just born, walks around touching things, putting chairs in place, and so on*)

MCCARTHY (*to* HARRY) Splendid. Splendid.

HARRY Then I go into this little routine. (*He demonstrates*)

KRUPP Is that good, Mac?

MCCARTHY It's awful, but it's honest and ambitious, like everything else in this great country.

HARRY Then I work along into this. (*He demonstrates*) And this is where I *really* get going. (*He finishes the dance*)

MCCARTHY Excellent. A most satisfying demonstration of the present state of the American body and soul. (*crossing to* HARRY *and shaking his hand*) Son, you're a genius.

HARRY (*delighted*) I go on in front of an audience for the first time in my life tonight.

MCCARTHY They'll be delighted. Where'd you learn to dance?

HARRY Never took a lesson in my life. I'm a natural-born dancer. And *comedian,* too.

MCCARTHY (*astounded*) You can make people *laugh?*

HARRY (*dumbly*) I can be funny, but they won't laugh.

MCCARTHY That's odd. Why not?

HARRY I don't know. They just won't laugh.

MCCARTHY Would you care to be funny now?

HARRY I'd like to try out a new monologue I've been thinking about.

MCCARTHY Please do. I promise you if it's funny I shall *roar* with laughter.

HARRY This is it. (*goes into the act, with much energy*) I'm up at Sharkey's on Turk Street. It's a quarter to nine, daylight saving. Wednesday, the eleventh. What I've got is a headache and a 1918 nickel. What I *want* is a cup of coffee. If I buy a cup of coffee with the nickel, I've got to walk home. I've got an eight-ball problem. George the Greek is shooting a game of snooker with Pedro the Filipino. *I'm in rags.* They're wearing thirty-five-dollar suits, made to order. I haven't got a cigarette. They're smoking Bobby Burns panatelas. I'm thinking it over, like I always do. George the Greek is in a tough spot. If I buy a cup of coffee, I'll want another cup. What happens? *My ear* aches! My ear. George the Greek takes the cue. Chalks it. Studies the table. Touches the cue ball delicately. Tick. What happens? He makes the three ball! What do I do? I get confused. *I go out and buy a morning paper.* What the hell do I want with a morning paper? What I *want* is a cup of coffee, and a good used car. I go out and buy a morning paper. Thursday, the twelfth. Maybe the headline's about *me.* I take a quick look. *No. The headline is not about me.* It's about Hitler. Seven thousand miles away. I'm here. Who the hell is Hitler? Who's behind the eight ball? I turn around. *Everybody's behind the eight ball! (pause.* KRUPP *moves toward* HARRY *as if to make an important arrest.* HARRY *moves to the swinging doors.* MCCARTHY *stops* KRUPP)

MCCARTHY   It's the funniest thing I've ever heard. Or *seen,* for that matter.

HARRY   Then, why don't you laugh?

MCCARTHY   I don't know, *yet.*

HARRY   I'm always getting funny ideas that nobody will laugh at.

MCCARTHY   It may be that you've stumbled headlong into a new kind of comedy.

HARRY   Well, what good is it if it doesn't make anybody laugh?

MCCARTHY   There are *kinds* of laughter, son. I must say, in all truth, that I *am* laughing, although not *out loud.*

HARRY   I want to *hear* people laugh. *Out loud.* That's why I keep thinking of funny things to say.

MCCARTHY   (*crossing to front right*)   Well. They may catch on in time. Let's go, Krupp. So long, Joe. (MCCARTHY *and* KRUPP *go out right*)

JOE   So long. (*after a moment's pause*) Hey, Nick.

NICK   Yeah. (HARRY *exits rear center.* DUDLEY *goes to bar and gets beer*)

JOE   Bet McCarthy in the last race.

NICK   You're crazy. That horse is a double-crossing, no-good—

JOE   Bet everything you've got on McCarthy.

NICK   I'm not betting a nickel on him. *You* bet everything you've got on McCarthy.

JOE   I don't need money.

NICK   What makes you think McCarthy's going to win?

JOE   McCarthy's name's McCarthy, isn't it?

NICK   Yeah, so what?

JOE   The *horse* named McCarthy is going to win, *that's all.* Today.

NICK   Why?

JOE   You do what I tell you, and everything will be all right.

NICK   McCarthy likes to talk, that's all. Where's Tom?

JOE   He'll be around. He'll be miserable, but he'll be around. Five or ten minutes more.

NICK   You don't believe that Kitty, do you? About being in burlesque?

JOE   (*very clearly*)   I believe dreams sooner than statistics.

NICK   (*remembering*)   She sure is somebody. Called me a dentist. (TOM, *turning about, confused, troubled, comes in, right, and hurries to* JOE'S *table*)

JOE   What's the matter?

TOM   (*giving* JOE *money*)   Here's your five, Joe. I'm in trouble again.

JOE   If it's not organic, it'll cure itself. If it *is* organic, science will cure it. What is it, organic or non-organic?

TOM   Joe, I don't know—(*He sits at right of table, buries his head on his arms and seems to be completely broken-down*)

JOE   What's eating you? I want you to go on an errand for me.

TOM   It's Kitty.

JOE   What about her?

TOM   She's up in her room, crying.

JOE   Crying?

TOM   Yeah, she's been crying for over an hour. I been talking to her all this time, but she won't stop.

JOE   What's she crying about?

TOM   I don't know. I couldn't understand anything. She kept crying and telling me about a big house and collie dogs all around and flowers and one of her brother's dead and the other one lost somewhere. Joe, I can't stand Kitty crying.

JOE   You want to marry the girl?

TOM   (*nodding*)   Yeah.

JOE   (*curious and sincere*)   Why?

TOM   I don't know why, exactly, Joe. (*pause*) Joe, I don't like to think of Kitty out in the streets. I guess I love her, that's all.

JOE   She's a nice girl.

TOM   She's like an angel. She's not like those other streetwalkers.

JOE   (*swiftly*)   Here. Take all this money and run next door to Frankie's and bet it on the nose of McCarthy.

TOM   (*swiftly*)   All this money, Joe? McCarthy?

JOE   Yeah. Hurry.

TOM (*going*) Ah, Joe. If McCarthy wins we'll be rich.

JOE Get going, will you? (TOM *runs out right and nearly knocks over the* ARAB *coming back in.* NICK *fills him a beer without a word*)

ARAB No foundation, anywhere. Whole world. No foundation. All the way down the line.

NICK (*angry*) McCarthy! Just because you got a little lucky this morning, you have to go to work and throw away eighty bucks.

JOE He wants to marry her.

NICK Suppose she doesn't want to marry *him*?

JOE (*amazed*) Oh, yeah. (*thinking*) Now, why wouldn't she want to marry a nice guy like Tom?

NICK She's been in burlesque. She's had flowers sent to her by European royalty. She's dined with young men of quality and social position. She's above Tom.

TOM (*comes running in, crossing to* JOE; *disgusted*) They were running when I got there. Frankie wouldn't take the bet. McCarthy didn't get a call till the stretch. I thought we were going to save all this money. Then McCarthy won by *two* lengths.

JOE What'd he pay, fifteen to one?

TOM Better, but Frankie wouldn't take the bet.

NICK (*throwing a dish towel across the room*) Well, for the love of Mike.

JOE Give me the money.

TOM (*giving back the money*) We would have had about a thousand five hundred dollars.

JOE (*pause; bored, displeased*) Go up to Schwabacher-Frey and get me the biggest Rand-McNally map of the nations of Europe they've got. On your way back stop at one of the pawn shops on Third Street, and buy me a good revolver and some cartridges.

TOM She's up in her room crying, Joe.

JOE Go get me those things.

NICK (*crossing to center table; gets glasses*) What are you going to do, study the map, and then go out and shoot somebody?

JOE I want to read the names of some European towns and rivers and valleys and mountains.

NICK What do you want with the revolver? (*goes to back of bar. Dries glasses*)

JOE I want to study it. I'm interested in things. Here's twenty dollars, Tom. Now go get them things.

TOM A big map of Europe. And a revolver.

JOE Get a good one. Tell the man you don't know anything about firearms and you're trusting him not to fool you. Don't pay more than ten dollars.

TOM Joe, you got something on your mind. Don't go fool with a revolver.

JOE Be sure it's a good one.

TOM Joe.

JOE What, Tom?

TOM Joe, what do you send me out for crazy things for all the time?

JOE They're not crazy, Tom. Now, get going.

TOM What about Kitty, Joe?

JOE Let her cry. It'll do her good.

TOM If she comes in here while I'm gone, talk to her, will you, Joe? Tell her about me.

JOE O.K. Get going. Don't load that gun. Just buy it and bring it here.

TOM (*going to stair landing, right*) You won't catch me loading any gun.

JOE Wait a minute. Take these toys away.

TOM (*crossing to right of* JOE) Where'll I take them?

JOE Give them to some kid. No. Take them up to Kitty. Toys stopped me from crying once. That's the reason I had you buy them. I wanted to see if I could find out *why* they stopped me from crying. I remember they seemed awfully stupid at the time.

TOM Shall I, Joe? Take them up to Kitty? Do you think they'd stop *her* from crying?

JOE They might. You get curious about the way they work and you forget whatever it is you're remembering that's making you cry. That's what they're for.

TOM Yeah. Sure. The girl at the store asked me what I wanted with toys. I'll take them up to Kitty. (*tragically*) She's like a little girl. (*He goes out right*)

WESLEY Mr. Nick, can I play the piano again?

NICK Sure. Practice all you like—until I tell you to stop.

WESLEY You going to pay me for playing the piano?

NICK Sure. I'll give you enough to get by on.

WESLEY (*amazed and delighted*) Get money for playing the piano? (*He goes to the piano and begins to play quietly.* HARRY *goes up on the little stage and listens to the music. After a while he begins a soft-shoe dance which is very quiet and relaxing*)

NICK What were you crying about?

JOE My mother.

NICK What about her?

JOE She was dead. I stopped crying when

they gave me the toys. (NICK'S MOTHER, *a little old woman of sixty or so, dressed plainly in black, her face shining, comes in briskly, chattering loudly in Italian, gesturing.* NICK *is delighted to see her*)

NICK'S MOTHER (*in Italian*)   Everything all right, Nickie?

NICK (*in Italian*)   Sure, Mamma. (NICK'S MOTHER *leaves as gaily and as noisily as she came*)

JOE   Who was that?

NICK (*to* JOE, *proudly and a little sadly*) My mother. (*still looking at the swinging doors*)

JOE   What'd she say?

NICK   Nothing. Just wanted to see me. What do you want with that gun?

JOE   I study things, Nick. (*An old man who looks like* KIT CARSON *staggers in right, looks around; edges to bar; reaction to* NICK; *goes to left and moves about aimlessly and finally goes to chair left of center table*)

KIT CARSON   Murphy's the name. Just an old trapper. Mind if I sit down?

JOE   Be delighted. What'll you drink?

KIT CARSON (*sitting down*)   Beer. Same as I've been drinking. And thanks.

JOE (*to* NICK)   Glass of beer, Nick. (NICK *brings the beer to the table, and goes back to bar.* KIT CARSON *swallows it in one swig, wipes his big white mustache with the back of his right hand*)

KIT CARSON (*moving in*)   I don't suppose you ever fell in love with a midget weighing thirty-nine pounds?

JOE   Can't say I have, but have another beer.

KIT CARSON (*intimately*)   Thanks, thanks. Down in Gallup, twenty years ago. Fellow by the name of Rufus Jenkins came to town with six white horses and two black ones. Said he wanted a man to break the horses for him because his left leg was wood and he couldn't do it. Had a meeting at Parker's Mercantile Store and finally came to blows, me and Henry Walpal. Bashed his head with a brass cuspidor and ran away to Mexico, but he didn't die. (SAILOR *enters right and goes to bar*) Couldn't speak a word. Took up with a cattle-breeder named Diego, educated in California. Spoke the language better than you and me. Said, "Your job, Murph, is to feed them prize bulls." I said, "Fine, what'll I feed them?" he said, "Hay, lettuce, salt, beer and aspirin." Came to blows two days later ·over an accordion he claimed I stole. I had *borrowed* it. During the fight I busted it over his head; ruined one of the finest accordions I ever saw. Grabbed a horse and rode back across the border. Texas. Got to talking with a fellow who looked honest. Turned out to be a Ranger who was looking for me.

(KILLER *enters right. Sits in front of bar*)

JOE   Yeah. You were saying, a thirty-nine-pound midget.

KIT CARSON   Will I ever forget that lady? Will I ever get over that amazon of small proportions?

JOE   Will you?

KIT CARSON   If I live to be sixty.

JOE   Sixty? You look more than sixty now.

KIT CARSON   That's trouble showing in my face. Trouble and complications. I was fifty-eight three months ago.

JOE   That accounts for it, then. Go ahead, tell me more.

KIT CARSON   Told the Texas Ranger my name was Rothstein, mining engineer from Pennsylvania, looking for something worth while. Mentioned two places in Houston. Nearly lost an eye early one morning, going down the stairs. (*rises*) Ran into a six-footer with an iron claw where his right hand was supposed to be. Said, "You broke up my home." Told him I was a stranger in Houston. The girls gathered at the top of the stairs to see a fight. Seven of them. Six feet and an iron claw. That's bad on the nerves. Kicked him in the mouth when he swung for my head with the claw. Would have lost an eye except for quick thinking. He rolled into the gutter and pulled a gun. Fired seven times. I was back upstairs. Left the place an hour later, dressed in silk and feathers, with a hat swung around over my face. Saw him standing on the corner, waiting. (*crossing left*) Said, "Care for a wiggle?" Said he didn't. I went on down the street and left town. I don't suppose you ever had to put a dress on to save your skin, did you? (*crosses to left of center table and sits*)

JOE (*signals* NICK *for beer*)   No, and I never fell in love with a midget weighing thirty-nine pounds. Have another beer?

KIT CARSON   Thanks. Ever try to herd cattle on a bicycle?

(NICK *crosses to left of center table with beer which* KIT *takes.* NICK *goes back to bar*)

JOE   No. I never got around to that.

KIT CARSON   Left Houston with sixty cents in my pocket, gift of a girl named Lucinda. Walked fourteen miles in fourteen hours. Big house with barbwire all around, and big dogs. One thing I never could get around. Walked past the gate, anyway, from hunger and thirst. Dogs jumped up and came for me. Walked right into them, growing older every second. Went up to the door and knocked. Big Negress opened the door, closed it quick. Said, "On your way, white trash." Knocked again. Said, "On your way." Again. "On your way." Again. This time the old man himself opened the door, ninety, if he was a day. Sawed-off shotgun, too. Said, "I ain't looking for trouble, Father. I'm hungry and thirsty, name's Cavanaugh." Took me in and made mint juleps for the two of us. Said, "Living here alone, Father?" Said, "Drink and ask no questions. Maybe I am and maybe I ain't. You saw the lady. Draw your own conclusions." I'd heard of that, but didn't wink out of tact. If I told you that old Southern gentleman was my grandfather, you wouldn't believe me, would you?

JOE   I might.

KIT CARSON   Well, it so happens he wasn't. Would have been romantic if he had been, though.

JOE   Where did you herd cattle on a bicycle?

KIT CARSON   Toledo, Ohio, 1918.

JOE   Toledo, Ohio? They don't herd cattle in Toledo.

KIT CARSON   They don't anymore. They did in 1918. One fellow did, least-a-ways. Bookkeeper named Sam Gold. Straight from the East Side, New York. Sombrero, lariats, Bull Durham, two head of cattle and two bicycles. Called his place The Gold Bar Ranch, two acres, just outside the city limits. That was the year of the War, you'll remember.

JOE   Yeah, I remember, but how about herding them two cows on a bicycle? How'd you do it?

KIT CARSON   Easiest thing in the world. Rode no hands. Had to, otherwise couldn't lasso the cows. Worked for Sam Gold till the cows ran away. Bicycles scared them. They went into Toledo. Never saw hide nor hair of them again. Advertised in every paper, but never got them back. Broke his heart. Sold both bikes and returned to New York. Took four aces from a deck of red cards and walked to town. Poker. Fellow in the game named Chuck Collins, liked to gamble. Told him with a smile I didn't suppose he'd care to bet a hundred dollars I wouldn't hold four aces the next hand. Called it. My cards were red on the blank side. The other cards were blue. Plumb forgot all about it. Showed him four aces. Ace of spades, ace of clubs, ace of diamonds, ace of hearts. I'll remember them four cards if I live to be sixty. Would have been killed on the spot except for the hurricane that year.

JOE   Hurricane?

KIT CARSON   You haven't forgotten the Toledo hurricane of 1918, have you?

JOE   No. There was no hurricane in Toledo in 1918, or any other year.

KIT CARSON   For the love of God, then what do you suppose that commotion was? And how come I came to in Chicago dream-walking down State Street?

JOE   I guess they scared you.

KIT CARSON   No, that wasn't it. You go back to the papers of November, 1918, and I think you'll find there was a hurricane in Toledo. I remember sitting on the roof of a two-story house, floating northwest.

JOE   (*seriously*)   Northwest?

KIT CARSON   Now, son, don't tell me *you* don't believe me, either?

JOE   (*very seriously, energetically and sharply*)   Of course I believe you. Living is an art. It's not bookkeeping. It takes a lot of rehearsing for a man to get to be himself.

KIT CARSON   (*thoughtfully, smiling*)   You're the first man I've ever met who believes me.

JOE   (*seriously*)   Have another beer. (TOM *comes in right with the Rand-McNally book, the revolver and the box of cartridges*)

JOE   (*to* TOM)   Did you give her the toys?

TOM   Yeah, I gave them to her.

JOE   Did she stop crying?

TOM   No. She started crying harder than ever.

JOE   That's funny. I wonder why.

TOM   Joe, if I was a minute earlier, Frankie would have taken the bet and now we'd have about a thousand five hundred dollars. How much of it would you have given me, Joe?

JOE   If she'd marry you—*all* of it.

TOM   Would you, Joe?

JOE   (*opening packages, examining book first, and revolver next*)   Sure. In this realm there's only one subject, and you're it. It's my duty to see that my subject is happy.

TOM   Joe, do you think we'll ever have eighty dollars for a race sometime again when there's a fifteen-to-one shot that we like, weather good, track fast, they get off to a good start, our horse doesn't get a call till the stretch, we think we're going to lose all that money, and then it wins, by a nose?

JOE   I didn't quite get that.

TOM   You know what I mean.

JOE   You mean the impossible. No, Tom, we won't. We were just a little late, that's all.

TOM   We might, Joe.

JOE   It's not likely.

TOM   Then how am I ever going to make enough money to marry her?

JOE   I don't know, Tom. Maybe you aren't.

TOM   Joe, I got to marry Kitty. (*shaking his head*) You ought to see the crazy room she lives in.

JOE   What kind of a room is it?

TOM   It's little. It crowds you in. It's bad, Joe. Kitty don't belong in a place like that.

JOE   You want to take her away from there?

TOM   Yeah. I want her to live in a house where there's room enough to live. Kitty ought to have a garden, or something.

JOE   You want to take care of her?

TOM   Yeah, sure, Joe. I ought to take care of somebody good that makes me feel like *I'm* somebody.

JOE   That means you'll have to get a job. What can you do?

TOM   I finished high school, but I don't know what I can do.

JOE   Sometimes when you think about it, what do you think you'd like to do?

TOM   Just sit around like you, Joe, and have somebody run errands for me and drink champagne and take things easy and never be broke and never worry about money.

JOE   That's a noble ambition.

NICK   How do you do it?

JOE   I really don't know, but I think you've got to have the full co-operation of the Good Lord.

NICK   I can't understand the way you talk.

TOM   Joe, shall I go back and see if I can get her to stop crying?

JOE   Give me a hand and I'll go with you.

TOM   (*amazed*)   What! You're going to get up already?

JOE   She's crying, isn't she?

TOM   She's crying. Worse than ever now.

JOE   I thought the toys would stop her.

TOM   I've seen you sit in one place from four in the morning till two the next morning.

JOE   At my best, Tom, I don't travel by foot. That's all. Come on. Give me a hand. I'll find some way to stop her from crying.

TOM   Joe, I never did tell you. You're a different kind of a guy.

JOE   Don't be silly. I don't understand things. I'm trying to understand them. (*TOM helps JOE up. He is a little drunk. They go out right together. The telephone rings. DUDLEY jumps to his feet and runs to it*)

ACT THREE

(*Scene: Room Twenty-one of The New York Hotel, around the corner from Nick's. This is* set inside the main set. There is a bed right; a screen above bed; a door back of screen; a window in back of bed. A dresser is painted on the screen. A small table above right of bed. KITTY DUVAL, *in a dress she has carried around with her from the early days in Ohio, is seated on the bed, tying a ribbon in her hair. She looks at herself in the mirror. She is deeply grieved at the change she sees in herself. She stares at the bare, desolate walls of the room. Looks into the mirror again. Takes off the ribbon, angry and hurt. She lifts a book from the bed and tries to read. She begins to sob again. Takes an old picture of herself from foot of bed and looks at it. And sobs harder than ever, falling on the bed and burying her face. She turns over on the other side, as if even with her eyes closed she cannot escape her sorrow. From one of the other rooms of the hotel is coming the voice of a young man singing "My Gal Sal." There is a knock at the door*)

KITTY   (*sobbing*)   Who is it?

TOM'S VOICE   Kitty, it's me. Tom. Me and Joe.

(KITTY *looks around the room, smiles at the remembrance of* TOM, *looks around the desolate room and falls back sobbing.* JOE, *followed by* TOM, *comes in quietly.* JOE *is holding a rather large toy carousel. He takes the room in swiftly. Amazed. He sets the toy carousel on the floor, at the foot of* KITTY's *bed*)

TOM   (*standing over* KITTY *and bending down close to her*)   Don't cry any more, Kitty.

KITTY   (*not looking up, sobbing*)   I don't like this life. (JOE *starts the carousel which makes a strange, sorrowful, tinkling music. The music begins slowly, becomes swift, gradually slows down, and ends.* JOE *himself is interested in the toy, watches and listens to it carefully*)

TOM   Kitty. Joe got up from his chair at Nick's just to get you a toy and come here. This one makes music. We rode all over town in a cab to get it. Listen.

(KITTY *sits up slowly, listening, while* TOM *watches her and* JOE. *Everything happens slowly and somberly.* KITTY *notices the photograph of herself when she was a little girl. Lifts it, and looks at it again*)

TOM   (*looking*)   Who's that little girl, Kitty?

KITTY   That's me. When I was seven.

(*hands the photo to* TOM)

TOM   Gee, you're pretty, Kitty. (JOE *reaches up for the photograph, which* TOM *hands to him.* TOM *returns to* KITTY *whom he finds as pretty now as she was at seven.* JOE *studies the photograph.* KITTY *looks up at* TOM. *There is no doubt that they really love one another.* JOE *looks up at them*)

KITTY   Tom?

TOM (*eagerly*)   Yeah, Kitty.

KITTY   Tom, when you were a little boy what did you want to be?

TOM (*a little bewildered, but eager to please her*)   What, Kitty?

KITTY   Do you remember when you were a little boy?

TOM (*thoughtfully*)   Yeah, I remember sometimes, Kitty.

KITTY   What did you want to be?

TOM (*looks at* JOE. JOE *holds* TOM's *eyes a moment; then* TOM *is able to speak*)   Sometimes I wanted to be a locomotive engineer. Sometimes I wanted to be a policeman.

KITTY   I wanted to be a great actress. (*She looks up into* TOM's *face*) Tom, didn't you ever want to be a doctor?

TOM (*looks at* JOE; JOE *holds* TOM's *eyes again, encouraging* TOM *by his serious expression to go on talking*)   Yeah, now I remember. Sure, Kitty. I wanted to be a doctor—*once.*

KITTY (*smiling sadly*)   I'm so glad. Because I wanted to be an actress and have a young doctor come to the theater and see me and fall in love with me and send me flowers. (JOE *pantomimes to* TOM, *demanding that he go on talking*)

TOM   I would do that, Kitty.

KITTY   I wouldn't know who it was, and then one day I'd see him in the street and fall in love with him. I wouldn't know *he* was the one who was in love with me. I'd think about him all the time. I'd dream about him. I'd dream of being near him the rest of my life. I'd dream of having children that looked like him. I wouldn't be an actress all the time. Only until I found him and fell in love with him. After that we'd take a train and go to beautiful cities and see the wonderful people everywhere and give money to the poor and whenever people were sick he'd go to them and make them well again. (TOM *looks at* JOE, *bewildered, confused, and full of sorrow.* KITTY *is deep in memory, almost in a trance*)

JOE (*gently*)   Talk to her, Tom. Be the wonderul young doctor she dreamed about and never found. Go ahead. Correct the errors of the world.

TOM   Joe. (*pathetically*)   I don't know what to say. (*There is rowdy singing in the hall. A loud young* VOICE *sings:* "Sailing, sailing, over the bounding main")

VOICE   Kitty. Oh, Kitty! (KITTY *stirs, shocked, coming out of the trance*) Where the hell are you? Oh, Kitty. (TOM *jumps up, furiously*)

WOMAN'S VOICE (*in the hall*)   Who are you looking for, Sailor Boy?

VOICE   The most beautiful lay in the world.

WOMAN'S VOICE   Don't go any further.

VOICE (*with impersonal contempt*)   You? No. Not you. Kitty. You stink.

WOMAN'S VOICE (*rasping, angry*)   Don't you dare talk to me that way. You pickpocket.

VOICE (*still impersonal, but louder*)   Oh, I see. Want to get tough, hey? Close the door. Go hide.

WOMAN'S VOICE   You pickpocket. All of you. (*The door slams*)

VOICE (*roaring with laughter which is very sad*)   Oh—Kitty. Room Twenty-one. Where the hell is that room?

TOM (*to* JOE)   Joe, I'll kill him.

KITTY (*fully herself again, terribly frightened*)   Who is it? (*She looks long and steadily at* TOM *and* JOE. TOM *is standing, excited and angry.* JOE *is completely at ease, his expression full of pity*)

JOE (*gently*)   Tom. Just take him away.

VOICE   Here it is. Number Twenty-one. Three naturals. Heaven. My blue heaven. The west, a nest, and you. Just Molly and me. (*tragically*) Ah, to hell with everything.

(*There is a loud knock at the door.* KITTY *turns away, as if seeking some place to be safe and protected.* JOE *doesn't even look toward the door.* TOM *opens the door.* JOE *turns and looks. In the doorway stands a young* SAILOR—*a good-looking boy of no more than twenty or so who is only drunk and lonely*)

SAILOR   Hiya, Kitty. (*pause*) Oh. Visitors. Sorry. A thousand apologies. I'll come back later.

TOM (*taking him by the shoulders, furiously*) If you do, I'll kill you. (*He pushes the frightened* SAILOR *away and closes the door*)

JOE   Tom, you stay with Kitty. I'm going down to Union Square to hire an automobile. I'll be back in a few minutes. We'll ride out to the ocean and watch the sun go down. Then we'll ride down the Great Highway to Half Moon Bay. We'll have supper down there, and you and Kitty can dance.

TOM (*stupefied, unable to express his amazement and gratitude*)   Joe, you mean you're going to go on an errand for me? You mean you're not going to send me?

JOE   That's right. (*He gestures toward* KITTY, *indicating that* TOM *shall talk to her, protect the innocence in her which is in so*

much danger when TOM *isn't near, which* TOM
loves so deeply)

ACT FOUR

(*Scene: Nick's again, a little later. We are
back to the time when* TOM *is helping* JOE *out
of the place, on their way to* KITTY'S. *They are
almost offstage when the lights are on.*

WESLEY, *the colored boy, is at the piano,
playing the same song—at the same place.*
HARRY *is on the little stage dancing.* WILLIE
is at marble game. NICK *is behind the bar.*
DUDLEY *is at table right. The* ARAB *is in his
place.* KIT CARSON *is asleep on his folded arms.*

DRUNK *comes in right, goes to the telephone
for nickel that might be in the return chute.*
NICK *goes to him.* DRUNK *shows money. Both
cross to bar.* NICK *to back of bar, hands* DRUNK
a shot glass and bottle)

DRUNK   To the old, God bless them. (*another*) To the new, God love them. (*another*)
To—children and small animals, like little dogs
that don't bite. (*another. Loudly*) To reforest-
ation. (*searches for money. Finds some*) To—
President Taft. (*He goes out right. The telephone rings.* KIT CARSON *jumps up and starts to
shadow box.* DUDLEY *runs to phone*)

KIT CARSON   Come on, *all* of you, if you're
looking for trouble. I never asked for quarter
and I always gave it.

NICK (*reproachfully*)   Hey, Kit Carson.

DUDLEY (*on the phone*)   Hello. Who? Nick?
Yes. He's here. (*to* NICK) It's for you. I think
it's important.

NICK (*crossing to the phone*)   Important!
What's important?

DUDLEY   He sounded like a big shot.

NICK   Big *what?* (*to* WESLEY *and* HARRY)
Hey, you. Quiet. I want to hear this important
stuff. (WESLEY *stops playing the piano.* HARRY
stops dancing. KIT CARSON *comes close to right
of* NICK)

KIT CARSON   If there's anything I can do,
name it. I'll do it for you. I'm fifty-eight years
old; been through three wars; married four
times; the father of countless children whose
names I don't even know. I've got no money. I
live from hand to mouth. But if there's anything I can do, name it. I'll do it.

NICK   Listen, Pop. For a moment, please sit
down and go back to sleep—*for me.*

KIT CARSON (*crossing to left of center table*)

I can do that, too. (*He sits down, folds his
arms, and puts his head into them. But not
for long. As* NICK *begins to talk, he listens carefully, gets to his feet, and then begins to express
in pantomime the moods of each of* NICK'S *remarks*)

NICK (*on phone*)   Yeah? (*pause*) Who? Oh,
I see. (*listens*) Why don't you leave them
alone? (*listens*) The church people? Well, to
hell with the church people. I'm a Catholic myself. (*listens*) All right. I'll send them away. I'll
tell them to lay low for a couple of days. Yeah,
I know how it is. (*is about to hang up.* NICK'S
daughter ANNA *comes in right shyly, looking
at her father, and stands unnoticed by the
piano*) What? (*very angry*) Listen. I don't like
that Blick. He was here this morning, and I
told him not to come back. I'll keep the girls
out of here. You keep Blick out of here. (*listens*) I know his brother-in-law is important,
but I don't want him to come down here. He
looks for trouble everywhere, and he always
finds it. I don't break any laws. I've got a dive
in the lousiest part of town. Five years nobody's
been robbed, murdered or gypped. I leave
people alone. Your swanky joints uptown make
trouble for you every night. (NICK *gestures to*
WESLEY—*keeps listening on the phone—puts
his hand over the mouthpiece. To* WESLEY *and*
HARRY) Start playing again. My ears have got
a headache. Go into your dance, son. (WESLEY
begins to play again. HARRY *begins to dance.*
NICK, *into mouthpiece*) Yeah. I'll keep them
out. Just see that Blick doesn't come around
and start something. O.K. (*He hangs up,
crosses to rear center*)

KIT CARSON (*following to left of* NICK)
Trouble coming?

NICK   That lousy Vice Squad again. It's
that gorilla Blick.

KIT CARSON   Anybody at all. You can count
on me. What kind of a gorilla is this gorilla
Blick?

NICK   Very dignified. Toenails on his fingers.

ANNA (*to* KIT CARSON, *with great, warm,
beautiful pride, pointing at* NICK)   That's my
father.

KIT CARSON (*leaping with amazement at the
beautiful voice, the wondrous face, the magnificent event*)   Well, bless your heart, child.
Bless your lovely heart. I had a little daughter
point me out in a crowd once.

NICK (*surprised*)   Anna. What the hell are
you doing here? Get back home where you
belong and help Grandma cook me some supper. (ANNA *smiles at her father, understanding
him, knowing that his words are words of love.
She turns and goes right, looking at him all the*

way out, as much as to say that she would cook for him the rest of her life. NICK *stares at the swinging doors.* KIT CARSON *moves toward them, two or three steps.* ANNA *pushes open one of the doors and peeks in, to look at her father again. She waves to him. Turns and runs.* NICK *is very sad. He doesn't know what to do. He gets a glass and a bottle. Pours himself a drink. Swallows some. It isn't enough, so he pours more and swallows the whole drink. To himself)* My beautiful, beautiful baby. Anna, she is you again. (*He brings out a handkerchief, touches his eyes, and blows his nose.* KIT CARSON *moves close to* NICK, *watching* NICK's *face.* NICK *looks at him. Loudly, almost making* KIT *jump)* You're broke, aren't you?

KIT CARSON   Always. *Always.*

NICK   All right. Go into the kitchen and give Sam a hand. Eat some food and when you come back you can have a couple of beers.

KIT CARSON (*studying* NICK) Anything at all. I know a good man when I see one.

(*He goes out back center.* ELSIE MANDELSPIEGEL *comes in right. She is a beautiful, dark girl, with a sorrowful, wise, dreaming face, almost on the verge of tears, and full of pity. There is an aura of dream about her. She moves softly and gently, as if everything around her were unreal and pathetic.* DUDLEY *doesn't notice her for a moment or two. When he does finally see her, he is so amazed, he can barely move or speak. Her presence has the effect of changing him completely. He gets up from his chair, as if in a trance, and walks toward her, smiling sadly)*

ELSIE (*crossing to chair right of center table*) Hello, Dudley.

DUDLEY   Elsie.

ELSIE (*sits*) I'm sorry. So many people are sick. Last night a little boy died. I love you, but—

DUDLEY (*crossing to chair left of center table*) Elsie. You'll never know how glad I am to see you. (*sits*) Just to *see* you. I was afraid I'd never see you again. It was driving me crazy. I didn't want to live. Honest. (*The* KILLER *and her* SIDEKICK *come in right and go to bar*) I know. You told me before, but I can't help it, Elsie. I love you.

ELSIE   I know you love me, and I love you, but don't you see love is impossible in this world?

DUDLEY   Maybe it isn't, Elsie.

ELSIE   Love is for birds. They have wings to fly away on when it's time for flying. For tigers in the jungle because they don't know their end. We know *our* end. Every night I watch over poor, dying men. I hear them breathing, crying, talking in their sleep. Crying for air and water and love, for mother and field and sunlight. *We* can never know love or greatness. We *should* know both.

DUDLEY   Elsie, I love you.

ELSIE   You want to live. *I* want to live, too, but where? Where can we escape our poor world?

DUDLEY   Elsie, we'll find a place.

ELSIE   All right. We'll try again. We'll go together to a room in a cheap hotel, and dream that the world is beautiful, and that living is full of love and greatness. But in the morning, can we forget debts, and duties, and the cost of ridiculous things?

DUDLEY   Sure, we can, Elsie.

ELSIE   All right, Dudley. Of course. (*rises*) Come on. The time for the new pathetic war has come. Let's hurry, before they dress you, stand you in line, hand you a gun, and have you kill and be killed. (*She leads him out right*)

KILLER   Nick, what the hell kind of a joint are you running?

NICK   Well, it's not out of the world. It's on a street in a city, and people come and go. They bring whatever they've got with them and they say what they must say.

THE OTHER STREETWALKER   It's floozies like her that raise hell with our racket.

NICK   Oh, yeah. Finnegan telephoned.

KILLER   That mouse in elephant's body?

THE OTHER STREETWALKER   What the hell does *he* want?

NICK   Spend your time at the movies for the next couple of days.

KILLER   They're all lousy. (*mincing and smoking*) All about love.

NICK   Lousy or not lousy, for a couple of days the flatfoots are going to be romancing you, so stay out of here, and lay low.

KILLER   I always was a pushover for a man in uniform, with a badge, a club and a gun. (KRUPP *comes in right. The* GIRLS *put down their drinks*)

NICK   O.K., get going. (*The* GIRLS *begin to leave and meet* KRUPP, *who pauses to look them over*)

THE OTHER STREETWALKER   We was just going.

KILLER   We was formerly models at Magnin's. (*They go out right*)

KRUPP (*at the bar*) The strike isn't enough, so they've got to put us on the tails of the girls, too. I don't know. I wish to God I was back in the Sunset holding the hands of kids going home from school, where I belong. I don't like trouble. Give me a beer. (NICK *gives him a beer. He drinks some*) Right now, McCarthy, my best friend, is with sixty strikers who want to stop the finks who are going to try to unload the *Mary Luckenbach* tonight. Why the hell McCarthy ever became a longshoreman instead of a professor of some kind is something I'll never know.

NICK   Cowboys and Indians, cops and robbers, longshoremen and finks.

KRUPP   They're all guys who are trying to be happy; trying to make a living; support a family; bring up children; enjoy sleep. Go to a movie; take a drive on Sunday. They're all good guys, so out of nowhere, comes trouble. All they want is a chance to get out of debt and relax in front of a radio while Amos and Andy go through their act. What the hell do they always want to make trouble for? I been thinking everything over, Nick, and you know what I think?

NICK   No. What?

KRUPP   I think we're all crazy. It came to me while I was on my way to Pier Twenty-seven. All of a sudden it hit me like a ton of bricks. A thing like that never happened to me before. Here we are in this wonderful world, full of all the wonderful things—here we are—all of us, and look at us. Just look at us. We're crazy. We're nuts. We've got everything, but we always feel lousy and dissatisfied just the same.

NICK   Of course we're crazy. Even so, we've got to go on living together.

KRUPP   There's no hope. I don't suppose it's right for an officer of the law to feel the way I feel, but, by God, right or not right, that's how I feel. Why are we all so lousy? This is a good world. It's wonderful to get up in the morning and go out for a little walk and smell the trees and see the streets and the kids going to school and the clouds in the sky. It's wonderful just to be able to move around and whistle a song if you feel like it, or maybe try to sing one. This is a nice world. So why do they make all the trouble?

NICK   I don't know. Why?

KRUPP   We're crazy, that's why. We're no good any more. All the corruption everywhere. The poor kids selling themselves. A couple of years ago they were in grammar school. Everybody trying to get a lot of money in a hurry. Everybody betting the horses. Nobody going quietly for a little walk to the ocean. Nobody taking things easy and not wanting to make some kind of a killing. Nick, I'm going to quit being a cop. Let somebody else keep law and

order. The stuff I hear about at headquarters. I'm thirty-seven years old, and I still can't get used to it. The only trouble is, the wife'll raise hell.

NICK   Ah, the wife.

KRUPP   She's a wonderful woman, Nick. We've got two of the swellest boys in the world. Twelve and seven years old.

NICK   I didn't know that. (ARAB, WESLEY *and* WILLIE *listen to* KRUPP)

KRUPP   Sure. But what'll I do? I've wanted to quit for seven years. I wanted to quit the day they began putting me through the school. I didn't quit. What'll I do if I quit? Where's money going to be coming in from?

NICK   That's one of the reasons we're all crazy. We don't know where it's going to be coming in from, except from wherever it happens to be coming in from at the time, which we don't usually like. (ARAB, WESLEY *and* WILLIE *go back to former interests*)

KRUPP   Every once in a while I catch myself being mean, hating people just because they're down and out, broke and hungry, sick or drunk. And then when I'm with the stuffed shirts at headquarters, all of a sudden I'm nice to them, trying to make an impression. On who? People I don't like. And I feel disgusted. (*with finality*) I'm going to quit. That's all. Quit. Out. I'm going to give them back the uniform and the gadgets that go with it. I don't want any part of it. (*takes off badge and slams it on bar*) This is a good world. What do they want to make all the trouble for all the time?

ARAB   No foundation. All the way down the line.

KRUPP   What?

ARAB   No foundation. No foundation.

KRUPP   I'll say there's no foundation.

ARAB   All the way down the line.

KRUPP   (*to* NICK)   Is that all he ever says?

NICK   That's all he's been saying *this* week.

KRUPP   What is he, anyway?

NICK   He's an Arab, or something like that.

KRUPP   No, I mean what's he do for a living?

NICK   (*to* ARAB)   What do you do for a living, brother?

ARAB   Work. Work all my life. All my life, work. From small boy to old man, work. In old country, work. In new country, work. In New York. Pittsburgh. Detroit. Chicago. Imperial Valley. San Francisco. Work. No beg. Work. For what? Nothing. Three boys in old country. Twenty years, not see. Lost. Dead. Who knows? What. What-not. No foundation. All the way down the line.

KRUPP   What'd he say last week?

NICK   Didn't say anything. Played the harmonica.

ARAB   Old country song, I play. (*He brings a harmonica from his back pocket and begins to play an old country song*)

KRUPP   Seems like a nice guy.

NICK   Nicest guy in the world.

KRUPP (*bitterly*)   But crazy. Just like all the rest of us. Stark raving mad.

(WESLEY *and* HARRY *long ago stopped playing and dancing. They sat at left center table together and talked for a while; then began playing casino or rummy. When the* ARAB *begins his solo on the harmonica, they stop their game to listen*)

WESLEY   You hear that?

HARRY   That's *something*.

WESLEY   That's crying. That's crying.

HARRY   I want to make people laugh.

WESLEY   That's deep, deep crying. That's crying a long time ago. That's crying a thousand years ago. Some place five thousand miles away.

HARRY   Do you think you can play to that?

WESLEY   I want to *sing* to that, but I can't sing.

HARRY   You try and play to that. I'll try to dance.

(WESLEY *goes to the piano, and after closer listening, he begins to accompany the harmonica solo.* HARRY *goes to the little stage and after a few efforts begins to dance to the song. This keeps up quietly for some time.* KRUPP *and* NICK *have been silent,* KRUPP *drinking a beer;* NICK *fooling around behind the bar*)

KRUPP   Well, anyhow, Nick. (*picks up badge and puts it on*)

NICK   Hmmmmmmmm?

KRUPP   What I said. Forget it.

NICK   Sure.

KRUPP   It gets me down once in a while.

NICK   No harm in talking.

KRUPP   Keep the girls out of here. (*starts for door right.* HARRY *starts double time whirl*)

NICK   Take it easy.

ACT FIVE

(*Scene: Nick's, that evening. Foghorns are heard throughout this scene. A* GENTLEMAN *in evening clothes and a top hat, and his* LADY *also in evening clothes, are entering right.*

WILLIE, *the marble-game maniac, is still at the marble game.* NICK *is behind the bar.* JOE *is at center table, looking at the book of maps of the countries of Europe. The box containing the revolver and the box containing cartridges are on the table, beside his glass. He is at peace, his hat tilted back on his head, a calm expression on his face.* TOM *is leaning against the bar, dreaming of love and* KITTY. *The* ARAB *is gone.* WESLEY *and* HARRY, *the comedian, are gone for the moment.* KIT CARSON *is watching the boy play the marble game.*

The MAN *and* LADY *take left center table. She sits right of it, he left.* NICK *gives them a menu.*

Outside, in the street, the Salvation Army people are playing a song. Big drum, cornet, big horn, and tambourine. They are singing too. "The Blood of the Lamb." The music and words come into the place faintly and comically. This is followed by an old sinner testifying; it's the DRUNK. *All his words are not intelligible, but his message is unmistakable. He is saved. He wants to sin no more. And so on*)

LADY   Oh, come on, please. (*The* GENTLEMAN *follows miserably*)

DRUNK (*testifying, unmistakably drunk*)   Brothers and sisters. I was a sinner. I chewed tobacco and chased women. Oh, I sinned, brothers and sisters. And then I was saved. Saved by the Salvation Army, God forgive me.

JOE   Let's see now. Here's a city. Pribor. Czechoslovakia. Little, lovely, lonely Czechoslovakia. I wonder what kind of a place Pribor was? (*calling*) Pribor! Pribor! (TOM *leaps*)

LADY   What's the matter with him?

MAN   Drunk.

TOM   Who you calling, Joe?

JOE   Pribor.

TOM   Who's Pribor?

JOE   He's a Czech. And a Slav. A Czechoslovakian.

LADY   How interesting.

MAN   He's drunk.

JOE   Tom, Pribor's a city in Czechoslovakia.

TOM   Oh. (*pause*) You sure were nice to her, Joe.

JOE   Kitty Duval? She's one of the finest people in the world.

TOM   It sure was nice of you to hire an automobile and take us for a drive along the ocean-front and down to Half Moon Bay.

JOE   Those three hours were the most delightful, the most somber, and the most beautiful I have ever known.

TOM   Why, Joe?

JOE   Why? I'm a student. (*lifting his voice*) Tom. (TOM *crosses and sits left of center table; quietly*) I'm a student. I study all things. All. All. And when my study reveals something of beauty in a place or in a person where by all rights only ugliness or death should be revealed, then I know how full of goodness this life is. And that's a good thing to know. That's a truth I shall always seek to verify.

LADY   Are you *sure* he's drunk?

MAN   He's either drunk, or just naturally crazy.

TOM   Joe?

JOE   Yeah.

TOM   You won't get sore or anything?

JOE   What is it, Tom?

TOM   Joe, where do you get all that money? You paid for the automobile. You paid for supper and the two bottles of champagne at the Half Moon Bay Restaurant. You moved Kitty out of The New York Hotel around the corner to the St. Francis Hotel on Powell Street. I saw you pay her rent. I saw you give her money for new clothes. Where do you get all that money, Joe? Three years now and I've never asked.

JOE   (*gestures the question aside impatiently. He smiles with some inner thought and suddenly lifts the box containing the gun, and the other with the cartridges. Looking at* TOM *sorrowfully, a little irritated, not so much with* TOM *as with the world and himself, his own superiority. He speaks clearly, slowly, and solemnly*)   Now don't be a fool, Tom. Listen carefully. If anybody's got any money—to hoard or to throw away—you can be sure he stole it from other people. Not from rich people who can spare it, but from poor people who can't. From their lives and from their dreams. I'm no exception. I *earned* the money I throw away. I stole it like everybody else does. I hurt people to get it. Loafing around this way, I *still* earn money. The money itself earns *more*. I *still* hurt people. I don't know who they are, or where they are. If I did, I'd feel worse than I do. I've got a Christian conscience in a world that's got no conscience at all. The world's trying to get some sort of a *social* conscience, but it's having a devil of a time trying to do *that*. I've got money. I'll always have money, as long as this world stays the way it is. I don't work. I don't make anything. (*He sips*) I drink. I worked when I was a kid. I worked *hard*. I mean hard, Tom. People are supposed to enjoy living. I got tired. (*He lifts the gun and looks at it while he talks*) I decided to get

even on the world. Well, you can't enjoy living unless you work. Unless you do something. I don't do anything. I don't *want* to do anything any more. There isn't anything I can do that won't make me feel embarrassed. Because I can't do simple, good things. I haven't the patience. And I'm too smart. Money is the guiltiest thing in the world. It stinks. Now, don't ever bother me about it again.

TOM   I didn't mean to make you feel bad, Joe.

JOE   (*slowly*)   Here. Take this gun out in the street and give it to some worthy holdup man.

LADY   What's he saying?

MAN   (*uncrosses legs*)   You wanted to visit a honky-tonk. Well, *this* is a honky-tonk. (*to the world*) Married twenty-eight years and she's still looking for adventure.

TOM   How should I know who's a holdup man?

JOE   Take it away. Give it to somebody.

TOM   (*bewildered*)   Do I *have* to *give* it to somebody?

JOE   Of course.

TOM   Can't I take it back and get some of our money?

JOE   Don't talk like a business man. Look around and find somebody who appears to be in need of a gun and give it to him. It's a good gun, isn't it?

TOM   The man said it was, but how can I tell who needs a gun?

JOE   Tom, you've seen good people who needed guns, haven't you?

TOM   I don't remember. Joe, I might give it to the wrong kind of guy. He might do something crazy.

JOE   All right. I'll find somebody myself. (TOM *rises*) Here's some money. Go get me this week's *Life, Liberty, Time*, and six or seven packages of chewing gum.

TOM   (*swiftly, in order to remember each item*)   *Life, Liberty, Time*, and six or seven packages of chewing gum.

JOE   That's right.

TOM   All that chewing gum? What kind?

JOE   Any kind. Mix 'em up. All kinds.

TOM   Licorice, too?

JOE   Licorice, by all means.

TOM   Juicy Fruit?

JOE   Juicy Fruit.

TOM   Tutti-frutti?

JOE   Is there such a gum?

TOM   I think so.

JOE   All right. Tutti-frutti, too. Get *all* the kinds. Get as many kinds as they're selling.

TOM   *Life, Liberty, Time,* and all the different kinds of gum. (*He begins to go right*)

JOE (*calling after him loudly*)   Get some jelly beans too. All the different colors.

TOM   All right, Joe.

JOE   And the longest panatela cigar you can find. Six of them.

TOM   Panatela. I got it.

JOE   Give a news-kid a dollar.

TOM   O.K., Joe.

JOE   Give some old man a dollar.

TOM   O.K., Joe.

JOE   Give them Salvation Army people in the street a couple of dollars and ask them to sing that song that goes—(*He sings loudly*) "Let the lower lights be burning, send a gleam across the wave."

TOM (*swiftly*)   "Let the lower lights be burning, send a gleam across the wave."

JOE   That's it. (*He goes on with the song, very loudly and religiously*) "Some poor, dying, struggling seaman, you may rescue, you may save." (*halts*)

TOM   O.K., Joe. I got it. *Life, Liberty, Time,* all the kinds of gum they're selling, jelly beans, six panatela cigars, a dollar for a news-kid, a dollar for an old man, two dollars for the Salvation Army. "Let the lower lights be burning, send a gleam across the wave."

JOE   That's it. (TOM *goes out right*)

LADY   He's absolutely insane.

MAN (*wearily*)   You asked me to take you to a honky-tonk, instead of to the Mark Hopkins. You're *here* in a honky-tonk. I can't help it if he's crazy. Do you want to go back to where people *aren't* crazy?

LADY   No, not just yet.

MAN   Well, all right then. Don't be telling me every minute that he's crazy.

LADY   You needn't be huffy about it. (MAN *refuses to answer. When* JOE *began to sing,* KIT CARSON *turned away from the marble game and listened. While the* MAN *and* LADY *are arguing he comes over to* JOE's *table*)

KIT CARSON   Presbyterian?

JOE   I attended a Presbyterian Sunday school.

KIT CARSON   Fond of singing?

JOE   On occasion. Have a drink?

KIT CARSON   Thanks.

JOE   Get a glass and sit down. (KIT CARSON *gets a glass from* NICK, *returns to the table, sits down,* JOE *pours him a drink, they touch glasses just as the Salvation Army people begin to fulfill the request. They sip some champagne, and at the proper moment begin to sing the song together, sipping champagne,* raising hell with the tune, swinging it, and so on) Always was fond of that song. Used to sing it at the top of my voice. Never saved a seaman in my life.

KIT CARSON   I saved a seaman once. Well, he wasn't exactly a seaman. He was a darky named Wellington. Heavy-set sort of a fellow. Nice personality, but no friends to speak of. Not until I came along, at any rate. In New Orleans. In the summer of the year 1899. No, '98. I was a lot younger of course, and had no mustache, but was regarded by many people as a man of means.

JOE   Know anything about guns?

KIT CARSON   All there is to know. Didn't fight the Ojibways for nothing. Up there in the Lake Takalooca Country, in Michigan. (*remembering*) Along about in 1881 or two. Fought 'em right up to the shore of the Lake. Made 'em swim for Canada. One fellow in particular, an Indian named Harry Daisy.

JOE (*opening the box containing the revolver*)   What sort of a gun would you say this is? Any good?

KIT CARSON (*at sight of gun, he is scared to death*)   Yep. That looks like a pretty nice hunk of shooting iron. That's a six-shooter. Shot a man with a six-shooter once. Got him through the palm of his right hand. Lifted his arm to wave to a friend. Thought it was a bird. Fellow named, I believe, Carroway. Larrimore Carroway.

JOE   Know how to work one of these things? (*He offers* KIT CARSON *the revolver, which is old and enormous*)

KIT CARSON (*laughing at the absurd question*)   Know how to work it? Hand me that little gun, son, and I'll show you all about it. (JOE *hands* KIT *the revolver. Obviously bluffing*) Let's see now. This is probably a new kind of six-shooter. After my time. Haven't nicked an Indian in years. I believe this here place is supposed to move out. (*He fools around and gets the barrel out for loading*) That's it. There it is.

JOE   Look all right?

KIT CARSON   It's a good gun. You've got a good gun there, son. I'll explain it to you. You see these holes? Well, that's where you put the cartridges.

JOE (*taking some cartridges out of the box*)   Here. Show me how it's done.

KIT CARSON (*scared to death but bluffing beautifully*)   Well, son, you take 'em one by one and put 'em in the holes, like this. There's one. Two. Three. Four. Five. Six. Then you get the barrel back in place. Then cock it.

Then all you got to do is aim and fire. (*He points the gun at the* LADY. *The gun is loaded, but uncocked*)

JOE   It's all set?

KIT CARSON   Ready to kill.

JOE   Let me hold it. (KIT *hands* JOE *the gun. The* LADY *and* MAN *are scared to death.* LADY *rises*)

KIT CARSON   Careful, now, son. Don't cock it. Many a man's lost an eye fooling with a loaded gun. Fellow I used to know named Danny Donovan lost a nose. Ruined his whole life. (LADY *sits*) Hold it firm. Squeeze the trigger. Don't snap it. Spoils your aim.

JOE   Thanks. Let's see if I can unload it. (*He begins to unload it*)

KIT CARSON   Of course you can.

(JOE *unloads the revolver, looks at it very closely, puts the cartridges back into the box and puts them away in his overcoat pocket*)

JOE (*looking at gun*)   I'm mighty grateful to you. Always wanted to see one of those things close up. Is it really a good one?

KIT CARSON   It's a beaut, son.

JOE (*aims the empty gun at a bottle on the bar*)   Bang! (*grinding of marble game*)

WILLIE (*at the marble game*)   Oh, boy! (*loudly, triumphantly*) There you are, Nick. Thought I couldn't do it, hey? *Now*, watch. (*The machine begins to make a special kind of noise. Lights go on and off. Some red, some green. A bell rings loudly six times*) One. Two. Three. Four. Five. Six. (*An American flag jumps up.* WILLIE *comes to attention. Salutes*) Oh, boy, what a beautiful country. (*a music-box version of the song* "America." *Singing*) "My country, 'tis of thee, sweet land of liberty, of thee I sing." (*Everything quiets down. The flag goes back into the machine.* WILLIE *is thrilled, amazed, delighted. Everybody has watched the performance of the defeated machine from wherever he happened to be when the performance began.* WILLIE, *looking around at everybody, as if they had all been on the side of the machine*) O.K. How's that? I knew I could do it. (*to* NICK) Six nickels. (NICK *hands him six nickels.* WILLIE *goes over to* JOE *and* KIT. *Exuberantly, pointing a finger, gesturing wildly*) Took me a little while, but I finally did it. It's scientific, really. With a little skill a man can make a modest living beating the marble games. Not that that's what I want to do. I just don't like the idea of anything getting the best of me. A machine or anything else. (*doubling his fist*) Myself, I'm the kind of guy who makes up his mind to do something, and then goes to work and does it. There's no

other way a man can be a success at anything. (*indicating the letter "F" on his sweater*) See that letter? That don't stand for some little-bitty high school somewhere. That stands for *me*. Faroughli. Willie Faroughli. I'm an Assyrian. We've got a civilization six or seven centuries old, I think. Somewhere along in there. Ever hear of Osman? Harold Osman? He's an Assyrian, too. He's got an orchestra down in Fresno. (*He goes to the* LADY *and* MAN) I've never seen you before in my life, but I can tell from the clothes you wear and the company you keep (*graciously indicating the* LADY) that you're a man who looks every problem straight in the eye, and then goes to work and *solves* it. (*He bangs his fist into his left palm violently*) I'm that way myself. (*three swift, ferocious bangs*) Well. (*He smiles beautifully*) It's been wonderful talking to a nicer type of people for a change. Well. I'll be seeing you. So long. (*He turns, takes two steps, returns to the table. Very politely and seriously*) Good-bye, lady. You've got a good man there. Take good care of him. (WILLIE *exits right, saluting* JOE *and the world.* NICK *goes into the kitchen, rear center*)

KIT CARSON (*to* JOE)   By God, for a while there I didn't think that young Assyrian was going to do it. That fellow's got something. (TOM *comes back right with the magazines and other stuff*)

JOE   Get it all?

TOM   Yeah. I had a little trouble finding the jelly beans.

JOE   Let's take a look at them.

TOM   These are the jelly beans. (JOE *puts his hand into the cellophane bag and takes out a handful of the jelly beans, looks at them, smiles and tosses a couple into his mouth*)

JOE   Same as ever. Have some. (*He offers the bag to* KIT)

KIT CARSON (*flirting*)   Thanks! I remember the first time I ever ate jelly beans. I was six, or at the most seven. Must have been in (*slowly*) 1877. Seven or eight. Baltimore.

JOE   Have some, Tom.

TOM (*takes some*)   Thanks, Joe.

JOE   Let's have some of that chewing gum. (*He dumps all the packages of gum out of the bag onto the table*)

KIT CARSON (*flirting*)   Me and a boy named Clark. Quinton Clark. Became a Senator.

JOE   Yeah. Tutti-frutti, all right. (*He opens a package and folds all five pieces into his mouth*) Always wanted to see how many I could chew at one time. Tell you what, Tom. I'll bet I can chew more at one time than you can.

TOM (*delighted*) All right. (*They both begin to fold gum into their mouths*)

KIT CARSON I'll referee. Now, one at a time. How many you got?

JOE Six.

KIT CARSON All right. Let Tom catch up with you.

JOE (*while* TOM's *catching up*) Did you give a dollar to a news-kid?

TOM Yeah, sure.

JOE What'd he say?

TOM Thanks.

JOE What sort of a kid was he?

TOM Little, dark kid. I guess he's Italian.

JOE Did he seemed pleased?

TOM Yeah.

JOE That's good. Did you give a dollar to an old man?

TOM Yeah.

JOE Was he pleased?

TOM Yeah.

JOE Good. How many you got in your mouth?

TOM Six.

JOE All right. I got six, too. (*folds one more in his mouth.* TOM *folds one too*)

KIT CARSON Seven. Seven each. (*They each fold one more into their mouths, very solemnly, chewing them into the main hunk of gum*) Eight. Nine. Ten.

JOE (*delighted*) Always wanted to do this. (*He picks up one of the magazines*) Let's see what's going on in the world. (*He turns the pages and keeps folding gum into his mouth and chewing*)

KIT CARSON Eleven. Twelve. (KIT *continues to count while* JOE *and* TOM *continue the contest. In spite of what they are doing, each is very serious*)

TOM Joe, what'd you want to move Kitty into the St. Francis Hotel for?

JOE She's a better woman than any of them tramp society dames that hang around that lobby.

TOM Yeah, but do you think she'll feel at home up there?

JOE Maybe not at first, but after a couple of days she'll be all right. A nice big room. A bed for sleeping in. Good clothes. Good food. She'll be all right, Tom.

TOM I hope so. Don't you think she'll get lonely up there with nobody to talk to?

JOE (*looking at* TOM *sharply, almost with admiration, pleased but severe*) There's nobody *anywhere* for *her* to talk to—except *you.*

TOM (*amazed and delighted*) *Me,* Joe?

JOE (*while* TOM *and* KIT CARSON *listen carefully,* KIT *with great appreciation*) Yes, you.

By the grace of God, you're the other half of that girl. Not the angry woman that swaggers into this waterfront dive and shouts because the world has kicked her around. *Anybody* can have *her.* You belong to the little kid in Ohio who once dreamed of living. Not with her carcass, for *money,* so she can have food and clothes, and pay rent. With *all* of her. I put her in that hotel, so she can have a chance to gather herself together again. She can't do that in The New York Hotel. You saw what happens there. There's nobody anywhere for her to talk to, except you. They all make her talk like a whore. After a while, she'll *believe* them. Then she won't be able to remember. She'll get lonely. Sure. People can get lonely for *misery,* even. I want her to go on being lonely for *you,* so she can come together again the way she was meant to be from the beginning. Loneliness is good for people. Right now it's the only thing for Kitty. Any more licorice?

TOM (*dazed*) What? Licorice? (*looking around busily*) I guess we've chewed all the licorice in. We still got Clove, Peppermint, Doublemint, Beechnut, Teaberry, and Juicy Fruit.

JOE Licorice used to be my favorite. Don't worry about her, Tom, she'll be all right. You really want to marry her, don't you?

TOM (*nodding*) Honest to God, Joe. (*pathetically*) Only, I haven't got any money.

JOE Couldn't you be a prize fighter or something like that?

TOM Naaaah. I couldn't hit a man if I wasn't sore at him. He'd have to do something that made me hate him.

JOE You've got to figure out something to do that you won't mind doing very much.

TOM I wish I could, Joe.

JOE (*thinking deeply, suddenly*) Tom, would you be embarrassed driving a truck?

TOM (*hit by a thunderbolt*) Joe, I never thought of that. I'd like that. Travel. Highways. Little towns. Coffee and hot cakes. Beautiful valleys and mountains and streams and trees and daybreak and sunset.

JOE There *is* poetry in it, at that.

TOM Joe, that's just the kind of work I *should* do. Just sit there and travel, and look, and smile, and bust out laughing. Could Kitty go with me, sometimes?

JOE I don't know. Get me the phone book. Can you drive a truck?

TOM (*crossing to phone*) Joe, you know I can drive a truck, or any kind of thing with a motor and wheels. (TOM *takes* JOE *the phone book.* JOE *turns the pages*)

JOE (*looking*) Here! Here it is. Tuxedo 7900. Here's a nickel. Get me that number. (TOM *goes to telephone, dials the number*)

TOM   Hello.

JOE   Ask for Mr. Keith.

TOM   I'd like to talk to Mr. Keith. (*pause*) Mr. Keith.

JOE   Take that gum out of your mouth for a minute.

TOM (*removes the gum*) Mr. Keith. Yeah. That's right. Hello, Mr. Keith?

JOE   Tell him to hold the line.

TOM   Hold the line, please.

JOE   Give me a hand, Tom. (TOM *helps* JOE *to the telephone. At phone, wad of gum in fingers delicately*) Keith? Joe. Yeah. Fine. Forget it. (*pause*) Have you got a place for a good driver? (*pause*) I don't think so. (*to* TOM) You haven't got a driver's license, have you?

TOM (*worried*) No. But I can get one, Joe.

JOE (*at phone*) No, but he can get one easy enough. To hell with the union. He'll join later. All right, call him a vice-president and say he drives for relaxation. Sure. What do you mean? Tonight? I don't know why not. San Diego? All right, let him start driving without a license. What the hell's the difference? Yeah. Sure. Look him over. Yeah. I'll send him right over. Right. (*He hangs up*) Thanks. (*to telephone*)

TOM (*helping* JOE *back to his seat*) Am I going to get the job?

JOE (*sits*) He wants to take a look at you.

TOM (*breaks to right*) Do I look all right, Joe?

JOE (*looking at him carefully*) Hold up your head. Stick out your chest. How do you feel?

TOM (*does these things*) Fine.

JOE   You *look* fine, too. (KIT CARSON *has now reached twenty-seven sticks each.* JOE *takes his wad of gum out of his mouth and wraps* Liberty *magazine around it*)

JOE   You win, Tom. Now, look. (*He bites off the tip of a very long panatela cigar, lights it, and hands one to* TOM, *and another to* KIT) Have yourselves a pleasant smoke. Here. (*He hands two more to* TOM) Give those slummers one each. (*He indicates the* LADY *and* MAN. TOM *goes over and without a word gives a cigar each to the* MAN *and the* LADY *then crosses to right of* JOE. *At first they are a little offended; then the* MAN *lights his cigar. The* LADY *looks at the cigar a moment, then bites off the tip the way* JOE *did*)

MAN   What do you think you're doing?

LADY   Really, dear. I'd like to.

MAN   Oh, this is too much.

LADY   I'd *really*, really like to, dear. (*turns to* KIT, *who rises and crosses to right of* LADY)

MAN (*loudly*) The mother of five grown men, and she's still looking for *romance*. (*The* LADY *timidly scratches a match, puts the cigar in her mouth;* KIT *lights it for her, and she begins to smoke, feeling wonderful*) No. I forbid it.

JOE (*shouting*) What's the matter with you? Why don't you leave her alone? What are you always pushing your women around for? (*almost without a pause*) Now, look, Tom. Here's ten bucks.

TOM   Ten bucks?

JOE   He may want you to get into a truck and begin driving to San Diego tonight.

TOM   Joe, I got to tell Kitty.

JOE   I'll tell her.

TOM   Joe, take care of her.

JOE   She'll be all right. Stop worrying about her. She's at the St. Francis Hotel. Now, look. Take a cab to Townsend and Fourth. You'll see the big sign. Keith Motor Transport Company. He'll be waiting for you.

TOM   O.K., Joe. (*trying hard*) Thanks, Joe.

JOE   Don't be silly. Get going. (TOM *goes out right.* LADY *starts puffing on cigar. As* TOM *goes,* WESLEY *and* HARRY *come in together, right, and cross to piano*)

NICK (*enters from rear center and goes behind bar*) Where the hell have you been? We've got to have some entertainment around here. Can't you see them fine people from uptown? (*He points at the* LADY *and* MAN)

WESLEY   You said to come back at ten for the second show.

NICK   Did I say that?

WESLEY   Yes, sir, Mr. Nick, that's exactly what you said.

HARRY   Was the first show all right?

NICK   That wasn't a show. There was no one here to see it. How can it be a show when no one sees it? People are afraid to come down to the waterfront.

HARRY   Yeah. We were just down to Pier Twenty-seven. One of the longshoremen and a cop had a fight and the cop hit him over the head with a blackjack. We saw it happen, didn't we?

WESLEY   Yes, sir, we was standing there looking when it happened.

NICK (*crossing from behind bar to center*) Anything else happen?

WESLEY   They was all talking.

HARRY   A man in a big car came up and said there was going to be a meeting right away and they hoped to satisfy everybody and stop the strike.

WESLEY   Right away. *Tonight.*

NICK   Well, it's about time. Them poor cops are liable to get nervous and—shoot somebody. (*to* HARRY) Come back here. I want you to tend bar for a while. I'm going to take a walk over to the pier.

HARRY   Yes, sir. (*crossing to back of bar*)

NICK   (*to the* LADY *and* MAN)   You society people made up your minds yet?

LADY   Have you champagne?

NICK   (*indicating* JOE)   What do you think he's pouring out of that bottle, water or something?

LADY   Have you a chill bottle?

NICK   I've got a dozen of them chilled. He's been drinking champagne here all day and all night for a month now.

LADY   May we have a bottle?

NICK   It's six dollars.

LADY   I think we can manage.

MAN   I don't know. I *know* I don't know.

(NICK *takes off his coat and helps* HARRY *into it.* HARRY *takes a bottle of champagne and two glasses to the* LADY *and the* MAN, *collects six dollars and goes back behind the bar.* NICK *gets his coat and hat*)

NICK   (*to* WESLEY)   Rattle the keys a little, son. Rattle the keys.

WESLEY   Yes, sir, Mr. Nick. (*starts piano.* NICK *is on his way out right. The* ARAB *enters and goes to his chair*)

NICK   Hiya, *Mahmed.*

ARAB   No foundation.

NICK   All the way down the line.

(*He goes out.* WESLEY *is at the piano, playing quietly. The* ARAB *swallows a glass of beer, takes out his harmonica, and begins to play.* WESLEY *fits his playing to the* ARAB'S. KITTY DUVAL, *strangely beautiful, in new clothes, comes in right. She walks shyly, as if she were embarrassed by the fine clothes, as if she had no right to wear them. The* LADY *and* MAN *are very impressed.* HARRY *looks at her with amazement.* JOE *is reading* Time *magazine.* KITTY *goes to his table.* JOE *looks up from the magazine, without the least amazement*)

JOE   Hello, Kitty.

KITTY   Hello, Joe.

JOE   It's nice seeing you again.

KITTY   I came in a cab.

JOE   You been crying again? (KITTY *can't answer. To* HARRY) Bring a glass. (HARRY *comes over with a glass and returns to bar.* JOE *pours* KITTY *a drink*)

KITTY   I've got to talk to you.

JOE   Have a drink.

KITTY   I've never been in burlesque. We were just poor.

JOE   Sit down, Kitty.

KITTY   (*sits down left of center table*)   I tried other things.

JOE   Here's to you, Katerina Koranovsky. Here's to you. And Tom.

KITTY   (*sorrowfully*)   Where *is* Tom?

JOE   He's getting a job tonight driving a truck. He'll be back in a couple of days.

KITTY   (*sadly*)   I told him I'd marry him.

JOE   He wanted to see you and say good-bye.

KITTY   He's too good for me. He's like a little boy. (*wearily*) I'm—Too many things have happened to me.

JOE   Kitty Duval, you're one of the few truly innocent people I have ever known. He'll be back in a couple of days. Go back to the hotel and wait for him.

KITTY   That's what I mean. I can't stand being alone. I'm no good. I tried very hard. I don't know what it is. I miss— (*She gestures*)

JOE   (*gently*)   Do you really want to come back here, Kitty?

KITTY   I don't know. I'm not sure. Everything *smells* different. I don't know how to feel, or what to think. (*gesturing pathetically*) I know I don't belong there. It's what I've wanted all my life, but it's too *late.* I try to be happy about it, but all I can do is remember everything and cry.

JOE   I don't know what to tell you, Kitty. I didn't mean to hurt you.

KITTY   You haven't hurt me. You're the only person who's ever been good to me. I've never known anybody like you. I'm not sure about love any more, but I know I love you, and I know I love Tom.

JOE   I love you too, Kitty Duval.

KITTY   He'll want babies. I know he will. I know *I* will, too. Of course I will. I can't— (*She shakes her head*)

JOE   Tom's a baby himself. You'll be very happy together. He wants you to ride with him in the truck. Tom's good for you. You're good for Tom.

KITTY   Do you want me to go back and wait for him?

JOE   I can't *tell* you what to do. I think it would be a good idea, though.

KITTY   I wish I could tell you how it makes me feel to be alone. It's almost worse.

JOE   It might take a whole week, Kitty. (*He looks at her sharply, at the arrival of an idea*) Didn't you speak of reading a book? A book of poems?

KITTY   I didn't know what I was saying.

JOE   (*trying to get up*)   Of course you knew. I think you'll like poetry. Wait here a minute, Kitty. I'll go see if I can find some books.

KITTY   All right, Joe.

(*He walks out of the place right, trying very hard not to wobble.* KITTY *looks at* LADY *and they exchange smiles. Foghorn. Music. The* NEWSBOY *comes in right. Looks for* JOE)

NEWSBOY   Paper?

MAN   No.

NEWSBOY   (*goes to the* ARAB)   Paper, Mister?

ARAB   No foundation.

NEWSBOY   What?

ARAB   (*very angry*)   No foundation.

NEWSBOY   (*starts out, turns, looks at the* ARAB, *shakes head*)   No foundation? How do you figure? (*goes out right as* BLICK *and* TWO COPS *enter. The* COPS *go to bar*)

NEWSBOY   (*to* BLICK)   Paper, Mister? (BLICK *pushes him aside. The* NEWSBOY *goes out right*)

BLICK   Where's Nick?

HARRY   He went for a walk.

BLICK   Who are you?

HARRY   Harry.

BLICK   (*to the* ARAB *who is playing harmonica*)   Hey, you. Shut up. (*The* ARAB *stops playing and exits right.* WESLEY *looks around, stops playing;* BLICK *studies* KITTY, *crosses to right of her*)   What's your name, sister?

KITTY   (*looking at him*)   Kitty Duval. What's it to you? (KITTY'S *voice is now like it was at the beginning of the play: tough, independent, bitter and hard*)

BLICK   (*angry*)   Don't give me any of your gutter lip. Just answer my questions.

KITTY   You go to hell, you.

BLICK   (*coming over, enraged*)   Where do you live?

KITTY   The New York Hotel. Room Twenty-one.

BLICK   Where do you work?

KITTY   I'm not working just now. I'm looking for work. (*lights cigarette*)

BLICK   What kind of work? (KITTY *can't answer*)   What kind of work? (KITTY *can't answer. Furiously*)   WHAT KIND OF WORK?

KIT CARSON   (*comes over to right of center table*)   You can't talk to a lady that way in *my* presence. (BLICK *turns and stares at* KIT. *The*

COPS *begin to move from the bar to back of* KIT CARSON)

BLICK   (*to the* COPS)   It's all right, boys. I'll take care of this. (*to* KIT)   *What'd you say?*

KIT CARSON   You got no right to hurt people. Who are *you?* (BLICK, *without a word, takes* KIT *out right to the street. Sounds of a blow and a groan.* BLICK *returns with his face flushed*)

BLICK   (*to the* COPS)   O.K., boys. You can go now. Take care of him. Put him on his feet and tell him to behave himself from now on. (*to* KITTY *again*)   Now answer my question. What kind of work?

KITTY   (*quietly*)   I'm a whore, you son of a bitch. You know what kind of work I do. And I know what kind you do.

MAN   (*rises; shocked and really hurt*)   Excuse me, officer, but it seems to me that your attitude—

BLICK   Shut up.

MAN   (*quietly*)   —is making the poor child say things that are not true.

BLICK   Shut up, I said.

LADY   Well. (*to the* MAN)   Are you going to stand for such insolence?

BLICK   (*crosses to right of* LADY; *to* MAN, *who is standing*)   Are you?

MAN   I'll get a divorce. I'll start life all over again. Come on. Get the hell out of here! (*The* MAN *hurries his* LADY *out of the place,* BLICK *watching them go. To left of* KITTY)

BLICK   (*to* KITTY)   Now. Let's begin again, and see that you tell the truth. What's your name?

KITTY   Kitty Duval.

BLICK   Where do you live?

KITTY   Until this evening I lived at The New York Hotel. Room Twenty-one. This evening I moved to the St. Francis Hotel.

BLICK   Oh. To the St. Francis Hotel. Nice place. Where do you work?

KITTY   I'm looking for work.

BLICK   What kind of work do you do?

KITTY   I'm an actress.

BLICK   I see. What movies have I seen you in?

KITTY   I've worked in burlesque.

BLICK   You're a liar.

KITTY   (*pathetically, as at the beginning of the play*)   It's the truth.

BLICK   What are you doing here?

KITTY   I came to see if I could get a job here.

BLICK   Doing what?

KITTY   Singing—and—dancing.

BLICK   You can't sing or dance. What are you lying for?

KITTY   I can. I sang and danced in burlesque all over the country.

BLICK   You're a liar.

KITTY   I said lines, too.

BLICK   So you danced in burlesque?

KITTY   Yes.

BLICK   All right. Let's see what you did.

KITTY   I can't. There's no music, and I haven't got the right clothes.

BLICK   There's music. (*to* WESLEY) Put a nickel in that phonograph. Come on. Put a nickel in that phonograph. (WESLEY *does so. To* KITTY) All right. Get up on that stage and do a hot little burlesque number. Get going, now. Let's see you dance the way you did in burlesque, all over the country. (KITTY *goes up on stage, sings a few lines and then tries to do a burlesque dance. It is beautiful in a tragic way, tragic and incredible*) All right, start taking them off! (KITTY *removes her hat and starts to remove her jacket.* JOE *enters right, crosses to center*)

JOE   (*hurrying to* KITTY)   Get down from there. (*He takes* KITTY *into his arms. She is crying. To* BLICK) What the hell do you think you're doing!

WESLEY   It's that man, Blick. He made her take off her clothes. He beat up the old man, too. (BLICK *pushes* WESLEY *off stage center and begins beating him*)

TOM   (*enters right*)   What's the matter, Joe? What's happened?

JOE   Is the truck out there?

TOM   Yeah, but what's happened? Kitty's crying again!

JOE   You driving to San Diego?

TOM   Yeah, Joe. But what's he doing to that poor colored boy?

JOE   Get going. Here's some money. Everything's O.K. (*to* KITTY) Dress in the truck. Take these books.

WESLEY'S VOICE   You can't hurt me. You'll get yours. You wait and see.

TOM   Joe, he's hurting that boy. I'll kill him!

JOE   Get out of here! Get married in San Diego. I'll see you when you get back. (TOM *and* KITTY *exit right.* NICK *enters and stands at the lower end of bar.* JOE *takes the revolver out of his pocket. Looks at it*) I've always wanted to kill somebody, but I never knew who it should be.

(*He cocks the revolver, stands real straight, holds it in front of him firmly and walks to the center door.* NICK *exits right. He stands a moment watching* BLICK, *aims very carefully, and pulls trigger. There is no shot. He cocks the pistol again and again presses the trigger.*

Again there is no shot. NICK *and* MCCARTHY *come in right.* JOE *is cocking the pistol again.* NICK *runs over and grabs the gun, and takes* JOE *aside*)

NICK   What the hell do you think you're doing?

JOE   (*casually, as if it were nothing*)   That dumb Tom. Buys a six-shooter that won't even shoot once. (NICK *hides the gun in a hurry.* BLICK *comes in center, panting for breath*)

NICK   (*looks at* BLICK, *infuriated*)   Blick! I told you to stay out of here! Now get out of here. (*starts to push* BLICK *off right*) If you come back again, I'm going to take you in that room where you've been beating up that colored boy, and I'm going to murder you—slowly—with my hands. Beat it! (*He pushes* BLICK *out right. To* HARRY) Go take care of the colored boy.

(HARRY *runs out center.* WILLIE *returns and doesn't sense that anything is changed.* WILLIE *puts another nickel into the machine, but he does so very violently. The consequence of this violence is that the flag comes up again.* WILLIE, *amazed, stands at attention and salutes. The flag goes down. He shakes his head*)

WILLIE   (*thoughtfully*)   As far as I'm concerned, this is the *only* country in the world. If you ask me, *nuts* to Europe! (*He is about to push the slide in again when the flag comes up again. Furiously, to* NICK, *while he salutes and stands at attention, pleadingly*) Hey, Nick. This machine is out of order.

NICK   (*somberly*)   Give it a whack on the side. (WILLIE *does so. A hell of a whack. The result is the flag comes up and down, and* WILLIE *keeps saluting*)

WILLIE   (*saluting*)   Hey, Nick. Something's wrong.

(*The machine quiets down abruptly.* WILLIE *very stealthily slides a new nickel in, and starts a new game. From a distance three shots are heard, each carefully timed.* NICK *runs out right followed by* MCCARTHY. *The* NEWSBOY *enters right, crosses to* JOE's *table, senses something is wrong*)

NEWSBOY   (*softly*)   Paper, Mister?

(JOE *takes them all, hands him money, shoves them off the table to floor without glancing at them.* ARAB *enters right, picks up paper, throws it down, crosses to right, sits down.* DRUNK *enters right, goes to bar.* NEWSBOY *backs to center, wishes he could cheer* JOE *up. Notices phonograph, goes to it and puts coin in it hoping it will make* JOE *happier.* NEWSBOY *sits down, left, he watches* JOE. *Music begins—* "The Missouri Waltz")

NICK (*enters, crosses to* JOE)   Joe, Blick's dead! Somebody just shot him, and none of the cops are trying to find out who. (JOE *looks up slowly. Shouting*) Joe.

JOE (*looking up*)   What?

NICK   Blick's dead.

JOE   Blick? Dead? Good! That goddamn gun wouldn't go off. I *told* Tom to get a good one.

NICK (*picking up gun and looking at it*) Joe, you wanted to kill that guy! (HARRY *returns*) I'm going to buy you a bottle of champagne. (NICK *goes to bar.* JOE *rises, takes hat from rack, puts coat on. The* NEWSBOY *jumps up, helps* JOE *with coat*) What's the matter, Joe?

JOE   Nothing. Nothing.

NICK   How about the champagne?

JOE   Thanks. (*crosses to center*)

NICK   It's not eleven yet. Where you going, Joe?

JOE   I don't know. Nowhere.

NICK   Will I see you tomorrow?

JOE   I don't know. I don't think so. (KIT CARSON *enters right, walks to* JOE)

JOE   Somebody just shot a man. How are you feeling?

KIT   Never felt better in my life. (*quietly*) I shot a man once. In San Francisco. Shot him two times. In 1939, I think it was. In October. Fellow named Blick or Glick or something like that. Couldn't stand the way he talked to ladies. Went up to my room and got my old pearl-handled revolver and waited for him on Pacific Street. Saw him walking, and let him have it, two times. Had to throw the beautiful revolver into the Bay.

(HARRY, NICK, *the* ARAB *and the* DRUNK *close in around him.* JOE *walks slowly to the stairs leading to the street, turns and waves. Exits*)

NOTE APPENDED

In the time of your life, live—so that in that good time there shall be no ugliness or death for yourself or for any life your life touches. Seek goodness everywhere, and when it is found, bring it out of its hiding-place and let it be free and unashamed. Place in matter and in flesh the least of the values, for these are the things that hold death and must pass away. Discover in all things that which shines and is beyond corruption. Encourage virtue in whatever heart it may have been driven into secrecy and sorrow by the shame and terror of the world. Ignore the obvious, for it is unworthy of the clear eye and the kindly heart. Be the inferior of no man, nor of any man be the superior. Remember that every man is a variation of yourself. No man's guilt is not yours, nor is any man's innocence a thing apart. Despise evil and ungodliness, but not men of ungodliness or evil. These, understand. Have no shame in being kindly and gentle, but if the time comes in the time of your life to kill, kill and have no regret. In the time of your life, live—so that in that wondrous time you shall not add to the misery and sorrow of the world, but shall smile to the infinite delight and mystery of it.

Thornton Wilder

1897-

SOME THOUGHTS ON PLAYWRITING

Four fundamental conditions of the drama separate it from the other arts. Each of these conditions has its advantages and disadvantages, each requires a particular aptitude from the dramatist, and from each there are a number of instructive consequences to be derived. These conditions are:

1. The theatre is an art which reposes upon the work of many collaborators;

2. It is addressed to the group-mind;

3. It is based upon a pretense and its very nature calls out a multiplication of pretenses;

4. Its action takes place in a perpetual present time.

I. THE THEATRE IS AN ART WHICH REPOSES UPON THE WORK OF MANY COLLABORATORS

We have been accustomed to think that a work of art is by definition the product of one governing selecting will.

A landscape by Cézanne consists of thousands of brushstrokes each commanded by one mind. *Paradise Lost* and *Pride and Prejudice,* even in cheap frayed copies, bear the immediate and exclusive message of one intelligence.

It is true that in musical performance we meet with intervening executants, but the element of intervention is slight compared to that which takes place in drama. Illustrations:

1. One of the finest productions of *The Merchant of Venice* in our time showed Sir Henry Irving as Shylock, a noble, wronged, and in-dignant being, of such stature that the Merchants of Venice dwindled before him into irresponsible schoolboys. He was confronted in court by a gracious, even queenly, Portia, Miss Ellen Terry. At the Odéon in Paris, however, Gémier played Shylock as a vengeful and hysterical buffoon, confronted in court by a Portia who was a *gamine* from the Paris streets with a lawyer's quill three feet long over her ear; at the close of the trial scene Shylock was driven screaming about the auditorium, behind the spectators' back and onto the stage again, in a wild Elizabethan revel. Yet for all their divergences both were admirable productions of the play.

2. If there were ever a play in which fidelity to the author's requirements were essential in the representation of the principal role, it would seem to be Ibsen's *Hedda Gabler,* for the play is primarily an exposition of her character. Ibsen's directions read: "Enter from the left Hedda Gabler. She is a woman of twenty-nine. Her face and figure show great refinement and distinction. Her complexion is pale and opaque. Her steel-gray eyes express an unruffled calm. Her hair is of an attractive medium brown, but is not particularly abundant; and she is dressed in a flowing loose-fitting morning gown." I once saw Eleonora Duse in this role. She was a woman of sixty and made no effort to conceal it. Her complexion was pale and transparent. Her hair was white, and she was dressed in a gown that suggested some medieval empress in mourning. And the performance was very fine.

One may well ask: why write for the theatre at all? Why not work in the novel where such deviations from one's intentions cannot take place?

There are two answers:

1. The theatre presents certain vitalities of its own so inviting and stimulating that the writer is willing to receive them in compensa-

tion for this inevitable variation from an exact image.

2. The dramatist through working in the theatre gradually learns not merely to take account of the presence of the collaborators, but to derive advantage from them; and he learns, above all, to organize the play in such a way that its strength lies not in appearances beyond his control, but in the succession of events and in the unfolding of an idea, in narration.

The gathered audience sits in a darkened room, one end of which is lighted. The nature of the transaction at which it is gazing is a succession of events illustrating a general idea— the stirring of the idea; the gradual feeding out of information; the shock and countershock of circumstances; the flow of action; the interruption of action; the moments of allusion to earlier events; the preparation of surprise, dread, or delight—all that is the author's and his alone.

For reasons to be discussed later—the expectancy of the group-mind, the problem of time on the stage, the absence of the narrator, the element of pretense—the theatre carries the art of narration to a higher power than the novel or the epic poem. The theatre is unfolding action and in the disposition of events the authors may exercise a governance so complete that the distortions effected by the physical appearance of actors, by the fancies of scene painters and the misunderstandings of directors, fall into relative insignificance. It is just because the theatre is an art of many collaborators, with the constant danger of grave misinterpretation, that the dramatist learns to turn his attention to the laws of narration, its logic and its deep necessity of presenting a unifying idea stronger than its mere collection of happenings. The dramatist must be by instinct a storyteller.

There is something mysterious about the endowment of the storyteller. Some very great writers possessed very little of it, and some others, lightly esteemed, possessed it in so large a measure that their books survive down the ages, to the confusion of severer critics. Alexandre Dumas had it to an extraordinary degree; while Melville, for all his splendid quality, had it barely sufficiently to raise his work from the realm of non-fiction. It springs, not, as some have said, from an aversion to general ideas, but from an instinctive coupling of idea and illustration; the idea, for a born storyteller, can only be expressed imbedded in its circumstantial illustration. The myth, the parable, the fable are the fountainhead of all fiction and in them is seen most clearly the didactic, moraliz-

ing employment of a story. Modern taste shrinks from emphasizing the central idea that hides behind the fiction, but it exists there nevertheless, supplying the unity to fantasizing, and offering a justification to what otherwise we would repudiate as mere arbitrary contrivance, pretentious lying, or individualistic emotional association spinning. For all their magnificent intellectual endowment, George Meredith and George Eliot were not born storytellers; they chose fiction as the vehicle for their reflections, and the passing of time is revealing their error in that choice. Jane Austen was pure storyteller and her works are outlasting those of apparently more formidable rivals. The theatre is more exacting than the novel in regard to this faculty, and its presence constitutes a force which compensates the dramatist for the deviations which are introduced into his work by the presence of his collaborators.

The chief of these collaborators are the actors.

The actor's gift is a combination of three separate faculties or endowments. Their presence to a high degree in any one person is extremely rare, although the ambition to possess them is common. Those who rise to the height of the profession represent a selection and a struggle for survival in one of the most difficult and cruel of the artistic activities. The three endowments that compose the gift are observation, imagination, and physical co-ordination.

1. An observant and analyzing eye for all modes of behavior about us, for dress and manner, and for the signs of thought and emotion in one's self and in others.

2. The strength of imagination and memory whereby the actor may, at the indication in the author's text, explore his store of observations and represent the details of appearance and the intensity of the emotions—joy, fear, surprise, grief, love, and hatred, and through imagination extend them to intenser degrees and to differing characterizations.

3. A physical co-ordination whereby the force of these inner realizations may be communicated to voice, face, and body.

An actor must *know* the appearances and the mental states; he must *apply* his knowledge to the role; and he must physically *express* his knowledge. Moreover, his concentration must be so great that he can effect this representation under conditions of peculiar difficulty —in abrupt transition from the non-imaginative conditions behind the stage; and in the presence of fellow-actors who may be momentarily destroying the reality of the action.

A dramatist prepares the characterization of

his personages in such a way that it will take advantage of the actor's gift.

Characterization in a novel is presented by the author's dogmatic assertion that the personage was such, and by an analysis of the personage with generally an account of his or her past. Since, in the drama, this is replaced by the actual presence of the personage before us and since there is no occasion for the intervening all-knowing author to instruct us as to his or her inner nature, a far greater share is given in a play to (1) highly characteristic utterances and (2) concrete occasions in which the character defines itself under action and (3) a conscious preparation of the text whereby the actor may build upon the suggestions in the role according to his own abilities.

Characterization in a play is like a blank check which the dramatist accords to the actor for him to fill in—not entirely blank, for a number of indications of individuality are already there, but to a far less definite and absolute degree than in the novel.

The dramatist's principal interest being the movement of the story, he is willing to resign the more detailed aspects of characterization to the actor and is often rewarded beyond his expectation.

The sleepwalking scene from *Macbeth* is a highly compressed selection of words whereby despair and remorse rise to the surface of indirect confession. It is to be assumed that had Shakespeare lived to see what the genius of Sarah Siddons could pour into the scene from that combination of observation, self-knowledge, imagination, and representational skill, even he might have exclaimed, "I never knew I wrote so well!"

II. THE THEATRE IS AN ART ADDRESSED TO A GROUP-MIND

Painting, sculpture, and the literature of the book are certainly solitary experiences; and it is likely that most people would agree that the audience seated shoulder to shoulder in a concert hall is not an essential element in musical enjoyment.

But a play presupposes a crowd. The reasons for this go deeper than (1) the economic necessity for the support of the play and (2) the fact that the temperament of actors is proverbially dependent on group attention.

It rests on the fact that (1) the pretense, the fiction, on the stage would fall to pieces and absurdity without the support accorded to it by a crowd, and (2) the excitement induced by pretending a fragment of life is such that it partakes of ritual and festival, and requires a throng.

Similarly the fiction that royal personages are of a mysteriously different nature from other people requires audiences, levees, and processions for its maintenance. Since the beginnings of society, satirists have occupied themselves with the descriptions of kings and queens in their intimacy and delighted in showing how the prerogatives of royalty become absurd when the crowd is not present to extend to them the enhancement of an imaginative awe.

The theatre partakes of the nature of festival. Life imitated is life raised to a higher power. In the case of comedy, the vitality of these pretended surprises, deceptions, and *contretemps* becomes so lively that before a spectator, solitary or regarding himself as solitary, the structure of so much event would inevitably expose the artificiality of the attempt and ring hollow and unjustified; and in the case of tragedy, the accumulation of woe and apprehension would soon fall short of conviction. All actors know the disturbing sensation of playing before a handful of spectators at a dress rehearsal or performance where only their interest in pure craftsmanship can barely sustain them. During the last rehearsals the phrase is often heard: "This play is hungry for an audience."

Since the theatre is directed to a group-mind, a number of consequences follow:

1. A group-mind presupposes, if not a lowering of standards, a broadening of the fields of interest. The other arts may presuppose an audience of connoisseurs trained in leisure and capable of being interested in certain rarefied aspects of life. The dramatist may be prevented from exhibiting, for example, detailed representations of certain moments in history that require specialized knowledge in the audience, or psychological states in the personages which are of insufficient general interest to evoke self-identification in the majority. In the Second Part of Goethe's *Faust* there are long passages dealing with the theory of paper money. The exposition of the nature of misanthropy (so much more drastic than Molière's) in Shakespeare's *Timon of Athens* has never been a success. The dramatist accepts this limitation in subject matter and realizes that the group-mind imposes upon him the necessity of treating material understandable by the larger number.

2. It is the presence of the group-mind that brings another requirement to the theatre—forward movement.

Maeterlinck said that there was more drama in the spectacle of an old man seated by a table than in the majority of plays offered to the public. He was juggling with the various meanings in the word "drama." In the sense whereby drama means the intensified concentration of life's diversity and significance he may well have been right; if he meant drama as a theatrical representation before an audience he was wrong. Drama on the stage is inseparable from forward movement, from action.

Many attempts have been made to present Plato's dialogues, Gobineau's [1] fine series of dialogues, *La Renaissance,* and the *Imaginary Conversations* of Landor; [2] but without success. Through some ingredient in the group-mind, and through the sheer weight of anticipation involved in the dressing up and the assumption of fictional roles, an action is required, and an action that is more than a mere progress in argumentation and debate.

III. THE THEATRE IS A WORLD OF PRETENSE

It lives by conventions: a convention is an agreed-upon falsehood, a permitted lie.

Illustrations: Consider at the first performance of the *Medea,* the passage where Medea meditates the murder of her children. An anecdote from antiquity tells us that the audience was so moved by this passage that considerable disturbance took place.

The following conventions were involved:

1. Medea was played by a man.

2. He wore a large mask on his face. In the lip of the mask was an acoustical device for projecting the voice. On his feet he wore shoes with soles and heels half a foot high.

3. His costume was so designed that it conveyed to the audience, by convention: woman of royal birth and Oriental origin.

4. The passage was in metric speech. All poetry is an "agreed-upon falsehood" in regard to speech.

5. The lines were sung in a kind of recitative. All opera involves this "permitted lie" in regard to speech.

Modern taste would say that the passage would convey much greater pathos if a woman "like Medea" had delivered it—with an uncovered face that exhibited all the emotions she was undergoing. For the Greeks, however, there was no pretense that Medea was on the stage. The mask, the costume, the mode of declamation, were a series of signs which the

spectator interpreted and reassembled in his own mind. Medea was being re-created within the imagination of each of the spectators.

The history of the theatre shows us that in its greatest ages the stage employed the greatest number of conventions. The stage is fundamental pretense and it thrives on the acceptance of that fact and in the multiplication of additional pretenses. When it tries to assert that the personages in the action "really are," really inhabit such and such rooms, really suffer such and such emotions, it loses rather than gains credibility. The modern world is inclined to laugh condescendingly at the fact that in the plays of Racine and Corneille the gods and heroes of antiquity were dressed like the courtiers under Louis XIV; that in the Elizabethan age scenery was replaced by placards notifying the audience of the location; and that a whip in the hand and a jogging motion of the body indicated that a man was on horseback in the Chinese theatre; these devices did not spring from naïveté, however, but from the vitality of the public imagination in those days and from an instinctive feeling as to where the essential and where the inessential lay in drama.

The convention has two functions:

1. It provokes the collaborative activity of the spectator's imagination; and

2. It raises the action from the specific to the general.

This second aspect is of even greater importance than the first.

If Juliet is represented as a girl "very like Juliet"—it was not merely a deference to contemporary prejudices that assigned this role to a boy in the Elizabethan age—moving about in a "real" house with marble staircases, rugs, lamps, and furniture, the impression is irresistibly conveyed that these events happened to this one girl, in one place, at one moment in time. When the play is staged as Shakespeare intended it, the bareness of the stage releases the events from the particular and the experience of Juliet partakes of that of all girls in love, in every time, place and language.

The stage continually strains to tell this generalized truth and it is the element of pretense that reinforces it. Out of the lie, the pretense, of the theatre proceeds a truth more compelling than the novel can attain, for the novel by its own laws is constrained to tell of an action that "once happened"—"once upon a time."

IV. THE ACTION ON THE STAGE TAKES PLACE IN A PERPETUAL PRESENT TIME

Novels are written in the past tense. The characters in them, it is true, are represented

---

[1] Joseph Arthur Gobineau (1816–1882), French man of letters and diplomat. The chief early French exponent of the theory of Nordic supremacy, he was strongly antidemocratic and anti-Semitic.

[2] Walter Savage Landor (1775–1864), British poet and author.

as living moment by moment their present time, but the constant running commentary of the novelist ("Tess slowly descended into the valley"; "Anna Karenina laughed") inevitably conveys to the reader the fact that these events are long since past and over.

The novel is a past reported in the present. On the stage it is always now. This confers upon the action an increased vitality which the novelist longs in vain to incorporate into his work.

This condition in the theatre brings with it another important element:

In the theatre we are not aware of the intervening storyteller. The speeches arise from the characters in an apparently pure spontaneity.

A play is what takes place.

A novel is what one person tells us took place.

A play visibly represents pure existing. A novel is what one mind, claiming to omniscience, asserts to have existed.

Many dramatists have regretted this absence of the narrator from the stage, with his point of view, his powers of analyzing the behavior of the characters, his ability to interfere and supply further facts about the past, about simultaneous actions not visible on the stage, and above *all* his function of pointing the moral and emphasizing the significance of the action. In some periods of the theatre he has been present as chorus, or prologue and epilogue or as *raisonneur*. But surely this absence constitutes an additional force to the form, as well as an additional tax upon the writer's skill. It is the task of the dramatist so to co-ordinate his play, through the selection of episodes and speeches, that, though he is himself not visible, his point of view and his governing intention will impose themselves on the spectator's attention, not as dogmatic assertion or motto, but as self-evident truth and inevitable deduction.

Imaginative narration—the invention of souls and destinies—is to a philosopher an all but indefensible activity.

Its justification lies in the fact that the communication of ideas from one mind to another inevitably reaches the point where exposition passes into illustration, into parable, metaphor, allegory, and myth.

It is no accident that when Plato arrived at the height of his argument and attempted to convey a theory of knowledge and a theory of the structure of man's nature he passed over into story telling, into the myths of the Cave and the Charioteer; and that the great religious teachers have constantly had recourse to the parable as a means of imparting their deepest intuitions.

The theatre offers to imaginative narration its highest possibilities. It has many pitfalls and its very vitality betrays it into service as mere diversion and the enhancement of insignificant matter; but it is well to remember that it was the theatre that rose to the highest place during those epochs that aftertime has chosen to call "great ages" and that the Athens of Pericles and the reigns of Elizabeth, Philip II, and Louis XIV were also the ages that gave to the world the greatest dramas it has known.

THE SKIN OF OUR TEETH

CAST OF CHARACTERS

ANNOUNCER
SABINA
MR. FITZPATRICK
MRS. ANTROBUS
DINOSAUR
MAMMOTH
TELEGRAPH BOY
GLADYS
HENRY
MR. ANTROBUS
DOCTOR
PROFESSOR
JUDGE (MOSES)
HOMER

MISS E. MUSE
MISS T. MUSE
MISS M. MUSE
TWO USHERS
TWO DRUM MAJORETTES
FORTUNE TELLER
TWO CHAIR PUSHERS
SIX CONVEENERS
BROADCAST OFFICIAL
DEFEATED CANDIDATE
MR. TREMAYNE
HESTER
IVY
FRED BAILEY

ACT   I: *Home, Excelsior, New Jersey*
ACT II: *Atlantic City Boardwalk*
ACT III: *Home, Excelsior, New Jersey*

ACT ONE

(*A projection screen in the middle of the curtain. The first lantern slide: the name of the theatre, and the words: NEWS EVENTS OF THE WORLD. An* ANNOUNCER's *voice is heard*)

ANNOUNCER   The management takes pleasure in bringing to you—The News Events of the World. (*slide of the sun appearing above the horizon*)

Freeport, Long Island: The sun rose this morning at 6:32 a.m. This gratifying event was first reported by Mrs. Dorothy Stetson of Freeport, Long Island, who promptly telephoned the Mayor.

The Society for Affirming the End of the

World at once went into a special session and postponed the arrival of that event for TWENTY-FOUR HOURS.

All honor to Mrs. Stetson for her public spirit.

New York City: (*slide of the front doors of the theatre in which this play is playing; three cleaning* WOMEN *with mops and pails*) The X Theatre. During the daily cleaning of this theatre a number of lost objects were collected as usual by Mesdames Simpson, Pateslewski, and Moriarty.

Among these objects found today was a wedding ring, inscribed: *To Eva from Adam. Genesis II: 18.*

The ring will be restored to the owner or owners, if their credentials are satisfactory.

Tippehatchee, Vermont: (*slide representing a glacier*) The unprecedented cold weather of this summer has produced a condition that has not yet been satisfactorily explained. There is a report that a wall of ice is moving southward across these counties. The disruption of communications by the cold wave now crossing the country has rendered exact information difficult, but little credence is given to the rumor that the ice had pushed the Cathedral of Montreal as far as St. Albans, Vermont.

For further information see your daily papers.

Excelsior, New Jersey: (*slide of a modest suburban home*) The home of Mr. George Antrobus, the inventor of the wheel. The discovery of the wheel, following so closely on the discovery of the lever, has centered the attention of the country on Mr. Antrobus of this attractive suburban residence district. This is his home, a commodious seven-room house, conveniently situated near a public school, a Methodist church, and a firehouse; it is right handy to an A. and P. (*slide of* MR. ANTROBUS *on his front steps, smiling and lifting his straw hat. He holds a wheel*) Mr. Antrobus, himself. He comes of very old stock and has made his way up from next to nothing.

It is reported that he was once a gardener, but left that situation under circumstances that have been variously reported.

Mr. Antrobus is a veteran of foreign wars, and bears a number of scars, front and back. (*slide of* MRS. ANTROBUS *holding some roses*) This is Mrs. Antrobus, the charming and gracious president of the Excelsior Mothers' Club.

Mrs. Antrobus is an excellent needlewoman; it is she who invented the apron on which so many interesting changes have been rung since. (*slide of the* FAMILY *and* SABINA) Here we see the Antrobuses with their two children, Henry and Gladys, and friend. The friend in the rear is Lily Sabina, the maid.

I know we all want to congratulate this typical American family on its enterprise. We all wish Mr. Antrobus a successful future. Now the management takes you to the interior of this home for a brief visit.

(*Curtain rises. Living room of a commuter's home.* SABINA—*straw-blonde, overrouged—is standing by the window back center, a feather duster under her elbow*)

SABINA Oh, oh, oh! Six o'clock and the master not home yet.

Pray God nothing serious has happened to him crossing the Hudson River. If anything happened to him, we would certainly be inconsolable and have to move into a less desirable residence district.

The fact is I don't know what'll become of us. Here it is the middle of August and the coldest day of the year. It's simply freezing; the dogs are sticking to the sidewalks; can anybody explain that? No.

But I'm not surprised. The whole world's at sixes and sevens, and why the house hasn't fallen down about our ears long ago is a miracle to me. (*A fragment of the right wall leans precariously over the stage.* SABINA *looks at it nervously and it slowly rights itself*) Every night this same anxiety as to whether the master will get home safely: whether he'll bring home anything to eat. In the midst of life we are in the midst of death, a truer word was never said. (*The fragment of scenery flies up into the lofts.* SABINA *is struck dumb with surprise, shrugs her shoulders and starts dusting* MR. ANTROBUS' *chair, including the under side*) Of course, Mr. Antrobus is a very fine man, an excellent husband and father, a pillar of the church, and has all the best interests of the community at heart. Of course, every muscle goes tight every time he passes a policeman; but what I think is that there are certain charges that ought not to be made, and I think I may add, ought not to be allowed to be made; we're all human; who isn't? (*She dusts* MRS. ANTROBUS' *rocking chair*) Mrs. Antrobus is as fine a woman as you could hope to see. She lives only for her children; and if it would be any benefit to her children she'd see the rest of us stretched out dead at her feet without turning a hair,—that's the truth. If you want to know anything more about Mrs. Antrobus, just go and look at a tigress, and look hard.

As to the children—

Well, Henry Antrobus is a real, clean-cut American boy. He'll graduate from High School one of these days, if they make the alphabet any easier.—Henry, when he has a stone in his hand, has a perfect aim; he can hit anything from a bird to an older brother—Oh! I didn't mean to say that!—but it certainly was an unfortunate accident, and it was very hard getting the police out of the house.

Mr. and Mrs. Antrobus' daughter is named Gladys. She'll make some good man a good wife some day, if he'll just come down off the movie screen and ask her.

So here we are!

We've managed to survive for some time now, catch as catch can, the fat and the lean, and if the dinosaurs don't trample us to death, and if the grasshoppers don't eat up our garden, we'll all live to see better days, knock on wood.

Each new child that's born to the Antrobuses seems to them to be sufficient reason for the whole universe's being set in motion; and each new child that dies seems to them to have been spared a whole world of sorrow, and what the end of it will be is still very much an open question.

We've rattled along, hot and cold, for some time now—(*A portion of the wall above the door, right, flies up into the air and disappears*)

—and my advice to you is not to inquire into why or whither, but just enjoy your ice cream while it's on your plate,—that's my philosophy.

Don't forget that a few years ago we came through the depression by the skin of our teeth! One more tight squeeze like that and where will we be? (*This is a cue line.* SABINA *looks angrily at the kitchen door and repeats*) . . . we came through the depression by the skin of our teeth; one more tight squeeze like that and where will we be? (*Flustered, she looks through the opening in the right wall; then goes to the window and reopens the Act*) Oh, oh, oh! Six o'clock and the master not home yet! Pray God nothing has happened to him crossing the Hudson. Here it is the middle of August and the coldest day of the year. It's simply freezing; the dogs are sticking. One more tight squeeze like that and where will we be?

VOICE (*offstage*) Make up something! Invent something!

SABINA Well . . . uh . . . this certainly is a fine American home . . . and—uh . . . everybody's very happy . . . and—uh . . . (*suddenly flings pretense to the winds and coming downstage says with indignation*) I can't invent any words for this play, and I'm glad I can't. I hate this play and every word in it.

As for me, I don't understand a single word of it, anyways,—all about the troubles the human race has gone through, there's a subject for you.

Besides, the author hasn't made up his silly mind as to whether we're all living back in caves or in New Jersey today, and that's the way it is all the way through.

Oh—why can't we have plays like we used to have—*Peg o' My Heart,* and *Smilin' Thru,* and *The Bat*—good entertainment with a message you can take home with you?

I took this hateful job because I had to. For two years I've sat up in my room living on a sandwich and a cup of tea a day, waiting for better things in the theatre. And look at me now: I—I who've played *Rain* and *The Barretts of Wimpole Street* and *First Lady*—God in Heaven!

(*The* STAGE MANAGER *puts his head out from the hole in the scenery*)

MR. FITZPATRICK Miss Somerset!! Miss Somerset!

SABINA Oh! Anyway—nothing matters! It'll all be the same in a hundred years. (*loudly*) We came through the depression by the skin of our teeth,—that's true!—one more tight

squeeze like that and where will we be? (*enter* MRS. ANTROBUS, *a mother*)

MRS. ANTROBUS Sabina, you've let the fire go out.

SABINA (*in a lather*) One-thing-and-another; don't-know-whether-my-wits-are-upside-or-down; might-as-well-be-dead-as-alive-in-a-house-all-sixes-and-sevens. . . .

MRS. ANTROBUS You've let the fire go out. Here it is the coldest day of the year right in the middle of August, and you've let the fire go out.

SABINA Mrs. Antrobus, I'd like to give my two weeks' notice, Mrs. Antrobus. A girl like I can get a situation in a home where they're rich enough to have a fire in every room, Mrs. Antrobus, and a girl don't have to carry the responsibility of the whole house on her two shoulders. And a home without children, Mrs. Antrobus, because children are a thing only a parent can stand, and a truer word was never said; and a home, Mrs. Antrobus, where the master of the house don't pinch decent, self-respecting girls when he meets them in a dark corridor. I mention no names and make no charges. So you have my notice, Mrs. Antrobus. I hope that's perfectly clear.

MRS. ANTROBUS You've let the fire go out!— Have you milked the mammoth?

SABINA I don't understand a word of this play.—Yes, I've milked the mammoth.

MRS. ANTROBUS Until Mr. Antrobus comes home we have no food and we have no fire. You'd better go over to the neighbors and borrow some fire.

SABINA Mrs. Antrobus! I can't! I'd die on the way, you know I would. It's worse than January. The dogs are sticking to the sidewalks. I'd die.

MRS. ANTROBUS Very well, I'll go.

SABINA (*even more distraught, coming forward and sinking on her knees*) You'd never come back alive; we'd all perish; if you weren't here, we'd just perish. How do we know Mr. Antrobus'll be back? We don't know. If you go out, I'll just kill myself.

MRS. ANTROBUS Get up, Sabina.

SABINA Every night it's the same thing. Will he come back safe, or won't he? Will we starve to death, or freeze to death, or boil to death or will we be killed by burglars? I don't know why we go on living. I don't know why we go on living at all. It's easier being dead.

(*She flings her arms on the table and buries her head in them. In each of the succeeding speeches she flings her head up—and some-*

times her hands—then quickly buries her head again)

MRS. ANTROBUS The same thing! Always throwing up the sponge, Sabina. Always announcing your own death. But give you a new hat—or a plate of ice cream—or a ticket to the movies, and you want to live forever.

SABINA You don't care whether we live or die; all you care about is those children. If it would be any benefit to them you'd be glad to see us all stretched out dead.

MRS. ANTROBUS Well, maybe I would.

SABINA And what do they care about? Themselves—that's all they care about. (*shrilly*) They make fun of you behind your back. Don't tell me: they're ashamed of you. Half the time, they pretend they're someone else's children. Little thanks you get from them.

MRS. ANTROBUS I'm not asking for any thanks.

SABINA And Mr. Antrobus—you don't understand *him*. All that work he does—trying to discover the alphabet and the multiplication table. Whenever he tries to learn anything you fight against it.

MRS. ANTROBUS Oh, Sabina, I know you. When Mr. Antrobus raped you home from your Sabine hills, he did it to insult me.

He did it for your pretty face, and to insult me.

You were the new wife, weren't you?

For a year or two you lay on your bed all day and polished the nails on your hands and feet.

You made puff-balls of the combings of your hair and you blew them up to the ceiling.

And I washed your underclothes and I made you chicken broths.

I bore children and between my very groans I stirred the cream that you'd put on your face.

But I knew you wouldn't last.

You didn't last.

SABINA But it was I who encouraged Mr. Antrobus to make the alphabet. I'm sorry to say it, Mrs. Antrobus, but you're not a beautiful woman, and you can never know what a man could do if he tried. It's girls like I who inspire the multiplication table.

I'm sorry to say it, but you're not a beautiful woman, Mrs. Antrobus, and that's the God's truth.

MRS. ANTROBUS And you didn't last—you sank to the kitchen. And what do you do there? *You let the fire go out!*

No wonder to you it seems easier being dead.

Reading and writing and counting on your fingers is all very well in their way,—but I keep the home going.—There's that dinosaur on the front lawn again.—Shoo! Go away. Go away.

(*The baby* DINOSAUR *puts his head in the window*)

DINOSAUR It's cold.

MRS. ANTROBUS You go around to the back of the house where you belong.

DINOSAUR It's cold.

(*The* DINOSAUR *disappears.* MRS. ANTROBUS *goes calmly out.* SABINA *slowly raises her head and speaks to the audience. The central portion of the center wall rises, pauses, and disappears into the loft*)

SABINA Now that you audience are listening to this, too, I understand it a little better.

I wish eleven o'clock were here; I don't want to be dragged through this whole play again. (*The* TELEGRAPH BOY *is seen entering along the back wall of the stage from the right. She catches sight of him and calls*) Mrs. Antrobus! Mrs. Antrobus! Help! There's a strange man coming to the house. He's coming up the walk, help!

(*Enter* MRS. ANTROBUS *in alarm, but efficient*)

MRS. ANTROBUS Help me quick! (*They barricade the door by piling the furniture against it*) Who is it? What do you want?

TELEGRAPH BOY A telegram for Mrs. Antrobus from Mr. Antrobus in the city.

SABINA Are you sure, are you sure? Maybe it's just a trap!

MRS. ANTROBUS I know his voice, Sabina. We can open the door. (*enter the* TELEGRAPH BOY, *12 years old, in uniform. The* DINOSAUR *and* MAMMOTH *slip by him into the room and settle down front right*) I'm sorry we kept you waiting. We have to be careful, you know. (*to the* ANIMALS) Hm! . . . Will you be quiet?

(*They nod*)

Have you had your supper? (*They nod*)

Are you *ready* to come in? (*They nod*)

Young man, have you any fire with you? Then light the grate, will you? (*He nods, produces something like a briquet; and kneels by the imagined fireplace, footlights center. Pause*) What are people saying about this cold weather? (*He makes a doubtful shrug with his shoulders*) Sabina, take this stick and go and light the stove.

SABINA Like I told you, Mrs. Antrobus; two weeks. That's the law. I hope that's perfectly clear.

MRS. ANTROBUS   What about this cold weather?

TELEGRAPH BOY   (*lowered eyes*)   Of course, I don't know anything . . . but they say there's a wall of ice moving down from the North, that's what they say. We can't get Boston by telegraph, and they're burning pianos in Hartford. . . . It moves everything in front of it, churches and post offices and city halls.

I live in Brooklyn myself.

MRS. ANTROBUS   What are people doing about it?

TELEGRAPH BOY   Well . . . uh . . . Talking, mostly.

Or just what you'd do a day in February.

There are some that are trying to go South and the roads are crowded; but you can't take old people and children very far in a cold like this.

MRS. ANTROBUS   What's this telegram you have for me?

TELEGRAPH BOY   (*fingertips to his forehead*) If you wait just a minute; I've got to remember it. (*The* ANIMALS *have left their corner and are nosing him. Presently they take their places on either side of him, leaning against his hips, like heraldic beasts*)

This telegram was flashed from Murray Hill to University Heights! And then by puffs of smoke from University Heights to Staten Island. And then by lantern from Staten Island to Plainfield, New Jersey. What hath God wrought! (*He clears his throat*)

"To Mrs. Antrobus, Excelsior, New Jersey: My dear wife, will be an hour late. Busy day at the office. Don't worry the children about the cold just keep them warm burn everything except Shakespeare."

MRS. ANTROBUS   Men!—He knows I'd burn ten Shakespeares to prevent a child of mine from having one cold in the head. What does it say next? (*enter* SABINA)

TELEGRAPH BOY   "Have made great discoveries today have separated em from en."

SABINA   I know what that is, that's the alphabet, yes it is. Mr. Antrobus is just the cleverest man. Why, when the alphabet's finished, we'll be able to tell the future and everything.

TELEGRAPH BOY   Then listen to this: "Ten tens make a hundred semi-colon consequences far-reaching." (*watches for effect*)

MRS. ANTROBUS   The earth's turning to ice, and all he can do is to make up new numbers.

TELEGRAPH BOY   Well, Mrs. Antrobus, like the head man at our office said: a few more discoveries like that and we'll be worth freezing.

MRS. ANTROBUS   What does he say next?

TELEGRAPH BOY   I . . . I can't do this last part very well. (*He clears his throat and sings*) "Happy w'dding ann'vers'ry to you, Happy ann'vers'ry to you—"

(*The* ANIMALS *begin to howl soulfully;* SABINA *screams with pleasure*)

MRS. ANTROBUS   Dolly! Frederick! Be quiet.

TELEGRAPH BOY   (*above the din*)   "Happy w'dding ann'vers'ry, dear Eva; happy w'dding ann'vers'ry to you."

MRS. ANTROBUS   Is that in the telegram? Are they singing telegrams now? (*He nods*) The earth's getting so silly no wonder the sun turns cold.

SABINA   Mrs. Antrobus, I want to take back the notice I gave you. Mrs. Antrobus, I don't want to leave a house that gets such interesting telegrams and I'm sorry for anything I said. I really am.

MRS. ANTROBUS   Young man, I'd like to give you something for all this trouble; Mr. Antrobus isn't home yet and I have no money and no food in the house—

TELEGRAPH BOY   Mrs. Antrobus . . . I don't like to . . . appear to . . . ask for anything, but . . .

MRS. ANTROBUS   What is it you'd like?

TELEGRAPH BOY   Do you happen to have an old needle you could spare? My wife just sits home all day thinking about needles.

SABINA   (*shrilly*)   We only got two in the house. Mrs. Antrobus, you know we only got two in the house.

MRS. ANTROBUS   (*after a look at* SABINA, *taking a needle from her collar*)   Why yes, I can spare this.

TELEGRAPH BOY   (*lowered eyes*)   Thank you, Mrs. Antrobus. Mrs. Antrobus, can I ask you something else? I have two sons of my own; if the cold gets worse, what should I do?

SABINA   I think we'll all perish, that's what I think. Cold like this in August is just the end of the whole world. (*silence*)

MRS. ANTROBUS   I don't know. After all, what does one do about anything? Just keep as warm as you can. And don't let your wife and children see that you're worried.

TELEGRAPH BOY   Yes. . . . Thank you, Mrs. Antrobus. Well, I'd better be going.—Oh, I forgot! There's one more sentence in the telegram. "Three cheers have invented the wheel."

MRS. ANTROBUS   A wheel? What's a wheel?

TELEGRAPH BOY   I don't know. That's what it said. The sign for it is like this. Well, goodbye.

(*The* WOMEN *see him to the door, with good-byes and injunctions to keep warm*)

SABINA (*apron to her eyes, wailing*) Mrs. Antrobus, it looks to me like all the nice men in the world are already married; I don't know why that is. (*exit*)

MRS. ANTROBUS (*thoughtful; to the* ANIMALS) Do you ever remember hearing tell of any cold like this in August? (*The* ANIMALS *shake their heads*) From your grandmothers or anyone? (*They shake their heads*) Have you any suggestions? (*They shake their heads. She pulls her shawl around, goes to the front door and opening it an inch calls*) Henry. Gladys. Children. Come right in and get warm. No, no, when mama says a thing she means it. Henry! *Henry.* Put down that stone. You know what happened last time. (*shriek*) Henry! Put down that stone! Gladys! Put down your dress!! Try and be a lady.

(*The* CHILDREN *bound in and dash to the fire. They take off their winter things and leave them in heaps on the floor*)

GLADYS Mama, I'm hungry. Mama, why is it so cold?

HENRY (*at the same time*) Mama, why doesn't it snow? Mama, when's supper ready? Maybe it'll snow and we can make snowballs.

GLADYS Mama, it's so cold that in one more minute I just couldn't of stood it.

MRS. ANTROBUS Settle down, both of you, I want to talk to you. (*She draws up a hassock and sits front center over the orchestra pit before the imaginary fire. The* CHILDREN *stretch out on the floor, leaning against her lap. Tableau by Raphael. The* ANIMALS *edge up and complete the triangle*) It's just a cold spell of some kind. Now listen to what I'm saying.

When your father comes home I want you to be extra quiet. He's had a hard day at the office and I don't know but what he may have one of his moods.

I just got a telegram from him very happy and excited, and you know what that means. Your father's temper's uneven; I guess you know that. (*shreik*) Henry! Henry!

Why—why can't you remember to keep your hair down over your forehead? You must keep that scar covered up. Don't you know that when your father sees it he loses all control over himself? He goes crazy. He wants to die. (*After a moment's despair she collects herself decisively, wets the hem of her apron in her mouth and starts polishing his forehead vigorously*) Lift your head up. Stop squirming. Blessed me, sometimes I think that it's going away—and then there it is: just as red as ever.

HENRY Mama, today at school two teachers forgot and called me by my old name. They forgot, Mama. You'd better write another letter to the principal, so that he'll tell them I've changed my name. Right out in class they called me: Cain.

MRS. ANTROBUS (*putting her hand on his mouth, too late; hoarsely*) Don't say it. (*polishing feverishly*) If you're good they'll forget it. Henry, you didn't hit anyone . . . today, did you?

HENRY Oh . . . no-o-o!

MRS. ANTROBUS (*still working, not looking at* GLADYS) And Gladys, I want you to be especially nice to your father tonight. You know what he calls you when you're good—his little angel, his little star. Keep your dress down like a little lady. And keep your voice nice and low. Gladys Antrobus!! What's that red stuff you have on your face? (*slaps her*) You're a filthy detestable child! (*rises in real, though temporary, repudiation and despair*) Get away from me, both of you! I wish I'd never seen sight or sound of you. Let the cold come! I can't stand it. I don't want to go on. (*She walks away*)

GLADYS (*weeping*) All the girls at school do, Mama.

MRS. ANTROBUS (*shrieking*) I'm through with you, that's all!—Sabina! Sabina!—Don't you know your father'd go crazy if he saw that paint on your face? Don't you know your father thinks you're perfect? Don't you know he couldn't live if he didn't think you were perfect?—Sabina! (*enter* SABINA)

SABINA Yes, Mrs. Antrobus!

MRS. ANTROBUS Take this girl out into the kitchen and wash her face with the scrubbing brush.

MR. ANTROBUS (*outside, roaring*) "I've been working on the railroad, all the livelong day . . ." etc.

(*The* ANIMALS *start running around in circles, bellowing.* SABINA *rushes to the window*)

MRS. ANTROBUS Sabina, what's that noise outside?

SABINA Oh, it's a drunken tramp. It's a giant, Mrs. Antrobus. We'll all be killed in our beds, I know it!

MRS. ANTROBUS Help me quick. Quick. Everybody. (*Again they stack all the furniture against the door.* MR. ANTROBUS *pounds and bellows*) Who is it? What do you want?—Sabina, have you any boiling water ready?—Who is it?

MR. ANTROBUS Broken-down camel of a pig's snout, open this door.

MRS. ANTROBUS God be praised! It's your

father.—Just a minute, George!—Sabina, clear the door, quick. Gladys, come here while I clean your nasty face!

MR. ANTROBUS She-bitch of a goat's gizzard, I'll break every bone in your body. Let me in or I'll tear the whole house down.

MRS. ANTROBUS Just a minute, George, something's the matter with the lock.

MR. ANTROBUS Open the door or I'll tear your livers out. I'll smash your brains on the ceiling, and Devil take the hindmost.

MRS. ANTROBUS Now, you can open the door, Sabina. I'm ready.

(*The door is flung open. Silence.* MR. ANTROBUS *—face of a Keystone Comedy Cop—stands there in fur cap and blanket. His arms are full of parcels, including a large stone wheel with a center in it. One hand carries a railroad man's lantern. Suddenly he bursts into joyous roar*)

MR. ANTROBUS Well, how's the whole crooked family? (*Relief. Laughter. Tears. Jumping up and down.* ANIMALS *cavorting.* ANTROBUS *throws the parcels on the ground. Hurls his cap and blanket after them. Heroic embraces. Melee of* HUMANS *and* ANIMALS, SABINA *included*) I'll be scalded and tarred if a man can't get a little welcome when he comes home. Well, Maggie, you old gunnysack, how's the broken down old weather hen?—Sabina, old fishbait, old skunkpot.—And the children, —how've the little smellers been?

GLADYS Papa, Papa, Papa, Papa, Papa.

MR. ANTROBUS How've they been, Maggie?

MRS. ANTROBUS Well, I must say they've been as good as gold. I haven't had to raise my voice once. I don't know what's the matter with them.

ANTROBUS (*kneeling before* GLADYS) Papa's little weasel, eh?—Sabina, there's some food for you.—Papa's little gopher?

GLADYS (*her arm around his neck*) Papa, you're always teasing me.

ANTROBUS And Henry? Nothing rash today, I hope. Nothing rash?

HENRY No, Papa.

ANTROBUS (*roaring*) Well that's good, that's good—I'll bet Sabina let the fire go out.

SABINA Mr. Antrobus, I've given my notice. I'm leaving two weeks from today. I'm sorry, but I'm leaving.

ANTROBUS (*roar*) Well, if you leave now you'll freeze to death, so go and cook the dinner.

SABINA Two weeks, that's the law. (*exit*)

ANTROBUS Did you get my telegram?

MRS. ANTROBUS Yes.—What's a wheel?

(*He indicates the wheel with a glance.* HENRY

is rolling it around the floor. Rapid, hoarse interchange: MRS. ANTROBUS: *What does this cold weather mean? It's below freezing.* ANTROBUS: *Not before the children!* MRS. ANTROBUS: *Shouldn't we do something about it?—start off, move?* ANTROBUS: *Not before the children!!!* He gives HENRY *a sharp slap*)

HENRY Papa, you hit me!

ANTROBUS Well, remember it. That's to make you remember today. Today. The day the alphabet's finished; and the day that we *saw* the hundred—the hundred, the hundred, the hundred, the hundred, the hundred— there's no end to 'em.

I've had a day at the office!

Take a look at that wheel, Maggie—when I've got that to rights: you'll see a sight.

There's a reward there for all the walking you've done.

MRS. ANTROBUS How do you mean?

ANTROBUS (*on the hassock looking into the fire; with awe*) Maggie, we've reached the top of the wave. There's not much more to be done. We're there!

MRS. ANTROBUS (*cutting across his mood sharply*) And the ice?

ANTROBUS The ice!

HENRY (*playing with the wheel*) Papa, you could put a chair on this.

ANTROBUS (*broodingly*) Ye-e-s, any booby can fool with it now,—but I thought of it first.

MRS. ANTROBUS Children, go out in the kitchen. I want to talk to your father alone.

(*The* CHILDREN *go out.* ANTROBUS *has moved his chair up left. He takes the goldfish bowl on his lap; pulls the canary cage down to the level of his face. Both the* ANIMALS *put their paws up on the arms of his chair.* MRS. ANTROBUS *faces him across the room, like a judge*)

MRS. ANTROBUS Well?

ANTROBUS (*shortly*) It's cold.—How things been, eh? Keck, keck, keck.—And you, Millicent?

MRS. ANTROBUS I know it's cold.

ANTROBUS (*to the canary*) No spilling of sunflower seed, eh? No singing after lights-out, y'know what I mean?

MRS. ANTROBUS You can try and prevent us freezing to death, can't you? You can do something? We can start moving. Or can we go on the animals' backs?

ANTROBUS The best thing about animals is that they don't talk much.

MAMMOTH It's cold.

ANTROBUS Eh, eh, eh! Watch that!— —By midnight we'd turn to ice. The roads are full of people now who can scarcely lift a foot from the ground. The grass out in front is like iron, —which reminds me, I have another needle for you.—The people up north—where are they? Frozen . . . crushed. . . .

MRS. ANTROBUS Is that what's going to happen to us?—Will you answer me?

ANTROBUS I don't know. I don't know anything. Some say that the ice is going slower. Some say that it's stopped. The sun's growing cold. What can I do about that? Nothing we can do but burn everything in the house, and the fenceposts and the barn. Keep the fire going. When we have no more fire, we die.

MRS. ANTROBUS Well, why didn't you say so in the first place?

(*She is about to march off when she catches sight of two* REFUGEES, *men, who have appeared against the back wall of the stage and who are soon joined by others*)

REFUGEES Mr. Antrobus! Mr. Antrobus! Mr. An-nn-tro-bus!

MRS. ANTROBUS Who's that? Who's that calling you?

ANTROBUS (*clearing his throat guiltily*) Hm —let me see.

(*Two* REFUGEES *come up to the window*)

REFUGEE Could we warm our hands for a moment, Mr. Antrobus? It's very cold, Mr. Antrobus.

ANOTHER REFUGEE Mr. Antrobus, I wonder if you have a piece of bread or something that you could spare.

(*Silence. They wait humbly.* MRS. ANTROBUS *stands rooted to the spot. Suddenly a knock at the door, then another hand knocking in short rapid blows*)

MRS. ANTROBUS Who are these people? Why, they're all over the front yard. What have they come *here* for? (*enter* SABINA)

SABINA Mrs. Antrobus! There are some tramps knocking at the back door.

MRS. ANTROBUS George, tell these people to go away. Tell them to move right along. I'll go and send them away from the back door. Sabina, come with me. (*She goes out energetically*)

ANTROBUS Sabina! Stay here! I have something to say to you. (*He goes to the door and opens it a crack and talks through it*) Ladies and gentlemen! I'll have to ask you to wait a few minutes longer. It'll be all right . . . while you're waiting you might each one pull up a stake of the fence. We'll need them all for the fireplace. There'll be coffee and sandwiches in a moment.

(SABINA *looks out door over his shoulder and*

suddenly extends her arm pointing, with a scream)

SABINA Mr. Antrobus, what's that??—that big white thing? Mr. Antrobus, it's ICE. It's ICE!!

ANTROBUS Sabina, I want you to go in the kitchen and make a lot of coffee. Make a whole pail full.

SABINA Pail full!!

ANTROBUS (*with gesture*) And sandwiches . . . piles of them . . . like this.

SABINA Mr. An . . . !! (*Suddenly she drops the play, and says in her own person as* MISS SOMERSET, *with surprise*) Oh, *I* see what this part of the play means now! This means refugees. (*She starts to cross the proscenium*) Oh, I don't like it. I don't like it. (*She leans against the proscenium and bursts into tears*)

ANTROBUS Miss Somerset!

VOICE OF THE STAGE MANAGER Miss Somerset!

SABINA (*energetically, to the audience*) Ladies and gentlemen! Don't take this play serious. The world's not coming to an end. You know it's not. People exaggerate! Most people really have enough to eat and a roof over their heads. Nobody actually starves— you can always eat grass or something. That ice-business—why, it was a long, long time ago. Besides they were only savages. Savages don't love their families—not like we do.

ANTROBUS AND STAGE MANAGER Miss Somerset!!

(*There is renewed knocking at the door*)

SABINA All right. I'll say the lines, but I won't think about the play.

(*Enter* MRS. ANTROBUS)

SABINA (*parting thrust at the audience*) And I advise *you* not to think about the play, either.

(*Exit* SABINA)

MRS. ANTROBUS George, these tramps say that you asked them to come to the house. What does this mean?

(*Knocking at the door*)

ANTROBUS Just . . . uh . . . These are a few friends, Maggie, I met on the road. Real nice, real useful people. . . .

MRS. ANTROBUS (*back to the door*) Now, don't you ask them in! George Antrobus, not another soul comes in here over my dead body.

ANTROBUS Maggie, there's a doctor there. Never hurt to have a good doctor in the house. We've lost a peck of children, one way and another. You can never tell when a child's throat will get stopped up. What you and I have seen—!!! (*He puts his fingers on his throat and imitates diphtheria*)

MRS. ANTROBUS Well, just one person then, the Doctor. The others can go right along the road.

ANTROBUS Maggie, there's an old man, particular friend of mine—

MRS. ANTROBUS I won't listen to you—

ANTROBUS It was he that really started off the A.B.C.'s.

MRS. ANTROBUS I don't care if he perishes. We can do without reading or writing. We can't do without food.

ANTROBUS Then let the ice come!! Drink your coffee!! I don't want any coffee if I can't drink it with some good people.

MRS. ANTROBUS Stop shouting. Who else is there trying to push us off the cliff?

ANTROBUS Well, there's the man . . . who makes all the laws. Judge Moses!

MRS. ANTROBUS Judges can't help us now.

ANTROBUS And if the ice melts? . . . and if we pull through? Have you and I been able to bring up Henry? What have we done?

MRS. ANTROBUS Who are those old women?

ANTROBUS (*coughs*) Up in town there are nine sisters. There are three or four of them here. They're sort of music teachers . . . and one of them recites and one of them—

MRS. ANTROBUS That's the end. A singing troupe! Well, take your choice, live or die. Starve your own children before your face.

ANTROBUS (*gently*) These people don't take much. They're used to starving. They'll sleep on the floor. Besides, Maggie, listen: no, listen: Who've we got in the house, but Sabina? Sabina's always afraid the worst will happen. Whose spirits can she keep up? Maggie, these people never give up. They think they'll live and work forever.

MRS. ANTROBUS (*walks slowly to the middle of the room*) All right, let them in. You're master here. (*softly*)—But these animals must go. Enough's enough. They'll soon be big enough to push the walls down, anyway. Take them away.

ANTROBUS (*sadly*) All right. The dinosaur and mammoth—! Come on, baby, come on, Frederick. Come for a walk. That's a good little fellow.

DINOSAUR It's cold.

ANTROBUS Yes, nice cold fresh air. Bracing. (*He holds the door open and the* ANIMALS *go out. He beckons to his friends. The* REFUGEES *are typical elderly out-of-works from the streets of New York today.* JUDGE MOSES *wears a skull cap.* HOMER *is a blind beggar with a guitar.*

The seedy crowd shuffles in and waits humbly and expectantly. ANTROBUS *introduces them to his wife, who bows to each with a stately bend of her head*) Make yourself at home. Maggie, this is the doctor . . . m . . . Coffee'll be here in a minute . . . Professor, this is my wife . . . And: . . . Judge . . . Maggie, you know the Judge. (*an old blind man with a guitar*) Maggie, you know . . . you know Homer?—Come right in, Judge.—Miss Muse—are some of your sisters here? Come right in. . . . Miss E. Muse, Miss T. Muse, Miss M. Muse.

MRS. ANTROBUS Pleased to meet you. Just . . . make yourself comfortable. Supper'll be ready in a minute.

(*She goes out, abruptly*)

ANTROBUS Make yourself at home, friends. I'll be right back.

(*He goes out. The* REFUGEES *stare about them in awe. Presently several voices start whispering* "Homer! Homer!" *All take it up.* HOMER *strikes a chord or two on his guitar, then starts to speak*)

HOMER Μῆνιν ἄειδε, θεά, Πηληϊάδεω ᾿Αχιλῆος, οὐλομένην, ἣ μυρί᾿ ᾿Αχαιοῖς ἄλγε ἔθηκε, πολλὰς δ᾿ ἰφθίμους ψυχὰς———[1]

(HOMER'S *face shows he is lost in thought and memory and the words die away on his lips. The* REFUGEES *likewise nod in dreamy recollection. Soon the whisper* "Moses, Moses!" *goes around. An aged Jew parts his beard and recites dramatically*)

MOSES

בְּרֵאשִׁית בָּרָא אֱלֹהִים אֵת הַשָּׁמַיִם וְאֵת הָאָרֶץ:
וְהָאָרֶץ הָיְתָה תֹהוּ וָבֹהוּ וְחֹשֶׁךְ עַל-פְּנֵי תְהוֹם
וְרוּחַ אֱלֹהִים מְרַחֶפֶת עַל-פְּנֵי הַמָּיִם:[2]

(*The same dying away of the words takes place, and on the part of the* REFUGEES *the same retreat into recollection. Some of them murmur,* "Yes, yes." *The mood is broken by the abrupt entrance of* MR. *and* MRS. ANTROBUS *and* SABINA *bearing platters of sandwiches and a pail of coffee.* SABINA *stops and stares at the guests*)

MR. ANTROBUS Sabina! Pass the sandwiches.

SABINA I thought I was working in a re-

---

[1] The first two and one-half lines of Homer's *Iliad*.

[2] "In the beginning God created the heaven and the earth. And the earth was without form and void, and darkness was upon the face of the deep. And the Spirit of God moved upon the face of the waters." *Genesis*, I, 2.

spectable house that had respectable guests. I'm giving my notice, Mr. Antrobus: two weeks, that's the law.

MR. ANTROBUS   Sabina! Pass the sandwiches.

SABINA   Two weeks, that's the law.

MR. ANTROBUS   There's the law. That's Moses.

SABINA (*stares*)   The Ten Commandments —faugh!!—(*to audience*) That's the worst line I've ever had to say on any stage.

ANTROBUS   I think the best thing to do is just not to stand on ceremony, but pass the sandwiches around from left to right.—Judge, help yourself to one of these.

MRS. ANTROBUS   The roads are crowded, I hear?

THE GUESTS (*all talking at once*)   Oh, ma'am, you can't imagine. . . . You can hardly put one foot before you . . . people are trampling one another.

(*Suddenly silence*)

MRS. ANTROBUS   Well, you know what I think it is,—I think it's sun-spots!

THE GUESTS (*discreet hubbub*)   Oh, you're right, Mrs. Antrobus . . . that's what it is. . . . That's what I was saying the other day.

(*Sudden silence*)

ANTROBUS   Well, I don't believe the whole world's going to turn to ice. (*All eyes are fixed on him, waiting*) I can't believe it, Judge! Have we worked for nothing? Professor! Have we just failed in the whole thing?

MRS. ANTROBUS   It is certainly very strange —well fortunately on both sides of the family we come of very hearty stock.—Doctor, I want you to meet my children. They're eating their supper now. And of course I want them to meet you.

MISS M. MUSE   How many children have you, Mrs. Antrobus?

MRS. ANTROBUS   I have two,—a boy and a girl.

MOSES (*softly*)   I understood you had two sons, Mrs. Antrobus.

MRS. ANTROBUS (*in blind suffering; she walks toward the footlights. In a low voice*)   Abel, Abel, my son, my son, Abel, my son, Abel, Abel, my son.

(*The* REFUGEES *move with few steps toward her as though in comfort, murmuring words in Greek, Hebrew, German, et cetera.*

*A piercing shriek from the kitchen,—*SABINA'S *voice. All heads turn*)

ANTROBUS   What's that?

(SABINA *enters, bursting with indignation, pulling on her gloves*)

SABINA   Mr. Antrobus—that son of yours, that boy Henry Antrobus—I don't stay in this house another moment!—He's not fit to live among respectable folks and that's a fact.

MRS. ANTROBUS   Don't say another word, Sabina. I'll be right back. (*Without waiting for an answer she goes past her into the kitchen*)

SABINA   Mr. Antrobus, Henry has thrown a stone again and if he hasn't killed the boy that lives next door, I'm very much mistaken. He finished his supper and went out to play; and I heard such a fight; and then I saw it. I saw it with my own eyes. And it looked to me like stark murder.

(MRS. ANTROBUS *appears at the kitchen door, shielding* HENRY, *who follows her. When she steps aside, we see on* HENRY'S *forehead a large ochre and scarlet scar in the shape of a* C. MR. ANTROBUS *starts toward him. A pause*)

HENRY (*under his breath*)   He was going to take the wheel away from me. He started to throw a stone at me first.

MRS. ANTROBUS   George, it was just a boyish impulse. Remember how young he is. (*louder, in an urgent wail*) George, he's only four thousand years old.

SABINA   And everything was going along so nicely!

(*Silence.* ANTROBUS *goes back to the fireplace*)

ANTROBUS   Put out the fire! Put out all the fires. (*violently*) No wonder the sun grows cold. (*He starts stamping on the fireplace*)

MRS. ANTROBUS   Doctor! Judge! Help me!— George, have you lost your mind?

ANTROBUS   There is no mind. We'll not try to live. (*to the* GUESTS) Give it up. Give up trying. (MRS. ANTROBUS *seizes him*)

SABINA   Mr. Antrobus! I'm downright ashamed of you.

MRS. ANTROBUS   George, have some more coffee.—Gladys! Where's Gladys gone?

(GLADYS *steps in, frightened*)

GLADYS   Here I am, Mama.

MRS. ANTROBUS   Go upstairs and bring your father's slippers. How could you forget a thing like that, when you know how tired he is? (ANTROBUS *sits in his chair. He covers his face with his hands.* MRS. ANTROBUS *turns to the* REFUGEES) Can't some of you sing? It's your business in life to sing, isn't it? Sabina! (*Several of the women clear their throats tentatively, and with frightened faces gather around* HOMER'S *guitar. He establishes a few chords. Almost inaudibly they start singing, led by* SABINA: *"Jingle Bells."* MRS. ANTROBUS *to* AN-TROBUS *in a low voice, while taking off his shoes*) George, remember all the other times.

When the volcanoes came right up in the front yard.

And the time the grasshoppers ate every single leaf and blade of grass, and all the grain and spinach you'd grown with your own hands. And the summer there were earthquakes every night.

ANTROBUS   Henry! Henry! (*puts his hand on his forehead*) Myself. All of us, we're covered with blood.

MRS. ANTROBUS   Then remember all the times you were pleased with him and when you were proud of yourself!—Henry! Henry! Come here and recite to your father the multiplication table that you do so nicely.

(HENRY *kneels on one knee beside his father and starts whispering the multiplication table*)

HENRY   (*finally*)   Two times six is twelve; three times six is eighteen—I don't think I know the sixes.

(*Enter* GLADYS *with the slippers.* MRS. ANTROBUS *makes stern gestures to her: Go in there and do your best. The* GUESTS *are now singing* "*Tenting Tonight.*")

GLADYS   (*putting slippers on his feet*)   Papa . . . Papa . . . I was very good in school today. Miss Conover said right out in class that if all the girls had as good manners as Gladys Antrobus, that the world would be a very different place to live in.

MRS. ANTROBUS   You recited a piece at assembly, didn't you? Recite it to your father.

GLADYS   Papa, do you want to hear what I recited in class? (*fierce directorial glance from her* MOTHER) "The Star" by Henry Wadsworth Longfellow.

MRS. ANTROBUS   Wait!!! The fire's going out. There isn't enough wood! Henry, go upstairs and bring down the chairs and start breaking up the beds.

(*Exit* HENRY. *The singers return to* "*Jingle Bells,*" *still very softly*)

GLADYS   Look, Papa, here's my report card. Lookit. Conduct A! Look, Papa. Papa, do you want to hear "The Star," by Henry Wadsworth Longfellow? Papa, you're not mad at me, are you?—I know it'll get warmer. Soon it'll be just like spring, and we can go to a picnic at the Hibernian Picnic Grounds like you always like to do, don't you remember? Papa, just look at me once.

(*Enter* HENRY *with some chairs*)

ANTROBUS   You recited in assembly, did you? (*She nods eagerly*) You didn't forget it?

GLADYS   No!!! I was perfect.

(*Pause. Then* ANTROBUS *rises, goes to the front*

door *and opens it. The* REFUGEES *draw back timidly; the song stops; he peers out of the door, then closes it*)

ANTROBUS   (*with decision, suddenly*)   Build up the fire. It's cold. Build up the fire. We'll do what we can. Sabina, get some more wood. Come around the fire, everybody. At least the young ones may pull through. Henry, have you eaten something?

HENRY   Yes, Papa.

ANTROBUS   Gladys, have you had some supper?

GLADYS   I ate in the kitchen, Papa.

ANTROBUS   If you do come through this— what'll you be able to do? What do you know? Henry, did you take a good look at that wheel?

HENRY   Yes, Papa.

ANTROBUS   (*sitting down in his chair*)   Six times two are—

HENRY   —twelve; six times three are eighteen; six times four are—Papa, it's hot and cold. It makes my head all funny. It makes me sleepy.

ANTROBUS   (*gives him a cuff*)   Wake up. I don't care if your head is sleepy. Six times four are twenty-four. Six times five are—

HENRY   Thirty. Papa!

ANTROBUS   Maggie, put something into Gladys' head on the chance she can use it.

MRS. ANTROBUS   What do you mean, George?

ANTROBUS   Six times six are thirty-six. Teach her the beginning of the Bible.

GLADYS   But, Mama, it's so cold and close. (HENRY *has all but drowsed off. His* FATHER *slaps him sharply and the lesson goes on*)

MRS. ANTROBUS   "In the beginning God created the heavens and the earth; and the earth was waste and void; and the darkness was upon the face of the deep—"

(*The singing starts up again louder.* SABINA *has returned with wood*)

SABINA   (*after placing wood on the fireplace comes down to the footlights and addresses the audience*)   Will you please start handing up your chairs? We'll need everything for this fire. Save the human race.—Ushers, will you pass the chairs up here? Thank you.

HENRY   Six times nine are fifty-four; six times ten are sixty.

(*In the back of the auditorium the sound of chairs being ripped up can be heard.* USHERS *rush down the aisles with chairs and hand them over*)

GLADYS   "And God called the light Day and the darkness he called Night."

SABINA Pass up your chairs, everybody. Save the human race.

ACT TWO

(*Toward the end of the intermission, though with the houselights still up, lantern slide projections begin to appear on the curtain. Time-tables for trains leaving Pennsylvania Station for Atlantic City. Advertisements of Atlantic City hotels, drugstores, churches, rug merchants; fortune tellers, bingo parlors.*

When the houselights go down, the voice of an ANNOUNCER *is heard*)

ANNOUNCER The Management now brings you the News Events of the World. Atlantic City, New Jersey:

(*Projection of a chrome postcard of the waterfront, trimmed in mica with the legend: FUN AT THE BEACH*)

This great convention city is playing host this week to the anniversary convocation of that great fraternal order,—the Ancient and Honorable Order of Mammals, Subdivision Humans. This great fraternal, militant and burial society is celebrating on the Boardwalk, ladies and gentlemen, its six-hundred-thousandth Annual Convention. It has just elected its president for the ensuing term,—(*projection of* MR. *and* MRS. ANTROBUS *posed as they will be shown a few moments later*) Mr. George Antrobus of Excelsior, New Jersey. We show you President Antrobus and his gracious and charming wife, every inch a mammal. Mr. Antrobus has had a long and chequered career. Credit has been paid to him for many useful enterprises including the introduction of the lever, of the wheel, and the brewing of beer. Credit has been also extended to President Antrobus' gracious and charming wife for many practical suggestions, including the hem, the gore, and the gusset; and the novelty of the year,—frying in oil. Before we show you Mr. Antrobus accepting the nomination, we have an important announcement to make. As many of you know, this great celebration of the Order of the Mammals has received delegations from the other rival Orders,—or shall we say: esteemed concurrent Orders: the WINGS, the FINS, the SHELLS, and so on. These Orders are holding their conventions also, in various parts of the world, and have sent representatives to our own, two of a kind.

Later in the day we will show you President Antrobus broadcasting his words of greeting and congratulation to the collected assemblies of the whole natural world.

Ladies and Gentlemen! We give you President Antrobus!

(*The screen becomes a transparency.* MR. ANTROBUS *stands beside a pedestal;* MRS. ANTROBUS *is seated wearing a corsage of orchids.* ANTROBUS *wears an untidy Prince Albert; spats; from a red rosette in his buttonhole hangs a fine long purple ribbon of honor. He wears a gay lodge hat,—something between a fez and a legionnaire's cap*)

ANTROBUS Fellow-mammals, fellow-vertebrates, fellow-humans, I thank you. Little did my parents think,—when they told me to stand on my own two feet,—that I'd arrive at this place.

My friends, we have come a long way.

During this week of happy celebration it is perhaps not fitting that we dwell on some of the difficult times we have been through. The dinosaur is extinct—(*applause*)—the ice has retreated; and the common cold is being pursued by every means within our power. (MRS. ANTROBUS *sneezes, laughs prettily, and murmurs: "I beg your pardon"*) In our memorial service yesterday we did honor to all our friends and relatives who are no longer with us, by reason of cold, earthquakes, plagues and . . . and (*coughs*) differences of opinion.

As our Bishop so ably said . . . uh . . . so ably said. . . .

MRS. ANTROBUS (*closed lips*) Gone, but not forgotten.

ANTROBUS "They are gone, but not forgotten." I think I can say, I think I can prophesy with complete . . . uh . . . with complete . . .

MRS. ANTROBUS Confidence.

ANTROBUS Thank you, my dear—With complete lack of confidence, that a new day of security is about to dawn. The watchword of the closing year was: Work. I give you the watchword for the future: Enjoy Yourselves.

MRS. ANTROBUS George, sit down!

ANTROBUS Before I close, however, I wish to answer one of those unjust and malicious accusations that were brought against me during this last electoral campaign.

Ladies and gentlemen, the charge was made that at various points in my career I leaned toward joining some of the rival orders,—that's a lie.

As I told reporters of the *Atlantic City Herald*, I do not deny that a few months before my birth I hesitated between . . . uh . . .

between pinfeathers and gill-breathing,—and so did many of us here,—but for the last million years I have been viviparous, hairy and diaphragmatic.

(*Applause. Cries of "Good old Antrobus," "The Prince Chap!" "Georgie," etc.*)

ANNOUNCER (*offstage*) Thank you. Thank you very much, Mr. Antrobus. Now I know that our visitors will wish to hear a word from that gracious and charming mammal, Mrs. Antrobus, wife and mother,—Mrs. Antrobus!

MRS. ANTROBUS (*rises, lays her program on her chair, bows and says*) Dear friends, I don't really think I should say anything. After all, it was my husband who was elected and not I.

Perhaps, as president of the Women's Auxiliary Bed and Board Society,—I had some notes here, oh, yes, here they are:—I should give a short report from some of our committees that have been meeting in this beautiful city.

Perhaps it may interest you to know that it has at last been decided that the tomato is edible. Can you all hear me? The tomato *is* edible.

A delegate from across the sea reports that the thread woven by the silkworm gives a cloth . . . I have a sample of it here . . . can you see it? smooth, elastic. I should say that it's rather attractive,—though personally I prefer less shiny surfaces. Should the windows of a sleeping apartment be open or shut? I know all mothers will follow our debates on this matter with close interest. I am sorry to say that the most expert authorities have not yet decided. It does seem to me that the night air would be bound to be unhealthy for our children, but there are many distinguished authorities on both sides. Well, I could go on talking forever,—as Shakespeare says: a woman's work is seldom done; but I think I'd better join my husband in saying thank you, and sit down. Thank you. (*She sits down*)

ANNOUNCER   Oh, Mrs. Antrobus!

MRS. ANTROBUS   Yes?

ANNOUNCER   We understand that you are about to celebrate a wedding anniversary. I know our listeners would like to extend their felicitations and hear a few words from you on that subject.

MRS. ANTROBUS   I have been asked by this kind gentleman . . . yes, my friends, this Spring Mr. Antrobus and I will be celebrating our five-thousandth wedding anniversary.

I don't know if I speak for my husband, but I can say that, as for me, I regret every moment of it. (*laughter of confusion*)

I beg your pardon. What I *mean* to say is that I do not regret one moment of it. I hope none of you catch my cold. We have two children. We've always had two children, though it hasn't always been the same two. But as I say, we have two fine children, and we're very grateful for that. Yes, Mr. Antrobus and I have been married five-thousand years. Each wedding anniversary reminds me of the times when there were no weddings. We had to crusade for marriage. Perhaps there are some women within the sound of my voice who remember that crusade and those struggles; we fought for it, didn't we? We chained ourselves to lampposts and we made disturbances in the Senate,—anyway, at last we women got the ring.

A few men helped us, but I must say that most men blocked our way at every step: they said we were unfeminine.

I only bring up these unpleasant memories, because I see some signs of backsliding from that great victory.

Oh, my fellow mammals, keep hold of that.

My husband says that the watchword for the year is Enjoy Yourselves. I think that's very open to misunderstanding. My watchword for the year is: Save the family. It's held together for over five thousand years: Save it! Thank you.

ANNOUNCER   Thank you, Mrs. Antrobus. (*the transparency disappears*) We had hoped to show you the Beauty Contest that took place here today. President Antrobus, an experienced judge of pretty girls, gave the title of Miss Atlantic City 1942, to Miss Lily-Sabina Fairweather, charming hostess of our Boardwalk Bingo Parlor. Unfortunately, however, our time is up, and I must take you to some views of the Convention City and conveeners,—enjoying themselves.

(*A burst of music; the curtain rises. The Boardwalk. The audience is sitting in the ocean. A handrail of scarlet cord stretches across the front of the stage. A ramp—also with scarlet hand rail—descends to the right corner of the orchestra pit where a great scarlet beach umbrella or a cabana stands. Front and right stage left are benches facing the sea; attached to each bench is a streetlamp. The only scenery is two cardboard cut-outs six feet high, representing shops at the back of the stage. Reading from left to right they are:* SALT WATER TAFFY; FORTUNE TELLER; *then the blank space;* BINGO PARLOR; TURKISH BATH. *They have practical doors, that of the Fortune Teller's being hung with bright gypsy curtains. By the left pro-*

scenium and rising from the orchestra pit is the weather signal; it is like the mast of a ship with cross bars. From time to time black discs are hung on it to indicate the storm and hurricane warnings. Three roller chairs, pushed by melancholy NEGROES *file by empty. Throughout the act they traverse the stage in both directions. From time to time,* CONVEENERS, *dressed like* MR. ANTROBUS, *cross the stage. Some walk sedately by; others engage in inane horseplay. The old gypsy* FORTUNE TELLER *is seated at the door of her shop, smoking a corncob pipe.*

From the Bingo Parlor comes the voice of the CALLER)

BINGO CALLER   A—nine; A—nine. C—twenty-six; C—twenty-six. A—four, A—four. B—twelve.

CHORUS (*backstage*)   Bingo!!!

(*The front of the Bingo Parlor shudders, rises a few feet in the air and returns to the ground trembling*)

FORTUNE TELLER (*mechanically, to the unconscious back of a passerby, pointing with her pipe*)   Bright's disease! Your partner's deceiving you in that Kansas City deal. You'll have six grandchildren. Avoid high places. (*She rises and shouts after another*) Cirrhosis of the liver!

(SABINA *appears at the door of the Bingo Parlor. She hugs about her a blue raincoat that almost conceals her red bathing suit. She tries to catch the* FORTUNE TELLER'S *attention*)

SABINA   Ssssst! Esmeralda! Ssssst!

FORTUNE TELLER   Keck!

SABINA   Has President Antrobus come along yet?

FORTUNE TELLER   No, no, no. Get back there. Hide yourself.

SABINA   I'm afraid I'll miss him. Oh, Esmeralda, if I fail in this, I'll die; I know I'll die. President Antrobus!!! And I'll be his wife! If it's the last thing I'll do, I'll be Mrs. George Antrobus.—Esmeralda, tell me my future.

FORTUNE TELLER   Keck!

SABINA   All right, I'll tell *you* my future. (*laughing dreamily and tracing it out with one finger on the palm of her hand*) I've won the Beauty Contest in Atlantic City,—well. I'll win the Beauty Contest of the whole world. I'll take President Antrobus away from that wife of his. Then I'll take every man away from his wife. I'll turn the whole earth upside down.

FORTUNE TELLER   Keck!

SABINA   When all those husbands just think about me they'll get dizzy. They'll faint in the streets. They'll have to lean against lampposts. —Esmeralda, who was Helen of Troy?

FORTUNE TELLER (*furiously*)   Shut your foolish mouth. When Mr. Antrobus comes along you can see what you can do. Until then, go away.

(SABINA *laughs. As she returns to the door of her Bingo Parlor a group of* CONVEENERS *rush over and smother her with attentions: "Oh, Miss Lily, you know me. You've known me for years"*)

SABINA   Go away, boys, go away. I'm after bigger fry than you are.—Why, Mr. Simpson!! How *dare* you!! I expect that even you nobodies must have girls to amuse you; but where you find them and what you do with them, is of absolutely no interest to me.

(*Exit. The* CONVEENERS *squeal with pleasure and stumble in after her. The* FORTUNE TELLER *rises, puts her pipe down on the stool, unfurls her voluminous skirts, gives a sharp wrench to her bodice and strolls toward the audience, swinging her hips like a young woman*)

FORTUNE TELLER   I tell the future. Keck. Nothing easier. Everybody's future is in their face. Nothing easier.

But who can tell your past,—eh? Nobody! Your youth,—where did it go? It slipped away while you weren't looking. While you were asleep. While you were drunk. Puh! You're like our friends, Mr. and Mrs. Antrobus; you lie awake nights trying to know your past. What did it mean? What was it trying to say to you?

Think! Think! Split your heads. I can't tell the past and neither can you. If anybody tries to tell you the past, take my word for it, they're charlatans! Charlatans! But I can tell the future. (*She suddenly barks at a passing chair-pusher*) Apoplexy! (*She returns to the audience*) Nobody listens.—Keck! I see a face among you now—I won't embarrass him by pointing him out, but, listen, it may be you: Next year the watchsprings inside you will crumple up. Death by regret,—Type Y. It's in the corners of your mouth. You'll decide that you should have lived for pleasure, but that you missed it. Death by regret,—Type Y. . . . Avoid mirrors. You'll try to be angry,—but no!—no anger. (*far forward, confidentially*) And now what's the immediate future of our friends, the Antrobuses? Oh, you've seen it as well as I have, keck,—that dizziness of the head; that Great Man dizziness? The inventor of beer and gunpowder? The sudden fits of temper and then the long stretches of inertia? "I'm a sultan; let my slave-girls fan me?"

You know as well as I what's coming. Rain. Rain. Rain in floods. The deluge. But first you'll see shameful things—shameful things. Some of you will be saying: "Let him drown. He's not worth saving. Give the whole thing up." I can see it in your faces. But you're wrong. Keep your doubts and despairs to yourselves.

Again there'll be the narrow escape. The survival of a handful. From destruction,—total destruction. (*She points sweeping with her hand to the stage*) Even of the animals, a few will be saved: two of a kind, male and female, two of a kind.

(*The heads of* CONVEENERS *appear about the stage and in the orchestra pit, jeering at her*)

CONVEENERS   Charlatan! Madam Kill-joy! Mrs. Jeremiah! Charlatan!

FORTUNE TELLER   And *you!* Mark my words before it's too late. Where'll *you* be?

CONVEENERS   The croaking raven. Old dust and ashes. Rags, bottles, sacks.

FORTUNE TELLER   Yes, stick out your tongues. You can't stick your tongues out far enough to lick the death-sweat from your foreheads. It's too late to work now—bail out the flood with your soup spoons. You've had your chance and you've lost.

CONVEENERS   Enjoy yourselves!!!

(*They disappear. The* FORTUNE TELLER *looks off left and puts her finger on her lip*)

FORTUNE TELLER   They're coming—the Antrobuses. Keck. Your hope. Your despair. Your selves.

(*Enter from the left,* MR. *and* MRS. ANTROBUS *and* GLADYS)

MRS. ANTROBUS   Gladys Antrobus, stick your stummick in.

GLADYS   But it's easier this way.

MRS. ANTROBUS   Well, it's too bad the new president has such a clumsy daughter, that's all I can say. Try and be a lady.

FORTUNE TELLER   Aijah! That's been said a hundred billion times.

MRS. ANTROBUS   Goodness! Where's Henry? He was here just a minute ago. Henry!

(*Sudden violent stir. A roller-chair appears from the left. About it are dancing in great excitement* HENRY *and a* NEGRO CHAIR-PUSHER)

HENRY (*slingshot in hand*)   I'll put your eye out. I'll make you yell, like you never yelled before.

NEGRO (*at the same time*)   Now, I warns you. I warns you. If you make me mad, you'll get hurt.

ANTROBUS   Henry! What is this? Put down that slingshot.

MRS. ANTROBUS (*at the same time*)   Henry! Henry! Behave yourself.

FORTUNE TELLER   That's right, young man. There are too many people in the world as it is. Everybody's in the way, except one's self.

HENRY   All I wanted to do was—have some fun.

NEGRO   Nobody can't touch my chair, nobody, without I allow 'em to. You get clean away from me and you get away fast. (*He pushes his chair off, muttering*)

ANTROBUS   What were you doing, Henry?

HENRY   Everybody's always getting mad. Everybody's always trying to push you around. I'll make him sorry for this; I'll make him sorry.

ANTROBUS   Give me that slingshot.

HENRY   I won't. I'm sorry I came to this place. I wish I weren't here. I wish I weren't anywhere.

MRS. ANTROBUS   Now, Henry, don't get so excited about nothing. I declare I don't know what we're going to do with you. Put your slingshot in your pocket, and don't try to take hold of things that don't belong to you.

ANTROBUS   After this you can stay home. I wash my hands of you.

MRS. ANTROBUS   Come now, let's forget all about it. Everybody take a good breath of that sea air and calm down. (*A passing* CONVEENER *bows to* ANTROBUS *who nods to him*) Who was that you spoke to, George?

ANTROBUS   Nobody, Maggie. Just the candidate who ran against me in the election.

MRS. ANTROBUS   The man who ran against you in the election!! (*She turns and waves her umbrella after the disappearing* CONVEENER) My husband didn't speak to you and he never will speak to you.

ANTROBUS   Now, Maggie.

MRS. ANTROBUS   After those lies you told about him in your speeches! Lies, that's what they were.

GLADYS AND HENRY   Mama, everybody's looking at you. Everybody's laughing at you.

MRS. ANTROBUS   If you must know, my husband's a Saint, a downright Saint, and you're not fit to speak to him on the street.

ANTROBUS   Now, Maggie, now, Maggie, that's enough of that.

MRS. ANTROBUS   George Antrobus, you're a perfect worm. If you won't stand up for yourself, I will.

GLADYS   Mama, you just act awful in public.

MRS. ANTROBUS (*laughing*)   Well, I must say I enjoyed it. I feel better. Wish his wife had been there to hear it. Children, what do you want to do?

GLADYS   Papa, can we ride in one of those

chairs? Mama, I want to ride in one of those chairs.

MRS. ANTROBUS   No, sir. If you're tired you just sit where you are. We have no money to spend on foolishness.

ANTROBUS   I guess we have money enough for a thing like that. It's one of the things you do at Atlantic City.

MRS. ANTROBUS   Oh, we have? I tell you it's a miracle my children have shoes to stand up in. I didn't think I'd ever live to see them pushed around in chairs.

ANTROBUS   We're on a vacation, aren't we? We have a right to some treats, I guess. Maggie, some day you're going to drive me crazy.

MRS. ANTROBUS   All right, go. I'll just sit here and laugh at you. And you can give me my dollar right in my hand. Mark my words, a rainy day is coming. There's a rainy day ahead of us. I feel it in my bones. Go on, throw your money around. I can starve. I've starved before. I know how.

(A CONVEENER *puts his head through Turkish Bath window, and says with raised eyebrows*)

CONVEENER   Hello, George. How are ya? I see where you brought the *whole* family along.

MRS. ANTROBUS   And what do you mean by that?

(CONVEENER *withdraws head and closes window*)

ANTROBUS   Maggie, I tell you there's a limit to what I can stand. God's Heaven, haven't I worked *enough*? Don't I get *any* vacation? Can't I even give my children so much as a ride in a roller-chair?

MRS. ANTROBUS   (*putting out her hand for raindrops*) Anyway, it's going to rain very soon and you have your broadcast to make.

ANTROBUS   Now, Maggie, I warn you. A man can stand a family only just so long. I'm warning you.

(Enter SABINA *from the Bingo Parlor. She wears a flounced red silk bathing suit, 1905. Red stockings, shoes, parasol. She bows demurely to* ANTROBUS *and starts down the ramp.* ANTROBUS *and the* CHILDREN *stare at her.* ANTROBUS *bows gallantly*)

MRS. ANTROBUS   Why, George Antrobus, how can you say such a thing! You have the best family in the world.

ANTROBUS   Good morning, Miss Fair-weather.

(SABINA *finally disappears behind the beach umbrella or in a cabana in the orchestra pit*)

MRS. ANTROBUS   Who on earth was that you spoke to, George?

ANTROBUS   (*complacent; mock-modest*) Hm . . . m . . . just a . . . solambaka keray.[1]

MRS. ANTROBUS   What? I can't understand you.

GLADYS   Mama, wasn't she beautiful?

HENRY   Papa, introduce her to me.

MRS. ANTROBUS   Children, will you be quiet while I ask your father a simple question?— Who did you say it was, George?

ANTROBUS   Why-uh . . . a friend of mine. Very nice refined girl.

MRS. ANTROBUS   I'm waiting.

ANTROBUS   Maggie, that's the girl I gave the prize to in the beauty contest,—that's Miss Atlantic City 1964.[2]

MRS. ANTROBUS   Hm! She looked like Sabina to me.

HENRY   (*at the railing*) Mama, the life-guard knows her, too. Mama, he knows her well.

ANTROBUS   Henry, come here.—She's a very nice girl in every way and the sole support of her aged mother.

MRS. ANTROBUS   So was Sabina, so was Sabina; and it took a wall of ice to open your eyes about Sabina.—Henry, come over and sit down on this bench.

ANTROBUS   She's a very different matter from Sabina. Miss Fairweather is a college graduate, Phi Beta Kappa.

MRS. ANTROBUS   Henry, you sit here by mama. Gladys—

ANTROBUS   (*sitting*) Reduced circumstances have required her taking a position as hostess in a Bingo Parlor; but there isn't a girl with higher principles in the country.

MRS. ANTROBUS   Well, let's not talk about it. —Henry, I haven't seen a whale yet.

ANTROBUS   She speaks seven languages and has more culture in her little finger than you've acquired in a lifetime.

MRS. ANTROBUS   (*assumed amiability*) All right, all right, George. I'm glad to know there are such superior girls in the Bingo Parlors.— Henry, what's that? (*pointing at the storm signal, which has one black disk*)

HENRY   What is it, Papa?

ANTROBUS   What? Oh, that's the storm signal. One of those black disks means bad weather; two means storm; three means hurricane; and four means the end of the world.

(As they watch it a second black disk rolls into place)

---

[1] A portmanteau word, in imitation of those found in *Finnegans Wake*.

[2] This date is changed to the year of performance.

MRS. ANTROBUS Goodness! I'm going this very minute to buy you all some raincoats.

GLADYS (*putting her cheek against her father's shoulder*) Mama, don't go yet. I like sitting this way. And the ocean coming in and coming in. Papa, don't you like it?

MRS. ANTROBUS Well, there's only one thing I lack to make me a perfectly happy woman: I'd like to see a whale.

HENRY Mama, we saw two. Right out there. They're delegates to the convention. I'll find you one.

GLADYS Papa, ask me something. Ask me a question.

ANTROBUS Well . . . how big's the ocean?

GLADYS Papa, you're teasing me. It's—three-hundred and sixty million square-miles — and — it — covers — three-fourths — of — the — earth's — surface — and — its — deepest — place — is — five — and — a — half — miles — deep — and — its — average — depth —is twelve-thousand—feet. No, Papa, ask me something hard, real hard.

MRS. ANTROBUS (*rising*) Now I'm going off to buy those raincoats. I think that bad weather's going to get worse and worse. I hope it doesn't come before your broadcast. I should think we have about an hour or so.

HENRY I hope it comes and zzzzzz everything before it. I hope it—

MRS. ANTROBUS Henry!—George, I think . . . maybe, it's one of those storms that are just as bad on land as on the sea. When you're just as safe and safer in a good stout boat.

HENRY There's a boat out at the end of the pier.

MRS. ANTROBUS Well, keep your eye on it. George, you shut your eyes and get a good rest before the broadcast.

ANTROBUS Thundering Judas, do I have to be told when to open and shut my eyes? Go and buy your raincoats.

MRS. ANTROBUS Now, children, you have ten minutes to walk around. Ten minutes. And, Henry: control yourself. Gladys, stick by your brother and don't get lost. (*They run off*)

MRS. ANTROBUS Will you be all right, George?

(CONVEENERS *suddenly stick their heads out of the Bingo Parlor and Salt Water Taffy store, and voices rise from the orchestra pit*)

CONVEENERS George. Geo-r-r-rge! George! Leave the old hen-coup at home, George. Do-mes-ticated Georgie!

MRS. ANTROBUS (*shaking her umbrella*) Low common oafs! That's what they are. Guess a man has a right to bring his wife to a con-vention, if he wants to. (*She starts off*) What's the matter with a family, I'd like to know. What else have they got to offer?

(*Exit.* ANTROBUS *has closed his eyes. The* FORTUNE TELLER *comes out of her shop and goes over to the left proscenium. She leans against it watching* SABINA *quizzically*)

FORTUNE TELLER Heh! Here she comes!

SABINA (*loud whisper*) What's he doing?

FORTUNE TELLER Oh, he's ready for you. Bite your lips, dear, take a long breath and come on up.

SABINA I'm nervous. My whole future depends on this. I'm nervous.

FORTUNE TELLER Don't be a fool. What more could you want? He's forty-five. His head's a little dizzy. He's just been elected president. He's never known any other woman than his wife. Whenever he looks at her he realizes that she knows every foolish thing he's ever done.

SABINA (*still whispering*) I don't know why it is, but every time I start one of these I'm nervous.

(*The* FORTUNE TELLER *stands in the center of the stage watching the following*)

FORTUNE TELLER You make me tired.

SABINA First tell me my fortune. (*The* FORTUNE TELLER *laughs drily and makes the gesture of brushing away a nonsensical question.* SABINA *coughs and says*) Oh, Mr. Antrobus,—dare I speak to you for a moment?

ANTROBUS What?—Oh, certainly, certainly, Miss Fairweather.

SABINA Mr. Antrobus . . . I've been so unhappy. I've wanted . . . I've wanted to make sure that you don't think that I'm the kind of girl who goes out for beauty contests.

FORTUNE TELLER That's the way!

ANTROBUS Oh, I understand. I understand perfectly.

FORTUNE TELLER Give it a little more. Lean on it.

SABINA I knew you would. My mother said to me this morning: Lily, she said, that fine Mr. Antrobus gave you the prize because he saw at once that you weren't the kind of girl who'd go in for a thing like that. But, honestly, Mr. Antrobus, in this world, honestly, a good girl doesn't know where to turn.

FORTUNE TELLER Now you've gone too far.

ANTROBUS My dear Miss Fairweather!

SABINA You wouldn't know how hard it is. With that lovely wife and daughter you have. Oh, I think Mrs. Antrobus is the finest woman I ever saw. I wish I were like her.

ANTROBUS There, there. There's . . . uh

. . . room for all kinds of people in the world, Miss Fairweather.

SABINA How wonderful of you to say that. How generous!—Mr. Antrobus, have you a moment free? . . . I'm afraid I may be a little conspicuous here . . . could you come down, for just a moment, to my beach cabana . . . ?

ANTROBUS Why-uh . . . yes, certainly . . . for a moment . . . just for a moment.

SABINA There's a deck chair there. Because: you know you *do* look tired. Just this morning my mother said to me: Lily, she said, I hope Mr. Antrobus is getting a good rest. His fine strong face has deep, deep lines in it. Now isn't it true, Mr. Antrobus: you work too hard?

FORTUNE TELLER Bingo! (*She goes into her shop*)

SABINA Now you will just stretch out. No, I shan't say a word, not a word. I shall just sit there,—privileged. That's what I am.

ANTROBUS (*taking her hand*) Miss Fairweather . . . you'll . . . spoil me.

SABINA Just a moment. I have something I wish to say to the audience.—Ladies and gentlemen. I'm not going to play this particular scene tonight. It's just a short scene and we're going to skip it. But I'll tell you what takes place and then we can continue the play from there on. Now in this scene—

ANTROBUS (*between his teeth*) But, Miss Somerset!

SABINA I'm sorry. I'm sorry. But I have to skip it. In this scene, I talk to Mr. Antrobus, and at the end of it he decides to leave his wife, get a divorce at Reno and marry me. That's all.

ANTROBUS Fitz!—Fitz!

SABINA So that now I've told you we can jump to the end of it,—where you say—

(*Enter in fury* MR. FITZPATRICK, *the stage manager*)

MR. FITZPATRICK Miss Somerset, we insist on your playing this scene.

SABINA I'm sorry, Mr. Fitzpatrick, but I can't and I won't. I've told the audience all they need to know and now we can go on.

(*Other* ACTORS *begin to appear on the stage, listening*)

MR. FITZPATRICK And *why* can't you play it?

SABINA Because there are some lines in that scene that would hurt some people's feelings and I don't think the theatre is a place where people's feelings ought to be hurt.

MR. FITZPATRICK Miss Somerset, you can pack up your things and go home. I shall call the understudy and I shall report you to Equity.

SABINA I sent the understudy up to the corner for a cup of coffee and if Equity tries to penalize me I'll drag the case right up to the Supreme Court. Now listen, everybody, there's no need to get excited.

MR. FITZPATRICK *and* ANTROBUS Why can't you play it? . . . what's the matter with the scene?

SABINA Well, if you must know, I have a personal guest in the audience tonight. Her life hasn't been exactly a happy one. I wouldn't have my friend hear some of these lines for the whole world. I don't suppose it occurred to the author that some other women might have gone through the experience of losing their husbands like this. Wild horses wouldn't drag from me the details of my friend's life, but . . . well, they'd been married twenty years, and before he got rich, why, she'd done the washing and everything.

MR. FITZPATRICK Miss Somerset, your friend will forgive you. We must play this scene.

SABINA Nothing, nothing will make me say some of those lines . . . about "a man outgrows a wife every seven years" and . . . and that one about "the Mohammedans being the only people who looked the subject square in the face." Nothing.

MR. FITZPATRICK Miss Somerset! Go to your dressing room. I'll *read* your lines.

SABINA Now everybody's nerves are on edge.

MR. ANTROBUS Skip the scene.

(MR. FITZPATRICK *and the other* ACTORS *go off*)

SABINA Thank you. I knew you'd understand. We'll do just what I said. So Mr. Antrobus is going to divorce his wife and marry me. Mr. Antrobus, you say: "It won't be easy to lay all this before my wife."

(*The* ACTORS *withdraw*)

ANTROBUS (*walks about, his hand to his forehead muttering*) Wait a minute. I can't get back into it as easily as all that. "My wife is a very obstinate woman." Hm . . . then you say . . . hm . . . Miss Fairweather, I mean Lily, it won't be easy to lay all this before my wife. It'll hurt her feelings a little.

SABINA Listen, George: *other* people haven't got feelings. Not in the same way that we have,—we who are presidents like you and prize-winners like me. Listen, other people haven't got feelings; they just imagine they have. Within two weeks they go back to playing bridge and going to the movies.

Listen, dear: everybody in the world except a few people like you and me are just people of straw. Most people have no insides at all. Now that you're president you'll see that. Listen, darling, there's a kind of secret society at the top of the world,—like you and me,—that know this. The world was made for us. What's life anyway? Except for two things, pleasure and power, what is life? Boredom! Foolishness. You know it is. Except for those two things, life's nau-se-at-ing. So,—come here! (*She moves close. They kiss*) So.

Now when your wife comes, it's really very simple; just tell her.

ANTROBUS   Lily, Lily: you're a wonderful woman.

SABINA   Of course I am.

(*They enter the cabana and it hides them from view. Distant roll of thunder. A third black disk appears on the weather signal. Distant thunder is heard.* MRS. ANTROBUS *appears carrying parcels. She looks about, seats herself on the bench left, and fans herself with her handkerchief. Enter* GLADYS *right, followed by two* CONVEENERS. *She is wearing red stockings*)

MRS. ANTROBUS   Gladys!

GLADYS   Mama, here I am.

MRS. ANTROBUS   Gladys Antrobus!!! Where did you get those dreadful things?

GLADYS   Wha-a-t? Papa liked the color.

MRS. ANTROBUS   You go back to the hotel this minute!

GLADYS   I won't. I won't. Papa liked the color.

MRS. ANTROBUS   All right. All right. You stay here. I've a good mind to let your father see you that way. You stay right here.

GLADYS   I . . . I don't want to stay if . . . if you don't think he'd like it.

MRS. ANTROBUS   Oh . . . it's all one to me. I don't care what happens. I don't care if the biggest storm in the whole world comes. Let it come. (*She folds her hands*) Where's your brother?

GLADYS   (*in a small voice*)   He'll be here.

MRS. ANTROBUS   Will he? Well, let him get into trouble. I don't care. I don't know where your father is, I'm sure.

(*Laughter from the cabana*)

GLADYS   (*leaning over the rail*)   I think he's . . . Mama, he's talking to the lady in the red dress.

MRS. ANTROBUS   Is that so? (*pause*) We'll wait till he's through. Sit down here beside me and stop fidgeting . . . what are you crying about?

(*Distant thunder. She covers* GLADYS' *stockings with a raincoat*)

GLADYS   You don't like my stockings.

(*Two* CONVEENERS *rush in with a microphone on a standard and various paraphernalia. The* FORTUNE TELLER *appears at the door of her shop. Other characters gradually gather*)

BROADCAST OFFICIAL   Mrs. Antrobus! Thank God we've found you at last. Where's Mr. Antrobus? We've been hunting everywhere for him. It's about time for the broadcast to the conventions of the world.

MRS. ANTROBUS   (*calm*)   I expect he'll be here in a minute.

BROADCAST OFFICIAL   Mrs. Antrobus, if he doesn't show up in time, I hope you will consent to broadcast in his place. It's the most important broadcast of the year.

(SABINA *enters from cabana followed by* ANTROBUS)

MRS. ANTROBUS   No, I shan't. I haven't one single thing to say.

BROADCAST OFFICIAL   Then won't you help us find him, Mrs. Antrobus? A storm's coming up. A hurricane. A deluge!

SECOND CONVEENER   (*who has sighted* ANTROBUS *over the rail*)   Joe! Joe! Here he is.

BROADCAST OFFICIAL   In the name of God, Mr. Antrobus, you're on the air in five minutes. Will you kindly please come and test the instrument? That's all we ask. If you just please begin the alphabet slowly.

(ANTROBUS, *with set face, comes ponderously up the ramp. He stops at the point where his waist is level with the stage and speaks authoritatively to the* OFFICIALS)

ANTROBUS   I'll be ready when the time comes. Until then, move away. Go away. I have something I wish to say to my wife.

BROADCAST OFFICIAL   (*whimpering*)   Mr. Antrobus! This is the most important broadcast of the year.

(*The* OFFICIALS *withdraw to the edge of the stage.* SABINA *glides up the ramp behind* ANTROBUS)

SABINA   (*whispering*)   Don't let her argue. Remember arguments have nothing to do with it.

ANTROBUS   Maggie, I'm moving out of the hotel. In fact, I'm moving out of everything. For good. I'm going to marry Miss Fairweather. I shall provide generously for you and the children. In a few years you'll be able to see that it's all for the best. That's all I have to say.

BROADCAST OFFICIAL   Mr. Antrobus! I hope you'll be ready. This is the most important broadcast of the year.

BINGO ANNOUNCER   A—nine; A—nine. D—forty-two; D—forty-two. C—thirty; C—thirty.

B—seventeen; B—seventeen. C—forty; C—forty.

GLADYS   What did Papa say, Mama? I didn't hear what Papa said.

CHORUS   Bingo!!

BROADCAST OFFICIAL   Mr. Antrobus. All we want to do is test your voice with the alphabet.

ANTROBUS   Go away. Clear out.

MRS. ANTROBUS   (*composedly with lowered eyes*)   George, I can't talk to you until you wipe those silly red marks off your face.

ANTROBUS   I think there's nothing to talk about. I've said what I have to say.

SABINA   Splendid!!

ANTROBUS   You're a fine woman, Maggie, but . . . but a man has his own life to lead in the world.

MRS. ANTROBUS   Well, after living with you for five thousand years I guess I have a right to a word or two, haven't I?

ANTROBUS   (*to* SABINA)   What can I answer to that?

SABINA   Tell her that conversation would only hurt her feelings. It's-kinder-in-the-long-run-to-do-it-short-and-quick.

ANTROBUS   I want to spare your feelings in every way I can, Maggie.

BROADCAST OFFICIAL   Mr. Antrobus, the hurricane signal's gone up. We could begin right now.

MRS. ANTROBUS   (*calmly, almost dreamily*)   I didn't marry you because you were perfect. I didn't even marry you because I loved you. I married you because you gave me a promise. (*She takes off her ring and looks at it*)   That promise made up for your faults. And the promise I gave you made up for mine. Two imperfect people got married and it was the promise that made the marriage.

ANTROBUS   Maggie, . . . I was only nineteen.

MRS. ANTROBUS   (*she puts her ring back on her finger*)   And when our children were growing up, it wasn't a house that protected them; and it wasn't our love that protected them—it was that promise.

And when that promise is broken—this can happen!

(*With a sweep of the hand she removes the raincoat from* GLADYS' *stockings*)

ANTROBUS   (*stretches out his arm, apoplectic*)   Gladys!! Have you gone crazy? Has everyone gone crazy? (*turning on* SABINA)   You did this. You gave them to her.

SABINA   I never said a word to her.

ANTROBUS   (*to* GLADYS)   You go back to the hotel and take those horrible things off.

GLADYS   (*pert*)   Before I go, I've got something to tell you,—it's about Henry.

MRS. ANTROBUS   (*claps her hands peremptorily*)   Stop your noise,—I'm taking her back to the hotel, George. Before I go I have a letter. . . . I have a message to throw into the ocean. (*fumbling in her handbag*)   Where is the plagued thing? Here it is. (*She flings something—invisible to us—far over the heads of the audience to the back of the auditorium*)   It's a bottle. And in the bottle's a letter. And in the letter is written all the things that a woman knows. It's never been told to any man and it's never been told to any woman, and if it finds its destination, a new time will come. We're not what books and plays say we are. We're not what advertisements say we are. We're not in the movies and we're not on the radio. We're not what you're all told and what you think we are: We're ourselves. And if any man can find one of us he'll learn why the whole universe was set in motion. And if any man harm any one of us, his soul—the only soul he's got—had better be at the bottom of that ocean,—and that's the only way to put it. Gladys, come here. We're going back to the hotel.

(*She drags* GLADYS *firmly off by the hand, but* GLADYS *breaks away and comes down to speak to her father*)

SABINA   Such goings-on. Don't give it a minute's thought.

GLADYS   Anyway, I think you ought to know that Henry hit a man with a stone. He hit one of those colored men that push the chairs and the man's very sick. Henry ran away and hid and some policemen are looking for him very hard. And I don't care a bit if you don't want to have anything to do with Mama and me, because I'll never like you again and I hope nobody ever likes you again,—so there!

(*She runs off.* ANTROBUS *starts after her*)

ANTROBUS   I . . . I have to go and see what I can do about this.

SABINA   You stay right here. Don't you go now while you're excited. Gracious sakes, all these things will be forgotten in a hundred years. Come, now, you're on the air. Just say anything,—it doesn't matter what. Just a lot of birds and fishes and things.

BROADCAST OFFICIAL   Thank you, Miss Fairweather. Thank you very much. Ready, Mr. Antrobus.

ANTROBUS   (*touching the microphone*)   What is it, what is it? Who am I talking to?

BROADCAST OFFICIAL   Why, Mr. Antrobus! To our order and to all the other orders.

ANTROBUS (*raising his head*) What are all those birds doing?

BROADCAST OFFICIAL Those are just a few of the birds. Those are the delegates to our convention,—two of a kind.

ANTROBUS (*pointing into the audience*) Look at the water. Look at them all. Those fishes jumping. The children should see this!—There's Maggie's whales!! Here are your whales, Maggie!!

BROADCAST OFFICIAL I hope you're ready, Mr. Antrobus.

ANTROBUS And look on the beach! You didn't tell me these would be here!

SABINA Yes, George. Those are the animals.

BROADCAST OFFICIAL (*busy with the apparatus*) Yes, Mr. Antrobus, those are the vertebrates. We hope the lion will have a word to say when you're through. Step right up, Mr. Antrobus, we're ready. We'll just have time before the storm. (*Pause. In a hoarse whisper*) They're wait-ing.

(*It has grown dark. Soon after he speaks a high whistling noise begins. Strange veering lights start whirling about the stage. The other characters disappear from the stage*)

ANTROBUS Friends. Cousins. Four score and ten billion years ago our forefather brought forth upon this planet the spark of life,—

(*He is drowned out by thunder. When the thunder stops the* FORTUNE TELLER *is seen standing beside him*)

FORTUNE TELLER Antrobus, there's not a minute to be lost. Don't you see the four disks on the weather signal? Take your family into that boat at the end of the pier.

ANTROBUS My family? I have no family. Maggie! Maggie! They won't come.

FORTUNE TELLER They'll come.—Antrobus! Take these animals into that boat with you. All of them,—two of each kind.

SABINA George, what's the matter with you? This is just a storm like any other storm.

ANTROBUS Maggie!

SABINA Stay with me, we'll go . . . (*losing conviction*) This is just another thunderstorm, —isn't it? Isn't it?

ANTROBUS Maggie!!!

(MRS. ANTROBUS *appears beside him with* GLADYS)

MRS. ANTROBUS (*matter-of-fact*) Here I am and here's Gladys.

ANTROBUS Where've you been? Where have you been? Quick, we're going into that boat out there.

MRS. ANTROBUS I know we are. But I haven't found Henry.

(*She wanders off into the darkness calling* "Henry!")

SABINA (*low urgent babbling, only occasionally raising her voice*) I don't believe it. I don't believe it's anything at all. I've seen hundreds of storms like this.

FORTUNE TELLER There's no time to lose. Go. Push the animals along before you. Start a new world. Begin again.

SABINA Esmeralda! George! Tell me,—is it really serious?

ANTROBUS (*suddenly very busy*) Elephants first. Gently, gently.—Look where you're going.

GLADYS (*leaning over the ramp and striking an animal on the back*) Stop it or you'll be left behind!

ANTROBUS Is the Kangaroo there? *There* you are! Take those turtles in your pouch, will you? (*to some other animals, pointing to his shoulder*) Here! You jump up here. You'll be trampled on.

GLADYS (*to her father, pointing below*) Papa, look,—the snakes!

MRS. ANTROBUS I can't find Henry. Hen-ry!

ANTROBUS Go along. Go along. Climb on their backs—Wolves! Jackals,—whatever you are,—tend to your own business!

GLADYS (*pointing, tenderly*) Papa,—look.

SABINA Mr. Antrobus—take me with you. Don't leave me here. I'll work. I'll help. I'll do anything.

(THREE CONVEENERS *cross the stage, marching with a banner*)

CONVEENERS George! What are you scared of?—George! Fellas, it looks like rain.—"Maggie, where's my umbrella?"—George, setting up for Barnum and Bailey.

ANTROBUS (*again catching his wife's hand*) Come on now, Maggie,—the pier's going to break any minute.

MRS. ANTROBUS I'm not going a step without Henry. Henry!

GLADYS (*on the ramp*) Mama! Papa! Hurry. The pier's cracking, Mama. It's going to break.

MRS. ANTROBUS Henry! Cain! CAIN!

(HENRY *dashes onto the stage and joins his mother*)

HENRY Here I am, Mama.

MRS. ANTROBUS Thank God!—now come quick.

HENRY I didn't think you wanted me.

MRS. ANTROBUS Quick! (*She pushes him down before her into the aisle*)

SABINA (*all the* ANTROBUSES *are now in the*

theatre aisle. SABINA *stands at the top of the ramp*) Mrs. Antrobus, take me. Don't you remember me? I'll work. I'll help. Don't leave me here!

MRS. ANTROBUS (*impatiently, but as though it were of no importance*) Yes, yes. There's a lot of work to be done. Only hurry.

FORTUNE TELLER (*now dominating the stage. To* SABINA *with a grim smile*) Yes, go—back to the kitchen with you.

SABINA (*half-down the ramp. To* FORTUNE TELLER) I don't know why my life's always being interrupted—just when everything's going fine!! (*She dashes up the aisle*)

(*Now the* CONVEENERS *emerge doing a serpentine dance on the stage. They jeer at the* FORTUNE TELLER)

CONVEENERS Get a canoe—there's not a minute to be lost! Tell me my future, Mrs. Croaker.

FORTUNE TELLER Paddle in the water, boys —enjoy yourselves.

VOICE FROM THE BINGO PARLOR A—nine; A—nine. C—twenty-four. C—twenty-four.

CONVEENERS Rags, bottles, and sacks.

FORTUNE TELLER Go back and climb on your roofs. Put rags in the cracks under your doors.—Nothing will keep out the flood. You've had your chance. You've had your day. You've failed. You've lost.

VOICE FROM THE BINGO PARLOR B—fifteen. B—fifteen.

FORTUNE TELLER (*shading her eyes and looking out to sea*) They're safe. George Antrobus! Think it over! A new world to make.—Think it over!

ACT THREE

(*Just before the curtain rises, two sounds are heard from the stage: a cracked bugle call.*

The curtain rises on almost total darkness. Almost all the flats composing the walls of MR. ANTROBUS' *house, as of Act One, are up, but they lean helter-skelter against one another, leaving irregular gaps. Among the flats missing are two in the back wall, leaving the frames of the window and door crazily out of line. Offstage, back right, some red Roman fire is burning. The bugle call is repeated. Enter* SABINA *through the tilted door. She is dressed as a Napoleonic camp follower, "la fille du regiment," in begrimed reds and blues*)

SABINA Mrs. Antrobus! Gladys! Where are you? The war's over. The war's over. You can come out. The peace treaty's been signed. Where are they?—Hmpf! Are they dead, too? Mrs. Annnntrobus! Glaaaadus! Mr. Antrobus'll be here this afternoon. I just saw him downtown. Huuuurry and put things in order. He says that now that the war's over we'll all have to settle down and be perfect.

(*Enter* MR. FITZPATRICK, *the stage manager, followed by the whole company, who stand waiting at the edges of the stage.* MR. FITZPATRICK *tries to interrupt* SABINA)

MR. FITZPATRICK Miss Somerset, we have to stop a moment.

SABINA They may be hiding out in the back—

MR. FITZPATRICK Miss Somerset! We have to stop a moment.

SABINA What's the matter?

MR. FITZPATRICK There's an explanation we have to make to the audience—Lights, please. (*to the actor who plays* MR. ANTROBUS) Will you explain the matter to the audience?

(*The lights go up. We now see that a balcony or elevated runway has been erected at the back of the stage, back of the wall of the Antrobus house. From its extreme right and left ends ladder-like steps descend to the floor of the stage*)

ANTROBUS Ladies and gentlemen, an unfortunate accident has taken place back stage. Perhaps I should say *another* unfortunate accident.

SABINA I'm sorry. I'm sorry.

ANTROBUS The management feels, in fact, we all feel that you are due an apology. And now we have to ask your indulgence for the most serious mishap of all. Seven of our actors have . . . have been taken ill. Apparently, it was something they ate. I'm not exactly clear what happened. (*All the actors start to talk at once.* ANTROBUS *raises his hand*) Now, now— not all at once. Fitz, do you know what it was?

MR. FITZPATRICK Why, it's perfectly clear. These seven actors had dinner together, and they ate something that disagreed with them.

SABINA Disagreed with them!!! They have ptomaine poisoning. They're in Bellevue Hospital this very minute in agony. They're having their stomachs pumped out this very minute, in perfect agony.

ANTROBUS Fortunately, we've just heard they'll all recover.

SABINA It'll be a miracle if they do, a downright miracle. It was the lemon meringue pie.

ACTORS It was the fish . . . it was the canned tomatoes . . . it was the fish.

SABINA It was the lemon meringue pie. I saw it with my own eyes; it had blue mould all over the bottom of it.

ANTROBUS Whatever it was, they're in no condition to take part in this performance. Naturally, we haven't enough understudies to fill all those roles; but we do have a number of splendid volunteers who have kindly consented to help us out. These friends have watched our rehearsals, and they assure me that they they know the lines and the business very well. Let me introduce them to you—my dresser, Mr. Tremayne,—himself a distinguished Shakespearean actor for many years; our wardrobe mistress, Hester; Miss Somerset's maid, Ivy; and Fred Bailey, captain of the ushers in this theatre. (*These persons bow modestly.* IVY *and* HESTER *are colored girls*) Now this scene takes place near the end of the act. And I'm sorry to say we'll need a short rehearsal, just a short run-through. And as some of it takes place in the auditorium, we'll have to keep the curtain up. Those of you who wish can go out in the lobby and smoke some more. The rest of you can listen to us, or . . . or just talk quietly among yourselves, as you choose. Thank you. Now will you take it over, Mr. Fitzpatrick?

MR. FITZPATRICK Thank you.—Now for those of you who are listening perhaps I should explain that at the end of this act, the men have come back from the War and the family's settled down in the house. And the author wants to show the hours of the night passing by over their heads, and the planets crossing the sky . . . uh . . . over their heads. And he he says—this is hard to explain—that each of the hours of the night is a philosopher, or a great thinker. Eleven o'clock, for instance, is Aristotle. And nine o'clock is Spinoza. Like that. I don't suppose it means anything. It's just a kind of poetic effect.

SABINA Not mean anything! Why, it certainly does. Twelve o'clock goes by saying those wonderful things. I think it means that when people are asleep they have all those lovely thoughts, much better than when they're awake.

IVY Excuse me, I think it means,—excuse me, Mr. Fitzpatrick—

SABINA What were you going to say, Ivy?

IVY Mr. Fitzpatrick, you let my father come to a rehearsal; and my father's a Baptist minister; and he said that the author meant that— just like the hours and stars go by over our heads at night, in the same way the ideas and

thoughts of the great men are in the air around us all the time and they're working on us, even when we don't know it.

MR. FITZPATRICK Well, well, maybe that's it. Thank you, Ivy. Anyway,—the hours of the night are philosophers. My friends, are you ready? Ivy, can you be eleven o'clock? "This good estate of the mind possessing its object in energy we call divine." Aristotle.

IVY Yes, sir. I know that and I know twelve o'clock and I know nine o'clock.

MR. FITZPATRICK Twelve o'clock? Mr. Tremayne, the Bible.

TREMAYNE Yes.

MR. FITZPATRICK Ten o'clock? Hester,— Plato? (*She nods eagerly*) Nine o'clock, Spinoza,—Fred?

BAILEY Yes, *sir*.

(FRED BAILEY *picks up a great gilded cardboard numeral IX and starts up the steps to the platform.* MR. FITZPATRICK *strikes his forehead*)

MR. FITZPATRICK The planets!! We forgot all about the planets.

SABINA O my God! The planets! Are they sick too?

(ACTORS *nod*)

MR. FITZPATRICK Ladies and gentlemen, the planets are singers. Of course, we can't replace them, so you'll have to imagine them singing in this scene. Saturn sings from the orchestra pit down here. The Moon is way up there. And Mars with a red lantern in his hand, stands in the aisle over there—Tz-tz-tz. It's too bad; it all makes a very fine effect. However! Ready— nine o'clock: Spinoza.

BAILEY (*walking slowly across the balcony, left to right*) "After experience had taught me that the common occurrences of daily life are vain and futile—"

FITZPATRICK Louder, Fred. "And I saw that all the objects of my desire and fear—"

BAILEY "And I saw that all the objects of my desire and fear were in themselves nothing good nor bad save insofar as· the mind was affected by them—"

FITZPATRICK Do you know the rest? All right. Ten o'clock. Hester. Plato.

HESTER "Then tell me, O Critias, how will a man choose the ruler that shall rule over him? Will he not—"

FITZPATRICK Thank you. Skip to the end, Hester.

HESTER ". . . can be multiplied a thousand fold in its effects among the citizens."

FITZPATRICK Thank you.—Aristotle, Ivy?

IVY "This good estate of the mind possessing its object in energy we call divine. This we mortals have occasionally and it is this energy which is pleasant and best. But God has it always. It is wonderful in us; but in Him how much more wonderful."

FITZPATRICK Midnight. Midnight, Mr. Tremayne. That's right,—you've done it before.— All right, everybody. You know what you have to do.—Lower the curtain. House lights up. Act Three of *The Skin of Our Teeth*. (*as the curtain descends he is heard saying*) You volunteers, just wear what you have on. Don't try to put on the costumes today.

(*House lights go down. The Act begins again. The Bugle call. Curtain rises. Enter* SABINA)

SABINA Mrs. Antrobus! Gladys! Where are you?

The war's over.—You've heard all this— (*She gabbles the main points*) Where—are— they? Are—they—dead, too, et cetera. I—just — saw — Mr. — Antrobus — downtown, et cetera. (*slowing up*) He says that now the war's over we'll all have to settle down and be perfect. They may be hiding out in the back somewhere. Mrs. An-tro-bus.

(*She wanders off. It has grown lighter. A trapdoor is cautiously raised and* MRS. ANTROBUS *emerges waist-high and listens. She is disheveled and worn; she wears a tattered dress and a shawl half covers her head. She talks down through the trapdoor*)

MRS. ANTROBUS It's getting light. There's something burning over there—Newark, or Jersey City. What? Yes, I could swear I heard someone moving about up here. But I can't see anybody. I say: I can't see anybody.

(*She starts to move about the stage.* GLADYS' *head appears at the trapdoor. She is holding a* BABY)

GLADYS Oh, Mama. Be careful.

MRS. ANTROBUS Now, Gladys, you stay out of sight.

GLADYS Well, let me stay here just a minute. I want the baby to get some of this fresh air.

MRS. ANTROBUS All right, but keep your eyes open. I'll see what I can find. I'll have a good hot plate of soup for you before you can say Jack Robinson. Gladys Antrobus! Do you know what I think I see? There's old Mr. Hawkins sweeping the sidewalk in front of his A. and P. store. Sweeping it with a broom. Why, he must have gone crazy, like the others! I see some other people moving about, too.

GLADYS Mama, come back, come back.

MRS. ANTROBUS (*returns to the trapdoor and listens*) Gladys, there's something in the air. Everybody's movement's sort of different.

I see some women walking right out in the middle of the street.

SABINA'S VOICE Mrs. An-tro-bus!

MRS. ANTROBUS AND GLADYS What's that?!!

SABINA'S VOICE. Glaaaadys! Mrs. An-tro-bus! (*enter* SABINA)

MRS. ANTROBUS Gladys, that's Sabina's voice as sure as I live—Sabina! Sabina!—Are you *alive*?!!

SABINA Of course, I'm alive. How've you girls been?—*Don't* try and kiss me. I never want to kiss another human being as long as I live. Sh-sh, there's nothing to get emotional about. Pull yourself together, the war's over. Take a deep breath,—the war's over.

MRS. ANTROBUS The war's over!! I don't believe you. I don't believe you. I can't believe you.

GLADYS Mama!

SABINA Who's that?

MRS. ANTROBUS That's Gladys and her baby. I don't believe you. Gladys, Sabina says the war's over. Oh, Sabina.

SABINA (*leaning over the* BABY) Goodness! Are there any babies left in the world? Can it *see*? And can it cry and everything?

GLADYS Yes, he can. He notices everything very well.

SABINA Where on earth did you get it? Oh, I won't ask.—Lord, I've lived all these seven years around camp and I've forgotten how to behave.—Now we've got to think about the men coming home.—Mrs. Antrobus, go and wash your face, I'm ashamed of you. Put your best clothes on. Mr. Antrobus'll be here this afternoon. I just saw him downtown.

MRS. ANTROBUS AND GLADYS He's alive!! He'll be here!! Sabina, you're not joking?

MRS. ANTROBUS And Henry?

SABINA (*dryly*) Yes, Henry's alive, too; that's what they say. Now don't stop to talk. Get yourselves fixed up. Gladys, you look terrible. Have you any decent clothes?

(SABINA *has pushed them toward the trapdoor*)

MRS. ANTROBUS (*half down*) Yes, I've something to wear just for this very day. But, Sabina,—who won the war?

SABINA Don't stop now,—just wash your face. (*A whistle sounds in the distance*) Oh, my God, what's that silly little noise?

MRS. ANTROBUS Why, it sounds like . . . it sounds like what used to be the noon whistle at the shoe-polish factory.

SABINA That's what it is. Seems to me like peacetime's coming along pretty fast— shoe polish!

GLADYS (*half down*) Sabina, how soon

after peacetime begins does the milkman start coming to the door?

SABINA   As soon as he catches a cow. Give him time to catch a cow, dear. (*exit* GLADYS.

SABINA *walks about a moment, thinking*) Shoe polish! My, I'd forgotten what peacetime was like. (*She shakes her head, then sits down by the trapdoor and starts talking down the hole*) Mrs. Antrobus, guess what I saw Mr. Antrobus doing this morning at dawn. He was tacking up a piece of paper on the door of the Town Hall. You'll die when you hear: it was a recipe for grass soup, for a grass soup that doesn't give you the diarrhea. Mr. Antrobus is still thinking up new things.—He told me to give you his love. He's got all sorts of ideas for peacetime, he says. No more laziness and idiocy, he says. And oh, yes! Where are his books? What? Well, pass them up. The first thing he wants to see are his books. He says if you've burnt those books, or if the rats have eaten them, he says it isn't worthwhile starting over again. Everybody's going to be beautiful, he says, and diligent, and very intelligent. (*A hand reaches up with two volumes*) What language is that? Pu-u-gh,—mould! And he's got such plans for you, Mrs. Antrobus. You're going to study history and algebra—and so are Gladys and I—and philosophy. You should hear him talk. (*taking two more volumes*) Well, these are in English, anyway.—To hear him talk, seems like he expects you to be a combination, Mrs. Antrobus, of a saint and a college professor, and a dancehall hostess, if you know what I mean. (*two more volumes*) Ugh. German! (*She is lying on the floor; one elbow bent, her cheek on her hand, meditatively*) Yes, peace will be here before we know it. In a week or two we'll be asking the Perkinses in for a quiet evening of bridge. We'll turn on the radio and hear how to be big successes with a new toothpaste. We'll trot down to the movies and see how girls with wax faces live—all *that* will begin again. Oh, Mrs. Antrobus, God forgive me but I enjoyed the war. Everybody's at their best in wartime. I'm sorry it's over. And, oh, I forgot! Mr. Antrobus sent you another message—can you hear me?—(*enter* HENRY, *blackened and sullen. He is wearing torn overalls, but has one gaudy admiral's epaulette hanging by a thread from his right shoulder, and there are vestiges of gold and scarlet braid running down his left trouser leg. He stands listening*) Listen! Henry's never to put foot in this house again, he says. He'll kill Henry on sight, if he sees him.

You don't know about Henry??? Well, where have you been? What? Well, Henry rose right to the top. Top of *what?* Listen, I'm telling you. Henry rose from corporal to captain, to major, to general.—I don't know how to say it, but the enemy is *Henry;* Henry *is* the enemy. Everybody knows that.

HENRY   He'll kill me, will he?

SABINA   Who are *you?* I'm not afraid of you. The war's over.

HENRY   I'll kill him so fast. I've spent seven years trying to find him; the others I killed were just substitutes.

SABINA   Goodness! It's Henry!—(*He makes an angry gesture*) Oh, I'm not afraid of you. The war's over, Henry Antrobus, and you're not any more important than any other unemployed. You go away and hide yourself, until we calm your father down.

HENRY   The first thing to do is to burn up those old books; it's the ideas he gets out of those old books that . . . that makes the whole world so you can't live in it.

(*He reels forward and starts kicking the books about, but suddenly falls down in a sitting position*)

SABINA   You leave those books alone!! Mr. Antrobus is looking forward to them a-special. —Gracious sakes, Henry, you're so tired you can't stand up. Your mother and sister'll be here in a minute and we'll think what to do about you.

HENRY   What did they ever care about me?

SABINA   There's that old whine again. All you people think you're not loved enough, nobody loves you. Well, you start being lovable and we'll love you.

HENRY   (*outraged*)   I don't want anybody to love me.

SABINA   Then stop talking about it all the time.

HENRY   I *never* talk about it. The last thing I want is anybody to pay any attention to me.

SABINA   I can hear it behind every word you say.

HENRY   I want everybody to hate me.

SABINA   Yes, you've decided that's second best, but it's still the same thing.—Mrs. Antrobus! Henry's here. He's so tired he can't stand up.

(MRS. ANTROBUS *and* GLADYS, *with her* BABY, *emerge. They are dressed as in Act One.* MRS. ANTROBUS *carries some objects in her apron, and* GLADYS *has a blanket over her shoulder*)

MRS. ANTROBUS AND GLADYS   Henry! Henry! Henry!

HENRY (*glaring at them*) Have you anything to eat?

MRS. ANTROBUS Yes, I have, Henry. I've been saving it for this very day,—two good baked potatoes. No! Henry! One of them's for your father. Henry!! Give me that other potato back this minute.

(SABINA *sidles up behind him and snatches the other potato away*)

SABINA He's so dog-tired he doesn't know what he's doing.

MRS. ANTROBUS Now you just rest there, Henry, until I can get your room ready. Eat that potato good and slow, so you can get all the nourishment out of it.

HENRY You all might as well know right now that I haven't come back here to live.

MRS. ANTROBUS Sh. . . . I'll put this coat over you. Your room's hardly damaged at all. Your football trophies are a little tarnished, but Sabina and I will polish them up tomorrow.

HENRY Did you hear me? I don't live here. I don't belong to anybody.

MRS. ANTROBUS Why, how can you say a thing like that! You certainly do belong right here. Where else would you want to go? Your forehead's feverish, Henry, seems to me. You'd better give me that gun, Henry. You won't need that any more.

GLADYS (*whispering*) Look, he's fallen asleep already, with his potato half-chewed.

SABINA Puh! The terror of the world.

MRS. ANTROBUS Sabina, you mind your own business, and start putting the room to rights.

(HENRY *has turned his face to the back of the sofa.* MRS. ANTROBUS *gingerly puts the revolver in her apron pocket, then helps* SABINA. SABINA *has found a rope hanging from the ceiling. Grunting, she hangs all her weight on it, and as she pulls the walls begin to move into their right places.* MRS. ANTROBUS *brings the overturned tables, chairs, and hassock into the positions of Act One*)

SABINA That's all we do—always beginning again! Over and over again. Always beginning again. (*She pulls on the rope and a part of the wall moves into place. She stops. Meditatively*) How do we know that it'll be any better than before? Why do we go on pretending? Some day the whole earth's going to have to turn cold anyway, and until that time all these other things'll be happening again: it will be more wars and more walls of ice and floods and earthquakes.

MRS. ANTROBUS Sabina!! Stop arguing and go on with your work.

SABINA All right. I'll go on just out of *habit*, but I won't believe in it.

MRS. ANTROBUS (*aroused*) Now, Sabina. I've let you talk long enough. I don't want to hear any more of it. Do I have to explain to you what everybody knows,—everybody who keeps a home going? Do I have to say to you what nobody should ever *have* to say, because they can read it in each other's eyes? Now listen to me: (MRS. ANTROBUS *takes hold of the rope*) I could live for seventy years in a cellar and make soup out of grass and bark, without ever doubting that this world has a work to do and will do it. Do you hear me?

SABINA (*frightened*) Yes, Mrs. Antrobus.

MRS. ANTROBUS Sabina, do you see this house,—216 Cedar Street,—do you see it?

SABINA Yes, Mrs. Antrobus.

MRS. ANTROBUS Well, just to have known this house is to have seen the idea of what we can do someday if we keep our wits about us. Too many people have suffered and died for my children for us to start reneging now. So we'll start putting this house to rights. Now, Sabina, go and see what you can do in the kitchen.

SABINA Kitchen! Why is it that however far I go away, I always find myself back in the kitchen? (*exit*)

MRS. ANTROBUS (*still thinking over her last speech, relaxes and says with a reminiscent smile*) Goodness gracious, wouldn't you know that my father was a parson? It was just like I heard his own voice speaking and he's been dead five-thousand years. There! I've gone and almost waked Henry up.

HENRY (*talking in his sleep, indistinctly*) Fellows . . . what have they done for us? . . . Blocked our way at every step. Kept everything in their own hands. And you've stood it. When are you going to wake up?

MRS. ANTROBUS Sh, Henry. Go to sleep. Go to sleep. Go to sleep.—Well, that looks better. Now let's go and help Sabina.

GLADYS Mama, I'm going out in the backyard and hold the baby right up in the air. And show him that we don't have to be afraid any more.

(*Exit* GLADYS *to the kitchen.* MRS. ANTROBUS *glances at* HENRY, *exits into kitchen.* HENRY *thrashes about in his sleep. Enter* ANTROBUS, *his arms full of bundles, chewing the end of a carrot. He has a slight limp. Over the suit of Act One he is wearing an overcoat too long for him, its skirts trailing on the ground. He lets his bundles fall and stands looking about. Presently his attention is fixed on* HENRY, *whose words grow clearer)*

HENRY   All right! What have you got to lose? What have they done for us? That's right—nothing. Tear everything down. I don't care what you smash. We'll begin again and we'll show 'em. (ANTROBUS *takes out his revolver and holds it pointing downwards. With his back towards the audience he moves toward the footlights.* HENRY's *voice grows louder and he wakes with a start. They stare at one another. Then* HENRY *sits up quickly. Throughout the following scene* HENRY *is played, not as a misunderstood or misguided young man, but as a representation of strong unreconciled evil)* All right! Do something. *(pause)* Don't think I'm afraid of you, either. All right, do what you were going to do. Do it. *(furiously)* Shoot me, I tell you. You don't have to think I'm any relation of yours. I haven't got any father or any mother, or brothers or sisters. And I don't want any. And what's more I haven't got anybody over me; and I never will have. I'm alone, and that's all I want to be: alone. So you can shoot me.

ANTROBUS   You're the last person I wanted to see. The sight of you dries up all my plans and hopes. I wish I were back at war still, because it's easier to fight you than to live with you. War's a pleasure—do you hear me?— War's a pleasure compared to what faces us now: trying to build up a peacetime with you in the middle of it. (ANTROBUS *walks up to the window)*

HENRY   I'm not going to be a part of any peacetime of yours. I'm going a long way from here and make my own world that's fit for man to live in. Where a man can be free, and have a chance, and do what he wants to do in his own way.

ANTROBUS   *(his attention arrested; thoughtfully. He throws the gun out of the window and turns wtih hope)* . . . Henry, let's try again.

HENRY   Try what? Living *here?*—Speaking polite downtown to all the old men like you? Standing like a sheep at the street corner until the red light turns to green? Being a good boy and a good sheep, like all the stinking ideas you get out of your books? Oh, no. I'll make a world, and I'll show you.

ANTROBUS   *(hard)*   How can you make a world for people to live in, unless you've first put order in yourself? Mark my words: I shall continue fighting you until my last breath as long as you mix up your idea of liberty with your idea of hogging everything for yourself.

I shall have no pity on you. I shall pursue you to the far corners of the earth. You and I want the same thing; but until you think of it as something that everyone has a right to, you are my deadly enemy and I will destroy you.—I hear your mother's voice in the kitchen. Have you seen her?

HENRY   I have no mother. Get it into your head. I don't belong here. I have nothing to do here. I have no home.

ANTROBUS   Then why did you come here? With the whole world to choose from, why did you come to this one place: 216 Cedar Street, Excelsior, New Jersey. . . . Well?

HENRY   What if I did? What if I wanted to look at it once more, to see if—

ANTROBUS   Oh, you're related, all right— When your mother comes in you must behave yourself. Do you hear me?

HENRY   *(wildly)*   What is this?—*must behave* yourself. Don't you say *must* to me.

ANTROBUS   Quiet.

(Enter MRS. ANTROBUS *and* SABINA*)*

HENRY   Nobody can say *must* to me. All my life everybody's been crossing me,—everybody, everything, all of you. I'm going to be free, even if I have to kill half the world for it. Right now, too. Let me get my hand on his throat. I'll show him. *(He advances toward* ANTROBUS. *Suddenly,* SABINA *jumps between them and calls out in her own person)*

SABINA   Stop! Stop! Don't play this scene. You know what happened last night. Stop the play. *(The men fall back, panting.* HENRY *covers his face with his hands)* Last night you almost strangled him. You became a regular savage. Stop it!

HENRY   It's true. I'm sorry. I don't know what comes over me. I have nothing against him personally. I respect him very much . . . I . . . I admire him. But something comes over me. It's like I become fifteen years old again. I . . . I . . . listen: my own father used to whip me and lock me up every Saturday night. I never had enough to eat. He never let me have enough money to buy decent clothes. I was ashamed to go downtown. I never could go to the dances. My father and my uncle put rules in the way of everything I wanted to do. They tried to prevent my living at all.—I'm sorry. I'm sorry.

MRS. ANTROBUS   *(quickly)*   No, go on. Finish what you were saying. Say it all.

HENRY   In this scene it's as though I were back in High School again. It's like I had some big emptiness inside me,—the emptiness of being hated and blocked at every turn. And the emptiness fills up with the one thought that you have to strike and fight and kill. Listen, it's as though you have to kill somebody else so as not to end up killing yourself.

SABINA That's not true. I knew your father and your uncle and your mother. You imagined all that. Why, they did everything they could for you. How can you say things like that? They didn't lock you up.

HENRY They did. They did. They wished I hadn't been born.

SABINA That's not true.

ANTROBUS (*in his own person, with self-condemnation, but cold and proud*) Wait a minute. I have something to say, too. It's not wholly his fault that he wants to strangle me in this scene. It's my fault, too. He wouldn't feel that way unless there were something in me that reminded him of all that. He talks about an emptiness. Well, there's an emptiness in me, too. Yes,—work, work, work,—that's all I do. I've ceased to *live*. No wonder he feels that anger coming over him.

MRS. ANTROBUS There! At last you've said it.

SABINA We're all just as wicked as we can be, and that's the God's truth.

MRS. ANTROBUS (*nods a moment, then comes forward; quietly*) Come. Come and put your head under some cold water.

SABINA (*in a whisper*) I'll go with him. I've known him a long while. You have to go on with the play. Come with me.

(HENRY *starts out with* SABINA, *but turns at the exit and says to* ANTROBUS)

HENRY Thanks. Thanks for what you said. I'll be all right tomorrow. I won't lose control in that place. I promise.

(*Exeunt* HENRY *and* SABINA. ANTROBUS *starts toward the front door, fastens it.* MRS. ANTROBUS *goes upstage and places the chair close to table*)

MRS. ANTROBUS George, do I see you limping?

ANTROBUS Yes, a little. My old wound from the other war started smarting again. I can manage.

MRS. ANTROBUS (*looking out of the window*) Some lights are coming on,—the first in seven years. People are walking up and down looking at them. Over in Hawkins' open lot they've built a bonfire to celebrate the peace. They're dancing around it like scarecrows.

ANTROBUS A bonfire! As though they hadn't seen enough things burning.—Maggie,—the dog died?

MRS. ANTROBUS Oh, yes. Long ago. There are no dogs left in Excelsior.—You're back again! All these years. I gave up counting on letters. The few that arrived were anywhere from six months to a year late.

ANTROBUS Yes, the ocean's full of letters, along with the other things.

MRS. ANTROBUS George, sit down, you're tired.

ANTROBUS No, you sit down. I'm tired but I'm restless. (*suddenly, as she comes forward*) Maggie! I've lost it. I've lost it.

MRS. ANTROBUS What, George? What have you lost?

ANTROBUS The most important thing of all: The desire to begin again, to start building.

MRS. ANTROBUS (*sitting in the chair right of the table*) Well, it will come back.

ANTROBUS (*at the window*) I've lost it. This minute I feel like all those people dancing around the bonfire—just relief. Just the desire to settle down; to slip into the old grooves and keep the neighbors from walking over my lawn.—Hm. But during the war,—in the middle of all that blood and dirt and hot and cold—every day and night, I'd have moments, Maggie, when I *saw* the things that we could do when it was over. When you're at war you think about a better life; when you're at peace you think about a more comfortable one. I've lost it. I feel sick and tired.

MRS. ANTROBUS Listen! The baby's crying. I hear Gladys talking. Probably she's quieting Henry again. George, while Gladys and I were living here—like moles, like rats, and when we were at our wits' end to save the baby's life— the only thought we clung to was that you were going to bring something good out of this suffering. In the night, in the dark, we'd whisper about it, starving and sick.—Oh, George, you'll have to get it back again. Think! What else kept us alive all these years? Even now, it's not comfort we want. We can suffer whatever's necessary; only give us back that promise.

(*Enter* SABINA *with a lighted lamp. She is dressed as in Act One*)

SABINA Mrs. Antrobus . . .

MRS. ANTROBUS Yes, Sabina?

SABINA Will you need me?

MRS. ANTROBUS No, Sabina, you can go to bed.

SABINA Mrs. Antrobus, if it's all right with you, I'd like to go to the bonfire and celebrate, seeing the war's over. And, Mrs. Antrobus, they've opened the Gem Movie Theatre and they're giving away a hand-painted soup tureen to every lady, and I though one of us ought to go.

ANTROBUS   Well, Sabina, I haven't any money. I haven't seen any money for quite a while.

SABINA   Oh, you don't need money. They're taking anything you can give them. And I have some . . . some . . . Mrs. Antrobus, promise you won't tell anyone. It's a little against the law. But I'll give you some, too.

ANTROBUS   What is it?

SABINA   I'll give you some, too. Yesterday I picked up a lot of . . . of beef-cubes!

MRS. ANTROBUS   (turns and says calmly) But, Sabina, you know you ought to give that in to the Center downtown. They know who needs them most.

SABINA   (outburst) Mrs. Antrobus, I didn't make this war. I didn't ask for it. And, in my opinion, after anybody's gone through what we've gone through, they have a right to grab what they can find. You're a very nice man, Mr. Antrobus, but you'd have got on better in the world if you'd realize that dog-eat-dog was the rule in the beginning and always will be. And most of all now. (in tears) Oh, the world's an awful place, and you know it is. I used to think something could be done about it; but I know better now. I hate it. I hate it. (She comes forward slowly and brings six cubes from the bag) All right. All right. You can have them.

ANTROBUS   Thank you, Sabina.

SABINA   Can I have . . . can I have one to go to the movies? (ANTROBUS in silence gives her one) Thank you.

ANTROBUS   Good night, Sabina.

SABINA   Mr. Antrobus, don't mind what I say. I'm just an ordinary girl, you know what I mean, I'm just an ordinary girl. But you're a bright man, you're a very bright man, and of course you invented the alphabet and the wheel, and, my God, a lot of things . . . and if you've got any other plans, my God, don't let me upset them. Only every now and then I've got to go to the movies. I mean my nerves can't stand it. But if you have any ideas about improving the crazy old world, I'm really with you. I really am. Because it's . . . it's . . . Good night. (She goes out. ANTROBUS starts laughing softly with exhilaration)

ANTROBUS   Now I remember what three things always went together when I was able to see things most clearly: three things. Three things: (He points to where SABINA has gone out) The voice of the people in their confusion and their need. And the thought of you and the children and this house. . . . And . . . Mag-

gie! I didn't dare ask you: my books! They haven't been lost, have they?

MRS. ANTROBUS   No. There are some of them right here. Kind of tattered.

ANTROBUS   Yes.—Remember, Maggie, we almost lost them once before? And when we finally did collect a few torn copies out of old cellars they ran in everyone's head like a fever. They as good as rebuilt the world. (pauses, book in hand, and looks up) Oh, I've never forgotten for long at a time that living is struggle. I know that every good and excellent thing in the world stands moment by moment on the razor-edge of danger and must be fought for—whether it's a field, or a home, or a country. All I ask is the chance to build new worlds and God has always given us that. And has given us (opening the book) voices to guide us; and the memory of our mistakes to warn us. Maggie, you and I will remember in peacetime all the resolves that were so clear to us in the days of war. We've come a long ways. We've learned. We're learning. And the steps of our journey are marked for us here. (He stands by the table turning the leaves of a book) Sometimes out there in the war,—standing all night on a hill—I'd try and remember some of the words in these books. Parts of them and phrases would come back to me. And after a while I used to give names to the hours of the night. (He sits, hunting for a passage in the book) Nine o'clock I used to call Spinoza. Where is it: "After experience had taught me—"

(The back wall has disappeared, revealing the platform. FRED BAILEY carrying his numeral has started from left to right. MRS. ANTROBUS sits by the table sewing)

BAILEY   "After experience had taught me that the common occurrences of daily life are vain and futile; and I saw that all the objects of my desire and fear were in themselves nothing good nor bad save insofar as the mind was affected by them; I at length determined to search out whether there was something truly good and communicable to man."

(Almost without break HESTER, carrying a large Roman numeral ten, starts crossing the platform. GLADYS appears at the kitchen door and moves towards her mother's chair)

HESTER   "Then tell me, O Critias, how will a man choose the ruler that shall rule over him? Will he not choose a man who has first established order in himself, knowing that any decision that has its spring from anger or pride or vanity can be multiplied a thousand fold in its effect upon the citizens?"

(HESTER *disappears and* IVY, *as eleven o'clock, starts speaking*)

IVY   "This good estate of the mind possessing its object in energy we call divine. This we mortals have occasionally and it is this energy which is pleasantest and best. But God has it always. It is wonderful in us; but in Him how much more wonderful."

(*As* MR. TREMAYNE *starts to speak,* HENRY *appears at the edge of the scene, brooding and unreconciled, but present*)

TREMAYNE   "In the beginning, God created the heavens and the earth; And the earth was waste and void; And the darkness was upon the face of the deep. And the Lord said let there be light and there was light."

(*Sudden black-out and silence, except for the last strokes of the midnight bell. Then just as suddenly the lights go up, and* SABINA *is standing at the window, as at the opening of the play*)

SABINA   Oh, oh, oh. Six o'clock and the master not home yet. Pray God nothing serious has happened to him crossing the Hudson River. But I wouldn't be surprised. The whole world's at sixes and sevens, and why the house hasn't fallen down about our ears long ago is a miracle to me. (*She comes down to the footlights*)

This is where you came in. We have to go on for ages and ages yet.

You go home.

The end of the play isn't written yet.

Mr. and Mrs. Antrobus! Their heads are full of plans and they're as confident as the first day they began,—and they told me to tell you: good night.

Tennessee Williams

1914-

THE TIMELESS WORLD
OF A PLAY

Carson McCullers concludes one of her lyric poems with the line: "Time, the endless idiot, runs screaming 'round the world." It is this continual rush of time, so violent that it appears to be screaming, that deprives our actual lives of so much dignity and meaning, and it is, perhaps more than anything else, the *arrest of time* which has taken place in a completed work of art that gives to certain plays their feeling of depth and significance. In the London notices of *Death of a Salesman* a certain notoriously skeptical critic made the remark that Willy Loman was the sort of man that almost any member of the audience would have kicked out of an office had he applied for a job or detained one for conversation about his troubles. The remark itself possibly holds some truth. But the implication that Willy Loman is consequently a character with whom we have no reason to concern ourselves in drama, reveals a strikingly false conception of what plays are. Contemplation is something that exists outside of time, and so is the tragic sense. Even in the actual world of commerce, there exists in some persons a sensibility to the unfortunate situations of others, a capacity for concern and compassion, surviving from a more tender period of life outside the present whirling wire-cage of business activity. Facing Willy Loman across an office desk, meeting his nervous glance and hearing his querulous voice, we would be very likely to glance at our wrist watch and our schedule of other appointments. We would

not kick him out of the office, no, but we would certainly *ease* him out with more expedition than Willy had feebly hoped for. But suppose there had been no wrist watch or office clock and suppose there had *not* been the schedule of pressing appointments, and suppose that we were not actually facing Willy across a desk—and facing a person is *not* the best way to *see* him!—suppose, in other words, that the meeting with Willy Loman had somehow occurred in a world *outside* of time. Then I think we would receive him with concern and kindness and even with respect. If the world of a play did not offer us this occasion to view its characters under that special condition of a *world without time*, then, indeed, the characters and occurrences of drama would become equally pointless, equally trivial, as corresponding meetings and happenings in life.

The classic tragedies of Greece had tremendous nobility. The actors wore great masks, movements were formal, dance-like, and the speeches had an epic quality which doubtless were as removed from the normal conversation of their contemporary society as they seem today. Yet they did not seem false to the Greek audiences: the magnitude of the events and the passions aroused by them did not seem ridiculously out of proportion to common experience. And I wonder if this was not because the Greek audiences knew, instinctively or by training, that the created world of a play is removed from that element which makes people *little* and their emotions fairly inconsequential.

Great sculpture often follows the lines of the human body: yet the repose of a great sculpture suddenly transmutes those human lines to something that has an absoluteness, a purity, a beauty, which would not be possible in a living mobile form.

A play may be violent, full of motion: yet it has that special kind of repose which allows contemplation and produces the climate in which tragic importance is a possible thing, provided that certain modern conditions are met.

In actual existence the moments of love are succeeded by the moments of satiety and sleep. The sincere remark is followed by a cynical distrust. Truth is fragmentary, at best: we love and betray each other not in quite the same breath but in two breaths that occur in fairly close sequence. But the fact that passion occurred in *passing*, that it then declined into a more familiar sense of indifference, should not be regarded as proof of its inconsequence. And this is the very truth that drama wishes to bring us . . .

Whether or not we admit it to ourselves, we are all haunted by a truly awful sense of impermanence. I have always had a particularly keen sense of this at New York cocktail parties, and perhaps that is why I drink the martinis almost as fast as I can snatch them from the tray. This sense is the febrile thing that hangs in the air. Horror of insincerity, of *not meaning*, overhangs these affairs like the cloud of cigarette smoke and the hectic chatter. This horror is the only thing, almost, that is left unsaid at such functions. All social functions involving a group of people not intimately known to each other are always under this shadow. They are almost always (in an unconscious way) like that last dinner of the condemned: where steak or turkey, whatever the doomed man wants, is served in his cell as a mockingly cruel reminder of what the great-big-little-transitory world had to offer.

In a play, time is arrested in the sense of being confined. By a sort of legerdemain, events are made to remain *events*, rather than being reduced so quickly to mere *occurrences*. The audience can sit back in a comforting dusk to watch a world which is flooded with light and in which emotion and action have a dimension and dignity that they would likewise have in real existence, if only the shattering intrusion of time could be locked out.

About their lives people ought to remember that when they are finished, everything in them will be contained in a marvelous state of repose which is the same as that which they unconsciously admired in drama. The rush is temporary. The great and only possible dignity of man lies in his power deliberately to choose certain moral values by which to live as steadfastly as if he, too, like a character in a play, were immured against the corrupting rush of time. Snatching the eternal out of the desperately fleeting is the great magic trick of human existence. As far as we know, as far as there exists any kind of empiric evidence, there is no

way to beat the game of *being* against *non-being*, in which non-being is the predestined victor on realistic levels.

Yet plays in the tragic tradition offer us a view of certain moral values in violent juxtaposition. Because we do not participate, except as spectators, we can view them clearly, within the limits of our emotional equipment. These people on the stage do not return our looks. We do not have to answer their questions nor make any sign of being in company with them, nor do we have to compete with their virtues nor resist their offenses. All at once, for this reason, we are able to *see* them! Our hearts are wrung by recognition and pity, so that the dusky shell of the auditorium where we are gathered anonymously together is flooded with an almost liquid warmth of unchecked human sympathies, relieved of self-consciousness, allowed to function . . .

Men pity and love each other more deeply than they permit themselves to know. The moment after the phone has been hung up, the hand reaches for a scratch pad and scrawls a notation: "Funeral Tuesday at five, Church of the Holy Redeemer, don't forget flowers." And the same hand is only a little shakier than usual as it reaches, some minutes later, for a highball glass that will pour a stupefaction over the kindled nerves. Fear and evasion are the two little beasts that chase each other's tails in the revolving wirecage of our nervous world. They distract us from feeling too much about things. Time rushes toward us with its hospital tray of infinitely varied narcotics, even while it is preparing us for its inevitably fatal operation . . .

So successfully have we disguised from ourselves the intensity of our own feelings, the sensibility of our own hearts, that plays in the tragic tradition have begun to seem untrue. For a couple of hours we may surrender ourselves to a world of fiercely illuminated values in conflict, but when the stage is covered and the auditorium lighted, almost immediately there is a recoil of disbelief. "Well, well!" we say as we shuffle back up the aisle, while the play dwindles behind us with the sudden perspective of an early Chirico [1] painting. By the time we have arrived at Sardi's, if not as soon as we have passed beneath the marquee, we have convinced ourselves once more that life

---

[1] Giorgio de Chirico (1888–   ), Italian painter and scene designer most famous for his use of distorted perspective, mannequin figures, empty space, and forms used out of context to create an atmosphere of mystery and loneliness.

has as little resemblance to the curiously stirring and meaningful occurrences on the stage as a jingle has to an elegy of Rilke.[2]

This modern condition of his theater audience is something that an author must know in advance. The diminishing influence of life's destroyer, time, must be somehow worked into the context of his play. Perhaps it is a certain foolery, a certain distortion toward the grotesque, which will solve the problem for him. Perhaps it is only restraint, putting a mute on the strings that would like to break all bounds. But almost surely, unless he contrives in some way to relate the dimensions of his tragedy to the dimensions of a world in which time is *included*—he will be left among his magnificent debris on a dark stage, muttering to himself: "Those fools . . ."

And if they could hear him above the clatter of tongues, glasses, chinaware and silver, they would give him this answer: "But you have shown us a world not ravaged by time. We admire your innocence. But we have seen our photographs, past and present. Yesterday evening we passed our first wife on the street. We smiled as we spoke but we didn't really see her! It's too bad, but we know what is true and not true, and at 3 a.m. your disgrace will be in print!"

---

[2] Rainer Maria Rilke (1875–1926), German mystic poet.

THE GLASS MENAGERIE

CAST OF CHARACTERS

AMANDA WINGFIELD, *the mother. A little woman of great but confused vitality clinging frantically to another time and place. Her characterization must be carefully created, not copied from type. She is not paranoiac, but her life is paranoia. There is much to admire in Amanda, and as much to love and pity as there is to laugh at. Certainly she has endurance and a kind of heroism, and though her foolishness makes her unwittingly cruel at times, there is tenderness in her slight person.*

LAURA WINGFIELD, *her daughter. Amanda, having failed to establish contact with reality, continues to live vitally in her illusions, but Laura's situation is even graver. A childhood illness has left her crippled, one leg slightly shorter than the other, and held in a brace. This defect need not be more than suggested on the stage. Stemming from this, Laura's separation increases till she is like a piece of her own glass collection, too exquisitely fragile to move from the shelf.*

TOM WINGFIELD, *her son, and the narrator of the play. A poet with a job in a warehouse. His nature is not remorseless, but to escape from a trap he has to act without pity.*

JIM O'CONNOR, *the gentleman caller. A nice, ordinary, young man.*

SCENE   *An Alley in St. Louis.*

PART I   *Preparation for a Gentleman Caller.*

PART II   *The Gentleman calls.*

TIME   *Now and the Past.*

Scene One

(*The Wingfield apartment is in the rear of the building, one of those vast hive-like conglomerations of cellular living-units that flower as warty growths in overcrowded urban centers of lower middle-class population and are symptomatic of the impulse of this largest and fundamentally enslaved section of American society to avoid fluidity and differentiation and to exist and function as one interfused mass of automatism.*

The apartment faces an alley and is entered by a fire escape, a structure whose name is a touch of accidental poetic truth, for all of these huge buildings are always burning with the slow and implacable fires of human desperation. The fire escape is included in the set— that is, the landing of it and steps descending from it.

The scene is memory and is therefore nonrealistic. Memory takes a lot of poetic license. It omits some details; others are exaggerated, according to the emotional value of the articles it touches, for memory is seated predominantly in the heart. The interior is therefore rather dim and poetic.

At the rise of the curtain, the audience is faced with the dark, grim rear wall of the Wingfield tenement. This building, which runs parallel to the footlights, is flanked on both sides by dark, narrow alleys which run into murky canyons of tangled clotheslines, garbage cans, and the sinister lattice-work of neighboring fire escapes. It is up and down these side alleys that exterior entrances and exits are made, during the play. At the end of TOM's *opening commentary, the dark tenement wall slowly reveals [by means of a transparency] the interior of the ground floor Wingfield apartment.*

Downstage is the living room, which also serves as a sleeping room for LAURA, *the sofa unfolding to make her bed. Upstage, center, and divided by a wide arch or second proscenium with transparent faded portieres [or second curtain], is the dining room. In an old-fashioned what-not in the living room are seen scores of transparent glass animals. A blown-up photograph of the father hangs on the wall of the living room, facing the audience, to the left of the archway. It is the face of a very handsome young man in a doughboy's First World War cap. He is gallantly smiling, ineluctably smiling, as if to say, "I will be smiling forever."*

The audience hears and sees the opening scene in the dining room through both the transparent fourth wall of the building and the transparent gauze portieres of the dining-room arch. It is during this revealing scene that the fourth wall slowly ascends, out of sight. This transparent exterior wall is not brought down again until the very end of the play, during TOM's *final speech.*

The narrator is an undisguised convention of the play. He takes whatever license with dramatic convention is convenient to his purposes.

TOM *enters dressed as a merchant sailor from alley, stage left, and strolls across the front of the stage to the fire escape. There he stops and lights a cigarette. He addresses the audience)*

TOM   Yes, I have tricks in my pocket, I have things up my sleeve. But I am the opposite of a stage magician. He gives you illusion that has the appearance of truth. I give you truth in the pleasant disguise of illusion.

To begin with, I turn back time. I reverse it to that quaint period, the thirties, when the huge middle class of America was matriculating in a school for the blind. Their eyes had failed them, or they had failed their eyes, and so they were having their fingers pressed forcibly down on the fiery Braille alphabet of a dissolving economy.

In Spain there was revolution. Here there was only shouting and confusion.

In Spain there was Guernica. Here there

were disturbances of labor, sometimes pretty violent, in otherwise peaceful cities such as Chicago, Cleveland, Saint Louis . . .

This is the social background of the play.

(*music*)

The play is memory.

Being a memory play, it is dimly lighted, it is sentimental, it is not realistic.

In memory everything seems to happen to music. That explains the fiddle in the wings.

I am the narrator of the play, and also a character in it.

The other characters are my mother, Amanda, my sister, Laura, and a gentleman caller who appears in the final scenes.

He is the most realistic character in the play, being an emissary from a world of reality that we were somehow set apart from.

But since I have a poet's weakness for symbols, I am using this character also as a symbol; he is the long delayed but always expected something that we live for.

There is a fifth character in the play who doesn't appear except in this larger-than-life-size photograph over the mantel.

This is our father who left us a long time ago.

He was a telephone man who fell in love with long distances; he gave up his job with the telephone company and skipped the light fantastic out of town . . .

The last we heard of him was a picture post-card from Mazatlan, on the Pacific coast of Mexico, containing a message of two words—

"Hello——Good-bye!" and no address.

I think the rest of the play will explain itself. . . .

(AMANDA's *voice becomes audible through the portieres.* LEGEND ON SCREEN: "OÙ SONT LES NEIGES?" *He divides the portieres and enters the upstage area.* AMANDA *and* LAURA *are seated at a drop-leaf table. Eating is indicated by gestures without food or utensils.* AMANDA *faces the audience.* TOM *and* LAURA *are seated in profile. The interior has lit up softly and through the scrim we see* AMANDA *and* LAURA *seated at the table in the upstage area)*

AMANDA   (*calling*)   Tom?

TOM   Yes, Mother.

AMANDA   We can't say grace until you come to the table!

TOM   Coming, Mother. (*He bows slightly and withdraws, reappearing a few moments later in his place at the table)*

AMANDA   (*to her son*)   Honey, don't *push* with your *fingers.* If you have to push with something, the thing to push with is a crust of bread. And chew—chew! Animals have sections in their stomachs which enable them to digest food without mastication, but human beings are supposed to chew their food before they swallow it down. Eat food leisurely, son, and really enjoy it. A well-cooked meal has lots of delicate flavors that have to be held in the mouth for appreciation. So chew your food and give your salivary glands a chance to function! (TOM *deliberately lays his imaginary fork down and pushes his chair back from the table*)

TOM   I haven't enjoyed one bite of this dinner because of your constant directions on how to eat it. It's you that make me rush through meals with your hawk-like attention to every bite I take. Sickening—spoils my appetite—all this discussion of—animals' secretion—salivary glands—mastication.

AMANDA   (*lightly*)   Temperament like a Metropolitan star! (*He rises and crosses downstage*) You're not excused from the table.

TOM   I'm getting a cigarette.

AMANDA   You smoke too much. (LAURA *rises*)

LAURA   I'll bring in the blanc mange. (*He remains standing with his cigarette by the portieres during the following*)

AMANDA   (*rising*)   No, sister, no, sister—you be the lady this time and I'll be the darky.

LAURA   I'm already up.

AMANDA   Resume your seat, little sister—I want you to stay fresh and pretty—for gentlemen callers!

LAURA   I'm not expecting any gentlemen callers.

AMANDA   (*crossing out to kitchenette. Airily*) Sometimes they come when they are least expected! Why, I remember one Sunday afternoon in Blue Mountain—(*enters kitchenette*)

TOM   I know what's coming!

LAURA   Yes. But let her tell it.

TOM   Again?

LAURA   She loves to tell it. (AMANDA *returns with bowl of dessert*)

AMANDA   One Sunday afternoon in Blue Mountain—your mother received—*seventeen!* —gentlemen callers! Why, sometimes there weren't chairs enough to accommodate them all. We had to send the nigger over to bring in folding chairs from the parish house.

TOM   (*remaining at portieres*)   How did you entertain those gentlemen callers?

AMANDA   I understood the art of conversation!

TOM   I bet you could talk.

AMANDA   Girls in those days *knew* how to talk, I can tell you.

TOM   Yes?

(IMAGE: AMANDA AS A GIRL ON A PORCH, GREETING CALLERS)

AMANDA   They knew how to entertain their gentlemen callers. It wasn't enough for a girl to be possessed of a pretty face and a graceful figure—although I wasn't slighted in either respect. She also needed to have a nimble wit and a tongue to meet all occasions.

TOM   What did you talk about?

AMANDA   Things of importance going on in the world! Never anything coarse or common or vulgar. (*She addresses* TOM *as though he were seated in the vacant chair at the table though he remains by portieres. He plays this scene as though he held the book*) My callers were gentlemen—all! Among my callers were some of the most prominent young planters of the Mississippi Delta—planters and sons of planters! (TOM *motions for music and a spot of light on* AMANDA. *Her eyes lift, her face glows, her voice becomes rich and elegiac.* SCREEN LEGEND: "OÙ SONT LES NEIGES?")

There was young Champ Laughlin, who later became vice-president of the Delta Planters Bank.

Hadley Stevenson, who was drowned in Moon Lake and left his widow one hundred and fifty thousand in Government bonds.

There were the Cutrere brothers, Wesley and Bates. Bates was one of my bright particular beaux! He got in a quarrel with that wild Wainwright boy. They shot it out on the floor of Moon Lake Casino. Bates was shot through the stomach. Died in the ambulance on his way to Memphis. His widow was also well-provided for, came into eight or ten thousand acres, that's all. She married him on the rebound—never loved her—carried my picture on him the night he died!

And there was that boy that every girl in the Delta had set her cap for! That beautiful, brilliant young Fitzhugh boy from Greene County!

TOM   What did he leave his widow?

AMANDA   He never married! Gracious, you talk as though all of my old admirers had turned up their toes to the daisies!

TOM   Isn't this the first you've mentioned that still survives?

AMANDA   That Fitzhugh boy went North and made a fortune—came to be known as the Wolf of Wall Street! He had the Midas touch, whatever he touched turned to gold!

And I could have been Mrs. Duncan J. Fitzhugh, mind you! But—I picked your *father!*

LAURA   (*rising*)   Mother, let me clear the table.

AMANDA No, dear, you go in front and study your typewriter chart. Or practice your shorthand a little. Stay fresh and pretty!—it's almost time for our gentlemen callers to start arriving. (*She flounces girlishly toward the kitchenette*) How many do you suppose we're going to entertain this afternoon? (TOM *throws down the paper and jumps up with a groan*)

LAURA (*alone in the dining room*)   I don't believe we're going to receive any, Mother.

AMANDA (*reappearing, airily*)   What? No one—not one? You must be joking! (LAURA *nervously echoes her laugh. She slips in a fugitive manner through the half-open portieres and draws them gently behind her. A shaft of very clear light is thrown on her face against the faded tapestry of the curtains.* MUSIC: "THE GLASS MENAGERIE" UNDER FAINTLY. *Lightly*) Not one gentleman caller? It can't be true! There must be a flood, there must have been a tornado!

LAURA   It isn't a flood, it's not a tornado, Mother. I'm just not popular like you were in Blue Mountain. . . . (TOM *utters another groan.* LAURA *glances at him with a faint, apologetic smile. Her voice catching a little*) Mother's afraid I'm going to be an old maid.

THE SCENE DIMS OUT WITH "GLASS MENAGERIE" MUSIC

Scene Two

(LEGEND: "LAURA, HAVEN'T YOU EVER LIKED SOME BOY?"

On the dark stage the screen is lighted with the image of blue roses.

Gradually LAURA's *figure becomes apparent and the screen goes out. The music subsides.*

LAURA *is seated in the delicate ivory chair at the small claw-foot table.*

She wears a dress of soft violet material for a kimono—her hair tied back from her forehead with a ribbon.

She is washing and polishing her collection of glass.

AMANDA *appears on the fire-escape steps. At the sound of her ascent,* LAURA *catches her breath, thrusts the bowl of ornaments away and seats herself stiffly before the diagram of the typewriter keyboard as though it held her spellbound.*

Something has happened to AMANDA. *It is*

written in her face as she climbs to the landing: a look that is grim and hopeless and a little absurd.

She has on one of those cheap or imitation velvety-looking cloth coats with imitation fur collar. Her hat is five or six years old, one of those dreadful cloche hats that were worn in the late twenties, and she is clasping an enormous black patent-leather pocketbook with nickel clasps and initials. This is her full-dress outfit, the one she usually wears to the D.A.R.

Before entering she looks through the door.

She purses her lips, opens her eyes very wide, rolls them upward and shakes her head.

Then she slowly lets herself in the door. Seeing her mother's expression LAURA *touches her lips with a nervous gesture*)

LAURA   Hello, Mother, I was—(*She makes a nervous gesture toward the chart on the wall.* AMANDA *leans against the shut door and stares at* LAURA *with a martyred look*)

AMANDA   Deception? Deception? (*She slowly removes her hat and gloves, continuing the sweet suffering stare. She lets the hat and gloves fall on the floor—a bit of acting*)

LAURA (*shakily*)   How was the D.A.R. meeting? (AMANDA *slowly opens her purse and removes a dainty white handkerchief which she shakes out delicately and delicately touches to her lips and nostrils*) Didn't you go to the D.A.R. meeting, Mother?

AMANDA (*faintly, almost inaudibly*)   —No. —No. (*then more forcibly*) I did not have the strength—to go to the D.A.R. In fact, I did not have the courage! I wanted to find a hole in the ground and hide myself in it forever! (*She crosses slowly to the wall and removes the diagram of the typewriter keyboard. She holds it in front of her for a second, staring at it sweetly and sorrowfully—then bites her lip and tears it in two pieces*)

LAURA (*faintly*)   Why did you do that, Mother? (AMANDA *repeats the same procedure with the chart of the Gregg Alphabet*) Why are you—

AMANDA   Why? Why? How old are you, Laura?

LAURA   Mother, you know my age.

AMANDA   I thought that you were an adult; it seems that I was mistaken. (*She crosses slowly to the sofa and sinks down and stares at* LAURA)

LAURA   Please don't stare at me, Mother. (AMANDA *closes her eyes and lowers her head. Count ten*)

AMANDA   What are we going to do, what is

going to become of us, what is the future? (*count ten*)

LAURA   Has something happened, Mother? (AMANDA *draws a long breath and takes out the handkerchief again. Dabbing process*) Mother, has—something happened?

AMANDA   I'll be all right in a minute, I'm just bewildered—(*count five*)—by life. . . .

LAURA   Mother, I wish that you would tell me what's happened!

AMANDA   As you know, I was supposed to be inducted into my office at the D.A.R. this afternoon. (IMAGE: A SWARM OF TYPEWRITERS) But I stopped off at Rubicam's Business College to speak to your teachers about your having a cold and ask them what progress they thought you were making down there.

LAURA   Oh. . . .

AMANDA   I went to the typing instructor and introduced myself as your mother. She didn't know who you were. Wingfield, she said. We don't have any such student enrolled at the school!

I assured her she did, that you had been going to classes since early in January.

"I wonder," she said, "if you could be talking about that terribly shy little girl who dropped out of school after only a few days' attendance?"

"No," I said, "Laura, my daughter, has been going to school every day for the past six weeks!"

"Excuse me," she said. She took the attendance book out and there was your name, unmistakably printed, and all the dates you were absent until they decided that you had dropped out of school.

I still said, "No, there must have been some mistake! There must have been some mix-up in the records!"

And she said, "No—I remember her perfectly now. Her hands shook so that she couldn't hit the right keys! The first time we gave a speed-test, she broke down completely —was sick at the stomach and almost had to be carried into the washroom! After that morning she never showed up any more. We phoned the house but never got any answer"—while I was working at Famous and Barr, I suppose, demonstrating those——Oh!

I felt so weak I could barely keep on my feet!

I had to sit down while they got me a glass of water!

Fifty dollars' tuition, all of our plans—my hopes and ambitions for you—just gone up the spout, just gone up the spout like that. (LAURA *draws a long breath and gets awkwardly to her feet. She crosses to the victrola and winds it up*)

What are you doing?

LAURA   Oh! (*She releases the handle and returns to her seat*)

AMANDA   Laura, where have you been going when you've gone out pretending that you were going to business college?

LAURA   I've just been going out walking.

AMANDA   That's not true.

LAURA   It is. I just went walking.

AMANDA   Walking? Walking? In winter? Deliberately courting pneumonia in that light coat? Where did you walk to, Laura?

LAURA   All sorts of places—mostly in the park.

AMANDA   Even after you'd started catching that cold?

LAURA   It was the lesser of two evils, Mother. (IMAGE: WINTER SCENE IN PARK) I couldn't go back up. I—threw up—on the floor!

AMANDA   From half past seven till after five every day you mean to tell me you walked around the park, because you wanted to make me think that you were still going to Rubicam's Business College?

LAURA   It wasn't as bad as it sounds. I went inside places to get warmed up.

AMANDA   Inside where?

LAURA   I went in the art museum and the bird-houses at the Zoo. I visited the penguins every day! Sometimes I did without lunch and went to the movies. Lately I've been spending most of my afternoons in the Jewel-box, that big glass house where they raise the tropical flowers.

AMANDA   You did all this to deceive me, just for deception? (LAURA *looks down*) Why?

LAURA   Mother, when you're disappointed, you get that awful suffering look on your face, like the picture of Jesus' mother in the museum!

AMANDA   Hush!

LAURA   I couldn't face it. (*Pause. A whisper of strings.* LEGEND: "THE CRUST OF HUMILITY")

AMANDA   (*hopelessly fingering the huge pocketbook*).   So what are we going to do the rest of our lives? Stay home and watch the parades go by? Amuse ourselves with the glass menagerie, darling? Eternally play those worn-out phonograph records your father left as a painful reminder of him?

We won't have a business career—we've given that up because it gave us nervous indigestion! (*laughs wearily*) What is there left but dependency all our lives? I know so well what becomes of unmarried women who aren't prepared to occupy a position. I've seen such pitiful cases in the South—barely tolerated spinsters living upon the grudging patronage of sister's husband or brother's wife!—stuck away in some little mouse-trap of a room—encouraged by one in-law to visit another—little bird-like women without any nest—eating the crust of humility all their life!

Is that the future that we've mapped out for ourselves?

I swear it's the only alternative I can think of!

It isn't a very pleasant alternative, is it?

Of course—some girls *do marry*. (LAURA *twists her hands nervously*)

Haven't you ever liked some boy?

LAURA   Yes. I liked one once. (*rises*) I came across his picture a while ago.

AMANDA (*with some interest*)   He gave you his picture?

LAURA   No, it's in the year-book.

AMANDA   (*disappointed*)   Oh—a high-school boy.

(SCREEN IMAGE: JIM AS HIGH-SCHOOL HERO BEARING A SILVER CUP)

LAURA   Yes. His name was Jim. (LAURA *lifts the heavy annual from the claw-foot table*) Here he is in *The Pirates of Penzance*.

AMANDA (*absently*)   The what?

LAURA   The operetta the senior class put on. He had a wonderful voice and we sat across the aisle from each other Mondays, Wednesdays, and Fridays in the Aud. Here he is with the silver cup for debating! See his grin?

AMANDA (*absently*)   He must have had a jolly disposition.

LAURA   He used to call me—Blue Roses.

(IMAGE: BLUE ROSES)

AMANDA   Why did he call you such a name as that?

LAURA   When I had that attack of pleurosis—he asked me what was the matter when I came back. I said pleurosis—he thought that I said Blue Roses! So that's what he always called me after that. Whenever he saw me, he'd holler, "Hello, Blue Roses!" I didn't care for the girl that he went out with. Emily Meisenbach. Emily was the best-dressed girl at Soldan. She never struck me, though, as being sincere . . . It says in the Personal Section—they're engaged. That's—six years ago! They must be married by now.

AMANDA   Girls that aren't cut out for business careers usually wind up married to some nice man. (*gets up with a spark of revival*) Sister, that's what you'll do! (LAURA *utters a startled, doubtful laugh. She reaches quickly for a piece of glass*)

LAURA   But, Mother—

AMANDA.   Yes? (*crossing to photograph*)

LAURA (*in a tone of frightened apology*) I'm—crippled! (IMAGE: SCREEN)

AMANDA   Nonsense! Laura, I've told you never, never to use that word. Why, you're not crippled, you just have a little defect—hardly noticeable, even! When people have some slight disadvantage like that, they cultivate other things to make up for it—develop charm—and vivacity—and—*charm!* That's all you have to do! (*She turns again to the photograph*) One thing your father had *plenty of*—was *charm!* (TOM *motions to the fiddle in the wings*)

THE SCENE FADES WITH MUSIC

Scene Three

(LEGEND ON SCREEN: "AFTER THE FIASCO—" TOM *speaks from the fire-escape landing*)

TOM   After the fiasco at Rubicam's Business College, the idea of getting a gentleman caller for Laura began to play a more and more important part in Mother's calculations.

It became an obsession. Like some archetype of the universal unconscious, the image of the gentleman caller haunted our small apartment. . . . (IMAGE: YOUNG MAN AT DOOR WITH FLOWERS)

An evening at home rarely passed without some allusion to this image, this spectre, this hope. . . .

Even when he wasn't mentioned, his presence hung in Mother's preoccupied look and in my sister's frightened, apologetic manner—hung like a sentence passed upon the Wingfields!

Mother was a woman of action as well as words.

She began to take logical steps in the planned direction.

Late that winter and in the early spring—realizing that extra money would be needed to properly feather the nest and plume the bird—she conducted a vigorous campaign on the telephone, roping in subscribers to one of those magazines for matrons called *The Homemaker's Companion*, the type of journal that features the serialized sublimations of ladies of letters who think in terms of delicate cup-like breasts, slim, tapering waists, rich, creamy thighs, eyes like wood-smoke in autumn, fingers that soothe and caress like strains of music, bodies as powerful as Etruscan sculpture.

(SCREEN IMAGE: GLAMOR MAGAZINE COVER. AMANDA *enters with phone on long extension cord. She is spotted in the dim stage*)

AMANDA   Ida Scott? This is Amanda Wing-field!

We *missed* you at the D.A.R. last Monday!

I said to myself: She's probably suffering with that sinus condition! How is that sinus condition?

Horrors! Heaven have mercy!—You're a Christian martyr, yes, that's what you are, a Christian martyr!

Well, I just now happened to notice that your subscription to the *Companion's* about to expire! Yes, it expires with the next issue, honey!—just when that wonderful new serial by Bessie Mae Hopper is getting off to such an exciting start. Oh, honey, it's something that you can't miss! You remember how *Gone With the Wind* took everybody by storm? You simply couldn't go out if you hadn't read it. All everybody *talked* was Scarlett O'Hara. Well, this is a book that critics already compare to *Gone With the Wind.* It's the *Gone With the Wind* of the post-World War generation!—What?—Burning?—Oh, honey, don't let them burn, go take a look in the oven and I'll hold the wire! Heavens—I think she's hung up!

DIM OUT

(LEGEND ON SCREEN: "YOU THINK I'M IN LOVE WITH CONTINENTAL SHOEMAKERS?" *Before the stage is lighted the violent voices of* TOM *and* AMANDA *are heard. They are quarreling behind the portieres. In front of them stands* LAURA *with clenched hands and panicky expression. A clear pool of light on her figure throughout this scene*)

TOM   What in Christ's name am I—
AMANDA   (*shrilly*)   Don't you use that—
TOM   Supposed to do!
AMANDA   Expression! Not in my—
TOM   Ohhh!
AMANDA   Presence! Have you gone out of your senses?
TOM   I have, that's true, *driven* out!
AMANDA   What is the matter with you, you —big—big—IDIOT!
TOM   Look!—I've got *no thing*, no single thing—
AMANDA   Lower your voice!

TOM   In my life here that I can call my own! Everything is—
AMANDA   Stop that shouting!
TOM   Yesterday you confiscated my books! You had the nerve to—
AMANDA   I took that horrible novel back to the library—yes! That hideous book by that insane Mr. Lawrence. (TOM *laughs wildly*) I cannot control the output of diseased minds or people who cater to them—(TOM *laughs still more wildly*) BUT I WON'T ALLOW SUCH FILTH BROUGHT INTO MY HOUSE! No, no, no, no, no!
TOM   House, house! Who pays rent on it, who makes a slave of himself to—
AMANDA   (*fairly screeching*)   Don't you DARE to—
TOM   No, no, *I* mustn't say things! *I've* got to just—
AMANDA   Let me tell you—
TOM   I don't want to hear any more! (*He tears the portieres open. The upstage area is lit with a turgid smoky red glow.* AMANDA's *hair is in metal curlers and she wears a very old bathrobe, much too large for her slight figure, a relic of the faithless Mr. Wingfield. An upright typewriter and a wild disarray of manuscripts is on the drop-leaf table. The quarrel was probably precipitated by* AMANDA's *interruption of his creative labor. A chair lying overthrown on the floor. Their gesticulating shadows are cast on the ceiling by the fiery glow*)
AMANDA   You *will* hear more, you—
TOM   No, I won't hear more, I'm going out!
AMANDA   You come right back in—
TOM   Out, out, out! Because I'm—
AMANDA   Come back here, Tom Wingfield! I'm not through talking to you!
TOM   Oh go—
LAURA   (*desperately*)   —Tom!
AMANDA   You're going to listen, and no more insolence from you! I'm at the end of my patience! (*He comes back toward her*)
TOM   What do you think I'm at? Aren't I supposed to have any patience to reach the end of, Mother? I know, I know. It seems unimportant to you, what I'm *doing*—what I *want* to do —having a little *difference* between them! You don't think that—
AMANDA   I think you've been doing things that you're ashamed of. That's why you act like this. I don't believe that you go every night to the movies. Nobody goes to the movies night after night. Nobody in their right minds goes to the movies as often as you pretend to. People don't go to the movies at nearly midnight, and movies don't let out at two A.M. Come in stumbling. Muttering to yourself like a maniac! You

get three hours' sleep and then go to work. Oh, I can picture the way you're doing down there. Moping, doping, because you're in no condition.

TOM (*wildly*)   No, I'm in no condition!

AMANDA   What right have you got to jeopardize your job? Jeopardize the security of us all? How do you think we'd manage if you were—

TOM   Listen! You think I'm crazy *about* the *warehouse*? (*He bends fiercely toward her slight figure*) You think I'm in love with the Continental Shoemakers? You think I want to spend fifty-five *years* down there in that—*celotex interior! with—fluorescent—tubes!* Look! I'd rather somebody picked up a crowbar and battered out my brains—than go back mornings! I *go*! Every time you come in yelling that goddamn "*Rise and Shine!*" "*Rise and Shine!*" I say to myself, "How *lucky dead* people are!" But I get up. I *go*! For sixty-five dollars a month I give up all that I dream of doing and being *ever*! And you say self—*self's* all I ever think of. Why listen, if self is what I thought of, Mother, I'd be where he is—GONE! (*pointing to father's picture*) As far as the system of transportation reaches! (*He starts past her. She grabs his arm*) Don't grab at me, Mother!

AMANDA   Where are you going?

TOM   I'm going to the *movies!*

AMANDA   I don't believe that lie!

TOM (*crouching toward her, overtowering her tiny figure. She backs away, gasping*)   I'm going to opium dens! Yes, opium dens, dens of vice and criminals' hang-outs, Mother. I've joined the Hogan gang, I'm a hired assassin, I carry a tommy-gun in a violin case! I run a string of cat-houses in the Valley! They call me Killer, Killer Wingfield, I'm leading a double-life: a simple, honest warehouse worker by day, by night a dynamic *czar* of the *underworld,* Mother. I go to gambling casinos, I spin away fortunes on the roulette table! I wear a patch over one eye and a false mustache; sometimes I put on green whiskers. On those occasions they call me—El Diablo! Oh, I could tell you things to make you sleepless! My enemies plan to dynamite this place. They're going to blow us all sky-high some night! I'll be glad, very happy, and so will you! You'll go up, up on a broomstick, over Blue Mountain with seventeen gentlemen callers! You ugly—babbling old—witch. . . . (*He goes through a series of violent, clumsy movements, seizing his overcoat, lunging to the door, pulling it fiercely open. The* WOMEN *watch him, aghast. His arm catches in the sleeve of the coat as he struggles*

to pull it on. For a moment he is pinioned by the bulky garment. With an outraged groan he tears the coat off again, splitting the shoulder of it, and hurls it across the room. It strikes against the shelf of* LAURA'S *glass collection, there is a tinkle of shattering glass.* LAURA *cries out as if wounded.* MUSIC. LEGEND: "THE GLASS MENAGERIE")

LAURA (*shrilly*)   My glass!—menagerie. . . . (*She covers her face and turns away. But* AMANDA *is still stunned and stupefied by the "ugly witch" so that she barely notices this occurrence. Now she recovers her speech*)

AMANDA (*in an awful voice*)   I won't speak to you—until you apologize! (*She crosses through portieres and draws them together behind her.* TOM *is left with* LAURA. LAURA *clings weakly to the mantel with her face averted.* TOM *stares at her stupidly for a moment. Then he crosses to shelf. Drops awkwardly on his knees to collect the fallen glass, glancing at* LAURA *as if he would speak but couldn't*)

"THE GLASS MENAGERIE" *steals in as*
THE SCENE DIMS OUT

Scene Four

(*The interior is dark. Faint light in the alley. A deep-voiced bell in a church is tolling the hour of five as the scene commences.* TOM *appears at the top of the alley. After each solemn boom of the bell in the tower, he shakes a little noise-maker or rattle as if to express the tiny spasm of man in contrast to the sustained power and dignity of the Almighty. This and the unsteadiness of his advance make it evident that he has been drinking.*

As he climbs the few steps to the fire-escape landing, light steals up inside. LAURA *appears in night-dress, observing* TOM'S *empty bed in the front room.*

TOM *fishes in his pockets for door key, removing a motley assortment of articles in the search, including a perfect shower of movie-ticket stubs and an empty bottle. At last he finds the key, but just as he is about to insert it, it slips from his fingers. He strikes a match and crouches below the door*)

TOM (*bitterly*)   One crack—and it falls through! (*LAURA opens the door*)

LAURA   Tom! Tom, what are you doing?

TOM   Looking for a door key.

LAURA   Where have you been all this time?

TOM   I have been to the movies.

LAURA All this time at the movies?

TOM There was a very long program. There was a Garbo picture and a Mickey Mouse and a travelogue and a newsreel and a preview of coming attractions. And there was an organ solo and a collection for the milk-fund—simultaneously—which ended up in a terrible fight between a fat lady and an usher!

LAURA (*innocently*) Did you have to stay through everything?

TOM Of course! And, oh, I forgot! There was a big stage show! The headliner on this stage show was Malvolio the Magician. He performed wonderful tricks, many of them, such as pouring water back and forth between pitchers. First it turned to wine and then it turned to beer and then it turned to whiskey. I know it was whiskey it finally turned into because he needed somebody to come up out of the audience to help him, and I came up— both shows! It was Kentucky Straight Bourbon. A very generous fellow, he gave souvenirs. (*He pulls from his back pocket a shimmering rainbow-colored scarf*) He gave me this. This is his magic scarf. You can have it, Laura. You wave it over a canary cage and you get a bowl of goldfish. You wave it over the goldfish bowl and they fly away canaries. . . . But the wonderfullest trick of all was the coffin trick. We nailed him into a coffin and he got out of the coffin without removing one nail. (*He has come inside*) There is a trick that would come in handy for me—get me out of this 2 by 4 situation! (*flops onto bed and starts removing shoes*)

LAURA Tom—Shhh!

TOM What are you shushing me for?

LAURA You'll wake up Mother.

TOM Goody, goody! Pay 'er back for all those "Rise and Shines." (*lies down, groaning*) You know it don't take much intelligence to get yourself into a nailed-up coffin, Laura. But who in hell ever got himself out of one without removing one nail? (*As if in answer, the father's grinning photograph lights up*)

SCENE DIMS OUT

(*Immediately following: The church bell is heard striking six. At the sixth stroke the alarm clock goes off in* AMANDA's *room, and after a few moments we hear her calling: "Rise and Shine! Rise and Shine! Laura, go tell your brother to rise and shine!"*)

TOM (*sitting up slowly*) I'll rise—but I won't shine. (*The light increases*)

AMANDA Laura, tell your brother his coffee is ready. (LAURA *slips into front room*)

LAURA Tom!—It's nearly seven. Don't make Mother nervous. (*He stares at her stupidly. Beseechingly*) Tom, speak to Mother this morning. Make up with her, apologize, speak to her!

TOM She won't to me. It's her that started not speaking.

LAURA If you just say you're sorry she'll start speaking.

TOM Her not speaking—is that such a tragedy?

LAURA Please—please!

AMANDA (*calling from kitchenette*) Laura, are you going to do what I asked you to do, or do I have to get dressed and go out myself?

LAURA Going, going—soon as I get on my coat! (*She pulls on a shapeless felt hat with nervous, jerky movement, pleadingly glancing at* TOM. *Rushes awkwardly for coat. The coat is one of* AMANDA's, *inaccurately made over, the sleeves too short for* LAURA) Butter and what else?

AMANDA (*entering upstage*) Just butter. Tell them to charge it.

LAURA Mother, they make such faces when I do that.

AMANDA Sticks and stones can break our bones, but the expression on Mr. Garfinkel's face won't harm us! Tell your brother his coffee is getting cold.

LAURA (*at door*) Do what I asked you, will you, will you, Tom? (*He looks sullenly away*)

AMANDA Laura, go now or just don't go at all!

LAURA (*rushing out*) Going—going! (*A second later she cries out.* TOM *springs up and crosses to door.* AMANDA *rushes anxiously in.* TOM *opens the door*)

TOM Laura?

LAURA I'm all right. I slipped, but I'm all right.

AMANDA (*peering anxiously after her*) If anyone breaks a leg on those fire-escape steps, the landlord ought to be sued for every cent he possesses!

(*She shuts door. Remembers she isn't speaking and returns to other room. As* TOM *enters listlessly for his coffee, she turns her back to him and stands rigidly facing the window on the gloomy gray vault of the areaway. Its light on her face with its aged but childish features is cruelly sharp, satirical as a Daumier print.* MUSIC UNDER: "AVE MARIA." TOM *glances sheepishly but sullenly at her averted figure and slumps at the table. The coffee is scalding hot; he sips it and gasps and spits it back in the cup. At his gasp,* AMANDA *catches her breath and half turns. Then catches herself and turns back to window.* TOM *blows on his coffee, glancing sidewise at his mother. She clears her throat.* TOM *clears his. He starts to rise. Sinks back down again, scratches his head, clears his throat again.* AMANDA *coughs.* TOM *raises his cup in both hands to blow on it, his eyes staring over the rim of it at his mother for several moments. Then he slowly sets the cup down and awkwardly and hesitantly rises from the chair)*

TOM (*hoarsely*) Mother. I—I apologize, Mother. (AMANDA *draws a quick, shuddering breath. Her face works grotesquely. She breaks into childlike tears)* I'm sorry for what I said, for everything that I said, I didn't mean it.

AMANDA (*sobbingly*) My devotion has made me a witch and so I make myself hateful to my children!

TOM *No,* you *don't.*

AMANDA I worry so much, don't sleep, it makes me nervous!

TOM (*gently*) I understand that.

AMANDA I've had to put up a solitary battle all these years. But you're my right-hand bower! Don't fall down, don't fail!

TOM (*gently*) I'll try, Mother.

AMANDA (*with great enthusiasm*) Try and you will SUCCEED! (*The notion makes her breathless*) Why, you—you're just *full* of natural endowments! Both of my children—they're *unusual* children! Don't you think I know it? I'm so—*proud!* Happy and—feel I've —so much to be thankful for but——Promise me one thing, Son!

TOM What, Mother?

AMANDA Promise, Son, you'll—never be a drunkard!

TOM (*turns to her, grinning*) I will never be a drunkard, Mother.

AMANDA That's what frightened me so, that you'd be drinking! Eat a bowl of Purina!

TOM Just coffee, Mother.

AMANDA Shredded wheat biscuit?

TOM No. No, Mother, just coffee.

AMANDA You can't put in a day's work on an empty stomach. You've got ten minutes—don't gulp! Drinking too-hot liquids makes cancer of the stomach. . . . Put cream in.

TOM No, thank you.

AMANDA To cool it.

TOM No! No, thank you, I want it black.

AMANDA I know, but it's not good for you. We have to do all that we can to build our-selves up. In these trying times we live in, all that we have to cling to is—each other. . . . That's why it's so important to—Tom, I—I

sent out your sister so I could discuss some-thing with you. If you hadn't spoken I would have spoken to you. (*sits down*)

TOM (*gently*) What is it, Mother, that you want to discuss?

AMANDA *Laura!* (TOM *puts his cup down slowly,* LEGEND ON SCREEN: "LAURA." MUSIC: "THE GLASS MENAGERIE")

TOM —Oh.—Laura . . .

AMANDA (*touching his sleeve*) You know how Laura is. So quiet but—still water runs deep! She notices things and I think she—broods about them. (TOM *looks up*) A few days ago I came in and she was crying.

TOM What about?

AMANDA You.

TOM Me?

AMANDA She has an idea that you're not happy here.

TOM What gave her that idea?

AMANDA What gives her any idea? How-ever, you do act strangely. I—I'm not criticiz-ing, understand *that!* I know your ambitions do not lie in the warehouse, that like every-body in the whole wide world—you've had to —make sacrifices, but—Tom—Tom—life's not easy, it calls for—Spartan endurance! There's so many things in my heart that I cannot de-scribe to you! I've never told you but I—*loved* your father. . . .

TOM (*gently*) I know that, Mother.

AMANDA And you—when I see you taking after his ways! Staying out late—and—well, you *had* been drinking the night you were in that—terrifying condition! Laura says that you hate the apartment and that you go out nights to get away from it! Is that true, Tom?

TOM No. You say there's so much in your heart that you can't describe to me. That's true of me, too. There's so much in my heart that I can't describe to *you!* So let's respect each other's—

AMANDA But, why—*why,* Tom—are you always so *restless?* Where do you *go* to, nights?

TOM I—go to the movies.

AMANDA Why do you go to the movies so much, Tom?

TOM I go to the movies because—I like adventure. Adventure is something I don't have much of at work, so I go to the movies.

AMANDA But, Tom, you go to the movies *entirely* too much!

TOM I like a lot of adventure. (AMANDA *looks baffled, then hurt. As the familiar inquisi-tion resumes he becomes hard and impatient again.* AMANDA *slips back into her querulous attitude toward him.* IMAGE ON SCREEN: SAIL-ING VESSEL WITH JOLLY ROGER)

AMANDA   Most young men find adventure in their careers.

TOM   Then most young men are not employed in a warehouse.

AMANDA   The world is full of young men employed in warehouses and offices and factories.

TOM   Do all of them find adventure in their careers?

AMANDA   They do or they do without it! Not everybody has a craze for adventure.

TOM   Man is by instinct a lover, a hunter, a fighter, and none of those instincts are given much play at the warehouse!

AMANDA   Man is by instinct! Don't quote instinct to me! Instinct is something that people have got away from! It belongs to animals! Christian adults don't want it!

TOM   What do Christian adults want, then, Mother?

AMANDA   Superior things! Things of the mind and the spirit! Only animals have to satisfy instincts! Surely your aims are somewhat higher than theirs! Than monkeys— pigs—

TOM   I reckon they're not.

AMANDA   You're joking. However, that isn't what I wanted to discuss.

TOM   (*rising*)   I haven't much time.

AMANDA   (*pushing his shoulders*)   Sit down.

TOM   You want me to punch in red at the warehouse, Mother?

AMANDA   You have five minutes. I want to talk about Laura.

(LEGEND: "PLANS AND PROVISIONS")

TOM   All right! What about Laura?

AMANDA   We have to be making some plans and provisions for her. She's older than you, two years, and nothing has happened. She just drifts along doing nothing. It frightens me terribly how she just drifts along.

TOM   I guess she's the type that people call home girls.

AMANDA   There's no such type, and if there is, it's a pity! That is unless the home is hers, with a husband!

TOM   What?

AMANDA   Oh, I can see the handwriting on the wall as plain as I see the nose in front of of my face! It's terrifying!

More and more you remind me of your father! He was out all hours without explanation!—Then *left!* Good-bye!

And me with the bag to hold. I saw that letter you got from the Merchant Marine. I know what you're dreaming of. I'm not standing here blindfolded.

Very well, then. Then *do* it!

But not till there's somebody to take your place.

TOM   What do you mean?

AMANDA   I mean that as soon as Laura has got somebody to take care of her, married, a home of her own, independent—why, then you'll be free to go wherever you please, on land, on sea, whichever way the wind blows you!

But until that time you've got to look out for your sister. I don't say me because I'm old and don't matter! I say for your sister because she's young and dependent.

I put her in business college—a dismal failure! Frightened her so it made her sick at the stomach.

I took her over to the Young People's League at the church. Another fiasco. She spoke to nobody, nobody spoke to her. Now all she does is fool with those pieces of glass and play those worn-out records. What kind of a life is that for a girl to lead?

TOM   What can I do about it?

AMANDA   Overcome selfishness!

Self, self, self is all that you ever think of! (TOM *springs up and crosses to get his coat. It is ugly and bulky. He pulls on a cap with earmuffs*) Where is your muffler? Put your wool muffler on! (*He snatches it angrily from the closet and tosses it around his neck and pulls both ends tight*) Tom! I haven't said what I had in mind to ask you.

TOM   I'm too late to—

AMANDA   (*catching his arm—very importunately. Then shyly*)   Down at the warehouse, aren't there some—nice young men?

TOM   No!

AMANDA   There *must* be—*some* . . .

TOM   Mother—(*gesture*)

AMANDA   Find out one that's clean-living —doesn't drink and—ask him out for sister!

TOM   What?

AMANDA   For *sister!* To *meet!* Get acquainted!

TOM   (*stamping to door*)   Oh, my go-osh!

AMANDA   Will you? (*He opens door. Imploringly*) Will you? (*He starts down*) Will you? *Will* you, dear?

TOM   (*calling back*)   YES!

(AMANDA *closes the door hesitantly and with a troubled but faintly hopeful expression.* SCREEN IMAGE: GLAMOR MAGAZINE COVER. *Spot* AMANDA *at phone*)

AMANDA   Ella Cartwright? This is Amanda Wingfield!

How are you, honey?

How is the kidney condition? (*count five*) *Horrors!* (*count five*)

You're a Christian martyr, yes, honey, that's what you are, a Christian martyr!

Well, I just now happened to notice in my little red book that your subscription to the *Companion* has just run out! I knew that you wouldn't want to miss out on the wonderful serial starting in this new issue. It's by Bessie Mae Hopper, the first thing she's written since *Honeymoon for Three.*

Wasn't that a strange and interesting story? Well, this one is even lovelier, I believe. It has a sophisticated, society background. It's all about the horsey set on Long Island!

FADE OUT

Scene Five

(LEGEND ON SCREEN: "ANNUNCIATION." *Fade with music.*

It is early dusk of a spring evening. Supper has just been finished in the Wingfield apartment. AMANDA *and* LAURA *in light-colored dresses are removing dishes from the table, in the upstage area, which is shadowy, their movements formalized almost as a dance or ritual, their moving forms as pale and silent as moths.*

TOM, *in white shirt and trousers, rises from the table and crosses toward the fire escape*)

AMANDA (*as he passes her*) Son, will you do me a favor?

TOM What?

AMANDA Comb your hair! You look so pretty when your hair is combed! (TOM *slouches on sofa with evening paper.* ENORMOUS CAPTION: "FRANCO TRIUMPHS") There is only one respect in which I would like you to emulate your father.

TOM What respect is that?

AMANDA The care he always took of his appearance. He never allowed himself to look untidy. (*He throws down the paper and crosses to fire escape*) Where are you going?

TOM I'm going out to smoke.

AMANDA You smoke too much. A pack a day at fifteen cents a pack. How much would that amount to in a month? Thirty times fifteen is how much, Tom? Figure it out and you will be astounded at what you could save. Enough to give you a night-school course in accounting at Washington U! Just think what a wonder-

ful thing that would be for you, Son! (TOM *is unmoved by the thought*)

TOM I'd rather smoke. (*He steps out on landing, letting the screen door slam*)

AMANDA (*sharply*) I know! That's the tragedy of it. . . . (*Alone, she turns to look at her husband's picture.* DANCE MUSIC: "ALL THE WORLD IS WAITING FOR THE SUNRISE!")

TOM (*to the audience*) Across the alley from us was the Paradise Dance Hall. On evenings in spring the windows and doors were open and the music came outdoors. Sometimes the lights were turned out except for a large glass sphere that hung from the ceiling. It would turn slowly about and filter the dusk with delicate rainbow colors. Then the orchestra played a waltz or a tango, something that had a slow and sensuous rhythm. Couples would come outside, to the relative privacy of the alley. You could see them kissing behind ash-pits and telephone poles.

This was the compensation for lives that passed like mine, without any change or adventure.

Adventure and change were imminent in this year. They were waiting around the corner for all these kids.

Suspended in the mist over Berchtesgaden, caught in the folds of Chamberlain's umbrella—

In Spain there was Guernica!

But here there was only hot swing music and liquor, dance halls, bars, and movies, and sex that hung in the gloom like a chandelier and flooded the world with brief, deceptive rainbows. . . .

All the world was waiting for bombardments!

(AMANDA *turns from the picture and comes outside*)

AMANDA (*sighing*) A fire-escape landing's a poor excuse for a porch. (*She spreads a newspaper on a step and sits down, gracefully and demurely as if she were settling into a swing on a Mississippi veranda*) What are you looking at?

TOM The moon.

AMANDA Is there a moon this evening?

TOM It's rising over Garfinkel's Delicatessen.

AMANDA So it is! A little silver slipper of a moon. Have you made a wish on it yet?

TOM Um-hum.

AMANDA What did you wish for?

TOM That's a secret.

AMANDA A secret, huh? Well, I won't tell mine either. I will be just as mysterious as you.

TOM   I bet I can guess what yours is.

AMANDA   Is my head so transparent?

TOM   You're not a sphinx.

AMANDA   No, I don't have secrets. I'll tell you what I wished for on the moon. Success and happiness for my precious children! I wish for that whenever there's a moon, and when there isn't a moon, I wish for it, too.

TOM   I thought perhaps you wished for a gentleman caller.

AMANDA   Why do you say that?

TOM   Don't you remember asking me to fetch one?

AMANDA   I remember suggesting that it would be nice for your sister if you brought home some nice young man from the warehouse. I think that I've made that suggestion more than once.

TOM   Yes, you have made it repeatedly.

AMANDA   Well?

TOM   We are going to have one.

AMANDA   *What?*

TOM   A gentleman caller! (*The annunciation is celebrated with music.* AMANDA *rises.* IMAGE ON SCREEN: CALLER WITH BOUQUET)

AMANDA   You mean you have asked some nice young man to come over?

TOM   Yep. I've asked him to dinner.

AMANDA   You really did?

TOM   I did!

AMANDA   You did, and did he—*accept?*

TOM   He did!

AMANDA   Well, well—well, well! That's —lovely!

TOM   I thought that you would be pleased.

AMANDA   It's definite, then?

TOM   Very definite.

AMANDA   Soon?

TOM   Very soon.

AMANDA   For heaven's sake, stop putting on and tell me some things, will you?

TOM   What things do you want me to tell you?

AMANDA   *Naturally* I would like to know when he's *coming!*

TOM   He's coming tomorrow.

AMANDA   *Tomorrow?*

TOM   Yep. Tomorrow.

AMANDA   But, Tom!

TOM   Yes, Mother?

AMANDA   Tomorrow gives me no time!

TOM   Time for what?

AMANDA   Preparations! Why didn't you phone me at once, as soon as you asked him, the minute that he accepted? Then, don't you see, I could have been getting ready!

TOM   You don't have to make any fuss.

AMANDA   Oh, Tom, Tom, Tom, of course I have to make a fuss! I want things nice, not sloppy! Not thrown together. I'll certainly have to do some fast thinking, won't I?

TOM   I don't see why you have to think at all.

AMANDA   You just don't know. We can't have a gentleman caller in a pig-sty! All my wedding silver has to be polished, monogrammed table linen ought to be laundered! The windows have to be washed and fresh curtains put up. And how about clothes? We have to *wear* something, don't we?

TOM   Mother, this boy is no one to make a fuss over!

AMANDA   Do you realize he's the first young man we've introduced to your sister?

It's terrible, dreadful, disgraceful that poor little sister has never received a single gentleman caller! Tom, come inside! (*She opens the screen door*)

TOM   What for?

AMANDA   I want to ask you some things.

TOM   If you're going to make such a fuss, I'll call it off, I'll tell him not to come!

AMANDA   You certainly won't do anything of the kind. Nothing offends people worse than broken engagements. It simply means I'll have to work like a Turk! We won't be brilliant, but we will pass inspection. Come on inside. (TOM *follows, groaning*) Sit down.

TOM   Any particular place you would like me to sit?

AMANDA   Thank heavens I've got that new sofa! I'm also making payments on a floor lamp I'll have sent out! And put the chintz covers on, they'll brighten things up! Of course I'd hoped to have these walls repapered. . . . What is the young man's name?

TOM   His name is O'Connor.

AMANDA   That, of course, means fish—tomorrow is Friday! I'll have that salmon loaf— with Durkee's dressing! What does he do? He works at the warehouse?

TOM   Of course! How else would I—

AMANDA   Tom, he—doesn't drink?

TOM   Why do you ask me that?

AMANDA   Your father *did!*

TOM   Don't get started on that!

AMANDA   He *does* drink, then?

TOM   Not that I know of!

AMANDA   Make sure, be certain! The last thing I want for my daughter's a boy who drinks!

TOM   Aren't you being a little premature? Mr. O'Connor has not yet appeared on the scene!

AMANDA   But will tomorrow. To meet your sister, and what do I know about his character? Nothing! Old maids are better off than wives of drunkards!

TOM   Oh, my God!

AMANDA   Be still!

TOM   (*leaning forward to whisper*)   Lots of fellows meet girls whom they don't marry!

AMANDA   Oh, talk sensibly, Tom—and don't be sarcastic! (*She has gotten a hairbrush*)

TOM   What are you doing?

AMANDA   I'm brushing that cow-lick down! What is this young man's position at the warehouse?

TOM   (*submitting grimly to the brush and the interrogation*)   This young man's position is that of a shipping clerk, Mother.

AMANDA   Sounds to me like a fairly responsible job, the sort of a job *you* would be in if you just had more *get-up*.

What is his salary? Have you any idea?

TOM   I would judge it to be approximately eighty-five dollars a month.

AMANDA   Well—not princely, but——

TOM   Twenty more than I make.

AMANDA   Yes, how well I know! But for a family man, eighty-five dollars a month is not much more than you can just get by on. . . .

TOM   Yes, but Mr. O'Connor is not a family man.

AMANDA   He might be, mightn't he? Some time in the future?

TOM   I see. Plans and provisions.

AMANDA   You are the only young man that I know of who ignores the fact that the future becomes the present, the present the past, and the past turns into everlasting regret if you don't plan for it!

TOM   I will think that over and see what I can make of it.

AMANDA   Don't be supercilious with your mother! Tell me some more about this—what do you call him?

TOM   James D. O'Connor. The D. is for Delaney.

AMANDA   Irish on *both* sides! *Gracious!* And doesn't drink?

TOM   Shall I call him up and ask him right this minute?

AMANDA   The only way to find out about those things is to make discreet inquiries at the proper moment. When I was a girl in Blue Mountain and it was suspected that a young man drank, the girl whose attentions he had been receiving, if any girl *was*, would sometimes speak to the minister of his church, or rather her father would if her father was living, and sort of feel him out on the young man's character. That is the way such things are dis-

creetly handled to keep a young woman from making a tragic mistake!

TOM   Then how did you happen to make a tragic mistake?

AMANDA   That innocent look of your father's had everyone fooled!

He *smiled*—the world was *enchanted!*

No girl can do worse than put herself at the mercy of a handsome appearance!

I hope that Mr. O'Connor is not too good-looking.

TOM   No, he's not too good-looking. He's covered with freckles and hasn't too much of a nose.

AMANDA   He's not right-down homely, though?

TOM   Not right-down homely. Just medium homely, I'd say.

AMANDA   Character's what to look for in a man.

TOM   That's what I've always said, Mother.

AMANDA   You've never said anything of the kind and I suspect you would never give it a thought.

TOM   Don't be so suspicious of me.

AMANDA   At least I hope he's the type that's up and coming.

TOM   I think he really goes in for self-improvement.

AMANDA   What reason have you to think so?

TOM   He goes to night school.

AMANDA   (*beaming*)   Splendid! What does he do, I mean study?

TOM   Radio engineering and public speaking!

AMANDA   Then he has visions of being advanced in the world!

Any young man who studies public speaking is aiming to have an executive job some day!

And radio engineering? A thing for the future!

Both of these facts are very illuminating. Those are the sort of things that a mother should know concerning any young man who comes to call on her daughter. Seriously or—not.

TOM   One little warning. He doesn't know about Laura, I didn't let on that we had dark ulterior motives. I just said, why don't you come and have dinner with us? He said okay and that was the whole conversation.

AMANDA   I bet it was! You're eloquent as an oyster.

However, he'll know about Laura when he gets here. When he sees how lovely and sweet and pretty she is, he'll thank his lucky stars he was asked to dinner.

TOM   Mother, you musn't expect too much of Laura.

AMANDA   What do you mean?

TOM   Laura seems all those things to you and me because she's ours and we love her. We don't even notice she's crippled any more.

AMANDA   Don't say crippled! You know that I never allow that word to be used!

TOM   But face facts, Mother. She is and— that's not all——

AMANDA   What do you mean "not all"?

TOM   Laura is very different from other girls.

AMANDA   I think the difference is all to her advantage.

TOM   Not quite all—in the eyes of others— stranger's—she's terribly shy and lives in a world of her own and those things make her seem a little peculiar to people outside the house.

AMANDA   Don't say peculiar.

TOM   Face the facts. She is.

(THE DANCE-HALL MUSIC CHANGES TO A TANGO THAT HAS A MINOR AND SOMEWHAT OMINOUS TONE)

AMANDA   In what way is she peculiar—may I ask?

TOM   (*gently*)   She lives in a world of her own—a world of—little glass ornaments, Mother. . . . (*Gets up.* AMANDA *remains holding brush, looking at him, troubled*) She plays old phonograph records and—that's about all——(*He glances at himself in the mirror and crosses to door*)

AMANDA   (*sharply*)   Where are you going?

TOM   I'm going to the movies. (*out screen door*)

AMANDA   Not to the movies, every night to the movies! (*follows quickly to screen door*) I don't believe you always go to the movies! (*He is gone.* AMANDA *looks worriedly after him for a moment. Then vitality and optimism return and she turns from the door. Crossing to portieres*) Laura! Laura! (LAURA *answers from kitchenette*)

LAURA   Yes, Mother.

AMANDA   Let those dishes go and come in front! (LAURA *appears with dish towel. Gaily*) Laura, come here and make a wish on the moon! (SCREEN IMAGE: MOON)

LAURA   (*entering*)   Moon—moon?

AMANDA   A little silver slipper of a moon. Look over your left shoulder, Laura, and make a wish! (LAURA *looks faintly puzzled as if called out of sleep.* AMANDA *seizes her shoulders and turns her at an angle by the door*)

Now!
Now, darling, *wish!*

LAURA   What shall I wish for, Mother?

AMANDA   (*her voice trembling and her eyes suddenly filling with tears*)   Happiness! Good fortune! (*The violin rises and the stage dims out*)

Scene Six

(IMAGE: HIGH-SCHOOL HERO)

TOM   And so the following evening I brought Jim home to dinner. I had known Jim slightly in high school. In high school Jim was a hero. He had tremendous Irish good nature and vitality with the scrubbed and polished look of white chinaware. He seemed to move in a continual spotlight. He was a star in basketball, captain of the debating club, president of the senior class and the glee club and he sang the male lead in the annual light operas. He was always running or bounding, never just walking. He seemed always at the point of defeating the law of gravity. He was shooting with such velocity through his adolescence that you would logically expect him to arrive at nothing short of the White House by the time he was thirty. But Jim apparently ran into more interference after his graduation from Soldan. His speed had definitely slowed. Six years after he left high school he was holding a job that wasn't much better than mine.

(IMAGE: CLERK)

He was the only one at the warehouse with whom I was on friendly terms. I was valuable to him as someone who could remember his former glory, who had seen him win basketball games and the silver cup in debating. He knew of my secret practice of retiring to a cabinet of the washroom to work on poems when business was slack in the warehouse. He called me Shakespeare. And while the other boys in the warehouse regarded me with suspicious hostility, Jim took a humorous attitude toward me. Gradually his attitude affected the others; their hostility wore off and they also began to smile at me as people smile at an oddly fashioned dog who trots across their path at some distance.

I knew that Jim and Laura had known each other at Soldan, and I had heard Laura speak admiringly of his voice. I didn't know if Jim remembered her or not. In high school Laura had been as unobtrusive as Jim had been astonishing. If he did remember Laura, it was not as my sister, for when I asked him to dinner, he grinned and said, "You know, Shakespeare, I never thought of you as having folks!"

He was about to discover that I did. . . .

(LIGHT UP STAGE. LEGEND ON SCREEN: "THE ACCENT OF A COMING FOOT." *Friday evening. It is about five o'clock of a late spring evening which comes "scattering poems in the sky." A delicate lemony light is in the Wingfield apartment.* AMANDA *has worked like a Turk in preparation for the gentleman caller. The results are astonishing. The new floor lamp with its rose-silk shade is in place, a colored paper lantern conceals the broken light fixture in the ceiling, new billowing white curtains are at the windows, chintz covers are on chairs and sofa, a pair of new sofa pillows make their initial appearance. Open boxes and tissue paper are scattered on the floor.* LAURA *stands in the middle with lifted arms while* AMANDA *crouches before her, adjusting the hem of the new dress, devout and ritualistic. The dress is colored and designed by memory. The arrangement of* LAURA's *hair is changed; it is softer and more becoming. A fragile, unearthly prettiness has come out in* LAURA: *she is like a piece of translucent glass touched by light, given a momentary radiance, not actual, not lasting)*

AMANDA (*impatiently*) Why are you trembling?

LAURA Mother, you've made me so nervous!

AMANDA How have I made you nervous?

LAURA By all this fuss! You make it seem so important!

AMANDA I don't understand you, Laura. You couldn't be satisfied with just sitting home, and yet whenever I try to arrange something for you, you seem to resist it. (*She gets up*)

Now take a look at yourself.

No, wait! Wait just a moment—I have an idea!

LAURA What is it now? (AMANDA *produces two powder puffs which she wraps in handkerchiefs and stuffs in* LAURA's *bosom*)

LAURA Mother, what are you doing?

AMANDA They call them "Gay Deceivers"!

LAURA I won't wear them!

AMANDA You will!

LAURA Why should I?

AMANDA Because, to be painfully honest, your chest is flat.

LAURA You make it seem like we were setting a trap.

AMANDA All pretty girls are a trap, a pretty trap, and men expect them to be. (LEGEND: "A PRETTY TRAP")

Now look at yourself, young lady. This is the prettiest you will ever be!

I've got to fix myself now! You're going to be surprised by your mother's appearance!

(*She crosses through portieres, humming gaily.* LAURA *moves slowly to the long mirror and stares solemnly at herself. A wind blows the white curtains inward in a slow, graceful motion and with a faint, sorrowful sighing*)

AMANDA (*offstage*) It isn't dark enough yet. (LAURA *turns slowly before the mirror with a troubled look.* LEGEND ON SCREEN: "THIS IS MY SISTER: CELEBRATE HER WITH STRINGS!" MUSIC)

AMANDA (*laughing, off*) I'm going to show you something. I'm going to make a spectacular appearance!

LAURA What is it, Mother?

AMANDA Possess your soul in patience—you will see!

Something I've resurrected from that old trunk! Styles haven't changed so terribly much after all. . . . (*She parts the portieres*)

Now just look at your mother! (*She wears a girlish frock of yellowed voile with a blue silk sash. She carries a bunch of jonquils—the legend of her youth is nearly revived. Feverishly*)

This is the dress in which I led the cotillion. Won the cakewalk twice at Sunset Hill, wore one spring to the Governor's ball in Jackson!

See how I sashayed around the ballroom, Laura? (*She raises her skirt and does a mincing step around the room*)

I wore it on Sundays for my gentlemen callers! I had it on the day I met your father——

I had malaria fever all that spring. The change of climate from East Tennessee to the Delta—weakened resistance—I had a little temperature all the time—not enough to be serious—just enough to make me restless and giddy!—Invitations poured in—parties all over the Delta!—"Stay in bed," said Mother, "you have fever!"—but I just wouldn't.—I took quinine but kept on going, going!—Evenings, dances!—Afternoons, long, long rides! Picnics—lovely!—So lovely, that country in May.—All lacy with dogwood, literally flooded with jonquils!—That was the spring I had the craze for jonquils. Jonquils became an absolute obsession. Mother said, "Honey, there's no more room for jonquils." And still I kept on bringing in more jonquils. Whenever, wherever I saw them, I'd say, "Stop! Stop! I see jonquils!" I made the young men help me gather the jonquils! It was a joke, Amanda and her jonquils!

Finally there were no more vases to hold them; every available space was filled with jonquils. No vases to hold them? All right, I'll hold them myself! And then I——(*She stops in front of the picture.* MUSIC) met your father!

Malaria fever and jonquils and then—this—boy. . . . (*She switches on the rose-colored lamp*)

I hope they get here before it starts to rain. (*She crosses upstage and places the jonquils in bowl on table*)

I gave your brother a little extra change so he and Mr. O'Connor could take the service car home.

LAURA (*with altered look*)   What did you say his name was?

AMANDA   O'Connor.

LAURA   What is his first name?

AMANDA   I don't remember. Oh, yes, I do. It was—Jim. (LAURA *sways slightly and catches hold of a chair.* LEGEND ON SCREEN: "NOT JIM!")

LAURA (*faintly*).   Not—Jim!

AMANDA   Yes, that was it, it was Jim! I've never known a Jim that wasn't nice! (MUSIC: OMINOUS)

LAURA   Are you sure his name is Jim O'Connor?

AMANDA   Yes. Why?

LAURA   Is he the one that Tom used to know in high school?

AMANDA   He didn't say so. I think he just got to know him at the warehouse.

LAURA   There was a Jim O'Connor we both knew in high school——(*then, with effort*) If that is the one that Tom is bringing to dinner—you'll have to excuse me, I won't come to the table.

AMANDA   What sort of nonsense is this?

LAURA   You asked me once if I'd ever liked a boy. Don't you remember I showed you this boy's picture?

AMANDA   You mean the boy you showed me in the year book?

LAURA   Yes, that boy.

AMANDA   Laura, Laura, were you in love with that boy?

LAURA   I don't know, Mother. All I know is I couldn't sit at the table if it was him!

AMANDA   It won't be him! It isn't the least bit likely. But whether it is or not, you will come to the table. You will not be excused.

LAURA   I'll have to be, Mother.

AMANDA   I don't intend to humor your silliness, Laura. I've had too much from you and your brother, both!

So just sit down and compose yourself till they come. Tom has forgotten his key so you'll have to let them in, when they arrive.

LAURA (*panicky*)   Oh, Mother—*you* answer the door!

AMANDA (*lightly*)   I'll be in the kitchen—busy!

LAURA   Oh, Mother, please answer the door, don't make me do it!

AMANDA (*crossing into kitchenette*)   I've got to fix the dressing for the salmon. Fuss, fuss—silliness!—over a gentleman caller!

(*Door swings shut.* LAURA *is left alone.* LEGEND: "TERROR!" *She utters a low moan and turns off the lamp—sits stiffly on the edge of the sofa, knotting her fingers together.* LEGEND ON SCREEN: "THE OPENING OF A DOOR!" TOM *and* JIM *appear on the fire-escape steps and climb to landing. Hearing their approach,* LAURA *rises with a panicky gesture. She retreats to the portieres. The doorbell.* LAURA *catches her breath and touches her throat. Low drums*)

AMANDA (*calling*)   Laura, sweetheart! the door! (LAURA *stares at it without moving*)

JIM   I think we just beat the rain.

TOM   Uh-huh. (*He rings again, nervously.* JIM *whistles and fishes for a cigarette*)

AMANDA (*very, very gaily*)   Laura, that is your brother and Mr. O'Connor! Will you let them in, darling? (LAURA *crosses toward kitchenette door*)

LAURA (*breathlessly*)   Mother—you go to the door! (AMANDA *steps out of kitchenette and stares furiously at* LAURA. *She points imperiously at the door*)

LAURA   Please, please!

AMANDA (*in a fierce whisper*)   What is the matter with you, you silly thing?

LAURA (*desperately*)   Please, you answer it, *please!*

AMANDA   I told you I wasn't going to humor you, Laura. Why have you chosen this moment to lose your mind?

LAURA   Please, please, please, you go!

AMANDA   You'll have to go to the door because I can't!

LAURA (*despairingly*)   I can't either!

AMANDA   *Why?*

LAURA   I'm *sick!*

AMANDA   I'm sick, too—of your nonsense! Why can't you and your brother be normal people? Fantastic whims and behavior! (TOM *gives a long ring*)

Preposterous goings on! Can you give me one reason—(*calls out lyrically*) COMING! JUST ONE SECOND!—why you should be afraid to open a door? Now you answer it, Laura!

LAURA   Oh, oh, oh . . . (*She returns through the portieres. Darts to the victrola and winds it frantically and turns it on*)

AMANDA   Laura Wingfield, you march right to that door!

LAURA   Yes—yes, Mother! (*A faraway, scratchy rendition of "Dardanella" softens the air and gives her strength to move through it. She slips to the door and draws it cautiously open.* TOM *enters with the caller,* JIM O'CONNOR)

TOM   Laura, this is Jim. Jim, this is my sister, Laura.

JIM   (*stepping inside*)   I didn't know that Shakespeare had a sister!

LAURA   (*retreating stiff and trembling from the door*)   How—how do you do?

JIM   (*heartily extending his hand*)   Okay! (LAURA *touches it hesitantly with hers*)

JIM   Your hand's *cold*, Laura!

LAURA   Yes, well—I've been playing the victrola. . . .

JIM   Must have been playing classical music on it! You ought to play a little hot swing music to warm you up!

LAURA   Excuse me—I haven't finished playing the victrola. . . . (*She turns awkwardly and hurries into the front room. She pauses a second by the victrola. Then catches her breath and darts through the portieres like a frightened deer*)

JIM   (*grinning*)   What was the matter?

TOM   Oh—with Laura? Laura is—terribly shy.

JIM   Shy, huh? It's unusual to meet a shy girl nowadays. I don't believe you ever mentioned you had a sister.

TOM   Well, now you know. I have one. Here is the *Post Dispatch*. You want a piece of it?

JIM   Uh-huh.

TOM   What piece? The comics?

JIM   Sports! (*glances at it*) Ole Dizzy Dean is on his bad behavior.

TOM   (*disinterested*)   Yeah? (*lights cigarette and crosses back to fire-escape door*)

JIM   Where are *you* going?

TOM   I'm going out on the terrace.

JIM   (*goes after him*)   You know, Shakespeare—I'm going to sell you a bill of goods!

TOM   What goods!

JIM   A course I'm taking.

TOM   Huh?

JIM   In public speaking! You and me, we're not the warehouse type.

TOM   Thanks—that's good news.

But what has public speaking got to do with it?

JIM   It fits you for—executive positions!

TOM   Awww.

JIM   I tell you it's done a helluva lot for me. (IMAGE: EXECUTIVE AT DESK)

TOM   In what respect?

JIM   In every! Ask yourself what is the difference between you an' me and men in the office down front? Brains?—No!—Ability?—No! Then what? Just one little thing—.

TOM   What is that one little thing?

JIM   Primarily it amounts to—social poise! Being able to square up to people and hold your own on any social level!

AMANDA   (*offstage*)   Tom?

TOM   Yes, Mother?

AMANDA   Is that you and Mr. O'Connor?

TOM   Yes, Mother?

AMANDA   Well, you just make yourselves comfortable in there.

TOM   Yes, Mother.

AMANDA   Ask Mr. O'Connor if he would like to wash his hands.

JIM   Aw, no—no—thank you—I took care of that at the warehouse. Tom—

TOM   Yes?

JIM   Mr. Mendoza was speaking to me about you.

TOM   Favorably?

JIM   What do you think?

TOM   Well—

JIM   You're going to be out of a job if you don't wake up.

TOM   I am waking up—

JIM   You show no signs.

TOM   The signs are interior. (IMAGE ON SCREEN: THE SAILING VESSEL WITH JOLLY ROGER AGAIN) I'm planning to change. (*He leans over the rail speaking with quiet exhilaration. The incandescent marquees and signs of the first-run movie houses light his face from across the alley. He looks like a voyager*) I'm right at the point of committing myself to a future that doesn't include the warehouse and Mr. Mendoza or even a night-school course in public speaking.

JIM   What are you gassing about?

TOM   I'm tired of the movies.

JIM   Movies!

TOM   Yes, movies! Look at them—(*a wave toward the marvels of Grand Avenue*) All of those glamorous people—having adventures—hogging it all, gobbling the whole thing up! You know what happens? People go to the *movies* instead of *moving!* Hollywood characters are supposed to have all the adventures for everybody in America, while everybody in America sits in a dark room and watches them have them! Yes, until there's a war. That's when adventure becomes available to the masses! *Everyone*'s dish, not only Gable's! Then the people in the dark room come out of the dark room to have some adventures themselves —Goody, goody!—It's our turn now, to go to the South Sea Islands—to make a safari—to be exotic, far-off!—But I'm not patient. I don't want to wait till then. I'm tired of the *movies* and I am *about* to *move!*

JIM (*incredulously*) Move?

TOM Yes.

JIM When?

TOM Soon!

JIM Where? Where? (THEME THREE MUSIC SEEMS TO ANSWER THE QUESTION, WHILE TOM THINKS IT OVER. HE SEARCHES AMONG HIS POCKETS)

TOM I'm starting to boil inside. I know I seem dreamy, but inside—well, I'm boiling!— Whenever I pick up a shoe, I shudder a little thinking how short life is and what I am doing!—Whatever that means, I know it doesn't mean shoes—except as something to wear on a traveler's feet! (*finds paper*) Look——

JIM What?

TOM I'm a member.

JIM (*reading*) The Union of Merchant Seamen.

TOM I paid my dues this month, instead of the light bill.

JIM You will regret it when they turn the lights off.

TOM I won't be here.

JIM How about your mother?

TOM I'm like my father. The bastard son of a bastard! See how he grins? And he's been absent going on sixteen years!

JIM You're just talking, you drip. How does your mother feel about it?

TOM Shhh!—Here comes Mother! Mother is not acquainted with my plans!

AMANDA (*enters portieres*) Where are you all?

TOM On the terrace, Mother.

(*They start inside. She advances to them.* TOM *is distinctly shocked at her appearance. Even* JIM *blinks a little. He is making his first contact with girlish Southern vivacity and in spite of the night-school course in public speaking is somewhat thrown off the beam by the unexpected outlay of social charm. Certain responses are attempted by* JIM *but are swept aside by* AMANDA's *gay laughter and chatter.*

TOM *is embarrassed but after the first shock* JIM *reacts very warmly. Grins and chuckles, is altogether won over.* IMAGE: AMANDA AS A GIRL)

AMANDA (*coyly smiling, shaking her girlish ringlets*) Well, well, well, so this is Mr. O'Connor. Introductions entirely unnecessary. I've heard so much about you from my boy. I finally said to him, Tom—good gracious!—why don't you bring this paragon to supper? I'd like to meet this nice young man at the warehouse! —Instead of just hearing him sing your praises so much!

I don't know why my son is so stand-offish— that's not Southern behavior!

Let's sit down and—I think we could stand a little more air in here! Tom, leave the door open. I felt a nice fresh breeze a moment ago. Where has it gone to?

Mmm, so warm already! And not quite summer, even. We're going to burn up when summer really gets started.

However, we're having—we're having a very light supper. I think light things are better fo' this time of year. The same as light clothes are. Light clothes an' light food are what warm weather calls fo'. You know our blood gets so thick during th' winter—it takes a while fo' us to *adjust* ou'selves!—when the season changes . . .

It's come so quick this year. I wasn't prepared. All of a sudden—heavens! Already summer!—I ran to the trunk an' pulled out this light dress—Terribly old! Historical almost! But feels so good—so good an' co-ol, y'know. . . .

TOM Mother——

AMANDA Yes, honey?

TOM How about—supper?

AMANDA Honey, you go ask Sister if supper is ready! You know that Sister is in full charge of supper!

Tell her you hungry boys are waiting for it. (*to* JIM)

Have you met Laura?

JIM She——

AMANDA Let you in? Oh, good, you've met already! It's rare for a girl as sweet an' pretty as Laura to be domestic! But Laura is, thank heavens, not only pretty but also very domestic. I'm not at all. I never was a bit. I never could make a thing but angel-food cake. Well, in the South we had so many servants. Gone, gone, gone. All vestige of gracious living! Gone completely! I wasn't prepared for what the future brought me. All of my gentlemen callers were sons of planters and so of course I assumed that I would be married to one and raise my family on a large piece of land with plenty of servants. But man proposes—and woman accepts the proposal!—To vary that old, old saying a little bit—I married no planter! I married a man who worked for the telephone company!—That gallantly smiling gentleman over there! (*points to the picture*) A telephone man who—fell in love with long-distance!—Now he travels and I don't even know where!—But what am I going on for about my—tribulations?

Tell me yours—I hope you don't have any! Tom?

TOM (*returning*) Yes, Mother?

AMANDA Is supper nearly ready?

TOM It looks to me like supper is on the table.

AMANDA Let me look—(*She rises prettily and looks through portieres*) Oh, lovely!—But where is Sister?

TOM Laura is not feeling well and she says that she thinks she'd better not come to the table.

AMANDA What?—Nonsense!—Laura? Oh, Laura!

LAURA (*offstage, faintly*) Yes, Mother.

AMANDA You really must come to the table. We won't be seated until you come to the table!

Come in, Mr. O'Connor. You sit over there, and I'll——

Laura? Laura Wingfield!

You're keeping us waiting, honey! We can't say grace until you come to the table!

(*The back door is pushed weakly open and* LAURA *comes in. She is obviously quite faint, her lips trembling, her eyes wide and staring. She moves unsteadily toward the table.* LEGEND: "TERROR!" *Outside a summer storm is coming abruptly. The white curtains billow inward at the windows and there is a sorrowful murmur and deep blue dusk.* LAURA *suddenly stumbles—she catches at a chair with a faint moan*)

TOM Laura!

AMANDA Laura! (*There is a clap of thunder.* LEGEND: "AH!" *Despairingly*)

Why, Laura, you *are* sick, darling! Tom, help your sister into the living room, dear!

Sit in the living room, Laura—rest on the sofa.

Well! (*to the gentleman caller*)

Standing over the hot stove made her ill!—I told her that it was just too warm this evening, but——(TOM *comes back in.* LAURA *is on the sofa*)

Is Laura all right now?

TOM Yes.

AMANDA What *is* that? Rain? A nice cool rain has come up! (*She gives the gentleman caller a frightened look*)

I think we may—have grace—now . . . (TOM *looks at her stupidly*)

Tom, honey—you say grace!

TOM Oh . . .

"For these and all thy mercies——(*They bow their heads,* AMANDA *stealing a nervous glance at* JIM. *In the living room* LAURA, *stretched on the sofa, clenches her hand to her lips, to hold back a shuddering sob*) God's Holy Name be praised"——

THE SCENE DIMS OUT

Scene Seven

(LEGEND: "A SOUVENIR"

Half an hour later. Dinner is just being finished in the upstage area which is concealed by the drawn portieres.

As the curtain rises LAURA *is still huddled upon the sofa, her feet drawn under her, her head resting on a pale blue pillow, her eyes wide and mysteriously watchful. The new floor lamp with its shade of rose-colored silk gives a soft, becoming light to her face, bringing out the fragile, unearthly prettiness which usually escapes attention. There is a steady murmur of rain, but it is slackening and stops soon after the scene begins; the air outside becomes pale and luminous as the moon breaks out.*

A moment after the curtain rises, the lights in both rooms flicker and go out)

JIM Hey, there, Mr. Light Bulb! (AMANDA *laughs nervously.* LEGEND: "SUSPENSION OF A PUBLIC SERVICE")

AMANDA Where was Moses when the lights when out? Ha-ha. Do you know the answer to that one, Mr. O'Connor?

JIM No, Ma'am, what's the answer?

AMANDA In the dark! (JIM *laughs appreciatively*)

Everybody sit still. I'll light the candles. Isn't it lucky we have them on the table? Where's a match? Which of you gentlemen can provide a match?

JIM Here.

AMANDA Thank you, sir.

JIM Not at all, Ma'am!

AMANDA I guess the fuse has burnt out. Mr. O'Connor, can you tell a burnt-out fuse? I know I can't and Tom is a total loss when it comes to mechanics. (SOUND: GETTING UP: VOICES RECEDE A LITTLE TO KITCHENETTE)

Oh, be careful you don't bump into something. We don't want our gentleman caller to break his neck. Now wouldn't that be a fine howdy-do?

JIM   Ha-ha!

Where is the fuse-box?

AMANDA   Right here next to the stove. Can you see anything?

JIM   Just a minute.

AMANDA   Isn't electricity a mysterious thing?

Wasn't it Benjamin Franklin who tied a key to a kite?

We live in such a mysterious universe, don't we? Some people say that science clears up all the mysteries for us. In my opinion it only creates more!

Have you found it yet?

JIM   No, Ma'am. All these fuses look okay to me.

AMANDA   Tom!

TOM   Yes, Mother?

AMANDA   That light bill I gave you several days ago. The one I told you we got the notices about? (LEGEND: "HA!")

TOM   Oh.—Yeah.

AMANDA   You didn't neglect to pay it by any chance?

TOM   Why, I—

AMANDA   Didn't! I might have known it!

JIM   Shakespeare probably wrote a poem on that light bill, Mrs. Wingfield.

AMANDA   I might have known better than to trust him with it! There's such a high price for negligence in this world!

JIM   Maybe the poem will win a ten-dollar prize.

AMANDA   We'll just have to spend the remainder of the evening in the nineteenth century, before Mr. Edison made the Mazda lamp!

JIM   Candlelight is my favorite kind of light.

AMANDA   That shows you're romantic! But that's no excuse for Tom.

Well, we got through dinner. Very considerate of them to let us get through dinner before they plunged us into everlasting darkness, wasn't it, Mr. O'Connor?

JIM   Ha-ha!

AMANDA   Tom, as a penalty for your carelessness you can help me with the dishes.

JIM   Let me give you a hand.

AMANDA   Indeed you will not!

JIM   I ought to be good for something.

AMANDA   Good for something? (*Her tone is rhapsodic*)

You? Why, Mr. O'Connor, nobody, *nobody's* given me this much entertainment in years—as you have!

JIM   Aw, now, Mrs. Wingfield!

AMANDA   I'm not exaggerating, not one bit! But Sister is all by her lonesome. You go keep her company in the parlor!

I'll give you this lovely old candelabrum that used to be on the altar at the Church of the Heavenly Rest. It was melted a little out of shape when the church burnt down. Lightning struck it one spring. Gypsy Jones was holding a revival at the time and he intimated that the church was destroyed because the Episcopalians gave card parties.

JIM   Ha-ha.

AMANDA   And how about you coaxing Sister to drink a little wine? I think it would be good for her! Can you carry both at once?

JIM   Sure. I'm Superman!

AMANDA   Now, Thomas, get into this apron!

(*The door of kitchenette swings closed on* AMANDA's *gay laughter; the flickering light approaches the portieres.* LAURA *sits up nervously as he enters. Her speech at first is low and breathless from the almost intolerable strain of being alone with a stranger.* THE LEGEND: "I DON'T SUPPOSE YOU REMEMBER ME AT ALL!" *In her first speeches in this scene, before* JIM's *warmth overcomes her paralyzing shyness,* LAURA's *voice is thin and breathless as though she has just run up a steep flight of stairs.* JIM's *attitude is gently humorous. In playing this scene it should be stressed that while the incident is apparently unimportant, it is to* LAURA *the climax of her secret life*)

JIM   Hello, there, Laura.

LAURA   (*faintly*) Hello. (*She clears her throat*)

JIM   How are you feeling now? Better?

LAURA   Yes. Yes, thank you.

JIM   This is for you. A little dandelion wine.

(*He extends it toward her with extravagant gallantry*)

LAURA   Thank you.

JIM   Drink it—but don't get drunk! (*He laughs heartily.* LAURA *takes the glass uncertainly, laughs shyly*)

Where shall I set the candles?

LAURA   Oh—oh, anywhere . . .

JIM   How about here on the floor? Any objections?

LAURA   No.

JIM   I'll spread a newspaper under to catch the drippings. I like to sit on the floor. Mind if I do?

LAURA   Oh, no.

JIM   Give me a pillow?

LAURA   What?

JIM   A pillow!

LAURA   Oh . . . (*hands him one quickly*)

JIM   How about you? Don't you like to sit on the floor?

LAURA   Oh—yes.

JIM   Why don't you, then?

LAURA   I—will.

JIM   Take a pillow!

(LAURA *does. Sits on the other side of the candelabrum.* JIM *crosses his legs and smiles engagingly at her*)   I can't hardly see you sitting way over there.

LAURA   I can—see you.

JIM   I know, but that's not fair; I'm in the limelight. (LAURA *moves her pillow closer*) Good! Now I can see you! Comfortable?

LAURA   Yes.

JIM   So am I. Comfortable as a cow! Will you have some gum?

LAURA   No, thank you.

JIM   I think that I will indulge, with your permission. (*musingly unwraps it and holds it up*) Think of the fortune made by the guy that invented the first piece of chewing gum. Amazing, huh? The Wrigley Building is one of the sights of Chicago.—I saw it summer before last when I went up to the Century of Progress. Did you take in the Century of Progress?

LAURA   No, I didn't.

JIM   Well, it was quite a wonderful exposition. What impressed me most was the Hall of Science. Gives you an idea of what the future will be in America, even more wonderful than the present time is! (*pause. Smiling at her*) Your brother tells me you're shy. Is that right, Laura?

LAURA   I—don't know.

JIM   I judge you to be an old-fashioned type of girl. Well, I think that's a pretty good type to be. Hope you don't think I'm being too personal—do you?

LAURA   (*hastily, out of embarrassment*)   I believe I *will* take a piece of gum, if you— don't mind. (*clearing her throat*) Mr. O'Connor, have you—kept up with your singing?

JIM   Singing? Me?

LAURA   Yes. I remember what a beautiful voice you had.

JIM   When did you hear me sing? (VOICE OFFSTAGE IN THE PAUSE)

VOICE   (*offstage*)

> O blow, ye winds, heigh-ho,
> A-roving I will go!
> > I'm off to my love
> > With a boxing glove—
> Ten thousand miles away!

JIM   You say you've heard me sing?

LAURA   Oh, yes! Yes, very often . . . I—don't suppose—you remember me—at all?

JIM   (*smiling doubtfully*)   You know I have an idea I've seen you before. I had that idea soon as you opened the door. It seemed almost like I was about to remember your name. But the name that I started to call you—wasn't a name! And so I stopped myself before I said it.

LAURA   Wasn't it—Blue Roses!

JIM   (*springs up. Grinning*)   Blue Roses!— My gosh, yes—Blue Roses!

That's what I had on my tongue when you opened the door!

Isn't it funny what tricks your memory plays? I didn't connect you with high school somehow or other.

But that's where it was; it was high school. I didn't even know you were Shakespeare's sister!

Gosh, I'm sorry.

LAURA   I didn't expect you to. You—barely knew me!

JIM   But we did have a speaking acquaintance, huh?

LAURA   Yes, we—spoke to each other.

JIM   When did you recognize me?

LAURA   Oh, right away!

JIM   Soon as I came in the door?

LAURA   When I heard your name I thought it was probably you. I knew that Tom used to know you a little in high school. So when you came in the door—

Well, then I was—sure.

JIM   Why didn't you *say* something, then?

LAURA   (*breathlessly*)   I didn't know what to say, I was—too surprised!

JIM   For goodness' sake! You know, this sure is funny!

LAURA   Yes! Yes, isn't it, though . . .

JIM   Didn't we have a class in something together?

LAURA   Yes, we did.

JIM   What class was that?

LAURA   It was—singing—Chorus!

JIM   Aw!

LAURA   I sat across the aisle from you in the Aud.

JIM   Aw.

LAURA   Mondays, Wednesdays, and Fridays.

JIM   Now I remember—you always came in late.

LAURA   Yes, it was so hard for me, getting upstairs. I had that brace on my leg—it clumped so loud!

JIM   I never heard any clumping.

LAURA   (*wincing at the recollection*)   To me it sounded like—thunder!

JIM   Well, well, well, I never even noticed.

LAURA   And everybody was seated before I came in. I had to walk in front of all those people. My seat was in the back row. I had to go clumping all the way up the aisle with everyone watching!

JIM   You shouldn't have been self-conscious.

LAURA   I know, but I was. It was always such a relief when the singing started.

JIM   Aw, yes, I've placed you now! I used to call you Blue Roses. How was it that I got started calling you that?

LAURA   I was out of school a little while with pleurosis. When I came back you asked me what was the matter. I said I had pleurosis—you thought I said Blue Roses. That's what you always called me after that!

JIM   I hope you didn't mind.

LAURA   Oh, no—I liked it. You see, I wasn't acquainted with many—people. . . .

JIM   As I remember you sort of stuck by yourself.

LAURA   I—I—never have had much luck at —making friends.

JIM   I don't see why you wouldn't.

LAURA   Well, I—started out badly.

JIM   You mean being—

LAURA   Yes, it sort of—stood between me—

JIM   You shouldn't have let it!

LAURA   I know, but it did, and—

JIM   You were shy with people!

LAURA   I tried not to be but never could—

JIM   Overcome it?

LAURA   No, I—I never could!

JIM   I guess being shy is something you have to work out of kind of gradually.

LAURA   (*sorrowfully*)   Yes—I guess it—

JIM   Takes time!

LAURA   Yes—

JIM   People are not so dreadful when you know them. That's what you have to remember! And everybody has problems, not just you, but practically everybody has got some problems. You think of yourself as having the only problems, as being the only one who is disappointed. But just look around you and you will see lots of people as disappointed as you are. For instance, I hoped when I was going to high school that I would be further along at this time, six years later, than I am now—You remember that wonderful write-up I had in *The Torch?*

LAURA   Yes! (*She rises and crosses to table*)

JIM   It said I was bound to succeed in anything I went into! (LAURA *returns with the annual*) Holy Jeez! *The Torch!*

(*He accepts it reverently. They smile across it with mutual wonder.* LAURA *crouches beside him and they begin to turn through it.* LAURA's *shyness is dissolving in his warmth*)

LAURA   Here you are in *The Pirates of Penzance!*

JIM   (*wistfully*)   I sang the baritone lead in that operetta.

LAURA   (*raptly*)   So—*beautifully!*

JIM   (*protesting*)   Aw—

LAURA   Yes, yes—beautifully—beautifully!

JIM   You heard me?

LAURA   All three times!

JIM   No!

LAURA   Yes!

JIM   All three performances?

LAURA   (*looking down*)   Yes.

JIM   Why?

LAURA   I—wanted to ask you to—autograph my program.

JIM   Why didn't you ask me to?

LAURA   You were always surrounded by your own friends so much that I never had a chance to.

JIM   You should have just—

LAURA   Well, I—thought you might think I was—

JIM   Thought I might think you was—what?

LAURA   Oh—

JIM   (*with reflective relish*)   I was beleaguered by females in those days.

LAURA   You were terribly popular!

JIM   Yeah—

LAURA   You had such a—friendly way—

JIM   I was spoiled in high school.

LAURA   Everybody—liked you!

JIM   Including you?

LAURA   I—yes, I—I did, too—(*She gently closes the book in her lap*)

JIM   Well, well, well!—Give me that program, Laura. (*She hands it to him. He signs it with a flourish*) There you are—better late than never!

LAURA   Oh, I—what a—surprise!

JIM   My signature isn't worth very much right now.

But some day—maybe—it will increase in value!

Being disappointed is one thing and being discouraged is something else. I am disappointed but I am not discouraged.

I'm twenty-three years old.

How old are you?

LAURA   I'll be twenty-four in June.

JIM   That's not old age!

LAURA   No, but—

JIM   You finished high school?

LAURA   (*with difficulty*)   I didn't go back.

JIM   You mean you dropped out?

LAURA   I made bad grades in my final examinations. (*She rises and replaces the book and the program. Her voice strained*)

How is—Emily Meisenbach getting along?

JIM   Oh, that kraut-head!

LAURA   Why do you call her that?

JIM   That's what she was.

LAURA   You're not still—going with her?

JIM   I never see her.

LAURA   It said in the Personal Section that you were—engaged!

JIM   I know, but I wasn't impressed by that—propaganda!

LAURA   It wasn't—the truth?

JIM   Only in Emily's optimistic opinion!

LAURA   Oh—

(LEGEND: "WHAT HAVE YOU DONE SINCE HIGH SCHOOL?" JIM *lights a cigarette and leans indolently back on his elbows smiling at* LAURA *with a warmth and charm which lights her inwardly with altar candles. She remains by the table and turns in her hands a piece of glass to cover her tumult*)

JIM   (*after several reflective puffs on a cigarette*)   What have you done since high school? (*She seems not to hear him*) Huh? (LAURA *looks up*) I said what have you done since high school, Laura?

LAURA   Nothing much.

JIM   You must have been doing something these six long years.

LAURA   Yes.

JIM   Well, then, such as what?

LAURA   I took a business course at business college—

JIM   How did that work out?

LAURA   Well, not very—well—I had to drop out, it gave me—indigestion—(JIM *laughs gently*)

JIM   What are you doing now?

LAURA   I don't do anything—much. Oh, please don't think I sit around doing nothing! My glass collection takes up a good deal of time. Glass is something you have to take good care of.

JIM   What did you say—about glass?

LAURA   Collection I said—I have one— (*She clears her throat and turns away again, acutely shy*)

JIM   (*abruptly*) You know what I judge to be the trouble with you?

Inferiority complex! Know what that is? That's what they call it when someone low-rates himself!

I understand it because I had it, too. Although my case was not so aggravated as yours seems to be. I had it until I took up public speaking, developed my voice, and learned that I had an aptitude for science. Before that time I never thought of myself as being outstanding in any way whatsoever!

Now I've never made a regular study of it, but I have a friend who says I can analyze people better than doctors that make a profession of it. I don't claim that to be necessarily true, but I can sure guess a person's psychology, Laura! (*takes out his gum*) Excuse me, Laura. I always take it out when the flavor is gone. I'll use this scrap of paper to wrap it in. I know how it is to get it stuck on a shoe.

Yep—that's what I judge to be your principal trouble. A lack of confidence in yourself as a person. You don't have the proper amount of faith in yourself. I'm basing that fact on a number of your remarks and also on certain observations I've made. For instance that clumping you thought was so awful in high school. You say that you even dreaded to walk into class. You see what you did? You dropped out of school, you gave up an education because of a clump, which as far as I know was practically non-existent! A little physical defect is what you have. Hardly noticeable even! Magnified thousands of times by imagination!

You know what my strong advice to you is? Think of yourself as *superior* in some way!

LAURA   In what way would I think?

JIM   Why, man alive, Laura! Just look about you a little. What do you see? A world full of common people! All of 'em born and all of 'em going to die!

Which of them has one-tenth of your good points? Or mine? Or anyone else's, as far as that goes—Gosh!

Everybody excels in some one thing. Some in many! (*unconsciously glances at himself in the mirror*)

All you've got to do is discover in *what!*

Take me, for instance. (*He adjusts his tie at the mirror*)

My interest happens to lie in electro-dynamics. I'm taking a course in radio engineering at night school, Laura, on top of a fairly responsible job at the warehouse. I'm taking that course and studying public speaking.

LAURA   Ohhhh.

JIM   Because I believe in the future of television! (*turning back to her*)

I wish to be ready to go up right along with it. Therefore I'm planning to get in on the ground floor. In fact I've already made the right connections and all that remains is for the industry itself to get under way! Full steam—(*His eyes are starry*)

Knowledge—Zzzzzp! *Money*—Zzzzzzp! *Power!*

That's the cycle democracy is built on! (*His attitude is convincingly dynamic.* LAURA *stares at him, even her shyness eclipsed in her absolute wonder. He suddenly grins*)

I guess you think I think a lot of myself!

LAURA No—o-o-o, I—

JIM Now how about you? Isn't there something you take more interest in than anything else?

LAURA Well, I do—as I said—have my— glass collection—(*a peal of girlish laughter from the kitchen*)

JIM I'm not right sure I know what you're talking about.

What kind of glass is it?

LAURA Little articles of it, they're ornaments mostly!

Most of them are little animals made out of glass, the tiniest little animals in the world. Mother calls them a glass menagerie!

Here's an example of one, if you'd like to see it!

This one is one of the oldest. It's nearly thirteen (MUSIC: "THE GLASS MENAGERIE." *He stretches out his hand*)

Oh, be careful—if you breathe, it breaks!

JIM I'd better not take it. I'm pretty clumsy with things.

LAURA Go on, I trust you with him! (*places it in his palm*)

There now—you're holding him gently!

Hold him over the light, he loves the light! You see how the light shines through him?

JIM It sure does shine!

LAURA I shouldn't be partial, but he is my favorite one.

JIM What kind of a thing is this one supposed to be?

LAURA Haven't you noticed the single horn on his forehead?

JIM A unicorn, huh?

LAURA Mmm-hmmm!

JIM Unicorns, aren't they extinct in the modern world?

LAURA I know!

JIM Poor little fellow, he must feel sort of lonesome.

LAURA (*smiling*) Well, if he does he doesn't complain about it. He stays on a shelf with some horses that don't have horns and all of them seem to get along nicely together.

JIM How do you know?

LAURA (*lightly*) I haven't heard any arguments among them!

JIM (*grinning*) No arguments, huh? Well, that's a pretty good sign!

Where shall I set him?

LAURA Put him on the table. They all like a change of scenery once in a while!

JIM (*stretching*) Well, well, well, well— Look how big my shadow is when I stretch!

LAURA Oh, oh, yes—it stretches across the ceiling!

JIM (*crossing to door*) I think it's stopped raining. (*opens fire-escape door*) Where does the music come from?

LAURA From the Paradise Dance Hall across the alley.

JIM How about cutting the rug a little, Miss Wingfield?

LAURA Oh, I—

JIM Or is your program filled up? Let me have a look at it. (*grasps imaginary card*) Why, every dance is taken! I'll just have to scratch some out. (WALTZ MUSIC: "LA GOLONDRINA") Ahh, a waltz! (*He executes some sweeping turns by himself then holds his arms toward* LAURA)

LAURA (*breathlessly*) I—can't dance!

JIM There you go, that inferiority stuff!

LAURA I've never danced in my life!

JIM Come on, try!

LAURA Oh, but I'd step on you!

JIM I'm not made out of glass.

LAURA How—how—how do we start?

JIM Just leave it to me. You hold your arms out a little.

LAURA Like this?

JIM A little bit higher. Right. Now don't tighten up, that's the main thing about it— relax.

LAURA (*laughing breathlessly*) It's hard not to.

JIM Okay.

LAURA I'm afraid you can't budge me.

JIM What do you bet I can't? (*He swings her into motion*)

LAURA Goodness, yes, you can!

JIM Let yourself go, now, Laura, just let yourself go.

LAURA I'm—

JIM Come on!

LAURA Trying!

JIM Not so stiff—Easy does it!

LAURA I know but I'm—

JIM Loosen th' backbone! There now, that's a lot better.

LAURA Am I?

JIM Lots, lots better! (*He moves her about the room in a clumsy waltz*)

LAURA Oh, my!

JIM Ha-ha!

LAURA Oh, my goodness!

JIM   Ha-ha-ha! (*They suddenly bump in to the table.* JIM *stops*) What did we hit on?
LAURA   Table.
JIM   Did something fall off it? I think—
LAURA   Yes.
JIM   I hope that it wasn't the little glass horse with the horn!
LAURA   Yes.
JIM   Aw, aw, aw. Is it broken?
LAURA   Now it is just like all the other horses.
JIM   It's lost its—
LAURA   Horn!
It doesn't matter. Maybe it's a blessing in disguise.
JIM   You'll never forgive me. I bet that that was your favorite piece of glass.
LAURA   I don't have favorites much. It's no tragedy, Freckles. Glass breaks so easily. No matter how careful you are. The traffic jars the shelves and things fall off them.
JIM   Still I'm awfully sorry that I was the cause.
LAURA (*smiling*)   I'll just imagine he had an operation.
The horn was removed to make him feel less—freakish! (*They both laugh*)
Now he will feel more at home with the other horses, the ones that don't have horns . . .
JIM   Ha-ha, that's very funny! (*suddenly serious*)
I'm glad to see that you have a sense of humor.
You know—you're—well—very different!
Surprisingly different from anyone else I know! (*His voice becomes soft and hesitant with a genuine feeling*)
Do you mind me telling you that? (LAURA *is abashed beyond speech*)
I mean it in a nice way . . . (LAURA *nods shyly, looking away*)
You make me feel sort of—I don't know how to put it!
I'm usually pretty good at expressing things, but—
This is something that I don't know how to say! (LAURA *touches her throat and clears it— turns the broken unicorn in her hands. Even softer*)
Has anyone ever told you that you were pretty? (PAUSE: MUSIC. LAURA *looks up slowly, with wonder, and shakes her head*)
Well, you are! In a very different way from anyone else.
And all the nicer because of the difference, too. (*His voice becomes low and husky.* LAURA *turns away, nearly faint with the novelty of her emotions*)

I wish that you were my sister. I'd teach you to have some confidence in yourself. The different people are not like other people, but being different is nothing to be ashamed of. Because other people are not such wonderful people. They're one hundred times one thousand. You're one times one! They walk all over the earth. You just stay here. They're common as—weeds, but—you—well, you're—*Blue Roses!* (IMAGE ON SCREEN: BLUE ROSES. MUSIC CHANGES)
LAURA   But blue is wrong for—roses . . .
JIM   It's right for you!—You're—pretty!
LAURA   In what respect am I pretty?
JIM   In all respects—believe me! Your eyes —your hair—are pretty! Your hands are pretty! (*He catches hold of her hand*)
You think I'm making this up because I'm invited to dinner and have to be nice. Oh, I could do that! I could put on an act for you, Laura, and say lots of things without being very sincere. But this time I am. I'm talking to you sincerely. I happened to notice you had this inferiority complex that keeps you from feeling comfortable with people. Somebody needs to build your confidence up and make you proud instead of shy and turning away and—blushing—
Somebody—ought to—
Ought to—*kiss* you, Laura! (*His hand slips slowly up her arm to her shoulder.* MUSIC SWELLS TUMULTUOUSLY. *He suddenly turns her about and kisses her on the lips. When he releases her,* LAURA *sinks on the sofa with a bright, dazed look.* JIM *backs away and fishes in his pocket for a cigarette.* LEGEND ON SCREEN: "SOUVENIR")
Stumble-john! (*He lights the cigarette, avoiding her look. There is a peal of girlish laughter from* AMANDA *in the kitchen.* LAURA *slowly raises and opens her hand. It still contains the little broken glass animal. She looks at it with a tender, bewildered expression*)
Stumble-john!
I shouldn't have done that—That was way off the beam.
You don't smoke, do you? (*She looks up, smiling, not hearing the question. He sits beside her a little gingerly. She looks at him speechlessly—waiting. He coughs decorously and moves a little farther aside as he considers the situation and senses her feelings, dimly, with perturbation. Gently*)
Would you—care for a—mint? (*She doesn't seem to hear him but her look grows brighter even*)
Peppermint—Life-Saver?

My pocket's a regular drug store—wherever I go . . .

(*He pops a mint in his mouth. Then gulps and decides to make a clean breast of it. He speaks slowly and gingerly*)

Laura, you know, if I had a sister like you, I'd do the same thing as Tom. I'd bring out fellows and—introduce her to them. The right type of boys of a type to—appreciate her.

Only—well—he made a mistake about me.

Maybe I've got no call to be saying this. That may not have been the idea in having me over. But what if it was?

There's nothing wrong about that. The only trouble is that in my case—I'm not in a situation to—do the right thing.

I can't take down your number and say I'll phone.

I can't call up next week and—ask for a date.

I thought I had better explain the situation in case you—misunderstood it and—hurt your feelings. . . . (*Pause. Slowly, very slowly, LAURA's look changes, her eyes returning slowly from his to the ornament in her palm. AMANDA utters another gay laugh in the kitchen*)

LAURA (*faintly*) You—won't—call again?

JIM No, Laura, I can't. (*He rises from the sofa*)

As I was just explaining, I've—got strings on me.

Laura, I've—been going steady!

I go out all of the time with a girl named Betty. She's a home-girl like you, and Catholic, and Irish, and in a great many ways we—get along fine.

I met her last summer on a moonlight boat trip up the river to Alton, on the *Majestic*.

Well—right away from the start it was—love! (*LEGEND: LOVE! LAURA sways slightly forward and grips the arm of the sofa. He fails to notice, now enrapt in his own comfortable being*)

Being in love has made a new man of me! (*Leaning stiffly forward, clutching the arm of the sofa, LAURA struggles visibly with her storm. But JIM is oblivious; she is a long way off*)

The power of love is really pretty tremendous!

Love is something that—changes the whole world, Laura! (*The storm abates a little and LAURA leans back. He notices her again*)

It happened that Betty's aunt took sick; she got a wire and had to go to Centralia. So Tom —when he asked me to dinner—I naturally just accepted the invitation, not knowing that you—that he—that I—(*He stops awkwardly*)

Huh—I'm a stumble-john! (*He flops back on the sofa. The holy candles in the altar of LAURA's face have been snuffed out. There is a look of almost infinite desolation. JIM glances at her uneasily*)

I wish that you would—say something. (*She bites her lip which was trembling and then bravely smiles. She opens her hand again on the broken glass ornament. Then she gently takes his hand and raises it level with her own. She carefully places the unicorn in the palm of his hand, then pushes his fingers closed upon it*) What are you—doing that for. You want me to have him?—Laura? (*She nods*) What for?

LAURA A—souvenir . . . (*She rises unsteadily and crouches beside the victrola to wind it up.* LEGEND ON SCREEN: "THINGS HAVE A WAY OF TURNING OUT SO BADLY!" OR IMAGE: "GENTLEMAN CALLER WAVING GOOD-BYE!— GAILY." *At this moment AMANDA rushes brightly back in the front room. She bears a pitcher of fruit punch in an old-fashioned cut-glass pitcher and a plate of macaroons. The plate has a gold border and poppies painted on it*)

AMANDA Well, well, well! Isn't the air delightful after the shower?

I've made you children a little liquid refreshment. (*turns gaily to the gentleman caller*)

Jim, do you know that song about lemonade?

"Lemonade, lemonade
Made in the shade and stirred with a
spade—
Good enough for any old maid!"

JIM (*uneasily*) Ha-ha! No—I never heard it.

AMANDA Why, Laura! You look so serious!

JIM We were having a serious conversation.

AMANDA Good! Now you're better acquainted!

JIM (*uncertainly*) Ha-ha! Yes.

AMANDA You modern young people are much more serious-minded than my generation. I was so gay as a girl!

JIM You haven't changed, Mrs. Wingfield.

AMANDA Tonight I'm rejuvenated! The gaiety of the occasion, Mr. O'Connor! (*She tosses her head with a peal of laughter. Spills lemonade*)

Oooo! I'm baptizing myself!

JIM Here—let me—

AMANDA (*setting the pitcher down*) There now. I discovered we had some maraschino cherries. I dumped them in, juice and all!

JIM You shouldn't have gone to that trouble, Mrs. Wingfield.

AMANDA Trouble, trouble? Why, it was loads of fun!

Didn't you hear me cutting up in the kitchen? I bet your ears were burning! I told Tom how outdone with him I was for keeping you to himself so long a time! He should have brought you over much, much sooner! Well, now that you've found your way, I want you to be a very frequent caller! Not just occasional but all the time.

Oh, we're going to have a lot of gay times together! I see them coming!

Mmm, just breathe that air! So fresh, and the moon's so pretty!

I'll skip back out—I know where my place is when young folks are having a—serious conversation!

JIM   Oh, don't go out, Mrs. Wingfield. The fact of the matter is I've got to be going.

AMANDA   Going, now? You're joking! Why, it's only the shank of the evening, Mr. O'Connor!

JIM   Well, you know how it is.

AMANDA   You mean you're a young workingman and have to keep workingmen's hours. We'll let you off early tonight. But only on the condition that next time you stay later.

What's the best night for you? Isn't Saturday night the best night for you workingmen?

JIM   I have a couple of time-clocks to punch, Mrs. Wingfield. One at morning, another one at night!

AMANDA   My, but you *are* ambitious! You work at night, too?

JIM   No, Ma'am, not work but—Betty! (*He crosses deliberately to pick up his hat. The band at the Paradise Dance Hall goes into a tender waltz*)

AMANDA   Betty? Betty? Who's—Betty? (*There is an ominous cracking sound in the sky*)

JIM   Oh, just a girl. The girl I go steady with! (*He smiles charmingly. The sky falls.* (LEGEND: "THE SKY FALLS")

AMANDA   (*a long-drawn exhalation*)   Ohhhh . . . Is it a serious romance, Mr. O'Connor?

JIM   We're going to be married the second Sunday in June.

AMANDA   Ohhhh—how nice!

Tom didn't mention that you were engaged to be married.

JIM   The cat's not out of the bag at the warehouse yet.

You know how they are. They call you Romeo and stuff like that. (*He stops at the oval mirror to put on his hat. He carefully shapes the brim and the crown to give a discreetly dashing effect*)

It's been a wonderful evening, Mrs. Wing-

field. I guess this is what they mean by Southern hospitality.

AMANDA   It really wasn't anything at all.

JIM   I hope it don't seem like I'm rushing off. But I promised Betty I'd pick her up at the Wabash depot, an' by the time I get my jalopy down there her train'll be in. Some women are pretty upset if you keep 'em waiting.

AMANDA   Yes, I know—The tyranny of women! (*extends her hand*)

Good-bye, Mr. O'Connor.

I wish you luck—and happiness—and success! All three of them, and so does Laura!— Don't you, Laura?

LAURA   Yes!

JIM   (*taking her hand*)   Good-bye, Laura. I'm certainly going to treasure that souvenir. And don't you forget the good advice I gave you. (*raises his voice to a cheery shout*)

So long, Shakespeare!

Thanks again, ladies—Good night!

(*He grins and ducks jauntily out. Still bravely grimacing,* AMANDA *closes the door on the gentleman caller. Then she turns back to the room with a puzzled expression. She and* LAURA *don't dare to face each other.* LAURA *crouches beside the victrola to wind it*)

AMANDA   (*faintly*)   Things have a way of turning out so badly.

I don't believe that I would play the victrola.

Well, well—well—

Our gentleman caller was engaged to be married!

Tom!

TOM   (*from back*)   Yes, Mother?

AMANDA   Come in here a minute. I want to tell you something awfully funny.

TOM   (*enters with macaroon and a glass of the lemonade*)   Has the gentleman caller gotten away already?

AMANDA   The gentleman caller has made an early departure.

What a wonderful joke you played on us!

TOM   How do you mean?

AMANDA   You didn't mention that he was engaged to be married.

TOM   Jim? Engaged?

AMANDA   That's what he just informed us.

TOM   I'll be jiggered! I didn't know about that.

AMANDA   That seems very peculiar.

TOM   What's peculiar about it?

AMANDA   Didn't you call him your best friend down at the warehouse?

TOM   He is, but how did I know?

AMANDA   It seems extremely peculiar that

you wouldn't know your best friend was going to be married!

TOM The warehouse is where I work, not where I know things about people!

AMANDA You don't know things anywhere! You live in a dream; you manufacture illusions! (*He crosses to the door*)

Where are you going?

TOM I'm going to the movies.

AMANDA That's right, now that you've had us make such fools of ourselves. The effort, the preparations, all the expense! The new floor lamp, the rug, the clothes for Laura! All for what? To entertain some other girl's fiancé!

Go to the movies, go! Don't think about us, a mother deserted, an unmarried sister who's crippled and has no job! Don't let anything interfere with your selfish pleasure!

Just go, go, go—to the movies!

TOM All right, I will! The more you shout about my selfishness to me the quicker I'll go, and I won't go to the movies!

AMANDA Go, then! Then go to the moon—you selfish dreamer!

(TOM *smashes his glass on the floor. He plunges out on the fire escape, slamming the door.* LAURA *screams—cut off by door. Dance-hall music up.* TOM *goes to the rail and grips it desperately, lifting his face in the chill white moonlight penetrating the narrow abyss of the alley.* LEGEND ON SCREEN: "AND SO GOOD-BYE . . ." TOM's *closing speech is timed with the interior pantomime. The interior scene is played as though viewed through soundproof glass.* AMANDA *appears to be making a comforting speech to* LAURA *who is huddled upon the sofa. Now that we cannot hear the mother's speech, her silliness is gone and she has dignity and tragic beauty.* LAURA's *dark hair hides her face until at the end of the speech she lifts it to smile at her mother.* AMANDA's *gestures are slow and graceful, almost dancelike, as she comforts the daughter. At the end of her speech she glances a moment at the father's picture—*

then withdraws through the portieres. At close of TOM's *speech,* LAURA *blows out the candles, ending the play*)

TOM I didn't go to the moon, I went much further—for time is the longest distance between two places—

Not long after that I was fired for writing a poem on the lid of a shoe-box.

I left Saint Louis. I descended the steps of this fire escape for the last time and followed, from then on, in my father's footsteps, attempting to find in motion what was lost in space—

I traveled around a great deal. The cities swept about me like dead leaves, leaves that were brightly colored but torn away from the branches.

I would have stopped, but I was pursued by something.

It always came upon me unawares, taking me altogether by surprise. Perhaps it was a familiar bit of music. Perhaps it was only a piece of transparent glass—

Perhaps I am walking along a street at night, in some strange city, before I have found companions. I pass the lighted window of a shop where perfume is sold. The window is filled with pieces of colored glass, tiny transparent bottles in delicate colors, like bits of a shattered rainbow.

Then all at once my sister touches my shoulder. I turn around and look into her eyes . . .

Oh, Laura, Laura, I tried to leave you behind me, but I am more faithful than I intended to be!

I reach for a cigarette, I cross the street, I run into the movies or a bar, I buy a drink, I speak to the nearest stranger—anything that can blow your candles out! (LAURA *bends over the candles*)—for nowadays the world is lit by lightning! Blow out your candles, Laura—and so good-bye. . . . (*She blows the candles out*)

THE SCENE DISSOLVES

Arthur Miller

1915-

TRAGEDY AND
THE COMMON MAN

In this age few tragedies are written. It has often been held that the lack is due to a paucity of heroes among us, or else that modern man has had the blood drawn out of his organs of belief by the skepticism of science, and the heroic attack on life cannot feed on an attitude of reserve and circumspection. For one reason or another, we are often held to be below tragedy—or tragedy above us. The inevitable conclusion is, of course, that the tragic mode is archaic, fit only for the very highly placed, the kings or the kingly, and where this admission is not made in so many words it is most often implied.

I believe that the common man is as apt a subject for tragedy in its highest sense as kings were. On the face of it this ought to be obvious in the light of modern psychiatry, which bases its analysis upon classic formulations, such as the Oedipus and Orestes complexes, for instances, which were enacted by royal beings, but which apply to everyone in similar emotional situations.

More simply, when the question of tragedy in art is not at issue, we never hesitate to attribute to the well-placed and the exalted the very same mental processes as the lowly. And finally, if the exaltation of tragic action were truly a property of the high-bred character alone, it is inconceivable that the mass of mankind should cherish tragedy above all other forms, let alone be capable of understanding it.

As a general rule, to which there may be

exceptions unknown to me, I think the tragic feeling is evoked in us when we are in the presence of a character who is ready to lay down his life, if need be, to secure one thing—his sense of personal dignity. From Orestes to Hamlet, Medea to Macbeth, the underlying struggle is that of the individual attempting to gain his "rightful" position in his society.

Sometimes he is one who has been displaced from it, sometimes one who seeks to attain it for the first time, but the fateful wound from which the inevitable events spiral is the wound of indignity, and its dominant force is indignation. Tragedy, then, is the consequence of a man's total compulsion to evaluate himself justly.

In the sense of having been initiated by the hero himself, the tale always reveals what has been called his "tragic flaw," a failing that is not peculiar to grand or elevated characters. Nor is it necessarily a weakness. The flaw, or crack in the character, is really nothing—and need be nothing, but his inherent unwillingness to remain passive in the face of what he conceives to be a challenge to his dignity, his image of his rightful status. Only the passive, only those who accept their lot without active retaliation, are "flawless." Most of us are in that category.

But there are among us today, as there always have been, those who act against the scheme of things that degrades them, and in the process of action everything we have accepted out of fear or insensitivity or ignorance is shaken before us and examined, and from this total onslaught by an individual against the seemingly stable cosmos surrounding us—from this total examination of the "unchangeable" environment—comes the terror and the fear that is classically associated with tragedy.

More important, from this total questioning of what has previously been unquestioned, we learn. And such a process is not beyond the common man. In revolutions around the world, these past thirty years, he has demonstrated again and again this inner dynamic of all tragedy.

Insistence upon the rank of the tragic hero, or the so-called nobility of his character, is really but a clinging to the outward forms of tragedy. If rank or nobility of character was indispensable, then it would follow that the problems of those with rank were the particular problems of tragedy. But surely the right of one monarch to capture the domain from another no longer raises our passions, nor are our concepts of justice what they were to the mind of an Elizabethan king.

The quality in such plays that does shake us, however, derives from the underlying fear of being displaced, the disaster inherent in being torn away from our chosen image of what and who we are in this world. Among us today this fear is as strong, and perhaps stronger, than it ever was. In fact, it is the common man who knows this fear best.

Now, if it is true that tragedy is the consequence of a man's total compulsion to evaluate himself justly, his destruction in the attempt posits a wrong or an evil in his environment. And this is precisely the morality of tragedy and its lesson. The discovery of the moral law, which is what the enlightenment of tragedy consists of, is not the discovery of some abstract or metaphysical quantity.

The tragic right is a condition of life, a condition in which the human personality is able to flower and realize itself. The wrong is the condition which suppresses man, perverts the flowing out of his love and creative instinct. Tragedy enlightens—and it must, in that it points the heroic finger at the enemy of man's freedom. The thrust for freedom is the quality in tragedy which exalts. The revolutionary questioning of the stable environment is what terrifies. In no way is the common man debarred from such thoughts or such actions.

Seen in this light, our lack of tragedy may be partially accounted for by the turn which modern literature has taken toward the purely psychiatric view of life, or the purely sociological. If all our miseries, our indignities, are born and bred within our minds, then all action, let alone the heroic action, is obviously impossible.

And if society alone is responsible for the cramping of our lives, then the protagonist must needs be so pure and faultless as to force us to deny his validity as a character. From neither of these views can tragedy derive, simply because neither represents a balanced

concept of life. Above all else, tragedy requires the finest appreciation by the writer of cause and effect.

No tragedy can therefore come about when its author fears to question absolutely everything, when he regards any institution, habit or custom as being either everlasting, immutable or inevitable. In the tragic view the need of man to wholly realize himself is the only fixed star, and whatever it is that hedges his nature and lowers it is ripe for attack and examination. Which is not to say that tragedy must preach revolution.

The Greeks could probe the very heavenly origin of their ways and return to confirm the rightness of laws. And Job could face God in anger, demanding his right and end in submission. But for a moment everything is in suspension, nothing is accepted, and in this stretching and tearing apart of the cosmos, in the very action of so doing, the character gains "size," the tragic stature which is spuriously attached to the royal or the high-born in our minds. The commonest of men may take on that stature to the extent of his willingness to throw all he has into the contest, the battle to secure his rightful place in his world.

There is a misconception of tragedy with which I have been struck in review after review, and in many conversations with writers and readers alike. It is the idea that tragedy is of necessity allied to pessimism. Even the dictionary says nothing more about the word than that it means a story with a sad or unhappy ending. This impression is so firmly fixed that I almost hesitate to claim that in truth tragedy implies more optimism in its author than does comedy, and that its final result ought to be the reinforcement of the onlooker's brightest opinions of the human animal.

For, if it is true to say that in essence the tragic hero is intent upon claiming his whole due as a personality, and if this struggle must be total and without reservation, then it automatically demonstrates the indestructible will of man to achieve his humanity.

The possibility of victory must be there in tragedy. Where pathos rules, where pathos is finally derived, a character has fought a battle he could not possibly have won. The pathetic is achieved when the protagonist is, by virtue of his witlessness, his insensitivity or the very air he gives off, incapable of grappling with a much superior force.

Pathos truly is the mode for the pessimist. But tragedy requires a nicer balance between what is possible and what is impossible. And it is curious, although edifying, that the plays we revere, century after century, are the tragedies. In them, and in them alone, lies the belief—optimistic, if you will, in the perfectibility of man.

It is time, I think, that we who are without kings, took up this bright thread of our history and followed it to the only place it can possibly lead in our time—the heart and spirit of the average man.

INTRODUCTION TO
A VIEW FROM THE BRIDGE

A play is rarely given a second chance. Unlike a novel, which may be received initially with less than enthusiasm, and then as time goes by be hailed by a large public, a play usually makes its mark right off or it vanishes into oblivion. Two of mine, *The Crucible* and *A View from the Bridge,* failed to find large audiences with their original Broadway productions. Both were regarded as rather cold plays at first. However, after a couple of years *The Crucible* was produced again off Broadway and ran two years, without a line being changed from the original. With McCarthy dead it was once again possible to feel warmly toward the play, whereas during his time of power it was suspected of being a special plea, a concoction and unaesthetic. On its second time around its humanity emerged and it could be enjoyed as drama.

At this writing I have not yet permitted a second New York production of *A View from the Bridge* principally because I have not had the desire to see it through the mill a second time. However, a year or so after its first production it was done with great success in London and then in Paris, where it ran two years. It is done everywhere in this country without any apparent difficulty in reaching the emotions of the audience. This play, however, unlike *The Crucible,* I have revised, and it was the revision which London and Paris saw. The nature of the revisions bears directly upon the questions of form and style which interest students and theater workers.

The original play produced on Broadway

was in one act. It was a hard, telegraphic, unadorned drama. Nothing was permitted which did not advance the progress of Eddie's catastrophe in a most direct way. In a Note to the published play, I wrote: "What struck me first about this tale when I heard it one night in my neighborhood was how directly, with what breathtaking simplicity, it did evolve. It seemed to me, finally, that its very bareness, its absolutely unswerving path, its exposed skeleton, so to speak, was its wisdom and even its charm and must not be tampered with. . . . These *qualities* of the events themselves, their texture, seemed to me more psychologically telling than a conventional investigation in width which would necessarily relax that clear, clean line of his catastrophe."

The explanation for this point of view lies in great part in the atmosphere of the time in which the play was written. It seemed to me then that the theater was retreating into an area of psycho-sexual romanticism, and this at the very moment when great events both at home and abroad cried out for recognition and analytic inspection. In a word, I was tired of mere sympathy in the theater. The spectacle of still another misunderstood victim left me impatient. The tender emotions, I felt, were being overworked. I wanted to write in a way that would call up the faculties of knowing as well as feeling. To bathe the audience in tears, to grip people by the age-old methods of suspense, to theatricalize life, in a word, seemed faintly absurd to me if not disgusting.

In *The Crucible* I had taken a step, I felt, toward a more self-aware drama. The Puritan not only felt, but constantly referred his feelings to concepts, to codes and ideas of social and ethical importance. Feeling, it seemed to me, had to be made of importance; the dramatic victory had to be more than a triumph over the audience's indifference. It must call up a concept, a new awareness.

I had known the story of *A View from the Bridge* for a long time. A water-front worker who had known Eddie's prototype told it to me. I had never thought to make a play of it because it was too complete, there was nothing I could add. And then a time came when its very completeness became appealing. It suddenly seemed to me that I ought to deliver it onto the stage as fact; that interpretation was inherent in the very existence of the tale in the first place. I saw that the reason I had not written it was that as a whole its meaning escaped me. I could not fit it into myself. It existed apart from me and seemed not to express anything within me. Yet it refused to disappear.

I wrote it in a mood of experiment—to see what it might mean. I kept to the *tale*, trying not to change its original shape. I wanted the audience to feel toward it as I had on hearing it for the first time—not so much with heart-wringing sympathy as with wonder. For when it was told to me I knew its ending a few minutes after the teller had begun to speak. I wanted to create suspense but not by withholding information. It must be suspenseful because one knew too well how it would come out, so that the basic feeling would be the desire to stop this man and tell him what he was really doing to his life. Thus, by knowing more than the hero, the audience would rather automatically see his life through conceptualized feelings.

As a consequence of this viewpoint, the characters were not permitted to talk about this and that before getting down to their functions in the tale; when a character entered he proceeded directly to serve the catastrophe. Thus, normal naturalistic acting techniques had to be modified. Excessive and arbitrary gestures were eliminated; the set itself was shorn of every adornment. An atmosphere was attempted in which nothing existed but the purpose of the tale.

The trouble was that neither the director, the actors, nor I had had any experience with this kind of staging. It was difficult to know how far to go. We were all aware that a strange style was called for which we were unsure how to provide.

About a year later in London new conditions created new solutions. Seemingly inconsequential details suggested these solutions at times. For one, the British actors could not reproduce the Brooklyn argot and had to create one that was never heard on heaven or earth. Already naturalism was evaporated by this much: the characters were slightly strange beings in a world of their own. Also, the pay scales of the London theater made it possible to do what I could not do in New York—hire a crowd.

These seemingly mundane facts had important consequences. The mind of Eddie Carbone is not comprehensible apart from its relation to his neighborhood, his fellow workers, his social situation. His self-esteem depends upon their estimate of him, and his value is created largely by his fidelity to the code of his culture. In New York we could have only four strategically placed actors to represent the community. In London there were at least twenty men and women surrounding the main action. Peter Brook, the British director, could then proceed to design a set which soared to the roof with fire escapes, passageways, suggested apartments, so that one sensed that Eddie was living out his horror in the midst of a certain normality, and that, invisibly and without having to speak of it, he was getting ready to invoke upon himself the wrath of his tribe. A certain size accrued to him as a result. The importance of his interior psychological dilemma was magnified to the size it would have in life. What had seemed like a mere aberration had now risen to a fatal violation of an ancient law. By the presence of his neighbors alone the play and Eddie were made more humanly understandable and moving. There was also the fact that the British cast, accustomed to playing Shakespeare, could incorporate into a seemingly realistic style the conception of the play—they moved easily into the larger-than-life attitude which the play demanded, and without the self-conscious awkwardness, the uncertain stylishness which hounds many actors without classic training.

As a consequence of not having to work at making the play seem as factual, as bare as I had conceived it, I felt now that it could afford to include elements of simple human motivation which I had rigorously excluded before—specifically, the viewpoint of Eddie's wife, and *her* dilemma in relation to him. This, in fact, accounts for almost all the added material which made it necessary to break the play in the middle for an intermission. In other words, once Eddie had been placed squarely in his social context, among his people, the mythlike feeling of the story emerged of itself, and he could be made more human and less a figure, a force. It thus seemed quite in keeping that certain details of realism should be allowed; a Christmas tree and decorations in the living room, for one, and a realistic make-up, which had been avoided in New York, where the actor was always much cleaner than a longshoreman ever is. In a word, the nature of the British actor and of the production there made it possible to concentrate more upon realistic characterization while the universality of Eddie's type was strengthened at the same time.

But it was not only external additions, such as a new kind of actor, sets, and so forth, which led to the expansion of the play. As I have said, the original was written in the hope that I would understand what it meant to me. It was only during the latter part of its run in New York that, while watching a performance one afternoon, I saw my own involvement in this story. Quite suddenly the play seemed to be "mine" and not merely a story I had heard. The revisions subsequently made were in part the result of that new awareness.

In general, then, I think it can be said that by the addition of significant psychological and behavioral detail the play became not only more human, warmer and less remote, but also a clearer statement. Eddie is still not a man to weep over; the play does not attempt to swamp an audience in tears. But it is more possible now to relate his actions to our own and thus to understand ourselves a little better not only as isolated psychological entities, but as we connect to our fellows and our long past together.

A VIEW FROM THE BRIDGE

CAST OF CHARACTERS

LOUIS
MIKE
ALFIERI
EDDIE
CATHERINE
BEATRICE
MARCO
TONY
RODOLPHO
FIRST IMMIGRATION OFFICER
SECOND IMMIGRATION
    OFFICER
MR. LIPARI
MRS. LIPARI
TWO "SUBMARINES"
NEIGHBORS

ACT ONE

(*The street and house front of a tenement building. The front is skeletal entirely. The main acting area is the living room–dining room of Eddie's apartment. It is a worker's flat, clean, sparse, homely. There is a rocker down front; a round dining table at center, with chairs; and a portable phonograph.*

At back are a bedroom door and an opening to the kitchen; none of these interiors are seen.

At the right, forestage, a desk. This is Mr. Alfieri's law office.

A *View from the Bridge* by Arthur Miller. Copyright 1955, © 1957 by Arthur Miller and reprinted by permission of The Viking Press, Inc. Inquiries concerning performance rights should be addressed to Ashley Famous Agency, 555 Madison Ave., N.Y.C. 22, N.Y. Lyrics from "Paper Doll" by Johnny Black copyright by Edward B. Marks Music Corp. Used by permission.

There is also a telephone booth. This is not used until the last scenes, so it may be covered or left in view.

A stairway leads up to the apartment, and then farther up to the next story, which is not seen.

Ramps, representing the street, run upstage and off to right and left.

As the curtain rises, LOUIS *and* MIKE, *longshoremen, are pitching coins against the building at left.*

A distant foghorn blows.

Enter ALFIERI, *a lawyer in his fifties turning gray; he is portly, good-humored, and thoughtful. The two pitchers nod to him as he passes. He crosses the stage to his desk, removes his hat, runs his fingers through his hair, and grinning, speaks to the audience*)

ALFIERI   You wouldn't have known it, but something amusing has just happened. You see how uneasily they nod to me? That's because I am a lawyer. In this neighborhood to meet a lawyer or a priest on the street is unlucky. We're only thought of in connection with disasters, and they'd rather not get too close.

I often think that behind that suspicious little nod of theirs lie three thousand years of distrust. A lawyer means the law, and in Sicily, from where their fathers came, the law has not been a friendly idea since the Greeks were beaten.

I am inclined to notice the ruins in things, perhaps because I was born in Italy. . . . I only came here when I was twenty-five. In those days, Al Capone, the greatest Carthaginian of all, was learning his trade on these pavements, and Frankie Yale himself was cut precisely in half by a machine gun on the corner of Union Street, two blocks away. Oh, there were many here who were justly shot by unjust men. Justice is very important here.

But this is Red Hook, not Sicily. This is the slum that faces the bay on the seaward side of Brooklyn Bridge. This is the gullet of New York swallowing the tonnage of the world. And now we are quite civilized, quite American. Now we settle for half, and I like it better. I no longer keep a pistol in my filing cabinet.

And my practice is entirely unromantic.

My wife has warned me, so have my friends; they tell me the people in this neighborhood lack elegance, glamour. After all, who have I dealt with in my life? Longshoremen and their wives, and fathers and grandfathers, compensation cases, evictions, family squabbles—the petty troubles of the poor—and yet . . . every few years there is still a case, and as the parties tell me what the trouble is, the flat air in my office suddenly washes in with the green scent of the sea, the dust in this air is blown away and the thought comes that in some Caesar's year, in Calabria perhaps or on the cliff at Syracuse, another lawyer, quite differently dressed, heard the same complaint and sat there as powerless as I, and watched it run its bloody course. (EDDIE *has appeared and has been pitching coins with the men and is highlighted among them. He is forty—a husky, slightly overweight longshoreman*)

This one's name was Eddie Carbone, a longshoreman working the docks from Brooklyn Bridge to the breakwater where the open sea begins. (ALFIERI *walks into darkness*)

EDDIE (*moving up steps into doorway*) Well, I'll see ya, fellas.

(CATHERINE *enters from kitchen, crosses down to window, looks out*)

LOUIS   You workin' tomorrow?

EDDIE   Yeah, there's another day yet on that ship. See ya, Louis. (EDDIE *goes into the house, as light rises in the apartment.* CATHERINE *is waving to* LOUIS *from the window and turns to him*)

CATHERINE   Hi, Eddie!

(EDDIE *is pleased and therefore shy about it; he hangs up his cap and jacket*)

EDDIE   Where you goin' all dressed up?

CATHERINE (*running her hands over her skirt*)   I just got it. You like it?

EDDIE   Yeah, it's nice. And what happened to your hair?

CATHERINE   You like it? I fixed it different (*calling to kitchen*) He's here, B.!

EDDIE   Beautiful. Turn around, lemme see in the back. (*She turns for him*) Oh, if your mother was alive to see you now! She wouldn't believe it.

CATHERINE   You like it, huh?

EDDIE   You look like one of them girls that went to college. Where you goin'?

CATHERINE (*taking his arm*) Wait'll B. comes in, I'll tell you something. Here, sit down. (*She is walking him to the armchair. Calling offstage*) Hurry up, will you, B.?

EDDIE (*sitting*)   What's goin' on?

CATHERINE   I'll get you a beer, all right?

EDDIE   Well, tell me what happened. Come over here, talk to me.

CATHERINE   I want to wait till B. comes in. (*She sits on her heels beside him*) Guess how much we paid for the skirt.

EDDIE   I think it's too short, ain't it?

CATHERINE (*standing*)   No! not when I stand up.

EDDIE   Yeah, but you gotta sit down sometimes.

CATHERINE   Eddie, it's the style now. (*She walks to show him*) I mean, if you see me walkin' down the street—

EDDIE   Listen, you been given' me the willies the way you walk down the street, I mean it.

CATHERINE   Why?

EDDIE   Catherine, I don't want to be a pest, but I'm tellin' you you're walkin' wavy.

CATHERINE   I'm walkin' wavy?

EDDIE   Now don't aggravate me, Katie, you are walkin' wavy! I don't like the looks they're givin' you in the candy store. And with them new high heels on the sidewalk—clack, clack, clack. The heads are turnin' like windmills.

CATHERINE   But those guys look at all the girls, you know that.

EDDIE   You ain't "all the girls."

CATHERINE (*almost in tears because he disapproves*)   What do you want me to do? You want me to—

EDDIE   Now don't get mad, kid.

CATHERINE   Well, I don't know what you want from me.

EDDIE   Katie, I promised your mother on her deathbed. I'm responsible for you. You're a baby, you don't understand these things. I mean like when you stand here by the window, wavin' outside.

CATHERINE   I was wavin' to Louis!

EDDIE   Listen, I could tell you things about Louis which you wouldn't wave to him no more.

CATHERINE (*trying to joke him out of his warning*)   Eddie, I wish there was one guy you couldn't tell me things about!

EDDIE   Catherine, do me a favor, will you? You're gettin' to be a big girl now, you gotta keep yourself more, you can't be so friendly, kid. (*calls*) Hey, B., what're you doin' in there?

(*to* CATHERINE) Get her in here, will you? I got news for her.

CATHERINE (*starting out*) What?

EDDIE Her cousins landed.

CATHERINE (*clapping her hands together*) No! (*She turns instantly and starts for the kitchen*) B.! Your cousins!

(BEATRICE *enters, wiping her hands with a towel*)

BEATRICE (*in the face of* CATHERINE's *shout*) What?

CATHERINE Your cousins got in!

BEATRICE (*astounded, turns to* EDDIE) What are you talkin' about? Where?

EDDIE I was just knockin' off work before and Tony Bereli come over to me; he says the ship is in the North River.

BEATRICE (*her hands are clasped at her breast; she seems half in fear, half in unutterable joy*) They're all right?

EDDIE He didn't see them yet, they're still on board. But as soon as they get off he'll meet them. He figures about ten o'clock they'll be here.

BEATRICE (*sits, almost weak from tension*) And they'll let them off the ship all right? That's fixed, heh?

EDDIE Sure, they give them regular seamen papers and they walk off with the crew. Don't worry about it, B., there's nothin' to it. Couple of hours they'll be here.

BEATRICE What happened? They wasn't supposed to be till next Thursday.

EDDIE I don't know; they put them on any ship they can get them out on. Maybe the other ship they was supposed to take there was some danger—What you cryin' about?

BEATRICE (*astounded and afraid*) I'm—I just—I can't believe it! I didn't even buy a new tablecloth; I was gonna wash the walls—

EDDIE Listen, they'll think it's a millionaire's house compared to the way they live. Don't worry about the walls. They'll be thankful. (*to* CATHERINE) Whyn't you run down buy a tablecloth. Go ahead, here. (*He is reaching into his pocket*)

CATHERINE There's no stores open now.

EDDIE (*to* BEATRICE) You was gonna put a new cover on the chair.

BEATRICE I know—well, I thought it was gonna be next week! I was gonna clean the walls, I was gonna wax the floors. (*She stands disturbed*)

CATHERINE (*pointing upward*) Maybe Mrs. Dondero upstairs—

BEATRICE (*of the tablecloth*) No, hers is worse than this one. (*suddenly*) My God, I don't even have nothin' to eat for them! (*She starts for the kitchen*)

EDDIE (*reaching out and grabbing her arm*) Hey, hey! Take it easy.

BEATRICE No, I'm just nervous, that's all. (*to* CATHERINE) I'll make the fish.

EDDIE You're savin' their lives, what're you worryin' about the tablecloth? They probably didn't see a tablecloth in their whole life where they come from.

BEATRICE (*looking into his eyes*) I'm just worried about you, that's all I'm worried.

EDDIE Listen, as long as they know where they're gonna sleep.

BEATRICE I told them in the letters. They're sleepin' on the floor.

EDDIE Beatrice, all I'm worried about is you got such a heart that I'll end up on the floor with you, and they'll be in our bed.

BEATRICE All right, stop it.

EDDIE Because as soon as you see a tired relative, I end up on the floor.

BEATRICE When did you end up on the floor?

EDDIE When your father's house burned down I didn't end up on the floor?

BEATRICE Well, their house burned down!

EDDIE Yeah, but it didn't keep burnin' for two weeks!

BEATRICE All right, look, I'll tell them to go someplace else. (*She starts into the kitchen*)

EDDIE Now wait a minute. Beatrice! (*She halts. He goes to her*) I just don't want you bein' pushed around, that's all. You got too big a heart. (*He touches her hand*) What're you so touchy?

BEATRICE I'm just afraid if it don't turn out good you'll be mad at me.

EDDIE Listen, if everybody keeps his mouth shut, nothin' can happen. They'll pay for their board.

BEATRICE Oh, I told them.

EDDIE Then what the hell. (*pause. He moves*) It's an honor, B. I mean it. I was just thinkin' before, comin' home, suppose my father didn't come to this country, and I was starvin' like them over there . . . and I had people in America could keep me a couple of months? The man would be honored to lend me a place to sleep.

BEATRICE (*there are tears in her eyes. She turns to* CATHERINE) You see what he is? (*She turns and grabs* EDDIE's *face in her hands*) Mmm! You're an angel! God'll bless you. (*He is gratefully smiling*) You'll see, you'll get a blessing for this!

EDDIE (*laughing*) I'll settle for my own bed.

BEATRICE Go, Baby, set the table.

CATHERINE We didn't tell him about me yet.

BEATRICE Let him eat first, then we'll tell him. Bring everything in. (*She hurries* CATHERINE *out*)

EDDIE (*sitting at the table*) What's all that about? Where's she goin'?

BEATRICE Noplace. It's very good news, Eddie. I want you to be happy.

EDDIE What's goin' on?

(CATHERINE *enters with plates, forks*)

BEATRICE She's got a job.

(*Pause.* EDDIE *looks at* CATHERINE, *then back to* BEATRICE)

EDDIE What job? She's gonna finish school.

CATHERINE Eddie, you won't believe it—

EDDIE No—no, you gonna finish school. What kinda job, what do you mean? All of a sudden you—

CATHERINE Listen a minute, it's wonderful.

EDDIE It's not wonderful. You'll never get nowheres unless you finish school. You can't take no job. Why didn't you ask me before you take a job?

BEATRICE She's askin' you now, she didn't take nothin' yet.

CATHERINE Listen a minute! I came to school this morning and the principal called me out of the class, see? To go to his office.

EDDIE Yeah?

CATHERINE So I went in and he says to me he's got my records, y'know? And there's a company wants a girl right away. It ain't exactly a secretary, it's a stenographer first, but pretty soon you get to be secretary. And he says to me that I'm the best student in the whole class—

BEATRICE You hear that?

EDDIE Well why not? Sure she's the best.

CATHERINE I'm the best student, he says, and if I want, I should take the job and the end of the year he'll let me take the examination and he'll give me the certificate. So I'll save practically a year!

EDDIE (*strangely nervous*) Where's the job? What company?

CATHERINE It's a big plumbing company over Nostrand Avenue.

EDDIE Nostrand Avenue and where?

CATHERINE It's someplace by the Navy Yard.

BEATRICE Fifty dollars a week, Eddie.

EDDIE (*to* CATHERINE, *surprised*) Fifty?

CATHERINE I swear.

(*Pause*)

EDDIE What about all the stuff you wouldn't learn this year, though?

CATHERINE There's nothin' more to learn, Eddie, I just gotta practice from now on. I know all the symbols and I know the keyboard. I'll just get faster, that's all. And when I'm workin' I'll keep gettin' better and better, you see?

BEATRICE Work is the best practice anyway.

EDDIE That ain't what I wanted, though.

CATHERINE Why! It's a great big company—

EDDIE I don't like that neighborhood over there.

CATHERINE It's a block and a half from the subway, he says.

EDDIE Near the Navy Yard plenty can happen in a block and a half. And a plumbin' company! That's one step over the water front. They're practically longshoremen.

BEATRICE Yeah, but she'll be in the office, Eddie.

EDDIE I know she'll be in the office, but that ain't what I had in mind.

BEATRICE Listen, she's gotta go to work sometime.

EDDIE Listen, B., she'll be with a lotta plumbers? And sailors up and down the street? So what did she go to school for?

CATHERINE But it's fifty a week, Eddie.

EDDIE Look, did I ask you for money? I supported you this long I support you a little more. Please, do me a favor, will ya? I want you to be with different kind of people. I want you to be in a nice office. Maybe a lawyer's office someplace in New York in one of them nice buildings. I mean if you're gonna get outa here then get out; don't go practically in the same kind of neighborhood.

(*Pause.* CATHERINE *lowers her eyes*)

BEATRICE Go, Baby, bring in the supper. (CATHERINE *goes out*) Think about it a little bit, Eddie. Please. She's crazy to start work. It's not a little shop, it's a big company. Some day she could be a secretary. They picked her out of the whole class. (*He is silent, staring down at the tablecloth, fingering the pattern*) What are you worried about? She could take care of herself. She'll get out of the subway and be in the office in two minutes.

EDDIE (*somehow sickened*) I know that neighborhood, B., I don't like it.

BEATRICE Listen, if nothin' happened to

her in this neighborhood it ain't gonna happen noplace else. (*She turns his face to her*) Look, you gotta get used to it, she's no baby no more. Tell her to take it. (*He turns his head away*) You hear me? (*She is angering*) I don't understand you; she's seventeen years old, you gonna keep her in the house all her life?

EDDIE (*insulted*) What kinda remark is that?

BEATRICE (*with sympathy but insistent force*) Well, I don't understand when it ends. First it was gonna be when she graduated high school, so she graduated high school. Then it was gonna be when she learned stenographer, so she learned stenographer. So what're we gonna wait for now? I mean it, Eddie, sometimes I don't understand you; they picked her out of the whole class, it's an honor for her.

(CATHERINE *enters with food, which she silently sets on the table. After a moment of watching her face,* EDDIE *breaks into a smile, but it almost seems that tears will form in his eyes*)

EDDIE With your hair that way you look like a madonna, you know that? You're the madonna type. (*She doesn't look at him, but continues ladling out food onto the plates*) You wanna go to work, heh, Madonna?

CATHERINE (*softly*) Yeah.

EDDIE (*with a sense of her childhood, her babyhood, and the years*) All right, go to work. (*She looks at him, then rushes and hugs him*) Hey, hey! Take it easy! (*He holds her face away from him to look at her*) What're you cryin' about? (*He is affected by her, but smiles his emotion away*)

CATHERINE (*sitting at her place*) I just— (*bursting out*) I'm gonna buy all new dishes with my first pay! (*They laugh warmly*) I mean it. I'll fix up the whole house! I'll buy a rug!

EDDIE And then you'll move away.

CATHERINE No, Eddie!

EDDIE (*grinning*) Why not? That's life. And you'll come visit on Sundays, then once a month, then Christmas and New Year's, finally.

CATHERINE (*grasping his arm to reassure him and to erase the accusation*) No, please!

EDDIE (*smiling but hurt*) I only ask you one thing—don't trust nobody. You got a good aunt but she's got too big a heart, you learned bad from her. Believe me.

BEATRICE Be the way you are, Katie, don't listen to him.

EDDIE (*to* BEATRICE—*strangely and quickly resentful*) You lived in a house all your life, what do you know about it? You never worked in your life.

BEATRICE She likes people. What's wrong with that?

EDDIE Because most people ain't people. She's goin' to work; plumbers; they'll chew her to pieces if she don't watch out. (*to* CATHERINE) Believe me, Katie, the less you trust, the less you be sorry. (EDDIE *crosses himself and the women do the same, and they eat*)

CATHERINE First thing I'll buy is a rug, heh, B.?

BEATRICE I don't mind. (*to* EDDIE) I smelled coffee all day today. You unloadin' coffee today?

EDDIE Yeah, a Brazil ship.

CATHERINE I smelled it too. It smelled all over the neighborhood.

EDDIE That's one time, boy, to be a longshoreman is a pleasure. I could work coffee ships twenty hours a day. You go down in the hold, y'know? It's like flowers, that smell. We'll bust a bag tomorrow, I'll bring you some.

BEATRICE Just be sure there's no spiders in it, will ya? I mean it. (*She directs this to* CATHERINE, *rolling her eyes upward*) I still remember that spider coming out of that bag he brung home. I nearly died.

EDDIE You call that a spider? You oughta see what comes outa the bananas sometimes.

BEATRICE Don't talk about it!

EDDIE I seen spiders could stop a Buick.

BEATRICE (*clapping her hands over her ears*) All right, shut up!

EDDIE (*laughing and taking a watch out of his pocket*) Well, who started with spiders?

BEATRICE All right, I'm sorry, I didn't mean it. Just don't bring none home again. What time is it?

EDDIE Quarter nine. (*Puts watch back in his pocket. They continue eating in silence*)

CATHERINE He's bringin' them ten o'clock, Tony?

EDDIE Around, yeah. (*He eats*)

CATHERINE Eddie, suppose somebody asks if they're livin' here. (*He looks at her as though already she had divulged something publicly. Defensively*) I mean if they ask.

EDDIE Now look, Baby, I can see we're gettin' mixed up again here.

CATHERINE No, I just mean . . . people'll see them goin' in and out.

EDDIE I don't care who sees them goin' in and out as long as you don't see them goin' in and out. And this goes for you too, B. You don't see nothin' and you don't know nothin'.

BEATRICE What do you mean? I understand.

EDDIE You don't understand; you still think you can talk about this to somebody just a little bit. Now lemme say it once and for all, because you're makin' me nervous again, both of you. I don't care if somebody comes in the house and sees them sleepin' on the floor, it never comes out of your mouth who they are or what they're doin' here.

BEATRICE Yeah, but my mother'll know—

EDDIE Sure she'll know, but just don't you be the one who told her, that's all. This is the United States government you're playin' with now, this is the Immigration Bureau. If you said it you knew it, if you didn't say it you didn't know it.

CATHERINE Yeah, but Eddie, suppose somebody—

EDDIE I don't care what question it is. You —don't—know—nothin'. They got stool pigeons all over this neighborhood they're payin' them every week for information, and you don't know who they are. It could be your best friend. You hear? (to BEATRICE) Like Vinny Bolzano, remember Vinny?

BEATRICE Oh, yeah. God forbid.

EDDIE Tell her about Vinny. (to CATHERINE) You think I'm blowin' steam here? (to BEATRICE) Go ahead, tell her. (to CATHERINE) You was a baby then. There was a family lived next door to her mother, he was about sixteen—

BEATRICE No, he was no more than fourteen, cause I was to his confirmation in Saint Agnes. But the family had an uncle that they were hidin' in the house, and he snitched to the Immigration.

CATHERINE The kid snitched?

EDDIE On his own uncle!

CATHERINE What, was he crazy?

EDDIE He was crazy after, I tell you that, boy.

BEATRICE Oh, it was terrible. He had five brothers and the old father. And they grabbed him in the kitchen and pulled him down the stairs—three flights his head was bouncin' like a coconut. And they spit on him in the street, his own father and his brothers. The whole neighborhood was cryin'.

CATHERINE Ts! So what happened to him?

BEATRICE I think he went away. (to EDDIE) I never seen him again, did you?

EDDIE (rises during this, taking out his watch) Him? You'll never see him no more, a guy do a thing like that? How's he gonna show his face? (to CATHERINE, as he gets up uneasily) Just remember, kid, you can quicker get back a million dollars that was stole than a

word that you gave away. (He is standing now, stretching his back)

CATHERINE Okay, I won't say a word to nobody, I swear.

EDDIE Gonna rain tomorrow. We'll be slidin' all over the decks. Maybe you oughta put something on for them, they be here soon.

BEATRICE I only got fish, I hate to spoil it if they ate already. I'll wait, it only takes a few minutes; I could broil it.

CATHERINE What happens, Eddie, when that ship pulls out and they ain't on it, though? Don't the captain say nothin'?

EDDIE (slicing an apple with his pocket knife) Captain's pieced off, what do you mean?

CATHERINE Even the Captain?

EDDIE What's the matter, the captain don't have to live? Captain gets a piece, maybe one of the mates, piece for the guy in Italy who fixed the papers for them, Tony here'll get a little bite. . . .

BEATRICE I just hope they get work here, that's all I hope.

EDDIE Oh, the syndicate'll fix jobs for them; till they pay 'em off they'll get them work every day. It's after the pay-off, then they'll have to scramble like the rest of us.

BEATRICE Well, it be better than they got there.

EDDIE Oh sure, well, listen. So you gonna start Monday, heh, Madonna?

CATHERINE (embarrassed) I'm supposed to, yeah.

(EDDIE is standing facing the two seated women. First BEATRICE smiles, then CATHERINE, for a powerful emotion is on him, a childish one and a knowing fear, and the tears show in his eyes—and they are shy before the avowal)

EDDIE (sadly smiling, yet somehow proud of her) Well . . . I hope you have good luck. I wish you the best. You know that, kid.

CATHERINE (rising, trying to laugh) You sound like I'm goin' a million miles.

EDDIE I know. I guess I just never figured on one thing.

CATHERINE (smiling) What?

EDDIE That you would ever grow up. (He utters a soundless laugh at himself, feeling his breast pocket of his shirt) I left a cigar in my other coat, I think. (He starts for the bedroom)

CATHERINE Stay there! I'll get it for you.

(She hurries out. There is a slight pause, and EDDIE turns to BEATRICE, who has been avoiding his gaze)

EDDIE What are you mad at me lately?

BEATRICE   Who's mad? (*She gets up, clearing the dishes*) I'm not mad. (*She picks up the dishes and turns to him*) You're the one is mad. (*She turns and goes into the kitchen as* CATHERINE *enters from the bedroom with a cigar and a pack of matches*)

CATHERINE   Here! I'll light it for you! (*She strikes a match and holds it to his cigar. He puffs. Quietly*) Don't worry about me, Eddie, heh?

EDDIE   Don't burn yourself. (*Just in time she blows out the match*) You better go in help her with the dishes. (CATHERINE *turns quickly to the table, and seeing the table cleared, she says, almost guiltily*) Oh! (*She hurries into the kitchen, and as she exits there*) I'll do the dishes, B.!

(*Alone,* EDDIE *stands looking toward the kitchen for a moment. Then he takes out his watch, glances at it, replaces it in his pocket, sits in the armchair, and stares at the smoke flowing out of his mouth.*

The lights go down, then come up on ALFIERI, *who has moved onto the forestage*)

ALFIERI   He was as good a man as he had to be in a life that was hard and even. He worked on the piers when there was work, he brought home his pay, and he lived. And toward ten o'clock of that night, after they had eaten, the cousins came.

(*The lights fade on* ALFIERI *and rise on the street.*

Enter TONY, *escorting* MARCO *and* RODOLPHO, *each with a valise.* TONY *halts, indicates the house. They stand for a moment looking at it*)

MARCO   (*he is a square-built peasant of thirty-two, suspicious, tender, and quiet-voiced*) Thank you.

TONY   You're on your own now. Just be careful, that's all. Ground floor.

MARCO   Thank you.

TONY   (*indicating the house*)   I'll see you on the pier tomorrow. You'll go to work.

(MARCO *nods.* TONY *continues on walking down the street*)

RODOLPHO   This will be the first house I ever walked into in America! Imagine! She said they were poor!

MARCO   Ssh! Come. (*They go to door*)

(MARCO *knocks. The lights rise in the room.* EDDIE *goes and opens the door. Enter* MARCO *and* RODOLPHO, *removing their caps.* BEATRICE *and* CATHERINE *enter from the kitchen. The lights fade in the street*)

EDDIE   You Marco?

MARCO   Marco.

EDDIE   Come on in! (*He shakes* MARCO's *hand*)

BEATRICE   Here, take the bags!

MARCO   (*nods, looks to the women and fixes on* BEATRICE. *Crosses to* BEATRICE)   Are you my cousin? (*She nods. He kisses her hand*)

BEATRICE   (*above the table, touching her chest with her hand*)   Beatrice. This is my husband, Eddie. (*all nod*) Catherine, my sister Nancy's daughter. (*The brothers nod*)

MARCO   (*indicating* RODOLPHO)   My brother. Rodolpho. (RODOLPHO *nods.* MARCO *comes with a certain formal stiffness to* EDDIE)   I want to tell you now Eddie—when you say go, we will go.

EDDIE   Oh, no . . . (*takes* MARCO's *bag*)

MARCO   I see it's a small house, but soon, maybe, we can have our own house.

EDDIE   You're welcome, Marco, we got plenty of room here. Katie, give them supper, heh? (*exits into bedroom with their bags*)

CATHERINE   Come here, sit down. I'll get you some soup.

MARCO   (*as they go to the table*)   We ate on the ship. Thank you. (*to* EDDIE, *calling off to bedroom*) Thank you.

BEATRICE   Get some coffee. We'll all have coffee. Come sit down.

(RODOLPHO *and* MARCO *sit, at the table*)

CATHERINE   (*wondrously*)   How come he's so dark and you're so light, Rodolpho?

RODOLPHO   (*ready to laugh*)   I don't know. A thousand years ago, they say, the Danes invaded Sicily.

(BEATRICE *kisses* RODOLPHO. *They laugh as* EDDIE *enters*)

CATHERINE   (*to* BEATRICE)   He's practically blond!

EDDIE   How's the coffee doin'?

CATHERINE   (*brought up*)   I'm gettin' it. (*She hurries out to kitchen*)

EDDIE   (*sits on his rocker*)   Yiz have a nice trip?

MARCO   The ocean is always rough. But we are good sailors.

EDDIE   No trouble gettin' here?

MARCO   No. The man brought us. Very nice man.

RODOLPHO   (*to* EDDIE)   He says we start to work tomorrow. Is he honest?

EDDIE   (*laughing*)   No. But as long as you owe them money, they'll get you plenty of work. (*to* MARCO) Yiz ever work on the piers in Italy?

MARCO   Piers? Ts!—no.

RODOLPHO   (*smiling at the smallness of his*

town) In our town there are no piers, only the beach, and little fishing boats.

BEATRICE So what kinda work did yiz do?

MARCO (*shrugging shyly, even embarrassed*) Whatever there is, anything.

RODOLPHO Sometimes they build a house, or if they fix the bridge—Marco is a mason and I bring him the cement. (*He laughs*) In harvest time we work in the fields . . . if there is work. Anything.

EDDIE Still bad there, heh?

MARCO Bad, yes.

RODOLPHO (*laughing*) It's terrible! We stand around all day in the piazza listening to the fountain like birds. Everybody waits only for the train.

BEATRICE What's on the train?

RODOLPHO Nothing. But if there are many passengers and you're lucky you make a few lire to push the taxi up the hill.

(*Enter* CATHERINE; *she listens*)

BEATRICE You gotta push a taxi?

RODOLPHO (*laughing*) Oh, sure! It's a feature in our town. The horses in our town are skinnier than goats. So if there are too many passengers we help to push the carriages up to the hotel. (*He laughs*) In our town the horses are only for show.

CATHERINE Why don't they have automobile taxis?

RODOLPHO There is one. We push that too. (*They laugh*) Everything in our town, you gotta push!

BEATRICE (*to* EDDIE) How do you like that!

EDDIE (*to* MARCO) So what're you wanna do, you gonna stay here in this country or you wanna go back?

MARCO (*surprised*) Go back?

EDDIE Well, you're married, ain't you?

MARCO Yes. I have three children.

BEATRICE Three! I thought only one.

MARCO Oh, no. I have three now. Four years, five years, six years.

BEATRICE Ah . . . I bet they're cryin' for you already, heh?

MARCO What can I do? The older one is sick in his chest. My wife—she feeds them from her own mouth. I tell you the truth, if I stay there they will never grow up. They eat the sunshine.

BEATRICE My God. So how long you want to stay?

MARCO With your permission, we will stay maybe a—

EDDIE She don't mean in this house, she means in the country.

MARCO Oh. Maybe four, five, six years, I think.

RODOLPHO (*smiling*) He trusts his wife.

BEATRICE Yeah, but maybe you'll get enough, you'll be able to go back quicker.

MARCO I hope. I don't know. (*to* EDDIE) I understand it's not so good here either.

EDDIE Oh, you guys'll be all right—till you pay them off, anyway. After that, you'll have to scramble, that's all. But you'll make better here than you could there.

RODOLPHO How much? We hear all kinds of figures. How much can a man make? We work hard, we'll work all day, all night—

(MARCO *raises a hand to hush him*)

EDDIE (*he is coming more and more to address* MARCO *only*) On the average a whole year? Maybe—well, it's hard to say, see. Sometimes we lay off, there's no ships three, four weeks.

MARCO Three, four weeks!—Ts!

EDDIE But I think you could probably—thirty, forty a week, over the whole twelve months of the year.

MARCO (*rises, crosses to* EDDIE) Dollars.

EDDIE Sure dollars.

(MARCO *puts an arm round* RODOLPHO *and they laugh*)

MARCO If we can stay here a few months, Beatrice—

BEATRICE Listen, you're welcome, Marco—

MARCO Because I could send them a little more if I stay here.

BEATRICE As long as you want, we got plenty a room.

MARCO (*his eyes are showing tears*) My wife—(*to* EDDIE) My wife—I want to send right away maybe twenty dollars—

EDDIE You could send them something next week already.

MARCO (*he is near tears*) Eduardo . . . (*He goes to* EDDIE, *offering his hand*)

EDDIE Don't thank me. Listen, what the hell, it's no skin off me. (*to* CATHERINE) What happened to the coffee?

CATHERINE I got it on. (*to* RODOLPHO) You married too? No.

RODOLPHO (*rises*) Oh, no . . .

BEATRICE (*to* CATHERINE) I told you he—

CATHERINE I know, I just thought maybe he got married recently.

RODOLPHO I have no money to get married. I have a nice face, but no money. (*He laughs*)

CATHERINE (*to* BEATRICE) He's a real blond!

BEATRICE (*to* RODOLPHO) You want to stay here too, heh? For good?

RODOLPHO Me? Yes, forever! Me, I want to be an American. And then I want to go back to Italy when I am rich, and I will buy a motorcycle. (*He smiles.* MARCO *shakes him affectionately*)

CATHERINE A motorcycle!

RODOLPHO With a motorcycle in Italy you will never starve any more.

BEATRICE I'll get you coffee. (*She exits to the kitchen*)

EDDIE What do you do with a motorcycle?

MARCO He dreams, he dreams.

RODOLPHO (*to* MARCO) Why? (*to* EDDIE) Messages! The rich people in the hotel always need someone who will carry a message. But quickly, and with a great noise. With a blue motorcycle I would station myself in the courtyard of the hotel, and in a little while I would have messages.

MARCO When you have no wife you have dreams.

EDDIE Why can't you just walk, or take a trolley or sump'm?

(*Enter* BEATRICE *with coffee*)

RODOLPHO Oh, no, the machine, the machine is necessary. A man comes into a great hotel and says, I am a messenger. Who is this man? He disappears walking, there is no noise, nothing. Maybe he will never come back, maybe he will never deliver the message. But a man who rides upon a great machine, this man is responsible, this man exists. He will be given messages. (*He helps* BEATRICE *set out the coffee things*) I am also a singer, though.

EDDIE You mean a regular—?

RODOLPHO Oh, yes. One night last year Andreola got sick. Baritone. And I took his place in the garden of the hotel. Three arias I sang without a mistake! Thousand-lire notes they threw from the tables, money was falling like a storm in the treasury. It was magnificent. We lived six months on that night, eh, Marco?

(MARCO *nods doubtfully*)

MARCO Two months.

(EDDIE *laughs*)

BEATRICE Can't you get a job in that place?

RODOLPHO Andreola got better. He's a baritone, very strong.

(BEATRICE *laughs*)

MARCO (*regretfully, to* BEATRICE) He sang too loud.

RODOLPHO Why too loud?

MARCO Too loud. The guests in that hotel are all Englishmen. They don't like too loud.

RODOLPHO (*to* CATHERINE) Nobody ever said it was too loud!

MARCO I say. It was too loud. (*to* BEATRICE) I knew it as soon as he started to sing. Too loud.

RODOLPHO Then why did they throw so much money?

MARCO They paid for your courage. The English like courage. But once is enough.

RODOLPHO (*to all but* MARCO) I never heard anybody say it was too loud.

CATHERINE Did you ever hear of jazz?

RODOLPHO Oh, sure! I *sing* jazz.

CATHERINE (*rises*) You could sing jazz?

RODOLPHO Oh, I sing Napolidan, jazz, bel canto—I sing "Paper Doll," you like "Paper Doll"?

CATHERINE Oh, sure, I'm crazy for "Paper Doll." Go ahead, sing it.

(RODOLPHO *takes his stance after getting a nod of permission from* MARCO, *and with a high tenor voice begins singing*)

> I'll tell you boys it's tough to be alone,
> And it's tough to love a doll that's
>   not your own.
> I'm through with all of them,
> I'll never fall again,
> Hey, boy, what you gonna do?
> I'm gonna buy a paper doll that I
>   can call my own,
> A doll that other fellows cannot steal.

(EDDIE *rises and moves upstage*)

> And then those flirty, flirty guys
> With their flirty, flirty eyes
> Will have to flirt with dollies that are
>   real—

EDDIE Hey, kid—hey, wait a minute—

CATHERINE (*enthralled*) Leave him finish, it's beautiful! (*to* BEATRICE) He's terrific! It's terrific, Rodolpho.

EDDIE Look, kid; you don't want to be picked up, do ya?

MARCO No—no! (*He rises*)

EDDIE (*indicating the rest of the building*) Because we never had no singers here . . . and all of a sudden there's a singer in the house, y'know what I mean?

MARCO Yes, yes. You'll be quiet, Rodolpho.

EDDIE (*he is flushed*) They got guys all over the place, Marco. I mean.

MARCO Yes. He'll be quiet. (*to* RODOLPHO) You'll be quiet.

(RODOLPHO *nods*)

(EDDIE *has risen, with iron control, even a smile. He moves to* CATHERINE)

EDDIE   What's the high heels for, Garbo?

CATHERINE   I figured for tonight—

EDDIE   Do me a favor, will you? Go ahead.

(*Embarrassed now, angered,* CATHERINE *goes out into the bedroom.* BEATRICE *watches her go and gets up; in passing, she gives* EDDIE *a cold look, restrained only by the strangers, and goes to the table to pour coffee*)

EDDIE (*striving to laugh, and to* MARCO, *but directed as much to* BEATRICE)   All actresses they want to be around here.

RODOLPHO (*happy about it*)   In Italy too! All the girls.

(CATHERINE *emerges from the bedroom in low-heel shoes, comes to the table.* RODOLPHO *is lifting a cup*)

EDDIE (*he is sizing up* RODOLPHO, *and there is a concealed suspicion*)   Yeah, heh?

RODOLPHO   Yes! (*laughs, indicating* CATHERINE)   Especially when they are so beautiful!

CATHERINE   You like sugar?

RODOLPHO   Sugar? Yes! I like sugar very much!

(EDDIE *is downstage, watching as she pours a spoonful of sugar into his cup, his face puffed with trouble, and the room dies.*

Lights rise on Alfieri)

ALFIERI   Who can ever know what will be discovered? Eddie Carbone had never expected to have a destiny. A man works, raises his family, goes bowling, eats, gets old, and then he dies. Now, as the weeks passed, there was a future, there was a trouble that would not go away.

(*The lights fade on* ALFIERI, *then rise on* EDDIE *standing at the doorway of the house.* BEATRICE *enters on the street. She sees* EDDIE, *smiles at him. He looks away.*

She starts to enter the house when EDDIE *speaks*)

EDDIE   It's after eight.

BEATRICE   Well, it's a long show at the Paramount.

EDDIE   They must've seen every picture in Brooklyn by now. He's supposed to stay in the house when he ain't working. He ain't supposed to go advertising himself.

BEATRICE   Well that's his trouble, what do you care? If they pick him up they pick him up, that's all. Come in the house.

EDDIE   What happened to the stenography? I don't see her practice no more.

BEATRICE   She'll get back to it. She's excited, Eddie.

EDDIE   She tell you anything?

BEATRICE (*comes to him, now the subject is opened*)   What's the matter with you? He's a nice kid, what do you want from him?

EDDIE   That's a nice kid? He gives me the heeby-jeebies.

BEATRICE (*smiling*)   Ah, go on, you're just jealous.

EDDIE   Of *him*? Boy, you don't think much of me.

BEATRICE   I don't understand you. What's so terrible about him?

EDDIE   You mean it's all right with you? That's gonna be her husband?

BEATRICE   Why? He's a nice fella, hard workin', he's a good-lookin' fella.

EDDIE   He sings on the ships, didja know that?

BEATRICE   What do you mean, he sings?

EDDIE   Just what I said, he sings. Right on the deck, all of a sudden, a whole song comes out of his mouth—with motions. You know what they're callin' him now? Paper Doll they're callin' him, Canary. He's like a weird. He comes out on the pier, one-two-three, it's a regular free show.

BEATRICE   Well, he's a kid; he don't know how to behave himself yet.

EDDIE   And with that wacky hair; he's like a chorus girl or sump'm.

BEATRICE   So he's blond, so—

EDDIE   I just hope that's his regular hair, that's all I hope.

BEATRICE   You crazy or sump'm? (*She tries to turn him to her*)

EDDIE (*he keeps his head turned away*)   What's so crazy? I don't like his whole way.

BEATRICE   Listen, you never seen a blond guy in your life? What about Whitey Balso?

EDDIE (*turning to her victoriously*)   Sure, but Whitey don't sing; he don't do like that on the ships.

BEATRICE   Well, maybe that's the way they do in Italy.

EDDIE   Then why don't his brother sing? Marco goes around like a man; nobody kids Marco. (*He moves from her, halts. She realizes there is a campaign solidified in him*)   I tell you the truth I'm surprised I have to tell you all this. I mean I'm surprised, B.

BEATRICE (*she goes to him with purpose now*)   Listen, you ain't gonna start nothin' here.

EDDIE   I ain't startin' nothin', but I ain't gonna stand around lookin' at that. For that character I didn't bring her up. I swear, B., I'm surprised at you; I sit there waitin' for you to wake up but everything is great with you.

BEATRICE   No, everything ain't great with me.

EDDIE   No?

BEATRICE   No. But I got other worries.

EDDIE   Yeah. (*He is already weakening*)

BEATRICE   Yeah, you want me to tell you?

EDDIE (*in retreat*)   Why? What worries you got?

BEATRICE   When am I gonna be a wife again, Eddie?

EDDIE   I ain't been feelin' good. They bother me since they came.

BEATRICE   It's almost three months you don't feel good; they're only here a couple of weeks. It's three months, Eddie.

EDDIE   I don't know, B. I don't want to talk about it.

BEATRICE   What's the matter, Eddie, you don't like me, heh?

EDDIE   What do you mean, I don't like you? I said I don't feel good, that's all.

BEATRICE   Well, tell me, am I doing something wrong? Talk to me.

EDDIE (*pause. He can't speak, then*)   I can't. I can't talk about it.

BEATRICE   Well tell me what—

EDDIE   I got nothin' to say about it!

(*She stands for a moment; he is looking off; she turns to go into the house*)

EDDIE   I'll be all right, B.; just lay off me, will ya? I'm worried about her.

BEATRICE   The girl is gonna be eighteen years old, it's time already.

EDDIE   B., he's taking her for a ride!

BEATRICE   All right, that's her ride. What're you gonna stand over her till she's forty? Eddie, I want you to cut it out now, you hear me? I don't like it! Now come in the house.

EDDIE   I want to take a walk, I'll be in right away.

BEATRICE   They ain't goin' to come any quicker if you stand in the street. It ain't nice, Eddie.

EDDIE   I'll be in right away. Go ahead. (*He walks off*)

(*She goes into the house.* EDDIE *glances up the street, sees* LOUIS *and* MIKE *coming, and sits on an iron railing.* LOUIS *and* MIKE *enter*)

LOUIS   Wanna go bowlin' tonight?

EDDIE   I'm too tired. Goin' to sleep.

LOUIS   How's your two submarines?

EDDIE   They're okay.

LOUIS   I see they're gettin' work allatime.

EDDIE   Oh yeah, they're doin' all right.

MIKE   That's what we oughta do. We oughta leave the country and come in under the water. Then we get work.

EDDIE   You ain't kiddin'.

LOUIS   Well, what the hell. Y'know?

EDDIE   Sure.

LOUIS (*sits on railing beside* EDDIE)   Believe me, Eddie, you got a lotta credit comin' to you.

EDDIE   Aah, they don't bother me, don't cost me nutt'n.

MIKE   That older one, boy, he's a regular bull. I seen him the other day liftin' coffee bags over the Matson Line. They leave him alone he woulda load the whole ship by himself.

EDDIE   Yeah, he's a strong guy, that guy. Their father was a regular giant, supposed to be.

LOUIS   Yeah, you could see. He's a regular slave.

MIKE (*grinning*)   That blond one, though— (EDDIE *looks at him*) He's got a sense of humor. (LOUIS *snickers*)

EDDIE (*searchingly*)   Yeah. He's funny—

MIKE (*starting to laugh*)   Well he ain't exackly funny, but he's always like makin' remarks like, y'know? He comes around, everybody's laughin'. (LOUIS *laughs*)

EDDIE (*uncomfortably, grinning*)   Yeah, well . . . he's got a sense of humor.

MIKE (*laughing*)   Yeah, I mean, he's always makin' like remarks, like, y'know?

EDDIE   Yeah, I know. But he's a kid yet, y'know? He—he's just a kid, that's all.

MIKE (*getting hysterical with* LOUIS)   I know. You take one look at him—everybody's happy. (LOUIS *laughs*) I worked one day with him last week over the Moore-MacCormack Line, I'm tellin' you they was all hysterical. (LOUIS *and he explode in laughter*)

EDDIE   Why? What'd he do?

MIKE   I don't know . . . he was just humorous. You never can remember what he says, y'know? But it's the way he says it. I mean he gives you a look sometimes and you start laughin'!

EDDIE   Yeah. (*troubled*) He's got a sense of humor.

MIKE (*gasping*)   Yeah.

LOUIS (*rising*)   Well, we see ya, Eddie.

EDDIE   Take it easy.

LOUIS   Yeah. See ya.

MIKE   If you wanna come bowlin' later we're goin' Flatbush Avenue.

(*Laughing, they move to exit, meeting* RO-DOLPHO *and* CATHERINE *entering on the street. Their laughter rises as they see* RODOLPHO, *who does not understand but joins in.* EDDIE *moves to enter the house as* LOUIS *and* MIKE *exit.* CATHERINE *stops him at the door*)

CATHERINE   Hey, Eddie—what a picture we saw! Did we laugh!

EDDIE (*he can't help smiling at sight of her*) Where'd you go?

CATHERINE Paramount. It was with those two guys, y'know? That—

EDDIE Brooklyn Paramount?

CATHERINE (*with an edge of anger, embarrassed before* RODOLPHO) Sure, the Brooklyn Paramount. I told you we wasn't goin' to New York.

EDDIE (*retreating before the threat of her anger*) All right, I only asked you. (*to* RODOLPHO) I just don't want her hangin' around Times Square, see? It's full of tramps over there.

RODOLPHO I would like to go to Broadway once, Eddie. I would like to walk with her once where the theatres are and the opera. Since I was a boy I see pictures of those lights.

EDDIE (*his little patience waning*) I want to talk to her a minute, Rodolpho. Go inside, will you?

RODOLPHO Eddie, we only walk together in the streets. She teaches me.

CATHERINE You know what he can't get over? That there's no fountains in Brooklyn!

EDDIE (*smiling unwillingly*) Fountains? (RODOLPHO *smiles at his own naïveté*)

CATHERINE In Italy he says, every town's got fountains, and they meet there. And you know what? They got oranges on the trees where he comes from, and lemons. Imagine—on the trees? I mean it's interesting. But he's crazy for New York.

RODOLPHO (*attempting familiarity*) Eddie, why can't we go once to Broadway—?

EDDIE Look, I gotta tell her something—

RODOLPHO Maybe you can come too. I want to see all those lights. (*He sees no response in* EDDIE'S *face. He glances at* CATHERINE) I'll walk by the river before I go to sleep. (*He walks off down the street*)

CATHERINE Why don't you talk to him, Eddie? He blesses you, and you don't talk to him hardly.

EDDIE (*enveloping her with his eyes*) I bless you and you don't talk to me. (*He tries to smile*)

CATHERINE *I* don't talk to you? (*She hits his arm*) What do you mean?

EDDIE I don't see you no more. I come home you're runnin' around someplace—

CATHERINE Well, he wants to see everything, that's all, so we go. . . . You mad at me?

EDDIE No. (*He moves from her, smiling sadly*) It's just I used to come home, you was always there. Now, I turn around, you're a big girl. I don't know how to talk to you.

CATHERINE Why?

EDDIE I don't know, you're runnin', you're runnin', Katie. I don't think you listening any more to me.

CATHERINE (*going to him*) Ah, Eddie, sure I am. What's the matter? You don't like him? (*Slight pause*)

EDDIE (*turns to her*) You like him, Katie?

CATHERINE (*with a blush but holding her ground*) Yeah. I like him.

EDDIE (*his smile goes*) You like him.

CATHERINE (*looking down*) Yeah. (*Now she looks at him for the consequences, smiling but tense. He looks at her like a lost boy*) What're you got against him? I don't understand. He only blesses you.

EDDIE (*turns away*) He don't bless me, Katie.

CATHERINE He does! You're like a father to him!

EDDIE (*turns to her*) Katie.

CATHERINE What, Eddie?

EDDIE You gonna marry him?

CATHERINE I don't know. We just been . . . goin' around, that's all. (*turns to him*) What're you got against him, Eddie? Please, tell me. What?

EDDIE He don't respect you.

CATHERINE Why?

EDDIE Katie . . . if you wasn't an orphan, wouldn't he ask your father's permission before he run around with you like this?

CATHERINE Oh, well, he didn't think you'd mind.

EDDIE He knows I mind, but it don't bother him if I mind, don't you see that?

CATHERINE No, Eddie, he's got all kinds of respect for me. And you too! We walk across the street he takes my arm—he almost bows to me! You got him all wrong, Eddie; I mean it, you—

EDDIE Katie, he's only bowin' to his passport.

CATHERINE His passport!

EDDIE That's right. He marries you he's got the right to be an American citizen. That's what's goin' on here. (*She is puzzled and surprised*) You understand what I'm tellin' you? The guy is lookin' for his break, that's all he's lookin' for.

CATHERINE (*pained*) Oh, no, Eddie, I don't think so.

EDDIE You don't think so! Katie, you're gonna make me cry here. Is that a workin' man? What does he do with his first money? A snappy new jacket he buys, records, a pointy pair new shoes and his brother's kids are starvin' over there with tuberculosis? That's a hit-and-run guy, baby; he's got bright lights in his head, Broadway. Them guys don't think of nobody but theirself! You marry him and the next time you see him it'll be for divorce!

CATHERINE (*steps toward him*) Eddie, he never said a word about his papers or—

EDDIE You mean he's supposed to tell you that?

CATHERINE I don't think he's even thinking about it.

EDDIE What's better for him to think about! He could be picked up any day here and he's back pushin' taxis up the hill!

CATHERINE No, I don't believe it.

EDDIE Katie, don't break my heart, listen to me.

CATHERINE I don't want to hear it.

EDDIE Katie, listen . . .

CATHERINE He loves me!

EDDIE (*with deep alarm*) Don't say that, for God's sake! This is the oldest racket in the country—

CATHERINE (*desperately, as though he had made his imprint*) I don't believe it! (*She rushes to the house*)

EDDIE (*following her*) They been pullin' this since the Immigration Law was put in! They grab a green kid that don't know nothin' and they—

CATHERINE (*sobbing*) I don't believe it and I wish to hell you'd stop it!

EDDIE Katie!

(*They enter the apartment. The lights in the living room have risen and* BEATRICE *is there. She looks past the sobbing* CATHERINE *at* EDDIE, *who in the presence of his wife, makes an awkward gesture of eroded command, indicating* CATHERINE)

EDDIE Why don't you straighten her out?

BEATRICE (*inwardly angered at his flowing emotion, which in itself alarms her*) When are you going to leave her alone?

EDDIE B., the guy is no good!

BEATRICE (*suddenly, with open fright and fury*) You going to leave her alone? Or you gonna drive me crazy? (*He turns, striving to retain his dignity, but nevertheless in guilt walks out of the house, into the street and away.* CATHERINE *starts into a bedroom*) Listen, Catherine. (CATHERINE *halts, turns to her sheepishly*) What are you going to do with yourself?

CATHERINE I don't know.

BEATRICE Don't tell me you don't know; you're not a baby any more, what are you going to do with yourself?

CATHERINE He won't listen to me.

BEATRICE I don't understand this. He's not your father, Catherine. I don't understand what's going on here.

CATHERINE (*as one who herself is trying to rationalize a buried impulse*) What am I going to do, just kick him in the face with it?

BEATRICE Look, honey, you wanna get married, or don't you wanna get married? What are you worried about, Katie?

CATHERINE (*quietly, trembling*) I don't know B. It just seems wrong if he's against it so much.

BEATRICE (*never losing her aroused alarm*) Sit down, honey, I want to tell you something. Here, sit down. Was there ever any fella he liked for you? There wasn't, was there?

CATHERINE But he says Rodolpho's just after his papers.

BEATRICE Look, he'll say anything. What does he care what he says? If it was a prince came here for you it would be no different. You know that, don't you?

CATHERINE Yeah, I guess.

BEATRICE So what does that mean?

CATHERINE (*slowly turns her head to* BEATRICE) What?

BEATRICE It means you gotta be your own self more. You still think you're a little girl, honey. But nobody else can make up your mind for you any more, you understand? You gotta give him to understand that he can't give you orders no more.

CATHERINE Yeah, but how am I going to do that? He thinks I'm a baby.

BEATRICE Because *you* think you're a baby. I told you fifty times already, you can't act the way you act. You still walk around in front of him in your slip—

CATHERINE Well I forgot.

BEATRICE Well you can't do it. Or like you sit on the edge of the bathtub talkin' to him when he's shavin' in his underwear.

CATHERINE When'd I do that?

BEATRICE I seen you in there this morning.

CATHERINE Oh . . . well, I wanted to tell him something and I—

BEATRICE I know, honey. But if you act like a baby and he be treatin' you like a baby. Like when he comes home sometimes you throw yourself at him like when you was twelve years old.

CATHERINE Well I like to see him and I'm happy so I—

BEATRICE Look, I'm not tellin' you what to do honey, but—

CATHERINE No, you could tell me, B.! Gee,

I'm all mixed up. See, I—He looks so sad now and it hurts me.

BEATRICE   Well look Katie, if it's goin' to hurt you so much you're gonna end up an old maid here.

CATHERINE   No!

BEATRICE   I'm tellin' you, I'm not makin' a joke. I tried to tell you a couple of times in the last year or so. That's why I was so happy you were going to go out and get work, you wouldn't be here so much, you'd be a little more independent. I mean it. It's wonderful for a whole family to love each other, but you're a grown woman and you're in the same house with a grown man. So you'll act different now, heh?

CATHERINE   Yeah, I will. I'll remember.

BEATRICE   Because it ain't only up to him, Katie, you understand? I told him the same thing already.

CATHERINE   (quickly)   What?

BEATRICE   That he should let you go. But, you see, if only I tell him, he thinks I'm just bawlin' him out, or maybe I'm jealous or somethin', you know?

CATHERINE   (astonished)   He said you was jealous?

BEATRICE   No, I'm just sayin' maybe that's what he thinks. (She reaches over to CATHERINE's hand; with a strained smile) You think I'm jealous of you, honey?

CATHERINE   No! It's the first I thought of it.

BEATRICE   (with a quiet sad laugh)   Well you should have thought of it before . . . but I'm not. We'll be all right. Just give him to understand; you don't have to fight, you're just —You're a woman, that's all, and you got a nice boy, and now the time came when you said good-bye. All right?

CATHERINE   (strangely moved at the prospect)   All right. . . . If I can.

BEATRICE   Honey . . . you gotta.

(CATHERINE, sensing now an imperious demand, turns with some fear, with a discovery, to BEATRICE. She is at the edge of tears, as though a familiar world had shattered)

CATHERINE   Okay.

(Lights out on them and up on ALFIERI, seated behind his desk)

ALFIERI   It was at this time that he first came to me. I had represented his father in an accident case some years before, and I was acquainted with the family in a casual way. I remember him now as he walked through my doorway—

(Enter EDDIE down right ramp)

His eyes were like tunnels; my first thought was that he had committed a crime, (EDDIE sits beside the desk, cap in hand, looking out) but soon I saw it was only a passion that had moved into his body, like a stranger. (ALFIERI pauses, looks down at his desk, then to EDDIE as though he were continuing a conversation with him) I don't quite understand what I can do for you. Is there a question of law somewhere?

EDDIE   That's what I want to ask you.

ALFIERI   Because there's nothing illegal about a girl falling in love with an immigrant.

EDDIE   Yeah, but what about it if the only reason for it is to get his papers?

ALFIERI   First of all you don't know that.

EDDIE   I see it in his eyes; he's laughin' at her and he's laughin' at me.

ALFIERI   Eddie, I'm a lawyer. I can only deal in what's provable. You understand that, don't you? Can you prove that?

EDDIE   I know what's in his mind, Mr. Alfieri!

ALFIERI   Eddie, even if you could prove that—

EDDIE   Listen . . . will you listen to me a minute? My father always said you was a smart man. I want you to listen to me.

ALFIERI   I'm only a lawyer, Eddie.

EDDIE   Will you listen a minute? I'm talkin' about the law. Lemme just bring out what I mean. A man, which he comes into the country illegal, don't it stand to reason he's gonna take every penny and put it in the sock? Because they don't know from one day to another, right?

ALFIERI   All right.

EDDIE   He's spendin'. Records he buys now. Shoes. Jackets. Y'understand me? This guy ain't worried. This guy is here. So it must be that he's got it all laid out in his mind already—he's stayin'. Right?

ALFIERI   Well? What about it?

EDDIE   All right. (He glances at ALFIERI, then down to the floor) I'm talking to you confidential, ain't I?

ALFIERI   Certainly.

EDDIE   I mean it don't go no place but here. Because I don't like to say this about anybody. Even my wife I didn't exactly say this.

ALFIERI   What is it?

EDDIE   (takes a breath and glances briefly over each shoulder)   The guy ain't right, Mr. Alfieri.

ALFIERI   What do you mean?

EDDIE   I mean he ain't right.

ALFIERI   I don't get you.

EDDIE   (*shifts to another position in the chair*)   Dja ever get a look at him?

ALFIERI   Not that I know of, no.

EDDIE   He's a blond guy. Like . . . platinum. You know what I mean?

ALFIERI   No.

EDDIE   I mean if you close the paper fast—you could blow him over.

ALFIERI   Well that doesn't mean—

EDDIE   Wait a minute, I'm tellin' you sump'm. He sings, see. Which is—I mean it's all right, but sometimes he hits a note, see. I turn around. I mean—high. You know what I mean?

ALFIERI   Well, that's a tenor.

EDDIE   I know a tenor, Mr. Alfieri. This ain't no tenor. I mean if you came in the house and you didn't know who was singin', you wouldn't be lookin' for him you be lookin' for her.

ALFIERI   Yes, but that's not—

EDDIE   I'm tellin' you sump'm, wait a minute. Please, Mr. Alfieri. I'm tryin' to bring out my thoughts here. Couple of nights ago my niece brings out a dress which it's too small for her, because she shot up like a light this last year. He takes the dress, lays it on the table, he cuts it up; one-two-three, he makes a new dress. I mean he looked so sweet there, like an angel—you could kiss him he was so sweet.

ALFIERI   Now look, Eddie—

EDDIE   Mr. Alfieri, they're laughin' at him on the piers. I'm ashamed. Paper Doll they call him. Blondie now. His brother thinks it's because he's got a sense of humor, see—which he's got—but that ain't what they're laughin'. Which they're not goin' to come out with it because they know he's my relative, which they have to see me if they make ,a crack, y'know? But I know what they're laughin' at, and when I think of that guy layin' his hands on her I could—I mean it's eatin' me out, Mr. Alfieri, because I struggled for that girl. And now he comes in my house and—

ALFIERI   Eddie, look—I have my own children. I understand you. But the law is very specific. The law does not . . .

EDDIE   (*with a fuller flow of indignation*) You mean to tell me that there's no law that a guy which he ain't right can go to work and marry a girl and—?

ALFIERI   You have no recourse in the law, Eddie.

EDDIE   Yeah, but if he ain't right, Mr. Alfieri, you mean to tell me—

ALFIERI   There is nothing you can do, Eddie, believe me.

EDDIE   Nothin'.

ALFIERI   Nothing at all. There's only one legal question here.

EDDIE   What?

ALFIERI   The manner in which they entered the country. But I don't think you want to do anything about that, do you?

EDDIE   You mean—?

ALFIERI   Well, they entered illegally.

EDDIE   Oh, Jesus, no, I wouldn't do nothin' about that, I mean—

ALFIERI   All right, then, let me talk now, eh?

EDDIE   Mr. Alfieri, I can't believe what you tell me. I mean there must be some kinda law which—

ALFIERI   Eddie, I want you to listen to me. (*pause*) You know, sometimes God mixes up the people. We all love somebody, the wife, the kids—every man's got somebody that he loves, heh? But sometimes . . . there's too much. You know? There's too much, and it goes where it mustn't. A man works hard, he brings up a child, sometimes it's a niece, sometimes even a daughter, and he never realizes it, but through the years—there is too much love for the daughter, there is too much love for the niece. Do you understand what I'm saying to you?

EDDIE   (*sardonically*)   What do you mean, I shouldn't look out for her good?

ALFIERI   Yes, but these things have to end, Eddie, that's all. The child has to grow up and go away, and the man has to learn to forget. Because after all, Eddie—what other way can it end? (*pause*) Let her go. That's my advice. You did your job, now it's her life; wish her luck, and let her go. (*pause*) Will you do that? Because there's no law, Eddie; make up your mind to it; the law is not interested in this.

EDDIE   You mean to tell me, even if he's a punk? If he's—

ALFIERI   There's nothing you can do.

(EDDIE *stands*)

EDDIE   Well, all right, thanks. Thanks very much.

ALFIERI   What are you going to do?

EDDIE   (*with a helpless but ironic gesture*) What can I do? I'm a patsy, what can a patsy do? I worked like a dog twenty years so a punk could have her, so that's what I done. I mean, in the worst times, in the worst, when there wasn't a ship comin' in the harbor, I didn't stand around lookin' for relief—I hustled. When there was empty piers in Brooklyn I went to Hoboken, Staten Island, the West Side, Jersey, all over—because I made a promise. I took out of my own mouth to give to her. I took out of my wife's mouth. I walked hungry plenty days in this city! (*It begins to break through*) And now I gotta sit in my own house and look at a son-of-a-bitch punk like that—which he came out of nowhere! I give him my house to sleep! I take the blankets off my bed for him, and he takes and puts his dirty filthy hands on her like a goddam thief!

ALFIERI (*rising*)   But, Eddie, she's a woman now.

EDDIE   He's stealing from me!

ALFIERI   She wants to get married, Eddie. She can't marry you, can she?

EDDIE (*furiously*)   What're you talkin' about, marry me! I don't know what the hell you're talkin' about!

(*Pause*)

ALFIERI   I gave you my advice, Eddie. That's it. (EDDIE *gathers himself. A pause*)

EDDIE   Well, thanks. Thanks very much. It just—it's breakin' my heart, y'know. I—

ALFIERI   I understand. Put it out of your mind. Can you do that?

EDDIE   I'm—(*He feels the threat of sobs, and with a helpless wave*) I'll see you around. (*He goes out up the right ramp*)

ALFIERI (*sits on desk*)   There are times when you want to spread an alarm, but nothing has happened. I knew, I knew then and there—I could have finished the whole story that afternoon. It wasn't as though there was a mystery to unravel. I could see every step coming, step after step, like a dark figure walking down a hall toward a certain door. I knew where he was heading for, I knew where he was going to end. And I sat here many afternoons asking myself why, being an intelligent man, I was so powerless to stop it. I even went to a certain old lady in the neighborhood, a very wise old woman, and I told her, and she only nodded, and said, "Pray for him . . ." And so I—waited here.

(*As lights go out on* ALFIERI, *they rise in the apartment where all are finishing dinner.* BEATRICE *and* CATHERINE *are clearing the table*)

CATHERINE   You know where they went?

BEATRICE   Where?

CATHERINE   They went to Africa once. On a fishing boat. (EDDIE *glances at her*) It's true, Eddie.

(BEATRICE *exits into the kitchen with dishes*)

EDDIE   I didn't say nothin'. (*He goes to his rocker, picks up a newspaper*)

CATHERINE   And I was never even in Staten Island.

EDDIE (*sitting with the paper*)   You didn't miss nothin'. (*pause.* CATHERINE *takes dishes out*) How long that take you, Marco—to get to Africa?

MARCO (*rising*)   Oh . . . two days. We go all over.

RODOLPHO (*rising*)   Once we went to Yugoslavia.

EDDIE (*to* MARCO)   They pay all right on them boats?

(BEATRICE *enters. She and* RODOLPHO *stack the remaining dishes*)

MARCO   If they catch fish they pay all right. (*sits on a stool*)

RODOLPHO   They're family boats, though. And nobody in our family owned one. So we only worked when one of the families was sick.

BEATRICE   Y'know, Marco, what I don't understand—there's an ocean full of fish and yiz are all starvin'.

EDDIE   They gotta have boats, nets, you need money.

(CATHERINE *enters*)

BEATRICE   Yeah, but couldn't they like fish from the beach? You see them down Coney Island—

MARCO   Sardines.

EDDIE   Sure. (*laughing*) How you gonna catch sardines on a hook?

BEATRICE   Oh, I didn't know they're sardines. (*to* CATHERINE) They're sardines!

CATHERINE   Yeah, they follow them all over the ocean, Africa, Yugoslavia . . . (*She sits and begins to look through a movie magazine.* RODOLPHO *joins her*)

BEATRICE (*to* EDDIE)   It's funny, y'know. You never think of it, that sardines are swimming in the ocean! (*She exits to kitchen with dishes*)

CATHERINE   I know. It's like oranges and lemons on a tree. (*to* EDDIE) I mean you ever think of oranges and lemons on a tree?

EDDIE   Yeah, I know. It's funny. (*to* MARCO) I heard that they paint the oranges to make them look orange.

(BEATRICE *enters*)

MARCO (*he has been reading a letter*) Paint?

EDDIE   Yeah, I heard that they grow like green.

MARCO   No, in Italy the oranges are orange.

RODOLPHO   Lemons are green.

EDDIE (*resenting his instruction*)   I know lemons are green, for Christ's sake, you see them in the store they're green sometimes. I said oranges they paint, I didn't say nothin' about lemons.

BEATRICE (*sitting; diverting their attention*) Your wife is gettin' the money all right, Marco?

MARCO Oh, yes. She bought medicine for my boy.

BEATRICE That's wonderful. You feel better, heh?

MARCO Oh, yes! But I'm lonesome.

BEATRICE I just hope you ain't gonna do like some of them around here. They're here twenty-five years, some men, and they didn't get enough together to go back twice.

MARCO Oh, I know. We have many families in our town, the children never saw the father. But I will go home. Three, four years, I think.

BEATRICE Maybe you should keep more here. Because maybe she thinks it comes so easy you'll never get ahead of yourself.

MARCO Oh, no, she saves. I send everything. My wife is very lonesome. (*He smiles shyly*)

BEATRICE She must be nice. She pretty? I bet, heh?

MARCO (*blushing*) No, but she understand everything.

RODOLPHO Oh, he's got a clever wife!

EDDIE I betcha there's plenty surprises sometimes when those guys get back there, heh?

MARCO Surprises?

EDDIE (*laughing*) I mean, you know—they count the kids and there's a couple extra than when they left?

MARCO No—no . . . The women wait, Eddie. Most. Most. Very few surprises.

RODOLPHO It's more strict in our town. (EDDIE *looks at him now*) It's not so free.

EDDIE (*rises, paces up and down*) It ain't so free here either, Rodolpho, like you think. I seen greenhorns sometimes get in trouble that way—they think just because a girl don't go around with a shawl over her head that she ain't strict, y'know? Girl don't have to wear black dress to be strict. Know what I mean?

RODOLPHO Well, I always have respect—

EDDIE I know, but in your town you wouldn't just drag off some girl without permission, I mean. (*He turns*) You know what I mean, Marco? It ain't that much different here.

MARCO (*cautiously*) Yes.

BEATRICE Well, he didn't exactly drag her off though, Eddie.

EDDIE I know, but I seen some of them get the wrong idea sometimes. (*to* RODOLPHO) I mean it might be a little more free here but it's just as strict.

RODOLPHO I have respect for her, Eddie. I do anything wrong?

EDDIE Look, kid, I ain't her father, I'm only her uncle—

BEATRICE Well then, be an uncle then. (EDDIE *looks at her, aware of her criticizing force*) I mean.

MARCO No, Beatrice, if he does wrong you must tell him. (*to* EDDIE) What does he do wrong?

EDDIE Well, Marco, till he came here she was never out on the street twelve o'clock at night.

MARCO (*to* RODOLPHO) You come home early now.

BEATRICE (*to* CATHERINE) Well, you said the movie ended late, didn't you?

CATHERINE Yeah.

BEATRICE Well, tell him, honey. (*to* EDDIE) The movie ended late.

EDDIE Look, B., I'm just sayin'—he thinks she always stayed out like that.

MARCO You come home early now, Rodolpho.

RODOLPHO (*embarrassed*) All right, sure. But I can't stay in the house all the time, Eddie.

EDDIE Look, kid, I'm not only talkin' about her. The more you run around like that the more chance you're takin'. (*to* BEATRICE) I mean suppose he gets hit by a car or something. (*to* MARCO) Where's his papers, who is he? Know what I mean?

BEATRICE Yeah, but who is he in the daytime, though? It's the same chance in the daytime.

EDDIE (*holding back a voice full of anger*) Yeah, but he don't have to go lookin' for it, Beatrice. If he's here to work, then he should work; if he's here for a good time then he could fool around! (*to* MARCO) But I understood, Marco, that you was both comin' to make a livin' for your family. You understand me, don't you, Marco? (*He goes to his rocker*)

MARCO I beg your pardon, Eddie.

EDDIE I mean, that's what I understood in the first place, see.

MARCO Yes. That's why we came.

EDDIE (*sits on his rocker*) Well, that's all I'm askin'.

(EDDIE *reads his paper. There is a pause, an awkwardness. Now* CATHERINE *gets up and puts a record on the phonograph—"Paper Doll"*)

CATHERINE (*flushed with revolt*) You wanna dance, Rodolpho?

(EDDIE *freezes*)

RODOLPHO (*in deference to* EDDIE) No, I— I'm tired.

BEATRICE Go ahead, dance, Rodolpho.

CATHERINE Ah, come on. They got a beautiful quartet, these guys. Come.

(*She has taken his hand and he stiffly rises, feeling* EDDIE'S *eyes on his back, and they dance*)

EDDIE (*to* CATHERINE)   What's that, a new record?

CATHERINE   It's the same one. We bought it the other day.

BEATRICE (*to* EDDIE)   They only bought three records. (*She watches them dance;* EDDIE *turns his head away.* MARCO *just sits there, waiting. Now* BEATRICE *turns to* EDDIE) Must be nice to go all over in one of them fishin' boats. I would like that myself. See all them other countries?

EDDIE   Yeah.

BEATRICE (*to* MARCO)   But the women don't go along, I bet.

MARCO   No, not on the boats. Hard work.

BEATRICE   What're you got, a regular kitchen and everything?

MARCO   Yes, we eat very good on the boats—especially when Rodolpho comes along; everybody gets fat.

BEATRICE   Oh, he cooks?

MARCO   Sure, very good cook. Rice, pasta, fish, everything.

(EDDIE *lowers his paper*)

EDDIE   He's a cook, too! (*looking at* RO-DOLPHO) He sings, he cooks . . .

(RODOLPHO *smiles thankfully*)

BEATRICE   Well it's good, he could always make a living.

EDDIE   It's wonderful. He sings, he cooks, he could make dresses . . .

CATHERINE   They get some high pay, them guys. The head chefs in all the big hotels are men. You read about them.

EDDIE   That's what I'm sayin'.

(CATHERINE *and* RODOLPHO *continue dancing*)

CATHERINE   Yeah, well, I mean.

EDDIE (*to* BEATRICE)   He's lucky, believe me. (*slight pause. He looks away, then back to* BEATRICE) That's why the water front is no place for him. (*They stop dancing.* RODOLPHO *turns off phonograph*) I mean like me—I can't cook, I can't sing, I can't make dresses, so I'm on the water front. But if I could cook, if I could sing, if I could make dresses, I wouldn't be on the water front. (*He has been uncon- sciously twisting the newspaper into a tight roll. They are all regarding him now; he senses he is exposing the issue and he is driven on*) I would be someplace else. I would be like in a dress store. (*He has bent the rolled paper and it suddenly tears in two. He suddenly gets*

up and pulls his pants up over his belly and goes to MARCO) What do you say, Marco, we go to the bouts next Saturday night. You never seen a fight, did you?

MARCO (*uneasily*)   Only in the moving pic- tures.

EDDIE (*going to* RODOLPHO)   I'll treat yiz. What do you say, Danish? You wanna come along? I'll buy the tickets.

RODOLPHO   Sure. I like to go.

CATHERINE (*goes to* EDDIE; *nervously happy now*)   I'll make some coffee, all right?

EDDIE   Go ahead, make some! Make it nice and strong. (*Mystified, she smiles and exits to kitchen. He is weirdly elated, rubbing his fists into his palms. He strides to* MARCO) You wait, Marco, you see some real fights here. You ever do any boxing?

MARCO   No, I never.

EDDIE (*to* RODOLPHO)   Betcha you have done some, heh?

RODOLPHO   No.

EDDIE   Well, come on, I'll teach you.

BEATRICE   What's he got to learn that for?

EDDIE   Ya can't tell, one of these days some- body's liable to step on his foot or sump'm. Come on, Rodolpho, I show you a couple a passes. (*He stands below table*)

BEATRICE   Go ahead, Rodolpho. He's a good boxer, he could teach you.

RODOLPHO (*embarrassed*)   Well, I don't know how to—(*He moves down to* EDDIE)

EDDIE   Just put your hands up. Like this, see? That's right. That's very good, keep your left up, because you lead with the left, see, like this. (*He gently moves his left into* RODOLPHO'S *face*) See? Now what you gotta do is you gotta block me, so when I come in like that you— (RODOLPHO *parries his left*) Hey, that's very good! (RODOLPHO *laughs*) All right, now come into me. Come on.

RODOLPHO   I don't want to hit you, Eddie.

EDDIE   Don't pity me, come on. Throw it, I'll show you how to block it. (RODOLPHO *jabs at him, laughing. The others join*) 'At's it. Come on again. For the jaw right here. (RODOLPHO *jabs with more assurance*) Very good!

BEATRICE (*to* MARCO)   He's very good!

(EDDIE *crosses directly upstage of* RODOLPHO)

EDDIE   Sure, he's great! Come on, kid, put sump'm behind it, you can't hurt me. (RO- DOLPHO, *more seriously, jabs at* EDDIE'S *jaw and grazes it*) Attaboy. (CATHERINE *comes from the kitchen, watches*) Now I'm gonna hit you, so block me, see?

CATHERINE (*with beginning alarm*)   What

are they doin'? (*They are lightly boxing now*)

BEATRICE (*she senses only the comradeship in it now*)   He's teachin' him; he's very good!

EDDIE   Sure, he's terrific! Look at him go! (RODOLPHO *lands a blow*) 'At's it! Now, watch out, here I come, Danish! (*He feints with his left hand and lands with his right. It mildly staggers* RODOLPHO. MARCO *rises*)

CATHERINE (*rushing to* RODOLPHO) Eddie!

EDDIE   Why? I didn't hurt him. Did I hurt you, kid? (*He rubs the back of his hand across his mouth*)

RODOLPHO   No, no, he didn't hurt me. (*to* EDDIE *with a certain gleam and a smile*) I was only surprised.

BEATRICE (*pulling* EDDIE *down into the rocker*)   That's enough, Eddie; he did pretty good, though.

EDDIE   Yeah. (*rubbing his fists together*) He could be very good, Marco. I'll teach him again. (MARCO *nods at him dubiously*)

RODOLPHO   Dance, Catherine. Come. (*He takes her hand; they go to phonograph and start it. It plays "Paper Doll"*)

(RODOLPHO *takes her in his arms. They dance.* EDDIE *in thought sits in his chair, and* MARCO *takes a chair, places it in front of* EDDIE, *and looks down at it.* BEATRICE *and* EDDIE *watch him*)

MARCO   Can you lift this chair?

EDDIE   What do you mean?

MARCO   From here. (*He gets on one knee with one hand behind his back, and grasps the bottom of one of the chair legs but does not raise it*)

EDDIE   Sure, why not? (*He comes to the chair, kneels, grasps the leg, raises the chair one inch, but it leans over to the floor*) Gee, that's hard, I never knew that. (*He tries again, and again fails*) It's on an angle, that's why, heh?

MARCO   Here.

(*He kneels, grasps, and with strain slowly raises the chair higher and higher, getting to his feet now.* RODOLPHO *and* CATHERINE *have stopped dancing as* MARCO *raises the chair over his head.*

MARCO *is face to face with* EDDIE, *a strained tension gripping his eyes and jaw, his neck stiff, the chair raised like a weapon over* EDDIE's *head—and he transforms what might appear like a glare of warning into a smile of triumph, and* EDDIE's *grin vanishes as he absorbs his look*)

ACT TWO

(*Light rises on* ALFIERI *at his desk*)

ALFIERI   On the twenty-third of that December a case of Scotch whisky slipped from a net while being unloaded—as a case of Scotch whisky is inclined to do on the twenty-third of December on Pier Forty-one. There was no snow, but it was cold, his wife was out shopping. Marco was still at work. The boy had not been hired that day; Catherine told me later that this was the first time they had been alone together in the house.

(*Light is rising on* CATHERINE *in the apartment.* RODOLPHO *is watching as she arranges a paper pattern on cloth spread on the table*)

CATHERINE   You hungry?

RODOLPHO   Not for anything to eat. (*pause*) I have nearly three hundred dollars. Catherine?

CATHERINE   I heard you.

RODOLPHO   You don't like to talk about it any more?

CATHERINE   Sure, I don't mind talkin' about it.

RODOLPHO   What worries you, Catherine?

CATHERINE   I been wantin' to ask you about something. Could I?

RODOLPHO   All the answers are in my eyes, Catherine. But you don't look in my eyes lately. You're full of secrets. (*She looks at him. She seems withdrawn*) What is the question?

CATHERINE   Suppose I wanted to live in Italy.

RODOLPHO (*smiling at the incongruity*)   You going to marry somebody rich?

CATHERINE   No, I mean live there—you and me.

RODOLPHO (*his smile vanishing*)   When?

CATHERINE   Well . . . when we get married.

RODOLPHO (*astonished*)   You want to be an Italian?

CATHERINE   No, but I could live there without being Italian. Americans live there.

RODOLPHO   Forever?

CATHERINE   Yeah.

RODOLPHO (*crosses to rocker*)   You're fooling.

CATHERINE   No, I mean it.

RODOLPHO   Where do you get such an idea?

CATHERINE   Well, you're always saying it's so beautiful there, with the mountains and the ocean and all the—

RODOLPHO   You're fooling me.

CATHERINE   I mean it.

RODOLPHO (*goes to her slowly*) Catherine, if I ever brought you home with no money, no business, nothing, they would call the priest and the doctor and they would say Rodolpho is crazy.

CATHERINE I know, but I think we would be happier there.

RODOLPHO Happier! What would you eat? You can't cook the view!

CATHERINE Maybe you could be a singer, like in Rome or—

RODOLPHO Rome! Rome is full of singers.

CATHERINE Well, I could work then.

RODOLPHO Where?

CATHERINE God, there must be jobs somewhere!

RODOLPHO There's nothing! Nothing, nothing, nothing. Now tell me what you're talking about. How can I bring you from a rich country to suffer in a poor country? What are you talking about? (*She searches for words*) I would be a criminal stealing your face. In two years you would have an old, hungry face. When my brother's babies cry they give them water, water that boiled a bone. Don't you believe that?

CATHERINE (*quietly*) I'm afraid of Eddie here.

(*Slight pause*)

RODOLPHO (*steps closer to her*) We wouldn't live here. Once I am a citizen I could work anywhere and I would find better jobs and we would have a house, Catherine. If I were not afraid to be arrested I would start to be something wonderful here!

CATHERINE (*steeling herself*) Tell me something. I mean just tell me, Rodolpho— would you still want to do it if it turned out we had to go live in Italy? I mean just if it turned out that way.

RODOLPHO This is your question or his question?

CATHERINE I would like to know, Rodolpho. I mean it.

RODOLPHO To go there with nothing.

CATHERINE Yeah.

RODOLPHO No. (*She looks at him wide-eyed*) No.

CATHERINE You wouldn't?

RODOLPHO No; I will not marry you to live in Italy. I want you to be my wife, and I want to be a citizen. Tell him that, or I will. Yes. (*He moves about angrily*) And tell him also, and tell yourself, please, that I am not a beggar, and you are not a horse, a gift, a favor for a poor immigrant.

CATHERINE Well, don't get mad!

RODOLPHO I am furious! (*goes to her*) Do you think I am so desperate? My brother is desperate, not me. You think I would carry on my back the rest of my life a woman I didn't love just to be an American? It's so wonderful? You think we have no tall buildings in Italy? Electric lights? No wide streets? No flags? No automobiles? Only work we don't have. I want to be an American so I can work, that is the only wonder here—work! How can you insult me, Catherine?

CATHERINE I didn't mean that—

RODOLPHO My heart dies to look at you. Why are you so afraid of him?

CATHERINE (*near tears*) I don't know!

RODOLPHO Do you trust me, Catherine? You?

CATHERINE It's only that I—He was good to me, Rodolpho. You don't know him; he was always the sweetest guy to me. Good. He razzes me all the time but he don't mean it. I know. I would—just feel ashamed if I made him sad. 'Cause I always dreamt that when I got married he would be happy at the wedding, and laughin'—and now he's—mad all the time and nasty—(*She is weeping*) Tell him you'd live in Italy—just tell him, and maybe he would start to trust you a little, see? Because I want him to be happy; I mean—I like him, Rodolpho—and I can't stand it!

RODOLPHO Oh, Catherine—oh, little girl.

CATHERINE I love you, Rodolpho, I love you.

RODOLPHO Then why are you afraid? That he'll spank you?

CATHERINE Don't, don't laugh at me! I've been here all my life. . . . Every day I saw him when he left in the morning and when he came home at night. You think it's so easy to turn around and say to a man he's nothin' to you no more?

RODOLPHO I know, but—

CATHERINE You don't know; nobody knows! I'm not a baby, I know a lot more than people think I know. Beatrice says to be a woman, but—

RODOLPHO Yes.

CATHERINE Then why don't she be a woman? If I was a wife I would make a man happy instead of goin' at him all the time. I can tell a block away when he's blue in his mind and just wants to talk to somebody quiet and nice. . . . I can tell when he's hungry or wants a beer before he even says anything. I know when his feet hurt him, I mean I *know* him and now I'm supposed to turn around and make a stranger out of him? I don't know why I have to do that, I mean.

RODOLPHO   Catherine. If I take in my hands a little bird. And she grows and wishes to fly. But I will not let her out of my hands because I love her so much, is that right for me to do? I don't say you must hate him; but anyway you must go, mustn't you? Catherine?

CATHERINE   (*softly*)   Hold me.

RODOLPHO   (*clasping her to him*)   Oh, my little girl.

CATHERINE   Teach me. (*She is weeping*) I don't know anything, teach me, Rodolpho, hold me.

RODOLPHO   There's nobody here now. Come inside. Come. (*He is leading her toward the bedrooms*) And don't cry any more.

(*Light rises on the street. In a moment* EDDIE *appears. He is unsteady, drunk. He mounts the stairs. He enters the apartment, looks around, takes out a bottle from one pocket, puts it on the table. Then another bottle from another pocket, and a third from an inside pocket. He sees the pattern and cloth, goes over to it and touches it, and turns toward upstage*)

EDDIE   Beatrice? (*He goes to the open kitchen door and looks in*) Beatrice? Beatrice?

(CATHERINE *enters from bedroom; under his gaze she adjusts her dress*)

CATHERINE   You got home early.

EDDIE   Knocked off for Christmas early. (*indicating the pattern*) Rodolpho makin' you a dress?

CATHERINE   No. I'm makin' a blouse.

(RODOLPHO *appears in the bedroom doorway.* EDDIE *sees him and his arm jerks slightly in shock.* RODOLPHO *nods to him testingly*)

RODOLPHO   Beatrice went to buy presents for her mother.

(*Pause*)

EDDIE   Pack it up. Go ahead. Get your stuff and get outa here. (CATHERINE *instantly turns and walks toward the bedroom, and* EDDIE *grabs her arm*) Where you goin'?

CATHERINE   (*trembling with fright*)   I think I have to get out of here, Eddie.

EDDIE   No, you ain't goin' nowheres, he's the one.

CATHERINE   I think I can't stay here no more. (*She frees her arm, steps back toward the bedroom*) I'm sorry, Eddie. (*She sees the tears in his eyes*) Well, don't cry. I'll be around the neighborhood; I'll see you. I just can't stay here no more. You know I can't. (*Her sobs of pity and love for him break her composure*) Don't

you know I can't? You know that, don't you? (*She goes to him*) Wish me luck. (*She clasps her hands prayerfully*) Oh, Eddie, don't be like that!

EDDIE   You ain't goin' nowheres.

CATHERINE   Eddie, I'm not gonna be a baby any more! You—

(*He reaches out suddenly, draws her to him, and as she strives to free herself he kisses her on the mouth*)

RODOLPHO   Don't! (*He pulls on* EDDIE's *arm*) Stop that! Have respect for her!

EDDIE   (*spun round by* RODOLPHO)   You want something?

RODOLPHO   Yes! She'll by my wife. That is what I want. My wife!

EDDIE   But what're you gonna be?

RODOLPHO   I show you what I be!

CATHERINE   Wait outside; don't argue with him!

EDDIE   Come on, show me! What're you gonna be? Show me!

RODOLPHO   (*with tears of rage*)   Don't say that to me!

(RODOLPHO *flies at him in attack.* EDDIE *pins his arms, laughing, and suddenly kisses him*)

CATHERINE   Eddie! Let go, ya hear me! I'll kill you! Leggo of him!

(*She tears at* EDDIE's *face and* EDDIE *releases* RODOLPHO. EDDIE *stands there with tears rolling down his face as he laughs mockingly at* RODOLPHO. *She is staring at him in horror.* RODOLPHO *is rigid. They are like animals that have torn at one another and broken up without a decision, each waiting for the other's mood*)

EDDIE   (*to* CATHERINE)   You see? (*to* RODOLPHO)   I give you till tomorrow, kid. Get outa here. Alone. You hear me? Alone.

CATHERINE   I'm going with him, Eddie. (*She starts toward* RODOLPHO)

EDDIE   (*indicating* RODOLPHO *with his head*) Not with that. (*She halts, frightened. He sits, still panting for breath, and they watch him helplessly as he leans toward them over the table*) Don't make me do nuttin', Catherine. Watch your step, submarine. By rights they oughta throw you back in the water. But I got pity for you. (*He moves unsteadily toward the door, always facing* RODOLPHO) Just get outa here and don't lay another hand on her unless you wanna go out feet first. (*He goes out of the apartment*)

(*The lights go down, as they rise on* ALFIERI)

ALFIERI   On December twenty-seventh I

saw him next. I normally go home well before six, but that day I sat around looking out my window at the bay, and when I saw him walking through my doorway, I knew why I had waited. And if I seem to tell this like a dream, it was that way. Several moments arrived in the course of the two talks we had when it occurred to me how—almost transfixed I had come to feel. I had lost my strength somewhere. (EDDIE *enters, removing his cap, sits in the chair, looks thoughtfully out*) I looked in his eyes more than I listened—in fact, I can hardly remember the conversation. But I will never forget how dark the room became when he looked at me; his eyes were like tunnels. I kept wanting to call the police, but nothing had happened. Nothing at all had really happened. (*He breaks off and looks down at the desk. Then he turns to* EDDIE) So in other words, he won't leave?

EDDIE   My wife is talkin' about renting a room upstairs for them. An old lady on the top floor is got an empty room.

ALFIERI   What does Marco say?

EDDIE   He just sits there. Marco don't say much.

ALFIERI   I guess they didn't tell him, heh? What happened?

EDDIE   I don't know; Marco don't say much.

ALFIERI   What does your wife say?

EDDIE   (*unwilling to pursue this*) Nobody's talkin' much in the house. So what about that?

ALFIERI   But you didn't prove anything about him. It sounds like he just wasn't strong enough to break your grip.

EDDIE   I'm tellin' you I know—he ain't right. Somebody that don't want it can break it. Even a mouse, if you catch a teeny mouse and you hold it in your hand, that mouse can give you the right kind of fight. He didn't give me the right kind of fight, I know it, Mr. Alfieri, the guy ain't right.

ALFIERI   What did you do that for, Eddie?

EDDIE   To show her what he is! So she would see, once and for all! Her mother'll turn over in the grave! (*He gathers himself almost peremptorily*) So what do I gotta do now? Tell me what to do.

ALFIERI   She actually said she's marrying him?

EDDIE   She told me, yeah. So what do I do?

(*Slight pause*)

ALFIERI   This is my last word, Eddie, take it or not, that's your business. Morally and legally you have no rights, you cannot stop it; she is a free agent.

EDDIE   (*angering*) Didn't you hear what I told you?

ALFIERI   (*with a tougher tone*) I heard what you told me, and I'm telling you what the answer is. I'm not only telling you now, I'm warning you—the law is nature. The law is only a word for what has a right to happen. When the law is wrong it's because it's unnatural, but in this case it is natural and a river will drown you if you buck it now. Let her go. And bless her. (*A phone booth begins to glow on the opposite side of the stage; a faint, lonely blue.* EDDIE *stands up, jaws clenched*) Somebody had to come for her, Eddie, sooner or later. (EDDIE *starts turning to go and* ALFIERI *rises with new anxiety*) You won't have a friend in the world, Eddie! Even those who understand will turn against you, even the ones who feel the same will despise you! (EDDIE *moves off*) Put it out of your mind! Eddie! (*He follows into the darkness, calling desperately*)

(EDDIE *is gone. The phone is glowing in light now. Light is out on* ALFIERI. EDDIE *has at the same time appeared beside the phone*)

EDDIE   Give me the number of the Immigration Bureau. Thanks. (*He dials*) I want to report something. Illegal immigrants. Two of them. That's right. Four-forty-one Saxon Street, Brooklyn, yeah. Ground floor. Heh? (*with greater difficulty*) I'm just around the neighborhood, that's all. Heh?

(*Evidently he is being questioned further, and he slowly hangs up. He leaves the phone just as* LOUIS *and* MIKE *come down the street*)

LOUIS   Go bowlin', Eddie?

EDDIE   No, I'm due home.

LOUIS   Well, take it easy.

EDDIE   I'll see yiz.

(*They leave him, exiting right, and he watches them go. He glances about, then goes up into the house. The lights go on in the apartment.* BEATRICE *is taking down Christmas decorations and packing them in a box*)

EDDIE   Where is everybody? (BEATRICE *does not answer*) I says where is everybody?

BEATRICE   (*looking up at him, wearied with it, and concealing a fear of him*) I decided to move them upstairs with Mrs. Dondero.

EDDIE   Oh, they're all moved up there already?

BEATRICE   Yeah.

EDDIE   Where's Catherine? She up there?

BEATRICE   Only to bring pillow cases.

EDDIE   She ain't movin' in with them.

BEATRICE   Look, I'm sick and tired of it. I'm sick and tired of it!

EDDIE All right, all right, take it easy.

BEATRICE I don't wanna hear no more about it, you understand? Nothin'!

EDDIE What're you blowin' off about? Who brought them in here?

BEATRICE All right, I'm sorry; I wish I'd a drop dead before I told them to come. In the ground I wish I was.

EDDIE Don't drop dead, just keep in mind who brought them in here, that's all. (*He moves about restlessly*) I mean I got a couple of rights here. (*He moves, wanting to beat down her evident disapproval of him*) This is my house here not their house.

BEATRICE What do you want from me? They're moved out; what do you want now?

EDDIE I want my respect!

BEATRICE So I moved them out, what more do you want? You got your house now, you got your respect.

EDDIE (*he moves about biting his lip*) I don't like the way you talk to me, Beatrice.

BEATRICE I'm just tellin' you I done what you want!

EDDIE I don't like it! The way you talk to me and the way you look at me. This is my house. And she is my niece and I'm responsible for her.

BEATRICE So that's why you done that to him?

EDDIE I done what to him?

BEATRICE What you done to him in front of her; you know what I'm talkin' about. She goes around shakin' all the time, she can't go to sleep! That's what you call responsible for her?

EDDIE (*quietly*) The guy ain't right, Beatrice. (*She is silent*) Did you hear what I said?

BEATRICE Look, I'm finished with it. That's all. (*She resumes her work*)

EDDIE (*helping her to pack the tinsel*) I'm gonna have it out with you one of these days, Beatrice.

BEATRICE Nothin' to have out with me, it's all settled. Now we gonna be like it never happened, that's all.

EDDIE I want my respect, Beatrice, and you know what I'm talkin' about.

BEATRICE What?

(*Pause*)

EDDIE (*finally his resolution hardens*) What I feel like doin' in the bed and what I don't feel like doin'. I don't want no—

BEATRICE When'd I say anything about that?

EDDIE You said, you said, I ain't deaf. I don't want no more conversations about that, Beatrice. I do what I feel like doin' or what I don't feel like doin'.

BEATRICE Okay.

(*Pause*)

EDDIE You used to be different, Beatrice. You had a whole different way.

BEATRICE *I'm* no different.

EDDIE You didn't used to jump me all the time about everything. The last year or two I come in the house I don't know what's gonna hit me. It's a shootin' gallery in here and I'm the pigeon.

BEATRICE Okay, okay.

EDDIE Don't tell me okay, okay, I'm tellin' you the truth. A wife is supposed to believe the husband. If I tell you that guy ain't right don't tell me he is right.

BEATRICE But how do you know?

EDDIE Because I know. I don't go around makin' accusations. He give me the heeby-jeebies the first minute I seen him. And I don't like you sayin' I don't want her marryin' anybody. I broke my back payin' her stenography lessons so she could go out and meet a better class of people. Would I do that if I didn't want her to get married? Sometimes you talk like I was a crazy man or sump'm.

BEATRICE But she likes him.

EDDIE Beatrice, she's a baby, how is she gonna know what she likes?

BEATRICE Well, you kept her a baby, you wouldn't let her go out. I told you a hundred times.

(*Pause*)

EDDIE All right. Let her go out, then.

BEATRICE She don't wanna go out now. It's too late, Eddie.

(*Pause*)

EDDIE Suppose I told her to go out. Suppose I—

BEATRICE They're going to get married next week, Eddie.

EDDIE (*his head jerks around to her*) She said that?

BEATRICE Eddie, if you want my advice, go to her and tell her good luck. I think maybe now that you had it out you learned better.

EDDIE What's the hurry next week?

BEATRICE Well, she's been worried about him bein' picked up; this way he could start to be a citizen. She loves him, Eddie. (*He gets up, moves about uneasily, restlessly*) Why don't you give her a good word? Because I still think she would like you to be a friend, y'know? (*He is standing, looking at the floor*) I mean like if you told her you'd go to the wedding.

EDDIE   She asked you that?

BEATRICE   I know she would like it. I'd like to make a party here for her. I mean there oughta be some kinda send-off. Heh? I mean she'll have trouble enough in her life, let's start it off happy. What do you say? 'Cause in her heart she still loves you, Eddie. I know it. (*He presses his fingers against his eyes*) What're you, cryin'? (*She goes to him, holds his face*) Go . . . whyn't you go tell her you're sorry? (CATHERINE *is seen on the upper landing of the stairway, and they hear her descending*) There . . . she's comin' down. Come on, shake hands with her.

EDDIE (*moving with suppressed suddenness*) No, I can't, I can't talk to her.

BEATRICE   Eddie, give her a break; a wedding should be happy!

EDDIE   I'm goin', I'm goin' for a walk. (*He goes upstage for his jacket.* CATHERINE *enters and starts for the bedroom door*)

BEATRICE   Katie? . . . Eddie, don't go, wait a minute. (*She embraces* EDDIE'S *arm with warmth*) Ask him, Katie. Come on, honey.

EDDIE   It's all right, I'm—(*He starts to go and she holds him*)

BEATRICE   No, she wants to ask you. Come on, Katie, ask him. We'll have a party! What're we gonna do, hate each other? Come on!

CATHERINE   I'm gonna get married, Eddie. So if you wanna come, the wedding be on Saturday.

(*Pause*)

EDDIE   Okay. I only wanted the best for you, Katie. I hope you know that.

CATHERINE   Okay. (*She starts out again*)

EDDIE   Catherine? (*She turns to him*) I was just tellin' Beatrice . . . if you wanna go out, like . . . I mean I realize maybe I kept you home too much. Because he's the first guy you ever knew, y'know? I mean now that you got a job, you might meet some fellas, and you get a different idea, y'know? I mean you could always come back to him, you're still only kids, the both of yiz. What's the hurry? Maybe you'll get around a little bit, you grow up a little more, maybe you'll see different in a couple of months. I mean you be surprised, it don't have to be him.

CATHERINE   No, we made it up already.

EDDIE (*with increasing anxiety*) Katie, wait a minute.

CATHERINE   No, I made up my mind.

EDDIE   But you never knew no other fella, Katie! How could you make up your mind?

CATHERINE   'Cause I did. I don't want nobody else.

EDDIE   But, Katie, suppose he gets picked up.

CATHERINE   That's why we gonna do it right away. Soon as we finish the wedding he's goin' right over and start to be a citizen. I made up my mind, Eddie. I'm sorry. (*to* BEATRICE) Could I take two more pillow cases for the other guys?

BEATRICE   Sure, go ahead. Only don't let her forget where they came from.

(CATHERINE *goes into a bedroom*)

EDDIE   She's got other boarders up there?

BEATRICE   Yeah, there's two guys that just came over.

EDDIE   What do you mean, came over?

BEATRICE   From Italy. Lipari the butcher—his nephew. They come from Bari, they just got here yesterday. I didn't even know till Marco and Rodolpho moved up there before. (CATHERINE *enters, going toward exit with two pillow cases*) It'll be nice, they could all talk together.

EDDIE   Catherine! (*She halts near the exit door. He takes in* BEATRICE *too*) What're you, got no brains? You put them up there with two other submarines?

CATHERINE   Why?

EDDIE (*in a driving fright and anger*)   Why! How do you know they're not trackin' these guys? They'll come up for them and find Marco and Rodolpho! Get them out of the house!

BEATRICE   But they been here so long already—

EDDIE   How do you know what enemies Lipari's got? Which they'd love to stab him in the back?

CATHERINE   Well what'll I do with them?

EDDIE   The neighborhood is full of rooms. Can't you stand to live a couple of blocks away from him? Get them out of the house!

CATHERINE   Well maybe tomorrow night I'll—

EDDIE   Not tomorrow, do it now. Catherine, you never mix yourself with somebody else's family! These guys get picked up, Lipari's liable to blame you or me and we got his whole family on our head. They got a temper, that family.

(*Two men in overcoats appear outside, start into the house*)

CATHERINE   How'm I gonna find a place tonight?

EDDIE   Will you stop arguin' with me and get them out! You think I'm always tryin' to fool you or sump'm? What's the matter with you, don't you believe I could think of your good? Did I ever ask sump'm for myself? You

think I got no feelin's? I never told you nothin'
in my life that wasn't for your good. Nothin'!
And look at the way you talk to me! Like I was
an enemy! Like I—(*A knock on the door. His
head swerves. They all stand motionless. Another knock.* EDDIE, *in a whisper, pointing
upstage*) Go up the fire escape, get them out
over the back fence.

(CATHERINE *stands motionless, uncomprehending*)

FIRST OFFICER (*in the hall*)   Immigration!
Open up in there!

EDDIE   Go, go. Hurry up! (*She stands a
moment staring at him in a realized horror*)
Well, what're you lookin' at!

FIRST OFFICER   Open up!

EDDIE (*calling toward door*)   Who's that
there?

FIRST OFFICER   Immigration, open up.

(EDDIE *turns, looks at* BEATRICE. *She sits. Then
he looks at* CATHERINE. *With a sob of fury*
CATHERINE *streaks into a bedroom.*

Knock is repeated)

EDDIE   All right, take it easy, take it easy.
(*He goes and opens the door. The* OFFICER
steps inside) What's all this?

FIRST OFFICER   Where are they?

(SECOND OFFICER *sweeps past and, glancing
about, goes into the kitchen*)

EDDIE   Where's who?

FIRST OFFICER   Come on, come on, where
are they? (*He hurries into the bedrooms*)

EDDIE   Who? We got nobody here. (*He
looks at* BEATRICE, *who turns her head away.
Pugnaciously, furious, he steps toward* BEA-
TRICE) What's the matter with *you?*

(FIRST OFFICER *enters from the bedroom, calls
to the kitchen*)

FIRST OFFICER   Dominick?

(*Enter* SECOND OFFICER *from kitchen*)

SECOND OFFICER   Maybe it's a different
apartment.

FIRST OFFICER   There's only two more floors
up there. I'll take the front, you go up the fire
escape. I'll let you in. Watch your step up there.

SECOND OFFICER   Okay, right, Charley.
(FIRST OFFICER *goes out apartment door and
runs up the stairs*) This is Four-forty-one, isn't
it?

EDDIE   That's right.

(SECOND OFFICER *goes out into the kitchen.*
EDDIE *turns to* BEATRICE. *She looks at him
now and sees his terror*)

BEATRICE (*weakened with fear*)   Oh, Jesus,
Eddie.

EDDIE   What's the matter with *you?*

BEATRICE (*pressing her palms against her
face*)   Oh, my God, my God.

EDDIE   What're you, accusin' me?

BEATRICE (*her final thrust is to turn toward
him instead of running from him*)   My God,
what did you do?

(*Many steps on the outer stair draw his attention. We see the* FIRST OFFICER *descending,
with* MARCO, *behind him* RODOLPHO, *and*
CATHERINE *and the two strange immigrants,
followed by* SECOND OFFICER. BEATRICE *hurries
to door*)

CATHERINE (*backing down stairs, fighting
with* FIRST OFFICER; *as they appear on the
stairs*)   What do yiz want from them? They
work, that's all. They're boarders upstairs, they
work on the piers.

BEATRICE (*to* FIRST OFFICER)   Ah, Mister,
what do you want from them, who do they
hurt?

CATHERINE (*pointing to* RODOLPHO)   They
ain't no submarines, he was born in Philadelphia.

FIRST OFFICER   Step aside, lady.

CATHERINE   What do you mean? You can't
just come in a house and—

FIRST OFFICER   All right, take it easy. (*to*
RODOLPHO) What street were you born in Philadelphia?

CATHERINE   What do you mean, what
street? Could you tell me what street you were
born?

FIRST OFFICER   Sure. Four blocks away,
One-eleven Union Street. Let's go fellas.

CATHERINE (*fending him off* RODOLPHO)
No, you can't! Now, get outa here!

FIRST OFFICER   Look, girlie, if they're all
right they'll be out tomorrow. If they're illegal
they go back where they came from. If you
want, get yourself a lawyer, although I'm tellin'
you now you're wasting your money. Let's get
them in the car, Dom. (*to the men*) Andiamo,
Andiamo, let's go. (*The men start, but* MARCO
hangs back)

BEATRICE (*from doorway*)   Who're they
hurtin', for God's sake, what do you want
from them? They're starvin' over there, what
do you want! Marco!

(MARCO *suddenly breaks from the group and
dashes into the room and faces* EDDIE; BEATRICE
and FIRST OFFICER *rush in as* MARCO *spits into*
EDDIE's *face.*

CATHERINE *runs into hallway and throws
herself into* RODOLPHO's *arms.* EDDIE, *with an
enraged cry, lunges for* MARCO)

EDDIE   Oh, you mother's—!

(FIRST OFFICER *quickly intercedes and pushes* EDDIE *from* MARCO, *who stands there accusingly*)

FIRST OFFICER (*between them, pushing* EDDIE *from* MARCO) Cut it out!

EDDIE (*over the* FIRST OFFICER'S *shoulder, to* MARCO) I'll kill you for that, you son of a bitch!

FIRST OFFICER Hey! (*shakes him*) Stay in here now, don't come out, don't bother him. You hear me? Don't come out, fella.

(*For an instant there is silence. Then* FIRST OFFICER *turns and takes* MARCO'S *arm and then gives a last, informative look at* EDDIE. *As he and* MARCO *are going out into the hall,* EDDIE *erupts*)

EDDIE I don't forget that, Marco! You hear what I'm sayin'?

(*Out in the hall,* FIRST OFFICER *and* MARCO *go down the stairs. Now, in the street,* LOUIS, MIKE, *and several neighbors including the butcher,* LIPARI—*a stout, intense, middle-aged man—are gathering around the stoop.*

LIPARI, *the butcher, walks over to the two strange men and kisses them. His wife, keening, goes and kisses their hands.* EDDIE *is emerging from the house shouting after* MARCO. BEATRICE *is trying to restrain him*)

EDDIE That's the thanks I get? Which I took the blankets off my bed for yiz? You gonna apologize to me, Marco! *Marco!*

FIRST OFFICER (*in the doorway with* MARCO) All right, lady, let them go. Get in the car, fellas, it's over there.

(RODOLPHO *is almost carrying the sobbing* CATHERINE *off up the street, left*)

CATHERINE He was born in Philadelphia! What do you want from him?

FIRST OFFICER Step aside, lady, come on now . . .

(*The* SECOND OFFICER *has moved off with the two strange men.* MARCO, *taking advantage of the* FIRST OFFICER'S *being occupied with* CATHERINE, *suddenly frees himself and points back at* EDDIE)

MARCO That one! I accuse that one!

(EDDIE *brushes* BEATRICE *aside and rushes out to the stoop*)

FIRST OFFICER (*grabbing him and moving him quickly off up the left street*) Come on!

MARCO (*as he is taken off, pointing back at* EDDIE) That one! He killed my children! That one stole the food from my children!

(MARCO *is gone. The crowd has turned to* EDDIE)

EDDIE (*to* LIPARI *and wife*) He's crazy! I give them the blankets off my bed. Six months I kept them like my own brothers!

(LIPARI, *the butcher, turns and starts up left with his arm around his wife*)

EDDIE Lipari! (*He follows* LIPARI *up left*) For Christ's sake, I kept them, I give them the blankets off my bed!

(LIPARI *and wife exit.* EDDIE *turns and starts crossing down right to* LOUIS *and* MIKE)

EDDIE Louis! *Louis!*

(LOUIS *barely turns, then walks off and exits down right with* MIKE. *Only* BEATRICE *is left on the stoop.* CATHERINE *now returns, blank-eyed, from offstage and the car.* EDDIE *calls after* LOUIS *and* MIKE)

EDDIE He's gonna take that back. He's gonna take that back or I'll kill him! You hear me? I'll kill him! I'll kill him! (*He exits up street calling*)

(*There is a pause of darkness before the lights rise, on the reception room of a prison.* MARCO *is seated;* ALFIERI, CATHERINE, *and* RODOLPHO *standing*)

ALFIERI I'm waiting, Marco, what do you say?

RODOLPHO Marco never hurt anybody.

ALFIERI I can bail you out until your hearing comes up. But I'm not going to do it, you understand me? Unless I have your promise. You're an honorable man, I will believe your promise. Now what do you say?

MARCO In my country he would be dead now. He would not live this long.

ALFIERI All right, Rodolpho—you come with me now.

RODOLPHO No! Please, Mister. Marco—promise the man. Please, I want you to watch the wedding. How can I be married and you're in here? Please, you're not going to do anything; you know you're not.

(MARCO *is silent*)

CATHERINE (*kneeling left of* MARCO) Marco, don't you understand? He can't bail you out if you're gonna do something bad. To hell with Eddie. Nobody is gonna talk to him again if he lives to a hundred. Everybody knows you spit in his face, that's enough, isn't it? Give me the satisfaction—I want you at the wedding. You got a wife and kids, Marco. You could be workin' till the hearing comes up, instead of layin' around here.

MARCO (*to* ALFIERI) I have no chance?

ALFIERI (*crosses to behind* MARCO) No, Marco. You're going back. The hearing is a formality, that's all.

MARCO   But him? There is a chance, eh?

ALFIERI   When she marries him he can start to become an American. They permit that, if the wife is born here.

MARCO   (*looking at* RODOLPHO)   Well—we did something. (*He lays a palm on* RODOLPHO'S *arm and* RODOLPHO *covers it*)

RODOLPHO   Marco, tell the man.

MARCO   (*pulling his hand away*)   What will I tell him? He knows such a promise is dishonorable.

ALFIERI   To promise not to kill is not dishonorable.

MARCO   (*looking at* ALFIERI)   No?

ALFIERI   No.

MARCO   (*gesturing with his head—this is a new idea*)   Then what is done with such a man?

ALFIERI   Nothing. If he obeys the law, he lives. That's all.

MARCO   (*rises, turns to* ALFIERI)   The law? All the law is not in a book.

ALFIERI   Yes. In a book. There is no other law.

MARCO   (*his anger rising*)   He degraded my brother. My blood. He robbed my children, he mocks my work. I work to come here, mister!

ALFIERI   I know, Marco—

MARCO   There is no law for that? Where is the law for that?

ALFIERI   There is none.

MARCO   (*shaking his head, sitting*)   I don't understand this country.

ALFIERI   Well? What is your answer? You have five or six weeks you could work. Or else you sit here. What do you say to me?

MARCO   (*lowers his eyes. It almost seems he is ashamed*)   All right.

ALFIERI   You won't touch him. This is your promise.

(*Slight pause*)

MARCO   Maybe he wants to apologize to me. (MARCO *is staring away.* ALFIERI *takes one of his hands*)

ALFIERI   This is not God, Marco. You hear? Only God makes justice.

MARCO   All right.

ALFIERI   (*nodding, not with assurance*) Good! Catherine, Rodolpho, Marco, let us go.

(CATHERINE *kisses* RODOLPHO *and* MARCO, *then kisses* ALFIERI'S *hand*)

CATHERINE   I'll get Beatrice and meet you at the church. (*She leaves quickly*)

(MARCO *rises.* RODOLPHO *suddenly embraces him.* MARCO *pats him on the back and* RODOLPHO *exits after* CATHERINE. MARCO *faces* ALFIERI)

ALFIERI   Only God, Marco.

(MARCO *turns and walks out.* ALFIERI *with a certain processional tread leaves the stage. The lights dim out.*

The lights rise in the apartment. EDDIE *is alone in the rocker, rocking back and forth in little surges. Pause. Now* BEATRICE *emerges from a bedroom. She is in her best clothes, wearing a hat*)

BEATRICE   (*with fear, going to* EDDIE)   I'll be back in about an hour, Eddie. All right?

EDDIE   (*quietly, almost inaudibly, as though drained*)   What, have I been talkin' to myself?

BEATRICE   Eddie, for God's sake, it's her wedding.

EDDIE   Didn't you hear what I told you? You walk out that door to that wedding you ain't comin' back here, Beatrice.

BEATRICE   Why! What do you want?

EDDIE   I want my respect. Didn't you ever hear of that? From my wife?

(CATHERINE *enters from bedroom*)

CATHERINE   It's after three; we're supposed to be there already, Beatrice. The priest won't wait.

BEATRICE   Eddie. It's her wedding. There'll be nobody there from her family. For my sister let me go. I'm goin' for my sister.

EDDIE   (*as though hurt*)   Look, I been arguin' with you all day already, Beatrice, and I said what I'm gonna say. He's gonna come here and apologize to me or nobody from this house is goin' into that church today. Now if that's more to you than I am, then go. But don't come back. You be on my side or on their side, that's all.

CATHERINE   (*suddenly*)   Who the hell do you think you are?

BEATRICE   Sssh!

CATHERINE   You got no more right to tell nobody nothin'! Nobody! The rest of your life, nobody!

BEATRICE   Shut up, Katie! (*She turns* CATHERINE *around*)

CATHERINE   You're gonna come with me!

BEATRICE   I can't Katie, I can't . . .

CATHERINE   How can you listen to him? This rat!

BEATRICE   (*shaking* CATHERINE)   Don't you call him that!

CATHERINE   (*clearing from* BEATRICE) What're you scared of? He's a rat! He belongs in the sewer!

BEATRICE   Stop it!

CATHERINE   (*weeping*)   He bites people when they sleep! He comes when nobody's lookin' and poisons decent people. In the garbage he belongs!

(EDDIE *seems about to pick up the table and fling it at her*)

BEATRICE   No, Eddie! Eddie! (*to* CATHERINE) Then we all belong in the garbage. You, and me too. Don't say that. Whatever happened we all done it, and don't you ever forget it, Catherine. (*She goes to* CATHERINE) Now go, go to your wedding, Katie, I'll stay home. Go. God bless you, God bless your children.

(*Enter* RODOLPHO)

RODOLPHO   Eddie?

EDDIE   Who said you could come in here? Get outa here!

RODOLPHO   Marco is coming, Eddie. (*pause.* BEATRICE *raises her hands in terror*) He's praying in the church. You understand? (*pause.* RODOLPHO *advances into the room*) Catherine, I think it is better we go. Come with me.

CATHERINE   Eddie, go away, please.

BEATRICE   (*quietly*) Eddie. Let's go someplace. Come. You and me. (*He has not moved*) I don't want you to be here when he comes. I'll get your coat.

EDDIE   Where? Where am I goin'? This is my house.

BEATRICE   (*crying out*)   What's the use of it! He's crazy now, you know the way they get, what good is it! You got nothin' against Marco, you always liked Marco!

EDDIE   I got nothin' against Marco? Which he called me a rat in front of the whole neighborhood? Which he said I killed his children! Where you been?

RODOLPHO   (*quite suddenly, stepping up to* EDDIE)   It is my fault, Eddie. Everything. I wish to apologize. It was wrong that I do not ask your permission. I kiss your hand. (*He reaches for* EDDIE's *hand, but* EDDIE *snaps it away from him*)

BEATRICE   Eddie, he's apologizing!

RODOLPHO   I have made all our troubles. But you have insult me too. Maybe God understands why you did that to me. Maybe you did not mean to insult me at all—

BEATRICE   Listen to him! Eddie, listen what he's tellin' you!

RODOLPHO   I think, maybe when Marco comes, if we can tell him we are comrades now, and we have no more argument between us. Then maybe Marco will not—

EDDIE   Now, listen—

CATHERINE   Eddie, give him a chance!

BEATRICE   What do you want! Eddie, what do you want!

EDDIE   I want my name! He didn't take my name; he's only a punk. Marco's got my name —(*to* RODOLPHO) and you can run tell him, kid, that he's gonna give it back to me in front of this neighborhood, or we have it out. (*hoisting up his pants*) Come on, where is he? Take me to him.

BEATRICE   Eddie, listen—

EDDIE   I heard enough! Come on, let's go!

BEATRICE   Only blood is good? He kissed your hand!

EDDIE   What he does don't mean nothin' to nobody! (*to* RODOLPHO) Come on!

BEATRICE   (*barring his way to the stairs*) What's gonna mean somethin'? Eddie, listen to me. Who could give you your name? Listen to me, I love you, I'm talkin' to you, I love you; if Marco'll kiss your hand outside, if he goes on his knees, what is he got to give you? That's not what you want.

EDDIE   Don't bother me!

BEATRICE   You want somethin' else, Eddie, and you can never have her!

CATHERINE   (*in horror*)   B.!

EDDIE   (*shocked, horrified, his fists clenching*)   Beatrice!

(MARCO *appears outside, walking toward the door from a distant point*)

BEATRICE   (*crying out, weeping*)   The truth is not as bad as blood, Eddie! I'm tellin' you the truth—tell her good-bye forever!

EDDIE   (*crying out in agony*)   That's what you think of me—that I would have such a thought? (*His fists clench his head as though it will burst*)

MARCO   (*calling near the door outside*)   Eddie Carbone!

(EDDIE *swerves about; all stand transfixed for an instant. People appear outside*)

EDDIE   (*as though flinging his challenge*) Yeah, Marco! Eddie Carbone. Eddie Carbone. Eddie Carbone. (*He goes up the stairs and emerges from the apartment.* RODOLPHO *streaks up and out past him and runs to* MARCO)

RODOLPHO   No, Marco, please! Eddie, please, he has children! You will kill a family!

BEATRICE   Go in the house! Eddie, go in the house!

EDDIE   (*he gradually comes to address the people*)   Maybe he come to apologize to me. Heh, Marco? For what you said about me in front of the neighborhood? (*He is incensing himself and little bits of laughter even escape him as his eyes are murderous and he cracks his knuckles in his hands with a strange sort of relaxation*) He knows that ain't right. To do like that? To a man? Which I put my roof over their head and my food in their mouth? Like in the Bible? Strangers I never seen in my whole life? To come out of the water and grab a girl for a passport? To go and take from your own family like from the stable—and never a word to me? And now accusations in the bargain! (*directly to* MARCO) Wipin' the neighborhood with my name like a dirty rag! I want my name, Marco. (*He is moving now, carefully, toward* MARCO) Now gimme my name and we go together to the wedding.

BEATRICE *and* CATHERINE (*keening*) Eddie! Eddie, don't! Eddie!

EDDIE No, Marco knows what's right from wrong. Tell the people, Marco, tell them what a liar you are! (*He has his arms spread and* MARCO *is spreading his*) Come on, liar, you know what you done! (*He lunges for* MARCO *as a great hushed shout goes up from the people*)

(MARCO *strikes* EDDIE *beside the neck*)

MARCO Animal! You go on your knees to me!

(EDDIE *goes down with the blow and* MARCO *starts to raise a foot to stomp him when* EDDIE *springs a knife into his hand and* MARCO *steps back.* LOUIS *rushes in toward* EDDIE)

LOUIS Eddie, for Christ's sake!

(EDDIE *raises the knife and* LOUIS *halts and steps back*)

EDDIE You lied about me, Marco. Now say it. Come on now, say it!

MARCO Anima-a-a-l!

(EDDIE *lunges with the knife.* MARCO *grabs his arm, turning the blade inward and pressing it home as the women and* LOUIS *and* MIKE *rush in and separate them, and* EDDIE, *the knife still in his hand, falls to his knees before* MARCO. *The two women support him for a moment, calling his name again and again*)

CATHERINE Eddie I never meant to do nothing bad to you.

EDDIE Then why—Oh, B.!

BEATRICE Yes, yes!

EDDIE My B.!

(*He dies in her arms, and* BEATRICE *covers him with her body.* ALFIERI, *who is in the crowd, turns out to the audience. The lights have gone down, leaving him in a glow, while behind him the dull prayers of the people and the keening of the women continue*)

ALFIERI Most of the time now we settle for half and I like it better. But the truth is holy, and even as I know how wrong he was, and his death useless, I tremble, for I confess that something perversely pure calls to me from his memory—not purely good, but himself purely, for he allowed himself to be wholly known and for that I think I will love him more than all my sensible clients. And yet, it is better to settle for half, it must be! And so I mourn him—I admit it—with a certain . . . alarm.

The Writers and Their Plays

Where no translations are known to exist, the plays' original titles are used.

BUECHNER, GEORG—1813–1837 (completion dates)

Danton's Death, 1835; Lenz, 1836; Leonce and Lena, 1836; Woyzeck, 1836.

HEBBEL, FRIEDERICH—1813–1863 (publication dates)

Judith, 1841; Genoveva, 1843; Maria Magdalena, 1844; Der Diamant, 1847; Herod and Mariamne, 1850; Der Rubin, 1851; Ein Trauerspiel in Sicilien, 1851; Julia, 1851; Michel Angelo, 1855; Agnes Bernauer, 1855; Gyges and His Ring, 1856; Der Nibelungen, 1862; Demetrius, 1864 (unfinished).

HAUPTMANN, GERHARDT—1862–1946 (publication dates)

Before Sunrise, 1889; The Festival of Peace, 1890; Lonely Lives, 1891; Colleague Crampton, 1892; The Weavers, 1892; The Beaver Coat, 1893; The Assumption of Hannele, 1893; Florian Geyer, 1894; Helios, 1896; The Sunken Bell, 1896; Elga, 1898; Pastoral, 1898; Drayman Henschel, 1898; Michael Kramer, 1900; The Conflagration (The Red Cock), 1901; Poor Heinrich, 1902; Rose Bernd, 1903; And Pippa Dances, 1906; The Maidens of Bischofsberg, 1907; Charlemagne's Hostage, 1908; Griselda, 1909; The Rats, 1911; Gabriel Schilling's Flight, 1912; The Festival Play, 1913; The Bow of Odysseus, 1914; Winter Ballad, 1917; The White Savior, 1920; Indipohdi, 1920; Peter Brauer, 1921; Veland, 1925; Dorothea Angermann, 1926; Witches' Ride, 1930; The Black Mask, 1930; Before Sunset, 1932; The Golden Harp, 1933; Hamlet at Wittenberg, 1935; Die Finsternisse, 1937; Ulrich of Lichtenstein, 1939; The Daughter of the Cathedral, 1939; Iphigenia in Delphi, 1941; Iphigenia in Aulis, 1944; Agamemnon's Death and Electra, 1948.

SCHNITZLER, ARTHUR—1862–1931 (publication dates)

Anatol, 1889; The Fairy Tale, 1891; Paracelsus, 1892; Light o' Love, 1895; Fair Game, 1896; Reigen (La Ronde), 1896; The Legacy, 1897; The Helpmate, 1898; The Green Cockatoo, 1899; The Veil of Beatrice, 1899; The Lady With the

Dagger, 1900; Living Hours, 1901; The Last Masks, 1901; Literature, 1902; The Puppet Player, 1902; Gallant Cassian, 1903; The Lonely Way, 1903; Intermezzo, 1905; The Great Show, 1905; The Call of Life, 1905; Countess Mizzi, 1909; Young Medarus, 1909; The Vast Domain, 1910; Professor Bernhardi, 1912; Frau Beate and Her Son, 1913; The Hour of Recognition, 1915; The Big Scene, 1915; The Festival of Bacchus, 1915; Fink and Fliederbusch, 1917; The Sisters, 1918; Seduction's Comedy, 1924; The Walk to the Pond, 1925; In the Play of Summer's Air, 1930.

WEDEKIND, FRANK—1864–1918 (publication dates)

Der Schnellmaler, oder Kunst und Mammon, 1887; Die junge, Welt oder Kinder und Narren, 1889; The Awakening of Spring, 1891; Fritz Schwigerling, 1892; The Earth Spirit, 1895; The Tenor, 1897; The Marquis of Keith, 1900; Such Is Life, 1902; Pandora's Box, 1904; Hidalla, 1904; Damnation, 1905; Music, 1906; Zensur, 1908; Der Stein der Weisen, 1909; Oaha (Till Eulenspiegel), 1909; Schloss Wetterstein, 1910; Franzisca, 1912; Simson, 1914; Bismarck, 1915; Herakles, 1919; The Solar Spectrum, 1921.

HOFMANNSTHAL, HUGO VON—1874–1929 (production dates)

Death and the Fool, 1893; The Emperor and the Witch, 1897; The Little Theatre of the World, 1897; The Marriage of Zobeide, 1900; Electra, 1904; Oedipus Rex, 1909; Everyman, 1911; The Man Who Was Difficult, 1918; Salzburg Great Theatre of the World, 1922; The Tower, 1925. (Operas: Electra, 1909; Der Rosenkavalier, 1911; Ariadne in Naxos, 1912; The Woman Without a Shadow, 1919; The Egyptian Helen, 1928; Arabella, 1933.)

BRECHT, BERTOLT—1898–1956 (production dates)

Baal, 1918; Drums in the Night, 1918; The Wedding, 1919; The Beggar, or The Dead Dog, 1919; He Exorcises a Devil, 1919; Light in Darkness, 1919; In the Jungle of Cities, 1923; Life of Edward II of England (with Lion Feuchtwanger),

1924; Calcutta, May 4, 1925; Man Equals Man, 1925; The Baby Elephant, 1925; The Threepenny Opera, 1928; Happy End (written with Elizabeth Hauptmann), 1929; The Flight of the Lindberghs, 1929; Downfall of the Egoist Johann Fatzer (unfinished), 1929; Rise and Fall of the City of Mahagonny, 1929; The Didactic Play of Baden: On Consent, 1929; He Who Says Yes, 1930; He Who Says No, 1930; The Bread Shop, 1930; St. Joan of the Stockyards, 1930; The Measures Taken, 1930; The Exception and the Rule, 1930; The Mother: Life of the Revolutionary Pelageya Vlasova from Tver, 1932; The Roundheads and the Peakheads, 1934; The Seven Deadly Sins of the Petty Bourgeois (Anna Anna), 1933; The Horatians and the Curiatians, 1934; Fear and Misery of the Third Reich (also known as The Private Life of the Master Race), 1938; Senora Carrar's Rifles, 1938; Mother Courage and Her Children, 1939; The Trial of Lucullus, 1939; Galileo, 1939; The Good Woman of Setzuan, 1940; Mr. Puntila and His Hired Man, Matti, 1941; The Resistable Rise of Arturo Ui, 1941; The Visions of Simone Machard, 1942; Schweik in the Second World War, 1944; Life of Confucius, 1944; The Caucasian Chalk Circle, 1945; The Antigone of Sophocles, 1948; The Days of the Commune, 1949; The Private Tutor, 1950; Report on Herrnburg, 1951; Trumpets and Drums (with Elizabeth Hauptmann and Benno Besson), 1956; Turandot, or the Congress of Whitewashers (unfinished), 1956.

FRISCH, MAX—1911–   (completion dates)
Santa Cruz, 1944; Now They Sing Again, 1945; The Chinese Wall, 1946 (revised 1955); A House in Berlin, 1948; Count Oederland, 1950; Don Juan, or The Love of Geometry, 1952; Biedermann and the Firebugs, 1956; The Great Rage of Philip Hotz, 1956; Andorra, 1961.

DUERRENMATT, FRIEDRICH—1921–   (completion dates)
It Is Written, 1947; The Blind Man, 1948; Romulus the Great, 1949; The Marriage of Mr. Mississippi (also translated as Fools Are Passing Through), 1952; An Angel Comes to Babylon, 1954; The Visit of the Old Lady, 1957; Frank the Fifth, 1959; The Physicists, 1962.

IBSEN, HENRIK—1828–1906 (completion dates)
Cataline, 1849; The Warrior's Barrow, 1850; St. John's Night, 1853; Lady Inger of Ostraat, 1855; The Feast at Solhaug, 1856; Olaf Liljekrans, 1857; The Vikings in Helgeland, 1858; Love's Comedy, 1862; The Pretenders, 1864; Brand, 1866; Peer Gynt, 1867; The League of Youth, 1869; Emperor and Galilean, 1873; The Pillars of Society, 1877; A Doll's House, 1879; Ghosts, 1881; An Enemy of the People, 1882; The Wild Duck, 1884; Rosmersholm, 1886; The Lady from the Sea, 1888; Hedda Gabler, 1890; The Master Builder, 1892; Little Eyolf, 1894; John Gabriel Borkman, 1896; When We Dead Awaken, 1899.

STRINDBERG, AUGUST—1849–1912 (publication dates)
The Outlaw, 1871; Master Olof, 1872 (fifth version, 1880); The Secret of the Guild, 1880; The Year Forty-Eight, 1881; The Wanderings of Lucky Per, 1881; Sir Bengt's Wife, 1882; The Father, 1887; Comrades, 1888; Miss Julie, 1888; Hemso Folk, 1889; Creditors, 1890; Pariah, 1890; Simoon, 1890; The Stronger, 1890; The Keys of Heaven, 1892; Facing Death, 1893; The First Warning, 1893; Debit and Credit, 1893; Mother Love, 1893; Playing With Fire, 1893; The Link, 1897; To Damascus, Parts I and II, 1898; There Are Crimes and Crimes, 1899; Advent, 1899; Gustavus Vasa, 1899; Eric XIV, 1899; The Saga of the Folkungs, 1899; Gustavus Adolphus, 1900; Caspar's Shrove Tuesday, 1900; Easter, 1901; Midsummer, 1901; The Dance of Death, Parts I and II, 1901; Englebrecht, 1901; Charles XII, 1901; The Bridal Crown, 1902; Swanwhite, 1902; The Dream Play, 1902; Christina, 1903; Gustavus III, 1903; The Nightingale of Wittenberg, 1904; To Damascus, Part III, 1904; Storm, 1907; The Burned Lot, 1907; The Ghost Sonata, 1907; The Pelican, 1907; The Slippers of Abou Casem, 1908; The Last Knight, 1908; The Regent, 1908; The Earl of Bjälbo, 1908; The Black Glove, 1909; The Great Highway, 1909; The Tooth, 1909; Moses, 1917; Greece or Socrates, 1918; The Lamb and the Wild Beast, or Christ, 1918.

CHEKHOV, ANTON PAVLOVITCH—1860–1904 (publication dates)
That Worthless Fellow Platonov (unfinished), 1881; On the High Road, 1884; Ivanov, 1887; The Tragedian in Spite of Himself, 1888; The Bear (The Boor), 1888; The Wood Demon, 1889; Tatyana Riepin, 1889; The Swan Song, 1889; The Proposal, 1889; The Sea Gull, 1896; Uncle Vanya, 1897; The Three Sisters, 1900; The Jubilee, 1903; The Wedding, 1903; The Cherry Orchard, 1904.

GORKI, MAXIM—1868–1936 (publication dates)
The Middle Class, 1900; The Lower Depths, 1902; Summer Folk, 1903; Children of the Sun, 1905; Barbarians, 1905; Odd People, 1910; Children, 1910; The Meeting, 1910; The Zykovs, 1913; The Judge (The Old Man), 1915; Enemies, 1916; The Last Ones, 1918; Cain and Artema, 1921; The Counterfeit Coin, 1926; Igor Bulichev and Others, 1932.

PIRANDELLO, LUIGI—1867–1936 (publication dates)
Scamandra, 1910; The Vise, 1913; Sicilian Limes, 1913; If Not Thus, 1915; Liola, 1916; Think It Over, Jimmy, 1916; Right You Are (If You Think So), 1916; At the Gate, 1916; The Pleasure of Honesty, 1917; Cap and Bells, 1917; Grafting, 1917; The Game as He Played It, 1918; He Didn't Mean It, 1918; Man, Beast, and Virtue, 1919; All for the Best, 1920; Floriani's Wife, 1920; Signora Morli, 1920; One and Two, 1920; By Judgment of the Court, 1920; The Other's Reason, 1921; Six Characters in Search of an Author, 1921; The

Mock Emperor (Enrico IV), 1922; Naked, 1922; The Life I Gave You, 1923; The Man with the Flower in His Mouth, 1923; Each in His Own Way, 1924; Our Lord of the Ship, 1925; The House with the Column, 1925; The Jar, 1925; Diana and Tuda, 1926; Friendship of Women, 1927; The New Colony, 1928; Lazarus, 1929; One's or Nobody's, 1929; As You Desire Me, 1930; Tonight We Improvise, 1930; The Phantoms, 1931; Finding Oneself, 1932; One Knows Not How, 1935; The Mountain Giants, 1937. (In addition, these undated but post-1913 plays: The Doctor's Duty, Chee-chee, The Imbecile.)

BETTI, UGO—1892–1953 (publication dates)
The Mistress, 1927; La Donna sullo Scudo, 1927; The House on the Water, 1929; L'Isola Meravigliosa, 1930; A Hotel on the Waterfront, 1933; Landslide at North Station, 1936; The Duck Hunter, 1937; A Beautiful Day in September, 1937; I Nostri Sogni, 1937; Summertime, 1942; Night in the House of a Rich Man, 1942; The Deluge, 1943; Night Wind, 1945; Inspection, 1947; Husband and Wife, 1947; Favola di Natale, 1948; Corruption in the Palace of Justice, 1949; Struggle Until Dawn, 1949; Irene the Innocent, 1950; Spiritism in the Old House, 1950; Crime on Goat Island, 1950; The Queen and the Rebels, 1951; The Gambler, 1951; The Inquisition, 1952; The Burnt Flowerbed, 1953; The Fugitives, 1953.

LORCA, FEDERICO GARCÍA—1899–1936 (completion dates)
The Spell of the Butterfly, 1920; The Girl Who Waters the Sweet Basil Flower and the Inquisitive Prince, 1923; Mariana Pineda, 1927; Chimera, 1928; The Lass, the Sailor, and the Student, 1928; Buster Keaton's Constitutional, 1928; The Puppet Farce of Don Cristóbal, 1930; The Shoemaker's Prodigious Wife, 1930; The Love of Don Perlimplín and Belisa in the Garden, 1931; If Five Years Pass, 1931; The Public, 1931; Blood Wedding, 1933; Yerma, 1934; The Tragi-comedy of Don Cristóbal, 1934; The House of Bernarda Alba, 1936.

SASTRE, ALFONSO—1926– (completion dates)
Cargo of Dreams, 1949; Uranium 235, 1949; Pathetic Prologue, 1949; The Condemned Squad, 1953; The Gag, 1954; Anna Kleiber, 1955; The Blood of God, 1955; Everyman's Bread, 1955; The Raven, 1958; Death in the Neighborhood, 1959; The Assault of Night, 1959; Sad Are the Eyes of William Tell, 1960; Red Earth, 1960; The Death Thrust, 1961; In the Net, 1961; Death Has Sounded, 1962.

JEAN GIRAUDOUX—1882–1944 (completion dates, except as noted)
Siegfried, 1928; Amphitryon 38, 1929; Judith, 1931; The Enchanted, 1933; Tessa, 1934; End of Siegfried, 1934; The Trojan War Will Not Take Place (Tiger at the Gates), 1935; Supplement to Cook's Voyage, 1937; Electra, 1937; The Impro-

visation of Paris, 1937; Song of Songs, 1938; Ondine, 1939; The Apollo of Bellac, 1942; Sodom and Gomorrha, 1943; The Madwoman of Chaillot, 1945 (production date); Duel of Angels, 1953 (production date).

JEAN ANOUILH—1910– (completion dates)
Humulus the Dumb, 1929; Mandarine, 1929; Attila the Magnificent, 1930; Hermine, 1931; Jezabel, 1932; Thieves' Carnival, 1932; The Savage, 1934; There Was a Prisoner, 1934; The Small Happiness, 1935; Traveler Without Baggage, 1936; The Rendezvous at Senlis, 1937; Léocadia, 1939; Eurydice (Legend of Lovers), 1941; Antigone, 1942; Romeo and Jeanette, 1945; Medea, 1946; Ring Round the Moon, 1947; Ardèle, 1948; Episode in an Author's Life, 1948; The School for Fathers, 1949; The Rehearsal, 1950; Colombe, 1950; Waltz of the Toreadors, 1951; The Lark, 1952; Ornifle, or The Current of Air, 1954; Poor Bitos, or The Dinner of Heads, 1956; The Fighting Cock, 1958; Becket, 1958; La Petite Molière, 1959; The Grotto, 1961.

SARTRE, JEAN-PAUL—1905– (completion dates)
The Flies, 1943; No Exit, 1944; The Victors, 1946; The Respectful Prostitute, 1946; Dirty Hands, 1948; The Devil and the Good Lord, 1951; Kean (adapted from a play by Dumas), 1954; Nekrassov, 1955; The Condemned of Altona, 1960.

GENÊT, JEAN—1910– (publication dates)
Deathwatch, 1948; The Maids, 1948; The Balcony, 1956; The Blacks, 1958; The Screens, 1961.

IONESCO, EUGÈNE—1912– (completion dates, except as noted)
The Bald Soprano, 1948; The Lesson, 1950; Jack, or Submission, 1950; The Chairs, 1951; The Motor Show, 1951 (production date); The Future Is in Eggs, or It Takes All Sorts to Make a World, 1951; Victims of Duty, 1952; Amédée, or How to Get Rid of It, 1953; The New Tenant, 1953; Les Grands Chaleurs (based on a play by Caragiale), 1953 (production); The Maid to Marry, 1953 (production); The Leader, 1953 (production); Le connaissez-vous, 1953 (production); La Nièce-Épouse, 1953 (production); Le rhume Onirique, 1953 (production); The Picture, 1955 (production); Improvisation, or The Shepherd's Chameleon, 1955; Impromptu pour la Duchesse de Windsor, 1957; The Killer, 1957; Rhinocerous, 1958; Foursome, 1959; The Pedestrian in the Air, 1962; Bedlam Galore, for Two or More, 1962; The King Dies, 1963.

BECKETT, SAMUEL—1906– (publication dates, except as noted)
Eleutheria, c. 1946 (unpublished, unproduced); Waiting for Godot, 1952; Endgame, 1957; All That Fall, 1957; Krapp's Last Tape, 1957; Embers, 1957; Act Without Words I, 1960; Act Without Words II, 1960; Happy Days, 1961; Play, 1964 (production date).

YEATS, WILLIAM BUTLER—1865–1939 (completion dates)

The Countess Cathleen, 1892; The Land of Heart's Desire, 1894; Cathleen Ni Houlihan, 1902; The Pot of Broth, 1904; The King's Threshold, 1904; On Baile's Stand, 1904; Deirdre, 1907; The Unicorn From the Stars, 1908; The Green Helmet, 1910; The Shadowy Waters, 1911; The Hour Glass, 1914; At the Hawk's Well, 1917; The Only Jealousy of Emer, 1919; The Dreaming of Bones, 1919; Calvary, 1920; The Player Queen, 1922; The Cat and the Moon, 1926; Sophocles' King Oedipus, 1928; The Resurrection, 1931; Sophocles' Oedipus at Colonus, 1934; The Words Upon the Window Pane, 1934; A Full Moon in March, 1935; The King of the Great Clock Tower, 1935; The Herne's Egg, 1938; Purgatory, 1939; The Death of Cuchulain, 1939.

SYNGE, JOHN MILLINGTON—1871–1909 (publication dates)

In the Shadow of the Glen, 1903; Riders to the Sea, 1904; The Well of the Saints, 1905; The Playboy of the Western World, 1907; The Tinker's Wedding, 1909 (written earlier); Deirdre of the Sorrows, 1910.

O'CASEY, SEAN—1880– (publication dates)

The Robe of Rosheen, 1918; The Shadow of a Gunman, 1923; Cathleen Listens In, 1923; The Cooing of the Doves, 1923; Juno and the Paycock, 1924; Nannie's Night Out, 1924; The Plough and the Stars, 1926; The Silver Tassie, 1928; Within the Gates, 1933; The End of the Beginning, 1935; The Star Turns Red, 1940; Purple Dust, 1940; Red Roses for Me, 1942; Oak Leaves and Lavender, 1946; A Pound on Demand, 1946; Cock-a-Doodle-Dandy, 1949; Hall of Healing, 1951; Bedtime Story, 1951; Time to Go, 1951; The Bishop's Bonfire, 1954; The Drums of Father Ned, 1958.

SHAW, GEORGE BERNARD—1856–1950 (completion dates)

Widowers' Houses, 1892; The Philanderer, 1893; Mrs. Warren's Profession, 1893; Arms and the Man, 1894; Candida, 1894; The Man of Destiny, 1895; You Never Can Tell, 1896; The Devil's Disciple, 1896; Caesar and Cleopatra, 1898; Captain Brassbound's Conversion, 1899; The Admirable Bashville, 1901; Man and Superman, 1903; John Bull's Other Island, 1904; How He Lied to Her Husband, 1904; Major Barbara, 1907; Passion, Poison, and Petrifaction, or The Fatal Gazogene, 1905; The Doctor's Dilemma, 1906; The Interlude at the Playhouse, 1907; Getting Married, 1908; The Shewing-up of Blanco Posnet, 1909; Press Cuttings, 1909; The Fascinating Foundling, 1909; The Glimpse of Reality, 1909; Misalliance, 1910; The Dark Lady of the Sonnets, 1910; Fanny's First Play, 1911; Androcles and the Lion, 1912; Overruled, 1912; Pygmalion, 1912; Great Catherine, 1913; The Music Cure, 1914; O'Flaherty, V.C., 1915; The Inca of Perusalem, 1916; Augustus Does His Bit, 1916; Annajanska, the Bolshevik Empress, 1916; Heartbreak House, 1919; Back to Methu-

selah, 1920; Jitta's Atonement, 1922; Saint Joan, 1923; The Apple Cart, 1929; Too True to Be Good, 1931; Village Wooing, 1933; On the Rocks, 1933; The Simpleton of the Unexpected Isles, 1934; The Six of Calais, 1934; The Millionairess, 1935; Cymbeline Refinished, 1937; Geneva, 1938; In Good King Charles's Golden Days, 1939; Buoyant Billions, 1948; Shakes Versus Shav (puppet play), 1949; Farfetched Fables, 1950; Why She Would Not, 1950 (unfinished).

ELIOT, THOMAS STEARNS—1888– (publication dates)

Sweeney Agonistes, 1932; The Rock, 1934; Murder in the Cathedral, 1935; The Family Reunion, 1939; The Cocktail Party, 1949; The Confidential Clerk, 1953; The Elder Statesman, 1958.

FRY, CHRISTOPHER—1907– (publication dates)

The Boy With a Cart, 1939; Cuthman, Saint of Sussex, 1939; The First Born, 1946; A Phoenix Too Frequent, 1946; Thor, With Angels, 1949; The Lady's Not for Burning, 1949; Venus Observed, 1950; A Sleep of Prisoners, 1951; The Dark Is Light Enough, 1954; Curtmantle, 1960. Also, Ring Round the Moon, 1950, and the Lark, 1955, adaptations of plays by Jean Anouilh; and Tiger at the Gates, 1955, and Duel of Angels, 1959, adaptations of plays by Jean Giraudoux.

O'NEILL, EUGENE GLADSTONE—1888–1953 (publication dates)

Thirst, The Web, Warnings, Fog, Recklessness, one-act plays published in 1914; Before Breakfast, 1916; The Sniper, 1917; In the Zone, 1917; The Long Voyage Home, 1917; Ile, 1917; The Rope, 1918; Where the Cross Is Made, 1918; The Moon of the Caribbees, 1918; The Dreamy Kid, 1919; Beyond the Horizon, 1920; Chris Christopherson (rewritten as Anna Christie), 1920; Exorcism, 1920; The Emperor Jones, 1920; Diff'rent, 1920; Gold, 1921; Anna Christie, 1921; The Straw, 1921; The First Man, 1922; The Hairy Ape, 1922; Welded, 1924; The Ancient Mariner, 1924; All God's Chillun Got Wings, 1924; Desire Under the Elms, 1924; S.S. Glencairn (containing The Moon of the Caribbees, The Long Voyage Home, In the Zone, and Bound East for Cardiff, united to form a single full-length play), 1924; The Fountain, 1925; The Great God Brown, 1926; Marco Millions, 1926; Lazarus Laughed, 1927; Strange Interlude, 1928; Dynamo, 1929; Mourning Becomes Electra, 1931; Ah, Wilderness, 1933; Days Without End, 1934; The Iceman Cometh, 1946; A Moon for the Misbegotten, 1947; A Long Day's Journey Into Night, 1956; A Touch of the Poet, 1956; Hughie, 1958; More Stately Mansions, 1964. In addition, his "Lost Plays" were published in 1950: Abortion; The Movie Man; The Sniper; Servitude; A Wife for Life.

HELLMAN, LILLIAN—1905– (production dates)

The Children's Hour, 1934; Days to Come, 1936;

The Little Foxes, 1939; Watch on the Rhine, 1941; The Searching Wind, 1944; Another Part of the Forest, 1946; The Autumn Garden, 1951; Toys in the Attic, 1960; My Mother, My Father and Me, 1963. A translation of Anouilh's The Lark, 1956.

SAROYAN, WILLIAM—1908– (completion dates)
Subway Circus, 1935; My Heart's in the Highlands, 1938; The Time of Your Life, 1939; Elmer and Lily, 1939; The Ping Pong Players, 1939; The Hungerers, 1939; Coming Through the Rye, 1940; Talking to You, 1940; Love's Old Sweet Song, 1940; Sweeney in the Trees, 1940; The Beautiful People, 1941; Jim Dandy, 1941; Hello Out There, 1941; Across the Board on Tomorrow Morning, 1941; Get Away, Old Man, 1943; Don't Go Away Mad, 1949; The Cave Dwellers, 1958.

WILDER, THORNTON NIVEN—1897– (publication dates)
The Trumpet Shall Sound, 1919; The Angel That Troubled the Waters (sixteen short plays), 1928; The Long Christmas Dinner (with five other short plays), 1931; Lucrece (translation of a play by Obey), 1932; Our Town, 1938; The Merchant of Yonkers (adapted from a play by Nestroy based on one by John Oxenford), 1938; The Skin of Our Teeth, 1942; Our Century, 1947; The Victors (translated from a play by Sartre), 1948; The Matchmaker (revision of The Merchant of Yon-

kers), 1954; A Life in the Sun, 1955; The Drunken Sisters, 1956; Bernice, 1957; The Wreck of the 5:25, 1957; Plays for Bleecker Street, 1961 (production).

WILLIAMS, TENNESSEE (THOMAS LANIER)—1914– (production dates)
Battle of Angels, 1940; You Touched Me, 1945; The Glass Menagerie, 1945; A Streetcar Named Desire, 1947; Summer and Smoke, 1948; The Rose Tattoo, 1951; Camino Real, 1953; Cat on a Hot Tin Roof, 1955; Orpheus Descending, 1957; Suddenly Last Summer, 1958; Sweet Bird of Youth, 1959; Period of Adjustment, 1960; The Night of the Iguana, 1961; The Milk Train Doesn't Stop Here Anymore, 1962. In addition, "27 Wagons Full of Cotton and Other Plays," a collection of one-act plays, was printed in 1945 and has been revised and added to since; and "American Blues," four short plays, was published in 1948.

MILLER, ARTHUR—1915– (production dates)
The Grass Still Grows, 1936; The Man Who Had All the Luck, 1944; All My Sons, 1947; Death of a Salesman, 1949; An Enemy of the People, 1950; The Crucible, 1953; A Memory of Two Mondays, 1955; A View from the Bridge, 1955; After the Fall, 1964. He also wrote in the Federal Theatre Project in the 1930's, for radio in the 1930's and 1940's, and the motion picture The Misfits, 1960.